W9-AWW-859

Couples' Devotional Bible

Couples' Devotional Bible

New International Version

ZONDERVAN™

GRAND RAPIDS, MICHIGAN 49530 USA

The Holy Bible, New International Version®
Copyright © 1973, 1978, 1984 by International Bible Society

ZONDERVAN™

NIV Couples' Devotional Bible, Revised and Updated
Copyright © 2000 by the Zondervan Corporation
All rights reserved.

Published by Zondervan
Grand Rapids, Michigan 49530, U.S.A.
www.zondervan.com

Library of Congress Catalog Card Number 9361898

The "NIV" and "New International Version" trademarks are registered in the United States Patent and Trademark Office by International Bible Society. Use of either trademark requires the permission of International Bible Society.

The NIV text may be quoted in any form (written, visual, electronic or audio), up to and inclusive of five hundred (500) verses without express written permission of the publisher, providing the verses quoted do not amount to a complete book of the Bible nor do the verses quoted account for 25 percent or more of the total text of the work in which they are quoted.

Notice of copyright must appear on the title or copyright page of the work as follows:

Scripture taken from the HOLY BIBLE, NEW INTERNATIONAL VERSION ®. Copyright © 1973, 1978, 1984 by International Bible Society. Used by permission of Zondervan. All rights reserved.

When quotations from the NIV text are used in non-saleable media, such as church bulletins, orders of service, posters, transparencies or similar media, a complete copyright notice is not required, but the initials (NIV) must appear at the end of each quotation.

Any commentary or other Biblical reference work produced for commercial sale that uses the New International Version must obtain written permission for use of the NIV text.

Permission requests for commercial use within the U.S. and Canada that exceed the above guidelines must be directed to, and approved in writing by, Zondervan, 5300 Patterson Avenue, S.E., Grand Rapids, MI 49530.

Permission requests for commercial use within the U.K., EEC, and EFTA countries that exceed the above guidelines must be directed to, and approved in writing by, Hodder & Stoughton Ltd., a member of the Hodder Headline Plc. Group, 338 Euston Road, London NW1 3BH, England.

Permission requests for non-commercial use that exceed the above guidelines must be directed to, and approved in writing by, International Bible Society, 1820 Jet Stream Drive, Colorado Springs, CO 80921.

Project Editors: Catherine DeVries and Paul Woods
Devotional material compiled and edited by Ron R. Lee, Annette LaPlaca and Lori McCullough
Interior Typesetting: Auto-Graphics, Inc.
Cover Design: Amy Peterman
Cover Photo: © 1999 Christopher Thomas/Tony Stone Images

Printed in the United States of America.

04 05 06 07 08 09 10/ DC / 13 12 11 10 9 8 7 6

You will be pleased to know that a portion of the purchase price of your new NIV Bible has been provided to International Bible Society to help spread the gospel of Jesus Christ around the world!

CONTENTS

Introduction vi
Preface to The New International Version viii

THE OLD TESTAMENT

Genesis 1
Exodus 58
Leviticus 101
Numbers 132
Deuteronomy 175
Joshua 214
Judges 238
Ruth 263
1 Samuel 269
2 Samuel 302
1 Kings 331
2 Kings 364
1 Chronicles 395
2 Chronicles 430
Ezra 467
Nehemiah 480
Esther 497
Job 506
Psalms 544
Proverbs 648
Ecclesiastes 695
Song of Songs 710
Isaiah 720
Jeremiah 797
Lamentations 866
Ezekiel 875
Daniel 926
Hosea 944
Joel 958
Amos 964
Obadiah 973
Jonah 977
Micah 981
Nahum 989
Habakkuk 993
Zephaniah 999
Haggai 1005
Zechariah 1008
Malachi 1018

THE NEW TESTAMENT

Matthew 1027
Mark 1071
Luke 1098
John 1145
Acts 1179
Romans 1220
1 Corinthians 1242
2 Corinthians 1266
Galatians 1281
Ephesians 1289
Philippians 1300
Colossians 1309
1 Thessalonians 1316
2 Thessalonians 1323
1 Timothy 1329
2 Timothy 1340
Titus 1346
Philemon 1350
Hebrews 1353
James 1370
1 Peter 1378
2 Peter 1388
1 John 1393
2 John 1401
3 John 1403
Jude 1405
Revelation 1408

Table of Weights & Measures 1427
Acknowledgments Index 1429
Reading Plan 1439
Author Biographies 1443
Subject Index 1453

INTRODUCTION—NIV COUPLES' DEVOTIONAL BIBLE

In the beginning, God created marriage.

Marriage wasn't the *first* thing God created, but since it was the first human relationship to appear in Scripture, God obviously considers it important.

However, in today's busy world, husbands and wives average about *six minutes per week* of in-depth communication. If you don't count discussions on money, children, neighbors, relatives and the weather, married couples average *less than one minute per day* of really talking to one another.

So how can you improve your communication and your marriage relationship? By using the *NIV Couples' Devotional Bible* on a regular basis. It helps you open up or improve the lines of communication with your spouse. If you use this Bible just a few minutes a day, the devotions will lead you through practical topics of concern in all marriages, enhancing your marriage as you apply the principles of Scripture to your lives.

The editors of *Marriage Partnership* magazine worked with more than 140 writers to produce the devotions in this Bible, most of which are based on material that first appeared in their magazine. With devotions written by people who know good communication, the *NIV Couple's Devotional Bible* will increase communication in your marriage. And it will strengthen your relationship with your spouse as you read the Bible and discuss questions relevant to your needs. Several features make this Bible the perfect source for separate or shared devotions:

The Bible

The NIV Couple's Devotional Bible features the complete text of the Holy Bible, New International Version. The NIV's accuracy and readability make it today's most popular modern translation.

The Introductions

The introduction to each of the 66 books of the Bible highlights that book's practical themes. Each introduction provides interesting facts and helpful background information, as well as practical applications to your daily life.

The Devotions

The devotions are designed to help you and your mate communicate better as you explore the guidance the Bible gives. Each of the weekday devotions includes "Marriage Builders"—questions designed to help you and your spouse talk about real issues within your own unique marriage relationship. At the end of each weekday devotion are additional Scripture references that can provide further insight into the day's topic.

The devotions follow the days of the week. No matter when you begin your reading, simply turn to a devotion for that day. To proceed to the next reading, look to the bottom of the devotion, where you will be directed to the page number for the next devotion.

Each Friday devotion will direct you to a "Weekending," which provides thought-provoking questions and quizzes. Each "Weekending" exercise will help you and your spouse explore together the various areas of your marriage, and will suggest Scripture passages to read on Saturday and Sunday. The end of every "Weekending" will direct you to the following Monday's devotion.

Reading Plan

On page 1439 you will find a plan to help you read through the entire Bible in one year. If you choose to follow this plan, you'll discover great riches as you read the Bible chapter by chapter and book by book.

Author Biographies

You will recognize the names of many of the men and women who contributed devotions to the *NIV Couples' Devotional Bible.* The author index, found on page 1443, provides background information about each author, as well as the page numbers where his or her devotions appear.

Subject Index

Whatever the circumstances of your marriage—too little time together, too much stress, too little romance—the subject index on page 1453 will direct you to a devotion on the topic you need help with. The wisdom contained in God's Word is *always* available to help you face the challenges and struggles of married life.

PREFACE

THE NEW INTERNATIONAL VERSION is a completely new translation of the Holy Bible made by over a hundred scholars working directly from the best available Hebrew, Aramaic and Greek texts. It had its beginning in 1965 when, after several years of exploratory study by committees from the Christian Reformed Church and the National Association of Evangelicals, a group of scholars met at Palos Heights, Illinois, and concurred in the need for a new translation of the Bible in contemporary English. This group, though not made up of official church representatives, was transdenominational. Its conclusion was endorsed by a large number of leaders from many denominations who met in Chicago in 1966.

Responsibility for the new version was delegated by the Palos Heights group to a self-governing body of fifteen, the Committee on Bible Translation, composed for the most part of biblical scholars from colleges, universities and seminaries. In 1967 the New York Bible Society (now the International Bible Society) generously undertook the financial sponsorship of the project—a sponsorship that made it possible to enlist the help of many distinguished scholars. The fact that participants from the United States, Great Britain, Canada, Australia and New Zealand worked together gave the project its international scope. That they were from many denominations—including Anglican, Assemblies of God, Baptist, Brethren, Christian Reformed, Church of Christ, Evangelical Free, Lutheran, Mennonite, Methodist, Nazarene, Presbyterian, Wesleyan and other churches—helped to safeguard the translation from sectarian bias.

How it was made helps to give the New International Version its distinctiveness. The translation of each book was assigned to a team of scholars. Next, one of the Intermediate Editorial Committees revised the initial translation, with constant reference to the Hebrew, Aramaic or Greek. Their work then went to one of the General Editorial Committees, which checked it in detail and made another thorough revision. This revision in turn was carefully reviewed by the Committee on Bible Translation, which made further changes and then released the final version for publication. In this way the entire Bible underwent three revisions, during each of which the translation was examined for its faithfulness to the original languages and for its English style.

All this involved many thousands of hours of research and discussion regarding the meaning of the texts and the precise way of putting them into English. It may well be that no other translation has been made by a more thorough process of review and revision from committee to committee than this one.

From the beginning of the project, the Committee on Bible Translation held to certain goals for the New International Version: that it would be an accurate translation and one that would have clarity and literary quality and so prove suitable for public and private reading, teaching, preaching, memorizing and liturgical use. The Committee also sought to preserve some measure of continuity with the long tradition of translating the Scriptures into English.

In working toward these goals, the translators were united in their commitment to the authority and infallibility of the Bible as God's Word in written form. They believe that it contains the divine answer to the deepest needs of humanity, that it sheds unique light on our path in a dark world, and that it sets forth the way to our eternal well-being.

The first concern of the translators has been the accuracy of the translation and its fidelity to the thought of the biblical writers. They have weighed the significance of the lexical and grammatical details of the Hebrew, Aramaic and Greek texts. At the same time, they have striven for more than a word-for-word translation. Because thought patterns and syntax differ from language to language, faithful communication of the meaning of the writers of the Bible demands frequent modifications in sentence structure and constant regard for the contextual meanings of words.

A sensitive feeling for style does not always accompany scholarship. Accordingly the Committee on Bible Translation submitted the developing version to a number of stylistic consultants. Two of them read every book of both Old and New Testaments twice—once before and once after the last major revision—and made invaluable suggestions. Samples of the translation were tested for clarity and ease of reading by various kinds of people—young and old, highly educated and less well educated, ministers and laymen.

Concern for clear and natural English—that the New International Version should be idiomatic but not idiosyncratic, contemporary but not dated—motivated the translators and consultants. At the same time, they tried to reflect the differing styles of the biblical writers. In view of the international use of English, the translators sought to avoid obvious Americanisms on the one hand and obvious Anglicisms on the other. A British edition reflects the comparatively few differences of significant idiom and of spelling.

As for the traditional pronouns "thou," "thee" and "thine" in reference to the Deity, the translators judged that to use these archaisms (along with the old verb forms such as "doest," "wouldest" and "hadst") would violate accuracy in translation. Neither Hebrew, Aramaic nor Greek uses special pronouns for the persons of the Godhead. A present-day translation is not enhanced by forms that in the time of the King James Version were used in everyday speech, whether referring to God or man.

For the Old Testament the standard Hebrew text, the Masoretic Text as published in the latest editions of *Biblia Hebraica,* was used throughout. The Dead Sea Scrolls contain material bearing on an earlier stage of the Hebrew text. They were consulted, as were the Samaritan Pentateuch and the ancient scribal traditions relating to textual changes. Sometimes a variant Hebrew reading in the margin of the Masoretic Text was followed instead of the text itself. Such instances, being variants within the Masoretic tradition, are not specified by footnotes. In rare cases, words in the consonantal text were divided differently from the way they appear in the Masoretic Text. Footnotes indicate this. The translators also consulted the more important early versions—the Septuagint; Aquila, Symmachus and Theodotion; the Vulgate; the Syriac Peshitta; the Targums; and for the Psalms the *Juxta Hebraica* of Jerome. Readings from these versions were occasionally followed where the Masoretic Text seemed doubtful and where accepted principles of textual criticism showed that one or more of these textual witnesses appeared to provide the correct reading. Such instances are footnoted. Sometimes vowel letters and vowel signs did not, in the judgment of the translators, represent the correct vowels for the original consonantal text. Accordingly some words were read with a different set of vowels. These instances are usually not indicated by footnotes.

The Greek text used in translating the New Testament was an eclectic one. No other piece of ancient literature has such an abundance of manuscript witnesses as does the New Testament. Where existing manuscripts differ, the translators made their choice of readings according to accepted principles of New Testament textual criticism. Footnotes call attention to places where there was uncertainty about what the original text was. The best current printed texts of the Greek New Testament were used.

There is a sense in which the work of translation is never wholly finished. This applies to all great literature and uniquely so to the Bible. In 1973 the New Testament in the New International Version was published. Since then, suggestions for corrections and revisions have been received from various sources. The Committee on Bible Translation carefully considered the suggestions and adopted a number of them. These were incorporated in the first printing of the entire Bible in 1978. Additional revisions were made by the Committee on Bible Translation in 1983 and appear in printings after that date.

As in other ancient documents, the precise meaning of the biblical texts is sometimes uncertain. This is more often the case with the Hebrew and Aramaic texts than with the Greek text. Although archaeological and linguistic discoveries in this century aid in understanding difficult passages, some uncertainties remain. The more significant of these have been called to the reader's attention in the footnotes.

In regard to the divine name *YHWH,* commonly referred to as the *Tetragrammaton,* the translators adopted the device used in most English versions of rendering that name as "LORD" in capital letters to distinguish it from *Adonai,* another Hebrew word rendered "Lord," for which small letters are used. Wherever the two names stand together in the Old Testament as a compound name of God, they are rendered "Sovereign LORD."

Because for most readers today the phrases "the LORD of hosts" and "God of hosts" have little meaning, this version renders them "the LORD Almighty" and "God Almighty." These renderings convey the sense of the Hebrew, namely, "he who is sovereign over all the 'hosts' (powers) in heaven and on earth, especially over the 'hosts' (armies) of Israel." For readers unacquainted with Hebrew this does not make clear the distinction between *Sabaoth* ("hosts" or "Almighty") and *Shaddai* (which can also be translated "Almighty"), but the latter occurs infrequently and is always footnoted. When *Adonai* and *YHWH Sabaoth* occur together, they are rendered "the Lord, the LORD Almighty."

As for other proper nouns, the familiar spellings of the King James Version are generally retained. Names traditionally spelled with "ch," except where it is final, are usually spelled in this translation with "k" or "c," since the biblical languages do not have the sound that "ch" frequently indicates in English—for example, in *chant*. For well-known names such as Zechariah, however, the traditional spelling has been retained. Variation in the spelling of names in the original languages has usually not been indicated. Where a person or place has two or more different names in the Hebrew, Aramaic or Greek texts, the more familiar one has generally been used, with footnotes where needed.

To achieve clarity the translators sometimes supplied words not in the original texts but required by the context. If there was uncertainty about such material, it is enclosed in brackets. Also for the sake of clarity or style, nouns, including some proper nouns, are sometimes substituted for pronouns, and vice versa. And though the Hebrew writers often shifted back and forth between first, second and third personal pronouns without change of antecedent, this translation often makes them uniform, in accordance with English style and without the use of footnotes.

Poetical passages are printed as poetry, that is, with indentation of lines and with separate stanzas. These are generally designed to reflect the structure of Hebrew poetry. This poetry is normally characterized by parallelism in balanced lines. Most of the poetry in the Bible is in the Old Testament, and scholars differ regarding the scansion of Hebrew lines. The translators determined the stanza divisions for the most part by analysis of the subject matter. The stanzas therefore serve as poetic paragraphs.

As an aid to the reader, italicized sectional headings are inserted in most of the books. They are not to be regarded as part of the NIV text, are not for oral reading, and are not intended to dictate the interpretation of the sections they head.

The footnotes in this version are of several kinds, most of which need no explanation. Those giving alternative translations begin with "Or" and generally introduce the alternative with the last word preceding it in the text, except when it is a single-word alternative; in poetry quoted in a footnote a slant mark indicates a line division. Footnotes introduced by "Or" do not have uniform significance. In some cases two possible translations were considered to have about equal validity. In other cases, though the translators were convinced that the translation in the text was correct, they judged that another interpretation was possible and of sufficient importance to be represented in a footnote.

In the New Testament, footnotes that refer to uncertainty regarding the original text are introduced by "Some manuscripts" or similar expressions. In the Old Testament, evidence for the reading chosen is given first and evidence for the alternative is added after a semicolon (for example: Septuagint; Hebrew *father*). In such notes the term "Hebrew" refers to the Masoretic Text.

It should be noted that minerals, flora and fauna, architectural details, articles of clothing and jewelry, musical instruments and other articles cannot always be identified with precision. Also measures of capacity in the biblical period are particularly uncertain (see the table of weights and measures following the text).

Like all translations of the Bible, made as they are by imperfect man, this one undoubtedly falls short of its goals. Yet we are grateful to God for the extent to which he has enabled us to realize these goals and for the strength he has given us and our colleagues to complete our task. We offer this version of the Bible to him in whose name and for whose glory it has been made. We pray that it will lead many into a better understanding of the Holy Scriptures and a fuller knowledge of Jesus Christ the incarnate Word, of whom the Scriptures so faithfully testify.

The Committee on Bible Translation

June 1978
(Revised August 1983)

Names of the translators and editors may be secured
from the International Bible Society,
translation sponsors of the New International Version,
1820 Jet Stream Drive, Colorado Springs, Colorado
80921-3696 U.S.A.

Old Testament

Old Testament

MOSES writes Genesis, a book of beginnings, to tell us how God creates the world, how sin comes into the world, and how God loves mankind in spite of his sin. He reports exciting stories about Adam, Noah, Abraham, Isaac, Jacob and Joseph, how God cares for them and stands beside them, no matter what they do. As you read this book, think about how God enters into a personal relationship with you, cares for you, and wants you to make serving him a priority in your life.

GENESIS

The Beginning

1 In the beginning God created the heavens and the earth. 2 Now the earth was[a] formless and empty, darkness was over the surface of the deep, and the Spirit of God was hovering over the waters.

3 And God said, "Let there be light," and there was light. 4 God saw that the light was good, and he separated the light from the darkness. 5 God called the light "day," and the darkness he called "night." And there was evening, and there was morning—the first day.

6 And God said, "Let there be an expanse between the waters to separate water from water." 7 So God made the expanse and separated the water under the expanse from the water above it. And it was so. 8 God called the expanse "sky." And there was evening, and there was morning—the second day.

[a] 2 Or possibly *became*

9And God said, "Let the water under the
sky be gathered to one place, and let
dry ground appear." And it was so.
10God called the dry ground "land,"
and the gathered waters he called
"seas." And God saw that it was good.
11Then God said, "Let the land pro-
duce vegetation: seed-bearing plants
and trees on the land that bear fruit
with seed in it, according to their vari-
ous kinds." And it was so. 12The land
produced vegetation: plants bearing
seed according to their kinds and
trees bearing fruit with seed in it ac-
cording to their kinds. And God saw
that it was good. 13And there was eve-
ning, and there was morning—the
third day.
14And God said, "Let there be lights in the
expanse of the sky to separate the day
from the night, and let them serve as
signs to mark seasons and days and
years, 15and let them be lights in the
expanse of the sky to give light on the
earth." And it was so. 16God made two
great lights—the greater light to gov-
ern the day and the lesser light to gov-
ern the night. He also made the stars.
17God set them in the expanse of the
sky to give light on the earth, 18to gov-
ern the day and the night, and to sepa-
rate light from darkness. And God
saw that it was good. 19And there was
evening, and there was morning—the
fourth day.
20And God said, "Let the water teem with
living creatures, and let birds fly
above the earth across the expanse of
the sky." 21So God created the great
creatures of the sea and every living
and moving thing with which the wa-
ter teems, according to their kinds,
and every winged bird according to its
kind. And God saw that it was good.
22God blessed them and said, "Be
fruitful and increase in number and
fill the water in the seas, and let the
birds increase on the earth." 23And
there was evening, and there was
morning—the fifth day.
24And God said, "Let the land produce liv-
ing creatures according to their kinds:
livestock, creatures that move along
the ground, and wild animals, each
according to its kind." And it was so.
25God made the wild animals accord-
ing to their kinds, the livestock ac-
cording to their kinds, and all the
creatures that move along the ground
according to their kinds. And God saw
that it was good.
26Then God said, "Let us make man
in our image, in our likeness, and let
them rule over the fish of the sea and
the birds of the air, over the livestock,
over all the earth,[a] and over all the
creatures that move along the
ground."
27So God created man in his own image,
in the image of God he created him;
male and female he created them.
28God blessed them and said to
them, "Be fruitful and increase in
number; fill the earth and subdue it.
Rule over the fish of the sea and the
birds of the air and over every living
creature that moves on the ground."
29Then God said, "I give you every
seed-bearing plant on the face of the
whole earth and every tree that has
fruit with seed in it. They will be
yours for food. 30And to all the beasts
of the earth and all the birds of the air
and all the creatures that move on the
ground—everything that has the
breath of life in it—I give every green
plant for food." And it was so.
31God saw all that he had made,
and it was very good. And there was
evening, and there was morning—the
sixth day.

2 Thus the heavens and the earth
were completed in all their vast
array.
2By the seventh day God had finished the
work he had been doing; so on the
seventh day he rested[b] from all his
work. 3And God blessed the seventh
day and made it holy, because on it he
rested from all the work of creating
that he had done.

Adam and Eye

4This is the account of the heavens and
the earth when they were created.

When the LORD God made the earth and
the heavens— 5and no shrub of the field
had yet appeared on the earth[c] and no
plant of the field had yet sprung up, for

[a]26 Hebrew; Syriac *all the wild animals* [b]2 Or *ceased*; also in verse 3 [c]5 Or *land*; also in verse 6

VERSE FOR THE DAY: Genesis 1:27

AUTHOR: Tim Stafford

PASSAGE FOR THE DAY: Genesis 1:1–31

God's Romance

The Bible's first marriage story (Genesis 1–2) begins, like all love stories, with a problem. The chapter reverberates with the regular drumbeat of "good" as God creates the universe. But then something is unsatisfactory. Having made Adam, God discovered something "not good" (Genesis 2:18). God's society was inadequate for Adam; he needed the company of another creature. So God made a partner for Adam—Eve—and presented her to him.

Adam's reaction was immediate and passionate. "This is now bone of my bones and flesh of my flesh." In effect, Adam exclaimed, "This one is family!" He was attracted because he felt kinship.

Sometimes it is claimed that marriage offers intimate possibilities because of the differences between the sexes—the way in which male and female, as opposites, complement each other. Genesis brings a very different emphasis: It was because of their similar make-up, not because of their differences, that they were able to become intimate partners.

No code of behavior could produce this; it was a gift from God. Something of God is seen in the unashamed nakedness of Adam and Eve. As Adam could delight in Eve because she was like him, so God finds particular delight in this man and woman because together they are like him. There is fellowship among the three. They feel mutual kinship, and they delight in one another.

MARRIAGE BUILDERS

♦ *You are probably well aware of your differences. But what are some of the ways you are similar?*

♦ *How have your differences and similarities strengthened your marriage?*

Additional Scripture Readings
Genesis 2:15–25; Proverbs 5:18; Song of Songs 2:3–4

Go to page 4 for your next devotional reading.

the LORD God had not sent rain on the
earth[a] and there was no man to work the
ground, 6but streams[b] came up from the
earth and watered the whole surface of
the ground— 7the LORD God formed the
man[c] from the dust of the ground and
breathed into his nostrils the breath of
life, and the man became a living being.
8Now the LORD God had planted a gar-
den in the east, in Eden; and there he put
the man he had formed. 9And the LORD
God made all kinds of trees grow out of
the ground—trees that were pleasing to
the eye and good for food. In the middle

[a]5 Or *land*; also in verse 6 [b]6 Or *mist* [c]7 The Hebrew for *man (adam)* sounds like and may be related to the Hebrew for *ground (adamah)*; it is also the name *Adam* (see Gen. 2:20).

TUESDAY

VERSE FOR THE DAY: Genesis 2:18

AUTHOR: Jeanne Hendricks

PASSAGE FOR THE DAY: Genesis 2:8–25

Blended Gifts

No matter what a wife or husband happens to be or do, marriage is teamwork. God doesn't give individual gifts to frustrate a marriage, but to enhance it. He doesn't lead two people into marriage to see sparks fly, to pull a husband and wife in two opposite directions. He leads them into marriage to blend and maximize their usefulness.

Much of the tension that I see in marriages comes from grasping and holding onto what we consider our individuality. No matter what our gifts, talents or personalities, when they are given to God, he will blend them with those of our spouse because that's what marriage is all about.

I think of a friend of mine who was a nursing instructor. It was her life. When her husband was called into vocational ministry, with great fear and trembling she quit her job at the school of nursing. The interesting outcome was that God gave her nursing back to her—wrapped in a bonus. Their move enabled her to use her nursing skills at a church-sponsored clinic. God moved both her and her husband into new areas of opportunity. But my friend had to be willing to trust God to do the blending.

MARRIAGE BUILDERS

♦ *Has there been a time when you put one of your individual dreams "on hold" so your spouse could pursue a dream? Was the eventual outcome positive for both of you?*

♦ *How has God "blended" you to maximize your usefulness for his kingdom? How can you both be more open to his blending?*

Additional Scripture Readings
Acts 18:1–3, 18–26; Ecclesiastes 4:9–10

Go to page 7 for your next devotional reading.

of the garden were the tree of life and the
tree of the knowledge of good and evil.
10A river watering the garden flowed
from Eden; from there it was separated
into four headwaters. 11The name of the
first is the Pishon; it winds through the en-
tire land of Havilah, where there is gold.
12(The gold of that land is good; aromatic
resin[a] and onyx are also there.) 13The
name of the second river is the Gihon; it
winds through the entire land of Cush.[b]
14The name of the third river is the Tigris;
it runs along the east side of Asshur. And
the fourth river is the Euphrates.
15The LORD God took the man and put
him in the Garden of Eden to work it and
take care of it. 16And the LORD God com-
manded the man, "You are free to eat from
any tree in the garden; 17but you must not
eat from the tree of the knowledge of good
and evil, for when you eat of it you will
surely die."
18The LORD God said, "It is not good for
the man to be alone. I will make a helper
suitable for him."
19Now the LORD God had formed out of
the ground all the beasts of the field and
all the birds of the air. He brought them to
the man to see what he would name them;
and whatever the man called each living
creature, that was its name. 20So the man
gave names to all the livestock, the birds
of the air and all the beasts of the field.
But for Adam[c] no suitable helper was
found. 21So the LORD God caused the man
to fall into a deep sleep; and while he was
sleeping, he took one of the man's ribs[d]
and closed up the place with flesh. 22Then
the LORD God made a woman from the
rib[e] he had taken out of the man, and he
brought her to the man.
23The man said,

"This is now bone of my bones
and flesh of my flesh;
she shall be called 'woman,[f]
for she was taken out of man."

24For this reason a man will leave his fa-
ther and mother and be united to his wife,
and they will become one flesh.
25The man and his wife were both na-
ked, and they felt no shame.

The Fall of Man

3 Now the serpent was more crafty than
any of the wild animals the LORD God
had made. He said to the woman, "Did
God really say, 'You must not eat from any
tree in the garden'?"
2The woman said to the serpent, "We
may eat fruit from the trees in the garden,
3but God did say, 'You must not eat fruit
from the tree that is in the middle of the
garden, and you must not touch it, or you
will die.' "
4"You will not surely die," the serpent
said to the woman. 5"For God knows that
when you eat of it your eyes will be
opened, and you will be like God, know-
ing good and evil."
6When the woman saw that the fruit of
the tree was good for food and pleasing to
the eye, and also desirable for gaining wis-
dom, she took some and ate it. She also
gave some to her husband, who was with
her, and he ate it. 7Then the eyes of both
of them were opened, and they realized
they were naked; so they sewed fig leaves
together and made coverings for them-
selves.
8Then the man and his wife heard the
sound of the LORD God as he was walking
in the garden in the cool of the day, and
they hid from the LORD God among the
trees of the garden. 9But the LORD God
called to the man, "Where are you?"
10He answered, "I heard you in the gar-
den, and I was afraid because I was naked;
so I hid."
11And he said, "Who told you that you
were naked? Have you eaten from the
tree that I commanded you not to eat
from?"
12The man said, "The woman you put
here with me—she gave me some fruit
from the tree, and I ate it."
13Then the LORD God said to the wom-
an, "What is this you have done?"
The woman said, "The serpent deceived
me, and I ate."
14So the LORD God said to the serpent,
"Because you have done this,

"Cursed are you above all the
livestock
and all the wild animals!
You will crawl on your belly
and you will eat dust
all the days of your life.
15And I will put enmity
between you and the woman,

[a]12 Or *good; pearls* [b]13 Possibly southeast Mesopotamia [c]20 Or *the man* [d]21 Or *took part of the man's side* [e]22 Or *part* [f]23 The Hebrew for *woman* sounds like the Hebrew for *man.*

and between your offspring[a] and hers;
he will crush[b] your head,
and you will strike his heel."

16To the woman he said,

"I will greatly increase your pains in childbearing;
with pain you will give birth to children.
Your desire will be for your husband,
and he will rule over you."

17To Adam he said, "Because you listened to your wife and ate from the tree about which I commanded you, 'You must not eat of it,'

"Cursed is the ground because of you;
through painful toil you will eat of it
all the days of your life.
18It will produce thorns and thistles for you,
and you will eat the plants of the field.
19By the sweat of your brow
you will eat your food
until you return to the ground,
since from it you were taken;
for dust you are
and to dust you will return."

20Adam[c] named his wife Eve,[d] because she would become the mother of all the living.

21The LORD God made garments of skin for Adam and his wife and clothed them. 22And the LORD God said, "The man has now become like one of us, knowing good and evil. He must not be allowed to reach out his hand and take also from the tree of life and eat, and live forever." 23So the LORD God banished him from the Garden of Eden to work the ground from which he had been taken. 24After he drove the man out, he placed on the east side[e] of the Garden of Eden cherubim and a flaming sword flashing back and forth to guard the way to the tree of life.

Cain and Abel

4 Adam[c] lay with his wife Eve, and she became pregnant and gave birth to Cain.[f] She said, "With the help of the LORD I have brought forth[g] a man." 2Later she gave birth to his brother Abel.

Now Abel kept flocks, and Cain worked the soil. 3In the course of time Cain brought some of the fruits of the soil as an offering to the LORD. 4But Abel brought fat portions from some of the firstborn of his flock. The LORD looked with favor on Abel and his offering, 5but on Cain and his offering he did not look with favor. So Cain was very angry, and his face was downcast.

6Then the LORD said to Cain, "Why are you angry? Why is your face downcast? 7If you do what is right, will you not be accepted? But if you do not do what is right, sin is crouching at your door; it desires to have you, but you must master it."

8Now Cain said to his brother Abel, "Let's go out to the field."[h] And while they were in the field, Cain attacked his brother Abel and killed him.

9Then the LORD said to Cain, "Where is your brother Abel?"

"I don't know," he replied. "Am I my brother's keeper?"

10The LORD said, "What have you done? Listen! Your brother's blood cries out to me from the ground. 11Now you are under a curse and driven from the ground, which opened its mouth to receive your brother's blood from your hand. 12When you work the ground, it will no longer yield its crops for you. You will be a restless wanderer on the earth."

13Cain said to the LORD, "My punishment is more than I can bear. 14Today you are driving me from the land, and I will be hidden from your presence; I will be a restless wanderer on the earth, and whoever finds me will kill me."

15But the LORD said to him, "Not so[i]; if anyone kills Cain, he will suffer vengeance seven times over." Then the LORD put a mark on Cain so that no one who found him would kill him. 16So Cain went out from the LORD's presence and lived in the land of Nod,[j] east of Eden.

17Cain lay with his wife, and she became pregnant and gave birth to Enoch. Cain was then building a city, and he named it after his son Enoch. 18To Enoch was born Irad, and Irad was the father of

[a] *15* Or *seed* [b] *15* Or *strike* [c] *20,1* Or *The man* [d] *20 Eve* probably means *living.* [e] *24* Or *placed in front* [f] *1 Cain* sounds like the Hebrew for *brought forth* or *acquired.* [g] *1* Or *have acquired* [h] *8* Samaritan Pentateuch, Septuagint, Vulgate and Syriac; Masoretic Text does not have *"Let's go out to the field."* [i] *15* Septuagint, Vulgate and Syriac; Hebrew *Very well* [j] *16 Nod* means *wandering* (see verses 12 and 14).

Mehujael, and Mehujael was the father of
Methushael, and Methushael was the father
of Lamech.
19Lamech married two women, one
named Adah and the other Zillah. 20Adah
gave birth to Jabal; he was the father of
those who live in tents and raise livestock.
21His brother's name was Jubal; he was
the father of all who play the harp and
flute. 22Zillah also had a son, Tubal-Cain,
who forged all kinds of tools out of[a]
bronze and iron. Tubal-Cain's sister was
Naamah.
23Lamech said to his wives,

[a]22 Or *who instructed all who work in*

VERSE FOR THE DAY: Genesis 4:4

AUTHOR: Ronald Blue

PASSAGE FOR THE DAY: Genesis 4:1–16

Charitable Giving

Giving money to help meet the needs of the church or to help feed the hungry can seem financially impossible, especially for cash-strapped newlyweds. That's why every couple needs to develop a giving plan that is consistent with the financial priorities set forth in the Bible. If we don't, then life's inevitable surprises (car repairs, illnesses, another bill in the mailbox) will consistently interfere with our desire—and our ability—to give.

Unfortunately, much of our giving is done with discretionary dollars—that is, the money that is left over after the bills are paid and our family is supplied with food, housing and clothing. The problem is that for most couples there simply *isn't* much money left over; and we feel frustrated and guilty that we aren't able to give more.

That's why it's good to avoid leaving the amount of your gift to whatever cash is left over at the end of the month. Instead, set aside a certain amount every week. When you do this, you are setting aside money—as a first priority—to be given away. And you are removing some of the temptation to regard those "giving dollars" as discretionary funds to be used for family or personal expenses.

MARRIAGE BUILDERS

♦ *How satisfied are you with your present level of charitable giving?*

♦ *How can you make giving a higher priority each month? each year?*

Additional Scripture Readings
Exodus 23:19; Proverbs 3:9;
2 Corinthians 9:6–9

Go to page 9 for your next devotional reading.

"Adah and Zillah, listen to me;
wives of Lamech, hear my words.
I have killed[a] a man for wounding me,
a young man for injuring me.
24If Cain is avenged seven times,
then Lamech seventy-seven times."

25Adam lay with his wife again, and she gave birth to a son and named him Seth,[b] saying, "God has granted me another child in place of Abel, since Cain killed him." 26Seth also had a son, and he named him Enosh.

At that time men began to call on[c] the name of the LORD.

From Adam to Noah

5 This is the written account of Adam's line.

When God created man, he made him in the likeness of God. 2He created them male and female and blessed them. And when they were created, he called them "man.[d]"

3When Adam had lived 130 years, he had a son in his own likeness, in his own image; and he named him Seth. 4After Seth was born, Adam lived 800 years and had other sons and daughters. 5Altogether, Adam lived 930 years, and then he died.

6When Seth had lived 105 years, he became the father[e] of Enosh. 7And after he became the father of Enosh, Seth lived 807 years and had other sons and daughters. 8Altogether, Seth lived 912 years, and then he died.

9When Enosh had lived 90 years, he became the father of Kenan. 10And after he became the father of Kenan, Enosh lived 815 years and had other sons and daughters. 11Altogether, Enosh lived 905 years, and then he died.

12When Kenan had lived 70 years, he became the father of Mahalalel. 13And after he became the father of Mahalalel, Kenan lived 840 years and had other sons and daughters. 14Altogether, Kenan lived 910 years, and then he died.

15When Mahalalel had lived 65 years, he became the father of Jared. 16And after he became the father of Jared, Mahalalel lived 830 years and had other sons and daughters. 17Altogether, Mahalalel lived 895 years, and then he died.

18When Jared had lived 162 years, he became the father of Enoch. 19And after he became the father of Enoch, Jared lived 800 years and had other sons and daughters. 20Altogether, Jared lived 962 years, and then he died.

21When Enoch had lived 65 years, he became the father of Methuselah. 22And after he became the father of Methuselah, Enoch walked with God 300 years and had other sons and daughters. 23Altogether, Enoch lived 365 years. 24Enoch walked with God; then he was no more, because God took him away.

25When Methuselah had lived 187 years, he became the father of Lamech. 26And after he became the father of Lamech, Methuselah lived 782 years and had other sons and daughters. 27Altogether, Methuselah lived 969 years, and then he died.

28When Lamech had lived 182 years, he had a son. 29He named him Noah[f] and said, "He will comfort us in the labor and painful toil of our hands caused by the ground the LORD has cursed." 30After Noah was born, Lamech lived 595 years and had other sons and daughters. 31Altogether, Lamech lived 777 years, and then he died.

32After Noah was 500 years old, he became the father of Shem, Ham and Japheth.

The Flood

6 When men began to increase in number on the earth and daughters were born to them, 2the sons of God saw that the daughters of men were beautiful, and they married any of them they chose. 3Then the LORD said, "My Spirit will not contend with[g] man forever, for he is mortal[h]; his days will be a hundred and twenty years."

4The Nephilim were on the earth in those days—and also afterward—when the sons of God went to the daughters of men and had children by them. They were the heroes of old, men of renown.

5The LORD saw how great man's wickedness on the earth had become, and that every inclination of the thoughts of his heart was only evil all the time. 6The LORD

[a]23 Or *I will kill* [b]25 *Seth* probably means *granted.* [c]26 Or *to proclaim* [d]2 Hebrew *adam*
[e]6 *Father* may mean *ancestor*; also in verses 7-26. [f]29 *Noah* sounds like the Hebrew for *comfort.*
[g]3 Or *My spirit will not remain in* [h]3 Or *corrupt*

was grieved that he had made man on the
earth, and his heart was filled with pain.
7So the LORD said, "I will wipe mankind,
whom I have created, from the face of the
earth—men and animals, and creatures
that move along the ground, and birds of
the air—for I am grieved that I have made
them." 8But Noah found favor in the eyes
of the LORD.

9This is the account of Noah.

Noah was a righteous man, blameless
among the people of his time, and he
walked with God. 10Noah had three sons:
Shem, Ham and Japheth.

11Now the earth was corrupt in God's
sight and was full of violence. 12God saw
how corrupt the earth had become, for all
the people on earth had corrupted their

VERSE FOR THE DAY: Genesis 6:9

AUTHOR: Kamilla Denman

PASSAGE FOR THE DAY: Genesis 6:5–22

Walking With God

I hadn't been reading my Bible long when I found what I had been looking for: "Abraham walked with God. . . . Noah walked with God. . . ." How could I walk with God?

Most of the time when walking, those partners who are walking together are silent. Certainly, they make comments, but there is a silent understanding that they are seeing the same sights and experiencing the same sounds and smells. In fact, the better I know the person I'm walking with, the less we have to say and the more we enjoy the walk.

But what about walking with God? I saw that I could pray without ceasing as simply as I breathe without ceasing. Prayer could encompass my nonverbal communication with God. Just as I reach out to touch my husband, I can reach out to God without words. Just as I smile at a close friend, I can offer a smile of appreciation to God.

As I began to focus on walk rather than talk, I sensed more keenly the times when I walked in my own direction. I discerned my distance from God more clearly. Now, it is harder for me to go on with business as usual when I am not at peace with God or with another person. For me to walk with God, my whole self—body, soul and spirit—needs to be in order.

MARRIAGE BUILDERS

♦ *In what ways do you reach out for fellowship with God?*
♦ *How would you characterize your "walk" with God—comfortable, close, distanced, awkward? What might make walking with God a more natural habit for you?*

Additional Scripture Readings
James 2:20–26; 1 Thessalonians 5:17; Galatians 5:25

Go to page 30 for your next devotional reading.

ways. 13So God said to Noah, "I am going
to put an end to all people, for the earth is
filled with violence because of them. I am
surely going to destroy both them and the
earth. 14So make yourself an ark of cy-
press[a] wood; make rooms in it and coat
it with pitch inside and out. 15This is how
you are to build it: The ark is to be 450 feet
long, 75 feet wide and 45 feet high.[b]
16Make a roof for it and finish[c] the ark to
within 18 inches[d] of the top. Put a door
in the side of the ark and make lower,
middle and upper decks. 17I am going to
bring floodwaters on the earth to destroy
all life under the heavens, every creature
that has the breath of life in it. Everything
on earth will perish. 18But I will establish
my covenant with you, and you will enter
the ark—you and your sons and your wife
and your sons' wives with you. 19You are
to bring into the ark two of all living cre-
atures, male and female, to keep them alive
with you. 20Two of every kind of bird, of
every kind of animal and of every kind of
creature that moves along the ground will
come to you to be kept alive. 21You are to
take every kind of food that is to be eaten
and store it away as food for you and for
them."

22Noah did everything just as God com-
manded him.

7 The LORD then said to Noah, "Go into
the ark, you and your whole family,
because I have found you righteous in this
generation. 2Take with you seven[e] of ev-
ery kind of clean animal, a male and its
mate, and two of every kind of unclean
animal, a male and its mate, 3and also sev-
en of every kind of bird, male and female,
to keep their various kinds alive through-
out the earth. 4Seven days from now I will
send rain on the earth for forty days and
forty nights, and I will wipe from the face
of the earth every living creature I have
made."

5And Noah did all that the LORD com-
manded him.

6Noah was six hundred years old when
the floodwaters came on the earth. 7And
Noah and his sons and his wife and his
sons' wives entered the ark to escape the
waters of the flood. 8Pairs of clean and un-
clean animals, of birds and of all creatures
that move along the ground, 9male and fe-
male, came to Noah and entered the ark,
as God had commanded Noah. 10And after
the seven days the floodwaters came on
the earth.

11In the six hundredth year of Noah's
life, on the seventeenth day of the second
month—on that day all the springs of the
great deep burst forth, and the floodgates
of the heavens were opened. 12And rain
fell on the earth forty days and forty
nights.

13On that very day Noah and his sons,
Shem, Ham and Japheth, together with his
wife and the wives of his three sons, en-
tered the ark. 14They had with them every
wild animal according to its kind, all live-
stock according to their kinds, every crea-
ture that moves along the ground accord-
ing to its kind and every bird according to
its kind, everything with wings. 15Pairs of
all creatures that have the breath of life in
them came to Noah and entered the ark.
16The animals going in were male and fe-
male of every living thing, as God had
commanded Noah. Then the LORD shut
him in.

17For forty days the flood kept coming
on the earth, and as the waters increased
they lifted the ark high above the earth.
18The waters rose and increased greatly
on the earth, and the ark floated on the
surface of the water. 19They rose greatly
on the earth, and all the high mountains
under the entire heavens were covered.
20The waters rose and covered the moun-
tains to a depth of more than twenty
feet.[f,g] 21Every living thing that moved
on the earth perished—birds, livestock,
wild animals, all the creatures that swarm
over the earth, and all mankind. 22Every-
thing on dry land that had the breath of
life in its nostrils died. 23Every living thing
on the face of the earth was wiped out;
men and animals and the creatures that
move along the ground and the birds of
the air were wiped from the earth. Only
Noah was left, and those with him in the
ark.

24The waters flooded the earth for a
hundred and fifty days.

8 But God remembered Noah and all
the wild animals and the livestock

[a] *14* The meaning of the Hebrew for this word is uncertain. [b] *15* Hebrew *300 cubits long, 50 cubits wide and 30 cubits high* (about 140 meters long, 23 meters wide and 13.5 meters high) [c] *16* Or *Make an opening for light by finishing* [d] *16* Hebrew *a cubit* (about 0.5 meter) [e] *2* Or *seven pairs*; also in verse 3 [f] *20* Hebrew *fifteen cubits* (about 6.9 meters) [g] *20* Or *rose more than twenty feet, and the mountains were covered*

that were with him in the ark, and he sent
a wind over the earth, and the waters re-
ceded. 2Now the springs of the deep and
the floodgates of the heavens had been
closed, and the rain had stopped falling
from the sky. 3The water receded steadily
from the earth. At the end of the hundred
and fifty days the water had gone down,
4and on the seventeenth day of the sev-
enth month the ark came to rest on the
mountains of Ararat. 5The waters contin-
ued to recede until the tenth month, and
on the first day of the tenth month the
tops of the mountains became visible.

6After forty days Noah opened the win-
dow he had made in the ark 7and sent out
a raven, and it kept flying back and forth
until the water had dried up from the
earth. 8Then he sent out a dove to see if
the water had receded from the surface of
the ground. 9But the dove could find no
place to set its feet because there was wa-
ter over all the surface of the earth; so it
returned to Noah in the ark. He reached
out his hand and took the dove and
brought it back to himself in the ark. 10He
waited seven more days and again sent
out the dove from the ark. 11When the
dove returned to him in the evening, there
in its beak was a freshly plucked olive
leaf! Then Noah knew that the water had
receded from the earth. 12He waited seven
more days and sent the dove out again,
but this time it did not return to him.

13By the first day of the first month of
Noah's six hundred and first year, the wa-
ter had dried up from the earth. Noah then
removed the covering from the ark and
saw that the surface of the ground was
dry. 14By the twenty-seventh day of the
second month the earth was completely
dry.

15Then God said to Noah, 16"Come out
of the ark, you and your wife and your
sons and their wives. 17Bring out every
kind of living creature that is with you—
the birds, the animals, and all the crea-
tures that move along the ground—so
they can multiply on the earth and be
fruitful and increase in number upon it."

18So Noah came out, together with his
sons and his wife and his sons' wives.
19All the animals and all the creatures that
move along the ground and all the birds—
everything that moves on the earth—
came out of the ark, one kind after an-
other.

20Then Noah built an altar to the LORD
and, taking some of all the clean animals
and clean birds, he sacrificed burnt offer-
ings on it. 21The LORD smelled the pleasing
aroma and said in his heart: "Never again
will I curse the ground because of man,
even though[a] every inclination of his
heart is evil from childhood. And never
again will I destroy all living creatures, as
I have done.

22"As long as the earth endures,
seedtime and harvest,
cold and heat,
summer and winter,
day and night
will never cease."

God's Covenant With Noah

9 Then God blessed Noah and his sons,
saying to them, "Be fruitful and in-
crease in number and fill the earth. 2The
fear and dread of you will fall upon all the
beasts of the earth and all the birds of the
air, upon every creature that moves along
the ground, and upon all the fish of the
sea; they are given into your hands. 3Ev-
erything that lives and moves will be food
for you. Just as I gave you the green
plants, I now give you everything.

4"But you must not eat meat that has its
lifeblood still in it. 5And for your lifeblood
I will surely demand an accounting. I will
demand an accounting from every animal.
And from each man, too, I will demand an
accounting for the life of his fellow man.

6"Whoever sheds the blood of man,
by man shall his blood be shed;
for in the image of God
has God made man.

7As for you, be fruitful and increase in
number; multiply on the earth and in-
crease upon it."

8Then God said to Noah and to his sons
with him: 9"I now establish my covenant
with you and with your descendants after
you 10and with every living creature that
was with you—the birds, the livestock
and all the wild animals, all those that
came out of the ark with you—every liv-
ing creature on earth. 11I establish my cov-
enant with you: Never again will all life be
cut off by the waters of a flood; never
again will there be a flood to destroy the
earth."

12And God said, "This is the sign of the

[a]21 Or *man, for*

covenant I am making between me and you and every living creature with you, a covenant for all generations to come: 13I have set my rainbow in the clouds, and it will be the sign of the covenant between me and the earth. 14Whenever I bring clouds over the earth and the rainbow appears in the clouds, 15I will remember my covenant between me and you and all living creatures of every kind. Never again will the waters become a flood to destroy all life. 16Whenever the rainbow appears in the clouds, I will see it and remember the everlasting covenant between God and all living creatures of every kind on the earth."

17So God said to Noah, "This is the sign of the covenant I have established between me and all life on the earth."

The Sons of Noah

18The sons of Noah who came out of the ark were Shem, Ham and Japheth. (Ham was the father of Canaan.) 19These were the three sons of Noah, and from them came the people who were scattered over the earth.

20Noah, a man of the soil, proceeded[a] to plant a vineyard. 21When he drank some of its wine, he became drunk and lay uncovered inside his tent. 22Ham, the father of Canaan, saw his father's nakedness and told his two brothers outside. 23But Shem and Japheth took a garment and laid it across their shoulders; then they walked in backward and covered their father's nakedness. Their faces were turned the other way so that they would not see their father's nakedness.

24When Noah awoke from his wine and found out what his youngest son had done to him, 25he said,

"Cursed be Canaan!
The lowest of slaves
will he be to his brothers."

26He also said,

"Blessed be the LORD, the God of Shem!
May Canaan be the slave of Shem.[b]
27May God extend the territory of Japheth[c];
may Japheth live in the tents of Shem,
and may Canaan be his[d] slave."

28After the flood Noah lived 350 years. 29Altogether, Noah lived 950 years, and then he died.

The Table of Nations

10 This is the account of Shem, Ham and Japheth, Noah's sons, who themselves had sons after the flood.

The Japhethites

2The sons[e] of Japheth:
Gomer, Magog, Madai, Javan, Tubal, Meshech and Tiras.
3The sons of Gomer:
Ashkenaz, Riphath and Togarmah.
4The sons of Javan:
Elishah, Tarshish, the Kittim and the Rodanim.[f] 5(From these the maritime peoples spread out into their territories by their clans within their nations, each with its own language.)

The Hamites

6The sons of Ham:
Cush, Mizraim,[g] Put and Canaan.
7The sons of Cush:
Seba, Havilah, Sabtah, Raamah and Sabteca.
The sons of Raamah:
Sheba and Dedan.

8Cush was the father[h] of Nimrod, who grew to be a mighty warrior on the earth. 9He was a mighty hunter before the LORD; that is why it is said, "Like Nimrod, a mighty hunter before the LORD." 10The first centers of his kingdom were Babylon, Erech, Akkad and Calneh, in[i] Shinar.[j] 11From that land he went to Assyria, where he built Nineveh, Rehoboth Ir,[k] Calah 12and Resen, which is between Nineveh and Calah; that is the great city.

13Mizraim was the father of
the Ludites, Anamites, Lehabites,

[a]20 Or *soil, was the first* [b]26 Or *be his slave* [c]27 *Japheth* sounds like the Hebrew for *extend.* [d]27 Or *their* [e]2 *Sons* may mean *descendants* or *successors* or *nations*; also in verses 3, 4, 6, 7, 20-23, 29 and 31. [f]4 Some manuscripts of the Masoretic Text and Samaritan Pentateuch (see also Septuagint and 1 Chron. 1:7); most manuscripts of the Masoretic Text *Dodanim* [g]6 That is, Egypt; also in verse 13 [h]8 *Father* may mean *ancestor* or *predecessor* or *founder*; also in verses 13, 15, 24 and 26. [i]10 Or *Erech and Akkad—all of them in* [j]10 That is, Babylonia [k]11 Or *Nineveh with its city squares*

Naphtuhites, 14Pathrusites, Casluhites (from whom the Philistines
came) and Caphtorites.
15Canaan was the father of
Sidon his firstborn,[a] and of the
Hittites, 16Jebusites, Amorites,
Girgashites, 17Hivites, Arkites, Sinites, 18Arvadites, Zemarites and
Hamathites.

Later the Canaanite clans scattered
19and the borders of Canaan reached from
Sidon toward Gerar as far as Gaza, and
then toward Sodom, Gomorrah, Admah
and Zeboiim, as far as Lasha.

20These are the sons of Ham by their
clans and languages, in their territories
and nations.

The Semites

21Sons were also born to Shem, whose
older brother was[b] Japheth; Shem was
the ancestor of all the sons of Eber.

22The sons of Shem:
Elam, Asshur, Arphaxad, Lud and
Aram.
23The sons of Aram:
Uz, Hul, Gether and Meshech.[c]
24Arphaxad was the father of[d] Shelah,
and Shelah the father of Eber.
25Two sons were born to Eber:
One was named Peleg,[e] because
in his time the earth was divided;
his brother was named Joktan.
26Joktan was the father of
Almodad, Sheleph, Hazarmaveth,
Jerah, 27Hadoram, Uzal, Diklah,
28Obal, Abimael, Sheba, 29Ophir,
Havilah and Jobab. All these were
sons of Joktan.

30The region where they lived stretched
from Mesha toward Sephar, in the eastern
hill country.

31These are the sons of Shem by their
clans and languages, in their territories
and nations.

32These are the clans of Noah's sons,
according to their lines of descent, within
their nations. From these the nations
spread out over the earth after the flood.

The Tower of Babel

11 Now the whole world had one language and a common speech. 2As
men moved eastward,[f] they found a
plain in Shinar[g] and settled there.

3They said to each other, "Come, let's
make bricks and bake them thoroughly."
They used brick instead of stone, and tar
for mortar. 4Then they said, "Come, let us
build ourselves a city, with a tower that
reaches to the heavens, so that we may
make a name for ourselves and not be
scattered over the face of the whole
earth."

5But the LORD came down to see the city
and the tower that the men were building.
6The LORD said, "If as one people speaking
the same language they have begun to do
this, then nothing they plan to do will be
impossible for them. 7Come, let us go
down and confuse their language so they
will not understand each other."

8So the LORD scattered them from there
over all the earth, and they stopped building the city. 9That is why it was called Babel[h]—because there the LORD confused
the language of the whole world. From
there the LORD scattered them over the
face of the whole earth.

From Shem to Abram

10This is the account of Shem.

Two years after the flood, when Shem
was 100 years old, he became the father[i]
of Arphaxad. 11And after he became the
father of Arphaxad, Shem lived 500 years
and had other sons and daughters.

12When Arphaxad had lived 35 years,
he became the father of Shelah. 13And after he became the father of Shelah, Arphaxad lived 403 years and had other sons
and daughters.[j]

14When Shelah had lived 30 years, he
became the father of Eber. 15And after he
became the father of Eber, Shelah lived
403 years and had other sons and daughters.

16When Eber had lived 34 years, he became the father of Peleg. 17And after he
became the father of Peleg, Eber lived 430

[a]*15* Or *of the Sidonians, the foremost* [b]*21* Or *Shem, the older brother of* [c]*23* See Septuagint and 1 Chron. 1:17; Hebrew *Mash* [d]*24* Hebrew; Septuagint *father of Cainan, and Cainan was the father of* [e]*25 Peleg* means *division.* [f]*2* Or *from the east*; or *in the east* [g]*2* That is, Babylonia [h]*9* That is, Babylon; *Babel* sounds like the Hebrew for *confused.* [i]*10 Father* may mean *ancestor*; also in verses 11-25. [j]*12,13* Hebrew; Septuagint (see also Luke 3:35, 36 and note at Gen. 10:24) *35 years, he became the father of Cainan.* 13*And after he became the father of Cainan, Arphaxad lived 430 years and had other sons and daughters, and then he died. When Cainan had lived 130 years, he became the father of Shelah. And after he became the father of Shelah, Cainan lived 330 years and had other sons and daughters*

years and had other sons and daughters.
18When Peleg had lived 30 years, he became the father of Reu. 19And after he became the father of Reu, Peleg lived 209 years and had other sons and daughters.
20When Reu had lived 32 years, he became the father of Serug. 21And after he became the father of Serug, Reu lived 207 years and had other sons and daughters.
22When Serug had lived 30 years, he became the father of Nahor. 23And after he became the father of Nahor, Serug lived 200 years and had other sons and daughters.
24When Nahor had lived 29 years, he became the father of Terah. 25And after he became the father of Terah, Nahor lived 119 years and had other sons and daughters.
26After Terah had lived 70 years, he became the father of Abram, Nahor and Haran.

27This is the account of Terah.

Terah became the father of Abram, Nahor and Haran. And Haran became the father of Lot. 28While his father Terah was still alive, Haran died in Ur of the Chaldeans, in the land of his birth. 29Abram and Nahor both married. The name of Abram's wife was Sarai, and the name of Nahor's wife was Milcah; she was the daughter of Haran, the father of both Milcah and Iscah. 30Now Sarai was barren; she had no children.
31Terah took his son Abram, his grandson Lot son of Haran, and his daughter-in-law Sarai, the wife of his son Abram, and together they set out from Ur of the Chaldeans to go to Canaan. But when they came to Haran, they settled there.
32Terah lived 205 years, and he died in Haran.

The Call of Abram

12 The Lord had said to Abram, "Leave your country, your people and your father's household and go to the land I will show you.

2"I will make you into a great nation
and I will bless you;
I will make your name great,
and you will be a blessing.
3I will bless those who bless you,
and whoever curses you I will
curse;
and all peoples on earth
will be blessed through you."

4So Abram left, as the Lord had told him; and Lot went with him. Abram was seventy-five years old when he set out from Haran. 5He took his wife Sarai, his nephew Lot, all the possessions they had accumulated and the people they had acquired in Haran, and they set out for the land of Canaan, and they arrived there.
6Abram traveled through the land as far as the site of the great tree of Moreh at Shechem. At that time the Canaanites were in the land. 7The Lord appeared to Abram and said, "To your offspring[a] I will give this land." So he built an altar there to the Lord, who had appeared to him.
8From there he went on toward the hills east of Bethel and pitched his tent, with Bethel on the west and Ai on the east. There he built an altar to the Lord and called on the name of the Lord. 9Then Abram set out and continued toward the Negev.

Abram in Egypt

10Now there was a famine in the land, and Abram went down to Egypt to live there for a while because the famine was severe. 11As he was about to enter Egypt, he said to his wife Sarai, "I know what a beautiful woman you are. 12When the Egyptians see you, they will say, 'This is his wife.' Then they will kill me but will let you live. 13Say you are my sister, so that I will be treated well for your sake and my life will be spared because of you."
14When Abram came to Egypt, the Egyptians saw that she was a very beautiful woman. 15And when Pharaoh's officials saw her, they praised her to Pharaoh, and she was taken into his palace. 16He treated Abram well for her sake, and Abram acquired sheep and cattle, male and female donkeys, menservants and maidservants, and camels.
17But the Lord inflicted serious diseases on Pharaoh and his household because of Abram's wife Sarai. 18So Pharaoh summoned Abram. "What have you done to me?" he said. "Why didn't you tell me she was your wife? 19Why did you say, 'She is my sister,' so that I took her to be my wife? Now then, here is your wife. Take her and go!" 20Then Pharaoh gave orders

[a] 7 Or *seed*

about Abram to his men, and they sent him on his way, with his wife and everything he had.

Abram and Lot Separate

13 So Abram went up from Egypt to the Negev, with his wife and everything he had, and Lot went with him. [2]Abram had become very wealthy in livestock and in silver and gold.

[3]From the Negev he went from place to place until he came to Bethel, to the place between Bethel and Ai where his tent had been earlier [4]and where he had first built an altar. There Abram called on the name of the LORD.

[5]Now Lot, who was moving about with Abram, also had flocks and herds and tents. [6]But the land could not support them while they stayed together, for their possessions were so great that they were not able to stay together. [7]And quarreling arose between Abram's herdsmen and the herdsmen of Lot. The Canaanites and Perizzites were also living in the land at that time.

[8]So Abram said to Lot, "Let's not have any quarreling between you and me, or between your herdsmen and mine, for we are brothers. [9]Is not the whole land before you? Let's part company. If you go to the left, I'll go to the right; if you go to the right, I'll go to the left."

[10]Lot looked up and saw that the whole plain of the Jordan was well watered, like the garden of the LORD, like the land of Egypt, toward Zoar. (This was before the LORD destroyed Sodom and Gomorrah.) [11]So Lot chose for himself the whole plain of the Jordan and set out toward the east. The two men parted company: [12]Abram lived in the land of Canaan, while Lot lived among the cities of the plain and pitched his tents near Sodom. [13]Now the men of Sodom were wicked and were sinning greatly against the LORD.

[14]The LORD said to Abram after Lot had parted from him, "Lift up your eyes from where you are and look north and south, east and west. [15]All the land that you see I will give to you and your offspring[a] forever. [16]I will make your offspring like the dust of the earth, so that if anyone could count the dust, then your offspring could be counted. [17]Go, walk through the length and breadth of the land, for I am giving it to you."

[18]So Abram moved his tents and went to live near the great trees of Mamre at Hebron, where he built an altar to the LORD.

Abram Rescues Lot

14 At this time Amraphel king of Shinar,[b] Arioch king of Ellasar, Kedorlaomer king of Elam and Tidal king of Goiim [2]went to war against Bera king of Sodom, Birsha king of Gomorrah, Shinab king of Admah, Shemeber king of Zeboiim, and the king of Bela (that is, Zoar). [3]All these latter kings joined forces in the Valley of Siddim (the Salt Sea[c]). [4]For twelve years they had been subject to Kedorlaomer, but in the thirteenth year they rebelled.

[5]In the fourteenth year, Kedorlaomer and the kings allied with him went out and defeated the Rephaites in Ashteroth Karnaim, the Zuzites in Ham, the Emites in Shaveh Kiriathaim [6]and the Horites in the hill country of Seir, as far as El Paran near the desert. [7]Then they turned back and went to En Mishpat (that is, Kadesh), and they conquered the whole territory of the Amalekites, as well as the Amorites who were living in Hazazon Tamar.

[8]Then the king of Sodom, the king of Gomorrah, the king of Admah, the king of Zeboiim and the king of Bela (that is, Zoar) marched out and drew up their battle lines in the Valley of Siddim [9]against Kedorlaomer king of Elam, Tidal king of Goiim, Amraphel king of Shinar and Arioch king of Ellasar—four kings against five. [10]Now the Valley of Siddim was full of tar pits, and when the kings of Sodom and Gomorrah fled, some of the men fell into them and the rest fled to the hills. [11]The four kings seized all the goods of Sodom and Gomorrah and all their food; then they went away. [12]They also carried off Abram's nephew Lot and his possessions, since he was living in Sodom.

[13]One who had escaped came and reported this to Abram the Hebrew. Now Abram was living near the great trees of Mamre the Amorite, a brother[d] of Eshcol and Aner, all of whom were allied with Abram. [14]When Abram heard that his relative had been taken captive, he called out the 318 trained men born in his household and went in pursuit as far as Dan.

[a] *15* Or *seed*; also in verse 16 [b] *1* That is, Babylonia; also in verse 9 [c] *3* That is, the Dead Sea
[d] *13* Or *a relative*; or *an ally*

15During the night Abram divided his men
to attack them and he routed them, pursu-
ing them as far as Hobah, north of Damas-
cus. 16He recovered all the goods and
brought back his relative Lot and his pos-
sessions, together with the women and
the other people.

17After Abram returned from defeating
Kedorlaomer and the kings allied with
him, the king of Sodom came out to meet
him in the Valley of Shaveh (that is, the
King's Valley).

18Then Melchizedek king of Salem[a]
brought out bread and wine. He was priest
of God Most High, 19and he blessed
Abram, saying,

"Blessed be Abram by God Most High,
Creator[b] of heaven and earth.
20And blessed be[c] God Most High,
who delivered your enemies into
your hand."

Then Abram gave him a tenth of every-
thing.

21The king of Sodom said to Abram,
"Give me the people and keep the goods
for yourself."

22But Abram said to the king of Sodom,
"I have raised my hand to the LORD, God
Most High, Creator of heaven and earth,
and have taken an oath 23that I will accept
nothing belonging to you, not even a
thread or the thong of a sandal, so that
you will never be able to say, 'I made
Abram rich.' 24I will accept nothing but
what my men have eaten and the share
that belongs to the men who went with
me—to Aner, Eshcol and Mamre. Let
them have their share."

God's Covenant With Abram

15 After this, the word of the LORD
came to Abram in a vision:

"Do not be afraid, Abram.
I am your shield,[d]
your very great reward.[e]"

2But Abram said, "O Sovereign LORD,
what can you give me since I remain
childless and the one who will inherit[f]
my estate is Eliezer of Damascus?" 3And
Abram said, "You have given me no chil-
dren; so a servant in my household will be
my heir."

4Then the word of the LORD came to
him: "This man will not be your heir, but
a son coming from your own body will be
your heir." 5He took him outside and said,
"Look up at the heavens and count the
stars—if indeed you can count them."
Then he said to him, "So shall your off-
spring be."

6Abram believed the LORD, and he cred-
ited it to him as righteousness.

7He also said to him, "I am the LORD,
who brought you out of Ur of the Chalde-
ans to give you this land to take posses-
sion of it."

8But Abram said, "O Sovereign LORD,
how can I know that I will gain possession
of it?"

9So the LORD said to him, "Bring me a
heifer, a goat and a ram, each three years
old, along with a dove and a young pi-
geon."

10Abram brought all these to him, cut
them in two and arranged the halves op-
posite each other; the birds, however, he
did not cut in half. 11Then birds of prey
came down on the carcasses, but Abram
drove them away.

12As the sun was setting, Abram fell
into a deep sleep, and a thick and dreadful
darkness came over him. 13Then the LORD
said to him, "Know for certain that your
descendants will be strangers in a country
not their own, and they will be enslaved
and mistreated four hundred years. 14But
I will punish the nation they serve as
slaves, and afterward they will come out
with great possessions. 15You, however,
will go to your fathers in peace and be
buried at a good old age. 16In the fourth
generation your descendants will come
back here, for the sin of the Amorites has
not yet reached its full measure."

17When the sun had set and darkness
had fallen, a smoking firepot with a blaz-
ing torch appeared and passed between
the pieces. 18On that day the LORD made a
covenant with Abram and said, "To your
descendants I give this land, from the riv-
er[g] of Egypt to the great river, the Eu-
phrates— 19the land of the Kenites, Ken-
izzites, Kadmonites, 20Hittites, Perizzites,
Rephaites, 21Amorites, Canaanites, Girga-
shites and Jebusites."

[a]18 That is, Jerusalem [b]19 Or *Possessor*; also in verse 22 [c]20 Or *And praise be to* [d]1 Or *sovereign* [e]1 Or *shield; / your reward will be very great* [f]2 The meaning of the Hebrew for this phrase is uncertain. [g]18 Or *Wadi*

Hagar and Ishmael

16 Now Sarai, Abram's wife, had borne him no children. But she had an Egyptian maidservant named Hagar; [2]so she said to Abram, "The LORD has kept me from having children. Go, sleep with my maidservant; perhaps I can build a family through her."

Abram agreed to what Sarai said. [3]So after Abram had been living in Canaan ten years, Sarai his wife took her Egyptian maidservant Hagar and gave her to her husband to be his wife. [4]He slept with Hagar, and she conceived.

When she knew she was pregnant, she began to despise her mistress. [5]Then Sarai said to Abram, "You are responsible for the wrong I am suffering. I put my servant in your arms, and now that she knows she is pregnant, she despises me. May the LORD judge between you and me."

[6]"Your servant is in your hands," Abram said. "Do with her whatever you think best." Then Sarai mistreated Hagar; so she fled from her.

[7]The angel of the LORD found Hagar near a spring in the desert; it was the spring that is beside the road to Shur. [8]And he said, "Hagar, servant of Sarai, where have you come from, and where are you going?"

"I'm running away from my mistress Sarai," she answered.

[9]Then the angel of the LORD told her, "Go back to your mistress and submit to her." [10]The angel added, "I will so increase your descendants that they will be too numerous to count."

[11]The angel of the LORD also said to her:

"You are now with child
and you will have a son.
You shall name him Ishmael,[a]
for the LORD has heard of your
misery.
[12]He will be a wild donkey of a man;
his hand will be against everyone
and everyone's hand against him,
and he will live in hostility
toward[b] all his brothers."

[13]She gave this name to the LORD who spoke to her: "You are the God who sees me," for she said, "I have now seen[c] the One who sees me." [14]That is why the well was called Beer Lahai Roi[d]; it is still there, between Kadesh and Bered.

[15]So Hagar bore Abram a son, and Abram gave the name Ishmael to the son she had borne. [16]Abram was eighty-six years old when Hagar bore him Ishmael.

The Covenant of Circumcision

17 When Abram was ninety-nine years old, the LORD appeared to him and said, "I am God Almighty[e]; walk before me and be blameless. [2]I will confirm my covenant between me and you and will greatly increase your numbers."

[3]Abram fell facedown, and God said to him, [4]"As for me, this is my covenant with you: You will be the father of many nations. [5]No longer will you be called Abram[f]; your name will be Abraham,[g] for I have made you a father of many nations. [6]I will make you very fruitful; I will make nations of you, and kings will come from you. [7]I will establish my covenant as an everlasting covenant between me and you and your descendants after you for the generations to come, to be your God and the God of your descendants after you. [8]The whole land of Canaan, where you are now an alien, I will give as an everlasting possession to you and your descendants after you; and I will be their God."

[9]Then God said to Abraham, "As for you, you must keep my covenant, you and your descendants after you for the generations to come. [10]This is my covenant with you and your descendants after you, the covenant you are to keep: Every male among you shall be circumcised. [11]You are to undergo circumcision, and it will be the sign of the covenant between me and you. [12]For the generations to come every male among you who is eight days old must be circumcised, including those born in your household or bought with money from a foreigner—those who are not your offspring. [13]Whether born in your household or bought with your money, they must be circumcised. My covenant in your flesh is to be an everlasting covenant. [14]Any uncircumcised male, who has not been circumcised in the flesh, will be cut off from his people; he has broken my covenant."

[15]God also said to Abraham, "As for Sa-

[a]11 *Ishmael* means *God hears.* [b]12 Or *live to the east / of* [c]13 Or *seen the back of* [d]14 *Beer Lahai Roi* means *well of the Living One who sees me.* [e]1 Hebrew *El-Shaddai* [f]5 *Abram* means *exalted father.* [g]5 *Abraham* means *father of many.*

rai your wife, you are no longer to call her
Sarai; her name will be Sarah. 16I will bless
her and will surely give you a son by her.
I will bless her so that she will be the
mother of nations; kings of peoples will
come from her."
17Abraham fell facedown; he laughed
and said to himself, "Will a son be born to
a man a hundred years old? Will Sarah
bear a child at the age of ninety?" 18And
Abraham said to God, "If only Ishmael
might live under your blessing!"
19Then God said, "Yes, but your wife
Sarah will bear you a son, and you will call
him Isaac.[a] I will establish my covenant
with him as an everlasting covenant for
his descendants after him. 20And as for
Ishmael, I have heard you: I will surely
bless him; I will make him fruitful and will
greatly increase his numbers. He will be
the father of twelve rulers, and I will make
him into a great nation. 21But my covenant I will establish with Isaac, whom
Sarah will bear to you by this time next
year." 22When he had finished speaking
with Abraham, God went up from him.
23On that very day Abraham took his
son Ishmael and all those born in his
household or bought with his money, every male in his household, and circumcised them, as God told him. 24Abraham
was ninety-nine years old when he was
circumcised, 25and his son Ishmael was
thirteen; 26Abraham and his son Ishmael
were both circumcised on that same day.
27And every male in Abraham's household, including those born in his household or bought from a foreigner, was circumcised with him.

The Three Visitors

18 The Lord appeared to Abraham
near the great trees of Mamre
while he was sitting at the entrance to his
tent in the heat of the day. 2Abraham
looked up and saw three men standing
nearby. When he saw them, he hurried
from the entrance of his tent to meet them
and bowed low to the ground.
3He said, "If I have found favor in your
eyes, my lord,[b] do not pass your servant
by. 4Let a little water be brought, and then
you may all wash your feet and rest under
this tree. 5Let me get you something to
eat, so you can be refreshed and then go
on your way—now that you have come to
your servant."
"Very well," they answered, "do as you
say."
6So Abraham hurried into the tent to
Sarah. "Quick," he said, "get three seahs[c]
of fine flour and knead it and bake some
bread."
7Then he ran to the herd and selected a
choice, tender calf and gave it to a servant,
who hurried to prepare it. 8He then
brought some curds and milk and the calf
that had been prepared, and set these before them. While they ate, he stood near
them under a tree.
9"Where is your wife Sarah?" they
asked him.
"There, in the tent," he said.
10Then the Lord[d] said, "I will surely return to you about this time next year, and
Sarah your wife will have a son."
Now Sarah was listening at the entrance
to the tent, which was behind him.
11Abraham and Sarah were already old
and well advanced in years, and Sarah
was past the age of childbearing. 12So Sarah laughed to herself as she thought, "After I am worn out and my master[e] is old,
will I now have this pleasure?"
13Then the Lord said to Abraham, "Why
did Sarah laugh and say, 'Will I really have
a child, now that I am old?' 14Is anything
too hard for the Lord? I will return to you
at the appointed time next year and Sarah
will have a son."
15Sarah was afraid, so she lied and said,
"I did not laugh."
But he said, "Yes, you did laugh."

Abraham Pleads for Sodom

16When the men got up to leave, they
looked down toward Sodom, and Abraham walked along with them to see them
on their way. 17Then the Lord said, "Shall
I hide from Abraham what I am about to
do? 18Abraham will surely become a great
and powerful nation, and all nations on
earth will be blessed through him. 19For I
have chosen him, so that he will direct his
children and his household after him to
keep the way of the Lord by doing what is
right and just, so that the Lord will bring
about for Abraham what he has promised
him."
20Then the Lord said, "The outcry
against Sodom and Gomorrah is so great

[a] 19 *Isaac* means *he laughs.* [b] 3 Or *O Lord* [c] 6 That is, probably about 20 quarts (about 22 liters)
[d] 10 Hebrew *Then he* [e] 12 Or *husband*

and their sin so grievous 21that I will go
down and see if what they have done is as
bad as the outcry that has reached me. If
not, I will know."

22The men turned away and went to-
ward Sodom, but Abraham remained
standing before the LORD.[a] 23Then Abra-
ham approached him and said: "Will you
sweep away the righteous with the wick-
ed? 24What if there are fifty righteous peo-
ple in the city? Will you really sweep it
away and not spare[b] the place for the
sake of the fifty righteous people in it?
25Far be it from you to do such a thing—to
kill the righteous with the wicked, treating
the righteous and the wicked alike. Far be
it from you! Will not the Judge[c] of all the
earth do right?"

26The LORD said, "If I find fifty righteous
people in the city of Sodom, I will spare
the whole place for their sake."

27Then Abraham spoke up again: "Now
that I have been so bold as to speak to the
Lord, though I am nothing but dust and
ashes, 28what if the number of the right-
eous is five less than fifty? Will you de-
stroy the whole city because of five peo-
ple?"

"If I find forty-five there," he said, "I will
not destroy it."

29Once again he spoke to him, "What if
only forty are found there?"

He said, "For the sake of forty, I will not
do it."

30Then he said, "May the Lord not be
angry, but let me speak. What if only thir-
ty can be found there?"

He answered, "I will not do it if I find
thirty there."

31Abraham said, "Now that I have been
so bold as to speak to the Lord, what if
only twenty can be found there?"

He said, "For the sake of twenty, I will
not destroy it."

32Then he said, "May the Lord not be
angry, but let me speak just once more.
What if only ten can be found there?"

He answered, "For the sake of ten, I will
not destroy it."

33When the LORD had finished speaking
with Abraham, he left, and Abraham re-
turned home.

Sodom and Gomorrah Destroyed

19 The two angels arrived at Sodom in
the evening, and Lot was sitting in
the gateway of the city. When he saw
them, he got up to meet them and bowed
down with his face to the ground. 2"My
lords," he said, "please turn aside to your
servant's house. You can wash your feet
and spend the night and then go on your
way early in the morning."

"No," they answered, "we will spend
the night in the square."

3But he insisted so strongly that they
did go with him and entered his house. He
prepared a meal for them, baking bread
without yeast, and they ate. 4Before they
had gone to bed, all the men from every
part of the city of Sodom—both young
and old—surrounded the house. 5They
called to Lot, "Where are the men who
came to you tonight? Bring them out to us
so that we can have sex with them."

6Lot went outside to meet them and
shut the door behind him 7and said, "No,
my friends. Don't do this wicked thing.
8Look, I have two daughters who have
never slept with a man. Let me bring them
out to you, and you can do what you like
with them. But don't do anything to these
men, for they have come under the pro-
tection of my roof."

9"Get out of our way," they replied. And
they said, "This fellow came here as an
alien, and now he wants to play the judge!
We'll treat you worse than them." They
kept bringing pressure on Lot and moved
forward to break down the door.

10But the men inside reached out and
pulled Lot back into the house and shut
the door. 11Then they struck the men who
were at the door of the house, young and
old, with blindness so that they could not
find the door.

12The two men said to Lot, "Do you
have anyone else here—sons-in-law, sons
or daughters, or anyone else in the city
who belongs to you? Get them out of here,
13because we are going to destroy this
place. The outcry to the LORD against its
people is so great that he has sent us to
destroy it."

14So Lot went out and spoke to his sons-
in-law, who were pledged to marry[d] his
daughters. He said, "Hurry and get out of
this place, because the LORD is about to
destroy the city!" But his sons-in-law
thought he was joking.

15With the coming of dawn, the angels
urged Lot, saying, "Hurry! Take your wife

[a]22 Masoretic Text; an ancient Hebrew scribal tradition *but the LORD remained standing before Abraham*
[b]24 Or *forgive*; also in verse 26 [c]25 Or *Ruler* [d]14 Or *were married to*

and your two daughters who are here, or
you will be swept away when the city is
punished."
16When he hesitated, the men grasped
his hand and the hands of his wife and of
his two daughters and led them safely out
of the city, for the LORD was merciful to
them. 17As soon as they had brought them
out, one of them said, "Flee for your lives!
Don't look back, and don't stop anywhere
in the plain! Flee to the mountains or you
will be swept away!"
18But Lot said to them, "No, my lords,[a]
please! 19Your[b] servant has found favor
in your[b] eyes, and you[b] have shown
great kindness to me in sparing my life.
But I can't flee to the mountains; this disaster will overtake me, and I'll die.
20Look, here is a town near enough to run
to, and it is small. Let me flee to it—it is
very small, isn't it? Then my life will be
spared."
21He said to him, "Very well, I will grant
this request too; I will not overthrow the
town you speak of. 22But flee there quickly, because I cannot do anything until you
reach it." (That is why the town was called
Zoar.[c])
23By the time Lot reached Zoar, the sun
had risen over the land. 24Then the LORD
rained down burning sulfur on Sodom
and Gomorrah—from the LORD out of the
heavens. 25Thus he overthrew those cities
and the entire plain, including all those
living in the cities—and also the vegetation in the land. 26But Lot's wife looked
back, and she became a pillar of salt.
27Early the next morning Abraham got
up and returned to the place where he had
stood before the LORD. 28He looked down
toward Sodom and Gomorrah, toward all
the land of the plain, and he saw dense
smoke rising from the land, like smoke
from a furnace.
29So when God destroyed the cities of
the plain, he remembered Abraham, and
he brought Lot out of the catastrophe that
overthrew the cities where Lot had lived.

Lot and His Daughters

30Lot and his two daughters left Zoar
and settled in the mountains, for he was
afraid to stay in Zoar. He and his two
daughters lived in a cave. 31One day the
older daughter said to the younger, "Our
father is old, and there is no man around
here to lie with us, as is the custom all
over the earth. 32Let's get our father to
drink wine and then lie with him and preserve our family line through our father."
33That night they got their father to
drink wine, and the older daughter went
in and lay with him. He was not aware of
it when she lay down or when she got up.
34The next day the older daughter said
to the younger, "Last night I lay with my
father. Let's get him to drink wine again
tonight, and you go in and lie with him so
we can preserve our family line through
our father." 35So they got their father to
drink wine that night also, and the younger daughter went and lay with him.
Again he was not aware of it when she lay
down or when she got up.
36So both of Lot's daughters became
pregnant by their father. 37The older
daughter had a son, and she named him
Moab[d]; he is the father of the Moabites of
today. 38The younger daughter also had a
son, and she named him Ben-Ammi[e]; he
is the father of the Ammonites of today.

Abraham and Abimelech

20 Now Abraham moved on from
there into the region of the Negev
and lived between Kadesh and Shur. For a
while he stayed in Gerar, 2and there Abraham said of his wife Sarah, "She is my sister." Then Abimelech king of Gerar sent
for Sarah and took her.
3But God came to Abimelech in a dream
one night and said to him, "You are as
good as dead because of the woman you
have taken; she is a married woman."
4Now Abimelech had not gone near her,
so he said, "Lord, will you destroy an innocent nation? 5Did he not say to me, 'She
is my sister,' and didn't she also say, 'He
is my brother'? I have done this with a
clear conscience and clean hands."
6Then God said to him in the dream,
"Yes, I know you did this with a clear conscience, and so I have kept you from sinning against me. That is why I did not let
you touch her. 7Now return the man's
wife, for he is a prophet, and he will pray
for you and you will live. But if you do not
return her, you may be sure that you and
all yours will die."
8Early the next morning Abimelech
summoned all his officials, and when he
told them all that had happened, they

[a]18 Or *No, Lord*; or *No, my lord* [b]19 The Hebrew is singular. [c]22 *Zoar* means *small.*
[d]37 *Moab* sounds like the Hebrew for *from father.* [e]38 *Ben-Ammi* means *son of my people.*

were very much afraid. 9Then Abimelech called Abraham in and said, "What have you done to us? How have I wronged you that you have brought such great guilt upon me and my kingdom? You have done things to me that should not be done." 10And Abimelech asked Abraham, "What was your reason for doing this?"

11Abraham replied, "I said to myself, 'There is surely no fear of God in this place, and they will kill me because of my wife.' 12Besides, she really is my sister, the daughter of my father though not of my mother; and she became my wife. 13And when God had me wander from my father's household, I said to her, 'This is how you can show your love to me: Everywhere we go, say of me, "He is my brother." ' "

14Then Abimelech brought sheep and cattle and male and female slaves and gave them to Abraham, and he returned Sarah his wife to him. 15And Abimelech said, "My land is before you; live wherever you like."

16To Sarah he said, "I am giving your brother a thousand shekels[a] of silver. This is to cover the offense against you before all who are with you; you are completely vindicated."

17Then Abraham prayed to God, and God healed Abimelech, his wife and his slave girls so they could have children again, 18for the LORD had closed up every womb in Abimelech's household because of Abraham's wife Sarah.

The Birth of Isaac

21 Now the LORD was gracious to Sarah as he had said, and the LORD did for Sarah what he had promised. 2Sarah became pregnant and bore a son to Abraham in his old age, at the very time God had promised him. 3Abraham gave the name Isaac[b] to the son Sarah bore him. 4When his son Isaac was eight days old, Abraham circumcised him, as God commanded him. 5Abraham was a hundred years old when his son Isaac was born to him.

6Sarah said, "God has brought me laughter, and everyone who hears about this will laugh with me." 7And she added, "Who would have said to Abraham that Sarah would nurse children? Yet I have borne him a son in his old age."

Hagar and Ishmael Sent Away

8The child grew and was weaned, and on the day Isaac was weaned Abraham held a great feast. 9But Sarah saw that the son whom Hagar the Egyptian had borne to Abraham was mocking, 10and she said to Abraham, "Get rid of that slave woman and her son, for that slave woman's son will never share in the inheritance with my son Isaac."

11The matter distressed Abraham greatly because it concerned his son. 12But God said to him, "Do not be so distressed about the boy and your maidservant. Listen to whatever Sarah tells you, because it is through Isaac that your offspring[c] will be reckoned. 13I will make the son of the maidservant into a nation also, because he is your offspring."

14Early the next morning Abraham took some food and a skin of water and gave them to Hagar. He set them on her shoulders and then sent her off with the boy. She went on her way and wandered in the desert of Beersheba.

15When the water in the skin was gone, she put the boy under one of the bushes. 16Then she went off and sat down nearby, about a bowshot away, for she thought, "I cannot watch the boy die." And as she sat there nearby, she[d] began to sob.

17God heard the boy crying, and the angel of God called to Hagar from heaven and said to her, "What is the matter, Hagar? Do not be afraid; God has heard the boy crying as he lies there. 18Lift the boy up and take him by the hand, for I will make him into a great nation."

19Then God opened her eyes and she saw a well of water. So she went and filled the skin with water and gave the boy a drink.

20God was with the boy as he grew up. He lived in the desert and became an archer. 21While he was living in the Desert of Paran, his mother got a wife for him from Egypt.

The Treaty at Beersheba

22At that time Abimelech and Phicol the commander of his forces said to Abraham, "God is with you in everything you do. 23Now swear to me here before God that you will not deal falsely with me or my children or my descendants. Show to me

[a] 16 That is, about 25 pounds (about 11.5 kilograms)
[b] 3 *Isaac* means *he laughs.*
[c] 12 Or *seed*
[d] 16 Hebrew; Septuagint *the child*

and the country where you are living as an
alien the same kindness I have shown to
you."
24Abraham said, "I swear it."
25Then Abraham complained to Abime-
lech about a well of water that Abime-
lech's servants had seized. 26But Abime-
lech said, "I don't know who has done
this. You did not tell me, and I heard
about it only today."
27So Abraham brought sheep and cattle
and gave them to Abimelech, and the two
men made a treaty. 28Abraham set apart
seven ewe lambs from the flock, 29and
Abimelech asked Abraham, "What is the
meaning of these seven ewe lambs you
have set apart by themselves?"
30He replied, "Accept these seven lambs
from my hand as a witness that I dug this
well."
31So that place was called Beersheba,[a]
because the two men swore an oath there.
32After the treaty had been made at Be-
ersheba, Abimelech and Phicol the com-
mander of his forces returned to the land
of the Philistines. 33Abraham planted a
tamarisk tree in Beersheba, and there he
called upon the name of the LORD, the
Eternal God. 34And Abraham stayed in the
land of the Philistines for a long time.

Abraham Tested

22 Some time later God tested Abra-
ham. He said to him, "Abraham!"
"Here I am," he replied.
2Then God said, "Take your son, your
only son, Isaac, whom you love, and go to
the region of Moriah. Sacrifice him there
as a burnt offering on one of the moun-
tains I will tell you about."
3Early the next morning Abraham got
up and saddled his donkey. He took with
him two of his servants and his son Isaac.
When he had cut enough wood for the
burnt offering, he set out for the place God
had told him about. 4On the third day
Abraham looked up and saw the place in
the distance. 5He said to his servants,
"Stay here with the donkey while I and the
boy go over there. We will worship and
then we will come back to you."
6Abraham took the wood for the burnt
offering and placed it on his son Isaac, and
he himself carried the fire and the knife.
As the two of them went on together,
7Isaac spoke up and said to his father
Abraham, "Father?"
"Yes, my son?" Abraham replied.
"The fire and wood are here," Isaac
said, "but where is the lamb for the burnt
offering?"
8Abraham answered, "God himself will
provide the lamb for the burnt offering,
my son." And the two of them went on to-
gether.
9When they reached the place God had
told him about, Abraham built an altar
there and arranged the wood on it. He
bound his son Isaac and laid him on the
altar, on top of the wood. 10Then he
reached out his hand and took the knife to
slay his son. 11But the angel of the LORD
called out to him from heaven, "Abraham!
Abraham!"
"Here I am," he replied.
12"Do not lay a hand on the boy," he
said. "Do not do anything to him. Now I
know that you fear God, because you have
not withheld from me your son, your only
son."
13Abraham looked up and there in a
thicket he saw a ram[b] caught by its
horns. He went over and took the ram and
sacrificed it as a burnt offering instead of
his son. 14So Abraham called that place
The LORD Will Provide. And to this day it
is said, "On the mountain of the LORD it
will be provided."
15The angel of the LORD called to Abra-
ham from heaven a second time 16and
said, "I swear by myself, declares the
LORD, that because you have done this and
have not withheld your son, your only
son, 17I will surely bless you and make
your descendants as numerous as the
stars in the sky and as the sand on the sea-
shore. Your descendants will take posses-
sion of the cities of their enemies, 18and
through your offspring[c] all nations on
earth will be blessed, because you have
obeyed me."
19Then Abraham returned to his ser-
vants, and they set off together for Beer-
sheba. And Abraham stayed in Beersheba.

Nahor's Sons

20Some time later Abraham was told,
"Milcah is also a mother; she has borne
sons to your brother Nahor: 21Uz the first-
born, Buz his brother, Kemuel (the father

[a]31 *Beersheba* can mean *well of seven* or *well of the oath.* [b]13 Many manuscripts of the Masoretic Text, Samaritan Pentateuch, Septuagint and Syriac; most manuscripts of the Masoretic Text *a ram behind him* [c]18 Or *seed*

of Aram), 22Kesed, Hazo, Pildash, Jidlaph
and Bethuel." 23Bethuel became the father
of Rebekah. Milcah bore these eight sons
to Abraham's brother Nahor. 24His concu-
bine, whose name was Reumah, also had
sons: Tebah, Gaham, Tahash and Maacah.

The Death of Sarah

23 Sarah lived to be a hundred and
twenty-seven years old. 2She died
at Kiriath Arba (that is, Hebron) in the
land of Canaan, and Abraham went to
mourn for Sarah and to weep over her.
3Then Abraham rose from beside his
dead wife and spoke to the Hittites.[a] He
said, 4"I am an alien and a stranger among
you. Sell me some property for a burial
site here so I can bury my dead."
5The Hittites replied to Abraham, 6"Sir,
listen to us. You are a mighty prince
among us. Bury your dead in the choicest
of our tombs. None of us will refuse you
his tomb for burying your dead."
7Then Abraham rose and bowed down
before the people of the land, the Hittites.
8He said to them, "If you are willing to let
me bury my dead, then listen to me and
intercede with Ephron son of Zohar on my
behalf 9so he will sell me the cave of
Machpelah, which belongs to him and is
at the end of his field. Ask him to sell it to
me for the full price as a burial site among
you."
10Ephron the Hittite was sitting among
his people and he replied to Abraham in
the hearing of all the Hittites who had
come to the gate of his city. 11"No, my
lord," he said. "Listen to me; I give[b] you
the field, and I give[b] you the cave that is
in it. I give[b] it to you in the presence of
my people. Bury your dead."
12Again Abraham bowed down before
the people of the land 13and he said to
Ephron in their hearing, "Listen to me, if
you will. I will pay the price of the field.
Accept it from me so I can bury my dead
there."
14Ephron answered Abraham, 15"Listen
to me, my lord; the land is worth four hun-
dred shekels[c] of silver, but what is that
between me and you? Bury your dead."
16Abraham agreed to Ephron's terms
and weighed out for him the price he had
named in the hearing of the Hittites: four
hundred shekels of silver, according to the
weight current among the merchants.
17So Ephron's field in Machpelah near
Mamre—both the field and the cave in it,
and all the trees within the borders of the
field—was deeded 18to Abraham as his
property in the presence of all the Hittites
who had come to the gate of the city. 19Af-
terward Abraham buried his wife Sarah in
the cave in the field of Machpelah near
Mamre (which is at Hebron) in the land of
Canaan. 20So the field and the cave in it
were deeded to Abraham by the Hittites as
a burial site.

Isaac and Rebekah

24 Abraham was now old and well ad-
vanced in years, and the LORD had
blessed him in every way. 2He said to the
chief[d] servant in his household, the one
in charge of all that he had, "Put your
hand under my thigh. 3I want you to
swear by the LORD, the God of heaven and
the God of earth, that you will not get a
wife for my son from the daughters of the
Canaanites, among whom I am living,
4but will go to my country and my own
relatives and get a wife for my son Isaac."
5The servant asked him, "What if the
woman is unwilling to come back with me
to this land? Shall I then take your son
back to the country you came from?"
6"Make sure that you do not take my
son back there," Abraham said. 7"The
LORD, the God of heaven, who brought me
out of my father's household and my na-
tive land and who spoke to me and prom-
ised me on oath, saying, 'To your off-
spring[e] I will give this land'—he will
send his angel before you so that you can
get a wife for my son from there. 8If the
woman is unwilling to come back with
you, then you will be released from this
oath of mine. Only do not take my son
back there." 9So the servant put his hand
under the thigh of his master Abraham
and swore an oath to him concerning this
matter.
10Then the servant took ten of his mas-
ter's camels and left, taking with him all
kinds of good things from his master. He
set out for Aram Naharaim[f] and made
his way to the town of Nahor. 11He had
the camels kneel down near the well out-
side the town; it was toward evening, the
time the women go out to draw water.
12Then he prayed, "O LORD, God of my
master Abraham, give me success today,

[a] 3 Or *the sons of Heth*; also in verses 5, 7, 10, 16, 18 and 20 [b] 11 Or *sell* [c] 15 That is, about 10 pounds (about 4.5 kilograms) [d] 2 Or *oldest* [e] 7 Or *seed* [f] 10 That is, Northwest Mesopotamia

and show kindness to my master Abraham. 13See, I am standing beside this
spring, and the daughters of the towns-
people are coming out to draw water.
14May it be that when I say to a girl,
'Please let down your jar that I may have
a drink,' and she says, 'Drink, and I'll wa-
ter your camels too'—let her be the one
you have chosen for your servant Isaac.
By this I will know that you have shown
kindness to my master."

15Before he had finished praying, Re-
bekah came out with her jar on her shoul-
der. She was the daughter of Bethuel son
of Milcah, who was the wife of Abraham's
brother Nahor. 16The girl was very beauti-
ful, a virgin; no man had ever lain with
her. She went down to the spring, filled
her jar and came up again.

17The servant hurried to meet her and
said, "Please give me a little water from
your jar."

18"Drink, my lord," she said, and quick-
ly lowered the jar to her hands and gave
him a drink.

19After she had given him a drink, she
said, "I'll draw water for your camels too,
until they have finished drinking." 20So
she quickly emptied her jar into the
trough, ran back to the well to draw more
water, and drew enough for all his camels.
21Without saying a word, the man
watched her closely to learn whether or
not the LORD had made his journey suc-
cessful.

22When the camels had finished drink-
ing, the man took out a gold nose ring
weighing a beka[a] and two gold bracelets
weighing ten shekels.[b] 23Then he asked,
"Whose daughter are you? Please tell me,
is there room in your father's house for us
to spend the night?"

24She answered him, "I am the daughter
of Bethuel, the son that Milcah bore to Na-
hor." 25And she added, "We have plenty of
straw and fodder, as well as room for you
to spend the night."

26Then the man bowed down and wor-
shiped the LORD, 27saying, "Praise be to
the LORD, the God of my master Abraham,
who has not abandoned his kindness and
faithfulness to my master. As for me, the
LORD has led me on the journey to the
house of my master's relatives."

28The girl ran and told her mother's
household about these things. 29Now Re-
bekah had a brother named Laban, and he
hurried out to the man at the spring. 30As
soon as he had seen the nose ring, and the
bracelets on his sister's arms, and had
heard Rebekah tell what the man said to
her, he went out to the man and found
him standing by the camels near the
spring. 31"Come, you who are blessed by
the LORD," he said. "Why are you standing
out here? I have prepared the house and a
place for the camels."

32So the man went to the house, and the
camels were unloaded. Straw and fodder
were brought for the camels, and water
for him and his men to wash their feet.
33Then food was set before him, but he
said, "I will not eat until I have told you
what I have to say."

"Then tell us," ⌊Laban⌋ said.

34So he said, "I am Abraham's servant.
35The LORD has blessed my master abun-
dantly, and he has become wealthy. He
has given him sheep and cattle, silver and
gold, menservants and maidservants, and
camels and donkeys. 36My master's wife
Sarah has borne him a son in her[c] old
age, and he has given him everything he
owns. 37And my master made me swear
an oath, and said, 'You must not get a wife
for my son from the daughters of the Ca-
naanites, in whose land I live, 38but go to
my father's family and to my own clan,
and get a wife for my son.'

39"Then I asked my master, 'What if the
woman will not come back with me?'

40"He replied, 'The LORD, before whom
I have walked, will send his angel with
you and make your journey a success, so
that you can get a wife for my son from
my own clan and from my father's family.
41Then, when you go to my clan, you will
be released from my oath even if they re-
fuse to give her to you—you will be re-
leased from my oath.'

42"When I came to the spring today, I
said, 'O LORD, God of my master Abra-
ham, if you will, please grant success to
the journey on which I have come. 43See,
I am standing beside this spring; if a maid-
en comes out to draw water and I say to
her, "Please let me drink a little water
from your jar," 44and if she says to me,
"Drink, and I'll draw water for your cam-
els too," let her be the one the LORD has
chosen for my master's son.'

45"Before I finished praying in my heart,

[a]22 That is, about 1/5 ounce (about 5.5 grams)
[b]22 That is, about 4 ounces (about 110 grams)
[c]36 Or *his*

Rebekah came out, with her jar on her shoulder. She went down to the spring and drew water, and I said to her, 'Please give me a drink.'

46"She quickly lowered her jar from her shoulder and said, 'Drink, and I'll water your camels too.' So I drank, and she watered the camels also.

47"I asked her, 'Whose daughter are you?'

"She said, 'The daughter of Bethuel son of Nahor, whom Milcah bore to him.'

"Then I put the ring in her nose and the bracelets on her arms, 48and I bowed down and worshiped the LORD. I praised the LORD, the God of my master Abraham, who had led me on the right road to get the granddaughter of my master's brother for his son. 49Now if you will show kindness and faithfulness to my master, tell me; and if not, tell me, so I may know which way to turn."

50Laban and Bethuel answered, "This is from the LORD; we can say nothing to you one way or the other. 51Here is Rebekah; take her and go, and let her become the wife of your master's son, as the LORD has directed."

52When Abraham's servant heard what they said, he bowed down to the ground before the LORD. 53Then the servant brought out gold and silver jewelry and articles of clothing and gave them to Rebekah; he also gave costly gifts to her brother and to her mother. 54Then he and the men who were with him ate and drank and spent the night there.

When they got up the next morning, he said, "Send me on my way to my master."

55But her brother and her mother replied, "Let the girl remain with us ten days or so; then you[a] may go."

56But he said to them, "Do not detain me, now that the LORD has granted success to my journey. Send me on my way so I may go to my master."

57Then they said, "Let's call the girl and ask her about it." 58So they called Rebekah and asked her, "Will you go with this man?"

"I will go," she said.

59So they sent their sister Rebekah on her way, along with her nurse and Abraham's servant and his men. 60And they blessed Rebekah and said to her,

"Our sister, may you increase
to thousands upon thousands;
may your offspring possess
the gates of their enemies."

61Then Rebekah and her maids got ready and mounted their camels and went back with the man. So the servant took Rebekah and left.

62Now Isaac had come from Beer Lahai Roi, for he was living in the Negev. 63He went out to the field one evening to meditate,[b] and as he looked up, he saw camels approaching. 64Rebekah also looked up and saw Isaac. She got down from her camel 65and asked the servant, "Who is that man in the field coming to meet us?"

"He is my master," the servant answered. So she took her veil and covered herself.

66Then the servant told Isaac all he had done. 67Isaac brought her into the tent of his mother Sarah, and he married Rebekah. So she became his wife, and he loved her; and Isaac was comforted after his mother's death.

The Death of Abraham

25 Abraham took[c] another wife, whose name was Keturah. 2She bore him Zimran, Jokshan, Medan, Midian, Ishbak and Shuah. 3Jokshan was the father of Sheba and Dedan; the descendants of Dedan were the Asshurites, the Letushites and the Leummites. 4The sons of Midian were Ephah, Epher, Hanoch, Abida and Eldaah. All these were descendants of Keturah.

5Abraham left everything he owned to Isaac. 6But while he was still living, he gave gifts to the sons of his concubines and sent them away from his son Isaac to the land of the east.

7Altogether, Abraham lived a hundred and seventy-five years. 8Then Abraham breathed his last and died at a good old age, an old man and full of years; and he was gathered to his people. 9His sons Isaac and Ishmael buried him in the cave of Machpelah near Mamre, in the field of Ephron son of Zohar the Hittite, 10the field Abraham had bought from the Hittites.[d] There Abraham was buried with his wife Sarah. 11After Abraham's death, God blessed his son Isaac, who then lived near Beer Lahai Roi.

[a] 55 Or *she* [b] 63 The meaning of the Hebrew for this word is uncertain. [c] 1 Or *had taken*
[d] 10 Or *the sons of Heth*

Ishmael's Sons

12This is the account of Abraham's son
Ishmael, whom Sarah's maidservant, Ha-
gar the Egyptian, bore to Abraham.

13These are the names of the sons of
Ishmael, listed in the order of their birth:
Nebaioth the firstborn of Ishmael, Kedar,
Adbeel, Mibsam, 14Mishma, Dumah, Mas-
sa, 15Hadad, Tema, Jetur, Naphish and
Kedemah. 16These were the sons of Ish-
mael, and these are the names of the
twelve tribal rulers according to their set-
tlements and camps. 17Altogether, Ishma-
el lived a hundred and thirty-seven years.
He breathed his last and died, and he was
gathered to his people. 18His descendants
settled in the area from Havilah to Shur,
near the border of Egypt, as you go toward
Asshur. And they lived in hostility to-
ward[a] all their brothers.

Jacob and Esau

19This is the account of Abraham's son
Isaac.

Abraham became the father of Isaac,
20and Isaac was forty years old when he
married Rebekah daughter of Bethuel the
Aramean from Paddan Aram[b] and sister
of Laban the Aramean.

21Isaac prayed to the LORD on behalf of
his wife, because she was barren. The
LORD answered his prayer, and his wife
Rebekah became pregnant. 22The babies
jostled each other within her, and she
said, "Why is this happening to me?" So
she went to inquire of the LORD.

23The LORD said to her,

"Two nations are in your womb,
and two peoples from within you
will be separated;
one people will be stronger than the
other,
and the older will serve the
younger."

24When the time came for her to give
birth, there were twin boys in her womb.
25The first to come out was red, and his
whole body was like a hairy garment; so
they named him Esau.[c] 26After this, his
brother came out, with his hand grasping
Esau's heel; so he was named Jacob.[d]
Isaac was sixty years old when Rebekah
gave birth to them.

27The boys grew up, and Esau became
a skillful hunter, a man of the open coun-
try, while Jacob was a quiet man, staying
among the tents. 28Isaac, who had a taste
for wild game, loved Esau, but Rebekah
loved Jacob.

29Once when Jacob was cooking some
stew, Esau came in from the open coun-
try, famished. 30He said to Jacob, "Quick,
let me have some of that red stew! I'm
famished!" (That is why he was also
called Edom.[e])

31Jacob replied, "First sell me your
birthright."

32"Look, I am about to die," Esau said.
"What good is the birthright to me?"

33But Jacob said, "Swear to me first." So
he swore an oath to him, selling his birth-
right to Jacob.

34Then Jacob gave Esau some bread
and some lentil stew. He ate and drank,
and then got up and left.

So Esau despised his birthright.

Isaac and Abimelech

26 Now there was a famine in the
land—besides the earlier famine of
Abraham's time—and Isaac went to
Abimelech king of the Philistines in Gerar.
2The LORD appeared to Isaac and said, "Do
not go down to Egypt; live in the land
where I tell you to live. 3Stay in this land
for a while, and I will be with you and will
bless you. For to you and your descen-
dants I will give all these lands and will
confirm the oath I swore to your father
Abraham. 4I will make your descendants
as numerous as the stars in the sky and
will give them all these lands, and through
your offspring[f] all nations on earth will
be blessed, 5because Abraham obeyed me
and kept my requirements, my com-
mands, my decrees and my laws." 6So
Isaac stayed in Gerar.

7When the men of that place asked him
about his wife, he said, "She is my sister,"
because he was afraid to say, "She is my
wife." He thought, "The men of this place
might kill me on account of Rebekah, be-
cause she is beautiful."

8When Isaac had been there a long
time, Abimelech king of the Philistines
looked down from a window and saw
Isaac caressing his wife Rebekah. 9So
Abimelech summoned Isaac and said,

[a] *18* Or *lived to the east of* [b] *20* That is, Northwest Mesopotamia [c] *25 Esau* may mean *hairy*; he was also called Edom, which means *red*. [d] *26 Jacob* means *he grasps the heel* (figuratively, *he deceives*). [e] *30 Edom* means *red*. [f] *4* Or *seed*

"She is really your wife! Why did you say,
'She is my sister'?"
Isaac answered him, "Because I thought
I might lose my life on account of her."
10Then Abimelech said, "What is this
you have done to us? One of the men
might well have slept with your wife, and
you would have brought guilt upon us."
11So Abimelech gave orders to all the
people: "Anyone who molests this man or
his wife shall surely be put to death."
12Isaac planted crops in that land and
the same year reaped a hundredfold, be-
cause the LORD blessed him. 13The man
became rich, and his wealth continued to
grow until he became very wealthy. 14He
had so many flocks and herds and ser-
vants that the Philistines envied him. 15So
all the wells that his father's servants had
dug in the time of his father Abraham, the
Philistines stopped up, filling them with
earth.
16Then Abimelech said to Isaac, "Move
away from us; you have become too pow-
erful for us."
17So Isaac moved away from there and
encamped in the Valley of Gerar and set-
tled there. 18Isaac reopened the wells that
had been dug in the time of his father
Abraham, which the Philistines had
stopped up after Abraham died, and he
gave them the same names his father had
given them.
19Isaac's servants dug in the valley and
discovered a well of fresh water there.
20But the herdsmen of Gerar quarreled
with Isaac's herdsmen and said, "The wa-
ter is ours!" So he named the well Esek,[a]
because they disputed with him. 21Then
they dug another well, but they quarreled
over that one also; so he named it Sit-
nah.[b] 22He moved on from there and dug
another well, and no one quarreled over
it. He named it Rehoboth,[c] saying, "Now
the LORD has given us room and we will
flourish in the land."
23From there he went up to Beersheba.
24That night the LORD appeared to him and
said, "I am the God of your father Abra-
ham. Do not be afraid, for I am with you;
I will bless you and will increase the num-
ber of your descendants for the sake of my
servant Abraham."
25Isaac built an altar there and called on
the name of the LORD. There he pitched
his tent, and there his servants dug a well.
26Meanwhile, Abimelech had come to
him from Gerar, with Ahuzzath his per-
sonal adviser and Phicol the commander
of his forces. 27Isaac asked them, "Why
have you come to me, since you were hos-
tile to me and sent me away?"
28They answered, "We saw clearly that
the LORD was with you; so we said, 'There
ought to be a sworn agreement between
us'—between us and you. Let us make a
treaty with you 29that you will do us no
harm, just as we did not molest you but
always treated you well and sent you
away in peace. And now you are blessed
by the LORD."
30Isaac then made a feast for them, and
they ate and drank. 31Early the next morn-
ing the men swore an oath to each other.
Then Isaac sent them on their way, and
they left him in peace.
32That day Isaac's servants came and
told him about the well they had dug.
They said, "We've found water!" 33He
called it Shibah,[d] and to this day the
name of the town has been Beersheba.[e]
34When Esau was forty years old, he
married Judith daughter of Beeri the Hit-
tite, and also Basemath daughter of Elon
the Hittite. 35They were a source of grief to
Isaac and Rebekah.

Jacob Gets Isaac's Blessing

27 When Isaac was old and his eyes
were so weak that he could no
longer see, he called for Esau his older son
and said to him, "My son."
"Here I am," he answered.
2Isaac said, "I am now an old man and
don't know the day of my death. 3Now
then, get your weapons—your quiver and
bow—and go out to the open country to
hunt some wild game for me. 4Prepare me
the kind of tasty food I like and bring it to
me to eat, so that I may give you my bless-
ing before I die."
5Now Rebekah was listening as Isaac
spoke to his son Esau. When Esau left for
the open country to hunt game and bring
it back, 6Rebekah said to her son Jacob,
"Look, I overheard your father say to your
brother Esau, 7'Bring me some game and
prepare me some tasty food to eat, so that
I may give you my blessing in the pres-
ence of the LORD before I die.' 8Now, my
son, listen carefully and do what I tell you:
9Go out to the flock and bring me two

[a]20 *Esek* means *dispute.* [b]21 *Sitnah* means *opposition.* [c]22 *Rehoboth* means *room.* [d]33 *Shibah* can mean *oath* or *seven.* [e]33 *Beersheba* can mean *well of the oath* or *well of seven.*

choice young goats, so I can prepare some tasty food for your father, just the way he likes it. 10Then take it to your father to eat, so that he may give you his blessing before he dies."

11Jacob said to Rebekah his mother, "But my brother Esau is a hairy man, and I'm a man with smooth skin. 12What if my father touches me? I would appear to be tricking him and would bring down a curse on myself rather than a blessing."

13His mother said to him, "My son, let the curse fall on me. Just do what I say; go and get them for me."

14So he went and got them and brought them to his mother, and she prepared some tasty food, just the way his father liked it. 15Then Rebekah took the best clothes of Esau her older son, which she had in the house, and put them on her younger son Jacob. 16She also covered his hands and the smooth part of his neck with the goatskins. 17Then she handed to her son Jacob the tasty food and the bread she had made.

18He went to his father and said, "My father."

"Yes, my son," he answered. "Who is it?"

19Jacob said to his father, "I am Esau your firstborn. I have done as you told me. Please sit up and eat some of my game so that you may give me your blessing."

20Isaac asked his son, "How did you find it so quickly, my son?"

"The LORD your God gave me success," he replied.

21Then Isaac said to Jacob, "Come near so I can touch you, my son, to know whether you really are my son Esau or not."

22Jacob went close to his father Isaac, who touched him and said, "The voice is the voice of Jacob, but the hands are the hands of Esau." 23He did not recognize him, for his hands were hairy like those of his brother Esau; so he blessed him. 24"Are you really my son Esau?" he asked.

"I am," he replied.

25Then he said, "My son, bring me some of your game to eat, so that I may give you my blessing."

Jacob brought it to him and he ate; and he brought some wine and he drank. 26Then his father Isaac said to him, "Come here, my son, and kiss me."

27So he went to him and kissed him. When Isaac caught the smell of his clothes, he blessed him and said,

"Ah, the smell of my son
is like the smell of a field
that the LORD has blessed.
28May God give you of heaven's dew
and of earth's richness—
an abundance of grain and new wine.
29May nations serve you
and peoples bow down to you.
Be lord over your brothers,
and may the sons of your mother bow down to you.
May those who curse you be cursed
and those who bless you be blessed."

30After Isaac finished blessing him and Jacob had scarcely left his father's presence, his brother Esau came in from hunting. 31He too prepared some tasty food and brought it to his father. Then he said to him, "My father, sit up and eat some of my game, so that you may give me your blessing."

32His father Isaac asked him, "Who are you?"

"I am your son," he answered, "your firstborn, Esau."

33Isaac trembled violently and said, "Who was it, then, that hunted game and brought it to me? I ate it just before you came and I blessed him—and indeed he will be blessed!"

34When Esau heard his father's words, he burst out with a loud and bitter cry and said to his father, "Bless me—me too, my father!"

35But he said, "Your brother came deceitfully and took your blessing."

36Esau said, "Isn't he rightly named Jacob[a]? He has deceived me these two times: He took my birthright, and now he's taken my blessing!" Then he asked, "Haven't you reserved any blessing for me?"

37Isaac answered Esau, "I have made him lord over you and have made all his relatives his servants, and I have sustained him with grain and new wine. So what can I possibly do for you, my son?"

38Esau said to his father, "Do you have only one blessing, my father? Bless me too, my father!" Then Esau wept aloud.

39His father Isaac answered him,

[a]36 *Jacob* means *he grasps the heel* (figuratively, *he deceives*).

"Your dwelling will be
away from the earth's richness,
away from the dew of heaven
above.
40You will live by the sword
and you will serve your brother.
But when you grow restless,
you will throw his yoke
from off your neck."

Jacob Flees to Laban

41Esau held a grudge against Jacob because of the blessing his father had given him. He said to himself, "The days of mourning for my father are near; then I will kill my brother Jacob."

42When Rebekah was told what her older son Esau had said, she sent for her younger son Jacob and said to him, "Your brother Esau is consoling himself with the thought of killing you. 43Now then, my son, do what I say: Flee at once to my brother Laban in Haran. 44Stay with him for a while until your brother's fury subsides. 45When your brother is no longer angry with you and forgets what you did to him, I'll send word for you to come back from there. Why should I lose both of you in one day?"

46Then Rebekah said to Isaac, "I'm disgusted with living because of these Hittite women. If Jacob takes a wife from among the women of this land, from Hittite women like these, my life will not be worth living."

28 So Isaac called for Jacob and blessed[a] him and commanded him: "Do not marry a Canaanite woman. 2Go at once to Paddan Aram,[b] to the house of your mother's father Bethuel. Take a wife for yourself there, from among the daughters of Laban, your mother's brother. 3May God Almighty[c] bless you and make you fruitful and increase your numbers until you become a community of peoples. 4May he give you and your descendants the blessing given to Abraham, so that you may take possession of the land where you now live as an alien, the land God gave to Abraham."

5Then Isaac sent Jacob on his way, and he went to Paddan Aram, to Laban son of Bethuel the Aramean, the brother of Rebekah, who was the mother of Jacob and Esau.

6Now Esau learned that Isaac had blessed Jacob and had sent him to Paddan Aram to take a wife from there, and that when he blessed him he commanded him, "Do not marry a Canaanite woman," 7and that Jacob had obeyed his father and mother and had gone to Paddan Aram. 8Esau then realized how displeasing the Canaanite women were to his father Isaac; 9so he went to Ishmael and married Mahalath, the sister of Nebaioth and daughter of Ishmael son of Abraham, in addition to the wives he already had.

Jacob's Dream at Bethel

10Jacob left Beersheba and set out for Haran. 11When he reached a certain place, he stopped for the night because the sun had set. Taking one of the stones there, he put it under his head and lay down to sleep. 12He had a dream in which he saw a stairway[d] resting on the earth, with its top reaching to heaven, and the angels of God were ascending and descending on it. 13There above it[e] stood the LORD, and he said: "I am the LORD, the God of your father Abraham and the God of Isaac. I will give you and your descendants the land on which you are lying. 14Your descendants will be like the dust of the earth, and you will spread out to the west and to the east, to the north and to the south. All peoples on earth will be blessed through you and your offspring. 15I am with you and will watch over you wherever you go, and I will bring you back to this land. I will not leave you until I have done what I have promised you."

16When Jacob awoke from his sleep, he thought, "Surely the LORD is in this place, and I was not aware of it." 17He was afraid and said, "How awesome is this place! This is none other than the house of God; this is the gate of heaven."

18Early the next morning Jacob took the stone he had placed under his head and set it up as a pillar and poured oil on top of it. 19He called that place Bethel,[f] though the city used to be called Luz.

20Then Jacob made a vow, saying, "If God will be with me and will watch over me on this journey I am taking and will give me food to eat and clothes to wear 21so that I return safely to my father's house, then the LORD[g] will be my God

[a] 1 Or *greeted* [b] 2 That is, Northwest Mesopotamia; also in verses 5, 6 and 7 [c] 3 Hebrew *El-Shaddai*
[d] 12 Or *ladder* [e] 13 Or *There beside him* [f] 19 *Bethel* means *house of God.* [g] 20,21 Or *Since God . . . father's house, the* LORD

22and[a] this stone that I have set up as a pillar will be God's house, and of all that you give me I will give you a tenth."

Jacob Arrives in Paddan Aram

29 Then Jacob continued on his journey and came to the land of the eastern peoples. 2There he saw a well in the field, with three flocks of sheep lying near it because the flocks were watered from that well. The stone over the mouth of the well was large. 3When all the flocks were gathered there, the shepherds would roll the stone away from the well's mouth

[a]21,22 Or *house, and the* LORD *will be my God,* 22*then*

VERSE FOR THE DAY: Genesis 28:16

AUTHOR: Anne Ortlund

PASSAGE FOR THE DAY: Genesis 28:10–17

Practice the Presence

My husband, Ray, and I were on vacation when we read Brother Lawrence's *The Practice of the Presence of God*. Suddenly, it hit us: We need to give God a time slot in our lives every day, but even more than that, God needs to be a presence in our lives all day long, every day.

Ray and I decided to establish a new habit—practicing the presence of God. Ray set his wristwatch alarm to sound every fifteen minutes. When he heard the tiny "d-d-ding," he'd stop to think on God. I wrote "Jesus" in huge print on a piece of paper and put it on the floor beside my bed, so that when I swung my feet out of bed in the morning I'd be reminded to turn my attention to him.

I began to be more aware of God. I talked to him about my tensions. I moved from knowing theoretically that Christ was in my heart to desiring intensely a conscious awareness of his nearness. I was like Jacob in Genesis 28:16 who said, "Surely the LORD is in this place, and I was not aware of it."

I still fall on my face. At times, my busyness and all my distractions take me far afield. In that place, away from his presence, I get uptight and ungodly. But by a deliberate act of my will, I return to his presence and think upon his Word.

MARRIAGE BUILDERS

♦ *Why is it that a sense of God's nearness is so difficult to keep foremost in our minds?*

♦ *What steps can you take to remind yourself to rejoice in God's presence all day long—as individuals, and as a couple?*

Additional Scripture Readings
Psalm 16:7–11; Joshua 1:5–9;
1 Chronicles 28:9

Go to page 42 for your next devotional reading.

and water the sheep. Then they would return the stone to its place over the mouth of the well.

4Jacob asked the shepherds, "My brothers, where are you from?"

"We're from Haran," they replied.

5He said to them, "Do you know Laban, Nahor's grandson?"

"Yes, we know him," they answered.

6Then Jacob asked them, "Is he well?"

"Yes, he is," they said, "and here comes his daughter Rachel with the sheep."

7"Look," he said, "the sun is still high; it is not time for the flocks to be gathered. Water the sheep and take them back to pasture."

8"We can't," they replied, "until all the flocks are gathered and the stone has been rolled away from the mouth of the well. Then we will water the sheep."

9While he was still talking with them, Rachel came with her father's sheep, for she was a shepherdess. 10When Jacob saw Rachel daughter of Laban, his mother's brother, and Laban's sheep, he went over and rolled the stone away from the mouth of the well and watered his uncle's sheep. 11Then Jacob kissed Rachel and began to weep aloud. 12He had told Rachel that he was a relative of her father and a son of Rebekah. So she ran and told her father.

13As soon as Laban heard the news about Jacob, his sister's son, he hurried to meet him. He embraced him and kissed him and brought him to his home, and there Jacob told him all these things. 14Then Laban said to him, "You are my own flesh and blood."

Jacob Marries Leah and Rachel

After Jacob had stayed with him for a whole month, 15Laban said to him, "Just because you are a relative of mine, should you work for me for nothing? Tell me what your wages should be."

16Now Laban had two daughters; the name of the older was Leah, and the name of the younger was Rachel. 17Leah had weak[a] eyes, but Rachel was lovely in form, and beautiful. 18Jacob was in love with Rachel and said, "I'll work for you seven years in return for your younger daughter Rachel."

19Laban said, "It's better that I give her to you than to some other man. Stay here with me." 20So Jacob served seven years to get Rachel, but they seemed like only a few days to him because of his love for her.

21Then Jacob said to Laban, "Give me my wife. My time is completed, and I want to lie with her."

22So Laban brought together all the people of the place and gave a feast. 23But when evening came, he took his daughter Leah and gave her to Jacob, and Jacob lay with her. 24And Laban gave his servant girl Zilpah to his daughter as her maidservant.

25When morning came, there was Leah! So Jacob said to Laban, "What is this you have done to me? I served you for Rachel, didn't I? Why have you deceived me?"

26Laban replied, "It is not our custom here to give the younger daughter in marriage before the older one. 27Finish this daughter's bridal week; then we will give you the younger one also, in return for another seven years of work."

28And Jacob did so. He finished the week with Leah, and then Laban gave him his daughter Rachel to be his wife. 29Laban gave his servant girl Bilhah to his daughter Rachel as her maidservant. 30Jacob lay with Rachel also, and he loved Rachel more than Leah. And he worked for Laban another seven years.

Jacob's Children

31When the LORD saw that Leah was not loved, he opened her womb, but Rachel was barren. 32Leah became pregnant and gave birth to a son. She named him Reuben,[b] for she said, "It is because the LORD has seen my misery. Surely my husband will love me now."

33She conceived again, and when she gave birth to a son she said, "Because the LORD heard that I am not loved, he gave me this one too." So she named him Simeon.[c]

34Again she conceived, and when she gave birth to a son she said, "Now at last my husband will become attached to me, because I have borne him three sons." So he was named Levi.[d]

35She conceived again, and when she gave birth to a son she said, "This time I will praise the LORD." So she named him

[a] *17* Or *delicate* [b] *32* *Reuben* sounds like the Hebrew for *he has seen my misery*; the name means *see, a son.* [c] *33* *Simeon* probably means *one who hears.* [d] *34* *Levi* sounds like and may be derived from the Hebrew for *attached.*

Judah.[a] Then she stopped having children.

30 When Rachel saw that she was not bearing Jacob any children, she became jealous of her sister. So she said to Jacob, "Give me children, or I'll die!"

2Jacob became angry with her and said, "Am I in the place of God, who has kept you from having children?"

3Then she said, "Here is Bilhah, my maidservant. Sleep with her so that she can bear children for me and that through her I too can build a family."

4So she gave him her servant Bilhah as a wife. Jacob slept with her, 5and she became pregnant and bore him a son. 6Then Rachel said, "God has vindicated me; he has listened to my plea and given me a son." Because of this she named him Dan.[b]

7Rachel's servant Bilhah conceived again and bore Jacob a second son. 8Then Rachel said, "I have had a great struggle with my sister, and I have won." So she named him Naphtali.[c]

9When Leah saw that she had stopped having children, she took her maidservant Zilpah and gave her to Jacob as a wife. 10Leah's servant Zilpah bore Jacob a son. 11Then Leah said, "What good fortune!"[d] So she named him Gad.[e]

12Leah's servant Zilpah bore Jacob a second son. 13Then Leah said, "How happy I am! The women will call me happy." So she named him Asher.[f]

14During wheat harvest, Reuben went out into the fields and found some mandrake plants, which he brought to his mother Leah. Rachel said to Leah, "Please give me some of your son's mandrakes."

15But she said to her, "Wasn't it enough that you took away my husband? Will you take my son's mandrakes too?"

"Very well," Rachel said, "he can sleep with you tonight in return for your son's mandrakes."

16So when Jacob came in from the fields that evening, Leah went out to meet him. "You must sleep with me," she said. "I have hired you with my son's mandrakes." So he slept with her that night.

17God listened to Leah, and she became pregnant and bore Jacob a fifth son. 18Then Leah said, "God has rewarded me for giving my maidservant to my husband." So she named him Issachar.[g]

19Leah conceived again and bore Jacob a sixth son. 20Then Leah said, "God has presented me with a precious gift. This time my husband will treat me with honor, because I have borne him six sons." So she named him Zebulun.[h]

21Some time later she gave birth to a daughter and named her Dinah.

22Then God remembered Rachel; he listened to her and opened her womb. 23She became pregnant and gave birth to a son and said, "God has taken away my disgrace." 24She named him Joseph,[i] and said, "May the LORD add to me another son."

Jacob's Flocks Increase

25After Rachel gave birth to Joseph, Jacob said to Laban, "Send me on my way so I can go back to my own homeland. 26Give me my wives and children, for whom I have served you, and I will be on my way. You know how much work I've done for you."

27But Laban said to him, "If I have found favor in your eyes, please stay. I have learned by divination that[j] the LORD has blessed me because of you." 28He added, "Name your wages, and I will pay them."

29Jacob said to him, "You know how I have worked for you and how your livestock has fared under my care. 30The little you had before I came has increased greatly, and the LORD has blessed you wherever I have been. But now, when may I do something for my own household?"

31"What shall I give you?" he asked.

"Don't give me anything," Jacob replied. "But if you will do this one thing for me, I will go on tending your flocks and watching over them: 32Let me go through all your flocks today and remove from them every speckled or spotted sheep, every dark-colored lamb and every spotted or speckled goat. They will be my wages. 33And my honesty will testify for me in the future, whenever you check on the wages you have paid me. Any goat in my posses-

[a]35 *Judah* sounds like and may be derived from the Hebrew for *praise.* [b]6 *Dan* here means *he has vindicated.* [c]8 *Naphtali* means *my struggle.* [d]11 Or *"A troop is coming!"* [e]11 *Gad* can mean *good fortune* or *a troop.* [f]13 *Asher* means *happy.* [g]18 *Issachar* sounds like the Hebrew for *reward.* [h]20 *Zebulun* probably means *honor.* [i]24 *Joseph* means *may he add.* [j]27 Or possibly *have become rich and*

sion that is not speckled or spotted, or any
lamb that is not dark-colored, will be con-
sidered stolen."
34"Agreed," said Laban. "Let it be as you
have said." 35That same day he removed
all the male goats that were streaked or
spotted, and all the speckled or spotted fe-
male goats (all that had white on them)
and all the dark-colored lambs, and he
placed them in the care of his sons.
36Then he put a three-day journey be-
tween himself and Jacob, while Jacob
continued to tend the rest of Laban's
flocks.
37Jacob, however, took fresh-cut
branches from poplar, almond and plane
trees and made white stripes on them by
peeling the bark and exposing the white
inner wood of the branches. 38Then he
placed the peeled branches in all the wa-
tering troughs, so that they would be di-
rectly in front of the flocks when they
came to drink. When the flocks were in
heat and came to drink, 39they mated in
front of the branches. And they bore
young that were streaked or speckled or
spotted. 40Jacob set apart the young of the
flock by themselves, but made the rest
face the streaked and dark-colored ani-
mals that belonged to Laban. Thus he
made separate flocks for himself and did
not put them with Laban's animals.
41Whenever the stronger females were in
heat, Jacob would place the branches in
the troughs in front of the animals so they
would mate near the branches, 42but if the
animals were weak, he would not place
them there. So the weak animals went to
Laban and the strong ones to Jacob. 43In
this way the man grew exceedingly pros-
perous and came to own large flocks, and
maidservants and menservants, and cam-
els and donkeys.

Jacob Flees From Laban

31 Jacob heard that Laban's sons
were saying, "Jacob has taken ev-
erything our father owned and has gained
all this wealth from what belonged to our
father." 2And Jacob noticed that Laban's
attitude toward him was not what it had
been.
3Then the LORD said to Jacob, "Go back
to the land of your fathers and to your rel-
atives, and I will be with you."
4So Jacob sent word to Rachel and Leah
to come out to the fields where his flocks
were. 5He said to them, "I see that your
father's attitude toward me is not what it
was before, but the God of my father has
been with me. 6You know that I've
worked for your father with all my
strength, 7yet your father has cheated me
by changing my wages ten times. Howev-
er, God has not allowed him to harm me.
8If he said, 'The speckled ones will be
your wages,' then all the flocks gave birth
to speckled young; and if he said, 'The
streaked ones will be your wages,' then all
the flocks bore streaked young. 9So God
has taken away your father's livestock and
has given them to me.
10"In breeding season I once had a
dream in which I looked up and saw that
the male goats mating with the flock were
streaked, speckled or spotted. 11The angel
of God said to me in the dream, 'Jacob.' I
answered, 'Here I am.' 12And he said,
'Look up and see that all the male goats
mating with the flock are streaked, speck-
led or spotted, for I have seen all that La-
ban has been doing to you. 13I am the God
of Bethel, where you anointed a pillar and
where you made a vow to me. Now leave
this land at once and go back to your na-
tive land.' "
14Then Rachel and Leah replied, "Do we
still have any share in the inheritance of
our father's estate? 15Does he not regard
us as foreigners? Not only has he sold us,
but he has used up what was paid for us.
16Surely all the wealth that God took away
from our father belongs to us and our chil-
dren. So do whatever God has told you."
17Then Jacob put his children and his
wives on camels, 18and he drove all his
livestock ahead of him, along with all the
goods he had accumulated in Paddan
Aram,[a] to go to his father Isaac in the
land of Canaan.
19When Laban had gone to shear his
sheep, Rachel stole her father's household
gods. 20Moreover, Jacob deceived Laban
the Aramean by not telling him he was
running away. 21So he fled with all he had,
and crossing the River,[b] he headed for
the hill country of Gilead.

Laban Pursues Jacob

22On the third day Laban was told that
Jacob had fled. 23Taking his relatives with
him, he pursued Jacob for seven days and
caught up with him in the hill country of
Gilead. 24Then God came to Laban the Ar-

[a] 18 That is, Northwest Mesopotamia [b] 21 That is, the Euphrates

amean in a dream at night and said to him,
"Be careful not to say anything to Jacob,
either good or bad."

25Jacob had pitched his tent in the hill
country of Gilead when Laban overtook
him, and Laban and his relatives camped
there too. 26Then Laban said to Jacob,
"What have you done? You've deceived
me, and you've carried off my daughters
like captives in war. 27Why did you run off
secretly and deceive me? Why didn't you
tell me, so I could send you away with joy
and singing to the music of tambourines
and harps? 28You didn't even let me kiss
my grandchildren and my daughters
good-by. You have done a foolish thing.
29I have the power to harm you; but last
night the God of your father said to me,
'Be careful not to say anything to Jacob,
either good or bad.' 30Now you have gone
off because you longed to return to your
father's house. But why did you steal my
gods?"

31Jacob answered Laban, "I was afraid,
because I thought you would take your
daughters away from me by force. 32But if
you find anyone who has your gods, he
shall not live. In the presence of our rela-
tives, see for yourself whether there is
anything of yours here with me; and if so,
take it." Now Jacob did not know that Ra-
chel had stolen the gods.

33So Laban went into Jacob's tent and
into Leah's tent and into the tent of the
two maidservants, but he found nothing.
After he came out of Leah's tent, he en-
tered Rachel's tent. 34Now Rachel had tak-
en the household gods and put them in-
side her camel's saddle and was sitting on
them. Laban searched through everything
in the tent but found nothing.

35Rachel said to her father, "Don't be
angry, my lord, that I cannot stand up in
your presence; I'm having my period." So
he searched but could not find the house-
hold gods.

36Jacob was angry and took Laban to
task. "What is my crime?" he asked Laban.
"What sin have I committed that you hunt
me down? 37Now that you have searched
through all my goods, what have you
found that belongs to your household?
Put it here in front of your relatives and
mine, and let them judge between the two
of us.

38"I have been with you for twenty
years now. Your sheep and goats have not
miscarried, nor have I eaten rams from
your flocks. 39I did not bring you animals
torn by wild beasts; I bore the loss myself.
And you demanded payment from me for
whatever was stolen by day or night.
40This was my situation: The heat con-
sumed me in the daytime and the cold at
night, and sleep fled from my eyes. 41It
was like this for the twenty years I was in
your household. I worked for you four-
teen years for your two daughters and six
years for your flocks, and you changed my
wages ten times. 42If the God of my father,
the God of Abraham and the Fear of Isaac,
had not been with me, you would surely
have sent me away empty-handed. But
God has seen my hardship and the toil of
my hands, and last night he rebuked you."

43Laban answered Jacob, "The women
are my daughters, the children are my
children, and the flocks are my flocks. All
you see is mine. Yet what can I do today
about these daughters of mine, or about
the children they have borne? 44Come
now, let's make a covenant, you and I, and
let it serve as a witness between us."

45So Jacob took a stone and set it up as
a pillar. 46He said to his relatives, "Gather
some stones." So they took stones and
piled them in a heap, and they ate there by
the heap. 47Laban called it Jegar Sahadu-
tha,[a] and Jacob called it Galeed.[b]

48Laban said, "This heap is a witness
between you and me today." That is why
it was called Galeed. 49It was also called
Mizpah,[c] because he said, "May the LORD
keep watch between you and me when we
are away from each other. 50If you mis-
treat my daughters or if you take any
wives besides my daughters, even though
no one is with us, remember that God is
a witness between you and me."

51Laban also said to Jacob, "Here is this
heap, and here is this pillar I have set up
between you and me. 52This heap is a wit-
ness, and this pillar is a witness, that I will
not go past this heap to your side to harm
you and that you will not go past this heap
and pillar to my side to harm me. 53May
the God of Abraham and the God of Na-
hor, the God of their father, judge be-
tween us."

So Jacob took an oath in the name of
the Fear of his father Isaac. 54He offered a
sacrifice there in the hill country and in-

[a]47 The Aramaic *Jegar Sahadutha* means *witness heap.*
[b]47 The Hebrew *Galeed* means *witness heap.*
[c]49 *Mizpah* means *watchtower.*

vited his relatives to a meal. After they had eaten, they spent the night there.

55Early the next morning Laban kissed his grandchildren and his daughters and blessed them. Then he left and returned home.

Jacob Prepares to Meet Esau

32 Jacob also went on his way, and the angels of God met him. 2When Jacob saw them, he said, "This is the camp of God!" So he named that place Mahanaim.[a]

3Jacob sent messengers ahead of him to his brother Esau in the land of Seir, the country of Edom. 4He instructed them: "This is what you are to say to my master Esau: 'Your servant Jacob says, I have been staying with Laban and have remained there till now. 5I have cattle and donkeys, sheep and goats, menservants and maidservants. Now I am sending this message to my lord, that I may find favor in your eyes.' "

6When the messengers returned to Jacob, they said, "We went to your brother Esau, and now he is coming to meet you, and four hundred men are with him."

7In great fear and distress Jacob divided the people who were with him into two groups,[b] and the flocks and herds and camels as well. 8He thought, "If Esau comes and attacks one group,[c] the group[c] that is left may escape."

9Then Jacob prayed, "O God of my father Abraham, God of my father Isaac, O LORD, who said to me, 'Go back to your country and your relatives, and I will make you prosper,' 10I am unworthy of all the kindness and faithfulness you have shown your servant. I had only my staff when I crossed this Jordan, but now I have become two groups. 11Save me, I pray, from the hand of my brother Esau, for I am afraid he will come and attack me, and also the mothers with their children. 12But you have said, 'I will surely make you prosper and will make your descendants like the sand of the sea, which cannot be counted.' "

13He spent the night there, and from what he had with him he selected a gift for his brother Esau: 14two hundred female goats and twenty male goats, two hundred ewes and twenty rams, 15thirty female camels with their young, forty cows and ten bulls, and twenty female donkeys and ten male donkeys. 16He put them in the care of his servants, each herd by itself, and said to his servants, "Go ahead of me, and keep some space between the herds."

17He instructed the one in the lead: "When my brother Esau meets you and asks, 'To whom do you belong, and where are you going, and who owns all these animals in front of you?' 18then you are to say, 'They belong to your servant Jacob. They are a gift sent to my lord Esau, and he is coming behind us.' "

19He also instructed the second, the third and all the others who followed the herds: "You are to say the same thing to Esau when you meet him. 20And be sure to say, 'Your servant Jacob is coming behind us.' " For he thought, "I will pacify him with these gifts I am sending on ahead; later, when I see him, perhaps he will receive me." 21So Jacob's gifts went on ahead of him, but he himself spent the night in the camp.

Jacob Wrestles With God

22That night Jacob got up and took his two wives, his two maidservants and his eleven sons and crossed the ford of the Jabbok. 23After he had sent them across the stream, he sent over all his possessions. 24So Jacob was left alone, and a man wrestled with him till daybreak. 25When the man saw that he could not overpower him, he touched the socket of Jacob's hip so that his hip was wrenched as he wrestled with the man. 26Then the man said, "Let me go, for it is daybreak."

But Jacob replied, "I will not let you go unless you bless me."

27The man asked him, "What is your name?"

"Jacob," he answered.

28Then the man said, "Your name will no longer be Jacob, but Israel,[d] because you have struggled with God and with men and have overcome."

29Jacob said, "Please tell me your name."

But he replied, "Why do you ask my name?" Then he blessed him there.

30So Jacob called the place Peniel,[e] saying, "It is because I saw God face to face, and yet my life was spared."

31The sun rose above him as he passed Peniel,[f] and he was limping because of

[a]2 *Mahanaim* means *two camps.* [b]7 Or *camps*; also in verse 10 [c]8 Or *camp* [d]28 *Israel* means *he struggles with God.* [e]30 *Peniel* means *face of God.* [f]31 Hebrew *Penuel*, a variant of *Peniel*

his hip. 32Therefore to this day the Israelites do not eat the tendon attached to the socket of the hip, because the socket of Jacob's hip was touched near the tendon.

Jacob Meets Esau

33 Jacob looked up and there was Esau, coming with his four hundred men; so he divided the children among Leah, Rachel and the two maidservants. 2He put the maidservants and their children in front, Leah and her children next, and Rachel and Joseph in the rear. 3He himself went on ahead and bowed down to the ground seven times as he approached his brother.

4But Esau ran to meet Jacob and embraced him; he threw his arms around his neck and kissed him. And they wept. 5Then Esau looked up and saw the women and children. "Who are these with you?" he asked.

Jacob answered, "They are the children God has graciously given your servant."

6Then the maidservants and their children approached and bowed down. 7Next, Leah and her children came and bowed down. Last of all came Joseph and Rachel, and they too bowed down.

8Esau asked, "What do you mean by all these droves I met?"

"To find favor in your eyes, my lord," he said.

9But Esau said, "I already have plenty, my brother. Keep what you have for yourself."

10"No, please!" said Jacob. "If I have found favor in your eyes, accept this gift from me. For to see your face is like seeing the face of God, now that you have received me favorably. 11Please accept the present that was brought to you, for God has been gracious to me and I have all I need." And because Jacob insisted, Esau accepted it.

12Then Esau said, "Let us be on our way; I'll accompany you."

13But Jacob said to him, "My lord knows that the children are tender and that I must care for the ewes and cows that are nursing their young. If they are driven hard just one day, all the animals will die. 14So let my lord go on ahead of his servant, while I move along slowly at the pace of the droves before me and that of the children, until I come to my lord in Seir."

15Esau said, "Then let me leave some of my men with you."

"But why do that?" Jacob asked. "Just let me find favor in the eyes of my lord."

16So that day Esau started on his way back to Seir. 17Jacob, however, went to Succoth, where he built a place for himself and made shelters for his livestock. That is why the place is called Succoth.[a]

18After Jacob came from Paddan Aram,[b] he arrived safely at the[c] city of Shechem in Canaan and camped within sight of the city. 19For a hundred pieces of silver,[d] he bought from the sons of Hamor, the father of Shechem, the plot of ground where he pitched his tent. 20There he set up an altar and called it El Elohe Israel.[e]

Dinah and the Shechemites

34 Now Dinah, the daughter Leah had borne to Jacob, went out to visit the women of the land. 2When Shechem son of Hamor the Hivite, the ruler of that area, saw her, he took her and violated her. 3His heart was drawn to Dinah daughter of Jacob, and he loved the girl and spoke tenderly to her. 4And Shechem said to his father Hamor, "Get me this girl as my wife."

5When Jacob heard that his daughter Dinah had been defiled, his sons were in the fields with his livestock; so he kept quiet about it until they came home.

6Then Shechem's father Hamor went out to talk with Jacob. 7Now Jacob's sons had come in from the fields as soon as they heard what had happened. They were filled with grief and fury, because Shechem had done a disgraceful thing in[f] Israel by lying with Jacob's daughter—a thing that should not be done.

8But Hamor said to them, "My son Shechem has his heart set on your daughter. Please give her to him as his wife. 9Intermarry with us; give us your daughters and take our daughters for yourselves. 10You can settle among us; the land is open to you. Live in it, trade[g] in it, and acquire property in it."

11Then Shechem said to Dinah's father

[a] 17 *Succoth* means *shelters.* [b] 18 That is, Northwest Mesopotamia [c] 18 Or *arrived at Shalem, a* [d] 19 Hebrew *hundred kesitahs*; a kesitah was a unit of money of unknown weight and value. [e] 20 *El Elohe Israel* can mean *God, the God of Israel* or *mighty is the God of Israel.* [f] 7 Or *against* [g] 10 Or *move about freely*; also in verse 21

and brothers, "Let me find favor in your
eyes, and I will give you whatever you ask.
12Make the price for the bride and the gift
I am to bring as great as you like, and I'll
pay whatever you ask me. Only give me
the girl as my wife."

13Because their sister Dinah had been
defiled, Jacob's sons replied deceitfully as
they spoke to Shechem and his father Ha-
mor. 14They said to them, "We can't do
such a thing; we can't give our sister to a
man who is not circumcised. That would
be a disgrace to us. 15We will give our con-
sent to you on one condition only: that
you become like us by circumcising all
your males. 16Then we will give you our
daughters and take your daughters for
ourselves. We'll settle among you and be-
come one people with you. 17But if you
will not agree to be circumcised, we'll take
our sister[a] and go."

18Their proposal seemed good to Ha-
mor and his son Shechem. 19The young
man, who was the most honored of all his
father's household, lost no time in doing
what they said, because he was delighted
with Jacob's daughter. 20So Hamor and
his son Shechem went to the gate of their
city to speak to their fellow townsmen.
21"These men are friendly toward us,"
they said. "Let them live in our land and
trade in it; the land has plenty of room for
them. We can marry their daughters and
they can marry ours. 22But the men will
consent to live with us as one people only
on the condition that our males be cir-
cumcised, as they themselves are. 23Won't
their livestock, their property and all their
other animals become ours? So let us give
our consent to them, and they will settle
among us."

24All the men who went out of the city
gate agreed with Hamor and his son She-
chem, and every male in the city was cir-
cumcised.

25Three days later, while all of them
were still in pain, two of Jacob's sons,
Simeon and Levi, Dinah's brothers, took
their swords and attacked the unsuspect-
ing city, killing every male. 26They put Ha-
mor and his son Shechem to the sword
and took Dinah from Shechem's house
and left. 27The sons of Jacob came upon
the dead bodies and looted the city
where[b] their sister had been defiled.
28They seized their flocks and herds and
donkeys and everything else of theirs in
the city and out in the fields. 29They car-
ried off all their wealth and all their wom-
en and children, taking as plunder every-
thing in the houses.

30Then Jacob said to Simeon and Levi,
"You have brought trouble on me by mak-
ing me a stench to the Canaanites and Per-
izzites, the people living in this land. We
are few in number, and if they join forces
against me and attack me, I and my house-
hold will be destroyed."

31But they replied, "Should he have
treated our sister like a prostitute?"

Jacob Returns to Bethel

35 Then God said to Jacob, "Go up to
Bethel and settle there, and build
an altar there to God, who appeared to
you when you were fleeing from your
brother Esau."

2So Jacob said to his household and to
all who were with him, "Get rid of the for-
eign gods you have with you, and purify
yourselves and change your clothes.
3Then come, let us go up to Bethel, where
I will build an altar to God, who answered
me in the day of my distress and who has
been with me wherever I have gone." 4So
they gave Jacob all the foreign gods they
had and the rings in their ears, and Jacob
buried them under the oak at Shechem.
5Then they set out, and the terror of God
fell upon the towns all around them so
that no one pursued them.

6Jacob and all the people with him
came to Luz (that is, Bethel) in the land of
Canaan. 7There he built an altar, and he
called the place El Bethel,[c] because it
was there that God revealed himself to
him when he was fleeing from his brother.

8Now Deborah, Rebekah's nurse, died
and was buried under the oak below Beth-
el. So it was named Allon Bacuth.[d]

9After Jacob returned from Paddan
Aram,[e] God appeared to him again and
blessed him. 10God said to him, "Your
name is Jacob,[f] but you will no longer be
called Jacob; your name will be Israel.[g]"
So he named him Israel.

11And God said to him, "I am God Al-
mighty[h]; be fruitful and increase in num-

[a] 17 Hebrew *daughter* [b] 27 Or *because* [c] 7 *El Bethel* means *God of Bethel.* [d] 8 *Allon Bacuth* means *oak of weeping.* [e] 9 That is, Northwest Mesopotamia; also in verse 26 [f] 10 *Jacob* means *he grasps the heel* (figuratively, *he deceives*). [g] 10 *Israel* means *he struggles with God.* [h] 11 Hebrew *El-Shaddai*

ber. A nation and a community of nations
will come from you, and kings will come
from your body. 12The land I gave to Abra-
ham and Isaac I also give to you, and I will
give this land to your descendants after
you." 13Then God went up from him at the
place where he had talked with him.
14Jacob set up a stone pillar at the place
where God had talked with him, and he
poured out a drink offering on it; he also
poured oil on it. 15Jacob called the place
where God had talked with him Bethel.[a]

The Deaths of Rachel and Isaac

16Then they moved on from Bethel.
While they were still some distance from
Ephrath, Rachel began to give birth and
had great difficulty. 17And as she was hav-
ing great difficulty in childbirth, the mid-
wife said to her, "Don't be afraid, for you
have another son." 18As she breathed her
last—for she was dying—she named her
son Ben-Oni.[b] But his father named him
Benjamin.[c]
19So Rachel died and was buried on the
way to Ephrath (that is, Bethlehem).
20Over her tomb Jacob set up a pillar, and
to this day that pillar marks Rachel's
tomb.
21Israel moved on again and pitched his
tent beyond Migdal Eder. 22While Israel
was living in that region, Reuben went in
and slept with his father's concubine Bil-
hah, and Israel heard of it.

Jacob had twelve sons:
23The sons of Leah:
Reuben the firstborn of Jacob,
Simeon, Levi, Judah, Issachar and
Zebulun.
24The sons of Rachel:
Joseph and Benjamin.
25The sons of Rachel's maidservant
Bilhah:
Dan and Naphtali.
26The sons of Leah's maidservant Zil-
pah:
Gad and Asher.
These were the sons of Jacob, who were
born to him in Paddan Aram.

27Jacob came home to his father Isaac
in Mamre, near Kiriath Arba (that is, He-
bron), where Abraham and Isaac had
stayed. 28Isaac lived a hundred and eighty
years. 29Then he breathed his last and
died and was gathered to his people, old
and full of years. And his sons Esau and
Jacob buried him.

Esau's Descendants

36 This is the account of Esau (that is,
Edom).
2Esau took his wives from the
women of Canaan: Adah daughter of
Elon the Hittite, and Oholibamah
daughter of Anah and granddaughter
of Zibeon the Hivite— 3also Base-
math daughter of Ishmael and sister
of Nebaioth.
4Adah bore Eliphaz to Esau, Base-
math bore Reuel, 5and Oholibamah
bore Jeush, Jalam and Korah. These
were the sons of Esau, who were
born to him in Canaan.
6Esau took his wives and sons and
daughters and all the members of his
household, as well as his livestock
and all his other animals and all the
goods he had acquired in Canaan,
and moved to a land some distance
from his brother Jacob. 7Their pos-
sessions were too great for them to
remain together; the land where they
were staying could not support them
both because of their livestock. 8So
Esau (that is, Edom) settled in the hill
country of Seir.

9This is the account of Esau the father
of the Edomites in the hill country of Seir.

10These are the names of Esau's sons:
Eliphaz, the son of Esau's wife
Adah, and Reuel, the son of Esau's
wife Basemath.
11The sons of Eliphaz:
Teman, Omar, Zepho, Gatam and
Kenaz.
12Esau's son Eliphaz also had a con-
cubine named Timna, who bore
him Amalek. These were grand-
sons of Esau's wife Adah.
13The sons of Reuel:
Nahath, Zerah, Shammah and
Mizzah. These were grandsons of
Esau's wife Basemath.
14The sons of Esau's wife Oholibamah
daughter of Anah and granddaugh-
ter of Zibeon, whom she bore to
Esau:
Jeush, Jalam and Korah.

[a] 15 *Bethel* means *house of God.* [b] 18 *Ben-Oni* means *son of my trouble.* [c] 18 *Benjamin* means *son of my right hand.*

15These were the chiefs among Esau's descendants:
The sons of Eliphaz the firstborn of Esau:
Chiefs Teman, Omar, Zepho, Kenaz, 16Korah,[a] Gatam and Amalek. These were the chiefs descended from Eliphaz in Edom; they were grandsons of Adah.
17The sons of Esau's son Reuel:
Chiefs Nahath, Zerah, Shammah and Mizzah. These were the chiefs descended from Reuel in Edom; they were grandsons of Esau's wife Basemath.
18The sons of Esau's wife Oholibamah:
Chiefs Jeush, Jalam and Korah. These were the chiefs descended from Esau's wife Oholibamah daughter of Anah.
19These were the sons of Esau (that is, Edom), and these were their chiefs.

20These were the sons of Seir the Horite, who were living in the region:
Lotan, Shobal, Zibeon, Anah, 21Dishon, Ezer and Dishan. These sons of Seir in Edom were Horite chiefs.
22The sons of Lotan:
Hori and Homam.[b] Timna was Lotan's sister.
23The sons of Shobal:
Alvan, Manahath, Ebal, Shepho and Onam.
24The sons of Zibeon:
Aiah and Anah. This is the Anah who discovered the hot springs[c] in the desert while he was grazing the donkeys of his father Zibeon.
25The children of Anah:
Dishon and Oholibamah daughter of Anah.
26The sons of Dishon[d]:
Hemdan, Eshban, Ithran and Keran.
27The sons of Ezer:
Bilhan, Zaavan and Akan.
28The sons of Dishan:
Uz and Aran.
29These were the Horite chiefs:
Lotan, Shobal, Zibeon, Anah, 30Dishon, Ezer and Dishan. These were the Horite chiefs, according to their divisions, in the land of Seir.

The Rulers of Edom

31These were the kings who reigned in Edom before any Israelite king reigned[e]:
32Bela son of Beor became king of Edom. His city was named Dinhabah.
33When Bela died, Jobab son of Zerah from Bozrah succeeded him as king.
34When Jobab died, Husham from the land of the Temanites succeeded him as king.
35When Husham died, Hadad son of Bedad, who defeated Midian in the country of Moab, succeeded him as king. His city was named Avith.
36When Hadad died, Samlah from Masrekah succeeded him as king.
37When Samlah died, Shaul from Rehoboth on the river[f] succeeded him as king.
38When Shaul died, Baal-Hanan son of Acbor succeeded him as king.
39When Baal-Hanan son of Acbor died, Hadad[g] succeeded him as king. His city was named Pau, and his wife's name was Mehetabel daughter of Matred, the daughter of Me-Zahab.

40These were the chiefs descended from Esau, by name, according to their clans and regions:
Timna, Alvah, Jetheth, 41Oholibamah, Elah, Pinon, 42Kenaz, Teman, Mibzar, 43Magdiel and Iram. These were the chiefs of Edom, according to their settlements in the land they occupied.

This was Esau the father of the Edomites.

Joseph's Dreams

37 Jacob lived in the land where his father had stayed, the land of Canaan.

2This is the account of Jacob.

[a]16 Masoretic Text; Samaritan Pentateuch (see also Gen. 36:11 and 1 Chron. 1:36) does not have *Korah.*
[b]22 Hebrew *Hemam,* a variant of *Homam* (see 1 Chron. 1:39) [c]24 Vulgate; Syriac *discovered water;* the meaning of the Hebrew for this word is uncertain. [d]26 Hebrew *Dishan,* a variant of *Dishon*
[e]31 Or *before an Israelite king reigned over them* [f]37 Possibly the Euphrates [g]39 Many manuscripts of the Masoretic Text, Samaritan Pentateuch and Syriac (see also 1 Chron. 1:50); most manuscripts of the Masoretic Text *Hadar*

Joseph, a young man of seventeen, was
tending the flocks with his brothers, the
sons of Bilhah and the sons of Zilpah, his
father's wives, and he brought their father
a bad report about them.

3Now Israel loved Joseph more than
any of his other sons, because he had
been born to him in his old age; and he
made a richly ornamented[a] robe for him.
4When his brothers saw that their father
loved him more than any of them, they
hated him and could not speak a kind
word to him.

5Joseph had a dream, and when he told
it to his brothers, they hated him all the
more. 6He said to them, "Listen to this
dream I had: 7We were binding sheaves of
grain out in the field when suddenly my
sheaf rose and stood upright, while your
sheaves gathered around mine and bowed
down to it."

8His brothers said to him, "Do you intend to reign over us? Will you actually
rule us?" And they hated him all the more
because of his dream and what he had
said.

9Then he had another dream, and he
told it to his brothers. "Listen," he said, "I
had another dream, and this time the sun
and moon and eleven stars were bowing
down to me."

10When he told his father as well as his
brothers, his father rebuked him and said,
"What is this dream you had? Will your
mother and I and your brothers actually
come and bow down to the ground before
you?" 11His brothers were jealous of him,
but his father kept the matter in mind.

Joseph Sold by His Brothers

12Now his brothers had gone to graze
their father's flocks near Shechem, 13and
Israel said to Joseph, "As you know, your
brothers are grazing the flocks near Shechem. Come, I am going to send you to
them."

"Very well," he replied.

14So he said to him, "Go and see if all is
well with your brothers and with the
flocks, and bring word back to me." Then
he sent him off from the Valley of Hebron.

When Joseph arrived at Shechem, 15a
man found him wandering around in the
fields and asked him, "What are you looking for?"

16He replied, "I'm looking for my brothers. Can you tell me where they are grazing their flocks?"

17"They have moved on from here," the
man answered. "I heard them say, 'Let's
go to Dothan.' "

So Joseph went after his brothers and
found them near Dothan. 18But they saw
him in the distance, and before he reached
them, they plotted to kill him.

19"Here comes that dreamer!" they said
to each other. 20"Come now, let's kill him
and throw him into one of these cisterns
and say that a ferocious animal devoured
him. Then we'll see what comes of his
dreams."

21When Reuben heard this, he tried to
rescue him from their hands. "Let's not
take his life," he said. 22"Don't shed any
blood. Throw him into this cistern here in
the desert, but don't lay a hand on him."
Reuben said this to rescue him from them
and take him back to his father.

23So when Joseph came to his brothers,
they stripped him of his robe—the richly
ornamented robe he was wearing— 24and
they took him and threw him into the cistern. Now the cistern was empty; there
was no water in it.

25As they sat down to eat their meal,
they looked up and saw a caravan of Ishmaelites coming from Gilead. Their camels were loaded with spices, balm and
myrrh, and they were on their way to take
them down to Egypt.

26Judah said to his brothers, "What will
we gain if we kill our brother and cover up
his blood? 27Come, let's sell him to the
Ishmaelites and not lay our hands on him;
after all, he is our brother, our own flesh
and blood." His brothers agreed.

28So when the Midianite merchants
came by, his brothers pulled Joseph up
out of the cistern and sold him for twenty
shekels[b] of silver to the Ishmaelites, who
took him to Egypt.

29When Reuben returned to the cistern
and saw that Joseph was not there, he tore
his clothes. 30He went back to his brothers
and said, "The boy isn't there! Where can
I turn now?"

31Then they got Joseph's robe, slaughtered a goat and dipped the robe in the
blood. 32They took the ornamented robe
back to their father and said, "We found
this. Examine it to see whether it is your
son's robe."

[a]3 The meaning of the Hebrew for *richly ornamented* is uncertain; also in verses 23 and 32. [b]28 That is, about 8 ounces (about 0.2 kilogram)

33He recognized it and said, "It is my
son's robe! Some ferocious animal has de-
voured him. Joseph has surely been torn
to pieces."
34Then Jacob tore his clothes, put on
sackcloth and mourned for his son many
days. 35All his sons and daughters came to
comfort him, but he refused to be com-
forted. "No," he said, "in mourning will I
go down to the grave[a] to my son." So his
father wept for him.
36Meanwhile, the Midianites[b] sold Jo-
seph in Egypt to Potiphar, one of Phar-
aoh's officials, the captain of the guard.

Judah and Tamar

38 At that time, Judah left his brothers
and went down to stay with a man
of Adullam named Hirah. 2There Judah
met the daughter of a Canaanite man
named Shua. He married her and lay with
her; 3she became pregnant and gave birth
to a son, who was named Er. 4She con-
ceived again and gave birth to a son and
named him Onan. 5She gave birth to still
another son and named him Shelah. It
was at Kezib that she gave birth to him.
6Judah got a wife for Er, his firstborn,
and her name was Tamar. 7But Er, Judah's
firstborn, was wicked in the LORD's sight;
so the LORD put him to death.
8Then Judah said to Onan, "Lie with
your brother's wife and fulfill your duty to
her as a brother-in-law to produce off-
spring for your brother." 9But Onan knew
that the offspring would not be his; so
whenever he lay with his brother's wife,
he spilled his semen on the ground to
keep from producing offspring for his
brother. 10What he did was wicked in the
LORD's sight; so he put him to death also.
11Judah then said to his daughter-in-law
Tamar, "Live as a widow in your father's
house until my son Shelah grows up." For
he thought, "He may die too, just like his
brothers." So Tamar went to live in her fa-
ther's house.
12After a long time Judah's wife, the
daughter of Shua, died. When Judah had
recovered from his grief, he went up to
Timnah, to the men who were shearing
his sheep, and his friend Hirah the Adul-
lamite went with him.
13When Tamar was told, "Your father-
in-law is on his way to Timnah to shear
his sheep," 14she took off her widow's
clothes, covered herself with a veil to dis-
guise herself, and then sat down at the en-
trance to Enaim, which is on the road to
Timnah. For she saw that, though Shelah
had now grown up, she had not been giv-
en to him as his wife.
15When Judah saw her, he thought she
was a prostitute, for she had covered her
face. 16Not realizing that she was his
daughter-in-law, he went over to her by
the roadside and said, "Come now, let me
sleep with you."
"And what will you give me to sleep
with you?" she asked.
17"I'll send you a young goat from my
flock," he said.
"Will you give me something as a
pledge until you send it?" she asked.
18He said, "What pledge should I give
you?"
"Your seal and its cord, and the staff in
your hand," she answered. So he gave
them to her and slept with her, and she
became pregnant by him. 19After she left,
she took off her veil and put on her wid-
ow's clothes again.
20Meanwhile Judah sent the young goat
by his friend the Adullamite in order to get
his pledge back from the woman, but he
did not find her. 21He asked the men who
lived there, "Where is the shrine prosti-
tute who was beside the road at Enaim?"
"There hasn't been any shrine prosti-
tute here," they said.
22So he went back to Judah and said, "I
didn't find her. Besides, the men who
lived there said, 'There hasn't been any
shrine prostitute here.' "
23Then Judah said, "Let her keep what
she has, or we will become a laughing-
stock. After all, I did send her this young
goat, but you didn't find her."
24About three months later Judah was
told, "Your daughter-in-law Tamar is
guilty of prostitution, and as a result she
is now pregnant."
Judah said, "Bring her out and have her
burned to death!"
25As she was being brought out, she
sent a message to her father-in-law. "I am
pregnant by the man who owns these,"
she said. And she added, "See if you rec-
ognize whose seal and cord and staff
these are."
26Judah recognized them and said, "She
is more righteous than I, since I wouldn't

[a]35 Hebrew *Sheol* [b]36 Samaritan Pentateuch, Septuagint, Vulgate and Syriac (see also verse 28); Masoretic Text *Medanites*

WEEKENDING

COMMUNICATION

Our *non*verbal communication accounts for 58 percent of the total message. Tone of voice—the *way* we say things—makes up 35 percent of the message. The actual words we say account for only seven percent of the total message.

Think about the ways you and your spouse communicate without using words. In the space below, list your mate's nonverbal actions in the left-hand column. Then write what you think each action means in the right-hand column. When you're finished, compare your lists with each other.

Husband's Nonverbal Actions	What Those Actions Mean
_____	_____
_____	_____
_____	_____

Wife's Nonverbal Actions	What Those Actions Mean
_____	_____
_____	_____
_____	_____

— Dave and Claudia Arp

REVIVE

Saturday: 1 John 3:11–24
Sunday: James 2:14–26

Go to page 50 for your next devotional reading.

give her to my son Shelah." And he did
not sleep with her again.
27When the time came for her to give
birth, there were twin boys in her womb.
28As she was giving birth, one of them put
out his hand; so the midwife took a scarlet
thread and tied it on his wrist and said,
"This one came out first." 29But when he
drew back his hand, his brother came out,
and she said, "So this is how you have bro-
ken out!" And he was named Perez.[a]
30Then his brother, who had the scarlet
thread on his wrist, came out and he was
given the name Zerah.[b]

Joseph and Potiphar's Wife

39 Now Joseph had been taken down
to Egypt. Potiphar, an Egyptian
who was one of Pharaoh's officials, the
captain of the guard, bought him from the
Ishmaelites who had taken him there.
2The LORD was with Joseph and he pros-
pered, and he lived in the house of his
Egyptian master. 3When his master saw
that the LORD was with him and that the
LORD gave him success in everything he
did, 4Joseph found favor in his eyes and
became his attendant. Potiphar put him in
charge of his household, and he entrusted
to his care everything he owned. 5From
the time he put him in charge of his
household and of all that he owned, the
LORD blessed the household of the Egyp-
tian because of Joseph. The blessing of
the LORD was on everything Potiphar had,
both in the house and in the field. 6So he
left in Joseph's care everything he had;
with Joseph in charge, he did not concern
himself with anything except the food he
ate.

Now Joseph was well-built and hand-
some, 7and after a while his master's wife
took notice of Joseph and said, "Come to
bed with me!"
8But he refused. "With me in charge,"
he told her, "my master does not concern
himself with anything in the house; every-
thing he owns he has entrusted to my
care. 9No one is greater in this house than
I am. My master has withheld nothing
from me except you, because you are his
wife. How then could I do such a wicked
thing and sin against God?" 10And though
she spoke to Joseph day after day, he re-
fused to go to bed with her or even be with
her.
11One day he went into the house to at-
tend to his duties, and none of the house-
hold servants was inside. 12She caught
him by his cloak and said, "Come to bed
with me!" But he left his cloak in her hand
and ran out of the house.
13When she saw that he had left his
cloak in her hand and had run out of the
house, 14she called her household ser-
vants. "Look," she said to them, "this He-
brew has been brought to us to make
sport of us! He came in here to sleep with
me, but I screamed. 15When he heard me
scream for help, he left his cloak beside
me and ran out of the house."
16She kept his cloak beside her until his
master came home. 17Then she told him
this story: "That Hebrew slave you
brought us came to me to make sport of
me. 18But as soon as I screamed for help,
he left his cloak beside me and ran out of
the house."
19When his master heard the story his
wife told him, saying, "This is how your
slave treated me," he burned with anger.
20Joseph's master took him and put him
in prison, the place where the king's pris-
oners were confined.

But while Joseph was there in the pris-
on, 21the LORD was with him; he showed
him kindness and granted him favor in the
eyes of the prison warden. 22So the war-
den put Joseph in charge of all those held
in the prison, and he was made responsi-
ble for all that was done there. 23The war-
den paid no attention to anything under
Joseph's care, because the LORD was with
Joseph and gave him success in whatever
he did.

The Cupbearer and the Baker

40 Some time later, the cupbearer and
the baker of the king of Egypt of-
fended their master, the king of Egypt.
2Pharaoh was angry with his two officials,
the chief cupbearer and the chief baker,
3and put them in custody in the house of
the captain of the guard, in the same pris-
on where Joseph was confined. 4The cap-
tain of the guard assigned them to Joseph,
and he attended them.

After they had been in custody for some
time, 5each of the two men—the cupbear-
er and the baker of the king of Egypt, who
were being held in prison—had a dream
the same night, and each dream had a
meaning of its own.
6When Joseph came to them the next

[a]29 *Perez* means *breaking out.* [b]30 *Zerah* can mean *scarlet* or *brightness.*

morning, he saw that they were dejected.
7So he asked Pharaoh's officials who were
in custody with him in his master's house,
"Why are your faces so sad today?"

8"We both had dreams," they answered,
"but there is no one to interpret them."

Then Joseph said to them, "Do not interpretations belong to God? Tell me your dreams."

9So the chief cupbearer told Joseph his dream. He said to him, "In my dream I saw a vine in front of me, 10and on the vine were three branches. As soon as it budded, it blossomed, and its clusters ripened into grapes. 11Pharaoh's cup was in my hand, and I took the grapes, squeezed them into Pharaoh's cup and put the cup in his hand."

12"This is what it means," Joseph said to him. "The three branches are three days. 13Within three days Pharaoh will lift up your head and restore you to your position, and you will put Pharaoh's cup in his hand, just as you used to do when you were his cupbearer. 14But when all goes well with you, remember me and show me kindness; mention me to Pharaoh and get me out of this prison. 15For I was forcibly carried off from the land of the Hebrews, and even here I have done nothing to deserve being put in a dungeon."

16When the chief baker saw that Joseph had given a favorable interpretation, he said to Joseph, "I too had a dream: On my head were three baskets of bread.[a] 17In the top basket were all kinds of baked goods for Pharaoh, but the birds were eating them out of the basket on my head."

18"This is what it means," Joseph said. "The three baskets are three days. 19Within three days Pharaoh will lift off your head and hang you on a tree.[b] And the birds will eat away your flesh."

20Now the third day was Pharaoh's birthday, and he gave a feast for all his officials. He lifted up the heads of the chief cupbearer and the chief baker in the presence of his officials: 21He restored the chief cupbearer to his position, so that he once again put the cup into Pharaoh's hand, 22but he hanged[c] the chief baker, just as Joseph had said to them in his interpretation.

23The chief cupbearer, however, did not remember Joseph; he forgot him.

Pharaoh's Dreams

41 When two full years had passed, Pharaoh had a dream: He was standing by the Nile, 2when out of the river there came up seven cows, sleek and fat, and they grazed among the reeds. 3After them, seven other cows, ugly and gaunt, came up out of the Nile and stood beside those on the riverbank. 4And the cows that were ugly and gaunt ate up the seven sleek, fat cows. Then Pharaoh woke up.

5He fell asleep again and had a second dream: Seven heads of grain, healthy and good, were growing on a single stalk. 6After them, seven other heads of grain sprouted—thin and scorched by the east wind. 7The thin heads of grain swallowed up the seven healthy, full heads. Then Pharaoh woke up; it had been a dream.

8In the morning his mind was troubled, so he sent for all the magicians and wise men of Egypt. Pharaoh told them his dreams, but no one could interpret them for him.

9Then the chief cupbearer said to Pharaoh, "Today I am reminded of my shortcomings. 10Pharaoh was once angry with his servants, and he imprisoned me and the chief baker in the house of the captain of the guard. 11Each of us had a dream the same night, and each dream had a meaning of its own. 12Now a young Hebrew was there with us, a servant of the captain of the guard. We told him our dreams, and he interpreted them for us, giving each man the interpretation of his dream. 13And things turned out exactly as he interpreted them to us: I was restored to my position, and the other man was hanged.[c]"

14So Pharaoh sent for Joseph, and he was quickly brought from the dungeon. When he had shaved and changed his clothes, he came before Pharaoh.

15Pharaoh said to Joseph, "I had a dream, and no one can interpret it. But I have heard it said of you that when you hear a dream you can interpret it."

16"I cannot do it," Joseph replied to Pharaoh, "but God will give Pharaoh the answer he desires."

17Then Pharaoh said to Joseph, "In my dream I was standing on the bank of the Nile, 18when out of the river there came up seven cows, fat and sleek, and they

[a]16 Or *three wicker baskets* [b]19 Or *and impale you on a pole* [c]22,13 Or *impaled*

grazed among the reeds. 19After them,
seven other cows came up—scrawny and
very ugly and lean. I had never seen such
ugly cows in all the land of Egypt. 20The
lean, ugly cows ate up the seven fat cows
that came up first. 21But even after they
ate them, no one could tell that they had
done so; they looked just as ugly as be-
fore. Then I woke up.

22"In my dreams I also saw seven heads
of grain, full and good, growing on a sin-
gle stalk. 23After them, seven other heads
sprouted—withered and thin and
scorched by the east wind. 24The thin
heads of grain swallowed up the seven
good heads. I told this to the magicians,
but none could explain it to me."

25Then Joseph said to Pharaoh, "The
dreams of Pharaoh are one and the same.
God has revealed to Pharaoh what he is
about to do. 26The seven good cows are
seven years, and the seven good heads of
grain are seven years; it is one and the
same dream. 27The seven lean, ugly cows
that came up afterward are seven years,
and so are the seven worthless heads of
grain scorched by the east wind: They are
seven years of famine.

28"It is just as I said to Pharaoh: God has
shown Pharaoh what he is about to do.
29Seven years of great abundance are
coming throughout the land of Egypt,
30but seven years of famine will follow
them. Then all the abundance in Egypt
will be forgotten, and the famine will rav-
age the land. 31The abundance in the land
will not be remembered, because the fam-
ine that follows it will be so severe. 32The
reason the dream was given to Pharaoh in
two forms is that the matter has been firm-
ly decided by God, and God will do it
soon.

33"And now let Pharaoh look for a dis-
cerning and wise man and put him in
charge of the land of Egypt. 34Let Pharaoh
appoint commissioners over the land to
take a fifth of the harvest of Egypt during
the seven years of abundance. 35They
should collect all the food of these good
years that are coming and store up the
grain under the authority of Pharaoh, to
be kept in the cities for food. 36This food
should be held in reserve for the country,
to be used during the seven years of fam-
ine that will come upon Egypt, so that the
country may not be ruined by the fam-
ine."

37The plan seemed good to Pharaoh and
to all his officials. 38So Pharaoh asked
them, "Can we find anyone like this man,
one in whom is the spirit of God[a]?"

39Then Pharaoh said to Joseph, "Since
God has made all this known to you, there
is no one so discerning and wise as you.
40You shall be in charge of my palace, and
all my people are to submit to your orders.
Only with respect to the throne will I be
greater than you."

Joseph in Charge of Egypt

41So Pharaoh said to Joseph, "I hereby
put you in charge of the whole land of
Egypt." 42Then Pharaoh took his signet
ring from his finger and put it on Joseph's
finger. He dressed him in robes of fine lin-
en and put a gold chain around his neck.
43He had him ride in a chariot as his sec-
ond-in-command,[b] and men shouted be-
fore him, "Make way[c]!" Thus he put him
in charge of the whole land of Egypt.

44Then Pharaoh said to Joseph, "I am
Pharaoh, but without your word no one
will lift hand or foot in all Egypt." 45Phar-
aoh gave Joseph the name Zaphenath-Pa-
neah and gave him Asenath daughter of
Potiphera, priest of On,[d] to be his wife.
And Joseph went throughout the land of
Egypt.

46Joseph was thirty years old when he
entered the service of Pharaoh king of
Egypt. And Joseph went out from Phar-
aoh's presence and traveled throughout
Egypt. 47During the seven years of abun-
dance the land produced plentifully. 48Jo-
seph collected all the food produced in
those seven years of abundance in Egypt
and stored it in the cities. In each city he
put the food grown in the fields surround-
ing it. 49Joseph stored up huge quantities
of grain, like the sand of the sea; it was so
much that he stopped keeping records be-
cause it was beyond measure.

50Before the years of famine came, two
sons were born to Joseph by Asenath
daughter of Potiphera, priest of On. 51Jo-
seph named his firstborn Manasseh[e] and
said, "It is because God has made me for-
get all my trouble and all my father's
household." 52The second son he named
Ephraim[f] and said, "It is because God

[a]38 Or *of the gods* [b]43 Or *in the chariot of his second-in-command*; or *in his second chariot*
[c]43 Or *Bow down* [d]45 That is, Heliopolis; also in verse 50 [e]51 *Manasseh* sounds like and may be derived from the Hebrew for *forget.* [f]52 *Ephraim* sounds like the Hebrew for *twice fruitful.*

has made me fruitful in the land of my suffering."

53The seven years of abundance in Egypt came to an end, 54and the seven years of famine began, just as Joseph had said. There was famine in all the other lands, but in the whole land of Egypt there was food. 55When all Egypt began to feel the famine, the people cried to Pharaoh for food. Then Pharaoh told all the Egyptians, "Go to Joseph and do what he tells you."

56When the famine had spread over the whole country, Joseph opened the storehouses and sold grain to the Egyptians, for the famine was severe throughout Egypt. 57And all the countries came to Egypt to buy grain from Joseph, because the famine was severe in all the world.

Joseph's Brothers Go to Egypt

42 When Jacob learned that there was grain in Egypt, he said to his sons, "Why do you just keep looking at each other?" 2He continued, "I have heard that there is grain in Egypt. Go down there and buy some for us, so that we may live and not die."

3Then ten of Joseph's brothers went down to buy grain from Egypt. 4But Jacob did not send Benjamin, Joseph's brother, with the others, because he was afraid that harm might come to him. 5So Israel's sons were among those who went to buy grain, for the famine was in the land of Canaan also.

6Now Joseph was the governor of the land, the one who sold grain to all its people. So when Joseph's brothers arrived, they bowed down to him with their faces to the ground. 7As soon as Joseph saw his brothers, he recognized them, but he pretended to be a stranger and spoke harshly to them. "Where do you come from?" he asked.

"From the land of Canaan," they replied, "to buy food."

8Although Joseph recognized his brothers, they did not recognize him. 9Then he remembered his dreams about them and said to them, "You are spies! You have come to see where our land is unprotected."

10"No, my lord," they answered. "Your servants have come to buy food. 11We are all the sons of one man. Your servants are honest men, not spies."

12"No!" he said to them. "You have come to see where our land is unprotected."

13But they replied, "Your servants were twelve brothers, the sons of one man, who lives in the land of Canaan. The youngest is now with our father, and one is no more."

14Joseph said to them, "It is just as I told you: You are spies! 15And this is how you will be tested: As surely as Pharaoh lives, you will not leave this place unless your youngest brother comes here. 16Send one of your number to get your brother; the rest of you will be kept in prison, so that your words may be tested to see if you are telling the truth. If you are not, then as surely as Pharaoh lives, you are spies!" 17And he put them all in custody for three days.

18On the third day, Joseph said to them, "Do this and you will live, for I fear God: 19If you are honest men, let one of your brothers stay here in prison, while the rest of you go and take grain back for your starving households. 20But you must bring your youngest brother to me, so that your words may be verified and that you may not die." This they proceeded to do.

21They said to one another, "Surely we are being punished because of our brother. We saw how distressed he was when he pleaded with us for his life, but we would not listen; that's why this distress has come upon us."

22Reuben replied, "Didn't I tell you not to sin against the boy? But you wouldn't listen! Now we must give an accounting for his blood." 23They did not realize that Joseph could understand them, since he was using an interpreter.

24He turned away from them and began to weep, but then turned back and spoke to them again. He had Simeon taken from them and bound before their eyes.

25Joseph gave orders to fill their bags with grain, to put each man's silver back in his sack, and to give them provisions for their journey. After this was done for them, 26they loaded their grain on their donkeys and left.

27At the place where they stopped for the night one of them opened his sack to get feed for his donkey, and he saw his silver in the mouth of his sack. 28"My silver has been returned," he said to his brothers. "Here it is in my sack."

Their hearts sank and they turned to each other trembling and said, "What is this that God has done to us?"

29When they came to their father Jacob
in the land of Canaan, they told him all
that had happened to them. They said,
30"The man who is lord over the land
spoke harshly to us and treated us as
though we were spying on the land. 31But
we said to him, 'We are honest men; we
are not spies. 32We were twelve brothers,
sons of one father. One is no more, and
the youngest is now with our father in Ca-
naan.'
33"Then the man who is lord over the
land said to us, 'This is how I will know
whether you are honest men: Leave one of
your brothers here with me, and take food
for your starving households and go.
34But bring your youngest brother to me
so I will know that you are not spies but
honest men. Then I will give your brother
back to you, and you can trade[a] in the
land.' "
35As they were emptying their sacks,
there in each man's sack was his pouch of
silver! When they and their father saw the
money pouches, they were frightened.
36Their father Jacob said to them, "You
have deprived me of my children. Joseph
is no more and Simeon is no more, and
now you want to take Benjamin. Every-
thing is against me!"
37Then Reuben said to his father, "You
may put both of my sons to death if I do
not bring him back to you. Entrust him to
my care, and I will bring him back."
38But Jacob said, "My son will not go
down there with you; his brother is dead
and he is the only one left. If harm comes
to him on the journey you are taking, you
will bring my gray head down to the
grave[b] in sorrow."

The Second Journey to Egypt

43 Now the famine was still severe in
the land. 2So when they had eaten
all the grain they had brought from Egypt,
their father said to them, "Go back and
buy us a little more food."
3But Judah said to him, "The man
warned us solemnly, 'You will not see my
face again unless your brother is with
you.' 4If you will send our brother along
with us, we will go down and buy food for
you. 5But if you will not send him, we will
not go down, because the man said to us,
'You will not see my face again unless
your brother is with you.' "
6Israel asked, "Why did you bring this
trouble on me by telling the man you had
another brother?"
7They replied, "The man questioned us
closely about ourselves and our family. 'Is
your father still living?' he asked us. 'Do
you have another brother?' We simply an-
swered his questions. How were we to
know he would say, 'Bring your brother
down here'?"
8Then Judah said to Israel his father,
"Send the boy along with me and we will
go at once, so that we and you and our
children may live and not die. 9I myself
will guarantee his safety; you can hold me
personally responsible for him. If I do not
bring him back to you and set him here
before you, I will bear the blame before
you all my life. 10As it is, if we had not de-
layed, we could have gone and returned
twice."
11Then their father Israel said to them,
"If it must be, then do this: Put some of
the best products of the land in your bags
and take them down to the man as a gift—
a little balm and a little honey, some
spices and myrrh, some pistachio nuts
and almonds. 12Take double the amount
of silver with you, for you must return the
silver that was put back into the mouths of
your sacks. Perhaps it was a mistake.
13Take your brother also and go back to
the man at once. 14And may God Al-
mighty[c] grant you mercy before the man
so that he will let your other brother and
Benjamin come back with you. As for me,
if I am bereaved, I am bereaved."
15So the men took the gifts and double
the amount of silver, and Benjamin also.
They hurried down to Egypt and present-
ed themselves to Joseph. 16When Joseph
saw Benjamin with them, he said to the
steward of his house, "Take these men to
my house, slaughter an animal and pre-
pare dinner; they are to eat with me at
noon."
17The man did as Joseph told him and
took the men to Joseph's house. 18Now
the men were frightened when they were
taken to his house. They thought, "We
were brought here because of the silver
that was put back into our sacks the first
time. He wants to attack us and overpow-
er us and seize us as slaves and take our
donkeys."
19So they went up to Joseph's steward
and spoke to him at the entrance to the
house. 20"Please, sir," they said, "we came

[a]34 Or *move about freely* [b]38 Hebrew *Sheol* [c]14 Hebrew *El-Shaddai*

down here the first time to buy food. 21But
at the place where we stopped for the
night we opened our sacks and each of us
found his silver—the exact weight—in
the mouth of his sack. So we have brought
it back with us. 22We have also brought
additional silver with us to buy food. We
don't know who put our silver in our
sacks."

23"It's all right," he said. "Don't be
afraid. Your God, the God of your father,
has given you treasure in your sacks; I re-
ceived your silver." Then he brought Sim-
eon out to them.

24The steward took the men into Jo-
seph's house, gave them water to wash
their feet and provided fodder for their
donkeys. 25They prepared their gifts for
Joseph's arrival at noon, because they had
heard that they were to eat there.

26When Joseph came home, they pre-
sented to him the gifts they had brought
into the house, and they bowed down be-
fore him to the ground. 27He asked them
how they were, and then he said, "How is
your aged father you told me about? Is he
still living?"

28They replied, "Your servant our father
is still alive and well." And they bowed
low to pay him honor.

29As he looked about and saw his broth-
er Benjamin, his own mother's son, he
asked, "Is this your youngest brother, the
one you told me about?" And he said,
"God be gracious to you, my son." 30Deep-
ly moved at the sight of his brother, Jo-
seph hurried out and looked for a place to
weep. He went into his private room and
wept there.

31After he had washed his face, he came
out and, controlling himself, said, "Serve
the food."

32They served him by himself, the
brothers by themselves, and the Egyptians
who ate with him by themselves, because
Egyptians could not eat with Hebrews, for
that is detestable to Egyptians. 33The men
had been seated before him in the order of
their ages, from the firstborn to the young-
est; and they looked at each other in as-
tonishment. 34When portions were served
to them from Joseph's table, Benjamin's
portion was five times as much as anyone
else's. So they feasted and drank freely
with him.

A Silver Cup in a Sack

44 Now Joseph gave these instruc-
tions to the steward of his house:
"Fill the men's sacks with as much food as
they can carry, and put each man's silver
in the mouth of his sack. 2Then put my
cup, the silver one, in the mouth of the
youngest one's sack, along with the silver
for his grain." And he did as Joseph said.

3As morning dawned, the men were
sent on their way with their donkeys.
4They had not gone far from the city when
Joseph said to his steward, "Go after those
men at once, and when you catch up with
them, say to them, 'Why have you repaid
good with evil? 5Isn't this the cup my mas-
ter drinks from and also uses for divina-
tion? This is a wicked thing you have
done.'"

6When he caught up with them, he re-
peated these words to them. 7But they
said to him, "Why does my lord say such
things? Far be it from your servants to do
anything like that! 8We even brought back
to you from the land of Canaan the silver
we found inside the mouths of our sacks.
So why would we steal silver or gold from
your master's house? 9If any of your ser-
vants is found to have it, he will die; and
the rest of us will become my lord's
slaves."

10"Very well, then," he said, "let it be as
you say. Whoever is found to have it will
become my slave; the rest of you will be
free from blame."

11Each of them quickly lowered his sack
to the ground and opened it. 12Then the
steward proceeded to search, beginning
with the oldest and ending with the young-
est. And the cup was found in Benja-
min's sack. 13At this, they tore their
clothes. Then they all loaded their don-
keys and returned to the city.

14Joseph was still in the house when Ju-
dah and his brothers came in, and they
threw themselves to the ground before
him. 15Joseph said to them, "What is this
you have done? Don't you know that a
man like me can find things out by divina-
tion?"

16"What can we say to my lord?" Judah
replied. "What can we say? How can we
prove our innocence? God has uncovered
your servants' guilt. We are now my lord's
slaves—we ourselves and the one who
was found to have the cup."

17But Joseph said, "Far be it from me to
do such a thing! Only the man who was
found to have the cup will become my
slave. The rest of you, go back to your fa-
ther in peace."

18Then Judah went up to him and said:

"Please, my lord, let your servant speak a
word to my lord. Do not be angry with
your servant, though you are equal to
Pharaoh himself. 19My lord asked his ser-
vants, 'Do you have a father or a brother?'
20And we answered, 'We have an aged fa-
ther, and there is a young son born to him
in his old age. His brother is dead, and he
is the only one of his mother's sons left,
and his father loves him.'
21"Then you said to your servants,
'Bring him down to me so I can see him
for myself.' 22And we said to my lord, 'The
boy cannot leave his father; if he leaves
him, his father will die.' 23But you told
your servants, 'Unless your youngest
brother comes down with you, you will
not see my face again.' 24When we went
back to your servant my father, we told
him what my lord had said.
25"Then our father said, 'Go back and
buy a little more food.' 26But we said, 'We
cannot go down. Only if our youngest
brother is with us will we go. We cannot
see the man's face unless our youngest
brother is with us.'
27"Your servant my father said to us,
'You know that my wife bore me two
sons. 28One of them went away from me,
and I said, "He has surely been torn to
pieces." And I have not seen him since.
29If you take this one from me too and
harm comes to him, you will bring my
gray head down to the grave[a] in misery.'
30"So now, if the boy is not with us
when I go back to your servant my father
and if my father, whose life is closely
bound up with the boy's life, 31sees that
the boy isn't there, he will die. Your ser-
vants will bring the gray head of our father
down to the grave in sorrow. 32Your ser-
vant guaranteed the boy's safety to my fa-
ther. I said, 'If I do not bring him back to
you, I will bear the blame before you, my
father, all my life!'
33"Now then, please let your servant re-
main here as my lord's slave in place of
the boy, and let the boy return with his
brothers. 34How can I go back to my father
if the boy is not with me? No! Do not let
me see the misery that would come upon
my father."

Joseph Makes Himself Known

45 Then Joseph could no longer con-
trol himself before all his atten-
dants, and he cried out, "Have everyone
leave my presence!" So there was no one
with Joseph when he made himself
known to his brothers. 2And he wept so
loudly that the Egyptians heard him, and
Pharaoh's household heard about it.
3Joseph said to his brothers, "I am Jo-
seph! Is my father still living?" But his
brothers were not able to answer him, be-
cause they were terrified at his presence.
4Then Joseph said to his brothers,
"Come close to me." When they had done
so, he said, "I am your brother Joseph, the
one you sold into Egypt! 5And now, do not
be distressed and do not be angry with
yourselves for selling me here, because it
was to save lives that God sent me ahead
of you. 6For two years now there has been
famine in the land, and for the next five
years there will not be plowing and reap-
ing. 7But God sent me ahead of you to pre-
serve for you a remnant on earth and to
save your lives by a great deliverance.[b]
8"So then, it was not you who sent me
here, but God. He made me father to Phar-
aoh, lord of his entire household and ruler
of all Egypt. 9Now hurry back to my father
and say to him, 'This is what your son Jo-
seph says: God has made me lord of all
Egypt. Come down to me; don't delay.
10You shall live in the region of Goshen
and be near me—you, your children and
grandchildren, your flocks and herds, and
all you have. 11I will provide for you there,
because five years of famine are still to
come. Otherwise you and your household
and all who belong to you will become
destitute.'
12"You can see for yourselves, and so
can my brother Benjamin, that it is really
I who am speaking to you. 13Tell my fa-
ther about all the honor accorded me in
Egypt and about everything you have
seen. And bring my father down here
quickly."
14Then he threw his arms around his
brother Benjamin and wept, and Benja-
min embraced him, weeping. 15And he
kissed all his brothers and wept over
them. Afterward his brothers talked with
him.
16When the news reached Pharaoh's
palace that Joseph's brothers had come,
Pharaoh and all his officials were pleased.
17Pharaoh said to Joseph, "Tell your
brothers, 'Do this: Load your animals and
return to the land of Canaan, 18and bring
your father and your families back to me.

[a] 29 Hebrew *Sheol*; also in verse 31 [b] 7 Or *save you as a great band of survivors*

I will give you the best of the land of Egypt
and you can enjoy the fat of the land.'
19"You are also directed to tell them,
'Do this: Take some carts from Egypt for
your children and your wives, and get
your father and come. 20Never mind
about your belongings, because the best
of all Egypt will be yours.' "
21So the sons of Israel did this. Joseph
gave them carts, as Pharaoh had com-
manded, and he also gave them provi-
sions for their journey. 22To each of them
he gave new clothing, but to Benjamin he
gave three hundred shekels[a] of silver and
five sets of clothes. 23And this is what he
sent to his father: ten donkeys loaded with
the best things of Egypt, and ten female
donkeys loaded with grain and bread and
other provisions for his journey. 24Then
he sent his brothers away, and as they

[a]22 That is, about 7 1/2 pounds (about 3.5 kilograms)

VERSE FOR THE DAY: Genesis 45:5

AUTHOR: Dr. John Trent

PASSAGE FOR THE DAY: Genesis 45:1–15

Break the Cycle

We are told in Genesis that "a man will leave his father and mother and be united to his wife." Yet if they come out of an unhealthy family background, that is, an upbringing that may have included alcoholism, verbal abuse or other chronic problems, they will have a hard time following this biblical mandate.

My dad was an alcoholic, and my parents were divorced. I never met my father until I was in high school, and then I hated him for many years after that. When I became a Christian, I knew it wasn't right to feel this way, so I buried my hatred. But when I got married, the strong negative feelings were still there, and they started to surface and poison my relationship with my wife. It wasn't until she confronted me about the way I was treating her that I began to work through the real issue—my unresolved anger toward my dad.

I harbored a lot of hatred toward my dad, but in resolving those feelings, I learned a real lesson in forgiveness, and that in itself has been a priceless gift. It broke the unhealthy cycle and opened the way to begin a healthy cycle of family relationships.

MARRIAGE BUILDERS

♦ *How has forgiveness been constructive in your own marriage?*
♦ *What issues in your relationship might be resolved through forgiveness?*

Additional Scripture Readings
Genesis 2:24; Exodus 20:5;
Isaiah 61:1, 3

Go to page 55 for your next devotional reading.

were leaving he said to them, "Don't quarrel on the way!"

25So they went up out of Egypt and came to their father Jacob in the land of Canaan. 26They told him, "Joseph is still alive! In fact, he is ruler of all Egypt." Jacob was stunned; he did not believe them. 27But when they told him everything Joseph had said to them, and when he saw the carts Joseph had sent to carry him back, the spirit of their father Jacob revived. 28And Israel said, "I'm convinced! My son Joseph is still alive. I will go and see him before I die."

Jacob Goes to Egypt

46 So Israel set out with all that was his, and when he reached Beersheba, he offered sacrifices to the God of his father Isaac.

2And God spoke to Israel in a vision at night and said, "Jacob! Jacob!"

"Here I am," he replied.

3"I am God, the God of your father," he said. "Do not be afraid to go down to Egypt, for I will make you into a great nation there. 4I will go down to Egypt with you, and I will surely bring you back again. And Joseph's own hand will close your eyes."

5Then Jacob left Beersheba, and Israel's sons took their father Jacob and their children and their wives in the carts that Pharaoh had sent to transport him. 6They also took with them their livestock and the possessions they had acquired in Canaan, and Jacob and all his offspring went to Egypt. 7He took with him to Egypt his sons and grandsons and his daughters and granddaughters—all his offspring.

8These are the names of the sons of Israel (Jacob and his descendants) who went to Egypt:

Reuben the firstborn of Jacob.
9The sons of Reuben:
Hanoch, Pallu, Hezron and Carmi.
10The sons of Simeon:
Jemuel, Jamin, Ohad, Jakin, Zohar and Shaul the son of a Canaanite woman.
11The sons of Levi:
Gershon, Kohath and Merari.
12The sons of Judah:
Er, Onan, Shelah, Perez and Zerah (but Er and Onan had died in the land of Canaan).
The sons of Perez:
Hezron and Hamul.
13The sons of Issachar:
Tola, Puah,[a] Jashub[b] and Shimron.
14The sons of Zebulun:
Sered, Elon and Jahleel.
15These were the sons Leah bore to Jacob in Paddan Aram,[c] besides his daughter Dinah. These sons and daughters of his were thirty-three in all.

16The sons of Gad:
Zephon,[d] Haggi, Shuni, Ezbon, Eri, Arodi and Areli.
17The sons of Asher:
Imnah, Ishvah, Ishvi and Beriah.
Their sister was Serah.
The sons of Beriah:
Heber and Malkiel.
18These were the children born to Jacob by Zilpah, whom Laban had given to his daughter Leah—sixteen in all.

19The sons of Jacob's wife Rachel:
Joseph and Benjamin. 20In Egypt, Manasseh and Ephraim were born to Joseph by Asenath daughter of Potiphera, priest of On.[e]
21The sons of Benjamin:
Bela, Beker, Ashbel, Gera, Naaman, Ehi, Rosh, Muppim, Huppim and Ard.
22These were the sons of Rachel who were born to Jacob—fourteen in all.

23The son of Dan:
Hushim.
24The sons of Naphtali:
Jahziel, Guni, Jezer and Shillem.
25These were the sons born to Jacob by Bilhah, whom Laban had given to his daughter Rachel—seven in all.

26All those who went to Egypt with Jacob—those who were his direct descendants, not counting his sons' wives—numbered sixty-six persons. 27With the two sons[f] who had been born to Joseph in Egypt, the members of Jacob's family,

[a] *13* Samaritan Pentateuch and Syriac (see also 1 Chron. 7:1); Masoretic Text *Puvah* [b] *13* Samaritan Pentateuch and some Septuagint manuscripts (see also Num. 26:24 and 1 Chron. 7:1); Masoretic Text *Iob* [c] *15* That is, Northwest Mesopotamia [d] *16* Samaritan Pentateuch and Septuagint (see also Num. 26:15); Masoretic Text *Ziphion* [e] *20* That is, Heliopolis [f] *27* Hebrew; Septuagint *the nine children*

which went to Egypt, were seventy[a] in all.

[28]Now Jacob sent Judah ahead of him to Joseph to get directions to Goshen. When they arrived in the region of Goshen, [29]Joseph had his chariot made ready and went to Goshen to meet his father Israel. As soon as Joseph appeared before him, he threw his arms around his father[b] and wept for a long time.

[30]Israel said to Joseph, "Now I am ready to die, since I have seen for myself that you are still alive."

[31]Then Joseph said to his brothers and to his father's household, "I will go up and speak to Pharaoh and will say to him, 'My brothers and my father's household, who were living in the land of Canaan, have come to me. [32]The men are shepherds; they tend livestock, and they have brought along their flocks and herds and everything they own.' [33]When Pharaoh calls you in and asks, 'What is your occupation?' [34]you should answer, 'Your servants have tended livestock from our boyhood on, just as our fathers did.' Then you will be allowed to settle in the region of Goshen, for all shepherds are detestable to the Egyptians."

47 Joseph went and told Pharaoh, "My father and brothers, with their flocks and herds and everything they own, have come from the land of Canaan and are now in Goshen." [2]He chose five of his brothers and presented them before Pharaoh.

[3]Pharaoh asked the brothers, "What is your occupation?"

"Your servants are shepherds," they replied to Pharaoh, "just as our fathers were." [4]They also said to him, "We have come to live here awhile, because the famine is severe in Canaan and your servants' flocks have no pasture. So now, please let your servants settle in Goshen."

[5]Pharaoh said to Joseph, "Your father and your brothers have come to you, [6]and the land of Egypt is before you; settle your father and your brothers in the best part of the land. Let them live in Goshen. And if you know of any among them with special ability, put them in charge of my own livestock."

[7]Then Joseph brought his father Jacob in and presented him before Pharaoh. After Jacob blessed[c] Pharaoh, [8]Pharaoh asked him, "How old are you?"

[9]And Jacob said to Pharaoh, "The years of my pilgrimage are a hundred and thirty. My years have been few and difficult, and they do not equal the years of the pilgrimage of my fathers." [10]Then Jacob blessed[d] Pharaoh and went out from his presence.

[11]So Joseph settled his father and his brothers in Egypt and gave them property in the best part of the land, the district of Rameses, as Pharaoh directed. [12]Joseph also provided his father and his brothers and all his father's household with food, according to the number of their children.

Joseph and the Famine

[13]There was no food, however, in the whole region because the famine was severe; both Egypt and Canaan wasted away because of the famine. [14]Joseph collected all the money that was to be found in Egypt and Canaan in payment for the grain they were buying, and he brought it to Pharaoh's palace. [15]When the money of the people of Egypt and Canaan was gone, all Egypt came to Joseph and said, "Give us food. Why should we die before your eyes? Our money is used up."

[16]"Then bring your livestock," said Joseph. "I will sell you food in exchange for your livestock, since your money is gone." [17]So they brought their livestock to Joseph, and he gave them food in exchange for their horses, their sheep and goats, their cattle and donkeys. And he brought them through that year with food in exchange for all their livestock.

[18]When that year was over, they came to him the following year and said, "We cannot hide from our lord the fact that since our money is gone and our livestock belongs to you, there is nothing left for our lord except our bodies and our land. [19]Why should we perish before your eyes—we and our land as well? Buy us and our land in exchange for food, and we with our land will be in bondage to Pharaoh. Give us seed so that we may live and not die, and that the land may not become desolate."

[20]So Joseph bought all the land in Egypt for Pharaoh. The Egyptians, one and all, sold their fields, because the famine was too severe for them. The land became

[a]27 Hebrew (see also Exodus 1:5 and footnote); Septuagint (see also Acts 7:14) *seventy-five*
[b]29 Hebrew *around him* [c]7 Or *greeted* [d]10 Or *said farewell to*

Pharaoh's, 21and Joseph reduced the people to servitude,[a] from one end of Egypt to the other. 22However, he did not buy the land of the priests, because they received a regular allotment from Pharaoh and had food enough from the allotment Pharaoh gave them. That is why they did not sell their land.

23Joseph said to the people, "Now that I have bought you and your land today for Pharaoh, here is seed for you so you can plant the ground. 24But when the crop comes in, give a fifth of it to Pharaoh. The other four-fifths you may keep as seed for the fields and as food for yourselves and your households and your children."

25"You have saved our lives," they said. "May we find favor in the eyes of our lord; we will be in bondage to Pharaoh."

26So Joseph established it as a law concerning land in Egypt—still in force today—that a fifth of the produce belongs to Pharaoh. It was only the land of the priests that did not become Pharaoh's.

27Now the Israelites settled in Egypt in the region of Goshen. They acquired property there and were fruitful and increased greatly in number.

28Jacob lived in Egypt seventeen years, and the years of his life were a hundred and forty-seven. 29When the time drew near for Israel to die, he called for his son Joseph and said to him, "If I have found favor in your eyes, put your hand under my thigh and promise that you will show me kindness and faithfulness. Do not bury me in Egypt, 30but when I rest with my fathers, carry me out of Egypt and bury me where they are buried."

"I will do as you say," he said.

31"Swear to me," he said. Then Joseph swore to him, and Israel worshiped as he leaned on the top of his staff.[b]

Manasseh and Ephraim

48 Some time later Joseph was told, "Your father is ill." So he took his two sons Manasseh and Ephraim along with him. 2When Jacob was told, "Your son Joseph has come to you," Israel rallied his strength and sat up on the bed.

3Jacob said to Joseph, "God Almighty[c] appeared to me at Luz in the land of Canaan, and there he blessed me 4and said to me, 'I am going to make you fruitful and will increase your numbers. I will make you a community of peoples, and I will give this land as an everlasting possession to your descendants after you.'

5"Now then, your two sons born to you in Egypt before I came to you here will be reckoned as mine; Ephraim and Manasseh will be mine, just as Reuben and Simeon are mine. 6Any children born to you after them will be yours; in the territory they inherit they will be reckoned under the names of their brothers. 7As I was returning from Paddan,[d] to my sorrow Rachel died in the land of Canaan while we were still on the way, a little distance from Ephrath. So I buried her there beside the road to Ephrath" (that is, Bethlehem).

8When Israel saw the sons of Joseph, he asked, "Who are these?"

9"They are the sons God has given me here," Joseph said to his father.

Then Israel said, "Bring them to me so I may bless them."

10Now Israel's eyes were failing because of old age, and he could hardly see. So Joseph brought his sons close to him, and his father kissed them and embraced them.

11Israel said to Joseph, "I never expected to see your face again, and now God has allowed me to see your children too."

12Then Joseph removed them from Israel's knees and bowed down with his face to the ground. 13And Joseph took both of them, Ephraim on his right toward Israel's left hand and Manasseh on his left toward Israel's right hand, and brought them close to him. 14But Israel reached out his right hand and put it on Ephraim's head, though he was the younger, and crossing his arms, he put his left hand on Manasseh's head, even though Manasseh was the firstborn.

15Then he blessed Joseph and said,

"May the God before whom my fathers
Abraham and Isaac walked,
the God who has been my shepherd
all my life to this day,
16the Angel who has delivered me from all harm
—may he bless these boys.
May they be called by my name

[a] 21 Samaritan Pentateuch and Septuagint (see also Vulgate); Masoretic Text *and he moved the people into the cities* [b] 31 Or *Israel bowed down at the head of his bed* [c] 3 Hebrew *El-Shaddai* [d] 7 That is, Northwest Mesopotamia

and the names of my fathers
Abraham and Isaac,
and may they increase greatly
upon the earth."

17When Joseph saw his father placing
his right hand on Ephraim's head he was
displeased; so he took hold of his father's
hand to move it from Ephraim's head to
Manasseh's head. 18Joseph said to him,
"No, my father, this one is the firstborn;
put your right hand on his head."
19But his father refused and said, "I
know, my son, I know. He too will become
a people, and he too will become great.
Nevertheless, his younger brother will be
greater than he, and his descendants will
become a group of nations." 20He blessed
them that day and said,

"In your[a] name will Israel pronounce
this blessing:
'May God make you like Ephraim
and Manasseh.' "

So he put Ephraim ahead of Manasseh.
21Then Israel said to Joseph, "I am
about to die, but God will be with you[b]
and take you[b] back to the land of your[b]
fathers. 22And to you, as one who is over
your brothers, I give the ridge of land[c] I
took from the Amorites with my sword
and my bow."

Jacob Blesses His Sons

49 Then Jacob called for his sons and
said: "Gather around so I can tell
you what will happen to you in days to
come.

2"Assemble and listen, sons of Jacob;
listen to your father Israel.

3"Reuben, you are my firstborn,
my might, the first sign of my
strength,
excelling in honor, excelling in
power.
4Turbulent as the waters, you will no
longer excel,
for you went up onto your father's
bed,
onto my couch and defiled it.

5"Simeon and Levi are brothers—
their swords[d] are weapons of
violence.
6Let me not enter their council,
let me not join their assembly,
for they have killed men in their anger
and hamstrung oxen as they
pleased.
7Cursed be their anger, so fierce,
and their fury, so cruel!
I will scatter them in Jacob
and disperse them in Israel.

8"Judah,[e] your brothers will praise
you;
your hand will be on the neck of
your enemies;
your father's sons will bow down to
you.
9You are a lion's cub, O Judah;
you return from the prey, my son.
Like a lion he crouches and lies down,
like a lioness—who dares to rouse
him?
10The scepter will not depart from
Judah,
nor the ruler's staff from between
his feet,
until he comes to whom it belongs[f]
and the obedience of the nations is
his.
11He will tether his donkey to a vine,
his colt to the choicest branch;
he will wash his garments in wine,
his robes in the blood of grapes.
12His eyes will be darker than wine,
his teeth whiter than milk.[g]

13"Zebulun will live by the seashore
and become a haven for ships;
his border will extend toward Sidon.

14"Issachar is a rawboned[h] donkey
lying down between two
saddlebags.[i]
15When he sees how good is his resting
place
and how pleasant is his land,
he will bend his shoulder to the
burden
and submit to forced labor.

16"Dan[j] will provide justice for his
people
as one of the tribes of Israel.
17Dan will be a serpent by the roadside,

[a] 20 The Hebrew is singular. [b] 21 The Hebrew is plural. [c] 22 Or *And to you I give one portion more than to your brothers—the portion* [d] 5 The meaning of the Hebrew for this word is uncertain. [e] 8 *Judah* sounds like and may be derived from the Hebrew for *praise.* [f] 10 Or *until Shiloh comes*; or *until he comes to whom tribute belongs* [g] 12 Or *will be dull from wine, / his teeth white from milk* [h] 14 Or *strong* [i] 14 Or *campfires* [j] 16 *Dan* here means *he provides justice.*

a viper along the path,
that bites the horse's heels
so that its rider tumbles backward.

18"I look for your deliverance, O LORD.

19"Gad[a] will be attacked by a band of raiders,
but he will attack them at their heels.

20"Asher's food will be rich;
he will provide delicacies fit for a king.

21"Naphtali is a doe set free
that bears beautiful fawns.[b]

22"Joseph is a fruitful vine,
a fruitful vine near a spring,

[a]19 *Gad* can mean *attack* and *band of raiders.* [b]21 Or *free; / he utters beautiful words*

VERSE FOR THE DAY: Genesis 49:28 | AUTHOR: Gary D. Chapman | PASSAGE FOR THE DAY: Genesis 49:1–28

A Spoken Blessing

Words of blessing communicate care and high regard for someone you love. Of all the ways spouses express love, speaking words of affirmation is one of the most important. Words of affirmation are statements that show you value your spouse: "You look nice today." "I love you." "Thanks for taking the garbage out." These statements focus either on something your spouse *does* or something he or she *is*.

People tell me, "I didn't grow up in a home where we did that. I'm just not a verbal person." There are a lot of things that don't come naturally to us, but we learn to do them anyway. Even if it's difficult, you can learn to express your feelings in words. Whenever you hear someone pay a compliment, for example, write it down. Or as you read things, pick out expressions of love and start making a list. Then practice reading your list out loud. After a while, it will begin to feel more comfortable.

Then, of course, start saying these things to your spouse. Once you start, it becomes much easier. Learning each other's love language is a real blessing, and it's one way you *both* can get what you need in marriage.

MARRIAGE BUILDERS

- *Tell one another three things that you value about each other.*
- *Describe to your mate the types of expressions that make you feel most loved and appreciated.*

Additional Scripture Readings
Proverbs 16:23; Ephesians 4:29–32

Go to page 60 for your next devotional reading.

whose branches climb over a wall.[a]
23With bitterness archers attacked him;
they shot at him with hostility.
24But his bow remained steady,
his strong arms stayed[b] limber,
because of the hand of the Mighty One of Jacob,
because of the Shepherd, the Rock of Israel,
25because of your father's God, who helps you,
because of the Almighty,[c] who blesses you
with blessings of the heavens above,
blessings of the deep that lies below,
blessings of the breast and womb.
26Your father's blessings are greater
than the blessings of the ancient mountains,
than[d] the bounty of the age-old hills.
Let all these rest on the head of Joseph,
on the brow of the prince among[e] his brothers.

27"Benjamin is a ravenous wolf;
in the morning he devours the prey,
in the evening he divides the plunder."

28All these are the twelve tribes of Israel, and this is what their father said to them when he blessed them, giving each the blessing appropriate to him.

The Death of Jacob

29Then he gave them these instructions: "I am about to be gathered to my people. Bury me with my fathers in the cave in the field of Ephron the Hittite, 30the cave in the field of Machpelah, near Mamre in Canaan, which Abraham bought as a burial place from Ephron the Hittite, along with the field. 31There Abraham and his wife Sarah were buried, there Isaac and his wife Rebekah were buried, and there I buried Leah. 32The field and the cave in it were bought from the Hittites.[f]"

33When Jacob had finished giving instructions to his sons, he drew his feet up into the bed, breathed his last and was gathered to his people.

50 Joseph threw himself upon his father and wept over him and kissed him. 2Then Joseph directed the physicians in his service to embalm his father Israel. So the physicians embalmed him, 3taking a full forty days, for that was the time required for embalming. And the Egyptians mourned for him seventy days.

4When the days of mourning had passed, Joseph said to Pharaoh's court, "If I have found favor in your eyes, speak to Pharaoh for me. Tell him, 5'My father made me swear an oath and said, "I am about to die; bury me in the tomb I dug for myself in the land of Canaan." Now let me go up and bury my father; then I will return.' "

6Pharaoh said, "Go up and bury your father, as he made you swear to do."

7So Joseph went up to bury his father. All Pharaoh's officials accompanied him—the dignitaries of his court and all the dignitaries of Egypt— 8besides all the members of Joseph's household and his brothers and those belonging to his father's household. Only their children and their flocks and herds were left in Goshen. 9Chariots and horsemen[g] also went up with him. It was a very large company.

10When they reached the threshing floor of Atad, near the Jordan, they lamented loudly and bitterly; and there Joseph observed a seven-day period of mourning for his father. 11When the Canaanites who lived there saw the mourning at the threshing floor of Atad, they said, "The Egyptians are holding a solemn ceremony of mourning." That is why that place near the Jordan is called Abel Mizraim.[h]

12So Jacob's sons did as he had commanded them: 13They carried him to the land of Canaan and buried him in the cave in the field of Machpelah, near Mamre, which Abraham had bought as a burial place from Ephron the Hittite, along with the field. 14After burying his father, Joseph returned to Egypt, together with his brothers and all the others who had gone with him to bury his father.

[a]22 Or *Joseph is a wild colt, / a wild colt near a spring, / a wild donkey on a terraced hill* [b]23,24 Or *archers will attack . . . will shoot . . . will remain . . . will stay* [c]25 Hebrew *Shaddai* [d]26 Or *of my progenitors, / as great as* [e]26 Or *the one separated from* [f]32 Or *the sons of Heth* [g]9 Or *charioteers* [h]11 *Abel Mizraim* means *mourning of the Egyptians.*

Joseph Reassures His Brothers

15When Joseph's brothers saw that
their father was dead, they said, "What if
Joseph holds a grudge against us and pays
us back for all the wrongs we did to him?"
16So they sent word to Joseph, saying,
"Your father left these instructions before
he died: 17'This is what you are to say to
Joseph: I ask you to forgive your brothers
the sins and the wrongs they committed
in treating you so badly.' Now please for-
give the sins of the servants of the God of
your father." When their message came to
him, Joseph wept.

18His brothers then came and threw
themselves down before him. "We are
your slaves," they said.

19But Joseph said to them, "Don't be
afraid. Am I in the place of God? 20You in-
tended to harm me, but God intended it
for good to accomplish what is now being
done, the saving of many lives. 21So then,
don't be afraid. I will provide for you and
your children." And he reassured them
and spoke kindly to them.

The Death of Joseph

22Joseph stayed in Egypt, along with all
his father's family. He lived a hundred and
ten years 23and saw the third generation
of Ephraim's children. Also the children of
Makir son of Manasseh were placed at
birth on Joseph's knees.[a]

24Then Joseph said to his brothers, "I
am about to die. But God will surely come
to your aid and take you up out of this
land to the land he promised on oath to
Abraham, Isaac and Jacob." 25And Joseph
made the sons of Israel swear an oath and
said, "God will surely come to your aid,
and then you must carry my bones up
from this place."

26So Joseph died at the age of a hundred
and ten. And after they embalmed him, he
was placed in a coffin in Egypt.

[a]23 That is, were counted as his

IN the first half of this book, Moses recounts the exciting story of God delivering his people from slavery in Egypt. In the second half he tells about their stay at Mount Sinai, where they receive God's law and build the tabernacle. As you read this book, think about how God miraculously delivers you from slavery to Satan and sin through the death of his Son Jesus and how he wants you to obey his will (especially the Ten Commandments) in your daily life.

EXODUS

The Israelites Oppressed

1 These are the names of the sons of Israel who went to Egypt with Jacob, each with his family: 2Reuben, Simeon, Levi and Judah; 3Issachar, Zebulun and Benjamin; 4Dan and Naphtali; Gad and Asher. 5The descendants of Jacob numbered seventy[a] in all; Joseph was already in Egypt.

6Now Joseph and all his brothers and all that generation died, 7but the Israelites were fruitful and multiplied greatly and became exceedingly numerous, so that the land was filled with them.

8Then a new king, who did not know about Joseph, came to power in Egypt. 9"Look," he said to his people, "the Israelites have become much too numerous for us. 10Come, we must deal shrewdly with them or they will become even more numerous and, if war breaks out, will join our enemies, fight against us and leave the country."

11So they put slave masters over them to oppress them with forced labor, and

[a]5 Masoretic Text (see also Gen. 46:27); Dead Sea Scrolls and Septuagint (see also Acts 7:14 and note at Gen. 46:27) *seventy-five*

they built Pithom and Rameses as store
cities for Pharaoh. 12But the more they
were oppressed, the more they multiplied
and spread; so the Egyptians came to
dread the Israelites 13and worked them
ruthlessly. 14They made their lives bitter
with hard labor in brick and mortar and
with all kinds of work in the fields; in all
their hard labor the Egyptians used them
ruthlessly.

15The king of Egypt said to the Hebrew
midwives, whose names were Shiphrah
and Puah, 16"When you help the Hebrew
women in childbirth and observe them on
the delivery stool, if it is a boy, kill him;
but if it is a girl, let her live." 17The mid-
wives, however, feared God and did not
do what the king of Egypt had told them
to do; they let the boys live. 18Then the
king of Egypt summoned the midwives
and asked them, "Why have you done
this? Why have you let the boys live?"

19The midwives answered Pharaoh,
"Hebrew women are not like Egyptian
women; they are vigorous and give birth
before the midwives arrive."

20So God was kind to the midwives and
the people increased and became even
more numerous. 21And because the mid-
wives feared God, he gave them families
of their own.

22Then Pharaoh gave this order to all
his people: "Every boy that is born[a] you
must throw into the Nile, but let every girl
live."

The Birth of Moses

2 Now a man of the house of Levi mar-
ried a Levite woman, 2and she became
pregnant and gave birth to a son. When
she saw that he was a fine child, she hid
him for three months. 3But when she
could hide him no longer, she got a papy-
rus basket for him and coated it with tar
and pitch. Then she placed the child in it
and put it among the reeds along the bank
of the Nile. 4His sister stood at a distance
to see what would happen to him.

5Then Pharaoh's daughter went down
to the Nile to bathe, and her attendants
were walking along the river bank. She
saw the basket among the reeds and sent
her slave girl to get it. 6She opened it and
saw the baby. He was crying, and she felt
sorry for him. "This is one of the Hebrew
babies," she said.

7Then his sister asked Pharaoh's daugh-
ter, "Shall I go and get one of the Hebrew
women to nurse the baby for you?"

8"Yes, go," she answered. And the girl
went and got the baby's mother. 9Phar-
aoh's daughter said to her, "Take this
baby and nurse him for me, and I will pay
you." So the woman took the baby and
nursed him. 10When the child grew older,
she took him to Pharaoh's daughter and
he became her son. She named him Mo-
ses,[b] saying, "I drew him out of the wa-
ter."

Moses Flees to Midian

11One day, after Moses had grown up,
he went out to where his own people were
and watched them at their hard labor. He
saw an Egyptian beating a Hebrew, one of
his own people. 12Glancing this way and
that and seeing no one, he killed the Egyp-
tian and hid him in the sand. 13The next
day he went out and saw two Hebrews
fighting. He asked the one in the wrong,
"Why are you hitting your fellow He-
brew?"

14The man said, "Who made you ruler
and judge over us? Are you thinking of
killing me as you killed the Egyptian?"
Then Moses was afraid and thought,
"What I did must have become known."

15When Pharaoh heard of this, he tried
to kill Moses, but Moses fled from Phar-
aoh and went to live in Midian, where he
sat down by a well. 16Now a priest of Midi-
an had seven daughters, and they came to
draw water and fill the troughs to water
their father's flock. 17Some shepherds
came along and drove them away, but Mo-
ses got up and came to their rescue and
watered their flock.

18When the girls returned to Reuel their
father, he asked them, "Why have you re-
turned so early today?"

19They answered, "An Egyptian rescued
us from the shepherds. He even drew wa-
ter for us and watered the flock."

20"And where is he?" he asked his
daughters. "Why did you leave him? In-
vite him to have something to eat."

21Moses agreed to stay with the man,
who gave his daughter Zipporah to Moses
in marriage. 22Zipporah gave birth to a
son, and Moses named him Gershom,[c]
saying, "I have become an alien in a for-
eign land."

[a]*22* Masoretic Text; Samaritan Pentateuch, Septuagint and Targums *born to the Hebrews* [b]*10 Moses* sounds like the Hebrew for *draw out.* [c]*22 Gershom* sounds like the Hebrew for *an alien there.*

VERSE FOR THE DAY: Exodus 3:10

AUTHOR: Marti Winchell Williams

PASSAGE FOR THE DAY: Exodus 2:11—3:10

The Hard Work of Waiting

My husband and I were living in a small furnished apartment, surrounded by someone else's taste. I was dusting *their* furniture, mopping *their* floors, vacuuming *their* carpets. I struggled with the mundaneness of everyday life.

As I searched the Scriptures for answers, I began to notice how distorted my attitude had become. I was focusing on my past accomplishments and the ministry my husband and I hoped to have. Why had God put us on hold?

Moses had the best education and training that was available in his day, yet he found himself out in the desert tending sheep. He was doing a job for which he was highly over-qualified. Forty years in a desert, tending a flock that belonged to someone else.

Given the advantage of 20/20 hindsight, we can see this period of Moses' life as a time of transition and preparation. Moses was learning the ways of the desert, the ways of surviving in the heat and sand, and maybe even the ways of "dumb sheep." How often, when he later led the children of Israel through the wilderness, he must have looked back at that earlier tiresome period and seen its value. It prepared him for leadership in ways the best schools in Egypt could not.

I have the responsibility to pursue what God wants to teach me during this time of seeming inactivity. My usefulness is not contingent on my education, my family or my possessions. My usefulness is dependent on my willingness to be used in *whatever* surroundings the Lord places me in.

MARRIAGE BUILDERS

♦ *When has your relationship with God encountered a "desert" period? How did you respond in that situation?*

♦ *What positive consequences can you identify as a result of going through a dry or difficult time in your marriage?*

Additional Scripture Readings
Numbers 14:26–35; Romans 8:28; Psalm 27:13–14

Go to page 77 for your next devotional reading.

23During that long period, the king of
Egypt died. The Israelites groaned in their
slavery and cried out, and their cry for
help because of their slavery went up to
God. 24God heard their groaning and he
remembered his covenant with Abraham,
with Isaac and with Jacob. 25So God
looked on the Israelites and was con-
cerned about them.

Moses and the Burning Bush

3 Now Moses was tending the flock of
Jethro his father-in-law, the priest of
Midian, and he led the flock to the far side
of the desert and came to Horeb, the
mountain of God. 2There the angel of the
LORD appeared to him in flames of fire
from within a bush. Moses saw that
though the bush was on fire it did not
burn up. 3So Moses thought, "I will go
over and see this strange sight—why the
bush does not burn up."

4When the LORD saw that he had gone
over to look, God called to him from with-
in the bush, "Moses! Moses!"

And Moses said, "Here I am."

5"Do not come any closer," God said.
"Take off your sandals, for the place
where you are standing is holy ground."
6Then he said, "I am the God of your fa-
ther, the God of Abraham, the God of
Isaac and the God of Jacob." At this, Mo-
ses hid his face, because he was afraid to
look at God.

7The LORD said, "I have indeed seen the
misery of my people in Egypt. I have
heard them crying out because of their
slave drivers, and I am concerned about
their suffering. 8So I have come down to
rescue them from the hand of the Egyp-
tians and to bring them up out of that land
into a good and spacious land, a land flow-
ing with milk and honey—the home of
the Canaanites, Hittites, Amorites, Peri-
zzites, Hivites and Jebusites. 9And now the
cry of the Israelites has reached me, and I
have seen the way the Egyptians are op-
pressing them. 10So now, go. I am sending
you to Pharaoh to bring my people the Is-
raelites out of Egypt."

11But Moses said to God, "Who am I,
that I should go to Pharaoh and bring the
Israelites out of Egypt?"

12And God said, "I will be with you. And
this will be the sign to you that it is I who
have sent you: When you have brought
the people out of Egypt, you[a] will wor-
ship God on this mountain."

13Moses said to God, "Suppose I go to
the Israelites and say to them, 'The God of
your fathers has sent me to you,' and they
ask me, 'What is his name?' Then what
shall I tell them?"

14God said to Moses, "I AM WHO I AM.[b]
This is what you are to say to the Israel-
ites: 'I AM has sent me to you.'"

15God also said to Moses, "Say to the Is-
raelites, 'The LORD,[c] the God of your fa-
thers—the God of Abraham, the God of
Isaac and the God of Jacob—has sent me
to you.' This is my name forever, the
name by which I am to be remembered
from generation to generation.

16"Go, assemble the elders of Israel and
say to them, 'The LORD, the God of your
fathers—the God of Abraham, Isaac and
Jacob—appeared to me and said: I have
watched over you and have seen what has
been done to you in Egypt. 17And I have
promised to bring you up out of your mis-
ery in Egypt into the land of the Canaan-
ites, Hittites, Amorites, Perizzites, Hivites
and Jebusites—a land flowing with milk
and honey.'

18"The elders of Israel will listen to you.
Then you and the elders are to go to the
king of Egypt and say to him, 'The LORD,
the God of the Hebrews, has met with us.
Let us take a three-day journey into the
desert to offer sacrifices to the LORD our
God.' 19But I know that the king of Egypt
will not let you go unless a mighty hand
compels him. 20So I will stretch out my
hand and strike the Egyptians with all the
wonders that I will perform among them.
After that, he will let you go.

21"And I will make the Egyptians favor-
ably disposed toward this people, so that
when you leave you will not go empty-
handed. 22Every woman is to ask her
neighbor and any woman living in her
house for articles of silver and gold and
for clothing, which you will put on your
sons and daughters. And so you will plun-
der the Egyptians."

Signs for Moses

4 Moses answered, "What if they do not
believe me or listen to me and say,
'The LORD did not appear to you'?"

2Then the LORD said to him, "What is
that in your hand?"

[a] 12 The Hebrew is plural. [b] 14 Or *I WILL BE WHAT I WILL BE* [c] 15 The Hebrew for *LORD* sounds like and may be derived from the Hebrew for *I AM* in verse 14.

"A staff," he replied.

3The LORD said, "Throw it on the ground."

Moses threw it on the ground and it became a snake, and he ran from it. 4Then the LORD said to him, "Reach out your hand and take it by the tail." So Moses reached out and took hold of the snake and it turned back into a staff in his hand. 5"This," said the LORD, "is so that they may believe that the LORD, the God of their fathers—the God of Abraham, the God of Isaac and the God of Jacob—has appeared to you."

6Then the LORD said, "Put your hand inside your cloak." So Moses put his hand into his cloak, and when he took it out, it was leprous,[a] like snow.

7"Now put it back into your cloak," he said. So Moses put his hand back into his cloak, and when he took it out, it was restored, like the rest of his flesh.

8Then the LORD said, "If they do not believe you or pay attention to the first miraculous sign, they may believe the second. 9But if they do not believe these two signs or listen to you, take some water from the Nile and pour it on the dry ground. The water you take from the river will become blood on the ground."

10Moses said to the LORD, "O Lord, I have never been eloquent, neither in the past nor since you have spoken to your servant. I am slow of speech and tongue."

11The LORD said to him, "Who gave man his mouth? Who makes him deaf or mute? Who gives him sight or makes him blind? Is it not I, the LORD? 12Now go; I will help you speak and will teach you what to say."

13But Moses said, "O Lord, please send someone else to do it."

14Then the LORD's anger burned against Moses and he said, "What about your brother, Aaron the Levite? I know he can speak well. He is already on his way to meet you, and his heart will be glad when he sees you. 15You shall speak to him and put words in his mouth; I will help both of you speak and will teach you what to do. 16He will speak to the people for you, and it will be as if he were your mouth and as if you were God to him. 17But take this staff in your hand so you can perform miraculous signs with it."

Moses Returns to Egypt

18Then Moses went back to Jethro his father-in-law and said to him, "Let me go back to my own people in Egypt to see if any of them are still alive."

Jethro said, "Go, and I wish you well."

19Now the LORD had said to Moses in Midian, "Go back to Egypt, for all the men who wanted to kill you are dead." 20So Moses took his wife and sons, put them on a donkey and started back to Egypt. And he took the staff of God in his hand.

21The LORD said to Moses, "When you return to Egypt, see that you perform before Pharaoh all the wonders I have given you the power to do. But I will harden his heart so that he will not let the people go. 22Then say to Pharaoh, 'This is what the LORD says: Israel is my firstborn son, 23and I told you, "Let my son go, so he may worship me." But you refused to let him go; so I will kill your firstborn son.' "

24At a lodging place on the way, the LORD met ⌊Moses⌋[b] and was about to kill him. 25But Zipporah took a flint knife, cut off her son's foreskin and touched ⌊Moses'⌋ feet with it.[c] "Surely you are a bridegroom of blood to me," she said. 26So the LORD let him alone. (At that time she said "bridegroom of blood," referring to circumcision.)

27The LORD said to Aaron, "Go into the desert to meet Moses." So he met Moses at the mountain of God and kissed him. 28Then Moses told Aaron everything the LORD had sent him to say, and also about all the miraculous signs he had commanded him to perform.

29Moses and Aaron brought together all the elders of the Israelites, 30and Aaron told them everything the LORD had said to Moses. He also performed the signs before the people, 31and they believed. And when they heard that the LORD was concerned about them and had seen their misery, they bowed down and worshiped.

Bricks Without Straw

5 Afterward Moses and Aaron went to Pharaoh and said, "This is what the LORD, the God of Israel, says: 'Let my people go, so that they may hold a festival to me in the desert.' "

2Pharaoh said, "Who is the LORD, that I should obey him and let Israel go? I do not

[a]6 The Hebrew word was used for various diseases affecting the skin—not necessarily leprosy. [b]24 Or ⌊*Moses' son*⌋; Hebrew *him* [c]25 Or *and drew near* ⌊*Moses'*⌋ *feet*

know the LORD and I will not let Israel go."
3Then they said, "The God of the Hebrews has met with us. Now let us take a three-day journey into the desert to offer sacrifices to the LORD our God, or he may strike us with plagues or with the sword."
4But the king of Egypt said, "Moses and Aaron, why are you taking the people away from their labor? Get back to your work!" 5Then Pharaoh said, "Look, the people of the land are now numerous, and you are stopping them from working."
6That same day Pharaoh gave this order to the slave drivers and foremen in charge of the people: 7"You are no longer to supply the people with straw for making bricks; let them go and gather their own straw. 8But require them to make the same number of bricks as before; don't reduce the quota. They are lazy; that is why they are crying out, 'Let us go and sacrifice to our God.' 9Make the work harder for the men so that they keep working and pay no attention to lies."
10Then the slave drivers and the foremen went out and said to the people, "This is what Pharaoh says: 'I will not give you any more straw. 11Go and get your own straw wherever you can find it, but your work will not be reduced at all.' "
12So the people scattered all over Egypt to gather stubble to use for straw. 13The slave drivers kept pressing them, saying, "Complete the work required of you for each day, just as when you had straw."
14The Israelite foremen appointed by Pharaoh's slave drivers were beaten and were asked, "Why didn't you meet your quota of bricks yesterday or today, as before?"
15Then the Israelite foremen went and appealed to Pharaoh: "Why have you treated your servants this way? 16Your servants are given no straw, yet we are told, 'Make bricks!' Your servants are being beaten, but the fault is with your own people."
17Pharaoh said, "Lazy, that's what you are—lazy! That is why you keep saying, 'Let us go and sacrifice to the LORD.' 18Now get to work. You will not be given any straw, yet you must produce your full quota of bricks."
19The Israelite foremen realized they were in trouble when they were told, "You are not to reduce the number of bricks required of you for each day." 20When they left Pharaoh, they found Moses and Aaron waiting to meet them, 21and they said, "May the LORD look upon you and judge you! You have made us a stench to Pharaoh and his officials and have put a sword in their hand to kill us."

God Promises Deliverance

22Moses returned to the LORD and said, "O Lord, why have you brought trouble upon this people? Is this why you sent me? 23Ever since I went to Pharaoh to speak in your name, he has brought trouble upon this people, and you have not rescued your people at all."

6 Then the LORD said to Moses, "Now you will see what I will do to Pharaoh: Because of my mighty hand he will let them go; because of my mighty hand he will drive them out of his country."
2God also said to Moses, "I am the LORD. 3I appeared to Abraham, to Isaac and to Jacob as God Almighty,[a] but by my name the LORD[b] I did not make myself known to them.[c] 4I also established my covenant with them to give them the land of Canaan, where they lived as aliens. 5Moreover, I have heard the groaning of the Israelites, whom the Egyptians are enslaving, and I have remembered my covenant.
6"Therefore, say to the Israelites: 'I am the LORD, and I will bring you out from under the yoke of the Egyptians. I will free you from being slaves to them, and I will redeem you with an outstretched arm and with mighty acts of judgment. 7I will take you as my own people, and I will be your God. Then you will know that I am the LORD your God, who brought you out from under the yoke of the Egyptians. 8And I will bring you to the land I swore with uplifted hand to give to Abraham, to Isaac and to Jacob. I will give it to you as a possession. I am the LORD.' "
9Moses reported this to the Israelites, but they did not listen to him because of their discouragement and cruel bondage.
10Then the LORD said to Moses, 11"Go, tell Pharaoh king of Egypt to let the Israelites go out of his country."
12But Moses said to the LORD, "If the Israelites will not listen to me, why would Pharaoh listen to me, since I speak with faltering lips[d]?"

[a] 3 Hebrew *El-Shaddai* [b] 3 See note at Exodus 3:15. [c] 3 Or *Almighty, and by my name the LORD did I not let myself be known to them?* [d] 12 Hebrew *I am uncircumcised of lips*; also in verse 30

Family Record of Moses and Aaron

13Now the LORD spoke to Moses and
Aaron about the Israelites and Pharaoh
king of Egypt, and he commanded them to
bring the Israelites out of Egypt.

14These were the heads of their fami-
lies[a]:

The sons of Reuben the firstborn
son of Israel were Hanoch and Pallu,
Hezron and Carmi. These were the
clans of Reuben.

15The sons of Simeon were Jemuel,
Jamin, Ohad, Jakin, Zohar and Shaul
the son of a Canaanite woman. These
were the clans of Simeon.

16These were the names of the
sons of Levi according to their
records: Gershon, Kohath and Mera-
ri. Levi lived 137 years.

17The sons of Gershon, by clans,
were Libni and Shimei.

18The sons of Kohath were Amram,
Izhar, Hebron and Uzziel. Kohath
lived 133 years.

19The sons of Merari were Mahli
and Mushi.

These were the clans of Levi ac-
cording to their records.

20Amram married his father's sister
Jochebed, who bore him Aaron and
Moses. Amram lived 137 years.

21The sons of Izhar were Korah,
Nepheg and Zicri.

22The sons of Uzziel were Mishael,
Elzaphan and Sithri.

23Aaron married Elisheba, daugh-
ter of Amminadab and sister of Nah-
shon, and she bore him Nadab and
Abihu, Eleazar and Ithamar.

24The sons of Korah were Assir, El-
kanah and Abiasaph. These were the
Korahite clans.

25Eleazar son of Aaron married one
of the daughters of Putiel, and she
bore him Phinehas.

These were the heads of the Levite
families, clan by clan.

26It was this same Aaron and Moses to
whom the LORD said, "Bring the Israelites
out of Egypt by their divisions." 27They
were the ones who spoke to Pharaoh king
of Egypt about bringing the Israelites out
of Egypt. It was the same Moses and
Aaron.

Aaron to Speak for Moses

28Now when the LORD spoke to Moses
in Egypt, 29he said to him, "I am the LORD.
Tell Pharaoh king of Egypt everything I
tell you."

30But Moses said to the LORD, "Since I
speak with faltering lips, why would Phar-
aoh listen to me?"

7 Then the LORD said to Moses, "See, I
have made you like God to Pharaoh,
and your brother Aaron will be your
prophet. 2You are to say everything I com-
mand you, and your brother Aaron is to
tell Pharaoh to let the Israelites go out of
his country. 3But I will harden Pharaoh's
heart, and though I multiply my miracu-
lous signs and wonders in Egypt, 4he will
not listen to you. Then I will lay my hand
on Egypt and with mighty acts of judg-
ment I will bring out my divisions, my
people the Israelites. 5And the Egyptians
will know that I am the LORD when I
stretch out my hand against Egypt and
bring the Israelites out of it."

6Moses and Aaron did just as the LORD
commanded them. 7Moses was eighty
years old and Aaron eighty-three when
they spoke to Pharaoh.

Aaron's Staff Becomes a Snake

8The LORD said to Moses and Aaron,
9"When Pharaoh says to you, 'Perform a
miracle,' then say to Aaron, 'Take your
staff and throw it down before Pharaoh,'
and it will become a snake."

10So Moses and Aaron went to Pharaoh
and did just as the LORD commanded. Aar-
on threw his staff down in front of Phar-
aoh and his officials, and it became a
snake. 11Pharaoh then summoned wise
men and sorcerers, and the Egyptian ma-
gicians also did the same things by their
secret arts: 12Each one threw down his
staff and it became a snake. But Aaron's
staff swallowed up their staffs. 13Yet Phar-
aoh's heart became hard and he would
not listen to them, just as the LORD had
said.

The Plague of Blood

14Then the LORD said to Moses, "Phar-
aoh's heart is unyielding; he refuses to let
the people go. 15Go to Pharaoh in the
morning as he goes out to the water. Wait
on the bank of the Nile to meet him, and
take in your hand the staff that was

[a] *14* The Hebrew for *families* here and in verse 25 refers to units larger than clans.

changed into a snake. 16Then say to him,
'The LORD, the God of the Hebrews, has
sent me to say to you: Let my people go,
so that they may worship me in the desert.
But until now you have not listened.
17This is what the LORD says: By this you
will know that I am the LORD: With the
staff that is in my hand I will strike the
water of the Nile, and it will be changed
into blood. 18The fish in the Nile will die,
and the river will stink; the Egyptians will
not be able to drink its water.' "

19The LORD said to Moses, "Tell Aaron,
'Take your staff and stretch out your hand
over the waters of Egypt—over the
streams and canals, over the ponds and all
the reservoirs'—and they will turn to
blood. Blood will be everywhere in Egypt,
even in the wooden buckets and stone
jars."

20Moses and Aaron did just as the LORD
had commanded. He raised his staff in the
presence of Pharaoh and his officials and
struck the water of the Nile, and all the
water was changed into blood. 21The fish
in the Nile died, and the river smelled so
bad that the Egyptians could not drink its
water. Blood was everywhere in Egypt.

22But the Egyptian magicians did the
same things by their secret arts, and Pharaoh's heart became hard; he would not listen to Moses and Aaron, just as the LORD
had said. 23Instead, he turned and went
into his palace, and did not take even this
to heart. 24And all the Egyptians dug along
the Nile to get drinking water, because
they could not drink the water of the river.

The Plague of Frogs

25Seven days passed after the LORD
8 struck the Nile. 1Then the LORD said to
Moses, "Go to Pharaoh and say to
him, 'This is what the LORD says: Let my
people go, so that they may worship me.
2If you refuse to let them go, I will plague
your whole country with frogs. 3The Nile
will teem with frogs. They will come up
into your palace and your bedroom and
onto your bed, into the houses of your officials and on your people, and into your
ovens and kneading troughs. 4The frogs
will go up on you and your people and all
your officials.' "

5Then the LORD said to Moses, "Tell Aaron, 'Stretch out your hand with your staff
over the streams and canals and ponds,
and make frogs come up on the land of
Egypt.' "

6So Aaron stretched out his hand over
the waters of Egypt, and the frogs came up
and covered the land. 7But the magicians
did the same things by their secret arts;
they also made frogs come up on the land
of Egypt.

8Pharaoh summoned Moses and Aaron
and said, "Pray to the LORD to take the
frogs away from me and my people, and I
will let your people go to offer sacrifices to
the LORD."

9Moses said to Pharaoh, "I leave to you
the honor of setting the time for me to
pray for you and your officials and your
people that you and your houses may be
rid of the frogs, except for those that remain in the Nile."

10"Tomorrow," Pharaoh said.

Moses replied, "It will be as you say, so
that you may know there is no one like the
LORD our God. 11The frogs will leave you
and your houses, your officials and your
people; they will remain only in the Nile."

12After Moses and Aaron left Pharaoh,
Moses cried out to the LORD about the
frogs he had brought on Pharaoh. 13And
the LORD did what Moses asked. The frogs
died in the houses, in the courtyards and
in the fields. 14They were piled into heaps,
and the land reeked of them. 15But when
Pharaoh saw that there was relief, he
hardened his heart and would not listen to
Moses and Aaron, just as the LORD had
said.

The Plague of Gnats

16Then the LORD said to Moses, "Tell
Aaron, 'Stretch out your staff and strike
the dust of the ground,' and throughout
the land of Egypt the dust will become
gnats." 17They did this, and when Aaron
stretched out his hand with the staff and
struck the dust of the ground, gnats came
upon men and animals. All the dust
throughout the land of Egypt became
gnats. 18But when the magicians tried to
produce gnats by their secret arts, they
could not. And the gnats were on men and
animals.

19The magicians said to Pharaoh, "This
is the finger of God." But Pharaoh's heart
was hard and he would not listen, just as
the LORD had said.

The Plague of Flies

20Then the LORD said to Moses, "Get up
early in the morning and confront Pharaoh as he goes to the water and say to
him, 'This is what the LORD says: Let my
people go, so that they may worship me.

21If you do not let my people go, I will
send swarms of flies on you and your offi-
cials, on your people and into your
houses. The houses of the Egyptians will
be full of flies, and even the ground where
they are.
22" 'But on that day I will deal different-
ly with the land of Goshen, where my peo-
ple live; no swarms of flies will be there,
so that you will know that I, the LORD, am
in this land. 23I will make a distinction[a]
between my people and your people. This
miraculous sign will occur tomorrow.' "
24And the LORD did this. Dense swarms
of flies poured into Pharaoh's palace and
into the houses of his officials, and
throughout Egypt the land was ruined by
the flies.
25Then Pharaoh summoned Moses and
Aaron and said, "Go, sacrifice to your God
here in the land."
26But Moses said, "That would not be
right. The sacrifices we offer the LORD our
God would be detestable to the Egyptians.
And if we offer sacrifices that are detest-
able in their eyes, will they not stone us?
27We must take a three-day journey into
the desert to offer sacrifices to the LORD
our God, as he commands us."
28Pharaoh said, "I will let you go to offer
sacrifices to the LORD your God in the
desert, but you must not go very far. Now
pray for me."
29Moses answered, "As soon as I leave
you, I will pray to the LORD, and tomorrow
the flies will leave Pharaoh and his offi-
cials and his people. Only be sure that
Pharaoh does not act deceitfully again by
not letting the people go to offer sacrifices
to the LORD."
30Then Moses left Pharaoh and prayed
to the LORD, 31and the LORD did what Mo-
ses asked: The flies left Pharaoh and his
officials and his people; not a fly re-
mained. 32But this time also Pharaoh
hardened his heart and would not let the
people go.

The Plague on Livestock

9 Then the LORD said to Moses, "Go to
Pharaoh and say to him, 'This is what
the LORD, the God of the Hebrews, says:
"Let my people go, so that they may wor-
ship me." 2If you refuse to let them go and
continue to hold them back, 3the hand of
the LORD will bring a terrible plague on
your livestock in the field—on your
horses and donkeys and camels and on
your cattle and sheep and goats. 4But the
LORD will make a distinction between the
livestock of Israel and that of Egypt, so
that no animal belonging to the Israelites
will die.' "
5The LORD set a time and said, "Tomor-
row the LORD will do this in the land."
6And the next day the LORD did it: All the
livestock of the Egyptians died, but not
one animal belonging to the Israelites
died. 7Pharaoh sent men to investigate
and found that not even one of the ani-
mals of the Israelites had died. Yet his
heart was unyielding and he would not let
the people go.

The Plague of Boils

8Then the LORD said to Moses and Aar-
on, "Take handfuls of soot from a furnace
and have Moses toss it into the air in the
presence of Pharaoh. 9It will become fine
dust over the whole land of Egypt, and fes-
tering boils will break out on men and ani-
mals throughout the land."
10So they took soot from a furnace and
stood before Pharaoh. Moses tossed it into
the air, and festering boils broke out on
men and animals. 11The magicians could
not stand before Moses because of the
boils that were on them and on all the
Egyptians. 12But the LORD hardened Phar-
aoh's heart and he would not listen to Mo-
ses and Aaron, just as the LORD had said to
Moses.

The Plague of Hail

13Then the LORD said to Moses, "Get up
early in the morning, confront Pharaoh
and say to him, 'This is what the LORD, the
God of the Hebrews, says: Let my people
go, so that they may worship me, 14or this
time I will send the full force of my
plagues against you and against your offi-
cials and your people, so you may know
that there is no one like me in all the earth.
15For by now I could have stretched out
my hand and struck you and your people
with a plague that would have wiped you
off the earth. 16But I have raised you up[b]
for this very purpose, that I might show
you my power and that my name might be
proclaimed in all the earth. 17You still set
yourself against my people and will not let
them go. 18Therefore, at this time tomor-
row I will send the worst hailstorm that
has ever fallen on Egypt, from the day it

[a]23 Septuagint and Vulgate; Hebrew *will put a deliverance* [b]16 Or *have spared you*

was founded till now. 19Give an order now
to bring your livestock and everything you
have in the field to a place of shelter, be-
cause the hail will fall on every man and
animal that has not been brought in and is
still out in the field, and they will die.' "
20Those officials of Pharaoh who feared
the word of the LORD hurried to bring their
slaves and their livestock inside. 21But
those who ignored the word of the LORD
left their slaves and livestock in the field.
22Then the LORD said to Moses, "Stretch
out your hand toward the sky so that hail
will fall all over Egypt—on men and ani-
mals and on everything growing in the
fields of Egypt." 23When Moses stretched
out his staff toward the sky, the LORD sent
thunder and hail, and lightning flashed
down to the ground. So the LORD rained
hail on the land of Egypt; 24hail fell and
lightning flashed back and forth. It was
the worst storm in all the land of Egypt
since it had become a nation. 25Through-
out Egypt hail struck everything in the
fields—both men and animals; it beat
down everything growing in the fields and
stripped every tree. 26The only place it did
not hail was the land of Goshen, where
the Israelites were.
27Then Pharaoh summoned Moses and
Aaron. "This time I have sinned," he said
to them. "The LORD is in the right, and I
and my people are in the wrong. 28Pray to
the LORD, for we have had enough thunder
and hail. I will let you go; you don't have
to stay any longer."
29Moses replied, "When I have gone out
of the city, I will spread out my hands in
prayer to the LORD. The thunder will stop
and there will be no more hail, so you may
know that the earth is the LORD's. 30But I
know that you and your officials still do
not fear the LORD God."
31(The flax and barley were destroyed,
since the barley had headed and the flax
was in bloom. 32The wheat and spelt,
however, were not destroyed, because
they ripen later.)
33Then Moses left Pharaoh and went
out of the city. He spread out his hands
toward the LORD; the thunder and hail
stopped, and the rain no longer poured
down on the land. 34When Pharaoh saw
that the rain and hail and thunder had
stopped, he sinned again: He and his offi-
cials hardened their hearts. 35So Phar-
aoh's heart was hard and he would not let
the Israelites go, just as the LORD had said
through Moses.

The Plague of Locusts

10 Then the LORD said to Moses, "Go
to Pharaoh, for I have hardened his
heart and the hearts of his officials so that
I may perform these miraculous signs of
mine among them 2that you may tell your
children and grandchildren how I dealt
harshly with the Egyptians and how I per-
formed my signs among them, and that
you may know that I am the LORD."
3So Moses and Aaron went to Pharaoh
and said to him, "This is what the LORD,
the God of the Hebrews, says: 'How long
will you refuse to humble yourself before
me? Let my people go, so that they may
worship me. 4If you refuse to let them go,
I will bring locusts into your country to-
morrow. 5They will cover the face of the
ground so that it cannot be seen. They will
devour what little you have left after the
hail, including every tree that is growing
in your fields. 6They will fill your houses
and those of all your officials and all the
Egyptians—something neither your fa-
thers nor your forefathers have ever seen
from the day they settled in this land till
now.' " Then Moses turned and left Phar-
aoh.
7Pharaoh's officials said to him, "How
long will this man be a snare to us? Let the
people go, so that they may worship the
LORD their God. Do you not yet realize that
Egypt is ruined?"
8Then Moses and Aaron were brought
back to Pharaoh. "Go, worship the LORD
your God," he said. "But just who will be
going?"
9Moses answered, "We will go with our
young and old, with our sons and daugh-
ters, and with our flocks and herds, be-
cause we are to celebrate a festival to the
LORD."
10Pharaoh said, "The LORD be with
you—if I let you go, along with your
women and children! Clearly you are bent
on evil.[a] 11No! Have only the men go;
and worship the LORD, since that's what
you have been asking for." Then Moses
and Aaron were driven out of Pharaoh's
presence.
12And the LORD said to Moses, "Stretch
out your hand over Egypt so that locusts
will swarm over the land and devour ev-

[a]10 Or *Be careful, trouble is in store for you!*

erything growing in the fields, everything
left by the hail."
13So Moses stretched out his staff over
Egypt, and the LORD made an east wind
blow across the land all that day and all
that night. By morning the wind had
brought the locusts; 14they invaded all
Egypt and settled down in every area of
the country in great numbers. Never be-
fore had there been such a plague of lo-
custs, nor will there ever be again. 15They
covered all the ground until it was black.
They devoured all that was left after the
hail—everything growing in the fields
and the fruit on the trees. Nothing green
remained on tree or plant in all the land of
Egypt.
16Pharaoh quickly summoned Moses
and Aaron and said, "I have sinned against
the LORD your God and against you.
17Now forgive my sin once more and pray
to the LORD your God to take this deadly
plague away from me."
18Moses then left Pharaoh and prayed
to the LORD. 19And the LORD changed the
wind to a very strong west wind, which
caught up the locusts and carried them
into the Red Sea.[a] Not a locust was left
anywhere in Egypt. 20But the LORD har-
dened Pharaoh's heart, and he would not
let the Israelites go.

The Plague of Darkness

21Then the LORD said to Moses, "Stretch
out your hand toward the sky so that dark-
ness will spread over Egypt—darkness
that can be felt." 22So Moses stretched out
his hand toward the sky, and total dark-
ness covered all Egypt for three days. 23No
one could see anyone else or leave his
place for three days. Yet all the Israelites
had light in the places where they lived.
24Then Pharaoh summoned Moses and
said, "Go, worship the LORD. Even your
women and children may go with you;
only leave your flocks and herds behind."
25But Moses said, "You must allow us to
have sacrifices and burnt offerings to
present to the LORD our God. 26Our live-
stock too must go with us; not a hoof is to
be left behind. We have to use some of
them in worshiping the LORD our God, and
until we get there we will not know what
we are to use to worship the LORD."
27But the LORD hardened Pharaoh's
heart, and he was not willing to let them
go. 28Pharaoh said to Moses, "Get out of
my sight! Make sure you do not appear
before me again! The day you see my face
you will die."
29"Just as you say," Moses replied, "I
will never appear before you again."

The Plague on the Firstborn

11 Now the LORD had said to Moses, "I
will bring one more plague on
Pharaoh and on Egypt. After that, he will
let you go from here, and when he does,
he will drive you out completely. 2Tell the
people that men and women alike are to
ask their neighbors for articles of silver
and gold." 3(The LORD made the Egyptians
favorably disposed toward the people,
and Moses himself was highly regarded in
Egypt by Pharaoh's officials and by the
people.)
4So Moses said, "This is what the LORD
says: 'About midnight I will go throughout
Egypt. 5Every firstborn son in Egypt will
die, from the firstborn son of Pharaoh,
who sits on the throne, to the firstborn
son of the slave girl, who is at her hand
mill, and all the firstborn of the cattle as
well. 6There will be loud wailing through-
out Egypt—worse than there has ever
been or ever will be again. 7But among the
Israelites not a dog will bark at any man or
animal.' Then you will know that the LORD
makes a distinction between Egypt and Is-
rael. 8All these officials of yours will come
to me, bowing down before me and say-
ing, 'Go, you and all the people who fol-
low you!' After that I will leave." Then
Moses, hot with anger, left Pharaoh.
9The LORD had said to Moses, "Pharaoh
will refuse to listen to you—so that my
wonders may be multiplied in Egypt."
10Moses and Aaron performed all these
wonders before Pharaoh, but the LORD
hardened Pharaoh's heart, and he would
not let the Israelites go out of his country.

The Passover

12 The LORD said to Moses and Aaron
in Egypt, 2"This month is to be for
you the first month, the first month of
your year. 3Tell the whole community of
Israel that on the tenth day of this month
each man is to take a lamb[b] for his fami-
ly, one for each household. 4If any house-
hold is too small for a whole lamb, they
must share one with their nearest neigh-

[a] 19 Hebrew *Yam Suph*; that is, Sea of Reeds

[b] 3 The Hebrew word can mean *lamb* or *kid*; also in verse 4.

bor, having taken into account the number of people there are. You are to determine the amount of lamb needed in accordance with what each person will eat. 5The animals you choose must be year-old males without defect, and you may take them from the sheep or the goats. 6Take care of them until the fourteenth day of the month, when all the people of the community of Israel must slaughter them at twilight. 7Then they are to take some of the blood and put it on the sides and tops of the doorframes of the houses where they eat the lambs. 8That same night they are to eat the meat roasted over the fire, along with bitter herbs, and bread made without yeast. 9Do not eat the meat raw or cooked in water, but roast it over the fire—head, legs and inner parts. 10Do not leave any of it till morning; if some is left till morning, you must burn it. 11This is how you are to eat it: with your cloak tucked into your belt, your sandals on your feet and your staff in your hand. Eat it in haste; it is the LORD's Passover.

12"On that same night I will pass through Egypt and strike down every firstborn—both men and animals—and I will bring judgment on all the gods of Egypt. I am the LORD. 13The blood will be a sign for you on the houses where you are; and when I see the blood, I will pass over you. No destructive plague will touch you when I strike Egypt.

14"This is a day you are to commemorate; for the generations to come you shall celebrate it as a festival to the LORD—a lasting ordinance. 15For seven days you are to eat bread made without yeast. On the first day remove the yeast from your houses, for whoever eats anything with yeast in it from the first day through the seventh must be cut off from Israel. 16On the first day hold a sacred assembly, and another one on the seventh day. Do no work at all on these days, except to prepare food for everyone to eat—that is all you may do.

17"Celebrate the Feast of Unleavened Bread, because it was on this very day that I brought your divisions out of Egypt. Celebrate this day as a lasting ordinance for the generations to come. 18In the first month you are to eat bread made without yeast, from the evening of the fourteenth day until the evening of the twenty-first day. 19For seven days no yeast is to be found in your houses. And whoever eats anything with yeast in it must be cut off from the community of Israel, whether he is an alien or native-born. 20Eat nothing made with yeast. Wherever you live, you must eat unleavened bread."

21Then Moses summoned all the elders of Israel and said to them, "Go at once and select the animals for your families and slaughter the Passover lamb. 22Take a bunch of hyssop, dip it into the blood in the basin and put some of the blood on the top and on both sides of the doorframe. Not one of you shall go out the door of his house until morning. 23When the LORD goes through the land to strike down the Egyptians, he will see the blood on the top and sides of the doorframe and will pass over that doorway, and he will not permit the destroyer to enter your houses and strike you down.

24"Obey these instructions as a lasting ordinance for you and your descendants. 25When you enter the land that the LORD will give you as he promised, observe this ceremony. 26And when your children ask you, 'What does this ceremony mean to you?' 27then tell them, 'It is the Passover sacrifice to the LORD, who passed over the houses of the Israelites in Egypt and spared our homes when he struck down the Egyptians.' " Then the people bowed down and worshiped. 28The Israelites did just what the LORD commanded Moses and Aaron.

29At midnight the LORD struck down all the firstborn in Egypt, from the firstborn of Pharaoh, who sat on the throne, to the firstborn of the prisoner, who was in the dungeon, and the firstborn of all the livestock as well. 30Pharaoh and all his officials and all the Egyptians got up during the night, and there was loud wailing in Egypt, for there was not a house without someone dead.

The Exodus

31During the night Pharaoh summoned Moses and Aaron and said, "Up! Leave my people, you and the Israelites! Go, worship the LORD as you have requested. 32Take your flocks and herds, as you have said, and go. And also bless me."

33The Egyptians urged the people to hurry and leave the country. "For otherwise," they said, "we will all die!" 34So the people took their dough before the yeast was added, and carried it on their shoulders in kneading troughs wrapped in clothing. 35The Israelites did as Moses instructed and asked the Egyptians for articles of silver and gold and for clothing. 36The LORD had made the Egyptians favorably disposed toward the people, and they gave them what they asked for; so they plundered the Egyptians.

37The Israelites journeyed from Rameses to Succoth. There were about six hundred thousand men on foot, besides women and children. 38Many other people went up with them, as well as large droves of livestock, both flocks and herds. 39With the dough they had brought from Egypt, they baked cakes of unleavened bread. The dough was without yeast because they had been driven out of Egypt and did not have time to prepare food for themselves.

40Now the length of time the Israelite people lived in Egypt[a] was 430 years. 41At the end of the 430 years, to the very day, all the LORD's divisions left Egypt. 42Because the LORD kept vigil that night to bring them out of Egypt, on this night all the Israelites are to keep vigil to honor the LORD for the generations to come.

Passover Restrictions

43The LORD said to Moses and Aaron, "These are the regulations for the Passover:

"No foreigner is to eat of it. 44Any slave you have bought may eat of it after you have circumcised him, 45but a temporary resident and a hired worker may not eat of it.

46"It must be eaten inside one house; take none of the meat outside the house. Do not break any of the bones. 47The whole community of Israel must celebrate it.

48"An alien living among you who wants to celebrate the LORD's Passover must have all the males in his household circumcised; then he may take part like one born in the land. No uncircumcised male may eat of it. 49The same law applies to the native-born and to the alien living among you."

50All the Israelites did just what the LORD had commanded Moses and Aaron. 51And on that very day the LORD brought the Israelites out of Egypt by their divisions.

Consecration of the Firstborn

13 The LORD said to Moses, 2"Consecrate to me every firstborn male. The first offspring of every womb among the Israelites belongs to me, whether man or animal."

3Then Moses said to the people, "Commemorate this day, the day you came out of Egypt, out of the land of slavery, because the LORD brought you out of it with a mighty hand. Eat nothing containing yeast. 4Today, in the month of Abib, you are leaving. 5When the LORD brings you into the land of the Canaanites, Hittites, Amorites, Hivites and Jebusites—the land he swore to your forefathers to give you, a land flowing with milk and honey—you are to observe this ceremony in this month: 6For seven days eat bread made without yeast and on the seventh day hold a festival to the LORD. 7Eat unleavened bread during those seven days; nothing with yeast in it is to be seen among you, nor shall any yeast be seen anywhere within your borders. 8On that day tell your son, 'I do this because of what the LORD did for me when I came out of Egypt.' 9This observance will be for you like a sign on your hand and a reminder on your forehead that the law of the LORD is to be on your lips. For the LORD brought you out of Egypt with his mighty hand. 10You must keep this ordinance at the appointed time year after year.

11"After the LORD brings you into the land of the Canaanites and gives it to you, as he promised on oath to you and your forefathers, 12you are to give over to the LORD the first offspring of every womb. All the firstborn males of your livestock belong to the LORD. 13Redeem with a lamb every firstborn donkey, but if you do not redeem it, break its neck. Redeem every firstborn among your sons.

14"In days to come, when your son asks you, 'What does this mean?' say to him, 'With a mighty hand the LORD brought us out of Egypt, out of the land of slavery. 15When Pharaoh stubbornly refused to let us go, the LORD killed every firstborn in Egypt, both man and animal. This is why I sacrifice to the LORD the first male offspring of every womb and redeem each of my firstborn sons.' 16And it will be like a sign on your hand and a symbol on your

[a]*40* Masoretic Text; Samaritan Pentateuch and Septuagint *Egypt and Canaan*

forehead that the LORD brought us out of Egypt with his mighty hand."

Crossing the Sea

17When Pharaoh let the people go, God did not lead them on the road through the Philistine country, though that was shorter. For God said, "If they face war, they might change their minds and return to Egypt." 18So God led the people around by the desert road toward the Red Sea.[a] The Israelites went up out of Egypt armed for battle.

19Moses took the bones of Joseph with him because Joseph had made the sons of Israel swear an oath. He had said, "God will surely come to your aid, and then you must carry my bones up with you from this place."[b]

20After leaving Succoth they camped at Etham on the edge of the desert. 21By day the LORD went ahead of them in a pillar of cloud to guide them on their way and by night in a pillar of fire to give them light, so that they could travel by day or night. 22Neither the pillar of cloud by day nor the pillar of fire by night left its place in front of the people.

14 Then the LORD said to Moses, 2"Tell the Israelites to turn back and encamp near Pi Hahiroth, between Migdol and the sea. They are to encamp by the sea, directly opposite Baal Zephon. 3Pharaoh will think, 'The Israelites are wandering around the land in confusion, hemmed in by the desert.' 4And I will harden Pharaoh's heart, and he will pursue them. But I will gain glory for myself through Pharaoh and all his army, and the Egyptians will know that I am the LORD." So the Israelites did this.

5When the king of Egypt was told that the people had fled, Pharaoh and his officials changed their minds about them and said, "What have we done? We have let the Israelites go and have lost their services!" 6So he had his chariot made ready and took his army with him. 7He took six hundred of the best chariots, along with all the other chariots of Egypt, with officers over all of them. 8The LORD hardened the heart of Pharaoh king of Egypt, so that he pursued the Israelites, who were marching out boldly. 9The Egyptians—all Pharaoh's horses and chariots, horsemen[c] and troops—pursued the Israelites and overtook them as they camped by the sea near Pi Hahiroth, opposite Baal Zephon.

10As Pharaoh approached, the Israelites looked up, and there were the Egyptians, marching after them. They were terrified and cried out to the LORD. 11They said to Moses, "Was it because there were no graves in Egypt that you brought us to the desert to die? What have you done to us by bringing us out of Egypt? 12Didn't we say to you in Egypt, 'Leave us alone; let us serve the Egyptians'? It would have been better for us to serve the Egyptians than to die in the desert!"

13Moses answered the people, "Do not be afraid. Stand firm and you will see the deliverance the LORD will bring you today. The Egyptians you see today you will never see again. 14The LORD will fight for you; you need only to be still."

15Then the LORD said to Moses, "Why are you crying out to me? Tell the Israelites to move on. 16Raise your staff and stretch out your hand over the sea to divide the water so that the Israelites can go through the sea on dry ground. 17I will harden the hearts of the Egyptians so that they will go in after them. And I will gain glory through Pharaoh and all his army, through his chariots and his horsemen. 18The Egyptians will know that I am the LORD when I gain glory through Pharaoh, his chariots and his horsemen."

19Then the angel of God, who had been traveling in front of Israel's army, withdrew and went behind them. The pillar of cloud also moved from in front and stood behind them, 20coming between the armies of Egypt and Israel. Throughout the night the cloud brought darkness to the one side and light to the other side; so neither went near the other all night long.

21Then Moses stretched out his hand over the sea, and all that night the LORD drove the sea back with a strong east wind and turned it into dry land. The waters were divided, 22and the Israelites went through the sea on dry ground, with a wall of water on their right and on their left.

23The Egyptians pursued them, and all Pharaoh's horses and chariots and horsemen followed them into the sea. 24During the last watch of the night the LORD looked down from the pillar of fire and cloud at the Egyptian army and threw it into confu-

[a] *18* Hebrew *Yam Suph*; that is, Sea of Reeds [b] *19* See Gen. 50:25. [c] *9* Or *charioteers*; also in verses 17, 18, 23, 26 and 28

sion. 25He made the wheels of their chariots come off[a] so that they had difficulty driving. And the Egyptians said, "Let's get away from the Israelites! The LORD is fighting for them against Egypt."

26Then the LORD said to Moses, "Stretch out your hand over the sea so that the waters may flow back over the Egyptians and their chariots and horsemen." 27Moses stretched out his hand over the sea, and at daybreak the sea went back to its place. The Egyptians were fleeing toward[b] it, and the LORD swept them into the sea. 28The water flowed back and covered the chariots and horsemen—the entire army of Pharaoh that had followed the Israelites into the sea. Not one of them survived.

29But the Israelites went through the sea on dry ground, with a wall of water on their right and on their left. 30That day the LORD saved Israel from the hands of the Egyptians, and Israel saw the Egyptians lying dead on the shore. 31And when the Israelites saw the great power the LORD displayed against the Egyptians, the people feared the LORD and put their trust in him and in Moses his servant.

The Song of Moses and Miriam

15 Then Moses and the Israelites sang this song to the LORD:

"I will sing to the LORD,
for he is highly exalted.
The horse and its rider
he has hurled into the sea.
2The LORD is my strength and my song;
he has become my salvation.
He is my God, and I will praise him,
my father's God, and I will exalt him.
3The LORD is a warrior;
the LORD is his name.
4Pharaoh's chariots and his army
he has hurled into the sea.
The best of Pharaoh's officers
are drowned in the Red Sea.[c]
5The deep waters have covered them;
they sank to the depths like a stone.
6"Your right hand, O LORD,
was majestic in power.
Your right hand, O LORD,
shattered the enemy.
7In the greatness of your majesty
you threw down those who opposed you.
You unleashed your burning anger;
it consumed them like stubble.
8By the blast of your nostrils
the waters piled up.
The surging waters stood firm like a wall;
the deep waters congealed in the heart of the sea.
9"The enemy boasted,
'I will pursue, I will overtake them.
I will divide the spoils;
I will gorge myself on them.
I will draw my sword
and my hand will destroy them.'
10But you blew with your breath,
and the sea covered them.
They sank like lead
in the mighty waters.
11"Who among the gods is like you, O LORD?
Who is like you—
majestic in holiness,
awesome in glory,
working wonders?
12You stretched out your right hand
and the earth swallowed them.
13"In your unfailing love you will lead
the people you have redeemed.
In your strength you will guide them
to your holy dwelling.
14The nations will hear and tremble;
anguish will grip the people of Philistia.
15The chiefs of Edom will be terrified,
the leaders of Moab will be seized with trembling,
the people[d] of Canaan will melt away;
16 terror and dread will fall upon them.
By the power of your arm
they will be as still as a stone—
until your people pass by, O LORD,
until the people you bought[e] pass by.
17You will bring them in and plant them
on the mountain of your inheritance—
the place, O LORD, you made for your dwelling,

[a]25 Or *He jammed the wheels of their chariots* (see Samaritan Pentateuch, Septuagint and Syriac)
[b]27 Or *from* [c]4 Hebrew *Yam Suph*; that is, Sea of Reeds; also in verse 22 [d]15 Or *rulers*
[e]16 Or *created*

the sanctuary, O Lord, your hands
established.
18The LORD will reign
for ever and ever."

19When Pharaoh's horses, chariots and horsemen[a] went into the sea, the LORD brought the waters of the sea back over them, but the Israelites walked through the sea on dry ground. 20Then Miriam the prophetess, Aaron's sister, took a tambourine in her hand, and all the women followed her, with tambourines and dancing. 21Miriam sang to them:

"Sing to the LORD,
for he is highly exalted.
The horse and its rider
he has hurled into the sea."

The Waters of Marah and Elim

22Then Moses led Israel from the Red Sea and they went into the Desert of Shur. For three days they traveled in the desert without finding water. 23When they came to Marah, they could not drink its water because it was bitter. (That is why the place is called Marah.[b]) 24So the people grumbled against Moses, saying, "What are we to drink?"

25Then Moses cried out to the LORD, and the LORD showed him a piece of wood. He threw it into the water, and the water became sweet.

There the LORD made a decree and a law for them, and there he tested them. 26He said, "If you listen carefully to the voice of the LORD your God and do what is right in his eyes, if you pay attention to his commands and keep all his decrees, I will not bring on you any of the diseases I brought on the Egyptians, for I am the LORD, who heals you."

27Then they came to Elim, where there were twelve springs and seventy palm trees, and they camped there near the water.

Manna and Quail

16 The whole Israelite community set out from Elim and came to the Desert of Sin, which is between Elim and Sinai, on the fifteenth day of the second month after they had come out of Egypt. 2In the desert the whole community grumbled against Moses and Aaron. 3The Israelites said to them, "If only we had died by the LORD's hand in Egypt! There we sat around pots of meat and ate all the food we wanted, but you have brought us out into this desert to starve this entire assembly to death."

4Then the LORD said to Moses, "I will rain down bread from heaven for you. The people are to go out each day and gather enough for that day. In this way I will test them and see whether they will follow my instructions. 5On the sixth day they are to prepare what they bring in, and that is to be twice as much as they gather on the other days."

6So Moses and Aaron said to all the Israelites, "In the evening you will know that it was the LORD who brought you out of Egypt, 7and in the morning you will see the glory of the LORD, because he has heard your grumbling against him. Who are we, that you should grumble against us?" 8Moses also said, "You will know that it was the LORD when he gives you meat to eat in the evening and all the bread you want in the morning, because he has heard your grumbling against him. Who are we? You are not grumbling against us, but against the LORD."

9Then Moses told Aaron, "Say to the entire Israelite community, 'Come before the LORD, for he has heard your grumbling.' "

10While Aaron was speaking to the whole Israelite community, they looked toward the desert, and there was the glory of the LORD appearing in the cloud.

11The LORD said to Moses, 12"I have heard the grumbling of the Israelites. Tell them, 'At twilight you will eat meat, and in the morning you will be filled with bread. Then you will know that I am the LORD your God.' "

13That evening quail came and covered the camp, and in the morning there was a layer of dew around the camp. 14When the dew was gone, thin flakes like frost on the ground appeared on the desert floor. 15When the Israelites saw it, they said to each other, "What is it?" For they did not know what it was.

Moses said to them, "It is the bread the LORD has given you to eat. 16This is what the LORD has commanded: 'Each one is to gather as much as he needs. Take an omer[c] for each person you have in your tent.' "

17The Israelites did as they were told;

[a]19 Or *charioteers* [b]23 *Marah* means *bitter.* [c]16 That is, probably about 2 quarts (about 2 liters); also in verses 18, 32, 33 and 36

some gathered much, some little. 18And when they measured it by the omer, he who gathered much did not have too much, and he who gathered little did not have too little. Each one gathered as much as he needed.

19Then Moses said to them, "No one is to keep any of it until morning."

20However, some of them paid no attention to Moses; they kept part of it until morning, but it was full of maggots and began to smell. So Moses was angry with them.

21Each morning everyone gathered as much as he needed, and when the sun grew hot, it melted away. 22On the sixth day, they gathered twice as much—two omers[a] for each person—and the leaders of the community came and reported this to Moses. 23He said to them, "This is what the LORD commanded: 'Tomorrow is to be a day of rest, a holy Sabbath to the LORD. So bake what you want to bake and boil what you want to boil. Save whatever is left and keep it until morning.' "

24So they saved it until morning, as Moses commanded, and it did not stink or get maggots in it. 25"Eat it today," Moses said, "because today is a Sabbath to the LORD. You will not find any of it on the ground today. 26Six days you are to gather it, but on the seventh day, the Sabbath, there will not be any."

27Nevertheless, some of the people went out on the seventh day to gather it, but they found none. 28Then the LORD said to Moses, "How long will you[b] refuse to keep my commands and my instructions? 29Bear in mind that the LORD has given you the Sabbath; that is why on the sixth day he gives you bread for two days. Everyone is to stay where he is on the seventh day; no one is to go out." 30So the people rested on the seventh day.

31The people of Israel called the bread manna.[c] It was white like coriander seed and tasted like wafers made with honey. 32Moses said, "This is what the LORD has commanded: 'Take an omer of manna and keep it for the generations to come, so they can see the bread I gave you to eat in the desert when I brought you out of Egypt.' "

33So Moses said to Aaron, "Take a jar and put an omer of manna in it. Then place it before the LORD to be kept for the generations to come."

34As the LORD commanded Moses, Aaron put the manna in front of the Testimony, that it might be kept. 35The Israelites ate manna forty years, until they came to a land that was settled; they ate manna until they reached the border of Canaan.

36(An omer is one tenth of an ephah.)

Water From the Rock

17 The whole Israelite community set out from the Desert of Sin, traveling from place to place as the LORD commanded. They camped at Rephidim, but there was no water for the people to drink. 2So they quarreled with Moses and said, "Give us water to drink."

Moses replied, "Why do you quarrel with me? Why do you put the LORD to the test?"

3But the people were thirsty for water there, and they grumbled against Moses. They said, "Why did you bring us up out of Egypt to make us and our children and livestock die of thirst?"

4Then Moses cried out to the LORD, "What am I to do with these people? They are almost ready to stone me."

5The LORD answered Moses, "Walk on ahead of the people. Take with you some of the elders of Israel and take in your hand the staff with which you struck the Nile, and go. 6I will stand there before you by the rock at Horeb. Strike the rock, and water will come out of it for the people to drink." So Moses did this in the sight of the elders of Israel. 7And he called the place Massah[d] and Meribah[e] because the Israelites quarreled and because they tested the LORD saying, "Is the LORD among us or not?"

The Amalekites Defeated

8The Amalekites came and attacked the Israelites at Rephidim. 9Moses said to Joshua, "Choose some of our men and go out to fight the Amalekites. Tomorrow I will stand on top of the hill with the staff of God in my hands."

10So Joshua fought the Amalekites as Moses had ordered, and Moses, Aaron and Hur went to the top of the hill. 11As long as Moses held up his hands, the Israelites were winning, but whenever he lowered his hands, the Amalekites were win-

[a]22 That is, probably about 4 quarts (about 4.5 liters) [b]28 The Hebrew is plural. [c]31 *Manna* means *What is it?* (see verse 15). [d]7 *Massah* means *testing.* [e]7 *Meribah* means *quarreling.*

ning. 12When Moses' hands grew tired,
they took a stone and put it under him and
he sat on it. Aaron and Hur held his hands
up—one on one side, one on the other—
so that his hands remained steady till sun-
set. 13So Joshua overcame the Amalekite
army with the sword.

14Then the LORD said to Moses, "Write
this on a scroll as something to be remem-
bered and make sure that Joshua hears it,
because I will completely blot out the
memory of Amalek from under heaven."

15Moses built an altar and called it The
LORD is my Banner. 16He said, "For hands
were lifted up to the throne of the LORD.
The[a] LORD will be at war against the Ama-
lekites from generation to generation."

Jethro Visits Moses

18 Now Jethro, the priest of Midian
and father-in-law of Moses, heard
of everything God had done for Moses and
for his people Israel, and how the LORD
had brought Israel out of Egypt.

2After Moses had sent away his wife
Zipporah, his father-in-law Jethro re-
ceived her 3and her two sons. One son
was named Gershom,[b] for Moses said, "I
have become an alien in a foreign land";
4and the other was named Eliezer,[c] for
he said, "My father's God was my helper;
he saved me from the sword of Pharaoh."

5Jethro, Moses' father-in-law, together
with Moses' sons and wife, came to him in
the desert, where he was camped near the
mountain of God. 6Jethro had sent word
to him, "I, your father-in-law Jethro, am
coming to you with your wife and her two
sons."

7So Moses went out to meet his father-
in-law and bowed down and kissed him.
They greeted each other and then went
into the tent. 8Moses told his father-in-law
about everything the LORD had done to
Pharaoh and the Egyptians for Israel's
sake and about all the hardships they had
met along the way and how the LORD had
saved them.

9Jethro was delighted to hear about all
the good things the LORD had done for Is-
rael in rescuing them from the hand of the
Egyptians. 10He said, "Praise be to the
LORD, who rescued you from the hand of
the Egyptians and of Pharaoh, and who
rescued the people from the hand of the
Egyptians. 11Now I know that the LORD is
greater than all other gods, for he did this
to those who had treated Israel arrogant-
ly." 12Then Jethro, Moses' father-in-law,
brought a burnt offering and other sacri-
fices to God, and Aaron came with all the
elders of Israel to eat bread with Moses'
father-in-law in the presence of God.

13The next day Moses took his seat to
serve as judge for the people, and they
stood around him from morning till eve-
ning. 14When his father-in-law saw all that
Moses was doing for the people, he said,
"What is this you are doing for the people?
Why do you alone sit as judge, while all
these people stand around you from
morning till evening?"

15Moses answered him, "Because the
people come to me to seek God's will.
16Whenever they have a dispute, it is
brought to me, and I decide between the
parties and inform them of God's decrees
and laws."

17Moses' father-in-law replied, "What
you are doing is not good. 18You and these
people who come to you will only wear
yourselves out. The work is too heavy for
you; you cannot handle it alone. 19Listen
now to me and I will give you some ad-
vice, and may God be with you. You must
be the people's representative before God
and bring their disputes to him. 20Teach
them the decrees and laws, and show
them the way to live and the duties they
are to perform. 21But select capable men
from all the people—men who fear God,
trustworthy men who hate dishonest
gain—and appoint them as officials over
thousands, hundreds, fifties and tens.
22Have them serve as judges for the peo-
ple at all times, but have them bring every
difficult case to you; the simple cases they
can decide themselves. That will make
your load lighter, because they will share
it with you. 23If you do this and God so
commands, you will be able to stand the
strain, and all these people will go home
satisfied."

24Moses listened to his father-in-law
and did everything he said. 25He chose ca-
pable men from all Israel and made them
leaders of the people, officials over thou-
sands, hundreds, fifties and tens. 26They
served as judges for the people at all
times. The difficult cases they brought to
Moses, but the simple ones they decided
themselves.

[a]16 Or *"Because a hand was against the throne of the* LORD, *the* for *an alien there.* [b]3 *Gershom* sounds like the Hebrew [c]4 *Eliezer* means *my God is helper.*

27Then Moses sent his father-in-law on
his way, and Jethro returned to his own
country.

At Mount Sinai

19 In the third month after the Israel-
ites left Egypt—on the very day—
they came to the Desert of Sinai. 2After
they set out from Rephidim, they entered
the Desert of Sinai, and Israel camped
there in the desert in front of the moun-
tain.
3Then Moses went up to God, and the
LORD called to him from the mountain and
said, "This is what you are to say to the
house of Jacob and what you are to tell the
people of Israel: 4'You yourselves have
seen what I did to Egypt, and how I carried
you on eagles' wings and brought you to
myself. 5Now if you obey me fully and
keep my covenant, then out of all nations
you will be my treasured possession. Al-
though the whole earth is mine, 6you[a]
will be for me a kingdom of priests and a
holy nation.' These are the words you are
to speak to the Israelites."
7So Moses went back and summoned
the elders of the people and set before
them all the words the LORD had com-
manded him to speak. 8The people all re-
sponded together, "We will do everything
the LORD has said." So Moses brought
their answer back to the LORD.
9The LORD said to Moses, "I am going to
come to you in a dense cloud, so that the
people will hear me speaking with you
and will always put their trust in you."
Then Moses told the LORD what the people
had said.
10And the LORD said to Moses, "Go to
the people and consecrate them today and
tomorrow. Have them wash their clothes
11and be ready by the third day, because
on that day the LORD will come down on
Mount Sinai in the sight of all the people.
12Put limits for the people around the
mountain and tell them, 'Be careful that
you do not go up the mountain or touch
the foot of it. Whoever touches the moun-
tain shall surely be put to death. 13He shall
surely be stoned or shot with arrows; not
a hand is to be laid on him. Whether man
or animal, he shall not be permitted to
live.' Only when the ram's horn sounds a
long blast may they go up to the moun-
tain."
14After Moses had gone down the
mountain to the people, he consecrated
them, and they washed their clothes.
15Then he said to the people, "Prepare
yourselves for the third day. Abstain from
sexual relations."
16On the morning of the third day there
was thunder and lightning, with a thick
cloud over the mountain, and a very loud
trumpet blast. Everyone in the camp trem-
bled. 17Then Moses led the people out of
the camp to meet with God, and they
stood at the foot of the mountain. 18Mount
Sinai was covered with smoke, because
the LORD descended on it in fire. The
smoke billowed up from it like smoke
from a furnace, the whole mountain[b]
trembled violently, 19and the sound of the
trumpet grew louder and louder. Then
Moses spoke and the voice of God an-
swered him.[c]
20The LORD descended to the top of
Mount Sinai and called Moses to the top of
the mountain. So Moses went up 21and
the LORD said to him, "Go down and warn
the people so they do not force their way
through to see the LORD and many of them
perish. 22Even the priests, who approach
the LORD, must consecrate themselves, or
the LORD will break out against them."
23Moses said to the LORD, "The people
cannot come up Mount Sinai, because you
yourself warned us, 'Put limits around the
mountain and set it apart as holy.'"
24The LORD replied, "Go down and bring
Aaron up with you. But the priests and the
people must not force their way through
to come up to the LORD, or he will break
out against them."
25So Moses went down to the people
and told them.

The Ten Commandments

20 And God spoke all these words:
2"I am the LORD your God, who
brought you out of Egypt, out of
the land of slavery.
3"You shall have no other gods be-
fore[d] me.
4"You shall not make for yourself an
idol in the form of anything in
heaven above or on the earth

[a]5,6 Or *possession, for the whole earth is mine.* [6]*You* [b]18 Most Hebrew manuscripts; a few Hebrew manuscripts and Septuagint *all the people* [c]19 Or *and God answered him with thunder* [d]3 Or *besides*

VERSE FOR THE DAY: Exodus 20:14

AUTHOR: Tim Stafford

PASSAGE FOR THE DAY: Exodus 20:1–17

The Damage of Adultery

No one seems invulnerable to sexual temptation, and an affair, however "meaningless," has the potential to ruin even the best marriage. Blumstein and Schwartz, in their study of American couples, found that "husbands and wives who had had extramarital sex were more likely to break up, whether the unfaithfulness happened at the beginning of the marriage or after many years."

Comparing couples who had affairs with those who didn't, they found few differences. Both kinds of couples claimed to be about equally pleased with their relationship generally. In one area, though, the researchers found a significant difference. Couples who had committed adultery were less committed to the future together.

A partner's infidelity is more than just a disappointing choice to prefer another person (for a night, or longer). It is a stab in the gut. Adultery threatens any relationship. It betrays the partner who has entrusted life, body and soul to another. It makes him or her into a sexual competitor.

Marriage demands, positively, that we make a pledge to love for life. Negatively, it demands that we abhor adultery. To brush past that rule, emphasizing the positive pledge without the negative command, is to kid ourselves.

Adultery is a marriage killer. That is why the Bible is so plain in its command: "You shall not commit adultery."

MARRIAGE BUILDERS

♦ *What effects has adultery had on the marriages of people you know?*

♦ *What practical steps can you take to "affair-proof" your marriage?*

Additional Scripture Readings
Genesis 39:1–23; Proverbs 7:1–27; 1 Corinthians 7:4–5

Go to page 81 for your next devotional reading.

beneath or in the waters below.
5You shall not bow down to
them or worship them; for I, the
LORD your God, am a jealous
God, punishing the children for
the sin of the fathers to the third
and fourth generation of those
who hate me, 6but showing love
to a thousand ⌊generations⌋ of
those who love me and keep my
commandments.
7"You shall not misuse the name of
the LORD your God, for the LORD
will not hold anyone guiltless
who misuses his name.
8"Remember the Sabbath day by
keeping it holy. 9Six days you
shall labor and do all your
work, 10but the seventh day is a
Sabbath to the LORD your God.
On it you shall not do any work,
neither you, nor your son or
daughter, nor your manservant
or maidservant, nor your ani-
mals, nor the alien within your
gates. 11For in six days the LORD
made the heavens and the
earth, the sea, and all that is in
them, but he rested on the sev-
enth day. Therefore the LORD
blessed the Sabbath day and
made it holy.
12"Honor your father and your moth-
er, so that you may live long in
the land the LORD your God is
giving you.
13"You shall not murder.
14"You shall not commit adultery.
15"You shall not steal.
16"You shall not give false testimony
against your neighbor.
17"You shall not covet your neighbor's
house. You shall not covet your
neighbor's wife, or his manser-
vant or maidservant, his ox or
donkey, or anything that be-
longs to your neighbor."

18When the people saw the thunder and lightning and heard the trumpet and saw the mountain in smoke, they trembled with fear. They stayed at a distance 19and said to Moses, "Speak to us yourself and we will listen. But do not have God speak to us or we will die."

20Moses said to the people, "Do not be afraid. God has come to test you, so that the fear of God will be with you to keep you from sinning."

21The people remained at a distance, while Moses approached the thick darkness where God was.

Idols and Altars

22Then the LORD said to Moses, "Tell the Israelites this: 'You have seen for yourselves that I have spoken to you from heaven: 23Do not make any gods to be alongside me; do not make for yourselves gods of silver or gods of gold.

24" 'Make an altar of earth for me and sacrifice on it your burnt offerings and fellowship offerings,[a] your sheep and goats and your cattle. Wherever I cause my name to be honored, I will come to you and bless you. 25If you make an altar of stones for me, do not build it with dressed stones, for you will defile it if you use a tool on it. 26And do not go up to my altar on steps, lest your nakedness be exposed on it.'

21

"These are the laws you are to set before them:

Hebrew Servants

2"If you buy a Hebrew servant, he is to serve you for six years. But in the seventh year, he shall go free, without paying anything. 3If he comes alone, he is to go free alone; but if he has a wife when he comes, she is to go with him. 4If his master gives him a wife and she bears him sons or daughters, the woman and her children shall belong to her master, and only the man shall go free.

5"But if the servant declares, 'I love my master and my wife and children and do not want to go free,' 6then his master must take him before the judges.[b] He shall take him to the door or the doorpost and pierce his ear with an awl. Then he will be his servant for life.

7"If a man sells his daughter as a servant, she is not to go free as menservants do. 8If she does not please the master who has selected her for himself,[c] he must let her be redeemed. He has no right to sell her to foreigners, because he has broken faith with her. 9If he selects her for his son, he must grant her the rights of a daughter. 10If he marries another woman, he must not deprive the first one of her food, clothing and marital rights. 11If he

[a] 24 Traditionally *peace offerings* [b] 6 Or *before God* [c] 8 Or *master so that he does not choose her*

does not provide her with these three things, she is to go free, without any payment of money.

Personal Injuries

12"Anyone who strikes a man and kills him shall surely be put to death. 13However, if he does not do it intentionally, but God lets it happen, he is to flee to a place I will designate. 14But if a man schemes and kills another man deliberately, take him away from my altar and put him to death.

15"Anyone who attacks[a] his father or his mother must be put to death.

16"Anyone who kidnaps another and either sells him or still has him when he is caught must be put to death.

17"Anyone who curses his father or mother must be put to death.

18"If men quarrel and one hits the other with a stone or with his fist[b] and he does not die but is confined to bed, 19the one who struck the blow will not be held responsible if the other gets up and walks around outside with his staff; however, he must pay the injured man for the loss of his time and see that he is completely healed.

20"If a man beats his male or female slave with a rod and the slave dies as a direct result, he must be punished, 21but he is not to be punished if the slave gets up after a day or two, since the slave is his property.

22"If men who are fighting hit a pregnant woman and she gives birth prematurely[c] but there is no serious injury, the offender must be fined whatever the woman's husband demands and the court allows. 23But if there is serious injury, you are to take life for life, 24eye for eye, tooth for tooth, hand for hand, foot for foot, 25burn for burn, wound for wound, bruise for bruise.

26"If a man hits a manservant or maidservant in the eye and destroys it, he must let the servant go free to compensate for the eye. 27And if he knocks out the tooth of a manservant or maidservant, he must let the servant go free to compensate for the tooth.

28"If a bull gores a man or a woman to death, the bull must be stoned to death, and its meat must not be eaten. But the owner of the bull will not be held responsible. 29If, however, the bull has had the habit of goring and the owner has been warned but has not kept it penned up and it kills a man or woman, the bull must be stoned and the owner also must be put to death. 30However, if payment is demanded of him, he may redeem his life by paying whatever is demanded. 31This law also applies if the bull gores a son or daughter. 32If the bull gores a male or female slave, the owner must pay thirty shekels[d] of silver to the master of the slave, and the bull must be stoned.

33"If a man uncovers a pit or digs one and fails to cover it and an ox or a donkey falls into it, 34the owner of the pit must pay for the loss; he must pay its owner, and the dead animal will be his.

35"If a man's bull injures the bull of another and it dies, they are to sell the live one and divide both the money and the dead animal equally. 36However, if it was known that the bull had the habit of goring, yet the owner did not keep it penned up, the owner must pay, animal for animal, and the dead animal will be his.

Protection of Property

22 "If a man steals an ox or a sheep and slaughters it or sells it, he must pay back five head of cattle for the ox and four sheep for the sheep.

2"If a thief is caught breaking in and is struck so that he dies, the defender is not guilty of bloodshed; 3but if it happens[e] after sunrise, he is guilty of bloodshed.

"A thief must certainly make restitution, but if he has nothing, he must be sold to pay for his theft.

4"If the stolen animal is found alive in his possession—whether ox or donkey or sheep—he must pay back double.

5"If a man grazes his livestock in a field or vineyard and lets them stray and they graze in another man's field, he must make restitution from the best of his own field or vineyard.

6"If a fire breaks out and spreads into thornbushes so that it burns shocks of grain or standing grain or the whole field, the one who started the fire must make restitution.

7"If a man gives his neighbor silver or goods for safekeeping and they are stolen from the neighbor's house, the thief, if he is caught, must pay back double. 8But if

[a] 15 Or *kills* [b] 18 Or *with a tool* [c] 22 Or *she has a miscarriage* [d] 32 That is, about 12 ounces (about 0.3 kilogram) [e] 3 Or *if he strikes him*

the thief is not found, the owner of the house must appear before the judges[a] to determine whether he has laid his hands on the other man's property. 9In all cases of illegal possession of an ox, a donkey, a sheep, a garment, or any other lost property about which somebody says, 'This is mine,' both parties are to bring their cases before the judges. The one whom the judges declare[b] guilty must pay back double to his neighbor.

10"If a man gives a donkey, an ox, a sheep or any other animal to his neighbor for safekeeping and it dies or is injured or is taken away while no one is looking, 11the issue between them will be settled by the taking of an oath before the LORD that the neighbor did not lay hands on the other person's property. The owner is to accept this, and no restitution is required. 12But if the animal was stolen from the neighbor, he must make restitution to the owner. 13If it was torn to pieces by a wild animal, he shall bring in the remains as evidence and he will not be required to pay for the torn animal.

14"If a man borrows an animal from his neighbor and it is injured or dies while the owner is not present, he must make restitution. 15But if the owner is with the animal, the borrower will not have to pay. If the animal was hired, the money paid for the hire covers the loss.

Social Responsibility

16"If a man seduces a virgin who is not pledged to be married and sleeps with her, he must pay the bride-price, and she shall be his wife. 17If her father absolutely refuses to give her to him, he must still pay the bride-price for virgins.

18"Do not allow a sorceress to live.

19"Anyone who has sexual relations with an animal must be put to death.

20"Whoever sacrifices to any god other than the LORD must be destroyed.[c]

21"Do not mistreat an alien or oppress him, for you were aliens in Egypt.

22"Do not take advantage of a widow or an orphan. 23If you do and they cry out to me, I will certainly hear their cry. 24My anger will be aroused, and I will kill you with the sword; your wives will become widows and your children fatherless.

25"If you lend money to one of my people among you who is needy, do not be like a moneylender; charge him no interest.[d] 26If you take your neighbor's cloak as a pledge, return it to him by sunset, 27because his cloak is the only covering he has for his body. What else will he sleep in? When he cries out to me, I will hear, for I am compassionate.

28"Do not blaspheme God[e] or curse the ruler of your people.

29"Do not hold back offerings from your granaries or your vats.[f]

"You must give me the firstborn of your sons. 30Do the same with your cattle and your sheep. Let them stay with their mothers for seven days, but give them to me on the eighth day.

31"You are to be my holy people. So do not eat the meat of an animal torn by wild beasts; throw it to the dogs.

Laws of Justice and Mercy

23 "Do not spread false reports. Do not help a wicked man by being a malicious witness.

2"Do not follow the crowd in doing wrong. When you give testimony in a lawsuit, do not pervert justice by siding with the crowd, 3and do not show favoritism to a poor man in his lawsuit.

4"If you come across your enemy's ox or donkey wandering off, be sure to take it back to him. 5If you see the donkey of someone who hates you fallen down under its load, do not leave it there; be sure you help him with it.

6"Do not deny justice to your poor people in their lawsuits. 7Have nothing to do with a false charge and do not put an innocent or honest person to death, for I will not acquit the guilty.

8"Do not accept a bribe, for a bribe blinds those who see and twists the words of the righteous.

9"Do not oppress an alien; you yourselves know how it feels to be aliens, because you were aliens in Egypt.

Sabbath Laws

10"For six years you are to sow your fields and harvest the crops, 11but during the seventh year let the land lie unplowed and unused. Then the poor among your

[a]8 Or *before God*; also in verse 9 [b]9 Or *whom God declares* [c]20 The Hebrew term refers to the irrevocable giving over of things or persons to the LORD, often by totally destroying them. [d]25 Or *excessive interest* [e]28 Or *Do not revile the judges* [f]29 The meaning of the Hebrew for this phrase is uncertain.

ree cups shaped like almond flowers
buds and blossoms are to be on one
nch, three on the next branch, and the
e for all six branches extending from
lampstand. 34And on the lampstand
ere are to be four cups shaped like al-
ond flowers with buds and blossoms.
One bud shall be under the first pair of
ranches extending from the lampstand, a
econd bud under the second pair, and a
hird bud under the third pair—six
branches in all. 36The buds and branches
shall all be of one piece with the lamp-
stand, hammered out of pure gold.

37"Then make its seven lamps and set them up on it so that they light the space in front of it. 38Its wick trimmers and trays are to be of pure gold. 39A talent[a] of pure gold is to be used for the lampstand and all these accessories. 40See that you make them according to the pattern shown you on the mountain.

The Tabernacle

26 "Make the tabernacle with ten curtains of finely twisted linen and blue, purple and scarlet yarn, with cherubim worked into them by a skilled craftsman. 2All the curtains are to be the same size—twenty-eight cubits long and four cubits wide.[b] 3Join five of the curtains together, and do the same with the other five. 4Make loops of blue material along the edge of the end curtain in one set, and do the same with the end curtain in the other set. 5Make fifty loops on one curtain and fifty loops on the end curtain of the other set, with the loops opposite each other. 6Then make fifty gold clasps and use them to fasten the curtains together so that the tabernacle is a unit.

7"Make curtains of goat hair for the tent over the tabernacle—eleven altogether. 8All eleven curtains are to be the same size—thirty cubits long and four cubits wide.[c] 9Join five of the curtains together into one set and the other six into another set. Fold the sixth curtain double at the front of the tent. 10Make fifty loops along the edge of the end curtain in one set and also along the edge of the end curtain in the other set. 11Then make fifty bronze clasps and put them in the loops to fasten the tent together as a unit. 12As for the additional length of the tent curtains, the half curtain that is left over is to hang down at the rear of the tabernacle. 13The tent curtains will be a cubit[d] longer on both sides; what is left will hang over the sides of the tabernacle so as to cover it. 14Make for the tent a covering of ram skins dyed red, and over that a covering of hides of sea cows.[e]

15"Make upright frames of acacia wood for the tabernacle. 16Each frame is to be ten cubits long and a cubit and a half wide,[f] 17with two projections set parallel to each other. Make all the frames of the tabernacle in this way. 18Make twenty frames for the south side of the tabernacle 19and make forty silver bases to go under them—two bases for each frame, one under each projection. 20For the other side, the north side of the tabernacle, make twenty frames 21and forty silver bases—two under each frame. 22Make six frames for the far end, that is, the west end of the tabernacle, 23and make two frames for the corners at the far end. 24At these two corners they must be double from the bottom all the way to the top, and fitted into a single ring; both shall be like that. 25So there will be eight frames and sixteen silver bases—two under each frame.

26"Also make crossbars of acacia wood: five for the frames on one side of the tabernacle, 27five for those on the other side, and five for the frames on the west, at the far end of the tabernacle. 28The center crossbar is to extend from end to end at the middle of the frames. 29Overlay the frames with gold and make gold rings to hold the crossbars. Also overlay the crossbars with gold.

30"Set up the tabernacle according to the plan shown you on the mountain.

31"Make a curtain of blue, purple and scarlet yarn and finely twisted linen, with cherubim worked into it by a skilled craftsman. 32Hang it with gold hooks on four posts of acacia wood overlaid with gold and standing on four silver bases. 33Hang the curtain from the clasps and place the ark of the Testimony behind the curtain. The curtain will separate the Holy Place from the Most Holy Place. 34Put the atonement cover on the ark of the Testimony in the Most Holy Place. 35Place the

[a]39 That is, about 75 pounds (about 34 kilograms) [b]2 That is, about 42 feet (about 12.5 meters) long and 6 feet (about 1.8 meters) wide [c]8 That is, about 45 feet (about 13.5 meters) long and 6 feet (about 1.8 meters) wide [d]13 That is, about 1 1/2 feet (about 0.5 meter) [e]14 That is, dugongs [f]16 That is, about 15 feet (about 4.5 meters) long and 2 1/4 feet (about 0.7 meter) wide

people may get food from it, and the wild animals may eat what they leave. Do the same with your vineyard and your olive grove.

12"Six days do your work, but on the seventh day do not work, so that your ox and your donkey may rest and the slave born in your household, and the alien as well, may be refreshed.

13"Be careful to do everything I have said to you. Do not invoke the names of other gods; do not let them be heard on your lips.

The Three Annual Festivals

14"Three times a year you are to celebrate a festival to me.

15"Celebrate the Feast of Unleavened

FRIDAY

VERSE FOR THE DAY: Exodus 23:10–11

AUTHOR: Paul A. Mickey

PASSAGE FOR THE DAY: Exodus 23:10–13

Time to Slow Down

The most relaxed marital relationships enjoy what I call periods of fallow time. "Fallow" means to lie dormant or idle, and it's a concept that has been applied most often to the land.

In biblical times, farmers used a rotation system of seven-year periods to revitalize their fields. For six years they would plant and harvest, but during the seventh year the field was allowed to lie fallow. The fallow year was a time to replenish and nourish.

We need to build this concept into our marriages. After we cram our minds full of information and fill our days with activity, we need to provide for fallow time and space in our closest relationships.

But a sabbatical every seven years won't do the trick. Instead, you need to include fallow time every week, time when you and your mate get off by yourselves and enjoy one another quietly, without any purpose or agenda other than being together.

To find fallow time you'll most likely have to cut out some other activity or commitment. But when you take that step, you may well find that your marriage responds like the lands of the ancient Hebrews. The time off will rejuvenate and nurture the two of you and move you toward a more complete state of unity.

MARRIAGE BUILDERS

♦ *What adjustments can you make in your weekly schedule to have regular time with your spouse?*

♦ *What benefits to your marriage might come from adhering to a regular "fallow" time together?*

Additional Scripture Readings
Isaiah 40:30–31; Matthew 11:28–30; Ephesians 4:2–3

Go to page 87 for your next devotional reading.

Bread; for seven days eat bread made
without yeast, as I commanded you. Do
this at the appointed time in the month of
Abib, for in that month you came out of
Egypt.

"No one is to appear before me empty-
handed.

16"Celebrate the Feast of Harvest with
the firstfruits of the crops you sow in your
field.

"Celebrate the Feast of Ingathering at
the end of the year, when you gather in
your crops from the field.

17"Three times a year all the men are to
appear before the Sovereign LORD.

18"Do not offer the blood of a sacrifice
to me along with anything containing
yeast.

"The fat of my festival offerings must
not be kept until morning.

19"Bring the best of the firstfruits of
your soil to the house of the LORD your
God.

"Do not cook a young goat in its moth-
er's milk.

God's Angel to Prepare the Way

20"See, I am sending an angel ahead of
you to guard you along the way and to
bring you to the place I have prepared.
21Pay attention to him and listen to what
he says. Do not rebel against him; he will
not forgive your rebellion, since my Name
is in him. 22If you listen carefully to what
he says and do all that I say, I will be an
enemy to your enemies and will oppose
those who oppose you. 23My angel will go
ahead of you and bring you into the land
of the Amorites, Hittites, Perizzites, Ca-
naanites, Hivites and Jebusites, and I will
wipe them out. 24Do not bow down before
their gods or worship them or follow their
practices. You must demolish them and
break their sacred stones to pieces. 25Wor-
ship the LORD your God, and his blessing
will be on your food and water. I will take
away sickness from among you, 26and
none will miscarry or be barren in your
land. I will give you a full life span.

27"I will send my terror ahead of you
and throw into confusion every nation
you encounter. I will make all your ene-
mies turn their backs and run. 28I will
send the hornet ahead of you to drive the
Hivites, Canaanites and Hittites out of
your way. 29But I will not drive them out
in a single year, because the land would
become desolate and the wild animals too
numerous for you. 30Little by little I will
drive them out before you, until you have
increased enough to take possession of
the land.

31"I will establish your borders from the
Red Sea[a] to the Sea of the Philistines,[b]
and from the desert to the River.[c] I will
hand over to you the people who live in
the land and you will drive them out be-
fore you. 32Do not make a covenant with
them or with their gods. 33Do not let them
live in your land, or they will cause you to
sin against me, because the worship of
their gods will certainly be a snare to
you."

The Covenant Confirmed

24 Then he said to Moses, "Come up
to the LORD, you and Aaron, Nadab
and Abihu, and seventy of the elders of Is-
rael. You are to worship at a distance, 2but
Moses alone is to approach the LORD; the
others must not come near. And the peo-
ple may not come up with him."

3When Moses went and told the people
all the LORD's words and laws, they re-
sponded with one voice, "Everything the
LORD has said we will do." 4Moses then
wrote down everything the LORD had said.

He got up early the next morning and
built an altar at the foot of the mountain
and set up twelve stone pillars represent-
ing the twelve tribes of Israel. 5Then he
sent young Israelite men, and they offered
burnt offerings and sacrificed young bulls
as fellowship offerings[d] to the LORD. 6Mo-
ses took half of the blood and put it in
bowls, and the other half he sprinkled on
the altar. 7Then he took the Book of the
Covenant and read it to the people. They
responded, "We will do everything the
LORD has said; we will obey."

8Moses then took the blood, sprinkled it
on the people and said, "This is the blood
of the covenant that the LORD has made
with you in accordance with all these
words."

9Moses and Aaron, Nadab and Abihu,
and the seventy elders of Israel went up
10and saw the God of Israel. Under his feet
was something like a pavement made of
sapphire,[e] clear as the sky itself. 11But
God did not raise his hand against these

[a]31 Hebrew *Yam Suph*; that is, Sea of Reeds [b]31 That is, the Mediterranean [c]31 That is, the Euphrates [d]5 Traditionally *peace offerings* [e]10 Or *lapis lazuli*

leaders of the Israelites; they saw God,
and they ate and drank.

12The LORD said to Moses, "Come up to
me on the mountain and stay here, and I
will give you the tablets of stone, with the
law and commands I have written for their
instruction."

13Then Moses set out with Joshua his
aide, and Moses went up on the mountain
of God. 14He said to the elders, "Wait here
for us until we come back to you. Aaron
and Hur are with you, and anyone in-
volved in a dispute can go to them."

15When Moses went up on the moun-
tain, the cloud covered it, 16and the glory
of the LORD settled on Mount Sinai. For six
days the cloud covered the mountain, and
on the seventh day the LORD called to Mo-
ses from within the cloud. 17To the Israel-
ites the glory of the LORD looked like a
consuming fire on top of the mountain.
18Then Moses entered the cloud as he
went on up the mountain. And he stayed
on the mountain forty days and forty
nights.

Offerings for the Tabernacle

25 The LORD said to Moses, 2"Tell the
Israelites to bring me an offering.
You are to receive the offering for me from
each man whose heart prompts him to
give. 3These are the offerings you are to
receive from them: gold, silver and
bronze; 4blue, purple and scarlet yarn and
fine linen; goat hair; 5ram skins dyed red
and hides of sea cows[a]; acacia wood; 6ol-
ive oil for the light; spices for the anoint-
ing oil and for the fragrant incense; 7and
onyx stones and other gems to be mount-
ed on the ephod and breastpiece.

8"Then have them make a sanctuary for
me, and I will dwell among them. 9Make
this tabernacle and all its furnishings ex-
actly like the pattern I will show you.

The Ark

10"Have them make a chest of acacia
wood—two and a half cubits long, a cubit
and a half wide, and a cubit and a half
high.[b] 11Overlay it with pure gold, both
inside and out, and make a gold molding
around it. 12Cast four gold rings for it and
fasten them to its four feet, with two rings
on one side and two rings
13Then make poles of acac
overlay them with gold. 14Ins
into the rings on the sides of
carry it. 15The poles are to re
rings of this ark; they are not
moved. 16Then put in the ark the
ny, which I will give you.

17"Make an atonement cover[c]
gold—two and a half cubits long a
bit and a half wide.[d] 18And mak
cherubim out of hammered gold
ends of the cover. 19Make one cheru
one end and the second cherub on
other; make the cherubim of one pi
with the cover, at the two ends. 20T
cherubim are to have their wings sprea
upward, overshadowing the cover wit
them. The cherubim are to face each oth
er, looking toward the cover. 21Place the
cover on top of the ark and put in the ark
the Testimony, which I will give you.
22There, above the cover between the two
cherubim that are over the ark of the Tes-
timony, I will meet with you and give you
all my commands for the Israelites.

The Table

23"Make a table of acacia wood—two
cubits long, a cubit wide and a cubit and
a half high.[e] 24Overlay it with pure gold
and make a gold molding around it. 25Also
make around it a rim a handbreadth[f]
wide and put a gold molding on the rim.
26Make four gold rings for the table and
fasten them to the four corners, where the
four legs are. 27The rings are to be close to
the rim to hold the poles used in carrying
the table. 28Make the poles of acacia
wood, overlay them with gold and carry
the table with them. 29And make its plates
and dishes of pure gold, as well as its
pitchers and bowls for the pouring out of
offerings. 30Put the bread of the Presence
on this table to be before me at all times.

The Lampstand

31"Make a lampstand of pure gold and
hammer it out, base and shaft; its flower-
like cups, buds and blossoms shall be of
one piece with it. 32Six branches are to ex-
tend from the sides of the lampstand—
three on one side and three on the other.

33Th
with
bra
sar
the
th
m
35
b
s

[a]5 That is, dugongs [b]10 That is, about 3 3/4 feet (about 1.1 meters) long and 2 1/4 feet (about 0.7 meter) wide and high [c]17 Traditionally *a mercy seat* [d]17 That is, about 3 3/4 feet (about 1.1 meters) long and 2 1/4 feet (about 0.7 meter) wide [e]23 That is, about 3 feet (about 0.9 meter) long and 1 1/2 feet (about 0.5 meter) wide and 2 1/4 feet (about 0.7 meter) high [f]25 That is, about 3 inches (about 8 centimeters)

table outside the curtain on the north side of the tabernacle and put the lampstand opposite it on the south side.

36"For the entrance to the tent make a curtain of blue, purple and scarlet yarn and finely twisted linen—the work of an embroiderer. 37Make gold hooks for this curtain and five posts of acacia wood overlaid with gold. And cast five bronze bases for them.

The Altar of Burnt Offering

27 "Build an altar of acacia wood, three cubits[a] high; it is to be square, five cubits long and five cubits wide.[b] 2Make a horn at each of the four corners, so that the horns and the altar are of one piece, and overlay the altar with bronze. 3Make all its utensils of bronze—its pots to remove the ashes, and its shovels, sprinkling bowls, meat forks and firepans. 4Make a grating for it, a bronze network, and make a bronze ring at each of the four corners of the network. 5Put it under the ledge of the altar so that it is halfway up the altar. 6Make poles of acacia wood for the altar and overlay them with bronze. 7The poles are to be inserted into the rings so they will be on two sides of the altar when it is carried. 8Make the altar hollow, out of boards. It is to be made just as you were shown on the mountain.

The Courtyard

9"Make a courtyard for the tabernacle. The south side shall be a hundred cubits[c] long and is to have curtains of finely twisted linen, 10with twenty posts and twenty bronze bases and with silver hooks and bands on the posts. 11The north side shall also be a hundred cubits long and is to have curtains, with twenty posts and twenty bronze bases and with silver hooks and bands on the posts.

12"The west end of the courtyard shall be fifty cubits[d] wide and have curtains, with ten posts and ten bases. 13On the east end, toward the sunrise, the courtyard shall also be fifty cubits wide. 14Curtains fifteen cubits[e] long are to be on one side of the entrance, with three posts and three bases, 15and curtains fifteen cubits long are to be on the other side, with three posts and three bases.

16"For the entrance to the courtyard, provide a curtain twenty cubits[f] long, of blue, purple and scarlet yarn and finely twisted linen—the work of an embroiderer—with four posts and four bases. 17All the posts around the courtyard are to have silver bands and hooks, and bronze bases. 18The courtyard shall be a hundred cubits long and fifty cubits wide,[g] with curtains of finely twisted linen five cubits[h] high, and with bronze bases. 19All the other articles used in the service of the tabernacle, whatever their function, including all the tent pegs for it and those for the courtyard, are to be of bronze.

Oil for the Lampstand

20"Command the Israelites to bring you clear oil of pressed olives for the light so that the lamps may be kept burning. 21In the Tent of Meeting, outside the curtain that is in front of the Testimony, Aaron and his sons are to keep the lamps burning before the LORD from evening till morning. This is to be a lasting ordinance among the Israelites for the generations to come.

The Priestly Garments

28 "Have Aaron your brother brought to you from among the Israelites, along with his sons Nadab and Abihu, Eleazar and Ithamar, so they may serve me as priests. 2Make sacred garments for your brother Aaron, to give him dignity and honor. 3Tell all the skilled men to whom I have given wisdom in such matters that they are to make garments for Aaron, for his consecration, so he may serve me as priest. 4These are the garments they are to make: a breastpiece, an ephod, a robe, a woven tunic, a turban and a sash. They are to make these sacred garments for your brother Aaron and his sons, so they may serve me as priests. 5Have them use gold, and blue, purple and scarlet yarn, and fine linen.

The Ephod

6"Make the ephod of gold, and of blue, purple and scarlet yarn, and of finely

[a] 1 That is, about 4 1/2 feet (about 1.3 meters) [b] 1 That is, about 7 1/2 feet (about 2.3 meters) long and wide [c] 9 That is, about 150 feet (about 46 meters); also in verse 11 [d] 12 That is, about 75 feet (about 23 meters); also in verse 13 [e] 14 That is, about 22 1/2 feet (about 6.9 meters); also in verse 15 [f] 16 That is, about 30 feet (about 9 meters) [g] 18 That is, about 150 feet (about 46 meters) long and 75 feet (about 23 meters) wide [h] 18 That is, about 7 1/2 feet (about 2.3 meters)

twisted linen—the work of a skilled
craftsman. 7It is to have two shoulder
pieces attached to two of its corners, so it
can be fastened. 8Its skillfully woven
waistband is to be like it—of one piece
with the ephod and made with gold, and
with blue, purple and scarlet yarn, and
with finely twisted linen.

9"Take two onyx stones and engrave on
them the names of the sons of Israel 10in
the order of their birth—six names on one
stone and the remaining six on the other.
11Engrave the names of the sons of Israel
on the two stones the way a gem cutter
engraves a seal. Then mount the stones in
gold filigree settings 12and fasten them on
the shoulder pieces of the ephod as memorial stones for the sons of Israel. Aaron
is to bear the names on his shoulders as a
memorial before the LORD. 13Make gold filigree settings 14and two braided chains of
pure gold, like a rope, and attach the
chains to the settings.

The Breastpiece

15"Fashion a breastpiece for making decisions—the work of a skilled craftsman.
Make it like the ephod: of gold, and of
blue, purple and scarlet yarn, and of finely
twisted linen. 16It is to be square—a
span[a] long and a span wide—and folded
double. 17Then mount four rows of precious stones on it. In the first row there
shall be a ruby, a topaz and a beryl; 18in
the second row a turquoise, a sapphire[b]
and an emerald; 19in the third row a jacinth, an agate and an amethyst; 20in
the fourth row a chrysolite, an onyx and a jasper.[c] Mount them in gold filigree settings. 21There are to be twelve stones, one
for each of the names of the sons of Israel,
each engraved like a seal with the name of
one of the twelve tribes.

22"For the breastpiece make braided
chains of pure gold, like a rope. 23Make
two gold rings for it and fasten them to
two corners of the breastpiece. 24Fasten
the two gold chains to the rings at the corners of the breastpiece, 25and the other
ends of the chains to the two settings, attaching them to the shoulder pieces of the
ephod at the front. 26Make two gold rings
and attach them to the other two corners
of the breastpiece on the inside edge next
to the ephod. 27Make two more gold rings
and attach them to the bottom of the
shoulder pieces on the front of the ephod,
close to the seam just above the waistband of the ephod. 28The rings of the
breastpiece are to be tied to the rings of
the ephod with blue cord, connecting it to
the waistband, so that the breastpiece will
not swing out from the ephod.

29"Whenever Aaron enters the Holy
Place, he will bear the names of the sons
of Israel over his heart on the breastpiece
of decision as a continuing memorial before the LORD. 30Also put the Urim and the
Thummim in the breastpiece, so they may
be over Aaron's heart whenever he enters
the presence of the LORD. Thus Aaron will
always bear the means of making decisions for the Israelites over his heart before the LORD.

Other Priestly Garments

31"Make the robe of the ephod entirely
of blue cloth, 32with an opening for the
head in its center. There shall be a woven
edge like a collar[d] around this opening,
so that it will not tear. 33Make pomegranates of blue, purple and scarlet yarn
around the hem of the robe, with gold
bells between them. 34The gold bells and
the pomegranates are to alternate around
the hem of the robe. 35Aaron must wear it
when he ministers. The sound of the bells
will be heard when he enters the Holy
Place before the LORD and when he comes
out, so that he will not die.

36"Make a plate of pure gold and engrave on it as on a seal: HOLY TO THE LORD.
37Fasten a blue cord to it to attach it to the
turban; it is to be on the front of the turban. 38It will be on Aaron's forehead, and
he will bear the guilt involved in the sacred gifts the Israelites consecrate, whatever their gifts may be. It will be on Aaron's forehead continually so that they will
be acceptable to the LORD.

39"Weave the tunic of fine linen and
make the turban of fine linen. The sash is
to be the work of an embroiderer. 40Make
tunics, sashes and headbands for Aaron's
sons, to give them dignity and honor. 41After you put these clothes on your brother
Aaron and his sons, anoint and ordain
them. Consecrate them so they may serve
me as priests.

42"Make linen undergarments as a cov-

[a] *16* That is, about 9 inches (about 22 centimeters) [b] *18* Or *lapis lazuli* [c] *20* The precise identification of some of these precious stones is uncertain. [d] *32* The meaning of the Hebrew for this word is uncertain.

WEEKENDING

UNITY

It's difficult to feel united as husband and wife when you don't share the same central priorities in life. Each of you write down answers to the following questions, then discuss together what each of your central priorities is—and where those priorities overlap and where they conflict.

1. What are the top five priorities in your life?

2. What are your mate's central priorities?

3. How do your top priorities differ from your spouse's?

4. Do they differ enough to create disunity?

5. If the two of you hold conflicting priorities, how can you realign your priorities to develop greater unity in your marriage?

— *The* Marriage Partnership *Staff*

REVIVE

Saturday: 1 Corinthians 9:24–27
Sunday: 1 Samuel 12:20–24

Go to page 93 for your next devotional reading.

ering for the body, reaching from the waist to the thigh. 43Aaron and his sons must wear them whenever they enter the Tent of Meeting or approach the altar to minister in the Holy Place, so that they will not incur guilt and die.

"This is to be a lasting ordinance for Aaron and his descendants.

Consecration of the Priests

29 "This is what you are to do to consecrate them, so they may serve me as priests: Take a young bull and two rams without defect. 2And from fine wheat flour, without yeast, make bread, and cakes mixed with oil, and wafers spread with oil. 3Put them in a basket and present them in it—along with the bull and the two rams. 4Then bring Aaron and his sons to the entrance to the Tent of Meeting and wash them with water. 5Take the garments and dress Aaron with the tunic, the robe of the ephod, the ephod itself and the breastpiece. Fasten the ephod on him by its skillfully woven waistband. 6Put the turban on his head and attach the sacred diadem to the turban. 7Take the anointing oil and anoint him by pouring it on his head. 8Bring his sons and dress them in tunics 9and put headbands on them. Then tie sashes on Aaron and his sons.[a] The priesthood is theirs by a lasting ordinance. In this way you shall ordain Aaron and his sons.

10"Bring the bull to the front of the Tent of Meeting, and Aaron and his sons shall lay their hands on its head. 11Slaughter it in the LORD's presence at the entrance to the Tent of Meeting. 12Take some of the bull's blood and put it on the horns of the altar with your finger, and pour out the rest of it at the base of the altar. 13Then take all the fat around the inner parts, the covering of the liver, and both kidneys with the fat on them, and burn them on the altar. 14But burn the bull's flesh and its hide and its offal outside the camp. It is a sin offering.

15"Take one of the rams, and Aaron and his sons shall lay their hands on its head. 16Slaughter it and take the blood and sprinkle it against the altar on all sides. 17Cut the ram into pieces and wash the inner parts and the legs, putting them with the head and the other pieces. 18Then burn the entire ram on the altar. It is a burnt offering to the LORD, a pleasing aroma, an offering made to the LORD by fire.

19"Take the other ram, and Aaron and his sons shall lay their hands on its head. 20Slaughter it, take some of its blood and put it on the lobes of the right ears of Aaron and his sons, on the thumbs of their right hands, and on the big toes of their right feet. Then sprinkle blood against the altar on all sides. 21And take some of the blood on the altar and some of the anointing oil and sprinkle it on Aaron and his garments and on his sons and their garments. Then he and his sons and their garments will be consecrated.

22"Take from this ram the fat, the fat tail, the fat around the inner parts, the covering of the liver, both kidneys with the fat on them, and the right thigh. (This is the ram for the ordination.) 23From the basket of bread made without yeast, which is before the LORD, take a loaf, and a cake made with oil, and a wafer. 24Put all these in the hands of Aaron and his sons and wave them before the LORD as a wave offering. 25Then take them from their hands and burn them on the altar along with the burnt offering for a pleasing aroma to the LORD, an offering made to the LORD by fire. 26After you take the breast of the ram for Aaron's ordination, wave it before the LORD as a wave offering, and it will be your share.

27"Consecrate those parts of the ordination ram that belong to Aaron and his sons: the breast that was waved and the thigh that was presented. 28This is always to be the regular share from the Israelites for Aaron and his sons. It is the contribution the Israelites are to make to the LORD from their fellowship offerings.[b]

29"Aaron's sacred garments will belong to his descendants so that they can be anointed and ordained in them. 30The son who succeeds him as priest and comes to the Tent of Meeting to minister in the Holy Place is to wear them seven days.

31"Take the ram for the ordination and cook the meat in a sacred place. 32At the entrance to the Tent of Meeting, Aaron and his sons are to eat the meat of the ram and the bread that is in the basket. 33They are to eat these offerings by which atonement was made for their ordination and consecration. But no one else may eat them, because they are sacred. 34And if any of the meat of the ordination ram or any bread is left over till morning, burn it

[a]9 Hebrew; Septuagint *on them* [b]28 Traditionally *peace offerings*

up. It must not be eaten, because it is sacred.

35"Do for Aaron and his sons everything
I have commanded you, taking seven days
to ordain them. 36Sacrifice a bull each day
as a sin offering to make atonement. Puri-
fy the altar by making atonement for it,
and anoint it to consecrate it. 37For seven
days make atonement for the altar and
consecrate it. Then the altar will be most
holy, and whatever touches it will be holy.

38"This is what you are to offer on the
altar regularly each day: two lambs a year
old. 39Offer one in the morning and the
other at twilight. 40With the first lamb of-
fer a tenth of an ephah[a] of fine flour
mixed with a quarter of a hin[b] of oil from
pressed olives, and a quarter of a hin of
wine as a drink offering. 41Sacrifice the
other lamb at twilight with the same grain
offering and its drink offering as in the
morning—a pleasing aroma, an offering
made to the LORD by fire.

42"For the generations to come this
burnt offering is to be made regularly at
the entrance to the Tent of Meeting before
the LORD. There I will meet you and speak
to you; 43there also I will meet with the
Israelites, and the place will be consecrat-
ed by my glory.

44"So I will consecrate the Tent of Meet-
ing and the altar and will consecrate Aar-
on and his sons to serve me as priests.
45Then I will dwell among the Israelites
and be their God. 46They will know that I
am the LORD their God, who brought them
out of Egypt so that I might dwell among
them. I am the LORD their God.

The Altar of Incense

30 "Make an altar of acacia wood for
burning incense. 2It is to be square,
a cubit long and a cubit wide, and two cu-
bits high[c]—its horns of one piece with it.
3Overlay the top and all the sides and the
horns with pure gold, and make a gold
molding around it. 4Make two gold rings
for the altar below the molding—two on
opposite sides—to hold the poles used to
carry it. 5Make the poles of acacia wood
and overlay them with gold. 6Put the altar
in front of the curtain that is before the ark
of the Testimony—before the atonement
cover that is over the Testimony—where
I will meet with you.

7"Aaron must burn fragrant incense on
the altar every morning when he tends the
lamps. 8He must burn incense again when
he lights the lamps at twilight so incense
will burn regularly before the LORD for the
generations to come. 9Do not offer on this
altar any other incense or any burnt offer-
ing or grain offering, and do not pour a
drink offering on it. 10Once a year Aaron
shall make atonement on its horns. This
annual atonement must be made with the
blood of the atoning sin offering for the
generations to come. It is most holy to the
LORD."

Atonement Money

11Then the LORD said to Moses,
12"When you take a census of the Israel-
ites to count them, each one must pay the
LORD a ransom for his life at the time he is
counted. Then no plague will come on
them when you number them. 13Each one
who crosses over to those already counted
is to give a half shekel,[d] according to the
sanctuary shekel, which weighs twenty
gerahs. This half shekel is an offering to
the LORD. 14All who cross over, those
twenty years old or more, are to give an
offering to the LORD. 15The rich are not to
give more than a half shekel and the poor
are not to give less when you make the of-
fering to the LORD to atone for your lives.
16Receive the atonement money from the
Israelites and use it for the service of the
Tent of Meeting. It will be a memorial for
the Israelites before the LORD, making
atonement for your lives."

Basin for Washing

17Then the LORD said to Moses, 18"Make
a bronze basin, with its bronze stand, for
washing. Place it between the Tent of
Meeting and the altar, and put water in it.
19Aaron and his sons are to wash their
hands and feet with water from it.
20Whenever they enter the Tent of Meet-
ing, they shall wash with water so that
they will not die. Also, when they ap-
proach the altar to minister by presenting
an offering made to the LORD by fire,
21they shall wash their hands and feet so
that they will not die. This is to be a last-
ing ordinance for Aaron and his descen-
dants for the generations to come."

[a]40 That is, probably about 2 quarts (about 2 liters) [b]40 That is, probably about 1 quart (about 1 liter) [c]2 That is, about 1 1/2 feet (about 0.5 meter) long and wide and about 3 feet (about 0.9 meter) high [d]13 That is, about 1/5 ounce (about 6 grams); also in verse 15

Anointing Oil

22Then the LORD said to Moses, 23"Take
the following fine spices: 500 shekels[a] of
liquid myrrh, half as much (that is, 250
shekels) of fragrant cinnamon, 250 shek-
els of fragrant cane, 24500 shekels of cas-
sia—all according to the sanctuary shek-
el—and a hin[b] of olive oil. 25Make these
into a sacred anointing oil, a fragrant
blend, the work of a perfumer. It will be
the sacred anointing oil. 26Then use it to
anoint the Tent of Meeting, the ark of the
Testimony, 27the table and all its articles,
the lampstand and its accessories, the al-
tar of incense, 28the altar of burnt offering
and all its utensils, and the basin with its
stand. 29You shall consecrate them so
they will be most holy, and whatever
touches them will be holy.
30"Anoint Aaron and his sons and con-
secrate them so they may serve me as
priests. 31Say to the Israelites, 'This is to
be my sacred anointing oil for the genera-
tions to come. 32Do not pour it on men's
bodies and do not make any oil with the
same formula. It is sacred, and you are to
consider it sacred. 33Whoever makes per-
fume like it and whoever puts it on any-
one other than a priest must be cut off
from his people.' "

Incense

34Then the LORD said to Moses, "Take
fragrant spices—gum resin, onycha and
galbanum—and pure frankincense, all in
equal amounts, 35and make a fragrant
blend of incense, the work of a perfumer.
It is to be salted and pure and sacred.
36Grind some of it to powder and place it
in front of the Testimony in the Tent of
Meeting, where I will meet with you. It
shall be most holy to you. 37Do not make
any incense with this formula for your-
selves; consider it holy to the LORD.
38Whoever makes any like it to enjoy its
fragrance must be cut off from his peo-
ple."

Bezalel and Oholiab

31 Then the LORD said to Moses,
2"See, I have chosen Bezalel son of
Uri, the son of Hur, of the tribe of Judah,
3and I have filled him with the Spirit of
God, with skill, ability and knowledge in
all kinds of crafts— 4to make artistic de-
signs for work in gold, silver and bronze,
5to cut and set stones, to work in wood,
and to engage in all kinds of craftsman-
ship. 6Moreover, I have appointed Oholiab
son of Ahisamach, of the tribe of Dan, to
help him. Also I have given skill to all the
craftsmen to make everything I have com-
manded you: 7the Tent of Meeting, the ark
of the Testimony with the atonement cov-
er on it, and all the other furnishings of
the tent— 8the table and its articles, the
pure gold lampstand and all its accesso-
ries, the altar of incense, 9the altar of
burnt offering and all its utensils, the ba-
sin with its stand— 10and also the woven
garments, both the sacred garments for
Aaron the priest and the garments for his
sons when they serve as priests, 11and the
anointing oil and fragrant incense for the
Holy Place. They are to make them just as
I commanded you."

The Sabbath

12Then the LORD said to Moses, 13"Say
to the Israelites, 'You must observe my
Sabbaths. This will be a sign between me
and you for the generations to come, so
you may know that I am the LORD, who
makes you holy.[c]
14" 'Observe the Sabbath, because it is
holy to you. Anyone who desecrates it
must be put to death; whoever does any
work on that day must be cut off from his
people. 15For six days, work is to be done,
but the seventh day is a Sabbath of rest,
holy to the LORD. Whoever does any work
on the Sabbath day must be put to death.
16The Israelites are to observe the Sab-
bath, celebrating it for the generations to
come as a lasting covenant. 17It will be a
sign between me and the Israelites forev-
er, for in six days the LORD made the heav-
ens and the earth, and on the seventh day
he abstained from work and rested.' "
18When the LORD finished speaking to
Moses on Mount Sinai, he gave him the
two tablets of the Testimony, the tablets
of stone inscribed by the finger of God.

The Golden Calf

32 When the people saw that Moses
was so long in coming down from
the mountain, they gathered around Aar-
on and said, "Come, make us gods[d] who
will go before us. As for this fellow Moses

[a] *23* That is, about 12 1/2 pounds (about 6 kilograms) [b] *24* That is, probably about 4 quarts (about 4 liters) [c] *13* Or *who sanctifies you*; or *who sets you apart as holy* [d] *1* Or *a god*; also in verses 23 and 31

who brought us up out of Egypt, we don't
know what has happened to him."
2Aaron answered them, "Take off the
gold earrings that your wives, your sons
and your daughters are wearing, and
bring them to me." 3So all the people took
off their earrings and brought them to
Aaron. 4He took what they handed him
and made it into an idol cast in the shape
of a calf, fashioning it with a tool. Then
they said, "These are your gods,[a] O Israel, who brought you up out of Egypt."
5When Aaron saw this, he built an altar
in front of the calf and announced, "Tomorrow there will be a festival to the
LORD." 6So the next day the people rose
early and sacrificed burnt offerings and
presented fellowship offerings.[b] Afterward they sat down to eat and drink and
got up to indulge in revelry.
7Then the LORD said to Moses, "Go
down, because your people, whom you
brought up out of Egypt, have become
corrupt. 8They have been quick to turn
away from what I commanded them and
have made themselves an idol cast in the
shape of a calf. They have bowed down to
it and sacrificed to it and have said, 'These
are your gods, O Israel, who brought you
up out of Egypt.'
9"I have seen these people," the LORD
said to Moses, "and they are a stiff-necked
people. 10Now leave me alone so that my
anger may burn against them and that I
may destroy them. Then I will make you
into a great nation."
11But Moses sought the favor of the
LORD his God. "O LORD," he said, "why
should your anger burn against your people, whom you brought out of Egypt with
great power and a mighty hand? 12Why
should the Egyptians say, 'It was with evil
intent that he brought them out, to kill
them in the mountains and to wipe them
off the face of the earth'? Turn from your
fierce anger; relent and do not bring disaster on your people. 13Remember your servants Abraham, Isaac and Israel, to whom
you swore by your own self: 'I will make
your descendants as numerous as the
stars in the sky and I will give your
descendants all this land I promised them,
and it will be their inheritance forever.' "
14Then the LORD relented and did not
bring on his people the disaster he had
threatened.
15Moses turned and went down the
mountain with the two tablets of the Testimony in his hands. They were inscribed
on both sides, front and back. 16The tablets were the work of God; the writing was
the writing of God, engraved on the tablets.
17When Joshua heard the noise of the
people shouting, he said to Moses, "There
is the sound of war in the camp."
18Moses replied:

"It is not the sound of victory,
it is not the sound of defeat;
it is the sound of singing that I
hear."

19When Moses approached the camp
and saw the calf and the dancing, his anger burned and he threw the tablets out of
his hands, breaking them to pieces at the
foot of the mountain. 20And he took the
calf they had made and burned it in the
fire; then he ground it to powder, scattered it on the water and made the Israelites drink it.
21He said to Aaron, "What did these
people do to you, that you led them into
such great sin?"
22"Do not be angry, my lord," Aaron answered. "You know how prone these people are to evil. 23They said to me, 'Make us
gods who will go before us. As for this fellow Moses who brought us up out of
Egypt, we don't know what has happened
to him.' 24So I told them, 'Whoever has
any gold jewelry, take it off.' Then they
gave me the gold, and I threw it into the
fire, and out came this calf!"
25Moses saw that the people were running wild and that Aaron had let them get
out of control and so become a laughingstock to their enemies. 26So he stood at
the entrance to the camp and said, "Whoever is for the LORD, come to me." And all
the Levites rallied to him.
27Then he said to them, "This is what
the LORD, the God of Israel, says: 'Each
man strap a sword to his side. Go back
and forth through the camp from one end
to the other, each killing his brother and
friend and neighbor.' " 28The Levites did
as Moses commanded, and that day about
three thousand of the people died. 29Then
Moses said, "You have been set apart to
the LORD today, for you were against your
own sons and brothers, and he has
blessed you this day."
30The next day Moses said to the peo-

[a]4 Or *This is your god*; also in verse 8 [b]6 Traditionally *peace offerings*

ple, "You have committed a great sin. But now I will go up to the LORD; perhaps I can make atonement for your sin."

31So Moses went back to the LORD and said, "Oh, what a great sin these people have committed! They have made themselves gods of gold. 32But now, please forgive their sin—but if not, then blot me out of the book you have written."

33The LORD replied to Moses, "Whoever has sinned against me I will blot out of my book. 34Now go, lead the people to the place I spoke of, and my angel will go before you. However, when the time comes for me to punish, I will punish them for their sin."

35And the LORD struck the people with a plague because of what they did with the calf Aaron had made.

33 Then the LORD said to Moses, "Leave this place, you and the people you brought up out of Egypt, and go up to the land I promised on oath to Abraham, Isaac and Jacob, saying, 'I will give it to your descendants.' 2I will send an angel before you and drive out the Canaanites, Amorites, Hittites, Perizzites, Hivites and Jebusites. 3Go up to the land flowing with milk and honey. But I will not go with you, because you are a stiff-necked people and I might destroy you on the way."

4When the people heard these distressing words, they began to mourn and no one put on any ornaments. 5For the LORD had said to Moses, "Tell the Israelites, 'You are a stiff-necked people. If I were to go with you even for a moment, I might destroy you. Now take off your ornaments and I will decide what to do with you.' " 6So the Israelites stripped off their ornaments at Mount Horeb.

The Tent of Meeting

7Now Moses used to take a tent and pitch it outside the camp some distance away, calling it the "tent of meeting." Anyone inquiring of the LORD would go to the tent of meeting outside the camp. 8And whenever Moses went out to the tent, all the people rose and stood at the entrances to their tents, watching Moses until he entered the tent. 9As Moses went into the tent, the pillar of cloud would come down and stay at the entrance, while the LORD spoke with Moses. 10Whenever the people saw the pillar of cloud standing at the entrance to the tent, they all stood and worshiped, each at the entrance to his tent. 11The LORD would speak to Moses face to face, as a man speaks with his friend. Then Moses would return to the camp, but his young aide Joshua son of Nun did not leave the tent.

Moses and the Glory of the LORD

12Moses said to the LORD, "You have been telling me, 'Lead these people,' but you have not let me know whom you will send with me. You have said, 'I know you by name and you have found favor with me.' 13If you are pleased with me, teach me your ways so I may know you and continue to find favor with you. Remember that this nation is your people."

14The LORD replied, "My Presence will go with you, and I will give you rest."

15Then Moses said to him, "If your Presence does not go with us, do not send us up from here. 16How will anyone know that you are pleased with me and with your people unless you go with us? What else will distinguish me and your people from all the other people on the face of the earth?"

17And the LORD said to Moses, "I will do the very thing you have asked, because I am pleased with you and I know you by name."

18Then Moses said, "Now show me your glory."

19And the LORD said, "I will cause all my goodness to pass in front of you, and I will proclaim my name, the LORD, in your presence. I will have mercy on whom I will have mercy, and I will have compassion on whom I will have compassion. 20But," he said, "you cannot see my face, for no one may see me and live."

21Then the LORD said, "There is a place near me where you may stand on a rock. 22When my glory passes by, I will put you in a cleft in the rock and cover you with my hand until I have passed by. 23Then I will remove my hand and you will see my back; but my face must not be seen."

The New Stone Tablets

34 The LORD said to Moses, "Chisel out two stone tablets like the first ones, and I will write on them the words that were on the first tablets, which you broke. 2Be ready in the morning, and then come up on Mount Sinai. Present yourself to me there on top of the mountain. 3No one is to come with you or be seen anywhere on the mountain; not even the

flocks and herds may graze in front of the mountain."

4So Moses chiseled out two stone tablets like the first ones and went up Mount Sinai early in the morning, as the LORD had commanded him; and he carried the two stone tablets in his hands. 5Then the LORD came down in the cloud and stood there with him and proclaimed his name, the LORD. 6And he passed in front of Moses, proclaiming, "The LORD, the LORD, the compassionate and gracious God, slow to anger, abounding in love and faithfulness, 7maintaining love to thousands, and forgiving wickedness, rebellion and sin. Yet he does not leave the guilty unpunished; he punishes the children and their children for the sin of the fathers to the third and fourth generation."

8Moses bowed to the ground at once and worshiped. 9"O Lord, if I have found favor in your eyes," he said, "then let the Lord go with us. Although this is a stiff-necked people, forgive our wickedness

VERSE FOR THE DAY: Exodus 33:14

AUTHOR: Bill Hybels

PASSAGE FOR THE DAY: Exodus 33:12–23

Crisis Mode

A few years ago, Lynne and I were living in a constant "crisis mode"—just above the point of total exhaustion. I realized I was "skimming" in life. To make energy available to keep my ministry afloat, I began to skim relationally, emotionally and spiritually.

When you're living in crisis mode, your spiritual life becomes a cry for God to help you sustain the treadmill of activity for yet another day. This is dangerous spiritually because you don't have time to reflect or to worship properly. You don't have time to confess your sins deeply. Pretty soon you're involved in mechanical Christianity.

If you're devoted to getting out of crisis-mode living, you'll be willing to make some difficult changes. I have a close friend who requested a demotion at work. It meant a huge financial loss but now his weekends are free, and he leaves the office at four o'clock instead of seven. He has his walk with Christ back. His marriage is growing. He's growing in his relationship with his kids. Those trade-offs may cost you dearly, but they become non-issues when you consider the reasons why you're making the adjustment.

MARRIAGE BUILDERS

♦ *How would you characterize your lifestyle?*
♦ *What changes—even drastic ones—might be necessary to maintain your priorities as a spouse and parent?*

Additional Scripture Readings
Isaiah 30:15; Psalm 62:1, 5; Psalm 91:1

Go to page 111 for your next devotional reading.

and our sin, and take us as your inheritance."

10Then the LORD said: "I am making a covenant with you. Before all your people I will do wonders never before done in any nation in all the world. The people you live among will see how awesome is the work that I, the LORD, will do for you. 11Obey what I command you today. I will drive out before you the Amorites, Canaanites, Hittites, Perizzites, Hivites and Jebusites. 12Be careful not to make a treaty with those who live in the land where you are going, or they will be a snare among you. 13Break down their altars, smash their sacred stones and cut down their Asherah poles.[a] 14Do not worship any other god, for the LORD, whose name is Jealous, is a jealous God.

15"Be careful not to make a treaty with those who live in the land; for when they prostitute themselves to their gods and sacrifice to them, they will invite you and you will eat their sacrifices. 16And when you choose some of their daughters as wives for your sons and those daughters prostitute themselves to their gods, they will lead your sons to do the same.

17"Do not make cast idols.

18"Celebrate the Feast of Unleavened Bread. For seven days eat bread made without yeast, as I commanded you. Do this at the appointed time in the month of Abib, for in that month you came out of Egypt.

19"The first offspring of every womb belongs to me, including all the firstborn males of your livestock, whether from herd or flock. 20Redeem the firstborn donkey with a lamb, but if you do not redeem it, break its neck. Redeem all your firstborn sons.

"No one is to appear before me empty-handed.

21"Six days you shall labor, but on the seventh day you shall rest; even during the plowing season and harvest you must rest.

22"Celebrate the Feast of Weeks with the firstfruits of the wheat harvest, and the Feast of Ingathering at the turn of the year.[b] 23Three times a year all your men are to appear before the Sovereign LORD, the God of Israel. 24I will drive out nations before you and enlarge your territory, and no one will covet your land when you go up three times each year to appear before the LORD your God.

25"Do not offer the blood of a sacrifice to me along with anything containing yeast, and do not let any of the sacrifice from the Passover Feast remain until morning.

26"Bring the best of the firstfruits of your soil to the house of the LORD your God.

"Do not cook a young goat in its mother's milk."

27Then the LORD said to Moses, "Write down these words, for in accordance with these words I have made a covenant with you and with Israel." 28Moses was there with the LORD forty days and forty nights without eating bread or drinking water. And he wrote on the tablets the words of the covenant—the Ten Commandments.

The Radiant Face of Moses

29When Moses came down from Mount Sinai with the two tablets of the Testimony in his hands, he was not aware that his face was radiant because he had spoken with the LORD. 30When Aaron and all the Israelites saw Moses, his face was radiant, and they were afraid to come near him. 31But Moses called to them; so Aaron and all the leaders of the community came back to him, and he spoke to them. 32Afterward all the Israelites came near him, and he gave them all the commands the LORD had given him on Mount Sinai.

33When Moses finished speaking to them, he put a veil over his face. 34But whenever he entered the LORD's presence to speak with him, he removed the veil until he came out. And when he came out and told the Israelites what he had been commanded, 35they saw that his face was radiant. Then Moses would put the veil back over his face until he went in to speak with the LORD.

Sabbath Regulations

35 Moses assembled the whole Israelite community and said to them, "These are the things the LORD has commanded you to do: 2For six days, work is to be done, but the seventh day shall be your holy day, a Sabbath of rest to the LORD. Whoever does any work on it must be put to death. 3Do not light a fire in any of your dwellings on the Sabbath day."

[a]13 That is, symbols of the goddess Asherah [b]22 That is, in the fall

Materials for the Tabernacle

4Moses said to the whole Israelite community, "This is what the LORD has commanded: 5From what you have, take an offering for the LORD. Everyone who is willing is to bring to the LORD an offering of gold, silver and bronze; 6blue, purple and scarlet yarn and fine linen; goat hair; 7ram skins dyed red and hides of sea cows[a]; acacia wood; 8olive oil for the light; spices for the anointing oil and for the fragrant incense; 9and onyx stones and other gems to be mounted on the ephod and breastpiece.

10"All who are skilled among you are to come and make everything the LORD has commanded: 11the tabernacle with its tent and its covering, clasps, frames, crossbars, posts and bases; 12the ark with its poles and the atonement cover and the curtain that shields it; 13the table with its poles and all its articles and the bread of the Presence; 14the lampstand that is for light with its accessories, lamps and oil for the light; 15the altar of incense with its poles, the anointing oil and the fragrant incense; the curtain for the doorway at the entrance to the tabernacle; 16the altar of burnt offering with its bronze grating, its poles and all its utensils; the bronze basin with its stand; 17the curtains of the courtyard with its posts and bases, and the curtain for the entrance to the courtyard; 18the tent pegs for the tabernacle and for the courtyard, and their ropes; 19the woven garments worn for ministering in the sanctuary—both the sacred garments for Aaron the priest and the garments for his sons when they serve as priests."

20Then the whole Israelite community withdrew from Moses' presence, 21and everyone who was willing and whose heart moved him came and brought an offering to the LORD for the work on the Tent of Meeting, for all its service, and for the sacred garments. 22All who were willing, men and women alike, came and brought gold jewelry of all kinds: brooches, earrings, rings and ornaments. They all presented their gold as a wave offering to the LORD. 23Everyone who had blue, purple or scarlet yarn or fine linen, or goat hair, ram skins dyed red or hides of sea cows brought them. 24Those presenting an offering of silver or bronze brought it as an offering to the LORD, and everyone who had acacia wood for any part of the work brought it. 25Every skilled woman spun with her hands and brought what she had spun—blue, purple or scarlet yarn or fine linen. 26And all the women who were willing and had the skill spun the goat hair. 27The leaders brought onyx stones and other gems to be mounted on the ephod and breastpiece. 28They also brought spices and olive oil for the light and for the anointing oil and for the fragrant incense. 29All the Israelite men and women who were willing brought to the LORD freewill offerings for all the work the LORD through Moses had commanded them to do.

Bezalel and Oholiab

30Then Moses said to the Israelites, "See, the LORD has chosen Bezalel son of Uri, the son of Hur, of the tribe of Judah, 31and he has filled him with the Spirit of God, with skill, ability and knowledge in all kinds of crafts— 32to make artistic designs for work in gold, silver and bronze, 33to cut and set stones, to work in wood and to engage in all kinds of artistic craftsmanship. 34And he has given both him and Oholiab son of Ahisamach, of the tribe of Dan, the ability to teach others. 35He has filled them with skill to do all kinds of work as craftsmen, designers, embroiderers in blue, purple and scarlet yarn and fine linen, and weavers—all of them master craftsmen and designers.

36 1So Bezalel, Oholiab and every skilled person to whom the LORD has given skill and ability to know how to carry out all the work of constructing the sanctuary are to do the work just as the Lord has commanded."

2Then Moses summoned Bezalel and Oholiab and every skilled person to whom the LORD had given ability and who was willing to come and do the work. 3They received from Moses all the offerings the Israelites had brought to carry out the work of constructing the sanctuary. And the people continued to bring freewill offerings morning after morning. 4So all the skilled craftsmen who were doing all the work on the sanctuary left their work 5and said to Moses, "The people are bringing more than enough for doing the work the LORD commanded to be done."

6Then Moses gave an order and they sent this word throughout the camp: "No man or woman is to make anything else as

[a]7 That is, dugongs; also in verse 23

an offering for the sanctuary." And so the people were restrained from bringing more, 7because what they already had was more than enough to do all the work.

The Tabernacle

8All the skilled men among the workmen made the tabernacle with ten curtains of finely twisted linen and blue, purple and scarlet yarn, with cherubim worked into them by a skilled craftsman. 9All the curtains were the same size—twenty-eight cubits long and four cubits wide.[a] 10They joined five of the curtains together and did the same with the other five. 11Then they made loops of blue material along the edge of the end curtain in one set, and the same was done with the end curtain in the other set. 12They also made fifty loops on one curtain and fifty loops on the end curtain of the other set, with the loops opposite each other. 13Then they made fifty gold clasps and used them to fasten the two sets of curtains together so that the tabernacle was a unit.

14They made curtains of goat hair for the tent over the tabernacle—eleven altogether. 15All eleven curtains were the same size—thirty cubits long and four cubits wide.[b] 16They joined five of the curtains into one set and the other six into another set. 17Then they made fifty loops along the edge of the end curtain in one set and also along the edge of the end curtain in the other set. 18They made fifty bronze clasps to fasten the tent together as a unit. 19Then they made for the tent a covering of ram skins dyed red, and over that a covering of hides of sea cows.[c]

20They made upright frames of acacia wood for the tabernacle. 21Each frame was ten cubits long and a cubit and a half wide,[d] 22with two projections set parallel to each other. They made all the frames of the tabernacle in this way. 23They made twenty frames for the south side of the tabernacle 24and made forty silver bases to go under them—two bases for each frame, one under each projection. 25For the other side, the north side of the tabernacle, they made twenty frames 26and forty silver bases—two under each frame. 27They made six frames for the far end, that is, the west end of the tabernacle, 28and two frames were made for the corners of the tabernacle at the far end. 29At these two corners the frames were double from the bottom all the way to the top and fitted into a single ring; both were made alike. 30So there were eight frames and sixteen silver bases—two under each frame.

31They also made crossbars of acacia wood: five for the frames on one side of the tabernacle, 32five for those on the other side, and five for the frames on the west, at the far end of the tabernacle. 33They made the center crossbar so that it extended from end to end at the middle of the frames. 34They overlaid the frames with gold and made gold rings to hold the crossbars. They also overlaid the crossbars with gold.

35They made the curtain of blue, purple and scarlet yarn and finely twisted linen, with cherubim worked into it by a skilled craftsman. 36They made four posts of acacia wood for it and overlaid them with gold. They made gold hooks for them and cast their four silver bases. 37For the entrance to the tent they made a curtain of blue, purple and scarlet yarn and finely twisted linen—the work of an embroiderer; 38and they made five posts with hooks for them. They overlaid the tops of the posts and their bands with gold and made their five bases of bronze.

The Ark

37 Bezalel made the ark of acacia wood—two and a half cubits long, a cubit and a half wide, and a cubit and a half high.[e] 2He overlaid it with pure gold, both inside and out, and made a gold molding around it. 3He cast four gold rings for it and fastened them to its four feet, with two rings on one side and two rings on the other. 4Then he made poles of acacia wood and overlaid them with gold. 5And he inserted the poles into the rings on the sides of the ark to carry it.

6He made the atonement cover of pure gold—two and a half cubits long and a cubit and a half wide.[f] 7Then he made two cherubim out of hammered gold at the

[a]9 That is, about 42 feet (about 12.5 meters) long and 6 feet (about 1.8 meters) wide [b]15 That is, about 45 feet (about 13.5 meters) long and 6 feet (about 1.8 meters) wide [c]19 That is, dugongs [d]21 That is, about 15 feet (about 4.5 meters) long and 2 1/4 feet (about 0.7 meter) wide [e]1 That is, about 3 3/4 feet (about 1.1 meters) long and 2 1/4 feet (about 0.7 meter) wide and high [f]6 That is, about 3 3/4 feet (about 1.1 meters) long and 2 1/4 feet (about 0.7 meter) wide

ends of the cover. 8He made one cherub
on one end and the second cherub on the
other; at the two ends he made them of
one piece with the cover. 9The cherubim
had their wings spread upward, overshad-
owing the cover with them. The cherubim
faced each other, looking toward the
cover.

The Table

10They[a] made the table of acacia
wood—two cubits long, a cubit wide, and
a cubit and a half high.[b] 11Then they
overlaid it with pure gold and made a gold
molding around it. 12They also made
around it a rim a handbreadth[c] wide and
put a gold molding on the rim. 13They cast
four gold rings for the table and fastened
them to the four corners, where the four
legs were. 14The rings were put close to
the rim to hold the poles used in carrying
the table. 15The poles for carrying the ta-
ble were made of acacia wood and were
overlaid with gold. 16And they made from
pure gold the articles for the table—its
plates and dishes and bowls and its pitch-
ers for the pouring out of drink offerings.

The Lampstand

17They made the lampstand of pure
gold and hammered it out, base and shaft;
its flowerlike cups, buds and blossoms
were of one piece with it. 18Six branches
extended from the sides of the lamp-
stand—three on one side and three on the
other. 19Three cups shaped like almond
flowers with buds and blossoms were on
one branch, three on the next branch and
the same for all six branches extending
from the lampstand. 20And on the lamp-
stand were four cups shaped like almond
flowers with buds and blossoms. 21One
bud was under the first pair of branches
extending from the lampstand, a second
bud under the second pair, and a third
bud under the third pair—six branches in
all. 22The buds and the branches were all
of one piece with the lampstand, ham-
mered out of pure gold.

23They made its seven lamps, as well as
its wick trimmers and trays, of pure gold.
24They made the lampstand and all its ac-
cessories from one talent[d] of pure gold.

The Altar of Incense

25They made the altar of incense out of
acacia wood. It was square, a cubit long
and a cubit wide, and two cubits high[e]—
its horns of one piece with it. 26They over-
laid the top and all the sides and the horns
with pure gold, and made a gold molding
around it. 27They made two gold rings be-
low the molding—two on opposite
sides—to hold the poles used to carry it.
28They made the poles of acacia wood and
overlaid them with gold.

29They also made the sacred anointing
oil and the pure, fragrant incense—the
work of a perfumer.

The Altar of Burnt Offering

38 They[f] built the altar of burnt of-
fering of acacia wood, three cu-
bits[g] high; it was square, five cubits long
and five cubits wide.[h] 2They made a horn
at each of the four corners, so that the
horns and the altar were of one piece, and
they overlaid the altar with bronze. 3They
made all its utensils of bronze—its pots,
shovels, sprinkling bowls, meat forks and
firepans. 4They made a grating for the al-
tar, a bronze network, to be under its
ledge, halfway up the altar. 5They cast
bronze rings to hold the poles for the four
corners of the bronze grating. 6They made
the poles of acacia wood and overlaid
them with bronze. 7They inserted the
poles into the rings so they would be on
the sides of the altar for carrying it. They
made it hollow, out of boards.

Basin for Washing

8They made the bronze basin and its
bronze stand from the mirrors of the
women who served at the entrance to the
Tent of Meeting.

The Courtyard

9Next they made the courtyard. The
south side was a hundred cubits[i] long
and had curtains of finely twisted linen,
10with twenty posts and twenty bronze
bases, and with silver hooks and bands on

[a] *10* Or *He*; also in verses 11-29 [b] *10* That is, about 3 feet (about 0.9 meter) long, 1 1/2 feet (about 0.5 meter) wide, and 2 1/4 feet (about 0.7 meter) high [c] *12* That is, about 3 inches (about 8 centimeters) [d] *24* That is, about 75 pounds (about 34 kilograms) [e] *25* That is, about 1 1/2 feet (about 0.5 meter) long and wide, and about 3 feet (about 0.9 meter) high [f] *1* Or *He*; also in verses 2-9 [g] *1* That is, about 4 1/2 feet (about 1.3 meters) [h] *1* That is, about 7 1/2 feet (about 2.3 meters) long and wide [i] *9* That is, about 150 feet (about 46 meters)

the posts. 11The north side was also a hundred cubits long and had twenty posts and twenty bronze bases, with silver hooks and bands on the posts.

12The west end was fifty cubits[a] wide and had curtains, with ten posts and ten bases, with silver hooks and bands on the posts. 13The east end, toward the sunrise, was also fifty cubits wide. 14Curtains fifteen cubits[b] long were on one side of the entrance, with three posts and three bases, 15and curtains fifteen cubits long were on the other side of the entrance to the courtyard, with three posts and three bases. 16All the curtains around the courtyard were of finely twisted linen. 17The bases for the posts were bronze. The hooks and bands on the posts were silver, and their tops were overlaid with silver; so all the posts of the courtyard had silver bands.

18The curtain for the entrance to the courtyard was of blue, purple and scarlet yarn and finely twisted linen—the work of an embroiderer. It was twenty cubits[c] long and, like the curtains of the courtyard, five cubits[d] high, 19with four posts and four bronze bases. Their hooks and bands were silver, and their tops were overlaid with silver. 20All the tent pegs of the tabernacle and of the surrounding courtyard were bronze.

The Materials Used

21These are the amounts of the materials used for the tabernacle, the tabernacle of the Testimony, which were recorded at Moses' command by the Levites under the direction of Ithamar son of Aaron, the priest. 22(Bezalel son of Uri, the son of Hur, of the tribe of Judah, made everything the LORD commanded Moses; 23with him was Oholiab son of Ahisamach, of the tribe of Dan—a craftsman and designer, and an embroiderer in blue, purple and scarlet yarn and fine linen.) 24The total amount of the gold from the wave offering used for all the work on the sanctuary was 29 talents and 730 shekels,[e] according to the sanctuary shekel.

25The silver obtained from those of the community who were counted in the census was 100 talents and 1,775 shekels,[f] according to the sanctuary shekel— 26one beka per person, that is, half a shekel,[g] according to the sanctuary shekel, from everyone who had crossed over to those counted, twenty years old or more, a total of 603,550 men. 27The 100 talents[h] of silver were used to cast the bases for the sanctuary and for the curtain—100 bases from the 100 talents, one talent for each base. 28They used the 1,775 shekels[i] to make the hooks for the posts, to overlay the tops of the posts, and to make their bands.

29The bronze from the wave offering was 70 talents and 2,400 shekels.[j] 30They used it to make the bases for the entrance to the Tent of Meeting, the bronze altar with its bronze grating and all its utensils, 31the bases for the surrounding courtyard and those for its entrance and all the tent pegs for the tabernacle and those for the surrounding courtyard.

The Priestly Garments

39 From the blue, purple and scarlet yarn they made woven garments for ministering in the sanctuary. They also made sacred garments for Aaron, as the LORD commanded Moses.

The Ephod

2They[k] made the ephod of gold, and of blue, purple and scarlet yarn, and of finely twisted linen. 3They hammered out thin sheets of gold and cut strands to be worked into the blue, purple and scarlet yarn and fine linen—the work of a skilled craftsman. 4They made shoulder pieces for the ephod, which were attached to two of its corners, so it could be fastened. 5Its skillfully woven waistband was like it—of one piece with the ephod and made with gold, and with blue, purple and scarlet yarn, and with finely twisted linen, as the LORD commanded Moses.

6They mounted the onyx stones in gold filigree settings and engraved them like a seal with the names of the sons of Israel. 7Then they fastened them on the shoulder pieces of the ephod as memorial stones for the sons of Israel, as the LORD commanded Moses.

[a]12 That is, about 75 feet (about 23 meters) [b]14 That is, about 22 1/2 feet (about 6.9 meters) [c]18 That is, about 30 feet (about 9 meters) [d]18 That is, about 7 1/2 feet (about 2.3 meters) [e]24 The weight of the gold was a little over one ton (about 1 metric ton). [f]25 The weight of the silver was a little over 3 3/4 tons (about 3.4 metric tons). [g]26 That is, about 1/5 ounce (about 5.5 grams) [h]27 That is, about 3 3/4 tons (about 3.4 metric tons) [i]28 That is, about 45 pounds (about 20 kilograms) [j]29 The weight of the bronze was about 2 1/2 tons (about 2.4 metric tons). [k]2 Or *He*; also in verses 7, 8 and 22

The Breastpiece

8They fashioned the breastpiece—the
work of a skilled craftsman. They made it
like the ephod: of gold, and of blue, purple
and scarlet yarn, and of finely twisted lin-
en. 9It was square—a span[a] long and a
span wide—and folded double. 10Then
they mounted four rows of precious
stones on it. In the first row there was a
ruby, a topaz and a beryl; 11in the second
row a turquoise, a sapphire[b] and an em-
erald; 12in the third row a jacinth, an agate
and an amethyst; 13in the fourth row a
chrysolite, an onyx and a jasper.[c] They
were mounted in gold filigree settings.
14There were twelve stones, one for each
of the names of the sons of Israel, each en-
graved like a seal with the name of one of
the twelve tribes.

15For the breastpiece they made braid-
ed chains of pure gold, like a rope. 16They
made two gold filigree settings and two
gold rings, and fastened the rings to two of
the corners of the breastpiece. 17They fas-
tened the two gold chains to the rings at
the corners of the breastpiece, 18and the
other ends of the chains to the two set-
tings, attaching them to the shoulder
pieces of the ephod at the front. 19They
made two gold rings and attached them to
the other two corners of the breastpiece
on the inside edge next to the ephod.
20Then they made two more gold rings
and attached them to the bottom of the
shoulder pieces on the front of the ephod,
close to the seam just above the waist-
band of the ephod. 21They tied the rings of
the breastpiece to the rings of the ephod
with blue cord, connecting it to the waist-
band so that the breastpiece would not
swing out from the ephod—as the LORD
commanded Moses.

Other Priestly Garments

22They made the robe of the ephod en-
tirely of blue cloth—the work of a weav-
er— 23with an opening in the center of the
robe like the opening of a collar,[d] and a
band around this opening, so that it would
not tear. 24They made pomegranates of
blue, purple and scarlet yarn and finely
twisted linen around the hem of the robe.
25And they made bells of pure gold and at-
tached them around the hem between the
pomegranates. 26The bells and pomegran-
ates alternated around the hem of the robe
to be worn for ministering, as the LORD
commanded Moses.

27For Aaron and his sons, they made tu-
nics of fine linen—the work of a weav-
er— 28and the turban of fine linen, the lin-
en headbands and the undergarments of
finely twisted linen. 29The sash was of
finely twisted linen and blue, purple and
scarlet yarn—the work of an embroider-
er—as the LORD commanded Moses.

30They made the plate, the sacred dia-
dem, out of pure gold and engraved on it,
like an inscription on a seal: HOLY TO THE
LORD. 31Then they fastened a blue cord to
it to attach it to the turban, as the LORD
commanded Moses.

Moses Inspects the Tabernacle

32So all the work on the tabernacle, the
Tent of Meeting, was completed. The Isra-
elites did everything just as the LORD com-
manded Moses. 33Then they brought the
tabernacle to Moses: the tent and all its
furnishings, its clasps, frames, crossbars,
posts and bases; 34the covering of ram
skins dyed red, the covering of hides of
sea cows[e] and the shielding curtain;
35the ark of the Testimony with its poles
and the atonement cover; 36the table with
all its articles and the bread of the Pres-
ence; 37the pure gold lampstand with its
row of lamps and all its accessories, and
the oil for the light; 38the gold altar, the
anointing oil, the fragrant incense, and the
curtain for the entrance to the tent; 39the
bronze altar with its bronze grating, its
poles and all its utensils; the basin with its
stand; 40the curtains of the courtyard with
its posts and bases, and the curtain for the
entrance to the courtyard; the ropes and
tent pegs for the courtyard; all the furnish-
ings for the tabernacle, the Tent of Meet-
ing; 41and the woven garments worn for
ministering in the sanctuary, both the sa-
cred garments for Aaron the priest and the
garments for his sons when serving as
priests.

42The Israelites had done all the work
just as the LORD had commanded Moses.
43Moses inspected the work and saw that
they had done it just as the LORD had com-
manded. So Moses blessed them.

[a]*9* That is, about 9 inches (about 22 centimeters) [b]*11* Or *lapis lazuli* [c]*13* The precise identification of some of these precious stones is uncertain. [d]*23* The meaning of the Hebrew for this word is uncertain. [e]*34* That is, dugongs

Setting Up the Tabernacle

40 Then the LORD said to Moses: 2"Set up the tabernacle, the Tent of Meeting, on the first day of the first month. 3Place the ark of the Testimony in it and shield the ark with the curtain. 4Bring in the table and set out what belongs on it. Then bring in the lampstand and set up its lamps. 5Place the gold altar of incense in front of the ark of the Testimony and put the curtain at the entrance to the tabernacle.

6"Place the altar of burnt offering in front of the entrance to the tabernacle, the Tent of Meeting; 7place the basin between the Tent of Meeting and the altar and put water in it. 8Set up the courtyard around it and put the curtain at the entrance to the courtyard.

9"Take the anointing oil and anoint the tabernacle and everything in it; consecrate it and all its furnishings, and it will be holy. 10Then anoint the altar of burnt offering and all its utensils; consecrate the altar, and it will be most holy. 11Anoint the basin and its stand and consecrate them.

12"Bring Aaron and his sons to the entrance to the Tent of Meeting and wash them with water. 13Then dress Aaron in the sacred garments, anoint him and consecrate him so he may serve me as priest. 14Bring his sons and dress them in tunics. 15Anoint them just as you anointed their father, so they may serve me as priests. Their anointing will be to a priesthood that will continue for all generations to come." 16Moses did everything just as the LORD commanded him.

17So the tabernacle was set up on the first day of the first month in the second year. 18When Moses set up the tabernacle, he put the bases in place, erected the frames, inserted the crossbars and set up the posts. 19Then he spread the tent over the tabernacle and put the covering over the tent, as the LORD commanded him.

20He took the Testimony and placed it in the ark, attached the poles to the ark and put the atonement cover over it. 21Then he brought the ark into the tabernacle and hung the shielding curtain and shielded the ark of the Testimony, as the LORD commanded him.

22Moses placed the table in the Tent of Meeting on the north side of the tabernacle outside the curtain 23and set out the bread on it before the LORD, as the LORD commanded him.

24He placed the lampstand in the Tent of Meeting opposite the table on the south side of the tabernacle 25and set up the lamps before the LORD, as the LORD commanded him.

26Moses placed the gold altar in the Tent of Meeting in front of the curtain 27and burned fragrant incense on it, as the LORD commanded him. 28Then he put up the curtain at the entrance to the tabernacle.

29He set the altar of burnt offering near the entrance to the tabernacle, the Tent of Meeting, and offered on it burnt offerings and grain offerings, as the LORD commanded him.

30He placed the basin between the Tent of Meeting and the altar and put water in it for washing, 31and Moses and Aaron and his sons used it to wash their hands and feet. 32They washed whenever they entered the Tent of Meeting or approached the altar, as the LORD commanded Moses.

33Then Moses set up the courtyard around the tabernacle and altar and put up the curtain at the entrance to the courtyard. And so Moses finished the work.

The Glory of the LORD

34Then the cloud covered the Tent of Meeting, and the glory of the LORD filled the tabernacle. 35Moses could not enter the Tent of Meeting because the cloud had settled upon it, and the glory of the LORD filled the tabernacle.

36In all the travels of the Israelites, whenever the cloud lifted from above the tabernacle, they would set out; 37but if the cloud did not lift, they did not set out—until the day it lifted. 38So the cloud of the LORD was over the tabernacle by day, and fire was in the cloud by night, in the sight of all the house of Israel during all their travels.

MOSES writes this book while the Israelites are in the wilderness, before they enter the promised land. In it he reports to them the numerous religious, civil and moral laws that God revealed to him on Mount Sinai. As you read this book, some of it may seem dull and boring. But think about how holy God is, how he wants you to serve him in every part of your life and in all you do.

LEVITICUS

The Burnt Offering

1 The LORD called to Moses and spoke
to him from the Tent of Meeting. He
said, 2"Speak to the Israelites and say to
them: 'When any of you brings an offering
to the LORD, bring as your offering an animal from either the herd or the flock.

3" 'If the offering is a burnt offering
from the herd, he is to offer a male without defect. He must present it at the entrance to the Tent of Meeting so that it[a]
will be acceptable to the LORD. 4He is to
lay his hand on the head of the burnt offering, and it will be accepted on his behalf to make atonement for him. 5He is to
slaughter the young bull before the LORD,
and then Aaron's sons the priests shall
bring the blood and sprinkle it against the
altar on all sides at the entrance to the
Tent of Meeting. 6He is to skin the burnt
offering and cut it into pieces. 7The sons
of Aaron the priest are to put fire on the
altar and arrange wood on the fire. 8Then
Aaron's sons the priests shall arrange the
pieces, including the head and the fat, on
the burning wood that is on the altar. 9He
is to wash the inner parts and the legs
with water, and the priest is to burn all of
it on the altar. It is a burnt offering, an offering made by fire, an aroma pleasing to
the LORD.

10" 'If the offering is a burnt offering
from the flock, from either the sheep or
the goats, he is to offer a male without de-

[a]3 Or *he*

fect. 11He is to slaughter it at the north
side of the altar before the LORD, and Aar-
on's sons the priests shall sprinkle its
blood against the altar on all sides. 12He is
to cut it into pieces, and the priest shall
arrange them, including the head and the
fat, on the burning wood that is on the al-
tar. 13He is to wash the inner parts and the
legs with water, and the priest is to bring
all of it and burn it on the altar. It is a
burnt offering, an offering made by fire,
an aroma pleasing to the LORD.

14" 'If the offering to the LORD is a burnt
offering of birds, he is to offer a dove or a
young pigeon. 15The priest shall bring it to
the altar, wring off the head and burn it on
the altar; its blood shall be drained out on
the side of the altar. 16He is to remove the
crop with its contents[a] and throw it to
the east side of the altar, where the ashes
are. 17He shall tear it open by the wings,
not severing it completely, and then the
priest shall burn it on the wood that is on
the fire on the altar. It is a burnt offering,
an offering made by fire, an aroma pleas-
ing to the LORD.

The Grain Offering

2 " 'When someone brings a grain offer-
ing to the LORD, his offering is to be of
fine flour. He is to pour oil on it, put in-
cense on it 2and take it to Aaron's sons the
priests. The priest shall take a handful of
the fine flour and oil, together with all the
incense, and burn this as a memorial por-
tion on the altar, an offering made by fire,
an aroma pleasing to the LORD. 3The rest
of the grain offering belongs to Aaron and
his sons; it is a most holy part of the offer-
ings made to the LORD by fire.

4" 'If you bring a grain offering baked in
an oven, it is to consist of fine flour: cakes
made without yeast and mixed with oil,
or[b] wafers made without yeast and
spread with oil. 5If your grain offering is
prepared on a griddle, it is to be made of
fine flour mixed with oil, and without
yeast. 6Crumble it and pour oil on it; it is
a grain offering. 7If your grain offering is
cooked in a pan, it is to be made of fine
flour and oil. 8Bring the grain offering
made of these things to the LORD; present
it to the priest, who shall take it to the al-
tar. 9He shall take out the memorial por-
tion from the grain offering and burn it on
the altar as an offering made by fire, an
aroma pleasing to the LORD. 10The rest of
the grain offering belongs to Aaron and
his sons; it is a most holy part of the offer-
ings made to the LORD by fire.

11" 'Every grain offering you bring to
the LORD must be made without yeast, for
you are not to burn any yeast or honey in
an offering made to the LORD by fire. 12You
may bring them to the LORD as an offering
of the firstfruits, but they are not to be of-
fered on the altar as a pleasing aroma.
13Season all your grain offerings with salt.
Do not leave the salt of the covenant of
your God out of your grain offerings; add
salt to all your offerings.

14" 'If you bring a grain offering of first-
fruits to the LORD, offer crushed heads of
new grain roasted in the fire. 15Put oil and
incense on it; it is a grain offering. 16The
priest shall burn the memorial portion of
the crushed grain and the oil, together
with all the incense, as an offering made
to the LORD by fire.

The Fellowship Offering

3 " 'If someone's offering is a fellowship
offering,[c] and he offers an animal
from the herd, whether male or female, he
is to present before the LORD an animal
without defect. 2He is to lay his hand on
the head of his offering and slaughter it at
the entrance to the Tent of Meeting. Then
Aaron's sons the priests shall sprinkle the
blood against the altar on all sides. 3From
the fellowship offering he is to bring a sac-
rifice made to the LORD by fire: all the fat
that covers the inner parts or is connected
to them, 4both kidneys with the fat on
them near the loins, and the covering of
the liver, which he will remove with the
kidneys. 5Then Aaron's sons are to burn it
on the altar on top of the burnt offering
that is on the burning wood, as an offering
made by fire, an aroma pleasing to the
LORD.

6" 'If he offers an animal from the flock
as a fellowship offering to the LORD, he is
to offer a male or female without defect.
7If he offers a lamb, he is to present it be-
fore the LORD. 8He is to lay his hand on the
head of his offering and slaughter it in
front of the Tent of Meeting. Then Aaron's
sons shall sprinkle its blood against the al-
tar on all sides. 9From the fellowship of-
fering he is to bring a sacrifice made to the

[a] 16 Or *crop and the feathers*; the meaning of the Hebrew for this word is uncertain. [b] 4 Or *and*
[c] 1 Traditionally *peace offering*; also in verses 3, 6 and 9

LORD by fire: its fat, the entire fat tail cut
off close to the backbone, all the fat that
covers the inner parts or is connected to
them, 10both kidneys with the fat on them
near the loins, and the covering of the liv-
er, which he will remove with the kidneys.
11The priest shall burn them on the altar
as food, an offering made to the LORD by
fire.

12" 'If his offering is a goat, he is to
present it before the LORD. 13He is to lay
his hand on its head and slaughter it in
front of the Tent of Meeting. Then Aaron's
sons shall sprinkle its blood against the al-
tar on all sides. 14From what he offers he
is to make this offering to the LORD by fire:
all the fat that covers the inner parts or is
connected to them, 15both kidneys with
the fat on them near the loins, and the
covering of the liver, which he will re-
move with the kidneys. 16The priest shall
burn them on the altar as food, an offering
made by fire, a pleasing aroma. All the fat
is the LORD's.

17" 'This is a lasting ordinance for the
generations to come, wherever you live:
You must not eat any fat or any blood.' "

The Sin Offering

4 The LORD said to Moses, 2"Say to the
Israelites: 'When anyone sins unin-
tentionally and does what is forbidden in
any of the LORD's commands—

3" 'If the anointed priest sins, bringing
guilt on the people, he must bring to the
LORD a young bull without defect as a sin
offering for the sin he has committed. 4He
is to present the bull at the entrance to the
Tent of Meeting before the LORD. He is to
lay his hand on its head and slaughter it
before the LORD. 5Then the anointed priest
shall take some of the bull's blood and
carry it into the Tent of Meeting. 6He is to
dip his finger into the blood and sprinkle
some of it seven times before the LORD, in
front of the curtain of the sanctuary. 7The
priest shall then put some of the blood on
the horns of the altar of fragrant incense
that is before the LORD in the Tent of Meet-
ing. The rest of the bull's blood he shall
pour out at the base of the altar of burnt
offering at the entrance to the Tent of
Meeting. 8He shall remove all the fat from
the bull of the sin offering—the fat that
covers the inner parts or is connected to
them, 9both kidneys with the fat on them
near the loins, and the covering of the liv-
er, which he will remove with the kid-
neys— 10just as the fat is removed from
the ox[a] sacrificed as a fellowship offer-
ing.[b] Then the priest shall burn them on
the altar of burnt offering. 11But the hide
of the bull and all its flesh, as well as the
head and legs, the inner parts and offal—
12that is, all the rest of the bull—he must
take outside the camp to a place cere-
monially clean, where the ashes are
thrown, and burn it in a wood fire on the
ash heap.

13" 'If the whole Israelite community
sins unintentionally and does what is for-
bidden in any of the LORD's commands,
even though the community is unaware of
the matter, they are guilty. 14When they
become aware of the sin they committed,
the assembly must bring a young bull as
a sin offering and present it before the
Tent of Meeting. 15The elders of the com-
munity are to lay their hands on the bull's
head before the LORD, and the bull shall be
slaughtered before the LORD. 16Then the
anointed priest is to take some of the
bull's blood into the Tent of Meeting. 17He
shall dip his finger into the blood and
sprinkle it before the LORD seven times in
front of the curtain. 18He is to put some of
the blood on the horns of the altar that is
before the LORD in the Tent of Meeting.
The rest of the blood he shall pour out at
the base of the altar of burnt offering at
the entrance to the Tent of Meeting. 19He
shall remove all the fat from it and burn it
on the altar, 20and do with this bull just as
he did with the bull for the sin offering. In
this way the priest will make atonement
for them, and they will be forgiven.
21Then he shall take the bull outside the
camp and burn it as he burned the first
bull. This is the sin offering for the com-
munity.

22" 'When a leader sins unintentionally
and does what is forbidden in any of the
commands of the LORD his God, he is
guilty. 23When he is made aware of the sin
he committed, he must bring as his offer-
ing a male goat without defect. 24He is to
lay his hand on the goat's head and
slaughter it at the place where the burnt
offering is slaughtered before the LORD. It
is a sin offering. 25Then the priest shall

[a] *10* The Hebrew word can include both male and female.

[b] *10* Traditionally *peace offering*; also in verses 26, 31 and 35

take some of the blood of the sin offering
with his finger and put it on the horns of
the altar of burnt offering and pour out the
rest of the blood at the base of the altar.
26He shall burn all the fat on the altar as
he burned the fat of the fellowship offer-
ing. In this way the priest will make atone-
ment for the man's sin, and he will be for-
given.

27" 'If a member of the community sins
unintentionally and does what is forbid-
den in any of the LORD's commands, he is
guilty. 28When he is made aware of the sin
he committed, he must bring as his offer-
ing for the sin he committed a female goat
without defect. 29He is to lay his hand on
the head of the sin offering and slaughter
it at the place of the burnt offering. 30Then
the priest is to take some of the blood with
his finger and put it on the horns of the
altar of burnt offering and pour out the
rest of the blood at the base of the altar.
31He shall remove all the fat, just as the fat
is removed from the fellowship offering,
and the priest shall burn it on the altar as
an aroma pleasing to the LORD. In this way
the priest will make atonement for him,
and he will be forgiven.

32" 'If he brings a lamb as his sin offer-
ing, he is to bring a female without defect.
33He is to lay his hand on its head and
slaughter it for a sin offering at the place
where the burnt offering is slaughtered.
34Then the priest shall take some of the
blood of the sin offering with his finger
and put it on the horns of the altar of
burnt offering and pour out the rest of the
blood at the base of the altar. 35He shall
remove all the fat, just as the fat is re-
moved from the lamb of the fellowship of-
fering, and the priest shall burn it on the
altar on top of the offerings made to the
LORD by fire. In this way the priest will
make atonement for him for the sin he has
committed, and he will be forgiven.

5 " 'If a person sins because he does not
speak up when he hears a public
charge to testify regarding something he
has seen or learned about, he will be held
responsible.

2" 'Or if a person touches anything cere-
monially unclean—whether the carcasses
of unclean wild animals or of unclean live-
stock or of unclean creatures that move
along the ground—even though he is un-
aware of it, he has become unclean and is
guilty.

3" 'Or if he touches human unclean-
ness—anything that would make him un-
clean—even though he is unaware of it,
when he learns of it he will be guilty.

4" 'Or if a person thoughtlessly takes an
oath to do anything, whether good or
evil—in any matter one might carelessly
swear about—even though he is unaware
of it, in any case when he learns of it he
will be guilty.

5" 'When anyone is guilty in any of
these ways, he must confess in what way
he has sinned 6and, as a penalty for the sin
he has committed, he must bring to the
LORD a female lamb or goat from the flock
as a sin offering; and the priest shall make
atonement for him for his sin.

7" 'If he cannot afford a lamb, he is to
bring two doves or two young pigeons to
the LORD as a penalty for his sin—one for
a sin offering and the other for a burnt of-
fering. 8He is to bring them to the priest,
who shall first offer the one for the sin of-
fering. He is to wring its head from its
neck, not severing it completely, 9and is to
sprinkle some of the blood of the sin offer-
ing against the side of the altar; the rest of
the blood must be drained out at the base
of the altar. It is a sin offering. 10The priest
shall then offer the other as a burnt offer-
ing in the prescribed way and make atone-
ment for him for the sin he has commit-
ted, and he will be forgiven.

11" 'If, however, he cannot afford two
doves or two young pigeons, he is to bring
as an offering for his sin a tenth of an
ephah[a] of fine flour for a sin offering. He
must not put oil or incense on it, because
it is a sin offering. 12He is to bring it to the
priest, who shall take a handful of it as a
memorial portion and burn it on the altar
on top of the offerings made to the LORD
by fire. It is a sin offering. 13In this way the
priest will make atonement for him for
any of these sins he has committed, and
he will be forgiven. The rest of the offering
will belong to the priest, as in the case of
the grain offering.' "

The Guilt Offering

14The LORD said to Moses: 15"When a
person commits a violation and sins unin-
tentionally in regard to any of the LORD's
holy things, he is to bring to the LORD as
a penalty a ram from the flock, one with-

[a] *11* That is, probably about 2 quarts (about 2 liters)

out defect and of the proper value in silver, according to the sanctuary shekel.[a] It is a guilt offering. 16He must make restitution for what he has failed to do in regard to the holy things, add a fifth of the value to that and give it all to the priest, who will make atonement for him with the ram as a guilt offering, and he will be forgiven.

17"If a person sins and does what is forbidden in any of the LORD's commands, even though he does not know it, he is guilty and will be held responsible. 18He is to bring to the priest as a guilt offering a ram from the flock, one without defect and of the proper value. In this way the priest will make atonement for him for the wrong he has committed unintentionally, and he will be forgiven. 19It is a guilt offering; he has been guilty of[b] wrongdoing against the LORD."

6 The LORD said to Moses: 2"If anyone sins and is unfaithful to the LORD by deceiving his neighbor about something entrusted to him or left in his care or stolen, or if he cheats him, 3or if he finds lost property and lies about it, or if he swears falsely, or if he commits any such sin that people may do— 4when he thus sins and becomes guilty, he must return what he has stolen or taken by extortion, or what was entrusted to him, or the lost property he found, 5or whatever it was he swore falsely about. He must make restitution in full, add a fifth of the value to it and give it all to the owner on the day he presents his guilt offering. 6And as a penalty he must bring to the priest, that is, to the LORD, his guilt offering, a ram from the flock, one without defect and of the proper value. 7In this way the priest will make atonement for him before the LORD, and he will be forgiven for any of these things he did that made him guilty."

The Burnt Offering

8The LORD said to Moses: 9"Give Aaron and his sons this command: 'These are the regulations for the burnt offering: The burnt offering is to remain on the altar hearth throughout the night, till morning, and the fire must be kept burning on the altar. 10The priest shall then put on his linen clothes, with linen undergarments next to his body, and shall remove the ashes of the burnt offering that the fire has consumed on the altar and place them beside the altar. 11Then he is to take off these clothes and put on others, and carry the ashes outside the camp to a place that is ceremonially clean. 12The fire on the altar must be kept burning; it must not go out. Every morning the priest is to add firewood and arrange the burnt offering on the fire and burn the fat of the fellowship offerings[c] on it. 13The fire must be kept burning on the altar continuously; it must not go out.

The Grain Offering

14" 'These are the regulations for the grain offering: Aaron's sons are to bring it before the LORD, in front of the altar. 15The priest is to take a handful of fine flour and oil, together with all the incense on the grain offering, and burn the memorial portion on the altar as an aroma pleasing to the LORD. 16Aaron and his sons shall eat the rest of it, but it is to be eaten without yeast in a holy place; they are to eat it in the courtyard of the Tent of Meeting. 17It must not be baked with yeast; I have given it as their share of the offerings made to me by fire. Like the sin offering and the guilt offering, it is most holy. 18Any male descendant of Aaron may eat it. It is his regular share of the offerings made to the LORD by fire for the generations to come. Whatever touches them will become holy.[d]' "

19The LORD also said to Moses, 20"This is the offering Aaron and his sons are to bring to the LORD on the day he[e] is anointed: a tenth of an ephah[f] of fine flour as a regular grain offering, half of it in the morning and half in the evening. 21Prepare it with oil on a griddle; bring it well-mixed and present the grain offering broken[g] in pieces as an aroma pleasing to the LORD. 22The son who is to succeed him as anointed priest shall prepare it. It is the LORD's regular share and is to be burned completely. 23Every grain offering of a priest shall be burned completely; it must not be eaten."

The Sin Offering

24The LORD said to Moses, 25"Say to Aaron and his sons: 'These are the regula-

[a] 15 That is, about 2/5 ounce (about 11.5 grams) [b] 19 Or *has made full expiation for his*
[c] 12 Traditionally *peace offerings* [d] 18 Or *Whoever touches them must be holy*; similarly in verse 27
[e] 20 Or *each* [f] 20 That is, probably about 2 quarts (about 2 liters) [g] 21 The meaning of the Hebrew for this word is uncertain.

tions for the sin offering: The sin offering
is to be slaughtered before the LORD in the
place the burnt offering is slaughtered; it
is most holy. 26The priest who offers it
shall eat it; it is to be eaten in a holy place,
in the courtyard of the Tent of Meeting.
27Whatever touches any of the flesh will
become holy, and if any of the blood is
spattered on a garment, you must wash it
in a holy place. 28The clay pot the meat is
cooked in must be broken; but if it is
cooked in a bronze pot, the pot is to be
scoured and rinsed with water. 29Any
male in a priest's family may eat it; it is
most holy. 30But any sin offering whose
blood is brought into the Tent of Meeting
to make atonement in the Holy Place must
not be eaten; it must be burned.

The Guilt Offering

7 " 'These are the regulations for the
guilt offering, which is most holy:
2The guilt offering is to be slaughtered in
the place where the burnt offering is
slaughtered, and its blood is to be sprin-
kled against the altar on all sides. 3All its
fat shall be offered: the fat tail and the fat
that covers the inner parts, 4both kidneys
with the fat on them near the loins, and
the covering of the liver, which is to be re-
moved with the kidneys. 5The priest shall
burn them on the altar as an offering
made to the LORD by fire. It is a guilt offer-
ing. 6Any male in a priest's family may eat
it, but it must be eaten in a holy place; it
is most holy.

7" 'The same law applies to both the sin
offering and the guilt offering: They be-
long to the priest who makes atonement
with them. 8The priest who offers a burnt
offering for anyone may keep its hide for
himself. 9Every grain offering baked in an
oven or cooked in a pan or on a griddle
belongs to the priest who offers it, 10and
every grain offering, whether mixed with
oil or dry, belongs equally to all the sons
of Aaron.

The Fellowship Offering

11" 'These are the regulations for the fel-
lowship offering[a] a person may present
to the LORD:

12" 'If he offers it as an expression of
thankfulness, then along with this thank
offering he is to offer cakes of bread made
without yeast and mixed with oil, wafers
made without yeast and spread with oil,
and cakes of fine flour well-kneaded and
mixed with oil. 13Along with his fellow-
ship offering of thanksgiving he is to
present an offering with cakes of bread
made with yeast. 14He is to bring one of
each kind as an offering, a contribution to
the LORD; it belongs to the priest who
sprinkles the blood of the fellowship offer-
ings. 15The meat of his fellowship offering
of thanksgiving must be eaten on the day
it is offered; he must leave none of it till
morning.

16" 'If, however, his offering is the result
of a vow or is a freewill offering, the sacri-
fice shall be eaten on the day he offers it,
but anything left over may be eaten on the
next day. 17Any meat of the sacrifice left
over till the third day must be burned up.
18If any meat of the fellowship offering is
eaten on the third day, it will not be ac-
cepted. It will not be credited to the one
who offered it, for it is impure; the person
who eats any of it will be held responsible.

19" 'Meat that touches anything cere-
monially unclean must not be eaten; it
must be burned up. As for other meat,
anyone ceremonially clean may eat it.
20But if anyone who is unclean eats any
meat of the fellowship offering belonging
to the LORD, that person must be cut off
from his people. 21If anyone touches
something unclean—whether human un-
cleanness or an unclean animal or any un-
clean, detestable thing—and then eats
any of the meat of the fellowship offering
belonging to the LORD, that person must
be cut off from his people.' "

Eating Fat and Blood Forbidden

22The LORD said to Moses, 23"Say to the
Israelites: 'Do not eat any of the fat of cat-
tle, sheep or goats. 24The fat of an animal
found dead or torn by wild animals may
be used for any other purpose, but you
must not eat it. 25Anyone who eats the fat
of an animal from which an offering by
fire may be[b] made to the LORD must be
cut off from his people. 26And wherever
you live, you must not eat the blood of
any bird or animal. 27If anyone eats blood,
that person must be cut off from his peo-
ple.' "

The Priests' Share

28The LORD said to Moses, 29"Say to the
Israelites: 'Anyone who brings a fellow-
ship offering to the LORD is to bring part of

[a] 11 Traditionally *peace offering*; also in verses 13-37

[b] 25 Or *fire is*

it as his sacrifice to the LORD. 30With his
own hands he is to bring the offering
made to the LORD by fire; he is to bring the
fat, together with the breast, and wave the
breast before the LORD as a wave offering.
31The priest shall burn the fat on the altar,
but the breast belongs to Aaron and his
sons. 32You are to give the right thigh of
your fellowship offerings to the priest as a
contribution. 33The son of Aaron who of-
fers the blood and the fat of the fellowship
offering shall have the right thigh as his
share. 34From the fellowship offerings of
the Israelites, I have taken the breast that
is waved and the thigh that is presented
and have given them to Aaron the priest
and his sons as their regular share from
the Israelites.' "

35This is the portion of the offerings
made to the LORD by fire that were allotted
to Aaron and his sons on the day they
were presented to serve the LORD as
priests. 36On the day they were anointed,
the LORD commanded that the Israelites
give this to them as their regular share for
the generations to come.

37These, then, are the regulations for
the burnt offering, the grain offering, the
sin offering, the guilt offering, the ordina-
tion offering and the fellowship offering,
38which the LORD gave Moses on Mount
Sinai on the day he commanded the Isra-
elites to bring their offerings to the LORD,
in the Desert of Sinai.

The Ordination of Aaron and His Sons

8 The LORD said to Moses, 2"Bring Aar-
on and his sons, their garments, the
anointing oil, the bull for the sin offering,
the two rams and the basket containing
bread made without yeast, 3and gather the
entire assembly at the entrance to the
Tent of Meeting." 4Moses did as the LORD
commanded him, and the assembly gath-
ered at the entrance to the Tent of Meet-
ing.

5Moses said to the assembly, "This is
what the LORD has commanded to be
done." 6Then Moses brought Aaron and
his sons forward and washed them with
water. 7He put the tunic on Aaron, tied the
sash around him, clothed him with the
robe and put the ephod on him. He also
tied the ephod to him by its skillfully wo-
ven waistband; so it was fastened on him.
8He placed the breastpiece on him and put
the Urim and Thummim in the breast-
piece. 9Then he placed the turban on Aar-
on's head and set the gold plate, the sa-
cred diadem, on the front of it, as the LORD
commanded Moses.

10Then Moses took the anointing oil
and anointed the tabernacle and every-
thing in it, and so consecrated them. 11He
sprinkled some of the oil on the altar sev-
en times, anointing the altar and all its
utensils and the basin with its stand, to
consecrate them. 12He poured some of the
anointing oil on Aaron's head and anoint-
ed him to consecrate him. 13Then he
brought Aaron's sons forward, put tunics
on them, tied sashes around them and put
headbands on them, as the LORD com-
manded Moses.

14He then presented the bull for the sin
offering, and Aaron and his sons laid their
hands on its head. 15Moses slaughtered
the bull and took some of the blood, and
with his finger he put it on all the horns of
the altar to purify the altar. He poured out
the rest of the blood at the base of the al-
tar. So he consecrated it to make atone-
ment for it. 16Moses also took all the fat
around the inner parts, the covering of the
liver, and both kidneys and their fat, and
burned it on the altar. 17But the bull with
its hide and its flesh and its offal he
burned up outside the camp, as the LORD
commanded Moses.

18He then presented the ram for the
burnt offering, and Aaron and his sons
laid their hands on its head. 19Then Moses
slaughtered the ram and sprinkled the
blood against the altar on all sides. 20He
cut the ram into pieces and burned the
head, the pieces and the fat. 21He washed
the inner parts and the legs with water
and burned the whole ram on the altar as
a burnt offering, a pleasing aroma, an of-
fering made to the LORD by fire, as the
LORD commanded Moses.

22He then presented the other ram, the
ram for the ordination, and Aaron and his
sons laid their hands on its head. 23Moses
slaughtered the ram and took some of its
blood and put it on the lobe of Aaron's
right ear, on the thumb of his right hand
and on the big toe of his right foot. 24Mo-
ses also brought Aaron's sons forward and
put some of the blood on the lobes of their
right ears, on the thumbs of their right
hands and on the big toes of their right
feet. Then he sprinkled blood against the
altar on all sides. 25He took the fat, the fat
tail, all the fat around the inner parts, the
covering of the liver, both kidneys and

their fat and the right thigh. 26Then from the basket of bread made without yeast, which was before the LORD, he took a cake of bread, and one made with oil, and a wafer; he put these on the fat portions and on the right thigh. 27He put all these in the hands of Aaron and his sons and waved them before the LORD as a wave offering. 28Then Moses took them from their hands and burned them on the altar on top of the burnt offering as an ordination offering, a pleasing aroma, an offering made to the LORD by fire. 29He also took the breast—Moses' share of the ordination ram—and waved it before the LORD as a wave offering, as the LORD commanded Moses.

30Then Moses took some of the anointing oil and some of the blood from the altar and sprinkled them on Aaron and his garments and on his sons and their garments. So he consecrated Aaron and his garments and his sons and their garments.

31Moses then said to Aaron and his sons, "Cook the meat at the entrance to the Tent of Meeting and eat it there with the bread from the basket of ordination offerings, as I commanded, saying,[a] 'Aaron and his sons are to eat it.' 32Then burn up the rest of the meat and the bread. 33Do not leave the entrance to the Tent of Meeting for seven days, until the days of your ordination are completed, for your ordination will last seven days. 34What has been done today was commanded by the LORD to make atonement for you. 35You must stay at the entrance to the Tent of Meeting day and night for seven days and do what the LORD requires, so you will not die; for that is what I have been commanded." 36So Aaron and his sons did everything the LORD commanded through Moses.

The Priests Begin Their Ministry

9 On the eighth day Moses summoned Aaron and his sons and the elders of Israel. 2He said to Aaron, "Take a bull calf for your sin offering and a ram for your burnt offering, both without defect, and present them before the LORD. 3Then say to the Israelites: 'Take a male goat for a sin offering, a calf and a lamb—both a year old and without defect—for a burnt offering, 4and an ox[b] and a ram for a fellowship offering[c] to sacrifice before the LORD, together with a grain offering mixed with oil. For today the LORD will appear to you.' "

5They took the things Moses commanded to the front of the Tent of Meeting, and the entire assembly came near and stood before the LORD. 6Then Moses said, "This is what the LORD has commanded you to do, so that the glory of the LORD may appear to you."

7Moses said to Aaron, "Come to the altar and sacrifice your sin offering and your burnt offering and make atonement for yourself and the people; sacrifice the offering that is for the people and make atonement for them, as the LORD has commanded."

8So Aaron came to the altar and slaughtered the calf as a sin offering for himself. 9His sons brought the blood to him, and he dipped his finger into the blood and put it on the horns of the altar; the rest of the blood he poured out at the base of the altar. 10On the altar he burned the fat, the kidneys and the covering of the liver from the sin offering, as the LORD commanded Moses; 11the flesh and the hide he burned up outside the camp.

12Then he slaughtered the burnt offering. His sons handed him the blood, and he sprinkled it against the altar on all sides. 13They handed him the burnt offering piece by piece, including the head, and he burned them on the altar. 14He washed the inner parts and the legs and burned them on top of the burnt offering on the altar.

15Aaron then brought the offering that was for the people. He took the goat for the people's sin offering and slaughtered it and offered it for a sin offering as he did with the first one.

16He brought the burnt offering and offered it in the prescribed way. 17He also brought the grain offering, took a handful of it and burned it on the altar in addition to the morning's burnt offering.

18He slaughtered the ox and the ram as the fellowship offering for the people. His sons handed him the blood, and he sprinkled it against the altar on all sides. 19But the fat portions of the ox and the ram—the fat tail, the layer of fat, the kidneys and the covering of the liver— 20these they laid on the breasts, and then Aaron burned the fat on the altar. 21Aaron waved the breasts and the right thigh before the

[a] 31 Or *I was commanded:* [b] 4 The Hebrew word can include both male and female; also in verses 18 and 19. [c] 4 Traditionally *peace offering*; also in verses 18 and 22

LORD as a wave offering, as Moses commanded.

22Then Aaron lifted his hands toward the people and blessed them. And having sacrificed the sin offering, the burnt offering and the fellowship offering, he stepped down.

23Moses and Aaron then went into the Tent of Meeting. When they came out, they blessed the people; and the glory of the LORD appeared to all the people. 24Fire came out from the presence of the LORD and consumed the burnt offering and the fat portions on the altar. And when all the people saw it, they shouted for joy and fell facedown.

The Death of Nadab and Abihu

10 Aaron's sons Nadab and Abihu took their censers, put fire in them and added incense; and they offered unauthorized fire before the LORD, contrary to his command. 2So fire came out from the presence of the LORD and consumed them, and they died before the LORD. 3Moses then said to Aaron, "This is what the LORD spoke of when he said:

" 'Among those who approach me
I will show myself holy;
in the sight of all the people
I will be honored.' "

Aaron remained silent.

4Moses summoned Mishael and Elzaphan, sons of Aaron's uncle Uzziel, and said to them, "Come here; carry your cousins outside the camp, away from the front of the sanctuary." 5So they came and carried them, still in their tunics, outside the camp, as Moses ordered.

6Then Moses said to Aaron and his sons Eleazar and Ithamar, "Do not let your hair become unkempt,[a] and do not tear your clothes, or you will die and the LORD will be angry with the whole community. But your relatives, all the house of Israel, may mourn for those the LORD has destroyed by fire. 7Do not leave the entrance to the Tent of Meeting or you will die, because the LORD's anointing oil is on you." So they did as Moses said.

8Then the LORD said to Aaron, 9"You and your sons are not to drink wine or other fermented drink whenever you go into the Tent of Meeting, or you will die. This is a lasting ordinance for the generations to come. 10You must distinguish between the holy and the common, between the unclean and the clean, 11and you must teach the Israelites all the decrees the LORD has given them through Moses."

12Moses said to Aaron and his remaining sons, Eleazar and Ithamar, "Take the grain offering left over from the offerings made to the LORD by fire and eat it prepared without yeast beside the altar, for it is most holy. 13Eat it in a holy place, because it is your share and your sons' share of the offerings made to the LORD by fire; for so I have been commanded. 14But you and your sons and your daughters may eat the breast that was waved and the thigh that was presented. Eat them in a ceremonially clean place; they have been given to you and your children as your share of the Israelites' fellowship offerings.[b] 15The thigh that was presented and the breast that was waved must be brought with the fat portions of the offerings made by fire, to be waved before the LORD as a wave offering. This will be the regular share for you and your children, as the LORD has commanded."

16When Moses inquired about the goat of the sin offering and found that it had been burned up, he was angry with Eleazar and Ithamar, Aaron's remaining sons, and asked, 17"Why didn't you eat the sin offering in the sanctuary area? It is most holy; it was given to you to take away the guilt of the community by making atonement for them before the LORD. 18Since its blood was not taken into the Holy Place, you should have eaten the goat in the sanctuary area, as I commanded."

19Aaron replied to Moses, "Today they sacrificed their sin offering and their burnt offering before the LORD, but such things as this have happened to me. Would the LORD have been pleased if I had eaten the sin offering today?" 20When Moses heard this, he was satisfied.

Clean and Unclean Food

11 The LORD said to Moses and Aaron, 2"Say to the Israelites: 'Of all the animals that live on land, these are the ones you may eat: 3You may eat any animal that has a split hoof completely divided and that chews the cud.

4" 'There are some that only chew the cud or only have a split hoof, but you must not eat them. The camel, though it chews the cud, does not have a split hoof;

[a]6 Or *Do not uncover your heads* [b]14 Traditionally *peace offerings*

it is ceremonially unclean for you. 5The
coney,[a] though it chews the cud, does
not have a split hoof; it is unclean for you.
6The rabbit, though it chews the cud, does
not have a split hoof; it is unclean for you.
7And the pig, though it has a split hoof
completely divided, does not chew the
cud; it is unclean for you. 8You must not
eat their meat or touch their carcasses;
they are unclean for you.

9" 'Of all the creatures living in the water of the seas and the streams, you may eat any that have fins and scales. 10But all creatures in the seas or streams that do not have fins and scales—whether among all the swarming things or among all the other living creatures in the water—you are to detest. 11And since you are to detest them, you must not eat their meat and you must detest their carcasses. 12Anything living in the water that does not have fins and scales is to be detestable to you.

13" 'These are the birds you are to detest and not eat because they are detestable: the eagle, the vulture, the black vulture, 14the red kite, any kind of black kite, 15any kind of raven, 16the horned owl, the screech owl, the gull, any kind of hawk, 17the little owl, the cormorant, the great owl, 18the white owl, the desert owl, the osprey, 19the stork, any kind of heron, the hoopoe and the bat.[b]

20" 'All flying insects that walk on all fours are to be detestable to you. 21There are, however, some winged creatures that walk on all fours that you may eat: those that have jointed legs for hopping on the ground. 22Of these you may eat any kind of locust, katydid, cricket or grasshopper. 23But all other winged creatures that have four legs you are to detest.

24" 'You will make yourselves unclean by these; whoever touches their carcasses will be unclean till evening. 25Whoever picks up one of their carcasses must wash his clothes, and he will be unclean till evening.

26" 'Every animal that has a split hoof not completely divided or that does not chew the cud is unclean for you; whoever touches ⌊the carcass of⌋ any of them will be unclean. 27Of all the animals that walk on all fours, those that walk on their paws are unclean for you; whoever touches their carcasses will be unclean till evening. 28Anyone who picks up their carcasses must wash his clothes, and he will be unclean till evening. They are unclean for you.

29" 'Of the animals that move about on the ground, these are unclean for you: the weasel, the rat, any kind of great lizard, 30the gecko, the monitor lizard, the wall lizard, the skink and the chameleon. 31Of all those that move along the ground, these are unclean for you. Whoever touches them when they are dead will be unclean till evening. 32When one of them dies and falls on something, that article, whatever its use, will be unclean, whether it is made of wood, cloth, hide or sackcloth. Put it in water; it will be unclean till evening, and then it will be clean. 33If one of them falls into a clay pot, everything in it will be unclean, and you must break the pot. 34Any food that could be eaten but has water on it from such a pot is unclean, and any liquid that could be drunk from it is unclean. 35Anything that one of their carcasses falls on becomes unclean; an oven or cooking pot must be broken up. They are unclean, and you are to regard them as unclean. 36A spring, however, or a cistern for collecting water remains clean, but anyone who touches one of these carcasses is unclean. 37If a carcass falls on any seeds that are to be planted, they remain clean. 38But if water has been put on the seed and a carcass falls on it, it is unclean for you.

39" 'If an animal that you are allowed to eat dies, anyone who touches the carcass will be unclean till evening. 40Anyone who eats some of the carcass must wash his clothes, and he will be unclean till evening. Anyone who picks up the carcass must wash his clothes, and he will be unclean till evening.

41" 'Every creature that moves about on the ground is detestable; it is not to be eaten. 42You are not to eat any creature that moves about on the ground, whether it moves on its belly or walks on all fours or on many feet; it is detestable. 43Do not defile yourselves by any of these creatures. Do not make yourselves unclean by means of them or be made unclean by them. 44I am the LORD your God; consecrate yourselves and be holy, because I am holy. Do not make yourselves unclean by any creature that moves about on the ground. 45I am the LORD who brought you

[a] 5 That is, the hyrax or rock badger

[b] 19 The precise identification of some of the birds, insects and animals in this chapter is uncertain.

up out of Egypt to be your God; therefore
be holy, because I am holy.
46" 'These are the regulations concern-
ing animals, birds, every living thing that
moves in the water and every creature
that moves about on the ground. 47You
must distinguish between the unclean
and the clean, between living creatures
that may be eaten and those that may not
be eaten.' "

Purification After Childbirth

12 The LORD said to Moses, 2"Say to
the Israelites: 'A woman who be-
comes pregnant and gives birth to a son
will be ceremonially unclean for seven
days, just as she is unclean during her
monthly period. 3On the eighth day the
boy is to be circumcised. 4Then the wom-
an must wait thirty-three days to be puri-
fied from her bleeding. She must not
touch anything sacred or go to the sanctu-
ary until the days of her purification are
over. 5If she gives birth to a daughter, for
two weeks the woman will be unclean, as
during her period. Then she must wait six-
ty-six days to be purified from her bleed-
ing.
6" 'When the days of her purification for
a son or daughter are over, she is to bring
to the priest at the entrance to the Tent of
Meeting a year-old lamb for a burnt offer-
ing and a young pigeon or a dove for a sin
offering. 7He shall offer them before the

VERSE FOR THE DAY: Leviticus 11:44

AUTHOR: Will Willimon

PASSAGE FOR THE DAY: Leviticus 11:41–47

Marriage Improves Us

It's clear that Christian faith demands change, but faith never begins in change. It begins in the devastating experience of God's graciousness toward us. The message of the cross is that God takes us before we change. Christians have found that we can't be in the presence of God's sacrificial love and not change. The same is true for the marriage relationship.

If someone asked you if being married has changed you, you would have to say, "Well, yes. My spouse has made me see things differently. He or she has told me where I've gone wrong. He or she has made me a better person."

Being married changes us, not because being changed is our goal, but because of who we are in relationship with. When someone truly loves and accepts you, your defenses go down and you're more likely to change.

MARRIAGE BUILDERS

♦ *How has your relationship with God changed you?*
♦ *How has being married to your spouse made you a better person?*

Additional Scripture Readings
1 Peter 1:16; 2 Peter 3:11

Go to page 120 for your next devotional reading.

LORD to make atonement for her, and then
she will be ceremonially clean from her
flow of blood.

" 'These are the regulations for the
woman who gives birth to a boy or a girl.
8If she cannot afford a lamb, she is to
bring two doves or two young pigeons,
one for a burnt offering and the other for
a sin offering. In this way the priest will
make atonement for her, and she will be
clean.' "

Regulations About Infectious Skin Diseases

13 The LORD said to Moses and Aaron,
2"When anyone has a swelling or a
rash or a bright spot on his skin that may
become an infectious skin disease,[a] he
must be brought to Aaron the priest or to
one of his sons[b] who is a priest. 3The
priest is to examine the sore on his skin,
and if the hair in the sore has turned white
and the sore appears to be more than skin
deep,[c] it is an infectious skin disease.
When the priest examines him, he shall
pronounce him ceremonially unclean. 4If
the spot on his skin is white but does not
appear to be more than skin deep and the
hair in it has not turned white, the priest
is to put the infected person in isolation
for seven days. 5On the seventh day the
priest is to examine him, and if he sees
that the sore is unchanged and has not
spread in the skin, he is to keep him in
isolation another seven days. 6On the sev-
enth day the priest is to examine him
again, and if the sore has faded and has
not spread in the skin, the priest shall pro-
nounce him clean; it is only a rash. The
man must wash his clothes, and he will be
clean. 7But if the rash does spread in his
skin after he has shown himself to the
priest to be pronounced clean, he must
appear before the priest again. 8The priest
is to examine him, and if the rash has
spread in the skin, he shall pronounce
him unclean; it is an infectious disease.

9"When anyone has an infectious skin
disease, he must be brought to the priest.
10The priest is to examine him, and if
there is a white swelling in the skin that
has turned the hair white and if there is
raw flesh in the swelling, 11it is a chronic
skin disease and the priest shall pro-
nounce him unclean. He is not to put him
in isolation, because he is already un-
clean.

12"If the disease breaks out all over his
skin and, so far as the priest can see, it
covers all the skin of the infected person
from head to foot, 13the priest is to exam-
ine him, and if the disease has covered his
whole body, he shall pronounce that per-
son clean. Since it has all turned white, he
is clean. 14But whenever raw flesh appears
on him, he will be unclean. 15When the
priest sees the raw flesh, he shall pro-
nounce him unclean. The raw flesh is un-
clean; he has an infectious disease.
16Should the raw flesh change and turn
white, he must go to the priest. 17The
priest is to examine him, and if the sores
have turned white, the priest shall pro-
nounce the infected person clean; then he
will be clean.

18"When someone has a boil on his skin
and it heals, 19and in the place where the
boil was, a white swelling or reddish-
white spot appears, he must present him-
self to the priest. 20The priest is to exam-
ine it, and if it appears to be more than
skin deep and the hair in it has turned
white, the priest shall pronounce him un-
clean. It is an infectious skin disease that
has broken out where the boil was. 21But
if, when the priest examines it, there is no
white hair in it and it is not more than skin
deep and has faded, then the priest is to
put him in isolation for seven days. 22If it
is spreading in the skin, the priest shall
pronounce him unclean; it is infectious.
23But if the spot is unchanged and has not
spread, it is only a scar from the boil, and
the priest shall pronounce him clean.

24"When someone has a burn on his
skin and a reddish-white or white spot ap-
pears in the raw flesh of the burn, 25the
priest is to examine the spot, and if the
hair in it has turned white, and it appears
to be more than skin deep, it is an infec-
tious disease that has broken out in the
burn. The priest shall pronounce him un-
clean; it is an infectious skin disease.
26But if the priest examines it and there is
no white hair in the spot and if it is not
more than skin deep and has faded, then
the priest is to put him in isolation for sev-
en days. 27On the seventh day the priest is
to examine him, and if it is spreading in
the skin, the priest shall pronounce him

[a] 2 Traditionally *leprosy*; the Hebrew word was used for various diseases affecting the skin—not necessarily leprosy; also elsewhere in this chapter. [b] 2 Or *descendants* [c] 3 Or *be lower than the rest of the skin*; also elsewhere in this chapter

unclean; it is an infectious skin disease.
28If, however, the spot is unchanged and
has not spread in the skin but has faded,
it is a swelling from the burn, and the
priest shall pronounce him clean; it is
only a scar from the burn.

29"If a man or woman has a sore on the
head or on the chin, 30the priest is to ex-
amine the sore, and if it appears to be
more than skin deep and the hair in it is
yellow and thin, the priest shall pro-
nounce that person unclean; it is an itch,
an infectious disease of the head or chin.
31But if, when the priest examines this
kind of sore, it does not seem to be more
than skin deep and there is no black hair
in it, then the priest is to put the infected
person in isolation for seven days. 32On
the seventh day the priest is to examine
the sore, and if the itch has not spread and
there is no yellow hair in it and it does not
appear to be more than skin deep, 33he
must be shaved except for the diseased
area, and the priest is to keep him in isola-
tion another seven days. 34On the seventh
day the priest is to examine the itch, and
if it has not spread in the skin and appears
to be no more than skin deep, the priest
shall pronounce him clean. He must wash
his clothes, and he will be clean. 35But if
the itch does spread in the skin after he is
pronounced clean, 36the priest is to exam-
ine him, and if the itch has spread in the
skin, the priest does not need to look for
yellow hair; the person is unclean. 37If,
however, in his judgment it is unchanged
and black hair has grown in it, the itch is
healed. He is clean, and the priest shall
pronounce him clean.

38"When a man or woman has white
spots on the skin, 39the priest is to exam-
ine them, and if the spots are dull white,
it is a harmless rash that has broken out
on the skin; that person is clean.

40"When a man has lost his hair and is
bald, he is clean. 41If he has lost his hair
from the front of his scalp and has a bald
forehead, he is clean. 42But if he has a red-
dish-white sore on his bald head or fore-
head, it is an infectious disease breaking
out on his head or forehead. 43The priest
is to examine him, and if the swollen sore
on his head or forehead is reddish-white
like an infectious skin disease, 44the man
is diseased and is unclean. The priest shall
pronounce him unclean because of the
sore on his head.

45"The person with such an infectious
disease must wear torn clothes, let his hair
be unkempt,[a] cover the lower part of his
face and cry out, 'Unclean! Unclean!' 46As
long as he has the infection he remains
unclean. He must live alone; he must live
outside the camp.

Regulations About Mildew

47"If any clothing is contaminated with
mildew—any woolen or linen clothing,
48any woven or knitted material of linen
or wool, any leather or anything made of
leather— 49and if the contamination in
the clothing, or leather, or woven or knit-
ted material, or any leather article, is
greenish or reddish, it is a spreading mil-
dew and must be shown to the priest.
50The priest is to examine the mildew and
isolate the affected article for seven days.
51On the seventh day he is to examine it,
and if the mildew has spread in the cloth-
ing, or the woven or knitted material, or
the leather, whatever its use, it is a de-
structive mildew; the article is unclean.
52He must burn up the clothing, or the wo-
ven or knitted material of wool or linen, or
any leather article that has the contamina-
tion in it, because the mildew is destruc-
tive; the article must be burned up.

53"But if, when the priest examines it,
the mildew has not spread in the clothing,
or the woven or knitted material, or the
leather article, 54he shall order that the
contaminated article be washed. Then he
is to isolate it for another seven days. 55Af-
ter the affected article has been washed,
the priest is to examine it, and if the mil-
dew has not changed its appearance, even
though it has not spread, it is unclean.
Burn it with fire, whether the mildew has
affected one side or the other. 56If, when
the priest examines it, the mildew has fad-
ed after the article has been washed, he is
to tear the contaminated part out of the
clothing, or the leather, or the woven or
knitted material. 57But if it reappears in
the clothing, or in the woven or knitted
material, or in the leather article, it is
spreading, and whatever has the mildew
must be burned with fire. 58The clothing,
or the woven or knitted material, or any
leather article that has been washed and is
rid of the mildew, must be washed again,
and it will be clean."

59These are the regulations concerning
contamination by mildew in woolen or

[a]45 Or *clothes, uncover his head*

linen clothing, woven or knitted material, or any leather article, for pronouncing them clean or unclean.

Cleansing From Infectious Skin Diseases

14 The LORD said to Moses, 2"These are the regulations for the diseased person at the time of his ceremonial cleansing, when he is brought to the priest: 3The priest is to go outside the camp and examine him. If the person has been healed of his infectious skin disease,[a] 4the priest shall order that two live clean birds and some cedar wood, scarlet yarn and hyssop be brought for the one to be cleansed. 5Then the priest shall order that one of the birds be killed over fresh water in a clay pot. 6He is then to take the live bird and dip it, together with the cedar wood, the scarlet yarn and the hyssop, into the blood of the bird that was killed over the fresh water. 7Seven times he shall sprinkle the one to be cleansed of the infectious disease and pronounce him clean. Then he is to release the live bird in the open fields.

8"The person to be cleansed must wash his clothes, shave off all his hair and bathe with water; then he will be ceremonially clean. After this he may come into the camp, but he must stay outside his tent for seven days. 9On the seventh day he must shave off all his hair; he must shave his head, his beard, his eyebrows and the rest of his hair. He must wash his clothes and bathe himself with water, and he will be clean.

10"On the eighth day he must bring two male lambs and one ewe lamb a year old, each without defect, along with three-tenths of an ephah[b] of fine flour mixed with oil for a grain offering, and one log[c] of oil. 11The priest who pronounces him clean shall present both the one to be cleansed and his offerings before the LORD at the entrance to the Tent of Meeting.

12"Then the priest is to take one of the male lambs and offer it as a guilt offering, along with the log of oil; he shall wave them before the LORD as a wave offering. 13He is to slaughter the lamb in the holy place where the sin offering and the burnt offering are slaughtered. Like the sin offering, the guilt offering belongs to the priest; it is most holy. 14The priest is to take some of the blood of the guilt offering and put it on the lobe of the right ear of the one to be cleansed, on the thumb of his right hand and on the big toe of his right foot. 15The priest shall then take some of the log of oil, pour it in the palm of his own left hand, 16dip his right forefinger into the oil in his palm, and with his finger sprinkle some of it before the LORD seven times. 17The priest is to put some of the oil remaining in his palm on the lobe of the right ear of the one to be cleansed, on the thumb of his right hand and on the big toe of his right foot, on top of the blood of the guilt offering. 18The rest of the oil in his palm the priest shall put on the head of the one to be cleansed and make atonement for him before the LORD.

19"Then the priest is to sacrifice the sin offering and make atonement for the one to be cleansed from his uncleanness. After that, the priest shall slaughter the burnt offering 20and offer it on the altar, together with the grain offering, and make atonement for him, and he will be clean.

21"If, however, he is poor and cannot afford these, he must take one male lamb as a guilt offering to be waved to make atonement for him, together with a tenth of an ephah[d] of fine flour mixed with oil for a grain offering, a log of oil, 22and two doves or two young pigeons, which he can afford, one for a sin offering and the other for a burnt offering.

23"On the eighth day he must bring them for his cleansing to the priest at the entrance to the Tent of Meeting, before the LORD. 24The priest is to take the lamb for the guilt offering, together with the log of oil, and wave them before the LORD as a wave offering. 25He shall slaughter the lamb for the guilt offering and take some of its blood and put it on the lobe of the right ear of the one to be cleansed, on the thumb of his right hand and on the big toe of his right foot. 26The priest is to pour some of the oil into the palm of his own left hand, 27and with his right forefinger sprinkle some of the oil from his palm seven times before the LORD. 28Some of the oil in his palm he is to put on the same places he put the blood of the guilt offering—on

[a] *3* Traditionally *leprosy*; the Hebrew word was used for various diseases affecting the skin—not necessarily leprosy; also elsewhere in this chapter. [b] *10* That is, probably about 6 quarts (about 6.5 liters) [c] *10* That is, probably about 2/3 pint (about 0.3 liter); also in verses 12, 15, 21 and 24
[d] *21* That is, probably about 2 quarts (about 2 liters)

the lobe of the right ear of the one to be cleansed, on the thumb of his right hand and on the big toe of his right foot. 29The rest of the oil in his palm the priest shall put on the head of the one to be cleansed, to make atonement for him before the LORD. 30Then he shall sacrifice the doves or the young pigeons, which the person can afford, 31one[a] as a sin offering and the other as a burnt offering, together with the grain offering. In this way the priest will make atonement before the LORD on behalf of the one to be cleansed."

32These are the regulations for anyone who has an infectious skin disease and who cannot afford the regular offerings for his cleansing.

Cleansing From Mildew

33The LORD said to Moses and Aaron, 34"When you enter the land of Canaan, which I am giving you as your possession, and I put a spreading mildew in a house in that land, 35the owner of the house must go and tell the priest, 'I have seen something that looks like mildew in my house.' 36The priest is to order the house to be emptied before he goes in to examine the mildew, so that nothing in the house will be pronounced unclean. After this the priest is to go in and inspect the house. 37He is to examine the mildew on the walls, and if it has greenish or reddish depressions that appear to be deeper than the surface of the wall, 38the priest shall go out the doorway of the house and close it up for seven days. 39On the seventh day the priest shall return to inspect the house. If the mildew has spread on the walls, 40he is to order that the contaminated stones be torn out and thrown into an unclean place outside the town. 41He must have all the inside walls of the house scraped and the material that is scraped off dumped into an unclean place outside the town. 42Then they are to take other stones to replace these and take new clay and plaster the house.

43"If the mildew reappears in the house after the stones have been torn out and the house scraped and plastered, 44the priest is to go and examine it and, if the mildew has spread in the house, it is a destructive mildew; the house is unclean. 45It must be torn down—its stones, timbers and all the plaster—and taken out of the town to an unclean place.

46"Anyone who goes into the house while it is closed up will be unclean till evening. 47Anyone who sleeps or eats in the house must wash his clothes.

48"But if the priest comes to examine it and the mildew has not spread after the house has been plastered, he shall pronounce the house clean, because the mildew is gone. 49To purify the house he is to take two birds and some cedar wood, scarlet yarn and hyssop. 50He shall kill one of the birds over fresh water in a clay pot. 51Then he is to take the cedar wood, the hyssop, the scarlet yarn and the live bird, dip them into the blood of the dead bird and the fresh water, and sprinkle the house seven times. 52He shall purify the house with the bird's blood, the fresh water, the live bird, the cedar wood, the hyssop and the scarlet yarn. 53Then he is to release the live bird in the open fields outside the town. In this way he will make atonement for the house, and it will be clean."

54These are the regulations for any infectious skin disease, for an itch, 55for mildew in clothing or in a house, 56and for a swelling, a rash or a bright spot, 57to determine when something is clean or unclean.

These are the regulations for infectious skin diseases and mildew.

Discharges Causing Uncleanness

15 The LORD said to Moses and Aaron, 2"Speak to the Israelites and say to them: 'When any man has a bodily discharge, the discharge is unclean. 3Whether it continues flowing from his body or is blocked, it will make him unclean. This is how his discharge will bring about uncleanness:

4" 'Any bed the man with a discharge lies on will be unclean, and anything he sits on will be unclean. 5Anyone who touches his bed must wash his clothes and bathe with water, and he will be unclean till evening. 6Whoever sits on anything that the man with a discharge sat on must wash his clothes and bathe with water, and he will be unclean till evening.

7" 'Whoever touches the man who has a discharge must wash his clothes and bathe with water, and he will be unclean till evening.

8" 'If the man with the discharge spits on someone who is clean, that person

[a] *31* Septuagint and Syriac; Hebrew *31such as the person can afford, one*

must wash his clothes and bathe with water, and he will be unclean till evening.

9" 'Everything the man sits on when riding will be unclean, 10and whoever touches any of the things that were under him will be unclean till evening; whoever picks up those things must wash his clothes and bathe with water, and he will be unclean till evening.

11" 'Anyone the man with a discharge touches without rinsing his hands with water must wash his clothes and bathe with water, and he will be unclean till evening.

12" 'A clay pot that the man touches must be broken, and any wooden article is to be rinsed with water.

13" 'When a man is cleansed from his discharge, he is to count off seven days for his ceremonial cleansing; he must wash his clothes and bathe himself with fresh water, and he will be clean. 14On the eighth day he must take two doves or two young pigeons and come before the LORD to the entrance to the Tent of Meeting and give them to the priest. 15The priest is to sacrifice them, the one for a sin offering and the other for a burnt offering. In this way he will make atonement before the LORD for the man because of his discharge.

16" 'When a man has an emission of semen, he must bathe his whole body with water, and he will be unclean till evening. 17Any clothing or leather that has semen on it must be washed with water, and it will be unclean till evening. 18When a man lies with a woman and there is an emission of semen, both must bathe with water, and they will be unclean till evening.

19" 'When a woman has her regular flow of blood, the impurity of her monthly period will last seven days, and anyone who touches her will be unclean till evening.

20" 'Anything she lies on during her period will be unclean, and anything she sits on will be unclean. 21Whoever touches her bed must wash his clothes and bathe with water, and he will be unclean till evening. 22Whoever touches anything she sits on must wash his clothes and bathe with water, and he will be unclean till evening. 23Whether it is the bed or anything she was sitting on, when anyone touches it, he will be unclean till evening.

24" 'If a man lies with her and her monthly flow touches him, he will be unclean for seven days; any bed he lies on will be unclean.

25" 'When a woman has a discharge of blood for many days at a time other than her monthly period or has a discharge that continues beyond her period, she will be unclean as long as she has the discharge, just as in the days of her period. 26Any bed she lies on while her discharge continues will be unclean, as is her bed during her monthly period, and anything she sits on will be unclean, as during her period. 27Whoever touches them will be unclean; he must wash his clothes and bathe with water, and he will be unclean till evening.

28" 'When she is cleansed from her discharge, she must count off seven days, and after that she will be ceremonially clean. 29On the eighth day she must take two doves or two young pigeons and bring them to the priest at the entrance to the Tent of Meeting. 30The priest is to sacrifice one for a sin offering and the other for a burnt offering. In this way he will make atonement for her before the LORD for the uncleanness of her discharge.

31" 'You must keep the Israelites separate from things that make them unclean, so they will not die in their uncleanness for defiling my dwelling place,[a] which is among them.' "

32These are the regulations for a man with a discharge, for anyone made unclean by an emission of semen, 33for a woman in her monthly period, for a man or a woman with a discharge, and for a man who lies with a woman who is ceremonially unclean.

The Day of Atonement

16 The LORD spoke to Moses after the death of the two sons of Aaron who died when they approached the LORD. 2The LORD said to Moses: "Tell your brother Aaron not to come whenever he chooses into the Most Holy Place behind the curtain in front of the atonement cover on the ark, or else he will die, because I appear in the cloud over the atonement cover.

3"This is how Aaron is to enter the sanctuary area: with a young bull for a sin offering and a ram for a burnt offering. 4He is to put on the sacred linen tunic, with linen undergarments next to his body; he is to tie the linen sash around him and put

[a]31 Or *my tabernacle*

on the linen turban. These are sacred garments; so he must bathe himself with water before he puts them on. 5From the Israelite community he is to take two male goats for a sin offering and a ram for a burnt offering.

6"Aaron is to offer the bull for his own sin offering to make atonement for himself and his household. 7Then he is to take the two goats and present them before the LORD at the entrance to the Tent of Meeting. 8He is to cast lots for the two goats—one lot for the LORD and the other for the scapegoat.[a] 9Aaron shall bring the goat whose lot falls to the LORD and sacrifice it for a sin offering. 10But the goat chosen by lot as the scapegoat shall be presented alive before the LORD to be used for making atonement by sending it into the desert as a scapegoat.

11"Aaron shall bring the bull for his own sin offering to make atonement for himself and his household, and he is to slaughter the bull for his own sin offering. 12He is to take a censer full of burning coals from the altar before the LORD and two handfuls of finely ground fragrant incense and take them behind the curtain. 13He is to put the incense on the fire before the LORD, and the smoke of the incense will conceal the atonement cover above the Testimony, so that he will not die. 14He is to take some of the bull's blood and with his finger sprinkle it on the front of the atonement cover; then he shall sprinkle some of it with his finger seven times before the atonement cover.

15"He shall then slaughter the goat for the sin offering for the people and take its blood behind the curtain and do with it as he did with the bull's blood: He shall sprinkle it on the atonement cover and in front of it. 16In this way he will make atonement for the Most Holy Place because of the uncleanness and rebellion of the Israelites, whatever their sins have been. He is to do the same for the Tent of Meeting, which is among them in the midst of their uncleanness. 17No one is to be in the Tent of Meeting from the time Aaron goes in to make atonement in the Most Holy Place until he comes out, having made atonement for himself, his household and the whole community of Israel.

18"Then he shall come out to the altar that is before the LORD and make atonement for it. He shall take some of the bull's blood and some of the goat's blood and put it on all the horns of the altar. 19He shall sprinkle some of the blood on it with his finger seven times to cleanse it and to consecrate it from the uncleanness of the Israelites.

20"When Aaron has finished making atonement for the Most Holy Place, the Tent of Meeting and the altar, he shall bring forward the live goat. 21He is to lay both hands on the head of the live goat and confess over it all the wickedness and rebellion of the Israelites—all their sins—and put them on the goat's head. He shall send the goat away into the desert in the care of a man appointed for the task. 22The goat will carry on itself all their sins to a solitary place; and the man shall release it in the desert.

23"Then Aaron is to go into the Tent of Meeting and take off the linen garments he put on before he entered the Most Holy Place, and he is to leave them there. 24He shall bathe himself with water in a holy place and put on his regular garments. Then he shall come out and sacrifice the burnt offering for himself and the burnt offering for the people, to make atonement for himself and for the people. 25He shall also burn the fat of the sin offering on the altar.

26"The man who releases the goat as a scapegoat must wash his clothes and bathe himself with water; afterward he may come into the camp. 27The bull and the goat for the sin offerings, whose blood was brought into the Most Holy Place to make atonement, must be taken outside the camp; their hides, flesh and offal are to be burned up. 28The man who burns them must wash his clothes and bathe himself with water; afterward he may come into the camp.

29"This is to be a lasting ordinance for you: On the tenth day of the seventh month you must deny yourselves[b] and not do any work—whether native-born or an alien living among you— 30because on this day atonement will be made for you, to cleanse you. Then, before the LORD, you will be clean from all your sins. 31It is a sabbath of rest, and you must deny yourselves; it is a lasting ordinance. 32The priest who is anointed and ordained to

[a]8 That is, the goat of removal; Hebrew *azazel*; also in verses 10 and 26 [b]29 Or *must fast*; also in verse 31

succeed his father as high priest is to make atonement. He is to put on the sacred linen garments 33and make atonement for the Most Holy Place, for the Tent of Meeting and the altar, and for the priests and all the people of the community.

34"This is to be a lasting ordinance for you: Atonement is to be made once a year for all the sins of the Israelites."

And it was done, as the LORD commanded Moses.

Eating Blood Forbidden

17 The LORD said to Moses, 2"Speak to Aaron and his sons and to all the Israelites and say to them: 'This is what the LORD has commanded: 3Any Israelite who sacrifices an ox,[a] a lamb or a goat in the camp or outside of it 4instead of bringing it to the entrance to the Tent of Meeting to present it as an offering to the LORD in front of the tabernacle of the LORD—that man shall be considered guilty of bloodshed; he has shed blood and must be cut off from his people. 5This is so the Israelites will bring to the LORD the sacrifices they are now making in the open fields. They must bring them to the priest, that is, to the LORD, at the entrance to the Tent of Meeting and sacrifice them as fellowship offerings.[b] 6The priest is to sprinkle the blood against the altar of the LORD at the entrance to the Tent of Meeting and burn the fat as an aroma pleasing to the LORD. 7They must no longer offer any of their sacrifices to the goat idols[c] to whom they prostitute themselves. This is to be a lasting ordinance for them and for the generations to come.'

8"Say to them: 'Any Israelite or any alien living among them who offers a burnt offering or sacrifice 9and does not bring it to the entrance to the Tent of Meeting to sacrifice it to the LORD—that man must be cut off from his people.

10" 'Any Israelite or any alien living among them who eats any blood—I will set my face against that person who eats blood and will cut him off from his people. 11For the life of a creature is in the blood, and I have given it to you to make atonement for yourselves on the altar; it is the blood that makes atonement for one's life. 12Therefore I say to the Israelites, "None of you may eat blood, nor may an alien living among you eat blood."

13" 'Any Israelite or any alien living among you who hunts any animal or bird that may be eaten must drain out the blood and cover it with earth, 14because the life of every creature is its blood. That is why I have said to the Israelites, "You must not eat the blood of any creature, because the life of every creature is its blood; anyone who eats it must be cut off."

15" 'Anyone, whether native-born or alien, who eats anything found dead or torn by wild animals must wash his clothes and bathe with water, and he will be ceremonially unclean till evening; then he will be clean. 16But if he does not wash his clothes and bathe himself, he will be held responsible.' "

Unlawful Sexual Relations

18 The LORD said to Moses, 2"Speak to the Israelites and say to them: 'I am the LORD your God. 3You must not do as they do in Egypt, where you used to live, and you must not do as they do in the land of Canaan, where I am bringing you. Do not follow their practices. 4You must obey my laws and be careful to follow my decrees. I am the LORD your God. 5Keep my decrees and laws, for the man who obeys them will live by them. I am the LORD.

6" 'No one is to approach any close relative to have sexual relations. I am the LORD.

7" 'Do not dishonor your father by having sexual relations with your mother. She is your mother; do not have relations with her.

8" 'Do not have sexual relations with your father's wife; that would dishonor your father.

9" 'Do not have sexual relations with your sister, either your father's daughter or your mother's daughter, whether she was born in the same home or elsewhere.

10" 'Do not have sexual relations with your son's daughter or your daughter's daughter; that would dishonor you.

11" 'Do not have sexual relations with the daughter of your father's wife, born to your father; she is your sister.

12" 'Do not have sexual relations with your father's sister; she is your father's close relative.

13" 'Do not have sexual relations with

[a] 3 The Hebrew word can include both male and female. [b] 5 Traditionally *peace offerings* [c] 7 Or *demons*

your mother's sister, because she is your mother's close relative.

14" 'Do not dishonor your father's brother by approaching his wife to have sexual relations; she is your aunt.

15" 'Do not have sexual relations with your daughter-in-law. She is your son's wife; do not have relations with her.

16" 'Do not have sexual relations with your brother's wife; that would dishonor your brother.

17" 'Do not have sexual relations with both a woman and her daughter. Do not have sexual relations with either her son's daughter or her daughter's daughter; they are her close relatives. That is wickedness.

18" 'Do not take your wife's sister as a rival wife and have sexual relations with her while your wife is living.

19" 'Do not approach a woman to have sexual relations during the uncleanness of her monthly period.

20" 'Do not have sexual relations with your neighbor's wife and defile yourself with her.

21" 'Do not give any of your children to be sacrificed[a] to Molech, for you must not profane the name of your God. I am the LORD.

22" 'Do not lie with a man as one lies with a woman; that is detestable.

23" 'Do not have sexual relations with an animal and defile yourself with it. A woman must not present herself to an animal to have sexual relations with it; that is a perversion.

24" 'Do not defile yourselves in any of these ways, because this is how the nations that I am going to drive out before you became defiled. 25Even the land was defiled; so I punished it for its sin, and the land vomited out its inhabitants. 26But you must keep my decrees and my laws. The native-born and the aliens living among you must not do any of these detestable things, 27for all these things were done by the people who lived in the land before you, and the land became defiled. 28And if you defile the land, it will vomit you out as it vomited out the nations that were before you.

29" 'Everyone who does any of these detestable things—such persons must be cut off from their people. 30Keep my requirements and do not follow any of the detestable customs that were practiced before you came and do not defile yourselves with them. I am the LORD your God.' "

Various Laws

19 The LORD said to Moses, 2"Speak to the entire assembly of Israel and say to them: 'Be holy because I, the LORD your God, am holy.

3" 'Each of you must respect his mother and father, and you must observe my Sabbaths. I am the LORD your God.

4" 'Do not turn to idols or make gods of cast metal for yourselves. I am the LORD your God.

5" 'When you sacrifice a fellowship offering[b] to the LORD, sacrifice it in such a way that it will be accepted on your behalf. 6It shall be eaten on the day you sacrifice it or on the next day; anything left over until the third day must be burned up. 7If any of it is eaten on the third day, it is impure and will not be accepted. 8Whoever eats it will be held responsible because he has desecrated what is holy to the LORD; that person must be cut off from his people.

9" 'When you reap the harvest of your land, do not reap to the very edges of your field or gather the gleanings of your harvest. 10Do not go over your vineyard a second time or pick up the grapes that have fallen. Leave them for the poor and the alien. I am the LORD your God.

11" 'Do not steal.

" 'Do not lie.

" 'Do not deceive one another.

12" 'Do not swear falsely by my name and so profane the name of your God. I am the LORD.

13" 'Do not defraud your neighbor or rob him.

" 'Do not hold back the wages of a hired man overnight.

14" 'Do not curse the deaf or put a stumbling block in front of the blind, but fear your God. I am the LORD.

15" 'Do not pervert justice; do not show partiality to the poor or favoritism to the great, but judge your neighbor fairly.

16" 'Do not go about spreading slander among your people.

" 'Do not do anything that endangers your neighbor's life. I am the LORD.

[a]21 Or *to be passed through [the fire]* [b]5 Traditionally *peace offering*

17" 'Do not hate your brother in your
heart. Rebuke your neighbor frankly so
you will not share in his guilt.
18" 'Do not seek revenge or bear a
grudge against one of your people, but
love your neighbor as yourself. I am the
LORD.
19" 'Keep my decrees.
" 'Do not mate different kinds of animals.
" 'Do not plant your field with two
kinds of seed.
" 'Do not wear clothing woven of two
kinds of material.
20" 'If a man sleeps with a woman who
is a slave girl promised to another man but
who has not been ransomed or given her
freedom, there must be due punishment.
Yet they are not to be put to death, because she had not been freed. 21 The man,
however, must bring a ram to the entrance
to the Tent of Meeting for a guilt offering
to the LORD. 22 With the ram of the guilt offering the priest is to make atonement for
him before the LORD for the sin he has
committed, and his sin will be forgiven.
23" 'When you enter the land and plant
any kind of fruit tree, regard its fruit as

VERSE FOR THE DAY: Leviticus 19:18

AUTHOR: Lewis Smedes

PASSAGE FOR THE DAY: Leviticus 19:9–18

The Forgiveness Process

When you forgive someone, you do three basic things: First, you surrender your right to get even. If you have been wronged, getting even is the natural impulse, but you resist that impulse.

Second, you revise your caricature of the person who hurt you. When you've been deeply wounded by your spouse, you redraw your picture of that person, making him or her not primarily your husband or wife, but rather "the person who hurt me." So in forgiving, you need to reconstruct that image and see the spouse as a flawed, weak human being—not much different from yourself—who hurt you as much out of weakness as out of ill will.

And third, you revise your feelings. Gradually your feelings of rage are transformed into a desire for that person's blessing and for that person's change.

This is a gradual process, of course. God can forgive in a single swoosh, but we are finite, temporal creatures for whom almost everything takes time.

MARRIAGE BUILDERS

♦ *What are some ways you quietly "get even" when your spouse hurts you?*

♦ *How can you handle the hurt more constructively?*

Additional Scripture Readings
Psalm 32:4–6; 51:10–12; Romans 12:18–21

Go to page 130 for your next devotional reading.

forbidden.[a] For three years you are to
consider it forbidden[a]; it must not be eat-
en. 24In the fourth year all its fruit will be
holy, an offering of praise to the LORD.
25But in the fifth year you may eat its fruit.
In this way your harvest will be increased.
I am the LORD your God.

26" 'Do not eat any meat with the blood
still in it.

" 'Do not practice divination or sorcery.

27" 'Do not cut the hair at the sides of
your head or clip off the edges of your
beard.

28" 'Do not cut your bodies for the dead
or put tattoo marks on yourselves. I am
the LORD.

29" 'Do not degrade your daughter by
making her a prostitute, or the land will
turn to prostitution and be filled with
wickedness.

30" 'Observe my Sabbaths and have rev-
erence for my sanctuary. I am the LORD.

31" 'Do not turn to mediums or seek out
spiritists, for you will be defiled by them.
I am the LORD your God.

32" 'Rise in the presence of the aged,
show respect for the elderly and revere
your God. I am the LORD.

33" 'When an alien lives with you in
your land, do not mistreat him. 34The
alien living with you must be treated as
one of your native-born. Love him as
yourself, for you were aliens in Egypt. I
am the LORD your God.

35" 'Do not use dishonest standards
when measuring length, weight or quanti-
ty. 36Use honest scales and honest
weights, an honest ephah[b] and an honest
hin.[c] I am the LORD your God, who
brought you out of Egypt.

37" 'Keep all my decrees and all my laws
and follow them. I am the LORD.' "

Punishments for Sin

20 The LORD said to Moses, 2"Say to
the Israelites: 'Any Israelite or any
alien living in Israel who gives[d] any of his
children to Molech must be put to death.
The people of the community are to stone
him. 3I will set my face against that man
and I will cut him off from his people; for
by giving his children to Molech, he has
defiled my sanctuary and profaned my
holy name. 4If the people of the community
close their eyes when that man gives
one of his children to Molech and they fail
to put him to death, 5I will set my face
against that man and his family and will
cut off from their people both him and all
who follow him in prostituting themselves
to Molech.

6" 'I will set my face against the person
who turns to mediums and spiritists to
prostitute himself by following them, and
I will cut him off from his people.

7" 'Consecrate yourselves and be holy,
because I am the LORD your God. 8Keep
my decrees and follow them. I am the
LORD, who makes you holy.[e]

9" 'If anyone curses his father or moth-
er, he must be put to death. He has cursed
his father or his mother, and his blood will
be on his own head.

10" 'If a man commits adultery with an-
other man's wife—with the wife of his
neighbor—both the adulterer and the
adulteress must be put to death.

11" 'If a man sleeps with his father's
wife, he has dishonored his father. Both
the man and the woman must be put to
death; their blood will be on their own
heads.

12" 'If a man sleeps with his daughter-
in-law, both of them must be put to death.
What they have done is a perversion; their
blood will be on their own heads.

13" 'If a man lies with a man as one lies
with a woman, both of them have done
what is detestable. They must be put to
death; their blood will be on their own
heads.

14" 'If a man marries both a woman and
her mother, it is wicked. Both he and they
must be burned in the fire, so that no
wickedness will be among you.

15" 'If a man has sexual relations with
an animal, he must be put to death, and
you must kill the animal.

16" 'If a woman approaches an animal to
have sexual relations with it, kill both the
woman and the animal. They must be put
to death; their blood will be on their own
heads.

17" 'If a man marries his sister, the
daughter of either his father or his moth-
er, and they have sexual relations, it is a
disgrace. They must be cut off before the
eyes of their people. He has dishonored
his sister and will be held responsible.

18" 'If a man lies with a woman during
her monthly period and has sexual rela-
tions with her, he has exposed the source

[a] 23 Hebrew *uncircumcised* [b] 36 An ephah was a dry measure. [c] 36 A hin was a liquid measure.
[d] 2 Or *sacrifices*; also in verses 3 and 4 [e] 8 Or *who sanctifies you*; or *who sets you apart as holy*

of her flow, and she has also uncovered it. Both of them must be cut off from their people.

19" 'Do not have sexual relations with the sister of either your mother or your father, for that would dishonor a close relative; both of you would be held responsible.

20" 'If a man sleeps with his aunt, he has dishonored his uncle. They will be held responsible; they will die childless.

21" 'If a man marries his brother's wife, it is an act of impurity; he has dishonored his brother. They will be childless.

22" 'Keep all my decrees and laws and follow them, so that the land where I am bringing you to live may not vomit you out. 23You must not live according to the customs of the nations I am going to drive out before you. Because they did all these things, I abhorred them. 24But I said to you, "You will possess their land; I will give it to you as an inheritance, a land flowing with milk and honey." I am the LORD your God, who has set you apart from the nations.

25" 'You must therefore make a distinction between clean and unclean animals and between unclean and clean birds. Do not defile yourselves by any animal or bird or anything that moves along the ground—those which I have set apart as unclean for you. 26You are to be holy to me[a] because I, the LORD, am holy, and I have set you apart from the nations to be my own.

27" 'A man or woman who is a medium or spiritist among you must be put to death. You are to stone them; their blood will be on their own heads.' "

Rules for Priests

21 The LORD said to Moses, "Speak to the priests, the sons of Aaron, and say to them: 'A priest must not make himself ceremonially unclean for any of his people who die, 2except for a close relative, such as his mother or father, his son or daughter, his brother, 3or an unmarried sister who is dependent on him since she has no husband—for her he may make himself unclean. 4He must not make himself unclean for people related to him by marriage,[b] and so defile himself.

5" 'Priests must not shave their heads or shave off the edges of their beards or cut their bodies. 6They must be holy to their God and must not profane the name of their God. Because they present the offerings made to the LORD by fire, the food of their God, they are to be holy.

7" 'They must not marry women defiled by prostitution or divorced from their husbands, because priests are holy to their God. 8Regard them as holy, because they offer up the food of your God. Consider them holy, because I the LORD am holy—I who make you holy.[c]

9" 'If a priest's daughter defiles herself by becoming a prostitute, she disgraces her father; she must be burned in the fire.

10" 'The high priest, the one among his brothers who has had the anointing oil poured on his head and who has been ordained to wear the priestly garments, must not let his hair become unkempt[d] or tear his clothes. 11He must not enter a place where there is a dead body. He must not make himself unclean, even for his father or mother, 12nor leave the sanctuary of his God or desecrate it, because he has been dedicated by the anointing oil of his God. I am the LORD.

13" 'The woman he marries must be a virgin. 14He must not marry a widow, a divorced woman, or a woman defiled by prostitution, but only a virgin from his own people, 15so he will not defile his offspring among his people. I am the LORD, who makes him holy.[e]' "

16The LORD said to Moses, 17"Say to Aaron: 'For the generations to come none of your descendants who has a defect may come near to offer the food of his God. 18No man who has any defect may come near: no man who is blind or lame, disfigured or deformed; 19no man with a crippled foot or hand, 20or who is hunchbacked or dwarfed, or who has any eye defect, or who has festering or running sores or damaged testicles. 21No descendant of Aaron the priest who has any defect is to come near to present the offerings made to the LORD by fire. He has a defect; he must not come near to offer the food of his God. 22He may eat the most holy food of his God, as well as the holy food; 23yet because of his defect, he must not go near the curtain or approach the al-

[a] 26 Or *be my holy ones who set you apart as holy him apart as holy*
[b] 4 Or *unclean as a leader among his people*
[c] 8 Or *who sanctify you*; or
[d] 10 Or *not uncover his head*
[e] 15 Or *who sanctifies him*; or *who sets*

tar, and so desecrate my sanctuary. I am the LORD, who makes them holy.[a]' "

24So Moses told this to Aaron and his sons and to all the Israelites.

22 The LORD said to Moses, 2"Tell Aaron and his sons to treat with respect the sacred offerings the Israelites consecrate to me, so they will not profane my holy name. I am the LORD.

3"Say to them: 'For the generations to come, if any of your descendants is ceremonially unclean and yet comes near the sacred offerings that the Israelites consecrate to the LORD, that person must be cut off from my presence. I am the LORD.

4" 'If a descendant of Aaron has an infectious skin disease[b] or a bodily discharge, he may not eat the sacred offerings until he is cleansed. He will also be unclean if he touches something defiled by a corpse or by anyone who has an emission of semen, 5or if he touches any crawling thing that makes him unclean, or any person who makes him unclean, whatever the uncleanness may be. 6The one who touches any such thing will be unclean till evening. He must not eat any of the sacred offerings unless he has bathed himself with water. 7When the sun goes down, he will be clean, and after that he may eat the sacred offerings, for they are his food. 8He must not eat anything found dead or torn by wild animals, and so become unclean through it. I am the LORD.

9" 'The priests are to keep my requirements so that they do not become guilty and die for treating them with contempt. I am the LORD, who makes them holy.[c]

10" 'No one outside a priest's family may eat the sacred offering, nor may the guest of a priest or his hired worker eat it. 11But if a priest buys a slave with money, or if a slave is born in his household, that slave may eat his food. 12If a priest's daughter marries anyone other than a priest, she may not eat any of the sacred contributions. 13But if a priest's daughter becomes a widow or is divorced, yet has no children, and she returns to live in her father's house as in her youth, she may eat of her father's food. No unauthorized person, however, may eat any of it.

14" 'If anyone eats a sacred offering by mistake, he must make restitution to the priest for the offering and add a fifth of the value to it. 15The priests must not desecrate the sacred offerings the Israelites present to the LORD 16by allowing them to eat the sacred offerings and so bring upon them guilt requiring payment. I am the LORD, who makes them holy.' "

Unacceptable Sacrifices

17The LORD said to Moses, 18"Speak to Aaron and his sons and to all the Israelites and say to them: 'If any of you—either an Israelite or an alien living in Israel—presents a gift for a burnt offering to the LORD, either to fulfill a vow or as a freewill offering, 19you must present a male without defect from the cattle, sheep or goats in order that it may be accepted on your behalf. 20Do not bring anything with a defect, because it will not be accepted on your behalf. 21When anyone brings from the herd or flock a fellowship offering[d] to the LORD to fulfill a special vow or as a freewill offering, it must be without defect or blemish to be acceptable. 22Do not offer to the LORD the blind, the injured or the maimed, or anything with warts or festering or running sores. Do not place any of these on the altar as an offering made to the LORD by fire. 23You may, however, present as a freewill offering an ox[e] or a sheep that is deformed or stunted, but it will not be accepted in fulfillment of a vow. 24You must not offer to the LORD an animal whose testicles are bruised, crushed, torn or cut. You must not do this in your own land, 25and you must not accept such animals from the hand of a foreigner and offer them as the food of your God. They will not be accepted on your behalf, because they are deformed and have defects.' "

26The LORD said to Moses, 27"When a calf, a lamb or a goat is born, it is to remain with its mother for seven days. From the eighth day on, it will be acceptable as an offering made to the LORD by fire. 28Do not slaughter a cow or a sheep and its young on the same day.

29"When you sacrifice a thank offering to the LORD, sacrifice it in such a way that it will be accepted on your behalf. 30It

[a] *23* Or *who sanctifies them*; or *who sets them apart as holy* [b] *4* Traditionally *leprosy*; the Hebrew word was used for various diseases affecting the skin—not necessarily leprosy. [c] *9* Or *who sanctifies them*; or *who sets them apart as holy*; also in verse 16 [d] *21* Traditionally *peace offering* [e] *23* The Hebrew word can include both male and female.

must be eaten that same day; leave none
of it till morning. I am the LORD.
31"Keep my commands and follow
them. I am the LORD. 32Do not profane my
holy name. I must be acknowledged as
holy by the Israelites. I am the LORD, who
makes[a] you holy[b] 33and who brought
you out of Egypt to be your God. I am the
LORD."

23 The LORD said to Moses, 2"Speak to
the Israelites and say to them:
'These are my appointed feasts, the ap-
pointed feasts of the LORD, which you are
to proclaim as sacred assemblies.

The Sabbath

3" 'There are six days when you may
work, but the seventh day is a Sabbath of
rest, a day of sacred assembly. You are not
to do any work; wherever you live, it is a
Sabbath to the LORD.

The Passover and Unleavened Bread

4" 'These are the LORD's appointed
feasts, the sacred assemblies you are to
proclaim at their appointed times: 5The
LORD's Passover begins at twilight on the
fourteenth day of the first month. 6On the
fifteenth day of that month the LORD's
Feast of Unleavened Bread begins; for sev-
en days you must eat bread made without
yeast. 7On the first day hold a sacred as-
sembly and do no regular work. 8For sev-
en days present an offering made to the
LORD by fire. And on the seventh day hold
a sacred assembly and do no regular
work.' "

Firstfruits

9The LORD said to Moses, 10"Speak to
the Israelites and say to them: 'When you
enter the land I am going to give you and
you reap its harvest, bring to the priest a
sheaf of the first grain you harvest. 11He is
to wave the sheaf before the LORD so it will
be accepted on your behalf; the priest is to
wave it on the day after the Sabbath. 12On
the day you wave the sheaf, you must sac-
rifice as a burnt offering to the LORD a
lamb a year old without defect, 13together
with its grain offering of two-tenths of an
ephah[c] of fine flour mixed with oil—an
offering made to the LORD by fire, a pleas-
ing aroma—and its drink offering of a
quarter of a hin[d] of wine. 14You must not
eat any bread, or roasted or new grain, un-
til the very day you bring this offering to
your God. This is to be a lasting ordinance
for the generations to come, wherever you
live.

Feast of Weeks

15" 'From the day after the Sabbath, the
day you brought the sheaf of the wave of-
fering, count off seven full weeks. 16Count
off fifty days up to the day after the sev-
enth Sabbath, and then present an offer-
ing of new grain to the LORD. 17From wher-
ever you live, bring two loaves made of
two-tenths of an ephah of fine flour,
baked with yeast, as a wave offering of
firstfruits to the LORD. 18Present with this
bread seven male lambs, each a year old
and without defect, one young bull and
two rams. They will be a burnt offering to
the LORD, together with their grain offer-
ings and drink offerings—an offering
made by fire, an aroma pleasing to the
LORD. 19Then sacrifice one male goat for a
sin offering and two lambs, each a year
old, for a fellowship offering.[e] 20The
priest is to wave the two lambs before the
LORD as a wave offering, together with the
bread of the firstfruits. They are a sacred
offering to the LORD for the priest. 21On
that same day you are to proclaim a sacred
assembly and do no regular work. This is
to be a lasting ordinance for the genera-
tions to come, wherever you live.

22" 'When you reap the harvest of your
land, do not reap to the very edges of your
field or gather the gleanings of your har-
vest. Leave them for the poor and the
alien. I am the LORD your God.' "

Feast of Trumpets

23The LORD said to Moses, 24"Say to the
Israelites: 'On the first day of the seventh
month you are to have a day of rest, a sa-
cred assembly commemorated with trum-
pet blasts. 25Do no regular work, but
present an offering made to the LORD by
fire.' "

Day of Atonement

26The LORD said to Moses, 27"The tenth
day of this seventh month is the Day of
Atonement. Hold a sacred assembly and
deny yourselves,[f] and present an offer-

[a]32 Or *made* [b]32 Or *who sanctifies you*; or *who sets you apart as holy* [c]13 That is, probably about 4 quarts (about 4.5 liters); also in verse 17 [d]13 That is, probably about 1 quart (about 1 liter) [e]19 Traditionally *peace offering* [f]27 Or *and fast*; also in verses 29 and 32

ing made to the LORD by fire. 28Do no work
on that day, because it is the Day of Atone-
ment, when atonement is made for you
before the LORD your God. 29Anyone who
does not deny himself on that day must be
cut off from his people. 30I will destroy
from among his people anyone who does
any work on that day. 31You shall do no
work at all. This is to be a lasting ordi-
nance for the generations to come, wher-
ever you live. 32It is a sabbath of rest for
you, and you must deny yourselves. From
the evening of the ninth day of the month
until the following evening you are to ob-
serve your sabbath."

Feast of Tabernacles

33The LORD said to Moses, 34"Say to the
Israelites: 'On the fifteenth day of the sev-
enth month the LORD's Feast of Taberna-
cles begins, and it lasts for seven days.
35The first day is a sacred assembly; do no
regular work. 36For seven days present of-
ferings made to the LORD by fire, and on
the eighth day hold a sacred assembly and
present an offering made to the LORD by
fire. It is the closing assembly; do no regu-
lar work.

37(" 'These are the LORD's appointed
feasts, which you are to proclaim as sa-
cred assemblies for bringing offerings
made to the LORD by fire—the burnt offer-
ings and grain offerings, sacrifices and
drink offerings required for each day.
38These offerings are in addition to those
for the LORD's Sabbaths and[a] in addition
to your gifts and whatever you have
vowed and all the freewill offerings you
give to the LORD.)

39" 'So beginning with the fifteenth day
of the seventh month, after you have gath-
ered the crops of the land, celebrate the
festival to the LORD for seven days; the
first day is a day of rest, and the eighth day
also is a day of rest. 40On the first day you
are to take choice fruit from the trees, and
palm fronds, leafy branches and poplars,
and rejoice before the LORD your God for
seven days. 41Celebrate this as a festival to
the LORD for seven days each year. This is
to be a lasting ordinance for the genera-
tions to come; celebrate it in the seventh
month. 42Live in booths for seven days:
All native-born Israelites are to live in
booths 43so your descendants will know
that I had the Israelites live in booths
when I brought them out of Egypt. I am
the LORD your God.' "

44So Moses announced to the Israelites
the appointed feasts of the LORD.

Oil and Bread Set Before the LORD

24 The LORD said to Moses, 2"Com-
mand the Israelites to bring you
clear oil of pressed olives for the light so
that the lamps may be kept burning con-
tinually. 3Outside the curtain of the Testi-
mony in the Tent of Meeting, Aaron is to
tend the lamps before the LORD from eve-
ning till morning, continually. This is to
be a lasting ordinance for the generations
to come. 4The lamps on the pure gold
lampstand before the LORD must be tend-
ed continually.

5"Take fine flour and bake twelve
loaves of bread, using two-tenths of an
ephah[b] for each loaf. 6Set them in two
rows, six in each row, on the table of pure
gold before the LORD. 7Along each row put
some pure incense as a memorial portion
to represent the bread and to be an offer-
ing made to the LORD by fire. 8This bread
is to be set out before the LORD regularly,
Sabbath after Sabbath, on behalf of the Is-
raelites, as a lasting covenant. 9It belongs
to Aaron and his sons, who are to eat it in
a holy place, because it is a most holy part
of their regular share of the offerings
made to the LORD by fire."

A Blasphemer Stoned

10Now the son of an Israelite mother
and an Egyptian father went out among
the Israelites, and a fight broke out in the
camp between him and an Israelite. 11The
son of the Israelite woman blasphemed
the Name with a curse; so they brought
him to Moses. (His mother's name was
Shelomith, the daughter of Dibri the Dan-
ite.) 12They put him in custody until the
will of the LORD should be made clear to
them.

13Then the LORD said to Moses: 14"Take
the blasphemer outside the camp. All
those who heard him are to lay their
hands on his head, and the entire assem-
bly is to stone him. 15Say to the Israelites:
'If anyone curses his God, he will be held
responsible; 16anyone who blasphemes
the name of the LORD must be put to
death. The entire assembly must stone
him. Whether an alien or native-born,

[a]38 Or *These feasts are in addition to the LORD's Sabbaths, and these offerings are*

[b]5 That is, probably about 4 quarts (about 4.5 liters)

when he blasphemes the Name, he must
be put to death.
17" 'If anyone takes the life of a human
being, he must be put to death. 18Anyone
who takes the life of someone's animal
must make restitution—life for life. 19If
anyone injures his neighbor, whatever he
has done must be done to him: 20fracture
for fracture, eye for eye, tooth for tooth.
As he has injured the other, so he is to be
injured. 21Whoever kills an animal must
make restitution, but whoever kills a man
must be put to death. 22You are to have
the same law for the alien and the native-
born. I am the LORD your God.' "
23Then Moses spoke to the Israelites,
and they took the blasphemer outside the
camp and stoned him. The Israelites did
as the LORD commanded Moses.

The Sabbath Year

25 The LORD said to Moses on Mount
Sinai, 2"Speak to the Israelites and
say to them: 'When you enter the land I
am going to give you, the land itself must
observe a sabbath to the LORD. 3For six
years sow your fields, and for six years
prune your vineyards and gather their
crops. 4But in the seventh year the land is
to have a sabbath of rest, a sabbath to the
LORD. Do not sow your fields or prune
your vineyards. 5Do not reap what grows
of itself or harvest the grapes of your un-
tended vines. The land is to have a year of
rest. 6Whatever the land yields during the
sabbath year will be food for you—for
yourself, your manservant and maidser-
vant, and the hired worker and temporary
resident who live among you, 7as well as
for your livestock and the wild animals in
your land. Whatever the land produces
may be eaten.

The Year of Jubilee

8" 'Count off seven sabbaths of years—
seven times seven years—so that the sev-
en sabbaths of years amount to a period of
forty-nine years. 9Then have the trumpet
sounded everywhere on the tenth day of
the seventh month; on the Day of Atone-
ment sound the trumpet throughout your
land. 10Consecrate the fiftieth year and
proclaim liberty throughout the land to all
its inhabitants. It shall be a jubilee for you;
each one of you is to return to his family
property and each to his own clan. 11The
fiftieth year shall be a jubilee for you; do
not sow and do not reap what grows of
itself or harvest the untended vines. 12For
it is a jubilee and is to be holy for you; eat
only what is taken directly from the fields.
13" 'In this Year of Jubilee everyone is to
return to his own property.
14" 'If you sell land to one of your coun-
trymen or buy any from him, do not take
advantage of each other. 15You are to buy
from your countryman on the basis of the
number of years since the Jubilee. And he
is to sell to you on the basis of the number
of years left for harvesting crops. 16When
the years are many, you are to increase
the price, and when the years are few, you
are to decrease the price, because what he
is really selling you is the number of
crops. 17Do not take advantage of each
other, but fear your God. I am the LORD
your God.
18" 'Follow my decrees and be careful to
obey my laws, and you will live safely in
the land. 19Then the land will yield its
fruit, and you will eat your fill and live
there in safety. 20You may ask, "What will
we eat in the seventh year if we do not
plant or harvest our crops?" 21I will send
you such a blessing in the sixth year that
the land will yield enough for three years.
22While you plant during the eighth year,
you will eat from the old crop and will
continue to eat from it until the harvest of
the ninth year comes in.
23" 'The land must not be sold perma-
nently, because the land is mine and you
are but aliens and my tenants. 24Through-
out the country that you hold as a posses-
sion, you must provide for the redemption
of the land.
25" 'If one of your countrymen becomes
poor and sells some of his property, his
nearest relative is to come and redeem
what his countryman has sold. 26If, how-
ever, a man has no one to redeem it for
him but he himself prospers and acquires
sufficient means to redeem it, 27he is to
determine the value for the years since he
sold it and refund the balance to the man
to whom he sold it; he can then go back
to his own property. 28But if he does not
acquire the means to repay him, what he
sold will remain in the possession of the
buyer until the Year of Jubilee. It will be
returned in the Jubilee, and he can then
go back to his property.
29" 'If a man sells a house in a walled
city, he retains the right of redemption a
full year after its sale. During that time he
may redeem it. 30If it is not redeemed be-
fore a full year has passed, the house in
the walled city shall belong permanently

to the buyer and his descendants. It is not
to be returned in the Jubilee. 31But houses
in villages without walls around them are
to be considered as open country. They
can be redeemed, and they are to be re-
turned in the Jubilee.

32" 'The Levites always have the right to
redeem their houses in the Levitical
towns, which they possess. 33So the prop-
erty of the Levites is redeemable—that is,
a house sold in any town they hold—and
is to be returned in the Jubilee, because
the houses in the towns of the Levites are
their property among the Israelites. 34But
the pastureland belonging to their towns
must not be sold; it is their permanent
possession.

35" 'If one of your countrymen becomes
poor and is unable to support himself
among you, help him as you would an
alien or a temporary resident, so he can
continue to live among you. 36Do not take
interest of any kind[a] from him, but fear
your God, so that your countryman may
continue to live among you. 37You must
not lend him money at interest or sell him
food at a profit. 38I am the LORD your God,
who brought you out of Egypt to give you
the land of Canaan and to be your God.

39" 'If one of your countrymen becomes
poor among you and sells himself to you,
do not make him work as a slave. 40He is
to be treated as a hired worker or a tempo-
rary resident among you; he is to work for
you until the Year of Jubilee. 41Then he
and his children are to be released, and he
will go back to his own clan and to the
property of his forefathers. 42Because the
Israelites are my servants, whom I
brought out of Egypt, they must not be
sold as slaves. 43Do not rule over them
ruthlessly, but fear your God.

44" 'Your male and female slaves are to
come from the nations around you; from
them you may buy slaves. 45You may also
buy some of the temporary residents liv-
ing among you and members of their
clans born in your country, and they will
become your property. 46You can will
them to your children as inherited proper-
ty and can make them slaves for life, but
you must not rule over your fellow Israel-
ites ruthlessly.

47" 'If an alien or a temporary resident
among you becomes rich and one of your
countrymen becomes poor and sells him-
self to the alien living among you or to a
member of the alien's clan, 48he retains
the right of redemption after he has sold
himself. One of his relatives may redeem
him: 49An uncle or a cousin or any blood
relative in his clan may redeem him. Or if
he prospers, he may redeem himself. 50He
and his buyer are to count the time from
the year he sold himself up to the Year of
Jubilee. The price for his release is to be
based on the rate paid to a hired man for
that number of years. 51If many years re-
main, he must pay for his redemption a
larger share of the price paid for him. 52If
only a few years remain until the Year of
Jubilee, he is to compute that and pay for
his redemption accordingly. 53He is to be
treated as a man hired from year to year;
you must see to it that his owner does not
rule over him ruthlessly.

54" 'Even if he is not redeemed in any of
these ways, he and his children are to be
released in the Year of Jubilee, 55for the
Israelites belong to me as servants. They
are my servants, whom I brought out of
Egypt. I am the LORD your God.

Reward for Obedience

26 " 'Do not make idols or set up an
image or a sacred stone for your-
selves, and do not place a carved stone in
your land to bow down before it. I am the
LORD your God.

2" 'Observe my Sabbaths and have rev-
erence for my sanctuary. I am the LORD.

3" 'If you follow my decrees and are
careful to obey my commands, 4I will
send you rain in its season, and the
ground will yield its crops and the trees of
the field their fruit. 5Your threshing will
continue until grape harvest and the grape
harvest will continue until planting, and
you will eat all the food you want and live
in safety in your land.

6" 'I will grant peace in the land, and
you will lie down and no one will make
you afraid. I will remove savage beasts
from the land, and the sword will not pass
through your country. 7You will pursue
your enemies, and they will fall by the
sword before you. 8Five of you will chase
a hundred, and a hundred of you will
chase ten thousand, and your enemies
will fall by the sword before you.

9" 'I will look on you with favor and
make you fruitful and increase your num-
bers, and I will keep my covenant with
you. 10You will still be eating last year's

[a]36 Or *take excessive interest*; similarly in verse 37

harvest when you will have to move it out
to make room for the new. 11I will put my
dwelling place[a] among you, and I will
not abhor you. 12I will walk among you
and be your God, and you will be my people.
13I am the LORD your God, who
brought you out of Egypt so that you
would no longer be slaves to the Egyptians;
I broke the bars of your yoke and
enabled you to walk with heads held high.

Punishment for Disobedience

14" 'But if you will not listen to me and
carry out all these commands, 15and if you
reject my decrees and abhor my laws and
fail to carry out all my commands and so
violate my covenant, 16then I will do this
to you: I will bring upon you sudden terror,
wasting diseases and fever that will
destroy your sight and drain away your
life. You will plant seed in vain, because
your enemies will eat it. 17I will set my
face against you so that you will be defeated
by your enemies; those who hate you
will rule over you, and you will flee even
when no one is pursuing you.

18" 'If after all this you will not listen to
me, I will punish you for your sins seven
times over. 19I will break down your stubborn
pride and make the sky above you
like iron and the ground beneath you like
bronze. 20Your strength will be spent in
vain, because your soil will not yield its
crops, nor will the trees of the land yield
their fruit.

21" 'If you remain hostile toward me
and refuse to listen to me, I will multiply
your afflictions seven times over, as your
sins deserve. 22I will send wild animals
against you, and they will rob you of your
children, destroy your cattle and make
you so few in number that your roads will
be deserted.

23" 'If in spite of these things you do not
accept my correction but continue to be
hostile toward me, 24I myself will be hostile
toward you and will afflict you for
your sins seven times over. 25And I will
bring the sword upon you to avenge the
breaking of the covenant. When you withdraw
into your cities, I will send a plague
among you, and you will be given into enemy
hands. 26When I cut off your supply
of bread, ten women will be able to bake
your bread in one oven, and they will dole
out the bread by weight. You will eat, but
you will not be satisfied.

27" 'If in spite of this you still do not listen
to me but continue to be hostile toward
me, 28then in my anger I will be hostile
toward you, and I myself will punish
you for your sins seven times over. 29You
will eat the flesh of your sons and the
flesh of your daughters. 30I will destroy
your high places, cut down your incense
altars and pile your dead bodies on the
lifeless forms of your idols, and I will abhor
you. 31I will turn your cities into ruins
and lay waste your sanctuaries, and I will
take no delight in the pleasing aroma of
your offerings. 32I will lay waste the land,
so that your enemies who live there will
be appalled. 33I will scatter you among the
nations and will draw out my sword and
pursue you. Your land will be laid waste,
and your cities will lie in ruins. 34Then the
land will enjoy its sabbath years all the
time that it lies desolate and you are in the
country of your enemies; then the land
will rest and enjoy its sabbaths. 35All the
time that it lies desolate, the land will have
the rest it did not have during the sabbaths
you lived in it.

36" 'As for those of you who are left, I
will make their hearts so fearful in the
lands of their enemies that the sound of a
windblown leaf will put them to flight.
They will run as though fleeing from the
sword, and they will fall, even though no
one is pursuing them. 37They will stumble
over one another as though fleeing from
the sword, even though no one is pursuing
them. So you will not be able to stand
before your enemies. 38You will perish
among the nations; the land of your enemies
will devour you. 39Those of you who
are left will waste away in the lands of
their enemies because of their sins; also
because of their fathers' sins they will
waste away.

40" 'But if they will confess their sins
and the sins of their fathers—their treachery
against me and their hostility toward
me, 41which made me hostile toward
them so that I sent them into the land of
their enemies—then when their uncircumcised
hearts are humbled and they
pay for their sin, 42I will remember my
covenant with Jacob and my covenant
with Isaac and my covenant with Abraham,
and I will remember the land. 43For
the land will be deserted by them and will
enjoy its sabbaths while it lies desolate
without them. They will pay for their sins

[a] 11 Or *my tabernacle*

because they rejected my laws and abhorred my decrees. 44Yet in spite of this, when they are in the land of their enemies, I will not reject them or abhor them so as to destroy them completely, breaking my covenant with them. I am the LORD their God. 45But for their sake I will remember the covenant with their ancestors whom I brought out of Egypt in the sight of the nations to be their God. I am the LORD.' "

46These are the decrees, the laws and the regulations that the LORD established on Mount Sinai between himself and the Israelites through Moses.

Redeeming What Is the LORD's

27 The LORD said to Moses, 2"Speak to the Israelites and say to them: 'If anyone makes a special vow to dedicate persons to the LORD by giving equivalent values, 3set the value of a male between the ages of twenty and sixty at fifty shekels[a] of silver, according to the sanctuary shekel[b]; 4and if it is a female, set her value at thirty shekels.[c] 5If it is a person between the ages of five and twenty, set the value of a male at twenty shekels[d] and of a female at ten shekels.[e] 6If it is a person between one month and five years, set the value of a male at five shekels[f] of silver and that of a female at three shekels[g] of silver. 7If it is a person sixty years old or more, set the value of a male at fifteen shekels[h] and of a female at ten shekels. 8If anyone making the vow is too poor to pay the specified amount, he is to present the person to the priest, who will set the value for him according to what the man making the vow can afford.

9" 'If what he vowed is an animal that is acceptable as an offering to the LORD, such an animal given to the LORD becomes holy. 10He must not exchange it or substitute a good one for a bad one, or a bad one for a good one; if he should substitute one animal for another, both it and the substitute become holy. 11If what he vowed is a ceremonially unclean animal—one that is not acceptable as an offering to the LORD—the animal must be presented to the priest, 12who will judge its quality as good or bad. Whatever value the priest then sets, that is what it will be. 13If the owner wishes to redeem the animal, he must add a fifth to its value.

14" 'If a man dedicates his house as something holy to the LORD, the priest will judge its quality as good or bad. Whatever value the priest then sets, so it will remain. 15If the man who dedicates his house redeems it, he must add a fifth to its value, and the house will again become his.

16" 'If a man dedicates to the LORD part of his family land, its value is to be set according to the amount of seed required for it—fifty shekels of silver to a homer[i] of barley seed. 17If he dedicates his field during the Year of Jubilee, the value that has been set remains. 18But if he dedicates his field after the Jubilee, the priest will determine the value according to the number of years that remain until the next Year of Jubilee, and its set value will be reduced. 19If the man who dedicates the field wishes to redeem it, he must add a fifth to its value, and the field will again become his. 20If, however, he does not redeem the field, or if he has sold it to someone else, it can never be redeemed. 21When the field is released in the Jubilee, it will become holy, like a field devoted to the LORD; it will become the property of the priests.[j]

22" 'If a man dedicates to the LORD a field he has bought, which is not part of his family land, 23the priest will determine its value up to the Year of Jubilee, and the man must pay its value on that day as something holy to the LORD. 24In the Year of Jubilee the field will revert to the person from whom he bought it, the one whose land it was. 25Every value is to be set according to the sanctuary shekel, twenty gerahs to the shekel.

26" 'No one, however, may dedicate the firstborn of an animal, since the firstborn already belongs to the LORD; whether an ox[k] or a sheep, it is the LORD's. 27If it is one of the unclean animals, he may buy it back at its set value, adding a fifth of the value to it. If he does not redeem it, it is to be sold at its set value.

28" 'But nothing that a man owns and

[a] 3 That is, about 1 1/4 pounds (about 0.6 kilogram); also in verse 16 [b] 3 That is, about 2/5 ounce (about 11.5 grams); also in verse 25 [c] 4 That is, about 12 ounces (about 0.3 kilogram) [d] 5 That is, about 8 ounces (about 0.2 kilogram) [e] 5 That is, about 4 ounces (about 110 grams); also in verse 7
[f] 6 That is, about 2 ounces (about 55 grams) [g] 6 That is, about 1 1/4 ounces (about 35 grams)
[h] 7 That is, about 6 ounces (about 170 grams) [i] 16 That is, probably about 6 bushels (about 220 liters)
[j] 21 Or *priest* [k] 26 The Hebrew word can include both male and female.

VERSE FOR THE DAY: Leviticus 27:30

AUTHOR: Ronald Blue

PASSAGE FOR THE DAY: Leviticus 27:30–34

Whose Money Is It?

I don't believe there is one single "right" level of giving—a "correct amount to tithe"—either in terms of a percentage of your income or a set dollar amount. But there *are* some biblical guidelines, as well as the convictions of your heart.

First, don't assume the financial resources entrusted to you are part yours and part God's. Your income is *all* God's, and the giving that you do should come from a personal conviction that recognizes his ownership of everything. By thinking and acting in that way, you and your spouse can eliminate some of the legalistic thoughts—and accompanying guilt—related to giving based on a set percentage of your income.

I view ten percent as a bare minimum, a goal upon which we can then build and increase our giving over time. However, God doesn't call us to be slaves to a set percentage, but to freely give back to him what our grateful hearts demand. Giving from the heart breaks the power of money, because the giver must first acknowledge the true Owner of the money and see himself or herself as merely a manager of those finances.

In serving God with our money, our motives—and ultimately our actions—will be different than if our lifestyle and material desires supersede all other priorities. The Bible calls us to "profane" the god of money by giving it away. And to do that, we must take Christ's famous exhortation and apply it to our checkbooks: "Where your treasure is," Jesus said, "there your heart will be also."

MARRIAGE BUILDERS

♦ *How would you characterize your giving "attitude"?*
♦ *What steps can the two of you take to change any attitudes that are not characterized by "cheerful giving"?*

Additional Scripture Readings
2 Corinthians 9:6–7; Proverbs 21:26; Luke 6:38

Go to page 149 for your next devotional reading.

devotes[a] to the LORD—whether man or animal or family land—may be sold or redeemed; everything so devoted is most holy to the LORD.

29" 'No person devoted to destruction[b] may be ransomed; he must be put to death.

30" 'A tithe of everything from the land, whether grain from the soil or fruit from the trees, belongs to the LORD; it is holy to the LORD. 31If a man redeems any of his tithe, he must add a fifth of the value to it. 32The entire tithe of the herd and flock—every tenth animal that passes under the shepherd's rod—will be holy to the LORD. 33He must not pick out the good from the bad or make any substitution. If he does make a substitution, both the animal and its substitute become holy and cannot be redeemed.' "

34These are the commands the LORD gave Moses on Mount Sinai for the Israelites.

[a]28 The Hebrew term refers to the irrevocable giving over of things or persons to the LORD. [b]29 The Hebrew term refers to the irrevocable giving over of things or persons to the LORD, often by totally destroying them.

MOSES records in this book the number of the Israelites and how he organizes them around the tabernacle. To this he adds an account of what happens as they wander in the wilderness. Note especially that in spite of their numerous rebellions, God still loves them and watches over them. As you read this book, rejoice in God's love and care in your life in spite of your sins; promise God that you will do your best to trust and obey him.

NUMBERS

The Census

1 The LORD spoke to Moses in the Tent
of Meeting in the Desert of Sinai on
the first day of the second month of the
second year after the Israelites came out
of Egypt. He said: 2"Take a census of the
whole Israelite community by their clans
and families, listing every man by name,
one by one. 3You and Aaron are to num-
ber by their divisions all the men in Israel
twenty years old or more who are able to
serve in the army. 4One man from each
tribe, each the head of his family, is to
help you. 5These are the names of the
men who are to assist you:
from Reuben, Elizur son of Shedeur;
6from Simeon, Shelumiel son of Zuri-
shaddai;
7from Judah, Nahshon son of Am-
minadab;
8from Issachar, Nethanel son of Zuar;
9from Zebulun, Eliab son of Helon;
10from the sons of Joseph:
from Ephraim, Elishama son of
Ammihud;
from Manasseh, Gamaliel son of
Pedahzur;
11from Benjamin, Abidan son of Gide-
oni;
12from Dan, Ahiezer son of Ammi-
shaddai;

[13]from Asher, Pagiel son of Ocran;
[14]from Gad, Eliasaph son of Deuel;
[15]from Naphtali, Ahira son of Enan."

[16]These were the men appointed from the community, the leaders of their ancestral tribes. They were the heads of the clans of Israel.

[17]Moses and Aaron took these men whose names had been given, [18]and they called the whole community together on the first day of the second month. The people indicated their ancestry by their clans and families, and the men twenty years old or more were listed by name, one by one, [19]as the LORD commanded Moses. And so he counted them in the Desert of Sinai:

[20]From the descendants of Reuben the firstborn son of Israel:
All the men twenty years old or more who were able to serve in the army were listed by name, one by one, according to the records of their clans and families. [21]The number from the tribe of Reuben was 46,500.

[22]From the descendants of Simeon:
All the men twenty years old or more who were able to serve in the army were counted and listed by name, one by one, according to the records of their clans and families. [23]The number from the tribe of Simeon was 59,300.

[24]From the descendants of Gad:
All the men twenty years old or more who were able to serve in the army were listed by name, according to the records of their clans and families. [25]The number from the tribe of Gad was 45,650.

[26]From the descendants of Judah:
All the men twenty years old or more who were able to serve in the army were listed by name, according to the records of their clans and families. [27]The number from the tribe of Judah was 74,600.

[28]From the descendants of Issachar:
All the men twenty years old or more who were able to serve in the army were listed by name, according to the records of their clans and families. [29]The number from the tribe of Issachar was 54,400.

[30]From the descendants of Zebulun:
All the men twenty years old or more who were able to serve in the army were listed by name, according to the records of their clans and families. [31]The number from the tribe of Zebulun was 57,400.

[32]From the sons of Joseph:
From the descendants of Ephraim:
All the men twenty years old or more who were able to serve in the army were listed by name, according to the records of their clans and families. [33]The number from the tribe of Ephraim was 40,500.

[34]From the descendants of Manasseh:
All the men twenty years old or more who were able to serve in the army were listed by name, according to the records of their clans and families. [35]The number from the tribe of Manasseh was 32,200.

[36]From the descendants of Benjamin:
All the men twenty years old or more who were able to serve in the army were listed by name, according to the records of their clans and families. [37]The number from the tribe of Benjamin was 35,400.

[38]From the descendants of Dan:
All the men twenty years old or more who were able to serve in the army were listed by name, according to the records of their clans and families. [39]The number from the tribe of Dan was 62,700.

[40]From the descendants of Asher:
All the men twenty years old or more who were able to serve in the army were listed by name, according to the records of their clans and families. [41]The number from the tribe of Asher was 41,500.

[42]From the descendants of Naphtali:
All the men twenty years old or more who were able to serve in the army were listed by name, according to the records of their clans and families. [43]The number

from the tribe of Naphtali was
53,400.

44These were the men counted by Moses and Aaron and the twelve leaders of Israel, each one representing his family. 45All the Israelites twenty years old or more who were able to serve in Israel's army were counted according to their families. 46The total number was 603,550.

47The families of the tribe of Levi, however, were not counted along with the others. 48The LORD had said to Moses: 49"You must not count the tribe of Levi or include them in the census of the other Israelites. 50Instead, appoint the Levites to be in charge of the tabernacle of the Testimony—over all its furnishings and everything belonging to it. They are to carry the tabernacle and all its furnishings; they are to take care of it and encamp around it. 51Whenever the tabernacle is to move, the Levites are to take it down, and whenever the tabernacle is to be set up, the Levites shall do it. Anyone else who goes near it shall be put to death. 52The Israelites are to set up their tents by divisions, each man in his own camp under his own standard. 53The Levites, however, are to set up their tents around the tabernacle of the Testimony so that wrath will not fall on the Israelite community. The Levites are to be responsible for the care of the tabernacle of the Testimony."

54The Israelites did all this just as the LORD commanded Moses.

The Arrangement of the Tribal Camps

2 The LORD said to Moses and Aaron: 2"The Israelites are to camp around the Tent of Meeting some distance from it, each man under his standard with the banners of his family."

3On the east, toward the sunrise, the divisions of the camp of Judah are to encamp under their standard. The leader of the people of Judah is Nahshon son of Amminadab. 4His division numbers 74,600.

5The tribe of Issachar will camp next to them. The leader of the people of Issachar is Nethanel son of Zuar. 6His division numbers 54,400.

7The tribe of Zebulun will be next. The leader of the people of Zebulun is Eliab son of Helon. 8His division numbers 57,400.

9All the men assigned to the camp of Judah, according to their divisions, number 186,400. They will set out first.

10On the south will be the divisions of the camp of Reuben under their standard. The leader of the people of Reuben is Elizur son of Shedeur. 11His division numbers 46,500.

12The tribe of Simeon will camp next to them. The leader of the people of Simeon is Shelumiel son of Zurishaddai. 13His division numbers 59,300.

14The tribe of Gad will be next. The leader of the people of Gad is Eliasaph son of Deuel.[a] 15His division numbers 45,650.

16All the men assigned to the camp of Reuben, according to their divisions, number 151,450. They will set out second.

17Then the Tent of Meeting and the camp of the Levites will set out in the middle of the camps. They will set out in the same order as they encamp, each in his own place under his standard.

18On the west will be the divisions of the camp of Ephraim under their standard. The leader of the people of Ephraim is Elishama son of Ammihud. 19His division numbers 40,500.

20The tribe of Manasseh will be next to them. The leader of the people of Manasseh is Gamaliel son of Pedahzur. 21His division numbers 32,200.

22The tribe of Benjamin will be next. The leader of the people of Benjamin is Abidan son of Gideoni. 23His division numbers 35,400.

24All the men assigned to the camp of Ephraim, according to their divisions, number 108,100. They will set out third.

25On the north will be the divisions of the camp of Dan, under their standard. The leader of the people of Dan is Ahiezer son of Ammishaddai. 26His division numbers 62,700.

27The tribe of Asher will camp next

[a] *14* Many manuscripts of the Masoretic Text, Samaritan Pentateuch and Vulgate (see also Num. 1:14); most manuscripts of the Masoretic Text *Reuel*

to them. The leader of the people of
Asher is Pagiel son of Ocran. 28His division numbers 41,500.
29The tribe of Naphtali will be next.
The leader of the people of Naphtali
is Ahira son of Enan. 30His division
numbers 53,400.
31All the men assigned to the camp
of Dan number 157,600. They will set
out last, under their standards.

32These are the Israelites, counted
according to their families. All those
in the camps, by their divisions, number 603,550. 33The Levites, however,
were not counted along with the other Israelites, as the LORD commanded
Moses.

34So the Israelites did everything the
LORD commanded Moses; that is the way
they encamped under their standards, and
that is the way they set out, each with his
clan and family.

The Levites

3 This is the account of the family of
Aaron and Moses at the time the LORD
talked with Moses on Mount Sinai.
2The names of the sons of Aaron were
Nadab the firstborn and Abihu, Eleazar
and Ithamar. 3Those were the names of
Aaron's sons, the anointed priests, who
were ordained to serve as priests. 4Nadab
and Abihu, however, fell dead before the
LORD when they made an offering with unauthorized fire before him in the Desert of
Sinai. They had no sons; so only Eleazar
and Ithamar served as priests during the
lifetime of their father Aaron.
5The LORD said to Moses, 6"Bring the
tribe of Levi and present them to Aaron
the priest to assist him. 7They are to perform duties for him and for the whole
community at the Tent of Meeting by doing the work of the tabernacle. 8They are
to take care of all the furnishings of the
Tent of Meeting, fulfilling the obligations
of the Israelites by doing the work of the
tabernacle. 9Give the Levites to Aaron and
his sons; they are the Israelites who are to
be given wholly to him.[a] 10Appoint Aaron and his sons to serve as priests; anyone
else who approaches the sanctuary must
be put to death."
11The LORD also said to Moses, 12"I have
taken the Levites from among the Israelites in place of the first male offspring of
every Israelite woman. The Levites are
mine, 13for all the firstborn are mine.
When I struck down all the firstborn in
Egypt, I set apart for myself every firstborn in Israel, whether man or animal.
They are to be mine. I am the LORD."
14The LORD said to Moses in the Desert
of Sinai, 15"Count the Levites by their families and clans. Count every male a month
old or more." 16So Moses counted them,
as he was commanded by the word of the
LORD.
17These were the names of the sons of
Levi:
Gershon, Kohath and Merari.
18These were the names of the Gershonite clans:
Libni and Shimei.
19The Kohathite clans:
Amram, Izhar, Hebron and Uzziel.
20The Merarite clans:
Mahli and Mushi.
These were the Levite clans, according
to their families.

21To Gershon belonged the clans of the
Libnites and Shimeites; these were the
Gershonite clans. 22The number of all the
males a month old or more who were
counted was 7,500. 23The Gershonite
clans were to camp on the west, behind
the tabernacle. 24The leader of the families of the Gershonites was Eliasaph son of
Lael. 25At the Tent of Meeting the Gershonites were responsible for the care of
the tabernacle and tent, its coverings, the
curtain at the entrance to the Tent of
Meeting, 26the curtains of the courtyard,
the curtain at the entrance to the courtyard surrounding the tabernacle and altar,
and the ropes—and everything related to
their use.

27To Kohath belonged the clans of the
Amramites, Izharites, Hebronites and Uzzielites; these were the Kohathite clans.
28The number of all the males a month old
or more was 8,600.[b] The Kohathites were
responsible for the care of the sanctuary.
29The Kohathite clans were to camp on
the south side of the tabernacle. 30The
leader of the families of the Kohathite
clans was Elizaphan son of Uzziel. 31They

[a]*9* Most manuscripts of the Masoretic Text; some manuscripts of the Masoretic Text, Samaritan Pentateuch and Septuagint (see also Num. 8:16) *to me*

[b]*28* Hebrew; some Septuagint manuscripts *8,300*

were responsible for the care of the ark, the table, the lampstand, the altars, the articles of the sanctuary used in ministering, the curtain, and everything related to their use. 32The chief leader of the Levites was Eleazar son of Aaron, the priest. He was appointed over those who were responsible for the care of the sanctuary.

33To Merari belonged the clans of the Mahlites and the Mushites; these were the Merarite clans. 34The number of all the males a month old or more who were counted was 6,200. 35The leader of the families of the Merarite clans was Zuriel son of Abihail; they were to camp on the north side of the tabernacle. 36The Merarites were appointed to take care of the frames of the tabernacle, its crossbars, posts, bases, all its equipment, and everything related to their use, 37as well as the posts of the surrounding courtyard with their bases, tent pegs and ropes.

38Moses and Aaron and his sons were to camp to the east of the tabernacle, toward the sunrise, in front of the Tent of Meeting. They were responsible for the care of the sanctuary on behalf of the Israelites. Anyone else who approached the sanctuary was to be put to death.

39The total number of Levites counted at the LORD's command by Moses and Aaron according to their clans, including every male a month old or more, was 22,000.

40The LORD said to Moses, "Count all the firstborn Israelite males who are a month old or more and make a list of their names. 41Take the Levites for me in place of all the firstborn of the Israelites, and the livestock of the Levites in place of all the firstborn of the livestock of the Israelites. I am the LORD."

42So Moses counted all the firstborn of the Israelites, as the LORD commanded him. 43The total number of firstborn males a month old or more, listed by name, was 22,273.

44The LORD also said to Moses, 45"Take the Levites in place of all the firstborn of Israel, and the livestock of the Levites in place of their livestock. The Levites are to be mine. I am the LORD. 46To redeem the 273 firstborn Israelites who exceed the number of the Levites, 47collect five shekels[a] for each one, according to the sanctuary shekel, which weighs twenty gerahs. 48Give the money for the redemption of the additional Israelites to Aaron and his sons."

49So Moses collected the redemption money from those who exceeded the number redeemed by the Levites. 50From the firstborn of the Israelites he collected silver weighing 1,365 shekels,[b] according to the sanctuary shekel. 51Moses gave the redemption money to Aaron and his sons, as he was commanded by the word of the LORD.

The Kohathites

4 The LORD said to Moses and Aaron: 2"Take a census of the Kohathite branch of the Levites by their clans and families. 3Count all the men from thirty to fifty years of age who come to serve in the work in the Tent of Meeting.

4"This is the work of the Kohathites in the Tent of Meeting: the care of the most holy things. 5When the camp is to move, Aaron and his sons are to go in and take down the shielding curtain and cover the ark of the Testimony with it. 6Then they are to cover this with hides of sea cows,[c] spread a cloth of solid blue over that and put the poles in place.

7"Over the table of the Presence they are to spread a blue cloth and put on it the plates, dishes and bowls, and the jars for drink offerings; the bread that is continually there is to remain on it. 8Over these they are to spread a scarlet cloth, cover that with hides of sea cows and put its poles in place.

9"They are to take a blue cloth and cover the lampstand that is for light, together with its lamps, its wick trimmers and trays, and all its jars for the oil used to supply it. 10Then they are to wrap it and all its accessories in a covering of hides of sea cows and put it on a carrying frame.

11"Over the gold altar they are to spread a blue cloth and cover that with hides of sea cows and put its poles in place.

12"They are to take all the articles used for ministering in the sanctuary, wrap them in a blue cloth, cover that with hides of sea cows and put them on a carrying frame.

13"They are to remove the ashes from

[a] *47* That is, about 2 ounces (about 55 grams) [b] *50* That is, about 35 pounds (about 15.5 kilograms)
[c] *6* That is, dugongs; also in verses 8, 10, 11, 12, 14 and 25

the bronze altar and spread a purple cloth over it. 14Then they are to place on it all the utensils used for ministering at the altar, including the firepans, meat forks, shovels and sprinkling bowls. Over it they are to spread a covering of hides of sea cows and put its poles in place.

15"After Aaron and his sons have finished covering the holy furnishings and all the holy articles, and when the camp is ready to move, the Kohathites are to come to do the carrying. But they must not touch the holy things or they will die. The Kohathites are to carry those things that are in the Tent of Meeting.

16"Eleazar son of Aaron, the priest, is to have charge of the oil for the light, the fragrant incense, the regular grain offering and the anointing oil. He is to be in charge of the entire tabernacle and everything in it, including its holy furnishings and articles."

17The LORD said to Moses and Aaron, 18"See that the Kohathite tribal clans are not cut off from the Levites. 19So that they may live and not die when they come near the most holy things, do this for them: Aaron and his sons are to go into the sanctuary and assign to each man his work and what he is to carry. 20But the Kohathites must not go in to look at the holy things, even for a moment, or they will die."

The Gershonites

21The LORD said to Moses, 22"Take a census also of the Gershonites by their families and clans. 23Count all the men from thirty to fifty years of age who come to serve in the work at the Tent of Meeting.

24"This is the service of the Gershonite clans as they work and carry burdens: 25They are to carry the curtains of the tabernacle, the Tent of Meeting, its covering and the outer covering of hides of sea cows, the curtains for the entrance to the Tent of Meeting, 26the curtains of the courtyard surrounding the tabernacle and altar, the curtain for the entrance, the ropes and all the equipment used in its service. The Gershonites are to do all that needs to be done with these things. 27All their service, whether carrying or doing other work, is to be done under the direction of Aaron and his sons. You shall assign to them as their responsibility all they are to carry. 28This is the service of the Gershonite clans at the Tent of Meeting. Their duties are to be under the direction of Ithamar son of Aaron, the priest.

The Merarites

29"Count the Merarites by their clans and families. 30Count all the men from thirty to fifty years of age who come to serve in the work at the Tent of Meeting. 31This is their duty as they perform service at the Tent of Meeting: to carry the frames of the tabernacle, its crossbars, posts and bases, 32as well as the posts of the surrounding courtyard with their bases, tent pegs, ropes, all their equipment and everything related to their use. Assign to each man the specific things he is to carry. 33This is the service of the Merarite clans as they work at the Tent of Meeting under the direction of Ithamar son of Aaron, the priest."

The Numbering of the Levite Clans

34Moses, Aaron and the leaders of the community counted the Kohathites by their clans and families. 35All the men from thirty to fifty years of age who came to serve in the work in the Tent of Meeting, 36counted by clans, were 2,750. 37This was the total of all those in the Kohathite clans who served in the Tent of Meeting. Moses and Aaron counted them according to the LORD's command through Moses.

38The Gershonites were counted by their clans and families. 39All the men from thirty to fifty years of age who came to serve in the work at the Tent of Meeting, 40counted by their clans and families, were 2,630. 41This was the total of those in the Gershonite clans who served at the Tent of Meeting. Moses and Aaron counted them according to the LORD's command.

42The Merarites were counted by their clans and families. 43All the men from thirty to fifty years of age who came to serve in the work at the Tent of Meeting, 44counted by their clans, were 3,200. 45This was the total of those in the Merarite clans. Moses and Aaron counted them according to the LORD's command through Moses.

46So Moses, Aaron and the leaders of Israel counted all the Levites by their clans and families. 47All the men from thirty to fifty years of age who came to do the work of serving and carrying the Tent of Meeting 48numbered 8,580. 49At the LORD's command through Moses, each was assigned his work and told what to carry.

Thus they were counted, as the LORD commanded Moses.

The Purity of the Camp

5 The LORD said to Moses, 2"Command the Israelites to send away from the camp anyone who has an infectious skin disease[a] or a discharge of any kind, or who is ceremonially unclean because of a dead body. 3Send away male and female alike; send them outside the camp so they will not defile their camp, where I dwell among them." 4The Israelites did this; they sent them outside the camp. They did just as the LORD had instructed Moses.

Restitution for Wrongs

5The LORD said to Moses, 6"Say to the Israelites: 'When a man or woman wrongs another in any way[b] and so is unfaithful to the LORD, that person is guilty 7and must confess the sin he has committed. He must make full restitution for his wrong, add one fifth to it and give it all to the person he has wronged. 8But if that person has no close relative to whom restitution can be made for the wrong, the restitution belongs to the LORD and must be given to the priest, along with the ram with which atonement is made for him. 9All the sacred contributions the Israelites bring to a priest will belong to him. 10Each man's sacred gifts are his own, but what he gives to the priest will belong to the priest.' "

The Test for an Unfaithful Wife

11Then the LORD said to Moses, 12"Speak to the Israelites and say to them: 'If a man's wife goes astray and is unfaithful to him 13by sleeping with another man, and this is hidden from her husband and her impurity is undetected (since there is no witness against her and she has not been caught in the act), 14and if feelings of jealousy come over her husband and he suspects his wife and she is impure—or if he is jealous and suspects her even though she is not impure— 15then he is to take his wife to the priest. He must also take an offering of a tenth of an ephah[c] of barley flour on her behalf. He must not pour oil on it or put incense on it, because it is a grain offering for jealousy, a reminder offering to draw attention to guilt.

16" 'The priest shall bring her and have her stand before the LORD. 17Then he shall take some holy water in a clay jar and put some dust from the tabernacle floor into the water. 18After the priest has had the woman stand before the LORD, he shall loosen her hair and place in her hands the reminder offering, the grain offering for jealousy, while he himself holds the bitter water that brings a curse. 19Then the priest shall put the woman under oath and say to her, "If no other man has slept with you and you have not gone astray and become impure while married to your husband, may this bitter water that brings a curse not harm you. 20But if you have gone astray while married to your husband and you have defiled yourself by sleeping with a man other than your husband"— 21here the priest is to put the woman under this curse of the oath—"may the LORD cause your people to curse and denounce you when he causes your thigh to waste away and your abdomen to swell.[d] 22May this water that brings a curse enter your body so that your abdomen swells and your thigh wastes away.[e]"

" 'Then the woman is to say, "Amen. So be it."

23" 'The priest is to write these curses on a scroll and then wash them off into the bitter water. 24He shall have the woman drink the bitter water that brings a curse, and this water will enter her and cause bitter suffering. 25The priest is to take from her hands the grain offering for jealousy, wave it before the LORD and bring it to the altar. 26The priest is then to take a handful of the grain offering as a memorial offering and burn it on the altar; after that, he is to have the woman drink the water. 27If she has defiled herself and been unfaithful to her husband, then when she is made to drink the water that brings a curse, it will go into her and cause bitter suffering; her abdomen will swell and her thigh waste away,[f] and she will become accursed among her people. 28If, however, the woman has not defiled herself and is free from impurity, she will be

[a]2 Traditionally *leprosy*; the Hebrew word was used for various diseases affecting the skin—not necessarily leprosy. [b]6 Or *woman commits any wrong common to mankind* [c]15 That is, probably about 2 quarts (about 2 liters) [d]21 Or *causes you to have a miscarrying womb and barrenness*
[e]22 Or *body and cause you to be barren and have a miscarrying womb* [f]27 Or *suffering; she will have barrenness and a miscarrying womb*

cleared of guilt and will be able to have children.

29" 'This, then, is the law of jealousy when a woman goes astray and defiles herself while married to her husband, 30or when feelings of jealousy come over a man because he suspects his wife. The priest is to have her stand before the LORD and is to apply this entire law to her. 31The husband will be innocent of any wrongdoing, but the woman will bear the consequences of her sin.' "

The Nazirite

6 The LORD said to Moses, 2"Speak to the Israelites and say to them: 'If a man or woman wants to make a special vow, a vow of separation to the LORD as a Nazirite, 3he must abstain from wine and other fermented drink and must not drink vinegar made from wine or from other fermented drink. He must not drink grape juice or eat grapes or raisins. 4As long as he is a Nazirite, he must not eat anything that comes from the grapevine, not even the seeds or skins.

5" 'During the entire period of his vow of separation no razor may be used on his head. He must be holy until the period of his separation to the LORD is over; he must let the hair of his head grow long. 6Throughout the period of his separation to the LORD he must not go near a dead body. 7Even if his own father or mother or brother or sister dies, he must not make himself ceremonially unclean on account of them, because the symbol of his separation to God is on his head. 8Throughout the period of his separation he is consecrated to the LORD.

9" 'If someone dies suddenly in his presence, thus defiling the hair he has dedicated, he must shave his head on the day of his cleansing—the seventh day. 10Then on the eighth day he must bring two doves or two young pigeons to the priest at the entrance to the Tent of Meeting. 11The priest is to offer one as a sin offering and the other as a burnt offering to make atonement for him because he sinned by being in the presence of the dead body. That same day he is to consecrate his head. 12He must dedicate himself to the LORD for the period of his separation and must bring a year-old male lamb as a guilt offering. The previous days do not count, because he became defiled during his separation.

13" 'Now this is the law for the Nazirite when the period of his separation is over. He is to be brought to the entrance to the Tent of Meeting. 14There he is to present his offerings to the LORD: a year-old male lamb without defect for a burnt offering, a year-old ewe lamb without defect for a sin offering, a ram without defect for a fellowship offering,[a] 15together with their grain offerings and drink offerings, and a basket of bread made without yeast—cakes made of fine flour mixed with oil, and wafers spread with oil.

16" 'The priest is to present them before the LORD and make the sin offering and the burnt offering. 17He is to present the basket of unleavened bread and is to sacrifice the ram as a fellowship offering to the LORD, together with its grain offering and drink offering.

18" 'Then at the entrance to the Tent of Meeting, the Nazirite must shave off the hair that he dedicated. He is to take the hair and put it in the fire that is under the sacrifice of the fellowship offering.

19" 'After the Nazirite has shaved off the hair of his dedication, the priest is to place in his hands a boiled shoulder of the ram, and a cake and a wafer from the basket, both made without yeast. 20The priest shall then wave them before the LORD as a wave offering; they are holy and belong to the priest, together with the breast that was waved and the thigh that was presented. After that, the Nazirite may drink wine.

21" 'This is the law of the Nazirite who vows his offering to the LORD in accordance with his separation, in addition to whatever else he can afford. He must fulfill the vow he has made, according to the law of the Nazirite.' "

The Priestly Blessing

22The LORD said to Moses, 23"Tell Aaron and his sons, 'This is how you are to bless the Israelites. Say to them:

24" ' "The LORD bless you
and keep you;
25the LORD make his face shine upon you
and be gracious to you;
26the LORD turn his face toward you
and give you peace." '

[a] 14 Traditionally *peace offering*; also in verses 17 and 18

27"So they will put my name on the Israelites, and I will bless them."

Offerings at the Dedication of the Tabernacle

7 When Moses finished setting up the tabernacle, he anointed it and consecrated it and all its furnishings. He also anointed and consecrated the altar and all its utensils. 2Then the leaders of Israel, the heads of families who were the tribal leaders in charge of those who were counted, made offerings. 3They brought as their gifts before the LORD six covered carts and twelve oxen—an ox from each leader and a cart from every two. These they presented before the tabernacle.

4The LORD said to Moses, 5"Accept these from them, that they may be used in the work at the Tent of Meeting. Give them to the Levites as each man's work requires."

6So Moses took the carts and oxen and gave them to the Levites. 7He gave two carts and four oxen to the Gershonites, as their work required, 8and he gave four carts and eight oxen to the Merarites, as their work required. They were all under the direction of Ithamar son of Aaron, the priest. 9But Moses did not give any to the Kohathites, because they were to carry on their shoulders the holy things, for which they were responsible.

10When the altar was anointed, the leaders brought their offerings for its dedication and presented them before the altar. 11For the LORD had said to Moses, "Each day one leader is to bring his offering for the dedication of the altar."

12The one who brought his offering on the first day was Nahshon son of Amminadab of the tribe of Judah.

13His offering was one silver plate weighing a hundred and thirty shekels,[a] and one silver sprinkling bowl weighing seventy shekels,[b] both according to the sanctuary shekel, each filled with fine flour mixed with oil as a grain offering; 14one gold dish weighing ten shekels,[c] filled with incense; 15one young bull, one ram and one male lamb a year old, for a burnt offering; 16one male goat for a sin offering; 17and two oxen, five rams, five male goats and five male lambs a year old, to be sacrificed as a fellowship offering.[d] This was the offering of Nahshon son of Amminadab.

18On the second day Nethanel son of Zuar, the leader of Issachar, brought his offering.

19The offering he brought was one silver plate weighing a hundred and thirty shekels, and one silver sprinkling bowl weighing seventy shekels, both according to the sanctuary shekel, each filled with fine flour mixed with oil as a grain offering; 20one gold dish weighing ten shekels, filled with incense; 21one young bull, one ram and one male lamb a year old, for a burnt offering; 22one male goat for a sin offering; 23and two oxen, five rams, five male goats and five male lambs a year old, to be sacrificed as a fellowship offering. This was the offering of Nethanel son of Zuar.

24On the third day, Eliab son of Helon, the leader of the people of Zebulun, brought his offering.

25His offering was one silver plate weighing a hundred and thirty shekels, and one silver sprinkling bowl weighing seventy shekels, both according to the sanctuary shekel, each filled with fine flour mixed with oil as a grain offering; 26one gold dish weighing ten shekels, filled with incense; 27one young bull, one ram and one male lamb a year old, for a burnt offering; 28one male goat for a sin offering; 29and two oxen, five rams, five male goats and five male lambs a year old, to be sacrificed as a fellowship offering. This was the offering of Eliab son of Helon.

30On the fourth day Elizur son of Shedeur, the leader of the people of Reuben, brought his offering.

31His offering was one silver plate weighing a hundred and thirty shekels, and one silver sprinkling bowl weighing seventy shekels, both according to the sanctuary shekel, each filled with fine flour mixed with oil as a grain offering; 32one gold dish weighing ten shekels, filled with in-

[a] *13* That is, about 3 1/4 pounds (about 1.5 kilograms); also elsewhere in this chapter [b] *13* That is, about 1 3/4 pounds (about 0.8 kilogram); also elsewhere in this chapter [c] *14* That is, about 4 ounces (about 110 grams); also elsewhere in this chapter [d] *17* Traditionally *peace offering*; also elsewhere in this chapter

cense; 33one young bull, one ram and
one male lamb a year old, for a burnt
offering; 34one male goat for a sin of-
fering; 35and two oxen, five rams, five
male goats and five male lambs a year
old, to be sacrificed as a fellowship
offering. This was the offering of Eli-
zur son of Shedeur.

36On the fifth day Shelumiel son of Zuri-
shaddai, the leader of the people of Sime-
on, brought his offering.
37His offering was one silver plate
weighing a hundred and thirty shek-
els, and one silver sprinkling bowl
weighing seventy shekels, both ac-
cording to the sanctuary shekel, each
filled with fine flour mixed with oil as
a grain offering; 38one gold dish
weighing ten shekels, filled with in-
cense; 39one young bull, one ram and
one male lamb a year old, for a burnt
offering; 40one male goat for a sin of-
fering; 41and two oxen, five rams, five
male goats and five male lambs a year
old, to be sacrificed as a fellowship
offering. This was the offering of She-
lumiel son of Zurishaddai.

42On the sixth day Eliasaph son of Deuel,
the leader of the people of Gad, brought
his offering.
43His offering was one silver plate
weighing a hundred and thirty shek-
els, and one silver sprinkling bowl
weighing seventy shekels, both ac-
cording to the sanctuary shekel, each
filled with fine flour mixed with oil as
a grain offering; 44one gold dish
weighing ten shekels, filled with in-
cense; 45one young bull, one ram and
one male lamb a year old, for a burnt
offering; 46one male goat for a sin of-
fering; 47and two oxen, five rams, five
male goats and five male lambs a year
old, to be sacrificed as a fellowship
offering. This was the offering of Elia-
saph son of Deuel.

48On the seventh day Elishama son of Am-
mihud, the leader of the people of Ephra-
im, brought his offering.
49His offering was one silver plate
weighing a hundred and thirty shek-
els, and one silver sprinkling bowl
weighing seventy shekels, both ac-
cording to the sanctuary shekel, each
filled with fine flour mixed with oil as
a grain offering; 50one gold dish
weighing ten shekels, filled with in-
cense; 51one young bull, one ram and
one male lamb a year old, for a burnt
offering; 52one male goat for a sin of-
fering; 53and two oxen, five rams, five
male goats and five male lambs a year
old, to be sacrificed as a fellowship
offering. This was the offering of
Elishama son of Ammihud.

54On the eighth day Gamaliel son of Pe-
dahzur, the leader of the people of Manas-
seh, brought his offering.
55His offering was one silver plate
weighing a hundred and thirty shek-
els, and one silver sprinkling bowl
weighing seventy shekels, both ac-
cording to the sanctuary shekel, each
filled with fine flour mixed with oil as
a grain offering; 56one gold dish
weighing ten shekels, filled with in-
cense; 57one young bull, one ram and
one male lamb a year old, for a burnt
offering; 58one male goat for a sin of-
fering; 59and two oxen, five rams, five
male goats and five male lambs a year
old, to be sacrificed as a fellowship
offering. This was the offering of Ga-
maliel son of Pedahzur.

60On the ninth day Abidan son of Gideoni,
the leader of the people of Benjamin,
brought his offering.
61His offering was one silver plate
weighing a hundred and thirty shek-
els, and one silver sprinkling bowl
weighing seventy shekels, both ac-
cording to the sanctuary shekel, each
filled with fine flour mixed with oil as
a grain offering; 62one gold dish
weighing ten shekels, filled with in-
cense; 63one young bull, one ram and
one male lamb a year old, for a burnt
offering; 64one male goat for a sin of-
fering; 65and two oxen, five rams, five
male goats and five male lambs a year
old, to be sacrificed as a fellowship
offering. This was the offering of Abi-
dan son of Gideoni.

66On the tenth day Ahiezer son of Ammi-
shaddai, the leader of the people of Dan,
brought his offering.
67His offering was one silver plate
weighing a hundred and thirty shek-
els, and one silver sprinkling bowl
weighing seventy shekels, both ac-
cording to the sanctuary shekel, each
filled with fine flour mixed with oil as
a grain offering; 68one gold dish
weighing ten shekels, filled with in-

cense; 69one young bull, one ram and
one male lamb a year old, for a burnt
offering; 70one male goat for a sin of-
fering; 71and two oxen, five rams, five
male goats and five male lambs a year
old, to be sacrificed as a fellowship
offering. This was the offering of Ahi-
ezer son of Ammishaddai.

72On the eleventh day Pagiel son of Ocran,
the leader of the people of Asher, brought
his offering.
73His offering was one silver plate
weighing a hundred and thirty shek-
els, and one silver sprinkling bowl
weighing seventy shekels, both ac-
cording to the sanctuary shekel, each
filled with fine flour mixed with oil as
a grain offering; 74one gold dish
weighing ten shekels, filled with in-
cense; 75one young bull, one ram and
one male lamb a year old, for a burnt
offering; 76one male goat for a sin of-
fering; 77and two oxen, five rams, five
male goats and five male lambs a year
old, to be sacrificed as a fellowship
offering. This was the offering of Pa-
giel son of Ocran.

78On the twelfth day Ahira son of Enan,
the leader of the people of Naphtali,
brought his offering.
79His offering was one silver plate
weighing a hundred and thirty shek-
els, and one silver sprinkling bowl
weighing seventy shekels, both ac-
cording to the sanctuary shekel, each
filled with fine flour mixed with oil as
a grain offering; 80one gold dish
weighing ten shekels, filled with in-
cense; 81one young bull, one ram and
one male lamb a year old, for a burnt
offering; 82one male goat for a sin of-
fering; 83and two oxen, five rams, five
male goats and five male lambs a year
old, to be sacrificed as a fellowship
offering. This was the offering of Ahi-
ra son of Enan.

84These were the offerings of the Israel-
ite leaders for the dedication of the altar
when it was anointed: twelve silver plates,
twelve silver sprinkling bowls and twelve
gold dishes. 85Each silver plate weighed a
hundred and thirty shekels, and each
sprinkling bowl seventy shekels. Alto-
gether, the silver dishes weighed two
thousand four hundred shekels,[a] accord-
ing to the sanctuary shekel. 86The twelve
gold dishes filled with incense weighed
ten shekels each, according to the sanctu-
ary shekel. Altogether, the gold dishes
weighed a hundred and twenty shekels.[b]
87The total number of animals for the
burnt offering came to twelve young bulls,
twelve rams and twelve male lambs a year
old, together with their grain offering.
Twelve male goats were used for the sin
offering. 88The total number of animals
for the sacrifice of the fellowship offering
came to twenty-four oxen, sixty rams, six-
ty male goats and sixty male lambs a year
old. These were the offerings for the ded-
ication of the altar after it was anointed.

89When Moses entered the Tent of
Meeting to speak with the LORD, he heard
the voice speaking to him from between
the two cherubim above the atonement
cover on the ark of the Testimony. And he
spoke with him.

Setting Up the Lamps

8 The LORD said to Moses, 2"Speak to
Aaron and say to him, 'When you set
up the seven lamps, they are to light the
area in front of the lampstand.' "

3Aaron did so; he set up the lamps so
that they faced forward on the lampstand,
just as the LORD commanded Moses. 4This
is how the lampstand was made: It was
made of hammered gold—from its base to
its blossoms. The lampstand was made
exactly like the pattern the LORD had
shown Moses.

The Setting Apart of the Levites

5The LORD said to Moses: 6"Take the Le-
vites from among the other Israelites and
make them ceremonially clean. 7To purify
them, do this: Sprinkle the water of
cleansing on them; then have them shave
their whole bodies and wash their clothes,
and so purify themselves. 8Have them
take a young bull with its grain offering of
fine flour mixed with oil; then you are to
take a second young bull for a sin offering.
9Bring the Levites to the front of the Tent
of Meeting and assemble the whole Israel-
ite community. 10You are to bring the Le-
vites before the LORD, and the Israelites
are to lay their hands on them. 11Aaron is
to present the Levites before the LORD as
a wave offering from the Israelites, so that
they may be ready to do the work of the
LORD.

[a] *85* That is, about 60 pounds (about 28 kilograms)

[b] *86* That is, about 3 pounds (about 1.4 kilograms)

12"After the Levites lay their hands on
the heads of the bulls, use the one for a sin
offering to the LORD and the other for a
burnt offering, to make atonement for the
Levites. 13Have the Levites stand in front
of Aaron and his sons and then present
them as a wave offering to the LORD. 14In
this way you are to set the Levites apart
from the other Israelites, and the Levites
will be mine.

15"After you have purified the Levites
and presented them as a wave offering,
they are to come to do their work at the
Tent of Meeting. 16They are the Israelites
who are to be given wholly to me. I have
taken them as my own in place of the first-
born, the first male offspring from every
Israelite woman. 17Every firstborn male in
Israel, whether man or animal, is mine.
When I struck down all the firstborn in
Egypt, I set them apart for myself. 18And
I have taken the Levites in place of all the
firstborn sons in Israel. 19Of all the Israel-
ites, I have given the Levites as gifts to
Aaron and his sons to do the work at the
Tent of Meeting on behalf of the Israelites
and to make atonement for them so that
no plague will strike the Israelites when
they go near the sanctuary."

20Moses, Aaron and the whole Israelite
community did with the Levites just as the
LORD commanded Moses. 21The Levites
purified themselves and washed their
clothes. Then Aaron presented them as a
wave offering before the LORD and made
atonement for them to purify them. 22After
that, the Levites came to do their work
at the Tent of Meeting under the supervi-
sion of Aaron and his sons. They did with
the Levites just as the LORD commanded
Moses.

23The LORD said to Moses, 24"This ap-
plies to the Levites: Men twenty-five years
old or more shall come to take part in the
work at the Tent of Meeting, 25but at the
age of fifty, they must retire from their
regular service and work no longer.
26They may assist their brothers in per-
forming their duties at the Tent of Meet-
ing, but they themselves must not do the
work. This, then, is how you are to assign
the responsibilities of the Levites."

The Passover

9 The LORD spoke to Moses in the
Desert of Sinai in the first month of
the second year after they came out of
Egypt. He said, 2"Have the Israelites cele-
brate the Passover at the appointed time.
3Celebrate it at the appointed time, at twi-
light on the fourteenth day of this month,
in accordance with all its rules and regula-
tions."

4So Moses told the Israelites to cele-
brate the Passover, 5and they did so in the
Desert of Sinai at twilight on the four-
teenth day of the first month. The Israel-
ites did everything just as the LORD com-
manded Moses.

6But some of them could not celebrate
the Passover on that day because they
were ceremonially unclean on account of
a dead body. So they came to Moses and
Aaron that same day 7and said to Moses,
"We have become unclean because of a
dead body, but why should we be kept
from presenting the LORD's offering with
the other Israelites at the appointed time?"

8Moses answered them, "Wait until I
find out what the LORD commands con-
cerning you."

9Then the LORD said to Moses, 10"Tell
the Israelites: 'When any of you or your
descendants are unclean because of a
dead body or are away on a journey, they
may still celebrate the LORD's Passover.
11They are to celebrate it on the four-
teenth day of the second month at twi-
light. They are to eat the lamb, together
with unleavened bread and bitter herbs.
12They must not leave any of it till morn-
ing or break any of its bones. When they
celebrate the Passover, they must follow
all the regulations. 13But if a man who is
ceremonially clean and not on a journey
fails to celebrate the Passover, that person
must be cut off from his people because
he did not present the LORD's offering at
the appointed time. That man will bear
the consequences of his sin.

14" 'An alien living among you who
wants to celebrate the LORD's Passover
must do so in accordance with its rules
and regulations. You must have the same
regulations for the alien and the native-
born.' "

The Cloud Above the Tabernacle

15On the day the tabernacle, the Tent of
the Testimony, was set up, the cloud cov-
ered it. From evening till morning the
cloud above the tabernacle looked like
fire. 16That is how it continued to be; the
cloud covered it, and at night it looked
like fire. 17Whenever the cloud lifted from
above the Tent, the Israelites set out;
wherever the cloud settled, the Israelites
encamped. 18At the LORD's command the

Israelites set out, and at his command they encamped. As long as the cloud stayed over the tabernacle, they remained in camp. 19When the cloud remained over the tabernacle a long time, the Israelites obeyed the LORD's order and did not set out. 20Sometimes the cloud was over the tabernacle only a few days; at the LORD's command they would encamp, and then at his command they would set out. 21Sometimes the cloud stayed only from evening till morning, and when it lifted in the morning, they set out. Whether by day or by night, whenever the cloud lifted, they set out. 22Whether the cloud stayed over the tabernacle for two days or a month or a year, the Israelites would remain in camp and not set out; but when it lifted, they would set out. 23At the LORD's command they encamped, and at the LORD's command they set out. They obeyed the LORD's order, in accordance with his command through Moses.

The Silver Trumpets

10 The LORD said to Moses: 2"Make two trumpets of hammered silver, and use them for calling the community together and for having the camps set out. 3When both are sounded, the whole community is to assemble before you at the entrance to the Tent of Meeting. 4If only one is sounded, the leaders—the heads of the clans of Israel—are to assemble before you. 5When a trumpet blast is sounded, the tribes camping on the east are to set out. 6At the sounding of a second blast, the camps on the south are to set out. The blast will be the signal for setting out. 7To gather the assembly, blow the trumpets, but not with the same signal.

8"The sons of Aaron, the priests, are to blow the trumpets. This is to be a lasting ordinance for you and the generations to come. 9When you go into battle in your own land against an enemy who is oppressing you, sound a blast on the trumpets. Then you will be remembered by the LORD your God and rescued from your enemies. 10Also at your times of rejoicing—your appointed feasts and New Moon festivals—you are to sound the trumpets over your burnt offerings and fellowship offerings,[a] and they will be a memorial for you before your God. I am the LORD your God."

The Israelites Leave Sinai

11On the twentieth day of the second month of the second year, the cloud lifted from above the tabernacle of the Testimony. 12Then the Israelites set out from the Desert of Sinai and traveled from place to place until the cloud came to rest in the Desert of Paran. 13They set out, this first time, at the LORD's command through Moses.

14The divisions of the camp of Judah went first, under their standard. Nahshon son of Amminadab was in command. 15Nethanel son of Zuar was over the division of the tribe of Issachar, 16and Eliab son of Helon was over the division of the tribe of Zebulun. 17Then the tabernacle was taken down, and the Gershonites and Merarites, who carried it, set out.

18The divisions of the camp of Reuben went next, under their standard. Elizur son of Shedeur was in command. 19Shelumiel son of Zurishaddai was over the division of the tribe of Simeon, 20and Eliasaph son of Deuel was over the division of the tribe of Gad. 21Then the Kohathites set out, carrying the holy things. The tabernacle was to be set up before they arrived.

22The divisions of the camp of Ephraim went next, under their standard. Elishama son of Ammihud was in command. 23Gamaliel son of Pedahzur was over the division of the tribe of Manasseh, 24and Abidan son of Gideoni was over the division of the tribe of Benjamin.

25Finally, as the rear guard for all the units, the divisions of the camp of Dan set out, under their standard. Ahiezer son of Ammishaddai was in command. 26Pagiel son of Ocran was over the division of the tribe of Asher, 27and Ahira son of Enan was over the division of the tribe of Naphtali. 28This was the order of march for the Israelite divisions as they set out.

29Now Moses said to Hobab son of Reuel the Midianite, Moses' father-in-law, "We are setting out for the place about which the LORD said, 'I will give it to you.' Come with us and we will treat you well, for the LORD has promised good things to Israel."

30He answered, "No, I will not go; I am going back to my own land and my own people."

31But Moses said, "Please do not leave us. You know where we should camp in

[a] 10 Traditionally *peace offerings*

the desert, and you can be our eyes. 32If
you come with us, we will share with you
whatever good things the LORD gives us."
33So they set out from the mountain of
the LORD and traveled for three days. The
ark of the covenant of the LORD went be-
fore them during those three days to find
them a place to rest. 34The cloud of the
LORD was over them by day when they set
out from the camp.
35Whenever the ark set out, Moses said,

"Rise up, O LORD!
May your enemies be scattered;
may your foes flee before you."

36Whenever it came to rest, he said,

"Return, O LORD,
to the countless thousands of
Israel."

Fire From the LORD

11 Now the people complained about
their hardships in the hearing of
the LORD, and when he heard them his an-
ger was aroused. Then fire from the LORD
burned among them and consumed some
of the outskirts of the camp. 2When the
people cried out to Moses, he prayed to
the LORD and the fire died down. 3So that
place was called Taberah,[a] because fire
from the LORD had burned among them.

Quail From the LORD

4The rabble with them began to crave
other food, and again the Israelites started
wailing and said, "If only we had meat to
eat! 5We remember the fish we ate in
Egypt at no cost—also the cucumbers,
melons, leeks, onions and garlic. 6But
now we have lost our appetite; we never
see anything but this manna!"
7The manna was like coriander seed
and looked like resin. 8The people went
around gathering it, and then ground it in
a handmill or crushed it in a mortar. They
cooked it in a pot or made it into cakes.
And it tasted like something made with ol-
ive oil. 9When the dew settled on the
camp at night, the manna also came
down.
10Moses heard the people of every fami-
ly wailing, each at the entrance to his tent.
The LORD became exceedingly angry, and
Moses was troubled. 11He asked the LORD,
"Why have you brought this trouble on
your servant? What have I done to dis-
please you that you put the burden of all
these people on me? 12Did I conceive all
these people? Did I give them birth? Why
do you tell me to carry them in my arms,
as a nurse carries an infant, to the land
you promised on oath to their forefathers?
13Where can I get meat for all these peo-
ple? They keep wailing to me, 'Give us
meat to eat!' 14I cannot carry all these peo-
ple by myself; the burden is too heavy for
me. 15If this is how you are going to treat
me, put me to death right now—if I have
found favor in your eyes—and do not let
me face my own ruin."
16The LORD said to Moses: "Bring me
seventy of Israel's elders who are known
to you as leaders and officials among the
people. Have them come to the Tent of
Meeting, that they may stand there with
you. 17I will come down and speak with
you there, and I will take of the Spirit that
is on you and put the Spirit on them. They
will help you carry the burden of the peo-
ple so that you will not have to carry it
alone.
18"Tell the people: 'Consecrate your-
selves in preparation for tomorrow, when
you will eat meat. The LORD heard you
when you wailed, "If only we had meat to
eat! We were better off in Egypt!" Now the
LORD will give you meat, and you will eat
it. 19You will not eat it for just one day, or
two days, or five, ten or twenty days, 20but
for a whole month—until it comes out of
your nostrils and you loathe it—because
you have rejected the LORD, who is among
you, and have wailed before him, saying,
"Why did we ever leave Egypt?" ' "
21But Moses said, "Here I am among six
hundred thousand men on foot, and you
say, 'I will give them meat to eat for a
whole month!' 22Would they have enough
if flocks and herds were slaughtered for
them? Would they have enough if all the
fish in the sea were caught for them?"
23The LORD answered Moses, "Is the
LORD's arm too short? You will now see
whether or not what I say will come true
for you."
24So Moses went out and told the peo-
ple what the LORD had said. He brought
together seventy of their elders and had
them stand around the Tent. 25Then the
LORD came down in the cloud and spoke
with him, and he took of the Spirit that
was on him and put the Spirit on the sev-
enty elders. When the Spirit rested on

[a]3 *Taberah* means *burning*.

them, they prophesied, but they did not do so again.[a]

26However, two men, whose names were Eldad and Medad, had remained in the camp. They were listed among the elders, but did not go out to the Tent. Yet the Spirit also rested on them, and they prophesied in the camp. 27A young man ran and told Moses, "Eldad and Medad are prophesying in the camp."

28Joshua son of Nun, who had been Moses' aide since youth, spoke up and said, "Moses, my lord, stop them!"

29But Moses replied, "Are you jealous for my sake? I wish that all the LORD's people were prophets and that the LORD would put his Spirit on them!" 30Then Moses and the elders of Israel returned to the camp.

31Now a wind went out from the LORD and drove quail in from the sea. It brought them[b] down all around the camp to about three feet[c] above the ground, as far as a day's walk in any direction. 32All that day and night and all the next day the people went out and gathered quail. No one gathered less than ten homers.[d] Then they spread them out all around the camp. 33But while the meat was still between their teeth and before it could be consumed, the anger of the LORD burned against the people, and he struck them with a severe plague. 34Therefore the place was named Kibroth Hattaavah,[e] because there they buried the people who had craved other food.

35From Kibroth Hattaavah the people traveled to Hazeroth and stayed there.

Miriam and Aaron Oppose Moses

12 Miriam and Aaron began to talk against Moses because of his Cushite wife, for he had married a Cushite. 2"Has the LORD spoken only through Moses?" they asked. "Hasn't he also spoken through us?" And the LORD heard this.

3(Now Moses was a very humble man, more humble than anyone else on the face of the earth.)

4At once the LORD said to Moses, Aaron and Miriam, "Come out to the Tent of Meeting, all three of you." So the three of them came out. 5Then the LORD came down in a pillar of cloud; he stood at the entrance to the Tent and summoned Aaron and Miriam. When both of them stepped forward, 6he said, "Listen to my words:

"When a prophet of the LORD is
among you,
I reveal myself to him in visions,
I speak to him in dreams.
7But this is not true of my servant
Moses;
he is faithful in all my house.
8With him I speak face to face,
clearly and not in riddles;
he sees the form of the LORD.
Why then were you not afraid
to speak against my servant Moses?"

9The anger of the LORD burned against them, and he left them.

10When the cloud lifted from above the Tent, there stood Miriam—leprous,[f] like snow. Aaron turned toward her and saw that she had leprosy; 11and he said to Moses, "Please, my lord, do not hold against us the sin we have so foolishly committed. 12Do not let her be like a stillborn infant coming from its mother's womb with its flesh half eaten away."

13So Moses cried out to the LORD, "O God, please heal her!"

14The LORD replied to Moses, "If her father had spit in her face, would she not have been in disgrace for seven days? Confine her outside the camp for seven days; after that she can be brought back." 15So Miriam was confined outside the camp for seven days, and the people did not move on till she was brought back.

16After that, the people left Hazeroth and encamped in the Desert of Paran.

Exploring Canaan

13 The LORD said to Moses, 2"Send some men to explore the land of Canaan, which I am giving to the Israelites. From each ancestral tribe send one of its leaders."

3So at the LORD's command Moses sent them out from the Desert of Paran. All of them were leaders of the Israelites. 4These are their names:

[a] *25* Or *prophesied and continued to do so* [b] *31* Or *They flew* [c] *31* Hebrew *two cubits* (about 1 meter) [d] *32* That is, probably about 60 bushels (about 2.2 kiloliters) [e] *34* *Kibroth Hattaavah* means *graves of craving.* [f] *10* The Hebrew word was used for various diseases affecting the skin—not necessarily leprosy.

from the tribe of Reuben, Shammua
son of Zaccur;
5from the tribe of Simeon, Shaphat
son of Hori;
6from the tribe of Judah, Caleb son of
Jephunneh;
7from the tribe of Issachar, Igal son of
Joseph;
8from the tribe of Ephraim, Hoshea
son of Nun;
9from the tribe of Benjamin, Palti son
of Raphu;
10from the tribe of Zebulun, Gaddiel
son of Sodi;
11from the tribe of Manasseh (a tribe
of Joseph), Gaddi son of Susi;
12from the tribe of Dan, Ammiel son of
Gemalli;
13from the tribe of Asher, Sethur son
of Michael;
14from the tribe of Naphtali, Nahbi son
of Vophsi;
15from the tribe of Gad, Geuel son of
Maki.

16These are the names of the men Moses sent to explore the land. (Moses gave Hoshea son of Nun the name Joshua.)

17When Moses sent them to explore Canaan, he said, "Go up through the Negev and on into the hill country. 18See what the land is like and whether the people who live there are strong or weak, few or many. 19What kind of land do they live in? Is it good or bad? What kind of towns do they live in? Are they unwalled or fortified? 20How is the soil? Is it fertile or poor? Are there trees on it or not? Do your best to bring back some of the fruit of the land." (It was the season for the first ripe grapes.)

21So they went up and explored the land from the Desert of Zin as far as Rehob, toward Lebo[a] Hamath. 22They went up through the Negev and came to Hebron, where Ahiman, Sheshai and Talmai, the descendants of Anak, lived. (Hebron had been built seven years before Zoan in Egypt.) 23When they reached the Valley of Eshcol,[b] they cut off a branch bearing a single cluster of grapes. Two of them carried it on a pole between them, along with some pomegranates and figs. 24That place was called the Valley of Eshcol because of the cluster of grapes the Israelites cut off there. 25At the end of forty days they returned from exploring the land.

Report on the Exploration

26They came back to Moses and Aaron and the whole Israelite community at Kadesh in the Desert of Paran. There they reported to them and to the whole assembly and showed them the fruit of the land. 27They gave Moses this account: "We went into the land to which you sent us, and it does flow with milk and honey! Here is its fruit. 28But the people who live there are powerful, and the cities are fortified and very large. We even saw descendants of Anak there. 29The Amalekites live in the Negev; the Hittites, Jebusites and Amorites live in the hill country; and the Canaanites live near the sea and along the Jordan."

30Then Caleb silenced the people before Moses and said, "We should go up and take possession of the land, for we can certainly do it."

31But the men who had gone up with him said, "We can't attack those people; they are stronger than we are." 32And they spread among the Israelites a bad report about the land they had explored. They said, "The land we explored devours those living in it. All the people we saw there are of great size. 33We saw the Nephilim there (the descendants of Anak come from the Nephilim). We seemed like grasshoppers in our own eyes, and we looked the same to them."

The People Rebel

14 That night all the people of the community raised their voices and wept aloud. 2All the Israelites grumbled against Moses and Aaron, and the whole assembly said to them, "If only we had died in Egypt! Or in this desert! 3Why is the LORD bringing us to this land only to let us fall by the sword? Our wives and children will be taken as plunder. Wouldn't it be better for us to go back to Egypt?" 4And they said to each other, "We should choose a leader and go back to Egypt."

5Then Moses and Aaron fell facedown in front of the whole Israelite assembly gathered there. 6Joshua son of Nun and Caleb son of Jephunneh, who were among those who had explored the land, tore their clothes 7and said to the entire Israelite assembly, "The land we passed through and explored is exceedingly

[a]21 Or *toward the entrance to*

[b]23 *Eshcol* means *cluster*; also in verse 24.

good. 8If the LORD is pleased with us, he
will lead us into that land, a land flowing
with milk and honey, and will give it to us.
9Only do not rebel against the LORD. And
do not be afraid of the people of the land,
because we will swallow them up. Their
protection is gone, but the LORD is with us.
Do not be afraid of them."

10But the whole assembly talked about
stoning them. Then the glory of the LORD
appeared at the Tent of Meeting to all the
Israelites. 11The LORD said to Moses, "How
long will these people treat me with con-
tempt? How long will they refuse to be-
lieve in me, in spite of all the miraculous
signs I have performed among them? 12I
will strike them down with a plague and
destroy them, but I will make you into a
nation greater and stronger than they."

13Moses said to the LORD, "Then the
Egyptians will hear about it! By your pow-
er you brought these people up from
among them. 14And they will tell the in-
habitants of this land about it. They have
already heard that you, O LORD, are with
these people and that you, O LORD, have
been seen face to face, that your cloud
stays over them, and that you go before
them in a pillar of cloud by day and a pil-
lar of fire by night. 15If you put these peo-
ple to death all at one time, the nations
who have heard this report about you will
say, 16'The LORD was not able to bring
these people into the land he promised
them on oath; so he slaughtered them in
the desert.'

17"Now may the Lord's strength be dis-
played, just as you have declared: 18'The
LORD is slow to anger, abounding in love
and forgiving sin and rebellion. Yet he
does not leave the guilty unpunished; he
punishes the children for the sin of the fa-
thers to the third and fourth generation.'
19In accordance with your great love, for-
give the sin of these people, just as you
have pardoned them from the time they
left Egypt until now."

20The LORD replied, "I have forgiven
them, as you asked. 21Nevertheless, as
surely as I live and as surely as the glory
of the LORD fills the whole earth, 22not one
of the men who saw my glory and the mi-
raculous signs I performed in Egypt and in
the desert but who disobeyed me and test-
ed me ten times— 23not one of them will
ever see the land I promised on oath to
their forefathers. No one who has treated
me with contempt will ever see it. 24But
because my servant Caleb has a different
spirit and follows me wholeheartedly, I
will bring him into the land he went to,
and his descendants will inherit it. 25Since
the Amalekites and Canaanites are living
in the valleys, turn back tomorrow and set
out toward the desert along the route to
the Red Sea.[a]"

26The LORD said to Moses and Aaron:
27"How long will this wicked community
grumble against me? I have heard the
complaints of these grumbling Israelites.
28So tell them, 'As surely as I live, declares
the LORD, I will do to you the very things
I heard you say: 29In this desert your bod-
ies will fall—every one of you twenty
years old or more who was counted in the
census and who has grumbled against me.
30Not one of you will enter the land I
swore with uplifted hand to make your
home, except Caleb son of Jephunneh and
Joshua son of Nun. 31As for your children
that you said would be taken as plunder,
I will bring them in to enjoy the land you
have rejected. 32But you—your bodies
will fall in this desert. 33Your children will
be shepherds here for forty years, suffer-
ing for your unfaithfulness, until the last
of your bodies lies in the desert. 34For for-
ty years—one year for each of the forty
days you explored the land—you will suf-
fer for your sins and know what it is like
to have me against you.' 35I, the LORD,
have spoken, and I will surely do these
things to this whole wicked community,
which has banded together against me.
They will meet their end in this desert;
here they will die."

36So the men Moses had sent to explore
the land, who returned and made the
whole community grumble against him
by spreading a bad report about it—
37these men responsible for spreading the
bad report about the land were struck
down and died of a plague before the
LORD. 38Of the men who went to explore
the land, only Joshua son of Nun and Ca-
leb son of Jephunneh survived.

39When Moses reported this to all the
Israelites, they mourned bitterly. 40Early
the next morning they went up toward the
high hill country. "We have sinned," they
said. "We will go up to the place the LORD
promised."

41But Moses said, "Why are you dis-
obeying the LORD's command? This will

[a]25 Hebrew *Yam Suph*; that is, Sea of Reeds

not succeed! 42Do not go up, because the
LORD is not with you. You will be defeated
by your enemies, 43for the Amalekites and
Canaanites will face you there. Because
you have turned away from the LORD, he
will not be with you and you will fall by
the sword."

44Nevertheless, in their presumption
they went up toward the high hill country,
though neither Moses nor the ark of the
LORD's covenant moved from the camp.
45Then the Amalekites and Canaanites
who lived in that hill country came down
and attacked them and beat them down
all the way to Hormah.

Supplementary Offerings

15 The LORD said to Moses, 2"Speak to
the Israelites and say to them: 'After
you enter the land I am giving you as
a home 3and you present to the LORD of-
ferings made by fire, from the herd or the
flock, as an aroma pleasing to the LORD—
whether burnt offerings or sacrifices, for

FRIDAY

VERSE FOR THE DAY: Numbers 14:18

AUTHOR: Scott M. Stanley

PASSAGE FOR THE DAY: Numbers 14:17–20

Slow to Anger

When someone criticizes you, your first impulse is to defend yourself. While turning the tables on your "attacker" is natural, it's potentially lethal to your marriage. That's how everyday events—like not getting household chores done—quickly turn into major blow-ups.

When you notice a disagreement is escalating, call an immediate cease-fire. Then agree on a specific time when you can resume the discussion. When you sit down later to talk, use a small object, such as a pen, to indicate whom the speaker is. The person holding the pen is the speaker. When the pen changes hands, the roles change. The speaker's job is to get his or her point across. The listener's job is to listen carefully and give feedback by paraphrasing what his or her mate has just said.

While this approach feels somewhat artificial, it greatly enhances communication by slowing things down and emphasizing listening and working together. It helps you to be "quick to hear, slow to speak and slow to become angry." Using a simple technique helps you avoid doing what comes naturally and choose to do what's good for your marriage.

MARRIAGE BUILDERS

- *When you get angry, do your arguments quickly get out of hand? How can you put a stop to that pattern?*
- *Try a pen-passing conversation on a nonthreatening topic.*

Additional Scripture Readings
Psalm 145:8-10; Jonah 4:2

Go to page 159 for your next devotional reading.

special vows or freewill offerings or festival offerings— 4then the one who brings his offering shall present to the LORD a grain offering of a tenth of an ephah[a] of fine flour mixed with a quarter of a hin[b] of oil. 5With each lamb for the burnt offering or the sacrifice, prepare a quarter of a hin of wine as a drink offering.

6" 'With a ram prepare a grain offering of two-tenths of an ephah[c] of fine flour mixed with a third of a hin[d] of oil, 7and a third of a hin of wine as a drink offering. Offer it as an aroma pleasing to the LORD.

8" 'When you prepare a young bull as a burnt offering or sacrifice, for a special vow or a fellowship offering[e] to the LORD, 9bring with the bull a grain offering of three-tenths of an ephah[f] of fine flour mixed with half a hin[g] of oil. 10Also bring half a hin of wine as a drink offering. It will be an offering made by fire, an aroma pleasing to the LORD. 11Each bull or ram, each lamb or young goat, is to be prepared in this manner. 12Do this for each one, for as many as you prepare.

13" 'Everyone who is native-born must do these things in this way when he brings an offering made by fire as an aroma pleasing to the LORD. 14For the generations to come, whenever an alien or anyone else living among you presents an offering made by fire as an aroma pleasing to the LORD, he must do exactly as you do. 15The community is to have the same rules for you and for the alien living among you; this is a lasting ordinance for the generations to come. You and the alien shall be the same before the LORD: 16The same laws and regulations will apply both to you and to the alien living among you.' "

17The LORD said to Moses, 18"Speak to the Israelites and say to them: 'When you enter the land to which I am taking you 19and you eat the food of the land, present a portion as an offering to the LORD. 20Present a cake from the first of your ground meal and present it as an offering from the threshing floor. 21Throughout the generations to come you are to give this offering to the LORD from the first of your ground meal.

Offerings for Unintentional Sins

22" 'Now if you unintentionally fail to keep any of these commands the LORD gave Moses— 23any of the LORD's commands to you through him, from the day the LORD gave them and continuing through the generations to come— 24and if this is done unintentionally without the community being aware of it, then the whole community is to offer a young bull for a burnt offering as an aroma pleasing to the LORD, along with its prescribed grain offering and drink offering, and a male goat for a sin offering. 25The priest is to make atonement for the whole Israelite community, and they will be forgiven, for it was not intentional and they have brought to the LORD for their wrong an offering made by fire and a sin offering. 26The whole Israelite community and the aliens living among them will be forgiven, because all the people were involved in the unintentional wrong.

27" 'But if just one person sins unintentionally, he must bring a year-old female goat for a sin offering. 28The priest is to make atonement before the LORD for the one who erred by sinning unintentionally, and when atonement has been made for him, he will be forgiven. 29One and the same law applies to everyone who sins unintentionally, whether he is a native-born Israelite or an alien.

30" 'But anyone who sins defiantly, whether native-born or alien, blasphemes the LORD, and that person must be cut off from his people. 31Because he has despised the LORD's word and broken his commands, that person must surely be cut off; his guilt remains on him.' "

The Sabbath-Breaker Put to Death

32While the Israelites were in the desert, a man was found gathering wood on the Sabbath day. 33Those who found him gathering wood brought him to Moses and Aaron and the whole assembly, 34and they kept him in custody, because it was not clear what should be done to him. 35Then the LORD said to Moses, "The man must die. The whole assembly must stone him outside the camp." 36So the assembly took him outside the camp and stoned

[a] 4 That is, probably about 2 quarts (about 2 liters) [b] 4 That is, probably about 1 quart (about 1 liter); also in verse 5 [c] 6 That is, probably about 4 quarts (about 4.5 liters) [d] 6 That is, probably about 1 1/4 quarts (about 1.2 liters); also in verse 7 [e] 8 Traditionally *peace offering* [f] 9 That is, probably about 6 quarts (about 6.5 liters) [g] 9 That is, probably about 2 quarts (about 2 liters); also in verse 10

him to death, as the LORD commanded Moses.

Tassels on Garments

37The LORD said to Moses, 38"Speak to the Israelites and say to them: 'Throughout the generations to come you are to make tassels on the corners of your garments, with a blue cord on each tassel. 39You will have these tassels to look at and so you will remember all the commands of the LORD, that you may obey them and not prostitute yourselves by going after the lusts of your own hearts and eyes. 40Then you will remember to obey all my commands and will be consecrated to your God. 41I am the LORD your God, who brought you out of Egypt to be your God. I am the LORD your God.' "

Korah, Dathan and Abiram

16 Korah son of Izhar, the son of Kohath, the son of Levi, and certain Reubenites—Dathan and Abiram, sons of Eliab, and On son of Peleth—became insolent[a] 2and rose up against Moses. With them were 250 Israelite men, well-known community leaders who had been appointed members of the council. 3They came as a group to oppose Moses and Aaron and said to them, "You have gone too far! The whole community is holy, every one of them, and the LORD is with them. Why then do you set yourselves above the LORD's assembly?"

4When Moses heard this, he fell facedown. 5Then he said to Korah and all his followers: "In the morning the LORD will show who belongs to him and who is holy, and he will have that person come near him. The man he chooses he will cause to come near him. 6You, Korah, and all your followers are to do this: Take censers 7and tomorrow put fire and incense in them before the LORD. The man the LORD chooses will be the one who is holy. You Levites have gone too far!"

8Moses also said to Korah, "Now listen, you Levites! 9Isn't it enough for you that the God of Israel has separated you from the rest of the Israelite community and brought you near himself to do the work at the LORD's tabernacle and to stand before the community and minister to them? 10He has brought you and all your fellow Levites near himself, but now you are trying to get the priesthood too. 11It is against the LORD that you and all your followers have banded together. Who is Aaron that you should grumble against him?"

12Then Moses summoned Dathan and Abiram, the sons of Eliab. But they said, "We will not come! 13Isn't it enough that you have brought us up out of a land flowing with milk and honey to kill us in the desert? And now you also want to lord it over us? 14Moreover, you haven't brought us into a land flowing with milk and honey or given us an inheritance of fields and vineyards. Will you gouge out the eyes of[b] these men? No, we will not come!"

15Then Moses became very angry and said to the LORD, "Do not accept their offering. I have not taken so much as a donkey from them, nor have I wronged any of them."

16Moses said to Korah, "You and all your followers are to appear before the LORD tomorrow—you and they and Aaron. 17Each man is to take his censer and put incense in it—250 censers in all—and present it before the LORD. You and Aaron are to present your censers also." 18So each man took his censer, put fire and incense in it, and stood with Moses and Aaron at the entrance to the Tent of Meeting. 19When Korah had gathered all his followers in opposition to them at the entrance to the Tent of Meeting, the glory of the LORD appeared to the entire assembly. 20The LORD said to Moses and Aaron, 21"Separate yourselves from this assembly so I can put an end to them at once."

22But Moses and Aaron fell facedown and cried out, "O God, God of the spirits of all mankind, will you be angry with the entire assembly when only one man sins?"

23Then the LORD said to Moses, 24"Say to the assembly, 'Move away from the tents of Korah, Dathan and Abiram.' "

25Moses got up and went to Dathan and Abiram, and the elders of Israel followed him. 26He warned the assembly, "Move back from the tents of these wicked men! Do not touch anything belonging to them, or you will be swept away because of all their sins." 27So they moved away from the tents of Korah, Dathan and Abiram. Dathan and Abiram had come out and were standing with their wives, children and little ones at the entrances to their tents.

28Then Moses said, "This is how you

[a] 1 Or *Peleth—took ⌊men⌋* [b] 14 Or *you make slaves of*; or *you deceive*

will know that the LORD has sent me to do
all these things and that it was not my
idea: 29If these men die a natural death
and experience only what usually hap-
pens to men, then the LORD has not sent
me. 30But if the LORD brings about some-
thing totally new, and the earth opens its
mouth and swallows them, with every-
thing that belongs to them, and they go
down alive into the grave,[a] then you will
know that these men have treated the
LORD with contempt."

31As soon as he finished saying all this,
the ground under them split apart 32and
the earth opened its mouth and swal-
lowed them, with their households and all
Korah's men and all their possessions.
33They went down alive into the grave,
with everything they owned; the earth
closed over them, and they perished and
were gone from the community. 34At their
cries, all the Israelites around them fled,
shouting, "The earth is going to swallow
us too!"

35And fire came out from the LORD and
consumed the 250 men who were offering
the incense.

36The LORD said to Moses, 37"Tell Elea-
zar son of Aaron, the priest, to take the
censers out of the smoldering remains
and scatter the coals some distance away,
for the censers are holy— 38the censers of
the men who sinned at the cost of their
lives. Hammer the censers into sheets to
overlay the altar, for they were presented
before the LORD and have become holy.
Let them be a sign to the Israelites."

39So Eleazar the priest collected the
bronze censers brought by those who had
been burned up, and he had them ham-
mered out to overlay the altar, 40as the
LORD directed him through Moses. This
was to remind the Israelites that no one
except a descendant of Aaron should
come to burn incense before the LORD, or
he would become like Korah and his fol-
lowers.

41The next day the whole Israelite com-
munity grumbled against Moses and Aar-
on. "You have killed the LORD's people,"
they said.

42But when the assembly gathered in
opposition to Moses and Aaron and
turned toward the Tent of Meeting, sud-
denly the cloud covered it and the glory of
the LORD appeared. 43Then Moses and
Aaron went to the front of the Tent of
Meeting, 44and the LORD said to Moses,
45"Get away from this assembly so I can
put an end to them at once." And they fell
facedown.

46Then Moses said to Aaron, "Take your
censer and put incense in it, along with
fire from the altar, and hurry to the assem-
bly to make atonement for them. Wrath
has come out from the LORD; the plague
has started." 47So Aaron did as Moses
said, and ran into the midst of the assem-
bly. The plague had already started
among the people, but Aaron offered the
incense and made atonement for them.
48He stood between the living and the
dead, and the plague stopped. 49But
14,700 people died from the plague, in ad-
dition to those who had died because of
Korah. 50Then Aaron returned to Moses at
the entrance to the Tent of Meeting, for
the plague had stopped.

The Budding of Aaron's Staff

17 The LORD said to Moses, 2"Speak to
the Israelites and get twelve staffs
from them, one from the leader of each of
their ancestral tribes. Write the name of
each man on his staff. 3On the staff of Levi
write Aaron's name, for there must be one
staff for the head of each ancestral tribe.
4Place them in the Tent of Meeting in
front of the Testimony, where I meet with
you. 5The staff belonging to the man I
choose will sprout, and I will rid myself of
this constant grumbling against you by
the Israelites."

6So Moses spoke to the Israelites, and
their leaders gave him twelve staffs, one
for the leader of each of their ancestral
tribes, and Aaron's staff was among them.
7Moses placed the staffs before the LORD
in the Tent of the Testimony.

8The next day Moses entered the Tent
of the Testimony and saw that Aaron's
staff, which represented the house of Levi,
had not only sprouted but had budded,
blossomed and produced almonds. 9Then
Moses brought out all the staffs from the
LORD's presence to all the Israelites. They
looked at them, and each man took his
own staff.

10The LORD said to Moses, "Put back
Aaron's staff in front of the Testimony, to
be kept as a sign to the rebellious. This
will put an end to their grumbling against
me, so that they will not die." 11Moses did
just as the LORD commanded him.

[a]30 Hebrew *Sheol*; also in verse 33

12The Israelites said to Moses, "We will
die! We are lost, we are all lost! 13Anyone
who even comes near the tabernacle of
the LORD will die. Are we all going to die?"

Duties of Priests and Levites

18 The LORD said to Aaron, "You, your
sons and your father's family are to
bear the responsibility for offenses against
the sanctuary, and you and your sons
alone are to bear the responsibility for of-
fenses against the priesthood. 2Bring your
fellow Levites from your ancestral tribe to
join you and assist you when you and
your sons minister before the Tent of the
Testimony. 3They are to be responsible to
you and are to perform all the duties of the
Tent, but they must not go near the fur-
nishings of the sanctuary or the altar, or
both they and you will die. 4They are to
join you and be responsible for the care of
the Tent of Meeting—all the work at the
Tent—and no one else may come near
where you are.

5"You are to be responsible for the care
of the sanctuary and the altar, so that
wrath will not fall on the Israelites again.
6I myself have selected your fellow Levites
from among the Israelites as a gift to you,
dedicated to the LORD to do the work at the
Tent of Meeting. 7But only you and your
sons may serve as priests in connection
with everything at the altar and inside the
curtain. I am giving you the service of the
priesthood as a gift. Anyone else who
comes near the sanctuary must be put to
death."

Offerings for Priests and Levites

8Then the LORD said to Aaron, "I myself
have put you in charge of the offerings
presented to me; all the holy offerings the
Israelites give me I give to you and your
sons as your portion and regular share.
9You are to have the part of the most holy
offerings that is kept from the fire. From
all the gifts they bring me as most holy of-
ferings, whether grain or sin or guilt offer-
ings, that part belongs to you and your
sons. 10Eat it as something most holy; ev-
ery male shall eat it. You must regard it as
holy.

11"This also is yours: whatever is set
aside from the gifts of all the wave offer-
ings of the Israelites. I give this to you and
your sons and daughters as your regular
share. Everyone in your household who is
ceremonially clean may eat it.

12"I give you all the finest olive oil and
all the finest new wine and grain they give
the LORD as the firstfruits of their harvest.
13All the land's firstfruits that they bring
to the LORD will be yours. Everyone in
your household who is ceremonially clean
may eat it.

14"Everything in Israel that is devoted[a]
to the LORD is yours. 15The first offspring
of every womb, both man and animal, that
is offered to the LORD is yours. But you
must redeem every firstborn son and ev-
ery firstborn male of unclean animals.
16When they are a month old, you must
redeem them at the redemption price set
at five shekels[b] of silver, according to the
sanctuary shekel, which weighs twenty
gerahs.

17"But you must not redeem the first-
born of an ox, a sheep or a goat; they are
holy. Sprinkle their blood on the altar and
burn their fat as an offering made by fire,
an aroma pleasing to the LORD. 18Their
meat is to be yours, just as the breast of
the wave offering and the right thigh are
yours. 19Whatever is set aside from the
holy offerings the Israelites present to the
LORD I give to you and your sons and
daughters as your regular share. It is an
everlasting covenant of salt before the
LORD for both you and your offspring."

20The LORD said to Aaron, "You will
have no inheritance in their land, nor will
you have any share among them; I am
your share and your inheritance among
the Israelites.

21"I give to the Levites all the tithes in
Israel as their inheritance in return for the
work they do while serving at the Tent of
Meeting. 22From now on the Israelites
must not go near the Tent of Meeting, or
they will bear the consequences of their
sin and will die. 23It is the Levites who are
to do the work at the Tent of Meeting and
bear the responsibility for offenses against
it. This is a lasting ordinance for the gen-
erations to come. They will receive no in-
heritance among the Israelites. 24Instead,
I give to the Levites as their inheritance
the tithes that the Israelites present as an
offering to the LORD. That is why I said
concerning them: 'They will have no in-
heritance among the Israelites.' "

25The LORD said to Moses, 26"Speak to

[a]14 The Hebrew term refers to the irrevocable giving over of things or persons to the LORD. [b]16 That is, about 2 ounces (about 55 grams)

the Levites and say to them: 'When you receive from the Israelites the tithe I give you as your inheritance, you must present a tenth of that tithe as the LORD's offering. 27Your offering will be reckoned to you as grain from the threshing floor or juice from the winepress. 28In this way you also will present an offering to the LORD from all the tithes you receive from the Israelites. From these tithes you must give the LORD's portion to Aaron the priest. 29You must present as the LORD's portion the best and holiest part of everything given to you.'

30"Say to the Levites: 'When you present the best part, it will be reckoned to you as the product of the threshing floor or the winepress. 31You and your households may eat the rest of it anywhere, for it is your wages for your work at the Tent of Meeting. 32By presenting the best part of it you will not be guilty in this matter; then you will not defile the holy offerings of the Israelites, and you will not die.' "

The Water of Cleansing

19 The LORD said to Moses and Aaron: 2"This is a requirement of the law that the LORD has commanded: Tell the Israelites to bring you a red heifer without defect or blemish and that has never been under a yoke. 3Give it to Eleazar the priest; it is to be taken outside the camp and slaughtered in his presence. 4Then Eleazar the priest is to take some of its blood on his finger and sprinkle it seven times toward the front of the Tent of Meeting. 5While he watches, the heifer is to be burned—its hide, flesh, blood and offal. 6The priest is to take some cedar wood, hyssop and scarlet wool and throw them onto the burning heifer. 7After that, the priest must wash his clothes and bathe himself with water. He may then come into the camp, but he will be ceremonially unclean till evening. 8The man who burns it must also wash his clothes and bathe with water, and he too will be unclean till evening.

9"A man who is clean shall gather up the ashes of the heifer and put them in a ceremonially clean place outside the camp. They shall be kept by the Israelite community for use in the water of cleansing; it is for purification from sin. 10The man who gathers up the ashes of the heifer must also wash his clothes, and he too will be unclean till evening. This will be a lasting ordinance both for the Israelites and for the aliens living among them.

11"Whoever touches the dead body of anyone will be unclean for seven days. 12He must purify himself with the water on the third day and on the seventh day; then he will be clean. But if he does not purify himself on the third and seventh days, he will not be clean. 13Whoever touches the dead body of anyone and fails to purify himself defiles the LORD's tabernacle. That person must be cut off from Israel. Because the water of cleansing has not been sprinkled on him, he is unclean; his uncleanness remains on him.

14"This is the law that applies when a person dies in a tent: Anyone who enters the tent and anyone who is in it will be unclean for seven days, 15and every open container without a lid fastened on it will be unclean.

16"Anyone out in the open who touches someone who has been killed with a sword or someone who has died a natural death, or anyone who touches a human bone or a grave, will be unclean for seven days.

17"For the unclean person, put some ashes from the burned purification offering into a jar and pour fresh water over them. 18Then a man who is ceremonially clean is to take some hyssop, dip it in the water and sprinkle the tent and all the furnishings and the people who were there. He must also sprinkle anyone who has touched a human bone or a grave or someone who has been killed or someone who has died a natural death. 19The man who is clean is to sprinkle the unclean person on the third and seventh days, and on the seventh day he is to purify him. The person being cleansed must wash his clothes and bathe with water, and that evening he will be clean. 20But if a person who is unclean does not purify himself, he must be cut off from the community, because he has defiled the sanctuary of the LORD. The water of cleansing has not been sprinkled on him, and he is unclean. 21This is a lasting ordinance for them.

"The man who sprinkles the water of cleansing must also wash his clothes, and anyone who touches the water of cleansing will be unclean till evening. 22Anything that an unclean person touches becomes unclean, and anyone who touches it becomes unclean till evening."

Water From the Rock

20 In the first month the whole Israelite community arrived at the Desert of Zin, and they stayed at Kadesh. There Miriam died and was buried.

2Now there was no water for the community, and the people gathered in opposition to Moses and Aaron. 3They quarreled with Moses and said, "If only we had died when our brothers fell dead before the LORD! 4Why did you bring the LORD's community into this desert, that we and our livestock should die here? 5Why did you bring us up out of Egypt to this terrible place? It has no grain or figs, grapevines or pomegranates. And there is no water to drink!"

6Moses and Aaron went from the assembly to the entrance to the Tent of Meeting and fell facedown, and the glory of the LORD appeared to them. 7The LORD said to Moses, 8"Take the staff, and you and your brother Aaron gather the assembly together. Speak to that rock before their eyes and it will pour out its water. You will bring water out of the rock for the community so they and their livestock can drink."

9So Moses took the staff from the LORD's presence, just as he commanded him. 10He and Aaron gathered the assembly together in front of the rock and Moses said to them, "Listen, you rebels, must we bring you water out of this rock?" 11Then Moses raised his arm and struck the rock twice with his staff. Water gushed out, and the community and their livestock drank.

12But the LORD said to Moses and Aaron, "Because you did not trust in me enough to honor me as holy in the sight of the Israelites, you will not bring this community into the land I give them."

13These were the waters of Meribah,[a] where the Israelites quarreled with the LORD and where he showed himself holy among them.

Edom Denies Israel Passage

14Moses sent messengers from Kadesh to the king of Edom, saying:

"This is what your brother Israel says: You know about all the hardships that have come upon us. 15Our forefathers went down into Egypt, and we lived there many years. The Egyptians mistreated us and our fathers, 16but when we cried out to the LORD, he heard our cry and sent an angel and brought us out of Egypt.

"Now we are here at Kadesh, a town on the edge of your territory. 17Please let us pass through your country. We will not go through any field or vineyard, or drink water from any well. We will travel along the king's highway and not turn to the right or to the left until we have passed through your territory."

18But Edom answered:

"You may not pass through here; if you try, we will march out and attack you with the sword."

19The Israelites replied:

"We will go along the main road, and if we or our livestock drink any of your water, we will pay for it. We only want to pass through on foot—nothing else."

20Again they answered:

"You may not pass through."

Then Edom came out against them with a large and powerful army. 21Since Edom refused to let them go through their territory, Israel turned away from them.

The Death of Aaron

22The whole Israelite community set out from Kadesh and came to Mount Hor. 23At Mount Hor, near the border of Edom, the LORD said to Moses and Aaron, 24"Aaron will be gathered to his people. He will not enter the land I give the Israelites, because both of you rebelled against my command at the waters of Meribah. 25Get Aaron and his son Eleazar and take them up Mount Hor. 26Remove Aaron's garments and put them on his son Eleazar, for Aaron will be gathered to his people; he will die there."

27Moses did as the LORD commanded: They went up Mount Hor in the sight of the whole community. 28Moses removed Aaron's garments and put them on his son Eleazar. And Aaron died there on top of the mountain. Then Moses and Eleazar came down from the mountain, 29and when the whole community learned that

[a] 13 *Meribah* means *quarreling.*

Aaron had died, the entire house of Israel mourned for him thirty days.

Arad Destroyed

21 When the Canaanite king of Arad, who lived in the Negev, heard that Israel was coming along the road to Atharim, he attacked the Israelites and captured some of them. 2Then Israel made this vow to the LORD: "If you will deliver these people into our hands, we will totally destroy[a] their cities." 3The LORD listened to Israel's plea and gave the Canaanites over to them. They completely destroyed them and their towns; so the place was named Hormah.[b]

The Bronze Snake

4They traveled from Mount Hor along the route to the Red Sea,[c] to go around Edom. But the people grew impatient on the way; 5they spoke against God and against Moses, and said, "Why have you brought us up out of Egypt to die in the desert? There is no bread! There is no water! And we detest this miserable food!"

6Then the LORD sent venomous snakes among them; they bit the people and many Israelites died. 7The people came to Moses and said, "We sinned when we spoke against the LORD and against you. Pray that the LORD will take the snakes away from us." So Moses prayed for the people.

8The LORD said to Moses, "Make a snake and put it up on a pole; anyone who is bitten can look at it and live." 9So Moses made a bronze snake and put it up on a pole. Then when anyone was bitten by a snake and looked at the bronze snake, he lived.

The Journey to Moab

10The Israelites moved on and camped at Oboth. 11Then they set out from Oboth and camped in Iye Abarim, in the desert that faces Moab toward the sunrise. 12From there they moved on and camped in the Zered Valley. 13They set out from there and camped alongside the Arnon, which is in the desert extending into Amorite territory. The Arnon is the border of Moab, between Moab and the Amorites.

14That is why the Book of the Wars of the LORD says:

"... Waheb in Suphah[d] and the ravines,
the Arnon 15and[e] the slopes of the ravines
that lead to the site of Ar
and lie along the border of Moab."

16From there they continued on to Beer, the well where the LORD said to Moses, "Gather the people together and I will give them water."

17Then Israel sang this song:

"Spring up, O well!
Sing about it,
18about the well that the princes dug,
that the nobles of the people sank—
the nobles with scepters and staffs."

Then they went from the desert to Mattanah, 19from Mattanah to Nahaliel, from Nahaliel to Bamoth, 20and from Bamoth to the valley in Moab where the top of Pisgah overlooks the wasteland.

Defeat of Sihon and Og

21Israel sent messengers to say to Sihon king of the Amorites:

22"Let us pass through your country. We will not turn aside into any field or vineyard, or drink water from any well. We will travel along the king's highway until we have passed through your territory."

23But Sihon would not let Israel pass through his territory. He mustered his entire army and marched out into the desert against Israel. When he reached Jahaz, he fought with Israel. 24Israel, however, put him to the sword and took over his land from the Arnon to the Jabbok, but only as far as the Ammonites, because their border was fortified. 25Israel captured all the cities of the Amorites and occupied them, including Heshbon and all its surrounding settlements. 26Heshbon was the city of Sihon king of the Amorites, who had fought against the former king of Moab and had taken from him all his land as far as the Arnon.

27That is why the poets say:

[a] *2* The Hebrew term refers to the irrevocable giving over of things or persons to the LORD, often by totally destroying them; also in verse 3. [b] *3* *Hormah* means *destruction.* [c] *4* Hebrew *Yam Suph*; that is, Sea of Reeds [d] *14* The meaning of the Hebrew for this phrase is uncertain. [e] *14,15* Or *"I have been given from Suphah and the ravines / of the Arnon* [15] *to*

"Come to Heshbon and let it be rebuilt;
let Sihon's city be restored.
28"Fire went out from Heshbon,
a blaze from the city of Sihon.
It consumed Ar of Moab,
the citizens of Arnon's heights.
29Woe to you, O Moab!
You are destroyed, O people of Chemosh!
He has given up his sons as fugitives
and his daughters as captives
to Sihon king of the Amorites.
30"But we have overthrown them;
Heshbon is destroyed all the way to Dibon.
We have demolished them as far as Nophah,
which extends to Medeba."

31So Israel settled in the land of the Amorites.

32After Moses had sent spies to Jazer, the Israelites captured its surrounding settlements and drove out the Amorites who were there. 33Then they turned and went up along the road toward Bashan, and Og king of Bashan and his whole army marched out to meet them in battle at Edrei.

34The LORD said to Moses, "Do not be afraid of him, for I have handed him over to you, with his whole army and his land. Do to him what you did to Sihon king of the Amorites, who reigned in Heshbon."

35So they struck him down, together with his sons and his whole army, leaving them no survivors. And they took possession of his land.

Balak Summons Balaam

22 Then the Israelites traveled to the plains of Moab and camped along the Jordan across from Jericho.[a]

2Now Balak son of Zippor saw all that Israel had done to the Amorites, 3and Moab was terrified because there were so many people. Indeed, Moab was filled with dread because of the Israelites.

4The Moabites said to the elders of Midian, "This horde is going to lick up everything around us, as an ox licks up the grass of the field."

So Balak son of Zippor, who was king of Moab at that time, 5sent messengers to summon Balaam son of Beor, who was at Pethor, near the River,[b] in his native land. Balak said:

"A people has come out of Egypt; they cover the face of the land and have settled next to me. 6Now come and put a curse on these people, because they are too powerful for me. Perhaps then I will be able to defeat them and drive them out of the country. For I know that those you bless are blessed, and those you curse are cursed."

7The elders of Moab and Midian left, taking with them the fee for divination. When they came to Balaam, they told him what Balak had said.

8"Spend the night here," Balaam said to them, "and I will bring you back the answer the LORD gives me." So the Moabite princes stayed with him.

9God came to Balaam and asked, "Who are these men with you?"

10Balaam said to God, "Balak son of Zippor, king of Moab, sent me this message: 11'A people that has come out of Egypt covers the face of the land. Now come and put a curse on them for me. Perhaps then I will be able to fight them and drive them away.' "

12But God said to Balaam, "Do not go with them. You must not put a curse on those people, because they are blessed."

13The next morning Balaam got up and said to Balak's princes, "Go back to your own country, for the LORD has refused to let me go with you."

14So the Moabite princes returned to Balak and said, "Balaam refused to come with us."

15Then Balak sent other princes, more numerous and more distinguished than the first. 16They came to Balaam and said:

"This is what Balak son of Zippor says: Do not let anything keep you from coming to me, 17because I will reward you handsomely and do whatever you say. Come and put a curse on these people for me."

18But Balaam answered them, "Even if Balak gave me his palace filled with silver and gold, I could not do anything great or small to go beyond the command of the LORD my God. 19Now stay here tonight as the others did, and I will find out what else the LORD will tell me."

[a] 1 Hebrew *Jordan of Jericho*; possibly an ancient name for the Jordan River [b] 5 That is, the Euphrates

[20]That night God came to Balaam and said, "Since these men have come to summon you, go with them, but do only what I tell you."

Balaam's Donkey

[21]Balaam got up in the morning, saddled his donkey and went with the princes of Moab. [22]But God was very angry when he went, and the angel of the LORD stood in the road to oppose him. Balaam was riding on his donkey, and his two servants were with him. [23]When the donkey saw the angel of the LORD standing in the road with a drawn sword in his hand, she turned off the road into a field. Balaam beat her to get her back on the road.

[24]Then the angel of the LORD stood in a narrow path between two vineyards, with walls on both sides. [25]When the donkey saw the angel of the LORD, she pressed close to the wall, crushing Balaam's foot against it. So he beat her again.

[26]Then the angel of the LORD moved on ahead and stood in a narrow place where there was no room to turn, either to the right or to the left. [27]When the donkey saw the angel of the LORD, she lay down under Balaam, and he was angry and beat her with his staff. [28]Then the LORD opened the donkey's mouth, and she said to Balaam, "What have I done to you to make you beat me these three times?"

[29]Balaam answered the donkey, "You have made a fool of me! If I had a sword in my hand, I would kill you right now."

[30]The donkey said to Balaam, "Am I not your own donkey, which you have always ridden, to this day? Have I been in the habit of doing this to you?"

"No," he said.

[31]Then the LORD opened Balaam's eyes, and he saw the angel of the LORD standing in the road with his sword drawn. So he bowed low and fell facedown.

[32]The angel of the LORD asked him, "Why have you beaten your donkey these three times? I have come here to oppose you because your path is a reckless one before me.[a] [33]The donkey saw me and turned away from me these three times. If she had not turned away, I would certainly have killed you by now, but I would have spared her."

[34]Balaam said to the angel of the LORD, "I have sinned. I did not realize you were standing in the road to oppose me. Now if you are displeased, I will go back."

[35]The angel of the LORD said to Balaam, "Go with the men, but speak only what I tell you." So Balaam went with the princes of Balak.

[36]When Balak heard that Balaam was coming, he went out to meet him at the Moabite town on the Arnon border, at the edge of his territory. [37]Balak said to Balaam, "Did I not send you an urgent summons? Why didn't you come to me? Am I really not able to reward you?"

[38]"Well, I have come to you now," Balaam replied. "But can I say just anything? I must speak only what God puts in my mouth."

[39]Then Balaam went with Balak to Kiriath Huzoth. [40]Balak sacrificed cattle and sheep, and gave some to Balaam and the princes who were with him. [41]The next morning Balak took Balaam up to Bamoth Baal, and from there he saw part of the people.

Balaam's First Oracle

23 Balaam said, "Build me seven altars here, and prepare seven bulls and seven rams for me." [2]Balak did as Balaam said, and the two of them offered a bull and a ram on each altar.

[3]Then Balaam said to Balak, "Stay here beside your offering while I go aside. Perhaps the LORD will come to meet with me. Whatever he reveals to me I will tell you." Then he went off to a barren height.

[4]God met with him, and Balaam said, "I have prepared seven altars, and on each altar I have offered a bull and a ram."

[5]The LORD put a message in Balaam's mouth and said, "Go back to Balak and give him this message."

[6]So he went back to him and found him standing beside his offering, with all the princes of Moab. [7]Then Balaam uttered his oracle:

"Balak brought me from Aram,
the king of Moab from the eastern mountains.
'Come,' he said, 'curse Jacob for me;
come, denounce Israel.'
[8]How can I curse
those whom God has not cursed?
How can I denounce
those whom the LORD has not denounced?

[a]32 The meaning of the Hebrew for this clause is uncertain.

WEEKENDING

SEX

What does your spouse *really* think about sex? Complete this exercise by circling the number after each question that best fits your feelings. (One indicates "agree strongly"; three is "no opinion"; and five means "disagree strongly".) After each of you has completed the questionnaire, discuss your respective answers.

1. A wife does not always have to have an orgasm every time she has intercourse.
   1 2 3 4 5

2. One of the strong messages of sexual intercourse is that it says you are wanted and needed.
   1 2 3 4 5

3. Sex is for oneness, and oneness really makes sex worthwhile. 1 2 3 4 5

4. A couple should take entire evenings and weekends to share together sensually and to develop their sex life. 1 2 3 4 5

5. I feel somewhat guilty about having sex in marriage. 1 2 3 4 5

— *Charles M. Sell*

REVIVE

Saturday: 1 Corinthians 7:1–11
Sunday: Song of Songs 8:5–14

Go to page 168 for your next devotional reading.

9From the rocky peaks I see them,
from the heights I view them.
I see a people who live apart
and do not consider themselves one
of the nations.
10Who can count the dust of Jacob
or number the fourth part of Israel?
Let me die the death of the righteous,
and may my end be like theirs!"

11Balak said to Balaam, "What have you done to me? I brought you to curse my enemies, but you have done nothing but bless them!"
12He answered, "Must I not speak what the LORD puts in my mouth?"

Balaam's Second Oracle

13Then Balak said to him, "Come with me to another place where you can see them; you will see only a part but not all of them. And from there, curse them for me." 14So he took him to the field of Zophim on the top of Pisgah, and there he built seven altars and offered a bull and a ram on each altar.
15Balaam said to Balak, "Stay here beside your offering while I meet with him over there."
16The LORD met with Balaam and put a message in his mouth and said, "Go back to Balak and give him this message."
17So he went to him and found him standing beside his offering, with the princes of Moab. Balak asked him, "What did the LORD say?"
18Then he uttered his oracle:

"Arise, Balak, and listen;
hear me, son of Zippor.
19God is not a man, that he should lie,
nor a son of man, that he should
change his mind.
Does he speak and then not act?
Does he promise and not fulfill?
20I have received a command to bless;
he has blessed, and I cannot change
it.

21"No misfortune is seen in Jacob,
no misery observed in Israel.[a]
The LORD their God is with them;
the shout of the King is among
them.
22God brought them out of Egypt;
they have the strength of a wild ox.
23There is no sorcery against Jacob,
no divination against Israel.
It will now be said of Jacob
and of Israel, 'See what God has
done!'
24The people rise like a lioness;
they rouse themselves like a lion
that does not rest till he devours his
prey
and drinks the blood of his victims."

25Then Balak said to Balaam, "Neither curse them at all nor bless them at all!"
26Balaam answered, "Did I not tell you I must do whatever the LORD says?"

Balaam's Third Oracle

27Then Balak said to Balaam, "Come, let me take you to another place. Perhaps it will please God to let you curse them for me from there." 28And Balak took Balaam to the top of Peor, overlooking the wasteland.
29Balaam said, "Build me seven altars here, and prepare seven bulls and seven rams for me." 30Balak did as Balaam had said, and offered a bull and a ram on each altar.

24 Now when Balaam saw that it pleased the LORD to bless Israel, he did not resort to sorcery as at other times, but turned his face toward the desert.
2When Balaam looked out and saw Israel encamped tribe by tribe, the Spirit of God came upon him 3and he uttered his oracle:

"The oracle of Balaam son of Beor,
the oracle of one whose eye sees
clearly,
4the oracle of one who hears the words
of God,
who sees a vision from the
Almighty,[b]
who falls prostrate, and whose eyes
are opened:

5"How beautiful are your tents,
O Jacob,
your dwelling places, O Israel!

6"Like valleys they spread out,
like gardens beside a river,
like aloes planted by the LORD,
like cedars beside the waters.
7Water will flow from their buckets;
their seed will have abundant water.

"Their king will be greater than Agag;
their kingdom will be exalted.

[a]21 Or *He has not looked on Jacob's offenses / or on the wrongs found in Israel.* [b]4 Hebrew *Shaddai*; also in verse 16

8"God brought them out of Egypt;
they have the strength of a wild ox.
They devour hostile nations
and break their bones in pieces;
with their arrows they pierce them.
9Like a lion they crouch and lie down,
like a lioness—who dares to rouse them?

"May those who bless you be blessed
and those who curse you be cursed!"

10Then Balak's anger burned against Balaam. He struck his hands together and said to him, "I summoned you to curse my enemies, but you have blessed them these three times. 11Now leave at once and go home! I said I would reward you handsomely, but the LORD has kept you from being rewarded."

12Balaam answered Balak, "Did I not tell the messengers you sent me, 13'Even if Balak gave me his palace filled with silver and gold, I could not do anything of my own accord, good or bad, to go beyond the command of the LORD—and I must say only what the LORD says'? 14Now I am going back to my people, but come, let me warn you of what this people will do to your people in days to come."

Balaam's Fourth Oracle

15Then he uttered his oracle:

"The oracle of Balaam son of Beor,
the oracle of one whose eye sees clearly,
16the oracle of one who hears the words of God,
who has knowledge from the Most High,
who sees a vision from the Almighty,
who falls prostrate, and whose eyes are opened:
17"I see him, but not now;
I behold him, but not near.
A star will come out of Jacob;
a scepter will rise out of Israel.
He will crush the foreheads of Moab,
the skulls[a] of[b] all the sons of Sheth.[c]
18Edom will be conquered;
Seir, his enemy, will be conquered,
but Israel will grow strong.
19A ruler will come out of Jacob
and destroy the survivors of the city."

Balaam's Final Oracles

20Then Balaam saw Amalek and uttered his oracle:

"Amalek was first among the nations,
but he will come to ruin at last."

21Then he saw the Kenites and uttered his oracle:

"Your dwelling place is secure,
your nest is set in a rock;
22yet you Kenites will be destroyed
when Asshur takes you captive."

23Then he uttered his oracle:

"Ah, who can live when God does this?[d]
24 Ships will come from the shores of Kittim;
they will subdue Asshur and Eber,
but they too will come to ruin."

25Then Balaam got up and returned home and Balak went his own way.

Moab Seduces Israel

25 While Israel was staying in Shittim, the men began to indulge in sexual immorality with Moabite women, 2who invited them to the sacrifices to their gods. The people ate and bowed down before these gods. 3So Israel joined in worshiping the Baal of Peor. And the LORD's anger burned against them.

4The LORD said to Moses, "Take all the leaders of these people, kill them and expose them in broad daylight before the LORD, so that the LORD's fierce anger may turn away from Israel."

5So Moses said to Israel's judges, "Each of you must put to death those of your men who have joined in worshiping the Baal of Peor."

6Then an Israelite man brought to his family a Midianite woman right before the eyes of Moses and the whole assembly of Israel while they were weeping at the entrance to the Tent of Meeting. 7When Phinehas son of Eleazar, the son of Aaron, the priest, saw this, he left the assembly, took a spear in his hand 8and followed the Israelite into the tent. He drove the spear through both of them—through the Isra-

[a]17 Samaritan Pentateuch (see also Jer. 48:45); the meaning of the word in the Masoretic Text is uncertain. [b]17 Or possibly *Moab, / batter* [c]17 Or *all the noisy boasters* [d]23 Masoretic Text; with a different word division of the Hebrew *A people will gather from the north.*

elite and into the woman's body. Then the
plague against the Israelites was stopped;
9but those who died in the plague num-
bered 24,000.

10The LORD said to Moses, 11"Phinehas
son of Eleazar, the son of Aaron, the
priest, has turned my anger away from the
Israelites; for he was as zealous as I am for
my honor among them, so that in my zeal
I did not put an end to them. 12Therefore
tell him I am making my covenant of
peace with him. 13He and his descendants
will have a covenant of a lasting priest-
hood, because he was zealous for the hon-
or of his God and made atonement for the
Israelites."

14The name of the Israelite who was
killed with the Midianite woman was Zim-
ri son of Salu, the leader of a Simeonite
family. 15And the name of the Midianite
woman who was put to death was Cozbi
daughter of Zur, a tribal chief of a Midian-
ite family.

16The LORD said to Moses, 17"Treat the
Midianites as enemies and kill them, 18be-
cause they treated you as enemies when
they deceived you in the affair of Peor
and their sister Cozbi, the daughter of a
Midianite leader, the woman who was
killed when the plague came as a result
of Peor."

The Second Census

26 After the plague the LORD said to
Moses and Eleazar son of Aaron,
the priest, 2"Take a census of the whole
Israelite community by families—all
those twenty years old or more who are
able to serve in the army of Israel." 3So on
the plains of Moab by the Jordan across
from Jericho,[a] Moses and Eleazar the
priest spoke with them and said, 4"Take a
census of the men twenty years old or
more, as the LORD commanded Moses."

These were the Israelites who came out
of Egypt:

5The descendants of Reuben, the firstborn
son of Israel, were:
through Hanoch, the Hanochite
clan;
through Pallu, the Palluite clan;
6through Hezron, the Hezronite clan;
through Carmi, the Carmite clan.
7These were the clans of Reuben; those
numbered were 43,730.

8The son of Pallu was Eliab, 9and the
sons of Eliab were Nemuel, Dathan and
Abiram. The same Dathan and Abiram
were the community officials who re-
belled against Moses and Aaron and were
among Korah's followers when they re-
belled against the LORD. 10The earth
opened its mouth and swallowed them
along with Korah, whose followers died
when the fire devoured the 250 men. And
they served as a warning sign. 11The line
of Korah, however, did not die out.

12The descendants of Simeon by their
clans were:
through Nemuel, the Nemuelite
clan;
through Jamin, the Jaminite clan;
through Jakin, the Jakinite clan;
13through Zerah, the Zerahite clan;
through Shaul, the Shaulite clan.
14These were the clans of Simeon; there
were 22,200 men.

15The descendants of Gad by their clans
were:
through Zephon, the Zephonite clan;
through Haggi, the Haggite clan;
through Shuni, the Shunite clan;
16through Ozni, the Oznite clan;
through Eri, the Erite clan;
17through Arodi,[b] the Arodite clan;
through Areli, the Arelite clan.
18These were the clans of Gad; those num-
bered were 40,500.

19Er and Onan were sons of Judah, but
they died in Canaan.
20The descendants of Judah by their clans
were:
through Shelah, the Shelanite clan;
through Perez, the Perezite clan;
through Zerah, the Zerahite clan.
21The descendants of Perez were:
through Hezron, the Hezronite
clan;
through Hamul, the Hamulite
clan.
22These were the clans of Judah; those
numbered were 76,500.

23The descendants of Issachar by their
clans were:
through Tola, the Tolaite clan;

[a] 3 Hebrew *Jordan of Jericho*; possibly an ancient name for the Jordan River; also in verse 63
[b] 17 Samaritan Pentateuch and Syriac (see also Gen. 46:16); Masoretic Text *Arod*

through Puah, the Puite[a] clan;
24 through Jashub, the Jashubite clan;
through Shimron, the Shimronite clan.
25 These were the clans of Issachar; those numbered were 64,300.

26 The descendants of Zebulun by their clans were:
through Sered, the Seredite clan;
through Elon, the Elonite clan;
through Jahleel, the Jahleelite clan.
27 These were the clans of Zebulun; those numbered were 60,500.

28 The descendants of Joseph by their clans through Manasseh and Ephraim were:

29 The descendants of Manasseh:
through Makir, the Makirite clan (Makir was the father of Gilead);
through Gilead, the Gileadite clan.
30 These were the descendants of Gilead:
through Iezer, the Iezerite clan;
through Helek, the Helekite clan;
31 through Asriel, the Asrielite clan;
through Shechem, the Shechemite clan;
32 through Shemida, the Shemidaite clan;
through Hepher, the Hepherite clan.
33 (Zelophehad son of Hepher had no sons; he had only daughters, whose names were Mahlah, Noah, Hoglah, Milcah and Tirzah.)
34 These were the clans of Manasseh; those numbered were 52,700.

35 These were the descendants of Ephraim by their clans:
through Shuthelah, the Shuthelahite clan;
through Beker, the Bekerite clan;
through Tahan, the Tahanite clan.
36 These were the descendants of Shuthelah:
through Eran, the Eranite clan.
37 These were the clans of Ephraim; those numbered were 32,500.

These were the descendants of Joseph by their clans.

38 The descendants of Benjamin by their clans were:
through Bela, the Belaite clan;
through Ashbel, the Ashbelite clan;
through Ahiram, the Ahiramite clan;
39 through Shupham,[b] the Shuphamite clan;
through Hupham, the Huphamite clan.
40 The descendants of Bela through Ard and Naaman were:
through Ard,[c] the Ardite clan;
through Naaman, the Naamite clan.
41 These were the clans of Benjamin; those numbered were 45,600.

42 These were the descendants of Dan by their clans:
through Shuham, the Shuhamite clan.
These were the clans of Dan: 43 All of them were Shuhamite clans; and those numbered were 64,400.

44 The descendants of Asher by their clans were:
through Imnah, the Imnite clan;
through Ishvi, the Ishvite clan;
through Beriah, the Beriite clan;
45 and through the descendants of Beriah:
through Heber, the Heberite clan;
through Malkiel, the Malkielite clan.
46 (Asher had a daughter named Serah.)
47 These were the clans of Asher; those numbered were 53,400.

48 The descendants of Naphtali by their clans were:
through Jahzeel, the Jahzeelite clan;
through Guni, the Gunite clan;
49 through Jezer, the Jezerite clan;
through Shillem, the Shillemite clan.
50 These were the clans of Naphtali; those numbered were 45,400.

51 The total number of the men of Israel was 601,730.

52 The LORD said to Moses, 53 "The land is to be allotted to them as an inheritance based on the number of names. 54 To a larger group give a larger inheritance, and

[a] *23* Samaritan Pentateuch, Septuagint, Vulgate and Syriac (see also 1 Chron. 7:1); Masoretic Text *through Puvah, the Punite* [b] *39* A few manuscripts of the Masoretic Text, Samaritan Pentateuch, Vulgate and Syriac (see also Septuagint); most manuscripts of the Masoretic Text *Shephupham* [c] *40* Samaritan Pentateuch and Vulgate (see also Septuagint); Masoretic Text does not have *through Ard.*

to a smaller group a smaller one; each is
to receive its inheritance according to the
number of those listed. 55Be sure that the
land is distributed by lot. What each
group inherits will be according to the
names for its ancestral tribe. 56Each inher-
itance is to be distributed by lot among
the larger and smaller groups."

57These were the Levites who were count-
ed by their clans:
through Gershon, the Gershonite
clan;
through Kohath, the Kohathite clan;
through Merari, the Merarite clan.
58These also were Levite clans:
the Libnite clan,
the Hebronite clan,
the Mahlite clan,
the Mushite clan,
the Korahite clan.
(Kohath was the forefather of Am-
ram; 59the name of Amram's wife was
Jochebed, a descendant of Levi, who
was born to the Levites[a] in Egypt. To
Amram she bore Aaron, Moses and
their sister Miriam. 60Aaron was the
father of Nadab and Abihu, Eleazar
and Ithamar. 61But Nadab and Abihu
died when they made an offering be-
fore the LORD with unauthorized
fire.)

62All the male Levites a month old or more
numbered 23,000. They were not counted
along with the other Israelites because
they received no inheritance among them.

63These are the ones counted by Moses
and Eleazar the priest when they counted
the Israelites on the plains of Moab by the
Jordan across from Jericho. 64Not one of
them was among those counted by Moses
and Aaron the priest when they counted
the Israelites in the Desert of Sinai. 65For
the LORD had told those Israelites they
would surely die in the desert, and not
one of them was left except Caleb son of
Jephunneh and Joshua son of Nun.

Zelophehad's Daughters

27 The daughters of Zelophehad son
of Hepher, the son of Gilead, the
son of Makir, the son of Manasseh, be-
longed to the clans of Manasseh son of Jo-
seph. The names of the daughters were
Mahlah, Noah, Hoglah, Milcah and Tir-
zah. They approached 2the entrance to the
Tent of Meeting and stood before Moses,
Eleazar the priest, the leaders and the
whole assembly, and said, 3"Our father
died in the desert. He was not among Ko-
rah's followers, who banded together
against the LORD, but he died for his own
sin and left no sons. 4Why should our fa-
ther's name disappear from his clan be-
cause he had no son? Give us property
among our father's relatives."

5So Moses brought their case before the
LORD 6and the LORD said to him, 7"What
Zelophehad's daughters are saying is
right. You must certainly give them prop-
erty as an inheritance among their father's
relatives and turn their father's inheri-
tance over to them.

8"Say to the Israelites, 'If a man dies and
leaves no son, turn his inheritance over to
his daughter. 9If he has no daughter, give
his inheritance to his brothers. 10If he has
no brothers, give his inheritance to his fa-
ther's brothers. 11If his father had no
brothers, give his inheritance to the near-
est relative in his clan, that he may pos-
sess it. This is to be a legal requirement for
the Israelites, as the LORD commanded
Moses.' "

Joshua to Succeed Moses

12Then the LORD said to Moses, "Go up
this mountain in the Abarim range and
see the land I have given the Israelites.
13After you have seen it, you too will be
gathered to your people, as your brother
Aaron was, 14for when the community re-
belled at the waters in the Desert of Zin,
both of you disobeyed my command to
honor me as holy before their eyes."
(These were the waters of Meribah Ka-
desh, in the Desert of Zin.)

15Moses said to the LORD, 16"May the
LORD, the God of the spirits of all mankind,
appoint a man over this community 17to
go out and come in before them, one who
will lead them out and bring them in, so
the LORD's people will not be like sheep
without a shepherd."

18So the LORD said to Moses, "Take
Joshua son of Nun, a man in whom is the
spirit,[b] and lay your hand on him. 19Have
him stand before Eleazar the priest and
the entire assembly and commission him
in their presence. 20Give him some of your
authority so the whole Israelite commun-
ity will obey him. 21He is to stand before
Eleazar the priest, who will obtain deci-

[a] 59 Or *Jochebed, a daughter of Levi, who was born to Levi*
[b] 18 Or *Spirit*

sions for him by inquiring of the Urim before the LORD. At his command he and the entire community of the Israelites will go out, and at his command they will come in."

22Moses did as the LORD commanded him. He took Joshua and had him stand before Eleazar the priest and the whole assembly. 23Then he laid his hands on him and commissioned him, as the LORD instructed through Moses.

Daily Offerings

28 The LORD said to Moses, 2"Give this command to the Israelites and say to them: 'See that you present to me at the appointed time the food for my offerings made by fire, as an aroma pleasing to me.' 3Say to them: 'This is the offering made by fire that you are to present to the LORD: two lambs a year old without defect, as a regular burnt offering each day. 4Prepare one lamb in the morning and the other at twilight, 5together with a grain offering of a tenth of an ephah[a] of fine flour mixed with a quarter of a hin[b] of oil from pressed olives. 6This is the regular burnt offering instituted at Mount Sinai as a pleasing aroma, an offering made to the LORD by fire. 7The accompanying drink offering is to be a quarter of a hin of fermented drink with each lamb. Pour out the drink offering to the LORD at the sanctuary. 8Prepare the second lamb at twilight, along with the same kind of grain offering and drink offering that you prepare in the morning. This is an offering made by fire, an aroma pleasing to the LORD.

Sabbath Offerings

9" 'On the Sabbath day, make an offering of two lambs a year old without defect, together with its drink offering and a grain offering of two-tenths of an ephah[c] of fine flour mixed with oil. 10This is the burnt offering for every Sabbath, in addition to the regular burnt offering and its drink offering.

Monthly Offerings

11" 'On the first of every month, present to the LORD a burnt offering of two young bulls, one ram and seven male lambs a year old, all without defect. 12With each bull there is to be a grain offering of three-tenths of an ephah[d] of fine flour mixed with oil; with the ram, a grain offering of two-tenths of an ephah of fine flour mixed with oil; 13and with each lamb, a grain offering of a tenth of an ephah of fine flour mixed with oil. This is for a burnt offering, a pleasing aroma, an offering made to the LORD by fire. 14With each bull there is to be a drink offering of half a hin[e] of wine; with the ram, a third of a hin[f]; and with each lamb, a quarter of a hin. This is the monthly burnt offering to be made at each new moon during the year. 15Besides the regular burnt offering with its drink offering, one male goat is to be presented to the LORD as a sin offering.

The Passover

16" 'On the fourteenth day of the first month the LORD's Passover is to be held. 17On the fifteenth day of this month there is to be a festival; for seven days eat bread made without yeast. 18On the first day hold a sacred assembly and do no regular work. 19Present to the LORD an offering made by fire, a burnt offering of two young bulls, one ram and seven male lambs a year old, all without defect. 20With each bull prepare a grain offering of three-tenths of an ephah of fine flour mixed with oil; with the ram, two-tenths; 21and with each of the seven lambs, one-tenth. 22Include one male goat as a sin offering to make atonement for you. 23Prepare these in addition to the regular morning burnt offering. 24In this way prepare the food for the offering made by fire every day for seven days as an aroma pleasing to the LORD; it is to be prepared in addition to the regular burnt offering and its drink offering. 25On the seventh day hold a sacred assembly and do no regular work.

Feast of Weeks

26" 'On the day of firstfruits, when you present to the LORD an offering of new grain during the Feast of Weeks, hold a sacred assembly and do no regular work. 27Present a burnt offering of two young bulls, one ram and seven male lambs a

[a] *5* That is, probably about 2 quarts (about 2 liters); also in verses 13, 21 and 29 [b] *5* That is, probably about 1 quart (about 1 liter); also in verses 7 and 14 [c] *9* That is, probably about 4 quarts (about 4.5 liters); also in verses 12, 20 and 28 [d] *12* That is, probably about 6 quarts (about 6.5 liters); also in verses 20 and 28 [e] *14* That is, probably about 2 quarts (about 2 liters) [f] *14* That is, probably about 1 1/4 quarts (about 1.2 liters)

year old as an aroma pleasing to the LORD.
28With each bull there is to be a grain of-
fering of three-tenths of an ephah of fine
flour mixed with oil; with the ram, two-
tenths; 29and with each of the seven
lambs, one-tenth. 30Include one male goat
to make atonement for you. 31Prepare
these together with their drink offerings,
in addition to the regular burnt offering
and its grain offering. Be sure the animals
are without defect.

Feast of Trumpets

29 " 'On the first day of the seventh
month hold a sacred assembly and
do no regular work. It is a day for you to
sound the trumpets. 2As an aroma pleas-
ing to the LORD, prepare a burnt offering of
one young bull, one ram and seven male
lambs a year old, all without defect. 3With
the bull prepare a grain offering of three-
tenths of an ephah[a] of fine flour mixed
with oil; with the ram, two-tenths[b]; 4and
with each of the seven lambs, one-tenth.[c]
5Include one male goat as a sin offering to
make atonement for you. 6These are in ad-
dition to the monthly and daily burnt of-
ferings with their grain offerings and
drink offerings as specified. They are of-
ferings made to the LORD by fire—a pleas-
ing aroma.

Day of Atonement

7" 'On the tenth day of this seventh
month hold a sacred assembly. You must
deny yourselves[d] and do no work.
8Present as an aroma pleasing to the LORD
a burnt offering of one young bull, one
ram and seven male lambs a year old, all
without defect. 9With the bull prepare a
grain offering of three-tenths of an ephah
of fine flour mixed with oil; with the ram,
two-tenths; 10and with each of the seven
lambs, one-tenth. 11Include one male goat
as a sin offering, in addition to the sin of-
fering for atonement and the regular burnt
offering with its grain offering, and their
drink offerings.

Feast of Tabernacles

12" 'On the fifteenth day of the seventh
month, hold a sacred assembly and do no
regular work. Celebrate a festival to the
LORD for seven days. 13Present an offering
made by fire as an aroma pleasing to the
LORD, a burnt offering of thirteen young
bulls, two rams and fourteen male lambs
a year old, all without defect. 14With each
of the thirteen bulls prepare a grain offer-
ing of three-tenths of an ephah of fine
flour mixed with oil; with each of the two
rams, two-tenths; 15and with each of the
fourteen lambs, one-tenth. 16Include one
male goat as a sin offering, in addition to
the regular burnt offering with its grain of-
fering and drink offering.

17" 'On the second day prepare twelve
young bulls, two rams and fourteen male
lambs a year old, all without defect.
18With the bulls, rams and lambs, prepare
their grain offerings and drink offerings
according to the number specified. 19In-
clude one male goat as a sin offering, in
addition to the regular burnt offering with
its grain offering, and their drink offer-
ings.

20" 'On the third day prepare eleven
bulls, two rams and fourteen male lambs
a year old, all without defect. 21With the
bulls, rams and lambs, prepare their grain
offerings and drink offerings according to
the number specified. 22Include one male
goat as a sin offering, in addition to the
regular burnt offering with its grain offer-
ing and drink offering.

23" 'On the fourth day prepare ten bulls,
two rams and fourteen male lambs a year
old, all without defect. 24With the bulls,
rams and lambs, prepare their grain offer-
ings and drink offerings according to the
number specified. 25Include one male
goat as a sin offering, in addition to the
regular burnt offering with its grain offer-
ing and drink offering.

26" 'On the fifth day prepare nine bulls,
two rams and fourteen male lambs a year
old, all without defect. 27With the bulls,
rams and lambs, prepare their grain offer-
ings and drink offerings according to the
number specified. 28Include one male
goat as a sin offering, in addition to the
regular burnt offering with its grain offer-
ing and drink offering.

29" 'On the sixth day prepare eight
bulls, two rams and fourteen male lambs
a year old, all without defect. 30With the
bulls, rams and lambs, prepare their grain
offerings and drink offerings according to
the number specified. 31Include one male
goat as a sin offering, in addition to the

[a] 3 That is, probably about 6 quarts (about 6.5 liters); also in verses 9 and 14 [b] 3 That is, probably about 4 quarts (about 4.5 liters); also in verses 9 and 14 [c] 4 That is, probably about 2 quarts (about 2 liters); also in verses 10 and 15 [d] 7 Or *must fast*

regular burnt offering with its grain offering and drink offering.

32"'On the seventh day prepare seven bulls, two rams and fourteen male lambs a year old, all without defect. 33With the bulls, rams and lambs, prepare their grain offerings and drink offerings according to the number specified. 34Include one male goat as a sin offering, in addition to the regular burnt offering with its grain offering and drink offering.

35"'On the eighth day hold an assembly and do no regular work. 36Present an offering made by fire as an aroma pleasing to the LORD, a burnt offering of one bull, one ram and seven male lambs a year old, all without defect. 37With the bull, the ram and the lambs, prepare their grain offerings and drink offerings according to the number specified. 38Include one male goat as a sin offering, in addition to the regular burnt offering with its grain offering and drink offering.

39"'In addition to what you vow and your freewill offerings, prepare these for the LORD at your appointed feasts: your burnt offerings, grain offerings, drink offerings and fellowship offerings.[a]'"

40Moses told the Israelites all that the LORD commanded him.

Vows

30 Moses said to the heads of the tribes of Israel: "This is what the LORD commands: 2When a man makes a vow to the LORD or takes an oath to obligate himself by a pledge, he must not break his word but must do everything he said.

3"When a young woman still living in her father's house makes a vow to the LORD or obligates herself by a pledge 4and her father hears about her vow or pledge but says nothing to her, then all her vows and every pledge by which she obligated herself will stand. 5But if her father forbids her when he hears about it, none of her vows or the pledges by which she obligated herself will stand; the LORD will release her because her father has forbidden her.

6"If she marries after she makes a vow or after her lips utter a rash promise by which she obligates herself 7and her husband hears about it but says nothing to her, then her vows or the pledges by which she obligated herself will stand. 8But if her husband forbids her when he hears about it, he nullifies the vow that obligates her or the rash promise by which she obligates herself, and the LORD will release her.

9"Any vow or obligation taken by a widow or divorced woman will be binding on her.

10"If a woman living with her husband makes a vow or obligates herself by a pledge under oath 11and her husband hears about it but says nothing to her and does not forbid her, then all her vows or the pledges by which she obligated herself will stand. 12But if her husband nullifies them when he hears about them, then none of the vows or pledges that came from her lips will stand. Her husband has nullified them, and the LORD will release her. 13Her husband may confirm or nullify any vow she makes or any sworn pledge to deny herself. 14But if her husband says nothing to her about it from day to day, then he confirms all her vows or the pledges binding on her. He confirms them by saying nothing to her when he hears about them. 15If, however, he nullifies them some time after he hears about them, then he is responsible for her guilt."

16These are the regulations the LORD gave Moses concerning relationships between a man and his wife, and between a father and his young daughter still living in his house.

Vengeance on the Midianites

31 The LORD said to Moses, 2"Take vengeance on the Midianites for the Israelites. After that, you will be gathered to your people."

3So Moses said to the people, "Arm some of your men to go to war against the Midianites and to carry out the LORD's vengeance on them. 4Send into battle a thousand men from each of the tribes of Israel." 5So twelve thousand men armed for battle, a thousand from each tribe, were supplied from the clans of Israel. 6Moses sent them into battle, a thousand from each tribe, along with Phinehas son of Eleazar, the priest, who took with him articles from the sanctuary and the trumpets for signaling.

7They fought against Midian, as the LORD commanded Moses, and killed every man. 8Among their victims were Evi, Re-

[a]39 Traditionally *peace offerings*

kem, Zur, Hur and Reba—the five kings of Midian. They also killed Balaam son of Beor with the sword. 9The Israelites captured the Midianite women and children and took all the Midianite herds, flocks and goods as plunder. 10They burned all the towns where the Midianites had settled, as well as all their camps. 11They took all the plunder and spoils, including the people and animals, 12and brought the captives, spoils and plunder to Moses and Eleazar the priest and the Israelite assembly at their camp on the plains of Moab, by the Jordan across from Jericho.[a]

13Moses, Eleazar the priest and all the leaders of the community went to meet them outside the camp. 14Moses was angry with the officers of the army—the commanders of thousands and commanders of hundreds—who returned from the battle.

15"Have you allowed all the women to live?" he asked them. 16"They were the ones who followed Balaam's advice and

[a]12 Hebrew *Jordan of Jericho*; possibly an ancient name for the Jordan River

VERSE FOR THE DAY: Numbers 30:2

AUTHOR: Janis Long Harris

PASSAGE FOR THE DAY: Numbers 30:1–2

One and Only One?

My husband believes in the "one right person" theory of marriage—that God specifically chose me for him, and him for me.

Does God have one—and only one—"right" person in mind for you to marry? When it comes to choosing a spouse, God rarely directs us by sending a vision. But the question changes once we are married. After we commit ourselves to another in marriage, we need to take our vows as seriously as God does. Jesus made it clear that God's intention is for a husband and a wife to stay together throughout their lives. Even when we marry someone who in retrospect may seem like a "wrong" person, God can redeem our choice.

I'm glad my husband believes that God picked me and only me as the "right one" for him. But what I'm really grateful for is the fact that he's committed to working things out—even on those days when I seem like the *wrong* one.

MARRIAGE BUILDERS

♦ *What problems or enticements might tempt you to break your marriage vows?*

♦ *Affirm to your spouse your commitment to remain together "for as long as you both shall live."*

Additional Scripture Readings
Psalm 15:4; Mark 10:1–9; Ephesians 1:11

Go to page 179 for your next devotional reading.

were the means of turning the Israelites
away from the LORD in what happened at
Peor, so that a plague struck the LORD's
people. 17Now kill all the boys. And kill
every woman who has slept with a man,
18but save for yourselves every girl who
has never slept with a man.
19"All of you who have killed anyone or
touched anyone who was killed must stay
outside the camp seven days. On the third
and seventh days you must purify your-
selves and your captives. 20Purify every
garment as well as everything made of
leather, goat hair or wood."
21Then Eleazar the priest said to the sol-
diers who had gone into battle, "This is
the requirement of the law that the LORD
gave Moses: 22Gold, silver, bronze, iron,
tin, lead 23and anything else that can with-
stand fire must be put through the fire,
and then it will be clean. But it must also
be purified with the water of cleansing.
And whatever cannot withstand fire must
be put through that water. 24On the sev-
enth day wash your clothes and you will
be clean. Then you may come into the
camp."

Dividing the Spoils

25The LORD said to Moses, 26"You and
Eleazar the priest and the family heads of
the community are to count all the people
and animals that were captured. 27Divide
the spoils between the soldiers who took
part in the battle and the rest of the com-
munity. 28From the soldiers who fought in
the battle, set apart as tribute for the LORD
one out of every five hundred, whether
persons, cattle, donkeys, sheep or goats.
29Take this tribute from their half share
and give it to Eleazar the priest as the
LORD's part. 30From the Israelites' half, se-
lect one out of every fifty, whether per-
sons, cattle, donkeys, sheep, goats or oth-
er animals. Give them to the Levites, who
are responsible for the care of the LORD's
tabernacle." 31So Moses and Eleazar the
priest did as the LORD commanded Moses.
32The plunder remaining from the
spoils that the soldiers took was 675,000
sheep, 33 72,000 cattle, 34 61,000 donkeys
35and 32,000 women who had never slept
with a man.
36The half share of those who fought in
the battle was:
337,500 sheep, 37of which the tribute
for the LORD was 675;
38 36,000 cattle, of which the tribute for
the LORD was 72;
39 30,500 donkeys, of which the tribute
for the LORD was 61;
40 16,000 people, of which the tribute
for the LORD was 32.
41Moses gave the tribute to Eleazar the
priest as the LORD's part, as the LORD com-
manded Moses.
42The half belonging to the Israelites,
which Moses set apart from that of the
fighting men— 43the community's half—
was 337,500 sheep, 44 36,000 cattle,
45 30,500 donkeys 46and 16,000 people.
47From the Israelites' half, Moses selected
one out of every fifty persons and animals,
as the LORD commanded him, and gave
them to the Levites, who were responsible
for the care of the LORD's tabernacle.
48Then the officers who were over the
units of the army—the commanders of
thousands and commanders of hun-
dreds—went to Moses 49and said to him,
"Your servants have counted the soldiers
under our command, and not one is miss-
ing. 50So we have brought as an offering to
the LORD the gold articles each of us ac-
quired—armlets, bracelets, signet rings,
earrings and necklaces—to make atone-
ment for ourselves before the LORD."
51Moses and Eleazar the priest accepted
from them the gold—all the crafted arti-
cles. 52All the gold from the commanders
of thousands and commanders of hun-
dreds that Moses and Eleazar presented as
a gift to the LORD weighed 16,750 shek-
els.[a] 53Each soldier had taken plunder for
himself. 54Moses and Eleazar the priest ac-
cepted the gold from the commanders of
thousands and commanders of hundreds
and brought it into the Tent of Meeting as
a memorial for the Israelites before the
LORD.

The Transjordan Tribes

32 The Reubenites and Gadites, who
had very large herds and flocks,
saw that the lands of Jazer and Gilead
were suitable for livestock. 2So they came
to Moses and Eleazar the priest and to the
leaders of the community, and said, 3"Ata-
roth, Dibon, Jazer, Nimrah, Heshbon, Ele-
aleh, Sebam, Nebo and Beon— 4the land
the LORD subdued before the people of Is-

[a]52 That is, about 420 pounds (about 190 kilograms)

rael—are suitable for livestock, and your
servants have livestock. 5If we have found
favor in your eyes," they said, "let this
land be given to your servants as our pos-
session. Do not make us cross the Jor-
dan."
6Moses said to the Gadites and Reuben-
ites, "Shall your countrymen go to war
while you sit here? 7Why do you discour-
age the Israelites from going over into the
land the LORD has given them? 8This is
what your fathers did when I sent them
from Kadesh Barnea to look over the land.
9After they went up to the Valley of Eshcol
and viewed the land, they discouraged the
Israelites from entering the land the LORD
had given them. 10The LORD's anger was
aroused that day and he swore this oath:
11'Because they have not followed me
wholeheartedly, not one of the men twen-
ty years old or more who came up out of
Egypt will see the land I promised on oath
to Abraham, Isaac and Jacob— 12not one
except Caleb son of Jephunneh the Keniz-
zite and Joshua son of Nun, for they fol-
lowed the LORD wholeheartedly.' 13The
LORD's anger burned against Israel and he
made them wander in the desert forty
years, until the whole generation of those
who had done evil in his sight was gone.
14"And here you are, a brood of sinners,
standing in the place of your fathers and
making the LORD even more angry with Is-
rael. 15If you turn away from following
him, he will again leave all this people in
the desert, and you will be the cause of
their destruction."
16Then they came up to him and said,
"We would like to build pens here for our
livestock and cities for our women and
children. 17But we are ready to arm our-
selves and go ahead of the Israelites until
we have brought them to their place.
Meanwhile our women and children will
live in fortified cities, for protection from
the inhabitants of the land. 18We will not
return to our homes until every Israelite
has received his inheritance. 19We will not
receive any inheritance with them on the
other side of the Jordan, because our in-
heritance has come to us on the east side
of the Jordan."
20Then Moses said to them, "If you will
do this—if you will arm yourselves before
the LORD for battle, 21and if all of you will
go armed over the Jordan before the LORD
until he has driven his enemies out before
him— 22then when the land is subdued
before the LORD, you may return and be
free from your obligation to the LORD and
to Israel. And this land will be your pos-
session before the LORD.
23"But if you fail to do this, you will be
sinning against the LORD; and you may be
sure that your sin will find you out.
24Build cities for your women and chil-
dren, and pens for your flocks, but do
what you have promised."
25The Gadites and Reubenites said to
Moses, "We your servants will do as our
lord commands. 26Our children and
wives, our flocks and herds will remain
here in the cities of Gilead. 27But your ser-
vants, every man armed for battle, will
cross over to fight before the LORD, just as
our lord says."
28Then Moses gave orders about them
to Eleazar the priest and Joshua son of
Nun and to the family heads of the Israel-
ite tribes. 29He said to them, "If the Gad-
ites and Reubenites, every man armed for
battle, cross over the Jordan with you be-
fore the LORD, then when the land is sub-
dued before you, give them the land of
Gilead as their possession. 30But if they do
not cross over with you armed, they must
accept their possession with you in Ca-
naan."
31The Gadites and Reubenites an-
swered, "Your servants will do what the
LORD has said. 32We will cross over before
the LORD into Canaan armed, but the prop-
erty we inherit will be on this side of the
Jordan."
33Then Moses gave to the Gadites, the
Reubenites and the half-tribe of Manasseh
son of Joseph the kingdom of Sihon king
of the Amorites and the kingdom of Og
king of Bashan—the whole land with its
cities and the territory around them.
34The Gadites built up Dibon, Ataroth,
Aroer, 35Atroth Shophan, Jazer, Jogbehah,
36Beth Nimrah and Beth Haran as fortified
cities, and built pens for their flocks.
37And the Reubenites rebuilt Heshbon,
Elealeh and Kiriathaim, 38as well as Nebo
and Baal Meon (these names were
changed) and Sibmah. They gave names
to the cities they rebuilt.
39The descendants of Makir son of Ma-
nasseh went to Gilead, captured it and
drove out the Amorites who were there.
40So Moses gave Gilead to the Makirites,
the descendants of Manasseh, and they
settled there. 41Jair, a descendant of Ma-
nasseh, captured their settlements and

called them Havvoth Jair.[a] 42And Nobah captured Kenath and its surrounding settlements and called it Nobah after himself.

Stages in Israel's Journey

33 Here are the stages in the journey of the Israelites when they came out of Egypt by divisions under the leadership of Moses and Aaron. 2At the LORD's command Moses recorded the stages in their journey. This is their journey by stages:

3The Israelites set out from Rameses on the fifteenth day of the first month, the day after the Passover. They marched out boldly in full view of all the Egyptians, 4who were burying all their firstborn, whom the LORD had struck down among them; for the LORD had brought judgment on their gods.

5The Israelites left Rameses and camped at Succoth.

6They left Succoth and camped at Etham, on the edge of the desert.

7They left Etham, turned back to Pi Hahiroth, to the east of Baal Zephon, and camped near Migdol.

8They left Pi Hahiroth[b] and passed through the sea into the desert, and when they had traveled for three days in the Desert of Etham, they camped at Marah.

9They left Marah and went to Elim, where there were twelve springs and seventy palm trees, and they camped there.

10They left Elim and camped by the Red Sea.[c]

11They left the Red Sea and camped in the Desert of Sin.

12They left the Desert of Sin and camped at Dophkah.

13They left Dophkah and camped at Alush.

14They left Alush and camped at Rephidim, where there was no water for the people to drink.

15They left Rephidim and camped in the Desert of Sinai.

16They left the Desert of Sinai and camped at Kibroth Hattaavah.

17They left Kibroth Hattaavah and camped at Hazeroth.

18They left Hazeroth and camped at Rithmah.

19They left Rithmah and camped at Rimmon Perez.

20They left Rimmon Perez and camped at Libnah.

21They left Libnah and camped at Rissah.

22They left Rissah and camped at Kehelathah.

23They left Kehelathah and camped at Mount Shepher.

24They left Mount Shepher and camped at Haradah.

25They left Haradah and camped at Makheloth.

26They left Makheloth and camped at Tahath.

27They left Tahath and camped at Terah.

28They left Terah and camped at Mithcah.

29They left Mithcah and camped at Hashmonah.

30They left Hashmonah and camped at Moseroth.

31They left Moseroth and camped at Bene Jaakan.

32They left Bene Jaakan and camped at Hor Haggidgad.

33They left Hor Haggidgad and camped at Jotbathah.

34They left Jotbathah and camped at Abronah.

35They left Abronah and camped at Ezion Geber.

36They left Ezion Geber and camped at Kadesh, in the Desert of Zin.

37They left Kadesh and camped at Mount Hor, on the border of Edom. 38At the LORD's command Aaron the priest went up Mount Hor, where he died on the first day of the fifth month of the fortieth year after the Israelites came out of Egypt. 39Aaron was a hundred and twenty-three years old when he died on Mount Hor.

40The Canaanite king of Arad, who lived in the Negev of Canaan, heard that the Israelites were coming.

41They left Mount Hor and camped at Zalmonah.

[a]41 Or *them the settlements of Jair* [b]8 Many manuscripts of the Masoretic Text, Samaritan Pentateuch and Vulgate; most manuscripts of the Masoretic Text *left from before Hahiroth* [c]10 Hebrew *Yam Suph*; that is, Sea of Reeds; also in verse 11

42They left Zalmonah and camped
at Punon.
43They left Punon and camped at
Oboth.
44They left Oboth and camped at
Iye Abarim, on the border of Moab.
45They left Iyim[a] and camped at
Dibon Gad.
46They left Dibon Gad and camped
at Almon Diblathaim.
47They left Almon Diblathaim and
camped in the mountains of Abarim,
near Nebo.
48They left the mountains of Abarim and camped on the plains of
Moab by the Jordan across from Jericho.[b] 49There on the plains of Moab
they camped along the Jordan from
Beth Jeshimoth to Abel Shittim.

50On the plains of Moab by the Jordan
across from Jericho the LORD said to Moses, 51"Speak to the Israelites and say to
them: 'When you cross the Jordan into
Canaan, 52drive out all the inhabitants of
the land before you. Destroy all their
carved images and their cast idols, and demolish all their high places. 53Take possession of the land and settle in it, for I
have given you the land to possess. 54Distribute the land by lot, according to your
clans. To a larger group give a larger inheritance, and to a smaller group a smaller
one. Whatever falls to them by lot will be
theirs. Distribute it according to your ancestral tribes.
55" 'But if you do not drive out the inhabitants of the land, those you allow to
remain will become barbs in your eyes
and thorns in your sides. They will give
you trouble in the land where you will
live. 56And then I will do to you what I
plan to do to them.' "

Boundaries of Canaan

34 The LORD said to Moses, 2"Command the Israelites and say to
them: 'When you enter Canaan, the land
that will be allotted to you as an inheritance will have these boundaries:

3" 'Your southern side will include
some of the Desert of Zin along the border
of Edom. On the east, your southern
boundary will start from the end of the
Salt Sea,[c] 4cross south of Scorpion[d]
Pass, continue on to Zin and go south of
Kadesh Barnea. Then it will go to Hazar
Addar and over to Azmon, 5where it will
turn, join the Wadi of Egypt and end at the
Sea.[e]
6" 'Your western boundary will be the
coast of the Great Sea. This will be your
boundary on the west.
7" 'For your northern boundary, run a
line from the Great Sea to Mount Hor 8and
from Mount Hor to Lebo[f] Hamath. Then
the boundary will go to Zedad, 9continue
to Ziphron and end at Hazar Enan. This
will be your boundary on the north.
10" 'For your eastern boundary, run a
line from Hazar Enan to Shepham. 11The
boundary will go down from Shepham to
Riblah on the east side of Ain and continue along the slopes east of the Sea of Kinnereth.[g] 12Then the boundary will go
down along the Jordan and end at the Salt
Sea.
" 'This will be your land, with its
boundaries on every side.' "
13Moses commanded the Israelites: "Assign this land by lot as an inheritance. The
LORD has ordered that it be given to the
nine and a half tribes, 14because the families of the tribe of Reuben, the tribe of Gad
and the half-tribe of Manasseh have received their inheritance. 15These two and
a half tribes have received their inheritance on the east side of the Jordan of Jericho,[h] toward the sunrise."
16The LORD said to Moses, 17"These are
the names of the men who are to assign
the land for you as an inheritance: Eleazar
the priest and Joshua son of Nun. 18And
appoint one leader from each tribe to help
assign the land. 19These are their names:

Caleb son of Jephunneh,
from the tribe of Judah;
20Shemuel son of Ammihud,
from the tribe of Simeon;
21Elidad son of Kislon,
from the tribe of Benjamin;
22Bukki son of Jogli,
the leader from the tribe of Dan;
23Hanniel son of Ephod,
the leader from the tribe of Manasseh son of Joseph;
24Kemuel son of Shiphtan,

[a]45 That is, Iye Abarim [b]48 Hebrew *Jordan of Jericho*; possibly an ancient name for the Jordan River; also in verse 50 [c]3 That is, the Dead Sea; also in verse 12 [d]4 Hebrew *Akrabbim* [e]5 That is, the Mediterranean; also in verses 6 and 7 [f]8 Or *to the entrance to* [g]11 That is, Galilee [h]15 *Jordan of Jericho* was possibly an ancient name for the Jordan River.

the leader from the tribe of Ephraim son of Joseph;
25Elizaphan son of Parnach,
the leader from the tribe of Zebulun;
26Paltiel son of Azzan,
the leader from the tribe of Issachar;
27Ahihud son of Shelomi,
the leader from the tribe of Asher;
28Pedahel son of Ammihud,
the leader from the tribe of Naphtali."
29These are the men the LORD commanded to assign the inheritance to the Israelites in the land of Canaan.

Towns for the Levites

35 On the plains of Moab by the Jordan across from Jericho,[a] the LORD said to Moses, 2"Command the Israelites to give the Levites towns to live in from the inheritance the Israelites will possess. And give them pasturelands around the towns. 3Then they will have towns to live in and pasturelands for their cattle, flocks and all their other livestock.
4"The pasturelands around the towns that you give the Levites will extend out fifteen hundred feet[b] from the town wall. 5Outside the town, measure three thousand feet[c] on the east side, three thousand on the south side, three thousand on the west and three thousand on the north, with the town in the center. They will have this area as pastureland for the towns.

Cities of Refuge

6"Six of the towns you give the Levites will be cities of refuge, to which a person who has killed someone may flee. In addition, give them forty-two other towns. 7In all you must give the Levites forty-eight towns, together with their pasturelands. 8The towns you give the Levites from the land the Israelites possess are to be given in proportion to the inheritance of each tribe: Take many towns from a tribe that has many, but few from one that has few."
9Then the LORD said to Moses: 10"Speak to the Israelites and say to them: 'When you cross the Jordan into Canaan, 11select some towns to be your cities of refuge, to which a person who has killed someone accidentally may flee. 12They will be places of refuge from the avenger, so that a person accused of murder may not die before he stands trial before the assembly. 13These six towns you give will be your cities of refuge. 14Give three on this side of the Jordan and three in Canaan as cities of refuge. 15These six towns will be a place of refuge for Israelites, aliens and any other people living among them, so that anyone who has killed another accidentally can flee there.
16" 'If a man strikes someone with an iron object so that he dies, he is a murderer; the murderer shall be put to death. 17Or if anyone has a stone in his hand that could kill, and he strikes someone so that he dies, he is a murderer; the murderer shall be put to death. 18Or if anyone has a wooden object in his hand that could kill, and he hits someone so that he dies, he is a murderer; the murderer shall be put to death. 19The avenger of blood shall put the murderer to death; when he meets him, he shall put him to death. 20If anyone with malice aforethought shoves another or throws something at him intentionally so that he dies 21or if in hostility he hits him with his fist so that he dies, that person shall be put to death; he is a murderer. The avenger of blood shall put the murderer to death when he meets him.
22" 'But if without hostility someone suddenly shoves another or throws something at him unintentionally 23or, without seeing him, drops a stone on him that could kill him, and he dies, then since he was not his enemy and he did not intend to harm him, 24the assembly must judge between him and the avenger of blood according to these regulations. 25The assembly must protect the one accused of murder from the avenger of blood and send him back to the city of refuge to which he fled. He must stay there until the death of the high priest, who was anointed with the holy oil.
26" 'But if the accused ever goes outside the limits of the city of refuge to which he has fled 27and the avenger of blood finds him outside the city, the avenger of blood may kill the accused without being guilty of murder. 28The accused must stay in his city of refuge until the death of the high priest; only after the death of the high priest may he return to his own property.
29" 'These are to be legal requirements

[a] 1 Hebrew *Jordan of Jericho*; possibly an ancient name for the Jordan River [b] 4 Hebrew *a thousand cubits* (about 450 meters) [c] 5 Hebrew *two thousand cubits* (about 900 meters)

for you throughout the generations to
come, wherever you live.
30" 'Anyone who kills a person is to be
put to death as a murderer only on the tes-
timony of witnesses. But no one is to be
put to death on the testimony of only one
witness.
31" 'Do not accept a ransom for the life
of a murderer, who deserves to die. He
must surely be put to death.
32" 'Do not accept a ransom for anyone
who has fled to a city of refuge and so al-
low him to go back and live on his own
land before the death of the high priest.
33" 'Do not pollute the land where you
are. Bloodshed pollutes the land, and
atonement cannot be made for the land on
which blood has been shed, except by the
blood of the one who shed it. 34Do not de-
file the land where you live and where I
dwell, for I, the LORD, dwell among the Is-
raelites.' "

Inheritance of Zelophehad's Daughters

36 The family heads of the clan of Gil-
ead son of Makir, the son of Ma-
nasseh, who were from the clans of the
descendants of Joseph, came and spoke
before Moses and the leaders, the heads of
the Israelite families. 2They said, "When
the LORD commanded my lord to give the
land as an inheritance to the Israelites by
lot, he ordered you to give the inheritance
of our brother Zelophehad to his daugh-
ters. 3Now suppose they marry men from
other Israelite tribes; then their inheri-
tance will be taken from our ancestral in-
heritance and added to that of the tribe
they marry into. And so part of the inheri-
tance allotted to us will be taken away.
4When the Year of Jubilee for the Israel-
ites comes, their inheritance will be added
to that of the tribe into which they marry,
and their property will be taken from the
tribal inheritance of our forefathers."
5Then at the LORD's command Moses
gave this order to the Israelites: "What the
tribe of the descendants of Joseph is say-
ing is right. 6This is what the LORD com-
mands for Zelophehad's daughters: They
may marry anyone they please as long as
they marry within the tribal clan of their
father. 7No inheritance in Israel is to pass
from tribe to tribe, for every Israelite shall
keep the tribal land inherited from his
forefathers. 8Every daughter who inherits
land in any Israelite tribe must marry
someone in her father's tribal clan, so that
every Israelite will possess the inheritance
of his fathers. 9No inheritance may pass
from tribe to tribe, for each Israelite tribe
is to keep the land it inherits."
10So Zelophehad's daughters did as the
LORD commanded Moses. 11Zelophehad's
daughters—Mahlah, Tirzah, Hoglah, Mil-
cah and Noah—married their cousins on
their father's side. 12They married within
the clans of the descendants of Manasseh
son of Joseph, and their inheritance re-
mained in their father's clan and tribe.
13These are the commands and regula-
tions the LORD gave through Moses to the
Israelites on the plains of Moab by the Jor-
dan across from Jericho.[a]

[a]13 Hebrew *Jordan of Jericho*; possibly an ancient name for the Jordan River

IN this book Moses records his farewell address to the nation of Israel as they wait on the bank of the Jordan River, ready to cross over into the land of Canaan. He reminds them of God's care in the past and of his laws, and he challenges them to rededicate their lives to serving the Lord. As you read this book, think about God's daily care in your life and his desire that you dedicate your life to serving him.

DEUTERONOMY

The Command to Leave Horeb

1 These are the words Moses spoke to all Israel in the desert east of the Jordan—that is, in the Arabah—opposite Suph, between Paran and Tophel, Laban, Hazeroth and Dizahab. [2](It takes eleven days to go from Horeb to Kadesh Barnea by the Mount Seir road.)

[3]In the fortieth year, on the first day of the eleventh month, Moses proclaimed to the Israelites all that the LORD had commanded him concerning them. [4]This was after he had defeated Sihon king of the Amorites, who reigned in Heshbon, and at Edrei had defeated Og king of Bashan, who reigned in Ashtaroth.

[5]East of the Jordan in the territory of Moab, Moses began to expound this law, saying:

[6]The LORD our God said to us at Horeb, "You have stayed long enough at this mountain. [7]Break camp and advance into the hill country of the Amorites; go to all the neighboring peoples in the Arabah, in the mountains, in the western foothills, in the Negev and along the coast, to the land of the Canaanites and to Lebanon, as far as the great river, the Euphrates. [8]See, I have given you this land. Go in and take possession of the land that the LORD swore he would give to your fathers—to Abraham, Isaac and Jacob—and to their descendants after them."

The Appointment of Leaders

9At that time I said to you, "You are too
heavy a burden for me to carry alone.
10The LORD your God has increased your
numbers so that today you are as many as
the stars in the sky. 11May the LORD, the
God of your fathers, increase you a thou-
sand times and bless you as he has prom-
ised! 12But how can I bear your problems
and your burdens and your disputes all by
myself? 13Choose some wise, understand-
ing and respected men from each of your
tribes, and I will set them over you."
14You answered me, "What you pro-
pose to do is good."
15So I took the leading men of your
tribes, wise and respected men, and ap-
pointed them to have authority over
you—as commanders of thousands, of
hundreds, of fifties and of tens and as trib-
al officials. 16And I charged your judges at
that time: Hear the disputes between your
brothers and judge fairly, whether the
case is between brother Israelites or be-
tween one of them and an alien. 17Do not
show partiality in judging; hear both small
and great alike. Do not be afraid of any
man, for judgment belongs to God. Bring
me any case too hard for you, and I will
hear it. 18And at that time I told you every-
thing you were to do.

Spies Sent Out

19Then, as the LORD our God command-
ed us, we set out from Horeb and went to-
ward the hill country of the Amorites
through all that vast and dreadful desert
that you have seen, and so we reached Ka-
desh Barnea. 20Then I said to you, "You
have reached the hill country of the Amo-
rites, which the LORD our God is giving us.
21See, the LORD your God has given you
the land. Go up and take possession of it
as the LORD, the God of your fathers, told
you. Do not be afraid; do not be dis-
couraged."
22Then all of you came to me and said,
"Let us send men ahead to spy out the
land for us and bring back a report about
the route we are to take and the towns we
will come to."
23The idea seemed good to me; so I se-
lected twelve of you, one man from each
tribe. 24They left and went up into the hill
country, and came to the Valley of Eshcol
and explored it. 25Taking with them some
of the fruit of the land, they brought it
down to us and reported, "It is a good land
that the LORD our God is giving us."

Rebellion Against the LORD

26But you were unwilling to go up; you
rebelled against the command of the LORD
your God. 27You grumbled in your tents
and said, "The LORD hates us; so he
brought us out of Egypt to deliver us into
the hands of the Amorites to destroy us.
28Where can we go? Our brothers have
made us lose heart. They say, 'The people
are stronger and taller than we are; the cit-
ies are large, with walls up to the sky. We
even saw the Anakites there.' "
29Then I said to you, "Do not be terri-
fied; do not be afraid of them. 30The LORD
your God, who is going before you, will
fight for you, as he did for you in Egypt,
before your very eyes, 31and in the desert.
There you saw how the LORD your God
carried you, as a father carries his son, all
the way you went until you reached this
place."
32In spite of this, you did not trust in the
LORD your God, 33who went ahead of you
on your journey, in fire by night and in a
cloud by day, to search out places for you
to camp and to show you the way you
should go.
34When the LORD heard what you said,
he was angry and solemnly swore: 35"Not
a man of this evil generation shall see the
good land I swore to give your forefathers,
36except Caleb son of Jephunneh. He will
see it, and I will give him and his descen-
dants the land he set his feet on, because
he followed the LORD wholeheartedly."
37Because of you the LORD became an-
gry with me also and said, "You shall not
enter it, either. 38But your assistant, Josh-
ua son of Nun, will enter it. Encourage
him, because he will lead Israel to inherit
it. 39And the little ones that you said
would be taken captive, your children
who do not yet know good from bad—
they will enter the land. I will give it to
them and they will take possession of it.
40But as for you, turn around and set out
toward the desert along the route to the
Red Sea.[a]"
41Then you replied, "We have sinned
against the LORD. We will go up and fight,
as the LORD our God commanded us." So
every one of you put on his weapons,

[a]40 Hebrew *Yam Suph*; that is, Sea of Reeds

thinking it easy to go up into the hill country.

42But the LORD said to me, "Tell them, 'Do not go up and fight, because I will not be with you. You will be defeated by your enemies.' "

43So I told you, but you would not listen. You rebelled against the LORD's command and in your arrogance you marched up into the hill country. 44The Amorites who lived in those hills came out against you; they chased you like a swarm of bees and beat you down from Seir all the way to Hormah. 45You came back and wept before the LORD, but he paid no attention to your weeping and turned a deaf ear to you. 46And so you stayed in Kadesh many days—all the time you spent there.

Wanderings in the Desert

2 Then we turned back and set out toward the desert along the route to the Red Sea,[a] as the LORD had directed me. For a long time we made our way around the hill country of Seir.

2Then the LORD said to me, 3"You have made your way around this hill country long enough; now turn north. 4Give the people these orders: 'You are about to pass through the territory of your brothers the descendants of Esau, who live in Seir. They will be afraid of you, but be very careful. 5Do not provoke them to war, for I will not give you any of their land, not even enough to put your foot on. I have given Esau the hill country of Seir as his own. 6You are to pay them in silver for the food you eat and the water you drink.' "

7The LORD your God has blessed you in all the work of your hands. He has watched over your journey through this vast desert. These forty years the LORD your God has been with you, and you have not lacked anything.

8So we went on past our brothers the descendants of Esau, who live in Seir. We turned from the Arabah road, which comes up from Elath and Ezion Geber, and traveled along the desert road of Moab.

9Then the LORD said to me, "Do not harass the Moabites or provoke them to war, for I will not give you any part of their land. I have given Ar to the descendants of Lot as a possession."

10(The Emites used to live there—a people strong and numerous, and as tall as the Anakites. 11Like the Anakites, they too were considered Rephaites, but the Moabites called them Emites. 12Horites used to live in Seir, but the descendants of Esau drove them out. They destroyed the Horites from before them and settled in their place, just as Israel did in the land the LORD gave them as their possession.)

13And the LORD said, "Now get up and cross the Zered Valley." So we crossed the valley.

14Thirty-eight years passed from the time we left Kadesh Barnea until we crossed the Zered Valley. By then, that entire generation of fighting men had perished from the camp, as the LORD had sworn to them. 15The LORD's hand was against them until he had completely eliminated them from the camp.

16Now when the last of these fighting men among the people had died, 17the LORD said to me, 18"Today you are to pass by the region of Moab at Ar. 19When you come to the Ammonites, do not harass them or provoke them to war, for I will not give you possession of any land belonging to the Ammonites. I have given it as a possession to the descendants of Lot."

20(That too was considered a land of the Rephaites, who used to live there; but the Ammonites called them Zamzummites. 21They were a people strong and numerous, and as tall as the Anakites. The LORD destroyed them from before the Ammonites, who drove them out and settled in their place. 22The LORD had done the same for the descendants of Esau, who lived in Seir, when he destroyed the Horites from before them. They drove them out and have lived in their place to this day. 23And as for the Avvites who lived in villages as far as Gaza, the Caphtorites coming out from Caphtor[b] destroyed them and settled in their place.)

Defeat of Sihon King of Heshbon

24"Set out now and cross the Arnon Gorge. See, I have given into your hand Sihon the Amorite, king of Heshbon, and his country. Begin to take possession of it and engage him in battle. 25This very day I will begin to put the terror and fear of you on all the nations under heaven. They will hear reports of you and will tremble and be in anguish because of you."

26From the desert of Kedemoth I sent messengers to Sihon king of Heshbon of-

[a] 1 Hebrew *Yam Suph*; that is, Sea of Reeds [b] 23 That is, Crete

fering peace and saying, 27"Let us pass
through your country. We will stay on the
main road; we will not turn aside to the
right or to the left. 28Sell us food to eat and
water to drink for their price in silver.
Only let us pass through on foot— 29as
the descendants of Esau, who live in Seir,
and the Moabites, who live in Ar, did for
us—until we cross the Jordan into the
land the LORD our God is giving us." 30But
Sihon king of Heshbon refused to let us
pass through. For the LORD your God had
made his spirit stubborn and his heart obstinate in order to give him into your
hands, as he has now done.

31The LORD said to me, "See, I have begun to deliver Sihon and his country over
to you. Now begin to conquer and possess
his land."

32When Sihon and all his army came
out to meet us in battle at Jahaz, 33the
LORD our God delivered him over to us
and we struck him down, together with
his sons and his whole army. 34At that
time we took all his towns and completely
destroyed[a] them—men, women and
children. We left no survivors. 35But the
livestock and the plunder from the towns
we had captured we carried off for ourselves. 36From Aroer on the rim of the Arnon Gorge, and from the town in the
gorge, even as far as Gilead, not one town
was too strong for us. The LORD our God
gave us all of them. 37But in accordance
with the command of the LORD our God,
you did not encroach on any of the land of
the Ammonites, neither the land along the
course of the Jabbok nor that around the
towns in the hills.

Defeat of Og King of Bashan

3 Next we turned and went up along the
road toward Bashan, and Og king of
Bashan with his whole army marched out
to meet us in battle at Edrei. 2The LORD
said to me, "Do not be afraid of him, for I
have handed him over to you with his
whole army and his land. Do to him what
you did to Sihon king of the Amorites,
who reigned in Heshbon."

3So the LORD our God also gave into our
hands Og king of Bashan and all his army.
We struck them down, leaving no survivors. 4At that time we took all his cities.
There was not one of the sixty cities that
we did not take from them—the whole region of Argob, Og's kingdom in Bashan.
5All these cities were fortified with high
walls and with gates and bars, and there
were also a great many unwalled villages.
6We completely destroyed[a] them, as we
had done with Sihon king of Heshbon, destroying[a] every city—men, women and
children. 7But all the livestock and the
plunder from their cities we carried off for
ourselves.

8So at that time we took from these two
kings of the Amorites the territory east of
the Jordan, from the Arnon Gorge as far as
Mount Hermon. 9(Hermon is called Sirion
by the Sidonians; the Amorites call it Senir.) 10We took all the towns on the plateau, and all Gilead, and all Bashan as far
as Salecah and Edrei, towns of Og's kingdom in Bashan. 11(Only Og king of Bashan
was left of the remnant of the Rephaites.
His bed[b] was made of iron and was more
than thirteen feet long and six feet wide.[c]
It is still in Rabbah of the Ammonites.)

Division of the Land

12Of the land that we took over at that
time, I gave the Reubenites and the Gadites the territory north of Aroer by the Arnon Gorge, including half the hill country
of Gilead, together with its towns. 13The
rest of Gilead and also all of Bashan, the
kingdom of Og, I gave to the half tribe of
Manasseh. (The whole region of Argob in
Bashan used to be known as a land of the
Rephaites. 14Jair, a descendant of Manasseh, took the whole region of Argob as far
as the border of the Geshurites and the
Maacathites; it was named after him, so
that to this day Bashan is called Havvoth
Jair.[d]) 15And I gave Gilead to Makir.
16But to the Reubenites and the Gadites I
gave the territory extending from Gilead
down to the Arnon Gorge (the middle of
the gorge being the border) and out to the
Jabbok River, which is the border of the
Ammonites. 17Its western border was the
Jordan in the Arabah, from Kinnereth to
the Sea of the Arabah (the Salt Sea[e]), below the slopes of Pisgah.

18I commanded you at that time: "The
LORD your God has given you this land to
take possession of it. But all your able-

[a] *34,6* The Hebrew term refers to the irrevocable giving over of things or persons to the LORD, often by totally destroying them. [b] *11* Or *sarcophagus* [c] *11* Hebrew *nine cubits long and four cubits wide* (about 4 meters long and 1.8 meters wide) [d] *14* Or *called the settlements of Jair* [e] *17* That is, the Dead Sea

bodied men, armed for battle, must cross
over ahead of your brother Israelites.
19However, your wives, your children and
your livestock (I know you have much
livestock) may stay in the towns I have
given you, 20until the LORD gives rest to
your brothers as he has to you, and they
too have taken over the land that the LORD
your God is giving them, across the Jor-
dan. After that, each of you may go back
to the possession I have given you."

Moses Forbidden to Cross the Jordan

21At that time I commanded Joshua:
"You have seen with your own eyes all
that the LORD your God has done to these
two kings. The LORD will do the same to all
the kingdoms over there where you are
going. 22Do not be afraid of them; the
LORD your God himself will fight for you."
23At that time I pleaded with the LORD:
24"O Sovereign LORD, you have begun to

VERSE FOR THE DAY: Deuteronomy 3:28 | AUTHOR: Beth Spring | PASSAGE FOR THE DAY: Deuteronomy 3:21–29

Get Out of the Dumps

I knew my husband's master's degree program was getting to him when he began calling his study room "the dungeon of doom." For three years Jeff had taken one or two evening classes each week while holding down a demanding full-time job.

For him, there was simply too much to do and too little time. Planning an evening out or saying "yes" to an invitation hinged on when midterms and finals were scheduled. And I had to do without the car regularly so Jeff would have a quicker commute. Our lifestyle adjustments became even more challenging after our son arrived, about a year before Jeff finished the master's program.

The week before his comprehensive exams, Jeff needed extra study time and encouragement. Uncertainty about the test plagued him, so I did all I could to keep him happy. I fixed a favorite dessert, and stocked his "dungeon" with late-night snacks. Finally the day arrived, and Jeff took the five-hour written exam. Afterward he came up the walk with a smile on his face. "No problem," was the verdict. And he presented me with a bouquet of flowers "for co-laboring with me."

For a moment, I forgot which one of us had earned the degree.

MARRIAGE BUILDERS

♦ *What challenges is your spouse facing for which your encouragement would provide a boost?*

♦ *What are two practical things you can do this week to encourage your spouse?*

Additional Scripture Readings
1 Thessalonians 5:12–15; Hebrews 3:13; 1 Peter 3:7

Go to page 181 for your next devotional reading.

show to your servant your greatness and
your strong hand. For what god is there in
heaven or on earth who can do the deeds
and mighty works you do? 25Let me go
over and see the good land beyond the
Jordan—that fine hill country and Leba-
non."

26But because of you the LORD was an-
gry with me and would not listen to me.
"That is enough," the LORD said. "Do not
speak to me anymore about this matter.
27Go up to the top of Pisgah and look west
and north and south and east. Look at the
land with your own eyes, since you are
not going to cross this Jordan. 28But com-
mission Joshua, and encourage and
strengthen him, for he will lead this peo-
ple across and will cause them to inherit
the land that you will see." 29So we stayed
in the valley near Beth Peor.

Obedience Commanded

4 Hear now, O Israel, the decrees and
laws I am about to teach you. Follow
them so that you may live and may go in
and take possession of the land that the
LORD, the God of your fathers, is giving
you. 2Do not add to what I command you
and do not subtract from it, but keep the
commands of the LORD your God that I
give you.

3You saw with your own eyes what the
LORD did at Baal Peor. The LORD your God
destroyed from among you everyone who
followed the Baal of Peor, 4but all of you
who held fast to the LORD your God are
still alive today.

5See, I have taught you decrees and
laws as the LORD my God commanded me,
so that you may follow them in the land
you are entering to take possession of it.
6Observe them carefully, for this will
show your wisdom and understanding to
the nations, who will hear about all these
decrees and say, "Surely this great nation
is a wise and understanding people."
7What other nation is so great as to have
their gods near them the way the LORD our
God is near us whenever we pray to him?
8And what other nation is so great as to
have such righteous decrees and laws as
this body of laws I am setting before you
today?

9Only be careful, and watch yourselves
closely so that you do not forget the things
your eyes have seen or let them slip from
your heart as long as you live. Teach them
to your children and to their children after
them. 10Remember the day you stood be-
fore the LORD your God at Horeb, when he
said to me, "Assemble the people before
me to hear my words so that they may
learn to revere me as long as they live in
the land and may teach them to their chil-
dren." 11You came near and stood at the
foot of the mountain while it blazed with
fire to the very heavens, with black clouds
and deep darkness. 12Then the LORD
spoke to you out of the fire. You heard the
sound of words but saw no form; there
was only a voice. 13He declared to you his
covenant, the Ten Commandments,
which he commanded you to follow and
then wrote them on two stone tablets.
14And the LORD directed me at that time to
teach you the decrees and laws you are to
follow in the land that you are crossing
the Jordan to possess.

Idolatry Forbidden

15You saw no form of any kind the day
the LORD spoke to you at Horeb out of the
fire. Therefore watch yourselves very
carefully, 16so that you do not become
corrupt and make for yourselves an idol,
an image of any shape, whether formed
like a man or a woman, 17or like any ani-
mal on earth or any bird that flies in the
air, 18or like any creature that moves
along the ground or any fish in the waters
below. 19And when you look up to the sky
and see the sun, the moon and the stars—
all the heavenly array—do not be enticed
into bowing down to them and worship-
ing things the LORD your God has appor-
tioned to all the nations under heaven.
20But as for you, the LORD took you and
brought you out of the iron-smelting fur-
nace, out of Egypt, to be the people of his
inheritance, as you now are.

21The LORD was angry with me because
of you, and he solemnly swore that I
would not cross the Jordan and enter the
good land the LORD your God is giving you
as your inheritance. 22I will die in this
land; I will not cross the Jordan; but you
are about to cross over and take posses-
sion of that good land. 23Be careful not to
forget the covenant of the LORD your God
that he made with you; do not make for
yourselves an idol in the form of anything
the LORD your God has forbidden. 24For
the LORD your God is a consuming fire, a
jealous God.

25After you have had children and
grandchildren and have lived in the land
a long time—if you then become corrupt
and make any kind of idol, doing evil in

the eyes of the LORD your God and provoking him to anger, [26]I call heaven and earth as witnesses against you this day that you will quickly perish from the land that you are crossing the Jordan to possess. You will not live there long but will certainly be destroyed. [27]The LORD will scatter you among the peoples, and only a few of you will survive among the nations to which the LORD will drive you. [28]There you will worship man-made gods of wood and stone, which cannot see or hear or eat or smell. [29]But if from there you seek the LORD your God, you will find him if you look for him with all your heart and with all your soul. [30]When you are in distress and all these things have happened to you, then in later days you will return to

VERSE FOR THE DAY: Deuteronomy 4:24

AUTHOR: Henri J. M. Nouwen

PASSAGE FOR THE DAY: Deuteronomy 4:9, 23–24

A Jealous God

When we have to wait for delayed airplanes we read *Time* and *Newsweek*, but do we pray? When we have a whole evening without concrete plans we watch TV, go to a movie, read a book, write some letters, or make phone calls, but do we pray? There appear to be empty hours in our lives to pray, so there must be something else getting in the way of prayer than just being too busy!

Our ambivalence about prayer reveals to us what kind of God our God is. We intuitively know that God is not someone who just seeks our occasional attention, and waits for our occasional prayers. God is not someone who can easily do without us and will be quite content when we are willing to spend a few hours of the weekend talking to him. If God were that kind of God we would not experience so many tensions when we enter into his presence to pray. No, our tensions come from the awareness that God is a jealous lover.

Moses said to his people, "The LORD your God is a consuming fire, a jealous God" (Deuteronomy 4:24), and Paul said to his brothers and sisters in Corinth that he loved them with the jealous love of God (2 Cor. 11:2). God is a lover who does not want to leave us alone for one second of our day or night. God is asking for our total, undivided attention.

MARRIAGE BUILDERS

♦ *How have you learned to fit times of prayer and focusing on God into spare moments of your day?*

♦ *What are regular times of prayer you share as a couple?*

Additional Scripture Readings
Deuteronomy 5:8–10; Exodus 20:4–6; 2 Corinthians 11:2

Go to page 184 for your next devotional reading.

the LORD your God and obey him. 31For the LORD your God is a merciful God; he will not abandon or destroy you or forget the covenant with your forefathers, which he confirmed to them by oath.

The LORD Is God

32Ask now about the former days, long before your time, from the day God created man on the earth; ask from one end of the heavens to the other. Has anything so great as this ever happened, or has anything like it ever been heard of? 33Has any other people heard the voice of God[a] speaking out of fire, as you have, and lived? 34Has any god ever tried to take for himself one nation out of another nation, by testings, by miraculous signs and wonders, by war, by a mighty hand and an outstretched arm, or by great and awesome deeds, like all the things the LORD your God did for you in Egypt before your very eyes?

35You were shown these things so that you might know that the LORD is God; besides him there is no other. 36From heaven he made you hear his voice to discipline you. On earth he showed you his great fire, and you heard his words from out of the fire. 37Because he loved your forefathers and chose their descendants after them, he brought you out of Egypt by his Presence and his great strength, 38to drive out before you nations greater and stronger than you and to bring you into their land to give it to you for your inheritance, as it is today.

39Acknowledge and take to heart this day that the LORD is God in heaven above and on the earth below. There is no other. 40Keep his decrees and commands, which I am giving you today, so that it may go well with you and your children after you and that you may live long in the land the LORD your God gives you for all time.

Cities of Refuge

41Then Moses set aside three cities east of the Jordan, 42to which anyone who had killed a person could flee if he had unintentionally killed his neighbor without malice aforethought. He could flee into one of these cities and save his life. 43The cities were these: Bezer in the desert plateau, for the Reubenites; Ramoth in Gilead, for the Gadites; and Golan in Bashan, for the Manassites.

Introduction to the Law

44This is the law Moses set before the Israelites. 45These are the stipulations, decrees and laws Moses gave them when they came out of Egypt 46and were in the valley near Beth Peor east of the Jordan, in the land of Sihon king of the Amorites, who reigned in Heshbon and was defeated by Moses and the Israelites as they came out of Egypt. 47They took possession of his land and the land of Og king of Bashan, the two Amorite kings east of the Jordan. 48This land extended from Aroer on the rim of the Arnon Gorge to Mount Siyon[b] (that is, Hermon), 49and included all the Arabah east of the Jordan, as far as the Sea of the Arabah,[c] below the slopes of Pisgah.

The Ten Commandments

5 Moses summoned all Israel and said: Hear, O Israel, the decrees and laws I declare in your hearing today. Learn them and be sure to follow them. 2The LORD our God made a covenant with us at Horeb. 3It was not with our fathers that the LORD made this covenant, but with us, with all of us who are alive here today. 4The LORD spoke to you face to face out of the fire on the mountain. 5(At that time I stood between the LORD and you to declare to you the word of the LORD, because you were afraid of the fire and did not go up the mountain.) And he said:

> 6"I am the LORD your God, who brought you out of Egypt, out of the land of slavery.
> 7"You shall have no other gods before[d] me.
> 8"You shall not make for yourself an idol in the form of anything in heaven above or on the earth beneath or in the waters below. 9You shall not bow down to them or worship them; for I, the LORD your God, am a jealous God, punishing the children for the sin of the fathers to the third and fourth generation of those who hate me, 10but showing love to a thousand ⌞generations⌟

[a]33 Or *of a god* [b]48 Hebrew; Syriac (see also Deut. 3:9) *Sirion* [c]49 That is, the Dead Sea
[d]7 Or *besides*

of those who love me and keep
my commandments.
11"You shall not misuse the name of
the LORD your God, for the LORD
will not hold anyone guiltless
who misuses his name.
12"Observe the Sabbath day by keep-
ing it holy, as the LORD your
God has commanded you. 13Six
days you shall labor and do all
your work, 14but the seventh
day is a Sabbath to the LORD
your God. On it you shall not do
any work, neither you, nor your
son or daughter, nor your man-
servant or maidservant, nor
your ox, your donkey or any of
your animals, nor the alien
within your gates, so that your
manservant and maidservant
may rest, as you do. 15Remem-
ber that you were slaves in
Egypt and that the LORD your
God brought you out of there
with a mighty hand and an out-
stretched arm. Therefore the
LORD your God has commanded
you to observe the Sabbath day.
16"Honor your father and your moth-
er, as the LORD your God has
commanded you, so that you
may live long and that it may go
well with you in the land the
LORD your God is giving you.
17"You shall not murder.
18"You shall not commit adultery.
19"You shall not steal.
20"You shall not give false testimony
against your neighbor.
21"You shall not covet your neighbor's
wife. You shall not set your de-
sire on your neighbor's house
or land, his manservant or
maidservant, his ox or donkey,
or anything that belongs to your
neighbor."

22These are the commandments the LORD proclaimed in a loud voice to your whole assembly there on the mountain from out of the fire, the cloud and the deep darkness; and he added nothing more. Then he wrote them on two stone tablets and gave them to me.

23When you heard the voice out of the darkness, while the mountain was ablaze with fire, all the leading men of your tribes and your elders came to me. 24And you said, "The LORD our God has shown us his glory and his majesty, and we have heard his voice from the fire. Today we have seen that a man can live even if God speaks with him. 25But now, why should we die? This great fire will consume us, and we will die if we hear the voice of the LORD our God any longer. 26For what mortal man has ever heard the voice of the living God speaking out of fire, as we have, and survived? 27Go near and listen to all that the LORD our God says. Then tell us whatever the LORD our God tells you. We will listen and obey."

28The LORD heard you when you spoke to me and the LORD said to me, "I have heard what this people said to you. Everything they said was good. 29Oh, that their hearts would be inclined to fear me and keep all my commands always, so that it might go well with them and their children forever!

30"Go, tell them to return to their tents. 31But you stay here with me so that I may give you all the commands, decrees and laws you are to teach them to follow in the land I am giving them to possess."

32So be careful to do what the LORD your God has commanded you; do not turn aside to the right or to the left. 33Walk in all the way that the LORD your God has commanded you, so that you may live and prosper and prolong your days in the land that you will possess.

Love the LORD Your God

6 These are the commands, decrees and laws the LORD your God directed me to teach you to observe in the land that you are crossing the Jordan to possess, 2so that you, your children and their children after them may fear the LORD your God as long as you live by keeping all his decrees and commands that I give you, and so that you may enjoy long life. 3Hear, O Israel, and be careful to obey so that it may go well with you and that you may increase greatly in a land flowing with milk and honey, just as the LORD, the God of your fathers, promised you.

4Hear, O Israel: The LORD our God, the LORD is one.[a] 5Love the LORD your God with all your heart and with all your soul and with all your strength. 6These com-

[a]4 Or *The LORD our God is one LORD*; or *The LORD is our God, the LORD is one*; or *The LORD is our God, the LORD alone*

mandments that I give you today are to be
upon your hearts. 7Impress them on your
children. Talk about them when you sit at
home and when you walk along the road,
when you lie down and when you get up.
8Tie them as symbols on your hands and
bind them on your foreheads. 9Write
them on the doorframes of your houses
and on your gates.

10When the LORD your God brings you
into the land he swore to your fathers, to
Abraham, Isaac and Jacob, to give you—a
land with large, flourishing cities you did
not build, 11houses filled with all kinds of
good things you did not provide, wells
you did not dig, and vineyards and olive
groves you did not plant—then when
you eat and are satisfied, 12be careful
that you do not forget the LORD, who
brought you out of Egypt, out of the land
of slavery.

13Fear the LORD your God, serve him
only and take your oaths in his name.
14Do not follow other gods, the gods of the
peoples around you; 15for the LORD your
God, who is among you, is a jealous God
and his anger will burn against you, and
he will destroy you from the face of the
land. 16Do not test the LORD your God as
you did at Massah. 17Be sure to keep the
commands of the LORD your God and the
stipulations and decrees he has given you.
18Do what is right and good in the LORD's
sight, so that it may go well with you and
you may go in and take over the good land
that the LORD promised on oath to your
forefathers, 19thrusting out all your ene-
mies before you, as the LORD said.

VERSE FOR THE DAY: Deuteronomy 6:4–5

AUTHOR: Larry Crabb

PASSAGE FOR THE DAY: Deuteronomy 6:1–9

Trusting God's Goodness

God asks us to trust him whether things are going well or going against us. It's always worthwhile to love my wife, even on days when I'd just as soon walk out. It's worthwhile to go to work every day, even though my boss might be driving me crazy.

Oswald Chambers wrote, "The root of all sin is the suspicion that God isn't good." Amid times of pain, questioning and anger, you need to say to God, "I'm not going to stop believing in your goodness, but I've got to know you better. I'm not demanding that you do anything for me. I'm coming to you just for you."

That's an appetite for God. That's seeking him with all your heart.

MARRIAGE BUILDERS

- *What troubling question do you wish God would answer for you?*
- *How can you practice coming to God just for him, without demands?*

Additional Scripture Readings
Psalm 25:1-3; Mark 12:28–34

Go to page 186 for your next devotional reading.

[20]In the future, when your son asks you, "What is the meaning of the stipulations, decrees and laws the LORD our God has commanded you?" [21]tell him: "We were slaves of Pharaoh in Egypt, but the LORD brought us out of Egypt with a mighty hand. [22]Before our eyes the LORD sent miraculous signs and wonders—great and terrible—upon Egypt and Pharaoh and his whole household. [23]But he brought us out from there to bring us in and give us the land that he promised on oath to our forefathers. [24]The LORD commanded us to obey all these decrees and to fear the LORD our God, so that we might always prosper and be kept alive, as is the case today. [25]And if we are careful to obey all this law before the LORD our God, as he has commanded us, that will be our righteousness."

Driving Out the Nations

7 When the LORD your God brings you into the land you are entering to possess and drives out before you many nations—the Hittites, Girgashites, Amorites, Canaanites, Perizzites, Hivites and Jebusites, seven nations larger and stronger than you— [2]and when the LORD your God has delivered them over to you and you have defeated them, then you must destroy them totally.[a] Make no treaty with them, and show them no mercy. [3]Do not intermarry with them. Do not give your daughters to their sons or take their daughters for your sons, [4]for they will turn your sons away from following me to serve other gods, and the LORD's anger will burn against you and will quickly destroy you. [5]This is what you are to do to them: Break down their altars, smash their sacred stones, cut down their Asherah poles[b] and burn their idols in the fire. [6]For you are a people holy to the LORD your God. The LORD your God has chosen you out of all the peoples on the face of the earth to be his people, his treasured possession.

[7]The LORD did not set his affection on you and choose you because you were more numerous than other peoples, for you were the fewest of all peoples. [8]But it was because the LORD loved you and kept the oath he swore to your forefathers that he brought you out with a mighty hand and redeemed you from the land of slavery, from the power of Pharaoh king of Egypt. [9]Know therefore that the LORD your God is God; he is the faithful God, keeping his covenant of love to a thousand generations of those who love him and keep his commands. [10]But

those who hate him he will repay to
their face by destruction;
he will not be slow to repay to their
face those who hate him.

[11]Therefore, take care to follow the commands, decrees and laws I give you today.

[12]If you pay attention to these laws and are careful to follow them, then the LORD your God will keep his covenant of love with you, as he swore to your forefathers. [13]He will love you and bless you and increase your numbers. He will bless the fruit of your womb, the crops of your land—your grain, new wine and oil—the calves of your herds and the lambs of your flocks in the land that he swore to your forefathers to give you. [14]You will be blessed more than any other people; none of your men or women will be childless, nor any of your livestock without young. [15]The LORD will keep you free from every disease. He will not inflict on you the horrible diseases you knew in Egypt, but he will inflict them on all who hate you. [16]You must destroy all the peoples the LORD your God gives over to you. Do not look on them with pity and do not serve their gods, for that will be a snare to you.

[17]You may say to yourselves, "These nations are stronger than we are. How can we drive them out?" [18]But do not be afraid of them; remember well what the LORD your God did to Pharaoh and to all Egypt. [19]You saw with your own eyes the great trials, the miraculous signs and wonders, the mighty hand and outstretched arm, with which the LORD your God brought you out. The LORD your God will do the same to all the peoples you now fear. [20]Moreover, the LORD your God will send the hornet among them until even the survivors who hide from you have perished. [21]Do not be terrified by them, for the LORD your God, who is among you, is a great and awesome God. [22]The LORD your God will drive out those nations before you, little by little. You will not be allowed to

[a]2 The Hebrew term refers to the irrevocable giving over of things or persons to the LORD, often by totally destroying them; also in verse 26. [b]5 That is, symbols of the goddess Asherah; here and elsewhere in Deuteronomy

eliminate them all at once, or the wild animals will multiply around you. 23But the LORD your God will deliver them over to you, throwing them into great confusion until they are destroyed. 24He will give their kings into your hand, and you will wipe out their names from under heaven. No one will be able to stand up against you; you will destroy them. 25The images of their gods you are to burn in the fire. Do not covet the silver and gold on them, and do not take it for yourselves, or you will be ensnared by it, for it is detestable to the LORD your God. 26Do not bring a detestable thing into your house or you, like it, will be set apart for destruction. Utterly abhor and detest it, for it is set apart for destruction.

Do Not Forget the LORD

8 Be careful to follow every command I am giving you today, so that you may live and increase and may enter and possess the land that the LORD promised on oath to your forefathers. 2Remember how the LORD your God led you all the way in

VERSE FOR THE DAY: Deuteronomy 8:6

AUTHOR: Gary Kinnaman

PASSAGE FOR THE DAY: Deuteronomy 8:1–20

Do Things God's Way

Too many Christians accept the cultural value of individualism. We prize independence so much that we fail to recognize the beauty and blessing of shared life. The solution involves turning our obsession to satisfy ourselves into love for others.

God doesn't tell us to live for our own convenience. Christianity is concerned with *interdependence.* One reason the Lord brings us together in marriage is to help us find real satisfaction and joy in serving others. Marriage is the first place to live out God's commands for serving, accepting, encouraging, forgiving and submitting to one another.

Marriage was never meant to be bent to our individual purposes. That's a shabby counterfeit. Real marriage is a God-given opportunity to live out love and commitment to another human being for a lifetime. When we weigh the options, we can trade the pursuit of short-lived personal happiness for the contentment that grows when we shape our marriage God's way.

MARRIAGE BUILDERS

♦ *Why is individualism so highly valued in our society?*
♦ *As a newlywed, have you found it hard to shift from independence to interdependence?*

Additional Scripture Readings
Psalm 119:137–144; Proverbs 3:1–6

Go to page 189 for your next devotional reading.

the desert these forty years, to humble
you and to test you in order to know what
was in your heart, whether or not you
would keep his commands. 3He humbled
you, causing you to hunger and then feed-
ing you with manna, which neither you
nor your fathers had known, to teach you
that man does not live on bread alone but
on every word that comes from the mouth
of the LORD. 4Your clothes did not wear
out and your feet did not swell during
these forty years. 5Know then in your
heart that as a man disciplines his son, so
the LORD your God disciplines you.

6Observe the commands of the LORD
your God, walking in his ways and rever-
ing him. 7For the LORD your God is bring-
ing you into a good land—a land with
streams and pools of water, with springs
flowing in the valleys and hills; 8a land
with wheat and barley, vines and fig trees,
pomegranates, olive oil and honey; 9a
land where bread will not be scarce and
you will lack nothing; a land where the
rocks are iron and you can dig copper out
of the hills.

10When you have eaten and are satis-
fied, praise the LORD your God for the
good land he has given you. 11Be careful
that you do not forget the LORD your God,
failing to observe his commands, his laws
and his decrees that I am giving you this
day. 12Otherwise, when you eat and are
satisfied, when you build fine houses and
settle down, 13and when your herds and
flocks grow large and your silver and gold
increase and all you have is multiplied,
14then your heart will become proud and
you will forget the LORD your God, who
brought you out of Egypt, out of the land
of slavery. 15He led you through the vast
and dreadful desert, that thirsty and wa-
terless land, with its venomous snakes
and scorpions. He brought you water out
of hard rock. 16He gave you manna to eat
in the desert, something your fathers had
never known, to humble and to test you
so that in the end it might go well with
you. 17You may say to yourself, "My pow-
er and the strength of my hands have pro-
duced this wealth for me." 18But remem-
ber the LORD your God, for it is he who
gives you the ability to produce wealth,
and so confirms his covenant, which he
swore to your forefathers, as it is today.

19If you ever forget the LORD your God
and follow other gods and worship and
bow down to them, I testify against you
today that you will surely be destroyed.
20Like the nations the LORD destroyed be-
fore you, so you will be destroyed for not
obeying the LORD your God.

Not Because of Israel's Righteousness

9 Hear, O Israel. You are now about to
cross the Jordan to go in and dispos-
sess nations greater and stronger than
you, with large cities that have walls up to
the sky. 2The people are strong and tall—
Anakites! You know about them and have
heard it said: "Who can stand up against
the Anakites?" 3But be assured today that
the LORD your God is the one who goes
across ahead of you like a devouring fire.
He will destroy them; he will subdue them
before you. And you will drive them out
and annihilate them quickly, as the LORD
has promised you.

4After the LORD your God has driven
them out before you, do not say to your-
self, "The LORD has brought me here to
take possession of this land because of my
righteousness." No, it is on account of the
wickedness of these nations that the LORD
is going to drive them out before you. 5It
is not because of your righteousness or
your integrity that you are going in to take
possession of their land; but on account of
the wickedness of these nations, the LORD
your God will drive them out before you,
to accomplish what he swore to your fa-
thers, to Abraham, Isaac and Jacob. 6Un-
derstand, then, that it is not because of
your righteousness that the LORD your
God is giving you this good land to pos-
sess, for you are a stiff-necked people.

The Golden Calf

7Remember this and never forget how
you provoked the LORD your God to anger
in the desert. From the day you left Egypt
until you arrived here, you have been re-
bellious against the LORD. 8At Horeb you
aroused the LORD's wrath so that he was
angry enough to destroy you. 9When I
went up on the mountain to receive the
tablets of stone, the tablets of the cov-
enant that the LORD had made with you, I
stayed on the mountain forty days and
forty nights; I ate no bread and drank no
water. 10The LORD gave me two stone tab-
lets inscribed by the finger of God. On
them were all the commandments the
LORD proclaimed to you on the mountain
out of the fire, on the day of the assembly.

11At the end of the forty days and forty
nights, the LORD gave me the two stone
tablets, the tablets of the covenant. 12Then

the LORD told me, "Go down from here at once, because your people whom you brought out of Egypt have become corrupt. They have turned away quickly from what I commanded them and have made a cast idol for themselves."

13And the LORD said to me, "I have seen this people, and they are a stiff-necked people indeed! 14Let me alone, so that I may destroy them and blot out their name from under heaven. And I will make you into a nation stronger and more numerous than they."

15So I turned and went down from the mountain while it was ablaze with fire. And the two tablets of the covenant were in my hands.[a] 16When I looked, I saw that you had sinned against the LORD your God; you had made for yourselves an idol cast in the shape of a calf. You had turned aside quickly from the way that the LORD had commanded you. 17So I took the two tablets and threw them out of my hands, breaking them to pieces before your eyes.

18Then once again I fell prostrate before the LORD for forty days and forty nights; I ate no bread and drank no water, because of all the sin you had committed, doing what was evil in the LORD's sight and so provoking him to anger. 19I feared the anger and wrath of the LORD, for he was angry enough with you to destroy you. But again the LORD listened to me. 20And the LORD was angry enough with Aaron to destroy him, but at that time I prayed for Aaron too. 21Also I took that sinful thing of yours, the calf you had made, and burned it in the fire. Then I crushed it and ground it to powder as fine as dust and threw the dust into a stream that flowed down the mountain.

22You also made the LORD angry at Taberah, at Massah and at Kibroth Hattaavah.

23And when the LORD sent you out from Kadesh Barnea, he said, "Go up and take possession of the land I have given you." But you rebelled against the command of the LORD your God. You did not trust him or obey him. 24You have been rebellious against the LORD ever since I have known you.

25I lay prostrate before the LORD those forty days and forty nights because the LORD had said he would destroy you. 26I prayed to the LORD and said, "O Sovereign LORD, do not destroy your people, your own inheritance that you redeemed by your great power and brought out of Egypt with a mighty hand. 27Remember your servants Abraham, Isaac and Jacob. Overlook the stubbornness of this people, their wickedness and their sin. 28Otherwise, the country from which you brought us will say, 'Because the LORD was not able to take them into the land he had promised them, and because he hated them, he brought them out to put them to death in the desert.' 29But they are your people, your inheritance that you brought out by your great power and your outstretched arm."

Tablets Like the First Ones

10 At that time the LORD said to me, "Chisel out two stone tablets like the first ones and come up to me on the mountain. Also make a wooden chest.[b] 2I will write on the tablets the words that were on the first tablets, which you broke. Then you are to put them in the chest."

3So I made the ark out of acacia wood and chiseled out two stone tablets like the first ones, and I went up on the mountain with the two tablets in my hands. 4The LORD wrote on these tablets what he had written before, the Ten Commandments he had proclaimed to you on the mountain, out of the fire, on the day of the assembly. And the LORD gave them to me. 5Then I came back down the mountain and put the tablets in the ark I had made, as the LORD commanded me, and they are there now.

6(The Israelites traveled from the wells of the Jaakanites to Moserah. There Aaron died and was buried, and Eleazar his son succeeded him as priest. 7From there they traveled to Gudgodah and on to Jotbathah, a land with streams of water. 8At that time the LORD set apart the tribe of Levi to carry the ark of the covenant of the LORD, to stand before the LORD to minister and to pronounce blessings in his name, as they still do today. 9That is why the Levites have no share or inheritance among their brothers; the LORD is their inheritance, as the LORD your God told them.)

10Now I had stayed on the mountain forty days and nights, as I did the first time, and the LORD listened to me at this time also. It was not his will to destroy you. 11"Go," the LORD said to me, "and lead the people on their way, so that they

[a] 15 Or *And I had the two tablets of the covenant with me, one in each hand*

[b] 1 That is, an ark

WEEKENDING

FRIENDSHIP

What do you contribute to the friendship between you? Using a rating system of usually (U), sometimes (S) and rarely (R), assign a value to each trait below, rating yourself as you think your spouse would rate you.

___ FUN-LOVING You can laugh at yourself and with others.
___ LOYAL You stand by your friends.
___ HELPFUL You are aware of and responsive to the needs of others.
___ CARING You offer emotional support and genuine concern.
___ LOVABLE You freely accept expressions of love.
___ SINCERE Others can assume you mean what you say.
___ TACTFUL You express yourself in a way that respects others' feelings.
___ GIVING You are unselfish with your time, money, energy.
___ FORGIVING You constructively handle hurts caused by others.
___ OPEN-MINDED You listen to and discuss opinions that differ from your own.
___ POSITIVE You maintain a hopeful, optimistic outlook.

— Richard Matteson and Janis Long Harris

REVIVE

Saturday: John 15:9-17
Sunday: Proverbs 27:1-11

Go to page 191 for your next devotional reading.

may enter and possess the land that I
swore to their fathers to give them."

Fear the Lord

12And now, O Israel, what does the
Lord your God ask of you but to fear the
Lord your God, to walk in all his ways, to
love him, to serve the Lord your God with
all your heart and with all your soul, 13and
to observe the Lord's commands and de-
crees that I am giving you today for your
own good?

14To the Lord your God belong the
heavens, even the highest heavens, the
earth and everything in it. 15Yet the Lord
set his affection on your forefathers and
loved them, and he chose you, their
descendants, above all the nations, as it is
today. 16Circumcise your hearts, there-
fore, and do not be stiff-necked any long-
er. 17For the Lord your God is God of gods
and Lord of lords, the great God, mighty
and awesome, who shows no partiality
and accepts no bribes. 18He defends the
cause of the fatherless and the widow, and
loves the alien, giving him food and cloth-
ing. 19And you are to love those who are
aliens, for you yourselves were aliens in
Egypt. 20Fear the Lord your God and serve
him. Hold fast to him and take your oaths
in his name. 21He is your praise; he is your
God, who performed for you those great
and awesome wonders you saw with your
own eyes. 22Your forefathers who went
down into Egypt were seventy in all, and
now the Lord your God has made you as
numerous as the stars in the sky.

Love and Obey the Lord

11 Love the Lord your God and keep
his requirements, his decrees, his
laws and his commands always. 2Remem-
ber today that your children were not the
ones who saw and experienced the disci-
pline of the Lord your God: his majesty,
his mighty hand, his outstretched arm;
3the signs he performed and the things he
did in the heart of Egypt, both to Pharaoh
king of Egypt and to his whole country;
4what he did to the Egyptian army, to its
horses and chariots, how he overwhelmed
them with the waters of the Red Sea[a] as
they were pursuing you, and how the
Lord brought lasting ruin on them. 5It was
not your children who saw what he did for
you in the desert until you arrived at this
place, 6and what he did to Dathan and
Abiram, sons of Eliab the Reubenite,
when the earth opened its mouth right in
the middle of all Israel and swallowed
them up with their households, their tents
and every living thing that belonged to
them. 7But it was your own eyes that saw
all these great things the Lord has done.

8Observe therefore all the commands I
am giving you today, so that you may
have the strength to go in and take over
the land that you are crossing the Jordan
to possess, 9and so that you may live long
in the land that the Lord swore to your
forefathers to give to them and their
descendants, a land flowing with milk and
honey. 10The land you are entering to take
over is not like the land of Egypt, from
which you have come, where you planted
your seed and irrigated it by foot as in a
vegetable garden. 11But the land you are
crossing the Jordan to take possession of
is a land of mountains and valleys that
drinks rain from heaven. 12It is a land the
Lord your God cares for; the eyes of the
Lord your God are continually on it from
the beginning of the year to its end.

13So if you faithfully obey the com-
mands I am giving you today—to love the
Lord your God and to serve him with all
your heart and with all your soul— 14then
I will send rain on your land in its season,
both autumn and spring rains, so that you
may gather in your grain, new wine and
oil. 15I will provide grass in the fields for
your cattle, and you will eat and be satis-
fied.

16Be careful, or you will be enticed to
turn away and worship other gods and
bow down to them. 17Then the Lord's an-
ger will burn against you, and he will shut
the heavens so that it will not rain and the
ground will yield no produce, and you will
soon perish from the good land the Lord
is giving you. 18Fix these words of mine in
your hearts and minds; tie them as sym-
bols on your hands and bind them on
your foreheads. 19Teach them to your
children, talking about them when you sit
at home and when you walk along the
road, when you lie down and when you
get up. 20Write them on the doorframes of
your houses and on your gates, 21so that
your days and the days of your children
may be many in the land that the Lord
swore to give your forefathers, as many as
the days that the heavens are above the
earth.

a4 Hebrew *Yam Suph*; that is, Sea of Reeds

VERSE FOR THE DAY: Deuteronomy 11:18–19

AUTHOR: Ravi Zacharias

PASSAGE FOR THE DAY: Deuteronomy 11:13–21

Open to the World

Inviting people into your home is one of the most effective ways to minister to others. Befriend people, let them get to know you. It's the backyard conversations you have, or the talk over coffee or tea with friends and neighbors, that create meaningful connections with others. People are lonely, and most of them are longing for a friendship nearby, a home where they can talk freely without the fear of a put-down. A Christian couple's home should convey peace to people when they come in. Where people sense that harmony, they will seek your feedback, even in subtle ways.

People have come to know the Lord in our home. One was a Hindu couple. I would love to think that happened because they sensed God in our home and in our marriage.

We befriended a woman—a clerk in a shop where my wife went to have a picture framed—who came to our home, where we prayed for her. Before she left, she remarked on the peace she sensed from being in a home where the gospel is at the heart of each member of the family. Our Christian homes must offer hope to those whose own homes are torn.

There is great hunger and anxiety in the world. Peace starts with the discipline of respecting your fellow human beings. Be kind to whomever you talk to, and be gentle and gracious in what you say. Add to that the love of Christ, which gives breadth to your kindness. When the love of Christ is in your heart, you're accountable to him for your actions toward others.

MARRIAGE BUILDERS

- *When have you sensed God's peace at work in your home?*
- *In what ways can you picture the two of you using your home to reach out to the lonely?*

Additional Scripture Readings
Romans 12:13; Hebrews 13:1–2

Go to page 215 for your next devotional reading.

22If you carefully observe all these commands I am giving you to follow—to love
the LORD your God, to walk in all his ways
and to hold fast to him— 23then the LORD
will drive out all these nations before you,
and you will dispossess nations larger and
stronger than you. 24Every place where
you set your foot will be yours: Your territory will extend from the desert to Lebanon, and from the Euphrates River to the
western sea.[a] 25No man will be able to
stand against you. The LORD your God, as
he promised you, will put the terror and
fear of you on the whole land, wherever
you go.

26See, I am setting before you today a
blessing and a curse— 27the blessing if
you obey the commands of the LORD your
God that I am giving you today; 28the
curse if you disobey the commands of the
LORD your God and turn from the way that
I command you today by following other
gods, which you have not known. 29When
the LORD your God has brought you into
the land you are entering to possess, you
are to proclaim on Mount Gerizim the
blessings, and on Mount Ebal the curses.
30As you know, these mountains are
across the Jordan, west of the road,[b] toward the setting sun, near the great trees
of Moreh, in the territory of those Canaanites living in the Arabah in the vicinity of
Gilgal. 31You are about to cross the Jordan
to enter and take possession of the land
the LORD your God is giving you. When
you have taken it over and are living there,
32be sure that you obey all the decrees and
laws I am setting before you today.

The One Place of Worship

12 These are the decrees and laws you
must be careful to follow in the
land that the LORD, the God of your fathers, has given you to possess—as long
as you live in the land. 2Destroy completely all the places on the high mountains
and on the hills and under every spreading tree where the nations you are dispossessing worship their gods. 3Break down
their altars, smash their sacred stones and
burn their Asherah poles in the fire; cut
down the idols of their gods and wipe out
their names from those places.

4You must not worship the LORD your
God in their way. 5But you are to seek the
place the LORD your God will choose from
among all your tribes to put his Name
there for his dwelling. To that place you
must go; 6there bring your burnt offerings
and sacrifices, your tithes and special
gifts, what you have vowed to give and
your freewill offerings, and the firstborn
of your herds and flocks. 7There, in the
presence of the LORD your God, you and
your families shall eat and shall rejoice in
everything you have put your hand to, because the LORD your God has blessed you.

8You are not to do as we do here today,
everyone as he sees fit, 9since you have
not yet reached the resting place and the
inheritance the LORD your God is giving
you. 10But you will cross the Jordan and
settle in the land the LORD your God is giving you as an inheritance, and he will give
you rest from all your enemies around
you so that you will live in safety. 11Then
to the place the LORD your God will choose
as a dwelling for his Name—there you are
to bring everything I command you: your
burnt offerings and sacrifices, your tithes
and special gifts, and all the choice possessions you have vowed to the LORD.
12And there rejoice before the LORD your
God, you, your sons and daughters, your
menservants and maidservants, and the
Levites from your towns, who have no allotment or inheritance of their own. 13Be
careful not to sacrifice your burnt offerings anywhere you please. 14Offer them
only at the place the LORD will choose in
one of your tribes, and there observe everything I command you.

15Nevertheless, you may slaughter your
animals in any of your towns and eat as
much of the meat as you want, as if it were
gazelle or deer, according to the blessing
the LORD your God gives you. Both the ceremonially unclean and the clean may eat
it. 16But you must not eat the blood; pour
it out on the ground like water. 17You
must not eat in your own towns the tithe
of your grain and new wine and oil, or the
firstborn of your herds and flocks, or
whatever you have vowed to give, or your
freewill offerings or special gifts. 18Instead, you are to eat them in the presence
of the LORD your God at the place the LORD
your God will choose—you, your sons
and daughters, your menservants and
maidservants, and the Levites from your
towns—and you are to rejoice before the
LORD your God in everything you put your
hand to. 19Be careful not to neglect the Levites as long as you live in your land.

[a]24 That is, the Mediterranean [b]30 Or *Jordan, westward*

[20]When the LORD your God has enlarged your territory as he promised you, and you crave meat and say, "I would like some meat," then you may eat as much of it as you want. [21]If the place where the LORD your God chooses to put his Name is too far away from you, you may slaughter animals from the herds and flocks the LORD has given you, as I have commanded you, and in your own towns you may eat as much of them as you want. [22]Eat them as you would gazelle or deer. Both the ceremonially unclean and the clean may eat. [23]But be sure you do not eat the blood, because the blood is the life, and you must not eat the life with the meat. [24]You must not eat the blood; pour it out on the ground like water. [25]Do not eat it, so that it may go well with you and your children after you, because you will be doing what is right in the eyes of the LORD.

[26]But take your consecrated things and whatever you have vowed to give, and go to the place the LORD will choose. [27]Present your burnt offerings on the altar of the LORD your God, both the meat and the blood. The blood of your sacrifices must be poured beside the altar of the LORD your God, but you may eat the meat. [28]Be careful to obey all these regulations I am giving you, so that it may always go well with you and your children after you, because you will be doing what is good and right in the eyes of the LORD your God.

[29]The LORD your God will cut off before you the nations you are about to invade and dispossess. But when you have driven them out and settled in their land, [30]and after they have been destroyed before you, be careful not to be ensnared by inquiring about their gods, saying, "How do these nations serve their gods? We will do the same." [31]You must not worship the LORD your God in their way, because in worshiping their gods, they do all kinds of detestable things the LORD hates. They even burn their sons and daughters in the fire as sacrifices to their gods.

[32]See that you do all I command you; do not add to it or take away from it.

Worshiping Other Gods

13 If a prophet, or one who foretells by dreams, appears among you and announces to you a miraculous sign or wonder, [2]and if the sign or wonder of which he has spoken takes place, and he says, "Let us follow other gods" (gods you have not known) "and let us worship them," [3]you must not listen to the words of that prophet or dreamer. The LORD your God is testing you to find out whether you love him with all your heart and with all your soul. [4]It is the LORD your God you must follow, and him you must revere. Keep his commands and obey him; serve him and hold fast to him. [5]That prophet or dreamer must be put to death, because he preached rebellion against the LORD your God, who brought you out of Egypt and redeemed you from the land of slavery; he has tried to turn you from the way the LORD your God commanded you to follow. You must purge the evil from among you.

[6]If your very own brother, or your son or daughter, or the wife you love, or your closest friend secretly entices you, saying, "Let us go and worship other gods" (gods that neither you nor your fathers have known, [7]gods of the peoples around you, whether near or far, from one end of the land to the other), [8]do not yield to him or listen to him. Show him no pity. Do not spare him or shield him. [9]You must certainly put him to death. Your hand must be the first in putting him to death, and then the hands of all the people. [10]Stone him to death, because he tried to turn you away from the LORD your God, who brought you out of Egypt, out of the land of slavery. [11]Then all Israel will hear and be afraid, and no one among you will do such an evil thing again.

[12]If you hear it said about one of the towns the LORD your God is giving you to live in [13]that wicked men have arisen among you and have led the people of their town astray, saying, "Let us go and worship other gods" (gods you have not known), [14]then you must inquire, probe and investigate it thoroughly. And if it is true and it has been proved that this detestable thing has been done among you, [15]you must certainly put to the sword all who live in that town. Destroy it completely,[a] both its people and its livestock. [16]Gather all the plunder of the town into the middle of the public square and completely burn the town and all its plunder as a whole burnt offering to the LORD your God. It is to remain a ruin forever, never to be rebuilt. [17]None of those condemned

[a]15 The Hebrew term refers to the irrevocable giving over of things or persons to the LORD, often by totally destroying them.

things[a] shall be found in your hands, so
that the LORD will turn from his fierce an-
ger; he will show you mercy, have com-
passion on you, and increase your num-
bers, as he promised on oath to your
forefathers, 18because you obey the LORD
your God, keeping all his commands that
I am giving you today and doing what is
right in his eyes.

Clean and Unclean Food

14 You are the children of the LORD
your God. Do not cut yourselves or
shave the front of your heads for the dead,
2for you are a people holy to the LORD your
God. Out of all the peoples on the face of
the earth, the LORD has chosen you to be
his treasured possession.

3Do not eat any detestable thing. 4These
are the animals you may eat: the ox, the
sheep, the goat, 5the deer, the gazelle, the
roe deer, the wild goat, the ibex, the ante-
lope and the mountain sheep.[b] 6You may
eat any animal that has a split hoof divid-
ed in two and that chews the cud. 7How-
ever, of those that chew the cud or that
have a split hoof completely divided you
may not eat the camel, the rabbit or the
coney.[c] Although they chew the cud,
they do not have a split hoof; they are cere-
monially unclean for you. 8The pig is
also unclean; although it has a split hoof,
it does not chew the cud. You are not to
eat their meat or touch their carcasses.

9Of all the creatures living in the water,
you may eat any that has fins and scales.
10But anything that does not have fins and
scales you may not eat; for you it is un-
clean.

11You may eat any clean bird. 12But
these you may not eat: the eagle, the vul-
ture, the black vulture, 13the red kite, the
black kite, any kind of falcon, 14any kind
of raven, 15the horned owl, the screech
owl, the gull, any kind of hawk, 16the little
owl, the great owl, the white owl, 17the
desert owl, the osprey, the cormorant,
18the stork, any kind of heron, the hoopoe
and the bat.

19All flying insects that swarm are un-
clean to you; do not eat them. 20But any
winged creature that is clean you may eat.

21Do not eat anything you find already
dead. You may give it to an alien living in
any of your towns, and he may eat it, or
you may sell it to a foreigner. But you are
a people holy to the LORD your God.

Do not cook a young goat in its moth-
er's milk.

Tithes

22Be sure to set aside a tenth of all that
your fields produce each year. 23Eat the
tithe of your grain, new wine and oil, and
the firstborn of your herds and flocks in
the presence of the LORD your God at the
place he will choose as a dwelling for his
Name, so that you may learn to revere the
LORD your God always. 24But if that place
is too distant and you have been blessed
by the LORD your God and cannot carry
your tithe (because the place where the
LORD will choose to put his Name is so far
away), 25then exchange your tithe for sil-
ver, and take the silver with you and go to
the place the LORD your God will choose.
26Use the silver to buy whatever you like:
cattle, sheep, wine or other fermented
drink, or anything you wish. Then you
and your household shall eat there in the
presence of the LORD your God and re-
joice. 27And do not neglect the Levites liv-
ing in your towns, for they have no allot-
ment or inheritance of their own.

28At the end of every three years, bring
all the tithes of that year's produce and
store it in your towns, 29so that the Levites
(who have no allotment or inheritance of
their own) and the aliens, the fatherless
and the widows who live in your towns
may come and eat and be satisfied, and so
that the LORD your God may bless you in
all the work of your hands.

The Year for Canceling Debts

15 At the end of every seven years you
must cancel debts. 2This is how it
is to be done: Every creditor shall cancel
the loan he has made to his fellow Israel-
ite. He shall not require payment from his
fellow Israelite or brother, because the
LORD's time for canceling debts has been
proclaimed. 3You may require payment
from a foreigner, but you must cancel any
debt your brother owes you. 4However,
there should be no poor among you, for in
the land the LORD your God is giving you
to possess as your inheritance, he will
richly bless you, 5if only you fully obey
the LORD your God and are careful to fol-

[a]17 The Hebrew term refers to the irrevocable giving over of things or persons to the LORD, often by totally destroying them. [b]5 The precise identification of some of the birds and animals in this chapter is uncertain. [c]7 That is, the hyrax or rock badger

low all these commands I am giving you
today. 6For the LORD your God will bless
you as he has promised, and you will lend
to many nations but will borrow from
none. You will rule over many nations but
none will rule over you.

7If there is a poor man among your
brothers in any of the towns of the land
that the LORD your God is giving you, do
not be hardhearted or tightfisted toward
your poor brother. 8Rather be openhand-
ed and freely lend him whatever he needs.
9Be careful not to harbor this wicked
thought: "The seventh year, the year for
canceling debts, is near," so that you do
not show ill will toward your needy broth-
er and give him nothing. He may then ap-
peal to the LORD against you, and you will
be found guilty of sin. 10Give generously
to him and do so without a grudging
heart; then because of this the LORD your
God will bless you in all your work and in
everything you put your hand to. 11There
will always be poor people in the land.
Therefore I command you to be open-
handed toward your brothers and toward
the poor and needy in your land.

Freeing Servants

12If a fellow Hebrew, a man or a wom-
an, sells himself to you and serves you six
years, in the seventh year you must let
him go free. 13And when you release him,
do not send him away empty-handed.
14Supply him liberally from your flock,
your threshing floor and your winepress.
Give to him as the LORD your God has
blessed you. 15Remember that you were
slaves in Egypt and the LORD your God re-
deemed you. That is why I give you this
command today.

16But if your servant says to you, "I do
not want to leave you," because he loves
you and your family and is well off with
you, 17then take an awl and push it
through his ear lobe into the door, and he
will become your servant for life. Do the
same for your maidservant.

18Do not consider it a hardship to set
your servant free, because his service to
you these six years has been worth twice
as much as that of a hired hand. And the
LORD your God will bless you in every-
thing you do.

The Firstborn Animals

19Set apart for the LORD your God every
firstborn male of your herds and flocks.
Do not put the firstborn of your oxen to
work, and do not shear the firstborn of
your sheep. 20Each year you and your
family are to eat them in the presence of
the LORD your God at the place he will
choose. 21If an animal has a defect, is lame
or blind, or has any serious flaw, you must
not sacrifice it to the LORD your God.
22You are to eat it in your own towns. Both
the ceremonially unclean and the clean
may eat it, as if it were gazelle or deer.
23But you must not eat the blood; pour it
out on the ground like water.

Passover

16 Observe the month of Abib and
celebrate the Passover of the LORD
your God, because in the month of Abib
he brought you out of Egypt by night.
2Sacrifice as the Passover to the LORD your
God an animal from your flock or herd at
the place the LORD will choose as a dwell-
ing for his Name. 3Do not eat it with bread
made with yeast, but for seven days eat
unleavened bread, the bread of affliction,
because you left Egypt in haste—so that
all the days of your life you may remem-
ber the time of your departure from Egypt.
4Let no yeast be found in your possession
in all your land for seven days. Do not let
any of the meat you sacrifice on the eve-
ning of the first day remain until morning.

5You must not sacrifice the Passover in
any town the LORD your God gives you
6except in the place he will choose as a
dwelling for his Name. There you must
sacrifice the Passover in the evening,
when the sun goes down, on the anniver-
sary[a] of your departure from Egypt.
7Roast it and eat it at the place the LORD
your God will choose. Then in the morn-
ing return to your tents. 8For six days eat
unleavened bread and on the seventh day
hold an assembly to the LORD your God
and do no work.

Feast of Weeks

9Count off seven weeks from the time
you begin to put the sickle to the standing
grain. 10Then celebrate the Feast of Weeks
to the LORD your God by giving a freewill
offering in proportion to the blessings the
LORD your God has given you. 11And re-
joice before the LORD your God at the
place he will choose as a dwelling for his
Name—you, your sons and daughters,

[a]6 Or *down, at the time of day*

your menservants and maidservants, the Levites in your towns, and the aliens, the fatherless and the widows living among you. 12Remember that you were slaves in Egypt, and follow carefully these decrees.

Feast of Tabernacles

13Celebrate the Feast of Tabernacles for seven days after you have gathered the produce of your threshing floor and your winepress. 14Be joyful at your Feast—you, your sons and daughters, your menservants and maidservants, and the Levites, the aliens, the fatherless and the widows who live in your towns. 15For seven days celebrate the Feast to the LORD your God at the place the LORD will choose. For the LORD your God will bless you in all your harvest and in all the work of your hands, and your joy will be complete.

16Three times a year all your men must appear before the LORD your God at the place he will choose: at the Feast of Unleavened Bread, the Feast of Weeks and the Feast of Tabernacles. No man should appear before the LORD empty-handed: 17Each of you must bring a gift in proportion to the way the LORD your God has blessed you.

Judges

18Appoint judges and officials for each of your tribes in every town the LORD your God is giving you, and they shall judge the people fairly. 19Do not pervert justice or show partiality. Do not accept a bribe, for a bribe blinds the eyes of the wise and twists the words of the righteous. 20Follow justice and justice alone, so that you may live and possess the land the LORD your God is giving you.

Worshiping Other Gods

21Do not set up any wooden Asherah pole[a] beside the altar you build to the LORD your God, 22and do not erect a sacred stone, for these the LORD your God hates.

17 Do not sacrifice to the LORD your God an ox or a sheep that has any defect or flaw in it, for that would be detestable to him.

2If a man or woman living among you in one of the towns the LORD gives you is found doing evil in the eyes of the LORD your God in violation of his covenant, 3and contrary to my command has worshiped other gods, bowing down to them or to the sun or the moon or the stars of the sky, 4and this has been brought to your attention, then you must investigate it thoroughly. If it is true and it has been proved that this detestable thing has been done in Israel, 5take the man or woman who has done this evil deed to your city gate and stone that person to death. 6On the testimony of two or three witnesses a man shall be put to death, but no one shall be put to death on the testimony of only one witness. 7The hands of the witnesses must be the first in putting him to death, and then the hands of all the people. You must purge the evil from among you.

Law Courts

8If cases come before your courts that are too difficult for you to judge—whether bloodshed, lawsuits or assaults—take them to the place the LORD your God will choose. 9Go to the priests, who are Levites, and to the judge who is in office at that time. Inquire of them and they will give you the verdict. 10You must act according to the decisions they give you at the place the LORD will choose. Be careful to do everything they direct you to do. 11Act according to the law they teach you and the decisions they give you. Do not turn aside from what they tell you, to the right or to the left. 12The man who shows contempt for the judge or for the priest who stands ministering there to the LORD your God must be put to death. You must purge the evil from Israel. 13All the people will hear and be afraid, and will not be contemptuous again.

The King

14When you enter the land the LORD your God is giving you and have taken possession of it and settled in it, and you say, "Let us set a king over us like all the nations around us," 15be sure to appoint over you the king the LORD your God chooses. He must be from among your own brothers. Do not place a foreigner over you, one who is not a brother Israelite. 16The king, moreover, must not acquire great numbers of horses for himself or make the people return to Egypt to get more of them, for the LORD has told you, "You are not to go back that way again." 17He must not take many wives, or his

[a]21 Or *Do not plant any tree dedicated to Asherah*

heart will be led astray. He must not accumulate large amounts of silver and gold.
18When he takes the throne of his kingdom, he is to write for himself on a scroll
a copy of this law, taken from that of the
priests, who are Levites. 19It is to be with
him, and he is to read it all the days of his
life so that he may learn to revere the LORD
his God and follow carefully all the words
of this law and these decrees 20and not
consider himself better than his brothers
and turn from the law to the right or to the
left. Then he and his descendants will
reign a long time over his kingdom in Israel.

Offerings for Priests and Levites

18 The priests, who are Levites—indeed the whole tribe of Levi—are
to have no allotment or inheritance with
Israel. They shall live on the offerings
made to the LORD by fire, for that is their
inheritance. 2They shall have no inheritance among their brothers; the LORD is
their inheritance, as he promised them.
3This is the share due the priests from
the people who sacrifice a bull or a sheep:
the shoulder, the jowls and the inner
parts. 4You are to give them the firstfruits
of your grain, new wine and oil, and the
first wool from the shearing of your sheep,
5for the LORD your God has chosen them
and their descendants out of all your
tribes to stand and minister in the LORD's
name always.
6If a Levite moves from one of your
towns anywhere in Israel where he is living, and comes in all earnestness to the
place the LORD will choose, 7he may minister in the name of the LORD his God like
all his fellow Levites who serve there in
the presence of the LORD. 8He is to share
equally in their benefits, even though he
has received money from the sale of family possessions.

Detestable Practices

9When you enter the land the LORD your
God is giving you, do not learn to imitate
the detestable ways of the nations there.
10Let no one be found among you who
sacrifices his son or daughter in[a] the fire,
who practices divination or sorcery, interprets omens, engages in witchcraft, 11or
casts spells, or who is a medium or spiritist or who consults the dead. 12Anyone
who does these things is detestable to the
LORD, and because of these detestable
practices the LORD your God will drive out
those nations before you. 13You must be
blameless before the LORD your God.

The Prophet

14The nations you will dispossess listen
to those who practice sorcery or divination. But as for you, the LORD your God
has not permitted you to do so. 15The
LORD your God will raise up for you a
prophet like me from among your own
brothers. You must listen to him. 16For
this is what you asked of the LORD your
God at Horeb on the day of the assembly
when you said, "Let us not hear the voice
of the LORD our God nor see this great fire
anymore, or we will die."
17The LORD said to me: "What they say
is good. 18I will raise up for them a prophet like you from among their brothers; I
will put my words in his mouth, and he
will tell them everything I command him.
19If anyone does not listen to my words
that the prophet speaks in my name, I myself will call him to account. 20But a
prophet who presumes to speak in my
name anything I have not commanded
him to say, or a prophet who speaks in the
name of other gods, must be put to
death."
21You may say to yourselves, "How can
we know when a message has not been
spoken by the LORD?" 22If what a prophet
proclaims in the name of the LORD does
not take place or come true, that is a message the LORD has not spoken. That prophet has spoken presumptuously. Do not be
afraid of him.

Cities of Refuge

19 When the LORD your God has destroyed the nations whose land he
is giving you, and when you have driven
them out and settled in their towns and
houses, 2then set aside for yourselves
three cities centrally located in the land
the LORD your God is giving you to possess. 3Build roads to them and divide into
three parts the land the LORD your God is
giving you as an inheritance, so that anyone who kills a man may flee there.
4This is the rule concerning the man
who kills another and flees there to save
his life—one who kills his neighbor unintentionally, without malice aforethought.
5For instance, a man may go into the for-

[a]10 Or *who makes his son or daughter pass through*

est with his neighbor to cut wood, and as
he swings his ax to fell a tree, the head
may fly off and hit his neighbor and kill
him. That man may flee to one of these
cities and save his life. 6Otherwise, the
avenger of blood might pursue him in a
rage, overtake him if the distance is too
great, and kill him even though he is not
deserving of death, since he did it to his
neighbor without malice aforethought.
7This is why I command you to set aside
for yourselves three cities.

8If the LORD your God enlarges your ter-
ritory, as he promised on oath to your
forefathers, and gives you the whole land
he promised them, 9because you carefully
follow all these laws I command you to-
day—to love the LORD your God and to
walk always in his ways—then you are to
set aside three more cities. 10Do this so
that innocent blood will not be shed in
your land, which the LORD your God is giv-
ing you as your inheritance, and so that
you will not be guilty of bloodshed.

11But if a man hates his neighbor and
lies in wait for him, assaults and kills him,
and then flees to one of these cities, 12the
elders of his town shall send for him,
bring him back from the city, and hand
him over to the avenger of blood to die.
13Show him no pity. You must purge from
Israel the guilt of shedding innocent
blood, so that it may go well with you.

14Do not move your neighbor's bound-
ary stone set up by your predecessors in
the inheritance you receive in the land the
LORD your God is giving you to possess.

Witnesses

15One witness is not enough to convict
a man accused of any crime or offense he
may have committed. A matter must be
established by the testimony of two or
three witnesses.

16If a malicious witness takes the stand
to accuse a man of a crime, 17the two men
involved in the dispute must stand in the
presence of the LORD before the priests
and the judges who are in office at the
time. 18The judges must make a thorough
investigation, and if the witness proves to
be a liar, giving false testimony against his
brother, 19then do to him as he intended
to do to his brother. You must purge the
evil from among you. 20The rest of the
people will hear of this and be afraid, and
never again will such an evil thing be done
among you. 21Show no pity: life for life,
eye for eye, tooth for tooth, hand for hand,
foot for foot.

Going to War

20 When you go to war against your
enemies and see horses and chari-
ots and an army greater than yours, do not
be afraid of them, because the LORD your
God, who brought you up out of Egypt,
will be with you. 2When you are about to
go into battle, the priest shall come for-
ward and address the army. 3He shall say:
"Hear, O Israel, today you are going into
battle against your enemies. Do not be
fainthearted or afraid; do not be terrified
or give way to panic before them. 4For the
LORD your God is the one who goes with
you to fight for you against your enemies
to give you victory."

5The officers shall say to the army: "Has
anyone built a new house and not dedicat-
ed it? Let him go home, or he may die in
battle and someone else may dedicate it.
6Has anyone planted a vineyard and not
begun to enjoy it? Let him go home, or he
may die in battle and someone else enjoy
it. 7Has anyone become pledged to a
woman and not married her? Let him go
home, or he may die in battle and some-
one else marry her." 8Then the officers
shall add, "Is any man afraid or faintheart-
ed? Let him go home so that his brothers
will not become disheartened too."
9When the officers have finished speaking
to the army, they shall appoint command-
ers over it.

10When you march up to attack a city,
make its people an offer of peace. 11If they
accept and open their gates, all the people
in it shall be subject to forced labor and
shall work for you. 12If they refuse to
make peace and they engage you in battle,
lay siege to that city. 13When the LORD
your God delivers it into your hand, put to
the sword all the men in it. 14As for the
women, the children, the livestock and ev-
erything else in the city, you may take
these as plunder for yourselves. And you
may use the plunder the LORD your God
gives you from your enemies. 15This is
how you are to treat all the cities that are
at a distance from you and do not belong
to the nations nearby.

16However, in the cities of the nations
the LORD your God is giving you as an in-
heritance, do not leave alive anything that

breathes. 17Completely destroy[a] them—
the Hittites, Amorites, Canaanites, Perizzites, Hivites and Jebusites—as the LORD
your God has commanded you. 18Otherwise, they will teach you to follow all the
detestable things they do in worshiping
their gods, and you will sin against the
LORD your God.

19When you lay siege to a city for a long
time, fighting against it to capture it, do
not destroy its trees by putting an ax to
them, because you can eat their fruit. Do
not cut them down. Are the trees of the
field people, that you should besiege
them?[b] 20However, you may cut down
trees that you know are not fruit trees and
use them to build siege works until the
city at war with you falls.

Atonement for an Unsolved Murder

21 If a man is found slain, lying in a
field in the land the LORD your God
is giving you to possess, and it is not
known who killed him, 2your elders and
judges shall go out and measure the distance from the body to the neighboring
towns. 3Then the elders of the town nearest the body shall take a heifer that has
never been worked and has never worn a
yoke 4and lead her down to a valley that
has not been plowed or planted and
where there is a flowing stream. There in
the valley they are to break the heifer's
neck. 5The priests, the sons of Levi, shall
step forward, for the LORD your God has
chosen them to minister and to pronounce blessings in the name of the LORD
and to decide all cases of dispute and assault. 6Then all the elders of the town
nearest the body shall wash their hands
over the heifer whose neck was broken in
the valley, 7and they shall declare: "Our
hands did not shed this blood, nor did our
eyes see it done. 8Accept this atonement
for your people Israel, whom you have redeemed, O LORD, and do not hold your
people guilty of the blood of an innocent
man." And the bloodshed will be atoned
for. 9So you will purge from yourselves
the guilt of shedding innocent blood,
since you have done what is right in the
eyes of the LORD.

Marrying a Captive Woman

10When you go to war against your enemies and the LORD your God delivers them
into your hands and you take captives, 11if
you notice among the captives a beautiful
woman and are attracted to her, you may
take her as your wife. 12Bring her into
your home and have her shave her head,
trim her nails 13and put aside the clothes
she was wearing when captured. After she
has lived in your house and mourned her
father and mother for a full month, then
you may go to her and be her husband
and she shall be your wife. 14If you are not
pleased with her, let her go wherever she
wishes. You must not sell her or treat her
as a slave, since you have dishonored her.

The Right of the Firstborn

15If a man has two wives, and he loves
one but not the other, and both bear him
sons but the firstborn is the son of the
wife he does not love, 16when he wills his
property to his sons, he must not give the
rights of the firstborn to the son of the
wife he loves in preference to his actual
firstborn, the son of the wife he does not
love. 17He must acknowledge the son of
his unloved wife as the firstborn by giving
him a double share of all he has. That son
is the first sign of his father's strength.
The right of the firstborn belongs to him.

A Rebellious Son

18If a man has a stubborn and rebellious
son who does not obey his father and
mother and will not listen to them when
they discipline him, 19his father and mother shall take hold of him and bring him to
the elders at the gate of his town. 20They
shall say to the elders, "This son of ours is
stubborn and rebellious. He will not obey
us. He is a profligate and a drunkard."
21Then all the men of his town shall stone
him to death. You must purge the evil
from among you. All Israel will hear of it
and be afraid.

Various Laws

22If a man guilty of a capital offense is
put to death and his body is hung on a
tree, 23you must not leave his body on the
tree overnight. Be sure to bury him that
same day, because anyone who is hung
on a tree is under God's curse. You must
not desecrate the land the LORD your God
is giving you as an inheritance.

22 If you see your brother's ox or
sheep straying, do not ignore it but

[a] *17* The Hebrew term refers to the irrevocable giving over of things or persons to the LORD, often by totally destroying them. [b] *19* Or *down to use in the siege, for the fruit trees are for the benefit of man.*

be sure to take it back to him. 2If the
brother does not live near you or if you do
not know who he is, take it home with you
and keep it until he comes looking for it.
Then give it back to him. 3Do the same if
you find your brother's donkey or his
cloak or anything he loses. Do not ignore it.

4If you see your brother's donkey or his
ox fallen on the road, do not ignore it.
Help him get it to its feet.

5A woman must not wear men's clothing, nor a man wear women's clothing, for
the LORD your God detests anyone who
does this.

6If you come across a bird's nest beside
the road, either in a tree or on the ground,
and the mother is sitting on the young or
on the eggs, do not take the mother with
the young. 7You may take the young, but
be sure to let the mother go, so that it may
go well with you and you may have a long
life.

8When you build a new house, make a
parapet around your roof so that you may
not bring the guilt of bloodshed on your
house if someone falls from the roof.

9Do not plant two kinds of seed in your
vineyard; if you do, not only the crops you
plant but also the fruit of the vineyard will
be defiled.[a]

10Do not plow with an ox and a donkey
yoked together.

11Do not wear clothes of wool and linen
woven together.

12Make tassels on the four corners of
the cloak you wear.

Marriage Violations

13If a man takes a wife and, after lying
with her, dislikes her 14and slanders her
and gives her a bad name, saying, "I married this woman, but when I approached
her, I did not find proof of her virginity,"
15then the girl's father and mother shall
bring proof that she was a virgin to the
town elders at the gate. 16The girl's father
will say to the elders, "I gave my daughter
in marriage to this man, but he dislikes
her. 17Now he has slandered her and said,
'I did not find your daughter to be a virgin.' But here is the proof of my daughter's virginity." Then her parents shall display the cloth before the elders of the
town, 18and the elders shall take the man
and punish him. 19They shall fine him a
hundred shekels of silver[b] and give them
to the girl's father, because this man has
given an Israelite virgin a bad name. She
shall continue to be his wife; he must not
divorce her as long as he lives.

20If, however, the charge is true and no
proof of the girl's virginity can be found,
21she shall be brought to the door of her
father's house and there the men of her
town shall stone her to death. She has
done a disgraceful thing in Israel by being
promiscuous while still in her father's
house. You must purge the evil from
among you.

22If a man is found sleeping with another man's wife, both the man who slept
with her and the woman must die. You
must purge the evil from Israel.

23If a man happens to meet in a town a
virgin pledged to be married and he sleeps
with her, 24you shall take both of them to
the gate of that town and stone them to
death—the girl because she was in a town
and did not scream for help, and the man
because he violated another man's wife.
You must purge the evil from among you.

25But if out in the country a man happens to meet a girl pledged to be married
and rapes her, only the man who has done
this shall die. 26Do nothing to the girl; she
has committed no sin deserving death.
This case is like that of someone who attacks and murders his neighbor, 27for the
man found the girl out in the country, and
though the betrothed girl screamed, there
was no one to rescue her.

28If a man happens to meet a virgin who
is not pledged to be married and rapes her
and they are discovered, 29he shall pay the
girl's father fifty shekels of silver.[c] He
must marry the girl, for he has violated
her. He can never divorce her as long as
he lives.

30A man is not to marry his father's
wife; he must not dishonor his father's
bed.

Exclusion From the Assembly

23 No one who has been emasculated
by crushing or cutting may enter
the assembly of the LORD.

2No one born of a forbidden marriage[d]
nor any of his descendants may enter the
assembly of the LORD, even down to the
tenth generation.

3No Ammonite or Moabite or any of his

[a] 9 Or *be forfeited to the sanctuary* [b] 19 That is, about 2 1/2 pounds (about 1 kilogram) [c] 29 That is, about 1 1/4 pounds (about 0.6 kilogram) [d] 2 Or *one of illegitimate birth*

descendants may enter the assembly of the LORD, even down to the tenth generation. 4For they did not come to meet you with bread and water on your way when you came out of Egypt, and they hired Balaam son of Beor from Pethor in Aram Naharaim[a] to pronounce a curse on you. 5However, the LORD your God would not listen to Balaam but turned the curse into a blessing for you, because the LORD your God loves you. 6Do not seek a treaty of friendship with them as long as you live.

7Do not abhor an Edomite, for he is your brother. Do not abhor an Egyptian, because you lived as an alien in his country. 8The third generation of children born to them may enter the assembly of the LORD.

Uncleanness in the Camp

9When you are encamped against your enemies, keep away from everything impure. 10If one of your men is unclean because of a nocturnal emission, he is to go outside the camp and stay there. 11But as evening approaches he is to wash himself, and at sunset he may return to the camp.

12Designate a place outside the camp where you can go to relieve yourself. 13As part of your equipment have something to dig with, and when you relieve yourself, dig a hole and cover up your excrement. 14For the LORD your God moves about in your camp to protect you and to deliver your enemies to you. Your camp must be holy, so that he will not see among you anything indecent and turn away from you.

Miscellaneous Laws

15If a slave has taken refuge with you, do not hand him over to his master. 16Let him live among you wherever he likes and in whatever town he chooses. Do not oppress him.

17No Israelite man or woman is to become a shrine prostitute. 18You must not bring the earnings of a female prostitute or of a male prostitute[b] into the house of the LORD your God to pay any vow, because the LORD your God detests them both.

19Do not charge your brother interest, whether on money or food or anything else that may earn interest. 20You may charge a foreigner interest, but not a brother Israelite, so that the LORD your God may bless you in everything you put your hand to in the land you are entering to possess.

21If you make a vow to the LORD your God, do not be slow to pay it, for the LORD your God will certainly demand it of you and you will be guilty of sin. 22But if you refrain from making a vow, you will not be guilty. 23Whatever your lips utter you must be sure to do, because you made your vow freely to the LORD your God with your own mouth.

24If you enter your neighbor's vineyard, you may eat all the grapes you want, but do not put any in your basket. 25If you enter your neighbor's grainfield, you may pick kernels with your hands, but you must not put a sickle to his standing grain.

24 If a man marries a woman who becomes displeasing to him because he finds something indecent about her, and he writes her a certificate of divorce, gives it to her and sends her from his house, 2and if after she leaves his house she becomes the wife of another man, 3and her second husband dislikes her and writes her a certificate of divorce, gives it to her and sends her from his house, or if he dies, 4then her first husband, who divorced her, is not allowed to marry her again after she has been defiled. That would be detestable in the eyes of the LORD. Do not bring sin upon the land the LORD your God is giving you as an inheritance.

5If a man has recently married, he must not be sent to war or have any other duty laid on him. For one year he is to be free to stay at home and bring happiness to the wife he has married.

6Do not take a pair of millstones—not even the upper one—as security for a debt, because that would be taking a man's livelihood as security.

7If a man is caught kidnapping one of his brother Israelites and treats him as a slave or sells him, the kidnapper must die. You must purge the evil from among you.

8In cases of leprous[c] diseases be very careful to do exactly as the priests, who are Levites, instruct you. You must follow carefully what I have commanded them. 9Remember what the LORD your God did to Miriam along the way after you came out of Egypt.

[a] 4 That is, Northwest Mesopotamia [b] 18 Hebrew *of a dog* [c] 8 The Hebrew word was used for various diseases affecting the skin—not necessarily leprosy.

[10]When you make a loan of any kind to your neighbor, do not go into his house to get what he is offering as a pledge. [11]Stay outside and let the man to whom you are making the loan bring the pledge out to you. [12]If the man is poor, do not go to sleep with his pledge in your possession. [13]Return his cloak to him by sunset so that he may sleep in it. Then he will thank you, and it will be regarded as a righteous act in the sight of the LORD your God.

[14]Do not take advantage of a hired man who is poor and needy, whether he is a brother Israelite or an alien living in one of your towns. [15]Pay him his wages each day before sunset, because he is poor and is counting on it. Otherwise he may cry to the LORD against you, and you will be guilty of sin.

[16]Fathers shall not be put to death for their children, nor children put to death for their fathers; each is to die for his own sin.

[17]Do not deprive the alien or the fatherless of justice, or take the cloak of the widow as a pledge. [18]Remember that you were slaves in Egypt and the LORD your God redeemed you from there. That is why I command you to do this.

[19]When you are harvesting in your field and you overlook a sheaf, do not go back to get it. Leave it for the alien, the fatherless and the widow, so that the LORD your God may bless you in all the work of your hands. [20]When you beat the olives from your trees, do not go over the branches a second time. Leave what remains for the alien, the fatherless and the widow. [21]When you harvest the grapes in your vineyard, do not go over the vines again. Leave what remains for the alien, the fatherless and the widow. [22]Remember that you were slaves in Egypt. That is why I command you to do this.

25 When men have a dispute, they are to take it to court and the judges will decide the case, acquitting the innocent and condemning the guilty. [2]If the guilty man deserves to be beaten, the judge shall make him lie down and have him flogged in his presence with the number of lashes his crime deserves, [3]but he must not give him more than forty lashes. If he is flogged more than that, your brother will be degraded in your eyes.

[4]Do not muzzle an ox while it is treading out the grain.

[5]If brothers are living together and one of them dies without a son, his widow must not marry outside the family. Her husband's brother shall take her and marry her and fulfill the duty of a brother-in-law to her. [6]The first son she bears shall carry on the name of the dead brother so that his name will not be blotted out from Israel.

[7]However, if a man does not want to marry his brother's wife, she shall go to the elders at the town gate and say, "My husband's brother refuses to carry on his brother's name in Israel. He will not fulfill the duty of a brother-in-law to me." [8]Then the elders of his town shall summon him and talk to him. If he persists in saying, "I do not want to marry her," [9]his brother's widow shall go up to him in the presence of the elders, take off one of his sandals, spit in his face and say, "This is what is done to the man who will not build up his brother's family line." [10]That man's line shall be known in Israel as The Family of the Unsandaled.

[11]If two men are fighting and the wife of one of them comes to rescue her husband from his assailant, and she reaches out and seizes him by his private parts, [12]you shall cut off her hand. Show her no pity.

[13]Do not have two differing weights in your bag—one heavy, one light. [14]Do not have two differing measures in your house—one large, one small. [15]You must have accurate and honest weights and measures, so that you may live long in the land the LORD your God is giving you. [16]For the LORD your God detests anyone who does these things, anyone who deals dishonestly.

[17]Remember what the Amalekites did to you along the way when you came out of Egypt. [18]When you were weary and worn out, they met you on your journey and cut off all who were lagging behind; they had no fear of God. [19]When the LORD your God gives you rest from all the enemies around you in the land he is giving you to possess as an inheritance, you shall blot out the memory of Amalek from under heaven. Do not forget!

Firstfruits and Tithes

26 When you have entered the land the LORD your God is giving you as an inheritance and have taken possession of it and settled in it, [2]take some of the firstfruits of all that you produce from the soil of the land the LORD your God is giving you and put them in a basket. Then go to the place the LORD your God will choose

as a dwelling for his Name [3]and say to the
priest in office at the time, "I declare today
to the LORD your God that I have come to
the land the LORD swore to our forefathers
to give us." [4]The priest shall take the bas-
ket from your hands and set it down in
front of the altar of the LORD your God.
[5]Then you shall declare before the LORD
your God: "My father was a wandering Ar-
amean, and he went down into Egypt with
a few people and lived there and became
a great nation, powerful and numerous.
[6]But the Egyptians mistreated us and
made us suffer, putting us to hard labor.
[7]Then we cried out to the LORD, the God of
our fathers, and the LORD heard our voice
and saw our misery, toil and oppression.
[8]So the LORD brought us out of Egypt with
a mighty hand and an outstretched arm,
with great terror and with miraculous
signs and wonders. [9]He brought us to this
place and gave us this land, a land flowing
with milk and honey; [10]and now I bring
the firstfruits of the soil that you, O LORD,
have given me." Place the basket before
the LORD your God and bow down before
him. [11]And you and the Levites and the
aliens among you shall rejoice in all the
good things the LORD your God has given
to you and your household.

[12]When you have finished setting aside
a tenth of all your produce in the third
year, the year of the tithe, you shall give
it to the Levite, the alien, the fatherless
and the widow, so that they may eat in
your towns and be satisfied. [13]Then say to
the LORD your God: "I have removed from
my house the sacred portion and have giv-
en it to the Levite, the alien, the fatherless
and the widow, according to all you com-
manded. I have not turned aside from
your commands nor have I forgotten any
of them. [14]I have not eaten any of the sa-
cred portion while I was in mourning, nor
have I removed any of it while I was un-
clean, nor have I offered any of it to the
dead. I have obeyed the LORD my God; I
have done everything you commanded
me. [15]Look down from heaven, your holy
dwelling place, and bless your people Isra-
el and the land you have given us as you
promised on oath to our forefathers, a
land flowing with milk and honey."

Follow the LORD's Commands

[16]The LORD your God commands you
this day to follow these decrees and laws;
carefully observe them with all your heart
and with all your soul. [17]You have de-
clared this day that the LORD is your God
and that you will walk in his ways, that
you will keep his decrees, commands and
laws, and that you will obey him. [18]And
the LORD has declared this day that you
are his people, his treasured possession as
he promised, and that you are to keep all
his commands. [19]He has declared that he
will set you in praise, fame and honor
high above all the nations he has made
and that you will be a people holy to the
LORD your God, as he promised.

The Altar on Mount Ebal

27 Moses and the elders of Israel com-
manded the people: "Keep all these
commands that I give you today. [2]When
you have crossed the Jordan into the land
the LORD your God is giving you, set up
some large stones and coat them with
plaster. [3]Write on them all the words of
this law when you have crossed over to
enter the land the LORD your God is giving
you, a land flowing with milk and honey,
just as the LORD, the God of your fathers,
promised you. [4]And when you have
crossed the Jordan, set up these stones on
Mount Ebal, as I command you today, and
coat them with plaster. [5]Build there an al-
tar to the LORD your God, an altar of
stones. Do not use any iron tool upon
them. [6]Build the altar of the LORD your
God with fieldstones and offer burnt offer-
ings on it to the LORD your God. [7]Sacrifice
fellowship offerings[a] there, eating them
and rejoicing in the presence of the LORD
your God. [8]And you shall write very clear-
ly all the words of this law on these stones
you have set up."

Curses From Mount Ebal

[9]Then Moses and the priests, who are
Levites, said to all Israel, "Be silent, O Isra-
el, and listen! You have now become the
people of the LORD your God. [10]Obey the
LORD your God and follow his commands
and decrees that I give you today."

[11]On the same day Moses commanded
the people:

[12]When you have crossed the Jordan,
these tribes shall stand on Mount Gerizim
to bless the people: Simeon, Levi, Judah,
Issachar, Joseph and Benjamin. [13]And
these tribes shall stand on Mount Ebal to

[a]7 Traditionally *peace offerings*

pronounce curses: Reuben, Gad, Asher, Zebulun, Dan and Naphtali.

14The Levites shall recite to all the people of Israel in a loud voice:

15"Cursed is the man who carves an image or casts an idol—a thing detestable to the LORD, the work of the craftsman's hands—and sets it up in secret."

Then all the people shall say, "Amen!"

16"Cursed is the man who dishonors his father or his mother."

Then all the people shall say, "Amen!"

17"Cursed is the man who moves his neighbor's boundary stone."

Then all the people shall say, "Amen!"

18"Cursed is the man who leads the blind astray on the road."

Then all the people shall say, "Amen!"

19"Cursed is the man who withholds justice from the alien, the fatherless or the widow."

Then all the people shall say, "Amen!"

20"Cursed is the man who sleeps with his father's wife, for he dishonors his father's bed."

Then all the people shall say, "Amen!"

21"Cursed is the man who has sexual relations with any animal."

Then all the people shall say, "Amen!"

22"Cursed is the man who sleeps with his sister, the daughter of his father or the daughter of his mother."

Then all the people shall say, "Amen!"

23"Cursed is the man who sleeps with his mother-in-law."

Then all the people shall say, "Amen!"

24"Cursed is the man who kills his neighbor secretly."

Then all the people shall say, "Amen!"

25"Cursed is the man who accepts a bribe to kill an innocent person."

Then all the people shall say, "Amen!"

26"Cursed is the man who does not uphold the words of this law by carrying them out."

Then all the people shall say, "Amen!"

Blessings for Obedience

28 If you fully obey the LORD your God and carefully follow all his commands I give you today, the LORD your God will set you high above all the nations on earth. 2All these blessings will come upon you and accompany you if you obey the LORD your God:

3You will be blessed in the city and blessed in the country.

4The fruit of your womb will be blessed, and the crops of your land and the young of your livestock—the calves of your herds and the lambs of your flocks.

5Your basket and your kneading trough will be blessed.

6You will be blessed when you come in and blessed when you go out.

7The LORD will grant that the enemies who rise up against you will be defeated before you. They will come at you from one direction but flee from you in seven.

8The LORD will send a blessing on your barns and on everything you put your hand to. The LORD your God will bless you in the land he is giving you.

9The LORD will establish you as his holy people, as he promised you on oath, if you keep the commands of the LORD your God and walk in his ways. 10Then all the peoples on earth will see that you are called by the name of the LORD, and they will fear you. 11The LORD will grant you abundant prosperity—in the fruit of your womb, the young of your livestock and the crops of your ground—in the land he swore to your forefathers to give you.

12The LORD will open the heavens, the storehouse of his bounty, to send rain on your land in season and to bless all the work of your hands. You will lend to many nations but will borrow from none. 13The LORD will make you the head, not the tail. If you pay attention to the commands of the LORD your God that I give you this day and carefully follow them, you will always be at the top, never at the bottom. 14Do not turn aside from any of the commands I give you today, to the right or to the left, following other gods and serving them.

Curses for Disobedience

15 However, if you do not obey the LORD
your God and do not carefully follow all
his commands and decrees I am giving
you today, all these curses will come upon
you and overtake you:

16 You will be cursed in the city and
cursed in the country.
17 Your basket and your kneading
trough will be cursed.
18 The fruit of your womb will be
cursed, and the crops of your land,
and the calves of your herds and the
lambs of your flocks.
19 You will be cursed when you
come in and cursed when you go out.

20 The LORD will send on you curses,
confusion and rebuke in everything you
put your hand to, until you are destroyed
and come to sudden ruin because of the
evil you have done in forsaking him.[a]
21 The LORD will plague you with diseases
until he has destroyed you from the land
you are entering to possess. 22 The LORD
will strike you with wasting disease, with
fever and inflammation, with scorching
heat and drought, with blight and mildew,
which will plague you until you perish.
23 The sky over your head will be bronze,
the ground beneath you iron. 24 The LORD
will turn the rain of your country into dust
and powder; it will come down from the
skies until you are destroyed.

25 The LORD will cause you to be defeat-
ed before your enemies. You will come at
them from one direction but flee from
them in seven, and you will become a
thing of horror to all the kingdoms on
earth. 26 Your carcasses will be food for all
the birds of the air and the beasts of the
earth, and there will be no one to frighten
them away. 27 The LORD will afflict you
with the boils of Egypt and with tumors,
festering sores and the itch, from which
you cannot be cured. 28 The LORD will af-
flict you with madness, blindness and
confusion of mind. 29 At midday you will
grope about like a blind man in the dark.
You will be unsuccessful in everything
you do; day after day you will be op-
pressed and robbed, with no one to rescue
you.

30 You will be pledged to be married to
a woman, but another will take her and
ravish her. You will build a house, but you
will not live in it. You will plant a vine-
yard, but you will not even begin to enjoy
its fruit. 31 Your ox will be slaughtered be-
fore your eyes, but you will eat none of it.
Your donkey will be forcibly taken from
you and will not be returned. Your sheep
will be given to your enemies, and no one
will rescue them. 32 Your sons and daugh-
ters will be given to another nation, and
you will wear out your eyes watching for
them day after day, powerless to lift a
hand. 33 A people that you do not know
will eat what your land and labor produce,
and you will have nothing but cruel op-
pression all your days. 34 The sights you
see will drive you mad. 35 The LORD will af-
flict your knees and legs with painful boils
that cannot be cured, spreading from the
soles of your feet to the top of your head.

36 The LORD will drive you and the king
you set over you to a nation unknown to
you or your fathers. There you will wor-
ship other gods, gods of wood and stone.
37 You will become a thing of horror and
an object of scorn and ridicule to all the
nations where the LORD will drive you.

38 You will sow much seed in the field
but you will harvest little, because locusts
will devour it. 39 You will plant vineyards
and cultivate them but you will not drink
the wine or gather the grapes, because
worms will eat them. 40 You will have olive
trees throughout your country but you
will not use the oil, because the olives will
drop off. 41 You will have sons and daugh-
ters but you will not keep them, because
they will go into captivity. 42 Swarms of lo-
custs will take over all your trees and the
crops of your land.

43 The alien who lives among you will
rise above you higher and higher, but you
will sink lower and lower. 44 He will lend
to you, but you will not lend to him. He
will be the head, but you will be the tail.

45 All these curses will come upon you.
They will pursue you and overtake you
until you are destroyed, because you did
not obey the LORD your God and observe
the commands and decrees he gave you.
46 They will be a sign and a wonder to you
and your descendants forever. 47 Because
you did not serve the LORD your God joy-
fully and gladly in the time of prosperity,
48 therefore in hunger and thirst, in naked-
ness and dire poverty, you will serve the
enemies the LORD sends against you. He

[a] 20 Hebrew *me*

will put an iron yoke on your neck until he has destroyed you.

49The LORD will bring a nation against you from far away, from the ends of the earth, like an eagle swooping down, a nation whose language you will not understand, 50a fierce-looking nation without respect for the old or pity for the young. 51They will devour the young of your livestock and the crops of your land until you are destroyed. They will leave you no grain, new wine or oil, nor any calves of your herds or lambs of your flocks until you are ruined. 52They will lay siege to all the cities throughout your land until the high fortified walls in which you trust fall down. They will besiege all the cities throughout the land the LORD your God is giving you.

53Because of the suffering that your enemy will inflict on you during the siege, you will eat the fruit of the womb, the flesh of the sons and daughters the LORD your God has given you. 54Even the most gentle and sensitive man among you will have no compassion on his own brother or the wife he loves or his surviving children, 55and he will not give to one of them any of the flesh of his children that he is eating. It will be all he has left because of the suffering your enemy will inflict on you during the siege[a] of all your cities. 56The most gentle and sensitive woman among you—so sensitive and gentle that she would not venture to touch the ground with the sole of her foot—will begrudge the husband she loves and her own son or daughter 57the afterbirth from her womb and the children she bears. For she intends to eat them secretly during the siege and in the distress that your enemy will inflict on you in your cities.

58If you do not carefully follow all the words of this law, which are written in this book, and do not revere this glorious and awesome name—the LORD your God— 59the LORD will send fearful plagues on you and your descendants, harsh and prolonged disasters, and severe and lingering illnesses. 60He will bring upon you all the diseases of Egypt that you dreaded, and they will cling to you. 61The LORD will also bring on you every kind of sickness and disaster not recorded in this Book of the Law, until you are destroyed. 62You who were as numerous as the stars in the sky will be left but few in number, because you did not obey the LORD your God. 63Just as it pleased the LORD to make you prosper and increase in number, so it will please him to ruin and destroy you. You will be uprooted from the land you are entering to possess.

64Then the LORD will scatter you among all nations, from one end of the earth to the other. There you will worship other gods—gods of wood and stone, which neither you nor your fathers have known. 65Among those nations you will find no repose, no resting place for the sole of your foot. There the LORD will give you an anxious mind, eyes weary with longing, and a despairing heart. 66You will live in constant suspense, filled with dread both night and day, never sure of your life. 67In the morning you will say, "If only it were evening!" and in the evening, "If only it were morning!"—because of the terror that will fill your hearts and the sights that your eyes will see. 68The LORD will send you back in ships to Egypt on a journey I said you should never make again. There you will offer yourselves for sale to your enemies as male and female slaves, but no one will buy you.

Renewal of the Covenant

29 These are the terms of the covenant the LORD commanded Moses to make with the Israelites in Moab, in addition to the covenant he had made with them at Horeb.

2Moses summoned all the Israelites and said to them:

Your eyes have seen all that the LORD did in Egypt to Pharaoh, to all his officials and to all his land. 3With your own eyes you saw those great trials, those miraculous signs and great wonders. 4But to this day the LORD has not given you a mind that understands or eyes that see or ears that hear. 5During the forty years that I led you through the desert, your clothes did not wear out, nor did the sandals on your feet. 6You ate no bread and drank no wine or other fermented drink. I did this so that you might know that I am the LORD your God.

7When you reached this place, Sihon king of Heshbon and Og king of Bashan came out to fight against us, but we defeated them. 8We took their land and gave it as an inheritance to the Reubenites, the Gadites and the half-tribe of Manasseh.

9Carefully follow the terms of this covenant, so that you may prosper in everything you do. 10All of you are standing to-

day in the presence of the LORD your
God—your leaders and chief men, your
elders and officials, and all the other men
of Israel, 11together with your children
and your wives, and the aliens living in
your camps who chop your wood and car-
ry your water. 12You are standing here in
order to enter into a covenant with the
LORD your God, a covenant the LORD is
making with you this day and sealing with
an oath, 13to confirm you this day as his
people, that he may be your God as he
promised you and as he swore to your fa-
thers, Abraham, Isaac and Jacob. 14I am
making this covenant, with its oath, not
only with you 15who are standing here
with us today in the presence of the LORD
our God but also with those who are not
here today.

16You yourselves know how we lived in
Egypt and how we passed through the
countries on the way here. 17You saw
among them their detestable images and
idols of wood and stone, of silver and
gold. 18Make sure there is no man or
woman, clan or tribe among you today
whose heart turns away from the LORD our
God to go and worship the gods of those
nations; make sure there is no root among
you that produces such bitter poison.

19When such a person hears the words
of this oath, he invokes a blessing on him-
self and therefore thinks, "I will be safe,
even though I persist in going my own
way." This will bring disaster on the wa-
tered land as well as the dry.[a] 20The LORD
will never be willing to forgive him; his
wrath and zeal will burn against that man.
All the curses written in this book will fall
upon him, and the LORD will blot out his
name from under heaven. 21The LORD will
single him out from all the tribes of Israel
for disaster, according to all the curses of
the covenant written in this Book of the
Law.

22Your children who follow you in later
generations and foreigners who come
from distant lands will see the calamities
that have fallen on the land and the dis-
eases with which the LORD has afflicted it.
23The whole land will be a burning waste
of salt and sulfur—nothing planted, noth-
ing sprouting, no vegetation growing on
it. It will be like the destruction of Sodom
and Gomorrah, Admah and Zeboiim,
which the LORD overthrew in fierce anger.
24All the nations will ask: "Why has the
LORD done this to this land? Why this
fierce, burning anger?"

25And the answer will be: "It is because
this people abandoned the covenant of
the LORD, the God of their fathers, the cov-
enant he made with them when he
brought them out of Egypt. 26They went
off and worshiped other gods and bowed
down to them, gods they did not know,
gods he had not given them. 27Therefore
the LORD's anger burned against this land,
so that he brought on it all the curses writ-
ten in this book. 28In furious anger and in
great wrath the LORD uprooted them from
their land and thrust them into another
land, as it is now."

29The secret things belong to the LORD
our God, but the things revealed belong to
us and to our children forever, that we
may follow all the words of this law.

Prosperity After Turning to the LORD

30 When all these blessings and
curses I have set before you come
upon you and you take them to heart
wherever the LORD your God disperses
you among the nations, 2and when you
and your children return to the LORD your
God and obey him with all your heart and
with all your soul according to everything
I command you today, 3then the LORD
your God will restore your fortunes[b] and
have compassion on you and gather you
again from all the nations where he scat-
tered you. 4Even if you have been ban-
ished to the most distant land under the
heavens, from there the LORD your God
will gather you and bring you back. 5He
will bring you to the land that belonged to
your fathers, and you will take possession
of it. He will make you more prosperous
and numerous than your fathers. 6The
LORD your God will circumcise your hearts
and the hearts of your descendants, so
that you may love him with all your heart
and with all your soul, and live. 7The LORD
your God will put all these curses on your
enemies who hate and persecute you.
8You will again obey the LORD and follow
all his commands I am giving you today.
9Then the LORD your God will make you
most prosperous in all the work of your
hands and in the fruit of your womb, the
young of your livestock and the crops of
your land. The LORD will again delight in
you and make you prosperous, just as he
delighted in your fathers, 10if you obey the

[a] 19 Or *way, in order to add drunkenness to thirst.*

[b] 3 Or *will bring you back from captivity*

LORD your God and keep his commands and decrees that are written in this Book of the Law and turn to the LORD your God with all your heart and with all your soul.

The Offer of Life or Death

[11]Now what I am commanding you today is not too difficult for you or beyond your reach. [12]It is not up in heaven, so that you have to ask, "Who will ascend into heaven to get it and proclaim it to us so we may obey it?" [13]Nor is it beyond the sea, so that you have to ask, "Who will cross the sea to get it and proclaim it to us so we may obey it?" [14]No, the word is very near you; it is in your mouth and in your heart so you may obey it.

[15]See, I set before you today life and prosperity, death and destruction. [16]For I command you today to love the LORD your God, to walk in his ways, and to keep his commands, decrees and laws; then you will live and increase, and the LORD your God will bless you in the land you are entering to possess.

[17]But if your heart turns away and you are not obedient, and if you are drawn away to bow down to other gods and worship them, [18]I declare to you this day that you will certainly be destroyed. You will not live long in the land you are crossing the Jordan to enter and possess.

[19]This day I call heaven and earth as witnesses against you that I have set before you life and death, blessings and curses. Now choose life, so that you and your children may live [20]and that you may love the LORD your God, listen to his voice, and hold fast to him. For the LORD is your life, and he will give you many years in the land he swore to give to your fathers, Abraham, Isaac and Jacob.

Joshua to Succeed Moses

31 Then Moses went out and spoke these words to all Israel: [2]"I am now a hundred and twenty years old and I am no longer able to lead you. The LORD has said to me, 'You shall not cross the Jordan.' [3]The LORD your God himself will cross over ahead of you. He will destroy these nations before you, and you will take possession of their land. Joshua also will cross over ahead of you, as the LORD said. [4]And the LORD will do to them what he did to Sihon and Og, the kings of the Amorites, whom he destroyed along with their land. [5]The LORD will deliver them to you, and you must do to them all that I have commanded you. [6]Be strong and courageous. Do not be afraid or terrified because of them, for the LORD your God goes with you; he will never leave you nor forsake you."

[7]Then Moses summoned Joshua and said to him in the presence of all Israel, "Be strong and courageous, for you must go with this people into the land that the LORD swore to their forefathers to give them, and you must divide it among them as their inheritance. [8]The LORD himself goes before you and will be with you; he will never leave you nor forsake you. Do not be afraid; do not be discouraged."

The Reading of the Law

[9]So Moses wrote down this law and gave it to the priests, the sons of Levi, who carried the ark of the covenant of the LORD, and to all the elders of Israel. [10]Then Moses commanded them: "At the end of every seven years, in the year for canceling debts, during the Feast of Tabernacles, [11]when all Israel comes to appear before the LORD your God at the place he will choose, you shall read this law before them in their hearing. [12]Assemble the people—men, women and children, and the aliens living in your towns—so they can listen and learn to fear the LORD your God and follow carefully all the words of this law. [13]Their children, who do not know this law, must hear it and learn to fear the LORD your God as long as you live in the land you are crossing the Jordan to possess."

Israel's Rebellion Predicted

[14]The LORD said to Moses, "Now the day of your death is near. Call Joshua and present yourselves at the Tent of Meeting, where I will commission him." So Moses and Joshua came and presented themselves at the Tent of Meeting.

[15]Then the LORD appeared at the Tent in a pillar of cloud, and the cloud stood over the entrance to the Tent. [16]And the LORD said to Moses: "You are going to rest with your fathers, and these people will soon prostitute themselves to the foreign gods of the land they are entering. They will forsake me and break the covenant I made with them. [17]On that day I will become angry with them and forsake them; I will hide my face from them, and they will be destroyed. Many disasters and difficulties will come upon them, and on that day they will ask, 'Have not these disasters

come upon us because our God is not with
us?' 18And I will certainly hide my face on
that day because of all their wickedness in
turning to other gods.
19"Now write down for yourselves this
song and teach it to the Israelites and have
them sing it, so that it may be a witness for
me against them. 20When I have brought
them into the land flowing with milk and
honey, the land I promised on oath to
their forefathers, and when they eat their
fill and thrive, they will turn to other gods
and worship them, rejecting me and
breaking my covenant. 21And when many
disasters and difficulties come upon them,
this song will testify against them, be-
cause it will not be forgotten by their
descendants. I know what they are dis-
posed to do, even before I bring them into
the land I promised them on oath." 22So
Moses wrote down this song that day and
taught it to the Israelites.
23The LORD gave this command to Josh-
ua son of Nun: "Be strong and coura-
geous, for you will bring the Israelites into
the land I promised them on oath, and I
myself will be with you."
24After Moses finished writing in a book
the words of this law from beginning to
end, 25he gave this command to the Le-
vites who carried the ark of the covenant
of the LORD: 26"Take this Book of the Law
and place it beside the ark of the covenant
of the LORD your God. There it will remain
as a witness against you. 27For I know
how rebellious and stiff-necked you are. If
you have been rebellious against the LORD
while I am still alive and with you, how
much more will you rebel after I die! 28As-
semble before me all the elders of your
tribes and all your officials, so that I can
speak these words in their hearing and
call heaven and earth to testify against
them. 29For I know that after my death
you are sure to become utterly corrupt
and to turn from the way I have com-
manded you. In days to come, disaster
will fall upon you because you will do evil
in the sight of the LORD and provoke him
to anger by what your hands have made."

The Song of Moses

30And Moses recited the words of this
song from beginning to end in the hearing
of the whole assembly of Israel:

32 Listen, O heavens, and I will
speak;
hear, O earth, the words of my
mouth.
2Let my teaching fall like rain
and my words descend like dew,
like showers on new grass,
like abundant rain on tender plants.

3I will proclaim the name of the LORD.
Oh, praise the greatness of our God!
4He is the Rock, his works are perfect,
and all his ways are just.
A faithful God who does no wrong,
upright and just is he.

5They have acted corruptly toward
him;
to their shame they are no longer
his children,
but a warped and crooked
generation.[a]
6Is this the way you repay the LORD,
O foolish and unwise people?
Is he not your Father, your Creator,[b]
who made you and formed you?

7Remember the days of old;
consider the generations long past.
Ask your father and he will tell you,
your elders, and they will explain to
you.
8When the Most High gave the nations
their inheritance,
when he divided all mankind,
he set up boundaries for the peoples
according to the number of the sons
of Israel.[c]
9For the LORD's portion is his people,
Jacob his allotted inheritance.

10In a desert land he found him,
in a barren and howling waste.
He shielded him and cared for him;
he guarded him as the apple of his
eye,
11like an eagle that stirs up its nest
and hovers over its young,
that spreads its wings to catch them
and carries them on its pinions.
12The LORD alone led him;
no foreign god was with him.

13He made him ride on the heights of
the land
and fed him with the fruit of the
fields.

[a]5 Or *Corrupt are they and not his children, / a generation warped and twisted to their shame* [b]6 Or *Father, who bought you* [c]8 Masoretic Text; Dead Sea Scrolls (see also Septuagint) *sons of God*

He nourished him with honey from
the rock,
and with oil from the flinty crag,
14 with curds and milk from herd and
flock
and with fattened lambs and goats,
with choice rams of Bashan
and the finest kernels of wheat.
You drank the foaming blood of the
grape.
15 Jeshurun[a] grew fat and kicked;
filled with food, he became heavy
and sleek.
He abandoned the God who made him
and rejected the Rock his Savior.
16 They made him jealous with their
foreign gods
and angered him with their
detestable idols.
17 They sacrificed to demons, which are
not God—
gods they had not known,
gods that recently appeared,
gods your fathers did not fear.
18 You deserted the Rock, who fathered
you;
you forgot the God who gave you
birth.

19 The LORD saw this and rejected them
because he was angered by his sons
and daughters.
20 "I will hide my face from them," he
said,
"and see what their end will be;
for they are a perverse generation,
children who are unfaithful.
21 They made me jealous by what is no
god
and angered me with their
worthless idols.
I will make them envious by those
who are not a people;
I will make them angry by a nation
that has no understanding.
22 For a fire has been kindled by my
wrath,
one that burns to the realm of
death[b] below.
It will devour the earth and its
harvests
and set afire the foundations of the
mountains.

23 "I will heap calamities upon them
and spend my arrows against them.
24 I will send wasting famine against
them,
consuming pestilence and deadly
plague;
I will send against them the fangs of
wild beasts,
the venom of vipers that glide in
the dust.
25 In the street the sword will make
them childless;
in their homes terror will reign.
Young men and young women will
perish,
infants and gray-haired men.
26 I said I would scatter them
and blot out their memory from
mankind,
27 but I dreaded the taunt of the enemy,
lest the adversary misunderstand
and say, 'Our hand has triumphed;
the LORD has not done all this.' "

28 They are a nation without sense,
there is no discernment in them.
29 If only they were wise and would
understand this
and discern what their end will be!
30 How could one man chase a
thousand,
or two put ten thousand to flight,
unless their Rock had sold them,
unless the LORD had given them up?
31 For their rock is not like our Rock,
as even our enemies concede.
32 Their vine comes from the vine of
Sodom
and from the fields of Gomorrah.
Their grapes are filled with poison,
and their clusters with bitterness.
33 Their wine is the venom of serpents,
the deadly poison of cobras.

34 "Have I not kept this in reserve
and sealed it in my vaults?
35 It is mine to avenge; I will repay.
In due time their foot will slip;
their day of disaster is near
and their doom rushes upon them."

36 The LORD will judge his people
and have compassion on his
servants
when he sees their strength is gone
and no one is left, slave or free.
37 He will say: "Now where are their
gods,
the rock they took refuge in,

[a] 15 *Jeshurun* means *the upright one*, that is, Israel.

[b] 22 Hebrew *to Sheol*

38the gods who ate the fat of their sacrifices
and drank the wine of their drink offerings?
Let them rise up to help you!
Let them give you shelter!

39"See now that I myself am He!
There is no god besides me.
I put to death and I bring to life,
I have wounded and I will heal,
and no one can deliver out of my hand.
40I lift my hand to heaven and declare:
As surely as I live forever,
41when I sharpen my flashing sword
and my hand grasps it in judgment,
I will take vengeance on my adversaries
and repay those who hate me.
42I will make my arrows drunk with blood,
while my sword devours flesh:
the blood of the slain and the captives,
the heads of the enemy leaders."

43Rejoice, O nations, with his people,[a,b]
for he will avenge the blood of his servants;
he will take vengeance on his enemies
and make atonement for his land and people.

44Moses came with Joshua[c] son of Nun and spoke all the words of this song in the hearing of the people. 45When Moses finished reciting all these words to all Israel, 46he said to them, "Take to heart all the words I have solemnly declared to you this day, so that you may command your children to obey carefully all the words of this law. 47They are not just idle words for you—they are your life. By them you will live long in the land you are crossing the Jordan to possess."

Moses to Die on Mount Nebo

48On that same day the LORD told Moses, 49"Go up into the Abarim Range to Mount Nebo in Moab, across from Jericho, and view Canaan, the land I am giving the Israelites as their own possession. 50There on the mountain that you have climbed you will die and be gathered to your people, just as your brother Aaron died on Mount Hor and was gathered to his people. 51This is because both of you broke faith with me in the presence of the Israelites at the waters of Meribah Kadesh in the Desert of Zin and because you did not uphold my holiness among the Israelites. 52Therefore, you will see the land only from a distance; you will not enter the land I am giving to the people of Israel."

Moses Blesses the Tribes

33 This is the blessing that Moses the man of God pronounced on the Israelites before his death. 2He said:

"The LORD came from Sinai
and dawned over them from Seir;
he shone forth from Mount Paran.
He came with[d] myriads of holy ones
from the south, from his mountain slopes.[e]
3Surely it is you who love the people;
all the holy ones are in your hand.
At your feet they all bow down,
and from you receive instruction,
4the law that Moses gave us,
the possession of the assembly of Jacob.
5He was king over Jeshurun[f]
when the leaders of the people assembled,
along with the tribes of Israel.

6"Let Reuben live and not die,
nor[g] his men be few."

7And this he said about Judah:

"Hear, O LORD, the cry of Judah;
bring him to his people.
With his own hands he defends his cause.
Oh, be his help against his foes!"

8About Levi he said:

"Your Thummim and Urim belong
to the man you favored.
You tested him at Massah;
you contended with him at the waters of Meribah.
9He said of his father and mother,
'I have no regard for them.'
He did not recognize his brothers
or acknowledge his own children,

[a]43 Or *Make his people rejoice, O nations* [b]43 Masoretic Text; Dead Sea Scrolls (see also Septuagint) *people, / and let all the angels worship him /* [c]44 Hebrew *Hoshea,* a variant of *Joshua* [d]2 Or *from* [e]2 The meaning of the Hebrew for this phrase is uncertain. [f]5 *Jeshurun* means *the upright one,* that is, Israel; also in verse 26. [g]6 Or *but let*

but he watched over your word
and guarded your covenant.
10He teaches your precepts to Jacob
and your law to Israel.
He offers incense before you
and whole burnt offerings on your altar.
11Bless all his skills, O LORD,
and be pleased with the work of his hands.
Smite the loins of those who rise up against him;
strike his foes till they rise no more."

12About Benjamin he said:

"Let the beloved of the LORD rest secure in him,
for he shields him all day long,
and the one the LORD loves rests between his shoulders."

13About Joseph he said:

"May the LORD bless his land
with the precious dew from heaven above
and with the deep waters that lie below;
14with the best the sun brings forth
and the finest the moon can yield;
15with the choicest gifts of the ancient mountains
and the fruitfulness of the everlasting hills;
16with the best gifts of the earth and its fullness
and the favor of him who dwelt in the burning bush.
Let all these rest on the head of Joseph,
on the brow of the prince among[a] his brothers.
17In majesty he is like a firstborn bull;
his horns are the horns of a wild ox.
With them he will gore the nations,
even those at the ends of the earth.
Such are the ten thousands of Ephraim;
such are the thousands of Manasseh."

18About Zebulun he said:

"Rejoice, Zebulun, in your going out,
and you, Issachar, in your tents.
19They will summon peoples to the mountain
and there offer sacrifices of righteousness;
they will feast on the abundance of the seas,
on the treasures hidden in the sand."

20About Gad he said:

"Blessed is he who enlarges Gad's domain!
Gad lives there like a lion,
tearing at arm or head.
21He chose the best land for himself;
the leader's portion was kept for him.
When the heads of the people assembled,
he carried out the LORD's righteous will,
and his judgments concerning Israel."

22About Dan he said:

"Dan is a lion's cub,
springing out of Bashan."

23About Naphtali he said:

"Naphtali is abounding with the favor of the LORD
and is full of his blessing;
he will inherit southward to the lake."

24About Asher he said:

"Most blessed of sons is Asher;
let him be favored by his brothers,
and let him bathe his feet in oil.
25The bolts of your gates will be iron and bronze,
and your strength will equal your days.
26"There is no one like the God of Jeshurun,
who rides on the heavens to help you
and on the clouds in his majesty.
27The eternal God is your refuge,
and underneath are the everlasting arms.
He will drive out your enemy before you,
saying, 'Destroy him!'
28So Israel will live in safety alone;
Jacob's spring is secure
in a land of grain and new wine,
where the heavens drop dew.

[a]16 Or *of the one separated from*

[29]Blessed are you, O Israel!
Who is like you,
a people saved by the LORD?
He is your shield and helper
and your glorious sword.
Your enemies will cower before you,
and you will trample down their
high places.[a]"

The Death of Moses

34 Then Moses climbed Mount Nebo from the plains of Moab to the top of Pisgah, across from Jericho. There the LORD showed him the whole land—from Gilead to Dan, [2]all of Naphtali, the territory of Ephraim and Manasseh, all the land of Judah as far as the western sea,[b] [3]the Negev and the whole region from the Valley of Jericho, the City of Palms, as far as Zoar. [4]Then the LORD said to him, "This is the land I promised on oath to Abraham, Isaac and Jacob when I said, 'I will give it to your descendants.' I have let you see it with your eyes, but you will not cross over into it."

[5]And Moses the servant of the LORD died there in Moab, as the LORD had said. [6]He buried him[c] in Moab, in the valley opposite Beth Peor, but to this day no one knows where his grave is. [7]Moses was a hundred and twenty years old when he died, yet his eyes were not weak nor his strength gone. [8]The Israelites grieved for Moses in the plains of Moab thirty days, until the time of weeping and mourning was over.

[9]Now Joshua son of Nun was filled with the spirit[d] of wisdom because Moses had laid his hands on him. So the Israelites listened to him and did what the LORD had commanded Moses.

[10]Since then, no prophet has risen in Israel like Moses, whom the LORD knew face to face, [11]who did all those miraculous signs and wonders the LORD sent him to do in Egypt—to Pharaoh and to all his officials and to his whole land. [12]For no one has ever shown the mighty power or performed the awesome deeds that Moses did in the sight of all Israel.

[a]29 Or *will tread upon their bodies* [b]2 That is, the Mediterranean [c]6 Or *He was buried* [d]9 Or *Spirit*

JOSHUA tells the story of how the Israelites conquer their enemies in the promised land and divide it up among the twelve tribes. As long as the people trust God and obey his will, he gives them victory in their battles. By the end of the book, the people choose to serve only the Lord. As you read this book, make your own choice to serve the Lord, to do his will, and to depend on him to give you victory over the evil one.

JOSHUA

The Lord Commands Joshua

1 After the death of Moses the servant
of the Lord, the Lord said to Joshua
son of Nun, Moses' aide: 2"Moses my ser-
vant is dead. Now then, you and all these
people, get ready to cross the Jordan River
into the land I am about to give to them—
to the Israelites. 3I will give you every
place where you set your foot, as I prom-
ised Moses. 4Your territory will extend
from the desert to Lebanon, and from the
great river, the Euphrates—all the Hittite
country—to the Great Sea[a] on the west.
5No one will be able to stand up against
you all the days of your life. As I was with
Moses, so I will be with you; I will never
leave you nor forsake you.

6"Be strong and courageous, because
you will lead these people to inherit the
land I swore to their forefathers to give
them. 7Be strong and very courageous. Be
careful to obey all the law my servant Mo-
ses gave you; do not turn from it to the
right or to the left, that you may be suc-
cessful wherever you go. 8Do not let this
Book of the Law depart from your mouth;
meditate on it day and night, so that you
may be careful to do everything written in
it. Then you will be prosperous and suc-
cessful. 9Have I not commanded you? Be

[a]4 That is, the Mediterranean

strong and courageous. Do not be terrified; do not be discouraged, for the LORD your God will be with you wherever you go."

10So Joshua ordered the officers of the people: 11"Go through the camp and tell the people, 'Get your supplies ready. Three days from now you will cross the Jordan here to go in and take possession of the land the LORD your God is giving you for your own.' "

12But to the Reubenites, the Gadites and the half-tribe of Manasseh, Joshua said, 13"Remember the command that Moses the servant of the LORD gave you: 'The LORD your God is giving you rest and has

VERSE FOR THE DAY: Joshua 1:9 | AUTHOR: Ruth Senter | PASSAGE FOR THE DAY: Joshua 1:1–9

Courageous Obedience

I was ten years old, and our family was driving through the Alabama pine wilderness headed to a two-week Bible school my parents were conducting. The night before, four drunk men—the Hall Brothers—had staggered across the road in front of our truck. Nobody in that area crossed the Hall brothers, but there my daddy stood, just inches from their rifle, while I crouched with my brothers in the back of the truck.

"No, we will not stay home tomorrow night. We are having Bible school in your community," I heard Daddy say. We held our breath and waited for the shot that never came. The Hall brothers finally lumbered off into the woods. And tonight we were back in the truck driving the dark, lonely roads back to the Crawford community.

"Aren't you scared, Daddy?" I finally blurted out when my fears had nearly overtaken me. "Of course I'm scared," he told me, "but that doesn't mean we won't go back." The Hall brothers never reappeared, and several months later Mrs. Hall apologized for the hard time her boys gave the preacher.

Today in the Crawford community a group of believers are walking with God as a result of that Bible school and a preacher who was willing to be afraid.

MARRIAGE BUILDERS

♦ *When have you gone ahead with something you knew was right, despite your fears?*

♦ *What anxieties do you hold about the future of your marriage, and how could your loving obedience to God help you face those fears?*

Additional Scripture Readings
2 Timothy 1:7; Psalm 56:4; Isaiah 12:2

Go to page 244 for your next devotional reading.

granted you this land.' [14]Your wives, your children and your livestock may stay in the land that Moses gave you east of the Jordan, but all your fighting men, fully armed, must cross over ahead of your brothers. You are to help your brothers [15]until the LORD gives them rest, as he has done for you, and until they too have taken possession of the land that the LORD your God is giving them. After that, you may go back and occupy your own land, which Moses the servant of the LORD gave you east of the Jordan toward the sunrise."

[16]Then they answered Joshua, "Whatever you have commanded us we will do, and wherever you send us we will go. [17]Just as we fully obeyed Moses, so we will obey you. Only may the LORD your God be with you as he was with Moses. [18]Whoever rebels against your word and does not obey your words, whatever you may command them, will be put to death. Only be strong and courageous!"

Rahab and the Spies

2 Then Joshua son of Nun secretly sent two spies from Shittim. "Go, look over the land," he said, "especially Jericho." So they went and entered the house of a prostitute[a] named Rahab and stayed there.

[2]The king of Jericho was told, "Look! Some of the Israelites have come here tonight to spy out the land." [3]So the king of Jericho sent this message to Rahab: "Bring out the men who came to you and entered your house, because they have come to spy out the whole land."

[4]But the woman had taken the two men and hidden them. She said, "Yes, the men came to me, but I did not know where they had come from. [5]At dusk, when it was time to close the city gate, the men left. I don't know which way they went. Go after them quickly. You may catch up with them." [6](But she had taken them up to the roof and hidden them under the stalks of flax she had laid out on the roof.) [7]So the men set out in pursuit of the spies on the road that leads to the fords of the Jordan, and as soon as the pursuers had gone out, the gate was shut.

[8]Before the spies lay down for the night, she went up on the roof [9]and said to them, "I know that the LORD has given this land to you and that a great fear of you has fallen on us, so that all who live in this country are melting in fear because of you. [10]We have heard how the LORD dried up the water of the Red Sea[b] for you when you came out of Egypt, and what you did to Sihon and Og, the two kings of the Amorites east of the Jordan, whom you completely destroyed.[c] [11]When we heard of it, our hearts melted and everyone's courage failed because of you, for the LORD your God is God in heaven above and on the earth below. [12]Now then, please swear to me by the LORD that you will show kindness to my family, because I have shown kindness to you. Give me a sure sign [13]that you will spare the lives of my father and mother, my brothers and sisters, and all who belong to them, and that you will save us from death."

[14]"Our lives for your lives!" the men assured her. "If you don't tell what we are doing, we will treat you kindly and faithfully when the LORD gives us the land."

[15]So she let them down by a rope through the window, for the house she lived in was part of the city wall. [16]Now she had said to them, "Go to the hills so the pursuers will not find you. Hide yourselves there three days until they return, and then go on your way."

[17]The men said to her, "This oath you made us swear will not be binding on us [18]unless, when we enter the land, you have tied this scarlet cord in the window through which you let us down, and unless you have brought your father and mother, your brothers and all your family into your house. [19]If anyone goes outside your house into the street, his blood will be on his own head; we will not be responsible. As for anyone who is in the house with you, his blood will be on our head if a hand is laid on him. [20]But if you tell what we are doing, we will be released from the oath you made us swear."

[21]"Agreed," she replied. "Let it be as you say." So she sent them away and they departed. And she tied the scarlet cord in the window.

[22]When they left, they went into the hills and stayed there three days, until the pursuers had searched all along the road and returned without finding them. [23]Then the two men started back. They went down out of the hills, forded the riv-

[a] 1 Or possibly *an innkeeper* [b] 10 Hebrew *Yam Suph*; that is, Sea of Reeds [c] 10 The Hebrew term refers to the irrevocable giving over of things or persons to the LORD, often by totally destroying them.

er and came to Joshua son of Nun and told him everything that had happened to them. 24They said to Joshua, "The LORD has surely given the whole land into our hands; all the people are melting in fear because of us."

Crossing the Jordan

3 Early in the morning Joshua and all the Israelites set out from Shittim and went to the Jordan, where they camped before crossing over. 2After three days the officers went throughout the camp, 3giving orders to the people: "When you see the ark of the covenant of the LORD your God, and the priests, who are Levites, carrying it, you are to move out from your positions and follow it. 4Then you will know which way to go, since you have never been this way before. But keep a distance of about a thousand yards[a] between you and the ark; do not go near it."

5Joshua told the people, "Consecrate yourselves, for tomorrow the LORD will do amazing things among you."

6Joshua said to the priests, "Take up the ark of the covenant and pass on ahead of the people." So they took it up and went ahead of them.

7And the LORD said to Joshua, "Today I will begin to exalt you in the eyes of all Israel, so they may know that I am with you as I was with Moses. 8Tell the priests who carry the ark of the covenant: 'When you reach the edge of the Jordan's waters, go and stand in the river.' "

9Joshua said to the Israelites, "Come here and listen to the words of the LORD your God. 10This is how you will know that the living God is among you and that he will certainly drive out before you the Canaanites, Hittites, Hivites, Perizzites, Girgashites, Amorites and Jebusites. 11See, the ark of the covenant of the Lord of all the earth will go into the Jordan ahead of you. 12Now then, choose twelve men from the tribes of Israel, one from each tribe. 13And as soon as the priests who carry the ark of the LORD—the Lord of all the earth—set foot in the Jordan, its waters flowing downstream will be cut off and stand up in a heap."

14So when the people broke camp to cross the Jordan, the priests carrying the ark of the covenant went ahead of them. 15Now the Jordan is at flood stage all during harvest. Yet as soon as the priests who carried the ark reached the Jordan and their feet touched the water's edge, 16the water from upstream stopped flowing. It piled up in a heap a great distance away, at a town called Adam in the vicinity of Zarethan, while the water flowing down to the Sea of the Arabah (the Salt Sea[b]) was completely cut off. So the people crossed over opposite Jericho. 17The priests who carried the ark of the covenant of the LORD stood firm on dry ground in the middle of the Jordan, while all Israel passed by until the whole nation had completed the crossing on dry ground.

4 When the whole nation had finished crossing the Jordan, the LORD said to Joshua, 2"Choose twelve men from among the people, one from each tribe, 3and tell them to take up twelve stones from the middle of the Jordan from right where the priests stood and to carry them over with you and put them down at the place where you stay tonight."

4So Joshua called together the twelve men he had appointed from the Israelites, one from each tribe, 5and said to them, "Go over before the ark of the LORD your God into the middle of the Jordan. Each of you is to take up a stone on his shoulder, according to the number of the tribes of the Israelites, 6to serve as a sign among you. In the future, when your children ask you, 'What do these stones mean?' 7tell them that the flow of the Jordan was cut off before the ark of the covenant of the LORD. When it crossed the Jordan, the waters of the Jordan were cut off. These stones are to be a memorial to the people of Israel forever."

8So the Israelites did as Joshua commanded them. They took twelve stones from the middle of the Jordan, according to the number of the tribes of the Israelites, as the LORD had told Joshua; and they carried them over with them to their camp, where they put them down. 9Joshua set up the twelve stones that had been[c] in the middle of the Jordan at the spot where the priests who carried the ark of the covenant had stood. And they are there to this day.

10Now the priests who carried the ark remained standing in the middle of the Jordan until everything the LORD had com-

[a]4 Hebrew *about two thousand cubits* (about 900 meters) [b]16 That is, the Dead Sea [c]9 Or *Joshua also set up twelve stones*

manded Joshua was done by the people,
just as Moses had directed Joshua. The
people hurried over, 11and as soon as all
of them had crossed, the ark of the LORD
and the priests came to the other side
while the people watched. 12The men of
Reuben, Gad and the half-tribe of Manas-
seh crossed over, armed, in front of the Is-
raelites, as Moses had directed them.
13About forty thousand armed for battle
crossed over before the LORD to the plains
of Jericho for war.

14That day the LORD exalted Joshua in
the sight of all Israel; and they revered
him all the days of his life, just as they had
revered Moses.

15Then the LORD said to Joshua,
16"Command the priests carrying the ark
of the Testimony to come up out of the
Jordan."

17So Joshua commanded the priests,
"Come up out of the Jordan."

18And the priests came up out of the riv-
er carrying the ark of the covenant of the
LORD. No sooner had they set their feet on
the dry ground than the waters of the Jor-
dan returned to their place and ran at
flood stage as before.

19On the tenth day of the first month the
people went up from the Jordan and
camped at Gilgal on the eastern border of
Jericho. 20And Joshua set up at Gilgal the
twelve stones they had taken out of the
Jordan. 21He said to the Israelites, "In the
future when your descendants ask their
fathers, 'What do these stones mean?'
22tell them, 'Israel crossed the Jordan on
dry ground.' 23For the LORD your God
dried up the Jordan before you until you
had crossed over. The LORD your God did
to the Jordan just what he had done to the
Red Sea[a] when he dried it up before us
until we had crossed over. 24He did this so
that all the peoples of the earth might
know that the hand of the LORD is power-
ful and so that you might always fear the
LORD your God."

Circumcision at Gilgal

5 Now when all the Amorite kings west
of the Jordan and all the Canaanite
kings along the coast heard how the LORD
had dried up the Jordan before the Israel-
ites until we had crossed over, their hearts
melted and they no longer had the cour-
age to face the Israelites.

2At that time the LORD said to Joshua,
"Make flint knives and circumcise the Is-
raelites again." 3So Joshua made flint
knives and circumcised the Israelites at
Gibeath Haaraloth.[b]

4Now this is why he did so: All those
who came out of Egypt—all the men of
military age—died in the desert on the
way after leaving Egypt. 5All the people
that came out had been circumcised, but
all the people born in the desert during
the journey from Egypt had not. 6The Isra-
elites had moved about in the desert forty
years until all the men who were of mili-
tary age when they left Egypt had died,
since they had not obeyed the LORD. For
the LORD had sworn to them that they
would not see the land that he had sol-
emnly promised their fathers to give us, a
land flowing with milk and honey. 7So he
raised up their sons in their place, and
these were the ones Joshua circumcised.
They were still uncircumcised because
they had not been circumcised on the
way. 8And after the whole nation had
been circumcised, they remained where
they were in camp until they were healed.

9Then the LORD said to Joshua, "Today
I have rolled away the reproach of Egypt
from you." So the place has been called
Gilgal[c] to this day.

10On the evening of the fourteenth day
of the month, while camped at Gilgal on
the plains of Jericho, the Israelites cele-
brated the Passover. 11The day after the
Passover, that very day, they ate some of
the produce of the land: unleavened bread
and roasted grain. 12The manna stopped
the day after[d] they ate this food from the
land; there was no longer any manna for
the Israelites, but that year they ate of the
produce of Canaan.

The Fall of Jericho

13Now when Joshua was near Jericho,
he looked up and saw a man standing in
front of him with a drawn sword in his
hand. Joshua went up to him and asked,
"Are you for us or for our enemies?"

14"Neither," he replied, "but as com-
mander of the army of the LORD I have
now come." Then Joshua fell facedown to
the ground in reverence, and asked him,
"What message does my Lord[e] have for
his servant?"

15The commander of the LORD's army

[a] 23 Hebrew *Yam Suph*; that is, Sea of Reeds
[b] 3 *Gibeath Haaraloth* means *hill of foreskins.*
[c] 9 *Gilgal* sounds like the Hebrew for *roll.*
[d] 12 Or *the day*
[e] 14 Or *lord*

replied, "Take off your sandals, for the place where you are standing is holy." And Joshua did so.

6 Now Jericho was tightly shut up because of the Israelites. No one went out and no one came in.

2 Then the LORD said to Joshua, "See, I have delivered Jericho into your hands, along with its king and its fighting men. 3 March around the city once with all the armed men. Do this for six days. 4 Have seven priests carry trumpets of rams' horns in front of the ark. On the seventh day, march around the city seven times, with the priests blowing the trumpets. 5 When you hear them sound a long blast on the trumpets, have all the people give a loud shout; then the wall of the city will collapse and the people will go up, every man straight in."

6 So Joshua son of Nun called the priests and said to them, "Take up the ark of the covenant of the LORD and have seven priests carry trumpets in front of it." 7 And he ordered the people, "Advance! March around the city, with the armed guard going ahead of the ark of the LORD."

8 When Joshua had spoken to the people, the seven priests carrying the seven trumpets before the LORD went forward, blowing their trumpets, and the ark of the LORD's covenant followed them. 9 The armed guard marched ahead of the priests who blew the trumpets, and the rear guard followed the ark. All this time the trumpets were sounding. 10 But Joshua had commanded the people, "Do not give a war cry, do not raise your voices, do not say a word until the day I tell you to shout. Then shout!" 11 So he had the ark of the LORD carried around the city, circling it once. Then the people returned to camp and spent the night there.

12 Joshua got up early the next morning and the priests took up the ark of the LORD. 13 The seven priests carrying the seven trumpets went forward, marching before the ark of the LORD and blowing the trumpets. The armed men went ahead of them and the rear guard followed the ark of the LORD, while the trumpets kept sounding. 14 So on the second day they marched around the city once and returned to the camp. They did this for six days.

15 On the seventh day, they got up at daybreak and marched around the city seven times in the same manner, except that on that day they circled the city seven times. 16 The seventh time around, when the priests sounded the trumpet blast, Joshua commanded the people, "Shout! For the LORD has given you the city! 17 The city and all that is in it are to be devoted[a] to the LORD. Only Rahab the prostitute[b] and all who are with her in her house shall be spared, because she hid the spies we sent. 18 But keep away from the devoted things, so that you will not bring about your own destruction by taking any of them. Otherwise you will make the camp of Israel liable to destruction and bring trouble on it. 19 All the silver and gold and the articles of bronze and iron are sacred to the LORD and must go into his treasury."

20 When the trumpets sounded, the people shouted, and at the sound of the trumpet, when the people gave a loud shout, the wall collapsed; so every man charged straight in, and they took the city. 21 They devoted the city to the LORD and destroyed with the sword every living thing in it—men and women, young and old, cattle, sheep and donkeys.

22 Joshua said to the two men who had spied out the land, "Go into the prostitute's house and bring her out and all who belong to her, in accordance with your oath to her." 23 So the young men who had done the spying went in and brought out Rahab, her father and mother and brothers and all who belonged to her. They brought out her entire family and put them in a place outside the camp of Israel.

24 Then they burned the whole city and everything in it, but they put the silver and gold and the articles of bronze and iron into the treasury of the LORD's house. 25 But Joshua spared Rahab the prostitute, with her family and all who belonged to her, because she hid the men Joshua had sent as spies to Jericho—and she lives among the Israelites to this day.

26 At that time Joshua pronounced this solemn oath: "Cursed before the LORD is the man who undertakes to rebuild this city, Jericho:

"At the cost of his firstborn son
will he lay its foundations;
at the cost of his youngest
will he set up its gates."

[a] 17 The Hebrew term refers to the irrevocable giving over of things or persons to the LORD, often by totally destroying them; also in verses 18 and 21. [b] 17 Or possibly *innkeeper*; also in verses 22 and 25

27 So the LORD was with Joshua, and his
fame spread throughout the land.

Achan's Sin

7 But the Israelites acted unfaithfully in
regard to the devoted things[a]; Achan
son of Carmi, the son of Zimri,[b] the son
of Zerah, of the tribe of Judah, took some
of them. So the LORD's anger burned
against Israel.

2 Now Joshua sent men from Jericho to
Ai, which is near Beth Aven to the east of
Bethel, and told them, "Go up and spy out
the region." So the men went up and spied
out Ai.

3 When they returned to Joshua, they
said, "Not all the people will have to go up
against Ai. Send two or three thousand
men to take it and do not weary all the
people, for only a few men are there." 4 So
about three thousand men went up; but
they were routed by the men of Ai, 5 who
killed about thirty-six of them. They
chased the Israelites from the city gate as
far as the stone quarries[c] and struck
them down on the slopes. At this the
hearts of the people melted and became
like water.

6 Then Joshua tore his clothes and fell
facedown to the ground before the ark of
the LORD, remaining there till evening.
The elders of Israel did the same, and
sprinkled dust on their heads. 7 And Josh-
ua said, "Ah, Sovereign LORD, why did you
ever bring this people across the Jordan to
deliver us into the hands of the Amorites
to destroy us? If only we had been content
to stay on the other side of the Jordan!
8 O Lord, what can I say, now that Israel
has been routed by its enemies? 9 The Ca-
naanites and the other people of the coun-
try will hear about this and they will sur-
round us and wipe out our name from the
earth. What then will you do for your own
great name?"

10 The LORD said to Joshua, "Stand up!
What are you doing down on your face?
11 Israel has sinned; they have violated my
covenant, which I commanded them to
keep. They have taken some of the devot-
ed things; they have stolen, they have lied,
they have put them with their own posses-
sions. 12 That is why the Israelites cannot
stand against their enemies; they turn
their backs and run because they have
been made liable to destruction. I will not
be with you anymore unless you destroy
whatever among you is devoted to de-
struction.

13 "Go, consecrate the people. Tell them,
'Consecrate yourselves in preparation for
tomorrow; for this is what the LORD, the
God of Israel, says: That which is devoted
is among you, O Israel. You cannot stand
against your enemies until you remove it.

14 " 'In the morning, present yourselves
tribe by tribe. The tribe that the LORD
takes shall come forward clan by clan; the
clan that the LORD takes shall come for-
ward family by family; and the family that
the LORD takes shall come forward man by
man. 15 He who is caught with the devoted
things shall be destroyed by fire, along
with all that belongs to him. He has violat-
ed the covenant of the LORD and has done
a disgraceful thing in Israel!' "

16 Early the next morning Joshua had Is-
rael come forward by tribes, and Judah
was taken. 17 The clans of Judah came for-
ward, and he took the Zerahites. He had
the clan of the Zerahites come forward by
families, and Zimri was taken. 18 Joshua
had his family come forward man by man,
and Achan son of Carmi, the son of Zimri,
the son of Zerah, of the tribe of Judah, was
taken.

19 Then Joshua said to Achan, "My son,
give glory to the LORD,[d] the God of Israel,
and give him the praise.[e] Tell me what
you have done; do not hide it from me."

20 Achan replied, "It is true! I have
sinned against the LORD, the God of Israel.
This is what I have done: 21 When I saw in
the plunder a beautiful robe from Babylo-
nia,[f] two hundred shekels[g] of silver and
a wedge of gold weighing fifty shekels,[h]
I coveted them and took them. They are
hidden in the ground inside my tent, with
the silver underneath."

22 So Joshua sent messengers, and they
ran to the tent, and there it was, hidden in
his tent, with the silver underneath.
23 They took the things from the tent,
brought them to Joshua and all the Israel-
ites and spread them out before the LORD.

24 Then Joshua, together with all Israel,

[a] 1 The Hebrew term refers to the irrevocable giving over of things or persons to the LORD, often by totally destroying them; also in verses 11, 12, 13 and 15. [b] 1 See Septuagint and 1 Chron. 2:6; Hebrew *Zabdi*; also in verses 17 and 18. [c] 5 Or *as far as Shebarim* [d] 19 A solemn charge to tell the truth [e] 19 Or *and confess to him* [f] 21 Hebrew *Shinar* [g] 21 That is, about 5 pounds (about 2.3 kilograms) [h] 21 That is, about 1 1/4 pounds (about 0.6 kilogram)

took Achan son of Zerah, the silver, the robe, the gold wedge, his sons and daughters, his cattle, donkeys and sheep, his tent and all that he had, to the Valley of Achor. 25Joshua said, "Why have you brought this trouble on us? The LORD will bring trouble on you today."

Then all Israel stoned him, and after they had stoned the rest, they burned them. 26Over Achan they heaped up a large pile of rocks, which remains to this day. Then the LORD turned from his fierce anger. Therefore that place has been called the Valley of Achor[a] ever since.

Ai Destroyed

8 Then the LORD said to Joshua, "Do not be afraid; do not be discouraged. Take the whole army with you, and go up and attack Ai. For I have delivered into your hands the king of Ai, his people, his city and his land. 2You shall do to Ai and its king as you did to Jericho and its king, except that you may carry off their plunder and livestock for yourselves. Set an ambush behind the city."

3So Joshua and the whole army moved out to attack Ai. He chose thirty thousand of his best fighting men and sent them out at night 4with these orders: "Listen carefully. You are to set an ambush behind the city. Don't go very far from it. All of you be on the alert. 5I and all those with me will advance on the city, and when the men come out against us, as they did before, we will flee from them. 6They will pursue us until we have lured them away from the city, for they will say, 'They are running away from us as they did before.' So when we flee from them, 7you are to rise up from ambush and take the city. The LORD your God will give it into your hand. 8When you have taken the city, set it on fire. Do what the LORD has commanded. See to it; you have my orders."

9Then Joshua sent them off, and they went to the place of ambush and lay in wait between Bethel and Ai, to the west of Ai—but Joshua spent that night with the people.

10Early the next morning Joshua mustered his men, and he and the leaders of Israel marched before them to Ai. 11The entire force that was with him marched up and approached the city and arrived in front of it. They set up camp north of Ai, with the valley between them and the city. 12Joshua had taken about five thousand men and set them in ambush between Bethel and Ai, to the west of the city. 13They had the soldiers take up their positions—all those in the camp to the north of the city and the ambush to the west of it. That night Joshua went into the valley.

14When the king of Ai saw this, he and all the men of the city hurried out early in the morning to meet Israel in battle at a certain place overlooking the Arabah. But he did not know that an ambush had been set against him behind the city. 15Joshua and all Israel let themselves be driven back before them, and they fled toward the desert. 16All the men of Ai were called to pursue them, and they pursued Joshua and were lured away from the city. 17Not a man remained in Ai or Bethel who did not go after Israel. They left the city open and went in pursuit of Israel.

18Then the LORD said to Joshua, "Hold out toward Ai the javelin that is in your hand, for into your hand I will deliver the city." So Joshua held out his javelin toward Ai. 19As soon as he did this, the men in the ambush rose quickly from their position and rushed forward. They entered the city and captured it and quickly set it on fire.

20The men of Ai looked back and saw the smoke of the city rising against the sky, but they had no chance to escape in any direction, for the Israelites who had been fleeing toward the desert had turned back against their pursuers. 21For when Joshua and all Israel saw that the ambush had taken the city and that smoke was going up from the city, they turned around and attacked the men of Ai. 22The men of the ambush also came out of the city against them, so that they were caught in the middle, with Israelites on both sides. Israel cut them down, leaving them neither survivors nor fugitives. 23But they took the king of Ai alive and brought him to Joshua.

24When Israel had finished killing all the men of Ai in the fields and in the desert where they had chased them, and when every one of them had been put to the sword, all the Israelites returned to Ai and killed those who were in it. 25Twelve thousand men and women fell that day—all the people of Ai. 26For Joshua did not draw back the hand that held out his jave-

[a]26 *Achor* means *trouble.*

lin until he had destroyed[a] all who lived
in Ai. 27But Israel did carry off for them-
selves the livestock and plunder of this
city, as the LORD had instructed Joshua.
28So Joshua burned Ai and made it a
permanent heap of ruins, a desolate place
to this day. 29He hung the king of Ai on a
tree and left him there until evening. At
sunset, Joshua ordered them to take his
body from the tree and throw it down at
the entrance of the city gate. And they
raised a large pile of rocks over it, which
remains to this day.

The Covenant Renewed at Mount Ebal

30Then Joshua built on Mount Ebal an
altar to the LORD, the God of Israel, 31as
Moses the servant of the LORD had com-
manded the Israelites. He built it accord-
ing to what is written in the Book of the
Law of Moses—an altar of uncut stones,
on which no iron tool had been used. On
it they offered to the LORD burnt offerings
and sacrificed fellowship offerings.[b]
32There, in the presence of the Israelites,
Joshua copied on stones the law of Moses,
which he had written. 33All Israel, aliens
and citizens alike, with their elders, offi-
cials and judges, were standing on both
sides of the ark of the covenant of the
LORD, facing those who carried it—the
priests, who were Levites. Half of the peo-
ple stood in front of Mount Gerizim and
half of them in front of Mount Ebal, as Mo-
ses the servant of the LORD had formerly
commanded when he gave instructions to
bless the people of Israel.
34Afterward, Joshua read all the words
of the law—the blessings and the
curses—just as it is written in the Book of
the Law. 35There was not a word of all that
Moses had commanded that Joshua did
not read to the whole assembly of Israel,
including the women and children, and
the aliens who lived among them.

The Gibeonite Deception

9 Now when all the kings west of the
Jordan heard about these things—
those in the hill country, in the western
foothills, and along the entire coast of the
Great Sea[c] as far as Lebanon (the kings of
the Hittites, Amorites, Canaanites, Periz-
zites, Hivites and Jebusites)—2they came
together to make war against Joshua and
Israel.
3However, when the people of Gibeon
heard what Joshua had done to Jericho
and Ai, 4they resorted to a ruse: They
went as a delegation whose donkeys were
loaded[d] with worn-out sacks and old
wineskins, cracked and mended. 5The
men put worn and patched sandals on
their feet and wore old clothes. All the
bread of their food supply was dry and
moldy. 6Then they went to Joshua in the
camp at Gilgal and said to him and the
men of Israel, "We have come from a dis-
tant country; make a treaty with us."
7The men of Israel said to the Hivites,
"But perhaps you live near us. How then
can we make a treaty with you?"
8"We are your servants," they said to
Joshua.
But Joshua asked, "Who are you and
where do you come from?"
9They answered: "Your servants have
come from a very distant country because
of the fame of the LORD your God. For we
have heard reports of him: all that he did
in Egypt, 10and all that he did to the two
kings of the Amorites east of the Jordan—
Sihon king of Heshbon, and Og king of Ba-
shan, who reigned in Ashtaroth. 11And
our elders and all those living in our coun-
try said to us, 'Take provisions for your
journey; go and meet them and say to
them, "We are your servants; make a trea-
ty with us."' 12This bread of ours was
warm when we packed it at home on the
day we left to come to you. But now see
how dry and moldy it is. 13And these
wineskins that we filled were new, but see
how cracked they are. And our clothes
and sandals are worn out by the very long
journey."
14The men of Israel sampled their provi-
sions but did not inquire of the LORD.
15Then Joshua made a treaty of peace with
them to let them live, and the leaders of
the assembly ratified it by oath.
16Three days after they made the treaty
with the Gibeonites, the Israelites heard
that they were neighbors, living near
them. 17So the Israelites set out and on the
third day came to their cities: Gibeon, Ke-
phirah, Beeroth and Kiriath Jearim. 18But

[a]26 The Hebrew term refers to the irrevocable giving over of things or persons to the LORD, often by totally destroying them. [b]31 Traditionally *peace offerings* [c]1 That is, the Mediterranean
[d]4 Most Hebrew manuscripts; some Hebrew manuscripts, Vulgate and Syriac (see also Septuagint) *They prepared provisions and loaded their donkeys*

the Israelites did not attack them, because the leaders of the assembly had sworn an oath to them by the LORD, the God of Israel.

The whole assembly grumbled against the leaders, 19but all the leaders answered, "We have given them our oath by the LORD, the God of Israel, and we cannot touch them now. 20This is what we will do to them: We will let them live, so that wrath will not fall on us for breaking the oath we swore to them." 21They continued, "Let them live, but let them be woodcutters and water carriers for the entire community." So the leaders' promise to them was kept.

22Then Joshua summoned the Gibeonites and said, "Why did you deceive us by saying, 'We live a long way from you,' while actually you live near us? 23You are now under a curse: You will never cease to serve as woodcutters and water carriers for the house of my God."

24They answered Joshua, "Your servants were clearly told how the LORD your God had commanded his servant Moses to give you the whole land and to wipe out all its inhabitants from before you. So we feared for our lives because of you, and that is why we did this. 25We are now in your hands. Do to us whatever seems good and right to you."

26So Joshua saved them from the Israelites, and they did not kill them. 27That day he made the Gibeonites woodcutters and water carriers for the community and for the altar of the LORD at the place the LORD would choose. And that is what they are to this day.

The Sun Stands Still

10 Now Adoni-Zedek king of Jerusalem heard that Joshua had taken Ai and totally destroyed[a] it, doing to Ai and its king as he had done to Jericho and its king, and that the people of Gibeon had made a treaty of peace with Israel and were living near them. 2He and his people were very much alarmed at this, because Gibeon was an important city, like one of the royal cities; it was larger than Ai, and all its men were good fighters. 3So Adoni-Zedek king of Jerusalem appealed to Hoham king of Hebron, Piram king of Jarmuth, Japhia king of Lachish and Debir king of Eglon. 4"Come up and help me attack Gibeon," he said, "because it has made peace with Joshua and the Israelites."

5Then the five kings of the Amorites—the kings of Jerusalem, Hebron, Jarmuth, Lachish and Eglon—joined forces. They moved up with all their troops and took up positions against Gibeon and attacked it.

6The Gibeonites then sent word to Joshua in the camp at Gilgal: "Do not abandon your servants. Come up to us quickly and save us! Help us, because all the Amorite kings from the hill country have joined forces against us."

7So Joshua marched up from Gilgal with his entire army, including all the best fighting men. 8The LORD said to Joshua, "Do not be afraid of them; I have given them into your hand. Not one of them will be able to withstand you."

9After an all-night march from Gilgal, Joshua took them by surprise. 10The LORD threw them into confusion before Israel, who defeated them in a great victory at Gibeon. Israel pursued them along the road going up to Beth Horon and cut them down all the way to Azekah and Makkedah. 11As they fled before Israel on the road down from Beth Horon to Azekah, the LORD hurled large hailstones down on them from the sky, and more of them died from the hailstones than were killed by the swords of the Israelites.

12On the day the LORD gave the Amorites over to Israel, Joshua said to the LORD in the presence of Israel:

"O sun, stand still over Gibeon,
O moon, over the Valley of Aijalon."
13So the sun stood still,
and the moon stopped,
till the nation avenged itself on[b] its enemies,

as it is written in the Book of Jashar.

The sun stopped in the middle of the sky and delayed going down about a full day. 14There has never been a day like it before or since, a day when the LORD listened to a man. Surely the LORD was fighting for Israel!

15Then Joshua returned with all Israel to the camp at Gilgal.

Five Amorite Kings Killed

16Now the five kings had fled and hid-

[a] *1* The Hebrew term refers to the irrevocable giving over of things or persons to the LORD, often by totally destroying them; also in verses 28, 35, 37, 39 and 40. [b] *13* Or *nation triumphed over*

den in the cave at Makkedah. [17]When
Joshua was told that the five kings had
been found hiding in the cave at Makke-
dah, [18]he said, "Roll large rocks up to the
mouth of the cave, and post some men
there to guard it. [19]But don't stop! Pursue
your enemies, attack them from the rear
and don't let them reach their cities, for
the LORD your God has given them into
your hand."

[20]So Joshua and the Israelites destroyed
them completely—almost to a man—but
the few who were left reached their forti-
fied cities. [21]The whole army then re-
turned safely to Joshua in the camp at
Makkedah, and no one uttered a word
against the Israelites.

[22]Joshua said, "Open the mouth of the
cave and bring those five kings out to me."
[23]So they brought the five kings out of the
cave—the kings of Jerusalem, Hebron,
Jarmuth, Lachish and Eglon. [24]When they
had brought these kings to Joshua, he
summoned all the men of Israel and said
to the army commanders who had come
with him, "Come here and put your feet
on the necks of these kings." So they came
forward and placed their feet on their
necks.

[25]Joshua said to them, "Do not be
afraid; do not be discouraged. Be strong
and courageous. This is what the LORD
will do to all the enemies you are going to
fight." [26]Then Joshua struck and killed the
kings and hung them on five trees, and
they were left hanging on the trees until
evening.

[27]At sunset Joshua gave the order and
they took them down from the trees and
threw them into the cave where they had
been hiding. At the mouth of the cave they
placed large rocks, which are there to this
day.

[28]That day Joshua took Makkedah. He
put the city and its king to the sword and
totally destroyed everyone in it. He left no
survivors. And he did to the king of Mak-
kedah as he had done to the king of Jeri-
cho.

Southern Cities Conquered

[29]Then Joshua and all Israel with him
moved on from Makkedah to Libnah and
attacked it. [30]The LORD also gave that city
and its king into Israel's hand. The city
and everyone in it Joshua put to the
sword. He left no survivors there. And he
did to its king as he had done to the king
of Jericho.

[31]Then Joshua and all Israel with him
moved on from Libnah to Lachish; he
took up positions against it and attacked
it. [32]The LORD handed Lachish over to Isra-
el, and Joshua took it on the second day.
The city and everyone in it he put to the
sword, just as he had done to Libnah.
[33]Meanwhile, Horam king of Gezer had
come up to help Lachish, but Joshua de-
feated him and his army—until no survi-
vors were left.

[34]Then Joshua and all Israel with him
moved on from Lachish to Eglon; they
took up positions against it and attacked
it. [35]They captured it that same day and
put it to the sword and totally destroyed
everyone in it, just as they had done to La-
chish.

[36]Then Joshua and all Israel with him
went up from Eglon to Hebron and at-
tacked it. [37]They took the city and put it to
the sword, together with its king, its vil-
lages and everyone in it. They left no sur-
vivors. Just as at Eglon, they totally de-
stroyed it and everyone in it.

[38]Then Joshua and all Israel with him
turned around and attacked Debir. [39]They
took the city, its king and its villages, and
put them to the sword. Everyone in it they
totally destroyed. They left no survivors.
They did to Debir and its king as they had
done to Libnah and its king and to He-
bron.

[40]So Joshua subdued the whole region,
including the hill country, the Negev, the
western foothills and the mountain
slopes, together with all their kings. He
left no survivors. He totally destroyed all
who breathed, just as the LORD, the God of
Israel, had commanded. [41]Joshua sub-
dued them from Kadesh Barnea to Gaza
and from the whole region of Goshen to
Gibeon. [42]All these kings and their lands
Joshua conquered in one campaign, be-
cause the LORD, the God of Israel, fought
for Israel.

[43]Then Joshua returned with all Israel
to the camp at Gilgal.

Northern Kings Defeated

11 When Jabin king of Hazor heard of
this, he sent word to Jobab king of
Madon, to the kings of Shimron and Ac-
shaph, [2]and to the northern kings who
were in the mountains, in the Arabah
south of Kinnereth, in the western foot-

hills and in Naphoth Dor[a] on the west;
3to the Canaanites in the east and west; to
the Amorites, Hittites, Perizzites and Jebusites in the hill country; and to the Hivites below Hermon in the region of Mizpah. 4They came out with all their troops
and a large number of horses and chariots—a huge army, as numerous as the
sand on the seashore. 5All these kings
joined forces and made camp together at
the Waters of Merom, to fight against Israel.

6The LORD said to Joshua, "Do not be
afraid of them, because by this time tomorrow I will hand all of them over to Israel, slain. You are to hamstring their
horses and burn their chariots."

7So Joshua and his whole army came
against them suddenly at the Waters of
Merom and attacked them, 8and the LORD
gave them into the hand of Israel. They
defeated them and pursued them all the
way to Greater Sidon, to Misrephoth
Maim, and to the Valley of Mizpah on the
east, until no survivors were left. 9Joshua
did to them as the LORD had directed: He
hamstrung their horses and burned their
chariots.

10At that time Joshua turned back and
captured Hazor and put its king to the
sword. (Hazor had been the head of all
these kingdoms.) 11Everyone in it they put
to the sword. They totally destroyed[b]
them, not sparing anything that breathed,
and he burned up Hazor itself.

12Joshua took all these royal cities and
their kings and put them to the sword. He
totally destroyed them, as Moses the servant of the LORD had commanded. 13Yet
Israel did not burn any of the cities built
on their mounds—except Hazor, which
Joshua burned. 14The Israelites carried off
for themselves all the plunder and livestock of these cities, but all the people
they put to the sword until they completely destroyed them, not sparing anyone
that breathed. 15As the LORD commanded
his servant Moses, so Moses commanded
Joshua, and Joshua did it; he left nothing
undone of all that the LORD commanded
Moses.

16So Joshua took this entire land: the
hill country, all the Negev, the whole region of Goshen, the western foothills, the
Arabah and the mountains of Israel with
their foothills, 17from Mount Halak, which
rises toward Seir, to Baal Gad in the Valley
of Lebanon below Mount Hermon. He
captured all their kings and struck them
down, putting them to death. 18Joshua
waged war against all these kings for a
long time. 19Except for the Hivites living
in Gibeon, not one city made a treaty of
peace with the Israelites, who took them
all in battle. 20For it was the LORD himself
who hardened their hearts to wage war
against Israel, so that he might destroy
them totally, exterminating them without
mercy, as the LORD had commanded Moses.

21At that time Joshua went and destroyed the Anakites from the hill country: from Hebron, Debir and Anab, from
all the hill country of Judah, and from all
the hill country of Israel. Joshua totally
destroyed them and their towns. 22No Anakites were left in Israelite territory; only
in Gaza, Gath and Ashdod did any survive. 23So Joshua took the entire land, just
as the LORD had directed Moses, and he
gave it as an inheritance to Israel according to their tribal divisions.

Then the land had rest from war.

List of Defeated Kings

12 These are the kings of the land
whom the Israelites had defeated
and whose territory they took over east of
the Jordan, from the Arnon Gorge to
Mount Hermon, including all the eastern
side of the Arabah:

2Sihon king of the Amorites,
who reigned in Heshbon. He ruled
from Aroer on the rim of the Arnon
Gorge—from the middle of the
gorge—to the Jabbok River, which is
the border of the Ammonites. This included half of Gilead. 3He also ruled
over the eastern Arabah from the Sea
of Kinnereth[c] to the Sea of the Arabah (the Salt Sea[d]), to Beth Jeshimoth, and then southward below the
slopes of Pisgah.

4And the territory of Og king of Bashan,
one of the last of the Rephaites, who
reigned in Ashtaroth and Edrei. 5He
ruled over Mount Hermon, Salecah,
all of Bashan to the border of the people of Geshur and Maacah, and half

[a]2 Or *in the heights of Dor* [b]11 The Hebrew term refers to the irrevocable giving over of things or persons to the LORD, often by totally destroying them; also in verses 12, 20 and 21. [c]3 That is, Galilee
[d]3 That is, the Dead Sea

of Gilead to the border of Sihon king of Heshbon.

[6]Moses, the servant of the LORD, and the Israelites conquered them. And Moses the servant of the LORD gave their land to the Reubenites, the Gadites and the half-tribe of Manasseh to be their possession.

[7]These are the kings of the land that Joshua and the Israelites conquered on the west side of the Jordan, from Baal Gad in the Valley of Lebanon to Mount Halak, which rises toward Seir (their lands Joshua gave as an inheritance to the tribes of Israel according to their tribal divisions—[8]the hill country, the western foothills, the Arabah, the mountain slopes, the desert and the Negev—the lands of the Hittites, Amorites, Canaanites, Perizzites, Hivites and Jebusites):

[9]the king of Jericho	one
the king of Ai (near Bethel)	one
[10]the king of Jerusalem	one
the king of Hebron	one
[11]the king of Jarmuth	one
the king of Lachish	one
[12]the king of Eglon	one
the king of Gezer	one
[13]the king of Debir	one
the king of Geder	one
[14]the king of Hormah	one
the king of Arad	one
[15]the king of Libnah	one
the king of Adullam	one
[16]the king of Makkedah	one
the king of Bethel	one
[17]the king of Tappuah	one
the king of Hepher	one
[18]the king of Aphek	one
the king of Lasharon	one
[19]the king of Madon	one
the king of Hazor	one
[20]the king of Shimron Meron	one
the king of Acshaph	one
[21]the king of Taanach	one
the king of Megiddo	one
[22]the king of Kedesh	one
the king of Jokneam in Carmel	one
[23]the king of Dor (in Naphoth Dor[a])	one
the king of Goyim in Gilgal	one
[24]the king of Tirzah	one

thirty-one kings in all.

Land Still to Be Taken

13 When Joshua was old and well advanced in years, the LORD said to him, "You are very old, and there are still very large areas of land to be taken over.

[2]"This is the land that remains: all the regions of the Philistines and Geshurites: [3]from the Shihor River on the east of Egypt to the territory of Ekron on the north, all of it counted as Canaanite (the territory of the five Philistine rulers in Gaza, Ashdod, Ashkelon, Gath and Ekron—that of the Avvites); [4]from the south, all the land of the Canaanites, from Arah of the Sidonians as far as Aphek, the region of the Amorites, [5]the area of the Gebalites[b]; and all Lebanon to the east, from Baal Gad below Mount Hermon to Lebo[c] Hamath.

[6]"As for all the inhabitants of the mountain regions from Lebanon to Misrephoth Maim, that is, all the Sidonians, I myself will drive them out before the Israelites. Be sure to allocate this land to Israel for an inheritance, as I have instructed you, [7]and divide it as an inheritance among the nine tribes and half of the tribe of Manasseh."

Division of the Land East of the Jordan

[8]The other half of Manasseh,[d] the Reubenites and the Gadites had received the inheritance that Moses had given them east of the Jordan, as he, the servant of the LORD, had assigned it to them.

[9]It extended from Aroer on the rim of the Arnon Gorge, and from the town in the middle of the gorge, and included the whole plateau of Medeba as far as Dibon, [10]and all the towns of Sihon king of the Amorites, who ruled in Heshbon, out to the border of the Ammonites. [11]It also included Gilead, the territory of the people of Geshur and Maacah, all of Mount Hermon and all Bashan as far as Salecah— [12]that is, the whole kingdom of Og in Bashan, who had reigned in Ashtaroth and Edrei and had survived as one of the last of the Rephaites. Moses had defeated them and taken over their land. [13]But the Israelites did not drive out the people of

[a]23 Or *in the heights of Dor* [b]5 That is, the area of Byblos [c]5 Or *to the entrance to*
[d]8 Hebrew *With it* (that is, with the other half of Manasseh)

Geshur and Maacah, so they continue
to live among the Israelites to this
day.

14But to the tribe of Levi he gave no in-
heritance, since the offerings made by fire
to the LORD, the God of Israel, are their in-
heritance, as he promised them.

15This is what Moses had given to the
tribe of Reuben, clan by clan:

16The territory from Aroer on the rim
of the Arnon Gorge, and from the
town in the middle of the gorge, and
the whole plateau past Medeba 17to
Heshbon and all its towns on the pla-
teau, including Dibon, Bamoth Baal,
Beth Baal Meon, 18Jahaz, Kedemoth,
Mephaath, 19Kiriathaim, Sibmah, Ze-
reth Shahar on the hill in the valley,
20Beth Peor, the slopes of Pisgah, and
Beth Jeshimoth 21—all the towns on
the plateau and the entire realm of Si-
hon king of the Amorites, who ruled
at Heshbon. Moses had defeated him
and the Midianite chiefs, Evi, Rekem,
Zur, Hur and Reba—princes allied
with Sihon—who lived in that coun-
try. 22In addition to those slain in bat-
tle, the Israelites had put to the sword
Balaam son of Beor, who practiced
divination. 23The boundary of the
Reubenites was the bank of the Jor-
dan. These towns and their villages
were the inheritance of the Reuben-
ites, clan by clan.

24This is what Moses had given to the
tribe of Gad, clan by clan:

25The territory of Jazer, all the towns
of Gilead and half the Ammonite
country as far as Aroer, near Rabbah;
26and from Heshbon to Ramath Miz-
pah and Betonim, and from Mahana-
im to the territory of Debir; 27and in
the valley, Beth Haram, Beth Nimrah,
Succoth and Zaphon with the rest of
the realm of Sihon king of Heshbon
(the east side of the Jordan, the terri-
tory up to the end of the Sea of Kinne-
reth[a]). 28These towns and their vil-
lages were the inheritance of the
Gadites, clan by clan.

29This is what Moses had given to the half-
tribe of Manasseh, that is, to half the fami-
ly of the descendants of Manasseh, clan
by clan:

30The territory extending from Maha-
naim and including all of Bashan, the
entire realm of Og king of Bashan—
all the settlements of Jair in Bashan,
sixty towns, 31half of Gilead, and Ash-
taroth and Edrei (the royal cities of
Og in Bashan). This was for the
descendants of Makir son of Manas-
seh—for half of the sons of Makir,
clan by clan.

32This is the inheritance Moses had giv-
en when he was in the plains of Moab
across the Jordan east of Jericho. 33But to
the tribe of Levi, Moses had given no in-
heritance; the LORD, the God of Israel, is
their inheritance, as he promised them.

Division of the Land West of the Jordan

14 Now these are the areas the Israel-
ites received as an inheritance in
the land of Canaan, which Eleazar the
priest, Joshua son of Nun and the heads of
the tribal clans of Israel allotted to them.
2Their inheritances were assigned by lot
to the nine-and-a-half tribes, as the LORD
had commanded through Moses. 3Moses
had granted the two-and-a-half tribes their
inheritance east of the Jordan but had not
granted the Levites an inheritance among
the rest, 4for the sons of Joseph had be-
come two tribes—Manasseh and Ephra-
im. The Levites received no share of the
land but only towns to live in, with pas-
turelands for their flocks and herds. 5So
the Israelites divided the land, just as the
LORD had commanded Moses.

Hebron Given to Caleb

6Now the men of Judah approached
Joshua at Gilgal, and Caleb son of Jephun-
neh the Kenizzite said to him, "You know
what the LORD said to Moses the man of
God at Kadesh Barnea about you and me.
7I was forty years old when Moses the ser-
vant of the LORD sent me from Kadesh Bar-
nea to explore the land. And I brought him
back a report according to my convic-
tions, 8but my brothers who went up with
me made the hearts of the people melt
with fear. I, however, followed the LORD
my God wholeheartedly. 9So on that day
Moses swore to me, 'The land on which
your feet have walked will be your inheri-
tance and that of your children forever,

[a]27 That is, Galilee

because you have followed the LORD my God wholeheartedly.'[a]

10"Now then, just as the LORD promised, he has kept me alive for forty-five years since the time he said this to Moses, while Israel moved about in the desert. So here I am today, eighty-five years old! 11I am still as strong today as the day Moses sent me out; I'm just as vigorous to go out to battle now as I was then. 12Now give me this hill country that the LORD promised me that day. You yourself heard then that the Anakites were there and their cities were large and fortified, but, the LORD helping me, I will drive them out just as he said."

13Then Joshua blessed Caleb son of Jephunneh and gave him Hebron as his inheritance. 14So Hebron has belonged to Caleb son of Jephunneh the Kenizzite ever since, because he followed the LORD, the God of Israel, wholeheartedly. 15(Hebron used to be called Kiriath Arba after Arba, who was the greatest man among the Anakites.)

Then the land had rest from war.

Allotment for Judah

15 The allotment for the tribe of Judah, clan by clan, extended down to the territory of Edom, to the Desert of Zin in the extreme south.

2Their southern boundary started from the bay at the southern end of the Salt Sea,[b] 3crossed south of Scorpion[c] Pass, continued on to Zin and went over to the south of Kadesh Barnea. Then it ran past Hezron up to Addar and curved around to Karka. 4It then passed along to Azmon and joined the Wadi of Egypt, ending at the sea. This is their[d] southern boundary.

5The eastern boundary is the Salt Sea as far as the mouth of the Jordan.

The northern boundary started from the bay of the sea at the mouth of the Jordan, 6went up to Beth Hoglah and continued north of Beth Arabah to the Stone of Bohan son of Reuben. 7The boundary then went up to Debir from the Valley of Achor and turned north to Gilgal, which faces the Pass of Adummim south of the gorge. It continued along to the waters of En Shemesh and came out at En Rogel. 8Then it ran up the Valley of Ben Hinnom along the southern slope of the Jebusite city (that is, Jerusalem). From there it climbed to the top of the hill west of the Hinnom Valley at the northern end of the Valley of Rephaim. 9From the hilltop the boundary headed toward the spring of the waters of Nephtoah, came out at the towns of Mount Ephron and went down toward Baalah (that is, Kiriath Jearim). 10Then it curved westward from Baalah to Mount Seir, ran along the northern slope of Mount Jearim (that is, Kesalon), continued down to Beth Shemesh and crossed to Timnah. 11It went to the northern slope of Ekron, turned toward Shikkeron, passed along to Mount Baalah and reached Jabneel. The boundary ended at the sea.

12The western boundary is the coastline of the Great Sea.[e]

These are the boundaries around the people of Judah by their clans.

13In accordance with the LORD's command to him, Joshua gave to Caleb son of Jephunneh a portion in Judah—Kiriath Arba, that is, Hebron. (Arba was the forefather of Anak.) 14From Hebron Caleb drove out the three Anakites—Sheshai, Ahiman and Talmai—descendants of Anak. 15From there he marched against the people living in Debir (formerly called Kiriath Sepher). 16And Caleb said, "I will give my daughter Acsah in marriage to the man who attacks and captures Kiriath Sepher." 17Othniel son of Kenaz, Caleb's brother, took it; so Caleb gave his daughter Acsah to him in marriage.

18One day when she came to Othniel, she urged him[f] to ask her father for a field. When she got off her donkey, Caleb asked her, "What can I do for you?"

19She replied, "Do me a special favor. Since you have given me land in the Negev, give me also springs of water." So Caleb gave her the upper and lower springs.

20This is the inheritance of the tribe of Judah, clan by clan:

21The southernmost towns of the tribe of

[a] 9 Deut. 1:36 [b] 2 That is, the Dead Sea; also in verse 5 [c] 3 Hebrew *Akrabbim* [d] 4 Hebrew *your*
[e] 12 That is, the Mediterranean; also in verse 47 [f] 18 Hebrew and some Septuagint manuscripts; other Septuagint manuscripts (see also note at Judges 1:14) *Othniel, he urged her*

Judah in the Negev toward the boundary of Edom were:

Kabzeel, Eder, Jagur, 22Kinah, Dimonah, Adadah, 23Kedesh, Hazor, Ithnan, 24Ziph, Telem, Bealoth, 25Hazor Hadattah, Kerioth Hezron (that is, Hazor), 26Amam, Shema, Moladah, 27Hazar Gaddah, Heshmon, Beth Pelet, 28Hazar Shual, Beersheba, Biziothiah, 29Baalah, Iim, Ezem, 30Eltolad, Kesil, Hormah, 31Ziklag, Madmannah, Sansannah, 32Lebaoth, Shilhim, Ain and Rimmon—a total of twenty-nine towns and their villages.

33In the western foothills:

Eshtaol, Zorah, Ashnah, 34Zanoah, En Gannim, Tappuah, Enam, 35Jarmuth, Adullam, Socoh, Azekah, 36Shaaraim, Adithaim and Gederah (or Gederothaim)[a]—fourteen towns and their villages.

37Zenan, Hadashah, Migdal Gad, 38Dilean, Mizpah, Joktheel, 39Lachish, Bozkath, Eglon, 40Cabbon, Lahmas, Kitlish, 41Gederoth, Beth Dagon, Naamah and Makkedah—sixteen towns and their villages.

42Libnah, Ether, Ashan, 43Iphtah, Ashnah, Nezib, 44Keilah, Aczib and Mareshah—nine towns and their villages.

45Ekron, with its surrounding settlements and villages; 46west of Ekron, all that were in the vicinity of Ashdod, together with their villages; 47Ashdod, its surrounding settlements and villages; and Gaza, its settlements and villages, as far as the Wadi of Egypt and the coastline of the Great Sea.

48In the hill country:

Shamir, Jattir, Socoh, 49Dannah, Kiriath Sannah (that is, Debir), 50Anab, Eshtemoh, Anim, 51Goshen, Holon and Giloh—eleven towns and their villages.

52Arab, Dumah, Eshan, 53Janim, Beth Tappuah, Aphekah, 54Humtah, Kiriath Arba (that is, Hebron) and Zior—nine towns and their villages.

55Maon, Carmel, Ziph, Juttah, 56Jezreel, Jokdeam, Zanoah, 57Kain, Gibeah and Timnah—ten towns and their villages.

58Halhul, Beth Zur, Gedor, 59Maarath, Beth Anoth and Eltekon—six towns and their villages.

60Kiriath Baal (that is, Kiriath Jearim) and Rabbah—two towns and their villages.

61In the desert:

Beth Arabah, Middin, Secacah, 62Nibshan, the City of Salt and En Gedi—six towns and their villages.

63Judah could not dislodge the Jebusites, who were living in Jerusalem; to this day the Jebusites live there with the people of Judah.

Allotment for Ephraim and Manasseh

16 The allotment for Joseph began at the Jordan of Jericho,[b] east of the waters of Jericho, and went up from there through the desert into the hill country of Bethel. 2It went on from Bethel (that is, Luz),[c] crossed over to the territory of the Arkites in Ataroth, 3descended westward to the territory of the Japhletites as far as the region of Lower Beth Horon and on to Gezer, ending at the sea.

4So Manasseh and Ephraim, the descendants of Joseph, received their inheritance.

5This was the territory of Ephraim, clan by clan:

The boundary of their inheritance went from Ataroth Addar in the east to Upper Beth Horon 6and continued to the sea. From Micmethath on the north it curved eastward to Taanath Shiloh, passing by it to Janoah on the east. 7Then it went down from Janoah to Ataroth and Naarah, touched Jericho and came out at the Jordan. 8From Tappuah the border went west to the Kanah Ravine and ended at the sea. This was the inheritance of the tribe of the Ephraimites, clan by clan. 9It also included all the towns and their villages that were set aside for the Ephraimites within the inheritance of the Manassites.

10They did not dislodge the Canaanites living in Gezer; to this day the Canaanites live among the people of Ephraim but are required to do forced labor.

[a]36 Or *Gederah and Gederothaim* [b]1 *Jordan of Jericho* was possibly an ancient name for the Jordan River. [c]2 Septuagint; Hebrew *Bethel to Luz*

17 This was the allotment for the tribe of Manasseh as Joseph's firstborn, that is, for Makir, Manasseh's firstborn. Makir was the ancestor of the Gileadites, who had received Gilead and Bashan because the Makirites were great soldiers. 2So this allotment was for the rest of the people of Manasseh—the clans of Abiezer, Helek, Asriel, Shechem, Hepher and Shemida. These are the other male descendants of Manasseh son of Joseph by their clans.

3Now Zelophehad son of Hepher, the son of Gilead, the son of Makir, the son of Manasseh, had no sons but only daughters, whose names were Mahlah, Noah, Hoglah, Milcah and Tirzah. 4They went to Eleazar the priest, Joshua son of Nun, and the leaders and said, "The LORD commanded Moses to give us an inheritance among our brothers." So Joshua gave them an inheritance along with the brothers of their father, according to the LORD's command. 5Manasseh's share consisted of ten tracts of land besides Gilead and Bashan east of the Jordan, 6because the daughters of the tribe of Manasseh received an inheritance among the sons. The land of Gilead belonged to the rest of the descendants of Manasseh.

7The territory of Manasseh extended from Asher to Micmethath east of Shechem. The boundary ran southward from there to include the people living at En Tappuah. 8(Manasseh had the land of Tappuah, but Tappuah itself, on the boundary of Manasseh, belonged to the Ephraimites.) 9Then the boundary continued south to the Kanah Ravine. There were towns belonging to Ephraim lying among the towns of Manasseh, but the boundary of Manasseh was the northern side of the ravine and ended at the sea. 10On the south the land belonged to Ephraim, on the north to Manasseh. The territory of Manasseh reached the sea and bordered Asher on the north and Issachar on the east.

11Within Issachar and Asher, Manasseh also had Beth Shan, Ibleam and the people of Dor, Endor, Taanach and Megiddo, together with their surrounding settlements (the third in the list is Naphoth[a]).

12Yet the Manassites were not able to occupy these towns, for the Canaanites were determined to live in that region. 13However, when the Israelites grew stronger, they subjected the Canaanites to forced labor but did not drive them out completely.

14The people of Joseph said to Joshua, "Why have you given us only one allotment and one portion for an inheritance? We are a numerous people and the LORD has blessed us abundantly."

15"If you are so numerous," Joshua answered, "and if the hill country of Ephraim is too small for you, go up into the forest and clear land for yourselves there in the land of the Perizzites and Rephaites."

16The people of Joseph replied, "The hill country is not enough for us, and all the Canaanites who live in the plain have iron chariots, both those in Beth Shan and its settlements and those in the Valley of Jezreel."

17But Joshua said to the house of Joseph—to Ephraim and Manasseh—"You are numerous and very powerful. You will have not only one allotment 18but the forested hill country as well. Clear it, and its farthest limits will be yours; though the Canaanites have iron chariots and though they are strong, you can drive them out."

Division of the Rest of the Land

18 The whole assembly of the Israelites gathered at Shiloh and set up the Tent of Meeting there. The country was brought under their control, 2but there were still seven Israelite tribes who had not yet received their inheritance.

3So Joshua said to the Israelites: "How long will you wait before you begin to take possession of the land that the LORD, the God of your fathers, has given you? 4Appoint three men from each tribe. I will send them out to make a survey of the land and to write a description of it, according to the inheritance of each. Then they will return to me. 5You are to divide the land into seven parts. Judah is to remain in its territory on the south and the house of Joseph in its territory on the north. 6After you have written descriptions of the seven parts of the land, bring them here to me and I will cast lots for you in the presence of the LORD our God. 7The Levites, however, do not get a portion among you, because the priestly service of the LORD is their inheritance. And Gad, Reuben and the half-tribe of Manasseh have already received their inheritance on

[a]11 That is, Naphoth Dor

the east side of the Jordan. Moses the servant of the LORD gave it to them."

8As the men started on their way to map out the land, Joshua instructed them, "Go and make a survey of the land and write a description of it. Then return to me, and I will cast lots for you here at Shiloh in the presence of the LORD." 9So the men left and went through the land. They wrote its description on a scroll, town by town, in seven parts, and returned to Joshua in the camp at Shiloh. 10Joshua then cast lots for them in Shiloh in the presence of the LORD, and there he distributed the land to the Israelites according to their tribal divisions.

Allotment for Benjamin

11The lot came up for the tribe of Benjamin, clan by clan. Their allotted territory lay between the tribes of Judah and Joseph:

12On the north side their boundary began at the Jordan, passed the northern slope of Jericho and headed west into the hill country, coming out at the desert of Beth Aven. 13From there it crossed to the south slope of Luz (that is, Bethel) and went down to Ataroth Addar on the hill south of Lower Beth Horon.

14From the hill facing Beth Horon on the south the boundary turned south along the western side and came out at Kiriath Baal (that is, Kiriath Jearim), a town of the people of Judah. This was the western side.

15The southern side began at the outskirts of Kiriath Jearim on the west, and the boundary came out at the spring of the waters of Nephtoah. 16The boundary went down to the foot of the hill facing the Valley of Ben Hinnom, north of the Valley of Rephaim. It continued down the Hinnom Valley along the southern slope of the Jebusite city and so to En Rogel. 17It then curved north, went to En Shemesh, continued to Geliloth, which faces the Pass of Adummim, and ran down to the Stone of Bohan son of Reuben. 18It continued to the northern slope of Beth Arabah[a] and on down into the Arabah. 19It then went to the northern slope of Beth Hoglah and came out at the northern bay of the Salt Sea,[b] at the mouth of the Jordan in the south. This was the southern boundary.

20The Jordan formed the boundary on the eastern side.

These were the boundaries that marked out the inheritance of the clans of Benjamin on all sides.

21The tribe of Benjamin, clan by clan, had the following cities:

Jericho, Beth Hoglah, Emek Keziz, 22Beth Arabah, Zemaraim, Bethel, 23Avvim, Parah, Ophrah, 24Kephar Ammoni, Ophni and Geba—twelve towns and their villages.

25Gibeon, Ramah, Beeroth, 26Mizpah, Kephirah, Mozah, 27Rekem, Irpeel, Taralah, 28Zelah, Haeleph, the Jebusite city (that is, Jerusalem), Gibeah and Kiriath—fourteen towns and their villages.

This was the inheritance of Benjamin for its clans.

Allotment for Simeon

19 The second lot came out for the tribe of Simeon, clan by clan. Their inheritance lay within the territory of Judah. 2It included:

Beersheba (or Sheba),[c] Moladah, 3Hazar Shual, Balah, Ezem, 4Eltolad, Bethul, Hormah, 5Ziklag, Beth Marcaboth, Hazar Susah, 6Beth Lebaoth and Sharuhen—thirteen towns and their villages;

7Ain, Rimmon, Ether and Ashan—four towns and their villages— 8and all the villages around these towns as far as Baalath Beer (Ramah in the Negev).

This was the inheritance of the tribe of the Simeonites, clan by clan. 9The inheritance of the Simeonites was taken from the share of Judah, because Judah's portion was more than they needed. So the Simeonites received their inheritance within the territory of Judah.

Allotment for Zebulun

10The third lot came up for Zebulun, clan by clan:

The boundary of their inheritance went as far as Sarid. 11Going west it ran to Maralah, touched Dabbesheth, and extended to the ravine near Jok-

[a] *18* Septuagint; Hebrew *slope facing the Arabah Sheba*; 1 Chron. 4:28 does not have *Sheba*.

[b] *19* That is, the Dead Sea

[c] *2* Or *Beersheba,*

neam. 12It turned east from Sarid toward the sunrise to the territory of Kisloth Tabor and went on to Daberath and up to Japhia. 13Then it continued eastward to Gath Hepher and Eth Kazin; it came out at Rimmon and turned toward Neah. 14There the boundary went around on the north to Hannathon and ended at the Valley of Iphtah El. 15Included were Kattath, Nahalal, Shimron, Idalah and Bethlehem. There were twelve towns and their villages.
16These towns and their villages were the inheritance of Zebulun, clan by clan.

Allotment for Issachar

17The fourth lot came out for Issachar, clan by clan. 18Their territory included:

Jezreel, Kesulloth, Shunem, 19Hapharaim, Shion, Anaharath, 20Rabbith, Kishion, Ebez, 21Remeth, En Gannim, En Haddah and Beth Pazzez. 22The boundary touched Tabor, Shahazumah and Beth Shemesh, and ended at the Jordan. There were sixteen towns and their villages.
23These towns and their villages were the inheritance of the tribe of Issachar, clan by clan.

Allotment for Asher

24The fifth lot came out for the tribe of Asher, clan by clan. 25Their territory included:

Helkath, Hali, Beten, Acshaph, 26Allammelech, Amad and Mishal. On the west the boundary touched Carmel and Shihor Libnath. 27It then turned east toward Beth Dagon, touched Zebulun and the Valley of Iphtah El, and went north to Beth Emek and Neiel, passing Cabul on the left. 28It went to Abdon,[a] Rehob, Hammon and Kanah, as far as Greater Sidon. 29The boundary then turned back toward Ramah and went to the fortified city of Tyre, turned toward Hosah and came out at the sea in the region of Aczib, 30Ummah, Aphek and Rehob. There were twenty-two towns and their villages.
31These towns and their villages were the inheritance of the tribe of Asher, clan by clan.

Allotment for Naphtali

32The sixth lot came out for Naphtali, clan by clan:

33Their boundary went from Heleph and the large tree in Zaanannim, passing Adami Nekeb and Jabneel to Lakkum and ending at the Jordan. 34The boundary ran west through Aznoth Tabor and came out at Hukkok. It touched Zebulun on the south, Asher on the west and the Jordan[b] on the east. 35The fortified cities were Ziddim, Zer, Hammath, Rakkath, Kinnereth, 36Adamah, Ramah, Hazor, 37Kedesh, Edrei, En Hazor, 38Iron, Migdal El, Horem, Beth Anath and Beth Shemesh. There were nineteen towns and their villages.
39These towns and their villages were the inheritance of the tribe of Naphtali, clan by clan.

Allotment for Dan

40The seventh lot came out for the tribe of Dan, clan by clan. 41The territory of their inheritance included:

Zorah, Eshtaol, Ir Shemesh, 42Shaalabbin, Aijalon, Ithlah, 43Elon, Timnah, Ekron, 44Eltekeh, Gibbethon, Baalath, 45Jehud, Bene Berak, Gath Rimmon, 46Me Jarkon and Rakkon, with the area facing Joppa.

47(But the Danites had difficulty taking possession of their territory, so they went up and attacked Leshem, took it, put it to the sword and occupied it. They settled in Leshem and named it Dan after their forefather.)
48These towns and their villages were the inheritance of the tribe of Dan, clan by clan.

Allotment for Joshua

49When they had finished dividing the land into its allotted portions, the Israelites gave Joshua son of Nun an inheritance among them, 50as the LORD had commanded. They gave him the town he asked for—Timnath Serah[c] in the hill country of Ephraim. And he built up the town and settled there.

51These are the territories that Eleazar the priest, Joshua son of Nun and the heads of the tribal clans of Israel assigned by lot at Shiloh in the presence of the LORD

[a] *28* Some Hebrew manuscripts (see also Joshua 21:30); most Hebrew manuscripts *Ebron*
[b] *34* Septuagint; Hebrew *west, and Judah, the Jordan,*
[c] *50* Also known as *Timnath Heres* (see Judges 2:9)

at the entrance to the Tent of Meeting.
And so they finished dividing the land.

Cities of Refuge

20 Then the LORD said to Joshua:
2"Tell the Israelites to designate
the cities of refuge, as I instructed you
through Moses, 3so that anyone who kills
a person accidentally and unintentionally
may flee there and find protection from
the avenger of blood.
4"When he flees to one of these cities,
he is to stand in the entrance of the city
gate and state his case before the elders of
that city. Then they are to admit him into
their city and give him a place to live with
them. 5If the avenger of blood pursues
him, they must not surrender the one ac-
cused, because he killed his neighbor
unintentionally and without malice afore-
thought. 6He is to stay in that city until he
has stood trial before the assembly and
until the death of the high priest who is
serving at that time. Then he may go back
to his own home in the town from which
he fled."
7So they set apart Kedesh in Galilee in
the hill country of Naphtali, Shechem in
the hill country of Ephraim, and Kiriath
Arba (that is, Hebron) in the hill country
of Judah. 8On the east side of the Jordan
of Jericho[a] they designated Bezer in the
desert on the plateau in the tribe of Reu-
ben, Ramoth in Gilead in the tribe of Gad,
and Golan in Bashan in the tribe of Manas-
seh. 9Any of the Israelites or any alien liv-
ing among them who killed someone acci-
dentally could flee to these designated
cities and not be killed by the avenger of
blood prior to standing trial before the as-
sembly.

Towns for the Levites

21 Now the family heads of the Le-
vites approached Eleazar the
priest, Joshua son of Nun, and the heads
of the other tribal families of Israel 2at Shi-
loh in Canaan and said to them, "The LORD
commanded through Moses that you give
us towns to live in, with pasturelands for
our livestock." 3So, as the LORD had com-
manded, the Israelites gave the Levites the
following towns and pasturelands out of
their own inheritance:
4The first lot came out for the Kohath-
ites, clan by clan. The Levites who were
descendants of Aaron the priest were al-
lotted thirteen towns from the tribes of Ju-
dah, Simeon and Benjamin. 5The rest of
Kohath's descendants were allotted ten
towns from the clans of the tribes of
Ephraim, Dan and half of Manasseh.
6The descendants of Gershon were al-
lotted thirteen towns from the clans of the
tribes of Issachar, Asher, Naphtali and the
half-tribe of Manasseh in Bashan.
7The descendants of Merari, clan by
clan, received twelve towns from the
tribes of Reuben, Gad and Zebulun.
8So the Israelites allotted to the Levites
these towns and their pasturelands, as the
LORD had commanded through Moses.

9From the tribes of Judah and Simeon
they allotted the following towns by name
10(these towns were assigned to the
descendants of Aaron who were from the
Kohathite clans of the Levites, because
the first lot fell to them):

11They gave them Kiriath Arba
(that is, Hebron), with its surround-
ing pastureland, in the hill country of
Judah. (Arba was the forefather of
Anak.) 12But the fields and villages
around the city they had given to Ca-
leb son of Jephunneh as his posses-
sion.

13So to the descendants of Aaron
the priest they gave Hebron (a city of
refuge for one accused of murder),
Libnah, 14Jattir, Eshtemoa, 15Holon,
Debir, 16Ain, Juttah and Beth She-
mesh, together with their pasture-
lands—nine towns from these two
tribes.

17And from the tribe of Benjamin
they gave them Gibeon, Geba, 18Ana-
thoth and Almon, together with their
pasturelands—four towns.

19All the towns for the priests, the descen-
dants of Aaron, were thirteen, together
with their pasturelands.

20The rest of the Kohathite clans of the Le-
vites were allotted towns from the tribe of
Ephraim:

21In the hill country of Ephraim
they were given Shechem (a city of
refuge for one accused of murder)
and Gezer, 22Kibzaim and Beth Ho-
ron, together with their pasture-
lands—four towns.

23Also from the tribe of Dan they
received Eltekeh, Gibbethon, 24Aija-

[a]8 *Jordan of Jericho* was possibly an ancient name for the Jordan River.

lon and Gath Rimmon, together with
their pasturelands—four towns.
[25]From half the tribe of Manasseh
they received Taanach and Gath Rim-
mon, together with their pasture-
lands—two towns.
[26]All these ten towns and their pasture-
lands were given to the rest of the Kohath-
ite clans.

[27]The Levite clans of the Gershonites were
given:
from the half-tribe of Manasseh,
Golan in Bashan (a city of refuge for
one accused of murder) and Be Esh-
tarah, together with their pasture-
lands—two towns;
[28]from the tribe of Issachar,
Kishion, Daberath, [29]Jarmuth and En
Gannim, together with their pasture-
lands—four towns;
[30]from the tribe of Asher,
Mishal, Abdon, [31]Helkath and Rehob,
together with their pasturelands—
four towns;
[32]from the tribe of Naphtali,
Kedesh in Galilee (a city of refuge for
one accused of murder), Hammoth
Dor and Kartan, together with their
pasturelands—three towns.
[33]All the towns of the Gershonite clans
were thirteen, together with their pasture-
lands.

[34]The Merarite clans (the rest of the Le-
vites) were given:
from the tribe of Zebulun,
Jokneam, Kartah, [35]Dimnah and Na-
halal, together with their pasture-
lands—four towns;
[36]from the tribe of Reuben,
Bezer, Jahaz, [37]Kedemoth and Meph-
aath, together with their pasture-
lands—four towns;
[38]from the tribe of Gad,
Ramoth in Gilead (a city of refuge for
one accused of murder), Mahanaim,
[39]Heshbon and Jazer, together with
their pasturelands—four towns in
all.
[40]All the towns allotted to the Merarite
clans, who were the rest of the Levites,
were twelve.

[41]The towns of the Levites in the territo-
ry held by the Israelites were forty-eight in
all, together with their pasturelands.
[42]Each of these towns had pasturelands
surrounding it; this was true for all these
towns.

[43]So the LORD gave Israel all the land he
had sworn to give their forefathers, and
they took possession of it and settled
there. [44]The LORD gave them rest on every
side, just as he had sworn to their forefa-
thers. Not one of their enemies withstood
them; the LORD handed all their enemies
over to them. [45]Not one of all the LORD's
good promises to the house of Israel
failed; every one was fulfilled.

Eastern Tribes Return Home

22 Then Joshua summoned the Reu-
benites, the Gadites and the half-
tribe of Manasseh [2]and said to them, "You
have done all that Moses the servant of
the LORD commanded, and you have
obeyed me in everything I commanded.
[3]For a long time now—to this very day—
you have not deserted your brothers but
have carried out the mission the LORD
your God gave you. [4]Now that the LORD
your God has given your brothers rest as
he promised, return to your homes in the
land that Moses the servant of the LORD
gave you on the other side of the Jordan.
[5]But be very careful to keep the com-
mandment and the law that Moses the ser-
vant of the LORD gave you: to love the LORD
your God, to walk in all his ways, to obey
his commands, to hold fast to him and to
serve him with all your heart and all your
soul."

[6]Then Joshua blessed them and sent
them away, and they went to their homes.
[7](To the half-tribe of Manasseh Moses had
given land in Bashan, and to the other half
of the tribe Joshua gave land on the west
side of the Jordan with their brothers.)
When Joshua sent them home, he blessed
them, [8]saying, "Return to your homes
with your great wealth—with large herds
of livestock, with silver, gold, bronze and
iron, and a great quantity of clothing—
and divide with your brothers the plunder
from your enemies."

[9]So the Reubenites, the Gadites and the
half-tribe of Manasseh left the Israelites at
Shiloh in Canaan to return to Gilead, their
own land, which they had acquired in ac-
cordance with the command of the LORD
through Moses.

[10]When they came to Geliloth near the
Jordan in the land of Canaan, the Reuben-
ites, the Gadites and the half-tribe of Ma-
nasseh built an imposing altar there by
the Jordan. [11]And when the Israelites
heard that they had built the altar on the
border of Canaan at Geliloth near the Jor-

dan on the Israelite side, 12the whole assembly of Israel gathered at Shiloh to go to war against them.

13So the Israelites sent Phinehas son of Eleazar, the priest, to the land of Gilead—to Reuben, Gad and the half-tribe of Manasseh. 14With him they sent ten of the chief men, one for each of the tribes of Israel, each the head of a family division among the Israelite clans.

15When they went to Gilead—to Reuben, Gad and the half-tribe of Manasseh—they said to them: 16"The whole assembly of the LORD says: 'How could you break faith with the God of Israel like this? How could you turn away from the LORD and build yourselves an altar in rebellion against him now? 17Was not the sin of Peor enough for us? Up to this very day we have not cleansed ourselves from that sin, even though a plague fell on the community of the LORD! 18And are you now turning away from the LORD?

" 'If you rebel against the LORD today, tomorrow he will be angry with the whole community of Israel. 19If the land you possess is defiled, come over to the LORD's land, where the LORD's tabernacle stands, and share the land with us. But do not rebel against the LORD or against us by building an altar for yourselves, other than the altar of the LORD our God. 20When Achan son of Zerah acted unfaithfully regarding the devoted things,[a] did not wrath come upon the whole community of Israel? He was not the only one who died for his sin.' "

21Then Reuben, Gad and the half-tribe of Manasseh replied to the heads of the clans of Israel: 22"The Mighty One, God, the LORD! The Mighty One, God, the LORD! He knows! And let Israel know! If this has been in rebellion or disobedience to the LORD, do not spare us this day. 23If we have built our own altar to turn away from the LORD and to offer burnt offerings and grain offerings, or to sacrifice fellowship offerings[b] on it, may the LORD himself call us to account.

24"No! We did it for fear that some day your descendants might say to ours, 'What do you have to do with the LORD, the God of Israel? 25The LORD has made the Jordan a boundary between us and you—you Reubenites and Gadites! You have no share in the LORD.' So your descendants might cause ours to stop fearing the LORD.

26"That is why we said, 'Let us get ready and build an altar—but not for burnt offerings or sacrifices.' 27On the contrary, it is to be a witness between us and you and the generations that follow, that we will worship the LORD at his sanctuary with our burnt offerings, sacrifices and fellowship offerings. Then in the future your descendants will not be able to say to ours, 'You have no share in the LORD.'

28"And we said, 'If they ever say this to us, or to our descendants, we will answer: Look at the replica of the LORD's altar, which our fathers built, not for burnt offerings and sacrifices, but as a witness between us and you.'

29"Far be it from us to rebel against the LORD and turn away from him today by building an altar for burnt offerings, grain offerings and sacrifices, other than the altar of the LORD our God that stands before his tabernacle."

30When Phinehas the priest and the leaders of the community—the heads of the clans of the Israelites—heard what Reuben, Gad and Manasseh had to say, they were pleased. 31And Phinehas son of Eleazar, the priest, said to Reuben, Gad and Manasseh, "Today we know that the LORD is with us, because you have not acted unfaithfully toward the LORD in this matter. Now you have rescued the Israelites from the LORD's hand."

32Then Phinehas son of Eleazar, the priest, and the leaders returned to Canaan from their meeting with the Reubenites and Gadites in Gilead and reported to the Israelites. 33They were glad to hear the report and praised God. And they talked no more about going to war against them to devastate the country where the Reubenites and the Gadites lived.

34And the Reubenites and the Gadites gave the altar this name: A Witness Between Us that the LORD is God.

Joshua's Farewell to the Leaders

23 After a long time had passed and the LORD had given Israel rest from all their enemies around them, Joshua, by then old and well advanced in years, 2summoned all Israel—their elders, leaders, judges and officials—and said to them: "I am old and well advanced in

[a] *20* The Hebrew term refers to the irrevocable giving over of things or persons to the LORD, often by totally destroying them. [b] *23* Traditionally *peace offerings*; also in verse 27

years. 3You yourselves have seen everything the LORD your God has done to all these nations for your sake; it was the LORD your God who fought for you. 4Remember how I have allotted as an inheritance for your tribes all the land of the nations that remain—the nations I conquered—between the Jordan and the Great Sea[a] in the west. 5The LORD your God himself will drive them out of your way. He will push them out before you, and you will take possession of their land, as the LORD your God promised you.

6"Be very strong; be careful to obey all that is written in the Book of the Law of Moses, without turning aside to the right or to the left. 7Do not associate with these nations that remain among you; do not invoke the names of their gods or swear by them. You must not serve them or bow down to them. 8But you are to hold fast to the LORD your God, as you have until now.

9"The LORD has driven out before you great and powerful nations; to this day no one has been able to withstand you. 10One of you routs a thousand, because the LORD your God fights for you, just as he promised. 11So be very careful to love the LORD your God.

12"But if you turn away and ally yourselves with the survivors of these nations that remain among you and if you intermarry with them and associate with them, 13then you may be sure that the LORD your God will no longer drive out these nations before you. Instead, they will become snares and traps for you, whips on your backs and thorns in your eyes, until you perish from this good land, which the LORD your God has given you.

14"Now I am about to go the way of all the earth. You know with all your heart and soul that not one of all the good promises the LORD your God gave you has failed. Every promise has been fulfilled; not one has failed. 15But just as every good promise of the LORD your God has come true, so the LORD will bring on you all the evil he has threatened, until he has destroyed you from this good land he has given you. 16If you violate the covenant of the LORD your God, which he commanded you, and go and serve other gods and bow down to them, the LORD's anger will burn against you, and you will quickly perish from the good land he has given you."

The Covenant Renewed at Shechem

24 Then Joshua assembled all the tribes of Israel at Shechem. He summoned the elders, leaders, judges and officials of Israel, and they presented themselves before God.

2Joshua said to all the people, "This is what the LORD, the God of Israel, says: 'Long ago your forefathers, including Terah the father of Abraham and Nahor, lived beyond the River[b] and worshiped other gods. 3But I took your father Abraham from the land beyond the River and led him throughout Canaan and gave him many descendants. I gave him Isaac, 4and to Isaac I gave Jacob and Esau. I assigned the hill country of Seir to Esau, but Jacob and his sons went down to Egypt.

5" 'Then I sent Moses and Aaron, and I afflicted the Egyptians by what I did there, and I brought you out. 6When I brought your fathers out of Egypt, you came to the sea, and the Egyptians pursued them with chariots and horsemen[c] as far as the Red Sea.[d] 7But they cried to the LORD for help, and he put darkness between you and the Egyptians; he brought the sea over them and covered them. You saw with your own eyes what I did to the Egyptians. Then you lived in the desert for a long time.

8" 'I brought you to the land of the Amorites who lived east of the Jordan. They fought against you, but I gave them into your hands. I destroyed them from before you, and you took possession of their land. 9When Balak son of Zippor, the king of Moab, prepared to fight against Israel, he sent for Balaam son of Beor to put a curse on you. 10But I would not listen to Balaam, so he blessed you again and again, and I delivered you out of his hand.

11" 'Then you crossed the Jordan and came to Jericho. The citizens of Jericho fought against you, as did also the Amorites, Perizzites, Canaanites, Hittites, Girgashites, Hivites and Jebusites, but I gave them into your hands. 12I sent the hornet ahead of you, which drove them out before you—also the two Amorite kings. You did not do it with your own sword and bow. 13So I gave you a land on which you did not toil and cities you did not build; and you live in them and eat from

[a] 4 That is, the Mediterranean [b] 2 That is, the Euphrates; also in verses 3, 14 and 15 [c] 6 Or *charioteers* [d] 6 Hebrew *Yam Suph*; that is, Sea of Reeds

vineyards and olive groves that you did
not plant.'
14"Now fear the LORD and serve him
with all faithfulness. Throw away the gods
your forefathers worshiped beyond the
River and in Egypt, and serve the LORD.
15But if serving the LORD seems undesir-
able to you, then choose for yourselves
this day whom you will serve, whether the
gods your forefathers served beyond the
River, or the gods of the Amorites, in
whose land you are living. But as for me
and my household, we will serve the
LORD."
16Then the people answered, "Far be it
from us to forsake the LORD to serve other
gods! 17It was the LORD our God himself
who brought us and our fathers up out of
Egypt, from that land of slavery, and per-
formed those great signs before our eyes.
He protected us on our entire journey and
among all the nations through which we
traveled. 18And the LORD drove out before
us all the nations, including the Amorites,
who lived in the land. We too will serve
the LORD, because he is our God."
19Joshua said to the people, "You are
not able to serve the LORD. He is a holy
God; he is a jealous God. He will not for-
give your rebellion and your sins. 20If you
forsake the LORD and serve foreign gods,
he will turn and bring disaster on you and
make an end of you, after he has been
good to you."
21But the people said to Joshua, "No!
We will serve the LORD."
22Then Joshua said, "You are witnesses
against yourselves that you have chosen
to serve the LORD."
"Yes, we are witnesses," they replied.
23"Now then," said Joshua, "throw
away the foreign gods that are among you
and yield your hearts to the LORD, the God
of Israel."
24And the people said to Joshua, "We
will serve the LORD our God and obey
him."
25On that day Joshua made a covenant
for the people, and there at Shechem he
drew up for them decrees and laws. 26And
Joshua recorded these things in the Book
of the Law of God. Then he took a large
stone and set it up there under the oak
near the holy place of the LORD.
27"See!" he said to all the people. "This
stone will be a witness against us. It has
heard all the words the LORD has said to
us. It will be a witness against you if you
are untrue to your God."

Buried in the Promised Land

28Then Joshua sent the people away,
each to his own inheritance.
29After these things, Joshua son of Nun,
the servant of the LORD, died at the age of
a hundred and ten. 30And they buried him
in the land of his inheritance, at Timnath
Serah[a] in the hill country of Ephraim,
north of Mount Gaash.
31Israel served the LORD throughout the
lifetime of Joshua and of the elders who
outlived him and who had experienced
everything the LORD had done for Israel.
32And Joseph's bones, which the Israel-
ites had brought up from Egypt, were bur-
ied at Shechem in the tract of land that Ja-
cob bought for a hundred pieces of
silver[b] from the sons of Hamor, the father
of Shechem. This became the inheritance
of Joseph's descendants.
33And Eleazar son of Aaron died and
was buried at Gibeah, which had been al-
lotted to his son Phinehas in the hill coun-
try of Ephraim.

[a]30 Also known as *Timnath Heres* (see Judges 2:9)

[b]32 Hebrew *hundred kesitahs*; a kesitah was a unit of money of unknown weight and value.

JUDGES recounts a regular pattern that develops for God's people in their new land: the people serve idols, God punishes them by an enemy invasion, they cry to the Lord, and he sends a judge (such as Deborah, Gideon, Jephthah or Samson) to save them. As you read this book, remember that only God can give you victory over sin and evil and that you will receive his help only when you serve him alone.

JUDGES

Israel Fights the Remaining Canaanites

1 After the death of Joshua, the Israelites asked the LORD, "Who will be the first to go up and fight for us against the Canaanites?"

2 The LORD answered, "Judah is to go; I have given the land into their hands."

3 Then the men of Judah said to the Simeonites their brothers, "Come up with us into the territory allotted to us, to fight against the Canaanites. We in turn will go with you into yours." So the Simeonites went with them.

4 When Judah attacked, the LORD gave the Canaanites and Perizzites into their hands and they struck down ten thousand men at Bezek. 5 It was there that they found Adoni-Bezek and fought against him, putting to rout the Canaanites and Perizzites. 6 Adoni-Bezek fled, but they chased him and caught him, and cut off his thumbs and big toes.

7 Then Adoni-Bezek said, "Seventy kings with their thumbs and big toes cut off have picked up scraps under my table. Now God has paid me back for what I did to them." They brought him to Jerusalem, and he died there.

8 The men of Judah attacked Jerusalem also and took it. They put the city to the sword and set it on fire.

9 After that, the men of Judah went down to fight against the Canaanites living in the hill country, the Negev and the

western foothills. 10They advanced against the Canaanites living in Hebron (formerly called Kiriath Arba) and defeated Sheshai, Ahiman and Talmai.

11From there they advanced against the people living in Debir (formerly called Kiriath Sepher). 12And Caleb said, "I will give my daughter Acsah in marriage to the man who attacks and captures Kiriath Sepher." 13Othniel son of Kenaz, Caleb's younger brother, took it; so Caleb gave his daughter Acsah to him in marriage.

14One day when she came to Othniel, she urged him[a] to ask her father for a field. When she got off her donkey, Caleb asked her, "What can I do for you?"

15She replied, "Do me a special favor. Since you have given me land in the Negev, give me also springs of water." Then Caleb gave her the upper and lower springs.

16The descendants of Moses' father-in-law, the Kenite, went up from the City of Palms[b] with the men of Judah to live among the people of the Desert of Judah in the Negev near Arad.

17Then the men of Judah went with the Simeonites their brothers and attacked the Canaanites living in Zephath, and they totally destroyed[c] the city. Therefore it was called Hormah.[d] 18The men of Judah also took[e] Gaza, Ashkelon and Ekron—each city with its territory.

19The LORD was with the men of Judah. They took possession of the hill country, but they were unable to drive the people from the plains, because they had iron chariots. 20As Moses had promised, Hebron was given to Caleb, who drove from it the three sons of Anak. 21The Benjamites, however, failed to dislodge the Jebusites, who were living in Jerusalem; to this day the Jebusites live there with the Benjamites.

22Now the house of Joseph attacked Bethel, and the LORD was with them. 23When they sent men to spy out Bethel (formerly called Luz), 24the spies saw a man coming out of the city and they said to him, "Show us how to get into the city and we will see that you are treated well." 25So he showed them, and they put the city to the sword but spared the man and his whole family. 26He then went to the land of the Hittites, where he built a city and called it Luz, which is its name to this day.

27But Manasseh did not drive out the people of Beth Shan or Taanach or Dor or Ibleam or Megiddo and their surrounding settlements, for the Canaanites were determined to live in that land. 28When Israel became strong, they pressed the Canaanites into forced labor but never drove them out completely. 29Nor did Ephraim drive out the Canaanites living in Gezer, but the Canaanites continued to live there among them. 30Neither did Zebulun drive out the Canaanites living in Kitron or Nahalol, who remained among them; but they did subject them to forced labor. 31Nor did Asher drive out those living in Acco or Sidon or Ahlab or Aczib or Helbah or Aphek or Rehob, 32and because of this the people of Asher lived among the Canaanite inhabitants of the land. 33Neither did Naphtali drive out those living in Beth Shemesh or Beth Anath; but the Naphtalites too lived among the Canaanite inhabitants of the land, and those living in Beth Shemesh and Beth Anath became forced laborers for them. 34The Amorites confined the Danites to the hill country, not allowing them to come down into the plain. 35And the Amorites were determined also to hold out in Mount Heres, Aijalon and Shaalbim, but when the power of the house of Joseph increased, they too were pressed into forced labor. 36The boundary of the Amorites was from Scorpion[f] Pass to Sela and beyond.

The Angel of the LORD at Bokim

2 The angel of the LORD went up from Gilgal to Bokim and said, "I brought you up out of Egypt and led you into the land that I swore to give to your forefathers. I said, 'I will never break my covenant with you, 2and you shall not make a covenant with the people of this land, but you shall break down their altars.' Yet you have disobeyed me. Why have you done this? 3Now therefore I tell you that I will not drive them out before you; they will be ⌊thorns⌋ in your sides and their gods will be a snare to you."

4When the angel of the LORD had spoken these things to all the Israelites, the

[a] 14 Hebrew; Septuagint and Vulgate *Othniel, he urged her* [b] 16 That is, Jericho [c] 17 The Hebrew term refers to the irrevocable giving over of things or persons to the LORD, often by totally destroying them. [d] 17 *Hormah* means *destruction.* [e] 18 Hebrew; Septuagint *Judah did not take*
[f] 36 Hebrew *Akrabbim*

people wept aloud, 5and they called that place Bokim.[a] There they offered sacrifices to the LORD.

Disobedience and Defeat

6After Joshua had dismissed the Israelites, they went to take possession of the land, each to his own inheritance. 7The people served the LORD throughout the lifetime of Joshua and of the elders who outlived him and who had seen all the great things the LORD had done for Israel.

8Joshua son of Nun, the servant of the LORD, died at the age of a hundred and ten. 9And they buried him in the land of his inheritance, at Timnath Heres[b] in the hill country of Ephraim, north of Mount Gaash.

10After that whole generation had been gathered to their fathers, another generation grew up, who knew neither the LORD nor what he had done for Israel. 11Then the Israelites did evil in the eyes of the LORD and served the Baals. 12They forsook the LORD, the God of their fathers, who had brought them out of Egypt. They followed and worshiped various gods of the peoples around them. They provoked the LORD to anger 13because they forsook him and served Baal and the Ashtoreths. 14In his anger against Israel the LORD handed them over to raiders who plundered them. He sold them to their enemies all around, whom they were no longer able to resist. 15Whenever Israel went out to fight, the hand of the LORD was against them to defeat them, just as he had sworn to them. They were in great distress.

16Then the LORD raised up judges,[c] who saved them out of the hands of these raiders. 17Yet they would not listen to their judges but prostituted themselves to other gods and worshiped them. Unlike their fathers, they quickly turned from the way in which their fathers had walked, the way of obedience to the LORD's commands. 18Whenever the LORD raised up a judge for them, he was with the judge and saved them out of the hands of their enemies as long as the judge lived; for the LORD had compassion on them as they groaned under those who oppressed and afflicted them. 19But when the judge died, the people returned to ways even more corrupt than those of their fathers, following other gods and serving and worshiping them. They refused to give up their evil practices and stubborn ways.

20Therefore the LORD was very angry with Israel and said, "Because this nation has violated the covenant that I laid down for their forefathers and has not listened to me, 21I will no longer drive out before them any of the nations Joshua left when he died. 22I will use them to test Israel and see whether they will keep the way of the LORD and walk in it as their forefathers did." 23The LORD had allowed those nations to remain; he did not drive them out at once by giving them into the hands of Joshua.

3 These are the nations the LORD left to test all those Israelites who had not experienced any of the wars in Canaan 2(he did this only to teach warfare to the descendants of the Israelites who had not had previous battle experience): 3the five rulers of the Philistines, all the Canaanites, the Sidonians, and the Hivites living in the Lebanon mountains from Mount Baal Hermon to Lebo[d] Hamath. 4They were left to test the Israelites to see whether they would obey the LORD's commands, which he had given their forefathers through Moses.

5The Israelites lived among the Canaanites, Hittites, Amorites, Perizzites, Hivites and Jebusites. 6They took their daughters in marriage and gave their own daughters to their sons, and served their gods.

Othniel

7The Israelites did evil in the eyes of the LORD; they forgot the LORD their God and served the Baals and the Asherahs. 8The anger of the LORD burned against Israel so that he sold them into the hands of Cushan-Rishathaim king of Aram Naharaim,[e] to whom the Israelites were subject for eight years. 9But when they cried out to the LORD, he raised up for them a deliverer, Othniel son of Kenaz, Caleb's younger brother, who saved them. 10The Spirit of the LORD came upon him, so that he became Israel's judge[f] and went to war. The LORD gave Cushan-Rishathaim king of Aram into the hands of Othniel, who overpowered him. 11So the land had peace for forty years, until Othniel son of Kenaz died.

[a]5 *Bokim* means *weepers.* [b]9 Also known as *Timnath Serah* (see Joshua 19:50 and 24:30) [c]16 Or *leaders*; similarly in verses 17-19 [d]3 Or *to the entrance to* [e]8 That is, Northwest Mesopotamia [f]10 Or *leader*

Ehud

12Once again the Israelites did evil in
the eyes of the LORD, and because they did
this evil the LORD gave Eglon king of Moab
power over Israel. 13Getting the Ammon-
ites and Amalekites to join him, Eglon
came and attacked Israel, and they took
possession of the City of Palms.[a] 14The
Israelites were subject to Eglon king of
Moab for eighteen years.

15Again the Israelites cried out to the
LORD, and he gave them a deliverer—
Ehud, a left-handed man, the son of Gera
the Benjamite. The Israelites sent him
with tribute to Eglon king of Moab. 16Now
Ehud had made a double-edged sword
about a foot and a half[b] long, which he
strapped to his right thigh under his cloth-
ing. 17He presented the tribute to Eglon
king of Moab, who was a very fat man.
18After Ehud had presented the tribute, he
sent on their way the men who had car-
ried it. 19At the idols[c] near Gilgal he him-
self turned back and said, "I have a secret
message for you, O king."

The king said, "Quiet!" And all his at-
tendants left him.

20Ehud then approached him while he
was sitting alone in the upper room of his
summer palace[d] and said, "I have a mes-
sage from God for you." As the king rose
from his seat, 21Ehud reached with his left
hand, drew the sword from his right thigh
and plunged it into the king's belly.
22Even the handle sank in after the blade,
which came out his back. Ehud did not
pull the sword out, and the fat closed in
over it. 23Then Ehud went out to the
porch[e]; he shut the doors of the upper
room behind him and locked them.

24After he had gone, the servants came
and found the doors of the upper room
locked. They said, "He must be relieving
himself in the inner room of the house."
25They waited to the point of embarrass-
ment, but when he did not open the doors
of the room, they took a key and unlocked
them. There they saw their lord fallen to
the floor, dead.

26While they waited, Ehud got away. He
passed by the idols and escaped to Seirah.
27When he arrived there, he blew a trum-
pet in the hill country of Ephraim, and the
Israelites went down with him from the
hills, with him leading them.

28"Follow me," he ordered, "for the
LORD has given Moab, your enemy, into
your hands." So they followed him down
and, taking possession of the fords of the
Jordan that led to Moab, they allowed no
one to cross over. 29At that time they
struck down about ten thousand Moab-
ites, all vigorous and strong; not a man es-
caped. 30That day Moab was made subject
to Israel, and the land had peace for eighty
years.

Shamgar

31After Ehud came Shamgar son of
Anath, who struck down six hundred Phi-
listines with an oxgoad. He too saved Is-
rael.

Deborah

4 After Ehud died, the Israelites once
again did evil in the eyes of the LORD.
2So the LORD sold them into the hands of
Jabin, a king of Canaan, who reigned in
Hazor. The commander of his army was
Sisera, who lived in Harosheth Haggoyim.
3Because he had nine hundred iron chari-
ots and had cruelly oppressed the Israel-
ites for twenty years, they cried to the
LORD for help.

4Deborah, a prophetess, the wife of Lap-
pidoth, was leading[f] Israel at that time.
5She held court under the Palm of Debo-
rah between Ramah and Bethel in the hill
country of Ephraim, and the Israelites
came to her to have their disputes decid-
ed. 6She sent for Barak son of Abinoam
from Kedesh in Naphtali and said to him,
"The LORD, the God of Israel, commands
you: 'Go, take with you ten thousand men
of Naphtali and Zebulun and lead the way
to Mount Tabor. 7I will lure Sisera, the
commander of Jabin's army, with his
chariots and his troops to the Kishon Riv-
er and give him into your hands.' "

8Barak said to her, "If you go with me,
I will go; but if you don't go with me, I
won't go."

9"Very well," Deborah said, "I will go
with you. But because of the way you are
going about this,[g] the honor will not be
yours, for the LORD will hand Sisera over
to a woman." So Deborah went with Barak

[a]13 That is, Jericho [b]16 Hebrew *a cubit* (about 0.5 meter) [c]19 Or *the stone quarries*; also in verse 26 [d]20 The meaning of the Hebrew for this phrase is uncertain. [e]23 The meaning of the Hebrew for this word is uncertain. [f]4 Traditionally *judging* [g]9 Or *But on the expedition you are undertaking*

to Kedesh, [10]where he summoned Zebulun and Naphtali. Ten thousand men followed him, and Deborah also went with him.

[11]Now Heber the Kenite had left the other Kenites, the descendants of Hobab, Moses' brother-in-law,[a] and pitched his tent by the great tree in Zaanannim near Kedesh.

[12]When they told Sisera that Barak son of Abinoam had gone up to Mount Tabor, [13]Sisera gathered together his nine hundred iron chariots and all the men with him, from Harosheth Haggoyim to the Kishon River.

[14]Then Deborah said to Barak, "Go! This is the day the LORD has given Sisera into your hands. Has not the LORD gone ahead of you?" So Barak went down Mount Tabor, followed by ten thousand men. [15]At Barak's advance, the LORD routed Sisera and all his chariots and army by the sword, and Sisera abandoned his chariot and fled on foot. [16]But Barak pursued the chariots and army as far as Harosheth Haggoyim. All the troops of Sisera fell by the sword; not a man was left.

[17]Sisera, however, fled on foot to the tent of Jael, the wife of Heber the Kenite, because there were friendly relations between Jabin king of Hazor and the clan of Heber the Kenite.

[18]Jael went out to meet Sisera and said to him, "Come, my lord, come right in. Don't be afraid." So he entered her tent, and she put a covering over him.

[19]"I'm thirsty," he said. "Please give me some water." She opened a skin of milk, gave him a drink, and covered him up.

[20]"Stand in the doorway of the tent," he told her. "If someone comes by and asks you, 'Is anyone here?' say 'No.' "

[21]But Jael, Heber's wife, picked up a tent peg and a hammer and went quietly to him while he lay fast asleep, exhausted. She drove the peg through his temple into the ground, and he died.

[22]Barak came by in pursuit of Sisera, and Jael went out to meet him. "Come," she said, "I will show you the man you're looking for." So he went in with her, and there lay Sisera with the tent peg through his temple—dead.

[23]On that day God subdued Jabin, the Canaanite king, before the Israelites. [24]And the hand of the Israelites grew stronger and stronger against Jabin, the Canaanite king, until they destroyed him.

The Song of Deborah

5 On that day Deborah and Barak son of Abinoam sang this song:

[2]"When the princes in Israel take the lead,
when the people willingly offer themselves—
praise the LORD!

[3]"Hear this, you kings! Listen, you rulers!
I will sing to[b] the LORD, I will sing;
I will make music to[c] the LORD, the God of Israel.

[4]"O LORD, when you went out from Seir,
when you marched from the land of Edom,
the earth shook, the heavens poured,
the clouds poured down water.
[5]The mountains quaked before the LORD, the One of Sinai,
before the LORD, the God of Israel.

[6]"In the days of Shamgar son of Anath,
in the days of Jael, the roads were abandoned;
travelers took to winding paths.
[7]Village life[d] in Israel ceased,
ceased until I,[e] Deborah, arose,
arose a mother in Israel.
[8]When they chose new gods,
war came to the city gates,
and not a shield or spear was seen among forty thousand in Israel.
[9]My heart is with Israel's princes,
with the willing volunteers among the people.
Praise the LORD!

[10]"You who ride on white donkeys,
sitting on your saddle blankets,
and you who walk along the road,
consider [11]the voice of the singers[f] at the watering places.
They recite the righteous acts of the LORD,
the righteous acts of his warriors[g] in Israel.

"Then the people of the LORD
went down to the city gates.
[12]'Wake up, wake up, Deborah!

[a]11 Or *father-in-law* [b]3 Or *of* [c]3 Or / *with song I will praise* [d]7 Or *Warriors* [e]7 Or *you*
[f]11 Or *archers*; the meaning of the Hebrew for this word is uncertain. [g]11 Or *villagers*

Wake up, wake up, break out in
song!
Arise, O Barak!
Take captive your captives, O son of
Abinoam.'

13"Then the men who were left
came down to the nobles;
the people of the LORD
came to me with the mighty.
14Some came from Ephraim, whose
roots were in Amalek;
Benjamin was with the people who
followed you.
From Makir captains came down,
from Zebulun those who bear a
commander's staff.
15The princes of Issachar were with
Deborah;
yes, Issachar was with Barak,
rushing after him into the valley.
In the districts of Reuben
there was much searching of heart.
16Why did you stay among the
campfires[a]
to hear the whistling for the flocks?
In the districts of Reuben
there was much searching of heart.
17Gilead stayed beyond the Jordan.
And Dan, why did he linger by the
ships?
Asher remained on the coast
and stayed in his coves.
18The people of Zebulun risked their
very lives;
so did Naphtali on the heights of
the field.

19"Kings came, they fought;
the kings of Canaan fought
at Taanach by the waters of Megiddo,
but they carried off no silver, no
plunder.
20From the heavens the stars fought,
from their courses they fought
against Sisera.
21The river Kishon swept them away,
the age-old river, the river Kishon.
March on, my soul; be strong!
22Then thundered the horses' hoofs—
galloping, galloping go his mighty
steeds.
23'Curse Meroz,' said the angel of the
LORD.
'Curse its people bitterly,
because they did not come to help the
LORD,
to help the LORD against the
mighty.'

24"Most blessed of women be Jael,
the wife of Heber the Kenite,
most blessed of tent-dwelling
women.
25He asked for water, and she gave him
milk;
in a bowl fit for nobles she brought
him curdled milk.
26Her hand reached for the tent peg,
her right hand for the workman's
hammer.
She struck Sisera, she crushed his
head,
she shattered and pierced his
temple.
27At her feet he sank,
he fell; there he lay.
At her feet he sank, he fell;
where he sank, there he fell—dead.

28"Through the window peered Sisera's
mother;
behind the lattice she cried out,
'Why is his chariot so long in coming?
Why is the clatter of his chariots
delayed?'
29The wisest of her ladies answer her;
indeed, she keeps saying to herself,
30'Are they not finding and dividing the
spoils:
a girl or two for each man,
colorful garments as plunder for
Sisera,
colorful garments embroidered,
highly embroidered garments for
my neck—
all this as plunder?'

31"So may all your enemies perish,
O LORD!
But may they who love you be like
the sun
when it rises in its strength."

Then the land had peace forty years.

Gideon

6 Again the Israelites did evil in the eyes of the LORD, and for seven years he gave them into the hands of the Midianites. 2Because the power of Midian was so oppressive, the Israelites prepared shelters for themselves in mountain clefts, caves and strongholds. 3Whenever the Israelites planted their crops, the Midian-

[a]16 Or *saddlebags*

ites, Amalekites and other eastern peoples
invaded the country. 4They camped on
the land and ruined the crops all the way
to Gaza and did not spare a living thing for
Israel, neither sheep nor cattle nor don-
keys. 5They came up with their livestock
and their tents like swarms of locusts. It
was impossible to count the men and their
camels; they invaded the land to ravage it.
6Midian so impoverished the Israelites
that they cried out to the LORD for help.
7When the Israelites cried to the LORD
because of Midian, 8he sent them a proph-
et, who said, "This is what the LORD, the
God of Israel, says: I brought you up out
of Egypt, out of the land of slavery. 9I
snatched you from the power of Egypt and
from the hand of all your oppressors. I
drove them from before you and gave you
their land. 10I said to you, 'I am the LORD

WEDNESDAY

VERSE FOR THE DAY:	AUTHOR:	PASSAGE FOR THE DAY:
Judges 6:14	David and Annette LaPlaca	Judges 6:6–16

Go in Strength

It was a familiar story. The Israelites had been flagrantly disobedient, and now they were under fire from one of their many enemies, the Midianites. In times like these, God would call forth a judge to lead his people back to righteous living and back into political peace.

But isn't it just like God to choose a person like Gideon, a regular, everyday kind of guy with a real self-confidence problem? When Gideon expressed his doubts, God commented, "Go in the strength you have. . . . Am I not sending you?" (Judges 6:14) and promised, "I will be with you" (6:16). Gideon still had doubts, and God was patient with him while Gideon gained the confidence to obey his Lord.

Everybody feels inadequate sometimes—as an employee on the job, as a spouse, as a Christian seeking to obey God. God's answer to our insecurities is "Go in the strength you have . . . I will be with you."

Annette's mom used to have a plaque on her kitchen wall that read, "The will of God will never lead you where the grace of God cannot keep you." We can tackle the responsibilities God has placed before us, while we hang onto that promise.

MARRIAGE BUILDERS

- *What task is before you that makes you feel inadequate?*
- *How can you encourage each other to go forward in obedience—with confidence?*

Additional Scripture Readings
Joshua 1:6–9; 2 Corinthians 12:9–10

Go to page 251 for your next devotional reading.

your God; do not worship the gods of the
Amorites, in whose land you live.' But you
have not listened to me."
11The angel of the LORD came and sat
down under the oak in Ophrah that be-
longed to Joash the Abiezrite, where his
son Gideon was threshing wheat in a
winepress to keep it from the Midianites.
12When the angel of the LORD appeared to
Gideon, he said, "The LORD is with you,
mighty warrior."
13"But sir," Gideon replied, "if the LORD
is with us, why has all this happened to
us? Where are all his wonders that our fa-
thers told us about when they said, 'Did
not the LORD bring us up out of Egypt?'
But now the LORD has abandoned us and
put us into the hand of Midian."
14The LORD turned to him and said, "Go
in the strength you have and save Israel
out of Midian's hand. Am I not sending
you?"
15"But Lord,[a]" Gideon asked, "how
can I save Israel? My clan is the weakest
in Manasseh, and I am the least in my
family."
16The LORD answered, "I will be with
you, and you will strike down all the Midi-
anites together."
17Gideon replied, "If now I have found
favor in your eyes, give me a sign that it
is really you talking to me. 18Please do not
go away until I come back and bring my
offering and set it before you."
And the LORD said, "I will wait until you
return."
19Gideon went in, prepared a young
goat, and from an ephah[b] of flour he
made bread without yeast. Putting the
meat in a basket and its broth in a pot, he
brought them out and offered them to him
under the oak.
20The angel of God said to him, "Take
the meat and the unleavened bread, place
them on this rock, and pour out the
broth." And Gideon did so. 21With the tip
of the staff that was in his hand, the angel
of the LORD touched the meat and the un-
leavened bread. Fire flared from the rock,
consuming the meat and the bread. And
the angel of the LORD disappeared.
22When Gideon realized that it was the an-
gel of the LORD, he exclaimed, "Ah, Sover-
eign LORD! I have seen the angel of the
LORD face to face!"
23But the LORD said to him, "Peace! Do
not be afraid. You are not going to die."
24So Gideon built an altar to the LORD
there and called it The LORD is Peace. To
this day it stands in Ophrah of the Abiez-
rites.
25That same night the LORD said to him,
"Take the second bull from your father's
herd, the one seven years old.[c] Tear
down your father's altar to Baal and cut
down the Asherah pole[d] beside it. 26Then
build a proper kind of[e] altar to the LORD
your God on the top of this height. Using
the wood of the Asherah pole that you cut
down, offer the second[f] bull as a burnt
offering."
27So Gideon took ten of his servants and
did as the LORD told him. But because he
was afraid of his family and the men of the
town, he did it at night rather than in the
daytime.
28In the morning when the men of the
town got up, there was Baal's altar, demol-
ished, with the Asherah pole beside it cut
down and the second bull sacrificed on
the newly built altar!
29They asked each other, "Who did
this?"
When they carefully investigated, they
were told, "Gideon son of Joash did it."
30The men of the town demanded of Jo-
ash, "Bring out your son. He must die, be-
cause he has broken down Baal's altar and
cut down the Asherah pole beside it."
31But Joash replied to the hostile crowd
around him, "Are you going to plead
Baal's cause? Are you trying to save him?
Whoever fights for him shall be put to
death by morning! If Baal really is a god,
he can defend himself when someone
breaks down his altar." 32So that day they
called Gideon "Jerub-Baal,[g]" saying, "Let
Baal contend with him," because he broke
down Baal's altar.
33Now all the Midianites, Amalekites
and other eastern peoples joined forces
and crossed over the Jordan and camped
in the Valley of Jezreel. 34Then the Spirit
of the LORD came upon Gideon, and he
blew a trumpet, summoning the Abiez-
rites to follow him. 35He sent messengers
throughout Manasseh, calling them to

[a]15 Or *sir* [b]19 That is, probably about 3/5 bushel (about 22 liters) [c]25 Or *Take a full-grown, mature bull from your father's herd* [d]25 That is, a symbol of the goddess Asherah; here and elsewhere in Judges [e]26 Or *build with layers of stone an* [f]26 Or *full-grown*; also in verse 28
[g]32 *Jerub-Baal* means *let Baal contend.*

arms, and also into Asher, Zebulun and
Naphtali, so that they too went up to meet
them.
36Gideon said to God, "If you will save
Israel by my hand as you have promised— 37look, I will place a wool fleece on
the threshing floor. If there is dew only on
the fleece and all the ground is dry, then
I will know that you will save Israel by my
hand, as you said." 38And that is what
happened. Gideon rose early the next day;
he squeezed the fleece and wrung out the
dew—a bowlful of water.
39Then Gideon said to God, "Do not be
angry with me. Let me make just one
more request. Allow me one more test
with the fleece. This time make the fleece
dry and the ground covered with dew."
40That night God did so. Only the fleece
was dry; all the ground was covered with
dew.

Gideon Defeats the Midianites

7 Early in the morning, Jerub-Baal (that
is, Gideon) and all his men camped at
the spring of Harod. The camp of Midian
was north of them in the valley near the
hill of Moreh. 2The Lord said to Gideon,
"You have too many men for me to deliver
Midian into their hands. In order that Israel may not boast against me that her own
strength has saved her, 3announce now to
the people, 'Anyone who trembles with
fear may turn back and leave Mount Gilead.' " So twenty-two thousand men left,
while ten thousand remained.
4But the Lord said to Gideon, "There
are still too many men. Take them down
to the water, and I will sift them for you
there. If I say, 'This one shall go with you,'
he shall go; but if I say, 'This one shall not
go with you,' he shall not go."
5So Gideon took the men down to the
water. There the Lord told him, "Separate
those who lap the water with their
tongues like a dog from those who kneel
down to drink." 6Three hundred men
lapped with their hands to their mouths.
All the rest got down on their knees to
drink.
7The Lord said to Gideon, "With the
three hundred men that lapped I will save
you and give the Midianites into your
hands. Let all the other men go, each to
his own place." 8So Gideon sent the rest of
the Israelites to their tents but kept the
three hundred, who took over the provisions and trumpets of the others.
Now the camp of Midian lay below him
in the valley. 9During that night the Lord
said to Gideon, "Get up, go down against
the camp, because I am going to give it
into your hands. 10If you are afraid to attack, go down to the camp with your servant Purah 11and listen to what they are
saying. Afterward, you will be encouraged
to attack the camp." So he and Purah his
servant went down to the outposts of the
camp. 12The Midianites, the Amalekites
and all the other eastern peoples had settled in the valley, thick as locusts. Their
camels could no more be counted than
the sand on the seashore.
13Gideon arrived just as a man was telling a friend his dream. "I had a dream," he
was saying. "A round loaf of barley bread
came tumbling into the Midianite camp. It
struck the tent with such force that the
tent overturned and collapsed."
14His friend responded, "This can be
nothing other than the sword of Gideon
son of Joash, the Israelite. God has given
the Midianites and the whole camp into
his hands."
15When Gideon heard the dream and its
interpretation, he worshiped God. He returned to the camp of Israel and called
out, "Get up! The Lord has given the Midianite camp into your hands." 16Dividing
the three hundred men into three companies, he placed trumpets and empty jars in
the hands of all of them, with torches inside.
17"Watch me," he told them. "Follow
my lead. When I get to the edge of the
camp, do exactly as I do. 18When I and all
who are with me blow our trumpets, then
from all around the camp blow yours and
shout, 'For the Lord and for Gideon.' "
19Gideon and the hundred men with
him reached the edge of the camp at the
beginning of the middle watch, just after
they had changed the guard. They blew
their trumpets and broke the jars that
were in their hands. 20The three companies blew the trumpets and smashed the
jars. Grasping the torches in their left
hands and holding in their right hands the
trumpets they were to blow, they shouted,
"A sword for the Lord and for Gideon!"
21While each man held his position
around the camp, all the Midianites ran,
crying out as they fled.
22When the three hundred trumpets
sounded, the Lord caused the men
throughout the camp to turn on each other with their swords. The army fled to
Beth Shittah toward Zererah as far as the

border of Abel Meholah near Tabbath.
23Israelites from Naphtali, Asher and all
Manasseh were called out, and they pur-
sued the Midianites. 24Gideon sent mes-
sengers throughout the hill country of
Ephraim, saying, "Come down against the
Midianites and seize the waters of the Jor-
dan ahead of them as far as Beth Barah."

So all the men of Ephraim were called
out and they took the waters of the Jordan
as far as Beth Barah. 25They also captured
two of the Midianite leaders, Oreb and
Zeeb. They killed Oreb at the rock of Oreb,
and Zeeb at the winepress of Zeeb. They
pursued the Midianites and brought the
heads of Oreb and Zeeb to Gideon, who
was by the Jordan.

Zebah and Zalmunna

8 Now the Ephraimites asked Gideon,
"Why have you treated us like this?
Why didn't you call us when you went to
fight Midian?" And they criticized him
sharply.

2But he answered them, "What have I
accomplished compared to you? Aren't
the gleanings of Ephraim's grapes better
than the full grape harvest of Abiezer?
3God gave Oreb and Zeeb, the Midianite
leaders, into your hands. What was I able
to do compared to you?" At this, their re-
sentment against him subsided.

4Gideon and his three hundred men, ex-
hausted yet keeping up the pursuit, came
to the Jordan and crossed it. 5He said to
the men of Succoth, "Give my troops
some bread; they are worn out, and I am
still pursuing Zebah and Zalmunna, the
kings of Midian."

6But the officials of Succoth said, "Do
you already have the hands of Zebah and
Zalmunna in your possession? Why
should we give bread to your troops?"

7Then Gideon replied, "Just for that,
when the LORD has given Zebah and Zal-
munna into my hand, I will tear your flesh
with desert thorns and briers."

8From there he went up to Peniel[a] and
made the same request of them, but they
answered as the men of Succoth had. 9So
he said to the men of Peniel, "When I re-
turn in triumph, I will tear down this
tower."

10Now Zebah and Zalmunna were in
Karkor with a force of about fifteen thou-
sand men, all that were left of the armies
of the eastern peoples; a hundred and
twenty thousand swordsmen had fallen.
11Gideon went up by the route of the no-
mads east of Nobah and Jogbehah and fell
upon the unsuspecting army. 12Zebah and
Zalmunna, the two kings of Midian, fled,
but he pursued them and captured them,
routing their entire army.

13Gideon son of Joash then returned
from the battle by the Pass of Heres. 14He
caught a young man of Succoth and ques-
tioned him, and the young man wrote
down for him the names of the seventy-
seven officials of Succoth, the elders of the
town. 15Then Gideon came and said to the
men of Succoth, "Here are Zebah and Zal-
munna, about whom you taunted me by
saying, 'Do you already have the hands of
Zebah and Zalmunna in your possession?
Why should we give bread to your ex-
hausted men?' " 16He took the elders of
the town and taught the men of Succoth a
lesson by punishing them with desert
thorns and briers. 17He also pulled down
the tower of Peniel and killed the men of
the town.

18Then he asked Zebah and Zalmunna,
"What kind of men did you kill at Tabor?"

"Men like you," they answered, "each
one with the bearing of a prince."

19Gideon replied, "Those were my
brothers, the sons of my own mother. As
surely as the LORD lives, if you had spared
their lives, I would not kill you." 20Turn-
ing to Jether, his oldest son, he said, "Kill
them!" But Jether did not draw his sword,
because he was only a boy and was afraid.

21Zebah and Zalmunna said, "Come, do
it yourself. 'As is the man, so is his
strength.' " So Gideon stepped forward
and killed them, and took the ornaments
off their camels' necks.

Gideon's Ephod

22The Israelites said to Gideon, "Rule
over us—you, your son and your grand-
son—because you have saved us out of
the hand of Midian."

23But Gideon told them, "I will not rule
over you, nor will my son rule over you.
The LORD will rule over you." 24And he
said, "I do have one request, that each of
you give me an earring from your share of
the plunder." (It was the custom of the
Ishmaelites to wear gold earrings.)

25They answered, "We'll be glad to give
them." So they spread out a garment, and
each man threw a ring from his plunder

[a]8 Hebrew *Penuel*, a variant of *Peniel*; also in verses 9 and 17

onto it. 26The weight of the gold rings he
asked for came to seventeen hundred
shekels,[a] not counting the ornaments,
the pendants and the purple garments
worn by the kings of Midian or the chains
that were on their camels' necks. 27Gideon
made the gold into an ephod, which he
placed in Ophrah, his town. All Israel
prostituted themselves by worshiping it
there, and it became a snare to Gideon
and his family.

Gideon's Death

28Thus Midian was subdued before the
Israelites and did not raise its head again.
During Gideon's lifetime, the land en-
joyed peace forty years.

29Jerub-Baal son of Joash went back
home to live. 30He had seventy sons of his
own, for he had many wives. 31His concu-
bine, who lived in Shechem, also bore him
a son, whom he named Abimelech. 32Gid-
eon son of Joash died at a good old age
and was buried in the tomb of his father
Joash in Ophrah of the Abiezrites.

33No sooner had Gideon died than the
Israelites again prostituted themselves to
the Baals. They set up Baal-Berith as their
god and 34did not remember the LORD
their God, who had rescued them from the
hands of all their enemies on every side.
35They also failed to show kindness to the
family of Jerub-Baal (that is, Gideon) for
all the good things he had done for them.

Abimelech

9 Abimelech son of Jerub-Baal went to
his mother's brothers in Shechem and
said to them and to all his mother's clan,
2"Ask all the citizens of Shechem, 'Which
is better for you: to have all seventy of Jer-
ub-Baal's sons rule over you, or just one
man?' Remember, I am your flesh and
blood."

3When the brothers repeated all this to
the citizens of Shechem, they were in-
clined to follow Abimelech, for they said,
"He is our brother." 4They gave him sev-
enty shekels[b] of silver from the temple of
Baal-Berith, and Abimelech used it to hire
reckless adventurers, who became his fol-
lowers. 5He went to his father's home in
Ophrah and on one stone murdered his
seventy brothers, the sons of Jerub-Baal.
But Jotham, the youngest son of Jerub-
Baal, escaped by hiding. 6Then all the citi-
zens of Shechem and Beth Millo gathered
beside the great tree at the pillar in She-
chem to crown Abimelech king.

7When Jotham was told about this, he
climbed up on the top of Mount Gerizim
and shouted to them, "Listen to me, citi-
zens of Shechem, so that God may listen
to you. 8One day the trees went out to
anoint a king for themselves. They said to
the olive tree, 'Be our king.'

9"But the olive tree answered, 'Should I
give up my oil, by which both gods and
men are honored, to hold sway over the
trees?'

10"Next, the trees said to the fig tree,
'Come and be our king.'

11"But the fig tree replied, 'Should I give
up my fruit, so good and sweet, to hold
sway over the trees?'

12"Then the trees said to the vine,
'Come and be our king.'

13"But the vine answered, 'Should I give
up my wine, which cheers both gods and
men, to hold sway over the trees?'

14"Finally all the trees said to the thorn-
bush, 'Come and be our king.'

15"The thornbush said to the trees, 'If
you really want to anoint me king over
you, come and take refuge in my shade;
but if not, then let fire come out of the
thornbush and consume the cedars of
Lebanon!'

16"Now if you have acted honorably
and in good faith when you made Abime-
lech king, and if you have been fair to Jer-
ub-Baal and his family, and if you have
treated him as he deserves— 17and to
think that my father fought for you, risked
his life to rescue you from the hand of
Midian 18(but today you have revolted
against my father's family, murdered his
seventy sons on a single stone, and made
Abimelech, the son of his slave girl, king
over the citizens of Shechem because he
is your brother)— 19if then you have act-
ed honorably and in good faith toward
Jerub-Baal and his family today, may
Abimelech be your joy, and may you be
his, too! 20But if you have not, let fire
come out from Abimelech and consume
you, citizens of Shechem and Beth Millo,
and let fire come out from you, citizens of
Shechem and Beth Millo, and consume
Abimelech!"

21Then Jotham fled, escaping to Beer,

[a]26 That is, about 43 pounds (about 19.5 kilograms)

[b]4 That is, about 1 3/4 pounds (about 0.8 kilogram)

and he lived there because he was afraid
of his brother Abimelech.
22After Abimelech had governed Israel
three years, 23God sent an evil spirit be-
tween Abimelech and the citizens of She-
chem, who acted treacherously against
Abimelech. 24God did this in order that
the crime against Jerub-Baal's seventy
sons, the shedding of their blood, might
be avenged on their brother Abimelech
and on the citizens of Shechem, who had
helped him murder his brothers. 25In op-
position to him these citizens of Shechem
set men on the hilltops to ambush and rob
everyone who passed by, and this was re-
ported to Abimelech.
26Now Gaal son of Ebed moved with his
brothers into Shechem, and its citizens
put their confidence in him. 27After they
had gone out into the fields and gathered
the grapes and trodden them, they held a
festival in the temple of their god. While
they were eating and drinking, they
cursed Abimelech. 28Then Gaal son of
Ebed said, "Who is Abimelech, and who is
Shechem, that we should be subject to
him? Isn't he Jerub-Baal's son, and isn't
Zebul his deputy? Serve the men of Ha-
mor, Shechem's father! Why should we
serve Abimelech? 29If only this people
were under my command! Then I would
get rid of him. I would say to Abimelech,
'Call out your whole army!' "[a]
30When Zebul the governor of the city
heard what Gaal son of Ebed said, he was
very angry. 31Under cover he sent messen-
gers to Abimelech, saying, "Gaal son of
Ebed and his brothers have come to She-
chem and are stirring up the city against
you. 32Now then, during the night you
and your men should come and lie in wait
in the fields. 33In the morning at sunrise,
advance against the city. When Gaal and
his men come out against you, do whatev-
er your hand finds to do."
34So Abimelech and all his troops set
out by night and took up concealed posi-
tions near Shechem in four companies.
35Now Gaal son of Ebed had gone out and
was standing at the entrance to the city
gate just as Abimelech and his soldiers
came out from their hiding place.
36When Gaal saw them, he said to Ze-
bul, "Look, people are coming down from
the tops of the mountains!"
Zebul replied, "You mistake the shad-
ows of the mountains for men."
37But Gaal spoke up again: "Look, peo-
ple are coming down from the center of
the land, and a company is coming from
the direction of the soothsayers' tree."
38Then Zebul said to him, "Where is
your big talk now, you who said, 'Who is
Abimelech that we should be subject to
him?' Aren't these the men you ridiculed?
Go out and fight them!"
39So Gaal led out[b] the citizens of She-
chem and fought Abimelech. 40Abimelech
chased him, and many fell wounded in
the flight—all the way to the entrance to
the gate. 41Abimelech stayed in Arumah,
and Zebul drove Gaal and his brothers out
of Shechem.
42The next day the people of Shechem
went out to the fields, and this was report-
ed to Abimelech. 43So he took his men, di-
vided them into three companies and set
an ambush in the fields. When he saw the
people coming out of the city, he rose to
attack them. 44Abimelech and the compa-
nies with him rushed forward to a posi-
tion at the entrance to the city gate. Then
two companies rushed upon those in the
fields and struck them down. 45All that
day Abimelech pressed his attack against
the city until he had captured it and killed
its people. Then he destroyed the city and
scattered salt over it.
46On hearing this, the citizens in the
tower of Shechem went into the strong-
hold of the temple of El-Berith. 47When
Abimelech heard that they had assembled
there, 48he and all his men went up Mount
Zalmon. He took an ax and cut off some
branches, which he lifted to his shoulders.
He ordered the men with him, "Quick! Do
what you have seen me do!" 49So all the
men cut branches and followed Abime-
lech. They piled them against the strong-
hold and set it on fire over the people in-
side. So all the people in the tower of
Shechem, about a thousand men and
women, also died.
50Next Abimelech went to Thebez and
besieged it and captured it. 51Inside the
city, however, was a strong tower, to
which all the men and women—all the
people of the city—fled. They locked
themselves in and climbed up on the tow-
er roof. 52Abimelech went to the tower
and stormed it. But as he approached the

[a]29 Septuagint; Hebrew *him." Then he said to Abimelech, "Call out your whole army!"* [b]39 Or *Gaal went out in the sight of*

entrance to the tower to set it on fire, 53a
woman dropped an upper millstone on
his head and cracked his skull.
54Hurriedly he called to his armor-bear-
er, "Draw your sword and kill me, so that
they can't say, 'A woman killed him.' " So
his servant ran him through, and he died.
55When the Israelites saw that Abimelech
was dead, they went home.
56Thus God repaid the wickedness that
Abimelech had done to his father by mur-
dering his seventy brothers. 57God also
made the men of Shechem pay for all their
wickedness. The curse of Jotham son of
Jerub-Baal came on them.

Tola

10 After the time of Abimelech a man
of Issachar, Tola son of Puah, the
son of Dodo, rose to save Israel. He lived
in Shamir, in the hill country of Ephraim.
2He led[a] Israel twenty-three years; then
he died, and was buried in Shamir.

Jair

3He was followed by Jair of Gilead, who
led Israel twenty-two years. 4He had thirty
sons, who rode thirty donkeys. They con-
trolled thirty towns in Gilead, which to
this day are called Havvoth Jair.[b] 5When
Jair died, he was buried in Kamon.

Jephthah

6Again the Israelites did evil in the eyes
of the LORD. They served the Baals and the
Ashtoreths, and the gods of Aram, the
gods of Sidon, the gods of Moab, the gods
of the Ammonites and the gods of the Phi-
listines. And because the Israelites for-
sook the LORD and no longer served him,
7he became angry with them. He sold
them into the hands of the Philistines and
the Ammonites, 8who that year shattered
and crushed them. For eighteen years
they oppressed all the Israelites on the
east side of the Jordan in Gilead, the land
of the Amorites. 9The Ammonites also
crossed the Jordan to fight against Judah,
Benjamin and the house of Ephraim; and
Israel was in great distress. 10Then the Is-
raelites cried out to the LORD, "We have
sinned against you, forsaking our God and
serving the Baals."
11The LORD replied, "When the Egyp-
tians, the Amorites, the Ammonites, the
Philistines, 12the Sidonians, the Amalek-
ites and the Maonites[c] oppressed you
and you cried to me for help, did I not save
you from their hands? 13But you have for-
saken me and served other gods, so I will
no longer save you. 14Go and cry out to
the gods you have chosen. Let them save
you when you are in trouble!"
15But the Israelites said to the LORD,
"We have sinned. Do with us whatever
you think best, but please rescue us now."
16Then they got rid of the foreign gods
among them and served the LORD. And he
could bear Israel's misery no longer.
17When the Ammonites were called to
arms and camped in Gilead, the Israelites
assembled and camped at Mizpah. 18The
leaders of the people of Gilead said to
each other, "Whoever will launch the at-
tack against the Ammonites will be the
head of all those living in Gilead."

11 Jephthah the Gileadite was a
mighty warrior. His father was Gil-
ead; his mother was a prostitute. 2Gilead's
wife also bore him sons, and when they
were grown up, they drove Jephthah
away. "You are not going to get any inheri-
tance in our family," they said, "because
you are the son of another woman." 3So
Jephthah fled from his brothers and set-
tled in the land of Tob, where a group of
adventurers gathered around him and fol-
lowed him.
4Some time later, when the Ammonites
made war on Israel, 5the elders of Gilead
went to get Jephthah from the land of
Tob. 6"Come," they said, "be our com-
mander, so we can fight the Ammonites."
7Jephthah said to them, "Didn't you
hate me and drive me from my father's
house? Why do you come to me now,
when you're in trouble?"
8The elders of Gilead said to him, "Nev-
ertheless, we are turning to you now;
come with us to fight the Ammonites, and
you will be our head over all who live in
Gilead."
9Jephthah answered, "Suppose you
take me back to fight the Ammonites and
the LORD gives them to me—will I really
be your head?"
10The elders of Gilead replied, "The
LORD is our witness; we will certainly do
as you say." 11So Jephthah went with the
elders of Gilead, and the people made him
head and commander over them. And he

[a] 2 Traditionally *judged*; also in verse 3 [b] 4 Or *called the settlements of Jair* [c] 12 Hebrew; some Septuagint manuscripts *Midianites*

repeated all his words before the LORD in
Mizpah.
12Then Jephthah sent messengers to
the Ammonite king with the question:
"What do you have against us that you
have attacked our country?"
13The king of the Ammonites answered
Jephthah's messengers, "When Israel
came up out of Egypt, they took away my
land from the Arnon to the Jabbok, all the
way to the Jordan. Now give it back peace-
ably."
14Jephthah sent back messengers to the
Ammonite king, 15saying:

"This is what Jephthah says: Israel
did not take the land of Moab or the
land of the Ammonites. 16But when

VERSE FOR THE DAY: Judges 10:6–7 | AUTHOR: Ron and Jeanette Lee | PASSAGE FOR THE DAY: Judges 10:6–16

God's Patience

God's patience with us is unfathomable. How many times did the people of Israel turn their backs on the Lord to worship foreign gods? And how many times did he punish them, only to welcome them back later with open arms?

We can learn two important lessons from God's patience with his wayward children. First, although our sin angers him, he always makes his mercy available to us when we seek his forgiveness. No matter how badly we fail him, he still desires an intimate relationship with us. And even when we are reaping the sour fruit of our misdeeds, he tries to draw us back into his waiting arms.

Second, we should extend the same kind of patience, and mercy, to our spouses. How many times do we say to each other, "I *told* you not to overdraw the checking account! Why do you keep forgetting?" Or, "You left the gas gauge on empty again! Why can't you remember to fill up on your way home?"

If a holy God can bear with us in spite of our daily transgressions, why can't we extend to each other a larger dose of mercy and acceptance? No matter how frustrated we may become with our spouse, approaching each other with open arms—rather than anger or silence—presents a clearer picture of God's patience with each of us.

MARRIAGE BUILDERS

♦ *What has your mate done or said in the past few weeks that really annoyed you?*
♦ *How can you communicate patience and mercy in your actions?*

Additional Scripture Readings
Deuteronomy 13:12–18;
1 Timothy 1:12–17

Go to page 264 for your next devotional reading.

they came up out of Egypt, Israel
went through the desert to the Red
Sea[a] and on to Kadesh. 17Then Israel
sent messengers to the king of Edom,
saying, 'Give us permission to go
through your country,' but the king
of Edom would not listen. They sent
also to the king of Moab, and he re-
fused. So Israel stayed at Kadesh.
18"Next they traveled through the
desert, skirted the lands of Edom and
Moab, passed along the eastern side
of the country of Moab, and camped
on the other side of the Arnon. They
did not enter the territory of Moab,
for the Arnon was its border.
19"Then Israel sent messengers to
Sihon king of the Amorites, who
ruled in Heshbon, and said to him,
'Let us pass through your country to
our own place.' 20Sihon, however, did
not trust Israel[b] to pass through his
territory. He mustered all his men
and encamped at Jahaz and fought
with Israel.
21"Then the LORD, the God of Israel,
gave Sihon and all his men into Isra-
el's hands, and they defeated them.
Israel took over all the land of the
Amorites who lived in that country,
22capturing all of it from the Arnon to
the Jabbok and from the desert to the
Jordan.
23"Now since the LORD, the God of
Israel, has driven the Amorites out
before his people Israel, what right
have you to take it over? 24Will you
not take what your god Chemosh
gives you? Likewise, whatever the
LORD our God has given us, we will
possess. 25Are you better than Balak
son of Zippor, king of Moab? Did he
ever quarrel with Israel or fight with
them? 26For three hundred years Isra-
el occupied Heshbon, Aroer, the sur-
rounding settlements and all the
towns along the Arnon. Why didn't
you retake them during that time? 27I
have not wronged you, but you are
doing me wrong by waging war
against me. Let the LORD, the Judge,[c]
decide the dispute this day between
the Israelites and the Ammonites."
28The king of Ammon, however, paid no
attention to the message Jephthah sent
him.
29Then the Spirit of the LORD came upon
Jephthah. He crossed Gilead and Manas-
seh, passed through Mizpah of Gilead,
and from there he advanced against the
Ammonites. 30And Jephthah made a vow
to the LORD: "If you give the Ammonites
into my hands, 31whatever comes out of
the door of my house to meet me when I
return in triumph from the Ammonites
will be the LORD's, and I will sacrifice it as
a burnt offering."
32Then Jephthah went over to fight the
Ammonites, and the LORD gave them into
his hands. 33He devastated twenty towns
from Aroer to the vicinity of Minnith, as
far as Abel Keramim. Thus Israel subdued
Ammon.
34When Jephthah returned to his home
in Mizpah, who should come out to meet
him but his daughter, dancing to the
sound of tambourines! She was an only
child. Except for her he had neither son
nor daughter. 35When he saw her, he tore
his clothes and cried, "Oh! My daughter!
You have made me miserable and wretch-
ed, because I have made a vow to the LORD
that I cannot break."
36"My father," she replied, "you have
given your word to the LORD. Do to me just
as you promised, now that the LORD has
avenged you of your enemies, the Am-
monites. 37But grant me this one request,"
she said. "Give me two months to roam
the hills and weep with my friends, be-
cause I will never marry."
38"You may go," he said. And he let her
go for two months. She and the girls went
into the hills and wept because she would
never marry. 39After the two months, she
returned to her father and he did to her as
he had vowed. And she was a virgin.
From this comes the Israelite custom
40that each year the young women of Isra-
el go out for four days to commemorate
the daughter of Jephthah the Gileadite.

Jephthah and Ephraim

12 The men of Ephraim called out
their forces, crossed over to Za-
phon and said to Jephthah, "Why did you
go to fight the Ammonites without calling
us to go with you? We're going to burn
down your house over your head."
2Jephthah answered, "I and my people

[a] 16 Hebrew *Yam Suph*; that is, Sea of Reeds
[b] 20 Or *however, would not make an agreement for Israel*
[c] 27 Or *Ruler*

were engaged in a great struggle with the Ammonites, and although I called, you didn't save me out of their hands. 3When I saw that you wouldn't help, I took my life in my hands and crossed over to fight the Ammonites, and the LORD gave me the victory over them. Now why have you come up today to fight me?"

4Jephthah then called together the men of Gilead and fought against Ephraim. The Gileadites struck them down because the Ephraimites had said, "You Gileadites are renegades from Ephraim and Manasseh." 5The Gileadites captured the fords of the Jordan leading to Ephraim, and whenever a survivor of Ephraim said, "Let me cross over," the men of Gilead asked him, "Are you an Ephraimite?" If he replied, "No," 6they said, "All right, say 'Shibboleth.' " If he said, "Sibboleth," because he could not pronounce the word correctly, they seized him and killed him at the fords of the Jordan. Forty-two thousand Ephraimites were killed at that time.

7Jephthah led[a] Israel six years. Then Jephthah the Gileadite died, and was buried in a town in Gilead.

Ibzan, Elon and Abdon

8After him, Ibzan of Bethlehem led Israel. 9He had thirty sons and thirty daughters. He gave his daughters away in marriage to those outside his clan, and for his sons he brought in thirty young women as wives from outside his clan. Ibzan led Israel seven years. 10Then Ibzan died, and was buried in Bethlehem.

11After him, Elon the Zebulunite led Israel ten years. 12Then Elon died, and was buried in Aijalon in the land of Zebulun.

13After him, Abdon son of Hillel, from Pirathon, led Israel. 14He had forty sons and thirty grandsons, who rode on seventy donkeys. He led Israel eight years. 15Then Abdon son of Hillel died, and was buried at Pirathon in Ephraim, in the hill country of the Amalekites.

The Birth of Samson

13 Again the Israelites did evil in the eyes of the LORD, so the LORD delivered them into the hands of the Philistines for forty years.

2A certain man of Zorah, named Manoah, from the clan of the Danites, had a wife who was sterile and remained childless. 3The angel of the LORD appeared to her and said, "You are sterile and childless, but you are going to conceive and have a son. 4Now see to it that you drink no wine or other fermented drink and that you do not eat anything unclean, 5because you will conceive and give birth to a son. No razor may be used on his head, because the boy is to be a Nazirite, set apart to God from birth, and he will begin the deliverance of Israel from the hands of the Philistines."

6Then the woman went to her husband and told him, "A man of God came to me. He looked like an angel of God, very awesome. I didn't ask him where he came from, and he didn't tell me his name. 7But he said to me, 'You will conceive and give birth to a son. Now then, drink no wine or other fermented drink and do not eat anything unclean, because the boy will be a Nazirite of God from birth until the day of his death.' "

8Then Manoah prayed to the LORD: "O Lord, I beg you, let the man of God you sent to us come again to teach us how to bring up the boy who is to be born."

9God heard Manoah, and the angel of God came again to the woman while she was out in the field; but her husband Manoah was not with her. 10The woman hurried to tell her husband, "He's here! The man who appeared to me the other day!"

11Manoah got up and followed his wife. When he came to the man, he said, "Are you the one who talked to my wife?"

"I am," he said.

12So Manoah asked him, "When your words are fulfilled, what is to be the rule for the boy's life and work?"

13The angel of the LORD answered, "Your wife must do all that I have told her. 14She must not eat anything that comes from the grapevine, nor drink any wine or other fermented drink nor eat anything unclean. She must do everything I have commanded her."

15Manoah said to the angel of the LORD, "We would like you to stay until we prepare a young goat for you."

16The angel of the LORD replied, "Even though you detain me, I will not eat any of your food. But if you prepare a burnt offering, offer it to the LORD." (Manoah did not realize that it was the angel of the LORD.)

17Then Manoah inquired of the angel of the LORD, "What is your name, so that we

[a]7 Traditionally *judged*; also in verses 8-14

may honor you when your word comes
true?"
18He replied, "Why do you ask my
name? It is beyond understanding.[a]"
19Then Manoah took a young goat, togeth-
er with the grain offering, and sacrificed it
on a rock to the LORD. And the LORD did an
amazing thing while Manoah and his wife
watched: 20As the flame blazed up from
the altar toward heaven, the angel of the
LORD ascended in the flame. Seeing this,
Manoah and his wife fell with their faces
to the ground. 21When the angel of the
LORD did not show himself again to Mano-
ah and his wife, Manoah realized that it
was the angel of the LORD.
22"We are doomed to die!" he said to his
wife. "We have seen God!"
23But his wife answered, "If the LORD
had meant to kill us, he would not have
accepted a burnt offering and grain offer-
ing from our hands, nor shown us all
these things or now told us this."
24The woman gave birth to a boy and
named him Samson. He grew and the
LORD blessed him, 25and the Spirit of the
LORD began to stir him while he was in
Mahaneh Dan, between Zorah and Esh-
taol.

Samson's Marriage

14 Samson went down to Timnah and
saw there a young Philistine wom-
an. 2When he returned, he said to his fa-
ther and mother, "I have seen a Philistine
woman in Timnah; now get her for me as
my wife."
3His father and mother replied, "Isn't
there an acceptable woman among your
relatives or among all our people? Must
you go to the uncircumcised Philistines to
get a wife?"
But Samson said to his father, "Get her
for me. She's the right one for me." 4(His
parents did not know that this was from
the LORD, who was seeking an occasion to
confront the Philistines; for at that time
they were ruling over Israel.) 5Samson
went down to Timnah together with his
father and mother. As they approached
the vineyards of Timnah, suddenly a
young lion came roaring toward him.
6The Spirit of the LORD came upon him in
power so that he tore the lion apart with
his bare hands as he might have torn a
young goat. But he told neither his father
nor his mother what he had done. 7Then
he went down and talked with the wom-
an, and he liked her.
8Some time later, when he went back to
marry her, he turned aside to look at the
lion's carcass. In it was a swarm of bees
and some honey, 9which he scooped out
with his hands and ate as he went along.
When he rejoined his parents, he gave
them some, and they too ate it. But he did
not tell them that he had taken the honey
from the lion's carcass.
10Now his father went down to see the
woman. And Samson made a feast there,
as was customary for bridegrooms.
11When he appeared, he was given thirty
companions.
12"Let me tell you a riddle," Samson
said to them. "If you can give me the an-
swer within the seven days of the feast, I
will give you thirty linen garments and
thirty sets of clothes. 13If you can't tell me
the answer, you must give me thirty linen
garments and thirty sets of clothes."
"Tell us your riddle," they said. "Let's
hear it."
14He replied,

"Out of the eater, something to eat;
out of the strong, something sweet."

For three days they could not give the an-
swer.
15On the fourth[b] day, they said to Sam-
son's wife, "Coax your husband into ex-
plaining the riddle for us, or we will burn
you and your father's household to death.
Did you invite us here to rob us?"
16Then Samson's wife threw herself on
him, sobbing, "You hate me! You don't
really love me. You've given my people a
riddle, but you haven't told me the an-
swer."
"I haven't even explained it to my father
or mother," he replied, "so why should I
explain it to you?" 17She cried the whole
seven days of the feast. So on the seventh
day he finally told her, because she con-
tinued to press him. She in turn explained
the riddle to her people.
18Before sunset on the seventh day the
men of the town said to him,

"What is sweeter than honey?
What is stronger than a lion?"

Samson said to them,

"If you had not plowed with my
heifer,

[a]18 Or *is wonderful* [b]15 Some Septuagint manuscripts and Syriac; Hebrew *seventh*

you would not have solved my
riddle."

19Then the Spirit of the LORD came upon
him in power. He went down to Ashkelon,
struck down thirty of their men, stripped
them of their belongings and gave their
clothes to those who had explained the
riddle. Burning with anger, he went up to
his father's house. 20And Samson's wife
was given to the friend who had attended
him at his wedding.

Samson's Vengeance on the Philistines

15 Later on, at the time of wheat harvest, Samson took a young goat
and went to visit his wife. He said, "I'm
going to my wife's room." But her father
would not let him go in.

2"I was so sure you thoroughly hated
her," he said, "that I gave her to your
friend. Isn't her younger sister more attractive? Take her instead."

3Samson said to them, "This time I have
a right to get even with the Philistines; I
will really harm them." 4So he went out
and caught three hundred foxes and tied
them tail to tail in pairs. He then fastened
a torch to every pair of tails, 5lit the
torches and let the foxes loose in the
standing grain of the Philistines. He
burned up the shocks and standing grain,
together with the vineyards and olive
groves.

6When the Philistines asked, "Who did
this?" they were told, "Samson, the Timnite's son-in-law, because his wife was
given to his friend."

So the Philistines went up and burned
her and her father to death. 7Samson said
to them, "Since you've acted like this, I
won't stop until I get my revenge on you."
8He attacked them viciously and slaughtered many of them. Then he went down
and stayed in a cave in the rock of Etam.

9The Philistines went up and camped in
Judah, spreading out near Lehi. 10The
men of Judah asked, "Why have you come
to fight us?"

"We have come to take Samson prisoner," they answered, "to do to him as he did
to us."

11Then three thousand men from Judah
went down to the cave in the rock of Etam
and said to Samson, "Don't you realize
that the Philistines are rulers over us?
What have you done to us?"

He answered, "I merely did to them
what they did to me."

12They said to him, "We've come to tie
you up and hand you over to the Philistines."

Samson said, "Swear to me that you
won't kill me yourselves."

13"Agreed," they answered. "We will
only tie you up and hand you over to
them. We will not kill you." So they bound
him with two new ropes and led him up
from the rock. 14As he approached Lehi,
the Philistines came toward him shouting.
The Spirit of the LORD came upon him in
power. The ropes on his arms became like
charred flax, and the bindings dropped
from his hands. 15Finding a fresh jawbone
of a donkey, he grabbed it and struck
down a thousand men.

16Then Samson said,

"With a donkey's jawbone
I have made donkeys of them.[a]
With a donkey's jawbone
I have killed a thousand men."

17When he finished speaking, he threw
away the jawbone; and the place was
called Ramath Lehi.[b]

18Because he was very thirsty, he cried
out to the LORD, "You have given your servant this great victory. Must I now die of
thirst and fall into the hands of the uncircumcised?" 19Then God opened up the
hollow place in Lehi, and water came out
of it. When Samson drank, his strength returned and he revived. So the spring was
called En Hakkore,[c] and it is still there in
Lehi.

20Samson led[d] Israel for twenty years
in the days of the Philistines.

Samson and Delilah

16 One day Samson went to Gaza,
where he saw a prostitute. He went
in to spend the night with her. 2The people of Gaza were told, "Samson is here!"
So they surrounded the place and lay in
wait for him all night at the city gate. They
made no move during the night, saying,
"At dawn we'll kill him."

3But Samson lay there only until the
middle of the night. Then he got up and
took hold of the doors of the city gate, together with the two posts, and tore them

[a]16 Or *made a heap or two*; the Hebrew for *donkey* sounds like the Hebrew for *heap*. [b]17 *Ramath Lehi* means *jawbone hill*. [c]19 *En Hakkore* means *caller's spring*. [d]20 Traditionally *judged*

loose, bar and all. He lifted them to his shoulders and carried them to the top of the hill that faces Hebron.

4Some time later, he fell in love with a woman in the Valley of Sorek whose name was Delilah. 5The rulers of the Philistines went to her and said, "See if you can lure him into showing you the secret of his great strength and how we can overpower him so we may tie him up and subdue him. Each one of us will give you eleven hundred shekels[a] of silver."

6So Delilah said to Samson, "Tell me the secret of your great strength and how you can be tied up and subdued."

7Samson answered her, "If anyone ties me with seven fresh thongs[b] that have not been dried, I'll become as weak as any other man."

8Then the rulers of the Philistines brought her seven fresh thongs that had not been dried, and she tied him with them. 9With men hidden in the room, she called to him, "Samson, the Philistines are upon you!" But he snapped the thongs as easily as a piece of string snaps when it comes close to a flame. So the secret of his strength was not discovered.

10Then Delilah said to Samson, "You have made a fool of me; you lied to me. Come now, tell me how you can be tied."

11He said, "If anyone ties me securely with new ropes that have never been used, I'll become as weak as any other man."

12So Delilah took new ropes and tied him with them. Then, with men hidden in the room, she called to him, "Samson, the Philistines are upon you!" But he snapped the ropes off his arms as if they were threads.

13Delilah then said to Samson, "Until now, you have been making a fool of me and lying to me. Tell me how you can be tied."

He replied, "If you weave the seven braids of my head into the fabric ⌊on the loom⌋ and tighten it with the pin, I'll become as weak as any other man." So while he was sleeping, Delilah took the seven braids of his head, wove them into the fabric 14and[c] tightened it with the pin.

Again she called to him, "Samson, the Philistines are upon you!" He awoke from his sleep and pulled up the pin and the loom, with the fabric.

15Then she said to him, "How can you say, 'I love you,' when you won't confide in me? This is the third time you have made a fool of me and haven't told me the secret of your great strength." 16With such nagging she prodded him day after day until he was tired to death.

17So he told her everything. "No razor has ever been used on my head," he said, "because I have been a Nazirite set apart to God since birth. If my head were shaved, my strength would leave me, and I would become as weak as any other man."

18When Delilah saw that he had told her everything, she sent word to the rulers of the Philistines, "Come back once more; he has told me everything." So the rulers of the Philistines returned with the silver in their hands. 19Having put him to sleep on her lap, she called a man to shave off the seven braids of his hair, and so began to subdue him.[d] And his strength left him.

20Then she called, "Samson, the Philistines are upon you!"

He awoke from his sleep and thought, "I'll go out as before and shake myself free." But he did not know that the LORD had left him.

21Then the Philistines seized him, gouged out his eyes and took him down to Gaza. Binding him with bronze shackles, they set him to grinding in the prison. 22But the hair on his head began to grow again after it had been shaved.

The Death of Samson

23Now the rulers of the Philistines assembled to offer a great sacrifice to Dagon their god and to celebrate, saying, "Our god has delivered Samson, our enemy, into our hands."

24When the people saw him, they praised their god, saying,

"Our god has delivered our enemy
into our hands,
the one who laid waste our land
and multiplied our slain."

25While they were in high spirits, they shouted, "Bring out Samson to entertain us." So they called Samson out of the prison, and he performed for them.

[a] 5 That is, about 28 pounds (about 13 kilograms)
[b] 7 Or *bowstrings*; also in verses 8 and 9
[c] 13,14 Some Septuagint manuscripts; Hebrew "*⌊I can⌋ if you weave the seven braids of my head into the fabric ⌊on the loom⌋.*" 14 *So she*
[d] 19 Hebrew; some Septuagint manuscripts *and he began to weaken*

When they stood him among the pillars, 26Samson said to the servant who
held his hand, "Put me where I can feel
the pillars that support the temple, so that
I may lean against them." 27Now the tem-
ple was crowded with men and women;
all the rulers of the Philistines were there,
and on the roof were about three thou-
sand men and women watching Samson
perform. 28Then Samson prayed to the
LORD, "O Sovereign LORD, remember me.
O God, please strengthen me just once
more, and let me with one blow get re-
venge on the Philistines for my two eyes."
29Then Samson reached toward the two
central pillars on which the temple stood.
Bracing himself against them, his right
hand on the one and his left hand on the
other, 30Samson said, "Let me die with the
Philistines!" Then he pushed with all his
might, and down came the temple on the
rulers and all the people in it. Thus he
killed many more when he died than
while he lived.

31Then his brothers and his father's
whole family went down to get him. They
brought him back and buried him be-
tween Zorah and Eshtaol in the tomb of
Manoah his father. He had led[a] Israel
twenty years.

Micah's Idols

17 Now a man named Micah from the
hill country of Ephraim 2said to his
mother, "The eleven hundred shekels[b] of
silver that were taken from you and about
which I heard you utter a curse—I have
that silver with me; I took it."

Then his mother said, "The LORD bless
you, my son!"

3When he returned the eleven hundred
shekels of silver to his mother, she said, "I
solemnly consecrate my silver to the LORD
for my son to make a carved image and a
cast idol. I will give it back to you."

4So he returned the silver to his mother,
and she took two hundred shekels[c] of sil-
ver and gave them to a silversmith, who
made them into the image and the idol.
And they were put in Micah's house.

5Now this man Micah had a shrine, and
he made an ephod and some idols and in-
stalled one of his sons as his priest. 6In
those days Israel had no king; everyone
did as he saw fit.

7A young Levite from Bethlehem in Ju-
dah, who had been living within the clan
of Judah, 8left that town in search of some
other place to stay. On his way[d] he came
to Micah's house in the hill country of
Ephraim.

9Micah asked him, "Where are you
from?"

"I'm a Levite from Bethlehem in Ju-
dah," he said, "and I'm looking for a place
to stay."

10Then Micah said to him, "Live with
me and be my father and priest, and I'll
give you ten shekels[e] of silver a year,
your clothes and your food." 11So the Le-
vite agreed to live with him, and the
young man was to him like one of his
sons. 12Then Micah installed the Levite,
and the young man became his priest and
lived in his house. 13And Micah said,
"Now I know that the LORD will be good to
me, since this Levite has become my
priest."

Danites Settle in Laish

18 In those days Israel had no king.
And in those days the tribe of the
Danites was seeking a place of their own
where they might settle, because they had
not yet come into an inheritance among
the tribes of Israel. 2So the Danites sent
five warriors from Zorah and Eshtaol to
spy out the land and explore it. These men
represented all their clans. They told
them, "Go, explore the land."

The men entered the hill country of
Ephraim and came to the house of Micah,
where they spent the night. 3When they
were near Micah's house, they recognized
the voice of the young Levite; so they
turned in there and asked him, "Who
brought you here? What are you doing in
this place? Why are you here?"

4He told them what Micah had done for
him, and said, "He has hired me and I am
his priest."

5Then they said to him, "Please inquire
of God to learn whether our journey will
be successful."

6The priest answered them, "Go in
peace. Your journey has the LORD's ap-
proval."

7So the five men left and came to Laish,
where they saw that the people were liv-
ing in safety, like the Sidonians, unsus-

[a] 31 Traditionally *judged* [b] 2 That is, about 28 pounds (about 13 kilograms) [c] 4 That is, about 5 pounds (about 2.3 kilograms) [d] 8 Or *To carry on his profession* [e] 10 That is, about 4 ounces (about 110 grams)

pecting and secure. And since their land lacked nothing, they were prosperous.[a] Also, they lived a long way from the Sidonians and had no relationship with anyone else.[b]

8When they returned to Zorah and Eshtaol, their brothers asked them, "How did you find things?"

9They answered, "Come on, let's attack them! We have seen that the land is very good. Aren't you going to do something? Don't hesitate to go there and take it over. 10When you get there, you will find an unsuspecting people and a spacious land that God has put into your hands, a land that lacks nothing whatever."

11Then six hundred men from the clan of the Danites, armed for battle, set out from Zorah and Eshtaol. 12On their way they set up camp near Kiriath Jearim in Judah. This is why the place west of Kiriath Jearim is called Mahaneh Dan[c] to this day. 13From there they went on to the hill country of Ephraim and came to Micah's house.

14Then the five men who had spied out the land of Laish said to their brothers, "Do you know that one of these houses has an ephod, other household gods, a carved image and a cast idol? Now you know what to do." 15So they turned in there and went to the house of the young Levite at Micah's place and greeted him. 16The six hundred Danites, armed for battle, stood at the entrance to the gate. 17The five men who had spied out the land went inside and took the carved image, the ephod, the other household gods and the cast idol while the priest and the six hundred armed men stood at the entrance to the gate.

18When these men went into Micah's house and took the carved image, the ephod, the other household gods and the cast idol, the priest said to them, "What are you doing?"

19They answered him, "Be quiet! Don't say a word. Come with us, and be our father and priest. Isn't it better that you serve a tribe and clan in Israel as priest rather than just one man's household?" 20Then the priest was glad. He took the ephod, the other household gods and the carved image and went along with the people. 21Putting their little children, their livestock and their possessions in front of them, they turned away and left.

22When they had gone some distance from Micah's house, the men who lived near Micah were called together and overtook the Danites. 23As they shouted after them, the Danites turned and said to Micah, "What's the matter with you that you called out your men to fight?"

24He replied, "You took the gods I made, and my priest, and went away. What else do I have? How can you ask, 'What's the matter with you?' "

25The Danites answered, "Don't argue with us, or some hot-tempered men will attack you, and you and your family will lose your lives." 26So the Danites went their way, and Micah, seeing that they were too strong for him, turned around and went back home.

27Then they took what Micah had made, and his priest, and went on to Laish, against a peaceful and unsuspecting people. They attacked them with the sword and burned down their city. 28There was no one to rescue them because they lived a long way from Sidon and had no relationship with anyone else. The city was in a valley near Beth Rehob.

The Danites rebuilt the city and settled there. 29They named it Dan after their forefather Dan, who was born to Israel—though the city used to be called Laish. 30There the Danites set up for themselves the idols, and Jonathan son of Gershom, the son of Moses,[d] and his sons were priests for the tribe of Dan until the time of the captivity of the land. 31They continued to use the idols Micah had made, all the time the house of God was in Shiloh.

A Levite and His Concubine

19 In those days Israel had no king. Now a Levite who lived in a remote area in the hill country of Ephraim took a concubine from Bethlehem in Judah. 2But she was unfaithful to him. She left him and went back to her father's house in Bethlehem, Judah. After she had been there four months, 3her husband went to her to persuade her to return. He had with him his servant and two donkeys. She took him into her father's house, and when her father saw him, he gladly welcomed him. 4His father-in-law, the girl's

[a]7 The meaning of the Hebrew for this clause is uncertain. [b]7 Hebrew; some Septuagint manuscripts *with the Arameans* [c]12 *Mahaneh Dan* means *Dan's camp.* [d]30 An ancient Hebrew scribal tradition, some Septuagint manuscripts and Vulgate; Masoretic Text *Manasseh*

father, prevailed upon him to stay; so he
remained with him three days, eating and
drinking, and sleeping there.
5On the fourth day they got up early
and he prepared to leave, but the girl's fa-
ther said to his son-in-law, "Refresh your-
self with something to eat; then you can
go." 6So the two of them sat down to eat
and drink together. Afterward the girl's fa-
ther said, "Please stay tonight and enjoy
yourself." 7And when the man got up to
go, his father-in-law persuaded him, so he
stayed there that night. 8On the morning
of the fifth day, when he rose to go, the
girl's father said, "Refresh yourself. Wait
till afternoon!" So the two of them ate to-
gether.
9Then when the man, with his concu-
bine and his servant, got up to leave, his
father-in-law, the girl's father, said, "Now
look, it's almost evening. Spend the night
here; the day is nearly over. Stay and en-
joy yourself. Early tomorrow morning you
can get up and be on your way home."
10But, unwilling to stay another night, the
man left and went toward Jebus (that is,
Jerusalem), with his two saddled donkeys
and his concubine.
11When they were near Jebus and the
day was almost gone, the servant said to
his master, "Come, let's stop at this city of
the Jebusites and spend the night."
12His master replied, "No. We won't go
into an alien city, whose people are not Is-
raelites. We will go on to Gibeah." 13He
added, "Come, let's try to reach Gibeah or
Ramah and spend the night in one of
those places." 14So they went on, and the
sun set as they neared Gibeah in Benja-
min. 15There they stopped to spend the
night. They went and sat in the city
square, but no one took them into his
home for the night.
16That evening an old man from the hill
country of Ephraim, who was living in
Gibeah (the men of the place were Benja-
mites), came in from his work in the
fields. 17When he looked and saw the trav-
eler in the city square, the old man asked,
"Where are you going? Where did you
come from?"
18He answered, "We are on our way
from Bethlehem in Judah to a remote area
in the hill country of Ephraim where I live.
I have been to Bethlehem in Judah and
now I am going to the house of the LORD.
No one has taken me into his house. 19We
have both straw and fodder for our don-
keys and bread and wine for ourselves
your servants—me, your maidservant,
and the young man with us. We don't
need anything."
20"You are welcome at my house," the
old man said. "Let me supply whatever
you need. Only don't spend the night in
the square." 21So he took him into his
house and fed his donkeys. After they had
washed their feet, they had something to
eat and drink.
22While they were enjoying themselves,
some of the wicked men of the city sur-
rounded the house. Pounding on the door,
they shouted to the old man who owned
the house, "Bring out the man who came
to your house so we can have sex with
him."
23The owner of the house went outside
and said to them, "No, my friends, don't
be so vile. Since this man is my guest,
don't do this disgraceful thing. 24Look,
here is my virgin daughter, and his concu-
bine. I will bring them out to you now,
and you can use them and do to them
whatever you wish. But to this man, don't
do such a disgraceful thing."
25But the men would not listen to him.
So the man took his concubine and sent
her outside to them, and they raped her
and abused her throughout the night, and
at dawn they let her go. 26At daybreak the
woman went back to the house where her
master was staying, fell down at the door
and lay there until daylight.
27When her master got up in the morn-
ing and opened the door of the house and
stepped out to continue on his way, there
lay his concubine, fallen in the doorway of
the house, with her hands on the thresh-
old. 28He said to her, "Get up; let's go." But
there was no answer. Then the man put
her on his donkey and set out for home.
29When he reached home, he took a
knife and cut up his concubine, limb by
limb, into twelve parts and sent them into
all the areas of Israel. 30Everyone who saw
it said, "Such a thing has never been seen
or done, not since the day the Israelites
came up out of Egypt. Think about it!
Consider it! Tell us what to do!"

Israelites Fight the Benjamites

20 Then all the Israelites from Dan to
Beersheba and from the land of
Gilead came out as one man and assem-
bled before the LORD in Mizpah. 2The
leaders of all the people of the tribes of Is-
rael took their places in the assembly of
the people of God, four hundred thousand

soldiers armed with swords. 3(The Benjamites heard that the Israelites had gone up to Mizpah.) Then the Israelites said, "Tell us how this awful thing happened."

4So the Levite, the husband of the murdered woman, said, "I and my concubine came to Gibeah in Benjamin to spend the night. 5During the night the men of Gibeah came after me and surrounded the house, intending to kill me. They raped my concubine, and she died. 6I took my concubine, cut her into pieces and sent one piece to each region of Israel's inheritance, because they committed this lewd and disgraceful act in Israel. 7Now, all you Israelites, speak up and give your verdict."

8All the people rose as one man, saying, "None of us will go home. No, not one of us will return to his house. 9But now this is what we'll do to Gibeah: We'll go up against it as the lot directs. 10We'll take ten men out of every hundred from all the tribes of Israel, and a hundred from a thousand, and a thousand from ten thousand, to get provisions for the army. Then, when the army arrives at Gibeah[a] in Benjamin, it can give them what they deserve for all this vileness done in Israel." 11So all the men of Israel got together and united as one man against the city.

12The tribes of Israel sent men throughout the tribe of Benjamin, saying, "What about this awful crime that was committed among you? 13Now surrender those wicked men of Gibeah so that we may put them to death and purge the evil from Israel."

But the Benjamites would not listen to their fellow Israelites. 14From their towns they came together at Gibeah to fight against the Israelites. 15At once the Benjamites mobilized twenty-six thousand swordsmen from their towns, in addition to seven hundred chosen men from those living in Gibeah. 16Among all these soldiers there were seven hundred chosen men who were left-handed, each of whom could sling a stone at a hair and not miss.

17Israel, apart from Benjamin, mustered four hundred thousand swordsmen, all of them fighting men.

18The Israelites went up to Bethel[b] and inquired of God. They said, "Who of us shall go first to fight against the Benjamites?"

The Lord replied, "Judah shall go first."

19The next morning the Israelites got up and pitched camp near Gibeah. 20The men of Israel went out to fight the Benjamites and took up battle positions against them at Gibeah. 21The Benjamites came out of Gibeah and cut down twenty-two thousand Israelites on the battlefield that day. 22But the men of Israel encouraged one another and again took up their positions where they had stationed themselves the first day. 23The Israelites went up and wept before the Lord until evening, and they inquired of the Lord. They said, "Shall we go up again to battle against the Benjamites, our brothers?"

The Lord answered, "Go up against them."

24Then the Israelites drew near to Benjamin the second day. 25This time, when the Benjamites came out from Gibeah to oppose them, they cut down another eighteen thousand Israelites, all of them armed with swords.

26Then the Israelites, all the people, went up to Bethel, and there they sat weeping before the Lord. They fasted that day until evening and presented burnt offerings and fellowship offerings[c] to the Lord. 27And the Israelites inquired of the Lord. (In those days the ark of the covenant of God was there, 28with Phinehas son of Eleazar, the son of Aaron, ministering before it.) They asked, "Shall we go up again to battle with Benjamin our brother, or not?"

The Lord responded, "Go, for tomorrow I will give them into your hands."

29Then Israel set an ambush around Gibeah. 30They went up against the Benjamites on the third day and took up positions against Gibeah as they had done before. 31The Benjamites came out to meet them and were drawn away from the city. They began to inflict casualties on the Israelites as before, so that about thirty men fell in the open field and on the roads—the one leading to Bethel and the other to Gibeah.

32While the Benjamites were saying, "We are defeating them as before," the Israelites were saying, "Let's retreat and draw them away from the city to the roads."

33All the men of Israel moved from their places and took up positions at Baal Tamar, and the Israelite ambush charged out

[a] *10* One Hebrew manuscript; most Hebrew manuscripts *Geba*, a variant of *Gibeah* [b] *18* Or *to the house of God*; also in verse 26 [c] *26* Traditionally *peace offerings*

of its place on the west[a] of Gibeah.[b]
34Then ten thousand of Israel's finest men
made a frontal attack on Gibeah. The
fighting was so heavy that the Benjamites
did not realize how near disaster was.
35The LORD defeated Benjamin before Israel, and on that day the Israelites struck
down 25,100 Benjamites, all armed with
swords. 36Then the Benjamites saw that
they were beaten.

Now the men of Israel had given way
before Benjamin, because they relied on
the ambush they had set near Gibeah.
37The men who had been in ambush
made a sudden dash into Gibeah, spread
out and put the whole city to the sword.
38The men of Israel had arranged with the
ambush that they should send up a great
cloud of smoke from the city, 39and then
the men of Israel would turn in the battle.

The Benjamites had begun to inflict casualties on the men of Israel (about thirty), and they said, "We are defeating them
as in the first battle." 40But when the column of smoke began to rise from the city,
the Benjamites turned and saw the smoke
of the whole city going up into the sky.
41Then the men of Israel turned on them,
and the men of Benjamin were terrified,
because they realized that disaster had
come upon them. 42So they fled before the
Israelites in the direction of the desert, but
they could not escape the battle. And the
men of Israel who came out of the towns
cut them down there. 43They surrounded
the Benjamites, chased them and easily[c]
overran them in the vicinity of Gibeah on
the east. 44Eighteen thousand Benjamites
fell, all of them valiant fighters. 45As they
turned and fled toward the desert to the
rock of Rimmon, the Israelites cut down
five thousand men along the roads. They
kept pressing after the Benjamites as far
as Gidom and struck down two thousand
more.

46On that day twenty-five thousand
Benjamite swordsmen fell, all of them valiant fighters. 47But six hundred men
turned and fled into the desert to the rock
of Rimmon, where they stayed four
months. 48The men of Israel went back to
Benjamin and put all the towns to the
sword, including the animals and everything else they found. All the towns they
came across they set on fire.

Wives for the Benjamites

21 The men of Israel had taken an
oath at Mizpah: "Not one of us will
give his daughter in marriage to a Benjamite."

2The people went to Bethel,[d] where
they sat before God until evening, raising
their voices and weeping bitterly.
3"O LORD, the God of Israel," they cried,
"why has this happened to Israel? Why
should one tribe be missing from Israel today?"

4Early the next day the people built an
altar and presented burnt offerings and
fellowship offerings.[e]
5Then the Israelites asked, "Who from
all the tribes of Israel has failed to assemble before the LORD?" For they had taken
a solemn oath that anyone who failed to
assemble before the LORD at Mizpah
should certainly be put to death.

6Now the Israelites grieved for their
brothers, the Benjamites. "Today one
tribe is cut off from Israel," they said.
7"How can we provide wives for those
who are left, since we have taken an oath
by the LORD not to give them any of our
daughters in marriage?" 8Then they
asked, "Which one of the tribes of Israel
failed to assemble before the LORD at Mizpah?" They discovered that no one from
Jabesh Gilead had come to the camp for
the assembly. 9For when they counted the
people, they found that none of the people
of Jabesh Gilead were there.

10So the assembly sent twelve thousand
fighting men with instructions to go to Jabesh Gilead and put to the sword those
living there, including the women and
children. 11"This is what you are to do,"
they said. "Kill every male and every
woman who is not a virgin." 12They found
among the people living in Jabesh Gilead
four hundred young women who had never slept with a man, and they took them to
the camp at Shiloh in Canaan.

13Then the whole assembly sent an offer of peace to the Benjamites at the rock
of Rimmon. 14So the Benjamites returned
at that time and were given the women of
Jabesh Gilead who had been spared. But
there were not enough for all of them.

15The people grieved for Benjamin, because the LORD had made a gap in the
tribes of Israel. 16And the elders of the as-

[a]33 Some Septuagint manuscripts and Vulgate; the meaning of the Hebrew for this word is uncertain.
[b]33 Hebrew *Geba*, a variant of *Gibeah*. [c]43 The meaning of the Hebrew for this word is uncertain.
[d]2 Or *to the house of God*. [e]4 Traditionally *peace offerings*

sembly said, "With the women of Benjamin destroyed, how shall we provide wives for the men who are left? [17]The Benjamite survivors must have heirs," they said, "so that a tribe of Israel will not be wiped out. [18]We can't give them our daughters as wives, since we Israelites have taken this oath: 'Cursed be anyone who gives a wife to a Benjamite.' [19]But look, there is the annual festival of the LORD in Shiloh, to the north of Bethel, and east of the road that goes from Bethel to Shechem, and to the south of Lebonah."

[20]So they instructed the Benjamites, saying, "Go and hide in the vineyards [21]and watch. When the girls of Shiloh come out to join in the dancing, then rush from the vineyards and each of you seize a wife from the girls of Shiloh and go to the land of Benjamin. [22]When their fathers or brothers complain to us, we will say to them, 'Do us a kindness by helping them, because we did not get wives for them during the war, and you are innocent, since you did not give your daughters to them.' "

[23]So that is what the Benjamites did. While the girls were dancing, each man caught one and carried her off to be his wife. Then they returned to their inheritance and rebuilt the towns and settled in them.

[24]At that time the Israelites left that place and went home to their tribes and clans, each to his own inheritance.

[25]In those days Israel had no king; everyone did as he saw fit.

RUTH'S story, occurring during the time of the judges, recalls the tragedy of Elimelech's family. They desert God's land during a famine, but God still cares about them. When Naomi returns to Judah, her daughter-in-law Ruth marries Boaz to carry on the family name and becomes an ancestor of David and Jesus. As you read this book, think about how God cares about you even when you sin and how wonderful it is that he sent Jesus, son of David, into the world.

RUTH

Naomi and Ruth

1 In the days when the judges ruled,[a] there was a famine in the land, and a man from Bethlehem in Judah, together with his wife and two sons, went to live for a while in the country of Moab. 2 The man's name was Elimelech, his wife's name Naomi, and the names of his two sons were Mahlon and Kilion. They were Ephrathites from Bethlehem, Judah. And they went to Moab and lived there.

3 Now Elimelech, Naomi's husband, died, and she was left with her two sons. 4 They married Moabite women, one named Orpah and the other Ruth. After they had lived there about ten years, 5 both Mahlon and Kilion also died, and Naomi was left without her two sons and her husband.

6 When she heard in Moab that the LORD had come to the aid of his people by providing food for them, Naomi and her daughters-in-law prepared to return home from there. 7 With her two daughters-in-law she left the place where she had been living and set out on the road that would take them back to the land of Judah.

8 Then Naomi said to her two daughters-

[a] 1 Traditionally *judged*

in-law, "Go back, each of you, to your mother's home. May the LORD show kindness to you, as you have shown to your dead and to me. 9May the LORD grant that each of you will find rest in the home of another husband."

Then she kissed them and they wept aloud 10and said to her, "We will go back with you to your people."

11But Naomi said, "Return home, my daughters. Why would you come with me? Am I going to have any more sons, who could become your husbands? 12Return home, my daughters; I am too old to have another husband. Even if I thought there was still hope for me—even if I had a husband tonight and then gave birth to sons— 13would you wait until they grew up? Would you remain unmarried for them? No, my daughters. It is more bitter for me than for you, because the LORD's hand has gone out against me!"

14At this they wept again. Then Orpah kissed her mother-in-law good-by, but Ruth clung to her.

15"Look," said Naomi, "your sister-in-law is going back to her people and her gods. Go back with her."

16But Ruth replied, "Don't urge me to leave you or to turn back from you. Where you go I will go, and where you stay I will stay. Your people will be my people and your God my God. 17Where you die I will die, and there I will be buried. May the

FRIDAY

VERSE FOR THE DAY: Ruth 1:16

AUTHOR: Ruth Senter

PASSAGE FOR THE DAY: Ruth 1:1–22

Risk, and Reward

Sometimes when all the changes in my life and in those around me become too unsettling, I think of a believer who, like me, is named Ruth. As a young woman she stepped out of her circle of security, crossed the hills to Bethlehem and took on a new country, new religion, new family, new everything. Little did she know that her daring move would place her directly into King David's royal lineup.

Change? Stress? Risk? Emphatically, yes. But for Ruth in the Old Testament, great risk brought with it great reward.

There will probably always be a part of me that wants to hold on to tradition, to the safe, the comfortable, the way it's always been. But like Ruth, I can trust that change—even unwanted change—can be the threshold to a new dimension of growth. And so can you.

MARRIAGE BUILDERS

- *What unsettling changes are you currently facing?*
- *Despite the risks of change, how can you look forward to new areas of growth?*

Additional Scripture Readings
Ruth 4:13–22; Isaiah 43:18–19; Jeremiah 29:11–13

Go to page 267 for your next devotional reading.

LORD deal with me, be it ever so severely,
if anything but death separates you and
me." 18When Naomi realized that Ruth
was determined to go with her, she
stopped urging her.

19So the two women went on until they
came to Bethlehem. When they arrived in
Bethlehem, the whole town was stirred
because of them, and the women ex-
claimed, "Can this be Naomi?"

20"Don't call me Naomi,[a]" she told
them. "Call me Mara,[b] because the Al-
mighty[c] has made my life very bitter. 21I
went away full, but the LORD has brought
me back empty. Why call me Naomi? The
LORD has afflicted[d] me; the Almighty has
brought misfortune upon me."

22So Naomi returned from Moab ac-
companied by Ruth the Moabitess, her
daughter-in-law, arriving in Bethlehem as
the barley harvest was beginning.

Ruth Meets Boaz

2 Now Naomi had a relative on her hus-
band's side, from the clan of Elime-
lech, a man of standing, whose name was
Boaz.

2And Ruth the Moabitess said to Naomi,
"Let me go to the fields and pick up the
leftover grain behind anyone in whose
eyes I find favor."

Naomi said to her, "Go ahead, my
daughter." 3So she went out and began to
glean in the fields behind the harvesters.
As it turned out, she found herself work-
ing in a field belonging to Boaz, who was
from the clan of Elimelech.

4Just then Boaz arrived from Bethlehem
and greeted the harvesters, "The LORD be
with you!"

"The LORD bless you!" they called back.

5Boaz asked the foreman of his harvest-
ers, "Whose young woman is that?"

6The foreman replied, "She is the Moab-
itess who came back from Moab with Na-
omi. 7She said, 'Please let me glean and
gather among the sheaves behind the har-
vesters.' She went into the field and has
worked steadily from morning till now,
except for a short rest in the shelter."

8So Boaz said to Ruth, "My daughter,
listen to me. Don't go and glean in another
field and don't go away from here. Stay
here with my servant girls. 9Watch the
field where the men are harvesting, and
follow along after the girls. I have told the
men not to touch you. And whenever you
are thirsty, go and get a drink from the wa-
ter jars the men have filled."

10At this, she bowed down with her face
to the ground. She exclaimed, "Why have
I found such favor in your eyes that you
notice me—a foreigner?"

11Boaz replied, "I've been told all about
what you have done for your mother-in-
law since the death of your husband—
how you left your father and mother and
your homeland and came to live with a
people you did not know before. 12May
the LORD repay you for what you have
done. May you be richly rewarded by the
LORD, the God of Israel, under whose
wings you have come to take refuge."

13"May I continue to find favor in your
eyes, my lord," she said. "You have given
me comfort and have spoken kindly to
your servant—though I do not have the
standing of one of your servant girls."

14At mealtime Boaz said to her, "Come
over here. Have some bread and dip it in
the wine vinegar."

When she sat down with the harvesters,
he offered her some roasted grain. She ate
all she wanted and had some left over.
15As she got up to glean, Boaz gave orders
to his men, "Even if she gathers among
the sheaves, don't embarrass her. 16Rath-
er, pull out some stalks for her from the
bundles and leave them for her to pick up,
and don't rebuke her."

17So Ruth gleaned in the field until eve-
ning. Then she threshed the barley she
had gathered, and it amounted to about an
ephah.[e] 18She carried it back to town,
and her mother-in-law saw how much she
had gathered. Ruth also brought out and
gave her what she had left over after she
had eaten enough.

19Her mother-in-law asked her, "Where
did you glean today? Where did you
work? Blessed be the man who took no-
tice of you!"

Then Ruth told her mother-in-law
about the one at whose place she had
been working. "The name of the man I
worked with today is Boaz," she said.

20"The LORD bless him!" Naomi said to
her daughter-in-law. "He has not stopped
showing his kindness to the living and the
dead." She added, "That man is our close
relative; he is one of our kinsman-redeem-
ers."

[a]20 *Naomi* means *pleasant*; also in verse 21. [b]20 *Mara* means *bitter*. [c]20 Hebrew *Shaddai*; also in verse 21 [d]21 Or *has testified against* [e]17 That is, probably about 3/5 bushel (about 22 liters)

21Then Ruth the Moabitess said, "He
even said to me, 'Stay with my workers
until they finish harvesting all my grain.' "
22Naomi said to Ruth her daughter-in-
law, "It will be good for you, my daughter,
to go with his girls, because in someone
else's field you might be harmed."
23So Ruth stayed close to the servant
girls of Boaz to glean until the barley and
wheat harvests were finished. And she
lived with her mother-in-law.

Ruth and Boaz at the Threshing Floor

3 One day Naomi her mother-in-law
said to her, "My daughter, should I
not try to find a home[a] for you, where
you will be well provided for? 2Is not
Boaz, with whose servant girls you have
been, a kinsman of ours? Tonight he will
be winnowing barley on the threshing
floor. 3Wash and perfume yourself, and
put on your best clothes. Then go down to
the threshing floor, but don't let him
know you are there until he has finished
eating and drinking. 4When he lies down,
note the place where he is lying. Then go
and uncover his feet and lie down. He will
tell you what to do."
5"I will do whatever you say," Ruth an-
swered. 6So she went down to the thresh-
ing floor and did everything her mother-
in-law told her to do.
7When Boaz had finished eating and
drinking and was in good spirits, he went
over to lie down at the far end of the grain
pile. Ruth approached quietly, uncovered
his feet and lay down. 8In the middle of
the night something startled the man, and
he turned and discovered a woman lying
at his feet.
9"Who are you?" he asked.
"I am your servant Ruth," she said.
"Spread the corner of your garment over
me, since you are a kinsman-redeemer."
10"The LORD bless you, my daughter,"
he replied. "This kindness is greater than
that which you showed earlier: You have
not run after the younger men, whether
rich or poor. 11And now, my daughter,
don't be afraid. I will do for you all you
ask. All my fellow townsmen know that
you are a woman of noble character. 12Al-
though it is true that I am near of kin,
there is a kinsman-redeemer nearer than I.
13Stay here for the night, and in the morn-
ing if he wants to redeem, good; let him
redeem. But if he is not willing, as surely
as the LORD lives I will do it. Lie here until
morning."
14So she lay at his feet until morning,
but got up before anyone could be recog-
nized; and he said, "Don't let it be known
that a woman came to the threshing
floor."
15He also said, "Bring me the shawl you
are wearing and hold it out." When she
did so, he poured into it six measures of
barley and put it on her. Then he[b] went
back to town.
16When Ruth came to her mother-in-
law, Naomi asked, "How did it go, my
daughter?"
Then she told her everything Boaz had
done for her 17and added, "He gave me
these six measures of barley, saying,
'Don't go back to your mother-in-law
empty-handed.' "
18Then Naomi said, "Wait, my daugh-
ter, until you find out what happens. For
the man will not rest until the matter is
settled today."

Boaz Marries Ruth

4 Meanwhile Boaz went up to the town
gate and sat there. When the kins-
man-redeemer he had mentioned came
along, Boaz said, "Come over here, my
friend, and sit down." So he went over and
sat down.
2Boaz took ten of the elders of the town
and said, "Sit here," and they did so.
3Then he said to the kinsman-redeemer,
"Naomi, who has come back from Moab,
is selling the piece of land that belonged
to our brother Elimelech. 4I thought I
should bring the matter to your attention
and suggest that you buy it in the pres-
ence of these seated here and in the pres-
ence of the elders of my people. If you will
redeem it, do so. But if you[c] will not, tell
me, so I will know. For no one has the
right to do it except you, and I am next in
line."
"I will redeem it," he said.
5Then Boaz said, "On the day you buy
the land from Naomi and from Ruth the
Moabitess, you acquire[d] the dead man's
widow, in order to maintain the name of
the dead with his property."

[a] 1 Hebrew *find rest* (see Ruth 1:9) [b] 15 Most Hebrew manuscripts; many Hebrew manuscripts, Vulgate and Syriac *she* [c] 4 Many Hebrew manuscripts, Septuagint, Vulgate and Syriac; most Hebrew manuscripts *he* [d] 5 Hebrew; Vulgate and Syriac *Naomi, you acquire Ruth the Moabitess,*

WEEKENDING

ROMANCE

Creating times of romance is important, even if the two of you approach romance differently. Talk about romance with your spouse, using these questions.

1. When it comes to romance:
   a. I am romantic. My mate is practical and realistic.
   b. My spouse is romantic. I am practical and realistic.
   c. Both of us are romantic, but in our own ways.
   d. Neither of us is romantic.
2. Sometimes I can't get romantic because:
   a. I am too critical of my spouse.
   b. I feel he or she is too critical of me.
   c. I am holding onto resentments from the past.
   d. My mind is elsewhere, like on practical concerns.
   e. I'm concerned my spouse might reject me or not respond when I become romantic.
   f. I like to get romantic first because I am more of an initiator than a responder.
3. One way I would like us to be romantic is . . .

— *H. Norman Wright*

REVIVE

Saturday: 1 John 4:1–12
Sunday: 2 John 1:4–6

Go to page 280 for your next devotional reading.

6At this, the kinsman-redeemer said,
"Then I cannot redeem it because I might
endanger my own estate. You redeem it
yourself. I cannot do it."
7(Now in earlier times in Israel, for the
redemption and transfer of property to be-
come final, one party took off his sandal
and gave it to the other. This was the
method of legalizing transactions in Is-
rael.)
8So the kinsman-redeemer said to Boaz,
"Buy it yourself." And he removed his
sandal.
9Then Boaz announced to the elders
and all the people, "Today you are wit-
nesses that I have bought from Naomi all
the property of Elimelech, Kilion and
Mahlon. 10I have also acquired Ruth the
Moabitess, Mahlon's widow, as my wife,
in order to maintain the name of the dead
with his property, so that his name will
not disappear from among his family or
from the town records. Today you are wit-
nesses!"
11Then the elders and all those at the
gate said, "We are witnesses. May the
LORD make the woman who is coming into
your home like Rachel and Leah, who to-
gether built up the house of Israel. May
you have standing in Ephrathah and be fa-
mous in Bethlehem. 12Through the off-
spring the LORD gives you by this young
woman, may your family be like that of
Perez, whom Tamar bore to Judah."

The Genealogy of David

13So Boaz took Ruth and she became
his wife. Then he went to her, and the
LORD enabled her to conceive, and she
gave birth to a son. 14The women said to
Naomi: "Praise be to the LORD, who this
day has not left you without a kinsman-re-
deemer. May he become famous through-
out Israel! 15He will renew your life and
sustain you in your old age. For your
daughter-in-law, who loves you and who
is better to you than seven sons, has given
him birth."
16Then Naomi took the child, laid him
in her lap and cared for him. 17The women
living there said, "Naomi has a son." And
they named him Obed. He was the father
of Jesse, the father of David.
18This, then, is the family line of Perez:

Perez was the father of Hezron,
19Hezron the father of Ram,
Ram the father of Amminadab,
20Amminadab the father of Nahshon,
Nahshon the father of Salmon,[a]
21Salmon the father of Boaz,
Boaz the father of Obed,
22Obed the father of Jesse,
and Jesse the father of David.

[a]20 A few Hebrew manuscripts, some Septuagint manuscripts and Vulgate (see also verse 21 and Septuagint of 1 Chron. 2:11); most Hebrew manuscripts *Salma*

THIS book tells the story of Samuel, the last judge, and of Saul, Israel's first king. Saul's sin and disobedience lead God to reject him and anoint David as Israel's second king. In spite of numerous threats to David's life from both the Philistines and from Saul, God keeps him safe. As you read this book, think how God will protect and bless you if you trust in him; be warned that if you disobey God, you may face many difficulties.

1 SAMUEL

The Birth of Samuel

1 There was a certain man from Ramathaim, a Zuphite[a] from the hill country of Ephraim, whose name was Elkanah son of Jeroham, the son of Elihu, the son of Tohu, the son of Zuph, an Ephraimite. [2]He had two wives; one was called Hannah and the other Peninnah. Peninnah had children, but Hannah had none.

[3]Year after year this man went up from his town to worship and sacrifice to the LORD Almighty at Shiloh, where Hophni and Phinehas, the two sons of Eli, were priests of the LORD. [4]Whenever the day came for Elkanah to sacrifice, he would give portions of the meat to his wife Peninnah and to all her sons and daughters. [5]But to Hannah he gave a double portion because he loved her, and the LORD had closed her womb. [6]And because the LORD had closed her womb, her rival kept provoking her in order to irritate her. [7]This went on year after year. Whenever Hannah went up to the house of the LORD, her rival provoked her till she wept and would not eat. [8]Elkanah her husband would say to her, "Hannah, why are you weeping? Why don't you eat? Why are you down-

[a]1 Or *from Ramathaim Zuphim*

hearted? Don't I mean more to you than
ten sons?"
9Once when they had finished eating
and drinking in Shiloh, Hannah stood up.
Now Eli the priest was sitting on a chair by
the doorpost of the LORD's temple.[a] 10In
bitterness of soul Hannah wept much and
prayed to the LORD. 11And she made a
vow, saying, "O LORD Almighty, if you will
only look upon your servant's misery and
remember me, and not forget your servant
but give her a son, then I will give him to
the LORD for all the days of his life, and no
razor will ever be used on his head."
12As she kept on praying to the LORD, Eli
observed her mouth. 13Hannah was pray-
ing in her heart, and her lips were moving
but her voice was not heard. Eli thought
she was drunk 14and said to her, "How
long will you keep on getting drunk? Get
rid of your wine."
15"Not so, my lord," Hannah replied, "I
am a woman who is deeply troubled. I
have not been drinking wine or beer; I was
pouring out my soul to the LORD. 16Do not
take your servant for a wicked woman; I
have been praying here out of my great
anguish and grief."
17Eli answered, "Go in peace, and may
the God of Israel grant you what you have
asked of him."
18She said, "May your servant find favor
in your eyes." Then she went her way and
ate something, and her face was no longer
downcast.
19Early the next morning they arose and
worshiped before the LORD and then went
back to their home at Ramah. Elkanah lay
with Hannah his wife, and the LORD re-
membered her. 20So in the course of time
Hannah conceived and gave birth to a son.
She named him Samuel,[b] saying, "Be-
cause I asked the LORD for him."

Hannah Dedicates Samuel

21When the man Elkanah went up with
all his family to offer the annual sacrifice
to the LORD and to fulfill his vow, 22Han-
nah did not go. She said to her husband,
"After the boy is weaned, I will take him
and present him before the LORD, and he
will live there always."
23"Do what seems best to you," Elkanah
her husband told her. "Stay here until you
have weaned him; only may the LORD
make good his[c] word." So the woman
stayed at home and nursed her son until
she had weaned him.
24After he was weaned, she took the
boy with her, young as he was, along with
a three-year-old bull,[d] an ephah[e] of
flour and a skin of wine, and brought him
to the house of the LORD at Shiloh. 25When
they had slaughtered the bull, they
brought the boy to Eli, 26and she said to
him, "As surely as you live, my lord, I am
the woman who stood here beside you
praying to the LORD. 27I prayed for this
child, and the LORD has granted me what
I asked of him. 28So now I give him to the
LORD. For his whole life he will be given
over to the LORD." And he worshiped the
LORD there.

Hannah's Prayer

2 Then Hannah prayed and said:

"My heart rejoices in the LORD;
in the LORD my horn[f] is lifted high.
My mouth boasts over my enemies,
for I delight in your deliverance.

2"There is no one holy[g] like the LORD;
there is no one besides you;
there is no Rock like our God.

3"Do not keep talking so proudly
or let your mouth speak such
arrogance,
for the LORD is a God who knows,
and by him deeds are weighed.

4"The bows of the warriors are broken,
but those who stumbled are armed
with strength.
5Those who were full hire themselves
out for food,
but those who were hungry hunger
no more.
She who was barren has borne seven
children,
but she who has had many sons
pines away.

6"The LORD brings death and makes
alive;
he brings down to the grave[h] and
raises up.
7The LORD sends poverty and wealth;
he humbles and he exalts.

[a]9 That is, tabernacle [b]20 *Samuel* sounds like the Hebrew for *heard of God.* [c]23 Masoretic Text; Dead Sea Scrolls, Septuagint and Syriac *your* [d]24 Dead Sea Scrolls, Septuagint and Syriac; Masoretic Text *with three bulls* [e]24 That is, probably about 3/5 bushel (about 22 liters) [f]1 *Horn* here symbolizes strength; also in verse 10. [g]2 Or *no Holy One* [h]6 Hebrew *Sheol*

8He raises the poor from the dust
and lifts the needy from the ash heap;
he seats them with princes
and has them inherit a throne of honor.

"For the foundations of the earth are the LORD's;
upon them he has set the world.
9He will guard the feet of his saints,
but the wicked will be silenced in darkness.

"It is not by strength that one prevails;
10 those who oppose the LORD will be shattered.
He will thunder against them from heaven;
the LORD will judge the ends of the earth.

"He will give strength to his king
and exalt the horn of his anointed."

11Then Elkanah went home to Ramah, but the boy ministered before the LORD under Eli the priest.

Eli's Wicked Sons

12Eli's sons were wicked men; they had no regard for the LORD. 13Now it was the practice of the priests with the people that whenever anyone offered a sacrifice and while the meat was being boiled, the servant of the priest would come with a three-pronged fork in his hand. 14He would plunge it into the pan or kettle or caldron or pot, and the priest would take for himself whatever the fork brought up. This is how they treated all the Israelites who came to Shiloh. 15But even before the fat was burned, the servant of the priest would come and say to the man who was sacrificing, "Give the priest some meat to roast; he won't accept boiled meat from you, but only raw."

16If the man said to him, "Let the fat be burned up first, and then take whatever you want," the servant would then answer, "No, hand it over now; if you don't, I'll take it by force."

17This sin of the young men was very great in the LORD's sight, for they[a] were treating the LORD's offering with contempt.

18But Samuel was ministering before the LORD—a boy wearing a linen ephod. 19Each year his mother made him a little robe and took it to him when she went up with her husband to offer the annual sacrifice. 20Eli would bless Elkanah and his wife, saying, "May the LORD give you children by this woman to take the place of the one she prayed for and gave to the LORD." Then they would go home. 21And the LORD was gracious to Hannah; she conceived and gave birth to three sons and two daughters. Meanwhile, the boy Samuel grew up in the presence of the LORD.

22Now Eli, who was very old, heard about everything his sons were doing to all Israel and how they slept with the women who served at the entrance to the Tent of Meeting. 23So he said to them, "Why do you do such things? I hear from all the people about these wicked deeds of yours. 24No, my sons; it is not a good report that I hear spreading among the LORD's people. 25If a man sins against another man, God[b] may mediate for him; but if a man sins against the LORD, who will intercede for him?" His sons, however, did not listen to their father's rebuke, for it was the LORD's will to put them to death.

26And the boy Samuel continued to grow in stature and in favor with the LORD and with men.

Prophecy Against the House of Eli

27Now a man of God came to Eli and said to him, "This is what the LORD says: 'Did I not clearly reveal myself to your father's house when they were in Egypt under Pharaoh? 28I chose your father out of all the tribes of Israel to be my priest, to go up to my altar, to burn incense, and to wear an ephod in my presence. I also gave your father's house all the offerings made with fire by the Israelites. 29Why do you[c] scorn my sacrifice and offering that I prescribed for my dwelling? Why do you honor your sons more than me by fattening yourselves on the choice parts of every offering made by my people Israel?'

30"Therefore the LORD, the God of Israel, declares: 'I promised that your house and your father's house would minister before me forever.' But now the LORD declares: 'Far be it from me! Those who honor me I will honor, but those who despise me will be disdained. 31The time is coming when I will cut short your strength and the strength of your father's house, so that

[a]17 Or *men* [b]25 Or *the judges* [c]29 The Hebrew is plural.

there will not be an old man in your family line 32and you will see distress in my dwelling. Although good will be done to Israel, in your family line there will never be an old man. 33Every one of you that I do not cut off from my altar will be spared only to blind your eyes with tears and to grieve your heart, and all your descendants will die in the prime of life.

34" 'And what happens to your two sons, Hophni and Phinehas, will be a sign to you—they will both die on the same day. 35I will raise up for myself a faithful priest, who will do according to what is in my heart and mind. I will firmly establish his house, and he will minister before my anointed one always. 36Then everyone left in your family line will come and bow down before him for a piece of silver and a crust of bread and plead, "Appoint me to some priestly office so I can have food to eat." ' "

The Lord Calls Samuel

3 The boy Samuel ministered before the Lord under Eli. In those days the word of the Lord was rare; there were not many visions.

2One night Eli, whose eyes were becoming so weak that he could barely see, was lying down in his usual place. 3The lamp of God had not yet gone out, and Samuel was lying down in the temple[a] of the Lord, where the ark of God was. 4Then the Lord called Samuel.

Samuel answered, "Here I am." 5And he ran to Eli and said, "Here I am; you called me."

But Eli said, "I did not call; go back and lie down." So he went and lay down.

6Again the Lord called, "Samuel!" And Samuel got up and went to Eli and said, "Here I am; you called me."

"My son," Eli said, "I did not call; go back and lie down."

7Now Samuel did not yet know the Lord: The word of the Lord had not yet been revealed to him.

8The Lord called Samuel a third time, and Samuel got up and went to Eli and said, "Here I am; you called me."

Then Eli realized that the Lord was calling the boy. 9So Eli told Samuel, "Go and lie down, and if he calls you, say, 'Speak, Lord, for your servant is listening.' " So Samuel went and lay down in his place.

10The Lord came and stood there, calling as at the other times, "Samuel! Samuel!"

Then Samuel said, "Speak, for your servant is listening."

11And the Lord said to Samuel: "See, I am about to do something in Israel that will make the ears of everyone who hears of it tingle. 12At that time I will carry out against Eli everything I spoke against his family—from beginning to end. 13For I told him that I would judge his family forever because of the sin he knew about; his sons made themselves contemptible,[b] and he failed to restrain them. 14Therefore, I swore to the house of Eli, 'The guilt of Eli's house will never be atoned for by sacrifice or offering.' "

15Samuel lay down until morning and then opened the doors of the house of the Lord. He was afraid to tell Eli the vision, 16but Eli called him and said, "Samuel, my son."

Samuel answered, "Here I am."

17"What was it he said to you?" Eli asked. "Do not hide it from me. May God deal with you, be it ever so severely, if you hide from me anything he told you." 18So Samuel told him everything, hiding nothing from him. Then Eli said, "He is the Lord; let him do what is good in his eyes."

19The Lord was with Samuel as he grew up, and he let none of his words fall to the ground. 20And all Israel from Dan to Beersheba recognized that Samuel was attested as a prophet of the Lord. 21The Lord continued to appear at Shiloh, and there he revealed himself to Samuel through his word.

4 And Samuel's word came to all Israel.

The Philistines Capture the Ark

Now the Israelites went out to fight against the Philistines. The Israelites camped at Ebenezer, and the Philistines at Aphek. 2The Philistines deployed their forces to meet Israel, and as the battle spread, Israel was defeated by the Philistines, who killed about four thousand of them on the battlefield. 3When the soldiers returned to camp, the elders of Israel asked, "Why did the Lord bring defeat upon us today before the Philistines? Let us bring the ark of the Lord's covenant from Shiloh, so that it[c] may go with us

[a] 3 That is, tabernacle [b] 13 Masoretic Text; an ancient Hebrew scribal tradition and Septuagint *sons blasphemed God* [c] 3 Or *he*

and save us from the hand of our enemies."

4So the people sent men to Shiloh, and they brought back the ark of the covenant of the LORD Almighty, who is enthroned between the cherubim. And Eli's two sons, Hophni and Phinehas, were there with the ark of the covenant of God.

5When the ark of the LORD's covenant came into the camp, all Israel raised such a great shout that the ground shook. 6Hearing the uproar, the Philistines asked, "What's all this shouting in the Hebrew camp?"

When they learned that the ark of the LORD had come into the camp, 7the Philistines were afraid. "A god has come into the camp," they said. "We're in trouble! Nothing like this has happened before. 8Woe to us! Who will deliver us from the hand of these mighty gods? They are the gods who struck the Egyptians with all kinds of plagues in the desert. 9Be strong, Philistines! Be men, or you will be subject to the Hebrews, as they have been to you. Be men, and fight!"

10So the Philistines fought, and the Israelites were defeated and every man fled to his tent. The slaughter was very great; Israel lost thirty thousand foot soldiers. 11The ark of God was captured, and Eli's two sons, Hophni and Phinehas, died.

Death of Eli

12That same day a Benjamite ran from the battle line and went to Shiloh, his clothes torn and dust on his head. 13When he arrived, there was Eli sitting on his chair by the side of the road, watching, because his heart feared for the ark of God. When the man entered the town and told what had happened, the whole town sent up a cry.

14Eli heard the outcry and asked, "What is the meaning of this uproar?"

The man hurried over to Eli, 15who was ninety-eight years old and whose eyes were set so that he could not see. 16He told Eli, "I have just come from the battle line; I fled from it this very day."

Eli asked, "What happened, my son?"

17The man who brought the news replied, "Israel fled before the Philistines, and the army has suffered heavy losses. Also your two sons, Hophni and Phinehas, are dead, and the ark of God has been captured."

18When he mentioned the ark of God, Eli fell backward off his chair by the side of the gate. His neck was broken and he died, for he was an old man and heavy. He had led[a] Israel forty years.

19His daughter-in-law, the wife of Phinehas, was pregnant and near the time of delivery. When she heard the news that the ark of God had been captured and that her father-in-law and her husband were dead, she went into labor and gave birth, but was overcome by her labor pains. 20As she was dying, the women attending her said, "Don't despair; you have given birth to a son." But she did not respond or pay any attention.

21She named the boy Ichabod,[b] saying, "The glory has departed from Israel"—because of the capture of the ark of God and the deaths of her father-in-law and her husband. 22She said, "The glory has departed from Israel, for the ark of God has been captured."

The Ark in Ashdod and Ekron

5 After the Philistines had captured the ark of God, they took it from Ebenezer to Ashdod. 2Then they carried the ark into Dagon's temple and set it beside Dagon. 3When the people of Ashdod rose early the next day, there was Dagon, fallen on his face on the ground before the ark of the LORD! They took Dagon and put him back in his place. 4But the following morning when they rose, there was Dagon, fallen on his face on the ground before the ark of the LORD! His head and hands had been broken off and were lying on the threshold; only his body remained. 5That is why to this day neither the priests of Dagon nor any others who enter Dagon's temple at Ashdod step on the threshold.

6The LORD's hand was heavy upon the people of Ashdod and its vicinity; he brought devastation upon them and afflicted them with tumors.[c] 7When the men of Ashdod saw what was happening, they said, "The ark of the god of Israel must not stay here with us, because his hand is heavy upon us and upon Dagon our god." 8So they called together all the rulers of the Philistines and asked them,

[a] 18 Traditionally *judged* [b] 21 *Ichabod* means *no glory.* [c] 6 Hebrew; Septuagint and Vulgate *tumors. And rats appeared in their land, and death and destruction were throughout the city*

"What shall we do with the ark of the god of Israel?"

They answered, "Have the ark of the god of Israel moved to Gath." So they moved the ark of the God of Israel.

9But after they had moved it, the LORD's hand was against that city, throwing it into a great panic. He afflicted the people of the city, both young and old, with an outbreak of tumors.[a] 10So they sent the ark of God to Ekron.

As the ark of God was entering Ekron, the people of Ekron cried out, "They have brought the ark of the god of Israel around to us to kill us and our people." 11So they called together all the rulers of the Philistines and said, "Send the ark of the god of Israel away; let it go back to its own place, or it[b] will kill us and our people." For death had filled the city with panic; God's hand was very heavy upon it. 12Those who did not die were afflicted with tumors, and the outcry of the city went up to heaven.

The Ark Returned to Israel

6 When the ark of the LORD had been in Philistine territory seven months, 2the Philistines called for the priests and the diviners and said, "What shall we do with the ark of the LORD? Tell us how we should send it back to its place."

3They answered, "If you return the ark of the god of Israel, do not send it away empty, but by all means send a guilt offering to him. Then you will be healed, and you will know why his hand has not been lifted from you."

4The Philistines asked, "What guilt offering should we send to him?"

They replied, "Five gold tumors and five gold rats, according to the number of the Philistine rulers, because the same plague has struck both you and your rulers. 5Make models of the tumors and of the rats that are destroying the country, and pay honor to Israel's god. Perhaps he will lift his hand from you and your gods and your land. 6Why do you harden your hearts as the Egyptians and Pharaoh did? When he[c] treated them harshly, did they not send the Israelites out so they could go on their way?

7"Now then, get a new cart ready, with two cows that have calved and have never been yoked. Hitch the cows to the cart, but take their calves away and pen them up. 8Take the ark of the LORD and put it on the cart, and in a chest beside it put the gold objects you are sending back to him as a guilt offering. Send it on its way, 9but keep watching it. If it goes up to its own territory, toward Beth Shemesh, then the LORD has brought this great disaster on us. But if it does not, then we will know that it was not his hand that struck us and that it happened to us by chance."

10So they did this. They took two such cows and hitched them to the cart and penned up their calves. 11They placed the ark of the LORD on the cart and along with it the chest containing the gold rats and the models of the tumors. 12Then the cows went straight up toward Beth Shemesh, keeping on the road and lowing all the way; they did not turn to the right or to the left. The rulers of the Philistines followed them as far as the border of Beth Shemesh.

13Now the people of Beth Shemesh were harvesting their wheat in the valley, and when they looked up and saw the ark, they rejoiced at the sight. 14The cart came to the field of Joshua of Beth Shemesh, and there it stopped beside a large rock. The people chopped up the wood of the cart and sacrificed the cows as a burnt offering to the LORD. 15The Levites took down the ark of the LORD, together with the chest containing the gold objects, and placed them on the large rock. On that day the people of Beth Shemesh offered burnt offerings and made sacrifices to the LORD. 16The five rulers of the Philistines saw all this and then returned that same day to Ekron.

17These are the gold tumors the Philistines sent as a guilt offering to the LORD—one each for Ashdod, Gaza, Ashkelon, Gath and Ekron. 18And the number of the gold rats was according to the number of Philistine towns belonging to the five rulers—the fortified towns with their country villages. The large rock, on which[d] they set the ark of the LORD, is a witness to this day in the field of Joshua of Beth Shemesh.

19But God struck down some of the men of Beth Shemesh, putting seventy[e] of them to death because they had looked

[a] *9* Or *with tumors in the groin* (see Septuagint) [b] *11* Or *he* [c] *6* That is, God [d] *18* A few Hebrew manuscripts (see also Septuagint); most Hebrew manuscripts *villages as far as Greater Abel, where*
[e] *19* A few Hebrew manuscripts; most Hebrew manuscripts and Septuagint *50,070*

into the ark of the LORD. The people
mourned because of the heavy blow the
LORD had dealt them, 20and the men of
Beth Shemesh asked, "Who can stand in
the presence of the LORD, this holy God?
To whom will the ark go up from here?"
21Then they sent messengers to the
people of Kiriath Jearim, saying, "The Philistines have returned the ark of the LORD.
Come down and take it up to your place."
7 1So the men of Kiriath Jearim came
and took up the ark of the LORD. They
took it to Abinadab's house on the hill and
consecrated Eleazar his son to guard the
ark of the LORD.

Samuel Subdues the Philistines at Mizpah

2It was a long time, twenty years in all,
that the ark remained at Kiriath Jearim,
and all the people of Israel mourned and
sought after the LORD. 3And Samuel said to
the whole house of Israel, "If you are returning to the LORD with all your hearts,
then rid yourselves of the foreign gods
and the Ashtoreths and commit yourselves to the LORD and serve him only, and
he will deliver you out of the hand of the
Philistines." 4So the Israelites put away
their Baals and Ashtoreths, and served the
LORD only.

5Then Samuel said, "Assemble all Israel
at Mizpah and I will intercede with the
LORD for you." 6When they had assembled
at Mizpah, they drew water and poured it
out before the LORD. On that day they fasted and there they confessed, "We have
sinned against the LORD." And Samuel was
leader[a] of Israel at Mizpah.

7When the Philistines heard that Israel
had assembled at Mizpah, the rulers of the
Philistines came up to attack them. And
when the Israelites heard of it, they were
afraid because of the Philistines. 8They
said to Samuel, "Do not stop crying out to
the LORD our God for us, that he may rescue us from the hand of the Philistines."
9Then Samuel took a suckling lamb and
offered it up as a whole burnt offering to
the LORD. He cried out to the LORD on Israel's behalf, and the LORD answered him.

10While Samuel was sacrificing the
burnt offering, the Philistines drew near to
engage Israel in battle. But that day the
LORD thundered with loud thunder against
the Philistines and threw them into such
a panic that they were routed before the
Israelites. 11The men of Israel rushed out
of Mizpah and pursued the Philistines,
slaughtering them along the way to a
point below Beth Car.

12Then Samuel took a stone and set it
up between Mizpah and Shen. He named
it Ebenezer,[b] saying, "Thus far has the
LORD helped us." 13So the Philistines were
subdued and did not invade Israelite territory again.

Throughout Samuel's lifetime, the hand
of the LORD was against the Philistines.
14The towns from Ekron to Gath that the
Philistines had captured from Israel were
restored to her, and Israel delivered the
neighboring territory from the power of
the Philistines. And there was peace between Israel and the Amorites.

15Samuel continued as judge over Israel
all the days of his life. 16From year to year
he went on a circuit from Bethel to Gilgal
to Mizpah, judging Israel in all those
places. 17But he always went back to Ramah, where his home was, and there he
also judged Israel. And he built an altar
there to the LORD.

Israel Asks for a King

8 When Samuel grew old, he appointed
his sons as judges for Israel. 2The
name of his firstborn was Joel and the
name of his second was Abijah, and they
served at Beersheba. 3But his sons did not
walk in his ways. They turned aside after
dishonest gain and accepted bribes and
perverted justice.

4So all the elders of Israel gathered together and came to Samuel at Ramah.
5They said to him, "You are old, and your
sons do not walk in your ways; now appoint a king to lead[c] us, such as all the
other nations have."

6But when they said, "Give us a king to
lead us," this displeased Samuel; so he
prayed to the LORD. 7And the LORD told
him: "Listen to all that the people are saying to you; it is not you they have rejected,
but they have rejected me as their king.
8As they have done from the day I brought
them up out of Egypt until this day, forsaking me and serving other gods, so they
are doing to you. 9Now listen to them; but
warn them solemnly and let them know
what the king who will reign over them
will do."

[a] 6 Traditionally *judge* and 20
[b] 12 *Ebenezer* means *stone of help.*
[c] 5 Traditionally *judge*; also in verses 6

10Samuel told all the words of the LORD
to the people who were asking him for a
king. 11He said, "This is what the king
who will reign over you will do: He will
take your sons and make them serve with
his chariots and horses, and they will run
in front of his chariots. 12Some he will as-
sign to be commanders of thousands and
commanders of fifties, and others to plow
his ground and reap his harvest, and still
others to make weapons of war and equip-
ment for his chariots. 13He will take your
daughters to be perfumers and cooks and
bakers. 14He will take the best of your
fields and vineyards and olive groves and
give them to his attendants. 15He will take
a tenth of your grain and of your vintage
and give it to his officials and attendants.
16Your menservants and maidservants
and the best of your cattle[a] and donkeys
he will take for his own use. 17He will take
a tenth of your flocks, and you yourselves
will become his slaves. 18When that day
comes, you will cry out for relief from the
king you have chosen, and the LORD will
not answer you in that day."

19But the people refused to listen to
Samuel. "No!" they said. "We want a king
over us. 20Then we will be like all the oth-
er nations, with a king to lead us and to go
out before us and fight our battles."

21When Samuel heard all that the peo-
ple said, he repeated it before the LORD.
22The LORD answered, "Listen to them and
give them a king."

Then Samuel said to the men of Israel,
"Everyone go back to his town."

Samuel Anoints Saul

9 There was a Benjamite, a man of
standing, whose name was Kish son
of Abiel, the son of Zeror, the son of Beco-
rath, the son of Aphiah of Benjamin. 2He
had a son named Saul, an impressive
young man without equal among the Isra-
elites—a head taller than any of the oth-
ers.

3Now the donkeys belonging to Saul's
father Kish were lost, and Kish said to his
son Saul, "Take one of the servants with
you and go and look for the donkeys." 4So
he passed through the hill country of
Ephraim and through the area around
Shalisha, but they did not find them. They
went on into the district of Shaalim, but
the donkeys were not there. Then he
passed through the territory of Benjamin,
but they did not find them.

5When they reached the district of
Zuph, Saul said to the servant who was
with him, "Come, let's go back, or my fa-
ther will stop thinking about the donkeys
and start worrying about us."

6But the servant replied, "Look, in this
town there is a man of God; he is highly
respected, and everything he says comes
true. Let's go there now. Perhaps he will
tell us what way to take."

7Saul said to his servant, "If we go, what
can we give the man? The food in our
sacks is gone. We have no gift to take to
the man of God. What do we have?"

8The servant answered him again.
"Look," he said, "I have a quarter of a
shekel[b] of silver. I will give it to the man
of God so that he will tell us what way to
take." 9(Formerly in Israel, if a man went
to inquire of God, he would say, "Come,
let us go to the seer," because the prophet
of today used to be called a seer.)

10"Good," Saul said to his servant.
"Come, let's go." So they set out for the
town where the man of God was.

11As they were going up the hill to the
town, they met some girls coming out to
draw water, and they asked them, "Is the
seer here?"

12"He is," they answered. "He's ahead
of you. Hurry now; he has just come to
our town today, for the people have a sac-
rifice at the high place. 13As soon as you
enter the town, you will find him before
he goes up to the high place to eat. The
people will not begin eating until he
comes, because he must bless the sacri-
fice; afterward, those who are invited will
eat. Go up now; you should find him
about this time."

14They went up to the town, and as they
were entering it, there was Samuel, com-
ing toward them on his way up to the high
place.

15Now the day before Saul came, the
LORD had revealed this to Samuel:
16"About this time tomorrow I will send
you a man from the land of Benjamin.
Anoint him leader over my people Israel;
he will deliver my people from the hand of
the Philistines. I have looked upon my
people, for their cry has reached me."

17When Samuel caught sight of Saul,
the LORD said to him, "This is the man I

[a]16 Septuagint; Hebrew *young men* [b]8 That is, about 1/10 ounce (about 3 grams)

spoke to you about; he will govern my people."

18Saul approached Samuel in the gateway and asked, "Would you please tell me where the seer's house is?"

19"I am the seer," Samuel replied. "Go up ahead of me to the high place, for today you are to eat with me, and in the morning I will let you go and will tell you all that is in your heart. 20As for the donkeys you lost three days ago, do not worry about them; they have been found. And to whom is all the desire of Israel turned, if not to you and all your father's family?"

21Saul answered, "But am I not a Benjamite, from the smallest tribe of Israel, and is not my clan the least of all the clans of the tribe of Benjamin? Why do you say such a thing to me?"

22Then Samuel brought Saul and his servant into the hall and seated them at the head of those who were invited—about thirty in number. 23Samuel said to the cook, "Bring the piece of meat I gave you, the one I told you to lay aside."

24So the cook took up the leg with what was on it and set it in front of Saul. Samuel said, "Here is what has been kept for you. Eat, because it was set aside for you for this occasion, from the time I said, 'I have invited guests.'" And Saul dined with Samuel that day.

25After they came down from the high place to the town, Samuel talked with Saul on the roof of his house. 26They rose about daybreak and Samuel called to Saul on the roof, "Get ready, and I will send you on your way." When Saul got ready, he and Samuel went outside together. 27As they were going down to the edge of the town, Samuel said to Saul, "Tell the servant to go on ahead of us"—and the servant did so—"but you stay here awhile, so that I may give you a message from God."

10 Then Samuel took a flask of oil and poured it on Saul's head and kissed him, saying, "Has not the LORD anointed you leader over his inheritance?[a] 2When you leave me today, you will meet two men near Rachel's tomb, at Zelzah on the border of Benjamin. They will say to you, 'The donkeys you set out to look for have been found. And now your father has stopped thinking about them and is worried about you. He is asking, "What shall I do about my son?"'

3"Then you will go on from there until you reach the great tree of Tabor. Three men going up to God at Bethel will meet you there. One will be carrying three young goats, another three loaves of bread, and another a skin of wine. 4They will greet you and offer you two loaves of bread, which you will accept from them.

5"After that you will go to Gibeah of God, where there is a Philistine outpost. As you approach the town, you will meet a procession of prophets coming down from the high place with lyres, tambourines, flutes and harps being played before them, and they will be prophesying. 6The Spirit of the LORD will come upon you in power, and you will prophesy with them; and you will be changed into a different person. 7Once these signs are fulfilled, do whatever your hand finds to do, for God is with you.

8"Go down ahead of me to Gilgal. I will surely come down to you to sacrifice burnt offerings and fellowship offerings,[b] but you must wait seven days until I come to you and tell you what you are to do."

Saul Made King

9As Saul turned to leave Samuel, God changed Saul's heart, and all these signs were fulfilled that day. 10When they arrived at Gibeah, a procession of prophets met him; the Spirit of God came upon him in power, and he joined in their prophesying. 11When all those who had formerly known him saw him prophesying with the prophets, they asked each other, "What is this that has happened to the son of Kish? Is Saul also among the prophets?"

12A man who lived there answered, "And who is their father?" So it became a saying: "Is Saul also among the prophets?" 13After Saul stopped prophesying, he went to the high place.

14Now Saul's uncle asked him and his servant, "Where have you been?"

"Looking for the donkeys," he said. "But when we saw they were not to be found, we went to Samuel."

15Saul's uncle said, "Tell me what Samuel said to you."

16Saul replied, "He assured us that the donkeys had been found." But he did not

[a] 1 Hebrew; Septuagint and Vulgate *over his people Israel? You will reign over the LORD's people and save them from the power of their enemies round about. And this will be a sign to you that the LORD has anointed you leader over his inheritance:* [b] 8 Traditionally *peace offerings*

tell his uncle what Samuel had said about the kingship.

17Samuel summoned the people of Israel to the LORD at Mizpah 18and said to them, "This is what the LORD, the God of Israel, says: 'I brought Israel up out of Egypt, and I delivered you from the power of Egypt and all the kingdoms that oppressed you.' 19But you have now rejected your God, who saves you out of all your calamities and distresses. And you have said, 'No, set a king over us.' So now present yourselves before the LORD by your tribes and clans."

20When Samuel brought all the tribes of Israel near, the tribe of Benjamin was chosen. 21Then he brought forward the tribe of Benjamin, clan by clan, and Matri's clan was chosen. Finally Saul son of Kish was chosen. But when they looked for him, he was not to be found. 22So they inquired further of the LORD, "Has the man come here yet?"

And the LORD said, "Yes, he has hidden himself among the baggage."

23They ran and brought him out, and as he stood among the people he was a head taller than any of the others. 24Samuel said to all the people, "Do you see the man the LORD has chosen? There is no one like him among all the people."

Then the people shouted, "Long live the king!"

25Samuel explained to the people the regulations of the kingship. He wrote them down on a scroll and deposited it before the LORD. Then Samuel dismissed the people, each to his own home.

26Saul also went to his home in Gibeah, accompanied by valiant men whose hearts God had touched. 27But some troublemakers said, "How can this fellow save us?" They despised him and brought him no gifts. But Saul kept silent.

Saul Rescues the City of Jabesh

11 Nahash the Ammonite went up and besieged Jabesh Gilead. And all the men of Jabesh said to him, "Make a treaty with us, and we will be subject to you."

2But Nahash the Ammonite replied, "I will make a treaty with you only on the condition that I gouge out the right eye of every one of you and so bring disgrace on all Israel."

3The elders of Jabesh said to him, "Give us seven days so we can send messengers throughout Israel; if no one comes to rescue us, we will surrender to you."

4When the messengers came to Gibeah of Saul and reported these terms to the people, they all wept aloud. 5Just then Saul was returning from the fields, behind his oxen, and he asked, "What is wrong with the people? Why are they weeping?" Then they repeated to him what the men of Jabesh had said.

6When Saul heard their words, the Spirit of God came upon him in power, and he burned with anger. 7He took a pair of oxen, cut them into pieces, and sent the pieces by messengers throughout Israel, proclaiming, "This is what will be done to the oxen of anyone who does not follow Saul and Samuel." Then the terror of the LORD fell on the people, and they turned out as one man. 8When Saul mustered them at Bezek, the men of Israel numbered three hundred thousand and the men of Judah thirty thousand.

9They told the messengers who had come, "Say to the men of Jabesh Gilead, 'By the time the sun is hot tomorrow, you will be delivered.' " When the messengers went and reported this to the men of Jabesh, they were elated. 10They said to the Ammonites, "Tomorrow we will surrender to you, and you can do to us whatever seems good to you."

11The next day Saul separated his men into three divisions; during the last watch of the night they broke into the camp of the Ammonites and slaughtered them until the heat of the day. Those who survived were scattered, so that no two of them were left together.

Saul Confirmed as King

12The people then said to Samuel, "Who was it that asked, 'Shall Saul reign over us?' Bring these men to us and we will put them to death."

13But Saul said, "No one shall be put to death today, for this day the LORD has rescued Israel."

14Then Samuel said to the people, "Come, let us go to Gilgal and there reaffirm the kingship." 15So all the people went to Gilgal and confirmed Saul as king in the presence of the LORD. There they sacrificed fellowship offerings[a] before the LORD, and Saul and all the Israelites held a great celebration.

[a]15 Traditionally *peace offerings*

Samuel's Farewell Speech

12 Samuel said to all Israel, "I have listened to everything you said to me
and have set a king over you. [2]Now you
have a king as your leader. As for me, I am
old and gray, and my sons are here with
you. I have been your leader from my
youth until this day. [3]Here I stand. Testify
against me in the presence of the LORD and
his anointed. Whose ox have I taken?
Whose donkey have I taken? Whom have
I cheated? Whom have I oppressed? From
whose hand have I accepted a bribe to
make me shut my eyes? If I have done any
of these, I will make it right."

[4]"You have not cheated or oppressed
us," they replied. "You have not taken
anything from anyone's hand."

[5]Samuel said to them, "The LORD is witness against you, and also his anointed is
witness this day, that you have not found
anything in my hand."

"He is witness," they said.

[6]Then Samuel said to the people, "It is
the LORD who appointed Moses and Aaron
and brought your forefathers up out of
Egypt. [7]Now then, stand here, because I
am going to confront you with evidence
before the LORD as to all the righteous acts
performed by the LORD for you and your
fathers.

[8]"After Jacob entered Egypt, they cried
to the LORD for help, and the LORD sent
Moses and Aaron, who brought your forefathers out of Egypt and settled them in
this place.

[9]"But they forgot the LORD their God; so
he sold them into the hand of Sisera, the
commander of the army of Hazor, and
into the hands of the Philistines and the
king of Moab, who fought against them.
[10]They cried out to the LORD and said, 'We
have sinned; we have forsaken the LORD
and served the Baals and the Ashtoreths.
But now deliver us from the hands of our
enemies, and we will serve you.' [11]Then
the LORD sent Jerub-Baal,[a] Barak,[b] Jephthah and Samuel,[c] and he delivered you
from the hands of your enemies on every
side, so that you lived securely.

[12]"But when you saw that Nahash king
of the Ammonites was moving against
you, you said to me, 'No, we want a king
to rule over us'—even though the LORD
your God was your king. [13]Now here is the
king you have chosen, the one you asked
for; see, the LORD has set a king over you.
[14]If you fear the LORD and serve and obey
him and do not rebel against his commands, and if both you and the king who
reigns over you follow the LORD your
God—good! [15]But if you do not obey the
LORD, and if you rebel against his commands, his hand will be against you, as it
was against your fathers.

[16]"Now then, stand still and see this
great thing the LORD is about to do before
your eyes! [17]Is it not wheat harvest now?
I will call upon the LORD to send thunder
and rain. And you will realize what an evil
thing you did in the eyes of the LORD when
you asked for a king."

[18]Then Samuel called upon the LORD,
and that same day the LORD sent thunder
and rain. So all the people stood in awe of
the LORD and of Samuel.

[19]The people all said to Samuel, "Pray
to the LORD your God for your servants so
that we will not die, for we have added to
all our other sins the evil of asking for a
king."

[20]"Do not be afraid," Samuel replied.
"You have done all this evil; yet do not
turn away from the LORD, but serve the
LORD with all your heart. [21]Do not turn
away after useless idols. They can do you
no good, nor can they rescue you, because
they are useless. [22]For the sake of his great
name the LORD will not reject his people,
because the LORD was pleased to make
you his own. [23]As for me, far be it from me
that I should sin against the LORD by failing to pray for you. And I will teach you
the way that is good and right. [24]But be
sure to fear the LORD and serve him faithfully with all your heart; consider what
great things he has done for you. [25]Yet if
you persist in doing evil, both you and
your king will be swept away."

Samuel Rebukes Saul

13 Saul was ⌊thirty⌋[d] years old when
he became king, and he reigned
over Israel ⌊forty-⌋[e] two years.

[2]Saul[f] chose three thousand men from
Israel; two thousand were with him at
Micmash and in the hill country of Bethel,
and a thousand were with Jonathan at

[a]11 Also called *Gideon* [b]11 Some Septuagint manuscripts and Syriac; Hebrew *Bedan* [c]11 Hebrew; some Septuagint manuscripts and Syriac *Samson* [d]1 A few late manuscripts of the Septuagint; Hebrew does not have *thirty.* [e]1 See the round number in Acts 13:21; Hebrew does not have *forty-.*
[f]1,2 Or *and when he had reigned over Israel two years,* [2]*he*

Gibeah in Benjamin. The rest of the men
he sent back to their homes.
3Jonathan attacked the Philistine out-
post at Geba, and the Philistines heard
about it. Then Saul had the trumpet blown
throughout the land and said, "Let the He-
brews hear!" 4So all Israel heard the news:
"Saul has attacked the Philistine outpost,
and now Israel has become a stench to the
Philistines." And the people were sum-
moned to join Saul at Gilgal.
5The Philistines assembled to fight Isra-
el, with three thousand[a] chariots, six
thousand charioteers, and soldiers as nu-
merous as the sand on the seashore. They
went up and camped at Micmash, east of
Beth Aven. 6When the men of Israel saw
that their situation was critical and that
their army was hard pressed, they hid in
caves and thickets, among the rocks, and
in pits and cisterns. 7Some Hebrews even
crossed the Jordan to the land of Gad and
Gilead.
Saul remained at Gilgal, and all the
troops with him were quaking with fear.
8He waited seven days, the time set by
Samuel; but Samuel did not come to Gil-
gal, and Saul's men began to scatter. 9So

[a]5 Some Septuagint manuscripts and Syriac; Hebrew *thirty thousand*

VERSE FOR THE DAY: 1 Samuel 12:24

AUTHOR: David Myers and Thomas Ludwig

PASSAGE FOR THE DAY: 1 Samuel 12:22–24

No Comparison

Whenever we feel deprived because of something that lies outside our power to control, we should accept our situation with calmness and equanimity. We can work to resist the tendency to compare ourselves with those higher on the success ladder and instead choose to remember those less fortunate. Earlier generations called it "counting your blessings." It's not a trite cliché.

We can avoid settings where we're surrounded by other people's luxury. We can even go out of our way to confront true poverty, to drown our relative deprivations in the absolute deprivation facing so many human beings. Some people's unmet needs—such as clean water, adequate nutrition, or medical care—are things we take for granted.

It's much easier, after seeing another's poverty, to thank God for all the ways in which he provides for our needs.

MARRIAGE BUILDERS

♦ *Does remembering God's goodness to you in the past affect your desire to serve him as a couple?*
♦ *How can you cultivate a habit of "counting your blessings"?*

Additional Scripture Readings
Ecclesiastes 4:1–6; Galatians 6:1–5; 2 Corinthians 10:12–18

Go to page 284 for your next devotional reading.

he said, "Bring me the burnt offering and the fellowship offerings.[a]" And Saul offered up the burnt offering. 10Just as he finished making the offering, Samuel arrived, and Saul went out to greet him.

11"What have you done?" asked Samuel.

Saul replied, "When I saw that the men were scattering, and that you did not come at the set time, and that the Philistines were assembling at Micmash, 12I thought, 'Now the Philistines will come down against me at Gilgal, and I have not sought the LORD's favor.' So I felt compelled to offer the burnt offering."

13"You acted foolishly," Samuel said. "You have not kept the command the LORD your God gave you; if you had, he would have established your kingdom over Israel for all time. 14But now your kingdom will not endure; the LORD has sought out a man after his own heart and appointed him leader of his people, because you have not kept the LORD's command."

15Then Samuel left Gilgal[b] and went up to Gibeah in Benjamin, and Saul counted the men who were with him. They numbered about six hundred.

Israel Without Weapons

16Saul and his son Jonathan and the men with them were staying in Gibeah[c] in Benjamin, while the Philistines camped at Micmash. 17Raiding parties went out from the Philistine camp in three detachments. One turned toward Ophrah in the vicinity of Shual, 18another toward Beth Horon, and the third toward the borderland overlooking the Valley of Zeboim facing the desert.

19Not a blacksmith could be found in the whole land of Israel, because the Philistines had said, "Otherwise the Hebrews will make swords or spears!" 20So all Israel went down to the Philistines to have their plowshares, mattocks, axes and sickles[d] sharpened. 21The price was two thirds of a shekel[e] for sharpening plowshares and mattocks, and a third of a shekel[f] for sharpening forks and axes and for repointing goads.

22So on the day of the battle not a soldier with Saul and Jonathan had a sword or spear in his hand; only Saul and his son Jonathan had them.

Jonathan Attacks the Philistines

23Now a detachment of Philistines had

14 gone out to the pass at Micmash. 1One day Jonathan son of Saul said to the young man bearing his armor, "Come, let's go over to the Philistine outpost on the other side." But he did not tell his father.

2Saul was staying on the outskirts of Gibeah under a pomegranate tree in Migron. With him were about six hundred men, 3among whom was Ahijah, who was wearing an ephod. He was a son of Ichabod's brother Ahitub son of Phinehas, the son of Eli, the LORD's priest in Shiloh. No one was aware that Jonathan had left.

4On each side of the pass that Jonathan intended to cross to reach the Philistine outpost was a cliff; one was called Bozez, and the other Seneh. 5One cliff stood to the north toward Micmash, the other to the south toward Geba.

6Jonathan said to his young armor-bearer, "Come, let's go over to the outpost of those uncircumcised fellows. Perhaps the LORD will act in our behalf. Nothing can hinder the LORD from saving, whether by many or by few."

7"Do all that you have in mind," his armor-bearer said. "Go ahead; I am with you heart and soul."

8Jonathan said, "Come, then; we will cross over toward the men and let them see us. 9If they say to us, 'Wait there until we come to you,' we will stay where we are and not go up to them. 10But if they say, 'Come up to us,' we will climb up, because that will be our sign that the LORD has given them into our hands."

11So both of them showed themselves to the Philistine outpost. "Look!" said the Philistines. "The Hebrews are crawling out of the holes they were hiding in." 12The men of the outpost shouted to Jonathan and his armor-bearer, "Come up to us and we'll teach you a lesson."

So Jonathan said to his armor-bearer, "Climb up after me; the LORD has given them into the hand of Israel."

[a]9 Traditionally *peace offerings* [b]15 Hebrew; Septuagint *Gilgal and went his way; the rest of the people went after Saul to meet the army, and they went out of Gilgal* [c]16 Two Hebrew manuscripts; most Hebrew manuscripts *Geba,* a variant of *Gibeah* [d]20 Septuagint; Hebrew *plowshares* [e]21 Hebrew *pim*; that is, about 1/4 ounce (about 8 grams) [f]21 That is, about 1/8 ounce (about 4 grams)

13Jonathan climbed up, using his hands
and feet, with his armor-bearer right be-
hind him. The Philistines fell before Jona-
than, and his armor-bearer followed and
killed behind him. 14In that first attack
Jonathan and his armor-bearer killed
some twenty men in an area of about half
an acre.[a]

Israel Routs the Philistines

15Then panic struck the whole army—
those in the camp and field, and those in
the outposts and raiding parties—and the
ground shook. It was a panic sent by
God.[b]
16Saul's lookouts at Gibeah in Benjamin
saw the army melting away in all direc-
tions. 17Then Saul said to the men who
were with him, "Muster the forces and see
who has left us." When they did, it was
Jonathan and his armor-bearer who were
not there.
18Saul said to Ahijah, "Bring the ark of
God." (At that time it was with the Israel-
ites.)[c] 19While Saul was talking to the
priest, the tumult in the Philistine camp
increased more and more. So Saul said to
the priest, "Withdraw your hand."
20Then Saul and all his men assembled
and went to the battle. They found the
Philistines in total confusion, striking
each other with their swords. 21Those He-
brews who had previously been with the
Philistines and had gone up with them to
their camp went over to the Israelites who
were with Saul and Jonathan. 22When all
the Israelites who had hidden in the hill
country of Ephraim heard that the Philis-
tines were on the run, they joined the bat-
tle in hot pursuit. 23So the LORD rescued
Israel that day, and the battle moved on
beyond Beth Aven.

Jonathan Eats Honey

24Now the men of Israel were in distress
that day, because Saul had bound the peo-
ple under an oath, saying, "Cursed be any
man who eats food before evening comes,
before I have avenged myself on my ene-
mies!" So none of the troops tasted food.
25The entire army[d] entered the woods,
and there was honey on the ground.
26When they went into the woods, they
saw the honey oozing out, yet no one put
his hand to his mouth, because they
feared the oath. 27But Jonathan had not
heard that his father had bound the peo-
ple with the oath, so he reached out the
end of the staff that was in his hand and
dipped it into the honeycomb. He raised
his hand to his mouth, and his eyes
brightened.[e] 28Then one of the soldiers
told him, "Your father bound the army un-
der a strict oath, saying, 'Cursed be any
man who eats food today!' That is why the
men are faint."
29Jonathan said, "My father has made
trouble for the country. See how my eyes
brightened[f] when I tasted a little of this
honey. 30How much better it would have
been if the men had eaten today some of
the plunder they took from their enemies.
Would not the slaughter of the Philistines
have been even greater?"
31That day, after the Israelites had
struck down the Philistines from Micmash
to Aijalon, they were exhausted. 32They
pounced on the plunder and, taking
sheep, cattle and calves, they butchered
them on the ground and ate them, togeth-
er with the blood. 33Then someone said to
Saul, "Look, the men are sinning against
the LORD by eating meat that has blood
in it."
"You have broken faith," he said. "Roll
a large stone over here at once." 34Then he
said, "Go out among the men and tell
them, 'Each of you bring me your cattle
and sheep, and slaughter them here and
eat them. Do not sin against the LORD by
eating meat with blood still in it.' "
So everyone brought his ox that night
and slaughtered it there. 35Then Saul built
an altar to the LORD; it was the first time he
had done this.
36Saul said, "Let us go down after the
Philistines by night and plunder them till
dawn, and let us not leave one of them
alive."
"Do whatever seems best to you," they
replied.
But the priest said, "Let us inquire of
God here."
37So Saul asked God, "Shall I go down
after the Philistines? Will you give them
into Israel's hand?" But God did not an-
swer him that day.
38Saul therefore said, "Come here, all

[a]14 Hebrew *half a yoke*; a "yoke" was the land plowed by a yoke of oxen in one day. [b]15 Or *a terrible panic* [c]18 Hebrew; Septuagint *"Bring the ephod." (At that time he wore the ephod before the Israelites.)* [d]25 Or *Now all the people of the land* [e]27 Or *his strength was renewed* [f]29 Or *my strength was renewed*

you who are leaders of the army, and let us find out what sin has been committed today. 39As surely as the LORD who rescues Israel lives, even if it lies with my son Jonathan, he must die." But not one of the men said a word.

40Saul then said to all the Israelites, "You stand over there; I and Jonathan my son will stand over here."

"Do what seems best to you," the men replied.

41Then Saul prayed to the LORD, the God of Israel, "Give me the right answer."[a] And Jonathan and Saul were taken by lot, and the men were cleared. 42Saul said, "Cast the lot between me and Jonathan my son." And Jonathan was taken.

43Then Saul said to Jonathan, "Tell me what you have done."

So Jonathan told him, "I merely tasted a little honey with the end of my staff. And now must I die?"

44Saul said, "May God deal with me, be it ever so severely, if you do not die, Jonathan."

45But the men said to Saul, "Should Jonathan die—he who has brought about this great deliverance in Israel? Never! As surely as the LORD lives, not a hair of his head will fall to the ground, for he did this today with God's help." So the men rescued Jonathan, and he was not put to death.

46Then Saul stopped pursuing the Philistines, and they withdrew to their own land.

47After Saul had assumed rule over Israel, he fought against their enemies on every side: Moab, the Ammonites, Edom, the kings[b] of Zobah, and the Philistines. Wherever he turned, he inflicted punishment on them.[c] 48He fought valiantly and defeated the Amalekites, delivering Israel from the hands of those who had plundered them.

Saul's Family

49Saul's sons were Jonathan, Ishvi and Malki-Shua. The name of his older daughter was Merab, and that of the younger was Michal. 50His wife's name was Ahinoam daughter of Ahimaaz. The name of the commander of Saul's army was Abner son of Ner, and Ner was Saul's uncle. 51Saul's father Kish and Abner's father Ner were sons of Abiel.

52All the days of Saul there was bitter war with the Philistines, and whenever Saul saw a mighty or brave man, he took him into his service.

The LORD Rejects Saul as King

15 Samuel said to Saul, "I am the one the LORD sent to anoint you king over his people Israel; so listen now to the message from the LORD. 2This is what the LORD Almighty says: 'I will punish the Amalekites for what they did to Israel when they waylaid them as they came up from Egypt. 3Now go, attack the Amalekites and totally destroy[d] everything that belongs to them. Do not spare them; put to death men and women, children and infants, cattle and sheep, camels and donkeys.' "

4So Saul summoned the men and mustered them at Telaim—two hundred thousand foot soldiers and ten thousand men from Judah. 5Saul went to the city of Amalek and set an ambush in the ravine. 6Then he said to the Kenites, "Go away, leave the Amalekites so that I do not destroy you along with them; for you showed kindness to all the Israelites when they came up out of Egypt." So the Kenites moved away from the Amalekites.

7Then Saul attacked the Amalekites all the way from Havilah to Shur, to the east of Egypt. 8He took Agag king of the Amalekites alive, and all his people he totally destroyed with the sword. 9But Saul and the army spared Agag and the best of the sheep and cattle, the fat calves[e] and lambs—everything that was good. These they were unwilling to destroy completely, but everything that was despised and weak they totally destroyed.

10Then the word of the LORD came to Samuel: 11"I am grieved that I have made Saul king, because he has turned away from me and has not carried out my instructions." Samuel was troubled, and he cried out to the LORD all that night.

12Early in the morning Samuel got up

[a]41 Hebrew; Septuagint *"Why have you not answered your servant today? If the fault is in me or my son Jonathan, respond with Urim, but if the men of Israel are at fault, respond with Thummim."*
[b]47 Masoretic Text; Dead Sea Scrolls and Septuagint *king* [c]47 Hebrew; Septuagint *he was victorious*
[d]3 The Hebrew term refers to the irrevocable giving over of things or persons to the LORD, often by totally destroying them; also in verses 8, 9, 15, 18, 20 and 21. [e]9 Or *the grown bulls*; the meaning of the Hebrew for this phrase is uncertain.

and went to meet Saul, but he was told,
"Saul has gone to Carmel. There he has set
up a monument in his own honor and has
turned and gone on down to Gilgal."
13When Samuel reached him, Saul said,
"The LORD bless you! I have carried out
the LORD's instructions."
14But Samuel said, "What then is this
bleating of sheep in my ears? What is this
lowing of cattle that I hear?"
15Saul answered, "The soldiers brought
them from the Amalekites; they spared
the best of the sheep and cattle to sacrifice
to the LORD your God, but we totally de-
stroyed the rest."
16"Stop!" Samuel said to Saul. "Let me
tell you what the LORD said to me last
night."
"Tell me," Saul replied.
17Samuel said, "Although you were
once small in your own eyes, did you not
become the head of the tribes of Israel?
The LORD anointed you king over Israel.
18And he sent you on a mission, saying,
'Go and completely destroy those wicked
people, the Amalekites; make war on
them until you have wiped them out.'
19Why did you not obey the LORD? Why
did you pounce on the plunder and do evil
in the eyes of the LORD?"
20"But I did obey the LORD," Saul said. "I
went on the mission the LORD assigned
me. I completely destroyed the Amalek-
ites and brought back Agag their king.
21The soldiers took sheep and cattle from
the plunder, the best of what was devoted
to God, in order to sacrifice them to the
LORD your God at Gilgal."
22But Samuel replied:

"Does the LORD delight in burnt
offerings and sacrifices
as much as in obeying the voice of
the LORD?

TUESDAY

VERSE FOR THE DAY: 1 Samuel 15:22
AUTHOR: Elizabeth Cody Newenhuyse
PASSAGE FOR THE DAY: 1 Samuel 15:1–35

It's Good to Ask God

My husband and I have been more or less consistent with our early-morning ritual of prayer. Usually we pray through a list of concerns, needs, confessions and praises. At times, it's hard not to feel perfunctory about this, as if we're quickly discharging a morning duty: brush teeth, shave, pray.

But "duty" isn't always a dirty word. Our prayer time gives us a refreshing pause in the morning rush; yet it has little to do, really, with what's good for us. It has everything to do with an old-fashioned word we don't hear much any more: obedience. It helps our marriage when we're obedient together.

MARRIAGE BUILDERS

♦ *What items would you like to pray about each day with each other?*

♦ *How might you create a time to pray together regularly?*

Additional Scripture Readings
Luke 11:28; 1 John 2:5; 5:3

Go to page 286 for your next devotional reading.

To obey is better than sacrifice,
and to heed is better than the fat of rams.
23For rebellion is like the sin of divination,
and arrogance like the evil of idolatry.
Because you have rejected the word of the LORD,
he has rejected you as king."

24Then Saul said to Samuel, "I have sinned. I violated the LORD's command and your instructions. I was afraid of the people and so I gave in to them. 25Now I beg you, forgive my sin and come back with me, so that I may worship the LORD."

26But Samuel said to him, "I will not go back with you. You have rejected the word of the LORD, and the LORD has rejected you as king over Israel!"

27As Samuel turned to leave, Saul caught hold of the hem of his robe, and it tore. 28Samuel said to him, "The LORD has torn the kingdom of Israel from you today and has given it to one of your neighbors—to one better than you. 29He who is the Glory of Israel does not lie or change his mind; for he is not a man, that he should change his mind."

30Saul replied, "I have sinned. But please honor me before the elders of my people and before Israel; come back with me, so that I may worship the LORD your God." 31So Samuel went back with Saul, and Saul worshiped the LORD.

32Then Samuel said, "Bring me Agag king of the Amalekites."

Agag came to him confidently,[a] thinking, "Surely the bitterness of death is past."

33But Samuel said,

"As your sword has made women childless,
so will your mother be childless among women."

And Samuel put Agag to death before the LORD at Gilgal.

34Then Samuel left for Ramah, but Saul went up to his home in Gibeah of Saul. 35Until the day Samuel died, he did not go to see Saul again, though Samuel mourned for him. And the LORD was grieved that he had made Saul king over Israel.

Samuel Anoints David

16 The LORD said to Samuel, "How long will you mourn for Saul, since I have rejected him as king over Israel? Fill your horn with oil and be on your way; I am sending you to Jesse of Bethlehem. I have chosen one of his sons to be king."

2But Samuel said, "How can I go? Saul will hear about it and kill me."

The LORD said, "Take a heifer with you and say, 'I have come to sacrifice to the LORD.' 3Invite Jesse to the sacrifice, and I will show you what to do. You are to anoint for me the one I indicate."

4Samuel did what the LORD said. When he arrived at Bethlehem, the elders of the town trembled when they met him. They asked, "Do you come in peace?"

5Samuel replied, "Yes, in peace; I have come to sacrifice to the LORD. Consecrate yourselves and come to the sacrifice with me." Then he consecrated Jesse and his sons and invited them to the sacrifice.

6When they arrived, Samuel saw Eliab and thought, "Surely the LORD's anointed stands here before the LORD."

7But the LORD said to Samuel, "Do not consider his appearance or his height, for I have rejected him. The LORD does not look at the things man looks at. Man looks at the outward appearance, but the LORD looks at the heart."

8Then Jesse called Abinadab and had him pass in front of Samuel. But Samuel said, "The LORD has not chosen this one either." 9Jesse then had Shammah pass by, but Samuel said, "Nor has the LORD chosen this one." 10Jesse had seven of his sons pass before Samuel, but Samuel said to him, "The LORD has not chosen these." 11So he asked Jesse, "Are these all the sons you have?"

"There is still the youngest," Jesse answered, "but he is tending the sheep."

Samuel said, "Send for him; we will not sit down[b] until he arrives."

12So he sent and had him brought in. He was ruddy, with a fine appearance and handsome features.

Then the LORD said, "Rise and anoint him; he is the one."

13So Samuel took the horn of oil and anointed him in the presence of his brothers, and from that day on the Spirit of the LORD came upon David in power. Samuel then went to Ramah.

[a]32 Or *him trembling, yet* [b]11 Some Septuagint manuscripts; Hebrew *not gather around*

David in Saul's Service

14 Now the Spirit of the LORD had departed from Saul, and an evil[a] spirit from the
LORD tormented him.
15 Saul's attendants said to him, "See, an
evil spirit from God is tormenting you.
16 Let our lord command his servants here
to search for someone who can play the
harp. He will play when the evil spirit
from God comes upon you, and you will
feel better."
17 So Saul said to his attendants, "Find

[a] 14 Or *injurious*; also in verses 15, 16 and 23

VERSE FOR THE DAY: 1 Samuel 16:7

AUTHOR: John Fischer

PASSAGE FOR THE DAY: 1 Samuel 16:1–13

Shedding the Image

I was speaking at an informal seminar. When one couple came in late, I couldn't help but notice that the girl was very attractive. The guy, however, was a prototype nerd. But they were obviously in love.

"What could she see in him?" I wondered. And then I realized she was blind.

What *did* she see in him? Everything that's important about who a person is . . . about what love is . . . about what a man is. She saw everything she needed to know about him. Blessed are the blind, for they can see people as they really are.

As two people grow more familiar in marriage, the excitement often fades. Why? In the early stages of a new relationship, we're usually seeing more of the *image* than we are of the real person. We've seen enough on the surface to know that our partner meets some of the requirements of the ideal we seek, and we project the rest of our ideal on the person. Sooner or later, however, the *real* person is going to start breaking through the image, and that's when disillusionment sets in. The success of a marriage comes not in finding the "right" person, but in the ability of both partners to adjust to the real person they married.

MARRIAGE BUILDERS

♦ *What is something you love about your spouse that you didn't even know about him or her when you first got married?*

♦ *What are some of the rewards of loving your* real *spouse instead of his or her image?*

Additional Scripture Readings
1 Peter 3:3–4; Psalm 139:1, 23–24; 1 Chronicles 28:9

Go to page 309 for your next devotional reading.

someone who plays well and bring him to me."

18One of the servants answered, "I have seen a son of Jesse of Bethlehem who knows how to play the harp. He is a brave man and a warrior. He speaks well and is a fine-looking man. And the LORD is with him."

19Then Saul sent messengers to Jesse and said, "Send me your son David, who is with the sheep." 20So Jesse took a donkey loaded with bread, a skin of wine and a young goat and sent them with his son David to Saul.

21David came to Saul and entered his service. Saul liked him very much, and David became one of his armor-bearers. 22Then Saul sent word to Jesse, saying, "Allow David to remain in my service, for I am pleased with him."

23Whenever the spirit from God came upon Saul, David would take his harp and play. Then relief would come to Saul; he would feel better, and the evil spirit would leave him.

David and Goliath

17 Now the Philistines gathered their forces for war and assembled at Socoh in Judah. They pitched camp at Ephes Dammim, between Socoh and Azekah. 2Saul and the Israelites assembled and camped in the Valley of Elah and drew up their battle line to meet the Philistines. 3The Philistines occupied one hill and the Israelites another, with the valley between them.

4A champion named Goliath, who was from Gath, came out of the Philistine camp. He was over nine feet[a] tall. 5He had a bronze helmet on his head and wore a coat of scale armor of bronze weighing five thousand shekels[b]; 6on his legs he wore bronze greaves, and a bronze javelin was slung on his back. 7His spear shaft was like a weaver's rod, and its iron point weighed six hundred shekels.[c] His shield bearer went ahead of him.

8Goliath stood and shouted to the ranks of Israel, "Why do you come out and line up for battle? Am I not a Philistine, and are you not the servants of Saul? Choose a man and have him come down to me. 9If he is able to fight and kill me, we will become your subjects; but if I overcome him and kill him, you will become our subjects and serve us." 10Then the Philistine said, "This day I defy the ranks of Israel! Give me a man and let us fight each other." 11On hearing the Philistine's words, Saul and all the Israelites were dismayed and terrified.

12Now David was the son of an Ephrathite named Jesse, who was from Bethlehem in Judah. Jesse had eight sons, and in Saul's time he was old and well advanced in years. 13Jesse's three oldest sons had followed Saul to the war: The firstborn was Eliab; the second, Abinadab; and the third, Shammah. 14David was the youngest. The three oldest followed Saul, 15but David went back and forth from Saul to tend his father's sheep at Bethlehem.

16For forty days the Philistine came forward every morning and evening and took his stand.

17Now Jesse said to his son David, "Take this ephah[d] of roasted grain and these ten loaves of bread for your brothers and hurry to their camp. 18Take along these ten cheeses to the commander of their unit.[e] See how your brothers are and bring back some assurance[f] from them. 19They are with Saul and all the men of Israel in the Valley of Elah, fighting against the Philistines."

20Early in the morning David left the flock with a shepherd, loaded up and set out, as Jesse had directed. He reached the camp as the army was going out to its battle positions, shouting the war cry. 21Israel and the Philistines were drawing up their lines facing each other. 22David left his things with the keeper of supplies, ran to the battle lines and greeted his brothers. 23As he was talking with them, Goliath, the Philistine champion from Gath, stepped out from his lines and shouted his usual defiance, and David heard it. 24When the Israelites saw the man, they all ran from him in great fear.

25Now the Israelites had been saying, "Do you see how this man keeps coming out? He comes out to defy Israel. The king will give great wealth to the man who kills him. He will also give him his daughter in marriage and will exempt his father's family from taxes in Israel."

26David asked the men standing near him, "What will be done for the man who

[a] *4* Hebrew *was six cubits and a span* (about 3 meters) [b] *5* That is, about 125 pounds (about 57 kilograms) [c] *7* That is, about 15 pounds (about 7 kilograms) [d] *17* That is, probably about 3/5 bushel (about 22 liters) [e] *18* Hebrew *thousand* [f] *18* Or *some token*; or *some pledge of spoils*

kills this Philistine and removes this disgrace from Israel? Who is this uncircumcised Philistine that he should defy the armies of the living God?"

27They repeated to him what they had been saying and told him, "This is what will be done for the man who kills him."

28When Eliab, David's oldest brother, heard him speaking with the men, he burned with anger at him and asked, "Why have you come down here? And with whom did you leave those few sheep in the desert? I know how conceited you are and how wicked your heart is; you came down only to watch the battle."

29"Now what have I done?" said David. "Can't I even speak?" 30He then turned away to someone else and brought up the same matter, and the men answered him as before. 31What David said was overheard and reported to Saul, and Saul sent for him.

32David said to Saul, "Let no one lose heart on account of this Philistine; your servant will go and fight him."

33Saul replied, "You are not able to go out against this Philistine and fight him; you are only a boy, and he has been a fighting man from his youth."

34But David said to Saul, "Your servant has been keeping his father's sheep. When a lion or a bear came and carried off a sheep from the flock, 35I went after it, struck it and rescued the sheep from its mouth. When it turned on me, I seized it by its hair, struck it and killed it. 36Your servant has killed both the lion and the bear; this uncircumcised Philistine will be like one of them, because he has defied the armies of the living God. 37The LORD who delivered me from the paw of the lion and the paw of the bear will deliver me from the hand of this Philistine."

Saul said to David, "Go, and the LORD be with you."

38Then Saul dressed David in his own tunic. He put a coat of armor on him and a bronze helmet on his head. 39David fastened on his sword over the tunic and tried walking around, because he was not used to them.

"I cannot go in these," he said to Saul, "because I am not used to them." So he took them off. 40Then he took his staff in his hand, chose five smooth stones from the stream, put them in the pouch of his shepherd's bag and, with his sling in his hand, approached the Philistine.

41Meanwhile, the Philistine, with his shield bearer in front of him, kept coming closer to David. 42He looked David over and saw that he was only a boy, ruddy and handsome, and he despised him. 43He said to David, "Am I a dog, that you come at me with sticks?" And the Philistine cursed David by his gods. 44"Come here," he said, "and I'll give your flesh to the birds of the air and the beasts of the field!"

45David said to the Philistine, "You come against me with sword and spear and javelin, but I come against you in the name of the LORD Almighty, the God of the armies of Israel, whom you have defied. 46This day the LORD will hand you over to me, and I'll strike you down and cut off your head. Today I will give the carcasses of the Philistine army to the birds of the air and the beasts of the earth, and the whole world will know that there is a God in Israel. 47All those gathered here will know that it is not by sword or spear that the LORD saves; for the battle is the LORD's, and he will give all of you into our hands."

48As the Philistine moved closer to attack him, David ran quickly toward the battle line to meet him. 49Reaching into his bag and taking out a stone, he slung it and struck the Philistine on the forehead. The stone sank into his forehead, and he fell facedown on the ground.

50So David triumphed over the Philistine with a sling and a stone; without a sword in his hand he struck down the Philistine and killed him.

51David ran and stood over him. He took hold of the Philistine's sword and drew it from the scabbard. After he killed him, he cut off his head with the sword.

When the Philistines saw that their hero was dead, they turned and ran. 52Then the men of Israel and Judah surged forward with a shout and pursued the Philistines to the entrance of Gath[a] and to the gates of Ekron. Their dead were strewn along the Shaaraim road to Gath and Ekron. 53When the Israelites returned from chasing the Philistines, they plundered their camp. 54David took the Philistine's head and brought it to Jerusalem, and he put the Philistine's weapons in his own tent.

55As Saul watched David going out to meet the Philistine, he said to Abner, com-

[a]52 Some Septuagint manuscripts; Hebrew *a valley*

mander of the army, "Abner, whose son is that young man?"

Abner replied, "As surely as you live, O king, I don't know."

56The king said, "Find out whose son this young man is."

57As soon as David returned from killing the Philistine, Abner took him and brought him before Saul, with David still holding the Philistine's head.

58"Whose son are you, young man?" Saul asked him.

David said, "I am the son of your servant Jesse of Bethlehem."

Saul's Jealousy of David

18 After David had finished talking with Saul, Jonathan became one in spirit with David, and he loved him as himself. 2From that day Saul kept David with him and did not let him return to his father's house. 3And Jonathan made a covenant with David because he loved him as himself. 4Jonathan took off the robe he was wearing and gave it to David, along with his tunic, and even his sword, his bow and his belt.

5Whatever Saul sent him to do, David did it so successfully[a] that Saul gave him a high rank in the army. This pleased all the people, and Saul's officers as well.

6When the men were returning home after David had killed the Philistine, the women came out from all the towns of Israel to meet King Saul with singing and dancing, with joyful songs and with tambourines and lutes. 7As they danced, they sang:

"Saul has slain his thousands,
and David his tens of thousands."

8Saul was very angry; this refrain galled him. "They have credited David with tens of thousands," he thought, "but me with only thousands. What more can he get but the kingdom?" 9And from that time on Saul kept a jealous eye on David.

10The next day an evil[b] spirit from God came forcefully upon Saul. He was prophesying in his house, while David was playing the harp, as he usually did. Saul had a spear in his hand 11and he hurled it, saying to himself, "I'll pin David to the wall." But David eluded him twice.

12Saul was afraid of David, because the LORD was with David but had left Saul. 13So he sent David away from him and gave him command over a thousand men, and David led the troops in their campaigns. 14In everything he did he had great success,[c] because the LORD was with him. 15When Saul saw how successful[d] he was, he was afraid of him. 16But all Israel and Judah loved David, because he led them in their campaigns.

17Saul said to David, "Here is my older daughter Merab. I will give her to you in marriage; only serve me bravely and fight the battles of the LORD." For Saul said to himself, "I will not raise a hand against him. Let the Philistines do that!"

18But David said to Saul, "Who am I, and what is my family or my father's clan in Israel, that I should become the king's son-in-law?" 19So[e] when the time came for Merab, Saul's daughter, to be given to David, she was given in marriage to Adriel of Meholah.

20Now Saul's daughter Michal was in love with David, and when they told Saul about it, he was pleased. 21"I will give her to him," he thought, "so that she may be a snare to him and so that the hand of the Philistines may be against him." So Saul said to David, "Now you have a second opportunity to become my son-in-law."

22Then Saul ordered his attendants: "Speak to David privately and say, 'Look, the king is pleased with you, and his attendants all like you; now become his son-in-law.' "

23They repeated these words to David. But David said, "Do you think it is a small matter to become the king's son-in-law? I'm only a poor man and little known."

24When Saul's servants told him what David had said, 25Saul replied, "Say to David, 'The king wants no other price for the bride than a hundred Philistine foreskins, to take revenge on his enemies.' " Saul's plan was to have David fall by the hands of the Philistines.

26When the attendants told David these things, he was pleased to become the king's son-in-law. So before the allotted time elapsed, 27David and his men went out and killed two hundred Philistines. He brought their foreskins and presented the full number to the king so that he might become the king's son-in-law. Then Saul gave him his daughter Michal in marriage.

28When Saul realized that the LORD was with David and that his daughter Michal loved David, 29Saul became still more

[a]5 Or *wisely* [b]10 Or *injurious* [c]14 Or *he was very wise* [d]15 Or *wise* [e]19 Or *However,*

afraid of him, and he remained his enemy the rest of his days.

30The Philistine commanders continued to go out to battle, and as often as they did, David met with more success[a] than the rest of Saul's officers, and his name became well known.

Saul Tries to Kill David

19 Saul told his son Jonathan and all the attendants to kill David. But Jonathan was very fond of David 2and warned him, "My father Saul is looking for a chance to kill you. Be on your guard tomorrow morning; go into hiding and stay there. 3I will go out and stand with my father in the field where you are. I'll speak to him about you and will tell you what I find out."

4Jonathan spoke well of David to Saul his father and said to him, "Let not the king do wrong to his servant David; he has not wronged you, and what he has done has benefited you greatly. 5He took his life in his hands when he killed the Philistine. The LORD won a great victory for all Israel, and you saw it and were glad. Why then would you do wrong to an innocent man like David by killing him for no reason?"

6Saul listened to Jonathan and took this oath: "As surely as the LORD lives, David will not be put to death."

7So Jonathan called David and told him the whole conversation. He brought him to Saul, and David was with Saul as before.

8Once more war broke out, and David went out and fought the Philistines. He struck them with such force that they fled before him.

9But an evil[b] spirit from the LORD came upon Saul as he was sitting in his house with his spear in his hand. While David was playing the harp, 10Saul tried to pin him to the wall with his spear, but David eluded him as Saul drove the spear into the wall. That night David made good his escape.

11Saul sent men to David's house to watch it and to kill him in the morning. But Michal, David's wife, warned him, "If you don't run for your life tonight, tomorrow you'll be killed." 12So Michal let David down through a window, and he fled and escaped. 13Then Michal took an idol[c] and laid it on the bed, covering it with a garment and putting some goats' hair at the head.

14When Saul sent the men to capture David, Michal said, "He is ill."

15Then Saul sent the men back to see David and told them, "Bring him up to me in his bed so that I may kill him." 16But when the men entered, there was the idol in the bed, and at the head was some goats' hair.

17Saul said to Michal, "Why did you deceive me like this and send my enemy away so that he escaped?"

Michal told him, "He said to me, 'Let me get away. Why should I kill you?' "

18When David had fled and made his escape, he went to Samuel at Ramah and told him all that Saul had done to him. Then he and Samuel went to Naioth and stayed there. 19Word came to Saul: "David is in Naioth at Ramah"; 20so he sent men to capture him. But when they saw a group of prophets prophesying, with Samuel standing there as their leader, the Spirit of God came upon Saul's men and they also prophesied. 21Saul was told about it, and he sent more men, and they prophesied too. Saul sent men a third time, and they also prophesied. 22Finally, he himself left for Ramah and went to the great cistern at Secu. And he asked, "Where are Samuel and David?"

"Over in Naioth at Ramah," they said.

23So Saul went to Naioth at Ramah. But the Spirit of God came even upon him, and he walked along prophesying until he came to Naioth. 24He stripped off his robes and also prophesied in Samuel's presence. He lay that way all that day and night. This is why people say, "Is Saul also among the prophets?"

David and Jonathan

20 Then David fled from Naioth at Ramah and went to Jonathan and asked, "What have I done? What is my crime? How have I wronged your father, that he is trying to take my life?"

2"Never!" Jonathan replied. "You are not going to die! Look, my father doesn't do anything, great or small, without confiding in me. Why would he hide this from me? It's not so!"

3But David took an oath and said, "Your father knows very well that I have found favor in your eyes, and he has said to himself, 'Jonathan must not know this or he

[a]30 Or *David acted more wisely* [b]9 Or *injurious* [c]13 Hebrew *teraphim*; also in verse 16

will be grieved.' Yet as surely as the LORD
lives and as you live, there is only a step
between me and death."
4Jonathan said to David, "Whatever you
want me to do, I'll do for you."
5So David said, "Look, tomorrow is the
New Moon festival, and I am supposed to
dine with the king; but let me go and hide
in the field until the evening of the day af-
ter tomorrow. 6If your father misses me at
all, tell him, 'David earnestly asked my
permission to hurry to Bethlehem, his
hometown, because an annual sacrifice is
being made there for his whole clan.' 7If
he says, 'Very well,' then your servant is
safe. But if he loses his temper, you can be
sure that he is determined to harm me.
8As for you, show kindness to your ser-
vant, for you have brought him into a cov-
enant with you before the LORD. If I am
guilty, then kill me yourself! Why hand
me over to your father?"
9"Never!" Jonathan said. "If I had the
least inkling that my father was deter-
mined to harm you, wouldn't I tell you?"
10David asked, "Who will tell me if your
father answers you harshly?"
11"Come," Jonathan said, "let's go out
into the field." So they went there to-
gether.
12Then Jonathan said to David: "By the
LORD, the God of Israel, I will surely sound
out my father by this time the day after
tomorrow! If he is favorably disposed to-
ward you, will I not send you word and let
you know? 13But if my father is inclined to
harm you, may the LORD deal with me, be
it ever so severely, if I do not let you know
and send you away safely. May the LORD
be with you as he has been with my fa-
ther. 14But show me unfailing kindness
like that of the LORD as long as I live, so
that I may not be killed, 15and do not ever
cut off your kindness from my family—
not even when the LORD has cut off every
one of David's enemies from the face of
the earth."
16So Jonathan made a covenant with
the house of David, saying, "May the LORD
call David's enemies to account." 17And
Jonathan had David reaffirm his oath out
of love for him, because he loved him as
he loved himself.
18Then Jonathan said to David: "Tomor-
row is the New Moon festival. You will be
missed, because your seat will be empty.
19The day after tomorrow, toward eve-
ning, go to the place where you hid when
this trouble began, and wait by the stone
Ezel. 20I will shoot three arrows to the side
of it, as though I were shooting at a target.
21Then I will send a boy and say, 'Go, find
the arrows.' If I say to him, 'Look, the ar-
rows are on this side of you; bring them
here,' then come, because, as surely as the
LORD lives, you are safe; there is no dan-
ger. 22But if I say to the boy, 'Look, the
arrows are beyond you,' then you must
go, because the LORD has sent you away.
23And about the matter you and I dis-
cussed—remember, the LORD is witness
between you and me forever."
24So David hid in the field, and when
the New Moon festival came, the king sat
down to eat. 25He sat in his customary
place by the wall, opposite Jonathan,[a]
and Abner sat next to Saul, but David's
place was empty. 26Saul said nothing that
day, for he thought, "Something must
have happened to David to make him cer-
emonially unclean—surely he is un-
clean." 27But the next day, the second day
of the month, David's place was empty
again. Then Saul said to his son Jonathan,
"Why hasn't the son of Jesse come to the
meal, either yesterday or today?"
28Jonathan answered, "David earnestly
asked me for permission to go to Bethle-
hem. 29He said, 'Let me go, because our
family is observing a sacrifice in the town
and my brother has ordered me to be
there. If I have found favor in your eyes,
let me get away to see my brothers.' That
is why he has not come to the king's ta-
ble."
30Saul's anger flared up at Jonathan and
he said to him, "You son of a perverse and
rebellious woman! Don't I know that you
have sided with the son of Jesse to your
own shame and to the shame of the moth-
er who bore you? 31As long as the son of
Jesse lives on this earth, neither you nor
your kingdom will be established. Now
send and bring him to me, for he must
die!"
32"Why should he be put to death?
What has he done?" Jonathan asked his
father. 33But Saul hurled his spear at him
to kill him. Then Jonathan knew that his
father intended to kill David.
34Jonathan got up from the table in
fierce anger; on that second day of the
month he did not eat, because he was

[a]25 Septuagint; Hebrew *wall. Jonathan arose*

grieved at his father's shameful treatment of David.

35In the morning Jonathan went out to the field for his meeting with David. He had a small boy with him, 36and he said to the boy, "Run and find the arrows I shoot." As the boy ran, he shot an arrow beyond him. 37When the boy came to the place where Jonathan's arrow had fallen, Jonathan called out after him, "Isn't the arrow beyond you?" 38Then he shouted, "Hurry! Go quickly! Don't stop!" The boy picked up the arrow and returned to his master. 39(The boy knew nothing of all this; only Jonathan and David knew.) 40Then Jonathan gave his weapons to the boy and said, "Go, carry them back to town."

41After the boy had gone, David got up from the south side ⌊of the stone⌋ and bowed down before Jonathan three times, with his face to the ground. Then they kissed each other and wept together—but David wept the most.

42Jonathan said to David, "Go in peace, for we have sworn friendship with each other in the name of the LORD, saying, 'The LORD is witness between you and me, and between your descendants and my descendants forever.' " Then David left, and Jonathan went back to the town.

David at Nob

21 David went to Nob, to Ahimelech the priest. Ahimelech trembled when he met him, and asked, "Why are you alone? Why is no one with you?"

2David answered Ahimelech the priest, "The king charged me with a certain matter and said to me, 'No one is to know anything about your mission and your instructions.' As for my men, I have told them to meet me at a certain place. 3Now then, what do you have on hand? Give me five loaves of bread, or whatever you can find."

4But the priest answered David, "I don't have any ordinary bread on hand; however, there is some consecrated bread here—provided the men have kept themselves from women."

5David replied, "Indeed women have been kept from us, as usual whenever[a] I set out. The men's things[b] are holy even on missions that are not holy. How much more so today!" 6So the priest gave him the consecrated bread, since there was no bread there except the bread of the Presence that had been removed from before the LORD and replaced by hot bread on the day it was taken away.

7Now one of Saul's servants was there that day, detained before the LORD; he was Doeg the Edomite, Saul's head shepherd.

8David asked Ahimelech, "Don't you have a spear or a sword here? I haven't brought my sword or any other weapon, because the king's business was urgent."

9The priest replied, "The sword of Goliath the Philistine, whom you killed in the Valley of Elah, is here; it is wrapped in a cloth behind the ephod. If you want it, take it; there is no sword here but that one."

David said, "There is none like it; give it to me."

David at Gath

10That day David fled from Saul and went to Achish king of Gath. 11But the servants of Achish said to him, "Isn't this David, the king of the land? Isn't he the one they sing about in their dances:

" 'Saul has slain his thousands,
and David his tens of thousands'?"

12David took these words to heart and was very much afraid of Achish king of Gath. 13So he pretended to be insane in their presence; and while he was in their hands he acted like a madman, making marks on the doors of the gate and letting saliva run down his beard.

14Achish said to his servants, "Look at the man! He is insane! Why bring him to me? 15Am I so short of madmen that you have to bring this fellow here to carry on like this in front of me? Must this man come into my house?"

David at Adullam and Mizpah

22 David left Gath and escaped to the cave of Adullam. When his brothers and his father's household heard about it, they went down to him there. 2All those who were in distress or in debt or discontented gathered around him, and he became their leader. About four hundred men were with him.

3From there David went to Mizpah in Moab and said to the king of Moab, "Would you let my father and mother come and stay with you until I learn what God will do for me?" 4So he left them with

[a]5 Or *from us in the past few days since* [b]5 Or *bodies*

the king of Moab, and they stayed with
him as long as David was in the stron-
ghold.
5But the prophet Gad said to David, "Do
not stay in the stronghold. Go into the
land of Judah." So David left and went to
the forest of Hereth.

Saul Kills the Priests of Nob

6Now Saul heard that David and his
men had been discovered. And Saul, spear
in hand, was seated under the tamarisk
tree on the hill at Gibeah, with all his offi-
cials standing around him. 7Saul said to
them, "Listen, men of Benjamin! Will the
son of Jesse give all of you fields and vine-
yards? Will he make all of you comman-
ders of thousands and commanders of hun-
dreds? 8Is that why you have all conspired
against me? No one tells me when my son
makes a covenant with the son of Jesse.
None of you is concerned about me or
tells me that my son has incited my ser-
vant to lie in wait for me, as he does to-
day."
9But Doeg the Edomite, who was stand-
ing with Saul's officials, said, "I saw the
son of Jesse come to Ahimelech son of
Ahitub at Nob. 10Ahimelech inquired of
the LORD for him; he also gave him provi-
sions and the sword of Goliath the Philis-
tine."
11Then the king sent for the priest
Ahimelech son of Ahitub and his father's
whole family, who were the priests at
Nob, and they all came to the king. 12Saul
said, "Listen now, son of Ahitub."
"Yes, my lord," he answered.
13Saul said to him, "Why have you con-
spired against me, you and the son of Jes-
se, giving him bread and a sword and in-
quiring of God for him, so that he has
rebelled against me and lies in wait for
me, as he does today?"
14Ahimelech answered the king, "Who
of all your servants is as loyal as David,
the king's son-in-law, captain of your
bodyguard and highly respected in your
household? 15Was that day the first time I
inquired of God for him? Of course not!
Let not the king accuse your servant or
any of his father's family, for your servant
knows nothing at all about this whole af-
fair."
16But the king said, "You will surely die,
Ahimelech, you and your father's whole
family."
17Then the king ordered the guards at
his side: "Turn and kill the priests of the
LORD, because they too have sided with
David. They knew he was fleeing, yet they
did not tell me."
But the king's officials were not willing
to raise a hand to strike the priests of the
LORD.
18The king then ordered Doeg, "You
turn and strike down the priests." So Doeg
the Edomite turned and struck them
down. That day he killed eighty-five men
who wore the linen ephod. 19He also put
to the sword Nob, the town of the priests,
with its men and women, its children and
infants, and its cattle, donkeys and sheep.
20But Abiathar, a son of Ahimelech son
of Ahitub, escaped and fled to join David.
21He told David that Saul had killed the
priests of the LORD. 22Then David said to
Abiathar: "That day, when Doeg the
Edomite was there, I knew he would be
sure to tell Saul. I am responsible for the
death of your father's whole family. 23Stay
with me; don't be afraid; the man who is
seeking your life is seeking mine also. You
will be safe with me."

David Saves Keilah

23 When David was told, "Look, the
Philistines are fighting against Kei-
lah and are looting the threshing floors,"
2he inquired of the LORD, saying, "Shall I
go and attack these Philistines?"
The LORD answered him, "Go, attack the
Philistines and save Keilah."
3But David's men said to him, "Here in
Judah we are afraid. How much more,
then, if we go to Keilah against the Philis-
tine forces!"
4Once again David inquired of the LORD,
and the LORD answered him, "Go down to
Keilah, for I am going to give the Philis-
tines into your hand." 5So David and his
men went to Keilah, fought the Philistines
and carried off their livestock. He inflicted
heavy losses on the Philistines and saved
the people of Keilah. 6(Now Abiathar son
of Ahimelech had brought the ephod
down with him when he fled to David at
Keilah.)

Saul Pursues David

7Saul was told that David had gone to
Keilah, and he said, "God has handed him
over to me, for David has imprisoned him-
self by entering a town with gates and
bars." 8And Saul called up all his forces for
battle, to go down to Keilah to besiege Da-
vid and his men.
9When David learned that Saul was

plotting against him, he said to Abiathar the priest, "Bring the ephod." 10David said, "O LORD, God of Israel, your servant has heard definitely that Saul plans to come to Keilah and destroy the town on account of me. 11Will the citizens of Keilah surrender me to him? Will Saul come down, as your servant has heard? O LORD, God of Israel, tell your servant."

And the LORD said, "He will."

12Again David asked, "Will the citizens of Keilah surrender me and my men to Saul?"

And the LORD said, "They will."

13So David and his men, about six hundred in number, left Keilah and kept moving from place to place. When Saul was told that David had escaped from Keilah, he did not go there.

14David stayed in the desert strongholds and in the hills of the Desert of Ziph. Day after day Saul searched for him, but God did not give David into his hands.

15While David was at Horesh in the Desert of Ziph, he learned that Saul had come out to take his life. 16And Saul's son Jonathan went to David at Horesh and helped him find strength in God. 17"Don't be afraid," he said. "My father Saul will not lay a hand on you. You will be king over Israel, and I will be second to you. Even my father Saul knows this." 18The two of them made a covenant before the LORD. Then Jonathan went home, but David remained at Horesh.

19The Ziphites went up to Saul at Gibeah and said, "Is not David hiding among us in the strongholds at Horesh, on the hill of Hakilah, south of Jeshimon? 20Now, O king, come down whenever it pleases you to do so, and we will be responsible for handing him over to the king."

21Saul replied, "The LORD bless you for your concern for me. 22Go and make further preparation. Find out where David usually goes and who has seen him there. They tell me he is very crafty. 23Find out about all the hiding places he uses and come back to me with definite information.[a] Then I will go with you; if he is in the area, I will track him down among all the clans of Judah."

24So they set out and went to Ziph ahead of Saul. Now David and his men were in the Desert of Maon, in the Arabah south of Jeshimon. 25Saul and his men began the search, and when David was told about it, he went down to the rock and stayed in the Desert of Maon. When Saul heard this, he went into the Desert of Maon in pursuit of David.

26Saul was going along one side of the mountain, and David and his men were on the other side, hurrying to get away from Saul. As Saul and his forces were closing in on David and his men to capture them, 27a messenger came to Saul, saying, "Come quickly! The Philistines are raiding the land." 28Then Saul broke off his pursuit of David and went to meet the Philistines. That is why they call this place Sela Hammahlekoth.[b] 29And David went up from there and lived in the strongholds of En Gedi.

David Spares Saul's Life

24 After Saul returned from pursuing the Philistines, he was told, "David is in the Desert of En Gedi." 2So Saul took three thousand chosen men from all Israel and set out to look for David and his men near the Crags of the Wild Goats.

3He came to the sheep pens along the way; a cave was there, and Saul went in to relieve himself. David and his men were far back in the cave. 4The men said, "This is the day the LORD spoke of when he said[c] to you, 'I will give your enemy into your hands for you to deal with as you wish.' " Then David crept up unnoticed and cut off a corner of Saul's robe.

5Afterward, David was conscience-stricken for having cut off a corner of his robe. 6He said to his men, "The LORD forbid that I should do such a thing to my master, the LORD's anointed, or lift my hand against him; for he is the anointed of the LORD." 7With these words David rebuked his men and did not allow them to attack Saul. And Saul left the cave and went his way.

8Then David went out of the cave and called out to Saul, "My lord the king!" When Saul looked behind him, David bowed down and prostrated himself with his face to the ground. 9He said to Saul, "Why do you listen when men say, 'David is bent on harming you'? 10This day you have seen with your own eyes how the LORD delivered you into my hands in the cave. Some urged me to kill you, but I spared you; I said, 'I will not lift my hand

[a]23 Or *me at Nacon* [b]28 *Sela Hammahlekoth* means *rock of parting.* [c]4 Or *"Today the LORD is saying*

against my master, because he is the LORD's anointed.' [11]See, my father, look at this piece of your robe in my hand! I cut off the corner of your robe but did not kill you. Now understand and recognize that I am not guilty of wrongdoing or rebellion. I have not wronged you, but you are hunting me down to take my life. [12]May the LORD judge between you and me. And may the LORD avenge the wrongs you have done to me, but my hand will not touch you. [13]As the old saying goes, 'From evildoers come evil deeds,' so my hand will not touch you.

[14]"Against whom has the king of Israel come out? Whom are you pursuing? A dead dog? A flea? [15]May the LORD be our judge and decide between us. May he consider my cause and uphold it; may he vindicate me by delivering me from your hand."

[16]When David finished saying this, Saul asked, "Is that your voice, David my son?" And he wept aloud. [17]"You are more righteous than I," he said. "You have treated me well, but I have treated you badly. [18]You have just now told me of the good you did to me; the LORD delivered me into your hands, but you did not kill me. [19]When a man finds his enemy, does he let him get away unharmed? May the LORD reward you well for the way you treated me today. [20]I know that you will surely be king and that the kingdom of Israel will be established in your hands. [21]Now swear to me by the LORD that you will not cut off my descendants or wipe out my name from my father's family."

[22]So David gave his oath to Saul. Then Saul returned home, but David and his men went up to the stronghold.

David, Nabal and Abigail

25 Now Samuel died, and all Israel assembled and mourned for him; and they buried him at his home in Ramah.

Then David moved down into the Desert of Maon.[a] [2]A certain man in Maon, who had property there at Carmel, was very wealthy. He had a thousand goats and three thousand sheep, which he was shearing in Carmel. [3]His name was Nabal and his wife's name was Abigail. She was an intelligent and beautiful woman, but her husband, a Calebite, was surly and mean in his dealings.

[4]While David was in the desert, he heard that Nabal was shearing sheep. [5]So he sent ten young men and said to them, "Go up to Nabal at Carmel and greet him in my name. [6]Say to him: 'Long life to you! Good health to you and your household! And good health to all that is yours!

[7]" 'Now I hear that it is sheep-shearing time. When your shepherds were with us, we did not mistreat them, and the whole time they were at Carmel nothing of theirs was missing. [8]Ask your own servants and they will tell you. Therefore be favorable toward my young men, since we come at a festive time. Please give your servants and your son David whatever you can find for them.' "

[9]When David's men arrived, they gave Nabal this message in David's name. Then they waited.

[10]Nabal answered David's servants, "Who is this David? Who is this son of Jesse? Many servants are breaking away from their masters these days. [11]Why should I take my bread and water, and the meat I have slaughtered for my shearers, and give it to men coming from who knows where?"

[12]David's men turned around and went back. When they arrived, they reported every word. [13]David said to his men, "Put on your swords!" So they put on their swords, and David put on his. About four hundred men went up with David, while two hundred stayed with the supplies.

[14]One of the servants told Nabal's wife Abigail: "David sent messengers from the desert to give our master his greetings, but he hurled insults at them. [15]Yet these men were very good to us. They did not mistreat us, and the whole time we were out in the fields near them nothing was missing. [16]Night and day they were a wall around us all the time we were herding our sheep near them. [17]Now think it over and see what you can do, because disaster is hanging over our master and his whole household. He is such a wicked man that no one can talk to him."

[18]Abigail lost no time. She took two hundred loaves of bread, two skins of wine, five dressed sheep, five seahs[b] of roasted grain, a hundred cakes of raisins and two hundred cakes of pressed figs,

[a] *1* Some Septuagint manuscripts; Hebrew *Paran*

[b] *18* That is, probably about a bushel (about 37 liters)

and loaded them on donkeys. 19Then she
told her servants, "Go on ahead; I'll follow
you." But she did not tell her husband Na-
bal.
20As she came riding her donkey into a
mountain ravine, there were David and
his men descending toward her, and she
met them. 21David had just said, "It's been
useless—all my watching over this fel-
low's property in the desert so that noth-
ing of his was missing. He has paid me
back evil for good. 22May God deal with
David,[a] be it ever so severely, if by morn-
ing I leave alive one male of all who be-
long to him!"
23When Abigail saw David, she quickly
got off her donkey and bowed down be-
fore David with her face to the ground.
24She fell at his feet and said: "My lord, let
the blame be on me alone. Please let your
servant speak to you; hear what your ser-
vant has to say. 25May my lord pay no at-
tention to that wicked man Nabal. He is
just like his name—his name is Fool, and
folly goes with him. But as for me, your
servant, I did not see the men my master
sent.
26"Now since the LORD has kept you, my
master, from bloodshed and from aveng-
ing yourself with your own hands, as sure-
ly as the LORD lives and as you live, may
your enemies and all who intend to harm
my master be like Nabal. 27And let this
gift, which your servant has brought to
my master, be given to the men who fol-
low you. 28Please forgive your servant's
offense, for the LORD will certainly make a
lasting dynasty for my master, because he
fights the LORD's battles. Let no wrongdo-
ing be found in you as long as you live.
29Even though someone is pursuing you
to take your life, the life of my master will
be bound securely in the bundle of the liv-
ing by the LORD your God. But the lives of
your enemies he will hurl away as from
the pocket of a sling. 30When the LORD has
done for my master every good thing he
promised concerning him and has ap-
pointed him leader over Israel, 31my mas-
ter will not have on his conscience the
staggering burden of needless bloodshed
or of having avenged himself. And when
the LORD has brought my master success,
remember your servant."
32David said to Abigail, "Praise be to the
LORD, the God of Israel, who has sent you
today to meet me. 33May you be blessed
for your good judgment and for keeping
me from bloodshed this day and from
avenging myself with my own hands.
34Otherwise, as surely as the LORD, the
God of Israel, lives, who has kept me from
harming you, if you had not come quickly
to meet me, not one male belonging to Na-
bal would have been left alive by day-
break."
35Then David accepted from her hand
what she had brought him and said, "Go
home in peace. I have heard your words
and granted your request."
36When Abigail went to Nabal, he was
in the house holding a banquet like that of
a king. He was in high spirits and very
drunk. So she told him nothing until day-
break. 37Then in the morning, when Nabal
was sober, his wife told him all these
things, and his heart failed him and he be-
came like a stone. 38About ten days later,
the LORD struck Nabal and he died.
39When David heard that Nabal was
dead, he said, "Praise be to the LORD, who
has upheld my cause against Nabal for
treating me with contempt. He has kept
his servant from doing wrong and has
brought Nabal's wrongdoing down on his
own head."
Then David sent word to Abigail, asking
her to become his wife. 40His servants
went to Carmel and said to Abigail, "David
has sent us to you to take you to become
his wife."
41She bowed down with her face to the
ground and said, "Here is your maidser-
vant, ready to serve you and wash the feet
of my master's servants." 42Abigail quick-
ly got on a donkey and, attended by her
five maids, went with David's messengers
and became his wife. 43David had also
married Ahinoam of Jezreel, and they
both were his wives. 44But Saul had given
his daughter Michal, David's wife, to Palti-
el[b] son of Laish, who was from Gallim.

David Again Spares Saul's Life

26 The Ziphites went to Saul at Gibe-
ah and said, "Is not David hiding
on the hill of Hakilah, which faces Jeshi-
mon?"
2So Saul went down to the Desert of
Ziph, with his three thousand chosen men
of Israel, to search there for David. 3Saul
made his camp beside the road on the hill
of Hakilah facing Jeshimon, but David
stayed in the desert. When he saw that

[a]22 Some Septuagint manuscripts; Hebrew *with David's enemies* [b]44 Hebrew *Palti*, a variant of *Paltiel*

Saul had followed him there, [4]he sent out scouts and learned that Saul had definitely arrived.[a]

[5]Then David set out and went to the place where Saul had camped. He saw where Saul and Abner son of Ner, the commander of the army, had lain down. Saul was lying inside the camp, with the army encamped around him.

[6]David then asked Ahimelech the Hittite and Abishai son of Zeruiah, Joab's brother, "Who will go down into the camp with me to Saul?"

"I'll go with you," said Abishai.

[7]So David and Abishai went to the army by night, and there was Saul, lying asleep inside the camp with his spear stuck in the ground near his head. Abner and the soldiers were lying around him.

[8]Abishai said to David, "Today God has delivered your enemy into your hands. Now let me pin him to the ground with one thrust of my spear; I won't strike him twice."

[9]But David said to Abishai, "Don't destroy him! Who can lay a hand on the LORD's anointed and be guiltless? [10]As surely as the LORD lives," he said, "the LORD himself will strike him; either his time will come and he will die, or he will go into battle and perish. [11]But the LORD forbid that I should lay a hand on the LORD's anointed. Now get the spear and water jug that are near his head, and let's go."

[12]So David took the spear and water jug near Saul's head, and they left. No one saw or knew about it, nor did anyone wake up. They were all sleeping, because the LORD had put them into a deep sleep.

[13]Then David crossed over to the other side and stood on top of the hill some distance away; there was a wide space between them. [14]He called out to the army and to Abner son of Ner, "Aren't you going to answer me, Abner?"

Abner replied, "Who are you who calls to the king?"

[15]David said, "You're a man, aren't you? And who is like you in Israel? Why didn't you guard your lord the king? Someone came to destroy your lord the king. [16]What you have done is not good. As surely as the LORD lives, you and your men deserve to die, because you did not guard your master, the LORD's anointed. Look around you. Where are the king's spear and water jug that were near his head?"

[17]Saul recognized David's voice and said, "Is that your voice, David my son?"

David replied, "Yes it is, my lord the king." [18]And he added, "Why is my lord pursuing his servant? What have I done, and what wrong am I guilty of? [19]Now let my lord the king listen to his servant's words. If the LORD has incited you against me, then may he accept an offering. If, however, men have done it, may they be cursed before the LORD! They have now driven me from my share in the LORD's inheritance and have said, 'Go, serve other gods.' [20]Now do not let my blood fall to the ground far from the presence of the LORD. The king of Israel has come out to look for a flea—as one hunts a partridge in the mountains."

[21]Then Saul said, "I have sinned. Come back, David my son. Because you considered my life precious today, I will not try to harm you again. Surely I have acted like a fool and have erred greatly."

[22]"Here is the king's spear," David answered. "Let one of your young men come over and get it. [23]The LORD rewards every man for his righteousness and faithfulness. The LORD delivered you into my hands today, but I would not lay a hand on the LORD's anointed. [24]As surely as I valued your life today, so may the LORD value my life and deliver me from all trouble."

[25]Then Saul said to David, "May you be blessed, my son David; you will do great things and surely triumph."

So David went on his way, and Saul returned home.

David Among the Philistines

27 But David thought to himself, "One of these days I will be destroyed by the hand of Saul. The best thing I can do is to escape to the land of the Philistines. Then Saul will give up searching for me anywhere in Israel, and I will slip out of his hand."

[2]So David and the six hundred men with him left and went over to Achish son of Maoch king of Gath. [3]David and his men settled in Gath with Achish. Each man had his family with him, and David had his two wives: Ahinoam of Jezreel and Abigail of Carmel, the widow of Nabal. [4]When Saul was told that David had

[a]4 Or *had come to Nacon*

fled to Gath, he no longer searched for him.

5Then David said to Achish, "If I have found favor in your eyes, let a place be assigned to me in one of the country towns, that I may live there. Why should your servant live in the royal city with you?"

6So on that day Achish gave him Ziklag, and it has belonged to the kings of Judah ever since. 7David lived in Philistine territory a year and four months.

8Now David and his men went up and raided the Geshurites, the Girzites and the Amalekites. (From ancient times these peoples had lived in the land extending to Shur and Egypt.) 9Whenever David attacked an area, he did not leave a man or woman alive, but took sheep and cattle, donkeys and camels, and clothes. Then he returned to Achish.

10When Achish asked, "Where did you go raiding today?" David would say, "Against the Negev of Judah" or "Against the Negev of Jerahmeel" or "Against the Negev of the Kenites." 11He did not leave a man or woman alive to be brought to Gath, for he thought, "They might inform on us and say, 'This is what David did.' " And such was his practice as long as he lived in Philistine territory. 12Achish trusted David and said to himself, "He has become so odious to his people, the Israelites, that he will be my servant forever."

Saul and the Witch of Endor

28 In those days the Philistines gathered their forces to fight against Israel. Achish said to David, "You must understand that you and your men will accompany me in the army."

2David said, "Then you will see for yourself what your servant can do."

Achish replied, "Very well, I will make you my bodyguard for life."

3Now Samuel was dead, and all Israel had mourned for him and buried him in his own town of Ramah. Saul had expelled the mediums and spiritists from the land.

4The Philistines assembled and came and set up camp at Shunem, while Saul gathered all the Israelites and set up camp at Gilboa. 5When Saul saw the Philistine army, he was afraid; terror filled his heart. 6He inquired of the LORD, but the LORD did not answer him by dreams or Urim or prophets. 7Saul then said to his attendants, "Find me a woman who is a medium, so I may go and inquire of her."

"There is one in Endor," they said.

8So Saul disguised himself, putting on other clothes, and at night he and two men went to the woman. "Consult a spirit for me," he said, "and bring up for me the one I name."

9But the woman said to him, "Surely you know what Saul has done. He has cut off the mediums and spiritists from the land. Why have you set a trap for my life to bring about my death?"

10Saul swore to her by the LORD, "As surely as the LORD lives, you will not be punished for this."

11Then the woman asked, "Whom shall I bring up for you?"

"Bring up Samuel," he said.

12When the woman saw Samuel, she cried out at the top of her voice and said to Saul, "Why have you deceived me? You are Saul!"

13The king said to her, "Don't be afraid. What do you see?"

The woman said, "I see a spirit[a] coming up out of the ground."

14"What does he look like?" he asked.

"An old man wearing a robe is coming up," she said.

Then Saul knew it was Samuel, and he bowed down and prostrated himself with his face to the ground.

15Samuel said to Saul, "Why have you disturbed me by bringing me up?"

"I am in great distress," Saul said. "The Philistines are fighting against me, and God has turned away from me. He no longer answers me, either by prophets or by dreams. So I have called on you to tell me what to do."

16Samuel said, "Why do you consult me, now that the LORD has turned away from you and become your enemy? 17The LORD has done what he predicted through me. The LORD has torn the kingdom out of your hands and given it to one of your neighbors—to David. 18Because you did not obey the LORD or carry out his fierce wrath against the Amalekites, the LORD has done this to you today. 19The LORD will hand over both Israel and you to the Philistines, and tomorrow you and your sons will be with me. The LORD will also hand over the army of Israel to the Philistines."

20Immediately Saul fell full length on

[a]13 Or *see spirits*; or *see gods*

the ground, filled with fear because of Samuel's words. His strength was gone, for he had eaten nothing all that day and night.

[21]When the woman came to Saul and saw that he was greatly shaken, she said, "Look, your maidservant has obeyed you. I took my life in my hands and did what you told me to do. [22]Now please listen to your servant and let me give you some food so you may eat and have the strength to go on your way."

[23]He refused and said, "I will not eat."

But his men joined the woman in urging him, and he listened to them. He got up from the ground and sat on the couch.

[24]The woman had a fattened calf at the house, which she butchered at once. She took some flour, kneaded it and baked bread without yeast. [25]Then she set it before Saul and his men, and they ate. That same night they got up and left.

Achish Sends David Back to Ziklag

29 The Philistines gathered all their forces at Aphek, and Israel camped by the spring in Jezreel. [2]As the Philistine rulers marched with their units of hundreds and thousands, David and his men were marching at the rear with Achish. [3]The commanders of the Philistines asked, "What about these Hebrews?"

Achish replied, "Is this not David, who was an officer of Saul king of Israel? He has already been with me for over a year, and from the day he left Saul until now, I have found no fault in him."

[4]But the Philistine commanders were angry with him and said, "Send the man back, that he may return to the place you assigned him. He must not go with us into battle, or he will turn against us during the fighting. How better could he regain his master's favor than by taking the heads of our own men? [5]Isn't this the David they sang about in their dances:

" 'Saul has slain his thousands,
and David his tens of thousands'?"

[6]So Achish called David and said to him, "As surely as the Lord lives, you have been reliable, and I would be pleased to have you serve with me in the army. From the day you came to me until now, I have found no fault in you, but the rulers don't approve of you. [7]Turn back and go in peace; do nothing to displease the Philistine rulers."

[8]"But what have I done?" asked David. "What have you found against your servant from the day I came to you until now? Why can't I go and fight against the enemies of my lord the king?"

[9]Achish answered, "I know that you have been as pleasing in my eyes as an angel of God; nevertheless, the Philistine commanders have said, 'He must not go up with us into battle.' [10]Now get up early, along with your master's servants who have come with you, and leave in the morning as soon as it is light."

[11]So David and his men got up early in the morning to go back to the land of the Philistines, and the Philistines went up to Jezreel.

David Destroys the Amalekites

30 David and his men reached Ziklag on the third day. Now the Amalekites had raided the Negev and Ziklag. They had attacked Ziklag and burned it, [2]and had taken captive the women and all who were in it, both young and old. They killed none of them, but carried them off as they went on their way.

[3]When David and his men came to Ziklag, they found it destroyed by fire and their wives and sons and daughters taken captive. [4]So David and his men wept aloud until they had no strength left to weep. [5]David's two wives had been captured—Ahinoam of Jezreel and Abigail, the widow of Nabal of Carmel. [6]David was greatly distressed because the men were talking of stoning him; each one was bitter in spirit because of his sons and daughters. But David found strength in the Lord his God.

[7]Then David said to Abiathar the priest, the son of Ahimelech, "Bring me the ephod." Abiathar brought it to him, [8]and David inquired of the Lord, "Shall I pursue this raiding party? Will I overtake them?"

"Pursue them," he answered. "You will certainly overtake them and succeed in the rescue."

[9]David and the six hundred men with him came to the Besor Ravine, where some stayed behind, [10]for two hundred men were too exhausted to cross the ravine. But David and four hundred men continued the pursuit.

[11]They found an Egyptian in a field and brought him to David. They gave him water to drink and food to eat— [12]part of a cake of pressed figs and two cakes of raisins. He ate and was revived, for he had not eaten any food or drunk any water for three days and three nights.

[13]David asked him, "To whom do you belong, and where do you come from?"

He said, "I am an Egyptian, the slave of an Amalekite. My master abandoned me when I became ill three days ago. [14]We raided the Negev of the Kerethites and the territory belonging to Judah and the Negev of Caleb. And we burned Ziklag."

[15]David asked him, "Can you lead me down to this raiding party?"

He answered, "Swear to me before God that you will not kill me or hand me over to my master, and I will take you down to them."

[16]He led David down, and there they were, scattered over the countryside, eating, drinking and reveling because of the great amount of plunder they had taken from the land of the Philistines and from Judah. [17]David fought them from dusk until the evening of the next day, and none of them got away, except four hundred young men who rode off on camels and fled. [18]David recovered everything the Amalekites had taken, including his two wives. [19]Nothing was missing: young or old, boy or girl, plunder or anything else they had taken. David brought everything back. [20]He took all the flocks and herds, and his men drove them ahead of the other livestock, saying, "This is David's plunder."

[21]Then David came to the two hundred men who had been too exhausted to follow him and who were left behind at the Besor Ravine. They came out to meet David and the people with him. As David and his men approached, he greeted them. [22]But all the evil men and troublemakers among David's followers said, "Because they did not go out with us, we will not share with them the plunder we recovered. However, each man may take his wife and children and go."

[23]David replied, "No, my brothers, you must not do that with what the LORD has given us. He has protected us and handed over to us the forces that came against us. [24]Who will listen to what you say? The share of the man who stayed with the supplies is to be the same as that of him who went down to the battle. All will share alike." [25]David made this a statute and ordinance for Israel from that day to this.

[26]When David arrived in Ziklag, he sent some of the plunder to the elders of Judah, who were his friends, saying, "Here is a present for you from the plunder of the LORD's enemies."

[27]He sent it to those who were in Bethel, Ramoth Negev and Jattir; [28]to those in Aroer, Siphmoth, Eshtemoa [29]and Racal; to those in the towns of the Jerahmeelites and the Kenites; [30]to those in Hormah, Bor Ashan, Athach [31]and Hebron; and to those in all the other places where David and his men had roamed.

Saul Takes His Life

31 Now the Philistines fought against Israel; the Israelites fled before them, and many fell slain on Mount Gilboa. [2]The Philistines pressed hard after Saul and his sons, and they killed his sons Jonathan, Abinadab and Malki-Shua. [3]The fighting grew fierce around Saul, and when the archers overtook him, they wounded him critically.

[4]Saul said to his armor-bearer, "Draw your sword and run me through, or these uncircumcised fellows will come and run me through and abuse me."

But his armor-bearer was terrified and would not do it; so Saul took his own sword and fell on it. [5]When the armor-bearer saw that Saul was dead, he too fell on his sword and died with him. [6]So Saul and his three sons and his armor-bearer and all his men died together that same day.

[7]When the Israelites along the valley and those across the Jordan saw that the Israelite army had fled and that Saul and his sons had died, they abandoned their towns and fled. And the Philistines came and occupied them.

[8]The next day, when the Philistines came to strip the dead, they found Saul and his three sons fallen on Mount Gilboa. [9]They cut off his head and stripped off his armor, and they sent messengers throughout the land of the Philistines to proclaim the news in the temple of their idols and among their people. [10]They put his armor in the temple of the Ashtoreths and fastened his body to the wall of Beth Shan.

[11]When the people of Jabesh Gilead heard of what the Philistines had done to

Saul, [12]all their valiant men journeyed through the night to Beth Shan. They took down the bodies of Saul and his sons from the wall of Beth Shan and went to Jabesh, where they burned them. [13]Then they took their bones and buried them under a tamarisk tree at Jabesh, and they fasted seven days.

THIS book tells the story of David's kingship over Israel, noting both his many victories and God's promise that his descendants will be on the throne forever. After David's shameful sin with Bathsheba, severe family problems threaten his kingdom. As you read this book, consider how terrible the consequences of sin can be, but also remember the faithfulness of God, who fulfills his promise by sending his Son to reign forever as David's true son.

2 SAMUEL

David Hears of Saul's Death

1 After the death of Saul, David returned from defeating the Amalekites
and stayed in Ziklag two days. 2On the
third day a man arrived from Saul's camp,
with his clothes torn and with dust on his
head. When he came to David, he fell to
the ground to pay him honor.

3"Where have you come from?" David
asked him.

He answered, "I have escaped from the
Israelite camp."

4"What happened?" David asked.
"Tell me."

He said, "The men fled from the battle.
Many of them fell and died. And Saul and
his son Jonathan are dead."

5Then David said to the young man
who brought him the report, "How do you
know that Saul and his son Jonathan are
dead?"

6"I happened to be on Mount Gilboa,"
the young man said, "and there was Saul,
leaning on his spear, with the chariots and
riders almost upon him. 7When he turned
around and saw me, he called out to me,
and I said, 'What can I do?'

8"He asked me, 'Who are you?'

" 'An Amalekite,' I answered.

9"Then he said to me, 'Stand over me

and kill me! I am in the throes of death,
but I'm still alive.'
10"So I stood over him and killed him,
because I knew that after he had fallen he
could not survive. And I took the crown
that was on his head and the band on his
arm and have brought them here to my
lord."
11Then David and all the men with him
took hold of their clothes and tore them.
12They mourned and wept and fasted till
evening for Saul and his son Jonathan,
and for the army of the LORD and the
house of Israel, because they had fallen by
the sword.
13David said to the young man who
brought him the report, "Where are you
from?"
"I am the son of an alien, an Amalekite,"
he answered.
14David asked him, "Why were you not
afraid to lift your hand to destroy the
LORD's anointed?"
15Then David called one of his men and
said, "Go, strike him down!" So he struck
him down, and he died. 16For David had
said to him, "Your blood be on your own
head. Your own mouth testified against
you when you said, 'I killed the LORD's
anointed.' "

David's Lament for Saul and Jonathan

17David took up this lament concerning
Saul and his son Jonathan, 18and ordered
that the men of Judah be taught this la-
ment of the bow (it is written in the Book
of Jashar):

19"Your glory, O Israel, lies slain on
your heights.
How the mighty have fallen!

20"Tell it not in Gath,
proclaim it not in the streets of
Ashkelon,
lest the daughters of the Philistines be
glad,
lest the daughters of the
uncircumcised rejoice.

21"O mountains of Gilboa,
may you have neither dew nor rain,
nor fields that yield offerings [of
grain].
For there the shield of the mighty was
defiled,
the shield of Saul—no longer
rubbed with oil.
22From the blood of the slain,
from the flesh of the mighty,
the bow of Jonathan did not turn
back,
the sword of Saul did not return
unsatisfied.

23"Saul and Jonathan—
in life they were loved and gracious,
and in death they were not parted.
They were swifter than eagles,
they were stronger than lions.

24"O daughters of Israel,
weep for Saul,
who clothed you in scarlet and finery,
who adorned your garments with
ornaments of gold.

25"How the mighty have fallen in battle!
Jonathan lies slain on your heights.
26I grieve for you, Jonathan my brother;
you were very dear to me.
Your love for me was wonderful,
more wonderful than that of
women.

27"How the mighty have fallen!
The weapons of war have
perished!"

David Anointed King Over Judah

2 In the course of time, David inquired
of the LORD. "Shall I go up to one of
the towns of Judah?" he asked.
The LORD said, "Go up."
David asked, "Where shall I go?"
"To Hebron," the LORD answered.
2So David went up there with his two
wives, Ahinoam of Jezreel and Abigail,
the widow of Nabal of Carmel. 3David also
took the men who were with him, each
with his family, and they settled in He-
bron and its towns. 4Then the men of Ju-
dah came to Hebron and there they
anointed David king over the house of Ju-
dah.
When David was told that it was the
men of Jabesh Gilead who had buried
Saul, 5he sent messengers to the men of
Jabesh Gilead to say to them, "The LORD
bless you for showing this kindness to
Saul your master by burying him. 6May
the LORD now show you kindness and
faithfulness, and I too will show you the
same favor because you have done this.
7Now then, be strong and brave, for Saul
your master is dead, and the house of Ju-
dah has anointed me king over them."

War Between the Houses of David and Saul

8Meanwhile, Abner son of Ner, the commander of Saul's army, had taken Ish-Bosheth son of Saul and brought him over to Mahanaim. 9He made him king over Gilead, Ashuri[a] and Jezreel, and also over Ephraim, Benjamin and all Israel.

10Ish-Bosheth son of Saul was forty years old when he became king over Israel, and he reigned two years. The house of Judah, however, followed David. 11The length of time David was king in Hebron over the house of Judah was seven years and six months.

12Abner son of Ner, together with the men of Ish-Bosheth son of Saul, left Mahanaim and went to Gibeon. 13Joab son of Zeruiah and David's men went out and met them at the pool of Gibeon. One group sat down on one side of the pool and one group on the other side.

14Then Abner said to Joab, "Let's have some of the young men get up and fight hand to hand in front of us."

"All right, let them do it," Joab said.

15So they stood up and were counted off—twelve men for Benjamin and Ish-Bosheth son of Saul, and twelve for David. 16Then each man grabbed his opponent by the head and thrust his dagger into his opponent's side, and they fell down together. So that place in Gibeon was called Helkath Hazzurim.[b]

17The battle that day was very fierce, and Abner and the men of Israel were defeated by David's men.

18The three sons of Zeruiah were there: Joab, Abishai and Asahel. Now Asahel was as fleet-footed as a wild gazelle. 19He chased Abner, turning neither to the right nor to the left as he pursued him. 20Abner looked behind him and asked, "Is that you, Asahel?"

"It is," he answered.

21Then Abner said to him, "Turn aside to the right or to the left; take on one of the young men and strip him of his weapons." But Asahel would not stop chasing him.

22Again Abner warned Asahel, "Stop chasing me! Why should I strike you down? How could I look your brother Joab in the face?"

23But Asahel refused to give up the pursuit; so Abner thrust the butt of his spear into Asahel's stomach, and the spear came out through his back. He fell there and died on the spot. And every man stopped when he came to the place where Asahel had fallen and died.

24But Joab and Abishai pursued Abner, and as the sun was setting, they came to the hill of Ammah, near Giah on the way to the wasteland of Gibeon. 25Then the men of Benjamin rallied behind Abner. They formed themselves into a group and took their stand on top of a hill.

26Abner called out to Joab, "Must the sword devour forever? Don't you realize that this will end in bitterness? How long before you order your men to stop pursuing their brothers?"

27Joab answered, "As surely as God lives, if you had not spoken, the men would have continued the pursuit of their brothers until morning.[c]"

28So Joab blew the trumpet, and all the men came to a halt; they no longer pursued Israel, nor did they fight anymore.

29All that night Abner and his men marched through the Arabah. They crossed the Jordan, continued through the whole Bithron[d] and came to Mahanaim.

30Then Joab returned from pursuing Abner and assembled all his men. Besides Asahel, nineteen of David's men were found missing. 31But David's men had killed three hundred and sixty Benjamites who were with Abner. 32They took Asahel and buried him in his father's tomb at Bethlehem. Then Joab and his men marched all night and arrived at Hebron by daybreak.

3 The war between the house of Saul and the house of David lasted a long time. David grew stronger and stronger, while the house of Saul grew weaker and weaker.

2Sons were born to David in Hebron:
His firstborn was Amnon the son of Ahinoam of Jezreel;
3his second, Kileab the son of Abigail the widow of Nabal of Carmel;
the third, Absalom the son of Maacah daughter of Talmai king of Geshur;

[a]9 Or *Asher* [b]16 *Helkath Hazzurim* means *field of daggers* or *field of hostilities.* [c]27 Or *spoken this morning, the men would not have taken up the pursuit of their brothers*; or *spoken, the men would have given up the pursuit of their brothers by morning* [d]29 Or *morning*; or *ravine*; the meaning of the Hebrew for this word is uncertain.

[4]the fourth, Adonijah the son of Haggith;
the fifth, Shephatiah the son of Abital;
[5]and the sixth, Ithream the son of David's wife Eglah.
These were born to David in Hebron.

Abner Goes Over to David

[6]During the war between the house of Saul and the house of David, Abner had been strengthening his own position in the house of Saul. [7]Now Saul had had a concubine named Rizpah daughter of Aiah. And Ish-Bosheth said to Abner, "Why did you sleep with my father's concubine?"

[8]Abner was very angry because of what Ish-Bosheth said and he answered, "Am I a dog's head—on Judah's side? This very day I am loyal to the house of your father Saul and to his family and friends. I haven't handed you over to David. Yet now you accuse me of an offense involving this woman! [9]May God deal with Abner, be it ever so severely, if I do not do for David what the LORD promised him on oath [10]and transfer the kingdom from the house of Saul and establish David's throne over Israel and Judah from Dan to Beersheba." [11]Ish-Bosheth did not dare to say another word to Abner, because he was afraid of him.

[12]Then Abner sent messengers on his behalf to say to David, "Whose land is it? Make an agreement with me, and I will help you bring all Israel over to you."

[13]"Good," said David. "I will make an agreement with you. But I demand one thing of you: Do not come into my presence unless you bring Michal daughter of Saul when you come to see me." [14]Then David sent messengers to Ish-Bosheth son of Saul, demanding, "Give me my wife Michal, whom I betrothed to myself for the price of a hundred Philistine foreskins."

[15]So Ish-Bosheth gave orders and had her taken away from her husband Paltiel son of Laish. [16]Her husband, however, went with her, weeping behind her all the way to Bahurim. Then Abner said to him, "Go back home!" So he went back.

[17]Abner conferred with the elders of Israel and said, "For some time you have wanted to make David your king. [18]Now do it! For the LORD promised David, 'By my servant David I will rescue my people Israel from the hand of the Philistines and from the hand of all their enemies.'"

[19]Abner also spoke to the Benjamites in person. Then he went to Hebron to tell David everything that Israel and the whole house of Benjamin wanted to do. [20]When Abner, who had twenty men with him, came to David at Hebron, David prepared a feast for him and his men. [21]Then Abner said to David, "Let me go at once and assemble all Israel for my lord the king, so that they may make a compact with you, and that you may rule over all that your heart desires." So David sent Abner away, and he went in peace.

Joab Murders Abner

[22]Just then David's men and Joab returned from a raid and brought with them a great deal of plunder. But Abner was no longer with David in Hebron, because David had sent him away, and he had gone in peace. [23]When Joab and all the soldiers with him arrived, he was told that Abner son of Ner had come to the king and that the king had sent him away and that he had gone in peace.

[24]So Joab went to the king and said, "What have you done? Look, Abner came to you. Why did you let him go? Now he is gone! [25]You know Abner son of Ner; he came to deceive you and observe your movements and find out everything you are doing."

[26]Joab then left David and sent messengers after Abner, and they brought him back from the well of Sirah. But David did not know it. [27]Now when Abner returned to Hebron, Joab took him aside into the gateway, as though to speak with him privately. And there, to avenge the blood of his brother Asahel, Joab stabbed him in the stomach, and he died.

[28]Later, when David heard about this, he said, "I and my kingdom are forever innocent before the LORD concerning the blood of Abner son of Ner. [29]May his blood fall upon the head of Joab and upon all his father's house! May Joab's house never be without someone who has a running sore or leprosy[a] or who leans on a crutch or who falls by the sword or who lacks food."

[30](Joab and his brother Abishai murdered Abner because he had killed their brother Asahel in the battle at Gibeon.)

[a]29 The Hebrew word was used for various diseases affecting the skin—not necessarily leprosy.

31Then David said to Joab and all the
people with him, "Tear your clothes and
put on sackcloth and walk in mourning in
front of Abner." King David himself
walked behind the bier. 32They buried Ab-
ner in Hebron, and the king wept aloud at
Abner's tomb. All the people wept also.
33The king sang this lament for Abner:

"Should Abner have died as the
lawless die?
34 Your hands were not bound,
your feet were not fettered.
You fell as one falls before wicked
men."

And all the people wept over him again.
35Then they all came and urged David
to eat something while it was still day; but
David took an oath, saying, "May God deal
with me, be it ever so severely, if I taste
bread or anything else before the sun
sets!"
36All the people took note and were
pleased; indeed, everything the king did
pleased them. 37So on that day all the peo-
ple and all Israel knew that the king had
no part in the murder of Abner son of Ner.
38Then the king said to his men, "Do
you not realize that a prince and a great
man has fallen in Israel this day? 39And to-
day, though I am the anointed king, I am
weak, and these sons of Zeruiah are too
strong for me. May the LORD repay the
evildoer according to his evil deeds!"

Ish-Bosheth Murdered

4 When Ish-Bosheth son of Saul heard
that Abner had died in Hebron, he lost
courage, and all Israel became alarmed.
2Now Saul's son had two men who were
leaders of raiding bands. One was named
Baanah and the other Recab; they were
sons of Rimmon the Beerothite from the
tribe of Benjamin—Beeroth is considered
part of Benjamin, 3because the people of
Beeroth fled to Gittaim and have lived
there as aliens to this day.
4(Jonathan son of Saul had a son who
was lame in both feet. He was five years
old when the news about Saul and Jona-
than came from Jezreel. His nurse picked
him up and fled, but as she hurried to
leave, he fell and became crippled. His
name was Mephibosheth.)
5Now Recab and Baanah, the sons of
Rimmon the Beerothite, set out for the
house of Ish-Bosheth, and they arrived
there in the heat of the day while he was
taking his noonday rest. 6They went into
the inner part of the house as if to get
some wheat, and they stabbed him in the
stomach. Then Recab and his brother Baa-
nah slipped away.
7They had gone into the house while he
was lying on the bed in his bedroom. After
they stabbed and killed him, they cut off
his head. Taking it with them, they trav-
eled all night by way of the Arabah. 8They
brought the head of Ish-Bosheth to David
at Hebron and said to the king, "Here is
the head of Ish-Bosheth son of Saul, your
enemy, who tried to take your life. This
day the LORD has avenged my lord the
king against Saul and his offspring."
9David answered Recab and his brother
Baanah, the sons of Rimmon the Beeroth-
ite, "As surely as the LORD lives, who has
delivered me out of all trouble, 10when a
man told me, 'Saul is dead,' and thought
he was bringing good news, I seized him
and put him to death in Ziklag. That was
the reward I gave him for his news! 11How
much more—when wicked men have
killed an innocent man in his own house
and on his own bed—should I not now
demand his blood from your hand and rid
the earth of you!"
12So David gave an order to his men,
and they killed them. They cut off their
hands and feet and hung the bodies by the
pool in Hebron. But they took the head of
Ish-Bosheth and buried it in Abner's tomb
at Hebron.

David Becomes King Over Israel

5 All the tribes of Israel came to David
at Hebron and said, "We are your own
flesh and blood. 2In the past, while Saul
was king over us, you were the one who
led Israel on their military campaigns.
And the LORD said to you, 'You will shep-
herd my people Israel, and you will be-
come their ruler.' "
3When all the elders of Israel had come
to King David at Hebron, the king made a
compact with them at Hebron before the
LORD, and they anointed David king over
Israel.
4David was thirty years old when he be-
came king, and he reigned forty years. 5In
Hebron he reigned over Judah seven years
and six months, and in Jerusalem he
reigned over all Israel and Judah thirty-
three years.

David Conquers Jerusalem

6The king and his men marched to Jeru-
salem to attack the Jebusites, who lived

there. The Jebusites said to David, "You will not get in here; even the blind and the lame can ward you off." They thought, "David cannot get in here." 7Nevertheless, David captured the fortress of Zion, the City of David.

8On that day, David said, "Anyone who conquers the Jebusites will have to use the water shaft[a] to reach those 'lame and blind' who are David's enemies.[b]" That is why they say, "The 'blind and lame' will not enter the palace."

9David then took up residence in the fortress and called it the City of David. He built up the area around it, from the supporting terraces[c] inward. 10And he became more and more powerful, because the LORD God Almighty was with him.

11Now Hiram king of Tyre sent messengers to David, along with cedar logs and carpenters and stonemasons, and they built a palace for David. 12And David knew that the LORD had established him as king over Israel and had exalted his kingdom for the sake of his people Israel.

13After he left Hebron, David took more concubines and wives in Jerusalem, and more sons and daughters were born to him. 14These are the names of the children born to him there: Shammua, Shobab, Nathan, Solomon, 15Ibhar, Elishua, Nepheg, Japhia, 16Elishama, Eliada and Eliphelet.

David Defeats the Philistines

17When the Philistines heard that David had been anointed king over Israel, they went up in full force to search for him, but David heard about it and went down to the stronghold. 18Now the Philistines had come and spread out in the Valley of Rephaim; 19so David inquired of the LORD, "Shall I go and attack the Philistines? Will you hand them over to me?"

The LORD answered him, "Go, for I will surely hand the Philistines over to you."

20So David went to Baal Perazim, and there he defeated them. He said, "As waters break out, the LORD has broken out against my enemies before me." So that place was called Baal Perazim.[d] 21The Philistines abandoned their idols there, and David and his men carried them off.

22Once more the Philistines came up and spread out in the Valley of Rephaim; 23so David inquired of the LORD, and he answered, "Do not go straight up, but circle around behind them and attack them in front of the balsam trees. 24As soon as you hear the sound of marching in the tops of the balsam trees, move quickly, because that will mean the LORD has gone out in front of you to strike the Philistine army." 25So David did as the LORD commanded him, and he struck down the Philistines all the way from Gibeon[e] to Gezer.

The Ark Brought to Jerusalem

6 David again brought together out of Israel chosen men, thirty thousand in all. 2He and all his men set out from Baalah of Judah[f] to bring up from there the ark of God, which is called by the Name,[g] the name of the LORD Almighty, who is enthroned between the cherubim that are on the ark. 3They set the ark of God on a new cart and brought it from the house of Abinadab, which was on the hill. Uzzah and Ahio, sons of Abinadab, were guiding the new cart 4with the ark of God on it,[h] and Ahio was walking in front of it. 5David and the whole house of Israel were celebrating with all their might before the LORD, with songs[i] and with harps, lyres, tambourines, sistrums and cymbals.

6When they came to the threshing floor of Nacon, Uzzah reached out and took hold of the ark of God, because the oxen stumbled. 7The LORD's anger burned against Uzzah because of his irreverent act; therefore God struck him down and he died there beside the ark of God.

8Then David was angry because the LORD's wrath had broken out against Uzzah, and to this day that place is called Perez Uzzah.[j]

9David was afraid of the LORD that day and said, "How can the ark of the LORD ever come to me?" 10He was not willing to take the ark of the LORD to be with him in the City of David. Instead, he took it aside to the house of Obed-Edom the Gittite. 11The ark of the LORD remained in the

[a] 8 Or *use scaling hooks* [b] 8 Or *are hated by David* [c] 9 Or *the Millo* [d] 20 *Baal Perazim* means *the lord who breaks out.* [e] 25 Septuagint (see also 1 Chron. 14:16); Hebrew *Geba* [f] 2 That is, Kiriath Jearim; Hebrew *Baale Judah*, a variant of *Baalah of Judah* [g] 2 Hebrew; Septuagint and Vulgate do not have *the Name.* [h] 3,4 Dead Sea Scrolls and some Septuagint manuscripts; Masoretic Text *cart* 4*and they brought it with the ark of God from the house of Abinadab, which was on the hill* [i] 5 See Dead Sea Scrolls, Septuagint and 1 Chronicles 13:8; Masoretic Text *celebrating before the* LORD *with all kinds of instruments made of pine.* [j] 8 *Perez Uzzah* means *outbreak against Uzzah.*

house of Obed-Edom the Gittite for three months, and the LORD blessed him and his entire household.

12Now King David was told, "The LORD has blessed the household of Obed-Edom and everything he has, because of the ark of God." So David went down and brought up the ark of God from the house of Obed-Edom to the City of David with rejoicing. 13When those who were carrying the ark of the LORD had taken six steps, he sacrificed a bull and a fattened calf. 14David, wearing a linen ephod, danced before the LORD with all his might, 15while he and the entire house of Israel brought up the ark of the LORD with shouts and the sound of trumpets.

16As the ark of the LORD was entering the City of David, Michal daughter of Saul watched from a window. And when she saw King David leaping and dancing before the LORD, she despised him in her heart.

17They brought the ark of the LORD and set it in its place inside the tent that David had pitched for it, and David sacrificed burnt offerings and fellowship offerings[a] before the LORD. 18After he had finished sacrificing the burnt offerings and fellowship offerings, he blessed the people in the name of the LORD Almighty. 19Then he gave a loaf of bread, a cake of dates and a cake of raisins to each person in the whole crowd of Israelites, both men and women. And all the people went to their homes.

20When David returned home to bless his household, Michal daughter of Saul came out to meet him and said, "How the king of Israel has distinguished himself today, disrobing in the sight of the slave girls of his servants as any vulgar fellow would!"

21David said to Michal, "It was before the LORD, who chose me rather than your father or anyone from his house when he appointed me ruler over the LORD's people Israel—I will celebrate before the LORD. 22I will become even more undignified than this, and I will be humiliated in my own eyes. But by these slave girls you spoke of, I will be held in honor."

23And Michal daughter of Saul had no children to the day of her death.

God's Promise to David

7 After the king was settled in his palace and the LORD had given him rest from all his enemies around him, 2he said to Nathan the prophet, "Here I am, living in a palace of cedar, while the ark of God remains in a tent."

3Nathan replied to the king, "Whatever you have in mind, go ahead and do it, for the LORD is with you."

4That night the word of the LORD came to Nathan, saying:

5"Go and tell my servant David, 'This is what the LORD says: Are you the one to build me a house to dwell in? 6I have not dwelt in a house from the day I brought the Israelites up out of Egypt to this day. I have been moving from place to place with a tent as my dwelling. 7Wherever I have moved with all the Israelites, did I ever say to any of their rulers whom I commanded to shepherd my people Israel, "Why have you not built me a house of cedar?" '

8"Now then, tell my servant David, 'This is what the LORD Almighty says: I took you from the pasture and from following the flock to be ruler over my people Israel. 9I have been with you wherever you have gone, and I have cut off all your enemies from before you. Now I will make your name great, like the names of the greatest men of the earth. 10And I will provide a place for my people Israel and will plant them so that they can have a home of their own and no longer be disturbed. Wicked people will not oppress them anymore, as they did at the beginning 11and have done ever since the time I appointed leaders[b] over my people Israel. I will also give you rest from all your enemies.

" 'The LORD declares to you that the LORD himself will establish a house for you: 12When your days are over and you rest with your fathers, I will raise up your offspring to succeed you, who will come from your own body, and I will establish his kingdom. 13He is the one who will build a house for my Name, and I will establish the throne of his kingdom forever. 14I will be his father, and he will be my son. When he does wrong, I will punish him with the rod of men, with floggings inflicted by men. 15But my love will never be taken away

[a] 17 Traditionally *peace offerings*; also in verse 18

[b] 11 Traditionally *judges*

from him, as I took it away from Saul,
whom I removed from before you.
16Your house and your kingdom will
endure forever before me[a]; your
throne will be established forever.'"

17Nathan reported to David all the
words of this entire revelation.

David's Prayer

18Then King David went in and sat be-
fore the LORD, and he said:
"Who am I, O Sovereign LORD, and
what is my family, that you have
brought me this far? 19And as if this
were not enough in your sight, O Sov-
ereign LORD, you have also spoken
about the future of the house of your
servant. Is this your usual way of
dealing with man, O Sovereign LORD?
20"What more can David say to
you? For you know your servant,
O Sovereign LORD. 21For the sake of
your word and according to your will,

[a]16 Some Hebrew manuscripts and Septuagint; most Hebrew manuscripts *you*

THURSDAY

VERSE FOR THE DAY:	AUTHOR:	PASSAGE FOR THE DAY:
2 Samuel 7:28–29	Ravi Zacharias	2 Samuel 7:18–29

Bless This House

Marriage is the first human relationship God instituted. Adam and Eve had no earthly parents. Their allegiance was first to God, then to each other, under God. Wedding vows are so sacred because they are rooted in God's first gift to humanity—a pure love, an exclusive love, an abiding love.

In our society of broken homes, where can people turn to see the reality of God's love if not to a Christian home? What they see there should show them that it will take more than human love to repair their own lives. Christian couples, in the honor and respect they give to one another, can have the privilege of showing God's power at work in their relationship.

Marriage ministry opens doors, because the average husband and wife want to honor each other. They just don't know how. Marriages are often in need of examples, and a marriage that reflects honor and commitment makes an impact on other homes.

MARRIAGE BUILDERS

♦ *How does your faith make your home different from the homes of some of your neighbors?*

♦ *When have you seen God open up conversations with others because of your marriage relationship, or vice versa?*

Additional Scripture Readings
John 13:34–35; 1 John 3:11–20

Go to page 326 for your next devotional reading.

you have done this great thing and made it known to your servant.

22"How great you are, O Sovereign LORD! There is no one like you, and there is no God but you, as we have heard with our own ears. 23And who is like your people Israel—the one nation on earth that God went out to redeem as a people for himself, and to make a name for himself, and to perform great and awesome wonders by driving out nations and their gods from before your people, whom you redeemed from Egypt?[a] 24You have established your people Israel as your very own forever, and you, O LORD, have become their God.

25"And now, LORD God, keep forever the promise you have made concerning your servant and his house. Do as you promised, 26so that your name will be great forever. Then men will say, 'The LORD Almighty is God over Israel!' And the house of your servant David will be established before you.

27"O LORD Almighty, God of Israel, you have revealed this to your servant, saying, 'I will build a house for you.' So your servant has found courage to offer you this prayer. 28O Sovereign LORD, you are God! Your words are trustworthy, and you have promised these good things to your servant. 29Now be pleased to bless the house of your servant, that it may continue forever in your sight; for you, O Sovereign LORD, have spoken, and with your blessing the house of your servant will be blessed forever."

David's Victories

8 In the course of time, David defeated the Philistines and subdued them, and he took Metheg Ammah from the control of the Philistines.

2David also defeated the Moabites. He made them lie down on the ground and measured them off with a length of cord. Every two lengths of them were put to death, and the third length was allowed to live. So the Moabites became subject to David and brought tribute.

3Moreover, David fought Hadadezer son of Rehob, king of Zobah, when he went to restore his control along the Euphrates River. 4David captured a thousand of his chariots, seven thousand charioteers[b] and twenty thousand foot soldiers. He hamstrung all but a hundred of the chariot horses.

5When the Arameans of Damascus came to help Hadadezer king of Zobah, David struck down twenty-two thousand of them. 6He put garrisons in the Aramean kingdom of Damascus, and the Arameans became subject to him and brought tribute. The LORD gave David victory wherever he went.

7David took the gold shields that belonged to the officers of Hadadezer and brought them to Jerusalem. 8From Tebah[c] and Berothai, towns that belonged to Hadadezer, King David took a great quantity of bronze.

9When Tou[d] king of Hamath heard that David had defeated the entire army of Hadadezer, 10he sent his son Joram[e] to King David to greet him and congratulate him on his victory in battle over Hadadezer, who had been at war with Tou. Joram brought with him articles of silver and gold and bronze.

11King David dedicated these articles to the LORD, as he had done with the silver and gold from all the nations he had subdued: 12Edom[f] and Moab, the Ammonites and the Philistines, and Amalek. He also dedicated the plunder taken from Hadadezer son of Rehob, king of Zobah.

13And David became famous after he returned from striking down eighteen thousand Edomites[g] in the Valley of Salt.

14He put garrisons throughout Edom, and all the Edomites became subject to David. The LORD gave David victory wherever he went.

David's Officials

15David reigned over all Israel, doing what was just and right for all his people. 16Joab son of Zeruiah was over the army; Jehoshaphat son of Ahilud was recorder;

[a]*23* See Septuagint and 1 Chron. 17:21; Hebrew *wonders for your land and before your people, whom you redeemed from Egypt, from the nations and their gods.* [b]*4* Septuagint (see also Dead Sea Scrolls and 1 Chron. 18:4); Masoretic Text *captured seventeen hundred of his charioteers* [c]*8* See some Septuagint manuscripts (see also 1 Chron. 18:8); Hebrew *Betah.* [d]*9* Hebrew *Toi,* a variant of *Tou;* also in verse 10 [e]*10* A variant of *Hadoram* [f]*12* Some Hebrew manuscripts, Septuagint and Syriac (see also 1 Chron. 18:11); most Hebrew manuscripts *Aram* [g]*13* A few Hebrew manuscripts, Septuagint and Syriac (see also 1 Chron. 18:12); most Hebrew manuscripts *Aram* (that is, Arameans)

17Zadok son of Ahitub and Ahimelech son
of Abiathar were priests; Seraiah was sec-
retary; 18Benaiah son of Jehoiada was
over the Kerethites and Pelethites; and
David's sons were royal advisers.[a]

David and Mephibosheth

9 David asked, "Is there anyone still left
of the house of Saul to whom I can
show kindness for Jonathan's sake?"
2Now there was a servant of Saul's
household named Ziba. They called him
to appear before David, and the king said
to him, "Are you Ziba?"
"Your servant," he replied.
3The king asked, "Is there no one still
left of the house of Saul to whom I can
show God's kindness?"
Ziba answered the king, "There is still a
son of Jonathan; he is crippled in both
feet."
4"Where is he?" the king asked.
Ziba answered, "He is at the house of
Makir son of Ammiel in Lo Debar."
5So King David had him brought from
Lo Debar, from the house of Makir son of
Ammiel.
6When Mephibosheth son of Jonathan,
the son of Saul, came to David, he bowed
down to pay him honor.
David said, "Mephibosheth!"
"Your servant," he replied.
7"Don't be afraid," David said to him,
"for I will surely show you kindness for
the sake of your father Jonathan. I will re-
store to you all the land that belonged to
your grandfather Saul, and you will al-
ways eat at my table."
8Mephibosheth bowed down and said,
"What is your servant, that you should no-
tice a dead dog like me?"
9Then the king summoned Ziba, Saul's
servant, and said to him, "I have given
your master's grandson everything that
belonged to Saul and his family. 10You
and your sons and your servants are to
farm the land for him and bring in the
crops, so that your master's grandson may
be provided for. And Mephibosheth,
grandson of your master, will always eat
at my table." (Now Ziba had fifteen sons
and twenty servants.)
11Then Ziba said to the king, "Your ser-
vant will do whatever my lord the king
commands his servant to do." So Mephib-
osheth ate at David's[b] table like one of
the king's sons.
12Mephibosheth had a young son
named Mica, and all the members of
Ziba's household were servants of Me-
phibosheth. 13And Mephibosheth lived in
Jerusalem, because he always ate at the
king's table, and he was crippled in both
feet.

David Defeats the Ammonites

10 In the course of time, the king of
the Ammonites died, and his son
Hanun succeeded him as king. 2David
thought, "I will show kindness to Hanun
son of Nahash, just as his father showed
kindness to me." So David sent a delega-
tion to express his sympathy to Hanun
concerning his father.
When David's men came to the land of
the Ammonites, 3the Ammonite nobles
said to Hanun their lord, "Do you think
David is honoring your father by sending
men to you to express sympathy? Hasn't
David sent them to you to explore the city
and spy it out and overthrow it?" 4So Ha-
nun seized David's men, shaved off half of
each man's beard, cut off their garments
in the middle at the buttocks, and sent
them away.
5When David was told about this, he
sent messengers to meet the men, for they
were greatly humiliated. The king said,
"Stay at Jericho till your beards have
grown, and then come back."
6When the Ammonites realized that
they had become a stench in David's nos-
trils, they hired twenty thousand Aramean
foot soldiers from Beth Rehob and Zobah,
as well as the king of Maacah with a thou-
sand men, and also twelve thousand men
from Tob.
7On hearing this, David sent Joab out
with the entire army of fighting men. 8The
Ammonites came out and drew up in bat-
tle formation at the entrance to their city
gate, while the Arameans of Zobah and
Rehob and the men of Tob and Maacah
were by themselves in the open country.
9Joab saw that there were battle lines in
front of him and behind him; so he select-
ed some of the best troops in Israel and
deployed them against the Arameans.
10He put the rest of the men under the
command of Abishai his brother and de-
ployed them against the Ammonites.
11Joab said, "If the Arameans are too
strong for me, then you are to come to my
rescue; but if the Ammonites are too

[a]18 Or *were priests* [b]11 Septuagint; Hebrew *my*

strong for you, then I will come to rescue
you. 12Be strong and let us fight bravely
for our people and the cities of our God.
The LORD will do what is good in his
sight."
13Then Joab and the troops with him
advanced to fight the Arameans, and they
fled before him. 14When the Ammonites
saw that the Arameans were fleeing, they
fled before Abishai and went inside the
city. So Joab returned from fighting the
Ammonites and came to Jerusalem.
15After the Arameans saw that they had
been routed by Israel, they regrouped.
16Hadadezer had Arameans brought from
beyond the River[a]; they went to Helam,
with Shobach the commander of Hadade-
zer's army leading them.
17When David was told of this, he gath-
ered all Israel, crossed the Jordan and
went to Helam. The Arameans formed
their battle lines to meet David and fought
against him. 18But they fled before Israel,
and David killed seven hundred of their
charioteers and forty thousand of their
foot soldiers.[b] He also struck down Sho-
bach the commander of their army, and
he died there. 19When all the kings who
were vassals of Hadadezer saw that they
had been defeated by Israel, they made
peace with the Israelites and became sub-
ject to them.

So the Arameans were afraid to help the
Ammonites anymore.

David and Bathsheba

11 In the spring, at the time when
kings go off to war, David sent Joab
out with the king's men and the whole Is-
raelite army. They destroyed the Ammon-
ites and besieged Rabbah. But David re-
mained in Jerusalem.
2One evening David got up from his bed
and walked around on the roof of the pal-
ace. From the roof he saw a woman bath-
ing. The woman was very beautiful, 3and
David sent someone to find out about her.
The man said, "Isn't this Bathsheba, the
daughter of Eliam and the wife of Uriah
the Hittite?" 4Then David sent messengers
to get her. She came to him, and he slept
with her. (She had purified herself from
her uncleanness.) Then[c] she went back
home. 5The woman conceived and sent
word to David, saying, "I am pregnant."
6So David sent this word to Joab: "Send
me Uriah the Hittite." And Joab sent him
to David. 7When Uriah came to him, Da-
vid asked him how Joab was, how the sol-
diers were and how the war was going.
8Then David said to Uriah, "Go down to
your house and wash your feet." So Uriah
left the palace, and a gift from the king
was sent after him. 9But Uriah slept at the
entrance to the palace with all his master's
servants and did not go down to his
house.
10When David was told, "Uriah did not
go home," he asked him, "Haven't you
just come from a distance? Why didn't
you go home?"
11Uriah said to David, "The ark and Isra-
el and Judah are staying in tents, and my
master Joab and my lord's men are
camped in the open fields. How could I go
to my house to eat and drink and lie with
my wife? As surely as you live, I will not
do such a thing!"
12Then David said to him, "Stay here
one more day, and tomorrow I will send
you back." So Uriah remained in Jerusa-
lem that day and the next. 13At David's in-
vitation, he ate and drank with him, and
David made him drunk. But in the evening
Uriah went out to sleep on his mat among
his master's servants; he did not go home.
14In the morning David wrote a letter to
Joab and sent it with Uriah. 15In it he
wrote, "Put Uriah in the front line where
the fighting is fiercest. Then withdraw
from him so he will be struck down and
die."
16So while Joab had the city under
siege, he put Uriah at a place where he
knew the strongest defenders were.
17When the men of the city came out and
fought against Joab, some of the men in
David's army fell; moreover, Uriah the
Hittite died.
18Joab sent David a full account of the
battle. 19He instructed the messenger:
"When you have finished giving the king
this account of the battle, 20the king's an-
ger may flare up, and he may ask you,
'Why did you get so close to the city to
fight? Didn't you know they would shoot
arrows from the wall? 21Who killed Abim-
elech son of Jerub-Besheth[d]? Didn't a
woman throw an upper millstone on him
from the wall, so that he died in Thebez?

[a]16 That is, the Euphrates [b]18 Some Septuagint manuscripts (see also 1 Chron. 19:18); Hebrew *horsemen* [c]4 Or *with her. When she purified herself from her uncleanness,* [d]21 Also known as *Jerub-Baal* (that is, Gideon)

Why did you get so close to the wall?' If he asks you this, then say to him, 'Also, your servant Uriah the Hittite is dead.' "

22The messenger set out, and when he arrived he told David everything Joab had sent him to say. 23The messenger said to David, "The men overpowered us and came out against us in the open, but we drove them back to the entrance to the city gate. 24Then the archers shot arrows at your servants from the wall, and some of the king's men died. Moreover, your servant Uriah the Hittite is dead."

25David told the messenger, "Say this to Joab: 'Don't let this upset you; the sword devours one as well as another. Press the attack against the city and destroy it.' Say this to encourage Joab."

26When Uriah's wife heard that her husband was dead, she mourned for him. 27After the time of mourning was over, David had her brought to his house, and she became his wife and bore him a son. But the thing David had done displeased the LORD.

Nathan Rebukes David

12 The LORD sent Nathan to David. When he came to him, he said, "There were two men in a certain town, one rich and the other poor. 2The rich man had a very large number of sheep and cattle, 3but the poor man had nothing except one little ewe lamb he had bought. He raised it, and it grew up with him and his children. It shared his food, drank from his cup and even slept in his arms. It was like a daughter to him.

4"Now a traveler came to the rich man, but the rich man refrained from taking one of his own sheep or cattle to prepare a meal for the traveler who had come to him. Instead, he took the ewe lamb that belonged to the poor man and prepared it for the one who had come to him."

5David burned with anger against the man and said to Nathan, "As surely as the LORD lives, the man who did this deserves to die! 6He must pay for that lamb four times over, because he did such a thing and had no pity."

7Then Nathan said to David, "You are the man! This is what the LORD, the God of Israel, says: 'I anointed you king over Israel, and I delivered you from the hand of Saul. 8I gave your master's house to you, and your master's wives into your arms. I gave you the house of Israel and Judah. And if all this had been too little, I would have given you even more. 9Why did you despise the word of the LORD by doing what is evil in his eyes? You struck down Uriah the Hittite with the sword and took his wife to be your own. You killed him with the sword of the Ammonites. 10Now, therefore, the sword will never depart from your house, because you despised me and took the wife of Uriah the Hittite to be your own.'

11"This is what the LORD says: 'Out of your own household I am going to bring calamity upon you. Before your very eyes I will take your wives and give them to one who is close to you, and he will lie with your wives in broad daylight. 12You did it in secret, but I will do this thing in broad daylight before all Israel.' "

13Then David said to Nathan, "I have sinned against the LORD."

Nathan replied, "The LORD has taken away your sin. You are not going to die. 14But because by doing this you have made the enemies of the LORD show utter contempt,[a] the son born to you will die."

15After Nathan had gone home, the LORD struck the child that Uriah's wife had borne to David, and he became ill. 16David pleaded with God for the child. He fasted and went into his house and spent the nights lying on the ground. 17The elders of his household stood beside him to get him up from the ground, but he refused, and he would not eat any food with them.

18On the seventh day the child died. David's servants were afraid to tell him that the child was dead, for they thought, "While the child was still living, we spoke to David but he would not listen to us. How can we tell him the child is dead? He may do something desperate."

19David noticed that his servants were whispering among themselves and he realized the child was dead. "Is the child dead?" he asked.

"Yes," they replied, "he is dead."

20Then David got up from the ground. After he had washed, put on lotions and changed his clothes, he went into the house of the LORD and worshiped. Then he went to his own house, and at his request they served him food, and he ate.

21His servants asked him, "Why are you acting this way? While the child was alive,

[a]14 Masoretic Text; an ancient Hebrew scribal tradition *this you have shown utter contempt for the LORD*

you fasted and wept, but now that the child is dead, you get up and eat!"

22He answered, "While the child was still alive, I fasted and wept. I thought, 'Who knows? The LORD may be gracious to me and let the child live.' 23But now that he is dead, why should I fast? Can I bring him back again? I will go to him, but he will not return to me."

24Then David comforted his wife Bathsheba, and he went to her and lay with her. She gave birth to a son, and they named him Solomon. The LORD loved him; 25and because the LORD loved him, he sent word through Nathan the prophet to name him Jedidiah.[a]

26Meanwhile Joab fought against Rabbah of the Ammonites and captured the royal citadel. 27Joab then sent messengers to David, saying, "I have fought against Rabbah and taken its water supply. 28Now muster the rest of the troops and besiege the city and capture it. Otherwise I will take the city, and it will be named after me."

29So David mustered the entire army and went to Rabbah, and attacked and captured it. 30He took the crown from the head of their king[b]—its weight was a talent[c] of gold, and it was set with precious stones—and it was placed on David's head. He took a great quantity of plunder from the city 31and brought out the people who were there, consigning them to labor with saws and with iron picks and axes, and he made them work at brickmaking.[d] He did this to all the Ammonite towns. Then David and his entire army returned to Jerusalem.

Amnon and Tamar

13 In the course of time, Amnon son of David fell in love with Tamar, the beautiful sister of Absalom son of David.

2Amnon became frustrated to the point of illness on account of his sister Tamar, for she was a virgin, and it seemed impossible for him to do anything to her.

3Now Amnon had a friend named Jonadab son of Shimeah, David's brother. Jonadab was a very shrewd man. 4He asked Amnon, "Why do you, the king's son, look so haggard morning after morning? Won't you tell me?"

Amnon said to him, "I'm in love with Tamar, my brother Absalom's sister."

5"Go to bed and pretend to be ill," Jonadab said. "When your father comes to see you, say to him, 'I would like my sister Tamar to come and give me something to eat. Let her prepare the food in my sight so I may watch her and then eat it from her hand.' "

6So Amnon lay down and pretended to be ill. When the king came to see him, Amnon said to him, "I would like my sister Tamar to come and make some special bread in my sight, so I may eat from her hand."

7David sent word to Tamar at the palace: "Go to the house of your brother Amnon and prepare some food for him." 8So Tamar went to the house of her brother Amnon, who was lying down. She took some dough, kneaded it, made the bread in his sight and baked it. 9Then she took the pan and served him the bread, but he refused to eat.

"Send everyone out of here," Amnon said. So everyone left him. 10Then Amnon said to Tamar, "Bring the food here into my bedroom so I may eat from your hand." And Tamar took the bread she had prepared and brought it to her brother Amnon in his bedroom. 11But when she took it to him to eat, he grabbed her and said, "Come to bed with me, my sister."

12"Don't, my brother!" she said to him. "Don't force me. Such a thing should not be done in Israel! Don't do this wicked thing. 13What about me? Where could I get rid of my disgrace? And what about you? You would be like one of the wicked fools in Israel. Please speak to the king; he will not keep me from being married to you." 14But he refused to listen to her, and since he was stronger than she, he raped her.

15Then Amnon hated her with intense hatred. In fact, he hated her more than he had loved her. Amnon said to her, "Get up and get out!"

16"No!" she said to him. "Sending me away would be a greater wrong than what you have already done to me."

But he refused to listen to her. 17He called his personal servant and said, "Get this woman out of here and bolt the door after her." 18So his servant put her out and bolted the door after her. She was wearing

[a]*25 Jedidiah* means *loved by the* LORD. [b]*30* Or *of Milcom* (that is, Molech) [c]*30* That is, about 75 pounds (about 34 kilograms) [d]*31* The meaning of the Hebrew for this clause is uncertain.

a richly ornamented[a] robe, for this was the kind of garment the virgin daughters of the king wore. 19Tamar put ashes on her head and tore the ornamented[b] robe she was wearing. She put her hand on her head and went away, weeping aloud as she went.

20Her brother Absalom said to her, "Has that Amnon, your brother, been with you? Be quiet now, my sister; he is your brother. Don't take this thing to heart." And Tamar lived in her brother Absalom's house, a desolate woman.

21When King David heard all this, he was furious. 22Absalom never said a word to Amnon, either good or bad; he hated Amnon because he had disgraced his sister Tamar.

Absalom Kills Amnon

23Two years later, when Absalom's sheepshearers were at Baal Hazor near the border of Ephraim, he invited all the king's sons to come there. 24Absalom went to the king and said, "Your servant has had shearers come. Will the king and his officials please join me?"

25"No, my son," the king replied. "All of us should not go; we would only be a burden to you." Although Absalom urged him, he still refused to go, but gave him his blessing.

26Then Absalom said, "If not, please let my brother Amnon come with us."

The king asked him, "Why should he go with you?" 27But Absalom urged him, so he sent with him Amnon and the rest of the king's sons.

28Absalom ordered his men, "Listen! When Amnon is in high spirits from drinking wine and I say to you, 'Strike Amnon down,' then kill him. Don't be afraid. Have not I given you this order? Be strong and brave." 29So Absalom's men did to Amnon what Absalom had ordered. Then all the king's sons got up, mounted their mules and fled.

30While they were on their way, the report came to David: "Absalom has struck down all the king's sons; not one of them is left." 31The king stood up, tore his clothes and lay down on the ground; and all his servants stood by with their clothes torn.

32But Jonadab son of Shimeah, David's brother, said, "My lord should not think that they killed all the princes; only Amnon is dead. This has been Absalom's expressed intention ever since the day Amnon raped his sister Tamar. 33My lord the king should not be concerned about the report that all the king's sons are dead. Only Amnon is dead."

34Meanwhile, Absalom had fled.

Now the man standing watch looked up and saw many people on the road west of him, coming down the side of the hill. The watchman went and told the king, "I see men in the direction of Horonaim, on the side of the hill."[c]

35Jonadab said to the king, "See, the king's sons are here; it has happened just as your servant said."

36As he finished speaking, the king's sons came in, wailing loudly. The king, too, and all his servants wept very bitterly.

37Absalom fled and went to Talmai son of Ammihud, the king of Geshur. But King David mourned for his son every day.

38After Absalom fled and went to Geshur, he stayed there three years. 39And the spirit of the king[d] longed to go to Absalom, for he was consoled concerning Amnon's death.

Absalom Returns to Jerusalem

14 Joab son of Zeruiah knew that the king's heart longed for Absalom. 2So Joab sent someone to Tekoa and had a wise woman brought from there. He said to her, "Pretend you are in mourning. Dress in mourning clothes, and don't use any cosmetic lotions. Act like a woman who has spent many days grieving for the dead. 3Then go to the king and speak these words to him." And Joab put the words in her mouth.

4When the woman from Tekoa went[e] to the king, she fell with her face to the ground to pay him honor, and she said, "Help me, O king!"

5The king asked her, "What is troubling you?"

She said, "I am indeed a widow; my husband is dead. 6I your servant had two sons. They got into a fight with each other in the field, and no one was there to separate them. One struck the other and killed

[a] *18* The meaning of the Hebrew for this phrase is uncertain. [b] *19* The meaning of the Hebrew for this word is uncertain. [c] *34* Septuagint; Hebrew does not have this sentence. [d] *39* Dead Sea Scrolls and some Septuagint manuscripts; Masoretic Text *But ‹the spirit of› David the king* [e] *4* Many Hebrew manuscripts, Septuagint, Vulgate and Syriac; most Hebrew manuscripts *spoke*

him. 7Now the whole clan has risen up
against your servant; they say, 'Hand over
the one who struck his brother down, so
that we may put him to death for the life
of his brother whom he killed; then we
will get rid of the heir as well.' They would
put out the only burning coal I have left,
leaving my husband neither name nor
descendant on the face of the earth."

8The king said to the woman, "Go
home, and I will issue an order in your be-
half."

9But the woman from Tekoa said to
him, "My lord the king, let the blame rest
on me and on my father's family, and let
the king and his throne be without guilt."

10The king replied, "If anyone says any-
thing to you, bring him to me, and he will
not bother you again."

11She said, "Then let the king invoke
the LORD his God to prevent the avenger of
blood from adding to the destruction, so
that my son will not be destroyed."

"As surely as the LORD lives," he said,
"not one hair of your son's head will fall
to the ground."

12Then the woman said, "Let your ser-
vant speak a word to my lord the king."

"Speak," he replied.

13The woman said, "Why then have you
devised a thing like this against the people
of God? When the king says this, does he
not convict himself, for the king has not
brought back his banished son? 14Like wa-
ter spilled on the ground, which cannot be
recovered, so we must die. But God does
not take away life; instead, he devises
ways so that a banished person may not
remain estranged from him.

15"And now I have come to say this to
my lord the king because the people have
made me afraid. Your servant thought, 'I
will speak to the king; perhaps he will do
what his servant asks. 16Perhaps the king
will agree to deliver his servant from the
hand of the man who is trying to cut off
both me and my son from the inheritance
God gave us.'

17"And now your servant says, 'May the
word of my lord the king bring me rest, for
my lord the king is like an angel of God in
discerning good and evil. May the LORD
your God be with you.' "

18Then the king said to the woman, "Do
not keep from me the answer to what I am
going to ask you."

"Let my lord the king speak," the wom-
an said.

19The king asked, "Isn't the hand of
Joab with you in all this?"

The woman answered, "As surely as
you live, my lord the king, no one can turn
to the right or to the left from anything my
lord the king says. Yes, it was your servant
Joab who instructed me to do this and
who put all these words into the mouth of
your servant. 20Your servant Joab did this
to change the present situation. My lord
has wisdom like that of an angel of God—
he knows everything that happens in the
land."

21The king said to Joab, "Very well, I
will do it. Go, bring back the young man
Absalom."

22Joab fell with his face to the ground to
pay him honor, and he blessed the king.
Joab said, "Today your servant knows that
he has found favor in your eyes, my lord
the king, because the king has granted his
servant's request."

23Then Joab went to Geshur and
brought Absalom back to Jerusalem. 24But
the king said, "He must go to his own
house; he must not see my face." So Absa-
lom went to his own house and did not
see the face of the king.

25In all Israel there was not a man so
highly praised for his handsome appear-
ance as Absalom. From the top of his head
to the sole of his foot there was no blem-
ish in him. 26Whenever he cut the hair of
his head—he used to cut his hair from
time to time when it became too heavy for
him—he would weigh it, and its weight
was two hundred shekels[a] by the royal
standard.

27Three sons and a daughter were born
to Absalom. The daughter's name was Ta-
mar, and she became a beautiful woman.

28Absalom lived two years in Jerusalem
without seeing the king's face. 29Then Ab-
salom sent for Joab in order to send him
to the king, but Joab refused to come to
him. So he sent a second time, but he re-
fused to come. 30Then he said to his ser-
vants, "Look, Joab's field is next to mine,
and he has barley there. Go and set it on
fire." So Absalom's servants set the field
on fire.

31Then Joab did go to Absalom's house
and he said to him, "Why have your ser-
vants set my field on fire?"

32Absalom said to Joab, "Look, I sent

[a]26 That is, about 5 pounds (about 2.3 kilograms)

word to you and said, 'Come here so I can send you to the king to ask, "Why have I come from Geshur? It would be better for me if I were still there!" ' Now then, I want to see the king's face, and if I am guilty of anything, let him put me to death."

33So Joab went to the king and told him this. Then the king summoned Absalom, and he came in and bowed down with his face to the ground before the king. And the king kissed Absalom.

Absalom's Conspiracy

15 In the course of time, Absalom provided himself with a chariot and horses and with fifty men to run ahead of him. 2He would get up early and stand by the side of the road leading to the city gate. Whenever anyone came with a complaint to be placed before the king for a decision, Absalom would call out to him, "What town are you from?" He would answer, "Your servant is from one of the tribes of Israel." 3Then Absalom would say to him, "Look, your claims are valid and proper, but there is no representative of the king to hear you." 4And Absalom would add, "If only I were appointed judge in the land! Then everyone who has a complaint or case could come to me and I would see that he gets justice."

5Also, whenever anyone approached him to bow down before him, Absalom would reach out his hand, take hold of him and kiss him. 6Absalom behaved in this way toward all the Israelites who came to the king asking for justice, and so he stole the hearts of the men of Israel.

7At the end of four[a] years, Absalom said to the king, "Let me go to Hebron and fulfill a vow I made to the LORD. 8While your servant was living at Geshur in Aram, I made this vow: 'If the LORD takes me back to Jerusalem, I will worship the LORD in Hebron.[b]' "

9The king said to him, "Go in peace." So he went to Hebron.

10Then Absalom sent secret messengers throughout the tribes of Israel to say, "As soon as you hear the sound of the trumpets, then say, 'Absalom is king in Hebron.' " 11Two hundred men from Jerusalem had accompanied Absalom. They had been invited as guests and went quite innocently, knowing nothing about the matter. 12While Absalom was offering sacrifices, he also sent for Ahithophel the Gilonite, David's counselor, to come from Giloh, his hometown. And so the conspiracy gained strength, and Absalom's following kept on increasing.

David Flees

13A messenger came and told David, "The hearts of the men of Israel are with Absalom."

14Then David said to all his officials who were with him in Jerusalem, "Come! We must flee, or none of us will escape from Absalom. We must leave immediately, or he will move quickly to overtake us and bring ruin upon us and put the city to the sword."

15The king's officials answered him, "Your servants are ready to do whatever our lord the king chooses."

16The king set out, with his entire household following him; but he left ten concubines to take care of the palace. 17So the king set out, with all the people following him, and they halted at a place some distance away. 18All his men marched past him, along with all the Kerethites and Pelethites; and all the six hundred Gittites who had accompanied him from Gath marched before the king.

19The king said to Ittai the Gittite, "Why should you come along with us? Go back and stay with King Absalom. You are a foreigner, an exile from your homeland. 20You came only yesterday. And today shall I make you wander about with us, when I do not know where I am going? Go back, and take your countrymen. May kindness and faithfulness be with you."

21But Ittai replied to the king, "As surely as the LORD lives, and as my lord the king lives, wherever my lord the king may be, whether it means life or death, there will your servant be."

22David said to Ittai, "Go ahead, march on." So Ittai the Gittite marched on with all his men and the families that were with him.

23The whole countryside wept aloud as all the people passed by. The king also crossed the Kidron Valley, and all the people moved on toward the desert.

24Zadok was there, too, and all the Levites who were with him were carrying the ark of the covenant of God. They set down the ark of God, and Abiathar offered

[a]7 Some Septuagint manuscripts, Syriac and Josephus; Hebrew *forty*
[b]8 Some Septuagint manuscripts; Hebrew does not have *in Hebron.*

sacrifices[a] until all the people had finished leaving the city.

[25]Then the king said to Zadok, "Take the ark of God back into the city. If I find favor in the LORD's eyes, he will bring me back and let me see it and his dwelling place again. [26]But if he says, 'I am not pleased with you,' then I am ready; let him do to me whatever seems good to him."

[27]The king also said to Zadok the priest, "Aren't you a seer? Go back to the city in peace, with your son Ahimaaz and Jonathan son of Abiathar. You and Abiathar take your two sons with you. [28]I will wait at the fords in the desert until word comes from you to inform me." [29]So Zadok and Abiathar took the ark of God back to Jerusalem and stayed there.

[30]But David continued up the Mount of Olives, weeping as he went; his head was covered and he was barefoot. All the people with him covered their heads too and were weeping as they went up. [31]Now David had been told, "Ahithophel is among the conspirators with Absalom." So David prayed, "O LORD, turn Ahithophel's counsel into foolishness."

[32]When David arrived at the summit, where people used to worship God, Hushai the Arkite was there to meet him, his robe torn and dust on his head. [33]David said to him, "If you go with me, you will be a burden to me. [34]But if you return to the city and say to Absalom, 'I will be your servant, O king; I was your father's servant in the past, but now I will be your servant,' then you can help me by frustrating Ahithophel's advice. [35]Won't the priests Zadok and Abiathar be there with you? Tell them anything you hear in the king's palace. [36]Their two sons, Ahimaaz son of Zadok and Jonathan son of Abiathar, are there with them. Send them to me with anything you hear."

[37]So David's friend Hushai arrived at Jerusalem as Absalom was entering the city.

David and Ziba

16 When David had gone a short distance beyond the summit, there was Ziba, the steward of Mephibosheth, waiting to meet him. He had a string of donkeys saddled and loaded with two hundred loaves of bread, a hundred cakes of raisins, a hundred cakes of figs and a skin of wine.

[2]The king asked Ziba, "Why have you brought these?"

Ziba answered, "The donkeys are for the king's household to ride on, the bread and fruit are for the men to eat, and the wine is to refresh those who become exhausted in the desert."

[3]The king then asked, "Where is your master's grandson?"

Ziba said to him, "He is staying in Jerusalem, because he thinks, 'Today the house of Israel will give me back my grandfather's kingdom.' "

[4]Then the king said to Ziba, "All that belonged to Mephibosheth is now yours."

"I humbly bow," Ziba said. "May I find favor in your eyes, my lord the king."

Shimei Curses David

[5]As King David approached Bahurim, a man from the same clan as Saul's family came out from there. His name was Shimei son of Gera, and he cursed as he came out. [6]He pelted David and all the king's officials with stones, though all the troops and the special guard were on David's right and left. [7]As he cursed, Shimei said, "Get out, get out, you man of blood, you scoundrel! [8]The LORD has repaid you for all the blood you shed in the household of Saul, in whose place you have reigned. The LORD has handed the kingdom over to your son Absalom. You have come to ruin because you are a man of blood!"

[9]Then Abishai son of Zeruiah said to the king, "Why should this dead dog curse my lord the king? Let me go over and cut off his head."

[10]But the king said, "What do you and I have in common, you sons of Zeruiah? If he is cursing because the LORD said to him, 'Curse David,' who can ask, 'Why do you do this?' "

[11]David then said to Abishai and all his officials, "My son, who is of my own flesh, is trying to take my life. How much more, then, this Benjamite! Leave him alone; let him curse, for the LORD has told him to. [12]It may be that the LORD will see my distress and repay me with good for the cursing I am receiving today."

[13]So David and his men continued along the road while Shimei was going along the hillside opposite him, cursing as he went and throwing stones at him and showering him with dirt. [14]The king and all the people with him arrived at their

[a]24 Or *Abiathar went up*

destination exhausted. And there he refreshed himself.

The Advice of Hushai and Ahithophel

15Meanwhile, Absalom and all the men
of Israel came to Jerusalem, and Ahitho-
phel was with him. 16Then Hushai the Ar-
kite, David's friend, went to Absalom and
said to him, "Long live the king! Long live
the king!"
17Absalom asked Hushai, "Is this the
love you show your friend? Why didn't
you go with your friend?"
18Hushai said to Absalom, "No, the one
chosen by the LORD, by these people, and
by all the men of Israel—his I will be, and
I will remain with him. 19Furthermore,
whom should I serve? Should I not serve
the son? Just as I served your father, so I
will serve you."
20Absalom said to Ahithophel, "Give us
your advice. What should we do?"
21Ahithophel answered, "Lie with your
father's concubines whom he left to take
care of the palace. Then all Israel will hear
that you have made yourself a stench in
your father's nostrils, and the hands of ev-
eryone with you will be strengthened."
22So they pitched a tent for Absalom on
the roof, and he lay with his father's con-
cubines in the sight of all Israel.
23Now in those days the advice Ahitho-
phel gave was like that of one who in-
quires of God. That was how both David
and Absalom regarded all of Ahithophel's
advice.

17 Ahithophel said to Absalom, "I
would[a] choose twelve thousand
men and set out tonight in pursuit of Da-
vid. 2I would[b] attack him while he is wea-
ry and weak. I would[b] strike him with
terror, and then all the people with him
will flee. I would[b] strike down only the
king 3and bring all the people back to you.
The death of the man you seek will mean
the return of all; all the people will be un-
harmed." 4This plan seemed good to Ab-
salom and to all the elders of Israel.
5But Absalom said, "Summon also Hu-
shai the Arkite, so we can hear what he
has to say." 6When Hushai came to him,
Absalom said, "Ahithophel has given this
advice. Should we do what he says? If not,
give us your opinion."
7Hushai replied to Absalom, "The ad-
vice Ahithophel has given is not good this
time. 8You know your father and his men;
they are fighters, and as fierce as a wild
bear robbed of her cubs. Besides, your fa-
ther is an experienced fighter; he will not
spend the night with the troops. 9Even
now, he is hidden in a cave or some other
place. If he should attack your troops
first,[c] whoever hears about it will say,
'There has been a slaughter among the
troops who follow Absalom.' 10Then even
the bravest soldier, whose heart is like the
heart of a lion, will melt with fear, for all
Israel knows that your father is a fighter
and that those with him are brave.
11"So I advise you: Let all Israel, from
Dan to Beersheba—as numerous as the
sand on the seashore—be gathered to
you, with you yourself leading them into
battle. 12Then we will attack him wher-
ever he may be found, and we will fall on
him as dew settles on the ground. Neither
he nor any of his men will be left alive. 13If
he withdraws into a city, then all Israel
will bring ropes to that city, and we will
drag it down to the valley until not even a
piece of it can be found."
14Absalom and all the men of Israel
said, "The advice of Hushai the Arkite is
better than that of Ahithophel." For the
LORD had determined to frustrate the good
advice of Ahithophel in order to bring di-
saster on Absalom.
15Hushai told Zadok and Abiathar, the
priests, "Ahithophel has advised Absalom
and the elders of Israel to do such and
such, but I have advised them to do so and
so. 16Now send a message immediately
and tell David, 'Do not spend the night at
the fords in the desert; cross over without
fail, or the king and all the people with
him will be swallowed up.' "
17Jonathan and Ahimaaz were staying
at En Rogel. A servant girl was to go and
inform them, and they were to go and tell
King David, for they could not risk being
seen entering the city. 18But a young man
saw them and told Absalom. So the two of
them left quickly and went to the house of
a man in Bahurim. He had a well in his
courtyard, and they climbed down into it.
19His wife took a covering and spread it
out over the opening of the well and scat-
tered grain over it. No one knew anything
about it.
20When Absalom's men came to the
woman at the house, they asked, "Where
are Ahimaaz and Jonathan?"

[a] 1 Or *Let me* [b] 2 Or *will* [c] 9 Or *When some of the men fall at the first attack*

The woman answered them, "They crossed over the brook."[a] The men searched but found no one, so they returned to Jerusalem.

21 After the men had gone, the two climbed out of the well and went to inform King David. They said to him, "Set out and cross the river at once; Ahithophel has advised such and such against you." 22 So David and all the people with him set out and crossed the Jordan. By daybreak, no one was left who had not crossed the Jordan.

23 When Ahithophel saw that his advice had not been followed, he saddled his donkey and set out for his house in his hometown. He put his house in order and then hanged himself. So he died and was buried in his father's tomb.

24 David went to Mahanaim, and Absalom crossed the Jordan with all the men of Israel. 25 Absalom had appointed Amasa over the army in place of Joab. Amasa was the son of a man named Jether,[b] an Israelite[c] who had married Abigail,[d] the daughter of Nahash and sister of Zeruiah the mother of Joab. 26 The Israelites and Absalom camped in the land of Gilead.

27 When David came to Mahanaim, Shobi son of Nahash from Rabbah of the Ammonites, and Makir son of Ammiel from Lo Debar, and Barzillai the Gileadite from Rogelim 28 brought bedding and bowls and articles of pottery. They also brought wheat and barley, flour and roasted grain, beans and lentils,[e] 29 honey and curds, sheep, and cheese from cows' milk for David and his people to eat. For they said, "The people have become hungry and tired and thirsty in the desert."

Absalom's Death

18 David mustered the men who were with him and appointed over them commanders of thousands and commanders of hundreds. 2 David sent the troops out—a third under the command of Joab, a third under Joab's brother Abishai son of Zeruiah, and a third under Ittai the Gittite. The king told the troops, "I myself will surely march out with you."

3 But the men said, "You must not go out; if we are forced to flee, they won't care about us. Even if half of us die, they won't care; but you are worth ten thousand of us.[f] It would be better now for you to give us support from the city."

4 The king answered, "I will do whatever seems best to you."

So the king stood beside the gate while all the men marched out in units of hundreds and of thousands. 5 The king commanded Joab, Abishai and Ittai, "Be gentle with the young man Absalom for my sake." And all the troops heard the king giving orders concerning Absalom to each of the commanders.

6 The army marched into the field to fight Israel, and the battle took place in the forest of Ephraim. 7 There the army of Israel was defeated by David's men, and the casualties that day were great—twenty thousand men. 8 The battle spread out over the whole countryside, and the forest claimed more lives that day than the sword.

9 Now Absalom happened to meet David's men. He was riding his mule, and as the mule went under the thick branches of a large oak, Absalom's head got caught in the tree. He was left hanging in midair, while the mule he was riding kept on going.

10 When one of the men saw this, he told Joab, "I just saw Absalom hanging in an oak tree."

11 Joab said to the man who had told him this, "What! You saw him? Why didn't you strike him to the ground right there? Then I would have had to give you ten shekels[g] of silver and a warrior's belt."

12 But the man replied, "Even if a thousand shekels[h] were weighed out into my hands, I would not lift my hand against the king's son. In our hearing the king commanded you and Abishai and Ittai, 'Protect the young man Absalom for my sake.'[i] 13 And if I had put my life in jeopardy[j]—and nothing is hidden from the king—you would have kept your distance from me."

[a] 20 Or *"They passed by the sheep pen toward the water."* [b] 25 Hebrew *Ithra*, a variant of *Jether*
[c] 25 Hebrew and some Septuagint manuscripts; other Septuagint manuscripts (see also 1 Chron. 2:17) *Ishmaelite* or *Jezreelite* [d] 25 Hebrew *Abigal*, a variant of *Abigail* [e] 28 Most Septuagint manuscripts and Syriac; Hebrew *lentils, and roasted grain* [f] 3 Two Hebrew manuscripts, some Septuagint manuscripts and Vulgate; most Hebrew manuscripts *care; for now there are ten thousand like us*
[g] 11 That is, about 4 ounces (about 115 grams) [h] 12 That is, about 25 pounds (about 11 kilograms)
[i] 12 A few Hebrew manuscripts, Septuagint, Vulgate and Syriac; most Hebrew manuscripts may be translated *Absalom, whoever you may be.* [j] 13 Or *Otherwise, if I had acted treacherously toward him*

14Joab said, "I'm not going to wait like
this for you." So he took three javelins in
his hand and plunged them into Absa-
lom's heart while Absalom was still alive
in the oak tree. 15And ten of Joab's armor-
bearers surrounded Absalom, struck him
and killed him.

16Then Joab sounded the trumpet, and
the troops stopped pursuing Israel, for
Joab halted them. 17They took Absalom,
threw him into a big pit in the forest and
piled up a large heap of rocks over him.
Meanwhile, all the Israelites fled to their
homes.

18During his lifetime Absalom had tak-
en a pillar and erected it in the King's Val-
ley as a monument to himself, for he
thought, "I have no son to carry on the
memory of my name." He named the pil-
lar after himself, and it is called Absalom's
Monument to this day.

David Mourns

19Now Ahimaaz son of Zadok said, "Let
me run and take the news to the king that
the LORD has delivered him from the hand
of his enemies."

20"You are not the one to take the news
today," Joab told him. "You may take the
news another time, but you must not do
so today, because the king's son is dead."

21Then Joab said to a Cushite, "Go, tell
the king what you have seen." The Cush-
ite bowed down before Joab and ran off.

22Ahimaaz son of Zadok again said to
Joab, "Come what may, please let me run
behind the Cushite."

But Joab replied, "My son, why do you
want to go? You don't have any news that
will bring you a reward."

23He said, "Come what may, I want to
run."

So Joab said, "Run!" Then Ahimaaz ran
by way of the plain[a] and outran the
Cushite.

24While David was sitting between the
inner and outer gates, the watchman went
up to the roof of the gateway by the wall.
As he looked out, he saw a man running
alone. 25The watchman called out to the
king and reported it.

The king said, "If he is alone, he must
have good news." And the man came clos-
er and closer.

26Then the watchman saw another man
running, and he called down to the gate-
keeper, "Look, another man running
alone!"

The king said, "He must be bringing
good news, too."

27The watchman said, "It seems to me
that the first one runs like Ahimaaz son of
Zadok."

"He's a good man," the king said. "He
comes with good news."

28Then Ahimaaz called out to the king,
"All is well!" He bowed down before the
king with his face to the ground and said,
"Praise be to the LORD your God! He has
delivered up the men who lifted their
hands against my lord the king."

29The king asked, "Is the young man
Absalom safe?"

Ahimaaz answered, "I saw great confu-
sion just as Joab was about to send the
king's servant and me, your servant, but I
don't know what it was."

30The king said, "Stand aside and wait
here." So he stepped aside and stood
there.

31Then the Cushite arrived and said,
"My lord the king, hear the good news!
The LORD has delivered you today from all
who rose up against you."

32The king asked the Cushite, "Is the
young man Absalom safe?"

The Cushite replied, "May the enemies
of my lord the king and all who rise up to
harm you be like that young man."

33The king was shaken. He went up to
the room over the gateway and wept. As
he went, he said: "O my son Absalom! My
son, my son Absalom! If only I had died
instead of you—O Absalom, my son, my
son!"

19 Joab was told, "The king is weep-
ing and mourning for Absalom."
2And for the whole army the victory that
day was turned into mourning, because
on that day the troops heard it said, "The
king is grieving for his son." 3The men
stole into the city that day as men steal in
who are ashamed when they flee from
battle. 4The king covered his face and
cried aloud, "O my son Absalom! O Absa-
lom, my son, my son!"

5Then Joab went into the house to the
king and said, "Today you have humiliat-
ed all your men, who have just saved your
life and the lives of your sons and daugh-
ters and the lives of your wives and concu-
bines. 6You love those who hate you and
hate those who love you. You have made

[a]23 That is, the plain of the Jordan

it clear today that the commanders and
their men mean nothing to you. I see that
you would be pleased if Absalom were
alive today and all of us were dead. 7Now
go out and encourage your men. I swear
by the LORD that if you don't go out, not a
man will be left with you by nightfall. This
will be worse for you than all the calami-
ties that have come upon you from your
youth till now."

8So the king got up and took his seat in
the gateway. When the men were told,
"The king is sitting in the gateway," they
all came before him.

David Returns to Jerusalem

Meanwhile, the Israelites had fled to
their homes. 9Throughout the tribes of Is-
rael, the people were all arguing with each
other, saying, "The king delivered us from
the hand of our enemies; he is the one
who rescued us from the hand of the Phi-
listines. But now he has fled the country
because of Absalom; 10and Absalom,
whom we anointed to rule over us, has
died in battle. So why do you say nothing
about bringing the king back?"

11King David sent this message to Za-
dok and Abiathar, the priests: "Ask the el-
ders of Judah, 'Why should you be the last
to bring the king back to his palace, since
what is being said throughout Israel has
reached the king at his quarters? 12You are
my brothers, my own flesh and blood. So
why should you be the last to bring back
the king?' 13And say to Amasa, 'Are you
not my own flesh and blood? May God
deal with me, be it ever so severely, if
from now on you are not the commander
of my army in place of Joab.' "

14He won over the hearts of all the men
of Judah as though they were one man.
They sent word to the king, "Return, you
and all your men." 15Then the king re-
turned and went as far as the Jordan.

Now the men of Judah had come to Gil-
gal to go out and meet the king and bring
him across the Jordan. 16Shimei son of
Gera, the Benjamite from Bahurim, hur-
ried down with the men of Judah to meet
King David. 17With him were a thousand
Benjamites, along with Ziba, the steward
of Saul's household, and his fifteen sons
and twenty servants. They rushed to the
Jordan, where the king was. 18They
crossed at the ford to take the king's
household over and to do whatever he
wished.

When Shimei son of Gera crossed the
Jordan, he fell prostrate before the king
19and said to him, "May my lord not hold
me guilty. Do not remember how your
servant did wrong on the day my lord the
king left Jerusalem. May the king put it
out of his mind. 20For I your servant know
that I have sinned, but today I have come
here as the first of the whole house of Jo-
seph to come down and meet my lord the
king."

21Then Abishai son of Zeruiah said,
"Shouldn't Shimei be put to death for this?
He cursed the LORD's anointed."

22David replied, "What do you and I
have in common, you sons of Zeruiah?
This day you have become my adversar-
ies! Should anyone be put to death in Isra-
el today? Do I not know that today I am
king over Israel?" 23So the king said to
Shimei, "You shall not die." And the king
promised him on oath.

24Mephibosheth, Saul's grandson, also
went down to meet the king. He had not
taken care of his feet or trimmed his mus-
tache or washed his clothes from the day
the king left until the day he returned safe-
ly. 25When he came from Jerusalem to
meet the king, the king asked him, "Why
didn't you go with me, Mephibosheth?"

26He said, "My lord the king, since I
your servant am lame, I said, 'I will have
my donkey saddled and will ride on it, so
I can go with the king.' But Ziba my ser-
vant betrayed me. 27And he has slandered
your servant to my lord the king. My lord
the king is like an angel of God; so do
whatever pleases you. 28All my grandfa-
ther's descendants deserved nothing but
death from my lord the king, but you gave
your servant a place among those who eat
at your table. So what right do I have to
make any more appeals to the king?"

29The king said to him, "Why say more?
I order you and Ziba to divide the fields."

30Mephibosheth said to the king, "Let
him take everything, now that my lord the
king has arrived home safely."

31Barzillai the Gileadite also came down
from Rogelim to cross the Jordan with the
king and to send him on his way from
there. 32Now Barzillai was a very old man,
eighty years of age. He had provided for
the king during his stay in Mahanaim, for
he was a very wealthy man. 33The king
said to Barzillai, "Cross over with me and
stay with me in Jerusalem, and I will pro-
vide for you."

34But Barzillai answered the king, "How
many more years will I live, that I should

go up to Jerusalem with the king? [35]I am now eighty years old. Can I tell the difference between what is good and what is not? Can your servant taste what he eats and drinks? Can I still hear the voices of men and women singers? Why should your servant be an added burden to my lord the king? [36]Your servant will cross over the Jordan with the king for a short distance, but why should the king reward me in this way? [37]Let your servant return, that I may die in my own town near the tomb of my father and mother. But here is your servant Kimham. Let him cross over with my lord the king. Do for him whatever pleases you."

[38]The king said, "Kimham shall cross over with me, and I will do for him whatever pleases you. And anything you desire from me I will do for you."

[39]So all the people crossed the Jordan, and then the king crossed over. The king kissed Barzillai and gave him his blessing, and Barzillai returned to his home.

[40]When the king crossed over to Gilgal, Kimham crossed with him. All the troops of Judah and half the troops of Israel had taken the king over.

[41]Soon all the men of Israel were coming to the king and saying to him, "Why did our brothers, the men of Judah, steal the king away and bring him and his household across the Jordan, together with all his men?"

[42]All the men of Judah answered the men of Israel, "We did this because the king is closely related to us. Why are you angry about it? Have we eaten any of the king's provisions? Have we taken anything for ourselves?"

[43]Then the men of Israel answered the men of Judah, "We have ten shares in the king; and besides, we have a greater claim on David than you have. So why do you treat us with contempt? Were we not the first to speak of bringing back our king?"

But the men of Judah responded even more harshly than the men of Israel.

Sheba Rebels Against David

20 Now a troublemaker named Sheba son of Bicri, a Benjamite, happened to be there. He sounded the trumpet and shouted,

"We have no share in David,
no part in Jesse's son!
Every man to his tent, O Israel!"

[2]So all the men of Israel deserted David to follow Sheba son of Bicri. But the men of Judah stayed by their king all the way from the Jordan to Jerusalem.

[3]When David returned to his palace in Jerusalem, he took the ten concubines he had left to take care of the palace and put them in a house under guard. He provided for them, but did not lie with them. They were kept in confinement till the day of their death, living as widows.

[4]Then the king said to Amasa, "Summon the men of Judah to come to me within three days, and be here yourself." [5]But when Amasa went to summon Judah, he took longer than the time the king had set for him.

[6]David said to Abishai, "Now Sheba son of Bicri will do us more harm than Absalom did. Take your master's men and pursue him, or he will find fortified cities and escape from us." [7]So Joab's men and the Kerethites and Pelethites and all the mighty warriors went out under the command of Abishai. They marched out from Jerusalem to pursue Sheba son of Bicri.

[8]While they were at the great rock in Gibeon, Amasa came to meet them. Joab was wearing his military tunic, and strapped over it at his waist was a belt with a dagger in its sheath. As he stepped forward, it dropped out of its sheath.

[9]Joab said to Amasa, "How are you, my brother?" Then Joab took Amasa by the beard with his right hand to kiss him. [10]Amasa was not on his guard against the dagger in Joab's hand, and Joab plunged it into his belly, and his intestines spilled out on the ground. Without being stabbed again, Amasa died. Then Joab and his brother Abishai pursued Sheba son of Bicri.

[11]One of Joab's men stood beside Amasa and said, "Whoever favors Joab, and whoever is for David, let him follow Joab!" [12]Amasa lay wallowing in his blood in the middle of the road, and the man saw that all the troops came to a halt there. When he realized that everyone who came up to Amasa stopped, he dragged him from the road into a field and threw a garment over him. [13]After Amasa had been removed from the road, all the men went on with Joab to pursue Sheba son of Bicri.

[14]Sheba passed through all the tribes of

Israel to Abel Beth Maacah[a] and through
the entire region of the Berites, who gath-
ered together and followed him. 15All the
troops with Joab came and besieged She-
ba in Abel Beth Maacah. They built a siege
ramp up to the city, and it stood against
the outer fortifications. While they were
battering the wall to bring it down, 16a
wise woman called from the city, "Listen!
Listen! Tell Joab to come here so I can
speak to him." 17He went toward her, and
she asked, "Are you Joab?"

"I am," he answered.

She said, "Listen to what your servant
has to say."

"I'm listening," he said.

18She continued, "Long ago they used
to say, 'Get your answer at Abel,' and that
settled it. 19We are the peaceful and faith-
ful in Israel. You are trying to destroy a
city that is a mother in Israel. Why do you
want to swallow up the LORD's inheri-
tance?"

20"Far be it from me!" Joab replied, "Far
be it from me to swallow up or destroy!
21That is not the case. A man named She-
ba son of Bicri, from the hill country of
Ephraim, has lifted up his hand against
the king, against David. Hand over this
one man, and I'll withdraw from the city."

The woman said to Joab, "His head will
be thrown to you from the wall."

22Then the woman went to all the peo-
ple with her wise advice, and they cut off
the head of Sheba son of Bicri and threw
it to Joab. So he sounded the trumpet, and
his men dispersed from the city, each re-
turning to his home. And Joab went back
to the king in Jerusalem.

23Joab was over Israel's entire army; Be-
naiah son of Jehoiada was over the Ker-
ethites and Pelethites; 24Adoniram[b] was
in charge of forced labor; Jehoshaphat son
of Ahilud was recorder; 25Sheva was sec-
retary; Zadok and Abiathar were priests;
26and Ira the Jairite was David's priest.

The Gibeonites Avenged

21 During the reign of David, there
was a famine for three successive
years; so David sought the face of the
LORD. The LORD said, "It is on account of
Saul and his blood-stained house; it is be-
cause he put the Gibeonites to death."

2The king summoned the Gibeonites
and spoke to them. (Now the Gibeonites
were not a part of Israel but were survi-
vors of the Amorites; the Israelites had
sworn to ⌊spare⌋ them, but Saul in his zeal
for Israel and Judah had tried to annihilate
them.) 3David asked the Gibeonites,
"What shall I do for you? How shall I make
amends so that you will bless the LORD's
inheritance?"

4The Gibeonites answered him, "We
have no right to demand silver or gold
from Saul or his family, nor do we have
the right to put anyone in Israel to death."

"What do you want me to do for you?"
David asked.

5They answered the king, "As for the
man who destroyed us and plotted against
us so that we have been decimated and
have no place anywhere in Israel, 6let sev-
en of his male descendants be given to us
to be killed and exposed before the LORD
at Gibeah of Saul—the LORD's chosen
one."

So the king said, "I will give them to
you."

7The king spared Mephibosheth son of
Jonathan, the son of Saul, because of the
oath before the LORD between David and
Jonathan son of Saul. 8But the king took
Armoni and Mephibosheth, the two sons
of Aiah's daughter Rizpah, whom she had
borne to Saul, together with the five sons
of Saul's daughter Merab,[c] whom she
had borne to Adriel son of Barzillai the
Meholathite. 9He handed them over to the
Gibeonites, who killed and exposed them
on a hill before the LORD. All seven of
them fell together; they were put to death
during the first days of the harvest, just as
the barley harvest was beginning.

10Rizpah daughter of Aiah took sack-
cloth and spread it out for herself on a
rock. From the beginning of the harvest
till the rain poured down from the heav-
ens on the bodies, she did not let the birds
of the air touch them by day or the wild
animals by night. 11When David was told
what Aiah's daughter Rizpah, Saul's con-
cubine, had done, 12he went and took the
bones of Saul and his son Jonathan from
the citizens of Jabesh Gilead. (They had
taken them secretly from the public
square at Beth Shan, where the Philistines
had hung them after they struck Saul
down on Gilboa.) 13David brought the

[a]*14* Or *Abel, even Beth Maacah*; also in verse 15 [b]*24* Some Septuagint manuscripts (see also 1 Kings 4:6 and 5:14); Hebrew *Adoram* [c]*8* Two Hebrew manuscripts, some Septuagint manuscripts and Syriac (see also 1 Samuel 18:19); most Hebrew and Septuagint manuscripts *Michal*

bones of Saul and his son Jonathan from there, and the bones of those who had been killed and exposed were gathered up.

14They buried the bones of Saul and his son Jonathan in the tomb of Saul's father Kish, at Zela in Benjamin, and did everything the king commanded. After that, God answered prayer in behalf of the land.

Wars Against the Philistines

15Once again there was a battle between the Philistines and Israel. David went down with his men to fight against the Philistines, and he became exhausted. 16And Ishbi-Benob, one of the descendants of Rapha, whose bronze spearhead weighed three hundred shekels[a] and who was armed with a new ⌊sword⌋, said he would kill David. 17But Abishai son of Zeruiah came to David's rescue; he struck the Philistine down and killed him. Then David's men swore to him, saying, "Never again will you go out with us to battle, so that the lamp of Israel will not be extinguished."

18In the course of time, there was another battle with the Philistines, at Gob. At that time Sibbecai the Hushathite killed Saph, one of the descendants of Rapha.

19In another battle with the Philistines at Gob, Elhanan son of Jaare-Oregim[b] the Bethlehemite killed Goliath[c] the Gittite, who had a spear with a shaft like a weaver's rod.

20In still another battle, which took place at Gath, there was a huge man with six fingers on each hand and six toes on each foot—twenty-four in all. He also was descended from Rapha. 21When he taunted Israel, Jonathan son of Shimeah, David's brother, killed him.

22These four were descendants of Rapha in Gath, and they fell at the hands of David and his men.

David's Song of Praise

22 David sang to the LORD the words of this song when the LORD delivered him from the hand of all his enemies and from the hand of Saul. 2He said:

"The LORD is my rock, my fortress and my deliverer;
3 my God is my rock, in whom I take refuge,
my shield and the horn[d] of my salvation.
He is my stronghold, my refuge and my savior—
from violent men you save me.
4I call to the LORD, who is worthy of praise,
and I am saved from my enemies.

5"The waves of death swirled about me;
the torrents of destruction overwhelmed me.
6The cords of the grave[e] coiled around me;
the snares of death confronted me.
7In my distress I called to the LORD;
I called out to my God.
From his temple he heard my voice;
my cry came to his ears.

8"The earth trembled and quaked,
the foundations of the heavens[f] shook;
they trembled because he was angry.
9Smoke rose from his nostrils;
consuming fire came from his mouth,
burning coals blazed out of it.
10He parted the heavens and came down;
dark clouds were under his feet.
11He mounted the cherubim and flew;
he soared[g] on the wings of the wind.
12He made darkness his canopy around him—
the dark[h] rain clouds of the sky.
13Out of the brightness of his presence
bolts of lightning blazed forth.
14The LORD thundered from heaven;
the voice of the Most High resounded.
15He shot arrows and scattered ⌊the enemies⌋,
bolts of lightning and routed them.
16The valleys of the sea were exposed
and the foundations of the earth laid bare

[a]16 That is, about 7 1/2 pounds (about 3.5 kilograms) [b]19 Or *son of Jair the weaver* [c]19 Hebrew and Septuagint; 1 Chron. 20:5 *son of Jair killed Lahmi the brother of Goliath* [d]3 *Horn* here symbolizes strength. [e]6 Hebrew *Sheol* [f]8 Hebrew; Vulgate and Syriac (see also Psalm 18:7) *mountains* [g]11 Many Hebrew manuscripts (see also Psalm 18:10); most Hebrew manuscripts *appeared* [h]12 Septuagint and Vulgate (see also Psalm 18:11); Hebrew *massed*

at the rebuke of the LORD,
at the blast of breath from his nostrils.

17"He reached down from on high and took hold of me;
he drew me out of deep waters.
18He rescued me from my powerful enemy,
from my foes, who were too strong for me.
19They confronted me in the day of my disaster,
but the LORD was my support.
20He brought me out into a spacious place;
he rescued me because he delighted in me.
21"The LORD has dealt with me according to my righteousness;
according to the cleanness of my hands he has rewarded me.
22For I have kept the ways of the LORD;
I have not done evil by turning from my God.
23All his laws are before me;
I have not turned away from his decrees.
24I have been blameless before him
and have kept myself from sin.
25The LORD has rewarded me according to my righteousness,
according to my cleanness[a] in his sight.
26"To the faithful you show yourself faithful,

[a]25 Hebrew; Septuagint and Vulgate (see also Psalm 18:24) *to the cleanness of my hands*

FRIDAY

VERSE FOR THE DAY: 2 Samuel 22:31

AUTHOR: Jill Briscoe

PASSAGE FOR THE DAY: 2 Samuel 22:1–51

A Green Pasture

Every family has a spot in their house through which everybody passes on their way in and out the door. It's the spot where everything gets dumped.

In our home, Stuart piles his papers there and wants them there when he comes looking for them two weeks later. I always have a Bible opened at that household intersection. As I pass by, I stop for a moment, glance at a verse and take it with me out the door. I don't think it's a travesty to nibble a bit of grass from the green pastures on your way past, do you?

MARRIAGE BUILDERS

♦ *When do portions of Scripture from your personal Bible reading or study resurface to influence your day-to-day life?*
♦ *In what ways do you remind yourselves and each other of important truths from God's Word?*

Additional Scripture Readings
Hebrews 4:12; 5:12–14; Psalm 119:103; Colossians 3:16

Go to page 334 for your next devotional reading.

to the blameless you show yourself
blameless,
27 to the pure you show yourself pure,
but to the crooked you show
yourself shrewd.
28 You save the humble,
but your eyes are on the haughty to
bring them low.
29 You are my lamp, O LORD;
the LORD turns my darkness into
light.
30 With your help I can advance against
a troop[a];
with my God I can scale a wall.

31 "As for God, his way is perfect;
the word of the LORD is flawless.
He is a shield
for all who take refuge in him.
32 For who is God besides the LORD?
And who is the Rock except our
God?
33 It is God who arms me with
strength[b]
and makes my way perfect.
34 He makes my feet like the feet of a
deer;
he enables me to stand on the
heights.
35 He trains my hands for battle;
my arms can bend a bow of bronze.
36 You give me your shield of victory;
you stoop down to make me great.
37 You broaden the path beneath me,
so that my ankles do not turn.

38 "I pursued my enemies and crushed
them;
I did not turn back till they were
destroyed.
39 I crushed them completely, and they
could not rise;
they fell beneath my feet.
40 You armed me with strength for
battle;
you made my adversaries bow at
my feet.
41 You made my enemies turn their
backs in flight,
and I destroyed my foes.
42 They cried for help, but there was no
one to save them—
to the LORD, but he did not answer.
43 I beat them as fine as the dust of the
earth;
I pounded and trampled them like
mud in the streets.

44 "You have delivered me from the
attacks of my people;
you have preserved me as the head
of nations.
People I did not know are subject to
me,
45 and foreigners come cringing to me;
as soon as they hear me, they obey
me.
46 They all lose heart;
they come trembling[c] from their
strongholds.

47 "The LORD lives! Praise be to my
Rock!
Exalted be God, the Rock, my
Savior!
48 He is the God who avenges me,
who puts the nations under me,
49 who sets me free from my enemies.
You exalted me above my foes;
from violent men you rescued me.
50 Therefore I will praise you, O LORD,
among the nations;
I will sing praises to your name.
51 He gives his king great victories;
he shows unfailing kindness to his
anointed,
to David and his descendants
forever."

The Last Words of David

23 These are the last words of David:
"The oracle of David son of Jesse,
the oracle of the man exalted by the
Most High,
the man anointed by the God of
Jacob,
Israel's singer of songs[d]:

2 "The Spirit of the LORD spoke through
me;
his word was on my tongue.
3 The God of Israel spoke,
the Rock of Israel said to me:
'When one rules over men in
righteousness,
when he rules in the fear of God,
4 he is like the light of morning at
sunrise
on a cloudless morning,
like the brightness after rain

[a] 30 Or *can run through a barricade* [b] 33 Dead Sea Scrolls, some Septuagint manuscripts, Vulgate and Syriac (see also Psalm 18:32); Masoretic Text *who is my strong refuge* [c] 46 Some Septuagint manuscripts and Vulgate (see also Psalm 18:45); Masoretic Text *they arm themselves.* [d] 1 Or *Israel's beloved singer*

that brings the grass from the
earth.'

5"Is not my house right with God?
Has he not made with me an
everlasting covenant,
arranged and secured in every part?
Will he not bring to fruition my
salvation
and grant me my every desire?
6But evil men are all to be cast aside
like thorns,
which are not gathered with the
hand.
7Whoever touches thorns
uses a tool of iron or the shaft of a
spear;
they are burned up where they lie."

David's Mighty Men

8These are the names of David's mighty men:

Josheb-Basshebeth,[a] a Tahkemonite,[b] was chief of the Three; he raised his spear against eight hundred men, whom he killed[c] in one encounter.

9Next to him was Eleazar son of Dodai the Ahohite. As one of the three mighty men, he was with David when they taunted the Philistines gathered ⌊at Pas Dammim⌋[d] for battle. Then the men of Israel retreated, 10but he stood his ground and struck down the Philistines till his hand grew tired and froze to the sword. The LORD brought about a great victory that day. The troops returned to Eleazar, but only to strip the dead.

11Next to him was Shammah son of Agee the Hararite. When the Philistines banded together at a place where there was a field full of lentils, Israel's troops fled from them. 12But Shammah took his stand in the middle of the field. He defended it and struck the Philistines down, and the LORD brought about a great victory.

13During harvest time, three of the thirty chief men came down to David at the cave of Adullam, while a band of Philistines was encamped in the Valley of Rephaim. 14At that time David was in the stronghold, and the Philistine garrison was at Bethlehem. 15David longed for water and said, "Oh, that someone would get me a drink of water from the well near the gate of Bethlehem!" 16So the three mighty men broke through the Philistine lines, drew water from the well near the gate of Bethlehem and carried it back to David. But he refused to drink it; instead, he poured it out before the LORD. 17"Far be it from me, O LORD, to do this!" he said. "Is it not the blood of men who went at the risk of their lives?" And David would not drink it.

Such were the exploits of the three mighty men.

18Abishai the brother of Joab son of Zeruiah was chief of the Three.[e] He raised his spear against three hundred men, whom he killed, and so he became as famous as the Three. 19Was he not held in greater honor than the Three? He became their commander, even though he was not included among them.

20Benaiah son of Jehoiada was a valiant fighter from Kabzeel, who performed great exploits. He struck down two of Moab's best men. He also went down into a pit on a snowy day and killed a lion. 21And he struck down a huge Egyptian. Although the Egyptian had a spear in his hand, Benaiah went against him with a club. He snatched the spear from the Egyptian's hand and killed him with his own spear. 22Such were the exploits of Benaiah son of Jehoiada; he too was as famous as the three mighty men. 23He was held in greater honor than any of the Thirty, but he was not included among the Three. And David put him in charge of his bodyguard.

24Among the Thirty were:
Asahel the brother of Joab,
Elhanan son of Dodo from Bethlehem,
25Shammah the Harodite,
Elika the Harodite,
26Helez the Paltite,
Ira son of Ikkesh from Tekoa,
27Abiezer from Anathoth,
Mebunnai[f] the Hushathite,
28Zalmon the Ahohite,
Maharai the Netophathite,

[a] 8 Hebrew; some Septuagint manuscripts suggest *Ish-Bosheth*, that is, *Esh-Baal* (see also 1 Chron. 11:11 *Jashobeam*). [b] 8 Probably a variant of *Hacmonite* (see 1 Chron. 11:11) [c] 8 Some Septuagint manuscripts (see also 1 Chron. 11:11); Hebrew and other Septuagint manuscripts *Three; it was Adino the Eznite who killed eight hundred men* [d] 9 See 1 Chron. 11:13; Hebrew *gathered there.* [e] 18 Most Hebrew manuscripts (see also 1 Chron. 11:20); two Hebrew manuscripts and Syriac *Thirty* [f] 27 Hebrew; some Septuagint manuscripts (see also 1 Chron. 11:29) *Sibbecai*

29Heled[a] son of Baanah the Netophathite,
Ithai son of Ribai from Gibeah in Benjamin,
30Benaiah the Pirathonite,
Hiddai[b] from the ravines of Gaash,
31Abi-Albon the Arbathite,
Azmaveth the Barhumite,
32Eliahba the Shaalbonite,
the sons of Jashen,
Jonathan 33son of[c] Shammah the Hararite,
Ahiam son of Sharar[d] the Hararite,
34Eliphelet son of Ahasbai the Maacathite,
Eliam son of Ahithophel the Gilonite,
35Hezro the Carmelite,
Paarai the Arbite,
36Igal son of Nathan from Zobah,
the son of Hagri,[e]
37Zelek the Ammonite,
Naharai the Beerothite, the armorbearer of Joab son of Zeruiah,
38Ira the Ithrite,
Gareb the Ithrite
39and Uriah the Hittite.
There were thirty-seven in all.

David Counts the Fighting Men

24 Again the anger of the LORD burned against Israel, and he incited David against them, saying, "Go and take a census of Israel and Judah."

2So the king said to Joab and the army commanders[f] with him, "Go throughout the tribes of Israel from Dan to Beersheba and enroll the fighting men, so that I may know how many there are."

3But Joab replied to the king, "May the LORD your God multiply the troops a hundred times over, and may the eyes of my lord the king see it. But why does my lord the king want to do such a thing?"

4The king's word, however, overruled Joab and the army commanders; so they left the presence of the king to enroll the fighting men of Israel.

5After crossing the Jordan, they camped near Aroer, south of the town in the gorge, and then went through Gad and on to Jazer. 6They went to Gilead and the region of Tahtim Hodshi, and on to Dan Jaan and around toward Sidon. 7Then they went toward the fortress of Tyre and all the towns of the Hivites and Canaanites. Finally, they went on to Beersheba in the Negev of Judah.

8After they had gone through the entire land, they came back to Jerusalem at the end of nine months and twenty days.

9Joab reported the number of the fighting men to the king: In Israel there were eight hundred thousand able-bodied men who could handle a sword, and in Judah five hundred thousand.

10David was conscience-stricken after he had counted the fighting men, and he said to the LORD, "I have sinned greatly in what I have done. Now, O LORD, I beg you, take away the guilt of your servant. I have done a very foolish thing."

11Before David got up the next morning, the word of the LORD had come to Gad the prophet, David's seer: 12"Go and tell David, 'This is what the LORD says: I am giving you three options. Choose one of them for me to carry out against you.' "

13So Gad went to David and said to him, "Shall there come upon you three[g] years of famine in your land? Or three months of fleeing from your enemies while they pursue you? Or three days of plague in your land? Now then, think it over and decide how I should answer the one who sent me."

14David said to Gad, "I am in deep distress. Let us fall into the hands of the LORD, for his mercy is great; but do not let me fall into the hands of men."

15So the LORD sent a plague on Israel from that morning until the end of the time designated, and seventy thousand of the people from Dan to Beersheba died. 16When the angel stretched out his hand to destroy Jerusalem, the LORD was grieved because of the calamity and said to the angel who was afflicting the people, "Enough! Withdraw your hand." The angel of the LORD was then at the threshing floor of Araunah the Jebusite.

17When David saw the angel who was

[a] *29* Some Hebrew manuscripts and Vulgate (see also 1 Chron. 11:30); most Hebrew manuscripts *Heleb*
[b] *30* Hebrew; some Septuagint manuscripts (see also 1 Chron. 11:32) *Hurai*
[c] *33* Some Septuagint manuscripts (see also 1 Chron. 11:34); Hebrew does not have *son of.*
[d] *33* Hebrew; some Septuagint manuscripts (see also 1 Chron. 11:35) *Sacar*
[e] *36* Some Septuagint manuscripts (see also 1 Chron. 11:38); Hebrew *Haggadi*
[f] *2* Septuagint (see also verse 4 and 1 Chron. 21:2); Hebrew *Joab the army commander*
[g] *13* Septuagint (see also 1 Chron. 21:12); Hebrew *seven*

striking down the people, he said to the LORD, "I am the one who has sinned and done wrong. These are but sheep. What have they done? Let your hand fall upon me and my family."

David Builds an Altar

18On that day Gad went to David and said to him, "Go up and build an altar to the LORD on the threshing floor of Araunah the Jebusite." 19So David went up, as the LORD had commanded through Gad. 20When Araunah looked and saw the king and his men coming toward him, he went out and bowed down before the king with his face to the ground.

21Araunah said, "Why has my lord the king come to his servant?"

"To buy your threshing floor," David answered, "so I can build an altar to the LORD, that the plague on the people may be stopped."

22Araunah said to David, "Let my lord the king take whatever pleases him and offer it up. Here are oxen for the burnt offering, and here are threshing sledges and ox yokes for the wood. 23O king, Araunah gives all this to the king." Araunah also said to him, "May the LORD your God accept you."

24But the king replied to Araunah, "No, I insist on paying you for it. I will not sacrifice to the LORD my God burnt offerings that cost me nothing."

So David bought the threshing floor and the oxen and paid fifty shekels[a] of silver for them. 25David built an altar to the LORD there and sacrificed burnt offerings and fellowship offerings.[b] Then the LORD answered prayer in behalf of the land, and the plague on Israel was stopped.

[a]24 That is, about 1 1/4 pounds (about 0.6 kilogram) [b]25 Traditionally *peace offerings*

THIS book begins by covering the excitement of Solomon's building of the temple, but it then goes on to describe the sad events that take place after Solomon begins serving other gods. The kingdom is divided into two nations, Israel and Judah. All of Israel's kings are wicked, half of Judah's are. God sends prophets (like Elijah) to preach God's word and to warn the rulers against idolatry. As you read this book, realize how severe it is to disobey God's word. Like the Israelites on Mount Carmel, confess, "The LORD—he is God" (1 Kings 18:39).

1 KINGS

Adonijah Sets Himself Up as King

1 When King David was old and well advanced in years, he could not keep warm even when they put covers over him. 2 So his servants said to him, "Let us look for a young virgin to attend the king and take care of him. She can lie beside him so that our lord the king may keep warm."

3 Then they searched throughout Israel for a beautiful girl and found Abishag, a Shunammite, and brought her to the king. 4 The girl was very beautiful; she took care of the king and waited on him, but the king had no intimate relations with her.

5 Now Adonijah, whose mother was Haggith, put himself forward and said, "I will be king." So he got chariots and horses[a] ready, with fifty men to run ahead of him. 6 (His father had never inter-

[a] 5 Or *charioteers*

fered with him by asking, "Why do you behave as you do?" He was also very handsome and was born next after Absalom.)

7Adonijah conferred with Joab son of Zeruiah and with Abiathar the priest, and they gave him their support. 8But Zadok the priest, Benaiah son of Jehoiada, Nathan the prophet, Shimei and Rei[a] and David's special guard did not join Adonijah.

9Adonijah then sacrificed sheep, cattle and fattened calves at the Stone of Zoheleth near En Rogel. He invited all his brothers, the king's sons, and all the men of Judah who were royal officials, 10but he did not invite Nathan the prophet or Benaiah or the special guard or his brother Solomon.

11Then Nathan asked Bathsheba, Solomon's mother, "Have you not heard that Adonijah, the son of Haggith, has become king without our lord David's knowing it? 12Now then, let me advise you how you can save your own life and the life of your son Solomon. 13Go in to King David and say to him, 'My lord the king, did you not swear to me your servant: "Surely Solomon your son shall be king after me, and he will sit on my throne"? Why then has Adonijah become king?' 14While you are still there talking to the king, I will come in and confirm what you have said."

15So Bathsheba went to see the aged king in his room, where Abishag the Shunammite was attending him. 16Bathsheba bowed low and knelt before the king.

"What is it you want?" the king asked.

17She said to him, "My lord, you yourself swore to me your servant by the LORD your God: 'Solomon your son shall be king after me, and he will sit on my throne.' 18But now Adonijah has become king, and you, my lord the king, do not know about it. 19He has sacrificed great numbers of cattle, fattened calves, and sheep, and has invited all the king's sons, Abiathar the priest and Joab the commander of the army, but he has not invited Solomon your servant. 20My lord the king, the eyes of all Israel are on you, to learn from you who will sit on the throne of my lord the king after him. 21Otherwise, as soon as my lord the king is laid to rest with his fathers, I and my son Solomon will be treated as criminals."

22While she was still speaking with the king, Nathan the prophet arrived. 23And they told the king, "Nathan the prophet is here." So he went before the king and bowed with his face to the ground.

24Nathan said, "Have you, my lord the king, declared that Adonijah shall be king after you, and that he will sit on your throne? 25Today he has gone down and sacrificed great numbers of cattle, fattened calves, and sheep. He has invited all the king's sons, the commanders of the army and Abiathar the priest. Right now they are eating and drinking with him and saying, 'Long live King Adonijah!' 26But me your servant, and Zadok the priest, and Benaiah son of Jehoiada, and your servant Solomon he did not invite. 27Is this something my lord the king has done without letting his servants know who should sit on the throne of my lord the king after him?"

David Makes Solomon King

28Then King David said, "Call in Bathsheba." So she came into the king's presence and stood before him.

29The king then took an oath: "As surely as the LORD lives, who has delivered me out of every trouble, 30I will surely carry out today what I swore to you by the LORD, the God of Israel: Solomon your son shall be king after me, and he will sit on my throne in my place."

31Then Bathsheba bowed low with her face to the ground and, kneeling before the king, said, "May my lord King David live forever!"

32King David said, "Call in Zadok the priest, Nathan the prophet and Benaiah son of Jehoiada." When they came before the king, 33he said to them: "Take your lord's servants with you and set Solomon my son on my own mule and take him down to Gihon. 34There have Zadok the priest and Nathan the prophet anoint him king over Israel. Blow the trumpet and shout, 'Long live King Solomon!' 35Then you are to go up with him, and he is to come and sit on my throne and reign in my place. I have appointed him ruler over Israel and Judah."

36Benaiah son of Jehoiada answered the king, "Amen! May the LORD, the God of my lord the king, so declare it. 37As the LORD was with my lord the king, so may he be with Solomon to make his throne

[a]8 Or *and his friends*

even greater than the throne of my lord
King David!"
38So Zadok the priest, Nathan the
prophet, Benaiah son of Jehoiada, the Ker-
ethites and the Pelethites went down and
put Solomon on King David's mule and
escorted him to Gihon. 39Zadok the priest
took the horn of oil from the sacred tent
and anointed Solomon. Then they sound-
ed the trumpet and all the people shouted,
"Long live King Solomon!" 40And all the
people went up after him, playing flutes
and rejoicing greatly, so that the ground
shook with the sound.
41Adonijah and all the guests who were
with him heard it as they were finishing
their feast. On hearing the sound of the
trumpet, Joab asked, "What's the mean-
ing of all the noise in the city?"
42Even as he was speaking, Jonathan
son of Abiathar the priest arrived. Adoni-
jah said, "Come in. A worthy man like you
must be bringing good news."
43"Not at all!" Jonathan answered. "Our
lord King David has made Solomon king.
44The king has sent with him Zadok the
priest, Nathan the prophet, Benaiah son of
Jehoiada, the Kerethites and the Pele-
thites, and they have put him on the
king's mule, 45and Zadok the priest and
Nathan the prophet have anointed him
king at Gihon. From there they have gone
up cheering, and the city resounds with it.
That's the noise you hear. 46Moreover,
Solomon has taken his seat on the royal
throne. 47Also, the royal officials have
come to congratulate our lord King David,
saying, 'May your God make Solomon's
name more famous than yours and his
throne greater than yours!' And the king
bowed in worship on his bed 48and said,
'Praise be to the LORD, the God of Israel,
who has allowed my eyes to see a succes-
sor on my throne today.' "
49At this, all Adonijah's guests rose in
alarm and dispersed. 50But Adonijah, in
fear of Solomon, went and took hold of
the horns of the altar. 51Then Solomon
was told, "Adonijah is afraid of King Solo-
mon and is clinging to the horns of the al-
tar. He says, 'Let King Solomon swear to
me today that he will not put his servant
to death with the sword.' "
52Solomon replied, "If he shows himself
to be a worthy man, not a hair of his head
will fall to the ground; but if evil is found
in him, he will die." 53Then King Solomon
sent men, and they brought him down
from the altar. And Adonijah came and
bowed down to King Solomon, and Solo-
mon said, "Go to your home."

David's Charge to Solomon

2 When the time drew near for David to
die, he gave a charge to Solomon his
son.
2"I am about to go the way of all the
earth," he said. "So be strong, show your-
self a man, 3and observe what the LORD
your God requires: Walk in his ways, and
keep his decrees and commands, his laws
and requirements, as written in the Law of
Moses, so that you may prosper in all you
do and wherever you go, 4and that the
LORD may keep his promise to me: 'If your
descendants watch how they live, and if
they walk faithfully before me with all
their heart and soul, you will never fail to
have a man on the throne of Israel.'
5"Now you yourself know what Joab
son of Zeruiah did to me—what he did to
the two commanders of Israel's armies,
Abner son of Ner and Amasa son of Je-
ther. He killed them, shedding their blood
in peacetime as if in battle, and with that
blood stained the belt around his waist
and the sandals on his feet. 6Deal with
him according to your wisdom, but do not
let his gray head go down to the grave[a] in
peace.
7"But show kindness to the sons of Bar-
zillai of Gilead and let them be among
those who eat at your table. They stood by
me when I fled from your brother Absa-
lom.
8"And remember, you have with you
Shimei son of Gera, the Benjamite from
Bahurim, who called down bitter curses
on me the day I went to Mahanaim. When
he came down to meet me at the Jordan,
I swore to him by the LORD: 'I will not put
you to death by the sword.' 9But now, do
not consider him innocent. You are a man
of wisdom; you will know what to do to
him. Bring his gray head down to the
grave in blood."
10Then David rested with his fathers
and was buried in the City of David. 11He
had reigned forty years over Israel—sev-
en years in Hebron and thirty-three in Je-
rusalem. 12So Solomon sat on the throne
of his father David, and his rule was firmly
established.

[a]6 Hebrew *Sheol*; also in verse 9

WEEKENDING

LONELINESS

Many people complain of loneliness, but some have only themselves to blame. If you realize that you need to take the initiative to spend more time in nurturing relationships, a first step might be to identify any tendencies that keep you from enjoying depth in your relationships.

For example, "I tend to talk to my friends about trivial or superficial matters" or "I should be less concerned about activities and more concerned about relationships." Use the space below to list any tendencies that fall into this category.

1. _____

2. _____

3. _____

4. _____

5. _____

With your spouse, brainstorm positive steps you could take to deepen your relationships.

— Dr. Les Carter and Dr. Frank Minirth

REVIVE

Saturday: Joshua 1:5–9
Sunday: Psalm 147:1–20

Go to page 337 for your next devotional reading.

Solomon's Throne Established

13Now Adonijah, the son of Haggith,
went to Bathsheba, Solomon's mother.
Bathsheba asked him, "Do you come
peacefully?"
He answered, "Yes, peacefully." 14Then
he added, "I have something to say to
you."
"You may say it," she replied.
15"As you know," he said, "the kingdom
was mine. All Israel looked to me as their
king. But things changed, and the king-
dom has gone to my brother; for it has
come to him from the LORD. 16Now I have
one request to make of you. Do not re-
fuse me."
"You may make it," she said.
17So he continued, "Please ask King Sol-
omon—he will not refuse you—to give
me Abishag the Shunammite as my wife."
18"Very well," Bathsheba replied, "I will
speak to the king for you."
19When Bathsheba went to King Solo-
mon to speak to him for Adonijah, the
king stood up to meet her, bowed down to
her and sat down on his throne. He had a
throne brought for the king's mother, and
she sat down at his right hand.
20"I have one small request to make of
you," she said. "Do not refuse me."
The king replied, "Make it, my mother;
I will not refuse you."
21So she said, "Let Abishag the Shu-
nammite be given in marriage to your
brother Adonijah."
22King Solomon answered his mother,
"Why do you request Abishag the Shu-
nammite for Adonijah? You might as well
request the kingdom for him—after all, he
is my older brother—yes, for him and for
Abiathar the priest and Joab son of Zeru-
iah!"
23Then King Solomon swore by the
LORD: "May God deal with me, be it ever
so severely, if Adonijah does not pay with
his life for this request! 24And now, as
surely as the LORD lives—he who has es-
tablished me securely on the throne of my
father David and has founded a dynasty
for me as he promised—Adonijah shall be
put to death today!" 25So King Solomon
gave orders to Benaiah son of Jehoiada,
and he struck down Adonijah and he died.
26To Abiathar the priest the king said,
"Go back to your fields in Anathoth. You
deserve to die, but I will not put you to
death now, because you carried the ark of
the Sovereign LORD before my father Da-
vid and shared all my father's hardships."
27So Solomon removed Abiathar from the
priesthood of the LORD, fulfilling the word
the LORD had spoken at Shiloh about the
house of Eli.
28When the news reached Joab, who
had conspired with Adonijah though not
with Absalom, he fled to the tent of the
LORD and took hold of the horns of the al-
tar. 29King Solomon was told that Joab
had fled to the tent of the LORD and was
beside the altar. Then Solomon ordered
Benaiah son of Jehoiada, "Go, strike him
down!"
30So Benaiah entered the tent of the
LORD and said to Joab, "The king says,
'Come out!' "
But he answered, "No, I will die here."
Benaiah reported to the king, "This is
how Joab answered me."
31Then the king commanded Benaiah,
"Do as he says. Strike him down and bury
him, and so clear me and my father's
house of the guilt of the innocent blood
that Joab shed. 32The LORD will repay him
for the blood he shed, because without
the knowledge of my father David he at-
tacked two men and killed them with the
sword. Both of them—Abner son of Ner,
commander of Israel's army, and Amasa
son of Jether, commander of Judah's
army—were better men and more upright
than he. 33May the guilt of their blood rest
on the head of Joab and his descendants
forever. But on David and his descen-
dants, his house and his throne, may there
be the LORD's peace forever."
34So Benaiah son of Jehoiada went up
and struck down Joab and killed him, and
he was buried on his own land[a] in the
desert. 35The king put Benaiah son of Je-
hoiada over the army in Joab's position
and replaced Abiathar with Zadok the
priest.
36Then the king sent for Shimei and
said to him, "Build yourself a house in Je-
rusalem and live there, but do not go any-
where else. 37The day you leave and cross
the Kidron Valley, you can be sure you
will die; your blood will be on your own
head."
38Shimei answered the king, "What you
say is good. Your servant will do as my
lord the king has said." And Shimei stayed
in Jerusalem for a long time.

[a]34 Or *buried in his tomb*

39But three years later, two of Shimei's
slaves ran off to Achish son of Maacah,
king of Gath, and Shimei was told, "Your
slaves are in Gath." 40At this, he saddled
his donkey and went to Achish at Gath in
search of his slaves. So Shimei went away
and brought the slaves back from Gath.

41When Solomon was told that Shimei
had gone from Jerusalem to Gath and had
returned, 42the king summoned Shimei
and said to him, "Did I not make you
swear by the LORD and warn you, 'On the
day you leave to go anywhere else, you
can be sure you will die'? At that time you
said to me, 'What you say is good. I will
obey.' 43Why then did you not keep your
oath to the LORD and obey the command
I gave you?"

44The king also said to Shimei, "You
know in your heart all the wrong you did
to my father David. Now the LORD will re-
pay you for your wrongdoing. 45But King
Solomon will be blessed, and David's
throne will remain secure before the LORD
forever."

46Then the king gave the order to Bena-
iah son of Jehoiada, and he went out and
struck Shimei down and killed him.

The kingdom was now firmly estab-
lished in Solomon's hands.

Solomon Asks for Wisdom

3 Solomon made an alliance with Phar-
aoh king of Egypt and married his
daughter. He brought her to the City of
David until he finished building his palace
and the temple of the LORD, and the wall
around Jerusalem. 2The people, however,
were still sacrificing at the high places, be-
cause a temple had not yet been built for
the Name of the LORD. 3Solomon showed
his love for the LORD by walking according
to the statutes of his father David, except
that he offered sacrifices and burned in-
cense on the high places.

4The king went to Gibeon to offer sacri-
fices, for that was the most important high
place, and Solomon offered a thousand
burnt offerings on that altar. 5At Gibeon
the LORD appeared to Solomon during the
night in a dream, and God said, "Ask for
whatever you want me to give you."

6Solomon answered, "You have shown
great kindness to your servant, my father
David, because he was faithful to you and
righteous and upright in heart. You have
continued this great kindness to him and
have given him a son to sit on his throne
this very day.

7"Now, O LORD my God, you have made
your servant king in place of my father
David. But I am only a little child and do
not know how to carry out my duties.
8Your servant is here among the people
you have chosen, a great people, too nu-
merous to count or number. 9So give your
servant a discerning heart to govern your
people and to distinguish between right
and wrong. For who is able to govern this
great people of yours?"

10The Lord was pleased that Solomon
had asked for this. 11So God said to him,
"Since you have asked for this and not for
long life or wealth for yourself, nor have
asked for the death of your enemies but
for discernment in administering justice,
12I will do what you have asked. I will give
you a wise and discerning heart, so that
there will never have been anyone like
you, nor will there ever be. 13Moreover, I
will give you what you have not asked
for—both riches and honor—so that in
your lifetime you will have no equal
among kings. 14And if you walk in my
ways and obey my statutes and com-
mands as David your father did, I will give
you a long life." 15Then Solomon awoke—
and he realized it had been a dream.

He returned to Jerusalem, stood before
the ark of the Lord's covenant and sacri-
ficed burnt offerings and fellowship offer-
ings.[a] Then he gave a feast for all his
court.

A Wise Ruling

16Now two prostitutes came to the king
and stood before him. 17One of them said,
"My lord, this woman and I live in the
same house. I had a baby while she was
there with me. 18The third day after my
child was born, this woman also had a
baby. We were alone; there was no one in
the house but the two of us.

19"During the night this woman's son
died because she lay on him. 20So she got
up in the middle of the night and took my
son from my side while I your servant was
asleep. She put him by her breast and put
her dead son by my breast. 21The next
morning, I got up to nurse my son—and
he was dead! But when I looked at him
closely in the morning light, I saw that it
wasn't the son I had borne."

22The other woman said, "No! The liv-

[a]15 Traditionally *peace offerings*

VERSE FOR THE DAY:
1 Kings 3:7–9

AUTHOR:
Ron and Jeanette Lee

PASSAGE FOR THE DAY:
1 Kings 3:5–12

Shifting the Focus

If you could have anything in the world simply by asking, what would you request? Perfect health? The ideal job? Tickets to the Superbowl?

That question might make for pleasant after-dinner conversation, but when was the last time someone came around to grant you all your wishes? Well, it happened to King Solomon. God appeared to him in a dream, asking him to name whatever it was that he desired. Solomon could have asked for victory over his enemies, a cooperative citizenry, personal riches. But instead, he asked for "a discerning heart" to govern God's people and to "distinguish between right and wrong." Solomon was asking for the tools he would need to do his job well.

If God were to ask you what you desire most for your marriage, what would you say? An end to your disagreements? The ability to get out of debt? Those are end results. Perhaps God wants us to focus instead on the qualities each of us needs in order to achieve the results he desires. And a good place to start is by seeking discernment.

Solomon sought the ability to distinguish between right and wrong so he could employ that wisdom in his dealings with the people of Israel. In our marriages, we need that same discernment in our dealings with each other. The success of our marriages depends on it.

MARRIAGE BUILDERS

♦ *If you could improve any two areas of your marriage, what would they be?*

♦ *In what ways do you need to change to help bring about those improvements?*

Additional Scripture Readings
2 Chronicles 1:6–12; 1 Kings 4:29–34; Deuteronomy 34:9–12

Go to page 345 for your next devotional reading.

ing one is my son; the dead one is yours."
But the first one insisted, "No! The dead one is yours; the living one is mine." And so they argued before the king.
23The king said, "This one says, 'My son is alive and your son is dead,' while that one says, 'No! Your son is dead and mine is alive.' "
24Then the king said, "Bring me a sword." So they brought a sword for the king. 25He then gave an order: "Cut the living child in two and give half to one and half to the other."
26The woman whose son was alive was filled with compassion for her son and said to the king, "Please, my lord, give her the living baby! Don't kill him!"
But the other said, "Neither I nor you shall have him. Cut him in two!"
27Then the king gave his ruling: "Give the living baby to the first woman. Do not kill him; she is his mother."
28When all Israel heard the verdict the king had given, they held the king in awe, because they saw that he had wisdom from God to administer justice.

Solomon's Officials and Governors

4 So King Solomon ruled over all Israel.
2And these were his chief officials:

Azariah son of Zadok—the priest;
3Elihoreph and Ahijah, sons of Shisha—secretaries;
Jehoshaphat son of Ahilud—recorder;
4Benaiah son of Jehoiada—commander in chief;
Zadok and Abiathar—priests;
5Azariah son of Nathan—in charge of the district officers;
Zabud son of Nathan—a priest and personal adviser to the king;
6Ahishar—in charge of the palace;
Adoniram son of Abda—in charge of forced labor.

7Solomon also had twelve district governors over all Israel, who supplied provisions for the king and the royal household. Each one had to provide supplies for one month in the year. 8These are their names:

Ben-Hur—in the hill country of Ephraim;
9Ben-Deker—in Makaz, Shaalbim, Beth Shemesh and Elon Bethhanan;
10Ben-Hesed—in Arubboth (Socoh and all the land of Hepher were his);
11Ben-Abinadab—in Naphoth Dor[a] (he was married to Taphath daughter of Solomon);
12Baana son of Ahilud—in Taanach and Megiddo, and in all of Beth Shan next to Zarethan below Jezreel, from Beth Shan to Abel Meholah across to Jokmeam;
13Ben-Geber—in Ramoth Gilead (the settlements of Jair son of Manasseh in Gilead were his, as well as the district of Argob in Bashan and its sixty large walled cities with bronze gate bars);
14Ahinadab son of Iddo—in Mahanaim;
15Ahimaaz—in Naphtali (he had married Basemath daughter of Solomon);
16Baana son of Hushai—in Asher and in Aloth;
17Jehoshaphat son of Paruah—in Issachar;
18Shimei son of Ela—in Benjamin;
19Geber son of Uri—in Gilead (the country of Sihon king of the Amorites and the country of Og king of Bashan). He was the only governor over the district.

Solomon's Daily Provisions

20The people of Judah and Israel were as numerous as the sand on the seashore; they ate, they drank and they were happy.
21And Solomon ruled over all the kingdoms from the River[b] to the land of the Philistines, as far as the border of Egypt. These countries brought tribute and were Solomon's subjects all his life.
22Solomon's daily provisions were thirty cors[c] of fine flour and sixty cors[d] of meal, 23ten head of stall-fed cattle, twenty of pasture-fed cattle and a hundred sheep and goats, as well as deer, gazelles, roebucks and choice fowl. 24For he ruled over all the kingdoms west of the River, from Tiphsah to Gaza, and had peace on all sides. 25During Solomon's lifetime Judah and Israel, from Dan to Beersheba, lived in safety, each man under his own vine and fig tree.

[a] *11* Or *in the heights of Dor* [b] *21* That is, the Euphrates; also in verse 24 [c] *22* That is, probably about 185 bushels (about 6.6 kiloliters) [d] *22* That is, probably about 375 bushels (about 13.2 kiloliters)

26Solomon had four[a] thousand stalls
for chariot horses, and twelve thousand
horses.[b]
27The district officers, each in his
month, supplied provisions for King Solo-
mon and all who came to the king's table.
They saw to it that nothing was lacking.
28They also brought to the proper place
their quotas of barley and straw for the
chariot horses and the other horses.

Solomon's Wisdom

29God gave Solomon wisdom and very
great insight, and a breadth of under-
standing as measureless as the sand on
the seashore. 30Solomon's wisdom was
greater than the wisdom of all the men of
the East, and greater than all the wisdom
of Egypt. 31He was wiser than any other
man, including Ethan the Ezrahite—wiser
than Heman, Calcol and Darda, the sons
of Mahol. And his fame spread to all the
surrounding nations. 32He spoke three
thousand proverbs and his songs num-
bered a thousand and five. 33He described
plant life, from the cedar of Lebanon to
the hyssop that grows out of walls. He also
taught about animals and birds, reptiles
and fish. 34Men of all nations came to lis-
ten to Solomon's wisdom, sent by all the
kings of the world, who had heard of his
wisdom.

Preparations for Building the Temple

5 When Hiram king of Tyre heard that
Solomon had been anointed king to
succeed his father David, he sent his en-
voys to Solomon, because he had always
been on friendly terms with David. 2Solo-
mon sent back this message to Hiram:

3"You know that because of the
wars waged against my father David
from all sides, he could not build a
temple for the Name of the LORD his
God until the LORD put his enemies
under his feet. 4But now the LORD my
God has given me rest on every side,
and there is no adversary or disaster.
5I intend, therefore, to build a temple
for the Name of the LORD my God, as
the LORD told my father David, when
he said, 'Your son whom I will put on
the throne in your place will build the
temple for my Name.'
6"So give orders that cedars of Leb-
anon be cut for me. My men will
work with yours, and I will pay you
for your men whatever wages you
set. You know that we have no one so
skilled in felling timber as the Sidoni-
ans."

7When Hiram heard Solomon's mes-
sage, he was greatly pleased and said,
"Praise be to the LORD today, for he has
given David a wise son to rule over this
great nation."
8So Hiram sent word to Solomon:

"I have received the message you
sent me and will do all you want in
providing the cedar and pine logs.
9My men will haul them down from
Lebanon to the sea, and I will float
them in rafts by sea to the place you
specify. There I will separate them
and you can take them away. And
you are to grant my wish by provid-
ing food for my royal household."

10In this way Hiram kept Solomon sup-
plied with all the cedar and pine logs he
wanted, 11and Solomon gave Hiram twen-
ty thousand cors[c] of wheat as food for his
household, in addition to twenty thou-
sand baths[d,e] of pressed olive oil. Solo-
mon continued to do this for Hiram year
after year. 12The LORD gave Solomon wis-
dom, just as he had promised him. There
were peaceful relations between Hiram
and Solomon, and the two of them made
a treaty.
13King Solomon conscripted laborers
from all Israel—thirty thousand men.
14He sent them off to Lebanon in shifts of
ten thousand a month, so that they spent
one month in Lebanon and two months at
home. Adoniram was in charge of the
forced labor. 15Solomon had seventy
thousand carriers and eighty thousand
stonecutters in the hills, 16as well as thir-
ty-three hundred[f] foremen who super-
vised the project and directed the work-
men. 17At the king's command they
removed from the quarry large blocks of
quality stone to provide a foundation of
dressed stone for the temple. 18The crafts-
men of Solomon and Hiram and the men
of Gebal[g] cut and prepared the timber
and stone for the building of the temple.

[a] *26* Some Septuagint manuscripts (see also 2 Chron. 9:25); Hebrew *forty* [b] *26* Or *charioteers*
[c] *11* That is, probably about 125,000 bushels (about 4,400 kiloliters) [d] *11* Septuagint (see also 2 Chron. 2:10); Hebrew *twenty cors* [e] *11* That is, about 115,000 gallons (about 440 kiloliters) [f] *16* Hebrew; some Septuagint manuscripts (see also 2 Chron. 2:2, 18) *thirty-six hundred* [g] *18* That is, Byblos

Solomon Builds the Temple

6 In the four hundred and eightieth[a] year after the Israelites had come out of Egypt, in the fourth year of Solomon's reign over Israel, in the month of Ziv, the second month, he began to build the temple of the LORD.

2 The temple that King Solomon built for the LORD was sixty cubits long, twenty wide and thirty high.[b] 3 The portico at the front of the main hall of the temple extended the width of the temple, that is twenty cubits,[c] and projected ten cubits[d] from the front of the temple. 4 He made narrow clerestory windows in the temple. 5 Against the walls of the main hall and inner sanctuary he built a structure around the building, in which there were side rooms. 6 The lowest floor was five cubits[e] wide, the middle floor six cubits[f] and the third floor seven.[g] He made offset ledges around the outside of the temple so that nothing would be inserted into the temple walls.

7 In building the temple, only blocks dressed at the quarry were used, and no hammer, chisel or any other iron tool was heard at the temple site while it was being built.

8 The entrance to the lowest[h] floor was on the south side of the temple; a stairway led up to the middle level and from there to the third. 9 So he built the temple and completed it, roofing it with beams and cedar planks. 10 And he built the side rooms all along the temple. The height of each was five cubits, and they were attached to the temple by beams of cedar.

11 The word of the LORD came to Solomon: 12 "As for this temple you are building, if you follow my decrees, carry out my regulations and keep all my commands and obey them, I will fulfill through you the promise I gave to David your father. 13 And I will live among the Israelites and will not abandon my people Israel."

14 So Solomon built the temple and completed it. 15 He lined its interior walls with cedar boards, paneling them from the floor of the temple to the ceiling, and covered the floor of the temple with planks of pine. 16 He partitioned off twenty cubits[c] at the rear of the temple with cedar boards from floor to ceiling to form within the temple an inner sanctuary, the Most Holy Place. 17 The main hall in front of this room was forty cubits[i] long. 18 The inside of the temple was cedar, carved with gourds and open flowers. Everything was cedar; no stone was to be seen.

19 He prepared the inner sanctuary within the temple to set the ark of the covenant of the LORD there. 20 The inner sanctuary was twenty cubits long, twenty wide and twenty high.[j] He overlaid the inside with pure gold, and he also overlaid the altar of cedar. 21 Solomon covered the inside of the temple with pure gold, and he extended gold chains across the front of the inner sanctuary, which was overlaid with gold. 22 So he overlaid the whole interior with gold. He also overlaid with gold the altar that belonged to the inner sanctuary.

23 In the inner sanctuary he made a pair of cherubim of olive wood, each ten cubits[d] high. 24 One wing of the first cherub was five cubits long, and the other wing five cubits—ten cubits from wing tip to wing tip. 25 The second cherub also measured ten cubits, for the two cherubim were identical in size and shape. 26 The height of each cherub was ten cubits. 27 He placed the cherubim inside the innermost room of the temple, with their wings spread out. The wing of one cherub touched one wall, while the wing of the other touched the other wall, and their wings touched each other in the middle of the room. 28 He overlaid the cherubim with gold.

29 On the walls all around the temple, in both the inner and outer rooms, he carved cherubim, palm trees and open flowers. 30 He also covered the floors of both the inner and outer rooms of the temple with gold.

31 For the entrance of the inner sanctuary he made doors of olive wood with five-sided jambs. 32 And on the two olive wood doors he carved cherubim, palm trees and open flowers, and overlaid the cherubim and palm trees with beaten gold. 33 In the same way he made four-sided jambs of ol-

[a] *1* Hebrew; Septuagint *four hundred and fortieth* [b] *2* That is, about 90 feet (about 27 meters) long and 30 feet (about 9 meters) wide and 45 feet (about 13.5 meters) high [c] *3,16* That is, about 30 feet (about 9 meters) [d] *3,23* That is, about 15 feet (about 4.5 meters) [e] *6* That is, about 7 1/2 feet (about 2.3 meters); also in verses 10 and 24 [f] *6* That is, about 9 feet (about 2.7 meters) [g] *6* That is, about 10 1/2 feet (about 3.1 meters) [h] *8* Septuagint; Hebrew *middle* [i] *17* That is, about 60 feet (about 18 meters) [j] *20* That is, about 30 feet (about 9 meters) long, wide and high

ive wood for the entrance to the main hall.
34He also made two pine doors, each hav-
ing two leaves that turned in sockets. 35He
carved cherubim, palm trees and open
flowers on them and overlaid them with
gold hammered evenly over the carvings.
36And he built the inner courtyard of
three courses of dressed stone and one
course of trimmed cedar beams.
37The foundation of the temple of the
LORD was laid in the fourth year, in the
month of Ziv. 38In the eleventh year in the
month of Bul, the eighth month, the tem-
ple was finished in all its details according
to its specifications. He had spent seven
years building it.

Solomon Builds His Palace

7 It took Solomon thirteen years, how-
ever, to complete the construction of
his palace. 2He built the Palace of the For-
est of Lebanon a hundred cubits long, fifty
wide and thirty high,[a] with four rows of
cedar columns supporting trimmed cedar
beams. 3It was roofed with cedar above
the beams that rested on the columns—
forty-five beams, fifteen to a row. 4Its win-
dows were placed high in sets of three,
facing each other. 5All the doorways had
rectangular frames; they were in the front
part in sets of three, facing each other.[b]
6He made a colonnade fifty cubits long
and thirty wide.[c] In front of it was a porti-
co, and in front of that were pillars and an
overhanging roof.
7He built the throne hall, the Hall of Jus-
tice, where he was to judge, and he cov-
ered it with cedar from floor to ceiling.[d]
8And the palace in which he was to live,
set farther back, was similar in design.
Solomon also made a palace like this hall
for Pharaoh's daughter, whom he had
married.
9All these structures, from the outside
to the great courtyard and from founda-
tion to eaves, were made of blocks of
high-grade stone cut to size and trimmed
with a saw on their inner and outer faces.
10The foundations were laid with large
stones of good quality, some measuring
ten cubits[e] and some eight.[f] 11Above
were high-grade stones, cut to size, and
cedar beams. 12The great courtyard was
surrounded by a wall of three courses of
dressed stone and one course of trimmed
cedar beams, as was the inner courtyard
of the temple of the LORD with its portico.

The Temple's Furnishings

13King Solomon sent to Tyre and
brought Huram,[g] 14whose mother was a
widow from the tribe of Naphtali and
whose father was a man of Tyre and a
craftsman in bronze. Huram was highly
skilled and experienced in all kinds of
bronze work. He came to King Solomon
and did all the work assigned to him.
15He cast two bronze pillars, each eigh-
teen cubits high and twelve cubits
around,[h] by line. 16He also made two
capitals of cast bronze to set on the tops
of the pillars; each capital was five cu-
bits[i] high. 17A network of interwoven
chains festooned the capitals on top of the
pillars, seven for each capital. 18He made
pomegranates in two rows[j] encircling
each network to decorate the capitals on
top of the pillars.[k] He did the same for
each capital. 19The capitals on top of the
pillars in the portico were in the shape of
lilies, four cubits[l] high. 20On the capitals
of both pillars, above the bowl-shaped
part next to the network, were the two
hundred pomegranates in rows all
around. 21He erected the pillars at the por-
tico of the temple. The pillar to the south
he named Jakin[m] and the one to the north
Boaz.[n] 22The capitals on top were in the
shape of lilies. And so the work on the pil-
lars was completed.
23He made the Sea of cast metal, circu-
lar in shape, measuring ten cubits[e] from
rim to rim and five cubits high. It took a
line of thirty cubits[o] to measure around
it. 24Below the rim, gourds encircled it—

[a] *2* That is, about 150 feet (about 46 meters) long, 75 feet (about 23 meters) wide and 45 feet (about 13.5 meters) high [b] *5* The meaning of the Hebrew for this verse is uncertain. [c] *6* That is, about 75 feet (about 23 meters) long and 45 feet (about 13.5 meters) wide [d] *7* Vulgate and Syriac; Hebrew *floor* [e] *10,23* That is, about 15 feet (about 4.5 meters) [f] *10* That is, about 12 feet (about 3.6 meters) [g] *13* Hebrew *Hiram*, a variant of *Huram*; also in verses 40 and 45 [h] *15* That is, about 27 feet (about 8.1 meters) high and 18 feet (about 5.4 meters) around [i] *16* That is, about 7 1/2 feet (about 2.3 meters); also in verse 23 [j] *18* Two Hebrew manuscripts and Septuagint; most Hebrew manuscripts *made the pillars, and there were two rows* [k] *18* Many Hebrew manuscripts and Syriac; most Hebrew manuscripts *pomegranates* [l] *19* That is, about 6 feet (about 1.8 meters); also in verse 38 [m] *21* *Jakin* probably means *he establishes.* [n] *21* *Boaz* probably means *in him is strength.* [o] *23* That is, about 45 feet (about 13.5 meters)

ten to a cubit. The gourds were cast in two rows in one piece with the Sea.

25The Sea stood on twelve bulls, three facing north, three facing west, three facing south and three facing east. The Sea rested on top of them, and their hindquarters were toward the center. 26It was a handbreadth[a] in thickness, and its rim was like the rim of a cup, like a lily blossom. It held two thousand baths.[b]

27He also made ten movable stands of bronze; each was four cubits long, four wide and three high.[c] 28This is how the stands were made: They had side panels attached to uprights. 29On the panels between the uprights were lions, bulls and cherubim—and on the uprights as well. Above and below the lions and bulls were wreaths of hammered work. 30Each stand had four bronze wheels with bronze axles, and each had a basin resting on four supports, cast with wreaths on each side. 31On the inside of the stand there was an opening that had a circular frame one cubit[d] deep. This opening was round, and with its basework it measured a cubit and a half.[e] Around its opening there was engraving. The panels of the stands were square, not round. 32The four wheels were under the panels, and the axles of the wheels were attached to the stand. The diameter of each wheel was a cubit and a half. 33The wheels were made like chariot wheels; the axles, rims, spokes and hubs were all of cast metal.

34Each stand had four handles, one on each corner, projecting from the stand. 35At the top of the stand there was a circular band half a cubit[f] deep. The supports and panels were attached to the top of the stand. 36He engraved cherubim, lions and palm trees on the surfaces of the supports and on the panels, in every available space, with wreaths all around. 37This is the way he made the ten stands. They were all cast in the same molds and were identical in size and shape.

38He then made ten bronze basins, each holding forty baths[g] and measuring four cubits across, one basin to go on each of the ten stands. 39He placed five of the stands on the south side of the temple and five on the north. He placed the Sea on the south side, at the southeast corner of the temple. 40He also made the basins and shovels and sprinkling bowls.

So Huram finished all the work he had undertaken for King Solomon in the temple of the LORD:

41the two pillars;
the two bowl-shaped capitals on top of the pillars;
the two sets of network decorating the two bowl-shaped capitals on top of the pillars;
42the four hundred pomegranates for the two sets of network (two rows of pomegranates for each network, decorating the bowl-shaped capitals on top of the pillars);
43the ten stands with their ten basins;
44the Sea and the twelve bulls under it;
45the pots, shovels and sprinkling bowls.

All these objects that Huram made for King Solomon for the temple of the LORD were of burnished bronze. 46The king had them cast in clay molds in the plain of the Jordan between Succoth and Zarethan. 47Solomon left all these things unweighed, because there were so many; the weight of the bronze was not determined.

48Solomon also made all the furnishings that were in the LORD's temple:

the golden altar;
the golden table on which was the bread of the Presence;
49the lampstands of pure gold (five on the right and five on the left, in front of the inner sanctuary);
the gold floral work and lamps and tongs;
50the pure gold basins, wick trimmers, sprinkling bowls, dishes and censers;
and the gold sockets for the doors of the innermost room, the Most Holy Place, and also for the doors of the main hall of the temple.

51When all the work King Solomon had done for the temple of the LORD was finished, he brought in the things his father David had dedicated—the silver and gold

[a] 26 That is, about 3 inches (about 8 centimeters) [b] 26 That is, probably about 11,500 gallons (about 44 kiloliters); the Septuagint does not have this sentence. [c] 27 That is, about 6 feet (about 1.8 meters) long and wide and about 4 1/2 feet (about 1.3 meters) high [d] 31 That is, about 1 1/2 feet (about 0.5 meter) [e] 31 That is, about 2 1/4 feet (about 0.7 meter); also in verse 32 [f] 35 That is, about 3/4 foot (about 0.2 meter) [g] 38 That is, about 230 gallons (about 880 liters)

and the furnishings—and he placed them in the treasuries of the LORD's temple.

The Ark Brought to the Temple

8 Then King Solomon summoned into his presence at Jerusalem the elders of Israel, all the heads of the tribes and the chiefs of the Israelite families, to bring up the ark of the LORD's covenant from Zion, the City of David. 2All the men of Israel came together to King Solomon at the time of the festival in the month of Ethanim, the seventh month.

3When all the elders of Israel had arrived, the priests took up the ark, 4and they brought up the ark of the LORD and the Tent of Meeting and all the sacred furnishings in it. The priests and Levites carried them up, 5and King Solomon and the entire assembly of Israel that had gathered about him were before the ark, sacrificing so many sheep and cattle that they could not be recorded or counted.

6The priests then brought the ark of the LORD's covenant to its place in the inner sanctuary of the temple, the Most Holy Place, and put it beneath the wings of the cherubim. 7The cherubim spread their wings over the place of the ark and overshadowed the ark and its carrying poles. 8These poles were so long that their ends could be seen from the Holy Place in front of the inner sanctuary, but not from outside the Holy Place; and they are still there today. 9There was nothing in the ark except the two stone tablets that Moses had placed in it at Horeb, where the LORD made a covenant with the Israelites after they came out of Egypt.

10When the priests withdrew from the Holy Place, the cloud filled the temple of the LORD. 11And the priests could not perform their service because of the cloud, for the glory of the LORD filled his temple.

12Then Solomon said, "The LORD has said that he would dwell in a dark cloud; 13I have indeed built a magnificent temple for you, a place for you to dwell forever."

14While the whole assembly of Israel was standing there, the king turned around and blessed them. 15Then he said:

"Praise be to the LORD, the God of Israel, who with his own hand has fulfilled what he promised with his own mouth to my father David. For he said, 16'Since the day I brought my people Israel out of Egypt, I have not chosen a city in any tribe of Israel to have a temple built for my Name to be there, but I have chosen David to rule my people Israel.'

17"My father David had it in his heart to build a temple for the Name of the LORD, the God of Israel. 18But the LORD said to my father David, 'Because it was in your heart to build a temple for my Name, you did well to have this in your heart. 19Nevertheless, you are not the one to build the temple, but your son, who is your own flesh and blood—he is the one who will build the temple for my Name.'

20"The LORD has kept the promise he made: I have succeeded David my father and now I sit on the throne of Israel, just as the LORD promised, and I have built the temple for the Name of the LORD, the God of Israel. 21I have provided a place there for the ark, in which is the covenant of the LORD that he made with our fathers when he brought them out of Egypt."

Solomon's Prayer of Dedication

22Then Solomon stood before the altar of the LORD in front of the whole assembly of Israel, spread out his hands toward heaven 23and said:

"O LORD, God of Israel, there is no God like you in heaven above or on earth below—you who keep your covenant of love with your servants who continue wholeheartedly in your way. 24You have kept your promise to your servant David my father; with your mouth you have promised and with your hand you have fulfilled it—as it is today.

25"Now LORD, God of Israel, keep for your servant David my father the promises you made to him when you said, 'You shall never fail to have a man to sit before me on the throne of Israel, if only your sons are careful in all they do to walk before me as you have done.' 26And now, O God of Israel, let your word that you promised your servant David my father come true.

27"But will God really dwell on earth? The heavens, even the highest heaven, cannot contain you. How much less this temple I have built! 28Yet give attention to your servant's prayer and his plea for mercy, O LORD

my God. Hear the cry and the prayer
that your servant is praying in your
presence this day. [29]May your eyes
be open toward this temple night and
day, this place of which you said, 'My
Name shall be there,' so that you will
hear the prayer your servant prays to-
ward this place. [30]Hear the supplica-
tion of your servant and of your peo-
ple Israel when they pray toward this
place. Hear from heaven, your dwell-
ing place, and when you hear, for-
give.

[31]"When a man wrongs his neigh-
bor and is required to take an oath
and he comes and swears the oath
before your altar in this temple,
[32]then hear from heaven and act.
Judge between your servants, con-
demning the guilty and bringing
down on his own head what he has
done. Declare the innocent not guilty,
and so establish his innocence.

[33]"When your people Israel have
been defeated by an enemy because
they have sinned against you, and
when they turn back to you and con-
fess your name, praying and making
supplication to you in this temple,
[34]then hear from heaven and forgive
the sin of your people Israel and
bring them back to the land you gave
to their fathers.

[35]"When the heavens are shut up
and there is no rain because your
people have sinned against you, and
when they pray toward this place and
confess your name and turn from
their sin because you have afflicted
them, [36]then hear from heaven and
forgive the sin of your servants, your
people Israel. Teach them the right
way to live, and send rain on the land
you gave your people for an inheri-
tance.

[37]"When famine or plague comes
to the land, or blight or mildew, lo-
custs or grasshoppers, or when an en-
emy besieges them in any of their cit-
ies, whatever disaster or disease may
come, [38]and when a prayer or plea is
made by any of your people Israel—
each one aware of the afflictions of
his own heart, and spreading out his
hands toward this temple— [39]then
hear from heaven, your dwelling
place. Forgive and act; deal with each
man according to all he does, since
you know his heart (for you alone
know the hearts of all men), [40]so that
they will fear you all the time they
live in the land you gave our fathers.

[41]"As for the foreigner who does
not belong to your people Israel but
has come from a distant land because
of your name— [42]for men will hear
of your great name and your mighty
hand and your outstretched arm—
when he comes and prays toward this
temple, [43]then hear from heaven,
your dwelling place, and do whatever
the foreigner asks of you, so that all
the peoples of the earth may know
your name and fear you, as do your
own people Israel, and may know
that this house I have built bears your
Name.

[44]"When your people go to war
against their enemies, wherever you
send them, and when they pray to the
LORD toward the city you have chosen
and the temple I have built for your
Name, [45]then hear from heaven their
prayer and their plea, and uphold
their cause.

[46]"When they sin against you—for
there is no one who does not sin—
and you become angry with them
and give them over to the enemy,
who takes them captive to his own
land, far away or near; [47]and if they
have a change of heart in the land
where they are held captive, and re-
pent and plead with you in the land
of their conquerors and say, 'We
have sinned, we have done wrong,
we have acted wickedly'; [48]and if
they turn back to you with all their
heart and soul in the land of their en-
emies who took them captive, and
pray to you toward the land you gave
their fathers, toward the city you
have chosen and the temple I have
built for your Name; [49]then from
heaven, your dwelling place, hear
their prayer and their plea, and up-
hold their cause. [50]And forgive your
people, who have sinned against you;
forgive all the offenses they have
committed against you, and cause
their conquerors to show them mer-
cy; [51]for they are your people and
your inheritance, whom you brought
out of Egypt, out of that iron-smelting
furnace.

[52]"May your eyes be open to your
servant's plea and to the plea of your
people Israel, and may you listen to

them whenever they cry out to you.
53For you singled them out from all
the nations of the world to be your
own inheritance, just as you declared
through your servant Moses when
you, O Sovereign LORD, brought our
fathers out of Egypt."
54When Solomon had finished all these
prayers and supplications to the LORD, he
rose from before the altar of the LORD,
where he had been kneeling with his
hands spread out toward heaven. 55He
stood and blessed the whole assembly of
Israel in a loud voice, saying:
56"Praise be to the LORD, who has
given rest to his people Israel just as

VERSE FOR THE DAY: 1 Kings 8:61 | AUTHOR: Andrea Midgett | PASSAGE FOR THE DAY: 1 Kings 8:54–61

Voluntary Love

It has been fifteen years since Judy and Len Vander Zee received the awful news that Judy had multiple sclerosis. "Sometimes I feel like a prisoner in my own home," Judy says. "I get jealous when I hear friends complain about how long it takes them to shop and how tired they get walking all over the mall. Or I get jealous when guests ooh and ahh over a meal that Len has prepared. I want to say, 'Yep, he did it, but I taught him everything he knows.' "

Len, a pastor, has his own moments of jealousy and discouragement. "Sometimes I feel angry with what has happened, sometimes I feel sorry for myself," he says. "But what has happened has deepened us. Judy's illness has forced me to be more oriented around the home than I would have been. I left a much larger church to come here, partly because the schedule and constant night meetings were too much for us. I would have perhaps been too career-oriented otherwise."

When they talk to couples who are thinking about marriage, Judy and Len say something like this: You're not going to feel in love forever. You'll love—as a voluntary action—forever, but you won't *feel* it forever. The feeling may leave for a period of time. But in spite of it, you love. For when you marry, you make a promise to love. You say, "Yes." And you cling to that word.

MARRIAGE BUILDERS

♦ *Recall a time when* feelings *failed you, and you loved because you had committed to love each other.*

♦ *How have others in your life shown the kind of love that is not swayed by circumstances or feelings?*

Additional Scripture Readings
Numbers 30:2; 2 Corinthians 1:20

Go to page 387 for your next devotional reading.

he promised. Not one word has failed
of all the good promises he gave
through his servant Moses. 57May the
LORD our God be with us as he was
with our fathers; may he never leave
us nor forsake us. 58May he turn our
hearts to him, to walk in all his ways
and to keep the commands, decrees
and regulations he gave our fathers.
59And may these words of mine,
which I have prayed before the LORD,
be near to the LORD our God day and
night, that he may uphold the cause
of his servant and the cause of his
people Israel according to each day's
need, 60so that all the peoples of the
earth may know that the LORD is God
and that there is no other. 61But your
hearts must be fully committed to the
LORD our God, to live by his decrees
and obey his commands, as at this
time."

The Dedication of the Temple

62Then the king and all Israel with him
offered sacrifices before the LORD. 63Solo-
mon offered a sacrifice of fellowship offer-
ings[a] to the LORD: twenty-two thousand
cattle and a hundred and twenty thousand
sheep and goats. So the king and all the
Israelites dedicated the temple of the
LORD.
64On that same day the king consecrat-
ed the middle part of the courtyard in
front of the temple of the LORD, and there
he offered burnt offerings, grain offerings
and the fat of the fellowship offerings, be-
cause the bronze altar before the LORD
was too small to hold the burnt offerings,
the grain offerings and the fat of the fel-
lowship offerings.
65So Solomon observed the festival at
that time, and all Israel with him—a vast
assembly, people from Lebo[b] Hamath to
the Wadi of Egypt. They celebrated it be-
fore the LORD our God for seven days and
seven days more, fourteen days in all.
66On the following day he sent the people
away. They blessed the king and then
went home, joyful and glad in heart for all
the good things the LORD had done for his
servant David and his people Israel.

The LORD Appears to Solomon

9 When Solomon had finished building
the temple of the LORD and the royal
palace, and had achieved all he had de-
sired to do, 2the LORD appeared to him a
second time, as he had appeared to him at
Gibeon. 3The LORD said to him:

"I have heard the prayer and plea
you have made before me; I have
consecrated this temple, which you
have built, by putting my Name there
forever. My eyes and my heart will al-
ways be there.
4"As for you, if you walk before me
in integrity of heart and uprightness,
as David your father did, and do all I
command and observe my decrees
and laws, 5I will establish your royal
throne over Israel forever, as I prom-
ised David your father when I said,
'You shall never fail to have a man on
the throne of Israel.'
6"But if you[c] or your sons turn
away from me and do not observe the
commands and decrees I have given
you[c] and go off to serve other gods
and worship them, 7then I will cut off
Israel from the land I have given
them and will reject this temple I
have consecrated for my Name. Israel
will then become a byword and an
object of ridicule among all peoples.
8And though this temple is now im-
posing, all who pass by will be ap-
palled and will scoff and say, 'Why
has the LORD done such a thing to this
land and to this temple?' 9People will
answer, 'Because they have forsaken
the LORD their God, who brought
their fathers out of Egypt, and have
embraced other gods, worshiping
and serving them—that is why the
LORD brought all this disaster on
them.' "

Solomon's Other Activities

10At the end of twenty years, during
which Solomon built these two build-
ings—the temple of the LORD and the roy-
al palace— 11King Solomon gave twenty
towns in Galilee to Hiram king of Tyre, be-
cause Hiram had supplied him with all the
cedar and pine and gold he wanted. 12But
when Hiram went from Tyre to see the
towns that Solomon had given him, he
was not pleased with them. 13"What kind
of towns are these you have given me, my
brother?" he asked. And he called them

[a]63 Traditionally *peace offerings*; also in verse 64
[b]65 Or *from the entrance to*
[c]6 The Hebrew is plural.

the Land of Cabul,[a] a name they have to
this day. 14Now Hiram had sent to the
king 120 talents[b] of gold.

15Here is the account of the forced labor
King Solomon conscripted to build the
LORD's temple, his own palace, the sup-
porting terraces,[c] the wall of Jerusalem,
and Hazor, Megiddo and Gezer. 16(Phar-
aoh king of Egypt had attacked and cap-
tured Gezer. He had set it on fire. He killed
its Canaanite inhabitants and then gave it
as a wedding gift to his daughter, Solo-
mon's wife. 17And Solomon rebuilt Ge-
zer.) He built up Lower Beth Horon, 18Ba-
alath, and Tadmor[d] in the desert, within
his land, 19as well as all his store cities and
the towns for his chariots and for his
horses[e]—whatever he desired to build in
Jerusalem, in Lebanon and throughout all
the territory he ruled.

20All the people left from the Amorites,
Hittites, Perizzites, Hivites and Jebusites
(these peoples were not Israelites), 21that
is, their descendants remaining in the
land, whom the Israelites could not exter-
minate[f]—these Solomon conscripted for
his slave labor force, as it is to this day.
22But Solomon did not make slaves of any
of the Israelites; they were his fighting
men, his government officials, his officers,
his captains, and the commanders of his
chariots and charioteers. 23They were also
the chief officials in charge of Solomon's
projects—550 officials supervising the
men who did the work.

24After Pharaoh's daughter had come
up from the City of David to the palace
Solomon had built for her, he constructed
the supporting terraces.

25Three times a year Solomon sacrificed
burnt offerings and fellowship offerings[g]
on the altar he had built for the LORD,
burning incense before the LORD along
with them, and so fulfilled the temple ob-
ligations.

26King Solomon also built ships at Ezi-
on Geber, which is near Elath in Edom, on
the shore of the Red Sea.[h] 27And Hiram
sent his men—sailors who knew the
sea—to serve in the fleet with Solomon's
men. 28They sailed to Ophir and brought
back 420 talents[i] of gold, which they de-
livered to King Solomon.

The Queen of Sheba Visits Solomon

10 When the queen of Sheba heard
about the fame of Solomon and his
relation to the name of the LORD, she came
to test him with hard questions. 2Arriving
at Jerusalem with a very great caravan—
with camels carrying spices, large quanti-
ties of gold, and precious stones—she
came to Solomon and talked with him
about all that she had on her mind. 3Solo-
mon answered all her questions; nothing
was too hard for the king to explain to her.
4When the queen of Sheba saw all the wis-
dom of Solomon and the palace he had
built, 5the food on his table, the seating of
his officials, the attending servants in
their robes, his cupbearers, and the burnt
offerings he made at[j] the temple of the
LORD, she was overwhelmed.

6She said to the king, "The report I
heard in my own country about your
achievements and your wisdom is true.
7But I did not believe these things until I
came and saw with my own eyes. Indeed,
not even half was told me; in wisdom and
wealth you have far exceeded the report I
heard. 8How happy your men must be!
How happy your officials, who continual-
ly stand before you and hear your wis-
dom! 9Praise be to the LORD your God,
who has delighted in you and placed you
on the throne of Israel. Because of the
LORD's eternal love for Israel, he has made
you king, to maintain justice and righ-
teousness."

10And she gave the king 120 talents[k] of
gold, large quantities of spices, and pre-
cious stones. Never again were so many
spices brought in as those the queen of
Sheba gave to King Solomon.

11(Hiram's ships brought gold from
Ophir; and from there they brought great
cargoes of almugwood[l] and precious
stones. 12The king used the almugwood to
make supports for the temple of the LORD
and for the royal palace, and to make
harps and lyres for the musicians. So
much almugwood has never been import-
ed or seen since that day.)

[a] *13 Cabul* sounds like the Hebrew for *good-for-nothing.* [b] *14* That is, about 4 1/2 tons (about 4 metric tons) [c] *15* Or *the Millo*; also in verse 24 [d] *18* The Hebrew may also be read *Tamar.* [e] *19* Or *charioteers* [f] *21* The Hebrew term refers to the irrevocable giving over of things or persons to the LORD, often by totally destroying them. [g] *25* Traditionally *peace offerings* [h] *26* Hebrew *Yam Suph*; that is, Sea of Reeds [i] *28* That is, about 16 tons (about 14.5 metric tons) [j] *5* Or *the ascent by which he went up to* [k] *10* That is, about 4 1/2 tons (about 4 metric tons) [l] *11* Probably a variant of *algumwood*; also in verse 12

13King Solomon gave the queen of Sheba all she desired and asked for, besides what he had given her out of his royal bounty. Then she left and returned with her retinue to her own country.

Solomon's Splendor

14The weight of the gold that Solomon received yearly was 666 talents,[a] 15not including the revenues from merchants and traders and from all the Arabian kings and the governors of the land.

16King Solomon made two hundred large shields of hammered gold; six hundred bekas[b] of gold went into each shield. 17He also made three hundred small shields of hammered gold, with three minas[c] of gold in each shield. The king put them in the Palace of the Forest of Lebanon.

18Then the king made a great throne inlaid with ivory and overlaid with fine gold. 19The throne had six steps, and its back had a rounded top. On both sides of the seat were armrests, with a lion standing beside each of them. 20Twelve lions stood on the six steps, one at either end of each step. Nothing like it had ever been made for any other kingdom. 21All King Solomon's goblets were gold, and all the household articles in the Palace of the Forest of Lebanon were pure gold. Nothing was made of silver, because silver was considered of little value in Solomon's days. 22The king had a fleet of trading ships[d] at sea along with the ships of Hiram. Once every three years it returned, carrying gold, silver and ivory, and apes and baboons.

23King Solomon was greater in riches and wisdom than all the other kings of the earth. 24The whole world sought audience with Solomon to hear the wisdom God had put in his heart. 25Year after year, everyone who came brought a gift—articles of silver and gold, robes, weapons and spices, and horses and mules.

26Solomon accumulated chariots and horses; he had fourteen hundred chariots and twelve thousand horses,[e] which he kept in the chariot cities and also with him in Jerusalem. 27The king made silver as common in Jerusalem as stones, and cedar as plentiful as sycamore-fig trees in the foothills. 28Solomon's horses were imported from Egypt[f] and from Kue[g]—the royal merchants purchased them from Kue. 29They imported a chariot from Egypt for six hundred shekels[h] of silver, and a horse for a hundred and fifty.[c] They also exported them to all the kings of the Hittites and of the Arameans.

Solomon's Wives

11 King Solomon, however, loved many foreign women besides Pharaoh's daughter—Moabites, Ammonites, Edomites, Sidonians and Hittites. 2They were from nations about which the LORD had told the Israelites, "You must not intermarry with them, because they will surely turn your hearts after their gods." Nevertheless, Solomon held fast to them in love. 3He had seven hundred wives of royal birth and three hundred concubines, and his wives led him astray. 4As Solomon grew old, his wives turned his heart after other gods, and his heart was not fully devoted to the LORD his God, as the heart of David his father had been. 5He followed Ashtoreth the goddess of the Sidonians, and Molech[i] the detestable god of the Ammonites. 6So Solomon did evil in the eyes of the LORD; he did not follow the LORD completely, as David his father had done.

7On a hill east of Jerusalem, Solomon built a high place for Chemosh the detestable god of Moab, and for Molech the detestable god of the Ammonites. 8He did the same for all his foreign wives, who burned incense and offered sacrifices to their gods.

9The LORD became angry with Solomon because his heart had turned away from the LORD, the God of Israel, who had appeared to him twice. 10Although he had forbidden Solomon to follow other gods, Solomon did not keep the LORD's command. 11So the LORD said to Solomon, "Since this is your attitude and you have not kept my covenant and my decrees, which I commanded you, I will most certainly tear the kingdom away from you and give it to one of your subordinates. 12Nevertheless, for the sake of David your

[a] *14* That is, about 25 tons (about 23 metric tons) [b] *16* That is, about 7 1/2 pounds (about 3.5 kilograms) [c] *17,29* That is, about 3 3/4 pounds (about 1.7 kilograms) [d] *22* Hebrew *of ships of Tarshish* [e] *26* Or *charioteers* [f] *28* Or possibly *Muzur*, a region in Cilicia; also in verse 29 [g] *28* Probably *Cilicia* [h] *29* That is, about 15 pounds (about 7 kilograms) [i] *5* Hebrew *Milcom*; also in verse 33

father, I will not do it during your lifetime.
I will tear it out of the hand of your son.
13Yet I will not tear the whole kingdom
from him, but will give him one tribe for
the sake of David my servant and for the
sake of Jerusalem, which I have chosen."

Solomon's Adversaries

14Then the LORD raised up against Solo-
mon an adversary, Hadad the Edomite,
from the royal line of Edom. 15Earlier
when David was fighting with Edom, Joab
the commander of the army, who had
gone up to bury the dead, had struck
down all the men in Edom. 16Joab and all
the Israelites stayed there for six months,
until they had destroyed all the men in
Edom. 17But Hadad, still only a boy, fled
to Egypt with some Edomite officials who
had served his father. 18They set out from
Midian and went to Paran. Then taking
men from Paran with them, they went to
Egypt, to Pharaoh king of Egypt, who gave
Hadad a house and land and provided him
with food.

19Pharaoh was so pleased with Hadad
that he gave him a sister of his own wife,
Queen Tahpenes, in marriage. 20The sister
of Tahpenes bore him a son named Genu-
bath, whom Tahpenes brought up in the
royal palace. There Genubath lived with
Pharaoh's own children.

21While he was in Egypt, Hadad heard
that David rested with his fathers and that
Joab the commander of the army was also
dead. Then Hadad said to Pharaoh, "Let
me go, that I may return to my own coun-
try."

22"What have you lacked here that you
want to go back to your own country?"
Pharaoh asked.

"Nothing," Hadad replied, "but do let
me go!"

23And God raised up against Solomon
another adversary, Rezon son of Eliada,
who had fled from his master, Hadadezer
king of Zobah. 24He gathered men around
him and became the leader of a band of
rebels when David destroyed the forces[a]
⌊of Zobah⌋; the rebels went to Damascus,
where they settled and took control. 25Re-
zon was Israel's adversary as long as Solo-
mon lived, adding to the trouble caused
by Hadad. So Rezon ruled in Aram and
was hostile toward Israel.

Jeroboam Rebels Against Solomon

26Also, Jeroboam son of Nebat rebelled
against the king. He was one of Solomon's
officials, an Ephraimite from Zeredah, and
his mother was a widow named Zeruah.

27Here is the account of how he rebelled
against the king: Solomon had built the
supporting terraces[b] and had filled in the
gap in the wall of the city of David his fa-
ther. 28Now Jeroboam was a man of stand-
ing, and when Solomon saw how well the
young man did his work, he put him in
charge of the whole labor force of the
house of Joseph.

29About that time Jeroboam was going
out of Jerusalem, and Ahijah the prophet
of Shiloh met him on the way, wearing a
new cloak. The two of them were alone
out in the country, 30and Ahijah took hold
of the new cloak he was wearing and tore
it into twelve pieces. 31Then he said to Jer-
oboam, "Take ten pieces for yourself, for
this is what the LORD, the God of Israel,
says: 'See, I am going to tear the kingdom
out of Solomon's hand and give you ten
tribes. 32But for the sake of my servant Da-
vid and the city of Jerusalem, which I have
chosen out of all the tribes of Israel, he
will have one tribe. 33I will do this because
they have[c] forsaken me and worshiped
Ashtoreth the goddess of the Sidonians,
Chemosh the god of the Moabites, and
Molech the god of the Ammonites, and
have not walked in my ways, nor done
what is right in my eyes, nor kept my stat-
utes and laws as David, Solomon's father,
did.

34" 'But I will not take the whole king-
dom out of Solomon's hand; I have made
him ruler all the days of his life for the
sake of David my servant, whom I chose
and who observed my commands and
statutes. 35I will take the kingdom from
his son's hands and give you ten tribes. 36I
will give one tribe to his son so that David
my servant may always have a lamp be-
fore me in Jerusalem, the city where I
chose to put my Name. 37However, as for
you, I will take you, and you will rule over
all that your heart desires; you will be
king over Israel. 38If you do whatever I
command you and walk in my ways and
do what is right in my eyes by keeping my
statutes and commands, as David my ser-
vant did, I will be with you. I will build

[a]24 Hebrew *destroyed them* [b]27 Or *the Millo* [c]33 Hebrew; Septuagint, Vulgate and Syriac *because he has*

you a dynasty as enduring as the one I
built for David and will give Israel to you.
39I will humble David's descendants be-
cause of this, but not forever.' "

40Solomon tried to kill Jeroboam, but
Jeroboam fled to Egypt, to Shishak the
king, and stayed there until Solomon's
death.

Solomon's Death

41As for the other events of Solomon's
reign—all he did and the wisdom he dis-
played—are they not written in the book
of the annals of Solomon? 42Solomon
reigned in Jerusalem over all Israel forty
years. 43Then he rested with his fathers
and was buried in the city of David his fa-
ther. And Rehoboam his son succeeded
him as king.

Israel Rebels Against Rehoboam

12 Rehoboam went to Shechem, for
all the Israelites had gone there to
make him king. 2When Jeroboam son of
Nebat heard this (he was still in Egypt,
where he had fled from King Solomon), he
returned from[a] Egypt. 3So they sent for
Jeroboam, and he and the whole assembly
of Israel went to Rehoboam and said to
him: 4"Your father put a heavy yoke on us,
but now lighten the harsh labor and the
heavy yoke he put on us, and we will
serve you."

5Rehoboam answered, "Go away for
three days and then come back to me." So
the people went away.

6Then King Rehoboam consulted the el-
ders who had served his father Solomon
during his lifetime. "How would you ad-
vise me to answer these people?" he
asked.

7They replied, "If today you will be a
servant to these people and serve them
and give them a favorable answer, they
will always be your servants."

8But Rehoboam rejected the advice the
elders gave him and consulted the young
men who had grown up with him and
were serving him. 9He asked them, "What
is your advice? How should we answer
these people who say to me, 'Lighten the
yoke your father put on us'?"

10The young men who had grown up
with him replied, "Tell these people who
have said to you, 'Your father put a heavy
yoke on us, but make our yoke lighter'—
tell them, 'My little finger is thicker than
my father's waist. 11My father laid on you
a heavy yoke; I will make it even heavier.
My father scourged you with whips; I will
scourge you with scorpions.' "

12Three days later Jeroboam and all the
people returned to Rehoboam, as the king
had said, "Come back to me in three
days." 13The king answered the people
harshly. Rejecting the advice given him by
the elders, 14he followed the advice of the
young men and said, "My father made
your yoke heavy; I will make it even
heavier. My father scourged you with
whips; I will scourge you with scorpions."
15So the king did not listen to the people,
for this turn of events was from the LORD,
to fulfill the word the LORD had spoken to
Jeroboam son of Nebat through Ahijah
the Shilonite.

16When all Israel saw that the king re-
fused to listen to them, they answered the
king:

"What share do we have in David,
what part in Jesse's son?
To your tents, O Israel!
Look after your own house,
O David!"

So the Israelites went home. 17But as for
the Israelites who were living in the towns
of Judah, Rehoboam still ruled over them.

18King Rehoboam sent out Adoniram,[b]
who was in charge of forced labor, but all
Israel stoned him to death. King Rehobo-
am, however, managed to get into his
chariot and escape to Jerusalem. 19So Isra-
el has been in rebellion against the house
of David to this day.

20When all the Israelites heard that Jer-
oboam had returned, they sent and called
him to the assembly and made him king
over all Israel. Only the tribe of Judah re-
mained loyal to the house of David.

21When Rehoboam arrived in Jerusa-
lem, he mustered the whole house of Ju-
dah and the tribe of Benjamin—a hun-
dred and eighty thousand fighting
men—to make war against the house of
Israel and to regain the kingdom for Reho-
boam son of Solomon.

22But this word of God came to Shema-
iah the man of God: 23"Say to Rehoboam
son of Solomon king of Judah, to the
whole house of Judah and Benjamin, and
to the rest of the people, 24'This is what

[a] 2 Or *he remained in*
[b] 18 Some Septuagint manuscripts and Syriac (see also 1 Kings 4:6 and 5:14); Hebrew *Adoram*

the LORD says: Do not go up to fight against your brothers, the Israelites. Go home, every one of you, for this is my doing.' " So they obeyed the word of the LORD and went home again, as the LORD had ordered.

Golden Calves at Bethel and Dan

25Then Jeroboam fortified Shechem in the hill country of Ephraim and lived there. From there he went out and built up Peniel.[a]

26Jeroboam thought to himself, "The kingdom will now likely revert to the house of David. 27If these people go up to offer sacrifices at the temple of the LORD in Jerusalem, they will again give their allegiance to their lord, Rehoboam king of Judah. They will kill me and return to King Rehoboam."

28After seeking advice, the king made two golden calves. He said to the people, "It is too much for you to go up to Jerusalem. Here are your gods, O Israel, who brought you up out of Egypt." 29One he set up in Bethel, and the other in Dan. 30And this thing became a sin; the people went even as far as Dan to worship the one there.

31Jeroboam built shrines on high places and appointed priests from all sorts of people, even though they were not Levites. 32He instituted a festival on the fifteenth day of the eighth month, like the festival held in Judah, and offered sacrifices on the altar. This he did in Bethel, sacrificing to the calves he had made. And at Bethel he also installed priests at the high places he had made. 33On the fifteenth day of the eighth month, a month of his own choosing, he offered sacrifices on the altar he had built at Bethel. So he instituted the festival for the Israelites and went up to the altar to make offerings.

The Man of God From Judah

13 By the word of the LORD a man of God came from Judah to Bethel, as Jeroboam was standing by the altar to make an offering. 2He cried out against the altar by the word of the LORD: "O altar, altar! This is what the LORD says: 'A son named Josiah will be born to the house of David. On you he will sacrifice the priests of the high places who now make offerings here, and human bones will be burned on you.' " 3That same day the man of God gave a sign: "This is the sign the LORD has declared: The altar will be split apart and the ashes on it will be poured out."

4When King Jeroboam heard what the man of God cried out against the altar at Bethel, he stretched out his hand from the altar and said, "Seize him!" But the hand he stretched out toward the man shriveled up, so that he could not pull it back. 5Also, the altar was split apart and its ashes poured out according to the sign given by the man of God by the word of the LORD.

6Then the king said to the man of God, "Intercede with the LORD your God and pray for me that my hand may be restored." So the man of God interceded with the LORD, and the king's hand was restored and became as it was before.

7The king said to the man of God, "Come home with me and have something to eat, and I will give you a gift."

8But the man of God answered the king, "Even if you were to give me half your possessions, I would not go with you, nor would I eat bread or drink water here. 9For I was commanded by the word of the LORD: 'You must not eat bread or drink water or return by the way you came.' " 10So he took another road and did not return by the way he had come to Bethel.

11Now there was a certain old prophet living in Bethel, whose sons came and told him all that the man of God had done there that day. They also told their father what he had said to the king. 12Their father asked them, "Which way did he go?" And his sons showed him which road the man of God from Judah had taken. 13So he said to his sons, "Saddle the donkey for me." And when they had saddled the donkey for him, he mounted it 14and rode after the man of God. He found him sitting under an oak tree and asked, "Are you the man of God who came from Judah?"

"I am," he replied.

15So the prophet said to him, "Come home with me and eat."

16The man of God said, "I cannot turn back and go with you, nor can I eat bread or drink water with you in this place. 17I have been told by the word of the LORD: 'You must not eat bread or drink water there or return by the way you came.' "

18The old prophet answered, "I too am a prophet, as you are. And an angel said to me by the word of the LORD: 'Bring him

[a]25 Hebrew *Penuel*, a variant of *Peniel*

back with you to your house so that he
may eat bread and drink water.' " (But he
was lying to him.) 19So the man of God re-
turned with him and ate and drank in his
house.

20While they were sitting at the table,
the word of the LORD came to the old
prophet who had brought him back. 21He
cried out to the man of God who had come
from Judah, "This is what the LORD says:
'You have defied the word of the LORD and
have not kept the command the LORD your
God gave you. 22You came back and ate
bread and drank water in the place where
he told you not to eat or drink. Therefore
your body will not be buried in the tomb
of your fathers.' "

23When the man of God had finished
eating and drinking, the prophet who had
brought him back saddled his donkey for
him. 24As he went on his way, a lion met
him on the road and killed him, and his
body was thrown down on the road, with
both the donkey and the lion standing be-
side it. 25Some people who passed by saw
the body thrown down there, with the lion
standing beside the body, and they went
and reported it in the city where the old
prophet lived.

26When the prophet who had brought
him back from his journey heard of it, he
said, "It is the man of God who defied the
word of the LORD. The LORD has given him
over to the lion, which has mauled him
and killed him, as the word of the LORD
had warned him."

27The prophet said to his sons, "Saddle
the donkey for me," and they did so.
28Then he went out and found the body
thrown down on the road, with the don-
key and the lion standing beside it. The
lion had neither eaten the body nor
mauled the donkey. 29So the prophet
picked up the body of the man of God, laid
it on the donkey, and brought it back to
his own city to mourn for him and bury
him. 30Then he laid the body in his own
tomb, and they mourned over him and
said, "Oh, my brother!"

31After burying him, he said to his sons,
"When I die, bury me in the grave where
the man of God is buried; lay my bones
beside his bones. 32For the message he de-
clared by the word of the LORD against the
altar in Bethel and against all the shrines
on the high places in the towns of Samaria
will certainly come true."

33Even after this, Jeroboam did not
change his evil ways, but once more ap-
pointed priests for the high places from all
sorts of people. Anyone who wanted to
become a priest he consecrated for the
high places. 34This was the sin of the
house of Jeroboam that led to its downfall
and to its destruction from the face of the
earth.

Ahijah's Prophecy Against Jeroboam

14 At that time Abijah son of Jerobo-
am became ill, 2and Jeroboam said
to his wife, "Go, disguise yourself, so you
won't be recognized as the wife of Jerobo-
am. Then go to Shiloh. Ahijah the prophet
is there—the one who told me I would be
king over this people. 3Take ten loaves of
bread with you, some cakes and a jar of
honey, and go to him. He will tell you
what will happen to the boy." 4So Jerobo-
am's wife did what he said and went to
Ahijah's house in Shiloh.

Now Ahijah could not see; his sight was
gone because of his age. 5But the LORD had
told Ahijah, "Jeroboam's wife is coming to
ask you about her son, for he is ill, and
you are to give her such and such an an-
swer. When she arrives, she will pretend
to be someone else."

6So when Ahijah heard the sound of her
footsteps at the door, he said, "Come in,
wife of Jeroboam. Why this pretense? I
have been sent to you with bad news. 7Go,
tell Jeroboam that this is what the LORD,
the God of Israel, says: 'I raised you up
from among the people and made you a
leader over my people Israel. 8I tore the
kingdom away from the house of David
and gave it to you, but you have not been
like my servant David, who kept my com-
mands and followed me with all his heart,
doing only what was right in my eyes.
9You have done more evil than all who
lived before you. You have made for your-
self other gods, idols made of metal; you
have provoked me to anger and thrust me
behind your back.

10" 'Because of this, I am going to bring
disaster on the house of Jeroboam. I will
cut off from Jeroboam every last male in
Israel—slave or free. I will burn up the
house of Jeroboam as one burns dung, un-
til it is all gone. 11Dogs will eat those be-
longing to Jeroboam who die in the city,
and the birds of the air will feed on those
who die in the country. The LORD has spo-
ken!'

12"As for you, go back home. When you
set foot in your city, the boy will die. 13All
Israel will mourn for him and bury him.

He is the only one belonging to Jeroboam
who will be buried, because he is the only
one in the house of Jeroboam in whom
the LORD, the God of Israel, has found any-
thing good.
14"The LORD will raise up for himself a
king over Israel who will cut off the family
of Jeroboam. This is the day! What? Yes,
even now.[a] 15And the LORD will strike Is-
rael, so that it will be like a reed swaying
in the water. He will uproot Israel from
this good land that he gave to their forefa-
thers and scatter them beyond the Riv-
er,[b] because they provoked the LORD to
anger by making Asherah poles.[c] 16And
he will give Israel up because of the sins
Jeroboam has committed and has caused
Israel to commit."
17Then Jeroboam's wife got up and left
and went to Tirzah. As soon as she
stepped over the threshold of the house,
the boy died. 18They buried him, and all
Israel mourned for him, as the LORD had
said through his servant the prophet Ahi-
jah.
19The other events of Jeroboam's reign,
his wars and how he ruled, are written in
the book of the annals of the kings of Isra-
el. 20He reigned for twenty-two years and
then rested with his fathers. And Nadab
his son succeeded him as king.

Rehoboam King of Judah

21Rehoboam son of Solomon was king
in Judah. He was forty-one years old when
he became king, and he reigned seventeen
years in Jerusalem, the city the LORD had
chosen out of all the tribes of Israel in
which to put his Name. His mother's
name was Naamah; she was an Ammon-
ite.
22Judah did evil in the eyes of the LORD.
By the sins they committed they stirred up
his jealous anger more than their fathers
had done. 23They also set up for them-
selves high places, sacred stones and
Asherah poles on every high hill and un-
der every spreading tree. 24There were
even male shrine prostitutes in the land;
the people engaged in all the detestable
practices of the nations the LORD had driv-
en out before the Israelites.
25In the fifth year of King Rehoboam,
Shishak king of Egypt attacked Jerusalem.
26He carried off the treasures of the tem-
ple of the LORD and the treasures of the
royal palace. He took everything, includ-
ing all the gold shields Solomon had
made. 27So King Rehoboam made bronze
shields to replace them and assigned
these to the commanders of the guard on
duty at the entrance to the royal palace.
28Whenever the king went to the LORD's
temple, the guards bore the shields, and
afterward they returned them to the
guardroom.
29As for the other events of Rehoboam's
reign, and all he did, are they not written
in the book of the annals of the kings of
Judah? 30There was continual warfare be-
tween Rehoboam and Jeroboam. 31And
Rehoboam rested with his fathers and was
buried with them in the City of David. His
mother's name was Naamah; she was an
Ammonite. And Abijah[d] his son succeed-
ed him as king.

Abijah King of Judah

15 In the eighteenth year of the reign
of Jeroboam son of Nebat, Abi-
jah[e] became king of Judah, 2and he
reigned in Jerusalem three years. His
mother's name was Maacah daughter of
Abishalom.[f]
3He committed all the sins his father
had done before him; his heart was not
fully devoted to the LORD his God, as the
heart of David his forefather had been.
4Nevertheless, for David's sake the LORD
his God gave him a lamp in Jerusalem by
raising up a son to succeed him and by
making Jerusalem strong. 5For David had
done what was right in the eyes of the
LORD and had not failed to keep any of the
LORD's commands all the days of his life—
except in the case of Uriah the Hittite.
6There was war between Rehoboam[g]
and Jeroboam throughout ⌊Abijah's⌋ life-
time. 7As for the other events of Abijah's
reign, and all he did, are they not written
in the book of the annals of the kings of
Judah? There was war between Abijah
and Jeroboam. 8And Abijah rested with
his fathers and was buried in the City of

[a] *14* The meaning of the Hebrew for this sentence is uncertain. [b] *15* That is, the Euphrates
[c] *15* That is, symbols of the goddess Asherah; here and elsewhere in 1 Kings [d] *31* Some Hebrew manuscripts and Septuagint (see also 2 Chron. 12:16); most Hebrew manuscripts *Abijam* [e] *1* Some Hebrew manuscripts and Septuagint (see also 2 Chron. 12:16); most Hebrew manuscripts *Abijam*; also in verses 7 and 8 [f] *2* A variant of *Absalom*; also in verse 10 [g] *6* Most Hebrew manuscripts; some Hebrew manuscripts and Syriac *Abijam* (that is, Abijah)

David. And Asa his son succeeded him as king.

Asa King of Judah

[9]In the twentieth year of Jeroboam king of Israel, Asa became king of Judah, [10]and he reigned in Jerusalem forty-one years. His grandmother's name was Maacah daughter of Abishalom.

[11]Asa did what was right in the eyes of the LORD, as his father David had done. [12]He expelled the male shrine prostitutes from the land and got rid of all the idols his fathers had made. [13]He even deposed his grandmother Maacah from her position as queen mother, because she had made a repulsive Asherah pole. Asa cut the pole down and burned it in the Kidron Valley. [14]Although he did not remove the high places, Asa's heart was fully committed to the LORD all his life. [15]He brought into the temple of the LORD the silver and gold and the articles that he and his father had dedicated.

[16]There was war between Asa and Baasha king of Israel throughout their reigns. [17]Baasha king of Israel went up against Judah and fortified Ramah to prevent anyone from leaving or entering the territory of Asa king of Judah.

[18]Asa then took all the silver and gold that was left in the treasuries of the LORD's temple and of his own palace. He entrusted it to his officials and sent them to Ben-Hadad son of Tabrimmon, the son of Hezion, the king of Aram, who was ruling in Damascus. [19]"Let there be a treaty between me and you," he said, "as there was between my father and your father. See, I am sending you a gift of silver and gold. Now break your treaty with Baasha king of Israel so he will withdraw from me."

[20]Ben-Hadad agreed with King Asa and sent the commanders of his forces against the towns of Israel. He conquered Ijon, Dan, Abel Beth Maacah and all Kinnereth in addition to Naphtali. [21]When Baasha heard this, he stopped building Ramah and withdrew to Tirzah. [22]Then King Asa issued an order to all Judah—no one was exempt—and they carried away from Ramah the stones and timber Baasha had been using there. With them King Asa built up Geba in Benjamin, and also Mizpah.

[23]As for all the other events of Asa's reign, all his achievements, all he did and the cities he built, are they not written in the book of the annals of the kings of Judah? In his old age, however, his feet became diseased. [24]Then Asa rested with his fathers and was buried with them in the city of his father David. And Jehoshaphat his son succeeded him as king.

Nadab King of Israel

[25]Nadab son of Jeroboam became king of Israel in the second year of Asa king of Judah, and he reigned over Israel two years. [26]He did evil in the eyes of the LORD, walking in the ways of his father and in his sin, which he had caused Israel to commit.

[27]Baasha son of Ahijah of the house of Issachar plotted against him, and he struck him down at Gibbethon, a Philistine town, while Nadab and all Israel were besieging it. [28]Baasha killed Nadab in the third year of Asa king of Judah and succeeded him as king.

[29]As soon as he began to reign, he killed Jeroboam's whole family. He did not leave Jeroboam anyone that breathed, but destroyed them all, according to the word of the LORD given through his servant Ahijah the Shilonite— [30]because of the sins Jeroboam had committed and had caused Israel to commit, and because he provoked the LORD, the God of Israel, to anger.

[31]As for the other events of Nadab's reign, and all he did, are they not written in the book of the annals of the kings of Israel? [32]There was war between Asa and Baasha king of Israel throughout their reigns.

Baasha King of Israel

[33]In the third year of Asa king of Judah, Baasha son of Ahijah became king of all Israel in Tirzah, and he reigned twenty-four years. [34]He did evil in the eyes of the LORD, walking in the ways of Jeroboam and in his sin, which he had caused Israel to commit.

16 Then the word of the LORD came to Jehu son of Hanani against Baasha: [2]"I lifted you up from the dust and made you leader of my people Israel, but you walked in the ways of Jeroboam and caused my people Israel to sin and to provoke me to anger by their sins. [3]So I am about to consume Baasha and his house, and I will make your house like that of Jeroboam son of Nebat. [4]Dogs will eat those belonging to Baasha who die in the city, and the birds of the air will feed on those who die in the country."

[5]As for the other events of Baasha's

reign, what he did and his achievements,
are they not written in the book of the an-
nals of the kings of Israel? 6Baasha rested
with his fathers and was buried in Tirzah.
And Elah his son succeeded him as king.
7Moreover, the word of the LORD came
through the prophet Jehu son of Hanani
to Baasha and his house, because of all the
evil he had done in the eyes of the LORD,
provoking him to anger by the things he
did, and becoming like the house of Jero-
boam—and also because he destroyed it.

Elah King of Israel

8In the twenty-sixth year of Asa king of
Judah, Elah son of Baasha became king of
Israel, and he reigned in Tirzah two years.
9Zimri, one of his officials, who had
command of half his chariots, plotted
against him. Elah was in Tirzah at the
time, getting drunk in the home of Arza,
the man in charge of the palace at Tirzah.
10Zimri came in, struck him down and
killed him in the twenty-seventh year of
Asa king of Judah. Then he succeeded
him as king.
11As soon as he began to reign and was
seated on the throne, he killed off Baa-
sha's whole family. He did not spare a sin-
gle male, whether relative or friend. 12So
Zimri destroyed the whole family of Baa-
sha, in accordance with the word of the
LORD spoken against Baasha through the
prophet Jehu— 13because of all the sins
Baasha and his son Elah had committed
and had caused Israel to commit, so that
they provoked the LORD, the God of Israel,
to anger by their worthless idols.
14As for the other events of Elah's reign,
and all he did, are they not written in the
book of the annals of the kings of Israel?

Zimri King of Israel

15In the twenty-seventh year of Asa
king of Judah, Zimri reigned in Tirzah sev-
en days. The army was encamped near
Gibbethon, a Philistine town. 16When the
Israelites in the camp heard that Zimri had
plotted against the king and murdered
him, they proclaimed Omri, the com-
mander of the army, king over Israel that
very day there in the camp. 17Then Omri
and all the Israelites with him withdrew
from Gibbethon and laid siege to Tirzah.
18When Zimri saw that the city was taken,
he went into the citadel of the royal palace
and set the palace on fire around him. So
he died, 19because of the sins he had com-
mitted, doing evil in the eyes of the LORD
and walking in the ways of Jeroboam and
in the sin he had committed and had
caused Israel to commit.
20As for the other events of Zimri's
reign, and the rebellion he carried out, are
they not written in the book of the annals
of the kings of Israel?

Omri King of Israel

21Then the people of Israel were split
into two factions; half supported Tibni
son of Ginath for king, and the other half
supported Omri. 22But Omri's followers
proved stronger than those of Tibni son of
Ginath. So Tibni died and Omri became
king.
23In the thirty-first year of Asa king of
Judah, Omri became king of Israel, and he
reigned twelve years, six of them in Tir-
zah. 24He bought the hill of Samaria from
Shemer for two talents[a] of silver and
built a city on the hill, calling it Samaria,
after Shemer, the name of the former own-
er of the hill.
25But Omri did evil in the eyes of the
LORD and sinned more than all those be-
fore him. 26He walked in all the ways of
Jeroboam son of Nebat and in his sin,
which he had caused Israel to commit, so
that they provoked the LORD, the God of
Israel, to anger by their worthless idols.
27As for the other events of Omri's
reign, what he did and the things he
achieved, are they not written in the book
of the annals of the kings of Israel? 28Omri
rested with his fathers and was buried in
Samaria. And Ahab his son succeeded
him as king.

Ahab Becomes King of Israel

29In the thirty-eighth year of Asa king of
Judah, Ahab son of Omri became king of
Israel, and he reigned in Samaria over Is-
rael twenty-two years. 30Ahab son of Omri
did more evil in the eyes of the LORD than
any of those before him. 31He not only
considered it trivial to commit the sins of
Jeroboam son of Nebat, but he also mar-
ried Jezebel daughter of Ethbaal king of
the Sidonians, and began to serve Baal
and worship him. 32He set up an altar for
Baal in the temple of Baal that he built in
Samaria. 33Ahab also made an Asherah
pole and did more to provoke the LORD,

[a]24 That is, about 150 pounds (about 70 kilograms)

the God of Israel, to anger than did all the kings of Israel before him.

34In Ahab's time, Hiel of Bethel rebuilt Jericho. He laid its foundations at the cost of his firstborn son Abiram, and he set up its gates at the cost of his youngest son Segub, in accordance with the word of the LORD spoken by Joshua son of Nun.

Elijah Fed by Ravens

17 Now Elijah the Tishbite, from Tishbe[a] in Gilead, said to Ahab, "As the LORD, the God of Israel, lives, whom I serve, there will be neither dew nor rain in the next few years except at my word."

2Then the word of the LORD came to Elijah: 3"Leave here, turn eastward and hide in the Kerith Ravine, east of the Jordan. 4You will drink from the brook, and I have ordered the ravens to feed you there."

5So he did what the LORD had told him. He went to the Kerith Ravine, east of the Jordan, and stayed there. 6The ravens brought him bread and meat in the morning and bread and meat in the evening, and he drank from the brook.

The Widow at Zarephath

7Some time later the brook dried up because there had been no rain in the land. 8Then the word of the LORD came to him: 9"Go at once to Zarephath of Sidon and stay there. I have commanded a widow in that place to supply you with food." 10So he went to Zarephath. When he came to the town gate, a widow was there gathering sticks. He called to her and asked, "Would you bring me a little water in a jar so I may have a drink?" 11As she was going to get it, he called, "And bring me, please, a piece of bread."

12"As surely as the LORD your God lives," she replied, "I don't have any bread—only a handful of flour in a jar and a little oil in a jug. I am gathering a few sticks to take home and make a meal for myself and my son, that we may eat it—and die."

13Elijah said to her, "Don't be afraid. Go home and do as you have said. But first make a small cake of bread for me from what you have and bring it to me, and then make something for yourself and your son. 14For this is what the LORD, the God of Israel, says: 'The jar of flour will not be used up and the jug of oil will not run dry until the day the LORD gives rain on the land.'"

15She went away and did as Elijah had told her. So there was food every day for Elijah and for the woman and her family. 16For the jar of flour was not used up and the jug of oil did not run dry, in keeping with the word of the LORD spoken by Elijah.

17Some time later the son of the woman who owned the house became ill. He grew worse and worse, and finally stopped breathing. 18She said to Elijah, "What do you have against me, man of God? Did you come to remind me of my sin and kill my son?"

19"Give me your son," Elijah replied. He took him from her arms, carried him to the upper room where he was staying, and laid him on his bed. 20Then he cried out to the LORD, "O LORD my God, have you brought tragedy also upon this widow I am staying with, by causing her son to die?" 21Then he stretched himself out on the boy three times and cried to the LORD, "O LORD my God, let this boy's life return to him!"

22The LORD heard Elijah's cry, and the boy's life returned to him, and he lived. 23Elijah picked up the child and carried him down from the room into the house. He gave him to his mother and said, "Look, your son is alive!"

24Then the woman said to Elijah, "Now I know that you are a man of God and that the word of the LORD from your mouth is the truth."

Elijah and Obadiah

18 After a long time, in the third year, the word of the LORD came to Elijah: "Go and present yourself to Ahab, and I will send rain on the land." 2So Elijah went to present himself to Ahab.

Now the famine was severe in Samaria, 3and Ahab had summoned Obadiah, who was in charge of his palace. (Obadiah was a devout believer in the LORD. 4While Jezebel was killing off the LORD's prophets, Obadiah had taken a hundred prophets and hidden them in two caves, fifty in each, and had supplied them with food and water.) 5Ahab had said to Obadiah, "Go through the land to all the springs and valleys. Maybe we can find some grass to keep the horses and mules alive so we will not have to kill any of our animals." 6So

[a] 1 Or *Tishbite, of the settlers*

they divided the land they were to cover,
Ahab going in one direction and Obadiah
in another.
7As Obadiah was walking along, Elijah
met him. Obadiah recognized him, bowed
down to the ground, and said, "Is it really
you, my lord Elijah?"
8"Yes," he replied. "Go tell your master,
'Elijah is here.' "
9"What have I done wrong," asked Oba-
diah, "that you are handing your servant
over to Ahab to be put to death? 10As sure-
ly as the LORD your God lives, there is not
a nation or kingdom where my master has
not sent someone to look for you. And
whenever a nation or kingdom claimed
you were not there, he made them swear
they could not find you. 11But now you
tell me to go to my master and say, 'Elijah
is here.' 12I don't know where the Spirit of
the LORD may carry you when I leave you.
If I go and tell Ahab and he doesn't find
you, he will kill me. Yet I your servant
have worshiped the LORD since my youth.
13Haven't you heard, my lord, what I did
while Jezebel was killing the prophets of
the LORD? I hid a hundred of the LORD's
prophets in two caves, fifty in each, and
supplied them with food and water. 14And
now you tell me to go to my master and
say, 'Elijah is here.' He will kill me!"
15Elijah said, "As the LORD Almighty
lives, whom I serve, I will surely present
myself to Ahab today."

Elijah on Mount Carmel

16So Obadiah went to meet Ahab and
told him, and Ahab went to meet Elijah.
17When he saw Elijah, he said to him, "Is
that you, you troubler of Israel?"
18"I have not made trouble for Israel,"
Elijah replied. "But you and your father's
family have. You have abandoned the
LORD's commands and have followed the
Baals. 19Now summon the people from all
over Israel to meet me on Mount Carmel.
And bring the four hundred and fifty
prophets of Baal and the four hundred
prophets of Asherah, who eat at Jezebel's
table."
20So Ahab sent word throughout all Is-
rael and assembled the prophets on
Mount Carmel. 21Elijah went before the
people and said, "How long will you wa-
ver between two opinions? If the LORD is
God, follow him; but if Baal is God, follow
him."
But the people said nothing.
22Then Elijah said to them, "I am the
only one of the LORD's prophets left, but
Baal has four hundred and fifty prophets.
23Get two bulls for us. Let them choose
one for themselves, and let them cut it
into pieces and put it on the wood but not
set fire to it. I will prepare the other bull
and put it on the wood but not set fire to
it. 24Then you call on the name of your
god, and I will call on the name of the
LORD. The god who answers by fire—he is
God."
Then all the people said, "What you say
is good."
25Elijah said to the prophets of Baal,
"Choose one of the bulls and prepare it
first, since there are so many of you. Call
on the name of your god, but do not light
the fire." 26So they took the bull given
them and prepared it.
Then they called on the name of Baal
from morning till noon. "O Baal, answer
us!" they shouted. But there was no re-
sponse; no one answered. And they
danced around the altar they had made.
27At noon Elijah began to taunt them.
"Shout louder!" he said. "Surely he is a
god! Perhaps he is deep in thought, or
busy, or traveling. Maybe he is sleeping
and must be awakened." 28So they shout-
ed louder and slashed themselves with
swords and spears, as was their custom,
until their blood flowed. 29Midday passed,
and they continued their frantic prophesy-
ing until the time for the evening sacrifice.
But there was no response, no one an-
swered, no one paid attention.
30Then Elijah said to all the people,
"Come here to me." They came to him,
and he repaired the altar of the LORD,
which was in ruins. 31Elijah took twelve
stones, one for each of the tribes descend-
ed from Jacob, to whom the word of the
LORD had come, saying, "Your name shall
be Israel." 32With the stones he built an
altar in the name of the LORD, and he dug
a trench around it large enough to hold
two seahs[a] of seed. 33He arranged the
wood, cut the bull into pieces and laid it
on the wood. Then he said to them, "Fill
four large jars with water and pour it on
the offering and on the wood."
34"Do it again," he said, and they did it
again.
"Do it a third time," he ordered, and
they did it the third time. 35The water ran

[a] *32* That is, probably about 13 quarts (about 15 liters)

down around the altar and even filled the trench.

36At the time of sacrifice, the prophet Elijah stepped forward and prayed: "O LORD, God of Abraham, Isaac and Israel, let it be known today that you are God in Israel and that I am your servant and have done all these things at your command. 37Answer me, O LORD, answer me, so these people will know that you, O LORD, are God, and that you are turning their hearts back again."

38Then the fire of the LORD fell and burned up the sacrifice, the wood, the stones and the soil, and also licked up the water in the trench.

39When all the people saw this, they fell prostrate and cried, "The LORD—he is God! The LORD—he is God!"

40Then Elijah commanded them, "Seize the prophets of Baal. Don't let anyone get away!" They seized them, and Elijah had them brought down to the Kishon Valley and slaughtered there.

41And Elijah said to Ahab, "Go, eat and drink, for there is the sound of a heavy rain." 42So Ahab went off to eat and drink, but Elijah climbed to the top of Carmel, bent down to the ground and put his face between his knees.

43"Go and look toward the sea," he told his servant. And he went up and looked.

"There is nothing there," he said.

Seven times Elijah said, "Go back."

44The seventh time the servant reported, "A cloud as small as a man's hand is rising from the sea."

So Elijah said, "Go and tell Ahab, 'Hitch up your chariot and go down before the rain stops you.' "

45Meanwhile, the sky grew black with clouds, the wind rose, a heavy rain came on and Ahab rode off to Jezreel. 46The power of the LORD came upon Elijah and, tucking his cloak into his belt, he ran ahead of Ahab all the way to Jezreel.

Elijah Flees to Horeb

19 Now Ahab told Jezebel everything Elijah had done and how he had killed all the prophets with the sword. 2So Jezebel sent a messenger to Elijah to say, "May the gods deal with me, be it ever so severely, if by this time tomorrow I do not make your life like that of one of them."

3Elijah was afraid[a] and ran for his life. When he came to Beersheba in Judah, he left his servant there, 4while he himself went a day's journey into the desert. He came to a broom tree, sat down under it and prayed that he might die. "I have had enough, LORD," he said. "Take my life; I am no better than my ancestors." 5Then he lay down under the tree and fell asleep.

All at once an angel touched him and said, "Get up and eat." 6He looked around, and there by his head was a cake of bread baked over hot coals, and a jar of water. He ate and drank and then lay down again.

7The angel of the LORD came back a second time and touched him and said, "Get up and eat, for the journey is too much for you." 8So he got up and ate and drank. Strengthened by that food, he traveled forty days and forty nights until he reached Horeb, the mountain of God. 9There he went into a cave and spent the night.

The LORD Appears to Elijah

And the word of the LORD came to him: "What are you doing here, Elijah?"

10He replied, "I have been very zealous for the LORD God Almighty. The Israelites have rejected your covenant, broken down your altars, and put your prophets to death with the sword. I am the only one left, and now they are trying to kill me too."

11The LORD said, "Go out and stand on the mountain in the presence of the LORD, for the LORD is about to pass by."

Then a great and powerful wind tore the mountains apart and shattered the rocks before the LORD, but the LORD was not in the wind. After the wind there was an earthquake, but the LORD was not in the earthquake. 12After the earthquake came a fire, but the LORD was not in the fire. And after the fire came a gentle whisper. 13When Elijah heard it, he pulled his cloak over his face and went out and stood at the mouth of the cave.

Then a voice said to him, "What are you doing here, Elijah?"

14He replied, "I have been very zealous for the LORD God Almighty. The Israelites have rejected your covenant, broken down your altars, and put your prophets to death with the sword. I am the only one left, and now they are trying to kill me too."

15The LORD said to him, "Go back the way you came, and go to the Desert of Da-

[a]3 Or *Elijah saw*

mascus. When you get there, anoint Hazael king over Aram. 16Also, anoint Jehu son of Nimshi king over Israel, and anoint Elisha son of Shaphat from Abel Meholah to succeed you as prophet. 17Jehu will put to death any who escape the sword of Hazael, and Elisha will put to death any who escape the sword of Jehu. 18Yet I reserve seven thousand in Israel—all whose knees have not bowed down to Baal and all whose mouths have not kissed him."

The Call of Elisha

19So Elijah went from there and found Elisha son of Shaphat. He was plowing with twelve yoke of oxen, and he himself was driving the twelfth pair. Elijah went up to him and threw his cloak around him. 20Elisha then left his oxen and ran after Elijah. "Let me kiss my father and mother good-by," he said, "and then I will come with you."

"Go back," Elijah replied. "What have I done to you?"

21So Elisha left him and went back. He took his yoke of oxen and slaughtered them. He burned the plowing equipment to cook the meat and gave it to the people, and they ate. Then he set out to follow Elijah and became his attendant.

Ben-Hadad Attacks Samaria

20 Now Ben-Hadad king of Aram mustered his entire army. Accompanied by thirty-two kings with their horses and chariots, he went up and besieged Samaria and attacked it. 2He sent messengers into the city to Ahab king of Israel, saying, "This is what Ben-Hadad says: 3'Your silver and gold are mine, and the best of your wives and children are mine.' "

4The king of Israel answered, "Just as you say, my lord the king. I and all I have are yours."

5The messengers came again and said, "This is what Ben-Hadad says: 'I sent to demand your silver and gold, your wives and your children. 6But about this time tomorrow I am going to send my officials to search your palace and the houses of your officials. They will seize everything you value and carry it away.' "

7The king of Israel summoned all the elders of the land and said to them, "See how this man is looking for trouble! When he sent for my wives and my children, my silver and my gold, I did not refuse him."

8The elders and the people all answered, "Don't listen to him or agree to his demands."

9So he replied to Ben-Hadad's messengers, "Tell my lord the king, 'Your servant will do all you demanded the first time, but this demand I cannot meet.' " They left and took the answer back to Ben-Hadad.

10Then Ben-Hadad sent another message to Ahab: "May the gods deal with me, be it ever so severely, if enough dust remains in Samaria to give each of my men a handful."

11The king of Israel answered, "Tell him: 'One who puts on his armor should not boast like one who takes it off.' "

12Ben-Hadad heard this message while he and the kings were drinking in their tents,[a] and he ordered his men: "Prepare to attack." So they prepared to attack the city.

Ahab Defeats Ben-Hadad

13Meanwhile a prophet came to Ahab king of Israel and announced, "This is what the LORD says: 'Do you see this vast army? I will give it into your hand today, and then you will know that I am the LORD.' "

14"But who will do this?" asked Ahab.

The prophet replied, "This is what the LORD says: 'The young officers of the provincial commanders will do it.' "

"And who will start the battle?" he asked.

The prophet answered, "You will."

15So Ahab summoned the young officers of the provincial commanders, 232 men. Then he assembled the rest of the Israelites, 7,000 in all. 16They set out at noon while Ben-Hadad and the 32 kings allied with him were in their tents getting drunk. 17The young officers of the provincial commanders went out first.

Now Ben-Hadad had dispatched scouts, who reported, "Men are advancing from Samaria."

18He said, "If they have come out for peace, take them alive; if they have come out for war, take them alive."

19The young officers of the provincial commanders marched out of the city with the army behind them 20and each one struck down his opponent. At that, the Ar-

[a]12 Or *in Succoth*; also in verse 16

ameans fled, with the Israelites in pursuit.
But Ben-Hadad king of Aram escaped on
horseback with some of his horsemen.
21The king of Israel advanced and over-
powered the horses and chariots and in-
flicted heavy losses on the Arameans.
22Afterward, the prophet came to the
king of Israel and said, "Strengthen your
position and see what must be done, be-
cause next spring the king of Aram will at-
tack you again."
23Meanwhile, the officials of the king of
Aram advised him, "Their gods are gods of
the hills. That is why they were too strong
for us. But if we fight them on the plains,
surely we will be stronger than they. 24Do
this: Remove all the kings from their com-
mands and replace them with other offi-
cers. 25You must also raise an army like
the one you lost—horse for horse and
chariot for chariot—so we can fight Israel
on the plains. Then surely we will be
stronger than they." He agreed with them
and acted accordingly.
26The next spring Ben-Hadad mustered
the Arameans and went up to Aphek to
fight against Israel. 27When the Israelites
were also mustered and given provisions,
they marched out to meet them. The Isra-
elites camped opposite them like two
small flocks of goats, while the Arameans
covered the countryside.
28The man of God came up and told the
king of Israel, "This is what the LORD says:
'Because the Arameans think the LORD is
a god of the hills and not a god of the val-
leys, I will deliver this vast army into your
hands, and you will know that I am the
LORD.' "
29For seven days they camped opposite
each other, and on the seventh day the
battle was joined. The Israelites inflicted a
hundred thousand casualties on the Ara-
mean foot soldiers in one day. 30The rest
of them escaped to the city of Aphek,
where the wall collapsed on twenty-seven
thousand of them. And Ben-Hadad fled to
the city and hid in an inner room.
31His officials said to him, "Look, we
have heard that the kings of the house of
Israel are merciful. Let us go to the king of
Israel with sackcloth around our waists
and ropes around our heads. Perhaps he
will spare your life."
32Wearing sackcloth around their
waists and ropes around their heads, they
went to the king of Israel and said, "Your
servant Ben-Hadad says: 'Please let me
live.' "
The king answered, "Is he still alive? He
is my brother."
33The men took this as a good sign and
were quick to pick up his word. "Yes, your
brother Ben-Hadad!" they said.
"Go and get him," the king said. When
Ben-Hadad came out, Ahab had him come
up into his chariot.
34"I will return the cities my father took
from your father," Ben-Hadad offered.
"You may set up your own market areas in
Damascus, as my father did in Samaria."
⌊Ahab said,⌋ "On the basis of a treaty I
will set you free." So he made a treaty with
him, and let him go.

A Prophet Condemns Ahab

35By the word of the LORD one of the
sons of the prophets said to his compan-
ion, "Strike me with your weapon," but
the man refused.
36So the prophet said, "Because you
have not obeyed the LORD, as soon as you
leave me a lion will kill you." And after the
man went away, a lion found him and
killed him.
37The prophet found another man and
said, "Strike me, please." So the man
struck him and wounded him. 38Then the
prophet went and stood by the road wait-
ing for the king. He disguised himself with
his headband down over his eyes. 39As the
king passed by, the prophet called out to
him, "Your servant went into the thick of
the battle, and someone came to me with
a captive and said, 'Guard this man. If he
is missing, it will be your life for his life,
or you must pay a talent[a] of silver.'
40While your servant was busy here and
there, the man disappeared."
"That is your sentence," the king of Is-
rael said. "You have pronounced it your-
self."
41Then the prophet quickly removed
the headband from his eyes, and the king
of Israel recognized him as one of the
prophets. 42He said to the king, "This is
what the LORD says: 'You have set free a
man I had determined should die.[b]
Therefore it is your life for his life, your
people for his people.' " 43Sullen and an-
gry, the king of Israel went to his palace in
Samaria.

[a]39 That is, about 75 pounds (about 34 kilograms)
[b]42 The Hebrew term refers to the irrevocable giving over of things or persons to the LORD, often by totally destroying them.

Naboth's Vineyard

21 Some time later there was an incident involving a vineyard belonging to Naboth the Jezreelite. The vineyard was in Jezreel, close to the palace of Ahab king of Samaria. [2]Ahab said to Naboth, "Let me have your vineyard to use for a vegetable garden, since it is close to my palace. In exchange I will give you a better vineyard or, if you prefer, I will pay you whatever it is worth."

[3]But Naboth replied, "The LORD forbid that I should give you the inheritance of my fathers."

[4]So Ahab went home, sullen and angry because Naboth the Jezreelite had said, "I will not give you the inheritance of my fathers." He lay on his bed sulking and refused to eat.

[5]His wife Jezebel came in and asked him, "Why are you so sullen? Why won't you eat?"

[6]He answered her, "Because I said to Naboth the Jezreelite, 'Sell me your vineyard; or if you prefer, I will give you another vineyard in its place.' But he said, 'I will not give you my vineyard.' "

[7]Jezebel his wife said, "Is this how you act as king over Israel? Get up and eat! Cheer up. I'll get you the vineyard of Naboth the Jezreelite."

[8]So she wrote letters in Ahab's name, placed his seal on them, and sent them to the elders and nobles who lived in Naboth's city with him. [9]In those letters she wrote:

> "Proclaim a day of fasting and seat Naboth in a prominent place among the people. [10]But seat two scoundrels opposite him and have them testify that he has cursed both God and the king. Then take him out and stone him to death."

[11]So the elders and nobles who lived in Naboth's city did as Jezebel directed in the letters she had written to them. [12]They proclaimed a fast and seated Naboth in a prominent place among the people. [13]Then two scoundrels came and sat opposite him and brought charges against Naboth before the people, saying, "Naboth has cursed both God and the king." So they took him outside the city and stoned him to death. [14]Then they sent word to Jezebel: "Naboth has been stoned and is dead."

[15]As soon as Jezebel heard that Naboth had been stoned to death, she said to Ahab, "Get up and take possession of the vineyard of Naboth the Jezreelite that he refused to sell you. He is no longer alive, but dead." [16]When Ahab heard that Naboth was dead, he got up and went down to take possession of Naboth's vineyard.

[17]Then the word of the LORD came to Elijah the Tishbite: [18]"Go down to meet Ahab king of Israel, who rules in Samaria. He is now in Naboth's vineyard, where he has gone to take possession of it. [19]Say to him, 'This is what the LORD says: Have you not murdered a man and seized his property?' Then say to him, 'This is what the LORD says: In the place where dogs licked up Naboth's blood, dogs will lick up your blood—yes, yours!' "

[20]Ahab said to Elijah, "So you have found me, my enemy!"

"I have found you," he answered, "because you have sold yourself to do evil in the eyes of the LORD. [21]'I am going to bring disaster on you. I will consume your descendants and cut off from Ahab every last male in Israel—slave or free. [22]I will make your house like that of Jeroboam son of Nebat and that of Baasha son of Ahijah, because you have provoked me to anger and have caused Israel to sin.'

[23]"And also concerning Jezebel the LORD says: 'Dogs will devour Jezebel by the wall of[a] Jezreel.'

[24]"Dogs will eat those belonging to Ahab who die in the city, and the birds of the air will feed on those who die in the country."

[25](There was never a man like Ahab, who sold himself to do evil in the eyes of the LORD, urged on by Jezebel his wife. [26]He behaved in the vilest manner by going after idols, like the Amorites the LORD drove out before Israel.)

[27]When Ahab heard these words, he tore his clothes, put on sackcloth and fasted. He lay in sackcloth and went around meekly.

[28]Then the word of the LORD came to Elijah the Tishbite: [29]"Have you noticed how Ahab has humbled himself before me? Because he has humbled himself, I will not bring this disaster in his day, but

[a]23 Most Hebrew manuscripts; a few Hebrew manuscripts, Vulgate and Syriac (see also 2 Kings 9:26) *the plot of ground at*

I will bring it on his house in the days of his son."

Micaiah Prophesies Against Ahab

22 For three years there was no war between Aram and Israel. 2But in the third year Jehoshaphat king of Judah went down to see the king of Israel. 3The king of Israel had said to his officials, "Don't you know that Ramoth Gilead belongs to us and yet we are doing nothing to retake it from the king of Aram?"

4So he asked Jehoshaphat, "Will you go with me to fight against Ramoth Gilead?"

Jehoshaphat replied to the king of Israel, "I am as you are, my people as your people, my horses as your horses." 5But Jehoshaphat also said to the king of Israel, "First seek the counsel of the LORD."

6So the king of Israel brought together the prophets—about four hundred men—and asked them, "Shall I go to war against Ramoth Gilead, or shall I refrain?"

"Go," they answered, "for the Lord will give it into the king's hand."

7But Jehoshaphat asked, "Is there not a prophet of the LORD here whom we can inquire of?"

8The king of Israel answered Jehoshaphat, "There is still one man through whom we can inquire of the LORD, but I hate him because he never prophesies anything good about me, but always bad. He is Micaiah son of Imlah."

"The king should not say that," Jehoshaphat replied.

9So the king of Israel called one of his officials and said, "Bring Micaiah son of Imlah at once."

10Dressed in their royal robes, the king of Israel and Jehoshaphat king of Judah were sitting on their thrones at the threshing floor by the entrance of the gate of Samaria, with all the prophets prophesying before them. 11Now Zedekiah son of Kenaanah had made iron horns and he declared, "This is what the LORD says: 'With these you will gore the Arameans until they are destroyed.' "

12All the other prophets were prophesying the same thing. "Attack Ramoth Gilead and be victorious," they said, "for the LORD will give it into the king's hand."

13The messenger who had gone to summon Micaiah said to him, "Look, as one man the other prophets are predicting success for the king. Let your word agree with theirs, and speak favorably."

14But Micaiah said, "As surely as the LORD lives, I can tell him only what the LORD tells me."

15When he arrived, the king asked him, "Micaiah, shall we go to war against Ramoth Gilead, or shall I refrain?"

"Attack and be victorious," he answered, "for the LORD will give it into the king's hand."

16The king said to him, "How many times must I make you swear to tell me nothing but the truth in the name of the LORD?"

17Then Micaiah answered, "I saw all Israel scattered on the hills like sheep without a shepherd, and the LORD said, 'These people have no master. Let each one go home in peace.' "

18The king of Israel said to Jehoshaphat, "Didn't I tell you that he never prophesies anything good about me, but only bad?"

19Micaiah continued, "Therefore hear the word of the LORD: I saw the LORD sitting on his throne with all the host of heaven standing around him on his right and on his left. 20And the LORD said, 'Who will entice Ahab into attacking Ramoth Gilead and going to his death there?'

"One suggested this, and another that. 21Finally, a spirit came forward, stood before the LORD and said, 'I will entice him.'

22" 'By what means?' the LORD asked.

" 'I will go out and be a lying spirit in the mouths of all his prophets,' he said.

" 'You will succeed in enticing him,' said the LORD. 'Go and do it.'

23"So now the LORD has put a lying spirit in the mouths of all these prophets of yours. The LORD has decreed disaster for you."

24Then Zedekiah son of Kenaanah went up and slapped Micaiah in the face. "Which way did the spirit from[a] the LORD go when he went from me to speak to you?" he asked.

25Micaiah replied, "You will find out on the day you go to hide in an inner room."

26The king of Israel then ordered, "Take Micaiah and send him back to Amon the ruler of the city and to Joash the king's son 27and say, 'This is what the king says: Put this fellow in prison and give him nothing but bread and water until I return safely.' "

28Micaiah declared, "If you ever return

[a]24 Or *Spirit of*

safely, the LORD has not spoken through me." Then he added, "Mark my words, all you people!"

Ahab Killed at Ramoth Gilead

29So the king of Israel and Jehoshaphat king of Judah went up to Ramoth Gilead. 30The king of Israel said to Jehoshaphat, "I will enter the battle in disguise, but you wear your royal robes." So the king of Israel disguised himself and went into battle.

31Now the king of Aram had ordered his thirty-two chariot commanders, "Do not fight with anyone, small or great, except the king of Israel." 32When the chariot commanders saw Jehoshaphat, they thought, "Surely this is the king of Israel." So they turned to attack him, but when Jehoshaphat cried out, 33the chariot commanders saw that he was not the king of Israel and stopped pursuing him.

34But someone drew his bow at random and hit the king of Israel between the sections of his armor. The king told his chariot driver, "Wheel around and get me out of the fighting. I've been wounded." 35All day long the battle raged, and the king was propped up in his chariot facing the Arameans. The blood from his wound ran onto the floor of the chariot, and that evening he died. 36As the sun was setting, a cry spread through the army: "Every man to his town; everyone to his land!"

37So the king died and was brought to Samaria, and they buried him there. 38They washed the chariot at a pool in Samaria (where the prostitutes bathed),[a] and the dogs licked up his blood, as the word of the LORD had declared.

39As for the other events of Ahab's reign, including all he did, the palace he built and inlaid with ivory, and the cities he fortified, are they not written in the book of the annals of the kings of Israel? 40Ahab rested with his fathers. And Ahaziah his son succeeded him as king.

Jehoshaphat King of Judah

41Jehoshaphat son of Asa became king of Judah in the fourth year of Ahab king of Israel. 42Jehoshaphat was thirty-five years old when he became king, and he reigned in Jerusalem twenty-five years. His mother's name was Azubah daughter of Shilhi. 43In everything he walked in the ways of his father Asa and did not stray from them; he did what was right in the eyes of the LORD. The high places, however, were not removed, and the people continued to offer sacrifices and burn incense there. 44Jehoshaphat was also at peace with the king of Israel.

45As for the other events of Jehoshaphat's reign, the things he achieved and his military exploits, are they not written in the book of the annals of the kings of Judah? 46He rid the land of the rest of the male shrine prostitutes who remained there even after the reign of his father Asa. 47There was then no king in Edom; a deputy ruled.

48Now Jehoshaphat built a fleet of trading ships[b] to go to Ophir for gold, but they never set sail—they were wrecked at Ezion Geber. 49At that time Ahaziah son of Ahab said to Jehoshaphat, "Let my men sail with your men," but Jehoshaphat refused.

50Then Jehoshaphat rested with his fathers and was buried with them in the city of David his father. And Jehoram his son succeeded him.

Ahaziah King of Israel

51Ahaziah son of Ahab became king of Israel in Samaria in the seventeenth year of Jehoshaphat king of Judah, and he reigned over Israel two years. 52He did evil in the eyes of the LORD, because he walked in the ways of his father and mother and in the ways of Jeroboam son of Nebat, who caused Israel to sin. 53He served and worshiped Baal and provoked the LORD, the God of Israel, to anger, just as his father had done.

[a]38 Or *Samaria and cleaned the weapons* [b]48 Hebrew *of ships of Tarshish*

THIS book continues the history of Israel and Judah begun in 1 Kings. When good kings reign, the people prosper; but after persistent idolatry, God finally allows the Assyrians to destroy the nation of Israel and the Babylonians to carry the nation of Judah into captivity. Yet God preserves the royal line because of the promise he made David (see 2 Kings 8:19). As you read this book, praise God for his faithful love to you in spite of your sins. But remember that God does eventually punish those who disobey.

2 KINGS

The Lord's Judgment on Ahaziah

1 After Ahab's death, Moab rebelled against Israel. 2 Now Ahaziah had fallen through the lattice of his upper room in Samaria and injured himself. So he sent messengers, saying to them, "Go and consult Baal-Zebub, the god of Ekron, to see if I will recover from this injury."

3 But the angel of the Lord said to Elijah the Tishbite, "Go up and meet the messengers of the king of Samaria and ask them, 'Is it because there is no God in Israel that you are going off to consult Baal-Zebub, the god of Ekron?' 4 Therefore this is what the Lord says: 'You will not leave the bed you are lying on. You will certainly die!'" So Elijah went.

5 When the messengers returned to the king, he asked them, "Why have you come back?"

6 "A man came to meet us," they replied. "And he said to us, 'Go back to the king who sent you and tell him, "This is what the Lord says: Is it because there is no God in Israel that you are sending men to consult Baal-Zebub, the god of Ekron?

Therefore you will not leave the bed you
are lying on. You will certainly die!'" "
7The king asked them, "What kind of
man was it who came to meet you and
told you this?"
8They replied, "He was a man with a
garment of hair and with a leather belt
around his waist."
The king said, "That was Elijah the
Tishbite."
9Then he sent to Elijah a captain with
his company of fifty men. The captain
went up to Elijah, who was sitting on the
top of a hill, and said to him, "Man of God,
the king says, 'Come down!' "
10Elijah answered the captain, "If I am a
man of God, may fire come down from
heaven and consume you and your fifty
men!" Then fire fell from heaven and con-
sumed the captain and his men.
11At this the king sent to Elijah another
captain with his fifty men. The captain
said to him, "Man of God, this is what the
king says, 'Come down at once!' "
12"If I am a man of God," Elijah replied,
"may fire come down from heaven and
consume you and your fifty men!" Then
the fire of God fell from heaven and con-
sumed him and his fifty men.
13So the king sent a third captain with
his fifty men. This third captain went up
and fell on his knees before Elijah. "Man
of God," he begged, "please have respect
for my life and the lives of these fifty men,
your servants! 14See, fire has fallen from
heaven and consumed the first two cap-
tains and all their men. But now have re-
spect for my life!"
15The angel of the LORD said to Elijah,
"Go down with him; do not be afraid of
him." So Elijah got up and went down
with him to the king.
16He told the king, "This is what the
LORD says: Is it because there is no God in
Israel for you to consult that you have sent
messengers to consult Baal-Zebub, the
god of Ekron? Because you have done
this, you will never leave the bed you are
lying on. You will certainly die!" 17So he
died, according to the word of the LORD
that Elijah had spoken.
Because Ahaziah had no son, Joram[a]
succeeded him as king in the second year
of Jehoram son of Jehoshaphat king of Ju-
dah. 18As for all the other events of Ahazi-
ah's reign, and what he did, are they not
written in the book of the annals of the
kings of Israel?

Elijah Taken Up to Heaven

2 When the LORD was about to take Eli-
jah up to heaven in a whirlwind, Eli-
jah and Elisha were on their way from Gil-
gal. 2Elijah said to Elisha, "Stay here; the
LORD has sent me to Bethel."
But Elisha said, "As surely as the LORD
lives and as you live, I will not leave you."
So they went down to Bethel.
3The company of the prophets at Bethel
came out to Elisha and asked, "Do you
know that the LORD is going to take your
master from you today?"
"Yes, I know," Elisha replied, "but do
not speak of it."
4Then Elijah said to him, "Stay here, Eli-
sha; the LORD has sent me to Jericho."
And he replied, "As surely as the LORD
lives and as you live, I will not leave you."
So they went to Jericho.
5The company of the prophets at Jeri-
cho went up to Elisha and asked him, "Do
you know that the LORD is going to take
your master from you today?"
"Yes, I know," he replied, "but do not
speak of it."
6Then Elijah said to him, "Stay here; the
LORD has sent me to the Jordan."
And he replied, "As surely as the LORD
lives and as you live, I will not leave you."
So the two of them walked on.
7Fifty men of the company of the proph-
ets went and stood at a distance, facing
the place where Elijah and Elisha had
stopped at the Jordan. 8Elijah took his
cloak, rolled it up and struck the water
with it. The water divided to the right and
to the left, and the two of them crossed
over on dry ground.
9When they had crossed, Elijah said to
Elisha, "Tell me, what can I do for you be-
fore I am taken from you?"
"Let me inherit a double portion of your
spirit," Elisha replied.
10"You have asked a difficult thing," Eli-
jah said, "yet if you see me when I am tak-
en from you, it will be yours—otherwise
not."
11As they were walking along and talk-
ing together, suddenly a chariot of fire and
horses of fire appeared and separated the
two of them, and Elijah went up to heaven
in a whirlwind. 12Elisha saw this and cried
out, "My father! My father! The chariots

[a] 17 Hebrew *Jehoram*, a variant of *Joram*

and horsemen of Israel!" And Elisha saw him no more. Then he took hold of his own clothes and tore them apart.

13He picked up the cloak that had fallen from Elijah and went back and stood on the bank of the Jordan. 14Then he took the cloak that had fallen from him and struck the water with it. "Where now is the LORD, the God of Elijah?" he asked. When he struck the water, it divided to the right and to the left, and he crossed over.

15The company of the prophets from Jericho, who were watching, said, "The spirit of Elijah is resting on Elisha." And they went to meet him and bowed to the ground before him. 16"Look," they said, "we your servants have fifty able men. Let them go and look for your master. Perhaps the Spirit of the LORD has picked him up and set him down on some mountain or in some valley."

"No," Elisha replied, "do not send them."

17But they persisted until he was too ashamed to refuse. So he said, "Send them." And they sent fifty men, who searched for three days but did not find him. 18When they returned to Elisha, who was staying in Jericho, he said to them, "Didn't I tell you not to go?"

Healing of the Water

19The men of the city said to Elisha, "Look, our lord, this town is well situated, as you can see, but the water is bad and the land is unproductive."

20"Bring me a new bowl," he said, "and put salt in it." So they brought it to him.

21Then he went out to the spring and threw the salt into it, saying, "This is what the LORD says: 'I have healed this water. Never again will it cause death or make the land unproductive.' " 22And the water has remained wholesome to this day, according to the word Elisha had spoken.

Elisha Is Jeered

23From there Elisha went up to Bethel. As he was walking along the road, some youths came out of the town and jeered at him. "Go on up, you baldhead!" they said. "Go on up, you baldhead!" 24He turned around, looked at them and called down a curse on them in the name of the LORD. Then two bears came out of the woods and mauled forty-two of the youths. 25And he went on to Mount Carmel and from there returned to Samaria.

Moab Revolts

3 Joram[a] son of Ahab became king of Israel in Samaria in the eighteenth year of Jehoshaphat king of Judah, and he reigned twelve years. 2He did evil in the eyes of the LORD, but not as his father and mother had done. He got rid of the sacred stone of Baal that his father had made. 3Nevertheless he clung to the sins of Jeroboam son of Nebat, which he had caused Israel to commit; he did not turn away from them.

4Now Mesha king of Moab raised sheep, and he had to supply the king of Israel with a hundred thousand lambs and with the wool of a hundred thousand rams. 5But after Ahab died, the king of Moab rebelled against the king of Israel. 6So at that time King Joram set out from Samaria and mobilized all Israel. 7He also sent this message to Jehoshaphat king of Judah: "The king of Moab has rebelled against me. Will you go with me to fight against Moab?"

"I will go with you," he replied. "I am as you are, my people as your people, my horses as your horses."

8"By what route shall we attack?" he asked.

"Through the Desert of Edom," he answered.

9So the king of Israel set out with the king of Judah and the king of Edom. After a roundabout march of seven days, the army had no more water for themselves or for the animals with them.

10"What!" exclaimed the king of Israel. "Has the LORD called us three kings together only to hand us over to Moab?"

11But Jehoshaphat asked, "Is there no prophet of the LORD here, that we may inquire of the LORD through him?"

An officer of the king of Israel answered, "Elisha son of Shaphat is here. He used to pour water on the hands of Elijah.[b]"

12Jehoshaphat said, "The word of the LORD is with him." So the king of Israel and Jehoshaphat and the king of Edom went down to him.

13Elisha said to the king of Israel, "What do we have to do with each other? Go to the prophets of your father and the prophets of your mother."

[a] 1 Hebrew *Jehoram*, a variant of *Joram*; also in verse 6

[b] 11 That is, he was Elijah's personal servant.

"No," the king of Israel answered, "because it was the LORD who called us three kings together to hand us over to Moab."
14Elisha said, "As surely as the LORD Almighty lives, whom I serve, if I did not have respect for the presence of Jehoshaphat king of Judah, I would not look at you or even notice you. 15But now bring me a harpist."

While the harpist was playing, the hand of the LORD came upon Elisha 16and he said, "This is what the LORD says: Make this valley full of ditches. 17For this is what the LORD says: You will see neither wind nor rain, yet this valley will be filled with water, and you, your cattle and your other animals will drink. 18This is an easy thing in the eyes of the LORD; he will also hand Moab over to you. 19You will overthrow every fortified city and every major town. You will cut down every good tree, stop up all the springs, and ruin every good field with stones."

20The next morning, about the time for offering the sacrifice, there it was—water flowing from the direction of Edom! And the land was filled with water.

21Now all the Moabites had heard that the kings had come to fight against them; so every man, young and old, who could bear arms was called up and stationed on the border. 22When they got up early in the morning, the sun was shining on the water. To the Moabites across the way, the water looked red—like blood. 23"That's blood!" they said. "Those kings must have fought and slaughtered each other. Now to the plunder, Moab!"

24But when the Moabites came to the camp of Israel, the Israelites rose up and fought them until they fled. And the Israelites invaded the land and slaughtered the Moabites. 25They destroyed the towns, and each man threw a stone on every good field until it was covered. They stopped up all the springs and cut down every good tree. Only Kir Hareseth was left with its stones in place, but men armed with slings surrounded it and attacked it as well.

26When the king of Moab saw that the battle had gone against him, he took with him seven hundred swordsmen to break through to the king of Edom, but they failed. 27Then he took his firstborn son, who was to succeed him as king, and offered him as a sacrifice on the city wall. The fury against Israel was great; they withdrew and returned to their own land.

The Widow's Oil

4 The wife of a man from the company of the prophets cried out to Elisha, "Your servant my husband is dead, and you know that he revered the LORD. But now his creditor is coming to take my two boys as his slaves."

2Elisha replied to her, "How can I help you? Tell me, what do you have in your house?"

"Your servant has nothing there at all," she said, "except a little oil."

3Elisha said, "Go around and ask all your neighbors for empty jars. Don't ask for just a few. 4Then go inside and shut the door behind you and your sons. Pour oil into all the jars, and as each is filled, put it to one side."

5She left him and afterward shut the door behind her and her sons. They brought the jars to her and she kept pouring. 6When all the jars were full, she said to her son, "Bring me another one."

But he replied, "There is not a jar left." Then the oil stopped flowing.

7She went and told the man of God, and he said, "Go, sell the oil and pay your debts. You and your sons can live on what is left."

The Shunammite's Son Restored to Life

8One day Elisha went to Shunem. And a well-to-do woman was there, who urged him to stay for a meal. So whenever he came by, he stopped there to eat. 9She said to her husband, "I know that this man who often comes our way is a holy man of God. 10Let's make a small room on the roof and put in it a bed and a table, a chair and a lamp for him. Then he can stay there whenever he comes to us."

11One day when Elisha came, he went up to his room and lay down there. 12He said to his servant Gehazi, "Call the Shunammite." So he called her, and she stood before him. 13Elisha said to him, "Tell her, 'You have gone to all this trouble for us. Now what can be done for you? Can we speak on your behalf to the king or the commander of the army?' "

She replied, "I have a home among my own people."

14"What can be done for her?" Elisha asked.

Gehazi said, "Well, she has no son and her husband is old."

15Then Elisha said, "Call her." So he

called her, and she stood in the doorway.
16"About this time next year," Elisha said,
"you will hold a son in your arms."
"No, my lord," she objected. "Don't
mislead your servant, O man of God!"
17But the woman became pregnant, and
the next year about that same time she
gave birth to a son, just as Elisha had told
her.
18The child grew, and one day he went
out to his father, who was with the reap-
ers. 19"My head! My head!" he said to his
father.
His father told a servant, "Carry him to
his mother." 20After the servant had lifted
him up and carried him to his mother, the
boy sat on her lap until noon, and then he
died. 21She went up and laid him on the
bed of the man of God, then shut the door
and went out.
22She called her husband and said,
"Please send me one of the servants and a
donkey so I can go to the man of God
quickly and return."
23"Why go to him today?" he asked.
"It's not the New Moon or the Sabbath."
"It's all right," she said.
24She saddled the donkey and said to
her servant, "Lead on; don't slow down
for me unless I tell you." 25So she set out
and came to the man of God at Mount Car-
mel.
When he saw her in the distance, the
man of God said to his servant Gehazi,
"Look! There's the Shunammite! 26Run to
meet her and ask her, 'Are you all right? Is
your husband all right? Is your child all
right?' "
"Everything is all right," she said.
27When she reached the man of God at
the mountain, she took hold of his feet.
Gehazi came over to push her away, but
the man of God said, "Leave her alone!
She is in bitter distress, but the LORD has
hidden it from me and has not told me
why."
28"Did I ask you for a son, my lord?" she
said. "Didn't I tell you, 'Don't raise my
hopes'?"
29Elisha said to Gehazi, "Tuck your
cloak into your belt, take my staff in your
hand and run. If you meet anyone, do not
greet him, and if anyone greets you, do
not answer. Lay my staff on the boy's
face."
30But the child's mother said, "As surely
as the LORD lives and as you live, I will not
leave you." So he got up and followed her.
31Gehazi went on ahead and laid the
staff on the boy's face, but there was no
sound or response. So Gehazi went back
to meet Elisha and told him, "The boy has
not awakened."
32When Elisha reached the house, there
was the boy lying dead on his couch. 33He
went in, shut the door on the two of them
and prayed to the LORD. 34Then he got on
the bed and lay upon the boy, mouth to
mouth, eyes to eyes, hands to hands. As
he stretched himself out upon him, the
boy's body grew warm. 35Elisha turned
away and walked back and forth in the
room and then got on the bed and
stretched out upon him once more. The
boy sneezed seven times and opened his
eyes.
36Elisha summoned Gehazi and said,
"Call the Shunammite." And he did. When
she came, he said, "Take your son." 37She
came in, fell at his feet and bowed to the
ground. Then she took her son and went
out.

Death in the Pot

38Elisha returned to Gilgal and there
was a famine in that region. While the
company of the prophets was meeting
with him, he said to his servant, "Put on
the large pot and cook some stew for these
men."
39One of them went out into the fields
to gather herbs and found a wild vine. He
gathered some of its gourds and filled the
fold of his cloak. When he returned, he
cut them up into the pot of stew, though
no one knew what they were. 40The stew
was poured out for the men, but as they
began to eat it, they cried out, "O man of
God, there is death in the pot!" And they
could not eat it.
41Elisha said, "Get some flour." He put
it into the pot and said, "Serve it to the
people to eat." And there was nothing
harmful in the pot.

Feeding of a Hundred

42A man came from Baal Shalishah,
bringing the man of God twenty loaves of
barley bread baked from the first ripe
grain, along with some heads of new
grain. "Give it to the people to eat," Elisha
said.
43"How can I set this before a hundred
men?" his servant asked.
But Elisha answered, "Give it to the peo-
ple to eat. For this is what the LORD says:
'They will eat and have some left over.' "
44Then he set it before them, and they ate

and had some left over, according to the
word of the LORD.

Naaman Healed of Leprosy

5 Now Naaman was commander of the
army of the king of Aram. He was a
great man in the sight of his master and
highly regarded, because through him the
LORD had given victory to Aram. He was a
valiant soldier, but he had leprosy.[a]
2 Now bands from Aram had gone out
and had taken captive a young girl from
Israel, and she served Naaman's wife.
3 She said to her mistress, "If only my mas-
ter would see the prophet who is in Sa-
maria! He would cure him of his leprosy."
4 Naaman went to his master and told
him what the girl from Israel had said.
5 "By all means, go," the king of Aram re-
plied. "I will send a letter to the king of
Israel." So Naaman left, taking with him
ten talents[b] of silver, six thousand shek-
els[c] of gold and ten sets of clothing. 6 The
letter that he took to the king of Israel
read: "With this letter I am sending my
servant Naaman to you so that you may
cure him of his leprosy."
7 As soon as the king of Israel read the
letter, he tore his robes and said, "Am I
God? Can I kill and bring back to life? Why
does this fellow send someone to me to be
cured of his leprosy? See how he is trying
to pick a quarrel with me!"
8 When Elisha the man of God heard
that the king of Israel had torn his robes,
he sent him this message: "Why have you
torn your robes? Have the man come to
me and he will know that there is a proph-
et in Israel." 9 So Naaman went with his
horses and chariots and stopped at the
door of Elisha's house. 10 Elisha sent a
messenger to say to him, "Go, wash your-
self seven times in the Jordan, and your
flesh will be restored and you will be
cleansed."
11 But Naaman went away angry and
said, "I thought that he would surely come
out to me and stand and call on the name
of the LORD his God, wave his hand over
the spot and cure me of my leprosy. 12 Are
not Abana and Pharpar, the rivers of Da-
mascus, better than any of the waters of
Israel? Couldn't I wash in them and be
cleansed?" So he turned and went off in a
rage.
13 Naaman's servants went to him and
said, "My father, if the prophet had told
you to do some great thing, would you not
have done it? How much more, then,
when he tells you, 'Wash and be
cleansed'!" 14 So he went down and
dipped himself in the Jordan seven times,
as the man of God had told him, and his
flesh was restored and became clean like
that of a young boy.
15 Then Naaman and all his attendants
went back to the man of God. He stood
before him and said, "Now I know that
there is no God in all the world except in
Israel. Please accept now a gift from your
servant."
16 The prophet answered, "As surely as
the LORD lives, whom I serve, I will not ac-
cept a thing." And even though Naaman
urged him, he refused.
17 "If you will not," said Naaman,
"please let me, your servant, be given as
much earth as a pair of mules can carry,
for your servant will never again make
burnt offerings and sacrifices to any other
god but the LORD. 18 But may the LORD for-
give your servant for this one thing: When
my master enters the temple of Rimmon
to bow down and he is leaning on my arm
and I bow there also—when I bow down
in the temple of Rimmon, may the LORD
forgive your servant for this."
19 "Go in peace," Elisha said.
After Naaman had traveled some dis-
tance, 20 Gehazi, the servant of Elisha the
man of God, said to himself, "My master
was too easy on Naaman, this Aramean,
by not accepting from him what he
brought. As surely as the LORD lives, I will
run after him and get something from
him."
21 So Gehazi hurried after Naaman.
When Naaman saw him running toward
him, he got down from the chariot to meet
him. "Is everything all right?" he asked.
22 "Everything is all right," Gehazi an-
swered. "My master sent me to say, 'Two
young men from the company of the
prophets have just come to me from the
hill country of Ephraim. Please give them
a talent[d] of silver and two sets of cloth-
ing.' "
23 "By all means, take two talents," said
Naaman. He urged Gehazi to accept them,
and then tied up the two talents of silver

[a] *1* The Hebrew word was used for various diseases affecting the skin—not necessarily leprosy; also in verses 3, 6, 7, 11 and 27. [b] *5* That is, about 750 pounds (about 340 kilograms) [c] *5* That is, about 150 pounds (about 70 kilograms) [d] *22* That is, about 75 pounds (about 34 kilograms)

in two bags, with two sets of clothing. He gave them to two of his servants, and they carried them ahead of Gehazi. 24When Gehazi came to the hill, he took the things from the servants and put them away in the house. He sent the men away and they left. 25Then he went in and stood before his master Elisha.

"Where have you been, Gehazi?" Elisha asked.

"Your servant didn't go anywhere," Gehazi answered.

26But Elisha said to him, "Was not my spirit with you when the man got down from his chariot to meet you? Is this the time to take money, or to accept clothes, olive groves, vineyards, flocks, herds, or menservants and maidservants? 27Naaman's leprosy will cling to you and to your descendants forever." Then Gehazi went from Elisha's presence and he was leprous, as white as snow.

An Axhead Floats

6 The company of the prophets said to Elisha, "Look, the place where we meet with you is too small for us. 2Let us go to the Jordan, where each of us can get a pole; and let us build a place there for us to live."

And he said, "Go."

3Then one of them said, "Won't you please come with your servants?"

"I will," Elisha replied. 4And he went with them.

They went to the Jordan and began to cut down trees. 5As one of them was cutting down a tree, the iron axhead fell into the water. "Oh, my lord," he cried out, "it was borrowed!"

6The man of God asked, "Where did it fall?" When he showed him the place, Elisha cut a stick and threw it there, and made the iron float. 7"Lift it out," he said. Then the man reached out his hand and took it.

Elisha Traps Blinded Arameans

8Now the king of Aram was at war with Israel. After conferring with his officers, he said, "I will set up my camp in such and such a place."

9The man of God sent word to the king of Israel: "Beware of passing that place, because the Arameans are going down there." 10So the king of Israel checked on the place indicated by the man of God. Time and again Elisha warned the king, so that he was on his guard in such places.

11This enraged the king of Aram. He summoned his officers and demanded of them, "Will you not tell me which of us is on the side of the king of Israel?"

12"None of us, my lord the king," said one of his officers, "but Elisha, the prophet who is in Israel, tells the king of Israel the very words you speak in your bedroom."

13"Go, find out where he is," the king ordered, "so I can send men and capture him." The report came back: "He is in Dothan." 14Then he sent horses and chariots and a strong force there. They went by night and surrounded the city.

15When the servant of the man of God got up and went out early the next morning, an army with horses and chariots had surrounded the city. "Oh, my lord, what shall we do?" the servant asked.

16"Don't be afraid," the prophet answered. "Those who are with us are more than those who are with them."

17And Elisha prayed, "O LORD, open his eyes so he may see." Then the LORD opened the servant's eyes, and he looked and saw the hills full of horses and chariots of fire all around Elisha.

18As the enemy came down toward him, Elisha prayed to the LORD, "Strike these people with blindness." So he struck them with blindness, as Elisha had asked.

19Elisha told them, "This is not the road and this is not the city. Follow me, and I will lead you to the man you are looking for." And he led them to Samaria.

20After they entered the city, Elisha said, "LORD, open the eyes of these men so they can see." Then the LORD opened their eyes and they looked, and there they were, inside Samaria.

21When the king of Israel saw them, he asked Elisha, "Shall I kill them, my father? Shall I kill them?"

22"Do not kill them," he answered. "Would you kill men you have captured with your own sword or bow? Set food and water before them so that they may eat and drink and then go back to their master." 23So he prepared a great feast for them, and after they had finished eating and drinking, he sent them away, and they returned to their master. So the bands from Aram stopped raiding Israel's territory.

Famine in Besieged Samaria

24Some time later, Ben-Hadad king of Aram mobilized his entire army and

marched up and laid siege to Samaria.
25 There was a great famine in the city; the
siege lasted so long that a donkey's head
sold for eighty shekels[a] of silver, and a
quarter of a cab[b] of seed pods[c] for five
shekels.[d]

26 As the king of Israel was passing by
on the wall, a woman cried to him, "Help
me, my lord the king!"

27 The king replied, "If the LORD does not
help you, where can I get help for you?
From the threshing floor? From the wine-
press?" 28 Then he asked her, "What's the
matter?"

She answered, "This woman said to me,
'Give up your son so we may eat him to-
day, and tomorrow we'll eat my son.' 29 So
we cooked my son and ate him. The next
day I said to her, 'Give up your son so we
may eat him,' but she had hidden him."

30 When the king heard the woman's
words, he tore his robes. As he went along
the wall, the people looked, and there, un-
derneath, he had sackcloth on his body.
31 He said, "May God deal with me, be it
ever so severely, if the head of Elisha son
of Shaphat remains on his shoulders to-
day!"

32 Now Elisha was sitting in his house,
and the elders were sitting with him. The
king sent a messenger ahead, but before
he arrived, Elisha said to the elders,
"Don't you see how this murderer is send-
ing someone to cut off my head? Look,
when the messenger comes, shut the door
and hold it shut against him. Is not the
sound of his master's footsteps behind
him?"

33 While he was still talking to them, the
messenger came down to him. And ⌊the
king⌋ said, "This disaster is from the LORD.
Why should I wait for the LORD any
longer?"

7 Elisha said, "Hear the word of the
LORD. This is what the LORD says:
About this time tomorrow, a seah[e] of
flour will sell for a shekel[f] and two
seahs[g] of barley for a shekel at the gate
of Samaria."

2 The officer on whose arm the king was
leaning said to the man of God, "Look,
even if the LORD should open the flood-
gates of the heavens, could this happen?"

"You will see it with your own eyes,"
answered Elisha, "but you will not eat any
of it!"

The Siege Lifted

3 Now there were four men with lepro-
sy[h] at the entrance of the city gate. They
said to each other, "Why stay here until
we die? 4 If we say, 'We'll go into the
city'—the famine is there, and we will die.
And if we stay here, we will die. So let's go
over to the camp of the Arameans and sur-
render. If they spare us, we live; if they kill
us, then we die."

5 At dusk they got up and went to the
camp of the Arameans. When they
reached the edge of the camp, not a man
was there, 6 for the Lord had caused the
Arameans to hear the sound of chariots
and horses and a great army, so that they
said to one another, "Look, the king of Is-
rael has hired the Hittite and Egyptian
kings to attack us!" 7 So they got up and
fled in the dusk and abandoned their tents
and their horses and donkeys. They left
the camp as it was and ran for their lives.

8 The men who had leprosy reached the
edge of the camp and entered one of the
tents. They ate and drank, and carried
away silver, gold and clothes, and went off
and hid them. They returned and entered
another tent and took some things from it
and hid them also.

9 Then they said to each other, "We're
not doing right. This is a day of good news
and we are keeping it to ourselves. If we
wait until daylight, punishment will over-
take us. Let's go at once and report this to
the royal palace."

10 So they went and called out to the city
gatekeepers and told them, "We went into
the Aramean camp and not a man was
there—not a sound of anyone—only teth-
ered horses and donkeys, and the tents
left just as they were." 11 The gatekeepers
shouted the news, and it was reported
within the palace.

12 The king got up in the night and said
to his officers, "I will tell you what the Ar-
ameans have done to us. They know we
are starving; so they have left the camp to

[a] 25 That is, about 2 pounds (about 1 kilogram) [b] 25 That is, probably about 1/2 pint (about 0.3 liter) [c] 25 Or *of doves' dung* [d] 25 That is, about 2 ounces (about 55 grams) [e] 1 That is, probably about 7 quarts (about 7.3 liters); also in verses 16 and 18 [f] 1 That is, about 2/5 ounce (about 11 grams); also in verses 16 and 18 [g] 1 That is, probably about 13 quarts (about 15 liters); also in verses 16 and 18 [h] 3 The Hebrew word is used for various diseases affecting the skin—not necessarily leprosy; also in verse 8.

hide in the countryside, thinking, 'They will surely come out, and then we will take them alive and get into the city.' "

13One of his officers answered, "Have some men take five of the horses that are left in the city. Their plight will be like that of all the Israelites left here—yes, they will only be like all these Israelites who are doomed. So let us send them to find out what happened."

14So they selected two chariots with their horses, and the king sent them after the Aramean army. He commanded the drivers, "Go and find out what has happened." 15They followed them as far as the Jordan, and they found the whole road strewn with the clothing and equipment the Arameans had thrown away in their headlong flight. So the messengers returned and reported to the king. 16Then the people went out and plundered the camp of the Arameans. So a seah of flour sold for a shekel, and two seahs of barley sold for a shekel, as the LORD had said.

17Now the king had put the officer on whose arm he leaned in charge of the gate, and the people trampled him in the gateway, and he died, just as the man of God had foretold when the king came down to his house. 18It happened as the man of God had said to the king: "About this time tomorrow, a seah of flour will sell for a shekel and two seahs of barley for a shekel at the gate of Samaria."

19The officer had said to the man of God, "Look, even if the LORD should open the floodgates of the heavens, could this happen?" The man of God had replied, "You will see it with your own eyes, but you will not eat any of it!" 20And that is exactly what happened to him, for the people trampled him in the gateway, and he died.

The Shunammite's Land Restored

8 Now Elisha had said to the woman whose son he had restored to life, "Go away with your family and stay for a while wherever you can, because the LORD has decreed a famine in the land that will last seven years." 2The woman proceeded to do as the man of God said. She and her family went away and stayed in the land of the Philistines seven years.

3At the end of the seven years she came back from the land of the Philistines and went to the king to beg for her house and land. 4The king was talking to Gehazi, the servant of the man of God, and had said, "Tell me about all the great things Elisha has done." 5Just as Gehazi was telling the king how Elisha had restored the dead to life, the woman whose son Elisha had brought back to life came to beg the king for her house and land.

Gehazi said, "This is the woman, my lord the king, and this is her son whom Elisha restored to life." 6The king asked the woman about it, and she told him.

Then he assigned an official to her case and said to him, "Give back everything that belonged to her, including all the income from her land from the day she left the country until now."

Hazael Murders Ben-Hadad

7Elisha went to Damascus, and Ben-Hadad king of Aram was ill. When the king was told, "The man of God has come all the way up here," 8he said to Hazael, "Take a gift with you and go to meet the man of God. Consult the LORD through him; ask him, 'Will I recover from this illness?' "

9Hazael went to meet Elisha, taking with him as a gift forty camel-loads of all the finest wares of Damascus. He went in and stood before him, and said, "Your son Ben-Hadad king of Aram has sent me to ask, 'Will I recover from this illness?' "

10Elisha answered, "Go and say to him, 'You will certainly recover'; but[a] the LORD has revealed to me that he will in fact die." 11He stared at him with a fixed gaze until Hazael felt ashamed. Then the man of God began to weep.

12"Why is my lord weeping?" asked Hazael.

"Because I know the harm you will do to the Israelites," he answered. "You will set fire to their fortified places, kill their young men with the sword, dash their little children to the ground, and rip open their pregnant women."

13Hazael said, "How could your servant, a mere dog, accomplish such a feat?"

"The LORD has shown me that you will become king of Aram," answered Elisha.

14Then Hazael left Elisha and returned to his master. When Ben-Hadad asked, "What did Elisha say to you?" Hazael replied, "He told me that you would certainly recover." 15But the next day he took a thick cloth, soaked it in water and spread

[a]*10* The Hebrew may also be read *Go and say, 'You will certainly not recover,' for.*

it over the king's face, so that he died. Then Hazael succeeded him as king.

Jehoram King of Judah

16In the fifth year of Joram son of Ahab king of Israel, when Jehoshaphat was king of Judah, Jehoram son of Jehoshaphat began his reign as king of Judah. 17He was thirty-two years old when he became king, and he reigned in Jerusalem eight years. 18He walked in the ways of the kings of Israel, as the house of Ahab had done, for he married a daughter of Ahab. He did evil in the eyes of the LORD. 19Nevertheless, for the sake of his servant David, the LORD was not willing to destroy Judah. He had promised to maintain a lamp for David and his descendants forever.

20In the time of Jehoram, Edom rebelled against Judah and set up its own king. 21So Jehoram[a] went to Zair with all his chariots. The Edomites surrounded him and his chariot commanders, but he rose up and broke through by night; his army, however, fled back home. 22To this day Edom has been in rebellion against Judah. Libnah revolted at the same time.

23As for the other events of Jehoram's reign, and all he did, are they not written in the book of the annals of the kings of Judah? 24Jehoram rested with his fathers and was buried with them in the City of David. And Ahaziah his son succeeded him as king.

Ahaziah King of Judah

25In the twelfth year of Joram son of Ahab king of Israel, Ahaziah son of Jehoram king of Judah began to reign. 26Ahaziah was twenty-two years old when he became king, and he reigned in Jerusalem one year. His mother's name was Athaliah, a granddaughter of Omri king of Israel. 27He walked in the ways of the house of Ahab and did evil in the eyes of the LORD, as the house of Ahab had done, for he was related by marriage to Ahab's family.

28Ahaziah went with Joram son of Ahab to war against Hazael king of Aram at Ramoth Gilead. The Arameans wounded Joram; 29so King Joram returned to Jezreel to recover from the wounds the Arameans had inflicted on him at Ramoth[b] in his battle with Hazael king of Aram.

Then Ahaziah son of Jehoram king of Judah went down to Jezreel to see Joram son of Ahab, because he had been wounded.

Jehu Anointed King of Israel

9 The prophet Elisha summoned a man from the company of the prophets and said to him, "Tuck your cloak into your belt, take this flask of oil with you and go to Ramoth Gilead. 2When you get there, look for Jehu son of Jehoshaphat, the son of Nimshi. Go to him, get him away from his companions and take him into an inner room. 3Then take the flask and pour the oil on his head and declare, 'This is what the LORD says: I anoint you king over Israel.' Then open the door and run; don't delay!"

4So the young man, the prophet, went to Ramoth Gilead. 5When he arrived, he found the army officers sitting together. "I have a message for you, commander," he said.

"For which of us?" asked Jehu.

"For you, commander," he replied.

6Jehu got up and went into the house. Then the prophet poured the oil on Jehu's head and declared, "This is what the LORD, the God of Israel, says: 'I anoint you king over the LORD's people Israel. 7You are to destroy the house of Ahab your master, and I will avenge the blood of my servants the prophets and the blood of all the LORD's servants shed by Jezebel. 8The whole house of Ahab will perish. I will cut off from Ahab every last male in Israel—slave or free. 9I will make the house of Ahab like the house of Jeroboam son of Nebat and like the house of Baasha son of Ahijah. 10As for Jezebel, dogs will devour her on the plot of ground at Jezreel, and no one will bury her.' " Then he opened the door and ran.

11When Jehu went out to his fellow officers, one of them asked him, "Is everything all right? Why did this madman come to you?"

"You know the man and the sort of things he says," Jehu replied.

12"That's not true!" they said. "Tell us."

Jehu said, "Here is what he told me: 'This is what the LORD says: I anoint you king over Israel.' "

13They hurried and took their cloaks and spread them under him on the bare

[a]21 Hebrew *Joram*, a variant of *Jehoram*; also in verses 23 and 24 [b]29 Hebrew *Ramah*, a variant of *Ramoth*

steps. Then they blew the trumpet and shouted, "Jehu is king!"

Jehu Kills Joram and Ahaziah

14So Jehu son of Jehoshaphat, the son of Nimshi, conspired against Joram. (Now Joram and all Israel had been defending Ramoth Gilead against Hazael king of Aram, 15but King Joram[a] had returned to Jezreel to recover from the wounds the Arameans had inflicted on him in the battle with Hazael king of Aram.) Jehu said, "If this is the way you feel, don't let anyone slip out of the city to go and tell the news in Jezreel." 16Then he got into his chariot and rode to Jezreel, because Joram was resting there and Ahaziah king of Judah had gone down to see him.

17When the lookout standing on the tower in Jezreel saw Jehu's troops approaching, he called out, "I see some troops coming."

"Get a horseman," Joram ordered. "Send him to meet them and ask, 'Do you come in peace?' "

18The horseman rode off to meet Jehu and said, "This is what the king says: 'Do you come in peace?' "

"What do you have to do with peace?" Jehu replied. "Fall in behind me."

The lookout reported, "The messenger has reached them, but he isn't coming back."

19So the king sent out a second horseman. When he came to them he said, "This is what the king says: 'Do you come in peace?' "

Jehu replied, "What do you have to do with peace? Fall in behind me."

20The lookout reported, "He has reached them, but he isn't coming back either. The driving is like that of Jehu son of Nimshi—he drives like a madman."

21"Hitch up my chariot," Joram ordered. And when it was hitched up, Joram king of Israel and Ahaziah king of Judah rode out, each in his own chariot, to meet Jehu. They met him at the plot of ground that had belonged to Naboth the Jezreelite. 22When Joram saw Jehu he asked, "Have you come in peace, Jehu?"

"How can there be peace," Jehu replied, "as long as all the idolatry and witchcraft of your mother Jezebel abound?"

23Joram turned about and fled, calling out to Ahaziah, "Treachery, Ahaziah!"

24Then Jehu drew his bow and shot Joram between the shoulders. The arrow pierced his heart and he slumped down in his chariot. 25Jehu said to Bidkar, his chariot officer, "Pick him up and throw him on the field that belonged to Naboth the Jezreelite. Remember how you and I were riding together in chariots behind Ahab his father when the LORD made this prophecy about him: 26'Yesterday I saw the blood of Naboth and the blood of his sons, declares the LORD, and I will surely make you pay for it on this plot of ground, declares the LORD.'[b] Now then, pick him up and throw him on that plot, in accordance with the word of the LORD."

27When Ahaziah king of Judah saw what had happened, he fled up the road to Beth Haggan.[c] Jehu chased him, shouting, "Kill him too!" They wounded him in his chariot on the way up to Gur near Ibleam, but he escaped to Megiddo and died there. 28His servants took him by chariot to Jerusalem and buried him with his fathers in his tomb in the City of David. 29(In the eleventh year of Joram son of Ahab, Ahaziah had become king of Judah.)

Jezebel Killed

30Then Jehu went to Jezreel. When Jezebel heard about it, she painted her eyes, arranged her hair and looked out of a window. 31As Jehu entered the gate, she asked, "Have you come in peace, Zimri, you murderer of your master?"[d]

32He looked up at the window and called out, "Who is on my side? Who?" Two or three eunuchs looked down at him. 33"Throw her down!" Jehu said. So they threw her down, and some of her blood spattered the wall and the horses as they trampled her underfoot.

34Jehu went in and ate and drank. "Take care of that cursed woman," he said, "and bury her, for she was a king's daughter." 35But when they went out to bury her, they found nothing except her skull, her feet and her hands. 36They went back and told Jehu, who said, "This is the word of the LORD that he spoke through his servant Elijah the Tishbite: On the plot of ground at Jezreel dogs will devour Jeze-

[a]15 Hebrew *Jehoram*, a variant of *Joram*; also in verses 17 and 21-24 [b]26 See 1 Kings 21:19.
[c]27 Or *fled by way of the garden house* [d]31 Or *"Did Zimri have peace, who murdered his master?"*

bel's flesh.[a] 37Jezebel's body will be like
refuse on the ground in the plot at Jezreel,
so that no one will be able to say, 'This is
Jezebel.' "

Ahab's Family Killed

10 Now there were in Samaria seven-
ty sons of the house of Ahab. So
Jehu wrote letters and sent them to Sa-
maria: to the officials of Jezreel,[b] to the
elders and to the guardians of Ahab's chil-
dren. He said, 2"As soon as this letter
reaches you, since your master's sons are
with you and you have chariots and
horses, a fortified city and weapons,
3choose the best and most worthy of your
master's sons and set him on his father's
throne. Then fight for your master's
house."

4But they were terrified and said, "If
two kings could not resist him, how
can we?"

5So the palace administrator, the city
governor, the elders and the guardians
sent this message to Jehu: "We are your
servants and we will do anything you say.
We will not appoint anyone as king; you
do whatever you think best."

6Then Jehu wrote them a second letter,
saying, "If you are on my side and will
obey me, take the heads of your master's
sons and come to me in Jezreel by this
time tomorrow."

Now the royal princes, seventy of them,
were with the leading men of the city, who
were rearing them. 7When the letter ar-
rived, these men took the princes and
slaughtered all seventy of them. They put
their heads in baskets and sent them to
Jehu in Jezreel. 8When the messenger ar-
rived, he told Jehu, "They have brought
the heads of the princes."

Then Jehu ordered, "Put them in two
piles at the entrance of the city gate until
morning."

9The next morning Jehu went out. He
stood before all the people and said, "You
are innocent. It was I who conspired
against my master and killed him, but
who killed all these? 10Know then, that not
a word the LORD has spoken against the
house of Ahab will fail. The LORD has done
what he promised through his servant Eli-
jah." 11So Jehu killed everyone in Jezreel
who remained of the house of Ahab, as
well as all his chief men, his close friends
and his priests, leaving him no survivor.

12Jehu then set out and went toward Sa-
maria. At Beth Eked of the Shepherds,
13he met some relatives of Ahaziah king of
Judah and asked, "Who are you?"

They said, "We are relatives of Ahaziah,
and we have come down to greet the fami-
lies of the king and of the queen mother."

14"Take them alive!" he ordered. So
they took them alive and slaughtered
them by the well of Beth Eked—forty-two
men. He left no survivor.

15After he left there, he came upon Je-
honadab son of Recab, who was on his
way to meet him. Jehu greeted him and
said, "Are you in accord with me, as I am
with you?"

"I am," Jehonadab answered.

"If so," said Jehu, "give me your hand."
So he did, and Jehu helped him up into
the chariot. 16Jehu said, "Come with me
and see my zeal for the LORD." Then he
had him ride along in his chariot.

17When Jehu came to Samaria, he killed
all who were left there of Ahab's family;
he destroyed them, according to the word
of the LORD spoken to Elijah.

Ministers of Baal Killed

18Then Jehu brought all the people to-
gether and said to them, "Ahab served
Baal a little; Jehu will serve him much.
19Now summon all the prophets of Baal,
all his ministers and all his priests. See
that no one is missing, because I am going
to hold a great sacrifice for Baal. Anyone
who fails to come will no longer live." But
Jehu was acting deceptively in order to de-
stroy the ministers of Baal.

20Jehu said, "Call an assembly in honor
of Baal." So they proclaimed it. 21Then he
sent word throughout Israel, and all the
ministers of Baal came; not one stayed
away. They crowded into the temple of
Baal until it was full from one end to the
other. 22And Jehu said to the keeper of the
wardrobe, "Bring robes for all the minis-
ters of Baal." So he brought out robes for
them.

23Then Jehu and Jehonadab son of Re-
cab went into the temple of Baal. Jehu
said to the ministers of Baal, "Look
around and see that no servants of the
LORD are here with you—only ministers of
Baal." 24So they went in to make sacrifices
and burnt offerings. Now Jehu had posted
eighty men outside with this warning: "If
one of you lets any of the men I am plac-

[a] 36 See 1 Kings 21:23. [b] 1 Hebrew; some Septuagint manuscripts and Vulgate *of the city*

ing in your hands escape, it will be your
life for his life."
25As soon as Jehu had finished making
the burnt offering, he ordered the guards
and officers: "Go in and kill them; let no
one escape." So they cut them down with
the sword. The guards and officers threw
the bodies out and then entered the inner
shrine of the temple of Baal. 26They
brought the sacred stone out of the temple
of Baal and burned it. 27They demolished
the sacred stone of Baal and tore down the
temple of Baal, and people have used it for
a latrine to this day.
28So Jehu destroyed Baal worship in Is-
rael. 29However, he did not turn away
from the sins of Jeroboam son of Nebat,
which he had caused Israel to commit—
the worship of the golden calves at Bethel
and Dan.
30The LORD said to Jehu, "Because you
have done well in accomplishing what is
right in my eyes and have done to the
house of Ahab all I had in mind to do,
your descendants will sit on the throne of
Israel to the fourth generation." 31Yet Jehu
was not careful to keep the law of the
LORD, the God of Israel, with all his heart.
He did not turn away from the sins of Jer-
oboam, which he had caused Israel to
commit.
32In those days the LORD began to re-
duce the size of Israel. Hazael overpow-
ered the Israelites throughout their territo-
ry 33east of the Jordan in all the land of
Gilead (the region of Gad, Reuben and
Manasseh), from Aroer by the Arnon
Gorge through Gilead to Bashan.
34As for the other events of Jehu's reign,
all he did, and all his achievements, are
they not written in the book of the annals
of the kings of Israel?
35Jehu rested with his fathers and was
buried in Samaria. And Jehoahaz his son
succeeded him as king. 36The time that
Jehu reigned over Israel in Samaria was
twenty-eight years.

Athaliah and Joash

11 When Athaliah the mother of Aha-
ziah saw that her son was dead,
she proceeded to destroy the whole royal
family. 2But Jehosheba, the daughter of
King Jehoram[a] and sister of Ahaziah,
took Joash son of Ahaziah and stole him
away from among the royal princes, who
were about to be murdered. She put him
and his nurse in a bedroom to hide him
from Athaliah; so he was not killed. 3He
remained hidden with his nurse at the
temple of the LORD for six years while Ath-
aliah ruled the land.
4In the seventh year Jehoiada sent for
the commanders of units of a hundred,
the Carites and the guards and had them
brought to him at the temple of the LORD.
He made a covenant with them and put
them under oath at the temple of the
LORD. Then he showed them the king's
son. 5He commanded them, saying, "This
is what you are to do: You who are in the
three companies that are going on duty on
the Sabbath—a third of you guarding the
royal palace, 6a third at the Sur Gate, and
a third at the gate behind the guard, who
take turns guarding the temple— 7and
you who are in the other two companies
that normally go off Sabbath duty are all
to guard the temple for the king. 8Station
yourselves around the king, each man
with his weapon in his hand. Anyone who
approaches your ranks[b] must be put to
death. Stay close to the king wherever he
goes."
9The commanders of units of a hundred
did just as Jehoiada the priest ordered.
Each one took his men—those who were
going on duty on the Sabbath and those
who were going off duty—and came to Je-
hoiada the priest. 10Then he gave the com-
manders the spears and shields that had
belonged to King David and that were in
the temple of the LORD. 11The guards, each
with his weapon in his hand, stationed
themselves around the king—near the al-
tar and the temple, from the south side to
the north side of the temple.
12Jehoiada brought out the king's son
and put the crown on him; he presented
him with a copy of the covenant and pro-
claimed him king. They anointed him,
and the people clapped their hands and
shouted, "Long live the king!"
13When Athaliah heard the noise made
by the guards and the people, she went to
the people at the temple of the LORD. 14She
looked and there was the king, standing
by the pillar, as the custom was. The offi-
cers and the trumpeters were beside the
king, and all the people of the land were
rejoicing and blowing trumpets. Then
Athaliah tore her robes and called out,
"Treason! Treason!"
15Jehoiada the priest ordered the com-

[a] 2 Hebrew *Joram*, a variant of *Jehoram* [b] 8 Or *approaches the precincts*

manders of units of a hundred, who were in charge of the troops: "Bring her out between the ranks[a] and put to the sword anyone who follows her." For the priest had said, "She must not be put to death in the temple of the LORD." [16]So they seized her as she reached the place where the horses enter the palace grounds, and there she was put to death.

[17]Jehoiada then made a covenant between the LORD and the king and people that they would be the LORD's people. He also made a covenant between the king and the people. [18]All the people of the land went to the temple of Baal and tore it down. They smashed the altars and idols to pieces and killed Mattan the priest of Baal in front of the altars.

Then Jehoiada the priest posted guards at the temple of the LORD. [19]He took with him the commanders of hundreds, the Carites, the guards and all the people of the land, and together they brought the king down from the temple of the LORD and went into the palace, entering by way of the gate of the guards. The king then took his place on the royal throne, [20]and all the people of the land rejoiced. And the city was quiet, because Athaliah had been slain with the sword at the palace.

[21]Joash[b] was seven years old when he began to reign.

Joash Repairs the Temple

12 In the seventh year of Jehu, Joash[c] became king, and he reigned in Jerusalem forty years. His mother's name was Zibiah; she was from Beersheba. [2]Joash did what was right in the eyes of the LORD all the years Jehoiada the priest instructed him. [3]The high places, however, were not removed; the people continued to offer sacrifices and burn incense there.

[4]Joash said to the priests, "Collect all the money that is brought as sacred offerings to the temple of the LORD—the money collected in the census, the money received from personal vows and the money brought voluntarily to the temple. [5]Let every priest receive the money from one of the treasurers, and let it be used to repair whatever damage is found in the temple."

[6]But by the twenty-third year of King Joash the priests still had not repaired the temple. [7]Therefore King Joash summoned Jehoiada the priest and the other priests and asked them, "Why aren't you repairing the damage done to the temple? Take no more money from your treasurers, but hand it over for repairing the temple." [8]The priests agreed that they would not collect any more money from the people and that they would not repair the temple themselves.

[9]Jehoiada the priest took a chest and bored a hole in its lid. He placed it beside the altar, on the right side as one enters the temple of the LORD. The priests who guarded the entrance put into the chest all the money that was brought to the temple of the LORD. [10]Whenever they saw that there was a large amount of money in the chest, the royal secretary and the high priest came, counted the money that had been brought into the temple of the LORD and put it into bags. [11]When the amount had been determined, they gave the money to the men appointed to supervise the work on the temple. With it they paid those who worked on the temple of the LORD—the carpenters and builders, [12]the masons and stonecutters. They purchased timber and dressed stone for the repair of the temple of the LORD, and met all the other expenses of restoring the temple.

[13]The money brought into the temple was not spent for making silver basins, wick trimmers, sprinkling bowls, trumpets or any other articles of gold or silver for the temple of the LORD; [14]it was paid to the workmen, who used it to repair the temple. [15]They did not require an accounting from those to whom they gave the money to pay the workers, because they acted with complete honesty. [16]The money from the guilt offerings and sin offerings was not brought into the temple of the LORD; it belonged to the priests.

[17]About this time Hazael king of Aram went up and attacked Gath and captured it. Then he turned to attack Jerusalem. [18]But Joash king of Judah took all the sacred objects dedicated by his fathers—Jehoshaphat, Jehoram and Ahaziah, the kings of Judah—and the gifts he himself had dedicated and all the gold found in the treasuries of the temple of the LORD and of the royal palace, and he sent them to Hazael king of Aram, who then withdrew from Jerusalem.

[19]As for the other events of the reign of

[a]15 Or *out from the precincts* [b]21 Hebrew *Jehoash*, a variant of *Joash* [c]1 Hebrew *Jehoash*, a variant of *Joash*; also in verses 2, 4, 6, 7 and 18

Joash, and all he did, are they not written
in the book of the annals of the kings of
Judah? 20His officials conspired against
him and assassinated him at Beth Millo,
on the road down to Silla. 21The officials
who murdered him were Jozabad son of
Shimeath and Jehozabad son of Shomer.
He died and was buried with his fathers in
the City of David. And Amaziah his son
succeeded him as king.

Jehoahaz King of Israel

13 In the twenty-third year of Joash
son of Ahaziah king of Judah, Je-
hoahaz son of Jehu became king of Israel
in Samaria, and he reigned seventeen
years. 2He did evil in the eyes of the LORD
by following the sins of Jeroboam son of
Nebat, which he had caused Israel to com-
mit, and he did not turn away from them.
3So the LORD's anger burned against Israel,
and for a long time he kept them under
the power of Hazael king of Aram and
Ben-Hadad his son.

4Then Jehoahaz sought the LORD's fa-
vor, and the LORD listened to him, for he
saw how severely the king of Aram was
oppressing Israel. 5The LORD provided a
deliverer for Israel, and they escaped from
the power of Aram. So the Israelites lived
in their own homes as they had before.
6But they did not turn away from the sins
of the house of Jeroboam, which he had
caused Israel to commit; they continued
in them. Also, the Asherah pole[a] re-
mained standing in Samaria.

7Nothing had been left of the army of
Jehoahaz except fifty horsemen, ten chari-
ots and ten thousand foot soldiers, for the
king of Aram had destroyed the rest and
made them like the dust at threshing time.

8As for the other events of the reign of
Jehoahaz, all he did and his achieve-
ments, are they not written in the book of
the annals of the kings of Israel? 9Jeho-
haz rested with his fathers and was buried
in Samaria. And Jehoash[b] his son suc-
ceeded him as king.

Jehoash King of Israel

10In the thirty-seventh year of Joash
king of Judah, Jehoash son of Jehoahaz
became king of Israel in Samaria, and he
reigned sixteen years. 11He did evil in the
eyes of the LORD and did not turn away
from any of the sins of Jeroboam son of
Nebat, which he had caused Israel to com-
mit; he continued in them.

12As for the other events of the reign of
Jehoash, all he did and his achievements,
including his war against Amaziah king of
Judah, are they not written in the book of
the annals of the kings of Israel? 13Jehoash
rested with his fathers, and Jeroboam suc-
ceeded him on the throne. Jehoash was
buried in Samaria with the kings of Israel.

14Now Elisha was suffering from the ill-
ness from which he died. Jehoash king of
Israel went down to see him and wept
over him. "My father! My father!" he
cried. "The chariots and horsemen of Is-
rael!"

15Elisha said, "Get a bow and some ar-
rows," and he did so. 16"Take the bow in
your hands," he said to the king of Israel.
When he had taken it, Elisha put his
hands on the king's hands.

17"Open the east window," he said, and
he opened it. "Shoot!" Elisha said, and he
shot. "The LORD's arrow of victory, the ar-
row of victory over Aram!" Elisha de-
clared. "You will completely destroy the
Arameans at Aphek."

18Then he said, "Take the arrows," and
the king took them. Elisha told him,
"Strike the ground." He struck it three
times and stopped. 19The man of God was
angry with him and said, "You should
have struck the ground five or six times;
then you would have defeated Aram and
completely destroyed it. But now you will
defeat it only three times."

20Elisha died and was buried.

Now Moabite raiders used to enter the
country every spring. 21Once while some
Israelites were burying a man, suddenly
they saw a band of raiders; so they threw
the man's body into Elisha's tomb. When
the body touched Elisha's bones, the man
came to life and stood up on his feet.

22Hazael king of Aram oppressed Israel
throughout the reign of Jehoahaz. 23But
the LORD was gracious to them and had
compassion and showed concern for them
because of his covenant with Abraham,
Isaac and Jacob. To this day he has been
unwilling to destroy them or banish them
from his presence.

24Hazael king of Aram died, and Ben-
Hadad his son succeeded him as king.
25Then Jehoash son of Jehoahaz recap-
tured from Ben-Hadad son of Hazael the

[a]6 That is, a symbol of the goddess Asherah; here and elsewhere in 2 Kings [b]9 Hebrew *Joash*, a variant of *Jehoash*; also in verses 12-14 and 25

towns he had taken in battle from his father Jehoahaz. Three times Jehoash defeated him, and so he recovered the Israelite towns.

Amaziah King of Judah

14 In the second year of Jehoash[a] son of Jehoahaz king of Israel, Amaziah son of Joash king of Judah began to reign. [2]He was twenty-five years old when he became king, and he reigned in Jerusalem twenty-nine years. His mother's name was Jehoaddin; she was from Jerusalem. [3]He did what was right in the eyes of the LORD, but not as his father David had done. In everything he followed the example of his father Joash. [4]The high places, however, were not removed; the people continued to offer sacrifices and burn incense there.

[5]After the kingdom was firmly in his grasp, he executed the officials who had murdered his father the king. [6]Yet he did not put the sons of the assassins to death, in accordance with what is written in the Book of the Law of Moses where the LORD commanded: "Fathers shall not be put to death for their children, nor children put to death for their fathers; each is to die for his own sins."[b]

[7]He was the one who defeated ten thousand Edomites in the Valley of Salt and captured Sela in battle, calling it Joktheel, the name it has to this day.

[8]Then Amaziah sent messengers to Jehoash son of Jehoahaz, the son of Jehu, king of Israel, with the challenge: "Come, meet me face to face."

[9]But Jehoash king of Israel replied to Amaziah king of Judah: "A thistle in Lebanon sent a message to a cedar in Lebanon, 'Give your daughter to my son in marriage.' Then a wild beast in Lebanon came along and trampled the thistle underfoot. [10]You have indeed defeated Edom and now you are arrogant. Glory in your victory, but stay at home! Why ask for trouble and cause your own downfall and that of Judah also?"

[11]Amaziah, however, would not listen, so Jehoash king of Israel attacked. He and Amaziah king of Judah faced each other at Beth Shemesh in Judah. [12]Judah was routed by Israel, and every man fled to his home. [13]Jehoash king of Israel captured Amaziah king of Judah, the son of Joash, the son of Ahaziah, at Beth Shemesh. Then Jehoash went to Jerusalem and broke down the wall of Jerusalem from the Ephraim Gate to the Corner Gate—a section about six hundred feet long.[c] [14]He took all the gold and silver and all the articles found in the temple of the LORD and in the treasuries of the royal palace. He also took hostages and returned to Samaria.

[15]As for the other events of the reign of Jehoash, what he did and his achievements, including his war against Amaziah king of Judah, are they not written in the book of the annals of the kings of Israel? [16]Jehoash rested with his fathers and was buried in Samaria with the kings of Israel. And Jeroboam his son succeeded him as king.

[17]Amaziah son of Joash king of Judah lived for fifteen years after the death of Jehoash son of Jehoahaz king of Israel. [18]As for the other events of Amaziah's reign, are they not written in the book of the annals of the kings of Judah?

[19]They conspired against him in Jerusalem, and he fled to Lachish, but they sent men after him to Lachish and killed him there. [20]He was brought back by horse and was buried in Jerusalem with his fathers, in the City of David.

[21]Then all the people of Judah took Azariah,[d] who was sixteen years old, and made him king in place of his father Amaziah. [22]He was the one who rebuilt Elath and restored it to Judah after Amaziah rested with his fathers.

Jeroboam II King of Israel

[23]In the fifteenth year of Amaziah son of Joash king of Judah, Jeroboam son of Jehoash king of Israel became king in Samaria, and he reigned forty-one years. [24]He did evil in the eyes of the LORD and did not turn away from any of the sins of Jeroboam son of Nebat, which he had caused Israel to commit. [25]He was the one who restored the boundaries of Israel from Lebo[e] Hamath to the Sea of the Arabah,[f] in accordance with the word of the LORD, the God of Israel, spoken through his servant Jonah son of Amittai, the prophet from Gath Hepher.

[26]The LORD had seen how bitterly every-

[a]*1* Hebrew *Joash*, a variant of *Jehoash*; also in verses 13, 23 and 27 [b]*6* Deut. 24:16 [c]*13* Hebrew *four hundred cubits* (about 180 meters) [d]*21* Also called *Uzziah* [e]*25* Or *from the entrance to* [f]*25* That is, the Dead Sea

one in Israel, whether slave or free, was suffering; there was no one to help them. 27And since the LORD had not said he would blot out the name of Israel from under heaven, he saved them by the hand of Jeroboam son of Jehoash.

28As for the other events of Jeroboam's reign, all he did, and his military achievements, including how he recovered for Israel both Damascus and Hamath, which had belonged to Yaudi,[a] are they not written in the book of the annals of the kings of Israel? 29Jeroboam rested with his fathers, the kings of Israel. And Zechariah his son succeeded him as king.

Azariah King of Judah

15 In the twenty-seventh year of Jeroboam king of Israel, Azariah son of Amaziah king of Judah began to reign. 2He was sixteen years old when he became king, and he reigned in Jerusalem fifty-two years. His mother's name was Jecoliah; she was from Jerusalem. 3He did what was right in the eyes of the LORD, just as his father Amaziah had done. 4The high places, however, were not removed; the people continued to offer sacrifices and burn incense there.

5The LORD afflicted the king with leprosy[b] until the day he died, and he lived in a separate house.[c] Jotham the king's son had charge of the palace and governed the people of the land.

6As for the other events of Azariah's reign, and all he did, are they not written in the book of the annals of the kings of Judah? 7Azariah rested with his fathers and was buried near them in the City of David. And Jotham his son succeeded him as king.

Zechariah King of Israel

8In the thirty-eighth year of Azariah king of Judah, Zechariah son of Jeroboam became king of Israel in Samaria, and he reigned six months. 9He did evil in the eyes of the LORD, as his fathers had done. He did not turn away from the sins of Jeroboam son of Nebat, which he had caused Israel to commit.

10Shallum son of Jabesh conspired against Zechariah. He attacked him in front of the people,[d] assassinated him and succeeded him as king. 11The other events of Zechariah's reign are written in the book of the annals of the kings of Israel. 12So the word of the LORD spoken to Jehu was fulfilled: "Your descendants will sit on the throne of Israel to the fourth generation."[e]

Shallum King of Israel

13Shallum son of Jabesh became king in the thirty-ninth year of Uzziah king of Judah, and he reigned in Samaria one month. 14Then Menahem son of Gadi went from Tirzah up to Samaria. He attacked Shallum son of Jabesh in Samaria, assassinated him and succeeded him as king.

15The other events of Shallum's reign, and the conspiracy he led, are written in the book of the annals of the kings of Israel.

16At that time Menahem, starting out from Tirzah, attacked Tiphsah and everyone in the city and its vicinity, because they refused to open their gates. He sacked Tiphsah and ripped open all the pregnant women.

Menahem King of Israel

17In the thirty-ninth year of Azariah king of Judah, Menahem son of Gadi became king of Israel, and he reigned in Samaria ten years. 18He did evil in the eyes of the LORD. During his entire reign he did not turn away from the sins of Jeroboam son of Nebat, which he had caused Israel to commit.

19Then Pul[f] king of Assyria invaded the land, and Menahem gave him a thousand talents[g] of silver to gain his support and strengthen his own hold on the kingdom. 20Menahem exacted this money from Israel. Every wealthy man had to contribute fifty shekels[h] of silver to be given to the king of Assyria. So the king of Assyria withdrew and stayed in the land no longer.

21As for the other events of Menahem's reign, and all he did, are they not written in the book of the annals of the kings of Israel? 22Menahem rested with his fathers. And Pekahiah his son succeeded him as king.

[a] *28* Or *Judah* [b] *5* The Hebrew word was used for various diseases affecting the skin—not necessarily leprosy. [c] *5* Or *in a house where he was relieved of responsibility* [d] *10* Hebrew; some Septuagint manuscripts *in Ibleam* [e] *12* 2 Kings 10:30 [f] *19* Also called *Tiglath-Pileser* [g] *19* That is, about 37 tons (about 34 metric tons) [h] *20* That is, about 1 1/4 pounds (about 0.6 kilogram)

Pekahiah King of Israel

23In the fiftieth year of Azariah king of
Judah, Pekahiah son of Menahem became
king of Israel in Samaria, and he reigned
two years. 24Pekahiah did evil in the eyes
of the LORD. He did not turn away from the
sins of Jeroboam son of Nebat, which he
had caused Israel to commit. 25One of his
chief officers, Pekah son of Remaliah, con-
spired against him. Taking fifty men of
Gilead with him, he assassinated Pekahi-
ah, along with Argob and Arieh, in the cit-
adel of the royal palace at Samaria. So Pe-
kah killed Pekahiah and succeeded him as
king.
26The other events of Pekahiah's reign,
and all he did, are written in the book of
the annals of the kings of Israel.

Pekah King of Israel

27In the fifty-second year of Azariah
king of Judah, Pekah son of Remaliah be-
came king of Israel in Samaria, and he
reigned twenty years. 28He did evil in the
eyes of the LORD. He did not turn away
from the sins of Jeroboam son of Nebat,
which he had caused Israel to commit.
29In the time of Pekah king of Israel,
Tiglath-Pileser king of Assyria came and
took Ijon, Abel Beth Maacah, Janoah, Ke-
desh and Hazor. He took Gilead and Gali-
lee, including all the land of Naphtali, and
deported the people to Assyria. 30Then
Hoshea son of Elah conspired against Pe-
kah son of Remaliah. He attacked and as-
sassinated him, and then succeeded him
as king in the twentieth year of Jotham
son of Uzziah.
31As for the other events of Pekah's
reign, and all he did, are they not written
in the book of the annals of the kings of
Israel?

Jotham King of Judah

32In the second year of Pekah son of
Remaliah king of Israel, Jotham son of Uz-
ziah king of Judah began to reign. 33He
was twenty-five years old when he be-
came king, and he reigned in Jerusalem
sixteen years. His mother's name was Je-
rusha daughter of Zadok. 34He did what
was right in the eyes of the LORD, just as
his father Uzziah had done. 35The high
places, however, were not removed; the
people continued to offer sacrifices and
burn incense there. Jotham rebuilt the Up-
per Gate of the temple of the LORD.
36As for the other events of Jotham's
reign, and what he did, are they not writ-
ten in the book of the annals of the kings
of Judah? 37(In those days the LORD began
to send Rezin king of Aram and Pekah son
of Remaliah against Judah.) 38Jotham
rested with his fathers and was buried
with them in the City of David, the city of
his father. And Ahaz his son succeeded
him as king.

Ahaz King of Judah

16 In the seventeenth year of Pekah
son of Remaliah, Ahaz son of Jo-
tham king of Judah began to reign. 2Ahaz
was twenty years old when he became
king, and he reigned in Jerusalem sixteen
years. Unlike David his father, he did not
do what was right in the eyes of the LORD
his God. 3He walked in the ways of the
kings of Israel and even sacrificed his son
in[a] the fire, following the detestable ways
of the nations the LORD had driven out be-
fore the Israelites. 4He offered sacrifices
and burned incense at the high places, on
the hilltops and under every spreading
tree.
5Then Rezin king of Aram and Pekah
son of Remaliah king of Israel marched up
to fight against Jerusalem and besieged
Ahaz, but they could not overpower him.
6At that time, Rezin king of Aram recov-
ered Elath for Aram by driving out the
men of Judah. Edomites then moved into
Elath and have lived there to this day.
7Ahaz sent messengers to say to Tig-
lath-Pileser king of Assyria, "I am your
servant and vassal. Come up and save me
out of the hand of the king of Aram and of
the king of Israel, who are attacking me."
8And Ahaz took the silver and gold found
in the temple of the LORD and in the trea-
suries of the royal palace and sent it as a
gift to the king of Assyria. 9The king of As-
syria complied by attacking Damascus
and capturing it. He deported its inhabi-
tants to Kir and put Rezin to death.
10Then King Ahaz went to Damascus to
meet Tiglath-Pileser king of Assyria. He
saw an altar in Damascus and sent to Uri-
ah the priest a sketch of the altar, with de-
tailed plans for its construction. 11So Uri-
ah the priest built an altar in accordance
with all the plans that King Ahaz had sent
from Damascus and finished it before

[a]3 Or *even made his son pass through*

King Ahaz returned. 12When the king
came back from Damascus and saw the al-
tar, he approached it and presented offer-
ings[a] on it. 13He offered up his burnt of-
fering and grain offering, poured out his
drink offering, and sprinkled the blood of
his fellowship offerings[b] on the altar.
14The bronze altar that stood before the
LORD he brought from the front of the tem-
ple—from between the new altar and the
temple of the LORD—and put it on the
north side of the new altar.

15King Ahaz then gave these orders to
Uriah the priest: "On the large new altar,
offer the morning burnt offering and the
evening grain offering, the king's burnt of-
fering and his grain offering, and the
burnt offering of all the people of the land,
and their grain offering and their drink of-
fering. Sprinkle on the altar all the blood
of the burnt offerings and sacrifices. But I
will use the bronze altar for seeking guid-
ance." 16And Uriah the priest did just as
King Ahaz had ordered.

17King Ahaz took away the side panels
and removed the basins from the movable
stands. He removed the Sea from the
bronze bulls that supported it and set it on
a stone base. 18He took away the Sabbath
canopy[c] that had been built at the temple
and removed the royal entryway outside
the temple of the LORD, in deference to the
king of Assyria.

19As for the other events of the reign of
Ahaz, and what he did, are they not writ-
ten in the book of the annals of the kings
of Judah? 20Ahaz rested with his fathers
and was buried with them in the City of
David. And Hezekiah his son succeeded
him as king.

Hoshea Last King of Israel

17 In the twelfth year of Ahaz king of
Judah, Hoshea son of Elah became
king of Israel in Samaria, and he reigned
nine years. 2He did evil in the eyes of the
LORD, but not like the kings of Israel who
preceded him.

3Shalmaneser king of Assyria came up
to attack Hoshea, who had been Shalman-
eser's vassal and had paid him tribute.
4But the king of Assyria discovered that
Hoshea was a traitor, for he had sent en-
voys to So[d] king of Egypt, and he no long-
er paid tribute to the king of Assyria, as he
had done year by year. Therefore Shal-
maneser seized him and put him in pris-
on. 5The king of Assyria invaded the en-
tire land, marched against Samaria and
laid siege to it for three years. 6In the ninth
year of Hoshea, the king of Assyria cap-
tured Samaria and deported the Israelites
to Assyria. He settled them in Halah, in
Gozan on the Habor River and in the
towns of the Medes.

Israel Exiled Because of Sin

7All this took place because the Israel-
ites had sinned against the LORD their God,
who had brought them up out of Egypt
from under the power of Pharaoh king of
Egypt. They worshiped other gods 8and
followed the practices of the nations the
LORD had driven out before them, as well
as the practices that the kings of Israel had
introduced. 9The Israelites secretly did
things against the LORD their God that
were not right. From watchtower to forti-
fied city they built themselves high places
in all their towns. 10They set up sacred
stones and Asherah poles on every high
hill and under every spreading tree. 11At
every high place they burned incense, as
the nations whom the LORD had driven out
before them had done. They did wicked
things that provoked the LORD to anger.
12They worshiped idols, though the LORD
had said, "You shall not do this."[e] 13The
LORD warned Israel and Judah through all
his prophets and seers: "Turn from your
evil ways. Observe my commands and de-
crees, in accordance with the entire Law
that I commanded your fathers to obey
and that I delivered to you through my
servants the prophets."

14But they would not listen and were as
stiff-necked as their fathers, who did not
trust in the LORD their God. 15They reject-
ed his decrees and the covenant he had
made with their fathers and the warnings
he had given them. They followed worth-
less idols and themselves became worth-
less. They imitated the nations around
them although the LORD had ordered
them, "Do not do as they do," and they did
the things the LORD had forbidden them
to do.

16They forsook all the commands of the
LORD their God and made for themselves
two idols cast in the shape of calves, and
an Asherah pole. They bowed down to all
the starry hosts, and they worshiped Baal.

[a] 12 Or *and went up* [b] 13 Traditionally *peace offerings* [c] 18 Or *the dais of his throne* (see Septuagint) [d] 4 Or *to Sais, to the*; *So* is possibly an abbreviation for *Osorkon*. [e] 12 Exodus 20:4, 5

17They sacrificed their sons and daughters in[a] the fire. They practiced divination
and sorcery and sold themselves to do evil
in the eyes of the LORD, provoking him to
anger.
18So the LORD was very angry with Israel
and removed them from his presence.
Only the tribe of Judah was left, 19and
even Judah did not keep the commands of
the LORD their God. They followed the
practices Israel had introduced. 20Therefore the LORD rejected all the people of Israel; he afflicted them and gave them into
the hands of plunderers, until he thrust
them from his presence.
21When he tore Israel away from the
house of David, they made Jeroboam son
of Nebat their king. Jeroboam enticed Israel away from following the LORD and
caused them to commit a great sin. 22The
Israelites persisted in all the sins of Jeroboam and did not turn away from them
23until the LORD removed them from his
presence, as he had warned through all
his servants the prophets. So the people of
Israel were taken from their homeland
into exile in Assyria, and they are still
there.

Samaria Resettled

24The king of Assyria brought people
from Babylon, Cuthah, Avva, Hamath and
Sepharvaim and settled them in the towns
of Samaria to replace the Israelites. They
took over Samaria and lived in its towns.
25When they first lived there, they did not
worship the LORD; so he sent lions among
them and they killed some of the people.
26It was reported to the king of Assyria:
"The people you deported and resettled in
the towns of Samaria do not know what
the god of that country requires. He has
sent lions among them, which are killing
them off, because the people do not know
what he requires."
27Then the king of Assyria gave this order: "Have one of the priests you took captive from Samaria go back to live there
and teach the people what the god of the
land requires." 28So one of the priests who
had been exiled from Samaria came to live
in Bethel and taught them how to worship
the LORD.
29Nevertheless, each national group
made its own gods in the several towns
where they settled, and set them up in the
shrines the people of Samaria had made at
the high places. 30The men from Babylon
made Succoth Benoth, the men from Cuthah made Nergal, and the men from Hamath made Ashima; 31the Avvites made
Nibhaz and Tartak, and the Sepharvites
burned their children in the fire as sacrifices to Adrammelech and Anammelech,
the gods of Sepharvaim. 32They worshiped the LORD, but they also appointed
all sorts of their own people to officiate for
them as priests in the shrines at the high
places. 33They worshiped the LORD, but
they also served their own gods in accordance with the customs of the nations
from which they had been brought.
34To this day they persist in their former practices. They neither worship the
LORD nor adhere to the decrees and ordinances, the laws and commands that the
LORD gave the descendants of Jacob,
whom he named Israel. 35When the LORD
made a covenant with the Israelites, he
commanded them: "Do not worship any
other gods or bow down to them, serve
them or sacrifice to them. 36But the LORD,
who brought you up out of Egypt with
mighty power and outstretched arm, is
the one you must worship. To him you
shall bow down and to him offer sacrifices. 37You must always be careful to
keep the decrees and ordinances, the laws
and commands he wrote for you. Do not
worship other gods. 38Do not forget the
covenant I have made with you, and do
not worship other gods. 39Rather, worship
the LORD your God; it is he who will deliver you from the hand of all your enemies."
40They would not listen, however, but
persisted in their former practices. 41Even
while these people were worshiping the
LORD, they were serving their idols. To this
day their children and grandchildren continue to do as their fathers did.

Hezekiah King of Judah

18 In the third year of Hoshea son of
Elah king of Israel, Hezekiah son of
Ahaz king of Judah began to reign. 2He
was twenty-five years old when he became king, and he reigned in Jerusalem
twenty-nine years. His mother's name
was Abijah[b] daughter of Zechariah. 3He
did what was right in the eyes of the LORD,
just as his father David had done. 4He removed the high places, smashed the sacred stones and cut down the Asherah
poles. He broke into pieces the bronze

[a] 17 Or *They made their sons and daughters pass through*
[b] 2 Hebrew *Abi*, a variant of *Abijah*

snake Moses had made, for up to that time the Israelites had been burning incense to it. (It was called[a] Nehushtan.[b])

5Hezekiah trusted in the LORD, the God of Israel. There was no one like him among all the kings of Judah, either before him or after him. 6He held fast to the LORD and did not cease to follow him; he kept the commands the LORD had given Moses. 7And the LORD was with him; he was successful in whatever he undertook. He rebelled against the king of Assyria and did not serve him. 8From watchtower to fortified city, he defeated the Philistines, as far as Gaza and its territory.

9In King Hezekiah's fourth year, which was the seventh year of Hoshea son of Elah king of Israel, Shalmaneser king of Assyria marched against Samaria and laid siege to it. 10At the end of three years the Assyrians took it. So Samaria was captured in Hezekiah's sixth year, which was the ninth year of Hoshea king of Israel. 11The king of Assyria deported Israel to Assyria and settled them in Halah, in Gozan on the Habor River and in towns of the Medes. 12This happened because they had not obeyed the LORD their God, but had violated his covenant—all that Moses the servant of the LORD commanded. They neither listened to the commands nor carried them out.

13In the fourteenth year of King Hezekiah's reign, Sennacherib king of Assyria attacked all the fortified cities of Judah and captured them. 14So Hezekiah king of Judah sent this message to the king of Assyria at Lachish: "I have done wrong. Withdraw from me, and I will pay whatever you demand of me." The king of Assyria exacted from Hezekiah king of Judah three hundred talents[c] of silver and thirty talents[d] of gold. 15So Hezekiah gave him all the silver that was found in the temple of the LORD and in the treasuries of the royal palace.

16At this time Hezekiah king of Judah stripped off the gold with which he had covered the doors and doorposts of the temple of the LORD, and gave it to the king of Assyria.

Sennacherib Threatens Jerusalem

17The king of Assyria sent his supreme commander, his chief officer and his field commander with a large army, from Lachish to King Hezekiah at Jerusalem. They came up to Jerusalem and stopped at the aqueduct of the Upper Pool, on the road to the Washerman's Field. 18They called for the king; and Eliakim son of Hilkiah the palace administrator, Shebna the secretary, and Joah son of Asaph the recorder went out to them.

19The field commander said to them, "Tell Hezekiah:

> " 'This is what the great king, the king of Assyria, says: On what are you basing this confidence of yours? 20You say you have strategy and military strength—but you speak only empty words. On whom are you depending, that you rebel against me? 21Look now, you are depending on Egypt, that splintered reed of a staff, which pierces a man's hand and wounds him if he leans on it! Such is Pharaoh king of Egypt to all who depend on him. 22And if you say to me, "We are depending on the LORD our God"—isn't he the one whose high places and altars Hezekiah removed, saying to Judah and Jerusalem, "You must worship before this altar in Jerusalem"?
>
> 23" 'Come now, make a bargain with my master, the king of Assyria: I will give you two thousand horses—if you can put riders on them! 24How can you repulse one officer of the least of my master's officials, even though you are depending on Egypt for chariots and horsemen[e]? 25Furthermore, have I come to attack and destroy this place without word from the LORD? The LORD himself told me to march against this country and destroy it.' "

26Then Eliakim son of Hilkiah, and Shebna and Joah said to the field commander, "Please speak to your servants in Aramaic, since we understand it. Don't speak to us in Hebrew in the hearing of the people on the wall."

27But the commander replied, "Was it only to your master and you that my master sent me to say these things, and not to the men sitting on the wall—who, like

[a] 4 Or *He called it* [b] 4 *Nehushtan* sounds like the Hebrew for *bronze* and *snake* and *unclean thing*.
[c] 14 That is, about 11 tons (about 10 metric tons) [d] 14 That is, about 1 ton (about 1 metric ton)
[e] 24 Or *charioteers*

you, will have to eat their own filth and drink their own urine?"

28Then the commander stood and called out in Hebrew: "Hear the word of the great king, the king of Assyria! 29This is what the king says: Do not let Hezekiah deceive you. He cannot deliver you from my hand. 30Do not let Hezekiah persuade you to trust in the LORD when he says, 'The LORD will surely deliver us; this city will not be given into the hand of the king of Assyria.'

31"Do not listen to Hezekiah. This is what the king of Assyria says: Make peace with me and come out to me. Then every one of you will eat from his own vine and fig tree and drink water from his own cistern, 32until I come and take you to a land like your own, a land of grain and new wine, a land of bread and vineyards, a land of olive trees and honey. Choose life and not death!

"Do not listen to Hezekiah, for he is misleading you when he says, 'The LORD will deliver us.' 33Has the god of any nation ever delivered his land from the hand of the king of Assyria? 34Where are the gods of Hamath and Arpad? Where are the gods of Sepharvaim, Hena and Ivvah? Have they rescued Samaria from my hand? 35Who of all the gods of these countries has been able to save his land from me? How then can the LORD deliver Jerusalem from my hand?"

36But the people remained silent and said nothing in reply, because the king had commanded, "Do not answer him."

37Then Eliakim son of Hilkiah the palace administrator, Shebna the secretary and Joah son of Asaph the recorder went to Hezekiah, with their clothes torn, and told him what the field commander had said.

Jerusalem's Deliverance Foretold

19 When King Hezekiah heard this, he tore his clothes and put on sackcloth and went into the temple of the LORD. 2He sent Eliakim the palace administrator, Shebna the secretary and the leading priests, all wearing sackcloth, to the prophet Isaiah son of Amoz. 3They told him, "This is what Hezekiah says: This day is a day of distress and rebuke and disgrace, as when children come to the point of birth and there is no strength to deliver them. 4It may be that the LORD your God will hear all the words of the field commander, whom his master, the king of Assyria, has sent to ridicule the living God, and that he will rebuke him for the words the LORD your God has heard. Therefore pray for the remnant that still survives."

5When King Hezekiah's officials came to Isaiah, 6Isaiah said to them, "Tell your master, 'This is what the LORD says: Do not be afraid of what you have heard—those words with which the underlings of the king of Assyria have blasphemed me. 7Listen! I am going to put such a spirit in him that when he hears a certain report, he will return to his own country, and there I will have him cut down with the sword.' "

8When the field commander heard that the king of Assyria had left Lachish, he withdrew and found the king fighting against Libnah.

9Now Sennacherib received a report that Tirhakah, the Cushite[a] king ⌊of Egypt⌋, was marching out to fight against him. So he again sent messengers to Hezekiah with this word: 10"Say to Hezekiah king of Judah: Do not let the god you depend on deceive you when he says, 'Jerusalem will not be handed over to the king of Assyria.' 11Surely you have heard what the kings of Assyria have done to all the countries, destroying them completely. And will you be delivered? 12Did the gods of the nations that were destroyed by my forefathers deliver them: the gods of Gozan, Haran, Rezeph and the people of Eden who were in Tel Assar? 13Where is the king of Hamath, the king of Arpad, the king of the city of Sepharvaim, or of Hena or Ivvah?"

Hezekiah's Prayer

14Hezekiah received the letter from the messengers and read it. Then he went up to the temple of the LORD and spread it out before the LORD. 15And Hezekiah prayed to the LORD: "O LORD, God of Israel, enthroned between the cherubim, you alone are God over all the kingdoms of the earth. You have made heaven and earth. 16Give ear, O LORD, and hear; open your eyes, O LORD, and see; listen to the words Sennacherib has sent to insult the living God.

17"It is true, O LORD, that the Assyrian kings have laid waste these nations and their lands. 18They have thrown their gods

[a]9 That is, from the upper Nile region

into the fire and destroyed them, for they
were not gods but only wood and stone,
fashioned by men's hands. [19]Now, O LORD
our God, deliver us from his hand, so that
all kingdoms on earth may know that you
alone, O LORD, are God."

Isaiah Prophesies Sennacherib's Fall

[20]Then Isaiah son of Amoz sent a message to Hezekiah: "This is what the LORD,
the God of Israel, says: I have heard your
prayer concerning Sennacherib king of
Assyria. [21]This is the word that the LORD
has spoken against him:

" 'The Virgin Daughter of Zion
despises you and mocks you.
The Daughter of Jerusalem
tosses her head as you flee.
[22]Who is it you have insulted and
blasphemed?
Against whom have you raised your
voice
and lifted your eyes in pride?
Against the Holy One of Israel!
[23]By your messengers
you have heaped insults on the
Lord.
And you have said,
"With my many chariots
I have ascended the heights of the
mountains,
the utmost heights of Lebanon.
I have cut down its tallest cedars,
the choicest of its pines.
I have reached its remotest parts,
the finest of its forests.
[24]I have dug wells in foreign lands
and drunk the water there.
With the soles of my feet
I have dried up all the streams of
Egypt."

[25]" 'Have you not heard?
Long ago I ordained it.
In days of old I planned it;
now I have brought it to pass,
that you have turned fortified cities
into piles of stone.
[26]Their people, drained of power,
are dismayed and put to shame.
They are like plants in the field,
like tender green shoots,
like grass sprouting on the roof,
scorched before it grows up.

[27]" 'But I know where you stay
and when you come and go
and how you rage against me.
[28]Because you rage against me
and your insolence has reached my
ears,
I will put my hook in your nose
and my bit in your mouth,
and I will make you return
by the way you came.'

[29]"This will be the sign for you,
O Hezekiah:

"This year you will eat what grows by
itself,
and the second year what springs
from that.
But in the third year sow and reap,
plant vineyards and eat their fruit.
[30]Once more a remnant of the house of
Judah
will take root below and bear fruit
above.
[31]For out of Jerusalem will come a
remnant,
and out of Mount Zion a band of
survivors.

The zeal of the LORD Almighty will accomplish this.

[32]"Therefore this is what the LORD says
concerning the king of Assyria:

"He will not enter this city
or shoot an arrow here.
He will not come before it with shield
or build a siege ramp against it.
[33]By the way that he came he will
return;
he will not enter this city,
declares the LORD.
[34]I will defend this city and save it,
for my sake and for the sake of
David my servant."

[35]That night the angel of the LORD went
out and put to death a hundred and
eighty-five thousand men in the Assyrian
camp. When the people got up the next
morning—there were all the dead bodies!
[36]So Sennacherib king of Assyria broke
camp and withdrew. He returned to Nineveh and stayed there.

[37]One day, while he was worshiping in
the temple of his god Nisroch, his sons
Adrammelech and Sharezer cut him down
with the sword, and they escaped to the
land of Ararat. And Esarhaddon his son
succeeded him as king.

Hezekiah's Illness

20 In those days Hezekiah became ill
and was at the point of death. The
prophet Isaiah son of Amoz went to him

and said, "This is what the LORD says: Put
your house in order, because you are go-
ing to die; you will not recover."
2Hezekiah turned his face to the wall
and prayed to the LORD, 3"Remember,
O LORD, how I have walked before you
faithfully and with wholehearted devotion
and have done what is good in your eyes."
And Hezekiah wept bitterly.
4Before Isaiah had left the middle court,
the word of the LORD came to him: 5"Go
back and tell Hezekiah, the leader of my
people, 'This is what the LORD, the God of
your father David, says: I have heard your
prayer and seen your tears; I will heal you.
On the third day from now you will go up
to the temple of the LORD. 6I will add fif-
teen years to your life. And I will deliver

VERSE FOR THE DAY: 2 Kings 20:3 | AUTHOR: Elizabeth Cody Newenhuyse | PASSAGE FOR THE DAY: 2 Kings 20:3

Sticking It Out

There is woven into the fabric of marriage a sense of something *ongoing*. One woman, one man, together for a lifetime. They don't have to be "communicating" or having fun or constantly setting goals. They do have to be together—and intend to stay that way. This is faithfulness to each other and to God.

Too many people think marriage should be fun, or fulfilling, or entertaining. Then they get married and find out it's not always like that. So they keep searching and find even more frustration with another marriage partner.

As I read Scripture, I don't see teachings on happiness as a first principle. Joy, yes—the kind of joy that flows from obedience, from service, from glimpses of the holy. God wants us to do that which glorifies him—to be faithful, to keep his commandments, to seek first his Kingdom. Sticking it out comes first in God's eyes—through the times when you're secretly thinking, "This is *life*? Why am I married to this person, anyway?"

Sticking it out means being faithful, and out of faithfulness there is peace. I see that peace in couples who have been married years and years. These are the couples who have come to terms with their choices, they accept each other wholly, and somewhere along the line they embraced sticking it out as a first principle.

MARRIAGE BUILDERS

♦ *What are the challenges you face as a Christian as you try to be faithful to God?*
♦ *What challenges are part of faithfulness in marriage?*

Additional Scripture Readings
Galatians 5:22–23; 1 Samuel 12:24

Go to page 390 for your next devotional reading.

you and this city from the hand of the king
of Assyria. I will defend this city for my
sake and for the sake of my servant Da-
vid.' "
7Then Isaiah said, "Prepare a poultice of
figs." They did so and applied it to the
boil, and he recovered.
8Hezekiah had asked Isaiah, "What will
be the sign that the LORD will heal me and
that I will go up to the temple of the LORD
on the third day from now?"
9Isaiah answered, "This is the LORD's
sign to you that the LORD will do what he
has promised: Shall the shadow go for-
ward ten steps, or shall it go back ten
steps?"
10"It is a simple matter for the shadow
to go forward ten steps," said Hezekiah.
"Rather, have it go back ten steps."
11Then the prophet Isaiah called upon
the LORD, and the LORD made the shadow
go back the ten steps it had gone down on
the stairway of Ahaz.

Envoys From Babylon

12At that time Merodach-Baladan son of
Baladan king of Babylon sent Hezekiah
letters and a gift, because he had heard of
Hezekiah's illness. 13Hezekiah received
the messengers and showed them all that
was in his storehouses—the silver, the
gold, the spices and the fine oil—his ar-
mory and everything found among his
treasures. There was nothing in his palace
or in all his kingdom that Hezekiah did
not show them.
14Then Isaiah the prophet went to King
Hezekiah and asked, "What did those
men say, and where did they come from?"
"From a distant land," Hezekiah re-
plied. "They came from Babylon."
15The prophet asked, "What did they
see in your palace?"
"They saw everything in my palace,"
Hezekiah said. "There is nothing among
my treasures that I did not show them."
16Then Isaiah said to Hezekiah, "Hear
the word of the LORD: 17The time will sure-
ly come when everything in your palace,
and all that your fathers have stored up
until this day, will be carried off to Bab-
ylon. Nothing will be left, says the LORD.
18And some of your descendants, your
own flesh and blood, that will be born to
you, will be taken away, and they will be-
come eunuchs in the palace of the king of
Babylon."
19"The word of the LORD you have spo-
ken is good," Hezekiah replied. For he
thought, "Will there not be peace and se-
curity in my lifetime?"
20As for the other events of Hezekiah's
reign, all his achievements and how he
made the pool and the tunnel by which he
brought water into the city, are they not
written in the book of the annals of the
kings of Judah? 21Hezekiah rested with
his fathers. And Manasseh his son suc-
ceeded him as king.

Manasseh King of Judah

21 Manasseh was twelve years old
when he became king, and he
reigned in Jerusalem fifty-five years. His
mother's name was Hephzibah. 2He did
evil in the eyes of the LORD, following the
detestable practices of the nations the
LORD had driven out before the Israelites.
3He rebuilt the high places his father Hez-
ekiah had destroyed; he also erected altars
to Baal and made an Asherah pole, as
Ahab king of Israel had done. He bowed
down to all the starry hosts and wor-
shiped them. 4He built altars in the temple
of the LORD, of which the LORD had said,
"In Jerusalem I will put my Name." 5In
both courts of the temple of the LORD, he
built altars to all the starry hosts. 6He sac-
rificed his own son in[a] the fire, practiced
sorcery and divination, and consulted me-
diums and spiritists. He did much evil in
the eyes of the LORD, provoking him to an-
ger.
7He took the carved Asherah pole he
had made and put it in the temple, of
which the LORD had said to David and to
his son Solomon, "In this temple and in
Jerusalem, which I have chosen out of all
the tribes of Israel, I will put my Name for-
ever. 8I will not again make the feet of the
Israelites wander from the land I gave
their forefathers, if only they will be care-
ful to do everything I commanded them
and will keep the whole Law that my ser-
vant Moses gave them." 9But the people
did not listen. Manasseh led them astray,
so that they did more evil than the nations
the LORD had destroyed before the Israel-
ites.
10The LORD said through his servants
the prophets: 11"Manasseh king of Judah
has committed these detestable sins. He
has done more evil than the Amorites who

[a]6 Or *He made his own son pass through*

preceded him and has led Judah into sin
with his idols. 12Therefore this is what the
LORD, the God of Israel, says: I am going to
bring such disaster on Jerusalem and Ju-
dah that the ears of everyone who hears of
it will tingle. 13I will stretch out over Jeru-
salem the measuring line used against Sa-
maria and the plumb line used against the
house of Ahab. I will wipe out Jerusalem
as one wipes a dish, wiping it and turning
it upside down. 14I will forsake the rem-
nant of my inheritance and hand them
over to their enemies. They will be looted
and plundered by all their foes, 15because
they have done evil in my eyes and have
provoked me to anger from the day their
forefathers came out of Egypt until this
day."

16Moreover, Manasseh also shed so
much innocent blood that he filled Jerusa-
lem from end to end—besides the sin that
he had caused Judah to commit, so that
they did evil in the eyes of the LORD.

17As for the other events of Manasseh's
reign, and all he did, including the sin he
committed, are they not written in the
book of the annals of the kings of Judah?
18Manasseh rested with his fathers and
was buried in his palace garden, the gar-
den of Uzza. And Amon his son succeed-
ed him as king.

Amon King of Judah

19Amon was twenty-two years old when
he became king, and he reigned in Jerusa-
lem two years. His mother's name was
Meshullemeth daughter of Haruz; she was
from Jotbah. 20He did evil in the eyes of
the LORD, as his father Manasseh had
done. 21He walked in all the ways of his
father; he worshiped the idols his father
had worshiped, and bowed down to them.
22He forsook the LORD, the God of his fa-
thers, and did not walk in the way of the
LORD.

23Amon's officials conspired against
him and assassinated the king in his pal-
ace. 24Then the people of the land killed
all who had plotted against King Amon,
and they made Josiah his son king in his
place.

25As for the other events of Amon's
reign, and what he did, are they not writ-
ten in the book of the annals of the kings
of Judah? 26He was buried in his grave in
the garden of Uzza. And Josiah his son
succeeded him as king.

The Book of the Law Found

22 Josiah was eight years old when he
became king, and he reigned in Je-
rusalem thirty-one years. His mother's
name was Jedidah daughter of Adaiah;
she was from Bozkath. 2He did what was
right in the eyes of the LORD and walked in
all the ways of his father David, not turn-
ing aside to the right or to the left.

3In the eighteenth year of his reign,
King Josiah sent the secretary, Shaphan
son of Azaliah, the son of Meshullam, to
the temple of the LORD. He said: 4"Go up
to Hilkiah the high priest and have him get
ready the money that has been brought
into the temple of the LORD, which the
doorkeepers have collected from the peo-
ple. 5Have them entrust it to the men ap-
pointed to supervise the work on the tem-
ple. And have these men pay the workers
who repair the temple of the LORD— 6the
carpenters, the builders and the masons.
Also have them purchase timber and
dressed stone to repair the temple. 7But
they need not account for the money en-
trusted to them, because they are acting
faithfully."

8Hilkiah the high priest said to Shaphan
the secretary, "I have found the Book of
the Law in the temple of the LORD." He
gave it to Shaphan, who read it. 9Then
Shaphan the secretary went to the king
and reported to him: "Your officials have
paid out the money that was in the temple
of the LORD and have entrusted it to the
workers and supervisors at the temple."
10Then Shaphan the secretary informed
the king, "Hilkiah the priest has given me
a book." And Shaphan read from it in the
presence of the king.

11When the king heard the words of the
Book of the Law, he tore his robes. 12He
gave these orders to Hilkiah the priest,
Ahikam son of Shaphan, Acbor son of Mi-
caiah, Shaphan the secretary and Asaiah
the king's attendant: 13"Go and inquire of
the LORD for me and for the people and for
all Judah about what is written in this
book that has been found. Great is the
LORD's anger that burns against us be-
cause our fathers have not obeyed the
words of this book; they have not acted in
accordance with all that is written there
concerning us."

14Hilkiah the priest, Ahikam, Acbor,
Shaphan and Asaiah went to speak to the
prophetess Huldah, who was the wife of
Shallum son of Tikvah, the son of Harhas,

keeper of the wardrobe. She lived in Jerusalem, in the Second District.

15She said to them, "This is what the LORD, the God of Israel, says: Tell the man who sent you to me, 16'This is what the LORD says: I am going to bring disaster on this place and its people, according to everything written in the book the king of Judah has read. 17Because they have forsaken me and burned incense to other gods and provoked me to anger by all the idols their hands have made,[a] my anger will burn against this place and will not be quenched.' 18Tell the king of Judah, who

[a]17 Or *by everything they have done*

VERSE FOR THE DAY: 2 Kings 22:1–2

AUTHOR: Leslie Parrott

PASSAGE FOR THE DAY: 2 Kings 21:19—22:2

Unfinished Business

Everyone, knowingly or not, marries with the hope that their mate and their marriage will heal past wounds. That's the unfinished business we bring into marriage. Many of us carry wounds from childhood. And sometimes, as in my case, the wounds come later in life.

Ever since my dad left my mom, I've recognized my heightened need for trust. I watched my father decide that his marriage was no longer worth the investment. I admit that sometimes I fear the same thing could happen to me. In light of the unfinished business I brought into my marriage, I long for certainty. I'm tempted to wonder if I'm "good enough" to prevent my marriage from following the same course as my parents'.

There are no quick fixes for the unfinished business we inherit from our parents. But my husband, Les, has given me time—even when it requires sacrifices on his part. He's allowed me time to heal, and it has restored my ability to trust.

I now see that my father's decision to leave Mom didn't make me heir to the disease of unfaithfulness. Their crisis simply brought me face-to-face with the world's oldest disease: sin. It revealed the hidden crevices of my marriage and gave me courage to face my own unfinished business.

MARRIAGE BUILDERS

♦ *Have you identified any unfinished business you inherited from your parents or other relatives?*

♦ *How can you help each other become strong in that area of weakness?*

Additional Scripture Readings
Ezekiel 36:24–28; Hebrews 12:1–13

Go to page 414 for your next devotional reading.

sent you to inquire of the LORD, 'This is what the LORD, the God of Israel, says concerning the words you heard: 19Because your heart was responsive and you humbled yourself before the LORD when you heard what I have spoken against this place and its people, that they would become accursed and laid waste, and because you tore your robes and wept in my presence, I have heard you, declares the LORD. 20Therefore I will gather you to your fathers, and you will be buried in peace. Your eyes will not see all the disaster I am going to bring on this place.' "

So they took her answer back to the king.

Josiah Renews the Covenant

23 Then the king called together all the elders of Judah and Jerusalem. 2He went up to the temple of the LORD with the men of Judah, the people of Jerusalem, the priests and the prophets—all the people from the least to the greatest. He read in their hearing all the words of the Book of the Covenant, which had been found in the temple of the LORD. 3The king stood by the pillar and renewed the covenant in the presence of the LORD—to follow the LORD and keep his commands, regulations and decrees with all his heart and all his soul, thus confirming the words of the covenant written in this book. Then all the people pledged themselves to the covenant.

4The king ordered Hilkiah the high priest, the priests next in rank and the doorkeepers to remove from the temple of the LORD all the articles made for Baal and Asherah and all the starry hosts. He burned them outside Jerusalem in the fields of the Kidron Valley and took the ashes to Bethel. 5He did away with the pagan priests appointed by the kings of Judah to burn incense on the high places of the towns of Judah and on those around Jerusalem—those who burned incense to Baal, to the sun and moon, to the constellations and to all the starry hosts. 6He took the Asherah pole from the temple of the LORD to the Kidron Valley outside Jerusalem and burned it there. He ground it to powder and scattered the dust over the graves of the common people. 7He also tore down the quarters of the male shrine prostitutes, which were in the temple of the LORD and where women did weaving for Asherah.

8Josiah brought all the priests from the towns of Judah and desecrated the high places, from Geba to Beersheba, where the priests had burned incense. He broke down the shrines[a] at the gates—at the entrance to the Gate of Joshua, the city governor, which is on the left of the city gate. 9Although the priests of the high places did not serve at the altar of the LORD in Jerusalem, they ate unleavened bread with their fellow priests.

10He desecrated Topheth, which was in the Valley of Ben Hinnom, so no one could use it to sacrifice his son or daughter in[b] the fire to Molech. 11He removed from the entrance to the temple of the LORD the horses that the kings of Judah had dedicated to the sun. They were in the court near the room of an official named Nathan-Melech. Josiah then burned the chariots dedicated to the sun.

12He pulled down the altars the kings of Judah had erected on the roof near the upper room of Ahaz, and the altars Manasseh had built in the two courts of the temple of the LORD. He removed them from there, smashed them to pieces and threw the rubble into the Kidron Valley. 13The king also desecrated the high places that were east of Jerusalem on the south of the Hill of Corruption—the ones Solomon king of Israel had built for Ashtoreth the vile goddess of the Sidonians, for Chemosh the vile god of Moab, and for Molech[c] the detestable god of the people of Ammon. 14Josiah smashed the sacred stones and cut down the Asherah poles and covered the sites with human bones.

15Even the altar at Bethel, the high place made by Jeroboam son of Nebat, who had caused Israel to sin—even that altar and high place he demolished. He burned the high place and ground it to powder, and burned the Asherah pole also. 16Then Josiah looked around, and when he saw the tombs that were there on the hillside, he had the bones removed from them and burned on the altar to defile it, in accordance with the word of the LORD proclaimed by the man of God who foretold these things.

17The king asked, "What is that tombstone I see?"

The men of the city said, "It marks the tomb of the man of God who came from

[a] 8 Or *high places* [b] 10 Or *to make his son or daughter pass through* [c] 13 Hebrew *Milcom*

Judah and pronounced against the altar of Bethel the very things you have done to it."

18"Leave it alone," he said. "Don't let anyone disturb his bones." So they spared his bones and those of the prophet who had come from Samaria.

19Just as he had done at Bethel, Josiah removed and defiled all the shrines at the high places that the kings of Israel had built in the towns of Samaria that had provoked the LORD to anger. 20Josiah slaughtered all the priests of those high places on the altars and burned human bones on them. Then he went back to Jerusalem.

21The king gave this order to all the people: "Celebrate the Passover to the LORD your God, as it is written in this Book of the Covenant." 22Not since the days of the judges who led Israel, nor throughout the days of the kings of Israel and the kings of Judah, had any such Passover been observed. 23But in the eighteenth year of King Josiah, this Passover was celebrated to the LORD in Jerusalem.

24Furthermore, Josiah got rid of the mediums and spiritists, the household gods, the idols and all the other detestable things seen in Judah and Jerusalem. This he did to fulfill the requirements of the law written in the book that Hilkiah the priest had discovered in the temple of the LORD. 25Neither before nor after Josiah was there a king like him who turned to the LORD as he did—with all his heart and with all his soul and with all his strength, in accordance with all the Law of Moses.

26Nevertheless, the LORD did not turn away from the heat of his fierce anger, which burned against Judah because of all that Manasseh had done to provoke him to anger. 27So the LORD said, "I will remove Judah also from my presence as I removed Israel, and I will reject Jerusalem, the city I chose, and this temple, about which I said, 'There shall my Name be.'[a]"

28As for the other events of Josiah's reign, and all he did, are they not written in the book of the annals of the kings of Judah?

29While Josiah was king, Pharaoh Neco king of Egypt went up to the Euphrates River to help the king of Assyria. King Josiah marched out to meet him in battle, but Neco faced him and killed him at Megiddo. 30Josiah's servants brought his body in a chariot from Megiddo to Jerusalem and buried him in his own tomb. And the people of the land took Jehoahaz son of Josiah and anointed him and made him king in place of his father.

Jehoahaz King of Judah

31Jehoahaz was twenty-three years old when he became king, and he reigned in Jerusalem three months. His mother's name was Hamutal daughter of Jeremiah; she was from Libnah. 32He did evil in the eyes of the LORD, just as his fathers had done. 33Pharaoh Neco put him in chains at Riblah in the land of Hamath[b] so that he might not reign in Jerusalem, and he imposed on Judah a levy of a hundred talents[c] of silver and a talent[d] of gold. 34Pharaoh Neco made Eliakim son of Josiah king in place of his father Josiah and changed Eliakim's name to Jehoiakim. But he took Jehoahaz and carried him off to Egypt, and there he died. 35Jehoiakim paid Pharaoh Neco the silver and gold he demanded. In order to do so, he taxed the land and exacted the silver and gold from the people of the land according to their assessments.

Jehoiakim King of Judah

36Jehoiakim was twenty-five years old when he became king, and he reigned in Jerusalem eleven years. His mother's name was Zebidah daughter of Pedaiah; she was from Rumah. 37And he did evil in the eyes of the LORD, just as his fathers had done.

24 During Jehoiakim's reign, Nebuchadnezzar king of Babylon invaded the land, and Jehoiakim became his vassal for three years. But then he changed his mind and rebelled against Nebuchadnezzar. 2The LORD sent Babylonian,[e] Aramean, Moabite and Ammonite raiders against him. He sent them to destroy Judah, in accordance with the word of the LORD proclaimed by his servants the prophets. 3Surely these things happened to Judah according to the LORD's command, in order to remove them from his presence because of the sins of Manasseh and all he had done, 4including the shedding of innocent blood. For he had filled

[a]27 1 Kings 8:29 [b]33 Hebrew; Septuagint (see also 2 Chron. 36:3) *Neco at Riblah in Hamath removed him* [c]33 That is, about 3 3/4 tons (about 3.4 metric tons) [d]33 That is, about 75 pounds (about 34 kilograms) [e]2 Or *Chaldean*

Jerusalem with innocent blood, and the LORD was not willing to forgive.

5As for the other events of Jehoiakim's reign, and all he did, are they not written in the book of the annals of the kings of Judah? 6Jehoiakim rested with his fathers. And Jehoiachin his son succeeded him as king.

7The king of Egypt did not march out from his own country again, because the king of Babylon had taken all his territory, from the Wadi of Egypt to the Euphrates River.

Jehoiachin King of Judah

8Jehoiachin was eighteen years old when he became king, and he reigned in Jerusalem three months. His mother's name was Nehushta daughter of Elnathan; she was from Jerusalem. 9He did evil in the eyes of the LORD, just as his father had done.

10At that time the officers of Nebuchadnezzar king of Babylon advanced on Jerusalem and laid siege to it, 11and Nebuchadnezzar himself came up to the city while his officers were besieging it. 12Jehoiachin king of Judah, his mother, his attendants, his nobles and his officials all surrendered to him.

In the eighth year of the reign of the king of Babylon, he took Jehoiachin prisoner. 13As the LORD had declared, Nebuchadnezzar removed all the treasures from the temple of the LORD and from the royal palace, and took away all the gold articles that Solomon king of Israel had made for the temple of the LORD. 14He carried into exile all Jerusalem: all the officers and fighting men, and all the craftsmen and artisans—a total of ten thousand. Only the poorest people of the land were left.

15Nebuchadnezzar took Jehoiachin captive to Babylon. He also took from Jerusalem to Babylon the king's mother, his wives, his officials and the leading men of the land. 16The king of Babylon also deported to Babylon the entire force of seven thousand fighting men, strong and fit for war, and a thousand craftsmen and artisans. 17He made Mattaniah, Jehoiachin's uncle, king in his place and changed his name to Zedekiah.

Zedekiah King of Judah

18Zedekiah was twenty-one years old when he became king, and he reigned in Jerusalem eleven years. His mother's name was Hamutal daughter of Jeremiah; she was from Libnah. 19He did evil in the eyes of the LORD, just as Jehoiakim had done. 20It was because of the LORD's anger that all this happened to Jerusalem and Judah, and in the end he thrust them from his presence.

The Fall of Jerusalem

Now Zedekiah rebelled against the king of Babylon.

25 So in the ninth year of Zedekiah's reign, on the tenth day of the tenth month, Nebuchadnezzar king of Babylon marched against Jerusalem with his whole army. He encamped outside the city and built siege works all around it. 2The city was kept under siege until the eleventh year of King Zedekiah. 3By the ninth day of the ⌊fourth⌋[a] month the famine in the city had become so severe that there was no food for the people to eat. 4Then the city wall was broken through, and the whole army fled at night through the gate between the two walls near the king's garden, though the Babylonians[b] were surrounding the city. They fled toward the Arabah,[c] 5but the Babylonian[d] army pursued the king and overtook him in the plains of Jericho. All his soldiers were separated from him and scattered, 6and he was captured. He was taken to the king of Babylon at Riblah, where sentence was pronounced on him. 7They killed the sons of Zedekiah before his eyes. Then they put out his eyes, bound him with bronze shackles and took him to Babylon.

8On the seventh day of the fifth month, in the nineteenth year of Nebuchadnezzar king of Babylon, Nebuzaradan commander of the imperial guard, an official of the king of Babylon, came to Jerusalem. 9He set fire to the temple of the LORD, the royal palace and all the houses of Jerusalem. Every important building he burned down. 10The whole Babylonian army, under the commander of the imperial guard, broke down the walls around Jerusalem. 11Nebuzaradan the commander of the guard carried into exile the people who remained in the city, along with the rest of

[a]3 See Jer. 52:6. [b]4 Or *Chaldeans*; also in verses 13, 25 and 26 [c]4 Or *the Jordan Valley* [d]5 Or *Chaldean*; also in verses 10 and 24

the populace and those who had gone over to the king of Babylon. 12But the commander left behind some of the poorest people of the land to work the vineyards and fields.

13The Babylonians broke up the bronze pillars, the movable stands and the bronze Sea that were at the temple of the LORD and they carried the bronze to Babylon. 14They also took away the pots, shovels, wick trimmers, dishes and all the bronze articles used in the temple service. 15The commander of the imperial guard took away the censers and sprinkling bowls—all that were made of pure gold or silver.

16The bronze from the two pillars, the Sea and the movable stands, which Solomon had made for the temple of the LORD, was more than could be weighed. 17Each pillar was twenty-seven feet[a] high. The bronze capital on top of one pillar was four and a half feet[b] high and was decorated with a network and pomegranates of bronze all around. The other pillar, with its network, was similar.

18The commander of the guard took as prisoners Seraiah the chief priest, Zephaniah the priest next in rank and the three doorkeepers. 19Of those still in the city, he took the officer in charge of the fighting men and five royal advisers. He also took the secretary who was chief officer in charge of conscripting the people of the land and sixty of his men who were found in the city. 20Nebuzaradan the commander took them all and brought them to the king of Babylon at Riblah. 21There at Riblah, in the land of Hamath, the king had them executed.

So Judah went into captivity, away from her land.

22Nebuchadnezzar king of Babylon appointed Gedaliah son of Ahikam, the son of Shaphan, to be over the people he had left behind in Judah. 23When all the army officers and their men heard that the king of Babylon had appointed Gedaliah as governor, they came to Gedaliah at Mizpah—Ishmael son of Nethaniah, Johanan son of Kareah, Seraiah son of Tanhumeth the Netophathite, Jaazaniah the son of the Maacathite, and their men. 24Gedaliah took an oath to reassure them and their men. "Do not be afraid of the Babylonian officials," he said. "Settle down in the land and serve the king of Babylon, and it will go well with you."

25In the seventh month, however, Ishmael son of Nethaniah, the son of Elishama, who was of royal blood, came with ten men and assassinated Gedaliah and also the men of Judah and the Babylonians who were with him at Mizpah. 26At this, all the people from the least to the greatest, together with the army officers, fled to Egypt for fear of the Babylonians.

Jehoiachin Released

27In the thirty-seventh year of the exile of Jehoiachin king of Judah, in the year Evil-Merodach[c] became king of Babylon, he released Jehoiachin from prison on the twenty-seventh day of the twelfth month. 28He spoke kindly to him and gave him a seat of honor higher than those of the other kings who were with him in Babylon. 29So Jehoiachin put aside his prison clothes and for the rest of his life ate regularly at the king's table. 30Day by day the king gave Jehoiachin a regular allowance as long as he lived.

[a] *17* Hebrew *eighteen cubits* (about 8.1 meters) [b] *17* Hebrew *three cubits* (about 1.3 meters)
[c] *27* Also called *Amel-Marduk*

THIS book, after listing the genealogies of God's people from Adam to David, describes in great detail how David conducts his administrative, military and religious affairs. Note David's desire for the true worship of God, shown by organizing the priests and Levites and by making extensive plans for building the temple. As you read this book, think about the importance of worshiping the Lord and the priority in your life that such worship deserves.

1 CHRONICLES

Historical Records From Adam to Abraham

To Noah's Sons

1 Adam, Seth, Enosh, 2Kenan, Mahalalel, Jared, 3Enoch, Methuselah, Lamech, Noah.

4The sons of Noah:[a]
Shem, Ham and Japheth.

The Japhethites

5The sons[b] of Japheth:
Gomer, Magog, Madai, Javan, Tubal, Meshech and Tiras.
6The sons of Gomer:
Ashkenaz, Riphath[c] and Togarmah.
7The sons of Javan:
Elishah, Tarshish, the Kittim and the Rodanim.

The Hamites

8The sons of Ham:
Cush, Mizraim,[d] Put and Canaan.
9The sons of Cush:

[a]4 Septuagint; Hebrew does not have *The sons of Noah:* [b]5 *Sons* may mean *descendants* or *successors* or *nations*; also in verses 6-10, 17 and 20. [c]6 Many Hebrew manuscripts and Vulgate (see also Septuagint and Gen. 10:3); most Hebrew manuscripts *Diphath* [d]8 That is, Egypt; also in verse 11

Seba, Havilah, Sabta, Raamah and
Sabteca.
The sons of Raamah:
Sheba and Dedan.
10Cush was the father[a] of
Nimrod, who grew to be a mighty
warrior on earth.
11Mizraim was the father of
the Ludites, Anamites, Lehabites,
Naphtuhites, 12Pathrusites, Caslu-
hites (from whom the Philistines
came) and Caphtorites.
13Canaan was the father of
Sidon his firstborn,[b] and of the
Hittites, 14Jebusites, Amorites,
Girgashites, 15Hivites, Arkites, Si-
nites, 16Arvadites, Zemarites and
Hamathites.

The Semites

17The sons of Shem:
Elam, Asshur, Arphaxad, Lud and
Aram.
The sons of Aram[c]:
Uz, Hul, Gether and Meshech.
18Arphaxad was the father of Shelah,
and Shelah the father of Eber.
19Two sons were born to Eber:
One was named Peleg,[d] because
in his time the earth was divided;
his brother was named Joktan.
20Joktan was the father of
Almodad, Sheleph, Hazarmaveth,
Jerah, 21Hadoram, Uzal, Diklah,
22Obal,[e] Abimael, Sheba, 23Ophir,
Havilah and Jobab. All these were
sons of Joktan.

24Shem, Arphaxad,[f] Shelah,
25Eber, Peleg, Reu,
26Serug, Nahor, Terah
27and Abram (that is, Abraham).

The Family of Abraham

28The sons of Abraham:
Isaac and Ishmael.

Descendants of Hagar

29These were their descendants:
Nebaioth the firstborn of Ishmael,
Kedar, Adbeel, Mibsam, 30Mish-
ma, Dumah, Massa, Hadad, Tema,
31Jetur, Naphish and Kedemah.
These were the sons of Ishmael.

Descendants of Keturah

32The sons born to Keturah, Abra-
ham's concubine:
Zimran, Jokshan, Medan, Midian,
Ishbak and Shuah.
The sons of Jokshan:
Sheba and Dedan.
33The sons of Midian:
Ephah, Epher, Hanoch, Abida and
Eldaah.
All these were descendants of Ketu-
rah.

Descendants of Sarah

34Abraham was the father of Isaac.
The sons of Isaac:
Esau and Israel.

Esau's Sons

35The sons of Esau:
Eliphaz, Reuel, Jeush, Jalam and
Korah.
36The sons of Eliphaz:
Teman, Omar, Zepho,[g] Gatam
and Kenaz;
by Timna: Amalek.[h]
37The sons of Reuel:
Nahath, Zerah, Shammah and
Mizzah.

The People of Seir in Edom

38The sons of Seir:
Lotan, Shobal, Zibeon, Anah, Di-
shon, Ezer and Dishan.
39The sons of Lotan:
Hori and Homam. Timna was Lo-
tan's sister.
40The sons of Shobal:
Alvan,[i] Manahath, Ebal, Shepho
and Onam.
The sons of Zibeon:
Aiah and Anah.
41The son of Anah:
Dishon.
The sons of Dishon:

[a] *10 Father* may mean *ancestor* or *predecessor* or *founder*; also in verses 11, 13, 18 and 20. [b] *13* Or *of the Sidonians, the foremost* [c] *17* One Hebrew manuscript and some Septuagint manuscripts (see also Gen. 10:23); most Hebrew manuscripts do not have this line. [d] *19 Peleg* means *division.* [e] *22* Some Hebrew manuscripts and Syriac (see also Gen. 10:28); most Hebrew manuscripts *Ebal* [f] *24* Hebrew; some Septuagint manuscripts *Arphaxad, Cainan* (see also note at Gen. 11:10) [g] *36* Many Hebrew manuscripts, some Septuagint manuscripts and Syriac (see also Gen. 36:11); most Hebrew manuscripts *Zephi* [h] *36* Some Septuagint manuscripts (see also Gen. 36:12); Hebrew *Gatam, Kenaz, Timna and Amalek* [i] *40* Many Hebrew manuscripts and some Septuagint manuscripts (see also Gen. 36:23); most Hebrew manuscripts *Alian*

Hemdan,[a] Eshban, Ithran and
Keran.
[42]The sons of Ezer:
Bilhan, Zaavan and Akan.[b]
The sons of Dishan[c]:
Uz and Aran.

The Rulers of Edom

[43]These were the kings who reigned in
Edom before any Israelite king
reigned[d]:
Bela son of Beor, whose city was
named Dinhabah.
[44]When Bela died, Jobab son of Zerah
from Bozrah succeeded him as
king.
[45]When Jobab died, Husham from the
land of the Temanites succeeded
him as king.
[46]When Husham died, Hadad son of
Bedad, who defeated Midian in
the country of Moab, succeeded
him as king. His city was named
Avith.
[47]When Hadad died, Samlah from
Masrekah succeeded him as king.
[48]When Samlah died, Shaul from Re-
hoboth on the river[e] succeeded
him as king.
[49]When Shaul died, Baal-Hanan son of
Acbor succeeded him as king.
[50]When Baal-Hanan died, Hadad suc-
ceeded him as king. His city was
named Pau,[f] and his wife's name
was Mehetabel daughter of Ma-
tred, the daughter of Me-Zahab.
[51]Hadad also died.

The chiefs of Edom were:
Timna, Alvah, Jetheth, [52]Oholiba-
mah, Elah, Pinon, [53]Kenaz, Te-
man, Mibzar, [54]Magdiel and Iram.
These were the chiefs of Edom.

Israel's Sons

2 These were the sons of Israel:
Reuben, Simeon, Levi, Judah, Is-
sachar, Zebulun, [2]Dan, Joseph,
Benjamin, Naphtali, Gad and
Asher.

Judah

To Hezron's Sons

[3]The sons of Judah:
Er, Onan and Shelah. These three
were born to him by a Canaanite
woman, the daughter of Shua. Er,
Judah's firstborn, was wicked in
the LORD's sight; so the LORD put
him to death. [4]Tamar, Judah's
daughter-in-law, bore him Perez
and Zerah. Judah had five sons in
all.

[5]The sons of Perez:
Hezron and Hamul.
[6]The sons of Zerah:
Zimri, Ethan, Heman, Calcol and
Darda[g]—five in all.
[7]The son of Carmi:
Achar,[h] who brought trouble on
Israel by violating the ban on tak-
ing devoted things.[i]
[8]The son of Ethan:
Azariah.
[9]The sons born to Hezron were:
Jerahmeel, Ram and Caleb.[j]

From Ram Son of Hezron

[10]Ram was the father of
Amminadab, and Amminadab the
father of Nahshon, the leader of
the people of Judah. [11]Nahshon
was the father of Salmon,[k] Sal-
mon the father of Boaz, [12]Boaz the
father of Obed and Obed the fa-
ther of Jesse.
[13]Jesse was the father of
Eliab his firstborn; the second son
was Abinadab, the third Shimea,
[14]the fourth Nethanel, the fifth
Raddai, [15]the sixth Ozem and the
seventh David. [16]Their sisters
were Zeruiah and Abigail. Zeru-
iah's three sons were Abishai, Joab
and Asahel. [17]Abigail was the

[a]41 Many Hebrew manuscripts and some Septuagint manuscripts (see also Gen. 36:26); most Hebrew manuscripts *Hamran* [b]42 Many Hebrew and Septuagint manuscripts (see also Gen. 36:27); most Hebrew manuscripts *Zaavan, Jaakan* [c]42 Hebrew *Dishon*, a variant of *Dishan* [d]43 Or *before an Israelite king reigned over them* [e]48 Possibly the Euphrates [f]50 Many Hebrew manuscripts, some Septuagint manuscripts, Vulgate and Syriac (see also Gen. 36:39); most Hebrew manuscripts *Pai* [g]6 Many Hebrew manuscripts, some Septuagint manuscripts and Syriac (see also 1 Kings 4:31); most Hebrew manuscripts *Dara* [h]7 *Achar* means *trouble*; *Achar* is called *Achan* in Joshua. [i]7 The Hebrew term refers to the irrevocable giving over of things or persons to the LORD, often by totally destroying them. [j]9 Hebrew *Kelubai*, a variant of *Caleb* [k]11 Septuagint (see also Ruth 4:21); Hebrew *Salma*

mother of Amasa, whose father
was Jether the Ishmaelite.

Caleb Son of Hezron

18 Caleb son of Hezron had children by
his wife Azubah (and by Jerioth).
These were her sons: Jesher, Sho-
bab and Ardon. 19 When Azubah
died, Caleb married Ephrath, who
bore him Hur. 20 Hur was the fa-
ther of Uri, and Uri the father of
Bezalel.
21 Later, Hezron lay with the daughter
of Makir the father of Gilead (he
had married her when he was six-
ty years old), and she bore him Se-
gub. 22 Segub was the father of
Jair, who controlled twenty-three
towns in Gilead. 23 (But Geshur
and Aram captured Havvoth
Jair,[a] as well as Kenath with its
surrounding settlements — sixty
towns.) All these were descen-
dants of Makir the father of Gil-
ead.

24 After Hezron died in Caleb Ephra-
thah, Abijah the wife of Hezron
bore him Ashhur the father[b] of
Tekoa.

Jerahmeel Son of Hezron

25 The sons of Jerahmeel the firstborn
of Hezron:
Ram his firstborn, Bunah, Oren,
Ozem and[c] Ahijah. 26 Jerahmeel
had another wife, whose name
was Atarah; she was the mother of
Onam.
27 The sons of Ram the firstborn of Je-
rahmeel:
Maaz, Jamin and Eker.
28 The sons of Onam:
Shammai and Jada.
The sons of Shammai:
Nadab and Abishur.
29 Abishur's wife was named Abihail,
who bore him Ahban and Molid.
30 The sons of Nadab:
Seled and Appaim. Seled died
without children.
31 The son of Appaim:
Ishi, who was the father of She-
shan.
Sheshan was the father of Ahlai.
32 The sons of Jada, Shammai's
brother:
Jether and Jonathan. Jether died
without children.
33 The sons of Jonathan:
Peleth and Zaza.
These were the descendants of Je-
rahmeel.
34 Sheshan had no sons — only daugh-
ters.
He had an Egyptian servant
named Jarha. 35 Sheshan gave his
daughter in marriage to his ser-
vant Jarha, and she bore him At-
tai.
36 Attai was the father of Nathan,
Nathan the father of Zabad,
37 Zabad the father of Ephlal,
Ephlal the father of Obed,
38 Obed the father of Jehu,
Jehu the father of Azariah,
39 Azariah the father of Helez,
Helez the father of Eleasah,
40 Eleasah the father of Sismai,
Sismai the father of Shallum,
41 Shallum the father of Jekamiah,
and Jekamiah the father of Elish-
ama.

The Clans of Caleb

42 The sons of Caleb the brother of Je-
rahmeel:
Mesha his firstborn, who was the
father of Ziph, and his son Mare-
shah,[d] who was the father of He-
bron.
43 The sons of Hebron:
Korah, Tappuah, Rekem and She-
ma. 44 Shema was the father of Ra-
ham, and Raham the father of Jor-
keam. Rekem was the father of
Shammai. 45 The son of Shammai
was Maon, and Maon was the fa-
ther of Beth Zur.
46 Caleb's concubine Ephah was the
mother of Haran, Moza and Ga-
zez. Haran was the father of Ga-
zez.
47 The sons of Jahdai:
Regem, Jotham, Geshan, Pelet,
Ephah and Shaaph.
48 Caleb's concubine Maacah was the
mother of Sheber and Tirhanah.
49 She also gave birth to Shaaph
the father of Madmannah and to

[a] 23 Or *captured the settlements of Jair* [b] 24 *Father* may mean *civic leader* or *military leader*; also in verses 42, 45, 49-52 and possibly elsewhere. [c] 25 Or *Oren and Ozem, by* [d] 42 The meaning of the Hebrew for this phrase is uncertain.

Sheva the father of Macbenah and
Gibea. Caleb's daughter was Ac-
sah. 50These were the descen-
dants of Caleb.

The sons of Hur the firstborn of Eph-
rathah:
Shobal the father of Kiriath Jea-
rim, 51Salma the father of Bethle-
hem, and Hareph the father of
Beth Gader.
52The descendants of Shobal the fa-
ther of Kiriath Jearim were:
Haroeh, half the Manahathites,
53and the clans of Kiriath Jearim:
the Ithrites, Puthites, Shumathites
and Mishraites. From these de-
scended the Zorathites and Eshta-
olites.
54The descendants of Salma:
Bethlehem, the Netophathites, At-
roth Beth Joab, half the Mana-
hathites, the Zorites, 55and the
clans of scribes[a] who lived at Ja-
bez: the Tirathites, Shimeathites
and Sucathites. These are the Ke-
nites who came from Hammath,
the father of the house of Recab.[b]

The Sons of David

3 These were the sons of David born to
him in Hebron:
The firstborn was Amnon the son
of Ahinoam of Jezreel;
the second, Daniel the son of Abi-
gail of Carmel;
2the third, Absalom the son of Maa-
cah daughter of Talmai king of Ge-
shur;
the fourth, Adonijah the son of
Haggith;
3the fifth, Shephatiah the son of
Abital;
and the sixth, Ithream, by his wife
Eglah.
4These six were born to David in
Hebron, where he reigned seven
years and six months.
David reigned in Jerusalem thirty-three
years, 5and these were the children born
to him there:
Shammua,[c] Shobab, Nathan and
Solomon. These four were by
Bathsheba[d] daughter of Ammiel.
6There were also Ibhar, Elishua,[e]
Eliphelet, 7Nogah, Nepheg, Ja-
phia, 8Elishama, Eliada and Eliph-
elet—nine in all. 9All these were
the sons of David, besides his sons
by his concubines. And Tamar
was their sister.

The Kings of Judah

10Solomon's son was Rehoboam,
Abijah his son,
Asa his son,
Jehoshaphat his son,
11Jehoram[f] his son,
Ahaziah his son,
Joash his son,
12Amaziah his son,
Azariah his son,
Jotham his son,
13Ahaz his son,
Hezekiah his son,
Manasseh his son,
14Amon his son,
Josiah his son.
15The sons of Josiah:
Johanan the firstborn,
Jehoiakim the second son,
Zedekiah the third,
Shallum the fourth.
16The successors of Jehoiakim:
Jehoiachin[g] his son,
and Zedekiah.

The Royal Line After the Exile

17The descendants of Jehoiachin the
captive:
Shealtiel his son, 18Malkiram, Pe-
daiah, Shenazzar, Jekamiah,
Hoshama and Nedabiah.
19The sons of Pedaiah:
Zerubbabel and Shimei.
The sons of Zerubbabel:
Meshullam and Hananiah.
Shelomith was their sister.
20There were also five others:
Hashubah, Ohel, Berekiah, Hasa-
diah and Jushab-Hesed.
21The descendants of Hananiah:
Pelatiah and Jeshaiah, and the
sons of Rephaiah, of Arnan, of
Obadiah and of Shecaniah.
22The descendants of Shecaniah:
Shemaiah and his sons:

[a]55 Or *of the Sopherites* [b]55 Or *father of Beth Recab* [c]5 Hebrew *Shimea*, a variant of *Shammua* [d]5 One Hebrew manuscript and Vulgate (see also Septuagint and 2 Samuel 11:3); most Hebrew manuscripts *Bathshua* [e]6 Two Hebrew manuscripts (see also 2 Samuel 5:15 and 1 Chron. 14:5); most Hebrew manuscripts *Elishama* [f]11 Hebrew *Joram*, a variant of *Jehoram* [g]16 Hebrew *Jeconiah*, a variant of *Jehoiachin*; also in verse 17

Hattush, Igal, Bariah, Neariah and
Shaphat—six in all.
23The sons of Neariah:
Elioenai, Hizkiah and Azrikam—
three in all.
24The sons of Elioenai:
Hodaviah, Eliashib, Pelaiah, Akkub, Johanan, Delaiah and Anani—seven in all.

Other Clans of Judah

4 The descendants of Judah:
Perez, Hezron, Carmi, Hur and
Shobal.
2Reaiah son of Shobal was the father
of Jahath, and Jahath the father of
Ahumai and Lahad. These were
the clans of the Zorathites.
3These were the sons[a] of Etam:
Jezreel, Ishma and Idbash. Their
sister was named Hazzelelponi.
4Penuel was the father of Gedor,
and Ezer the father of Hushah.
These were the descendants of Hur,
the firstborn of Ephrathah and father[b] of Bethlehem.
5Ashhur the father of Tekoa had two
wives, Helah and Naarah.
6Naarah bore him Ahuzzam, Hepher,
Temeni and Haahashtari. These
were the descendants of Naarah.
7The sons of Helah:
Zereth, Zohar, Ethnan, 8and Koz,
who was the father of Anub and
Hazzobebah and of the clans of
Aharhel son of Harum.

9Jabez was more honorable than his brothers. His mother had named him Jabez,[c] saying, "I gave birth to him in pain." 10Jabez cried out to the God of Israel, "Oh, that you would bless me and enlarge my territory! Let your hand be with me, and keep me from harm so that I will be free from pain." And God granted his request.

11Kelub, Shuhah's brother, was the father of Mehir, who was the father
of Eshton. 12Eshton was the father
of Beth Rapha, Paseah and Tehinnah the father of Ir Nahash.[d]
These were the men of Recah.
13The sons of Kenaz:
Othniel and Seraiah.
The sons of Othniel:
Hathath and Meonothai.[e] 14Meonothai was the father of Ophrah.
Seraiah was the father of Joab,
the father of Ge Harashim.[f] It
was called this because its people
were craftsmen.
15The sons of Caleb son of Jephunneh:
Iru, Elah and Naam.
The son of Elah:
Kenaz.
16The sons of Jehallelel:
Ziph, Ziphah, Tiria and Asarel.
17The sons of Ezrah:
Jether, Mered, Epher and Jalon.
One of Mered's wives gave birth to
Miriam, Shammai and Ishbah the
father of Eshtemoa. 18(His Judean
wife gave birth to Jered the father
of Gedor, Heber the father of Soco,
and Jekuthiel the father of Zanoah.) These were the children of
Pharaoh's daughter Bithiah,
whom Mered had married.
19The sons of Hodiah's wife, the sister
of Naham:
the father of Keilah the Garmite,
and Eshtemoa the Maacathite.
20The sons of Shimon:
Amnon, Rinnah, Ben-Hanan and
Tilon.
The descendants of Ishi:
Zoheth and Ben-Zoheth.
21The sons of Shelah son of Judah:
Er the father of Lecah, Laadah the
father of Mareshah and the clans
of the linen workers at Beth Ashbea, 22Jokim, the men of Cozeba,
and Joash and Saraph, who ruled
in Moab and Jashubi Lehem.
(These records are from ancient
times.) 23They were the potters
who lived at Netaim and Gederah;
they stayed there and worked for
the king.

Simeon

24The descendants of Simeon:
Nemuel, Jamin, Jarib, Zerah and
Shaul;
25Shallum was Shaul's son, Mibsam
his son and Mishma his son.
26The descendants of Mishma:

[a]3 Some Septuagint manuscripts (see also Vulgate); Hebrew *father* [b]4 *Father* may mean *civic leader* or *military leader*; also in verses 12, 14, 17, 18 and possibly elsewhere. [c]9 *Jabez* sounds like the Hebrew for *pain*. [d]12 Or *of the city of Nahash* [e]13 Some Septuagint manuscripts and Vulgate; Hebrew does not have *and Meonothai*. [f]14 *Ge Harashim* means *valley of craftsmen*.

Hammuel his son, Zaccur his son
and Shimei his son.
27Shimei had sixteen sons and six
daughters, but his brothers did not have
many children; so their entire clan did not
become as numerous as the people of Ju-
dah. 28They lived in Beersheba, Moladah,
Hazar Shual, 29Bilhah, Ezem, Tolad, 30Be-
thuel, Hormah, Ziklag, 31Beth Marcaboth,
Hazar Susim, Beth Biri and Shaaraim.
These were their towns until the reign of
David. 32Their surrounding villages were
Etam, Ain, Rimmon, Token and Ashan—
five towns— 33and all the villages around
these towns as far as Baalath.[a] These
were their settlements. And they kept a
genealogical record.

34Meshobab, Jamlech, Joshah son of
Amaziah, 35Joel, Jehu son of Joshibi-
ah, the son of Seraiah, the son of Asi-
el, 36also Elioenai, Jaakobah, Jesho-
haiah, Asaiah, Adiel, Jesimiel,
Benaiah, 37and Ziza son of Shiphi, the
son of Allon, the son of Jedaiah, the
son of Shimri, the son of Shemaiah.

38The men listed above by name were
leaders of their clans. Their families in-
creased greatly, 39and they went to the
outskirts of Gedor to the east of the valley
in search of pasture for their flocks.
40They found rich, good pasture, and the
land was spacious, peaceful and quiet.
Some Hamites had lived there formerly.
41The men whose names were listed
came in the days of Hezekiah king of Ju-
dah. They attacked the Hamites in their
dwellings and also the Meunites who
were there and completely destroyed[b]
them, as is evident to this day. Then they
settled in their place, because there was
pasture for their flocks. 42And five hun-
dred of these Simeonites, led by Pelatiah,
Neariah, Rephaiah and Uzziel, the sons of
Ishi, invaded the hill country of Seir.
43They killed the remaining Amalekites
who had escaped, and they have lived
there to this day.

Reuben

5 The sons of Reuben the firstborn of Is-
rael (he was the firstborn, but when
he defiled his father's marriage bed, his
rights as firstborn were given to the sons
of Joseph son of Israel; so he could not be
listed in the genealogical record in accor-
dance with his birthright, 2and though Ju-
dah was the strongest of his brothers and
a ruler came from him, the rights of the
firstborn belonged to Joseph) — 3the sons
of Reuben the firstborn of Israel:
Hanoch, Pallu, Hezron and Carmi.
4The descendants of Joel:
Shemaiah his son, Gog his son,
Shimei his son, 5Micah his son,
Reaiah his son, Baal his son,
6and Beerah his son, whom Tig-
lath-Pileser[c] king of Assyria took
into exile. Beerah was a leader of
the Reubenites.
7Their relatives by clans, listed ac-
cording to their genealogical
records:
Jeiel the chief, Zechariah, 8and
Bela son of Azaz, the son of She-
ma, the son of Joel. They settled in
the area from Aroer to Nebo and
Baal Meon. 9To the east they occu-
pied the land up to the edge of the
desert that extends to the Euphra-
tes River, because their livestock
had increased in Gilead.
10During Saul's reign they waged
war against the Hagrites, who were
defeated at their hands; they occu-
pied the dwellings of the Hagrites
throughout the entire region east of
Gilead.

Gad

11The Gadites lived next to them in Ba-
shan, as far as Salecah:
12Joel was the chief, Shapham the
second, then Janai and Shaphat,
in Bashan.
13Their relatives, by families, were:
Michael, Meshullam, Sheba, Jorai,
Jacan, Zia and Eber—seven in all.
14These were the sons of Abihail
son of Huri, the son of Jaroah, the
son of Gilead, the son of Michael,
the son of Jeshishai, the son of
Jahdo, the son of Buz.
15Ahi son of Abdiel, the son of Guni,
was head of their family.
16The Gadites lived in Gilead, in Ba-
shan and its outlying villages, and
on all the pasturelands of Sharon
as far as they extended.
17All these were entered in the gene-

[a]33 Some Septuagint manuscripts (see also Joshua 19:8); Hebrew *Baal*
[b]41 The Hebrew term refers to the irrevocable giving over of things or persons to the LORD, often by totally destroying them.
[c]6 Hebrew *Tilgath-Pilneser*, a variant of *Tiglath-Pileser*; also in verse 26

alogical records during the reigns of Jotham king of Judah and Jeroboam king of Israel.

18The Reubenites, the Gadites and the half-tribe of Manasseh had 44,760 men ready for military service—able-bodied men who could handle shield and sword, who could use a bow, and who were trained for battle. 19They waged war against the Hagrites, Jetur, Naphish and Nodab. 20They were helped in fighting them, and God handed the Hagrites and all their allies over to them, because they cried out to him during the battle. He answered their prayers, because they trusted in him. 21They seized the livestock of the Hagrites—fifty thousand camels, two hundred fifty thousand sheep and two thousand donkeys. They also took one hundred thousand people captive, 22and many others fell slain, because the battle was God's. And they occupied the land until the exile.

The Half-Tribe of Manasseh

23The people of the half-tribe of Manasseh were numerous; they settled in the land from Bashan to Baal Hermon, that is, to Senir (Mount Hermon).

24These were the heads of their families: Epher, Ishi, Eliel, Azriel, Jeremiah, Hodaviah and Jahdiel. They were brave warriors, famous men, and heads of their families. 25But they were unfaithful to the God of their fathers and prostituted themselves to the gods of the peoples of the land, whom God had destroyed before them. 26So the God of Israel stirred up the spirit of Pul king of Assyria (that is, Tiglath-Pileser king of Assyria), who took the Reubenites, the Gadites and the half-tribe of Manasseh into exile. He took them to Halah, Habor, Hara and the river of Gozan, where they are to this day.

Levi

6 The sons of Levi:
Gershon, Kohath and Merari.
2The sons of Kohath:
Amram, Izhar, Hebron and Uzziel.
3The children of Amram:
Aaron, Moses and Miriam.
The sons of Aaron:
Nadab, Abihu, Eleazar and Ithamar.
4Eleazar was the father of Phinehas,
Phinehas the father of Abishua,
5Abishua the father of Bukki,
Bukki the father of Uzzi,
6Uzzi the father of Zerahiah,
Zerahiah the father of Meraioth,
7Meraioth the father of Amariah,
Amariah the father of Ahitub,
8Ahitub the father of Zadok,
Zadok the father of Ahimaaz,
9Ahimaaz the father of Azariah,
Azariah the father of Johanan,
10Johanan the father of Azariah (it was he who served as priest in the temple Solomon built in Jerusalem),
11Azariah the father of Amariah,
Amariah the father of Ahitub,
12Ahitub the father of Zadok,
Zadok the father of Shallum,
13Shallum the father of Hilkiah,
Hilkiah the father of Azariah,
14Azariah the father of Seraiah,
and Seraiah the father of Jehozadak.
15Jehozadak was deported when the LORD sent Judah and Jerusalem into exile by the hand of Nebuchadnezzar.

16The sons of Levi:
Gershon,[a] Kohath and Merari.
17These are the names of the sons of Gershon:
Libni and Shimei.
18The sons of Kohath:
Amram, Izhar, Hebron and Uzziel.
19The sons of Merari:
Mahli and Mushi.
These are the clans of the Levites listed according to their fathers:
20Of Gershon:
Libni his son, Jehath his son,
Zimmah his son, 21Joah his son,
Iddo his son, Zerah his son
and Jeatherai his son.
22The descendants of Kohath:
Amminadab his son, Korah his son,
Assir his son, 23Elkanah his son,
Ebiasaph his son, Assir his son,
24Tahath his son, Uriel his son,
Uzziah his son and Shaul his son.
25The descendants of Elkanah:
Amasai, Ahimoth,

[a]16 Hebrew *Gershom*, a variant of *Gershon*; also in verses 17, 20, 43, 62 and 71

26Elkanah his son,[a] Zophai his son,
Nahath his son, 27Eliab his son,
Jeroham his son, Elkanah his son
and Samuel his son.[b]
28The sons of Samuel:
Joel[c] the firstborn
and Abijah the second son.
29The descendants of Merari:
Mahli, Libni his son,
Shimei his son, Uzzah his son,
30Shimea his son, Haggiah his son
and Asaiah his son.

The Temple Musicians

31These are the men David put in
charge of the music in the house of the
LORD after the ark came to rest there.
32They ministered with music before the
tabernacle, the Tent of Meeting, until Solomon built the temple of the LORD in Jerusalem. They performed their duties according to the regulations laid down for them.
33Here are the men who served, together with their sons:
From the Kohathites:
Heman, the musician,
the son of Joel, the son of Samuel,
34the son of Elkanah, the son of Jeroham,
the son of Eliel, the son of Toah,
35the son of Zuph, the son of Elkanah,
the son of Mahath, the son of Amasai,
36the son of Elkanah, the son of Joel,
the son of Azariah, the son of Zephaniah,
37the son of Tahath, the son of Assir,
the son of Ebiasaph, the son of Korah,
38the son of Izhar, the son of Kohath,
the son of Levi, the son of Israel;
39and Heman's associate Asaph, who
served at his right hand:
Asaph son of Berekiah, the son of Shimea,
40the son of Michael, the son of Baaseiah,[d]
the son of Malkijah, 41the son of Ethni,
the son of Zerah, the son of Adaiah,
42the son of Ethan, the son of Zimmah,
the son of Shimei, 43the son of Jahath,
the son of Gershon, the son of Levi;
44and from their associates, the Merarites, at his left hand:
Ethan son of Kishi, the son of Abdi,
the son of Malluch, 45the son of Hashabiah,
the son of Amaziah, the son of Hilkiah,
46the son of Amzi, the son of Bani,
the son of Shemer, 47the son of Mahli,
the son of Mushi, the son of Merari,
the son of Levi.

48Their fellow Levites were assigned to
all the other duties of the tabernacle, the
house of God. 49But Aaron and his descendants were the ones who presented offerings on the altar of burnt offering and on the altar of incense in connection with all that was done in the Most Holy Place, making atonement for Israel, in accordance with all that Moses the servant of God had commanded.

50These were the descendants of
Aaron:
Eleazar his son, Phinehas his son,
Abishua his son, 51Bukki his son,
Uzzi his son, Zerahiah his son,
52Meraioth his son, Amariah his son,
Ahitub his son, 53Zadok his son
and Ahimaaz his son.

54These were the locations of their settlements allotted as their territory (they were assigned to the descendants of Aaron who were from the Kohathite clan, because the first lot was for them):
55They were given Hebron in Judah with its surrounding pasturelands. 56But the fields and villages around the city were given to Caleb son of Jephunneh.
57So the descendants of Aaron

[a]*26* Some Hebrew manuscripts, Septuagint and Syriac; most Hebrew manuscripts *Ahimoth* 26*and Elkanah. The sons of Elkanah:* [b]*27* Some Septuagint manuscripts (see also 1 Samuel 1:19,20 and 1 Chron. 6:33,34); Hebrew does not have *and Samuel his son.* [c]*28* Some Septuagint manuscripts and Syriac (see also 1 Samuel 8:2 and 1 Chron. 6:33); Hebrew does not have *Joel.* [d]*40* Most Hebrew manuscripts; some Hebrew manuscripts, one Septuagint manuscript and Syriac *Maaseiah*

were given Hebron (a city of refuge),
and Libnah,[a] Jattir, Eshtemoa, [58]Hi-
len, Debir, [59]Ashan, Juttah[b] and
Beth Shemesh, together with their
pasturelands. [60]And from the tribe of
Benjamin they were given Gibeon,[c]
Geba, Alemeth and Anathoth, togeth-
er with their pasturelands.

These towns, which were distribut-
ed among the Kohathite clans, were
thirteen in all.

[61]The rest of Kohath's descendants
were allotted ten towns from the clans of
half the tribe of Manasseh.

[62]The descendants of Gershon, clan by
clan, were allotted thirteen towns from
the tribes of Issachar, Asher and Naphtali,
and from the part of the tribe of Manasseh
that is in Bashan.

[63]The descendants of Merari, clan by
clan, were allotted twelve towns from the
tribes of Reuben, Gad and Zebulun.

[64]So the Israelites gave the Levites these
towns and their pasturelands. [65]From the
tribes of Judah, Simeon and Benjamin
they allotted the previously named towns.

[66]Some of the Kohathite clans were giv-
en as their territory towns from the tribe
of Ephraim.

[67]In the hill country of Ephraim
they were given Shechem (a city of
refuge), and Gezer,[d] [68]Jokmeam,
Beth Horon, [69]Aijalon and Gath Rim-
mon, together with their pastures-
lands.

[70]And from half the tribe of Manas-
seh the Israelites gave Aner and Bile-
am, together with their pasturelands,
to the rest of the Kohathite clans.

[71]The Gershonites received the follow-
ing:

From the clan of the half-tribe of Ma-
nasseh
they received Golan in Bashan
and also Ashtaroth, together with
their pasturelands;

[72]from the tribe of Issachar
they received Kedesh, Daberath,
[73]Ramoth and Anem, together
with their pasturelands;

[74]from the tribe of Asher
they received Mashal, Abdon,
[75]Hukok and Rehob, together with
their pasturelands;

[76]and from the tribe of Naphtali
they received Kedesh in Galilee,
Hammon and Kiriathaim, together
with their pasturelands.

[77]The Merarites (the rest of the Le-
vites) received the following:

From the tribe of Zebulun
they received Jokneam, Kartah,[e]
Rimmono and Tabor, together
with their pasturelands;

[78]from the tribe of Reuben across the
Jordan east of Jericho
they received Bezer in the desert,
Jahzah, [79]Kedemoth and Mepha-
ath, together with their pastures-
lands;

[80]and from the tribe of Gad
they received Ramoth in Gilead,
Mahanaim, [81]Heshbon and Jazer,
together with their pasturelands.

Issachar

7 The sons of Issachar:
Tola, Puah, Jashub and Shim-
ron—four in all.

[2]The sons of Tola:
Uzzi, Rephaiah, Jeriel, Jahmai, Ib-
sam and Samuel—heads of their
families. During the reign of Da-
vid, the descendants of Tola listed
as fighting men in their genealogy
numbered 22,600.

[3]The son of Uzzi:
Izrahiah.

The sons of Izrahiah:
Michael, Obadiah, Joel and Isshi-
ah. All five of them were chiefs.
[4]According to their family genea-
logy, they had 36,000 men ready
for battle, for they had many
wives and children.

[5]The relatives who were fighting men
belonging to all the clans of Issa-
char, as listed in their genealogy,
were 87,000 in all.

Benjamin

[6]Three sons of Benjamin:
Bela, Beker and Jediael.

[7]The sons of Bela:
Ezbon, Uzzi, Uzziel, Jerimoth and
Iri, heads of families—five in all.
Their genealogical record listed
22,034 fighting men.

[a]57 See Joshua 21:13; Hebrew *given the cities of refuge: Hebron, Libnah.* [b]59 Syriac (see also Septuagint and Joshua 21:16); Hebrew does not have *Juttah.* [c]60 See Joshua 21:17; Hebrew does not have *Gibeon.* [d]67 See Joshua 21:21; Hebrew *given the cities of refuge: Shechem, Gezer.* [e]77 See Septuagint and Joshua 21:34; Hebrew does not have *Jokneam, Kartah.*

8The sons of Beker:
Zemirah, Joash, Eliezer, Elioenai,
Omri, Jeremoth, Abijah, Anathoth
and Alemeth. All these were the
sons of Beker. 9Their genealogical
record listed the heads of families
and 20,200 fighting men.
10The son of Jediael:
Bilhan.
The sons of Bilhan:
Jeush, Benjamin, Ehud, Kenaa-
nah, Zethan, Tarshish and Ahisha-
har. 11All these sons of Jediael
were heads of families. There
were 17,200 fighting men ready to
go out to war.
12The Shuppites and Huppites were
the descendants of Ir, and the Hu-
shites the descendants of Aher.

Naphtali

13The sons of Naphtali:
Jahziel, Guni, Jezer and Shil-
lem[a]—the descendants of Bil-
hah.

Manasseh

14The descendants of Manasseh:
Asriel was his descendant through
his Aramean concubine. She gave
birth to Makir the father of Gilead.
15Makir took a wife from among the
Huppites and Shuppites. His sister's
name was Maacah.
Another descendant was named
Zelophehad, who had only daugh-
ters.
16Makir's wife Maacah gave birth
to a son and named him Peresh. His
brother was named Sheresh, and his
sons were Ulam and Rakem.
17The son of Ulam:
Bedan.
These were the sons of Gilead son of
Makir, the son of Manasseh. 18His
sister Hammoleketh gave birth to
Ishhod, Abiezer and Mahlah.
19The sons of Shemida were:
Ahian, Shechem, Likhi and
Aniam.

Ephraim

20The descendants of Ephraim:
Shuthelah, Bered his son,
Tahath his son, Eleadah his son,
Tahath his son, 21Zabad his son
and Shuthelah his son.
Ezer and Elead were killed by the
native-born men of Gath, when they
went down to seize their livestock.
22Their father Ephraim mourned for
them many days, and his relatives
came to comfort him. 23Then he lay
with his wife again, and she became
pregnant and gave birth to a son. He
named him Beriah,[b] because there
had been misfortune in his family.
24His daughter was Sheerah, who
built Lower and Upper Beth Horon
as well as Uzzen Sheerah.
25Rephah was his son, Resheph his
son,[c]
Telah his son, Tahan his son,
26Ladan his son, Ammihud his son,
Elishama his son, 27Nun his son
and Joshua his son.
28Their lands and settlements included
Bethel and its surrounding villages, Naa-
ran to the east, Gezer and its villages to
the west, and Shechem and its villages all
the way to Ayyah and its villages. 29Along
the borders of Manasseh were Beth Shan,
Taanach, Megiddo and Dor, together with
their villages. The descendants of Joseph
son of Israel lived in these towns.

Asher

30The sons of Asher:
Imnah, Ishvah, Ishvi and Beriah.
Their sister was Serah.
31The sons of Beriah:
Heber and Malkiel, who was the
father of Birzaith.
32Heber was the father of Japhlet, Sho-
mer and Hotham and of their sis-
ter Shua.
33The sons of Japhlet:
Pasach, Bimhal and Ashvath.
These were Japhlet's sons.
34The sons of Shomer:
Ahi, Rohgah,[d] Hubbah and
Aram.
35The sons of his brother Helem:
Zophah, Imna, Shelesh and Amal.
36The sons of Zophah:
Suah, Harnepher, Shual, Beri, Im-
rah, 37Bezer, Hod, Shamma, Shil-
shah, Ithran[e] and Beera.

[a]13 Some Hebrew and Septuagint manuscripts (see also Gen. 46:24 and Num. 26:49); most Hebrew manuscripts *Shallum* [b]23 *Beriah* sounds like the Hebrew for *misfortune.* [c]25 Some Septuagint manuscripts; Hebrew does not have *his son.* [d]34 Or *of his brother Shomer: Rohgah* [e]37 Possibly a variant of *Jether*

38The sons of Jether:
Jephunneh, Pispah and Ara.
39The sons of Ulla:
Arah, Hanniel and Rizia.
40All these were descendants of Asher—heads of families, choice men, brave warriors and outstanding leaders. The number of men ready for battle, as listed in their genealogy, was 26,000.

The Genealogy of Saul the Benjamite

8 Benjamin was the father of Bela his firstborn,
Ashbel the second son, Aharah the third,
2Nohah the fourth and Rapha the fifth.
3The sons of Bela were:
Addar, Gera, Abihud,[a] 4Abishua, Naaman, Ahoah, 5Gera, Shephuphan and Huram.
6These were the descendants of Ehud, who were heads of families of those living in Geba and were deported to Manahath:
7Naaman, Ahijah, and Gera, who deported them and who was the father of Uzza and Ahihud.
8Sons were born to Shaharaim in Moab after he had divorced his wives Hushim and Baara. 9By his wife Hodesh he had Jobab, Zibia, Mesha, Malcam, 10Jeuz, Sakia and Mirmah. These were his sons, heads of families. 11By Hushim he had Abitub and Elpaal.
12The sons of Elpaal:
Eber, Misham, Shemed (who built Ono and Lod with its surrounding villages), 13and Beriah and Shema, who were heads of families of those living in Aijalon and who drove out the inhabitants of Gath.
14Ahio, Shashak, Jeremoth, 15Zebadiah, Arad, Eder, 16Michael, Ishpah and Joha were the sons of Beriah.
17Zebadiah, Meshullam, Hizki, Heber, 18Ishmerai, Izliah and Jobab were the sons of Elpaal.
19Jakim, Zicri, Zabdi, 20Elienai, Zillethai, Eliel, 21Adaiah, Beraiah and Shimrath were the sons of Shimei.
22Ishpan, Eber, Eliel, 23Abdon, Zicri, Hanan, 24Hananiah, Elam, Anthothijah, 25Iphdeiah and Penuel were the sons of Shashak.
26Shamsherai, Shehariah, Athaliah, 27Jaareshiah, Elijah and Zicri were the sons of Jeroham.
28All these were heads of families, chiefs as listed in their genealogy, and they lived in Jerusalem.

29Jeiel[b] the father[c] of Gibeon lived in Gibeon.
His wife's name was Maacah, 30and his firstborn son was Abdon, followed by Zur, Kish, Baal, Ner,[d] Nadab, 31Gedor, Ahio, Zeker 32and Mikloth, who was the father of Shimeah. They too lived near their relatives in Jerusalem.
33Ner was the father of Kish, Kish the father of Saul, and Saul the father of Jonathan, Malki-Shua, Abinadab and Esh-Baal.[e]
34The son of Jonathan:
Merib-Baal,[f] who was the father of Micah.
35The sons of Micah:
Pithon, Melech, Tarea and Ahaz.
36Ahaz was the father of Jehoaddah, Jehoaddah was the father of Alemeth, Azmaveth and Zimri, and Zimri was the father of Moza. 37Moza was the father of Binea; Raphah was his son, Eleasah his son and Azel his son.
38Azel had six sons, and these were their names:
Azrikam, Bokeru, Ishmael, Sheariah, Obadiah and Hanan. All these were the sons of Azel.
39The sons of his brother Eshek:
Ulam his firstborn, Jeush the second son and Eliphelet the third. 40The sons of Ulam were brave warriors who could handle the bow. They had many sons and grandsons—150 in all.
All these were the descendants of Benjamin.

9 All Israel was listed in the genealogies recorded in the book of the kings of Israel.

[a]3 Or *Gera the father of Ehud* [b]29 Some Septuagint manuscripts (see also 1 Chron. 9:35); Hebrew does not have *Jeiel.* [c]29 *Father* may mean *civic leader* or *military leader.* [d]30 Some Septuagint manuscripts (see also 1 Chron. 9:36); Hebrew does not have *Ner.* [e]33 Also known as *Ish-Bosheth* [f]34 Also known as *Mephibosheth*

The People in Jerusalem

The people of Judah were taken captive
to Babylon because of their unfaithful-
ness. [2]Now the first to resettle on their
own property in their own towns were
some Israelites, priests, Levites and tem-
ple servants.
[3]Those from Judah, from Benjamin,
and from Ephraim and Manasseh who
lived in Jerusalem were:
[4]Uthai son of Ammihud, the son of
Omri, the son of Imri, the son of
Bani, a descendant of Perez son
of Judah.
[5]Of the Shilonites:
Asaiah the firstborn and his sons.
[6]Of the Zerahites:
Jeuel.
The people from Judah numbered
690.
[7]Of the Benjamites:
Sallu son of Meshullam, the son of
Hodaviah, the son of Hassenuah;
[8]Ibneiah son of Jeroham; Elah son
of Uzzi, the son of Micri; and Me-
shullam son of Shephatiah, the
son of Reuel, the son of Ibnijah.
[9]The people from Benjamin, as list-
ed in their genealogy, numbered
956. All these men were heads of
their families.
[10]Of the priests:
Jedaiah; Jehoiarib; Jakin;
[11]Azariah son of Hilkiah, the son of
Meshullam, the son of Zadok, the
son of Meraioth, the son of Ahi-
tub, the official in charge of the
house of God;
[12]Adaiah son of Jeroham, the son of
Pashhur, the son of Malkijah; and
Maasai son of Adiel, the son of
Jahzerah, the son of Meshullam,
the son of Meshillemith, the son
of Immer.
[13]The priests, who were heads of
families, numbered 1,760. They
were able men, responsible for
ministering in the house of God.
[14]Of the Levites:
Shemaiah son of Hasshub, the son
of Azrikam, the son of Hashabiah,
a Merarite; [15]Bakbakkar, Heresh,
Galal and Mattaniah son of Mica,
the son of Zicri, the son of Asaph;
[16]Obadiah son of Shemaiah, the
son of Galal, the son of Jeduthun;
and Berekiah son of Asa, the son
of Elkanah, who lived in the vil-
lages of the Netophathites.
[17]The gatekeepers:
Shallum, Akkub, Talmon, Ahiman
and their brothers, Shallum their
chief [18]being stationed at the
King's Gate on the east, up to the
present time. These were the gate-
keepers belonging to the camp of
the Levites. [19]Shallum son of
Kore, the son of Ebiasaph, the son
of Korah, and his fellow gatekeep-
ers from his family (the Korahites)
were responsible for guarding the
thresholds of the Tent[a] just as
their fathers had been responsible
for guarding the entrance to the
dwelling of the LORD. [20]In earlier
times Phinehas son of Eleazar was
in charge of the gatekeepers, and
the LORD was with him. [21]Zechari-
ah son of Meshelemiah was the
gatekeeper at the entrance to the
Tent of Meeting.
[22]Altogether, those chosen to be gate-
keepers at the thresholds numbered 212.
They were registered by genealogy in
their villages. The gatekeepers had been
assigned to their positions of trust by Da-
vid and Samuel the seer. [23]They and their
descendants were in charge of guarding
the gates of the house of the LORD—the
house called the Tent. [24]The gatekeepers
were on the four sides: east, west, north
and south. [25]Their brothers in their vil-
lages had to come from time to time and
share their duties for seven-day periods.
[26]But the four principal gatekeepers, who
were Levites, were entrusted with the re-
sponsibility for the rooms and treasuries
in the house of God. [27]They would spend
the night stationed around the house of
God, because they had to guard it; and
they had charge of the key for opening it
each morning.
[28]Some of them were in charge of the
articles used in the temple service; they
counted them when they were brought in
and when they were taken out. [29]Others
were assigned to take care of the furnish-
ings and all the other articles of the sanc-
tuary, as well as the flour and wine, and
the oil, incense and spices. [30]But some of
the priests took care of mixing the spices.
[31]A Levite named Mattithiah, the firstborn
son of Shallum the Korahite, was entrust-

[a] *19* That is, the temple; also in verses 21 and 23

ed with the responsibility for baking the offering bread. [32]Some of their Kohathite brothers were in charge of preparing for every Sabbath the bread set out on the table.

[33]Those who were musicians, heads of Levite families, stayed in the rooms of the temple and were exempt from other duties because they were responsible for the work day and night.

[34]All these were heads of Levite families, chiefs as listed in their genealogy, and they lived in Jerusalem.

The Genealogy of Saul

[35]Jeiel the father[a] of Gibeon lived in Gibeon.
His wife's name was Maacah,
[36]and his firstborn son was Abdon, followed by Zur, Kish, Baal, Ner, Nadab, [37]Gedor, Ahio, Zechariah and Mikloth. [38]Mikloth was the father of Shimeam. They too lived near their relatives in Jerusalem.

[39]Ner was the father of Kish, Kish the father of Saul, and Saul the father of Jonathan, Malki-Shua, Abinadab and Esh-Baal.[b]

[40]The son of Jonathan:
Merib-Baal,[c] who was the father of Micah.

[41]The sons of Micah:
Pithon, Melech, Tahrea and Ahaz.[d]

[42]Ahaz was the father of Jadah, Jadah[e] was the father of Alemeth, Azmaveth and Zimri, and Zimri was the father of Moza. [43]Moza was the father of Binea; Rephaiah was his son, Eleasah his son and Azel his son.

[44]Azel had six sons, and these were their names:
Azrikam, Bokeru, Ishmael, Sheariah, Obadiah and Hanan. These were the sons of Azel.

Saul Takes His Life

10 Now the Philistines fought against Israel; the Israelites fled before them, and many fell slain on Mount Gilboa. [2]The Philistines pressed hard after Saul and his sons, and they killed his sons Jonathan, Abinadab and Malki-Shua. [3]The fighting grew fierce around Saul, and when the archers overtook him, they wounded him.

[4]Saul said to his armor-bearer, "Draw your sword and run me through, or these uncircumcised fellows will come and abuse me."

But his armor-bearer was terrified and would not do it; so Saul took his own sword and fell on it. [5]When the armor-bearer saw that Saul was dead, he too fell on his sword and died. [6]So Saul and his three sons died, and all his house died together.

[7]When all the Israelites in the valley saw that the army had fled and that Saul and his sons had died, they abandoned their towns and fled. And the Philistines came and occupied them.

[8]The next day, when the Philistines came to strip the dead, they found Saul and his sons fallen on Mount Gilboa. [9]They stripped him and took his head and his armor, and sent messengers throughout the land of the Philistines to proclaim the news among their idols and their people. [10]They put his armor in the temple of their gods and hung up his head in the temple of Dagon.

[11]When all the inhabitants of Jabesh Gilead heard of everything the Philistines had done to Saul, [12]all their valiant men went and took the bodies of Saul and his sons and brought them to Jabesh. Then they buried their bones under the great tree in Jabesh, and they fasted seven days.

[13]Saul died because he was unfaithful to the LORD; he did not keep the word of the LORD and even consulted a medium for guidance, [14]and did not inquire of the LORD. So the LORD put him to death and turned the kingdom over to David son of Jesse.

David Becomes King Over Israel

11 All Israel came together to David at Hebron and said, "We are your own flesh and blood. [2]In the past, even while Saul was king, you were the one who led Israel on their military campaigns. And the LORD your God said to you, 'You will shepherd my people Israel, and you will become their ruler.' "

[a]*35 Father* may mean *civic leader* or *military leader.* [b]*39* Also known as *Ish-Bosheth* [c]*40* Also known as *Mephibosheth* [d]*41* Vulgate and Syriac (see also Septuagint and 1 Chron. 8:35); Hebrew does not have *and Ahaz.* [e]*42* Some Hebrew manuscripts and Septuagint (see also 1 Chron. 8:36); most Hebrew manuscripts *Jarah, Jarah*

3When all the elders of Israel had come
to King David at Hebron, he made a com-
pact with them at Hebron before the LORD,
and they anointed David king over Israel,
as the LORD had promised through Sam-
uel.

David Conquers Jerusalem

4David and all the Israelites marched to
Jerusalem (that is, Jebus). The Jebusites
who lived there 5said to David, "You will
not get in here." Nevertheless, David cap-
tured the fortress of Zion, the City of Da-
vid.

6David had said, "Whoever leads the at-
tack on the Jebusites will become com-
mander-in-chief." Joab son of Zeruiah
went up first, and so he received the com-
mand.

7David then took up residence in the
fortress, and so it was called the City of
David. 8He built up the city around it,
from the supporting terraces[a] to the sur-
rounding wall, while Joab restored the
rest of the city. 9And David became more
and more powerful, because the LORD Al-
mighty was with him.

David's Mighty Men

10These were the chiefs of David's
mighty men—they, together with all Isra-
el, gave his kingship strong support to ex-
tend it over the whole land, as the LORD
had promised— 11this is the list of David's
mighty men:

Jashobeam,[b] a Hacmonite, was chief of
the officers[c]; he raised his spear against
three hundred men, whom he killed in
one encounter.

12Next to him was Eleazar son of Dodai
the Ahohite, one of the three mighty men.
13He was with David at Pas Dammim
when the Philistines gathered there for
battle. At a place where there was a field
full of barley, the troops fled from the Phi-
listines. 14But they took their stand in the
middle of the field. They defended it and
struck the Philistines down, and the LORD
brought about a great victory.

15Three of the thirty chiefs came down
to David to the rock at the cave of Adul-
lam, while a band of Philistines was en-
camped in the Valley of Rephaim. 16At
that time David was in the stronghold, and
the Philistine garrison was at Bethlehem.
17David longed for water and said, "Oh,
that someone would get me a drink of wa-
ter from the well near the gate of Bethle-
hem!" 18So the Three broke through the
Philistine lines, drew water from the well
near the gate of Bethlehem and carried it
back to David. But he refused to drink it;
instead, he poured it out before the LORD.
19"God forbid that I should do this!" he
said. "Should I drink the blood of these
men who went at the risk of their lives?"
Because they risked their lives to bring it
back, David would not drink it.

Such were the exploits of the three
mighty men.

20Abishai the brother of Joab was chief
of the Three. He raised his spear against
three hundred men, whom he killed, and
so he became as famous as the Three.
21He was doubly honored above the Three
and became their commander, even
though he was not included among them.

22Benaiah son of Jehoiada was a valiant
fighter from Kabzeel, who performed
great exploits. He struck down two of
Moab's best men. He also went down into
a pit on a snowy day and killed a lion.
23And he struck down an Egyptian who
was seven and a half feet[d] tall. Although
the Egyptian had a spear like a weaver's
rod in his hand, Benaiah went against him
with a club. He snatched the spear from
the Egyptian's hand and killed him with
his own spear. 24Such were the exploits of
Benaiah son of Jehoiada; he too was as fa-
mous as the three mighty men. 25He was
held in greater honor than any of the Thir-
ty, but he was not included among the
Three. And David put him in charge of his
bodyguard.

26The mighty men were:
Asahel the brother of Joab,
Elhanan son of Dodo from Bethle-
hem,
27Shammoth the Harorite,
Helez the Pelonite,
28Ira son of Ikkesh from Tekoa,
Abiezer from Anathoth,
29Sibbecai the Hushathite,
Ilai the Ahohite,
30Maharai the Netophathite,
Heled son of Baanah the Netopha-
thite,
31Ithai son of Ribai from Gibeah in
Benjamin,
Benaiah the Pirathonite,

[a]8 Or *the Millo* [b]11 Possibly a variant of *Jashob-Baal* [c]11 Or *Thirty*; some Septuagint manuscripts *Three* (see also 2 Samuel 23:8) [d]23 Hebrew *five cubits* (about 2.3 meters)

[32]Hurai from the ravines of Gaash,
Abiel the Arbathite,
[33]Azmaveth the Baharumite,
Eliahba the Shaalbonite,
[34]the sons of Hashem the Gizonite,
Jonathan son of Shagee the Hararite,
[35]Ahiam son of Sacar the Hararite,
Eliphal son of Ur,
[36]Hepher the Mekerathite,
Ahijah the Pelonite,
[37]Hezro the Carmelite,
Naarai son of Ezbai,
[38]Joel the brother of Nathan,
Mibhar son of Hagri,
[39]Zelek the Ammonite,
Naharai the Berothite, the armor-bearer of Joab son of Zeruiah,
[40]Ira the Ithrite,
Gareb the Ithrite,
[41]Uriah the Hittite,
Zabad son of Ahlai,
[42]Adina son of Shiza the Reubenite, who was chief of the Reubenites, and the thirty with him,
[43]Hanan son of Maacah,
Joshaphat the Mithnite,
[44]Uzzia the Ashterathite,
Shama and Jeiel the sons of Hotham the Aroerite,
[45]Jediael son of Shimri,
his brother Joha the Tizite,
[46]Eliel the Mahavite,
Jeribai and Joshaviah the sons of Elnaam,
Ithmah the Moabite,
[47]Eliel, Obed and Jaasiel the Mezobaite.

Warriors Join David

12 These were the men who came to David at Ziklag, while he was banished from the presence of Saul son of Kish (they were among the warriors who helped him in battle; [2]they were armed with bows and were able to shoot arrows or to sling stones right-handed or left-handed; they were kinsmen of Saul from the tribe of Benjamin):

[3]Ahiezer their chief and Joash the sons of Shemaah the Gibeathite; Jeziel and Pelet the sons of Azmaveth; Beracah, Jehu the Anathothite, [4]and Ishmaiah the Gibeonite, a mighty man among the Thirty, who was a leader of the Thirty; Jeremiah, Jahaziel, Johanan, Jozabad the Gederathite, [5]Eluzai, Jerimoth, Bealiah, Shemariah and Shephatiah the Haruphite; [6]Elkanah, Isshiah, Azarel, Joezer and Jashobeam the Korahites; [7]and Joelah and Zebadiah the sons of Jeroham from Gedor.

[8]Some Gadites defected to David at his stronghold in the desert. They were brave warriors, ready for battle and able to handle the shield and spear. Their faces were the faces of lions, and they were as swift as gazelles in the mountains.

[9]Ezer was the chief,
Obadiah the second in command,
Eliab the third,
[10]Mishmannah the fourth, Jeremiah the fifth,
[11]Attai the sixth, Eliel the seventh,
[12]Johanan the eighth, Elzabad the ninth,
[13]Jeremiah the tenth and Macbannai the eleventh.

[14]These Gadites were army commanders; the least was a match for a hundred, and the greatest for a thousand. [15]It was they who crossed the Jordan in the first month when it was overflowing all its banks, and they put to flight everyone living in the valleys, to the east and to the west.

[16]Other Benjamites and some men from Judah also came to David in his stronghold. [17]David went out to meet them and said to them, "If you have come to me in peace, to help me, I am ready to have you unite with me. But if you have come to betray me to my enemies when my hands are free from violence, may the God of our fathers see it and judge you."

[18]Then the Spirit came upon Amasai, chief of the Thirty, and he said:

"We are yours, O David!
We are with you, O son of Jesse!
Success, success to you,
and success to those who help you,
for your God will help you."

So David received them and made them leaders of his raiding bands.

[19]Some of the men of Manasseh defected to David when he went with the Philistines to fight against Saul. (He and his men did not help the Philistines because, after consultation, their rulers sent him away. They said, "It will cost us our heads if he deserts to his master Saul.") [20]When David went to Ziklag, these were the men of Manasseh who defected to him: Adnah, Jozabad, Jediael, Michael, Jozabad, Elihu

and Zillethai, leaders of units of a thousand in Manasseh. [21]They helped David against raiding bands, for all of them were brave warriors, and they were commanders in his army. [22]Day after day men came to help David, until he had a great army, like the army of God.[a]

Others Join David at Hebron

[23]These are the numbers of the men armed for battle who came to David at Hebron to turn Saul's kingdom over to him, as the LORD had said:

[24]men of Judah, carrying shield and spear—6,800 armed for battle;
[25]men of Simeon, warriors ready for battle—7,100;
[26]men of Levi—4,600, [27]including Jehoiada, leader of the family of Aaron, with 3,700 men, [28]and Zadok, a brave young warrior, with 22 officers from his family;
[29]men of Benjamin, Saul's kinsmen—3,000, most of whom had remained loyal to Saul's house until then;
[30]men of Ephraim, brave warriors, famous in their own clans—20,800;
[31]men of half the tribe of Manasseh, designated by name to come and make David king—18,000;
[32]men of Issachar, who understood the times and knew what Israel should do—200 chiefs, with all their relatives under their command;
[33]men of Zebulun, experienced soldiers prepared for battle with every type of weapon, to help David with undivided loyalty—50,000;
[34]men of Naphtali—1,000 officers, together with 37,000 men carrying shields and spears;
[35]men of Dan, ready for battle—28,600;
[36]men of Asher, experienced soldiers prepared for battle—40,000;
[37]and from east of the Jordan, men of Reuben, Gad and the half-tribe of Manasseh, armed with every type of weapon—120,000.

[38]All these were fighting men who volunteered to serve in the ranks. They came to Hebron fully determined to make David king over all Israel. All the rest of the Israelites were also of one mind to make David king. [39]The men spent three days there with David, eating and drinking, for their families had supplied provisions for them. [40]Also, their neighbors from as far away as Issachar, Zebulun and Naphtali came bringing food on donkeys, camels, mules and oxen. There were plentiful supplies of flour, fig cakes, raisin cakes, wine, oil, cattle and sheep, for there was joy in Israel.

Bringing Back the Ark

13 David conferred with each of his officers, the commanders of thousands and commanders of hundreds. [2]He then said to the whole assembly of Israel, "If it seems good to you and if it is the will of the LORD our God, let us send word far and wide to the rest of our brothers throughout the territories of Israel, and also to the priests and Levites who are with them in their towns and pastureland, to come and join us. [3]Let us bring the ark of our God back to us, for we did not inquire of[b] it[c] during the reign of Saul." [4]The whole assembly agreed to do this, because it seemed right to all the people.

[5]So David assembled all the Israelites, from the Shihor River in Egypt to Lebo[d] Hamath, to bring the ark of God from Kiriath Jearim. [6]David and all the Israelites with him went to Baalah of Judah (Kiriath Jearim) to bring up from there the ark of God the LORD, who is enthroned between the cherubim—the ark that is called by the Name.

[7]They moved the ark of God from Abinadab's house on a new cart, with Uzzah and Ahio guiding it. [8]David and all the Israelites were celebrating with all their might before God, with songs and with harps, lyres, tambourines, cymbals and trumpets.

[9]When they came to the threshing floor of Kidon, Uzzah reached out his hand to steady the ark, because the oxen stumbled. [10]The LORD's anger burned against Uzzah, and he struck him down because he had put his hand on the ark. So he died there before God.

[11]Then David was angry because the LORD's wrath had broken out against Uzzah, and to this day that place is called Perez Uzzah.[e]

[12]David was afraid of God that day and

[a]22 Or *a great and mighty army* [b]3 Or *we neglected* [c]3 Or *him* [d]5 Or *to the entrance to*
[e]11 *Perez Uzzah* means *outbreak against Uzzah.*

asked, "How can I ever bring the ark of God to me?" [13]He did not take the ark to be with him in the City of David. Instead, he took it aside to the house of Obed-Edom the Gittite. [14]The ark of God remained with the family of Obed-Edom in his house for three months, and the LORD blessed his household and everything he had.

David's House and Family

14 Now Hiram king of Tyre sent messengers to David, along with cedar logs, stonemasons and carpenters to build a palace for him. [2]And David knew that the LORD had established him as king over Israel and that his kingdom had been highly exalted for the sake of his people Israel.

[3]In Jerusalem David took more wives and became the father of more sons and daughters. [4]These are the names of the children born to him there: Shammua, Shobab, Nathan, Solomon, [5]Ibhar, Elishua, Elpelet, [6]Nogah, Nepheg, Japhia, [7]Elishama, Beeliada[a] and Eliphelet.

David Defeats the Philistines

[8]When the Philistines heard that David had been anointed king over all Israel, they went up in full force to search for him, but David heard about it and went out to meet them. [9]Now the Philistines had come and raided the Valley of Rephaim; [10]so David inquired of God: "Shall I go and attack the Philistines? Will you hand them over to me?"

The LORD answered him, "Go, I will hand them over to you."

[11]So David and his men went up to Baal Perazim, and there he defeated them. He said, "As waters break out, God has broken out against my enemies by my hand." So that place was called Baal Perazim.[b] [12]The Philistines had abandoned their gods there, and David gave orders to burn them in the fire.

[13]Once more the Philistines raided the valley; [14]so David inquired of God again, and God answered him, "Do not go straight up, but circle around them and attack them in front of the balsam trees. [15]As soon as you hear the sound of marching in the tops of the balsam trees, move out to battle, because that will mean God has gone out in front of you to strike the Philistine army." [16]So David did as God commanded him, and they struck down the Philistine army, all the way from Gibeon to Gezer.

[17]So David's fame spread throughout every land, and the LORD made all the nations fear him.

The Ark Brought to Jerusalem

15 After David had constructed buildings for himself in the City of David, he prepared a place for the ark of God and pitched a tent for it. [2]Then David said, "No one but the Levites may carry the ark of God, because the LORD chose them to carry the ark of the LORD and to minister before him forever."

[3]David assembled all Israel in Jerusalem to bring up the ark of the LORD to the place he had prepared for it. [4]He called together the descendants of Aaron and the Levites:

[5]From the descendants of Kohath,
Uriel the leader and 120 relatives;
[6]from the descendants of Merari,
Asaiah the leader and 220 relatives;
[7]from the descendants of Gershon,[c]
Joel the leader and 130 relatives;
[8]from the descendants of Elizaphan,
Shemaiah the leader and 200 relatives;
[9]from the descendants of Hebron,
Eliel the leader and 80 relatives;
[10]from the descendants of Uzziel,
Amminadab the leader and 112 relatives.

[11]Then David summoned Zadok and Abiathar the priests, and Uriel, Asaiah, Joel, Shemaiah, Eliel and Amminadab the Levites. [12]He said to them, "You are the heads of the Levitical families; you and your fellow Levites are to consecrate yourselves and bring up the ark of the LORD, the God of Israel, to the place I have prepared for it. [13]It was because you, the Levites, did not bring it up the first time that the LORD our God broke out in anger against us. We did not inquire of him about how to do it in the prescribed way." [14]So the priests and Levites consecrated themselves in order to bring up the ark of the LORD, the God of Israel. [15]And the Levites carried the ark of God with the poles on their shoulders, as Moses had com-

[a]7 A variant of *Eliada* [b]11 *Baal Perazim* means *the lord who breaks out.* [c]7 Hebrew *Gershom,* a variant of *Gershon*

manded in accordance with the word of the LORD.

16David told the leaders of the Levites to appoint their brothers as singers to sing joyful songs, accompanied by musical instruments: lyres, harps and cymbals.

17So the Levites appointed Heman son of Joel; from his brothers, Asaph son of Berekiah; and from their brothers the Merarites, Ethan son of Kushaiah; 18and with them their brothers next in rank: Zechariah,[a] Jaaziel, Shemiramoth, Jehiel, Unni, Eliab, Benaiah, Maaseiah, Mattithiah, Eliphelehu, Mikneiah, Obed-Edom and Jeiel,[b] the gatekeepers.

19The musicians Heman, Asaph and Ethan were to sound the bronze cymbals; 20Zechariah, Aziel, Shemiramoth, Jehiel, Unni, Eliab, Maaseiah and Benaiah were to play the lyres according to *alamoth,*[c] 21and Mattithiah, Eliphelehu, Mikneiah, Obed-Edom, Jeiel and Azaziah were to play the harps, directing according to *sheminith.*[c] 22Kenaniah the head Levite was in charge of the singing; that was his responsibility because he was skillful at it.

23Berekiah and Elkanah were to be doorkeepers for the ark. 24Shebaniah, Joshaphat, Nethanel, Amasai, Zechariah, Benaiah and Eliezer the priests were to blow trumpets before the ark of God. Obed-Edom and Jehiah were also to be doorkeepers for the ark.

25So David and the elders of Israel and the commanders of units of a thousand went to bring up the ark of the covenant of the LORD from the house of Obed-Edom, with rejoicing. 26Because God had helped the Levites who were carrying the ark of the covenant of the LORD, seven bulls and seven rams were sacrificed. 27Now David was clothed in a robe of fine linen, as were all the Levites who were carrying the ark, and as were the singers, and Kenaniah, who was in charge of the singing of the choirs. David also wore a linen ephod. 28So all Israel brought up the ark of the covenant of the LORD with shouts, with the sounding of rams' horns and trumpets, and of cymbals, and the playing of lyres and harps.

29As the ark of the covenant of the LORD was entering the City of David, Michal daughter of Saul watched from a window. And when she saw King David dancing and celebrating, she despised him in her heart.

16 They brought the ark of God and set it inside the tent that David had pitched for it, and they presented burnt offerings and fellowship offerings[d] before God. 2After David had finished sacrificing the burnt offerings and fellowship offerings, he blessed the people in the name of the LORD. 3Then he gave a loaf of bread, a cake of dates and a cake of raisins to each Israelite man and woman.

4He appointed some of the Levites to minister before the ark of the LORD, to make petition, to give thanks, and to praise the LORD, the God of Israel: 5Asaph was the chief, Zechariah second, then Jeiel, Shemiramoth, Jehiel, Mattithiah, Eliab, Benaiah, Obed-Edom and Jeiel. They were to play the lyres and harps, Asaph was to sound the cymbals, 6and Benaiah and Jahaziel the priests were to blow the trumpets regularly before the ark of the covenant of God.

David's Psalm of Thanks

7That day David first committed to Asaph and his associates this psalm of thanks to the LORD:

8Give thanks to the LORD, call on his name;
make known among the nations what he has done.
9Sing to him, sing praise to him;
tell of all his wonderful acts.
10Glory in his holy name;
let the hearts of those who seek the LORD rejoice.
11Look to the LORD and his strength;
seek his face always.
12Remember the wonders he has done,
his miracles, and the judgments he pronounced,
13O descendants of Israel his servant,
O sons of Jacob, his chosen ones.

14He is the LORD our God;
his judgments are in all the earth.
15He remembers[e] his covenant forever,
the word he commanded, for a thousand generations,
16the covenant he made with Abraham,

[a] *18* Three Hebrew manuscripts and most Septuagint manuscripts (see also verse 20 and 1 Chron. 16:5); most Hebrew manuscripts *Zechariah son and* or *Zechariah, Ben and* [b] *18* Hebrew; Septuagint (see also verse 21) *Jeiel and Azaziah* [c] *20,21* Probably a musical term [d] *1* Traditionally *peace offerings*; also in verse 2 [e] *15* Some Septuagint manuscripts (see also Psalm 105:8); Hebrew *Remember*

the oath he swore to Isaac.
17 He confirmed it to Jacob as a decree,
to Israel as an everlasting covenant:
18 "To you I will give the land of Canaan
as the portion you will inherit."

19 When they were but few in number,
few indeed, and strangers in it,
20 they[a] wandered from nation to
nation,
from one kingdom to another.
21 He allowed no man to oppress them;
for their sake he rebuked kings:
22 "Do not touch my anointed ones;
do my prophets no harm."

23 Sing to the LORD, all the earth;
proclaim his salvation day after day.
24 Declare his glory among the nations,
his marvelous deeds among all
peoples.
25 For great is the LORD and most worthy
of praise;
he is to be feared above all gods.
26 For all the gods of the nations are
idols,
but the LORD made the heavens.
27 Splendor and majesty are before him;
strength and joy in his dwelling
place.
28 Ascribe to the LORD, O families of
nations,
ascribe to the LORD glory and
strength,
29 ascribe to the LORD the glory due
his name.
Bring an offering and come before
him;
worship the LORD in the splendor of
his[b] holiness.
30 Tremble before him, all the earth!

[a] *18-20* One Hebrew manuscript, Septuagint and Vulgate (see also Psalm 105:12); most Hebrew manuscripts *inherit, / 19 though you are but few in number, / few indeed, and strangers in it." / 20 They*
[b] *29* Or LORD *with the splendor of*

FRIDAY

VERSE FOR THE DAY:	AUTHOR:	PASSAGE FOR THE DAY:
1 Chronicles 16:11	Calvin Miller	1 Chronicles 16:8–29

Adore the Savior

The best way to deal with sin is not to attempt reform but to adore the Savior. Winning over our lower nature is made positive by adoration. While we worship the enthroned and inner Christ, we cannot be intrigued by negative preoccupations with sin. Rules, instead of limiting our sin, define sin, rivet our attention to it and lead us to desire it. Worship, on the other hand, avoids all interest in sin, pointing our hearts and minds in a totally different direction.

MARRIAGE BUILDERS

♦ *Apart from Sunday worship at church, how do you incorporate personal times of worshiping God into your life?*
♦ *Why does worship have an effect on your sinful behaviors?*

Additional Scripture Readings
Hebrews 12:1–3; Psalm 42:1–2, 8

Go to page 418 for your next devotional reading.

The world is firmly established; it
cannot be moved.
31Let the heavens rejoice, let the earth
be glad;
let them say among the nations,
"The LORD reigns!"
32Let the sea resound, and all that is in
it;
let the fields be jubilant, and
everything in them!
33Then the trees of the forest will sing,
they will sing for joy before the
LORD,
for he comes to judge the earth.

34Give thanks to the LORD, for he is
good;
his love endures forever.
35Cry out, "Save us, O God our Savior;
gather us and deliver us from the
nations,
that we may give thanks to your holy
name,
that we may glory in your praise."
36Praise be to the LORD, the God of
Israel,
from everlasting to everlasting.

Then all the people said "Amen" and "Praise the LORD."

37David left Asaph and his associates before the ark of the covenant of the LORD to minister there regularly, according to each day's requirements. 38He also left Obed-Edom and his sixty-eight associates to minister with them. Obed-Edom son of Jeduthun, and also Hosah, were gatekeepers.

39David left Zadok the priest and his fellow priests before the tabernacle of the LORD at the high place in Gibeon 40to present burnt offerings to the LORD on the altar of burnt offering regularly, morning and evening, in accordance with everything written in the Law of the LORD, which he had given Israel. 41With them were Heman and Jeduthun and the rest of those chosen and designated by name to give thanks to the LORD, "for his love endures forever." 42Heman and Jeduthun were responsible for the sounding of the trumpets and cymbals and for the playing of the other instruments for sacred song. The sons of Jeduthun were stationed at the gate.

43Then all the people left, each for his own home, and David returned home to bless his family.

God's Promise to David

17 After David was settled in his palace, he said to Nathan the prophet, "Here I am, living in a palace of cedar, while the ark of the covenant of the LORD is under a tent."

2Nathan replied to David, "Whatever you have in mind, do it, for God is with you."

3That night the word of God came to Nathan, saying:

4"Go and tell my servant David, 'This is what the LORD says: You are not the one to build me a house to dwell in. 5I have not dwelt in a house from the day I brought Israel up out of Egypt to this day. I have moved from one tent site to another, from one dwelling place to another. 6Wherever I have moved with all the Israelites, did I ever say to any of their leaders[a] whom I commanded to shepherd my people, "Why have you not built me a house of cedar?" '

7"Now then, tell my servant David, 'This is what the LORD Almighty says: I took you from the pasture and from following the flock, to be ruler over my people Israel. 8I have been with you wherever you have gone, and I have cut off all your enemies from before you. Now I will make your name like the names of the greatest men of the earth. 9And I will provide a place for my people Israel and will plant them so that they can have a home of their own and no longer be disturbed. Wicked people will not oppress them anymore, as they did at the beginning 10and have done ever since the time I appointed leaders over my people Israel. I will also subdue all your enemies.

" 'I declare to you that the LORD will build a house for you: 11When your days are over and you go to be with your fathers, I will raise up your offspring to succeed you, one of your own sons, and I will establish his kingdom. 12He is the one who will build a house for me, and I will establish his throne forever. 13I will be his father, and he will be my son. I will

[a]6 Traditionally *judges*; also in verse 10

never take my love away from him, as
I took it away from your predecessor.
14I will set him over my house and
my kingdom forever; his throne will
be established forever.' "

15Nathan reported to David all the
words of this entire revelation.

David's Prayer

16Then King David went in and sat be-
fore the LORD, and he said:

"Who am I, O LORD God, and what
is my family, that you have brought
me this far? 17And as if this were not
enough in your sight, O God, you
have spoken about the future of the
house of your servant. You have
looked on me as though I were the
most exalted of men, O LORD God.
18"What more can David say to you
for honoring your servant? For you
know your servant, 19O LORD. For the
sake of your servant and according to
your will, you have done this great
thing and made known all these great
promises.
20"There is no one like you,
O LORD, and there is no God but you,
as we have heard with our own ears.
21And who is like your people Isra-
el—the one nation on earth whose
God went out to redeem a people for
himself, and to make a name for
yourself, and to perform great and
awesome wonders by driving out na-
tions from before your people, whom
you redeemed from Egypt? 22You
made your people Israel your very
own forever, and you, O LORD, have
become their God.
23"And now, LORD, let the promise
you have made concerning your ser-
vant and his house be established for-
ever. Do as you promised, 24so that it
will be established and that your
name will be great forever. Then men
will say, 'The LORD Almighty, the God
over Israel, is Israel's God!' And the
house of your servant David will be
established before you.
25"You, my God, have revealed to
your servant that you will build a
house for him. So your servant has
found courage to pray to you.
26O LORD, you are God! You have
promised these good things to your
servant. 27Now you have been
pleased to bless the house of your
servant, that it may continue forever
in your sight; for you, O LORD, have
blessed it, and it will be blessed for-
ever."

David's Victories

18 In the course of time, David defeat-
ed the Philistines and subdued
them, and he took Gath and its surround-
ing villages from the control of the Philis-
tines.
2David also defeated the Moabites, and
they became subject to him and brought
tribute.
3Moreover, David fought Hadadezer
king of Zobah, as far as Hamath, when he
went to establish his control along the Eu-
phrates River. 4David captured a thousand
of his chariots, seven thousand chario-
teers and twenty thousand foot soldiers.
He hamstrung all but a hundred of the
chariot horses.
5When the Arameans of Damascus
came to help Hadadezer king of Zobah,
David struck down twenty-two thousand
of them. 6He put garrisons in the Aramean
kingdom of Damascus, and the Arameans
became subject to him and brought trib-
ute. The LORD gave David victory every-
where he went.
7David took the gold shields carried by
the officers of Hadadezer and brought
them to Jerusalem. 8From Tebah[a] and
Cun, towns that belonged to Hadadezer,
David took a great quantity of bronze,
which Solomon used to make the bronze
Sea, the pillars and various bronze arti-
cles.
9When Tou king of Hamath heard that
David had defeated the entire army of
Hadadezer king of Zobah, 10he sent his
son Hadoram to King David to greet him
and congratulate him on his victory in bat-
tle over Hadadezer, who had been at war
with Tou. Hadoram brought all kinds of
articles of gold and silver and bronze.
11King David dedicated these articles to
the LORD, as he had done with the silver
and gold he had taken from all these na-
tions: Edom and Moab, the Ammonites
and the Philistines, and Amalek.
12Abishai son of Zeruiah struck down
eighteen thousand Edomites in the Valley
of Salt. 13He put garrisons in Edom, and all
the Edomites became subject to David.

[a]8 Hebrew *Tibhath*, a variant of *Tebah*

The LORD gave David victory everywhere he went.

David's Officials

[14]David reigned over all Israel, doing what was just and right for all his people. [15]Joab son of Zeruiah was over the army; Jehoshaphat son of Ahilud was recorder; [16]Zadok son of Ahitub and Ahimelech[a] son of Abiathar were priests; Shavsha was secretary; [17]Benaiah son of Jehoiada was over the Kerethites and Pelethites; and David's sons were chief officials at the king's side.

The Battle Against the Ammonites

19 In the course of time, Nahash king of the Ammonites died, and his son succeeded him as king. [2]David thought, "I will show kindness to Hanun son of Nahash, because his father showed kindness to me." So David sent a delegation to express his sympathy to Hanun concerning his father.

When David's men came to Hanun in the land of the Ammonites to express sympathy to him, [3]the Ammonite nobles said to Hanun, "Do you think David is honoring your father by sending men to you to express sympathy? Haven't his men come to you to explore and spy out the country and overthrow it?" [4]So Hanun seized David's men, shaved them, cut off their garments in the middle at the buttocks, and sent them away.

[5]When someone came and told David about the men, he sent messengers to meet them, for they were greatly humiliated. The king said, "Stay at Jericho till your beards have grown, and then come back."

[6]When the Ammonites realized that they had become a stench in David's nostrils, Hanun and the Ammonites sent a thousand talents[b] of silver to hire chariots and charioteers from Aram Naharaim,[c] Aram Maacah and Zobah. [7]They hired thirty-two thousand chariots and charioteers, as well as the king of Maacah with his troops, who came and camped near Medeba, while the Ammonites were mustered from their towns and moved out for battle.

[8]On hearing this, David sent Joab out with the entire army of fighting men. [9]The Ammonites came out and drew up in battle formation at the entrance to their city, while the kings who had come were by themselves in the open country.

[10]Joab saw that there were battle lines in front of him and behind him; so he selected some of the best troops in Israel and deployed them against the Arameans. [11]He put the rest of the men under the command of Abishai his brother, and they were deployed against the Ammonites. [12]Joab said, "If the Arameans are too strong for me, then you are to rescue me; but if the Ammonites are too strong for you, then I will rescue you. [13]Be strong and let us fight bravely for our people and the cities of our God. The LORD will do what is good in his sight."

[14]Then Joab and the troops with him advanced to fight the Arameans, and they fled before him. [15]When the Ammonites saw that the Arameans were fleeing, they too fled before his brother Abishai and went inside the city. So Joab went back to Jerusalem.

[16]After the Arameans saw that they had been routed by Israel, they sent messengers and had Arameans brought from beyond the River,[d] with Shophach the commander of Hadadezer's army leading them.

[17]When David was told of this, he gathered all Israel and crossed the Jordan; he advanced against them and formed his battle lines opposite them. David formed his lines to meet the Arameans in battle, and they fought against him. [18]But they fled before Israel, and David killed seven thousand of their charioteers and forty thousand of their foot soldiers. He also killed Shophach the commander of their army.

[19]When the vassals of Hadadezer saw that they had been defeated by Israel, they made peace with David and became subject to him.

So the Arameans were not willing to help the Ammonites anymore.

The Capture of Rabbah

20 In the spring, at the time when kings go off to war, Joab led out the armed forces. He laid waste the land of the Ammonites and went to Rabbah and besieged it, but David remained in Jerusalem. Joab attacked Rabbah and left it in

[a]16 Some Hebrew manuscripts, Vulgate and Syriac (see also 2 Samuel 8:17); most Hebrew manuscripts *Abimelech* [b]6 That is, about 37 tons (about 34 metric tons) [c]6 That is, Northwest Mesopotamia
[d]16 That is, the Euphrates

WEEKENDING

BREAKAWAY

Nobody piles the pressure on us as well as we do it to ourselves! Discuss the possibility of trying some of these activities to give yourselves a refreshing break.

1. Retreat for a day. Take a long walk, avoid noise and keep your schedule free and unhurried.

2. Make a list of things that give you pleasure. Remember how much joy God has put into your world.

3. Surround yourself with nature's beauty.

4. Spend some time watching children.

5. Write a note of encouragement to someone.

6. Subtract one. Consider removing one outside responsibility from your list.

7. Change only one negative personal trait at a time.

8. Let go of a difficult memory.

— *Jan Dargatz*

REVIVE

Saturday: Proverbs 11:25
Sunday: Psalm 51:10–12

Go to page 421 for your next devotional reading.

ruins. 2David took the crown from the
head of their king[a]—its weight was
found to be a talent[b] of gold, and it was
set with precious stones—and it was
placed on David's head. He took a great
quantity of plunder from the city 3and
brought out the people who were there,
consigning them to labor with saws and
with iron picks and axes. David did this to
all the Ammonite towns. Then David and
his entire army returned to Jerusalem.

War With the Philistines

4In the course of time, war broke out
with the Philistines, at Gezer. At that time
Sibbecai the Hushathite killed Sippai, one
of the descendants of the Rephaites, and
the Philistines were subjugated.
5In another battle with the Philistines,
Elhanan son of Jair killed Lahmi the
brother of Goliath the Gittite, who had a
spear with a shaft like a weaver's rod.
6In still another battle, which took place
at Gath, there was a huge man with six fingers on each hand and six toes on each
foot—twenty-four in all. He also was descended from Rapha. 7When he taunted
Israel, Jonathan son of Shimea, David's
brother, killed him.
8These were descendants of Rapha in
Gath, and they fell at the hands of David
and his men.

David Numbers the Fighting Men

21 Satan rose up against Israel and incited David to take a census of Israel. 2So David said to Joab and the commanders of the troops, "Go and count the
Israelites from Beersheba to Dan. Then report back to me so that I may know how
many there are."
3But Joab replied, "May the LORD multiply his troops a hundred times over. My
lord the king, are they not all my lord's
subjects? Why does my lord want to do
this? Why should he bring guilt on Israel?"
4The king's word, however, overruled
Joab; so Joab left and went throughout Israel and then came back to Jerusalem.
5Joab reported the number of the fighting
men to David: In all Israel there were one
million one hundred thousand men who
could handle a sword, including four hundred and seventy thousand in Judah.
6But Joab did not include Levi and Benjamin in the numbering, because the
king's command was repulsive to him.
7This command was also evil in the sight
of God; so he punished Israel.
8Then David said to God, "I have sinned
greatly by doing this. Now, I beg you, take
away the guilt of your servant. I have done
a very foolish thing."
9The LORD said to Gad, David's seer,
10"Go and tell David, 'This is what the
LORD says: I am giving you three options.
Choose one of them for me to carry out
against you.' "
11So Gad went to David and said to him,
"This is what the LORD says: 'Take your
choice: 12three years of famine, three
months of being swept away[c] before
your enemies, with their swords overtaking you, or three days of the sword of the
LORD—days of plague in the land, with
the angel of the LORD ravaging every part
of Israel.' Now then, decide how I should
answer the one who sent me."
13David said to Gad, "I am in deep distress. Let me fall into the hands of the
LORD, for his mercy is very great; but do
not let me fall into the hands of men."
14So the LORD sent a plague on Israel,
and seventy thousand men of Israel fell
dead. 15And God sent an angel to destroy
Jerusalem. But as the angel was doing so,
the LORD saw it and was grieved because
of the calamity and said to the angel who
was destroying the people, "Enough!
Withdraw your hand." The angel of the
LORD was then standing at the threshing
floor of Araunah[d] the Jebusite.
16David looked up and saw the angel of
the LORD standing between heaven and
earth, with a drawn sword in his hand extended over Jerusalem. Then David and
the elders, clothed in sackcloth, fell face-
down.
17David said to God, "Was it not I who
ordered the fighting men to be counted? I
am the one who has sinned and done
wrong. These are but sheep. What have
they done? O LORD my God, let your hand
fall upon me and my family, but do not let
this plague remain on your people."
18Then the angel of the LORD ordered
Gad to tell David to go up and build an
altar to the LORD on the threshing floor of
Araunah the Jebusite. 19So David went up

[a]2 Or *of Milcom*, that is, Molech [b]2 That is, about 75 pounds (about 34 kilograms) [c]12 Hebrew; Septuagint and Vulgate (see also 2 Samuel 24:13) *of fleeing* [d]15 Hebrew *Ornan*, a variant of *Araunah*; also in verses 18-28

in obedience to the word that Gad had spoken in the name of the LORD.

20While Araunah was threshing wheat, he turned and saw the angel; his four sons who were with him hid themselves. 21Then David approached, and when Araunah looked and saw him, he left the threshing floor and bowed down before David with his face to the ground.

22David said to him, "Let me have the site of your threshing floor so I can build an altar to the LORD, that the plague on the people may be stopped. Sell it to me at the full price."

23Araunah said to David, "Take it! Let my lord the king do whatever pleases him. Look, I will give the oxen for the burnt offerings, the threshing sledges for the wood, and the wheat for the grain offering. I will give all this."

24But King David replied to Araunah, "No, I insist on paying the full price. I will not take for the LORD what is yours, or sacrifice a burnt offering that costs me nothing."

25So David paid Araunah six hundred shekels[a] of gold for the site. 26David built an altar to the LORD there and sacrificed burnt offerings and fellowship offerings.[b] He called on the LORD, and the LORD answered him with fire from heaven on the altar of burnt offering.

27Then the LORD spoke to the angel, and he put his sword back into its sheath. 28At that time, when David saw that the LORD had answered him on the threshing floor of Araunah the Jebusite, he offered sacrifices there. 29The tabernacle of the LORD, which Moses had made in the desert, and the altar of burnt offering were at that time on the high place at Gibeon. 30But David could not go before it to inquire of God, because he was afraid of the sword of the angel of the LORD.

22 Then David said, "The house of the LORD God is to be here, and also the altar of burnt offering for Israel."

Preparations for the Temple

2So David gave orders to assemble the aliens living in Israel, and from among them he appointed stonecutters to prepare dressed stone for building the house of God. 3He provided a large amount of iron to make nails for the doors of the gateways and for the fittings, and more bronze than could be weighed. 4He also provided more cedar logs than could be counted, for the Sidonians and Tyrians had brought large numbers of them to David.

5David said, "My son Solomon is young and inexperienced, and the house to be built for the LORD should be of great magnificence and fame and splendor in the sight of all the nations. Therefore I will make preparations for it." So David made extensive preparations before his death.

6Then he called for his son Solomon and charged him to build a house for the LORD, the God of Israel. 7David said to Solomon: "My son, I had it in my heart to build a house for the Name of the LORD my God. 8But this word of the LORD came to me: 'You have shed much blood and have fought many wars. You are not to build a house for my Name, because you have shed much blood on the earth in my sight. 9But you will have a son who will be a man of peace and rest, and I will give him rest from all his enemies on every side. His name will be Solomon,[c] and I will grant Israel peace and quiet during his reign. 10He is the one who will build a house for my Name. He will be my son, and I will be his father. And I will establish the throne of his kingdom over Israel forever.'

11"Now, my son, the LORD be with you, and may you have success and build the house of the LORD your God, as he said you would. 12May the LORD give you discretion and understanding when he puts you in command over Israel, so that you may keep the law of the LORD your God. 13Then you will have success if you are careful to observe the decrees and laws that the LORD gave Moses for Israel. Be strong and courageous. Do not be afraid or discouraged.

14"I have taken great pains to provide for the temple of the LORD a hundred thousand talents[d] of gold, a million talents[e] of silver, quantities of bronze and iron too great to be weighed, and wood and stone. And you may add to them. 15You have many workmen: stonecutters, masons and carpenters, as well as men skilled in

[a] *25* That is, about 15 pounds (about 7 kilograms) [b] *26* Traditionally *peace offerings* [c] *9 Solomon* sounds like and may be derived from the Hebrew for *peace.* [d] *14* That is, about 3,750 tons (about 3,450 metric tons) [e] *14* That is, about 37,500 tons (about 34,500 metric tons)

every kind of work [16]in gold and silver,
bronze and iron—craftsmen beyond
number. Now begin the work, and the
LORD be with you."

[17]Then David ordered all the leaders of
Israel to help his son Solomon. [18]He said
to them, "Is not the LORD your God with
you? And has he not granted you rest on
every side? For he has handed the inhabi-
tants of the land over to me, and the land
is subject to the LORD and to his people.
[19]Now devote your heart and soul to seek-
ing the LORD your God. Begin to build the
sanctuary of the LORD God, so that you
may bring the ark of the covenant of the
LORD and the sacred articles belonging to
God into the temple that will be built for
the Name of the LORD."

VERSE FOR THE DAY: 1 Chronicles 22:13

AUTHOR: Ernest Boyer

PASSAGE FOR THE DAY: 1 Chronicles 22:6–13

A Courageous Vow

Marriage is the most remarkable and most courageous of all human acts—the promise of two human beings to share life together on all levels, physical, economic, spiritual—a promise made in the face of the certainty of death, the certainty of change and the uncertainty of everything else. There is nothing else we might choose to do that is quite like this act, nothing so foolish or so profound.

Much of marriage is a struggle. One of the partners may buckle under the strain and need to lean against the other for support. Later the role may be reversed and the other partner may need to be carried by the first. In these periods the one doing the supporting may begin to think, "I am not being helped by this person, only held back." But because of that foolish, extraordinary marriage vow, he or she keeps going.

Both partners see two of their spouse's many faces—that of the afflicted and that of the comforter of the afflicted. And only after seeing both of those faces on the same person and knowing that they themselves had worn them as well, can each begin to really understand the nature of the divine. Love matures through the ordinary pains and sharing of day-to-day life into a love very close to God's own.

MARRIAGE BUILDERS

♦ *How has your love for each other, and for God, been deepened as a result of persevering through past struggles in your marriage?*

♦ *Which one of you needs the most help now, and how can the other best provide the help that is needed?*

Additional Scripture Readings
Ecclesiastes 4:9–12; 1 Corinthians 13:7; Philippians 2:3–7

Go to page 435 for your next devotional reading.

The Levites

23 When David was old and full of years, he made his son Solomon king over Israel.

[2]He also gathered together all the leaders of Israel, as well as the priests and Levites. [3]The Levites thirty years old or more were counted, and the total number of men was thirty-eight thousand. [4]David said, "Of these, twenty-four thousand are to supervise the work of the temple of the LORD and six thousand are to be officials and judges. [5]Four thousand are to be gatekeepers and four thousand are to praise the LORD with the musical instruments I have provided for that purpose."

[6]David divided the Levites into groups corresponding to the sons of Levi: Gershon, Kohath and Merari.

Gershonites

[7]Belonging to the Gershonites:
Ladan and Shimei.
[8]The sons of Ladan:
Jehiel the first, Zetham and Joel—three in all.
[9]The sons of Shimei:
Shelomoth, Haziel and Haran—three in all.
These were the heads of the families of Ladan.
[10]And the sons of Shimei:
Jahath, Ziza,[a] Jeush and Beriah.
These were the sons of Shimei—four in all.
[11]Jahath was the first and Ziza the second, but Jeush and Beriah did not have many sons; so they were counted as one family with one assignment.

Kohathites

[12]The sons of Kohath:
Amram, Izhar, Hebron and Uzziel—four in all.
[13]The sons of Amram:
Aaron and Moses.
Aaron was set apart, he and his descendants forever, to consecrate the most holy things, to offer sacrifices before the LORD, to minister before him and to pronounce blessings in his name forever.
[14]The sons of Moses the man of God were counted as part of the tribe of Levi.
[15]The sons of Moses:
Gershom and Eliezer.
[16]The descendants of Gershom:
Shubael was the first.
[17]The descendants of Eliezer:
Rehabiah was the first.
Eliezer had no other sons, but the sons of Rehabiah were very numerous.
[18]The sons of Izhar:
Shelomith was the first.
[19]The sons of Hebron:
Jeriah the first, Amariah the second, Jahaziel the third and Jekameam the fourth.
[20]The sons of Uzziel:
Micah the first and Isshiah the second.

Merarites

[21]The sons of Merari:
Mahli and Mushi.
The sons of Mahli:
Eleazar and Kish.
[22]Eleazar died without having sons: he had only daughters. Their cousins, the sons of Kish, married them.
[23]The sons of Mushi:
Mahli, Eder and Jerimoth—three in all.

[24]These were the descendants of Levi by their families—the heads of families as they were registered under their names and counted individually, that is, the workers twenty years old or more who served in the temple of the LORD. [25]For David had said, "Since the LORD, the God of Israel, has granted rest to his people and has come to dwell in Jerusalem forever, [26]the Levites no longer need to carry the tabernacle or any of the articles used in its service." [27]According to the last instructions of David, the Levites were counted from those twenty years old or more.

[28]The duty of the Levites was to help Aaron's descendants in the service of the temple of the LORD: to be in charge of the courtyards, the side rooms, the purification of all sacred things and the performance of other duties at the house of God. [29]They were in charge of the bread set out on the table, the flour for the grain offerings, the unleavened wafers, the baking and the mixing, and all measurements of quantity and size. [30]They were also to

[a]10 One Hebrew manuscript, Septuagint and Vulgate (see also verse 11); most Hebrew manuscripts *Zina*

stand every morning to thank and praise
the LORD. They were to do the same in the
evening [31]and whenever burnt offerings
were presented to the LORD on Sabbaths
and at New Moon festivals and at appoint-
ed feasts. They were to serve before the
LORD regularly in the proper number and
in the way prescribed for them.
[32]And so the Levites carried out their re-
sponsibilities for the Tent of Meeting, for
the Holy Place and, under their brothers
the descendants of Aaron, for the service
of the temple of the LORD.

The Divisions of Priests

24 These were the divisions of the
sons of Aaron:
The sons of Aaron were Nadab, Abihu,
Eleazar and Ithamar. [2]But Nadab and Abi-
hu died before their father did, and they
had no sons; so Eleazar and Ithamar
served as the priests. [3]With the help of Za-
dok a descendant of Eleazar and Ahime-
lech a descendant of Ithamar, David sepa-
rated them into divisions for their
appointed order of ministering. [4]A larger
number of leaders were found among Ele-
azar's descendants than among Ithamar's,
and they were divided accordingly: six-
teen heads of families from Eleazar's
descendants and eight heads of families
from Ithamar's descendants. [5]They divid-
ed them impartially by drawing lots, for
there were officials of the sanctuary and
officials of God among the descendants of
both Eleazar and Ithamar.
[6]The scribe Shemaiah son of Nethanel,
a Levite, recorded their names in the pres-
ence of the king and of the officials: Zadok
the priest, Ahimelech son of Abiathar and
the heads of families of the priests and of
the Levites—one family being taken from
Eleazar and then one from Ithamar.

[7]The first lot fell to Jehoiarib,
the second to Jedaiah,
[8]the third to Harim,
the fourth to Seorim,
[9]the fifth to Malkijah,
the sixth to Mijamin,
[10]the seventh to Hakkoz,
the eighth to Abijah,
[11]the ninth to Jeshua,
the tenth to Shecaniah,
[12]the eleventh to Eliashib,
the twelfth to Jakim,
[13]the thirteenth to Huppah,
the fourteenth to Jeshebeab,
[14]the fifteenth to Bilgah,
the sixteenth to Immer,
[15]the seventeenth to Hezir,
the eighteenth to Happizzez,
[16]the nineteenth to Pethahiah,
the twentieth to Jehezkel,
[17]the twenty-first to Jakin,
the twenty-second to Gamul,
[18]the twenty-third to Delaiah
and the twenty-fourth to Maaziah.

[19]This was their appointed order of
ministering when they entered the temple
of the LORD, according to the regulations
prescribed for them by their forefather
Aaron, as the LORD, the God of Israel, had
commanded him.

The Rest of the Levites

[20]As for the rest of the descendants of
Levi:
from the sons of Amram: Shubael;
from the sons of Shubael: Jehdeiah.
[21]As for Rehabiah, from his sons:
Isshiah was the first.
[22]From the Izharites: Shelomoth;
from the sons of Shelomoth: Jahath.
[23]The sons of Hebron: Jeriah the
first,[a] Amariah the second, Jahaziel the third and Jekameam the
fourth.
[24]The son of Uzziel: Micah;
from the sons of Micah: Shamir.
[25]The brother of Micah: Isshiah;
from the sons of Isshiah: Zechariah.
[26]The sons of Merari: Mahli and Mushi.
The son of Jaaziah: Beno.
[27]The sons of Merari:
from Jaaziah: Beno, Shoham, Zaccur and Ibri.
[28]From Mahli: Eleazar, who had no
sons.
[29]From Kish: the son of Kish:
Jerahmeel.
[30]And the sons of Mushi: Mahli, Eder
and Jerimoth.

These were the Levites, according to
their families. [31]They also cast lots, just as
their brothers the descendants of Aaron
did, in the presence of King David and of

[a]*23* Two Hebrew manuscripts and some Septuagint manuscripts (see also 1 Chron. 23:19); most Hebrew manuscripts *The sons of Jeriah:*

Zadok, Ahimelech, and the heads of families of the priests and of the Levites. The families of the oldest brother were treated the same as those of the youngest.

The Singers

25 David, together with the commanders of the army, set apart some of the sons of Asaph, Heman and Jeduthun for the ministry of prophesying, accompanied by harps, lyres and cymbals. Here is the list of the men who performed this service:

2 From the sons of Asaph:
Zaccur, Joseph, Nethaniah and Asarelah. The sons of Asaph were under the supervision of Asaph, who prophesied under the king's supervision.

3 As for Jeduthun, from his sons:
Gedaliah, Zeri, Jeshaiah, Shimei,[a] Hashabiah and Mattithiah, six in all, under the supervision of their father Jeduthun, who prophesied, using the harp in thanking and praising the LORD.

4 As for Heman, from his sons:
Bukkiah, Mattaniah, Uzziel, Shubael and Jerimoth; Hananiah, Hanani, Eliathah, Giddalti and Romamti-Ezer; Joshbekashah, Mallothi, Hothir and Mahazioth. 5 All these were sons of Heman the king's seer. They were given him through the promises of God to exalt him.[b] God gave Heman fourteen sons and three daughters.

6 All these men were under the supervision of their fathers for the music of the temple of the LORD, with cymbals, lyres and harps, for the ministry at the house of God. Asaph, Jeduthun and Heman were under the supervision of the king. 7 Along with their relatives—all of them trained and skilled in music for the LORD—they numbered 288. 8 Young and old alike, teacher as well as student, cast lots for their duties.

9 The first lot, which was for
Asaph, fell to Joseph,
his sons and relatives,[c] 12[d]
the second to Gedaliah,
he and his relatives and
sons, 12
10 the third to Zaccur,
his sons and relatives, 12
11 the fourth to Izri,[e]
his sons and relatives, 12
12 the fifth to Nethaniah,
his sons and relatives, 12
13 the sixth to Bukkiah,
his sons and relatives, 12
14 the seventh to Jesarelah,[f]
his sons and relatives, 12
15 the eighth to Jeshaiah,
his sons and relatives, 12
16 the ninth to Mattaniah,
his sons and relatives, 12
17 the tenth to Shimei,
his sons and relatives, 12
18 the eleventh to Azarel,[g]
his sons and relatives, 12
19 the twelfth to Hashabiah,
his sons and relatives, 12
20 the thirteenth to Shubael,
his sons and relatives, 12
21 the fourteenth to
Mattithiah,
his sons and relatives, 12
22 the fifteenth to Jerimoth,
his sons and relatives, 12
23 the sixteenth to Hananiah,
his sons and relatives, 12
24 the seventeenth to
Joshbekashah,
his sons and relatives, 12
25 the eighteenth to Hanani,
his sons and relatives, 12
26 the nineteenth to Mallothi,
his sons and relatives, 12
27 the twentieth to Eliathah,
his sons and relatives, 12
28 the twenty-first to Hothir,
his sons and relatives, 12
29 the twenty-second to
Giddalti,
his sons and relatives, 12
30 the twenty-third to
Mahazioth,
his sons and relatives, 12
31 the twenty-fourth to
Romamti-Ezer,
his sons and relatives, 12

The Gatekeepers

26 The divisions of the gatekeepers:
From the Korahites: Meshelemiah

[a] 3 One Hebrew manuscript and some Septuagint manuscripts (see also verse 17); most Hebrew manuscripts do not have *Shimei.* [b] 5 Hebrew *exalt the horn* [c] 9 See Septuagint; Hebrew does not have *his sons and relatives.* [d] 9 See the total in verse 7; Hebrew does not have *twelve.* [e] 11 A variant of *Zeri* [f] 14 A variant of *Asarelah* [g] 18 A variant of *Uzziel*

son of Kore, one of the sons of
Asaph.
2Meshelemiah had sons:
Zechariah the firstborn,
Jediael the second,
Zebadiah the third,
Jathniel the fourth,
3Elam the fifth,
Jehohanan the sixth
and Eliehoenai the seventh.
4Obed-Edom also had sons:
Shemaiah the firstborn,
Jehozabad the second,
Joah the third,
Sacar the fourth,
Nethanel the fifth,
5Ammiel the sixth,
Issachar the seventh
and Peullethai the eighth.
(For God had blessed Obed-Edom.)

6His son Shemaiah also had sons, who were leaders in their father's family because they were very capable men. 7The sons of Shemaiah: Othni, Rephael, Obed and Elzabad; his relatives Elihu and Semakiah were also able men. 8All these were descendants of Obed-Edom; they and their sons and their relatives were capable men with the strength to do the work—descendants of Obed-Edom, 62 in all.

9Meshelemiah had sons and relatives, who were able men—18 in all.

10Hosah the Merarite had sons: Shimri the first (although he was not the firstborn, his father had appointed him the first), 11Hilkiah the second, Tabaliah the third and Zechariah the fourth. The sons and relatives of Hosah were 13 in all.

12These divisions of the gatekeepers, through their chief men, had duties for ministering in the temple of the LORD, just as their relatives had. 13Lots were cast for each gate, according to their families, young and old alike.

14The lot for the East Gate fell to Shelemiah.[a] Then lots were cast for his son Zechariah, a wise counselor, and the lot for the North Gate fell to him. 15The lot for the South Gate fell to Obed-Edom, and the lot for the storehouse fell to his sons. 16The lots for the West Gate and the Shalleketh Gate on the upper road fell to Shuppim and Hosah.

Guard was alongside of guard: 17There were six Levites a day on the east, four a day on the north, four a day on the south and two at a time at the storehouse. 18As for the court to the west, there were four at the road and two at the court itself.

19These were the divisions of the gatekeepers who were descendants of Korah and Merari.

The Treasurers and Other Officials

20Their fellow Levites were[b] in charge of the treasuries of the house of God and the treasuries for the dedicated things.

21The descendants of Ladan, who were Gershonites through Ladan and who were heads of families belonging to Ladan the Gershonite, were Jehieli, 22the sons of Jehieli, Zetham and his brother Joel. They were in charge of the treasuries of the temple of the LORD.

23From the Amramites, the Izharites, the Hebronites and the Uzzielites:

24Shubael, a descendant of Gershom son of Moses, was the officer in charge of the treasuries. 25His relatives through Eliezer: Rehabiah his son, Jeshaiah his son, Joram his son, Zicri his son and Shelomith his son. 26Shelomith and his relatives were in charge of all the treasuries for the things dedicated by King David, by the heads of families who were the commanders of thousands and commanders of hundreds, and by the other army commanders. 27Some of the plunder taken in battle they dedicated for the repair of the temple of the LORD. 28And everything dedicated by Samuel the seer and by Saul son of Kish, Abner son of Ner and Joab son of Zeruiah, and all the other dedicated things were in the care of Shelomith and his relatives.

29From the Izharites: Kenaniah and his sons were assigned duties away from the temple, as officials and judges over Israel.

30From the Hebronites: Hashabiah and his relatives—seventeen hundred able men—were responsible in Israel west of the Jordan for all

[a] 14 A variant of *Meshelemiah* [b] 20 Septuagint; Hebrew *As for the Levites, Ahijah was*

the work of the LORD and for the king's service. [31]As for the Hebronites, Jeriah was their chief according to the genealogical records of their families. In the fortieth year of David's reign a search was made in the records, and capable men among the Hebronites were found at Jazer in Gilead. [32]Jeriah had twenty-seven hundred relatives, who were able men and heads of families, and King David put them in charge of the Reubenites, the Gadites and the half-tribe of Manasseh for every matter pertaining to God and for the affairs of the king.

Army Divisions

27 This is the list of the Israelites—heads of families, commanders of thousands and commanders of hundreds, and their officers, who served the king in all that concerned the army divisions that were on duty month by month throughout the year. Each division consisted of 24,000 men.

[2]In charge of the first division, for the first month, was Jashobeam son of Zabdiel. There were 24,000 men in his division. [3]He was a descendant of Perez and chief of all the army officers for the first month.

[4]In charge of the division for the second month was Dodai the Ahohite; Mikloth was the leader of his division. There were 24,000 men in his division.

[5]The third army commander, for the third month, was Benaiah son of Jehoiada the priest. He was chief and there were 24,000 men in his division. [6]This was the Benaiah who was a mighty man among the Thirty and was over the Thirty. His son Ammizabad was in charge of his division.

[7]The fourth, for the fourth month, was Asahel the brother of Joab; his son Zebadiah was his successor. There were 24,000 men in his division.

[8]The fifth, for the fifth month, was the commander Shamhuth the Izrahite. There were 24,000 men in his division.

[9]The sixth, for the sixth month, was Ira the son of Ikkesh the Tekoite. There were 24,000 men in his division.

[10]The seventh, for the seventh month, was Helez the Pelonite, an Ephraimite. There were 24,000 men in his division.

[11]The eighth, for the eighth month, was Sibbecai the Hushathite, a Zerahite. There were 24,000 men in his division.

[12]The ninth, for the ninth month, was Abiezer the Anathothite, a Benjamite. There were 24,000 men in his division.

[13]The tenth, for the tenth month, was Maharai the Netophathite, a Zerahite. There were 24,000 men in his division.

[14]The eleventh, for the eleventh month, was Benaiah the Pirathonite, an Ephraimite. There were 24,000 men in his division.

[15]The twelfth, for the twelfth month, was Heldai the Netophathite, from the family of Othniel. There were 24,000 men in his division.

Officers of the Tribes

[16]The officers over the tribes of Israel:

over the Reubenites: Eliezer son of Zicri;
over the Simeonites: Shephatiah son of Maacah;
[17]over Levi: Hashabiah son of Kemuel;
over Aaron: Zadok;
[18]over Judah: Elihu, a brother of David;
over Issachar: Omri son of Michael;
[19]over Zebulun: Ishmaiah son of Obadiah;
over Naphtali: Jerimoth son of Azriel;
[20]over the Ephraimites: Hoshea son of Azaziah;
over half the tribe of Manasseh: Joel son of Pedaiah;
[21]over the half-tribe of Manasseh in Gilead: Iddo son of Zechariah;
over Benjamin: Jaasiel son of Abner;
[22]over Dan: Azarel son of Jeroham.

These were the officers over the tribes of Israel.

[23]David did not take the number of the men twenty years old or less, because the LORD had promised to make Israel as numerous as the stars in the sky. [24]Joab son of Zeruiah began to count the men but did not finish. Wrath came on Israel on account of this numbering, and the number

was not entered in the book[a] of the annals of King David.

The King's Overseers

25Azmaveth son of Adiel was in charge of the royal storehouses.

Jonathan son of Uzziah was in charge of the storehouses in the outlying districts, in the towns, the villages and the watchtowers.

26Ezri son of Kelub was in charge of the field workers who farmed the land.

27Shimei the Ramathite was in charge of the vineyards.

Zabdi the Shiphmite was in charge of the produce of the vineyards for the wine vats.

28Baal-Hanan the Gederite was in charge of the olive and sycamore-fig trees in the western foothills.

Joash was in charge of the supplies of olive oil.

29Shitrai the Sharonite was in charge of the herds grazing in Sharon.

Shaphat son of Adlai was in charge of the herds in the valleys.

30Obil the Ishmaelite was in charge of the camels.

Jehdeiah the Meronothite was in charge of the donkeys.

31Jaziz the Hagrite was in charge of the flocks.

All these were the officials in charge of King David's property.

32Jonathan, David's uncle, was a counselor, a man of insight and a scribe. Jehiel son of Hacmoni took care of the king's sons.

33Ahithophel was the king's counselor.

Hushai the Arkite was the king's friend. 34Ahithophel was succeeded by Jehoiada son of Benaiah and by Abiathar.

Joab was the commander of the royal army.

David's Plans for the Temple

28 David summoned all the officials of Israel to assemble at Jerusalem: the officers over the tribes, the commanders of the divisions in the service of the king, the commanders of thousands and commanders of hundreds, and the officials in charge of all the property and livestock belonging to the king and his sons, together with the palace officials, the mighty men and all the brave warriors.

2King David rose to his feet and said: "Listen to me, my brothers and my people. I had it in my heart to build a house as a place of rest for the ark of the covenant of the Lord, for the footstool of our God, and I made plans to build it. 3But God said to me, 'You are not to build a house for my Name, because you are a warrior and have shed blood.'

4"Yet the Lord, the God of Israel, chose me from my whole family to be king over Israel forever. He chose Judah as leader, and from the house of Judah he chose my family, and from my father's sons he was pleased to make me king over all Israel. 5Of all my sons—and the Lord has given me many—he has chosen my son Solomon to sit on the throne of the kingdom of the Lord over Israel. 6He said to me: 'Solomon your son is the one who will build my house and my courts, for I have chosen him to be my son, and I will be his father. 7I will establish his kingdom forever if he is unswerving in carrying out my commands and laws, as is being done at this time.'

8"So now I charge you in the sight of all Israel and of the assembly of the Lord, and in the hearing of our God: Be careful to follow all the commands of the Lord your God, that you may possess this good land and pass it on as an inheritance to your descendants forever.

9"And you, my son Solomon, acknowledge the God of your father, and serve him with wholehearted devotion and with a willing mind, for the Lord searches every heart and understands every motive behind the thoughts. If you seek him, he will be found by you; but if you forsake him, he will reject you forever. 10Consider now, for the Lord has chosen you to build a temple as a sanctuary. Be strong and do the work."

11Then David gave his son Solomon the plans for the portico of the temple, its buildings, its storerooms, its upper parts, its inner rooms and the place of atonement. 12He gave him the plans of all that the Spirit had put in his mind for the courts of the temple of the Lord and all the surrounding rooms, for the treasuries of the temple of God and for the treasuries for the dedicated things. 13He gave him instructions for the divisions of the priests and Levites, and for all the work of serving in the temple of the Lord, as well as for all

[a]24 Septuagint; Hebrew *number*

the articles to be used in its service. 14He
designated the weight of gold for all the
gold articles to be used in various kinds of
service, and the weight of silver for all the
silver articles to be used in various kinds
of service: 15the weight of gold for the gold
lampstands and their lamps, with the
weight for each lampstand and its lamps;
and the weight of silver for each silver
lampstand and its lamps, according to the
use of each lampstand; 16the weight of
gold for each table for consecrated bread;
the weight of silver for the silver tables;
17the weight of pure gold for the forks,
sprinkling bowls and pitchers; the weight
of gold for each gold dish; the weight of
silver for each silver dish; 18and the
weight of the refined gold for the altar of
incense. He also gave him the plan for the
chariot, that is, the cherubim of gold that
spread their wings and shelter the ark of
the covenant of the LORD.

19"All this," David said, "I have in writing from the hand of the LORD upon me, and he gave me understanding in all the details of the plan."

20David also said to Solomon his son, "Be strong and courageous, and do the work. Do not be afraid or discouraged, for the LORD God, my God, is with you. He will not fail you or forsake you until all the work for the service of the temple of the LORD is finished. 21The divisions of the priests and Levites are ready for all the work on the temple of God, and every willing man skilled in any craft will help you in all the work. The officials and all the people will obey your every command."

Gifts for Building the Temple

29 Then King David said to the whole assembly: "My son Solomon, the one whom God has chosen, is young and inexperienced. The task is great, because this palatial structure is not for man but for the LORD God. 2With all my resources I have provided for the temple of my God—gold for the gold work, silver for the silver, bronze for the bronze, iron for the iron and wood for the wood, as well as onyx for the settings, turquoise,[a] stones of various colors, and all kinds of fine stone and marble—all of these in large quantities. 3Besides, in my devotion to the temple of my God I now give my personal treasures of gold and silver for the temple of my God, over and above everything I have provided for this holy temple: 4three thousand talents[b] of gold (gold of Ophir) and seven thousand talents[c] of refined silver, for the overlaying of the walls of the buildings, 5for the gold work and the silver work, and for all the work to be done by the craftsmen. Now, who is willing to consecrate himself today to the LORD?"

6Then the leaders of families, the officers of the tribes of Israel, the commanders of thousands and commanders of hundreds, and the officials in charge of the king's work gave willingly. 7They gave toward the work on the temple of God five thousand talents[d] and ten thousand darics[e] of gold, ten thousand talents[f] of silver, eighteen thousand talents[g] of bronze and a hundred thousand talents[h] of iron. 8Any who had precious stones gave them to the treasury of the temple of the LORD in the custody of Jehiel the Gershonite. 9The people rejoiced at the willing response of their leaders, for they had given freely and wholeheartedly to the LORD. David the king also rejoiced greatly.

David's Prayer

10David praised the LORD in the presence of the whole assembly, saying,

"Praise be to you, O LORD,
God of our father Israel,
from everlasting to everlasting.
11Yours, O LORD, is the greatness and
the power
and the glory and the majesty and
the splendor,
for everything in heaven and earth
is yours.
Yours, O LORD, is the kingdom;
you are exalted as head over all.
12Wealth and honor come from you;
you are the ruler of all things.
In your hands are strength and power
to exalt and give strength to all.
13Now, our God, we give you thanks,
and praise your glorious name.

14"But who am I, and who are my peo-

[a] 2 The meaning of the Hebrew for this word is uncertain. [b] 4 That is, about 110 tons (about 100 metric tons) [c] 4 That is, about 260 tons (about 240 metric tons) [d] 7 That is, about 190 tons (about 170 metric tons) [e] 7 That is, about 185 pounds (about 84 kilograms) [f] 7 That is, about 375 tons (about 345 metric tons) [g] 7 That is, about 675 tons (about 610 metric tons) [h] 7 That is, about 3,750 tons (about 3,450 metric tons)

ple, that we should be able to give as generously as this? Everything comes from you, and we have given you only what comes from your hand. [15]We are aliens and strangers in your sight, as were all our forefathers. Our days on earth are like a shadow, without hope. [16]O LORD our God, as for all this abundance that we have provided for building you a temple for your Holy Name, it comes from your hand, and all of it belongs to you. [17]I know, my God, that you test the heart and are pleased with integrity. All these things have I given willingly and with honest intent. And now I have seen with joy how willingly your people who are here have given to you. [18]O LORD, God of our fathers Abraham, Isaac and Israel, keep this desire in the hearts of your people forever, and keep their hearts loyal to you. [19]And give my son Solomon the wholehearted devotion to keep your commands, requirements and decrees and to do everything to build the palatial structure for which I have provided."

[20]Then David said to the whole assembly, "Praise the LORD your God." So they all praised the LORD, the God of their fathers; they bowed low and fell prostrate before the LORD and the king.

Solomon Acknowledged as King

[21]The next day they made sacrifices to the LORD and presented burnt offerings to him: a thousand bulls, a thousand rams and a thousand male lambs, together with their drink offerings, and other sacrifices in abundance for all Israel. [22]They ate and drank with great joy in the presence of the LORD that day.

Then they acknowledged Solomon son of David as king a second time, anointing him before the LORD to be ruler and Zadok to be priest. [23]So Solomon sat on the throne of the LORD as king in place of his father David. He prospered and all Israel obeyed him. [24]All the officers and mighty men, as well as all of King David's sons, pledged their submission to King Solomon.

[25]The LORD highly exalted Solomon in the sight of all Israel and bestowed on him royal splendor such as no king over Israel ever had before.

The Death of David

[26]David son of Jesse was king over all Israel. [27]He ruled over Israel forty years—seven in Hebron and thirty-three in Jerusalem. [28]He died at a good old age, having enjoyed long life, wealth and honor. His son Solomon succeeded him as king.

[29]As for the events of King David's reign, from beginning to end, they are written in the records of Samuel the seer, the records of Nathan the prophet and the records of Gad the seer, [30]together with the details of his reign and power, and the circumstances that surrounded him and Israel and the kingdoms of all the other lands.

THIS book continues the history of God's people begun in 1 Chronicles, concentrating exclusively on the nation of Judah. It stresses God's powerful presence in the lives of those kings who believe the word of the Lord and obey his laws. Even though the people are eventually carried away to Babylon, the book ends with a reminder of God's faithfulness in bringing them back. As you read this book, think about how God keeps his promise to surround you with his love in spite of your sin.

2 CHRONICLES

Solomon Asks for Wisdom

1 Solomon son of David established himself firmly over his kingdom, for the LORD his God was with him and made him exceedingly great.

2 Then Solomon spoke to all Israel—to the commanders of thousands and commanders of hundreds, to the judges and to all the leaders in Israel, the heads of families— 3 and Solomon and the whole assembly went to the high place at Gibeon, for God's Tent of Meeting was there, which Moses the LORD's servant had made in the desert. 4 Now David had brought up the ark of God from Kiriath Jearim to the place he had prepared for it, because he had pitched a tent for it in Jerusalem. 5 But the bronze altar that Bezalel son of Uri, the son of Hur, had made was in Gibeon in front of the tabernacle of the LORD; so Solomon and the assembly inquired of him there. 6 Solomon went up to the bronze altar before the LORD in the Tent of Meeting and offered a thousand burnt offerings on it.

7 That night God appeared to Solomon and said to him, "Ask for whatever you want me to give you."

8 Solomon answered God, "You have shown great kindness to David my father

and have made me king in his place.
9Now, LORD God, let your promise to my
father David be confirmed, for you have
made me king over a people who are as
numerous as the dust of the earth. 10Give
me wisdom and knowledge, that I may
lead this people, for who is able to govern
this great people of yours?"

11God said to Solomon, "Since this is
your heart's desire and you have not
asked for wealth, riches or honor, nor for
the death of your enemies, and since you
have not asked for a long life but for wis-
dom and knowledge to govern my people
over whom I have made you king, 12there-
fore wisdom and knowledge will be given
you. And I will also give you wealth,
riches and honor, such as no king who
was before you ever had and none after
you will have."

13Then Solomon went to Jerusalem
from the high place at Gibeon, from be-
fore the Tent of Meeting. And he reigned
over Israel.

14Solomon accumulated chariots and
horses; he had fourteen hundred chariots
and twelve thousand horses,[a] which he
kept in the chariot cities and also with him
in Jerusalem. 15The king made silver and
gold as common in Jerusalem as stones,
and cedar as plentiful as sycamore-fig
trees in the foothills. 16Solomon's horses
were imported from Egypt[b] and from
Kue[c]—the royal merchants purchased
them from Kue. 17They imported a chariot
from Egypt for six hundred shekels[d] of
silver, and a horse for a hundred and fif-
ty.[e] They also exported them to all the
kings of the Hittites and of the Arameans.

Preparations for Building the Temple

2 Solomon gave orders to build a tem-
ple for the Name of the LORD and a
royal palace for himself. 2He conscripted
seventy thousand men as carriers and
eighty thousand as stonecutters in the
hills and thirty-six hundred as foremen
over them.

3Solomon sent this message to Hiram[f]
king of Tyre:

"Send me cedar logs as you did for
my father David when you sent him
cedar to build a palace to live in.
4Now I am about to build a temple for
the Name of the LORD my God and to
dedicate it to him for burning fra-
grant incense before him, for setting
out the consecrated bread regularly,
and for making burnt offerings every
morning and evening and on Sab-
baths and New Moons and at the ap-
pointed feasts of the LORD our God.
This is a lasting ordinance for Israel.

5"The temple I am going to build
will be great, because our God is
greater than all other gods. 6But who
is able to build a temple for him,
since the heavens, even the highest
heavens, cannot contain him? Who
then am I to build a temple for him,
except as a place to burn sacrifices
before him?

7"Send me, therefore, a man skilled
to work in gold and silver, bronze
and iron, and in purple, crimson and
blue yarn, and experienced in the art
of engraving, to work in Judah and
Jerusalem with my skilled craftsmen,
whom my father David provided.

8"Send me also cedar, pine and al-
gum[g] logs from Lebanon, for I know
that your men are skilled in cutting
timber there. My men will work with
yours 9to provide me with plenty of
lumber, because the temple I build
must be large and magnificent. 10I
will give your servants, the woods-
men who cut the timber, twenty
thousand cors[h] of ground wheat,
twenty thousand cors of barley,
twenty thousand baths[i] of wine and
twenty thousand baths of olive oil."

11Hiram king of Tyre replied by letter to
Solomon:

"Because the LORD loves his peo-
ple, he has made you their king."

12And Hiram added:

"Praise be to the LORD, the God of
Israel, who made heaven and earth!
He has given King David a wise son,
endowed with intelligence and dis-
cernment, who will build a temple for
the LORD and a palace for himself.

[a] 14 Or *charioteers* [b] 16 Or possibly *Muzur*, a region in Cilicia; also in verse 17 [c] 16 Probably Cilicia
[d] 17 That is, about 15 pounds (about 7 kilograms) [e] 17 That is, about 3 3/4 pounds (about 1.7 kilograms) [f] 3 Hebrew *Huram*, a variant of *Hiram*; also in verses 11 and 12 [g] 8 Probably a variant of *almug*; possibly juniper [h] 10 That is, probably about 125,000 bushels (about 4,400 kiloliters)
[i] 10 That is, probably about 115,000 gallons (about 440 kiloliters)

13"I am sending you Huram-Abi, a
man of great skill, 14whose mother
was from Dan and whose father was
from Tyre. He is trained to work in
gold and silver, bronze and iron,
stone and wood, and with purple and
blue and crimson yarn and fine linen.
He is experienced in all kinds of en-
graving and can execute any design
given to him. He will work with your
craftsmen and with those of my lord,
David your father.
15"Now let my lord send his ser-
vants the wheat and barley and the
olive oil and wine he promised, 16and
we will cut all the logs from Lebanon
that you need and will float them in
rafts by sea down to Joppa. You can
then take them up to Jerusalem."

17Solomon took a census of all the aliens who were in Israel, after the census his father David had taken; and they were found to be 153,600. 18He assigned 70,000 of them to be carriers and 80,000 to be stonecutters in the hills, with 3,600 foremen over them to keep the people working.

Solomon Builds the Temple

3 Then Solomon began to build the temple of the LORD in Jerusalem on Mount Moriah, where the LORD had appeared to his father David. It was on the threshing floor of Araunah[a] the Jebusite, the place provided by David. 2He began building on the second day of the second month in the fourth year of his reign.

3The foundation Solomon laid for building the temple of God was sixty cubits long and twenty cubits wide[b] (using the cubit of the old standard). 4The portico at the front of the temple was twenty cubits[c] long across the width of the building and twenty cubits[d] high.

He overlaid the inside with pure gold. 5He paneled the main hall with pine and covered it with fine gold and decorated it with palm tree and chain designs. 6He adorned the temple with precious stones. And the gold he used was gold of Parvaim. 7He overlaid the ceiling beams, doorframes, walls and doors of the temple with gold, and he carved cherubim on the walls.

8He built the Most Holy Place, its length corresponding to the width of the temple—twenty cubits long and twenty cubits wide. He overlaid the inside with six hundred talents[e] of fine gold. 9The gold nails weighed fifty shekels.[f] He also overlaid the upper parts with gold.

10In the Most Holy Place he made a pair of sculptured cherubim and overlaid them with gold. 11The total wingspan of the cherubim was twenty cubits. One wing of the first cherub was five cubits[g] long and touched the temple wall, while its other wing, also five cubits long, touched the wing of the other cherub. 12Similarly one wing of the second cherub was five cubits long and touched the other temple wall, and its other wing, also five cubits long, touched the wing of the first cherub. 13The wings of these cherubim extended twenty cubits. They stood on their feet, facing the main hall.[h]

14He made the curtain of blue, purple and crimson yarn and fine linen, with cherubim worked into it.

15In the front of the temple he made two pillars, which ⌊together⌋ were thirty-five cubits[i] long, each with a capital on top measuring five cubits. 16He made interwoven chains[j] and put them on top of the pillars. He also made a hundred pomegranates and attached them to the chains. 17He erected the pillars in the front of the temple, one to the south and one to the north. The one to the south he named Jakin[k] and the one to the north Boaz.[l]

The Temple's Furnishings

4 He made a bronze altar twenty cubits long, twenty cubits wide and ten cubits high.[m] 2He made the Sea of cast metal, circular in shape, measuring ten cubits from rim to rim and five cubits[n] high. It

[a] *1* Hebrew *Ornan*, a variant of *Araunah* [b] *3* That is, about 90 feet (about 27 meters) long and 30 feet (about 9 meters) wide [c] *4* That is, about 30 feet (about 9 meters); also in verses 8, 11 and 13 [d] *4* Some Septuagint and Syriac manuscripts; Hebrew *and a hundred and twenty* [e] *8* That is, about 23 tons (about 21 metric tons) [f] *9* That is, about 1 1/4 pounds (about 0.6 kilogram) [g] *11* That is, about 7 1/2 feet (about 2.3 meters); also in verse 15 [h] *13* Or *facing inward* [i] *15* That is, about 52 feet (about 16 meters) [j] *16* Or possibly *made chains in the inner sanctuary*; the meaning of the Hebrew for this phrase is uncertain. [k] *17* *Jakin* probably means *he establishes.* [l] *17* *Boaz* probably means *in him is strength.* [m] *1* That is, about 30 feet (about 9 meters) long and wide, and about 15 feet (about 4.5 meters) high [n] *2* That is, about 7 1/2 feet (about 2.3 meters)

took a line of thirty cubits[a] to measure around it. 3Below the rim, figures of bulls encircled it—ten to a cubit.[b] The bulls were cast in two rows in one piece with the Sea.

4The Sea stood on twelve bulls, three facing north, three facing west, three facing south and three facing east. The Sea rested on top of them, and their hindquarters were toward the center. 5It was a handbreadth[c] in thickness, and its rim was like the rim of a cup, like a lily blossom. It held three thousand baths.[d]

6He then made ten basins for washing and placed five on the south side and five on the north. In them the things to be used for the burnt offerings were rinsed, but the Sea was to be used by the priests for washing.

7He made ten gold lampstands according to the specifications for them and placed them in the temple, five on the south side and five on the north.

8He made ten tables and placed them in the temple, five on the south side and five on the north. He also made a hundred gold sprinkling bowls.

9He made the courtyard of the priests, and the large court and the doors for the court, and overlaid the doors with bronze. 10He placed the Sea on the south side, at the southeast corner.

11He also made the pots and shovels and sprinkling bowls.

So Huram finished the work he had undertaken for King Solomon in the temple of God:

12the two pillars;
the two bowl-shaped capitals on top of the pillars;
the two sets of network decorating the two bowl-shaped capitals on top of the pillars;
13the four hundred pomegranates for the two sets of network (two rows of pomegranates for each network, decorating the bowl-shaped capitals on top of the pillars);
14the stands with their basins;
15the Sea and the twelve bulls under it;
16the pots, shovels, meat forks and all related articles.

All the objects that Huram-Abi made for King Solomon for the temple of the LORD were of polished bronze. 17The king had them cast in clay molds in the plain of the Jordan between Succoth and Zarethan.[e] 18All these things that Solomon made amounted to so much that the weight of the bronze was not determined.

19Solomon also made all the furnishings that were in God's temple:

the golden altar;
the tables on which was the bread of the Presence;
20the lampstands of pure gold with their lamps, to burn in front of the inner sanctuary as prescribed;
21the gold floral work and lamps and tongs (they were solid gold);
22the pure gold wick trimmers, sprinkling bowls, dishes and censers;
and the gold doors of the temple: the inner doors to the Most Holy Place and the doors of the main hall.

5 When all the work Solomon had done for the temple of the LORD was finished, he brought in the things his father David had dedicated—the silver and gold and all the furnishings—and he placed them in the treasuries of God's temple.

The Ark Brought to the Temple

2Then Solomon summoned to Jerusalem the elders of Israel, all the heads of the tribes and the chiefs of the Israelite families, to bring up the ark of the LORD's covenant from Zion, the City of David. 3And all the men of Israel came together to the king at the time of the festival in the seventh month.

4When all the elders of Israel had arrived, the Levites took up the ark, 5and they brought up the ark and the Tent of Meeting and all the sacred furnishings in it. The priests, who were Levites, carried them up; 6and King Solomon and the entire assembly of Israel that had gathered about him were before the ark, sacrificing so many sheep and cattle that they could not be recorded or counted.

7The priests then brought the ark of the LORD's covenant to its place in the inner sanctuary of the temple, the Most Holy Place, and put it beneath the wings of the cherubim. 8The cherubim spread their

[a] 2 That is, about 45 feet (about 13.5 meters)
[b] 3 That is, about 1 1/2 feet (about 0.5 meter)
[c] 5 That is, about 3 inches (about 8 centimeters)
[d] 5 That is, about 17,500 gallons (about 66 kiloliters)
[e] 17 Hebrew *Zeredatha,* a variant of *Zarethan*

wings over the place of the ark and covered the ark and its carrying poles. 9These poles were so long that their ends, extending from the ark, could be seen from in front of the inner sanctuary, but not from outside the Holy Place; and they are still there today. 10There was nothing in the ark except the two tablets that Moses had placed in it at Horeb, where the LORD made a covenant with the Israelites after they came out of Egypt.

11The priests then withdrew from the Holy Place. All the priests who were there had consecrated themselves, regardless of their divisions. 12All the Levites who were musicians—Asaph, Heman, Jeduthun and their sons and relatives—stood on the east side of the altar, dressed in fine linen and playing cymbals, harps and lyres. They were accompanied by 120 priests sounding trumpets. 13The trumpeters and singers joined in unison, as with one voice, to give praise and thanks to the LORD. Accompanied by trumpets, cymbals and other instruments, they raised their voices in praise to the LORD and sang:

"He is good;
his love endures forever."

Then the temple of the LORD was filled with a cloud, 14and the priests could not perform their service because of the cloud, for the glory of the LORD filled the temple of God.

6 Then Solomon said, "The LORD has said that he would dwell in a dark cloud; 2I have built a magnificent temple for you, a place for you to dwell forever."

3While the whole assembly of Israel was standing there, the king turned around and blessed them. 4Then he said:

"Praise be to the LORD, the God of Israel, who with his hands has fulfilled what he promised with his mouth to my father David. For he said, 5'Since the day I brought my people out of Egypt, I have not chosen a city in any tribe of Israel to have a temple built for my Name to be there, nor have I chosen anyone to be the leader over my people Israel. 6But now I have chosen Jerusalem for my Name to be there, and I have chosen David to rule my people Israel.'

7"My father David had it in his heart to build a temple for the Name of the LORD, the God of Israel. 8But the LORD said to my father David, 'Because it was in your heart to build a temple for my Name, you did well to have this in your heart. 9Nevertheless, you are not the one to build the temple, but your son, who is your own flesh and blood—he is the one who will build the temple for my Name.'

10"The LORD has kept the promise he made. I have succeeded David my father and now I sit on the throne of Israel, just as the LORD promised, and I have built the temple for the Name of the LORD, the God of Israel. 11There I have placed the ark, in which is the covenant of the LORD that he made with the people of Israel."

Solomon's Prayer of Dedication

12Then Solomon stood before the altar of the LORD in front of the whole assembly of Israel and spread out his hands. 13Now he had made a bronze platform, five cubits[a] long, five cubits wide and three cubits[b] high, and had placed it in the center of the outer court. He stood on the platform and then knelt down before the whole assembly of Israel and spread out his hands toward heaven. 14He said:

"O LORD, God of Israel, there is no God like you in heaven or on earth—you who keep your covenant of love with your servants who continue wholeheartedly in your way. 15You have kept your promise to your servant David my father; with your mouth you have promised and with your hand you have fulfilled it—as it is today.

16"Now LORD, God of Israel, keep for your servant David my father the promises you made to him when you said, 'You shall never fail to have a man to sit before me on the throne of Israel, if only your sons are careful in all they do to walk before me according to my law, as you have done.' 17And now, O LORD, God of Israel, let your word that you promised your servant David come true.

18"But will God really dwell on earth with men? The heavens, even the highest heavens, cannot contain

[a] 13 That is, about 7 1/2 feet (about 2.3 meters) [b] 13 That is, about 4 1/2 feet (about 1.3 meters)

you. How much less this temple I
have built! 19Yet give attention to
your servant's prayer and his plea for
mercy, O LORD my God. Hear the cry
and the prayer that your servant is
praying in your presence. 20May your
eyes be open toward this temple day
and night, this place of which you
said you would put your Name there.
May you hear the prayer your servant
prays toward this place. 21Hear the
supplications of your servant and of
your people Israel when they pray to-
ward this place. Hear from heaven,
your dwelling place; and when you
hear, forgive.

22"When a man wrongs his neigh-
bor and is required to take an oath
and he comes and swears the oath
before your altar in this temple,
23then hear from heaven and act.
Judge between your servants, repay-
ing the guilty by bringing down on
his own head what he has done. De-
clare the innocent not guilty and so
establish his innocence.

24"When your people Israel have
been defeated by an enemy because
they have sinned against you and
when they turn back and confess
your name, praying and making sup-
plication before you in this temple,

VERSE FOR THE DAY: 2 Chronicles 6:14

AUTHOR: Susan Alexander Yates

PASSAGE FOR THE DAY: 2 Chronicles 6:12–21

Just a Beginning

Marriage is a covenant relationship—not a contract. By covenant, I mean marriage is a permanent commitment. Viewing marriage this way gives us security and freedom. Under covenant, I have a lifetime to learn how to bond together as one with my husband. The "I do" I said on my wedding day was not the *culmination* of a relationship, but the *beginning* of a new commitment to work on my relationship with my husband for the rest of my life.

Covenant provides us with the challenge to grow in our marriage. If I'm committed for the long haul, I can either live in solitude, emotionally divorcing myself, or I can build friendship with my husband by working on communication and continuing to discover new things about him.

In a sense, then, covenant encourages me to know my husband—and my husband to know me. And it gives us a lifetime to grow together in deep friendship.

MARRIAGE BUILDERS

- *Describe the difference between a covenant and a contract.*
- *Why does a binding agreement like the marriage covenant actually provide a context of freedom for you and your spouse?*

Additional Scripture Readings
Malachi 2:13–16; 2 Corinthians 1:20

Go to page 438 for your next devotional reading.

[25]then hear from heaven and forgive the sin of your people Israel and bring them back to the land you gave to them and their fathers.

[26]"When the heavens are shut up and there is no rain because your people have sinned against you, and when they pray toward this place and confess your name and turn from their sin because you have afflicted them, [27]then hear from heaven and forgive the sin of your servants, your people Israel. Teach them the right way to live, and send rain on the land you gave your people for an inheritance.

[28]"When famine or plague comes to the land, or blight or mildew, locusts or grasshoppers, or when enemies besiege them in any of their cities, whatever disaster or disease may come, [29]and when a prayer or plea is made by any of your people Israel—each one aware of his afflictions and pains, and spreading out his hands toward this temple— [30]then hear from heaven, your dwelling place. Forgive, and deal with each man according to all he does, since you know his heart (for you alone know the hearts of men), [31]so that they will fear you and walk in your ways all the time they live in the land you gave our fathers.

[32]"As for the foreigner who does not belong to your people Israel but has come from a distant land because of your great name and your mighty hand and your outstretched arm—when he comes and prays toward this temple, [33]then hear from heaven, your dwelling place, and do whatever the foreigner asks of you, so that all the peoples of the earth may know your name and fear you, as do your own people Israel, and may know that this house I have built bears your Name.

[34]"When your people go to war against their enemies, wherever you send them, and when they pray to you toward this city you have chosen and the temple I have built for your Name, [35]then hear from heaven their prayer and their plea, and uphold their cause.

[36]"When they sin against you—for there is no one who does not sin—and you become angry with them and give them over to the enemy, who takes them captive to a land far away or near; [37]and if they have a change of heart in the land where they are held captive, and repent and plead with you in the land of their captivity and say, 'We have sinned, we have done wrong and acted wickedly'; [38]and if they turn back to you with all their heart and soul in the land of their captivity where they were taken, and pray toward the land you gave their fathers, toward the city you have chosen and toward the temple I have built for your Name; [39]then from heaven, your dwelling place, hear their prayer and their pleas, and uphold their cause. And forgive your people, who have sinned against you.

[40]"Now, my God, may your eyes be open and your ears attentive to the prayers offered in this place.

[41]"Now arise, O LORD God, and
come to your resting place,
you and the ark of your might.
May your priests, O LORD God, be
clothed with salvation,
may your saints rejoice in your
goodness.
[42]O LORD God, do not reject your
anointed one.
Remember the great love
promised to David your
servant."

The Dedication of the Temple

7 When Solomon finished praying, fire came down from heaven and consumed the burnt offering and the sacrifices, and the glory of the LORD filled the temple. [2]The priests could not enter the temple of the LORD because the glory of the LORD filled it. [3]When all the Israelites saw the fire coming down and the glory of the LORD above the temple, they knelt on the pavement with their faces to the ground, and they worshiped and gave thanks to the LORD, saying,

"He is good;
his love endures forever."

[4]Then the king and all the people offered sacrifices before the LORD. [5]And King Solomon offered a sacrifice of twenty-two thousand head of cattle and a hundred and twenty thousand sheep and goats. So the king and all the people dedicated the

temple of God. 6The priests took their positions, as did the Levites with the LORD's musical instruments, which King David had made for praising the LORD and which were used when he gave thanks, saying, "His love endures forever." Opposite the Levites, the priests blew their trumpets, and all the Israelites were standing.

7Solomon consecrated the middle part of the courtyard in front of the temple of the LORD, and there he offered burnt offerings and the fat of the fellowship offerings,[a] because the bronze altar he had made could not hold the burnt offerings, the grain offerings and the fat portions.

8So Solomon observed the festival at that time for seven days, and all Israel with him—a vast assembly, people from Lebo[b] Hamath to the Wadi of Egypt. 9On the eighth day they held an assembly, for they had celebrated the dedication of the altar for seven days and the festival for seven days more. 10On the twenty-third day of the seventh month he sent the people to their homes, joyful and glad in heart for the good things the LORD had done for David and Solomon and for his people Israel.

The LORD Appears to Solomon

11When Solomon had finished the temple of the LORD and the royal palace, and had succeeded in carrying out all he had in mind to do in the temple of the LORD and in his own palace, 12the LORD appeared to him at night and said:

"I have heard your prayer and have chosen this place for myself as a temple for sacrifices.

13"When I shut up the heavens so that there is no rain, or command locusts to devour the land or send a plague among my people, 14if my people, who are called by my name, will humble themselves and pray and seek my face and turn from their wicked ways, then will I hear from heaven and will forgive their sin and will heal their land. 15Now my eyes will be open and my ears attentive to the prayers offered in this place. 16I have chosen and consecrated this temple so that my Name may be there forever. My eyes and my heart will always be there.

17"As for you, if you walk before me as David your father did, and do all I command, and observe my decrees and laws, 18I will establish your royal throne, as I covenanted with David your father when I said, 'You shall never fail to have a man to rule over Israel.'

19"But if you[c] turn away and forsake the decrees and commands I have given you[c] and go off to serve other gods and worship them, 20then I will uproot Israel from my land, which I have given them, and will reject this temple I have consecrated for my Name. I will make it a byword and an object of ridicule among all peoples. 21And though this temple is now so imposing, all who pass by will be appalled and say, 'Why has the LORD done such a thing to this land and to this temple?' 22People will answer, 'Because they have forsaken the LORD, the God of their fathers, who brought them out of Egypt, and have embraced other gods, worshiping and serving them—that is why he brought all this disaster on them.' "

Solomon's Other Activities

8 At the end of twenty years, during which Solomon built the temple of the LORD and his own palace, 2Solomon rebuilt the villages that Hiram[d] had given him, and settled Israelites in them. 3Solomon then went to Hamath Zobah and captured it. 4He also built up Tadmor in the desert and all the store cities he had built in Hamath. 5He rebuilt Upper Beth Horon and Lower Beth Horon as fortified cities, with walls and with gates and bars, 6as well as Baalath and all his store cities, and all the cities for his chariots and for his horses[e]—whatever he desired to build in Jerusalem, in Lebanon and throughout all the territory he ruled.

7All the people left from the Hittites, Amorites, Perizzites, Hivites and Jebusites (these peoples were not Israelites), 8that is, their descendants remaining in the land, whom the Israelites had not destroyed—these Solomon conscripted for his slave labor force, as it is to this day. 9But Solomon did not make slaves of the Israelites for his work; they were his fighting men, commanders of his captains, and

[a] 7 Traditionally *peace offerings* [b] 8 Or *from the entrance to* [c] 19 The Hebrew is plural.
[d] 2 Hebrew *Huram*, a variant of *Hiram*; also in verse 18 [e] 6 Or *charioteers*

commanders of his chariots and charioteers. [10]They were also King Solomon's chief officials—two hundred and fifty officials supervising the men.

[11]Solomon brought Pharaoh's daughter up from the City of David to the palace he had built for her, for he said, "My wife must not live in the palace of David king of Israel, because the places the ark of the LORD has entered are holy."

[12]On the altar of the LORD that he had built in front of the portico, Solomon sacrificed burnt offerings to the LORD, [13]according to the daily requirement for offerings commanded by Moses for Sabbaths, New Moons and the three annual feasts—the Feast of Unleavened Bread, the Feast of Weeks and the Feast of Tabernacles. [14]In keeping with the ordinance of his father David, he appointed the divisions of the priests for their duties, and the Levites to lead the praise and to assist the priests according to each day's requirement. He also appointed the gatekeepers by divisions for the various gates, because this was what David the man of God had or-

VERSE FOR THE DAY: 2 Chronicles 7:14

AUTHOR: Win Couchman

PASSAGE FOR THE DAY: 2 Chronicles 7:11–16

Shared Prayer

After we had been married nineteen years, Bob began to take his relationship with God much more seriously. We were anxious to build a mutual devotional life because we wanted to grow in our relationship with God and with each other. Our challenge was to find a prayer style that wouldn't squelch me or overwhelm or bore Bob. God gave me an idea to "interview" Bob. By asking him in the morning what he would be doing that day and what he'd like me to pray about, I could intercede for him in a way of his choosing.

Soon Bob picked up the pattern and began to interview me. In the process, he learned a great deal about what I did in the hours we were apart. If I had a difficult meeting ahead of me, I found relief in asking Bob to pray. His kind, affirming prayer would seem like an echo of my heavenly Father's encouragement.

The prayer-interview is a rich extra in our marriage. And as a result, our friendship as husband and wife has deepened.

MARRIAGE BUILDERS

♦ *Does each of you feel that the other supports you in prayer? In what ways does that lighten your burdens?*

♦ *When have you felt sure of God's presence as you prayed together? Have you recognized God's answers to those prayers?*

Additional Scripture Readings
Matthew 18:19–20; 1 John 5:14–15; 1 Timothy 2:1–4

Go to page 447 for your next devotional reading.

dered. 15They did not deviate from the
king's commands to the priests or to the
Levites in any matter, including that of the
treasuries.
16All Solomon's work was carried out,
from the day the foundation of the temple
of the LORD was laid until its completion.
So the temple of the LORD was finished.
17Then Solomon went to Ezion Geber
and Elath on the coast of Edom. 18And Hi-
ram sent him ships commanded by his
own officers, men who knew the sea.
These, with Solomon's men, sailed to
Ophir and brought back four hundred and
fifty talents[a] of gold, which they deliv-
ered to King Solomon.

The Queen of Sheba Visits Solomon

9 When the queen of Sheba heard of
Solomon's fame, she came to Jerusa-
lem to test him with hard questions. Arriv-
ing with a very great caravan—with cam-
els carrying spices, large quantities of
gold, and precious stones—she came to
Solomon and talked with him about all
she had on her mind. 2Solomon answered
all her questions; nothing was too hard for
him to explain to her. 3When the queen of
Sheba saw the wisdom of Solomon, as
well as the palace he had built, 4the food
on his table, the seating of his officials, the
attending servants in their robes, the cup-
bearers in their robes and the burnt offer-
ings he made at[b] the temple of the LORD,
she was overwhelmed.
5She said to the king, "The report I
heard in my own country about your
achievements and your wisdom is true.
6But I did not believe what they said until
I came and saw with my own eyes. In-
deed, not even half the greatness of your
wisdom was told me; you have far exceed-
ed the report I heard. 7How happy your
men must be! How happy your officials,
who continually stand before you and
hear your wisdom! 8Praise be to the LORD
your God, who has delighted in you and
placed you on his throne as king to rule
for the LORD your God. Because of the love
of your God for Israel and his desire to up-
hold them forever, he has made you king
over them, to maintain justice and righ-
teousness."
9Then she gave the king 120 talents[c] of
gold, large quantities of spices, and pre-
cious stones. There had never been such
spices as those the queen of Sheba gave to
King Solomon.
10(The men of Hiram and the men of
Solomon brought gold from Ophir; they
also brought algumwood[d] and precious
stones. 11The king used the algumwood to
make steps for the temple of the LORD and
for the royal palace, and to make harps
and lyres for the musicians. Nothing like
them had ever been seen in Judah.)
12King Solomon gave the queen of She-
ba all she desired and asked for; he gave
her more than she had brought to him.
Then she left and returned with her reti-
nue to her own country.

Solomon's Splendor

13The weight of the gold that Solomon
received yearly was 666 talents,[e] 14not
including the revenues brought in by mer-
chants and traders. Also all the kings of
Arabia and the governors of the land
brought gold and silver to Solomon.
15King Solomon made two hundred
large shields of hammered gold; six hun-
dred bekas[f] of hammered gold went into
each shield. 16He also made three hun-
dred small shields of hammered gold,
with three hundred bekas[g] of gold in
each shield. The king put them in the Pal-
ace of the Forest of Lebanon.
17Then the king made a great throne in-
laid with ivory and overlaid with pure
gold. 18The throne had six steps, and a
footstool of gold was attached to it. On
both sides of the seat were armrests, with
a lion standing beside each of them.
19Twelve lions stood on the six steps, one
at either end of each step. Nothing like it
had ever been made for any other king-
dom. 20All King Solomon's goblets were
gold, and all the household articles in the
Palace of the Forest of Lebanon were pure
gold. Nothing was made of silver, because
silver was considered of little value in Sol-
omon's day. 21The king had a fleet of trad-
ing ships[h] manned by Hiram's[i] men.
Once every three years it returned, carry-
ing gold, silver and ivory, and apes and
baboons.

[a] *18* That is, about 17 tons (about 16 metric tons)
[b] *4* Or *the ascent by which he went up to*
[c] *9* That is, about 4 1/2 tons (about 4 metric tons)
[d] *10* Probably a variant of *almugwood*
[e] *13* That is, about 25 tons (about 23 metric tons)
[f] *15* That is, about 7 1/2 pounds (about 3.5 kilograms)
[g] *16* That is, about 3 3/4 pounds (about 1.7 kilograms)
[h] *21* Hebrew *of ships that could go to Tarshish*
[i] *21* Hebrew *Huram,* a variant of *Hiram*

22King Solomon was greater in riches
and wisdom than all the other kings of the
earth. 23All the kings of the earth sought
audience with Solomon to hear the wis-
dom God had put in his heart. 24Year after
year, everyone who came brought a gift—
articles of silver and gold, and robes,
weapons and spices, and horses and
mules.
25Solomon had four thousand stalls for
horses and chariots, and twelve thousand
horses,[a] which he kept in the chariot cit-
ies and also with him in Jerusalem. 26He
ruled over all the kings from the River[b]
to the land of the Philistines, as far as the
border of Egypt. 27The king made silver as
common in Jerusalem as stones, and ce-
dar as plentiful as sycamore-fig trees in
the foothills. 28Solomon's horses were im-
ported from Egypt[c] and from all other
countries.

Solomon's Death

29As for the other events of Solomon's
reign, from beginning to end, are they
not written in the records of Nathan
the prophet, in the prophecy of Ahijah the
Shilonite and in the visions of Iddo the
seer concerning Jeroboam son of Nebat?
30Solomon reigned in Jerusalem over all
Israel forty years. 31Then he rested with
his fathers and was buried in the city of
David his father. And Rehoboam his son
succeeded him as king.

Israel Rebels Against Rehoboam

10 Rehoboam went to Shechem, for
all the Israelites had gone there to
make him king. 2When Jeroboam son of
Nebat heard this (he was in Egypt, where
he had fled from King Solomon), he re-
turned from Egypt. 3So they sent for Jero-
boam, and he and all Israel went to Reho-
boam and said to him: 4"Your father put a
heavy yoke on us, but now lighten the
harsh labor and the heavy yoke he put on
us, and we will serve you."
5Rehoboam answered, "Come back to
me in three days." So the people went
away.
6Then King Rehoboam consulted the el-
ders who had served his father Solomon
during his lifetime. "How would you ad-
vise me to answer these people?" he
asked.
7They replied, "If you will be kind to
these people and please them and give
them a favorable answer, they will always
be your servants."
8But Rehoboam rejected the advice the
elders gave him and consulted the young
men who had grown up with him and
were serving him. 9He asked them, "What
is your advice? How should we answer
these people who say to me, 'Lighten the
yoke your father put on us'?"
10The young men who had grown up
with him replied, "Tell the people who
have said to you, 'Your father put a heavy
yoke on us, but make our yoke lighter'—
tell them, 'My little finger is thicker than
my father's waist. 11My father laid on you
a heavy yoke; I will make it even heavier.
My father scourged you with whips; I will
scourge you with scorpions.' "
12Three days later Jeroboam and all the
people returned to Rehoboam, as the king
had said, "Come back to me in three
days." 13The king answered them harshly.
Rejecting the advice of the elders, 14he fol-
lowed the advice of the young men and
said, "My father made your yoke heavy; I
will make it even heavier. My father
scourged you with whips; I will scourge
you with scorpions." 15So the king did not
listen to the people, for this turn of events
was from God, to fulfill the word the LORD
had spoken to Jeroboam son of Nebat
through Ahijah the Shilonite.
16When all Israel saw that the king re-
fused to listen to them, they answered the
king:

"What share do we have in David,
what part in Jesse's son?
To your tents, O Israel!
Look after your own house,
O David!"

So all the Israelites went home. 17But as
for the Israelites who were living in the
towns of Judah, Rehoboam still ruled over
them.
18King Rehoboam sent out Adoniram,[d]
who was in charge of forced labor, but the
Israelites stoned him to death. King Reho-
boam, however, managed to get into his
chariot and escape to Jerusalem. 19So Isra-
el has been in rebellion against the house
of David to this day.
11 When Rehoboam arrived in Jeru-
salem, he mustered the house of
Judah and Benjamin—a hundred and

[a] 25 Or *charioteers* [b] 26 That is, the Euphrates
[c] 28 Or possibly *Muzur*, a region in Cilicia
[d] 18 Hebrew *Hadoram*, a variant of *Adoniram*

eighty thousand fighting men—to make war against Israel and to regain the kingdom for Rehoboam.

[2]But this word of the LORD came to Shemaiah the man of God: [3]"Say to Rehoboam son of Solomon king of Judah and to all the Israelites in Judah and Benjamin, [4]'This is what the LORD says: Do not go up to fight against your brothers. Go home, every one of you, for this is my doing.'" So they obeyed the words of the LORD and turned back from marching against Jeroboam.

Rehoboam Fortifies Judah

[5]Rehoboam lived in Jerusalem and built up towns for defense in Judah: [6]Bethlehem, Etam, Tekoa, [7]Beth Zur, Soco, Adullam, [8]Gath, Mareshah, Ziph, [9]Adoraim, Lachish, Azekah, [10]Zorah, Aijalon and Hebron. These were fortified cities in Judah and Benjamin. [11]He strengthened their defenses and put commanders in them, with supplies of food, olive oil and wine. [12]He put shields and spears in all the cities, and made them very strong. So Judah and Benjamin were his.

[13]The priests and Levites from all their districts throughout Israel sided with him. [14]The Levites even abandoned their pasturelands and property, and came to Judah and Jerusalem because Jeroboam and his sons had rejected them as priests of the LORD. [15]And he appointed his own priests for the high places and for the goat and calf idols he had made. [16]Those from every tribe of Israel who set their hearts on seeking the LORD, the God of Israel, followed the Levites to Jerusalem to offer sacrifices to the LORD, the God of their fathers. [17]They strengthened the kingdom of Judah and supported Rehoboam son of Solomon three years, walking in the ways of David and Solomon during this time.

Rehoboam's Family

[18]Rehoboam married Mahalath, who was the daughter of David's son Jerimoth and of Abihail, the daughter of Jesse's son Eliab. [19]She bore him sons: Jeush, Shemariah and Zaham. [20]Then he married Maacah daughter of Absalom, who bore him Abijah, Attai, Ziza and Shelomith. [21]Rehoboam loved Maacah daughter of Absalom more than any of his other wives and concubines. In all, he had eighteen wives and sixty concubines, twenty-eight sons and sixty daughters.

[22]Rehoboam appointed Abijah son of Maacah to be the chief prince among his brothers, in order to make him king. [23]He acted wisely, dispersing some of his sons throughout the districts of Judah and Benjamin, and to all the fortified cities. He gave them abundant provisions and took many wives for them.

Shishak Attacks Jerusalem

12 After Rehoboam's position as king was established and he had become strong, he and all Israel[a] with him abandoned the law of the LORD. [2]Because they had been unfaithful to the LORD, Shishak king of Egypt attacked Jerusalem in the fifth year of King Rehoboam. [3]With twelve hundred chariots and sixty thousand horsemen and the innumerable troops of Libyans, Sukkites and Cushites[b] that came with him from Egypt, [4]he captured the fortified cities of Judah and came as far as Jerusalem.

[5]Then the prophet Shemaiah came to Rehoboam and to the leaders of Judah who had assembled in Jerusalem for fear of Shishak, and he said to them, "This is what the LORD says, 'You have abandoned me; therefore, I now abandon you to Shishak.'"

[6]The leaders of Israel and the king humbled themselves and said, "The LORD is just."

[7]When the LORD saw that they humbled themselves, this word of the LORD came to Shemaiah: "Since they have humbled themselves, I will not destroy them but will soon give them deliverance. My wrath will not be poured out on Jerusalem through Shishak. [8]They will, however, become subject to him, so that they may learn the difference between serving me and serving the kings of other lands."

[9]When Shishak king of Egypt attacked Jerusalem, he carried off the treasures of the temple of the LORD and the treasures of the royal palace. He took everything, including the gold shields Solomon had made. [10]So King Rehoboam made bronze shields to replace them and assigned these to the commanders of the guard on duty at the entrance to the royal palace. [11]Whenever the king went to the LORD's temple, the guards went with him, bearing

[a] *1* That is, Judah, as frequently in 2 Chronicles [b] *3* That is, people from the upper Nile region

the shields, and afterward they returned them to the guardroom.

12Because Rehoboam humbled himself, the LORD's anger turned from him, and he was not totally destroyed. Indeed, there was some good in Judah.

13King Rehoboam established himself firmly in Jerusalem and continued as king. He was forty-one years old when he became king, and he reigned seventeen years in Jerusalem, the city the LORD had chosen out of all the tribes of Israel in which to put his Name. His mother's name was Naamah; she was an Ammonite. 14He did evil because he had not set his heart on seeking the LORD.

15As for the events of Rehoboam's reign, from beginning to end, are they not written in the records of Shemaiah the prophet and of Iddo the seer that deal with genealogies? There was continual warfare between Rehoboam and Jeroboam. 16Rehoboam rested with his fathers and was buried in the City of David. And Abijah his son succeeded him as king.

Abijah King of Judah

13 In the eighteenth year of the reign of Jeroboam, Abijah became king of Judah, 2and he reigned in Jerusalem three years. His mother's name was Maacah,[a] a daughter[b] of Uriel of Gibeah.

There was war between Abijah and Jeroboam. 3Abijah went into battle with a force of four hundred thousand able fighting men, and Jeroboam drew up a battle line against him with eight hundred thousand able troops.

4Abijah stood on Mount Zemaraim, in the hill country of Ephraim, and said, "Jeroboam and all Israel, listen to me! 5Don't you know that the LORD, the God of Israel, has given the kingship of Israel to David and his descendants forever by a covenant of salt? 6Yet Jeroboam son of Nebat, an official of Solomon son of David, rebelled against his master. 7Some worthless scoundrels gathered around him and opposed Rehoboam son of Solomon when he was young and indecisive and not strong enough to resist them.

8"And now you plan to resist the kingdom of the LORD, which is in the hands of David's descendants. You are indeed a vast army and have with you the golden calves that Jeroboam made to be your gods. 9But didn't you drive out the priests of the LORD, the sons of Aaron, and the Levites, and make priests of your own as the peoples of other lands do? Whoever comes to consecrate himself with a young bull and seven rams may become a priest of what are not gods.

10"As for us, the LORD is our God, and we have not forsaken him. The priests who serve the LORD are sons of Aaron, and the Levites assist them. 11Every morning and evening they present burnt offerings and fragrant incense to the LORD. They set out the bread on the ceremonially clean table and light the lamps on the gold lampstand every evening. We are observing the requirements of the LORD our God. But you have forsaken him. 12God is with us; he is our leader. His priests with their trumpets will sound the battle cry against you. Men of Israel, do not fight against the LORD, the God of your fathers, for you will not succeed."

13Now Jeroboam had sent troops around to the rear, so that while he was in front of Judah the ambush was behind them. 14Judah turned and saw that they were being attacked at both front and rear. Then they cried out to the LORD. The priests blew their trumpets 15and the men of Judah raised the battle cry. At the sound of their battle cry, God routed Jeroboam and all Israel before Abijah and Judah. 16The Israelites fled before Judah, and God delivered them into their hands. 17Abijah and his men inflicted heavy losses on them, so that there were five hundred thousand casualties among Israel's able men. 18The men of Israel were subdued on that occasion, and the men of Judah were victorious because they relied on the LORD, the God of their fathers.

19Abijah pursued Jeroboam and took from him the towns of Bethel, Jeshanah and Ephron, with their surrounding villages. 20Jeroboam did not regain power during the time of Abijah. And the LORD struck him down and he died.

21But Abijah grew in strength. He married fourteen wives and had twenty-two sons and sixteen daughters.

22The other events of Abijah's reign, what he did and what he said, are written in the annotations of the prophet Iddo.

14 And Abijah rested with his fathers and was buried in the City of Da-

[a] 2 Most Septuagint manuscripts and Syriac (see also 2 Chron. 11:20 and 1 Kings 15:2); Hebrew *Micaiah*
[b] 2 Or *granddaughter*

vid. Asa his son succeeded him as king,
and in his days the country was at peace
for ten years.

Asa King of Judah

2Asa did what was good and right in the
eyes of the LORD his God. 3He removed the
foreign altars and the high places,
smashed the sacred stones and cut down
the Asherah poles.[a] 4He commanded Ju-
dah to seek the LORD, the God of their fa-
thers, and to obey his laws and com-
mands. 5He removed the high places and
incense altars in every town in Judah, and
the kingdom was at peace under him. 6He
built up the fortified cities of Judah, since
the land was at peace. No one was at war
with him during those years, for the LORD
gave him rest.

7"Let us build up these towns," he said
to Judah, "and put walls around them,
with towers, gates and bars. The land is
still ours, because we have sought the
LORD our God; we sought him and he has
given us rest on every side." So they built
and prospered.

8Asa had an army of three hundred
thousand men from Judah, equipped with
large shields and with spears, and two
hundred and eighty thousand from Benja-
min, armed with small shields and with
bows. All these were brave fighting men.

9Zerah the Cushite marched out against
them with a vast army[b] and three hun-
dred chariots, and came as far as Mare-
shah. 10Asa went out to meet him, and
they took up battle positions in the Valley
of Zephathah near Mareshah.

11Then Asa called to the LORD his God
and said, "LORD, there is no one like you
to help the powerless against the mighty.
Help us, O LORD our God, for we rely on
you, and in your name we have come
against this vast army. O LORD, you are
our God; do not let man prevail against
you."

12The LORD struck down the Cushites
before Asa and Judah. The Cushites fled,
13and Asa and his army pursued them as
far as Gerar. Such a great number of Cush-
ites fell that they could not recover; they
were crushed before the LORD and his
forces. The men of Judah carried off a
large amount of plunder. 14They de-
stroyed all the villages around Gerar, for
the terror of the LORD had fallen upon
them. They plundered all these villages,
since there was much booty there. 15They
also attacked the camps of the herdsmen
and carried off droves of sheep and goats
and camels. Then they returned to Jerusa-
lem.

Asa's Reform

15 The Spirit of God came upon Azari-
ah son of Oded. 2He went out to
meet Asa and said to him, "Listen to me,
Asa and all Judah and Benjamin. The LORD
is with you when you are with him. If you
seek him, he will be found by you, but if
you forsake him, he will forsake you. 3For
a long time Israel was without the true
God, without a priest to teach and without
the law. 4But in their distress they turned
to the LORD, the God of Israel, and sought
him, and he was found by them. 5In those
days it was not safe to travel about, for all
the inhabitants of the lands were in great
turmoil. 6One nation was being crushed
by another and one city by another, be-
cause God was troubling them with every
kind of distress. 7But as for you, be strong
and do not give up, for your work will be
rewarded."

8When Asa heard these words and the
prophecy of Azariah son of[c] Oded the
prophet, he took courage. He removed the
detestable idols from the whole land of Ju-
dah and Benjamin and from the towns he
had captured in the hills of Ephraim. He
repaired the altar of the LORD that was in
front of the portico of the LORD's temple.

9Then he assembled all Judah and Ben-
jamin and the people from Ephraim, Ma-
nasseh and Simeon who had settled
among them, for large numbers had come
over to him from Israel when they saw
that the LORD his God was with him.

10They assembled at Jerusalem in the
third month of the fifteenth year of Asa's
reign. 11At that time they sacrificed to the
LORD seven hundred head of cattle and
seven thousand sheep and goats from the
plunder they had brought back. 12They
entered into a covenant to seek the LORD,
the God of their fathers, with all their
heart and soul. 13All who would not seek
the LORD, the God of Israel, were to be put
to death, whether small or great, man or
woman. 14They took an oath to the LORD

[a]3 That is, symbols of the goddess Asherah; here and elsewhere in 2 Chronicles
[b]9 Hebrew *with an army of a thousand thousands* or *with an army of thousands upon thousands* (see also Septuagint and verse 1); Hebrew does not have *Azariah son of.*
[c]8 Vulgate and Syriac

with loud acclamation, with shouting and with trumpets and horns. 15All Judah rejoiced about the oath because they had sworn it wholeheartedly. They sought God eagerly, and he was found by them. So the LORD gave them rest on every side.

16King Asa also deposed his grandmother Maacah from her position as queen mother, because she had made a repulsive Asherah pole. Asa cut the pole down, broke it up and burned it in the Kidron Valley. 17Although he did not remove the high places from Israel, Asa's heart was fully committed ⌊to the LORD⌋ all his life. 18He brought into the temple of God the silver and gold and the articles that he and his father had dedicated.

19There was no more war until the thirty-fifth year of Asa's reign.

Asa's Last Years

16 In the thirty-sixth year of Asa's reign Baasha king of Israel went up against Judah and fortified Ramah to prevent anyone from leaving or entering the territory of Asa king of Judah.

2Asa then took the silver and gold out of the treasuries of the LORD's temple and of his own palace and sent it to Ben-Hadad king of Aram, who was ruling in Damascus. 3"Let there be a treaty between me and you," he said, "as there was between my father and your father. See, I am sending you silver and gold. Now break your treaty with Baasha king of Israel so he will withdraw from me."

4Ben-Hadad agreed with King Asa and sent the commanders of his forces against the towns of Israel. They conquered Ijon, Dan, Abel Maim[a] and all the store cities of Naphtali. 5When Baasha heard this, he stopped building Ramah and abandoned his work. 6Then King Asa brought all the men of Judah, and they carried away from Ramah the stones and timber Baasha had been using. With them he built up Geba and Mizpah.

7At that time Hanani the seer came to Asa king of Judah and said to him: "Because you relied on the king of Aram and not on the LORD your God, the army of the king of Aram has escaped from your hand. 8Were not the Cushites[b] and Libyans a mighty army with great numbers of chariots and horsemen[c]? Yet when you relied on the LORD, he delivered them into your hand. 9For the eyes of the LORD range throughout the earth to strengthen those whose hearts are fully committed to him. You have done a foolish thing, and from now on you will be at war."

10Asa was angry with the seer because of this; he was so enraged that he put him in prison. At the same time Asa brutally oppressed some of the people.

11The events of Asa's reign, from beginning to end, are written in the book of the kings of Judah and Israel. 12In the thirty-ninth year of his reign Asa was afflicted with a disease in his feet. Though his disease was severe, even in his illness he did not seek help from the LORD, but only from the physicians. 13Then in the forty-first year of his reign Asa died and rested with his fathers. 14They buried him in the tomb that he had cut out for himself in the City of David. They laid him on a bier covered with spices and various blended perfumes, and they made a huge fire in his honor.

Jehoshaphat King of Judah

17 Jehoshaphat his son succeeded him as king and strengthened himself against Israel. 2He stationed troops in all the fortified cities of Judah and put garrisons in Judah and in the towns of Ephraim that his father Asa had captured.

3The LORD was with Jehoshaphat because in his early years he walked in the ways his father David had followed. He did not consult the Baals 4but sought the God of his father and followed his commands rather than the practices of Israel. 5The LORD established the kingdom under his control; and all Judah brought gifts to Jehoshaphat, so that he had great wealth and honor. 6His heart was devoted to the ways of the LORD; furthermore, he removed the high places and the Asherah poles from Judah.

7In the third year of his reign he sent his officials Ben-Hail, Obadiah, Zechariah, Nethanel and Micaiah to teach in the towns of Judah. 8With them were certain Levites—Shemaiah, Nethaniah, Zebadiah, Asahel, Shemiramoth, Jehonathan, Adonijah, Tobijah and Tob-Adonijah—and the priests Elishama and Jehoram. 9They taught throughout Judah, taking with them the Book of the Law of the

[a]4 Also known as *Abel Beth Maacah* [b]8 That is, people from the upper Nile region [c]8 Or *charioteers*

LORD; they went around to all the towns of Judah and taught the people.

10The fear of the LORD fell on all the kingdoms of the lands surrounding Judah, so that they did not make war with Jehoshaphat. 11Some Philistines brought Jehoshaphat gifts and silver as tribute, and the Arabs brought him flocks: seven thousand seven hundred rams and seven thousand seven hundred goats.

12Jehoshaphat became more and more powerful; he built forts and store cities in Judah 13and had large supplies in the towns of Judah. He also kept experienced fighting men in Jerusalem. 14Their enrollment by families was as follows:

From Judah, commanders of units of 1,000:
Adnah the commander, with 300,000 fighting men;
15next, Jehohanan the commander, with 280,000;
16next, Amasiah son of Zicri, who volunteered himself for the service of the LORD, with 200,000.
17From Benjamin:
Eliada, a valiant soldier, with 200,000 men armed with bows and shields;
18next, Jehozabad, with 180,000 men armed for battle.

19These were the men who served the king, besides those he stationed in the fortified cities throughout Judah.

Micaiah Prophesies Against Ahab

18 Now Jehoshaphat had great wealth and honor, and he allied himself with Ahab by marriage. 2Some years later he went down to visit Ahab in Samaria. Ahab slaughtered many sheep and cattle for him and the people with him and urged him to attack Ramoth Gilead. 3Ahab king of Israel asked Jehoshaphat king of Judah, "Will you go with me against Ramoth Gilead?"

Jehoshaphat replied, "I am as you are, and my people as your people; we will join you in the war." 4But Jehoshaphat also said to the king of Israel, "First seek the counsel of the LORD."

5So the king of Israel brought together the prophets—four hundred men—and asked them, "Shall we go to war against Ramoth Gilead, or shall I refrain?"

"Go," they answered, "for God will give it into the king's hand."

6But Jehoshaphat asked, "Is there not a prophet of the LORD here whom we can inquire of?"

7The king of Israel answered Jehoshaphat, "There is still one man through whom we can inquire of the LORD, but I hate him because he never prophesies anything good about me, but always bad. He is Micaiah son of Imlah."

"The king should not say that," Jehoshaphat replied.

8So the king of Israel called one of his officials and said, "Bring Micaiah son of Imlah at once."

9Dressed in their royal robes, the king of Israel and Jehoshaphat king of Judah were sitting on their thrones at the threshing floor by the entrance to the gate of Samaria, with all the prophets prophesying before them. 10Now Zedekiah son of Kenaanah had made iron horns, and he declared, "This is what the LORD says: 'With these you will gore the Arameans until they are destroyed.' "

11All the other prophets were prophesying the same thing. "Attack Ramoth Gilead and be victorious," they said, "for the LORD will give it into the king's hand."

12The messenger who had gone to summon Micaiah said to him, "Look, as one man the other prophets are predicting success for the king. Let your word agree with theirs, and speak favorably."

13But Micaiah said, "As surely as the LORD lives, I can tell him only what my God says."

14When he arrived, the king asked him, "Micaiah, shall we go to war against Ramoth Gilead, or shall I refrain?"

"Attack and be victorious," he answered, "for they will be given into your hand."

15The king said to him, "How many times must I make you swear to tell me nothing but the truth in the name of the LORD?"

16Then Micaiah answered, "I saw all Israel scattered on the hills like sheep without a shepherd, and the LORD said, 'These people have no master. Let each one go home in peace.' "

17The king of Israel said to Jehoshaphat, "Didn't I tell you that he never prophesies anything good about me, but only bad?"

18Micaiah continued, "Therefore hear the word of the LORD: I saw the LORD sitting on his throne with all the host of heaven standing on his right and on his left. 19And the LORD said, 'Who will entice

Ahab king of Israel into attacking Ramoth Gilead and going to his death there?'

"One suggested this, and another that. 20Finally, a spirit came forward, stood before the LORD and said, 'I will entice him.'

" 'By what means?' the LORD asked.

21" 'I will go and be a lying spirit in the mouths of all his prophets,' he said.

" 'You will succeed in enticing him,' said the LORD. 'Go and do it.'

22"So now the LORD has put a lying spirit in the mouths of these prophets of yours. The LORD has decreed disaster for you."

23Then Zedekiah son of Kenaanah went up and slapped Micaiah in the face. "Which way did the spirit from[a] the LORD go when he went from me to speak to you?" he asked.

24Micaiah replied, "You will find out on the day you go to hide in an inner room."

25The king of Israel then ordered, "Take Micaiah and send him back to Amon the ruler of the city and to Joash the king's son, 26and say, 'This is what the king says: Put this fellow in prison and give him nothing but bread and water until I return safely.' "

27Micaiah declared, "If you ever return safely, the LORD has not spoken through me." Then he added, "Mark my words, all you people!"

Ahab Killed at Ramoth Gilead

28So the king of Israel and Jehoshaphat king of Judah went up to Ramoth Gilead. 29The king of Israel said to Jehoshaphat, "I will enter the battle in disguise, but you wear your royal robes." So the king of Israel disguised himself and went into battle.

30Now the king of Aram had ordered his chariot commanders, "Do not fight with anyone, small or great, except the king of Israel." 31When the chariot commanders saw Jehoshaphat, they thought, "This is the king of Israel." So they turned to attack him, but Jehoshaphat cried out, and the LORD helped him. God drew them away from him, 32for when the chariot commanders saw that he was not the king of Israel, they stopped pursuing him.

33But someone drew his bow at random and hit the king of Israel between the sections of his armor. The king told the chariot driver, "Wheel around and get me out of the fighting. I've been wounded." 34All day long the battle raged, and the king of Israel propped himself up in his chariot facing the Arameans until evening. Then at sunset he died.

19 When Jehoshaphat king of Judah returned safely to his palace in Jerusalem, 2Jehu the seer, the son of Hanani, went out to meet him and said to the king, "Should you help the wicked and love[b] those who hate the LORD? Because of this, the wrath of the LORD is upon you. 3There is, however, some good in you, for you have rid the land of the Asherah poles and have set your heart on seeking God."

Jehoshaphat Appoints Judges

4Jehoshaphat lived in Jerusalem, and he went out again among the people from Beersheba to the hill country of Ephraim and turned them back to the LORD, the God of their fathers. 5He appointed judges in the land, in each of the fortified cities of Judah. 6He told them, "Consider carefully what you do, because you are not judging for man but for the LORD, who is with you whenever you give a verdict. 7Now let the fear of the LORD be upon you. Judge carefully, for with the LORD our God there is no injustice or partiality or bribery."

8In Jerusalem also, Jehoshaphat appointed some of the Levites, priests and heads of Israelite families to administer the law of the LORD and to settle disputes. And they lived in Jerusalem. 9He gave them these orders: "You must serve faithfully and wholeheartedly in the fear of the LORD. 10In every case that comes before you from your fellow countrymen who live in the cities—whether bloodshed or other concerns of the law, commands, decrees or ordinances—you are to warn them not to sin against the LORD; otherwise his wrath will come on you and your brothers. Do this, and you will not sin.

11"Amariah the chief priest will be over you in any matter concerning the LORD, and Zebadiah son of Ishmael, the leader of the tribe of Judah, will be over you in any matter concerning the king, and the Levites will serve as officials before you. Act with courage, and may the LORD be with those who do well."

Jehoshaphat Defeats Moab and Ammon

20 After this, the Moabites and Ammonites with some of the Meu-

[a]23 Or *Spirit of* [b]2 Or *and make alliances with*

VERSE FOR THE DAY: 2 Chronicles 19:7

AUTHOR: Kathy Tippett Henderson

PASSAGE FOR THE DAY: 2 Chronicles 19:4–11

Judge-and-Jury Syndrome

I was at the local pool when I noticed a frightened adolescent taking swimming lessons. "No! No, please, I can't!" she begged. She stood a head taller than the rest of the beginner swim class, but she sobbed like a four-year-old.

"Jump in, I'll catch you!" her teacher called. The girl bawled, "No! I can't!"

"Why do they pamper her?" I said to my friend. "Her fear only gets worse the longer they delay."

A third coach tossed the weary instructor a life preserver. It took both adults to drag the girl to the water and lower her into the arms of her teacher.

"Well, it's about time!" I thought. "They should have done that fifteen minutes ago."

Another instructor appeared beside me. "That girl went boating with her parents and brother last summer. The boat capsized, and her father managed to save only her. She watched her mother and brother drown. Now her father insists she learn to swim."

Those words stung. I looked at the drenched child as she climbed out of the pool. I had not witnessed typical childish fear—I'd just seen a young girl cross a terrifying mountain.

Forgive me, child.

Forgive me, Lord.

MARRIAGE BUILDERS

♦ *Have you ever discovered that your perception of your mate's attitudes or actions was inaccurate? What did you learn from that experience?*

♦ *Though we cannot be omniscient, as God is, how can you employ wisdom in your discernment about others?*

Additional Scripture Readings
Matthew 7:1–6; Luke 6:37–42;
1 Corinthians 4:3–5

Go to page 458 for your next devotional reading.

nites[a] came to make war on Jehoshaphat.
2Some men came and told Jehoshaphat,
"A vast army is coming against you from
Edom,[b] from the other side of the Sea.[c]
It is already in Hazazon Tamar" (that is,
En Gedi). 3Alarmed, Jehoshaphat resolved
to inquire of the LORD, and he proclaimed
a fast for all Judah. 4The people of Judah
came together to seek help from the LORD;
indeed, they came from every town in Judah to seek him.

5Then Jehoshaphat stood up in the assembly of Judah and Jerusalem at the
temple of the LORD in the front of the new
courtyard 6and said:

"O LORD, God of our fathers, are
you not the God who is in heaven?
You rule over all the kingdoms of the
nations. Power and might are in your
hand, and no one can withstand you.
7O our God, did you not drive out the
inhabitants of this land before your
people Israel and give it forever to the
descendants of Abraham your friend?
8They have lived in it and have built
in it a sanctuary for your Name, saying, 9'If calamity comes upon us,
whether the sword of judgment, or
plague or famine, we will stand in
your presence before this temple that
bears your Name and will cry out to
you in our distress, and you will hear
us and save us.'
10"But now here are men from Ammon, Moab and Mount Seir, whose
territory you would not allow Israel
to invade when they came from
Egypt; so they turned away from
them and did not destroy them. 11See
how they are repaying us by coming
to drive us out of the possession you
gave us as an inheritance. 12O our
God, will you not judge them? For we
have no power to face this vast army
that is attacking us. We do not know
what to do, but our eyes are upon
you."

13All the men of Judah, with their wives
and children and little ones, stood there
before the LORD.

14Then the Spirit of the LORD came upon
Jahaziel son of Zechariah, the son of Benaiah, the son of Jeiel, the son of Mattaniah, a Levite and descendant of Asaph, as
he stood in the assembly.

15He said: "Listen, King Jehoshaphat
and all who live in Judah and Jerusalem!
This is what the LORD says to you: 'Do not
be afraid or discouraged because of this
vast army. For the battle is not yours, but
God's. 16Tomorrow march down against
them. They will be climbing up by the
Pass of Ziz, and you will find them at the
end of the gorge in the Desert of Jeruel.
17You will not have to fight this battle.
Take up your positions; stand firm and
see the deliverance the LORD will give you,
O Judah and Jerusalem. Do not be afraid;
do not be discouraged. Go out to face
them tomorrow, and the LORD will be with
you.' "

18Jehoshaphat bowed with his face to
the ground, and all the people of Judah
and Jerusalem fell down in worship before the LORD. 19Then some Levites from
the Kohathites and Korahites stood up
and praised the LORD, the God of Israel,
with very loud voice.

20Early in the morning they left for the
Desert of Tekoa. As they set out, Jehoshaphat stood and said, "Listen to me, Judah
and people of Jerusalem! Have faith in the
LORD your God and you will be upheld;
have faith in his prophets and you will be
successful." 21After consulting the people,
Jehoshaphat appointed men to sing to the
LORD and to praise him for the splendor of
his[d] holiness as they went out at the head
of the army, saying:

"Give thanks to the LORD,
for his love endures forever."

22As they began to sing and praise, the
LORD set ambushes against the men of
Ammon and Moab and Mount Seir who
were invading Judah, and they were defeated. 23The men of Ammon and Moab
rose up against the men from Mount Seir
to destroy and annihilate them. After they
finished slaughtering the men from Seir,
they helped to destroy one another.

24When the men of Judah came to the
place that overlooks the desert and looked
toward the vast army, they saw only dead
bodies lying on the ground; no one had
escaped. 25So Jehoshaphat and his men
went to carry off their plunder, and they
found among them a great amount of

[a] 1 Some Septuagint manuscripts; Hebrew *Ammonites* [b] 2 One Hebrew manuscript; most Hebrew manuscripts, Septuagint and Vulgate *Aram* [c] 2 That is, the Dead Sea [d] 21 Or *him with the splendor of*

equipment and clothing[a] and also articles of value—more than they could take away. There was so much plunder that it took three days to collect it. 26On the fourth day they assembled in the Valley of Beracah, where they praised the LORD. This is why it is called the Valley of Beracah[b] to this day.

27Then, led by Jehoshaphat, all the men of Judah and Jerusalem returned joyfully to Jerusalem, for the LORD had given them cause to rejoice over their enemies. 28They entered Jerusalem and went to the temple of the LORD with harps and lutes and trumpets.

29The fear of God came upon all the kingdoms of the countries when they heard how the LORD had fought against the enemies of Israel. 30And the kingdom of Jehoshaphat was at peace, for his God had given him rest on every side.

The End of Jehoshaphat's Reign

31So Jehoshaphat reigned over Judah. He was thirty-five years old when he became king of Judah, and he reigned in Jerusalem twenty-five years. His mother's name was Azubah daughter of Shilhi. 32He walked in the ways of his father Asa and did not stray from them; he did what was right in the eyes of the LORD. 33The high places, however, were not removed, and the people still had not set their hearts on the God of their fathers.

34The other events of Jehoshaphat's reign, from beginning to end, are written in the annals of Jehu son of Hanani, which are recorded in the book of the kings of Israel.

35Later, Jehoshaphat king of Judah made an alliance with Ahaziah king of Israel, who was guilty of wickedness. 36He agreed with him to construct a fleet of trading ships.[c] After these were built at Ezion Geber, 37Eliezer son of Dodavahu of Mareshah prophesied against Jehoshaphat, saying, "Because you have made an alliance with Ahaziah, the LORD will destroy what you have made." The ships were wrecked and were not able to set sail to trade.[d]

21 Then Jehoshaphat rested with his fathers and was buried with them in the City of David. And Jehoram his son succeeded him as king. 2Jehoram's brothers, the sons of Jehoshaphat, were Azariah, Jehiel, Zechariah, Azariahu, Michael and Shephatiah. All these were sons of Jehoshaphat king of Israel.[e] 3Their father had given them many gifts of silver and gold and articles of value, as well as fortified cities in Judah, but he had given the kingdom to Jehoram because he was his firstborn son.

Jehoram King of Judah

4When Jehoram established himself firmly over his father's kingdom, he put all his brothers to the sword along with some of the princes of Israel. 5Jehoram was thirty-two years old when he became king, and he reigned in Jerusalem eight years. 6He walked in the ways of the kings of Israel, as the house of Ahab had done, for he married a daughter of Ahab. He did evil in the eyes of the LORD. 7Nevertheless, because of the covenant the LORD had made with David, the LORD was not willing to destroy the house of David. He had promised to maintain a lamp for him and his descendants forever.

8In the time of Jehoram, Edom rebelled against Judah and set up its own king. 9So Jehoram went there with his officers and all his chariots. The Edomites surrounded him and his chariot commanders, but he rose up and broke through by night. 10To this day Edom has been in rebellion against Judah.

Libnah revolted at the same time, because Jehoram had forsaken the LORD, the God of his fathers. 11He had also built high places on the hills of Judah and had caused the people of Jerusalem to prostitute themselves and had led Judah astray.

12Jehoram received a letter from Elijah the prophet, which said:

> "This is what the LORD, the God of your father David, says: 'You have not walked in the ways of your father Jehoshaphat or of Asa king of Judah. 13But you have walked in the ways of the kings of Israel, and you have led Judah and the people of Jerusalem to prostitute themselves, just as the house of Ahab did. You have also murdered your own brothers, members of your father's house, men who were better than you. 14So now the

[a]25 Some Hebrew manuscripts and Vulgate; most Hebrew manuscripts *corpses* [b]26 *Beracah* means *praise.* [c]36 Hebrew *of ships that could go to Tarshish* [d]37 Hebrew *sail for Tarshish* [e]2 That is, Judah, as frequently in 2 Chronicles

LORD is about to strike your people,
your sons, your wives and everything
that is yours, with a heavy blow.
15You yourself will be very ill with a
lingering disease of the bowels, until
the disease causes your bowels to
come out.' "

16The LORD aroused against Jehoram
the hostility of the Philistines and of the
Arabs who lived near the Cushites. 17They
attacked Judah, invaded it and carried off
all the goods found in the king's palace,
together with his sons and wives. Not a
son was left to him except Ahaziah,[a] the
youngest.

18After all this, the LORD afflicted Jeho-
ram with an incurable disease of the bow-
els. 19In the course of time, at the end of
the second year, his bowels came out be-
cause of the disease, and he died in great
pain. His people made no fire in his honor,
as they had for his fathers.

20Jehoram was thirty-two years old
when he became king, and he reigned in
Jerusalem eight years. He passed away, to
no one's regret, and was buried in the City
of David, but not in the tombs of the
kings.

Ahaziah King of Judah

22 The people of Jerusalem made
Ahaziah, Jehoram's youngest son,
king in his place, since the raiders, who
came with the Arabs into the camp, had
killed all the older sons. So Ahaziah son of
Jehoram king of Judah began to reign.

2Ahaziah was twenty-two[b] years old
when he became king, and he reigned in
Jerusalem one year. His mother's name
was Athaliah, a granddaughter of Omri.

3He too walked in the ways of the house
of Ahab, for his mother encouraged him
in doing wrong. 4He did evil in the eyes of
the LORD, as the house of Ahab had done,
for after his father's death they became his
advisers, to his undoing. 5He also fol-
lowed their counsel when he went with
Joram[c] son of Ahab king of Israel to war
against Hazael king of Aram at Ramoth
Gilead. The Arameans wounded Joram;
6so he returned to Jezreel to recover from
the wounds they had inflicted on him at
Ramoth[d] in his battle with Hazael king of
Aram.

Then Ahaziah[e] son of Jehoram king of
Judah went down to Jezreel to see Joram
son of Ahab because he had been
wounded.

7Through Ahaziah's visit to Joram, God
brought about Ahaziah's downfall. When
Ahaziah arrived, he went out with Joram
to meet Jehu son of Nimshi, whom the
LORD had anointed to destroy the house of
Ahab. 8While Jehu was executing judg-
ment on the house of Ahab, he found the
princes of Judah and the sons of Ahazi-
ah's relatives, who had been attending
Ahaziah, and he killed them. 9He then
went in search of Ahaziah, and his men
captured him while he was hiding in Sa-
maria. He was brought to Jehu and put to
death. They buried him, for they said, "He
was a son of Jehoshaphat, who sought the
LORD with all his heart." So there was no
one in the house of Ahaziah powerful
enough to retain the kingdom.

Athaliah and Joash

10When Athaliah the mother of Ahaziah
saw that her son was dead, she proceeded
to destroy the whole royal family of the
house of Judah. 11But Jehosheba,[f] the
daughter of King Jehoram, took Joash son
of Ahaziah and stole him away from
among the royal princes who were about
to be murdered and put him and his nurse
in a bedroom. Because Jehosheba,[f] the
daughter of King Jehoram and wife of the
priest Jehoiada, was Ahaziah's sister, she
hid the child from Athaliah so she could
not kill him. 12He remained hidden with
them at the temple of God for six years
while Athaliah ruled the land.

23 In the seventh year Jehoiada
showed his strength. He made a
covenant with the commanders of units of
a hundred: Azariah son of Jeroham, Ish-
mael son of Jehohanan, Azariah son of
Obed, Maaseiah son of Adaiah, and Elish-
aphat son of Zicri. 2They went throughout
Judah and gathered the Levites and the
heads of Israelite families from all the
towns. When they came to Jerusalem,
3the whole assembly made a covenant
with the king at the temple of God.

[a] 17 Hebrew *Jehoahaz*, a variant of *Ahaziah* [b] 2 Some Septuagint manuscripts and Syriac (see also 2 Kings 8:26); Hebrew *forty-two* [c] 5 Hebrew *Jehoram*, a variant of *Joram*; also in verses 6 and 7 [d] 6 Hebrew *Ramah*, a variant of *Ramoth* [e] 6 Some Hebrew manuscripts, Septuagint, Vulgate and Syriac (see also 2 Kings 8:29); most Hebrew manuscripts *Azariah* [f] 11 Hebrew *Jehoshabeath*, a variant of *Jehosheba*

Jehoiada said to them, "The king's son shall reign, as the LORD promised concerning the descendants of David. 4Now this is what you are to do: A third of you priests and Levites who are going on duty on the Sabbath are to keep watch at the doors, 5a third of you at the royal palace and a third at the Foundation Gate, and all the other men are to be in the courtyards of the temple of the LORD. 6No one is to enter the temple of the LORD except the priests and Levites on duty; they may enter because they are consecrated, but all the other men are to guard what the LORD has assigned to them.[a] 7The Levites are to station themselves around the king, each man with his weapons in his hand. Anyone who enters the temple must be put to death. Stay close to the king wherever he goes."

8The Levites and all the men of Judah did just as Jehoiada the priest ordered. Each one took his men—those who were going on duty on the Sabbath and those who were going off duty—for Jehoiada the priest had not released any of the divisions. 9Then he gave the commanders of units of a hundred the spears and the large and small shields that had belonged to King David and that were in the temple of God. 10He stationed all the men, each with his weapon in his hand, around the king—near the altar and the temple, from the south side to the north side of the temple.

11Jehoiada and his sons brought out the king's son and put the crown on him; they presented him with a copy of the covenant and proclaimed him king. They anointed him and shouted, "Long live the king!"

12When Athaliah heard the noise of the people running and cheering the king, she went to them at the temple of the LORD. 13She looked, and there was the king, standing by his pillar at the entrance. The officers and the trumpeters were beside the king, and all the people of the land were rejoicing and blowing trumpets, and singers with musical instruments were leading the praises. Then Athaliah tore her robes and shouted, "Treason! Treason!"

14Jehoiada the priest sent out the commanders of units of a hundred, who were in charge of the troops, and said to them: "Bring her out between the ranks[b] and put to the sword anyone who follows her." For the priest had said, "Do not put her to death at the temple of the LORD." 15So they seized her as she reached the entrance of the Horse Gate on the palace grounds, and there they put her to death.

16Jehoiada then made a covenant that he and the people and the king[c] would be the LORD's people. 17All the people went to the temple of Baal and tore it down. They smashed the altars and idols and killed Mattan the priest of Baal in front of the altars.

18Then Jehoiada placed the oversight of the temple of the LORD in the hands of the priests, who were Levites, to whom David had made assignments in the temple, to present the burnt offerings of the LORD as written in the Law of Moses, with rejoicing and singing, as David had ordered. 19He also stationed doorkeepers at the gates of the LORD's temple so that no one who was in any way unclean might enter.

20He took with him the commanders of hundreds, the nobles, the rulers of the people and all the people of the land and brought the king down from the temple of the LORD. They went into the palace through the Upper Gate and seated the king on the royal throne, 21and all the people of the land rejoiced. And the city was quiet, because Athaliah had been slain with the sword.

Joash Repairs the Temple

24 Joash was seven years old when he became king, and he reigned in Jerusalem forty years. His mother's name was Zibiah; she was from Beersheba. 2Joash did what was right in the eyes of the LORD all the years of Jehoiada the priest. 3Jehoiada chose two wives for him, and he had sons and daughters.

4Some time later Joash decided to restore the temple of the LORD. 5He called together the priests and Levites and said to them, "Go to the towns of Judah and collect the money due annually from all Israel, to repair the temple of your God. Do it now." But the Levites did not act at once.

6Therefore the king summoned Jehoiada the chief priest and said to him, "Why haven't you required the Levites to bring in from Judah and Jerusalem the tax imposed by Moses the servant of the LORD

[a] 6 Or *to observe the LORD's command ⌜not to enter⌝*
[b] 14 Or *out from the precincts*
[c] 16 Or *covenant between ⌜the LORD⌝ and the people and the king that they* (see 2 Kings 11:17)

and by the assembly of Israel for the Tent of the Testimony?"

7Now the sons of that wicked woman Athaliah had broken into the temple of God and had used even its sacred objects for the Baals.

8At the king's command, a chest was made and placed outside, at the gate of the temple of the LORD. 9A proclamation was then issued in Judah and Jerusalem that they should bring to the LORD the tax that Moses the servant of God had required of Israel in the desert. 10All the officials and all the people brought their contributions gladly, dropping them into the chest until it was full. 11Whenever the chest was brought in by the Levites to the king's officials and they saw that there was a large amount of money, the royal secretary and the officer of the chief priest would come and empty the chest and carry it back to its place. They did this regularly and collected a great amount of money. 12The king and Jehoiada gave it to the men who carried out the work required for the temple of the LORD. They hired masons and carpenters to restore the LORD's temple, and also workers in iron and bronze to repair the temple.

13The men in charge of the work were diligent, and the repairs progressed under them. They rebuilt the temple of God according to its original design and reinforced it. 14When they had finished, they brought the rest of the money to the king and Jehoiada, and with it were made articles for the LORD's temple: articles for the service and for the burnt offerings, and also dishes and other objects of gold and silver. As long as Jehoiada lived, burnt offerings were presented continually in the temple of the LORD.

15Now Jehoiada was old and full of years, and he died at the age of a hundred and thirty. 16He was buried with the kings in the City of David, because of the good he had done in Israel for God and his temple.

The Wickedness of Joash

17After the death of Jehoiada, the officials of Judah came and paid homage to the king, and he listened to them. 18They abandoned the temple of the LORD, the God of their fathers, and worshiped Asherah poles and idols. Because of their guilt, God's anger came upon Judah and Jerusalem. 19Although the LORD sent prophets to the people to bring them back to him, and though they testified against them, they would not listen.

20Then the Spirit of God came upon Zechariah son of Jehoiada the priest. He stood before the people and said, "This is what God says: 'Why do you disobey the LORD's commands? You will not prosper. Because you have forsaken the LORD, he has forsaken you.' "

21But they plotted against him, and by order of the king they stoned him to death in the courtyard of the LORD's temple. 22King Joash did not remember the kindness Zechariah's father Jehoiada had shown him but killed his son, who said as he lay dying, "May the LORD see this and call you to account."

23At the turn of the year,[a] the army of Aram marched against Joash; it invaded Judah and Jerusalem and killed all the leaders of the people. They sent all the plunder to their king in Damascus. 24Although the Aramean army had come with only a few men, the LORD delivered into their hands a much larger army. Because Judah had forsaken the LORD, the God of their fathers, judgment was executed on Joash. 25When the Arameans withdrew, they left Joash severely wounded. His officials conspired against him for murdering the son of Jehoiada the priest, and they killed him in his bed. So he died and was buried in the City of David, but not in the tombs of the kings.

26Those who conspired against him were Zabad,[b] son of Shimeath an Ammonite woman, and Jehozabad, son of Shimrith[c] a Moabite woman. 27The account of his sons, the many prophecies about him, and the record of the restoration of the temple of God are written in the annotations on the book of the kings. And Amaziah his son succeeded him as king.

Amaziah King of Judah

25 Amaziah was twenty-five years old when he became king, and he reigned in Jerusalem twenty-nine years. His mother's name was Jehoaddin[d]; she was from Jerusalem. 2He did what was right in the eyes of the LORD, but not wholeheartedly. 3After the kingdom was firmly in his control, he executed the offi-

[a]23 Probably in the spring [b]26 A variant of *Jozabad* [c]26 A variant of *Shomer* [d]1 Hebrew *Jehoaddan*, a variant of *Jehoaddin*

cials who had murdered his father the king. 4Yet he did not put their sons to death, but acted in accordance with what is written in the Law, in the Book of Moses, where the LORD commanded: "Fathers shall not be put to death for their children, nor children put to death for their fathers; each is to die for his own sins."[a]

5Amaziah called the people of Judah together and assigned them according to their families to commanders of thousands and commanders of hundreds for all Judah and Benjamin. He then mustered those twenty years old or more and found that there were three hundred thousand men ready for military service, able to handle the spear and shield. 6He also hired a hundred thousand fighting men from Israel for a hundred talents[b] of silver.

7But a man of God came to him and said, "O king, these troops from Israel must not march with you, for the LORD is not with Israel—not with any of the people of Ephraim. 8Even if you go and fight courageously in battle, God will overthrow you before the enemy, for God has the power to help or to overthrow."

9Amaziah asked the man of God, "But what about the hundred talents I paid for these Israelite troops?"

The man of God replied, "The LORD can give you much more than that."

10So Amaziah dismissed the troops who had come to him from Ephraim and sent them home. They were furious with Judah and left for home in a great rage.

11Amaziah then marshaled his strength and led his army to the Valley of Salt, where he killed ten thousand men of Seir. 12The army of Judah also captured ten thousand men alive, took them to the top of a cliff and threw them down so that all were dashed to pieces.

13Meanwhile the troops that Amaziah had sent back and had not allowed to take part in the war raided Judean towns from Samaria to Beth Horon. They killed three thousand people and carried off great quantities of plunder.

14When Amaziah returned from slaughtering the Edomites, he brought back the gods of the people of Seir. He set them up as his own gods, bowed down to them and burned sacrifices to them. 15The anger of the LORD burned against Amaziah, and he sent a prophet to him, who said, "Why do you consult this people's gods, which could not save their own people from your hand?"

16While he was still speaking, the king said to him, "Have we appointed you an adviser to the king? Stop! Why be struck down?"

So the prophet stopped but said, "I know that God has determined to destroy you, because you have done this and have not listened to my counsel."

17After Amaziah king of Judah consulted his advisers, he sent this challenge to Jehoash[c] son of Jehoahaz, the son of Jehu, king of Israel: "Come, meet me face to face."

18But Jehoash king of Israel replied to Amaziah king of Judah: "A thistle in Lebanon sent a message to a cedar in Lebanon, 'Give your daughter to my son in marriage.' Then a wild beast in Lebanon came along and trampled the thistle underfoot. 19You say to yourself that you have defeated Edom, and now you are arrogant and proud. But stay at home! Why ask for trouble and cause your own downfall and that of Judah also?"

20Amaziah, however, would not listen, for God so worked that he might hand them over to ⌊Jehoash⌋, because they sought the gods of Edom. 21So Jehoash king of Israel attacked. He and Amaziah king of Judah faced each other at Beth Shemesh in Judah. 22Judah was routed by Israel, and every man fled to his home. 23Jehoash king of Israel captured Amaziah king of Judah, the son of Joash, the son of Ahaziah,[d] at Beth Shemesh. Then Jehoash brought him to Jerusalem and broke down the wall of Jerusalem from the Ephraim Gate to the Corner Gate—a section about six hundred feet[e] long. 24He took all the gold and silver and all the articles found in the temple of God that had been in the care of Obed-Edom, together with the palace treasures and the hostages, and returned to Samaria.

25Amaziah son of Joash king of Judah lived for fifteen years after the death of Jehoash son of Jehoahaz king of Israel. 26As for the other events of Amaziah's reign, from beginning to end, are they not written in the book of the kings of Judah and

[a] 4 Deut. 24:16 [b] 6 That is, about 3 3/4 tons (about 3.4 metric tons); also in verse 9 [c] 17 Hebrew *Joash*, a variant of *Jehoash*; also in verses 18, 21, 23 and 25 [d] 23 Hebrew *Jehoahaz*, a variant of *Ahaziah* [e] 23 Hebrew *four hundred cubits* (about 180 meters)

Israel? 27From the time that Amaziah
turned away from following the LORD,
they conspired against him in Jerusalem
and he fled to Lachish, but they sent men
after him to Lachish and killed him there.
28He was brought back by horse and was
buried with his fathers in the City of Ju-
dah.

Uzziah King of Judah

26 Then all the people of Judah took
Uzziah,[a] who was sixteen years
old, and made him king in place of his fa-
ther Amaziah. 2He was the one who re-
built Elath and restored it to Judah after
Amaziah rested with his fathers.

3Uzziah was sixteen years old when he
became king, and he reigned in Jerusalem
fifty-two years. His mother's name was
Jecoliah; she was from Jerusalem. 4He did
what was right in the eyes of the LORD, just
as his father Amaziah had done. 5He
sought God during the days of Zechariah,
who instructed him in the fear[b] of God.
As long as he sought the LORD, God gave
him success.

6He went to war against the Philistines
and broke down the walls of Gath, Jabneh
and Ashdod. He then rebuilt towns near
Ashdod and elsewhere among the Philis-
tines. 7God helped him against the Philis-
tines and against the Arabs who lived in
Gur Baal and against the Meunites. 8The
Ammonites brought tribute to Uzziah,
and his fame spread as far as the border of
Egypt, because he had become very pow-
erful.

9Uzziah built towers in Jerusalem at the
Corner Gate, at the Valley Gate and at the
angle of the wall, and he fortified them.
10He also built towers in the desert and
dug many cisterns, because he had much
livestock in the foothills and in the plain.
He had people working his fields and
vineyards in the hills and in the fertile
lands, for he loved the soil.

11Uzziah had a well-trained army, ready
to go out by divisions according to their
numbers as mustered by Jeiel the secre-
tary and Maaseiah the officer under the di-
rection of Hananiah, one of the royal offi-
cials. 12The total number of family leaders
over the fighting men was 2,600. 13Under
their command was an army of 307,500
men trained for war, a powerful force to
support the king against his enemies.
14Uzziah provided shields, spears, hel-
mets, coats of armor, bows and sling-
stones for the entire army. 15In Jerusalem
he made machines designed by skillful
men for use on the towers and on the cor-
ner defenses to shoot arrows and hurl
large stones. His fame spread far and
wide, for he was greatly helped until he
became powerful.

16But after Uzziah became powerful, his
pride led to his downfall. He was unfaith-
ful to the LORD his God, and entered the
temple of the LORD to burn incense on the
altar of incense. 17Azariah the priest with
eighty other courageous priests of the
LORD followed him in. 18They confronted
him and said, "It is not right for you, Uzzi-
ah, to burn incense to the LORD. That is for
the priests, the descendants of Aaron,
who have been consecrated to burn in-
cense. Leave the sanctuary, for you have
been unfaithful; and you will not be hon-
ored by the LORD God."

19Uzziah, who had a censer in his hand
ready to burn incense, became angry.
While he was raging at the priests in their
presence before the incense altar in the
LORD's temple, leprosy[c] broke out on his
forehead. 20When Azariah the chief priest
and all the other priests looked at him,
they saw that he had leprosy on his fore-
head, so they hurried him out. Indeed, he
himself was eager to leave, because the
LORD had afflicted him.

21King Uzziah had leprosy until the day
he died. He lived in a separate house[d]—
leprous, and excluded from the temple of
the LORD. Jotham his son had charge of
the palace and governed the people of the
land.

22The other events of Uzziah's reign,
from beginning to end, are recorded by
the prophet Isaiah son of Amoz. 23Uzziah
rested with his fathers and was buried
near them in a field for burial that be-
longed to the kings, for people said, "He
had leprosy." And Jotham his son suc-
ceeded him as king.

Jotham King of Judah

27 Jotham was twenty-five years old
when he became king, and he

[a] 1 Also called *Azariah* [b] 5 Many Hebrew manuscripts, Septuagint and Syriac; other Hebrew manuscripts *vision* [c] 19 The Hebrew word was used for various diseases affecting the skin—not necessarily leprosy; also in verses 20, 21 and 23. [d] 21 Or *in a house where he was relieved of responsibilities*

reigned in Jerusalem sixteen years. His mother's name was Jerusha daughter of Zadok. 2He did what was right in the eyes of the LORD, just as his father Uzziah had done, but unlike him he did not enter the temple of the LORD. The people, however, continued their corrupt practices. 3Jotham rebuilt the Upper Gate of the temple of the LORD and did extensive work on the wall at the hill of Ophel. 4He built towns in the Judean hills and forts and towers in the wooded areas.

5Jotham made war on the king of the Ammonites and conquered them. That year the Ammonites paid him a hundred talents[a] of silver, ten thousand cors[b] of wheat and ten thousand cors of barley. The Ammonites brought him the same amount also in the second and third years.

6Jotham grew powerful because he walked steadfastly before the LORD his God.

7The other events in Jotham's reign, including all his wars and the other things he did, are written in the book of the kings of Israel and Judah. 8He was twenty-five years old when he became king, and he reigned in Jerusalem sixteen years. 9Jotham rested with his fathers and was buried in the City of David. And Ahaz his son succeeded him as king.

Ahaz King of Judah

28 Ahaz was twenty years old when he became king, and he reigned in Jerusalem sixteen years. Unlike David his father, he did not do what was right in the eyes of the LORD. 2He walked in the ways of the kings of Israel and also made cast idols for worshiping the Baals. 3He burned sacrifices in the Valley of Ben Hinnom and sacrificed his sons in the fire, following the detestable ways of the nations the LORD had driven out before the Israelites. 4He offered sacrifices and burned incense at the high places, on the hilltops and under every spreading tree.

5Therefore the LORD his God handed him over to the king of Aram. The Arameans defeated him and took many of his people as prisoners and brought them to Damascus.

He was also given into the hands of the king of Israel, who inflicted heavy casualties on him. 6In one day Pekah son of Remaliah killed a hundred and twenty thousand soldiers in Judah—because Judah had forsaken the LORD, the God of their fathers. 7Zicri, an Ephraimite warrior, killed Maaseiah the king's son, Azrikam the officer in charge of the palace, and Elkanah, second to the king. 8The Israelites took captive from their kinsmen two hundred thousand wives, sons and daughters. They also took a great deal of plunder, which they carried back to Samaria.

9But a prophet of the LORD named Oded was there, and he went out to meet the army when it returned to Samaria. He said to them, "Because the LORD, the God of your fathers, was angry with Judah, he gave them into your hand. But you have slaughtered them in a rage that reaches to heaven. 10And now you intend to make the men and women of Judah and Jerusalem your slaves. But aren't you also guilty of sins against the LORD your God? 11Now listen to me! Send back your fellow countrymen you have taken as prisoners, for the LORD's fierce anger rests on you."

12Then some of the leaders in Ephraim—Azariah son of Jehohanan, Berekiah son of Meshillemoth, Jehizkiah son of Shallum, and Amasa son of Hadlai—confronted those who were arriving from the war. 13"You must not bring those prisoners here," they said, "or we will be guilty before the LORD. Do you intend to add to our sin and guilt? For our guilt is already great, and his fierce anger rests on Israel."

14So the soldiers gave up the prisoners and plunder in the presence of the officials and all the assembly. 15The men designated by name took the prisoners, and from the plunder they clothed all who were naked. They provided them with clothes and sandals, food and drink, and healing balm. All those who were weak they put on donkeys. So they took them back to their fellow countrymen at Jericho, the City of Palms, and returned to Samaria.

16At that time King Ahaz sent to the king[c] of Assyria for help. 17The Edomites had again come and attacked Judah and carried away prisoners, 18while the Philistines had raided towns in the foothills and in the Negev of Judah. They captured and occupied Beth Shemesh, Aijalon and Ge-

[a]5 That is, about 3 3/4 tons (about 3.4 metric tons) [b]5 That is, probably about 62,000 bushels (about 2,200 kiloliters) [c]16 One Hebrew manuscript, Septuagint and Vulgate (see also 2 Kings 16:7); most Hebrew manuscripts *kings*

deroth, as well as Soco, Timnah and Gimzo, with their surrounding villages. 19The LORD had humbled Judah because of Ahaz king of Israel,[a] for he had promoted wickedness in Judah and had been most unfaithful to the LORD. 20Tiglath-Pileser[b] king of Assyria came to him, but he gave him trouble instead of help. 21Ahaz took some of the things from the temple of the LORD and from the royal palace and from the princes and presented them to the king of Assyria, but that did not help him.

22In his time of trouble King Ahaz became even more unfaithful to the LORD. 23He offered sacrifices to the gods of Damascus, who had defeated him; for he thought, "Since the gods of the kings of Aram have helped them, I will sacrifice to them so they will help me." But they were his downfall and the downfall of all Israel.

24Ahaz gathered together the furnishings from the temple of God and took them away.[c] He shut the doors of the LORD's temple and set up altars at every street corner in Jerusalem. 25In every town in Judah he built high places to burn sacrifices to other gods and provoked the LORD, the God of his fathers, to anger.

26The other events of his reign and all his ways, from beginning to end, are written in the book of the kings of Judah and Israel. 27Ahaz rested with his fathers and was buried in the city of Jerusalem, but he was not placed in the tombs of the kings of Israel. And Hezekiah his son succeeded him as king.

Hezekiah Purifies the Temple

29 Hezekiah was twenty-five years old when he became king, and he reigned in Jerusalem twenty-nine years. His mother's name was Abijah daughter of Zechariah. 2He did what was right in the eyes of the LORD, just as his father David had done.

3In the first month of the first year of his reign, he opened the doors of the temple of the LORD and repaired them. 4He brought in the priests and the Levites, assembled them in the square on the east side 5and said: "Listen to me, Levites! Consecrate yourselves now and consecrate the temple of the LORD, the God of your fathers. Remove all defilement from the sanctuary. 6Our fathers were unfaithful; they did evil in the eyes of the LORD our God and forsook him. They turned their faces away from the LORD's dwelling place and turned their backs on him. 7They also shut the doors of the portico and put out the lamps. They did not burn incense or present any burnt offerings at the sanctuary to the God of Israel. 8Therefore, the anger of the LORD has fallen on Judah and Jerusalem; he has made them an object of dread and horror and scorn, as you can see with your own eyes. 9This is why our fathers have fallen by the sword and why our sons and daughters and our wives are in captivity. 10Now I intend to make a covenant with the LORD, the God of Israel, so that his fierce anger will turn away from us. 11My sons, do not be negligent now, for the LORD has chosen you to stand before him and serve him, to minister before him and to burn incense."

12Then these Levites set to work:
from the Kohathites,
Mahath son of Amasai and Joel son of Azariah;
from the Merarites,
Kish son of Abdi and Azariah son of Jehallelel;
from the Gershonites,
Joah son of Zimmah and Eden son of Joah;
13from the descendants of Elizaphan,
Shimri and Jeiel;
from the descendants of Asaph,
Zechariah and Mattaniah;
14from the descendants of Heman,
Jehiel and Shimei;
from the descendants of Jeduthun,
Shemaiah and Uzziel.

15When they had assembled their brothers and consecrated themselves, they went in to purify the temple of the LORD, as the king had ordered, following the word of the LORD. 16The priests went into the sanctuary of the LORD to purify it. They brought out to the courtyard of the LORD's temple everything unclean that they found in the temple of the LORD. The Levites took it and carried it out to the Kidron Valley. 17They began the consecration on the first day of the first month, and by the eighth day of the month they reached the portico of the LORD. For eight more days they consecrated the temple of the LORD itself, finishing on the sixteenth day of the first month.

18Then they went in to King Hezekiah

[a] *19* That is, Judah, as frequently in 2 Chronicles [b] *20* Hebrew *Tilgath-Pilneser*, a variant of *Tiglath-Pileser* [c] *24* Or *and cut them up*

and reported: "We have purified the entire
temple of the LORD, the altar of burnt of-
fering with all its utensils, and the table
for setting out the consecrated bread, with
all its articles. 19We have prepared and
consecrated all the articles that King Ahaz
removed in his unfaithfulness while he
was king. They are now in front of the
LORD's altar."
20Early the next morning King Hezekiah
gathered the city officials together and
went up to the temple of the LORD. 21They
brought seven bulls, seven rams, seven
male lambs and seven male goats as a sin
offering for the kingdom, for the sanctu-
ary and for Judah. The king commanded
the priests, the descendants of Aaron, to
offer these on the altar of the LORD. 22So
they slaughtered the bulls, and the priests
took the blood and sprinkled it on the al-
tar; next they slaughtered the rams and
sprinkled their blood on the altar; then
they slaughtered the lambs and sprinkled
their blood on the altar. 23The goats for
the sin offering were brought before the
king and the assembly, and they laid their
hands on them. 24The priests then slaugh-
tered the goats and presented their blood
on the altar for a sin offering to atone for
all Israel, because the king had ordered
the burnt offering and the sin offering for
all Israel.
25He stationed the Levites in the temple
of the LORD with cymbals, harps and lyres
in the way prescribed by David and Gad
the king's seer and Nathan the prophet;
this was commanded by the LORD through
his prophets. 26So the Levites stood ready
with David's instruments, and the priests
with their trumpets.
27Hezekiah gave the order to sacrifice
the burnt offering on the altar. As the of-
fering began, singing to the LORD began
also, accompanied by trumpets and the
instruments of David king of Israel. 28The
whole assembly bowed in worship, while
the singers sang and the trumpeters
played. All this continued until the sacri-
fice of the burnt offering was completed.
29When the offerings were finished, the
king and everyone present with him knelt
down and worshiped. 30King Hezekiah
and his officials ordered the Levites to
praise the LORD with the words of David
and of Asaph the seer. So they sang
praises with gladness and bowed their
heads and worshiped.
31Then Hezekiah said, "You have now
dedicated yourselves to the LORD. Come
and bring sacrifices and thank offerings to
the temple of the LORD." So the assembly
brought sacrifices and thank offerings,
and all whose hearts were willing brought
burnt offerings.
32The number of burnt offerings the as-
sembly brought was seventy bulls, a hun-
dred rams and two hundred male lambs —
all of them for burnt offerings to the LORD.
33The animals consecrated as sacrifices
amounted to six hundred bulls and three
thousand sheep and goats. 34The priests,
however, were too few to skin all the
burnt offerings; so their kinsmen the Le-
vites helped them until the task was fin-
ished and until other priests had been
consecrated, for the Levites had been
more conscientious in consecrating them-
selves than the priests had been. 35There
were burnt offerings in abundance, to-
gether with the fat of the fellowship offer-
ings[a] and the drink offerings that accom-
panied the burnt offerings.
So the service of the temple of the LORD
was reestablished. 36Hezekiah and all the
people rejoiced at what God had brought
about for his people, because it was done
so quickly.

Hezekiah Celebrates the Passover

30 Hezekiah sent word to all Israel
and Judah and also wrote letters to
Ephraim and Manasseh, inviting them to
come to the temple of the LORD in Jerusa-
lem and celebrate the Passover to the
LORD, the God of Israel. 2The king and his
officials and the whole assembly in Jeru-
salem decided to celebrate the Passover in
the second month. 3They had not been
able to celebrate it at the regular time be-
cause not enough priests had consecrated
themselves and the people had not assem-
bled in Jerusalem. 4The plan seemed right
both to the king and to the whole assem-
bly. 5They decided to send a proclamation
throughout Israel, from Beersheba to Dan,
calling the people to come to Jerusalem
and celebrate the Passover to the LORD,
the God of Israel. It had not been celebrat-
ed in large numbers according to what
was written.
6At the king's command, couriers went
throughout Israel and Judah with letters
from the king and from his officials, which
read:

[a]35 Traditionally *peace offerings*

"People of Israel, return to the LORD, the God of Abraham, Isaac and Israel, that he may return to you who are left, who have escaped from the hand of the kings of Assyria. 7Do not be like your fathers and brothers, who were unfaithful to the LORD, the God of their fathers, so that he made them an object of horror, as you see. 8Do not be stiff-necked, as your fathers were; submit to the LORD. Come to the sanctuary, which he has consecrated forever. Serve the LORD your God, so that his fierce anger will turn away from you. 9If you return to the LORD, then your brothers and your children will be shown compassion by their captors and will come back to this land, for the LORD your God is gracious and compassionate. He will not turn his face from you if you return to him."

10The couriers went from town to town in Ephraim and Manasseh, as far as Zebulun, but the people scorned and ridiculed

VERSE FOR THE DAY: 2 Chronicles 30:12

AUTHOR: Howard and Jeanne Hendricks

PASSAGE FOR THE DAY: 2 Chronicles 30:1–27

A Shared Purpose

There's a dental school in Dallas just down the street from the seminary, and some of the wives there have taken out "insurance policies" to protect them in case of divorce. These contracts say, "If I put you through dental school and you divorce me, I get a rebate on the investment." The problem is they are in a marriage in terms only, not in spirit.

We have wives at Dallas Seminary who say, "Hey, I married you, but I didn't sign on for a church or the mission field." Often times those wives are the ones who have not been given an opportunity to be a part of the decision-making process. The husband feels called, but forgets that his wife is a part of that call.

Somehow we've gotten the marriage concept confused. We think God's direction to one spouse is somehow going to minimize or obliterate the other. That's a pretty mean concept of God. God is in the business of improving people through marriage—not destroying them through marriage.

MARRIAGE BUILDERS

♦ *How have you handled it when one of you began to feel God calling you to some change in your lives?*

♦ *As God has blended you as a couple, how have each of you improved as individuals?*

Additional Scripture Readings
Romans 12:4–5; 2 Thessalonians 2:16–17

Go to page 471 for your next devotional reading.

them. 11Nevertheless, some men of Asher,
Manasseh and Zebulun humbled them-
selves and went to Jerusalem. 12Also in
Judah the hand of God was on the people
to give them unity of mind to carry out
what the king and his officials had or-
dered, following the word of the LORD.

13A very large crowd of people assem-
bled in Jerusalem to celebrate the Feast of
Unleavened Bread in the second month.
14They removed the altars in Jerusalem
and cleared away the incense altars and
threw them into the Kidron Valley.

15They slaughtered the Passover lamb
on the fourteenth day of the second
month. The priests and the Levites were
ashamed and consecrated themselves and
brought burnt offerings to the temple of
the LORD. 16Then they took up their regu-
lar positions as prescribed in the Law of
Moses the man of God. The priests sprin-
kled the blood handed to them by the Le-
vites. 17Since many in the crowd had not
consecrated themselves, the Levites had
to kill the Passover lambs for all those
who were not ceremonially clean and
could not consecrate ⌊their lambs⌋ to the
LORD. 18Although most of the many peo-
ple who came from Ephraim, Manasseh,
Issachar and Zebulun had not purified
themselves, yet they ate the Passover,
contrary to what was written. But Hezeki-
ah prayed for them, saying, "May the
LORD, who is good, pardon everyone
19who sets his heart on seeking God—the
LORD, the God of his fathers—even if he is
not clean according to the rules of the
sanctuary." 20And the LORD heard Hezeki-
ah and healed the people.

21The Israelites who were present in Je-
rusalem celebrated the Feast of Unleav-
ened Bread for seven days with great re-
joicing, while the Levites and priests sang
to the LORD every day, accompanied by
the LORD's instruments of praise.[a]

22Hezekiah spoke encouragingly to all
the Levites, who showed good under-
standing of the service of the LORD. For the
seven days they ate their assigned portion
and offered fellowship offerings[b] and
praised the LORD, the God of their fathers.

23The whole assembly then agreed to
celebrate the festival seven more days; so
for another seven days they celebrated
joyfully. 24Hezekiah king of Judah provid-
ed a thousand bulls and seven thousand
sheep and goats for the assembly, and the
officials provided them with a thousand
bulls and ten thousand sheep and goats. A
great number of priests consecrated them-
selves. 25The entire assembly of Judah re-
joiced, along with the priests and Levites
and all who had assembled from Israel, in-
cluding the aliens who had come from Is-
rael and those who lived in Judah. 26There
was great joy in Jerusalem, for since the
days of Solomon son of David king of Isra-
el there had been nothing like this in Jeru-
salem. 27The priests and the Levites stood
to bless the people, and God heard them,
for their prayer reached heaven, his holy
dwelling place.

31 When all this had ended, the Isra-
elites who were there went out to
the towns of Judah, smashed the sacred
stones and cut down the Asherah poles.
They destroyed the high places and the al-
tars throughout Judah and Benjamin and
in Ephraim and Manasseh. After they had
destroyed all of them, the Israelites re-
turned to their own towns and to their
own property.

Contributions for Worship

2Hezekiah assigned the priests and Le-
vites to divisions—each of them accord-
ing to their duties as priests or Levites—to
offer burnt offerings and fellowship offer-
ings,[b] to minister, to give thanks and to
sing praises at the gates of the LORD's
dwelling. 3The king contributed from his
own possessions for the morning and eve-
ning burnt offerings and for the burnt of-
ferings on the Sabbaths, New Moons and
appointed feasts as written in the Law of
the LORD. 4He ordered the people living in
Jerusalem to give the portion due the
priests and Levites so they could devote
themselves to the Law of the LORD. 5As
soon as the order went out, the Israelites
generously gave the firstfruits of their
grain, new wine, oil and honey and all that
the fields produced. They brought a great
amount, a tithe of everything. 6The men of
Israel and Judah who lived in the towns of
Judah also brought a tithe of their herds
and flocks and a tithe of the holy things
dedicated to the LORD their God, and they
piled them in heaps. 7They began doing
this in the third month and finished in the
seventh month. 8When Hezekiah and his
officials came and saw the heaps, they

[a] 21 Or *priests praised the* LORD *every day with resounding instruments belonging to the* LORD
[b] 22,2 Traditionally *peace offerings*

praised the LORD and blessed his people Israel.

9Hezekiah asked the priests and Levites about the heaps; 10and Azariah the chief priest, from the family of Zadok, answered, "Since the people began to bring their contributions to the temple of the LORD, we have had enough to eat and plenty to spare, because the LORD has blessed his people, and this great amount is left over."

11Hezekiah gave orders to prepare storerooms in the temple of the LORD, and this was done. 12Then they faithfully brought in the contributions, tithes and dedicated gifts. Conaniah, a Levite, was in charge of these things, and his brother Shimei was next in rank. 13Jehiel, Azaziah, Nahath, Asahel, Jerimoth, Jozabad, Eliel, Ismakiah, Mahath and Benaiah were supervisors under Conaniah and Shimei his brother, by appointment of King Hezekiah and Azariah the official in charge of the temple of God.

14Kore son of Imnah the Levite, keeper of the East Gate, was in charge of the freewill offerings given to God, distributing the contributions made to the LORD and also the consecrated gifts. 15Eden, Miniamin, Jeshua, Shemaiah, Amariah and Shecaniah assisted him faithfully in the towns of the priests, distributing to their fellow priests according to their divisions, old and young alike.

16In addition, they distributed to the males three years old or more whose names were in the genealogical records—all who would enter the temple of the LORD to perform the daily duties of their various tasks, according to their responsibilities and their divisions. 17And they distributed to the priests enrolled by their families in the genealogical records and likewise to the Levites twenty years old or more, according to their responsibilities and their divisions. 18They included all the little ones, the wives, and the sons and daughters of the whole community listed in these genealogical records. For they were faithful in consecrating themselves.

19As for the priests, the descendants of Aaron, who lived on the farm lands around their towns or in any other towns, men were designated by name to distribute portions to every male among them and to all who were recorded in the genealogies of the Levites.

20This is what Hezekiah did throughout Judah, doing what was good and right and faithful before the LORD his God. 21In everything that he undertook in the service of God's temple and in obedience to the law and the commands, he sought his God and worked wholeheartedly. And so he prospered.

Sennacherib Threatens Jerusalem

32 After all that Hezekiah had so faithfully done, Sennacherib king of Assyria came and invaded Judah. He laid siege to the fortified cities, thinking to conquer them for himself. 2When Hezekiah saw that Sennacherib had come and that he intended to make war on Jerusalem, 3he consulted with his officials and military staff about blocking off the water from the springs outside the city, and they helped him. 4A large force of men assembled, and they blocked all the springs and the stream that flowed through the land. "Why should the kings[a] of Assyria come and find plenty of water?" they said. 5Then he worked hard repairing all the broken sections of the wall and building towers on it. He built another wall outside that one and reinforced the supporting terraces[b] of the City of David. He also made large numbers of weapons and shields.

6He appointed military officers over the people and assembled them before him in the square at the city gate and encouraged them with these words: 7"Be strong and courageous. Do not be afraid or discouraged because of the king of Assyria and the vast army with him, for there is a greater power with us than with him. 8With him is only the arm of flesh, but with us is the LORD our God to help us and to fight our battles." And the people gained confidence from what Hezekiah the king of Judah said.

9Later, when Sennacherib king of Assyria and all his forces were laying siege to Lachish, he sent his officers to Jerusalem with this message for Hezekiah king of Judah and for all the people of Judah who were there:

10"This is what Sennacherib king of Assyria says: On what are you basing your confidence, that you remain in Jerusalem under siege? 11When Hezekiah says, 'The LORD our God

[a]4 Hebrew; Septuagint and Syriac *king* [b]5 Or *the Millo*

will save us from the hand of the king
of Assyria,' he is misleading you, to
let you die of hunger and thirst. 12Did
not Hezekiah himself remove this
god's high places and altars, saying to
Judah and Jerusalem, 'You must wor-
ship before one altar and burn sacri-
fices on it'?
13"Do you not know what I and my
fathers have done to all the peoples of
the other lands? Were the gods of
those nations ever able to deliver
their land from my hand? 14Who of
all the gods of these nations that my
fathers destroyed has been able to
save his people from me? How then
can your god deliver you from my
hand? 15Now do not let Hezekiah de-
ceive you and mislead you like this.
Do not believe him, for no god of any
nation or kingdom has been able to
deliver his people from my hand or
the hand of my fathers. How much
less will your god deliver you from
my hand!"

16Sennacherib's officers spoke further against the LORD God and against his servant Hezekiah. 17The king also wrote letters insulting the LORD, the God of Israel, and saying this against him: "Just as the gods of the peoples of the other lands did not rescue their people from my hand, so the god of Hezekiah will not rescue his people from my hand." 18Then they called out in Hebrew to the people of Jerusalem who were on the wall, to terrify them and make them afraid in order to capture the city. 19They spoke about the God of Jerusalem as they did about the gods of the other peoples of the world—the work of men's hands.

20King Hezekiah and the prophet Isaiah son of Amoz cried out in prayer to heaven about this. 21And the LORD sent an angel, who annihilated all the fighting men and the leaders and officers in the camp of the Assyrian king. So he withdrew to his own land in disgrace. And when he went into the temple of his god, some of his sons cut him down with the sword.

22So the LORD saved Hezekiah and the people of Jerusalem from the hand of Sennacherib king of Assyria and from the hand of all others. He took care of them[a] on every side. 23Many brought offerings to Jerusalem for the LORD and valuable gifts for Hezekiah king of Judah. From then on he was highly regarded by all the nations.

Hezekiah's Pride, Success and Death

24In those days Hezekiah became ill and was at the point of death. He prayed to the LORD, who answered him and gave him a miraculous sign. 25But Hezekiah's heart was proud and he did not respond to the kindness shown him; therefore the LORD's wrath was on him and on Judah and Jerusalem. 26Then Hezekiah repented of the pride of his heart, as did the people of Jerusalem; therefore the LORD's wrath did not come upon them during the days of Hezekiah.

27Hezekiah had very great riches and honor, and he made treasuries for his silver and gold and for his precious stones, spices, shields and all kinds of valuables. 28He also made buildings to store the harvest of grain, new wine and oil; and he made stalls for various kinds of cattle, and pens for the flocks. 29He built villages and acquired great numbers of flocks and herds, for God had given him very great riches.

30It was Hezekiah who blocked the upper outlet of the Gihon spring and channeled the water down to the west side of the City of David. He succeeded in everything he undertook. 31But when envoys were sent by the rulers of Babylon to ask him about the miraculous sign that had occurred in the land, God left him to test him and to know everything that was in his heart.

32The other events of Hezekiah's reign and his acts of devotion are written in the vision of the prophet Isaiah son of Amoz in the book of the kings of Judah and Israel. 33Hezekiah rested with his fathers and was buried on the hill where the tombs of David's descendants are. All Judah and the people of Jerusalem honored him when he died. And Manasseh his son succeeded him as king.

Manasseh King of Judah

33 Manasseh was twelve years old when he became king, and he reigned in Jerusalem fifty-five years. 2He did evil in the eyes of the LORD, following the detestable practices of the nations the LORD had driven out before the Israelites. 3He rebuilt the high places his father Hezekiah had demolished; he also erected al-

[a]22 Hebrew; Septuagint and Vulgate *He gave them rest*

tars to the Baals and made Asherah poles. He bowed down to all the starry hosts and worshiped them. 4He built altars in the temple of the LORD, of which the LORD had said, "My Name will remain in Jerusalem forever." 5In both courts of the temple of the LORD, he built altars to all the starry hosts. 6He sacrificed his sons in[a] the fire in the Valley of Ben Hinnom, practiced sorcery, divination and witchcraft, and consulted mediums and spiritists. He did much evil in the eyes of the LORD, provoking him to anger.

7He took the carved image he had made and put it in God's temple, of which God had said to David and to his son Solomon, "In this temple and in Jerusalem, which I have chosen out of all the tribes of Israel, I will put my Name forever. 8I will not again make the feet of the Israelites leave the land I assigned to your forefathers, if only they will be careful to do everything I commanded them concerning all the laws, decrees and ordinances given through Moses." 9But Manasseh led Judah and the people of Jerusalem astray, so that they did more evil than the nations the LORD had destroyed before the Israelites.

10The LORD spoke to Manasseh and his people, but they paid no attention. 11So the LORD brought against them the army commanders of the king of Assyria, who took Manasseh prisoner, put a hook in his nose, bound him with bronze shackles and took him to Babylon. 12In his distress he sought the favor of the LORD his God and humbled himself greatly before the God of his fathers. 13And when he prayed to him, the LORD was moved by his entreaty and listened to his plea; so he brought him back to Jerusalem and to his kingdom. Then Manasseh knew that the LORD is God.

14Afterward he rebuilt the outer wall of the City of David, west of the Gihon spring in the valley, as far as the entrance of the Fish Gate and encircling the hill of Ophel; he also made it much higher. He stationed military commanders in all the fortified cities in Judah.

15He got rid of the foreign gods and removed the image from the temple of the LORD, as well as all the altars he had built on the temple hill and in Jerusalem; and he threw them out of the city. 16Then he restored the altar of the LORD and sacrificed fellowship offerings[b] and thank offerings on it, and told Judah to serve the LORD, the God of Israel. 17The people, however, continued to sacrifice at the high places, but only to the LORD their God.

18The other events of Manasseh's reign, including his prayer to his God and the words the seers spoke to him in the name of the LORD, the God of Israel, are written in the annals of the kings of Israel.[c] 19His prayer and how God was moved by his entreaty, as well as all his sins and unfaithfulness, and the sites where he built high places and set up Asherah poles and idols before he humbled himself—all are written in the records of the seers.[d] 20Manasseh rested with his fathers and was buried in his palace. And Amon his son succeeded him as king.

Amon King of Judah

21Amon was twenty-two years old when he became king, and he reigned in Jerusalem two years. 22He did evil in the eyes of the LORD, as his father Manasseh had done. Amon worshiped and offered sacrifices to all the idols Manasseh had made. 23But unlike his father Manasseh, he did not humble himself before the LORD; Amon increased his guilt.

24Amon's officials conspired against him and assassinated him in his palace. 25Then the people of the land killed all who had plotted against King Amon, and they made Josiah his son king in his place.

Josiah's Reforms

34 Josiah was eight years old when he became king, and he reigned in Jerusalem thirty-one years. 2He did what was right in the eyes of the LORD and walked in the ways of his father David, not turning aside to the right or to the left.

3In the eighth year of his reign, while he was still young, he began to seek the God of his father David. In his twelfth year he began to purge Judah and Jerusalem of high places, Asherah poles, carved idols and cast images. 4Under his direction the altars of the Baals were torn down; he cut to pieces the incense altars that were above them, and smashed the Asherah poles, the idols and the images. These he

[a]6 Or *He made his sons pass through* [b]16 Traditionally *peace offerings* [c]18 That is, Judah, as frequently in 2 Chronicles [d]19 One Hebrew manuscript and Septuagint; most Hebrew manuscripts *of Hozai*

broke to pieces and scattered over the graves of those who had sacrificed to them. 5He burned the bones of the priests on their altars, and so he purged Judah and Jerusalem. 6In the towns of Manasseh, Ephraim and Simeon, as far as Naphtali, and in the ruins around them, 7he tore down the altars and the Asherah poles and crushed the idols to powder and cut to pieces all the incense altars throughout Israel. Then he went back to Jerusalem.

8In the eighteenth year of Josiah's reign, to purify the land and the temple, he sent Shaphan son of Azaliah and Maaseiah the ruler of the city, with Joah son of Joahaz, the recorder, to repair the temple of the LORD his God.

9They went to Hilkiah the high priest and gave him the money that had been brought into the temple of God, which the Levites who were the doorkeepers had collected from the people of Manasseh, Ephraim and the entire remnant of Israel and from all the people of Judah and Benjamin and the inhabitants of Jerusalem. 10Then they entrusted it to the men appointed to supervise the work on the LORD's temple. These men paid the workers who repaired and restored the temple. 11They also gave money to the carpenters and builders to purchase dressed stone, and timber for joists and beams for the buildings that the kings of Judah had allowed to fall into ruin.

12The men did the work faithfully. Over them to direct them were Jahath and Obadiah, Levites descended from Merari, and Zechariah and Meshullam, descended from Kohath. The Levites—all who were skilled in playing musical instruments—13had charge of the laborers and supervised all the workers from job to job. Some of the Levites were secretaries, scribes and doorkeepers.

The Book of the Law Found

14While they were bringing out the money that had been taken into the temple of the LORD, Hilkiah the priest found the Book of the Law of the LORD that had been given through Moses. 15Hilkiah said to Shaphan the secretary, "I have found the Book of the Law in the temple of the LORD." He gave it to Shaphan.

16Then Shaphan took the book to the king and reported to him: "Your officials are doing everything that has been committed to them. 17They have paid out the money that was in the temple of the LORD and have entrusted it to the supervisors and workers." 18Then Shaphan the secretary informed the king, "Hilkiah the priest has given me a book." And Shaphan read from it in the presence of the king.

19When the king heard the words of the Law, he tore his robes. 20He gave these orders to Hilkiah, Ahikam son of Shaphan, Abdon son of Micah,[a] Shaphan the secretary and Asaiah the king's attendant: 21"Go and inquire of the LORD for me and for the remnant in Israel and Judah about what is written in this book that has been found. Great is the LORD's anger that is poured out on us because our fathers have not kept the word of the LORD; they have not acted in accordance with all that is written in this book."

22Hilkiah and those the king had sent with him[b] went to speak to the prophetess Huldah, who was the wife of Shallum son of Tokhath,[c] the son of Hasrah,[d] keeper of the wardrobe. She lived in Jerusalem, in the Second District.

23She said to them, "This is what the LORD, the God of Israel, says: Tell the man who sent you to me, 24'This is what the LORD says: I am going to bring disaster on this place and its people—all the curses written in the book that has been read in the presence of the king of Judah. 25Because they have forsaken me and burned incense to other gods and provoked me to anger by all that their hands have made,[e] my anger will be poured out on this place and will not be quenched.' 26Tell the king of Judah, who sent you to inquire of the LORD, 'This is what the LORD, the God of Israel, says concerning the words you heard: 27Because your heart was responsive and you humbled yourself before God when you heard what he spoke against this place and its people, and because you humbled yourself before me and tore your robes and wept in my presence, I have heard you, declares the LORD. 28Now I will gather you to your fathers, and you will be buried in peace. Your eyes will not see all the disaster I am going to

[a]20 Also called *Acbor son of Micaiah* [b]22 One Hebrew manuscript, Vulgate and Syriac; most Hebrew manuscripts do not have *had sent with him.* [c]22 Also called *Tikvah* [d]22 Also called *Harhas*
[e]25 Or *by everything they have done*

bring on this place and on those who live here.' "

So they took her answer back to the king.

[29]Then the king called together all the elders of Judah and Jerusalem. [30]He went up to the temple of the LORD with the men of Judah, the people of Jerusalem, the priests and the Levites—all the people from the least to the greatest. He read in their hearing all the words of the Book of the Covenant, which had been found in the temple of the LORD. [31]The king stood by his pillar and renewed the covenant in the presence of the LORD—to follow the LORD and keep his commands, regulations and decrees with all his heart and all his soul, and to obey the words of the covenant written in this book.

[32]Then he had everyone in Jerusalem and Benjamin pledge themselves to it; the people of Jerusalem did this in accordance with the covenant of God, the God of their fathers.

[33]Josiah removed all the detestable idols from all the territory belonging to the Israelites, and he had all who were present in Israel serve the LORD their God. As long as he lived, they did not fail to follow the LORD, the God of their fathers.

Josiah Celebrates the Passover

35 Josiah celebrated the Passover to the LORD in Jerusalem, and the Passover lamb was slaughtered on the fourteenth day of the first month. [2]He appointed the priests to their duties and encouraged them in the service of the LORD's temple. [3]He said to the Levites, who instructed all Israel and who had been consecrated to the LORD: "Put the sacred ark in the temple that Solomon son of David king of Israel built. It is not to be carried about on your shoulders. Now serve the LORD your God and his people Israel. [4]Prepare yourselves by families in your divisions, according to the directions written by David king of Israel and by his son Solomon.

[5]"Stand in the holy place with a group of Levites for each subdivision of the families of your fellow countrymen, the lay people. [6]Slaughter the Passover lambs, consecrate yourselves and prepare ⌊the lambs⌋ for your fellow countrymen, doing what the LORD commanded through Moses."

[7]Josiah provided for all the lay people who were there a total of thirty thousand sheep and goats for the Passover offerings, and also three thousand cattle—all from the king's own possessions.

[8]His officials also contributed voluntarily to the people and the priests and Levites. Hilkiah, Zechariah and Jehiel, the administrators of God's temple, gave the priests twenty-six hundred Passover offerings and three hundred cattle. [9]Also Conaniah along with Shemaiah and Nethanel, his brothers, and Hashabiah, Jeiel and Jozabad, the leaders of the Levites, provided five thousand Passover offerings and five hundred head of cattle for the Levites.

[10]The service was arranged and the priests stood in their places with the Levites in their divisions as the king had ordered. [11]The Passover lambs were slaughtered, and the priests sprinkled the blood handed to them, while the Levites skinned the animals. [12]They set aside the burnt offerings to give them to the subdivisions of the families of the people to offer to the LORD, as is written in the Book of Moses. They did the same with the cattle. [13]They roasted the Passover animals over the fire as prescribed, and boiled the holy offerings in pots, caldrons and pans and served them quickly to all the people. [14]After this, they made preparations for themselves and for the priests, because the priests, the descendants of Aaron, were sacrificing the burnt offerings and the fat portions until nightfall. So the Levites made preparations for themselves and for the Aaronic priests.

[15]The musicians, the descendants of Asaph, were in the places prescribed by David, Asaph, Heman and Jeduthun the king's seer. The gatekeepers at each gate did not need to leave their posts, because their fellow Levites made the preparations for them.

[16]So at that time the entire service of the LORD was carried out for the celebration of the Passover and the offering of burnt offerings on the altar of the LORD, as King Josiah had ordered. [17]The Israelites who were present celebrated the Passover at that time and observed the Feast of Unleavened Bread for seven days. [18]The Passover had not been observed like this in Israel since the days of the prophet Samuel; and none of the kings of Israel had ever celebrated such a Passover as did Josiah, with the priests, the Levites and all Judah and Israel who were there with the people of Jerusalem. [19]This Passover was

celebrated in the eighteenth year of Josiah's reign.

The Death of Josiah

20After all this, when Josiah had set the
temple in order, Neco king of Egypt went
up to fight at Carchemish on the Euphra-
tes, and Josiah marched out to meet him
in battle. 21But Neco sent messengers to
him, saying, "What quarrel is there be-
tween you and me, O king of Judah? It is
not you I am attacking at this time, but the
house with which I am at war. God has
told me to hurry; so stop opposing God,
who is with me, or he will destroy you."
22Josiah, however, would not turn away
from him, but disguised himself to engage
him in battle. He would not listen to what
Neco had said at God's command but
went to fight him on the plain of Megiddo.
23Archers shot King Josiah, and he told
his officers, "Take me away; I am badly
wounded." 24So they took him out of his
chariot, put him in the other chariot he
had and brought him to Jerusalem, where
he died. He was buried in the tombs of his
fathers, and all Judah and Jerusalem
mourned for him.
25Jeremiah composed laments for Josi-
ah, and to this day all the men and women
singers commemorate Josiah in the la-
ments. These became a tradition in Israel
and are written in the Laments.
26The other events of Josiah's reign and
his acts of devotion, according to what is
written in the Law of the LORD— 27all the
events, from beginning to end, are written
in the book of the kings of Israel and Ju-
36 dah. 1And the people of the land
took Jehoahaz son of Josiah and
made him king in Jerusalem in place of
his father.

Jehoahaz King of Judah

2Jehoahaz[a] was twenty-three years old
when he became king, and he reigned in
Jerusalem three months. 3The king of
Egypt dethroned him in Jerusalem and
imposed on Judah a levy of a hundred tal-
ents[b] of silver and a talent[c] of gold. 4The
king of Egypt made Eliakim, a brother of
Jehoahaz, king over Judah and Jerusalem
and changed Eliakim's name to Jehoia-
kim. But Neco took Eliakim's brother Je-
hoahaz and carried him off to Egypt.

Jehoiakim King of Judah

5Jehoiakim was twenty-five years old
when he became king, and he reigned in
Jerusalem eleven years. He did evil in the
eyes of the LORD his God. 6Nebuchadnez-
zar king of Babylon attacked him and
bound him with bronze shackles to take
him to Babylon. 7Nebuchadnezzar also
took to Babylon articles from the temple
of the LORD and put them in his temple[d]
there.
8The other events of Jehoiakim's reign,
the detestable things he did and all that
was found against him, are written in the
book of the kings of Israel and Judah. And
Jehoiachin his son succeeded him as king.

Jehoiachin King of Judah

9Jehoiachin was eighteen[e] years old
when he became king, and he reigned in
Jerusalem three months and ten days. He
did evil in the eyes of the LORD. 10In the
spring, King Nebuchadnezzar sent for
him and brought him to Babylon, together
with articles of value from the temple of
the LORD, and he made Jehoiachin's un-
cle,[f] Zedekiah, king over Judah and Jeru-
salem.

Zedekiah King of Judah

11Zedekiah was twenty-one years old
when he became king, and he reigned in
Jerusalem eleven years. 12He did evil in
the eyes of the LORD his God and did not
humble himself before Jeremiah the
prophet, who spoke the word of the LORD.
13He also rebelled against King Nebuchad-
nezzar, who had made him take an oath in
God's name. He became stiff-necked and
hardened his heart and would not turn to
the LORD, the God of Israel. 14Further-
more, all the leaders of the priests and
the people became more and more unfaithful,
following all the detestable practices of
the nations and defiling the temple of the
LORD, which he had consecrated in Jerusa-
lem.

The Fall of Jerusalem

15The LORD, the God of their fathers,
sent word to them through his messen-

[a] 2 Hebrew *Joahaz*, a variant of *Jehoahaz*; also in verse 4 [b] 3 That is, about 3 3/4 tons (about 3.4 metric tons) [c] 3 That is, about 75 pounds (about 34 kilograms) [d] 7 Or *palace* [e] 9 One Hebrew manuscript, some Septuagint manuscripts and Syriac (see also 2 Kings 24:8); most Hebrew manuscripts *eight* [f] 10 Hebrew *brother*, that is, relative (see 2 Kings 24:17)

gers again and again, because he had pity
on his people and on his dwelling place.
16But they mocked God's messengers, de-
spised his words and scoffed at his proph-
ets until the wrath of the LORD was
aroused against his people and there was
no remedy. 17He brought up against them
the king of the Babylonians,[a] who killed
their young men with the sword in the
sanctuary, and spared neither young man
nor young woman, old man or aged. God
handed all of them over to Nebuchadnez-
zar. 18He carried to Babylon all the articles
from the temple of God, both large and
small, and the treasures of the LORD's tem-
ple and the treasures of the king and his
officials. 19They set fire to God's temple
and broke down the wall of Jerusalem;
they burned all the palaces and destroyed
everything of value there.

20He carried into exile to Babylon the
remnant, who escaped from the sword,
and they became servants to him and his
sons until the kingdom of Persia came to
power. 21The land enjoyed its sabbath
rests; all the time of its desolation it rest-
ed, until the seventy years were complet-
ed in fulfillment of the word of the LORD
spoken by Jeremiah.

22In the first year of Cyrus king of Per-
sia, in order to fulfill the word of the LORD
spoken by Jeremiah, the LORD moved the
heart of Cyrus king of Persia to make a
proclamation throughout his realm and to
put it in writing:

23"This is what Cyrus king of Persia
says:

" 'The LORD, the God of heaven, has
given me all the kingdoms of the
earth and he has appointed me to
build a temple for him at Jerusalem
in Judah. Anyone of his people
among you—may the LORD his God
be with him, and let him go up.' "

[a] 17 Or *Chaldeans*

EZRA tells how God helps two groups return from Babylon to the promised land, the second group led by Ezra himself. The temple of the Lord is rebuilt despite opposition, the worship of the Lord resumes, and the people realize they must not sin through mixed marriages as their ancestors did. As you read this book, rejoice that God always gives you a second chance to serve him; promise to do your best to remain faithful to his Word.

EZRA

Cyrus Helps the Exiles to Return

1 In the first year of Cyrus king of Persia, in order to fulfill the word of the LORD spoken by Jeremiah, the LORD moved the heart of Cyrus king of Persia to make a proclamation throughout his realm and to put it in writing:

2"This is what Cyrus king of Persia says:

" 'The LORD, the God of heaven, has given me all the kingdoms of the earth and he has appointed me to build a temple for him at Jerusalem in Judah. 3Anyone of his people among you—may his God be with him, and let him go up to Jerusalem in Judah and build the temple of the LORD, the God of Israel, the God who is in Jerusalem. 4And the people of any place where survivors may now be living are to provide him with silver and gold, with goods and livestock, and with freewill offerings for the temple of God in Jerusalem.' "

5Then the family heads of Judah and Benjamin, and the priests and Levites—everyone whose heart God had moved—prepared to go up and build the house of the LORD in Jerusalem. 6All their neighbors assisted them with articles of silver and gold, with goods and livestock, and with valuable gifts, in addition to all the freewill offerings. 7Moreover, King Cyrus brought out the articles belonging to the temple of the LORD, which Nebuchadnezzar had carried away from Jerusalem and had placed in the temple of his god.[a] 8Cyrus king of Persia had them brought by Mithredath the treasurer, who counted them out to Sheshbazzar the prince of Judah.

9This was the inventory:

gold dishes	30
silver dishes	1,000
silver pans[b]	29
10gold bowls	30
matching silver bowls	410
other articles	1,000

11In all, there were 5,400 articles of gold and of silver. Sheshbazzar brought all these along when the exiles came up from Babylon to Jerusalem.

The List of the Exiles Who Returned

2 Now these are the people of the province who came up from the captivity of the exiles, whom Nebuchadnezzar king of Babylon had taken captive to Babylon (they returned to Jerusalem and Judah, each to his own town, 2in company with Zerubbabel, Jeshua, Nehemiah, Seraiah, Reelaiah, Mordecai, Bilshan, Mispar, Bigvai, Rehum and Baanah):

The list of the men of the people of Israel:

3the descendants of Parosh	2,172
4of Shephatiah	372
5of Arah	775
6of Pahath-Moab (through the line of Jeshua and Joab)	2,812
7of Elam	1,254
8of Zattu	945
9of Zaccai	760
10of Bani	642
11of Bebai	623
12of Azgad	1,222
13of Adonikam	666
14of Bigvai	2,056
15of Adin	454
16of Ater (through Hezekiah)	98
17of Bezai	323
18of Jorah	112
19of Hashum	223
20of Gibbar	95
21the men of Bethlehem	123
22of Netophah	56
23of Anathoth	128
24of Azmaveth	42
25of Kiriath Jearim,[c] Kephirah and Beeroth	743
26of Ramah and Geba	621
27of Micmash	122
28of Bethel and Ai	223
29of Nebo	52
30of Magbish	156
31of the other Elam	1,254
32of Harim	320
33of Lod, Hadid and Ono	725
34of Jericho	345
35of Senaah	3,630

36The priests:

the descendants of Jedaiah (through the family of Jeshua)	973
37of Immer	1,052
38of Pashhur	1,247
39of Harim	1,017

40The Levites:

the descendants of Jeshua and Kadmiel (through the line of Hodaviah)	74

41The singers:

the descendants of Asaph	128

42The gatekeepers of the temple:

the descendants of Shallum, Ater, Talmon, Akkub, Hatita and Shobai	139

43The temple servants:

the descendants of
Ziha, Hasupha, Tabbaoth,
44Keros, Siaha, Padon,
45Lebanah, Hagabah, Akkub,
46Hagab, Shalmai, Hanan,
47Giddel, Gahar, Reaiah,
48Rezin, Nekoda, Gazzam,
49Uzza, Paseah, Besai,
50Asnah, Meunim, Nephussim,
51Bakbuk, Hakupha, Harhur,
52Bazluth, Mehida, Harsha,
53Barkos, Sisera, Temah,
54Neziah and Hatipha

55The descendants of the servants of Solomon:

the descendants of

[a]7 Or *gods* [b]9 The meaning of the Hebrew for this word is uncertain. [c]25 See Septuagint (see also Neh. 7:29); Hebrew *Kiriath Arim.*

Sotai, Hassophereth, Peruda,
56Jaala, Darkon, Giddel,
57Shephatiah, Hattil,
Pokereth-Hazzebaim and Ami

58The temple servants and the
descendants of the servants
of Solomon 392

59The following came up from the towns of Tel Melah, Tel Harsha, Kerub, Addon and Immer, but they could not show that their families were descended from Israel:

60The descendants of
Delaiah, Tobiah and
Nekoda 652

61And from among the priests:

The descendants of
Hobaiah, Hakkoz and Barzillai
(a man who had married a
daughter of Barzillai the
Gileadite and was called by that
name).

62These searched for their family records, but they could not find them and so were excluded from the priesthood as unclean. 63The governor ordered them not to eat any of the most sacred food until there was a priest ministering with the Urim and Thummim.

64The whole company numbered 42,360, 65besides their 7,337 menservants and maidservants; and they also had 200 men and women singers. 66They had 736 horses, 245 mules, 67435 camels and 6,720 donkeys.

68When they arrived at the house of the LORD in Jerusalem, some of the heads of the families gave freewill offerings toward the rebuilding of the house of God on its site. 69According to their ability they gave to the treasury for this work 61,000 drachmas[a] of gold, 5,000 minas[b] of silver and 100 priestly garments.

70The priests, the Levites, the singers, the gatekeepers and the temple servants settled in their own towns, along with some of the other people, and the rest of the Israelites settled in their towns.

Rebuilding the Altar

3 When the seventh month came and the Israelites had settled in their towns, the people assembled as one man in Jerusalem. 2Then Jeshua son of Jozadak and his fellow priests and Zerubbabel son of Shealtiel and his associates began to build the altar of the God of Israel to sacrifice burnt offerings on it, in accordance with what is written in the Law of Moses the man of God. 3Despite their fear of the peoples around them, they built the altar on its foundation and sacrificed burnt offerings on it to the LORD, both the morning and evening sacrifices. 4Then in accordance with what is written, they celebrated the Feast of Tabernacles with the required number of burnt offerings prescribed for each day. 5After that, they presented the regular burnt offerings, the New Moon sacrifices and the sacrifices for all the appointed sacred feasts of the LORD, as well as those brought as freewill offerings to the LORD. 6On the first day of the seventh month they began to offer burnt offerings to the LORD, though the foundation of the LORD's temple had not yet been laid.

Rebuilding the Temple

7Then they gave money to the masons and carpenters, and gave food and drink and oil to the people of Sidon and Tyre, so that they would bring cedar logs by sea from Lebanon to Joppa, as authorized by Cyrus king of Persia.

8In the second month of the second year after their arrival at the house of God in Jerusalem, Zerubbabel son of Shealtiel, Jeshua son of Jozadak and the rest of their brothers (the priests and the Levites and all who had returned from the captivity to Jerusalem) began the work, appointing Levites twenty years of age and older to supervise the building of the house of the LORD. 9Jeshua and his sons and brothers and Kadmiel and his sons (descendants of Hodaviah[c]) and the sons of Henadad and their sons and brothers—all Levites—joined together in supervising those working on the house of God.

10When the builders laid the foundation of the temple of the LORD, the priests in their vestments and with trumpets, and the Levites (the sons of Asaph) with cym-

[a]69 That is, about 1,100 pounds (about 500 kilograms) [b]69 That is, about 3 tons (about 2.9 metric tons) [c]9 Hebrew *Yehudah*, probably a variant of *Hodaviah*

bals, took their places to praise the LORD, as prescribed by David king of Israel. 11With praise and thanksgiving they sang to the LORD:

"He is good;
his love to Israel endures forever."

And all the people gave a great shout of praise to the LORD, because the foundation of the house of the LORD was laid. 12But many of the older priests and Levites and family heads, who had seen the former temple, wept aloud when they saw the foundation of this temple being laid, while many others shouted for joy. 13No one could distinguish the sound of the shouts of joy from the sound of weeping, because the people made so much noise. And the sound was heard far away.

Opposition to the Rebuilding

4 When the enemies of Judah and Benjamin heard that the exiles were building a temple for the LORD, the God of Israel, 2they came to Zerubbabel and to the heads of the families and said, "Let us help you build because, like you, we seek your God and have been sacrificing to him since the time of Esarhaddon king of Assyria, who brought us here."

3But Zerubbabel, Jeshua and the rest of the heads of the families of Israel answered, "You have no part with us in building a temple to our God. We alone will build it for the LORD, the God of Israel, as King Cyrus, the king of Persia, commanded us."

4Then the peoples around them set out to discourage the people of Judah and make them afraid to go on building.[a] 5They hired counselors to work against them and frustrate their plans during the entire reign of Cyrus king of Persia and down to the reign of Darius king of Persia.

Later Opposition Under Xerxes and Artaxerxes

6At the beginning of the reign of Xerxes,[b] they lodged an accusation against the people of Judah and Jerusalem.

7And in the days of Artaxerxes king of Persia, Bishlam, Mithredath, Tabeel and the rest of his associates wrote a letter to Artaxerxes. The letter was written in Aramaic script and in the Aramaic language.[c,d]

8Rehum the commanding officer and Shimshai the secretary wrote a letter against Jerusalem to Artaxerxes the king as follows:

9Rehum the commanding officer and Shimshai the secretary, together with the rest of their associates—the judges and officials over the men from Tripolis, Persia,[e] Erech and Babylon, the Elamites of Susa, 10and the other people whom the great and honorable Ashurbanipal[f] deported and settled in the city of Samaria and elsewhere in Trans-Euphrates.

11(This is a copy of the letter they sent him.)

To King Artaxerxes,

From your servants, the men of Trans-Euphrates:

12The king should know that the Jews who came up to us from you have gone to Jerusalem and are rebuilding that rebellious and wicked city. They are restoring the walls and repairing the foundations.

13Furthermore, the king should know that if this city is built and its walls are restored, no more taxes, tribute or duty will be paid, and the royal revenues will suffer. 14Now since we are under obligation to the palace and it is not proper for us to see the king dishonored, we are sending this message to inform the king, 15so that a search may be made in the archives of your predecessors. In these records you will find that this city is a rebellious city, troublesome to kings and provinces, a place of rebellion from ancient times. That is why this city was destroyed. 16We inform the king that if this city is built and its walls are restored, you will be left with nothing in Trans-Euphrates.

17The king sent this reply:

To Rehum the commanding officer, Shimshai the secretary and the rest of

[a] 4 Or *and troubled them as they built*
[b] 6 Hebrew *Ahasuerus*, a variant of Xerxes' Persian name
[c] 7 Or *written in Aramaic and translated*
[d] 7 The text of Ezra 4:8—6:18 is in Aramaic.
[e] 9 Or *officials, magistrates and governors over the men from*
[f] 10 Aramaic *Osnappar*, a variant of *Ashurbanipal*

WEEKENDING

DECISION-MAKING

The next time you and your spouse face a major decision, answer yes or no to each question below before settling on a course of action. Practice by working through any decision facing you now.

1. Is the contemplated action in accordance with the Ten Commandments? Is it consistent with Jesus' commandment to "love one another as I have loved you"?

2. Is it something we would want everyone to know about?

3. Five or ten years from now, will both of us be pleased to have done this?

4. Is it something Jesus would do?

5. Will either of us feel regret or gratitude after the deed is done? If it is left undone?

6. Have we prayed about this decision?

7. Would this be hurtful to either one of us, to our marriage or to others? Would it be helpful to either one of us, to our marriage or to others?

— Lowell and Carol Erdahl

REVIVE

Saturday: Deuteronomy 5:1–22
Sunday: John 13:31–35

Go to page 476 for your next devotional reading.

their associates living in Samaria and elsewhere in Trans-Euphrates:

Greetings.

18The letter you sent us has been read and translated in my presence. 19I issued an order and a search was made, and it was found that this city has a long history of revolt against kings and has been a place of rebellion and sedition. 20Jerusalem has had powerful kings ruling over the whole of Trans-Euphrates, and taxes, tribute and duty were paid to them. 21Now issue an order to these men to stop work, so that this city will not be rebuilt until I so order. 22Be careful not to neglect this matter. Why let this threat grow, to the detriment of the royal interests?

23As soon as the copy of the letter of King Artaxerxes was read to Rehum and Shimshai the secretary and their associates, they went immediately to the Jews in Jerusalem and compelled them by force to stop.

24Thus the work on the house of God in Jerusalem came to a standstill until the second year of the reign of Darius king of Persia.

Tattenai's Letter to Darius

5 Now Haggai the prophet and Zechariah the prophet, a descendant of Iddo, prophesied to the Jews in Judah and Jerusalem in the name of the God of Israel, who was over them. 2Then Zerubbabel son of Shealtiel and Jeshua son of Jozadak set to work to rebuild the house of God in Jerusalem. And the prophets of God were with them, helping them.

3At that time Tattenai, governor of Trans-Euphrates, and Shethar-Bozenai and their associates went to them and asked, "Who authorized you to rebuild this temple and restore this structure?" 4They also asked, "What are the names of the men constructing this building?"[a] 5But the eye of their God was watching over the elders of the Jews, and they were not stopped until a report could go to Darius and his written reply be received.

6This is a copy of the letter that Tattenai, governor of Trans-Euphrates, and Shethar-Bozenai and their associates, the officials of Trans-Euphrates, sent to King Darius. 7The report they sent him read as follows:

To King Darius:

Cordial greetings.

8The king should know that we went to the district of Judah, to the temple of the great God. The people are building it with large stones and placing the timbers in the walls. The work is being carried on with diligence and is making rapid progress under their direction.

9We questioned the elders and asked them, "Who authorized you to rebuild this temple and restore this structure?" 10We also asked them their names, so that we could write down the names of their leaders for your information.

11This is the answer they gave us:

"We are the servants of the God of heaven and earth, and we are rebuilding the temple that was built many years ago, one that a great king of Israel built and finished. 12But because our fathers angered the God of heaven, he handed them over to Nebuchadnezzar the Chaldean, king of Babylon, who destroyed this temple and deported the people to Babylon.

13"However, in the first year of Cyrus king of Babylon, King Cyrus issued a decree to rebuild this house of God. 14He even removed from the temple[b] of Babylon the gold and silver articles of the house of God, which Nebuchadnezzar had taken from the temple in Jerusalem and brought to the temple[b] in Babylon.

"Then King Cyrus gave them to a man named Sheshbazzar, whom he had appointed governor, 15and he told him, 'Take these articles and go and deposit them in the temple in Jerusalem. And rebuild the house of God on its site.' 16So this Sheshbazzar came and laid the foundations of the house of God in Jerusalem. From that day to the present it has been under construction but is not yet finished."

[a]4 See Septuagint; Aramaic *4We told them the names of the men constructing this building.* [b]14 Or *palace*

17Now if it pleases the king, let a
search be made in the royal archives
of Babylon to see if King Cyrus did in
fact issue a decree to rebuild this
house of God in Jerusalem. Then let
the king send us his decision in this
matter.

The Decree of Darius

6 King Darius then issued an order, and
they searched in the archives stored
in the treasury at Babylon. 2A scroll was
found in the citadel of Ecbatana in the
province of Media, and this was written
on it:

Memorandum:

3In the first year of King Cyrus, the
king issued a decree concerning the
temple of God in Jerusalem:

Let the temple be rebuilt as a place
to present sacrifices, and let its foun-
dations be laid. It is to be ninety
feet[a] high and ninety feet wide,
4with three courses of large stones
and one of timbers. The costs are to
be paid by the royal treasury. 5Also,
the gold and silver articles of the
house of God, which Nebuchadnez-
zar took from the temple in Jerusa-
lem and brought to Babylon, are to be
returned to their places in the temple
in Jerusalem; they are to be deposited
in the house of God.

6Now then, Tattenai, governor of
Trans-Euphrates, and Shethar-Boze-
nai and you, their fellow officials of
that province, stay away from there.
7Do not interfere with the work on
this temple of God. Let the governor
of the Jews and the Jewish elders re-
build this house of God on its site.

8Moreover, I hereby decree what
you are to do for these elders of the
Jews in the construction of this house
of God:

The expenses of these men are to
be fully paid out of the royal treasury,
from the revenues of Trans-Euphra-
tes, so that the work will not stop.
9Whatever is needed—young bulls,
rams, male lambs for burnt offerings
to the God of heaven, and wheat, salt,
wine and oil, as requested by the
priests in Jerusalem—must be given
them daily without fail, 10so that they
may offer sacrifices pleasing to the
God of heaven and pray for the well-
being of the king and his sons.

11Furthermore, I decree that if any-
one changes this edict, a beam is to
be pulled from his house and he is to
be lifted up and impaled on it. And
for this crime his house is to be made
a pile of rubble. 12May God, who has
caused his Name to dwell there, over-
throw any king or people who lifts a
hand to change this decree or to de-
stroy this temple in Jerusalem.

I Darius have decreed it. Let it be
carried out with diligence.

Completion and Dedication of the Temple

13Then, because of the decree King Da-
rius had sent, Tattenai, governor of Trans-
Euphrates, and Shethar-Bozenai and their
associates carried it out with diligence.
14So the elders of the Jews continued to
build and prosper under the preaching of
Haggai the prophet and Zechariah, a
descendant of Iddo. They finished build-
ing the temple according to the command
of the God of Israel and the decrees of Cy-
rus, Darius and Artaxerxes, kings of Per-
sia. 15The temple was completed on the
third day of the month Adar, in the sixth
year of the reign of King Darius.

16Then the people of Israel—the
priests, the Levites and the rest of the ex-
iles—celebrated the dedication of the
house of God with joy. 17For the dedica-
tion of this house of God they offered a
hundred bulls, two hundred rams, four
hundred male lambs and, as a sin offering
for all Israel, twelve male goats, one for
each of the tribes of Israel. 18And they in-
stalled the priests in their divisions and
the Levites in their groups for the service
of God at Jerusalem, according to what is
written in the Book of Moses.

The Passover

19On the fourteenth day of the first
month, the exiles celebrated the Passover.
20The priests and Levites had purified
themselves and were all ceremonially
clean. The Levites slaughtered the Pass-
over lamb for all the exiles, for their broth-
ers the priests and for themselves. 21So
the Israelites who had returned from the
exile ate it, together with all who had sep-

[a]3 Aramaic *sixty cubits* (about 27 meters)

arated themselves from the unclean practices of their Gentile neighbors in order to seek the LORD, the God of Israel. 22For seven days they celebrated with joy the Feast of Unleavened Bread, because the LORD had filled them with joy by changing the attitude of the king of Assyria, so that he assisted them in the work on the house of God, the God of Israel.

Ezra Comes to Jerusalem

7 After these things, during the reign of Artaxerxes king of Persia, Ezra son of Seraiah, the son of Azariah, the son of Hilkiah, 2the son of Shallum, the son of Zadok, the son of Ahitub, 3the son of Amariah, the son of Azariah, the son of Meraioth, 4the son of Zerahiah, the son of Uzzi, the son of Bukki, 5the son of Abishua, the son of Phinehas, the son of Eleazar, the son of Aaron the chief priest—6this Ezra came up from Babylon. He was a teacher well versed in the Law of Moses, which the LORD, the God of Israel, had given. The king had granted him everything he asked, for the hand of the LORD his God was on him. 7Some of the Israelites, including priests, Levites, singers, gatekeepers and temple servants, also came up to Jerusalem in the seventh year of King Artaxerxes.

8Ezra arrived in Jerusalem in the fifth month of the seventh year of the king. 9He had begun his journey from Babylon on the first day of the first month, and he arrived in Jerusalem on the first day of the fifth month, for the gracious hand of his God was on him. 10For Ezra had devoted himself to the study and observance of the Law of the LORD, and to teaching its decrees and laws in Israel.

King Artaxerxes' Letter to Ezra

11This is a copy of the letter King Artaxerxes had given to Ezra the priest and teacher, a man learned in matters concerning the commands and decrees of the LORD for Israel:

12[a]Artaxerxes, king of kings,

To Ezra the priest, a teacher of the Law of the God of heaven:

Greetings.

13Now I decree that any of the Israelites in my kingdom, including priests and Levites, who wish to go to Jerusalem with you, may go. 14You are sent by the king and his seven advisers to inquire about Judah and Jerusalem with regard to the Law of your God, which is in your hand. 15Moreover, you are to take with you the silver and gold that the king and his advisers have freely given to the God of Israel, whose dwelling is in Jerusalem, 16together with all the silver and gold you may obtain from the province of Babylon, as well as the freewill offerings of the people and priests for the temple of their God in Jerusalem. 17With this money be sure to buy bulls, rams and male lambs, together with their grain offerings and drink offerings, and sacrifice them on the altar of the temple of your God in Jerusalem.

18You and your brother Jews may then do whatever seems best with the rest of the silver and gold, in accordance with the will of your God. 19Deliver to the God of Jerusalem all the articles entrusted to you for worship in the temple of your God. 20And anything else needed for the temple of your God that you may have occasion to supply, you may provide from the royal treasury.

21Now I, King Artaxerxes, order all the treasurers of Trans-Euphrates to provide with diligence whatever Ezra the priest, a teacher of the Law of the God of heaven, may ask of you—22up to a hundred talents[b] of silver, a hundred cors[c] of wheat, a hundred baths[d] of wine, a hundred baths[d] of olive oil, and salt without limit. 23Whatever the God of heaven has prescribed, let it be done with diligence for the temple of the God of heaven. Why should there be wrath against the realm of the king and of his sons? 24You are also to know that you have no authority to impose taxes, tribute or duty on any of the priests, Levites, singers, gatekeepers, temple servants or other workers at this house of God.

25And you, Ezra, in accordance with the wisdom of your God, which

[a]12 The text of Ezra 7:12-26 is in Aramaic. [b]22 That is, about 3 3/4 tons (about 3.4 metric tons) [c]22 That is, probably about 600 bushels (about 22 kiloliters) [d]22 That is, probably about 600 gallons (about 2.2 kiloliters)

you possess, appoint magistrates and judges to administer justice to all the people of Trans-Euphrates—all who know the laws of your God. And you are to teach any who do not know them. [26]Whoever does not obey the law of your God and the law of the king must surely be punished by death, banishment, confiscation of property, or imprisonment.

[27]Praise be to the LORD, the God of our fathers, who has put it into the king's heart to bring honor to the house of the LORD in Jerusalem in this way [28]and who has extended his good favor to me before the king and his advisers and all the king's powerful officials. Because the hand of the LORD my God was on me, I took courage and gathered leading men from Israel to go up with me.

List of the Family Heads Returning With Ezra

8 These are the family heads and those registered with them who came up with me from Babylon during the reign of King Artaxerxes:

[2]of the descendants of Phinehas, Gershom;
of the descendants of Ithamar, Daniel;
of the descendants of David, Hattush
[3]of the descendants of Shecaniah;
of the descendants of Parosh, Zechariah, and with him were registered 150 men;
[4]of the descendants of Pahath-Moab, Eliehoenai son of Zerahiah, and with him 200 men;
[5]of the descendants of Zattu,[a] Shecaniah son of Jahaziel, and with him 300 men;
[6]of the descendants of Adin, Ebed son of Jonathan, and with him 50 men;
[7]of the descendants of Elam, Jeshaiah son of Athaliah, and with him 70 men;
[8]of the descendants of Shephatiah, Zebadiah son of Michael, and with him 80 men;
[9]of the descendants of Joab, Obadiah son of Jehiel, and with him 218 men;
[10]of the descendants of Bani,[b] Shelomith son of Josiphiah, and with him 160 men;
[11]of the descendants of Bebai, Zechariah son of Bebai, and with him 28 men;
[12]of the descendants of Azgad, Johanan son of Hakkatan, and with him 110 men;
[13]of the descendants of Adonikam, the last ones, whose names were Eliphelet, Jeuel and Shemaiah, and with them 60 men;
[14]of the descendants of Bigvai, Uthai and Zaccur, and with them 70 men.

The Return to Jerusalem

[15]I assembled them at the canal that flows toward Ahava, and we camped there three days. When I checked among the people and the priests, I found no Levites there. [16]So I summoned Eliezer, Ariel, Shemaiah, Elnathan, Jarib, Elnathan, Nathan, Zechariah and Meshullam, who were leaders, and Joiarib and Elnathan, who were men of learning, [17]and I sent them to Iddo, the leader in Casiphia. I told them what to say to Iddo and his kinsmen, the temple servants in Casiphia, so that they might bring attendants to us for the house of our God. [18]Because the gracious hand of our God was on us, they brought us Sherebiah, a capable man, from the descendants of Mahli son of Levi, the son of Israel, and Sherebiah's sons and brothers, 18 men; [19]and Hashabiah, together with Jeshaiah from the descendants of Merari, and his brothers and nephews, 20 men. [20]They also brought 220 of the temple servants—a body that David and the officials had established to assist the Levites. All were registered by name.

[21]There, by the Ahava Canal, I proclaimed a fast, so that we might humble ourselves before our God and ask him for a safe journey for us and our children, with all our possessions. [22]I was ashamed to ask the king for soldiers and horsemen to protect us from enemies on the road, because we had told the king, "The gracious hand of our God is on everyone who looks to him, but his great anger is against all who forsake him." [23]So we fasted and petitioned our God about this, and he answered our prayer.

[a]5 Some Septuagint manuscripts (also 1 Esdras 8:32); Hebrew does not have *Zattu*. [b]10 Some Septuagint manuscripts (also 1 Esdras 8:36); Hebrew does not have *Bani*.

24Then I set apart twelve of the leading
priests, together with Sherebiah, Hashabi-
ah and ten of their brothers, 25and I
weighed out to them the offering of silver
and gold and the articles that the king, his
advisers, his officials and all Israel present
there had donated for the house of our
God. 26I weighed out to them 650 talents[a]
of silver, silver articles weighing 100 tal-
ents,[b] 100 talents[b] of gold, 27 20 bowls of

[a]26 That is, about 25 tons (about 22 metric tons)

[b]26 That is, about 3 3/4 tons (about 3.4 metric tons)

VERSE FOR THE DAY: Ezra 8:23

AUTHOR: Les and Leslie Parrott

PASSAGE FOR THE DAY: Ezra 8:21–23

Praying Heart to Heart

No amount of being religious can replace the time a couple spends in shared prayer. Research shows that couples who frequently pray together are twice as likely as those who pray less often to describe their marriages as being highly romantic. And couples who pray together are 90 percent more likely to report higher satisfaction with sex than couples who don't pray together. Because of the vulnerability it demands, prayer draws a couple closer.

If prayer is so good for marriage, why don't more couples do it? Because it's not easy and the price of that vulnerability can seem too high. Praying together hasn't always been easy for us, either. At times we've fallen into the trap of preaching through our prayers, subtly jabbing each other with our good intentions. But we're learning.

Often we thank God rather than praying about needs or difficulties. Occasionally we say the Lord's Prayer together. Sometimes one of us initiates a time of silent prayer or brief sentence prayers. There is no right or wrong way to pray together. Every attempt to commune with God in shared prayer nurtures the soul of our marriage.

We've become convinced that the most desperate need in many marriages is not for more excitement or activity, but for depth. Try sojourning together toward communion with God. Then your aching urge to be connected—soul to soul—will be satisfied.

MARRIAGE BUILDERS

- *Recall a time when you felt close to each other during prayer.*
- *What time of day would work best for regularly sharing a time of prayer?*

Additional Scripture Readings
Matthew 18:19–20; 1 John 5:13–15

Go to page 481 for your next devotional reading.

gold valued at 1,000 darics,[a] and two fine
articles of polished bronze, as precious as
gold.
[28]I said to them, "You as well as these
articles are consecrated to the LORD. The
silver and gold are a freewill offering to
the LORD, the God of your fathers. [29]Guard
them carefully until you weigh them out
in the chambers of the house of the LORD
in Jerusalem before the leading priests
and the Levites and the family heads of Is-
rael." [30]Then the priests and Levites re-
ceived the silver and gold and sacred arti-
cles that had been weighed out to be taken
to the house of our God in Jerusalem.
[31]On the twelfth day of the first month
we set out from the Ahava Canal to go to
Jerusalem. The hand of our God was on
us, and he protected us from enemies and
bandits along the way. [32]So we arrived in
Jerusalem, where we rested three days.
[33]On the fourth day, in the house of our
God, we weighed out the silver and gold
and the sacred articles into the hands of
Meremoth son of Uriah, the priest. Eleazar
son of Phinehas was with him, and so
were the Levites Jozabad son of Jeshua
and Noadiah son of Binnui. [34]Everything
was accounted for by number and weight,
and the entire weight was recorded at that
time.
[35]Then the exiles who had returned
from captivity sacrificed burnt offerings to
the God of Israel: twelve bulls for all Isra-
el, ninety-six rams, seventy-seven male
lambs and, as a sin offering, twelve male
goats. All this was a burnt offering to the
LORD. [36]They also delivered the king's or-
ders to the royal satraps and to the gover-
nors of Trans-Euphrates, who then gave
assistance to the people and to the house
of God.

Ezra's Prayer About Intermarriage

9 After these things had been done, the
leaders came to me and said, "The
people of Israel, including the priests and
the Levites, have not kept themselves sep-
arate from the neighboring peoples with
their detestable practices, like those of the
Canaanites, Hittites, Perizzites, Jebusites,
Ammonites, Moabites, Egyptians and Am-
orites. [2]They have taken some of their
daughters as wives for themselves and
their sons, and have mingled the holy race
with the peoples around them. And the
leaders and officials have led the way in
this unfaithfulness."
[3]When I heard this, I tore my tunic and
cloak, pulled hair from my head and beard
and sat down appalled. [4]Then everyone
who trembled at the words of the God of
Israel gathered around me because of this
unfaithfulness of the exiles. And I sat
there appalled until the evening sacrifice.
[5]Then, at the evening sacrifice, I rose
from my self-abasement, with my tunic
and cloak torn, and fell on my knees with
my hands spread out to the LORD my God
[6]and prayed:

> "O my God, I am too ashamed and
> disgraced to lift up my face to you,
> my God, because our sins are higher
> than our heads and our guilt has
> reached to the heavens. [7]From the
> days of our forefathers until now, our
> guilt has been great. Because of our
> sins, we and our kings and our priests
> have been subjected to the sword and
> captivity, to pillage and humiliation
> at the hand of foreign kings, as it is
> today.
> [8]"But now, for a brief moment, the
> LORD our God has been gracious in
> leaving us a remnant and giving us a
> firm place in his sanctuary, and so
> our God gives light to our eyes and a
> little relief in our bondage. [9]Though
> we are slaves, our God has not deser-
> ted us in our bondage. He has shown
> us kindness in the sight of the kings
> of Persia: He has granted us new life
> to rebuild the house of our God and
> repair its ruins, and he has given us a
> wall of protection in Judah and Jeru-
> salem.
> [10]"But now, O our God, what can
> we say after this? For we have disre-
> garded the commands [11]you gave
> through your servants the prophets
> when you said: 'The land you are en-
> tering to possess is a land polluted by
> the corruption of its peoples. By their
> detestable practices they have filled it
> with their impurity from one end to
> the other. [12]Therefore, do not give
> your daughters in marriage to their
> sons or take their daughters for your
> sons. Do not seek a treaty of friend-
> ship with them at any time, that you
> may be strong and eat the good
> things of the land and leave it to your

[a]27 That is, about 19 pounds (about 8.5 kilograms)

children as an everlasting inheritance.'

[13]"What has happened to us is a result of our evil deeds and our great guilt, and yet, our God, you have punished us less than our sins have deserved and have given us a remnant like this. [14]Shall we again break your commands and intermarry with the peoples who commit such detestable practices? Would you not be angry enough with us to destroy us, leaving us no remnant or survivor? [15]O LORD, God of Israel, you are righteous! We are left this day as a remnant. Here we are before you in our guilt, though because of it not one of us can stand in your presence."

The People's Confession of Sin

10 While Ezra was praying and confessing, weeping and throwing himself down before the house of God, a large crowd of Israelites—men, women and children—gathered around him. They too wept bitterly. [2]Then Shecaniah son of Jehiel, one of the descendants of Elam, said to Ezra, "We have been unfaithful to our God by marrying foreign women from the peoples around us. But in spite of this, there is still hope for Israel. [3]Now let us make a covenant before our God to send away all these women and their children, in accordance with the counsel of my lord and of those who fear the commands of our God. Let it be done according to the Law. [4]Rise up; this matter is in your hands. We will support you, so take courage and do it."

[5]So Ezra rose up and put the leading priests and Levites and all Israel under oath to do what had been suggested. And they took the oath. [6]Then Ezra withdrew from before the house of God and went to the room of Jehohanan son of Eliashib. While he was there, he ate no food and drank no water, because he continued to mourn over the unfaithfulness of the exiles.

[7]A proclamation was then issued throughout Judah and Jerusalem for all the exiles to assemble in Jerusalem. [8]Anyone who failed to appear within three days would forfeit all his property, in accordance with the decision of the officials and elders, and would himself be expelled from the assembly of the exiles.

[9]Within the three days, all the men of Judah and Benjamin had gathered in Jerusalem. And on the twentieth day of the ninth month, all the people were sitting in the square before the house of God, greatly distressed by the occasion and because of the rain. [10]Then Ezra the priest stood up and said to them, "You have been unfaithful; you have married foreign women, adding to Israel's guilt. [11]Now make confession to the LORD, the God of your fathers, and do his will. Separate yourselves from the peoples around you and from your foreign wives."

[12]The whole assembly responded with a loud voice: "You are right! We must do as you say. [13]But there are many people here and it is the rainy season; so we cannot stand outside. Besides, this matter cannot be taken care of in a day or two, because we have sinned greatly in this thing. [14]Let our officials act for the whole assembly. Then let everyone in our towns who has married a foreign woman come at a set time, along with the elders and judges of each town, until the fierce anger of our God in this matter is turned away from us." [15]Only Jonathan son of Asahel and Jahzeiah son of Tikvah, supported by Meshullam and Shabbethai the Levite, opposed this.

[16]So the exiles did as was proposed. Ezra the priest selected men who were family heads, one from each family division, and all of them designated by name. On the first day of the tenth month they sat down to investigate the cases, [17]and by the first day of the first month they finished dealing with all the men who had married foreign women.

Those Guilty of Intermarriage

[18]Among the descendants of the priests, the following had married foreign women:

From the descendants of Jeshua son of Jozadak, and his brothers: Maaseiah, Eliezer, Jarib and Gedaliah. [19](They all gave their hands in pledge to put away their wives, and for their guilt they each presented a ram from the flock as a guilt offering.)

[20]From the descendants of Immer: Hanani and Zebadiah.

[21]From the descendants of Harim: Maaseiah, Elijah, Shemaiah, Jehiel and Uzziah.

22From the descendants of Pashhur:
Elioenai, Maaseiah, Ishmael, Nethanel, Jozabad and Elasah.

23Among the Levites:

Jozabad, Shimei, Kelaiah (that is, Kelita), Pethahiah, Judah and Eliezer.

24From the singers:
Eliashib.
From the gatekeepers:
Shallum, Telem and Uri.

25And among the other Israelites:

From the descendants of Parosh:
Ramiah, Izziah, Malkijah, Mijamin, Eleazar, Malkijah and Benaiah.

26From the descendants of Elam:
Mattaniah, Zechariah, Jehiel, Abdi, Jeremoth and Elijah.

27From the descendants of Zattu:
Elioenai, Eliashib, Mattaniah, Jeremoth, Zabad and Aziza.

28From the descendants of Bebai:
Jehohanan, Hananiah, Zabbai and Athlai.

29From the descendants of Bani:
Meshullam, Malluch, Adaiah, Jashub, Sheal and Jeremoth.

30From the descendants of Pahath-Moab:
Adna, Kelal, Benaiah, Maaseiah, Mattaniah, Bezalel, Binnui and Manasseh.

31From the descendants of Harim:
Eliezer, Ishijah, Malkijah, Shemaiah, Shimeon, 32Benjamin, Malluch and Shemariah.

33From the descendants of Hashum:
Mattenai, Mattattah, Zabad, Eliphelet, Jeremai, Manasseh and Shimei.

34From the descendants of Bani:
Maadai, Amram, Uel, 35Benaiah, Bedeiah, Keluhi, 36Vaniah, Meremoth, Eliashib, 37Mattaniah, Mattenai and Jaasu.

38From the descendants of Binnui:[a]
Shimei, 39Shelemiah, Nathan, Adaiah, 40Macnadebai, Shashai, Sharai, 41Azarel, Shelemiah, Shemariah, 42Shallum, Amariah and Joseph.

43From the descendants of Nebo:
Jeiel, Mattithiah, Zabad, Zebina, Jaddai, Joel and Benaiah.

44All these had married foreign women, and some of them had children by these wives.[b]

[a]*37,38* See Septuagint (also 1 Esdras 9:34); Hebrew *Jaasu* 38*and Bani and Binnui,*

[b]*44* Or *and they sent them away with their children*

THE book of Nehemiah recounts Nehemiah's time as governor of Canaan when God's people were returning from Babylon. He rebuilds the walls of Jerusalem, along with Ezra he leads God's people in worship, and he administers their affairs. Important to his daily work is prayer, through which he expresses his dependence on God. As you read this book, ask yourself how God wants you to serve his people; be sure that everything you do is accompanied by prayer.

NEHEMIAH

Nehemiah's Prayer

1 The words of Nehemiah son of Hacaliah:

In the month of Kislev in the twentieth year, while I was in the citadel of Susa, [2]Hanani, one of my brothers, came from Judah with some other men, and I questioned them about the Jewish remnant that survived the exile, and also about Jerusalem.

[3]They said to me, "Those who survived the exile and are back in the province are in great trouble and disgrace. The wall of Jerusalem is broken down, and its gates have been burned with fire."

[4]When I heard these things, I sat down and wept. For some days I mourned and fasted and prayed before the God of heaven. [5]Then I said:

"O LORD, God of heaven, the great and awesome God, who keeps his covenant of love with those who love him and obey his commands, [6]let your ear be attentive and your eyes open to hear the prayer your servant is praying before you day and night for your servants, the people of Israel. I confess the sins we Israelites, including myself and my father's

house, have committed against you.
7We have acted very wickedly toward
you. We have not obeyed the com-
mands, decrees and laws you gave
your servant Moses.
8"Remember the instruction you
gave your servant Moses, saying, 'If
you are unfaithful, I will scatter you
among the nations, 9but if you return
to me and obey my commands, then
even if your exiled people are at the
farthest horizon, I will gather them
from there and bring them to the
place I have chosen as a dwelling for
my Name.'
10"They are your servants and your
people, whom you redeemed by your
great strength and your mighty hand.

VERSE FOR THE DAY:	AUTHOR:	PASSAGE FOR THE DAY:
Nehemiah 1:5–6	Henri J. M. Nouwen	Nehemiah 1:3–11

Hiding From God

I am convinced that the real reason we pray so little is fear: fear of facing God, fear also of facing our own and others' brokenness. Our hearts are saying: "Can I really trust God? Will he really show me his love when I don't keep anything hidden from him—or will I be crushed by his anger and lose the little bit of freedom I have so carefully carved out for myself?"

"Do not be afraid." Those are the first words to those who want to come close to God. They were spoken by angels to Zechariah, Mary, the shepherds in the fields, and the women at the empty tomb.

Yes, God is a jealous God, but God's jealousy is not filled with possessiveness and suspicion, as is our human jealousy. There is not a tinge of hatred, resentment or revenge in God. God loves us with a perfect love, a love that casts out all fear and allows us to approach God and his people in complete freedom. God indeed loves us so much that he passionately desires our love in response.

So let us pray without fear, let us enter God's presence with a vulnerable openness. Let us dare to be silent in his presence so that he can first speak to us and reveal us to ourselves as men and women created in love and created free to love. Then we can respond with a full "yes," affirming from the depth of our hearts that we are indeed made in the image and likeness of God.

MARRIAGE BUILDERS

- *What fears keep you from sharing openly with your spouse?*
- *What fears keep you from feeling free to approach God in prayer?*

Additional Scripture Readings
Deuteronomy 4:24; 5:8–10; Exodus 20:4–6; 1 John 4:18; 5:1–5

Go to page 490 for your next devotional reading.

[11]O Lord, let your ear be attentive to
the prayer of this your servant and to
the prayer of your servants who de-
light in revering your name. Give
your servant success today by grant-
ing him favor in the presence of this
man."

I was cupbearer to the king.

Artaxerxes Sends Nehemiah to Jerusalem

2 In the month of Nisan in the twentieth year of King Artaxerxes, when wine was brought for him, I took the wine and gave it to the king. I had not been sad in his presence before; [2]so the king asked me, "Why does your face look so sad when you are not ill? This can be nothing but sadness of heart."

I was very much afraid, [3]but I said to the king, "May the king live forever! Why should my face not look sad when the city where my fathers are buried lies in ruins, and its gates have been destroyed by fire?"

[4]The king said to me, "What is it you want?"

Then I prayed to the God of heaven, [5]and I answered the king, "If it pleases the king and if your servant has found favor in his sight, let him send me to the city in Judah where my fathers are buried so that I can rebuild it."

[6]Then the king, with the queen sitting beside him, asked me, "How long will your journey take, and when will you get back?" It pleased the king to send me; so I set a time.

[7]I also said to him, "If it pleases the king, may I have letters to the governors of Trans-Euphrates, so that they will provide me safe-conduct until I arrive in Judah? [8]And may I have a letter to Asaph, keeper of the king's forest, so he will give me timber to make beams for the gates of the citadel by the temple and for the city wall and for the residence I will occupy?" And because the gracious hand of my God was upon me, the king granted my requests. [9]So I went to the governors of Trans-Euphrates and gave them the king's letters. The king had also sent army officers and cavalry with me.

[10]When Sanballat the Horonite and Tobiah the Ammonite official heard about this, they were very much disturbed that someone had come to promote the welfare of the Israelites.

Nehemiah Inspects Jerusalem's Walls

[11]I went to Jerusalem, and after staying there three days [12]I set out during the night with a few men. I had not told anyone what my God had put in my heart to do for Jerusalem. There were no mounts with me except the one I was riding on.

[13]By night I went out through the Valley Gate toward the Jackal[a] Well and the Dung Gate, examining the walls of Jerusalem, which had been broken down, and its gates, which had been destroyed by fire. [14]Then I moved on toward the Fountain Gate and the King's Pool, but there was not enough room for my mount to get through; [15]so I went up the valley by night, examining the wall. Finally, I turned back and reentered through the Valley Gate. [16]The officials did not know where I had gone or what I was doing, because as yet I had said nothing to the Jews or the priests or nobles or officials or any others who would be doing the work.

[17]Then I said to them, "You see the trouble we are in: Jerusalem lies in ruins, and its gates have been burned with fire. Come, let us rebuild the wall of Jerusalem, and we will no longer be in disgrace." [18]I also told them about the gracious hand of my God upon me and what the king had said to me.

They replied, "Let us start rebuilding." So they began this good work.

[19]But when Sanballat the Horonite, Tobiah the Ammonite official and Geshem the Arab heard about it, they mocked and ridiculed us. "What is this you are doing?" they asked. "Are you rebelling against the king?"

[20]I answered them by saying, "The God of heaven will give us success. We his servants will start rebuilding, but as for you, you have no share in Jerusalem or any claim or historic right to it."

Builders of the Wall

3 Eliashib the high priest and his fellow priests went to work and rebuilt the Sheep Gate. They dedicated it and set its doors in place, building as far as the Tower of the Hundred, which they dedicated, and as far as the Tower of Hananel. [2]The men of Jericho built the adjoining section,

[a]13 Or *Serpent* or *Fig*

and Zaccur son of Imri built next to them.

3The Fish Gate was rebuilt by the sons
of Hassenaah. They laid its beams and put
its doors and bolts and bars in place.
4Meremoth son of Uriah, the son of Hak-
koz, repaired the next section. Next to
him Meshullam son of Berekiah, the son
of Meshezabel, made repairs, and next to
him Zadok son of Baana also made re-
pairs. 5The next section was repaired by
the men of Tekoa, but their nobles would
not put their shoulders to the work under
their supervisors.[a]

6The Jeshanah[b] Gate was repaired by
Joiada son of Paseah and Meshullam son
of Besodeiah. They laid its beams and put
its doors and bolts and bars in place.
7Next to them, repairs were made by men
from Gibeon and Mizpah—Melatiah of
Gibeon and Jadon of Meronoth—places
under the authority of the governor of
Trans-Euphrates. 8Uzziel son of Harhaiah,
one of the goldsmiths, repaired the next
section; and Hananiah, one of the per-
fume-makers, made repairs next to that.
They restored[c] Jerusalem as far as the
Broad Wall. 9Rephaiah son of Hur, ruler of
a half-district of Jerusalem, repaired the
next section. 10Adjoining this, Jedaiah son
of Harumaph made repairs opposite his
house, and Hattush son of Hashabneiah
made repairs next to him. 11Malkijah son
of Harim and Hasshub son of Pahath-
Moab repaired another section and the
Tower of the Ovens. 12Shallum son of Hal-
lohesh, ruler of a half-district of Jerusa-
lem, repaired the next section with the
help of his daughters.

13The Valley Gate was repaired by Ha-
nun and the residents of Zanoah. They re-
built it and put its doors and bolts and
bars in place. They also repaired five hun-
dred yards[d] of the wall as far as the Dung
Gate.

14The Dung Gate was repaired by Mal-
kijah son of Recab, ruler of the district of
Beth Hakkerem. He rebuilt it and put its
doors and bolts and bars in place.

15The Fountain Gate was repaired by
Shallun son of Col-Hozeh, ruler of the dis-
trict of Mizpah. He rebuilt it, roofing it
over and putting its doors and bolts and
bars in place. He also repaired the wall of
the Pool of Siloam,[e] by the King's Gar-
den, as far as the steps going down from
the City of David. 16Beyond him, Nehemi-
ah son of Azbuk, ruler of a half-district of
Beth Zur, made repairs up to a point oppo-
site the tombs[f] of David, as far as the arti-
ficial pool and the House of the Heroes.

17Next to him, the repairs were made by
the Levites under Rehum son of Bani. Be-
side him, Hashabiah, ruler of half the dis-
trict of Keilah, carried out repairs for his
district. 18Next to him, the repairs were
made by their countrymen under Binnui[g]
son of Henadad, ruler of the other
half-district of Keilah. 19Next to him, Ezer
son of Jeshua, ruler of Mizpah, repaired
another section, from a point facing the
ascent to the armory as far as the angle.
20Next to him, Baruch son of Zabbai zeal-
ously repaired another section, from the
angle to the entrance of the house of Elia-
shib the high priest. 21Next to him, Mere-
moth son of Uriah, the son of Hakkoz, re-
paired another section, from the entrance
of Eliashib's house to the end of it.

22The repairs next to him were made by
the priests from the surrounding region.
23Beyond them, Benjamin and Hasshub
made repairs in front of their house; and
next to them, Azariah son of Maaseiah,
the son of Ananiah, made repairs beside
his house. 24Next to him, Binnui son of
Henadad repaired another section, from
Azariah's house to the angle and the cor-
ner, 25and Palal son of Uzai worked oppo-
site the angle and the tower projecting
from the upper palace near the court of
the guard. Next to him, Pedaiah son of Pa-
rosh 26and the temple servants living on
the hill of Ophel made repairs up to a
point opposite the Water Gate toward the
east and the projecting tower. 27Next to
them, the men of Tekoa repaired another
section, from the great projecting tower to
the wall of Ophel.

28Above the Horse Gate, the priests
made repairs, each in front of his own
house. 29Next to them, Zadok son of Im-
mer made repairs opposite his house.
Next to him, Shemaiah son of Shecaniah,
the guard at the East Gate, made repairs.
30Next to him, Hananiah son of Shelemi-
ah, and Hanun, the sixth son of Zalaph,

[a]5 Or *their Lord* or *the governor* [b]6 Or *Old* [c]8 Or *They left out part of* [d]13 Hebrew *a thousand cubits* (about 450 meters) [e]15 Hebrew *Shelah,* a variant of *Shiloah,* that is, Siloam [f]16 Hebrew; Septuagint, some Vulgate manuscripts and Syriac *tomb* [g]18 Two Hebrew manuscripts and Syriac (see also Septuagint and verse 24); most Hebrew manuscripts *Bavvai*

repaired another section. Next to them, Meshullam son of Berekiah made repairs opposite his living quarters. [31]Next to him, Malkijah, one of the goldsmiths, made repairs as far as the house of the temple servants and the merchants, opposite the Inspection Gate, and as far as the room above the corner; [32]and between the room above the corner and the Sheep Gate the goldsmiths and merchants made repairs.

Opposition to the Rebuilding

4 When Sanballat heard that we were rebuilding the wall, he became angry and was greatly incensed. He ridiculed the Jews, [2]and in the presence of his associates and the army of Samaria, he said, "What are those feeble Jews doing? Will they restore their wall? Will they offer sacrifices? Will they finish in a day? Can they bring the stones back to life from those heaps of rubble—burned as they are?"

[3]Tobiah the Ammonite, who was at his side, said, "What they are building—if even a fox climbed up on it, he would break down their wall of stones!"

[4]Hear us, O our God, for we are despised. Turn their insults back on their own heads. Give them over as plunder in a land of captivity. [5]Do not cover up their guilt or blot out their sins from your sight, for they have thrown insults in the face of[a] the builders.

[6]So we rebuilt the wall till all of it reached half its height, for the people worked with all their heart.

[7]But when Sanballat, Tobiah, the Arabs, the Ammonites and the men of Ashdod heard that the repairs to Jerusalem's walls had gone ahead and that the gaps were being closed, they were very angry. [8]They all plotted together to come and fight against Jerusalem and stir up trouble against it. [9]But we prayed to our God and posted a guard day and night to meet this threat.

[10]Meanwhile, the people in Judah said, "The strength of the laborers is giving out, and there is so much rubble that we cannot rebuild the wall."

[11]Also our enemies said, "Before they know it or see us, we will be right there among them and will kill them and put an end to the work."

[12]Then the Jews who lived near them came and told us ten times over, "Wherever you turn, they will attack us."

[13]Therefore I stationed some of the people behind the lowest points of the wall at the exposed places, posting them by families, with their swords, spears and bows. [14]After I looked things over, I stood up and said to the nobles, the officials and the rest of the people, "Don't be afraid of them. Remember the Lord, who is great and awesome, and fight for your brothers, your sons and your daughters, your wives and your homes."

[15]When our enemies heard that we were aware of their plot and that God had frustrated it, we all returned to the wall, each to his own work.

[16]From that day on, half of my men did the work, while the other half were equipped with spears, shields, bows and armor. The officers posted themselves behind all the people of Judah [17]who were building the wall. Those who carried materials did their work with one hand and held a weapon in the other, [18]and each of the builders wore his sword at his side as he worked. But the man who sounded the trumpet stayed with me.

[19]Then I said to the nobles, the officials and the rest of the people, "The work is extensive and spread out, and we are widely separated from each other along the wall. [20]Wherever you hear the sound of the trumpet, join us there. Our God will fight for us!"

[21]So we continued the work with half the men holding spears, from the first light of dawn till the stars came out. [22]At that time I also said to the people, "Have every man and his helper stay inside Jerusalem at night, so they can serve us as guards by night and workmen by day." [23]Neither I nor my brothers nor my men nor the guards with me took off our clothes; each had his weapon, even when he went for water.[b]

Nehemiah Helps the Poor

5 Now the men and their wives raised a great outcry against their Jewish brothers. [2]Some were saying, "We and our sons and daughters are numerous; in order for us to eat and stay alive, we must get grain."

[3]Others were saying, "We are mortgaging our fields, our vineyards and our homes to get grain during the famine."

[a]5 Or *have provoked you to anger before*

[b]23 The meaning of the Hebrew for this clause is uncertain.

4Still others were saying, "We have had
to borrow money to pay the king's tax on
our fields and vineyards. 5Although we
are of the same flesh and blood as our
countrymen and though our sons are as
good as theirs, yet we have to subject our
sons and daughters to slavery. Some of
our daughters have already been en-
slaved, but we are powerless, because our
fields and our vineyards belong to others."
6When I heard their outcry and these
charges, I was very angry. 7I pondered
them in my mind and then accused the
nobles and officials. I told them, "You are
exacting usury from your own country-
men!" So I called together a large meeting
to deal with them 8and said: "As far as
possible, we have bought back our Jewish
brothers who were sold to the Gentiles.
Now you are selling your brothers, only
for them to be sold back to us!" They kept
quiet, because they could find nothing to
say.
9So I continued, "What you are doing is
not right. Shouldn't you walk in the fear of
our God to avoid the reproach of our Gen-
tile enemies? 10I and my brothers and my
men are also lending the people money
and grain. But let the exacting of usury
stop! 11Give back to them immediately
their fields, vineyards, olive groves and
houses, and also the usury you are charg-
ing them—the hundredth part of the
money, grain, new wine and oil."
12"We will give it back," they said. "And
we will not demand anything more from
them. We will do as you say."
Then I summoned the priests and made
the nobles and officials take an oath to do
what they had promised. 13I also shook
out the folds of my robe and said, "In this
way may God shake out of his house and
possessions every man who does not keep
this promise. So may such a man be shak-
en out and emptied!"
At this the whole assembly said,
"Amen," and praised the LORD. And the
people did as they had promised.
14Moreover, from the twentieth year of
King Artaxerxes, when I was appointed to
be their governor in the land of Judah, un-
til his thirty-second year—twelve years—
neither I nor my brothers ate the food al-
lotted to the governor. 15But the earlier
governors—those preceding me—placed
a heavy burden on the people and took
forty shekels[a] of silver from them in ad-
dition to food and wine. Their assistants
also lorded it over the people. But out of
reverence for God I did not act like that.
16Instead, I devoted myself to the work on
this wall. All my men were assembled
there for the work; we[b] did not acquire
any land.
17Furthermore, a hundred and fifty
Jews and officials ate at my table, as well
as those who came to us from the sur-
rounding nations. 18Each day one ox, six
choice sheep and some poultry were pre-
pared for me, and every ten days an abun-
dant supply of wine of all kinds. In spite
of all this, I never demanded the food al-
lotted to the governor, because the de-
mands were heavy on the people.
19Remember me with favor, O my God,
for all I have done for these people.

Further Opposition to the Rebuilding

6 When word came to Sanballat, Tobi-
ah, Geshem the Arab and the rest of
our enemies that I had rebuilt the wall and
not a gap was left in it—though up to that
time I had not set the doors in the gates—
2Sanballat and Geshem sent me this mes-
sage: "Come, let us meet together in one
of the villages[c] on the plain of Ono."
But they were scheming to harm me;
3so I sent messengers to them with this re-
ply: "I am carrying on a great project and
cannot go down. Why should the work
stop while I leave it and go down to you?"
4Four times they sent me the same mes-
sage, and each time I gave them the same
answer.
5Then, the fifth time, Sanballat sent his
aide to me with the same message, and in
his hand was an unsealed letter 6in which
was written:

> "It is reported among the na-
> tions—and Geshem[d] says it is
> true—that you and the Jews are plot-
> ting to revolt, and therefore you are
> building the wall. Moreover, accord-
> ing to these reports you are about to
> become their king 7and have even ap-
> pointed prophets to make this procla-
> mation about you in Jerusalem:
> 'There is a king in Judah!' Now this

[a] 15 That is, about 1 pound (about 0.5 kilogram)
[b] 16 Most Hebrew manuscripts; some Hebrew manuscripts, Septuagint, Vulgate and Syriac *I*
[c] 2 Or *in Kephirim*
[d] 6 Hebrew *Gashmu*, a variant of *Geshem*

report will get back to the king; so
come, let us confer together."

8I sent him this reply: "Nothing like
what you are saying is happening; you are
just making it up out of your head."
9They were all trying to frighten us,
thinking, "Their hands will get too weak
for the work, and it will not be com-
pleted."
⌊But I prayed,⌋ "Now strengthen my
hands."
10One day I went to the house of She-
maiah son of Delaiah, the son of Mehetabel, who was shut in at his home. He said,
"Let us meet in the house of God, inside
the temple, and let us close the temple
doors, because men are coming to kill
you—by night they are coming to kill
you."
11But I said, "Should a man like me run
away? Or should one like me go into the
temple to save his life? I will not go!" 12I
realized that God had not sent him, but
that he had prophesied against me be-
cause Tobiah and Sanballat had hired
him. 13He had been hired to intimidate me
so that I would commit a sin by doing this,
and then they would give me a bad name
to discredit me.

14Remember Tobiah and Sanballat,
O my God, because of what they have
done; remember also the prophetess Noadiah and the rest of the prophets who
have been trying to intimidate me.

The Completion of the Wall

15So the wall was completed on the
twenty-fifth of Elul, in fifty-two days.
16When all our enemies heard about this,
all the surrounding nations were afraid
and lost their self-confidence, because
they realized that this work had been
done with the help of our God.
17Also, in those days the nobles of Judah were sending many letters to Tobiah,
and replies from Tobiah kept coming to
them. 18For many in Judah were under
oath to him, since he was son-in-law to
Shecaniah son of Arah, and his son Jehohanan had married the daughter of Meshullam son of Berekiah. 19Moreover, they
kept reporting to me his good deeds and
then telling him what I said. And Tobiah
sent letters to intimidate me.

7 After the wall had been rebuilt and I
had set the doors in place, the gatekeepers and the singers and the Levites
were appointed. 2I put in charge of Jerusalem my brother Hanani, along with[a] Hananiah the commander of the citadel, because he was a man of integrity and feared
God more than most men do. 3I said to
them, "The gates of Jerusalem are not to
be opened until the sun is hot. While the
gatekeepers are still on duty, have them
shut the doors and bar them. Also appoint
residents of Jerusalem as guards, some at
their posts and some near their own
houses."

The List of the Exiles Who Returned

4Now the city was large and spacious,
but there were few people in it, and the
houses had not yet been rebuilt. 5So my
God put it into my heart to assemble the
nobles, the officials and the common people for registration by families. I found the
genealogical record of those who had
been the first to return. This is what I
found written there:

6These are the people of the province who came up from the captivity
of the exiles whom Nebuchadnezzar
king of Babylon had taken captive
(they returned to Jerusalem and Judah, each to his own town, 7in company with Zerubbabel, Jeshua, Nehemiah, Azariah, Raamiah, Nahamani,
Mordecai, Bilshan, Mispereth, Bigvai,
Nehum and Baanah):

The list of the men of Israel:

8the descendants of Parosh	2,172
9of Shephatiah	372
10of Arah	652
11of Pahath-Moab (through the line of Jeshua and Joab)	2,818
12of Elam	1,254
13of Zattu	845
14of Zaccai	760
15of Binnui	648
16of Bebai	628
17of Azgad	2,322
18of Adonikam	667
19of Bigvai	2,067
20of Adin	655
21of Ater (through Hezekiah)	98
22of Hashum	328
23of Bezai	324
24of Hariph	112
25of Gibeon	95

[a]2 Or *Hanani, that is,*

26the men of Bethlehem and Netophah 188
27of Anathoth 128
28of Beth Azmaveth 42
29of Kiriath Jearim, Kephirah and Beeroth 743
30of Ramah and Geba 621
31of Micmash 122
32of Bethel and Ai 123
33of the other Nebo 52
34of the other Elam 1,254
35of Harim 320
36of Jericho 345
37of Lod, Hadid and Ono 721
38of Senaah 3,930

39The priests:

the descendants of Jedaiah (through the family of Jeshua) 973
40of Immer 1,052
41of Pashhur 1,247
42of Harim 1,017

43The Levites:

the descendants of Jeshua (through Kadmiel through the line of Hodaviah) 74

44The singers:

the descendants of Asaph 148

45The gatekeepers:

the descendants of Shallum, Ater, Talmon, Akkub, Hatita and Shobai 138

46The temple servants:

the descendants of Ziha, Hasupha, Tabbaoth,
47Keros, Sia, Padon,
48Lebana, Hagaba, Shalmai,
49Hanan, Giddel, Gahar,
50Reaiah, Rezin, Nekoda,
51Gazzam, Uzza, Paseah,
52Besai, Meunim, Nephussim,
53Bakbuk, Hakupha, Harhur,
54Bazluth, Mehida, Harsha,
55Barkos, Sisera, Temah,
56Neziah and Hatipha

57The descendants of the servants of Solomon:

the descendants of Sotai, Sophereth, Perida,
58Jaala, Darkon, Giddel,
59Shephatiah, Hattil, Pokereth-Hazzebaim and Amon

60The temple servants and the descendants of the servants of Solomon 392

61The following came up from the towns of Tel Melah, Tel Harsha, Kerub, Addon and Immer, but they could not show that their families were descended from Israel:

62the descendants of Delaiah, Tobiah and Nekoda 642

63And from among the priests:

the descendants of Hobaiah, Hakkoz and Barzillai (a man who had married a daughter of Barzillai the Gileadite and was called by that name).

64These searched for their family records, but they could not find them and so were excluded from the priesthood as unclean. 65The governor, therefore, ordered them not to eat any of the most sacred food until there should be a priest ministering with the Urim and Thummim.

66The whole company numbered 42,360, 67besides their 7,337 menservants and maidservants; and they also had 245 men and women singers. 68There were 736 horses, 245 mules,[a] 69435 camels and 6,720 donkeys.

70Some of the heads of the families contributed to the work. The governor gave to the treasury 1,000 drachmas[b] of gold, 50 bowls and 530 garments for priests. 71Some of the heads of the families gave to the treasury for the work 20,000 drachmas[c] of gold and 2,200 minas[d] of silver. 72The total given by the rest of the people was 20,000 drachmas of gold, 2,000 minas[e] of silver and 67 garments for priests.

73The priests, the Levites, the gatekeepers, the singers and the temple

[a] *68* Some Hebrew manuscripts (see also Ezra 2:66); most Hebrew manuscripts do not have this verse. [b] *70* That is, about 19 pounds (about 8.5 kilograms) [c] *71* That is, about 375 pounds (about 170 kilograms); also in verse 72 [d] *71* That is, about 1 1/3 tons (about 1.2 metric tons) [e] *72* That is, about 1 1/4 tons (about 1.1 metric tons)

servants, along with certain of the people and the rest of the Israelites, settled in their own towns.

Ezra Reads the Law

8 When the seventh month came and the Israelites had settled in their towns, [1]all the people assembled as one man in the square before the Water Gate. They told Ezra the scribe to bring out the Book of the Law of Moses, which the LORD had commanded for Israel.

[2]So on the first day of the seventh month Ezra the priest brought the Law before the assembly, which was made up of men and women and all who were able to understand. [3]He read it aloud from daybreak till noon as he faced the square before the Water Gate in the presence of the men, women and others who could understand. And all the people listened attentively to the Book of the Law.

[4]Ezra the scribe stood on a high wooden platform built for the occasion. Beside him on his right stood Mattithiah, Shema, Anaiah, Uriah, Hilkiah and Maaseiah; and on his left were Pedaiah, Mishael, Malkijah, Hashum, Hashbaddanah, Zechariah and Meshullam.

[5]Ezra opened the book. All the people could see him because he was standing above them; and as he opened it, the people all stood up. [6]Ezra praised the LORD, the great God; and all the people lifted their hands and responded, "Amen! Amen!" Then they bowed down and worshiped the LORD with their faces to the ground.

[7]The Levites—Jeshua, Bani, Sherebiah, Jamin, Akkub, Shabbethai, Hodiah, Maaseiah, Kelita, Azariah, Jozabad, Hanan and Pelaiah—instructed the people in the Law while the people were standing there. [8]They read from the Book of the Law of God, making it clear[a] and giving the meaning so that the people could understand what was being read.

[9]Then Nehemiah the governor, Ezra the priest and scribe, and the Levites who were instructing the people said to them all, "This day is sacred to the LORD your God. Do not mourn or weep." For all the people had been weeping as they listened to the words of the Law.

[10]Nehemiah said, "Go and enjoy choice food and sweet drinks, and send some to those who have nothing prepared. This day is sacred to our Lord. Do not grieve, for the joy of the LORD is your strength."

[11]The Levites calmed all the people, saying, "Be still, for this is a sacred day. Do not grieve."

[12]Then all the people went away to eat and drink, to send portions of food and to celebrate with great joy, because they now understood the words that had been made known to them.

[13]On the second day of the month, the heads of all the families, along with the priests and the Levites, gathered around Ezra the scribe to give attention to the words of the Law. [14]They found written in the Law, which the LORD had commanded through Moses, that the Israelites were to live in booths during the feast of the seventh month [15]and that they should proclaim this word and spread it throughout their towns and in Jerusalem: "Go out into the hill country and bring back branches from olive and wild olive trees, and from myrtles, palms and shade trees, to make booths"—as it is written.[b]

[16]So the people went out and brought back branches and built themselves booths on their own roofs, in their courtyards, in the courts of the house of God and in the square by the Water Gate and the one by the Gate of Ephraim. [17]The whole company that had returned from exile built booths and lived in them. From the days of Joshua son of Nun until that day, the Israelites had not celebrated it like this. And their joy was very great.

[18]Day after day, from the first day to the last, Ezra read from the Book of the Law of God. They celebrated the feast for seven days, and on the eighth day, in accordance with the regulation, there was an assembly.

The Israelites Confess Their Sins

9 On the twenty-fourth day of the same month, the Israelites gathered together, fasting and wearing sackcloth and having dust on their heads. [2]Those of Israelite descent had separated themselves from all foreigners. They stood in their places and confessed their sins and the wickedness of their fathers. [3]They stood where they were and read from the Book of the Law of the LORD their God for a quarter of the day, and spent another quarter in confession and in worshiping the LORD their God. [4]Standing on the stairs were the Le-

[a]8 Or *God, translating it* [b]15 See Lev. 23:37-40.

vites—Jeshua, Bani, Kadmiel, Shebaniah, Bunni, Sherebiah, Bani and Kenani—who called with loud voices to the LORD their God. 5And the Levites—Jeshua, Kadmiel, Bani, Hashabneiah, Sherebiah, Hodiah, Shebaniah and Pethahiah—said: "Stand up and praise the LORD your God, who is from everlasting to everlasting.[a]"

"Blessed be your glorious name, and may it be exalted above all blessing and praise. 6You alone are the LORD. You made the heavens, even the highest heavens, and all their starry host, the earth and all that is on it, the seas and all that is in them. You give life to everything, and the multitudes of heaven worship you.

7"You are the LORD God, who chose Abram and brought him out of Ur of the Chaldeans and named him Abraham. 8You found his heart faithful to you, and you made a covenant with him to give to his descendants the land of the Canaanites, Hittites, Amorites, Perizzites, Jebusites and Girgashites. You have kept your promise because you are righteous.

9"You saw the suffering of our forefathers in Egypt; you heard their cry at the Red Sea.[b] 10You sent miraculous signs and wonders against Pharaoh, against all his officials and all the people of his land, for you knew how arrogantly the Egyptians treated them. You made a name for yourself, which remains to this day. 11You divided the sea before them, so that they passed through it on dry ground, but you hurled their pursuers into the depths, like a stone into mighty waters. 12By day you led them with a pillar of cloud, and by night with a pillar of fire to give them light on the way they were to take.

13"You came down on Mount Sinai; you spoke to them from heaven. You gave them regulations and laws that are just and right, and decrees and commands that are good. 14You made known to them your holy Sabbath and gave them commands, decrees and laws through your servant Moses. 15In their hunger you gave them bread from heaven and in their thirst you brought them water from the rock; you told them to go in and take possession of the land you had sworn with uplifted hand to give them.

16"But they, our forefathers, became arrogant and stiff-necked, and did not obey your commands. 17They refused to listen and failed to remember the miracles you performed among them. They became stiff-necked and in their rebellion appointed a leader in order to return to their slavery. But you are a forgiving God, gracious and compassionate, slow to anger and abounding in love. Therefore you did not desert them, 18even when they cast for themselves an image of a calf and said, 'This is your god, who brought you up out of Egypt,' or when they committed awful blasphemies.

19"Because of your great compassion you did not abandon them in the desert. By day the pillar of cloud did not cease to guide them on their path, nor the pillar of fire by night to shine on the way they were to take. 20You gave your good Spirit to instruct them. You did not withhold your manna from their mouths, and you gave them water for their thirst. 21For forty years you sustained them in the desert; they lacked nothing, their clothes did not wear out nor did their feet become swollen.

22"You gave them kingdoms and nations, allotting to them even the remotest frontiers. They took over the country of Sihon[c] king of Heshbon and the country of Og king of Bashan. 23You made their sons as numerous as the stars in the sky, and you brought them into the land that you told their fathers to enter and possess. 24Their sons went in and took possession of the land. You subdued before them the Canaanites, who lived in the land; you handed the Canaanites over to them, along with their kings and the peoples of the land, to deal with them as they pleased. 25They captured fortified cities and fertile land; they took possession of houses filled with all kinds of good things, wells already dug, vineyards, olive groves and fruit trees in

[a]5 Or *God for ever and ever* [b]9 Hebrew *Yam Suph*; that is, Sea of Reeds [c]22 One Hebrew manuscript and Septuagint; most Hebrew manuscripts *Sihon, that is, the country of the*

VERSE FOR THE DAY: Nehemiah 9:17

AUTHOR: Martha Russi

PASSAGE FOR THE DAY: Nehemiah 9:5–25

Beyond "I'm Sorry"

Greg and I couldn't resolve our differences, and I felt we needed some outside input. He finally conceded and I made the appointment.

I told the counselor of instances in which I felt Greg had broken our trust, mostly with regard to how he handled our money. As much as I wanted to be rid of those past hurts, my mind remained fixed on bitter memories. Greg had apologized to me, and he couldn't understand why I couldn't forget incidents that had taken place months, even years, before.

The counselor asked a question that began to change our whole perspective. "Martha," he said, "has Greg ever asked for your forgiveness?"

"No," I said. "He never has."

The counselor explained that saying "I'm sorry" is a unilateral act. It doesn't require a response from the offended party. But asking someone to forgive you involves a two-way act of confession and, hopefully, forgiveness.

Later that night, Greg asked for my forgiveness, and I was able to forgive him and let go of my hold on the past. When hurtful actions or words test the very core of your relationship, taking the additional step of asking for your spouse's forgiveness can be a road to healing.

MARRIAGE BUILDERS

♦ *On a day-to-day basis, you probably forgive many minor things without ever discussing the forgiveness. What are the more major areas that you feel forgiveness needs to be asked for, and communicated?*

♦ *How does forgiving free you to let go of the past and look ahead to the future?*

Additional Scripture Readings
Matthew 6:14–15; Ephesians 4:26, 29–32

Go to page 502 for your next devotional reading.

abundance. They ate to the full and
were well-nourished; they reveled in
your great goodness.
26"But they were disobedient and
rebelled against you; they put your
law behind their backs. They killed
your prophets, who had admonished
them in order to turn them back to
you; they committed awful blasphe-
mies. 27So you handed them over to
their enemies, who oppressed them.
But when they were oppressed they
cried out to you. From heaven you
heard them, and in your great com-
passion you gave them deliverers,
who rescued them from the hand of
their enemies.
28"But as soon as they were at rest,
they again did what was evil in your
sight. Then you abandoned them to
the hand of their enemies so that they
ruled over them. And when they
cried out to you again, you heard
from heaven, and in your compas-
sion you delivered them time after
time.
29"You warned them to return to
your law, but they became arrogant
and disobeyed your commands. They
sinned against your ordinances, by
which a man will live if he obeys
them. Stubbornly they turned their
backs on you, became stiff-necked
and refused to listen. 30For many
years you were patient with them. By
your Spirit you admonished them
through your prophets. Yet they paid
no attention, so you handed them
over to the neighboring peoples.
31But in your great mercy you did not
put an end to them or abandon them,
for you are a gracious and merciful
God.
32"Now therefore, O our God, the
great, mighty and awesome God, who
keeps his covenant of love, do not let
all this hardship seem trifling in your
eyes—the hardship that has come
upon us, upon our kings and leaders,
upon our priests and prophets, upon
our fathers and all your people, from
the days of the kings of Assyria until
today. 33In all that has happened to
us, you have been just; you have act-
ed faithfully, while we did wrong.
34Our kings, our leaders, our priests
and our fathers did not follow your
law; they did not pay attention to
your commands or the warnings you
gave them. 35Even while they were in
their kingdom, enjoying your great
goodness to them in the spacious and
fertile land you gave them, they did
not serve you or turn from their evil
ways.
36"But see, we are slaves today,
slaves in the land you gave our forefa-
thers so they could eat its fruit and
the other good things it produces.
37Because of our sins, its abundant
harvest goes to the kings you have
placed over us. They rule over our
bodies and our cattle as they please.
We are in great distress.

The Agreement of the People

38"In view of all this, we are making a
binding agreement, putting it in writing,
and our leaders, our Levites and our
priests are affixing their seals to it."

10 Those who sealed it were:

Nehemiah the governor, the son of
Hacaliah.

Zedekiah, 2Seraiah, Azariah, Jere-
miah,
3Pashhur, Amariah, Malkijah,
4Hattush, Shebaniah, Malluch,
5Harim, Meremoth, Obadiah,
6Daniel, Ginnethon, Baruch,
7Meshullam, Abijah, Mijamin,
8Maaziah, Bilgai and Shemaiah.
These were the priests.

9The Levites:

Jeshua son of Azaniah, Binnui of the
sons of Henadad, Kadmiel,
10and their associates: Shebaniah,
Hodiah, Kelita, Pelaiah, Hanan,
11Mica, Rehob, Hashabiah,
12Zaccur, Sherebiah, Shebaniah,
13Hodiah, Bani and Beninu.

14The leaders of the people:

Parosh, Pahath-Moab, Elam, Zattu,
Bani,
15Bunni, Azgad, Bebai,
16Adonijah, Bigvai, Adin,
17Ater, Hezekiah, Azzur,
18Hodiah, Hashum, Bezai,
19Hariph, Anathoth, Nebai,
20Magpiash, Meshullam, Hezir,
21Meshezabel, Zadok, Jaddua,
22Pelatiah, Hanan, Anaiah,
23Hoshea, Hananiah, Hasshub,
24Hallohesh, Pilha, Shobek,
25Rehum, Hashabnah, Maaseiah,

26Ahiah, Hanan, Anan,
27Malluch, Harim and Baanah.

28"The rest of the people—priests, Levites, gatekeepers, singers, temple servants and all who separated themselves from the neighboring peoples for the sake of the Law of God, together with their wives and all their sons and daughters who are able to understand— 29all these now join their brothers the nobles, and bind themselves with a curse and an oath to follow the Law of God given through Moses the servant of God and to obey carefully all the commands, regulations and decrees of the LORD our Lord.

30"We promise not to give our daughters in marriage to the peoples around us or take their daughters for our sons.

31"When the neighboring peoples bring merchandise or grain to sell on the Sabbath, we will not buy from them on the Sabbath or on any holy day. Every seventh year we will forgo working the land and will cancel all debts.

32"We assume the responsibility for carrying out the commands to give a third of a shekel[a] each year for the service of the house of our God: 33for the bread set out on the table; for the regular grain offerings and burnt offerings; for the offerings on the Sabbaths, New Moon festivals and appointed feasts; for the holy offerings; for sin offerings to make atonement for Israel; and for all the duties of the house of our God.

34"We—the priests, the Levites and the people—have cast lots to determine when each of our families is to bring to the house of our God at set times each year a contribution of wood to burn on the altar of the LORD our God, as it is written in the Law.

35"We also assume responsibility for bringing to the house of the LORD each year the firstfruits of our crops and of every fruit tree.

36"As it is also written in the Law, we will bring the firstborn of our sons and of our cattle, of our herds and of our flocks to the house of our God, to the priests ministering there.

37"Moreover, we will bring to the storerooms of the house of our God, to the priests, the first of our ground meal, of our ⌊grain⌋ offerings, of the fruit of all our trees and of our new wine and oil. And we will bring a tithe of our crops to the Levites, for it is the Levites who collect the tithes in all the towns where we work. 38A priest descended from Aaron is to accompany the Levites when they receive the tithes, and the Levites are to bring a tenth of the tithes up to the house of our God, to the storerooms of the treasury. 39The people of Israel, including the Levites, are to bring their contributions of grain, new wine and oil to the storerooms where the articles for the sanctuary are kept and where the ministering priests, the gatekeepers and the singers stay.

"We will not neglect the house of our God."

The New Residents of Jerusalem

11 Now the leaders of the people settled in Jerusalem, and the rest of the people cast lots to bring one out of every ten to live in Jerusalem, the holy city, while the remaining nine were to stay in their own towns. 2The people commended all the men who volunteered to live in Jerusalem.

3These are the provincial leaders who settled in Jerusalem (now some Israelites, priests, Levites, temple servants and descendants of Solomon's servants lived in the towns of Judah, each on his own property in the various towns, 4while other people from both Judah and Benjamin lived in Jerusalem):

From the descendants of Judah:

Athaiah son of Uzziah, the son of Zechariah, the son of Amariah, the son of Shephatiah, the son of Mahalalel, a descendant of Perez; 5and Maaseiah son of Baruch, the son of Col-Hozeh, the son of Hazaiah, the son of Adaiah, the son of Joiarib, the son of Zechariah, a descendant of Shelah. 6The descendants of Perez who lived in Jerusalem totaled 468 able men.

7From the descendants of Benjamin:

Sallu son of Meshullam, the son of Joed, the son of Pedaiah, the son of

[a] 32 That is, about 1/8 ounce (about 4 grams)

Kolaiah, the son of Maaseiah, the son of Ithiel, the son of Jeshaiah, 8and his followers, Gabbai and Sallai—928 men. 9Joel son of Zicri was their chief officer, and Judah son of Hassenuah was over the Second District of the city.

10From the priests:

Jedaiah; the son of Joiarib; Jakin; 11Seraiah son of Hilkiah, the son of Meshullam, the son of Zadok, the son of Meraioth, the son of Ahitub, supervisor in the house of God, 12and their associates, who carried on work for the temple—822 men; Adaiah son of Jeroham, the son of Pelaliah, the son of Amzi, the son of Zechariah, the son of Pashhur, the son of Malkijah, 13and his associates, who were heads of families—242 men; Amashsai son of Azarel, the son of Ahzai, the son of Meshillemoth, the son of Immer, 14and his[a] associates, who were able men—128. Their chief officer was Zabdiel son of Haggedolim.

15From the Levites:

Shemaiah son of Hasshub, the son of Azrikam, the son of Hashabiah, the son of Bunni; 16Shabbethai and Jozabad, two of the heads of the Levites, who had charge of the outside work of the house of God; 17Mattaniah son of Mica, the son of Zabdi, the son of Asaph, the director who led in thanksgiving and prayer; Bakbukiah, second among his associates; and Abda son of Shammua, the son of Galal, the son of Jeduthun. 18The Levites in the holy city totaled 284.

19The gatekeepers:

Akkub, Talmon and their associates, who kept watch at the gates—172 men.

20The rest of the Israelites, with the priests and Levites, were in all the towns of Judah, each on his ancestral property. 21The temple servants lived on the hill of Ophel, and Ziha and Gishpa were in charge of them.

22The chief officer of the Levites in Jerusalem was Uzzi son of Bani, the son of Hashabiah, the son of Mattaniah, the son of Mica. Uzzi was one of Asaph's descendants, who were the singers responsible for the service of the house of God. 23The singers were under the king's orders, which regulated their daily activity.

24Pethahiah son of Meshezabel, one of the descendants of Zerah son of Judah, was the king's agent in all affairs relating to the people.

25As for the villages with their fields, some of the people of Judah lived in Kiriath Arba and its surrounding settlements, in Dibon and its settlements, in Jekabzeel and its villages, 26in Jeshua, in Moladah, in Beth Pelet, 27in Hazar Shual, in Beersheba and its settlements, 28in Ziklag, in Meconah and its settlements, 29in En Rimmon, in Zorah, in Jarmuth, 30Zanoah, Adullam and their villages, in Lachish and its fields, and in Azekah and its settlements. So they were living all the way from Beersheba to the Valley of Hinnom.

31The descendants of the Benjamites from Geba lived in Micmash, Aija, Bethel and its settlements, 32in Anathoth, Nob and Ananiah, 33in Hazor, Ramah and Gittaim, 34in Hadid, Zeboim and Neballat, 35in Lod and Ono, and in the Valley of the Craftsmen.

36Some of the divisions of the Levites of Judah settled in Benjamin.

Priests and Levites

12 These were the priests and Levites who returned with Zerubbabel son of Shealtiel and with Jeshua:

Seraiah, Jeremiah, Ezra,
2Amariah, Malluch, Hattush,
3Shecaniah, Rehum, Meremoth,
4Iddo, Ginnethon,[b] Abijah,
5Mijamin,[c] Moadiah, Bilgah,
6Shemaiah, Joiarib, Jedaiah,
7Sallu, Amok, Hilkiah and Jedaiah.

These were the leaders of the priests and their associates in the days of Jeshua.

8The Levites were Jeshua, Binnui, Kadmiel, Sherebiah, Judah, and also Mattaniah, who, together with his associates, was in charge of the songs of thanksgiving. 9Bakbukiah and Unni, their associates, stood opposite them in the services.

10Jeshua was the father of Joiakim, Joiakim the father of Eliashib, Eliashib the father of Joiada, 11Joiada the father of Jonathan, and Jonathan the father of Jaddua.

[a]14 Most Septuagint manuscripts; Hebrew *their* Neh. 12:16); most Hebrew manuscripts *Ginnethoi*

[b]4 Many Hebrew manuscripts and Vulgate (see also

[c]5 A variant of *Miniamin*

12In the days of Joiakim, these were the
heads of the priestly families:
of Seraiah's family, Meraiah;
of Jeremiah's, Hananiah;
13of Ezra's, Meshullam;
of Amariah's, Jehohanan;
14of Malluch's, Jonathan;
of Shecaniah's,[a] Joseph;
15of Harim's, Adna;
of Meremoth's,[b] Helkai;
16of Iddo's, Zechariah;
of Ginnethon's, Meshullam;
17of Abijah's, Zicri;
of Miniamin's and of Moadiah's, Piltai;
18of Bilgah's, Shammua;
of Shemaiah's, Jehonathan;
19of Joiarib's, Mattenai;
of Jedaiah's, Uzzi;
20of Sallu's, Kallai;
of Amok's, Eber;
21of Hilkiah's, Hashabiah;
of Jedaiah's, Nethanel.

22The family heads of the Levites in the days of Eliashib, Joiada, Johanan and Jaddua, as well as those of the priests, were recorded in the reign of Darius the Persian. 23The family heads among the descendants of Levi up to the time of Johanan son of Eliashib were recorded in the book of the annals. 24And the leaders of the Levites were Hashabiah, Sherebiah, Jeshua son of Kadmiel, and their associates, who stood opposite them to give praise and thanksgiving, one section responding to the other, as prescribed by David the man of God.

25Mattaniah, Bakbukiah, Obadiah, Meshullam, Talmon and Akkub were gatekeepers who guarded the storerooms at the gates. 26They served in the days of Joiakim son of Jeshua, the son of Jozadak, and in the days of Nehemiah the governor and of Ezra the priest and scribe.

Dedication of the Wall of Jerusalem

27At the dedication of the wall of Jerusalem, the Levites were sought out from where they lived and were brought to Jerusalem to celebrate joyfully the dedication with songs of thanksgiving and with the music of cymbals, harps and lyres. 28The singers also were brought together from the region around Jerusalem—from the villages of the Netophathites, 29from Beth Gilgal, and from the area of Geba and Azmaveth, for the singers had built villages for themselves around Jerusalem. 30When the priests and Levites had purified themselves ceremonially, they purified the people, the gates and the wall.

31I had the leaders of Judah go up on top[c] of the wall. I also assigned two large choirs to give thanks. One was to proceed on top[d] of the wall to the right, toward the Dung Gate. 32Hoshaiah and half the leaders of Judah followed them, 33along with Azariah, Ezra, Meshullam, 34Judah, Benjamin, Shemaiah, Jeremiah, 35as well as some priests with trumpets, and also Zechariah son of Jonathan, the son of Shemaiah, the son of Mattaniah, the son of Micaiah, the son of Zaccur, the son of Asaph, 36and his associates—Shemaiah, Azarel, Milalai, Gilalai, Maai, Nethanel, Judah and Hanani—with musical instruments ⌊prescribed by⌋ David the man of God. Ezra the scribe led the procession. 37At the Fountain Gate they continued directly up the steps of the City of David on the ascent to the wall and passed above the house of David to the Water Gate on the east.

38The second choir proceeded in the opposite direction. I followed them on top[e] of the wall, together with half the people—past the Tower of the Ovens to the Broad Wall, 39over the Gate of Ephraim, the Jeshanah[f] Gate, the Fish Gate, the Tower of Hananel and the Tower of the Hundred, as far as the Sheep Gate. At the Gate of the Guard they stopped.

40The two choirs that gave thanks then took their places in the house of God; so did I, together with half the officials, 41as well as the priests—Eliakim, Maaseiah, Miniamin, Micaiah, Elioenai, Zechariah and Hananiah with their trumpets—42and also Maaseiah, Shemaiah, Eleazar, Uzzi, Jehohanan, Malkijah, Elam and Ezer. The choirs sang under the direction of Jezrahiah. 43And on that day they offered great sacrifices, rejoicing because God had given them great joy. The women and children also rejoiced. The sound of rejoicing in Jerusalem could be heard far away.

44At that time men were appointed to be

[a] *14* Very many Hebrew manuscripts, some Septuagint manuscripts and Syriac (see also Neh. 12:3); most Hebrew manuscripts *Shebaniah's* [b] *15* Some Septuagint manuscripts (see also Neh. 12:3); Hebrew *Meraioth's* [c] *31* Or *go alongside* [d] *31* Or *proceed alongside* [e] *38* Or *them alongside* [f] *39* Or *Old*

in charge of the storerooms for the contributions, firstfruits and tithes. From the fields around the towns they were to bring into the storerooms the portions required by the Law for the priests and the Levites, for Judah was pleased with the ministering priests and Levites. [45]They performed the service of their God and the service of purification, as did also the singers and gatekeepers, according to the commands of David and his son Solomon. [46]For long ago, in the days of David and Asaph, there had been directors for the singers and for the songs of praise and thanksgiving to God. [47]So in the days of Zerubbabel and of Nehemiah, all Israel contributed the daily portions for the singers and gatekeepers. They also set aside the portion for the other Levites, and the Levites set aside the portion for the descendants of Aaron.

Nehemiah's Final Reforms

13 On that day the Book of Moses was read aloud in the hearing of the people and there it was found written that no Ammonite or Moabite should ever be admitted into the assembly of God, [2]because they had not met the Israelites with food and water but had hired Balaam to call a curse down on them. (Our God, however, turned the curse into a blessing.) [3]When the people heard this law, they excluded from Israel all who were of foreign descent.

[4]Before this, Eliashib the priest had been put in charge of the storerooms of the house of our God. He was closely associated with Tobiah, [5]and he had provided him with a large room formerly used to store the grain offerings and incense and temple articles, and also the tithes of grain, new wine and oil prescribed for the Levites, singers and gatekeepers, as well as the contributions for the priests.

[6]But while all this was going on, I was not in Jerusalem, for in the thirty-second year of Artaxerxes king of Babylon I had returned to the king. Some time later I asked his permission [7]and came back to Jerusalem. Here I learned about the evil thing Eliashib had done in providing Tobiah a room in the courts of the house of God. [8]I was greatly displeased and threw all Tobiah's household goods out of the room. [9]I gave orders to purify the rooms, and then I put back into them the equipment of the house of God, with the grain offerings and the incense.

[10]I also learned that the portions assigned to the Levites had not been given to them, and that all the Levites and singers responsible for the service had gone back to their own fields. [11]So I rebuked the officials and asked them, "Why is the house of God neglected?" Then I called them together and stationed them at their posts.

[12]All Judah brought the tithes of grain, new wine and oil into the storerooms. [13]I put Shelemiah the priest, Zadok the scribe, and a Levite named Pedaiah in charge of the storerooms and made Hanan son of Zaccur, the son of Mattaniah, their assistant, because these men were considered trustworthy. They were made responsible for distributing the supplies to their brothers.

[14]Remember me for this, O my God, and do not blot out what I have so faithfully done for the house of my God and its services.

[15]In those days I saw men in Judah treading winepresses on the Sabbath and bringing in grain and loading it on donkeys, together with wine, grapes, figs and all other kinds of loads. And they were bringing all this into Jerusalem on the Sabbath. Therefore I warned them against selling food on that day. [16]Men from Tyre who lived in Jerusalem were bringing in fish and all kinds of merchandise and selling them in Jerusalem on the Sabbath to the people of Judah. [17]I rebuked the nobles of Judah and said to them, "What is this wicked thing you are doing—desecrating the Sabbath day? [18]Didn't your forefathers do the same things, so that our God brought all this calamity upon us and upon this city? Now you are stirring up more wrath against Israel by desecrating the Sabbath."

[19]When evening shadows fell on the gates of Jerusalem before the Sabbath, I ordered the doors to be shut and not opened until the Sabbath was over. I stationed some of my own men at the gates so that no load could be brought in on the Sabbath day. [20]Once or twice the merchants and sellers of all kinds of goods spent the night outside Jerusalem. [21]But I warned them and said, "Why do you spend the night by the wall? If you do this again, I will lay hands on you." From that time on they no longer came on the Sabbath. [22]Then I commanded the Levites to purify themselves and go and guard the

gates in order to keep the Sabbath day holy.

Remember me for this also, O my God, and show mercy to me according to your great love.

[23]Moreover, in those days I saw men of Judah who had married women from Ashdod, Ammon and Moab. [24]Half of their children spoke the language of Ashdod or the language of one of the other peoples, and did not know how to speak the language of Judah. [25]I rebuked them and called curses down on them. I beat some of the men and pulled out their hair. I made them take an oath in God's name and said: "You are not to give your daughters in marriage to their sons, nor are you to take their daughters in marriage for your sons or for yourselves. [26]Was it not because of marriages like these that Solomon king of Israel sinned? Among the many nations there was no king like him. He was loved by his God, and God made him king over all Israel, but even he was led into sin by foreign women. [27]Must we hear now that you too are doing all this terrible wickedness and are being unfaithful to our God by marrying foreign women?"

[28]One of the sons of Joiada son of Eliashib the high priest was son-in-law to Sanballat the Horonite. And I drove him away from me.

[29]Remember them, O my God, because they defiled the priestly office and the covenant of the priesthood and of the Levites.

[30]So I purified the priests and the Levites of everything foreign, and assigned them duties, each to his own task. [31]I also made provision for contributions of wood at designated times, and for the firstfruits.

Remember me with favor, O my God.

ESTHER records God's remarkable, providential care of his exiled people when their enemies threaten to destroy them completely. Though his name is not actually mentioned in the book, God is in control, using Esther's position as queen to reverse the plan of wicked Haman. As you read this book, think how God takes care of you in your everyday life, even making good come out of evil.

ESTHER

Queen Vashti Deposed

1 This is what happened during the time of Xerxes,[a] the Xerxes who ruled over 127 provinces stretching from India to Cush[b]: 2At that time King Xerxes reigned from his royal throne in the citadel of Susa, 3and in the third year of his reign he gave a banquet for all his nobles and officials. The military leaders of Persia and Media, the princes, and the nobles of the provinces were present.

4For a full 180 days he displayed the vast wealth of his kingdom and the splendor and glory of his majesty. 5When these days were over, the king gave a banquet, lasting seven days, in the enclosed garden of the king's palace, for all the people from the least to the greatest, who were in the citadel of Susa. 6The garden had hangings of white and blue linen, fastened with cords of white linen and purple material to silver rings on marble pillars. There were couches of gold and silver on a mosaic pavement of porphyry, marble, mother-of-pearl and other costly stones. 7Wine was served in goblets of gold, each one different from the other, and the royal wine was abundant, in keeping with the king's liberality. 8By the king's command each guest was allowed to drink in his own way, for the king instructed all the wine stewards to serve each man what he wished.

9Queen Vashti also gave a banquet for

[a] 1 Hebrew *Ahasuerus*, a variant of Xerxes' Persian name; here and throughout Esther

[b] 1 That is, the upper Nile region

the women in the royal palace of King Xerxes.

10On the seventh day, when King Xerxes was in high spirits from wine, he commanded the seven eunuchs who served him—Mehuman, Biztha, Harbona, Bigtha, Abagtha, Zethar and Carcas— 11to bring before him Queen Vashti, wearing her royal crown, in order to display her beauty to the people and nobles, for she was lovely to look at. 12But when the attendants delivered the king's command, Queen Vashti refused to come. Then the king became furious and burned with anger.

13Since it was customary for the king to consult experts in matters of law and justice, he spoke with the wise men who understood the times 14and were closest to the king—Carshena, Shethar, Admatha, Tarshish, Meres, Marsena and Memucan, the seven nobles of Persia and Media who had special access to the king and were highest in the kingdom.

15"According to law, what must be done to Queen Vashti?" he asked. "She has not obeyed the command of King Xerxes that the eunuchs have taken to her."

16Then Memucan replied in the presence of the king and the nobles, "Queen Vashti has done wrong, not only against the king but also against all the nobles and the peoples of all the provinces of King Xerxes. 17For the queen's conduct will become known to all the women, and so they will despise their husbands and say, 'King Xerxes commanded Queen Vashti to be brought before him, but she would not come.' 18This very day the Persian and Median women of the nobility who have heard about the queen's conduct will respond to all the king's nobles in the same way. There will be no end of disrespect and discord.

19"Therefore, if it pleases the king, let him issue a royal decree and let it be written in the laws of Persia and Media, which cannot be repealed, that Vashti is never again to enter the presence of King Xerxes. Also let the king give her royal position to someone else who is better than she. 20Then when the king's edict is proclaimed throughout all his vast realm, all the women will respect their husbands, from the least to the greatest."

21The king and his nobles were pleased with this advice, so the king did as Memucan proposed. 22He sent dispatches to all parts of the kingdom, to each province in its own script and to each people in its own language, proclaiming in each people's tongue that every man should be ruler over his own household.

Esther Made Queen

2 Later when the anger of King Xerxes had subsided, he remembered Vashti and what she had done and what he had decreed about her. 2Then the king's personal attendants proposed, "Let a search be made for beautiful young virgins for the king. 3Let the king appoint commissioners in every province of his realm to bring all these beautiful girls into the harem at the citadel of Susa. Let them be placed under the care of Hegai, the king's eunuch, who is in charge of the women; and let beauty treatments be given to them. 4Then let the girl who pleases the king be queen instead of Vashti." This advice appealed to the king, and he followed it.

5Now there was in the citadel of Susa a Jew of the tribe of Benjamin, named Mordecai son of Jair, the son of Shimei, the son of Kish, 6who had been carried into exile from Jerusalem by Nebuchadnezzar king of Babylon, among those taken captive with Jehoiachin[a] king of Judah. 7Mordecai had a cousin named Hadassah, whom he had brought up because she had neither father nor mother. This girl, who was also known as Esther, was lovely in form and features, and Mordecai had taken her as his own daughter when her father and mother died.

8When the king's order and edict had been proclaimed, many girls were brought to the citadel of Susa and put under the care of Hegai. Esther also was taken to the king's palace and entrusted to Hegai, who had charge of the harem. 9The girl pleased him and won his favor. Immediately he provided her with her beauty treatments and special food. He assigned to her seven maids selected from the king's palace and moved her and her maids into the best place in the harem.

10Esther had not revealed her nationality and family background, because Mordecai had forbidden her to do so. 11Every day he walked back and forth near the courtyard of the harem to find out how Es-

[a]6 Hebrew *Jeconiah*, a variant of *Jehoiachin*

ther was and what was happening to her.
12Before a girl's turn came to go in to
King Xerxes, she had to complete twelve
months of beauty treatments prescribed
for the women, six months with oil of
myrrh and six with perfumes and cosmet-
ics. 13And this is how she would go to the
king: Anything she wanted was given her
to take with her from the harem to the
king's palace. 14In the evening she would
go there and in the morning return to an-
other part of the harem to the care of Sha-
ashgaz, the king's eunuch who was in
charge of the concubines. She would not
return to the king unless he was pleased
with her and summoned her by name.
15When the turn came for Esther (the
girl Mordecai had adopted, the daughter
of his uncle Abihail) to go to the king, she
asked for nothing other than what Hegai,
the king's eunuch who was in charge of
the harem, suggested. And Esther won the
favor of everyone who saw her. 16She was
taken to King Xerxes in the royal resi-
dence in the tenth month, the month of
Tebeth, in the seventh year of his reign.
17Now the king was attracted to Esther
more than to any of the other women, and
she won his favor and approval more than
any of the other virgins. So he set a royal
crown on her head and made her queen
instead of Vashti. 18And the king gave a
great banquet, Esther's banquet, for all his
nobles and officials. He proclaimed a holi-
day throughout the provinces and distrib-
uted gifts with royal liberality.

Mordecai Uncovers a Conspiracy

19When the virgins were assembled a
second time, Mordecai was sitting at the
king's gate. 20But Esther had kept secret
her family background and nationality
just as Mordecai had told her to do, for she
continued to follow Mordecai's instruc-
tions as she had done when he was bring-
ing her up.
21During the time Mordecai was sitting
at the king's gate, Bigthana[a] and Teresh,
two of the king's officers who guarded the
doorway, became angry and conspired to
assassinate King Xerxes. 22But Mordecai
found out about the plot and told Queen
Esther, who in turn reported it to the king,
giving credit to Mordecai. 23And when the
report was investigated and found to be
true, the two officials were hanged on a
gallows.[b] All this was recorded in the
book of the annals in the presence of the
king.

Haman's Plot to Destroy the Jews

3 After these events, King Xerxes hon-
ored Haman son of Hammedatha, the
Agagite, elevating him and giving him a
seat of honor higher than that of all the
other nobles. 2All the royal officials at the
king's gate knelt down and paid honor to
Haman, for the king had commanded this
concerning him. But Mordecai would not
kneel down or pay him honor.
3Then the royal officials at the king's
gate asked Mordecai, "Why do you dis-
obey the king's command?" 4Day after day
they spoke to him but he refused to com-
ply. Therefore they told Haman about it to
see whether Mordecai's behavior would
be tolerated, for he had told them he was
a Jew.
5When Haman saw that Mordecai
would not kneel down or pay him honor,
he was enraged. 6Yet having learned who
Mordecai's people were, he scorned the
idea of killing only Mordecai. Instead Ha-
man looked for a way to destroy all Mor-
decai's people, the Jews, throughout the
whole kingdom of Xerxes.
7In the twelfth year of King Xerxes, in
the first month, the month of Nisan, they
cast the *pur* (that is, the lot) in the pres-
ence of Haman to select a day and month.
And the lot fell on[c] the twelfth month,
the month of Adar.
8Then Haman said to King Xerxes,
"There is a certain people dispersed and
scattered among the peoples in all the
provinces of your kingdom whose cus-
toms are different from those of all other
people and who do not obey the king's
laws; it is not in the king's best interest to
tolerate them. 9If it pleases the king, let a
decree be issued to destroy them, and I
will put ten thousand talents[d] of silver
into the royal treasury for the men who
carry out this business."
10So the king took his signet ring from
his finger and gave it to Haman son of
Hammedatha, the Agagite, the enemy of
the Jews. 11"Keep the money," the king
said to Haman, "and do with the people as
you please."

[a]21 Hebrew *Bigthan*, a variant of *Bigthana* elsewhere in Esther [b]23 Or *were hung* (or *impaled*) *on poles*; similarly [c]7 Septuagint; Hebrew does not have *And the lot fell on.* [d]9 That is, about 375 tons (about 345 metric tons)

12Then on the thirteenth day of the first
month the royal secretaries were sum-
moned. They wrote out in the script of
each province and in the language of each
people all Haman's orders to the king's sa-
traps, the governors of the various prov-
inces and the nobles of the various peo-
ples. These were written in the name of
King Xerxes himself and sealed with his
own ring. 13Dispatches were sent by cou-
riers to all the king's provinces with the
order to destroy, kill and annihilate all the
Jews—young and old, women and little
children—on a single day, the thirteenth
day of the twelfth month, the month of
Adar, and to plunder their goods. 14A copy
of the text of the edict was to be issued as
law in every province and made known to
the people of every nationality so they
would be ready for that day.

15Spurred on by the king's command,
the couriers went out, and the edict was
issued in the citadel of Susa. The king and
Haman sat down to drink, but the city of
Susa was bewildered.

Mordecai Persuades Esther to Help

4 When Mordecai learned of all that had
been done, he tore his clothes, put on
sackcloth and ashes, and went out into the
city, wailing loudly and bitterly. 2But he
went only as far as the king's gate, be-
cause no one clothed in sackcloth was al-
lowed to enter it. 3In every province to
which the edict and order of the king
came, there was great mourning among
the Jews, with fasting, weeping and wail-
ing. Many lay in sackcloth and ashes.

4When Esther's maids and eunuchs
came and told her about Mordecai, she
was in great distress. She sent clothes for
him to put on instead of his sackcloth, but
he would not accept them. 5Then Esther
summoned Hathach, one of the king's eu-
nuchs assigned to attend her, and ordered
him to find out what was troubling Mor-
decai and why.

6So Hathach went out to Mordecai in
the open square of the city in front of the
king's gate. 7Mordecai told him every-
thing that had happened to him, including
the exact amount of money Haman had
promised to pay into the royal treasury for
the destruction of the Jews. 8He also gave
him a copy of the text of the edict for their
annihilation, which had been published in
Susa, to show to Esther and explain it to
her, and he told him to urge her to go into
the king's presence to beg for mercy and
plead with him for her people.

9Hathach went back and reported to Es-
ther what Mordecai had said. 10Then she
instructed him to say to Mordecai, 11"All
the king's officials and the people of the
royal provinces know that for any man or
woman who approaches the king in the
inner court without being summoned the
king has but one law: that he be put to
death. The only exception to this is for the
king to extend the gold scepter to him and
spare his life. But thirty days have passed
since I was called to go to the king."

12When Esther's words were reported
to Mordecai, 13he sent back this answer:
"Do not think that because you are in the
king's house you alone of all the Jews will
escape. 14For if you remain silent at this
time, relief and deliverance for the Jews
will arise from another place, but you and
your father's family will perish. And who
knows but that you have come to royal
position for such a time as this?"

15Then Esther sent this reply to Morde-
cai: 16"Go, gather together all the Jews
who are in Susa, and fast for me. Do not
eat or drink for three days, night or day. I
and my maids will fast as you do. When
this is done, I will go to the king, even
though it is against the law. And if I per-
ish, I perish."

17So Mordecai went away and carried
out all of Esther's instructions.

Esther's Request to the King

5 On the third day Esther put on her
royal robes and stood in the inner
court of the palace, in front of the king's
hall. The king was sitting on his royal
throne in the hall, facing the entrance.
2When he saw Queen Esther standing in
the court, he was pleased with her and
held out to her the gold scepter that was
in his hand. So Esther approached and
touched the tip of the scepter.

3Then the king asked, "What is it,
Queen Esther? What is your request? Even
up to half the kingdom, it will be given
you."

4"If it pleases the king," replied Esther,
"let the king, together with Haman, come
today to a banquet I have prepared for
him."

5"Bring Haman at once," the king said,
"so that we may do what Esther asks."

So the king and Haman went to the ban-
quet Esther had prepared. 6As they were
drinking wine, the king again asked Es-

ther, "Now what is your petition? It will be given you. And what is your request? Even up to half the kingdom, it will be granted."

7Esther replied, "My petition and my request is this: 8If the king regards me with favor and if it pleases the king to grant my petition and fulfill my request, let the king and Haman come tomorrow to the banquet I will prepare for them. Then I will answer the king's question."

Haman's Rage Against Mordecai

9Haman went out that day happy and in high spirits. But when he saw Mordecai at the king's gate and observed that he neither rose nor showed fear in his presence, he was filled with rage against Mordecai. 10Nevertheless, Haman restrained himself and went home.

Calling together his friends and Zeresh, his wife, 11Haman boasted to them about his vast wealth, his many sons, and all the ways the king had honored him and how he had elevated him above the other nobles and officials. 12"And that's not all," Haman added. "I'm the only person Queen Esther invited to accompany the king to the banquet she gave. And she has invited me along with the king tomorrow. 13But all this gives me no satisfaction as long as I see that Jew Mordecai sitting at the king's gate."

14His wife Zeresh and all his friends said to him, "Have a gallows built, seventy-five feet[a] high, and ask the king in the morning to have Mordecai hanged on it. Then go with the king to the dinner and be happy." This suggestion delighted Haman, and he had the gallows built.

Mordecai Honored

6 That night the king could not sleep; so he ordered the book of the chronicles, the record of his reign, to be brought in and read to him. 2It was found recorded there that Mordecai had exposed Bigthana and Teresh, two of the king's officers who guarded the doorway, who had conspired to assassinate King Xerxes.

3"What honor and recognition has Mordecai received for this?" the king asked.

"Nothing has been done for him," his attendants answered.

4The king said, "Who is in the court?" Now Haman had just entered the outer court of the palace to speak to the king about hanging Mordecai on the gallows he had erected for him.

5His attendants answered, "Haman is standing in the court."

"Bring him in," the king ordered.

6When Haman entered, the king asked him, "What should be done for the man the king delights to honor?"

Now Haman thought to himself, "Who is there that the king would rather honor than me?" 7So he answered the king, "For the man the king delights to honor, 8have them bring a royal robe the king has worn and a horse the king has ridden, one with a royal crest placed on its head. 9Then let the robe and horse be entrusted to one of the king's most noble princes. Let them robe the man the king delights to honor, and lead him on the horse through the city streets, proclaiming before him, 'This is what is done for the man the king delights to honor!' "

10"Go at once," the king commanded Haman. "Get the robe and the horse and do just as you have suggested for Mordecai the Jew, who sits at the king's gate. Do not neglect anything you have recommended."

11So Haman got the robe and the horse. He robed Mordecai, and led him on horseback through the city streets, proclaiming before him, "This is what is done for the man the king delights to honor!"

12Afterward Mordecai returned to the king's gate. But Haman rushed home, with his head covered in grief, 13and told Zeresh his wife and all his friends everything that had happened to him.

His advisers and his wife Zeresh said to him, "Since Mordecai, before whom your downfall has started, is of Jewish origin, you cannot stand against him—you will surely come to ruin!" 14While they were still talking with him, the king's eunuchs arrived and hurried Haman away to the banquet Esther had prepared.

Haman Hanged

7 So the king and Haman went to dine with Queen Esther, 2and as they were drinking wine on that second day, the king again asked, "Queen Esther, what is your petition? It will be given you. What is your request? Even up to half the kingdom, it will be granted."

3Then Queen Esther answered, "If I have found favor with you, O king, and if

[a]14 Hebrew *fifty cubits* (about 23 meters)

it pleases your majesty, grant me my
life—this is my petition. And spare my
people—this is my request. [4]For I and my
people have been sold for destruction and
slaughter and annihilation. If we had
merely been sold as male and female
slaves, I would have kept quiet, because
no such distress would justify disturbing
the king.[a]"

[5]King Xerxes asked Queen Esther,
"Who is he? Where is the man who has
dared to do such a thing?"

[a]4 Or *quiet, but the compensation our adversary offers cannot be compared with the loss the king would suffer*

VERSE FOR THE DAY:	AUTHOR:	PASSAGE FOR THE DAY:
Esther 7:2	Annette LaPlaca	Esther 7:1–10

Don't Manipulate

Before David and I were married—even before we were engaged—he made me laugh one day when he abruptly asked me, "So, do you manipulate me?" He remembered hearing one of his female cousins talking about how she and her friends got guys to ask them out or do what they wanted. I had to admit that an ability to "handle" men is often a polished skill of girlfriends and wives. But I had always been very forthright with David, so I could tell him honestly that I didn't *think* I had ever manipulated him—at least I hadn't yet.

Esther, the Old Testament queen, showed some real insight and political savvy in the way she approached her husband in order to defeat Haman, the enemy who threatened to destroy the Jewish people. Her convoluted arrangements seem to border on manipulation, but I give Esther a lot of credit. She honored and pleased her husband, while at the same time making her great personal desire—to save her people—his desire as well.

I would never recommend that one spouse resort to manipulation to get what he or she wants. But I am pleased to discover this biblical model for honoring a spouse, and a model for communicating and sharing personal goals in marriage.

MARRIAGE BUILDERS

♦ *Have you ever gotten something you wanted from your spouse by using manipulative tactics?*

♦ *How can you respect your spouse at the same time you communicate what you need and want?*

Additional Scripture Readings
Genesis 27:1–36; Acts 13:10

Go to page 507 for your next devotional reading.

6Esther said, "The adversary and enemy
is this vile Haman."
Then Haman was terrified before the
king and queen. 7The king got up in a
rage, left his wine and went out into the
palace garden. But Haman, realizing that
the king had already decided his fate,
stayed behind to beg Queen Esther for his
life.
8Just as the king returned from the pal-
ace garden to the banquet hall, Haman
was falling on the couch where Esther was
reclining.
The king exclaimed, "Will he even mo-
lest the queen while she is with me in the
house?"
As soon as the word left the king's
mouth, they covered Haman's face. 9Then
Harbona, one of the eunuchs attending
the king, said, "A gallows seventy-five
feet[a] high stands by Haman's house. He
had it made for Mordecai, who spoke up
to help the king."
The king said, "Hang him on it!" 10So
they hanged Haman on the gallows he had
prepared for Mordecai. Then the king's
fury subsided.

The King's Edict in Behalf of the Jews

8 That same day King Xerxes gave
Queen Esther the estate of Haman, the
enemy of the Jews. And Mordecai came
into the presence of the king, for Esther
had told how he was related to her. 2The
king took off his signet ring, which he had
reclaimed from Haman, and presented it
to Mordecai. And Esther appointed him
over Haman's estate.
3Esther again pleaded with the king,
falling at his feet and weeping. She begged
him to put an end to the evil plan of Ha-
man the Agagite, which he had devised
against the Jews. 4Then the king extended
the gold scepter to Esther and she arose
and stood before him.
5"If it pleases the king," she said, "and
if he regards me with favor and thinks it
the right thing to do, and if he is pleased
with me, let an order be written overruling
the dispatches that Haman son of Ham-
medatha, the Agagite, devised and wrote
to destroy the Jews in all the king's prov-
inces. 6For how can I bear to see disaster
fall on my people? How can I bear to see
the destruction of my family?"
7King Xerxes replied to Queen Esther
and to Mordecai the Jew, "Because Ha-
man attacked the Jews, I have given his
estate to Esther, and they have hanged
him on the gallows. 8Now write another
decree in the king's name in behalf of the
Jews as seems best to you, and seal it with
the king's signet ring—for no document
written in the king's name and sealed with
his ring can be revoked."
9At once the royal secretaries were
summoned—on the twenty-third day of
the third month, the month of Sivan. They
wrote out all Mordecai's orders to the
Jews, and to the satraps, governors and
nobles of the 127 provinces stretching
from India to Cush.[b] These orders were
written in the script of each province and
the language of each people and also to
the Jews in their own script and language.
10Mordecai wrote in the name of King Xer-
xes, sealed the dispatches with the king's
signet ring, and sent them by mounted
couriers, who rode fast horses especially
bred for the king.
11The king's edict granted the Jews in
every city the right to assemble and pro-
tect themselves; to destroy, kill and anni-
hilate any armed force of any nationality
or province that might attack them and
their women and children; and to plunder
the property of their enemies. 12The day
appointed for the Jews to do this in all the
provinces of King Xerxes was the thir-
teenth day of the twelfth month, the
month of Adar. 13A copy of the text of the
edict was to be issued as law in every
province and made known to the people
of every nationality so that the Jews
would be ready on that day to avenge
themselves on their enemies.
14The couriers, riding the royal horses,
raced out, spurred on by the king's com-
mand. And the edict was also issued in the
citadel of Susa.
15Mordecai left the king's presence
wearing royal garments of blue and white,
a large crown of gold and a purple robe of
fine linen. And the city of Susa held a joy-
ous celebration. 16For the Jews it was a
time of happiness and joy, gladness and
honor. 17In every province and in every
city, wherever the edict of the king went,
there was joy and gladness among the
Jews, with feasting and celebrating. And
many people of other nationalities be-
came Jews because fear of the Jews had
seized them.

[a]9 Hebrew *fifty cubits* (about 23 meters) [b]9 That is, the upper Nile region

Triumph of the Jews

9 On the thirteenth day of the twelfth month, the month of Adar, the edict commanded by the king was to be carried out. On this day the enemies of the Jews had hoped to overpower them, but now the tables were turned and the Jews got the upper hand over those who hated them. 2The Jews assembled in their cities in all the provinces of King Xerxes to attack those seeking their destruction. No one could stand against them, because the people of all the other nationalities were afraid of them. 3And all the nobles of the provinces, the satraps, the governors and the king's administrators helped the Jews, because fear of Mordecai had seized them. 4Mordecai was prominent in the palace; his reputation spread throughout the provinces, and he became more and more powerful.

5The Jews struck down all their enemies with the sword, killing and destroying them, and they did what they pleased to those who hated them. 6In the citadel of Susa, the Jews killed and destroyed five hundred men. 7They also killed Parshandatha, Dalphon, Aspatha, 8Poratha, Adalia, Aridatha, 9Parmashta, Arisai, Aridai and Vaizatha, 10the ten sons of Haman son of Hammedatha, the enemy of the Jews. But they did not lay their hands on the plunder.

11The number of those slain in the citadel of Susa was reported to the king that same day. 12The king said to Queen Esther, "The Jews have killed and destroyed five hundred men and the ten sons of Haman in the citadel of Susa. What have they done in the rest of the king's provinces? Now what is your petition? It will be given you. What is your request? It will also be granted."

13"If it pleases the king," Esther answered, "give the Jews in Susa permission to carry out this day's edict tomorrow also, and let Haman's ten sons be hanged on gallows."

14So the king commanded that this be done. An edict was issued in Susa, and they hanged the ten sons of Haman. 15The Jews in Susa came together on the fourteenth day of the month of Adar, and they put to death in Susa three hundred men, but they did not lay their hands on the plunder.

16Meanwhile, the remainder of the Jews who were in the king's provinces also assembled to protect themselves and get relief from their enemies. They killed seventy-five thousand of them but did not lay their hands on the plunder. 17This happened on the thirteenth day of the month of Adar, and on the fourteenth they rested and made it a day of feasting and joy.

Purim Celebrated

18The Jews in Susa, however, had assembled on the thirteenth and fourteenth, and then on the fifteenth they rested and made it a day of feasting and joy.

19That is why rural Jews—those living in villages—observe the fourteenth of the month of Adar as a day of joy and feasting, a day for giving presents to each other.

20Mordecai recorded these events, and he sent letters to all the Jews throughout the provinces of King Xerxes, near and far, 21to have them celebrate annually the fourteenth and fifteenth days of the month of Adar 22as the time when the Jews got relief from their enemies, and as the month when their sorrow was turned into joy and their mourning into a day of celebration. He wrote them to observe the days as days of feasting and joy and giving presents of food to one another and gifts to the poor.

23So the Jews agreed to continue the celebration they had begun, doing what Mordecai had written to them. 24For Haman son of Hammedatha, the Agagite, the enemy of all the Jews, had plotted against the Jews to destroy them and had cast the *pur* (that is, the lot) for their ruin and destruction. 25But when the plot came to the king's attention,[a] he issued written orders that the evil scheme Haman had devised against the Jews should come back onto his own head, and that he and his sons should be hanged on the gallows. 26(Therefore these days were called Purim, from the word *pur*.) Because of everything written in this letter and because of what they had seen and what had happened to them, 27the Jews took it upon themselves to establish the custom that they and their descendants and all who join them should without fail observe these two days every year, in the way prescribed and at the time appointed. 28These days should be remembered and observed in every generation by every family, and

[a]25 Or *when Esther came before the king*

in every province and in every city. And these days of Purim should never cease to be celebrated by the Jews, nor should the memory of them die out among their descendants.

[29]So Queen Esther, daughter of Abihail, along with Mordecai the Jew, wrote with full authority to confirm this second letter concerning Purim. [30]And Mordecai sent letters to all the Jews in the 127 provinces of the kingdom of Xerxes—words of goodwill and assurance— [31]to establish these days of Purim at their designated times, as Mordecai the Jew and Queen Esther had decreed for them, and as they had established for themselves and their descendants in regard to their times of fasting and lamentation. [32]Esther's decree confirmed these regulations about Purim, and it was written down in the records.

The Greatness of Mordecai

10 King Xerxes imposed tribute throughout the empire, to its distant shores. [2]And all his acts of power and might, together with a full account of the greatness of Mordecai to which the king had raised him, are they not written in the book of the annals of the kings of Media and Persia? [3]Mordecai the Jew was second in rank to King Xerxes, preeminent among the Jews, and held in high esteem by his many fellow Jews, because he worked for the good of his people and spoke up for the welfare of all the Jews.

JOB presents a striking example of the news behind the news—of God at work behind the scenes of human suffering. After numerous attempts by Job and his friends to uncover the reasons for his suffering, God himself enters the dialogue with a majestic description of his power and love. As you read this book, realize that God may not answer all your questions about life's suffering; realize too that God does control Satan, who can go no farther than the Lord allows.

JOB

Prologue

1 In the land of Uz there lived a man whose name was Job. This man was blameless and upright; he feared God and shunned evil. [2]He had seven sons and three daughters, [3]and he owned seven thousand sheep, three thousand camels, five hundred yoke of oxen and five hundred donkeys, and had a large number of servants. He was the greatest man among all the people of the East.

[4]His sons used to take turns holding feasts in their homes, and they would invite their three sisters to eat and drink with them. [5]When a period of feasting had run its course, Job would send and have them purified. Early in the morning he would sacrifice a burnt offering for each of them, thinking, "Perhaps my children have sinned and cursed God in their hearts." This was Job's regular custom.

Job's First Test

[6]One day the angels[a] came to present themselves before the LORD, and Satan[b] also came with them. [7]The LORD said to Satan, "Where have you come from?"

Satan answered the LORD, "From roam-

[a]6 Hebrew *the sons of God* [b]6 *Satan* means *accuser.*

ing through the earth and going back and
forth in it."
8Then the LORD said to Satan, "Have you
considered my servant Job? There is no
one on earth like him; he is blameless and
upright, a man who fears God and shuns
evil."
9"Does Job fear God for nothing?" Satan
replied. 10"Have you not put a hedge
around him and his household and every-
thing he has? You have blessed the work
of his hands, so that his flocks and herds
are spread throughout the land. 11But
stretch out your hand and strike every-
thing he has, and he will surely curse you
to your face."
12The LORD said to Satan, "Very well,
then, everything he has is in your hands,
but on the man himself do not lay a fin-
ger."
Then Satan went out from the presence
of the LORD.
13One day when Job's sons and daugh-
ters were feasting and drinking wine at
the oldest brother's house, 14a messenger
came to Job and said, "The oxen were
plowing and the donkeys were grazing
nearby, 15and the Sabeans attacked and

VERSE FOR THE DAY: Job 1:20–21 | AUTHOR: Ben Patterson | PASSAGE FOR THE DAY: Job 1:1–21

Job's Essential Lesson

Job's name has become a synonym for the suffering of life's derailments. Actually "derailment" is too weak a word to describe what happened. He lost everything: children, health, riches, the support of his friends and wife, and apparently the love of the God he had trusted and loved for so long.

What did he do when life ground to a halt? The Bible says he "got up and tore his robe and shaved his head. Then he fell to the ground in worship and said: 'Naked I came from my mother's womb, and naked I will depart. The LORD gave and the Lord has taken away; may the name of the LORD be praised' " (Job 1:20–21).

Job's perspective wiped the "why me?" question from his mind. He recognized that he had nothing when he arrived on this planet, and he would have nothing when he left it. His nakedness was a dress rehearsal for his death and a remembrance of his birth. In the end it will have gone full circle and he would be back where he started: with nothing and no one but God.

MARRIAGE BUILDERS

♦ *What are some of the struggles and losses you're experiencing right now?*

♦ *How are you able to love and trust God, despite these painful experiences?*

Additional Scripture Readings
Matthew 6:19; Colossians 1:16–17

Go to page 510 for your next devotional reading.

carried them off. They put the servants to the sword, and I am the only one who has escaped to tell you!"

16While he was still speaking, another messenger came and said, "The fire of God fell from the sky and burned up the sheep and the servants, and I am the only one who has escaped to tell you!"

17While he was still speaking, another messenger came and said, "The Chaldeans formed three raiding parties and swept down on your camels and carried them off. They put the servants to the sword, and I am the only one who has escaped to tell you!"

18While he was still speaking, yet another messenger came and said, "Your sons and daughters were feasting and drinking wine at the oldest brother's house, 19when suddenly a mighty wind swept in from the desert and struck the four corners of the house. It collapsed on them and they are dead, and I am the only one who has escaped to tell you!"

20At this, Job got up and tore his robe and shaved his head. Then he fell to the ground in worship 21and said:

"Naked I came from my mother's
womb,
and naked I will depart.[a]
The LORD gave and the LORD has taken
away;
may the name of the LORD be
praised."

22In all this, Job did not sin by charging God with wrongdoing.

Job's Second Test

2 On another day the angels[b] came to present themselves before the LORD, and Satan also came with them to present himself before him. 2And the LORD said to Satan, "Where have you come from?"

Satan answered the LORD, "From roaming through the earth and going back and forth in it."

3Then the LORD said to Satan, "Have you considered my servant Job? There is no one on earth like him; he is blameless and upright, a man who fears God and shuns evil. And he still maintains his integrity, though you incited me against him to ruin him without any reason."

4"Skin for skin!" Satan replied. "A man will give all he has for his own life. 5But stretch out your hand and strike his flesh and bones, and he will surely curse you to your face."

6The LORD said to Satan, "Very well, then, he is in your hands; but you must spare his life."

7So Satan went out from the presence of the LORD and afflicted Job with painful sores from the soles of his feet to the top of his head. 8Then Job took a piece of broken pottery and scraped himself with it as he sat among the ashes.

9His wife said to him, "Are you still holding on to your integrity? Curse God and die!"

10He replied, "You are talking like a foolish[c] woman. Shall we accept good from God, and not trouble?"

In all this, Job did not sin in what he said.

Job's Three Friends

11When Job's three friends, Eliphaz the Temanite, Bildad the Shuhite and Zophar the Naamathite, heard about all the troubles that had come upon him, they set out from their homes and met together by agreement to go and sympathize with him and comfort him. 12When they saw him from a distance, they could hardly recognize him; they began to weep aloud, and they tore their robes and sprinkled dust on their heads. 13Then they sat on the ground with him for seven days and seven nights. No one said a word to him, because they saw how great his suffering was.

Job Speaks

3 After this, Job opened his mouth and cursed the day of his birth. 2He said:

3"May the day of my birth perish,
and the night it was said, 'A boy is
born!'
4That day—may it turn to darkness;
may God above not care about it;
may no light shine upon it.
5May darkness and deep shadow[d]
claim it once more;
may a cloud settle over it;
may blackness overwhelm its light.
6That night—may thick darkness seize
it;
may it not be included among the
days of the year

[a] 21 Or *will return there* denotes moral deficiency. [b] 1 Hebrew *the sons of God* [c] 10 The Hebrew word rendered *foolish* [d] 5 Or *and the shadow of death*

nor be entered in any of the months.
7 May that night be barren;
may no shout of joy be heard in it.
8 May those who curse days[a] curse that day,
those who are ready to rouse Leviathan.
9 May its morning stars become dark;
may it wait for daylight in vain
and not see the first rays of dawn,
10 for it did not shut the doors of the womb on me
to hide trouble from my eyes.

11 "Why did I not perish at birth,
and die as I came from the womb?
12 Why were there knees to receive me
and breasts that I might be nursed?
13 For now I would be lying down in peace;
I would be asleep and at rest
14 with kings and counselors of the earth,
who built for themselves places now lying in ruins,
15 with rulers who had gold,
who filled their houses with silver.
16 Or why was I not hidden in the ground like a stillborn child,
like an infant who never saw the light of day?
17 There the wicked cease from turmoil,
and there the weary are at rest.
18 Captives also enjoy their ease;
they no longer hear the slave driver's shout.
19 The small and the great are there,
and the slave is freed from his master.

20 "Why is light given to those in misery,
and life to the bitter of soul,
21 to those who long for death that does not come,
who search for it more than for hidden treasure,
22 who are filled with gladness
and rejoice when they reach the grave?
23 Why is life given to a man
whose way is hidden,
whom God has hedged in?
24 For sighing comes to me instead of food;
my groans pour out like water.
25 What I feared has come upon me;
what I dreaded has happened to me.
26 I have no peace, no quietness;
I have no rest, but only turmoil."

Eliphaz

4 Then Eliphaz the Temanite replied:
2 "If someone ventures a word with you, will you be impatient?
But who can keep from speaking?
3 Think how you have instructed many,
how you have strengthened feeble hands.
4 Your words have supported those who stumbled;
you have strengthened faltering knees.
5 But now trouble comes to you, and you are discouraged;
it strikes you, and you are dismayed.
6 Should not your piety be your confidence
and your blameless ways your hope?

7 "Consider now: Who, being innocent, has ever perished?
Where were the upright ever destroyed?
8 As I have observed, those who plow evil
and those who sow trouble reap it.
9 At the breath of God they are destroyed;
at the blast of his anger they perish.
10 The lions may roar and growl,
yet the teeth of the great lions are broken.
11 The lion perishes for lack of prey,
and the cubs of the lioness are scattered.

12 "A word was secretly brought to me,
my ears caught a whisper of it.
13 Amid disquieting dreams in the night,
when deep sleep falls on men,
14 fear and trembling seized me
and made all my bones shake.
15 A spirit glided past my face,
and the hair on my body stood on end.
16 It stopped,
but I could not tell what it was.
A form stood before my eyes,
and I heard a hushed voice:
17 'Can a mortal be more righteous than God?

[a] 8 Or *the sea*

WEEKENDING

LISTENING

Good listening is essential in maintaining a healthy marriage. This quiz will help you gauge how well you're doing. If you discover areas where either of you needs improvement, begin to make a concerted effort toward developing better skills. Realizing there is room for improvement is the first step toward building a stronger marriage.

On a scale of one (hardly ever) to five (almost always), rate yourself on the *frequency* of each of the following good-listening habits.

___ I maintain direct eye contact.

___ I focus my attention on what my partner is saying rather than on what I'm going to say next.

___ I listen for feelings as well as facts.

___ I avoid letting my mind wander.

___ I tune in instead of tune out when difficult or controversial issues come up.

___ I think first, then respond.

___ I think of questions to ask and ask them.

— Paul W. Swets

REVIVE

Saturday: Proverbs 18:1–13
Sunday: Proverbs 4:1–27

Go to page 512 for your next devotional reading.

Can a man be more pure than his Maker?
18 If God places no trust in his servants,
if he charges his angels with error,
19 how much more those who live in houses of clay,
whose foundations are in the dust,
who are crushed more readily than a moth!
20 Between dawn and dusk they are broken to pieces;
unnoticed, they perish forever.
21 Are not the cords of their tent pulled up,
so that they die without wisdom?'[a]

5 "Call if you will, but who will answer you?
To which of the holy ones will you turn?
2 Resentment kills a fool,
and envy slays the simple.
3 I myself have seen a fool taking root,
but suddenly his house was cursed.
4 His children are far from safety,
crushed in court without a defender.
5 The hungry consume his harvest,
taking it even from among thorns,
and the thirsty pant after his wealth.
6 For hardship does not spring from the soil,
nor does trouble sprout from the ground.
7 Yet man is born to trouble
as surely as sparks fly upward.

8 "But if it were I, I would appeal to God;
I would lay my cause before him.
9 He performs wonders that cannot be fathomed,
miracles that cannot be counted.
10 He bestows rain on the earth;
he sends water upon the countryside.
11 The lowly he sets on high,
and those who mourn are lifted to safety.
12 He thwarts the plans of the crafty,
so that their hands achieve no success.
13 He catches the wise in their craftiness,
and the schemes of the wily are swept away.
14 Darkness comes upon them in the daytime;
at noon they grope as in the night.
15 He saves the needy from the sword in their mouth;
he saves them from the clutches of the powerful.
16 So the poor have hope,
and injustice shuts its mouth.

17 "Blessed is the man whom God corrects;
so do not despise the discipline of the Almighty.[b]
18 For he wounds, but he also binds up;
he injures, but his hands also heal.
19 From six calamities he will rescue you;
in seven no harm will befall you.
20 In famine he will ransom you from death,
and in battle from the stroke of the sword.
21 You will be protected from the lash of the tongue,
and need not fear when destruction comes.
22 You will laugh at destruction and famine,
and need not fear the beasts of the earth.
23 For you will have a covenant with the stones of the field,
and the wild animals will be at peace with you.
24 You will know that your tent is secure;
you will take stock of your property and find nothing missing.
25 You will know that your children will be many,
and your descendants like the grass of the earth.
26 You will come to the grave in full vigor,
like sheaves gathered in season.

27 "We have examined this, and it is true.
So hear it and apply it to yourself."

Job

6 Then Job replied:
2 "If only my anguish could be weighed
and all my misery be placed on the scales!
3 It would surely outweigh the sand of the seas—

[a] 21 Some interpreters end the quotation after verse 17.
[b] 17 Hebrew *Shaddai*; here and throughout Job

VERSE FOR THE DAY: Job 6:24

AUTHOR: David L. Goetz

PASSAGE FOR THE DAY: Job 6:24–30

Truth and Consequences

My wife, Jana, was forking the last bite of an order of banana pancakes into her mouth when our conversation screeched to a halt.

"We've been having this same conversation for the past two years," she said, having listened to my frustrations about my father who had turned down our request for a loan. "Every time you talk about your family, your face gets red and you pound the table. I don't know what to say anymore. I think you need to see a counselor."

I felt hurt, even betrayed. But my wife's truthtelling launched me on a journey that invited the presence of Christ into a back corner of my soul. She had exercised an unpleasant kindness; she had served me by telling the truth. And it cost her something. She had to endure my angry response, and then my sullenness. But Jana's insistence that I had a problem with my anger was a beautiful expression of her love for me, no matter how difficult it was for me to accept.

There isn't always a pain-free way to tell the truth, but the alternative is a marriage built around a series of covert compromises. Truth may initially douse the fires of passion, but over time it creates new possibilities for genuine intimacy—the intimacy that comes with being fully known by another. The gust of God's grace now blowing through our marriage is experienced in a little more transparency, a little more honesty and, consequently, a little more intimacy.

MARRIAGE BUILDERS

♦ *When have you struggled to tell your spouse the truth about something? What happened when you spoke up?*

♦ *When has it been hard for you to accept something your spouse said about you? In the long run, did that truth help or hurt?*

Additional Scripture Readings
Proverbs 15:4; Ephesians 4:25–27

Go to page 519 for your next devotional reading.

no wonder my words have been impetuous.
4 The arrows of the Almighty are in me,
my spirit drinks in their poison;
God's terrors are marshaled against me.
5 Does a wild donkey bray when it has grass,
or an ox bellow when it has fodder?
6 Is tasteless food eaten without salt,
or is there flavor in the white of an egg[a]?
7 I refuse to touch it;
such food makes me ill.

8 "Oh, that I might have my request,
that God would grant what I hope for,
9 that God would be willing to crush me,
to let loose his hand and cut me off!
10 Then I would still have this consolation—
my joy in unrelenting pain—
that I had not denied the words of the Holy One.

11 "What strength do I have, that I should still hope?
What prospects, that I should be patient?
12 Do I have the strength of stone?
Is my flesh bronze?
13 Do I have any power to help myself,
now that success has been driven from me?

14 "A despairing man should have the devotion of his friends,
even though he forsakes the fear of the Almighty.
15 But my brothers are as undependable as intermittent streams,
as the streams that overflow
16 when darkened by thawing ice
and swollen with melting snow,
17 but that cease to flow in the dry season,
and in the heat vanish from their channels.
18 Caravans turn aside from their routes;
they go up into the wasteland and perish.
19 The caravans of Tema look for water,
the traveling merchants of Sheba look in hope.
20 They are distressed, because they had been confident;
they arrive there, only to be disappointed.
21 Now you too have proved to be of no help;
you see something dreadful and are afraid.
22 Have I ever said, 'Give something on my behalf,
pay a ransom for me from your wealth,
23 deliver me from the hand of the enemy,
ransom me from the clutches of the ruthless'?

24 "Teach me, and I will be quiet;
show me where I have been wrong.
25 How painful are honest words!
But what do your arguments prove?
26 Do you mean to correct what I say,
and treat the words of a despairing man as wind?
27 You would even cast lots for the fatherless
and barter away your friend.

28 "But now be so kind as to look at me.
Would I lie to your face?
29 Relent, do not be unjust;
reconsider, for my integrity is at stake.[b]
30 Is there any wickedness on my lips?
Can my mouth not discern malice?

7 "Does not man have hard service on earth?
Are not his days like those of a hired man?
2 Like a slave longing for the evening shadows,
or a hired man waiting eagerly for his wages,
3 so I have been allotted months of futility,
and nights of misery have been assigned to me.
4 When I lie down I think, 'How long before I get up?'
The night drags on, and I toss till dawn.
5 My body is clothed with worms and scabs,
my skin is broken and festering.

6 "My days are swifter than a weaver's shuttle,

[a] 6 The meaning of the Hebrew for this phrase is uncertain. [b] 29 Or *my righteousness still stands*

and they come to an end without
hope.
7Remember, O God, that my life is but
a breath;
my eyes will never see happiness
again.
8The eye that now sees me will see me
no longer;
you will look for me, but I will be
no more.
9As a cloud vanishes and is gone,
so he who goes down to the grave[a]
does not return.
10He will never come to his house
again;
his place will know him no more.

11"Therefore I will not keep silent;
I will speak out in the anguish of
my spirit,
I will complain in the bitterness of
my soul.
12Am I the sea, or the monster of the
deep,
that you put me under guard?
13When I think my bed will comfort me
and my couch will ease my
complaint,
14even then you frighten me with
dreams
and terrify me with visions,
15so that I prefer strangling and death,
rather than this body of mine.
16I despise my life; I would not live
forever.
Let me alone; my days have no
meaning.

17"What is man that you make so much
of him,
that you give him so much
attention,
18that you examine him every morning
and test him every moment?
19Will you never look away from me,
or let me alone even for an instant?
20If I have sinned, what have I done to
you,
O watcher of men?
Why have you made me your target?
Have I become a burden to you?[b]
21Why do you not pardon my offenses
and forgive my sins?
For I will soon lie down in the dust;
you will search for me, but I will be
no more."

Bildad

8 Then Bildad the Shuhite replied:

2"How long will you say such things?
Your words are a blustering wind.
3Does God pervert justice?
Does the Almighty pervert what is
right?
4When your children sinned against
him,
he gave them over to the penalty of
their sin.
5But if you will look to God
and plead with the Almighty,
6if you are pure and upright,
even now he will rouse himself on
your behalf
and restore you to your rightful
place.
7Your beginnings will seem humble,
so prosperous will your future be.

8"Ask the former generations
and find out what their fathers
learned,
9for we were born only yesterday and
know nothing,
and our days on earth are but a
shadow.
10Will they not instruct you and tell
you?
Will they not bring forth words
from their understanding?
11Can papyrus grow tall where there is
no marsh?
Can reeds thrive without water?
12While still growing and uncut,
they wither more quickly than
grass.
13Such is the destiny of all who forget
God;
so perishes the hope of the godless.
14What he trusts in is fragile[c];
what he relies on is a spider's web.
15He leans on his web, but it gives way;
he clings to it, but it does not hold.
16He is like a well-watered plant in the
sunshine,
spreading its shoots over the
garden;
17it entwines its roots around a pile of
rocks
and looks for a place among the
stones.
18But when it is torn from its spot,

[a]9 Hebrew *Sheol* [b]20 A few manuscripts of the Masoretic Text, an ancient Hebrew scribal tradition and Septuagint; most manuscripts of the Masoretic Text *I have become a burden to myself.* [c]14 The meaning of the Hebrew for this word is uncertain.

that place disowns it and says, 'I
never saw you.'
19Surely its life withers away,
and[a] from the soil other plants
grow.
20"Surely God does not reject a
blameless man
or strengthen the hands of
evildoers.
21He will yet fill your mouth with
laughter
and your lips with shouts of joy.
22Your enemies will be clothed in
shame,
and the tents of the wicked will be
no more."

Job

9 Then Job replied:
2"Indeed, I know that this is true.
But how can a mortal be righteous
before God?
3Though one wished to dispute with
him,
he could not answer him one time
out of a thousand.
4His wisdom is profound, his power is
vast.
Who has resisted him and come out
unscathed?
5He moves mountains without their
knowing it
and overturns them in his anger.
6He shakes the earth from its place
and makes its pillars tremble.
7He speaks to the sun and it does not
shine;
he seals off the light of the stars.
8He alone stretches out the heavens
and treads on the waves of the sea.
9He is the Maker of the Bear and
Orion,
the Pleiades and the constellations
of the south.
10He performs wonders that cannot be
fathomed,
miracles that cannot be counted.
11When he passes me, I cannot see him;
when he goes by, I cannot perceive
him.
12If he snatches away, who can stop
him?
Who can say to him, 'What are you
doing?'
13God does not restrain his anger;
even the cohorts of Rahab cowered
at his feet.
14"How then can I dispute with him?
How can I find words to argue with
him?
15Though I were innocent, I could not
answer him;
I could only plead with my Judge
for mercy.
16Even if I summoned him and he
responded,
I do not believe he would give me a
hearing.
17He would crush me with a storm
and multiply my wounds for no
reason.
18He would not let me regain my breath
but would overwhelm me with
misery.
19If it is a matter of strength, he is
mighty!
And if it is a matter of justice, who
will summon him[b]?
20Even if I were innocent, my mouth
would condemn me;
if I were blameless, it would
pronounce me guilty.
21"Although I am blameless,
I have no concern for myself;
I despise my own life.
22It is all the same; that is why I say,
'He destroys both the blameless and
the wicked.'
23When a scourge brings sudden death,
he mocks the despair of the
innocent.
24When a land falls into the hands of
the wicked,
he blindfolds its judges.
If it is not he, then who is it?
25"My days are swifter than a runner;
they fly away without a glimpse of
joy.
26They skim past like boats of papyrus,
like eagles swooping down on their
prey.
27If I say, 'I will forget my complaint,
I will change my expression, and
smile,'
28I still dread all my sufferings,
for I know you will not hold me
innocent.
29Since I am already found guilty,
why should I struggle in vain?
30Even if I washed myself with soap[c]

[a] 19 Or *Surely all the joy it has / is that* [b] 19 See Septuagint; Hebrew *me.* [c] 30 Or *snow*

and my hands with washing soda,
31 you would plunge me into a slime pit
so that even my clothes would
detest me.
32 "He is not a man like me that I might
answer him,
that we might confront each other
in court.
33 If only there were someone to
arbitrate between us,
to lay his hand upon us both,
34 someone to remove God's rod from
me,
so that his terror would frighten me
no more.
35 Then I would speak up without fear of
him,
but as it now stands with me, I
cannot.

10 "I loathe my very life;
therefore I will give free rein to
my complaint
and speak out in the bitterness of
my soul.
2 I will say to God: Do not condemn
me,
but tell me what charges you have
against me.
3 Does it please you to oppress me,
to spurn the work of your hands,
while you smile on the schemes of
the wicked?
4 Do you have eyes of flesh?
Do you see as a mortal sees?
5 Are your days like those of a mortal
or your years like those of a man,
6 that you must search out my faults
and probe after my sin—
7 though you know that I am not guilty
and that no one can rescue me from
your hand?
8 "Your hands shaped me and made me.
Will you now turn and destroy me?
9 Remember that you molded me like
clay.
Will you now turn me to dust
again?
10 Did you not pour me out like milk
and curdle me like cheese,
11 clothe me with skin and flesh
and knit me together with bones
and sinews?
12 You gave me life and showed me
kindness,
and in your providence watched
over my spirit.
13 "But this is what you concealed in
your heart,
and I know that this was in your
mind:
14 If I sinned, you would be watching me
and would not let my offense go
unpunished.
15 If I am guilty—woe to me!
Even if I am innocent, I cannot lift
my head,
for I am full of shame
and drowned in[a] my affliction.
16 If I hold my head high, you stalk me
like a lion
and again display your awesome
power against me.
17 You bring new witnesses against me
and increase your anger toward me;
your forces come against me wave
upon wave.
18 "Why then did you bring me out of
the womb?
I wish I had died before any eye
saw me.
19 If only I had never come into being,
or had been carried straight from
the womb to the grave!
20 Are not my few days almost over?
Turn away from me so I can have a
moment's joy
21 before I go to the place of no return,
to the land of gloom and deep
shadow,[b]
22 to the land of deepest night,
of deep shadow and disorder,
where even the light is like
darkness."

Zophar

11 Then Zophar the Naamathite replied:
2 "Are all these words to go
unanswered?
Is this talker to be vindicated?
3 Will your idle talk reduce men to
silence?
Will no one rebuke you when you
mock?
4 You say to God, 'My beliefs are
flawless
and I am pure in your sight.'
5 Oh, how I wish that God would speak,

[a] 15 Or *and aware of* [b] 21 Or *and the shadow of death*; also in verse 22

that he would open his lips against you
[6]and disclose to you the secrets of wisdom,
for true wisdom has two sides.
Know this: God has even forgotten some of your sin.

[7]"Can you fathom the mysteries of God?
Can you probe the limits of the Almighty?
[8]They are higher than the heavens—what can you do?
They are deeper than the depths of the grave[a]—what can you know?
[9]Their measure is longer than the earth and wider than the sea.

[10]"If he comes along and confines you in prison
and convenes a court, who can oppose him?
[11]Surely he recognizes deceitful men;
and when he sees evil, does he not take note?
[12]But a witless man can no more become wise
than a wild donkey's colt can be born a man.[b]

[13]"Yet if you devote your heart to him
and stretch out your hands to him,
[14]if you put away the sin that is in your hand
and allow no evil to dwell in your tent,
[15]then you will lift up your face without shame;
you will stand firm and without fear.
[16]You will surely forget your trouble,
recalling it only as waters gone by.
[17]Life will be brighter than noonday,
and darkness will become like morning.
[18]You will be secure, because there is hope;
you will look about you and take your rest in safety.
[19]You will lie down, with no one to make you afraid,
and many will court your favor.
[20]But the eyes of the wicked will fail,
and escape will elude them;
their hope will become a dying gasp."

Job

12 Then Job replied:

[2]"Doubtless you are the people,
and wisdom will die with you!
[3]But I have a mind as well as you;
I am not inferior to you.
Who does not know all these things?

[4]"I have become a laughingstock to my friends,
though I called upon God and he answered—
a mere laughingstock, though righteous and blameless!
[5]Men at ease have contempt for misfortune
as the fate of those whose feet are slipping.
[6]The tents of marauders are undisturbed,
and those who provoke God are secure—
those who carry their god in their hands.[c]

[7]"But ask the animals, and they will teach you,
or the birds of the air, and they will tell you;
[8]or speak to the earth, and it will teach you,
or let the fish of the sea inform you.
[9]Which of all these does not know
that the hand of the LORD has done this?
[10]In his hand is the life of every creature
and the breath of all mankind.
[11]Does not the ear test words
as the tongue tastes food?
[12]Is not wisdom found among the aged?
Does not long life bring understanding?

[13]"To God belong wisdom and power;
counsel and understanding are his.
[14]What he tears down cannot be rebuilt;
the man he imprisons cannot be released.
[15]If he holds back the waters, there is drought;

[a]8 Hebrew *than Sheol* [b]12 Or *wild donkey can be born tame* [c]6 Or *secure / in what God's hand brings them*

if he lets them loose, they devastate
the land.
16To him belong strength and victory;
both deceived and deceiver are his.
17He leads counselors away stripped
and makes fools of judges.
18He takes off the shackles put on by
kings
and ties a loincloth[a] around their
waist.
19He leads priests away stripped
and overthrows men long
established.
20He silences the lips of trusted advisers
and takes away the discernment of
elders.
21He pours contempt on nobles
and disarms the mighty.
22He reveals the deep things of darkness
and brings deep shadows into the
light.
23He makes nations great, and destroys
them;
he enlarges nations, and disperses
them.
24He deprives the leaders of the earth of
their reason;
he sends them wandering through a
trackless waste.
25They grope in darkness with no light;
he makes them stagger like
drunkards.

13 "My eyes have seen all this,
my ears have heard and
understood it.
2What you know, I also know;
I am not inferior to you.
3But I desire to speak to the Almighty
and to argue my case with God.
4You, however, smear me with lies;
you are worthless physicians, all of
you!
5If only you would be altogether silent!
For you, that would be wisdom.
6Hear now my argument;
listen to the plea of my lips.
7Will you speak wickedly on God's
behalf?
Will you speak deceitfully for him?
8Will you show him partiality?
Will you argue the case for God?
9Would it turn out well if he examined
you?
Could you deceive him as you
might deceive men?
10He would surely rebuke you
if you secretly showed partiality.
11Would not his splendor terrify you?
Would not the dread of him fall on
you?
12Your maxims are proverbs of ashes;
your defenses are defenses of clay.

13"Keep silent and let me speak;
then let come to me what may.
14Why do I put myself in jeopardy
and take my life in my hands?
15Though he slay me, yet will I hope in
him;
I will surely[b] defend my ways to
his face.
16Indeed, this will turn out for my
deliverance,
for no godless man would dare
come before him!
17Listen carefully to my words;
let your ears take in what I say.
18Now that I have prepared my case,
I know I will be vindicated.
19Can anyone bring charges against me?
If so, I will be silent and die.

20"Only grant me these two things,
O God,
and then I will not hide from you:
21Withdraw your hand far from me,
and stop frightening me with your
terrors.
22Then summon me and I will answer,
or let me speak, and you reply.
23How many wrongs and sins have I
committed?
Show me my offense and my sin.
24Why do you hide your face
and consider me your enemy?
25Will you torment a windblown leaf?
Will you chase after dry chaff?
26For you write down bitter things
against me
and make me inherit the sins of my
youth.
27You fasten my feet in shackles;
you keep close watch on all my
paths
by putting marks on the soles of my
feet.

28"So man wastes away like something
rotten,
like a garment eaten by moths.

14 "Man born of woman
is of few days and full of trouble.
2He springs up like a flower and
withers away;

[a]18 Or *shackles of kings / and ties a belt*

[b]15 Or *He will surely slay me; I have no hope — / yet I will*

like a fleeting shadow, he does not endure.
[3]Do you fix your eye on such a one?
Will you bring him[a] before you for judgment?
[4]Who can bring what is pure from the impure?
No one!
[5]Man's days are determined;
you have decreed the number of his months
and have set limits he cannot exceed.
[6]So look away from him and let him alone,
till he has put in his time like a hired man.
[7]"At least there is hope for a tree:
If it is cut down, it will sprout again,
and its new shoots will not fail.
[8]Its roots may grow old in the ground
and its stump die in the soil,
[9]yet at the scent of water it will bud
and put forth shoots like a plant.

[a]3 Septuagint, Vulgate and Syriac; Hebrew *me*

VERSE FOR THE DAY: Job 13:15 | AUTHOR: Jim Conway | PASSAGE FOR THE DAY: Job 13:15

Crisis of Faith

Sally and I went through a time when my faith was challenged to the very core of my being. When our daughter Becki developed cancer in 1978, I believed God would answer my prayers to heal her. When that didn't happen, I became very angry at God. I was totally devastated.

After the doctor told us he would have to amputate Becki's leg, I turned to Sally and said, "We're going to have to be very strong from now on because God isn't going to care for us." I was ready to leave the ministry.

Sally was busy helping Becki after the surgery, but fortunately I had three close friends who let me pour out my grief. They stood by me and let me ventilate for hours on end. It ultimately came to a point where I had to say, "I'm either going to trust myself, or I am going to trust God blindly." I realized if I trusted myself there would be nothing but despair, because I could not control life. So the only viable option was to trust God.

MARRIAGE BUILDERS

♦ *How have you worked through a time of spiritual doubting, a time when you questioned God's love, or goodness or presence?*
♦ *Who might provide much-needed support if you encounter such a time in the future?*

Additional Scripture Readings
Isaiah 26:3–4; John 14:1

Go to page 537 for your next devotional reading.

10 But man dies and is laid low;
he breathes his last and is no more.
11 As water disappears from the sea
or a riverbed becomes parched and dry,
12 so man lies down and does not rise;
till the heavens are no more, men will not awake
or be roused from their sleep.
13 "If only you would hide me in the grave[a]
and conceal me till your anger has passed!
If only you would set me a time
and then remember me!
14 If a man dies, will he live again?
All the days of my hard service
I will wait for my renewal[b] to come.
15 You will call and I will answer you;
you will long for the creature your hands have made.
16 Surely then you will count my steps
but not keep track of my sin.
17 My offenses will be sealed up in a bag;
you will cover over my sin.
18 "But as a mountain erodes and crumbles
and as a rock is moved from its place,
19 as water wears away stones
and torrents wash away the soil,
so you destroy man's hope.
20 You overpower him once for all, and he is gone;
you change his countenance and send him away.
21 If his sons are honored, he does not know it;
if they are brought low, he does not see it.
22 He feels but the pain of his own body
and mourns only for himself."

Eliphaz

15 Then Eliphaz the Temanite replied:

2 "Would a wise man answer with empty notions
or fill his belly with the hot east wind?
3 Would he argue with useless words,
with speeches that have no value?
4 But you even undermine piety
and hinder devotion to God.
5 Your sin prompts your mouth;
you adopt the tongue of the crafty.
6 Your own mouth condemns you, not mine;
your own lips testify against you.
7 "Are you the first man ever born?
Were you brought forth before the hills?
8 Do you listen in on God's council?
Do you limit wisdom to yourself?
9 What do you know that we do not know?
What insights do you have that we do not have?
10 The gray-haired and the aged are on our side,
men even older than your father.
11 Are God's consolations not enough for you,
words spoken gently to you?
12 Why has your heart carried you away,
and why do your eyes flash,
13 so that you vent your rage against God
and pour out such words from your mouth?
14 "What is man, that he could be pure,
or one born of woman, that he could be righteous?
15 If God places no trust in his holy ones,
if even the heavens are not pure in his eyes,
16 how much less man, who is vile and corrupt,
who drinks up evil like water!
17 "Listen to me and I will explain to you;
let me tell you what I have seen,
18 what wise men have declared,
hiding nothing received from their fathers
19 (to whom alone the land was given
when no alien passed among them):
20 All his days the wicked man suffers torment,
the ruthless through all the years stored up for him.
21 Terrifying sounds fill his ears;
when all seems well, marauders attack him.
22 He despairs of escaping the darkness;

[a] 13 Hebrew *Sheol* [b] 14 Or *release*

he is marked for the sword.
23He wanders about—food for vultures[a];
he knows the day of darkness is at hand.
24Distress and anguish fill him with terror;
they overwhelm him, like a king poised to attack,
25because he shakes his fist at God
and vaunts himself against the Almighty,
26defiantly charging against him
with a thick, strong shield.

27"Though his face is covered with fat
and his waist bulges with flesh,
28he will inhabit ruined towns
and houses where no one lives,
houses crumbling to rubble.
29He will no longer be rich and his wealth will not endure,
nor will his possessions spread over the land.
30He will not escape the darkness;
a flame will wither his shoots,
and the breath of God's mouth will carry him away.
31Let him not deceive himself by trusting what is worthless,
for he will get nothing in return.
32Before his time he will be paid in full,
and his branches will not flourish.
33He will be like a vine stripped of its unripe grapes,
like an olive tree shedding its blossoms.
34For the company of the godless will be barren,
and fire will consume the tents of those who love bribes.
35They conceive trouble and give birth to evil;
their womb fashions deceit."

Job

16 Then Job replied:
2"I have heard many things like these;
miserable comforters are you all!
3Will your long-winded speeches never end?
What ails you that you keep on arguing?
4I also could speak like you,
if you were in my place;
I could make fine speeches against you
and shake my head at you.
5But my mouth would encourage you;
comfort from my lips would bring you relief.

6"Yet if I speak, my pain is not relieved;
and if I refrain, it does not go away.
7Surely, O God, you have worn me out;
you have devastated my entire household.
8You have bound me—and it has become a witness;
my gauntness rises up and testifies against me.
9God assails me and tears me in his anger
and gnashes his teeth at me;
my opponent fastens on me his piercing eyes.
10Men open their mouths to jeer at me;
they strike my cheek in scorn
and unite together against me.
11God has turned me over to evil men
and thrown me into the clutches of the wicked.
12All was well with me, but he shattered me;
he seized me by the neck and crushed me.
He has made me his target;
13 his archers surround me.
Without pity, he pierces my kidneys
and spills my gall on the ground.
14Again and again he bursts upon me;
he rushes at me like a warrior.

15"I have sewed sackcloth over my skin
and buried my brow in the dust.
16My face is red with weeping,
deep shadows ring my eyes;
17yet my hands have been free of violence
and my prayer is pure.

18"O earth, do not cover my blood;
may my cry never be laid to rest!
19Even now my witness is in heaven;
my advocate is on high.
20My intercessor is my friend[b]
as my eyes pour out tears to God;
21on behalf of a man he pleads with God
as a man pleads for his friend.

22"Only a few years will pass

[a]23 Or *about, looking for food* [b]20 Or *My friends treat me with scorn*

before I go on the journey of no
return.

17 [1]My spirit is broken,
my days are cut short,
the grave awaits me.
[2]Surely mockers surround me;
my eyes must dwell on their
hostility.

[3]"Give me, O God, the pledge you
demand.
Who else will put up security for
me?
[4]You have closed their minds to
understanding;
therefore you will not let them
triumph.
[5]If a man denounces his friends for
reward,
the eyes of his children will fail.

[6]"God has made me a byword to
everyone,
a man in whose face people spit.
[7]My eyes have grown dim with grief;
my whole frame is but a shadow.
[8]Upright men are appalled at this;
the innocent are aroused against the
ungodly.
[9]Nevertheless, the righteous will hold
to their ways,
and those with clean hands will
grow stronger.

[10]"But come on, all of you, try again!
I will not find a wise man among
you.
[11]My days have passed, my plans are
shattered,
and so are the desires of my heart.
[12]These men turn night into day;
in the face of darkness they say,
'Light is near.'
[13]If the only home I hope for is the
grave,[a]
if I spread out my bed in darkness,
[14]if I say to corruption, 'You are my
father,'
and to the worm, 'My mother' or
'My sister,'
[15]where then is my hope?
Who can see any hope for me?
[16]Will it go down to the gates of
death[a]?
Will we descend together into the
dust?"

Bildad

18 Then Bildad the Shuhite replied:

[2]"When will you end these speeches?
Be sensible, and then we can talk.
[3]Why are we regarded as cattle
and considered stupid in your sight?
[4]You who tear yourself to pieces in
your anger,
is the earth to be abandoned for
your sake?
Or must the rocks be moved from
their place?

[5]"The lamp of the wicked is snuffed
out;
the flame of his fire stops burning.
[6]The light in his tent becomes dark;
the lamp beside him goes out.
[7]The vigor of his step is weakened;
his own schemes throw him down.
[8]His feet thrust him into a net
and he wanders into its mesh.
[9]A trap seizes him by the heel;
a snare holds him fast.
[10]A noose is hidden for him on the
ground;
a trap lies in his path.
[11]Terrors startle him on every side
and dog his every step.
[12]Calamity is hungry for him;
disaster is ready for him when he
falls.
[13]It eats away parts of his skin;
death's firstborn devours his limbs.
[14]He is torn from the security of his tent
and marched off to the king of
terrors.
[15]Fire resides[b] in his tent;
burning sulfur is scattered over his
dwelling.
[16]His roots dry up below
and his branches wither above.
[17]The memory of him perishes from the
earth;
he has no name in the land.
[18]He is driven from light into darkness
and is banished from the world.
[19]He has no offspring or descendants
among his people,
no survivor where once he lived.
[20]Men of the west are appalled at his
fate;
men of the east are seized with
horror.
[21]Surely such is the dwelling of an evil
man;

[a] *13,16* Hebrew *Sheol* [b] *15* Or *Nothing he had remains*

such is the place of one who knows
not God."

Job

19 Then Job replied:

2"How long will you torment me
and crush me with words?
3Ten times now you have reproached
me;
shamelessly you attack me.
4If it is true that I have gone astray,
my error remains my concern alone.
5If indeed you would exalt yourselves
above me
and use my humiliation against me,
6then know that God has wronged me
and drawn his net around me.

7"Though I cry, 'I've been wronged!' I
get no response;
though I call for help, there is no
justice.
8He has blocked my way so I cannot
pass;
he has shrouded my paths in
darkness.
9He has stripped me of my honor
and removed the crown from my
head.
10He tears me down on every side till I
am gone;
he uproots my hope like a tree.
11His anger burns against me;
he counts me among his enemies.
12His troops advance in force;
they build a siege ramp against me
and encamp around my tent.

13"He has alienated my brothers from
me;
my acquaintances are completely
estranged from me.
14My kinsmen have gone away;
my friends have forgotten me.
15My guests and my maidservants count
me a stranger;
they look upon me as an alien.
16I summon my servant, but he does
not answer,
though I beg him with my own
mouth.
17My breath is offensive to my wife;
I am loathsome to my own brothers.
18Even the little boys scorn me;
when I appear, they ridicule me.
19All my intimate friends detest me;
those I love have turned against me.
20I am nothing but skin and bones;
I have escaped with only the skin of
my teeth.[a]

21"Have pity on me, my friends, have
pity,
for the hand of God has struck me.
22Why do you pursue me as God does?
Will you never get enough of my
flesh?

23"Oh, that my words were recorded,
that they were written on a scroll,
24that they were inscribed with an iron
tool on[b] lead,
or engraved in rock forever!
25I know that my Redeemer[c] lives,
and that in the end he will stand
upon the earth.[d]
26And after my skin has been destroyed,
yet[e] in[f] my flesh I will see God;
27I myself will see him
with my own eyes—I, and not
another.
How my heart yearns within me!

28"If you say, 'How we will hound him,
since the root of the trouble lies in
him,[g]'
29you should fear the sword yourselves;
for wrath will bring punishment by
the sword,
and then you will know that there
is judgment.[h]"

Zophar

20 Then Zophar the Naamathite replied:

2"My troubled thoughts prompt me to
answer
because I am greatly disturbed.
3I hear a rebuke that dishonors me,
and my understanding inspires me
to reply.

4"Surely you know how it has been
from of old,
ever since man[i] was placed on the
earth,
5that the mirth of the wicked is brief,
the joy of the godless lasts but a
moment.

[a]20 Or *only my gums* [b]24 Or *and* [c]25 Or *defender* [d]25 Or *upon my grave* [e]26 Or *And after I awake, / though this ⌊body⌋ has been destroyed, / then* [f]26 Or / *apart from* [g]28 Many Hebrew manuscripts, Septuagint and Vulgate; most Hebrew manuscripts *me* [h]29 Or / *that you may come to know the Almighty* [i]4 Or *Adam*

6Though his pride reaches to the heavens
and his head touches the clouds,
7he will perish forever, like his own dung;
those who have seen him will say, 'Where is he?'
8Like a dream he flies away, no more to be found,
banished like a vision of the night.
9The eye that saw him will not see him again;
his place will look on him no more.
10His children must make amends to the poor;
his own hands must give back his wealth.
11The youthful vigor that fills his bones
will lie with him in the dust.

12"Though evil is sweet in his mouth
and he hides it under his tongue,
13though he cannot bear to let it go
and keeps it in his mouth,
14yet his food will turn sour in his stomach;
it will become the venom of serpents within him.
15He will spit out the riches he swallowed;
God will make his stomach vomit them up.
16He will suck the poison of serpents;
the fangs of an adder will kill him.
17He will not enjoy the streams,
the rivers flowing with honey and cream.
18What he toiled for he must give back uneaten;
he will not enjoy the profit from his trading.
19For he has oppressed the poor and left them destitute;
he has seized houses he did not build.
20"Surely he will have no respite from his craving;
he cannot save himself by his treasure.
21Nothing is left for him to devour;
his prosperity will not endure.
22In the midst of his plenty, distress will overtake him;
the full force of misery will come upon him.
23When he has filled his belly,
God will vent his burning anger against him
and rain down his blows upon him.
24Though he flees from an iron weapon,
a bronze-tipped arrow pierces him.
25He pulls it out of his back,
the gleaming point out of his liver.
Terrors will come over him;
26 total darkness lies in wait for his treasures.
A fire unfanned will consume him
and devour what is left in his tent.
27The heavens will expose his guilt;
the earth will rise up against him.
28A flood will carry off his house,
rushing waters[a] on the day of God's wrath.
29Such is the fate God allots the wicked,
the heritage appointed for them by God."

Job

21 Then Job replied:
2"Listen carefully to my words;
let this be the consolation you give me.
3Bear with me while I speak,
and after I have spoken, mock on.

4"Is my complaint directed to man?
Why should I not be impatient?
5Look at me and be astonished;
clap your hand over your mouth.
6When I think about this, I am terrified;
trembling seizes my body.
7Why do the wicked live on,
growing old and increasing in power?
8They see their children established around them,
their offspring before their eyes.
9Their homes are safe and free from fear;
the rod of God is not upon them.
10Their bulls never fail to breed;
their cows calve and do not miscarry.
11They send forth their children as a flock;
their little ones dance about.
12They sing to the music of tambourine and harp;
they make merry to the sound of the flute.
13They spend their years in prosperity

[a]28 Or *The possessions in his house will be carried off, / washed away*

and go down to the grave[a] in
peace.[b]
14Yet they say to God, 'Leave us alone!
We have no desire to know your
ways.
15Who is the Almighty, that we should
serve him?
What would we gain by praying to
him?'
16But their prosperity is not in their
own hands,
so I stand aloof from the counsel of
the wicked.

17"Yet how often is the lamp of the
wicked snuffed out?
How often does calamity come
upon them,
the fate God allots in his anger?
18How often are they like straw before
the wind,
like chaff swept away by a gale?
19⌊It is said,⌋ 'God stores up a man's
punishment for his sons.'
Let him repay the man himself, so
that he will know it!
20Let his own eyes see his destruction;
let him drink of the wrath of the
Almighty.[c]
21For what does he care about the
family he leaves behind
when his allotted months come to
an end?

22"Can anyone teach knowledge to God,
since he judges even the highest?
23One man dies in full vigor,
completely secure and at ease,
24his body[d] well nourished,
his bones rich with marrow.
25Another man dies in bitterness of
soul,
never having enjoyed anything
good.
26Side by side they lie in the dust,
and worms cover them both.

27"I know full well what you are
thinking,
the schemes by which you would
wrong me.
28You say, 'Where now is the great
man's house,
the tents where wicked men lived?'
29Have you never questioned those who
travel?
Have you paid no regard to their
accounts—
30that the evil man is spared from the
day of calamity,
that he is delivered from[e] the day
of wrath?
31Who denounces his conduct to his
face?
Who repays him for what he has
done?
32He is carried to the grave,
and watch is kept over his tomb.
33The soil in the valley is sweet to him;
all men follow after him,
and a countless throng goes[f]
before him.

34"So how can you console me with
your nonsense?
Nothing is left of your answers but
falsehood!"

Eliphaz

22 Then Eliphaz the Temanite replied:

2"Can a man be of benefit to God?
Can even a wise man benefit him?
3What pleasure would it give the
Almighty if you were righteous?
What would he gain if your ways
were blameless?

4"Is it for your piety that he rebukes
you
and brings charges against you?
5Is not your wickedness great?
Are not your sins endless?
6You demanded security from your
brothers for no reason;
you stripped men of their clothing,
leaving them naked.
7You gave no water to the weary
and you withheld food from the
hungry,
8though you were a powerful man,
owning land—
an honored man, living on it.
9And you sent widows away
empty-handed
and broke the strength of the
fatherless.
10That is why snares are all around you,
why sudden peril terrifies you,
11why it is so dark you cannot see,

[a] *13* Hebrew *Sheol* [b] *13* Or *in an instant* [c] *17-20* Verses 17 and 18 may be taken as exclamations and 19 and 20 as declarations. [d] *24* The meaning of the Hebrew for this word is uncertain. [e] *30* Or *man is reserved for the day of calamity, / that he is brought forth to* [f] *33* Or / *as a countless throng went*

and why a flood of water covers
you.
12"Is not God in the heights of heaven?
And see how lofty are the highest
stars!
13Yet you say, 'What does God know?
Does he judge through such
darkness?
14Thick clouds veil him, so he does not
see us
as he goes about in the vaulted
heavens.'
15Will you keep to the old path
that evil men have trod?
16They were carried off before their
time,
their foundations washed away by a
flood.
17They said to God, 'Leave us alone!
What can the Almighty do to us?'
18Yet it was he who filled their houses
with good things,
so I stand aloof from the counsel of
the wicked.

19"The righteous see their ruin and
rejoice;
the innocent mock them, saying,
20'Surely our foes are destroyed,
and fire devours their wealth.'

21"Submit to God and be at peace with
him;
in this way prosperity will come to
you.
22Accept instruction from his mouth
and lay up his words in your heart.
23If you return to the Almighty, you will
be restored:
If you remove wickedness far from
your tent
24and assign your nuggets to the dust,
your gold of Ophir to the rocks in
the ravines,
25then the Almighty will be your gold,
the choicest silver for you.
26Surely then you will find delight in
the Almighty
and will lift up your face to God.
27You will pray to him, and he will hear
you,
and you will fulfill your vows.
28What you decide on will be done,
and light will shine on your ways.
29When men are brought low and you
say, 'Lift them up!'
then he will save the downcast.
30He will deliver even one who is not
innocent,
who will be delivered through the
cleanness of your hands."

Job

23 Then Job replied:
2"Even today my complaint is bitter;
his hand[a] is heavy in spite of[b] my
groaning.
3If only I knew where to find him;
if only I could go to his dwelling!
4I would state my case before him
and fill my mouth with arguments.
5I would find out what he would
answer me,
and consider what he would say.
6Would he oppose me with great
power?
No, he would not press charges
against me.
7There an upright man could present
his case before him,
and I would be delivered forever
from my judge.

8"But if I go to the east, he is not
there;
if I go to the west, I do not find
him.
9When he is at work in the north, I do
not see him;
when he turns to the south, I catch
no glimpse of him.
10But he knows the way that I take;
when he has tested me, I will come
forth as gold.
11My feet have closely followed his
steps;
I have kept to his way without
turning aside.
12I have not departed from the
commands of his lips;
I have treasured the words of his
mouth more than my daily
bread.

13"But he stands alone, and who can
oppose him?
He does whatever he pleases.
14He carries out his decree against me,
and many such plans he still has in
store.
15That is why I am terrified before him;
when I think of all this, I fear him.
16God has made my heart faint;
the Almighty has terrified me.

[a] 2 Septuagint and Syriac; Hebrew / *the hand on me*

[b] 2 Or *heavy on me in*

17Yet I am not silenced by the darkness,
by the thick darkness that covers
my face.

24 "Why does the Almighty not set
times for judgment?
Why must those who know him
look in vain for such days?
2Men move boundary stones;
they pasture flocks they have stolen.
3They drive away the orphan's donkey
and take the widow's ox in pledge.
4They thrust the needy from the path
and force all the poor of the land
into hiding.
5Like wild donkeys in the desert,
the poor go about their labor of
foraging food;
the wasteland provides food for
their children.
6They gather fodder in the fields
and glean in the vineyards of the
wicked.
7Lacking clothes, they spend the night
naked;
they have nothing to cover
themselves in the cold.
8They are drenched by mountain rains
and hug the rocks for lack of
shelter.
9The fatherless child is snatched from
the breast;
the infant of the poor is seized for a
debt.
10Lacking clothes, they go about naked;
they carry the sheaves, but still go
hungry.
11They crush olives among the
terraces[a];
they tread the winepresses, yet
suffer thirst.
12The groans of the dying rise from the
city,
and the souls of the wounded cry
out for help.
But God charges no one with
wrongdoing.

13"There are those who rebel against the
light,
who do not know its ways
or stay in its paths.
14When daylight is gone, the murderer
rises up
and kills the poor and needy;
in the night he steals forth like a
thief.
15The eye of the adulterer watches for
dusk;
he thinks, 'No eye will see me,'
and he keeps his face concealed.
16In the dark, men break into houses,
but by day they shut themselves in;
they want nothing to do with the
light.
17For all of them, deep darkness is their
morning[b];
they make friends with the terrors
of darkness.[c]

18"Yet they are foam on the surface of
the water;
their portion of the land is cursed,
so that no one goes to the
vineyards.
19As heat and drought snatch away the
melted snow,
so the grave[d] snatches away those
who have sinned.
20The womb forgets them,
the worm feasts on them;
evil men are no longer remembered
but are broken like a tree.
21They prey on the barren and childless
woman,
and to the widow show no
kindness.
22But God drags away the mighty by his
power;
though they become established,
they have no assurance of life.
23He may let them rest in a feeling of
security,
but his eyes are on their ways.
24For a little while they are exalted, and
then they are gone;
they are brought low and gathered
up like all others;
they are cut off like heads of grain.

25"If this is not so, who can prove me
false
and reduce my words to nothing?"

Bildad

25 Then Bildad the Shuhite replied:
2"Dominion and awe belong to God;
he establishes order in the heights
of heaven.
3Can his forces be numbered?
Upon whom does his light not rise?

[a] 11 Or *olives between the millstones*; the meaning of the Hebrew for this word is uncertain. [b] 17 Or *them, their morning is like the shadow of death* [c] 17 Or *of the shadow of death* [d] 19 Hebrew *Sheol*

4How then can a man be righteous
before God?
How can one born of woman be
pure?
5If even the moon is not bright
and the stars are not pure in his
eyes,
6how much less man, who is but a
maggot—
a son of man, who is only a worm!"

Job

26 Then Job replied:

2"How you have helped the powerless!
How you have saved the arm that is
feeble!
3What advice you have offered to one
without wisdom!
And what great insight you have
displayed!
4Who has helped you utter these
words?
And whose spirit spoke from your
mouth?

5"The dead are in deep anguish,
those beneath the waters and all
that live in them.
6Death[a] is naked before God;
Destruction[b] lies uncovered.
7He spreads out the northern ⌊skies⌋
over empty space;
he suspends the earth over nothing.
8He wraps up the waters in his clouds,
yet the clouds do not burst under
their weight.
9He covers the face of the full moon,
spreading his clouds over it.
10He marks out the horizon on the face
of the waters
for a boundary between light and
darkness.
11The pillars of the heavens quake,
aghast at his rebuke.
12By his power he churned up the sea;
by his wisdom he cut Rahab to
pieces.
13By his breath the skies became fair;
his hand pierced the gliding serpent.
14And these are but the outer fringe of
his works;
how faint the whisper we hear of
him!
Who then can understand the
thunder of his power?"

27 And Job continued his discourse:

2"As surely as God lives, who has
denied me justice,
the Almighty, who has made me
taste bitterness of soul,
3as long as I have life within me,
the breath of God in my nostrils,
4my lips will not speak wickedness,
and my tongue will utter no deceit.
5I will never admit you are in the right;
till I die, I will not deny my
integrity.
6I will maintain my righteousness and
never let go of it;
my conscience will not reproach me
as long as I live.

7"May my enemies be like the wicked,
my adversaries like the unjust!
8For what hope has the godless when
he is cut off,
when God takes away his life?
9Does God listen to his cry
when distress comes upon him?
10Will he find delight in the Almighty?
Will he call upon God at all times?

11"I will teach you about the power of
God;
the ways of the Almighty I will not
conceal.
12You have all seen this yourselves.
Why then this meaningless talk?

13"Here is the fate God allots to the
wicked,
the heritage a ruthless man receives
from the Almighty:
14However many his children, their fate
is the sword;
his offspring will never have enough
to eat.
15The plague will bury those who
survive him,
and their widows will not weep for
them.
16Though he heaps up silver like dust
and clothes like piles of clay,
17what he lays up the righteous will
wear,
and the innocent will divide his
silver.
18The house he builds is like a moth's
cocoon,
like a hut made by a watchman.
19He lies down wealthy, but will do so
no more;

[a]6 Hebrew *Sheol* [b]6 Hebrew *Abaddon*

when he opens his eyes, all is gone.
20 Terrors overtake him like a flood;
a tempest snatches him away in the night.
21 The east wind carries him off, and he is gone;
it sweeps him out of his place.
22 It hurls itself against him without mercy
as he flees headlong from its power.
23 It claps its hands in derision
and hisses him out of his place.

28 "There is a mine for silver
and a place where gold is refined.
2 Iron is taken from the earth,
and copper is smelted from ore.
3 Man puts an end to the darkness;
he searches the farthest recesses
for ore in the blackest darkness.
4 Far from where people dwell he cuts a shaft,
in places forgotten by the foot of man;
far from men he dangles and sways.
5 The earth, from which food comes,
is transformed below as by fire;
6 sapphires[a] come from its rocks,
and its dust contains nuggets of gold.
7 No bird of prey knows that hidden path,
no falcon's eye has seen it.
8 Proud beasts do not set foot on it,
and no lion prowls there.
9 Man's hand assaults the flinty rock
and lays bare the roots of the mountains.
10 He tunnels through the rock;
his eyes see all its treasures.
11 He searches[b] the sources of the rivers
and brings hidden things to light.

12 "But where can wisdom be found?
Where does understanding dwell?
13 Man does not comprehend its worth;
it cannot be found in the land of the living.
14 The deep says, 'It is not in me';
the sea says, 'It is not with me.'
15 It cannot be bought with the finest gold,
nor can its price be weighed in silver.
16 It cannot be bought with the gold of Ophir,
with precious onyx or sapphires.
17 Neither gold nor crystal can compare with it,
nor can it be had for jewels of gold.
18 Coral and jasper are not worthy of mention;
the price of wisdom is beyond rubies.
19 The topaz of Cush cannot compare with it;
it cannot be bought with pure gold.

20 "Where then does wisdom come from?
Where does understanding dwell?
21 It is hidden from the eyes of every living thing,
concealed even from the birds of the air.
22 Destruction[c] and Death say,
'Only a rumor of it has reached our ears.'
23 God understands the way to it
and he alone knows where it dwells,
24 for he views the ends of the earth
and sees everything under the heavens.
25 When he established the force of the wind
and measured out the waters,
26 when he made a decree for the rain
and a path for the thunderstorm,
27 then he looked at wisdom and appraised it;
he confirmed it and tested it.
28 And he said to man,
'The fear of the Lord—that is wisdom,
and to shun evil is understanding.' "

29 Job continued his discourse:
2 "How I long for the months gone by,
for the days when God watched over me,
3 when his lamp shone upon my head
and by his light I walked through darkness!
4 Oh, for the days when I was in my prime,
when God's intimate friendship blessed my house,
5 when the Almighty was still with me
and my children were around me,
6 when my path was drenched with cream

[a] 6 Or *lapis lazuli*; also in verse 16 [b] 11 Septuagint, Aquila and Vulgate; Hebrew *He dams up*
[c] 22 Hebrew *Abaddon*

and the rock poured out for me
streams of olive oil.

7"When I went to the gate of the city
and took my seat in the public
square,
8the young men saw me and stepped
aside
and the old men rose to their feet;
9the chief men refrained from speaking
and covered their mouths with their
hands;
10the voices of the nobles were hushed,
and their tongues stuck to the roof
of their mouths.
11Whoever heard me spoke well of me,
and those who saw me commended
me,
12because I rescued the poor who cried
for help,
and the fatherless who had none to
assist him.
13The man who was dying blessed me;
I made the widow's heart sing.
14I put on righteousness as my clothing;
justice was my robe and my turban.
15I was eyes to the blind
and feet to the lame.
16I was a father to the needy;
I took up the case of the stranger.
17I broke the fangs of the wicked
and snatched the victims from their
teeth.

18"I thought, 'I will die in my own
house,
my days as numerous as the grains
of sand.
19My roots will reach to the water,
and the dew will lie all night on my
branches.
20My glory will remain fresh in me,
the bow ever new in my hand.'

21"Men listened to me expectantly,
waiting in silence for my counsel.
22After I had spoken, they spoke no
more;
my words fell gently on their ears.
23They waited for me as for showers
and drank in my words as the
spring rain.
24When I smiled at them, they scarcely
believed it;
the light of my face was precious to
them.[a]
25I chose the way for them and sat as
their chief;
I dwelt as a king among his troops;
I was like one who comforts
mourners.

30 "But now they mock me,
men younger than I,
whose fathers I would have disdained
to put with my sheep dogs.
2Of what use was the strength of their
hands to me,
since their vigor had gone from
them?
3Haggard from want and hunger,
they roamed[b] the parched land
in desolate wastelands at night.
4In the brush they gathered salt herbs,
and their food[c] was the root of the
broom tree.
5They were banished from their fellow
men,
shouted at as if they were thieves.
6They were forced to live in the dry
stream beds,
among the rocks and in holes in the
ground.
7They brayed among the bushes
and huddled in the undergrowth.
8A base and nameless brood,
they were driven out of the land.

9"And now their sons mock me in
song;
I have become a byword among
them.
10They detest me and keep their
distance;
they do not hesitate to spit in my
face.
11Now that God has unstrung my bow
and afflicted me,
they throw off restraint in my
presence.
12On my right the tribe[d] attacks;
they lay snares for my feet,
they build their siege ramps against
me.
13They break up my road;
they succeed in destroying me—
without anyone's helping them.[e]
14They advance as through a gaping
breach;
amid the ruins they come rolling in.
15Terrors overwhelm me;

[a] 24 The meaning of the Hebrew for this clause is uncertain.
[b] 3 Or *gnawed*
[c] 4 Or *fuel*
[d] 12 The meaning of the Hebrew for this word is uncertain.
[e] 13 Or *me. / 'No one can help him,' they say.*

my dignity is driven away as by the wind,
my safety vanishes like a cloud.

16"And now my life ebbs away;
days of suffering grip me.
17Night pierces my bones;
my gnawing pains never rest.
18In his great power ⌊God⌋ becomes like clothing to me[a];
he binds me like the neck of my garment.
19He throws me into the mud,
and I am reduced to dust and ashes.

20"I cry out to you, O God, but you do not answer;
I stand up, but you merely look at me.
21You turn on me ruthlessly;
with the might of your hand you attack me.
22You snatch me up and drive me before the wind;
you toss me about in the storm.
23I know you will bring me down to death,
to the place appointed for all the living.

24"Surely no one lays a hand on a broken man
when he cries for help in his distress.
25Have I not wept for those in trouble?
Has not my soul grieved for the poor?
26Yet when I hoped for good, evil came;
when I looked for light, then came darkness.
27The churning inside me never stops;
days of suffering confront me.
28I go about blackened, but not by the sun;
I stand up in the assembly and cry for help.
29I have become a brother of jackals,
a companion of owls.
30My skin grows black and peels;
my body burns with fever.
31My harp is tuned to mourning,
and my flute to the sound of wailing.

31 "I made a covenant with my eyes
not to look lustfully at a girl.
2For what is man's lot from God above,
his heritage from the Almighty on high?
3Is it not ruin for the wicked,
disaster for those who do wrong?
4Does he not see my ways
and count my every step?

5"If I have walked in falsehood
or my foot has hurried after deceit—
6let God weigh me in honest scales
and he will know that I am blameless—
7if my steps have turned from the path,
if my heart has been led by my eyes,
or if my hands have been defiled,
8then may others eat what I have sown,
and may my crops be uprooted.

9"If my heart has been enticed by a woman,
or if I have lurked at my neighbor's door,
10then may my wife grind another man's grain,
and may other men sleep with her.
11For that would have been shameful,
a sin to be judged.
12It is a fire that burns to Destruction[b];
it would have uprooted my harvest.

13"If I have denied justice to my menservants and maidservants
when they had a grievance against me,
14what will I do when God confronts me?
What will I answer when called to account?
15Did not he who made me in the womb make them?
Did not the same one form us both within our mothers?

16"If I have denied the desires of the poor
or let the eyes of the widow grow weary,
17if I have kept my bread to myself,
not sharing it with the fatherless—
18but from my youth I reared him as would a father,
and from my birth I guided the widow—
19if I have seen anyone perishing for lack of clothing,
or a needy man without a garment,
20and his heart did not bless me

[a] 18 Hebrew; Septuagint ⌊God⌋ *grasps my clothing*

[b] 12 Hebrew *Abaddon*

for warming him with the fleece
from my sheep,
21 if I have raised my hand against the
fatherless,
knowing that I had influence in
court,
22 then let my arm fall from the
shoulder,
let it be broken off at the joint.
23 For I dreaded destruction from God,
and for fear of his splendor I could
not do such things.

24 "If I have put my trust in gold
or said to pure gold, 'You are my
security,'
25 if I have rejoiced over my great
wealth,
the fortune my hands had gained,
26 if I have regarded the sun in its
radiance
or the moon moving in splendor,
27 so that my heart was secretly enticed
and my hand offered them a kiss of
homage,
28 then these also would be sins to be
judged,
for I would have been unfaithful to
God on high.

29 "If I have rejoiced at my enemy's
misfortune
or gloated over the trouble that
came to him—
30 I have not allowed my mouth to sin
by invoking a curse against his
life—
31 if the men of my household have
never said,
'Who has not had his fill of Job's
meat?'—
32 but no stranger had to spend the night
in the street,
for my door was always open to the
traveler—
33 if I have concealed my sin as men
do,[a]
by hiding my guilt in my heart
34 because I so feared the crowd
and so dreaded the contempt of the
clans
that I kept silent and would not go
outside

35 ("Oh, that I had someone to hear me!
I sign now my defense—let the
Almighty answer me;
let my accuser put his indictment in
writing.
36 Surely I would wear it on my
shoulder,
I would put it on like a crown.
37 I would give him an account of my
every step;
like a prince I would approach
him.)—

38 "if my land cries out against me
and all its furrows are wet with
tears,
39 if I have devoured its yield without
payment
or broken the spirit of its tenants,
40 then let briers come up instead of
wheat
and weeds instead of barley."

The words of Job are ended.

Elihu

32 So these three men stopped answering Job, because he was righteous in his own eyes. 2 But Elihu son of Barakel the Buzite, of the family of Ram, became very angry with Job for justifying himself rather than God. 3 He was also angry with the three friends, because they had found no way to refute Job, and yet had condemned him.[b] 4 Now Elihu had waited before speaking to Job because they were older than he. 5 But when he saw that the three men had nothing more to say, his anger was aroused.

6 So Elihu son of Barakel the Buzite said:

"I am young in years,
and you are old;
that is why I was fearful,
not daring to tell you what I know.
7 I thought, 'Age should speak;
advanced years should teach
wisdom.'
8 But it is the spirit[c] in a man,
the breath of the Almighty, that
gives him understanding.
9 It is not only the old[d] who are wise,
not only the aged who understand
what is right.

10 "Therefore I say: Listen to me;
I too will tell you what I know.
11 I waited while you spoke,
I listened to your reasoning;
while you were searching for words,
12 I gave you my full attention.

[a] 33 Or *as Adam did* [b] 3 Masoretic Text; an ancient Hebrew scribal tradition *Job, and so had condemned God* [c] 8 Or *Spirit*; also in verse 18 [d] 9 Or *many*; or *great*

But not one of you has proved Job wrong;
none of you has answered his arguments.
13 Do not say, 'We have found wisdom;
let God refute him, not man.'
14 But Job has not marshaled his words against me,
and I will not answer him with your arguments.

15 "They are dismayed and have no more to say;
words have failed them.
16 Must I wait, now that they are silent,
now that they stand there with no reply?
17 I too will have my say;
I too will tell what I know.
18 For I am full of words,
and the spirit within me compels me;
19 inside I am like bottled-up wine,
like new wineskins ready to burst.
20 I must speak and find relief;
I must open my lips and reply.
21 I will show partiality to no one,
nor will I flatter any man;
22 for if I were skilled in flattery,
my Maker would soon take me away.

33 "But now, Job, listen to my words;
pay attention to everything I say.
2 I am about to open my mouth;
my words are on the tip of my tongue.
3 My words come from an upright heart;
my lips sincerely speak what I know.
4 The Spirit of God has made me;
the breath of the Almighty gives me life.
5 Answer me then, if you can;
prepare yourself and confront me.
6 I am just like you before God;
I too have been taken from clay.
7 No fear of me should alarm you,
nor should my hand be heavy upon you.

8 "But you have said in my hearing—
I heard the very words—
9 'I am pure and without sin;
I am clean and free from guilt.
10 Yet God has found fault with me;
he considers me his enemy.
11 He fastens my feet in shackles;
he keeps close watch on all my paths.'

12 "But I tell you, in this you are not right,
for God is greater than man.
13 Why do you complain to him
that he answers none of man's words[a]?
14 For God does speak—now one way, now another—
though man may not perceive it.
15 In a dream, in a vision of the night,
when deep sleep falls on men
as they slumber in their beds,
16 he may speak in their ears
and terrify them with warnings,
17 to turn man from wrongdoing
and keep him from pride,
18 to preserve his soul from the pit,[b]
his life from perishing by the sword.[c]
19 Or a man may be chastened on a bed of pain
with constant distress in his bones,
20 so that his very being finds food repulsive
and his soul loathes the choicest meal.
21 His flesh wastes away to nothing,
and his bones, once hidden, now stick out.
22 His soul draws near to the pit,[d]
and his life to the messengers of death.[e]

23 "Yet if there is an angel on his side
as a mediator, one out of a thousand,
to tell a man what is right for him,
24 to be gracious to him and say,
'Spare him from going down to the pit[f];
I have found a ransom for him'—
25 then his flesh is renewed like a child's;
it is restored as in the days of his youth.
26 He prays to God and finds favor with him,
he sees God's face and shouts for joy;
he is restored by God to his righteous state.

[a] 13 Or *that he does not answer for any of his actions* [b] 18 Or *preserve him from the grave* [c] 18 Or *from crossing the River* [d] 22 Or *He draws near to the grave* [e] 22 Or *to the dead* [f] 24 Or *grave*

27Then he comes to men and says,
'I sinned, and perverted what was right,
but I did not get what I deserved.
28He redeemed my soul from going down to the pit,[a]
and I will live to enjoy the light.'

29"God does all these things to a man—
twice, even three times—
30to turn back his soul from the pit,[b]
that the light of life may shine on him.

31"Pay attention, Job, and listen to me;
be silent, and I will speak.
32If you have anything to say, answer me;
speak up, for I want you to be cleared.
33But if not, then listen to me;
be silent, and I will teach you wisdom."

34

Then Elihu said:

2"Hear my words, you wise men;
listen to me, you men of learning.
3For the ear tests words
as the tongue tastes food.
4Let us discern for ourselves what is right;
let us learn together what is good.

5"Job says, 'I am innocent,
but God denies me justice.
6Although I am right,
I am considered a liar;
although I am guiltless,
his arrow inflicts an incurable wound.'
7What man is like Job,
who drinks scorn like water?
8He keeps company with evildoers;
he associates with wicked men.
9For he says, 'It profits a man nothing
when he tries to please God.'

10"So listen to me, you men of understanding.
Far be it from God to do evil,
from the Almighty to do wrong.
11He repays a man for what he has done;
he brings upon him what his conduct deserves.
12It is unthinkable that God would do wrong,
that the Almighty would pervert justice.
13Who appointed him over the earth?
Who put him in charge of the whole world?
14If it were his intention
and he withdrew his spirit[c] and breath,
15all mankind would perish together
and man would return to the dust.

16"If you have understanding, hear this;
listen to what I say.
17Can he who hates justice govern?
Will you condemn the just and mighty One?
18Is he not the One who says to kings,
'You are worthless,'
and to nobles, 'You are wicked,'
19who shows no partiality to princes
and does not favor the rich over the poor,
for they are all the work of his hands?
20They die in an instant, in the middle of the night;
the people are shaken and they pass away;
the mighty are removed without human hand.

21"His eyes are on the ways of men;
he sees their every step.
22There is no dark place, no deep shadow,
where evildoers can hide.
23God has no need to examine men further,
that they should come before him for judgment.
24Without inquiry he shatters the mighty
and sets up others in their place.
25Because he takes note of their deeds,
he overthrows them in the night
and they are crushed.
26He punishes them for their wickedness
where everyone can see them,
27because they turned from following him
and had no regard for any of his ways.
28They caused the cry of the poor to come before him,
so that he heard the cry of the needy.

[a]28 Or *redeemed me from going down to the grave*
[b]30 Or *turn him back from the grave*
[c]14 Or *Spirit*

29 But if he remains silent, who can condemn him?
If he hides his face, who can see him?
Yet he is over man and nation alike,
30 to keep a godless man from ruling,
from laying snares for the people.

31 "Suppose a man says to God,
'I am guilty but will offend no more.
32 Teach me what I cannot see;
if I have done wrong, I will not do so again.'
33 Should God then reward you on your terms,
when you refuse to repent?
You must decide, not I;
so tell me what you know.

34 "Men of understanding declare,
wise men who hear me say to me,
35 'Job speaks without knowledge;
his words lack insight.'
36 Oh, that Job might be tested to the utmost
for answering like a wicked man!
37 To his sin he adds rebellion;
scornfully he claps his hands among us
and multiplies his words against God."

35

Then Elihu said:

2 "Do you think this is just?
You say, 'I will be cleared by God.[a]'
3 Yet you ask him, 'What profit is it to me,[b]
and what do I gain by not sinning?'

4 "I would like to reply to you
and to your friends with you.
5 Look up at the heavens and see;
gaze at the clouds so high above you.
6 If you sin, how does that affect him?
If your sins are many, what does that do to him?
7 If you are righteous, what do you give to him,
or what does he receive from your hand?
8 Your wickedness affects only a man like yourself,
and your righteousness only the sons of men.

9 "Men cry out under a load of oppression;
they plead for relief from the arm of the powerful.
10 But no one says, 'Where is God my Maker,
who gives songs in the night,
11 who teaches more to us than to[c] the beasts of the earth
and makes us wiser than[d] the birds of the air?'
12 He does not answer when men cry out
because of the arrogance of the wicked.
13 Indeed, God does not listen to their empty plea;
the Almighty pays no attention to it.
14 How much less, then, will he listen
when you say that you do not see him,
that your case is before him
and you must wait for him,
15 and further, that his anger never punishes
and he does not take the least notice of wickedness.[e]
16 So Job opens his mouth with empty talk;
without knowledge he multiplies words."

36

Elihu continued:

2 "Bear with me a little longer and I will show you
that there is more to be said in God's behalf.
3 I get my knowledge from afar;
I will ascribe justice to my Maker.
4 Be assured that my words are not false;
one perfect in knowledge is with you.

5 "God is mighty, but does not despise men;
he is mighty, and firm in his purpose.
6 He does not keep the wicked alive
but gives the afflicted their rights.
7 He does not take his eyes off the righteous;
he enthrones them with kings

[a] 2 Or *My righteousness is more than God's* [b] 3 Or *you* [c] 11 Or *teaches us by* [d] 11 Or *us wise by*
[e] 15 Symmachus, Theodotion and Vulgate; the meaning of the Hebrew for this word is uncertain.

and exalts them forever.
8 But if men are bound in chains,
held fast by cords of affliction,
9 he tells them what they have done—
that they have sinned arrogantly.
10 He makes them listen to correction
and commands them to repent of their evil.
11 If they obey and serve him,
they will spend the rest of their days in prosperity
and their years in contentment.
12 But if they do not listen,
they will perish by the sword[a]
and die without knowledge.

13 "The godless in heart harbor resentment;
even when he fetters them, they do not cry for help.
14 They die in their youth,
among male prostitutes of the shrines.
15 But those who suffer he delivers in their suffering;
he speaks to them in their affliction.

16 "He is wooing you from the jaws of distress
to a spacious place free from restriction,
to the comfort of your table laden with choice food.
17 But now you are laden with the judgment due the wicked;
judgment and justice have taken hold of you.
18 Be careful that no one entices you by riches;
do not let a large bribe turn you aside.
19 Would your wealth
or even all your mighty efforts
sustain you so you would not be in distress?
20 Do not long for the night,
to drag people away from their homes.[b]
21 Beware of turning to evil,
which you seem to prefer to affliction.

22 "God is exalted in his power.
Who is a teacher like him?
23 Who has prescribed his ways for him,
or said to him, 'You have done wrong'?
24 Remember to extol his work,
which men have praised in song.
25 All mankind has seen it;
men gaze on it from afar.
26 How great is God—beyond our understanding!
The number of his years is past finding out.

27 "He draws up the drops of water,
which distill as rain to the streams[c];
28 the clouds pour down their moisture
and abundant showers fall on mankind.
29 Who can understand how he spreads out the clouds,
how he thunders from his pavilion?
30 See how he scatters his lightning about him,
bathing the depths of the sea.
31 This is the way he governs[d] the nations
and provides food in abundance.
32 He fills his hands with lightning
and commands it to strike its mark.
33 His thunder announces the coming storm;
even the cattle make known its approach.[e]

37 "At this my heart pounds
and leaps from its place.
2 Listen! Listen to the roar of his voice,
to the rumbling that comes from his mouth.
3 He unleashes his lightning beneath the whole heaven
and sends it to the ends of the earth.
4 After that comes the sound of his roar;
he thunders with his majestic voice.
When his voice resounds,
he holds nothing back.
5 God's voice thunders in marvelous ways;
he does great things beyond our understanding.
6 He says to the snow, 'Fall on the earth,'
and to the rain shower, 'Be a mighty downpour.'

[a] 12 Or *will cross the River against evil*
[b] 20 The meaning of the Hebrew for verses 18-20 is uncertain.
[c] 27 Or *distill from the mist as rain*
[d] 31 Or *nourishes*
[e] 33 Or *announces his coming— / the One zealous*

7So that all men he has made may
know his work,
he stops every man from his
labor.[a]
8The animals take cover;
they remain in their dens.
9The tempest comes out from its
chamber,
the cold from the driving winds.
10The breath of God produces ice,
and the broad waters become
frozen.
11He loads the clouds with moisture;
he scatters his lightning through
them.
12At his direction they swirl around
over the face of the whole earth
to do whatever he commands them.
13He brings the clouds to punish men,
or to water his earth[b] and show his
love.
14"Listen to this, Job;
stop and consider God's wonders.
15Do you know how God controls the
clouds
and makes his lightning flash?

[a]7 Or */ he fills all men with fear by his power*
[b]13 Or *to favor them*

VERSE FOR THE DAY: Job 37:23 | AUTHOR: Philip Yancey | PASSAGE FOR THE DAY: Job 37:1–24

Forgiveness Is Unfair

At its core, forgiveness remains unfair. There *is* something unjust about a person's dastardly deeds going unpunished.

Such thoughts nagged at me until one day I came across an admonition from the apostle Paul tucked away in Romans 12. Hate evil, be joyful, live in harmony, do not be conceited—the list goes on and on. Then appears this verse: "Do not take revenge, my friends, but leave room for God's wrath, for it is written: 'It is mine to avenge; I will repay,' says the Lord" (v. 19).

At last I understood: In the final analysis, forgiveness is an act of faith. By forgiving another, I am simply trusting that God is a better justice maker than I am. By forgiving, I leave issues of fairness for God to work out. I defer to him the scales of justice.

Wrong does not disappear when I forgive. But it loses its grip on me, and is taken over by God. *He* knows what to do.

MARRIAGE BUILDERS

♦ *Why is it hard not to "get back" at your spouse in small ways when he or she has hurt you?*

♦ *How can you trust God to handle the situation when others wrong you?*

Additional Scripture Readings
Deuteronomy 32:35; Romans 12:19

Go to page 542 for your next devotional reading.

16Do you know how the clouds hang
poised,
those wonders of him who is
perfect in knowledge?
17You who swelter in your clothes
when the land lies hushed under
the south wind,
18can you join him in spreading out the
skies,
hard as a mirror of cast bronze?

19"Tell us what we should say to him;
we cannot draw up our case
because of our darkness.
20Should he be told that I want to
speak?
Would any man ask to be
swallowed up?
21Now no one can look at the sun,
bright as it is in the skies
after the wind has swept them
clean.
22Out of the north he comes in golden
splendor;
God comes in awesome majesty.
23The Almighty is beyond our reach and
exalted in power;
in his justice and great
righteousness, he does not
oppress.
24Therefore, men revere him,
for does he not have regard for all
the wise in heart?[a]"

The Lord Speaks

38 Then the Lord answered Job out of the storm. He said:

2"Who is this that darkens my counsel
with words without knowledge?
3Brace yourself like a man;
I will question you,
and you shall answer me.

4"Where were you when I laid the
earth's foundation?
Tell me, if you understand.
5Who marked off its dimensions?
Surely you know!
Who stretched a measuring line
across it?
6On what were its footings set,
or who laid its cornerstone—
7while the morning stars sang together
and all the angels[b] shouted for joy?

8"Who shut up the sea behind doors
when it burst forth from the womb,
9when I made the clouds its garment
and wrapped it in thick darkness,
10when I fixed limits for it
and set its doors and bars in place,
11when I said, 'This far you may come
and no farther;
here is where your proud waves
halt'?

12"Have you ever given orders to the
morning,
or shown the dawn its place,
13that it might take the earth by the
edges
and shake the wicked out of it?
14The earth takes shape like clay under
a seal;
its features stand out like those of a
garment.
15The wicked are denied their light,
and their upraised arm is broken.

16"Have you journeyed to the springs of
the sea
or walked in the recesses of the
deep?
17Have the gates of death been shown
to you?
Have you seen the gates of the
shadow of death[c]?
18Have you comprehended the vast
expanses of the earth?
Tell me, if you know all this.

19"What is the way to the abode of
light?
And where does darkness reside?
20Can you take them to their places?
Do you know the paths to their
dwellings?
21Surely you know, for you were
already born!
You have lived so many years!

22"Have you entered the storehouses of
the snow
or seen the storehouses of the hail,
23which I reserve for times of trouble,
for days of war and battle?
24What is the way to the place where
the lightning is dispersed,
or the place where the east winds
are scattered over the earth?
25Who cuts a channel for the torrents of
rain,
and a path for the thunderstorm,
26to water a land where no man lives,
a desert with no one in it,

[a]24 Or *for he does not have regard for any who think they are wise.* [b]7 Hebrew *the sons of God*
[c]17 Or *gates of deep shadows*

27to satisfy a desolate wasteland
and make it sprout with grass?
28Does the rain have a father?
Who fathers the drops of dew?
29From whose womb comes the ice?
Who gives birth to the frost from the heavens
30when the waters become hard as stone,
when the surface of the deep is frozen?

31"Can you bind the beautiful[a] Pleiades?
Can you loose the cords of Orion?
32Can you bring forth the constellations in their seasons[b]
or lead out the Bear[c] with its cubs?
33Do you know the laws of the heavens?
Can you set up ⌊God's[d]⌋ dominion over the earth?

34"Can you raise your voice to the clouds
and cover yourself with a flood of water?
35Do you send the lightning bolts on their way?
Do they report to you, 'Here we are'?
36Who endowed the heart[e] with wisdom
or gave understanding to the mind[e]?
37Who has the wisdom to count the clouds?
Who can tip over the water jars of the heavens
38when the dust becomes hard
and the clods of earth stick together?

39"Do you hunt the prey for the lioness
and satisfy the hunger of the lions
40when they crouch in their dens
or lie in wait in a thicket?
41Who provides food for the raven
when its young cry out to God
and wander about for lack of food?

39 "Do you know when the mountain goats give birth?
Do you watch when the doe bears her fawn?
2Do you count the months till they bear?
Do you know the time they give birth?
3They crouch down and bring forth their young;
their labor pains are ended.
4Their young thrive and grow strong in the wilds;
they leave and do not return.

5"Who let the wild donkey go free?
Who untied his ropes?
6I gave him the wasteland as his home,
the salt flats as his habitat.
7He laughs at the commotion in the town;
he does not hear a driver's shout.
8He ranges the hills for his pasture
and searches for any green thing.

9"Will the wild ox consent to serve you?
Will he stay by your manger at night?
10Can you hold him to the furrow with a harness?
Will he till the valleys behind you?
11Will you rely on him for his great strength?
Will you leave your heavy work to him?
12Can you trust him to bring in your grain
and gather it to your threshing floor?

13"The wings of the ostrich flap joyfully,
but they cannot compare with the pinions and feathers of the stork.
14She lays her eggs on the ground
and lets them warm in the sand,
15unmindful that a foot may crush them,
that some wild animal may trample them.
16She treats her young harshly, as if they were not hers;
she cares not that her labor was in vain,
17for God did not endow her with wisdom
or give her a share of good sense.
18Yet when she spreads her feathers to run,
she laughs at horse and rider.

19"Do you give the horse his strength
or clothe his neck with a flowing mane?
20Do you make him leap like a locust,

[a]31 Or *the twinkling*; or *the chains of the* [b]32 Or *the morning star in its season* [c]32 Or *out Leo*
[d]33 Or *his*; or *their* [e]36 The meaning of the Hebrew for this word is uncertain.

striking terror with his proud
snorting?
21He paws fiercely, rejoicing in his
strength,
and charges into the fray.
22He laughs at fear, afraid of nothing;
he does not shy away from the
sword.
23The quiver rattles against his side,
along with the flashing spear and
lance.
24In frenzied excitement he eats up the
ground;
he cannot stand still when the
trumpet sounds.
25At the blast of the trumpet he snorts,
'Aha!'
He catches the scent of battle from
afar,
the shout of commanders and the
battle cry.

26"Does the hawk take flight by your
wisdom
and spread his wings toward the
south?
27Does the eagle soar at your command
and build his nest on high?
28He dwells on a cliff and stays there at
night;
a rocky crag is his stronghold.
29From there he seeks out his food;
his eyes detect it from afar.
30His young ones feast on blood,
and where the slain are, there is
he."

40 The LORD said to Job:

2"Will the one who contends with the
Almighty correct him?
Let him who accuses God answer
him!"

3Then Job answered the LORD:

4"I am unworthy—how can I reply to
you?
I put my hand over my mouth.
5I spoke once, but I have no answer—
twice, but I will say no more."

6Then the LORD spoke to Job out of the
storm:

7"Brace yourself like a man;
I will question you,
and you shall answer me.
8"Would you discredit my justice?
Would you condemn me to justify
yourself?
9Do you have an arm like God's,
and can your voice thunder like his?
10Then adorn yourself with glory and
splendor,
and clothe yourself in honor and
majesty.
11Unleash the fury of your wrath,
look at every proud man and bring
him low,
12look at every proud man and humble
him,
crush the wicked where they stand.
13Bury them all in the dust together;
shroud their faces in the grave.
14Then I myself will admit to you
that your own right hand can save
you.

15"Look at the behemoth,[a]
which I made along with you
and which feeds on grass like an
ox.
16What strength he has in his loins,
what power in the muscles of his
belly!
17His tail[b] sways like a cedar;
the sinews of his thighs are
close-knit.
18His bones are tubes of bronze,
his limbs like rods of iron.
19He ranks first among the works of
God,
yet his Maker can approach him
with his sword.
20The hills bring him their produce,
and all the wild animals play
nearby.
21Under the lotus plants he lies,
hidden among the reeds in the
marsh.
22The lotuses conceal him in their
shadow;
the poplars by the stream surround
him.
23When the river rages, he is not
alarmed;
he is secure, though the Jordan
should surge against his mouth.
24Can anyone capture him by the
eyes,[c]
or trap him and pierce his nose?

41 "Can you pull in the leviathan[d]
with a fishhook

[a] 15 Possibly the hippopotamus or the elephant
[b] 17 Possibly trunk
[c] 24 Or *by a water hole*
[d] 1 Possibly the crocodile

or tie down his tongue with a rope?
2 Can you put a cord through his nose
or pierce his jaw with a hook?
3 Will he keep begging you for mercy?
Will he speak to you with gentle words?
4 Will he make an agreement with you
for you to take him as your slave for life?
5 Can you make a pet of him like a bird
or put him on a leash for your girls?
6 Will traders barter for him?
Will they divide him up among the merchants?
7 Can you fill his hide with harpoons
or his head with fishing spears?
8 If you lay a hand on him,
you will remember the struggle and never do it again!
9 Any hope of subduing him is false;
the mere sight of him is overpowering.
10 No one is fierce enough to rouse him.
Who then is able to stand against me?
11 Who has a claim against me that I must pay?
Everything under heaven belongs to me.
12 "I will not fail to speak of his limbs,
his strength and his graceful form.
13 Who can strip off his outer coat?
Who would approach him with a bridle?
14 Who dares open the doors of his mouth,
ringed about with his fearsome teeth?
15 His back has[a] rows of shields
tightly sealed together;
16 each is so close to the next
that no air can pass between.
17 They are joined fast to one another;
they cling together and cannot be parted.
18 His snorting throws out flashes of light;
his eyes are like the rays of dawn.
19 Firebrands stream from his mouth;
sparks of fire shoot out.
20 Smoke pours from his nostrils
as from a boiling pot over a fire of reeds.
21 His breath sets coals ablaze,
and flames dart from his mouth.
22 Strength resides in his neck;
dismay goes before him.
23 The folds of his flesh are tightly joined;
they are firm and immovable.
24 His chest is hard as rock,
hard as a lower millstone.
25 When he rises up, the mighty are terrified;
they retreat before his thrashing.
26 The sword that reaches him has no effect,
nor does the spear or the dart or the javelin.
27 Iron he treats like straw
and bronze like rotten wood.
28 Arrows do not make him flee;
slingstones are like chaff to him.
29 A club seems to him but a piece of straw;
he laughs at the rattling of the lance.
30 His undersides are jagged potsherds,
leaving a trail in the mud like a threshing sledge.
31 He makes the depths churn like a boiling caldron
and stirs up the sea like a pot of ointment.
32 Behind him he leaves a glistening wake;
one would think the deep had white hair.
33 Nothing on earth is his equal—
a creature without fear.
34 He looks down on all that are haughty;
he is king over all that are proud."

Job

42 Then Job replied to the Lord:
2 "I know that you can do all things;
no plan of yours can be thwarted.
3 ⌊You asked,⌋ 'Who is this that obscures my counsel without knowledge?'
Surely I spoke of things I did not understand,
things too wonderful for me to know.
4 ⌊"You said,⌋ 'Listen now, and I will speak;
I will question you,
and you shall answer me.'

[a] 15 Or *His pride is his*

[5]My ears had heard of you
but now my eyes have seen you.
[6]Therefore I despise myself
and repent in dust and ashes."

Epilogue

[7]After the LORD had said these things to Job, he said to Eliphaz the Temanite, "I am angry with you and your two friends, because you have not spoken of me what is right, as my servant Job has. [8]So now take seven bulls and seven rams and go to my servant Job and sacrifice a burnt offering for yourselves. My servant Job will pray for you, and I will accept his prayer and not deal with you according to your folly. You have not spoken of me what is right, as my servant Job has." [9]So Eliphaz the Temanite, Bildad the Shuhite and Zophar the Naamathite did what the LORD told them; and the LORD accepted Job's prayer.

[10]After Job had prayed for his friends, the LORD made him prosperous again and gave him twice as much as he had before. [11]All his brothers and sisters and everyone who had known him before came and ate with him in his house. They comforted and consoled him over all the trouble the LORD had brought upon him, and each one

VERSE FOR THE DAY: Job 42:5

AUTHOR: Ruth Senter

PASSAGE FOR THE DAY: Job 42:1–6

The Opportunity of Change

Change points are stress points. My ten-year-old loses his childhood innocence. My skin takes on some wrinkles. And Mark, my husband, leaves the pastorate to teach at a seminary.

Sometimes change is a package I'd rather return to the sender. I watch as a four-year-old neighbor succumbs to leukemia's wasteland. I watch as a friend's marriage turns sour. And I grieve over the change.

In my quest for stability, I remember Job, caught in chaotic upheavals—currents of change that blew hard against all that he had and was. I'm sure Job didn't glibly sing his way from gentleman farmer to the ash heap. In fact, he probably muttered under his breath all the way. But when all his muttering was done, he came face-to-face with his changeless God. "My ears had heard of you, but now my eyes have seen you" (Job 42:5). The changes in Job's life moved him toward God. Stress points? Yes, but also opportunities to discover new dimensions of God.

MARRIAGE BUILDERS

- *When has a period of instability been uncomfortable?*
- *When has change been an opportunity for growth?*

Additional Scripture Readings
Philippians 3:8–10; Deuteronomy 4:29; Jeremiah 29:13

Go to page 545 for your next devotional reading.

gave him a piece of silver[a] and a gold ring.

12The LORD blessed the latter part of Job's life more than the first. He had fourteen thousand sheep, six thousand camels, a thousand yoke of oxen and a thousand donkeys. 13And he also had seven sons and three daughters. 14The first daughter he named Jemimah, the second Keziah and the third Keren-Happuch. 15Nowhere in all the land were there found women as beautiful as Job's daughters, and their father granted them an inheritance along with their brothers.

16After this, Job lived a hundred and forty years; he saw his children and their children to the fourth generation. 17And so he died, old and full of years.

[a] *11* Hebrew *him a kesitah*; a kesitah was a unit of money of unknown weight and value.

DAVID, the shepherd boy and Israel's greatest king, writes most of the psalms. Together these 150 songs form the greatest collection of prayers ever written. A wide range of human emotion is expressed—joy, excitement, compassion, love, anger, grief, depression. As you read this book, remember that no matter what you are feeling, God wants to hear about it in your prayers to him. He promises to listen to all your concerns and to answer them for Jesus' sake.

PSALMS

BOOK I

Psalms 1–41

Psalm 1

1Blessed is the man
who does not walk in the counsel of the wicked
or stand in the way of sinners
or sit in the seat of mockers.
2But his delight is in the law of the LORD,
and on his law he meditates day and night.
3He is like a tree planted by streams of water,
which yields its fruit in season
and whose leaf does not wither.
Whatever he does prospers.

4Not so the wicked!
They are like chaff
that the wind blows away.
5Therefore the wicked will not stand in the judgment,
nor sinners in the assembly of the righteous.

6For the LORD watches over the way of the righteous,
but the way of the wicked will perish.

Psalm 2

1 Why do the nations conspire[a]
and the peoples plot in vain?
2 The kings of the earth take their stand
and the rulers gather together
against the LORD
and against his Anointed One.[b]
3 "Let us break their chains," they say,
"and throw off their fetters."

4 The One enthroned in heaven laughs;
the Lord scoffs at them.
5 Then he rebukes them in his anger
and terrifies them in his wrath,
saying,
6 "I have installed my King[c]
on Zion, my holy hill."

7 I will proclaim the decree of the LORD:

He said to me, "You are my Son[d];
today I have become your Father.[e]
8 Ask of me,

[a] 1 Hebrew; Septuagint *rage* [b] 2 Or *anointed one* [c] 6 Or *king* [d] 7 Or *son*; also in verse 12
[e] 7 Or *have begotten you*

FRIDAY

VERSE FOR THE DAY:	AUTHOR:	PASSAGE FOR THE DAY:
Psalm 1:2	Martha Reapsome	Psalm 1:1–6

Christian Meditation

I was studying Psalm 1, and a question presented itself that led me to a new discovery. According to the passage, the individual who is rooted like a tree (deep, stable, mature) is characterized by something he does: He meditates on God's law day and night.

"How do I follow this example?" I asked myself. I began to think about the word "meditate." Meditating is a great way to retain the Word. But how do I learn to meditate in a world so full of distractions? For me, meditating on the Word often necessitates turning off the radio and TV while I do housework or drive. Silence gives me freedom to mull over what I've studied and pray it into my life or the lives of others.

Meditating on the Word also means I will have spiritual "meat" to offer to my spouse. What I have studied and meditated on—developed in my own mind—may be the exact insight my husband needs.

MARRIAGE BUILDERS

♦ *How do you manage to reflect on what you've learned from Scripture when you're constantly battling distractions?*
♦ *What is something you've recently learned from God's Word that you might share with your spouse this week?*

Additional Scripture Readings
Psalm 19:1; 104:33–34; 119:15, 48, 97, 103

Go to page 547 for your next devotional reading.

and I will make the nations your
inheritance,
the ends of the earth your
possession.
9You will rule them with an iron
scepter[a];
you will dash them to pieces like
pottery."

10Therefore, you kings, be wise;
be warned, you rulers of the earth.
11Serve the LORD with fear
and rejoice with trembling.
12Kiss the Son, lest he be angry
and you be destroyed in your
way,
for his wrath can flare up in a
moment.
Blessed are all who take refuge in
him.

Psalm 3

A psalm of David. When he fled from
his son Absalom.

1O LORD, how many are my foes!
How many rise up against me!
2Many are saying of me,
"God will not deliver him." *Selah*[b]

3But you are a shield around me,
O LORD;
you bestow glory on me and lift[c]
up my head.
4To the LORD I cry aloud,
and he answers me from his holy
hill. *Selah*

5I lie down and sleep;
I wake again, because the LORD
sustains me.
6I will not fear the tens of thousands
drawn up against me on every
side.

7Arise, O LORD!
Deliver me, O my God!
Strike all my enemies on the jaw;
break the teeth of the wicked.

8From the LORD comes deliverance.
May your blessing be on your
people. *Selah*

Psalm 4

For the director of music. With stringed
instruments. A psalm of David.

1Answer me when I call to you,
O my righteous God.
Give me relief from my distress;
be merciful to me and hear my
prayer.

2How long, O men, will you turn my
glory into shame[d]?
How long will you love delusions
and seek false gods[e]? *Selah*
3Know that the LORD has set apart the
godly for himself;
the LORD will hear when I call to
him.

4In your anger do not sin;
when you are on your beds,
search your hearts and be silent.
Selah
5Offer right sacrifices
and trust in the LORD.

6Many are asking, "Who can show us
any good?"
Let the light of your face shine
upon us, O LORD.
7You have filled my heart with greater
joy
than when their grain and new wine
abound.
8I will lie down and sleep in peace,
for you alone, O LORD,
make me dwell in safety.

Psalm 5

For the director of music. For flutes.
A psalm of David.

1Give ear to my words, O LORD,
consider my sighing.
2Listen to my cry for help,
my King and my God,
for to you I pray.
3In the morning, O LORD, you hear my
voice;
in the morning I lay my requests
before you
and wait in expectation.

4You are not a God who takes pleasure
in evil;
with you the wicked cannot dwell.

[a]9 Or *will break them with a rod of iron* [b]2 A word of uncertain meaning, occurring frequently in the Psalms; possibly a musical term [c]3 Or *LORD, / my Glorious One, who lifts* [d]2 Or *you dishonor my Glorious One* [e]2 Or *seek lies*

WEEKENDING

APPRECIATION

If you had only five minutes to express your appreciation to your spouse, what would you say to him or her? Reflect on your spouse's character qualities, achievements, skills and talents, and the special things he or she does for you. Then use the space below to write your thoughts down.

Husband's List

Wife's List

When you have completed your list, consider putting it in the form of a letter or poem and give it to your spouse. Or keep your list and use it to give your mate one honest compliment each day in the coming week.

— Dave and Claudia Arp

REVIVE

Saturday: Philippians 1:1–11
Sunday: Philemon 1–7

Go to page 548 for your next devotional reading.

[5]The arrogant cannot stand in your presence;
you hate all who do wrong.
[6]You destroy those who tell lies;
bloodthirsty and deceitful men
the LORD abhors.
[7]But I, by your great mercy,
will come into your house;
in reverence will I bow down
toward your holy temple.
[8]Lead me, O LORD, in your righteousness
because of my enemies—
make straight your way before me.
[9]Not a word from their mouth can be trusted;
their heart is filled with destruction.
Their throat is an open grave;
with their tongue they speak deceit.
[10]Declare them guilty, O God!

MONDAY

VERSE FOR THE DAY: Psalm 4:8

AUTHOR: Hannah Whitall Smith

PASSAGE FOR THE DAY: Psalm 4:1–8

Delicious Rest

Have you felt the delicious sense of rest upon going to bed at night? How delightful was the sensation of relaxing every muscle and letting your body go in a perfect abandonment of ease and comfort. The strain of the day had ceased, for a few hours at least. You no longer had to hold up an aching head or a weary back. You trusted yourself to the bed in an absolute confidence and it held you up without effort or strain. You rested!

But suppose you had doubted the strength or the stability of your bed, and had dreaded each moment to find it giving way beneath you. Could you have rested then? Would not every muscle have been strained in a fruitless effort to hold yourself up, and would not the weariness have been greater than if you had not gone to bed at all?

Let this analogy teach you what it means to rest in the Lord. Let your souls lie down upon the couch of his will. Relax every strain, and lay off every burden. Let yourself go in a perfect abandonment of ease and comfort, sure that, since he holds you up, you are perfectly safe. Your part is simply to rest. His part is to sustain you; and he cannot fail.

MARRIAGE BUILDERS

♦ *Is there an area or issue in your life in which you need to experience God's rest and peace?*

♦ *When have you felt a God-given rest or peace after particularly difficult times?*

Additional Scripture Readings
Psalm 62:1–2; Isaiah 62:3–4; Psalm 91:1

Go to page 558 for your next devotional reading.

Let their intrigues be their downfall.
Banish them for their many sins,
for they have rebelled against you.

11 But let all who take refuge in you be glad;
let them ever sing for joy.
Spread your protection over them,
that those who love your name may rejoice in you.
12 For surely, O LORD, you bless the righteous;
you surround them with your favor as with a shield.

Psalm 6

For the director of music. With stringed instruments. According to *sheminith.*[a]
A psalm of David.

1 O LORD, do not rebuke me in your anger
or discipline me in your wrath.
2 Be merciful to me, LORD, for I am faint;
O LORD, heal me, for my bones are in agony.
3 My soul is in anguish.
How long, O LORD, how long?

4 Turn, O LORD, and deliver me;
save me because of your unfailing love.
5 No one remembers you when he is dead.
Who praises you from the grave[b]?

6 I am worn out from groaning;
all night long I flood my bed with weeping
and drench my couch with tears.
7 My eyes grow weak with sorrow;
they fail because of all my foes.

8 Away from me, all you who do evil,
for the LORD has heard my weeping.
9 The LORD has heard my cry for mercy;
the LORD accepts my prayer.
10 All my enemies will be ashamed and dismayed;
they will turn back in sudden disgrace.

Psalm 7

A *shiggaion*[c] of David, which he sang to the LORD concerning Cush, a Benjamite.

1 O LORD my God, I take refuge in you;
save and deliver me from all who pursue me,
2 or they will tear me like a lion
and rip me to pieces with no one to rescue me.

3 O LORD my God, if I have done this
and there is guilt on my hands—
4 if I have done evil to him who is at peace with me
or without cause have robbed my foe—
5 then let my enemy pursue and overtake me;
let him trample my life to the ground
and make me sleep in the dust.
Selah

6 Arise, O LORD, in your anger;
rise up against the rage of my enemies.
Awake, my God; decree justice.
7 Let the assembled peoples gather around you.
Rule over them from on high;
8 let the LORD judge the peoples.
Judge me, O LORD, according to my righteousness,
according to my integrity, O Most High.
9 O righteous God,
who searches minds and hearts,
bring to an end the violence of the wicked
and make the righteous secure.

10 My shield[d] is God Most High,
who saves the upright in heart.
11 God is a righteous judge,
a God who expresses his wrath every day.
12 If he does not relent,
he[e] will sharpen his sword;
he will bend and string his bow.
13 He has prepared his deadly weapons;
he makes ready his flaming arrows.

[a] Title: Probably a musical term [b] 5 Hebrew *Sheol* [c] Title: Probably a literary or musical term
[d] 10 Or *sovereign* [e] 12 Or *If a man does not repent, / God*

14He who is pregnant with evil
and conceives trouble gives birth to disillusionment.
15He who digs a hole and scoops it out
falls into the pit he has made.
16The trouble he causes recoils on himself;
his violence comes down on his own head.

17I will give thanks to the LORD because of his righteousness
and will sing praise to the name of the LORD Most High.

Psalm 8

For the director of music. According to *gittith.*[a] A psalm of David.

1O LORD, our Lord,
how majestic is your name in all the earth!

You have set your glory
above the heavens.
2From the lips of children and infants
you have ordained praise[b]
because of your enemies,
to silence the foe and the avenger.

3When I consider your heavens,
the work of your fingers,
the moon and the stars,
which you have set in place,
4what is man that you are mindful of him,
the son of man that you care for him?
5You made him a little lower than the heavenly beings[c]
and crowned him with glory and honor.

6You made him ruler over the works of your hands;
you put everything under his feet:
7all flocks and herds,
and the beasts of the field,
8the birds of the air,
and the fish of the sea,
all that swim the paths of the seas.

9O LORD, our Lord,
how majestic is your name in all the earth!

Psalm 9[d]

For the director of music. To ⌊the tune of⌋ "The Death of the Son." A psalm of David.

1I will praise you, O LORD, with all my heart;
I will tell of all your wonders.
2I will be glad and rejoice in you;
I will sing praise to your name, O Most High.

3My enemies turn back;
they stumble and perish before you.
4For you have upheld my right and my cause;
you have sat on your throne, judging righteously.
5You have rebuked the nations and destroyed the wicked;
you have blotted out their name for ever and ever.
6Endless ruin has overtaken the enemy,
you have uprooted their cities;
even the memory of them has perished.

7The LORD reigns forever;
he has established his throne for judgment.
8He will judge the world in righteousness;
he will govern the peoples with justice.
9The LORD is a refuge for the oppressed,
a stronghold in times of trouble.
10Those who know your name will trust in you,
for you, LORD, have never forsaken those who seek you.

11Sing praises to the LORD, enthroned in Zion;
proclaim among the nations what he has done.
12For he who avenges blood remembers;
he does not ignore the cry of the afflicted.

13O LORD, see how my enemies persecute me!
Have mercy and lift me up from the gates of death,
14that I may declare your praises
in the gates of the Daughter of Zion

[a]Title: Probably a musical term [b]2 Or *strength* [c]5 Or *than God* [d]Psalms 9 and 10 may have been originally a single acrostic poem, the stanzas of which begin with the successive letters of the Hebrew alphabet. In the Septuagint they constitute one psalm.

and there rejoice in your salvation.
15The nations have fallen into the pit
they have dug;
their feet are caught in the net they
have hidden.
16The LORD is known by his justice;
the wicked are ensnared by the
work of their hands.
Higgaion.[a] *Selah*
17The wicked return to the grave,[b]
all the nations that forget God.
18But the needy will not always be
forgotten,
nor the hope of the afflicted ever
perish.

19Arise, O LORD, let not man triumph;
let the nations be judged in your
presence.
20Strike them with terror, O LORD;
let the nations know they are but
men. *Selah*

Psalm 10[c]

1Why, O LORD, do you stand far off?
Why do you hide yourself in times
of trouble?

2In his arrogance the wicked man
hunts down the weak,
who are caught in the schemes he
devises.
3He boasts of the cravings of his heart;
he blesses the greedy and reviles
the LORD.
4In his pride the wicked does not seek
him;
in all his thoughts there is no room
for God.
5His ways are always prosperous;
he is haughty and your laws are far
from him;
he sneers at all his enemies.
6He says to himself, "Nothing will
shake me;
I'll always be happy and never have
trouble."
7His mouth is full of curses and lies
and threats;
trouble and evil are under his
tongue.
8He lies in wait near the villages;
from ambush he murders the
innocent,
watching in secret for his victims.
9He lies in wait like a lion in cover;
he lies in wait to catch the helpless;
he catches the helpless and drags
them off in his net.
10His victims are crushed, they collapse;
they fall under his strength.
11He says to himself, "God has
forgotten;
he covers his face and never sees."

12Arise, LORD! Lift up your hand, O God.
Do not forget the helpless.
13Why does the wicked man revile God?
Why does he say to himself,
"He won't call me to account"?
14But you, O God, do see trouble and
grief;
you consider it to take it in hand.
The victim commits himself to you;
you are the helper of the fatherless.
15Break the arm of the wicked and evil
man;
call him to account for his
wickedness
that would not be found out.

16The LORD is King for ever and ever;
the nations will perish from his
land.
17You hear, O LORD, the desire of the
afflicted;
you encourage them, and you listen
to their cry,
18defending the fatherless and the
oppressed,
in order that man, who is of the
earth, may terrify no more.

Psalm 11

For the director of music. Of David.

1In the LORD I take refuge.
How then can you say to me:
"Flee like a bird to your mountain.
2For look, the wicked bend their bows;
they set their arrows against the
strings
to shoot from the shadows
at the upright in heart.
3When the foundations are being
destroyed,
what can the righteous do[d]?"

4The LORD is in his holy temple;
the LORD is on his heavenly throne.
He observes the sons of men;

[a]16 Or *Meditation*; possibly a musical notation [b]17 Hebrew *Sheol* [c]Psalms 9 and 10 may have been originally a single acrostic poem, the stanzas of which begin with the successive letters of the Hebrew alphabet. In the Septuagint they constitute one psalm. [d]3 Or *what is the Righteous One doing*

his eyes examine them.
5The LORD examines the righteous,
but the wicked[a] and those who love violence
his soul hates.
6On the wicked he will rain
fiery coals and burning sulfur;
a scorching wind will be their lot.

7For the LORD is righteous,
he loves justice;
upright men will see his face.

Psalm 12

For the director of music. According to *sheminith.*[b] A psalm of David.

1Help, LORD, for the godly are no more;
the faithful have vanished from among men.
2Everyone lies to his neighbor;
their flattering lips speak with deception.

3May the LORD cut off all flattering lips
and every boastful tongue
4that says, "We will triumph with our tongues;
we own our lips[c]—who is our master?"

5"Because of the oppression of the weak
and the groaning of the needy,
I will now arise," says the LORD.
"I will protect them from those who malign them."
6And the words of the LORD are flawless,
like silver refined in a furnace of clay,
purified seven times.

7O LORD, you will keep us safe
and protect us from such people forever.
8The wicked freely strut about
when what is vile is honored among men.

Psalm 13

For the director of music. A psalm of David.

1How long, O LORD? Will you forget me forever?
How long will you hide your face from me?
2How long must I wrestle with my thoughts
and every day have sorrow in my heart?
How long will my enemy triumph over me?

3Look on me and answer, O LORD my God.
Give light to my eyes, or I will sleep in death;
4my enemy will say, "I have overcome him,"
and my foes will rejoice when I fall.

5But I trust in your unfailing love;
my heart rejoices in your salvation.
6I will sing to the LORD,
for he has been good to me.

Psalm 14

For the director of music. Of David.

1The fool[d] says in his heart,
"There is no God."
They are corrupt, their deeds are vile;
there is no one who does good.

2The LORD looks down from heaven
on the sons of men
to see if there are any who understand,
any who seek God.
3All have turned aside,
they have together become corrupt;
there is no one who does good,
not even one.

4Will evildoers never learn—
those who devour my people as men eat bread
and who do not call on the LORD?
5There they are, overwhelmed with dread,
for God is present in the company of the righteous.
6You evildoers frustrate the plans of the poor,
but the LORD is their refuge.

7Oh, that salvation for Israel would come out of Zion!
When the LORD restores the fortunes of his people,
let Jacob rejoice and Israel be glad!

[a]5 Or *The LORD, the Righteous One, examines the wicked, / / our lips are our plowshares* [b]Title: Probably a musical term [c]4 Or [d]1 The Hebrew words rendered *fool* in Psalms denote one who is morally deficient.

Psalm 15

A psalm of David.

1 LORD, who may dwell in your
sanctuary?
Who may live on your holy hill?

2 He whose walk is blameless
and who does what is righteous,
who speaks the truth from his heart
3 and has no slander on his tongue,
who does his neighbor no wrong
and casts no slur on his fellowman,
4 who despises a vile man
but honors those who fear the LORD,
who keeps his oath
even when it hurts,
5 who lends his money without usury
and does not accept a bribe against
the innocent.
He who does these things
will never be shaken.

Psalm 16

A *miktam*[a] of David.

1 Keep me safe, O God,
for in you I take refuge.

2 I said to the LORD, "You are my Lord;
apart from you I have no good
thing."
3 As for the saints who are in the land,
they are the glorious ones in whom
is all my delight.[b]
4 The sorrows of those will increase
who run after other gods.
I will not pour out their libations of
blood
or take up their names on my lips.

5 LORD, you have assigned me my
portion and my cup;
you have made my lot secure.
6 The boundary lines have fallen for me
in pleasant places;
surely I have a delightful
inheritance.

7 I will praise the LORD, who counsels
me;
even at night my heart instructs me.
8 I have set the LORD always before me.
Because he is at my right hand,
I will not be shaken.

9 Therefore my heart is glad and my
tongue rejoices;
my body also will rest secure,
10 because you will not abandon me to
the grave,[c]
nor will you let your Holy One[d]
see decay.
11 You have made[e] known to me the
path of life;
you will fill me with joy in your
presence,
with eternal pleasures at your right
hand.

Psalm 17

A prayer of David.

1 Hear, O LORD, my righteous plea;
listen to my cry.
Give ear to my prayer—
it does not rise from deceitful lips.
2 May my vindication come from you;
may your eyes see what is right.

3 Though you probe my heart and
examine me at night,
though you test me, you will find
nothing;
I have resolved that my mouth will
not sin.
4 As for the deeds of men—
by the word of your lips
I have kept myself
from the ways of the violent.
5 My steps have held to your paths;
my feet have not slipped.

6 I call on you, O God, for you will
answer me;
give ear to me and hear my prayer.
7 Show the wonder of your great love,
you who save by your right hand
those who take refuge in you from
their foes.
8 Keep me as the apple of your eye;
hide me in the shadow of your
wings
9 from the wicked who assail me,
from my mortal enemies who
surround me.

10 They close up their callous hearts,
and their mouths speak with
arrogance.
11 They have tracked me down, they
now surround me,

[a] Title: Probably a literary or musical term [b] 3 Or *As for the pagan priests who are in the land / and the nobles in whom all delight, I said:* [c] 10 Hebrew *Sheol* [d] 10 Or *your faithful one* [e] 11 Or *You will make*

with eyes alert, to throw me to the ground.
12 They are like a lion hungry for prey,
like a great lion crouching in cover.

13 Rise up, O LORD, confront them, bring them down;
rescue me from the wicked by your sword.
14 O LORD, by your hand save me from such men,
from men of this world whose reward is in this life.

You still the hunger of those you cherish;
their sons have plenty,
and they store up wealth for their children.
15 And I—in righteousness I will see your face;
when I awake, I will be satisfied with seeing your likeness.

Psalm 18

For the director of music. Of David the servant of the LORD. He sang to the LORD the words of this song when the LORD delivered him from the hand of all his enemies and from the hand of Saul. He said:

1 I love you, O LORD, my strength.

2 The LORD is my rock, my fortress and my deliverer;
my God is my rock, in whom I take refuge.
He is my shield and the horn[a] of my salvation, my stronghold.
3 I call to the LORD, who is worthy of praise,
and I am saved from my enemies.

4 The cords of death entangled me;
the torrents of destruction overwhelmed me.
5 The cords of the grave[b] coiled around me;
the snares of death confronted me.
6 In my distress I called to the LORD;
I cried to my God for help.
From his temple he heard my voice;
my cry came before him, into his ears.

7 The earth trembled and quaked,
and the foundations of the mountains shook;
they trembled because he was angry.
8 Smoke rose from his nostrils;
consuming fire came from his mouth,
burning coals blazed out of it.
9 He parted the heavens and came down;
dark clouds were under his feet.
10 He mounted the cherubim and flew;
he soared on the wings of the wind.
11 He made darkness his covering, his canopy around him—
the dark rain clouds of the sky.
12 Out of the brightness of his presence clouds advanced,
with hailstones and bolts of lightning.
13 The LORD thundered from heaven;
the voice of the Most High resounded.[c]
14 He shot his arrows and scattered ⌊the enemies⌋,
great bolts of lightning and routed them.
15 The valleys of the sea were exposed
and the foundations of the earth laid bare
at your rebuke, O LORD,
at the blast of breath from your nostrils.

16 He reached down from on high and took hold of me;
he drew me out of deep waters.
17 He rescued me from my powerful enemy,
from my foes, who were too strong for me.
18 They confronted me in the day of my disaster,
but the LORD was my support.
19 He brought me out into a spacious place;
he rescued me because he delighted in me.

20 The LORD has dealt with me according to my righteousness;
according to the cleanness of my hands he has rewarded me.
21 For I have kept the ways of the LORD;
I have not done evil by turning from my God.

[a] 2 *Horn* here symbolizes strength. [b] 5 Hebrew *Sheol* [c] 13 Some Hebrew manuscripts and Septuagint (see also 2 Samuel 22:14); most Hebrew manuscripts *resounded, / amid hailstones and bolts of lightning*

22All his laws are before me;
I have not turned away from his decrees.
23I have been blameless before him
and have kept myself from sin.
24The LORD has rewarded me according to my righteousness,
according to the cleanness of my hands in his sight.

25To the faithful you show yourself faithful,
to the blameless you show yourself blameless,
26to the pure you show yourself pure,
but to the crooked you show yourself shrewd.
27You save the humble
but bring low those whose eyes are haughty.
28You, O LORD, keep my lamp burning;
my God turns my darkness into light.
29With your help I can advance against a troop[a];
with my God I can scale a wall.

30As for God, his way is perfect;
the word of the LORD is flawless.
He is a shield
for all who take refuge in him.
31For who is God besides the LORD?
And who is the Rock except our God?
32It is God who arms me with strength
and makes my way perfect.
33He makes my feet like the feet of a deer;
he enables me to stand on the heights.
34He trains my hands for battle;
my arms can bend a bow of bronze.
35You give me your shield of victory,
and your right hand sustains me;
you stoop down to make me great.
36You broaden the path beneath me,
so that my ankles do not turn.

37I pursued my enemies and overtook them;
I did not turn back till they were destroyed.
38I crushed them so that they could not rise;
they fell beneath my feet.
39You armed me with strength for battle;
you made my adversaries bow at my feet.
40You made my enemies turn their backs in flight,
and I destroyed my foes.
41They cried for help, but there was no one to save them—
to the LORD, but he did not answer.
42I beat them as fine as dust borne on the wind;
I poured them out like mud in the streets.

43You have delivered me from the attacks of the people;
you have made me the head of nations;
people I did not know are subject to me.
44As soon as they hear me, they obey me;
foreigners cringe before me.
45They all lose heart;
they come trembling from their strongholds.

46The LORD lives! Praise be to my Rock!
Exalted be God my Savior!
47He is the God who avenges me,
who subdues nations under me,
48 who saves me from my enemies.
You exalted me above my foes;
from violent men you rescued me.
49Therefore I will praise you among the nations, O LORD;
I will sing praises to your name.
50He gives his king great victories;
he shows unfailing kindness to his anointed,
to David and his descendants forever.

Psalm 19

For the director of music. A psalm of David.

1The heavens declare the glory of God;
the skies proclaim the work of his hands.
2Day after day they pour forth speech;
night after night they display knowledge.
3There is no speech or language
where their voice is not heard.[b]
4Their voice[c] goes out into all the earth,

[a]29 Or *can run through a barricade* [b]3 Or *They have no speech, there are no words; / no sound is heard from them* [c]4 Septuagint, Jerome and Syriac; Hebrew *line*

their words to the ends of the world.
In the heavens he has pitched a tent for the sun,
5 which is like a bridegroom coming forth from his pavilion,
like a champion rejoicing to run his course.
6It rises at one end of the heavens
and makes its circuit to the other;
nothing is hidden from its heat.

7The law of the LORD is perfect,
reviving the soul.
The statutes of the LORD are trustworthy,
making wise the simple.
8The precepts of the LORD are right,
giving joy to the heart.
The commands of the LORD are radiant,
giving light to the eyes.
9The fear of the LORD is pure,
enduring forever.
The ordinances of the LORD are sure
and altogether righteous.
10They are more precious than gold,
than much pure gold;
they are sweeter than honey,
than honey from the comb.
11By them is your servant warned;
in keeping them there is great reward.

12Who can discern his errors?
Forgive my hidden faults.
13Keep your servant also from willful sins;
may they not rule over me.
Then will I be blameless,
innocent of great transgression.

14May the words of my mouth and the meditation of my heart
be pleasing in your sight,
O LORD, my Rock and my Redeemer.

Psalm 20

For the director of music. A psalm of David.

1May the LORD answer you when you are in distress;
may the name of the God of Jacob protect you.
2May he send you help from the sanctuary
and grant you support from Zion.
3May he remember all your sacrifices
and accept your burnt offerings. *Selah*
4May he give you the desire of your heart
and make all your plans succeed.
5We will shout for joy when you are victorious
and will lift up our banners in the name of our God.
May the LORD grant all your requests.

6Now I know that the LORD saves his anointed;
he answers him from his holy heaven
with the saving power of his right hand.
7Some trust in chariots and some in horses,
but we trust in the name of the LORD our God.
8They are brought to their knees and fall,
but we rise up and stand firm.

9O LORD, save the king!
Answer[a] us when we call!

Psalm 21

For the director of music. A psalm of David.

1O LORD, the king rejoices in your strength.
How great is his joy in the victories you give!
2You have granted him the desire of his heart
and have not withheld the request of his lips. *Selah*
3You welcomed him with rich blessings
and placed a crown of pure gold on his head.
4He asked you for life, and you gave it to him—
length of days, for ever and ever.
5Through the victories you gave, his glory is great;
you have bestowed on him splendor and majesty.
6Surely you have granted him eternal blessings

[a]9 Or *save! / O King, answer*

and made him glad with the joy of
your presence.
7For the king trusts in the LORD;
through the unfailing love of the
Most High
he will not be shaken.
8Your hand will lay hold on all your
enemies;
your right hand will seize your foes.
9At the time of your appearing
you will make them like a fiery
furnace.
In his wrath the LORD will swallow
them up,
and his fire will consume them.
10You will destroy their descendants
from the earth,
their posterity from mankind.
11Though they plot evil against you
and devise wicked schemes, they
cannot succeed;
12for you will make them turn their
backs
when you aim at them with drawn
bow.

13Be exalted, O LORD, in your strength;
we will sing and praise your might.

Psalm 22

For the director of music. To ⌊the tune
of⌋ "The Doe of the Morning." A psalm
of David.

1My God, my God, why have you
forsaken me?
Why are you so far from saving me,
so far from the words of my
groaning?
2O my God, I cry out by day, but you
do not answer,
by night, and am not silent.

3Yet you are enthroned as the Holy
One;
you are the praise of Israel.[a]
4In you our fathers put their trust;
they trusted and you delivered
them.
5They cried to you and were saved;
in you they trusted and were not
disappointed.

6But I am a worm and not a man,
scorned by men and despised by
the people.
7All who see me mock me;
they hurl insults, shaking their
heads:
8"He trusts in the LORD;
let the LORD rescue him.
Let him deliver him,
since he delights in him."

9Yet you brought me out of the womb;
you made me trust in you
even at my mother's breast.
10From birth I was cast upon you;
from my mother's womb you have
been my God.
11Do not be far from me,
for trouble is near
and there is no one to help.

12Many bulls surround me;
strong bulls of Bashan encircle me.
13Roaring lions tearing their prey
open their mouths wide against me.
14I am poured out like water,
and all my bones are out of joint.
My heart has turned to wax;
it has melted away within me.
15My strength is dried up like a
potsherd,
and my tongue sticks to the roof of
my mouth;
you lay me[b] in the dust of death.
16Dogs have surrounded me;
a band of evil men has encircled
me,
they have pierced[c] my hands and
my feet.
17I can count all my bones;
people stare and gloat over me.
18They divide my garments among them
and cast lots for my clothing.

19But you, O LORD, be not far off;
O my Strength, come quickly to
help me.
20Deliver my life from the sword,
my precious life from the power of
the dogs.
21Rescue me from the mouth of the
lions;
save[d] me from the horns of the
wild oxen.

22I will declare your name to my
brothers;

[a]3 Or *Yet you are holy, / enthroned on the praises of Israel* [b]15 Or / *I am laid* [c]16 Some Hebrew manuscripts, Septuagint and Syriac; most Hebrew manuscripts / *like the lion,* [d]21 Or / *you have heard*

in the congregation I will praise
you.
23 You who fear the LORD, praise him!
All you descendants of Jacob, honor
him!
Revere him, all you descendants of
Israel!
24 For he has not despised or disdained
the suffering of the afflicted one;
he has not hidden his face from him
but has listened to his cry for help.
25 From you comes the theme of my
praise in the great assembly;

VERSE FOR THE DAY: Psalm 22:5 | AUTHOR: Elizabeth Cody Newenhuyse | PASSAGE FOR THE DAY: Psalm 22:1–31

Conquering Disappointment

Disappointment can corrode a marriage like rust eats away at a car. Any number of things—a spouse's unemployment, a chronic illness, a serious betrayal—these things often kill marriages.

This is where a spiritual perspective may not only help—but be essential. Faith does not deny disappointment. Some things really are awful. But look for answers we must. Dr. Paul Brand may have the best answer to this conundrum. Renowned for his work with leprosy patients, Brand responded to the question, "Where is God when it hurts?" with this: "He is in *you*, the one hurting, not in *it*, the thing that hurts."

We may find ourselves placing our hope in many things: our spouse, our careers, our health. Yet these things have their limitations. Spouses, being human, will disappoint. Careers change; health fades.

But God doesn't. Ultimately, our hope is in him. It's important to remember he is in us when we hurt. It is, perhaps, even more important to remember he is also in our spouse. The couples I have observed who have come through disappointment have done so first by God's grace, and second by holding firmly to each other. They have affirmed that the "we" is stronger than the "it" of disappointment. And their marriages are better for it.

MARRIAGE BUILDERS

♦ *How does your "ultimate hope" carry you in times of disappointment or discouragement?*
♦ *How does having two of you to cope with troubles give you courage as you face the future?*

Additional Scripture Readings
Lamentations 3:21; Romans 5:5; 1 Corinthians 15:19

Go to page 560 for your next devotional reading.

before those who fear you[a] will I
fulfill my vows.
26 The poor will eat and be satisfied;
they who seek the LORD will praise him—
may your hearts live forever!
27 All the ends of the earth
will remember and turn to the LORD,
and all the families of the nations
will bow down before him,
28 for dominion belongs to the LORD
and he rules over the nations.

29 All the rich of the earth will feast and worship;
all who go down to the dust will kneel before him—
those who cannot keep themselves alive.
30 Posterity will serve him;
future generations will be told about the Lord.
31 They will proclaim his righteousness
to a people yet unborn—
for he has done it.

Psalm 23

A psalm of David.

1 The LORD is my shepherd, I shall not be in want.
2 He makes me lie down in green pastures,
he leads me beside quiet waters,
3 he restores my soul.
He guides me in paths of righteousness
for his name's sake.
4 Even though I walk
through the valley of the shadow of death,[b]
I will fear no evil,
for you are with me;
your rod and your staff,
they comfort me.

5 You prepare a table before me
in the presence of my enemies.
You anoint my head with oil;
my cup overflows.
6 Surely goodness and love will follow me
all the days of my life,
and I will dwell in the house of the LORD
forever.

Psalm 24

Of David. A psalm.

1 The earth is the LORD's, and everything in it,
the world, and all who live in it;
2 for he founded it upon the seas
and established it upon the waters.

3 Who may ascend the hill of the LORD?
Who may stand in his holy place?
4 He who has clean hands and a pure heart,
who does not lift up his soul to an idol
or swear by what is false.[c]
5 He will receive blessing from the LORD
and vindication from God his Savior.
6 Such is the generation of those who seek him,
who seek your face, O God of Jacob.[d] *Selah*

7 Lift up your heads, O you gates;
be lifted up, you ancient doors,
that the King of glory may come in.
8 Who is this King of glory?
The LORD strong and mighty,
the LORD mighty in battle.
9 Lift up your heads, O you gates;
lift them up, you ancient doors,
that the King of glory may come in.
10 Who is he, this King of glory?
The LORD Almighty—
he is the King of glory. *Selah*

Psalm 25[e]

Of David.

1 To you, O LORD, I lift up my soul;
2 in you I trust, O my God.
Do not let me be put to shame,
nor let my enemies triumph over me.
3 No one whose hope is in you
will ever be put to shame,
but they will be put to shame
who are treacherous without excuse.

[a] 25 Hebrew *him* [b] 4 Or *through the darkest valley* [c] 4 Or *swear falsely* [d] 6 Two Hebrew manuscripts and Syriac (see also Septuagint); most Hebrew manuscripts *face, Jacob* [e] This psalm is an acrostic poem, the verses of which begin with the successive letters of the Hebrew alphabet.

4Show me your ways, O LORD,
teach me your paths;
5guide me in your truth and teach me,
for you are God my Savior,
and my hope is in you all day long.
6Remember, O LORD, your great mercy
and love,
for they are from of old.
7Remember not the sins of my youth
and my rebellious ways;
according to your love remember me,
for you are good, O LORD.
8Good and upright is the LORD;
therefore he instructs sinners in his
ways.
9He guides the humble in what is right
and teaches them his way.
10All the ways of the LORD are loving
and faithful
for those who keep the demands of
his covenant.

VERSE FOR THE DAY: Psalm 25:5 | AUTHOR: Jill Briscoe | PASSAGE FOR THE DAY: Psalm 25:1–22

Finding Help

Opening my Bible is a little like going to the library: I know where to go for certain things. Sometimes when I come to Scripture, I sense a deep need in my life.

Some days I may feel I'm in the pits. I remember the story of Joseph, who was in a pit too. So I go to Genesis 37 and read how Joseph was rejected by his brothers. Then I come to that beautiful verse in Genesis 50:20 where Joseph said to his brothers, "You intended to harm me, but God intended it for good to accomplish what is now being done, the saving of many lives." I am encouraged by Joseph's perspective on the pain in his life.

Perhaps I've just had a tough meeting, and I don't feel that I did a very good job in the contributions I made. I need encouragement, so I turn to the Psalms. I know that David was discouraged too. Reading his prayers ministers to my need for encouragement. Or I've been criticized, so I go to 1 Corinthians 3, where Paul talks about divisions and disunity in the church and gives advice for what to do about it.

If God is going to speak directly to my needs, it makes sense to know where to go for help.

MARRIAGE BUILDERS

♦ *What are some favorite Scripture passages that you find yourself returning to over and over?*
♦ *What personal needs do they address for you?*

Additional Scripture Readings
Genesis 37:1–36; Genesis 50:20;
1 Corinthians 3

Go to page 563 for your next devotional reading.

11For the sake of your name, O LORD,
forgive my iniquity, though it is great.
12Who, then, is the man that fears the LORD?
He will instruct him in the way chosen for him.
13He will spend his days in prosperity,
and his descendants will inherit the land.
14The LORD confides in those who fear him;
he makes his covenant known to them.
15My eyes are ever on the LORD,
for only he will release my feet from the snare.

16Turn to me and be gracious to me,
for I am lonely and afflicted.
17The troubles of my heart have multiplied;
free me from my anguish.
18Look upon my affliction and my distress
and take away all my sins.
19See how my enemies have increased
and how fiercely they hate me!
20Guard my life and rescue me;
let me not be put to shame,
for I take refuge in you.
21May integrity and uprightness protect me,
because my hope is in you.
22Redeem Israel, O God,
from all their troubles!

Psalm 26

Of David.

1Vindicate me, O LORD,
for I have led a blameless life;
I have trusted in the LORD
without wavering.
2Test me, O LORD, and try me,
examine my heart and my mind;
3for your love is ever before me,
and I walk continually in your truth.
4I do not sit with deceitful men,
nor do I consort with hypocrites;
5I abhor the assembly of evildoers
and refuse to sit with the wicked.
6I wash my hands in innocence,
and go about your altar, O LORD,
7proclaiming aloud your praise
and telling of all your wonderful deeds.
8I love the house where you live, O LORD,
the place where your glory dwells.

9Do not take away my soul along with sinners,
my life with bloodthirsty men,
10in whose hands are wicked schemes,
whose right hands are full of bribes.
11But I lead a blameless life;
redeem me and be merciful to me.

12My feet stand on level ground;
in the great assembly I will praise the LORD.

Psalm 27

Of David.

1The LORD is my light and my salvation—
whom shall I fear?
The LORD is the stronghold of my life—
of whom shall I be afraid?
2When evil men advance against me
to devour my flesh,[a]
when my enemies and my foes attack me,
they will stumble and fall.
3Though an army besiege me,
my heart will not fear;
though war break out against me,
even then will I be confident.

4One thing I ask of the LORD,
this is what I seek:
that I may dwell in the house of the LORD
all the days of my life,
to gaze upon the beauty of the LORD
and to seek him in his temple.
5For in the day of trouble
he will keep me safe in his dwelling;
he will hide me in the shelter of his tabernacle
and set me high upon a rock.
6Then my head will be exalted
above the enemies who surround me;
at his tabernacle will I sacrifice with shouts of joy;
I will sing and make music to the LORD.

[a]2 Or *to slander me*

7Hear my voice when I call, O LORD;
be merciful to me and answer me.
8My heart says of you, "Seek his[a] face!"
Your face, LORD, I will seek.
9Do not hide your face from me,
do not turn your servant away in anger;
you have been my helper.
Do not reject me or forsake me,
O God my Savior.
10Though my father and mother forsake me,
the LORD will receive me.
11Teach me your way, O LORD;
lead me in a straight path
because of my oppressors.
12Do not turn me over to the desire of my foes,
for false witnesses rise up against me,
breathing out violence.

13I am still confident of this:
I will see the goodness of the LORD
in the land of the living.
14Wait for the LORD;
be strong and take heart
and wait for the LORD.

Psalm 28

Of David.

1To you I call, O LORD my Rock;
do not turn a deaf ear to me.
For if you remain silent,
I will be like those who have gone down to the pit.
2Hear my cry for mercy
as I call to you for help,
as I lift up my hands
toward your Most Holy Place.

3Do not drag me away with the wicked,
with those who do evil,
who speak cordially with their neighbors
but harbor malice in their hearts.
4Repay them for their deeds
and for their evil work;
repay them for what their hands have done
and bring back upon them what they deserve.
5Since they show no regard for the works of the LORD
and what his hands have done,
he will tear them down
and never build them up again.

6Praise be to the LORD,
for he has heard my cry for mercy.
7The LORD is my strength and my shield;
my heart trusts in him, and I am helped.
My heart leaps for joy
and I will give thanks to him in song.

8The LORD is the strength of his people,
a fortress of salvation for his anointed one.
9Save your people and bless your inheritance;
be their shepherd and carry them forever.

Psalm 29

A psalm of David.

1Ascribe to the LORD, O mighty ones,
ascribe to the LORD glory and strength.
2Ascribe to the LORD the glory due his name;
worship the LORD in the splendor of his[b] holiness.

3The voice of the LORD is over the waters;
the God of glory thunders,
the LORD thunders over the mighty waters.
4The voice of the LORD is powerful;
the voice of the LORD is majestic.
5The voice of the LORD breaks the cedars;
the LORD breaks in pieces the cedars of Lebanon.
6He makes Lebanon skip like a calf,
Sirion[c] like a young wild ox.
7The voice of the LORD strikes
with flashes of lightning.
8The voice of the LORD shakes the desert;
the LORD shakes the Desert of Kadesh.

[a] 8 Or *To you, O my heart, he has said, "Seek my*
[b] 2 Or *LORD with the splendor of*
[c] 6 That is, Mount Hermon

9The voice of the LORD twists the oaks[a]
and strips the forests bare.
And in his temple all cry, "Glory!"

10The LORD sits[b] enthroned over the flood;
the LORD is enthroned as King forever.
11The LORD gives strength to his people;
the LORD blesses his people with peace.

[a]9 Or *LORD makes the deer give birth* [b]10 Or *sat*

Psalm 30

A psalm. A song. For the dedication of the temple.[c] Of David.

1I will exalt you, O LORD,
for you lifted me out of the depths
and did not let my enemies gloat over me.
2O LORD my God, I called to you for help
and you healed me.
3O LORD, you brought me up from the grave[d];

[c]Title: Or *palace* [d]3 Hebrew *Sheol*

VERSE FOR THE DAY: Psalm 30:5

AUTHOR: Lewis Smedes

PASSAGE FOR THE DAY: Psalm 30:1–12

Quick to Forgive

When forgiveness is necessary, don't wait too long. We must begin to forgive, because without forgiving, we choke off our own joy; we kill our own soul. People carrying hate and resentment can invest themselves so deeply in that resentment that they gradually define themselves in terms of it.

The longer you wait, the more you risk becoming a person *defined by* your anger, rather than simply a person who has a grievance. The offense and the resultant anger begin to possess you, until your identity is practically demonized by resentment.

So, when forgiveness is truly necessary, forgive as quickly as you can, because forgiving has two good results: The first is your own release, and the second is the possibility of reconciliation between you and your mate.

MARRIAGE BUILDERS

♦ *Have you ever known a person whose anger was his or her defining characteristic? How was that person's anger a handicap to him or her?*

♦ *What difference would "quick" forgiveness make in the atmosphere of your home?*

Additional Scripture Readings
Matthew 5:23–26; Ephesians 4:26, 32

Go to page 571 for your next devotional reading.

you spared me from going down
into the pit.

4Sing to the LORD, you saints of his;
praise his holy name.
5For his anger lasts only a moment,
but his favor lasts a lifetime;
weeping may remain for a night,
but rejoicing comes in the morning.

6When I felt secure, I said,
"I will never be shaken."
7O LORD, when you favored me,
you made my mountain[a] stand
firm;
but when you hid your face,
I was dismayed.

8To you, O LORD, I called;
to the Lord I cried for mercy:
9"What gain is there in my
destruction,[b]
in my going down into the pit?
Will the dust praise you?
Will it proclaim your faithfulness?
10Hear, O LORD, and be merciful to me;
O LORD, be my help."

11You turned my wailing into dancing;
you removed my sackcloth and
clothed me with joy,
12that my heart may sing to you and
not be silent.
O LORD my God, I will give you
thanks forever.

Psalm 31

For the director of music. A psalm
of David.

1In you, O LORD, I have taken refuge;
let me never be put to shame;
deliver me in your righteousness.
2Turn your ear to me,
come quickly to my rescue;
be my rock of refuge,
a strong fortress to save me.
3Since you are my rock and my
fortress,
for the sake of your name lead and
guide me.
4Free me from the trap that is set for
me,
for you are my refuge.
5Into your hands I commit my spirit;
redeem me, O LORD, the God of
truth.

6I hate those who cling to worthless
idols;
I trust in the LORD.
7I will be glad and rejoice in your love,
for you saw my affliction
and knew the anguish of my soul.
8You have not handed me over to the
enemy
but have set my feet in a spacious
place.

9Be merciful to me, O LORD, for I am in
distress;
my eyes grow weak with sorrow,
my soul and my body with grief.
10My life is consumed by anguish
and my years by groaning;
my strength fails because of my
affliction,[c]
and my bones grow weak.
11Because of all my enemies,
I am the utter contempt of my
neighbors;
I am a dread to my friends—
those who see me on the street flee
from me.
12I am forgotten by them as though I
were dead;
I have become like broken pottery.
13For I hear the slander of many;
there is terror on every side;
they conspire against me
and plot to take my life.

14But I trust in you, O LORD;
I say, "You are my God."
15My times are in your hands;
deliver me from my enemies
and from those who pursue me.
16Let your face shine on your servant;
save me in your unfailing love.
17Let me not be put to shame, O LORD,
for I have cried out to you;
but let the wicked be put to shame
and lie silent in the grave.[d]
18Let their lying lips be silenced,
for with pride and contempt
they speak arrogantly against the
righteous.

19How great is your goodness,
which you have stored up for those
who fear you,
which you bestow in the sight of men
on those who take refuge in you.
20In the shelter of your presence you
hide them
from the intrigues of men;

[a]7 Or *hill country* [b]9 Or *there if I am silenced* [c]10 Or *guilt* [d]17 Hebrew *Sheol*

in your dwelling you keep them safe
from accusing tongues.
21 Praise be to the LORD,
for he showed his wonderful love to me
when I was in a besieged city.
22 In my alarm I said,
"I am cut off from your sight!"
Yet you heard my cry for mercy
when I called to you for help.

23 Love the LORD, all his saints!
The LORD preserves the faithful,
but the proud he pays back in full.
24 Be strong and take heart,
all you who hope in the LORD.

Psalm 32

Of David. A *maskil.*[a]

1 Blessed is he
whose transgressions are forgiven,
whose sins are covered.
2 Blessed is the man
whose sin the LORD does not count against him
and in whose spirit is no deceit.

3 When I kept silent,
my bones wasted away
through my groaning all day long.
4 For day and night
your hand was heavy upon me;
my strength was sapped
as in the heat of summer. *Selah*
5 Then I acknowledged my sin to you
and did not cover up my iniquity.
I said, "I will confess
my transgressions to the LORD"—
and you forgave
the guilt of my sin. *Selah*

6 Therefore let everyone who is godly pray to you
while you may be found;
surely when the mighty waters rise,
they will not reach him.
7 You are my hiding place;
you will protect me from trouble
and surround me with songs of deliverance. *Selah*

8 I will instruct you and teach you in the way you should go;
I will counsel you and watch over you.
9 Do not be like the horse or the mule,
which have no understanding
but must be controlled by bit and bridle
or they will not come to you.
10 Many are the woes of the wicked,
but the LORD's unfailing love
surrounds the man who trusts in him.

11 Rejoice in the LORD and be glad, you righteous;
sing, all you who are upright in heart!

Psalm 33

1 Sing joyfully to the LORD, you righteous;
it is fitting for the upright to praise him.
2 Praise the LORD with the harp;
make music to him on the ten-stringed lyre.
3 Sing to him a new song;
play skillfully, and shout for joy.

4 For the word of the LORD is right and true;
he is faithful in all he does.
5 The LORD loves righteousness and justice;
the earth is full of his unfailing love.

6 By the word of the LORD were the heavens made,
their starry host by the breath of his mouth.
7 He gathers the waters of the sea into jars[b];
he puts the deep into storehouses.
8 Let all the earth fear the LORD;
let all the people of the world revere him.
9 For he spoke, and it came to be;
he commanded, and it stood firm.
10 The LORD foils the plans of the nations;
he thwarts the purposes of the peoples.
11 But the plans of the LORD stand firm forever,
the purposes of his heart through all generations.

12 Blessed is the nation whose God is the LORD,
the people he chose for his inheritance.

[a] Title: Probably a literary or musical term [b] 7 Or *sea as into a heap*

13From heaven the LORD looks down
and sees all mankind;
14from his dwelling place he watches
all who live on earth—
15he who forms the hearts of all,
who considers everything they do.
16No king is saved by the size of his
army;
no warrior escapes by his great
strength.
17A horse is a vain hope for deliverance;
despite all its great strength it
cannot save.
18But the eyes of the LORD are on those
who fear him,
on those whose hope is in his
unfailing love,
19to deliver them from death
and keep them alive in famine.

20We wait in hope for the LORD;
he is our help and our shield.
21In him our hearts rejoice,
for we trust in his holy name.
22May your unfailing love rest upon us,
O LORD,
even as we put our hope in you.

Psalm 34[a]

Of David. When he pretended to be insane before Abimelech, who drove him away, and he left.

1I will extol the LORD at all times;
his praise will always be on my lips.
2My soul will boast in the LORD;
let the afflicted hear and rejoice.
3Glorify the LORD with me;
let us exalt his name together.

4I sought the LORD, and he answered
me;
he delivered me from all my fears.
5Those who look to him are radiant;
their faces are never covered with
shame.
6This poor man called, and the LORD
heard him;
he saved him out of all his troubles.
7The angel of the LORD encamps
around those who fear him,
and he delivers them.

8Taste and see that the LORD is good;
blessed is the man who takes refuge
in him.
9Fear the LORD, you his saints,
for those who fear him lack
nothing.
10The lions may grow weak and hungry,
but those who seek the LORD lack
no good thing.

11Come, my children, listen to me;
I will teach you the fear of the
LORD.
12Whoever of you loves life
and desires to see many good days,
13keep your tongue from evil
and your lips from speaking lies.
14Turn from evil and do good;
seek peace and pursue it.

15The eyes of the LORD are on the
righteous
and his ears are attentive to their
cry;
16the face of the LORD is against those
who do evil,
to cut off the memory of them from
the earth.

17The righteous cry out, and the LORD
hears them;
he delivers them from all their
troubles.
18The LORD is close to the
brokenhearted
and saves those who are crushed in
spirit.

19A righteous man may have many
troubles,
but the LORD delivers him from
them all;
20he protects all his bones,
not one of them will be broken.

21Evil will slay the wicked;
the foes of the righteous will be
condemned.
22The LORD redeems his servants;
no one will be condemned who
takes refuge in him.

Psalm 35

Of David.

1Contend, O LORD, with those who
contend with me;
fight against those who fight against
me.
2Take up shield and buckler;
arise and come to my aid.
3Brandish spear and javelin[b]

[a]This psalm is an acrostic poem, the verses of which begin with the successive letters of the Hebrew alphabet. [b]3 Or *and block the way*

against those who pursue me.
Say to my soul,
"I am your salvation."

4May those who seek my life
be disgraced and put to shame;
may those who plot my ruin
be turned back in dismay.
5May they be like chaff before the wind,
with the angel of the LORD driving them away;
6may their path be dark and slippery,
with the angel of the LORD pursuing them.
7Since they hid their net for me without cause
and without cause dug a pit for me,
8may ruin overtake them by surprise—
may the net they hid entangle them,
may they fall into the pit, to their ruin.
9Then my soul will rejoice in the LORD
and delight in his salvation.
10My whole being will exclaim,
"Who is like you, O LORD?
You rescue the poor from those too strong for them,
the poor and needy from those who rob them."

11Ruthless witnesses come forward;
they question me on things I know nothing about.
12They repay me evil for good
and leave my soul forlorn.
13Yet when they were ill, I put on sackcloth
and humbled myself with fasting.
When my prayers returned to me unanswered,
14 I went about mourning
as though for my friend or brother.
I bowed my head in grief
as though weeping for my mother.
15But when I stumbled, they gathered in glee;
attackers gathered against me when I was unaware.
They slandered me without ceasing.
16Like the ungodly they maliciously mocked[a];
they gnashed their teeth at me.
17O Lord, how long will you look on?
Rescue my life from their ravages,
my precious life from these lions.
18I will give you thanks in the great assembly;
among throngs of people I will praise you.
19Let not those gloat over me
who are my enemies without cause;
let not those who hate me without reason
maliciously wink the eye.
20They do not speak peaceably,
but devise false accusations
against those who live quietly in the land.
21They gape at me and say, "Aha! Aha!
With our own eyes we have seen it."
22O LORD, you have seen this; be not silent.
Do not be far from me, O Lord.
23Awake, and rise to my defense!
Contend for me, my God and Lord.
24Vindicate me in your righteousness,
O LORD my God;
do not let them gloat over me.
25Do not let them think, "Aha, just what we wanted!"
or say, "We have swallowed him up."

26May all who gloat over my distress
be put to shame and confusion;
may all who exalt themselves over me
be clothed with shame and disgrace.
27May those who delight in my vindication
shout for joy and gladness;
may they always say, "The LORD be exalted,
who delights in the well-being of his servant."
28My tongue will speak of your righteousness
and of your praises all day long.

Psalm 36

For the director of music. Of David the servant of the LORD.

1An oracle is within my heart
concerning the sinfulness of the wicked:[b]
There is no fear of God
before his eyes.
2For in his own eyes he flatters himself
too much to detect or hate his sin.

[a] 16 Septuagint; Hebrew may mean *ungodly circle of mockers.*
[b] 1 Or *heart: / Sin proceeds from the wicked.*

3The words of his mouth are wicked
and deceitful;
he has ceased to be wise and to do
good.
4Even on his bed he plots evil;
he commits himself to a sinful
course
and does not reject what is wrong.

5Your love, O LORD, reaches to the
heavens,
your faithfulness to the skies.
6Your righteousness is like the mighty
mountains,
your justice like the great deep.
O LORD, you preserve both man and
beast.
7 How priceless is your unfailing
love!
Both high and low among men
find[a] refuge in the shadow of your
wings.
8They feast on the abundance of your
house;
you give them drink from your river
of delights.
9For with you is the fountain of life;
in your light we see light.

10Continue your love to those who
know you,
your righteousness to the upright in
heart.
11May the foot of the proud not come
against me,
nor the hand of the wicked drive
me away.
12See how the evildoers lie fallen—
thrown down, not able to rise!

Psalm 37[b]

Of David.

1Do not fret because of evil men
or be envious of those who do
wrong;
2for like the grass they will soon
wither,
like green plants they will soon die
away.

3Trust in the LORD and do good;
dwell in the land and enjoy safe
pasture.
4Delight yourself in the LORD
and he will give you the desires of
your heart.

5Commit your way to the LORD;
trust in him and he will do this:
6He will make your righteousness shine
like the dawn,
the justice of your cause like the
noonday sun.

7Be still before the LORD and wait
patiently for him;
do not fret when men succeed in
their ways,
when they carry out their wicked
schemes.

8Refrain from anger and turn from
wrath;
do not fret—it leads only to evil.
9For evil men will be cut off,
but those who hope in the LORD will
inherit the land.

10A little while, and the wicked will be
no more;
though you look for them, they will
not be found.
11But the meek will inherit the land
and enjoy great peace.

12The wicked plot against the righteous
and gnash their teeth at them;
13but the Lord laughs at the wicked,
for he knows their day is coming.

14The wicked draw the sword
and bend the bow
to bring down the poor and needy,
to slay those whose ways are
upright.
15But their swords will pierce their own
hearts,
and their bows will be broken.

16Better the little that the righteous have
than the wealth of many wicked;
17for the power of the wicked will be
broken,
but the LORD upholds the righteous.

18The days of the blameless are known
to the LORD,
and their inheritance will endure
forever.
19In times of disaster they will not
wither;
in days of famine they will enjoy
plenty.

20But the wicked will perish:
The LORD's enemies will be like the
beauty of the fields,

[a]7 Or *love, O God! / Men find*; or *love! / Both heavenly beings and men / find* [b]This psalm is an acrostic poem, the stanzas of which begin with the successive letters of the Hebrew alphabet.

they will vanish—vanish like
smoke.
21The wicked borrow and do not repay,
but the righteous give generously;
22those the LORD blesses will inherit the
land,
but those he curses will be cut off.

23If the LORD delights in a man's way,
he makes his steps firm;
24though he stumble, he will not fall,
for the LORD upholds him with his
hand.

25I was young and now I am old,
yet I have never seen the righteous
forsaken
or their children begging bread.
26They are always generous and lend
freely;
their children will be blessed.

27Turn from evil and do good;
then you will dwell in the land
forever.
28For the LORD loves the just
and will not forsake his faithful
ones.

They will be protected forever,
but the offspring of the wicked will
be cut off;
29the righteous will inherit the land
and dwell in it forever.

30The mouth of the righteous man
utters wisdom,
and his tongue speaks what is just.
31The law of his God is in his heart;
his feet do not slip.

32The wicked lie in wait for the
righteous,
seeking their very lives;
33but the LORD will not leave them in
their power
or let them be condemned when
brought to trial.

34Wait for the LORD
and keep his way.
He will exalt you to inherit the land;
when the wicked are cut off, you
will see it.

35I have seen a wicked and ruthless
man
flourishing like a green tree in its
native soil,
36but he soon passed away and was no
more;
though I looked for him, he could
not be found.

37Consider the blameless, observe the
upright;
there is a future[a] for the man of
peace.
38But all sinners will be destroyed;
the future[b] of the wicked will be
cut off.

39The salvation of the righteous comes
from the LORD;
he is their stronghold in time of
trouble.
40The LORD helps them and delivers
them;
he delivers them from the wicked
and saves them,
because they take refuge in him.

Psalm 38

A psalm of David. A petition.

1O LORD, do not rebuke me in your
anger
or discipline me in your wrath.
2For your arrows have pierced me,
and your hand has come down
upon me.
3Because of your wrath there is no
health in my body;
my bones have no soundness
because of my sin.
4My guilt has overwhelmed me
like a burden too heavy to bear.
5My wounds fester and are loathsome
because of my sinful folly.
6I am bowed down and brought very
low;
all day long I go about mourning.
7My back is filled with searing pain;
there is no health in my body.
8I am feeble and utterly crushed;
I groan in anguish of heart.

9All my longings lie open before you,
O Lord;
my sighing is not hidden from you.
10My heart pounds, my strength fails
me;
even the light has gone from my
eyes.
11My friends and companions avoid me
because of my wounds;

[a]37 Or *there will be posterity* [b]38 Or *posterity*

my neighbors stay far away.
12Those who seek my life set their traps,
those who would harm me talk of my ruin;
all day long they plot deception.

13I am like a deaf man, who cannot hear,
like a mute, who cannot open his mouth;
14I have become like a man who does not hear,
whose mouth can offer no reply.
15I wait for you, O LORD;
you will answer, O Lord my God.
16For I said, "Do not let them gloat
or exalt themselves over me when my foot slips."

17For I am about to fall,
and my pain is ever with me.
18I confess my iniquity;
I am troubled by my sin.
19Many are those who are my vigorous enemies;
those who hate me without reason are numerous.
20Those who repay my good with evil
slander me when I pursue what is good.

21O LORD, do not forsake me;
be not far from me, O my God.
22Come quickly to help me,
O Lord my Savior.

Psalm 39

For the director of music. For Jeduthun. A psalm of David.

1I said, "I will watch my ways
and keep my tongue from sin;
I will put a muzzle on my mouth
as long as the wicked are in my presence."
2But when I was silent and still,
not even saying anything good,
my anguish increased.
3My heart grew hot within me,
and as I meditated, the fire burned;
then I spoke with my tongue:

4"Show me, O LORD, my life's end
and the number of my days;
let me know how fleeting is my life.
5You have made my days a mere handbreadth;
the span of my years is as nothing before you.
Each man's life is but a breath. *Selah*

6Man is a mere phantom as he goes to and fro:
He bustles about, but only in vain;
he heaps up wealth, not knowing who will get it.

7"But now, Lord, what do I look for?
My hope is in you.
8Save me from all my transgressions;
do not make me the scorn of fools.
9I was silent; I would not open my mouth,
for you are the one who has done this.
10Remove your scourge from me;
I am overcome by the blow of your hand.
11You rebuke and discipline men for their sin;
you consume their wealth like a moth—
each man is but a breath. *Selah*

12"Hear my prayer, O LORD,
listen to my cry for help;
be not deaf to my weeping.
For I dwell with you as an alien,
a stranger, as all my fathers were.
13Look away from me, that I may rejoice again
before I depart and am no more."

Psalm 40

For the director of music. Of David. A psalm.

1I waited patiently for the LORD;
he turned to me and heard my cry.
2He lifted me out of the slimy pit,
out of the mud and mire;
he set my feet on a rock
and gave me a firm place to stand.
3He put a new song in my mouth,
a hymn of praise to our God.
Many will see and fear
and put their trust in the LORD.

4Blessed is the man
who makes the LORD his trust,
who does not look to the proud,
to those who turn aside to false gods.[a]
5Many, O LORD my God,
are the wonders you have done.

[a]4 Or *to falsehood*

The things you planned for us
no one can recount to you;
were I to speak and tell of them,
they would be too many to declare.

6Sacrifice and offering you did not
desire,
but my ears you have pierced[a,b];
burnt offerings and sin offerings
you did not require.
7Then I said, "Here I am, I have
come—
it is written about me in the
scroll.[c]
8I desire to do your will, O my God;
your law is within my heart."

[a]6 Hebrew; Septuagint *but a body you have prepared for me* (see also Symmachus and Theodotion)
[b]6 Or *opened* [c]7 Or *come / with the scroll written for me*

VERSE FOR THE DAY: Psalm 40:3 | AUTHOR: Max Lucado | PASSAGE FOR THE DAY: Psalm 40:1–8

A New Song

There's a cascading effect to God's grace: As we grow in understanding its power in our lives, we can turn around and give it to others. My wife, Denalyn, is a true gift of grace—one I never expected and certainly didn't deserve.

I met Denalyn while we were in college. She was a sincere, godly woman, and I never dreamed she'd be interested in a guy like me. I didn't become a committed Christian until I was out of high school. In the years preceding that commitment, I had relationships with women that were out of control physically. When God got hold of me, I repented of my sin. But I had so much remorse that I grew accustomed to the idea that I would live out my life as a single man.

God brought Denalyn and me together anyway. And in spite of my past, she saw me as a new creation and extended grace to me. I was overwhelmed by God's goodness, which was shown through the love and acceptance of this woman. In fact, the thought that he would entrust me with such a treasure as Denalyn still astounds me. I feel like a pauper who got to marry a princess.

MARRIAGE BUILDERS

- *How does your spouse show God's grace to you?*
- *If you were on the outside looking in, do you think you'd see "grace" in your marriage?*

Additional Scripture Readings
Romans 5:6–11; 1 Peter 1:3–9

Go to page 574 for your next devotional reading.

9I proclaim righteousness in the great assembly;
I do not seal my lips,
as you know, O LORD.
10I do not hide your righteousness in my heart;
I speak of your faithfulness and salvation.
I do not conceal your love and your truth
from the great assembly.

11Do not withhold your mercy from me, O LORD;
may your love and your truth always protect me.
12For troubles without number surround me;
my sins have overtaken me, and I cannot see.
They are more than the hairs of my head,
and my heart fails within me.

13Be pleased, O LORD, to save me;
O LORD, come quickly to help me.
14May all who seek to take my life
be put to shame and confusion;
may all who desire my ruin
be turned back in disgrace.
15May those who say to me, "Aha! Aha!"
be appalled at their own shame.
16But may all who seek you
rejoice and be glad in you;
may those who love your salvation always say,
"The LORD be exalted!"

17Yet I am poor and needy;
may the Lord think of me.
You are my help and my deliverer;
O my God, do not delay.

Psalm 41

For the director of music. A psalm of David.

1Blessed is he who has regard for the weak;
the LORD delivers him in times of trouble.
2The LORD will protect him and preserve his life;
he will bless him in the land
and not surrender him to the desire of his foes.
3The LORD will sustain him on his sickbed
and restore him from his bed of illness.

4I said, "O LORD, have mercy on me;
heal me, for I have sinned against you."
5My enemies say of me in malice,
"When will he die and his name perish?"
6Whenever one comes to see me,
he speaks falsely, while his heart gathers slander;
then he goes out and spreads it abroad.

7All my enemies whisper together against me;
they imagine the worst for me, saying,
8"A vile disease has beset him;
he will never get up from the place where he lies."
9Even my close friend, whom I trusted,
he who shared my bread,
has lifted up his heel against me.

10But you, O LORD, have mercy on me;
raise me up, that I may repay them.
11I know that you are pleased with me,
for my enemy does not triumph over me.
12In my integrity you uphold me
and set me in your presence forever.

13Praise be to the LORD, the God of Israel,
from everlasting to everlasting.
Amen and Amen.

BOOK II

Psalms 42–72

Psalm 42[a]

For the director of music. A *maskil*[b] of the Sons of Korah.

1As the deer pants for streams of water,
so my soul pants for you, O God.
2My soul thirsts for God, for the living God.
When can I go and meet with God?
3My tears have been my food

[a]In many Hebrew manuscripts Psalms 42 and 43 constitute one psalm. [b]Title: Probably a literary or musical term

day and night,
while men say to me all day long,
"Where is your God?"
4 These things I remember
as I pour out my soul:
how I used to go with the multitude,
leading the procession to the house of God,
with shouts of joy and thanksgiving
among the festive throng.

5 Why are you downcast, O my soul?
Why so disturbed within me?
Put your hope in God,
for I will yet praise him,
my Savior and 6 my God.

My[a] soul is downcast within me;
therefore I will remember you
from the land of the Jordan,
the heights of Hermon—from Mount Mizar.
7 Deep calls to deep
in the roar of your waterfalls;
all your waves and breakers
have swept over me.

8 By day the LORD directs his love,
at night his song is with me—
a prayer to the God of my life.

9 I say to God my Rock,
"Why have you forgotten me?
Why must I go about mourning,
oppressed by the enemy?"
10 My bones suffer mortal agony
as my foes taunt me,
saying to me all day long,
"Where is your God?"

11 Why are you downcast, O my soul?
Why so disturbed within me?
Put your hope in God,
for I will yet praise him,
my Savior and my God.

Psalm 43[b]

1 Vindicate me, O God,
and plead my cause against an ungodly nation;
rescue me from deceitful and wicked men.
2 You are God my stronghold.
Why have you rejected me?
Why must I go about mourning,
oppressed by the enemy?
3 Send forth your light and your truth,
let them guide me;
let them bring me to your holy mountain,
to the place where you dwell.
4 Then will I go to the altar of God,
to God, my joy and my delight.
I will praise you with the harp,
O God, my God.

5 Why are you downcast, O my soul?
Why so disturbed within me?
Put your hope in God,
for I will yet praise him,
my Savior and my God.

Psalm 44

For the director of music. Of the Sons of Korah. A *maskil.*[c]

1 We have heard with our ears, O God;
our fathers have told us
what you did in their days,
in days long ago.
2 With your hand you drove out the nations
and planted our fathers;
you crushed the peoples
and made our fathers flourish.
3 It was not by their sword that they won the land,
nor did their arm bring them victory;
it was your right hand, your arm,
and the light of your face, for you loved them.

4 You are my King and my God,
who decrees[d] victories for Jacob.
5 Through you we push back our enemies;
through your name we trample our foes.
6 I do not trust in my bow,
my sword does not bring me victory;
7 but you give us victory over our enemies,
you put our adversaries to shame.
8 In God we make our boast all day long,
and we will praise your name forever. *Selah*

[a] *5,6* A few Hebrew manuscripts, Septuagint and Syriac; most Hebrew manuscripts *praise him for his saving help.* / [6] *O my God, my* [b] In many Hebrew manuscripts Psalms 42 and 43 constitute one psalm.
[c] Title: Probably a literary or musical term [d] *4* Septuagint, Aquila and Syriac; Hebrew *King, O God;* / *command*

WEEKENDING

GOALS

The longer you're married, the easier it is for goal-setting to take a back seat. But you can develop a stronger sense of shared purpose in marriage by setting goals for the year ahead. Use these questions to explore ways you could improve your marriage in the coming months.

1. Are you content with the depth and effectiveness of your marital communication? If not, what needs to be changed?

2. Are you satisfied with the way you resolve disagreements?

3. Do you feel you spend enough time together when no one else is around, and are you satisfied with how you use that time?

4. Are you satisfied with the frequency and quality of your physical intimacy?

Set aside an evening six months from now to review together how you're doing on reaching your goals. Use that time to evaluate and reshape your goals, as needed.

— *The* Marriage Partnership *Staff*

REVIVE

Saturday: Jeremiah 29:11–14
Sunday: Hebrews 11:1–16

Go to page 577 for your next devotional reading.

9But now you have rejected and
humbled us;
you no longer go out with our
armies.
10You made us retreat before the
enemy,
and our adversaries have plundered
us.
11You gave us up to be devoured like
sheep
and have scattered us among the
nations.
12You sold your people for a pittance,
gaining nothing from their sale.

13You have made us a reproach to our
neighbors,
the scorn and derision of those
around us.
14You have made us a byword among
the nations;
the peoples shake their heads at us.
15My disgrace is before me all day long,
and my face is covered with shame
16at the taunts of those who reproach
and revile me,
because of the enemy, who is bent
on revenge.

17All this happened to us,
though we had not forgotten you
or been false to your covenant.
18Our hearts had not turned back;
our feet had not strayed from your
path.
19But you crushed us and made us a
haunt for jackals
and covered us over with deep
darkness.

20If we had forgotten the name of our
God
or spread out our hands to a foreign
god,
21would not God have discovered it,
since he knows the secrets of the
heart?
22Yet for your sake we face death all
day long;
we are considered as sheep to be
slaughtered.

23Awake, O Lord! Why do you sleep?
Rouse yourself! Do not reject us
forever.
24Why do you hide your face
and forget our misery and
oppression?
25We are brought down to the dust;
our bodies cling to the ground.
26Rise up and help us;
redeem us because of your unfailing
love.

Psalm 45

For the director of music. To ¡the tune
of¡ "Lilies." Of the Sons of Korah. A
maskil.[a] A wedding song.

1My heart is stirred by a noble theme
as I recite my verses for the king;
my tongue is the pen of a skillful
writer.

2You are the most excellent of men
and your lips have been anointed
with grace,
since God has blessed you forever.
3Gird your sword upon your side,
O mighty one;
clothe yourself with splendor and
majesty.
4In your majesty ride forth victoriously
in behalf of truth, humility and
righteousness;
let your right hand display awesome
deeds.
5Let your sharp arrows pierce the
hearts of the king's enemies;
let the nations fall beneath your
feet.
6Your throne, O God, will last for ever
and ever;
a scepter of justice will be the
scepter of your kingdom.
7You love righteousness and hate
wickedness;
therefore God, your God, has set
you above your companions
by anointing you with the oil of joy.
8All your robes are fragrant with myrrh
and aloes and cassia;
from palaces adorned with ivory
the music of the strings makes you
glad.
9Daughters of kings are among your
honored women;
at your right hand is the royal bride
in gold of Ophir.

10Listen, O daughter, consider and give
ear:
Forget your people and your father's
house.
11The king is enthralled by your beauty;

[a]Title: Probably a literary or musical term

honor him, for he is your lord.
12The Daughter of Tyre will come with a gift,[a]
men of wealth will seek your favor.

13All glorious is the princess within her chamber;
her gown is interwoven with gold.
14In embroidered garments she is led to the king;
her virgin companions follow her
and are brought to you.
15They are led in with joy and gladness;
they enter the palace of the king.

16Your sons will take the place of your fathers;
you will make them princes throughout the land.
17I will perpetuate your memory through all generations;
therefore the nations will praise you for ever and ever.

Psalm 46

For the director of music. Of the Sons of Korah. According to *alamoth.*[b] A song.

1God is our refuge and strength,
an ever-present help in trouble.
2Therefore we will not fear, though the earth give way
and the mountains fall into the heart of the sea,
3though its waters roar and foam
and the mountains quake with their surging. *Selah*

4There is a river whose streams make glad the city of God,
the holy place where the Most High dwells.
5God is within her, she will not fall;
God will help her at break of day.
6Nations are in uproar, kingdoms fall;
he lifts his voice, the earth melts.

7The LORD Almighty is with us;
the God of Jacob is our fortress. *Selah*

8Come and see the works of the LORD,
the desolations he has brought on the earth.
9He makes wars cease to the ends of the earth;
he breaks the bow and shatters the spear,
he burns the shields[c] with fire.
10"Be still, and know that I am God;
I will be exalted among the nations,
I will be exalted in the earth."

11The LORD Almighty is with us;
the God of Jacob is our fortress. *Selah*

Psalm 47

For the director of music. Of the Sons of Korah. A psalm.

1Clap your hands, all you nations;
shout to God with cries of joy.
2How awesome is the LORD Most High,
the great King over all the earth!
3He subdued nations under us,
peoples under our feet.
4He chose our inheritance for us,
the pride of Jacob, whom he loved. *Selah*

5God has ascended amid shouts of joy,
the LORD amid the sounding of trumpets.
6Sing praises to God, sing praises;
sing praises to our King, sing praises.

7For God is the King of all the earth;
sing to him a psalm[d] of praise.
8God reigns over the nations;
God is seated on his holy throne.
9The nobles of the nations assemble
as the people of the God of Abraham,
for the kings[e] of the earth belong to God;
he is greatly exalted.

Psalm 48

A song. A psalm of the Sons of Korah.

1Great is the LORD, and most worthy of praise,
in the city of our God, his holy mountain.
2It is beautiful in its loftiness,
the joy of the whole earth.
Like the utmost heights of Zaphon[f] is Mount Zion,
the[g] city of the Great King.

[a]12 Or *A Tyrian robe is among the gifts* [b]Title: Probably a musical term [c]9 Or *chariots* [d]7 Or *a maskil* (probably a literary or musical term) [e]9 Or *shields* [f]2 *Zaphon* can refer to a sacred mountain or the direction north. [g]2 Or *earth, / Mount Zion, on the northern side / of the*

[3]God is in her citadels;
he has shown himself to be her
fortress.

[4]When the kings joined forces,
when they advanced together,
[5]they saw ⌊her⌋ and were astounded;
they fled in terror.
[6]Trembling seized them there,
pain like that of a woman in labor.
[7]You destroyed them like ships of
Tarshish
shattered by an east wind.

[8]As we have heard,
so have we seen
in the city of the LORD Almighty,
in the city of our God:
God makes her secure forever. *Selah*

[9]Within your temple, O God,
we meditate on your unfailing
love.
[10]Like your name, O God,

VERSE FOR THE DAY: Psalm 46:10

AUTHOR: Gregg Lewis

PASSAGE FOR THE DAY: Psalm 46:1–11

Good Marriages Take Time

Some days I think men, especially, inherit a double dose of impatience. That could explain why so many of us despise shopping and mutter when the driver in front of us balks at turning right on red. More than once, my wife, Debi, has said: "Sometimes I just don't understand you at all!" Well, I haven't completely figured her out, either. After more than twenty years of marriage, there's so much more we need to learn about living and loving as husband and wife. And it takes time.

But why is that so exasperating? My guess is it's part of human nature. A congenital hurry-bone of contention inherited from Adam and Eve who started the whole business by eating an apple guaranteed to give them instant knowledge.

When we live by the false "faster is better" creed, we lose sight of the contrasting truth: Relationships take lots of time to develop and nurture. They demand long hours and years and even decades of work.

But when you stop to consider the alternative, it's clear that marriage is worth the time. Why hurry to divorce court when you can take your time and nurture a deep commitment for the rest of your life?

MARRIAGE BUILDERS

- *Have you ever felt that your marriage should be better faster?*
- *Why is it hard to be patient as relationships develop?*

Additional Scripture Readings
Genesis 3:1–19; Psalm 90:12;
James 1:2–5

Go to page 580 for your next devotional reading.

your praise reaches to the ends of
the earth;
your right hand is filled with
righteousness.
11Mount Zion rejoices,
the villages of Judah are glad
because of your judgments.

12Walk about Zion, go around her,
count her towers,
13consider well her ramparts,
view her citadels,
that you may tell of them to the
next generation.
14For this God is our God for ever and
ever;
he will be our guide even to the
end.

Psalm 49

For the director of music. Of the Sons of Korah. A psalm.

1Hear this, all you peoples;
listen, all who live in this world,
2both low and high,
rich and poor alike:
3My mouth will speak words of
wisdom;
the utterance from my heart will
give understanding.
4I will turn my ear to a proverb;
with the harp I will expound my
riddle:

5Why should I fear when evil days
come,
when wicked deceivers surround
me—
6those who trust in their wealth
and boast of their great riches?
7No man can redeem the life of
another
or give to God a ransom for him—
8the ransom for a life is costly,
no payment is ever enough—
9that he should live on forever
and not see decay.

10For all can see that wise men die;
the foolish and the senseless alike
perish
and leave their wealth to others.
11Their tombs will remain their
houses[a] forever,
their dwellings for endless
generations,
though they had[b] named lands
after themselves.

12But man, despite his riches, does not
endure;
he is[c] like the beasts that perish.

13This is the fate of those who trust in
themselves,
and of their followers, who approve
their sayings. *Selah*
14Like sheep they are destined for the
grave,[d]
and death will feed on them.
The upright will rule over them in the
morning;
their forms will decay in the
grave,[d]
far from their princely mansions.
15But God will redeem my life[e] from
the grave;
he will surely take me to himself.
Selah

16Do not be overawed when a man
grows rich,
when the splendor of his house
increases;
17for he will take nothing with him
when he dies,
his splendor will not descend with
him.
18Though while he lived he counted
himself blessed—
and men praise you when you
prosper—
19he will join the generation of his
fathers,
who will never see the light ⌊of life⌋.

20A man who has riches without
understanding
is like the beasts that perish.

Psalm 50

A psalm of Asaph.

1The Mighty One, God, the LORD,
speaks and summons the earth
from the rising of the sun to the
place where it sets.
2From Zion, perfect in beauty,
God shines forth.
3Our God comes and will not be silent;

[a] 11 Septuagint and Syriac; Hebrew *In their thoughts their houses will remain* [b] 11 Or / *for they have*
[c] 12 Hebrew; Septuagint and Syriac read verse 12 the same as verse 20. [d] 14 Hebrew *Sheol*; also in verse 15 [e] 15 Or *soul*

a fire devours before him,
and around him a tempest rages.
4He summons the heavens above,
and the earth, that he may judge his people:
5"Gather to me my consecrated ones,
who made a covenant with me by sacrifice."
6And the heavens proclaim his righteousness,
for God himself is judge. *Selah*

7"Hear, O my people, and I will speak,
O Israel, and I will testify against you:
I am God, your God.
8I do not rebuke you for your sacrifices
or your burnt offerings, which are ever before me.
9I have no need of a bull from your stall
or of goats from your pens,
10for every animal of the forest is mine,
and the cattle on a thousand hills.
11I know every bird in the mountains,
and the creatures of the field are mine.
12If I were hungry I would not tell you,
for the world is mine, and all that is in it.
13Do I eat the flesh of bulls
or drink the blood of goats?
14Sacrifice thank offerings to God,
fulfill your vows to the Most High,
15and call upon me in the day of trouble;
I will deliver you, and you will honor me."

16But to the wicked, God says:

"What right have you to recite my laws
or take my covenant on your lips?
17You hate my instruction
and cast my words behind you.
18When you see a thief, you join with him;
you throw in your lot with adulterers.
19You use your mouth for evil
and harness your tongue to deceit.
20You speak continually against your brother
and slander your own mother's son.
21These things you have done and I kept silent;
you thought I was altogether[a] like you.
But I will rebuke you
and accuse you to your face.

22"Consider this, you who forget God,
or I will tear you to pieces, with none to rescue:
23He who sacrifices thank offerings honors me,
and he prepares the way
so that I may show him[b] the salvation of God."

Psalm 51

For the director of music. A psalm of David. When the prophet Nathan came to him after David had committed adultery with Bathsheba.

1Have mercy on me, O God,
according to your unfailing love;
according to your great compassion
blot out my transgressions.
2Wash away all my iniquity
and cleanse me from my sin.

3For I know my transgressions,
and my sin is always before me.
4Against you, you only, have I sinned
and done what is evil in your sight,
so that you are proved right when you speak
and justified when you judge.
5Surely I was sinful at birth,
sinful from the time my mother conceived me.
6Surely you desire truth in the inner parts[c];
you teach[d] me wisdom in the inmost place.

7Cleanse me with hyssop, and I will be clean;
wash me, and I will be whiter than snow.
8Let me hear joy and gladness;
let the bones you have crushed rejoice.
9Hide your face from my sins
and blot out all my iniquity.

10Create in me a pure heart, O God,
and renew a steadfast spirit within me.
11Do not cast me from your presence
or take your Holy Spirit from me.

[a]21 Or *thought the 'I AM' was* [b]23 Or *and to him who considers his way / I will show* [c]6 The meaning of the Hebrew for this phrase is uncertain. [d]6 Or *you desired . . . ; / you taught*

VERSE FOR THE DAY: Psalm 51:12

AUTHOR: Elizabeth Cody Newenhuyse

PASSAGE FOR THE DAY: Psalm 51:1–17

Fighting Fatigue

Constant fatigue and busyness can sap our joy in the Lord. It imperils everyone, including the Christian who gets so busy and carries so many responsibilities that he or she barely has time to sleep. Life begins to feel flat, marriage seems stale. We can even wonder if God really cares about the burdens we bear.

Recently I was looking up some Psalms. And as so often happens, the Word not only spoke, but shouted at me! What struck me with special force was David's longing for deliverance from his constant fatigue. Here are his words:

"I am feeble and utterly crushed; I groan in anguish of heart" (Psalm 38:8).

"Save me, O God, for the waters have come up to my neck. I sink in the miry depths, where there is no foothold" (Psalm 69:1–2).

These are the cries of a tired and defeated man searching for his God. Who *wouldn't* feel exhausted? Yet Psalm 69 continues:

"You who seek God, may your hearts live! The LORD hears the needy and does not despise his captive people" (Psalm 69:32–33).

This is the great "even though" of the Psalms: Even though I am weary and discouraged, yet I will praise you! David spoke to the Lord in terms both personal and reverent, intimate and majestic.

And like David, we also can, through continuous awareness of God's presence, pray very specifically: "Give me energy for this task, Lord."

MARRIAGE BUILDERS

♦ *When has constant busyness sapped your joy as a Christian? How did you respond?*

♦ *What activities refresh you rather than fatigue you?*

Additional Scripture Readings
Hosea 6:1–3; Psalm 69:1–33

Go to page 583 for your next devotional reading.

12Restore to me the joy of your salvation
and grant me a willing spirit, to sustain me.
13Then I will teach transgressors your ways,
and sinners will turn back to you.
14Save me from bloodguilt, O God,
the God who saves me,
and my tongue will sing of your righteousness.
15O Lord, open my lips,
and my mouth will declare your praise.
16You do not delight in sacrifice, or I would bring it;
you do not take pleasure in burnt offerings.
17The sacrifices of God are[a] a broken spirit;
a broken and contrite heart,
O God, you will not despise.
18In your good pleasure make Zion prosper;
build up the walls of Jerusalem.
19Then there will be righteous sacrifices,
whole burnt offerings to delight you;
then bulls will be offered on your altar.

Psalm 52

For the director of music. A *maskil*[b] of David. When Doeg the Edomite had gone to Saul and told him: "David has gone to the house of Ahimelech."

1Why do you boast of evil, you mighty man?
Why do you boast all day long,
you who are a disgrace in the eyes of God?
2Your tongue plots destruction;
it is like a sharpened razor,
you who practice deceit.
3You love evil rather than good,
falsehood rather than speaking the truth. *Selah*
4You love every harmful word,
O you deceitful tongue!
5Surely God will bring you down to everlasting ruin:
He will snatch you up and tear you from your tent;
he will uproot you from the land of the living. *Selah*
6The righteous will see and fear;
they will laugh at him, saying,
7"Here now is the man
who did not make God his stronghold
but trusted in his great wealth
and grew strong by destroying others!"
8But I am like an olive tree
flourishing in the house of God;
I trust in God's unfailing love
for ever and ever.
9I will praise you forever for what you have done;
in your name I will hope, for your name is good.
I will praise you in the presence of your saints.

Psalm 53

For the director of music. According to *mahalath*.[c] A *maskil*[b] of David.

1The fool says in his heart,
"There is no God."
They are corrupt, and their ways are vile;
there is no one who does good.
2God looks down from heaven
on the sons of men
to see if there are any who understand,
any who seek God.
3Everyone has turned away,
they have together become corrupt;
there is no one who does good,
not even one.
4Will the evildoers never learn—
those who devour my people as men eat bread
and who do not call on God?
5There they were, overwhelmed with dread,
where there was nothing to dread.
God scattered the bones of those who attacked you;
you put them to shame, for God despised them.
6Oh, that salvation for Israel would come out of Zion!

[a]17 Or *My sacrifice, O God, is*
[b]Title: Probably a literary or musical term
[c]Title: Probably a musical term

When God restores the fortunes of
his people,
let Jacob rejoice and Israel be glad!

Psalm 54

For the director of music. With stringed instruments. A *maskil*[a] of David. When the Ziphites had gone to Saul and said, "Is not David hiding among us?"

1Save me, O God, by your name;
vindicate me by your might.
2Hear my prayer, O God;
listen to the words of my mouth.

3Strangers are attacking me;
ruthless men seek my life—
men without regard for God. *Selah*

4Surely God is my help;
the Lord is the one who sustains
me.

5Let evil recoil on those who slander
me;
in your faithfulness destroy them.

6I will sacrifice a freewill offering to
you;
I will praise your name, O LORD,
for it is good.
7For he has delivered me from all my
troubles,
and my eyes have looked in
triumph on my foes.

Psalm 55

For the director of music. With stringed instruments. A *maskil*[a] of David.

1Listen to my prayer, O God,
do not ignore my plea;
2 hear me and answer me.
My thoughts trouble me and I am
distraught
3 at the voice of the enemy,
at the stares of the wicked;
for they bring down suffering upon
me
and revile me in their anger.

4My heart is in anguish within me;
the terrors of death assail me.
5Fear and trembling have beset me;
horror has overwhelmed me.
6I said, "Oh, that I had the wings of a
dove!
I would fly away and be at rest—
7I would flee far away
and stay in the desert; *Selah*
8I would hurry to my place of shelter,
far from the tempest and storm."

9Confuse the wicked, O Lord, confound
their speech,
for I see violence and strife in the
city.
10Day and night they prowl about on its
walls;
malice and abuse are within it.
11Destructive forces are at work in the
city;
threats and lies never leave its
streets.

12If an enemy were insulting me,
I could endure it;
if a foe were raising himself against
me,
I could hide from him.
13But it is you, a man like myself,
my companion, my close friend,
14with whom I once enjoyed sweet
fellowship
as we walked with the throng at the
house of God.

15Let death take my enemies by
surprise;
let them go down alive to the
grave,[b]
for evil finds lodging among them.

16But I call to God,
and the LORD saves me.
17Evening, morning and noon
I cry out in distress,
and he hears my voice.
18He ransoms me unharmed
from the battle waged against me,
even though many oppose me.
19God, who is enthroned forever,
will hear them and afflict them—
Selah
men who never change their ways
and have no fear of God.

20My companion attacks his friends;
he violates his covenant.
21His speech is smooth as butter,
yet war is in his heart;
his words are more soothing than oil,
yet they are drawn swords.

22Cast your cares on the LORD
and he will sustain you;

[a]Title: Probably a literary or musical term [b]15 Hebrew *Sheol*

he will never let the righteous fall.
23 But you, O God, will bring down the wicked
into the pit of corruption;
bloodthirsty and deceitful men
will not live out half their days.

But as for me, I trust in you.

[a] Title: Probably a literary or musical term

Psalm 56

For the director of music. To the tune of "A Dove on Distant Oaks." Of David. A *miktam.*[a] When the Philistines had seized him in Gath.

1 Be merciful to me, O God, for men
hotly pursue me;

VERSE FOR THE DAY: Psalm 55:6, 8

AUTHOR: Lyn Cryderman

PASSAGE FOR THE DAY: Psalm 55:4–8

Escape from Togetherness

Solitude is an indispensable aspect of a healthy marriage. An hour alone in a library or a leisurely walk can provide needed time to reflect, time to dream, even time to grow spiritually.

But there are valid reasons why it's not that easy. For one thing, the very nature of marriage is togetherness. Esther and I got married because, among other things, we didn't want to spend the rest of our lives alone. And it is sometimes difficult to balance this yearning to experience life together with that basic need for solitude.

However, good marriages don't restrict you from continuing to grow. And often that growth requires time away from each other. Ethicist Lewis B. Smedes has written of the need for couples to allow each other to be who they are—to trust each other enough to let go. That's what we do when we protect each other's private moments. We relinquish control in favor of allowing our loved one to retain those characteristics that attracted us in the first place.

Maybe it's time for spouses to admit they harbor a strong desire to just get away occasionally. Maybe it's time to kindly say those three little words: "Leave me alone!"

MARRIAGE BUILDERS

♦ *What is the best balance for you for time together and time apart?*

♦ *What are two times this week when you can offer your spouse the gift of solitude?*

Additional Scripture Readings
Mark 1:35–42; Matthew 14:23; Luke 5:16

Go to page 587 for your next devotional reading.

all day long they press their attack.
2My slanderers pursue me all day long;
many are attacking me in their pride.
3When I am afraid,
I will trust in you.
4In God, whose word I praise,
in God I trust; I will not be afraid.
What can mortal man do to me?

5All day long they twist my words;
they are always plotting to harm me.
6They conspire, they lurk,
they watch my steps,
eager to take my life.

7On no account let them escape;
in your anger, O God, bring down the nations.
8Record my lament;
list my tears on your scroll[a]—
are they not in your record?

9Then my enemies will turn back
when I call for help.
By this I will know that God is for me.
10In God, whose word I praise,
in the LORD, whose word I praise—
11in God I trust; I will not be afraid.
What can man do to me?

12I am under vows to you, O God;
I will present my thank offerings to you.
13For you have delivered me[b] from death
and my feet from stumbling,
that I may walk before God
in the light of life.[c]

Psalm 57

For the director of music. ⌊To the tune of⌋ "Do Not Destroy." Of David. A *miktam.*[d] When he had fled from Saul into the cave.

1Have mercy on me, O God, have mercy on me,
for in you my soul takes refuge.
I will take refuge in the shadow of your wings
until the disaster has passed.
2I cry out to God Most High,
to God, who fulfills ⌊his purpose⌋ for me.
3He sends from heaven and saves me,
rebuking those who hotly pursue me; *Selah*
God sends his love and his faithfulness.

4I am in the midst of lions;
I lie among ravenous beasts—
men whose teeth are spears and arrows,
whose tongues are sharp swords.

5Be exalted, O God, above the heavens;
let your glory be over all the earth.

6They spread a net for my feet—
I was bowed down in distress.
They dug a pit in my path—
but they have fallen into it themselves. *Selah*

7My heart is steadfast, O God,
my heart is steadfast;
I will sing and make music.
8Awake, my soul!
Awake, harp and lyre!
I will awaken the dawn.

9I will praise you, O Lord, among the nations;
I will sing of you among the peoples.
10For great is your love, reaching to the heavens;
your faithfulness reaches to the skies.

11Be exalted, O God, above the heavens;
let your glory be over all the earth.

Psalm 58

For the director of music. ⌊To the tune of⌋ "Do Not Destroy." Of David. A *miktam.*[d]

1Do you rulers indeed speak justly?
Do you judge uprightly among men?
2No, in your heart you devise injustice,
and your hands mete out violence on the earth.
3Even from birth the wicked go astray;
from the womb they are wayward and speak lies.

[a]8 Or / *put my tears in your wineskin* [b]13 Or *my soul* [c]13 Or *the land of the living* [d]Title: Probably a literary or musical term

4Their venom is like the venom of a snake,
like that of a cobra that has stopped its ears,
5that will not heed the tune of the charmer,
however skillful the enchanter may be.

6Break the teeth in their mouths, O God;
tear out, O LORD, the fangs of the lions!
7Let them vanish like water that flows away;
when they draw the bow, let their arrows be blunted.
8Like a slug melting away as it moves along,
like a stillborn child, may they not see the sun.

9Before your pots can feel ⌊the heat of⌋ the thorns—
whether they be green or dry—the wicked will be swept away.[a]
10The righteous will be glad when they are avenged,
when they bathe their feet in the blood of the wicked.
11Then men will say,
"Surely the righteous still are rewarded;
surely there is a God who judges the earth."

Psalm 59

For the director of music. ⌊To the tune of⌋ "Do Not Destroy." Of David. A *miktam.*[b] When Saul had sent men to watch David's house in order to kill him.

1Deliver me from my enemies, O God;
protect me from those who rise up against me.
2Deliver me from evildoers
and save me from bloodthirsty men.

3See how they lie in wait for me!
Fierce men conspire against me
for no offense or sin of mine, O LORD.
4I have done no wrong, yet they are ready to attack me.
Arise to help me; look on my plight!
5O LORD God Almighty, the God of Israel,
rouse yourself to punish all the nations;
show no mercy to wicked traitors. *Selah*

6They return at evening,
snarling like dogs,
and prowl about the city.
7See what they spew from their mouths—
they spew out swords from their lips,
and they say, "Who can hear us?"
8But you, O LORD, laugh at them;
you scoff at all those nations.
9O my Strength, I watch for you;
you, O God, are my fortress, 10my loving God.

God will go before me
and will let me gloat over those who slander me.
11But do not kill them, O Lord our shield,[c]
or my people will forget.
In your might make them wander about,
and bring them down.
12For the sins of their mouths,
for the words of their lips,
let them be caught in their pride.
For the curses and lies they utter,
13 consume them in wrath,
consume them till they are no more.
Then it will be known to the ends of the earth
that God rules over Jacob. *Selah*

14They return at evening,
snarling like dogs,
and prowl about the city.
15They wander about for food
and howl if not satisfied.
16But I will sing of your strength,
in the morning I will sing of your love;
for you are my fortress,
my refuge in times of trouble.
17O my Strength, I sing praise to you;
you, O God, are my fortress, my loving God.

[a]9 The meaning of the Hebrew for this verse is uncertain.
[b]Title: Probably a literary or musical term
[c]11 Or *sovereign*

Psalm 60

For the director of music. To the tune of "The Lily of the Covenant." A *miktam*[a] of David. For teaching. When he fought Aram Naharaim[b] and Aram Zobah,[c] and when Joab returned and struck down twelve thousand Edomites in the Valley of Salt.

1 You have rejected us, O God, and burst forth upon us;
you have been angry—now restore us!
2 You have shaken the land and torn it open;
mend its fractures, for it is quaking.
3 You have shown your people desperate times;
you have given us wine that makes us stagger.

4 But for those who fear you, you have raised a banner
to be unfurled against the bow. *Selah*

5 Save us and help us with your right hand,
that those you love may be delivered.
6 God has spoken from his sanctuary:
"In triumph I will parcel out Shechem
and measure off the Valley of Succoth.
7 Gilead is mine, and Manasseh is mine;
Ephraim is my helmet,
Judah my scepter.
8 Moab is my washbasin,
upon Edom I toss my sandal;
over Philistia I shout in triumph."

9 Who will bring me to the fortified city?
Who will lead me to Edom?
10 Is it not you, O God, you who have rejected us
and no longer go out with our armies?
11 Give us aid against the enemy,
for the help of man is worthless.
12 With God we will gain the victory,
and he will trample down our enemies.

Psalm 61

For the director of music. With stringed instruments. Of David.

1 Hear my cry, O God;
listen to my prayer.

2 From the ends of the earth I call to you,
I call as my heart grows faint;
lead me to the rock that is higher than I.
3 For you have been my refuge,
a strong tower against the foe.

4 I long to dwell in your tent forever
and take refuge in the shelter of your wings. *Selah*
5 For you have heard my vows, O God;
you have given me the heritage of those who fear your name.

6 Increase the days of the king's life,
his years for many generations.
7 May he be enthroned in God's presence forever;
appoint your love and faithfulness to protect him.

8 Then will I ever sing praise to your name
and fulfill my vows day after day.

Psalm 62

For the director of music. For Jeduthun. A psalm of David.

1 My soul finds rest in God alone;
my salvation comes from him.
2 He alone is my rock and my salvation;
he is my fortress, I will never be shaken.

3 How long will you assault a man?
Would all of you throw him down—
this leaning wall, this tottering fence?
4 They fully intend to topple him
from his lofty place;
they take delight in lies.
With their mouths they bless,
but in their hearts they curse. *Selah*

[a] Title: Probably a literary or musical term
[b] Title: That is, Arameans of Northwest Mesopotamia
[c] Title: That is, Arameans of central Syria

5Find rest, O my soul, in God alone;
my hope comes from him.
6He alone is my rock and my salvation;
he is my fortress, I will not be
shaken.
7My salvation and my honor depend
on God[a];
he is my mighty rock, my refuge.
8Trust in him at all times, O people;
pour out your hearts to him,
for God is our refuge. *Selah*
9Lowborn men are but a breath,
the highborn are but a lie;
if weighed on a balance, they are
nothing;
together they are only a breath.
10Do not trust in extortion
or take pride in stolen goods;
though your riches increase,
do not set your heart on them.
11One thing God has spoken,
two things have I heard:
that you, O God, are strong,
12 and that you, O Lord, are loving.
Surely you will reward each person
according to what he has done.

[a]7 Or / *God Most High is my salvation and my honor*

VERSE FOR THE DAY: Psalm 62:1

AUTHOR: Ruth Ann Polston

PASSAGE FOR THE DAY: Psalm 62:1–12

Arrivals and Departures

St. Augustine prayed, "Thou hast formed us for Thyself, and our hearts are restless till they find rest in Thee." After my husband and I moved from one state to another, I began to see that my restlessness was the "part" longing for the "whole." My mistake was that I was looking for home in places other than God.

The soul is at rest with God. Not with a particular city, a church, a house, friends or even family. The psalmist had found the secret. He once said, "My soul finds rest in God alone . . ." (Ps. 62:1). To commit myself to other allegiances is to make myself vulnerable to the pain of change.

Our lives are like airport concourses, filled with arrivals and departures. But God abides. We need not worry that we'll leave him in some cherished place we're moving away from. He's always there waiting for us at our next stop.

MARRIAGE BUILDERS

♦ *How does the prospect of change affect you?*
♦ *Think of one time when change was difficult for you. How did your spouse and your faith help you deal with that change?*

Additional Scripture Readings
Psalm 87:7; John 15:4;
Joshua 1:5

Go to page 590 for your next devotional reading.

Psalm 63

A psalm of David. When he was in the Desert of Judah.

1O God, you are my God,
earnestly I seek you;
my soul thirsts for you,
my body longs for you,
in a dry and weary land
where there is no water.

2I have seen you in the sanctuary
and beheld your power and your glory.
3Because your love is better than life,
my lips will glorify you.
4I will praise you as long as I live,
and in your name I will lift up my hands.
5My soul will be satisfied as with the richest of foods;
with singing lips my mouth will praise you.

6On my bed I remember you;
I think of you through the watches of the night.
7Because you are my help,
I sing in the shadow of your wings.
8My soul clings to you;
your right hand upholds me.

9They who seek my life will be destroyed;
they will go down to the depths of the earth.
10They will be given over to the sword
and become food for jackals.

11But the king will rejoice in God;
all who swear by God's name will praise him,
while the mouths of liars will be silenced.

Psalm 64

For the director of music. A psalm of David.

1Hear me, O God, as I voice my complaint;
protect my life from the threat of the enemy.
2Hide me from the conspiracy of the wicked,
from that noisy crowd of evildoers.
3They sharpen their tongues like swords
and aim their words like deadly arrows.
4They shoot from ambush at the innocent man;
they shoot at him suddenly, without fear.
5They encourage each other in evil plans,
they talk about hiding their snares;
they say, "Who will see them[a]?"
6They plot injustice and say,
"We have devised a perfect plan!"
Surely the mind and heart of man are cunning.

7But God will shoot them with arrows;
suddenly they will be struck down.
8He will turn their own tongues against them
and bring them to ruin;
all who see them will shake their heads in scorn.

9All mankind will fear;
they will proclaim the works of God
and ponder what he has done.
10Let the righteous rejoice in the LORD
and take refuge in him;
let all the upright in heart praise him!

Psalm 65

For the director of music. A psalm of David. A song.

1Praise awaits[b] you, O God, in Zion;
to you our vows will be fulfilled.
2O you who hear prayer,
to you all men will come.
3When we were overwhelmed by sins,
you forgave[c] our transgressions.
4Blessed are those you choose
and bring near to live in your courts!
We are filled with the good things of your house,
of your holy temple.

5You answer us with awesome deeds of righteousness,
O God our Savior,
the hope of all the ends of the earth
and of the farthest seas,

[a]5 Or *us* [b]1 Or *befits*; the meaning of the Hebrew for this word is uncertain. [c]3 Or *made atonement for*

6who formed the mountains by your power,
having armed yourself with strength,
7who stilled the roaring of the seas,
the roaring of their waves,
and the turmoil of the nations.
8Those living far away fear your wonders;
where morning dawns and evening fades
you call forth songs of joy.

9You care for the land and water it;
you enrich it abundantly.
The streams of God are filled with water
to provide the people with grain,
for so you have ordained it.[a]
10You drench its furrows
and level its ridges;
you soften it with showers
and bless its crops.
11You crown the year with your bounty,
and your carts overflow with abundance.
12The grasslands of the desert overflow;
the hills are clothed with gladness.
13The meadows are covered with flocks
and the valleys are mantled with grain;
they shout for joy and sing.

Psalm 66

For the director of music. A song. A psalm.

1Shout with joy to God, all the earth!
2 Sing the glory of his name;
make his praise glorious!
3Say to God, "How awesome are your deeds!
So great is your power
that your enemies cringe before you.
4All the earth bows down to you;
they sing praise to you,
they sing praise to your name." *Selah*

5Come and see what God has done,
how awesome his works in man's behalf!
6He turned the sea into dry land,
they passed through the waters on foot—
come, let us rejoice in him.
7He rules forever by his power,
his eyes watch the nations—
let not the rebellious rise up against him. *Selah*

8Praise our God, O peoples,
let the sound of his praise be heard;
9he has preserved our lives
and kept our feet from slipping.
10For you, O God, tested us;
you refined us like silver.
11You brought us into prison
and laid burdens on our backs.
12You let men ride over our heads;
we went through fire and water,
but you brought us to a place of abundance.

13I will come to your temple with burnt offerings
and fulfill my vows to you—
14vows my lips promised and my mouth spoke
when I was in trouble.
15I will sacrifice fat animals to you
and an offering of rams;
I will offer bulls and goats. *Selah*

16Come and listen, all you who fear God;
let me tell you what he has done for me.
17I cried out to him with my mouth;
his praise was on my tongue.
18If I had cherished sin in my heart,
the Lord would not have listened;
19but God has surely listened
and heard my voice in prayer.
20Praise be to God,
who has not rejected my prayer
or withheld his love from me!

Psalm 67

For the director of music. With stringed instruments. A psalm. A song.

1May God be gracious to us and bless us
and make his face shine upon us, *Selah*
2that your ways may be known on earth,
your salvation among all nations.

3May the peoples praise you, O God;
may all the peoples praise you.

[a]9 Or *for that is how you prepare the land*

[4]May the nations be glad and sing for
joy,
for you rule the peoples justly
and guide the nations of the earth.
Selah
[5]May the peoples praise you, O God;
may all the peoples praise you.

[6]Then the land will yield its harvest,
and God, our God, will bless us.
[7]God will bless us,
and all the ends of the earth will
fear him.

Psalm 68

For the director of music. Of David.
A psalm. A song.

[1]May God arise, may his enemies be
scattered;
may his foes flee before him.
[2]As smoke is blown away by the wind,
may you blow them away;
as wax melts before the fire,
may the wicked perish before God.
[3]But may the righteous be glad

FRIDAY

VERSE FOR THE DAY:	AUTHOR:	PASSAGE FOR THE DAY:
Psalm 66:18	Evelyn Christenson	Psalm 66:1–20

Unconfessed Sin

I had been a pastor's wife for years when I realized that if I were going to see any effects of my prayer, I must first deal with unconfessed sin in my life. I had been praying regularly with a group of women, and one day we read Psalm 66:18. We couldn't get around the hard truth of that verse: "If I had cherished sin in my heart, the Lord would not have listened." We were humbled, and we were forced to be honest with one another.

It was also tough on my ego. I had to be willing to confess my sins—to admit that I didn't have my act all together, and that Satan's darts hit me too. Effective prayer meant I had to lay aside my self-sufficiency, and come to God in confession.

As I began to be honest about my needs and my shortcomings, the other women in the prayer group began to be honest about theirs. It was hard work for us all, because it meant assuming a servant's role. It meant being supportive of each other in our needs.

The key to powerful praying is the confession of sin.

MARRIAGE BUILDERS

♦ *How does self-sufficiency have a damaging effect on effective prayer life?*

♦ *What role does confession of sin play in your times of shared prayer?*

Additional Scripture Readings
1 John 1:9–10; Psalm 32:4–6; 139:23–24

Go to page 591 for your next devotional reading.

WEEKENDING

SOLUTIONS

This checklist will help you see how well you're doing in developing marriage-keeping attitudes and skills.

1. How do you handle problems? The mark of a good marriage isn't the absence of problems but what you do with them. Working through a difficulty can produce confidence: If you did it once, you can do it again!

2. What do you do when warm feelings ebb? It's easy to panic and fall into all-or-nothing thinking. Remember that it's normal for intense feelings of love to come and go.

3. Where is your focus? Instead of thinking about your problems, focus on what's going well.

4. Do you tap into available resources? Get involved with other Christian couples, especially older ones who can offer needed wisdom.

5. What do you do when you feel you're at the end of your rope? Remember whose hand is holding the other end! With Almighty God on your team, your marriage is stronger than either of you can fathom.

— *Nancy Kennedy*

REVIVE

Saturday: Psalm 91:1–16
Sunday: Hebrews 6:13–20

Go to page 592 for your next devotional reading.

and rejoice before God;
may they be happy and joyful.

4Sing to God, sing praise to his name,
extol him who rides on the clouds[a]—
his name is the LORD—
and rejoice before him.
5A father to the fatherless, a defender of widows,
is God in his holy dwelling.
6God sets the lonely in families,[b]
he leads forth the prisoners with singing;
but the rebellious live in a sun-scorched land.

7When you went out before your people, O God,

[a]4 Or / *prepare the way for him who rides through the deserts*

[b]6 Or *the desolate in a homeland*

VERSE FOR THE DAY: Psalm 68:6

AUTHOR: Beverly J. Burch

PASSAGE FOR THE DAY: Psalm 68:1–35

Independence and Intimacy

"We used to talk," Jen told me. "Now I can't pry him away from the TV."

"Before we were married, she thought I was great," Mike responded. "Now she complains all the time."

Mike and Jen, still newlyweds, had expected their Velcro stage—that sense of being two perfectly interlocking parts of a whole—to last forever. But finding the right balance of closeness and distance is a trial-and-error process. Mike, accustomed to dealing with things on his own, used TV as a buffer when he felt smothered by Jen. Jen felt threatened by that distance and expressed her fears by criticizing.

Then they learned how to talk without defensiveness. Instead of accusing Mike of watching too much TV, Jen told him: "I feel shut out. I'm scared you don't love me anymore." Then Mike's old defensive line of "I do not!" became "I still love you. But when I'm under pressure at work, I need to escape a little."

Recognizing each other's vulnerabilities was scary because it meant they could no longer expect the other to fill in their own gaps. But Mike and Jen discovered a deeper sense of empathy and connectedness.

MARRIAGE BUILDERS

- *Do you ever feel shut out from each other, or smothered?*
- *What do you think is a good balance of independence and interdependence in marriage?*

Additional Scripture Readings
1 Corinthians 11:2–12; Galatians 5:13–15

Go to page 594 for your next devotional reading.

when you marched through the
wasteland, *Selah*
8the earth shook,
the heavens poured down rain,
before God, the One of Sinai,
before God, the God of Israel.
9You gave abundant showers, O God;
you refreshed your weary
inheritance.
10Your people settled in it,
and from your bounty, O God, you
provided for the poor.

11The Lord announced the word,
and great was the company of those
who proclaimed it:
12"Kings and armies flee in haste;
in the camps men divide the
plunder.
13Even while you sleep among the
campfires,[a]
the wings of ⌊my⌋ dove are sheathed
with silver,
its feathers with shining gold."
14When the Almighty[b] scattered the
kings in the land,
it was like snow fallen on Zalmon.

15The mountains of Bashan are majestic
mountains;
rugged are the mountains of
Bashan.
16Why gaze in envy, O rugged
mountains,
at the mountain where God chooses
to reign,
where the LORD himself will dwell
forever?
17The chariots of God are tens of
thousands
and thousands of thousands;
the Lord ⌊has come⌋ from Sinai into
his sanctuary.
18When you ascended on high,
you led captives in your train;
you received gifts from men,
even from[c] the rebellious—
that you,[d] O LORD God, might
dwell there.

19Praise be to the Lord, to God our
Savior,
who daily bears our burdens. *Selah*
20Our God is a God who saves;
from the Sovereign LORD comes
escape from death.

21Surely God will crush the heads of his
enemies,
the hairy crowns of those who go
on in their sins.
22The Lord says, "I will bring them from
Bashan;
I will bring them from the depths of
the sea,
23that you may plunge your feet in the
blood of your foes,
while the tongues of your dogs have
their share."

24Your procession has come into view,
O God,
the procession of my God and King
into the sanctuary.
25In front are the singers, after them the
musicians;
with them are the maidens playing
tambourines.
26Praise God in the great congregation;
praise the LORD in the assembly of
Israel.
27There is the little tribe of Benjamin,
leading them,
there the great throng of Judah's
princes,
and there the princes of Zebulun
and of Naphtali.

28Summon your power, O God[e];
show us your strength, O God, as
you have done before.
29Because of your temple at Jerusalem
kings will bring you gifts.
30Rebuke the beast among the reeds,
the herd of bulls among the calves
of the nations.
Humbled, may it bring bars of silver.
Scatter the nations who delight in
war.
31Envoys will come from Egypt;
Cush[f] will submit herself to God.

32Sing to God, O kingdoms of the earth,
sing praise to the Lord, *Selah*
33to him who rides the ancient skies
above,
who thunders with mighty voice.
34Proclaim the power of God,
whose majesty is over Israel,
whose power is in the skies.
35You are awesome, O God, in your
sanctuary;

[a]13 Or *saddlebags* [b]14 Hebrew *Shaddai* [c]18 Or *gifts for men, / even* [d]18 Or *they*
[e]28 Many Hebrew manuscripts, Septuagint and Syriac; most Hebrew manuscripts *Your God has summoned power for you* [f]31 That is, the upper Nile region

the God of Israel gives power and
strength to his people.

Praise be to God!

Psalm 69

For the director of music. To [the tune
of] "Lilies." Of David.

[1]Save me, O God,
for the waters have come up to my
neck.
[2]I sink in the miry depths,
where there is no foothold.
I have come into the deep waters;
the floods engulf me.
[3]I am worn out calling for help;
my throat is parched.
My eyes fail,
looking for my God.
[4]Those who hate me without reason
outnumber the hairs of my head;
many are my enemies without cause,
those who seek to destroy me.
I am forced to restore
what I did not steal.

VERSE FOR THE DAY: Psalm 69:9

AUTHOR: Diana and David Garland

PASSAGE FOR THE DAY: Psalm 69:1–18

Anger Into Intimacy

A couple may find that conflict leads to the destruction of their love and commitment, or it may be a source of creative change that brings them closer together. One of the deciding factors is the way they handle their anger toward each other.

One way to deal constructively with anger is to see it as a powerful tool for truth. When Jesus overturned the tables and drove the money changers out of the temple, his goal was not to get the anger out of his system so he would feel better. Instead, he was using his righteous anger to communicate to the temple authorities a message from God. When anger is used to confront the problems in a relationship, it can be a constructive force. When it is used to exalt oneself and humiliate another person, it destroys.

We should pray continually about our anger, and we need to ask God's help in taking seriously the problems that face us as couples. Thinking through our anger can help prepare us to talk with each other in ways that will turn anger into intimacy and conflict into creative change.

MARRIAGE BUILDERS

♦ *What would it take for your angry times to be productive times for your relationship?*

♦ *Remember the last time the two of you expressed your anger to one another. Was it constructive? Why or why not?*

Additional Scripture Readings
John 2:12–17; Ephesians 4:26–27;
Proverbs 22:24; 1 Corinthians 13:5

Go to page 606 for your next devotional reading.

5You know my folly, O God;
my guilt is not hidden from you.

6May those who hope in you
not be disgraced because of me,
O Lord, the LORD Almighty;
may those who seek you
not be put to shame because of me,
O God of Israel.
7For I endure scorn for your sake,
and shame covers my face.
8I am a stranger to my brothers,
an alien to my own mother's sons;
9for zeal for your house consumes me,
and the insults of those who insult
you fall on me.
10When I weep and fast,
I must endure scorn;
11when I put on sackcloth,
people make sport of me.
12Those who sit at the gate mock me,
and I am the song of the drunkards.

13But I pray to you, O LORD,
in the time of your favor;
in your great love, O God,
answer me with your sure salvation.
14Rescue me from the mire,
do not let me sink;
deliver me from those who hate me,
from the deep waters.
15Do not let the floodwaters engulf me
or the depths swallow me up
or the pit close its mouth over me.
16Answer me, O LORD, out of the
goodness of your love;
in your great mercy turn to me.
17Do not hide your face from your
servant;
answer me quickly, for I am in
trouble.
18Come near and rescue me;
redeem me because of my foes.

19You know how I am scorned,
disgraced and shamed;
all my enemies are before you.
20Scorn has broken my heart
and has left me helpless;
I looked for sympathy, but there was
none,
for comforters, but I found none.
21They put gall in my food
and gave me vinegar for my thirst.

22May the table set before them become
a snare;
may it become retribution and[a] a
trap.
23May their eyes be darkened so they
cannot see,
and their backs be bent forever.
24Pour out your wrath on them;
let your fierce anger overtake them.
25May their place be deserted;
let there be no one to dwell in their
tents.
26For they persecute those you wound
and talk about the pain of those you
hurt.
27Charge them with crime upon crime;
do not let them share in your
salvation.
28May they be blotted out of the book
of life
and not be listed with the righteous.

29I am in pain and distress;
may your salvation, O God, protect
me.

30I will praise God's name in song
and glorify him with thanksgiving.
31This will please the LORD more than
an ox,
more than a bull with its horns and
hoofs.
32The poor will see and be glad—
you who seek God, may your hearts
live!
33The LORD hears the needy
and does not despise his captive
people.

34Let heaven and earth praise him,
the seas and all that move in them,
35for God will save Zion
and rebuild the cities of Judah.
Then people will settle there and
possess it;
36 the children of his servants will
inherit it,
and those who love his name will
dwell there.

Psalm 70

For the director of music. Of David.
A petition.

1Hasten, O God, to save me;
O LORD, come quickly to help me.
2May those who seek my life
be put to shame and confusion;
may all who desire my ruin
be turned back in disgrace.
3May those who say to me, "Aha!
Aha!"

[a]22 Or *snare / and their fellowship become*

turn back because of their shame.
4But may all who seek you
rejoice and be glad in you;
may those who love your salvation
always say,
"Let God be exalted!"
5Yet I am poor and needy;
come quickly to me, O God.
You are my help and my deliverer;
O LORD, do not delay.

Psalm 71

1In you, O LORD, I have taken refuge;
let me never be put to shame.
2Rescue me and deliver me in your
righteousness;
turn your ear to me and save me.
3Be my rock of refuge,
to which I can always go;
give the command to save me,
for you are my rock and my
fortress.
4Deliver me, O my God, from the hand
of the wicked,
from the grasp of evil and cruel
men.
5For you have been my hope,
O Sovereign LORD,
my confidence since my youth.
6From birth I have relied on you;
you brought me forth from my
mother's womb.
I will ever praise you.
7I have become like a portent to many,
but you are my strong refuge.
8My mouth is filled with your praise,
declaring your splendor all day
long.

9Do not cast me away when I am old;
do not forsake me when my
strength is gone.
10For my enemies speak against me;
those who wait to kill me conspire
together.
11They say, "God has forsaken him;
pursue him and seize him,
for no one will rescue him."
12Be not far from me, O God;
come quickly, O my God, to help
me.
13May my accusers perish in shame;
may those who want to harm me
be covered with scorn and disgrace.
14But as for me, I will always have
hope;
I will praise you more and more.
15My mouth will tell of your
righteousness,
of your salvation all day long,
though I know not its measure.
16I will come and proclaim your mighty
acts, O Sovereign LORD;
I will proclaim your righteousness,
yours alone.
17Since my youth, O God, you have
taught me,
and to this day I declare your
marvelous deeds.
18Even when I am old and gray,
do not forsake me, O God,
till I declare your power to the next
generation,
your might to all who are to come.

19Your righteousness reaches to the
skies, O God,
you who have done great things.
Who, O God, is like you?
20Though you have made me see
troubles, many and bitter,
you will restore my life again;
from the depths of the earth
you will again bring me up.
21You will increase my honor
and comfort me once again.

22I will praise you with the harp
for your faithfulness, O my God;
I will sing praise to you with the lyre,
O Holy One of Israel.
23My lips will shout for joy
when I sing praise to you—
I, whom you have redeemed.
24My tongue will tell of your righteous
acts
all day long,
for those who wanted to harm me
have been put to shame and
confusion.

Psalm 72

Of Solomon.

1Endow the king with your justice,
O God,
the royal son with your
righteousness.
2He will[a] judge your people in
righteousness,
your afflicted ones with justice.

[a]2 Or *May he*; similarly in verses 3-11 and 17

3 The mountains will bring prosperity to the people,
the hills the fruit of righteousness.
4 He will defend the afflicted among the people
and save the children of the needy;
he will crush the oppressor.

5 He will endure[a] as long as the sun,
as long as the moon, through all generations.
6 He will be like rain falling on a mown field,
like showers watering the earth.
7 In his days the righteous will flourish;
prosperity will abound till the moon is no more.
8 He will rule from sea to sea
and from the River[b] to the ends of the earth.[c]
9 The desert tribes will bow before him
and his enemies will lick the dust.
10 The kings of Tarshish and of distant shores
will bring tribute to him;
the kings of Sheba and Seba
will present him gifts.
11 All kings will bow down to him
and all nations will serve him.

12 For he will deliver the needy who cry out,
the afflicted who have no one to help.
13 He will take pity on the weak and the needy
and save the needy from death.
14 He will rescue them from oppression and violence,
for precious is their blood in his sight.

15 Long may he live!
May gold from Sheba be given him.
May people ever pray for him
and bless him all day long.
16 Let grain abound throughout the land;
on the tops of the hills may it sway.
Let its fruit flourish like Lebanon;
let it thrive like the grass of the field.
17 May his name endure forever;
may it continue as long as the sun.

All nations will be blessed through him,
and they will call him blessed.

18 Praise be to the LORD God, the God of Israel,
who alone does marvelous deeds.
19 Praise be to his glorious name forever;
may the whole earth be filled with his glory.
Amen and Amen.

20 This concludes the prayers of David son of Jesse.

BOOK III

Psalms 73–89

Psalm 73

A psalm of Asaph.

1 Surely God is good to Israel,
to those who are pure in heart.

2 But as for me, my feet had almost slipped;
I had nearly lost my foothold.
3 For I envied the arrogant
when I saw the prosperity of the wicked.

4 They have no struggles;
their bodies are healthy and strong.[d]
5 They are free from the burdens common to man;
they are not plagued by human ills.
6 Therefore pride is their necklace;
they clothe themselves with violence.
7 From their callous hearts comes iniquity[e];
the evil conceits of their minds know no limits.
8 They scoff, and speak with malice;
in their arrogance they threaten oppression.
9 Their mouths lay claim to heaven,
and their tongues take possession of the earth.
10 Therefore their people turn to them
and drink up waters in abundance.[f]
11 They say, "How can God know?
Does the Most High have knowledge?"

[a] 5 Septuagint; Hebrew *You will be feared* [b] 8 That is, the Euphrates [c] 8 Or *the end of the land*
[d] 4 With a different word division of the Hebrew; Masoretic Text *struggles at their death; / their bodies are healthy* [e] 7 Syriac (see also Septuagint); Hebrew *Their eyes bulge with fat* [f] 10 The meaning of the Hebrew for this verse is uncertain.

12This is what the wicked are like—
always carefree, they increase in wealth.

13Surely in vain have I kept my heart pure;
in vain have I washed my hands in innocence.
14All day long I have been plagued;
I have been punished every morning.

15If I had said, "I will speak thus,"
I would have betrayed your children.
16When I tried to understand all this,
it was oppressive to me
17till I entered the sanctuary of God;
then I understood their final destiny.

18Surely you place them on slippery ground;
you cast them down to ruin.
19How suddenly are they destroyed,
completely swept away by terrors!
20As a dream when one awakes,
so when you arise, O Lord,
you will despise them as fantasies.

21When my heart was grieved
and my spirit embittered,
22I was senseless and ignorant;
I was a brute beast before you.

23Yet I am always with you;
you hold me by my right hand.
24You guide me with your counsel,
and afterward you will take me into glory.
25Whom have I in heaven but you?
And earth has nothing I desire besides you.
26My flesh and my heart may fail,
but God is the strength of my heart
and my portion forever.

27Those who are far from you will perish;
you destroy all who are unfaithful to you.
28But as for me, it is good to be near God.
I have made the Sovereign LORD my refuge;
I will tell of all your deeds.

[a]Title: Probably a literary or musical term

Psalm 74

A *maskil*[a] of Asaph.

1Why have you rejected us forever, O God?
Why does your anger smolder against the sheep of your pasture?
2Remember the people you purchased of old,
the tribe of your inheritance, whom you redeemed—
Mount Zion, where you dwelt.
3Turn your steps toward these everlasting ruins,
all this destruction the enemy has brought on the sanctuary.

4Your foes roared in the place where you met with us;
they set up their standards as signs.
5They behaved like men wielding axes
to cut through a thicket of trees.
6They smashed all the carved paneling
with their axes and hatchets.
7They burned your sanctuary to the ground;
they defiled the dwelling place of your Name.
8They said in their hearts, "We will crush them completely!"
They burned every place where God was worshiped in the land.
9We are given no miraculous signs;
no prophets are left,
and none of us knows how long this will be.

10How long will the enemy mock you, O God?
Will the foe revile your name forever?
11Why do you hold back your hand, your right hand?
Take it from the folds of your garment and destroy them!

12But you, O God, are my king from of old;
you bring salvation upon the earth.
13It was you who split open the sea by your power;
you broke the heads of the monster in the waters.
14It was you who crushed the heads of Leviathan

and gave him as food to the
creatures of the desert.
15 It was you who opened up springs
and streams;
you dried up the ever flowing
rivers.
16 The day is yours, and yours also the
night;
you established the sun and moon.
17 It was you who set all the boundaries
of the earth;
you made both summer and winter.

18 Remember how the enemy has
mocked you, O LORD,
how foolish people have reviled
your name.
19 Do not hand over the life of your dove
to wild beasts;
do not forget the lives of your
afflicted people forever.
20 Have regard for your covenant,
because haunts of violence fill the
dark places of the land.
21 Do not let the oppressed retreat in
disgrace;
may the poor and needy praise your
name.

22 Rise up, O God, and defend your
cause;
remember how fools mock you all
day long.
23 Do not ignore the clamor of your
adversaries,
the uproar of your enemies, which
rises continually.

Psalm 75

For the director of music. ¸To the tune of¸ "Do Not Destroy." A psalm of Asaph. A song.

1 We give thanks to you, O God,
we give thanks, for your Name is
near;
men tell of your wonderful deeds.

2 You say, "I choose the appointed time;
it is I who judge uprightly.
3 When the earth and all its people
quake,
it is I who hold its pillars firm.
Selah
4 To the arrogant I say, 'Boast no more,'
and to the wicked, 'Do not lift up
your horns.
5 Do not lift your horns against heaven;
do not speak with outstretched
neck.' "

6 No one from the east or the west
or from the desert can exalt a man.
7 But it is God who judges:
He brings one down, he exalts
another.
8 In the hand of the LORD is a cup
full of foaming wine mixed with
spices;
he pours it out, and all the wicked of
the earth
drink it down to its very dregs.

9 As for me, I will declare this forever;
I will sing praise to the God of
Jacob.
10 I will cut off the horns of all the
wicked,
but the horns of the righteous will
be lifted up.

Psalm 76

For the director of music. With stringed instruments. A psalm of Asaph. A song.

1 In Judah God is known;
his name is great in Israel.
2 His tent is in Salem,
his dwelling place in Zion.
3 There he broke the flashing arrows,
the shields and the swords, the
weapons of war. *Selah*

4 You are resplendent with light,
more majestic than mountains rich
with game.
5 Valiant men lie plundered,
they sleep their last sleep;
not one of the warriors
can lift his hands.
6 At your rebuke, O God of Jacob,
both horse and chariot lie still.
7 You alone are to be feared.
Who can stand before you when
you are angry?
8 From heaven you pronounced
judgment,
and the land feared and was
quiet—
9 when you, O God, rose up to judge,
to save all the afflicted of the land.
Selah
10 Surely your wrath against men brings
you praise,
and the survivors of your wrath are
restrained.[a]

[a] 10 Or *Surely the wrath of men brings you praise, / and with the remainder of wrath you arm yourself*

11Make vows to the LORD your God and
fulfill them;
let all the neighboring lands
bring gifts to the One to be feared.
12He breaks the spirit of rulers;
he is feared by the kings of the
earth.

Psalm 77

For the director of music. For Jeduthun.
Of Asaph. A psalm.

1I cried out to God for help;
I cried out to God to hear me.
2When I was in distress, I sought the
Lord;
at night I stretched out untiring
hands
and my soul refused to be
comforted.

3I remembered you, O God, and I
groaned;
I mused, and my spirit grew faint.
Selah
4You kept my eyes from closing;
I was too troubled to speak.
5I thought about the former days,
the years of long ago;
6I remembered my songs in the night.
My heart mused and my spirit
inquired:

7"Will the Lord reject forever?
Will he never show his favor again?
8Has his unfailing love vanished
forever?
Has his promise failed for all time?
9Has God forgotten to be merciful?
Has he in anger withheld his
compassion?" *Selah*

10Then I thought, "To this I will appeal:
the years of the right hand of the
Most High."
11I will remember the deeds of the
LORD;
yes, I will remember your miracles
of long ago.
12I will meditate on all your works
and consider all your mighty deeds.

13Your ways, O God, are holy.
What god is so great as our God?
14You are the God who performs
miracles;
you display your power among the
peoples.
15With your mighty arm you redeemed
your people,
the descendants of Jacob and
Joseph. *Selah*

16The waters saw you, O God,
the waters saw you and writhed;
the very depths were convulsed.
17The clouds poured down water,
the skies resounded with thunder;
your arrows flashed back and forth.
18Your thunder was heard in the
whirlwind,
your lightning lit up the world;
the earth trembled and quaked.
19Your path led through the sea,
your way through the mighty
waters,
though your footprints were not
seen.

20You led your people like a flock
by the hand of Moses and Aaron.

Psalm 78

A *maskil*[a] of Asaph.

1O my people, hear my teaching;
listen to the words of my mouth.
2I will open my mouth in parables,
I will utter hidden things, things
from of old—
3what we have heard and known,
what our fathers have told us.
4We will not hide them from their
children;
we will tell the next generation
the praiseworthy deeds of the LORD,
his power, and the wonders he has
done.
5He decreed statutes for Jacob
and established the law in Israel,
which he commanded our forefathers
to teach their children,
6so the next generation would know
them,
even the children yet to be born,
and they in turn would tell their
children.
7Then they would put their trust in
God
and would not forget his deeds
but would keep his commands.
8They would not be like their
forefathers—
a stubborn and rebellious
generation,

[a]Title: Probably a literary or musical term

whose hearts were not loyal to God,
whose spirits were not faithful to him.
9 The men of Ephraim, though armed with bows,
turned back on the day of battle;
10 they did not keep God's covenant
and refused to live by his law.
11 They forgot what he had done,
the wonders he had shown them.
12 He did miracles in the sight of their fathers
in the land of Egypt, in the region of Zoan.
13 He divided the sea and led them through;
he made the water stand firm like a wall.
14 He guided them with the cloud by day
and with light from the fire all night.
15 He split the rocks in the desert
and gave them water as abundant as the seas;
16 he brought streams out of a rocky crag
and made water flow down like rivers.
17 But they continued to sin against him,
rebelling in the desert against the Most High.
18 They willfully put God to the test
by demanding the food they craved.
19 They spoke against God, saying,
"Can God spread a table in the desert?
20 When he struck the rock, water gushed out,
and streams flowed abundantly.
But can he also give us food?
Can he supply meat for his people?"
21 When the LORD heard them, he was very angry;
his fire broke out against Jacob,
and his wrath rose against Israel,
22 for they did not believe in God
or trust in his deliverance.
23 Yet he gave a command to the skies above
and opened the doors of the heavens;
24 he rained down manna for the people to eat,
he gave them the grain of heaven.
25 Men ate the bread of angels;
he sent them all the food they could eat.
26 He let loose the east wind from the heavens
and led forth the south wind by his power.
27 He rained meat down on them like dust,
flying birds like sand on the seashore.
28 He made them come down inside their camp,
all around their tents.
29 They ate till they had more than enough,
for he had given them what they craved.
30 But before they turned from the food they craved,
even while it was still in their mouths,
31 God's anger rose against them;
he put to death the sturdiest among them,
cutting down the young men of Israel.

32 In spite of all this, they kept on sinning;
in spite of his wonders, they did not believe.
33 So he ended their days in futility
and their years in terror.
34 Whenever God slew them, they would seek him;
they eagerly turned to him again.
35 They remembered that God was their Rock,
that God Most High was their Redeemer.
36 But then they would flatter him with their mouths,
lying to him with their tongues;
37 their hearts were not loyal to him,
they were not faithful to his covenant.
38 Yet he was merciful;
he forgave their iniquities
and did not destroy them.
Time after time he restrained his anger
and did not stir up his full wrath.
39 He remembered that they were but flesh,
a passing breeze that does not return.

40 How often they rebelled against him in the desert
and grieved him in the wasteland!
41 Again and again they put God to the test;

they vexed the Holy One of Israel.
42They did not remember his power—
the day he redeemed them from the oppressor,
43the day he displayed his miraculous signs in Egypt,
his wonders in the region of Zoan.
44He turned their rivers to blood;
they could not drink from their streams.
45He sent swarms of flies that devoured them,
and frogs that devastated them.
46He gave their crops to the grasshopper,
their produce to the locust.
47He destroyed their vines with hail
and their sycamore-figs with sleet.
48He gave over their cattle to the hail,
their livestock to bolts of lightning.
49He unleashed against them his hot anger,
his wrath, indignation and hostility—
a band of destroying angels.
50He prepared a path for his anger;
he did not spare them from death
but gave them over to the plague.
51He struck down all the firstborn of Egypt,
the firstfruits of manhood in the tents of Ham.
52But he brought his people out like a flock;
he led them like sheep through the desert.
53He guided them safely, so they were unafraid;
but the sea engulfed their enemies.
54Thus he brought them to the border of his holy land,
to the hill country his right hand had taken.
55He drove out nations before them
and allotted their lands to them as an inheritance;
he settled the tribes of Israel in their homes.

56But they put God to the test
and rebelled against the Most High;
they did not keep his statutes.
57Like their fathers they were disloyal and faithless,
as unreliable as a faulty bow.
58They angered him with their high places;
they aroused his jealousy with their idols.
59When God heard them, he was very angry;
he rejected Israel completely.
60He abandoned the tabernacle of Shiloh,
the tent he had set up among men.
61He sent ⌊the ark of⌋ his might into captivity,
his splendor into the hands of the enemy.
62He gave his people over to the sword;
he was very angry with his inheritance.
63Fire consumed their young men,
and their maidens had no wedding songs;
64their priests were put to the sword,
and their widows could not weep.

65Then the Lord awoke as from sleep,
as a man wakes from the stupor of wine.
66He beat back his enemies;
he put them to everlasting shame.
67Then he rejected the tents of Joseph,
he did not choose the tribe of Ephraim;
68but he chose the tribe of Judah,
Mount Zion, which he loved.
69He built his sanctuary like the heights,
like the earth that he established forever.
70He chose David his servant
and took him from the sheep pens;
71from tending the sheep he brought him
to be the shepherd of his people Jacob,
of Israel his inheritance.
72And David shepherded them with integrity of heart;
with skillful hands he led them.

Psalm 79

A psalm of Asaph.

1O God, the nations have invaded your inheritance;
they have defiled your holy temple,
they have reduced Jerusalem to rubble.
2They have given the dead bodies of your servants
as food to the birds of the air,
the flesh of your saints to the beasts of the earth.
3They have poured out blood like water

all around Jerusalem,
and there is no one to bury the dead.
4We are objects of reproach to our neighbors,
of scorn and derision to those around us.

5How long, O LORD? Will you be angry forever?
How long will your jealousy burn like fire?
6Pour out your wrath on the nations
that do not acknowledge you,
on the kingdoms
that do not call on your name;
7for they have devoured Jacob
and destroyed his homeland.
8Do not hold against us the sins of the fathers;
may your mercy come quickly to meet us,
for we are in desperate need.

9Help us, O God our Savior,
for the glory of your name;
deliver us and forgive our sins
for your name's sake.
10Why should the nations say,
"Where is their God?"
Before our eyes, make known among the nations
that you avenge the outpoured blood of your servants.
11May the groans of the prisoners come before you;
by the strength of your arm
preserve those condemned to die.

12Pay back into the laps of our neighbors seven times
the reproach they have hurled at you, O Lord.
13Then we your people, the sheep of your pasture,
will praise you forever;
from generation to generation
we will recount your praise.

Psalm 80

For the director of music. To ⌊the tune of⌋ "The Lilies of the Covenant."
Of Asaph. A psalm.

1Hear us, O Shepherd of Israel,
you who lead Joseph like a flock;
you who sit enthroned between the cherubim, shine forth
2 before Ephraim, Benjamin and Manasseh.
Awaken your might;
come and save us.

3Restore us, O God;
make your face shine upon us,
that we may be saved.

4O LORD God Almighty,
how long will your anger smolder
against the prayers of your people?
5You have fed them with the bread of tears;
you have made them drink tears by the bowlful.
6You have made us a source of contention to our neighbors,
and our enemies mock us.

7Restore us, O God Almighty;
make your face shine upon us,
that we may be saved.

8You brought a vine out of Egypt;
you drove out the nations and planted it.
9You cleared the ground for it,
and it took root and filled the land.
10The mountains were covered with its shade,
the mighty cedars with its branches.
11It sent out its boughs to the Sea,[a]
its shoots as far as the River.[b]

12Why have you broken down its walls
so that all who pass by pick its grapes?
13Boars from the forest ravage it
and the creatures of the field feed on it.
14Return to us, O God Almighty!
Look down from heaven and see!
Watch over this vine,
15 the root your right hand has planted,
the son[c] you have raised up for yourself.

16Your vine is cut down, it is burned with fire;
at your rebuke your people perish.
17Let your hand rest on the man at your right hand,
the son of man you have raised up for yourself.
18Then we will not turn away from you;
revive us, and we will call on your name.

[a] *11* Probably the Mediterranean [b] *11* That is, the Euphrates [c] *15* Or *branch*

19 Restore us, O LORD God Almighty;
make your face shine upon us,
that we may be saved.

Psalm 81

For the director of music. According to *gittith.*[a] Of Asaph.

1 Sing for joy to God our strength;
shout aloud to the God of Jacob!
2 Begin the music, strike the tambourine,
play the melodious harp and lyre.
3 Sound the ram's horn at the New Moon,
and when the moon is full, on the day of our Feast;
4 this is a decree for Israel,
an ordinance of the God of Jacob.
5 He established it as a statute for Joseph
when he went out against Egypt,
where we heard a language we did not understand.[b]
6 He says, "I removed the burden from their shoulders;
their hands were set free from the basket.
7 In your distress you called and I rescued you,
I answered you out of a thundercloud;
I tested you at the waters of Meribah. *Selah*
8 "Hear, O my people, and I will warn you—
if you would but listen to me, O Israel!
9 You shall have no foreign god among you;
you shall not bow down to an alien god.
10 I am the LORD your God,
who brought you up out of Egypt.
Open wide your mouth and I will fill it.
11 "But my people would not listen to me;
Israel would not submit to me.
12 So I gave them over to their stubborn hearts
to follow their own devices.
13 "If my people would but listen to me,
if Israel would follow my ways,
14 how quickly would I subdue their enemies
and turn my hand against their foes!
15 Those who hate the LORD would cringe before him,
and their punishment would last forever.
16 But you would be fed with the finest of wheat;
with honey from the rock I would satisfy you."

Psalm 82

A psalm of Asaph.

1 God presides in the great assembly;
he gives judgment among the "gods":
2 "How long will you[c] defend the unjust
and show partiality to the wicked? *Selah*
3 Defend the cause of the weak and fatherless;
maintain the rights of the poor and oppressed.
4 Rescue the weak and needy;
deliver them from the hand of the wicked.
5 "They know nothing, they understand nothing.
They walk about in darkness;
all the foundations of the earth are shaken.
6 "I said, 'You are "gods";
you are all sons of the Most High.'
7 But you will die like mere men;
you will fall like every other ruler."
8 Rise up, O God, judge the earth,
for all the nations are your inheritance.

Psalm 83

A song. A psalm of Asaph.

1 O God, do not keep silent;
be not quiet, O God, be not still.
2 See how your enemies are astir,
how your foes rear their heads.

[a] Title: Probably a musical term [b] 5 Or / *and we heard a voice we had not known* [c] 2 The Hebrew is plural.

3With cunning they conspire against
your people;
they plot against those you cherish.
4"Come," they say, "let us destroy them
as a nation,
that the name of Israel be
remembered no more."
5With one mind they plot together;
they form an alliance against you—
6the tents of Edom and the Ishmaelites,
of Moab and the Hagrites,
7Gebal,[a] Ammon and Amalek,
Philistia, with the people of Tyre.
8Even Assyria has joined them
to lend strength to the descendants
of Lot. *Selah*
9Do to them as you did to Midian,
as you did to Sisera and Jabin at the
river Kishon,
10who perished at Endor
and became like refuse on the
ground.
11Make their nobles like Oreb and Zeeb,
all their princes like Zebah and
Zalmunna,
12who said, "Let us take possession
of the pasturelands of God."
13Make them like tumbleweed, O my
God,
like chaff before the wind.
14As fire consumes the forest
or a flame sets the mountains
ablaze,
15so pursue them with your tempest
and terrify them with your storm.
16Cover their faces with shame
so that men will seek your name,
O LORD.
17May they ever be ashamed and
dismayed;
may they perish in disgrace.
18Let them know that you, whose name
is the LORD—
that you alone are the Most High
over all the earth.

Psalm 84

For the director of music. According to *gittith.*[b] Of the Sons of Korah. A psalm.

1How lovely is your dwelling place,
O LORD Almighty!
2My soul yearns, even faints,
for the courts of the LORD;
my heart and my flesh cry out
for the living God.
3Even the sparrow has found a home,
and the swallow a nest for herself,
where she may have her young—
a place near your altar,
O LORD Almighty, my King and my
God.
4Blessed are those who dwell in your
house;
they are ever praising you. *Selah*
5Blessed are those whose strength is in
you,
who have set their hearts on
pilgrimage.
6As they pass through the Valley of
Baca,
they make it a place of springs;
the autumn rains also cover it with
pools.[c]
7They go from strength to strength,
till each appears before God in Zion.
8Hear my prayer, O LORD God
Almighty;
listen to me, O God of Jacob. *Selah*
9Look upon our shield,[d] O God;
look with favor on your anointed
one.
10Better is one day in your courts
than a thousand elsewhere;
I would rather be a doorkeeper in the
house of my God
than dwell in the tents of the
wicked.
11For the LORD God is a sun and shield;
the LORD bestows favor and honor;
no good thing does he withhold
from those whose walk is blameless.
12O LORD Almighty,
blessed is the man who trusts in
you.

Psalm 85

For the director of music. Of the Sons of Korah. A psalm.

1You showed favor to your land,
O LORD;
you restored the fortunes of Jacob.
2You forgave the iniquity of your
people
and covered all their sins. *Selah*
3You set aside all your wrath
and turned from your fierce anger.

[a]7 That is, Byblos [b]Title: Probably a musical term [c]6 Or *blessings* [d]9 Or *sovereign*

4 Restore us again, O God our Savior,
and put away your displeasure
toward us.
5 Will you be angry with us forever?
Will you prolong your anger
through all generations?
6 Will you not revive us again,
that your people may rejoice in you?
7 Show us your unfailing love, O LORD,
and grant us your salvation.
8 I will listen to what God the LORD will say;
he promises peace to his people, his saints—
but let them not return to folly.

VERSE FOR THE DAY: Psalm 84:10 | AUTHOR: Charlie Wedemeyer | PASSAGE FOR THE DAY: Psalm 84:1–12

What About Tomorrow?

When doctors discovered I had Lou Gehrig's Disease (ALS) in 1978, they gave me only a year to live. In the years since then, ALS has destroyed my voluntary muscle control.

One day when friends were waiting for me in the living room and my wife, Lucy, was helping me get ready, I suffered a bad coughing spell. I couldn't catch my breath, and I realized again what a terrible burden I was on my family. Tears of humiliation welled up, and I expressed to Lucy what I'd felt for a long time: "You and the children would be better off if I died."

But Lucy responded, "We would rather have you like this than not have you at all." I didn't know then how many times the memory of Lucy's words would give me the will to fight for my next breath.

Many loving husbands honestly say, "I couldn't live without my wife," but for me every single day I live is a testimony to God's grace and Lucy's devotion. If there's one thing Lucy and I have learned, it's this: Tomorrow is not promised to anyone. We're all terminal. Every day is a gift. And it's up to us to make the most of it.

MARRIAGE BUILDERS

♦ *For what things in your marriage are you thankful on a day-to-day basis?*

♦ *When you realize you're "terminal"—that at any time you might be in heaven with God—how does it affect the decisions you make in your marriage and family?*

Additional Scripture Readings
Proverbs 27:1; James 4:13–17

Go to page 617 for your next devotional reading.

9Surely his salvation is near those who
fear him,
that his glory may dwell in our
land.

10Love and faithfulness meet together;
righteousness and peace kiss each
other.
11Faithfulness springs forth from the
earth,
and righteousness looks down from
heaven.
12The LORD will indeed give what is
good,
and our land will yield its harvest.
13Righteousness goes before him
and prepares the way for his steps.

Psalm 86

A prayer of David.

1Hear, O LORD, and answer me,
for I am poor and needy.
2Guard my life, for I am devoted to
you.
You are my God; save your servant
who trusts in you.
3Have mercy on me, O Lord,
for I call to you all day long.
4Bring joy to your servant,
for to you, O Lord,
I lift up my soul.

5You are forgiving and good, O Lord,
abounding in love to all who call to
you.
6Hear my prayer, O LORD;
listen to my cry for mercy.
7In the day of my trouble I will call to
you,
for you will answer me.

8Among the gods there is none like
you, O Lord;
no deeds can compare with yours.
9All the nations you have made
will come and worship before you,
O Lord;
they will bring glory to your name.
10For you are great and do marvelous
deeds;
you alone are God.

11Teach me your way, O LORD,
and I will walk in your truth;
give me an undivided heart,
that I may fear your name.
12I will praise you, O Lord my God,
with all my heart;
I will glorify your name forever.
13For great is your love toward me;
you have delivered me from the
depths of the grave.[a]

14The arrogant are attacking me, O God;
a band of ruthless men seeks my
life—
men without regard for you.
15But you, O Lord, are a compassionate
and gracious God,
slow to anger, abounding in love
and faithfulness.
16Turn to me and have mercy on me;
grant your strength to your servant
and save the son of your
maidservant.[b]
17Give me a sign of your goodness,
that my enemies may see it and be
put to shame,
for you, O LORD, have helped me
and comforted me.

Psalm 87

Of the Sons of Korah. A psalm. A song.

1He has set his foundation on the holy
mountain;
2 the LORD loves the gates of Zion
more than all the dwellings of
Jacob.
3Glorious things are said of you,
O city of God: *Selah*
4"I will record Rahab[c] and Babylon
among those who acknowledge
me—
Philistia too, and Tyre, along with
Cush[d]—
and will say, 'This[e] one was born
in Zion.' "

5Indeed, of Zion it will be said,
"This one and that one were born
in her,
and the Most High himself will
establish her."
6The LORD will write in the register of
the peoples:
"This one was born in Zion." *Selah*
7As they make music they will sing,
"All my fountains are in you."

[a] 13 Hebrew *Sheol* [b] 16 Or *save your faithful son* [c] 4 A poetic name for Egypt [d] 4 That is, the upper Nile region [e] 4 Or *"O Rahab and Babylon, / Philistia, Tyre and Cush, / I will record concerning those who acknowledge me: / 'This*

Psalm 88

A song. A psalm of the Sons of Korah.
For the director of music. According to
mahalath leannoth.[a] A *maskil*[b] of
Heman the Ezrahite.

1O LORD, the God who saves me,
day and night I cry out before you.
2May my prayer come before you;
turn your ear to my cry.

3For my soul is full of trouble
and my life draws near the grave.[c]
4I am counted among those who go
down to the pit;
I am like a man without strength.
5I am set apart with the dead,
like the slain who lie in the grave,
whom you remember no more,
who are cut off from your care.

6You have put me in the lowest pit,
in the darkest depths.
7Your wrath lies heavily upon me;
you have overwhelmed me with all
your waves. *Selah*
8You have taken from me my closest
friends
and have made me repulsive to
them.
I am confined and cannot escape;
9 my eyes are dim with grief.

I call to you, O LORD, every day;
I spread out my hands to you.
10Do you show your wonders to the
dead?
Do those who are dead rise up and
praise you? *Selah*
11Is your love declared in the grave,
your faithfulness in Destruction[d]?
12Are your wonders known in the place
of darkness,
or your righteous deeds in the land
of oblivion?

13But I cry to you for help, O LORD;
in the morning my prayer comes
before you.
14Why, O LORD, do you reject me
and hide your face from me?

15From my youth I have been afflicted
and close to death;
I have suffered your terrors and am
in despair.
16Your wrath has swept over me;
your terrors have destroyed me.
17All day long they surround me like a
flood;
they have completely engulfed me.
18You have taken my companions and
loved ones from me;
the darkness is my closest friend.

Psalm 89

A *maskil*[b] of Ethan the Ezrahite.

1I will sing of the LORD's great love
forever;
with my mouth I will make your
faithfulness known through all
generations.
2I will declare that your love stands
firm forever,
that you established your
faithfulness in heaven itself.

3You said, "I have made a covenant
with my chosen one,
I have sworn to David my servant,
4'I will establish your line forever
and make your throne firm through
all generations.' " *Selah*

5The heavens praise your wonders,
O LORD,
your faithfulness too, in the
assembly of the holy ones.
6For who in the skies above can
compare with the LORD?
Who is like the LORD among the
heavenly beings?
7In the council of the holy ones God is
greatly feared;
he is more awesome than all who
surround him.
8O LORD God Almighty, who is like
you?
You are mighty, O LORD, and your
faithfulness surrounds you.

9You rule over the surging sea;
when its waves mount up, you still
them.
10You crushed Rahab like one of the
slain;
with your strong arm you scattered
your enemies.
11The heavens are yours, and yours also
the earth;
you founded the world and all that
is in it.
12You created the north and the south;

[a]Title: Possibly a tune, "The Suffering of Affliction"
[b]Title: Probably a literary or musical term
[c]3 Hebrew *Sheol* [d]11 Hebrew *Abaddon*

Tabor and Hermon sing for joy at
your name.
13Your arm is endued with power;
your hand is strong, your right hand
exalted.
14Righteousness and justice are the
foundation of your throne;
love and faithfulness go before you.
15Blessed are those who have learned to
acclaim you,
who walk in the light of your
presence, O LORD.
16They rejoice in your name all day
long;
they exult in your righteousness.
17For you are their glory and strength,
and by your favor you exalt our
horn.[a]
18Indeed, our shield[b] belongs to the
LORD,
our king to the Holy One of Israel.

19Once you spoke in a vision,
to your faithful people you said:
"I have bestowed strength on a
warrior;
I have exalted a young man from
among the people.
20I have found David my servant;
with my sacred oil I have anointed
him.
21My hand will sustain him;
surely my arm will strengthen him.
22No enemy will subject him to tribute;
no wicked man will oppress him.
23I will crush his foes before him
and strike down his adversaries.
24My faithful love will be with him,
and through my name his horn[c]
will be exalted.
25I will set his hand over the sea,
his right hand over the rivers.
26He will call out to me, 'You are my
Father,
my God, the Rock my Savior.'
27I will also appoint him my firstborn,
the most exalted of the kings of the
earth.
28I will maintain my love to him
forever,
and my covenant with him will
never fail.
29I will establish his line forever,
his throne as long as the heavens
endure.

30"If his sons forsake my law
and do not follow my statutes,
31if they violate my decrees
and fail to keep my commands,
32I will punish their sin with the rod,
their iniquity with flogging;
33but I will not take my love from him,
nor will I ever betray my
faithfulness.
34I will not violate my covenant
or alter what my lips have uttered.
35Once for all, I have sworn by my
holiness—
and I will not lie to David—
36that his line will continue forever
and his throne endure before me
like the sun;
37it will be established forever like the
moon,
the faithful witness in the sky."
Selah

38But you have rejected, you have
spurned,
you have been very angry with your
anointed one.
39You have renounced the covenant
with your servant
and have defiled his crown in the
dust.
40You have broken through all his walls
and reduced his strongholds to
ruins.
41All who pass by have plundered him;
he has become the scorn of his
neighbors.
42You have exalted the right hand of his
foes;
you have made all his enemies
rejoice.
43You have turned back the edge of his
sword
and have not supported him in
battle.
44You have put an end to his splendor
and cast his throne to the ground.
45You have cut short the days of his
youth;
you have covered him with a
mantle of shame. *Selah*
46How long, O LORD? Will you hide
yourself forever?
How long will your wrath burn like
fire?
47Remember how fleeting is my life.
For what futility you have created
all men!
48What man can live and not see death,

[a]17 *Horn* here symbolizes strong one. [b]18 Or *sovereign* [c]24 *Horn* here symbolizes strength.

or save himself from the power of
the grave[a]? *Selah*
49O Lord, where is your former great
love,
which in your faithfulness you
swore to David?
50Remember, Lord, how your servant
has[b] been mocked,
how I bear in my heart the taunts
of all the nations,
51the taunts with which your enemies
have mocked, O LORD,
with which they have mocked every
step of your anointed one.

52Praise be to the LORD forever!
Amen and Amen.

BOOK IV

Psalms 90–106

Psalm 90

A prayer of Moses the man of God.

1Lord, you have been our dwelling
place
throughout all generations.
2Before the mountains were born
or you brought forth the earth and
the world,
from everlasting to everlasting you
are God.

3You turn men back to dust,
saying, "Return to dust, O sons of
men."
4For a thousand years in your sight
are like a day that has just gone by,
or like a watch in the night.
5You sweep men away in the sleep of
death;
they are like the new grass of the
morning—
6though in the morning it springs up
new,
by evening it is dry and withered.

7We are consumed by your anger
and terrified by your indignation.
8You have set our iniquities before
you,
our secret sins in the light of your
presence.
9All our days pass away under your
wrath;
we finish our years with a moan.

10The length of our days is seventy
years—
or eighty, if we have the strength;
yet their span[c] is but trouble and
sorrow,
for they quickly pass, and we fly
away.

11Who knows the power of your anger?
For your wrath is as great as the
fear that is due you.
12Teach us to number our days aright,
that we may gain a heart of
wisdom.

13Relent, O LORD! How long will it be?
Have compassion on your servants.
14Satisfy us in the morning with your
unfailing love,
that we may sing for joy and be
glad all our days.
15Make us glad for as many days as you
have afflicted us,
for as many years as we have seen
trouble.
16May your deeds be shown to your
servants,
your splendor to their children.

17May the favor[d] of the Lord our God
rest upon us;
establish the work of our hands for
us—
yes, establish the work of our
hands.

Psalm 91

1He who dwells in the shelter of the
Most High
will rest in the shadow of the
Almighty.[e]
2I will say[f] of the LORD, "He is my
refuge and my fortress,
my God, in whom I trust."

3Surely he will save you from the
fowler's snare
and from the deadly pestilence.
4He will cover you with his feathers,
and under his wings you will find
refuge;
his faithfulness will be your shield
and rampart.
5You will not fear the terror of night,
nor the arrow that flies by day,
6nor the pestilence that stalks in the
darkness,

[a] 48 Hebrew *Sheol* [b] 50 Or *your servants have* [c] 10 Or *yet the best of them* [d] 17 Or *beauty*
[e] 1 Hebrew *Shaddai* [f] 2 Or *He says*

nor the plague that destroys at
midday.
7A thousand may fall at your side,
ten thousand at your right hand,
but it will not come near you.
8You will only observe with your eyes
and see the punishment of the
wicked.

9If you make the Most High your
dwelling—
even the LORD, who is my refuge—
10then no harm will befall you,
no disaster will come near your
tent.
11For he will command his angels
concerning you
to guard you in all your ways;
12they will lift you up in their hands,
so that you will not strike your foot
against a stone.
13You will tread upon the lion and the
cobra;
you will trample the great lion and
the serpent.

14"Because he loves me," says the LORD,
"I will rescue him;
I will protect him, for he
acknowledges my name.
15He will call upon me, and I will
answer him;
I will be with him in trouble,
I will deliver him and honor him.
16With long life will I satisfy him
and show him my salvation."

Psalm 92

A psalm. A song. For the Sabbath day.

1It is good to praise the LORD
and make music to your name,
O Most High,
2to proclaim your love in the morning
and your faithfulness at night,
3to the music of the ten-stringed lyre
and the melody of the harp.

4For you make me glad by your deeds,
O LORD;
I sing for joy at the works of your
hands.
5How great are your works, O LORD,
how profound your thoughts!
6The senseless man does not know,
fools do not understand,
7that though the wicked spring up like
grass
and all evildoers flourish,
they will be forever destroyed.

8But you, O LORD, are exalted forever.

9For surely your enemies, O LORD,
surely your enemies will perish;
all evildoers will be scattered.
10You have exalted my horn[a] like that
of a wild ox;
fine oils have been poured upon
me.
11My eyes have seen the defeat of my
adversaries;
my ears have heard the rout of my
wicked foes.

12The righteous will flourish like a palm
tree,
they will grow like a cedar of
Lebanon;
13planted in the house of the LORD,
they will flourish in the courts of
our God.
14They will still bear fruit in old age,
they will stay fresh and green,
15proclaiming, "The LORD is upright;
he is my Rock, and there is no
wickedness in him."

Psalm 93

1The LORD reigns, he is robed in
majesty;
the LORD is robed in majesty
and is armed with strength.
The world is firmly established;
it cannot be moved.
2Your throne was established long ago;
you are from all eternity.

3The seas have lifted up, O LORD,
the seas have lifted up their voice;
the seas have lifted up their
pounding waves.
4Mightier than the thunder of the great
waters,
mightier than the breakers of the
sea—
the LORD on high is mighty.

5Your statutes stand firm;
holiness adorns your house
for endless days, O LORD.

[a]10 *Horn* here symbolizes strength.

Psalm 94

1O LORD, the God who avenges,
O God who avenges, shine forth.
2Rise up, O Judge of the earth;
pay back to the proud what they deserve.
3How long will the wicked, O LORD,
how long will the wicked be jubilant?
4They pour out arrogant words;
all the evildoers are full of boasting.
5They crush your people, O LORD;
they oppress your inheritance.
6They slay the widow and the alien;
they murder the fatherless.
7They say, "The LORD does not see;
the God of Jacob pays no heed."

8Take heed, you senseless ones among the people;
you fools, when will you become wise?
9Does he who implanted the ear not hear?
Does he who formed the eye not see?
10Does he who disciplines nations not punish?
Does he who teaches man lack knowledge?
11The LORD knows the thoughts of man;
he knows that they are futile.

12Blessed is the man you discipline, O LORD,
the man you teach from your law;
13you grant him relief from days of trouble,
till a pit is dug for the wicked.
14For the LORD will not reject his people;
he will never forsake his inheritance.
15Judgment will again be founded on righteousness,
and all the upright in heart will follow it.
16Who will rise up for me against the wicked?
Who will take a stand for me against evildoers?
17Unless the LORD had given me help,
I would soon have dwelt in the silence of death.
18When I said, "My foot is slipping,"
your love, O LORD, supported me.
19When anxiety was great within me,
your consolation brought joy to my soul.
20Can a corrupt throne be allied with you—
one that brings on misery by its decrees?
21They band together against the righteous
and condemn the innocent to death.
22But the LORD has become my fortress,
and my God the rock in whom I take refuge.
23He will repay them for their sins
and destroy them for their wickedness;
the LORD our God will destroy them.

Psalm 95

1Come, let us sing for joy to the LORD;
let us shout aloud to the Rock of our salvation.
2Let us come before him with thanksgiving
and extol him with music and song.
3For the LORD is the great God,
the great King above all gods.
4In his hand are the depths of the earth,
and the mountain peaks belong to him.
5The sea is his, for he made it,
and his hands formed the dry land.

6Come, let us bow down in worship,
let us kneel before the LORD our Maker;
7for he is our God
and we are the people of his pasture,
the flock under his care.

Today, if you hear his voice,
8 do not harden your hearts as you did at Meribah,[a]
as you did that day at Massah[b] in the desert,
9where your fathers tested and tried me,
though they had seen what I did.
10For forty years I was angry with that generation;
I said, "They are a people whose hearts go astray,
and they have not known my ways."

[a]8 *Meribah* means *quarreling.* [b]8 *Massah* means *testing.*

11 So I declared on oath in my anger,
"They shall never enter my rest."

Psalm 96

1 Sing to the LORD a new song;
sing to the LORD, all the earth.
2 Sing to the LORD, praise his name;
proclaim his salvation day after day.
3 Declare his glory among the nations,
his marvelous deeds among all peoples.

4 For great is the LORD and most worthy of praise;
he is to be feared above all gods.
5 For all the gods of the nations are idols,
but the LORD made the heavens.
6 Splendor and majesty are before him;
strength and glory are in his sanctuary.

7 Ascribe to the LORD, O families of nations,
ascribe to the LORD glory and strength.
8 Ascribe to the LORD the glory due his name;
bring an offering and come into his courts.
9 Worship the LORD in the splendor of his[a] holiness;
tremble before him, all the earth.

10 Say among the nations, "The LORD reigns."
The world is firmly established, it cannot be moved;
he will judge the peoples with equity.
11 Let the heavens rejoice, let the earth be glad;
let the sea resound, and all that is in it;
12 let the fields be jubilant, and everything in them.
Then all the trees of the forest will sing for joy;
13 they will sing before the LORD, for he comes,
he comes to judge the earth.
He will judge the world in righteousness
and the peoples in his truth.

Psalm 97

1 The LORD reigns, let the earth be glad;
let the distant shores rejoice.

2 Clouds and thick darkness surround him;
righteousness and justice are the foundation of his throne.
3 Fire goes before him
and consumes his foes on every side.
4 His lightning lights up the world;
the earth sees and trembles.
5 The mountains melt like wax before the LORD,
before the Lord of all the earth.
6 The heavens proclaim his righteousness,
and all the peoples see his glory.

7 All who worship images are put to shame,
those who boast in idols—
worship him, all you gods!

8 Zion hears and rejoices
and the villages of Judah are glad
because of your judgments, O LORD.
9 For you, O LORD, are the Most High over all the earth;
you are exalted far above all gods.

10 Let those who love the LORD hate evil,
for he guards the lives of his faithful ones
and delivers them from the hand of the wicked.
11 Light is shed upon the righteous
and joy on the upright in heart.
12 Rejoice in the LORD, you who are righteous,
and praise his holy name.

Psalm 98

A psalm.

1 Sing to the LORD a new song,
for he has done marvelous things;
his right hand and his holy arm
have worked salvation for him.
2 The LORD has made his salvation known
and revealed his righteousness to the nations.
3 He has remembered his love
and his faithfulness to the house of Israel;

[a] 9 Or *LORD with the splendor of*

all the ends of the earth have seen
the salvation of our God.

4Shout for joy to the LORD, all the earth,
burst into jubilant song with music;
5make music to the LORD with the harp,
with the harp and the sound of singing,
6with trumpets and the blast of the ram's horn—
shout for joy before the LORD, the King.

7Let the sea resound, and everything in it,
the world, and all who live in it.
8Let the rivers clap their hands,
let the mountains sing together for joy;
9let them sing before the LORD,
for he comes to judge the earth.
He will judge the world in righteousness
and the peoples with equity.

Psalm 99

1The LORD reigns,
let the nations tremble;
he sits enthroned between the cherubim,
let the earth shake.
2Great is the LORD in Zion;
he is exalted over all the nations.
3Let them praise your great and awesome name—
he is holy.

4The King is mighty, he loves justice—
you have established equity;
in Jacob you have done
what is just and right.
5Exalt the LORD our God
and worship at his footstool;
he is holy.

6Moses and Aaron were among his priests,
Samuel was among those who called on his name;
they called on the LORD
and he answered them.
7He spoke to them from the pillar of cloud;
they kept his statutes and the decrees he gave them.
8O LORD our God,
you answered them;
you were to Israel[a] a forgiving God,
though you punished their misdeeds.[b]
9Exalt the LORD our God
and worship at his holy mountain,
for the LORD our God is holy.

Psalm 100

A psalm. For giving thanks.

1Shout for joy to the LORD, all the earth.
2 Worship the LORD with gladness;
come before him with joyful songs.
3Know that the LORD is God.
It is he who made us, and we are his[c];
we are his people, the sheep of his pasture.

4Enter his gates with thanksgiving
and his courts with praise;
give thanks to him and praise his name.
5For the LORD is good and his love endures forever;
his faithfulness continues through all generations.

Psalm 101

Of David. A psalm.

1I will sing of your love and justice;
to you, O LORD, I will sing praise.
2I will be careful to lead a blameless life—
when will you come to me?

I will walk in my house
with blameless heart.
3I will set before my eyes
no vile thing.

The deeds of faithless men I hate;
they will not cling to me.
4Men of perverse heart shall be far from me;
I will have nothing to do with evil.

5Whoever slanders his neighbor in secret,
him will I put to silence;
whoever has haughty eyes and a proud heart,
him will I not endure.

[a]8 Hebrew *them* [b]8 Or / *an avenger of the wrongs done to them* [c]3 Or *and not we ourselves*

6My eyes will be on the faithful in the land,
that they may dwell with me;
he whose walk is blameless
will minister to me.

7No one who practices deceit
will dwell in my house;
no one who speaks falsely
will stand in my presence.

8Every morning I will put to silence
all the wicked in the land;
I will cut off every evildoer
from the city of the LORD.

Psalm 102

A prayer of an afflicted man. When he is faint and pours out his lament before the LORD.

1Hear my prayer, O LORD;
let my cry for help come to you.
2Do not hide your face from me
when I am in distress.
Turn your ear to me;
when I call, answer me quickly.

3For my days vanish like smoke;
my bones burn like glowing embers.
4My heart is blighted and withered like grass;
I forget to eat my food.
5Because of my loud groaning
I am reduced to skin and bones.
6I am like a desert owl,
like an owl among the ruins.
7I lie awake; I have become
like a bird alone on a roof.
8All day long my enemies taunt me;
those who rail against me use my name as a curse.
9For I eat ashes as my food
and mingle my drink with tears
10because of your great wrath,
for you have taken me up and thrown me aside.
11My days are like the evening shadow;
I wither away like grass.

12But you, O LORD, sit enthroned forever;
your renown endures through all generations.
13You will arise and have compassion on Zion,
for it is time to show favor to her;
the appointed time has come.
14For her stones are dear to your servants;
her very dust moves them to pity.
15The nations will fear the name of the LORD,
all the kings of the earth will revere your glory.
16For the LORD will rebuild Zion
and appear in his glory.
17He will respond to the prayer of the destitute;
he will not despise their plea.

18Let this be written for a future generation,
that a people not yet created may praise the LORD:
19"The LORD looked down from his sanctuary on high,
from heaven he viewed the earth,
20to hear the groans of the prisoners
and release those condemned to death."
21So the name of the LORD will be declared in Zion
and his praise in Jerusalem
22when the peoples and the kingdoms
assemble to worship the LORD.

23In the course of my life[a] he broke my strength;
he cut short my days.
24So I said:
"Do not take me away, O my God,
in the midst of my days;
your years go on through all generations.
25In the beginning you laid the foundations of the earth,
and the heavens are the work of your hands.
26They will perish, but you remain;
they will all wear out like a garment.
Like clothing you will change them
and they will be discarded.
27But you remain the same,
and your years will never end.
28The children of your servants will live in your presence;
their descendants will be established before you."

[a]23 Or *By his power*

Psalm 103

Of David.

1 Praise the LORD, O my soul;
all my inmost being, praise his holy name.
2 Praise the LORD, O my soul,
and forget not all his benefits—
3 who forgives all your sins
and heals all your diseases,
4 who redeems your life from the pit
and crowns you with love and compassion,
5 who satisfies your desires with good things
so that your youth is renewed like the eagle's.

6 The LORD works righteousness
and justice for all the oppressed.

7 He made known his ways to Moses,
his deeds to the people of Israel:
8 The LORD is compassionate and gracious,
slow to anger, abounding in love.
9 He will not always accuse,
nor will he harbor his anger forever;
10 he does not treat us as our sins deserve
or repay us according to our iniquities.
11 For as high as the heavens are above the earth,
so great is his love for those who fear him;
12 as far as the east is from the west,
so far has he removed our transgressions from us.
13 As a father has compassion on his children,
so the LORD has compassion on those who fear him;
14 for he knows how we are formed,
he remembers that we are dust.
15 As for man, his days are like grass,
he flourishes like a flower of the field;
16 the wind blows over it and it is gone,
and its place remembers it no more.
17 But from everlasting to everlasting
the LORD's love is with those who fear him,
and his righteousness with their children's children—
18 with those who keep his covenant
and remember to obey his precepts.
19 The LORD has established his throne in heaven,
and his kingdom rules over all.

20 Praise the LORD, you his angels,
you mighty ones who do his bidding,
who obey his word.
21 Praise the LORD, all his heavenly hosts,
you his servants who do his will.
22 Praise the LORD, all his works
everywhere in his dominion.

Praise the LORD, O my soul.

Psalm 104

1 Praise the LORD, O my soul.

O LORD my God, you are very great;
you are clothed with splendor and majesty.
2 He wraps himself in light as with a garment;
he stretches out the heavens like a tent
3 and lays the beams of his upper chambers on their waters.
He makes the clouds his chariot
and rides on the wings of the wind.
4 He makes winds his messengers,[a]
flames of fire his servants.

5 He set the earth on its foundations;
it can never be moved.
6 You covered it with the deep as with a garment;
the waters stood above the mountains.
7 But at your rebuke the waters fled,
at the sound of your thunder they took to flight;
8 they flowed over the mountains,
they went down into the valleys,
to the place you assigned for them.
9 You set a boundary they cannot cross;
never again will they cover the earth.

10 He makes springs pour water into the ravines;
it flows between the mountains.
11 They give water to all the beasts of the field;
the wild donkeys quench their thirst.
12 The birds of the air nest by the waters;
they sing among the branches.

[a] 4 Or *angels*

13He waters the mountains from his
upper chambers;
the earth is satisfied by the fruit of
his work.
14He makes grass grow for the cattle,
and plants for man to cultivate—
bringing forth food from the earth:
15wine that gladdens the heart of
man,
oil to make his face shine,
and bread that sustains his heart.
16The trees of the LORD are well
watered,
the cedars of Lebanon that he
planted.
17There the birds make their nests;
the stork has its home in the pine
trees.

THURSDAY

VERSE FOR THE DAY:	AUTHOR:	PASSAGE FOR THE DAY:
Psalm 103:8	Gary Smalley	Psalm 103:1–22

Honor: The Anger Antidote

Anger is such an unsettling emotion that we're tempted to shove it aside and not deal with it. But it won't just go away. If we don't take responsibility for our own anger, it will come back later to haunt us.

One way to battle anger is to forgive, basing that on how much you yourself have been forgiven by God. It helps to understand that people who offend us usually carry around a lot of pain in their own hearts. Another way is to learn to deal with disappointment over not getting what we expect, because we'll never get everything we want. A third principle is to remember we can't choose what others will do—we can't keep someone from hurting us.

In our marriages, honoring is the opposite of being angry. We all need to focus on honor, which means placing a high value on your spouse. When my wife, Norma, does something I don't like, I may react negatively at first. But as soon as I can, I start honoring her in my mind. I pray, "God, would you help me be a source of encouragement to my wife—this woman I value so highly? Will you show me how I can help her?" It's a matter of taking control of your attitudes and emotions and steering them away from an angry response.

MARRIAGE BUILDERS

♦ *Generally speaking, do you tend to deal with your anger or shove it aside?*

♦ *What characteristics of your spouse do you find easy to honor (place high value on)?*

Additional Scripture Readings
Proverbs 29:11; 1 Thessalonians 5:16–18

Go to page 621 for your next devotional reading.

18 The high mountains belong to the wild goats;
the crags are a refuge for the coneys.[a]

19 The moon marks off the seasons,
and the sun knows when to go down.
20 You bring darkness, it becomes night,
and all the beasts of the forest prowl.
21 The lions roar for their prey
and seek their food from God.
22 The sun rises, and they steal away;
they return and lie down in their dens.
23 Then man goes out to his work,
to his labor until evening.

24 How many are your works, O LORD!
In wisdom you made them all;
the earth is full of your creatures.
25 There is the sea, vast and spacious,
teeming with creatures beyond number—
living things both large and small.
26 There the ships go to and fro,
and the leviathan, which you formed to frolic there.

27 These all look to you
to give them their food at the proper time.
28 When you give it to them,
they gather it up;
when you open your hand,
they are satisfied with good things.
29 When you hide your face,
they are terrified;
when you take away their breath,
they die and return to the dust.
30 When you send your Spirit,
they are created,
and you renew the face of the earth.

31 May the glory of the LORD endure forever;
may the LORD rejoice in his works—
32 he who looks at the earth, and it trembles,
who touches the mountains, and they smoke.

33 I will sing to the LORD all my life;
I will sing praise to my God as long as I live.
34 May my meditation be pleasing to him,
as I rejoice in the LORD.
35 But may sinners vanish from the earth
and the wicked be no more.

Praise the LORD, O my soul.

Praise the LORD.[b]

Psalm 105

1 Give thanks to the LORD, call on his name;
make known among the nations what he has done.
2 Sing to him, sing praise to him;
tell of all his wonderful acts.
3 Glory in his holy name;
let the hearts of those who seek the LORD rejoice.
4 Look to the LORD and his strength;
seek his face always.

5 Remember the wonders he has done,
his miracles, and the judgments he pronounced,
6 O descendants of Abraham his servant,
O sons of Jacob, his chosen ones.
7 He is the LORD our God;
his judgments are in all the earth.

8 He remembers his covenant forever,
the word he commanded, for a thousand generations,
9 the covenant he made with Abraham,
the oath he swore to Isaac.
10 He confirmed it to Jacob as a decree,
to Israel as an everlasting covenant:
11 "To you I will give the land of Canaan
as the portion you will inherit."

12 When they were but few in number,
few indeed, and strangers in it,
13 they wandered from nation to nation,
from one kingdom to another.
14 He allowed no one to oppress them;
for their sake he rebuked kings:
15 "Do not touch my anointed ones;
do my prophets no harm."

16 He called down famine on the land
and destroyed all their supplies of food;
17 and he sent a man before them—
Joseph, sold as a slave.
18 They bruised his feet with shackles,
his neck was put in irons,
19 till what he foretold came to pass,

[a] 18 That is, the hyrax or rock badger
[b] 35 Hebrew *Hallelu Yah*; in the Septuagint this line stands at the beginning of Psalm 105.

till the word of the LORD proved him true.
20 The king sent and released him,
the ruler of peoples set him free.
21 He made him master of his household,
ruler over all he possessed,
22 to instruct his princes as he pleased
and teach his elders wisdom.

23 Then Israel entered Egypt;
Jacob lived as an alien in the land of Ham.
24 The LORD made his people very fruitful;
he made them too numerous for their foes,
25 whose hearts he turned to hate his people,
to conspire against his servants.
26 He sent Moses his servant,
and Aaron, whom he had chosen.
27 They performed his miraculous signs among them,
his wonders in the land of Ham.
28 He sent darkness and made the land dark—
for had they not rebelled against his words?
29 He turned their waters into blood,
causing their fish to die.
30 Their land teemed with frogs,
which went up into the bedrooms of their rulers.
31 He spoke, and there came swarms of flies,
and gnats throughout their country.
32 He turned their rain into hail,
with lightning throughout their land;
33 he struck down their vines and fig trees
and shattered the trees of their country.
34 He spoke, and the locusts came,
grasshoppers without number;
35 they ate up every green thing in their land,
ate up the produce of their soil.
36 Then he struck down all the firstborn in their land,
the firstfruits of all their manhood.

37 He brought out Israel, laden with silver and gold,
and from among their tribes no one faltered.
38 Egypt was glad when they left,
because dread of Israel had fallen on them.
39 He spread out a cloud as a covering,
and a fire to give light at night.
40 They asked, and he brought them quail
and satisfied them with the bread of heaven.
41 He opened the rock, and water gushed out;
like a river it flowed in the desert.

42 For he remembered his holy promise
given to his servant Abraham.
43 He brought out his people with rejoicing,
his chosen ones with shouts of joy;
44 he gave them the lands of the nations,
and they fell heir to what others had toiled for—
45 that they might keep his precepts
and observe his laws.

Praise the LORD.[a]

Psalm 106

1 Praise the LORD.[b]

Give thanks to the LORD, for he is good;
his love endures forever.
2 Who can proclaim the mighty acts of the LORD
or fully declare his praise?
3 Blessed are they who maintain justice,
who constantly do what is right.
4 Remember me, O LORD, when you show favor to your people,
come to my aid when you save them,
5 that I may enjoy the prosperity of your chosen ones,
that I may share in the joy of your nation
and join your inheritance in giving praise.

6 We have sinned, even as our fathers did;
we have done wrong and acted wickedly.
7 When our fathers were in Egypt,
they gave no thought to your miracles;
they did not remember your many kindnesses,

[a] 45 Hebrew *Hallelu Yah* [b] 1 Hebrew *Hallelu Yah*; also in verse 48

and they rebelled by the sea, the
Red Sea.[a]
8Yet he saved them for his name's
sake,
to make his mighty power known.
9He rebuked the Red Sea, and it dried
up;
he led them through the depths as
through a desert.
10He saved them from the hand of the
foe;
from the hand of the enemy he
redeemed them.
11The waters covered their adversaries;
not one of them survived.
12Then they believed his promises
and sang his praise.

13But they soon forgot what he had
done
and did not wait for his counsel.
14In the desert they gave in to their
craving;
in the wasteland they put God to
the test.
15So he gave them what they asked for,
but sent a wasting disease upon
them.

16In the camp they grew envious of
Moses
and of Aaron, who was consecrated
to the LORD.
17The earth opened up and swallowed
Dathan;
it buried the company of Abiram.
18Fire blazed among their followers;
a flame consumed the wicked.

19At Horeb they made a calf
and worshiped an idol cast from
metal.
20They exchanged their Glory
for an image of a bull, which eats
grass.
21They forgot the God who saved them,
who had done great things in Egypt,
22miracles in the land of Ham
and awesome deeds by the Red Sea.
23So he said he would destroy them—
had not Moses, his chosen one,
stood in the breach before him
to keep his wrath from destroying
them.

24Then they despised the pleasant land;
they did not believe his promise.
25They grumbled in their tents
and did not obey the LORD.
26So he swore to them with uplifted
hand
that he would make them fall in the
desert,
27make their descendants fall among the
nations
and scatter them throughout the
lands.

28They yoked themselves to the Baal of
Peor
and ate sacrifices offered to lifeless
gods;
29they provoked the LORD to anger by
their wicked deeds,
and a plague broke out among
them.
30But Phinehas stood up and intervened,
and the plague was checked.
31This was credited to him as
righteousness
for endless generations to come.

32By the waters of Meribah they
angered the LORD,
and trouble came to Moses because
of them;
33for they rebelled against the Spirit of
God,
and rash words came from Moses'
lips.[b]

34They did not destroy the peoples
as the LORD had commanded them,
35but they mingled with the nations
and adopted their customs.
36They worshiped their idols,
which became a snare to them.
37They sacrificed their sons
and their daughters to demons.
38They shed innocent blood,
the blood of their sons and
daughters,
whom they sacrificed to the idols of
Canaan,
and the land was desecrated by
their blood.
39They defiled themselves by what they
did;
by their deeds they prostituted
themselves.

40Therefore the LORD was angry with his
people
and abhorred his inheritance.
41He handed them over to the nations,
and their foes ruled over them.

[a]7 Hebrew *Yam Suph*; that is, Sea of Reeds; also in verses 9 and 22 [b]33 Or *against his spirit, / and rash words came from his lips*

42Their enemies oppressed them
and subjected them to their power.
43Many times he delivered them,
but they were bent on rebellion
and they wasted away in their sin.

44But he took note of their distress
when he heard their cry;
45for their sake he remembered his covenant
and out of his great love he relented.
46He caused them to be pitied
by all who held them captive.

47Save us, O LORD our God,
and gather us from the nations,
that we may give thanks to your holy name
and glory in your praise.

48Praise be to the LORD, the God of Israel,
from everlasting to everlasting.
Let all the people say, "Amen!"
Praise the LORD.

BOOK V

Psalms 107–150

Psalm 107

1Give thanks to the LORD, for he is good;
his love endures forever.
2Let the redeemed of the LORD say this—
those he redeemed from the hand of the foe,
3those he gathered from the lands,

VERSE FOR THE DAY: Psalm 107:8–9

AUTHOR: Ben Patterson

PASSAGE FOR THE DAY: Psalm 107:1–22

Joyful Gratitude

There is no single area where the faith of the Bible is more at odds with 20th-century American culture than Job losing everything that he used to call his own. Americans believe they have certain rights: the right to be happy; the right to an acceptable standard of living; the right to a satisfying marriage and a fulfilling job.

But according to the Bible, we have no rights! Whatever we do have we have because God in his grace and generosity has given it to us. When we realize this, there comes into our lives a joyful gratitude for what we have, and we are freed from resentment and anxiety over what we don't have.

MARRIAGE BUILDERS

♦ *How does gratitude free you from anxiety over what you don't have?*

♦ *How can giving up those false expectations actually help you meet each other's needs even better in the future?*

Additional Scripture Readings
Job 1:21; Colossians 3:15

Go to page 626 for your next devotional reading.

from east and west, from north and
south.[a]

4Some wandered in desert wastelands,
finding no way to a city where they
could settle.
5They were hungry and thirsty,
and their lives ebbed away.
6Then they cried out to the LORD in
their trouble,
and he delivered them from their
distress.
7He led them by a straight way
to a city where they could settle.
8Let them give thanks to the LORD for
his unfailing love
and his wonderful deeds for men,
9for he satisfies the thirsty
and fills the hungry with good
things.

10Some sat in darkness and the deepest
gloom,
prisoners suffering in iron chains,
11for they had rebelled against the
words of God
and despised the counsel of the
Most High.
12So he subjected them to bitter labor;
they stumbled, and there was no
one to help.
13Then they cried to the LORD in their
trouble,
and he saved them from their
distress.
14He brought them out of darkness and
the deepest gloom
and broke away their chains.
15Let them give thanks to the LORD for
his unfailing love
and his wonderful deeds for men,
16for he breaks down gates of bronze
and cuts through bars of iron.

17Some became fools through their
rebellious ways
and suffered affliction because of
their iniquities.
18They loathed all food
and drew near the gates of death.
19Then they cried to the LORD in their
trouble,
and he saved them from their
distress.
20He sent forth his word and healed
them;
he rescued them from the grave.
21Let them give thanks to the LORD for
his unfailing love
and his wonderful deeds for men.
22Let them sacrifice thank offerings
and tell of his works with songs of
joy.

23Others went out on the sea in ships;
they were merchants on the mighty
waters.
24They saw the works of the LORD,
his wonderful deeds in the deep.
25For he spoke and stirred up a tempest
that lifted high the waves.
26They mounted up to the heavens and
went down to the depths;
in their peril their courage melted
away.
27They reeled and staggered like
drunken men;
they were at their wits' end.
28Then they cried out to the LORD in
their trouble,
and he brought them out of their
distress.
29He stilled the storm to a whisper;
the waves of the sea were hushed.
30They were glad when it grew calm,
and he guided them to their desired
haven.
31Let them give thanks to the LORD for
his unfailing love
and his wonderful deeds for men.
32Let them exalt him in the assembly of
the people
and praise him in the council of the
elders.

33He turned rivers into a desert,
flowing springs into thirsty ground,
34and fruitful land into a salt waste,
because of the wickedness of those
who lived there.
35He turned the desert into pools of
water
and the parched ground into
flowing springs;
36there he brought the hungry to live,
and they founded a city where they
could settle.
37They sowed fields and planted
vineyards
that yielded a fruitful harvest;
38he blessed them, and their numbers
greatly increased,
and he did not let their herds
diminish.

[a]3 Hebrew *north and the sea*

39Then their numbers decreased, and they were humbled
by oppression, calamity and sorrow;
40he who pours contempt on nobles
made them wander in a trackless waste.
41But he lifted the needy out of their affliction
and increased their families like flocks.
42The upright see and rejoice,
but all the wicked shut their mouths.

43Whoever is wise, let him heed these things
and consider the great love of the LORD.

Psalm 108

A song. A psalm of David.

1My heart is steadfast, O God;
I will sing and make music with all my soul.
2Awake, harp and lyre!
I will awaken the dawn.
3I will praise you, O LORD, among the nations;
I will sing of you among the peoples.
4For great is your love, higher than the heavens;
your faithfulness reaches to the skies.
5Be exalted, O God, above the heavens,
and let your glory be over all the earth.

6Save us and help us with your right hand,
that those you love may be delivered.
7God has spoken from his sanctuary:
"In triumph I will parcel out Shechem
and measure off the Valley of Succoth.
8Gilead is mine, Manasseh is mine;
Ephraim is my helmet,
Judah my scepter.
9Moab is my washbasin,
upon Edom I toss my sandal;
over Philistia I shout in triumph."

10Who will bring me to the fortified city?
Who will lead me to Edom?
11Is it not you, O God, you who have rejected us
and no longer go out with our armies?
12Give us aid against the enemy,
for the help of man is worthless.
13With God we will gain the victory,
and he will trample down our enemies.

Psalm 109

For the director of music. Of David. A psalm.

1O God, whom I praise,
do not remain silent,
2for wicked and deceitful men
have opened their mouths against me;
they have spoken against me with lying tongues.
3With words of hatred they surround me;
they attack me without cause.
4In return for my friendship they accuse me,
but I am a man of prayer.
5They repay me evil for good,
and hatred for my friendship.

6Appoint[a] an evil man[b] to oppose him;
let an accuser[c] stand at his right hand.
7When he is tried, let him be found guilty,
and may his prayers condemn him.
8May his days be few;
may another take his place of leadership.
9May his children be fatherless
and his wife a widow.
10May his children be wandering beggars;
may they be driven[d] from their ruined homes.
11May a creditor seize all he has;
may strangers plunder the fruits of his labor.
12May no one extend kindness to him
or take pity on his fatherless children.
13May his descendants be cut off,
their names blotted out from the next generation.

[a]6 Or ¿*They say:*¿ "*Appoint* (with quotation marks at the end of verse 19) [b]6 Or *the Evil One* [c]6 Or *let Satan* [d]10 Septuagint; Hebrew *sought*

14 May the iniquity of his fathers be
remembered before the LORD;
may the sin of his mother never be
blotted out.
15 May their sins always remain before
the LORD,
that he may cut off the memory of
them from the earth.

16 For he never thought of doing a
kindness,
but hounded to death the poor
and the needy and the
brokenhearted.
17 He loved to pronounce a curse—
may it[a] come on him;
he found no pleasure in blessing—
may it be[b] far from him.
18 He wore cursing as his garment;
it entered into his body like water,
into his bones like oil.
19 May it be like a cloak wrapped about
him,
like a belt tied forever around him.
20 May this be the LORD's payment to my
accusers,
to those who speak evil of me.

21 But you, O Sovereign LORD,
deal well with me for your name's
sake;
out of the goodness of your love,
deliver me.
22 For I am poor and needy,
and my heart is wounded within
me.
23 I fade away like an evening shadow;
I am shaken off like a locust.
24 My knees give way from fasting;
my body is thin and gaunt.
25 I am an object of scorn to my
accusers;
when they see me, they shake their
heads.

26 Help me, O LORD my God;
save me in accordance with your
love.
27 Let them know that it is your hand,
that you, O LORD, have done it.
28 They may curse, but you will bless;
when they attack they will be put to
shame,
but your servant will rejoice.
29 My accusers will be clothed with
disgrace
and wrapped in shame as in a
cloak.

30 With my mouth I will greatly extol the
LORD;
in the great throng I will praise him.
31 For he stands at the right hand of the
needy one,
to save his life from those who
condemn him.

Psalm 110

Of David. A psalm.

1 The LORD says to my Lord:
"Sit at my right hand
until I make your enemies
a footstool for your feet."

2 The LORD will extend your mighty
scepter from Zion;
you will rule in the midst of your
enemies.
3 Your troops will be willing
on your day of battle.
Arrayed in holy majesty,
from the womb of the dawn
you will receive the dew of your
youth.[c]

4 The LORD has sworn
and will not change his mind:
"You are a priest forever,
in the order of Melchizedek."

5 The Lord is at your right hand;
he will crush kings on the day of
his wrath.
6 He will judge the nations, heaping up
the dead
and crushing the rulers of the whole
earth.
7 He will drink from a brook beside the
way[d];
therefore he will lift up his head.

Psalm 111[e]

1 Praise the LORD.[f]

I will extol the LORD with all my heart
in the council of the upright and in
the assembly.

2 Great are the works of the LORD;
they are pondered by all who
delight in them.

[a] 17 Or *curse, / and it has* [b] 17 Or *blessing, / and it is like the dew* [c] 3 Or / *your young men will come to you* [d] 7 Or / *The One who grants succession will set him in authority* [e] This psalm is an acrostic poem, the lines of which begin with the successive letters of the Hebrew alphabet. [f] 1 Hebrew *Hallelu Yah*

3Glorious and majestic are his deeds,
and his righteousness endures
forever.
4He has caused his wonders to be
remembered;
the LORD is gracious and
compassionate.
5He provides food for those who fear
him;
he remembers his covenant forever.
6He has shown his people the power of
his works,
giving them the lands of other
nations.
7The works of his hands are faithful
and just;
all his precepts are trustworthy.
8They are steadfast for ever and ever,
done in faithfulness and
uprightness.
9He provided redemption for his
people;
he ordained his covenant forever—
holy and awesome is his name.

10The fear of the LORD is the beginning
of wisdom;
all who follow his precepts have
good understanding.
To him belongs eternal praise.

Psalm 112[a]

1Praise the LORD.[b]

Blessed is the man who fears the
LORD,
who finds great delight in his
commands.

2His children will be mighty in the
land;
the generation of the upright will be
blessed.
3Wealth and riches are in his house,
and his righteousness endures
forever.
4Even in darkness light dawns for the
upright,
for the gracious and compassionate
and righteous man.[c]
5Good will come to him who is
generous and lends freely,
who conducts his affairs with
justice.
6Surely he will never be shaken;
a righteous man will be
remembered forever.
7He will have no fear of bad news;
his heart is steadfast, trusting in the
LORD.
8His heart is secure, he will have no
fear;
in the end he will look in triumph
on his foes.
9He has scattered abroad his gifts to
the poor,
his righteousness endures forever;
his horn[d] will be lifted high in
honor.

10The wicked man will see and be
vexed,
he will gnash his teeth and waste
away;
the longings of the wicked will
come to nothing.

Psalm 113

1Praise the LORD.[e]

Praise, O servants of the LORD,
praise the name of the LORD.
2Let the name of the LORD be praised,
both now and forevermore.
3From the rising of the sun to the place
where it sets,
the name of the LORD is to be
praised.

4The LORD is exalted over all the
nations,
his glory above the heavens.
5Who is like the LORD our God,
the One who sits enthroned on
high,
6who stoops down to look
on the heavens and the earth?

7He raises the poor from the dust
and lifts the needy from the ash
heap;
8he seats them with princes,
with the princes of their people.
9He settles the barren woman in her
home
as a happy mother of children.

Praise the LORD.

[a]This psalm is an acrostic poem, the lines of which begin with the successive letters of the Hebrew alphabet. [b]1 Hebrew *Hallelu Yah* [c]4 Or / *for* ⌊*the* LORD⌋ *is gracious and compassionate and righteous* [d]9 *Horn* here symbolizes dignity. [e]1 Hebrew *Hallelu Yah*; also in verse 9

WEEKENDING

IN-LAWS

Despite the fact that mother-in-law jokes still abound, the responsibility for making in-law relationships work belongs to all of us. Discuss how these guidelines might make you a better daughter- and son-in-law.

1. Make your in-laws feel that they are important to you.

2. Do not blame your in-laws for problems you are having with your spouse.

3. Encourage your in-laws to talk about themselves. This is a great way to understand what they are really like.

4. Express interest in their interests.

5. Don't expect instant warmth and bonding; a solid relationship takes time.

6. Solicit their help in finding a comfortable way of addressing them ("Mom" or "Mother Giordano," "Dad" or "Russell").

7. Maintain direct contact with your in-laws; don't use your spouse as a go-between.

8. Act real and authentic; be yourself.

— *Penny Bilofsky and Fredda Sacharow*

REVIVE

Saturday: Ruth 1:1–19
Sunday: Ephesians 6:2–3

Go to page 629 for your next devotional reading.

Psalm 114

1When Israel came out of Egypt,
the house of Jacob from a people of foreign tongue,
2Judah became God's sanctuary,
Israel his dominion.

3The sea looked and fled,
the Jordan turned back;
4the mountains skipped like rams,
the hills like lambs.

5Why was it, O sea, that you fled,
O Jordan, that you turned back,
6you mountains, that you skipped like rams,
you hills, like lambs?

7Tremble, O earth, at the presence of the Lord,
at the presence of the God of Jacob,
8who turned the rock into a pool,
the hard rock into springs of water.

Psalm 115

1Not to us, O LORD, not to us
but to your name be the glory,
because of your love and faithfulness.

2Why do the nations say,
"Where is their God?"
3Our God is in heaven;
he does whatever pleases him.
4But their idols are silver and gold,
made by the hands of men.
5They have mouths, but cannot speak,
eyes, but they cannot see;
6they have ears, but cannot hear,
noses, but they cannot smell;
7they have hands, but cannot feel,
feet, but they cannot walk;
nor can they utter a sound with their throats.
8Those who make them will be like them,
and so will all who trust in them.

9O house of Israel, trust in the LORD—
he is their help and shield.
10O house of Aaron, trust in the LORD—
he is their help and shield.
11You who fear him, trust in the LORD—
he is their help and shield.

12The LORD remembers us and will bless us:
He will bless the house of Israel,
he will bless the house of Aaron,
13he will bless those who fear the LORD—
small and great alike.

14May the LORD make you increase,
both you and your children.
15May you be blessed by the LORD,
the Maker of heaven and earth.

16The highest heavens belong to the LORD,
but the earth he has given to man.
17It is not the dead who praise the LORD,
those who go down to silence;
18it is we who extol the LORD,
both now and forevermore.

Praise the LORD.[a]

Psalm 116

1I love the LORD, for he heard my voice;
he heard my cry for mercy.
2Because he turned his ear to me,
I will call on him as long as I live.

3The cords of death entangled me,
the anguish of the grave[b] came upon me;
I was overcome by trouble and sorrow.
4Then I called on the name of the LORD:
"O LORD, save me!"

5The LORD is gracious and righteous;
our God is full of compassion.
6The LORD protects the simplehearted;
when I was in great need, he saved me.

7Be at rest once more, O my soul,
for the LORD has been good to you.

8For you, O LORD, have delivered my soul from death,
my eyes from tears,
my feet from stumbling,
9that I may walk before the LORD
in the land of the living.
10I believed; therefore[c] I said,
"I am greatly afflicted."
11And in my dismay I said,
"All men are liars."

12How can I repay the LORD
for all his goodness to me?
13I will lift up the cup of salvation
and call on the name of the LORD.

[a]18 Hebrew *Hallelu Yah* [b]3 Hebrew *Sheol* [c]10 Or *believed even when*

14 I will fulfill my vows to the LORD
in the presence of all his people.

15 Precious in the sight of the LORD
is the death of his saints.
16 O LORD, truly I am your servant;
I am your servant, the son of your maidservant[a];
you have freed me from my chains.

17 I will sacrifice a thank offering to you
and call on the name of the LORD.
18 I will fulfill my vows to the LORD
in the presence of all his people,
19 in the courts of the house of the LORD—
in your midst, O Jerusalem.

Praise the LORD.[b]

Psalm 117

1 Praise the LORD, all you nations;
extol him, all you peoples.
2 For great is his love toward us,
and the faithfulness of the LORD endures forever.

Praise the LORD.[b]

Psalm 118

1 Give thanks to the LORD, for he is good;
his love endures forever.

2 Let Israel say:
"His love endures forever."
3 Let the house of Aaron say:
"His love endures forever."
4 Let those who fear the LORD say:
"His love endures forever."

5 In my anguish I cried to the LORD,
and he answered by setting me free.
6 The LORD is with me; I will not be afraid.
What can man do to me?
7 The LORD is with me; he is my helper.
I will look in triumph on my enemies.

8 It is better to take refuge in the LORD
than to trust in man.
9 It is better to take refuge in the LORD
than to trust in princes.

10 All the nations surrounded me,
but in the name of the LORD I cut them off.
11 They surrounded me on every side,
but in the name of the LORD I cut them off.
12 They swarmed around me like bees,
but they died out as quickly as burning thorns;
in the name of the LORD I cut them off.

13 I was pushed back and about to fall,
but the LORD helped me.
14 The LORD is my strength and my song;
he has become my salvation.

15 Shouts of joy and victory
resound in the tents of the righteous:
"The LORD's right hand has done mighty things!
16 The LORD's right hand is lifted high;
the LORD's right hand has done mighty things!"

17 I will not die but live,
and will proclaim what the LORD has done.
18 The LORD has chastened me severely,
but he has not given me over to death.

19 Open for me the gates of righteousness;
I will enter and give thanks to the LORD.
20 This is the gate of the LORD
through which the righteous may enter.
21 I will give you thanks, for you answered me;
you have become my salvation.

22 The stone the builders rejected
has become the capstone;
23 the LORD has done this,
and it is marvelous in our eyes.
24 This is the day the LORD has made;
let us rejoice and be glad in it.

25 O LORD, save us;
O LORD, grant us success.
26 Blessed is he who comes in the name of the LORD.
From the house of the LORD we bless you.[c]
27 The LORD is God,
and he has made his light shine upon us.
With boughs in hand, join in the festal procession
up[d] to the horns of the altar.

[a] 16 Or *servant, your faithful son* [b] 19,2 Hebrew *Hallelu Yah* [c] 26 The Hebrew is plural.
[d] 27 Or *Bind the festal sacrifice with ropes / and take it*

VERSE FOR THE DAY: Psalm 118:24

AUTHOR: David and Claudia Arp

PASSAGE FOR THE DAY: Psalm 118:1–29

Rejoice and Be Glad

Fun is a crucial element in a strong, healthy marriage. If you're having fun together, your spouse becomes your friend—you'll want to be together. Having fun really is divorce protection.

Life is so busy that you need to find those moments of fun and relaxation or the accumulated stress will overpower you. And sometimes a "moment" is all you can find. Fifteen minutes of fun here or there can make a world of difference.

It's vital for husbands and wives to laugh together and not take themselves too seriously. So cultivate a habit of looking for the humor in any situation—good or bad. In the middle of the hard times, you'll be glad you learned to laugh together. As Christians we're instructed to be joyful in times of trial or difficulty. We can do that because Scripture tells us the Lord is with us in every circumstance. That joy in companionship applies in marriage, too. In times of difficulty, there's joy—and peace—in knowing the two of you are in it together.

Joy is an attitude, while fun is something you can—and should—plan. The fun times can contribute to the joy, but the joy goes deeper. When you know that you're married to someone who understands you and cares how you feel, you can face any difficulty more easily.

To help you both deal with the tough parts of marriage, never lose your sense of joy or fun as you grow together.

MARRIAGE BUILDERS

♦ *What do the two of you do for fun together? Do you need to plan more fun into your relationship?*

♦ *How does joy in your relationship differ from the fun in it?*

Additional Scripture Readings
Philippians 2:1-4; Philemon 7

Go to page 637 for your next devotional reading.

28 You are my God, and I will give you thanks;
you are my God, and I will exalt you.

29 Give thanks to the LORD, for he is good;
his love endures forever.

Psalm 119[a]

א Aleph

1 Blessed are they whose ways are blameless,
who walk according to the law of the LORD.
2 Blessed are they who keep his statutes
and seek him with all their heart.
3 They do nothing wrong;
they walk in his ways.
4 You have laid down precepts
that are to be fully obeyed.
5 Oh, that my ways were steadfast
in obeying your decrees!
6 Then I would not be put to shame
when I consider all your commands.
7 I will praise you with an upright heart
as I learn your righteous laws.
8 I will obey your decrees;
do not utterly forsake me.

ב Beth

9 How can a young man keep his way pure?
By living according to your word.
10 I seek you with all my heart;
do not let me stray from your commands.
11 I have hidden your word in my heart
that I might not sin against you.
12 Praise be to you, O LORD;
teach me your decrees.
13 With my lips I recount
all the laws that come from your mouth.
14 I rejoice in following your statutes
as one rejoices in great riches.
15 I meditate on your precepts
and consider your ways.
16 I delight in your decrees;
I will not neglect your word.

ג Gimel

17 Do good to your servant, and I will live;
I will obey your word.
18 Open my eyes that I may see
wonderful things in your law.
19 I am a stranger on earth;
do not hide your commands from me.
20 My soul is consumed with longing
for your laws at all times.
21 You rebuke the arrogant, who are cursed
and who stray from your commands.
22 Remove from me scorn and contempt,
for I keep your statutes.
23 Though rulers sit together and slander me,
your servant will meditate on your decrees.
24 Your statutes are my delight;
they are my counselors.

ד Daleth

25 I am laid low in the dust;
preserve my life according to your word.
26 I recounted my ways and you answered me;
teach me your decrees.
27 Let me understand the teaching of your precepts;
then I will meditate on your wonders.
28 My soul is weary with sorrow;
strengthen me according to your word.
29 Keep me from deceitful ways;
be gracious to me through your law.
30 I have chosen the way of truth;
I have set my heart on your laws.
31 I hold fast to your statutes, O LORD;
do not let me be put to shame.
32 I run in the path of your commands,
for you have set my heart free.

ה He

33 Teach me, O LORD, to follow your decrees;
then I will keep them to the end.
34 Give me understanding, and I will keep your law
and obey it with all my heart.

[a] This psalm is an acrostic poem; the verses of each stanza begin with the same letter of the Hebrew alphabet.

35Direct me in the path of your commands,
for there I find delight.
36Turn my heart toward your statutes
and not toward selfish gain.
37Turn my eyes away from worthless things;
preserve my life according to your word.[a]
38Fulfill your promise to your servant,
so that you may be feared.
39Take away the disgrace I dread,
for your laws are good.
40How I long for your precepts!
Preserve my life in your righteousness.

ו Waw

41May your unfailing love come to me, O LORD,
your salvation according to your promise;
42then I will answer the one who taunts me,
for I trust in your word.
43Do not snatch the word of truth from my mouth,
for I have put my hope in your laws.
44I will always obey your law,
for ever and ever.
45I will walk about in freedom,
for I have sought out your precepts.
46I will speak of your statutes before kings
and will not be put to shame,
47for I delight in your commands
because I love them.
48I lift up my hands to[b] your commands, which I love,
and I meditate on your decrees.

ז Zayin

49Remember your word to your servant,
for you have given me hope.
50My comfort in my suffering is this:
Your promise preserves my life.
51The arrogant mock me without restraint,
but I do not turn from your law.
52I remember your ancient laws, O LORD,
and I find comfort in them.
53Indignation grips me because of the wicked,
who have forsaken your law.
54Your decrees are the theme of my song
wherever I lodge.
55In the night I remember your name, O LORD,
and I will keep your law.
56This has been my practice:
I obey your precepts.

ח Heth

57You are my portion, O LORD;
I have promised to obey your words.
58I have sought your face with all my heart;
be gracious to me according to your promise.
59I have considered my ways
and have turned my steps to your statutes.
60I will hasten and not delay
to obey your commands.
61Though the wicked bind me with ropes,
I will not forget your law.
62At midnight I rise to give you thanks
for your righteous laws.
63I am a friend to all who fear you,
to all who follow your precepts.
64The earth is filled with your love, O LORD;
teach me your decrees.

ט Teth

65Do good to your servant
according to your word, O LORD.
66Teach me knowledge and good judgment,
for I believe in your commands.
67Before I was afflicted I went astray,
but now I obey your word.
68You are good, and what you do is good;
teach me your decrees.
69Though the arrogant have smeared me with lies,
I keep your precepts with all my heart.
70Their hearts are callous and unfeeling,
but I delight in your law.
71It was good for me to be afflicted
so that I might learn your decrees.
72The law from your mouth is more precious to me
than thousands of pieces of silver and gold.

[a]37 Two manuscripts of the Masoretic Text and Dead Sea Scrolls; most manuscripts of the Masoretic Text *life in your way* [b]48 Or *for*

י Yodh

73 Your hands made me and formed me;
give me understanding to learn your commands.
74 May those who fear you rejoice when they see me,
for I have put my hope in your word.
75 I know, O LORD, that your laws are righteous,
and in faithfulness you have afflicted me.
76 May your unfailing love be my comfort,
according to your promise to your servant.
77 Let your compassion come to me that I may live,
for your law is my delight.
78 May the arrogant be put to shame for wronging me without cause;
but I will meditate on your precepts.
79 May those who fear you turn to me,
those who understand your statutes.
80 May my heart be blameless toward your decrees,
that I may not be put to shame.

כ Kaph

81 My soul faints with longing for your salvation,
but I have put my hope in your word.
82 My eyes fail, looking for your promise;
I say, "When will you comfort me?"
83 Though I am like a wineskin in the smoke,
I do not forget your decrees.
84 How long must your servant wait?
When will you punish my persecutors?
85 The arrogant dig pitfalls for me,
contrary to your law.
86 All your commands are trustworthy;
help me, for men persecute me without cause.
87 They almost wiped me from the earth,
but I have not forsaken your precepts.
88 Preserve my life according to your love,
and I will obey the statutes of your mouth.

ל Lamedh

89 Your word, O LORD, is eternal;
it stands firm in the heavens.
90 Your faithfulness continues through all generations;
you established the earth, and it endures.
91 Your laws endure to this day,
for all things serve you.
92 If your law had not been my delight,
I would have perished in my affliction.
93 I will never forget your precepts,
for by them you have preserved my life.
94 Save me, for I am yours;
I have sought out your precepts.
95 The wicked are waiting to destroy me,
but I will ponder your statutes.
96 To all perfection I see a limit;
but your commands are boundless.

מ Mem

97 Oh, how I love your law!
I meditate on it all day long.
98 Your commands make me wiser than my enemies,
for they are ever with me.
99 I have more insight than all my teachers,
for I meditate on your statutes.
100 I have more understanding than the elders,
for I obey your precepts.
101 I have kept my feet from every evil path
so that I might obey your word.
102 I have not departed from your laws,
for you yourself have taught me.
103 How sweet are your words to my taste,
sweeter than honey to my mouth!
104 I gain understanding from your precepts;
therefore I hate every wrong path.

נ Nun

105 Your word is a lamp to my feet
and a light for my path.
106 I have taken an oath and confirmed it,
that I will follow your righteous laws.
107 I have suffered much;
preserve my life, O LORD, according to your word.
108 Accept, O LORD, the willing praise of my mouth,

and teach me your laws.
109Though I constantly take my life in my hands,
I will not forget your law.
110The wicked have set a snare for me,
but I have not strayed from your precepts.
111Your statutes are my heritage forever;
they are the joy of my heart.
112My heart is set on keeping your decrees
to the very end.

ס Samekh

113I hate double-minded men,
but I love your law.
114You are my refuge and my shield;
I have put my hope in your word.
115Away from me, you evildoers,
that I may keep the commands of my God!
116Sustain me according to your promise, and I will live;
do not let my hopes be dashed.
117Uphold me, and I will be delivered;
I will always have regard for your decrees.
118You reject all who stray from your decrees,
for their deceitfulness is in vain.
119All the wicked of the earth you discard like dross;
therefore I love your statutes.
120My flesh trembles in fear of you;
I stand in awe of your laws.

ע Ayin

121I have done what is righteous and just;
do not leave me to my oppressors.
122Ensure your servant's well-being;
let not the arrogant oppress me.
123My eyes fail, looking for your salvation,
looking for your righteous promise.
124Deal with your servant according to your love
and teach me your decrees.
125I am your servant; give me discernment
that I may understand your statutes.
126It is time for you to act, O Lord;
your law is being broken.
127Because I love your commands
more than gold, more than pure gold,
128and because I consider all your precepts right,
I hate every wrong path.

פ Pe

129Your statutes are wonderful;
therefore I obey them.
130The unfolding of your words gives light;
it gives understanding to the simple.
131I open my mouth and pant,
longing for your commands.
132Turn to me and have mercy on me,
as you always do to those who love your name.
133Direct my footsteps according to your word;
let no sin rule over me.
134Redeem me from the oppression of men,
that I may obey your precepts.
135Make your face shine upon your servant
and teach me your decrees.
136Streams of tears flow from my eyes,
for your law is not obeyed.

צ Tsadhe

137Righteous are you, O Lord,
and your laws are right.
138The statutes you have laid down are righteous;
they are fully trustworthy.
139My zeal wears me out,
for my enemies ignore your words.
140Your promises have been thoroughly tested,
and your servant loves them.
141Though I am lowly and despised,
I do not forget your precepts.
142Your righteousness is everlasting
and your law is true.
143Trouble and distress have come upon me,
but your commands are my delight.
144Your statutes are forever right;
give me understanding that I may live.

ק Qoph

145I call with all my heart; answer me, O Lord,
and I will obey your decrees.
146I call out to you; save me
and I will keep your statutes.
147I rise before dawn and cry for help;
I have put my hope in your word.
148My eyes stay open through the watches of the night,
that I may meditate on your promises.

149Hear my voice in accordance with
your love;
preserve my life, O LORD, according
to your laws.
150Those who devise wicked schemes
are near,
but they are far from your law.
151Yet you are near, O LORD,
and all your commands are true.
152Long ago I learned from your statutes
that you established them to last
forever.

ר Resh

153Look upon my suffering and
deliver me,
for I have not forgotten your law.
154Defend my cause and redeem me;
preserve my life according to your
promise.
155Salvation is far from the wicked,
for they do not seek out your
decrees.
156Your compassion is great, O LORD;
preserve my life according to your
laws.
157Many are the foes who persecute me,
but I have not turned from your
statutes.
158I look on the faithless with loathing,
for they do not obey your word.
159See how I love your precepts;
preserve my life, O LORD, according
to your love.
160All your words are true;
all your righteous laws are eternal.

ש Sin and Shin

161Rulers persecute me without cause,
but my heart trembles at your word.
162I rejoice in your promise
like one who finds great spoil.
163I hate and abhor falsehood
but I love your law.
164Seven times a day I praise you
for your righteous laws.
165Great peace have they who love your
law,
and nothing can make them
stumble.
166I wait for your salvation, O LORD,
and I follow your commands.
167I obey your statutes,
for I love them greatly.
168I obey your precepts and your
statutes,
for all my ways are known to you.

ת Taw

169May my cry come before you,
O LORD;
give me understanding according to
your word.
170May my supplication come before
you;
deliver me according to your
promise.
171May my lips overflow with praise,
for you teach me your decrees.
172May my tongue sing of your word,
for all your commands are
righteous.
173May your hand be ready to help me,
for I have chosen your precepts.
174I long for your salvation, O LORD,
and your law is my delight.
175Let me live that I may praise you,
and may your laws sustain me.
176I have strayed like a lost sheep.
Seek your servant,
for I have not forgotten your
commands.

Psalm 120

A song of ascents.

1I call on the LORD in my distress,
and he answers me.
2Save me, O LORD, from lying lips
and from deceitful tongues.

3What will he do to you,
and what more besides, O deceitful
tongue?
4He will punish you with a warrior's
sharp arrows,
with burning coals of the broom
tree.

5Woe to me that I dwell in Meshech,
that I live among the tents of Kedar!
6Too long have I lived
among those who hate peace.
7I am a man of peace;
but when I speak, they are for war.

Psalm 121

A song of ascents.

1I lift up my eyes to the hills—
where does my help come from?
2My help comes from the LORD,
the Maker of heaven and earth.

3He will not let your foot slip—

he who watches over you will not slumber;
4indeed, he who watches over Israel
will neither slumber nor sleep.

5The LORD watches over you—
the LORD is your shade at your right hand;
6the sun will not harm you by day,
nor the moon by night.

7The LORD will keep you from all harm—
he will watch over your life;
8the LORD will watch over your coming and going
both now and forevermore.

Psalm 122

A song of ascents. Of David.

1I rejoiced with those who said to me,
"Let us go to the house of the LORD."
2Our feet are standing
in your gates, O Jerusalem.

3Jerusalem is built like a city
that is closely compacted together.
4That is where the tribes go up,
the tribes of the LORD,
to praise the name of the LORD
according to the statute given to Israel.
5There the thrones for judgment stand,
the thrones of the house of David.

6Pray for the peace of Jerusalem:
"May those who love you be secure.
7May there be peace within your walls
and security within your citadels."
8For the sake of my brothers and friends,
I will say, "Peace be within you."
9For the sake of the house of the LORD our God,
I will seek your prosperity.

Psalm 123

A song of ascents.

1I lift up my eyes to you,
to you whose throne is in heaven.
2As the eyes of slaves look to the hand of their master,
as the eyes of a maid look to the hand of her mistress,
so our eyes look to the LORD our God,
till he shows us his mercy.

3Have mercy on us, O LORD, have mercy on us,
for we have endured much contempt.
4We have endured much ridicule from the proud,
much contempt from the arrogant.

Psalm 124

A song of ascents. Of David.

1If the LORD had not been on our side—
let Israel say—
2if the LORD had not been on our side
when men attacked us,
3when their anger flared against us,
they would have swallowed us alive;
4the flood would have engulfed us,
the torrent would have swept over us,
5the raging waters
would have swept us away.

6Praise be to the LORD,
who has not let us be torn by their teeth.
7We have escaped like a bird
out of the fowler's snare;
the snare has been broken,
and we have escaped.
8Our help is in the name of the LORD,
the Maker of heaven and earth.

Psalm 125

A song of ascents.

1Those who trust in the LORD are like Mount Zion,
which cannot be shaken but endures forever.
2As the mountains surround Jerusalem,
so the LORD surrounds his people
both now and forevermore.

3The scepter of the wicked will not remain
over the land allotted to the righteous,
for then the righteous might use
their hands to do evil.

4Do good, O LORD, to those who are good,
to those who are upright in heart.

5But those who turn to crooked ways
the LORD will banish with the
evildoers.

Peace be upon Israel.

Psalm 126

A song of ascents.

1When the LORD brought back the
captives to[a] Zion,
we were like men who dreamed.[b]
2Our mouths were filled with laughter,
our tongues with songs of joy.
Then it was said among the nations,
"The LORD has done great things for
them."
3The LORD has done great things for us,
and we are filled with joy.

4Restore our fortunes,[c] O LORD,
like streams in the Negev.
5Those who sow in tears
will reap with songs of joy.
6He who goes out weeping,
carrying seed to sow,
will return with songs of joy,
carrying sheaves with him.

Psalm 127

A song of ascents. Of Solomon.

1Unless the LORD builds the house,
its builders labor in vain.
Unless the LORD watches over the
city,
the watchmen stand guard in
vain.
2In vain you rise early
and stay up late,
toiling for food to eat—
for he grants sleep to[d] those he
loves.

3Sons are a heritage from the LORD,
children a reward from him.
4Like arrows in the hands of a warrior
are sons born in one's youth.
5Blessed is the man
whose quiver is full of them.
They will not be put to shame
when they contend with their
enemies in the gate.

Psalm 128

A song of ascents.

1Blessed are all who fear the LORD,
who walk in his ways.
2You will eat the fruit of your labor;
blessings and prosperity will be
yours.
3Your wife will be like a fruitful vine
within your house;
your sons will be like olive shoots
around your table.
4Thus is the man blessed
who fears the LORD.

5May the LORD bless you from Zion
all the days of your life;
may you see the prosperity of
Jerusalem,
6 and may you live to see your
children's children.

Peace be upon Israel.

Psalm 129

A song of ascents.

1They have greatly oppressed me from
my youth—
let Israel say—
2they have greatly oppressed me from
my youth,
but they have not gained the victory
over me.
3Plowmen have plowed my back
and made their furrows long.
4But the LORD is righteous;
he has cut me free from the cords
of the wicked.

5May all who hate Zion
be turned back in shame.
6May they be like grass on the roof,
which withers before it can grow;
7with it the reaper cannot fill his
hands,
nor the one who gathers fill his
arms.
8May those who pass by not say,
"The blessing of the LORD be upon
you;
we bless you in the name of the
LORD."

[a] 1 Or *LORD restored the fortunes of* [b] 1 Or *men restored to health* [c] 4 Or *Bring back our captives*
[d] 2 Or *eat— / for while they sleep he provides for*

Psalm 130

A song of ascents.

1 Out of the depths I cry to you,
O LORD;
2 O Lord, hear my voice.
Let your ears be attentive
to my cry for mercy.
3 If you, O LORD, kept a record of sins,
O Lord, who could stand?
4 But with you there is forgiveness;
therefore you are feared.
5 I wait for the LORD, my soul waits,
and in his word I put my hope.
6 My soul waits for the Lord
more than watchmen wait for the morning,
more than watchmen wait for the morning.
7 O Israel, put your hope in the LORD,

TUESDAY

VERSE FOR THE DAY:	AUTHOR:	PASSAGE FOR THE DAY:
Psalm 130:3	Walter Wangerin, Jr.	Psalm 130:1–8

The Freedom of Forgiveness

Forgiveness is marriage's lifeblood, and it renews daily. It's like your blood keeps pumping through your body, picking up fresh oxygen. If that renewal stops, death begins. Sin will destroy a marriage.

One big marital crisis that Thanne and I endured actually created a lasting atmosphere of forgiveness. And my wife's forgiveness wasn't a pragmatic decision—she didn't do it to save our marriage. Forgiveness doesn't remove all the hurt feelings. Fears and anger can remain, but something new—God's intrusion of grace—comes in to energize your relationship.

Jesus' presence in a marriage can become power to forgive. When you're too angry or too exhausted to deal with things, God can be the source of a divine ability to forgive.

Now when tension arises between Thanne and me, I retain a trust that God will enable us to forgive each other. We don't underplay problems or sweep them under the rug. We now know that God will bring our marriage along another step beyond our problems. Every instance of significant forgiveness and grace in marriage makes trust and hope grow. Trust and hope in your spouse, and trust and hope in God.

MARRIAGE BUILDERS

♦ *During courtship or the first months of marriage, what was the most significant exchange of forgiveness between you?*
♦ *How can forgiveness give you confidence for the future?*

Additional Scripture Readings
Matthew 6:14–15; Ephesians 4:31—5:2

Go to page 644 for your next devotional reading.

for with the LORD is unfailing love
and with him is full redemption.
8He himself will redeem Israel
from all their sins.

Psalm 131

A song of ascents. Of David.

1My heart is not proud, O LORD,
my eyes are not haughty;
I do not concern myself with great matters
or things too wonderful for me.
2But I have stilled and quieted my soul;
like a weaned child with its mother,
like a weaned child is my soul within me.

3O Israel, put your hope in the LORD
both now and forevermore.

Psalm 132

A song of ascents.

1O LORD, remember David
and all the hardships he endured.

2He swore an oath to the LORD
and made a vow to the Mighty One of Jacob:
3"I will not enter my house
or go to my bed—
4I will allow no sleep to my eyes,
no slumber to my eyelids,
5till I find a place for the LORD,
a dwelling for the Mighty One of Jacob."

6We heard it in Ephrathah,
we came upon it in the fields of Jaar[a:b]
7"Let us go to his dwelling place;
let us worship at his footstool—
8arise, O LORD, and come to your resting place,
you and the ark of your might.
9May your priests be clothed with righteousness;
may your saints sing for joy."

10For the sake of David your servant,
do not reject your anointed one.

11The LORD swore an oath to David,
a sure oath that he will not revoke:
"One of your own descendants
I will place on your throne—
12if your sons keep my covenant
and the statutes I teach them,
then their sons will sit
on your throne for ever and ever."

13For the LORD has chosen Zion,
he has desired it for his dwelling:
14"This is my resting place for ever and ever;
here I will sit enthroned, for I have desired it—
15I will bless her with abundant provisions;
her poor will I satisfy with food.
16I will clothe her priests with salvation,
and her saints will ever sing for joy.

17"Here I will make a horn[c] grow for David
and set up a lamp for my anointed one.
18I will clothe his enemies with shame,
but the crown on his head will be resplendent."

Psalm 133

A song of ascents. Of David.

1How good and pleasant it is
when brothers live together in unity!
2It is like precious oil poured on the head,
running down on the beard,
running down on Aaron's beard,
down upon the collar of his robes.
3It is as if the dew of Hermon
were falling on Mount Zion.
For there the LORD bestows his blessing,
even life forevermore.

Psalm 134

A song of ascents.

1Praise the LORD, all you servants of the LORD
who minister by night in the house of the LORD.
2Lift up your hands in the sanctuary
and praise the LORD.

3May the LORD, the Maker of heaven and earth,
bless you from Zion.

[a]6 That is, Kiriath Jearim [b]6 Or *heard of it in Ephrathah, / we found it in the fields of Jaar.* (And no quotes around verses 7-9) [c]17 *Horn* here symbolizes strong one, that is, king.

Psalm 135

1 Praise the LORD.[a]

Praise the name of the LORD;
praise him, you servants of the LORD,
2 you who minister in the house of the LORD,
in the courts of the house of our God.

3 Praise the LORD, for the LORD is good;
sing praise to his name, for that is pleasant.
4 For the LORD has chosen Jacob to be his own,
Israel to be his treasured possession.

5 I know that the LORD is great,
that our Lord is greater than all gods.
6 The LORD does whatever pleases him,
in the heavens and on the earth,
in the seas and all their depths.
7 He makes clouds rise from the ends of the earth;
he sends lightning with the rain
and brings out the wind from his storehouses.

8 He struck down the firstborn of Egypt,
the firstborn of men and animals.
9 He sent his signs and wonders into your midst, O Egypt,
against Pharaoh and all his servants.
10 He struck down many nations
and killed mighty kings—
11 Sihon king of the Amorites,
Og king of Bashan
and all the kings of Canaan—
12 and he gave their land as an inheritance,
an inheritance to his people Israel.

13 Your name, O LORD, endures forever,
your renown, O LORD, through all generations.
14 For the LORD will vindicate his people
and have compassion on his servants.

15 The idols of the nations are silver and gold,
made by the hands of men.
16 They have mouths, but cannot speak,
eyes, but they cannot see;
17 they have ears, but cannot hear,
nor is there breath in their mouths.
18 Those who make them will be like them,
and so will all who trust in them.

19 O house of Israel, praise the LORD;
O house of Aaron, praise the LORD;
20 O house of Levi, praise the LORD;
you who fear him, praise the LORD.
21 Praise be to the LORD from Zion,
to him who dwells in Jerusalem.

Praise the LORD.

Psalm 136

1 Give thanks to the LORD, for he is good.
His love endures forever.
2 Give thanks to the God of gods.
His love endures forever.
3 Give thanks to the Lord of lords:
His love endures forever.

4 to him who alone does great wonders,
His love endures forever.
5 who by his understanding made the heavens,
His love endures forever.
6 who spread out the earth upon the waters,
His love endures forever.
7 who made the great lights—
His love endures forever.
8 the sun to govern the day,
His love endures forever.
9 the moon and stars to govern the night;
His love endures forever.

10 to him who struck down the firstborn of Egypt
His love endures forever.
11 and brought Israel out from among them
His love endures forever.
12 with a mighty hand and outstretched arm;
His love endures forever.

13 to him who divided the Red Sea[b] asunder
His love endures forever.
14 and brought Israel through the midst of it,
His love endures forever.

[a] 1 Hebrew *Hallelu Yah*; also in verses 3 and 21
[b] 13 Hebrew *Yam Suph*; that is, Sea of Reeds; also in verse 15

15but swept Pharaoh and his army into
the Red Sea;
His love endures forever.
16to him who led his people through the
desert,
His love endures forever.
17who struck down great kings,
His love endures forever.
18and killed mighty kings—
His love endures forever.
19Sihon king of the Amorites
His love endures forever.
20and Og king of Bashan—
His love endures forever.
21and gave their land as an inheritance,
His love endures forever.
22an inheritance to his servant Israel;
His love endures forever.
23to the One who remembered us in our
low estate
His love endures forever.
24and freed us from our enemies,
His love endures forever.
25and who gives food to every creature.
His love endures forever.
26Give thanks to the God of heaven.
His love endures forever.

Psalm 137

1By the rivers of Babylon we sat and
wept
when we remembered Zion.
2There on the poplars
we hung our harps,
3for there our captors asked us for
songs,
our tormentors demanded songs of
joy;
they said, "Sing us one of the songs
of Zion!"
4How can we sing the songs of the
LORD
while in a foreign land?
5If I forget you, O Jerusalem,
may my right hand forget ⌊its skill⌋.
6May my tongue cling to the roof of
my mouth
if I do not remember you,
if I do not consider Jerusalem
my highest joy.
7Remember, O LORD, what the
Edomites did
on the day Jerusalem fell.
"Tear it down," they cried,
"tear it down to its foundations!"
8O Daughter of Babylon, doomed to
destruction,
happy is he who repays you
for what you have done to us—
9he who seizes your infants
and dashes them against the rocks.

Psalm 138

Of David.

1I will praise you, O LORD, with all my
heart;
before the "gods" I will sing your
praise.
2I will bow down toward your holy
temple
and will praise your name
for your love and your faithfulness,
for you have exalted above all things
your name and your word.
3When I called, you answered me;
you made me bold and
stouthearted.
4May all the kings of the earth praise
you, O LORD,
when they hear the words of your
mouth.
5May they sing of the ways of the
LORD,
for the glory of the LORD is great.
6Though the LORD is on high, he looks
upon the lowly,
but the proud he knows from afar.
7Though I walk in the midst of trouble,
you preserve my life;
you stretch out your hand against the
anger of my foes,
with your right hand you save me.
8The LORD will fulfill ⌊his purpose⌋ for
me;
your love, O LORD, endures
forever—
do not abandon the works of your
hands.

Psalm 139

For the director of music. Of David.
A psalm.

1O LORD, you have searched me
and you know me.
2You know when I sit and when I rise;
you perceive my thoughts from afar.
3You discern my going out and my
lying down;
you are familiar with all my ways.

4Before a word is on my tongue
you know it completely, O LORD.
5You hem me in—behind and before;
you have laid your hand upon me.
6Such knowledge is too wonderful for me,
too lofty for me to attain.

7Where can I go from your Spirit?
Where can I flee from your presence?
8If I go up to the heavens, you are there;
if I make my bed in the depths,[a]
you are there.
9If I rise on the wings of the dawn,
if I settle on the far side of the sea,
10even there your hand will guide me,
your right hand will hold me fast.

11If I say, "Surely the darkness will hide me
and the light become night around me,"
12even the darkness will not be dark to you;
the night will shine like the day,
for darkness is as light to you.

13For you created my inmost being;
you knit me together in my mother's womb.
14I praise you because I am fearfully and wonderfully made;
your works are wonderful,
I know that full well.
15My frame was not hidden from you
when I was made in the secret place.
When I was woven together in the depths of the earth,
16 your eyes saw my unformed body.
All the days ordained for me
were written in your book
before one of them came to be.

17How precious to[b] me are your thoughts, O God!
How vast is the sum of them!
18Were I to count them,
they would outnumber the grains of sand.
When I awake,
I am still with you.

19If only you would slay the wicked, O God!
Away from me, you bloodthirsty men!
20They speak of you with evil intent;
your adversaries misuse your name.
21Do I not hate those who hate you, O LORD,
and abhor those who rise up against you?
22I have nothing but hatred for them;
I count them my enemies.

23Search me, O God, and know my heart;
test me and know my anxious thoughts.
24See if there is any offensive way in me,
and lead me in the way everlasting.

Psalm 140

For the director of music. A psalm of David.

1Rescue me, O LORD, from evil men;
protect me from men of violence,
2who devise evil plans in their hearts
and stir up war every day.
3They make their tongues as sharp as a serpent's;
the poison of vipers is on their lips. *Selah*

4Keep me, O LORD, from the hands of the wicked;
protect me from men of violence
who plan to trip my feet.
5Proud men have hidden a snare for me;
they have spread out the cords of their net
and have set traps for me along my path. *Selah*

6O LORD, I say to you, "You are my God."
Hear, O LORD, my cry for mercy.
7O Sovereign LORD, my strong deliverer,
who shields my head in the day of battle—
8do not grant the wicked their desires, O LORD;
do not let their plans succeed,
or they will become proud. *Selah*

9Let the heads of those who surround me
be covered with the trouble their lips have caused.
10Let burning coals fall upon them;
may they be thrown into the fire,

[a]8 Hebrew *Sheol* [b]17 Or *concerning*

into miry pits, never to rise.
11Let slanderers not be established in the land;
may disaster hunt down men of violence.

12I know that the LORD secures justice for the poor
and upholds the cause of the needy.
13Surely the righteous will praise your name
and the upright will live before you.

Psalm 141

A psalm of David.

1O LORD, I call to you; come quickly to me.
Hear my voice when I call to you.
2May my prayer be set before you like incense;
may the lifting up of my hands be like the evening sacrifice.

3Set a guard over my mouth, O LORD;
keep watch over the door of my lips.
4Let not my heart be drawn to what is evil,
to take part in wicked deeds
with men who are evildoers;
let me not eat of their delicacies.

5Let a righteous man[a] strike me—it is a kindness;
let him rebuke me—it is oil on my head.
My head will not refuse it.

Yet my prayer is ever against the deeds of evildoers;
6 their rulers will be thrown down from the cliffs,
and the wicked will learn that my words were well spoken.
7⌞They will say,⌟ "As one plows and breaks up the earth,
so our bones have been scattered at the mouth of the grave.[b]"

8But my eyes are fixed on you, O Sovereign LORD;
in you I take refuge—do not give me over to death.
9Keep me from the snares they have laid for me,
from the traps set by evildoers.
10Let the wicked fall into their own nets,
while I pass by in safety.

Psalm 142

A *maskil*[c] of David. When he was in the cave. A prayer.

1I cry aloud to the LORD;
I lift up my voice to the LORD for mercy.
2I pour out my complaint before him;
before him I tell my trouble.

3When my spirit grows faint within me,
it is you who know my way.
In the path where I walk
men have hidden a snare for me.
4Look to my right and see;
no one is concerned for me.
I have no refuge;
no one cares for my life.

5I cry to you, O LORD;
I say, "You are my refuge,
my portion in the land of the living."
6Listen to my cry,
for I am in desperate need;
rescue me from those who pursue me,
for they are too strong for me.
7Set me free from my prison,
that I may praise your name.

Then the righteous will gather about me
because of your goodness to me.

Psalm 143

A psalm of David.

1O LORD, hear my prayer,
listen to my cry for mercy;
in your faithfulness and righteousness
come to my relief.
2Do not bring your servant into judgment,
for no one living is righteous before you.

3The enemy pursues me,
he crushes me to the ground;
he makes me dwell in darkness
like those long dead.
4So my spirit grows faint within me;
my heart within me is dismayed.

5I remember the days of long ago;

[a]5 Or *Let the Righteous One* [b]7 Hebrew *Sheol* [c]Title: Probably a literary or musical term

I meditate on all your works
and consider what your hands have done.
6 I spread out my hands to you;
my soul thirsts for you like a parched land. *Selah*

7 Answer me quickly, O LORD;
my spirit fails.
Do not hide your face from me
or I will be like those who go down to the pit.
8 Let the morning bring me word of your unfailing love,
for I have put my trust in you.
Show me the way I should go,
for to you I lift up my soul.
9 Rescue me from my enemies, O LORD,
for I hide myself in you.
10 Teach me to do your will,
for you are my God;
may your good Spirit
lead me on level ground.

11 For your name's sake, O LORD,
preserve my life;
in your righteousness, bring me out of trouble.
12 In your unfailing love, silence my enemies;
destroy all my foes,
for I am your servant.

Psalm 144

Of David.

1 Praise be to the LORD my Rock,
who trains my hands for war,
my fingers for battle.
2 He is my loving God and my fortress,
my stronghold and my deliverer,
my shield, in whom I take refuge,
who subdues peoples[a] under me.

3 O LORD, what is man that you care for him,
the son of man that you think of him?
4 Man is like a breath;
his days are like a fleeting shadow.

5 Part your heavens, O LORD, and come down;
touch the mountains, so that they smoke.
6 Send forth lightning and scatter ⌊the enemies⌋;
shoot your arrows and rout them.
7 Reach down your hand from on high;
deliver me and rescue me
from the mighty waters,
from the hands of foreigners
8 whose mouths are full of lies,
whose right hands are deceitful.

9 I will sing a new song to you, O God;
on the ten-stringed lyre I will make music to you,
10 to the One who gives victory to kings,
who delivers his servant David from the deadly sword.

11 Deliver me and rescue me
from the hands of foreigners
whose mouths are full of lies,
whose right hands are deceitful.

12 Then our sons in their youth
will be like well-nurtured plants,
and our daughters will be like pillars
carved to adorn a palace.
13 Our barns will be filled
with every kind of provision.
Our sheep will increase by thousands,
by tens of thousands in our fields;
14 our oxen will draw heavy loads.[b]
There will be no breaching of walls,
no going into captivity,
no cry of distress in our streets.

15 Blessed are the people of whom this is true;
blessed are the people whose God is the LORD.

Psalm 145[c]

A psalm of praise. Of David.

1 I will exalt you, my God the King;
I will praise your name for ever and ever.
2 Every day I will praise you
and extol your name for ever and ever.

3 Great is the LORD and most worthy of praise;
his greatness no one can fathom.
4 One generation will commend your works to another;

[a] 2 Many manuscripts of the Masoretic Text, Dead Sea Scrolls, Aquila, Jerome and Syriac; most manuscripts of the Masoretic Text *subdues my people* [b] 14 Or *our chieftains will be firmly established*
[c] This psalm is an acrostic poem, the verses of which (including verse 13b) begin with the successive letters of the Hebrew alphabet.

they will tell of your mighty acts.
5They will speak of the glorious
splendor of your majesty,
and I will meditate on your
wonderful works.[a]
6They will tell of the power of your
awesome works,
and I will proclaim your great
deeds.
7They will celebrate your abundant
goodness
and joyfully sing of your
righteousness.
8The LORD is gracious and
compassionate,
slow to anger and rich in love.
9The LORD is good to all;
he has compassion on all he has
made.
10All you have made will praise you,
O LORD;
your saints will extol you.

[a]5 Dead Sea Scrolls and Syriac (see also Septuagint); Masoretic Text *On the glorious splendor of your majesty / and on your wonderful works I will meditate*

VERSE FOR THE DAY: Psalm 145:13–14

AUTHOR: Elizabeth Cody Newenhuyse

PASSAGE FOR THE DAY: Psalm 145:1–21

Fatigue and Rest

When I'm running on empty, my husband helps fill my tank, and he checks me if I'm taking on too much. I do the same for him.

Perhaps what a mate can do best is provide comfort, a place of welcome and solace when the discouragement piles up. One of us can send the other to bed early and say, "Get some sleep and don't worry about a thing. I'm praying for you."

I'm almost always too busy. But God sends people to help fill me up so I'm no longer simply running on fumes. Now I'm trying to learn to look for God's provision in all things, to keep my sensors out to feel his hand brushing me, and that's something we all can do—*before* we run out of gas.

The world tells us that busyness is good, that the most successful people are those who learn to live with little sleep and can accomplish fifty things in a day. But God says something else. Are we listening?

MARRIAGE BUILDERS

♦ *Why do you think the myth that busyness is always good is so pervasive?*

♦ *How do you and your spouse provide "breathing" time for each other?*

Additional Scripture Readings
1 Timothy 6:17; Proverbs 11:25

Go to page 650 for your next devotional reading.

11They will tell of the glory of your kingdom
and speak of your might,
12so that all men may know of your mighty acts
and the glorious splendor of your kingdom.
13Your kingdom is an everlasting kingdom,
and your dominion endures through all generations.

The LORD is faithful to all his promises
and loving toward all he has made.[a]
14The LORD upholds all those who fall
and lifts up all who are bowed down.
15The eyes of all look to you,
and you give them their food at the proper time.
16You open your hand
and satisfy the desires of every living thing.

17The LORD is righteous in all his ways
and loving toward all he has made.
18The LORD is near to all who call on him,
to all who call on him in truth.
19He fulfills the desires of those who fear him;
he hears their cry and saves them.
20The LORD watches over all who love him,
but all the wicked he will destroy.

21My mouth will speak in praise of the LORD.
Let every creature praise his holy name
for ever and ever.

Psalm 146

1Praise the LORD.[b]

Praise the LORD, O my soul.
2 I will praise the LORD all my life;
I will sing praise to my God as long as I live.
3Do not put your trust in princes,
in mortal men, who cannot save.
4When their spirit departs, they return to the ground;
on that very day their plans come to nothing.

5Blessed is he whose help is the God of Jacob,
whose hope is in the LORD his God,
6the Maker of heaven and earth,
the sea, and everything in them—
the LORD, who remains faithful forever.
7He upholds the cause of the oppressed
and gives food to the hungry.
The LORD sets prisoners free,
8 the LORD gives sight to the blind,
the LORD lifts up those who are bowed down,
the LORD loves the righteous.
9The LORD watches over the alien
and sustains the fatherless and the widow,
but he frustrates the ways of the wicked.

10The LORD reigns forever,
your God, O Zion, for all generations.

Praise the LORD.

Psalm 147

1Praise the LORD.[c]

How good it is to sing praises to our God,
how pleasant and fitting to praise him!

2The LORD builds up Jerusalem;
he gathers the exiles of Israel.
3He heals the brokenhearted
and binds up their wounds.

4He determines the number of the stars
and calls them each by name.
5Great is our Lord and mighty in power;
his understanding has no limit.
6The LORD sustains the humble
but casts the wicked to the ground.

7Sing to the LORD with thanksgiving;
make music to our God on the harp.
8He covers the sky with clouds;
he supplies the earth with rain
and makes grass grow on the hills.
9He provides food for the cattle
and for the young ravens when they call.

[a]13 One manuscript of the Masoretic Text, Dead Sea Scrolls and Syriac (see also Septuagint); most manuscripts of the Masoretic Text do not have the last two lines of verse 13. [b]1 Hebrew *Hallelu Yah*; also in verse 10 [c]1 Hebrew *Hallelu Yah*; also in verse 20

[10]His pleasure is not in the strength of the horse,
nor his delight in the legs of a man;
[11]the LORD delights in those who fear him,
who put their hope in his unfailing love.

[12]Extol the LORD, O Jerusalem;
praise your God, O Zion,
[13]for he strengthens the bars of your gates
and blesses your people within you.
[14]He grants peace to your borders
and satisfies you with the finest of wheat.

[15]He sends his command to the earth;
his word runs swiftly.
[16]He spreads the snow like wool
and scatters the frost like ashes.
[17]He hurls down his hail like pebbles.
Who can withstand his icy blast?
[18]He sends his word and melts them;
he stirs up his breezes, and the waters flow.

[19]He has revealed his word to Jacob,
his laws and decrees to Israel.
[20]He has done this for no other nation;
they do not know his laws.

Praise the LORD.

Psalm 148

[1]Praise the LORD.[a]

Praise the LORD from the heavens,
praise him in the heights above.
[2]Praise him, all his angels,
praise him, all his heavenly hosts.
[3]Praise him, sun and moon,
praise him, all you shining stars.
[4]Praise him, you highest heavens
and you waters above the skies.
[5]Let them praise the name of the LORD,
for he commanded and they were created.
[6]He set them in place for ever and ever;
he gave a decree that will never pass away.

[7]Praise the LORD from the earth,
you great sea creatures and all ocean depths,
[8]lightning and hail, snow and clouds,
stormy winds that do his bidding,
[9]you mountains and all hills,
fruit trees and all cedars,
[10]wild animals and all cattle,
small creatures and flying birds,
[11]kings of the earth and all nations,
you princes and all rulers on earth,
[12]young men and maidens,
old men and children.

[13]Let them praise the name of the LORD,
for his name alone is exalted;
his splendor is above the earth and the heavens.
[14]He has raised up for his people a horn,[b]
the praise of all his saints,
of Israel, the people close to his heart.

Praise the LORD.

Psalm 149

[1]Praise the LORD.[c]

Sing to the LORD a new song,
his praise in the assembly of the saints.

[2]Let Israel rejoice in their Maker;
let the people of Zion be glad in their King.
[3]Let them praise his name with dancing
and make music to him with tambourine and harp.
[4]For the LORD takes delight in his people;
he crowns the humble with salvation.
[5]Let the saints rejoice in this honor
and sing for joy on their beds.

[6]May the praise of God be in their mouths
and a double-edged sword in their hands,
[7]to inflict vengeance on the nations
and punishment on the peoples,
[8]to bind their kings with fetters,
their nobles with shackles of iron,
[9]to carry out the sentence written against them.
This is the glory of all his saints.

Praise the LORD.

[a] *1* Hebrew *Hallelu Yah*; also in verse 14
[b] *14* *Horn* here symbolizes strong one, that is, king.
[c] *1* Hebrew *Hallelu Yah*; also in verse 9

Psalm 150

1 Praise the LORD.[a]

Praise God in his sanctuary;
praise him in his mighty heavens.
2 Praise him for his acts of power;
praise him for his surpassing greatness.
3 Praise him with the sounding of the trumpet,
praise him with the harp and lyre,
4 praise him with tambourine and dancing,
praise him with the strings and flute,
5 praise him with the clash of cymbals,
praise him with resounding cymbals.

6 Let everything that has breath praise the LORD.

Praise the LORD.

[a] 1 Hebrew *Hallelu Yah*; also in verse 6

SOLOMON "spoke three thousand proverbs" (1 Kings 4:32), many of which are collected in this book. These wise sayings describe patterns that operate in everyday life, offering us advice on how to conduct ourselves in various situations. Solomon's fundamental instruction is to fear and trust the Lord. As you read this book, remember that God has something to say about every aspect of your life; seek his wisdom in the decisions you must make each day.

PROVERBS

Prologue: Purpose and Theme

1 The proverbs of Solomon son of David, king of Israel:

2 for attaining wisdom and discipline;
for understanding words of insight;
3 for acquiring a disciplined and prudent life,
doing what is right and just and fair;
4 for giving prudence to the simple,
knowledge and discretion to the young—
5 let the wise listen and add to their learning,
and let the discerning get guidance—
6 for understanding proverbs and parables,
the sayings and riddles of the wise.

7 The fear of the LORD is the beginning of knowledge,
but fools[a] despise wisdom and discipline.

[a] 7 The Hebrew words rendered *fool* in Proverbs, and often elsewhere in the Old Testament, denote one who is morally deficient.

Exhortations to Embrace Wisdom

Warning Against Enticement

8 Listen, my son, to your father's instruction
and do not forsake your mother's teaching.
9 They will be a garland to grace your head
and a chain to adorn your neck.

10 My son, if sinners entice you,
do not give in to them.
11 If they say, "Come along with us;
let's lie in wait for someone's blood,
let's waylay some harmless soul;
12 let's swallow them alive, like the grave,[a]
and whole, like those who go down to the pit;
13 we will get all sorts of valuable things
and fill our houses with plunder;
14 throw in your lot with us,
and we will share a common purse"—
15 my son, do not go along with them,
do not set foot on their paths;
16 for their feet rush into sin,
they are swift to shed blood.
17 How useless to spread a net
in full view of all the birds!
18 These men lie in wait for their own blood;
they waylay only themselves!
19 Such is the end of all who go after ill-gotten gain;
it takes away the lives of those who get it.

Warning Against Rejecting Wisdom

20 Wisdom calls aloud in the street,
she raises her voice in the public squares;
21 at the head of the noisy streets[b] she cries out,
in the gateways of the city she makes her speech:

22 "How long will you simple ones[c] love your simple ways?
How long will mockers delight in mockery
and fools hate knowledge?
23 If you had responded to my rebuke,
I would have poured out my heart to you
and made my thoughts known to you.
24 But since you rejected me when I called
and no one gave heed when I stretched out my hand,
25 since you ignored all my advice
and would not accept my rebuke,
26 I in turn will laugh at your disaster;
I will mock when calamity overtakes you—
27 when calamity overtakes you like a storm,
when disaster sweeps over you like a whirlwind,
when distress and trouble overwhelm you.

28 "Then they will call to me but I will not answer;
they will look for me but will not find me.
29 Since they hated knowledge
and did not choose to fear the LORD,
30 since they would not accept my advice
and spurned my rebuke,
31 they will eat the fruit of their ways
and be filled with the fruit of their schemes.
32 For the waywardness of the simple will kill them,
and the complacency of fools will destroy them;
33 but whoever listens to me will live in safety
and be at ease, without fear of harm."

Moral Benefits of Wisdom

2 My son, if you accept my words
and store up my commands within you,
2 turning your ear to wisdom
and applying your heart to understanding,
3 and if you call out for insight
and cry aloud for understanding,
4 and if you look for it as for silver
and search for it as for hidden treasure,
5 then you will understand the fear of the LORD
and find the knowledge of God.
6 For the LORD gives wisdom,

[a] 12 Hebrew *Sheol* [b] 21 Hebrew; Septuagint / *on the tops of the walls* [c] 22 The Hebrew word rendered *simple* in Proverbs generally denotes one without moral direction and inclined to evil.

and from his mouth come
knowledge and understanding.
7He holds victory in store for the
upright,
he is a shield to those whose walk
is blameless,
8for he guards the course of the just
and protects the way of his faithful
ones.
9Then you will understand what is
right and just
and fair—every good path.
10For wisdom will enter your heart,
and knowledge will be pleasant to
your soul.
11Discretion will protect you,
and understanding will guard
you.

VERSE FOR THE DAY: Proverbs 2:1–2, 5

AUTHOR: Ruth Senter

PASSAGE FOR THE DAY: Proverbs 2:1–22

Between Young and Old

I was a city girl from Chicago in Navajo country on a service project. Bai'Azzi was a Navajo woman who didn't speak English. Yet she taught me you can love God simply. She didn't know how to read or write, but her dark eyes sparkled as she listened to the Bible stories I taught through an interpreter. When offering time came, she always untied her little velvet pouch and gave of her all to the Lord.

After the services (even if she had to shift her sleeping baby to someone else's arms), Bai'Azzi was the one who stayed behind to pick up the song books and stack them neatly beside the piano. Once I saw her wipe off the benches with her shawl so worshipers wouldn't have to sit in dust. Today, more than twenty-five years later, I think of Bai'Azzi as my mentor and friend.

"Every man is in some way my superior," Abraham Lincoln said, "therefore every man is in some way my teacher." The linkage of youth with age may be God's continuing provision for our support, our growth and development. We all, young and old, need to share our joys, sit at the feet of wisdom and learn from those who are a few steps further down the path.

MARRIAGE BUILDERS

♦ *In your life, who have been your models for godliness and service? What specific attitudes or actions impressed you?*

♦ *What godly attitudes and behaviors have you seen in your spouse? How have you been able to incorporate some of them into your own life?*

Additional Scripture Readings
Titus 2:3–4; Psalm 37:25;
Proverbs 1:8–9

Go to page 652 for your next devotional reading.

12Wisdom will save you from the ways
of wicked men,
from men whose words are
perverse,
13who leave the straight paths
to walk in dark ways,
14who delight in doing wrong
and rejoice in the perverseness of
evil,
15whose paths are crooked
and who are devious in their ways.

16It will save you also from the
adulteress,
from the wayward wife with her
seductive words,
17who has left the partner of her youth
and ignored the covenant she made
before God.[a]
18For her house leads down to death
and her paths to the spirits of the
dead.
19None who go to her return
or attain the paths of life.

20Thus you will walk in the ways of
good men
and keep to the paths of the
righteous.
21For the upright will live in the land,
and the blameless will remain in it;
22but the wicked will be cut off from
the land,
and the unfaithful will be torn from
it.

Further Benefits of Wisdom

3 My son, do not forget my teaching,
but keep my commands in your
heart,
2for they will prolong your life many
years
and bring you prosperity.

3Let love and faithfulness never leave
you;
bind them around your neck,
write them on the tablet of your
heart.
4Then you will win favor and a good
name
in the sight of God and man.

5Trust in the LORD with all your heart
and lean not on your own
understanding;
6in all your ways acknowledge him,
and he will make your paths
straight.[b]

7Do not be wise in your own eyes;
fear the LORD and shun evil.
8This will bring health to your body
and nourishment to your bones.

9Honor the LORD with your wealth,
with the firstfruits of all your crops;
10then your barns will be filled to
overflowing,
and your vats will brim over with
new wine.

11My son, do not despise the LORD's
discipline
and do not resent his rebuke,
12because the LORD disciplines those he
loves,
as a father[c] the son he delights in.

13Blessed is the man who finds wisdom,
the man who gains understanding,
14for she is more profitable than silver
and yields better returns than gold.
15She is more precious than rubies;
nothing you desire can compare
with her.
16Long life is in her right hand;
in her left hand are riches and
honor.
17Her ways are pleasant ways,
and all her paths are peace.
18She is a tree of life to those who
embrace her;
those who lay hold of her will be
blessed.

19By wisdom the LORD laid the earth's
foundations,
by understanding he set the
heavens in place;
20by his knowledge the deeps were
divided,
and the clouds let drop the dew.

21My son, preserve sound judgment and
discernment,
do not let them out of your sight;
22they will be life for you,
an ornament to grace your neck.
23Then you will go on your way in
safety,
and your foot will not stumble;
24when you lie down, you will not be
afraid;
when you lie down, your sleep will
be sweet.

[a]17 Or *covenant of her God*
[b]6 Or *will direct your paths*
[c]12 Hebrew; Septuagint / *and he punishes*

25 Have no fear of sudden disaster
or of the ruin that overtakes the wicked,
26 for the LORD will be your confidence
and will keep your foot from being snared.
27 Do not withhold good from those who deserve it,
when it is in your power to act.
28 Do not say to your neighbor,
"Come back later; I'll give it tomorrow"—
when you now have it with you.
29 Do not plot harm against your neighbor,
who lives trustfully near you.

FRIDAY

VERSE FOR THE DAY: Proverbs 3:3–4

AUTHOR: Ed Wheat, M.D., and Gloria Okes Perkins

PASSAGE FOR THE DAY: Proverbs 3:1–8

Remaining Faithful

The ongoing choice to be faithful to your spouse makes all the difference between an empty relationship and a vital, intimate relationship, which continues to grow in the security of steadfast love. It is also a continuing call to action. If you don't express it and demonstrate it in your daily life, it can't be faithfulness.

One couple was married only a year when the wife became ill with multiple sclerosis. Unable to bear the thought of being a burden to her husband, she decided she would "set him free." But her husband refused to leave. Instead, he showered tender care and love on her as long as she lived. Why did he do it? "Because," he said, "when I vowed before God 'in sickness and in health,' I meant it. And God made both of us unbelievably happy."

In contrast, consider another husband whose wife came to the last months of her terminal illness. He decided he couldn't give her all the attention she needed, because he felt it necessary to live his own life, which must come first. Both of these men had made their vows, but only one continued to choose faithfulness under difficult circumstances.

There is great comfort when you can count on each other to be faithful, no matter what.

MARRIAGE BUILDERS

♦ *What difficult circumstances are you facing that require you to choose to be faithful?*

♦ *How can you demonstrate love and faithfulness to your spouse in new ways this week?*

Additional Scripture Readings
Genesis 2:24; Lamentations 3:22–23; Matthew 5:3–10

Go to page 653 for your next devotional reading.

WEEKENDING

COMMUNICATION

Do a personal inventory of your talking-and-listening skills. Could these ten commandments for better communication improve your relationship?

1. Express your feelings and frustrations honestly, without accusing or attacking.

2. Choose words, expressions and a tone of voice that are kind and gentle.

3. Do not exaggerate, distort or stretch the truth. Avoid extreme words like "never" and "always."

4. Give specific examples; stay away from generalities.

5. Seek solutions rather than merely airing grievances.

6. Listen to what your spouse is saying, feeling and needing.

7. Refuse to indulge bitterness, anger, withdrawal or argument.

8. Acknowledge your own failure, and don't hesitate to forgive.

9. Keep communicating until you both understand what the other is saying and feeling.

10. Train your mouth and heart to say the right thing at the right time in the right way for the right reasons!

— *Gary and Betsy Ricucci*

REVIVE

Saturday: Ephesians 4:29–32

Sunday: James 3:1–12

Go to page 655 for your next devotional reading.

30Do not accuse a man for no reason—
when he has done you no harm.

31Do not envy a violent man
or choose any of his ways,
32for the LORD detests a perverse man
but takes the upright into his confidence.

33The LORD's curse is on the house of the wicked,
but he blesses the home of the righteous.
34He mocks proud mockers
but gives grace to the humble.
35The wise inherit honor,
but fools he holds up to shame.

Wisdom Is Supreme

4 Listen, my sons, to a father's instruction;
pay attention and gain understanding.
2I give you sound learning,
so do not forsake my teaching.
3When I was a boy in my father's house,
still tender, and an only child of my mother,
4he taught me and said,
"Lay hold of my words with all your heart;
keep my commands and you will live.
5Get wisdom, get understanding;
do not forget my words or swerve from them.
6Do not forsake wisdom, and she will protect you;
love her, and she will watch over you.
7Wisdom is supreme; therefore get wisdom.
Though it cost all you have,[a] get understanding.
8Esteem her, and she will exalt you;
embrace her, and she will honor you.
9She will set a garland of grace on your head
and present you with a crown of splendor."

10Listen, my son, accept what I say,
and the years of your life will be many.
11I guide you in the way of wisdom
and lead you along straight paths.
12When you walk, your steps will not be hampered;
when you run, you will not stumble.
13Hold on to instruction, do not let it go;
guard it well, for it is your life.
14Do not set foot on the path of the wicked
or walk in the way of evil men.
15Avoid it, do not travel on it;
turn from it and go on your way.
16For they cannot sleep till they do evil;
they are robbed of slumber till they make someone fall.
17They eat the bread of wickedness
and drink the wine of violence.

18The path of the righteous is like the first gleam of dawn,
shining ever brighter till the full light of day.
19But the way of the wicked is like deep darkness;
they do not know what makes them stumble.

20My son, pay attention to what I say;
listen closely to my words.
21Do not let them out of your sight,
keep them within your heart;
22for they are life to those who find them
and health to a man's whole body.
23Above all else, guard your heart,
for it is the wellspring of life.
24Put away perversity from your mouth;
keep corrupt talk far from your lips.
25Let your eyes look straight ahead,
fix your gaze directly before you.
26Make level[b] paths for your feet
and take only ways that are firm.
27Do not swerve to the right or the left;
keep your foot from evil.

Warning Against Adultery

5 My son, pay attention to my wisdom,
listen well to my words of insight,
2that you may maintain discretion
and your lips may preserve knowledge.
3For the lips of an adulteress drip honey,
and her speech is smoother than oil;
4but in the end she is bitter as gall,
sharp as a double-edged sword.

[a]7 Or *Whatever else you get* [b]26 Or *Consider the*

VERSE FOR THE DAY: Proverbs 4:7

AUTHOR: Jeanne Hendricks

PASSAGE FOR THE DAY: Proverbs 4:1–27

The Good Observer

Years ago, when Howie was going through a period of depression, I sometimes got angry with him. It's hard not to be upset when you are trying to help, and in return you get a husband who comes home and tightens up the whole happy, relaxed atmosphere of the home.

One night I was praying for some kind of insight. I remembered a course in child psychology that I had taken in college, which taught me how to ask questions in a non-threatening way. I began asking Howie questions about his childhood, and I realized how much fear had been a part of his background. He began to tell me things he had never talked about before. Slowly I began to piece together some valid reasons for his depression.

Howie needed my help, but not in a condescending way. So instead of telling the children to tiptoe around Daddy, we just went about life as usual. We ate our meals, played our games, read our books and hoped that soon Daddy would join us. And eventually he did. Slowly depression became a thing of the past and God's grace enabled us to move beyond it.

One of the secrets to a healthy marriage is for both partners to be good observers. I have learned how important it is for me to listen to Howie. To hear what kinds of things he says when he's not even aware I'm listening. To find the activities that relax and slow him down. I learn a lot about my husband when I take the time to observe.

MARRIAGE BUILDERS

♦ *What have you learned about your spouse that you picked up just by watching him or her?*

♦ *How could you be a better observer of your spouse?*

Additional Scripture Readings
Job 32:8; Psalm 119:129–130

Go to page 657 for your next devotional reading.

5Her feet go down to death;
her steps lead straight to the grave.[a]
6She gives no thought to the way of life;
her paths are crooked, but she knows it not.

7Now then, my sons, listen to me;
do not turn aside from what I say.
8Keep to a path far from her,
do not go near the door of her house,
9lest you give your best strength to others
and your years to one who is cruel,
10lest strangers feast on your wealth
and your toil enrich another man's house.
11At the end of your life you will groan,
when your flesh and body are spent.
12You will say, "How I hated discipline!
How my heart spurned correction!
13I would not obey my teachers
or listen to my instructors.
14I have come to the brink of utter ruin
in the midst of the whole assembly."

15Drink water from your own cistern,
running water from your own well.
16Should your springs overflow in the streets,
your streams of water in the public squares?
17Let them be yours alone,
never to be shared with strangers.
18May your fountain be blessed,
and may you rejoice in the wife of your youth.
19A loving doe, a graceful deer—
may her breasts satisfy you always,
may you ever be captivated by her love.
20Why be captivated, my son, by an adulteress?
Why embrace the bosom of another man's wife?

21For a man's ways are in full view of the LORD,
and he examines all his paths.
22The evil deeds of a wicked man ensnare him;
the cords of his sin hold him fast.
23He will die for lack of discipline,
led astray by his own great folly.

Warnings Against Folly

6 My son, if you have put up security for your neighbor,
if you have struck hands in pledge for another,
2if you have been trapped by what you said,
ensnared by the words of your mouth,
3then do this, my son, to free yourself,
since you have fallen into your neighbor's hands:
Go and humble yourself;
press your plea with your neighbor!
4Allow no sleep to your eyes,
no slumber to your eyelids.
5Free yourself, like a gazelle from the hand of the hunter,
like a bird from the snare of the fowler.

6Go to the ant, you sluggard;
consider its ways and be wise!
7It has no commander,
no overseer or ruler,
8yet it stores its provisions in summer
and gathers its food at harvest.

9How long will you lie there, you sluggard?
When will you get up from your sleep?
10A little sleep, a little slumber,
a little folding of the hands to rest—
11and poverty will come on you like a bandit
and scarcity like an armed man.[b]

12A scoundrel and villain,
who goes about with a corrupt mouth,
13 who winks with his eye,
signals with his feet
and motions with his fingers,
14 who plots evil with deceit in his heart—
he always stirs up dissension.
15Therefore disaster will overtake him in an instant;
he will suddenly be destroyed—without remedy.

16There are six things the LORD hates,
seven that are detestable to him:
17 haughty eyes,
a lying tongue,
hands that shed innocent blood,

[a]5 Hebrew *Sheol* [b]11 Or *like a vagrant / and scarcity like a beggar*

VERSE FOR THE DAY: Proverbs 5:18

AUTHOR: Harold B. Smith

PASSAGE FOR THE DAY: Proverbs 5:15–21

Faithful Brain, Faithful Body

When standing at the altar saying "I do," emotional fidelity is probably the last thing on the minds of a bride and groom. After all, it's the physical act that usually fills their immediate expectations. And they assume—if they even think of it—that emotional faithfulness will follow.

No wonder. Our culture insists on thinking of sexuality solely in physical terms. Society insists on defining it in a simple, measurable way—avoiding intercourse with anyone other than your spouse. But Christ pushed his followers way beyond "measurable fidelity" to a fuller measure: "You have heard that it was said, 'Do not commit adultery.' But I tell you that anyone who looks at a woman lustfully has already committed adultery with her in his heart" (Matt. 5:27–28). In other words, "People, fidelity goes far beyond a physical definition. It demands that your sexual attitudes and attentions be directed solely, wholly to your husband or wife."

This mind, body and soul fidelity means I must rely on God. Not by my might, but only by his alone, can I withstand the forces that would rob me of the pleasure of experiencing the mystery of oneness with my mate. If God demands total fidelity—and he does—then he will provide the means whereby fidelity can truly characterize marital relationships.

Admittedly, the Biblical mandate for mind, body and soul fidelity is radical when compared to society's standards. But those who practice it find a freedom in oneness that is truly liberating.

MARRIAGE BUILDERS

♦ *How do your words, thoughts and attitudes contribute to your sexual fidelity?*

♦ *What safeguards can you put into place to help you avoid sexual temptations?*

Additional Scripture Readings
Song of Songs 8:6; Colossians 3:5–14

Go to page 662 for your next devotional reading.

18 a heart that devises wicked schemes,
feet that are quick to rush into evil,
19 a false witness who pours out lies
and a man who stirs up dissension among brothers.

Warning Against Adultery

20My son, keep your father's commands
and do not forsake your mother's teaching.
21Bind them upon your heart forever;
fasten them around your neck.
22When you walk, they will guide you;
when you sleep, they will watch over you;
when you awake, they will speak to you.
23For these commands are a lamp,
this teaching is a light,
and the corrections of discipline are the way to life,
24keeping you from the immoral woman,
from the smooth tongue of the wayward wife.
25Do not lust in your heart after her beauty
or let her captivate you with her eyes,
26for the prostitute reduces you to a loaf of bread,
and the adulteress preys upon your very life.
27Can a man scoop fire into his lap
without his clothes being burned?
28Can a man walk on hot coals
without his feet being scorched?
29So is he who sleeps with another man's wife;
no one who touches her will go unpunished.

30Men do not despise a thief if he steals
to satisfy his hunger when he is starving.
31Yet if he is caught, he must pay sevenfold,
though it costs him all the wealth of his house.
32But a man who commits adultery lacks judgment;
whoever does so destroys himself.
33Blows and disgrace are his lot,
and his shame will never be wiped away;
34for jealousy arouses a husband's fury,
and he will show no mercy when he takes revenge.
35He will not accept any compensation;
he will refuse the bribe, however great it is.

Warning Against the Adulteress

7 My son, keep my words
and store up my commands within you.
2Keep my commands and you will live;
guard my teachings as the apple of your eye.
3Bind them on your fingers;
write them on the tablet of your heart.
4Say to wisdom, "You are my sister,"
and call understanding your kinsman;
5they will keep you from the adulteress,
from the wayward wife with her seductive words.

6At the window of my house
I looked out through the lattice.
7I saw among the simple,
I noticed among the young men,
a youth who lacked judgment.
8He was going down the street near her corner,
walking along in the direction of her house
9at twilight, as the day was fading,
as the dark of night set in.

10Then out came a woman to meet him,
dressed like a prostitute and with crafty intent.
11(She is loud and defiant,
her feet never stay at home;
12now in the street, now in the squares,
at every corner she lurks.)
13She took hold of him and kissed him
and with a brazen face she said:

14"I have fellowship offerings[a] at home;
today I fulfilled my vows.
15So I came out to meet you;
I looked for you and have found you!
16I have covered my bed
with colored linens from Egypt.
17I have perfumed my bed
with myrrh, aloes and cinnamon.
18Come, let's drink deep of love till morning;

[a]14 Traditionally *peace offerings*

let's enjoy ourselves with love!
19My husband is not at home;
he has gone on a long journey.
20He took his purse filled with money
and will not be home till full
moon."

21With persuasive words she led him
astray;
she seduced him with her smooth
talk.
22All at once he followed her
like an ox going to the slaughter,
like a deer[a] stepping into a noose[b]
23 till an arrow pierces his liver,
like a bird darting into a snare,
little knowing it will cost him his
life.

24Now then, my sons, listen to me;
pay attention to what I say.
25Do not let your heart turn to her ways
or stray into her paths.
26Many are the victims she has brought
down;
her slain are a mighty throng.
27Her house is a highway to the grave,[c]
leading down to the chambers of
death.

Wisdom's Call

8 Does not wisdom call out?
Does not understanding raise her
voice?
2On the heights along the way,
where the paths meet, she takes her
stand;
3beside the gates leading into the city,
at the entrances, she cries aloud:
4"To you, O men, I call out;
I raise my voice to all mankind.
5You who are simple, gain prudence;
you who are foolish, gain
understanding.
6Listen, for I have worthy things to say;
I open my lips to speak what is
right.
7My mouth speaks what is true,
for my lips detest wickedness.
8All the words of my mouth are just;
none of them is crooked or
perverse.
9To the discerning all of them are
right;
they are faultless to those who have
knowledge.
10Choose my instruction instead of
silver,
knowledge rather than choice gold,
11for wisdom is more precious than
rubies,
and nothing you desire can compare
with her.

12"I, wisdom, dwell together with
prudence;
I possess knowledge and discretion.
13To fear the LORD is to hate evil;
I hate pride and arrogance,
evil behavior and perverse speech.
14Counsel and sound judgment are
mine;
I have understanding and power.
15By me kings reign
and rulers make laws that are just;
16by me princes govern,
and all nobles who rule on earth.[d]
17I love those who love me,
and those who seek me find me.
18With me are riches and honor,
enduring wealth and prosperity.
19My fruit is better than fine gold;
what I yield surpasses choice silver.
20I walk in the way of righteousness,
along the paths of justice,
21bestowing wealth on those who love
me
and making their treasuries full.

22"The LORD brought me forth as the
first of his works,[e,f]
before his deeds of old;
23I was appointed[g] from eternity,
from the beginning, before the
world began.
24When there were no oceans, I was
given birth,
when there were no springs
abounding with water;
25before the mountains were settled in
place,
before the hills, I was given birth,
26before he made the earth or its fields
or any of the dust of the world.
27I was there when he set the heavens
in place,
when he marked out the horizon on
the face of the deep,

[a]22 Syriac (see also Septuagint); Hebrew *fool* [b]22 The meaning of the Hebrew for this line is uncertain. [c]27 Hebrew *Sheol* [d]16 Many Hebrew manuscripts and Septuagint; most Hebrew manuscripts *and nobles—all righteous rulers* [e]22 Or *way*; or *dominion* [f]22 Or *The LORD possessed me at the beginning of his work*; or *The LORD brought me forth at the beginning of his work* [g]23 Or *fashioned*

28 when he established the clouds above
and fixed securely the fountains of
the deep,
29 when he gave the sea its boundary
so the waters would not overstep
his command,
and when he marked out the
foundations of the earth.
30 Then I was the craftsman at his
side.
I was filled with delight day after day,
rejoicing always in his presence,
31 rejoicing in his whole world
and delighting in mankind.

32 "Now then, my sons, listen to me;
blessed are those who keep my
ways.
33 Listen to my instruction and be wise;
do not ignore it.
34 Blessed is the man who listens to me,
watching daily at my doors,
waiting at my doorway.
35 For whoever finds me finds life
and receives favor from the LORD.
36 But whoever fails to find me harms
himself;
all who hate me love death."

Invitations of Wisdom and of Folly

9 Wisdom has built her house;
she has hewn out its seven pillars.
2 She has prepared her meat and mixed
her wine;
she has also set her table.
3 She has sent out her maids, and she
calls
from the highest point of the city.
4 "Let all who are simple come in here!"
she says to those who lack
judgment.
5 "Come, eat my food
and drink the wine I have mixed.
6 Leave your simple ways and you will
live;
walk in the way of understanding.

7 "Whoever corrects a mocker invites
insult;
whoever rebukes a wicked man
incurs abuse.
8 Do not rebuke a mocker or he will
hate you;
rebuke a wise man and he will love
you.
9 Instruct a wise man and he will be
wiser still;
teach a righteous man and he will
add to his learning.

10 "The fear of the LORD is the beginning
of wisdom,
and knowledge of the Holy One is
understanding.
11 For through me your days will be
many,
and years will be added to your life.
12 If you are wise, your wisdom will
reward you;
if you are a mocker, you alone will
suffer."

13 The woman Folly is loud;
she is undisciplined and without
knowledge.
14 She sits at the door of her house,
on a seat at the highest point of the
city,
15 calling out to those who pass by,
who go straight on their way.
16 "Let all who are simple come in here!"
she says to those who lack
judgment.
17 "Stolen water is sweet;
food eaten in secret is delicious!"
18 But little do they know that the dead
are there,
that her guests are in the depths of
the grave.[a]

Proverbs of Solomon

10 The proverbs of Solomon:

A wise son brings joy to his father,
but a foolish son grief to his
mother.

2 Ill-gotten treasures are of no value,
but righteousness delivers from
death.

3 The LORD does not let the righteous go
hungry
but he thwarts the craving of the
wicked.

4 Lazy hands make a man poor,
but diligent hands bring wealth.

5 He who gathers crops in summer is a
wise son,
but he who sleeps during harvest is
a disgraceful son.

6 Blessings crown the head of the
righteous,

[a] 18 Hebrew *Sheol*

but violence overwhelms the mouth
of the wicked.[a]

7The memory of the righteous will be a
blessing,
but the name of the wicked will rot.

8The wise in heart accept commands,
but a chattering fool comes to ruin.

9The man of integrity walks securely,
but he who takes crooked paths will
be found out.

10He who winks maliciously causes
grief,
and a chattering fool comes to ruin.

11The mouth of the righteous is a
fountain of life,
but violence overwhelms the mouth
of the wicked.

12Hatred stirs up dissension,
but love covers over all wrongs.

13Wisdom is found on the lips of the
discerning,
but a rod is for the back of him
who lacks judgment.

14Wise men store up knowledge,
but the mouth of a fool invites ruin.

15The wealth of the rich is their fortified
city,
but poverty is the ruin of the poor.

16The wages of the righteous bring them
life,
but the income of the wicked brings
them punishment.

17He who heeds discipline shows the
way to life,
but whoever ignores correction
leads others astray.

18He who conceals his hatred has lying
lips,
and whoever spreads slander is a
fool.

19When words are many, sin is not
absent,
but he who holds his tongue is
wise.

20The tongue of the righteous is choice
silver,
but the heart of the wicked is of
little value.

21The lips of the righteous nourish
many,
but fools die for lack of judgment.

22The blessing of the LORD brings
wealth,
and he adds no trouble to it.

23A fool finds pleasure in evil conduct,
but a man of understanding delights
in wisdom.

24What the wicked dreads will overtake
him;
what the righteous desire will be
granted.

25When the storm has swept by, the
wicked are gone,
but the righteous stand firm forever.

26As vinegar to the teeth and smoke to
the eyes,
so is a sluggard to those who send
him.

27The fear of the LORD adds length to
life,
but the years of the wicked are cut
short.

28The prospect of the righteous is joy,
but the hopes of the wicked come
to nothing.

29The way of the LORD is a refuge for
the righteous,
but it is the ruin of those who do
evil.

30The righteous will never be uprooted,
but the wicked will not remain in
the land.

31The mouth of the righteous brings
forth wisdom,
but a perverse tongue will be cut
out.

32The lips of the righteous know what is
fitting,
but the mouth of the wicked only
what is perverse.

11 The LORD abhors dishonest
scales,
but accurate weights are his delight.

2When pride comes, then comes
disgrace,
but with humility comes wisdom.

3The integrity of the upright guides
them,

[a]6 Or *but the mouth of the wicked conceals violence*; also in verse 11

but the unfaithful are destroyed by
their duplicity.

4 Wealth is worthless in the day of
wrath,
but righteousness delivers from
death.

5 The righteousness of the blameless
makes a straight way for them,
but the wicked are brought down
by their own wickedness.

6 The righteousness of the upright
delivers them,
but the unfaithful are trapped by
evil desires.

7 When a wicked man dies, his hope
perishes;
all he expected from his power
comes to nothing.

8 The righteous man is rescued from
trouble,
and it comes on the wicked instead.

9 With his mouth the godless destroys
his neighbor,
but through knowledge the
righteous escape.

10 When the righteous prosper, the city
rejoices;

VERSE FOR THE DAY: Proverbs 11:16

AUTHOR: Jim Conway

PASSAGE FOR THE DAY: Proverbs 11:1–31

R-E-S-P-E-C-T

Respect means you not only value your mate, but you let your mate teach you. If your mate has important God-given abilities you don't have, his or her contribution to your life is essential.

I have found that the more I respect Sally for her abilities, the more I am able to trust her. The more I trust her, the more she is free to exercise her gifts, which, in turn, gains my respect.

Recently we were speaking at a couples' retreat in California. We had shared equally in all of the sessions until the Sunday-morning meeting when I was expected to speak alone.

I told Sally I thought we ought to lead the session together. She had heard me speak several times from the Scripture passage I was going to use, and she agreed to join me. I was delighted as she contributed new and important ideas to our talk. The overall impact of the message was heightened and so was my respect for my wife.

MARRIAGE BUILDERS

♦ *How does your respect for your spouse encourage him or her to make the most of talents and gifts?*

♦ *How has your spouse's respect encouraged you?*

Additional Scripture Readings
Ephesians 5:33; 1 Peter 3:7

Go to page 664 for your next devotional reading.

when the wicked perish, there are
shouts of joy.

11 Through the blessing of the upright a
city is exalted,
but by the mouth of the wicked it is
destroyed.

12 A man who lacks judgment derides
his neighbor,
but a man of understanding holds
his tongue.

13 A gossip betrays a confidence,
but a trustworthy man keeps a
secret.

14 For lack of guidance a nation falls,
but many advisers make victory
sure.

15 He who puts up security for another
will surely suffer,
but whoever refuses to strike hands
in pledge is safe.

16 A kindhearted woman gains respect,
but ruthless men gain only wealth.

17 A kind man benefits himself,
but a cruel man brings trouble on
himself.

18 The wicked man earns deceptive
wages,
but he who sows righteousness
reaps a sure reward.

19 The truly righteous man attains life,
but he who pursues evil goes to his
death.

20 The LORD detests men of perverse
heart
but he delights in those whose ways
are blameless.

21 Be sure of this: The wicked will not
go unpunished,
but those who are righteous will go
free.

22 Like a gold ring in a pig's snout
is a beautiful woman who shows no
discretion.

23 The desire of the righteous ends only
in good,
but the hope of the wicked only in
wrath.

24 One man gives freely, yet gains even
more;
another withholds unduly, but
comes to poverty.

25 A generous man will prosper;
he who refreshes others will himself
be refreshed.

26 People curse the man who hoards
grain,
but blessing crowns him who is
willing to sell.

27 He who seeks good finds goodwill,
but evil comes to him who searches
for it.

28 Whoever trusts in his riches will fall,
but the righteous will thrive like a
green leaf.

29 He who brings trouble on his family
will inherit only wind,
and the fool will be servant to the
wise.

30 The fruit of the righteous is a tree of
life,
and he who wins souls is wise.

31 If the righteous receive their due on
earth,
how much more the ungodly and
the sinner!

12 Whoever loves discipline loves
knowledge,
but he who hates correction is
stupid.

2 A good man obtains favor from the
LORD,
but the LORD condemns a crafty
man.

3 A man cannot be established through
wickedness,
but the righteous cannot be
uprooted.

4 A wife of noble character is her
husband's crown,
but a disgraceful wife is like decay
in his bones.

5 The plans of the righteous are just,
but the advice of the wicked is
deceitful.

6 The words of the wicked lie in wait
for blood,
but the speech of the upright
rescues them.

7 Wicked men are overthrown and are
no more,
but the house of the righteous
stands firm.

VERSE FOR THE DAY: Proverbs 12:4

AUTHOR: Dave Roever and Harold Fickett

PASSAGE FOR THE DAY: Proverbs 12:1–28

Welcome Home

The first time I looked into a mirror after I was wounded in Vietnam, I saw a monster. My face was covered with charred skin. My left eye seemed to bug out of its socket. The right half of my nose was gone, and my right eye was gray and lacked an eyelid.

I couldn't imagine that Brenda, my wife, could play beauty to the beast I had become. At Brooke Army Medical Center in San Antonio, I spent four weeks in an intensive-care unit and another eight months in the burn ward. That's where Brenda first came to visit me. I waited for her arrival, wondering if she could accept me. I felt as though my whole identity, my life itself depended on the look on her face when she saw me.

Brenda walked straight up to my bed, paused at the chart and looked right at me. Showing not the slightest tremor of horror or shock, she bent down and kissed me on what was left of my face. Then she looked me in my good eye, smiled, and said, "Welcome home, Davey. I love you." By using her term of endearment for me, she said, "You are my husband. You will always be my husband. You are still my man."

How could she look at a creature composed of inflammation and charred bone and yet act as though I were the man of her dreams come home? Only God could put it in a woman to love a man the way my wife did.

MARRIAGE BUILDERS

♦ *When, in the course of your marriage, has your spouse looked beyond your flaws and conveyed God's unconditional love? How did it make you feel?*

♦ *How could you help develop a climate of unconditional acceptance in your marriage?*

Additional Scripture Readings
1 Corinthians 11:11–12; Genesis 3:16; Proverbs 31:10–11

Go to page 668 for your next devotional reading.

8A man is praised according to his wisdom,
but men with warped minds are despised.

9Better to be a nobody and yet have a servant
than pretend to be somebody and have no food.

10A righteous man cares for the needs of his animal,
but the kindest acts of the wicked are cruel.

11He who works his land will have abundant food,
but he who chases fantasies lacks judgment.

12The wicked desire the plunder of evil men,
but the root of the righteous flourishes.

13An evil man is trapped by his sinful talk,
but a righteous man escapes trouble.

14From the fruit of his lips a man is filled with good things
as surely as the work of his hands rewards him.

15The way of a fool seems right to him,
but a wise man listens to advice.

16A fool shows his annoyance at once,
but a prudent man overlooks an insult.

17A truthful witness gives honest testimony,
but a false witness tells lies.

18Reckless words pierce like a sword,
but the tongue of the wise brings healing.

19Truthful lips endure forever,
but a lying tongue lasts only a moment.

20There is deceit in the hearts of those who plot evil,
but joy for those who promote peace.

21No harm befalls the righteous,
but the wicked have their fill of trouble.

22The LORD detests lying lips,
but he delights in men who are truthful.

23A prudent man keeps his knowledge to himself,
but the heart of fools blurts out folly.

24Diligent hands will rule,
but laziness ends in slave labor.

25An anxious heart weighs a man down,
but a kind word cheers him up.

26A righteous man is cautious in friendship,[a]
but the way of the wicked leads them astray.

27The lazy man does not roast[b] his game,
but the diligent man prizes his possessions.

28In the way of righteousness there is life;
along that path is immortality.

13 A wise son heeds his father's instruction,
but a mocker does not listen to rebuke.

2From the fruit of his lips a man enjoys good things,
but the unfaithful have a craving for violence.

3He who guards his lips guards his life,
but he who speaks rashly will come to ruin.

4The sluggard craves and gets nothing,
but the desires of the diligent are fully satisfied.

5The righteous hate what is false,
but the wicked bring shame and disgrace.

6Righteousness guards the man of integrity,
but wickedness overthrows the sinner.

7One man pretends to be rich, yet has nothing;
another pretends to be poor, yet has great wealth.

8A man's riches may ransom his life,
but a poor man hears no threat.

[a]26 Or *man is a guide to his neighbor*

[b]27 The meaning of the Hebrew for this word is uncertain.

9The light of the righteous shines
brightly,
but the lamp of the wicked is
snuffed out.

10Pride only breeds quarrels,
but wisdom is found in those who
take advice.

11Dishonest money dwindles away,
but he who gathers money little by
little makes it grow.

12Hope deferred makes the heart sick,
but a longing fulfilled is a tree of
life.

13He who scorns instruction will pay for
it,
but he who respects a command is
rewarded.

14The teaching of the wise is a fountain
of life,
turning a man from the snares of
death.

15Good understanding wins favor,
but the way of the unfaithful is
hard.[a]

16Every prudent man acts out of
knowledge,
but a fool exposes his folly.

17A wicked messenger falls into trouble,
but a trustworthy envoy brings
healing.

18He who ignores discipline comes to
poverty and shame,
but whoever heeds correction is
honored.

19A longing fulfilled is sweet to the soul,
but fools detest turning from evil.

20He who walks with the wise grows
wise,
but a companion of fools suffers
harm.

21Misfortune pursues the sinner,
but prosperity is the reward of the
righteous.

22A good man leaves an inheritance for
his children's children,
but a sinner's wealth is stored up
for the righteous.

23A poor man's field may produce
abundant food,
but injustice sweeps it away.

24He who spares the rod hates his son,
but he who loves him is careful to
discipline him.

25The righteous eat to their hearts'
content,
but the stomach of the wicked goes
hungry.

14 The wise woman builds her
house,
but with her own hands the foolish
one tears hers down.

2He whose walk is upright fears the
LORD,
but he whose ways are devious
despises him.

3A fool's talk brings a rod to his back,
but the lips of the wise protect
them.

4Where there are no oxen, the manger
is empty,
but from the strength of an ox
comes an abundant harvest.

5A truthful witness does not deceive,
but a false witness pours out lies.

6The mocker seeks wisdom and finds
none,
but knowledge comes easily to the
discerning.

7Stay away from a foolish man,
for you will not find knowledge on
his lips.

8The wisdom of the prudent is to give
thought to their ways,
but the folly of fools is deception.

9Fools mock at making amends for sin,
but goodwill is found among the
upright.

10Each heart knows its own bitterness,
and no one else can share its joy.

11The house of the wicked will be
destroyed,
but the tent of the upright will
flourish.

12There is a way that seems right to a
man,
but in the end it leads to death.

13Even in laughter the heart may ache,
and joy may end in grief.

[a]15 Or *unfaithful does not endure*

14 The faithless will be fully repaid for
their ways,
and the good man rewarded for his.

15 A simple man believes anything,
but a prudent man gives thought to
his steps.

16 A wise man fears the LORD and shuns
evil,
but a fool is hotheaded and
reckless.

17 A quick-tempered man does foolish
things,
and a crafty man is hated.

18 The simple inherit folly,
but the prudent are crowned with
knowledge.

19 Evil men will bow down in the
presence of the good,
and the wicked at the gates of the
righteous.

20 The poor are shunned even by their
neighbors,
but the rich have many friends.

21 He who despises his neighbor sins,
but blessed is he who is kind to the
needy.

22 Do not those who plot evil go astray?
But those who plan what is good
find[a] love and faithfulness.

23 All hard work brings a profit,
but mere talk leads only to poverty.

24 The wealth of the wise is their crown,
but the folly of fools yields folly.

25 A truthful witness saves lives,
but a false witness is deceitful.

26 He who fears the LORD has a secure
fortress,
and for his children it will be a
refuge.

27 The fear of the LORD is a fountain of
life,
turning a man from the snares of
death.

28 A large population is a king's glory,
but without subjects a prince is
ruined.

29 A patient man has great
understanding,
but a quick-tempered man displays
folly.

30 A heart at peace gives life to the body,
but envy rots the bones.

31 He who oppresses the poor shows
contempt for their Maker,
but whoever is kind to the needy
honors God.

32 When calamity comes, the wicked are
brought down,
but even in death the righteous
have a refuge.

33 Wisdom reposes in the heart of the
discerning
and even among fools she lets
herself be known.[b]

34 Righteousness exalts a nation,
but sin is a disgrace to any people.

35 A king delights in a wise servant,
but a shameful servant incurs his
wrath.

15 A gentle answer turns away
wrath,
but a harsh word stirs up anger.

2 The tongue of the wise commends
knowledge,
but the mouth of the fool gushes
folly.

3 The eyes of the LORD are everywhere,
keeping watch on the wicked and
the good.

4 The tongue that brings healing is a
tree of life,
but a deceitful tongue crushes the
spirit.

5 A fool spurns his father's discipline,
but whoever heeds correction shows
prudence.

6 The house of the righteous contains
great treasure,
but the income of the wicked brings
them trouble.

7 The lips of the wise spread
knowledge;
not so the hearts of fools.

8 The LORD detests the sacrifice of the
wicked,
but the prayer of the upright pleases
him.

[a] 22 Or *show* [b] 33 Hebrew; Septuagint and Syriac / *but in the heart of fools she is not known*

9The LORD detests the way of the wicked
but he loves those who pursue righteousness.

10Stern discipline awaits him who leaves the path;
he who hates correction will die.

11Death and Destruction[a] lie open before the LORD—
how much more the hearts of men!

12A mocker resents correction;
he will not consult the wise.

13A happy heart makes the face cheerful,

[a] 11 Hebrew *Sheol and Abaddon*

FRIDAY

VERSE FOR THE DAY: Proverbs 15:22

AUTHOR: Alison A. McCaughan

PASSAGE FOR THE DAY: Proverbs 15:1–33

Research God's Will

The challenge to "find God's will" can become a consuming passion. Should we accept a job offer, buy a home, start a family?

From reading the Proverbs, it's clear that careful research plays a part in discerning God's guidance. "Plans fail for lack of counsel, but with many advisers they succeed" (Proverbs 15:22). Decisions are best made in the light of as many facts as possible.

Our attachment to a neighborhood, a church or extended family may hinder our openness to God's guidance. It's easy to give our hearts to a place or a group of people, but our hearts belong to God. That's why it is important in transition times to maintain a sense of humor and a proper sense of our importance. "The One enthroned in heaven laughs . . . ," Psalm 2:4 says. I suspect he may laugh at the antics of men and women who think the future of the world—or their neighborhood or church—depends only on them.

We need to realize that God is far more interested in who we *are* than in what we *do*. When my husband and I were in a time of job transition, God guided us, and through it all he brought us to trust him more fully. God continually wants to lead his children through various staging-posts in this world as he prepares us for a better place.

MARRIAGE BUILDERS

♦ *How have research and seeking the counsel of others helped you make major decisions?*

♦ *How does staying in close relationship to God help you make the best decisions?*

Additional Scripture Readings
Isaiah 30:21; 2 Timothy 2:7; Hebrews 13:14

Go to page 670 for your next devotional reading.

but heartache crushes the spirit.

14 The discerning heart seeks knowledge,
but the mouth of a fool feeds on folly.

15 All the days of the oppressed are wretched,
but the cheerful heart has a continual feast.

16 Better a little with the fear of the LORD
than great wealth with turmoil.

17 Better a meal of vegetables where there is love
than a fattened calf with hatred.

18 A hot-tempered man stirs up dissension,
but a patient man calms a quarrel.

19 The way of the sluggard is blocked with thorns,
but the path of the upright is a highway.

20 A wise son brings joy to his father,
but a foolish man despises his mother.

21 Folly delights a man who lacks judgment,
but a man of understanding keeps a straight course.

22 Plans fail for lack of counsel,
but with many advisers they succeed.

23 A man finds joy in giving an apt reply—
and how good is a timely word!

24 The path of life leads upward for the wise
to keep him from going down to the grave.[a]

25 The LORD tears down the proud man's house
but he keeps the widow's boundaries intact.

26 The LORD detests the thoughts of the wicked,
but those of the pure are pleasing to him.

27 A greedy man brings trouble to his family,
but he who hates bribes will live.

28 The heart of the righteous weighs its answers,
but the mouth of the wicked gushes evil.

29 The LORD is far from the wicked
but he hears the prayer of the righteous.

30 A cheerful look brings joy to the heart,
and good news gives health to the bones.

31 He who listens to a life-giving rebuke
will be at home among the wise.

32 He who ignores discipline despises himself,
but whoever heeds correction gains understanding.

33 The fear of the LORD teaches a man wisdom,[b]
and humility comes before honor.

16 To man belong the plans of the heart,
but from the LORD comes the reply of the tongue.

2 All a man's ways seem innocent to him,
but motives are weighed by the LORD.

3 Commit to the LORD whatever you do,
and your plans will succeed.

4 The LORD works out everything for his own ends—
even the wicked for a day of disaster.

5 The LORD detests all the proud of heart.
Be sure of this: They will not go unpunished.

6 Through love and faithfulness sin is atoned for;
through the fear of the LORD a man avoids evil.

7 When a man's ways are pleasing to the LORD,
he makes even his enemies live at peace with him.

8 Better a little with righteousness
than much gain with injustice.

9 In his heart a man plans his course,
but the LORD determines his steps.

[a] 24 Hebrew *Sheol* [b] 33 Or *Wisdom teaches the fear of the LORD*

WEEKENDING

CHARACTER

It's common for the things that first attracted two people to each other to become sources of irritation. In the space below, list the characteristics that attracted you to your mate. Talk about how you've changed and how you're the same. Appreciate each other's improvements!

Husband's List

1. _____
2. _____
3. _____
4. _____
5. _____

Wife's List

1. _____
2. _____
3. _____
4. _____
5. _____

— *The* Marriage Partnership *Staff*

REVIVE

Saturday: 1 Peter 4:7–11
Sunday: 2 Peter 1:3–10

Go to page 672 for your next devotional reading.

10 The lips of a king speak as an oracle,
and his mouth should not betray justice.

11 Honest scales and balances are from the LORD;
all the weights in the bag are of his making.

12 Kings detest wrongdoing,
for a throne is established through righteousness.

13 Kings take pleasure in honest lips;
they value a man who speaks the truth.

14 A king's wrath is a messenger of death,
but a wise man will appease it.

15 When a king's face brightens, it means life;
his favor is like a rain cloud in spring.

16 How much better to get wisdom than gold,
to choose understanding rather than silver!

17 The highway of the upright avoids evil;
he who guards his way guards his life.

18 Pride goes before destruction,
a haughty spirit before a fall.

19 Better to be lowly in spirit and among the oppressed
than to share plunder with the proud.

20 Whoever gives heed to instruction prospers,
and blessed is he who trusts in the LORD.

21 The wise in heart are called discerning,
and pleasant words promote instruction.[a]

22 Understanding is a fountain of life to those who have it,
but folly brings punishment to fools.

23 A wise man's heart guides his mouth,
and his lips promote instruction.[b]

24 Pleasant words are a honeycomb,
sweet to the soul and healing to the bones.

25 There is a way that seems right to a man,
but in the end it leads to death.

26 The laborer's appetite works for him;
his hunger drives him on.

27 A scoundrel plots evil,
and his speech is like a scorching fire.

28 A perverse man stirs up dissension,
and a gossip separates close friends.

29 A violent man entices his neighbor
and leads him down a path that is not good.

30 He who winks with his eye is plotting perversity;
he who purses his lips is bent on evil.

31 Gray hair is a crown of splendor;
it is attained by a righteous life.

32 Better a patient man than a warrior,
a man who controls his temper than one who takes a city.

33 The lot is cast into the lap,
but its every decision is from the LORD.

17 Better a dry crust with peace and quiet
than a house full of feasting,[c] with strife.

2 A wise servant will rule over a disgraceful son,
and will share the inheritance as one of the brothers.

3 The crucible for silver and the furnace for gold,
but the LORD tests the heart.

4 A wicked man listens to evil lips;
a liar pays attention to a malicious tongue.

5 He who mocks the poor shows contempt for their Maker;
whoever gloats over disaster will not go unpunished.

[a] 21 Or *words make a man persuasive* [b] 23 Or *mouth / and makes his lips persuasive* [c] 1 Hebrew *sacrifices*

6Children's children are a crown to the aged,
and parents are the pride of their children.

7Arrogant[a] lips are unsuited to a fool—
how much worse lying lips to a ruler!

8A bribe is a charm to the one who gives it;
wherever he turns, he succeeds.

9He who covers over an offense promotes love,
but whoever repeats the matter separates close friends.

[a]7 Or *Eloquent*

MONDAY

VERSE FOR THE DAY:	AUTHOR:	PASSAGE FOR THE DAY:
Proverbs 17:22	Dennis and Lucy Guernsey	Proverbs 17:1–28

Have Some Fun!

Marriage is similar to a 400-meter sprint. Long sprinters know how to pace themselves for the race so they can push when they need to. If they run at 110 percent all the time, they end up with no reserves. Likewise in marriage, learning to relax and have fun along the way is key to making your commitment work.

One of the main distractions that prevents couples from developing a habit of having fun and relaxing is the commitment to careers. In many cases, both husband and wife are in the midst of escalating, demanding careers, and at the same time are committed to establishing a healthy home and a thriving marriage. Such high stakes tend to breed intense relationships.

Sex is another example. It's impossible to have a delightful sexual experience without being able to have fun, to laugh and relax. Yet our culture has elevated expectations so high that couples commonly approach sex as a task to be mastered with the same prowess as every other successful experience. The results are often disappointing. But a little less seriousness and a bit more playfulness will make a big difference.

Even if you have to "work" at getting more fun into your marriage, the effort is more than worth it.

MARRIAGE BUILDERS

♦ *How long has it been since you did something together solely for enjoyment, with no other objectives?*

♦ *Are you and your mate having enough fun together? If not, what can you do this month to enjoy each other more?*

Additional Scripture Readings
Proverbs 15:13; 1 Samuel 18:6–7; Philippians 4:4

Go to page 674 for your next devotional reading.

10 A rebuke impresses a man of discernment
more than a hundred lashes a fool.

11 An evil man is bent only on rebellion;
a merciless official will be sent against him.

12 Better to meet a bear robbed of her cubs
than a fool in his folly.

13 If a man pays back evil for good,
evil will never leave his house.

14 Starting a quarrel is like breaching a dam;
so drop the matter before a dispute breaks out.

15 Acquitting the guilty and condemning the innocent—
the LORD detests them both.

16 Of what use is money in the hand of a fool,
since he has no desire to get wisdom?

17 A friend loves at all times,
and a brother is born for adversity.

18 A man lacking in judgment strikes hands in pledge
and puts up security for his neighbor.

19 He who loves a quarrel loves sin;
he who builds a high gate invites destruction.

20 A man of perverse heart does not prosper;
he whose tongue is deceitful falls into trouble.

21 To have a fool for a son brings grief;
there is no joy for the father of a fool.

22 A cheerful heart is good medicine,
but a crushed spirit dries up the bones.

23 A wicked man accepts a bribe in secret
to pervert the course of justice.

24 A discerning man keeps wisdom in view,
but a fool's eyes wander to the ends of the earth.

25 A foolish son brings grief to his father
and bitterness to the one who bore him.

26 It is not good to punish an innocent man,
or to flog officials for their integrity.

27 A man of knowledge uses words with restraint,
and a man of understanding is even-tempered.

28 Even a fool is thought wise if he keeps silent,
and discerning if he holds his tongue.

18 An unfriendly man pursues selfish ends;
he defies all sound judgment.

2 A fool finds no pleasure in understanding
but delights in airing his own opinions.

3 When wickedness comes, so does contempt,
and with shame comes disgrace.

4 The words of a man's mouth are deep waters,
but the fountain of wisdom is a bubbling brook.

5 It is not good to be partial to the wicked
or to deprive the innocent of justice.

6 A fool's lips bring him strife,
and his mouth invites a beating.

7 A fool's mouth is his undoing,
and his lips are a snare to his soul.

8 The words of a gossip are like choice morsels;
they go down to a man's inmost parts.

9 One who is slack in his work
is brother to one who destroys.

10 The name of the LORD is a strong tower;
the righteous run to it and are safe.

11 The wealth of the rich is their fortified city;
they imagine it an unscalable wall.

12 Before his downfall a man's heart is proud,
but humility comes before honor.

13 He who answers before listening—
that is his folly and his shame.

14 A man's spirit sustains him in sickness,

but a crushed spirit who can bear?

15 The heart of the discerning acquires knowledge;
the ears of the wise seek it out.

16 A gift opens the way for the giver
and ushers him into the presence of the great.

17 The first to present his case seems right,
till another comes forward and questions him.

18 Casting the lot settles disputes
and keeps strong opponents apart.

19 An offended brother is more unyielding than a fortified city,
and disputes are like the barred gates of a citadel.

20 From the fruit of his mouth a man's stomach is filled;

VERSE FOR THE DAY: Proverbs 18:22

AUTHOR: Jim and Sally Conway

PASSAGE FOR THE DAY: Proverbs 18:1–24

What Men Need

Communication between a woman and a man is very different from what happens when two women talk. When two women get together, they do a lot of explaining and restating until the other person understands what is being said.

But a man may say something vague, such as, "I don't know. I guess my job is really tough." After making that short statement, he may drop it. His wife assumes it must not be a big problem since he didn't say more than two sentences. But she needs to pick up on the little phrase that he *did* say. He's feeling a great loss, but he's not expressing it. Women need to listen to the small phrases that their husbands are saying and then respond accordingly.

A man needs a wife who cares enough to listen to the brief, sometimes weak, signals that he gives off. And then respond with gentle questions to draw him out, not by taking the opportunity to describe her own struggles. When one spouse is drawn away by someone outside the marriage, it's usually not that he's being drawn away by love. More often, he is drawn away because someone else showed they *cared*.

MARRIAGE BUILDERS

♦ *What are the different ways the two of you express problems or feelings?*

♦ *Over the years of your marriage, how have you come to understand each other's communication style better?*

Additional Scripture Readings
Proverbs 12:4; James 3:1–12

Go to page 679 for your next devotional reading.

with the harvest from his lips he is satisfied.

21 The tongue has the power of life and death,
and those who love it will eat its fruit.

22 He who finds a wife finds what is good
and receives favor from the LORD.

23 A poor man pleads for mercy,
but a rich man answers harshly.

24 A man of many companions may come to ruin,
but there is a friend who sticks closer than a brother.

19 Better a poor man whose walk is blameless
than a fool whose lips are perverse.

2 It is not good to have zeal without knowledge,
nor to be hasty and miss the way.

3 A man's own folly ruins his life,
yet his heart rages against the LORD.

4 Wealth brings many friends,
but a poor man's friend deserts him.

5 A false witness will not go unpunished,
and he who pours out lies will not go free.

6 Many curry favor with a ruler,
and everyone is the friend of a man who gives gifts.

7 A poor man is shunned by all his relatives—
how much more do his friends avoid him!
Though he pursues them with pleading,
they are nowhere to be found.[a]

8 He who gets wisdom loves his own soul;
he who cherishes understanding prospers.

9 A false witness will not go unpunished,
and he who pours out lies will perish.

10 It is not fitting for a fool to live in luxury—
how much worse for a slave to rule over princes!

11 A man's wisdom gives him patience;
it is to his glory to overlook an offense.

12 A king's rage is like the roar of a lion,
but his favor is like dew on the grass.

13 A foolish son is his father's ruin,
and a quarrelsome wife is like a constant dripping.

14 Houses and wealth are inherited from parents,
but a prudent wife is from the LORD.

15 Laziness brings on deep sleep,
and the shiftless man goes hungry.

16 He who obeys instructions guards his life,
but he who is contemptuous of his ways will die.

17 He who is kind to the poor lends to the LORD,
and he will reward him for what he has done.

18 Discipline your son, for in that there is hope;
do not be a willing party to his death.

19 A hot-tempered man must pay the penalty;
if you rescue him, you will have to do it again.

20 Listen to advice and accept instruction,
and in the end you will be wise.

21 Many are the plans in a man's heart,
but it is the LORD's purpose that prevails.

22 What a man desires is unfailing love[b];
better to be poor than a liar.

23 The fear of the LORD leads to life:
Then one rests content, untouched by trouble.

24 The sluggard buries his hand in the dish;
he will not even bring it back to his mouth!

[a] 7 The meaning of the Hebrew for this sentence is uncertain.

[b] 22 Or *A man's greed is his shame*

25Flog a mocker, and the simple will
learn prudence;
rebuke a discerning man, and he
will gain knowledge.

26He who robs his father and drives out
his mother
is a son who brings shame and
disgrace.

27Stop listening to instruction, my son,
and you will stray from the words
of knowledge.

28A corrupt witness mocks at justice,
and the mouth of the wicked gulps
down evil.

29Penalties are prepared for mockers,
and beatings for the backs of fools.

20 Wine is a mocker and beer a
brawler;
whoever is led astray by them is not
wise.

2A king's wrath is like the roar of a
lion;
he who angers him forfeits his life.

3It is to a man's honor to avoid strife,
but every fool is quick to quarrel.

4A sluggard does not plow in season;
so at harvest time he looks but
finds nothing.

5The purposes of a man's heart are
deep waters,
but a man of understanding draws
them out.

6Many a man claims to have unfailing
love,
but a faithful man who can find?

7The righteous man leads a blameless
life;
blessed are his children after him.

8When a king sits on his throne to
judge,
he winnows out all evil with his
eyes.

9Who can say, "I have kept my heart
pure;
I am clean and without sin"?

10Differing weights and differing
measures—
the LORD detests them both.

11Even a child is known by his actions,
by whether his conduct is pure and
right.

12Ears that hear and eyes that see—
the LORD has made them both.

13Do not love sleep or you will grow
poor;
stay awake and you will have food
to spare.

14"It's no good, it's no good!" says the
buyer;
then off he goes and boasts about
his purchase.

15Gold there is, and rubies in
abundance,
but lips that speak knowledge are a
rare jewel.

16Take the garment of one who puts up
security for a stranger;
hold it in pledge if he does it for a
wayward woman.

17Food gained by fraud tastes sweet to a
man,
but he ends up with a mouth full of
gravel.

18Make plans by seeking advice;
if you wage war, obtain guidance.

19A gossip betrays a confidence;
so avoid a man who talks too much.

20If a man curses his father or mother,
his lamp will be snuffed out in
pitch darkness.

21An inheritance quickly gained at the
beginning
will not be blessed at the end.

22Do not say, "I'll pay you back for this
wrong!"
Wait for the LORD, and he will
deliver you.

23The LORD detests differing weights,
and dishonest scales do not please
him.

24A man's steps are directed by the
LORD.
How then can anyone understand
his own way?

25It is a trap for a man to dedicate
something rashly
and only later to consider his vows.

26A wise king winnows out the wicked;
he drives the threshing wheel over
them.

27 The lamp of the LORD searches the
spirit of a man[a];
it searches out his inmost being.

28 Love and faithfulness keep a king
safe;
through love his throne is made
secure.

29 The glory of young men is their
strength,
gray hair the splendor of the old.

30 Blows and wounds cleanse away evil,
and beatings purge the inmost
being.

21 The king's heart is in the hand of
the LORD;
he directs it like a watercourse
wherever he pleases.

2 All a man's ways seem right to him,
but the LORD weighs the heart.

3 To do what is right and just
is more acceptable to the LORD than
sacrifice.

4 Haughty eyes and a proud heart,
the lamp of the wicked, are sin!

5 The plans of the diligent lead to profit
as surely as haste leads to poverty.

6 A fortune made by a lying tongue
is a fleeting vapor and a deadly
snare.[b]

7 The violence of the wicked will drag
them away,
for they refuse to do what is right.

8 The way of the guilty is devious,
but the conduct of the innocent is
upright.

9 Better to live on a corner of the roof
than share a house with a
quarrelsome wife.

10 The wicked man craves evil;
his neighbor gets no mercy from
him.

11 When a mocker is punished, the
simple gain wisdom;
when a wise man is instructed, he
gets knowledge.

12 The Righteous One[c] takes note of the
house of the wicked
and brings the wicked to ruin.

13 If a man shuts his ears to the cry of
the poor,
he too will cry out and not be
answered.

14 A gift given in secret soothes anger,
and a bribe concealed in the cloak
pacifies great wrath.

15 When justice is done, it brings joy to
the righteous
but terror to evildoers.

16 A man who strays from the path of
understanding
comes to rest in the company of the
dead.

17 He who loves pleasure will become
poor;
whoever loves wine and oil will
never be rich.

18 The wicked become a ransom for the
righteous,
and the unfaithful for the upright.

19 Better to live in a desert
than with a quarrelsome and
ill-tempered wife.

20 In the house of the wise are stores of
choice food and oil,
but a foolish man devours all he
has.

21 He who pursues righteousness and
love
finds life, prosperity[d] and honor.

22 A wise man attacks the city of the
mighty
and pulls down the stronghold in
which they trust.

23 He who guards his mouth and his
tongue
keeps himself from calamity.

24 The proud and arrogant man—
"Mocker" is his name;
he behaves with overweening pride.

25 The sluggard's craving will be the
death of him,
because his hands refuse to work.

26 All day long he craves for more,
but the righteous give without
sparing.

27 The sacrifice of the wicked is
detestable—

[a] 27 Or *The spirit of man is the LORD's lamp* [b] 6 Some Hebrew manuscripts, Septuagint and Vulgate; most Hebrew manuscripts *vapor for those who seek death* [c] 12 Or *The righteous man* [d] 21 Or *righteousness*

how much more so when brought
with evil intent!

28 A false witness will perish,
and whoever listens to him will be
destroyed forever.[a]

29 A wicked man puts up a bold front,
but an upright man gives thought to
his ways.

30 There is no wisdom, no insight, no
plan
that can succeed against the LORD.

31 The horse is made ready for the day
of battle,
but victory rests with the LORD.

22 A good name is more desirable
than great riches;
to be esteemed is better than silver
or gold.

2 Rich and poor have this in common:
The LORD is the Maker of them all.

3 A prudent man sees danger and takes
refuge,
but the simple keep going and
suffer for it.

4 Humility and the fear of the LORD
bring wealth and honor and life.

5 In the paths of the wicked lie thorns
and snares,
but he who guards his soul stays far
from them.

6 Train[b] a child in the way he should
go,
and when he is old he will not turn
from it.

7 The rich rule over the poor,
and the borrower is servant to the
lender.

8 He who sows wickedness reaps
trouble,
and the rod of his fury will be
destroyed.

9 A generous man will himself be
blessed,
for he shares his food with the
poor.

10 Drive out the mocker, and out goes
strife;
quarrels and insults are ended.

11 He who loves a pure heart and whose
speech is gracious
will have the king for his friend.

12 The eyes of the LORD keep watch over
knowledge,
but he frustrates the words of the
unfaithful.

13 The sluggard says, "There is a lion
outside!"
or, "I will be murdered in the
streets!"

14 The mouth of an adulteress is a deep
pit;
he who is under the LORD's wrath
will fall into it.

15 Folly is bound up in the heart of a
child,
but the rod of discipline will drive it
far from him.

16 He who oppresses the poor to increase
his wealth
and he who gives gifts to the rich—
both come to poverty.

Sayings of the Wise

17 Pay attention and listen to the sayings
of the wise;
apply your heart to what I teach,
18 for it is pleasing when you keep them
in your heart
and have all of them ready on your
lips.
19 So that your trust may be in the LORD,
I teach you today, even you.
20 Have I not written thirty[c] sayings for
you,
sayings of counsel and knowledge,
21 teaching you true and reliable words,
so that you can give sound answers
to him who sent you?

22 Do not exploit the poor because they
are poor
and do not crush the needy in
court,
23 for the LORD will take up their case
and will plunder those who plunder
them.

24 Do not make friends with a
hot-tempered man,
do not associate with one easily
angered,
25 or you may learn his ways

[a] 28 Or / *but the words of an obedient man will live on* or *not written excellent*

[b] 6 Or *Start*

[c] 20 Or *not formerly written;*

VERSE FOR THE DAY: Proverbs 21:9

AUTHOR: Scott M. Stanley

PASSAGE FOR THE DAY: Proverbs 21:1–31

Lovers' Quarrels

Alicia and Joe are newlyweds who argue repeatedly—and heatedly—about Alicia's family. Recently, just as they were leaving for a movie, Alicia's mother called. The conversation dragged on as they discussed how to get Alicia's dad to go to the doctor. Joe repeatedly pointed to his watch. Alicia looked away, thinking, "It would be rude to tell Mom I have to hang up."

She finally got off the phone, but she and Joe didn't go to the movie. Instead, they spent the night fighting.

For Joe, this was just one more example of Alicia putting her family ahead of him. To Alicia, their argument confirmed that Joe hated her parents. They are no different from many couples who, early in marriage, argue most frequently about in-laws. For other couples, arguments center around ties to old friends or old flames. Arguments rooted in jealousy are common at this stage.

Such disagreements underscore the need for newlywed couples to develop a clear identity as a couple. In part, they define "who's in" and "who's out" of their relationship.

After they define who they are as a couple, newlyweds next face decisions about how their roles and duties will be divided up. This is a challenging task that requires honest communication so they can work together on the best solutions. The couples who come out of the newlywed stage the strongest are the ones who develop a clear and stable sense of "us" so they can approach life as a team.

MARRIAGE BUILDERS

♦ *What "outsider" issues give you trouble (in-laws, friends, old boyfriends or girlfriends)?*

♦ *What would help you approach these outside relationships as a team?*

Additional Scripture Readings
Genesis 2:22–25; 1 Corinthians 13:4–6

Go to page 682 for your next devotional reading.

and get yourself ensnared.

26 Do not be a man who strikes hands in pledge
or puts up security for debts;
27 if you lack the means to pay,
your very bed will be snatched from under you.

28 Do not move an ancient boundary stone
set up by your forefathers.

29 Do you see a man skilled in his work?
He will serve before kings;
he will not serve before obscure men.

23 When you sit to dine with a ruler,
note well what[a] is before you,
2 and put a knife to your throat
if you are given to gluttony.
3 Do not crave his delicacies,
for that food is deceptive.

4 Do not wear yourself out to get rich;
have the wisdom to show restraint.
5 Cast but a glance at riches, and they are gone,
for they will surely sprout wings
and fly off to the sky like an eagle.

6 Do not eat the food of a stingy man,
do not crave his delicacies;
7 for he is the kind of man
who is always thinking about the cost.[b]
"Eat and drink," he says to you,
but his heart is not with you.
8 You will vomit up the little you have eaten
and will have wasted your compliments.

9 Do not speak to a fool,
for he will scorn the wisdom of your words.

10 Do not move an ancient boundary stone
or encroach on the fields of the fatherless,
11 for their Defender is strong;
he will take up their case against you.

12 Apply your heart to instruction
and your ears to words of knowledge.

13 Do not withhold discipline from a child;
if you punish him with the rod, he will not die.
14 Punish him with the rod
and save his soul from death.[c]

15 My son, if your heart is wise,
then my heart will be glad;
16 my inmost being will rejoice
when your lips speak what is right.

17 Do not let your heart envy sinners,
but always be zealous for the fear of the LORD.
18 There is surely a future hope for you,
and your hope will not be cut off.

19 Listen, my son, and be wise,
and keep your heart on the right path.
20 Do not join those who drink too much wine
or gorge themselves on meat,
21 for drunkards and gluttons become poor,
and drowsiness clothes them in rags.

22 Listen to your father, who gave you life,
and do not despise your mother when she is old.
23 Buy the truth and do not sell it;
get wisdom, discipline and understanding.
24 The father of a righteous man has great joy;
he who has a wise son delights in him.
25 May your father and mother be glad;
may she who gave you birth rejoice!

26 My son, give me your heart
and let your eyes keep to my ways,
27 for a prostitute is a deep pit
and a wayward wife is a narrow well.
28 Like a bandit she lies in wait,
and multiplies the unfaithful among men.

29 Who has woe? Who has sorrow?
Who has strife? Who has complaints?
Who has needless bruises? Who has bloodshot eyes?
30 Those who linger over wine,

[a] 1 Or *who* [b] 7 Or *for as he thinks within himself, / so he is*; or *for as he puts on a feast, / so he is*
[c] 14 Hebrew *Sheol*

who go to sample bowls of mixed wine.
31 Do not gaze at wine when it is red,
when it sparkles in the cup,
when it goes down smoothly!
32 In the end it bites like a snake
and poisons like a viper.
33 Your eyes will see strange sights
and your mind imagine confusing things.
34 You will be like one sleeping on the high seas,
lying on top of the rigging.
35 "They hit me," you will say, "but I'm not hurt!
They beat me, but I don't feel it!
When will I wake up
so I can find another drink?"

24 Do not envy wicked men,
do not desire their company;
2 for their hearts plot violence,
and their lips talk about making trouble.

3 By wisdom a house is built,
and through understanding it is established;
4 through knowledge its rooms are filled
with rare and beautiful treasures.

5 A wise man has great power,
and a man of knowledge increases strength;
6 for waging war you need guidance,
and for victory many advisers.

7 Wisdom is too high for a fool;
in the assembly at the gate he has nothing to say.

8 He who plots evil
will be known as a schemer.
9 The schemes of folly are sin,
and men detest a mocker.

10 If you falter in times of trouble,
how small is your strength!

11 Rescue those being led away to death;
hold back those staggering toward slaughter.
12 If you say, "But we knew nothing about this,"
does not he who weighs the heart perceive it?
Does not he who guards your life know it?
Will he not repay each person according to what he has done?

13 Eat honey, my son, for it is good;
honey from the comb is sweet to your taste.
14 Know also that wisdom is sweet to your soul;
if you find it, there is a future hope for you,
and your hope will not be cut off.

15 Do not lie in wait like an outlaw against a righteous man's house,
do not raid his dwelling place;
16 for though a righteous man falls seven times, he rises again,
but the wicked are brought down by calamity.

17 Do not gloat when your enemy falls;
when he stumbles, do not let your heart rejoice,
18 or the Lord will see and disapprove
and turn his wrath away from him.

19 Do not fret because of evil men
or be envious of the wicked,
20 for the evil man has no future hope,
and the lamp of the wicked will be snuffed out.

21 Fear the Lord and the king, my son,
and do not join with the rebellious,
22 for those two will send sudden destruction upon them,
and who knows what calamities they can bring?

Further Sayings of the Wise

23 These also are sayings of the wise:

To show partiality in judging is not good:
24 Whoever says to the guilty, "You are innocent"—
peoples will curse him and nations denounce him.
25 But it will go well with those who convict the guilty,
and rich blessing will come upon them.

26 An honest answer
is like a kiss on the lips.

27 Finish your outdoor work
and get your fields ready;
after that, build your house.

28 Do not testify against your neighbor without cause,
or use your lips to deceive.
29 Do not say, "I'll do to him as he has done to me;

I'll pay that man back for what he
did."
30I went past the field of the sluggard,
past the vineyard of the man who
lacks judgment;
31thorns had come up everywhere,
the ground was covered with weeds,
and the stone wall was in ruins.
32I applied my heart to what I observed
and learned a lesson from what I
saw:
33A little sleep, a little slumber,
a little folding of the hands to
rest—
34and poverty will come on you like a
bandit
and scarcity like an armed man.[a]

More Proverbs of Solomon

25 These are more proverbs of Solomon, copied by the men of Hezekiah king of Judah:

2It is the glory of God to conceal a
matter;

[a]34 Or *like a vagrant / and scarcity like a beggar*

VERSE FOR THE DAY: Proverbs 25:11 | AUTHOR: Elisa Morgan | PASSAGE FOR THE DAY: Proverbs 25:1–15

How Listening Can Help

A while back, on the way home from a party that my husband and I had attended, Evan commented on my conversational style. I had hopped from person to person all evening, and there had been a definite lack of substance in my dialogue. As we drove home, Evan turned to me and asked, "What were you after with all your socializing?"

I had thought I was just being friendly. But my husband's question prompted me to look more closely at my conversations. I realized that there had been times when, rather than being genuinely interested in someone, I had slipped into a "what-are-they-thinking-about-my-ability-to-ask-questions" discourse—as though I were competing in a popularity contest. There are times when I can't hear myself until someone else first hears what I'm saying and draws my attention to it.

MARRIAGE BUILDERS

♦ *Who is the best listener you know? What is that person doing that works?*

♦ *How could you be more open and willing to receiving helpful criticism from your spouse?*

Additional Scripture Readings
Proverbs 15:23; James 3:3–12

Go to page 686 for your next devotional reading.

to search out a matter is the glory
of kings.

3As the heavens are high and the earth
is deep,
so the hearts of kings are
unsearchable.

4Remove the dross from the silver,
and out comes material for[a] the
silversmith;
5remove the wicked from the king's
presence,
and his throne will be established
through righteousness.

6Do not exalt yourself in the king's
presence,
and do not claim a place among
great men;
7it is better for him to say to you,
"Come up here,"
than for him to humiliate you
before a nobleman.

What you have seen with your eyes
8 do not bring[b] hastily to court,
for what will you do in the end
if your neighbor puts you to shame?

9If you argue your case with a
neighbor,
do not betray another man's
confidence,
10or he who hears it may shame you
and you will never lose your bad
reputation.

11A word aptly spoken
is like apples of gold in settings of
silver.

12Like an earring of gold or an
ornament of fine gold
is a wise man's rebuke to a listening
ear.

13Like the coolness of snow at harvest
time
is a trustworthy messenger to those
who send him;
he refreshes the spirit of his
masters.

14Like clouds and wind without rain
is a man who boasts of gifts he
does not give.

15Through patience a ruler can be
persuaded,
and a gentle tongue can break a
bone.

16If you find honey, eat just enough—
too much of it, and you will vomit.
17Seldom set foot in your neighbor's
house—
too much of you, and he will hate
you.

18Like a club or a sword or a sharp
arrow
is the man who gives false
testimony against his neighbor.

19Like a bad tooth or a lame foot
is reliance on the unfaithful in times
of trouble.

20Like one who takes away a garment
on a cold day,
or like vinegar poured on soda,
is one who sings songs to a heavy
heart.

21If your enemy is hungry, give him
food to eat;
if he is thirsty, give him water to
drink.
22In doing this, you will heap burning
coals on his head,
and the LORD will reward you.

23As a north wind brings rain,
so a sly tongue brings angry looks.

24Better to live on a corner of the roof
than share a house with a
quarrelsome wife.

25Like cold water to a weary soul
is good news from a distant land.

26Like a muddied spring or a polluted
well
is a righteous man who gives way
to the wicked.

27It is not good to eat too much honey,
nor is it honorable to seek one's
own honor.

28Like a city whose walls are broken
down
is a man who lacks self-control.

26 Like snow in summer or rain in
harvest,
honor is not fitting for a fool.

2Like a fluttering sparrow or a darting
swallow,
an undeserved curse does not come
to rest.

[a]4 Or *comes a vessel from* [b]7,8 Or *nobleman / on whom you had set your eyes.* / 8*Do not go*

3A whip for the horse, a halter for the donkey,
and a rod for the backs of fools!

4Do not answer a fool according to his folly,
or you will be like him yourself.

5Answer a fool according to his folly,
or he will be wise in his own eyes.

6Like cutting off one's feet or drinking violence
is the sending of a message by the hand of a fool.

7Like a lame man's legs that hang limp
is a proverb in the mouth of a fool.

8Like tying a stone in a sling
is the giving of honor to a fool.

9Like a thornbush in a drunkard's hand
is a proverb in the mouth of a fool.

10Like an archer who wounds at random
is he who hires a fool or any passer-by.

11As a dog returns to its vomit,
so a fool repeats his folly.

12Do you see a man wise in his own eyes?
There is more hope for a fool than for him.

13The sluggard says, "There is a lion in the road,
a fierce lion roaming the streets!"

14As a door turns on its hinges,
so a sluggard turns on his bed.

15The sluggard buries his hand in the dish;
he is too lazy to bring it back to his mouth.

16The sluggard is wiser in his own eyes
than seven men who answer discreetly.

17Like one who seizes a dog by the ears
is a passer-by who meddles in a quarrel not his own.

18Like a madman shooting firebrands or deadly arrows
19is a man who deceives his neighbor
and says, "I was only joking!"

20Without wood a fire goes out;
without gossip a quarrel dies down.

21As charcoal to embers and as wood to fire,
so is a quarrelsome man for kindling strife.

22The words of a gossip are like choice morsels;
they go down to a man's inmost parts.

23Like a coating of glaze[a] over earthenware
are fervent lips with an evil heart.

24A malicious man disguises himself with his lips,
but in his heart he harbors deceit.
25Though his speech is charming, do not believe him,
for seven abominations fill his heart.

26His malice may be concealed by deception,
but his wickedness will be exposed in the assembly.

27If a man digs a pit, he will fall into it;
if a man rolls a stone, it will roll back on him.

28A lying tongue hates those it hurts,
and a flattering mouth works ruin.

27 Do not boast about tomorrow,
for you do not know what a day may bring forth.

2Let another praise you, and not your own mouth;
someone else, and not your own lips.

3Stone is heavy and sand a burden,
but provocation by a fool is heavier than both.

4Anger is cruel and fury overwhelming,
but who can stand before jealousy?

5Better is open rebuke
than hidden love.

6Wounds from a friend can be trusted,
but an enemy multiplies kisses.

7He who is full loathes honey,
but to the hungry even what is bitter tastes sweet.

8Like a bird that strays from its nest
is a man who strays from his home.

9Perfume and incense bring joy to the heart,

[a]23 With a different word division of the Hebrew; Masoretic Text *of silver dross*

and the pleasantness of one's friend
springs from his earnest
counsel.

10Do not forsake your friend and the
friend of your father,
and do not go to your brother's
house when disaster strikes
you—
better a neighbor nearby than a
brother far away.

11Be wise, my son, and bring joy to my
heart;
then I can answer anyone who
treats me with contempt.

12The prudent see danger and take
refuge,
but the simple keep going and
suffer for it.

13Take the garment of one who puts up
security for a stranger;
hold it in pledge if he does it for a
wayward woman.

14If a man loudly blesses his neighbor
early in the morning,
it will be taken as a curse.

15A quarrelsome wife is like
a constant dripping on a rainy day;
16restraining her is like restraining the
wind
or grasping oil with the hand.

17As iron sharpens iron,
so one man sharpens another.

18He who tends a fig tree will eat its
fruit,
and he who looks after his master
will be honored.

19As water reflects a face,
so a man's heart reflects the man.

20Death and Destruction[a] are never
satisfied,
and neither are the eyes of man.

21The crucible for silver and the furnace
for gold,
but man is tested by the praise he
receives.

22Though you grind a fool in a mortar,
grinding him like grain with a
pestle,
you will not remove his folly from
him.

23Be sure you know the condition of
your flocks,
give careful attention to your herds;
24for riches do not endure forever,
and a crown is not secure for all
generations.

25When the hay is removed and new
growth appears
and the grass from the hills is
gathered in,
26the lambs will provide you with
clothing,
and the goats with the price of a
field.

27You will have plenty of goats' milk
to feed you and your family
and to nourish your servant girls.

28 The wicked man flees though no
one pursues,
but the righteous are as bold as a
lion.

2When a country is rebellious, it has
many rulers,
but a man of understanding and
knowledge maintains order.

3A ruler[b] who oppresses the poor
is like a driving rain that leaves no
crops.

4Those who forsake the law praise the
wicked,
but those who keep the law resist
them.

5Evil men do not understand justice,
but those who seek the LORD
understand it fully.

6Better a poor man whose walk is
blameless
than a rich man whose ways are
perverse.

7He who keeps the law is a discerning
son,
but a companion of gluttons
disgraces his father.

8He who increases his wealth by
exorbitant interest
amasses it for another, who will be
kind to the poor.

9If anyone turns a deaf ear to the law,
even his prayers are detestable.

10He who leads the upright along an
evil path
will fall into his own trap,

[a]20 Hebrew *Sheol and Abaddon* [b]3 Or *A poor man*

but the blameless will receive a
good inheritance.
11 A rich man may be wise in his own
eyes,
but a poor man who has
discernment sees through him.
12 When the righteous triumph, there is
great elation;
but when the wicked rise to power,
men go into hiding.
13 He who conceals his sins does not
prosper,
but whoever confesses and
renounces them finds mercy.
14 Blessed is the man who always fears
the LORD,

VERSE FOR THE DAY: Proverbs 27:17 | AUTHOR: Marian Liautaud | PASSAGE FOR THE DAY: Proverbs 27:15–19

Dan's Best One-Liner

Dan says he fell in love with me because I learned to spell his last name the first day I met him. I liked the fact that he reeled off jokes like a stand-up comic. Of course, his best one-liner was when he asked me to marry him. I was quick to say yes because I sensed an integrity and spirituality that were authentic. Marriage was not just a union for our own happiness, but more important, it carried the weight of ministering to each other as a brother and sister in Christ.

Never was this concept of spiritual sharpening more evident than when Dan and I decided to join a new church near our home. Making the switch forced us to think about our lives as Christians. And it gave each of us a better understanding of where the other is spiritually.

God has affirmed our decision to change churches in many ways. But the biggest sign is coming from Dan. For the first time he is experiencing the benefits of knowing what it means to really belong to a church family. And he feels inspired to serve.

Seeing Dan's renewed commitment to Christ has reminded me again just why I married him. But it made me aware of something even more important: God was working in each of us—even as we stood at the altar unpolished in our faith.

MARRIAGE BUILDERS

- *What first attracted you to your spouse?*
- *How has your spouse's spiritual growth contributed to your own?*

Additional Scripture Readings
Philippians 1:3–6; Jude 24–25

Go to page 687 for your next devotional reading.

WEEKENDING

DECISION-MAKING

Most couples easily negotiate the everyday give-and-take of marriage, but what happens if you disagree on a major decision? Try these suggestions for working through an impasse:

1. Seek a win-win solution. It's human nature to resent solutions that are imposed on you, so seek a mutual victory.

2. Listen more than you talk. Your genuine empathy may elicit a reciprocal response.

3. Solve the problem; don't conquer your spouse. Your spouse is not the problem; your problem is the problem.

4. Take time for big decisions. If you feel a sense of urgency about an important decision, it could be a product of your own emotions or imagination.

5. Get some advice. Seek the counsel of a person or couple you both respect.

6. Pray about it. God can see the end from the beginning. He knows the true impact your choices will have on your future.

— *Bob Moeller*

REVIVE

Saturday: James 1:2–18
Sunday: Isaiah 55:6–13

Go to page 689 for your next devotional reading.

but he who hardens his heart falls
into trouble.

15Like a roaring lion or a charging bear
is a wicked man ruling over a
helpless people.

16A tyrannical ruler lacks judgment,
but he who hates ill-gotten gain will
enjoy a long life.

17A man tormented by the guilt of
murder
will be a fugitive till death;
let no one support him.

18He whose walk is blameless is kept
safe,
but he whose ways are perverse will
suddenly fall.

19He who works his land will have
abundant food,
but the one who chases fantasies
will have his fill of poverty.

20A faithful man will be richly blessed,
but one eager to get rich will not go
unpunished.

21To show partiality is not good—
yet a man will do wrong for a piece
of bread.

22A stingy man is eager to get rich
and is unaware that poverty awaits
him.

23He who rebukes a man will in the end
gain more favor
than he who has a flattering tongue.

24He who robs his father or mother
and says, "It's not wrong"—
he is partner to him who destroys.

25A greedy man stirs up dissension,
but he who trusts in the LORD will
prosper.

26He who trusts in himself is a fool,
but he who walks in wisdom is kept
safe.

27He who gives to the poor will lack
nothing,
but he who closes his eyes to them
receives many curses.

28When the wicked rise to power,
people go into hiding;
but when the wicked perish, the
righteous thrive.

29 A man who remains stiff-necked
after many rebukes
will suddenly be destroyed—
without remedy.

2When the righteous thrive, the people
rejoice;
when the wicked rule, the people
groan.

3A man who loves wisdom brings joy
to his father,
but a companion of prostitutes
squanders his wealth.

4By justice a king gives a country
stability,
but one who is greedy for bribes
tears it down.

5Whoever flatters his neighbor
is spreading a net for his feet.

6An evil man is snared by his own sin,
but a righteous one can sing and be
glad.

7The righteous care about justice for
the poor,
but the wicked have no such
concern.

8Mockers stir up a city,
but wise men turn away anger.

9If a wise man goes to court with a
fool,
the fool rages and scoffs, and there
is no peace.

10Bloodthirsty men hate a man of
integrity
and seek to kill the upright.

11A fool gives full vent to his anger,
but a wise man keeps himself under
control.

12If a ruler listens to lies,
all his officials become wicked.

13The poor man and the oppressor have
this in common:
The LORD gives sight to the eyes of
both.

14If a king judges the poor with fairness,
his throne will always be secure.

15The rod of correction imparts wisdom,
but a child left to himself disgraces
his mother.

16When the wicked thrive, so does sin,
but the righteous will see their
downfall.

17 Discipline your son, and he will give you peace;
he will bring delight to your soul.
18 Where there is no revelation, the people cast off restraint;
but blessed is he who keeps the law.
19 A servant cannot be corrected by mere words;
though he understands, he will not respond.
20 Do you see a man who speaks in haste?
There is more hope for a fool than for him.

VERSE FOR THE DAY: Proverbs 29:11

AUTHOR: Charles R. Swindoll

PASSAGE FOR THE DAY: Proverbs 29:1–27

How to Fight Clean

Most marriages have their periodic skirmishes—and, occasionally, an all-out war. We can't stamp out fighting completely, but we can learn how to fight clean. Here are biblical ground rules for marital battles.

First, commit yourselves to honesty and mutual respect. Have you committed yourself, verbally and honestly in your soul, to being authentic and honest with your partner—viewing him or her with respect?

Next, lay down your deadly weapons. A temper that slips out of control is sinful. Anger that means to hurt is sin.

Third, agree with your mate that the time is right. *Both* partners should sense when to talk. There are times to disagree, and there are times not to disagree.

Fourth, after you take a verbal swing, be ready with a solution. When you come to your mate with justified criticism, be quick with a suggested solution.

Fifth, watch your words and guard your tone. The louder our voices, the less our mate will hear; the uglier the words, the less we will communicate.

Finally, when it's all over, help clean up the mess. Be compassionate enough to weep with the one who's hurt from the fight.

MARRIAGE BUILDERS

♦ *How do you and your spouse come to an agreement about when it's time to talk about a problem?*

♦ *How could you incorporate these ground rules as you seek solutions to your disagreements?*

Additional Scripture Readings
Ephesians 4:32; Proverbs 15:1;
2 Timothy 2:23; Philippians 2:14

Go to page 691 for your next devotional reading.

21 If a man pampers his servant from youth,
he will bring grief[a] in the end.

22 An angry man stirs up dissension,
and a hot-tempered one commits many sins.

23 A man's pride brings him low,
but a man of lowly spirit gains honor.

24 The accomplice of a thief is his own enemy;
he is put under oath and dare not testify.

25 Fear of man will prove to be a snare,
but whoever trusts in the LORD is kept safe.

26 Many seek an audience with a ruler,
but it is from the LORD that man gets justice.

27 The righteous detest the dishonest;
the wicked detest the upright.

Sayings of Agur

30 The sayings of Agur son of Jakeh—an oracle[b]:

This man declared to Ithiel,
to Ithiel and to Ucal:[c]

2 "I am the most ignorant of men;
I do not have a man's understanding.
3 I have not learned wisdom,
nor have I knowledge of the Holy One.
4 Who has gone up to heaven and come down?
Who has gathered up the wind in the hollow of his hands?
Who has wrapped up the waters in his cloak?
Who has established all the ends of the earth?
What is his name, and the name of his son?
Tell me if you know!

5 "Every word of God is flawless;
he is a shield to those who take refuge in him.
6 Do not add to his words,
or he will rebuke you and prove you a liar.

7 "Two things I ask of you, O LORD;
do not refuse me before I die:
8 Keep falsehood and lies far from me;
give me neither poverty nor riches,
but give me only my daily bread.
9 Otherwise, I may have too much and disown you
and say, 'Who is the LORD?'
Or I may become poor and steal,
and so dishonor the name of my God.

10 "Do not slander a servant to his master,
or he will curse you, and you will pay for it.

11 "There are those who curse their fathers
and do not bless their mothers;
12 those who are pure in their own eyes
and yet are not cleansed of their filth;
13 those whose eyes are ever so haughty,
whose glances are so disdainful;
14 those whose teeth are swords
and whose jaws are set with knives
to devour the poor from the earth,
the needy from among mankind.

15 "The leech has two daughters.
'Give! Give!' they cry.

"There are three things that are never satisfied,
four that never say, 'Enough!':
16 the grave,[d] the barren womb,
land, which is never satisfied with water,
and fire, which never says, 'Enough!'

17 "The eye that mocks a father,
that scorns obedience to a mother,
will be pecked out by the ravens of the valley,
will be eaten by the vultures.

18 "There are three things that are too amazing for me,
four that I do not understand:
19 the way of an eagle in the sky,
the way of a snake on a rock,
the way of a ship on the high seas,

[a] 21 The meaning of the Hebrew for this word is uncertain. [b] 1 Or *Jakeh of Massa* [c] 1 Masoretic Text; with a different word division of the Hebrew *declared, "I am weary, O God; / I am weary, O God, and faint.* [d] 16 Hebrew *Sheol*

and the way of a man with a
maiden.
20"This is the way of an adulteress:
She eats and wipes her mouth
and says, 'I've done nothing wrong.'
21"Under three things the earth
trembles,
under four it cannot bear up:
22a servant who becomes king,
a fool who is full of food,
23an unloved woman who is married,
and a maidservant who displaces
her mistress.
24"Four things on earth are small,
yet they are extremely wise:
25Ants are creatures of little strength,
yet they store up their food in the
summer;

VERSE FOR THE DAY: Proverbs 30:21, 23

AUTHOR: Ron Hutchcraft

PASSAGE FOR THE DAY: Proverbs 30:1–33

Making Time

Spending time with God is the time to listen to the most important voice in heaven. Likewise, freeing up time with my wife is a time to listen to the most important voice on earth. My marriage commitment implies putting Karen first, and that's almost impossible to do if she cannot get on my agenda regularly.

If Karen feels unheard, she will eventually feel unloved. And that is a dangerous state. The Bible warns "Under three things the earth trembles, under four it cannot bear up: . . . an unloved woman who is married" (Proverbs 30:21, 23).

Karen will not *feel* loved if I don't spend time with her. She craves a oneness that can only be built through daily debriefings. But as delays go from days to weeks, the postponed agendas pile up and the volcano starts to rumble. Finally, a conversation starts out slowly, then it picks up momentum, knocking loose a score of larger thoughts. Every item she shares with me reminds her of another. Before long, I'm buried in an avalanche! I ask her, "Why did you wait so long to tell me all this?"

She doesn't need to answer. She tried, but I was traveling too fast to hear, or I didn't leave any time in which she could even try.

MARRIAGE BUILDERS

♦ *Are you a person who lets things pile up until there's an avalanche of emotions? What about your spouse?*

♦ *What time of day would be best for a "daily debriefing" between you and your mate?*

Additional Scripture Readings
Genesis 2:20–24; Ephesians 4:25–32

Go to page 693 for your next devotional reading.

26coneys[a] are creatures of little power,
yet they make their home in the crags;
27locusts have no king,
yet they advance together in ranks;
28a lizard can be caught with the hand,
yet it is found in kings' palaces.

29"There are three things that are stately in their stride,
four that move with stately bearing:
30a lion, mighty among beasts,
who retreats before nothing;
31a strutting rooster, a he-goat,
and a king with his army around him.[b]

32"If you have played the fool and exalted yourself,
or if you have planned evil,
clap your hand over your mouth!
33For as churning the milk produces butter,
and as twisting the nose produces blood,
so stirring up anger produces strife."

Sayings of King Lemuel

31 The sayings of King Lemuel—an oracle[c] his mother taught him:

2"O my son, O son of my womb,
O son of my vows,[d]
3do not spend your strength on women,
your vigor on those who ruin kings.

4"It is not for kings, O Lemuel—
not for kings to drink wine,
not for rulers to crave beer,
5lest they drink and forget what the law decrees,
and deprive all the oppressed of their rights.
6Give beer to those who are perishing,
wine to those who are in anguish;
7let them drink and forget their poverty
and remember their misery no more.

8"Speak up for those who cannot speak for themselves,
for the rights of all who are destitute.
9Speak up and judge fairly;
defend the rights of the poor and needy."

Epilogue: The Wife of Noble Character

10[e]A wife of noble character who can find?
She is worth far more than rubies.
11Her husband has full confidence in her
and lacks nothing of value.
12She brings him good, not harm,
all the days of her life.
13She selects wool and flax
and works with eager hands.
14She is like the merchant ships,
bringing her food from afar.
15She gets up while it is still dark;
she provides food for her family
and portions for her servant girls.
16She considers a field and buys it;
out of her earnings she plants a vineyard.
17She sets about her work vigorously;
her arms are strong for her tasks.
18She sees that her trading is profitable,
and her lamp does not go out at night.
19In her hand she holds the distaff
and grasps the spindle with her fingers.
20She opens her arms to the poor
and extends her hands to the needy.
21When it snows, she has no fear for her household;
for all of them are clothed in scarlet.
22She makes coverings for her bed;
she is clothed in fine linen and purple.
23Her husband is respected at the city gate,
where he takes his seat among the elders of the land.
24She makes linen garments and sells them,
and supplies the merchants with sashes.
25She is clothed with strength and dignity;
she can laugh at the days to come.
26She speaks with wisdom,
and faithful instruction is on her tongue.

[a]*26* That is, the hyrax or rock badger [b]*31* Or *king secure against revolt* [c]*1* Or *of Lemuel king of Massa, which* [d]*2* Or / *the answer to my prayers* [e]*10* Verses 10-31 are an acrostic, each verse beginning with a successive letter of the Hebrew alphabet.

VERSE FOR THE DAY: Proverbs 31:12

AUTHOR: Win Couchman

PASSAGE FOR THE DAY: Proverbs 31:10–31

Not Our *Goodness*

Bob and I were married in the middle of World War II. After a short honeymoon we began a year-and-a-half-long "paper marriage" while Bob returned to war in the Pacific.

I wrote often and passionately of my love. Then Bob came home and I had to begin living out what I had sincerely, but naively, portrayed in my letters. Bob quickly got to know the selfish, immature, not-so-good wife who had never shown up in our wartime correspondence.

As my hopes of appearing good faded, my longing to *be* good grew. Bible verses haunted me. For example: Proverbs 31:12. "She brings him good, not harm, all the days of her life." The other verse that caught my attention was in Matthew 19, where Jesus asks, "Why do you ask me about what is good? . . . There is only One who is good" (v. 17).

During the years we were neck-deep in raising four children, Bob and I were struggling in our relationship. We were disappointed—in ourselves, and in each other. A study of Romans began to reveal the fact that God's Spirit lived in us. In all our years as Christians, neither of us had heard a message on the Spirit of God! We hadn't realized that God wanted to express *his* goodness in and through us.

We began to lean on the in-dwelling God to change us, and our marriage was transformed. The understanding that we could live out of God's resources changed the dynamics of how we related to each other. Now we both want to demonstrate the loveliness of Jesus in our lives, and we know he will help us do that.

MARRIAGE BUILDERS

♦ *What makes it impossible for spouses always to "look good" to one another?*

♦ *How can you come together in depending on God to bring "goodness" into your relationship?*

Additional Scripture Readings
Matthew 19:17; Romans 8:9–14; Zechariah 4:6

Go to page 697 for your next devotional reading.

[27]She watches over the affairs of her household
and does not eat the bread of idleness.
[28]Her children arise and call her blessed;
her husband also, and he praises her:
[29]"Many women do noble things,
but you surpass them all."
[30]Charm is deceptive, and beauty is fleeting;
but a woman who fears the LORD is to be praised.
[31]Give her the reward she has earned,
and let her works bring her praise at the city gate.

THE Teacher, a king in Jerusalem, searches in this book for a purpose to his life. After various pursuits, frustrated by not finding satisfactory answers, he discovers that happiness is in the Lord and in obeying his word (Ecclesiastes 12:11–14). As you read this book, think about how life without God has no meaning but how life regulated by God and his word is wonderful indeed. Be sure to dedicate your life to the Lord when you are young (Ecclesiastes 12:1).

ECCLESIASTES

Everything Is Meaningless

1 The words of the Teacher,[a] son of
David, king in Jerusalem:

2"Meaningless! Meaningless!"
says the Teacher.
"Utterly meaningless!
Everything is meaningless."

3What does man gain from all his labor
at which he toils under the sun?
4Generations come and generations go,
but the earth remains forever.
5The sun rises and the sun sets,
and hurries back to where it rises.
6The wind blows to the south
and turns to the north;
round and round it goes,
ever returning on its course.
7All streams flow into the sea,
yet the sea is never full.
To the place the streams come from,
there they return again.
8All things are wearisome,
more than one can say.
The eye never has enough of seeing,
nor the ear its fill of hearing.
9What has been will be again,
what has been done will be done
again;

[a] 1 Or *leader of the assembly*; also in verses 2 and 12

there is nothing new under the sun.
10 Is there anything of which one can say,
"Look! This is something new"?
It was here already, long ago;
it was here before our time.
11 There is no remembrance of men of old,
and even those who are yet to come
will not be remembered
by those who follow.

Wisdom Is Meaningless

12 I, the Teacher, was king over Israel in Jerusalem. 13 I devoted myself to study and to explore by wisdom all that is done under heaven. What a heavy burden God has laid on men! 14 I have seen all the things that are done under the sun; all of them are meaningless, a chasing after the wind.

15 What is twisted cannot be straightened;
what is lacking cannot be counted.

16 I thought to myself, "Look, I have grown and increased in wisdom more than anyone who has ruled over Jerusalem before me; I have experienced much of wisdom and knowledge." 17 Then I applied myself to the understanding of wisdom, and also of madness and folly, but I learned that this, too, is a chasing after the wind.

18 For with much wisdom comes much sorrow;
the more knowledge, the more grief.

Pleasures Are Meaningless

2 I thought in my heart, "Come now, I will test you with pleasure to find out what is good." But that also proved to be meaningless. 2 "Laughter," I said, "is foolish. And what does pleasure accomplish?" 3 I tried cheering myself with wine, and embracing folly—my mind still guiding me with wisdom. I wanted to see what was worthwhile for men to do under heaven during the few days of their lives.

4 I undertook great projects: I built houses for myself and planted vineyards. 5 I made gardens and parks and planted all kinds of fruit trees in them. 6 I made reservoirs to water groves of flourishing trees. 7 I bought male and female slaves and had other slaves who were born in my house. I also owned more herds and flocks than anyone in Jerusalem before me. 8 I amassed silver and gold for myself, and the treasure of kings and provinces. I acquired men and women singers, and a harem[a] as well—the delights of the heart of man. 9 I became greater by far than anyone in Jerusalem before me. In all this my wisdom stayed with me.

10 I denied myself nothing my eyes desired;
I refused my heart no pleasure.
My heart took delight in all my work,
and this was the reward for all my labor.
11 Yet when I surveyed all that my hands had done
and what I had toiled to achieve,
everything was meaningless, a chasing after the wind;
nothing was gained under the sun.

Wisdom and Folly Are Meaningless

12 Then I turned my thoughts to consider wisdom,
and also madness and folly.
What more can the king's successor do
than what has already been done?
13 I saw that wisdom is better than folly,
just as light is better than darkness.
14 The wise man has eyes in his head,
while the fool walks in the darkness;
but I came to realize
that the same fate overtakes them both.

15 Then I thought in my heart,
"The fate of the fool will overtake me also.
What then do I gain by being wise?"
I said in my heart,
"This too is meaningless."
16 For the wise man, like the fool, will not be long remembered;
in days to come both will be forgotten.
Like the fool, the wise man too must die!

Toil Is Meaningless

17 So I hated life, because the work that is done under the sun was grievous to me. All of it is meaningless, a chasing after the

[a] 8 The meaning of the Hebrew for this phrase is uncertain.

wind. 18I hated all the things I had toiled
for under the sun, because I must leave
them to the one who comes after me.
19And who knows whether he will be a
wise man or a fool? Yet he will have con-
trol over all the work into which I have
poured my effort and skill under the sun.
This too is meaningless. 20So my heart be-
gan to despair over all my toilsome labor
under the sun. 21For a man may do his
work with wisdom, knowledge and skill,
and then he must leave all he owns to
someone who has not worked for it. This
too is meaningless and a great misfortune.
22What does a man get for all the toil and
anxious striving with which he labors un-
der the sun? 23All his days his work is pain
and grief; even at night his mind does not
rest. This too is meaningless.
24A man can do nothing better than to
eat and drink and find satisfaction in his
work. This too, I see, is from the hand of
God, 25for without him, who can eat or
find enjoyment? 26To the man who
pleases him, God gives wisdom, knowl-
edge and happiness, but to the sinner he
gives the task of gathering and storing up
wealth to hand it over to the one who

VERSE FOR THE DAY: Ecclesiastes 2:13

AUTHOR: Elizabeth Cody Newenhuyse

PASSAGE FOR THE DAY: Ecclesiastes 2:1–16

Doomsday Paranoia

Some astronomers have theorized that a giant asteroid may be hurtling our way. "Eventually," they say, "it will hit and be catastrophic." How catastrophic? Try the end of agriculture as we know it. And that's just for starters.

The more one watches TV and reads the newspapers, and the less one thinks, the more fear is created. Studies have in fact shown that people who watch a lot of television think the world is more dangerous than it really is. And if roving bands of armed youths don't get you first, that rare disease the *New England Journal of Medicine* just reported on will.

Whatever happened to wisdom, to discernment, to trust in a merciful and all-sovereign God? It's time we refuse to live our lives according to the doomsayers. Instead, let's choose to live in the spirit of 2 Timothy 1:7: "For God did not give us a spirit of timidity, but a spirit of power, of love and of self-discipline."

MARRIAGE BUILDERS

♦ *What are the things that discourage you? How does the discouragement affect your marriage?*

♦ *How can Christians live with confidence, despite disheartening trends?*

Additional Scripture Readings
2 Timothy 1:7; 1 John 4:18

Go to page 699 for your next devotional reading.

pleases God. This too is meaningless, a chasing after the wind.

A Time for Everything

3 There is a time for everything,
and a season for every activity
under heaven:

2 a time to be born and a time to die,
a time to plant and a time to
uproot,
3 a time to kill and a time to heal,
a time to tear down and a time to
build,
4 a time to weep and a time to laugh,
a time to mourn and a time to
dance,
5 a time to scatter stones and a time
to gather them,
a time to embrace and a time to
refrain,
6 a time to search and a time to give
up,
a time to keep and a time to throw
away,
7 a time to tear and a time to mend,
a time to be silent and a time to
speak,
8 a time to love and a time to hate,
a time for war and a time for peace.

9What does the worker gain from his toil? 10I have seen the burden God has laid on men. 11He has made everything beautiful in its time. He has also set eternity in the hearts of men; yet they cannot fathom what God has done from beginning to end. 12I know that there is nothing better for men than to be happy and do good while they live. 13That everyone may eat and drink, and find satisfaction in all his toil—this is the gift of God. 14I know that everything God does will endure forever; nothing can be added to it and nothing taken from it. God does it so that men will revere him.

15Whatever is has already been,
and what will be has been before;
and God will call the past to
account.[a]

16And I saw something else under the sun:

In the place of judgment—wickedness
was there,
in the place of justice—wickedness
was there.

17I thought in my heart,

"God will bring to judgment
both the righteous and the wicked,
for there will be a time for every
activity,
a time for every deed."

18I also thought, "As for men, God tests them so that they may see that they are like the animals. 19Man's fate is like that of the animals; the same fate awaits them both: As one dies, so dies the other. All have the same breath[b]; man has no advantage over the animal. Everything is meaningless. 20All go to the same place; all come from dust, and to dust all return. 21Who knows if the spirit of man rises upward and if the spirit of the animal[c] goes down into the earth?"

22So I saw that there is nothing better for a man than to enjoy his work, because that is his lot. For who can bring him to see what will happen after him?

Oppression, Toil, Friendlessness

4 Again I looked and saw all the oppression that was taking place under the sun:

I saw the tears of the oppressed—
and they have no comforter;
power was on the side of their
oppressors—
and they have no comforter.
2And I declared that the dead,
who had already died,
are happier than the living,
who are still alive.
3But better than both
is he who has not yet been,
who has not seen the evil
that is done under the sun.

4And I saw that all labor and all achievement spring from man's envy of his neighbor. This too is meaningless, a chasing after the wind.

5The fool folds his hands
and ruins himself.
6Better one handful with tranquillity
than two handfuls with toil
and chasing after the wind.

[a] 15 Or *God calls back the past* [b] 19 Or *spirit* [c] 21 Or *Who knows the spirit of man, which rises upward, or the spirit of the animal, which*

7Again I saw something meaningless
under the sun:

8There was a man all alone;
he had neither son nor brother.
There was no end to his toil,
yet his eyes were not content with
his wealth.
"For whom am I toiling," he asked,
"and why am I depriving myself of
enjoyment?"
This too is meaningless—
a miserable business!

9Two are better than one,
because they have a good return for
their work:
10If one falls down,
his friend can help him up.
But pity the man who falls
and has no one to help him up!
11Also, if two lie down together, they
will keep warm.
But how can one keep warm alone?

VERSE FOR THE DAY: Ecclesiastes 4:9–10

AUTHOR: Les and Leslie Parrott

PASSAGE FOR THE DAY: Ecclesiastes 4:9–12

It Takes Two

"I never knew how selfish I was until I got married," said Gary. He was telling us about his wife, Paula, who volunteered at a retirement center one night a week.

"At first I resented her being away from me," he told us. "But a couple of months ago she needed a lift, so I went with her." Gary kept returning to the center, and soon he realized that volunteering with his wife was the highlight of his week. "It brings Paula and me closer together," he said. "As a team we make a difference."

There are hundreds of ways to incorporate shared service into your marriage. As a team, our mentoring friends, Dennis and Lucy Guernsey, always maintained an open home and were generous with others. Their home became a hub of celebration and delicious dinners. The key is to find something that fits your personal style. Not all your service needs to be done in front of others. We've found that the soul of our marriage is nourished most when we do something anonymously. Secretly observing the results of our service brings deeper devotion and intimacy.

MARRIAGE BUILDERS

♦ *Describe a time when your spouse's support enabled you to serve the Lord.*

♦ *What are some of the strengths that make the two of you a good team?*

Additional Scripture Readings
1 Corinthians 12:27–31; Ephesians 2:14–22

Go to page 701 for your next devotional reading.

12Though one may be overpowered,
two can defend themselves.
A cord of three strands is not quickly
broken.

Advancement Is Meaningless

13Better a poor but wise youth than an
old but foolish king who no longer knows
how to take warning. 14The youth may
have come from prison to the kingship, or
he may have been born in poverty within
his kingdom. 15I saw that all who lived
and walked under the sun followed the
youth, the king's successor. 16There was
no end to all the people who were before
them. But those who came later were not
pleased with the successor. This too is
meaningless, a chasing after the wind.

Stand in Awe of God

5 Guard your steps when you go to the
house of God. Go near to listen rather
than to offer the sacrifice of fools, who do
not know that they do wrong.

2Do not be quick with your mouth,
do not be hasty in your heart
to utter anything before God.
God is in heaven
and you are on earth,
so let your words be few.
3As a dream comes when there are
many cares,
so the speech of a fool when there
are many words.

4When you make a vow to God, do not
delay in fulfilling it. He has no pleasure in
fools; fulfill your vow. 5It is better not to
vow than to make a vow and not fulfill it.
6Do not let your mouth lead you into sin.
And do not protest to the ⌊temple⌋ messen-
ger, "My vow was a mistake." Why should
God be angry at what you say and destroy
the work of your hands? 7Much dreaming
and many words are meaningless. There-
fore stand in awe of God.

Riches Are Meaningless

8If you see the poor oppressed in a dis-
trict, and justice and rights denied, do not
be surprised at such things; for one offi-
cial is eyed by a higher one, and over them
both are others higher still. 9The increase
from the land is taken by all; the king him-
self profits from the fields.

10Whoever loves money never has
money enough;
whoever loves wealth is never
satisfied with his income.
This too is meaningless.

11As goods increase,
so do those who consume them.
And what benefit are they to the
owner
except to feast his eyes on them?

12The sleep of a laborer is sweet,
whether he eats little or much,
but the abundance of a rich man
permits him no sleep.

13I have seen a grievous evil under the
sun:

wealth hoarded to the harm of its
owner,
14 or wealth lost through some
misfortune,
so that when he has a son
there is nothing left for him.
15Naked a man comes from his mother's
womb,
and as he comes, so he departs.
He takes nothing from his labor
that he can carry in his hand.

16This too is a grievous evil:

As a man comes, so he departs,
and what does he gain,
since he toils for the wind?
17All his days he eats in darkness,
with great frustration, affliction and
anger.

18Then I realized that it is good and
proper for a man to eat and drink, and to
find satisfaction in his toilsome labor un-
der the sun during the few days of life God
has given him—for this is his lot. 19More-
over, when God gives any man wealth and
possessions, and enables him to enjoy
them, to accept his lot and be happy in his
work—this is a gift of God. 20He seldom
reflects on the days of his life, because
God keeps him occupied with gladness of
heart.

6 I have seen another evil under the
sun, and it weighs heavily on men:
2God gives a man wealth, possessions and
honor, so that he lacks nothing his heart
desires, but God does not enable him to
enjoy them, and a stranger enjoys them
instead. This is meaningless, a grievous
evil.

3A man may have a hundred children
and live many years; yet no matter how
long he lives, if he cannot enjoy his pros-

WEEKENDING

ENCOURAGEMENT

Couples can build their relationships by focusing on each other's needs, and championing their spouses' self-esteem. Here are four ways you could build trust and intimacy and express your love and appreciation for each other. Talk about each of these with your spouse to see which of these would encourage him or her most.

1. Don't let your spouse neglect his or her own needs. Rearrange your time—and, if necessary, your financial priorities—to allow your spouse personal time to pursue a hobby or other outside interest.

2. Let your spouse's past mistakes and failures stay in the past; don't bring them up again.

3. Emphasize the fact that we are all created by God; and remind your spouse of God's tenderness and forgiveness toward us.

4. Pray together about any problem areas or recurring difficulties in your marriage.

— *The* Marriage Partnership *Staff*

REVIVE

Saturday: Ephesians 4:29–32
Sunday: Philippians 3:12–21

Go to page 703 for your next devotional reading.

perity and does not receive proper burial,
I say that a stillborn child is better off than
he. [4]It comes without meaning, it departs
in darkness, and in darkness its name is
shrouded. [5]Though it never saw the sun
or knew anything, it has more rest than
does that man— [6]even if he lives a thou-
sand years twice over but fails to enjoy his
prosperity. Do not all go to the same
place?

[7]All man's efforts are for his mouth,
yet his appetite is never satisfied.
[8]What advantage has a wise man
over a fool?
What does a poor man gain
by knowing how to conduct himself
before others?
[9]Better what the eye sees
than the roving of the appetite.
This too is meaningless,
a chasing after the wind.

[10]Whatever exists has already been
named,
and what man is has been known;
no man can contend
with one who is stronger than he.
[11]The more the words,
the less the meaning,
and how does that profit anyone?

[12]For who knows what is good for a
man in life, during the few and meaning-
less days he passes through like a shad-
ow? Who can tell him what will happen
under the sun after he is gone?

Wisdom

7 A good name is better than fine
perfume,
and the day of death better than the
day of birth.
[2]It is better to go to a house of
mourning
than to go to a house of feasting,
for death is the destiny of every man;
the living should take this to heart.
[3]Sorrow is better than laughter,
because a sad face is good for the
heart.
[4]The heart of the wise is in the house
of mourning,
but the heart of fools is in the
house of pleasure.
[5]It is better to heed a wise man's
rebuke
than to listen to the song of fools.
[6]Like the crackling of thorns under the
pot,
so is the laughter of fools.
This too is meaningless.

[7]Extortion turns a wise man into a fool,
and a bribe corrupts the heart.

[8]The end of a matter is better than its
beginning,
and patience is better than pride.
[9]Do not be quickly provoked in your
spirit,
for anger resides in the lap of fools.

[10]Do not say, "Why were the old days
better than these?"
For it is not wise to ask such
questions.

[11]Wisdom, like an inheritance, is a good
thing
and benefits those who see the sun.
[12]Wisdom is a shelter
as money is a shelter,
but the advantage of knowledge is
this:
that wisdom preserves the life of its
possessor.

[13]Consider what God has done:

Who can straighten
what he has made crooked?
[14]When times are good, be happy;
but when times are bad, consider:
God has made the one
as well as the other.
Therefore, a man cannot discover
anything about his future.

[15]In this meaningless life of mine I have
seen both of these:

a righteous man perishing in his
righteousness,
and a wicked man living long in his
wickedness.
[16]Do not be overrighteous,
neither be overwise—
why destroy yourself?
[17]Do not be overwicked,
and do not be a fool—
why die before your time?
[18]It is good to grasp the one
and not let go of the other.
The man who fears God will avoid
all ⌞extremes⌟.[a]

[a]18 Or *will follow them both*

19 Wisdom makes one wise man more powerful
than ten rulers in a city.

20 There is not a righteous man on earth
who does what is right and never sins.

21 Do not pay attention to every word people say,
or you may hear your servant cursing you—
22 for you know in your heart
that many times you yourself have cursed others.

23 All this I tested by wisdom and I said,
"I am determined to be wise"—
but this was beyond me.

24 Whatever wisdom may be,
it is far off and most profound—
who can discover it?
25 So I turned my mind to understand,
to investigate and to search out wisdom and the scheme of things
and to understand the stupidity of wickedness
and the madness of folly.

26 I find more bitter than death
the woman who is a snare,
whose heart is a trap
and whose hands are chains.
The man who pleases God will escape her,
but the sinner she will ensnare.

VERSE FOR THE DAY: Ecclesiastes 7:10

AUTHOR: Jill Briscoe

PASSAGE FOR THE DAY: Ecclesiastes 7:1–14

The Good Old Days?

Recently, while reading through Ecclesiastes, I came across a verse that I'd never seen before. It was chapter 7, verse 10: "Do not say, 'Why were the old days better than these?' For it is not wise to ask such questions." It was a verse that made me say, "And here, all along, I thought the good old days were better than today."

I took that verse with me into my day, and when at our deaconess meeting that night we started talking about what we used to do and how much better it was that way, I thought of my verse. I shared it with the women. But God had given it to me for my need first. Once I had made it mine, then the opportunity came to pass it along to help someone else.

MARRIAGE BUILDERS

♦ *As you look back on your courtship and the early years of your marriage, what are some highlights?*
♦ *Why is it helpful to look at the future in positive terms?*

Additional Scripture Readings
Isaiah 43:18–19; 2 Timothy 3:16–17; Hebrews 12:1–2

Go to page 705 for your next devotional reading.

27"Look," says the Teacher,[a] "this is
what I have discovered:

"Adding one thing to another to
discover the scheme of
things—
28 while I was still searching
but not finding—
I found one upright man among a
thousand,
but not one upright woman among
them all.
29This only have I found:
God made mankind upright,
but men have gone in search of
many schemes."

8 Who is like the wise man?
Who knows the explanation of
things?
Wisdom brightens a man's face
and changes its hard appearance.

Obey the King

2Obey the king's command, I say, because you took an oath before God. 3Do not be in a hurry to leave the king's presence. Do not stand up for a bad cause, for he will do whatever he pleases. 4Since a king's word is supreme, who can say to him, "What are you doing?"

5Whoever obeys his command will
come to no harm,
and the wise heart will know the
proper time and procedure.
6For there is a proper time and
procedure for every matter,
though a man's misery weighs
heavily upon him.

7Since no man knows the future,
who can tell him what is to come?
8No man has power over the wind to
contain it[b];
so no one has power over the day
of his death.
As no one is discharged in time of
war,
so wickedness will not release those
who practice it.

9All this I saw, as I applied my mind to everything done under the sun. There is a time when a man lords it over others to his own[c] hurt. 10Then too, I saw the wicked buried—those who used to come and go from the holy place and receive praise[d] in the city where they did this. This too is meaningless.

11When the sentence for a crime is not quickly carried out, the hearts of the people are filled with schemes to do wrong. 12Although a wicked man commits a hundred crimes and still lives a long time, I know that it will go better with God-fearing men, who are reverent before God. 13Yet because the wicked do not fear God, it will not go well with them, and their days will not lengthen like a shadow.

14There is something else meaningless that occurs on earth: righteous men who get what the wicked deserve, and wicked men who get what the righteous deserve. This too, I say, is meaningless. 15So I commend the enjoyment of life, because nothing is better for a man under the sun than to eat and drink and be glad. Then joy will accompany him in his work all the days of the life God has given him under the sun.

16When I applied my mind to know wisdom and to observe man's labor on earth—his eyes not seeing sleep day or night— 17then I saw all that God has done. No one can comprehend what goes on under the sun. Despite all his efforts to search it out, man cannot discover its meaning. Even if a wise man claims he knows, he cannot really comprehend it.

A Common Destiny for All

9 So I reflected on all this and concluded that the righteous and the wise and what they do are in God's hands, but no man knows whether love or hate awaits him. 2All share a common destiny—the righteous and the wicked, the good and the bad,[e] the clean and the unclean, those who offer sacrifices and those who do not.

As it is with the good man,
so with the sinner;
as it is with those who take oaths,
so with those who are afraid to take
them.

3This is the evil in everything that happens under the sun: The same destiny overtakes all. The hearts of men, moreover, are full of evil and there is madness in their hearts while they live, and afterward they join the dead. 4Anyone who is

[a]27 Or *leader of the assembly* [b]8 Or *over his spirit to retain it* [c]9 Or *to their* [d]10 Some Hebrew manuscripts and Septuagint (Aquila); most Hebrew manuscripts *and are forgotten*
[e]2 Septuagint (Aquila), Vulgate and Syriac; Hebrew does not have *and the bad.*

among the living has hope[a]—even a live
dog is better off than a dead lion!

5For the living know that they will die,
but the dead know nothing;
they have no further reward,
and even the memory of them is
forgotten.

6Their love, their hate
and their jealousy have long since
vanished;
never again will they have a part
in anything that happens under the
sun.

7Go, eat your food with gladness, and

[a]4 Or *What then is to be chosen? With all who live, there is hope*

TUESDAY

VERSE FOR THE DAY: Ecclesiastes 9:17

AUTHOR: Will Willimon

PASSAGE FOR THE DAY: Ecclesiastes 9:1–18

Growth and Pain

Somebody did a study of men in marriage and found that when asked, "What is it you've gotten out of marriage?" they would often say, "My wife has shown me parts of my personality I didn't know were there. She's helped me express things I didn't know I felt." They expressed a sense of gratitude. They were better people; they were changed people.

But significant human growth occurs only with truthfulness and with some pain. Marriage is our most omnipresent experience of failure because we don't love our mates like we should. It's humiliating to have to go back and ask for forgiveness again and again. But radical change doesn't occur for most of us without somebody there to tell us the truth in love.

The traditional wedding vows say very clearly that humans change. We repeat promises such as "for better, for worse; for richer, for poorer." But standing there at the altar you have two people in the prime of their lives. So a minister really should stand in front of them and say, "in baldness, impotency, alcoholism, menopause" and so forth. In its wisdom, the church knows we don't remain nineteen forever. That's why we make promises. If you are true to the promises of marriage, you'll change in ways you never dreamed.

MARRIAGE BUILDERS

♦ *What are some of the "better" and "worse" things the two of you have encountered in your marriage?*

♦ *How has your spouse helped you improve as a person?*

Additional Scripture Readings
Ephesians 4:15, 29; 1 Corinthians 8:1

Go to page 707 for your next devotional reading.

drink your wine with a joyful heart, for it
is now that God favors what you do. 8Al-
ways be clothed in white, and always
anoint your head with oil. 9Enjoy life with
your wife, whom you love, all the days of
this meaningless life that God has given
you under the sun— all your meaningless
days. For this is your lot in life and in your
toilsome labor under the sun. 10Whatever
your hand finds to do, do it with all your
might, for in the grave,[a] where you are
going, there is neither working nor plan-
ning nor knowledge nor wisdom.

11I have seen something else under the
sun:

The race is not to the swift
or the battle to the strong,
nor does food come to the wise
or wealth to the brilliant
or favor to the learned;
but time and chance happen to them
all.

12Moreover, no man knows when his
hour will come:

As fish are caught in a cruel net,
or birds are taken in a snare,
so men are trapped by evil times
that fall unexpectedly upon them.

Wisdom Better Than Folly

13I also saw under the sun this example
of wisdom that greatly impressed me:
14There was once a small city with only a
few people in it. And a powerful king
came against it, surrounded it and built
huge siegeworks against it. 15Now there
lived in that city a man poor but wise, and
he saved the city by his wisdom. But no-
body remembered that poor man. 16So I
said, "Wisdom is better than strength."
But the poor man's wisdom is despised,
and his words are no longer heeded.

17The quiet words of the wise are more
to be heeded
than the shouts of a ruler of fools.
18Wisdom is better than weapons of
war,
but one sinner destroys much good.

10 As dead flies give perfume a bad
smell,
so a little folly outweighs wisdom
and honor.
2The heart of the wise inclines to the
right,
but the heart of the fool to the left.
3Even as he walks along the road,
the fool lacks sense
and shows everyone how stupid he
is.
4If a ruler's anger rises against you,
do not leave your post;
calmness can lay great errors to
rest.

5There is an evil I have seen under the
sun,
the sort of error that arises from a
ruler:
6Fools are put in many high positions,
while the rich occupy the low ones.
7I have seen slaves on horseback,
while princes go on foot like slaves.

8Whoever digs a pit may fall into it;
whoever breaks through a wall may
be bitten by a snake.
9Whoever quarries stones may be
injured by them;
whoever splits logs may be
endangered by them.

10If the ax is dull
and its edge unsharpened,
more strength is needed
but skill will bring success.

11If a snake bites before it is charmed,
there is no profit for the charmer.

12Words from a wise man's mouth are
gracious,
but a fool is consumed by his own
lips.
13At the beginning his words are folly;
at the end they are wicked
madness—
14 and the fool multiplies words.

No one knows what is coming—
who can tell him what will happen
after him?

15A fool's work wearies him;
he does not know the way to town.

16Woe to you, O land whose king was a
servant[b]
and whose princes feast in the
morning.
17Blessed are you, O land whose king is
of noble birth
and whose princes eat at a proper
time—
for strength and not for
drunkenness.

[a] 10 Hebrew *Sheol* [b] 16 Or *king is a child*

18 If a man is lazy, the rafters sag;
if his hands are idle, the house leaks.

19 A feast is made for laughter,
and wine makes life merry,
but money is the answer for everything.

20 Do not revile the king even in your thoughts,
or curse the rich in your bedroom,
because a bird of the air may carry your words,
and a bird on the wing may report what you say.

Bread Upon the Waters

11 Cast your bread upon the waters,
for after many days you will find it again.

2 Give portions to seven, yes to eight,
for you do not know what disaster
may come upon the land.

3 If clouds are full of water,
they pour rain upon the earth.
Whether a tree falls to the south or to the north,
in the place where it falls, there will it lie.

4 Whoever watches the wind will not plant;
whoever looks at the clouds will not reap.

5 As you do not know the path of the wind,

VERSE FOR THE DAY: Ecclesiastes 10:12

AUTHOR: Jeanette and Robert Lauer

PASSAGE FOR THE DAY: Ecclesiastes 10:1–20

A Bridled Tongue

Husbands and wives need to consider what they say in an effort to be honest. The tongue should be a monitor, rather than an open channel, of our thoughts. Perhaps we can't keep hurtful thoughts from coming into our minds, but we can refuse to speak those thoughts that might bring pain to another.

In a healthy marriage, you can tell your spouse anything, but you aren't obligated to tell your spouse *everything*. Whenever you wonder whether to tell your spouse something, stop and ask who will benefit if you share it. A tongue that speaks the truth in love—rather than total honesty about every feeling that you have—is the surest route to intimacy in marriage.

MARRIAGE BUILDERS

♦ *Do you think married partners should tell each other everything? What are some things that might be considered off-limits?*
♦ *When can total honesty be cruel or harmful?*

Additional Scripture Readings
Ephesians 4:15; James 1:26

Go to page 708 for your next devotional reading.

or how the body is formed[a] in a
mother's womb,
so you cannot understand the work of
God,
the Maker of all things.

6 Sow your seed in the morning,
and at evening let not your hands
be idle,
for you do not know which will
succeed,
whether this or that,
or whether both will do equally
well.

Remember Your Creator While Young

7 Light is sweet,
and it pleases the eyes to see the sun.

[a] 5 Or *know how life* (or *the spirit*) / *enters the body being formed*

VERSE FOR THE DAY: Ecclesiastes 12:1, 7

AUTHOR: Luci Shaw

PASSAGE FOR THE DAY: Ecclesiastes 12:1–7

'Til Death Us Do Part

There are white flowers in the bride's hands. In the groom's eyes is the tender glint of promise. The organ music vibrates with joy; the very air in the church celebrates. The vows fill our ears: "I take you to be my wedded husband, my wedded wife . . . to have and to hold, from this day forward, until death us do part."

But today, no one is thinking about death. The bride and groom are young, healthy, good-looking, happy, romantic, ambitious. Death is a discordant note. Don't even think about it! And so they don't think about it. Or talk about it. And sometimes death separates them so suddenly, like a tree split by lightning, that they are torn apart without preparation.

The knowledge that at some point every couple will experience the inevitable separation of death is a fact we must look in the face and act on. Real, bone-deep love will choose to face mortality. Don't dodge the reality. Begin to face your inevitable separation together, *now*. Prepare on spiritual, emotional and practical levels. Look into each other's eyes, hear it from each other's lips: "Because I love you so much, I want you to be ready to live alone if I die. Let's work on it together. Now."

MARRIAGE BUILDERS

♦ *What are some of your long-term goals for yourselves and for your marriage?*

♦ *What are the things the two of you need to do right away to prepare for possible loss through death?*

Additional Scripture Readings
Psalm 89:48; 1 Corinthians 15:55–57

Go to page 715 for your next devotional reading.

[8]However many years a man may live,
let him enjoy them all.
But let him remember the days of darkness,
for they will be many.
Everything to come is meaningless.

[9]Be happy, young man, while you are young,
and let your heart give you joy in the days of your youth.
Follow the ways of your heart
and whatever your eyes see,
but know that for all these things
God will bring you to judgment.
[10]So then, banish anxiety from your heart
and cast off the troubles of your body,
for youth and vigor are meaningless.

12 Remember your Creator
in the days of your youth,
before the days of trouble come
and the years approach when you will say,
"I find no pleasure in them"—
[2]before the sun and the light
and the moon and the stars grow dark,
and the clouds return after the rain;
[3]when the keepers of the house tremble,
and the strong men stoop,
when the grinders cease because they are few,
and those looking through the windows grow dim;
[4]when the doors to the street are closed
and the sound of grinding fades;
when men rise up at the sound of birds,
but all their songs grow faint;
[5]when men are afraid of heights
and of dangers in the streets;
when the almond tree blossoms
and the grasshopper drags himself along
and desire no longer is stirred.
Then man goes to his eternal home
and mourners go about the streets.

[6]Remember him—before the silver cord is severed,
or the golden bowl is broken;
before the pitcher is shattered at the spring,
or the wheel broken at the well,
[7]and the dust returns to the ground it came from,
and the spirit returns to God who gave it.

[8]"Meaningless! Meaningless!" says the Teacher.[a]
"Everything is meaningless!"

The Conclusion of the Matter

[9]Not only was the Teacher wise, but also he imparted knowledge to the people. He pondered and searched out and set in order many proverbs. [10]The Teacher searched to find just the right words, and what he wrote was upright and true.

[11]The words of the wise are like goads, their collected sayings like firmly embedded nails—given by one Shepherd. [12]Be warned, my son, of anything in addition to them.

Of making many books there is no end, and much study wearies the body.

[13]Now all has been heard;
here is the conclusion of the matter:
Fear God and keep his commandments,
for this is the whole ⌜duty⌟ of man.
[14]For God will bring every deed into judgment,
including every hidden thing,
whether it is good or evil.

[a]8 Or *the leader of the assembly*; also in verses 9 and 10

SOLOMON'S "songs numbered a thousand and five" (1 Kings 4:32), of which this is one. It focuses on the spontaneous and exclusive love between a lover and his beloved, demonstrating at the same time the sort of love Christ has for his beloved bride, the church. As you read this book, rejoice not only in the love that can exist between a man and woman, but also bask in the warmth of a personal love relationship with Christ.

SONG OF SONGS

1 Solomon's Song of Songs.

Beloved[a]

2 Let him kiss me with the kisses of his mouth—
for your love is more delightful than wine.
3 Pleasing is the fragrance of your perfumes;
your name is like perfume poured out.
No wonder the maidens love you!
4 Take me away with you—let us hurry!
Let the king bring me into his chambers.

Friends

We rejoice and delight in you[b];
we will praise your love more than wine.

Beloved

How right they are to adore you!
5 Dark am I, yet lovely,

[a] Primarily on the basis of the gender of the Hebrew pronouns used, male and female speakers are indicated in the margins by the captions *Lover* and *Beloved* respectively. The words of others are marked *Friends*. In some instances the divisions and their captions are debatable. [b] 4 The Hebrew is masculine singular.

O daughters of Jerusalem,
dark like the tents of Kedar,
like the tent curtains of Solomon.[a]
6Do not stare at me because I am dark,
because I am darkened by the sun.
My mother's sons were angry with me
and made me take care of the vineyards;
my own vineyard I have neglected.
7Tell me, you whom I love, where you graze your flock
and where you rest your sheep at midday.
Why should I be like a veiled woman
beside the flocks of your friends?

Friends

8If you do not know, most beautiful of women,
follow the tracks of the sheep
and graze your young goats
by the tents of the shepherds.

Lover

9I liken you, my darling, to a mare
harnessed to one of the chariots of Pharaoh.
10Your cheeks are beautiful with earrings,
your neck with strings of jewels.
11We will make you earrings of gold,
studded with silver.

Beloved

12While the king was at his table,
my perfume spread its fragrance.
13My lover is to me a sachet of myrrh
resting between my breasts.
14My lover is to me a cluster of henna blossoms
from the vineyards of En Gedi.

Lover

15How beautiful you are, my darling!
Oh, how beautiful!
Your eyes are doves.

Beloved

16How handsome you are, my lover!
Oh, how charming!
And our bed is verdant.

Lover

17The beams of our house are cedars;
our rafters are firs.

Beloved[b]

2 I am a rose[c] of Sharon,
a lily of the valleys.

Lover

2Like a lily among thorns
is my darling among the maidens.

Beloved

3Like an apple tree among the trees of the forest
is my lover among the young men.
I delight to sit in his shade,
and his fruit is sweet to my taste.
4He has taken me to the banquet hall,
and his banner over me is love.
5Strengthen me with raisins,
refresh me with apples,
for I am faint with love.
6His left arm is under my head,
and his right arm embraces me.
7Daughters of Jerusalem, I charge you
by the gazelles and by the does of the field:
Do not arouse or awaken love
until it so desires.

8Listen! My lover!
Look! Here he comes,
leaping across the mountains,
bounding over the hills.
9My lover is like a gazelle or a young stag.
Look! There he stands behind our wall,
gazing through the windows,
peering through the lattice.
10My lover spoke and said to me,
"Arise, my darling,
my beautiful one, and come with me.
11See! The winter is past;
the rains are over and gone.
12Flowers appear on the earth;
the season of singing has come,
the cooing of doves
is heard in our land.
13The fig tree forms its early fruit;
the blossoming vines spread their fragrance.
Arise, come, my darling;
my beautiful one, come with me."

Lover

14My dove in the clefts of the rock,
in the hiding places on the mountainside,

[a] 5 Or *Salma* [b] 1 Or *Lover* [c] 1 Possibly a member of the crocus family

show me your face,
let me hear your voice;
for your voice is sweet,
and your face is lovely.
15Catch for us the foxes,
the little foxes
that ruin the vineyards,
our vineyards that are in bloom.

Beloved

16My lover is mine and I am his;
he browses among the lilies.
17Until the day breaks
and the shadows flee,
turn, my lover,
and be like a gazelle
or like a young stag
on the rugged hills.[a]

3 All night long on my bed
I looked for the one my heart loves;
I looked for him but did not find him.
2I will get up now and go about the city,
through its streets and squares;
I will search for the one my heart loves.
So I looked for him but did not find him.
3The watchmen found me
as they made their rounds in the city.
"Have you seen the one my heart loves?"
4Scarcely had I passed them
when I found the one my heart loves.
I held him and would not let him go
till I had brought him to my mother's house,
to the room of the one who conceived me.
5Daughters of Jerusalem, I charge you
by the gazelles and by the does of the field:
Do not arouse or awaken love
until it so desires.

6Who is this coming up from the desert
like a column of smoke,
perfumed with myrrh and incense
made from all the spices of the merchant?
7Look! It is Solomon's carriage,
escorted by sixty warriors,
the noblest of Israel,
8all of them wearing the sword,
all experienced in battle,
each with his sword at his side,
prepared for the terrors of the night.
9King Solomon made for himself the carriage;
he made it of wood from Lebanon.
10Its posts he made of silver,
its base of gold.
Its seat was upholstered with purple,
its interior lovingly inlaid
by[b] the daughters of Jerusalem.
11Come out, you daughters of Zion,
and look at King Solomon wearing the crown,
the crown with which his mother crowned him
on the day of his wedding,
the day his heart rejoiced.

Lover

4 How beautiful you are, my darling!
Oh, how beautiful!
Your eyes behind your veil are doves.
Your hair is like a flock of goats
descending from Mount Gilead.
2Your teeth are like a flock of sheep just shorn,
coming up from the washing.
Each has its twin;
not one of them is alone.
3Your lips are like a scarlet ribbon;
your mouth is lovely.
Your temples behind your veil
are like the halves of a pomegranate.
4Your neck is like the tower of David,
built with elegance[c];
on it hang a thousand shields,
all of them shields of warriors.
5Your two breasts are like two fawns,
like twin fawns of a gazelle
that browse among the lilies.
6Until the day breaks
and the shadows flee,
I will go to the mountain of myrrh
and to the hill of incense.
7All beautiful you are, my darling;
there is no flaw in you.

8Come with me from Lebanon, my bride,
come with me from Lebanon.
Descend from the crest of Amana,

[a]17 Or *the hills of Bether* [b]10 Or *its inlaid interior a gift of love / from* [c]4 The meaning of the Hebrew for this word is uncertain.

from the top of Senir, the summit of Hermon,
from the lions' dens
and the mountain haunts of the leopards.
9You have stolen my heart, my sister, my bride;
you have stolen my heart
with one glance of your eyes,
with one jewel of your necklace.
10How delightful is your love, my sister, my bride!
How much more pleasing is your love than wine,
and the fragrance of your perfume than any spice!
11Your lips drop sweetness as the honeycomb, my bride;
milk and honey are under your tongue.
The fragrance of your garments is like that of Lebanon.
12You are a garden locked up, my sister, my bride;
you are a spring enclosed, a sealed fountain.
13Your plants are an orchard of pomegranates
with choice fruits,
with henna and nard,
14 nard and saffron,
calamus and cinnamon,
with every kind of incense tree,
with myrrh and aloes
and all the finest spices.
15You are[a] a garden fountain,
a well of flowing water
streaming down from Lebanon.

Beloved

16Awake, north wind,
and come, south wind!
Blow on my garden,
that its fragrance may spread abroad.
Let my lover come into his garden
and taste its choice fruits.

Lover

5 I have come into my garden, my sister, my bride;
I have gathered my myrrh with my spice.
I have eaten my honeycomb and my honey;
I have drunk my wine and my milk.

Friends

Eat, O friends, and drink;
drink your fill, O lovers.

Beloved

2I slept but my heart was awake.
Listen! My lover is knocking:
"Open to me, my sister, my darling,
my dove, my flawless one.
My head is drenched with dew,
my hair with the dampness of the night."
3I have taken off my robe—
must I put it on again?
I have washed my feet—
must I soil them again?
4My lover thrust his hand through the latch-opening;
my heart began to pound for him.
5I arose to open for my lover,
and my hands dripped with myrrh,
my fingers with flowing myrrh,
on the handles of the lock.
6I opened for my lover,
but my lover had left; he was gone.
My heart sank at his departure.[b]
I looked for him but did not find him.
I called him but he did not answer.
7The watchmen found me
as they made their rounds in the city.
They beat me, they bruised me;
they took away my cloak,
those watchmen of the walls!
8O daughters of Jerusalem, I charge you—
if you find my lover,
what will you tell him?
Tell him I am faint with love.

Friends

9How is your beloved better than others,
most beautiful of women?
How is your beloved better than others,
that you charge us so?

Beloved

10My lover is radiant and ruddy,
outstanding among ten thousand.
11His head is purest gold;
his hair is wavy
and black as a raven.
12His eyes are like doves
by the water streams,

[a]15 Or *I am* (spoken by the *Beloved*) [b]6 Or *heart had gone out to him when he spoke*

washed in milk,
mounted like jewels.
13His cheeks are like beds of spice
yielding perfume.
His lips are like lilies
dripping with myrrh.
14His arms are rods of gold
set with chrysolite.
His body is like polished ivory
decorated with sapphires.[a]
15His legs are pillars of marble
set on bases of pure gold.
His appearance is like Lebanon,
choice as its cedars.
16His mouth is sweetness itself;
he is altogether lovely.
This is my lover, this my friend,
O daughters of Jerusalem.

Friends

6 Where has your lover gone,
most beautiful of women?
Which way did your lover turn,
that we may look for him with you?

Beloved

2My lover has gone down to his
garden,
to the beds of spices,
to browse in the gardens
and to gather lilies.
3I am my lover's and my lover is mine;
he browses among the lilies.

Lover

4You are beautiful, my darling, as
Tirzah,
lovely as Jerusalem,
majestic as troops with banners.
5Turn your eyes from me;
they overwhelm me.
Your hair is like a flock of goats
descending from Gilead.
6Your teeth are like a flock of sheep
coming up from the washing.
Each has its twin,
not one of them is alone.
7Your temples behind your veil
are like the halves of a
pomegranate.
8Sixty queens there may be,
and eighty concubines,
and virgins beyond number;
9but my dove, my perfect one, is
unique,
the only daughter of her mother,
the favorite of the one who bore
her.
The maidens saw her and called her
blessed;
the queens and concubines praised
her.

Friends

10Who is this that appears like the
dawn,
fair as the moon, bright as the sun,
majestic as the stars in procession?

Lover

11I went down to the grove of nut trees
to look at the new growth in the
valley,
to see if the vines had budded
or the pomegranates were in bloom.
12Before I realized it,
my desire set me among the royal
chariots of my people.[b]

Friends

13Come back, come back,
O Shulammite;
come back, come back, that we may
gaze on you!

Lover

Why would you gaze on the
Shulammite
as on the dance of Mahanaim?

7 How beautiful your sandaled feet,
O prince's daughter!
Your graceful legs are like jewels,
the work of a craftsman's hands.
2Your navel is a rounded goblet
that never lacks blended wine.
Your waist is a mound of wheat
encircled by lilies.
3Your breasts are like two fawns,
twins of a gazelle.
4Your neck is like an ivory tower.
Your eyes are the pools of Heshbon
by the gate of Bath Rabbim.
Your nose is like the tower of
Lebanon
looking toward Damascus.
5Your head crowns you like Mount
Carmel.
Your hair is like royal tapestry;
the king is held captive by its
tresses.

[a]14 Or *lapis lazuli*
[b]12 Or *among the chariots of Amminadab*; or *among the chariots of the people of the prince*

VERSE FOR THE DAY: Song of Songs 7:10

AUTHOR: Jim Smith

PASSAGE FOR THE DAY: Song of Songs 7:1–13

Sexual Differences

Men and women bring two different sets of expectations to the way they view sex. Studies indicate that a woman's libido rises and falls according to her twenty-eight-day ovulation cycle. The typical male, on the other hand, has sexual thoughts every few minutes. I tell couples, women especially, that sometimes they will need to offer the gift of availability to their spouse out of love and sensitivity to their partner's needs (1 Corinthians 7:5).

Most women place a higher priority on romance and affection than men do. Not that men don't want these things too, it's just that they don't usually rate them at the top of their needs list. And both approaches are valid. The senior pastor of our church used to describe sex like eating: Sometimes you sit down to a gourmet feast with candlelight, soft music, seven courses. Other times it's a snack on the run. Neither would be healthy all the time.

Spouses need to be realistic about their sex life and willing to accommodate each other's desires. Granted, not every sexual experience is going to be equally satisfying and fulfilling for both partners. But good communication helps ensure that you know what your spouse wants in bed. And it keeps sex from becoming mechanical.

MARRIAGE BUILDERS

♦ *How do your expectations about your sexual life seem to be different from those of your spouse?*

♦ *The pastor uses the metaphor of eating for sex. Because of busy lifestyles, couples increasingly only have time for that "snack on the run." When was the last time you and your spouse had a "gourmet feast"?*

Additional Scripture Readings
1 Corinthians 7:3–5; Proverbs 5:18–23

Go to page 717 for your next devotional reading.

6 How beautiful you are and how pleasing,
O love, with your delights!
7 Your stature is like that of the palm,
and your breasts like clusters of fruit.
8 I said, "I will climb the palm tree;
I will take hold of its fruit."
May your breasts be like the clusters of the vine,
the fragrance of your breath like apples,
9 and your mouth like the best wine.

Beloved

May the wine go straight to my lover,
flowing gently over lips and teeth.[a]
10 I belong to my lover,
and his desire is for me.
11 Come, my lover, let us go to the countryside,
let us spend the night in the villages.[b]
12 Let us go early to the vineyards
to see if the vines have budded,
if their blossoms have opened,
and if the pomegranates are in bloom—
there I will give you my love.
13 The mandrakes send out their fragrance,
and at our door is every delicacy,
both new and old,
that I have stored up for you, my lover.

8 If only you were to me like a brother,
who was nursed at my mother's breasts!
Then, if I found you outside,
I would kiss you,
and no one would despise me.
2 I would lead you
and bring you to my mother's house—
she who has taught me.
I would give you spiced wine to drink,
the nectar of my pomegranates.
3 His left arm is under my head
and his right arm embraces me.
4 Daughters of Jerusalem, I charge you:
Do not arouse or awaken love
until it so desires.

Friends

5 Who is this coming up from the desert
leaning on her lover?

Beloved

Under the apple tree I roused you;
there your mother conceived you,
there she who was in labor gave you birth.
6 Place me like a seal over your heart,
like a seal on your arm;
for love is as strong as death,
its jealousy[c] unyielding as the grave.[d]
It burns like blazing fire,
like a mighty flame.[e]
7 Many waters cannot quench love;
rivers cannot wash it away.
If one were to give
all the wealth of his house for love,
it[f] would be utterly scorned.

Friends

8 We have a young sister,
and her breasts are not yet grown.
What shall we do for our sister
for the day she is spoken for?
9 If she is a wall,
we will build towers of silver on her.
If she is a door,
we will enclose her with panels of cedar.

Beloved

10 I am a wall,
and my breasts are like towers.
Thus I have become in his eyes
like one bringing contentment.
11 Solomon had a vineyard in Baal Hamon;

[a] 9 Septuagint, Aquila, Vulgate and Syriac; Hebrew *lips of sleepers* [b] 11 Or *henna bushes* [c] 6 Or *ardor* [d] 6 Hebrew *Sheol* [e] 6 Or / *like the very flame of the* LORD [f] 7 Or *he*

WEEKENDING

CREATIVITY

What makes romance? Try incorporating the following ingredients into your personal romantic style.

1. *The element of the unexpected.* Anything that is repeated month after month, year after year, can easily become humdrum.

2. *The element of dating.* Laugh and enjoy each other and be a little crazy.

3. *The element of the impractical.* Impractical romantic events create moments to remember.

4. *The element of creativity.* Discover what delights your partner and then make those delights happen in creative ways.

5. *The element of the daily.* Romance involves daily acts of care, concern, love, listening and giving each other your personal attention.

6. *The element of commitment.* If commitment to each other is at the heart of your marriage, romance will thrive.

— *H. Norman Wright*

REVIVE

Saturday: 1 Peter 4:7–11
Sunday: Hosea 2:19–23

Go to page 719 for your next devotional reading.

he let out his vineyard to
tenants.
Each was to bring for its fruit
a thousand shekels[a] of silver.
12But my own vineyard is mine to
give;
the thousand shekels are for you,
O Solomon,
and two hundred[b] are for those
who tend its fruit.

Lover

13You who dwell in the gardens
with friends in attendance,
let me hear your voice!

Beloved

14Come away, my lover,
and be like a gazelle
or like a young stag
on the spice-laden mountains.

[a] *11* That is, about 25 pounds (about 11.5 kilograms); also in verse 12 [b] *12* That is, about 5 pounds (about 2.3 kilograms)

VERSE FOR THE DAY: Song of Songs 8:7

AUTHOR: Tim Stafford

PASSAGE FOR THE DAY: Song of Songs 8:5–14

Unshakable Love

My friend has been married for almost ten years, and she and her husband continue to have a hard marriage. If the purpose of marriage were purely to provide loving intimacy, their marriage might be considered purposeless. But they have stayed married largely because they were brought up to believe that marriage is for life. And they really do love each other. They just haven't figured out how to translate that into happiness.

It is clear, however, that happiness is not the chief point of marriage. Marriages are important to God not so much for what they are, as for what they teach. Marriage teaches us what God's kingdom is like. As his kingdom is about love, it is natural that marriage should teach us about love. It does this in two ways.

The first way is seen in "easy" marriages, which shine with the beauty of intimate love, the kind of natural, heartfelt, spontaneous love that was seen in Eden. For many of us, marriages—our own or others'—are the closest we ever come to understanding such love. Even if we experience it imperfectly, we understand, through marriage, something about the love of God.

But the other way of love is what I see in my friend's marriage. It is love that will not let go, the love of passionate demands and passionate tears, the love that will not accept defeat. Marriages like my friend's are not happiness, nor are they peace. But they are certainly a sign of something wonderful: an unshakable love.

MARRIAGE BUILDERS

- *What do you think is the chief purpose of marriage?*
- *When you come to a period in your marriage that isn't happy or peaceful, how can you keep alive your commitment to stay together?*

Additional Scripture Readings
Romans 8:35–39; 1 Corinthians 13:7–8; Jeremiah 31:3

Go to page 731 for your next devotional reading.

ISAIAH ministers during the events recorded in 2 Chronicles 26–32. He portrays graphically the sins of the kingdom of Judah (idolatry, hypocrisy, materialism, and oppression of the poor) and prophesies that severe judgment is coming. At the same time, he extends to God's people the promise of redemption, offering hope for a glorious future, particularly when the Messiah comes. As you read this book, listen to God's offer to redeem you through Jesus, the Messiah; express your own Christian joy by singing one of Isaiah's songs of thanksgiving.

ISAIAH

1 The vision concerning Judah and Jerusalem that Isaiah son of Amoz saw during the reigns of Uzziah, Jotham, Ahaz and Hezekiah, kings of Judah.

A Rebellious Nation

2 Hear, O heavens! Listen, O earth!
For the LORD has spoken:
"I reared children and brought them up,
but they have rebelled against me.
3 The ox knows his master,
the donkey his owner's manger,
but Israel does not know,
my people do not understand."

4 Ah, sinful nation,
a people loaded with guilt,
a brood of evildoers,
children given to corruption!
They have forsaken the LORD;
they have spurned the Holy One of Israel
and turned their backs on him.

5 Why should you be beaten anymore?
Why do you persist in rebellion?
Your whole head is injured,
your whole heart afflicted.
6 From the sole of your foot to the top of your head
there is no soundness—
only wounds and welts
and open sores,
not cleansed or bandaged
or soothed with oil.

7 Your country is desolate,
your cities burned with fire;
your fields are being stripped by foreigners
right before you,
laid waste as when overthrown by strangers.
8 The Daughter of Zion is left
like a shelter in a vineyard,
like a hut in a field of melons,
like a city under siege.
9 Unless the LORD Almighty
had left us some survivors,
we would have become like Sodom,
we would have been like Gomorrah.

10 Hear the word of the LORD,
you rulers of Sodom;
listen to the law of our God,
you people of Gomorrah!
11 "The multitude of your sacrifices—
what are they to me?" says the LORD.
"I have more than enough of burnt offerings,
of rams and the fat of fattened animals;
I have no pleasure
in the blood of bulls and lambs and goats.
12 When you come to appear before me,
who has asked this of you,
this trampling of my courts?
13 Stop bringing meaningless offerings!
Your incense is detestable to me.
New Moons, Sabbaths and convocations—
I cannot bear your evil assemblies.
14 Your New Moon festivals and your appointed feasts
my soul hates.
They have become a burden to me;
I am weary of bearing them.
15 When you spread out your hands in prayer,
I will hide my eyes from you;
even if you offer many prayers,
I will not listen.
Your hands are full of blood;
16 wash and make yourselves clean.
Take your evil deeds
out of my sight!
Stop doing wrong,
17 learn to do right!
Seek justice,
encourage the oppressed.[a]
Defend the cause of the fatherless,
plead the case of the widow.

18 "Come now, let us reason together,"
says the LORD.
"Though your sins are like scarlet,
they shall be as white as snow;
though they are red as crimson,
they shall be like wool.
19 If you are willing and obedient,
you will eat the best from the land;
20 but if you resist and rebel,
you will be devoured by the sword."
For the mouth of the LORD has spoken.

21 See how the faithful city
has become a harlot!
She once was full of justice;
righteousness used to dwell in her—
but now murderers!
22 Your silver has become dross,
your choice wine is diluted with water.
23 Your rulers are rebels,
companions of thieves;
they all love bribes
and chase after gifts.
They do not defend the cause of the fatherless;
the widow's case does not come before them.
24 Therefore the Lord, the LORD Almighty,
the Mighty One of Israel, declares:
"Ah, I will get relief from my foes
and avenge myself on my enemies.
25 I will turn my hand against you;
I will thoroughly purge away your dross
and remove all your impurities.
26 I will restore your judges as in days of old,
your counselors as at the beginning.
Afterward you will be called
the City of Righteousness,
the Faithful City."

[a] 17 Or / *rebuke the oppressor*

27Zion will be redeemed with justice,
her penitent ones with
righteousness.
28But rebels and sinners will both be
broken,
and those who forsake the LORD will
perish.

29"You will be ashamed because of the
sacred oaks
in which you have delighted;
you will be disgraced because of the
gardens
that you have chosen.
30You will be like an oak with fading
leaves,
like a garden without water.
31The mighty man will become tinder
and his work a spark;
both will burn together,
with no one to quench the fire."

The Mountain of the LORD

2 This is what Isaiah son of Amoz saw
concerning Judah and Jerusalem:

2In the last days

the mountain of the LORD's temple will
be established
as chief among the mountains;
it will be raised above the hills,
and all nations will stream to it.

3Many peoples will come and say,

"Come, let us go up to the mountain
of the LORD,
to the house of the God of Jacob.
He will teach us his ways,
so that we may walk in his paths."
The law will go out from Zion,
the word of the LORD from
Jerusalem.
4He will judge between the nations
and will settle disputes for many
peoples.
They will beat their swords into
plowshares
and their spears into pruning hooks.
Nation will not take up sword against
nation,
nor will they train for war anymore.

5Come, O house of Jacob,
let us walk in the light of the LORD.

The Day of the LORD

6You have abandoned your people,
the house of Jacob.
They are full of superstitions from the
East;
they practice divination like the
Philistines
and clasp hands with pagans.
7Their land is full of silver and gold;
there is no end to their treasures.
Their land is full of horses;
there is no end to their chariots.
8Their land is full of idols;
they bow down to the work of their
hands,
to what their fingers have made.
9So man will be brought low
and mankind humbled—
do not forgive them.[a]

10Go into the rocks,
hide in the ground
from dread of the LORD
and the splendor of his majesty!
11The eyes of the arrogant man will be
humbled
and the pride of men brought low;
the LORD alone will be exalted in that
day.

12The LORD Almighty has a day in store
for all the proud and lofty,
for all that is exalted
(and they will be humbled),
13for all the cedars of Lebanon, tall and
lofty,
and all the oaks of Bashan,
14for all the towering mountains
and all the high hills,
15for every lofty tower
and every fortified wall,
16for every trading ship[b]
and every stately vessel.
17The arrogance of man will be brought
low
and the pride of men humbled;
the LORD alone will be exalted in that
day,
18 and the idols will totally disappear.

19Men will flee to caves in the rocks
and to holes in the ground
from dread of the LORD
and the splendor of his majesty,
when he rises to shake the earth.
20In that day men will throw away
to the rodents and bats
their idols of silver and idols of gold,
which they made to worship.
21They will flee to caverns in the rocks
and to the overhanging crags

[a]9 Or *not raise them up* [b]16 Hebrew *every ship of Tarshish*

from dread of the LORD
and the splendor of his majesty,
when he rises to shake the earth.

22 Stop trusting in man,
who has but a breath in his nostrils.
Of what account is he?

Judgment on Jerusalem and Judah

3 See now, the Lord,
the LORD Almighty,
is about to take from Jerusalem and Judah
both supply and support:
all supplies of food and all supplies of water,
2 the hero and warrior,
the judge and prophet,
the soothsayer and elder,
3 the captain of fifty and man of rank,
the counselor, skilled craftsman and clever enchanter.

4 I will make boys their officials;
mere children will govern them.
5 People will oppress each other—
man against man, neighbor against neighbor.
The young will rise up against the old,
the base against the honorable.

6 A man will seize one of his brothers
at his father's home, and say,
"You have a cloak, you be our leader;
take charge of this heap of ruins!"
7 But in that day he will cry out,
"I have no remedy.
I have no food or clothing in my house;
do not make me the leader of the people."

8 Jerusalem staggers,
Judah is falling;
their words and deeds are against the LORD,
defying his glorious presence.
9 The look on their faces testifies against them;
they parade their sin like Sodom;
they do not hide it.
Woe to them!
They have brought disaster upon themselves.

10 Tell the righteous it will be well with them,
for they will enjoy the fruit of their deeds.
11 Woe to the wicked! Disaster is upon them!
They will be paid back for what their hands have done.

12 Youths oppress my people,
women rule over them.
O my people, your guides lead you astray;
they turn you from the path.

13 The LORD takes his place in court;
he rises to judge the people.
14 The LORD enters into judgment
against the elders and leaders of his people:
"It is you who have ruined my vineyard;
the plunder from the poor is in your houses.
15 What do you mean by crushing my people
and grinding the faces of the poor?"
declares the Lord,
the LORD Almighty.

16 The LORD says,
"The women of Zion are haughty,
walking along with outstretched necks,
flirting with their eyes,
tripping along with mincing steps,
with ornaments jingling on their ankles.
17 Therefore the Lord will bring sores on the heads of the women of Zion;
the LORD will make their scalps bald."

18 In that day the Lord will snatch away their finery: the bangles and headbands and crescent necklaces, 19 the earrings and bracelets and veils, 20 the headdresses and ankle chains and sashes, the perfume bottles and charms, 21 the signet rings and nose rings, 22 the fine robes and the capes and cloaks, the purses 23 and mirrors, and the linen garments and tiaras and shawls.

24 Instead of fragrance there will be a stench;
instead of a sash, a rope;
instead of well-dressed hair, baldness;
instead of fine clothing, sackcloth;
instead of beauty, branding.
25 Your men will fall by the sword,
your warriors in battle.
26 The gates of Zion will lament and mourn;
destitute, she will sit on the ground.

4 In that day seven women
will take hold of one man

and say, "We will eat our own food
and provide our own clothes;
only let us be called by your name.
Take away our disgrace!"

The Branch of the Lord

2In that day the Branch of the Lord will
be beautiful and glorious, and the fruit of
the land will be the pride and glory of the
survivors in Israel. 3Those who are left in
Zion, who remain in Jerusalem, will be
called holy, all who are recorded among
the living in Jerusalem. 4The Lord will
wash away the filth of the women of Zion;
he will cleanse the bloodstains from Jeru-
salem by a spirit[a] of judgment and a spir-
it[a] of fire. 5Then the Lord will create over
all of Mount Zion and over those who as-
semble there a cloud of smoke by day and
a glow of flaming fire by night; over all the
glory will be a canopy. 6It will be a shelter
and shade from the heat of the day, and a
refuge and hiding place from the storm
and rain.

The Song of the Vineyard

5 I will sing for the one I love
a song about his vineyard:
My loved one had a vineyard
on a fertile hillside.
2He dug it up and cleared it of stones
and planted it with the choicest
vines.
He built a watchtower in it
and cut out a winepress as well.
Then he looked for a crop of good
grapes,
but it yielded only bad fruit.
3"Now you dwellers in Jerusalem and
men of Judah,
judge between me and my vineyard.
4What more could have been done for
my vineyard
than I have done for it?
When I looked for good grapes,
why did it yield only bad?
5Now I will tell you
what I am going to do to my
vineyard:
I will take away its hedge,
and it will be destroyed;
I will break down its wall,
and it will be trampled.
6I will make it a wasteland,
neither pruned nor cultivated,
and briers and thorns will grow
there.
I will command the clouds
not to rain on it."
7The vineyard of the Lord Almighty
is the house of Israel,
and the men of Judah
are the garden of his delight.
And he looked for justice, but saw
bloodshed;
for righteousness, but heard cries of
distress.

Woes and Judgments

8Woe to you who add house to house
and join field to field
till no space is left
and you live alone in the land.
9The Lord Almighty has declared in my
hearing:
"Surely the great houses will become
desolate,
the fine mansions left without
occupants.
10A ten-acre[b] vineyard will produce
only a bath[c] of wine,
a homer[d] of seed only an ephah[e]
of grain."
11Woe to those who rise early in the
morning
to run after their drinks,
who stay up late at night
till they are inflamed with wine.
12They have harps and lyres at their
banquets,
tambourines and flutes and wine,
but they have no regard for the deeds
of the Lord,
no respect for the work of his
hands.
13Therefore my people will go into exile
for lack of understanding;
their men of rank will die of hunger
and their masses will be parched
with thirst.
14Therefore the grave[f] enlarges its
appetite
and opens its mouth without limit;
into it will descend their nobles and
masses
with all their brawlers and revelers.
15So man will be brought low

[a] 4 Or *the Spirit* [b] 10 Hebrew *ten-yoke,* that is, the land plowed by 10 yoke of oxen in one day
[c] 10 That is, probably about 6 gallons (about 22 liters) [d] 10 That is, probably about 6 bushels (about 220 liters) [e] 10 That is, probably about 3/5 bushel (about 22 liters) [f] 14 Hebrew *Sheol*

and mankind humbled,
the eyes of the arrogant humbled.
16But the LORD Almighty will be exalted
by his justice,
and the holy God will show himself
holy by his righteousness.
17Then sheep will graze as in their own
pasture;
lambs will feed[a] among the ruins
of the rich.

18Woe to those who draw sin along
with cords of deceit,
and wickedness as with cart ropes,
19to those who say, "Let God hurry,
let him hasten his work
so we may see it.
Let it approach,
let the plan of the Holy One of
Israel come,
so we may know it."

20Woe to those who call evil good
and good evil,
who put darkness for light
and light for darkness,
who put bitter for sweet
and sweet for bitter.

21Woe to those who are wise in their
own eyes
and clever in their own sight.

22Woe to those who are heroes at
drinking wine
and champions at mixing drinks,
23who acquit the guilty for a bribe,
but deny justice to the innocent.
24Therefore, as tongues of fire lick up
straw
and as dry grass sinks down in the
flames,
so their roots will decay
and their flowers blow away like
dust;
for they have rejected the law of the
LORD Almighty
and spurned the word of the Holy
One of Israel.
25Therefore the LORD's anger burns
against his people;
his hand is raised and he strikes
them down.
The mountains shake,
and the dead bodies are like refuse
in the streets.

Yet for all this, his anger is not turned
away,
his hand is still upraised.

26He lifts up a banner for the distant
nations,
he whistles for those at the ends of
the earth.
Here they come,
swiftly and speedily!
27Not one of them grows tired or
stumbles,
not one slumbers or sleeps;
not a belt is loosened at the waist,
not a sandal thong is broken.
28Their arrows are sharp,
all their bows are strung;
their horses' hoofs seem like flint,
their chariot wheels like a
whirlwind.
29Their roar is like that of the lion,
they roar like young lions;
they growl as they seize their prey
and carry it off with no one to
rescue.
30In that day they will roar over it
like the roaring of the sea.
And if one looks at the land,
he will see darkness and distress;
even the light will be darkened by
the clouds.

Isaiah's Commission

6 In the year that King Uzziah died, I saw the Lord seated on a throne, high and exalted, and the train of his robe filled the temple. 2Above him were seraphs, each with six wings: With two wings they covered their faces, with two they covered their feet, and with two they were flying. 3And they were calling to one another:

"Holy, holy, holy is the LORD
Almighty;
the whole earth is full of his glory."

4At the sound of their voices the doorposts and thresholds shook and the temple was filled with smoke.

5"Woe to me!" I cried. "I am ruined! For I am a man of unclean lips, and I live among a people of unclean lips, and my eyes have seen the King, the LORD Almighty."

6Then one of the seraphs flew to me with a live coal in his hand, which he had taken with tongs from the altar. 7With it he touched my mouth and said, "See, this has touched your lips; your guilt is taken away and your sin atoned for."

[a]17 Septuagint; Hebrew / *strangers will eat*

8Then I heard the voice of the Lord saying, "Whom shall I send? And who will go
for us?"
And I said, "Here am I. Send me!"
9He said, "Go and tell this people:

" 'Be ever hearing, but never
understanding;
be ever seeing, but never
perceiving.'
10Make the heart of this people
calloused;
make their ears dull
and close their eyes.[a]
Otherwise they might see with their
eyes,
hear with their ears,
understand with their hearts,
and turn and be healed."

11Then I said, "For how long, O Lord?"
And he answered:

"Until the cities lie ruined
and without inhabitant,
until the houses are left deserted
and the fields ruined and ravaged,
12until the LORD has sent everyone far
away
and the land is utterly forsaken.
13And though a tenth remains in the
land,
it will again be laid waste.
But as the terebinth and oak
leave stumps when they are cut
down,
so the holy seed will be the stump
in the land."

The Sign of Immanuel

7 When Ahaz son of Jotham, the son of Uzziah, was king of Judah, King Rezin of Aram and Pekah son of Remaliah king of Israel marched up to fight against Jerusalem, but they could not overpower it.

2Now the house of David was told, "Aram has allied itself with[b] Ephraim"; so the hearts of Ahaz and his people were shaken, as the trees of the forest are shaken by the wind.

3Then the LORD said to Isaiah, "Go out, you and your son Shear-Jashub,[c] to meet Ahaz at the end of the aqueduct of the Upper Pool, on the road to the Washerman's Field. 4Say to him, 'Be careful, keep calm and don't be afraid. Do not lose heart because of these two smoldering stubs of firewood—because of the fierce anger of Rezin and Aram and of the son of Remaliah. 5Aram, Ephraim and Remaliah's son have plotted your ruin, saying, 6"Let us invade Judah; let us tear it apart and divide it among ourselves, and make the son of Tabeel king over it." 7Yet this is what the Sovereign LORD says:

" 'It will not take place,
it will not happen,
8for the head of Aram is Damascus,
and the head of Damascus is only
Rezin.
Within sixty-five years
Ephraim will be too shattered to be
a people.
9The head of Ephraim is Samaria,
and the head of Samaria is only
Remaliah's son.
If you do not stand firm in your faith,
you will not stand at all.' "

10Again the LORD spoke to Ahaz, 11"Ask the LORD your God for a sign, whether in the deepest depths or in the highest heights."

12But Ahaz said, "I will not ask; I will not put the LORD to the test."

13Then Isaiah said, "Hear now, you house of David! Is it not enough to try the patience of men? Will you try the patience of my God also? 14Therefore the Lord himself will give you[d] a sign: The virgin will be with child and will give birth to a son, and[e] will call him Immanuel.[f] 15He will eat curds and honey when he knows enough to reject the wrong and choose the right. 16But before the boy knows enough to reject the wrong and choose the right, the land of the two kings you dread will be laid waste. 17The LORD will bring on you and on your people and on the house of your father a time unlike any since Ephraim broke away from Judah—he will bring the king of Assyria."

18In that day the LORD will whistle for flies from the distant streams of Egypt and for bees from the land of Assyria. 19They will all come and settle in the steep ravines and in the crevices in the rocks, on all the thornbushes and at all the water

[a] *9,10* Hebrew; Septuagint *'You will be ever hearing, but never understanding; / you will be ever seeing, but never perceiving.' / 10This people's heart has become calloused; / they hardly hear with their ears, / and they have closed their eyes* [b] *2* Or *has set up camp in* [c] *3 Shear-Jashub* means *a remnant will return.* [d] *14* The Hebrew is plural. [e] *14* Masoretic Text; Dead Sea Scrolls *and he* or *and they*
[f] *14 Immanuel* means *God with us.*

holes. 20In that day the Lord will use a razor hired from beyond the River[a]—the
king of Assyria—to shave your head and
the hair of your legs, and to take off your
beards also. 21In that day, a man will keep
alive a young cow and two goats. 22And
because of the abundance of the milk they
give, he will have curds to eat. All who remain in the land will eat curds and honey.
23In that day, in every place where there
were a thousand vines worth a thousand
silver shekels,[b] there will be only briers
and thorns. 24Men will go there with bow
and arrow, for the land will be covered
with briers and thorns. 25As for all the
hills once cultivated by the hoe, you will
no longer go there for fear of the briers
and thorns; they will become places
where cattle are turned loose and where
sheep run.

Assyria, the Lord's Instrument

8 The Lord said to me, "Take a large
scroll and write on it with an ordinary
pen: Maher-Shalal-Hash-Baz.[c] 2And I will
call in Uriah the priest and Zechariah son
of Jeberekiah as reliable witnesses
for me."

3Then I went to the prophetess, and she
conceived and gave birth to a son. And the
Lord said to me, "Name him Maher-Shal-
al-Hash-Baz. 4Before the boy knows how
to say 'My father' or 'My mother,' the
wealth of Damascus and the plunder of
Samaria will be carried off by the king of
Assyria."

5The Lord spoke to me again:

6"Because this people has rejected
the gently flowing waters of Shiloah
and rejoices over Rezin
and the son of Remaliah,
7therefore the Lord is about to bring
against them
the mighty floodwaters of the
River[a]—
the king of Assyria with all his
pomp.
It will overflow all its channels,
run over all its banks
8and sweep on into Judah, swirling
over it,
passing through it and reaching up
to the neck.
Its outspread wings will cover the
breadth of your land,
O Immanuel[d]!"

9Raise the war cry,[e] you nations, and
be shattered!
Listen, all you distant lands.
Prepare for battle, and be shattered!
Prepare for battle, and be shattered!
10Devise your strategy, but it will be
thwarted;
propose your plan, but it will not
stand,
for God is with us.[f]

Fear God

11The Lord spoke to me with his strong
hand upon me, warning me not to follow
the way of this people. He said:

12"Do not call conspiracy
everything that these people call
conspiracy[g];
do not fear what they fear,
and do not dread it.
13The Lord Almighty is the one you are
to regard as holy,
he is the one you are to fear,
he is the one you are to dread,
14and he will be a sanctuary;
but for both houses of Israel he will
be
a stone that causes men to stumble
and a rock that makes them fall.
And for the people of Jerusalem he
will be
a trap and a snare.
15Many of them will stumble;
they will fall and be broken,
they will be snared and captured."

16Bind up the testimony
and seal up the law among my
disciples.
17I will wait for the Lord,
who is hiding his face from the
house of Jacob.
I will put my trust in him.

18Here am I, and the children the Lord
has given me. We are signs and symbols
in Israel from the Lord Almighty, who
dwells on Mount Zion.

19When men tell you to consult mediums and spiritists, who whisper and mutter, should not a people inquire of their

[a] *20,7* That is, the Euphrates [b] *23* That is, about 25 pounds (about 11.5 kilograms)
[c] *1 Maher-Shalal-Hash-Baz* means *quick to the plunder, swift to the spoil*; also in verse 3. [d] *8 Immanuel* means *God with us.* [e] *9* Or *Do your worst* [f] *10* Hebrew *Immanuel* [g] *12* Or *Do not call for a treaty / every time these people call for a treaty*

God? Why consult the dead on behalf of
the living? 20To the law and to the testimo-
ny! If they do not speak according to this
word, they have no light of dawn. 21Dis-
tressed and hungry, they will roam
through the land; when they are fam-
ished, they will become enraged and,
looking upward, will curse their king and
their God. 22Then they will look toward
the earth and see only distress and dark-
ness and fearful gloom, and they will be
thrust into utter darkness.

To Us a Child Is Born

9 Nevertheless, there will be no more
gloom for those who were in distress.
In the past he humbled the land of Zebu-
lun and the land of Naphtali, but in the
future he will honor Galilee of the Gen-
tiles, by the way of the sea, along the Jor-
dan—

2The people walking in darkness
have seen a great light;
on those living in the land of the
shadow of death[a]
a light has dawned.
3You have enlarged the nation
and increased their joy;
they rejoice before you
as people rejoice at the harvest,
as men rejoice
when dividing the plunder.
4For as in the day of Midian's defeat,
you have shattered
the yoke that burdens them,
the bar across their shoulders,
the rod of their oppressor.
5Every warrior's boot used in battle
and every garment rolled in blood
will be destined for burning,
will be fuel for the fire.
6For to us a child is born,
to us a son is given,
and the government will be on his
shoulders.
And he will be called
Wonderful Counselor,[b] Mighty
God,
Everlasting Father, Prince of Peace.
7Of the increase of his government and
peace
there will be no end.
He will reign on David's throne
and over his kingdom,
establishing and upholding it
with justice and righteousness
from that time on and forever.
The zeal of the LORD Almighty
will accomplish this.

The LORD's Anger Against Israel

8The Lord has sent a message against
Jacob;
it will fall on Israel.
9All the people will know it—
Ephraim and the inhabitants of
Samaria—
who say with pride
and arrogance of heart,
10"The bricks have fallen down,
but we will rebuild with dressed
stone;
the fig trees have been felled,
but we will replace them with
cedars."
11But the LORD has strengthened Rezin's
foes against them
and has spurred their enemies on.
12Arameans from the east and
Philistines from the west
have devoured Israel with open
mouth.

Yet for all this, his anger is not turned
away,
his hand is still upraised.

13But the people have not returned to
him who struck them,
nor have they sought the LORD
Almighty.
14So the LORD will cut off from Israel
both head and tail,
both palm branch and reed in a
single day;
15the elders and prominent men are the
head,
the prophets who teach lies are the
tail.
16Those who guide this people mislead
them,
and those who are guided are led
astray.
17Therefore the Lord will take no
pleasure in the young men,
nor will he pity the fatherless and
widows,
for everyone is ungodly and wicked,
every mouth speaks vileness.

Yet for all this, his anger is not turned
away,
his hand is still upraised.

18Surely wickedness burns like a fire;

[a]2 Or *land of darkness* [b]6 Or *Wonderful, Counselor*

it consumes briers and thorns,
it sets the forest thickets ablaze,
so that it rolls upward in a column
of smoke.
19By the wrath of the LORD Almighty
the land will be scorched
and the people will be fuel for the
fire;
no one will spare his brother.
20On the right they will devour,
but still be hungry;
on the left they will eat,
but not be satisfied.
Each will feed on the flesh of his own
offspring[a]:
21 Manasseh will feed on Ephraim, and
Ephraim on Manasseh;
together they will turn against
Judah.
Yet for all this, his anger is not turned
away,
his hand is still upraised.

10 Woe to those who make unjust
laws,
to those who issue oppressive
decrees,
2to deprive the poor of their rights
and withhold justice from the
oppressed of my people,
making widows their prey
and robbing the fatherless.
3What will you do on the day of
reckoning,
when disaster comes from afar?
To whom will you run for help?
Where will you leave your riches?
4Nothing will remain but to cringe
among the captives
or fall among the slain.
Yet for all this, his anger is not turned
away,
his hand is still upraised.

God's Judgment on Assyria

5"Woe to the Assyrian, the rod of my
anger,
in whose hand is the club of my
wrath!
6I send him against a godless nation,
I dispatch him against a people who
anger me,
to seize loot and snatch plunder,
and to trample them down like mud
in the streets.
7But this is not what he intends,
this is not what he has in mind;
his purpose is to destroy,
to put an end to many nations.
8'Are not my commanders all kings?'
he says.
9 'Has not Calno fared like
Carchemish?
Is not Hamath like Arpad,
and Samaria like Damascus?
10As my hand seized the kingdoms of
the idols,
kingdoms whose images excelled
those of Jerusalem and
Samaria—
11shall I not deal with Jerusalem and
her images
as I dealt with Samaria and her
idols?' "
12When the Lord has finished all his work against Mount Zion and Jerusalem, he will say, "I will punish the king of Assyria for the willful pride of his heart and the haughty look in his eyes. 13For he says:

" 'By the strength of my hand I have
done this,
and by my wisdom, because I have
understanding.
I removed the boundaries of nations,
I plundered their treasures;
like a mighty one I subdued[b] their
kings.
14As one reaches into a nest,
so my hand reached for the wealth
of the nations;
as men gather abandoned eggs,
so I gathered all the countries;
not one flapped a wing,
or opened its mouth to chirp.' "

15Does the ax raise itself above him
who swings it,
or the saw boast against him who
uses it?
As if a rod were to wield him who
lifts it up,
or a club brandish him who is not
wood!
16Therefore, the Lord, the LORD
Almighty,
will send a wasting disease upon his
sturdy warriors;
under his pomp a fire will be kindled
like a blazing flame.
17The Light of Israel will become a fire,
their Holy One a flame;

[a]20 Or *arm* [b]13 Or / *I subdued the mighty,*

in a single day it will burn and consume
his thorns and his briers.
18 The splendor of his forests and fertile fields
it will completely destroy,
as when a sick man wastes away.
19 And the remaining trees of his forests will be so few
that a child could write them down.

The Remnant of Israel

20 In that day the remnant of Israel,
the survivors of the house of Jacob,
will no longer rely on him
who struck them down
but will truly rely on the LORD,
the Holy One of Israel.
21 A remnant will return,[a] a remnant of Jacob
will return to the Mighty God.
22 Though your people, O Israel, be like the sand by the sea,
only a remnant will return.
Destruction has been decreed,
overwhelming and righteous.
23 The Lord, the LORD Almighty, will carry out
the destruction decreed upon the whole land.

24 Therefore, this is what the Lord, the LORD Almighty, says:

"O my people who live in Zion,
do not be afraid of the Assyrians,
who beat you with a rod
and lift up a club against you, as Egypt did.
25 Very soon my anger against you will end
and my wrath will be directed to their destruction."

26 The LORD Almighty will lash them with a whip,
as when he struck down Midian at the rock of Oreb;
and he will raise his staff over the waters,
as he did in Egypt.
27 In that day their burden will be lifted from your shoulders,
their yoke from your neck;
the yoke will be broken
because you have grown so fat.[b]

28 They enter Aiath;
they pass through Migron;
they store supplies at Micmash.
29 They go over the pass, and say,
"We will camp overnight at Geba."
Ramah trembles;
Gibeah of Saul flees.
30 Cry out, O Daughter of Gallim!
Listen, O Laishah!
Poor Anathoth!
31 Madmenah is in flight;
the people of Gebim take cover.
32 This day they will halt at Nob;
they will shake their fist
at the mount of the Daughter of Zion,
at the hill of Jerusalem.

33 See, the Lord, the LORD Almighty,
will lop off the boughs with great power.
The lofty trees will be felled,
the tall ones will be brought low.
34 He will cut down the forest thickets with an ax;
Lebanon will fall before the Mighty One.

The Branch From Jesse

11 A shoot will come up from the stump of Jesse;
from his roots a Branch will bear fruit.
2 The Spirit of the LORD will rest on him—
the Spirit of wisdom and of understanding,
the Spirit of counsel and of power,
the Spirit of knowledge and of the fear of the LORD—
3 and he will delight in the fear of the LORD.

He will not judge by what he sees with his eyes,
or decide by what he hears with his ears;
4 but with righteousness he will judge the needy,
with justice he will give decisions for the poor of the earth.
He will strike the earth with the rod of his mouth;
with the breath of his lips he will slay the wicked.
5 Righteousness will be his belt
and faithfulness the sash around his waist.

6 The wolf will live with the lamb,

[a] 21 Hebrew *shear-jashub*; also in verse 22
[b] 27 Hebrew; Septuagint *broken / from your shoulders*

the leopard will lie down with the goat,
the calf and the lion and the yearling[a] together;
and a little child will lead them.
7The cow will feed with the bear,
their young will lie down together,
and the lion will eat straw like the ox.
8The infant will play near the hole of the cobra,
and the young child put his hand into the viper's nest.
9They will neither harm nor destroy on all my holy mountain,
for the earth will be full of the knowledge of the LORD
as the waters cover the sea.

10In that day the Root of Jesse will stand as a banner for the peoples; the nations will rally to him, and his place of rest will be glorious. 11In that day the Lord will

[a]6 Hebrew; Septuagint *lion will feed*

VERSE FOR THE DAY: Isaiah 11:2 | AUTHOR: Bonnie Shipley Rice | PASSAGE FOR THE DAY: Isaiah 11:1–9

The Spirit's Gentle Ministry

Spiritual discipline has many forms. In his book *Celebration of Discipline*, Richard Foster lists twelve disciplines: meditation, prayer, fasting, study, simplicity, solitude, submission, service, confession, worship, guidance and celebration.

The responsibility to exercise these disciplines lies with us, but we should not think of them as our efforts to force ourselves to be better. Instead, we are submitting ourselves to a process whereby we will be changed. As we submit to Christ, as we allow him to work in us, we gain new insights into his reality, and the new person we become is shaped by our response to the gentle ministry of his Spirit.

From the disciplines, new habits develop that strengthen us and bring a hunger for more and more knowledge of God. We, his children, can be assured that he who delights in us and knows us perfectly is working in us to bring about spiritual vitality and wholeness.

MARRIAGE BUILDERS

♦ *Which of the twelve spiritual disciplines listed above have you consciously worked to incorporate into your spiritual life?*
♦ *Which additional spiritual discipline would you like to have? How can you begin to incorporate it into your daily life?*

Additional Scripture Readings
Philippians 1:3–6; 2:13;
2 Corinthians 3:18

Go to page 733 for your next devotional reading.

reach out his hand a second time to reclaim the remnant that is left of his people
from Assyria, from Lower Egypt, from Upper Egypt,[a] from Cush,[b] from Elam,
from Babylonia,[c] from Hamath and from
the islands of the sea.

12 He will raise a banner for the nations
and gather the exiles of Israel;
he will assemble the scattered people of Judah
from the four quarters of the earth.
13 Ephraim's jealousy will vanish,
and Judah's enemies[d] will be cut off;
Ephraim will not be jealous of Judah,
nor Judah hostile toward Ephraim.
14 They will swoop down on the slopes of Philistia to the west;
together they will plunder the people to the east.
They will lay hands on Edom and Moab,
and the Ammonites will be subject to them.
15 The LORD will dry up
the gulf of the Egyptian sea;
with a scorching wind he will sweep his hand
over the Euphrates River.[e]
He will break it up into seven streams
so that men can cross over in sandals.
16 There will be a highway for the remnant of his people
that is left from Assyria,
as there was for Israel
when they came up from Egypt.

Songs of Praise

12 In that day you will say:
"I will praise you, O LORD.
Although you were angry with me,
your anger has turned away
and you have comforted me.
2 Surely God is my salvation;
I will trust and not be afraid.
The LORD, the LORD, is my strength and my song;
he has become my salvation."
3 With joy you will draw water
from the wells of salvation.

4 In that day you will say:
"Give thanks to the LORD, call on his name;
make known among the nations what he has done,
and proclaim that his name is exalted.
5 Sing to the LORD, for he has done glorious things;
let this be known to all the world.
6 Shout aloud and sing for joy, people of Zion,
for great is the Holy One of Israel among you."

A Prophecy Against Babylon

13 An oracle concerning Babylon that Isaiah son of Amoz saw:

2 Raise a banner on a bare hilltop,
shout to them;
beckon to them
to enter the gates of the nobles.
3 I have commanded my holy ones;
I have summoned my warriors to carry out my wrath—
those who rejoice in my triumph.

4 Listen, a noise on the mountains,
like that of a great multitude!
Listen, an uproar among the kingdoms,
like nations massing together!
The LORD Almighty is mustering
an army for war.
5 They come from faraway lands,
from the ends of the heavens—
the LORD and the weapons of his wrath—
to destroy the whole country.

6 Wail, for the day of the LORD is near;
it will come like destruction from the Almighty.[f]
7 Because of this, all hands will go limp,
every man's heart will melt.
8 Terror will seize them,
pain and anguish will grip them;
they will writhe like a woman in labor.
They will look aghast at each other,
their faces aflame.

9 See, the day of the LORD is coming
—a cruel day, with wrath and fierce anger—
to make the land desolate
and destroy the sinners within it.

[a] 11 Hebrew *from Pathros* [b] 11 That is, the upper Nile region [c] 11 Hebrew *Shinar* [d] 13 Or *hostility* [e] 15 Hebrew *the River* [f] 6 Hebrew *Shaddai*

10 The stars of heaven and their constellations
will not show their light.
The rising sun will be darkened
and the moon will not give its light.
11 I will punish the world for its evil,
the wicked for their sins.
I will put an end to the arrogance of the haughty
and will humble the pride of the ruthless.
12 I will make man scarcer than pure gold,
more rare than the gold of Ophir.

VERSE FOR THE DAY: Isaiah 12:2

AUTHOR: Henri J. M. Nouwen

PASSAGE FOR THE DAY: Isaiah 12:1–6

Stronger Than Fear

When we look at the increasing loneliness, inner anguish, hunger, violence and war in this world we should not hesitate to confess that the powers of darkness are very active among us, but we should also dare to face them in the conviction that our Lord has overcome them through his suffering. Look at Jesus quietly, confidently and trustingly, and you will find a joy and peace you did not dare to dream of. Even on the road to the cross you will find that love is stronger than fear, and life—God's life—stronger than death.

I have seen this among the poor Indians of Peru, Bolivia and Guatemala. Their eyes are radiant with light and hope, though they have suffered more than any one of us imagines. If anyone taught me to pray it was these Indians in whom I could see the self-portrait of Jesus come alive.

There is so much dullness among us Christians, so much lukewarm carelessness, so much tiptoeing around the hard places. Do not be afraid of the Father who created you in love, nor of the Son who set you free to journey to the Father's house, nor of the Holy Spirit who gives you the joy and peace of God's dwelling place. Let the jealous God be your God and all will be well.

MARRIAGE BUILDERS

♦ *When have you experienced supernatural joy and peace, even when surrounded by troubles?*

♦ *What things have you been able to share with your spouse simply because you know he or she loves you and is committed to you, no matter what?*

Additional Scripture Readings
1 John 4:18–19; Song of Songs 8:6–7; Psalm 46:1

Go to page 750 for your next devotional reading.

13 Therefore I will make the heavens tremble;
and the earth will shake from its place
at the wrath of the LORD Almighty,
in the day of his burning anger.

14 Like a hunted gazelle,
like sheep without a shepherd,
each will return to his own people,
each will flee to his native land.
15 Whoever is captured will be thrust through;
all who are caught will fall by the sword.
16 Their infants will be dashed to pieces before their eyes;
their houses will be looted and their wives ravished.

17 See, I will stir up against them the Medes,
who do not care for silver
and have no delight in gold.
18 Their bows will strike down the young men;
they will have no mercy on infants
nor will they look with compassion on children.
19 Babylon, the jewel of kingdoms,
the glory of the Babylonians'[a] pride,
will be overthrown by God
like Sodom and Gomorrah.
20 She will never be inhabited
or lived in through all generations;
no Arab will pitch his tent there,
no shepherd will rest his flocks there.
21 But desert creatures will lie there,
jackals will fill her houses;
there the owls will dwell,
and there the wild goats will leap about.
22 Hyenas will howl in her strongholds,
jackals in her luxurious palaces.
Her time is at hand,
and her days will not be prolonged.

14 The LORD will have compassion on Jacob;
once again he will choose Israel
and will settle them in their own land.
Aliens will join them
and unite with the house of Jacob.
2 Nations will take them
and bring them to their own place.
And the house of Israel will possess the nations
as menservants and maidservants in the LORD's land.
They will make captives of their captors
and rule over their oppressors.

3 On the day the LORD gives you relief from suffering and turmoil and cruel bondage, 4 you will take up this taunt against the king of Babylon:

How the oppressor has come to an end!
How his fury[b] has ended!
5 The LORD has broken the rod of the wicked,
the scepter of the rulers,
6 which in anger struck down peoples
with unceasing blows,
and in fury subdued nations
with relentless aggression.
7 All the lands are at rest and at peace;
they break into singing.
8 Even the pine trees and the cedars of Lebanon
exult over you and say,
"Now that you have been laid low,
no woodsman comes to cut us down."

9 The grave[c] below is all astir
to meet you at your coming;
it rouses the spirits of the departed to greet you—
all those who were leaders in the world;
it makes them rise from their thrones—
all those who were kings over the nations.
10 They will all respond,
they will say to you,
"You also have become weak, as we are;
you have become like us."
11 All your pomp has been brought down to the grave,
along with the noise of your harps;
maggots are spread out beneath you
and worms cover you.

12 How you have fallen from heaven,
O morning star, son of the dawn!
You have been cast down to the earth,
you who once laid low the nations!

[a] 19 Or *Chaldeans'* [b] 4 Dead Sea Scrolls, Septuagint and Syriac; the meaning of the word in the Masoretic Text is uncertain. [c] 9 Hebrew *Sheol*; also in verses 11 and 15

13You said in your heart,
"I will ascend to heaven;
I will raise my throne
above the stars of God;
I will sit enthroned on the mount of assembly,
on the utmost heights of the sacred mountain.[a]
14I will ascend above the tops of the clouds;
I will make myself like the Most High."
15But you are brought down to the grave,
to the depths of the pit.

16Those who see you stare at you,
they ponder your fate:
"Is this the man who shook the earth
and made kingdoms tremble,
17the man who made the world a desert,
who overthrew its cities
and would not let his captives go home?"

18All the kings of the nations lie in state,
each in his own tomb.
19But you are cast out of your tomb
like a rejected branch;
you are covered with the slain,
with those pierced by the sword,
those who descend to the stones of the pit.
Like a corpse trampled underfoot,
20 you will not join them in burial,
for you have destroyed your land
and killed your people.

The offspring of the wicked
will never be mentioned again.
21Prepare a place to slaughter his sons
for the sins of their forefathers;
they are not to rise to inherit the land
and cover the earth with their cities.

22"I will rise up against them,"
declares the LORD Almighty.
"I will cut off from Babylon her name and survivors,
her offspring and descendants,"
declares the LORD.
23"I will turn her into a place for owls
and into swampland;
I will sweep her with the broom of destruction,"
declares the LORD Almighty.

A Prophecy Against Assyria

24The LORD Almighty has sworn,

"Surely, as I have planned, so it will be,
and as I have purposed, so it will stand.
25I will crush the Assyrian in my land;
on my mountains I will trample him down.
His yoke will be taken from my people,
and his burden removed from their shoulders."

26This is the plan determined for the whole world;
this is the hand stretched out over all nations.
27For the LORD Almighty has purposed,
and who can thwart him?
His hand is stretched out, and who can turn it back?

A Prophecy Against the Philistines

28This oracle came in the year King Ahaz died:

29Do not rejoice, all you Philistines,
that the rod that struck you is broken;
from the root of that snake will spring up a viper,
its fruit will be a darting, venomous serpent.
30The poorest of the poor will find pasture,
and the needy will lie down in safety.
But your root I will destroy by famine;
it will slay your survivors.

31Wail, O gate! Howl, O city!
Melt away, all you Philistines!
A cloud of smoke comes from the north,
and there is not a straggler in its ranks.
32What answer shall be given
to the envoys of that nation?
"The LORD has established Zion,
and in her his afflicted people will find refuge."

A Prophecy Against Moab

15 An oracle concerning Moab:
Ar in Moab is ruined,

[a]13 Or *the north*; Hebrew *Zaphon*

destroyed in a night!
Kir in Moab is ruined,
destroyed in a night!
2Dibon goes up to its temple,
to its high places to weep;
Moab wails over Nebo and Medeba.
Every head is shaved
and every beard cut off.
3In the streets they wear sackcloth;
on the roofs and in the public squares
they all wail,
prostrate with weeping.
4Heshbon and Elealeh cry out,
their voices are heard all the way to Jahaz.
Therefore the armed men of Moab cry out,
and their hearts are faint.

5My heart cries out over Moab;
her fugitives flee as far as Zoar,
as far as Eglath Shelishiyah.
They go up the way to Luhith,
weeping as they go;
on the road to Horonaim
they lament their destruction.
6The waters of Nimrim are dried up
and the grass is withered;
the vegetation is gone
and nothing green is left.
7So the wealth they have acquired and stored up
they carry away over the Ravine of the Poplars.
8Their outcry echoes along the border of Moab;
their wailing reaches as far as Eglaim,
their lamentation as far as Beer Elim.
9Dimon's[a] waters are full of blood,
but I will bring still more upon Dimon[a]—
a lion upon the fugitives of Moab
and upon those who remain in the land.

16 Send lambs as tribute
to the ruler of the land,
from Sela, across the desert,
to the mount of the Daughter of Zion.
2Like fluttering birds
pushed from the nest,
so are the women of Moab
at the fords of the Arnon.
3"Give us counsel,
render a decision.
Make your shadow like night—
at high noon.
Hide the fugitives,
do not betray the refugees.
4Let the Moabite fugitives stay with you;
be their shelter from the destroyer."

The oppressor will come to an end,
and destruction will cease;
the aggressor will vanish from the land.
5In love a throne will be established;
in faithfulness a man will sit on it—
one from the house[b] of David—
one who in judging seeks justice
and speeds the cause of righteousness.

6We have heard of Moab's pride—
her overweening pride and conceit,
her pride and her insolence—
but her boasts are empty.
7Therefore the Moabites wail,
they wail together for Moab.
Lament and grieve
for the men[c] of Kir Hareseth.
8The fields of Heshbon wither,
the vines of Sibmah also.
The rulers of the nations
have trampled down the choicest vines,
which once reached Jazer
and spread toward the desert.
Their shoots spread out
and went as far as the sea.
9So I weep, as Jazer weeps,
for the vines of Sibmah.
O Heshbon, O Elealeh,
I drench you with tears!
The shouts of joy over your ripened fruit
and over your harvests have been stilled.
10Joy and gladness are taken away from the orchards;
no one sings or shouts in the vineyards;
no one treads out wine at the presses,
for I have put an end to the shouting.
11My heart laments for Moab like a harp,

[a]9 Masoretic Text; Dead Sea Scrolls, some Septuagint manuscripts and Vulgate *Dibon*
[b]5 Hebrew *tent*
[c]7 Or "*raisin cakes*," a wordplay

my inmost being for Kir Hareseth.
12When Moab appears at her high place,
she only wears herself out;
when she goes to her shrine to pray,
it is to no avail.

13This is the word the LORD has already spoken concerning Moab. 14But now the LORD says: "Within three years, as a servant bound by contract would count them, Moab's splendor and all her many people will be despised, and her survivors will be very few and feeble."

An Oracle Against Damascus

17 An oracle concerning Damascus:
"See, Damascus will no longer be a city
but will become a heap of ruins.
2The cities of Aroer will be deserted
and left to flocks, which will lie down,
with no one to make them afraid.
3The fortified city will disappear from Ephraim,
and royal power from Damascus;
the remnant of Aram will be
like the glory of the Israelites,"
declares the LORD Almighty.

4"In that day the glory of Jacob will fade;
the fat of his body will waste away.
5It will be as when a reaper gathers the standing grain
and harvests the grain with his arm—
as when a man gleans heads of grain
in the Valley of Rephaim.
6Yet some gleanings will remain,
as when an olive tree is beaten,
leaving two or three olives on the topmost branches,
four or five on the fruitful boughs,"
declares the LORD, the God of Israel.

7In that day men will look to their Maker
and turn their eyes to the Holy One of Israel.
8They will not look to the altars,
the work of their hands,
and they will have no regard for the Asherah poles[a]
and the incense altars their fingers have made.

9In that day their strong cities, which they left because of the Israelites, will be like places abandoned to thickets and undergrowth. And all will be desolation.

10You have forgotten God your Savior;
you have not remembered the Rock, your fortress.
Therefore, though you set out the finest plants
and plant imported vines,
11though on the day you set them out, you make them grow,
and on the morning when you plant them, you bring them to bud,
yet the harvest will be as nothing
in the day of disease and incurable pain.

12Oh, the raging of many nations—
they rage like the raging sea!
Oh, the uproar of the peoples—
they roar like the roaring of great waters!
13Although the peoples roar like the roar of surging waters,
when he rebukes them they flee far away,
driven before the wind like chaff on the hills,
like tumbleweed before a gale.
14In the evening, sudden terror!
Before the morning, they are gone!
This is the portion of those who loot us,
the lot of those who plunder us.

A Prophecy Against Cush

18 Woe to the land of whirring wings[b]
along the rivers of Cush,[c]
2which sends envoys by sea
in papyrus boats over the water.

Go, swift messengers,
to a people tall and smooth-skinned,
to a people feared far and wide,
an aggressive nation of strange speech,
whose land is divided by rivers.

3All you people of the world,
you who live on the earth,
when a banner is raised on the mountains,
you will see it,
and when a trumpet sounds,
you will hear it.
4This is what the LORD says to me:

[a]8 That is, symbols of the goddess Asherah [b]1 Or *of locusts* [c]1 That is, the upper Nile region

"I will remain quiet and will look
on from my dwelling place,
like shimmering heat in the sunshine,
like a cloud of dew in the heat of
harvest."
5For, before the harvest, when the
blossom is gone
and the flower becomes a ripening
grape,
he will cut off the shoots with pruning
knives,
and cut down and take away the
spreading branches.
6They will all be left to the mountain
birds of prey
and to the wild animals;
the birds will feed on them all
summer,
the wild animals all winter.

7At that time gifts will be brought to the LORD Almighty

from a people tall and
smooth-skinned,
from a people feared far and wide,
an aggressive nation of strange
speech,
whose land is divided by rivers—

the gifts will be brought to Mount Zion, the place of the Name of the LORD Almighty.

A Prophecy About Egypt

19 An oracle concerning Egypt:

See, the LORD rides on a swift cloud
and is coming to Egypt.
The idols of Egypt tremble before him,
and the hearts of the Egyptians melt
within them.

2"I will stir up Egyptian against
Egyptian—
brother will fight against brother,
neighbor against neighbor,
city against city,
kingdom against kingdom.
3The Egyptians will lose heart,
and I will bring their plans to
nothing;
they will consult the idols and the
spirits of the dead,
the mediums and the spiritists.
4I will hand the Egyptians over
to the power of a cruel master,
and a fierce king will rule over them,"
declares the Lord, the LORD
Almighty.

5The waters of the river will dry up,
and the riverbed will be parched
and dry.
6The canals will stink;
the streams of Egypt will dwindle
and dry up.
The reeds and rushes will wither,
7 also the plants along the Nile,
at the mouth of the river.
Every sown field along the Nile
will become parched, will blow
away and be no more.
8The fishermen will groan and lament,
all who cast hooks into the Nile;
those who throw nets on the water
will pine away.
9Those who work with combed flax
will despair,
the weavers of fine linen will lose
hope.
10The workers in cloth will be dejected,
and all the wage earners will be sick
at heart.

11The officials of Zoan are nothing but
fools;
the wise counselors of Pharaoh give
senseless advice.
How can you say to Pharaoh,
"I am one of the wise men,
a disciple of the ancient kings"?

12Where are your wise men now?
Let them show you and make
known
what the LORD Almighty
has planned against Egypt.
13The officials of Zoan have become
fools,
the leaders of Memphis[a] are
deceived;
the cornerstones of her peoples
have led Egypt astray.
14The LORD has poured into them
a spirit of dizziness;
they make Egypt stagger in all that
she does,
as a drunkard staggers around in
his vomit.
15There is nothing Egypt can do—
head or tail, palm branch or reed.

16In that day the Egyptians will be like women. They will shudder with fear at the uplifted hand that the LORD Almighty raises against them. 17And the land of Ju-

[a]13 Hebrew *Noph*

dah will bring terror to the Egyptians; everyone to whom Judah is mentioned will be terrified, because of what the LORD Almighty is planning against them.

18 In that day five cities in Egypt will speak the language of Canaan and swear allegiance to the LORD Almighty. One of them will be called the City of Destruction.[a]

19 In that day there will be an altar to the LORD in the heart of Egypt, and a monument to the LORD at its border. 20 It will be a sign and witness to the LORD Almighty in the land of Egypt. When they cry out to the LORD because of their oppressors, he will send them a savior and defender, and he will rescue them. 21 So the LORD will make himself known to the Egyptians, and in that day they will acknowledge the LORD. They will worship with sacrifices and grain offerings; they will make vows to the LORD and keep them. 22 The LORD will strike Egypt with a plague; he will strike them and heal them. They will turn to the LORD, and he will respond to their pleas and heal them.

23 In that day there will be a highway from Egypt to Assyria. The Assyrians will go to Egypt and the Egyptians to Assyria. The Egyptians and Assyrians will worship together. 24 In that day Israel will be the third, along with Egypt and Assyria, a blessing on the earth. 25 The LORD Almighty will bless them, saying, "Blessed be Egypt my people, Assyria my handiwork, and Israel my inheritance."

A Prophecy Against Egypt and Cush

20 In the year that the supreme commander, sent by Sargon king of Assyria, came to Ashdod and attacked and captured it— 2 at that time the LORD spoke through Isaiah son of Amoz. He said to him, "Take off the sackcloth from your body and the sandals from your feet." And he did so, going around stripped and barefoot.

3 Then the LORD said, "Just as my servant Isaiah has gone stripped and barefoot for three years, as a sign and portent against Egypt and Cush,[b] 4 so the king of Assyria will lead away stripped and barefoot the Egyptian captives and Cushite exiles, young and old, with buttocks bared—to Egypt's shame. 5 Those who trusted in Cush and boasted in Egypt will be afraid and put to shame. 6 In that day the people who live on this coast will say, 'See what has happened to those we relied on, those we fled to for help and deliverance from the king of Assyria! How then can we escape?' "

A Prophecy Against Babylon

21 An oracle concerning the Desert by the Sea:

Like whirlwinds sweeping through the southland,
an invader comes from the desert,
from a land of terror.

2 A dire vision has been shown to me:
The traitor betrays, the looter takes loot.
Elam, attack! Media, lay siege!
I will bring to an end all the groaning she caused.

3 At this my body is racked with pain,
pangs seize me, like those of a woman in labor;
I am staggered by what I hear,
I am bewildered by what I see.
4 My heart falters,
fear makes me tremble;
the twilight I longed for
has become a horror to me.

5 They set the tables,
they spread the rugs,
they eat, they drink!
Get up, you officers,
oil the shields!

6 This is what the Lord says to me:

"Go, post a lookout
and have him report what he sees.
7 When he sees chariots
with teams of horses,
riders on donkeys
or riders on camels,
let him be alert,
fully alert."

8 And the lookout[c] shouted,

"Day after day, my lord, I stand on the watchtower;
every night I stay at my post.
9 Look, here comes a man in a chariot
with a team of horses.
And he gives back the answer:

[a] 18 Most manuscripts of the Masoretic Text; some manuscripts of the Masoretic Text, Dead Sea Scrolls and Vulgate *City of the Sun* (that is, Heliopolis) [b] 3 That is, the upper Nile region; also in verse 5
[c] 8 Dead Sea Scrolls and Syriac; Masoretic Text *A lion*

'Babylon has fallen, has fallen!
All the images of its gods
lie shattered on the ground!'"
10O my people, crushed on the
threshing floor,
I tell you what I have heard
from the LORD Almighty,
from the God of Israel.

A Prophecy Against Edom

11An oracle concerning Dumah[a]:
Someone calls to me from Seir,
"Watchman, what is left of the
night?
Watchman, what is left of the
night?"
12The watchman replies,
"Morning is coming, but also the
night.
If you would ask, then ask;
and come back yet again."

A Prophecy Against Arabia

13An oracle concerning Arabia:
You caravans of Dedanites,
who camp in the thickets of Arabia,
14 bring water for the thirsty;
you who live in Tema,
bring food for the fugitives.
15They flee from the sword,
from the drawn sword,
from the bent bow
and from the heat of battle.

16This is what the Lord says to me: "Within one year, as a servant bound by contract would count it, all the pomp of Kedar will come to an end. 17The survivors of the bowmen, the warriors of Kedar, will be few." The LORD, the God of Israel, has spoken.

A Prophecy About Jerusalem

22 An oracle concerning the Valley of Vision:
What troubles you now,
that you have all gone up on the
roofs,
2O town full of commotion,
O city of tumult and revelry?
Your slain were not killed by the
sword,
nor did they die in battle.
3All your leaders have fled together;
they have been captured without
using the bow.
All you who were caught were taken
prisoner together,
having fled while the enemy was
still far away.
4Therefore I said, "Turn away from me;
let me weep bitterly.
Do not try to console me
over the destruction of my people."

5The Lord, the LORD Almighty, has a
day
of tumult and trampling and terror
in the Valley of Vision,
a day of battering down walls
and of crying out to the mountains.
6Elam takes up the quiver,
with her charioteers and horses;
Kir uncovers the shield.
7Your choicest valleys are full of
chariots,
and horsemen are posted at the city
gates;
8 the defenses of Judah are stripped
away.

And you looked in that day
to the weapons in the Palace of the
Forest;
9you saw that the City of David
had many breaches in its defenses;
you stored up water
in the Lower Pool.
10You counted the buildings in
Jerusalem
and tore down houses to strengthen
the wall.
11You built a reservoir between the two
walls
for the water of the Old Pool,
but you did not look to the One who
made it,
or have regard for the One who
planned it long ago.

12The Lord, the LORD Almighty,
called you on that day
to weep and to wail,
to tear out your hair and put on
sackcloth.
13But see, there is joy and revelry,
slaughtering of cattle and killing of
sheep,
eating of meat and drinking of
wine!
"Let us eat and drink," you say,
"for tomorrow we die!"

[a]11 *Dumah* means *silence* or *stillness*, a wordplay on *Edom*.

[14]The LORD Almighty has revealed this
in my hearing: "Till your dying day this
sin will not be atoned for," says the Lord,
the LORD Almighty.

[15]This is what the Lord, the LORD Al-
mighty, says:

"Go, say to this steward,
to Shebna, who is in charge of the
palace:
[16]What are you doing here and who
gave you permission
to cut out a grave for yourself here,
hewing your grave on the height
and chiseling your resting place in
the rock?

[17]"Beware, the LORD is about to take
firm hold of you
and hurl you away, O you mighty
man.
[18]He will roll you up tightly like a ball
and throw you into a large country.
There you will die
and there your splendid chariots
will remain—
you disgrace to your master's
house!
[19]I will depose you from your office,
and you will be ousted from your
position.

[20]"In that day I will summon my ser-
vant, Eliakim son of Hilkiah. [21]I will clothe
him with your robe and fasten your sash
around him and hand your authority over
to him. He will be a father to those who
live in Jerusalem and to the house of Ju-
dah. [22]I will place on his shoulder the key
to the house of David; what he opens no
one can shut, and what he shuts no one
can open. [23]I will drive him like a peg into
a firm place; he will be a seat[a] of honor
for the house of his father. [24]All the glory
of his family will hang on him: its off-
spring and offshoots—all its lesser ves-
sels, from the bowls to all the jars.

[25]"In that day," declares the LORD Al-
mighty, "the peg driven into the firm place
will give way; it will be sheared off and
will fall, and the load hanging on it will be
cut down." The LORD has spoken.

A Prophecy About Tyre

23 An oracle concerning Tyre:
Wail, O ships of Tarshish!
For Tyre is destroyed
and left without house or harbor.
From the land of Cyprus[b]
word has come to them.

[2]Be silent, you people of the island
and you merchants of Sidon,
whom the seafarers have enriched.
[3]On the great waters
came the grain of the Shihor;
the harvest of the Nile[c] was the
revenue of Tyre,
and she became the marketplace of
the nations.
[4]Be ashamed, O Sidon, and you,
O fortress of the sea,
for the sea has spoken:
"I have neither been in labor nor
given birth;
I have neither reared sons nor
brought up daughters."
[5]When word comes to Egypt,
they will be in anguish at the report
from Tyre.

[6]Cross over to Tarshish;
wail, you people of the island.
[7]Is this your city of revelry,
the old, old city,
whose feet have taken her
to settle in far-off lands?
[8]Who planned this against Tyre,
the bestower of crowns,
whose merchants are princes,
whose traders are renowned in the
earth?
[9]The LORD Almighty planned it,
to bring low the pride of all glory
and to humble all who are
renowned on the earth.

[10]Till[d] your land as along the Nile,
O Daughter of Tarshish,
for you no longer have a harbor.
[11]The LORD has stretched out his hand
over the sea
and made its kingdoms tremble.
He has given an order concerning
Phoenicia[e]
that her fortresses be destroyed.
[12]He said, "No more of your reveling,

[a]23 Or *throne* [b]1 Hebrew *Kittim* [c]2,3 Masoretic Text; one Dead Sea Scroll *Sidon, / who cross over the sea; / your envoys* [3]*are on the great waters. / The grain of the Shihor, / the harvest of the Nile,* [d]10 Dead Sea Scrolls and some Septuagint manuscripts; Masoretic Text *Go through* [e]11 Hebrew *Canaan*

O Virgin Daughter of Sidon, now
crushed!

"Up, cross over to Cyprus[a];
even there you will find no rest."
13Look at the land of the Babylonians,[b]
this people that is now of no
account!
The Assyrians have made it
a place for desert creatures;
they raised up their siege towers,
they stripped its fortresses bare
and turned it into a ruin.

14Wail, you ships of Tarshish;
your fortress is destroyed!

15At that time Tyre will be forgotten for seventy years, the span of a king's life. But at the end of these seventy years, it will happen to Tyre as in the song of the prostitute:

16"Take up a harp, walk through the
city,
O prostitute forgotten;
play the harp well, sing many a song,
so that you will be remembered."

17At the end of seventy years, the LORD will deal with Tyre. She will return to her hire as a prostitute and will ply her trade with all the kingdoms on the face of the earth. 18Yet her profit and her earnings will be set apart for the LORD; they will not be stored up or hoarded. Her profits will go to those who live before the LORD, for abundant food and fine clothes.

The LORD's Devastation of the Earth

24 See, the LORD is going to lay
waste the earth
and devastate it;
he will ruin its face
and scatter its inhabitants—
2it will be the same
for priest as for people,
for master as for servant,
for mistress as for maid,
for seller as for buyer,
for borrower as for lender,
for debtor as for creditor.
3The earth will be completely laid
waste
and totally plundered.
The LORD has spoken this word.

4The earth dries up and withers,
the world languishes and withers,
the exalted of the earth languish.
5The earth is defiled by its people;
they have disobeyed the laws,
violated the statutes
and broken the everlasting
covenant.
6Therefore a curse consumes the earth;
its people must bear their guilt.
Therefore earth's inhabitants are
burned up,
and very few are left.
7The new wine dries up and the vine
withers;
all the merrymakers groan.
8The gaiety of the tambourines is
stilled,
the noise of the revelers has
stopped,
the joyful harp is silent.
9No longer do they drink wine with a
song;
the beer is bitter to its drinkers.
10The ruined city lies desolate;
the entrance to every house is
barred.
11In the streets they cry out for wine;
all joy turns to gloom,
all gaiety is banished from the
earth.
12The city is left in ruins,
its gate is battered to pieces.
13So will it be on the earth
and among the nations,
as when an olive tree is beaten,
or as when gleanings are left after
the grape harvest.

14They raise their voices, they shout for
joy;
from the west they acclaim the
LORD's majesty.
15Therefore in the east give glory to the
LORD;
exalt the name of the LORD, the God
of Israel,
in the islands of the sea.
16From the ends of the earth we hear
singing:
"Glory to the Righteous One."

But I said, "I waste away, I waste
away!
Woe to me!
The treacherous betray!
With treachery the treacherous
betray!"
17Terror and pit and snare await you,
O people of the earth.
18Whoever flees at the sound of terror

[a]12 Hebrew *Kittim* [b]13 Or *Chaldeans*

will fall into a pit;
whoever climbs out of the pit
will be caught in a snare.

The floodgates of the heavens are opened,
the foundations of the earth shake.
19The earth is broken up,
the earth is split asunder,
the earth is thoroughly shaken.
20The earth reels like a drunkard,
it sways like a hut in the wind;
so heavy upon it is the guilt of its rebellion
that it falls—never to rise again.

21In that day the LORD will punish
the powers in the heavens above
and the kings on the earth below.
22They will be herded together
like prisoners bound in a dungeon;
they will be shut up in prison
and be punished[a] after many days.
23The moon will be abashed, the sun ashamed;
for the LORD Almighty will reign
on Mount Zion and in Jerusalem,
and before its elders, gloriously.

Praise to the LORD

25 O LORD, you are my God;
I will exalt you and praise your name,
for in perfect faithfulness
you have done marvelous things,
things planned long ago.
2You have made the city a heap of rubble,
the fortified town a ruin,
the foreigners' stronghold a city no more;
it will never be rebuilt.
3Therefore strong peoples will honor you;
cities of ruthless nations will revere you.
4You have been a refuge for the poor,
a refuge for the needy in his distress,
a shelter from the storm
and a shade from the heat.
For the breath of the ruthless
is like a storm driving against a wall
5 and like the heat of the desert.
You silence the uproar of foreigners;
as heat is reduced by the shadow of a cloud,
so the song of the ruthless is stilled.

6On this mountain the LORD Almighty will prepare
a feast of rich food for all peoples,
a banquet of aged wine—
the best of meats and the finest of wines.
7On this mountain he will destroy
the shroud that enfolds all peoples,
the sheet that covers all nations;
8 he will swallow up death forever.
The Sovereign LORD will wipe away the tears
from all faces;
he will remove the disgrace of his people
from all the earth.
The LORD has spoken.

9In that day they will say,

"Surely this is our God;
we trusted in him, and he saved us.
This is the LORD, we trusted in him;
let us rejoice and be glad in his salvation."

10The hand of the LORD will rest on this mountain;
but Moab will be trampled under him
as straw is trampled down in the manure.
11They will spread out their hands in it,
as a swimmer spreads out his hands to swim.
God will bring down their pride
despite the cleverness[b] of their hands.
12He will bring down your high fortified walls
and lay them low;
he will bring them down to the ground,
to the very dust.

A Song of Praise

26 In that day this song will be sung in the land of Judah:

We have a strong city;
God makes salvation
its walls and ramparts.
2Open the gates
that the righteous nation may enter,
the nation that keeps faith.
3You will keep in perfect peace
him whose mind is steadfast,
because he trusts in you.
4Trust in the LORD forever,

[a] 22 Or *released* [b] 11 The meaning of the Hebrew for this word is uncertain.

for the LORD, the LORD, is the Rock
eternal.
5He humbles those who dwell on high,
he lays the lofty city low;
he levels it to the ground
and casts it down to the dust.
6Feet trample it down—
the feet of the oppressed,
the footsteps of the poor.

7The path of the righteous is level;
O upright One, you make the way
of the righteous smooth.
8Yes, LORD, walking in the way of your
laws,[a]
we wait for you;
your name and renown
are the desire of our hearts.
9My soul yearns for you in the night;
in the morning my spirit longs for
you.
When your judgments come upon the
earth,
the people of the world learn
righteousness.
10Though grace is shown to the wicked,
they do not learn righteousness;
even in a land of uprightness they go
on doing evil
and regard not the majesty of the
LORD.
11O LORD, your hand is lifted high,
but they do not see it.
Let them see your zeal for your
people and be put to shame;
let the fire reserved for your
enemies consume them.
12LORD, you establish peace for us;
all that we have accomplished you
have done for us.
13O LORD, our God, other lords besides
you have ruled over us,
but your name alone do we honor.
14They are now dead, they live no
more;
those departed spirits do not rise.
You punished them and brought them
to ruin;
you wiped out all memory of them.
15You have enlarged the nation, O LORD;
you have enlarged the nation.
You have gained glory for yourself;
you have extended all the borders
of the land.

16LORD, they came to you in their
distress;
when you disciplined them,
they could barely whisper a
prayer.[b]
17As a woman with child and about to
give birth
writhes and cries out in her pain,
so were we in your presence,
O LORD.
18We were with child, we writhed in
pain,
but we gave birth to wind.
We have not brought salvation to the
earth;
we have not given birth to people of
the world.

19But your dead will live;
their bodies will rise.
You who dwell in the dust,
wake up and shout for joy.
Your dew is like the dew of the
morning;
the earth will give birth to her dead.

20Go, my people, enter your rooms
and shut the doors behind you;
hide yourselves for a little while
until his wrath has passed by.
21See, the LORD is coming out of his
dwelling
to punish the people of the earth for
their sins.
The earth will disclose the blood shed
upon her;
she will conceal her slain no longer.

Deliverance of Israel

27 In that day,
the LORD will punish with his sword,
his fierce, great and powerful sword,
Leviathan the gliding serpent,
Leviathan the coiling serpent;
he will slay the monster of the sea.

2In that day—
"Sing about a fruitful vineyard:
3 I, the LORD, watch over it;
I water it continually.
I guard it day and night
so that no one may harm it.
4 I am not angry.
If only there were briers and thorns
confronting me!
I would march against them in
battle;
I would set them all on fire.

[a]8 Or *judgments* [b]16 The meaning of the Hebrew for this clause is uncertain.

5Or else let them come to me for
refuge;
let them make peace with me,
yes, let them make peace with me."

6In days to come Jacob will take root,
Israel will bud and blossom
and fill all the world with fruit.

7Has ⌊the LORD⌋ struck her
as he struck down those who struck
her?
Has she been killed
as those were killed who killed
her?
8By warfare[a] and exile you contend
with her—
with his fierce blast he drives her
out,
as on a day the east wind blows.
9By this, then, will Jacob's guilt be
atoned for,
and this will be the full fruitage of
the removal of his sin:
When he makes all the altar stones
to be like chalk stones crushed to
pieces,
no Asherah poles[b] or incense altars
will be left standing.
10The fortified city stands desolate,
an abandoned settlement, forsaken
like the desert;
there the calves graze,
there they lie down;
they strip its branches bare.
11When its twigs are dry, they are
broken off
and women come and make fires
with them.
For this is a people without
understanding;
so their Maker has no compassion
on them,
and their Creator shows them no
favor.

12In that day the LORD will thresh from the flowing Euphrates[c] to the Wadi of Egypt, and you, O Israelites, will be gathered up one by one. 13And in that day a great trumpet will sound. Those who were perishing in Assyria and those who were exiled in Egypt will come and worship the LORD on the holy mountain in Jerusalem.

Woe to Ephraim

28 Woe to that wreath, the pride of
Ephraim's drunkards,
to the fading flower, his glorious
beauty,
set on the head of a fertile valley—
to that city, the pride of those laid
low by wine!
2See, the Lord has one who is powerful
and strong.
Like a hailstorm and a destructive
wind,
like a driving rain and a flooding
downpour,
he will throw it forcefully to the
ground.
3That wreath, the pride of Ephraim's
drunkards,
will be trampled underfoot.
4That fading flower, his glorious
beauty,
set on the head of a fertile valley,
will be like a fig ripe before harvest—
as soon as someone sees it and
takes it in his hand,
he swallows it.

5In that day the LORD Almighty
will be a glorious crown,
a beautiful wreath
for the remnant of his people.
6He will be a spirit of justice
to him who sits in judgment,
a source of strength
to those who turn back the battle at
the gate.

7And these also stagger from wine
and reel from beer:
Priests and prophets stagger from beer
and are befuddled with wine;
they reel from beer,
they stagger when seeing visions,
they stumble when rendering
decisions.
8All the tables are covered with vomit
and there is not a spot without filth.

9"Who is it he is trying to teach?
To whom is he explaining his
message?
To children weaned from their milk,
to those just taken from the breast?
10For it is:
Do and do, do and do,
rule on rule, rule on rule[d];

[a]8 See Septuagint; the meaning of the Hebrew for this word is uncertain. [b]9 That is, symbols of the goddess Asherah [c]12 Hebrew *River* [d]10 Hebrew / *sav lasav sav lasav / kav lakav kav lakav* (possibly meaningless sounds; perhaps a mimicking of the prophet's words); also in verse 13

a little here, a little there."

11Very well then, with foreign lips and strange tongues
God will speak to this people,
12to whom he said,
"This is the resting place, let the weary rest";
and, "This is the place of repose"—
but they would not listen.
13So then, the word of the LORD to them will become:
Do and do, do and do,
rule on rule, rule on rule;
a little here, a little there—
so that they will go and fall backward,
be injured and snared and captured.

14Therefore hear the word of the LORD, you scoffers
who rule this people in Jerusalem.
15You boast, "We have entered into a covenant with death,
with the grave[a] we have made an agreement.
When an overwhelming scourge sweeps by,
it cannot touch us,
for we have made a lie our refuge
and falsehood[b] our hiding place."

16So this is what the Sovereign LORD says:

"See, I lay a stone in Zion,
a tested stone,
a precious cornerstone for a sure foundation;
the one who trusts will never be dismayed.
17I will make justice the measuring line
and righteousness the plumb line;
hail will sweep away your refuge, the lie,
and water will overflow your hiding place.
18Your covenant with death will be annulled;
your agreement with the grave will not stand.
When the overwhelming scourge sweeps by,
you will be beaten down by it.
19As often as it comes it will carry you away;
morning after morning, by day and by night,
it will sweep through."
The understanding of this message will bring sheer terror.
20The bed is too short to stretch out on,
the blanket too narrow to wrap around you.
21The LORD will rise up as he did at Mount Perazim,
he will rouse himself as in the Valley of Gibeon—
to do his work, his strange work,
and perform his task, his alien task.
22Now stop your mocking,
or your chains will become heavier;
the Lord, the LORD Almighty, has told me
of the destruction decreed against the whole land.

23Listen and hear my voice;
pay attention and hear what I say.
24When a farmer plows for planting,
does he plow continually?
Does he keep on breaking up and harrowing the soil?
25When he has leveled the surface,
does he not sow caraway and scatter cummin?
Does he not plant wheat in its place,[c]
barley in its plot,[c]
and spelt in its field?
26His God instructs him
and teaches him the right way.

27Caraway is not threshed with a sledge,
nor is a cartwheel rolled over cummin;
caraway is beaten out with a rod,
and cummin with a stick.
28Grain must be ground to make bread;
so one does not go on threshing it forever.
Though he drives the wheels of his threshing cart over it,
his horses do not grind it.
29All this also comes from the LORD Almighty,
wonderful in counsel and magnificent in wisdom.

Woe to David's City

29 Woe to you, Ariel, Ariel,
the city where David settled!
Add year to year
and let your cycle of festivals go on.
2Yet I will besiege Ariel;
she will mourn and lament,

[a] 15 Hebrew *Sheol*; also in verse 18 [b] 15 Or *false gods* [c] 25 The meaning of the Hebrew for this word is uncertain.

she will be to me like an altar
hearth.[a]
3 I will encamp against you all around;
I will encircle you with towers
and set up my siege works against
you.
4 Brought low, you will speak from the
ground;
your speech will mumble out of the
dust.
Your voice will come ghostlike from
the earth;
out of the dust your speech will
whisper.

5 But your many enemies will become
like fine dust,
the ruthless hordes like blown chaff.
Suddenly, in an instant,
6 the LORD Almighty will come
with thunder and earthquake and
great noise,
with windstorm and tempest and
flames of a devouring fire.
7 Then the hordes of all the nations that
fight against Ariel,
that attack her and her fortress and
besiege her,
will be as it is with a dream,
with a vision in the night—
8 as when a hungry man dreams that he
is eating,
but he awakens, and his hunger
remains;
as when a thirsty man dreams that he
is drinking,
but he awakens faint, with his thirst
unquenched.
So will it be with the hordes of all the
nations
that fight against Mount Zion.

9 Be stunned and amazed,
blind yourselves and be sightless;
be drunk, but not from wine,
stagger, but not from beer.
10 The LORD has brought over you a deep
sleep:
He has sealed your eyes (the
prophets);
he has covered your heads (the
seers).

11 For you this whole vision is nothing
but words sealed in a scroll. And if you
give the scroll to someone who can read,
and say to him, "Read this, please," he will
answer, "I can't; it is sealed." 12 Or if you
give the scroll to someone who cannot
read, and say, "Read this, please," he will
answer, "I don't know how to read."

13 The Lord says:

"These people come near to me with
their mouth
and honor me with their lips,
but their hearts are far from me.
Their worship of me
is made up only of rules taught by
men.[b]
14 Therefore once more I will astound
these people
with wonder upon wonder;
the wisdom of the wise will perish,
the intelligence of the intelligent
will vanish."
15 Woe to those who go to great depths
to hide their plans from the LORD,
who do their work in darkness and
think,
"Who sees us? Who will know?"
16 You turn things upside down,
as if the potter were thought to be
like the clay!
Shall what is formed say to him who
formed it,
"He did not make me"?
Can the pot say of the potter,
"He knows nothing"?

17 In a very short time, will not Lebanon
be turned into a fertile field
and the fertile field seem like a
forest?
18 In that day the deaf will hear the
words of the scroll,
and out of gloom and darkness
the eyes of the blind will see.
19 Once more the humble will rejoice in
the LORD;
the needy will rejoice in the Holy
One of Israel.
20 The ruthless will vanish,
the mockers will disappear,
and all who have an eye for evil
will be cut down—
21 those who with a word make a man
out to be guilty,
who ensnare the defender in court
and with false testimony deprive the
innocent of justice.

22 Therefore this is what the LORD, who

[a] 2 The Hebrew for *altar hearth* sounds like the Hebrew for *Ariel.*
[b] 13 Hebrew; Septuagint *They worship me in vain; / their teachings are but rules taught by men*

redeemed Abraham, says to the house of Jacob:

"No longer will Jacob be ashamed;
no longer will their faces grow pale.
23 When they see among them their children,
the work of my hands,
they will keep my name holy;
they will acknowledge the holiness of the Holy One of Jacob,
and will stand in awe of the God of Israel.
24 Those who are wayward in spirit will gain understanding;
those who complain will accept instruction."

Woe to the Obstinate Nation

30 "Woe to the obstinate children," declares the LORD,
"to those who carry out plans that are not mine,
forming an alliance, but not by my Spirit,
heaping sin upon sin;
2 who go down to Egypt
without consulting me;
who look for help to Pharaoh's protection,
to Egypt's shade for refuge.
3 But Pharaoh's protection will be to your shame,
Egypt's shade will bring you disgrace.
4 Though they have officials in Zoan
and their envoys have arrived in Hanes,
5 everyone will be put to shame
because of a people useless to them,
who bring neither help nor advantage,
but only shame and disgrace."

6 An oracle concerning the animals of the Negev:

Through a land of hardship and distress,
of lions and lionesses,
of adders and darting snakes,
the envoys carry their riches on donkeys' backs,
their treasures on the humps of camels,
to that unprofitable nation,
7 to Egypt, whose help is utterly useless.
Therefore I call her
Rahab the Do-Nothing.

8 Go now, write it on a tablet for them,
inscribe it on a scroll,
that for the days to come
it may be an everlasting witness.
9 These are rebellious people, deceitful children,
children unwilling to listen to the LORD's instruction.
10 They say to the seers,
"See no more visions!"
and to the prophets,
"Give us no more visions of what is right!
Tell us pleasant things,
prophesy illusions.
11 Leave this way,
get off this path,
and stop confronting us
with the Holy One of Israel!"

12 Therefore, this is what the Holy One of Israel says:

"Because you have rejected this message,
relied on oppression
and depended on deceit,
13 this sin will become for you
like a high wall, cracked and bulging,
that collapses suddenly, in an instant.
14 It will break in pieces like pottery,
shattered so mercilessly
that among its pieces not a fragment will be found
for taking coals from a hearth
or scooping water out of a cistern."

15 This is what the Sovereign LORD, the Holy One of Israel, says:

"In repentance and rest is your salvation,
in quietness and trust is your strength,
but you would have none of it.
16 You said, 'No, we will flee on horses.'
Therefore you will flee!
You said, 'We will ride off on swift horses.'
Therefore your pursuers will be swift!
17 A thousand will flee
at the threat of one;
at the threat of five
you will all flee away,
till you are left
like a flagstaff on a mountaintop,
like a banner on a hill."

18Yet the LORD longs to be gracious to
you;
he rises to show you compassion.
For the LORD is a God of justice.
Blessed are all who wait for him!

19O people of Zion, who live in Jerusalem, you will weep no more. How gracious he will be when you cry for help! As soon as he hears, he will answer you. 20Although the Lord gives you the bread of adversity and the water of affliction, your teachers will be hidden no more; with your own eyes you will see them. 21Whether you turn to the right or to the left, your ears will hear a voice behind you, saying, "This is the way; walk in it." 22Then you will defile your idols overlaid with silver and your images covered with gold; you will throw them away like a menstrual cloth and say to them, "Away with you!"

23He will also send you rain for the seed you sow in the ground, and the food that comes from the land will be rich and plentiful. In that day your cattle will graze in broad meadows. 24The oxen and donkeys that work the soil will eat fodder and mash, spread out with fork and shovel. 25In the day of great slaughter, when the towers fall, streams of water will flow on every high mountain and every lofty hill. 26The moon will shine like the sun, and the sunlight will be seven times brighter, like the light of seven full days, when the LORD binds up the bruises of his people and heals the wounds he inflicted.

27See, the Name of the LORD comes
from afar,
with burning anger and dense
clouds of smoke;
his lips are full of wrath,
and his tongue is a consuming fire.
28His breath is like a rushing torrent,
rising up to the neck.
He shakes the nations in the sieve of
destruction;
he places in the jaws of the peoples
a bit that leads them astray.
29And you will sing
as on the night you celebrate a holy
festival;
your hearts will rejoice
as when people go up with flutes
to the mountain of the LORD,
to the Rock of Israel.
30The LORD will cause men to hear his
majestic voice
and will make them see his arm
coming down
with raging anger and consuming fire,
with cloudburst, thunderstorm and
hail.
31The voice of the LORD will shatter
Assyria;
with his scepter he will strike them
down.
32Every stroke the LORD lays on them
with his punishing rod
will be to the music of tambourines
and harps,
as he fights them in battle with the
blows of his arm.
33Topheth has long been prepared;
it has been made ready for the king.
Its fire pit has been made deep and
wide,
with an abundance of fire and
wood;
the breath of the LORD,
like a stream of burning sulfur,
sets it ablaze.

Woe to Those Who Rely on Egypt

31 Woe to those who go down to
Egypt for help,
who rely on horses,
who trust in the multitude of their
chariots
and in the great strength of their
horsemen,
but do not look to the Holy One of
Israel,
or seek help from the LORD.
2Yet he too is wise and can bring
disaster;
he does not take back his words.
He will rise up against the house of
the wicked,
against those who help evildoers.
3But the Egyptians are men and not
God;
their horses are flesh and not spirit.
When the LORD stretches out his hand,
he who helps will stumble,
he who is helped will fall;
both will perish together.

4This is what the LORD says to me:

"As a lion growls,
a great lion over his prey—
and though a whole band of
shepherds
is called together against him,
he is not frightened by their shouts
or disturbed by their clamor—
so the LORD Almighty will come down

VERSE FOR THE DAY: Isaiah 30:21

AUTHOR: Ruth Stafford Peale

PASSAGE FOR THE DAY: Isaiah 30:18–21

Hard Decisions

How can you be sure you're receiving God's guidance? One indication is when the answer that comes is not the one you prefer.

Soon after Norman and I were married—when he was pastoring a church in Syracuse, New York—he received calls from two churches. One was the largest Methodist congregation in the country (in Los Angeles), and the other, Marble Collegiate Church in New York City. Norman would make up his mind and then unmake it. Finally I said, "We're going to put it in God's hands and ask for his guidance. We'll wait and listen until we get it."

We knelt, held hands and prayed. Norman paced. We turned the pages of the Bible. But no answer seemed to come. Norman was pleased and flattered by the thought of preaching to the country's largest Methodist church, and he doubted his ability to reach a sophisticated New York congregation. But we tried to surrender any shred of personal preference and leave the decision up to God.

Finally the atmosphere in the room seemed to change. Norman looked at me and asked, "Do you have an answer?" "Yes," I said, "but you must make this decision. Have you an answer?"

Norman said firmly, "I think God wants us to go to New York." I agreed. After days of anguished indecision, we felt an amazing calmness, an acceptance of being led and guided in the right direction.

MARRIAGE BUILDERS

♦ *When have you clearly felt the distinct leading of God? Was God's leading taking you in a direction you might naturally have avoided if it were left entirely up to you?*

♦ *What important decisions are you facing right now? What role does joint prayer play in the decision-making process?*

Additional Scripture Readings
Proverbs 3:5–6; Psalm 119:105; John 8:12

Go to page 751 for your next devotional reading.

to do battle on Mount Zion and on
its heights.
5Like birds hovering overhead,
the LORD Almighty will shield
Jerusalem;
he will shield it and deliver it,
he will 'pass over' it and will rescue
it."

6Return to him you have so greatly revolted against, O Israelites. 7For in that day every one of you will reject the idols of silver and gold your sinful hands have made.

8"Assyria will fall by a sword that is
not of man;
a sword, not of mortals, will devour
them.
They will flee before the sword
and their young men will be put to
forced labor.
9Their stronghold will fall because of
terror;
at sight of the battle standard their
commanders will panic,"
declares the LORD,
whose fire is in Zion,
whose furnace is in Jerusalem.

The Kingdom of Righteousness

32 See, a king will reign in
righteousness
and rulers will rule with justice.
2Each man will be like a shelter from
the wind
and a refuge from the storm,
like streams of water in the desert
and the shadow of a great rock in a
thirsty land.

3Then the eyes of those who see will
no longer be closed,

VERSE FOR THE DAY: Isaiah 32:18 | AUTHOR: Ron Hutchcraft | PASSAGE FOR THE DAY: Isaiah 32:1–20

A Safe Harbor

My wife, Karen, and I work hard at providing a harbor for each other. All day long we find ourselves masking deep feelings from others—our children, the people at work, friends.

Time at home with your mate should be a place to unload, to unmask, to laugh, to cry, to work out grudges, to come to the end of your rope and know you will still be accepted and loved. The marriage harbor should be a place where each partner unloads burdens and loads up on encouragement. We are created for safe harbors.

MARRIAGE BUILDERS

♦ *What does your spouse do that makes you feel safe and accepted?*

♦ *If you could change one thing about your home life to make it more of a "safe harbor" for you, what would it be?*

Additional Scripture Readings
Galatians 6:2; Romans 15:5–7

Go to page 756 for your next devotional reading.

and the ears of those who hear will listen.
4 The mind of the rash will know and understand,
and the stammering tongue will be fluent and clear.
5 No longer will the fool be called noble
nor the scoundrel be highly respected.
6 For the fool speaks folly,
his mind is busy with evil:
He practices ungodliness
and spreads error concerning the LORD;
the hungry he leaves empty
and from the thirsty he withholds water.
7 The scoundrel's methods are wicked,
he makes up evil schemes
to destroy the poor with lies,
even when the plea of the needy is just.
8 But the noble man makes noble plans,
and by noble deeds he stands.

The Women of Jerusalem

9 You women who are so complacent,
rise up and listen to me;
you daughters who feel secure,
hear what I have to say!
10 In little more than a year
you who feel secure will tremble;
the grape harvest will fail,
and the harvest of fruit will not come.
11 Tremble, you complacent women;
shudder, you daughters who feel secure!
Strip off your clothes,
put sackcloth around your waists.
12 Beat your breasts for the pleasant fields,
for the fruitful vines
13 and for the land of my people,
a land overgrown with thorns and briers—
yes, mourn for all houses of merriment
and for this city of revelry.
14 The fortress will be abandoned,
the noisy city deserted;
citadel and watchtower will become a wasteland forever,
the delight of donkeys, a pasture for flocks,
15 till the Spirit is poured upon us from on high,
and the desert becomes a fertile field,
and the fertile field seems like a forest.
16 Justice will dwell in the desert
and righteousness live in the fertile field.
17 The fruit of righteousness will be peace;
the effect of righteousness will be quietness and confidence forever.
18 My people will live in peaceful dwelling places,
in secure homes,
in undisturbed places of rest.
19 Though hail flattens the forest
and the city is leveled completely,
20 how blessed you will be,
sowing your seed by every stream,
and letting your cattle and donkeys range free.

Distress and Help

33 Woe to you, O destroyer,
you who have not been destroyed!
Woe to you, O traitor,
you who have not been betrayed!
When you stop destroying,
you will be destroyed;
when you stop betraying,
you will be betrayed.

2 O LORD, be gracious to us;
we long for you.
Be our strength every morning,
our salvation in time of distress.
3 At the thunder of your voice, the peoples flee;
when you rise up, the nations scatter.
4 Your plunder, O nations, is harvested as by young locusts;
like a swarm of locusts men pounce on it.

5 The LORD is exalted, for he dwells on high;
he will fill Zion with justice and righteousness.
6 He will be the sure foundation for your times,
a rich store of salvation and wisdom and knowledge;
the fear of the LORD is the key to this treasure.[a]

[a] 6 Or *is a treasure from him*

7Look, their brave men cry aloud in the streets;
the envoys of peace weep bitterly.
8The highways are deserted,
no travelers are on the roads.
The treaty is broken,
its witnesses[a] are despised,
no one is respected.
9The land mourns[b] and wastes away,
Lebanon is ashamed and withers;
Sharon is like the Arabah,
and Bashan and Carmel drop their leaves.

10"Now will I arise," says the LORD.
"Now will I be exalted;
now will I be lifted up.
11You conceive chaff,
you give birth to straw;
your breath is a fire that consumes you.
12The peoples will be burned as if to lime;
like cut thornbushes they will be set ablaze."

13You who are far away, hear what I have done;
you who are near, acknowledge my power!
14The sinners in Zion are terrified;
trembling grips the godless:
"Who of us can dwell with the consuming fire?
Who of us can dwell with everlasting burning?"
15He who walks righteously
and speaks what is right,
who rejects gain from extortion
and keeps his hand from accepting bribes,
who stops his ears against plots of murder
and shuts his eyes against contemplating evil—
16this is the man who will dwell on the heights,
whose refuge will be the mountain fortress.
His bread will be supplied,
and water will not fail him.

17Your eyes will see the king in his beauty
and view a land that stretches afar.
18In your thoughts you will ponder the former terror:
"Where is that chief officer?
Where is the one who took the revenue?
Where is the officer in charge of the towers?"
19You will see those arrogant people no more,
those people of an obscure speech,
with their strange, incomprehensible tongue.

20Look upon Zion, the city of our festivals;
your eyes will see Jerusalem,
a peaceful abode, a tent that will not be moved;
its stakes will never be pulled up,
nor any of its ropes broken.
21There the LORD will be our Mighty One.
It will be like a place of broad rivers and streams.
No galley with oars will ride them,
no mighty ship will sail them.
22For the LORD is our judge,
the LORD is our lawgiver,
the LORD is our king;
it is he who will save us.

23Your rigging hangs loose:
The mast is not held secure,
the sail is not spread.
Then an abundance of spoils will be divided
and even the lame will carry off plunder.
24No one living in Zion will say, "I am ill";
and the sins of those who dwell there will be forgiven.

Judgment Against the Nations

34 Come near, you nations, and listen;
pay attention, you peoples!
Let the earth hear, and all that is in it,
the world, and all that comes out of it!
2The LORD is angry with all nations;
his wrath is upon all their armies.
He will totally destroy[c] them,
he will give them over to slaughter.
3Their slain will be thrown out,
their dead bodies will send up a stench;
the mountains will be soaked with their blood.

[a]8 Dead Sea Scrolls; Masoretic Text / *the cities* [b]9 Or *dries up* [c]2 The Hebrew term refers to the irrevocable giving over of things or persons to the LORD, often by totally destroying them; also in verse 5.

4All the stars of the heavens will be dissolved
and the sky rolled up like a scroll;
all the starry host will fall
like withered leaves from the vine,
like shriveled figs from the fig tree.

5My sword has drunk its fill in the heavens;
see, it descends in judgment on Edom,
the people I have totally destroyed.
6The sword of the LORD is bathed in blood,
it is covered with fat—
the blood of lambs and goats,
fat from the kidneys of rams.
For the LORD has a sacrifice in Bozrah
and a great slaughter in Edom.
7And the wild oxen will fall with them,
the bull calves and the great bulls.
Their land will be drenched with blood,
and the dust will be soaked with fat.

8For the LORD has a day of vengeance,
a year of retribution, to uphold Zion's cause.
9Edom's streams will be turned into pitch,
her dust into burning sulfur;
her land will become blazing pitch!
10It will not be quenched night and day;
its smoke will rise forever.
From generation to generation it will lie desolate;
no one will ever pass through it again.
11The desert owl[a] and screech owl[a] will possess it;
the great owl[a] and the raven will nest there.
God will stretch out over Edom
the measuring line of chaos
and the plumb line of desolation.
12Her nobles will have nothing there to be called a kingdom,
all her princes will vanish away.
13Thorns will overrun her citadels,
nettles and brambles her strongholds.
She will become a haunt for jackals,
a home for owls.
14Desert creatures will meet with hyenas,
and wild goats will bleat to each other;
there the night creatures will also repose
and find for themselves places of rest.
15The owl will nest there and lay eggs,
she will hatch them, and care for her young under the shadow of her wings;
there also the falcons will gather,
each with its mate.

16Look in the scroll of the LORD and read:

None of these will be missing,
not one will lack her mate.
For it is his mouth that has given the order,
and his Spirit will gather them together.
17He allots their portions;
his hand distributes them by measure.
They will possess it forever
and dwell there from generation to generation.

Joy of the Redeemed

35 The desert and the parched land will be glad;
the wilderness will rejoice and blossom.
Like the crocus, 2it will burst into bloom;
it will rejoice greatly and shout for joy.
The glory of Lebanon will be given to it,
the splendor of Carmel and Sharon;
they will see the glory of the LORD,
the splendor of our God.

3Strengthen the feeble hands,
steady the knees that give way;
4say to those with fearful hearts,
"Be strong, do not fear;
your God will come,
he will come with vengeance;
with divine retribution
he will come to save you."

5Then will the eyes of the blind be opened
and the ears of the deaf unstopped.
6Then will the lame leap like a deer,
and the mute tongue shout for joy.
Water will gush forth in the wilderness
and streams in the desert.

[a]11 The precise identification of these birds is uncertain.

7The burning sand will become a pool,
the thirsty ground bubbling springs.
In the haunts where jackals once lay,
grass and reeds and papyrus will grow.

8And a highway will be there;
it will be called the Way of Holiness.
The unclean will not journey on it;
it will be for those who walk in that Way;
wicked fools will not go about on it.[a]
9No lion will be there,
nor will any ferocious beast get up on it;
they will not be found there.
But only the redeemed will walk there,
10 and the ransomed of the LORD will return.
They will enter Zion with singing;
everlasting joy will crown their heads.
Gladness and joy will overtake them,
and sorrow and sighing will flee away.

Sennacherib Threatens Jerusalem

36 In the fourteenth year of King Hezekiah's reign, Sennacherib king of Assyria attacked all the fortified cities of Judah and captured them. 2Then the king of Assyria sent his field commander with a large army from Lachish to King Hezekiah at Jerusalem. When the commander stopped at the aqueduct of the Upper Pool, on the road to the Washerman's Field, 3Eliakim son of Hilkiah the palace administrator, Shebna the secretary, and Joah son of Asaph the recorder went out to him.

4The field commander said to them, "Tell Hezekiah,

" 'This is what the great king, the king of Assyria, says: On what are you basing this confidence of yours? 5You say you have strategy and military strength—but you speak only empty words. On whom are you depending, that you rebel against me? 6Look now, you are depending on Egypt, that splintered reed of a staff, which pierces a man's hand and wounds him if he leans on it! Such is Pharaoh king of Egypt to all who depend on him. 7And if you say to me, "We are depending on the LORD our God"—isn't he the one whose high places and altars Hezekiah removed, saying to Judah and Jerusalem, "You must worship before this altar"?

8" 'Come now, make a bargain with my master, the king of Assyria: I will give you two thousand horses—if you can put riders on them! 9How then can you repulse one officer of the least of my master's officials, even though you are depending on Egypt for chariots and horsemen? 10Furthermore, have I come to attack and destroy this land without the LORD? The LORD himself told me to march against this country and destroy it.' "

11Then Eliakim, Shebna and Joah said to the field commander, "Please speak to your servants in Aramaic, since we understand it. Don't speak to us in Hebrew in the hearing of the people on the wall."

12But the commander replied, "Was it only to your master and you that my master sent me to say these things, and not to the men sitting on the wall—who, like you, will have to eat their own filth and drink their own urine?"

13Then the commander stood and called out in Hebrew, "Hear the words of the great king, the king of Assyria! 14This is what the king says: Do not let Hezekiah deceive you. He cannot deliver you! 15Do not let Hezekiah persuade you to trust in the LORD when he says, 'The LORD will surely deliver us; this city will not be given into the hand of the king of Assyria.'

16"Do not listen to Hezekiah. This is what the king of Assyria says: Make peace with me and come out to me. Then every one of you will eat from his own vine and fig tree and drink water from his own cistern, 17until I come and take you to a land like your own—a land of grain and new wine, a land of bread and vineyards.

18"Do not let Hezekiah mislead you when he says, 'The LORD will deliver us.' Has the god of any nation ever delivered his land from the hand of the king of Assyria? 19Where are the gods of Hamath and Arpad? Where are the gods of Sepharvaim? Have they rescued Samaria from my hand? 20Who of all the gods of these countries has been able to save his land

[a]8 Or / *the simple will not stray from it*

WEEKENDING

LEISURE

When setting goals for your marriage, don't forget to plan leisure time together. Time for fun and relaxation is part of building intimacy and that strong sense of shared purpose. These questions might help you set any needed goals.

1. Is enough leisure time scheduled into our calendar? If not, how can we work it in?

2. Is our available free time left unstructured, or is it filled with specific activities?

3. Are we satisfied with the amount of time we devote to each other—without friends or relatives being involved?

4. Would we like to have more dates, take more weekend getaways or a special vacation? If so, when can we begin?

— *The* Marriage Partnership *Staff*

REVIVE

Saturday: Genesis 1:1—2:2
Sunday: Acts 3:19–20

Go to page 760 for your next devotional reading.

from me? How then can the LORD deliver
Jerusalem from my hand?"
21But the people remained silent and
said nothing in reply, because the king
had commanded, "Do not answer him."
22Then Eliakim son of Hilkiah the pal-
ace administrator, Shebna the secretary,
and Joah son of Asaph the recorder went
to Hezekiah, with their clothes torn, and
told him what the field commander had
said.

Jerusalem's Deliverance Foretold

37 When King Hezekiah heard this,
he tore his clothes and put on sack-
cloth and went into the temple of the
LORD. 2He sent Eliakim the palace admin-
istrator, Shebna the secretary, and the
leading priests, all wearing sackcloth, to
the prophet Isaiah son of Amoz. 3They
told him, "This is what Hezekiah says:
This day is a day of distress and rebuke
and disgrace, as when children come to
the point of birth and there is no strength
to deliver them. 4It may be that the LORD
your God will hear the words of the field
commander, whom his master, the king of
Assyria, has sent to ridicule the living
God, and that he will rebuke him for the
words the LORD your God has heard.
Therefore pray for the remnant that still
survives."
5When King Hezekiah's officials came
to Isaiah, 6Isaiah said to them, "Tell your
master, 'This is what the LORD says: Do
not be afraid of what you have heard—
those words with which the underlings of
the king of Assyria have blasphemed me.
7Listen! I am going to put a spirit in him
so that when he hears a certain report, he
will return to his own country, and there
I will have him cut down with the
sword.' "
8When the field commander heard that
the king of Assyria had left Lachish, he
withdrew and found the king fighting
against Libnah.
9Now Sennacherib received a report
that Tirhakah, the Cushite[a] king ⌊of
Egypt⌋, was marching out to fight against
him. When he heard it, he sent messen-
gers to Hezekiah with this word: 10"Say to
Hezekiah king of Judah: Do not let the god
you depend on deceive you when he says,
'Jerusalem will not be handed over to the
king of Assyria.' 11Surely you have heard
what the kings of Assyria have done to all
the countries, destroying them complete-
ly. And will you be delivered? 12Did the
gods of the nations that were destroyed by
my forefathers deliver them—the gods of
Gozan, Haran, Rezeph and the people of
Eden who were in Tel Assar? 13Where is
the king of Hamath, the king of Arpad, the
king of the city of Sepharvaim, or of Hena
or Ivvah?"

Hezekiah's Prayer

14Hezekiah received the letter from the
messengers and read it. Then he went up
to the temple of the LORD and spread it out
before the LORD. 15And Hezekiah prayed
to the LORD: 16"O LORD Almighty, God of
Israel, enthroned between the cherubim,
you alone are God over all the kingdoms
of the earth. You have made heaven and
earth. 17Give ear, O LORD, and hear; open
your eyes, O LORD, and see; listen to all
the words Sennacherib has sent to insult
the living God.
18"It is true, O LORD, that the Assyrian
kings have laid waste all these peoples
and their lands. 19They have thrown their
gods into the fire and destroyed them, for
they were not gods but only wood and
stone, fashioned by human hands. 20Now,
O LORD our God, deliver us from his hand,
so that all kingdoms on earth may know
that you alone, O LORD, are God.[b]"

Sennacherib's Fall

21Then Isaiah son of Amoz sent a mes-
sage to Hezekiah: "This is what the LORD,
the God of Israel, says: Because you have
prayed to me concerning Sennacherib
king of Assyria, 22this is the word the LORD
has spoken against him:

"The Virgin Daughter of Zion
despises and mocks you.
The Daughter of Jerusalem
tosses her head as you flee.
23Who is it you have insulted and
blasphemed?
Against whom have you raised your
voice
and lifted your eyes in pride?
Against the Holy One of Israel!
24By your messengers
you have heaped insults on the
Lord.
And you have said,

[a]9 That is, from the upper Nile region
[b]20 Dead Sea Scrolls (see also 2 Kings 19:19); Masoretic Text *alone are the LORD*

'With my many chariots
I have ascended the heights of the mountains,
the utmost heights of Lebanon.
I have cut down its tallest cedars,
the choicest of its pines.
I have reached its remotest heights,
the finest of its forests.
25I have dug wells in foreign lands[a]
and drunk the water there.
With the soles of my feet
I have dried up all the streams of Egypt.'

26"Have you not heard?
Long ago I ordained it.
In days of old I planned it;
now I have brought it to pass,
that you have turned fortified cities
into piles of stone.
27Their people, drained of power,
are dismayed and put to shame.
They are like plants in the field,
like tender green shoots,
like grass sprouting on the roof,
scorched[b] before it grows up.

28"But I know where you stay
and when you come and go
and how you rage against me.
29Because you rage against me
and because your insolence has reached my ears,
I will put my hook in your nose
and my bit in your mouth,
and I will make you return
by the way you came.

30"This will be the sign for you, O Hezekiah:

"This year you will eat what grows by itself,
and the second year what springs from that.
But in the third year sow and reap,
plant vineyards and eat their fruit.
31Once more a remnant of the house of Judah
will take root below and bear fruit above.
32For out of Jerusalem will come a remnant,
and out of Mount Zion a band of survivors.
The zeal of the LORD Almighty
will accomplish this.

33"Therefore this is what the LORD says concerning the king of Assyria:

"He will not enter this city
or shoot an arrow here.
He will not come before it with shield
or build a siege ramp against it.
34By the way that he came he will return;
he will not enter this city,"
declares the LORD.
35"I will defend this city and save it,
for my sake and for the sake of David my servant!"

36Then the angel of the LORD went out and put to death a hundred and eighty-five thousand men in the Assyrian camp. When the people got up the next morning—there were all the dead bodies! 37So Sennacherib king of Assyria broke camp and withdrew. He returned to Nineveh and stayed there.

38One day, while he was worshiping in the temple of his god Nisroch, his sons Adrammelech and Sharezer cut him down with the sword, and they escaped to the land of Ararat. And Esarhaddon his son succeeded him as king.

Hezekiah's Illness

38 In those days Hezekiah became ill and was at the point of death. The prophet Isaiah son of Amoz went to him and said, "This is what the LORD says: Put your house in order, because you are going to die; you will not recover."

2Hezekiah turned his face to the wall and prayed to the LORD, 3"Remember, O LORD, how I have walked before you faithfully and with wholehearted devotion and have done what is good in your eyes." And Hezekiah wept bitterly.

4Then the word of the LORD came to Isaiah: 5"Go and tell Hezekiah, 'This is what the LORD, the God of your father David, says: I have heard your prayer and seen your tears; I will add fifteen years to your life. 6And I will deliver you and this city from the hand of the king of Assyria. I will defend this city.

7" 'This is the LORD's sign to you that the LORD will do what he has promised: 8I will make the shadow cast by the sun go back the ten steps it has gone down on the

[a]25 Dead Sea Scrolls (see also 2 Kings 19:24); Masoretic Text does not have *in foreign lands.*
[b]27 Some manuscripts of the Masoretic Text, Dead Sea Scrolls and some Septuagint manuscripts (see also 2 Kings 19:26); most manuscripts of the Masoretic Text *roof / and terraced fields*

stairway of Ahaz.' " So the sunlight went back the ten steps it had gone down.

9A writing of Hezekiah king of Judah after his illness and recovery:

10I said, "In the prime of my life
must I go through the gates of death[a]
and be robbed of the rest of my years?"
11I said, "I will not again see the LORD,
the LORD, in the land of the living;
no longer will I look on mankind,
or be with those who now dwell in this world.[b]
12Like a shepherd's tent my house
has been pulled down and taken from me.
Like a weaver I have rolled up my life,
and he has cut me off from the loom;
day and night you made an end of me.
13I waited patiently till dawn,
but like a lion he broke all my bones;
day and night you made an end of me.
14I cried like a swift or thrush,
I moaned like a mourning dove.
My eyes grew weak as I looked to the heavens.
I am troubled; O Lord, come to my aid!"

15But what can I say?
He has spoken to me, and he himself has done this.
I will walk humbly all my years
because of this anguish of my soul.
16Lord, by such things men live;
and my spirit finds life in them too.
You restored me to health
and let me live.
17Surely it was for my benefit
that I suffered such anguish.
In your love you kept me
from the pit of destruction;
you have put all my sins
behind your back.
18For the grave[a] cannot praise you,
death cannot sing your praise;
those who go down to the pit
cannot hope for your faithfulness.
19The living, the living—they praise you,
as I am doing today;
fathers tell their children
about your faithfulness.

20The LORD will save me,
and we will sing with stringed instruments
all the days of our lives
in the temple of the LORD.

21Isaiah had said, "Prepare a poultice of figs and apply it to the boil, and he will recover."

22Hezekiah had asked, "What will be the sign that I will go up to the temple of the LORD?"

Envoys From Babylon

39 At that time Merodach-Baladan son of Baladan king of Babylon sent Hezekiah letters and a gift, because he had heard of his illness and recovery. 2Hezekiah received the envoys gladly and showed them what was in his storehouses—the silver, the gold, the spices, the fine oil, his entire armory and everything found among his treasures. There was nothing in his palace or in all his kingdom that Hezekiah did not show them.

3Then Isaiah the prophet went to King Hezekiah and asked, "What did those men say, and where did they come from?"

"From a distant land," Hezekiah replied. "They came to me from Babylon."

4The prophet asked, "What did they see in your palace?"

"They saw everything in my palace," Hezekiah said. "There is nothing among my treasures that I did not show them."

5Then Isaiah said to Hezekiah, "Hear the word of the LORD Almighty: 6The time will surely come when everything in your palace, and all that your fathers have stored up until this day, will be carried off to Babylon. Nothing will be left, says the LORD. 7And some of your descendants, your own flesh and blood who will be born to you, will be taken away, and they will become eunuchs in the palace of the king of Babylon."

8"The word of the LORD you have spoken is good," Hezekiah replied. For he thought, "There will be peace and security in my lifetime."

[a] *10,18* Hebrew *Sheol* [b] *11* A few Hebrew manuscripts; most Hebrew manuscripts *in the place of cessation*

Comfort for God's People

40 Comfort, comfort my people,
says your God.
[2]Speak tenderly to Jerusalem,
and proclaim to her
that her hard service has been
completed,
that her sin has been paid for,
that she has received from the LORD's
hand
double for all her sins.
[3]A voice of one calling:
"In the desert prepare
the way for the LORD[a];
make straight in the wilderness
a highway for our God.[b]
[4]Every valley shall be raised up,
every mountain and hill made low;
the rough ground shall become level,
the rugged places a plain.

[a]3 Or *A voice of one calling in the desert: / "Prepare the way for the LORD*
[b]3 Hebrew; Septuagint *make straight the paths of our God*

VERSE FOR THE DAY: Isaiah 40:31 | AUTHOR: Les and Leslie Parrott | PASSAGE FOR THE DAY: Isaiah 40:25–31

The Lord Will Carry You

What is it that makes couples happy? You'll be surprised to find out what it's not! Money, success, health, beauty, intelligence or power have little to do with a couple's subjective feelings of well-being. Research has shown that the level of a couple's joy is determined by each partner's ability to *adjust to things beyond his or her control.* Happy couples learn to find the right attitude in spite of the conditions they're in.

When trials come your way, you have a choice. You can throw up your hands in frustration, give in to self-pity and become mired in resentment and defeat. Or you can raise your hands to God in prayer, search out alternatives, move ahead and ultimately trust the Lord to carry you through.

If your hearts are heavy, do what you can to meet one another's needs. Then rely on God to get you through your beyond-belief ordeal. Your capacity to adjust to undesirable circumstances is the real secret to building the happy marriage that you both desire.

MARRIAGE BUILDERS

- *What big difficulties have you already encountered as a couple?*
- *When you reached the end of your own ability to "fix" the situation, were you able to rely on God?*

Additional Scripture Readings
2 Corinthians 4:16–18; Hebrews 12:1–3

Go to page 763 for your next devotional reading.

5And the glory of the LORD will be
revealed,
and all mankind together will see it.
For the mouth of the LORD
has spoken."

6A voice says, "Cry out."
And I said, "What shall I cry?"

"All men are like grass,
and all their glory is like the flowers
of the field.
7The grass withers and the flowers fall,
because the breath of the LORD
blows on them.
Surely the people are grass.
8The grass withers and the flowers fall,
but the word of our God stands
forever."

9You who bring good tidings to Zion,
go up on a high mountain.
You who bring good tidings to
Jerusalem,[a]
lift up your voice with a shout,
lift it up, do not be afraid;
say to the towns of Judah,
"Here is your God!"
10See, the Sovereign LORD comes with
power,
and his arm rules for him.
See, his reward is with him,
and his recompense accompanies
him.
11He tends his flock like a shepherd:
He gathers the lambs in his arms
and carries them close to his heart;
he gently leads those that have
young.

12Who has measured the waters in the
hollow of his hand,
or with the breadth of his hand
marked off the heavens?
Who has held the dust of the earth in
a basket,
or weighed the mountains on the
scales
and the hills in a balance?
13Who has understood the mind[b] of
the LORD,
or instructed him as his counselor?
14Whom did the LORD consult to
enlighten him,
and who taught him the right way?
Who was it that taught him
knowledge
or showed him the path of
understanding?

15Surely the nations are like a drop in a
bucket;
they are regarded as dust on the
scales;
he weighs the islands as though
they were fine dust.
16Lebanon is not sufficient for altar
fires,
nor its animals enough for burnt
offerings.
17Before him all the nations are as
nothing;
they are regarded by him as
worthless
and less than nothing.

18To whom, then, will you compare
God?
What image will you compare him
to?
19As for an idol, a craftsman casts it,
and a goldsmith overlays it with
gold
and fashions silver chains for it.
20A man too poor to present such an
offering
selects wood that will not rot.
He looks for a skilled craftsman
to set up an idol that will not
topple.

21Do you not know?
Have you not heard?
Has it not been told you from the
beginning?
Have you not understood since the
earth was founded?
22He sits enthroned above the circle of
the earth,
and its people are like grasshoppers.
He stretches out the heavens like a
canopy,
and spreads them out like a tent to
live in.
23He brings princes to naught
and reduces the rulers of this world
to nothing.
24No sooner are they planted,
no sooner are they sown,
no sooner do they take root in the
ground,
than he blows on them and they
wither,

[a]9 Or *O Zion, bringer of good tidings, / go up on a high mountain. / O Jerusalem, bringer of good tidings*
[b]13 Or *Spirit*; or *spirit*

and a whirlwind sweeps them away
like chaff.

25"To whom will you compare me?
Or who is my equal?" says the Holy
One.
26Lift your eyes and look to the
heavens:
Who created all these?
He who brings out the starry host one
by one,
and calls them each by name.
Because of his great power and
mighty strength,
not one of them is missing.

27Why do you say, O Jacob,
and complain, O Israel,
"My way is hidden from the LORD;
my cause is disregarded by my
God"?
28Do you not know?
Have you not heard?
The LORD is the everlasting God,
the Creator of the ends of the earth.
He will not grow tired or weary,
and his understanding no one can
fathom.
29He gives strength to the weary
and increases the power of the
weak.
30Even youths grow tired and weary,
and young men stumble and fall;
31but those who hope in the LORD
will renew their strength.
They will soar on wings like eagles;
they will run and not grow weary,
they will walk and not be faint.

The Helper of Israel

41 "Be silent before me, you islands!
Let the nations renew their
strength!
Let them come forward and speak;
let us meet together at the place of
judgment.

2"Who has stirred up one from the
east,
calling him in righteousness to his
service[a]?
He hands nations over to him
and subdues kings before him.
He turns them to dust with his sword,
to windblown chaff with his bow.
3He pursues them and moves on
unscathed,
by a path his feet have not traveled
before.
4Who has done this and carried it
through,
calling forth the generations from
the beginning?
I, the LORD—with the first of them
and with the last—I am he."

5The islands have seen it and fear;
the ends of the earth tremble.
They approach and come forward;
6 each helps the other
and says to his brother, "Be strong!"
7The craftsman encourages the
goldsmith,
and he who smooths with the
hammer
spurs on him who strikes the anvil.
He says of the welding, "It is good."
He nails down the idol so it will not
topple.

8"But you, O Israel, my servant,
Jacob, whom I have chosen,
you descendants of Abraham my
friend,
9I took you from the ends of the earth,
from its farthest corners I called
you.
I said, 'You are my servant';
I have chosen you and have not
rejected you.
10So do not fear, for I am with you;
do not be dismayed, for I am your
God.
I will strengthen you and help you;
I will uphold you with my righteous
right hand.

11"All who rage against you
will surely be ashamed and
disgraced;
those who oppose you
will be as nothing and perish.
12Though you search for your enemies,
you will not find them.
Those who wage war against you
will be as nothing at all.
13For I am the LORD, your God,
who takes hold of your right hand
and says to you, Do not fear;
I will help you.
14Do not be afraid, O worm Jacob,
O little Israel,
for I myself will help you," declares
the LORD,

[a]2 Or / *whom victory meets at every step*

your Redeemer, the Holy One of
Israel.
15"See, I will make you into a threshing
sledge,
new and sharp, with many teeth.
You will thresh the mountains and
crush them,
and reduce the hills to chaff.
16You will winnow them, the wind will
pick them up,
and a gale will blow them away.
But you will rejoice in the LORD
and glory in the Holy One of Israel.
17"The poor and needy search for
water,
but there is none;
their tongues are parched with
thirst.
But I the LORD will answer them;
I, the God of Israel, will not forsake
them.
18I will make rivers flow on barren
heights,
and springs within the valleys.
I will turn the desert into pools of
water,

VERSE FOR THE DAY: Isaiah 41:10

AUTHOR: Betsey Glavach

PASSAGE FOR THE DAY: Isaiah 41:10–20

God Provides

My husband, Vic, had been out of work for more than a year, and I had begun questioning beliefs about God that I had held since childhood. What if none of it was true? But when I moved beyond the negative emotions and could see things rationally, I found it was easier to believe in a creative, loving God than it was to discard my beliefs. And I was able to look back and see God's care, his provision and his timing in so many of the things that happened during our long ordeal.

Several weeks after Vic received his last regular paycheck, he got a short-term consulting job that carried us over Christmas and into the next year. And shortly after that, a friend from church offered Vic a job installing locks. So in the eighteen months that Vic searched for a job, there were less than four months when he didn't have *some* source of income. It wasn't as much money as he was making before, but there was always just enough to pay each week's bills.

God's provision for us when we needed it most was clear proof of his care for us, and it erased my doubts.

MARRIAGE BUILDERS

♦ *When have you seen God provide for your physical needs like food and clothing and housing?*

♦ *How did those times serve to strengthen your faith for the future?*

Additional Scripture Readings
Psalm 11:1–4; 1 Timothy 6:17

Go to page 766 for your next devotional reading.

and the parched ground into
springs.
19 I will put in the desert
the cedar and the acacia, the myrtle
and the olive.
I will set pines in the wasteland,
the fir and the cypress together,
20 so that people may see and know,
may consider and understand,
that the hand of the LORD has done
this,
that the Holy One of Israel has
created it.

21 "Present your case," says the LORD.
"Set forth your arguments," says
Jacob's King.
22 "Bring in ⌊your idols⌋ to tell us
what is going to happen.
Tell us what the former things were,
so that we may consider them
and know their final outcome.
Or declare to us the things to come,
23 tell us what the future holds,
so we may know that you are gods.
Do something, whether good or bad,
so that we will be dismayed and
filled with fear.
24 But you are less than nothing
and your works are utterly
worthless;
he who chooses you is detestable.

25 "I have stirred up one from the north,
and he comes—
one from the rising sun who calls
on my name.
He treads on rulers as if they were
mortar,
as if he were a potter treading the
clay.
26 Who told of this from the beginning,
so we could know,
or beforehand, so we could say, 'He
was right'?
No one told of this,
no one foretold it,
no one heard any words from you.
27 I was the first to tell Zion, 'Look, here
they are!'
I gave to Jerusalem a messenger of
good tidings.
28 I look but there is no one—
no one among them to give counsel,
no one to give answer when I ask
them.
29 See, they are all false!
Their deeds amount to nothing;
their images are but wind and
confusion.

The Servant of the LORD

42 "Here is my servant, whom I
uphold,
my chosen one in whom I delight;
I will put my Spirit on him
and he will bring justice to the
nations.
2 He will not shout or cry out,
or raise his voice in the streets.
3 A bruised reed he will not break,
and a smoldering wick he will not
snuff out.
In faithfulness he will bring forth
justice;
4 he will not falter or be discouraged
till he establishes justice on earth.
In his law the islands will put their
hope."

5 This is what God the LORD says—
he who created the heavens and
stretched them out,
who spread out the earth and all
that comes out of it,
who gives breath to its people,
and life to those who walk on it:
6 "I, the LORD, have called you in
righteousness;
I will take hold of your hand.
I will keep you and will make you
to be a covenant for the people
and a light for the Gentiles,
7 to open eyes that are blind,
to free captives from prison
and to release from the dungeon
those who sit in darkness.

8 "I am the LORD; that is my name!
I will not give my glory to another
or my praise to idols.
9 See, the former things have taken
place,
and new things I declare;
before they spring into being
I announce them to you."

Song of Praise to the LORD

10 Sing to the LORD a new song,
his praise from the ends of the
earth,
you who go down to the sea, and all
that is in it,
you islands, and all who live in
them.
11 Let the desert and its towns raise their
voices;
let the settlements where Kedar
lives rejoice.
Let the people of Sela sing for joy;

let them shout from the
mountaintops.
12Let them give glory to the LORD
and proclaim his praise in the
islands.
13The LORD will march out like a mighty
man,
like a warrior he will stir up his
zeal;
with a shout he will raise the battle
cry
and will triumph over his enemies.

14"For a long time I have kept silent,
I have been quiet and held myself
back.
But now, like a woman in childbirth,
I cry out, I gasp and pant.
15I will lay waste the mountains and
hills
and dry up all their vegetation;
I will turn rivers into islands
and dry up the pools.
16I will lead the blind by ways they
have not known,
along unfamiliar paths I will guide
them;
I will turn the darkness into light
before them
and make the rough places smooth.
These are the things I will do;
I will not forsake them.
17But those who trust in idols,
who say to images, 'You are our
gods,'
will be turned back in utter shame.

Israel Blind and Deaf

18"Hear, you deaf;
look, you blind, and see!
19Who is blind but my servant,
and deaf like the messenger I send?
Who is blind like the one committed
to me,
blind like the servant of the LORD?
20You have seen many things, but have
paid no attention;
your ears are open, but you hear
nothing."
21It pleased the LORD
for the sake of his righteousness
to make his law great and glorious.
22But this is a people plundered and
looted,
all of them trapped in pits
or hidden away in prisons.
They have become plunder,
with no one to rescue them;
they have been made loot,
with no one to say, "Send them
back."

23Which of you will listen to this
or pay close attention in time to
come?
24Who handed Jacob over to become
loot,
and Israel to the plunderers?
Was it not the LORD,
against whom we have sinned?
For they would not follow his ways;
they did not obey his law.
25So he poured out on them his burning
anger,
the violence of war.
It enveloped them in flames, yet they
did not understand;
it consumed them, but they did not
take it to heart.

Israel's Only Savior

43 But now, this is what the LORD
says—
he who created you, O Jacob,
he who formed you, O Israel:
"Fear not, for I have redeemed you;
I have summoned you by name;
you are mine.
2When you pass through the waters,
I will be with you;
and when you pass through the rivers,
they will not sweep over you.
When you walk through the fire,
you will not be burned;
the flames will not set you ablaze.
3For I am the LORD, your God,
the Holy One of Israel, your Savior;
I give Egypt for your ransom,
Cush[a] and Seba in your stead.
4Since you are precious and honored in
my sight,
and because I love you,
I will give men in exchange for you,
and people in exchange for your
life.
5Do not be afraid, for I am with you;
I will bring your children from the
east
and gather you from the west.
6I will say to the north, 'Give them up!'
and to the south, 'Do not hold them
back.'
Bring my sons from afar

[a]3 That is, the upper Nile region

and my daughters from the ends of
the earth—
7everyone who is called by my name,
whom I created for my glory,
whom I formed and made."

8Lead out those who have eyes but are
blind,
who have ears but are deaf.
9All the nations gather together
and the peoples assemble.
Which of them foretold this
and proclaimed to us the former
things?
Let them bring in their witnesses to
prove they were right,
so that others may hear and say, "It
is true."

VERSE FOR THE DAY: Isaiah 43:2 | AUTHOR: Diane Eble | PASSAGE FOR THE DAY: Isaiah 43:1–13

God Will Be There

I know of a couple who took their toddler to the doctor for what appeared to be a virus. An examination revealed a heart condition requiring surgery. After surgery, the child died. One day a virus, the next day surgery, and then she was gone. Another true story: A man went into his attic to repair some wiring. When his wife returned home, she found him electrocuted.

These are people of faith, and their faith hasn't spared them the agonies of a world shot through with tragedy. I asked my husband, "How do you face the possibility of something terrible happening to us?" His answer: "The only way is to tell myself I won't go through it alone."

Faith tells us that God will be with us no matter what happens. Isaiah 43:2: "When you pass through the waters, I will be with you; and when you pass through the rivers, they will not sweep over you. When you walk through the fire, you will not be burned; the flames will not set you ablaze." Not *if* you pass through the waters. It's *when* you pass through the waters, the rivers, the fire.

It's unhealthy to dwell on what *might* happen before it does. Whenever that voice whispers, "What would you do if . . . ?", we can remind ourselves that God will be there.

MARRIAGE BUILDERS

♦ *What kinds of "deep water" or "fire" have you already navigated successfully, with God's help?*

♦ *How was God's presence real and comforting to you in those times?*

Additional Scripture Readings
2 Corinthians 4:16–17; Revelation 7:17

Go to page 771 for your next devotional reading.

10"You are my witnesses," declares the LORD,
"and my servant whom I have chosen,
so that you may know and believe me
and understand that I am he.
Before me no god was formed,
nor will there be one after me.
11I, even I, am the LORD,
and apart from me there is no savior.
12I have revealed and saved and proclaimed—
I, and not some foreign god among you.
You are my witnesses," declares the LORD, "that I am God.
13 Yes, and from ancient days I am he.
No one can deliver out of my hand.
When I act, who can reverse it?"

God's Mercy and Israel's Unfaithfulness

14This is what the LORD says—
your Redeemer, the Holy One of Israel:
"For your sake I will send to Babylon
and bring down as fugitives all the Babylonians,[a]
in the ships in which they took pride.
15I am the LORD, your Holy One,
Israel's Creator, your King."

16This is what the LORD says—
he who made a way through the sea,
a path through the mighty waters,
17who drew out the chariots and horses,
the army and reinforcements together,
and they lay there, never to rise again,
extinguished, snuffed out like a wick:
18"Forget the former things;
do not dwell on the past.
19See, I am doing a new thing!
Now it springs up; do you not perceive it?
I am making a way in the desert
and streams in the wasteland.
20The wild animals honor me,
the jackals and the owls,
because I provide water in the desert
and streams in the wasteland,
to give drink to my people, my chosen,
21 the people I formed for myself
that they may proclaim my praise.

22"Yet you have not called upon me, O Jacob,
you have not wearied yourselves for me, O Israel.
23You have not brought me sheep for burnt offerings,
nor honored me with your sacrifices.
I have not burdened you with grain offerings
nor wearied you with demands for incense.
24You have not bought any fragrant calamus for me,
or lavished on me the fat of your sacrifices.
But you have burdened me with your sins
and wearied me with your offenses.

25"I, even I, am he who blots out
your transgressions, for my own sake,
and remembers your sins no more.
26Review the past for me,
let us argue the matter together;
state the case for your innocence.
27Your first father sinned;
your spokesmen rebelled against me.
28So I will disgrace the dignitaries of your temple,
and I will consign Jacob to destruction[b]
and Israel to scorn.

Israel the Chosen

44 "But now listen, O Jacob, my servant,
Israel, whom I have chosen.
2This is what the LORD says—
he who made you, who formed you in the womb,
and who will help you:
Do not be afraid, O Jacob, my servant,
Jeshurun, whom I have chosen.
3For I will pour water on the thirsty land,
and streams on the dry ground;
I will pour out my Spirit on your offspring,

[a]14 Or *Chaldeans* [b]28 The Hebrew term refers to the irrevocable giving over of things or persons to the LORD, often by totally destroying them.

and my blessing on your
descendants.
4 They will spring up like grass in a
meadow,
like poplar trees by flowing streams.
5 One will say, 'I belong to the LORD';
another will call himself by the
name of Jacob;
still another will write on his hand,
'The LORD's,'
and will take the name Israel.

The LORD, Not Idols

6 "This is what the LORD says—
Israel's King and Redeemer, the
LORD Almighty:
I am the first and I am the last;
apart from me there is no God.
7 Who then is like me? Let him
proclaim it.
Let him declare and lay out before
me
what has happened since I established
my ancient people,
and what is yet to come—
yes, let him foretell what will come.
8 Do not tremble, do not be afraid.
Did I not proclaim this and foretell
it long ago?
You are my witnesses. Is there any
God besides me?
No, there is no other Rock; I know
not one."
9 All who make idols are nothing,
and the things they treasure are
worthless.
Those who would speak up for them
are blind;
they are ignorant, to their own
shame.
10 Who shapes a god and casts an idol,
which can profit him nothing?
11 He and his kind will be put to shame;
craftsmen are nothing but men.
Let them all come together and take
their stand;
they will be brought down to terror
and infamy.

12 The blacksmith takes a tool
and works with it in the coals;
he shapes an idol with hammers,
he forges it with the might of his
arm.
He gets hungry and loses his strength;
he drinks no water and grows faint.
13 The carpenter measures with a line
and makes an outline with a
marker;
he roughs it out with chisels
and marks it with compasses.
He shapes it in the form of man,
of man in all his glory,
that it may dwell in a shrine.
14 He cut down cedars,
or perhaps took a cypress or oak.
He let it grow among the trees of the
forest,
or planted a pine, and the rain
made it grow.
15 It is man's fuel for burning;
some of it he takes and warms
himself,
he kindles a fire and bakes bread.
But he also fashions a god and
worships it;
he makes an idol and bows down to
it.
16 Half of the wood he burns in the fire;
over it he prepares his meal,
he roasts his meat and eats his fill.
He also warms himself and says,
"Ah! I am warm; I see the fire."
17 From the rest he makes a god, his
idol;
he bows down to it and worships.
He prays to it and says,
"Save me; you are my god."
18 They know nothing, they understand
nothing;
their eyes are plastered over so they
cannot see,
and their minds closed so they
cannot understand.
19 No one stops to think,
no one has the knowledge or
understanding to say,
"Half of it I used for fuel;
I even baked bread over its coals,
I roasted meat and I ate.
Shall I make a detestable thing from
what is left?
Shall I bow down to a block of
wood?"
20 He feeds on ashes, a deluded heart
misleads him;
he cannot save himself, or say,
"Is not this thing in my right hand a
lie?"

21 "Remember these things, O Jacob,
for you are my servant, O Israel.
I have made you, you are my servant;
O Israel, I will not forget you.
22 I have swept away your offenses like a
cloud,
your sins like the morning mist.
Return to me,

for I have redeemed you."

23 Sing for joy, O heavens, for the LORD
has done this;
shout aloud, O earth beneath.
Burst into song, you mountains,
you forests and all your trees,
for the LORD has redeemed Jacob,
he displays his glory in Israel.

Jerusalem to Be Inhabited

24 "This is what the LORD says—
your Redeemer, who formed you in the womb:

I am the LORD,
who has made all things,
who alone stretched out the heavens,
who spread out the earth by myself,

25 who foils the signs of false prophets
and makes fools of diviners,
who overthrows the learning of the wise
and turns it into nonsense,
26 who carries out the words of his servants
and fulfills the predictions of his messengers,

who says of Jerusalem, 'It shall be inhabited,'
of the towns of Judah, 'They shall be built,'
and of their ruins, 'I will restore them,'
27 who says to the watery deep, 'Be dry,
and I will dry up your streams,'
28 who says of Cyrus, 'He is my shepherd
and will accomplish all that I please;
he will say of Jerusalem, "Let it be rebuilt,"
and of the temple, "Let its foundations be laid."'

45 "This is what the LORD says to his anointed,
to Cyrus, whose right hand I take hold of
to subdue nations before him
and to strip kings of their armor,
to open doors before him
so that gates will not be shut:
2 I will go before you
and will level the mountains[a];
I will break down gates of bronze
and cut through bars of iron.
3 I will give you the treasures of darkness,
riches stored in secret places,
so that you may know that I am the LORD,
the God of Israel, who summons you by name.
4 For the sake of Jacob my servant,
of Israel my chosen,
I summon you by name
and bestow on you a title of honor,
though you do not acknowledge me.
5 I am the LORD, and there is no other;
apart from me there is no God.
I will strengthen you,
though you have not acknowledged me,
6 so that from the rising of the sun
to the place of its setting
men may know there is none besides me.
I am the LORD, and there is no other.
7 I form the light and create darkness,
I bring prosperity and create disaster;
I, the LORD, do all these things.

8 "You heavens above, rain down righteousness;
let the clouds shower it down.
Let the earth open wide,
let salvation spring up,
let righteousness grow with it;
I, the LORD, have created it.

9 "Woe to him who quarrels with his Maker,
to him who is but a potsherd among the potsherds on the ground.
Does the clay say to the potter,
'What are you making?'
Does your work say,
'He has no hands'?
10 Woe to him who says to his father,
'What have you begotten?'
or to his mother,
'What have you brought to birth?'

11 "This is what the LORD says—
the Holy One of Israel, and its Maker:
Concerning things to come,
do you question me about my children,
or give me orders about the work of my hands?

[a] 2 Dead Sea Scrolls and Septuagint; the meaning of the word in the Masoretic Text is uncertain.

12It is I who made the earth
and created mankind upon it.
My own hands stretched out the heavens;
I marshaled their starry hosts.
13I will raise up Cyrus[a] in my righteousness:
I will make all his ways straight.
He will rebuild my city
and set my exiles free,
but not for a price or reward,
says the LORD Almighty."

14This is what the LORD says:

"The products of Egypt and the merchandise of Cush,[b]
and those tall Sabeans—
they will come over to you
and will be yours;
they will trudge behind you,
coming over to you in chains.
They will bow down before you
and plead with you, saying,
'Surely God is with you, and there is no other;
there is no other god.' "

15Truly you are a God who hides himself,
O God and Savior of Israel.
16All the makers of idols will be put to shame and disgraced;
they will go off into disgrace together.
17But Israel will be saved by the LORD
with an everlasting salvation;
you will never be put to shame or disgraced,
to ages everlasting.

18For this is what the LORD says—
he who created the heavens,
he is God;
he who fashioned and made the earth,
he founded it;
he did not create it to be empty,
but formed it to be inhabited—
he says:
"I am the LORD,
and there is no other.
19I have not spoken in secret,
from somewhere in a land of darkness;
I have not said to Jacob's descendants,
'Seek me in vain.'
I, the LORD, speak the truth;
I declare what is right.

20"Gather together and come;
assemble, you fugitives from the nations.
Ignorant are those who carry about idols of wood,
who pray to gods that cannot save.
21Declare what is to be, present it—
let them take counsel together.
Who foretold this long ago,
who declared it from the distant past?
Was it not I, the LORD?
And there is no God apart from me,
a righteous God and a Savior;
there is none but me.

22"Turn to me and be saved,
all you ends of the earth;
for I am God, and there is no other.
23By myself I have sworn,
my mouth has uttered in all integrity
a word that will not be revoked:
Before me every knee will bow;
by me every tongue will swear.
24They will say of me, 'In the LORD alone
are righteousness and strength.' "
All who have raged against him
will come to him and be put to shame.
25But in the LORD all the descendants of Israel
will be found righteous and will exult.

Gods of Babylon

46 Bel bows down, Nebo stoops low;
their idols are borne by beasts of burden.[c]
The images that are carried about are burdensome,
a burden for the weary.
2They stoop and bow down together;
unable to rescue the burden,
they themselves go off into captivity.

3"Listen to me, O house of Jacob,
all you who remain of the house of Israel,
you whom I have upheld since you were conceived,
and have carried since your birth.
4Even to your old age and gray hairs
I am he, I am he who will sustain you.

[a] *13* Hebrew *him* [b] *14* That is, the upper Nile region [c] *1* Or *are but beasts and cattle*

VERSE FOR THE DAY: Isaiah 46:4

AUTHOR: Les and Leslie Parrott

PASSAGE FOR THE DAY: Isaiah 46:1–13

Start to Finish

The frequent expressions of affection and approval that couples give each other during courtship and in the honeymoon stage can dwindle in the first years of marriage. You may still love each other just as much, but you start to talk about it less.

Contrary to the fairy tales we were weaned on, romance always fades. But you can keep your romantic love alive long after the honeymoon has ended. The secret is simple: Do everything you can now to establish lasting habits of loving behavior.

The habits you develop now can lead either to actions that will nurture lifelong love or to behaviors that will sabotage your love. The little things you do now—without thinking—will shape your relationship for years to come. So pay attention to those little things.

We tend to think about romance on a grand scale—such as the perfect, once-a-year getaway—and neglect the little opportunities that present themselves every day. Consider how you greet one another after work, or how well you incorporate common courtesies like saying "please" and "thank you." Be sure to maintain a dating habit, too, to keep your marriage from falling into the doldrums of working all week and coming home to collapse on the weekends.

Keep love alive—starting now—by establishing daily habits of romance, passion and intimacy. Your honeymoon will become more than just a memory. It will become a way of life.

MARRIAGE BUILDERS

♦ *Which of your spouse's everyday behaviors seem "romantic" to you?*

♦ *What are one or two "common courtesies" that you could put back into your relationship, starting this week?*

Additional Scripture Readings
Proverbs 3:3–23; Matthew 25:14–30

Go to page 779 for your next devotional reading.

I have made you and I will carry you;
I will sustain you and I will rescue you.

5"To whom will you compare me or count me equal?
To whom will you liken me that we may be compared?
6Some pour out gold from their bags
and weigh out silver on the scales;
they hire a goldsmith to make it into a god,
and they bow down and worship it.
7They lift it to their shoulders and carry it;
they set it up in its place, and there it stands.
From that spot it cannot move.
Though one cries out to it, it does not answer;
it cannot save him from his troubles.

8"Remember this, fix it in mind,
take it to heart, you rebels.
9Remember the former things, those of long ago;
I am God, and there is no other;
I am God, and there is none like me.
10I make known the end from the beginning,
from ancient times, what is still to come.
I say: My purpose will stand,
and I will do all that I please.
11From the east I summon a bird of prey;
from a far-off land, a man to fulfill my purpose.
What I have said, that will I bring about;
what I have planned, that will I do.
12Listen to me, you stubborn-hearted,
you who are far from righteousness.
13I am bringing my righteousness near,
it is not far away;
and my salvation will not be delayed.
I will grant salvation to Zion,
my splendor to Israel.

The Fall of Babylon

47 "Go down, sit in the dust,
Virgin Daughter of Babylon;
sit on the ground without a throne,
Daughter of the Babylonians.[a]
No more will you be called
tender or delicate.
2Take millstones and grind flour;
take off your veil.
Lift up your skirts, bare your legs,
and wade through the streams.
3Your nakedness will be exposed
and your shame uncovered.
I will take vengeance;
I will spare no one."

4Our Redeemer—the LORD Almighty is his name—
is the Holy One of Israel.

5"Sit in silence, go into darkness,
Daughter of the Babylonians;
no more will you be called
queen of kingdoms.
6I was angry with my people
and desecrated my inheritance;
I gave them into your hand,
and you showed them no mercy.
Even on the aged
you laid a very heavy yoke.
7You said, 'I will continue forever—
the eternal queen!'
But you did not consider these things
or reflect on what might happen.

8"Now then, listen, you wanton creature,
lounging in your security
and saying to yourself,
'I am, and there is none besides me.
I will never be a widow
or suffer the loss of children.'
9Both of these will overtake you
in a moment, on a single day:
loss of children and widowhood.
They will come upon you in full measure,
in spite of your many sorceries
and all your potent spells.
10You have trusted in your wickedness
and have said, 'No one sees me.'
Your wisdom and knowledge mislead you
when you say to yourself,
'I am, and there is none besides me.'
11Disaster will come upon you,
and you will not know how to conjure it away.
A calamity will fall upon you
that you cannot ward off with a ransom;
a catastrophe you cannot foresee
will suddenly come upon you.

[a] 1 Or *Chaldeans*; also in verse 5

12"Keep on, then, with your magic spells
and with your many sorceries,
which you have labored at since
childhood.
Perhaps you will succeed,
perhaps you will cause terror.
13All the counsel you have received has
only worn you out!
Let your astrologers come forward,
those stargazers who make predictions
month by month,
let them save you from what is
coming upon you.
14Surely they are like stubble;
the fire will burn them up.
They cannot even save themselves
from the power of the flame.
Here are no coals to warm anyone;
here is no fire to sit by.
15That is all they can do for you—
these you have labored with
and trafficked with since childhood.
Each of them goes on in his error;
there is not one that can save you.

Stubborn Israel

48 "Listen to this, O house of Jacob,
you who are called by the name
of Israel
and come from the line of Judah,
you who take oaths in the name of
the LORD
and invoke the God of Israel—
but not in truth or righteousness—
2you who call yourselves citizens of
the holy city
and rely on the God of Israel—
the LORD Almighty is his name:
3I foretold the former things long ago,
my mouth announced them and I
made them known;
then suddenly I acted, and they
came to pass.
4For I knew how stubborn you were;
the sinews of your neck were iron,
your forehead was bronze.
5Therefore I told you these things long
ago;
before they happened I announced
them to you
so that you could not say,
'My idols did them;
my wooden image and metal god
ordained them.'
6You have heard these things; look at
them all.
Will you not admit them?
"From now on I will tell you of new
things,
of hidden things unknown to you.
7They are created now, and not long
ago;
you have not heard of them before
today.
So you cannot say,
'Yes, I knew of them.'
8You have neither heard nor
understood;
from of old your ear has not been
open.
Well do I know how treacherous you
are;
you were called a rebel from birth.
9For my own name's sake I delay my
wrath;
for the sake of my praise I hold it
back from you,
so as not to cut you off.
10See, I have refined you, though not as
silver;
I have tested you in the furnace of
affliction.
11For my own sake, for my own sake, I
do this.
How can I let myself be defamed?
I will not yield my glory to another.

Israel Freed

12"Listen to me, O Jacob,
Israel, whom I have called:
I am he;
I am the first and I am the last.
13My own hand laid the foundations of
the earth,
and my right hand spread out the
heavens;
when I summon them,
they all stand up together.

14"Come together, all of you, and listen:
Which of ⌊the idols⌋ has foretold
these things?
The LORD's chosen ally
will carry out his purpose against
Babylon;
his arm will be against the
Babylonians.[a]
15I, even I, have spoken;
yes, I have called him.
I will bring him,
and he will succeed in his mission.

16"Come near me and listen to this:

[a]14 Or *Chaldeans*; also in verse 20

"From the first announcement I have not spoken in secret;
at the time it happens, I am there."

And now the Sovereign LORD has sent me,
with his Spirit.

17This is what the LORD says—
your Redeemer, the Holy One of Israel:
"I am the LORD your God,
who teaches you what is best for you,
who directs you in the way you should go.
18If only you had paid attention to my commands,
your peace would have been like a river,
your righteousness like the waves of the sea.
19Your descendants would have been like the sand,
your children like its numberless grains;
their name would never be cut off nor destroyed from before me."

20Leave Babylon,
flee from the Babylonians!
Announce this with shouts of joy and proclaim it.
Send it out to the ends of the earth;
say, "The LORD has redeemed his servant Jacob."
21They did not thirst when he led them through the deserts;
he made water flow for them from the rock;
he split the rock and water gushed out.

22"There is no peace," says the LORD, "for the wicked."

The Servant of the LORD

49 Listen to me, you islands;
hear this, you distant nations:
Before I was born the LORD called me;
from my birth he has made mention of my name.
2He made my mouth like a sharpened sword,
in the shadow of his hand he hid me;
he made me into a polished arrow and concealed me in his quiver.
3He said to me, "You are my servant, Israel, in whom I will display my splendor."
4But I said, "I have labored to no purpose;
I have spent my strength in vain and for nothing.
Yet what is due me is in the LORD's hand,
and my reward is with my God."

5And now the LORD says—
he who formed me in the womb to be his servant
to bring Jacob back to him and gather Israel to himself,
for I am honored in the eyes of the LORD
and my God has been my strength—
6he says:
"It is too small a thing for you to be my servant
to restore the tribes of Jacob and bring back those of Israel I have kept.
I will also make you a light for the Gentiles,
that you may bring my salvation to the ends of the earth."

7This is what the LORD says—
the Redeemer and Holy One of Israel—
to him who was despised and abhorred by the nation,
to the servant of rulers:
"Kings will see you and rise up,
princes will see and bow down,
because of the LORD, who is faithful,
the Holy One of Israel, who has chosen you."

Restoration of Israel

8This is what the LORD says:

"In the time of my favor I will answer you,
and in the day of salvation I will help you;
I will keep you and will make you to be a covenant for the people,
to restore the land
and to reassign its desolate inheritances,
9to say to the captives, 'Come out,'
and to those in darkness, 'Be free!'

"They will feed beside the roads
and find pasture on every barren hill.
10They will neither hunger nor thirst,
nor will the desert heat or the sun beat upon them.

He who has compassion on them will
guide them
and lead them beside springs of
water.
11 I will turn all my mountains into
roads,
and my highways will be raised up.
12 See, they will come from afar—
some from the north, some from the
west,
some from the region of Aswan.[a]"

13 Shout for joy, O heavens;
rejoice, O earth;
burst into song, O mountains!
For the LORD comforts his people
and will have compassion on his
afflicted ones.

14 But Zion said, "The LORD has forsaken
me,
the Lord has forgotten me."

15 "Can a mother forget the baby at her
breast
and have no compassion on the
child she has borne?
Though she may forget,
I will not forget you!
16 See, I have engraved you on the palms
of my hands;
your walls are ever before me.
17 Your sons hasten back,
and those who laid you waste
depart from you.
18 Lift up your eyes and look around;
all your sons gather and come to
you.
As surely as I live," declares the LORD,
"you will wear them all as
ornaments;
you will put them on, like a bride.

19 "Though you were ruined and made
desolate
and your land laid waste,
now you will be too small for your
people,
and those who devoured you will
be far away.
20 The children born during your
bereavement
will yet say in your hearing,
'This place is too small for us;
give us more space to live in.'
21 Then you will say in your heart,
'Who bore me these?
I was bereaved and barren;
I was exiled and rejected.
Who brought these up?
I was left all alone,
but these—where have they come
from?' "

22 This is what the Sovereign LORD says:

"See, I will beckon to the Gentiles,
I will lift up my banner to the
peoples;
they will bring your sons in their arms
and carry your daughters on their
shoulders.
23 Kings will be your foster fathers,
and their queens your nursing
mothers.
They will bow down before you with
their faces to the ground;
they will lick the dust at your feet.
Then you will know that I am the
LORD;
those who hope in me will not be
disappointed."

24 Can plunder be taken from warriors,
or captives rescued from the
fierce[b]?

25 But this is what the LORD says:

"Yes, captives will be taken from
warriors,
and plunder retrieved from the
fierce;
I will contend with those who contend
with you,
and your children I will save.
26 I will make your oppressors eat their
own flesh;
they will be drunk on their own
blood, as with wine.
Then all mankind will know
that I, the LORD, am your Savior,
your Redeemer, the Mighty One of
Jacob."

Israel's Sin and the Servant's Obedience

50 This is what the LORD says:
"Where is your mother's certificate of
divorce
with which I sent her away?
Or to which of my creditors
did I sell you?
Because of your sins you were sold;

[a] 12 Dead Sea Scrolls; Masoretic Text *Sinim*
[b] 24 Dead Sea Scrolls, Vulgate and Syriac (see also Septuagint and verse 25); Masoretic Text *righteous*

because of your transgressions your
mother was sent away.
2When I came, why was there no one?
When I called, why was there no
one to answer?
Was my arm too short to ransom you?
Do I lack the strength to rescue
you?
By a mere rebuke I dry up the sea,
I turn rivers into a desert;
their fish rot for lack of water
and die of thirst.
3I clothe the sky with darkness
and make sackcloth its covering."

4The Sovereign Lord has given me an
instructed tongue,
to know the word that sustains the
weary.
He wakens me morning by morning,
wakens my ear to listen like one
being taught.
5The Sovereign Lord has opened my
ears,
and I have not been rebellious;
I have not drawn back.
6I offered my back to those who beat
me,
my cheeks to those who pulled out
my beard;
I did not hide my face
from mocking and spitting.
7Because the Sovereign Lord helps me,
I will not be disgraced.
Therefore have I set my face like flint,
and I know I will not be put to
shame.
8He who vindicates me is near.
Who then will bring charges against
me?
Let us face each other!
Who is my accuser?
Let him confront me!
9It is the Sovereign Lord who helps
me.
Who is he that will condemn me?
They will all wear out like a garment;
the moths will eat them up.

10Who among you fears the Lord
and obeys the word of his servant?
Let him who walks in the dark,
who has no light,
trust in the name of the Lord
and rely on his God.
11But now, all you who light fires
and provide yourselves with flaming
torches,
go, walk in the light of your fires
and of the torches you have set
ablaze.
This is what you shall receive from
my hand:
You will lie down in torment.

Everlasting Salvation for Zion

51 "Listen to me, you who pursue
righteousness
and who seek the Lord:
Look to the rock from which you were
cut
and to the quarry from which you
were hewn;
2look to Abraham, your father,
and to Sarah, who gave you birth.
When I called him he was but one,
and I blessed him and made him
many.
3The Lord will surely comfort Zion
and will look with compassion on
all her ruins;
he will make her deserts like Eden,
her wastelands like the garden of
the Lord.
Joy and gladness will be found in her,
thanksgiving and the sound of
singing.
4"Listen to me, my people;
hear me, my nation:
The law will go out from me;
my justice will become a light to
the nations.
5My righteousness draws near speedily,
my salvation is on the way,
and my arm will bring justice to the
nations.
The islands will look to me
and wait in hope for my arm.
6Lift up your eyes to the heavens,
look at the earth beneath;
the heavens will vanish like smoke,
the earth will wear out like a
garment
and its inhabitants die like flies.
But my salvation will last forever,
my righteousness will never fail.
7"Hear me, you who know what is
right,
you people who have my law in
your hearts:
Do not fear the reproach of men
or be terrified by their insults.
8For the moth will eat them up like a
garment;
the worm will devour them like
wool.
But my righteousness will last forever,

my salvation through all
generations."

9Awake, awake! Clothe yourself with
strength,
O arm of the LORD;
awake, as in days gone by,
as in generations of old.
Was it not you who cut Rahab to
pieces,
who pierced that monster through?
10Was it not you who dried up the sea,
the waters of the great deep,
who made a road in the depths of the
sea
so that the redeemed might cross
over?
11The ransomed of the LORD will return.
They will enter Zion with singing;
everlasting joy will crown their
heads.
Gladness and joy will overtake them,
and sorrow and sighing will flee
away.

12"I, even I, am he who comforts you.
Who are you that you fear mortal
men,
the sons of men, who are but grass,
13that you forget the LORD your Maker,
who stretched out the heavens
and laid the foundations of the
earth,
that you live in constant terror every
day
because of the wrath of the
oppressor,
who is bent on destruction?
For where is the wrath of the
oppressor?
14 The cowering prisoners will soon be
set free;
they will not die in their dungeon,
nor will they lack bread.
15For I am the LORD your God,
who churns up the sea so that its
waves roar—
the LORD Almighty is his name.
16I have put my words in your mouth
and covered you with the shadow of
my hand—
I who set the heavens in place,
who laid the foundations of the
earth,
and who say to Zion, 'You are my
people.' "

The Cup of the LORD's Wrath

17Awake, awake!
Rise up, O Jerusalem,
you who have drunk from the hand of
the LORD
the cup of his wrath,
you who have drained to its dregs
the goblet that makes men stagger.
18Of all the sons she bore
there was none to guide her;
of all the sons she reared
there was none to take her by the
hand.
19These double calamities have come
upon you—
who can comfort you?—
ruin and destruction, famine and
sword—
who can[a] console you?
20Your sons have fainted;
they lie at the head of every street,
like antelope caught in a net.
They are filled with the wrath of the
LORD
and the rebuke of your God.
21Therefore hear this, you afflicted one,
made drunk, but not with wine.
22This is what your Sovereign LORD
says,
your God, who defends his people:
"See, I have taken out of your hand
the cup that made you stagger;
from that cup, the goblet of my wrath,
you will never drink again.
23I will put it into the hands of your
tormentors,
who said to you,
'Fall prostrate that we may walk
over you.'
And you made your back like the
ground,
like a street to be walked over."

52 Awake, awake, O Zion,
clothe yourself with strength.
Put on your garments of splendor,
O Jerusalem, the holy city.
The uncircumcised and defiled
will not enter you again.
2Shake off your dust;
rise up, sit enthroned, O Jerusalem.
Free yourself from the chains on your
neck,
O captive Daughter of Zion.

3For this is what the LORD says:

[a] 19 Dead Sea Scrolls, Septuagint, Vulgate and Syriac; Masoretic Text / *how can I*

"You were sold for nothing,
and without money you will be redeemed."

4For this is what the Sovereign LORD says:

"At first my people went down to Egypt to live;
lately, Assyria has oppressed them.

5"And now what do I have here?" declares the LORD.

"For my people have been taken away for nothing,
and those who rule them mock,[a]" declares the LORD.
"And all day long
my name is constantly blasphemed.
6Therefore my people will know my name;
therefore in that day they will know
that it is I who foretold it.
Yes, it is I."

7How beautiful on the mountains
are the feet of those who bring good news,
who proclaim peace,
who bring good tidings,
who proclaim salvation,
who say to Zion,
"Your God reigns!"
8Listen! Your watchmen lift up their voices;
together they shout for joy.
When the LORD returns to Zion,
they will see it with their own eyes.
9Burst into songs of joy together,
you ruins of Jerusalem,
for the LORD has comforted his people,
he has redeemed Jerusalem.
10The LORD will lay bare his holy arm
in the sight of all the nations,
and all the ends of the earth will see
the salvation of our God.

11Depart, depart, go out from there!
Touch no unclean thing!
Come out from it and be pure,
you who carry the vessels of the LORD.
12But you will not leave in haste
or go in flight;
for the LORD will go before you,
the God of Israel will be your rear guard.

The Suffering and Glory of the Servant

13See, my servant will act wisely[b];
he will be raised and lifted up and highly exalted.
14Just as there were many who were appalled at him[c]—
his appearance was so disfigured beyond that of any man
and his form marred beyond human likeness—
15so will he sprinkle many nations,[d]
and kings will shut their mouths because of him.
For what they were not told, they will see,
and what they have not heard, they will understand.

53 Who has believed our message
and to whom has the arm of the LORD been revealed?
2He grew up before him like a tender shoot,
and like a root out of dry ground.
He had no beauty or majesty to attract us to him,
nothing in his appearance that we should desire him.
3He was despised and rejected by men,
a man of sorrows, and familiar with suffering.
Like one from whom men hide their faces
he was despised, and we esteemed him not.

4Surely he took up our infirmities
and carried our sorrows,
yet we considered him stricken by God,
smitten by him, and afflicted.
5But he was pierced for our transgressions,
he was crushed for our iniquities;
the punishment that brought us peace was upon him,
and by his wounds we are healed.
6We all, like sheep, have gone astray,
each of us has turned to his own way;
and the LORD has laid on him
the iniquity of us all.

7He was oppressed and afflicted,

[a]5 Dead Sea Scrolls and Vulgate; Masoretic Text *wail* [b]13 Or *will prosper* [c]14 Hebrew *you*
[d]15 Hebrew; Septuagint *so will many nations marvel at him*

yet he did not open his mouth;
he was led like a lamb to the slaughter,
and as a sheep before her shearers is silent,
so he did not open his mouth.

[8]By oppression[a] and judgment he was taken away.
And who can speak of his descendants?
For he was cut off from the land of the living;

[a]8 Or *From arrest*

VERSE FOR THE DAY: Isaiah 53:3

AUTHOR: Diane M. Langberg

PASSAGE FOR THE DAY: Isaiah 53:1–6

Rejection and Acceptance

It's true that acceptance is something we all need, want and enjoy, but it is not our goal. It's important to remember that the Lord we follow was not accepted. He knew the feelings of rejection and aloneness. He lived with pressing crowds, irregular hours and the lack of a place to lay his head. Others did not always understand him.

Yet Scripture gives us a clear picture of how Christ responded in the face of rejection. He walked humbly, not regarding equality with God a thing to be grasped (Philippians 2:6). He did not draw attention to his credentials or to his successes.

Not everyone will be accepting and responsive to you. But one friendship blessed by common goals and oneness in the Spirit of God can insulate against the pain of isolation you may feel from others. Your spouse, of course, can be the friend who gives you support and strength.

When we experience feelings of isolation, we need to continually ask ourselves: "How can I love this person? How can I minister to that person's needs?" This will not eliminate loneliness; it will not even always remove the pain of isolation. It will, however, keep your focus on your walk before others rather than on their approval or disapproval.

MARRIAGE BUILDERS

♦ *It takes a radical love to serve and support someone who hurts you. When in your life has someone loved you with that kind of accepting love?*

♦ *When you are feeling isolated or lonely, how do you communicate your trouble to your spouse?*

Additional Scripture Readings
Philippians 2:6; 1 Peter 2:4–7

Go to page 781 for your next devotional reading.

for the transgression of my people
he was stricken.[a]
9He was assigned a grave with the
wicked,
and with the rich in his death,
though he had done no violence,
nor was any deceit in his mouth.

10Yet it was the LORD's will to crush him
and cause him to suffer,
and though the LORD makes[b] his
life a guilt offering,
he will see his offspring and prolong
his days,
and the will of the LORD will
prosper in his hand.
11After the suffering of his soul,
he will see the light ⌊of life⌋[c] and be
satisfied[d];
by his knowledge[e] my righteous
servant will justify many,
and he will bear their iniquities.
12Therefore I will give him a portion
among the great,[f]
and he will divide the spoils with
the strong,[g]
because he poured out his life unto
death,
and was numbered with the
transgressors.
For he bore the sin of many,
and made intercession for the
transgressors.

The Future Glory of Zion

54 "Sing, O barren woman,
you who never bore a child;
burst into song, shout for joy,
you who were never in labor;
because more are the children of the
desolate woman
than of her who has a husband,"
says the LORD.
2"Enlarge the place of your tent,
stretch your tent curtains wide,
do not hold back;
lengthen your cords,
strengthen your stakes.
3For you will spread out to the right
and to the left;
your descendants will dispossess
nations
and settle in their desolate cities.

4"Do not be afraid; you will not suffer
shame.
Do not fear disgrace; you will not
be humiliated.
You will forget the shame of your
youth
and remember no more the
reproach of your widowhood.
5For your Maker is your husband—
the LORD Almighty is his name—
the Holy One of Israel is your
Redeemer;
he is called the God of all the earth.
6The LORD will call you back
as if you were a wife deserted and
distressed in spirit—
a wife who married young,
only to be rejected," says your God.
7"For a brief moment I abandoned you,
but with deep compassion I will
bring you back.
8In a surge of anger
I hid my face from you for a
moment,
but with everlasting kindness
I will have compassion on you,"
says the LORD your Redeemer.

9"To me this is like the days of Noah,
when I swore that the waters of
Noah would never again cover
the earth.
So now I have sworn not to be angry
with you,
never to rebuke you again.
10Though the mountains be shaken
and the hills be removed,
yet my unfailing love for you will not
be shaken
nor my covenant of peace be
removed,"
says the LORD, who has compassion
on you.

11"O afflicted city, lashed by storms and
not comforted,
I will build you with stones of
turquoise,[h]
your foundations with sapphires.[i]

[a]8 Or *away. / Yet who of his generation considered / that he was cut off from the land of the living / for the transgression of my people, / to whom the blow was due?* [b]10 Hebrew *though you make* [c]11 Dead Sea Scrolls (see also Septuagint); Masoretic Text does not have *the light ⌊of life⌋.* [d]11 Or (with Masoretic Text) [11]*He will see the result of the suffering of his soul / and be satisfied* [e]11 Or *by knowledge of him* [f]12 Or *many* [g]12 Or *numerous* [h]11 The meaning of the Hebrew for this word is uncertain. [i]11 Or *lapis lazuli*

WEEKENDING

PARENTS

You know your parents pretty well, but when was the last time they shared their hopes, dreams and memories with you? Here are questions that might spur such a conversation. Or, if you are a parent, answer these questions for your children.

1. What surprises you the most about getting older?
2. Who was your best friend in school?
3. When you were twelve, what did you want to be when you grew up?
4. Where were you the first time you saw TV?
5. What's the scariest thing that ever happened to you?
6. Before air conditioning, how did you keep cool?
7. What was the hardest part of rearing children?
8. What was the first car you ever drove?
9. Did you ever have a hero? Who was it?
10. In your opinion, what has been the biggest change over the past fifty years?

— Todd Temple and Tracy Green

REVIVE

Saturday: Leviticus 19:1–32
Sunday: Proverbs 17:1–20

Go to page 782 for your next devotional reading.

12 I will make your battlements of rubies,
your gates of sparkling jewels,
and all your walls of precious stones.
13 All your sons will be taught by the LORD,
and great will be your children's peace.
14 In righteousness you will be established:
Tyranny will be far from you;
you will have nothing to fear.
Terror will be far removed;

VERSE FOR THE DAY: Isaiah 55:7

AUTHOR: Louis McBurney, M.D.

PASSAGE FOR THE DAY: Isaiah 55:10–17

Free Pardon

People often mistake forgiveness for a feeling, but fundamentally it's a choice, an act of the will. Forgiving involves acknowledging your hurt, releasing your thoughts about the violation and giving up the desire to pay the offender back. If your spouse has wronged you, it may seem strange that the burden of restoring your relationship by forgiving should fall on you. But forgiving has more to do with your own spiritual and mental health than it does with your spouse's. Forgiving releases your spouse from your wrath, but—more importantly—it frees you from the bondage of unforgiveness.

Soon after Becky found an X-rated video that her husband, Andy, had hidden in a closet, Andy confessed to a long-term porn addiction. They went to counseling, where Andy acknowledged the shame and hurt his addiction had caused his wife.

For a time, Becky got stuck in a painful recycling of Andy's betrayal, complete with her imagined scenarios of revenge. She finally left behind the rehearsal of Andy's betrayal by choosing, again and again, to shut out negative, angry thoughts. She asked God to keep those images from dominating her thinking. In their place, she substituted good memories and feelings about her relationship with Andy.

Forgiveness is much tougher if your spouse doesn't acknowledge his or her sin and the pain it has caused you. But even then, it's still necessary.

MARRIAGE BUILDERS

♦ *When have you forgiven your spouse by an act of the will—by choosing to forgive?*

♦ *What painful memories need to be replaced with positive ones?*

Additional Scripture Readings
Psalm 34:11–22; Matthew 18:21–35

Go to page 786 for your next devotional reading.

it will not come near you.
15 If anyone does attack you, it will not be my doing;
whoever attacks you will surrender to you.

16 "See, it is I who created the blacksmith
who fans the coals into flame
and forges a weapon fit for its work.
And it is I who have created the destroyer to work havoc;
17 no weapon forged against you will prevail,
and you will refute every tongue that accuses you.
This is the heritage of the servants of the LORD,
and this is their vindication from me,"
declares the LORD.

Invitation to the Thirsty

55 "Come, all you who are thirsty, come to the waters;
and you who have no money,
come, buy and eat!
Come, buy wine and milk
without money and without cost.
2 Why spend money on what is not bread,
and your labor on what does not satisfy?
Listen, listen to me, and eat what is good,
and your soul will delight in the richest of fare.
3 Give ear and come to me;
hear me, that your soul may live.
I will make an everlasting covenant with you,
my faithful love promised to David.
4 See, I have made him a witness to the peoples,
a leader and commander of the peoples.
5 Surely you will summon nations you know not,
and nations that do not know you will hasten to you,
because of the LORD your God,
the Holy One of Israel,
for he has endowed you with splendor."

6 Seek the LORD while he may be found;
call on him while he is near.
7 Let the wicked forsake his way
and the evil man his thoughts.
Let him turn to the LORD, and he will have mercy on him,
and to our God, for he will freely pardon.

8 "For my thoughts are not your thoughts,
neither are your ways my ways,"
declares the LORD.
9 "As the heavens are higher than the earth,
so are my ways higher than your ways
and my thoughts than your thoughts.
10 As the rain and the snow
come down from heaven,
and do not return to it
without watering the earth
and making it bud and flourish,
so that it yields seed for the sower
and bread for the eater,
11 so is my word that goes out from my mouth:
It will not return to me empty,
but will accomplish what I desire
and achieve the purpose for which I sent it.
12 You will go out in joy
and be led forth in peace;
the mountains and hills
will burst into song before you,
and all the trees of the field
will clap their hands.
13 Instead of the thornbush will grow the pine tree,
and instead of briers the myrtle will grow.
This will be for the LORD's renown,
for an everlasting sign,
which will not be destroyed."

Salvation for Others

56 This is what the LORD says:
"Maintain justice
and do what is right,
for my salvation is close at hand
and my righteousness will soon be revealed.
2 Blessed is the man who does this,
the man who holds it fast,
who keeps the Sabbath without desecrating it,
and keeps his hand from doing any evil."

3 Let no foreigner who has bound himself to the LORD say,

"The LORD will surely exclude me
from his people."
And let not any eunuch complain,
"I am only a dry tree."

4For this is what the LORD says:

"To the eunuchs who keep my
Sabbaths,
who choose what pleases me
and hold fast to my covenant—
5to them I will give within my temple
and its walls
a memorial and a name
better than sons and daughters;
I will give them an everlasting name
that will not be cut off.
6And foreigners who bind themselves
to the LORD
to serve him,
to love the name of the LORD,
and to worship him,
all who keep the Sabbath without
desecrating it
and who hold fast to my
covenant—
7these I will bring to my holy
mountain
and give them joy in my house of
prayer.
Their burnt offerings and sacrifices
will be accepted on my altar;
for my house will be called
a house of prayer for all nations."
8The Sovereign LORD declares—
he who gathers the exiles of Israel:
"I will gather still others to them
besides those already gathered."

God's Accusation Against the Wicked

9Come, all you beasts of the field,
come and devour, all you beasts of
the forest!
10Israel's watchmen are blind,
they all lack knowledge;
they are all mute dogs,
they cannot bark;
they lie around and dream,
they love to sleep.
11They are dogs with mighty appetites;
they never have enough.
They are shepherds who lack
understanding;
they all turn to their own way,
each seeks his own gain.
12"Come," each one cries, "let me get
wine!
Let us drink our fill of beer!
And tomorrow will be like today,
or even far better."

57 The righteous perish,
and no one ponders it in his
heart;
devout men are taken away,
and no one understands
that the righteous are taken away
to be spared from evil.
2Those who walk uprightly
enter into peace;
they find rest as they lie in death.

3"But you—come here, you sons of a
sorceress,
you offspring of adulterers and
prostitutes!
4Whom are you mocking?
At whom do you sneer
and stick out your tongue?
Are you not a brood of rebels,
the offspring of liars?
5You burn with lust among the oaks
and under every spreading tree;
you sacrifice your children in the
ravines
and under the overhanging crags.
6⌊The idols⌋ among the smooth stones
of the ravines are your portion;
they, they are your lot.
Yes, to them you have poured out
drink offerings
and offered grain offerings.
In the light of these things, should I
relent?
7You have made your bed on a high
and lofty hill;
there you went up to offer your
sacrifices.
8Behind your doors and your doorposts
you have put your pagan symbols.
Forsaking me, you uncovered your
bed,
you climbed into it and opened it
wide;
you made a pact with those whose
beds you love,
and you looked on their nakedness.
9You went to Molech[a] with olive oil
and increased your perfumes.
You sent your ambassadors[b] far
away;
you descended to the grave[c] itself!
10You were wearied by all your ways,
but you would not say, 'It is
hopeless.'

[a]9 Or *to the king* [b]9 Or *idols* [c]9 Hebrew *Sheol*

You found renewal of your strength,
and so you did not faint.
11"Whom have you so dreaded and feared
that you have been false to me,
and have neither remembered me
nor pondered this in your hearts?
Is it not because I have long been silent
that you do not fear me?
12I will expose your righteousness and your works,
and they will not benefit you.
13When you cry out for help,
let your collection ⌊of idols⌋ save you!
The wind will carry all of them off,
a mere breath will blow them away.
But the man who makes me his refuge
will inherit the land
and possess my holy mountain."

Comfort for the Contrite

14And it will be said:

"Build up, build up, prepare the road!
Remove the obstacles out of the way of my people."
15For this is what the high and lofty One says—
he who lives forever, whose name is holy:
"I live in a high and holy place,
but also with him who is contrite and lowly in spirit,
to revive the spirit of the lowly
and to revive the heart of the contrite.
16I will not accuse forever,
nor will I always be angry,
for then the spirit of man would grow faint before me—
the breath of man that I have created.
17I was enraged by his sinful greed;
I punished him, and hid my face in anger,
yet he kept on in his willful ways.
18I have seen his ways, but I will heal him;
I will guide him and restore comfort to him,
19 creating praise on the lips of the mourners in Israel.
Peace, peace, to those far and near,"
says the LORD. "And I will heal them."
20But the wicked are like the tossing sea,
which cannot rest,
whose waves cast up mire and mud.
21"There is no peace," says my God,
"for the wicked."

True Fasting

58 "Shout it aloud, do not hold back.
Raise your voice like a trumpet.
Declare to my people their rebellion
and to the house of Jacob their sins.
2For day after day they seek me out;
they seem eager to know my ways,
as if they were a nation that does what is right
and has not forsaken the commands of its God.
They ask me for just decisions
and seem eager for God to come near them.
3'Why have we fasted,' they say,
'and you have not seen it?
Why have we humbled ourselves,
and you have not noticed?'
"Yet on the day of your fasting, you do as you please
and exploit all your workers.
4Your fasting ends in quarreling and strife,
and in striking each other with wicked fists.
You cannot fast as you do today
and expect your voice to be heard on high.
5Is this the kind of fast I have chosen,
only a day for a man to humble himself?
Is it only for bowing one's head like a reed
and for lying on sackcloth and ashes?
Is that what you call a fast,
a day acceptable to the LORD?
6"Is not this the kind of fasting I have chosen:
to loose the chains of injustice
and untie the cords of the yoke,
to set the oppressed free
and break every yoke?
7Is it not to share your food with the hungry
and to provide the poor wanderer with shelter—
when you see the naked, to clothe him,
and not to turn away from your own flesh and blood?

8 Then your light will break forth like
the dawn,
and your healing will quickly
appear;
then your righteousness[a] will go
before you,
and the glory of the LORD will be
your rear guard.

9 Then you will call, and the LORD will
answer;
you will cry for help, and he will
say: Here am I.

"If you do away with the yoke of
oppression,
with the pointing finger and
malicious talk,

[a] 8 Or *your righteous One*

VERSE FOR THE DAY: Isaiah 58:11

AUTHOR: Jim and Sally Conway

PASSAGE FOR THE DAY: Isaiah 58:1–14

How to Meet Needs

Our work with mid-life couples confirms the fact that people stay together in marriage because their needs are being met. At first glance, that idea appears to be self-centered. But we've discovered that couples whose marriages are tenuous can experience a deepening sense of commitment, a desire to stay together, and an ability to express affection as they understand each other's needs and specifically focus on meeting those needs.

Sometimes at marriage conferences we give time for couples to go for a walk together and talk about their most important needs. We've first asked each of them to write down four of their own needs and then what they think are their mate's four most important needs.

We encourage them to compare their lists to see how well they understand each other. Beyond that, they are to explain the meaning of each of these needs by talking about the feelings associated with those needs. Then they are to talk about practical ways they could more adequately meet each other's major needs.

Understanding your mate's needs and trying to meet those needs is a powerful way to serve your mate and strengthen your marriage.

MARRIAGE BUILDERS

♦ *What do you think are your spouse's top three needs? Make a guess, then check with him or her to see if you were right.*

♦ *What practical steps can you take to meet your spouse's most important needs?*

Additional Scripture Readings
Philippians 4:9; Hebrews 4:16

Go to page 788 for your next devotional reading.

10and if you spend yourselves in behalf
of the hungry
and satisfy the needs of the
oppressed,
then your light will rise in the
darkness,
and your night will become like the
noonday.
11The LORD will guide you always;
he will satisfy your needs in a
sun-scorched land
and will strengthen your frame.
You will be like a well-watered
garden,
like a spring whose waters never
fail.
12Your people will rebuild the ancient
ruins
and will raise up the age-old
foundations;
you will be called Repairer of Broken
Walls,
Restorer of Streets with Dwellings.

13"If you keep your feet from breaking
the Sabbath
and from doing as you please on
my holy day,
if you call the Sabbath a delight
and the LORD's holy day honorable,
and if you honor it by not going your
own way
and not doing as you please or
speaking idle words,
14then you will find your joy in the
LORD,
and I will cause you to ride on the
heights of the land
and to feast on the inheritance of
your father Jacob."
The mouth of the LORD
has spoken.

Sin, Confession and Redemption

59 Surely the arm of the LORD is not
too short to save,
nor his ear too dull to hear.
2But your iniquities have separated
you from your God;
your sins have hidden his face from
you,
so that he will not hear.
3For your hands are stained with
blood,
your fingers with guilt.
Your lips have spoken lies,
and your tongue mutters wicked
things.
4No one calls for justice;
no one pleads his case with
integrity.
They rely on empty arguments and
speak lies;
they conceive trouble and give birth
to evil.
5They hatch the eggs of vipers
and spin a spider's web.
Whoever eats their eggs will die,
and when one is broken, an adder
is hatched.
6Their cobwebs are useless for
clothing;
they cannot cover themselves with
what they make.
Their deeds are evil deeds,
and acts of violence are in their
hands.
7Their feet rush into sin;
they are swift to shed innocent
blood.
Their thoughts are evil thoughts;
ruin and destruction mark their
ways.
8The way of peace they do not know;
there is no justice in their paths.
They have turned them into crooked
roads;
no one who walks in them will
know peace.

9So justice is far from us,
and righteousness does not reach
us.
We look for light, but all is darkness;
for brightness, but we walk in deep
shadows.
10Like the blind we grope along the
wall,
feeling our way like men without
eyes.
At midday we stumble as if it were
twilight;
among the strong, we are like the
dead.
11We all growl like bears;
we moan mournfully like doves.
We look for justice, but find none;
for deliverance, but it is far away.

12For our offenses are many in your
sight,
and our sins testify against us.
Our offenses are ever with us,
and we acknowledge our iniquities:
13rebellion and treachery against the
LORD,

turning our backs on our God,
fomenting oppression and revolt,
uttering lies our hearts have
conceived.
14 So justice is driven back,
and righteousness stands at a
distance;
truth has stumbled in the streets,
honesty cannot enter.
15 Truth is nowhere to be found,
and whoever shuns evil becomes a
prey.
The LORD looked and was displeased
that there was no justice.
16 He saw that there was no one,
he was appalled that there was no
one to intervene;
so his own arm worked salvation for
him,
and his own righteousness
sustained him.
17 He put on righteousness as his
breastplate,
and the helmet of salvation on his
head;
he put on the garments of vengeance
and wrapped himself in zeal as in a
cloak.
18 According to what they have done,
so will he repay
wrath to his enemies

VERSE FOR THE DAY: Isaiah 59:1

AUTHOR: Elisa Morgan

PASSAGE FOR THE DAY: Isaiah 59:1–21

Take the Back Seat

When I think of good listening habits, I think in terms of being a passenger in a car. For example, when I "listen from the back seat," I allow my husband to air his feelings in an open and accepting atmosphere. I simply listen, without correcting, evaluating or judging.

I admit that "back-seat listening" goes against my fix-it nature. But if I can put a leash on my goals long enough to listen to my husband, I gain terrific benefits. For example, listening from the "back seat" can provide a kind of oasis where your mate can be him- or herself and still feel accepted.

In our world of conditional acceptance, competition and performance, such a safe place is crucial. If a healthy hearing can't be had in marriage, where will spouses go to be heard?

MARRIAGE BUILDERS

♦ *What are the clues, verbal or nonverbal, that your spouse gives that help you know he or she is really hearing what you say?*
♦ *Analyze your own listening style. Do you think your conversational habits are creating an "oasis" for your spouse?*

Additional Scripture Readings
Colossians 3:12; 1 Peter 5:5

Go to page 791 for your next devotional reading.

and retribution to his foes;
he will repay the islands their due.
19 From the west, men will fear the
name of the LORD,
and from the rising of the sun, they
will revere his glory.
For he will come like a pent-up flood
that the breath of the LORD drives
along.[a]

20 "The Redeemer will come to Zion,
to those in Jacob who repent of
their sins,"
declares the LORD.

21 "As for me, this is my covenant with them," says the LORD. "My Spirit, who is on you, and my words that I have put in your mouth will not depart from your mouth, or from the mouths of your children, or from the mouths of their descendants from this time on and forever," says the LORD.

The Glory of Zion

60 "Arise, shine, for your light has
come,
and the glory of the LORD rises upon
you.
2 See, darkness covers the earth
and thick darkness is over the
peoples,
but the LORD rises upon you
and his glory appears over you.
3 Nations will come to your light,
and kings to the brightness of your
dawn.

4 "Lift up your eyes and look about
you:
All assemble and come to you;
your sons come from afar,
and your daughters are carried on
the arm.
5 Then you will look and be radiant,
your heart will throb and swell with
joy;
the wealth on the seas will be brought
to you,
to you the riches of the nations will
come.
6 Herds of camels will cover your land,
young camels of Midian and Ephah.
And all from Sheba will come,
bearing gold and incense
and proclaiming the praise of the
LORD.

7 All Kedar's flocks will be gathered to
you,
the rams of Nebaioth will serve you;
they will be accepted as offerings on
my altar,
and I will adorn my glorious
temple.

8 "Who are these that fly along like
clouds,
like doves to their nests?
9 Surely the islands look to me;
in the lead are the ships of
Tarshish,[b]
bringing your sons from afar,
with their silver and gold,
to the honor of the LORD your God,
the Holy One of Israel,
for he has endowed you with
splendor.

10 "Foreigners will rebuild your walls,
and their kings will serve you.
Though in anger I struck you,
in favor I will show you
compassion.
11 Your gates will always stand open,
they will never be shut, day or
night,
so that men may bring you the wealth
of the nations—
their kings led in triumphal
procession.
12 For the nation or kingdom that will
not serve you will perish;
it will be utterly ruined.

13 "The glory of Lebanon will come to
you,
the pine, the fir and the cypress
together,
to adorn the place of my sanctuary;
and I will glorify the place of my
feet.
14 The sons of your oppressors will come
bowing before you;
all who despise you will bow down
at your feet
and will call you the City of the LORD,
Zion of the Holy One of Israel.

15 "Although you have been forsaken
and hated,
with no one traveling through,
I will make you the everlasting pride
and the joy of all generations.
16 You will drink the milk of nations

[a] 19 Or *When the enemy comes in like a flood, / the Spirit of the LORD will put him to flight*
[b] 9 Or *the trading ships*

and be nursed at royal breasts.
Then you will know that I, the LORD,
am your Savior,
your Redeemer, the Mighty One of
Jacob.
17 Instead of bronze I will bring you
gold,
and silver in place of iron.
Instead of wood I will bring you
bronze,
and iron in place of stones.
I will make peace your governor
and righteousness your ruler.
18 No longer will violence be heard in
your land,
nor ruin or destruction within your
borders,
but you will call your walls Salvation
and your gates Praise.
19 The sun will no more be your light by
day,
nor will the brightness of the moon
shine on you,
for the LORD will be your everlasting
light,
and your God will be your glory.
20 Your sun will never set again,
and your moon will wane no more;
the LORD will be your everlasting light,
and your days of sorrow will end.
21 Then will all your people be righteous
and they will possess the land
forever.
They are the shoot I have planted,
the work of my hands,
for the display of my splendor.
22 The least of you will become a
thousand,
the smallest a mighty nation.
I am the LORD;
in its time I will do this swiftly."

The Year of the LORD's Favor

61 The Spirit of the Sovereign LORD
is on me,
because the LORD has anointed me
to preach good news to the poor.
He has sent me to bind up the
brokenhearted,
to proclaim freedom for the captives
and release from darkness for the
prisoners,[a]
2 to proclaim the year of the LORD's
favor
and the day of vengeance of our
God,
to comfort all who mourn,
3 and provide for those who grieve in
Zion—
to bestow on them a crown of beauty
instead of ashes,
the oil of gladness
instead of mourning,
and a garment of praise
instead of a spirit of despair.
They will be called oaks of
righteousness,
a planting of the LORD
for the display of his splendor.

4 They will rebuild the ancient ruins
and restore the places long
devastated;
they will renew the ruined cities
that have been devastated for
generations.
5 Aliens will shepherd your flocks;
foreigners will work your fields and
vineyards.
6 And you will be called priests of the
LORD,
you will be named ministers of our
God.
You will feed on the wealth of
nations,
and in their riches you will boast.

7 Instead of their shame
my people will receive a double
portion,
and instead of disgrace
they will rejoice in their inheritance;
and so they will inherit a double
portion in their land,
and everlasting joy will be theirs.

8 "For I, the LORD, love justice;
I hate robbery and iniquity.
In my faithfulness I will reward them
and make an everlasting covenant
with them.
9 Their descendants will be known
among the nations
and their offspring among the
peoples.
All who see them will acknowledge
that they are a people the LORD has
blessed."

10 I delight greatly in the LORD;
my soul rejoices in my God.
For he has clothed me with garments
of salvation
and arrayed me in a robe of
righteousness,

[a] 1 Hebrew; Septuagint *the blind*

VERSE FOR THE DAY: Isaiah 61:1, 3

AUTHOR: Mary Ellen Williams Ton

PASSAGE FOR THE DAY: Isaiah 61:1–11

Beauty for Ashes

As I rushed out the door, I never guessed that before evening I would wake up in a hospital burn center. Trapped in a fire in the church where I worked as bookkeeper, my face was now disfigured, my hands deformed and burn scars covered my body. How could my husband possibly want me for his wife now that I looked this way? In the midst of my despair, I began to learn an invaluable lesson about self-esteem.

Part of my daily routine was to exercise. I began to ride an exercise bike, and as my damaged skin was stretched, it responded with painful, burning sensations. To distract my mind and endure the pain a bit longer each day, I began to sing my way through the hymnal.

Slowly, and very faintly at first, I began to hear the words of *another* song. This song came from that part of me made in the image of God. And this is what the voice said: "God loves me. God loves me. God loves me." When I began to go out in public and people stared, or whispered, or laughed, I sang those words. "Jesus loves me; this I know."

I don't have to look perfect or accomplish great things. I am created in the image of God; that makes me unique and valuable.

Some days, when I feel down about myself, I remember the lesson of the exercise bike. I have a choice. I can decide what I will do with my feelings and that inner song will come bursting through—"Jesus loves me; this I know!"

MARRIAGE BUILDERS

♦ *When in your life have you most needed the assurance that you were loved by God?*

♦ *How can you communicate "unconditional love" to each other on a regular basis?*

Additional Scripture Readings
1 Samuel 16:7; John 6:27–29; Jude 24–25

Go to page 799 for your next devotional reading.

as a bridegroom adorns his head like
a priest,
and as a bride adorns herself with
her jewels.
11For as the soil makes the sprout come
up
and a garden causes seeds to grow,
so the Sovereign LORD will make
righteousness and praise
spring up before all nations.

Zion's New Name

62 For Zion's sake I will not keep
silent,
for Jerusalem's sake I will not
remain quiet,
till her righteousness shines out like
the dawn,
her salvation like a blazing torch.
2The nations will see your
righteousness,
and all kings your glory;
you will be called by a new name
that the mouth of the LORD will
bestow.
3You will be a crown of splendor in the
LORD's hand,
a royal diadem in the hand of your
God.
4No longer will they call you Deserted,
or name your land Desolate.
But you will be called Hephzibah,[a]
and your land Beulah[b];
for the LORD will take delight in you,
and your land will be married.
5As a young man marries a maiden,
so will your sons[c] marry you;
as a bridegroom rejoices over his
bride,
so will your God rejoice over you.

6I have posted watchmen on your
walls, O Jerusalem;
they will never be silent day or
night.
You who call on the LORD,
give yourselves no rest,
7and give him no rest till he establishes
Jerusalem
and makes her the praise of the
earth.

8The LORD has sworn by his right hand
and by his mighty arm:
"Never again will I give your grain
as food for your enemies,
and never again will foreigners drink
the new wine
for which you have toiled;
9but those who harvest it will eat it
and praise the LORD,
and those who gather the grapes will
drink it
in the courts of my sanctuary."

10Pass through, pass through the gates!
Prepare the way for the people.
Build up, build up the highway!
Remove the stones.
Raise a banner for the nations.

11The LORD has made proclamation
to the ends of the earth:
"Say to the Daughter of Zion,
'See, your Savior comes!
See, his reward is with him,
and his recompense accompanies
him.' "
12They will be called the Holy People,
the Redeemed of the LORD;
and you will be called Sought After,
the City No Longer Deserted.

God's Day of Vengeance and Redemption

63 Who is this coming from Edom,
from Bozrah, with his garments
stained crimson?
Who is this, robed in splendor,
striding forward in the greatness of
his strength?

"It is I, speaking in righteousness,
mighty to save."

2Why are your garments red,
like those of one treading the
winepress?

3"I have trodden the winepress alone;
from the nations no one was with
me.
I trampled them in my anger
and trod them down in my wrath;
their blood spattered my garments,
and I stained all my clothing.
4For the day of vengeance was in my
heart,
and the year of my redemption has
come.
5I looked, but there was no one to
help,
I was appalled that no one gave
support;
so my own arm worked salvation for
me,
and my own wrath sustained me.

[a]4 *Hephzibah* means *my delight is in her.* [b]4 *Beulah* means *married.* [c]5 Or *Builder*

[6]I trampled the nations in my anger;
in my wrath I made them drunk
and poured their blood on the ground."

Praise and Prayer

[7]I will tell of the kindnesses of the LORD,
the deeds for which he is to be praised,
according to all the LORD has done for us—
yes, the many good things he has done
for the house of Israel,
according to his compassion and many kindnesses.
[8]He said, "Surely they are my people,
sons who will not be false to me";
and so he became their Savior.
[9]In all their distress he too was distressed,
and the angel of his presence saved them.
In his love and mercy he redeemed them;
he lifted them up and carried them
all the days of old.
[10]Yet they rebelled
and grieved his Holy Spirit.
So he turned and became their enemy
and he himself fought against them.
[11]Then his people recalled[a] the days of old,
the days of Moses and his people—
where is he who brought them through the sea,
with the shepherd of his flock?
Where is he who set
his Holy Spirit among them,
[12]who sent his glorious arm of power
to be at Moses' right hand,
who divided the waters before them,
to gain for himself everlasting renown,
[13]who led them through the depths?
Like a horse in open country,
they did not stumble;
[14]like cattle that go down to the plain,
they were given rest by the Spirit of the LORD.
This is how you guided your people
to make for yourself a glorious name.
[15]Look down from heaven and see
from your lofty throne, holy and glorious.
Where are your zeal and your might?
Your tenderness and compassion are withheld from us.
[16]But you are our Father,
though Abraham does not know us
or Israel acknowledge us;
you, O LORD, are our Father,
our Redeemer from of old is your name.
[17]Why, O LORD, do you make us wander from your ways
and harden our hearts so we do not revere you?
Return for the sake of your servants,
the tribes that are your inheritance.
[18]For a little while your people possessed your holy place,
but now our enemies have trampled down your sanctuary.
[19]We are yours from of old;
but you have not ruled over them,
they have not been called by your name.[b]

64 Oh, that you would rend the heavens and come down,
that the mountains would tremble before you!
[2]As when fire sets twigs ablaze
and causes water to boil,
come down to make your name known to your enemies
and cause the nations to quake before you!
[3]For when you did awesome things that we did not expect,
you came down, and the mountains trembled before you.
[4]Since ancient times no one has heard,
no ear has perceived,
no eye has seen any God besides you,
who acts on behalf of those who wait for him.
[5]You come to the help of those who gladly do right,
who remember your ways.
But when we continued to sin against them,
you were angry.
How then can we be saved?
[6]All of us have become like one who is unclean,
and all our righteous acts are like filthy rags;

[a]11 Or *But may he recall*
[b]19 Or *We are like those you have never ruled, / like those never called by your name*

we all shrivel up like a leaf,
and like the wind our sins sweep us away.
7No one calls on your name
or strives to lay hold of you;
for you have hidden your face from us
and made us waste away because of our sins.

8Yet, O LORD, you are our Father.
We are the clay, you are the potter;
we are all the work of your hand.
9Do not be angry beyond measure, O LORD;
do not remember our sins forever.
Oh, look upon us, we pray,
for we are all your people.
10Your sacred cities have become a desert;
even Zion is a desert, Jerusalem a desolation.
11Our holy and glorious temple, where our fathers praised you,
has been burned with fire,
and all that we treasured lies in ruins.
12After all this, O LORD, will you hold yourself back?
Will you keep silent and punish us beyond measure?

Judgment and Salvation

65 "I revealed myself to those who did not ask for me;
I was found by those who did not seek me.
To a nation that did not call on my name,
I said, 'Here am I, here am I.'
2All day long I have held out my hands
to an obstinate people,
who walk in ways not good,
pursuing their own imaginations—
3a people who continually provoke me
to my very face,
offering sacrifices in gardens
and burning incense on altars of brick;
4who sit among the graves
and spend their nights keeping secret vigil;
who eat the flesh of pigs,
and whose pots hold broth of unclean meat;
5who say, 'Keep away; don't come near me,
for I am too sacred for you!'
Such people are smoke in my nostrils,
a fire that keeps burning all day.
6"See, it stands written before me:
I will not keep silent but will pay back in full;
I will pay it back into their laps—
7both your sins and the sins of your fathers,"
says the LORD.
"Because they burned sacrifices on the mountains
and defied me on the hills,
I will measure into their laps
the full payment for their former deeds."

8This is what the LORD says:

"As when juice is still found in a cluster of grapes
and men say, 'Don't destroy it,
there is yet some good in it,'
so will I do in behalf of my servants;
I will not destroy them all.
9I will bring forth descendants from Jacob,
and from Judah those who will possess my mountains;
my chosen people will inherit them,
and there will my servants live.
10Sharon will become a pasture for flocks,
and the Valley of Achor a resting place for herds,
for my people who seek me.

11"But as for you who forsake the LORD
and forget my holy mountain,
who spread a table for Fortune
and fill bowls of mixed wine for Destiny,
12I will destine you for the sword,
and you will all bend down for the slaughter;
for I called but you did not answer,
I spoke but you did not listen.
You did evil in my sight
and chose what displeases me."

13Therefore this is what the Sovereign LORD says:

"My servants will eat,
but you will go hungry;
my servants will drink,
but you will go thirsty;
my servants will rejoice,
but you will be put to shame.
14My servants will sing
out of the joy of their hearts,
but you will cry out
from anguish of heart
and wail in brokenness of spirit.

15 You will leave your name
to my chosen ones as a curse;
the Sovereign LORD will put you to death,
but to his servants he will give another name.
16 Whoever invokes a blessing in the land
will do so by the God of truth;
he who takes an oath in the land
will swear by the God of truth.
For the past troubles will be forgotten
and hidden from my eyes.

New Heavens and a New Earth

17 "Behold, I will create
new heavens and a new earth.
The former things will not be remembered,
nor will they come to mind.
18 But be glad and rejoice forever
in what I will create,
for I will create Jerusalem to be a delight
and its people a joy.
19 I will rejoice over Jerusalem
and take delight in my people;
the sound of weeping and of crying
will be heard in it no more.

20 "Never again will there be in it
an infant who lives but a few days,
or an old man who does not live out his years;
he who dies at a hundred
will be thought a mere youth;
he who fails to reach[a] a hundred
will be considered accursed.
21 They will build houses and dwell in them;
they will plant vineyards and eat their fruit.
22 No longer will they build houses and others live in them,
or plant and others eat.
For as the days of a tree,
so will be the days of my people;
my chosen ones will long enjoy
the works of their hands.
23 They will not toil in vain
or bear children doomed to misfortune;
for they will be a people blessed by the LORD,
they and their descendants with them.
24 Before they call I will answer;
while they are still speaking I will hear.
25 The wolf and the lamb will feed together,
and the lion will eat straw like the ox,
but dust will be the serpent's food.
They will neither harm nor destroy
on all my holy mountain,"
says the LORD.

Judgment and Hope

66 This is what the LORD says:
"Heaven is my throne,
and the earth is my footstool.
Where is the house you will build for me?
Where will my resting place be?
2 Has not my hand made all these things,
and so they came into being?"
declares the LORD.

"This is the one I esteem:
he who is humble and contrite in spirit,
and trembles at my word.
3 But whoever sacrifices a bull
is like one who kills a man,
and whoever offers a lamb,
like one who breaks a dog's neck;
whoever makes a grain offering
is like one who presents pig's blood,
and whoever burns memorial incense,
like one who worships an idol.
They have chosen their own ways,
and their souls delight in their abominations;
4 so I also will choose harsh treatment for them
and will bring upon them what they dread.
For when I called, no one answered,
when I spoke, no one listened.
They did evil in my sight
and chose what displeases me."

5 Hear the word of the LORD,
you who tremble at his word:
"Your brothers who hate you,
and exclude you because of my name, have said,
'Let the LORD be glorified,
that we may see your joy!'
Yet they will be put to shame.
6 Hear that uproar from the city,
hear that noise from the temple!

[a] 20 Or / *the sinner who reaches*

It is the sound of the LORD
repaying his enemies all they
deserve.

7"Before she goes into labor,
she gives birth;
before the pains come upon her,
she delivers a son.
8Who has ever heard of such a thing?
Who has ever seen such things?
Can a country be born in a day
or a nation be brought forth in a
moment?
Yet no sooner is Zion in labor
than she gives birth to her children.
9Do I bring to the moment of birth
and not give delivery?" says the
LORD.
"Do I close up the womb
when I bring to delivery?" says your
God.
10"Rejoice with Jerusalem and be glad
for her,
all you who love her;
rejoice greatly with her,
all you who mourn over her.
11For you will nurse and be satisfied
at her comforting breasts;
you will drink deeply
and delight in her overflowing
abundance."

12For this is what the LORD says:

"I will extend peace to her like a river,
and the wealth of nations like a
flooding stream;
you will nurse and be carried on her
arm
and dandled on her knees.
13As a mother comforts her child,
so will I comfort you;
and you will be comforted over
Jerusalem."

14When you see this, your heart will
rejoice
and you will flourish like grass;
the hand of the LORD will be made
known to his servants,
but his fury will be shown to his
foes.
15See, the LORD is coming with fire,
and his chariots are like a
whirlwind;
he will bring down his anger with
fury,
and his rebuke with flames of fire.
16For with fire and with his sword
the LORD will execute judgment
upon all men,
and many will be those slain by the
LORD.

17"Those who consecrate and purify themselves to go into the gardens, following the one in the midst of[a] those who eat the flesh of pigs and rats and other abominable things—they will meet their end together," declares the LORD.

18"And I, because of their actions and their imaginations, am about to come[b] and gather all nations and tongues, and they will come and see my glory.

19"I will set a sign among them, and I will send some of those who survive to the nations—to Tarshish, to the Libyans[c] and Lydians (famous as archers), to Tubal and Greece, and to the distant islands that have not heard of my fame or seen my glory. They will proclaim my glory among the nations. 20And they will bring all your brothers, from all the nations, to my holy mountain in Jerusalem as an offering to the LORD—on horses, in chariots and wagons, and on mules and camels," says the LORD. "They will bring them, as the Israelites bring their grain offerings, to the temple of the LORD in ceremonially clean vessels. 21And I will select some of them also to be priests and Levites," says the LORD.

22"As the new heavens and the new earth that I make will endure before me," declares the LORD, "so will your name and descendants endure. 23From one New Moon to another and from one Sabbath to another, all mankind will come and bow down before me," says the LORD. 24"And they will go out and look upon the dead bodies of those who rebelled against me; their worm will not die, nor will their fire be quenched, and they will be loathsome to all mankind."

[a] 17 Or *gardens behind one of your temples, and* uncertain. [b] 18 The meaning of the Hebrew for this clause is [c] 19 Some Septuagint manuscripts *Put* (Libyans); Hebrew *Pul*

JEREMIAH prophesies in the kingdom of Judah as Jerusalem is being destroyed and God's people are being carried away into Babylon because of their sins (see 2 Chronicles 36). It is a time of judgment and of suffering for all the people and for Jeremiah personally. But Jeremiah also cites God's promise of restoration after seventy years, assuring the people of a coming new covenant. As you read this book, remember that sin has its consequences but also that through Jesus, your mediator, God's last word is forgiveness and eternal life.

JEREMIAH

1 The words of Jeremiah son of Hilkiah,
one of the priests at Anathoth in the
territory of Benjamin. 2 The word of the
LORD came to him in the thirteenth year of
the reign of Josiah son of Amon king of
Judah, 3 and through the reign of Jehoia-
kim son of Josiah king of Judah, down to
the fifth month of the eleventh year of
Zedekiah son of Josiah king of Judah,
when the people of Jerusalem went into
exile.

The Call of Jeremiah

4 The word of the LORD came to me, saying,

5 "Before I formed you in the womb I
knew[a] you,
before you were born I set you
apart;
I appointed you as a prophet to the
nations."

6 "Ah, Sovereign LORD," I said, "I do not

[a] 5 Or *chose*

know how to speak; I am only a child."
7But the LORD said to me, "Do not say,
'I am only a child.' You must go to every-
one I send you to and say whatever I com-
mand you. 8Do not be afraid of them, for
I am with you and will rescue you," de-
clares the LORD.
9Then the LORD reached out his hand
and touched my mouth and said to me,
"Now, I have put my words in your
mouth. 10See, today I appoint you over na-
tions and kingdoms to uproot and tear
down, to destroy and overthrow, to build
and to plant."
11The word of the LORD came to me:
"What do you see, Jeremiah?"
"I see the branch of an almond tree," I
replied.
12The LORD said to me, "You have seen
correctly, for I am watching[a] to see that
my word is fulfilled."
13The word of the LORD came to me
again: "What do you see?"
"I see a boiling pot, tilting away from
the north," I answered.
14The LORD said to me, "From the north
disaster will be poured out on all who live
in the land. 15I am about to summon all
the peoples of the northern kingdoms,"
declares the LORD.

"Their kings will come and set up
their thrones
in the entrance of the gates of
Jerusalem;
they will come against all her
surrounding walls
and against all the towns of Judah.
16I will pronounce my judgments on my
people
because of their wickedness in
forsaking me,
in burning incense to other gods
and in worshiping what their hands
have made.

17"Get yourself ready! Stand up and say
to them whatever I command you. Do not
be terrified by them, or I will terrify you
before them. 18Today I have made you a
fortified city, an iron pillar and a bronze
wall to stand against the whole land—
against the kings of Judah, its officials, its
priests and the people of the land. 19They
will fight against you but will not over-
come you, for I am with you and will res-
cue you," declares the LORD.

Israel Forsakes God

2 The word of the LORD came to me:
2"Go and proclaim in the hearing of
Jerusalem:

" 'I remember the devotion of your
youth,
how as a bride you loved me
and followed me through the desert,
through a land not sown.
3Israel was holy to the LORD,
the firstfruits of his harvest;
all who devoured her were held guilty,
and disaster overtook them,' "
declares the LORD.

4Hear the word of the LORD, O house of
Jacob,
all you clans of the house of Israel.

5This is what the LORD says:

"What fault did your fathers find in
me,
that they strayed so far from me?
They followed worthless idols
and became worthless themselves.
6They did not ask, 'Where is the LORD,
who brought us up out of Egypt
and led us through the barren
wilderness,
through a land of deserts and rifts,
a land of drought and darkness,[b]
a land where no one travels and no
one lives?'
7I brought you into a fertile land
to eat its fruit and rich produce.
But you came and defiled my land
and made my inheritance
detestable.
8The priests did not ask,
'Where is the LORD?'
Those who deal with the law did not
know me;
the leaders rebelled against me.
The prophets prophesied by Baal,
following worthless idols.

9"Therefore I bring charges against you
again,"
declares the LORD.
"And I will bring charges against
your children's children.
10Cross over to the coasts of Kittim[c]
and look,

[a]12 The Hebrew for *watching* sounds like the Hebrew for *almond tree.* [b]6 Or *and the shadow of death* [c]10 That is, Cyprus and western coastlands

VERSE FOR THE DAY: Jeremiah 2:19

AUTHOR: Tim Stafford

PASSAGE FOR THE DAY: Jeremiah 2:1–2, 13–19

God's Adulterous Bride

The Old Testament tells the story of God's marriage to his people. The most notable characteristic of this marriage is the unfaithfulness of the bride and the passionate, tortured response of the Husband.

Jeremiah cites God's accusations against his beloved. " 'I remember the devotion of your youth, how as a bride you loved me and followed me through the desert. . . . Consider then and realize how evil and bitter it is for you when you forsake the Lord your God and have no awe of me,' declares the Lord, the Lord Almighty. . . . 'You have lived as a prostitute with many lovers—would you now return to me?' declares the Lord" (Jeremiah 2:19; 3:3).

Yet these terrible words are interlaced with pleading love: " 'Return, faithless Israel,' declares the LORD, 'I will frown on you no longer, for I am merciful,' declares the LORD, 'I will not be angry forever. Only acknowledge your guilt. . . . Return, faithless people,' declares the Lord, 'for I am your husband' " (Jeremiah 3:12–14).

If you consider the entire Bible, you cannot help but see that despite God's passionate anger and jealousy, it is his love and humility that dominate. He threatens, pleads, blusters, shouts, he even sends his bride off into exile. But in the end he always brings her back. At the slightest sign of genuine repentance, he throws his arms open to her. Hope persistently rises in the background.

MARRIAGE BUILDERS

♦ *Think back over times when you have forgiven—and been forgiven by—each other. How did those experiences strengthen your marriage?*

♦ *What might you need to forgive now?*

Additional Scripture Readings
Jeremiah 3:3, 12–14; Ezekiel 16:32, 37, 40; Isaiah 62:5

Go to page 803 for your next devotional reading.

send to Kedar[a] and observe
closely;
see if there has ever been anything
like this:
11 Has a nation ever changed its gods?
(Yet they are not gods at all.)
But my people have exchanged their[b]
Glory
for worthless idols.
12 Be appalled at this, O heavens,
and shudder with great horror,"
declares the LORD.
13 "My people have committed two sins:
They have forsaken me,
the spring of living water,
and have dug their own cisterns,
broken cisterns that cannot hold
water.
14 Is Israel a servant, a slave by birth?
Why then has he become plunder?
15 Lions have roared;
they have growled at him.
They have laid waste his land;
his towns are burned and deserted.
16 Also, the men of Memphis[c] and
Tahpanhes
have shaved the crown of your
head.[d]
17 Have you not brought this on
yourselves
by forsaking the LORD your God
when he led you in the way?
18 Now why go to Egypt
to drink water from the Shihor[e]?
And why go to Assyria
to drink water from the River[f]?
19 Your wickedness will punish you;
your backsliding will rebuke you.
Consider then and realize
how evil and bitter it is for you
when you forsake the LORD your God
and have no awe of me,"
declares the Lord,
the LORD Almighty.

20 "Long ago you broke off your yoke
and tore off your bonds;
you said, 'I will not serve you!'
Indeed, on every high hill
and under every spreading tree
you lay down as a prostitute.
21 I had planted you like a choice vine
of sound and reliable stock.
How then did you turn against me
into a corrupt, wild vine?
22 Although you wash yourself with soda
and use an abundance of soap,
the stain of your guilt is still before
me,"
declares the Sovereign LORD.
23 "How can you say, 'I am not defiled;
I have not run after the Baals'?
See how you behaved in the valley;
consider what you have done.
You are a swift she-camel
running here and there,
24 a wild donkey accustomed to the
desert,
sniffing the wind in her craving—
in her heat who can restrain her?
Any males that pursue her need not
tire themselves;
at mating time they will find her.
25 Do not run until your feet are bare
and your throat is dry.
But you said, 'It's no use!
I love foreign gods,
and I must go after them.'

26 "As a thief is disgraced when he is
caught,
so the house of Israel is disgraced—
they, their kings and their officials,
their priests and their prophets.
27 They say to wood, 'You are my
father,'
and to stone, 'You gave me birth.'
They have turned their backs to me
and not their faces;
yet when they are in trouble, they say,
'Come and save us!'
28 Where then are the gods you made for
yourselves?
Let them come if they can save you
when you are in trouble!
For you have as many gods
as you have towns, O Judah.

29 "Why do you bring charges against
me?
You have all rebelled against me,"
declares the LORD.
30 "In vain I punished your people;
they did not respond to correction.
Your sword has devoured your
prophets
like a ravening lion.

31 "You of this generation, consider the
word of the LORD:

"Have I been a desert to Israel

[a] 10 The home of Bedouin tribes in the Syro-Arabian desert [b] 11 Masoretic Text; an ancient Hebrew scribal tradition *my* [c] 16 Hebrew *Noph* [d] 16 Or *have cracked your skull* [e] 18 That is, a branch of the Nile [f] 18 That is, the Euphrates

or a land of great darkness?
Why do my people say, 'We are free to roam;
we will come to you no more'?
32Does a maiden forget her jewelry,
a bride her wedding ornaments?
Yet my people have forgotten me,
days without number.
33How skilled you are at pursuing love!
Even the worst of women can learn from your ways.
34On your clothes men find
the lifeblood of the innocent poor,
though you did not catch them breaking in.
Yet in spite of all this
35 you say, 'I am innocent;
he is not angry with me.'
But I will pass judgment on you
because you say, 'I have not sinned.'
36Why do you go about so much,
changing your ways?
You will be disappointed by Egypt
as you were by Assyria.
37You will also leave that place
with your hands on your head,
for the LORD has rejected those you trust;
you will not be helped by them.

3 "If a man divorces his wife
and she leaves him and marries another man,
should he return to her again?
Would not the land be completely defiled?
But you have lived as a prostitute with many lovers—
would you now return to me?"
declares the LORD.
2"Look up to the barren heights and see.
Is there any place where you have not been ravished?
By the roadside you sat waiting for lovers,
sat like a nomad[a] in the desert.
You have defiled the land
with your prostitution and wickedness.
3Therefore the showers have been withheld,
and no spring rains have fallen.
Yet you have the brazen look of a prostitute;
you refuse to blush with shame.
4Have you not just called to me:
'My Father, my friend from my youth,
5will you always be angry?
Will your wrath continue forever?'
This is how you talk,
but you do all the evil you can."

Unfaithful Israel

6During the reign of King Josiah, the LORD said to me, "Have you seen what faithless Israel has done? She has gone up on every high hill and under every spreading tree and has committed adultery there. 7I thought that after she had done all this she would return to me but she did not, and her unfaithful sister Judah saw it. 8I gave faithless Israel her certificate of divorce and sent her away because of all her adulteries. Yet I saw that her unfaithful sister Judah had no fear; she also went out and committed adultery. 9Because Israel's immorality mattered so little to her, she defiled the land and committed adultery with stone and wood. 10In spite of all this, her unfaithful sister Judah did not return to me with all her heart, but only in pretense," declares the LORD.

11The LORD said to me, "Faithless Israel is more righteous than unfaithful Judah. 12Go, proclaim this message toward the north:

" 'Return, faithless Israel,' declares the LORD,
'I will frown on you no longer,
for I am merciful,' declares the LORD,
'I will not be angry forever.
13Only acknowledge your guilt—
you have rebelled against the LORD your God,
you have scattered your favors to foreign gods
under every spreading tree,
and have not obeyed me,' "
declares the LORD.

14"Return, faithless people," declares the LORD, "for I am your husband. I will choose you—one from a town and two from a clan—and bring you to Zion. 15Then I will give you shepherds after my own heart, who will lead you with knowledge and understanding. 16In those days, when your numbers have increased greatly in the land," declares the LORD, "men will no longer say, 'The ark of the covenant of the LORD.' It will never enter their

[a]2 Or *an Arab*

minds or be remembered; it will not be
missed, nor will another one be made.
17At that time they will call Jerusalem The
Throne of the LORD, and all nations will
gather in Jerusalem to honor the name of
the LORD. No longer will they follow the
stubbornness of their evil hearts. 18In
those days the house of Judah will join the
house of Israel, and together they will
come from a northern land to the land I
gave your forefathers as an inheritance.
19"I myself said,

" 'How gladly would I treat you like
sons
and give you a desirable land,
the most beautiful inheritance of
any nation.'
I thought you would call me 'Father'
and not turn away from following
me.
20But like a woman unfaithful to her
husband,
so you have been unfaithful to me,
O house of Israel,"
declares the LORD.

21A cry is heard on the barren heights,
the weeping and pleading of the
people of Israel,
because they have perverted their
ways
and have forgotten the LORD their
God.

22"Return, faithless people;
I will cure you of backsliding."

"Yes, we will come to you,
for you are the LORD our God.
23Surely the ⌊idolatrous⌋ commotion on
the hills
and mountains is a deception;
surely in the LORD our God
is the salvation of Israel.
24From our youth shameful gods have
consumed
the fruits of our fathers' labor—
their flocks and herds,
their sons and daughters.
25Let us lie down in our shame,
and let our disgrace cover us.
We have sinned against the LORD our
God,
both we and our fathers;
from our youth till this day
we have not obeyed the LORD our
God."

4 "If you will return, O Israel,
return to me,"
declares the LORD.
"If you put your detestable idols out
of my sight
and no longer go astray,
2and if in a truthful, just and righteous
way
you swear, 'As surely as the LORD
lives,'
then the nations will be blessed by
him
and in him they will glory."

3This is what the LORD says to the men
of Judah and to Jerusalem:

"Break up your unplowed ground
and do not sow among thorns.
4Circumcise yourselves to the LORD,
circumcise your hearts,
you men of Judah and people of
Jerusalem,
or my wrath will break out and burn
like fire
because of the evil you have
done—
burn with no one to quench it.

Disaster From the North

5"Announce in Judah and proclaim in
Jerusalem and say:
'Sound the trumpet throughout the
land!'
Cry aloud and say:
'Gather together!
Let us flee to the fortified cities!'
6Raise the signal to go to Zion!
Flee for safety without delay!
For I am bringing disaster from the
north,
even terrible destruction."

7A lion has come out of his lair;
a destroyer of nations has set out.
He has left his place
to lay waste your land.
Your towns will lie in ruins
without inhabitant.
8So put on sackcloth,
lament and wail,
for the fierce anger of the LORD
has not turned away from us.

9"In that day," declares the LORD,
"the king and the officials will lose
heart,
the priests will be horrified,
and the prophets will be appalled."

10Then I said, "Ah, Sovereign LORD, how

WEEKENDING

CONVERSATION

Once you're married to each other and living together every day, it's sometimes easy to feel like there's nothing left to say. Try these questions to jump-start some lively discussions between you.

1. If you could keep just one memory, which memory would you keep?

2. How would you describe your ideal day? your ideal weekend? your ideal vacation?

3. If you could spend one uninterrupted hour with any person alive, who would it be? Why?

4. If our house caught fire (and everyone was safely out), what three things would you most want to save? Why?

5. What do you want your life to be like at 70?

— *Dennis and Barbara Rainey*

REVIVE

Saturday: Colossians 4:6
Sunday: Ephesians 5:19–20

Go to page 805 for your next devotional reading.

completely you have deceived this people
and Jerusalem by saying, 'You will have
peace,' when the sword is at our throats."
11At that time this people and Jerusa-
lem will be told, "A scorching wind from
the barren heights in the desert blows to-
ward my people, but not to winnow or
cleanse; 12a wind too strong for that
comes from me.[a] Now I pronounce my
judgments against them."

13Look! He advances like the clouds,
his chariots come like a whirlwind,
his horses are swifter than eagles.
Woe to us! We are ruined!
14O Jerusalem, wash the evil from your
heart and be saved.
How long will you harbor wicked
thoughts?
15A voice is announcing from Dan,
proclaiming disaster from the hills
of Ephraim.
16"Tell this to the nations,
proclaim it to Jerusalem:
'A besieging army is coming from a
distant land,
raising a war cry against the cities
of Judah.
17They surround her like men guarding
a field,
because she has rebelled against
me,' "
declares the LORD.
18"Your own conduct and actions
have brought this upon you.
This is your punishment.
How bitter it is!
How it pierces to the heart!"

19Oh, my anguish, my anguish!
I writhe in pain.
Oh, the agony of my heart!
My heart pounds within me,
I cannot keep silent.
For I have heard the sound of the
trumpet;
I have heard the battle cry.
20Disaster follows disaster;
the whole land lies in ruins.
In an instant my tents are destroyed,
my shelter in a moment.
21How long must I see the battle
standard
and hear the sound of the trumpet?

22"My people are fools;
they do not know me.
They are senseless children;
they have no understanding.
They are skilled in doing evil;
they know not how to do good."

23I looked at the earth,
and it was formless and empty;
and at the heavens,
and their light was gone.
24I looked at the mountains,
and they were quaking;
all the hills were swaying.
25I looked, and there were no people;
every bird in the sky had flown
away.
26I looked, and the fruitful land was a
desert;
all its towns lay in ruins
before the LORD, before his fierce
anger.
27This is what the LORD says:
"The whole land will be ruined,
though I will not destroy it
completely.
28Therefore the earth will mourn
and the heavens above grow dark,
because I have spoken and will not
relent,
I have decided and will not turn
back."
29At the sound of horsemen and archers
every town takes to flight.
Some go into the thickets;
some climb up among the rocks.
All the towns are deserted;
no one lives in them.

30What are you doing, O devastated
one?
Why dress yourself in scarlet
and put on jewels of gold?
Why shade your eyes with paint?
You adorn yourself in vain.
Your lovers despise you;
they seek your life.

31I hear a cry as of a woman in labor,
a groan as of one bearing her first
child—
the cry of the Daughter of Zion
gasping for breath,
stretching out her hands and saying,
"Alas! I am fainting;
my life is given over to murderers."

Not One Is Upright

5 "Go up and down the streets of
Jerusalem,

[a]12 Or *comes at my command*

look around and consider,
search through her squares.
If you can find but one person
who deals honestly and seeks the truth,
I will forgive this city.
2 Although they say, 'As surely as the LORD lives,'
still they are swearing falsely."

3 O LORD, do not your eyes look for truth?
You struck them, but they felt no pain;
you crushed them, but they refused correction.
They made their faces harder than stone
and refused to repent.

VERSE FOR THE DAY: Jeremiah 5:1 | AUTHOR: Charles Colson | PASSAGE FOR THE DAY: Jeremiah 5:1–31

The Best Policy

As the Watergate storm thundered around me, I was subpoenaed by grand juries, summoned before congressional committees, interrogated by special prosecutors and the FBI. The real crucible came the day I was hauled before a grand jury. Most of the questions were designed to embarrass and entrap me.

My first instinct was to evade, maybe even shade the truth a bit, and throw them off the track. But another voice—my father's—sounded in my mind: "Always tell the truth. It's the right thing to do."

Those words and my dad's faithful example over the years stayed with me. So that day in the courthouse, I took a few deep breaths, sat up straight in my chair and gave truthful answers. I did the same thing the forty-four other times I was called to testify under oath during Watergate—and, as it turned out, I was the only major Watergate figure not charged with perjury.

That didn't keep me out of jail, however. As I was being sentenced, my dad's question to me was, "Have you told the truth?" I told him I had. He looked at me with a confident smile. "Then you'll be all right." And he was right.

MARRIAGE BUILDERS

♦ *Has there ever been a time when it seemed like a lie could make your life a lot simpler? What did you do?*
♦ *What person in your life is your best model of honesty or integrity?*

Additional Scripture Readings
Proverbs 6:16–17; Proverbs 12:19, 22;
2 Corinthians 6:4–7

Go to page 808 for your next devotional reading.

4I thought, "These are only the poor;
they are foolish,
for they do not know the way of the LORD,
the requirements of their God.
5So I will go to the leaders
and speak to them;
surely they know the way of the LORD,
the requirements of their God."
But with one accord they too had broken off the yoke
and torn off the bonds.
6Therefore a lion from the forest will attack them,
a wolf from the desert will ravage them,
a leopard will lie in wait near their towns
to tear to pieces any who venture out,
for their rebellion is great
and their backslidings many.

7"Why should I forgive you?
Your children have forsaken me
and sworn by gods that are not gods.
I supplied all their needs,
yet they committed adultery
and thronged to the houses of prostitutes.
8They are well-fed, lusty stallions,
each neighing for another man's wife.
9Should I not punish them for this?"
declares the LORD.
"Should I not avenge myself
on such a nation as this?

10"Go through her vineyards and ravage them,
but do not destroy them completely.
Strip off her branches,
for these people do not belong to the LORD.
11The house of Israel and the house of Judah
have been utterly unfaithful to me,"
declares the LORD.

12They have lied about the LORD;
they said, "He will do nothing!
No harm will come to us;
we will never see sword or famine.
13The prophets are but wind
and the word is not in them;
so let what they say be done to them."

14Therefore this is what the LORD God Almighty says:
"Because the people have spoken these words,
I will make my words in your mouth a fire
and these people the wood it consumes.
15O house of Israel," declares the LORD,
"I am bringing a distant nation against you—
an ancient and enduring nation,
a people whose language you do not know,
whose speech you do not understand.
16Their quivers are like an open grave;
all of them are mighty warriors.
17They will devour your harvests and food,
devour your sons and daughters;
they will devour your flocks and herds,
devour your vines and fig trees.
With the sword they will destroy
the fortified cities in which you trust.

18"Yet even in those days," declares the LORD, "I will not destroy you completely.
19And when the people ask, 'Why has the LORD our God done all this to us?' you will tell them, 'As you have forsaken me and served foreign gods in your own land, so now you will serve foreigners in a land not your own.'

20"Announce this to the house of Jacob
and proclaim it in Judah:
21Hear this, you foolish and senseless people,
who have eyes but do not see,
who have ears but do not hear:
22Should you not fear me?" declares the LORD.
"Should you not tremble in my presence?
I made the sand a boundary for the sea,
an everlasting barrier it cannot cross.
The waves may roll, but they cannot prevail;
they may roar, but they cannot cross it.
23But these people have stubborn and rebellious hearts;
they have turned aside and gone away.
24They do not say to themselves,
'Let us fear the LORD our God,

who gives autumn and spring rains in season,
who assures us of the regular weeks of harvest.'
25 Your wrongdoings have kept these away;
your sins have deprived you of good.

26 "Among my people are wicked men
who lie in wait like men who snare birds
and like those who set traps to catch men.
27 Like cages full of birds,
their houses are full of deceit;
they have become rich and powerful
28 and have grown fat and sleek.
Their evil deeds have no limit;
they do not plead the case of the fatherless to win it,
they do not defend the rights of the poor.
29 Should I not punish them for this?"
declares the LORD.
"Should I not avenge myself
on such a nation as this?

30 "A horrible and shocking thing
has happened in the land:
31 The prophets prophesy lies,
the priests rule by their own authority,
and my people love it this way.
But what will you do in the end?

Jerusalem Under Siege

6 "Flee for safety, people of Benjamin!
Flee from Jerusalem!
Sound the trumpet in Tekoa!
Raise the signal over Beth Hakkerem!
For disaster looms out of the north,
even terrible destruction.
2 I will destroy the Daughter of Zion,
so beautiful and delicate.
3 Shepherds with their flocks will come against her;
they will pitch their tents around her,
each tending his own portion."

4 "Prepare for battle against her!
Arise, let us attack at noon!
But, alas, the daylight is fading,
and the shadows of evening grow long.
5 So arise, let us attack at night
and destroy her fortresses!"

6 This is what the LORD Almighty says:

"Cut down the trees
and build siege ramps against Jerusalem.
This city must be punished;
it is filled with oppression.
7 As a well pours out its water,
so she pours out her wickedness.
Violence and destruction resound in her;
her sickness and wounds are ever before me.
8 Take warning, O Jerusalem,
or I will turn away from you
and make your land desolate
so no one can live in it."

9 This is what the LORD Almighty says:

"Let them glean the remnant of Israel
as thoroughly as a vine;
pass your hand over the branches again,
like one gathering grapes."

10 To whom can I speak and give warning?
Who will listen to me?
Their ears are closed[a]
so they cannot hear.
The word of the LORD is offensive to them;
they find no pleasure in it.
11 But I am full of the wrath of the LORD,
and I cannot hold it in.

"Pour it out on the children in the street
and on the young men gathered together;
both husband and wife will be caught in it,
and the old, those weighed down with years.
12 Their houses will be turned over to others,
together with their fields and their wives,
when I stretch out my hand
against those who live in the land,"
declares the LORD.
13 "From the least to the greatest,
all are greedy for gain;
prophets and priests alike,
all practice deceit.
14 They dress the wound of my people

[a] 10 Hebrew *uncircumcised*

as though it were not serious.
'Peace, peace,' they say,
when there is no peace.
15 Are they ashamed of their loathsome
conduct?
No, they have no shame at all;
they do not even know how to
blush.
So they will fall among the fallen;
they will be brought down when I
punish them,"
says the LORD.
16 This is what the LORD says:
"Stand at the crossroads and look;
ask for the ancient paths,

VERSE FOR THE DAY: Jeremiah 6:16 | AUTHOR: Diane Eble | PASSAGE FOR THE DAY: Jeremiah 6:1–16

Why We Stay Married

My husband and I reached a crisis point, dealing with an issue that had to be resolved one way or the other. I wasn't sure how I could stay in the marriage if things continued as they were.

We sought the help of a counselor, and I was surprised when he asked, "Do you know why you're staying together, or is it just an unquestioned sense of duty? Why have you chosen to stick it out?"

Staying together, I realized, was not the same as "sticking it out, no matter what." In sticking things out, we only seemed to remain stuck. But I believed that God could do anything, didn't I? Was I really trusting him with my marriage?

My husband and I came to the point where we could focus on working through our problems with all the energy and commitment we had. I chose our marriage above all the other possibilities—leaving, ignoring the problems, going my own way while living under the same roof—and I continue to make that choice every day.

Love is both risky and immensely rewarding precisely because it is something freely chosen and freely given. Remove the element of choice and you cut out the very heart of love. Marriage that does not rest on this kind of love may be tight-lipped commitment, but it's not all that God had in mind when he created marriage.

MARRIAGE BUILDERS

- *What are the risks of loving?*
- *What makes the difference between "sticking it out" and staying together with a better future in mind?*

Additional Scripture Readings
Joshua 24:15; Malachi 2:14–16

Go to page 821 for your next devotional reading.

ask where the good way is, and walk
in it,
and you will find rest for your
souls.
But you said, 'We will not walk in
it.'
17I appointed watchmen over you and
said,
'Listen to the sound of the trumpet!'
But you said, 'We will not listen.'
18Therefore hear, O nations;
observe, O witnesses,
what will happen to them.
19Hear, O earth:
I am bringing disaster on this people,
the fruit of their schemes,
because they have not listened to my
words
and have rejected my law.
20What do I care about incense from
Sheba
or sweet calamus from a distant
land?
Your burnt offerings are not
acceptable;
your sacrifices do not please me."

21Therefore this is what the LORD says:

"I will put obstacles before this
people.
Fathers and sons alike will stumble
over them;
neighbors and friends will perish."

22This is what the LORD says:

"Look, an army is coming
from the land of the north;
a great nation is being stirred up
from the ends of the earth.
23They are armed with bow and spear;
they are cruel and show no mercy.
They sound like the roaring sea
as they ride on their horses;
they come like men in battle
formation
to attack you, O Daughter of Zion."
24We have heard reports about them,
and our hands hang limp.
Anguish has gripped us,
pain like that of a woman in labor.
25Do not go out to the fields
or walk on the roads,
for the enemy has a sword,
and there is terror on every side.
26O my people, put on sackcloth
and roll in ashes;
mourn with bitter wailing
as for an only son,
for suddenly the destroyer
will come upon us.
27"I have made you a tester of metals
and my people the ore,
that you may observe
and test their ways.
28They are all hardened rebels,
going about to slander.
They are bronze and iron;
they all act corruptly.
29The bellows blow fiercely
to burn away the lead with fire,
but the refining goes on in vain;
the wicked are not purged out.
30They are called rejected silver,
because the LORD has rejected
them."

False Religion Worthless

7 This is the word that came to Jeremiah from the LORD: 2"Stand at the gate of the LORD's house and there proclaim this message:

" 'Hear the word of the LORD, all you people of Judah who come through these gates to worship the LORD. 3This is what the LORD Almighty, the God of Israel, says: Reform your ways and your actions, and I will let you live in this place. 4Do not trust in deceptive words and say, "This is the temple of the LORD, the temple of the LORD, the temple of the LORD!" 5If you really change your ways and your actions and deal with each other justly, 6if you do not oppress the alien, the fatherless or the widow and do not shed innocent blood in this place, and if you do not follow other gods to your own harm, 7then I will let you live in this place, in the land I gave your forefathers for ever and ever. 8But look, you are trusting in deceptive words that are worthless.

9" 'Will you steal and murder, commit adultery and perjury,[a] burn incense to Baal and follow other gods you have not known, 10and then come and stand before me in this house, which bears my Name, and say, "We are safe"—safe to do all these detestable things? 11Has this house, which bears my Name, become a den of robbers to you? But I have been watching! declares the LORD.

12" 'Go now to the place in Shiloh where I first made a dwelling for my Name, and

[a]9 Or *and swear by false gods*

see what I did to it because of the wickedness of my people Israel. [13]While you were doing all these things, declares the LORD, I spoke to you again and again, but you did not listen; I called you, but you did not answer. [14]Therefore, what I did to Shiloh I will now do to the house that bears my Name, the temple you trust in, the place I gave to you and your fathers. [15]I will thrust you from my presence, just as I did all your brothers, the people of Ephraim.'

[16]"So do not pray for this people nor offer any plea or petition for them; do not plead with me, for I will not listen to you. [17]Do you not see what they are doing in the towns of Judah and in the streets of Jerusalem? [18]The children gather wood, the fathers light the fire, and the women knead the dough and make cakes of bread for the Queen of Heaven. They pour out drink offerings to other gods to provoke me to anger. [19]But am I the one they are provoking? declares the LORD. Are they not rather harming themselves, to their own shame?

[20]" 'Therefore this is what the Sovereign LORD says: My anger and my wrath will be poured out on this place, on man and beast, on the trees of the field and on the fruit of the ground, and it will burn and not be quenched.

[21]" 'This is what the LORD Almighty, the God of Israel, says: Go ahead, add your burnt offerings to your other sacrifices and eat the meat yourselves! [22]For when I brought your forefathers out of Egypt and spoke to them, I did not just give them commands about burnt offerings and sacrifices, [23]but I gave them this command: Obey me, and I will be your God and you will be my people. Walk in all the ways I command you, that it may go well with you. [24]But they did not listen or pay attention; instead, they followed the stubborn inclinations of their evil hearts. They went backward and not forward. [25]From the time your forefathers left Egypt until now, day after day, again and again I sent you my servants the prophets. [26]But they did not listen to me or pay attention. They were stiff-necked and did more evil than their forefathers.'

[27]"When you tell them all this, they will not listen to you; when you call to them, they will not answer. [28]Therefore say to them, 'This is the nation that has not obeyed the LORD its God or responded to correction. Truth has perished; it has vanished from their lips. [29]Cut off your hair and throw it away; take up a lament on the barren heights, for the LORD has rejected and abandoned this generation that is under his wrath.

The Valley of Slaughter

[30]" 'The people of Judah have done evil in my eyes, declares the LORD. They have set up their detestable idols in the house that bears my Name and have defiled it. [31]They have built the high places of Topheth in the Valley of Ben Hinnom to burn their sons and daughters in the fire—something I did not command, nor did it enter my mind. [32]So beware, the days are coming, declares the LORD, when people will no longer call it Topheth or the Valley of Ben Hinnom, but the Valley of Slaughter, for they will bury the dead in Topheth until there is no more room. [33]Then the carcasses of this people will become food for the birds of the air and the beasts of the earth, and there will be no one to frighten them away. [34]I will bring an end to the sounds of joy and gladness and to the voices of bride and bridegroom in the towns of Judah and the streets of Jerusalem, for the land will become desolate.

8 " 'At that time, declares the LORD, the bones of the kings and officials of Judah, the bones of the priests and prophets, and the bones of the people of Jerusalem will be removed from their graves. [2]They will be exposed to the sun and the moon and all the stars of the heavens, which they have loved and served and which they have followed and consulted and worshiped. They will not be gathered up or buried, but will be like refuse lying on the ground. [3]Wherever I banish them, all the survivors of this evil nation will prefer death to life, declares the LORD Almighty.'

Sin and Punishment

[4]"Say to them, 'This is what the LORD says:

" 'When men fall down, do they not
get up?
When a man turns away, does he
not return?
[5]Why then have these people turned
away?
Why does Jerusalem always turn
away?
They cling to deceit;
they refuse to return.

6I have listened attentively,
but they do not say what is right.
No one repents of his wickedness,
saying, "What have I done?"
Each pursues his own course
like a horse charging into battle.
7Even the stork in the sky
knows her appointed seasons,
and the dove, the swift and the thrush
observe the time of their migration.
But my people do not know
the requirements of the LORD.

8" 'How can you say, "We are wise,
for we have the law of the LORD,"
when actually the lying pen of the scribes
has handled it falsely?
9The wise will be put to shame;
they will be dismayed and trapped.
Since they have rejected the word of the LORD,
what kind of wisdom do they have?
10Therefore I will give their wives to other men
and their fields to new owners.
From the least to the greatest,
all are greedy for gain;
prophets and priests alike,
all practice deceit.
11They dress the wound of my people
as though it were not serious.
"Peace, peace," they say,
when there is no peace.
12Are they ashamed of their loathsome conduct?
No, they have no shame at all;
they do not even know how to blush.
So they will fall among the fallen;
they will be brought down when they are punished,
says the LORD.

13" 'I will take away their harvest,
declares the LORD.
There will be no grapes on the vine.
There will be no figs on the tree,
and their leaves will wither.
What I have given them
will be taken from them.[a]' "

14"Why are we sitting here?
Gather together!
Let us flee to the fortified cities
and perish there!
For the LORD our God has doomed us to perish
and given us poisoned water to drink,
because we have sinned against him.
15We hoped for peace
but no good has come,
for a time of healing
but there was only terror.
16The snorting of the enemy's horses
is heard from Dan;
at the neighing of their stallions
the whole land trembles.
They have come to devour
the land and everything in it,
the city and all who live there."

17"See, I will send venomous snakes among you,
vipers that cannot be charmed,
and they will bite you,"
declares the LORD.

18O my Comforter[b] in sorrow,
my heart is faint within me.
19Listen to the cry of my people
from a land far away:
"Is the LORD not in Zion?
Is her King no longer there?"

"Why have they provoked me to anger with their images,
with their worthless foreign idols?"

20"The harvest is past,
the summer has ended,
and we are not saved."

21Since my people are crushed, I am crushed;
I mourn, and horror grips me.
22Is there no balm in Gilead?
Is there no physician there?
Why then is there no healing
for the wound of my people?

9 1Oh, that my head were a spring of water
and my eyes a fountain of tears!
I would weep day and night
for the slain of my people.
2Oh, that I had in the desert
a lodging place for travelers,
so that I might leave my people
and go away from them;
for they are all adulterers,
a crowd of unfaithful people.

3"They make ready their tongue

[a] 13 The meaning of the Hebrew for this sentence is uncertain.
[b] 18 The meaning of the Hebrew for this word is uncertain.

like a bow, to shoot lies;
it is not by truth
that they triumph[a] in the land.
They go from one sin to another;
they do not acknowledge me,"
declares the LORD.
4"Beware of your friends;
do not trust your brothers.
For every brother is a deceiver,[b]
and every friend a slanderer.
5Friend deceives friend,
and no one speaks the truth.
They have taught their tongues to lie;
they weary themselves with sinning.
6You[c] live in the midst of deception;
in their deceit they refuse to
acknowledge me,"
declares the LORD.

7Therefore this is what the LORD Almighty says:

"See, I will refine and test them,
for what else can I do
because of the sin of my people?
8Their tongue is a deadly arrow;
it speaks with deceit.
With his mouth each speaks cordially
to his neighbor,
but in his heart he sets a trap for
him.
9Should I not punish them for this?"
declares the LORD.
"Should I not avenge myself
on such a nation as this?"

10I will weep and wail for the
mountains
and take up a lament concerning
the desert pastures.
They are desolate and untraveled,
and the lowing of cattle is not
heard.
The birds of the air have fled
and the animals are gone.
11"I will make Jerusalem a heap of
ruins,
a haunt of jackals;
and I will lay waste the towns of
Judah
so no one can live there."

12What man is wise enough to understand this? Who has been instructed by the LORD and can explain it? Why has the land been ruined and laid waste like a desert that no one can cross?

13The LORD said, "It is because they have forsaken my law, which I set before them; they have not obeyed me or followed my law. 14Instead, they have followed the stubbornness of their hearts; they have followed the Baals, as their fathers taught them." 15Therefore, this is what the LORD Almighty, the God of Israel, says: "See, I will make this people eat bitter food and drink poisoned water. 16I will scatter them among nations that neither they nor their fathers have known, and I will pursue them with the sword until I have destroyed them."

17This is what the LORD Almighty says:

"Consider now! Call for the wailing
women to come;
send for the most skillful of them.
18Let them come quickly
and wail over us
till our eyes overflow with tears
and water streams from our eyelids.
19The sound of wailing is heard from
Zion:
'How ruined we are!
How great is our shame!
We must leave our land
because our houses are in ruins.' "

20Now, O women, hear the word of the
LORD;
open your ears to the words of his
mouth.
Teach your daughters how to wail;
teach one another a lament.
21Death has climbed in through our
windows
and has entered our fortresses;
it has cut off the children from the
streets
and the young men from the public
squares.

22Say, "This is what the LORD declares:

" 'The dead bodies of men will lie
like refuse on the open field,
like cut grain behind the reaper,
with no one to gather them.' "

23This is what the LORD says:

"Let not the wise man boast of his
wisdom
or the strong man boast of his
strength
or the rich man boast of his riches,

[a] 3 Or *lies; / they are not valiant for truth*
[b] 4 Or *a deceiving Jacob*
[c] 6 That is, Jeremiah (the Hebrew is singular)

24but let him who boasts boast about this:
that he understands and knows me,
that I am the LORD, who exercises kindness,
justice and righteousness on earth,
for in these I delight,"
declares the LORD.

25"The days are coming," declares the LORD, "when I will punish all who are circumcised only in the flesh— 26Egypt, Judah, Edom, Ammon, Moab and all who live in the desert in distant places.[a] For all these nations are really uncircumcised, and even the whole house of Israel is uncircumcised in heart."

God and Idols

10 Hear what the LORD says to you, O house of Israel. 2This is what the LORD says:

"Do not learn the ways of the nations
or be terrified by signs in the sky,
though the nations are terrified by them.
3For the customs of the peoples are worthless;
they cut a tree out of the forest,
and a craftsman shapes it with his chisel.
4They adorn it with silver and gold;
they fasten it with hammer and nails
so it will not totter.
5Like a scarecrow in a melon patch,
their idols cannot speak;
they must be carried
because they cannot walk.
Do not fear them;
they can do no harm
nor can they do any good."

6No one is like you, O LORD;
you are great,
and your name is mighty in power.
7Who should not revere you,
O King of the nations?
This is your due.
Among all the wise men of the nations
and in all their kingdoms,
there is no one like you.
8They are all senseless and foolish;
they are taught by worthless wooden idols.
9Hammered silver is brought from Tarshish
and gold from Uphaz.
What the craftsman and goldsmith have made
is then dressed in blue and purple—
all made by skilled workers.
10But the LORD is the true God;
he is the living God, the eternal King.
When he is angry, the earth trembles;
the nations cannot endure his wrath.

11"Tell them this: 'These gods, who did not make the heavens and the earth, will perish from the earth and from under the heavens.' "[b]

12But God made the earth by his power;
he founded the world by his wisdom
and stretched out the heavens by his understanding.
13When he thunders, the waters in the heavens roar;
he makes clouds rise from the ends of the earth.
He sends lightning with the rain
and brings out the wind from his storehouses.
14Everyone is senseless and without knowledge;
every goldsmith is shamed by his idols.
His images are a fraud;
they have no breath in them.
15They are worthless, the objects of mockery;
when their judgment comes, they will perish.
16He who is the Portion of Jacob is not like these,
for he is the Maker of all things,
including Israel, the tribe of his inheritance—
the LORD Almighty is his name.

Coming Destruction

17Gather up your belongings to leave the land,
you who live under siege.
18For this is what the LORD says:
"At this time I will hurl out those who live in this land;
I will bring distress on them

[a]26 Or *desert and who clip the hair by their foreheads*

[b]11 The text of this verse is in Aramaic.

so that they may be captured."

19Woe to me because of my injury!
My wound is incurable!
Yet I said to myself,
"This is my sickness, and I must endure it."
20My tent is destroyed;
all its ropes are snapped.
My sons are gone from me and are no more;
no one is left now to pitch my tent
or to set up my shelter.
21The shepherds are senseless
and do not inquire of the LORD;
so they do not prosper
and all their flock is scattered.
22Listen! The report is coming—
a great commotion from the land of the north!
It will make the towns of Judah desolate,
a haunt of jackals.

Jeremiah's Prayer

23I know, O LORD, that a man's life is not his own;
it is not for man to direct his steps.
24Correct me, LORD, but only with justice—
not in your anger,
lest you reduce me to nothing.
25Pour out your wrath on the nations
that do not acknowledge you,
on the peoples who do not call on your name.
For they have devoured Jacob;
they have devoured him completely
and destroyed his homeland.

The Covenant Is Broken

11 This is the word that came to Jeremiah from the LORD: 2"Listen to the terms of this covenant and tell them to the people of Judah and to those who live in Jerusalem. 3Tell them that this is what the LORD, the God of Israel, says: 'Cursed is the man who does not obey the terms of this covenant— 4the terms I commanded your forefathers when I brought them out of Egypt, out of the iron-smelting furnace.' I said, 'Obey me and do everything I command you, and you will be my people, and I will be your God. 5Then I will fulfill the oath I swore to your forefathers, to give them a land flowing with milk and honey'—the land you possess today."

I answered, "Amen, LORD."

6The LORD said to me, "Proclaim all these words in the towns of Judah and in the streets of Jerusalem: 'Listen to the terms of this covenant and follow them. 7From the time I brought your forefathers up from Egypt until today, I warned them again and again, saying, "Obey me." 8But they did not listen or pay attention; instead, they followed the stubbornness of their evil hearts. So I brought on them all the curses of the covenant I had commanded them to follow but that they did not keep.' "

9Then the LORD said to me, "There is a conspiracy among the people of Judah and those who live in Jerusalem. 10They have returned to the sins of their forefathers, who refused to listen to my words. They have followed other gods to serve them. Both the house of Israel and the house of Judah have broken the covenant I made with their forefathers. 11Therefore this is what the LORD says: 'I will bring on them a disaster they cannot escape. Although they cry out to me, I will not listen to them. 12The towns of Judah and the people of Jerusalem will go and cry out to the gods to whom they burn incense, but they will not help them at all when disaster strikes. 13You have as many gods as you have towns, O Judah; and the altars you have set up to burn incense to that shameful god Baal are as many as the streets of Jerusalem.'

14"Do not pray for this people nor offer any plea or petition for them, because I will not listen when they call to me in the time of their distress.

15"What is my beloved doing in my temple
as she works out her evil schemes with many?
Can consecrated meat avert ⌞your punishment⌟?
When you engage in your wickedness,
then you rejoice.[a]"

16The LORD called you a thriving olive tree
with fruit beautiful in form.
But with the roar of a mighty storm
he will set it on fire,
and its branches will be broken.

17The LORD Almighty, who planted you, has decreed disaster for you, because the

[a]15 Or *Could consecrated meat avert your punishment? / Then you would rejoice*

house of Israel and the house of Judah
have done evil and provoked me to anger
by burning incense to Baal.

Plot Against Jeremiah

18Because the LORD revealed their plot
to me, I knew it, for at that time he
showed me what they were doing. 19I had
been like a gentle lamb led to the slaughter; I did not realize that they had plotted
against me, saying,

"Let us destroy the tree and its fruit;
let us cut him off from the land of
the living,
that his name be remembered no
more."
20But, O LORD Almighty, you who judge
righteously
and test the heart and mind,
let me see your vengeance upon them,
for to you I have committed my
cause.

21"Therefore this is what the LORD says
about the men of Anathoth who are seeking your life and saying, 'Do not prophesy
in the name of the LORD or you will die by
our hands'— 22therefore this is what the
LORD Almighty says: 'I will punish them.
Their young men will die by the sword,
their sons and daughters by famine. 23Not
even a remnant will be left to them, because I will bring disaster on the men of
Anathoth in the year of their punishment.' "

Jeremiah's Complaint

12 You are always righteous,
O LORD,
when I bring a case before you.
Yet I would speak with you about
your justice:
Why does the way of the wicked
prosper?
Why do all the faithless live at ease?
2You have planted them, and they have
taken root;
they grow and bear fruit.
You are always on their lips
but far from their hearts.
3Yet you know me, O LORD;
you see me and test my thoughts
about you.
Drag them off like sheep to be
butchered!
Set them apart for the day of
slaughter!
4How long will the land lie parched[a]
and the grass in every field be
withered?
Because those who live in it are
wicked,
the animals and birds have
perished.
Moreover, the people are saying,
"He will not see what happens to
us."

God's Answer

5"If you have raced with men on foot
and they have worn you out,
how can you compete with horses?
If you stumble in safe country,[b]
how will you manage in the thickets
by[c] the Jordan?
6Your brothers, your own family—
even they have betrayed you;
they have raised a loud cry against
you.
Do not trust them,
though they speak well of you.

7"I will forsake my house,
abandon my inheritance;
I will give the one I love
into the hands of her enemies.
8My inheritance has become to me
like a lion in the forest.
She roars at me;
therefore I hate her.
9Has not my inheritance become to me
like a speckled bird of prey
that other birds of prey surround
and attack?
Go and gather all the wild beasts;
bring them to devour.
10Many shepherds will ruin my vineyard
and trample down my field;
they will turn my pleasant field
into a desolate wasteland.
11It will be made a wasteland,
parched and desolate before me;
the whole land will be laid waste
because there is no one who cares.
12Over all the barren heights in the
desert
destroyers will swarm,
for the sword of the LORD will devour
from one end of the land to the
other;
no one will be safe.
13They will sow wheat but reap thorns;
they will wear themselves out but
gain nothing.

[a]4 Or *land mourn* [b]5 Or *If you put your trust in a land of safety* [c]5 Or *the flooding of*

So bear the shame of your harvest
because of the LORD's fierce anger."

14This is what the LORD says: "As for all
my wicked neighbors who seize the inheritance I gave my people Israel, I will uproot them from their lands and I will uproot the house of Judah from among them. 15But after I uproot them, I will again have compassion and will bring each of them back to his own inheritance and his own country. 16And if they learn well the ways of my people and swear by my name, saying, 'As surely as the LORD lives'—even as they once taught my people to swear by Baal—then they will be established among my people. 17But if any nation does not listen, I will completely uproot and destroy it," declares the LORD.

A Linen Belt

13 This is what the LORD said to me: "Go and buy a linen belt and put it around your waist, but do not let it touch water." 2So I bought a belt, as the LORD directed, and put it around my waist.

3Then the word of the LORD came to me a second time: 4"Take the belt you bought and are wearing around your waist, and go now to Perath[a] and hide it there in a crevice in the rocks." 5So I went and hid it at Perath, as the LORD told me.

6Many days later the LORD said to me, "Go now to Perath and get the belt I told you to hide there." 7So I went to Perath and dug up the belt and took it from the place where I had hidden it, but now it was ruined and completely useless.

8Then the word of the LORD came to me: 9"This is what the LORD says: 'In the same way I will ruin the pride of Judah and the great pride of Jerusalem. 10These wicked people, who refuse to listen to my words, who follow the stubbornness of their hearts and go after other gods to serve and worship them, will be like this belt—completely useless! 11For as a belt is bound around a man's waist, so I bound the whole house of Israel and the whole house of Judah to me,' declares the LORD, 'to be my people for my renown and praise and honor. But they have not listened.'

Wineskins

12"Say to them: 'This is what the LORD, the God of Israel, says: Every wineskin should be filled with wine.' And if they say to you, 'Don't we know that every wineskin should be filled with wine?' 13then tell them, 'This is what the LORD says: I am going to fill with drunkenness all who live in this land, including the kings who sit on David's throne, the priests, the prophets and all those living in Jerusalem. 14I will smash them one against the other, fathers and sons alike, declares the LORD. I will allow no pity or mercy or compassion to keep me from destroying them.' "

Threat of Captivity

15Hear and pay attention,
do not be arrogant,
for the LORD has spoken.
16Give glory to the LORD your God
before he brings the darkness,
before your feet stumble
on the darkening hills.
You hope for light,
but he will turn it to thick darkness
and change it to deep gloom.
17But if you do not listen,
I will weep in secret
because of your pride;
my eyes will weep bitterly,
overflowing with tears,
because the LORD's flock will be
taken captive.

18Say to the king and to the queen
mother,
"Come down from your thrones,
for your glorious crowns
will fall from your heads."
19The cities in the Negev will be shut
up,
and there will be no one to open
them.
All Judah will be carried into exile,
carried completely away.

20Lift up your eyes and see
those who are coming from the
north.
Where is the flock that was entrusted
to you,
the sheep of which you boasted?
21What will you say when ⌊the LORD⌋
sets over you
those you cultivated as your special
allies?
Will not pain grip you
like that of a woman in labor?
22And if you ask yourself,

[a]4 Or possibly *the Euphrates*; also in verses 5-7

"Why has this happened to me?"—
it is because of your many sins
that your skirts have been torn off
and your body mistreated.
23Can the Ethiopian[a] change his skin
or the leopard its spots?
Neither can you do good
who are accustomed to doing evil.

24"I will scatter you like chaff
driven by the desert wind.
25This is your lot,
the portion I have decreed for you,"
declares the LORD,
"because you have forgotten me
and trusted in false gods.
26I will pull up your skirts over your face
that your shame may be seen—
27your adulteries and lustful neighings,
your shameless prostitution!
I have seen your detestable acts
on the hills and in the fields.
Woe to you, O Jerusalem!
How long will you be unclean?"

Drought, Famine, Sword

14 This is the word of the LORD to Jeremiah concerning the drought:

2"Judah mourns,
her cities languish;
they wail for the land,
and a cry goes up from Jerusalem.
3The nobles send their servants for water;
they go to the cisterns
but find no water.
They return with their jars unfilled;
dismayed and despairing,
they cover their heads.
4The ground is cracked
because there is no rain in the land;
the farmers are dismayed
and cover their heads.
5Even the doe in the field
deserts her newborn fawn
because there is no grass.
6Wild donkeys stand on the barren heights
and pant like jackals;
their eyesight fails
for lack of pasture."

7Although our sins testify against us,
O LORD, do something for the sake of your name.
For our backsliding is great;
we have sinned against you.
8O Hope of Israel,
its Savior in times of distress,
why are you like a stranger in the land,
like a traveler who stays only a night?
9Why are you like a man taken by surprise,
like a warrior powerless to save?
You are among us, O LORD,
and we bear your name;
do not forsake us!

10This is what the LORD says about this people:

"They greatly love to wander;
they do not restrain their feet.
So the LORD does not accept them;
he will now remember their wickedness
and punish them for their sins."

11Then the LORD said to me, "Do not pray for the well-being of this people. 12Although they fast, I will not listen to their cry; though they offer burnt offerings and grain offerings, I will not accept them. Instead, I will destroy them with the sword, famine and plague."

13But I said, "Ah, Sovereign LORD, the prophets keep telling them, 'You will not see the sword or suffer famine. Indeed, I will give you lasting peace in this place.' "

14Then the LORD said to me, "The prophets are prophesying lies in my name. I have not sent them or appointed them or spoken to them. They are prophesying to you false visions, divinations, idolatries[b] and the delusions of their own minds. 15Therefore, this is what the LORD says about the prophets who are prophesying in my name: I did not send them, yet they are saying, 'No sword or famine will touch this land.' Those same prophets will perish by sword and famine. 16And the people they are prophesying to will be thrown out into the streets of Jerusalem because of the famine and sword. There will be no one to bury them or their wives, their sons or their daughters. I will pour out on them the calamity they deserve.

17"Speak this word to them:

" 'Let my eyes overflow with tears

[a]23 Hebrew *Cushite* (probably a person from the upper Nile region) [b]14 Or *visions, worthless divinations*

night and day without ceasing;
for my virgin daughter—my people—
has suffered a grievous wound,
a crushing blow.
18If I go into the country,
I see those slain by the sword;
if I go into the city,
I see the ravages of famine.
Both prophet and priest
have gone to a land they know
not.' "

19Have you rejected Judah completely?
Do you despise Zion?
Why have you afflicted us
so that we cannot be healed?
We hoped for peace
but no good has come,
for a time of healing
but there is only terror.
20O LORD, we acknowledge our
wickedness
and the guilt of our fathers;
we have indeed sinned against you.
21For the sake of your name do not
despise us;
do not dishonor your glorious
throne.
Remember your covenant with us
and do not break it.
22Do any of the worthless idols of the
nations bring rain?
Do the skies themselves send down
showers?
No, it is you, O LORD our God.
Therefore our hope is in you,
for you are the one who does all
this.

15 Then the LORD said to me: "Even if Moses and Samuel were to stand before me, my heart would not go out to this people. Send them away from my presence! Let them go! 2And if they ask you, 'Where shall we go?' tell them, 'This is what the LORD says:

" 'Those destined for death, to death;
those for the sword, to the sword;
those for starvation, to starvation;
those for captivity, to captivity.'

3"I will send four kinds of destroyers against them," declares the LORD, "the sword to kill and the dogs to drag away and the birds of the air and the beasts of the earth to devour and destroy. 4I will make them abhorrent to all the kingdoms of the earth because of what Manasseh son of Hezekiah king of Judah did in Jerusalem.

5"Who will have pity on you,
O Jerusalem?
Who will mourn for you?
Who will stop to ask how you are?
6You have rejected me," declares the
LORD.
"You keep on backsliding.
So I will lay hands on you and destroy
you;
I can no longer show compassion.
7I will winnow them with a winnowing
fork
at the city gates of the land.
I will bring bereavement and
destruction on my people,
for they have not changed their
ways.
8I will make their widows more
numerous
than the sand of the sea.
At midday I will bring a destroyer
against the mothers of their young
men;
suddenly I will bring down on them
anguish and terror.
9The mother of seven will grow faint
and breathe her last.
Her sun will set while it is still day;
she will be disgraced and
humiliated.
I will put the survivors to the sword
before their enemies,"
declares the LORD.

10Alas, my mother, that you gave me
birth,
a man with whom the whole land
strives and contends!
I have neither lent nor borrowed,
yet everyone curses me.

11The LORD said,

"Surely I will deliver you for a good
purpose;
surely I will make your enemies
plead with you
in times of disaster and times of
distress.

12"Can a man break iron—
iron from the north—or bronze?
13Your wealth and your treasures
I will give as plunder, without
charge,
because of all your sins
throughout your country.
14I will enslave you to your enemies

in[a] a land you do not know,
for my anger will kindle a fire
that will burn against you."

15You understand, O LORD;
remember me and care for me.
Avenge me on my persecutors.
You are long-suffering—do not take me away;
think of how I suffer reproach for your sake.
16When your words came, I ate them;
they were my joy and my heart's delight,
for I bear your name,
O LORD God Almighty.
17I never sat in the company of revelers,
never made merry with them;
I sat alone because your hand was on me
and you had filled me with indignation.
18Why is my pain unending
and my wound grievous and incurable?
Will you be to me like a deceptive brook,
like a spring that fails?

19Therefore this is what the LORD says:

"If you repent, I will restore you
that you may serve me;
if you utter worthy, not worthless, words,
you will be my spokesman.
Let this people turn to you,
but you must not turn to them.
20I will make you a wall to this people,
a fortified wall of bronze;
they will fight against you
but will not overcome you,
for I am with you
to rescue and save you,"
declares the LORD.
21"I will save you from the hands of the wicked
and redeem you from the grasp of the cruel."

Day of Disaster

16 Then the word of the LORD came to me: 2"You must not marry and have sons or daughters in this place." 3For this is what the LORD says about the sons and daughters born in this land and about the women who are their mothers and the men who are their fathers: 4"They will die of deadly diseases. They will not be mourned or buried but will be like refuse lying on the ground. They will perish by sword and famine, and their dead bodies will become food for the birds of the air and the beasts of the earth."

5For this is what the LORD says: "Do not enter a house where there is a funeral meal; do not go to mourn or show sympathy, because I have withdrawn my blessing, my love and my pity from this people," declares the LORD. 6"Both high and low will die in this land. They will not be buried or mourned, and no one will cut himself or shave his head for them. 7No one will offer food to comfort those who mourn for the dead—not even for a father or a mother—nor will anyone give them a drink to console them.

8"And do not enter a house where there is feasting and sit down to eat and drink. 9For this is what the LORD Almighty, the God of Israel, says: Before your eyes and in your days I will bring an end to the sounds of joy and gladness and to the voices of bride and bridegroom in this place.

10"When you tell these people all this and they ask you, 'Why has the LORD decreed such a great disaster against us? What wrong have we done? What sin have we committed against the LORD our God?' 11then say to them, 'It is because your fathers forsook me,' declares the LORD, 'and followed other gods and served and worshiped them. They forsook me and did not keep my law. 12But you have behaved more wickedly than your fathers. See how each of you is following the stubbornness of his evil heart instead of obeying me. 13So I will throw you out of this land into a land neither you nor your fathers have known, and there you will serve other gods day and night, for I will show you no favor.'

14"However, the days are coming," declares the LORD, "when men will no longer say, 'As surely as the LORD lives, who brought the Israelites up out of Egypt,' 15but they will say, 'As surely as the LORD lives, who brought the Israelites up out of the land of the north and out of all the countries where he had banished them.' For I will restore them to the land I gave their forefathers.

[a]14 Some Hebrew manuscripts, Septuagint and Syriac (see also Jer. 17:4); most Hebrew manuscripts *I will cause your enemies to bring you / into*

16"But now I will send for many fishermen," declares the LORD, "and they will
catch them. After that I will send for many
hunters, and they will hunt them down on
every mountain and hill and from the
crevices of the rocks. 17My eyes are on all
their ways; they are not hidden from me,
nor is their sin concealed from my eyes.
18I will repay them double for their wick-
edness and their sin, because they have
defiled my land with the lifeless forms of
their vile images and have filled my inher-
itance with their detestable idols."

19O LORD, my strength and my fortress,
my refuge in time of distress,
to you the nations will come
from the ends of the earth and say,
"Our fathers possessed nothing but
false gods,
worthless idols that did them no
good.
20Do men make their own gods?
Yes, but they are not gods!"

21"Therefore I will teach them—
this time I will teach them
my power and might.
Then they will know
that my name is the LORD.

17 "Judah's sin is engraved with an
iron tool,
inscribed with a flint point,
on the tablets of their hearts
and on the horns of their altars.
2Even their children remember
their altars and Asherah poles[a]
beside the spreading trees
and on the high hills.
3My mountain in the land
and your[b] wealth and all your
treasures
I will give away as plunder,
together with your high places,
because of sin throughout your
country.
4Through your own fault you will lose
the inheritance I gave you.
I will enslave you to your enemies
in a land you do not know,
for you have kindled my anger,
and it will burn forever."

5This is what the LORD says:
"Cursed is the one who trusts in man,
who depends on flesh for his
strength
and whose heart turns away from
the LORD.
6He will be like a bush in the
wastelands;
he will not see prosperity when it
comes.
He will dwell in the parched places of
the desert,
in a salt land where no one lives.

7"But blessed is the man who trusts in
the LORD,
whose confidence is in him.
8He will be like a tree planted by the
water
that sends out its roots by the
stream.
It does not fear when heat comes;
its leaves are always green.
It has no worries in a year of drought
and never fails to bear fruit."

9The heart is deceitful above all things
and beyond cure.
Who can understand it?

10"I the LORD search the heart
and examine the mind,
to reward a man according to his
conduct,
according to what his deeds
deserve."

11Like a partridge that hatches eggs it
did not lay
is the man who gains riches by
unjust means.
When his life is half gone, they will
desert him,
and in the end he will prove to be a
fool.

12A glorious throne, exalted from the
beginning,
is the place of our sanctuary.
13O LORD, the hope of Israel,
all who forsake you will be put to
shame.
Those who turn away from you will
be written in the dust
because they have forsaken the
LORD,
the spring of living water.

14Heal me, O LORD, and I will be healed;
save me and I will be saved,
for you are the one I praise.
15They keep saying to me,
"Where is the word of the LORD?
Let it now be fulfilled!"

[a]2 That is, symbols of the goddess Asherah [b]2,3 Or *hills* / 3*and the mountains of the land.* / *Your*

VERSE FOR THE DAY: Jeremiah 17:14

AUTHOR: Mark Lewis

PASSAGE FOR THE DAY: Jeremiah 17:1–18

Lessons From a Hurricane

Angela and I were living on the island of St. Croix when Hurricane Hugo struck. We took our two young daughters into the shower stall of our bathroom and huddled together while the sounds of destruction raged outside.

I've been through some scary moments in my life where I experienced intense fear. But I've never felt anything like those hours of relentless terror. I prayed repeatedly for wisdom to know what to do and the courage to do it. I envisioned God's hands around the house, protecting us and holding up the walls. And finally, I prayed that Angela and the girls would be spared. I was so uncertain that I would survive, that I told Angela if she was trapped in the shower after the storm, she could easily kick the slats out of the louvered door and crawl out.

As the storm finally lost strength, I risked a one-man reconnaissance trip to inspect the damage. Our living room had blown away. And our possessions looked like they'd been blenderized with equal parts glass, wood, assorted building materials and rainwater to create an ugly hurricane stew.

This experience put the day-to-day struggles of marriage into perspective. Angela and I are now more tolerant of petty differences and irritations. And we have a new appreciation for each other. After surviving a devastating hurricane, we have a new marriage. And we give all the thanks to God.

MARRIAGE BUILDERS

♦ *What day-to-day annoyances and problems seem trivial when placed against a backdrop of life and death?*

♦ *How can you let petty differences and irritations go instead of letting them cause trouble in your relationship?*

Additional Scripture Readings
Psalm 68:20; Daniel 3:17

Go to page 827 for your next devotional reading.

16 I have not run away from being your
shepherd;
you know I have not desired the
day of despair.
What passes my lips is open before
you.
17 Do not be a terror to me;
you are my refuge in the day of
disaster.
18 Let my persecutors be put to shame,
but keep me from shame;
let them be terrified,
but keep me from terror.
Bring on them the day of disaster;
destroy them with double
destruction.

Keeping the Sabbath Holy

19 This is what the LORD said to me: "Go and stand at the gate of the people, through which the kings of Judah go in and out; stand also at all the other gates of Jerusalem. 20 Say to them, 'Hear the word of the LORD, O kings of Judah and all people of Judah and everyone living in Jerusalem who come through these gates. 21 This is what the LORD says: Be careful not to carry a load on the Sabbath day or bring it through the gates of Jerusalem. 22 Do not bring a load out of your houses or do any work on the Sabbath, but keep the Sabbath day holy, as I commanded your forefathers. 23 Yet they did not listen or pay attention; they were stiff-necked and would not listen or respond to discipline. 24 But if you are careful to obey me, declares the LORD, and bring no load through the gates of this city on the Sabbath, but keep the Sabbath day holy by not doing any work on it, 25 then kings who sit on David's throne will come through the gates of this city with their officials. They and their officials will come riding in chariots and on horses, accompanied by the men of Judah and those living in Jerusalem, and this city will be inhabited forever. 26 People will come from the towns of Judah and the villages around Jerusalem, from the territory of Benjamin and the western foothills, from the hill country and the Negev, bringing burnt offerings and sacrifices, grain offerings, incense and thank offerings to the house of the LORD. 27 But if you do not obey me to keep the Sabbath day holy by not carrying any load as you come through the gates of Jerusalem on the Sabbath day, then I will kindle an unquenchable fire in the gates of Jerusalem that will consume her fortresses.' "

At the Potter's House

18 This is the word that came to Jeremiah from the LORD: 2 "Go down to the potter's house, and there I will give you my message." 3 So I went down to the potter's house, and I saw him working at the wheel. 4 But the pot he was shaping from the clay was marred in his hands; so the potter formed it into another pot, shaping it as seemed best to him.

5 Then the word of the LORD came to me: 6 "O house of Israel, can I not do with you as this potter does?" declares the LORD. "Like clay in the hand of the potter, so are you in my hand, O house of Israel. 7 If at any time I announce that a nation or kingdom is to be uprooted, torn down and destroyed, 8 and if that nation I warned repents of its evil, then I will relent and not inflict on it the disaster I had planned. 9 And if at another time I announce that a nation or kingdom is to be built up and planted, 10 and if it does evil in my sight and does not obey me, then I will reconsider the good I had intended to do for it.

11 "Now therefore say to the people of Judah and those living in Jerusalem, 'This is what the LORD says: Look! I am preparing a disaster for you and devising a plan against you. So turn from your evil ways, each one of you, and reform your ways and your actions.' 12 But they will reply, 'It's no use. We will continue with our own plans; each of us will follow the stubbornness of his evil heart.' "

13 Therefore this is what the LORD says:

"Inquire among the nations:
Who has ever heard anything like
this?
A most horrible thing has been done
by Virgin Israel.
14 Does the snow of Lebanon
ever vanish from its rocky slopes?
Do its cool waters from distant
sources
ever cease to flow?[a]
15 Yet my people have forgotten me;
they burn incense to worthless
idols,
which made them stumble in their
ways
and in the ancient paths.

[a] 14 The meaning of the Hebrew for this sentence is uncertain.

They made them walk in bypaths
and on roads not built up.
16Their land will be laid waste,
an object of lasting scorn;
all who pass by will be appalled
and will shake their heads.
17Like a wind from the east,
I will scatter them before their enemies;
I will show them my back and not my face
in the day of their disaster."

18They said, "Come, let's make plans against Jeremiah; for the teaching of the law by the priest will not be lost, nor will counsel from the wise, nor the word from the prophets. So come, let's attack him with our tongues and pay no attention to anything he says."

19Listen to me, O LORD;
hear what my accusers are saying!
20Should good be repaid with evil?
Yet they have dug a pit for me.
Remember that I stood before you
and spoke in their behalf
to turn your wrath away from them.
21So give their children over to famine;
hand them over to the power of the sword.
Let their wives be made childless and widows;
let their men be put to death,
their young men slain by the sword in battle.
22Let a cry be heard from their houses
when you suddenly bring invaders against them,
for they have dug a pit to capture me
and have hidden snares for my feet.
23But you know, O LORD,
all their plots to kill me.
Do not forgive their crimes
or blot out their sins from your sight.
Let them be overthrown before you;
deal with them in the time of your anger.

19 This is what the LORD says: "Go and buy a clay jar from a potter. Take along some of the elders of the people and of the priests 2and go out to the Valley of Ben Hinnom, near the entrance of the Potsherd Gate. There proclaim the words I tell you, 3and say, 'Hear the word of the LORD, O kings of Judah and people of Jerusalem. This is what the LORD Almighty, the God of Israel, says: Listen! I am going to bring a disaster on this place that will make the ears of everyone who hears of it tingle. 4For they have forsaken me and made this a place of foreign gods; they have burned sacrifices in it to gods that neither they nor their fathers nor the kings of Judah ever knew, and they have filled this place with the blood of the innocent. 5They have built the high places of Baal to burn their sons in the fire as offerings to Baal—something I did not command or mention, nor did it enter my mind. 6So beware, the days are coming, declares the LORD, when people will no longer call this place Topheth or the Valley of Ben Hinnom, but the Valley of Slaughter.

7" 'In this place I will ruin[a] the plans of Judah and Jerusalem. I will make them fall by the sword before their enemies, at the hands of those who seek their lives, and I will give their carcasses as food to the birds of the air and the beasts of the earth. 8I will devastate this city and make it an object of scorn; all who pass by will be appalled and will scoff because of all its wounds. 9I will make them eat the flesh of their sons and daughters, and they will eat one another's flesh during the stress of the siege imposed on them by the enemies who seek their lives.'

10"Then break the jar while those who go with you are watching, 11and say to them, 'This is what the LORD Almighty says: I will smash this nation and this city just as this potter's jar is smashed and cannot be repaired. They will bury the dead in Topheth until there is no more room. 12This is what I will do to this place and to those who live here, declares the LORD. I will make this city like Topheth. 13The houses in Jerusalem and those of the kings of Judah will be defiled like this place, Topheth—all the houses where they burned incense on the roofs to all the starry hosts and poured out drink offerings to other gods.' "

14Jeremiah then returned from Topheth, where the LORD had sent him to prophesy, and stood in the court of the LORD's temple and said to all the people, 15"This is what the LORD Almighty, the God of Israel, says: 'Listen! I am going to bring on this city and the villages around it every disaster I pronounced against

[a]7 The Hebrew for *ruin* sounds like the Hebrew for *jar* (see verses 1 and 10).

them, because they were stiff-necked and
would not listen to my words.' "

Jeremiah and Pashhur

20 When the priest Pashhur son of
Immer, the chief officer in the temple of the LORD, heard Jeremiah prophesying these things, [2]he had Jeremiah the
prophet beaten and put in the stocks at
the Upper Gate of Benjamin at the LORD's
temple. [3]The next day, when Pashhur released him from the stocks, Jeremiah said
to him, "The LORD's name for you is not
Pashhur, but Magor-Missabib.[a] [4]For this
is what the LORD says: 'I will make you a
terror to yourself and to all your friends;
with your own eyes you will see them fall
by the sword of their enemies. I will hand
all Judah over to the king of Babylon, who
will carry them away to Babylon or put
them to the sword. [5]I will hand over to
their enemies all the wealth of this city—
all its products, all its valuables and all the
treasures of the kings of Judah. They will
take it away as plunder and carry it off to
Babylon. [6]And you, Pashhur, and all who
live in your house will go into exile to Babylon. There you will die and be buried,
you and all your friends to whom you
have prophesied lies.' "

Jeremiah's Complaint

[7]O LORD, you deceived[b] me, and I was
deceived[b];
you overpowered me and prevailed.
I am ridiculed all day long;
everyone mocks me.
[8]Whenever I speak, I cry out
proclaiming violence and
destruction.
So the word of the LORD has brought
me
insult and reproach all day long.
[9]But if I say, "I will not mention him
or speak any more in his name,"
his word is in my heart like a fire,
a fire shut up in my bones.
I am weary of holding it in;
indeed, I cannot.
[10]I hear many whispering,
"Terror on every side!
Report him! Let's report him!"
All my friends
are waiting for me to slip, saying,
"Perhaps he will be deceived;
then we will prevail over him
and take our revenge on him."
[11]But the LORD is with me like a mighty
warrior;
so my persecutors will stumble and
not prevail.
They will fail and be thoroughly
disgraced;
their dishonor will never be
forgotten.
[12]O LORD Almighty, you who examine
the righteous
and probe the heart and mind,
let me see your vengeance upon them,
for to you I have committed my
cause.
[13]Sing to the LORD!
Give praise to the LORD!
He rescues the life of the needy
from the hands of the wicked.
[14]Cursed be the day I was born!
May the day my mother bore me
not be blessed!
[15]Cursed be the man who brought my
father the news,
who made him very glad, saying,
"A child is born to you—a son!"
[16]May that man be like the towns
the LORD overthrew without pity.
May he hear wailing in the morning,
a battle cry at noon.
[17]For he did not kill me in the womb,
with my mother as my grave,
her womb enlarged forever.
[18]Why did I ever come out of the womb
to see trouble and sorrow
and to end my days in shame?

God Rejects Zedekiah's Request

21 The word came to Jeremiah from
the LORD when King Zedekiah sent
to him Pashhur son of Malkijah and the
priest Zephaniah son of Maaseiah. They
said: [2]"Inquire now of the LORD for us because Nebuchadnezzar[c] king of Babylon
is attacking us. Perhaps the LORD will perform wonders for us as in times past so
that he will withdraw from us."
[3]But Jeremiah answered them, "Tell
Zedekiah, [4]'This is what the LORD, the God
of Israel, says: I am about to turn against
you the weapons of war that are in your
hands, which you are using to fight the

[a]3 *Magor-Missabib* means *terror on every side.* [b]7 Or *persuaded* [c]2 Hebrew *Nebuchadrezzar,* of which *Nebuchadnezzar* is a variant; here and often in Jeremiah and Ezekiel

king of Babylon and the Babylonians[a]
who are outside the wall besieging you.
And I will gather them inside this city. 5I
myself will fight against you with an out-
stretched hand and a mighty arm in anger
and fury and great wrath. 6I will strike
down those who live in this city—both
men and animals—and they will die of a
terrible plague. 7After that, declares the
LORD, I will hand over Zedekiah king of Ju-
dah, his officials and the people in this
city who survive the plague, sword and
famine, to Nebuchadnezzar king of Bab-
ylon and to their enemies who seek their
lives. He will put them to the sword; he
will show them no mercy or pity or com-
passion.'

8"Furthermore, tell the people, 'This is
what the LORD says: See, I am setting be-
fore you the way of life and the way of
death. 9Whoever stays in this city will die
by the sword, famine or plague. But who-
ever goes out and surrenders to the Bab-
ylonians who are besieging you will live;
he will escape with his life. 10I have deter-
mined to do this city harm and not good,
declares the LORD. It will be given into the
hands of the king of Babylon, and he will
destroy it with fire.'

11"Moreover, say to the royal house of
Judah, 'Hear the word of the LORD;
12O house of David, this is what the LORD
says:

" 'Administer justice every morning;
rescue from the hand of his
oppressor
the one who has been robbed,
or my wrath will break out and burn
like fire
because of the evil you have
done—
burn with no one to quench it.
13I am against you, ⌊Jerusalem,⌋
you who live above this valley
on the rocky plateau,
declares the LORD—
you who say, "Who can come against
us?
Who can enter our refuge?"
14I will punish you as your deeds
deserve,
declares the LORD.
I will kindle a fire in your forests
that will consume everything
around you.' "

Judgment Against Evil Kings

22 This is what the LORD says: "Go
down to the palace of the king of
Judah and proclaim this message there:
2'Hear the word of the LORD, O king of Ju-
dah, you who sit on David's throne—you,
your officials and your people who come
through these gates. 3This is what the
LORD says: Do what is just and right. Res-
cue from the hand of his oppressor the
one who has been robbed. Do no wrong or
violence to the alien, the fatherless or the
widow, and do not shed innocent blood in
this place. 4For if you are careful to carry
out these commands, then kings who sit
on David's throne will come through the
gates of this palace, riding in chariots and
on horses, accompanied by their officials
and their people. 5But if you do not obey
these commands, declares the LORD, I
swear by myself that this palace will be-
come a ruin.' "

6For this is what the LORD says about
the palace of the king of Judah:

"Though you are like Gilead to me,
like the summit of Lebanon,
I will surely make you like a desert,
like towns not inhabited.
7I will send destroyers against you,
each man with his weapons,
and they will cut up your fine cedar
beams
and throw them into the fire.

8"People from many nations will pass
by this city and will ask one another,
'Why has the LORD done such a thing to
this great city?' 9And the answer will be:
'Because they have forsaken the covenant
of the LORD their God and have worshiped
and served other gods.' "

10Do not weep for the dead ⌊king⌋ or
mourn his loss;
rather, weep bitterly for him who is
exiled,
because he will never return
nor see his native land again.

11For this is what the LORD says about
Shallum[b] son of Josiah, who succeeded
his father as king of Judah but has gone
from this place: "He will never return.
12He will die in the place where they have
led him captive; he will not see this land
again."

[a]4 Or *Chaldeans*; also in verse 9 [b]11 Also called *Jehoahaz*

13"Woe to him who builds his palace by
unrighteousness,
his upper rooms by injustice,
making his countrymen work for
nothing,
not paying them for their labor.
14He says, 'I will build myself a great
palace
with spacious upper rooms.'
So he makes large windows in it,
panels it with cedar
and decorates it in red.

15"Does it make you a king
to have more and more cedar?
Did not your father have food and
drink?
He did what was right and just,
so all went well with him.
16He defended the cause of the poor
and needy,
and so all went well.
Is that not what it means to know
me?"
declares the LORD.
17"But your eyes and your heart
are set only on dishonest gain,
on shedding innocent blood
and on oppression and extortion."

18Therefore this is what the LORD says
about Jehoiakim son of Josiah king of Judah:

"They will not mourn for him:
'Alas, my brother! Alas, my sister!'
They will not mourn for him:
'Alas, my master! Alas, his
splendor!'
19He will have the burial of a donkey—
dragged away and thrown
outside the gates of Jerusalem."

20"Go up to Lebanon and cry out,
let your voice be heard in Bashan,
cry out from Abarim,
for all your allies are crushed.
21I warned you when you felt secure,
but you said, 'I will not listen!'
This has been your way from your
youth;
you have not obeyed me.
22The wind will drive all your shepherds
away,
and your allies will go into exile.
Then you will be ashamed and
disgraced
because of all your wickedness.
23You who live in 'Lebanon,[a]'
who are nestled in cedar buildings,
how you will groan when pangs come
upon you,
pain like that of a woman in labor!

24"As surely as I live," declares the LORD, "even if you, Jehoiachin[b] son of Jehoiakim king of Judah, were a signet ring on my right hand, I would still pull you off. 25I will hand you over to those who seek your life, those you fear—to Nebuchadnezzar king of Babylon and to the Babylonians.[c] 26I will hurl you and the mother who gave you birth into another country, where neither of you was born, and there you both will die. 27You will never come back to the land you long to return to."

28Is this man Jehoiachin a despised,
broken pot,
an object no one wants?
Why will he and his children be
hurled out,
cast into a land they do not know?
29O land, land, land,
hear the word of the LORD!
30This is what the LORD says:
"Record this man as if childless,
a man who will not prosper in his
lifetime,
for none of his offspring will prosper,
none will sit on the throne of David
or rule anymore in Judah."

The Righteous Branch

23 "Woe to the shepherds who are destroying and scattering the sheep of my pasture!" declares the LORD. 2Therefore this is what the LORD, the God of Israel, says to the shepherds who tend my people: "Because you have scattered my flock and driven them away and have not bestowed care on them, I will bestow punishment on you for the evil you have done," declares the LORD. 3"I myself will gather the remnant of my flock out of all the countries where I have driven them and will bring them back to their pasture, where they will be fruitful and increase in number. 4I will place shepherds over them who will tend them, and they will no longer be afraid or terrified, nor will any be missing," declares the LORD.

[a]23 That is, the palace in Jerusalem (see 1 Kings 7:2) also in verse 28 [b]24 Hebrew *Coniah*, a variant of *Jehoiachin*; [c]25 Or *Chaldeans*

5"The days are coming," declares the LORD,
"when I will raise up to David[a] a righteous Branch,
a King who will reign wisely
and do what is just and right in the land.
6In his days Judah will be saved
and Israel will live in safety.
This is the name by which he will be called:
The LORD Our Righteousness.

7"So then, the days are coming," declares the LORD, "when people will no longer say, 'As surely as the LORD lives, who brought the Israelites up out of Egypt,' 8but they will say, 'As surely as the LORD lives, who brought the descendants of Israel up out of the land of the north and out of all the countries where he had banished them.' Then they will live in their own land."

Lying Prophets

9Concerning the prophets:

My heart is broken within me;
all my bones tremble.
I am like a drunken man,
like a man overcome by wine,
because of the LORD
and his holy words.
10The land is full of adulterers;

[a]5 Or *up from David's line*

VERSE FOR THE DAY: Jeremiah 23:24 | AUTHOR: Howard Hendricks | PASSAGE FOR THE DAY: Jeremiah 23:1–24

Unconditional Acceptance

I came from a broken home. My father was a military man who brought me up with military discipline. I was painfully aware of the times I didn't measure up.

When I came to marriage, I was afraid that if Jeanne really found out what I was like, she wouldn't love me anymore. Rejection was one thing I knew I couldn't handle. It was at about the ten-year point in our marriage that I began to realize that I didn't have to prove myself or earn her love. Knowing of her unconditional acceptance, I was then free to make the drastic changes in myself that I needed to make in terms of being the partner God wanted me to be in our marriage.

MARRIAGE BUILDERS

♦ *Be completely honest with each other: Does either of you feel a lack of acceptance in any area of your marriage?*
♦ *How does your spouse's acceptance of you make it easier for you to become the mate God wants you to be?*

Additional Scripture Readings
Psalm 19:12; 139:1–4, 23–24

Go to page 834 for your next devotional reading.

because of the curse[a] the land lies
parched[b]
and the pastures in the desert are
withered.
The ⌊prophets⌋ follow an evil course
and use their power unjustly.

11"Both prophet and priest are godless;
even in my temple I find their
wickedness,"
declares the LORD.
12"Therefore their path will become
slippery;
they will be banished to darkness
and there they will fall.
I will bring disaster on them
in the year they are punished,"
declares the LORD.

13"Among the prophets of Samaria
I saw this repulsive thing:
They prophesied by Baal
and led my people Israel astray.
14And among the prophets of Jerusalem
I have seen something horrible:
They commit adultery and live a lie.
They strengthen the hands of
evildoers,
so that no one turns from his
wickedness.
They are all like Sodom to me;
the people of Jerusalem are like
Gomorrah."

15Therefore, this is what the LORD Almighty says concerning the prophets:

"I will make them eat bitter food
and drink poisoned water,
because from the prophets of
Jerusalem
ungodliness has spread throughout
the land."

16This is what the LORD Almighty says:

"Do not listen to what the prophets
are prophesying to you;
they fill you with false hopes.
They speak visions from their own
minds,
not from the mouth of the LORD.
17They keep saying to those who
despise me,
'The LORD says: You will have
peace.'
And to all who follow the
stubbornness of their hearts
they say, 'No harm will come to
you.'

18But which of them has stood in the
council of the LORD
to see or to hear his word?
Who has listened and heard his
word?
19See, the storm of the LORD
will burst out in wrath,
a whirlwind swirling down
on the heads of the wicked.
20The anger of the LORD will not turn
back
until he fully accomplishes
the purposes of his heart.
In days to come
you will understand it clearly.
21I did not send these prophets,
yet they have run with their
message;
I did not speak to them,
yet they have prophesied.
22But if they had stood in my council,
they would have proclaimed my
words to my people
and would have turned them from
their evil ways
and from their evil deeds.

23"Am I only a God nearby,"
declares the LORD,
"and not a God far away?
24Can anyone hide in secret places
so that I cannot see him?"
declares the LORD.
"Do not I fill heaven and earth?"
declares the LORD.

25"I have heard what the prophets say who prophesy lies in my name. They say, 'I had a dream! I had a dream!' 26How long will this continue in the hearts of these lying prophets, who prophesy the delusions of their own minds? 27They think the dreams they tell one another will make my people forget my name, just as their fathers forgot my name through Baal worship. 28Let the prophet who has a dream tell his dream, but let the one who has my word speak it faithfully. For what has straw to do with grain?" declares the LORD. 29"Is not my word like fire," declares the LORD, "and like a hammer that breaks a rock in pieces?

30"Therefore," declares the LORD, "I am against the prophets who steal from one another words supposedly from me. 31Yes," declares the LORD, "I am against the prophets who wag their own tongues and yet declare, 'The LORD declares.' 32In-

[a] 10 Or *because of these things* [b] 10 Or *land mourns*

deed, I am against those who prophesy
false dreams," declares the LORD. "They
tell them and lead my people astray with
their reckless lies, yet I did not send or ap-
point them. They do not benefit these
people in the least," declares the LORD.

False Oracles and False Prophets

33"When these people, or a prophet or a
priest, ask you, 'What is the oracle[a] of the
LORD?' say to them, 'What oracle?[b] I will
forsake you, declares the LORD.' 34If a
prophet or a priest or anyone else claims,
'This is the oracle of the LORD,' I will pun-
ish that man and his household. 35This is
what each of you keeps on saying to his
friend or relative: 'What is the LORD's an-
swer?' or 'What has the LORD spoken?'
36But you must not mention 'the oracle of
the LORD' again, because every man's own
word becomes his oracle and so you dis-
tort the words of the living God, the LORD
Almighty, our God. 37This is what you
keep saying to a prophet: 'What is the
LORD's answer to you?' or 'What has the
LORD spoken?' 38Although you claim,
'This is the oracle of the LORD,' this is what
the LORD says: You used the words, 'This
is the oracle of the LORD,' even though I
told you that you must not claim, 'This is
the oracle of the LORD.' 39Therefore, I will
surely forget you and cast you out of my
presence along with the city I gave to you
and your fathers. 40I will bring upon you
everlasting disgrace—everlasting shame
that will not be forgotten."

Two Baskets of Figs

24 After Jehoiachin[c] son of Jehoia-
kim king of Judah and the officials,
the craftsmen and the artisans of Judah
were carried into exile from Jerusalem to
Babylon by Nebuchadnezzar king of Bab-
ylon, the LORD showed me two baskets of
figs placed in front of the temple of the
LORD. 2One basket had very good figs, like
those that ripen early; the other basket
had very poor figs, so bad they could not
be eaten.

3Then the LORD asked me, "What do
you see, Jeremiah?"

"Figs," I answered. "The good ones are
very good, but the poor ones are so bad
they cannot be eaten."

4Then the word of the LORD came to me:
5"This is what the LORD, the God of Israel,
says: 'Like these good figs, I regard as
good the exiles from Judah, whom I sent
away from this place to the land of the
Babylonians.[d] 6My eyes will watch over
them for their good, and I will bring them
back to this land. I will build them up and
not tear them down; I will plant them and
not uproot them. 7I will give them a heart
to know me, that I am the LORD. They will
be my people, and I will be their God, for
they will return to me with all their heart.

8" 'But like the poor figs, which are so
bad they cannot be eaten,' says the LORD,
'so will I deal with Zedekiah king of Ju-
dah, his officials and the survivors from
Jerusalem, whether they remain in this
land or live in Egypt. 9I will make them
abhorrent and an offense to all the king-
doms of the earth, a reproach and a by-
word, an object of ridicule and cursing,
wherever I banish them. 10I will send the
sword, famine and plague against them
until they are destroyed from the land I
gave to them and their fathers.' "

Seventy Years of Captivity

25 The word came to Jeremiah con-
cerning all the people of Judah in
the fourth year of Jehoiakim son of Josiah
king of Judah, which was the first year of
Nebuchadnezzar king of Babylon. 2So Jer-
emiah the prophet said to all the people of
Judah and to all those living in Jerusalem:
3For twenty-three years—from the thir-
teenth year of Josiah son of Amon king of
Judah until this very day—the word of the
LORD has come to me and I have spoken to
you again and again, but you have not lis-
tened.

4And though the LORD has sent all his
servants the prophets to you again and
again, you have not listened or paid any
attention. 5They said, "Turn now, each of
you, from your evil ways and your evil
practices, and you can stay in the land the
LORD gave to you and your fathers for ever
and ever. 6Do not follow other gods to
serve and worship them; do not provoke
me to anger with what your hands have
made. Then I will not harm you."

7"But you did not listen to me," declares
the LORD, "and you have provoked me
with what your hands have made, and you
have brought harm to yourselves."

[a] 33 Or *burden* (see Septuagint and Vulgate) (The Hebrew for *oracle* and *burden* is the same.)
[b] 33 Hebrew; Septuagint and Vulgate *'You are the burden.*
[c] 1 Hebrew *Jeconiah,* a variant of *Jehoiachin*
[d] 5 Or *Chaldeans*

8Therefore the LORD Almighty says this:
"Because you have not listened to my
words, 9I will summon all the peoples of
the north and my servant Nebuchadnez-
zar king of Babylon," declares the LORD,
"and I will bring them against this land
and its inhabitants and against all the sur-
rounding nations. I will completely de-
stroy[a] them and make them an object of
horror and scorn, and an everlasting ruin.
10I will banish from them the sounds of
joy and gladness, the voices of bride and
bridegroom, the sound of millstones and
the light of the lamp. 11This whole coun-
try will become a desolate wasteland, and
these nations will serve the king of Ba-
bylon seventy years.

12"But when the seventy years are ful-
filled, I will punish the king of Babylon
and his nation, the land of the Babylonians,[b] for their guilt," declares the LORD,
"and will make it desolate forever. 13I will
bring upon that land all the things I have
spoken against it, all that are written in
this book and prophesied by Jeremiah
against all the nations. 14They themselves
will be enslaved by many nations and
great kings; I will repay them according to
their deeds and the work of their hands."

The Cup of God's Wrath

15This is what the LORD, the God of Israel, said to me: "Take from my hand this
cup filled with the wine of my wrath and
make all the nations to whom I send you
drink it. 16When they drink it, they will
stagger and go mad because of the sword
I will send among them."

17So I took the cup from the LORD's
hand and made all the nations to whom
he sent me drink it: 18Jerusalem and the
towns of Judah, its kings and officials, to
make them a ruin and an object of horror
and scorn and cursing, as they are today;
19Pharaoh king of Egypt, his attendants,
his officials and all his people, 20and all
the foreign people there; all the kings of
Uz; all the kings of the Philistines (those
of Ashkelon, Gaza, Ekron, and the people
left at Ashdod); 21Edom, Moab and Am-
mon; 22all the kings of Tyre and Sidon; the
kings of the coastlands across the sea;
23Dedan, Tema, Buz and all who are in
distant places[c]; 24all the kings of Arabia
and all the kings of the foreign people who
live in the desert; 25all the kings of Zimri,
Elam and Media; 26and all the kings of the
north, near and far, one after the other—
all the kingdoms on the face of the earth.
And after all of them, the king of Sheshach[d] will drink it too.

27"Then tell them, 'This is what the
LORD Almighty, the God of Israel, says:
Drink, get drunk and vomit, and fall to rise
no more because of the sword I will send
among you.' 28But if they refuse to take
the cup from your hand and drink, tell
them, 'This is what the LORD Almighty
says: You must drink it! 29See, I am begin-
ning to bring disaster on the city that
bears my Name, and will you indeed go
unpunished? You will not go unpunished,
for I am calling down a sword upon all
who live on the earth, declares the LORD
Almighty.'

30"Now prophesy all these words
against them and say to them:

" 'The LORD will roar from on high;
he will thunder from his holy
dwelling
and roar mightily against his land.
He will shout like those who tread the
grapes,
shout against all who live on the
earth.
31The tumult will resound to the ends
of the earth,
for the LORD will bring charges
against the nations;
he will bring judgment on all mankind
and put the wicked to the sword,' "
declares the LORD.

32This is what the LORD Almighty says:

"Look! Disaster is spreading
from nation to nation;
a mighty storm is rising
from the ends of the earth."

33At that time those slain by the LORD will
be everywhere—from one end of the
earth to the other. They will not be
mourned or gathered up or buried, but
will be like refuse lying on the ground.

34Weep and wail, you shepherds;
roll in the dust, you leaders of the
flock.
For your time to be slaughtered has
come;

[a]9 The Hebrew term refers to the irrevocable giving over of things or persons to the LORD, often by totally destroying them. [b]12 Or *Chaldeans* [c]23 Or *who clip the hair by their foreheads* [d]26 *Sheshach* is a cryptogram for Babylon.

you will fall and be shattered like
fine pottery.
35The shepherds will have nowhere to
flee,
the leaders of the flock no place to
escape.
36Hear the cry of the shepherds,
the wailing of the leaders of the
flock,
for the LORD is destroying their
pasture.
37The peaceful meadows will be laid
waste
because of the fierce anger of the
LORD.
38Like a lion he will leave his lair,
and their land will become desolate
because of the sword[a] of the
oppressor
and because of the LORD's fierce
anger.

Jeremiah Threatened With Death

26 Early in the reign of Jehoiakim son of Josiah king of Judah, this word came from the LORD: 2"This is what the LORD says: Stand in the courtyard of the LORD's house and speak to all the people of the towns of Judah who come to worship in the house of the LORD. Tell them everything I command you; do not omit a word. 3Perhaps they will listen and each will turn from his evil way. Then I will relent and not bring on them the disaster I was planning because of the evil they have done. 4Say to them, 'This is what the LORD says: If you do not listen to me and follow my law, which I have set before you, 5and if you do not listen to the words of my servants the prophets, whom I have sent to you again and again (though you have not listened), 6then I will make this house like Shiloh and this city an object of cursing among all the nations of the earth.' "

7The priests, the prophets and all the people heard Jeremiah speak these words in the house of the LORD. 8But as soon as Jeremiah finished telling all the people everything the LORD had commanded him to say, the priests, the prophets and all the people seized him and said, "You must die! 9Why do you prophesy in the LORD's name that this house will be like Shiloh and this city will be desolate and deserted?" And all the people crowded around Jeremiah in the house of the LORD.

10When the officials of Judah heard about these things, they went up from the royal palace to the house of the LORD and took their places at the entrance of the New Gate of the LORD's house. 11Then the priests and the prophets said to the officials and all the people, "This man should be sentenced to death because he has prophesied against this city. You have heard it with your own ears!"

12Then Jeremiah said to all the officials and all the people: "The LORD sent me to prophesy against this house and this city all the things you have heard. 13Now reform your ways and your actions and obey the LORD your God. Then the LORD will relent and not bring the disaster he has pronounced against you. 14As for me, I am in your hands; do with me whatever you think is good and right. 15Be assured, however, that if you put me to death, you will bring the guilt of innocent blood on yourselves and on this city and on those who live in it, for in truth the LORD has sent me to you to speak all these words in your hearing."

16Then the officials and all the people said to the priests and the prophets, "This man should not be sentenced to death! He has spoken to us in the name of the LORD our God."

17Some of the elders of the land stepped forward and said to the entire assembly of people, 18"Micah of Moresheth prophesied in the days of Hezekiah king of Judah. He told all the people of Judah, 'This is what the LORD Almighty says:

" 'Zion will be plowed like a field,
Jerusalem will become a heap of
rubble,
the temple hill a mound overgrown
with thickets.'[b]

19"Did Hezekiah king of Judah or anyone else in Judah put him to death? Did not Hezekiah fear the LORD and seek his favor? And did not the LORD relent, so that he did not bring the disaster he pronounced against them? We are about to bring a terrible disaster on ourselves!"

20(Now Uriah son of Shemaiah from Kiriath Jearim was another man who prophesied in the name of the LORD; he prophesied the same things against this

[a]*38* Some Hebrew manuscripts and Septuagint (see also Jer. 46:16 and 50:16); most Hebrew manuscripts *anger* [b]*18* Micah 3:12

city and this land as Jeremiah did. 21When
King Jehoiakim and all his officers and of-
ficials heard his words, the king sought to
put him to death. But Uriah heard of it and
fled in fear to Egypt. 22King Jehoiakim,
however, sent Elnathan son of Acbor to
Egypt, along with some other men. 23They
brought Uriah out of Egypt and took him
to King Jehoiakim, who had him struck
down with a sword and his body thrown
into the burial place of the common peo-
ple.)

24Furthermore, Ahikam son of Shaphan
supported Jeremiah, and so he was not
handed over to the people to be put to
death.

Judah to Serve Nebuchadnezzar

27 Early in the reign of Zedekiah[a]
son of Josiah king of Judah, this
word came to Jeremiah from the LORD:
2This is what the LORD said to me: "Make
a yoke out of straps and crossbars and put
it on your neck. 3Then send word to the
kings of Edom, Moab, Ammon, Tyre and
Sidon through the envoys who have come
to Jerusalem to Zedekiah king of Judah.
4Give them a message for their masters
and say, 'This is what the LORD Almighty,
the God of Israel, says: "Tell this to your
masters: 5With my great power and out-
stretched arm I made the earth and its
people and the animals that are on it, and
I give it to anyone I please. 6Now I will
hand all your countries over to my servant
Nebuchadnezzar king of Babylon; I will
make even the wild animals subject to
him. 7All nations will serve him and his
son and his grandson until the time for his
land comes; then many nations and great
kings will subjugate him.

8" ' "If, however, any nation or kingdom
will not serve Nebuchadnezzar king of
Babylon or bow its neck under his yoke,
I will punish that nation with the sword,
famine and plague, declares the LORD, un-
til I destroy it by his hand. 9So do not lis-
ten to your prophets, your diviners, your
interpreters of dreams, your mediums or
your sorcerers who tell you, 'You will not
serve the king of Babylon.' 10They prophe-
sy lies to you that will only serve to re-
move you far from your lands; I will ban-
ish you and you will perish. 11But if any
nation will bow its neck under the yoke of
the king of Babylon and serve him, I will
let that nation remain in its own land to
till it and to live there, declares the
LORD." ' "

12I gave the same message to Zedekiah
king of Judah. I said, "Bow your neck un-
der the yoke of the king of Babylon; serve
him and his people, and you will live.
13Why will you and your people die by the
sword, famine and plague with which the
LORD has threatened any nation that will
not serve the king of Babylon? 14Do not
listen to the words of the prophets who
say to you, 'You will not serve the king of
Babylon,' for they are prophesying lies to
you. 15'I have not sent them,' declares the
LORD. 'They are prophesying lies in my
name. Therefore, I will banish you and
you will perish, both you and the prophets
who prophesy to you.' "

16Then I said to the priests and all these
people, "This is what the LORD says: Do
not listen to the prophets who say, 'Very
soon now the articles from the LORD's
house will be brought back from Bab-
ylon.' They are prophesying lies to you.
17Do not listen to them. Serve the king of
Babylon, and you will live. Why should
this city become a ruin? 18If they are
prophets and have the word of the LORD,
let them plead with the LORD Almighty
that the furnishings remaining in the
house of the LORD and in the palace of the
king of Judah and in Jerusalem not be tak-
en to Babylon. 19For this is what the LORD
Almighty says about the pillars, the Sea,
the movable stands and the other furnish-
ings that are left in this city, 20which Neb-
uchadnezzar king of Babylon did not take
away when he carried Jehoiachin[b] son of
Jehoiakim king of Judah into exile from
Jerusalem to Babylon, along with all the
nobles of Judah and Jerusalem— 21yes,
this is what the LORD Almighty, the God of
Israel, says about the things that are left in
the house of the LORD and in the palace of
the king of Judah and in Jerusalem:
22'They will be taken to Babylon and there
they will remain until the day I come for
them,' declares the LORD. 'Then I will
bring them back and restore them to this
place.' "

[a]*1* A few Hebrew manuscripts and Syriac (see also Jer. 27:3, 12 and 28:1); most Hebrew manuscripts *Jehoiakim* (Most Septuagint manuscripts do not have this verse.) [b]*20* Hebrew *Jeconiah,* a variant of *Jehoiachin*

The False Prophet Hananiah

28 In the fifth month of that same year, the fourth year, early in the reign of Zedekiah king of Judah, the prophet Hananiah son of Azzur, who was from Gibeon, said to me in the house of the LORD in the presence of the priests and all the people: 2"This is what the LORD Almighty, the God of Israel, says: 'I will break the yoke of the king of Babylon. 3Within two years I will bring back to this place all the articles of the LORD's house that Nebuchadnezzar king of Babylon removed from here and took to Babylon. 4I will also bring back to this place Jehoiachin[a] son of Jehoiakim king of Judah and all the other exiles from Judah who went to Babylon,' declares the LORD, 'for I will break the yoke of the king of Babylon.' "

5Then the prophet Jeremiah replied to the prophet Hananiah before the priests and all the people who were standing in the house of the LORD. 6He said, "Amen! May the LORD do so! May the LORD fulfill the words you have prophesied by bringing the articles of the LORD's house and all the exiles back to this place from Babylon. 7Nevertheless, listen to what I have to say in your hearing and in the hearing of all the people: 8From early times the prophets who preceded you and me have prophesied war, disaster and plague against many countries and great kingdoms. 9But the prophet who prophesies peace will be recognized as one truly sent by the LORD only if his prediction comes true."

10Then the prophet Hananiah took the yoke off the neck of the prophet Jeremiah and broke it, 11and he said before all the people, "This is what the LORD says: 'In the same way will I break the yoke of Nebuchadnezzar king of Babylon off the neck of all the nations within two years.' " At this, the prophet Jeremiah went on his way.

12Shortly after the prophet Hananiah had broken the yoke off the neck of the prophet Jeremiah, the word of the LORD came to Jeremiah: 13"Go and tell Hananiah, 'This is what the LORD says: You have broken a wooden yoke, but in its place you will get a yoke of iron. 14This is what the LORD Almighty, the God of Israel, says: I will put an iron yoke on the necks of all these nations to make them serve Nebuchadnezzar king of Babylon, and they will serve him. I will even give him control over the wild animals.' "

15Then the prophet Jeremiah said to Hananiah the prophet, "Listen, Hananiah! The LORD has not sent you, yet you have persuaded this nation to trust in lies. 16Therefore, this is what the LORD says: 'I am about to remove you from the face of the earth. This very year you are going to die, because you have preached rebellion against the LORD.' "

17In the seventh month of that same year, Hananiah the prophet died.

A Letter to the Exiles

29 This is the text of the letter that the prophet Jeremiah sent from Jerusalem to the surviving elders among the exiles and to the priests, the prophets and all the other people Nebuchadnezzar had carried into exile from Jerusalem to Babylon. 2(This was after King Jehoiachin[a] and the queen mother, the court officials and the leaders of Judah and Jerusalem, the craftsmen and the artisans had gone into exile from Jerusalem.) 3He entrusted the letter to Elasah son of Shaphan and to Gemariah son of Hilkiah, whom Zedekiah king of Judah sent to King Nebuchadnezzar in Babylon. It said:

> 4This is what the LORD Almighty, the God of Israel, says to all those I carried into exile from Jerusalem to Babylon: 5"Build houses and settle down; plant gardens and eat what they produce. 6Marry and have sons and daughters; find wives for your sons and give your daughters in marriage, so that they too may have sons and daughters. Increase in number there; do not decrease. 7Also, seek the peace and prosperity of the city to which I have carried you into exile. Pray to the LORD for it, because if it prospers, you too will prosper." 8Yes, this is what the LORD Almighty, the God of Israel, says: "Do not let the prophets and diviners among you deceive you. Do not listen to the dreams you encourage them to have. 9They are prophesying lies to you in my name. I have not sent them," declares the LORD.
>
> 10This is what the LORD says: "When seventy years are completed

[a]4,2 Hebrew *Jeconiah*, a variant of *Jehoiachin*

for Babylon, I will come to you and
fulfill my gracious promise to bring
you back to this place. 11For I know
the plans I have for you," declares the
LORD, "plans to prosper you and not
to harm you, plans to give you hope
and a future. 12Then you will call
upon me and come and pray to me,
and I will listen to you. 13You will
seek me and find me when you seek
me with all your heart. 14I will be
found by you," declares the LORD,
"and will bring you back from captiv-
ity.[a] I will gather you from all the na-
tions and places where I have ban-
ished you," declares the LORD, "and

[a]14 Or *will restore your fortunes*

VERSE FOR THE DAY: Jeremiah 29:11 | AUTHOR: Ben Patterson | PASSAGE FOR THE DAY: Jeremiah 29:1–32

Waiting

One Monday morning I awoke with a stabbing pain shooting down my right leg. The diagnosis: a ruptured disc in the lower back. The treatment: four to six weeks of complete bed rest. That was going to be difficult. Weeks of bed rest would be a blatant suspension of my own "sovereign" plans for my life. Yet I had no choice. For six weeks, all I had to do was lie there, listen to music and think.

Eventually, out of sheer desperation and boredom, I spent hours in prayer. When we pray, we relinquish in a radical way our so-called sovereignty over the purposes of our lives. We subordinate our plans, schedules and life scenarios to the infinitely wiser and more joyful work of God's hands.

And contrary to what we like to think, God's view of our lives doesn't always square with our own dreams. But how can we get our lives—and our dreams—more in line with what God desires? Much of the answer, I came to realize, involves *not* taking action, but instead doing the hard work of waiting. Waiting isn't just the thing we do until we get what we're hoping for; it's a critical part of the process of *becoming* what we hope for.

MARRIAGE BUILDERS

♦ *How is waiting a part of lining up your goals and dreams with what God desires for you?*

♦ *When was a time when a period of waiting on God was actually productive for you?*

Additional Scripture Readings
Psalm 27:13–14; 33:20–22

Go to page 837 for your next devotional reading.

will bring you back to the place from which I carried you into exile."

15You may say, "The LORD has raised up prophets for us in Babylon," 16but this is what the LORD says about the king who sits on David's throne and all the people who remain in this city, your countrymen who did not go with you into exile— 17yes, this is what the LORD Almighty says: "I will send the sword, famine and plague against them and I will make them like poor figs that are so bad they cannot be eaten. 18I will pursue them with the sword, famine and plague and will make them abhorrent to all the kingdoms of the earth and an object of cursing and horror, of scorn and reproach, among all the nations where I drive them. 19For they have not listened to my words," declares the LORD, "words that I sent to them again and again by my servants the prophets. And you exiles have not listened either," declares the LORD.

20Therefore, hear the word of the LORD, all you exiles whom I have sent away from Jerusalem to Babylon. 21This is what the LORD Almighty, the God of Israel, says about Ahab son of Kolaiah and Zedekiah son of Maaseiah, who are prophesying lies to you in my name: "I will hand them over to Nebuchadnezzar king of Babylon, and he will put them to death before your very eyes. 22Because of them, all the exiles from Judah who are in Babylon will use this curse: 'The LORD treat you like Zedekiah and Ahab, whom the king of Babylon burned in the fire.' 23For they have done outrageous things in Israel; they have committed adultery with their neighbors' wives and in my name have spoken lies, which I did not tell them to do. I know it and am a witness to it," declares the LORD.

Message to Shemaiah

24Tell Shemaiah the Nehelamite, 25"This is what the LORD Almighty, the God of Israel, says: You sent letters in your own name to all the people in Jerusalem, to Zephaniah son of Maaseiah the priest, and to all the other priests. You said to Zephaniah, 26'The LORD has appointed you priest in place of Jehoiada to be in charge of the house of the LORD; you should put any madman who acts like a prophet into the stocks and neck-irons. 27So why have you not reprimanded Jeremiah from Anathoth, who poses as a prophet among you? 28He has sent this message to us in Babylon: It will be a long time. Therefore build houses and settle down; plant gardens and eat what they produce.' "

29Zephaniah the priest, however, read the letter to Jeremiah the prophet. 30Then the word of the LORD came to Jeremiah: 31"Send this message to all the exiles: 'This is what the LORD says about Shemaiah the Nehelamite: Because Shemaiah has prophesied to you, even though I did not send him, and has led you to believe a lie, 32this is what the LORD says: I will surely punish Shemaiah the Nehelamite and his descendants. He will have no one left among this people, nor will he see the good things I will do for my people, declares the LORD, because he has preached rebellion against me.' "

Restoration of Israel

30 This is the word that came to Jeremiah from the LORD: 2"This is what the LORD, the God of Israel, says: 'Write in a book all the words I have spoken to you. 3The days are coming,' declares the LORD, 'when I will bring my people Israel and Judah back from captivity[a] and restore them to the land I gave their forefathers to possess,' says the LORD."

4These are the words the LORD spoke concerning Israel and Judah: 5"This is what the LORD says:

" 'Cries of fear are heard—
terror, not peace.
6Ask and see:
Can a man bear children?
Then why do I see every strong man
with his hands on his stomach like
a woman in labor,
every face turned deathly pale?
7How awful that day will be!
None will be like it.
It will be a time of trouble for Jacob,
but he will be saved out of it.

8" 'In that day,' declares the LORD
Almighty,
'I will break the yoke off their necks
and will tear off their bonds;

[a]3 Or *will restore the fortunes of my people Israel and Judah*

no longer will foreigners enslave them.
9 Instead, they will serve the LORD their God
and David their king,
whom I will raise up for them.

10 " 'So do not fear, O Jacob my servant;
do not be dismayed, O Israel,'
declares the LORD.
'I will surely save you out of a distant place,
your descendants from the land of their exile.
Jacob will again have peace and security,
and no one will make him afraid.
11 I am with you and will save you,'
declares the LORD.
'Though I completely destroy all the nations
among which I scatter you,
I will not completely destroy you.
I will discipline you but only with justice;
I will not let you go entirely unpunished.'

12 "This is what the LORD says:

" 'Your wound is incurable,
your injury beyond healing.
13 There is no one to plead your cause,
no remedy for your sore,
no healing for you.
14 All your allies have forgotten you;
they care nothing for you.
I have struck you as an enemy would
and punished you as would the cruel,
because your guilt is so great
and your sins so many.
15 Why do you cry out over your wound,
your pain that has no cure?
Because of your great guilt and many sins
I have done these things to you.

16 " 'But all who devour you will be devoured;
all your enemies will go into exile.
Those who plunder you will be plundered;
all who make spoil of you I will despoil.
17 But I will restore you to health
and heal your wounds,'
declares the LORD,
'because you are called an outcast,
Zion for whom no one cares.'

18 "This is what the LORD says:

" 'I will restore the fortunes of Jacob's tents
and have compassion on his dwellings;
the city will be rebuilt on her ruins,
and the palace will stand in its proper place.
19 From them will come songs of thanksgiving
and the sound of rejoicing.
I will add to their numbers,
and they will not be decreased;
I will bring them honor,
and they will not be disdained.
20 Their children will be as in days of old,
and their community will be established before me;
I will punish all who oppress them.
21 Their leader will be one of their own;
their ruler will arise from among them.
I will bring him near and he will come close to me,
for who is he who will devote himself
to be close to me?'
declares the LORD.
22 " 'So you will be my people,
and I will be your God.' "

23 See, the storm of the LORD
will burst out in wrath,
a driving wind swirling down
on the heads of the wicked.
24 The fierce anger of the LORD will not turn back
until he fully accomplishes
the purposes of his heart.
In days to come
you will understand this.

31 "At that time," declares the LORD, "I will be the God of all the clans of Israel, and they will be my people."
2 This is what the LORD says:

"The people who survive the sword
will find favor in the desert;
I will come to give rest to Israel."

3 The LORD appeared to us in the past,[a]
saying:

"I have loved you with an everlasting love;

[a] 3 Or *LORD has appeared to us from afar*

WEEKENDING

SPIRITUALITY

Too often, the demanding responsibilities of marriage and family result in our investing too little time in the spiritual dimension of our lives. Discuss these issues together to help you gain a greater understanding of why God called the two of you together.

In what ways are you working to develop a deeper faith and Christian spirituality as a couple?

☐ Attending church.

☐ Reading the Bible together on a regular basis.

☐ Setting aside time to pray together regularly.

☐ Participating in a small-group Bible study.

☐ Discussing spiritual issues with each other.

☐ Helping out someone who is in need.

☐ Giving a portion of our income to the church and other charitable causes.

☐ Serving together on church committees, team teaching Sunday school, co-leading a Bible study group, etc.

☐ Other: _____

— *The* Marriage Partnership *Staff*

REVIVE

Saturday: Matthew 18:1–20
Sunday: Acts 2:42–47

Go to page 842 for your next devotional reading.

I have drawn you with
loving-kindness.
4I will build you up again
and you will be rebuilt, O Virgin
Israel.
Again you will take up your
tambourines
and go out to dance with the joyful.
5Again you will plant vineyards
on the hills of Samaria;
the farmers will plant them
and enjoy their fruit.
6There will be a day when watchmen
cry out
on the hills of Ephraim,
'Come, let us go up to Zion,
to the LORD our God.' "

7This is what the LORD says:

"Sing with joy for Jacob;
shout for the foremost of the
nations.
Make your praises heard, and say,
'O LORD, save your people,
the remnant of Israel.'
8See, I will bring them from the land of
the north
and gather them from the ends of
the earth.
Among them will be the blind and the
lame,
expectant mothers and women in
labor;
a great throng will return.
9They will come with weeping;
they will pray as I bring them back.
I will lead them beside streams of
water
on a level path where they will not
stumble,
because I am Israel's father,
and Ephraim is my firstborn son.

10"Hear the word of the LORD,
O nations;
proclaim it in distant coastlands:
'He who scattered Israel will gather
them
and will watch over his flock like a
shepherd.'
11For the LORD will ransom Jacob
and redeem them from the hand of
those stronger than they.
12They will come and shout for joy on
the heights of Zion;
they will rejoice in the bounty of
the LORD—
the grain, the new wine and the oil,
the young of the flocks and herds.
They will be like a well-watered
garden,
and they will sorrow no more.
13Then maidens will dance and be glad,
young men and old as well.
I will turn their mourning into
gladness;
I will give them comfort and joy
instead of sorrow.
14I will satisfy the priests with
abundance,
and my people will be filled with
my bounty,"
declares the LORD.

15This is what the LORD says:

"A voice is heard in Ramah,
mourning and great weeping,
Rachel weeping for her children
and refusing to be comforted,
because her children are no more."

16This is what the LORD says:

"Restrain your voice from weeping
and your eyes from tears,
for your work will be rewarded,"
declares the LORD.
"They will return from the land of
the enemy.
17So there is hope for your future,"
declares the LORD.
"Your children will return to their
own land.

18"I have surely heard Ephraim's
moaning:
'You disciplined me like an unruly
calf,
and I have been disciplined.
Restore me, and I will return,
because you are the LORD my God.
19After I strayed,
I repented;
after I came to understand,
I beat my breast.
I was ashamed and humiliated
because I bore the disgrace of my
youth.'
20Is not Ephraim my dear son,
the child in whom I delight?
Though I often speak against him,
I still remember him.
Therefore my heart yearns for him;
I have great compassion for him,"
declares the LORD.

21"Set up road signs;
put up guideposts.
Take note of the highway,
the road that you take.

Return, O Virgin Israel,
return to your towns.
22 How long will you wander,
O unfaithful daughter?
The LORD will create a new thing on earth—
a woman will surround[a] a man."

23 This is what the LORD Almighty, the God of Israel, says: "When I bring them back from captivity,[b] the people in the land of Judah and in its towns will once again use these words: 'The LORD bless you, O righteous dwelling, O sacred mountain.' 24 People will live together in Judah and all its towns—farmers and those who move about with their flocks. 25 I will refresh the weary and satisfy the faint."

26 At this I awoke and looked around. My sleep had been pleasant to me.

27 "The days are coming," declares the LORD, "when I will plant the house of Israel and the house of Judah with the offspring of men and of animals. 28 Just as I watched over them to uproot and tear down, and to overthrow, destroy and bring disaster, so I will watch over them to build and to plant," declares the LORD. 29 "In those days people will no longer say,

'The fathers have eaten sour grapes,
and the children's teeth are set on edge.'

30 Instead, everyone will die for his own sin; whoever eats sour grapes—his own teeth will be set on edge.

31 "The time is coming," declares the LORD,
"when I will make a new covenant
with the house of Israel
and with the house of Judah.
32 It will not be like the covenant
I made with their forefathers
when I took them by the hand
to lead them out of Egypt,
because they broke my covenant,
though I was a husband to[c] them,[d]"
declares the LORD.
33 "This is the covenant I will make with the house of Israel
after that time," declares the LORD.
"I will put my law in their minds
and write it on their hearts.
I will be their God,
and they will be my people.
34 No longer will a man teach his neighbor,
or a man his brother, saying, 'Know the LORD,'
because they will all know me,
from the least of them to the greatest,"
declares the LORD.
"For I will forgive their wickedness
and will remember their sins no more."

35 This is what the LORD says,

he who appoints the sun
to shine by day,
who decrees the moon and stars
to shine by night,
who stirs up the sea
so that its waves roar—
the LORD Almighty is his name:
36 "Only if these decrees vanish from my sight,"
declares the LORD,
"will the descendants of Israel ever cease
to be a nation before me."

37 This is what the LORD says:

"Only if the heavens above can be measured
and the foundations of the earth below be searched out
will I reject all the descendants of Israel
because of all they have done,"
declares the LORD.

38 "The days are coming," declares the LORD, "when this city will be rebuilt for me from the Tower of Hananel to the Corner Gate. 39 The measuring line will stretch from there straight to the hill of Gareb and then turn to Goah. 40 The whole valley where dead bodies and ashes are thrown, and all the terraces out to the Kidron Valley on the east as far as the corner of the Horse Gate, will be holy to the LORD. The city will never again be uprooted or demolished."

Jeremiah Buys a Field

32 This is the word that came to Jeremiah from the LORD in the tenth year of Zedekiah king of Judah, which was the eighteenth year of Nebuchadnez-

[a] 22 Or *will go about* ‹seeking›; or *will protect* Septuagint and Syriac / *and I turned away from*
[b] 23 Or *I restore their fortunes*
[c] 32 Hebrew;
[d] 32 Or *was their master*

zar. 2The army of the king of Babylon was
then besieging Jerusalem, and Jeremiah
the prophet was confined in the courtyard
of the guard in the royal palace of Judah.
3Now Zedekiah king of Judah had im-
prisoned him there, saying, "Why do you
prophesy as you do? You say, 'This is
what the LORD says: I am about to hand
this city over to the king of Babylon, and
he will capture it. 4Zedekiah king of Judah
will not escape out of the hands of the
Babylonians[a] but will certainly be hand-
ed over to the king of Babylon, and will
speak with him face to face and see him
with his own eyes. 5He will take Zedekiah
to Babylon, where he will remain until I
deal with him, declares the LORD. If you
fight against the Babylonians, you will not
succeed.' "
6Jeremiah said, "The word of the LORD
came to me: 7Hanamel son of Shallum
your uncle is going to come to you and
say, 'Buy my field at Anathoth, because as
nearest relative it is your right and duty to
buy it.'
8"Then, just as the LORD had said, my
cousin Hanamel came to me in the court-
yard of the guard and said, 'Buy my field
at Anathoth in the territory of Benjamin.
Since it is your right to redeem it and pos-
sess it, buy it for yourself.'
"I knew that this was the word of the
LORD; 9so I bought the field at Anathoth
from my cousin Hanamel and weighed
out for him seventeen shekels[b] of silver.
10I signed and sealed the deed, had it wit-
nessed, and weighed out the silver on the
scales. 11I took the deed of purchase—the
sealed copy containing the terms and con-
ditions, as well as the unsealed copy—
12and I gave this deed to Baruch son of Ne-
riah, the son of Mahseiah, in the presence
of my cousin Hanamel and of the wit-
nesses who had signed the deed and of all
the Jews sitting in the courtyard of the
guard.
13"In their presence I gave Baruch these
instructions: 14'This is what the LORD Al-
mighty, the God of Israel, says: Take these
documents, both the sealed and unsealed
copies of the deed of purchase, and put
them in a clay jar so they will last a long
time. 15For this is what the LORD Almighty,
the God of Israel, says: Houses, fields and
vineyards will again be bought in this
land.'
16"After I had given the deed of pur-
chase to Baruch son of Neriah, I prayed to
the LORD:

17"Ah, Sovereign LORD, you have
made the heavens and the earth by
your great power and outstretched
arm. Nothing is too hard for you.
18You show love to thousands but
bring the punishment for the fathers'
sins into the laps of their children af-
ter them. O great and powerful God,
whose name is the LORD Almighty,
19great are your purposes and mighty
are your deeds. Your eyes are open to
all the ways of men; you reward ev-
eryone according to his conduct and
as his deeds deserve. 20You per-
formed miraculous signs and won-
ders in Egypt and have continued
them to this day, both in Israel and
among all mankind, and have gained
the renown that is still yours. 21You
brought your people Israel out of
Egypt with signs and wonders, by a
mighty hand and an outstretched
arm and with great terror. 22You gave
them this land you had sworn to give
their forefathers, a land flowing with
milk and honey. 23They came in and
took possession of it, but they did not
obey you or follow your law; they did
not do what you commanded them to
do. So you brought all this disaster
upon them.
24"See how the siege ramps are
built up to take the city. Because of
the sword, famine and plague, the
city will be handed over to the Bab-
ylonians who are attacking it. What
you said has happened, as you now
see. 25And though the city will be
handed over to the Babylonians, you,
O Sovereign LORD, say to me, 'Buy
the field with silver and have the
transaction witnessed.' "

26Then the word of the LORD came to
Jeremiah: 27"I am the LORD, the God of all
mankind. Is anything too hard for me?
28Therefore, this is what the LORD says: I
am about to hand this city over to the Bab-
ylonians and to Nebuchadnezzar king of
Babylon, who will capture it. 29The Bab-
ylonians who are attacking this city will
come in and set it on fire; they will burn
it down, along with the houses where the
people provoked me to anger by burning

[a]4 Or *Chaldeans*; also in verses 5, 24, 25, 28, 29 and 43

[b]9 That is, about 7 ounces (about 200 grams)

incense on the roofs to Baal and by pouring out drink offerings to other gods.

30"The people of Israel and Judah have done nothing but evil in my sight from their youth; indeed, the people of Israel have done nothing but provoke me with what their hands have made, declares the LORD. 31From the day it was built until now, this city has so aroused my anger and wrath that I must remove it from my sight. 32The people of Israel and Judah have provoked me by all the evil they have done—they, their kings and officials, their priests and prophets, the men of Judah and the people of Jerusalem. 33They turned their backs to me and not their faces; though I taught them again and again, they would not listen or respond to discipline. 34They set up their abominable idols in the house that bears my Name and defiled it. 35They built high places for Baal in the Valley of Ben Hinnom to sacrifice their sons and daughters[a] to Molech, though I never commanded, nor did it enter my mind, that they should do such a detestable thing and so make Judah sin.

36"You are saying about this city, 'By the sword, famine and plague it will be handed over to the king of Babylon'; but this is what the LORD, the God of Israel, says: 37I will surely gather them from all the lands where I banish them in my furious anger and great wrath; I will bring them back to this place and let them live in safety. 38They will be my people, and I will be their God. 39I will give them singleness of heart and action, so that they will always fear me for their own good and the good of their children after them. 40I will make an everlasting covenant with them: I will never stop doing good to them, and I will inspire them to fear me, so that they will never turn away from me. 41I will rejoice in doing them good and will assuredly plant them in this land with all my heart and soul.

42"This is what the LORD says: As I have brought all this great calamity on this people, so I will give them all the prosperity I have promised them. 43Once more fields will be bought in this land of which you say, 'It is a desolate waste, without men or animals, for it has been handed over to the Babylonians.' 44Fields will be bought for silver, and deeds will be signed, sealed and witnessed in the territory of Benjamin, in the villages around Jerusalem, in the towns of Judah and in the towns of the hill country, of the western foothills and of the Negev, because I will restore their fortunes,[b] declares the LORD."

Promise of Restoration

33 While Jeremiah was still confined in the courtyard of the guard, the word of the LORD came to him a second time: 2"This is what the LORD says, he who made the earth, the LORD who formed it and established it—the LORD is his name: 3'Call to me and I will answer you and tell you great and unsearchable things you do not know.' 4For this is what the LORD, the God of Israel, says about the houses in this city and the royal palaces of Judah that have been torn down to be used against the siege ramps and the sword 5in the fight with the Babylonians[c]: 'They will be filled with the dead bodies of the men I will slay in my anger and wrath. I will hide my face from this city because of all its wickedness.

6" 'Nevertheless, I will bring health and healing to it; I will heal my people and will let them enjoy abundant peace and security. 7I will bring Judah and Israel back from captivity[d] and will rebuild them as they were before. 8I will cleanse them from all the sin they have committed against me and will forgive all their sins of rebellion against me. 9Then this city will bring me renown, joy, praise and honor before all nations on earth that hear of all the good things I do for it; and they will be in awe and will tremble at the abundant prosperity and peace I provide for it.'

10"This is what the LORD says: 'You say about this place, "It is a desolate waste, without men or animals." Yet in the towns of Judah and the streets of Jerusalem that are deserted, inhabited by neither men nor animals, there will be heard once more 11the sounds of joy and gladness, the voices of bride and bridegroom, and the voices of those who bring thank offerings to the house of the LORD, saying,

"Give thanks to the LORD Almighty,
for the LORD is good;
his love endures forever."

For I will restore the fortunes of the land as they were before,' says the LORD.

[a]35 Or *to make their sons and daughters pass through the fire,* [b]44 Or *will bring them back from captivity* [c]5 Or *Chaldeans* [d]7 Or *will restore the fortunes of Judah and Israel*

VERSE FOR THE DAY: Jeremiah 33:10–11

AUTHOR: John W. Kennedy

PASSAGE FOR THE DAY: Jeremiah 33:1–11

God's Sovereign Purposes

Conventional wisdom says the wedded state should confer a long list of attractive benefits—a lifetime of companionship and emotional support, a partner who will gladly share in activities and interests. But marriage is not solely a pragmatic arrangement. Its purposes exceed mere comfort and convenience.

When Patty and I stood at the altar and recited our vows for better or worse, in sickness and in health, we never imagined the outcome. Now Patty suffers from a physical malady that has left her fatigued and weak. Her debilitating illness has changed our lives dramatically. My wife can no longer sing on the church worship team; we can no longer play tennis together; she can't drive a car.

But our love endures. God can still work through her weakened body, for her soul is what's important. As we face an unknown future, the Lord is reinforcing those qualities that marriage is all about: patience, trust, unconditional love. With Patty's illness, we are seeing some of our old dreams, once taken for granted, now taking on new meaning.

Most couples shortchange what God has ordained by defining marriage as a fulfilling, mutually beneficial arrangement, rather than seeing it as God's gift to us no matter how difficult the terms become.

In this world, nothing is guaranteed. But we know God brings one man and one woman together for life. The outcome is in his hands. For us, the blessing is in being together.

MARRIAGE BUILDERS

♦ *How have you been strong for your spouse in a time of illness, loss or fatigue?*

♦ *What can you do now to prepare for life's future trials?*

Additional Scripture Readings
Lamentations 3:22–33; Romans 8:35–39

Go to page 871 for your next devotional reading.

12"This is what the LORD Almighty says:
'In this place, desolate and without men
or animals—in all its towns there will
again be pastures for shepherds to rest
their flocks. 13In the towns of the hill
country, of the western foothills and of
the Negev, in the territory of Benjamin, in
the villages around Jerusalem and in the
towns of Judah, flocks will again pass un-
der the hand of the one who counts them,'
says the LORD.
14" 'The days are coming,' declares the
LORD, 'when I will fulfill the gracious
promise I made to the house of Israel and
to the house of Judah.

15" 'In those days and at that time
I will make a righteous Branch
sprout from David's line;
he will do what is just and right in
the land.
16In those days Judah will be saved
and Jerusalem will live in safety.
This is the name by which it[a] will be
called:
The LORD Our Righteousness.'

17For this is what the LORD says: 'David
will never fail to have a man to sit on the
throne of the house of Israel, 18nor will the
priests, who are Levites, ever fail to have
a man to stand before me continually to
offer burnt offerings, to burn grain offer-
ings and to present sacrifices.' "
19The word of the LORD came to Jeremi-
ah: 20"This is what the LORD says: 'If you
can break my covenant with the day and
my covenant with the night, so that day
and night no longer come at their appoint-
ed time, 21then my covenant with David
my servant—and my covenant with the
Levites who are priests ministering before
me—can be broken and David will no
longer have a descendant to reign on his
throne. 22I will make the descendants of
David my servant and the Levites who
minister before me as countless as the
stars of the sky and as measureless as the
sand on the seashore.' "
23The word of the LORD came to Jeremi-
ah: 24"Have you not noticed that these
people are saying, 'The LORD has rejected
the two kingdoms[b] he chose'? So they de-
spise my people and no longer regard
them as a nation. 25This is what the LORD
says: 'If I have not established my cove-
nant with day and night and the fixed
laws of heaven and earth, 26then I will re-
ject the descendants of Jacob and David
my servant and will not choose one of his
sons to rule over the descendants of Abra-
ham, Isaac and Jacob. For I will restore
their fortunes[c] and have compassion on
them.' "

Warning to Zedekiah

34 While Nebuchadnezzar king of
Babylon and all his army and all
the kingdoms and peoples in the empire
he ruled were fighting against Jerusalem
and all its surrounding towns, this word
came to Jeremiah from the LORD: 2"This is
what the LORD, the God of Israel, says: Go
to Zedekiah king of Judah and tell him,
'This is what the LORD says: I am about to
hand this city over to the king of Babylon,
and he will burn it down. 3You will not es-
cape from his grasp but will surely be cap-
tured and handed over to him. You will
see the king of Babylon with your own
eyes, and he will speak with you face to
face. And you will go to Babylon.
4" 'Yet hear the promise of the LORD,
O Zedekiah king of Judah. This is what
the LORD says concerning you: You will
not die by the sword; 5you will die peace-
fully. As people made a funeral fire in
honor of your fathers, the former kings
who preceded you, so they will make a
fire in your honor and lament, "Alas,
O master!" I myself make this promise,
declares the LORD.' "
6Then Jeremiah the prophet told all this
to Zedekiah king of Judah, in Jerusalem,
7while the army of the king of Babylon
was fighting against Jerusalem and
the other cities of Judah that were still hold-
ing out—Lachish and Azekah. These
were the only fortified cities left in Judah.

Freedom for Slaves

8The word came to Jeremiah from the
LORD after King Zedekiah had made a cov-
enant with all the people in Jerusalem to
proclaim freedom for the slaves. 9Every-
one was to free his Hebrew slaves, both
male and female; no one was to hold a fel-
low Jew in bondage. 10So all the officials
and people who entered into this cov-
enant agreed that they would free their
male and female slaves and no longer
hold them in bondage. They agreed, and
set them free. 11But afterward they
changed their minds and took back the

[a]16 Or *he* [b]24 Or *families* [c]26 Or *will bring them back from captivity*

slaves they had freed and enslaved them again.

12Then the word of the LORD came to Jeremiah: 13"This is what the LORD, the God of Israel, says: I made a covenant with your forefathers when I brought them out of Egypt, out of the land of slavery. I said, 14'Every seventh year each of you must free any fellow Hebrew who has sold himself to you. After he has served you six years, you must let him go free.'[a] Your fathers, however, did not listen to me or pay attention to me. 15Recently you repented and did what is right in my sight: Each of you proclaimed freedom to his countrymen. You even made a covenant before me in the house that bears my Name. 16But now you have turned around and profaned my name; each of you has taken back the male and female slaves you had set free to go where they wished. You have forced them to become your slaves again.

17"Therefore, this is what the LORD says: You have not obeyed me; you have not proclaimed freedom for your fellow countrymen. So I now proclaim 'freedom' for you, declares the LORD—'freedom' to fall by the sword, plague and famine. I will make you abhorrent to all the kingdoms of the earth. 18The men who have violated my covenant and have not fulfilled the terms of the covenant they made before me, I will treat like the calf they cut in two and then walked between its pieces. 19The leaders of Judah and Jerusalem, the court officials, the priests and all the people of the land who walked between the pieces of the calf, 20I will hand over to their enemies who seek their lives. Their dead bodies will become food for the birds of the air and the beasts of the earth.

21"I will hand Zedekiah king of Judah and his officials over to their enemies who seek their lives, to the army of the king of Babylon, which has withdrawn from you. 22I am going to give the order, declares the LORD, and I will bring them back to this city. They will fight against it, take it and burn it down. And I will lay waste the towns of Judah so no one can live there."

The Recabites

35 This is the word that came to Jeremiah from the LORD during the reign of Jehoiakim son of Josiah king of Judah: 2"Go to the Recabite family and invite them to come to one of the side rooms of the house of the LORD and give them wine to drink."

3So I went to get Jaazaniah son of Jeremiah, the son of Habazziniah, and his brothers and all his sons—the whole family of the Recabites. 4I brought them into the house of the LORD, into the room of the sons of Hanan son of Igdaliah the man of God. It was next to the room of the officials, which was over that of Maaseiah son of Shallum the doorkeeper. 5Then I set bowls full of wine and some cups before the men of the Recabite family and said to them, "Drink some wine."

6But they replied, "We do not drink wine, because our forefather Jonadab son of Recab gave us this command: 'Neither you nor your descendants must ever drink wine. 7Also you must never build houses, sow seed or plant vineyards; you must never have any of these things, but must always live in tents. Then you will live a long time in the land where you are nomads.' 8We have obeyed everything our forefather Jonadab son of Recab commanded us. Neither we nor our wives nor our sons and daughters have ever drunk wine 9or built houses to live in or had vineyards, fields or crops. 10We have lived in tents and have fully obeyed everything our forefather Jonadab commanded us. 11But when Nebuchadnezzar king of Babylon invaded this land, we said, 'Come, we must go to Jerusalem to escape the Babylonian[b] and Aramean armies.' So we have remained in Jerusalem."

12Then the word of the LORD came to Jeremiah, saying: 13"This is what the LORD Almighty, the God of Israel, says: Go and tell the men of Judah and the people of Jerusalem, 'Will you not learn a lesson and obey my words?' declares the LORD. 14'Jonadab son of Recab ordered his sons not to drink wine and this command has been kept. To this day they do not drink wine, because they obey their forefather's command. But I have spoken to you again and again, yet you have not obeyed me. 15Again and again I sent all my servants the prophets to you. They said, "Each of you must turn from your wicked ways and reform your actions; do not follow other gods to serve them. Then you will live in the land I have given to you and your fathers." But you have not paid attention or listened to me. 16The descendants of Jona-

[a] 14 Deut. 15:12 [b] 11 Or *Chaldean*

dab son of Recab have carried out the
command their forefather gave them, but
these people have not obeyed me.'
17"Therefore, this is what the LORD God
Almighty, the God of Israel, says: 'Listen!
I am going to bring on Judah and on ev-
eryone living in Jerusalem every disaster
I pronounced against them. I spoke to
them, but they did not listen; I called to
them, but they did not answer.' "
18Then Jeremiah said to the family of
the Recabites, "This is what the LORD Al-
mighty, the God of Israel, says: 'You have
obeyed the command of your forefather
Jonadab and have followed all his instruc-
tions and have done everything he or-
dered.' 19Therefore, this is what the LORD
Almighty, the God of Israel, says: 'Jona-
dab son of Recab will never fail to have a
man to serve me.' "

Jehoiakim Burns Jeremiah's Scroll

36 In the fourth year of Jehoiakim son
of Josiah king of Judah, this word
came to Jeremiah from the LORD: 2"Take a
scroll and write on it all the words I have
spoken to you concerning Israel, Judah
and all the other nations from the time I
began speaking to you in the reign of Josi-
ah till now. 3Perhaps when the people of
Judah hear about every disaster I plan to
inflict on them, each of them will turn
from his wicked way; then I will forgive
their wickedness and their sin."
4So Jeremiah called Baruch son of Neri-
ah, and while Jeremiah dictated all the
words the LORD had spoken to him, Ba-
ruch wrote them on the scroll. 5Then Jere-
miah told Baruch, "I am restricted; I can-
not go to the LORD's temple. 6So you go to
the house of the LORD on a day of fasting
and read to the people from the scroll the
words of the LORD that you wrote as I dic-
tated. Read them to all the people of Judah
who come in from their towns. 7Perhaps
they will bring their petition before the
LORD, and each will turn from his wicked
ways, for the anger and wrath pronounced
against this people by the LORD are great."
8Baruch son of Neriah did everything
Jeremiah the prophet told him to do; at
the LORD's temple he read the words of the
LORD from the scroll. 9In the ninth month
of the fifth year of Jehoiakim son of Josiah
king of Judah, a time of fasting before the
LORD was proclaimed for all the people in
Jerusalem and those who had come from
the towns of Judah. 10From the room of
Gemariah son of Shaphan the secretary,
which was in the upper courtyard at the
entrance of the New Gate of the temple,
Baruch read to all the people at the LORD's
temple the words of Jeremiah from the
scroll.
11When Micaiah son of Gemariah, the
son of Shaphan, heard all the words of the
LORD from the scroll, 12he went down to
the secretary's room in the royal palace,
where all the officials were sitting: Elisha-
ma the secretary, Delaiah son of Shema-
iah, Elnathan son of Acbor, Gemariah son
of Shaphan, Zedekiah son of Hananiah,
and all the other officials. 13After Micaiah
told them everything he had heard Baruch
read to the people from the scroll, 14all the
officials sent Jehudi son of Nethaniah, the
son of Shelemiah, the son of Cushi, to say
to Baruch, "Bring the scroll from which
you have read to the people and come." So
Baruch son of Neriah went to them with
the scroll in his hand. 15They said to him,
"Sit down, please, and read it to us."
So Baruch read it to them. 16When they
heard all these words, they looked at each
other in fear and said to Baruch, "We must
report all these words to the king." 17Then
they asked Baruch, "Tell us, how did you
come to write all this? Did Jeremiah dic-
tate it?"
18"Yes," Baruch replied, "he dictated all
these words to me, and I wrote them in
ink on the scroll."
19Then the officials said to Baruch,
"You and Jeremiah, go and hide. Don't let
anyone know where you are."
20After they put the scroll in the room of
Elishama the secretary, they went to the
king in the courtyard and reported every-
thing to him. 21The king sent Jehudi to get
the scroll, and Jehudi brought it from the
room of Elishama the secretary and read it
to the king and all the officials standing
beside him. 22It was the ninth month and
the king was sitting in the winter apart-
ment, with a fire burning in the firepot in
front of him. 23Whenever Jehudi had read
three or four columns of the scroll, the
king cut them off with a scribe's knife and
threw them into the firepot, until the en-
tire scroll was burned in the fire. 24The
king and all his attendants who heard all
these words showed no fear, nor did they
tear their clothes. 25Even though Elna-
than, Delaiah and Gemariah urged the
king not to burn the scroll, he would not
listen to them. 26Instead, the king com-
manded Jerahmeel, a son of the king, Se-
raiah son of Azriel and Shelemiah son of

Abdeel to arrest Baruch the scribe and Jeremiah the prophet. But the LORD had hidden them.

27After the king burned the scroll containing the words that Baruch had written at Jeremiah's dictation, the word of the LORD came to Jeremiah: 28"Take another scroll and write on it all the words that were on the first scroll, which Jehoiakim king of Judah burned up. 29Also tell Jehoiakim king of Judah, 'This is what the LORD says: You burned that scroll and said, "Why did you write on it that the king of Babylon would certainly come and destroy this land and cut off both men and animals from it?" 30Therefore, this is what the LORD says about Jehoiakim king of Judah: He will have no one to sit on the throne of David; his body will be thrown out and exposed to the heat by day and the frost by night. 31I will punish him and his children and his attendants for their wickedness; I will bring on them and those living in Jerusalem and the people of Judah every disaster I pronounced against them, because they have not listened.' "

32So Jeremiah took another scroll and gave it to the scribe Baruch son of Neriah, and as Jeremiah dictated, Baruch wrote on it all the words of the scroll that Jehoiakim king of Judah had burned in the fire. And many similar words were added to them.

Jeremiah in Prison

37 Zedekiah son of Josiah was made king of Judah by Nebuchadnezzar king of Babylon; he reigned in place of Jehoiachin[a] son of Jehoiakim. 2Neither he nor his attendants nor the people of the land paid any attention to the words the LORD had spoken through Jeremiah the prophet.

3King Zedekiah, however, sent Jehucal son of Shelemiah with the priest Zephaniah son of Maaseiah to Jeremiah the prophet with this message: "Please pray to the LORD our God for us."

4Now Jeremiah was free to come and go among the people, for he had not yet been put in prison. 5Pharaoh's army had marched out of Egypt, and when the Babylonians[b] who were besieging Jerusalem heard the report about them, they withdrew from Jerusalem.

6Then the word of the LORD came to Jeremiah the prophet: 7"This is what the LORD, the God of Israel, says: Tell the king of Judah, who sent you to inquire of me, 'Pharaoh's army, which has marched out to support you, will go back to its own land, to Egypt. 8Then the Babylonians will return and attack this city; they will capture it and burn it down.'

9"This is what the LORD says: Do not deceive yourselves, thinking, 'The Babylonians will surely leave us.' They will not! 10Even if you were to defeat the entire Babylonian[c] army that is attacking you and only wounded men were left in their tents, they would come out and burn this city down."

11After the Babylonian army had withdrawn from Jerusalem because of Pharaoh's army, 12Jeremiah started to leave the city to go to the territory of Benjamin to get his share of the property among the people there. 13But when he reached the Benjamin Gate, the captain of the guard, whose name was Irijah son of Shelemiah, the son of Hananiah, arrested him and said, "You are deserting to the Babylonians!"

14"That's not true!" Jeremiah said. "I am not deserting to the Babylonians." But Irijah would not listen to him; instead, he arrested Jeremiah and brought him to the officials. 15They were angry with Jeremiah and had him beaten and imprisoned in the house of Jonathan the secretary, which they had made into a prison.

16Jeremiah was put into a vaulted cell in a dungeon, where he remained a long time. 17Then King Zedekiah sent for him and had him brought to the palace, where he asked him privately, "Is there any word from the LORD?"

"Yes," Jeremiah replied, "you will be handed over to the king of Babylon."

18Then Jeremiah said to King Zedekiah, "What crime have I committed against you or your officials or this people, that you have put me in prison? 19Where are your prophets who prophesied to you, 'The king of Babylon will not attack you or this land'? 20But now, my lord the king, please listen. Let me bring my petition before you: Do not send me back to the house of Jonathan the secretary, or I will die there."

21King Zedekiah then gave orders for

[a] *1* Hebrew *Coniah*, a variant of *Jehoiachin*
[b] *5* Or *Chaldeans*; also in verses 8, 9, 13 and 14
[c] *10* Or *Chaldean*; also in verse 11

Jeremiah to be placed in the courtyard of the guard and given bread from the street of the bakers each day until all the bread in the city was gone. So Jeremiah remained in the courtyard of the guard.

Jeremiah Thrown Into a Cistern

38 Shephatiah son of Mattan, Gedaliah son of Pashhur, Jehucal[a] son of Shelemiah, and Pashhur son of Malkijah heard what Jeremiah was telling all the people when he said, **2**"This is what the LORD says: 'Whoever stays in this city will die by the sword, famine or plague, but whoever goes over to the Babylonians[b] will live. He will escape with his life; he will live.' **3**And this is what the LORD says: 'This city will certainly be handed over to the army of the king of Babylon, who will capture it.' "

4Then the officials said to the king, "This man should be put to death. He is discouraging the soldiers who are left in this city, as well as all the people, by the things he is saying to them. This man is not seeking the good of these people but their ruin."

5"He is in your hands," King Zedekiah answered. "The king can do nothing to oppose you."

6So they took Jeremiah and put him into the cistern of Malkijah, the king's son, which was in the courtyard of the guard. They lowered Jeremiah by ropes into the cistern; it had no water in it, only mud, and Jeremiah sank down into the mud.

7But Ebed-Melech, a Cushite,[c] an official[d] in the royal palace, heard that they had put Jeremiah into the cistern. While the king was sitting in the Benjamin Gate, **8**Ebed-Melech went out of the palace and said to him, **9**"My lord the king, these men have acted wickedly in all they have done to Jeremiah the prophet. They have thrown him into a cistern, where he will starve to death when there is no longer any bread in the city."

10Then the king commanded Ebed-Melech the Cushite, "Take thirty men from here with you and lift Jeremiah the prophet out of the cistern before he dies."

11So Ebed-Melech took the men with him and went to a room under the treasury in the palace. He took some old rags and worn-out clothes from there and let them down with ropes to Jeremiah in the cistern. **12**Ebed-Melech the Cushite said to Jeremiah, "Put these old rags and worn-out clothes under your arms to pad the ropes." Jeremiah did so, **13**and they pulled him up with the ropes and lifted him out of the cistern. And Jeremiah remained in the courtyard of the guard.

Zedekiah Questions Jeremiah Again

14Then King Zedekiah sent for Jeremiah the prophet and had him brought to the third entrance to the temple of the LORD. "I am going to ask you something," the king said to Jeremiah. "Do not hide anything from me."

15Jeremiah said to Zedekiah, "If I give you an answer, will you not kill me? Even if I did give you counsel, you would not listen to me."

16But King Zedekiah swore this oath secretly to Jeremiah: "As surely as the LORD lives, who has given us breath, I will neither kill you nor hand you over to those who are seeking your life."

17Then Jeremiah said to Zedekiah, "This is what the LORD God Almighty, the God of Israel, says: 'If you surrender to the officers of the king of Babylon, your life will be spared and this city will not be burned down; you and your family will live. **18**But if you will not surrender to the officers of the king of Babylon, this city will be handed over to the Babylonians and they will burn it down; you yourself will not escape from their hands.' "

19King Zedekiah said to Jeremiah, "I am afraid of the Jews who have gone over to the Babylonians, for the Babylonians may hand me over to them and they will mistreat me."

20"They will not hand you over," Jeremiah replied. "Obey the LORD by doing what I tell you. Then it will go well with you, and your life will be spared. **21**But if you refuse to surrender, this is what the LORD has revealed to me: **22**All the women left in the palace of the king of Judah will be brought out to the officials of the king of Babylon. Those women will say to you:

" 'They misled you and overcame
you—
those trusted friends of yours.
Your feet are sunk in the mud;
your friends have deserted you.'

[a] 1 Hebrew *Jucal*, a variant of *Jehucal* [b] 2 Or *Chaldeans*; also in verses 18, 19 and 23 [c] 7 Probably from the upper Nile region [d] 7 Or *a eunuch*

23"All your wives and children will be
brought out to the Babylonians. You your-
self will not escape from their hands but
will be captured by the king of Babylon;
and this city will[a] be burned down."
24Then Zedekiah said to Jeremiah, "Do
not let anyone know about this conversa-
tion, or you may die. 25If the officials hear
that I talked with you, and they come to
you and say, 'Tell us what you said to the
king and what the king said to you; do not
hide it from us or we will kill you,' 26then
tell them, 'I was pleading with the king
not to send me back to Jonathan's house
to die there.' "
27All the officials did come to Jeremiah
and question him, and he told them every-
thing the king had ordered him to say. So
they said no more to him, for no one had
heard his conversation with the king.
28And Jeremiah remained in the court-
yard of the guard until the day Jerusalem
was captured.

The Fall of Jerusalem

39 This is how Jerusalem was taken:
1In the ninth year of Zedekiah king
of Judah, in the tenth month, Nebuchad-
nezzar king of Babylon marched against
Jerusalem with his whole army and laid
siege to it. 2And on the ninth day of the
fourth month of Zedekiah's eleventh year,
the city wall was broken through. 3Then
all the officials of the king of Babylon
came and took seats in the Middle Gate:
Nergal-Sharezer of Samgar, Nebo-Sarse-
kim[b] a chief officer, Nergal-Sharezer a
high official and all the other officials of
the king of Babylon. 4When Zedekiah king
of Judah and all the soldiers saw them,
they fled; they left the city at night by way
of the king's garden, through the gate be-
tween the two walls, and headed toward
the Arabah.[c]
5But the Babylonian[d] army pursued
them and overtook Zedekiah in the plains
of Jericho. They captured him and took
him to Nebuchadnezzar king of Babylon
at Riblah in the land of Hamath, where he
pronounced sentence on him. 6There at
Riblah the king of Babylon slaughtered
the sons of Zedekiah before his eyes and
also killed all the nobles of Judah. 7Then
he put out Zedekiah's eyes and bound
him with bronze shackles to take him to
Babylon.
8The Babylonians[e] set fire to the royal
palace and the houses of the people and
broke down the walls of Jerusalem. 9Neb-
uzaradan commander of the imperial
guard carried into exile to Babylon the
people who remained in the city, along
with those who had gone over to him, and
the rest of the people. 10But Nebuzaradan
the commander of the guard left behind in
the land of Judah some of the poor people,
who owned nothing; and at that time he
gave them vineyards and fields.
11Now Nebuchadnezzar king of Bab-
ylon had given these orders about Jerem-
iah through Nebuzaradan commander of
the imperial guard: 12"Take him and look
after him; don't harm him but do for him
whatever he asks." 13So Nebuzaradan the
commander of the guard, Nebushazban a
chief officer, Nergal-Sharezer a high offi-
cial and all the other officers of the king of
Babylon 14sent and had Jeremiah taken
out of the courtyard of the guard. They
turned him over to Gedaliah son of Ahi-
kam, the son of Shaphan, to take him back
to his home. So he remained among his
own people.
15While Jeremiah had been confined in
the courtyard of the guard, the word of the
LORD came to him: 16"Go and tell Ebed-
Melech the Cushite, 'This is what the LORD
Almighty, the God of Israel, says: I am
about to fulfill my words against this city
through disaster, not prosperity. At that
time they will be fulfilled before your
eyes. 17But I will rescue you on that day,
declares the LORD; you will not be handed
over to those you fear. 18I will save you;
you will not fall by the sword but will es-
cape with your life, because you trust in
me, declares the LORD.' "

Jeremiah Freed

40 The word came to Jeremiah from
the LORD after Nebuzaradan com-
mander of the imperial guard had released
him at Ramah. He had found Jeremiah
bound in chains among all the captives
from Jerusalem and Judah who were be-
ing carried into exile to Babylon. 2When
the commander of the guard found Jere-
miah, he said to him, "The LORD your God
decreed this disaster for this place. 3And
now the LORD has brought it about; he has
done just as he said he would. All this
happened because you people sinned

[a]23 Or *and you will cause this city to* [b]3 Or *Nergal-Sharezer, Samgar-Nebo, Sarsekim* [c]4 Or *the Jordan Valley* [d]5 Or *Chaldean* [e]8 Or *Chaldeans*

against the LORD and did not obey him.
4But today I am freeing you from the
chains on your wrists. Come with me to
Babylon, if you like, and I will look after
you; but if you do not want to, then don't
come. Look, the whole country lies before
you; go wherever you please." 5However,
before Jeremiah turned to go,[a] Nebuzar-
adan added, "Go back to Gedaliah son of
Ahikam, the son of Shaphan, whom the
king of Babylon has appointed over the
towns of Judah, and live with him among
the people, or go anywhere else you
please."

Then the commander gave him provi-
sions and a present and let him go. 6So
Jeremiah went to Gedaliah son of Ahikam
at Mizpah and stayed with him among the
people who were left behind in the land.

Gedaliah Assassinated

7When all the army officers and their
men who were still in the open country
heard that the king of Babylon had ap-
pointed Gedaliah son of Ahikam as gover-
nor over the land and had put him in
charge of the men, women and children
who were the poorest in the land and who
had not been carried into exile to Babylon,
8they came to Gedaliah at Mizpah—Ish-
mael son of Nethaniah, Johanan and Jona-
than the sons of Kareah, Seraiah son of
Tanhumeth, the sons of Ephai the Ne-
tophathite, and Jaazaniah[b] the son of the
Maacathite, and their men. 9Gedaliah son
of Ahikam, the son of Shaphan, took an
oath to reassure them and their men. "Do
not be afraid to serve the Babylonians,[c]"
he said. "Settle down in the land and serve
the king of Babylon, and it will go well
with you. 10I myself will stay at Mizpah to
represent you before the Babylonians who
come to us, but you are to harvest the
wine, summer fruit and oil, and put them
in your storage jars, and live in the towns
you have taken over."

11When all the Jews in Moab, Ammon,
Edom and all the other countries heard
that the king of Babylon had left a rem-
nant in Judah and had appointed Gedaliah
son of Ahikam, the son of Shaphan, as
governor over them, 12they all came back
to the land of Judah, to Gedaliah at Miz-
pah, from all the countries where they had
been scattered. And they harvested an
abundance of wine and summer fruit.

13Johanan son of Kareah and all the
army officers still in the open country
came to Gedaliah at Mizpah 14and said to
him, "Don't you know that Baalis king of
the Ammonites has sent Ishmael son of
Nethaniah to take your life?" But Gedaliah
son of Ahikam did not believe them.

15Then Johanan son of Kareah said pri-
vately to Gedaliah in Mizpah, "Let me go
and kill Ishmael son of Nethaniah, and no
one will know it. Why should he take your
life and cause all the Jews who are gath-
ered around you to be scattered and the
remnant of Judah to perish?"

16But Gedaliah son of Ahikam said to
Johanan son of Kareah, "Don't do such a
thing! What you are saying about Ishmael
is not true."

41 In the seventh month Ishmael son
of Nethaniah, the son of Elishama,
who was of royal blood and had been one
of the king's officers, came with ten men
to Gedaliah son of Ahikam at Mizpah.
While they were eating together there,
2Ishmael son of Nethaniah and the ten
men who were with him got up and struck
down Gedaliah son of Ahikam, the son of
Shaphan, with the sword, killing the one
whom the king of Babylon had appointed
as governor over the land. 3Ishmael also
killed all the Jews who were with Gedali-
ah at Mizpah, as well as the Babylonian[d]
soldiers who were there.

4The day after Gedaliah's assassination,
before anyone knew about it, 5eighty men
who had shaved off their beards, torn
their clothes and cut themselves came
from Shechem, Shiloh and Samaria, bring-
ing grain offerings and incense with them
to the house of the LORD. 6Ishmael son of
Nethaniah went out from Mizpah to meet
them, weeping as he went. When he met
them, he said, "Come to Gedaliah son of
Ahikam." 7When they went into the city,
Ishmael son of Nethaniah and the men
who were with him slaughtered them and
threw them into a cistern. 8But ten of
them said to Ishmael, "Don't kill us! We
have wheat and barley, oil and honey, hid-
den in a field." So he let them alone and
did not kill them with the others. 9Now
the cistern where he threw all the bodies
of the men he had killed along with Geda-
liah was the one King Asa had made as
part of his defense against Baasha king of

[a]5 Or *Jeremiah answered* [b]8 Hebrew *Jezaniah*, a variant of *Jaazaniah* [c]9 Or *Chaldeans*; also in verse 10 [d]3 Or *Chaldean*

Israel. Ishmael son of Nethaniah filled it with the dead.

10Ishmael made captives of all the rest of the people who were in Mizpah—the king's daughters along with all the others who were left there, over whom Nebuzaradan commander of the imperial guard had appointed Gedaliah son of Ahikam. Ishmael son of Nethaniah took them captive and set out to cross over to the Ammonites.

11When Johanan son of Kareah and all the army officers who were with him heard about all the crimes Ishmael son of Nethaniah had committed, 12they took all their men and went to fight Ishmael son of Nethaniah. They caught up with him near the great pool in Gibeon. 13When all the people Ishmael had with him saw Johanan son of Kareah and the army officers who were with him, they were glad. 14All the people Ishmael had taken captive at Mizpah turned and went over to Johanan son of Kareah. 15But Ishmael son of Nethaniah and eight of his men escaped from Johanan and fled to the Ammonites.

Flight to Egypt

16Then Johanan son of Kareah and all the army officers who were with him led away all the survivors from Mizpah whom he had recovered from Ishmael son of Nethaniah after he had assassinated Gedaliah son of Ahikam: the soldiers, women, children and court officials he had brought from Gibeon. 17And they went on, stopping at Geruth Kimham near Bethlehem on their way to Egypt 18to escape the Babylonians.[a] They were afraid of them because Ishmael son of Nethaniah had killed Gedaliah son of Ahikam, whom the king of Babylon had appointed as governor over the land.

42 Then all the army officers, including Johanan son of Kareah and Jezaniah[b] son of Hoshaiah, and all the people from the least to the greatest approached 2Jeremiah the prophet and said to him, "Please hear our petition and pray to the LORD your God for this entire remnant. For as you now see, though we were once many, now only a few are left. 3Pray that the LORD your God will tell us where we should go and what we should do."

4"I have heard you," replied Jeremiah the prophet. "I will certainly pray to the LORD your God as you have requested; I will tell you everything the LORD says and will keep nothing back from you."

5Then they said to Jeremiah, "May the LORD be a true and faithful witness against us if we do not act in accordance with everything the LORD your God sends you to tell us. 6Whether it is favorable or unfavorable, we will obey the LORD our God, to whom we are sending you, so that it will go well with us, for we will obey the LORD our God."

7Ten days later the word of the LORD came to Jeremiah. 8So he called together Johanan son of Kareah and all the army officers who were with him and all the people from the least to the greatest. 9He said to them, "This is what the LORD, the God of Israel, to whom you sent me to present your petition, says: 10'If you stay in this land, I will build you up and not tear you down; I will plant you and not uproot you, for I am grieved over the disaster I have inflicted on you. 11Do not be afraid of the king of Babylon, whom you now fear. Do not be afraid of him, declares the LORD, for I am with you and will save you and deliver you from his hands. 12I will show you compassion so that he will have compassion on you and restore you to your land.'

13"However, if you say, 'We will not stay in this land,' and so disobey the LORD your God, 14and if you say, 'No, we will go and live in Egypt, where we will not see war or hear the trumpet or be hungry for bread,' 15then hear the word of the LORD, O remnant of Judah. This is what the LORD Almighty, the God of Israel, says: 'If you are determined to go to Egypt and you do go to settle there, 16then the sword you fear will overtake you there, and the famine you dread will follow you into Egypt, and there you will die. 17Indeed, all who are determined to go to Egypt to settle there will die by the sword, famine and plague; not one of them will survive or escape the disaster I will bring on them.' 18This is what the LORD Almighty, the God of Israel, says: 'As my anger and wrath have been poured out on those who lived in Jerusalem, so will my wrath be poured out on you when you go to Egypt. You will be an object of cursing and horror, of condemnation and reproach; you will never see this place again.'

19"O remnant of Judah, the LORD has

[a] 18 Or *Chaldeans* [b] 1 Hebrew; Septuagint (see also 43:2) *Azariah*

told you, 'Do not go to Egypt.' Be sure of
this: I warn you today 20that you made a
fatal mistake[a] when you sent me to the
LORD your God and said, 'Pray to the LORD
our God for us; tell us everything he says
and we will do it.' 21I have told you today,
but you still have not obeyed the LORD
your God in all he sent me to tell you. 22So
now, be sure of this: You will die by the
sword, famine and plague in the place
where you want to go to settle."

43 When Jeremiah finished telling the
people all the words of the LORD
their God—everything the LORD had sent
him to tell them— 2Azariah son of Hosha-
iah and Johanan son of Kareah and all the
arrogant men said to Jeremiah, "You are
lying! The LORD our God has not sent you
to say, 'You must not go to Egypt to settle
there.' 3But Baruch son of Neriah is incit-
ing you against us to hand us over to the
Babylonians,[b] so they may kill us or car-
ry us into exile to Babylon."

4So Johanan son of Kareah and all the
army officers and all the people disobeyed
the LORD's command to stay in the land of
Judah. 5Instead, Johanan son of Kareah
and all the army officers led away all the
remnant of Judah who had come back to
live in the land of Judah from all the na-
tions where they had been scattered.
6They also led away all the men, women
and children and the king's daughters
whom Nebuzaradan commander of the
imperial guard had left with Gedaliah son
of Ahikam, the son of Shaphan, and Jere-
miah the prophet and Baruch son of Neri-
ah. 7So they entered Egypt in disobedi-
ence to the LORD and went as far as
Tahpanhes.

8In Tahpanhes the word of the LORD
came to Jeremiah: 9"While the Jews are
watching, take some large stones with you
and bury them in clay in the brick pave-
ment at the entrance to Pharaoh's palace
in Tahpanhes. 10Then say to them, 'This is
what the LORD Almighty, the God of Israel,
says: I will send for my servant Nebuchad-
nezzar king of Babylon, and I will set his
throne over these stones I have buried
here; he will spread his royal canopy
above them. 11He will come and attack
Egypt, bringing death to those destined
for death, captivity to those destined for
captivity, and the sword to those destined
for the sword. 12He[c] will set fire to the
temples of the gods of Egypt; he will burn
their temples and take their gods captive.
As a shepherd wraps his garment around
him, so will he wrap Egypt around himself
and depart from there unscathed. 13There
in the temple of the sun[d] in Egypt he will
demolish the sacred pillars and will burn
down the temples of the gods of Egypt.' "

Disaster Because of Idolatry

44 This word came to Jeremiah con-
cerning all the Jews living in Lower
Egypt—in Migdol, Tahpanhes and Mem-
phis[e]—and in Upper Egypt[f]: 2"This is
what the LORD Almighty, the God of Israel,
says: You saw the great disaster I brought
on Jerusalem and on all the towns of Ju-
dah. Today they lie deserted and in ruins
3because of the evil they have done. They
provoked me to anger by burning incense
and by worshiping other gods that neither
they nor you nor your fathers ever knew.
4Again and again I sent my servants the
prophets, who said, 'Do not do this detest-
able thing that I hate!' 5But they did not
listen or pay attention; they did not turn
from their wickedness or stop burning in-
cense to other gods. 6Therefore, my fierce
anger was poured out; it raged against the
towns of Judah and the streets of Jerusa-
lem and made them the desolate ruins
they are today.

7"Now this is what the LORD God Al-
mighty, the God of Israel, says: Why bring
such great disaster on yourselves by cut-
ting off from Judah the men and women,
the children and infants, and so leave
yourselves without a remnant? 8Why pro-
voke me to anger with what your hands
have made, burning incense to other gods
in Egypt, where you have come to live?
You will destroy yourselves and make
yourselves an object of cursing and re-
proach among all the nations on earth.
9Have you forgotten the wickedness com-
mitted by your fathers and by the kings
and queens of Judah and the wickedness
committed by you and your wives in the
land of Judah and the streets of Jerusa-
lem? 10To this day they have not humbled
themselves or shown reverence, nor have
they followed my law and the decrees I set
before you and your fathers.

11"Therefore, this is what the LORD Al-
mighty, the God of Israel, says: I am deter-
mined to bring disaster on you and to de-

[a] 20 Or *you erred in your hearts* [b] 3 Or *Chaldeans* [c] 12 Or *I* [d] 13 Or *in Heliopolis*
[e] 1 Hebrew *Noph* [f] 1 Hebrew *in Pathros*

stroy all Judah. 12I will take away the remnant of Judah who were determined to go to Egypt to settle there. They will all perish in Egypt; they will fall by the sword or die from famine. From the least to the greatest, they will die by sword or famine. They will become an object of cursing and horror, of condemnation and reproach. 13I will punish those who live in Egypt with the sword, famine and plague, as I punished Jerusalem. 14None of the remnant of Judah who have gone to live in Egypt will escape or survive to return to the land of Judah, to which they long to return and live; none will return except a few fugitives."

15Then all the men who knew that their wives were burning incense to other gods, along with all the women who were present—a large assembly—and all the people living in Lower and Upper Egypt,[a] said to Jeremiah, 16"We will not listen to the message you have spoken to us in the name of the LORD! 17We will certainly do everything we said we would: We will burn incense to the Queen of Heaven and will pour out drink offerings to her just as we and our fathers, our kings and our officials did in the towns of Judah and in the streets of Jerusalem. At that time we had plenty of food and were well off and suffered no harm. 18But ever since we stopped burning incense to the Queen of Heaven and pouring out drink offerings to her, we have had nothing and have been perishing by sword and famine."

19The women added, "When we burned incense to the Queen of Heaven and poured out drink offerings to her, did not our husbands know that we were making cakes like her image and pouring out drink offerings to her?"

20Then Jeremiah said to all the people, both men and women, who were answering him, 21"Did not the LORD remember and think about the incense burned in the towns of Judah and the streets of Jerusalem by you and your fathers, your kings and your officials and the people of the land? 22When the LORD could no longer endure your wicked actions and the detestable things you did, your land became an object of cursing and a desolate waste without inhabitants, as it is today. 23Because you have burned incense and have sinned against the LORD and have not obeyed him or followed his law or his decrees or his stipulations, this disaster has come upon you, as you now see."

24Then Jeremiah said to all the people, including the women, "Hear the word of the LORD, all you people of Judah in Egypt. 25This is what the LORD Almighty, the God of Israel, says: You and your wives have shown by your actions what you promised when you said, 'We will certainly carry out the vows we made to burn incense and pour out drink offerings to the Queen of Heaven.'

"Go ahead then, do what you promised! Keep your vows! 26But hear the word of the LORD, all Jews living in Egypt: 'I swear by my great name,' says the LORD, 'that no one from Judah living anywhere in Egypt will ever again invoke my name or swear, "As surely as the Sovereign LORD lives." 27For I am watching over them for harm, not for good; the Jews in Egypt will perish by sword and famine until they are all destroyed. 28Those who escape the sword and return to the land of Judah from Egypt will be very few. Then the whole remnant of Judah who came to live in Egypt will know whose word will stand—mine or theirs.

29" 'This will be the sign to you that I will punish you in this place,' declares the LORD, 'so that you will know that my threats of harm against you will surely stand.' 30This is what the LORD says: 'I am going to hand Pharaoh Hophra king of Egypt over to his enemies who seek his life, just as I handed Zedekiah king of Judah over to Nebuchadnezzar king of Babylon, the enemy who was seeking his life.' "

A Message to Baruch

45 This is what Jeremiah the prophet told Baruch son of Neriah in the fourth year of Jehoiakim son of Josiah king of Judah, after Baruch had written on a scroll the words Jeremiah was then dictating: 2"This is what the LORD, the God of Israel, says to you, Baruch: 3You said, 'Woe to me! The LORD has added sorrow to my pain; I am worn out with groaning and find no rest.' "

4⌊The LORD said,⌋ "Say this to him: 'This is what the LORD says: I will overthrow what I have built and uproot what I have planted, throughout the land. 5Should you then seek great things for yourself? Seek them not. For I will bring disaster on all

[a]15 Hebrew *in Egypt and Pathros*

people, declares the LORD, but wherever you go I will let you escape with your life.' "

A Message About Egypt

46 This is the word of the LORD that came to Jeremiah the prophet concerning the nations:

2Concerning Egypt:

This is the message against the army of Pharaoh Neco king of Egypt, which was defeated at Carchemish on the Euphrates River by Nebuchadnezzar king of Babylon in the fourth year of Jehoiakim son of Josiah king of Judah:

3"Prepare your shields, both large and small,
and march out for battle!
4Harness the horses,
mount the steeds!
Take your positions
with helmets on!
Polish your spears,
put on your armor!
5What do I see?
They are terrified,
they are retreating,
their warriors are defeated.
They flee in haste
without looking back,
and there is terror on every side,"
declares the LORD.
6"The swift cannot flee
nor the strong escape.
In the north by the River Euphrates
they stumble and fall.

7"Who is this that rises like the Nile,
like rivers of surging waters?
8Egypt rises like the Nile,
like rivers of surging waters.
She says, 'I will rise and cover the earth;
I will destroy cities and their people.'
9Charge, O horses!
Drive furiously, O charioteers!
March on, O warriors—
men of Cush[a] and Put who carry shields,
men of Lydia who draw the bow.
10But that day belongs to the Lord, the LORD Almighty—
a day of vengeance, for vengeance on his foes.
The sword will devour till it is satisfied,
till it has quenched its thirst with blood.
For the Lord, the LORD Almighty, will offer sacrifice
in the land of the north by the River Euphrates.

11"Go up to Gilead and get balm,
O Virgin Daughter of Egypt.
But you multiply remedies in vain;
there is no healing for you.
12The nations will hear of your shame;
your cries will fill the earth.
One warrior will stumble over another;
both will fall down together."

13This is the message the LORD spoke to Jeremiah the prophet about the coming of Nebuchadnezzar king of Babylon to attack Egypt:

14"Announce this in Egypt, and proclaim it in Migdol;
proclaim it also in Memphis[b] and Tahpanhes:
'Take your positions and get ready,
for the sword devours those around you.'
15Why will your warriors be laid low?
They cannot stand, for the LORD will push them down.
16They will stumble repeatedly;
they will fall over each other.
They will say, 'Get up, let us go back
to our own people and our native lands,
away from the sword of the oppressor.'
17There they will exclaim,
'Pharaoh king of Egypt is only a loud noise;
he has missed his opportunity.'

18"As surely as I live," declares the King,
whose name is the LORD Almighty,
"one will come who is like Tabor among the mountains,
like Carmel by the sea.
19Pack your belongings for exile,
you who live in Egypt,
for Memphis will be laid waste
and lie in ruins without inhabitant.
20"Egypt is a beautiful heifer,
but a gadfly is coming

[a]9 That is, the upper Nile region [b]14 Hebrew *Noph*; also in verse 19

against her from the north.
21 The mercenaries in her ranks
are like fattened calves.
They too will turn and flee together,
they will not stand their ground,
for the day of disaster is coming upon them,
the time for them to be punished.
22 Egypt will hiss like a fleeing serpent
as the enemy advances in force;
they will come against her with axes,
like men who cut down trees.
23 They will chop down her forest,"
declares the LORD,
"dense though it be.
They are more numerous than locusts,
they cannot be counted.
24 The Daughter of Egypt will be put to shame,
handed over to the people of the north."

25 The LORD Almighty, the God of Israel, says: "I am about to bring punishment on Amon god of Thebes,[a] on Pharaoh, on Egypt and her gods and her kings, and on those who rely on Pharaoh. 26 I will hand them over to those who seek their lives, to Nebuchadnezzar king of Babylon and his officers. Later, however, Egypt will be inhabited as in times past," declares the LORD.

27 "Do not fear, O Jacob my servant;
do not be dismayed, O Israel.
I will surely save you out of a distant place,
your descendants from the land of their exile.
Jacob will again have peace and security,
and no one will make him afraid.
28 Do not fear, O Jacob my servant,
for I am with you," declares the LORD.
"Though I completely destroy all the nations
among which I scatter you,
I will not completely destroy you.
I will discipline you but only with justice;
I will not let you go entirely unpunished."

A Message About the Philistines

47 This is the word of the LORD that came to Jeremiah the prophet concerning the Philistines before Pharaoh attacked Gaza:

2 This is what the LORD says:

"See how the waters are rising in the north;
they will become an overflowing torrent.
They will overflow the land and everything in it,
the towns and those who live in them.
The people will cry out;
all who dwell in the land will wail
3 at the sound of the hoofs of galloping steeds,
at the noise of enemy chariots
and the rumble of their wheels.
Fathers will not turn to help their children;
their hands will hang limp.
4 For the day has come
to destroy all the Philistines
and to cut off all survivors
who could help Tyre and Sidon.
The LORD is about to destroy the Philistines,
the remnant from the coasts of Caphtor.[b]
5 Gaza will shave her head in mourning;
Ashkelon will be silenced.
O remnant on the plain,
how long will you cut yourselves?

6 "'Ah, sword of the LORD,' ⌊you cry,⌋
'how long till you rest?
Return to your scabbard;
cease and be still.'
7 But how can it rest
when the LORD has commanded it,
when he has ordered it
to attack Ashkelon and the coast?"

A Message About Moab

48 Concerning Moab:

This is what the LORD Almighty, the God of Israel, says:

"Woe to Nebo, for it will be ruined.
Kiriathaim will be disgraced and captured;
the stronghold[c] will be disgraced and shattered.
2 Moab will be praised no more;
in Heshbon[d] men will plot her downfall:

[a] 25 Hebrew *No* [b] 4 That is, Crete [c] 1 Or / *Misgab* [d] 2 The Hebrew for *Heshbon* sounds like the Hebrew for *plot*.

'Come, let us put an end to that
nation.'
You too, O Madmen,[a] will be
silenced;
the sword will pursue you.
3Listen to the cries from Horonaim,
cries of great havoc and destruction.
4Moab will be broken;
her little ones will cry out.[b]
5They go up the way to Luhith,
weeping bitterly as they go;
on the road down to Horonaim
anguished cries over the destruction
are heard.
6Flee! Run for your lives;
become like a bush[c] in the desert.
7Since you trust in your deeds and
riches,
you too will be taken captive,
and Chemosh will go into exile,
together with his priests and
officials.
8The destroyer will come against every
town,
and not a town will escape.
The valley will be ruined
and the plateau destroyed,
because the LORD has spoken.
9Put salt on Moab,
for she will be laid waste[d];
her towns will become desolate,
with no one to live in them.

10"A curse on him who is lax in doing
the LORD's work!
A curse on him who keeps his
sword from bloodshed!

11"Moab has been at rest from youth,
like wine left on its dregs,
not poured from one jar to another—
she has not gone into exile.
So she tastes as she did,
and her aroma is unchanged.
12But days are coming,"
declares the LORD,
"when I will send men who pour from
jars,
and they will pour her out;
they will empty her jars
and smash her jugs.
13Then Moab will be ashamed of
Chemosh,
as the house of Israel was ashamed
when they trusted in Bethel.
14"How can you say, 'We are warriors,
men valiant in battle'?
15Moab will be destroyed and her towns
invaded;
her finest young men will go down
in the slaughter,"
declares the King, whose name is
the LORD Almighty.
16"The fall of Moab is at hand;
her calamity will come quickly.
17Mourn for her, all who live around
her,
all who know her fame;
say, 'How broken is the mighty
scepter,
how broken the glorious staff!'

18"Come down from your glory
and sit on the parched ground,
O inhabitants of the Daughter of
Dibon,
for he who destroys Moab
will come up against you
and ruin your fortified cities.
19Stand by the road and watch,
you who live in Aroer.
Ask the man fleeing and the woman
escaping,
ask them, 'What has happened?'
20Moab is disgraced, for she is
shattered.
Wail and cry out!
Announce by the Arnon
that Moab is destroyed.
21Judgment has come to the plateau—
to Holon, Jahzah and Mephaath,
22 to Dibon, Nebo and Beth
Diblathaim,
23 to Kiriathaim, Beth Gamul and Beth
Meon,
24 to Kerioth and Bozrah—
to all the towns of Moab, far and
near.
25Moab's horn[e] is cut off;
her arm is broken,"
declares the LORD.

26"Make her drunk,
for she has defied the LORD.
Let Moab wallow in her vomit;
let her be an object of ridicule.
27Was not Israel the object of your
ridicule?
Was she caught among thieves,
that you shake your head in scorn
whenever you speak of her?

[a]2 The name of the Moabite town Madmen sounds like the Hebrew for *be silenced.* [b]4 Hebrew; Septuagint / *proclaim it to Zoar* [c]6 Or *like Aroer* [d]9 Or *Give wings to Moab, / for she will fly away* [e]25 *Horn* here symbolizes strength.

28 Abandon your towns and dwell among
the rocks,
you who live in Moab.
Be like a dove that makes its nest
at the mouth of a cave.

29 "We have heard of Moab's pride—
her overweening pride and conceit,
her pride and arrogance
and the haughtiness of her heart.
30 I know her insolence but it is futile,"
declares the LORD,
"and her boasts accomplish nothing.
31 Therefore I wail over Moab,
for all Moab I cry out,
I moan for the men of Kir Hareseth.
32 I weep for you, as Jazer weeps,
O vines of Sibmah.
Your branches spread as far as the
sea;
they reached as far as the sea of
Jazer.
The destroyer has fallen
on your ripened fruit and grapes.
33 Joy and gladness are gone
from the orchards and fields of
Moab.
I have stopped the flow of wine from
the presses;
no one treads them with shouts of
joy.
Although there are shouts,
they are not shouts of joy.

34 "The sound of their cry rises
from Heshbon to Elealeh and Jahaz,
from Zoar as far as Horonaim and
Eglath Shelishiyah,
for even the waters of Nimrim are
dried up.
35 In Moab I will put an end
to those who make offerings on the
high places
and burn incense to their gods,"
declares the LORD.
36 "So my heart laments for Moab like a
flute;
it laments like a flute for the men of
Kir Hareseth.
The wealth they acquired is gone.
37 Every head is shaved
and every beard cut off;
every hand is slashed
and every waist is covered with
sackcloth.
38 On all the roofs in Moab
and in the public squares
there is nothing but mourning,
for I have broken Moab
like a jar that no one wants,"
declares the LORD.
39 "How shattered she is! How they wail!
How Moab turns her back in
shame!
Moab has become an object of
ridicule,
an object of horror to all those
around her."

40 This is what the LORD says:
"Look! An eagle is swooping down,
spreading its wings over Moab.
41 Kerioth[a] will be captured
and the strongholds taken.
In that day the hearts of Moab's
warriors
will be like the heart of a woman in
labor.
42 Moab will be destroyed as a nation
because she defied the LORD.
43 Terror and pit and snare await you,
O people of Moab,"
declares the LORD.
44 "Whoever flees from the terror
will fall into a pit,
whoever climbs out of the pit
will be caught in a snare;
for I will bring upon Moab
the year of her punishment,"
declares the LORD.

45 "In the shadow of Heshbon
the fugitives stand helpless,
for a fire has gone out from Heshbon,
a blaze from the midst of Sihon;
it burns the foreheads of Moab,
the skulls of the noisy boasters.
46 Woe to you, O Moab!
The people of Chemosh are
destroyed;
your sons are taken into exile
and your daughters into captivity.
47 "Yet I will restore the fortunes of
Moab
in days to come,"
declares the LORD.

Here ends the judgment on Moab.

A Message About Ammon

49 Concerning the Ammonites:
This is what the LORD says:
"Has Israel no sons?
Has she no heirs?

[a] 41 Or *The cities*

Why then has Molech[a] taken
possession of Gad?
Why do his people live in its towns?
2But the days are coming,"
declares the LORD,
"when I will sound the battle cry
against Rabbah of the Ammonites;
it will become a mound of ruins,
and its surrounding villages will be
set on fire.
Then Israel will drive out
those who drove her out,"
says the LORD.
3"Wail, O Heshbon, for Ai is destroyed!
Cry out, O inhabitants of Rabbah!
Put on sackcloth and mourn;
rush here and there inside the
walls,
for Molech will go into exile,
together with his priests and
officials.
4Why do you boast of your valleys,
boast of your valleys so fruitful?
O unfaithful daughter,
you trust in your riches and say,
'Who will attack me?'
5I will bring terror on you
from all those around you,"
declares the Lord,
the LORD Almighty.
"Every one of you will be driven
away,
and no one will gather the fugitives.
6"Yet afterward, I will restore the
fortunes of the Ammonites,"
declares the LORD.

A Message About Edom

7Concerning Edom:

This is what the LORD Almighty says:
"Is there no longer wisdom in Teman?
Has counsel perished from the
prudent?
Has their wisdom decayed?
8Turn and flee, hide in deep caves,
you who live in Dedan,
for I will bring disaster on Esau
at the time I punish him.
9If grape pickers came to you,
would they not leave a few grapes?
If thieves came during the night,
would they not steal only as much
as they wanted?
10But I will strip Esau bare;
I will uncover his hiding places,
so that he cannot conceal himself.
His children, relatives and neighbors
will perish,
and he will be no more.
11Leave your orphans; I will protect
their lives.
Your widows too can trust in me."

12This is what the LORD says: "If those who do not deserve to drink the cup must drink it, why should you go unpunished? You will not go unpunished, but must drink it. 13I swear by myself," declares the LORD, "that Bozrah will become a ruin and an object of horror, of reproach and of cursing; and all its towns will be in ruins forever."

14I have heard a message from the LORD:
An envoy was sent to the nations to
say,
"Assemble yourselves to attack it!
Rise up for battle!"
15"Now I will make you small among
the nations,
despised among men.
16The terror you inspire
and the pride of your heart have
deceived you,
you who live in the clefts of the rocks,
who occupy the heights of the hill.
Though you build your nest as high
as the eagle's,
from there I will bring you down,"
declares the LORD.
17"Edom will become an object of
horror;
all who pass by will be appalled
and will scoff
because of all its wounds.
18As Sodom and Gomorrah were
overthrown,
along with their neighboring
towns,"
says the LORD,
"so no one will live there;
no man will dwell in it.
19"Like a lion coming up from Jordan's
thickets
to a rich pastureland,
I will chase Edom from its land in an
instant.
Who is the chosen one I will
appoint for this?
Who is like me and who can
challenge me?

[a] 1 Or *their king*; Hebrew *malcam*; also in verse 3

And what shepherd can stand
against me?"
20 Therefore, hear what the LORD has
planned against Edom,
what he has purposed against those
who live in Teman:
The young of the flock will be
dragged away;
he will completely destroy their
pasture because of them.
21 At the sound of their fall the earth
will tremble;
their cry will resound to the Red
Sea.[a]
22 Look! An eagle will soar and swoop
down,
spreading its wings over Bozrah.
In that day the hearts of Edom's
warriors
will be like the heart of a woman in
labor.

A Message About Damascus

23 Concerning Damascus:

"Hamath and Arpad are dismayed,
for they have heard bad news.
They are disheartened,
troubled like[b] the restless sea.
24 Damascus has become feeble,
she has turned to flee
and panic has gripped her;
anguish and pain have seized her,
pain like that of a woman in labor.
25 Why has the city of renown not been
abandoned,
the town in which I delight?
26 Surely, her young men will fall in the
streets;
all her soldiers will be silenced in
that day,"
declares the LORD Almighty.
27 "I will set fire to the walls of
Damascus;
it will consume the fortresses of
Ben-Hadad."

A Message About Kedar and Hazor

28 Concerning Kedar and the kingdoms
of Hazor, which Nebuchadnezzar king of
Babylon attacked:

This is what the LORD says:

"Arise, and attack Kedar
and destroy the people of the East.
29 Their tents and their flocks will be
taken;
their shelters will be carried off
with all their goods and camels.
Men will shout to them,
'Terror on every side!'

30 "Flee quickly away!
Stay in deep caves, you who live in
Hazor,"
declares the LORD.
"Nebuchadnezzar king of Babylon has
plotted against you;
he has devised a plan against you.

31 "Arise and attack a nation at ease,
which lives in confidence,"
declares the LORD,
"a nation that has neither gates nor
bars;
its people live alone.
32 Their camels will become plunder,
and their large herds will be booty.
I will scatter to the winds those who
are in distant places[c]
and will bring disaster on them
from every side,"
declares the LORD.
33 "Hazor will become a haunt of jackals,
a desolate place forever.
No one will live there;
no man will dwell in it."

A Message About Elam

34 This is the word of the LORD that came
to Jeremiah the prophet concerning Elam,
early in the reign of Zedekiah king of Judah:

35 This is what the LORD Almighty says:

"See, I will break the bow of Elam,
the mainstay of their might.
36 I will bring against Elam the four
winds
from the four quarters of the
heavens;
I will scatter them to the four winds,
and there will not be a nation
where Elam's exiles do not go.
37 I will shatter Elam before their foes,
before those who seek their lives;
I will bring disaster upon them,
even my fierce anger,"
declares the LORD.
"I will pursue them with the sword
until I have made an end of them.
38 I will set my throne in Elam

[a] 21 Hebrew *Yam Suph*; that is, Sea of Reeds [b] 23 Hebrew *on* or *by* [c] 32 Or *who clip the hair by their foreheads*

and destroy her king and officials,"
declares the LORD.
39"Yet I will restore the fortunes of Elam
in days to come,"
declares the LORD.

A Message About Babylon

50 This is the word the LORD spoke
through Jeremiah the prophet con-
cerning Babylon and the land of the Bab-
ylonians[a]:

2"Announce and proclaim among the
nations,
lift up a banner and proclaim it;
keep nothing back, but say,
'Babylon will be captured;
Bel will be put to shame,
Marduk filled with terror.
Her images will be put to shame
and her idols filled with terror.'
3A nation from the north will attack
her
and lay waste her land.
No one will live in it;
both men and animals will flee
away.

4"In those days, at that time,"
declares the LORD,
"the people of Israel and the people of
Judah together
will go in tears to seek the LORD
their God.
5They will ask the way to Zion
and turn their faces toward it.
They will come and bind themselves
to the LORD
in an everlasting covenant
that will not be forgotten.

6"My people have been lost sheep;
their shepherds have led them
astray
and caused them to roam on the
mountains.
They wandered over mountain and
hill
and forgot their own resting place.
7Whoever found them devoured them;
their enemies said, 'We are not
guilty,
for they sinned against the LORD, their
true pasture,
the LORD, the hope of their fathers.'

8"Flee out of Babylon;
leave the land of the Babylonians,
and be like the goats that lead the
flock.
9For I will stir up and bring against
Babylon
an alliance of great nations from the
land of the north.
They will take up their positions
against her,
and from the north she will be
captured.
Their arrows will be like skilled
warriors
who do not return empty-handed.
10So Babylonia[b] will be plundered;
all who plunder her will have their
fill,"
declares the LORD.

11"Because you rejoice and are glad,
you who pillage my inheritance,
because you frolic like a heifer
threshing grain
and neigh like stallions,
12your mother will be greatly ashamed;
she who gave you birth will be
disgraced.
She will be the least of the nations—
a wilderness, a dry land, a desert.
13Because of the LORD's anger she will
not be inhabited
but will be completely desolate.
All who pass Babylon will be horrified
and scoff
because of all her wounds.

14"Take up your positions around
Babylon,
all you who draw the bow.
Shoot at her! Spare no arrows,
for she has sinned against the LORD.
15Shout against her on every side!
She surrenders, her towers fall,
her walls are torn down.
Since this is the vengeance of the
LORD,
take vengeance on her;
do to her as she has done to others.
16Cut off from Babylon the sower,
and the reaper with his sickle at
harvest.
Because of the sword of the oppressor
let everyone return to his own
people,
let everyone flee to his own land.

17"Israel is a scattered flock
that lions have chased away.
The first to devour him

[a] 1 Or *Chaldeans*; also in verses 8, 25, 35 and 45

[b] 10 Or *Chaldea*

was the king of Assyria;
the last to crush his bones
was Nebuchadnezzar king of Babylon."

18 Therefore this is what the LORD Almighty, the God of Israel, says:

"I will punish the king of Babylon and his land
as I punished the king of Assyria.
19 But I will bring Israel back to his own pasture
and he will graze on Carmel and Bashan;
his appetite will be satisfied
on the hills of Ephraim and Gilead.
20 In those days, at that time,"
declares the LORD,
"search will be made for Israel's guilt,
but there will be none,
and for the sins of Judah,
but none will be found,
for I will forgive the remnant I spare.

21 "Attack the land of Merathaim
and those who live in Pekod.
Pursue, kill and completely destroy[a] them,"
declares the LORD.
"Do everything I have commanded you.
22 The noise of battle is in the land,
the noise of great destruction!
23 How broken and shattered
is the hammer of the whole earth!
How desolate is Babylon
among the nations!
24 I set a trap for you, O Babylon,
and you were caught before you knew it;
you were found and captured
because you opposed the LORD.
25 The LORD has opened his arsenal
and brought out the weapons of his wrath,
for the Sovereign LORD Almighty has work to do
in the land of the Babylonians.
26 Come against her from afar.
Break open her granaries;
pile her up like heaps of grain.
Completely destroy her
and leave her no remnant.
27 Kill all her young bulls;
let them go down to the slaughter!
Woe to them! For their day has come,
the time for them to be punished.
28 Listen to the fugitives and refugees from Babylon
declaring in Zion
how the LORD our God has taken vengeance,
vengeance for his temple.

29 "Summon archers against Babylon,
all those who draw the bow.
Encamp all around her;
let no one escape.
Repay her for her deeds;
do to her as she has done.
For she has defied the LORD,
the Holy One of Israel.
30 Therefore, her young men will fall in the streets;
all her soldiers will be silenced in that day,"
declares the LORD.
31 "See, I am against you, O arrogant one,"
declares the Lord, the LORD Almighty,
"for your day has come,
the time for you to be punished.
32 The arrogant one will stumble and fall
and no one will help her up;
I will kindle a fire in her towns
that will consume all who are around her."

33 This is what the LORD Almighty says:

"The people of Israel are oppressed,
and the people of Judah as well.
All their captors hold them fast,
refusing to let them go.
34 Yet their Redeemer is strong;
the LORD Almighty is his name.
He will vigorously defend their cause
so that he may bring rest to their land,
but unrest to those who live in Babylon.

35 "A sword against the Babylonians!"
declares the LORD—
"against those who live in Babylon
and against her officials and wise men!
36 A sword against her false prophets!
They will become fools.
A sword against her warriors!
They will be filled with terror.

[a] 21 The Hebrew term refers to the irrevocable giving over of things or persons to the LORD, often by totally destroying them; also in verse 26.

37A sword against her horses and chariots
and all the foreigners in her ranks!
They will become women.
A sword against her treasures!
They will be plundered.
38A drought on[a] her waters!
They will dry up.
For it is a land of idols,
idols that will go mad with terror.

39"So desert creatures and hyenas will live there,
and there the owl will dwell.
It will never again be inhabited
or lived in from generation to generation.
40As God overthrew Sodom and Gomorrah
along with their neighboring towns,"
declares the LORD,
"so no one will live there;
no man will dwell in it.

41"Look! An army is coming from the north;
a great nation and many kings
are being stirred up from the ends of the earth.
42They are armed with bows and spears;
they are cruel and without mercy.
They sound like the roaring sea
as they ride on their horses;
they come like men in battle formation
to attack you, O Daughter of Babylon.
43The king of Babylon has heard reports about them,
and his hands hang limp.
Anguish has gripped him,
pain like that of a woman in labor.
44Like a lion coming up from Jordan's thickets
to a rich pastureland,
I will chase Babylon from its land in an instant.
Who is the chosen one I will appoint for this?
Who is like me and who can challenge me?
And what shepherd can stand against me?"
45Therefore, hear what the LORD has planned against Babylon,
what he has purposed against the land of the Babylonians:
The young of the flock will be dragged away;
he will completely destroy their pasture because of them.
46At the sound of Babylon's capture the earth will tremble;
its cry will resound among the nations.

51 This is what the LORD says:
"See, I will stir up the spirit of a destroyer
against Babylon and the people of Leb Kamai.[b]
2I will send foreigners to Babylon
to winnow her and to devastate her land;
they will oppose her on every side
in the day of her disaster.
3Let not the archer string his bow,
nor let him put on his armor.
Do not spare her young men;
completely destroy[c] her army.
4They will fall down slain in Babylon,[d]
fatally wounded in her streets.
5For Israel and Judah have not been forsaken
by their God, the LORD Almighty,
though their land[e] is full of guilt
before the Holy One of Israel.

6"Flee from Babylon!
Run for your lives!
Do not be destroyed because of her sins.
It is time for the LORD's vengeance;
he will pay her what she deserves.
7Babylon was a gold cup in the LORD's hand;
she made the whole earth drunk.
The nations drank her wine;
therefore they have now gone mad.
8Babylon will suddenly fall and be broken.
Wail over her!
Get balm for her pain;
perhaps she can be healed.

9" 'We would have healed Babylon,
but she cannot be healed;
let us leave her and each go to his own land,

[a]38 Or *A sword against* [b]1 *Leb Kamai* is a cryptogram for Chaldea, that is, Babylonia. [c]3 The Hebrew term refers to the irrevocable giving over of things or persons to the LORD, often by totally destroying them. [d]4 Or *Chaldea* [e]5 Or / *and the land ⌞of the Babylonians⌟*

for her judgment reaches to the skies,
it rises as high as the clouds.'

10" 'The LORD has vindicated us;
come, let us tell in Zion
what the LORD our God has done.'

11"Sharpen the arrows,
take up the shields!
The LORD has stirred up the kings of the Medes,
because his purpose is to destroy Babylon.
The LORD will take vengeance,
vengeance for his temple.
12Lift up a banner against the walls of Babylon!
Reinforce the guard,
station the watchmen,
prepare an ambush!
The LORD will carry out his purpose,
his decree against the people of Babylon.
13You who live by many waters
and are rich in treasures,
your end has come,
the time for you to be cut off.
14The LORD Almighty has sworn by himself:
I will surely fill you with men, as with a swarm of locusts,
and they will shout in triumph over you.

15"He made the earth by his power;
he founded the world by his wisdom
and stretched out the heavens by his understanding.
16When he thunders, the waters in the heavens roar;
he makes clouds rise from the ends of the earth.
He sends lightning with the rain
and brings out the wind from his storehouses.

17"Every man is senseless and without knowledge;
every goldsmith is shamed by his idols.
His images are a fraud;
they have no breath in them.
18They are worthless, the objects of mockery;
when their judgment comes, they will perish.
19He who is the Portion of Jacob is not like these,
for he is the Maker of all things,
including the tribe of his inheritance—
the LORD Almighty is his name.

20"You are my war club,
my weapon for battle—
with you I shatter nations,
with you I destroy kingdoms,
21with you I shatter horse and rider,
with you I shatter chariot and driver,
22with you I shatter man and woman,
with you I shatter old man and youth,
with you I shatter young man and maiden,
23with you I shatter shepherd and flock,
with you I shatter farmer and oxen,
with you I shatter governors and officials.

24"Before your eyes I will repay Babylon and all who live in Babylonia[a] for all the wrong they have done in Zion," declares the LORD.

25"I am against you, O destroying mountain,
you who destroy the whole earth," declares the LORD.
"I will stretch out my hand against you,
roll you off the cliffs,
and make you a burned-out mountain.
26No rock will be taken from you for a cornerstone,
nor any stone for a foundation,
for you will be desolate forever," declares the LORD.

27"Lift up a banner in the land!
Blow the trumpet among the nations!
Prepare the nations for battle against her;
summon against her these kingdoms:
Ararat, Minni and Ashkenaz.
Appoint a commander against her;
send up horses like a swarm of locusts.
28Prepare the nations for battle against her—
the kings of the Medes,
their governors and all their officials,

[a]24 Or *Chaldea*; also in verse 35

and all the countries they rule.
29The land trembles and writhes,
for the LORD's purposes against Babylon stand—
to lay waste the land of Babylon
so that no one will live there.
30Babylon's warriors have stopped fighting;
they remain in their strongholds.
Their strength is exhausted;
they have become like women.
Her dwellings are set on fire;
the bars of her gates are broken.
31One courier follows another
and messenger follows messenger
to announce to the king of Babylon
that his entire city is captured,
32the river crossings seized,
the marshes set on fire,
and the soldiers terrified."

33This is what the LORD Almighty, the God of Israel, says:

"The Daughter of Babylon is like a threshing floor
at the time it is trampled;
the time to harvest her will soon come."

34"Nebuchadnezzar king of Babylon has devoured us,
he has thrown us into confusion,
he has made us an empty jar.
Like a serpent he has swallowed us
and filled his stomach with our delicacies,
and then has spewed us out.
35May the violence done to our flesh[a] be upon Babylon,"
say the inhabitants of Zion.
"May our blood be on those who live in Babylonia,"
says Jerusalem.

36Therefore, this is what the LORD says:

"See, I will defend your cause
and avenge you;
I will dry up her sea
and make her springs dry.
37Babylon will be a heap of ruins,
a haunt of jackals,
an object of horror and scorn,
a place where no one lives.
38Her people all roar like young lions,
they growl like lion cubs.
39But while they are aroused,
I will set out a feast for them
and make them drunk,
so that they shout with laughter—
then sleep forever and not awake,"
declares the LORD.
40"I will bring them down
like lambs to the slaughter,
like rams and goats.

41"How Sheshach[b] will be captured,
the boast of the whole earth seized!
What a horror Babylon will be among the nations!
42The sea will rise over Babylon;
its roaring waves will cover her.
43Her towns will be desolate,
a dry and desert land,
a land where no one lives,
through which no man travels.
44I will punish Bel in Babylon
and make him spew out what he has swallowed.
The nations will no longer stream to him.
And the wall of Babylon will fall.

45"Come out of her, my people!
Run for your lives!
Run from the fierce anger of the LORD.
46Do not lose heart or be afraid
when rumors are heard in the land;
one rumor comes this year, another the next,
rumors of violence in the land
and of ruler against ruler.
47For the time will surely come
when I will punish the idols of Babylon;
her whole land will be disgraced
and her slain will all lie fallen within her.
48Then heaven and earth and all that is in them
will shout for joy over Babylon,
for out of the north
destroyers will attack her,"
declares the LORD.

49"Babylon must fall because of Israel's slain,
just as the slain in all the earth
have fallen because of Babylon.
50You who have escaped the sword,
leave and do not linger!
Remember the LORD in a distant land,
and think on Jerusalem."

51"We are disgraced,
for we have been insulted

[a]35 Or *done to us and to our children* [b]41 *Sheshach* is a cryptogram for Babylon.

and shame covers our faces,
because foreigners have entered
the holy places of the LORD's
house."

52"But days are coming," declares the
LORD,
"when I will punish her idols,
and throughout her land
the wounded will groan.
53Even if Babylon reaches the sky
and fortifies her lofty stronghold,
I will send destroyers against her,"
declares the LORD.

54"The sound of a cry comes from
Babylon,
the sound of great destruction
from the land of the Babylonians.[a]
55The LORD will destroy Babylon;
he will silence her noisy din.
Waves ⌊of enemies⌋ will rage like great
waters;
the roar of their voices will resound.
56A destroyer will come against
Babylon;
her warriors will be captured,
and their bows will be broken.
For the LORD is a God of retribution;
he will repay in full.
57I will make her officials and wise men
drunk,
her governors, officers and warriors
as well;
they will sleep forever and not
awake,"
declares the King, whose name is
the LORD Almighty.

58This is what the LORD Almighty says:

"Babylon's thick wall will be leveled
and her high gates set on fire;
the peoples exhaust themselves for
nothing,
the nations' labor is only fuel for
the flames."

59This is the message Jeremiah gave to the staff officer Seraiah son of Neriah, the son of Mahseiah, when he went to Babylon with Zedekiah king of Judah in the fourth year of his reign. 60Jeremiah had written on a scroll about all the disasters that would come upon Babylon—all that had been recorded concerning Babylon. 61He said to Seraiah, "When you get to Babylon, see that you read all these words aloud. 62Then say, 'O LORD, you have said you will destroy this place, so that neither man nor animal will live in it; it will be desolate forever.' 63When you finish reading this scroll, tie a stone to it and throw it into the Euphrates. 64Then say, 'So will Babylon sink to rise no more because of the disaster I will bring upon her. And her people will fall.' "

The words of Jeremiah end here.

The Fall of Jerusalem

52 Zedekiah was twenty-one years old when he became king, and he reigned in Jerusalem eleven years. His mother's name was Hamutal daughter of Jeremiah; she was from Libnah. 2He did evil in the eyes of the LORD, just as Jehoiakim had done. 3It was because of the LORD's anger that all this happened to Jerusalem and Judah, and in the end he thrust them from his presence.

Now Zedekiah rebelled against the king of Babylon.

4So in the ninth year of Zedekiah's reign, on the tenth day of the tenth month, Nebuchadnezzar king of Babylon marched against Jerusalem with his whole army. They camped outside the city and built siege works all around it. 5The city was kept under siege until the eleventh year of King Zedekiah.

6By the ninth day of the fourth month the famine in the city had become so severe that there was no food for the people to eat. 7Then the city wall was broken through, and the whole army fled. They left the city at night through the gate between the two walls near the king's garden, though the Babylonians[b] were surrounding the city. They fled toward the Arabah,[c] 8but the Babylonian[d] army pursued King Zedekiah and overtook him in the plains of Jericho. All his soldiers were separated from him and scattered, 9and he was captured.

He was taken to the king of Babylon at Riblah in the land of Hamath, where he pronounced sentence on him. 10There at Riblah the king of Babylon slaughtered the sons of Zedekiah before his eyes; he also killed all the officials of Judah. 11Then he put out Zedekiah's eyes, bound him with bronze shackles and took him to

[a]54 Or *Chaldeans* [b]7 Or *Chaldeans*; also in verse 17 [c]7 Or *the Jordan Valley* [d]8 Or *Chaldean*; also in verse 14

Babylon, where he put him in prison till the day of his death.

12On the tenth day of the fifth month, in the nineteenth year of Nebuchadnezzar king of Babylon, Nebuzaradan commander of the imperial guard, who served the king of Babylon, came to Jerusalem. 13He set fire to the temple of the LORD, the royal palace and all the houses of Jerusalem. Every important building he burned down. 14The whole Babylonian army under the commander of the imperial guard broke down all the walls around Jerusalem. 15Nebuzaradan the commander of the guard carried into exile some of the poorest people and those who remained in the city, along with the rest of the craftsmen[a] and those who had gone over to the king of Babylon. 16But Nebuzaradan left behind the rest of the poorest people of the land to work the vineyards and fields.

17The Babylonians broke up the bronze pillars, the movable stands and the bronze Sea that were at the temple of the LORD and they carried all the bronze to Babylon. 18They also took away the pots, shovels, wick trimmers, sprinkling bowls, dishes and all the bronze articles used in the temple service. 19The commander of the imperial guard took away the basins, censers, sprinkling bowls, pots, lampstands, dishes and bowls used for drink offerings—all that were made of pure gold or silver.

20The bronze from the two pillars, the Sea and the twelve bronze bulls under it, and the movable stands, which King Solomon had made for the temple of the LORD, was more than could be weighed. 21Each of the pillars was eighteen cubits high and twelve cubits in circumference[b]; each was four fingers thick, and hollow. 22The bronze capital on top of the one pillar was five cubits[c] high and was decorated with a network and pomegranates of bronze all around. The other pillar, with its pomegranates, was similar. 23There were ninety-six pomegranates on the sides; the total number of pomegranates above the surrounding network was a hundred.

24The commander of the guard took as prisoners Seraiah the chief priest, Zephaniah the priest next in rank and the three doorkeepers. 25Of those still in the city, he took the officer in charge of the fighting men, and seven royal advisers. He also took the secretary who was chief officer in charge of conscripting the people of the land and sixty of his men who were found in the city. 26Nebuzaradan the commander took them all and brought them to the king of Babylon at Riblah. 27There at Riblah, in the land of Hamath, the king had them executed.

So Judah went into captivity, away from her land. 28This is the number of the people Nebuchadnezzar carried into exile:

in the seventh year, 3,023 Jews;
29in Nebuchadnezzar's eighteenth year,
832 people from Jerusalem;
30in his twenty-third year,
745 Jews taken into exile by Nebuzaradan the commander of the imperial guard.
There were 4,600 people in all.

Jehoiachin Released

31In the thirty-seventh year of the exile of Jehoiachin king of Judah, in the year Evil-Merodach[d] became king of Babylon, he released Jehoiachin king of Judah and freed him from prison on the twenty-fifth day of the twelfth month. 32He spoke kindly to him and gave him a seat of honor higher than those of the other kings who were with him in Babylon. 33So Jehoiachin put aside his prison clothes and for the rest of his life ate regularly at the king's table. 34Day by day the king of Babylon gave Jehoiachin a regular allowance as long as he lived, till the day of his death.

[a] *15* Or *populace* [b] *21* That is, about 27 feet (about 8.1 meters) high and 18 feet (about 5.4 meters) in circumference [c] *22* That is, about 7 1/2 feet (about 2.3 meters) [d] *31* Also called *Amel-Marduk*

JEREMIAH writes these laments as he watches the intense suffering of God's people and the utter devastation of Jerusalem and the temple. He does not question God's justice in sending this suffering; instead, in the middle of the suffering, he celebrates God's faithfulness and unfailing love (Lamentations 3:22–32). As you read this book, think about what Jesus suffered to pay the penalty for your sins and rejoice in the incredible love of the God who offers you salvation.

LAMENTATIONS

1[a] How deserted lies the city,
once so full of people!
How like a widow is she,
who once was great among the nations!
She who was queen among the provinces
has now become a slave.

2 Bitterly she weeps at night,
tears are upon her cheeks.
Among all her lovers
there is none to comfort her.
All her friends have betrayed her;
they have become her enemies.

3 After affliction and harsh labor,
Judah has gone into exile.
She dwells among the nations;
she finds no resting place.
All who pursue her have overtaken her
in the midst of her distress.

4 The roads to Zion mourn,

[a] This chapter is an acrostic poem, the verses of which begin with the successive letters of the Hebrew alphabet.

for no one comes to her appointed feasts.
All her gateways are desolate,
her priests groan,
her maidens grieve,
and she is in bitter anguish.

5 Her foes have become her masters;
her enemies are at ease.
The LORD has brought her grief
because of her many sins.
Her children have gone into exile,
captive before the foe.

6 All the splendor has departed
from the Daughter of Zion.
Her princes are like deer
that find no pasture;
in weakness they have fled
before the pursuer.

7 In the days of her affliction and wandering
Jerusalem remembers all the treasures
that were hers in days of old.
When her people fell into enemy hands,
there was no one to help her.
Her enemies looked at her
and laughed at her destruction.

8 Jerusalem has sinned greatly
and so has become unclean.
All who honored her despise her,
for they have seen her nakedness;
she herself groans
and turns away.

9 Her filthiness clung to her skirts;
she did not consider her future.
Her fall was astounding;
there was none to comfort her.
"Look, O LORD, on my affliction,
for the enemy has triumphed."

10 The enemy laid hands
on all her treasures;
she saw pagan nations
enter her sanctuary—
those you had forbidden
to enter your assembly.

11 All her people groan
as they search for bread;
they barter their treasures for food
to keep themselves alive.
"Look, O LORD, and consider,
for I am despised."

12 "Is it nothing to you, all you who pass by?
Look around and see.
Is any suffering like my suffering
that was inflicted on me,
that the LORD brought on me
in the day of his fierce anger?

13 "From on high he sent fire,
sent it down into my bones.
He spread a net for my feet
and turned me back.
He made me desolate,
faint all the day long.

14 "My sins have been bound into a yoke[a];
by his hands they were woven together.
They have come upon my neck
and the Lord has sapped my strength.
He has handed me over
to those I cannot withstand.

15 "The Lord has rejected
all the warriors in my midst;
he has summoned an army against me
to[b] crush my young men.
In his winepress the Lord has trampled
the Virgin Daughter of Judah.

16 "This is why I weep
and my eyes overflow with tears.
No one is near to comfort me,
no one to restore my spirit.
My children are destitute
because the enemy has prevailed."

17 Zion stretches out her hands,
but there is no one to comfort her.
The LORD has decreed for Jacob
that his neighbors become his foes;
Jerusalem has become
an unclean thing among them.

18 "The LORD is righteous,
yet I rebelled against his command.
Listen, all you peoples;
look upon my suffering.
My young men and maidens
have gone into exile.

19 "I called to my allies
but they betrayed me.
My priests and my elders
perished in the city
while they searched for food

[a] 14 Most Hebrew manuscripts; Septuagint *He kept watch over my sins* [b] 15 Or *has set a time for me / when he will*

to keep themselves alive.

20"See, O LORD, how distressed I am!
I am in torment within,
and in my heart I am disturbed,
for I have been most rebellious.
Outside, the sword bereaves;
inside, there is only death.

21"People have heard my groaning,
but there is no one to comfort me.
All my enemies have heard of my distress;
they rejoice at what you have done.
May you bring the day you have announced
so they may become like me.

22"Let all their wickedness come before you;
deal with them
as you have dealt with me
because of all my sins.
My groans are many
and my heart is faint."

2 [a] How the Lord has covered the Daughter of Zion
with the cloud of his anger[b]!
He has hurled down the splendor of Israel
from heaven to earth;
he has not remembered his footstool
in the day of his anger.

2Without pity the Lord has swallowed up
all the dwellings of Jacob;
in his wrath he has torn down
the strongholds of the Daughter of Judah.
He has brought her kingdom and its princes
down to the ground in dishonor.

3In fierce anger he has cut off
every horn[c] of Israel.
He has withdrawn his right hand
at the approach of the enemy.
He has burned in Jacob like a flaming fire
that consumes everything around it.

4Like an enemy he has strung his bow;
his right hand is ready.
Like a foe he has slain
all who were pleasing to the eye;
he has poured out his wrath like fire
on the tent of the Daughter of Zion.

5The Lord is like an enemy;
he has swallowed up Israel.
He has swallowed up all her palaces
and destroyed her strongholds.
He has multiplied mourning and lamentation
for the Daughter of Judah.

6He has laid waste his dwelling like a garden;
he has destroyed his place of meeting.
The LORD has made Zion forget
her appointed feasts and her Sabbaths;
in his fierce anger he has spurned
both king and priest.

7The Lord has rejected his altar
and abandoned his sanctuary.
He has handed over to the enemy
the walls of her palaces;
they have raised a shout in the house of the LORD
as on the day of an appointed feast.

8The LORD determined to tear down
the wall around the Daughter of Zion.
He stretched out a measuring line
and did not withhold his hand from destroying.
He made ramparts and walls lament;
together they wasted away.

9Her gates have sunk into the ground;
their bars he has broken and destroyed.
Her king and her princes are exiled among the nations,
the law is no more,
and her prophets no longer find
visions from the LORD.

10The elders of the Daughter of Zion
sit on the ground in silence;
they have sprinkled dust on their heads
and put on sackcloth.
The young women of Jerusalem
have bowed their heads to the ground.

11My eyes fail from weeping,
I am in torment within,
my heart is poured out on the ground

[a] This chapter is an acrostic poem, the verses of which begin with the successive letters of the Hebrew alphabet. [b] 1 Or *How the Lord in his anger / has treated the Daughter of Zion with contempt / all the strength*; or *every king*; *horn* here symbolizes strength. [c] 3 Or

because my people are destroyed,
because children and infants faint
in the streets of the city.

12 They say to their mothers,
"Where is bread and wine?"
as they faint like wounded men
in the streets of the city,
as their lives ebb away
in their mothers' arms.

13 What can I say for you?
With what can I compare you,
O Daughter of Jerusalem?
To what can I liken you,
that I may comfort you,
O Virgin Daughter of Zion?
Your wound is as deep as the sea.
Who can heal you?

14 The visions of your prophets
were false and worthless;
they did not expose your sin
to ward off your captivity.
The oracles they gave you
were false and misleading.

15 All who pass your way
clap their hands at you;
they scoff and shake their heads
at the Daughter of Jerusalem:
"Is this the city that was called
the perfection of beauty,
the joy of the whole earth?"

16 All your enemies open their mouths
wide against you;
they scoff and gnash their teeth
and say, "We have swallowed her up.
This is the day we have waited for;
we have lived to see it."

17 The LORD has done what he planned;
he has fulfilled his word,
which he decreed long ago.
He has overthrown you without pity,
he has let the enemy gloat over you,
he has exalted the horn[a] of your foes.

18 The hearts of the people
cry out to the Lord.
O wall of the Daughter of Zion,
let your tears flow like a river
day and night;
give yourself no relief,
your eyes no rest.

19 Arise, cry out in the night,
as the watches of the night begin;
pour out your heart like water
in the presence of the Lord.
Lift up your hands to him
for the lives of your children,
who faint from hunger
at the head of every street.

20 "Look, O LORD, and consider:
Whom have you ever treated like this?
Should women eat their offspring,
the children they have cared for?
Should priest and prophet be killed
in the sanctuary of the Lord?

21 "Young and old lie together
in the dust of the streets;
my young men and maidens
have fallen by the sword.
You have slain them in the day of your anger;
you have slaughtered them without pity.

22 "As you summon to a feast day,
so you summoned against me terrors on every side.
In the day of the LORD's anger
no one escaped or survived;
those I cared for and reared,
my enemy has destroyed."

3 [b] I am the man who has seen affliction
by the rod of his wrath.
2 He has driven me away and made me walk
in darkness rather than light;
3 indeed, he has turned his hand against me
again and again, all day long.

4 He has made my skin and my flesh grow old
and has broken my bones.
5 He has besieged me and surrounded me
with bitterness and hardship.
6 He has made me dwell in darkness
like those long dead.

7 He has walled me in so I cannot escape;

[a] 17 *Horn* here symbolizes strength. [b] This chapter is an acrostic poem; the verses of each stanza begin with the successive letters of the Hebrew alphabet, and the verses within each stanza begin with the same letter.

he has weighed me down with
chains.
8Even when I call out or cry for help,
he shuts out my prayer.
9He has barred my way with blocks of
stone;
he has made my paths crooked.

10Like a bear lying in wait,
like a lion in hiding,
11he dragged me from the path and
mangled me
and left me without help.
12He drew his bow
and made me the target for his
arrows.

13He pierced my heart
with arrows from his quiver.
14I became the laughingstock of all my
people;
they mock me in song all day long.
15He has filled me with bitter herbs
and sated me with gall.

16He has broken my teeth with gravel;
he has trampled me in the dust.
17I have been deprived of peace;
I have forgotten what prosperity is.
18So I say, "My splendor is gone
and all that I had hoped from the
LORD."

19I remember my affliction and my
wandering,
the bitterness and the gall.
20I well remember them,
and my soul is downcast within me.
21Yet this I call to mind
and therefore I have hope:

22Because of the LORD's great love we
are not consumed,
for his compassions never fail.
23They are new every morning;
great is your faithfulness.
24I say to myself, "The LORD is my
portion;
therefore I will wait for him."

25The LORD is good to those whose hope
is in him,
to the one who seeks him;
26it is good to wait quietly
for the salvation of the LORD.
27It is good for a man to bear the yoke
while he is young.

28Let him sit alone in silence,
for the LORD has laid it on him.
29Let him bury his face in the dust—
there may yet be hope.
30Let him offer his cheek to one who
would strike him,
and let him be filled with disgrace.

31For men are not cast off
by the Lord forever.
32Though he brings grief, he will show
compassion,
so great is his unfailing love.
33For he does not willingly bring
affliction
or grief to the children of men.

34To crush underfoot
all prisoners in the land,
35to deny a man his rights
before the Most High,
36to deprive a man of justice—
would not the Lord see such things?

37Who can speak and have it happen
if the Lord has not decreed it?
38Is it not from the mouth of the Most
High
that both calamities and good things
come?
39Why should any living man complain
when punished for his sins?

40Let us examine our ways and test
them,
and let us return to the LORD.
41Let us lift up our hearts and our
hands
to God in heaven, and say:
42"We have sinned and rebelled
and you have not forgiven.

43"You have covered yourself with anger
and pursued us;
you have slain without pity.
44You have covered yourself with a
cloud
so that no prayer can get through.
45You have made us scum and refuse
among the nations.

46"All our enemies have opened their
mouths
wide against us.
47We have suffered terror and pitfalls,
ruin and destruction."
48Streams of tears flow from my eyes
because my people are destroyed.

49My eyes will flow unceasingly,
without relief,
50until the LORD looks down
from heaven and sees.
51What I see brings grief to my soul
because of all the women of my
city.

VERSE FOR THE DAY:
Lamentations 3:22–23

AUTHOR:
Ruth Senter

PASSAGE FOR THE DAY:
Lamentations 3:19–33

Fairy Tale Marriage?

As a child I was captivated by fairy tales—the idea that a plain-clothed kitchen maid could turn into a dazzling Cinderella, commanding the heart of Prince Charming, who carried her off into a land where they lived happily ever after.

Then I grew up, got married and found that marriage involves a lifetime of adjusting to reality. The white horse never came galloping out of my sunset. Instead, our Corvair broke down on the interstate just outside Baltimore, and Mark and I spent part of our honeymoon in a garage. Over the years since our wedding day, Mark and I haven't galloped anywhere much. Instead, we've gotten up in the morning and put one foot in front of the other. My prince charming is fighting a losing battle with a fluctuating hair line, and our noble quest for love . . . Well, we sometimes forget to light the candles.

Marriage has been a lifetime of learning to live without magic. No fairy godmother has ever waved her wand over cluttered desks, forgotten grocery lists and jogging clothes on the shelf instead of in the drawers. Magic words have never provided my husband with a wife who can sit down after dinner and watch the news with him instead of rushing off to clean up the kitchen.

But I am a stronger person because magic wands have never waved for me. As a result, I have had the opportunity to know more about the grace of God in my marriage.

MARRIAGE BUILDERS

♦ *Before you were married, what were your expectations of what marriage would be like?*

♦ *How have the realities of marriage ended up showing you God's grace?*

Additional Scripture Readings
Proverbs 3:34; 1 Peter 5:5–7

Go to page 873 for your next devotional reading.

52Those who were my enemies without cause
hunted me like a bird.
53They tried to end my life in a pit
and threw stones at me;
54the waters closed over my head,
and I thought I was about to be cut off.

55I called on your name, O LORD,
from the depths of the pit.
56You heard my plea: "Do not close your ears
to my cry for relief."
57You came near when I called you,
and you said, "Do not fear."

58O Lord, you took up my case;
you redeemed my life.
59You have seen, O LORD, the wrong done to me.
Uphold my cause!
60You have seen the depth of their vengeance,
all their plots against me.

61O LORD, you have heard their insults,
all their plots against me—
62what my enemies whisper and mutter
against me all day long.
63Look at them! Sitting or standing,
they mock me in their songs.

64Pay them back what they deserve,
O LORD,
for what their hands have done.
65Put a veil over their hearts,
and may your curse be on them!
66Pursue them in anger and destroy them
from under the heavens of the LORD.

4 [a] How the gold has lost its luster,
the fine gold become dull!
The sacred gems are scattered
at the head of every street.

2How the precious sons of Zion,
once worth their weight in gold,
are now considered as pots of clay,
the work of a potter's hands!

3Even jackals offer their breasts
to nurse their young,
but my people have become heartless
like ostriches in the desert.

4Because of thirst the infant's tongue
sticks to the roof of its mouth;
the children beg for bread,
but no one gives it to them.

5Those who once ate delicacies
are destitute in the streets.
Those nurtured in purple
now lie on ash heaps.

6The punishment of my people
is greater than that of Sodom,
which was overthrown in a moment
without a hand turned to help her.

7Their princes were brighter than snow
and whiter than milk,
their bodies more ruddy than rubies,
their appearance like sapphires.[b]

8But now they are blacker than soot;
they are not recognized in the streets.
Their skin has shriveled on their bones;
it has become as dry as a stick.

9Those killed by the sword are better off
than those who die of famine;
racked with hunger, they waste away
for lack of food from the field.

10With their own hands compassionate women
have cooked their own children,
who became their food
when my people were destroyed.

11The LORD has given full vent to his wrath;
he has poured out his fierce anger.
He kindled a fire in Zion
that consumed her foundations.

12The kings of the earth did not believe,
nor did any of the world's people,
that enemies and foes could enter
the gates of Jerusalem.

13But it happened because of the sins of her prophets
and the iniquities of her priests,
who shed within her
the blood of the righteous.

14Now they grope through the streets
like men who are blind.
They are so defiled with blood
that no one dares to touch their garments.

[a] This chapter is an acrostic poem, the verses of which begin with the successive letters of the Hebrew alphabet. [b] 7 Or *lapis lazuli*

VERSE FOR THE DAY: Lamentations 5:21

AUTHOR: Jay Kesler

PASSAGE FOR THE DAY: Lamentations 5:1–22

The Work of Forgiveness

A man once confided to me that his wife had been unfaithful. He had forgiven her, but people at church were treating her like an outcast, which made it harder for them to rebuild their marriage.

I suggested that he share their struggle with a small group of trusted friends, perhaps a few members of their Sunday school class or a small-group Bible study. "Tell them you're struggling with the perception that your wife is being rejected by others," I told him, "and that you and she would appreciate their understanding and support. Also, ask them to pray for you as you rebuild your lives together."

This type of candor and openness can melt the hearts of Christians and lead to a new chapter in relationships among couples in the church. A small group of trusted friends can become your allies who will tell others: "We need to pray for these people, not discuss them. They have straightened this out in their marriage. We need to be on their side as they rebuild their marriage."

Facing the problem candidly not only speeds the healing process, but it also models a healthy way to handle tough problems. The message of the Gospel is still true—there really is full forgiveness and redemption and the chance to start afresh when we repent of sin.

MARRIAGE BUILDERS

♦ *Have you ever experienced a time when you knew God had forgiven you for something, but felt that others had not?*

♦ *How do you communicate your forgiveness and acceptance within your marriage?*

Additional Scripture Readings
Galatians 6:1; Ephesians 4:32

Go to page 883 for your next devotional reading.

15"Go away! You are unclean!" men cry
to them.
"Away! Away! Don't touch us!"
When they flee and wander about,
people among the nations say,
"They can stay here no longer."

16The LORD himself has scattered them;
he no longer watches over them.
The priests are shown no honor,
the elders no favor.

17Moreover, our eyes failed,
looking in vain for help;
from our towers we watched
for a nation that could not save us.

18Men stalked us at every step,
so we could not walk in our streets.
Our end was near, our days were
numbered,
for our end had come.

19Our pursuers were swifter
than eagles in the sky;
they chased us over the mountains
and lay in wait for us in the desert.

20The LORD's anointed, our very life
breath,
was caught in their traps.
We thought that under his shadow
we would live among the nations.

21Rejoice and be glad, O Daughter of
Edom,
you who live in the land of Uz.
But to you also the cup will be
passed;
you will be drunk and stripped
naked.

22O Daughter of Zion, your punishment
will end;
he will not prolong your exile.
But, O Daughter of Edom, he will
punish your sin
and expose your wickedness.

5 Remember, O LORD, what has
happened to us;
look, and see our disgrace.
2Our inheritance has been turned over
to aliens,
our homes to foreigners.
3We have become orphans and
fatherless,
our mothers like widows.
4We must buy the water we drink;
our wood can be had only at a
price.
5Those who pursue us are at our heels;
we are weary and find no rest.
6We submitted to Egypt and Assyria
to get enough bread.
7Our fathers sinned and are no more,
and we bear their punishment.
8Slaves rule over us,
and there is none to free us from
their hands.
9We get our bread at the risk of our
lives
because of the sword in the desert.
10Our skin is hot as an oven,
feverish from hunger.
11Women have been ravished in Zion,
and virgins in the towns of Judah.
12Princes have been hung up by their
hands;
elders are shown no respect.
13Young men toil at the millstones;
boys stagger under loads of wood.
14The elders are gone from the city gate;
the young men have stopped their
music.
15Joy is gone from our hearts;
our dancing has turned to
mourning.
16The crown has fallen from our head.
Woe to us, for we have sinned!
17Because of this our hearts are faint,
because of these things our eyes
grow dim
18for Mount Zion, which lies desolate,
with jackals prowling over it.

19You, O LORD, reign forever;
your throne endures from
generation to generation.
20Why do you always forget us?
Why do you forsake us so long?
21Restore us to yourself, O LORD, that
we may return;
renew our days as of old
22unless you have utterly rejected us
and are angry with us beyond
measure.

EZEKIEL, living among the exiles in Babylon, wants the people to know that God is everywhere. He reminds them that worshiping false gods has brought about this catastrophe, he emphasizes the need for a new personal relationship with God, and he assures them that God wants a new covenant of peace with them. As you read this book, think of the Prince of Peace who has come to give you eternal life in his name. Be sure to make your own personal commitment to Jesus Christ.

EZEKIEL

The Living Creatures and the Glory of the LORD

1 In the[a] thirtieth year, in the fourth month on the fifth day, while I was among the exiles by the Kebar River, the heavens were opened and I saw visions of God.

2 On the fifth of the month—it was the fifth year of the exile of King Jehoiachin—
3 the word of the LORD came to Ezekiel the priest, the son of Buzi,[b] by the Kebar River in the land of the Babylonians.[c] There the hand of the LORD was upon him.

4 I looked, and I saw a windstorm coming out of the north—an immense cloud with flashing lightning and surrounded by brilliant light. The center of the fire looked like glowing metal, 5 and in the fire was what looked like four living creatures. In appearance their form was that of a man, 6 but each of them had four faces and four wings. 7 Their legs were straight; their feet were like those of a calf and gleamed like burnished bronze. 8 Under their wings on

[a] 1 Or ⌊my⌋ [b] 3 Or *Ezekiel son of Buzi the priest* [c] 3 Or *Chaldeans*

their four sides they had the hands of a man. All four of them had faces and wings, 9and their wings touched one another. Each one went straight ahead; they did not turn as they moved.

10Their faces looked like this: Each of the four had the face of a man, and on the right side each had the face of a lion, and on the left the face of an ox; each also had the face of an eagle. 11Such were their faces. Their wings were spread out upward; each had two wings, one touching the wing of another creature on either side, and two wings covering its body. 12Each one went straight ahead. Wherever the spirit would go, they would go, without turning as they went. 13The appearance of the living creatures was like burning coals of fire or like torches. Fire moved back and forth among the creatures; it was bright, and lightning flashed out of it. 14The creatures sped back and forth like flashes of lightning.

15As I looked at the living creatures, I saw a wheel on the ground beside each creature with its four faces. 16This was the appearance and structure of the wheels: They sparkled like chrysolite, and all four looked alike. Each appeared to be made like a wheel intersecting a wheel. 17As they moved, they would go in any one of the four directions the creatures faced; the wheels did not turn about[a] as the creatures went. 18Their rims were high and awesome, and all four rims were full of eyes all around.

19When the living creatures moved, the wheels beside them moved; and when the living creatures rose from the ground, the wheels also rose. 20Wherever the spirit would go, they would go, and the wheels would rise along with them, because the spirit of the living creatures was in the wheels. 21When the creatures moved, they also moved; when the creatures stood still, they also stood still; and when the creatures rose from the ground, the wheels rose along with them, because the spirit of the living creatures was in the wheels.

22Spread out above the heads of the living creatures was what looked like an expanse, sparkling like ice, and awesome. 23Under the expanse their wings were stretched out one toward the other, and each had two wings covering its body. 24When the creatures moved, I heard the sound of their wings, like the roar of rushing waters, like the voice of the Almighty,[b] like the tumult of an army. When they stood still, they lowered their wings.

25Then there came a voice from above the expanse over their heads as they stood with lowered wings. 26Above the expanse over their heads was what looked like a throne of sapphire,[c] and high above on the throne was a figure like that of a man. 27I saw that from what appeared to be his waist up he looked like glowing metal, as if full of fire, and that from there down he looked like fire; and brilliant light surrounded him. 28Like the appearance of a rainbow in the clouds on a rainy day, so was the radiance around him.

This was the appearance of the likeness of the glory of the LORD. When I saw it, I fell facedown, and I heard the voice of one speaking.

Ezekiel's Call

2 He said to me, "Son of man, stand up on your feet and I will speak to you." 2As he spoke, the Spirit came into me and raised me to my feet, and I heard him speaking to me.

3He said: "Son of man, I am sending you to the Israelites, to a rebellious nation that has rebelled against me; they and their fathers have been in revolt against me to this very day. 4The people to whom I am sending you are obstinate and stubborn. Say to them, 'This is what the Sovereign LORD says.' 5And whether they listen or fail to listen—for they are a rebellious house—they will know that a prophet has been among them. 6And you, son of man, do not be afraid of them or their words. Do not be afraid, though briers and thorns are all around you and you live among scorpions. Do not be afraid of what they say or terrified by them, though they are a rebellious house. 7You must speak my words to them, whether they listen or fail to listen, for they are rebellious. 8But you, son of man, listen to what I say to you. Do not rebel like that rebellious house; open your mouth and eat what I give you."

9Then I looked, and I saw a hand stretched out to me. In it was a scroll, 10which he unrolled before me. On both sides of it were written words of lament and mourning and woe.

[a]17 Or *aside* [b]24 Hebrew *Shaddai* [c]26 Or *lapis lazuli*

3 And he said to me, "Son of man, eat
what is before you, eat this scroll;
then go and speak to the house of Israel."
2So I opened my mouth, and he gave me
the scroll to eat.
3Then he said to me, "Son of man, eat
this scroll I am giving you and fill your
stomach with it." So I ate it, and it tasted
as sweet as honey in my mouth.
4He then said to me: "Son of man, go
now to the house of Israel and speak my
words to them. 5You are not being sent to
a people of obscure speech and difficult
language, but to the house of Israel— 6not
to many peoples of obscure speech and
difficult language, whose words you can-
not understand. Surely if I had sent you to
them, they would have listened to you.
7But the house of Israel is not willing to
listen to you because they are not willing
to listen to me, for the whole house of Is-
rael is hardened and obstinate. 8But I will
make you as unyielding and hardened as
they are. 9I will make your forehead like
the hardest stone, harder than flint. Do
not be afraid of them or terrified by them,
though they are a rebellious house."
10And he said to me, "Son of man, listen
carefully and take to heart all the words I
speak to you. 11Go now to your country-
men in exile and speak to them. Say to
them, 'This is what the Sovereign LORD
says,' whether they listen or fail to listen."
12Then the Spirit lifted me up, and I
heard behind me a loud rumbling
sound—May the glory of the LORD be
praised in his dwelling place!— 13the
sound of the wings of the living creatures
brushing against each other and the
sound of the wheels beside them, a loud
rumbling sound. 14The Spirit then lifted
me up and took me away, and I went in
bitterness and in the anger of my spirit,
with the strong hand of the LORD upon me.
15I came to the exiles who lived at Tel
Abib near the Kebar River. And there,
where they were living, I sat among them
for seven days—overwhelmed.

Warning to Israel

16At the end of seven days the word of
the LORD came to me: 17"Son of man, I
have made you a watchman for the house
of Israel; so hear the word I speak and give
them warning from me. 18When I say to a
wicked man, 'You will surely die,' and you
do not warn him or speak out to dissuade
him from his evil ways in order to save his
life, that wicked man will die for[a] his sin,
and I will hold you accountable for his
blood. 19But if you do warn the wicked
man and he does not turn from his wick-
edness or from his evil ways, he will die
for his sin; but you will have saved your-
self.
20"Again, when a righteous man turns
from his righteousness and does evil, and
I put a stumbling block before him, he will
die. Since you did not warn him, he will
die for his sin. The righteous things he did
will not be remembered, and I will hold
you accountable for his blood. 21But if you
do warn the righteous man not to sin and
he does not sin, he will surely live because
he took warning, and you will have saved
yourself."
22The hand of the LORD was upon me
there, and he said to me, "Get up and go
out to the plain, and there I will speak to
you." 23So I got up and went out to the
plain. And the glory of the LORD was
standing there, like the glory I had seen by
the Kebar River, and I fell facedown.
24Then the Spirit came into me and
raised me to my feet. He spoke to me and
said: "Go, shut yourself inside your house.
25And you, son of man, they will tie with
ropes; you will be bound so that you can-
not go out among the people. 26I will make
your tongue stick to the roof of your
mouth so that you will be silent and un-
able to rebuke them, though they are a re-
bellious house. 27But when I speak to you,
I will open your mouth and you shall say
to them, 'This is what the Sovereign LORD
says.' Whoever will listen let him listen,
and whoever will refuse let him refuse; for
they are a rebellious house.

Siege of Jerusalem Symbolized

4 "Now, son of man, take a clay tablet,
put it in front of you and draw the city
of Jerusalem on it. 2Then lay siege to it:
Erect siege works against it, build a ramp
up to it, set up camps against it and put
battering rams around it. 3Then take an
iron pan, place it as an iron wall between
you and the city and turn your face to-
ward it. It will be under siege, and you
shall besiege it. This will be a sign to the
house of Israel.
4"Then lie on your left side and put the
sin of the house of Israel upon yourself.[b]
You are to bear their sin for the number of

[a] 18 Or *in*; also in verses 19 and 20 [b] 4 Or *your side*

days you lie on your side. 5I have assigned
you the same number of days as the years
of their sin. So for 390 days you will bear
the sin of the house of Israel.

6"After you have finished this, lie down
again, this time on your right side, and
bear the sin of the house of Judah. I have
assigned you 40 days, a day for each year.
7Turn your face toward the siege of Jeru-
salem and with bared arm prophesy
against her. 8I will tie you up with ropes so
that you cannot turn from one side to the
other until you have finished the days of
your siege.

9"Take wheat and barley, beans and
lentils, millet and spelt; put them in a stor-
age jar and use them to make bread for
yourself. You are to eat it during the 390
days you lie on your side. 10Weigh out
twenty shekels[a] of food to eat each day
and eat it at set times. 11Also measure out
a sixth of a hin[b] of water and drink it at
set times. 12Eat the food as you would a
barley cake; bake it in the sight of the peo-
ple, using human excrement for fuel."
13The LORD said, "In this way the people of
Israel will eat defiled food among the na-
tions where I will drive them."

14Then I said, "Not so, Sovereign LORD!
I have never defiled myself. From my
youth until now I have never eaten any-
thing found dead or torn by wild animals.
No unclean meat has ever entered my
mouth."

15"Very well," he said, "I will let you
bake your bread over cow manure instead
of human excrement."

16He then said to me: "Son of man, I will
cut off the supply of food in Jerusalem.
The people will eat rationed food in anxi-
ety and drink rationed water in despair,
17for food and water will be scarce. They
will be appalled at the sight of each other
and will waste away because of[c] their
sin.

5 "Now, son of man, take a sharp sword
and use it as a barber's razor to shave
your head and your beard. Then take a set
of scales and divide up the hair. 2When
the days of your siege come to an end,
burn a third of the hair with fire inside the
city. Take a third and strike it with the
sword all around the city. And scatter a
third to the wind. For I will pursue them
with drawn sword. 3But take a few strands
of hair and tuck them away in the folds of
your garment. 4Again, take a few of these
and throw them into the fire and burn
them up. A fire will spread from there to
the whole house of Israel.

5"This is what the Sovereign LORD says:
This is Jerusalem, which I have set in the
center of the nations, with countries all
around her. 6Yet in her wickedness she
has rebelled against my laws and decrees
more than the nations and countries
around her. She has rejected my laws and
has not followed my decrees.

7"Therefore this is what the Sovereign
LORD says: You have been more unruly
than the nations around you and have not
followed my decrees or kept my laws. You
have not even[d] conformed to the stan-
dards of the nations around you.

8"Therefore this is what the Sovereign
LORD says: I myself am against you, Jeru-
salem, and I will inflict punishment on
you in the sight of the nations. 9Because of
all your detestable idols, I will do to you
what I have never done before and will
never do again. 10Therefore in your midst
fathers will eat their children, and chil-
dren will eat their fathers. I will inflict
punishment on you and will scatter all
your survivors to the winds. 11Therefore
as surely as I live, declares the Sovereign
LORD, because you have defiled my sanc-
tuary with all your vile images and detest-
able practices, I myself will withdraw my
favor; I will not look on you with pity or
spare you. 12A third of your people will die
of the plague or perish by famine inside
you; a third will fall by the sword outside
your walls; and a third I will scatter to the
winds and pursue with drawn sword.

13"Then my anger will cease and my
wrath against them will subside, and I will
be avenged. And when I have spent my
wrath upon them, they will know that I
the LORD have spoken in my zeal.

14"I will make you a ruin and a reproach
among the nations around you, in the
sight of all who pass by. 15You will be a
reproach and a taunt, a warning and an
object of horror to the nations around you
when I inflict punishment on you in anger
and in wrath and with stinging rebuke. I
the LORD have spoken. 16When I shoot at
you with my deadly and destructive ar-
rows of famine, I will shoot to destroy
you. I will bring more and more famine
upon you and cut off your supply of food.

[a] 10 That is, about 8 ounces (about 0.2 kilogram)
[b] 11 That is, about 2/3 quart (about 0.6 liter)
[c] 17 Or *away in*
[d] 7 Most Hebrew manuscripts; some Hebrew manuscripts and Syriac *You have*

17I will send famine and wild beasts
against you, and they will leave you child-
less. Plague and bloodshed will sweep
through you, and I will bring the sword
against you. I the LORD have spoken."

A Prophecy Against the Mountains of Israel

6 The word of the LORD came to me:
2"Son of man, set your face against
the mountains of Israel; prophesy against
them 3and say: 'O mountains of Israel,
hear the word of the Sovereign LORD. This
is what the Sovereign LORD says to the
mountains and hills, to the ravines and
valleys: I am about to bring a sword
against you, and I will destroy your high
places. 4Your altars will be demolished
and your incense altars will be smashed;
and I will slay your people in front of your
idols. 5I will lay the dead bodies of the Is-
raelites in front of their idols, and I will
scatter your bones around your altars.
6Wherever you live, the towns will be laid
waste and the high places demolished, so
that your altars will be laid waste and dev-
astated, your idols smashed and ruined,
your incense altars broken down, and
what you have made wiped out. 7Your
people will fall slain among you, and you
will know that I am the LORD.

8" 'But I will spare some, for some of
you will escape the sword when you are
scattered among the lands and nations.
9Then in the nations where they have
been carried captive, those who escape
will remember me—how I have been
grieved by their adulterous hearts, which
have turned away from me, and by their
eyes, which have lusted after their idols.
They will loathe themselves for the evil
they have done and for all their detestable
practices. 10And they will know that I am
the LORD; I did not threaten in vain to
bring this calamity on them.

11" 'This is what the Sovereign LORD
says: Strike your hands together and
stamp your feet and cry out "Alas!" be-
cause of all the wicked and detestable
practices of the house of Israel, for they
will fall by the sword, famine and plague.
12He that is far away will die of the plague,
and he that is near will fall by the sword,
and he that survives and is spared will die
of famine. So will I spend my wrath upon
them. 13And they will know that I am the
LORD, when their people lie slain among
their idols around their altars, on every
high hill and on all the mountaintops, un-
der every spreading tree and every leafy
oak—places where they offered fragrant
incense to all their idols. 14And I will
stretch out my hand against them and
make the land a desolate waste from the
desert to Diblah[a]—wherever they live.
Then they will know that I am the LORD.' "

The End Has Come

7 The word of the LORD came to me:
2"Son of man, this is what the Sover-
eign LORD says to the land of Israel: The
end! The end has come upon the four cor-
ners of the land. 3The end is now upon
you and I will unleash my anger against
you. I will judge you according to your
conduct and repay you for all your detest-
able practices. 4I will not look on you with
pity or spare you; I will surely repay you
for your conduct and the detestable prac-
tices among you. Then you will know that
I am the LORD.

5"This is what the Sovereign LORD says:
Disaster! An unheard-of[b] disaster is com-
ing. 6The end has come! The end has
come! It has roused itself against you. It
has come! 7Doom has come upon you—
you who dwell in the land. The time has
come, the day is near; there is panic, not
joy, upon the mountains. 8I am about to
pour out my wrath on you and spend my
anger against you; I will judge you accor-
ding to your conduct and repay you for all
your detestable practices. 9I will not look
on you with pity or spare you; I will repay
you in accordance with your conduct and
the detestable practices among you. Then
you will know that it is I the LORD who
strikes the blow.

10"The day is here! It has come! Doom
has burst forth, the rod has budded, arro-
gance has blossomed! 11Violence has
grown into[c] a rod to punish wickedness;
none of the people will be left, none of
that crowd—no wealth, nothing of value.
12The time has come, the day has arrived.
Let not the buyer rejoice nor the seller
grieve, for wrath is upon the whole crowd.
13The seller will not recover the land he
has sold as long as both of them live, for
the vision concerning the whole crowd
will not be reversed. Because of their sins,
not one of them will preserve his life.

[a] *14* Most Hebrew manuscripts; a few Hebrew manuscripts *Riblah* [b] *5* Most Hebrew manuscripts; some Hebrew manuscripts and Syriac *Disaster after* [c] *11* Or *The violent one has become*

14Though they blow the trumpet and get
everything ready, no one will go into bat-
tle, for my wrath is upon the whole crowd.
15"Outside is the sword, inside are
plague and famine; those in the country
will die by the sword, and those in the city
will be devoured by famine and plague.
16All who survive and escape will be in the
mountains, moaning like doves of the val-
leys, each because of his sins. 17Every
hand will go limp, and every knee will be-
come as weak as water. 18They will put on
sackcloth and be clothed with terror.
Their faces will be covered with shame
and their heads will be shaved. 19They
will throw their silver into the streets, and
their gold will be an unclean thing. Their
silver and gold will not be able to save
them in the day of the LORD's wrath. They
will not satisfy their hunger or fill their
stomachs with it, for it has made them
stumble into sin. 20They were proud of
their beautiful jewelry and used it to make
their detestable idols and vile images.
Therefore I will turn these into an unclean
thing for them. 21I will hand it all over as
plunder to foreigners and as loot to the
wicked of the earth, and they will defile it.
22I will turn my face away from them, and
they will desecrate my treasured place;
robbers will enter it and desecrate it.
23"Prepare chains, because the land is
full of bloodshed and the city is full of vio-
lence. 24I will bring the most wicked of the
nations to take possession of their houses;
I will put an end to the pride of the
mighty, and their sanctuaries will be dese-
crated. 25When terror comes, they will
seek peace, but there will be none. 26Ca-
lamity upon calamity will come, and ru-
mor upon rumor. They will try to get a vi-
sion from the prophet; the teaching of the
law by the priest will be lost, as will the
counsel of the elders. 27The king will
mourn, the prince will be clothed with de-
spair, and the hands of the people of the
land will tremble. I will deal with them ac-
cording to their conduct, and by their own
standards I will judge them. Then they
will know that I am the LORD."

Idolatry in the Temple

8 In the sixth year, in the sixth month
on the fifth day, while I was sitting in
my house and the elders of Judah were
sitting before me, the hand of the Sover-
eign LORD came upon me there. 2I looked,
and I saw a figure like that of a man.[a]
From what appeared to be his waist down
he was like fire, and from there up his ap-
pearance was as bright as glowing metal.
3He stretched out what looked like a hand
and took me by the hair of my head. The
Spirit lifted me up between earth and
heaven and in visions of God he took me
to Jerusalem, to the entrance to the north
gate of the inner court, where the idol that
provokes to jealousy stood. 4And there be-
fore me was the glory of the God of Israel,
as in the vision I had seen in the plain.
5Then he said to me, "Son of man, look
toward the north." So I looked, and in the
entrance north of the gate of the altar I
saw this idol of jealousy.
6And he said to me, "Son of man, do
you see what they are doing—the utterly
detestable things the house of Israel is do-
ing here, things that will drive me far from
my sanctuary? But you will see things that
are even more detestable."
7Then he brought me to the entrance to
the court. I looked, and I saw a hole in the
wall. 8He said to me, "Son of man, now dig
into the wall." So I dug into the wall and
saw a doorway there.
9And he said to me, "Go in and see the
wicked and detestable things they are do-
ing here." 10So I went in and looked, and
I saw portrayed all over the walls all kinds
of crawling things and detestable animals
and all the idols of the house of Israel. 11In
front of them stood seventy elders of the
house of Israel, and Jaazaniah son of Sha-
phan was standing among them. Each had
a censer in his hand, and a fragrant cloud
of incense was rising.
12He said to me, "Son of man, have you
seen what the elders of the house of Israel
are doing in the darkness, each at the
shrine of his own idol? They say, 'The
LORD does not see us; the LORD has forsak-
en the land.' " 13Again, he said, "You will
see them doing things that are even more
detestable."
14Then he brought me to the entrance
to the north gate of the house of the LORD,
and I saw women sitting there, mourning
for Tammuz. 15He said to me, "Do you see
this, son of man? You will see things that
are even more detestable than this."
16He then brought me into the inner
court of the house of the LORD, and there
at the entrance to the temple, between the
portico and the altar, were about twenty-

[a]2 Or *saw a fiery figure*

five men. With their backs toward the temple of the LORD and their faces toward the east, they were bowing down to the sun in the east.

17He said to me, "Have you seen this, son of man? Is it a trivial matter for the house of Judah to do the detestable things they are doing here? Must they also fill the land with violence and continually provoke me to anger? Look at them putting the branch to their nose! 18Therefore I will deal with them in anger; I will not look on them with pity or spare them. Although they shout in my ears, I will not listen to them."

Idolaters Killed

9 Then I heard him call out in a loud voice, "Bring the guards of the city here, each with a weapon in his hand." 2And I saw six men coming from the direction of the upper gate, which faces north, each with a deadly weapon in his hand. With them was a man clothed in linen who had a writing kit at his side. They came in and stood beside the bronze altar.

3Now the glory of the God of Israel went up from above the cherubim, where it had been, and moved to the threshold of the temple. Then the LORD called to the man clothed in linen who had the writing kit at his side 4and said to him, "Go throughout the city of Jerusalem and put a mark on the foreheads of those who grieve and lament over all the detestable things that are done in it."

5As I listened, he said to the others, "Follow him through the city and kill, without showing pity or compassion. 6Slaughter old men, young men and maidens, women and children, but do not touch anyone who has the mark. Begin at my sanctuary." So they began with the elders who were in front of the temple.

7Then he said to them, "Defile the temple and fill the courts with the slain. Go!" So they went out and began killing throughout the city. 8While they were killing and I was left alone, I fell facedown, crying out, "Ah, Sovereign LORD! Are you going to destroy the entire remnant of Israel in this outpouring of your wrath on Jerusalem?"

9He answered me, "The sin of the house of Israel and Judah is exceedingly great; the land is full of bloodshed and the city is full of injustice. They say, 'The LORD has forsaken the land; the LORD does not see.' 10So I will not look on them with pity or spare them, but I will bring down on their own heads what they have done."

11Then the man in linen with the writing kit at his side brought back word, saying, "I have done as you commanded."

The Glory Departs From the Temple

10 I looked, and I saw the likeness of a throne of sapphire[a] above the expanse that was over the heads of the cherubim. 2The LORD said to the man clothed in linen, "Go in among the wheels beneath the cherubim. Fill your hands with burning coals from among the cherubim and scatter them over the city." And as I watched, he went in.

3Now the cherubim were standing on the south side of the temple when the man went in, and a cloud filled the inner court. 4Then the glory of the LORD rose from above the cherubim and moved to the threshold of the temple. The cloud filled the temple, and the court was full of the radiance of the glory of the LORD. 5The sound of the wings of the cherubim could be heard as far away as the outer court, like the voice of God Almighty[b] when he speaks.

6When the LORD commanded the man in linen, "Take fire from among the wheels, from among the cherubim," the man went in and stood beside a wheel. 7Then one of the cherubim reached out his hand to the fire that was among them. He took up some of it and put it into the hands of the man in linen, who took it and went out. 8(Under the wings of the cherubim could be seen what looked like the hands of a man.)

9I looked, and I saw beside the cherubim four wheels, one beside each of the cherubim; the wheels sparkled like chrysolite. 10As for their appearance, the four of them looked alike; each was like a wheel intersecting a wheel. 11As they moved, they would go in any one of the four directions the cherubim faced; the wheels did not turn about[c] as the cherubim went. The cherubim went in whatever direction the head faced, without turning as they went. 12Their entire bodies, including their backs, their hands and their wings, were completely full of eyes, as were their four wheels. 13I heard the wheels being called "the whirling wheels." 14Each of the

[a] 1 Or *lapis lazuli* [b] 5 Hebrew *El-Shaddai* [c] 11 Or *aside*

cherubim had four faces: One face was that of a cherub, the second the face of a man, the third the face of a lion, and the fourth the face of an eagle.

15Then the cherubim rose upward. These were the living creatures I had seen by the Kebar River. 16When the cherubim moved, the wheels beside them moved; and when the cherubim spread their wings to rise from the ground, the wheels did not leave their side. 17When the cherubim stood still, they also stood still; and when the cherubim rose, they rose with them, because the spirit of the living creatures was in them.

18Then the glory of the LORD departed from over the threshold of the temple and stopped above the cherubim. 19While I watched, the cherubim spread their wings and rose from the ground, and as they went, the wheels went with them. They stopped at the entrance to the east gate of the LORD's house, and the glory of the God of Israel was above them.

20These were the living creatures I had seen beneath the God of Israel by the Kebar River, and I realized that they were cherubim. 21Each had four faces and four wings, and under their wings was what looked like the hands of a man. 22Their faces had the same appearance as those I had seen by the Kebar River. Each one went straight ahead.

Judgment on Israel's Leaders

11 Then the Spirit lifted me up and brought me to the gate of the house of the LORD that faces east. There at the entrance to the gate were twenty-five men, and I saw among them Jaazaniah son of Azzur and Pelatiah son of Benaiah, leaders of the people. 2The LORD said to me, "Son of man, these are the men who are plotting evil and giving wicked advice in this city. 3They say, 'Will it not soon be time to build houses?[a] This city is a cooking pot, and we are the meat.' 4Therefore prophesy against them; prophesy, son of man."

5Then the Spirit of the LORD came upon me, and he told me to say: "This is what the LORD says: That is what you are saying, O house of Israel, but I know what is going through your mind. 6You have killed many people in this city and filled its streets with the dead.

7"Therefore this is what the Sovereign LORD says: The bodies you have thrown there are the meat and this city is the pot, but I will drive you out of it. 8You fear the sword, and the sword is what I will bring against you, declares the Sovereign LORD. 9I will drive you out of the city and hand you over to foreigners and inflict punishment on you. 10You will fall by the sword, and I will execute judgment on you at the borders of Israel. Then you will know that I am the LORD. 11This city will not be a pot for you, nor will you be the meat in it; I will execute judgment on you at the borders of Israel. 12And you will know that I am the LORD, for you have not followed my decrees or kept my laws but have conformed to the standards of the nations around you."

13Now as I was prophesying, Pelatiah son of Benaiah died. Then I fell facedown and cried out in a loud voice, "Ah, Sovereign LORD! Will you completely destroy the remnant of Israel?"

14The word of the LORD came to me: 15"Son of man, your brothers—your brothers who are your blood relatives[b] and the whole house of Israel—are those of whom the people of Jerusalem have said, 'They are[c] far away from the LORD; this land was given to us as our possession.'

Promised Return of Israel

16"Therefore say: 'This is what the Sovereign LORD says: Although I sent them far away among the nations and scattered them among the countries, yet for a little while I have been a sanctuary for them in the countries where they have gone.'

17"Therefore say: 'This is what the Sovereign LORD says: I will gather you from the nations and bring you back from the countries where you have been scattered, and I will give you back the land of Israel again.'

18"They will return to it and remove all its vile images and detestable idols. 19I will give them an undivided heart and put a new spirit in them; I will remove from them their heart of stone and give them a heart of flesh. 20Then they will follow my decrees and be careful to keep my laws. They will be my people, and I will be their

[a] 3 Or *This is not the time to build houses.* [b] 15 Or *are in exile with you* (see Septuagint and Syriac)
[c] 15 Or *those to whom the people of Jerusalem have said, 'Stay*

God. 21But as for those whose hearts are
devoted to their vile images and detest-
able idols, I will bring down on their own
heads what they have done, declares the
Sovereign LORD."

22Then the cherubim, with the wheels
beside them, spread their wings, and the
glory of the God of Israel was above them.
23The glory of the LORD went up from
within the city and stopped above the
mountain east of it. 24The Spirit lifted me
up and brought me to the exiles in Babylo-
nia[a] in the vision given by the Spirit of
God.

Then the vision I had seen went up
from me, 25and I told the exiles everything
the LORD had shown me.

The Exile Symbolized

12 The word of the LORD came to me:
2"Son of man, you are living
among a rebellious people. They have
eyes to see but do not see and ears to hear
but do not hear, for they are a rebellious
people.

3"Therefore, son of man, pack your be-
longings for exile and in the daytime, as
they watch, set out and go from where
you are to another place. Perhaps they
will understand, though they are a rebel-
lious house. 4During the daytime, while
they watch, bring out your belongings
packed for exile. Then in the evening,
while they are watching, go out like those
who go into exile. 5While they watch, dig

[a]24 Or *Chaldea*

VERSE FOR THE DAY: Ezekiel 11:19

AUTHOR: Lewis Smedes

PASSAGE FOR THE DAY: Ezekiel 11:17–25

Forgiveness's First Step

The most effective and sometimes the most necessary first step in forgiving a spouse is to get on your knees and let God's forgiveness of you seep into your feelings—not into your intellect, but into the deepest recesses of your emotions. You may have to get alone by yourself and give yourself time—maybe several weekends—in which you do nothing but wait for God to get through to your deepest feelings. It's when you become overcome with gratitude for being forgiven for your own contributions to whatever went wrong—even if you don't know what those contributions are—that the power of resentment and rage gradually erodes, and it becomes much easier to forgive.

MARRIAGE BUILDERS

♦ *Why is it helpful to be in fellowship with God before going on to make things right with your spouse?*

♦ *How could a habit of forgiveness between you result in a spirit of freedom and peace in your marriage?*

Additional Scripture Readings
Ephesians 4:31–32; Colossians 3:8

Go to page 909 for your next devotional reading.

through the wall and take your belongings
out through it. 6Put them on your shoul-
der as they are watching and carry them
out at dusk. Cover your face so that you
cannot see the land, for I have made you
a sign to the house of Israel."
7So I did as I was commanded. During
the day I brought out my things packed
for exile. Then in the evening I dug
through the wall with my hands. I took
my belongings out at dusk, carrying them
on my shoulders while they watched.
8In the morning the word of the LORD
came to me: 9"Son of man, did not that re-
bellious house of Israel ask you, 'What are
you doing?'
10"Say to them, 'This is what the Sover-
eign LORD says: This oracle concerns the
prince in Jerusalem and the whole house
of Israel who are there.' 11Say to them, 'I
am a sign to you.'
"As I have done, so it will be done to
them. They will go into exile as captives.
12"The prince among them will put his
things on his shoulder at dusk and leave,
and a hole will be dug in the wall for him
to go through. He will cover his face so
that he cannot see the land. 13I will spread
my net for him, and he will be caught in
my snare; I will bring him to Babylonia,
the land of the Chaldeans, but he will not
see it, and there he will die. 14I will scatter
to the winds all those around him—his
staff and all his troops—and I will pursue
them with drawn sword.
15"They will know that I am the LORD,
when I disperse them among the nations
and scatter them through the countries.
16But I will spare a few of them from the
sword, famine and plague, so that in the
nations where they go they may acknowl-
edge all their detestable practices. Then
they will know that I am the LORD."
17The word of the LORD came to me:
18"Son of man, tremble as you eat your
food, and shudder in fear as you drink
your water. 19Say to the people of the
land: 'This is what the Sovereign LORD
says about those living in Jerusalem and
in the land of Israel: They will eat their
food in anxiety and drink their water in
despair, for their land will be stripped of
everything in it because of the violence of
all who live there. 20The inhabited towns
will be laid waste and the land will be des-
olate. Then you will know that I am the
LORD.' "
21The word of the LORD came to me:
22"Son of man, what is this proverb you
have in the land of Israel: 'The days go by
and every vision comes to nothing'? 23Say
to them, 'This is what the Sovereign LORD
says: I am going to put an end to this prov-
erb, and they will no longer quote it in Is-
rael.' Say to them, 'The days are near
when every vision will be fulfilled. 24For
there will be no more false visions or flat-
tering divinations among the people of Is-
rael. 25But I the LORD will speak what I
will, and it shall be fulfilled without delay.
For in your days, you rebellious house, I
will fulfill whatever I say, declares the
Sovereign LORD.' "
26The word of the LORD came to me:
27"Son of man, the house of Israel is say-
ing, 'The vision he sees is for many years
from now, and he prophesies about the
distant future.'
28"Therefore say to them, 'This is what
the Sovereign LORD says: None of my
words will be delayed any longer; whatev-
er I say will be fulfilled, declares the Sov-
ereign LORD.' "

False Prophets Condemned

13 The word of the LORD came to me:
2"Son of man, prophesy against the
prophets of Israel who are now prophesy-
ing. Say to those who prophesy out of
their own imagination: 'Hear the word of
the LORD! 3This is what the Sovereign
LORD says: Woe to the foolish[a] prophets
who follow their own spirit and have seen
nothing! 4Your prophets, O Israel, are like
jackals among ruins. 5You have not gone
up to the breaks in the wall to repair it for
the house of Israel so that it will stand firm
in the battle on the day of the LORD. 6Their
visions are false and their divinations a lie.
They say, "The LORD declares," when the
LORD has not sent them; yet they expect
their words to be fulfilled. 7Have you not
seen false visions and uttered lying divina-
tions when you say, "The LORD declares,"
though I have not spoken?
8" 'Therefore this is what the Sovereign
LORD says: Because of your false words
and lying visions, I am against you, de-
clares the Sovereign LORD. 9My hand will
be against the prophets who see false vi-
sions and utter lying divinations. They
will not belong to the council of my peo-
ple or be listed in the records of the house
of Israel, nor will they enter the land of

[a]3 Or *wicked*

its roots remained under it. So it became
a vine and produced branches and put out
leafy boughs.

7" 'But there was another great eagle
with powerful wings and full plumage.
The vine now sent out its roots toward
him from the plot where it was planted
and stretched out its branches to him for
water. 8It had been planted in good soil by
abundant water so that it would produce
branches, bear fruit and become a splen-
did vine.'

9"Say to them, 'This is what the Sover-
eign LORD says: Will it thrive? Will it not
be uprooted and stripped of its fruit so
that it withers? All its new growth will
wither. It will not take a strong arm or
many people to pull it up by the roots.
10Even if it is transplanted, will it thrive?
Will it not wither completely when the
east wind strikes it—wither away in the
plot where it grew?' "

11Then the word of the LORD came to
me: 12"Say to this rebellious house, 'Do
you not know what these things mean?'
Say to them: 'The king of Babylon went to
Jerusalem and carried off her king and her
nobles, bringing them back with him to
Babylon. 13Then he took a member of the
royal family and made a treaty with him,
putting him under oath. He also carried
away the leading men of the land, 14so
that the kingdom would be brought low,
unable to rise again, surviving only by
keeping his treaty. 15But the king rebelled
against him by sending his envoys to
Egypt to get horses and a large army. Will
he succeed? Will he who does such things
escape? Will he break the treaty and yet
escape?

16" 'As surely as I live, declares the Sov-
ereign LORD, he shall die in Babylon, in the
land of the king who put him on the
throne, whose oath he despised and
whose treaty he broke. 17Pharaoh with his
mighty army and great horde will be of no
help to him in war, when ramps are built
and siege works erected to destroy many
lives. 18He despised the oath by breaking
the covenant. Because he had given his
hand in pledge and yet did all these
things, he shall not escape.

19" 'Therefore this is what the Sovereign
LORD says: As surely as I live, I will bring
down on his head my oath that he de-
spised and my covenant that he broke. 20I
will spread my net for him, and he will be
caught in my snare. I will bring him to
Babylon and execute judgment upon him
there because he was unfaithful to me.
21All his fleeing troops will fall by the
sword, and the survivors will be scattered
to the winds. Then you will know that I
the LORD have spoken.

22" 'This is what the Sovereign LORD
says: I myself will take a shoot from the
very top of a cedar and plant it; I will
break off a tender sprig from its topmost
shoots and plant it on a high and lofty
mountain. 23On the mountain heights of
Israel I will plant it; it will produce
branches and bear fruit and become a
splendid cedar. Birds of every kind will
nest in it; they will find shelter in the
shade of its branches. 24All the trees of the
field will know that I the LORD bring down
the tall tree and make the low tree grow
tall. I dry up the green tree and make the
dry tree flourish.

" 'I the LORD have spoken, and I will
do it.' "

The Soul Who Sins Will Die

18 The word of the LORD came to me:
2"What do you people mean by
quoting this proverb about the land of Is-
rael:

" 'The fathers eat sour grapes,
and the children's teeth are set on
edge'?

3"As surely as I live, declares the Sover-
eign LORD, you will no longer quote this
proverb in Israel. 4For every living soul be-
longs to me, the father as well as the
son—both alike belong to me. The soul
who sins is the one who will die.

5"Suppose there is a righteous man
who does what is just and right.
6He does not eat at the mountain
shrines
or look to the idols of the house of
Israel.
He does not defile his neighbor's wife
or lie with a woman during her
period.
7He does not oppress anyone,
but returns what he took in pledge
for a loan.
He does not commit robbery
but gives his food to the hungry
and provides clothing for the naked.
8He does not lend at usury

or take excessive interest.[a]
He withholds his hand from doing wrong
and judges fairly between man and man.
9He follows my decrees
and faithfully keeps my laws.
That man is righteous;
he will surely live,
declares the Sovereign LORD.

10"Suppose he has a violent son, who sheds blood or does any of these other things[b] 11(though the father has done none of them):

"He eats at the mountain shrines.
He defiles his neighbor's wife.
12He oppresses the poor and needy.
He commits robbery.
He does not return what he took in pledge.
He looks to the idols.
He does detestable things.
13He lends at usury and takes excessive interest.

Will such a man live? He will not! Because he has done all these detestable things, he will surely be put to death and his blood will be on his own head.

14"But suppose this son has a son who sees all the sins his father commits, and though he sees them, he does not do such things:

15"He does not eat at the mountain shrines
or look to the idols of the house of Israel.
He does not defile his neighbor's wife.
16He does not oppress anyone
or require a pledge for a loan.
He does not commit robbery
but gives his food to the hungry
and provides clothing for the naked.
17He withholds his hand from sin[c]
and takes no usury or excessive interest.
He keeps my laws and follows my decrees.

He will not die for his father's sin; he will surely live. 18But his father will die for his own sin, because he practiced extortion, robbed his brother and did what was wrong among his people.

19"Yet you ask, 'Why does the son not share the guilt of his father?' Since the son has done what is just and right and has been careful to keep all my decrees, he will surely live. 20The soul who sins is the one who will die. The son will not share the guilt of the father, nor will the father share the guilt of the son. The righteousness of the righteous man will be credited to him, and the wickedness of the wicked will be charged against him.

21"But if a wicked man turns away from all the sins he has committed and keeps all my decrees and does what is just and right, he will surely live; he will not die. 22None of the offenses he has committed will be remembered against him. Because of the righteous things he has done, he will live. 23Do I take any pleasure in the death of the wicked? declares the Sovereign LORD. Rather, am I not pleased when they turn from their ways and live?

24"But if a righteous man turns from his righteousness and commits sin and does the same detestable things the wicked man does, will he live? None of the righteous things he has done will be remembered. Because of the unfaithfulness he is guilty of and because of the sins he has committed, he will die.

25"Yet you say, 'The way of the Lord is not just.' Hear, O house of Israel: Is my way unjust? Is it not your ways that are unjust? 26If a righteous man turns from his righteousness and commits sin, he will die for it; because of the sin he has committed he will die. 27But if a wicked man turns away from the wickedness he has committed and does what is just and right, he will save his life. 28Because he considers all the offenses he has committed and turns away from them, he will surely live; he will not die. 29Yet the house of Israel says, 'The way of the Lord is not just.' Are my ways unjust, O house of Israel? Is it not your ways that are unjust?

30"Therefore, O house of Israel, I will judge you, each one according to his ways, declares the Sovereign LORD. Repent! Turn away from all your offenses; then sin will not be your downfall. 31Rid yourselves of all the offenses you have committed, and get a new heart and a new spirit. Why will you die, O house of Israel? 32For I take no pleasure in the death of anyone, declares the Sovereign LORD. Repent and live!

[a]8 Or *take interest*; similarly in verses 13 and 17 also verse 8); Hebrew *from the poor*

[b]10 Or *things to a brother*

[c]17 Septuagint (see

A Lament for Israel's Princes

19 "Take up a lament concerning the
princes of Israel [2]and say:

" 'What a lioness was your mother
among the lions!
She lay down among the young lions
and reared her cubs.
[3]She brought up one of her cubs,
and he became a strong lion.
He learned to tear the prey
and he devoured men.
[4]The nations heard about him,
and he was trapped in their pit.
They led him with hooks
to the land of Egypt.

[5]" 'When she saw her hope unfulfilled,
her expectation gone,
she took another of her cubs
and made him a strong lion.
[6]He prowled among the lions,
for he was now a strong lion.
He learned to tear the prey
and he devoured men.
[7]He broke down[a] their strongholds
and devastated their towns.
The land and all who were in it
were terrified by his roaring.
[8]Then the nations came against him,
those from regions round about.
They spread their net for him,
and he was trapped in their pit.
[9]With hooks they pulled him into a
cage
and brought him to the king of
Babylon.
They put him in prison,
so his roar was heard no longer
on the mountains of Israel.

[10]" 'Your mother was like a vine in your
vineyard[b]
planted by the water;
it was fruitful and full of branches
because of abundant water.
[11]Its branches were strong,
fit for a ruler's scepter.
It towered high
above the thick foliage,
conspicuous for its height
and for its many branches.
[12]But it was uprooted in fury
and thrown to the ground.
The east wind made it shrivel,
it was stripped of its fruit;
its strong branches withered
and fire consumed them.
[13]Now it is planted in the desert,
in a dry and thirsty land.
[14]Fire spread from one of its main[c]
branches
and consumed its fruit.
No strong branch is left on it
fit for a ruler's scepter.'

This is a lament and is to be used as a lament."

Rebellious Israel

20 In the seventh year, in the fifth month on the tenth day, some of the elders of Israel came to inquire of the LORD, and they sat down in front of me.

[2]Then the word of the LORD came to me: [3]"Son of man, speak to the elders of Israel and say to them, 'This is what the Sovereign LORD says: Have you come to inquire of me? As surely as I live, I will not let you inquire of me, declares the Sovereign LORD.'

[4]"Will you judge them? Will you judge them, son of man? Then confront them with the detestable practices of their fathers [5]and say to them: 'This is what the Sovereign LORD says: On the day I chose Israel, I swore with uplifted hand to the descendants of the house of Jacob and revealed myself to them in Egypt. With uplifted hand I said to them, "I am the LORD your God." [6]On that day I swore to them that I would bring them out of Egypt into a land I had searched out for them, a land flowing with milk and honey, the most beautiful of all lands. [7]And I said to them, "Each of you, get rid of the vile images you have set your eyes on, and do not defile yourselves with the idols of Egypt. I am the LORD your God."

[8]" 'But they rebelled against me and would not listen to me; they did not get rid of the vile images they had set their eyes on, nor did they forsake the idols of Egypt. So I said I would pour out my wrath on them and spend my anger against them in Egypt. [9]But for the sake of my name I did what would keep it from being profaned in the eyes of the nations they lived among and in whose sight I had revealed myself to the Israelites by bringing them out of Egypt. [10]Therefore I led them out of Egypt and brought them into the desert. [11]I gave them my decrees and made

[a]7 Targum (see Septuagint); Hebrew *He knew* [b]10 Two Hebrew manuscripts; most Hebrew manuscripts *your blood* [c]14 Or *from under its*

known to them my laws, for the man who
obeys them will live by them. 12Also I gave
them my Sabbaths as a sign between us,
so they would know that I the LORD made
them holy.

13" 'Yet the people of Israel rebelled
against me in the desert. They did not fol-
low my decrees but rejected my laws—al-
though the man who obeys them will live
by them—and they utterly desecrated my
Sabbaths. So I said I would pour out my
wrath on them and destroy them in the
desert. 14But for the sake of my name I did
what would keep it from being profaned
in the eyes of the nations in whose sight
I had brought them out. 15Also with uplift-
ed hand I swore to them in the desert that
I would not bring them into the land I had
given them—a land flowing with milk and
honey, most beautiful of all lands— 16be-
cause they rejected my laws and did not
follow my decrees and desecrated my Sab-
baths. For their hearts were devoted to
their idols. 17Yet I looked on them with
pity and did not destroy them or put an
end to them in the desert. 18I said to their
children in the desert, "Do not follow the
statutes of your fathers or keep their laws
or defile yourselves with their idols. 19I am
the LORD your God; follow my decrees and
be careful to keep my laws. 20Keep my
Sabbaths holy, that they may be a sign be-
tween us. Then you will know that I am
the LORD your God."

21" 'But the children rebelled against
me: They did not follow my decrees, they
were not careful to keep my laws—al-
though the man who obeys them will live
by them—and they desecrated my Sab-
baths. So I said I would pour out my wrath
on them and spend my anger against
them in the desert. 22But I withheld my
hand, and for the sake of my name I did
what would keep it from being profaned
in the eyes of the nations in whose sight
I had brought them out. 23Also with uplift-
ed hand I swore to them in the desert that
I would disperse them among the nations
and scatter them through the countries,
24because they had not obeyed my laws
but had rejected my decrees and desecrat-
ed my Sabbaths, and their eyes ⌊lusted⌋ af-
ter their fathers' idols. 25I also gave them
over to statutes that were not good and
laws they could not live by; 26I let them
become defiled through their gifts—the
sacrifice of every firstborn[a]—that I
might fill them with horror so they would
know that I am the LORD.'

27"Therefore, son of man, speak to the
people of Israel and say to them, 'This is
what the Sovereign LORD says: In this also
your fathers blasphemed me by forsaking
me: 28When I brought them into the land
I had sworn to give them and they saw any
high hill or any leafy tree, there they of-
fered their sacrifices, made offerings that
provoked me to anger, presented their fra-
grant incense and poured out their drink
offerings. 29Then I said to them: What is
this high place you go to?' " (It is called
Bamah[b] to this day.)

Judgment and Restoration

30"Therefore say to the house of Israel:
'This is what the Sovereign LORD says:
Will you defile yourselves the way your
fathers did and lust after their vile images?
31When you offer your gifts—the sacrifice
of your sons in[c] the fire—you continue
to defile yourselves with all your idols to
this day. Am I to let you inquire of me,
O house of Israel? As surely as I live, de-
clares the Sovereign LORD, I will not let
you inquire of me.

32" 'You say, "We want to be like the na-
tions, like the peoples of the world, who
serve wood and stone." But what you have
in mind will never happen. 33As surely as
I live, declares the Sovereign LORD, I will
rule over you with a mighty hand and an
outstretched arm and with outpoured
wrath. 34I will bring you from the nations
and gather you from the countries where
you have been scattered—with a mighty
hand and an outstretched arm and with
outpoured wrath. 35I will bring you into
the desert of the nations and there, face to
face, I will execute judgment upon you.
36As I judged your fathers in the desert of
the land of Egypt, so I will judge you, de-
clares the Sovereign LORD. 37I will take
note of you as you pass under my rod, and
I will bring you into the bond of the cov-
enant. 38I will purge you of those who re-
volt and rebel against me. Although I will
bring them out of the land where they are
living, yet they will not enter the land of
Israel. Then you will know that I am the
LORD.

39" 'As for you, O house of Israel, this is
what the Sovereign LORD says: Go and

[a]26 Or —*making every firstborn pass through* ⌊*the fire*⌋ —*making your sons pass through*

[b]29 *Bamah* means *high place.*

[c]31 Or

serve your idols, every one of you! But afterward you will surely listen to me and
no longer profane my holy name with
your gifts and idols. 40For on my holy
mountain, the high mountain of Israel, de-
clares the Sovereign LORD, there in the
land the entire house of Israel will serve
me, and there I will accept them. There I
will require your offerings and your
choice gifts,[a] along with all your holy
sacrifices. 41I will accept you as fragrant
incense when I bring you out from the na-
tions and gather you from the countries
where you have been scattered, and I will
show myself holy among you in the sight
of the nations. 42Then you will know that
I am the LORD, when I bring you into the
land of Israel, the land I had sworn with
uplifted hand to give to your fathers.
43There you will remember your conduct
and all the actions by which you have de-
filed yourselves, and you will loathe your-
selves for all the evil you have done. 44You
will know that I am the LORD, when I deal
with you for my name's sake and not ac-
cording to your evil ways and your cor-
rupt practices, O house of Israel, declares
the Sovereign LORD.' "

Prophecy Against the South

45The word of the LORD came to me:
46"Son of man, set your face toward the
south; preach against the south and
prophesy against the forest of the south-
land. 47Say to the southern forest: 'Hear
the word of the LORD. This is what the Sov-
ereign LORD says: I am about to set fire to
you, and it will consume all your trees,
both green and dry. The blazing flame will
not be quenched, and every face from
south to north will be scorched by it. 48Ev-
eryone will see that I the LORD have kin-
dled it; it will not be quenched.' "

49Then I said, "Ah, Sovereign LORD!
They are saying of me, 'Isn't he just telling
parables?' "

Babylon, God's Sword of Judgment

21 The word of the LORD came to me:
2"Son of man, set your face against
Jerusalem and preach against the sanctu-
ary. Prophesy against the land of Israel
3and say to her: 'This is what the LORD
says: I am against you. I will draw my
sword from its scabbard and cut off from
you both the righteous and the wicked.
4Because I am going to cut off the righ-
teous and the wicked, my sword will be
unsheathed against everyone from south
to north. 5Then all people will know that
I the LORD have drawn my sword from its
scabbard; it will not return again.'

6"Therefore groan, son of man! Groan
before them with broken heart and bitter
grief. 7And when they ask you, 'Why are
you groaning?' you shall say, 'Because of
the news that is coming. Every heart will
melt and every hand go limp; every spirit
will become faint and every knee become
as weak as water.' It is coming! It will
surely take place, declares the Sovereign
LORD."

8The word of the LORD came to me:
9"Son of man, prophesy and say, 'This is
what the Lord says:

" 'A sword, a sword,
sharpened and polished—
10sharpened for the slaughter,
polished to flash like lightning!

" 'Shall we rejoice in the scepter of my
son ⌊Judah⌋? The sword despises every
such stick.

11" 'The sword is appointed to be
polished,
to be grasped with the hand;
it is sharpened and polished,
made ready for the hand of the
slayer.
12Cry out and wail, son of man,
for it is against my people;
it is against all the princes of Israel.
They are thrown to the sword
along with my people.
Therefore beat your breast.

13" 'Testing will surely come. And what
if the scepter ⌊of Judah⌋, which the sword
despises, does not continue? declares the
Sovereign LORD.'

14"So then, son of man, prophesy
and strike your hands together.
Let the sword strike twice,
even three times.
It is a sword for slaughter—
a sword for great slaughter,
closing in on them from every side.
15So that hearts may melt
and the fallen be many,
I have stationed the sword for
slaughter[b]

[a]40 Or *and the gifts of your firstfruits*
[b]15 Septuagint; the meaning of the Hebrew for this word is uncertain.

at all their gates.
Oh! It is made to flash like lightning,
it is grasped for slaughter.
16O sword, slash to the right,
then to the left,
wherever your blade is turned.
17I too will strike my hands together,
and my wrath will subside.
I the LORD have spoken."

18The word of the LORD came to me:
19"Son of man, mark out two roads for the sword of the king of Babylon to take, both starting from the same country. Make a signpost where the road branches off to the city. 20Mark out one road for the sword to come against Rabbah of the Ammonites and another against Judah and fortified Jerusalem. 21For the king of Babylon will stop at the fork in the road, at the junction of the two roads, to seek an omen: He will cast lots with arrows, he will consult his idols, he will examine the liver. 22Into his right hand will come the lot for Jerusalem, where he is to set up battering rams, to give the command to slaughter, to sound the battle cry, to set battering rams against the gates, to build a ramp and to erect siege works. 23It will seem like a false omen to those who have sworn allegiance to him, but he will remind them of their guilt and take them captive.

24"Therefore this is what the Sovereign LORD says: 'Because you people have brought to mind your guilt by your open rebellion, revealing your sins in all that you do—because you have done this, you will be taken captive.

25" 'O profane and wicked prince of Israel, whose day has come, whose time of punishment has reached its climax, 26this is what the Sovereign LORD says: Take off the turban, remove the crown. It will not be as it was: The lowly will be exalted and the exalted will be brought low. 27A ruin! A ruin! I will make it a ruin! It will not be restored until he comes to whom it rightfully belongs; to him I will give it.'

28"And you, son of man, prophesy and say, 'This is what the Sovereign LORD says about the Ammonites and their insults:

" 'A sword, a sword,
drawn for the slaughter,
polished to consume
and to flash like lightning!
29Despite false visions concerning you
and lying divinations about you,
it will be laid on the necks
of the wicked who are to be slain,
whose day has come,
whose time of punishment has
reached its climax.
30Return the sword to its scabbard.
In the place where you were
created,
in the land of your ancestry,
I will judge you.
31I will pour out my wrath upon you
and breathe out my fiery anger
against you;
I will hand you over to brutal men,
men skilled in destruction.
32You will be fuel for the fire,
your blood will be shed in your
land,
you will be remembered no more;
for I the LORD have spoken.' "

Jerusalem's Sins

22 The word of the LORD came to me:
2"Son of man, will you judge her? Will you judge this city of bloodshed? Then confront her with all her detestable practices 3and say: 'This is what the Sovereign LORD says: O city that brings on herself doom by shedding blood in her midst and defiles herself by making idols, 4you have become guilty because of the blood you have shed and have become defiled by the idols you have made. You have brought your days to a close, and the end of your years has come. Therefore I will make you an object of scorn to the nations and a laughingstock to all the countries. 5Those who are near and those who are far away will mock you, O infamous city, full of turmoil.

6" 'See how each of the princes of Israel who are in you uses his power to shed blood. 7In you they have treated father and mother with contempt; in you they have oppressed the alien and mistreated the fatherless and the widow. 8You have despised my holy things and desecrated my Sabbaths. 9In you are slanderous men bent on shedding blood; in you are those who eat at the mountain shrines and commit lewd acts. 10In you are those who dishonor their fathers' bed; in you are those who violate women during their period, when they are ceremonially unclean. 11In you one man commits a detestable offense with his neighbor's wife, another shamefully defiles his daughter-in-law, and another violates his sister, his own father's daughter. 12In you men accept bribes to shed blood; you take usury and

excessive interest[a] and make unjust gain
from your neighbors by extortion. And
you have forgotten me, declares the Sov-
ereign LORD.
13" 'I will surely strike my hands togeth-
er at the unjust gain you have made and
at the blood you have shed in your midst.
14Will your courage endure or your hands
be strong in the day I deal with you? I the
LORD have spoken, and I will do it. 15I will
disperse you among the nations and scat-
ter you through the countries; and I will
put an end to your uncleanness. 16When
you have been defiled[b] in the eyes of the
nations, you will know that I am the
LORD.' "
17Then the word of the LORD came to
me: 18"Son of man, the house of Israel has
become dross to me; all of them are the
copper, tin, iron and lead left inside a fur-
nace. They are but the dross of silver.
19Therefore this is what the Sovereign
LORD says: 'Because you have all become
dross, I will gather you into Jerusalem.
20As men gather silver, copper, iron, lead
and tin into a furnace to melt it with a fiery
blast, so will I gather you in my anger and
my wrath and put you inside the city and
melt you. 21I will gather you and I will
blow on you with my fiery wrath, and you
will be melted inside her. 22As silver is
melted in a furnace, so you will be melted
inside her, and you will know that I the
LORD have poured out my wrath upon
you.' "
23Again the word of the LORD came to
me: 24"Son of man, say to the land, 'You
are a land that has had no rain or show-
ers[c] in the day of wrath.' 25There is a con-
spiracy of her princes[d] within her like a
roaring lion tearing its prey; they devour
people, take treasures and precious things
and make many widows within her. 26Her
priests do violence to my law and profane
my holy things; they do not distinguish
between the holy and the common; they
teach that there is no difference between
the unclean and the clean; and they shut
their eyes to the keeping of my Sabbaths,
so that I am profaned among them. 27Her
officials within her are like wolves tearing
their prey; they shed blood and kill people
to make unjust gain. 28Her prophets
whitewash these deeds for them by false
visions and lying divinations. They say,
'This is what the Sovereign LORD says'—
when the LORD has not spoken. 29The peo-
ple of the land practice extortion and com-
mit robbery; they oppress the poor and
needy and mistreat the alien, denying
them justice.
30"I looked for a man among them who
would build up the wall and stand before
me in the gap on behalf of the land so I
would not have to destroy it, but I found
none. 31So I will pour out my wrath on
them and consume them with my fiery an-
ger, bringing down on their own heads all
they have done, declares the Sovereign
LORD."

Two Adulterous Sisters

23 The word of the LORD came to me:
2"Son of man, there were two
women, daughters of the same mother.
3They became prostitutes in Egypt, engag-
ing in prostitution from their youth. In
that land their breasts were fondled and
their virgin bosoms caressed. 4The older
was named Oholah, and her sister was
Oholibah. They were mine and gave birth
to sons and daughters. Oholah is Samaria,
and Oholibah is Jerusalem.
5"Oholah engaged in prostitution while
she was still mine; and she lusted after her
lovers, the Assyrians—warriors 6clothed
in blue, governors and commanders, all of
them handsome young men, and mount-
ed horsemen. 7She gave herself as a pros-
titute to all the elite of the Assyrians and
defiled herself with all the idols of every-
one she lusted after. 8She did not give up
the prostitution she began in Egypt, when
during her youth men slept with her, ca-
ressed her virgin bosom and poured out
their lust upon her.
9"Therefore I handed her over to her
lovers, the Assyrians, for whom she lust-
ed. 10They stripped her naked, took away
her sons and daughters and killed her
with the sword. She became a byword
among women, and punishment was in-
flicted on her.
11"Her sister Oholibah saw this, yet in
her lust and prostitution she was more de-
praved than her sister. 12She too lusted af-
ter the Assyrians—governors and com-
manders, warriors in full dress, mounted
horsemen, all handsome young men. 13I
saw that she too defiled herself; both of
them went the same way.
14"But she carried her prostitution still

[a] 12 Or *usury and interest* [b] 16 Or *When I have allotted you your inheritance* [c] 24 Septuagint; Hebrew *has not been cleansed or rained on* [d] 25 Septuagint; Hebrew *prophets*

further. She saw men portrayed on a wall,
figures of Chaldeans[a] portrayed in red,
15with belts around their waists and flow-
ing turbans on their heads; all of them
looked like Babylonian chariot officers,
natives of Chaldea.[b] 16As soon as she saw
them, she lusted after them and sent mes-
sengers to them in Chaldea. 17Then the
Babylonians came to her, to the bed of
love, and in their lust they defiled her. Af-
ter she had been defiled by them, she
turned away from them in disgust.
18When she carried on her prostitution
openly and exposed her nakedness, I
turned away from her in disgust, just as I
had turned away from her sister. 19Yet she
became more and more promiscuous as
she recalled the days of her youth, when
she was a prostitute in Egypt. 20There she
lusted after her lovers, whose genitals
were like those of donkeys and whose
emission was like that of horses. 21So you
longed for the lewdness of your youth,
when in Egypt your bosom was caressed
and your young breasts fondled.[c]

22"Therefore, Oholibah, this is what the
Sovereign LORD says: I will stir up your
lovers against you, those you turned away
from in disgust, and I will bring them
against you from every side— 23the Bab-
ylonians and all the Chaldeans, the men of
Pekod and Shoa and Koa, and all the As-
syrians with them, handsome young men,
all of them governors and commanders,
chariot officers and men of high rank, all
mounted on horses. 24They will come
against you with weapons,[d] chariots and
wagons and with a throng of people; they
will take up positions against you on ev-
ery side with large and small shields and
with helmets. I will turn you over to them
for punishment, and they will punish you
according to their standards. 25I will direct
my jealous anger against you, and they
will deal with you in fury. They will cut off
your noses and your ears, and those of
you who are left will fall by the sword.
They will take away your sons and daugh-
ters, and those of you who are left will be
consumed by fire. 26They will also strip
you of your clothes and take your fine
jewelry. 27So I will put a stop to the lewd-
ness and prostitution you began in Egypt.
You will not look on these things with
longing or remember Egypt anymore.

28"For this is what the Sovereign LORD
says: I am about to hand you over to those
you hate, to those you turned away from
in disgust. 29They will deal with you in ha-
tred and take away everything you have
worked for. They will leave you naked
and bare, and the shame of your prostitu-
tion will be exposed. Your lewdness and
promiscuity 30have brought this upon
you, because you lusted after the nations
and defiled yourself with their idols.
31You have gone the way of your sister; so
I will put her cup into your hand.

32"This is what the Sovereign LORD says:

"You will drink your sister's cup,
a cup large and deep;
it will bring scorn and derision,
for it holds so much.
33You will be filled with drunkenness
and sorrow,
the cup of ruin and desolation,
the cup of your sister Samaria.
34You will drink it and drain it dry;
you will dash it to pieces
and tear your breasts.

I have spoken, declares the Sovereign
LORD.

35"Therefore this is what the Sovereign
LORD says: Since you have forgotten me
and thrust me behind your back, you
must bear the consequences of your lewd-
ness and prostitution."

36The LORD said to me: "Son of man,
will you judge Oholah and Oholibah?
Then confront them with their detestable
practices, 37for they have committed adul-
tery and blood is on their hands. They
committed adultery with their idols; they
even sacrificed their children, whom
they bore to me,[e] as food for them.
38They have also done this to me: At that
same time they defiled my sanctuary and
desecrated my Sabbaths. 39On the very
day they sacrificed their children to their
idols, they entered my sanctuary and des-
ecrated it. That is what they did in my
house.

40"They even sent messengers for men
who came from far away, and when they
arrived you bathed yourself for them,
painted your eyes and put on your jewel-
ry. 41You sat on an elegant couch, with a
table spread before it on which you had

[a] 14 Or *Babylonians* [b] 15 Or *Babylonia*; also in verse 16 [c] 21 Syriac (see also verse 3); Hebrew *caressed because of your young breasts* [d] 24 The meaning of the Hebrew for this word is uncertain. [e] 37 Or *even made the children they bore to me pass through the fire*

placed the incense and oil that belonged
to me.
42"The noise of a carefree crowd was
around her; Sabeans[a] were brought from
the desert along with men from the
rabble, and they put bracelets on the arms
of the woman and her sister and beautiful
crowns on their heads. 43Then I said about
the one worn out by adultery, 'Now let
them use her as a prostitute, for that is all
she is.' 44And they slept with her. As men
sleep with a prostitute, so they slept with
those lewd women, Oholah and Oholibah.
45But righteous men will sentence them to
the punishment of women who commit
adultery and shed blood, because they are
adulterous and blood is on their hands.
46"This is what the Sovereign LORD says:
Bring a mob against them and give them
over to terror and plunder. 47The mob will
stone them and cut them down with their
swords; they will kill their sons and
daughters and burn down their houses.
48"So I will put an end to lewdness in
the land, that all women may take warn-
ing and not imitate you. 49You will suffer
the penalty for your lewdness and bear
the consequences of your sins of idolatry.
Then you will know that I am the Sover-
eign LORD."

The Cooking Pot

24 In the ninth year, in the tenth
month on the tenth day, the word
of the LORD came to me: 2"Son of man,
record this date, this very date, because
the king of Babylon has laid siege to Jeru-
salem this very day. 3Tell this rebellious
house a parable and say to them: 'This is
what the Sovereign LORD says:

" 'Put on the cooking pot; put it on
and pour water into it.
4Put into it the pieces of meat,
all the choice pieces—the leg and
the shoulder.
Fill it with the best of these bones;
5 take the pick of the flock.
Pile wood beneath it for the bones;
bring it to a boil
and cook the bones in it.

6" 'For this is what the Sovereign LORD
says:

" 'Woe to the city of bloodshed,
to the pot now encrusted,
whose deposit will not go away!
Empty it piece by piece
without casting lots for them.

7" 'For the blood she shed is in her
midst:
She poured it on the bare rock;
she did not pour it on the ground,
where the dust would cover it.
8To stir up wrath and take revenge
I put her blood on the bare rock,
so that it would not be covered.

9" 'Therefore this is what the Sovereign
LORD says:

" 'Woe to the city of bloodshed!
I, too, will pile the wood high.
10So heap on the wood
and kindle the fire.
Cook the meat well,
mixing in the spices;
and let the bones be charred.
11Then set the empty pot on the coals
till it becomes hot and its copper
glows
so its impurities may be melted
and its deposit burned away.
12It has frustrated all efforts;
its heavy deposit has not been
removed,
not even by fire.

13" 'Now your impurity is lewdness. Be-
cause I tried to cleanse you but you would
not be cleansed from your impurity, you
will not be clean again until my wrath
against you has subsided.

14" 'I the LORD have spoken. The time
has come for me to act. I will not hold
back; I will not have pity, nor will I relent.
You will be judged according to your con-
duct and your actions, declares the Sover-
eign LORD.' "

Ezekiel's Wife Dies

15The word of the LORD came to me:
16"Son of man, with one blow I am about
to take away from you the delight of your
eyes. Yet do not lament or weep or shed
any tears. 17Groan quietly; do not mourn
for the dead. Keep your turban fastened
and your sandals on your feet; do not cov-
er the lower part of your face or eat the
customary food ⌊of mourners⌋."
18So I spoke to the people in the morn-
ing, and in the evening my wife died. The
next morning I did as I had been com-
manded.

[a]42 Or *drunkards*

19Then the people asked me, "Won't
you tell us what these things have to do
with us?"
20So I said to them, "The word of the
LORD came to me: 21Say to the house of
Israel, 'This is what the Sovereign LORD
says: I am about to desecrate my sanctu-
ary—the stronghold in which you take
pride, the delight of your eyes, the object
of your affection. The sons and daughters
you left behind will fall by the sword.
22And you will do as I have done. You will
not cover the lower part of your face or eat
the customary food ⌊of mourners⌋. 23You
will keep your turbans on your heads and
your sandals on your feet. You will not
mourn or weep but will waste away be-
cause of[a] your sins and groan among
yourselves. 24Ezekiel will be a sign to you;
you will do just as he has done. When this
happens, you will know that I am the Sov-
ereign LORD.'
25"And you, son of man, on the day I
take away their stronghold, their joy and
glory, the delight of their eyes, their
heart's desire, and their sons and daugh-
ters as well— 26on that day a fugitive will
come to tell you the news. 27At that time
your mouth will be opened; you will
speak with him and will no longer be si-
lent. So you will be a sign to them, and
they will know that I am the LORD."

A Prophecy Against Ammon

25 The word of the LORD came to me:
2"Son of man, set your face against
the Ammonites and prophesy against
them. 3Say to them, 'Hear the word of the
Sovereign LORD. This is what the Sover-
eign LORD says: Because you said "Aha!"
over my sanctuary when it was desecrated
and over the land of Israel when it was
laid waste and over the people of Judah
when they went into exile, 4therefore I am
going to give you to the people of the East
as a possession. They will set up their
camps and pitch their tents among you;
they will eat your fruit and drink your
milk. 5I will turn Rabbah into a pasture for
camels and Ammon into a resting place
for sheep. Then you will know that I am
the LORD. 6For this is what the Sovereign
LORD says: Because you have clapped your
hands and stamped your feet, rejoicing
with all the malice of your heart against
the land of Israel, 7therefore I will stretch
out my hand against you and give you as
plunder to the nations. I will cut you off
from the nations and exterminate you
from the countries. I will destroy you, and
you will know that I am the LORD.' "

A Prophecy Against Moab

8"This is what the Sovereign LORD says:
'Because Moab and Seir said, "Look, the
house of Judah has become like all the
other nations," 9therefore I will expose the
flank of Moab, beginning at its frontier
towns—Beth Jeshimoth, Baal Meon and
Kiriathaim—the glory of that land. 10I will
give Moab along with the Ammonites to
the people of the East as a possession, so
that the Ammonites will not be remem-
bered among the nations; 11and I will in-
flict punishment on Moab. Then they will
know that I am the LORD.' "

A Prophecy Against Edom

12"This is what the Sovereign LORD says:
'Because Edom took revenge on the house
of Judah and became very guilty by doing
so, 13therefore this is what the Sovereign
LORD says: I will stretch out my hand
against Edom and kill its men and their
animals. I will lay it waste, and from Te-
man to Dedan they will fall by the sword.
14I will take vengeance on Edom by the
hand of my people Israel, and they will
deal with Edom in accordance with my
anger and my wrath; they will know
my vengeance, declares the Sovereign
LORD.' "

A Prophecy Against Philistia

15"This is what the Sovereign LORD says:
'Because the Philistines acted in ven-
geance and took revenge with malice in
their hearts, and with ancient hostility
sought to destroy Judah, 16therefore this
is what the Sovereign LORD says: I am
about to stretch out my hand against the
Philistines, and I will cut off the Kerethites
and destroy those remaining along the
coast. 17I will carry out great vengeance on
them and punish them in my wrath. Then
they will know that I am the LORD, when
I take vengeance on them.' "

A Prophecy Against Tyre

26 In the eleventh year, on the first
day of the month, the word of the
LORD came to me: 2"Son of man, because
Tyre has said of Jerusalem, 'Aha! The gate
to the nations is broken, and its doors

[a]23 Or *away in*

have swung open to me; now that she lies
in ruins I will prosper,' [3]therefore this is
what the Sovereign LORD says: I am
against you, O Tyre, and I will bring many
nations against you, like the sea casting
up its waves. [4]They will destroy the walls
of Tyre and pull down her towers; I will
scrape away her rubble and make her a
bare rock. [5]Out in the sea she will become
a place to spread fishnets, for I have spo-
ken, declares the Sovereign LORD. She will
become plunder for the nations, [6]and her
settlements on the mainland will be rav-
aged by the sword. Then they will know
that I am the LORD.

[7]"For this is what the Sovereign LORD
says: From the north I am going to bring
against Tyre Nebuchadnezzar[a] king of
Babylon, king of kings, with horses and
chariots, with horsemen and a great army.
[8]He will ravage your settlements on the
mainland with the sword; he will set up
siege works against you, build a ramp up
to your walls and raise his shields against
you. [9]He will direct the blows of his bat-
tering rams against your walls and demol-
ish your towers with his weapons. [10]His
horses will be so many that they will cover
you with dust. Your walls will tremble at
the noise of the war horses, wagons and
chariots when he enters your gates as men
enter a city whose walls have been broken
through. [11]The hoofs of his horses will
trample all your streets; he will kill your
people with the sword, and your strong
pillars will fall to the ground. [12]They will
plunder your wealth and loot your mer-
chandise; they will break down your walls
and demolish your fine houses and throw
your stones, timber and rubble into the
sea. [13]I will put an end to your noisy
songs, and the music of your harps will be
heard no more. [14]I will make you a bare
rock, and you will become a place to
spread fishnets. You will never be rebuilt,
for I the LORD have spoken, declares the
Sovereign LORD.

[15]"This is what the Sovereign LORD says
to Tyre: Will not the coastlands tremble at
the sound of your fall, when the wounded
groan and the slaughter takes place in
you? [16]Then all the princes of the coast
will step down from their thrones and lay
aside their robes and take off their em-
broidered garments. Clothed with terror,
they will sit on the ground, trembling ev-
ery moment, appalled at you. [17]Then they
will take up a lament concerning you and
say to you:

" 'How you are destroyed, O city of
renown,
peopled by men of the sea!
You were a power on the seas,
you and your citizens;
you put your terror
on all who lived there.
[18]Now the coastlands tremble
on the day of your fall;
the islands in the sea
are terrified at your collapse.'

[19]"This is what the Sovereign LORD says:
When I make you a desolate city, like cit-
ies no longer inhabited, and when I bring
the ocean depths over you and its vast wa-
ters cover you, [20]then I will bring you
down with those who go down to the pit,
to the people of long ago. I will make you
dwell in the earth below, as in ancient ru-
ins, with those who go down to the pit,
and you will not return or take your
place[b] in the land of the living. [21]I will
bring you to a horrible end and you will be
no more. You will be sought, but you will
never again be found, declares the Sover-
eign LORD."

A Lament for Tyre

27 The word of the LORD came to me:
[2]"Son of man, take up a lament
concerning Tyre. [3]Say to Tyre, situated at
the gateway to the sea, merchant of peo-
ples on many coasts, 'This is what the
Sovereign LORD says:

" 'You say, O Tyre,
"I am perfect in beauty."
[4]Your domain was on the high seas;
your builders brought your beauty
to perfection.
[5]They made all your timbers
of pine trees from Senir[c];
they took a cedar from Lebanon
to make a mast for you.
[6]Of oaks from Bashan
they made your oars;
of cypress wood[d] from the coasts of
Cyprus[e]
they made your deck, inlaid with
ivory.

[a]7 Hebrew *Nebuchadrezzar*, of which *Nebuchadnezzar* is a variant; here and often in Ezekiel and Jeremiah
[b]20 Septuagint; Hebrew *return, and I will give glory* [c]5 That is, Hermon [d]6 Targum; the Masoretic Text has a different division of the consonants. [e]6 Hebrew *Kittim*

7Fine embroidered linen from Egypt
was your sail
and served as your banner;
your awnings were of blue and purple
from the coasts of Elishah.
8Men of Sidon and Arvad were your
oarsmen;
your skilled men, O Tyre, were
aboard as your seamen.
9Veteran craftsmen of Gebal[a] were on
board
as shipwrights to caulk your seams.
All the ships of the sea and their
sailors
came alongside to trade for your
wares.

10" 'Men of Persia, Lydia and Put
served as soldiers in your army.
They hung their shields and helmets
on your walls,
bringing you splendor.
11Men of Arvad and Helech
manned your walls on every side;
men of Gammad
were in your towers.
They hung their shields around your
walls;
they brought your beauty to
perfection.

12" 'Tarshish did business with you because of your great wealth of goods; they exchanged silver, iron, tin and lead for your merchandise.

13" 'Greece, Tubal and Meshech traded with you; they exchanged slaves and articles of bronze for your wares.

14" 'Men of Beth Togarmah exchanged work horses, war horses and mules for your merchandise.

15" 'The men of Rhodes[b] traded with you, and many coastlands were your customers; they paid you with ivory tusks and ebony.

16" 'Aram[c] did business with you because of your many products; they exchanged turquoise, purple fabric, embroidered work, fine linen, coral and rubies for your merchandise.

17" 'Judah and Israel traded with you; they exchanged wheat from Minnith and confections,[d] honey, oil and balm for your wares.

18" 'Damascus, because of your many products and great wealth of goods, did business with you in wine from Helbon and wool from Zahar.

19" 'Danites and Greeks from Uzal bought your merchandise; they exchanged wrought iron, cassia and calamus for your wares.

20" 'Dedan traded in saddle blankets with you.

21" 'Arabia and all the princes of Kedar were your customers; they did business with you in lambs, rams and goats.

22" 'The merchants of Sheba and Raamah traded with you; for your merchandise they exchanged the finest of all kinds of spices and precious stones, and gold.

23" 'Haran, Canneh and Eden and merchants of Sheba, Asshur and Kilmad traded with you. 24In your marketplace they traded with you beautiful garments, blue fabric, embroidered work and multicolored rugs with cords twisted and tightly knotted.

25" 'The ships of Tarshish serve
as carriers for your wares.
You are filled with heavy cargo
in the heart of the sea.
26Your oarsmen take you
out to the high seas.
But the east wind will break you to
pieces
in the heart of the sea.
27Your wealth, merchandise and wares,
your mariners, seamen and
shipwrights,
your merchants and all your soldiers,
and everyone else on board
will sink into the heart of the sea
on the day of your shipwreck.
28The shorelands will quake
when your seamen cry out.
29All who handle the oars
will abandon their ships;
the mariners and all the seamen
will stand on the shore.
30They will raise their voice
and cry bitterly over you;
they will sprinkle dust on their heads
and roll in ashes.
31They will shave their heads because of
you
and will put on sackcloth.
They will weep over you with anguish
of soul
and with bitter mourning.
32As they wail and mourn over you,

[a]9 That is, Byblos [b]15 Septuagint; Hebrew *Dedan* [c]16 Most Hebrew manuscripts; some Hebrew manuscripts and Syriac *Edom* [d]17 The meaning of the Hebrew for this word is uncertain.

they will take up a lament
concerning you:
"Who was ever silenced like Tyre,
surrounded by the sea?"
33When your merchandise went out on
the seas,
you satisfied many nations;
with your great wealth and your wares
you enriched the kings of the earth.
34Now you are shattered by the sea
in the depths of the waters;
your wares and all your company
have gone down with you.
35All who live in the coastlands
are appalled at you;
their kings shudder with horror
and their faces are distorted with
fear.
36The merchants among the nations hiss
at you;
you have come to a horrible end
and will be no more.' "

A Prophecy Against the King of Tyre

28 The word of the LORD came to me:
2"Son of man, say to the ruler of
Tyre, 'This is what the Sovereign LORD
says:

" 'In the pride of your heart
you say, "I am a god;
I sit on the throne of a god
in the heart of the seas."
But you are a man and not a god,
though you think you are as wise as
a god.
3Are you wiser than Daniel[a]?
Is no secret hidden from you?
4By your wisdom and understanding
you have gained wealth for yourself
and amassed gold and silver
in your treasuries.
5By your great skill in trading
you have increased your wealth,
and because of your wealth
your heart has grown proud.

6" 'Therefore this is what the Sovereign
LORD says:

" 'Because you think you are wise,
as wise as a god,
7I am going to bring foreigners against
you,
the most ruthless of nations;
they will draw their swords against
your beauty and wisdom
and pierce your shining splendor.
8They will bring you down to the pit,
and you will die a violent death
in the heart of the seas.
9Will you then say, "I am a god,"
in the presence of those who kill
you?
You will be but a man, not a god,
in the hands of those who slay you.
10You will die the death of the
uncircumcised
at the hands of foreigners.

I have spoken, declares the Sovereign
LORD.' "

11The word of the LORD came to me:
12"Son of man, take up a lament concerning the king of Tyre and say to him: 'This is what the Sovereign LORD says:

" 'You were the model of perfection,
full of wisdom and perfect in
beauty.
13You were in Eden,
the garden of God;
every precious stone adorned you:
ruby, topaz and emerald,
chrysolite, onyx and jasper,
sapphire,[b] turquoise and beryl.[c]
Your settings and mountings[d] were
made of gold;
on the day you were created they
were prepared.
14You were anointed as a guardian
cherub,
for so I ordained you.
You were on the holy mount of God;
you walked among the fiery stones.
15You were blameless in your ways
from the day you were created
till wickedness was found in you.
16Through your widespread trade
you were filled with violence,
and you sinned.
So I drove you in disgrace from the
mount of God,
and I expelled you, O guardian
cherub,
from among the fiery stones.
17Your heart became proud
on account of your beauty,
and you corrupted your wisdom
because of your splendor.

[a] 3 Or *Danel*; the Hebrew spelling may suggest a person other than the prophet Daniel. [b] 13 Or *lapis lazuli* [c] 13 The precise identification of some of these precious stones is uncertain. [d] 13 The meaning of the Hebrew for this phrase is uncertain.

So I threw you to the earth;
I made a spectacle of you before kings.
18By your many sins and dishonest trade
you have desecrated your sanctuaries.
So I made a fire come out from you,
and it consumed you,
and I reduced you to ashes on the ground
in the sight of all who were watching.
19All the nations who knew you
are appalled at you;
you have come to a horrible end
and will be no more.' "

A Prophecy Against Sidon

20The word of the LORD came to me:
21"Son of man, set your face against Sidon; prophesy against her 22and say: 'This is what the Sovereign LORD says:

" 'I am against you, O Sidon,
and I will gain glory within you.
They will know that I am the LORD,
when I inflict punishment on her
and show myself holy within her.
23I will send a plague upon her
and make blood flow in her streets.
The slain will fall within her,
with the sword against her on every side.
Then they will know that I am the LORD.

24" 'No longer will the people of Israel have malicious neighbors who are painful briers and sharp thorns. Then they will know that I am the Sovereign LORD.

25" 'This is what the Sovereign LORD says: When I gather the people of Israel from the nations where they have been scattered, I will show myself holy among them in the sight of the nations. Then they will live in their own land, which I gave to my servant Jacob. 26They will live there in safety and will build houses and plant vineyards; they will live in safety when I inflict punishment on all their neighbors who maligned them. Then they will know that I am the LORD their God.' "

A Prophecy Against Egypt

29 In the tenth year, in the tenth month on the twelfth day, the word of the LORD came to me: 2"Son of man, set your face against Pharaoh king of Egypt and prophesy against him and against all Egypt. 3Speak to him and say: 'This is what the Sovereign LORD says:

" 'I am against you, Pharaoh king of Egypt,
you great monster lying among your streams.
You say, "The Nile is mine;
I made it for myself."
4But I will put hooks in your jaws
and make the fish of your streams stick to your scales.
I will pull you out from among your streams,
with all the fish sticking to your scales.
5I will leave you in the desert,
you and all the fish of your streams.
You will fall on the open field
and not be gathered or picked up.
I will give you as food
to the beasts of the earth and the birds of the air.

6Then all who live in Egypt will know that I am the LORD.

" 'You have been a staff of reed for the house of Israel. 7When they grasped you with their hands, you splintered and you tore open their shoulders; when they leaned on you, you broke and their backs were wrenched.[a]

8" 'Therefore this is what the Sovereign LORD says: I will bring a sword against you and kill your men and their animals. 9Egypt will become a desolate wasteland. Then they will know that I am the LORD.

" 'Because you said, "The Nile is mine; I made it," 10therefore I am against you and against your streams, and I will make the land of Egypt a ruin and a desolate waste from Migdol to Aswan, as far as the border of Cush.[b] 11No foot of man or animal will pass through it; no one will live there for forty years. 12I will make the land of Egypt desolate among devastated lands, and her cities will lie desolate forty years among ruined cities. And I will disperse the Egyptians among the nations and scatter them through the countries.

13" 'Yet this is what the Sovereign LORD says: At the end of forty years I will gather the Egyptians from the nations where they

[a] 7 Syriac (see also Septuagint and Vulgate); Hebrew *and you caused their backs to stand* [b] 10 That is, the upper Nile region

were scattered. 14I will bring them back
from captivity and return them to Upper
Egypt,[a] the land of their ancestry. There
they will be a lowly kingdom. 15It will be
the lowliest of kingdoms and will never
again exalt itself above the other nations.
I will make it so weak that it will never
again rule over the nations. 16Egypt will
no longer be a source of confidence for
the people of Israel but will be a reminder
of their sin in turning to her for help. Then
they will know that I am the Sovereign
LORD.' "

17In the twenty-seventh year, in the first
month on the first day, the word of the
LORD came to me: 18"Son of man, Nebu-
chadnezzar king of Babylon drove his
army in a hard campaign against Tyre; ev-
ery head was rubbed bare and every
shoulder made raw. Yet he and his army
got no reward from the campaign he led
against Tyre. 19Therefore this is what the
Sovereign LORD says: I am going to give
Egypt to Nebuchadnezzar king of Bab-
ylon, and he will carry off its wealth. He
will loot and plunder the land as pay for
his army. 20I have given him Egypt as a
reward for his efforts because he and his
army did it for me, declares the Sovereign
LORD.

21"On that day I will make a horn[b]
grow for the house of Israel, and I will
open your mouth among them. Then they
will know that I am the LORD."

A Lament for Egypt

30 The word of the LORD came to me:
2"Son of man, prophesy and say:
'This is what the Sovereign LORD says:

" 'Wail and say,
"Alas for that day!"
3For the day is near,
the day of the LORD is near—
a day of clouds,
a time of doom for the nations.
4A sword will come against Egypt,
and anguish will come upon
Cush.[c]
When the slain fall in Egypt,
her wealth will be carried away
and her foundations torn down.
5Cush and Put, Lydia and all Arabia, Lib-
ya[d] and the people of the covenant land
will fall by the sword along with Egypt.
6" 'This is what the LORD says:

" 'The allies of Egypt will fall
and her proud strength will fail.
From Migdol to Aswan
they will fall by the sword within
her,
declares the Sovereign LORD.
7" 'They will be desolate
among desolate lands,
and their cities will lie
among ruined cities.
8Then they will know that I am the
LORD,
when I set fire to Egypt
and all her helpers are crushed.

9" 'On that day messengers will go out
from me in ships to frighten Cush out of
her complacency. Anguish will take hold
of them on the day of Egypt's doom, for it
is sure to come.

10" 'This is what the Sovereign LORD
says:

" 'I will put an end to the hordes of
Egypt
by the hand of Nebuchadnezzar
king of Babylon.
11He and his army—the most ruthless
of nations—
will be brought in to destroy the
land.
They will draw their swords against
Egypt
and fill the land with the slain.
12I will dry up the streams of the Nile
and sell the land to evil men;
by the hand of foreigners
I will lay waste the land and
everything in it.

I the LORD have spoken.

13" 'This is what the Sovereign LORD
says:

" 'I will destroy the idols
and put an end to the images in
Memphis.[e]
No longer will there be a prince in
Egypt,
and I will spread fear throughout
the land.
14I will lay waste Upper Egypt,[f]

[a] 14 Hebrew *to Pathros* [b] 21 *Horn* here symbolizes strength. [c] 4 That is, the upper Nile region; also in verses 5 and 9 [d] 5 Hebrew *Cub* [e] 13 Hebrew *Noph*; also in verse 16 [f] 14 Hebrew *waste Pathros*

set fire to Zoan
and inflict punishment on Thebes.[a]
15I will pour out my wrath on
Pelusium,[b]
the stronghold of Egypt,
and cut off the hordes of Thebes.
16I will set fire to Egypt;
Pelusium will writhe in agony.
Thebes will be taken by storm;
Memphis will be in constant
distress.
17The young men of Heliopolis[c] and
Bubastis[d]
will fall by the sword,
and the cities themselves will go
into captivity.
18Dark will be the day at Tahpanhes
when I break the yoke of Egypt;
there her proud strength will come
to an end.
She will be covered with clouds,
and her villages will go into
captivity.
19So I will inflict punishment on
Egypt,
and they will know that I am
the LORD.' "

20In the eleventh year, in the first month on the seventh day, the word of the LORD came to me: 21"Son of man, I have broken the arm of Pharaoh king of Egypt. It has not been bound up for healing or put in a splint so as to become strong enough to hold a sword. 22Therefore this is what the Sovereign LORD says: I am against Pharaoh king of Egypt. I will break both his arms, the good arm as well as the broken one, and make the sword fall from his hand. 23I will disperse the Egyptians among the nations and scatter them through the countries. 24I will strengthen the arms of the king of Babylon and put my sword in his hand, but I will break the arms of Pharaoh, and he will groan before him like a mortally wounded man. 25I will strengthen the arms of the king of Babylon, but the arms of Pharaoh will fall limp. Then they will know that I am the LORD, when I put my sword into the hand of the king of Babylon and he brandishes it against Egypt. 26I will disperse the Egyptians among the nations and scatter them through the countries. Then they will know that I am the LORD."

A Cedar in Lebanon

31 In the eleventh year, in the third month on the first day, the word of the LORD came to me: 2"Son of man, say to Pharaoh king of Egypt and to his hordes:

" 'Who can be compared with you in
majesty?
3Consider Assyria, once a cedar in
Lebanon,
with beautiful branches
overshadowing the forest;
it towered on high,
its top above the thick foliage.
4The waters nourished it,
deep springs made it grow tall;
their streams flowed
all around its base
and sent their channels
to all the trees of the field.
5So it towered higher
than all the trees of the field;
its boughs increased
and its branches grew long,
spreading because of abundant
waters.
6All the birds of the air
nested in its boughs,
all the beasts of the field
gave birth under its branches;
all the great nations
lived in its shade.
7It was majestic in beauty,
with its spreading boughs,
for its roots went down
to abundant waters.
8The cedars in the garden of God
could not rival it,
nor could the pine trees
equal its boughs,
nor could the plane trees
compare with its branches—
no tree in the garden of God
could match its beauty.
9I made it beautiful
with abundant branches,
the envy of all the trees of Eden
in the garden of God.

10" 'Therefore this is what the Sovereign LORD says: Because it towered on high, lifting its top above the thick foliage, and because it was proud of its height, 11I handed it over to the ruler of the nations, for him to deal with according to its wickedness. I cast it aside, 12and the most ruth-

[a]14 Hebrew *No*; also in verses 15 and 16 [b]15 Hebrew *Sin*; also in verse 16 [c]17 Hebrew *Awen* (or *On*) [d]17 Hebrew *Pi Beseth*

less of foreign nations cut it down and left it. Its boughs fell on the mountains and in all the valleys; its branches lay broken in all the ravines of the land. All the nations of the earth came out from under its shade and left it. 13All the birds of the air settled on the fallen tree, and all the beasts of the field were among its branches. 14Therefore no other trees by the waters are ever to tower proudly on high, lifting their tops above the thick foliage. No other trees so well-watered are ever to reach such a height; they are all destined for death, for the earth below, among mortal men, with those who go down to the pit.

15" 'This is what the Sovereign LORD says: On the day it was brought down to the grave[a] I covered the deep springs with mourning for it; I held back its streams, and its abundant waters were restrained. Because of it I clothed Lebanon with gloom, and all the trees of the field withered away. 16I made the nations tremble at the sound of its fall when I brought it down to the grave with those who go down to the pit. Then all the trees of Eden, the choicest and best of Lebanon, all the trees that were well-watered, were consoled in the earth below. 17Those who lived in its shade, its allies among the nations, had also gone down to the grave with it, joining those killed by the sword.

18" 'Which of the trees of Eden can be compared with you in splendor and majesty? Yet you, too, will be brought down with the trees of Eden to the earth below; you will lie among the uncircumcised, with those killed by the sword.

" 'This is Pharaoh and all his hordes, declares the Sovereign LORD.' "

A Lament for Pharaoh

32 In the twelfth year, in the twelfth month on the first day, the word of the LORD came to me: 2"Son of man, take up a lament concerning Pharaoh king of Egypt and say to him:

" 'You are like a lion among the nations;
you are like a monster in the seas
thrashing about in your streams,
churning the water with your feet
and muddying the streams.

3" 'This is what the Sovereign LORD says:

" 'With a great throng of people
I will cast my net over you,
and they will haul you up in my net.
4I will throw you on the land
and hurl you on the open field.
I will let all the birds of the air settle on you
and all the beasts of the earth gorge themselves on you.
5I will spread your flesh on the mountains
and fill the valleys with your remains.
6I will drench the land with your flowing blood
all the way to the mountains,
and the ravines will be filled with your flesh.
7When I snuff you out, I will cover the heavens
and darken their stars;
I will cover the sun with a cloud,
and the moon will not give its light.
8All the shining lights in the heavens
I will darken over you;
I will bring darkness over your land, declares the Sovereign LORD.
9I will trouble the hearts of many peoples
when I bring about your destruction among the nations,
among[b] lands you have not known.
10I will cause many peoples to be appalled at you,
and their kings will shudder with horror because of you
when I brandish my sword before them.
On the day of your downfall
each of them will tremble
every moment for his life.

11" 'For this is what the Sovereign LORD says:

" 'The sword of the king of Babylon
will come against you.
12I will cause your hordes to fall
by the swords of mighty men—
the most ruthless of all nations.
They will shatter the pride of Egypt,
and all her hordes will be overthrown.
13I will destroy all her cattle
from beside abundant waters

[a] 15 Hebrew *Sheol*; also in verses 16 and 17
[b] 9 Hebrew; Septuagint *bring you into captivity among the nations, / to*

no longer to be stirred by the foot of man
or muddied by the hoofs of cattle.
14Then I will let her waters settle
and make her streams flow like oil,
declares the Sovereign LORD.
15When I make Egypt desolate
and strip the land of everything in it,
when I strike down all who live there,
then they will know that I am the LORD.'

16"This is the lament they will chant for her. The daughters of the nations will chant it; for Egypt and all her hordes they will chant it, declares the Sovereign LORD."

17In the twelfth year, on the fifteenth day of the month, the word of the LORD came to me: 18"Son of man, wail for the hordes of Egypt and consign to the earth below both her and the daughters of mighty nations, with those who go down to the pit. 19Say to them, 'Are you more favored than others? Go down and be laid among the uncircumcised.' 20They will fall among those killed by the sword. The sword is drawn; let her be dragged off with all her hordes. 21From within the grave[a] the mighty leaders will say of Egypt and her allies, 'They have come down and they lie with the uncircumcised, with those killed by the sword.'

22"Assyria is there with her whole army; she is surrounded by the graves of all her slain, all who have fallen by the sword. 23Their graves are in the depths of the pit and her army lies around her grave. All who had spread terror in the land of the living are slain, fallen by the sword.

24"Elam is there, with all her hordes around her grave. All of them are slain, fallen by the sword. All who had spread terror in the land of the living went down uncircumcised to the earth below. They bear their shame with those who go down to the pit. 25A bed is made for her among the slain, with all her hordes around her grave. All of them are uncircumcised, killed by the sword. Because their terror had spread in the land of the living, they bear their shame with those who go down to the pit; they are laid among the slain.

26"Meshech and Tubal are there, with all their hordes around their graves. All of them are uncircumcised, killed by the sword because they spread their terror in the land of the living. 27Do they not lie with the other uncircumcised warriors who have fallen, who went down to the grave with their weapons of war, whose swords were placed under their heads? The punishment for their sins rested on their bones, though the terror of these warriors had stalked through the land of the living.

28"You too, O Pharaoh, will be broken and will lie among the uncircumcised, with those killed by the sword.

29"Edom is there, her kings and all her princes; despite their power, they are laid with those killed by the sword. They lie with the uncircumcised, with those who go down to the pit.

30"All the princes of the north and all the Sidonians are there; they went down with the slain in disgrace despite the terror caused by their power. They lie uncircumcised with those killed by the sword and bear their shame with those who go down to the pit.

31"Pharaoh—he and all his army—will see them and he will be consoled for all his hordes that were killed by the sword, declares the Sovereign LORD. 32Although I had him spread terror in the land of the living, Pharaoh and all his hordes will be laid among the uncircumcised, with those killed by the sword, declares the Sovereign LORD."

Ezekiel a Watchman

33 The word of the LORD came to me: 2"Son of man, speak to your countrymen and say to them: 'When I bring the sword against a land, and the people of the land choose one of their men and make him their watchman, 3and he sees the sword coming against the land and blows the trumpet to warn the people, 4then if anyone hears the trumpet but does not take warning and the sword comes and takes his life, his blood will be on his own head. 5Since he heard the sound of the trumpet but did not take warning, his blood will be on his own head. If he had taken warning, he would have saved himself. 6But if the watchman sees the sword coming and does not blow the trumpet to warn the people and the sword comes and takes the life of one of them, that man will be taken away because of his sin, but I will hold the watchman accountable for his blood.'

[a]21 Hebrew *Sheol*; also in verse 27

7"Son of man, I have made you a watchman for the house of Israel; so hear the
word I speak and give them warning from
me. 8When I say to the wicked, 'O wicked
man, you will surely die,' and you do not
speak out to dissuade him from his ways,
that wicked man will die for[a] his sin, and
I will hold you accountable for his blood.
9But if you do warn the wicked man to
turn from his ways and he does not do so,
he will die for his sin, but you will have
saved yourself.

10"Son of man, say to the house of Israel, 'This is what you are saying: "Our offenses and sins weigh us down, and we are wasting away because of[b] them. How then can we live?" ' 11Say to them, 'As surely as I live, declares the Sovereign LORD, I take no pleasure in the death of the wicked, but rather that they turn from their ways and live. Turn! Turn from your evil ways! Why will you die, O house of Israel?'

12"Therefore, son of man, say to your countrymen, 'The righteousness of the righteous man will not save him when he disobeys, and the wickedness of the wicked man will not cause him to fall when he turns from it. The righteous man, if he sins, will not be allowed to live because of his former righteousness.' 13If I tell the righteous man that he will surely live, but then he trusts in his righteousness and does evil, none of the righteous things he has done will be remembered; he will die for the evil he has done. 14And if I say to the wicked man, 'You will surely die,' but he then turns away from his sin and does what is just and right— 15if he gives back what he took in pledge for a loan, returns what he has stolen, follows the decrees that give life, and does no evil, he will surely live; he will not die. 16None of the sins he has committed will be remembered against him. He has done what is just and right; he will surely live.

17"Yet your countrymen say, 'The way of the Lord is not just.' But it is their way that is not just. 18If a righteous man turns from his righteousness and does evil, he will die for it. 19And if a wicked man turns away from his wickedness and does what is just and right, he will live by doing so. 20Yet, O house of Israel, you say, 'The way of the Lord is not just.' But I will judge each of you according to his own ways."

Jerusalem's Fall Explained

21In the twelfth year of our exile, in the tenth month on the fifth day, a man who had escaped from Jerusalem came to me and said, "The city has fallen!" 22Now the evening before the man arrived, the hand of the LORD was upon me, and he opened my mouth before the man came to me in the morning. So my mouth was opened and I was no longer silent.

23Then the word of the LORD came to me: 24"Son of man, the people living in those ruins in the land of Israel are saying, 'Abraham was only one man, yet he possessed the land. But we are many; surely the land has been given to us as our possession.' 25Therefore say to them, 'This is what the Sovereign LORD says: Since you eat meat with the blood still in it and look to your idols and shed blood, should you then possess the land? 26You rely on your sword, you do detestable things, and each of you defiles his neighbor's wife. Should you then possess the land?'

27"Say this to them: 'This is what the Sovereign LORD says: As surely as I live, those who are left in the ruins will fall by the sword, those out in the country I will give to the wild animals to be devoured, and those in strongholds and caves will die of a plague. 28I will make the land a desolate waste, and her proud strength will come to an end, and the mountains of Israel will become desolate so that no one will cross them. 29Then they will know that I am the LORD, when I have made the land a desolate waste because of all the detestable things they have done.'

30"As for you, son of man, your countrymen are talking together about you by the walls and at the doors of the houses, saying to each other, 'Come and hear the message that has come from the LORD.' 31My people come to you, as they usually do, and sit before you to listen to your words, but they do not put them into practice. With their mouths they express devotion, but their hearts are greedy for unjust gain. 32Indeed, to them you are nothing more than one who sings love songs with a beautiful voice and plays an instrument well, for they hear your words but do not put them into practice.

33"When all this comes true—and it surely will—then they will know that a prophet has been among them."

[a]8 Or *in*; also in verse 9 [b]10 Or *away in*

Shepherds and Sheep

34 The word of the LORD came to me:
2"Son of man, prophesy against the
shepherds of Israel; prophesy and say to
them: 'This is what the Sovereign LORD
says: Woe to the shepherds of Israel who
only take care of themselves! Should not
shepherds take care of the flock? 3You eat
the curds, clothe yourselves with the wool
and slaughter the choice animals, but you
do not take care of the flock. 4You have
not strengthened the weak or healed the
sick or bound up the injured. You have
not brought back the strays or searched
for the lost. You have ruled them harshly
and brutally. 5So they were scattered be-
cause there was no shepherd, and when
they were scattered they became food for
all the wild animals. 6My sheep wandered
over all the mountains and on every high
hill. They were scattered over the whole
earth, and no one searched or looked for
them.

7" 'Therefore, you shepherds, hear the
word of the LORD: 8As surely as I live, de-
clares the Sovereign LORD, because my
flock lacks a shepherd and so has been
plundered and has become food for all the
wild animals, and because my shepherds
did not search for my flock but cared for
themselves rather than for my flock,
9therefore, O shepherds, hear the word of
the LORD: 10This is what the Sovereign
LORD says: I am against the shepherds and
will hold them accountable for my flock.
I will remove them from tending the flock
so that the shepherds can no longer feed
themselves. I will rescue my flock from
their mouths, and it will no longer be food
for them.

11" 'For this is what the Sovereign LORD
says: I myself will search for my sheep
and look after them. 12As a shepherd
looks after his scattered flock when he is
with them, so will I look after my sheep.
I will rescue them from all the places
where they were scattered on a day of
clouds and darkness. 13I will bring them
out from the nations and gather them
from the countries, and I will bring them
into their own land. I will pasture them on
the mountains of Israel, in the ravines and
in all the settlements in the land. 14I will
tend them in a good pasture, and the
mountain heights of Israel will be their
grazing land. There they will lie down in
good grazing land, and there they will
feed in a rich pasture on the mountains of
Israel. 15I myself will tend my sheep and
have them lie down, declares the Sover-
eign LORD. 16I will search for the lost and
bring back the strays. I will bind up the
injured and strengthen the weak, but the
sleek and the strong I will destroy. I will
shepherd the flock with justice.

17" 'As for you, my flock, this is what
the Sovereign LORD says: I will judge be-
tween one sheep and another, and be-
tween rams and goats. 18Is it not enough
for you to feed on the good pasture? Must
you also trample the rest of your pasture
with your feet? Is it not enough for you to
drink clear water? Must you also muddy
the rest with your feet? 19Must my flock
feed on what you have trampled and drink
what you have muddied with your feet?

20" 'Therefore this is what the Sovereign
LORD says to them: See, I myself will judge
between the fat sheep and the lean sheep.
21Because you shove with flank and
shoulder, butting all the weak sheep with
your horns until you have driven them
away, 22I will save my flock, and they will
no longer be plundered. I will judge be-
tween one sheep and another. 23I will
place over them one shepherd, my servant
David, and he will tend them; he will tend
them and be their shepherd. 24I the LORD
will be their God, and my servant David
will be prince among them. I the LORD
have spoken.

25" 'I will make a covenant of peace
with them and rid the land of wild beasts
so that they may live in the desert and
sleep in the forests in safety. 26I will bless
them and the places surrounding my
hill.[a] I will send down showers in season;
there will be showers of blessing. 27The
trees of the field will yield their fruit and
the ground will yield its crops; the people
will be secure in their land. They will
know that I am the LORD, when I break the
bars of their yoke and rescue them from
the hands of those who enslaved them.
28They will no longer be plundered by the
nations, nor will wild animals devour
them. They will live in safety, and no one
will make them afraid. 29I will provide for
them a land renowned for its crops, and
they will no longer be victims of famine in
the land or bear the scorn of the nations.
30Then they will know that I, the LORD
their God, am with them and that they, the

[a]26 Or *I will make them and the places surrounding my hill a blessing*

house of Israel, are my people, declares
the Sovereign LORD. 31You my sheep, the
sheep of my pasture, are people, and I am
your God, declares the Sovereign LORD.' "

A Prophecy Against Edom

35 The word of the LORD came to me:
2"Son of man, set your face against
Mount Seir; prophesy against it 3and say:
'This is what the Sovereign LORD says: I
am against you, Mount Seir, and I will
stretch out my hand against you and make
you a desolate waste. 4I will turn your
towns into ruins and you will be desolate.
Then you will know that I am the LORD.
5" 'Because you harbored an ancient
hostility and delivered the Israelites over
to the sword at the time of their calamity,
the time their punishment reached its climax, 6therefore as surely as I live, declares
the Sovereign LORD, I will give you over to
bloodshed and it will pursue you. Since
you did not hate bloodshed, bloodshed
will pursue you. 7I will make Mount Seir
a desolate waste and cut off from it all
who come and go. 8I will fill your moun-

FRIDAY

VERSE FOR THE DAY: Ezekiel 34:26

AUTHOR: David and Annette LaPlaca

PASSAGE FOR THE DAY: Ezekiel 34:22–31

Showers of Blessing

We both grew up singing—and loving—the great hymns. One childhood favorite began, "There will be showers of blessing, this is the promise of God!" Later we discovered the passage of Scripture this verse comes from: Ezekiel 34. Most of Ezekiel is a diatribe against the sins of Israel and Egypt, but here in the middle of all God's anger, he stops to draw his metaphor of the loving Shepherd and his needy sheep.

Jesus called himself our Shepherd (John 10), once again reflecting the care of a sovereign God over his needy people. In Ezekiel, God calls his people "the sheep of his pasture" and promises "showers of blessing." These "showers" include peace, safety in the wilderness, fruitful trees and bountiful crops, national security and, best of all, a relationship with their Shepherd: "Then they will know that I, the LORD their God, am with them."

As God's people, we are the recipients of God's great blessings and, best of all, a relationship with the Shepherd himself.

MARRIAGE BUILDERS

- *What are some of the blessings God has "showered" on you and your spouse?*
- *How does a relationship with the Shepherd benefit your marriage relationship?*

Additional Scripture Readings
John 10:1–18, 27–30; 21:15–17

Go to page 922 for your next devotional reading.

tains with the slain; those killed by the
sword will fall on your hills and in your
valleys and in all your ravines. 9I will
make you desolate forever; your towns
will not be inhabited. Then you will know
that I am the LORD.

10" 'Because you have said, "These two
nations and countries will be ours and we
will take possession of them," even
though I the LORD was there, 11therefore
as surely as I live, declares the Sovereign
LORD, I will treat you in accordance with
the anger and jealousy you showed in
your hatred of them and I will make my-
self known among them when I judge
you. 12Then you will know that I the LORD
have heard all the contemptible things
you have said against the mountains of Is-
rael. You said, "They have been laid waste
and have been given over to us to devour."
13You boasted against me and spoke
against me without restraint, and I heard
it. 14This is what the Sovereign LORD says:
While the whole earth rejoices, I will
make you desolate. 15Because you re-
joiced when the inheritance of the house
of Israel became desolate, that is how I
will treat you. You will be desolate,
O Mount Seir, you and all of Edom. Then
they will know that I am the LORD.' "

A Prophecy to the Mountains of Israel

36 "Son of man, prophesy to the
mountains of Israel and say,
'O mountains of Israel, hear the word of
the LORD. 2This is what the Sovereign LORD
says: The enemy said of you, "Aha! The
ancient heights have become our posses-
sion." ' 3Therefore prophesy and say,
'This is what the Sovereign LORD says: Be-
cause they ravaged and hounded you
from every side so that you became the
possession of the rest of the nations and
the object of people's malicious talk and
slander, 4therefore, O mountains of Israel,
hear the word of the Sovereign LORD: This
is what the Sovereign LORD says to the
mountains and hills, to the ravines and
valleys, to the desolate ruins and the de-
serted towns that have been plundered
and ridiculed by the rest of the nations
around you— 5this is what the Sovereign
LORD says: In my burning zeal I have spo-
ken against the rest of the nations, and
against all Edom, for with glee and with
malice in their hearts they made my land
their own possession so that they might
plunder its pastureland.' 6Therefore
prophesy concerning the land of Israel
and say to the mountains and hills, to the
ravines and valleys: 'This is what the Sov-
ereign LORD says: I speak in my jealous
wrath because you have suffered the
scorn of the nations. 7Therefore this is
what the Sovereign LORD says: I swear
with uplifted hand that the nations
around you will also suffer scorn.

8" 'But you, O mountains of Israel, will
produce branches and fruit for my people
Israel, for they will soon come home. 9I
am concerned for you and will look on
you with favor; you will be plowed and
sown, 10and I will multiply the number of
people upon you, even the whole house of
Israel. The towns will be inhabited and
the ruins rebuilt. 11I will increase the
number of men and animals upon you,
and they will be fruitful and become nu-
merous. I will settle people on you as in
the past and will make you prosper more
than before. Then you will know that I am
the LORD. 12I will cause people, my people
Israel, to walk upon you. They will pos-
sess you, and you will be their inherit-
tance; you will never again deprive them
of their children.

13" 'This is what the Sovereign LORD
says: Because people say to you, "You de-
vour men and deprive your nation of its
children," 14therefore you will no longer
devour men or make your nation child-
less, declares the Sovereign LORD. 15No
longer will I make you hear the taunts of
the nations, and no longer will you suffer
the scorn of the peoples or cause your na-
tion to fall, declares the Sovereign LORD.' "

16Again the word of the LORD came to
me: 17"Son of man, when the people of Is-
rael were living in their own land, they de-
filed it by their conduct and their actions.
Their conduct was like a woman's month-
ly uncleanness in my sight. 18So I poured
out my wrath on them because they had
shed blood in the land and because they
had defiled it with their idols. 19I dis-
persed them among the nations, and they
were scattered through the countries; I
judged them according to their conduct
and their actions. 20And wherever they
went among the nations they profaned my
holy name, for it was said of them, 'These
are the LORD's people, and yet they had to
leave his land.' 21I had concern for my
holy name, which the house of Israel pro-
faned among the nations where they had
gone.

22"Therefore say to the house of Israel,
'This is what the Sovereign LORD says: It is
not for your sake, O house of Israel, that
I am going to do these things, but for the
sake of my holy name, which you have
profaned among the nations where you
have gone. 23I will show the holiness of
my great name, which has been profaned
among the nations, the name you have
profaned among them. Then the nations
will know that I am the LORD, declares the
Sovereign LORD, when I show myself holy
through you before their eyes.

24" 'For I will take you out of the na-
tions; I will gather you from all the coun-
tries and bring you back into your own
land. 25I will sprinkle clean water on you,
and you will be clean; I will cleanse you
from all your impurities and from all your
idols. 26I will give you a new heart and put
a new spirit in you; I will remove from you
your heart of stone and give you a heart of
flesh. 27And I will put my Spirit in you and
move you to follow my decrees and be
careful to keep my laws. 28You will live in
the land I gave your forefathers; you will
be my people, and I will be your God. 29I
will save you from all your uncleanness. I
will call for the grain and make it plentiful
and will not bring famine upon you. 30I
will increase the fruit of the trees and the
crops of the field, so that you will no long-
er suffer disgrace among the nations be-
cause of famine. 31Then you will remem-
ber your evil ways and wicked deeds, and
you will loathe yourselves for your sins
and detestable practices. 32I want you to
know that I am not doing this for your
sake, declares the Sovereign LORD. Be
ashamed and disgraced for your conduct,
O house of Israel!

33" 'This is what the Sovereign LORD
says: On the day I cleanse you from all
your sins, I will resettle your towns, and
the ruins will be rebuilt. 34The desolate
land will be cultivated instead of lying
desolate in the sight of all who pass
through it. 35They will say, "This land that
was laid waste has become like the garden
of Eden; the cities that were lying in ruins,
desolate and destroyed, are now fortified
and inhabited." 36Then the nations
around you that remain will know that I
the LORD have rebuilt what was destroyed
and have replanted what was desolate. I
the LORD have spoken, and I will do it.'

37"This is what the Sovereign LORD says:
Once again I will yield to the plea of the
house of Israel and do this for them: I will
make their people as numerous as sheep,
38as numerous as the flocks for offerings
at Jerusalem during her appointed feasts.
So will the ruined cities be filled with
flocks of people. Then they will know that
I am the LORD."

The Valley of Dry Bones

37 The hand of the LORD was upon
me, and he brought me out by the
Spirit of the LORD and set me in the middle
of a valley; it was full of bones. 2He led me
back and forth among them, and I saw a
great many bones on the floor of the val-
ley, bones that were very dry. 3He asked
me, "Son of man, can these bones live?"
I said, "O Sovereign LORD, you alone
know."

4Then he said to me, "Prophesy to these
bones and say to them, 'Dry bones, hear
the word of the LORD! 5This is what the
Sovereign LORD says to these bones: I will
make breath[a] enter you, and you will
come to life. 6I will attach tendons to you
and make flesh come upon you and cover
you with skin; I will put breath in you, and
you will come to life. Then you will know
that I am the LORD.' "

7So I prophesied as I was commanded.
And as I was prophesying, there was a
noise, a rattling sound, and the bones
came together, bone to bone. 8I looked,
and tendons and flesh appeared on them
and skin covered them, but there was no
breath in them.

9Then he said to me, "Prophesy to the
breath; prophesy, son of man, and say to
it, 'This is what the Sovereign LORD says:
Come from the four winds, O breath, and
breathe into these slain, that they may
live.' " 10So I prophesied as he command-
ed me, and breath entered them; they
came to life and stood up on their feet—a
vast army.

11Then he said to me: "Son of man,
these bones are the whole house of Israel.
They say, 'Our bones are dried up and our
hope is gone; we are cut off.' 12Therefore
prophesy and say to them: 'This is what
the Sovereign LORD says: O my people, I
am going to open your graves and bring
you up from them; I will bring you back to
the land of Israel. 13Then you, my people,
will know that I am the LORD, when I open
your graves and bring you up from them.

[a]5 The Hebrew for this word can also mean *wind* or *spirit* (see verses 6-14).

14I will put my Spirit in you and you will
live, and I will settle you in your own land.
Then you will know that I the LORD have
spoken, and I have done it, declares the
LORD.' "

One Nation Under One King

15The word of the LORD came to me:
16"Son of man, take a stick of wood and
write on it, 'Belonging to Judah and the
Israelites associated with him.' Then take
another stick of wood, and write on it,
'Ephraim's stick, belonging to Joseph and
all the house of Israel associated with
him.' 17Join them together into one stick
so that they will become one in your
hand.

18"When your countrymen ask you,
'Won't you tell us what you mean by this?'
19say to them, 'This is what the Sovereign
LORD says: I am going to take the stick of
Joseph—which is in Ephraim's hand—
and of the Israelite tribes associated with
him, and join it to Judah's stick, making
them a single stick of wood, and they will
become one in my hand.' 20Hold before
their eyes the sticks you have written on
21and say to them, 'This is what the Sover-
eign LORD says: I will take the Israelites
out of the nations where they have gone.
I will gather them from all around and
bring them back into their own land. 22I
will make them one nation in the land, on
the mountains of Israel. There will be one
king over all of them and they will never
again be two nations or be divided into
two kingdoms. 23They will no longer de-
file themselves with their idols and vile
images or with any of their offenses, for I
will save them from all their sinful back-
sliding,[a] and I will cleanse them. They
will be my people, and I will be their God.

24" 'My servant David will be king over
them, and they will all have one shepherd.
They will follow my laws and be careful to
keep my decrees. 25They will live in the
land I gave to my servant Jacob, the land
where your fathers lived. They and their
children and their children's children will
live there forever, and David my servant
will be their prince forever. 26I will make
a covenant of peace with them; it will be
an everlasting covenant. I will establish
them and increase their numbers, and I
will put my sanctuary among them forev-
er. 27My dwelling place will be with them;
I will be their God, and they will be my
people. 28Then the nations will know that
I the LORD make Israel holy, when my
sanctuary is among them forever.' "

A Prophecy Against Gog

38 The word of the LORD came to me:
2"Son of man, set your face against
Gog, of the land of Magog, the chief prince
of[b] Meshech and Tubal; prophesy
against him 3and say: 'This is what the
Sovereign LORD says: I am against you,
O Gog, chief prince of[c] Meshech and Tu-
bal. 4I will turn you around, put hooks in
your jaws and bring you out with your
whole army—your horses, your horse-
men fully armed, and a great horde with
large and small shields, all of them bran-
dishing their swords. 5Persia, Cush[d] and
Put will be with them, all with shields and
helmets, 6also Gomer with all its troops,
and Beth Togarmah from the far north
with all its troops—the many nations with
you.

7" 'Get ready; be prepared, you and all
the hordes gathered about you, and take
command of them. 8After many days you
will be called to arms. In future years you
will invade a land that has recovered from
war, whose people were gathered from
many nations to the mountains of Israel,
which had long been desolate. They had
been brought out from the nations, and
now all of them live in safety. 9You and all
your troops and the many nations with
you will go up, advancing like a storm;
you will be like a cloud covering the land.

10" 'This is what the Sovereign LORD
says: On that day thoughts will come into
your mind and you will devise an evil
scheme. 11You will say, "I will invade a
land of unwalled villages; I will attack a
peaceful and unsuspecting people—all of
them living without walls and without
gates and bars. 12I will plunder and loot
and turn my hand against the resettled ru-
ins and the people gathered from the na-
tions, rich in livestock and goods, living at
the center of the land." 13Sheba and De-
dan and the merchants of Tarshish and all
her villages[e] will say to you, "Have you
come to plunder? Have you gathered your
hordes to loot, to carry off silver and gold,

[a]23 Many Hebrew manuscripts (see also Septuagint); most Hebrew manuscripts *all their dwelling places where they sinned* [b]2 Or *the prince of Rosh,* [c]3 Or *Gog, prince of Rosh,* [d]5 That is, the upper Nile region [e]13 Or *her strong lions*

to take away livestock and goods and to
seize much plunder?" '

14"Therefore, son of man, prophesy and
say to Gog: 'This is what the Sovereign
LORD says: In that day, when my people
Israel are living in safety, will you not take
notice of it? 15You will come from your
place in the far north, you and many na-
tions with you, all of them riding on
horses, a great horde, a mighty army.
16You will advance against my people Is-
rael like a cloud that covers the land. In
days to come, O Gog, I will bring you
against my land, so that the nations may
know me when I show myself holy
through you before their eyes.

17" 'This is what the Sovereign LORD
says: Are you not the one I spoke of in for-
mer days by my servants the prophets of
Israel? At that time they prophesied for
years that I would bring you against them.
18This is what will happen in that day:
When Gog attacks the land of Israel, my
hot anger will be aroused, declares the
Sovereign LORD. 19In my zeal and fiery
wrath I declare that at that time there shall
be a great earthquake in the land of Israel.
20The fish of the sea, the birds of the air,
the beasts of the field, every creature that
moves along the ground, and all the peo-
ple on the face of the earth will tremble at
my presence. The mountains will be over-
turned, the cliffs will crumble and every
wall will fall to the ground. 21I will sum-
mon a sword against Gog on all my moun-
tains, declares the Sovereign LORD. Every
man's sword will be against his brother.
22I will execute judgment upon him with
plague and bloodshed; I will pour down
torrents of rain, hailstones and burning
sulfur on him and on his troops and on
the many nations with him. 23And so I will
show my greatness and my holiness, and
I will make myself known in the sight of
many nations. Then they will know that I
am the LORD.'

39 "Son of man, prophesy against Gog
and say: 'This is what the Sover-
eign LORD says: I am against you, O Gog,
chief prince of[a] Meshech and Tubal. 2I
will turn you around and drag you along.
I will bring you from the far north and
send you against the mountains of Israel.
3Then I will strike your bow from your left
hand and make your arrows drop from
your right hand. 4On the mountains of Is-
rael you will fall, you and all your troops
and the nations with you. I will give you
as food to all kinds of carrion birds and to
the wild animals. 5You will fall in the open
field, for I have spoken, declares the Sov-
ereign LORD. 6I will send fire on Magog
and on those who live in safety in the
coastlands, and they will know that I am
the LORD.

7" 'I will make known my holy name
among my people Israel. I will no longer
let my holy name be profaned, and the na-
tions will know that I the LORD am the
Holy One in Israel. 8It is coming! It will
surely take place, declares the Sovereign
LORD. This is the day I have spoken of.

9" 'Then those who live in the towns of
Israel will go out and use the weapons for
fuel and burn them up—the small and
large shields, the bows and arrows, the
war clubs and spears. For seven years
they will use them for fuel. 10They will not
need to gather wood from the fields or cut
it from the forests, because they will use
the weapons for fuel. And they will plun-
der those who plundered them and loot
those who looted them, declares the Sov-
ereign LORD.

11" 'On that day I will give Gog a burial
place in Israel, in the valley of those who
travel east toward[b] the Sea.[c] It will block
the way of travelers, because Gog and all
his hordes will be buried there. So it will
be called the Valley of Hamon Gog.[d]

12" 'For seven months the house of Isra-
el will be burying them in order to cleanse
the land. 13All the people of the land will
bury them, and the day I am glorified will
be a memorable day for them, declares the
Sovereign LORD.

14" 'Men will be regularly employed to
cleanse the land. Some will go throughout
the land and, in addition to them, others
will bury those that remain on the ground.
At the end of the seven months they will
begin their search. 15As they go through
the land and one of them sees a human
bone, he will set up a marker beside it un-
til the gravediggers have buried it in the
Valley of Hamon Gog. 16(Also a town
called Hamonah[e] will be there.) And so
they will cleanse the land.'

17"Son of man, this is what the Sover-
eign LORD says: Call out to every kind of
bird and all the wild animals: 'Assemble
and come together from all around to the

[a] 1 Or *Gog, prince of Rosh,* [b] 11 Or *of* [c] 11 That is, the Dead Sea [d] 11 *Hamon Gog* means *hordes of Gog.* [e] 16 *Hamonah* means *horde.*

sacrifice I am preparing for you, the great sacrifice on the mountains of Israel. There you will eat flesh and drink blood. 18You will eat the flesh of mighty men and drink the blood of the princes of the earth as if they were rams and lambs, goats and bulls—all of them fattened animals from Bashan. 19At the sacrifice I am preparing for you, you will eat fat till you are glutted and drink blood till you are drunk. 20At my table you will eat your fill of horses and riders, mighty men and soldiers of every kind,' declares the Sovereign LORD.

21"I will display my glory among the nations, and all the nations will see the punishment I inflict and the hand I lay upon them. 22From that day forward the house of Israel will know that I am the LORD their God. 23And the nations will know that the people of Israel went into exile for their sin, because they were unfaithful to me. So I hid my face from them and handed them over to their enemies, and they all fell by the sword. 24I dealt with them according to their uncleanness and their offenses, and I hid my face from them.

25"Therefore this is what the Sovereign LORD says: I will now bring Jacob back from captivity[a] and will have compassion on all the people of Israel, and I will be zealous for my holy name. 26They will forget their shame and all the unfaithfulness they showed toward me when they lived in safety in their land with no one to make them afraid. 27When I have brought them back from the nations and have gathered them from the countries of their enemies, I will show myself holy through them in the sight of many nations. 28Then they will know that I am the LORD their God, for though I sent them into exile among the nations, I will gather them to their own land, not leaving any behind. 29I will no longer hide my face from them, for I will pour out my Spirit on the house of Israel, declares the Sovereign LORD."

The New Temple Area

40 In the twenty-fifth year of our exile, at the beginning of the year, on the tenth of the month, in the fourteenth year after the fall of the city—on that very day the hand of the LORD was upon me and he took me there. 2In visions of God he took me to the land of Israel and set me on a very high mountain, on whose south side were some buildings that looked like a city. 3He took me there, and I saw a man whose appearance was like bronze; he was standing in the gateway with a linen cord and a measuring rod in his hand. 4The man said to me, "Son of man, look with your eyes and hear with your ears and pay attention to everything I am going to show you, for that is why you have been brought here. Tell the house of Israel everything you see."

The East Gate to the Outer Court

5I saw a wall completely surrounding the temple area. The length of the measuring rod in the man's hand was six long cubits, each of which was a cubit[b] and a handbreadth.[c] He measured the wall; it was one measuring rod thick and one rod high.

6Then he went to the gate facing east. He climbed its steps and measured the threshold of the gate; it was one rod deep.[d] 7The alcoves for the guards were one rod long and one rod wide, and the projecting walls between the alcoves were five cubits thick. And the threshold of the gate next to the portico facing the temple was one rod deep.

8Then he measured the portico of the gateway; 9it[e] was eight cubits deep and its jambs were two cubits thick. The portico of the gateway faced the temple.

10Inside the east gate were three alcoves on each side; the three had the same measurements, and the faces of the projecting walls on each side had the same measurements. 11Then he measured the width of the entrance to the gateway; it was ten cubits and its length was thirteen cubits. 12In front of each alcove was a wall one cubit high, and the alcoves were six cubits square. 13Then he measured the gateway from the top of the rear wall of one alcove to the top of the opposite one; the distance was twenty-five cubits from one parapet opening to the opposite one. 14He measured along the faces of the projecting walls all around the inside of the gateway—sixty cubits. The measurement was

[a]25 Or *now restore the fortunes of Jacob* [b]5 The common cubit was about 1 1/2 feet (about 0.5 meter). [c]5 That is, about 3 inches (about 8 centimeters) [d]6 Septuagint; Hebrew *deep, the first threshold, one rod deep* [e]8,9 Many Hebrew manuscripts, Septuagint, Vulgate and Syriac; most Hebrew manuscripts *gateway facing the temple; it was one rod deep.* 9*Then he measured the portico of the gateway; it*

up to the portico[a] facing the courtyard.[b]
15The distance from the entrance of the
gateway to the far end of its portico was
fifty cubits. 16The alcoves and the project-
ing walls inside the gateway were sur-
mounted by narrow parapet openings all
around, as was the portico; the openings
all around faced inward. The faces of the
projecting walls were decorated with
palm trees.

The Outer Court

17Then he brought me into the outer
court. There I saw some rooms and a
pavement that had been constructed all
around the court; there were thirty rooms
along the pavement. 18It abutted the sides
of the gateways and was as wide as they
were long; this was the lower pavement.
19Then he measured the distance from the
inside of the lower gateway to the outside
of the inner court; it was a hundred cubits
on the east side as well as on the north.

The North Gate

20Then he measured the length and
width of the gate facing north, leading into
the outer court. 21Its alcoves—three on
each side—its projecting walls and its
portico had the same measurements as
those of the first gateway. It was fifty cu-
bits long and twenty-five cubits wide. 22Its
openings, its portico and its palm tree dec-
orations had the same measurements as
those of the gate facing east. Seven steps
led up to it, with its portico opposite them.
23There was a gate to the inner court fac-
ing the north gate, just as there was on the
east. He measured from one gate to the
opposite one; it was a hundred cubits.

The South Gate

24Then he led me to the south side and
I saw a gate facing south. He measured its
jambs and its portico, and they had the
same measurements as the others. 25The
gateway and its portico had narrow open-
ings all around, like the openings of the
others. It was fifty cubits long and twenty-
five cubits wide. 26Seven steps led up to it,
with its portico opposite them; it had palm
tree decorations on the faces of the pro-
jecting walls on each side. 27The inner
court also had a gate facing south, and he
measured from this gate to the outer gate
on the south side; it was a hundred cubits.

Gates to the Inner Court

28Then he brought me into the inner
court through the south gate, and he mea-
sured the south gate; it had the same mea-
surements as the others. 29Its alcoves, its
projecting walls and its portico had the
same measurements as the others. The
gateway and its portico had openings all
around. It was fifty cubits long and twen-
ty-five cubits wide. 30(The porticoes of the
gateways around the inner court were
twenty-five cubits wide and five cubits
deep.) 31Its portico faced the outer court;
palm trees decorated its jambs, and eight
steps led up to it.

32Then he brought me to the inner court
on the east side, and he measured the
gateway; it had the same measurements
as the others. 33Its alcoves, its projecting
walls and its portico had the same mea-
surements as the others. The gateway and
its portico had openings all around. It was
fifty cubits long and twenty-five cubits
wide. 34Its portico faced the outer court;
palm trees decorated the jambs on either
side, and eight steps led up to it.

35Then he brought me to the north gate
and measured it. It had the same measure-
ments as the others, 36as did its alcoves,
its projecting walls and its portico, and it
had openings all around. It was fifty cubits
long and twenty-five cubits wide. 37Its
portico[c] faced the outer court; palm trees
decorated the jambs on either side, and
eight steps led up to it.

The Rooms for Preparing Sacrifices

38A room with a doorway was by the
portico in each of the inner gateways,
where the burnt offerings were washed.
39In the portico of the gateway were two
tables on each side, on which the burnt
offerings, sin offerings and guilt offerings
were slaughtered. 40By the outside wall of
the portico of the gateway, near the steps
at the entrance to the north gateway were
two tables, and on the other side of the
steps were two tables. 41So there were
four tables on one side of the gateway and
four on the other—eight tables in all—on
which the sacrifices were slaughtered.
42There were also four tables of dressed
stone for the burnt offerings, each a cubit
and a half long, a cubit and a half wide
and a cubit high. On them were placed the

[a] 14 Septuagint; Hebrew *projecting wall* [b] 14 The meaning of the Hebrew for this verse is uncertain.
[c] 37 Septuagint (see also verses 31 and 34); Hebrew *jambs*

utensils for slaughtering the burnt offerings and the other sacrifices. 43And double-pronged hooks, each a handbreadth long, were attached to the wall all around. The tables were for the flesh of the offerings.

Rooms for the Priests

44Outside the inner gate, within the inner court, were two rooms, one[a] at the side of the north gate and facing south, and another at the side of the south[b] gate and facing north. 45He said to me, "The room facing south is for the priests who have charge of the temple, 46and the room facing north is for the priests who have charge of the altar. These are the sons of Zadok, who are the only Levites who may draw near to the LORD to minister before him."

47Then he measured the court: It was square—a hundred cubits long and a hundred cubits wide. And the altar was in front of the temple.

The Temple

48He brought me to the portico of the temple and measured the jambs of the portico; they were five cubits wide on either side. The width of the entrance was fourteen cubits and its projecting walls were[c] three cubits wide on either side. 49The portico was twenty cubits wide, and twelve[d] cubits from front to back. It was reached by a flight of stairs,[e] and there were pillars on each side of the jambs.

41 Then the man brought me to the outer sanctuary and measured the jambs; the width of the jambs was six cubits[f] on each side.[g] 2The entrance was ten cubits wide, and the projecting walls on each side of it were five cubits wide. He also measured the outer sanctuary; it was forty cubits long and twenty cubits wide.

3Then he went into the inner sanctuary and measured the jambs of the entrance; each was two cubits wide. The entrance was six cubits wide, and the projecting walls on each side of it were seven cubits wide. 4And he measured the length of the inner sanctuary; it was twenty cubits, and its width was twenty cubits across the end of the outer sanctuary. He said to me, "This is the Most Holy Place."

5Then he measured the wall of the temple; it was six cubits thick, and each side room around the temple was four cubits wide. 6The side rooms were on three levels, one above another, thirty on each level. There were ledges all around the wall of the temple to serve as supports for the side rooms, so that the supports were not inserted into the wall of the temple. 7The side rooms all around the temple were wider at each successive level. The structure surrounding the temple was built in ascending stages, so that the rooms widened as one went upward. A stairway went up from the lowest floor to the top floor through the middle floor.

8I saw that the temple had a raised base all around it, forming the foundation of the side rooms. It was the length of the rod, six long cubits. 9The outer wall of the side rooms was five cubits thick. The open area between the side rooms of the temple 10and the ⌊priests'⌋ rooms was twenty cubits wide all around the temple. 11There were entrances to the side rooms from the open area, one on the north and another on the south; and the base adjoining the open area was five cubits wide all around.

12The building facing the temple courtyard on the west side was seventy cubits wide. The wall of the building was five cubits thick all around, and its length was ninety cubits.

13Then he measured the temple; it was a hundred cubits long, and the temple courtyard and the building with its walls were also a hundred cubits long. 14The width of the temple courtyard on the east, including the front of the temple, was a hundred cubits.

15Then he measured the length of the building facing the courtyard at the rear of the temple, including its galleries on each side; it was a hundred cubits.

The outer sanctuary, the inner sanctuary and the portico facing the court, 16as well as the thresholds and the narrow windows and galleries around the three of them—everything beyond and including the threshold was covered with wood. The floor, the wall up to the windows, and the windows were covered. 17In the space above the outside of the entrance to the inner sanctuary and on the walls at regu-

[a]44 Septuagint; Hebrew *were rooms for singers, which were* [b]44 Septuagint; Hebrew *east* [c]48 Septuagint; Hebrew *entrance was* [d]49 Septuagint; Hebrew *eleven* [e]49 Hebrew; Septuagint *Ten steps led up to it* [f]1 The common cubit was about 1 1/2 feet (about 0.5 meter). [g]1 One Hebrew manuscript and Septuagint; most Hebrew manuscripts *side, the width of the tent*

lar intervals all around the inner and outer sanctuary [18]were carved cherubim and palm trees. Palm trees alternated with cherubim. Each cherub had two faces: [19]the face of a man toward the palm tree on one side and the face of a lion toward the palm tree on the other. They were carved all around the whole temple. [20]From the floor to the area above the entrance, cherubim and palm trees were carved on the wall of the outer sanctuary.

[21]The outer sanctuary had a rectangular doorframe, and the one at the front of the Most Holy Place was similar. [22]There was a wooden altar three cubits high and two cubits square[a]; its corners, its base[b] and its sides were of wood. The man said to me, "This is the table that is before the LORD." [23]Both the outer sanctuary and the Most Holy Place had double doors. [24]Each door had two leaves—two hinged leaves for each door. [25]And on the doors of the outer sanctuary were carved cherubim and palm trees like those carved on the walls, and there was a wooden overhang on the front of the portico. [26]On the sidewalls of the portico were narrow windows with palm trees carved on each side. The side rooms of the temple also had overhangs.

Rooms for the Priests

42 Then the man led me northward into the outer court and brought me to the rooms opposite the temple courtyard and opposite the outer wall on the north side. [2]The building whose door faced north was a hundred cubits[c] long and fifty cubits wide. [3]Both in the section twenty cubits from the inner court and in the section opposite the pavement of the outer court, gallery faced gallery at the three levels. [4]In front of the rooms was an inner passageway ten cubits wide and a hundred cubits[d] long. Their doors were on the north. [5]Now the upper rooms were narrower, for the galleries took more space from them than from the rooms on the lower and middle floors of the building. [6]The rooms on the third floor had no pillars, as the courts had; so they were smaller in floor space than those on the lower and middle floors. [7]There was an outer wall parallel to the rooms and the outer court; it extended in front of the rooms for fifty cubits. [8]While the row of rooms on the side next to the outer court was fifty cubits long, the row on the side nearest the sanctuary was a hundred cubits long. [9]The lower rooms had an entrance on the east side as one enters them from the outer court.

[10]On the south side[e] along the length of the wall of the outer court, adjoining the temple courtyard and opposite the outer wall, were rooms [11]with a passageway in front of them. These were like the rooms on the north; they had the same length and width, with similar exits and dimensions. Similar to the doorways on the north [12]were the doorways of the rooms on the south. There was a doorway at the beginning of the passageway that was parallel to the corresponding wall extending eastward, by which one enters the rooms.

[13]Then he said to me, "The north and south rooms facing the temple courtyard are the priests' rooms, where the priests who approach the LORD will eat the most holy offerings. There they will put the most holy offerings—the grain offerings, the sin offerings and the guilt offerings—for the place is holy. [14]Once the priests enter the holy precincts, they are not to go into the outer court until they leave behind the garments in which they minister, for these are holy. They are to put on other clothes before they go near the places that are for the people."

[15]When he had finished measuring what was inside the temple area, he led me out by the east gate and measured the area all around: [16]He measured the east side with the measuring rod; it was five hundred cubits.[f] [17]He measured the north side; it was five hundred cubits[g] by the measuring rod. [18]He measured the south side; it was five hundred cubits by the measuring rod. [19]Then he turned to the west side and measured; it was five hundred cubits by the measuring rod. [20]So he measured the area on all four sides. It had a wall around it, five hundred cubits long and five hundred cubits wide, to separate the holy from the common.

[a]22 Septuagint; Hebrew *long* [b]22 Septuagint; Hebrew *length* [c]2 The common cubit was about 1 1/2 feet (about 0.5 meter). [d]4 Septuagint and Syriac; Hebrew *and one cubit* [e]10 Septuagint; Hebrew *Eastward* [f]16 See Septuagint of verse 17; Hebrew *rods*; also in verses 18 and 19. [g]17 Septuagint; Hebrew *rods*

The Glory Returns to the Temple

43 Then the man brought me to the gate facing east, 2and I saw the glory of the God of Israel coming from the east. His voice was like the roar of rushing waters, and the land was radiant with his glory. 3The vision I saw was like the vision I had seen when he[a] came to destroy the city and like the visions I had seen by the Kebar River, and I fell facedown. 4The glory of the LORD entered the temple through the gate facing east. 5Then the Spirit lifted me up and brought me into the inner court, and the glory of the LORD filled the temple.

6While the man was standing beside me, I heard someone speaking to me from inside the temple. 7He said: "Son of man, this is the place of my throne and the place for the soles of my feet. This is where I will live among the Israelites forever. The house of Israel will never again defile my holy name—neither they nor their kings—by their prostitution[b] and the lifeless idols[c] of their kings at their high places. 8When they placed their threshold next to my threshold and their doorposts beside my doorposts, with only a wall between me and them, they defiled my holy name by their detestable practices. So I destroyed them in my anger. 9Now let them put away from me their prostitution and the lifeless idols of their kings, and I will live among them forever.

10"Son of man, describe the temple to the people of Israel, that they may be ashamed of their sins. Let them consider the plan, 11and if they are ashamed of all they have done, make known to them the design of the temple—its arrangement, its exits and entrances—its whole design and all its regulations[d] and laws. Write these down before them so that they may be faithful to its design and follow all its regulations.

12"This is the law of the temple: All the surrounding area on top of the mountain will be most holy. Such is the law of the temple.

The Altar

13"These are the measurements of the altar in long cubits, that cubit being a cubit[e] and a handbreadth[f]: Its gutter is a cubit deep and a cubit wide, with a rim of one span[g] around the edge. And this is the height of the altar: 14From the gutter on the ground up to the lower ledge it is two cubits high and a cubit wide, and from the smaller ledge up to the larger ledge it is four cubits high and a cubit wide. 15The altar hearth is four cubits high, and four horns project upward from the hearth. 16The altar hearth is square, twelve cubits long and twelve cubits wide. 17The upper ledge also is square, fourteen cubits long and fourteen cubits wide, with a rim of half a cubit and a gutter of a cubit all around. The steps of the altar face east."

18Then he said to me, "Son of man, this is what the Sovereign LORD says: These will be the regulations for sacrificing burnt offerings and sprinkling blood upon the altar when it is built: 19You are to give a young bull as a sin offering to the priests, who are Levites, of the family of Zadok, who come near to minister before me, declares the Sovereign LORD. 20You are to take some of its blood and put it on the four horns of the altar and on the four corners of the upper ledge and all around the rim, and so purify the altar and make atonement for it. 21You are to take the bull for the sin offering and burn it in the designated part of the temple area outside the sanctuary.

22"On the second day you are to offer a male goat without defect for a sin offering, and the altar is to be purified as it was purified with the bull. 23When you have finished purifying it, you are to offer a young bull and a ram from the flock, both without defect. 24You are to offer them before the LORD, and the priests are to sprinkle salt on them and sacrifice them as a burnt offering to the LORD.

25"For seven days you are to provide a male goat daily for a sin offering; you are also to provide a young bull and a ram from the flock, both without defect. 26For seven days they are to make atonement for the altar and cleanse it; thus they will dedicate it. 27At the end of these days, from the eighth day on, the priests are to present your burnt offerings and fellow-

[a] 3 Some Hebrew manuscripts and Vulgate; most Hebrew manuscripts *I* [b] 7 Or *their spiritual adultery*; also in verse 9 [c] 7 Or *the corpses*; also in verse 9 [d] 11 Some Hebrew manuscripts and Septuagint; most Hebrew manuscripts *regulations and its whole design* [e] 13 The common cubit was about 1 1/2 feet (about 0.5 meter). [f] 13 That is, about 3 inches (about 8 centimeters) [g] 13 That is, about 9 inches (about 22 centimeters)

ship offerings[a] on the altar. Then I will accept you, declares the Sovereign LORD."

The Prince, the Levites, the Priests

44 Then the man brought me back to the outer gate of the sanctuary, the one facing east, and it was shut. [2]The LORD said to me, "This gate is to remain shut. It must not be opened; no one may enter through it. It is to remain shut because the LORD, the God of Israel, has entered through it. [3]The prince himself is the only one who may sit inside the gateway to eat in the presence of the LORD. He is to enter by way of the portico of the gateway and go out the same way."

[4]Then the man brought me by way of the north gate to the front of the temple. I looked and saw the glory of the LORD filling the temple of the LORD, and I fell face-down.

[5]The LORD said to me, "Son of man, look carefully, listen closely and give attention to everything I tell you concerning all the regulations regarding the temple of the LORD. Give attention to the entrance of the temple and all the exits of the sanctuary. [6]Say to the rebellious house of Israel, 'This is what the Sovereign LORD says: Enough of your detestable practices, O house of Israel! [7]In addition to all your other detestable practices, you brought foreigners uncircumcised in heart and flesh into my sanctuary, desecrating my temple while you offered me food, fat and blood, and you broke my covenant. [8]Instead of carrying out your duty in regard to my holy things, you put others in charge of my sanctuary. [9]This is what the Sovereign LORD says: No foreigner uncircumcised in heart and flesh is to enter my sanctuary, not even the foreigners who live among the Israelites.

[10]" 'The Levites who went far from me when Israel went astray and who wandered from me after their idols must bear the consequences of their sin. [11]They may serve in my sanctuary, having charge of the gates of the temple and serving in it; they may slaughter the burnt offerings and sacrifices for the people and stand before the people and serve them. [12]But because they served them in the presence of their idols and made the house of Israel fall into sin, therefore I have sworn with uplifted hand that they must bear the consequences of their sin, declares the Sovereign LORD. [13]They are not to come near to serve me as priests or come near any of my holy things or my most holy offerings; they must bear the shame of their detestable practices. [14]Yet I will put them in charge of the duties of the temple and all the work that is to be done in it.

[15]" 'But the priests, who are Levites and descendants of Zadok and who faithfully carried out the duties of my sanctuary when the Israelites went astray from me, are to come near to minister before me; they are to stand before me to offer sacrifices of fat and blood, declares the Sovereign LORD. [16]They alone are to enter my sanctuary; they alone are to come near my table to minister before me and perform my service.

[17]" 'When they enter the gates of the inner court, they are to wear linen clothes; they must not wear any woolen garment while ministering at the gates of the inner court or inside the temple. [18]They are to wear linen turbans on their heads and linen undergarments around their waists. They must not wear anything that makes them perspire. [19]When they go out into the outer court where the people are, they are to take off the clothes they have been ministering in and are to leave them in the sacred rooms, and put on other clothes, so that they do not consecrate the people by means of their garments.

[20]" 'They must not shave their heads or let their hair grow long, but they are to keep the hair of their heads trimmed. [21]No priest is to drink wine when he enters the inner court. [22]They must not marry widows or divorced women; they may marry only virgins of Israelite descent or widows of priests. [23]They are to teach my people the difference between the holy and the common and show them how to distinguish between the unclean and the clean.

[24]" 'In any dispute, the priests are to serve as judges and decide it according to my ordinances. They are to keep my laws and my decrees for all my appointed feasts, and they are to keep my Sabbaths holy.

[25]" 'A priest must not defile himself by going near a dead person; however, if the dead person was his father or mother, son or daughter, brother or unmarried sister, then he may defile himself. [26]After he is cleansed, he must wait seven days. [27]On the day he goes into the inner court of the

[a]27 Traditionally *peace offerings*

sanctuary to minister in the sanctuary, he is to offer a sin offering for himself, declares the Sovereign LORD.

28"'I am to be the only inheritance the priests have. You are to give them no possession in Israel; I will be their possession. 29They will eat the grain offerings, the sin offerings and the guilt offerings; and everything in Israel devoted[a] to the LORD will belong to them. 30The best of all the firstfruits and of all your special gifts will belong to the priests. You are to give them the first portion of your ground meal so that a blessing may rest on your household. 31The priests must not eat anything, bird or animal, found dead or torn by wild animals.

Division of the Land

45 "'When you allot the land as an inheritance, you are to present to the LORD a portion of the land as a sacred district, 25,000 cubits long and 20,000[b] cubits wide; the entire area will be holy. 2Of this, a section 500 cubits square is to be for the sanctuary, with 50 cubits around it for open land. 3In the sacred district, measure off a section 25,000 cubits[c] long and 10,000 cubits[d] wide. In it will be the sanctuary, the Most Holy Place. 4It will be the sacred portion of the land for the priests, who minister in the sanctuary and who draw near to minister before the LORD. It will be a place for their houses as well as a holy place for the sanctuary. 5An area 25,000 cubits long and 10,000 cubits wide will belong to the Levites, who serve in the temple, as their possession for towns to live in.[e]

6"'You are to give the city as its property an area 5,000 cubits wide and 25,000 cubits long, adjoining the sacred portion; it will belong to the whole house of Israel.

7"'The prince will have the land bordering each side of the area formed by the sacred district and the property of the city. It will extend westward from the west side and eastward from the east side, running lengthwise from the western to the eastern border parallel to one of the tribal portions. 8This land will be his possession in Israel. And my princes will no longer oppress my people but will allow the house of Israel to possess the land according to their tribes.

9"'This is what the Sovereign LORD says: You have gone far enough, O princes of Israel! Give up your violence and oppression and do what is just and right. Stop dispossessing my people, declares the Sovereign LORD. 10You are to use accurate scales, an accurate ephah[f] and an accurate bath.[g] 11The ephah and the bath are to be the same size, the bath containing a tenth of a homer[h] and the ephah a tenth of a homer; the homer is to be the standard measure for both. 12The shekel[i] is to consist of twenty gerahs. Twenty shekels plus twenty-five shekels plus fifteen shekels equal one mina.[j]

Offerings and Holy Days

13"'This is the special gift you are to offer: a sixth of an ephah from each homer of wheat and a sixth of an ephah from each homer of barley. 14The prescribed portion of oil, measured by the bath, is a tenth of a bath from each cor (which consists of ten baths or one homer, for ten baths are equivalent to a homer). 15Also one sheep is to be taken from every flock of two hundred from the well-watered pastures of Israel. These will be used for the grain offerings, burnt offerings and fellowship offerings[k] to make atonement for the people, declares the Sovereign LORD. 16All the people of the land will participate in this special gift for the use of the prince in Israel. 17It will be the duty of the prince to provide the burnt offerings, grain offerings and drink offerings at the festivals, the New Moons and the Sabbaths—at all the appointed feasts of the house of Israel. He will provide the sin offerings, grain offerings, burnt offerings and fellowship offerings to make atonement for the house of Israel.

18"'This is what the Sovereign LORD says: In the first month on the first day you are to take a young bull without defect and purify the sanctuary. 19The priest is to take some of the blood of the sin offering and put it on the doorposts of the temple, on the four corners of the upper

[a] *29* The Hebrew term refers to the irrevocable giving over of things or persons to the LORD.
[b] *1* Septuagint (see also verses 3 and 5 and 48:9); Hebrew *10,000*
[c] *3* That is, about 7 miles (about 12 kilometers)
[d] *3* That is, about 3 miles (about 5 kilometers)
[e] *5* Septuagint; Hebrew *temple; they will have as their possession 20 rooms*
[f] *10* An ephah was a dry measure.
[g] *10* A bath was a liquid measure.
[h] *11* A homer was a dry measure.
[i] *12* A shekel weighed about 2/5 ounce (about 11.5 grams).
[j] *12* That is, 60 shekels; the common mina was 50 shekels.
[k] *15* Traditionally *peace offerings*; also in verse 17

ledge of the altar and on the gateposts of the inner court. 20You are to do the same on the seventh day of the month for anyone who sins unintentionally or through ignorance; so you are to make atonement for the temple.

21" 'In the first month on the fourteenth day you are to observe the Passover, a feast lasting seven days, during which you shall eat bread made without yeast. 22On that day the prince is to provide a bull as a sin offering for himself and for all the people of the land. 23Every day during the seven days of the Feast he is to provide seven bulls and seven rams without defect as a burnt offering to the LORD, and a male goat for a sin offering. 24He is to provide as a grain offering an ephah for each bull and an ephah for each ram, along with a hin[a] of oil for each ephah.

25" 'During the seven days of the Feast, which begins in the seventh month on the fifteenth day, he is to make the same provision for sin offerings, burnt offerings, grain offerings and oil.

46 " 'This is what the Sovereign LORD says: The gate of the inner court facing east is to be shut on the six working days, but on the Sabbath day and on the day of the New Moon it is to be opened. 2The prince is to enter from the outside through the portico of the gateway and stand by the gatepost. The priests are to sacrifice his burnt offering and his fellowship offerings.[b] He is to worship at the threshold of the gateway and then go out, but the gate will not be shut until evening. 3On the Sabbaths and New Moons the people of the land are to worship in the presence of the LORD at the entrance to that gateway. 4The burnt offering the prince brings to the LORD on the Sabbath day is to be six male lambs and a ram, all without defect. 5The grain offering given with the ram is to be an ephah,[c] and the grain offering with the lambs is to be as much as he pleases, along with a hin[a] of oil for each ephah. 6On the day of the New Moon he is to offer a young bull, six lambs and a ram, all without defect. 7He is to provide as a grain offering one ephah with the bull, one ephah with the ram, and with the lambs as much as he wants to give, along with a hin of oil with each ephah. 8When the prince enters, he is to go in through the portico of the gateway, and he is to come out the same way.

9" 'When the people of the land come before the LORD at the appointed feasts, whoever enters by the north gate to worship is to go out the south gate; and whoever enters by the south gate is to go out the north gate. No one is to return through the gate by which he entered, but each is to go out the opposite gate. 10The prince is to be among them, going in when they go in and going out when they go out.

11" 'At the festivals and the appointed feasts, the grain offering is to be an ephah with a bull, an ephah with a ram, and with the lambs as much as one pleases, along with a hin of oil for each ephah. 12When the prince provides a freewill offering to the LORD—whether a burnt offering or fellowship offerings—the gate facing east is to be opened for him. He shall offer his burnt offering or his fellowship offerings as he does on the Sabbath day. Then he shall go out, and after he has gone out, the gate will be shut.

13" 'Every day you are to provide a year-old lamb without defect for a burnt offering to the LORD; morning by morning you shall provide it. 14You are also to provide with it morning by morning a grain offering, consisting of a sixth of an ephah with a third of a hin of oil to moisten the flour. The presenting of this grain offering to the LORD is a lasting ordinance. 15So the lamb and the grain offering and the oil shall be provided morning by morning for a regular burnt offering.

16" 'This is what the Sovereign LORD says: If the prince makes a gift from his inheritance to one of his sons, it will also belong to his descendants; it is to be their property by inheritance. 17If, however, he makes a gift from his inheritance to one of his servants, the servant may keep it until the year of freedom; then it will revert to the prince. His inheritance belongs to his sons only; it is theirs. 18The prince must not take any of the inheritance of the people, driving them off their property. He is to give his sons their inheritance out of his own property, so that none of my people will be separated from his property.' "

19Then the man brought me through the entrance at the side of the gate to the sacred rooms facing north, which belonged to the priests, and showed me a

[a] 24,5 That is, probably about 4 quarts (about 4 liters)
[b] 2 Traditionally *peace offerings*; also in verse 12
[c] 5 That is, probably about 3/5 bushel (about 22 liters)

WEEKENDING

HOUSEWORK

Household chores and roles in marriage can easily become the source of a couple's most common arguments. To help reach agreement in this area, talk about your "before" and "after" expectations regarding who would carry out the following tasks. What did you expect before you got married? Who do you expect to handle these tasks now—husband, wife or both of you?

1. Work outside the home
2. Prepare meals
3. Clean house
4. Wash dishes
5. Pay bills
6. Take out the trash
7. Repair the car
8. Mow the lawn
9. Do laundry
10. Handle other household tasks

How did your premarital expectations compare with reality? Are you both satisfied with your current balance of responsibilities?

— *Kaye V. Cook*

REVIVE

Saturday: 2 Thessalonians 3:6–13
Sunday: Galatians 6:7–10

Go to page 932 for your next devotional reading.

place at the western end. 20He said to me, "This is the place where the priests will cook the guilt offering and the sin offering and bake the grain offering, to avoid bringing them into the outer court and consecrating the people."

21He then brought me to the outer court and led me around to its four corners, and I saw in each corner another court. 22In the four corners of the outer court were enclosed[a] courts, forty cubits long and thirty cubits wide; each of the courts in the four corners was the same size. 23Around the inside of each of the four courts was a ledge of stone, with places for fire built all around under the ledge. 24He said to me, "These are the kitchens where those who minister at the temple will cook the sacrifices of the people."

The River From the Temple

47 The man brought me back to the entrance of the temple, and I saw water coming out from under the threshold of the temple toward the east (for the temple faced east). The water was coming down from under the south side of the temple, south of the altar. 2He then brought me out through the north gate and led me around the outside to the outer gate facing east, and the water was flowing from the south side.

3As the man went eastward with a measuring line in his hand, he measured off a thousand cubits[b] and then led me through water that was ankle-deep. 4He measured off another thousand cubits and led me through water that was knee-deep. He measured off another thousand and led me through water that was up to the waist. 5He measured off another thousand, but now it was a river that I could not cross, because the water had risen and was deep enough to swim in—a river that no one could cross. 6He asked me, "Son of man, do you see this?"

Then he led me back to the bank of the river. 7When I arrived there, I saw a great number of trees on each side of the river. 8He said to me, "This water flows toward the eastern region and goes down into the Arabah,[c] where it enters the Sea.[d] When it empties into the Sea,[d] the water there becomes fresh. 9Swarms of living creatures will live wherever the river flows. There will be large numbers of fish, because this water flows there and makes the salt water fresh; so where the river flows everything will live. 10Fishermen will stand along the shore; from En Gedi to En Eglaim there will be places for spreading nets. The fish will be of many kinds—like the fish of the Great Sea.[e] 11But the swamps and marshes will not become fresh; they will be left for salt. 12Fruit trees of all kinds will grow on both banks of the river. Their leaves will not wither, nor will their fruit fail. Every month they will bear, because the water from the sanctuary flows to them. Their fruit will serve for food and their leaves for healing."

The Boundaries of the Land

13This is what the Sovereign LORD says: "These are the boundaries by which you are to divide the land for an inheritance among the twelve tribes of Israel, with two portions for Joseph. 14You are to divide it equally among them. Because I swore with uplifted hand to give it to your forefathers, this land will become your inheritance.

15"This is to be the boundary of the land:

"On the north side it will run from the Great Sea by the Hethlon road past Lebo[f] Hamath to Zedad, 16Berothah[g] and Sibraim (which lies on the border between Damascus and Hamath), as far as Hazer Hatticon, which is on the border of Hauran. 17The boundary will extend from the sea to Hazar Enan,[h] along the northern border of Damascus, with the border of Hamath to the north. This will be the north boundary.

18"On the east side the boundary will run between Hauran and Damascus, along the Jordan between Gilead and the land of Israel, to the eastern sea and as far as Tamar.[i] This will be the east boundary.

19"On the south side it will run from Tamar as far as the waters of Meribah

[a]22 The meaning of the Hebrew for this word is uncertain. [b]3 That is, about 1,500 feet (about 450 meters) [c]8 Or *the Jordan Valley* [d]8 That is, the Dead Sea [e]10 That is, the Mediterranean; also in verses 15, 19 and 20 [f]15 Or *past the entrance to* [g]15,16 See Septuagint and Ezekiel 48:1; Hebrew *road to go into Zedad,* 16*Hamath, Berothah* [h]17 Hebrew *Enon,* a variant of *Enan* [i]18 Septuagint and Syriac; Hebrew *Israel. You will measure to the eastern sea*

Kadesh, then along the Wadi ⌊of Egypt⌋
to the Great Sea. This will be the
south boundary.
20"On the west side, the Great Sea will be
the boundary to a point opposite
Lebo[a] Hamath. This will be the west
boundary.

21"You are to distribute this land among yourselves according to the tribes of Israel. 22You are to allot it as an inheritance for yourselves and for the aliens who have settled among you and who have children. You are to consider them as native-born Israelites; along with you they are to be allotted an inheritance among the tribes of Israel. 23In whatever tribe the alien settles, there you are to give him his inheritance," declares the Sovereign LORD.

The Division of the Land

48 "These are the tribes, listed by name: At the northern frontier, Dan will have one portion; it will follow the Hethlon road to Lebo[b] Hamath; Hazar Enan and the northern border of Damascus next to Hamath will be part of its border from the east side to the west side.

2"Asher will have one portion; it will border the territory of Dan from east to west.

3"Naphtali will have one portion; it will border the territory of Asher from east to west.

4"Manasseh will have one portion; it will border the territory of Naphtali from east to west.

5"Ephraim will have one portion; it will border the territory of Manasseh from east to west.

6"Reuben will have one portion; it will border the territory of Ephraim from east to west.

7"Judah will have one portion; it will border the territory of Reuben from east to west.

8"Bordering the territory of Judah from east to west will be the portion you are to present as a special gift. It will be 25,000 cubits[c] wide, and its length from east to west will equal one of the tribal portions; the sanctuary will be in the center of it.

9"The special portion you are to offer to the LORD will be 25,000 cubits long and 10,000 cubits[d] wide. 10This will be the sacred portion for the priests. It will be 25,000 cubits long on the north side, 10,000 cubits wide on the west side, 10,000 cubits wide on the east side and 25,000 cubits long on the south side. In the center of it will be the sanctuary of the LORD. 11This will be for the consecrated priests, the Zadokites, who were faithful in serving me and did not go astray as the Levites did when the Israelites went astray. 12It will be a special gift to them from the sacred portion of the land, a most holy portion, bordering the territory of the Levites.

13"Alongside the territory of the priests, the Levites will have an allotment 25,000 cubits long and 10,000 cubits wide. Its total length will be 25,000 cubits and its width 10,000 cubits. 14They must not sell or exchange any of it. This is the best of the land and must not pass into other hands, because it is holy to the LORD.

15"The remaining area, 5,000 cubits wide and 25,000 cubits long, will be for the common use of the city, for houses and for pastureland. The city will be in the center of it 16and will have these measurements: the north side 4,500 cubits, the south side 4,500 cubits, the east side 4,500 cubits, and the west side 4,500 cubits. 17The pastureland for the city will be 250 cubits on the north, 250 cubits on the south, 250 cubits on the east, and 250 cubits on the west. 18What remains of the area, bordering on the sacred portion and running the length of it, will be 10,000 cubits on the east side and 10,000 cubits on the west side. Its produce will supply food for the workers of the city. 19The workers from the city who farm it will come from all the tribes of Israel. 20The entire portion will be a square, 25,000 cubits on each side. As a special gift you will set aside the sacred portion, along with the property of the city.

21"What remains on both sides of the area formed by the sacred portion and the city property will belong to the prince. It will extend eastward from the 25,000 cubits of the sacred portion to the eastern border, and westward from the 25,000 cubits to the western border. Both these areas running the length of the tribal portions will belong to the prince, and the

[a] 20 Or *opposite the entrance to* [b] 1 Or *to the entrance to* [c] 8 That is, about 7 miles (about 12 kilometers) [d] 9 That is, about 3 miles (about 5 kilometers)

sacred portion with the temple sanctuary will be in the center of them. 22So the property of the Levites and the property of the city will lie in the center of the area that belongs to the prince. The area belonging to the prince will lie between the border of Judah and the border of Benjamin.

23"As for the rest of the tribes: Benjamin will have one portion; it will extend from the east side to the west side.

24"Simeon will have one portion; it will border the territory of Benjamin from east to west.

25"Issachar will have one portion; it will border the territory of Simeon from east to west.

26"Zebulun will have one portion; it will border the territory of Issachar from east to west.

27"Gad will have one portion; it will border the territory of Zebulun from east to west.

28"The southern boundary of Gad will run south from Tamar to the waters of Meribah Kadesh, then along the Wadi ⌊of Egypt⌋ to the Great Sea.[a]

29"This is the land you are to allot as an inheritance to the tribes of Israel, and these will be their portions," declares the Sovereign LORD.

The Gates of the City

30"These will be the exits of the city: Beginning on the north side, which is 4,500 cubits long, 31the gates of the city will be named after the tribes of Israel. The three gates on the north side will be the gate of Reuben, the gate of Judah and the gate of Levi.

32"On the east side, which is 4,500 cubits long, will be three gates: the gate of Joseph, the gate of Benjamin and the gate of Dan.

33"On the south side, which measures 4,500 cubits, will be three gates: the gate of Simeon, the gate of Issachar and the gate of Zebulun.

34"On the west side, which is 4,500 cubits long, will be three gates: the gate of Gad, the gate of Asher and the gate of Naphtali.

35"The distance all around will be 18,000 cubits.

"And the name of the city from that time on will be:

THE LORD IS THERE."

[a]28 That is, the Mediterranean

DANIEL, writing from Babylon during the time of the exile, wants us to know that God controls everything and that the victory always belongs to the Lord and to those who do his will. Even the pagan kings in Babylon must admit this truth. As you read this book, think about how God controls your life and how you will win out over the forces of evil because you obey the Lord.

DANIEL

Daniel's Training in Babylon

1 In the third year of the reign of Jehoiakim king of Judah, Nebuchadnezzar king of Babylon came to Jerusalem and besieged it. 2 And the Lord delivered Jehoiakim king of Judah into his hand, along with some of the articles from the temple of God. These he carried off to the temple of his god in Babylonia[a] and put in the treasure house of his god.

3 Then the king ordered Ashpenaz, chief of his court officials, to bring in some of the Israelites from the royal family and the nobility— 4 young men without any physical defect, handsome, showing aptitude for every kind of learning, well informed, quick to understand, and qualified to serve in the king's palace. He was to teach them the language and literature of the Babylonians.[b] 5 The king assigned them a daily amount of food and wine from the king's table. They were to be trained for three years, and after that they were to enter the king's service.

6 Among these were some from Judah: Daniel, Hananiah, Mishael and Azariah. 7 The chief official gave them new names: to Daniel, the name Belteshazzar; to Hananiah, Shadrach; to Mishael, Meshach; and to Azariah, Abednego.

8 But Daniel resolved not to defile himself with the royal food and wine, and he asked the chief official for permission not to defile himself this way. 9 Now God had caused the official to show favor and sym-

[a] 2 Hebrew *Shinar* [b] 4 Or *Chaldeans*

pathy to Daniel, [10]but the official told Daniel, "I am afraid of my lord the king, who has assigned your[a] food and drink. Why should he see you looking worse than the other young men your age? The king would then have my head because of you."

[11]Daniel then said to the guard whom the chief official had appointed over Daniel, Hananiah, Mishael and Azariah, [12]"Please test your servants for ten days: Give us nothing but vegetables to eat and water to drink. [13]Then compare our appearance with that of the young men who eat the royal food, and treat your servants in accordance with what you see." [14]So he agreed to this and tested them for ten days.

[15]At the end of the ten days they looked healthier and better nourished than any of the young men who ate the royal food. [16]So the guard took away their choice food and the wine they were to drink and gave them vegetables instead.

[17]To these four young men God gave knowledge and understanding of all kinds of literature and learning. And Daniel could understand visions and dreams of all kinds.

[18]At the end of the time set by the king to bring them in, the chief official presented them to Nebuchadnezzar. [19]The king talked with them, and he found none equal to Daniel, Hananiah, Mishael and Azariah; so they entered the king's service. [20]In every matter of wisdom and understanding about which the king questioned them, he found them ten times better than all the magicians and enchanters in his whole kingdom.

[21]And Daniel remained there until the first year of King Cyrus.

Nebuchadnezzar's Dream

2 In the second year of his reign, Nebuchadnezzar had dreams; his mind was troubled and he could not sleep. [2]So the king summoned the magicians, enchanters, sorcerers and astrologers[b] to tell him what he had dreamed. When they came in and stood before the king, [3]he said to them, "I have had a dream that troubles me and I want to know what it means.[c]"

[4]Then the astrologers answered the king in Aramaic,[d] "O king, live forever! Tell your servants the dream, and we will interpret it."

[5]The king replied to the astrologers, "This is what I have firmly decided: If you do not tell me what my dream was and interpret it, I will have you cut into pieces and your houses turned into piles of rubble. [6]But if you tell me the dream and explain it, you will receive from me gifts and rewards and great honor. So tell me the dream and interpret it for me."

[7]Once more they replied, "Let the king tell his servants the dream, and we will interpret it."

[8]Then the king answered, "I am certain that you are trying to gain time, because you realize that this is what I have firmly decided: [9]If you do not tell me the dream, there is just one penalty for you. You have conspired to tell me misleading and wicked things, hoping the situation will change. So then, tell me the dream, and I will know that you can interpret it for me."

[10]The astrologers answered the king, "There is not a man on earth who can do what the king asks! No king, however great and mighty, has ever asked such a thing of any magician or enchanter or astrologer. [11]What the king asks is too difficult. No one can reveal it to the king except the gods, and they do not live among men."

[12]This made the king so angry and furious that he ordered the execution of all the wise men of Babylon. [13]So the decree was issued to put the wise men to death, and men were sent to look for Daniel and his friends to put them to death.

[14]When Arioch, the commander of the king's guard, had gone out to put to death the wise men of Babylon, Daniel spoke to him with wisdom and tact. [15]He asked the king's officer, "Why did the king issue such a harsh decree?" Arioch then explained the matter to Daniel. [16]At this, Daniel went in to the king and asked for time, so that he might interpret the dream for him.

[17]Then Daniel returned to his house and explained the matter to his friends Hananiah, Mishael and Azariah. [18]He urged them to plead for mercy from the God of heaven concerning this mystery, so that he and his friends might not be executed with the rest of the wise men of

[a] *10* The Hebrew for *your* and *you* in this verse is plural. [b] *2* Or *Chaldeans*; also in verses 4, 5 and 10
[c] *3* Or *was* [d] *4* The text from here through chapter 7 is in Aramaic.

Babylon. [19]During the night the mystery
was revealed to Daniel in a vision. Then
Daniel praised the God of heaven [20]and
said:

"Praise be to the name of God for ever
and ever;
wisdom and power are his.
[21]He changes times and seasons;
he sets up kings and deposes them.
He gives wisdom to the wise
and knowledge to the discerning.
[22]He reveals deep and hidden things;
he knows what lies in darkness,
and light dwells with him.
[23]I thank and praise you, O God of my
fathers:
You have given me wisdom and
power,
you have made known to me what we
asked of you,
you have made known to us the
dream of the king."

Daniel Interprets the Dream

[24]Then Daniel went to Arioch, whom
the king had appointed to execute the
wise men of Babylon, and said to him, "Do
not execute the wise men of Babylon.
Take me to the king, and I will interpret
his dream for him."

[25]Arioch took Daniel to the king at once
and said, "I have found a man among the
exiles from Judah who can tell the king
what his dream means."

[26]The king asked Daniel (also called
Belteshazzar), "Are you able to tell me
what I saw in my dream and interpret it?"

[27]Daniel replied, "No wise man, en-
chanter, magician or diviner can explain
to the king the mystery he has asked
about, [28]but there is a God in heaven who
reveals mysteries. He has shown King
Nebuchadnezzar what will happen in
days to come. Your dream and the visions
that passed through your mind as you lay
on your bed are these:

[29]"As you were lying there, O king,
your mind turned to things to come, and
the revealer of mysteries showed you
what is going to happen. [30]As for me, this
mystery has been revealed to me, not be-
cause I have greater wisdom than other
living men, but so that you, O king, may
know the interpretation and that you may
understand what went through your
mind.

[31]"You looked, O king, and there before
you stood a large statue—an enormous,
dazzling statue, awesome in appearance.
[32]The head of the statue was made of pure
gold, its chest and arms of silver, its belly
and thighs of bronze, [33]its legs of iron, its
feet partly of iron and partly of baked clay.
[34]While you were watching, a rock was
cut out, but not by human hands. It struck
the statue on its feet of iron and clay and
smashed them. [35]Then the iron, the clay,
the bronze, the silver and the gold were
broken to pieces at the same time and be-
came like chaff on a threshing floor in the
summer. The wind swept them away
without leaving a trace. But the rock that
struck the statue became a huge mountain
and filled the whole earth.

[36]"This was the dream, and now we will
interpret it to the king. [37]You, O king, are
the king of kings. The God of heaven has
given you dominion and power and might
and glory; [38]in your hands he has placed
mankind and the beasts of the field and
the birds of the air. Wherever they live, he
has made you ruler over them all. You are
that head of gold.

[39]"After you, another kingdom will rise,
inferior to yours. Next, a third kingdom,
one of bronze, will rule over the whole
earth. [40]Finally, there will be a fourth
kingdom, strong as iron—for iron breaks
and smashes everything—and as iron
breaks things to pieces, so it will crush
and break all the others. [41]Just as you saw
that the feet and toes were partly of baked
clay and partly of iron, so this will be a
divided kingdom; yet it will have some of
the strength of iron in it, even as you saw
iron mixed with clay. [42]As the toes were
partly iron and partly clay, so this king-
dom will be partly strong and partly brit-
tle. [43]And just as you saw the iron mixed
with baked clay, so the people will be a
mixture and will not remain united, any
more than iron mixes with clay.

[44]"In the time of those kings, the God of
heaven will set up a kingdom that will
never be destroyed, nor will it be left to
another people. It will crush all those
kingdoms and bring them to an end, but
it will itself endure forever. [45]This is the
meaning of the vision of the rock cut out
of a mountain, but not by human hands—
a rock that broke the iron, the bronze, the
clay, the silver and the gold to pieces.

"The great God has shown the king
what will take place in the future. The
dream is true and the interpretation is
trustworthy."

[46]Then King Nebuchadnezzar fell pros-

trate before Daniel and paid him honor
and ordered that an offering and incense
be presented to him. 47The king said to
Daniel, "Surely your God is the God of
gods and the Lord of kings and a revealer
of mysteries, for you were able to reveal
this mystery."
48Then the king placed Daniel in a high
position and lavished many gifts on him.
He made him ruler over the entire prov-
ince of Babylon and placed him in charge
of all its wise men. 49Moreover, at Daniel's
request the king appointed Shadrach, Me-
shach and Abednego administrators over
the province of Babylon, while Daniel
himself remained at the royal court.

The Image of Gold and the Fiery Furnace

3 King Nebuchadnezzar made an image
of gold, ninety feet high and nine
feet[a] wide, and set it up on the plain of
Dura in the province of Babylon. 2He then
summoned the satraps, prefects, gover-
nors, advisers, treasurers, judges, magis-
trates and all the other provincial officials
to come to the dedication of the image he
had set up. 3So the satraps, prefects, gov-
ernors, advisers, treasurers, judges, mag-
istrates and all the other provincial offi-
cials assembled for the dedication of the
image that King Nebuchadnezzar had set
up, and they stood before it.
4Then the herald loudly proclaimed,
"This is what you are commanded to do,
O peoples, nations and men of every lan-
guage: 5As soon as you hear the sound of
the horn, flute, zither, lyre, harp, pipes
and all kinds of music, you must fall down
and worship the image of gold that King
Nebuchadnezzar has set up. 6Whoever
does not fall down and worship will im-
mediately be thrown into a blazing fur-
nace."
7Therefore, as soon as they heard the
sound of the horn, flute, zither, lyre, harp
and all kinds of music, all the peoples, na-
tions and men of every language fell down
and worshiped the image of gold that King
Nebuchadnezzar had set up.
8At this time some astrologers[b] came
forward and denounced the Jews. 9They
said to King Nebuchadnezzar, "O king,
live forever! 10You have issued a decree, O
king, that everyone who hears the sound
of the horn, flute, zither, lyre, harp, pipes
and all kinds of music must fall down and
worship the image of gold, 11and that
whoever does not fall down and worship
will be thrown into a blazing furnace.
12But there are some Jews whom you have
set over the affairs of the province of Bab-
ylon—Shadrach, Meshach and Abedne-
go—who pay no attention to you, O king.
They neither serve your gods nor worship
the image of gold you have set up."
13Furious with rage, Nebuchadnezzar
summoned Shadrach, Meshach and Abed-
nego. So these men were brought before
the king, 14and Nebuchadnezzar said to
them, "Is it true, Shadrach, Meshach and
Abednego, that you do not serve my gods
or worship the image of gold I have set
up? 15Now when you hear the sound of
the horn, flute, zither, lyre, harp, pipes
and all kinds of music, if you are ready to
fall down and worship the image I made,
very good. But if you do not worship it,
you will be thrown immediately into a
blazing furnace. Then what god will be
able to rescue you from my hand?"
16Shadrach, Meshach and Abednego re-
plied to the king, "O Nebuchadnezzar, we
do not need to defend ourselves before
you in this matter. 17If we are thrown into
the blazing furnace, the God we serve is
able to save us from it, and he will rescue
us from your hand, O king. 18But even if
he does not, we want you to know,
O king, that we will not serve your gods or
worship the image of gold you have
set up."
19Then Nebuchadnezzar was furious
with Shadrach, Meshach and Abednego,
and his attitude toward them changed. He
ordered the furnace heated seven times
hotter than usual 20and commanded some
of the strongest soldiers in his army to tie
up Shadrach, Meshach and Abednego and
throw them into the blazing furnace. 21So
these men, wearing their robes, trousers,
turbans and other clothes, were bound
and thrown into the blazing furnace.
22The king's command was so urgent and
the furnace so hot that the flames of the
fire killed the soldiers who took up Sha-
drach, Meshach and Abednego, 23and
these three men, firmly tied, fell into the
blazing furnace.

[a] 1 Aramaic *sixty cubits high and six cubits wide* (about 27 meters high and 2.7 meters wide) [b] 8 Or *Chaldeans*

24Then King Nebuchadnezzar leaped to
his feet in amazement and asked his ad-
visers, "Weren't there three men that we
tied up and threw into the fire?"
They replied, "Certainly, O king."
25He said, "Look! I see four men walk-
ing around in the fire, unbound and un-
harmed, and the fourth looks like a son of
the gods."
26Nebuchadnezzar then approached
the opening of the blazing furnace and
shouted, "Shadrach, Meshach and Abed-
nego, servants of the Most High God,
come out! Come here!"
So Shadrach, Meshach and Abednego
came out of the fire, 27and the satraps,
prefects, governors and royal advisers
crowded around them. They saw that the
fire had not harmed their bodies, nor was
a hair of their heads singed; their robes
were not scorched, and there was no smell
of fire on them.
28Then Nebuchadnezzar said, "Praise
be to the God of Shadrach, Meshach and
Abednego, who has sent his angel and res-
cued his servants! They trusted in him
and defied the king's command and were
willing to give up their lives rather than
serve or worship any god except their own
God. 29Therefore I decree that the people
of any nation or language who say any-
thing against the God of Shadrach, Me-
shach and Abednego be cut into pieces
and their houses be turned into piles of
rubble, for no other god can save in this
way."
30Then the king promoted Shadrach,
Meshach and Abednego in the province of
Babylon.

Nebuchadnezzar's Dream of a Tree

4 King Nebuchadnezzar,

To the peoples, nations and men of
every language, who live in all the
world:

May you prosper greatly!

2It is my pleasure to tell you about
the miraculous signs and wonders
that the Most High God has per-
formed for me.

3How great are his signs,
how mighty his wonders!
His kingdom is an eternal
kingdom;
his dominion endures from
generation to generation.

4I, Nebuchadnezzar, was at home
in my palace, contented and prosper-
ous. 5I had a dream that made me
afraid. As I was lying in my bed, the
images and visions that passed
through my mind terrified me. 6So I
commanded that all the wise men of
Babylon be brought before me to in-
terpret the dream for me. 7When the
magicians, enchanters, astrologers[a]
and diviners came, I told them the
dream, but they could not interpret it
for me. 8Finally, Daniel came into my
presence and I told him the dream.
(He is called Belteshazzar, after the
name of my god, and the spirit of the
holy gods is in him.)
9I said, "Belteshazzar, chief of the
magicians, I know that the spirit of
the holy gods is in you, and no mys-
tery is too difficult for you. Here is
my dream; interpret it for me.
10These are the visions I saw while ly-
ing in my bed: I looked, and there be-
fore me stood a tree in the middle of
the land. Its height was enormous.
11The tree grew large and strong and
its top touched the sky; it was visible
to the ends of the earth. 12Its leaves
were beautiful, its fruit abundant,
and on it was food for all. Under it the
beasts of the field found shelter, and
the birds of the air lived in its
branches; from it every creature was
fed.
13"In the visions I saw while lying
in my bed, I looked, and there before
me was a messenger,[b] a holy one,
coming down from heaven. 14He
called in a loud voice: 'Cut down the
tree and trim off its branches; strip off
its leaves and scatter its fruit. Let the
animals flee from under it and the
birds from its branches. 15But let the
stump and its roots, bound with iron
and bronze, remain in the ground, in
the grass of the field.
" 'Let him be drenched with the
dew of heaven, and let him live with
the animals among the plants of the
earth. 16Let his mind be changed
from that of a man and let him be giv-

[a]7 Or *Chaldeans* [b]13 Or *watchman*; also in verses 17 and 23

en the mind of an animal, till seven times[a] pass by for him.

17" 'The decision is announced by messengers, the holy ones declare the verdict, so that the living may know that the Most High is sovereign over the kingdoms of men and gives them to anyone he wishes and sets over them the lowliest of men.'

18"This is the dream that I, King Nebuchadnezzar, had. Now, Belteshazzar, tell me what it means, for none of the wise men in my kingdom can interpret it for me. But you can, because the spirit of the holy gods is in you."

Daniel Interprets the Dream

19Then Daniel (also called Belteshazzar) was greatly perplexed for a time, and his thoughts terrified him. So the king said, "Belteshazzar, do not let the dream or its meaning alarm you."

Belteshazzar answered, "My lord, if only the dream applied to your enemies and its meaning to your adversaries! 20The tree you saw, which grew large and strong, with its top touching the sky, visible to the whole earth, 21with beautiful leaves and abundant fruit, providing food for all, giving shelter to the beasts of the field, and having nesting places in its branches for the birds of the air—22you, O king, are that tree! You have become great and strong; your greatness has grown until it reaches the sky, and your dominion extends to distant parts of the earth.

23"You, O king, saw a messenger, a holy one, coming down from heaven and saying, 'Cut down the tree and destroy it, but leave the stump, bound with iron and bronze, in the grass of the field, while its roots remain in the ground. Let him be drenched with the dew of heaven; let him live like the wild animals, until seven times pass by for him.'

24"This is the interpretation, O king, and this is the decree the Most High has issued against my lord the king: 25You will be driven away from people and will live with the wild animals; you will eat grass like cattle and be drenched with the dew of heaven. Seven times will pass by for you until you acknowledge that the Most High is sovereign over the kingdoms of men and gives them to anyone he wishes. 26The command to leave the stump of the tree with its roots means that your kingdom will be restored to you when you acknowledge that Heaven rules. 27Therefore, O king, be pleased to accept my advice: Renounce your sins by doing what is right, and your wickedness by being kind to the oppressed. It may be that then your prosperity will continue."

The Dream Is Fulfilled

28All this happened to King Nebuchadnezzar. 29Twelve months later, as the king was walking on the roof of the royal palace of Babylon, 30he said, "Is not this the great Babylon I have built as the royal residence, by my mighty power and for the glory of my majesty?"

31The words were still on his lips when a voice came from heaven, "This is what is decreed for you, King Nebuchadnezzar: Your royal authority has been taken from you. 32You will be driven away from people and will live with the wild animals; you will eat grass like cattle. Seven times will pass by for you until you acknowledge that the Most High is sovereign over the kingdoms of men and gives them to anyone he wishes."

33Immediately what had been said about Nebuchadnezzar was fulfilled. He was driven away from people and ate grass like cattle. His body was drenched with the dew of heaven until his hair grew like the feathers of an eagle and his nails like the claws of a bird.

34At the end of that time, I, Nebuchadnezzar, raised my eyes toward heaven, and my sanity was restored. Then I praised the Most High; I honored and glorified him who lives forever.

His dominion is an eternal dominion;
his kingdom endures from
generation to generation.
35All the peoples of the earth
are regarded as nothing.

[a]16 Or *years*; also in verses 23, 25 and 32

He does as he pleases
with the powers of heaven
and the peoples of the earth.
No one can hold back his hand
or say to him: "What have you
done?"

36At the same time that my sanity
was restored, my honor and splendor
were returned to me for the glory of
my kingdom. My advisers and nobles
sought me out, and I was restored to
my throne and became even greater
than before. 37Now I, Nebuchadnez-
zar, praise and exalt and glorify the
King of heaven, because everything
he does is right and all his ways are
just. And those who walk in pride he
is able to humble.

The Writing on the Wall

5 King Belshazzar gave a great banquet
for a thousand of his nobles and
drank wine with them. 2While Belshazzar
was drinking his wine, he gave orders to
bring in the gold and silver goblets that

VERSE FOR THE DAY: Daniel 5:12

AUTHOR: Jim and Sally Conway

PASSAGE FOR THE DAY: Daniel 5:1–30

Communicating About Decisions

One big difference between men and women is the way they arrive at decisions. Women tend to think out loud: They talk through their thinking process. But men generally make decisions—especially regarding their own personal growth—very privately. Typically, a man doesn't express his decision to make a change until it has already been finalized in his mind.

One of the most tragic consequences of this difference in communication style shows up when one spouses realizes the marriage is in trouble. If the woman senses the trouble, she'll verbalize what she's feeling over a number of months, maybe even years. But if the husband senses that all is not right, he very often won't say anything. Then one day he'll come home and announce that he's moving out. By the time he expresses his feelings, he's already made the decision.

If each spouse, from day to day, would work harder at communicating in ways their mate can understand, many marital breakups could be avoided.

MARRIAGE BUILDERS

♦ *How do each of you communicate during the decision-making process?*

♦ *How could you communicate more effectively with each other when things are bothering you?*

Additional Scripture Readings
Proverbs 3:5–6; Joshua 24:15

Go to page 935 for your next devotional reading.

Nebuchadnezzar his father[a] had taken from the temple in Jerusalem, so that the king and his nobles, his wives and his concubines might drink from them. 3So they brought in the gold goblets that had been taken from the temple of God in Jerusalem, and the king and his nobles, his wives and his concubines drank from them. 4As they drank the wine, they praised the gods of gold and silver, of bronze, iron, wood and stone.

5Suddenly the fingers of a human hand appeared and wrote on the plaster of the wall, near the lampstand in the royal palace. The king watched the hand as it wrote. 6His face turned pale and he was so frightened that his knees knocked together and his legs gave way.

7The king called out for the enchanters, astrologers[b] and diviners to be brought and said to these wise men of Babylon, "Whoever reads this writing and tells me what it means will be clothed in purple and have a gold chain placed around his neck, and he will be made the third highest ruler in the kingdom."

8Then all the king's wise men came in, but they could not read the writing or tell the king what it meant. 9So King Belshazzar became even more terrified and his face grew more pale. His nobles were baffled.

10The queen,[c] hearing the voices of the king and his nobles, came into the banquet hall. "O king, live forever!" she said. "Don't be alarmed! Don't look so pale! 11There is a man in your kingdom who has the spirit of the holy gods in him. In the time of your father he was found to have insight and intelligence and wisdom like that of the gods. King Nebuchadnezzar your father—your father the king, I say—appointed him chief of the magicians, enchanters, astrologers and diviners. 12This man Daniel, whom the king called Belteshazzar, was found to have a keen mind and knowledge and understanding, and also the ability to interpret dreams, explain riddles and solve difficult problems. Call for Daniel, and he will tell you what the writing means."

13So Daniel was brought before the king, and the king said to him, "Are you Daniel, one of the exiles my father the king brought from Judah? 14I have heard that the spirit of the gods is in you and that you have insight, intelligence and outstanding wisdom. 15The wise men and enchanters were brought before me to read this writing and tell me what it means, but they could not explain it. 16Now I have heard that you are able to give interpretations and to solve difficult problems. If you can read this writing and tell me what it means, you will be clothed in purple and have a gold chain placed around your neck, and you will be made the third highest ruler in the kingdom."

17Then Daniel answered the king, "You may keep your gifts for yourself and give your rewards to someone else. Nevertheless, I will read the writing for the king and tell him what it means.

18"O king, the Most High God gave your father Nebuchadnezzar sovereignty and greatness and glory and splendor. 19Because of the high position he gave him, all the peoples and nations and men of every language dreaded and feared him. Those the king wanted to put to death, he put to death; those he wanted to spare, he spared; those he wanted to promote, he promoted; and those he wanted to humble, he humbled. 20But when his heart became arrogant and hardened with pride, he was deposed from his royal throne and stripped of his glory. 21He was driven away from people and given the mind of an animal; he lived with the wild donkeys and ate grass like cattle; and his body was drenched with the dew of heaven, until he acknowledged that the Most High God is sovereign over the kingdoms of men and sets over them anyone he wishes.

22"But you his son,[d] O Belshazzar, have not humbled yourself, though you knew all this. 23Instead, you have set yourself up against the Lord of heaven. You had the goblets from his temple brought to you, and you and your nobles, your wives and your concubines drank wine from them. You praised the gods of silver and gold, of bronze, iron, wood and stone, which cannot see or hear or understand. But you did not honor the God who holds in his hand your life and all your ways. 24Therefore he sent the hand that wrote the inscription.

25"This is the inscription that was written:

[a] 2 Or *ancestor*; or *predecessor*; also in verses 11, 13 and 18
[b] 7 Or *Chaldeans*; also in verse 11
[c] 10 Or *queen mother*
[d] 22 Or *descendant*; or *successor*

MENE, MENE, TEKEL, PARSIN[a]

26"This is what these words mean:

Mene[b]: God has numbered the
days of your reign and
brought it to an end.
27*Tekel*[c]: You have been weighed
on the scales and found
wanting.
28*Peres*[d]: Your kingdom is divided
and given to the Medes and
Persians."

29Then at Belshazzar's command, Daniel was clothed in purple, a gold chain was placed around his neck, and he was proclaimed the third highest ruler in the kingdom.

30That very night Belshazzar, king of the Babylonians,[e] was slain, 31and Darius the Mede took over the kingdom, at the age of sixty-two.

Daniel in the Den of Lions

6 It pleased Darius to appoint 120 satraps to rule throughout the kingdom, 2with three administrators over them, one of whom was Daniel. The satraps were made accountable to them so that the king might not suffer loss. 3Now Daniel so distinguished himself among the administrators and the satraps by his exceptional qualities that the king planned to set him over the whole kingdom. 4At this, the administrators and the satraps tried to find grounds for charges against Daniel in his conduct of government affairs, but they were unable to do so. They could find no corruption in him, because he was trustworthy and neither corrupt nor negligent. 5Finally these men said, "We will never find any basis for charges against this man Daniel unless it has something to do with the law of his God."

6So the administrators and the satraps went as a group to the king and said: "O King Darius, live forever! 7The royal administrators, prefects, satraps, advisers and governors have all agreed that the king should issue an edict and enforce the decree that anyone who prays to any god or man during the next thirty days, except to you, O king, shall be thrown into the lions' den. 8Now, O king, issue the decree and put it in writing so that it cannot be altered—in accordance with the laws of the Medes and Persians, which cannot be repealed." 9So King Darius put the decree in writing.

10Now when Daniel learned that the decree had been published, he went home to his upstairs room where the windows opened toward Jerusalem. Three times a day he got down on his knees and prayed, giving thanks to his God, just as he had done before. 11Then these men went as a group and found Daniel praying and asking God for help. 12So they went to the king and spoke to him about his royal decree: "Did you not publish a decree that during the next thirty days anyone who prays to any god or man except to you, O king, would be thrown into the lions' den?"

The king answered, "The decree stands—in accordance with the laws of the Medes and Persians, which cannot be repealed."

13Then they said to the king, "Daniel, who is one of the exiles from Judah, pays no attention to you, O king, or to the decree you put in writing. He still prays three times a day." 14When the king heard this, he was greatly distressed; he was determined to rescue Daniel and made every effort until sundown to save him.

15Then the men went as a group to the king and said to him, "Remember, O king, that according to the law of the Medes and Persians no decree or edict that the king issues can be changed."

16So the king gave the order, and they brought Daniel and threw him into the lions' den. The king said to Daniel, "May your God, whom you serve continually, rescue you!"

17A stone was brought and placed over the mouth of the den, and the king sealed it with his own signet ring and with the rings of his nobles, so that Daniel's situation might not be changed. 18Then the king returned to his palace and spent the night without eating and without any entertainment being brought to him. And he could not sleep.

19At the first light of dawn, the king got up and hurried to the lions' den. 20When he came near the den, he called to Daniel in an anguished voice, "Daniel, servant of the living God, has your God, whom you

[a]25 Aramaic *UPARSIN* (that is, *AND PARSIN*) [b]26 *Mene* can mean *numbered* or *mina* (a unit of money). [c]27 *Tekel* can mean *weighed* or *shekel.* [d]28 *Peres* (the singular of *Parsin*) can mean *divided* or *Persia* or *a half mina* or *a half shekel.* [e]30 Or *Chaldeans*

serve continually, been able to rescue you
from the lions?"
21Daniel answered, "O king, live forever! 22My God sent his angel, and he shut
the mouths of the lions. They have not
hurt me, because I was found innocent in
his sight. Nor have I ever done any wrong
before you, O king."
23The king was overjoyed and gave orders to lift Daniel out of the den. And
when Daniel was lifted from the den, no
wound was found on him, because he had
trusted in his God.
24At the king's command, the men who
had falsely accused Daniel were brought
in and thrown into the lions' den, along
with their wives and children. And before
they reached the floor of the den, the lions
overpowered them and crushed all their
bones.
25Then King Darius wrote to all the peoples, nations and men of every language
throughout the land:

"May you prosper greatly!

26"I issue a decree that in every
part of my kingdom people must fear
and reverence the God of Daniel.

"For he is the living God

VERSE FOR THE DAY: Daniel 6:10

AUTHOR: Calvin Miller

PASSAGE FOR THE DAY: Daniel 6:2–23

No Hurry

One barrier to full intimacy with the Savior is hurriedness. Intimacy may not be rushed. To meet with the Son of God takes time. We can't dash into his presence and choke down spiritual inwardness before we hurry to our one o'clock appointment. Inwardness is time-consuming, open only to minds willing to sample spirituality in small bites, savoring each one.

Intimacy with Christ comes from entering his presence with inner peace rather than bursting into his presence from the hassles of life. A relaxed contemplation of the indwelling Christ allows for an inner communion impossible to achieve while oppressed by busyness and care.

Holy living is not abrupt living. No one who hurries into the presence of God is content to remain for long. Those who hurry in, hurry out.

MARRIAGE BUILDERS

♦ *When you take time out of a hectic day to spend time with God, what things help you to forget your busy schedule and focus on him?*

♦ *What difference does inner peace make in the daily pace of your life?*

Additional Scripture Readings
Psalm 46:10; 90:14; Isaiah 30:15

Go to page 938 for your next devotional reading.

and he endures forever;
his kingdom will not be destroyed,
his dominion will never end.
27He rescues and he saves;
he performs signs and wonders
in the heavens and on the earth.
He has rescued Daniel
from the power of the lions."

28So Daniel prospered during the reign of Darius and the reign of Cyrus[a] the Persian.

Daniel's Dream of Four Beasts

7 In the first year of Belshazzar king of Babylon, Daniel had a dream, and visions passed through his mind as he was lying on his bed. He wrote down the substance of his dream.

2Daniel said: "In my vision at night I looked, and there before me were the four winds of heaven churning up the great sea. 3Four great beasts, each different from the others, came up out of the sea.

4"The first was like a lion, and it had the wings of an eagle. I watched until its wings were torn off and it was lifted from the ground so that it stood on two feet like a man, and the heart of a man was given to it.

5"And there before me was a second beast, which looked like a bear. It was raised up on one of its sides, and it had three ribs in its mouth between its teeth. It was told, 'Get up and eat your fill of flesh!'

6"After that, I looked, and there before me was another beast, one that looked like a leopard. And on its back it had four wings like those of a bird. This beast had four heads, and it was given authority to rule.

7"After that, in my vision at night I looked, and there before me was a fourth beast—terrifying and frightening and very powerful. It had large iron teeth; it crushed and devoured its victims and trampled underfoot whatever was left. It was different from all the former beasts, and it had ten horns.

8"While I was thinking about the horns, there before me was another horn, a little one, which came up among them; and three of the first horns were uprooted before it. This horn had eyes like the eyes of a man and a mouth that spoke boastfully.

9"As I looked,
"thrones were set in place,
and the Ancient of Days took his seat.
His clothing was as white as snow;
the hair of his head was white like wool.
His throne was flaming with fire,
and its wheels were all ablaze.
10A river of fire was flowing,
coming out from before him.
Thousands upon thousands attended him;
ten thousand times ten thousand stood before him.
The court was seated,
and the books were opened.

11"Then I continued to watch because of the boastful words the horn was speaking. I kept looking until the beast was slain and its body destroyed and thrown into the blazing fire. 12(The other beasts had been stripped of their authority, but were allowed to live for a period of time.)

13"In my vision at night I looked, and there before me was one like a son of man, coming with the clouds of heaven. He approached the Ancient of Days and was led into his presence. 14He was given authority, glory and sovereign power; all peoples, nations and men of every language worshiped him. His dominion is an everlasting dominion that will not pass away, and his kingdom is one that will never be destroyed.

The Interpretation of the Dream

15"I, Daniel, was troubled in spirit, and the visions that passed through my mind disturbed me. 16I approached one of those standing there and asked him the true meaning of all this.

"So he told me and gave me the interpretation of these things: 17'The four great beasts are four kingdoms that will rise from the earth. 18But the saints of the Most High will receive the kingdom and will possess it forever—yes, for ever and ever.'

19"Then I wanted to know the true meaning of the fourth beast, which was different from all the others and most terrifying, with its iron teeth and bronze claws—the beast that crushed and devoured its victims and trampled underfoot whatever was left. 20I also wanted to know about the ten horns on its head and about

[a]28 Or *Darius, that is, the reign of Cyrus*

the other horn that came up, before which
three of them fell—the horn that looked
more imposing than the others and that
had eyes and a mouth that spoke boastfully. 21As I watched, this horn was waging
war against the saints and defeating them,
22until the Ancient of Days came and pronounced judgment in favor of the saints of
the Most High, and the time came when
they possessed the kingdom.

23"He gave me this explanation: 'The
fourth beast is a fourth kingdom that will
appear on earth. It will be different from
all the other kingdoms and will devour the
whole earth, trampling it down and crushing it. 24The ten horns are ten kings who
will come from this kingdom. After them
another king will arise, different from the
earlier ones; he will subdue three kings.
25He will speak against the Most High and
oppress his saints and try to change the
set times and the laws. The saints will be
handed over to him for a time, times and
half a time.[a]

26" 'But the court will sit, and his power
will be taken away and completely destroyed forever. 27Then the sovereignty,
power and greatness of the kingdoms under the whole heaven will be handed over
to the saints, the people of the Most High.
His kingdom will be an everlasting kingdom, and all rulers will worship and obey
him.'

28"This is the end of the matter. I, Daniel, was deeply troubled by my thoughts,
and my face turned pale, but I kept the
matter to myself."

Daniel's Vision of a Ram and a Goat

8 In the third year of King Belshazzar's
reign, I, Daniel, had a vision, after the
one that had already appeared to me. 2In
my vision I saw myself in the citadel of
Susa in the province of Elam; in the vision
I was beside the Ulai Canal. 3I looked up,
and there before me was a ram with two
horns, standing beside the canal, and the
horns were long. One of the horns was
longer than the other but grew up later. 4I
watched the ram as he charged toward the
west and the north and the south. No animal could stand against him, and none
could rescue from his power. He did as he
pleased and became great.

5As I was thinking about this, suddenly
a goat with a prominent horn between his
eyes came from the west, crossing the
whole earth without touching the ground.
6He came toward the two-horned ram I
had seen standing beside the canal and
charged at him in great rage. 7I saw him
attack the ram furiously, striking the ram
and shattering his two horns. The ram
was powerless to stand against him; the
goat knocked him to the ground and trampled on him, and none could rescue the
ram from his power. 8The goat became
very great, but at the height of his power
his large horn was broken off, and in its
place four prominent horns grew up toward the four winds of heaven.

9Out of one of them came another horn,
which started small but grew in power to
the south and to the east and toward the
Beautiful Land. 10It grew until it reached
the host of the heavens, and it threw some
of the starry host down to the earth and
trampled on them. 11It set itself up to be
as great as the Prince of the host; it took
away the daily sacrifice from him, and the
place of his sanctuary was brought low.
12Because of rebellion, the host [of the
saints,][b] and the daily sacrifice were given
over to it. It prospered in everything it did,
and truth was thrown to the ground.

13Then I heard a holy one speaking, and
another holy one said to him, "How long
will it take for the vision to be fulfilled—
the vision concerning the daily sacrifice,
the rebellion that causes desolation, and
the surrender of the sanctuary and of the
host that will be trampled underfoot?"

14He said to me, "It will take 2,300 evenings and mornings; then the sanctuary
will be reconsecrated."

The Interpretation of the Vision

15While I, Daniel, was watching the vision and trying to understand it, there before me stood one who looked like a man.
16And I heard a man's voice from the Ulai
calling, "Gabriel, tell this man the meaning of the vision."

17As he came near the place where I was
standing, I was terrified and fell prostrate.
"Son of man," he said to me, "understand
that the vision concerns the time of the
end."

18While he was speaking to me, I was in
a deep sleep, with my face to the ground.
Then he touched me and raised me to my
feet.

19He said: "I am going to tell you what
will happen later in the time of wrath, be-

[a]25 Or *for a year, two years and half a year*
[b]12 Or *rebellion, the armies*

cause the vision concerns the appointed time of the end.[a] 20The two-horned ram that you saw represents the kings of Media and Persia. 21The shaggy goat is the king of Greece, and the large horn between his eyes is the first king. 22The four horns that replaced the one that was broken off represent four kingdoms that will emerge from his nation but will not have the same power.

23"In the latter part of their reign, when rebels have become completely wicked, a stern-faced king, a master of intrigue, will arise. 24He will become very strong, but not by his own power. He will cause astounding devastation and will succeed in whatever he does. He will destroy the mighty men and the holy people. 25He will cause deceit to prosper, and he will consider himself superior. When they feel secure, he will destroy many and take his stand against the Prince of princes. Yet he will be destroyed, but not by human power.

26"The vision of the evenings and mornings that has been given you is true, but seal up the vision, for it concerns the distant future."

27I, Daniel, was exhausted and lay ill for several days. Then I got up and went about the king's business. I was appalled by the vision; it was beyond understanding.

Daniel's Prayer

9 In the first year of Darius son of Xerxes[b] (a Mede by descent), who was made ruler over the Babylonian[c] kingdom— 2in the first year of his reign, I, Daniel, understood from the Scriptures,

[a] 19 Or *because the end will be at the appointed time*

[b] 1 Hebrew *Ahasuerus*

[c] 1 Or *Chaldean*

VERSE FOR THE DAY:
Daniel 9:4

AUTHOR:
Jill and Stuart Briscoe

PASSAGE FOR THE DAY:
Daniel 9:1–19

The Diplomacy of Prayer

Couples often fail to pray together because there's a shyness—especially when one spouse has been on the Christian pilgrimage longer than the other. The less experienced spouse may feel intimidated about praying out loud with another person. And sometimes one spouse pushes the other into spiritual exercises that he or she isn't ready for. This is unwise. Before they begin, both must recognize the value of praying together. If one person is not convinced it's important, then it's an imposition.

MARRIAGE BUILDERS

♦ *Is one of you more comfortable with praying out loud than the other?*

♦ *What topics would you feel most comfortable praying about together?*

Additional Scripture Readings
Romans 14:1; 1 Thessalonians 5:16–18

Go to page 942 for your next devotional reading.

according to the word of the LORD given to
Jeremiah the prophet, that the desolation
of Jerusalem would last seventy years. 3So
I turned to the Lord God and pleaded with
him in prayer and petition, in fasting, and
in sackcloth and ashes.
4I prayed to the LORD my God and con-
fessed:

"O Lord, the great and awesome
God, who keeps his covenant of love
with all who love him and obey his
commands, 5we have sinned and
done wrong. We have been wicked
and have rebelled; we have turned
away from your commands and laws.
6We have not listened to your ser-
vants the prophets, who spoke in
your name to our kings, our princes
and our fathers, and to all the people
of the land.
7"Lord, you are righteous, but this
day we are covered with shame—the
men of Judah and people of Jerusa-
lem and all Israel, both near and far,
in all the countries where you have
scattered us because of our unfaith-
fulness to you. 8O LORD, we and our
kings, our princes and our fathers are
covered with shame because we have
sinned against you. 9The Lord our
God is merciful and forgiving, even
though we have rebelled against him;
10we have not obeyed the LORD our
God or kept the laws he gave us
through his servants the prophets.
11All Israel has transgressed your law
and turned away, refusing to obey
you.
"Therefore the curses and sworn
judgments written in the Law of Mo-
ses, the servant of God, have been
poured out on us, because we have
sinned against you. 12You have ful-
filled the words spoken against us
and against our rulers by bringing
upon us great disaster. Under the
whole heaven nothing has ever been
done like what has been done to Jeru-
salem. 13Just as it is written in the
Law of Moses, all this disaster has
come upon us, yet we have not
sought the favor of the LORD our God
by turning from our sins and giving
attention to your truth. 14The LORD
did not hesitate to bring the disaster
upon us, for the LORD our God is righ-
teous in everything he does; yet we
have not obeyed him.
15"Now, O Lord our God, who
brought your people out of Egypt
with a mighty hand and who made
for yourself a name that endures to
this day, we have sinned, we have
done wrong. 16O Lord, in keeping
with all your righteous acts, turn
away your anger and your wrath
from Jerusalem, your city, your holy
hill. Our sins and the iniquities of our
fathers have made Jerusalem and
your people an object of scorn to all
those around us.
17"Now, our God, hear the prayers
and petitions of your servant. For
your sake, O Lord, look with favor on
your desolate sanctuary. 18Give ear,
O God, and hear; open your eyes and
see the desolation of the city that
bears your Name. We do not make
requests of you because we are righ-
teous, but because of your great mer-
cy. 19O Lord, listen! O Lord, forgive!
O Lord, hear and act! For your sake,
O my God, do not delay, because
your city and your people bear your
Name."

The Seventy "Sevens"

20While I was speaking and praying,
confessing my sin and the sin of my peo-
ple Israel and making my request to the
LORD my God for his holy hill— 21while I
was still in prayer, Gabriel, the man I had
seen in the earlier vision, came to me in
swift flight about the time of the evening
sacrifice. 22He instructed me and said to
me, "Daniel, I have now come to give you
insight and understanding. 23As soon as
you began to pray, an answer was given,
which I have come to tell you, for you are
highly esteemed. Therefore, consider the
message and understand the vision:
24"Seventy 'sevens'[a] are decreed for
your people and your holy city to finish[b]
transgression, to put an end to sin, to
atone for wickedness, to bring in everlast-
ing righteousness, to seal up vision and
prophecy and to anoint the most holy.[c]
25"Know and understand this: From the
issuing of the decree[d] to restore and re-
build Jerusalem until the Anointed One,[e]
the ruler, comes, there will be seven 'sev-

[a]24 Or *'weeks'*; also in verses 25 and 26 [b]24 Or *restrain* [c]24 Or *Most Holy Place*; or *most holy One* [d]25 Or *word* [e]25 Or *an anointed one*; also in verse 26

ens,' and sixty-two 'sevens.' It will be rebuilt with streets and a trench, but in times of trouble. 26After the sixty-two 'sevens,' the Anointed One will be cut off and will have nothing.[a] The people of the ruler who will come will destroy the city and the sanctuary. The end will come like a flood: War will continue until the end, and desolations have been decreed. 27He will confirm a covenant with many for one 'seven.'[b] In the middle of the 'seven'[b] he will put an end to sacrifice and offering. And on a wing ⌊of the temple⌋ he will set up an abomination that causes desolation, until the end that is decreed is poured out on him.[c]"[d]

Daniel's Vision of a Man

10 In the third year of Cyrus king of Persia, a revelation was given to Daniel (who was called Belteshazzar). Its message was true and it concerned a great war.[e] The understanding of the message came to him in a vision.

2At that time I, Daniel, mourned for three weeks. 3I ate no choice food; no meat or wine touched my lips; and I used no lotions at all until the three weeks were over.

4On the twenty-fourth day of the first month, as I was standing on the bank of the great river, the Tigris, 5I looked up and there before me was a man dressed in linen, with a belt of the finest gold around his waist. 6His body was like chrysolite, his face like lightning, his eyes like flaming torches, his arms and legs like the gleam of burnished bronze, and his voice like the sound of a multitude.

7I, Daniel, was the only one who saw the vision; the men with me did not see it, but such terror overwhelmed them that they fled and hid themselves. 8So I was left alone, gazing at this great vision; I had no strength left, my face turned deathly pale and I was helpless. 9Then I heard him speaking, and as I listened to him, I fell into a deep sleep, my face to the ground.

10A hand touched me and set me trembling on my hands and knees. 11He said, "Daniel, you who are highly esteemed, consider carefully the words I am about to speak to you, and stand up, for I have now been sent to you." And when he said this to me, I stood up trembling.

12Then he continued, "Do not be afraid, Daniel. Since the first day that you set your mind to gain understanding and to humble yourself before your God, your words were heard, and I have come in response to them. 13But the prince of the Persian kingdom resisted me twenty-one days. Then Michael, one of the chief princes, came to help me, because I was detained there with the king of Persia. 14Now I have come to explain to you what will happen to your people in the future, for the vision concerns a time yet to come."

15While he was saying this to me, I bowed with my face toward the ground and was speechless. 16Then one who looked like a man[f] touched my lips, and I opened my mouth and began to speak. I said to the one standing before me, "I am overcome with anguish because of the vision, my lord, and I am helpless. 17How can I, your servant, talk with you, my lord? My strength is gone and I can hardly breathe."

18Again the one who looked like a man touched me and gave me strength. 19"Do not be afraid, O man highly esteemed," he said. "Peace! Be strong now; be strong."

When he spoke to me, I was strengthened and said, "Speak, my lord, since you have given me strength."

20So he said, "Do you know why I have come to you? Soon I will return to fight against the prince of Persia, and when I go, the prince of Greece will come; 21but first I will tell you what is written in the Book of Truth. (No one supports me against them except Michael, your prince.

11 1And in the first year of Darius the Mede, I took my stand to support and protect him.)

The Kings of the South and the North

2"Now then, I tell you the truth: Three more kings will appear in Persia, and then a fourth, who will be far richer than all the others. When he has gained power by his wealth, he will stir up everyone against the kingdom of Greece. 3Then a mighty

[a] 26 Or *off and will have no one*; or *off, but not for himself* [b] 27 Or *'week'* [c] 27 Or *it* [d] 27 Or *And one who causes desolation will come upon the pinnacle of the abominable ⌊temple⌋ until the end that is decreed is poured out on the desolated ⌊city⌋* [e] 1 Or *true and burdensome* [f] 16 Most manuscripts of the Masoretic Text; one manuscript of the Masoretic Text, Dead Sea Scrolls and Septuagint *Then something that looked like a man's hand*

king will appear, who will rule with great
power and do as he pleases. 4After he has
appeared, his empire will be broken up
and parceled out toward the four winds of
heaven. It will not go to his descendants,
nor will it have the power he exercised,
because his empire will be uprooted and
given to others.

5"The king of the South will become
strong, but one of his commanders will
become even stronger than he and will
rule his own kingdom with great power.
6After some years, they will become allies.
The daughter of the king of the South will
go to the king of the North to make an alli-
ance, but she will not retain her power,
and he and his power[a] will not last. In
those days she will be handed over, to-
gether with her royal escort and her fa-
ther[b] and the one who supported her.

7"One from her family line will arise to
take her place. He will attack the forces of
the king of the North and enter his for-
tress; he will fight against them and be
victorious. 8He will also seize their gods,
their metal images and their valuable arti-
cles of silver and gold and carry them off
to Egypt. For some years he will leave the
king of the North alone. 9Then the king of
the North will invade the realm of the king
of the South but will retreat to his own
country. 10His sons will prepare for war
and assemble a great army, which will
sweep on like an irresistible flood and car-
ry the battle as far as his fortress.

11"Then the king of the South will
march out in a rage and fight against the
king of the North, who will raise a large
army, but it will be defeated. 12When the
army is carried off, the king of the South
will be filled with pride and will slaughter
many thousands, yet he will not remain
triumphant. 13For the king of the North
will muster another army, larger than the
first; and after several years, he will ad-
vance with a huge army fully equipped.

14"In those times many will rise against
the king of the South. The violent men
among your own people will rebel in ful-
fillment of the vision, but without success.
15Then the king of the North will come
and build up siege ramps and will capture
a fortified city. The forces of the South will
be powerless to resist; even their best
troops will not have the strength to stand.
16The invader will do as he pleases; no
one will be able to stand against him. He
will establish himself in the Beautiful
Land and will have the power to destroy
it. 17He will determine to come with the
might of his entire kingdom and will make
an alliance with the king of the South. And
he will give him a daughter in marriage in
order to overthrow the kingdom, but his
plans[c] will not succeed or help him.
18Then he will turn his attention to the
coastlands and will take many of them,
but a commander will put an end to his
insolence and will turn his insolence back
upon him. 19After this, he will turn back
toward the fortresses of his own country
but will stumble and fall, to be seen no
more.

20"His successor will send out a tax col-
lector to maintain the royal splendor. In a
few years, however, he will be destroyed,
yet not in anger or in battle.

21"He will be succeeded by a contempt-
ible person who has not been given the
honor of royalty. He will invade the king-
dom when its people feel secure, and he
will seize it through intrigue. 22Then an
overwhelming army will be swept away
before him; both it and a prince of the cov-
enant will be destroyed. 23After coming to
an agreement with him, he will act deceit-
fully, and with only a few people he will
rise to power. 24When the richest prov-
inces feel secure, he will invade them and
will achieve what neither his fathers nor
his forefathers did. He will distribute
plunder, loot and wealth among his fol-
lowers. He will plot the overthrow of for-
tresses—but only for a time.

25"With a large army he will stir up his
strength and courage against the king of
the South. The king of the South will wage
war with a large and very powerful army,
but he will not be able to stand because of
the plots devised against him. 26Those
who eat from the king's provisions will try
to destroy him; his army will be swept
away, and many will fall in battle. 27The
two kings, with their hearts bent on evil,
will sit at the same table and lie to each
other, but to no avail, because an end will
still come at the appointed time. 28The
king of the North will return to his own
country with great wealth, but his heart
will be set against the holy covenant. He
will take action against it and then return
to his own country.

29"At the appointed time he will invade
the South again, but this time the outcome

[a]6 Or *offspring* [b]6 Or *child* (see Vulgate and Syriac) [c]17 Or *but she*

will be different from what it was before.
30Ships of the western coastlands[a] will
oppose him, and he will lose heart. Then
he will turn back and vent his fury against
the holy covenant. He will return and
show favor to those who forsake the holy
covenant.

31"His armed forces will rise up to desecrate the temple fortress and will abolish
the daily sacrifice. Then they will set up
the abomination that causes desolation.
32With flattery he will corrupt those who
have violated the covenant, but the people
who know their God will firmly resist him.

33"Those who are wise will instruct
many, though for a time they will fall by
the sword or be burned or captured or
plundered. 34When they fall, they will receive a little help, and many who are not
sincere will join them. 35Some of the wise
will stumble, so that they may be refined,
purified and made spotless until the time
of the end, for it will still come at the appointed time.

The King Who Exalts Himself

36"The king will do as he pleases. He
will exalt and magnify himself above every god and will say unheard-of things
against the God of gods. He will be successful until the time of wrath is completed, for what has been determined must

[a]30 Hebrew *of Kittim*

VERSE FOR THE DAY: Daniel 12:3 | AUTHOR: Stuart Briscoe | PASSAGE FOR THE DAY: Daniel 12:1–4

Serving as a Team

When Jill and I first met, we were already committed to a lifestyle of service. We remind each other that we are here to serve. And we have helped each other see the boundless opportunities that stretch before us.

I know many couples don't reach that point until fifteen years into their marriage. At first, they might be more interested in having a comfortable life. But until the joint commitment to serve God becomes an underlying attitude between you, all the efforts to serve or use your gifts won't make any sense.

By definition, a Christian is a servant. So by definition, a Christian marriage is a serving team. The paradox is that we find fullness of life in being expendable and available. The prerequisite to a resurrection is the cross. There's no such thing as spirituality without some degree of cost.

MARRIAGE BUILDERS

- *Where are you in your joint commitment to serve the Lord?*
- *Are there specific areas in which you would like to serve?*

Additional Scripture Readings
Luke 9:23; 1 Samuel 12:24

Go to page 946 for your next devotional reading.

take place. 37He will show no regard for
the gods of his fathers or for the one de-
sired by women, nor will he regard any
god, but will exalt himself above them all.
38Instead of them, he will honor a god of
fortresses; a god unknown to his fathers
he will honor with gold and silver, with
precious stones and costly gifts. 39He will
attack the mightiest fortresses with the
help of a foreign god and will greatly hon-
or those who acknowledge him. He will
make them rulers over many people and
will distribute the land at a price.[a]

40"At the time of the end the king of the
South will engage him in battle, and the
king of the North will storm out against
him with chariots and cavalry and a great
fleet of ships. He will invade many coun-
tries and sweep through them like a flood.
41He will also invade the Beautiful Land.
Many countries will fall, but Edom, Moab
and the leaders of Ammon will be deliv-
ered from his hand. 42He will extend his
power over many countries; Egypt will
not escape. 43He will gain control of the
treasures of gold and silver and all the
riches of Egypt, with the Libyans and Nu-
bians in submission. 44But reports from
the east and the north will alarm him, and
he will set out in a great rage to destroy
and annihilate many. 45He will pitch his
royal tents between the seas at[b] the beau-
tiful holy mountain. Yet he will come to
his end, and no one will help him.

The End Times

12 "At that time Michael, the great
prince who protects your people,
will arise. There will be a time of distress
such as has not happened from the begin-
ning of nations until then. But at that time
your people—everyone whose name is
found written in the book—will be deliv-
ered. 2Multitudes who sleep in the dust of
the earth will awake: some to everlasting
life, others to shame and everlasting con-
tempt. 3Those who are wise[c] will shine
like the brightness of the heavens, and
those who lead many to righteousness,
like the stars for ever and ever. 4But you,
Daniel, close up and seal the words of the
scroll until the time of the end. Many will
go here and there to increase knowledge."

5Then I, Daniel, looked, and there be-
fore me stood two others, one on this
bank of the river and one on the opposite
bank. 6One of them said to the man
clothed in linen, who was above the wa-
ters of the river, "How long will it be be-
fore these astonishing things are ful-
filled?"

7The man clothed in linen, who was
above the waters of the river, lifted his
right hand and his left hand toward heav-
en, and I heard him swear by him who
lives forever, saying, "It will be for a time,
times and half a time.[d] When the power
of the holy people has been finally bro-
ken, all these things will be completed."

8I heard, but I did not understand. So I
asked, "My lord, what will the outcome of
all this be?"

9He replied, "Go your way, Daniel, be-
cause the words are closed up and sealed
until the time of the end. 10Many will be
purified, made spotless and refined, but
the wicked will continue to be wicked.
None of the wicked will understand, but
those who are wise will understand.

11"From the time that the daily sacrifice
is abolished and the abomination that
causes desolation is set up, there will
be 1,290 days. 12Blessed is the one who
waits for and reaches the end of the 1,335
days.

13"As for you, go your way till the end.
You will rest, and then at the end of the
days you will rise to receive your allotted
inheritance."

[a]39 Or *land for a reward* [b]45 Or *the sea and* [c]3 Or *who impart wisdom* [d]7 Or *a year, two years and half a year*

HOSEA prophesies during the last days of Israel (see 2 Kings 14:23–17:41), focusing on her sin of spiritual adultery (that is, idolatry). He warns them that God will punish them unless they change their ways. But he also reminds them of God's incredible love, pleading with them to repent. As you read this book, think of God's love in sending his Son Jesus to die for you, in spite of your sins. Repent of your unfaithfulness to the Lord and turn to him.

HOSEA

1 The word of the LORD that came to Hosea son of Beeri during the reigns of Uzziah, Jotham, Ahaz and Hezekiah, kings of Judah, and during the reign of Jeroboam son of Jehoash[a] king of Israel:

Hosea's Wife and Children

2 When the LORD began to speak through Hosea, the LORD said to him, "Go, take to yourself an adulterous wife and children of unfaithfulness, because the land is guilty of the vilest adultery in departing from the LORD." 3 So he married Gomer daughter of Diblaim, and she conceived and bore him a son.

4 Then the LORD said to Hosea, "Call him Jezreel, because I will soon punish the house of Jehu for the massacre at Jezreel, and I will put an end to the kingdom of Israel. 5 In that day I will break Israel's bow in the Valley of Jezreel."

6 Gomer conceived again and gave birth to a daughter. Then the LORD said to Hosea, "Call her Lo-Ruhamah,[b] for I will no longer show love to the house of Israel, that I should at all forgive them. 7 Yet I will show love to the house of Judah; and I will

[a] 1 Hebrew *Joash*, a variant of *Jehoash*

[b] 6 *Lo-Ruhamah* means *not loved*.

save them—not by bow, sword or battle,
or by horses and horsemen, but by the LORD their God."
8After she had weaned Lo-Ruhamah,
Gomer had another son. 9Then the LORD
said, "Call him Lo-Ammi,[a] for you are not
my people, and I am not your God.
10"Yet the Israelites will be like the sand
on the seashore, which cannot be measured or counted. In the place where it
was said to them, 'You are not my people,'
they will be called 'sons of the living God.'
11The people of Judah and the people of
Israel will be reunited, and they will appoint one leader and will come up out of
the land, for great will be the day of Jezreel.

2 "Say of your brothers, 'My people,'
and of your sisters, 'My loved one.'

Israel Punished and Restored

2"Rebuke your mother, rebuke her,
for she is not my wife,
and I am not her husband.
Let her remove the adulterous look
from her face
and the unfaithfulness from
between her breasts.
3Otherwise I will strip her naked
and make her as bare as on the day
she was born;
I will make her like a desert,
turn her into a parched land,
and slay her with thirst.
4I will not show my love to her
children,
because they are the children of
adultery.
5Their mother has been unfaithful
and has conceived them in disgrace.
She said, 'I will go after my lovers,
who give me my food and my
water,
my wool and my linen, my oil and
my drink.'
6Therefore I will block her path with
thornbushes;
I will wall her in so that she cannot
find her way.
7She will chase after her lovers but not
catch them;
she will look for them but not find
them.
Then she will say,
'I will go back to my husband as at
first,
for then I was better off than now.'
8She has not acknowledged that I was
the one
who gave her the grain, the new
wine and oil,
who lavished on her the silver and
gold—
which they used for Baal.

9"Therefore I will take away my grain
when it ripens,
and my new wine when it is ready.
I will take back my wool and my
linen,
intended to cover her nakedness.
10So now I will expose her lewdness
before the eyes of her lovers;
no one will take her out of my
hands.
11I will stop all her celebrations:
her yearly festivals, her New Moons,
her Sabbath days—all her appointed
feasts.
12I will ruin her vines and her fig trees,
which she said were her pay from
her lovers;
I will make them a thicket,
and wild animals will devour them.
13I will punish her for the days
she burned incense to the Baals;
she decked herself with rings and
jewelry,
and went after her lovers,
but me she forgot,"
declares the LORD.

14"Therefore I am now going to allure
her;
I will lead her into the desert
and speak tenderly to her.
15There I will give her back her
vineyards,
and will make the Valley of Achor[b]
a door of hope.
There she will sing[c] as in the days of
her youth,
as in the day she came up out of
Egypt.

16"In that day," declares the LORD,
"you will call me 'my husband';
you will no longer call me 'my
master.[d]'
17I will remove the names of the Baals
from her lips;
no longer will their names be
invoked.

[a]9 *Lo-Ammi* means *not my people.* [b]15 *Achor* means *trouble.* [c]15 Or *respond* [d]16 Hebrew *baal*

VERSE FOR THE DAY:
Hosea 2:19–20

AUTHOR:
Jim Smith

PASSAGE FOR THE DAY:
Hosea 2:16–23

Preventative Medicine

When I perform a wedding, I list five words—each beginning with "C"—that represent critical areas in marriage. If these are left untended, it opens the door to sexual vulnerability.

The first "C" is *calendar.* Couples need to block out time exclusively for each other—no friends, no family. Just the two of you.

The second "C" is *communication*—sharing both feelings and thoughts. People frequently admit they had an affair because they found someone else who would talk and listen to them.

The third area is *caring.* The more effort you put into meeting each other's needs, the less likely either of you will be to go outside the marriage to get your needs met.

The fourth area is *courtship.* I see too many spouses stop being affectionate and sensitive to each other. Invariably, the neglected mate gets angry and begins to shut down emotionally. Then, instead of approaching life as a team, they turn into adversaries.

The last "C" is *commitment,* especially during those times when you feel disillusioned with marriage. And of course, in a Christian marriage the couple is committed to Christ, as well as to each other.

No list of reminders can completely ward off the possibility of an affair. That's why couples should establish boundaries for behavior and relationships with others. In any male/female friendship, a person needs to ask: "What deep need is being met by this friendship?" If the answer is a need that only your spouse should be fulfilling, you should re-evaluate that friendship.

Any time you enjoy another person's company more than your mate's, and you continue to cultivate that relationship, you are a prime candidate for an affair.

MARRIAGE BUILDERS

♦ *On which of the five "C" areas are you and your spouse already doing well?*

♦ *Brainstorm one or two things you might do to improve your relationship in each of these five categories.*

Additional Scripture Readings
Exodus 20:14; Matthew 5:27–28;
1 Corinthians 6:18–20

Go to page 948 for your next devotional reading.

18 In that day I will make a covenant for them
with the beasts of the field and the birds of the air
and the creatures that move along the ground.
Bow and sword and battle
I will abolish from the land,
so that all may lie down in safety.
19 I will betroth you to me forever;
I will betroth you in[a] righteousness and justice,
in[b] love and compassion.
20 I will betroth you in faithfulness,
and you will acknowledge the LORD.

21 "In that day I will respond,"
declares the LORD—
"I will respond to the skies,
and they will respond to the earth;
22 and the earth will respond to the grain,
the new wine and oil,
and they will respond to Jezreel.[c]
23 I will plant her for myself in the land;
I will show my love to the one I called 'Not my loved one.[d]'
I will say to those called 'Not my people,[e]' 'You are my people';
and they will say, 'You are my God.' "

Hosea's Reconciliation With His Wife

3 The LORD said to me, "Go, show your love to your wife again, though she is loved by another and is an adulteress. Love her as the LORD loves the Israelites, though they turn to other gods and love the sacred raisin cakes."

2 So I bought her for fifteen shekels[f] of silver and about a homer and a lethek[g] of barley. 3 Then I told her, "You are to live with[h] me many days; you must not be a prostitute or be intimate with any man, and I will live with[h] you."

4 For the Israelites will live many days without king or prince, without sacrifice or sacred stones, without ephod or idol. 5 Afterward the Israelites will return and seek the LORD their God and David their king. They will come trembling to the LORD and to his blessings in the last days.

The Charge Against Israel

4 Hear the word of the LORD, you Israelites,
because the LORD has a charge to bring
against you who live in the land:
"There is no faithfulness, no love,
no acknowledgment of God in the land.
2 There is only cursing,[i] lying and murder,
stealing and adultery;
they break all bounds,
and bloodshed follows bloodshed.
3 Because of this the land mourns,[j]
and all who live in it waste away;
the beasts of the field and the birds of the air
and the fish of the sea are dying.

4 "But let no man bring a charge,
let no man accuse another,
for your people are like those
who bring charges against a priest.
5 You stumble day and night,
and the prophets stumble with you.
So I will destroy your mother—
6 my people are destroyed from lack of knowledge.

"Because you have rejected knowledge,
I also reject you as my priests;
because you have ignored the law of your God,
I also will ignore your children.
7 The more the priests increased,
the more they sinned against me;
they exchanged[k] their[l] Glory for something disgraceful.
8 They feed on the sins of my people
and relish their wickedness.
9 And it will be: Like people, like priests.
I will punish both of them for their ways
and repay them for their deeds.

10 "They will eat but not have enough;
they will engage in prostitution but not increase,
because they have deserted the LORD
to give themselves 11 to prostitution,
to old wine and new,

[a] 19 Or *with*; also in verse 20 [b] 19 Or *with* [c] 22 *Jezreel* means *God plants.* [d] 23 Hebrew *Lo-Ruhamah* [e] 23 Hebrew *Lo-Ammi* [f] 2 That is, about 6 ounces (about 170 grams) [g] 2 That is, probably about 10 bushels (about 330 liters) [h] 3 Or *wait for* [i] 2 That is, to pronounce a curse upon [j] 3 Or *dries up* [k] 7 Syriac and an ancient Hebrew scribal tradition; Masoretic Text *I will exchange* [l] 7 Masoretic Text; an ancient Hebrew scribal tradition *my*

WEEKENDING

WORK

It's true that work eats up great amounts of our time and energy. But there are clear benefits to working, as well. To help pinpoint those benefits, discuss your responses to the following statements.

1. My work provides opportunities for personal growth.

2. I have learned something beneficial about myself through my work.

3. I have learned something beneficial about my mate through his or her work.

4. I would turn down a promotion if accepting it would be detrimental to my marriage.

5. I would be willing to change jobs for my spouse's and/or children's benefit.

Discuss your responses. Pray together that God will show both of you ways to make your jobs a force for good in your marriage.

— *The* Marriage Partnership *Staff*

REVIVE

Saturday: Colossians 3:18—4:1
Sunday: 2 Timothy 3:10–17

Go to page 951 for your next devotional reading.

which take away the understanding
12of my people.
They consult a wooden idol
and are answered by a stick of wood.
A spirit of prostitution leads them astray;
they are unfaithful to their God.
13They sacrifice on the mountaintops
and burn offerings on the hills,
under oak, poplar and terebinth,
where the shade is pleasant.
Therefore your daughters turn to prostitution
and your daughters-in-law to adultery.

14"I will not punish your daughters
when they turn to prostitution,
nor your daughters-in-law
when they commit adultery,
because the men themselves consort with harlots
and sacrifice with shrine prostitutes—
a people without understanding will come to ruin!

15"Though you commit adultery, O Israel,
let not Judah become guilty.

"Do not go to Gilgal;
do not go up to Beth Aven.[a]
And do not swear, 'As surely as the LORD lives!'
16The Israelites are stubborn,
like a stubborn heifer.
How then can the LORD pasture them
like lambs in a meadow?
17Ephraim is joined to idols;
leave him alone!
18Even when their drinks are gone,
they continue their prostitution;
their rulers dearly love shameful ways.
19A whirlwind will sweep them away,
and their sacrifices will bring them shame.

Judgment Against Israel

5 "Hear this, you priests!
Pay attention, you Israelites!
Listen, O royal house!
This judgment is against you:
You have been a snare at Mizpah,
a net spread out on Tabor.
2The rebels are deep in slaughter.
I will discipline all of them.
3I know all about Ephraim;
Israel is not hidden from me.
Ephraim, you have now turned to prostitution;
Israel is corrupt.

4"Their deeds do not permit them
to return to their God.
A spirit of prostitution is in their heart;
they do not acknowledge the LORD.
5Israel's arrogance testifies against them;
the Israelites, even Ephraim, stumble in their sin;
Judah also stumbles with them.
6When they go with their flocks and herds
to seek the LORD,
they will not find him;
he has withdrawn himself from them.
7They are unfaithful to the LORD;
they give birth to illegitimate children.
Now their New Moon festivals
will devour them and their fields.

8"Sound the trumpet in Gibeah,
the horn in Ramah.
Raise the battle cry in Beth Aven[a];
lead on, O Benjamin.
9Ephraim will be laid waste
on the day of reckoning.
Among the tribes of Israel
I proclaim what is certain.
10Judah's leaders are like those
who move boundary stones.
I will pour out my wrath on them
like a flood of water.
11Ephraim is oppressed,
trampled in judgment,
intent on pursuing idols.[b]
12I am like a moth to Ephraim,
like rot to the people of Judah.

13"When Ephraim saw his sickness,
and Judah his sores,
then Ephraim turned to Assyria,
and sent to the great king for help.
But he is not able to cure you,
not able to heal your sores.
14For I will be like a lion to Ephraim,
like a great lion to Judah.

[a] *15,8 Beth Aven* means *house of wickedness* (a name for Bethel, which means *house of God*). [b] *11* The meaning of the Hebrew for this word is uncertain.

I will tear them to pieces and go
away;
I will carry them off, with no one to
rescue them.
15Then I will go back to my place
until they admit their guilt.
And they will seek my face;
in their misery they will earnestly
seek me."

Israel Unrepentant

6 "Come, let us return to the LORD.
He has torn us to pieces
but he will heal us;
he has injured us
but he will bind up our wounds.
2After two days he will revive us;
on the third day he will restore us,
that we may live in his presence.
3Let us acknowledge the LORD;
let us press on to acknowledge him.
As surely as the sun rises,
he will appear;
he will come to us like the winter
rains,
like the spring rains that water the
earth."

4"What can I do with you, Ephraim?
What can I do with you, Judah?
Your love is like the morning mist,
like the early dew that disappears.
5Therefore I cut you in pieces with my
prophets,
I killed you with the words of my
mouth;
my judgments flashed like lightning
upon you.
6For I desire mercy, not sacrifice,
and acknowledgment of God rather
than burnt offerings.
7Like Adam,[a] they have broken the
covenant—
they were unfaithful to me there.
8Gilead is a city of wicked men,
stained with footprints of blood.
9As marauders lie in ambush for a
man,
so do bands of priests;
they murder on the road to Shechem,
committing shameful crimes.
10I have seen a horrible thing
in the house of Israel.
There Ephraim is given to prostitution
and Israel is defiled.

11"Also for you, Judah,
a harvest is appointed.
"Whenever I would restore the
fortunes of my people,
7 1whenever I would heal Israel,
the sins of Ephraim are exposed
and the crimes of Samaria revealed.
They practice deceit,
thieves break into houses,
bandits rob in the streets;
2but they do not realize
that I remember all their evil deeds.
Their sins engulf them;
they are always before me.

3"They delight the king with their
wickedness,
the princes with their lies.
4They are all adulterers,
burning like an oven
whose fire the baker need not stir
from the kneading of the dough till
it rises.
5On the day of the festival of our king
the princes become inflamed with
wine,
and he joins hands with the
mockers.
6Their hearts are like an oven;
they approach him with intrigue.
Their passion smolders all night;
in the morning it blazes like a
flaming fire.
7All of them are hot as an oven;
they devour their rulers.
All their kings fall,
and none of them calls on me.

8"Ephraim mixes with the nations;
Ephraim is a flat cake not turned
over.
9Foreigners sap his strength,
but he does not realize it.
His hair is sprinkled with gray,
but he does not notice.
10Israel's arrogance testifies against him,
but despite all this
he does not return to the LORD his
God
or search for him.

11"Ephraim is like a dove,
easily deceived and senseless—
now calling to Egypt,
now turning to Assyria.
12When they go, I will throw my net
over them;
I will pull them down like birds of
the air.
When I hear them flocking together,

[a]7 Or *As at Adam*; or *Like men*

VERSE FOR THE DAY: Hosea 6:3

AUTHOR: Joni Eareckson Tada

PASSAGE FOR THE DAY: Hosea 6:1–3

Surprised by Grace

Ken and I just had a quarrel. An hour passes, and Ken enters the room. "I can't stand it when you come on with that strong-willed tone of yours," he says. "I know it's because you're a survivor, a fighter. But I just can't handle you like that."

"I feel like every time the slightest conflict surfaces, you back off," I tell him, "and I'm the one who's supposed to walk on eggshells."

"Maybe the only thing to do now is pray," Ken suggests. He mumbles a few phrases, mechanically saying things about God's greatness, holiness and mercy. But I hear his heart begin to soften, and his quiet voice wrenches and pleads as he finishes.

My prayer begins just as hollow-sounding as his. But after several moments I too sense my heart beginning to melt. I ask for mercy.

Ken prays again, then he stops and takes a deep breath. "I can't believe this," he says. "A load of concrete is off of me. I feel so light."

"That's amazing," I tell him. "Just seconds ago I felt the same peace and contentment." Without thinking I utter the words, "I love you." Ken embraces me, burying his head into my shoulder. We feel a sense of wonder at how strong Ken is when I am weak; at how weak Ken is when I am strong; and how God, with his strength, keeps us both from falling from grace.

MARRIAGE BUILDERS

♦ *Think back to a recent disagreement or quarrel. What things did each of you do to bring the conflict to an end?*

♦ *How does praying together help you and your spouse resolve conflict?*

Additional Scripture Readings
Psalm 51:17; 1 Corinthians 10:13

Go to page 956 for your next devotional reading.

I will catch them.
13Woe to them,
because they have strayed from me!
Destruction to them,
because they have rebelled against me!
I long to redeem them
but they speak lies against me.
14They do not cry out to me from their hearts
but wail upon their beds.
They gather together[a] for grain and new wine
but turn away from me.
15I trained them and strengthened them,
but they plot evil against me.
16They do not turn to the Most High;
they are like a faulty bow.
Their leaders will fall by the sword
because of their insolent words.
For this they will be ridiculed
in the land of Egypt.

Israel to Reap the Whirlwind

8 "Put the trumpet to your lips!
An eagle is over the house of the LORD
because the people have broken my covenant
and rebelled against my law.
2Israel cries out to me,
'O our God, we acknowledge you!'
3But Israel has rejected what is good;
an enemy will pursue him.
4They set up kings without my consent;
they choose princes without my approval.
With their silver and gold
they make idols for themselves
to their own destruction.
5Throw out your calf-idol, O Samaria!
My anger burns against them.
How long will they be incapable of purity?
6 They are from Israel!
This calf—a craftsman has made it;
it is not God.
It will be broken in pieces,
that calf of Samaria.

7"They sow the wind
and reap the whirlwind.
The stalk has no head;
it will produce no flour.
Were it to yield grain,
foreigners would swallow it up.
8Israel is swallowed up;
now she is among the nations
like a worthless thing.
9For they have gone up to Assyria
like a wild donkey wandering alone.
Ephraim has sold herself to lovers.
10Although they have sold themselves among the nations,
I will now gather them together.
They will begin to waste away
under the oppression of the mighty king.

11"Though Ephraim built many altars for sin offerings,
these have become altars for sinning.
12I wrote for them the many things of my law,
but they regarded them as something alien.
13They offer sacrifices given to me
and they eat the meat,
but the LORD is not pleased with them.
Now he will remember their wickedness
and punish their sins:
They will return to Egypt.
14Israel has forgotten his Maker
and built palaces;
Judah has fortified many towns.
But I will send fire upon their cities
that will consume their fortresses."

Punishment for Israel

9 Do not rejoice, O Israel;
do not be jubilant like the other nations.
For you have been unfaithful to your God;
you love the wages of a prostitute
at every threshing floor.
2Threshing floors and winepresses will not feed the people;
the new wine will fail them.
3They will not remain in the LORD's land;
Ephraim will return to Egypt
and eat unclean[b] food in Assyria.
4They will not pour out wine offerings to the LORD,
nor will their sacrifices please him.
Such sacrifices will be to them like the bread of mourners;

[a] 14 Most Hebrew manuscripts; some Hebrew manuscripts and Septuagint *They slash themselves*
[b] 3 That is, ceremonially unclean

all who eat them will be unclean.
This food will be for themselves;
it will not come into the temple of the LORD.

5What will you do on the day of your appointed feasts,
on the festival days of the LORD?
6Even if they escape from destruction,
Egypt will gather them,
and Memphis will bury them.
Their treasures of silver will be taken over by briers,
and thorns will overrun their tents.
7The days of punishment are coming,
the days of reckoning are at hand.
Let Israel know this.
Because your sins are so many
and your hostility so great,
the prophet is considered a fool,
the inspired man a maniac.
8The prophet, along with my God,
is the watchman over Ephraim,[a]
yet snares await him on all his paths,
and hostility in the house of his God.
9They have sunk deep into corruption,
as in the days of Gibeah.
God will remember their wickedness
and punish them for their sins.

10"When I found Israel,
it was like finding grapes in the desert;
when I saw your fathers,
it was like seeing the early fruit on the fig tree.
But when they came to Baal Peor,
they consecrated themselves to that shameful idol
and became as vile as the thing they loved.
11Ephraim's glory will fly away like a bird—
no birth, no pregnancy, no conception.
12Even if they rear children,
I will bereave them of every one.
Woe to them
when I turn away from them!
13I have seen Ephraim, like Tyre,
planted in a pleasant place.
But Ephraim will bring out
their children to the slayer."

14Give them, O LORD—
what will you give them?
Give them wombs that miscarry
and breasts that are dry.

15"Because of all their wickedness in Gilgal,
I hated them there.
Because of their sinful deeds,
I will drive them out of my house.
I will no longer love them;
all their leaders are rebellious.
16Ephraim is blighted,
their root is withered,
they yield no fruit.
Even if they bear children,
I will slay their cherished offspring."

17My God will reject them
because they have not obeyed him;
they will be wanderers among the nations.

10 Israel was a spreading vine;
he brought forth fruit for himself.
As his fruit increased,
he built more altars;
as his land prospered,
he adorned his sacred stones.
2Their heart is deceitful,
and now they must bear their guilt.
The LORD will demolish their altars
and destroy their sacred stones.

3Then they will say, "We have no king
because we did not revere the LORD.
But even if we had a king,
what could he do for us?"
4They make many promises,
take false oaths
and make agreements;
therefore lawsuits spring up
like poisonous weeds in a plowed field.
5The people who live in Samaria fear
for the calf-idol of Beth Aven.[b]
Its people will mourn over it,
and so will its idolatrous priests,
those who had rejoiced over its splendor,
because it is taken from them into exile.
6It will be carried to Assyria
as tribute for the great king.
Ephraim will be disgraced;
Israel will be ashamed of its wooden idols.[c]
7Samaria and its king will float away

[a]8 Or *The prophet is the watchman over Ephraim, / the people of my God* [b]5 *Beth Aven* means *house of wickedness* (a name for Bethel, which means *house of God*). [c]6 Or *its counsel*

like a twig on the surface of the waters.
8 The high places of wickedness[a] will be destroyed—
it is the sin of Israel.
Thorns and thistles will grow up and cover their altars.
Then they will say to the mountains, "Cover us!"
and to the hills, "Fall on us!"

9 "Since the days of Gibeah, you have sinned, O Israel,
and there you have remained.[b]
Did not war overtake the evildoers in Gibeah?
10 When I please, I will punish them;
nations will be gathered against them
to put them in bonds for their double sin.
11 Ephraim is a trained heifer
that loves to thresh;
so I will put a yoke on her fair neck.
I will drive Ephraim,
Judah must plow,
and Jacob must break up the ground.
12 Sow for yourselves righteousness,
reap the fruit of unfailing love,
and break up your unplowed ground;
for it is time to seek the LORD,
until he comes
and showers righteousness on you.
13 But you have planted wickedness,
you have reaped evil,
you have eaten the fruit of deception.
Because you have depended on your own strength
and on your many warriors,
14 the roar of battle will rise against your people,
so that all your fortresses will be devastated—
as Shalman devastated Beth Arbel on the day of battle,
when mothers were dashed to the ground with their children.
15 Thus will it happen to you, O Bethel,
because your wickedness is great.
When that day dawns,
the king of Israel will be completely destroyed.

God's Love for Israel

11 "When Israel was a child, I loved him,
and out of Egypt I called my son.
2 But the more I[c] called Israel,
the further they went from me.[d]
They sacrificed to the Baals
and they burned incense to images.
3 It was I who taught Ephraim to walk,
taking them by the arms;
but they did not realize
it was I who healed them.
4 I led them with cords of human kindness,
with ties of love;
I lifted the yoke from their neck
and bent down to feed them.

5 "Will they not return to Egypt
and will not Assyria rule over them
because they refuse to repent?
6 Swords will flash in their cities,
will destroy the bars of their gates
and put an end to their plans.
7 My people are determined to turn from me.
Even if they call to the Most High,
he will by no means exalt them.

8 "How can I give you up, Ephraim?
How can I hand you over, Israel?
How can I treat you like Admah?
How can I make you like Zeboiim?
My heart is changed within me;
all my compassion is aroused.
9 I will not carry out my fierce anger,
nor will I turn and devastate Ephraim.
For I am God, and not man—
the Holy One among you.
I will not come in wrath.[e]
10 They will follow the LORD;
he will roar like a lion.
When he roars,
his children will come trembling from the west.
11 They will come trembling
like birds from Egypt,
like doves from Assyria.
I will settle them in their homes,"
declares the LORD.

Israel's Sin

12 Ephraim has surrounded me with lies,
the house of Israel with deceit.
And Judah is unruly against God,

[a] 8 Hebrew *aven*, a reference to Beth Aven (a derogatory name for Bethel) [b] 9 Or *there a stand was taken* [c] 2 Some Septuagint manuscripts; Hebrew *they* [d] 2 Septuagint; Hebrew *them* [e] 9 Or *come against any city*

even against the faithful Holy One.

12 [1]Ephraim feeds on the wind;
he pursues the east wind all day
and multiplies lies and violence.
He makes a treaty with Assyria
and sends olive oil to Egypt.
[2]The LORD has a charge to bring
against Judah;
he will punish Jacob[a] according to
his ways
and repay him according to his
deeds.
[3]In the womb he grasped his brother's
heel;
as a man he struggled with God.
[4]He struggled with the angel and
overcame him;
he wept and begged for his favor.
He found him at Bethel
and talked with him there—
[5]the LORD God Almighty,
the LORD is his name of renown!
[6]But you must return to your God;
maintain love and justice,
and wait for your God always.

[7]The merchant uses dishonest scales;
he loves to defraud.
[8]Ephraim boasts,
"I am very rich; I have become
wealthy.
With all my wealth they will not find
in me
any iniquity or sin."

[9]"I am the LORD your God,
⌊who brought you⌋ out of[b] Egypt;
I will make you live in tents again,
as in the days of your appointed
feasts.
[10]I spoke to the prophets,
gave them many visions
and told parables through them."

[11]Is Gilead wicked?
Its people are worthless!
Do they sacrifice bulls in Gilgal?
Their altars will be like piles of
stones
on a plowed field.
[12]Jacob fled to the country of Aram[c];
Israel served to get a wife,
and to pay for her he tended sheep.
[13]The LORD used a prophet to bring
Israel up from Egypt,
by a prophet he cared for him.
[14]But Ephraim has bitterly provoked
him to anger;
his Lord will leave upon him the
guilt of his bloodshed
and will repay him for his
contempt.

The LORD's Anger Against Israel

13 When Ephraim spoke, men
trembled;
he was exalted in Israel.
But he became guilty of Baal
worship and died.
[2]Now they sin more and more;
they make idols for themselves from
their silver,
cleverly fashioned images,
all of them the work of craftsmen.
It is said of these people,
"They offer human sacrifice
and kiss[d] the calf-idols."
[3]Therefore they will be like the
morning mist,
like the early dew that disappears,
like chaff swirling from a threshing
floor,
like smoke escaping through a
window.

[4]"But I am the LORD your God,
⌊who brought you⌋ out of[b] Egypt.
You shall acknowledge no God but
me,
no Savior except me.
[5]I cared for you in the desert,
in the land of burning heat.
[6]When I fed them, they were satisfied;
when they were satisfied, they
became proud;
then they forgot me.
[7]So I will come upon them like a lion,
like a leopard I will lurk by the
path.
[8]Like a bear robbed of her cubs,
I will attack them and rip them
open.
Like a lion I will devour them;
a wild animal will tear them apart.

[9]"You are destroyed, O Israel,
because you are against me, against
your helper.
[10]Where is your king, that he may save
you?
Where are your rulers in all your
towns,
of whom you said,

[a]2 *Jacob* means *he grasps the heel* (figuratively, *he deceives*). [b]9,4 Or *God / ever since you were in*
[c]12 That is, Northwest Mesopotamia [d]2 Or *"Men who sacrifice / kiss*

VERSE FOR THE DAY: Hosea 14:4

AUTHOR: Tim Stafford

PASSAGE FOR THE DAY: Hosea 14:1–9

Love's Last Word

Stories are most profitable when used as mirrors for seeing ourselves. The story of Eden, for instance, helps us remember why we married. It calls us back to our original idealism and delight in each other (see Gen. 1–2).

Our marriages may have been made in Eden, but they have not stayed there. They are filled with jealousy, anger, frustration. Is there any possibility that the unashamed nakedness and passionate delight of Eden can be restored?

Let us look in the mirror of God and Israel. Israel had become bored with her first love. But God perseveres, in spite of the pain of rejection. Can this marriage between God and his unfaithful people be saved? From a human point of view, never. But this story tells us that something more than a human point of view is involved. Somehow, God will make his marriage like the original in Eden, and even better. He wants to save marriages—to make them whole again.

To believe in this possibility takes faith. That is one reason to tell the story of God and his love for Israel. Love stories can get behind our defenses and call our hearts toward what we were meant to be. We were meant to be lovers like Adam and Eve—passionate, unashamed. We were meant to be lovers like God—passionate, unwavering even in pain.

MARRIAGE BUILDERS

♦ *What is your favorite story of another couple whose marriage nearly failed but was wonderfully saved? Tell it to your spouse.*

♦ *What attributes of God made him so passionate and persistent, despite his troubles with his unfaithful Bride—Israel?*

Additional Scripture Readings
Genesis 2:15–25; Isaiah 62:5; Jeremiah 3:12–14; Matthew 25:1–13

Go to page 962 for your next devotional reading.

'Give me a king and princes'?
11 So in my anger I gave you a king,
and in my wrath I took him away.
12 The guilt of Ephraim is stored up,
his sins are kept on record.
13 Pains as of a woman in childbirth
come to him,
but he is a child without wisdom;
when the time arrives,
he does not come to the opening of
the womb.

14 "I will ransom them from the power
of the grave[a];
I will redeem them from death.
Where, O death, are your plagues?
Where, O grave,[a] is your
destruction?

"I will have no compassion,
15 even though he thrives among his
brothers.
An east wind from the LORD will
come,
blowing in from the desert;
his spring will fail
and his well dry up.
His storehouse will be plundered
of all its treasures.
16 The people of Samaria must bear their
guilt,
because they have rebelled against
their God.
They will fall by the sword;
their little ones will be dashed to
the ground,
their pregnant women ripped open."

Repentance to Bring Blessing

14 Return, O Israel, to the LORD your
God.
Your sins have been your downfall!
2 Take words with you
and return to the LORD.
Say to him:
"Forgive all our sins
and receive us graciously,
that we may offer the fruit of our
lips.[b]
3 Assyria cannot save us;
we will not mount war-horses.
We will never again say 'Our gods'
to what our own hands have made,
for in you the fatherless find
compassion."

4 "I will heal their waywardness
and love them freely,
for my anger has turned away from
them.
5 I will be like the dew to Israel;
he will blossom like a lily.
Like a cedar of Lebanon
he will send down his roots;
6 his young shoots will grow.
His splendor will be like an olive tree,
his fragrance like a cedar of
Lebanon.
7 Men will dwell again in his shade.
He will flourish like the grain.
He will blossom like a vine,
and his fame will be like the wine
from Lebanon.
8 O Ephraim, what more have I[c] to do
with idols?
I will answer him and care for him.
I am like a green pine tree;
your fruitfulness comes from me."

9 Who is wise? He will realize these
things.
Who is discerning? He will
understand them.
The ways of the LORD are right;
the righteous walk in them,
but the rebellious stumble in them.

[a] 14 Hebrew *Sheol* [b] 2 Or *offer our lips as sacrifices of bulls* [c] 8 Or *What more has Ephraim*

JOEL uses a famine (due to a devastating plague of locusts) to picture the coming day of the Lord. He calls on God's people to repent and turn to the Lord, promising that everyone who does so will be saved and will receive God's Spirit. As you read this book, listen to God's call to repent of your sins, so that you may be saved and be filled with the Holy Spirit.

JOEL

1 The word of the LORD that came to
Joel son of Pethuel.

An Invasion of Locusts

2 Hear this, you elders;
listen, all who live in the land.
Has anything like this ever happened
in your days
or in the days of your forefathers?
3 Tell it to your children,
and let your children tell it to their
children,
and their children to the next
generation.
4 What the locust swarm has left
the great locusts have eaten;
what the great locusts have left
the young locusts have eaten;
what the young locusts have left
other locusts[a] have eaten.

5 Wake up, you drunkards, and weep!
Wail, all you drinkers of wine;
wail because of the new wine,
for it has been snatched from your
lips.
6 A nation has invaded my land,
powerful and without number;
it has the teeth of a lion,
the fangs of a lioness.
7 It has laid waste my vines
and ruined my fig trees.
It has stripped off their bark
and thrown it away,
leaving their branches white.

8 Mourn like a virgin[b] in sackcloth

[a] 4 The precise meaning of the four Hebrew words used here for locusts is uncertain. [b] 8 Or *young woman*

grieving for the husband[a] of her
youth.
9Grain offerings and drink offerings
are cut off from the house of the
LORD.
The priests are in mourning,
those who minister before the LORD.
10The fields are ruined,
the ground is dried up[b];
the grain is destroyed,
the new wine is dried up,
the oil fails.
11Despair, you farmers,
wail, you vine growers;
grieve for the wheat and the barley,
because the harvest of the field is
destroyed.
12The vine is dried up
and the fig tree is withered;
the pomegranate, the palm and the
apple tree—
all the trees of the field—are dried
up.
Surely the joy of mankind
is withered away.

A Call to Repentance

13Put on sackcloth, O priests, and
mourn;
wail, you who minister before the
altar.
Come, spend the night in sackcloth,
you who minister before my God;
for the grain offerings and drink
offerings
are withheld from the house of your
God.
14Declare a holy fast;
call a sacred assembly.
Summon the elders
and all who live in the land
to the house of the LORD your God,
and cry out to the LORD.

15Alas for that day!
For the day of the LORD is near;
it will come like destruction from
the Almighty.[c]

16Has not the food been cut off
before our very eyes—
joy and gladness
from the house of our God?
17The seeds are shriveled
beneath the clods.[d]
The storehouses are in ruins,
the granaries have been broken
down,
for the grain has dried up.
18How the cattle moan!
The herds mill about
because they have no pasture;
even the flocks of sheep are
suffering.

19To you, O LORD, I call,
for fire has devoured the open
pastures
and flames have burned up all the
trees of the field.
20Even the wild animals pant for you;
the streams of water have dried up
and fire has devoured the open
pastures.

An Army of Locusts

2 Blow the trumpet in Zion;
sound the alarm on my holy hill.
Let all who live in the land tremble,
for the day of the LORD is coming.
It is close at hand—
2 a day of darkness and gloom,
a day of clouds and blackness.
Like dawn spreading across the
mountains
a large and mighty army comes,
such as never was of old
nor ever will be in ages to come.

3Before them fire devours,
behind them a flame blazes.
Before them the land is like the
garden of Eden,
behind them, a desert waste—
nothing escapes them.
4They have the appearance of horses;
they gallop along like cavalry.
5With a noise like that of chariots
they leap over the mountaintops,
like a crackling fire consuming
stubble,
like a mighty army drawn up for
battle.

6At the sight of them, nations are in
anguish;
every face turns pale.
7They charge like warriors;
they scale walls like soldiers.
They all march in line,
not swerving from their course.
8They do not jostle each other;
each marches straight ahead.

[a]8 Or *betrothed* [b]10 Or *ground mourns* [c]15 Hebrew *Shaddai* [d]17 The meaning of the Hebrew for this word is uncertain.

They plunge through defenses
without breaking ranks.
9They rush upon the city;
they run along the wall.
They climb into the houses;
like thieves they enter through the windows.

10Before them the earth shakes,
the sky trembles,
the sun and moon are darkened,
and the stars no longer shine.
11The LORD thunders
at the head of his army;
his forces are beyond number,
and mighty are those who obey his command.
The day of the LORD is great;
it is dreadful.
Who can endure it?

Rend Your Heart

12"Even now," declares the LORD,
"return to me with all your heart,
with fasting and weeping and mourning."

13Rend your heart
and not your garments.
Return to the LORD your God,
for he is gracious and compassionate,
slow to anger and abounding in love,
and he relents from sending calamity.
14Who knows? He may turn and have pity
and leave behind a blessing—
grain offerings and drink offerings
for the LORD your God.

15Blow the trumpet in Zion,
declare a holy fast,
call a sacred assembly.
16Gather the people,
consecrate the assembly;
bring together the elders,
gather the children,
those nursing at the breast.
Let the bridegroom leave his room
and the bride her chamber.
17Let the priests, who minister before the LORD,
weep between the temple porch and the altar.
Let them say, "Spare your people, O LORD.
Do not make your inheritance an object of scorn,
a byword among the nations.
Why should they say among the peoples,
'Where is their God?' "

The LORD's Answer

18Then the LORD will be jealous for his land
and take pity on his people.

19The LORD will reply[a] to them:

"I am sending you grain, new wine and oil,
enough to satisfy you fully;
never again will I make you
an object of scorn to the nations.

20"I will drive the northern army far from you,
pushing it into a parched and barren land,
with its front columns going into the eastern sea[b]
and those in the rear into the western sea.[c]
And its stench will go up;
its smell will rise."

Surely he has done great things.[d]
21 Be not afraid, O land;
be glad and rejoice.
Surely the LORD has done great things.
22 Be not afraid, O wild animals,
for the open pastures are becoming green.
The trees are bearing their fruit;
the fig tree and the vine yield their riches.
23Be glad, O people of Zion,
rejoice in the LORD your God,
for he has given you
the autumn rains in righteousness.[e]
He sends you abundant showers,
both autumn and spring rains, as before.
24The threshing floors will be filled with grain;
the vats will overflow with new wine and oil.

25"I will repay you for the years the locusts have eaten—

[a] *18,19* Or *LORD was jealous . . . / and took pity . . . / 19The LORD replied* [b] *20* That is, the Dead Sea
[c] *20* That is, the Mediterranean [d] *20* Or *rise. / Surely it has done great things."* [e] *23* Or */ the teacher for righteousness:*

the great locust and the young
locust,
the other locusts and the locust
swarm[a]—
my great army that I sent among you.
26You will have plenty to eat, until you
are full,
and you will praise the name of the
LORD your God,
who has worked wonders for you;
never again will my people be
shamed.
27Then you will know that I am in
Israel,
that I am the LORD your God,
and that there is no other;
never again will my people be
shamed.

The Day of the LORD

28"And afterward,
I will pour out my Spirit on all
people.
Your sons and daughters will
prophesy,
your old men will dream dreams,
your young men will see visions.
29Even on my servants, both men and
women,
I will pour out my Spirit in those
days.
30I will show wonders in the heavens
and on the earth,
blood and fire and billows of
smoke.
31The sun will be turned to darkness
and the moon to blood
before the coming of the great and
dreadful day of the LORD.
32And everyone who calls
on the name of the LORD will be
saved;
for on Mount Zion and in Jerusalem
there will be deliverance,
as the LORD has said,
among the survivors
whom the LORD calls.

The Nations Judged

3 "In those days and at that time,
when I restore the fortunes of Judah
and Jerusalem,
2I will gather all nations
and bring them down to the Valley
of Jehoshaphat.[b]
There I will enter into judgment
against them
concerning my inheritance, my
people Israel,
for they scattered my people among
the nations
and divided up my land.
3They cast lots for my people
and traded boys for prostitutes;
they sold girls for wine
that they might drink.

4"Now what have you against me, O Tyre and Sidon and all you regions of Philistia? Are you repaying me for something I have done? If you are paying me back, I will swiftly and speedily return on your own heads what you have done. 5For you took my silver and my gold and carried off my finest treasures to your temples. 6You sold the people of Judah and Jerusalem to the Greeks, that you might send them far from their homeland.

7"See, I am going to rouse them out of the places to which you sold them, and I will return on your own heads what you have done. 8I will sell your sons and daughters to the people of Judah, and they will sell them to the Sabeans, a nation far away." The LORD has spoken.

9Proclaim this among the nations:
Prepare for war!
Rouse the warriors!
Let all the fighting men draw near
and attack.
10Beat your plowshares into swords
and your pruning hooks into spears.
Let the weakling say,
"I am strong!"
11Come quickly, all you nations from
every side,
and assemble there.

Bring down your warriors, O LORD!

12"Let the nations be roused;
let them advance into the Valley of
Jehoshaphat,
for there I will sit
to judge all the nations on every
side.
13Swing the sickle,
for the harvest is ripe.
Come, trample the grapes,
for the winepress is full
and the vats overflow—
so great is their wickedness!"

[a]25 The precise meaning of the four Hebrew words used here for locusts is uncertain. [b]2 *Jehoshaphat* means *the LORD judges*; also in verse 12.

14 Multitudes, multitudes
in the valley of decision!
For the day of the LORD is near
in the valley of decision.
15 The sun and moon will be darkened,
and the stars no longer shine.
16 The LORD will roar from Zion
and thunder from Jerusalem;
the earth and the sky will tremble.
But the LORD will be a refuge for his people,
a stronghold for the people of Israel.

Blessings for God's People

17 "Then you will know that I, the LORD your God,
dwell in Zion, my holy hill.
Jerusalem will be holy;

VERSE FOR THE DAY: Joel 2:32

AUTHOR: Keith Stonehocker

PASSAGE FOR THE DAY: Joel 2:28–32

S.O.S.

A couple very close to us announced that their marriage was in trouble. They had been married only four years, but there had been problems from the start and they saw little hope for rebuilding their relationship. The sad part was that all of us close to them were taken completely by surprise.

By God's providence, we found out soon enough to come alongside in their moment of crisis and help them sort through the long-term implications of divorce. They've been able to stop the stone from rolling all the way down the hill—now comes the arduous task of rolling it back up.

This experience reinforced the critical role we can play in the lives of couples around us. It's easy to be so preoccupied with the crush of living that we don't even see the cracks in our own marriages, let alone in others'. Or when we do sense our friends' relationships floundering, we find it easiest to look the other way.

But survey after survey affirms that couples in trouble will hint of their pain to friends long before seeking professional help. Are we keeping our antennae tuned for those S.O.S. signals, or is the ship lost before the pleas for help are ever heard?

MARRIAGE BUILDERS

♦ *How has the divorce of close friends or family members affected your relationship?*

♦ *How can you "call on the name of the LORD" on behalf of your married friends and loved ones?*

Additional Scripture Readings
Daniel 12:3; Matthew 10:42; Jude 23–24

Go to page 967 for your next devotional reading.

never again will foreigners invade
her.

18"In that day the mountains will drip
new wine,
and the hills will flow with milk;
all the ravines of Judah will run
with water.
A fountain will flow out of the LORD's
house
and will water the valley of
acacias.[a]

19But Egypt will be desolate,
Edom a desert waste,
because of violence done to the
people of Judah,
in whose land they shed innocent
blood.

20Judah will be inhabited forever
and Jerusalem through all
generations.

21Their bloodguilt, which I have not
pardoned,
I will pardon."

The LORD dwells in Zion!

[a]18 Or *Valley of Shittim*

AMOS prophesies during the time of Jeroboam II (2 Kings 14:23–29), a time of prosperity for some but extreme poverty for many others. He reprimands those who oppress the poor and make them suffer even more. As you read this book, think about how angry God becomes when you show more interest in your wealth than in obeying him. Remember, though, that God will forgive you, if you confess your sins and seek to do his will.

AMOS

1 The words of Amos, one of the shepherds of Tekoa—what he saw concerning Israel two years before the earthquake, when Uzziah was king of Judah and Jeroboam son of Jehoash[a] was king of Israel.

2 He said:

"The LORD roars from Zion
and thunders from Jerusalem;
the pastures of the shepherds dry up,[b]
and the top of Carmel withers."

Judgment on Israel's Neighbors

3 This is what the LORD says:

"For three sins of Damascus,
even for four, I will not turn back
⌊my wrath⌋.
Because she threshed Gilead
with sledges having iron teeth,
4 I will send fire upon the house of Hazael
that will consume the fortresses of Ben-Hadad.
5 I will break down the gate of Damascus;

[a] 1 Hebrew *Joash*, a variant of *Jehoash* [b] 2 Or *shepherds mourn*

I will destroy the king who is in[a]
the Valley of Aven[b]
and the one who holds the scepter in
Beth Eden.
The people of Aram will go into
exile to Kir,"
says the LORD.

6This is what the LORD says:

"For three sins of Gaza,
even for four, I will not turn back
⌊my wrath⌋.
Because she took captive whole
communities
and sold them to Edom,
7I will send fire upon the walls of Gaza
that will consume her fortresses.
8I will destroy the king[c] of Ashdod
and the one who holds the scepter
in Ashkelon.
I will turn my hand against Ekron,
till the last of the Philistines is
dead,"
says the Sovereign LORD.

9This is what the LORD says:

"For three sins of Tyre,
even for four, I will not turn back
⌊my wrath⌋.
Because she sold whole communities
of captives to Edom,
disregarding a treaty of
brotherhood,
10I will send fire upon the walls of Tyre
that will consume her fortresses."

11This is what the LORD says:

"For three sins of Edom,
even for four, I will not turn back
⌊my wrath⌋.
Because he pursued his brother with a
sword,
stifling all compassion,[d]
because his anger raged continually
and his fury flamed unchecked,
12I will send fire upon Teman
that will consume the fortresses of
Bozrah."

13This is what the LORD says:

"For three sins of Ammon,
even for four, I will not turn back
⌊my wrath⌋.
Because he ripped open the pregnant
women of Gilead
in order to extend his borders,
14I will set fire to the walls of Rabbah
that will consume her fortresses
amid war cries on the day of battle,
amid violent winds on a stormy
day.
15Her king[e] will go into exile,
he and his officials together,"
says the LORD.

2 This is what the LORD says:

"For three sins of Moab,
even for four, I will not turn back
⌊my wrath⌋.
Because he burned, as if to lime,
the bones of Edom's king,
2I will send fire upon Moab
that will consume the fortresses of
Kerioth.[f]
Moab will go down in great tumult
amid war cries and the blast of the
trumpet.
3I will destroy her ruler
and kill all her officials with him,"
says the LORD.

4This is what the LORD says:

"For three sins of Judah,
even for four, I will not turn back
⌊my wrath⌋.
Because they have rejected the law of
the LORD
and have not kept his decrees,
because they have been led astray by
false gods,[g]
the gods[h] their ancestors followed,
5I will send fire upon Judah
that will consume the fortresses of
Jerusalem."

Judgment on Israel

6This is what the LORD says:

"For three sins of Israel,
even for four, I will not turn back
⌊my wrath⌋.
They sell the righteous for silver,
and the needy for a pair of sandals.
7They trample on the heads of the poor
as upon the dust of the ground
and deny justice to the oppressed.
Father and son use the same girl
and so profane my holy name.
8They lie down beside every altar
on garments taken in pledge.

[a]5 Or *the inhabitants of* [b]5 *Aven* means *wickedness.* [c]8 Or *inhabitants* [d]11 Or *sword / and destroyed his allies* [e]15 Or / *Molech*; Hebrew *malcam* [f]2 Or *of her cities* [g]4 Or *by lies* [h]4 Or *lies*

In the house of their god
they drink wine taken as fines.

9"I destroyed the Amorite before them,
though he was tall as the cedars
and strong as the oaks.
I destroyed his fruit above
and his roots below.

10"I brought you up out of Egypt,
and I led you forty years in the desert
to give you the land of the Amorites.
11I also raised up prophets from among your sons
and Nazirites from among your young men.
Is this not true, people of Israel?"
declares the LORD.
12"But you made the Nazirites drink wine
and commanded the prophets not to prophesy.

13"Now then, I will crush you
as a cart crushes when loaded with grain.
14The swift will not escape,
the strong will not muster their strength,
and the warrior will not save his life.
15The archer will not stand his ground,
the fleet-footed soldier will not get away,
and the horseman will not save his life.
16Even the bravest warriors
will flee naked on that day,"
declares the LORD.

Witnesses Summoned Against Israel

3 Hear this word the LORD has spoken against you, O people of Israel—against the whole family I brought up out of Egypt:

2"You only have I chosen
of all the families of the earth;
therefore I will punish you
for all your sins."

3Do two walk together
unless they have agreed to do so?
4Does a lion roar in the thicket
when he has no prey?
Does he growl in his den
when he has caught nothing?
5Does a bird fall into a trap on the ground
where no snare has been set?
Does a trap spring up from the earth
when there is nothing to catch?
6When a trumpet sounds in a city,
do not the people tremble?
When disaster comes to a city,
has not the LORD caused it?

7Surely the Sovereign LORD does nothing
without revealing his plan
to his servants the prophets.

8The lion has roared—
who will not fear?
The Sovereign LORD has spoken—
who can but prophesy?

9Proclaim to the fortresses of Ashdod
and to the fortresses of Egypt:
"Assemble yourselves on the mountains of Samaria;
see the great unrest within her
and the oppression among her people."

10"They do not know how to do right,"
declares the LORD,
"who hoard plunder and loot in their fortresses."

11Therefore this is what the Sovereign LORD says:

"An enemy will overrun the land;
he will pull down your strongholds
and plunder your fortresses."

12This is what the LORD says:

"As a shepherd saves from the lion's mouth
only two leg bones or a piece of an ear,
so will the Israelites be saved,
those who sit in Samaria
on the edge of their beds
and in Damascus on their couches.[a]"

13"Hear this and testify against the house of Jacob," declares the Lord, the LORD God Almighty.

14"On the day I punish Israel for her sins,
I will destroy the altars of Bethel;
the horns of the altar will be cut off
and fall to the ground.
15I will tear down the winter house

[a] 12 The meaning of the Hebrew for this line is uncertain.

along with the summer house;
the houses adorned with ivory will be destroyed
and the mansions will be demolished,"
declares the LORD.

Israel Has Not Returned to God

4 Hear this word, you cows of Bashan
on Mount Samaria,
you women who oppress the poor
and crush the needy
and say to your husbands, "Bring us some drinks!"
[2]The Sovereign LORD has sworn by his holiness:
"The time will surely come
when you will be taken away with hooks,
the last of you with fishhooks.
[3]You will each go straight out

VERSE FOR THE DAY: Amos 3:3 | AUTHOR: Richard Capen, Jr. | PASSAGE FOR THE DAY: Amos 3:1–7

Feed the Fire

"The flame just went out. It was as simple as that."

My friend was "explaining away" the death of his 22-year marriage. There had been no bitter dispute, no extramarital affair. My friend and his wife had simply drifted apart—bored, indifferent, uncommitted.

Without commitment, no marriage can succeed. When my wife, Joan, and I were married, we made an unconditional commitment to each other in the presence of God. Our wedding vow was not a promise "if," it was a promise "always." Over the years, our mutual love and respect have grown, and God's presence in our marriage has made the difference.

The traumas of life—crisis, disappointment, failure—can undermine even the strongest relationships. Success in marriage must be a conscious choice, not a thing left to chance. It requires hard work, compromise, patience and a willingness to grow. For the flame of marriage to be kept alive, the marriage relationship must be nurtured. If it is not, then it will flicker out—as it did for my friend.

MARRIAGE BUILDERS

♦ *Identify a time in your marriage when you did what was right, even though you didn't* feel *like doing it. What was the outcome?*

♦ *Repeat your wedding promise to your spouse—with a commitment of "always."*

Additional Scripture Readings
1 Corinthians 13:7–8; Joshua 24:15

Go to page 974 for your next devotional reading.

through breaks in the wall,
and you will be cast out toward
Harmon,[a]"
declares the LORD.

4"Go to Bethel and sin;
go to Gilgal and sin yet more.
Bring your sacrifices every morning,
your tithes every three years.[b]
5Burn leavened bread as a thank
offering
and brag about your freewill
offerings—
boast about them, you Israelites,
for this is what you love to do,"
declares the Sovereign LORD.

6"I gave you empty stomachs[c] in
every city
and lack of bread in every town,
yet you have not returned to me,"
declares the LORD.

7"I also withheld rain from you
when the harvest was still three
months away.
I sent rain on one town,
but withheld it from another.
One field had rain;
another had none and dried up.
8People staggered from town to town
for water
but did not get enough to drink,
yet you have not returned to me,"
declares the LORD.

9"Many times I struck your gardens
and vineyards,
I struck them with blight and
mildew.
Locusts devoured your fig and olive
trees,
yet you have not returned to me,"
declares the LORD.

10"I sent plagues among you
as I did to Egypt.
I killed your young men with the
sword,
along with your captured horses.
I filled your nostrils with the stench of
your camps,
yet you have not returned to me,"
declares the LORD.

11"I overthrew some of you
as I[d] overthrew Sodom and
Gomorrah.
You were like a burning stick
snatched from the fire,
yet you have not returned to me,"
declares the LORD.

12"Therefore this is what I will do to
you, Israel,
and because I will do this to you,
prepare to meet your God, O Israel."

13He who forms the mountains,
creates the wind,
and reveals his thoughts to man,
he who turns dawn to darkness,
and treads the high places of the
earth—
the LORD God Almighty is his name.

A Lament and Call to Repentance

5 Hear this word, O house of Israel, this
lament I take up concerning you:

2"Fallen is Virgin Israel,
never to rise again,
deserted in her own land,
with no one to lift her up."

3This is what the Sovereign LORD says:

"The city that marches out a thousand
strong for Israel
will have only a hundred left;
the town that marches out a hundred
strong
will have only ten left."

4This is what the LORD says to the house
of Israel:

"Seek me and live;
5 do not seek Bethel,
do not go to Gilgal,
do not journey to Beersheba.
For Gilgal will surely go into exile,
and Bethel will be reduced to
nothing.[e]"

6Seek the LORD and live,
or he will sweep through the house
of Joseph like a fire;
it will devour,
and Bethel will have no one to
quench it.

7You who turn justice into bitterness
and cast righteousness to the
ground
8(he who made the Pleiades and Orion,
who turns blackness into dawn
and darkens day into night,

[a]3 Masoretic Text; with a different word division of the Hebrew (see Septuagint) *out, O mountain of oppression* [b]4 Or *tithes on the third day* [c]6 Hebrew *you cleanness of teeth* [d]11 Hebrew *God*
[e]5 Or *grief*; or *wickedness*; Hebrew *aven*, a reference to Beth Aven (a derogatory name for Bethel)

who calls for the waters of the sea
and pours them out over the face of the land—
the LORD is his name—
9he flashes destruction on the stronghold
and brings the fortified city to ruin),
10you hate the one who reproves in court
and despise him who tells the truth.

11You trample on the poor
and force him to give you grain.
Therefore, though you have built stone mansions,
you will not live in them;
though you have planted lush vineyards,
you will not drink their wine.
12For I know how many are your offenses
and how great your sins.

You oppress the righteous and take bribes
and you deprive the poor of justice in the courts.
13Therefore the prudent man keeps quiet in such times,
for the times are evil.

14Seek good, not evil,
that you may live.
Then the LORD God Almighty will be with you,
just as you say he is.
15Hate evil, love good;
maintain justice in the courts.
Perhaps the LORD God Almighty will have mercy
on the remnant of Joseph.

16Therefore this is what the Lord, the LORD God Almighty, says:

"There will be wailing in all the streets
and cries of anguish in every public square.
The farmers will be summoned to weep
and the mourners to wail.
17There will be wailing in all the vineyards,
for I will pass through your midst,"
says the LORD.

The Day of the LORD

18Woe to you who long
for the day of the LORD!
Why do you long for the day of the LORD?
That day will be darkness, not light.
19It will be as though a man fled from a lion
only to meet a bear,
as though he entered his house
and rested his hand on the wall
only to have a snake bite him.
20Will not the day of the LORD be darkness, not light—
pitch-dark, without a ray of brightness?

21"I hate, I despise your religious feasts;
I cannot stand your assemblies.
22Even though you bring me burnt offerings and grain offerings,
I will not accept them.
Though you bring choice fellowship offerings,[a]
I will have no regard for them.
23Away with the noise of your songs!
I will not listen to the music of your harps.
24But let justice roll on like a river,
righteousness like a never-failing stream!

25"Did you bring me sacrifices and offerings
forty years in the desert, O house of Israel?
26You have lifted up the shrine of your king,
the pedestal of your idols,
the star of your god[b]—
which you made for yourselves.
27Therefore I will send you into exile beyond Damascus,"
says the LORD, whose name is God Almighty.

Woe to the Complacent

6 Woe to you who are complacent in Zion,
and to you who feel secure on Mount Samaria,
you notable men of the foremost nation,
to whom the people of Israel come!
2Go to Calneh and look at it;
go from there to great Hamath,

[a]22 Traditionally *peace offerings* [b]26 Or *lifted up Sakkuth your king / and Kaiwan your idols, / your star-gods*; Septuagint *lifted up the shrine of Molech / and the star of your god Rephan, / their idols*

and then go down to Gath in
Philistia.
Are they better off than your two
kingdoms?
Is their land larger than yours?
3You put off the evil day
and bring near a reign of terror.
4You lie on beds inlaid with ivory
and lounge on your couches.
You dine on choice lambs
and fattened calves.
5You strum away on your harps like
David
and improvise on musical
instruments.
6You drink wine by the bowlful
and use the finest lotions,
but you do not grieve over the ruin
of Joseph.
7Therefore you will be among the first
to go into exile;
your feasting and lounging will end.

The Lord Abhors the Pride of Israel

8The Sovereign Lord has sworn by himself—the Lord God Almighty declares:

"I abhor the pride of Jacob
and detest his fortresses;
I will deliver up the city
and everything in it."

9If ten men are left in one house, they too will die. 10And if a relative who is to burn the bodies comes to carry them out of the house and asks anyone still hiding there, "Is anyone with you?" and he says, "No," then he will say, "Hush! We must not mention the name of the Lord."

11For the Lord has given the command,
and he will smash the great house
into pieces
and the small house into bits.

12Do horses run on the rocky crags?
Does one plow there with oxen?
But you have turned justice into
poison
and the fruit of righteousness into
bitterness—
13you who rejoice in the conquest of Lo
Debar[a]
and say, "Did we not take
Karnaim[b] by our own
strength?"

14For the Lord God Almighty declares,
"I will stir up a nation against you,
O house of Israel,
that will oppress you all the way
from Lebo[c] Hamath to the valley of
the Arabah."

Locusts, Fire and a Plumb Line

7 This is what the Sovereign Lord showed me: He was preparing swarms of locusts after the king's share had been harvested and just as the second crop was coming up. 2When they had stripped the land clean, I cried out, "Sovereign Lord, forgive! How can Jacob survive? He is so small!"

3So the Lord relented.

"This will not happen," the Lord said.

4This is what the Sovereign Lord showed me: The Sovereign Lord was calling for judgment by fire; it dried up the great deep and devoured the land. 5Then I cried out, "Sovereign Lord, I beg you, stop! How can Jacob survive? He is so small!"

6So the Lord relented.

"This will not happen either," the Sovereign Lord said.

7This is what he showed me: The Lord was standing by a wall that had been built true to plumb, with a plumb line in his hand. 8And the Lord asked me, "What do you see, Amos?"

"A plumb line," I replied.

Then the Lord said, "Look, I am setting a plumb line among my people Israel; I will spare them no longer.

9"The high places of Isaac will be
destroyed
and the sanctuaries of Israel will be
ruined;
with my sword I will rise against
the house of Jeroboam."

Amos and Amaziah

10Then Amaziah the priest of Bethel sent a message to Jeroboam king of Israel: "Amos is raising a conspiracy against you in the very heart of Israel. The land cannot bear all his words. 11For this is what Amos is saying:

" 'Jeroboam will die by the sword,
and Israel will surely go into exile,
away from their native land.' "

12Then Amaziah said to Amos, "Get out,

[a]13 *Lo Debar* means *nothing.* [b]13 *Karnaim* means *horns; horn* here symbolizes strength. [c]14 Or *from the entrance to*

you seer! Go back to the land of Judah.
Earn your bread there and do your prophesying there. 13Don't prophesy anymore
at Bethel, because this is the king's sanctuary and the temple of the kingdom."
14Amos answered Amaziah, "I was neither a prophet nor a prophet's son, but I
was a shepherd, and I also took care of sycamore-fig trees. 15But the LORD took
me from tending the flock and said to me,
'Go, prophesy to my people Israel.' 16Now
then, hear the word of the LORD. You say,

" 'Do not prophesy against Israel,
and stop preaching against the
house of Isaac.'

17"Therefore this is what the LORD says:

" 'Your wife will become a prostitute
in the city,
and your sons and daughters will
fall by the sword.
Your land will be measured and
divided up,
and you yourself will die in a
pagan[a] country.
And Israel will certainly go into exile,
away from their native land.' "

A Basket of Ripe Fruit

8 This is what the Sovereign LORD
showed me: a basket of ripe fruit.
2"What do you see, Amos?" he asked.
"A basket of ripe fruit," I answered.
Then the LORD said to me, "The time is
ripe for my people Israel; I will spare them
no longer.
3"In that day," declares the Sovereign
LORD, "the songs in the temple will turn to
wailing.[b] Many, many bodies—flung everywhere! Silence!"

4Hear this, you who trample the needy
and do away with the poor of the
land,

5saying,

"When will the New Moon be over
that we may sell grain,
and the Sabbath be ended
that we may market wheat?"—
skimping the measure,
boosting the price
and cheating with dishonest scales,
6buying the poor with silver
and the needy for a pair of sandals,
selling even the sweepings with the
wheat.

7The LORD has sworn by the Pride of Jacob: "I will never forget anything they
have done.

8"Will not the land tremble for this,
and all who live in it mourn?
The whole land will rise like the Nile;
it will be stirred up and then sink
like the river of Egypt.

9"In that day," declares the Sovereign
LORD,

"I will make the sun go down at noon
and darken the earth in broad
daylight.
10I will turn your religious feasts into
mourning
and all your singing into weeping.
I will make all of you wear sackcloth
and shave your heads.
I will make that time like mourning
for an only son
and the end of it like a bitter day.

11"The days are coming," declares the
Sovereign LORD,
"when I will send a famine through
the land—
not a famine of food or a thirst for
water,
but a famine of hearing the words
of the LORD.
12Men will stagger from sea to sea
and wander from north to east,
searching for the word of the LORD,
but they will not find it.

13"In that day

"the lovely young women and strong
young men
will faint because of thirst.
14They who swear by the shame[c] of
Samaria,
or say, 'As surely as your god lives,
O Dan,'
or, 'As surely as the god[d] of
Beersheba lives'—
they will fall,
never to rise again."

Israel to Be Destroyed

9 I saw the Lord standing by the altar,
and he said:

"Strike the tops of the pillars

[a] 17 Hebrew *an unclean* [b] 3 Or *"the temple singers will wail* [c] 14 Or *by Ashima*; or *by the idol*
[d] 14 Or *power*

so that the thresholds shake.
Bring them down on the heads of all the people;
those who are left I will kill with the sword.
Not one will get away,
none will escape.
2 Though they dig down to the depths of the grave,[a]
from there my hand will take them.
Though they climb up to the heavens,
from there I will bring them down.
3 Though they hide themselves on the top of Carmel,
there I will hunt them down and seize them.
Though they hide from me at the bottom of the sea,
there I will command the serpent to bite them.
4 Though they are driven into exile by their enemies,
there I will command the sword to slay them.
I will fix my eyes upon them
for evil and not for good."
5 The Lord, the Lord Almighty,
he who touches the earth and it melts,
and all who live in it mourn—
the whole land rises like the Nile,
then sinks like the river of Egypt—
6 he who builds his lofty palace[b] in the heavens
and sets its foundation[c] on the earth,
who calls for the waters of the sea
and pours them out over the face of the land—
the Lord is his name.
7 "Are not you Israelites
the same to me as the Cushites[d]?"
declares the Lord.
"Did I not bring Israel up from Egypt,
the Philistines from Caphtor[e]
and the Arameans from Kir?
8 "Surely the eyes of the Sovereign Lord
are on the sinful kingdom.
I will destroy it
from the face of the earth—
yet I will not totally destroy
the house of Jacob,"
declares the Lord.
9 "For I will give the command,
and I will shake the house of Israel among all the nations
as grain is shaken in a sieve,
and not a pebble will reach the ground.
10 All the sinners among my people
will die by the sword,
all those who say,
'Disaster will not overtake or meet us.'

Israel's Restoration

11 "In that day I will restore
David's fallen tent.
I will repair its broken places,
restore its ruins,
and build it as it used to be,
12 so that they may possess the remnant of Edom
and all the nations that bear my name,[f]"
declares the Lord, who will do these things.

13 "The days are coming," declares the Lord,
"when the reaper will be overtaken by the plowman
and the planter by the one treading grapes.
New wine will drip from the mountains
and flow from all the hills.
14 I will bring back my exiled[g] people Israel;
they will rebuild the ruined cities and live in them.
They will plant vineyards and drink their wine;
they will make gardens and eat their fruit.
15 I will plant Israel in their own land,
never again to be uprooted
from the land I have given them,"
says the Lord your God.

[a] 2 Hebrew *to Sheol* [b] 6 The meaning of the Hebrew for this phrase is uncertain. [c] 6 The meaning of the Hebrew for this word is uncertain. [d] 7 That is, people from the upper Nile region [e] 7 That is, Crete [f] 12 Hebrew; Septuagint *so that the remnant of men / and all the nations that bear my name may seek the Lord,* [g] 14 Or *will restore the fortunes of my*

OBADIAH prophesies judgment against Edom for her violence against Israel, promising that God will restore his people. As you read this book, remember that no one can fight against God's people and hope to win in the end. The final victory belongs to Christ and his church.

OBADIAH

1 The vision of Obadiah.

This is what the Sovereign LORD says
about Edom—

We have heard a message from the
LORD:
An envoy was sent to the nations to
say,
"Rise, and let us go against her for
battle"—

2 "See, I will make you small among the
nations;
you will be utterly despised.
3 The pride of your heart has deceived
you,
you who live in the clefts of the
rocks[a]
and make your home on the
heights,
you who say to yourself,
'Who can bring me down to the
ground?'
4 Though you soar like the eagle
and make your nest among the
stars,
from there I will bring you down,"
declares the LORD.
5 "If thieves came to you,
if robbers in the night—
Oh, what a disaster awaits you—
would they not steal only as much
as they wanted?
If grape pickers came to you,
would they not leave a few grapes?
6 But how Esau will be ransacked,
his hidden treasures pillaged!
7 All your allies will force you to the
border;
your friends will deceive and
overpower you;
those who eat your bread will set a
trap for you,[b]

[a] 3 Or *of Sela* [b] 7 The meaning of the Hebrew for this clause is uncertain.

but you will not detect it.
8"In that day," declares the LORD,
"will I not destroy the wise men of Edom,
men of understanding in the mountains of Esau?
9Your warriors, O Teman, will be terrified,
and everyone in Esau's mountains
will be cut down in the slaughter.
10Because of the violence against your brother Jacob,
you will be covered with shame;
you will be destroyed forever.
11On the day you stood aloof
while strangers carried off his wealth
and foreigners entered his gates

VERSE FOR THE DAY: Obadiah 3

AUTHOR: Ron R. Lee

PASSAGE FOR THE DAY: Obadiah 3–4

Sins of Omission

Your wife came home early from work with the flu. By bedtime, she seemed to be feeling better, but in the middle of the night you hear her in the bathroom. You know that if you lie quietly, she'll think you're asleep. What's the harm in staying in bed? She can take care of herself.

Your husband is worried about losing his job. His department failed to meet its quota for the second consecutive quarter, and his boss called him on the carpet. You consider preparing his favorite meal for dinner, but you've had a rough week at work yourself. Giving in to fatigue, you decide to microwave some leftovers instead.

Because of pride, we carry an internal debate over whose welfare we should seek—our own or that of others. Pride can cause us to refuse to do what is right, to ignore God's promptings to show kindness or offer help to our spouse. We frequently resist God's leading because we're too tired, too busy or too distracted by seemingly more important matters.

When we become aware of these silent sins, we realize once again our need to submit to God's rule in our lives. Only then will we find the strength to sacrifice our own needs to serve one another, and only then will our marriages truly thrive.

MARRIAGE BUILDERS

♦ *When was the last time you chose to stick with your previous plans rather than offer to help your mate?*
♦ *What impact did that decision have on your marriage?*

Additional Scripture Readings
Proverbs 11:2–6; James 4:17

Go to page 975 for your next devotional reading.

WEEKENDING

CHERISHING

Husbands and wives commonly express and receive love differently. Use this ranking system to identify your "love language." If the listed behavior is something that makes you feel loved and cherished, circle the number three. If you feel neutral about that behavior, circle the number two. If you feel the action is an ineffective indicator of love, circle the number one. After each of you has circled the appropriate numbers, discuss each other's answers.

Hearing expressions of love	1 2 3
Reading expressions of love	1 2 3
Receiving help	1 2 3
Being served	1 2 3
Being touched	1 2 3
Being provided for	1 2 3
Receiving a gift	1 2 3
Being challenged	1 2 3
Having time devoted to me	1 2 3

— *Harold B. Smith*

REVIVE

Saturday: Proverbs 5:1–23
Sunday: 1 John 4:7–21

Go to page 978 for your next devotional reading.

and cast lots for Jerusalem,
you were like one of them.
12 You should not look down on your brother
in the day of his misfortune,
nor rejoice over the people of Judah
in the day of their destruction,
nor boast so much
in the day of their trouble.
13 You should not march through the gates of my people
in the day of their disaster,
nor look down on them in their calamity
in the day of their disaster,
nor seize their wealth
in the day of their disaster.
14 You should not wait at the crossroads
to cut down their fugitives,
nor hand over their survivors
in the day of their trouble.
15 "The day of the LORD is near
for all nations.
As you have done, it will be done to you;
your deeds will return upon your own head.
16 Just as you drank on my holy hill,
so all the nations will drink continually;
they will drink and drink
and be as if they had never been.
17 But on Mount Zion will be deliverance;
it will be holy,
and the house of Jacob
will possess its inheritance.
18 The house of Jacob will be a fire
and the house of Joseph a flame;
the house of Esau will be stubble,
and they will set it on fire and consume it.
There will be no survivors
from the house of Esau."
The LORD has spoken.
19 People from the Negev will occupy
the mountains of Esau,
and people from the foothills will possess
the land of the Philistines.
They will occupy the fields of Ephraim and Samaria,
and Benjamin will possess Gilead.
20 This company of Israelite exiles who are in Canaan
will possess ⌊the land⌋ as far as Zarephath;
the exiles from Jerusalem who are in Sepharad
will possess the towns of the Negev.
21 Deliverers will go up on[a] Mount Zion
to govern the mountains of Esau.
And the kingdom will be the LORD's.

[a] 21 Or *from*

JONAH is sent by God to Nineveh, the city of the enemy of God's people during the time of Jeroboam II (2 Kings 14:23–29). After he tries to run away, God gives him a second chance to prophesy, for the Lord wants the whole world to hear the message of his grace. As you read this book, think about how many times God gives you a second opportunity. Don't forget to tell others about your Lord.

JONAH

Jonah Flees From the Lord

1 The word of the Lord came to Jonah
son of Amittai: 2"Go to the great city
of Nineveh and preach against it, because
its wickedness has come up before me."
3But Jonah ran away from the Lord and
headed for Tarshish. He went down to
Joppa, where he found a ship bound for
that port. After paying the fare, he went
aboard and sailed for Tarshish to flee from
the Lord.
4Then the Lord sent a great wind on the
sea, and such a violent storm arose that
the ship threatened to break up. 5All the
sailors were afraid and each cried out to
his own god. And they threw the cargo
into the sea to lighten the ship.

But Jonah had gone below deck, where
he lay down and fell into a deep sleep.
6The captain went to him and said, "How
can you sleep? Get up and call on your
god! Maybe he will take notice of us, and
we will not perish."
7Then the sailors said to each other,
"Come, let us cast lots to find out who is
responsible for this calamity." They cast
lots and the lot fell on Jonah.
8So they asked him, "Tell us, who is re-
sponsible for making all this trouble for
us? What do you do? Where do you come
from? What is your country? From what
people are you?"
9He answered, "I am a Hebrew and I
worship the Lord, the God of heaven, who
made the sea and the land."

VERSE FOR THE DAY:
Jonah 1:1–3

AUTHOR:
Wonda Layton

PASSAGE FOR THE DAY:
Jonah 1:1–2:10

God's Responsibilities

Each of us needs to determine what we can and cannot change, and then act accordingly. Sorting out the matters for which we are responsible—and relaxing about the things that are unchangeable—not only puts the events of life into perspective and relieves us from immense burdens of guilt, but it also liberates us to act within God's will.

The prophet Jonah had a difficult time taking care of his own business and leaving God's business to God. God assigned to Jonah the task of proclaiming the Word of the Lord to Nineveh—meanwhile, God's own business was to bring Nineveh to repentance. It took a violent storm, a great fish, a vine, a worm and sunstroke before Jonah finally separated the two effectively and the city of Nineveh was saved.

In another era, the Corinthian church had the issues so blurred that they were ignoring the important questions before the body. Paul gave considerable space to this concern in his first letter to them, clarifying each person's part in God's scheme. Paul finally said, "What, after all, is Apollos? And what is Paul? Only servants, through whom you came to believe—as the Lord assigned to each his task. I planted the seed, Apollos watered it, but God made it grow" (1 Corinthians 3:5–6). Paul knew who was responsible for what. And we would do ourselves a favor if we figured out the same in our own lives.

MARRIAGE BUILDERS

♦ *What responsibilities are you carrying that more rightly belong to God?*

♦ *How can you relax and trust God in those areas?*

Additional Scripture Readings
1 Corinthians 3:1–9; Romans 12:1–2; James 4:17

Go to page 986 for your next devotional reading.

10This terrified them and they asked,
"What have you done?" (They knew he
was running away from the LORD, because
he had already told them so.)
11The sea was getting rougher and
rougher. So they asked him, "What should
we do to you to make the sea calm down
for us?"
12"Pick me up and throw me into the
sea," he replied, "and it will become calm.
I know that it is my fault that this great
storm has come upon you."
13Instead, the men did their best to row
back to land. But they could not, for the
sea grew even wilder than before. 14Then
they cried to the LORD, "O LORD, please do
not let us die for taking this man's life. Do
not hold us accountable for killing an in-
nocent man, for you, O LORD, have done
as you pleased." 15Then they took Jonah
and threw him overboard, and the raging
sea grew calm. 16At this the men greatly
feared the LORD, and they offered a sacri-
fice to the LORD and made vows to him.
17But the LORD provided a great fish to
swallow Jonah, and Jonah was inside the
fish three days and three nights.

Jonah's Prayer

2 From inside the fish Jonah prayed to
the LORD his God. 2He said:

"In my distress I called to the LORD,
and he answered me.
From the depths of the grave[a] I
called for help,
and you listened to my cry.
3You hurled me into the deep,
into the very heart of the seas,
and the currents swirled about me;
all your waves and breakers
swept over me.
4I said, 'I have been banished
from your sight;
yet I will look again
toward your holy temple.'
5The engulfing waters threatened me,[b]
the deep surrounded me;
seaweed was wrapped around my
head.
6To the roots of the mountains I sank
down;
the earth beneath barred me in
forever.
But you brought my life up from the
pit,
O LORD my God.
7"When my life was ebbing away,
I remembered you, LORD,
and my prayer rose to you,
to your holy temple.
8"Those who cling to worthless idols
forfeit the grace that could be theirs.
9But I, with a song of thanksgiving,
will sacrifice to you.
What I have vowed I will make good.
Salvation comes from the LORD."

10And the LORD commanded the fish,
and it vomited Jonah onto dry land.

Jonah Goes to Nineveh

3 Then the word of the LORD came to Jo-
nah a second time: 2"Go to the great
city of Nineveh and proclaim to it the mes-
sage I give you."
3Jonah obeyed the word of the LORD
and went to Nineveh. Now Nineveh was a
very important city—a visit required
three days. 4On the first day, Jonah started
into the city. He proclaimed: "Forty more
days and Nineveh will be overturned."
5The Ninevites believed God. They de-
clared a fast, and all of them, from the
greatest to the least, put on sackcloth.
6When the news reached the king of
Nineveh, he rose from his throne, took off
his royal robes, covered himself with
sackcloth and sat down in the dust. 7Then
he issued a proclamation in Nineveh:

"By the decree of the king and his no-
bles:

Do not let any man or beast, herd
or flock, taste anything; do not let
them eat or drink. 8But let man and
beast be covered with sackcloth. Let
everyone call urgently on God. Let
them give up their evil ways and their
violence. 9Who knows? God may yet
relent and with compassion turn
from his fierce anger so that we will
not perish."

10When God saw what they did and
how they turned from their evil ways, he
had compassion and did not bring upon
them the destruction he had threatened.

Jonah's Anger at the LORD's Compassion

4 But Jonah was greatly displeased and
became angry. 2He prayed to the
LORD, "O LORD, is this not what I said

[a]2 Hebrew *Sheol* [b]5 Or *waters were at my throat*

when I was still at home? That is why I
was so quick to flee to Tarshish. I knew
that you are a gracious and compassion-
ate God, slow to anger and abounding
in love, a God who relents from sending
calamity. 3Now, O LORD, take away my
life, for it is better for me to die than to
live."

4But the LORD replied, "Have you any
right to be angry?"

5Jonah went out and sat down at a place
east of the city. There he made himself a
shelter, sat in its shade and waited to see
what would happen to the city. 6Then the
LORD God provided a vine and made it
grow up over Jonah to give shade for his
head to ease his discomfort, and Jonah
was very happy about the vine. 7But at
dawn the next day God provided a worm,
which chewed the vine so that it withered.
8When the sun rose, God provided a
scorching east wind, and the sun blazed
on Jonah's head so that he grew faint. He
wanted to die, and said, "It would be bet-
ter for me to die than to live."

9But God said to Jonah, "Do you have a
right to be angry about the vine?"

"I do," he said. "I am angry enough to
die."

10But the LORD said, "You have been
concerned about this vine, though you did
not tend it or make it grow. It sprang up
overnight and died overnight. 11But Nine-
veh has more than a hundred and twenty
thousand people who cannot tell their
right hand from their left, and many cattle
as well. Should I not be concerned about
that great city?"

MICAH prophesies during the time of Jotham and Ahaz (2 Chronicles 27–28) against the numerous sins of the kingdom of Judah, insisting that God wants justice in society. He inspires hope by speaking of the coming Messiah and his kingdom of peace. As you read this book, promise the Lord that your lifestyle will be one of justice, mercy and peace in his Son Jesus Christ.

MICAH

1 The word of the LORD that came to Micah of Moresheth during the reigns of Jotham, Ahaz and Hezekiah, kings of Judah—the vision he saw concerning Samaria and Jerusalem.

2 Hear, O peoples, all of you,
listen, O earth and all who are in it,
that the Sovereign LORD may witness against you,
the Lord from his holy temple.

Judgment Against Samaria and Jerusalem

3 Look! The LORD is coming from his dwelling place;
he comes down and treads the high places of the earth.
4 The mountains melt beneath him
and the valleys split apart,
like wax before the fire,
like water rushing down a slope.
5 All this is because of Jacob's transgression,
because of the sins of the house of Israel.
What is Jacob's transgression?
Is it not Samaria?
What is Judah's high place?
Is it not Jerusalem?

6 "Therefore I will make Samaria a heap of rubble,
a place for planting vineyards.
I will pour her stones into the valley
and lay bare her foundations.
7 All her idols will be broken to pieces;
all her temple gifts will be burned with fire;
I will destroy all her images.

Since she gathered her gifts from the wages of prostitutes,
as the wages of prostitutes they will again be used."

Weeping and Mourning

8Because of this I will weep and wail;
I will go about barefoot and naked.
I will howl like a jackal
and moan like an owl.
9For her wound is incurable;
it has come to Judah.
It[a] has reached the very gate of my people,
even to Jerusalem itself.
10Tell it not in Gath[b];
weep not at all.[c]
In Beth Ophrah[d]
roll in the dust.
11Pass on in nakedness and shame,
you who live in Shaphir.[e]
Those who live in Zaanan[f]
will not come out.
Beth Ezel is in mourning;
its protection is taken from you.
12Those who live in Maroth[g] writhe in pain,
waiting for relief,
because disaster has come from the LORD,
even to the gate of Jerusalem.
13You who live in Lachish,[h]
harness the team to the chariot.
You were the beginning of sin
to the Daughter of Zion,
for the transgressions of Israel
were found in you.
14Therefore you will give parting gifts
to Moresheth Gath.
The town of Aczib[i] will prove deceptive
to the kings of Israel.
15I will bring a conqueror against you
who live in Mareshah.[j]
He who is the glory of Israel
will come to Adullam.
16Shave your heads in mourning
for the children in whom you delight;
make yourselves as bald as the vulture,
for they will go from you into exile.

Man's Plans and God's

2 Woe to those who plan iniquity,
to those who plot evil on their beds!
At morning's light they carry it out
because it is in their power to do it.
2They covet fields and seize them,
and houses, and take them.
They defraud a man of his home,
a fellowman of his inheritance.

3Therefore, the LORD says:

"I am planning disaster against this people,
from which you cannot save yourselves.
You will no longer walk proudly,
for it will be a time of calamity.
4In that day men will ridicule you;
they will taunt you with this mournful song:
'We are utterly ruined;
my people's possession is divided up.
He takes it from me!
He assigns our fields to traitors.' "

5Therefore you will have no one in the assembly of the LORD
to divide the land by lot.

False Prophets

6"Do not prophesy," their prophets say.
"Do not prophesy about these things;
disgrace will not overtake us."
7Should it be said, O house of Jacob:
"Is the Spirit of the LORD angry?
Does he do such things?"

"Do not my words do good
to him whose ways are upright?
8Lately my people have risen up
like an enemy.
You strip off the rich robe
from those who pass by without a care,
like men returning from battle.
9You drive the women of my people
from their pleasant homes.
You take away my blessing
from their children forever.
10Get up, go away!
For this is not your resting place,

[a] 9 Or *He* [b] 10 *Gath* sounds like the Hebrew for *tell.* [c] 10 Hebrew; Septuagint may suggest *not in Acco.* The Hebrew for *in Acco* sounds like the Hebrew for *weep.* [d] 10 *Beth Ophrah* means *house of dust.* [e] 11 *Shaphir* means *pleasant.* [f] 11 *Zaanan* sounds like the Hebrew for *come out.* [g] 12 *Maroth* sounds like the Hebrew for *bitter.* [h] 13 *Lachish* sounds like the Hebrew for *team.* [i] 14 *Aczib* means *deception.* [j] 15 *Mareshah* sounds like the Hebrew for *conqueror.*

because it is defiled,
it is ruined, beyond all remedy.
11If a liar and deceiver comes and says,
'I will prophesy for you plenty of wine and beer,'
he would be just the prophet for this people!

Deliverance Promised

12"I will surely gather all of you, O Jacob;
I will surely bring together the remnant of Israel.
I will bring them together like sheep in a pen,
like a flock in its pasture;
the place will throng with people.
13One who breaks open the way will go up before them;
they will break through the gate and go out.
Their king will pass through before them,
the LORD at their head."

Leaders and Prophets Rebuked

3 Then I said,
"Listen, you leaders of Jacob,
you rulers of the house of Israel.
Should you not know justice,
2 you who hate good and love evil;
who tear the skin from my people
and the flesh from their bones;
3who eat my people's flesh,
strip off their skin
and break their bones in pieces;
who chop them up like meat for the pan,
like flesh for the pot?"

4Then they will cry out to the LORD,
but he will not answer them.
At that time he will hide his face from them
because of the evil they have done.

5This is what the LORD says:

"As for the prophets
who lead my people astray,
if one feeds them,
they proclaim 'peace';
if he does not,
they prepare to wage war against him.
6Therefore night will come over you, without visions,
and darkness, without divination.
The sun will set for the prophets,
and the day will go dark for them.
7The seers will be ashamed
and the diviners disgraced.
They will all cover their faces
because there is no answer from God."

8But as for me, I am filled with power,
with the Spirit of the LORD,
and with justice and might,
to declare to Jacob his transgression,
to Israel his sin.
9Hear this, you leaders of the house of Jacob,
you rulers of the house of Israel,
who despise justice
and distort all that is right;
10who build Zion with bloodshed,
and Jerusalem with wickedness.
11Her leaders judge for a bribe,
her priests teach for a price,
and her prophets tell fortunes for money.
Yet they lean upon the LORD and say,
"Is not the LORD among us?
No disaster will come upon us."
12Therefore because of you,
Zion will be plowed like a field,
Jerusalem will become a heap of rubble,
the temple hill a mound overgrown with thickets.

The Mountain of the LORD

4 In the last days
the mountain of the LORD's temple will be established
as chief among the mountains;
it will be raised above the hills,
and peoples will stream to it.

2Many nations will come and say,

"Come, let us go up to the mountain of the LORD,
to the house of the God of Jacob.
He will teach us his ways,
so that we may walk in his paths."
The law will go out from Zion,
the word of the LORD from Jerusalem.
3He will judge between many peoples
and will settle disputes for strong nations far and wide.
They will beat their swords into plowshares
and their spears into pruning hooks.
Nation will not take up sword against nation,

nor will they train for war anymore.
4 Every man will sit under his own vine
and under his own fig tree,
and no one will make them afraid,
for the LORD Almighty has spoken.
5 All the nations may walk
in the name of their gods;
we will walk in the name of the LORD
our God for ever and ever.

The LORD's Plan

6 "In that day," declares the LORD,
"I will gather the lame;
I will assemble the exiles
and those I have brought to grief.
7 I will make the lame a remnant,
those driven away a strong nation.
The LORD will rule over them in
Mount Zion
from that day and forever.
8 As for you, O watchtower of the flock,
O stronghold[a] of the Daughter of
Zion,
the former dominion will be restored
to you;
kingship will come to the Daughter
of Jerusalem."

9 Why do you now cry aloud—
have you no king?
Has your counselor perished,
that pain seizes you like that of a
woman in labor?
10 Writhe in agony, O Daughter of Zion,
like a woman in labor,
for now you must leave the city
to camp in the open field.
You will go to Babylon;
there you will be rescued.
There the LORD will redeem you
out of the hand of your enemies.

11 But now many nations
are gathered against you.
They say, "Let her be defiled,
let our eyes gloat over Zion!"
12 But they do not know
the thoughts of the LORD;
they do not understand his plan,
he who gathers them like sheaves to
the threshing floor.

13 "Rise and thresh, O Daughter of Zion,
for I will give you horns of iron;
I will give you hoofs of bronze
and you will break to pieces many
nations."
You will devote their ill-gotten gains
to the LORD,
their wealth to the Lord of all the
earth.

A Promised Ruler From Bethlehem

5 Marshal your troops, O city of
troops,[b]
for a siege is laid against us.
They will strike Israel's ruler
on the cheek with a rod.

2 "But you, Bethlehem Ephrathah,
though you are small among the
clans[c] of Judah,
out of you will come for me
one who will be ruler over Israel,
whose origins[d] are from of old,
from ancient times.[e]"

3 Therefore Israel will be abandoned
until the time when she who is in
labor gives birth
and the rest of his brothers return
to join the Israelites.

4 He will stand and shepherd his flock
in the strength of the LORD,
in the majesty of the name of the
LORD his God.
And they will live securely, for then
his greatness
will reach to the ends of the earth.
5 And he will be their peace.

Deliverance and Destruction

When the Assyrian invades our land
and marches through our fortresses,
we will raise against him seven
shepherds,
even eight leaders of men.
6 They will rule[f] the land of Assyria
with the sword,
the land of Nimrod with drawn
sword.[g]
He will deliver us from the Assyrian
when he invades our land
and marches into our borders.

7 The remnant of Jacob will be
in the midst of many peoples
like dew from the LORD,
like showers on the grass,
which do not wait for man
or linger for mankind.
8 The remnant of Jacob will be among
the nations,
in the midst of many peoples,

[a] 8 Or *hill* [b] 1 Or *Strengthen your walls, O walled city* [c] 2 Or *rulers* [d] 2 Hebrew *goings out*
[e] 2 Or *from days of eternity* [f] 6 Or *crush* [g] 6 Or *Nimrod in its gates*

like a lion among the beasts of the forest,
like a young lion among flocks of sheep,
which mauls and mangles as it goes,
and no one can rescue.
9Your hand will be lifted up in triumph over your enemies,
and all your foes will be destroyed.

10"In that day," declares the LORD,
"I will destroy your horses from among you
and demolish your chariots.
11I will destroy the cities of your land
and tear down all your strongholds.
12I will destroy your witchcraft
and you will no longer cast spells.
13I will destroy your carved images
and your sacred stones from among you;
you will no longer bow down
to the work of your hands.
14I will uproot from among you your Asherah poles[a]
and demolish your cities.
15I will take vengeance in anger and wrath
upon the nations that have not obeyed me."

The LORD's Case Against Israel

6 Listen to what the LORD says:
"Stand up, plead your case before the mountains;
let the hills hear what you have to say.
2Hear, O mountains, the LORD's accusation;
listen, you everlasting foundations of the earth.
For the LORD has a case against his people;
he is lodging a charge against Israel.

3"My people, what have I done to you?
How have I burdened you? Answer me.
4I brought you up out of Egypt
and redeemed you from the land of slavery.
I sent Moses to lead you,
also Aaron and Miriam.
5My people, remember
what Balak king of Moab counseled
and what Balaam son of Beor answered.
Remember ⌊your journey⌋ from Shittim to Gilgal,
that you may know the righteous acts of the LORD."

6With what shall I come before the LORD
and bow down before the exalted God?
Shall I come before him with burnt offerings,
with calves a year old?
7Will the LORD be pleased with thousands of rams,
with ten thousand rivers of oil?
Shall I offer my firstborn for my transgression,
the fruit of my body for the sin of my soul?
8He has showed you, O man, what is good.
And what does the LORD require of you?
To act justly and to love mercy
and to walk humbly with your God.

Israel's Guilt and Punishment

9Listen! The LORD is calling to the city—
and to fear your name is wisdom—
"Heed the rod and the One who appointed it.[b]
10Am I still to forget, O wicked house,
your ill-gotten treasures
and the short ephah,[c] which is accursed?
11Shall I acquit a man with dishonest scales,
with a bag of false weights?
12Her rich men are violent;
her people are liars
and their tongues speak deceitfully.
13Therefore, I have begun to destroy you,
to ruin you because of your sins.
14You will eat but not be satisfied;
your stomach will still be empty.[d]
You will store up but save nothing,
because what you save I will give to the sword.
15You will plant but not harvest;

[a]14 That is, symbols of the goddess Asherah [b]9 The meaning of the Hebrew for this line is uncertain.
[c]10 An ephah was a dry measure. [d]14 The meaning of the Hebrew for this word is uncertain.

you will press olives but not use the
oil on yourselves,
you will crush grapes but not drink
the wine.
16 You have observed the statutes of
Omri
and all the practices of Ahab's
house,
and you have followed their
traditions.
Therefore I will give you over to ruin
and your people to derision;
you will bear the scorn of the
nations.[a]"

[a] 16 Septuagint; Hebrew *scorn due my people*

Israel's Misery

7 What misery is mine!
I am like one who gathers summer
fruit
at the gleaning of the vineyard;
there is no cluster of grapes to eat,
none of the early figs that I crave.
2 The godly have been swept from the
land;
not one upright man remains.
All men lie in wait to shed blood;
each hunts his brother with a net.
3 Both hands are skilled in doing evil;
the ruler demands gifts,

VERSE FOR THE DAY: Micah 6:8 | AUTHOR: Charlene Ann Baumbich | PASSAGE FOR THE DAY: Micah 6:1–8

Feelings Will Follow

Simply reading a good book on marriage or watching an instructional video won't fix a hurting relationship. You also have to *work*—relentlessly. Our natural bent is to wait for good feelings to return before we'll act in a loving manner toward our mate. But marriage counselors commonly urge couples to reverse that sequence: Take positive steps first, then, hopefully, the positive feelings will follow.

Commitment to a *marriage* is different from commitment to a *relationship*. Commitment to marriage alone is static, like throwing out an anchor—you're stuck there. Commitment to a relationship is dynamic: Together you chart your course, navigate through the channels and work to stay afloat.

With God's help, my husband and I have done that. So have multitudes of other couples. And so can you.

MARRIAGE BUILDERS

♦ *How does it prove "commitment" for you to* do *what is right, even when you don't* feel *like it?*

♦ *Why is commitment dynamic (renewed day by day) instead of static (a one-time promise)?*

Additional Scripture Readings
Isaiah 1:17; Colossians 3:12–14

Go to page 987 for your next devotional reading.

the judge accepts bribes,
the powerful dictate what they desire—
they all conspire together.
4The best of them is like a brier,
the most upright worse than a thorn hedge.
The day of your watchmen has come,
the day God visits you.
Now is the time of their confusion.
5Do not trust a neighbor;
put no confidence in a friend.
Even with her who lies in your embrace
be careful of your words.
6For a son dishonors his father,
a daughter rises up against her mother,
a daughter-in-law against her mother-in-law—
a man's enemies are the members of his own household.

VERSE FOR THE DAY: Micah 7:18 | AUTHOR: Max Lucado | PASSAGE FOR THE DAY: Micah 7:1–20

Fabulous Forgiveness

In a *Reader's Digest* story that I love, a husband and wife call a time-out during a quarrel to retire to separate corners. There, they write down everything about the other person that they don't like.

She notices he's writing feverishly and then erasing as he goes along. She thinks he's perfecting his list of criticisms, so she makes a list that will outdo his.

Later, when they exchange notepads, he's confronted by a comprehensive inventory of his failings: "You snore. You come home late. You don't appreciate me."

She finds that he had begun writing down her flaws but had gone back and erased everything except the last words: "but I love you anyway."

That's a great example of what God—through his grace—has done for us. He isn't blind to our sin, but he loves us in spite of it. He doesn't expect us to overlook our mate's faults, either. But he commands us to love each other in spite of those flaws. As a grateful recipient of God's grace, I want to extend that same grace to my wife.

MARRIAGE BUILDERS

♦ *If you've been keeping a mental inventory of your spouse's irksome habits, go back and try erasing it all.*
♦ *Tell your spouse about a time when you recieved God's grace.*

Additional Scripture Readings
Psalm 103:8–13; Jeremiah 31:34

Go to page 990 for your next devotional reading.

7 But as for me, I watch in hope for the LORD,
I wait for God my Savior;
my God will hear me.

Israel Will Rise

8 Do not gloat over me, my enemy!
Though I have fallen, I will rise.
Though I sit in darkness,
the LORD will be my light.
9 Because I have sinned against him,
I will bear the LORD's wrath,
until he pleads my case
and establishes my right.
He will bring me out into the light;
I will see his righteousness.
10 Then my enemy will see it
and will be covered with shame,
she who said to me,
"Where is the LORD your God?"
My eyes will see her downfall;
even now she will be trampled underfoot
like mire in the streets.

11 The day for building your walls will come,
the day for extending your boundaries.
12 In that day people will come to you
from Assyria and the cities of Egypt,
even from Egypt to the Euphrates
and from sea to sea
and from mountain to mountain.
13 The earth will become desolate because of its inhabitants,
as the result of their deeds.

Prayer and Praise

14 Shepherd your people with your staff,
the flock of your inheritance,
which lives by itself in a forest,
in fertile pasturelands.[a]
Let them feed in Bashan and Gilead
as in days long ago.
15 "As in the days when you came out of Egypt,
I will show them my wonders."

16 Nations will see and be ashamed,
deprived of all their power.
They will lay their hands on their mouths
and their ears will become deaf.
17 They will lick dust like a snake,
like creatures that crawl on the ground.
They will come trembling out of their dens;
they will turn in fear to the LORD our God
and will be afraid of you.
18 Who is a God like you,
who pardons sin and forgives the transgression
of the remnant of his inheritance?
You do not stay angry forever
but delight to show mercy.
19 You will again have compassion on us;
you will tread our sins underfoot
and hurl all our iniquities into the depths of the sea.
20 You will be true to Jacob,
and show mercy to Abraham,
as you pledged on oath to our fathers
in days long ago.

[a] 14 Or *in the middle of Carmel*

NAHUM prophesies against the wicked and cruel nation of Assyria, probably during the time of Josiah (2 Kings 22–23). In so doing he testifies that God, as the judge of the nations, is in control of all that happens. As you read this book, be comforted (Nahum means "comfort") by the thought that God is Lord of history.

NAHUM

1 An oracle concerning Nineveh. The book of the vision of Nahum the Elkoshite.

The Lord's Anger Against Nineveh

2 The Lord is a jealous and avenging God;
the Lord takes vengeance and is filled with wrath.
The Lord takes vengeance on his foes
and maintains his wrath against his enemies.
3 The Lord is slow to anger and great in power;
the Lord will not leave the guilty unpunished.
His way is in the whirlwind and the storm,
and clouds are the dust of his feet.
4 He rebukes the sea and dries it up;
he makes all the rivers run dry.
Bashan and Carmel wither
and the blossoms of Lebanon fade.
5 The mountains quake before him
and the hills melt away.
The earth trembles at his presence,
the world and all who live in it.
6 Who can withstand his indignation?
Who can endure his fierce anger?
His wrath is poured out like fire;
the rocks are shattered before him.

7 The Lord is good,
a refuge in times of trouble.
He cares for those who trust in him,
8 but with an overwhelming flood
he will make an end of ⌊Nineveh⌋;
he will pursue his foes into darkness.

9 Whatever they plot against the Lord
he[a] will bring to an end;

[a] 9 Or *What do you foes plot against the Lord? / He*

trouble will not come a second
time.
10They will be entangled among thorns
and drunk from their wine;
they will be consumed like dry
stubble.[a]
11From you, ⌞O Nineveh,⌟ has one come
forth
who plots evil against the LORD
and counsels wickedness.
12This is what the LORD says:
"Although they have allies and are
numerous,
they will be cut off and pass away.
Although I have afflicted you,
⌞O Judah,⌟
I will afflict you no more.
13Now I will break their yoke from your
neck
and tear your shackles away."

[a]10 The meaning of the Hebrew for this verse is uncertain.

VERSE FOR THE DAY: Nahum 1:7 | AUTHOR: Charles R. Swindoll | PASSAGE FOR THE DAY: Nahum 1:1–15

Trouble and Grace

Without wanting to come across as the Ebenezer Scrooge of wedding bells, I must say that *troubles in marriage are inevitable*. The list is endless. Trouble from calamities, from disease, from the old nature. Trouble from children and family squabbles. Trouble from differing viewpoints about time, temperature and trips. Trouble from neighbors. Trouble because of finances. Trouble due to pressure at work that you can't turn off.

It will require grace for the two of you to endure. Grace to accept, to forgive, to laugh much of it off. Grace to keep going, to encourage the other in the midst of the paths that lead through conflict and disagreement.

I don't know how many times my wife, Cynthia, has taken my hand, looked me in the eye, and said, "Honey, we'll make it through this." That took grace, and it lifted my spirit. On other occasions I had the grace to help her. Without the grace to let each other be, our marriage would be stormy and full of struggles.

Grace gives us tolerance. And it just may save our marriages.

MARRIAGE BUILDERS

♦ *Why do you think some couples are surprised when troubles come to their marriage?*

♦ *What role does a sense of humor play in handling the common troubles that are part of your married life?*

Additional Scripture Readings
Ecclesiastes 4:9–10; 2 Corinthians 12:9; Titus 2:11–14

Go to page 995 for your next devotional reading.

14The LORD has given a command
concerning you, ⌊Nineveh⌋:
"You will have no descendants to
bear your name.
I will destroy the carved images and
cast idols
that are in the temple of your gods.
I will prepare your grave,
for you are vile."

15Look, there on the mountains,
the feet of one who brings good
news,
who proclaims peace!
Celebrate your festivals, O Judah,
and fulfill your vows.
No more will the wicked invade you;
they will be completely destroyed.

Nineveh to Fall

2 An attacker advances against you,
⌊Nineveh⌋.
Guard the fortress,
watch the road,
brace yourselves,
marshal all your strength!

2The LORD will restore the splendor of
Jacob
like the splendor of Israel,
though destroyers have laid them
waste
and have ruined their vines.

3The shields of his soldiers are red;
the warriors are clad in scarlet.
The metal on the chariots flashes
on the day they are made ready;
the spears of pine are brandished.[a]
4The chariots storm through the
streets,
rushing back and forth through the
squares.
They look like flaming torches;
they dart about like lightning.

5He summons his picked troops,
yet they stumble on their way.
They dash to the city wall;
the protective shield is put in place.
6The river gates are thrown open
and the palace collapses.
7It is decreed[b] that ⌊the city⌋
be exiled and carried away.
Its slave girls moan like doves
and beat upon their breasts.
8Nineveh is like a pool,
and its water is draining away.
"Stop! Stop!" they cry,
but no one turns back.
9Plunder the silver!
Plunder the gold!
The supply is endless,
the wealth from all its treasures!
10She is pillaged, plundered, stripped!
Hearts melt, knees give way,
bodies tremble, every face grows
pale.

11Where now is the lions' den,
the place where they fed their
young,
where the lion and lioness went,
and the cubs, with nothing to fear?
12The lion killed enough for his cubs
and strangled the prey for his mate,
filling his lairs with the kill
and his dens with the prey.

13"I am against you,"
declares the LORD Almighty.
"I will burn up your chariots in
smoke,
and the sword will devour your
young lions.
I will leave you no prey on the
earth.
The voices of your messengers
will no longer be heard."

Woe to Nineveh

3 Woe to the city of blood,
full of lies,
full of plunder,
never without victims!
2The crack of whips,
the clatter of wheels,
galloping horses
and jolting chariots!
3Charging cavalry,
flashing swords
and glittering spears!
Many casualties,
piles of dead,
bodies without number,
people stumbling over the
corpses—
4all because of the wanton lust of a
harlot,
alluring, the mistress of sorceries,
who enslaved nations by her
prostitution
and peoples by her witchcraft.

[a]3 Hebrew; Septuagint and Syriac / *the horsemen rush to and fro*
[b]7 The meaning of the Hebrew for this word is uncertain.

5"I am against you," declares the LORD
Almighty.
"I will lift your skirts over your face.
I will show the nations your
nakedness
and the kingdoms your shame.
6I will pelt you with filth,
I will treat you with contempt
and make you a spectacle.
7All who see you will flee from you
and say,
'Nineveh is in ruins—who will
mourn for her?'
Where can I find anyone to comfort
you?"

8Are you better than Thebes,[a]
situated on the Nile,
with water around her?
The river was her defense,
the waters her wall.
9Cush[b] and Egypt were her boundless
strength;
Put and Libya were among her
allies.
10Yet she was taken captive
and went into exile.
Her infants were dashed to pieces
at the head of every street.
Lots were cast for her nobles,
and all her great men were put in
chains.
11You too will become drunk;
you will go into hiding
and seek refuge from the enemy.

12All your fortresses are like fig trees
with their first ripe fruit;
when they are shaken,
the figs fall into the mouth of the
eater.
13Look at your troops—
they are all women!
The gates of your land
are wide open to your enemies;
fire has consumed their bars.

14Draw water for the siege,
strengthen your defenses!
Work the clay,
tread the mortar,
repair the brickwork!
15There the fire will devour you;
the sword will cut you down
and, like grasshoppers, consume
you.
Multiply like grasshoppers,
multiply like locusts!
16You have increased the number of
your merchants
till they are more than the stars of
the sky,
but like locusts they strip the land
and then fly away.
17Your guards are like locusts,
your officials like swarms of locusts
that settle in the walls on a cold
day—
but when the sun appears they fly
away,
and no one knows where.

18O king of Assyria, your shepherds[c]
slumber;
your nobles lie down to rest.
Your people are scattered on the
mountains
with no one to gather them.
19Nothing can heal your wound;
your injury is fatal.
Everyone who hears the news about
you
claps his hands at your fall,
for who has not felt
your endless cruelty?

[a]8 Hebrew *No Amon* [b]9 That is, the upper Nile region [c]18 Or *rulers*

HABAKKUK prophesies in Judah when the power of Babylon is growing (2 Chronicles 35:20–36:8). When he questions God's justice in allowing evil to go unchecked, he receives the answer that God knows what he is doing, leading to a concluding celebration of God's glory and power. As you read this book, remember that the majestic God is in control of your life, no matter what happens to you.

HABAKKUK

1 The oracle that Habakkuk the prophet received.

Habakkuk's Complaint

2 How long, O LORD, must I call for help,
but you do not listen?
Or cry out to you, "Violence!"
but you do not save?
3 Why do you make me look at injustice?
Why do you tolerate wrong?
Destruction and violence are before me;
there is strife, and conflict abounds.
4 Therefore the law is paralyzed,
and justice never prevails.
The wicked hem in the righteous,
so that justice is perverted.

The LORD's Answer

5 "Look at the nations and watch—
and be utterly amazed.
For I am going to do something in your days
that you would not believe,
even if you were told.
6 I am raising up the Babylonians,[a]
that ruthless and impetuous people,
who sweep across the whole earth
to seize dwelling places not their own.

[a] 6 Or *Chaldeans*

7They are a feared and dreaded people;
they are a law to themselves
and promote their own honor.
8Their horses are swifter than leopards,
fiercer than wolves at dusk.
Their cavalry gallops headlong;
their horsemen come from afar.
They fly like a vulture swooping to
devour;
9 they all come bent on violence.
Their hordes[a] advance like a desert
wind
and gather prisoners like sand.
10They deride kings
and scoff at rulers.
They laugh at all fortified cities;
they build earthen ramps and
capture them.
11Then they sweep past like the wind
and go on—
guilty men, whose own strength is
their god."

Habakkuk's Second Complaint

12O LORD, are you not from everlasting?
My God, my Holy One, we will not
die.
O LORD, you have appointed them to
execute judgment;
O Rock, you have ordained them to
punish.
13Your eyes are too pure to look on
evil;
you cannot tolerate wrong.
Why then do you tolerate the
treacherous?
Why are you silent while the
wicked
swallow up those more righteous
than themselves?
14You have made men like fish in the
sea,
like sea creatures that have no ruler.
15The wicked foe pulls all of them up
with hooks,
he catches them in his net,
he gathers them up in his dragnet;
and so he rejoices and is glad.
16Therefore he sacrifices to his net
and burns incense to his dragnet,
for by his net he lives in luxury
and enjoys the choicest food.
17Is he to keep on emptying his net,
destroying nations without mercy?

2 I will stand at my watch
and station myself on the ramparts;
I will look to see what he will say to
me,
and what answer I am to give to
this complaint.[b]

The LORD's Answer

2Then the LORD replied:

"Write down the revelation
and make it plain on tablets
so that a herald[c] may run with it.
3For the revelation awaits an appointed
time;
it speaks of the end
and will not prove false.
Though it linger, wait for it;
it[d] will certainly come and will not
delay.

4"See, he is puffed up;
his desires are not upright—
but the righteous will live by his
faith[e]—
5indeed, wine betrays him;
he is arrogant and never at rest.
Because he is as greedy as the grave[f]
and like death is never satisfied,
he gathers to himself all the nations
and takes captive all the peoples.

6"Will not all of them taunt him with
ridicule and scorn, saying,

" 'Woe to him who piles up stolen
goods
and makes himself wealthy by
extortion!
How long must this go on?'
7Will not your debtors[g] suddenly
arise?
Will they not wake up and make
you tremble?
Then you will become their victim.
8Because you have plundered many
nations,
the peoples who are left will
plunder you.
For you have shed man's blood;
you have destroyed lands and cities
and everyone in them.

9"Woe to him who builds his realm by
unjust gain
to set his nest on high,

[a]9 The meaning of the Hebrew for this word is uncertain. [b]1 Or *and what to answer when I am rebuked* [c]2 Or *so that whoever reads it* [d]3 Or *Though he linger, wait for him; / he* [e]4 Or *faithfulness* [f]5 Hebrew *Sheol* [g]7 Or *creditors*

to escape the clutches of ruin!
10You have plotted the ruin of many peoples,
shaming your own house and forfeiting your life.
11The stones of the wall will cry out,
and the beams of the woodwork will echo it.

12"Woe to him who builds a city with bloodshed
and establishes a town by crime!
13Has not the LORD Almighty determined
that the people's labor is only fuel for the fire,
that the nations exhaust themselves for nothing?
14For the earth will be filled with the knowledge of the glory of the LORD,
as the waters cover the sea.

15"Woe to him who gives drink to his neighbors,
pouring it from the wineskin till they are drunk,
so that he can gaze on their naked bodies.
16You will be filled with shame instead of glory.
Now it is your turn! Drink and be exposed[a]!
The cup from the LORD's right hand is coming around to you,

[a] 16 Masoretic Text; Dead Sea Scrolls, Aquila, Vulgate and Syriac (see also Septuagint) *and stagger*

FRIDAY

VERSE FOR THE DAY:	AUTHOR:	PASSAGE FOR THE DAY:
Habakkuk 2:20	Thomas à Kempis	Habakkuk 2:1–20

Silent Lessons

Someone has said: "Whenever I have been among men, I have returned a lesser man." We often experience this when we have spent a long time in conversation. For it is easier to be completely silent, than not to exceed in speech. It is easier to lie hidden at home than to be able sufficiently to guard oneself abroad. He, therefore, who seeks to reach that which is hidden and spiritual must with Jesus slip away from the crowd. No one can safely appear in public who does not enjoy seclusion. No one safely talks but he who gladly keeps silent. No one safely rules but he who is glad to be subordinate. No one safely commands but he who has learned well to obey.

MARRIAGE BUILDERS

♦ *What obstacles prevent you from finding times of quiet before God?*

♦ *How could each of you help the other create personal quiet times?*

Additional Scripture Readings
Ecclesiastes 3:7; Psalm 5:1–12; Matthew 14:23

Go to page 997 for your next devotional reading.

and disgrace will cover your glory.
17 The violence you have done to
Lebanon will overwhelm you,
and your destruction of animals will
terrify you.
For you have shed man's blood;
you have destroyed lands and cities
and everyone in them.
18 "Of what value is an idol, since a man
has carved it?
Or an image that teaches lies?
For he who makes it trusts in his own
creation;
he makes idols that cannot speak.
19 Woe to him who says to wood, 'Come
to life!'
Or to lifeless stone, 'Wake up!'
Can it give guidance?
It is covered with gold and silver;
there is no breath in it.
20 But the LORD is in his holy temple;
let all the earth be silent before
him."

Habakkuk's Prayer

3 A prayer of Habakkuk the prophet. On *shigionoth.*[a]

2 LORD, I have heard of your fame;
I stand in awe of your deeds,
O LORD.
Renew them in our day,
in our time make them known;
in wrath remember mercy.
3 God came from Teman,
the Holy One from Mount Paran.
Selah[b]
His glory covered the heavens
and his praise filled the earth.
4 His splendor was like the sunrise;
rays flashed from his hand,
where his power was hidden.
5 Plague went before him;
pestilence followed his steps.
6 He stood, and shook the earth;
he looked, and made the nations
tremble.
The ancient mountains crumbled
and the age-old hills collapsed.
His ways are eternal.
7 I saw the tents of Cushan in distress,
the dwellings of Midian in anguish.
8 Were you angry with the rivers,
O LORD?
Was your wrath against the
streams?
Did you rage against the sea
when you rode with your horses
and your victorious chariots?
9 You uncovered your bow,
you called for many arrows. *Selah*
You split the earth with rivers;
10 the mountains saw you and
writhed.
Torrents of water swept by;
the deep roared
and lifted its waves on high.
11 Sun and moon stood still in the
heavens
at the glint of your flying arrows,
at the lightning of your flashing
spear.
12 In wrath you strode through the
earth
and in anger you threshed the
nations.
13 You came out to deliver your people,
to save your anointed one.
You crushed the leader of the land of
wickedness,
you stripped him from head to foot.
Selah
14 With his own spear you pierced his
head
when his warriors stormed out to
scatter us,
gloating as though about to devour
the wretched who were in hiding.
15 You trampled the sea with your
horses,
churning the great waters.
16 I heard and my heart pounded,
my lips quivered at the sound;
decay crept into my bones,
and my legs trembled.
Yet I will wait patiently for the day of
calamity
to come on the nation invading us.
17 Though the fig tree does not bud
and there are no grapes on the
vines,
though the olive crop fails
and the fields produce no food,

[a] *1* Probably a literary or musical term in verses 9 and 13

[b] *3* A word of uncertain meaning; possibly a musical term; also

WEEKENDING

SEX

It's often said that the most important sex organ is the one between your ears—namely, your brain. What we *think* about sex—our attitudes, fears, misconceptions—has a far-reaching impact on our lovemaking. That's why it's good to talk openly with your spouse to clear up any misunderstandings and to better understand the sources of each other's sexual attitudes. Each of you finish the following sentences. Let your discussion help you feel comfortable talking together about your sex life.

1. Thinking back to childhood, I wish my parents had talked to me more about sex to help clarify . . .

2. I sometimes feel uncomfortable talking about sex because of . . .

3. Sometimes I feel that our sex life is less than satisfactory because . . .

— *Jeron Frame*

REVIVE

Saturday: Proverbs 5:15–23
Sunday: Song of Songs 7:1–13

Go to page 1001 for your next devotional reading.

though there are no sheep in the pen
and no cattle in the stalls,
18 yet I will rejoice in the LORD,
I will be joyful in God my Savior.

19 The Sovereign LORD is my strength;
he makes my feet like the feet of a deer,
he enables me to go on the heights.

For the director of music. On my stringed instruments.

ZEPHANIAH, early in Josiah's reign and before his reforms (2 Chronicles 34:1–13), prophesies about a coming devastating day of the Lord. But he promises a wonderful future to those who humble themselves, seek the Lord, and live righteously. As you read this book, remember that a day of judgment is coming but that you can escape by turning to the Lord Jesus Christ.

ZEPHANIAH

1 The word of the LORD that came to
Zephaniah son of Cushi, the son of
Gedaliah, the son of Amariah, the son of
Hezekiah, during the reign of Josiah son
of Amon king of Judah:

Warning of Coming Destruction

2"I will sweep away everything
from the face of the earth,"
declares the LORD.
3"I will sweep away both men and
animals;
I will sweep away the birds of the
air
and the fish of the sea.
The wicked will have only heaps of
rubble[a]
when I cut off man from the face of
the earth,"
declares the LORD.

Against Judah

4"I will stretch out my hand against
Judah
and against all who live in
Jerusalem.
I will cut off from this place every
remnant of Baal,
the names of the pagan and the
idolatrous priests—
5those who bow down on the roofs
to worship the starry host,
those who bow down and swear by
the LORD
and who also swear by Molech,[b]

[a]3 The meaning of the Hebrew for this line is uncertain.

[b]5 Hebrew *Malcam*, that is, Milcom

[6]those who turn back from following
the LORD
and neither seek the LORD nor
inquire of him.
[7]Be silent before the Sovereign LORD,
for the day of the LORD is near.
The LORD has prepared a sacrifice;
he has consecrated those he has
invited.
[8]On the day of the LORD's sacrifice
I will punish the princes
and the king's sons
and all those clad
in foreign clothes.
[9]On that day I will punish
all who avoid stepping on the
threshold,[a]
who fill the temple of their gods
with violence and deceit.

[10]"On that day," declares the LORD,
"a cry will go up from the Fish
Gate,
wailing from the New Quarter,
and a loud crash from the hills.
[11]Wail, you who live in the market
district[b];
all your merchants will be wiped
out,
all who trade with[c] silver will be
ruined.
[12]At that time I will search Jerusalem
with lamps
and punish those who are
complacent,
who are like wine left on its dregs,
who think, 'The LORD will do nothing,
either good or bad.'
[13]Their wealth will be plundered,
their houses demolished.
They will build houses
but not live in them;
they will plant vineyards
but not drink the wine.

The Great Day of the LORD

[14]"The great day of the LORD is near—
near and coming quickly.
Listen! The cry on the day of the LORD
will be bitter,
the shouting of the warrior there.
[15]That day will be a day of wrath,
a day of distress and anguish,
a day of trouble and ruin,
a day of darkness and gloom,
a day of clouds and blackness,
[16]a day of trumpet and battle cry
against the fortified cities
and against the corner towers.
[17]I will bring distress on the people
and they will walk like blind men,
because they have sinned against
the LORD.
Their blood will be poured out like
dust
and their entrails like filth.
[18]Neither their silver nor their gold
will be able to save them
on the day of the LORD's wrath.
In the fire of his jealousy
the whole world will be consumed,
for he will make a sudden end
of all who live in the earth."

2 Gather together, gather together,
O shameful nation,
[2]before the appointed time arrives
and that day sweeps on like chaff,
before the fierce anger of the LORD
comes upon you,
before the day of the LORD's wrath
comes upon you.
[3]Seek the LORD, all you humble of the
land,
you who do what he commands.
Seek righteousness, seek humility;
perhaps you will be sheltered
on the day of the LORD's anger.

Against Philistia

[4]Gaza will be abandoned
and Ashkelon left in ruins.
At midday Ashdod will be emptied
and Ekron uprooted.
[5]Woe to you who live by the sea,
O Kerethite people;
the word of the LORD is against you,
O Canaan, land of the Philistines.

"I will destroy you,
and none will be left."

[6]The land by the sea, where the
Kerethites[d] dwell,
will be a place for shepherds and
sheep pens.
[7]It will belong to the remnant of the
house of Judah;
there they will find pasture.
In the evening they will lie down
in the houses of Ashkelon.
The LORD their God will care for them;
he will restore their fortunes.[e]

[a]9 See 1 Samuel 5:5. [b]11 Or *the Mortar* [c]11 Or *in* [d]6 The meaning of the Hebrew for this word is uncertain. [e]7 Or *will bring back their captives*

Against Moab and Ammon

8"I have heard the insults of Moab
and the taunts of the Ammonites,
who insulted my people
and made threats against their land.
9Therefore, as surely as I live,"
declares the LORD Almighty, the God
of Israel,
"surely Moab will become like Sodom,
the Ammonites like Gomorrah—
a place of weeds and salt pits,
a wasteland forever.
The remnant of my people will
plunder them;
the survivors of my nation will
inherit their land."

VERSE FOR THE DAY: Zephaniah 2:3

AUTHOR: Charlene Ann Baumbich

PASSAGE FOR THE DAY: Zephaniah 2:1–3

This Can *Get Better*

Before divorce can happen, it has to first become an option. That's why somewhere among the constricting tentacles of discontent, anger and the conviction that "I just can't stand it anymore," couples need to hold on to one vision: This marriage can get better.

If you ever get the feeling your mate is "never going to change," you need to take the step of honest self-assessment. You can look inside yourself and decide that the one thing you can change is yourself. But, of course, that's not easy.

Years ago, my husband, George, and I sought counseling for a crisis we were in. As I sat in the therapist's office, I couldn't wait for him to explain to George why he was making our marriage a miserable place to be. Thank God I also had enough sense to pray about the sessions, and to be sensitive to God's leading. I had a humbling shock in store for me: I owned a major piece of our problem. It took an outside mediator to bring a sense of balance, hope, reality and direction to our relationship.

We all need to reduce our criticism and start noticing what's *right* about our mates. And we need to recognize the ways we are contributing to the problems in our marriages. We can change *ourselves*, and that's an important first step to finding a solution.

MARRIAGE BUILDERS

♦ *Concerning what issues do you currently feel critical of your spouse?*

♦ *For each area of criticism, can you think of one way that* you *could change to help alleviate the problem?*

Additional Scripture Readings
Proverbs 14:8; Matthew 7:1–2;
1 Peter 5:5–7

Go to page 1003 for your next devotional reading.

10This is what they will get in return for
their pride,
for insulting and mocking the
people of the LORD Almighty.
11The LORD will be awesome to them
when he destroys all the gods of the
land.
The nations on every shore will
worship him,
every one in its own land.

Against Cush

12"You too, O Cushites,[a]
will be slain by my sword."

Against Assyria

13He will stretch out his hand against
the north
and destroy Assyria,
leaving Nineveh utterly desolate
and dry as the desert.
14Flocks and herds will lie down there,
creatures of every kind.
The desert owl and the screech owl
will roost on her columns.
Their calls will echo through the
windows,
rubble will be in the doorways,
the beams of cedar will be exposed.
15This is the carefree city
that lived in safety.
She said to herself,
"I am, and there is none besides
me."
What a ruin she has become,
a lair for wild beasts!
All who pass by her scoff
and shake their fists.

The Future of Jerusalem

3 Woe to the city of oppressors,
rebellious and defiled!
2She obeys no one,
she accepts no correction.
She does not trust in the LORD,
she does not draw near to her God.
3Her officials are roaring lions,
her rulers are evening wolves,
who leave nothing for the morning.
4Her prophets are arrogant;
they are treacherous men.
Her priests profane the sanctuary
and do violence to the law.
5The LORD within her is righteous;
he does no wrong.
Morning by morning he dispenses his
justice,
and every new day he does not fail,
yet the unrighteous know no
shame.
6"I have cut off nations;
their strongholds are demolished.
I have left their streets deserted,
with no one passing through.
Their cities are destroyed;
no one will be left—no one at all.
7I said to the city,
'Surely you will fear me
and accept correction!'
Then her dwelling would not be cut
off,
nor all my punishments come upon
her.
But they were still eager
to act corruptly in all they did.
8Therefore wait for me," declares the
LORD,
"for the day I will stand up to
testify.[b]
I have decided to assemble the
nations,
to gather the kingdoms
and to pour out my wrath on them—
all my fierce anger.
The whole world will be consumed
by the fire of my jealous anger.
9"Then will I purify the lips of the
peoples,
that all of them may call on the
name of the LORD
and serve him shoulder to shoulder.
10From beyond the rivers of Cush[c]
my worshipers, my scattered people,
will bring me offerings.
11On that day you will not be put to
shame
for all the wrongs you have done to
me,
because I will remove from this city
those who rejoice in their pride.
Never again will you be haughty
on my holy hill.
12But I will leave within you
the meek and humble,
who trust in the name of the LORD.
13The remnant of Israel will do no
wrong;
they will speak no lies,
nor will deceit be found in their
mouths.

[a]12 That is, people from the upper Nile region
[b]8 Septuagint and Syriac; Hebrew *will rise up to plunder*
[c]10 That is, the upper Nile region

They will eat and lie down
and no one will make them afraid."

14Sing, O Daughter of Zion;
shout aloud, O Israel!
Be glad and rejoice with all your heart,
O Daughter of Jerusalem!
15The LORD has taken away your punishment,
he has turned back your enemy.
The LORD, the King of Israel, is with you;
never again will you fear any harm.
16On that day they will say to Jerusalem,
"Do not fear, O Zion;
do not let your hands hang limp.
17The LORD your God is with you,
he is mighty to save.
He will take great delight in you,
he will quiet you with his love,
he will rejoice over you with singing."

18"The sorrows for the appointed feasts
I will remove from you;
they are a burden and a reproach to you.[a]

[a]18 Or *"I will gather you who mourn for the appointed feasts; / your reproach is a burden to you*

VERSE FOR THE DAY: Zephaniah 3:17

AUTHOR: Paul Stevens

PASSAGE FOR THE DAY: Zephaniah 3:8–20

Earthy Spirituality

Being married can play havoc with your spiritual life. Many people feel they were better friends in Christ before they got married.

Said one man: "I come home from a prayer meeting in seventh heaven and she informs me that the toilet is plugged." A tired homemaker sighs, "I'm just drifting off to sleep, my last thoughts about the goodness of God, and he reaches over to touch me. I know what this means!"

To be married means to have our privacy invaded, to live dangerously close to another sinner, to be interfered with by someone who claims to love us but does not always know how. Yet to be married also means to celebrate a sacrament every day, all day, through everything we share, even when we are not together.

Marriage is a risky business, but one that is fraught with the deepest kind of joy.

MARRIAGE BUILDERS

♦ *How do the nitty-gritty details of life as two married people sometimes interfere with your desire to be close spiritually?*
♦ *What are some of the blessings that come because marriage offers a unique opportunity for spiritual friendship?*

Additional Scripture Readings
Micah 6:8; Romans 12:1

Go to page 1006 for your next devotional reading.

19 At that time I will deal
with all who oppressed you;
I will rescue the lame
and gather those who have been
scattered.
I will give them praise and honor
in every land where they were put
to shame.

20 At that time I will gather you;
at that time I will bring you
home.
I will give you honor and praise
among all the peoples of the earth
when I restore your fortunes[a]
before your very eyes,"
says the LORD.

[a] 20 Or *I bring back your captives*

HAGGAI encourages the returning exiles (Ezra 4:24–5:2) to set proper priorities by rebuilding the temple of the Lord before they rebuild their own houses. He goes on to envision a time when all nations will come to the temple. As you read this book, decide to seek God's kingdom first, and rejoice in his promise of a new world when people everywhere will worship the Lord together.

HAGGAI

A Call to Build the House of the Lord

1 In the second year of King Darius, on the first day of the sixth month, the word of the Lord came through the prophet Haggai to Zerubbabel son of Shealtiel, governor of Judah, and to Joshua[a] son of Jehozadak, the high priest:

2 This is what the Lord Almighty says: "These people say, 'The time has not yet come for the Lord's house to be built.'"

3 Then the word of the Lord came through the prophet Haggai: 4 "Is it a time for you yourselves to be living in your paneled houses, while this house remains a ruin?"

5 Now this is what the Lord Almighty says: "Give careful thought to your ways. 6 You have planted much, but have harvested little. You eat, but never have enough. You drink, but never have your fill. You put on clothes, but are not warm. You earn wages, only to put them in a purse with holes in it."

7 This is what the Lord Almighty says: "Give careful thought to your ways. 8 Go up into the mountains and bring down timber and build the house, so that I may take pleasure in it and be honored," says the Lord. 9 "You expected much, but see, it turned out to be little. What you brought home, I blew away. Why?" declares the Lord Almighty. "Because of my house, which remains a ruin, while each of you is busy with his own house. 10 Therefore, because of you the heavens have withheld

[a] 1 A variant of *Jeshua*; here and elsewhere in Haggai

their dew and the earth its crops. [11]I called
for a drought on the fields and the mountains, on the grain, the new wine, the oil
and whatever the ground produces, on
men and cattle, and on the labor of your
hands."

[12]Then Zerubbabel son of Shealtiel,
Joshua son of Jehozadak, the high priest,
and the whole remnant of the people
obeyed the voice of the LORD their God
and the message of the prophet Haggai,
because the LORD their God had sent him.
And the people feared the LORD.

[13]Then Haggai, the LORD's messenger,
gave this message of the LORD to the people: "I am with you," declares the LORD.
[14]So the LORD stirred up the spirit of Ze-

VERSE FOR THE DAY: Haggai 1:6–7 | AUTHOR: Ron and Jeanette Lee | PASSAGE FOR THE DAY: Haggai 1:3–9

First Things First

When God's people returned from exile, they quickly began building houses to live in. Sounds reasonable, but it sure didn't make sense to God. He wasn't pleased that people were pouring so much energy into building homes while his house—the temple—stood in ruins (v. 9).

The Hebrews of Haggai's time were distracted by an extremely good thing—creating a home for those closest to them. A similar thing happens today. It's so exciting to begin a new life together, and there is so much involved in getting off to a great start that good things can distract us from the best thing—the Kingdom of God. And it's not just learning how to live together as husband and wife. There are the added challenges of getting established in careers, working out finances and keeping in touch with friends. There's a place for all of these things, but the key is knowing what that place is.

Once God's people listened to his voice and set to work rebuilding the temple, the Lord honored their obedience in two ways. First, he encouraged them with his presence (2:4). Second, he blessed them (2:19). What more could we want than God's presence and his blessing as we begin married life? We can enjoy those gifts by keeping sight of his legitimate claim to be first in our lives.

MARRIAGE BUILDERS

♦ *In the fun of getting your marriage started, has God slipped out of the central position of your shared focus?*

♦ *How are you sensing God's presence and blessing in your marriage?*

Additional Scripture Readings
2 Chronicles 2:1–6; Matthew 6:28-33

Go to page 1011 for your next devotional reading.

rubbabel son of Shealtiel, governor of Judah, and the spirit of Joshua son of Jehozadak, the high priest, and the spirit of the whole remnant of the people. They came and began to work on the house of the LORD Almighty, their God, 15on the twenty-fourth day of the sixth month in the second year of King Darius.

The Promised Glory of the New House

2 On the twenty-first day of the seventh month, the word of the LORD came through the prophet Haggai: 2"Speak to Zerubbabel son of Shealtiel, governor of Judah, to Joshua son of Jehozadak, the high priest, and to the remnant of the people. Ask them, 3'Who of you is left who saw this house in its former glory? How does it look to you now? Does it not seem to you like nothing? 4But now be strong, O Zerubbabel,' declares the LORD. 'Be strong, O Joshua son of Jehozadak, the high priest. Be strong, all you people of the land,' declares the LORD, 'and work. For I am with you,' declares the LORD Almighty. 5'This is what I covenanted with you when you came out of Egypt. And my Spirit remains among you. Do not fear.'

6"This is what the LORD Almighty says: 'In a little while I will once more shake the heavens and the earth, the sea and the dry land. 7I will shake all nations, and the desired of all nations will come, and I will fill this house with glory,' says the LORD Almighty. 8'The silver is mine and the gold is mine,' declares the LORD Almighty. 9'The glory of this present house will be greater than the glory of the former house,' says the LORD Almighty. 'And in this place I will grant peace,' declares the LORD Almighty."

Blessings for a Defiled People

10On the twenty-fourth day of the ninth month, in the second year of Darius, the word of the LORD came to the prophet Haggai: 11"This is what the LORD Almighty says: 'Ask the priests what the law says: 12If a person carries consecrated meat in the fold of his garment, and that fold touches some bread or stew, some wine, oil or other food, does it become consecrated?' "

The priests answered, "No."

13Then Haggai said, "If a person defiled by contact with a dead body touches one of these things, does it become defiled?"

"Yes," the priests replied, "it becomes defiled."

14Then Haggai said, " 'So it is with this people and this nation in my sight,' declares the LORD. 'Whatever they do and whatever they offer there is defiled.

15" 'Now give careful thought to this from this day on[a]—consider how things were before one stone was laid on another in the LORD's temple. 16When anyone came to a heap of twenty measures, there were only ten. When anyone went to a wine vat to draw fifty measures, there were only twenty. 17I struck all the work of your hands with blight, mildew and hail, yet you did not turn to me,' declares the LORD. 18'From this day on, from this twenty-fourth day of the ninth month, give careful thought to the day when the foundation of the LORD's temple was laid. Give careful thought: 19Is there yet any seed left in the barn? Until now, the vine and the fig tree, the pomegranate and the olive tree have not borne fruit.

" 'From this day on I will bless you.' "

Zerubbabel the LORD's Signet Ring

20The word of the LORD came to Haggai a second time on the twenty-fourth day of the month: 21"Tell Zerubbabel governor of Judah that I will shake the heavens and the earth. 22I will overturn royal thrones and shatter the power of the foreign kingdoms. I will overthrow chariots and their drivers; horses and their riders will fall, each by the sword of his brother.

23" 'On that day,' declares the LORD Almighty, 'I will take you, my servant Zerubbabel son of Shealtiel,' declares the LORD, 'and I will make you like my signet ring, for I have chosen you,' declares the LORD Almighty."

[a]15 Or *to the days past*

ZECHARIAH writes to inspire the returning exiles to turn to the Lord and continue rebuilding the temple in Jerusalem (Ezra 4:24–5:2). He encourages them with his visions that show God's control over everything and the coming new kingdom of the Messiah. As you read this book, be sure you have turned to the Lord and let these visions of hope inspire you to continue serving the Lord.

ZECHARIAH

A Call to Return to the Lord

1 In the eighth month of the second year of Darius, the word of the Lord came to the prophet Zechariah son of Berekiah, the son of Iddo:

2"The Lord was very angry with your forefathers. 3Therefore tell the people: This is what the Lord Almighty says: 'Return to me,' declares the Lord Almighty, 'and I will return to you,' says the Lord Almighty. 4Do not be like your forefathers, to whom the earlier prophets proclaimed: This is what the Lord Almighty says: 'Turn from your evil ways and your evil practices.' But they would not listen or pay attention to me, declares the Lord. 5Where are your forefathers now? And the prophets, do they live forever? 6But did not my words and my decrees, which I commanded my servants the prophets, overtake your forefathers?

"Then they repented and said, 'The Lord Almighty has done to us what our ways and practices deserve, just as he determined to do.' "

The Man Among the Myrtle Trees

7On the twenty-fourth day of the eleventh month, the month of Shebat, in the second year of Darius, the word of the Lord came to the prophet Zechariah son of Berekiah, the son of Iddo.

8During the night I had a vision—and there before me was a man riding a red horse! He was standing among the myrtle trees in a ravine. Behind him were red, brown and white horses.

9I asked, "What are these, my lord?"

The angel who was talking with me answered, "I will show you what they are."

10Then the man standing among the myrtle trees explained, "They are the ones the LORD has sent to go throughout the earth."

11And they reported to the angel of the LORD, who was standing among the myrtle trees, "We have gone throughout the earth and found the whole world at rest and in peace."

12Then the angel of the LORD said, "LORD Almighty, how long will you withhold mercy from Jerusalem and from the towns of Judah, which you have been angry with these seventy years?" 13So the LORD spoke kind and comforting words to the angel who talked with me.

14Then the angel who was speaking to me said, "Proclaim this word: This is what the LORD Almighty says: 'I am very jealous for Jerusalem and Zion, 15but I am very angry with the nations that feel secure. I was only a little angry, but they added to the calamity.'

16"Therefore, this is what the LORD says: 'I will return to Jerusalem with mercy, and there my house will be rebuilt. And the measuring line will be stretched out over Jerusalem,' declares the LORD Almighty.

17"Proclaim further: This is what the LORD Almighty says: 'My towns will again overflow with prosperity, and the LORD will again comfort Zion and choose Jerusalem.' "

Four Horns and Four Craftsmen

18Then I looked up—and there before me were four horns! 19I asked the angel who was speaking to me, "What are these?"

He answered me, "These are the horns that scattered Judah, Israel and Jerusalem."

20Then the LORD showed me four craftsmen. 21I asked, "What are these coming to do?"

He answered, "These are the horns that scattered Judah so that no one could raise his head, but the craftsmen have come to terrify them and throw down these horns of the nations who lifted up their horns against the land of Judah to scatter its people."

A Man With a Measuring Line

2 Then I looked up—and there before me was a man with a measuring line in his hand! 2I asked, "Where are you going?"

He answered me, "To measure Jerusalem, to find out how wide and how long it is."

3Then the angel who was speaking to me left, and another angel came to meet him 4and said to him: "Run, tell that young man, 'Jerusalem will be a city without walls because of the great number of men and livestock in it. 5And I myself will be a wall of fire around it,' declares the LORD, 'and I will be its glory within.'

6"Come! Come! Flee from the land of the north," declares the LORD, "for I have scattered you to the four winds of heaven," declares the LORD.

7"Come, O Zion! Escape, you who live in the Daughter of Babylon!" 8For this is what the LORD Almighty says: "After he has honored me and has sent me against the nations that have plundered you—for whoever touches you touches the apple of his eye— 9I will surely raise my hand against them so that their slaves will plunder them.[a] Then you will know that the LORD Almighty has sent me.

10"Shout and be glad, O Daughter of Zion. For I am coming, and I will live among you," declares the LORD. 11"Many nations will be joined with the LORD in that day and will become my people. I will live among you and you will know that the LORD Almighty has sent me to you. 12The LORD will inherit Judah as his portion in the holy land and will again choose Jerusalem. 13Be still before the LORD, all mankind, because he has roused himself from his holy dwelling."

Clean Garments for the High Priest

3 Then he showed me Joshua[b] the high priest standing before the angel of the LORD, and Satan[c] standing at his right side to accuse him. 2The LORD said to Satan, "The LORD rebuke you, Satan! The LORD, who has chosen Jerusalem, rebuke you! Is not this man a burning stick snatched from the fire?"

3Now Joshua was dressed in filthy

[a] *8,9* Or *says after . . . eye: 9"I . . . plunder them."*

[b] *1* A variant of *Jeshua*; here and elsewhere in Zechariah

[c] *1* *Satan* means *accuser.*

clothes as he stood before the angel. 4The angel said to those who were standing before him, "Take off his filthy clothes."

Then he said to Joshua, "See, I have taken away your sin, and I will put rich garments on you."

5Then I said, "Put a clean turban on his head." So they put a clean turban on his head and clothed him, while the angel of the LORD stood by.

6The angel of the LORD gave this charge to Joshua: 7"This is what the LORD Almighty says: 'If you will walk in my ways and keep my requirements, then you will govern my house and have charge of my courts, and I will give you a place among these standing here.

8" 'Listen, O high priest Joshua and your associates seated before you, who are men symbolic of things to come: I am going to bring my servant, the Branch. 9See, the stone I have set in front of Joshua! There are seven eyes[a] on that one stone, and I will engrave an inscription on it,' says the LORD Almighty, 'and I will remove the sin of this land in a single day.

10" 'In that day each of you will invite his neighbor to sit under his vine and fig tree,' declares the LORD Almighty."

The Gold Lampstand and the Two Olive Trees

4 Then the angel who talked with me returned and wakened me, as a man is wakened from his sleep. 2He asked me, "What do you see?"

I answered, "I see a solid gold lampstand with a bowl at the top and seven lights on it, with seven channels to the lights. 3Also there are two olive trees by it, one on the right of the bowl and the other on its left."

4I asked the angel who talked with me, "What are these, my lord?"

5He answered, "Do you not know what these are?"

"No, my lord," I replied.

6So he said to me, "This is the word of the LORD to Zerubbabel: 'Not by might nor by power, but by my Spirit,' says the LORD Almighty.

7"What[b] are you, O mighty mountain? Before Zerubbabel you will become level ground. Then he will bring out the capstone to shouts of 'God bless it! God bless it!' "

8Then the word of the LORD came to me: 9"The hands of Zerubbabel have laid the foundation of this temple; his hands will also complete it. Then you will know that the LORD Almighty has sent me to you.

10"Who despises the day of small things? Men will rejoice when they see the plumb line in the hand of Zerubbabel.

"(These seven are the eyes of the LORD, which range throughout the earth.)"

11Then I asked the angel, "What are these two olive trees on the right and the left of the lampstand?"

12Again I asked him, "What are these two olive branches beside the two gold pipes that pour out golden oil?"

13He replied, "Do you not know what these are?"

"No, my lord," I said.

14So he said, "These are the two who are anointed to[c] serve the Lord of all the earth."

The Flying Scroll

5 I looked again—and there before me was a flying scroll!

2He asked me, "What do you see?"

I answered, "I see a flying scroll, thirty feet long and fifteen feet wide.[d]"

3And he said to me, "This is the curse that is going out over the whole land; for according to what it says on one side, every thief will be banished, and according to what it says on the other, everyone who swears falsely will be banished. 4The LORD Almighty declares, 'I will send it out, and it will enter the house of the thief and the house of him who swears falsely by my name. It will remain in his house and destroy it, both its timbers and its stones.' "

The Woman in a Basket

5Then the angel who was speaking to me came forward and said to me, "Look up and see what this is that is appearing."

6I asked, "What is it?"

He replied, "It is a measuring basket.[e]" And he added, "This is the iniquity[f] of the people throughout the land."

7Then the cover of lead was raised, and there in the basket sat a woman! 8He said,

[a]9 Or *facets* [b]7 Or *Who* [c]14 Or *two who bring oil and* [d]2 Hebrew *twenty cubits long and ten cubits wide* (about 9 meters long and 4.5 meters wide) [e]6 Hebrew *an ephah*; also in verses 7-11 [f]6 Or *appearance*

"This is wickedness," and he pushed her
back into the basket and pushed the lead
cover down over its mouth.
9Then I looked up—and there before
me were two women, with the wind in
their wings! They had wings like those of
a stork, and they lifted up the basket be-
tween heaven and earth.
10"Where are they taking the basket?" I
asked the angel who was speaking to me.
11He replied, "To the country of Babylo-
nia[a] to build a house for it. When it is

[a] 11 Hebrew *Shinar*

VERSE FOR THE DAY: Zechariah 4:6

AUTHOR: Win Couchman

PASSAGE FOR THE DAY: Zechariah 4:6

Supportive Partners

After Bob retired, we decided God was calling us to be missionaries. We knew we'd be suffering from "adjustment stress," so we made a deal with each other and knew God would help us keep it. No matter what one of us did (lose our airline tickets and passports, miss flights, drive on the wrong side of the road), we would not blame each other but would support one another and pray as partners, asking God to help us out of our trouble.

The first time we tested this agreement was on a flight to Australia. Fifteen minutes into the flight, I tried to remember whether I had packed all sorts of absolute essentials. I glanced at Bob, and his face looked like it had been carved out of stone. "Uh-oh," I thought. "He's having an anxiety attack, too."

I punched him softly in the arm, and he looked at me. I said, "Are you as sure as I am that we've left behind everything we really need, and have brought along tons of nonessentials?" He nodded, miserable. Then we remembered the deal we had made. We clasped hands and murmured our brief prayer for help. We looked at each other and laughed. What do you know? It was going to work!

God, indeed, is good.

MARRIAGE BUILDERS

♦ *You face many challenges in your life together. How do you face them as partners?*

♦ *Can you make a deal with one another, similar to that of the Couchmans, not to blame each other when problems come up but to "pray as partners"?*

Additional Scripture Readings
Romans 8:26–28; 1 Corinthians 2:2–5; 2 Corinthians 12:9

Go to page 1019 for your next devotional reading.

ready, the basket will be set there in its place."

Four Chariots

6 I looked up again—and there before me were four chariots coming out from between two mountains—mountains of bronze! [2]The first chariot had red horses, the second black, [3]the third white, and the fourth dappled—all of them powerful. [4]I asked the angel who was speaking to me, "What are these, my lord?"

[5]The angel answered me, "These are the four spirits[a] of heaven, going out from standing in the presence of the Lord of the whole world. [6]The one with the black horses is going toward the north country, the one with the white horses toward the west,[b] and the one with the dappled horses toward the south."

[7]When the powerful horses went out, they were straining to go throughout the earth. And he said, "Go throughout the earth!" So they went throughout the earth.

[8]Then he called to me, "Look, those going toward the north country have given my Spirit[c] rest in the land of the north."

A Crown for Joshua

[9]The word of the LORD came to me: [10]"Take ⌊silver and gold⌋ from the exiles Heldai, Tobijah and Jedaiah, who have arrived from Babylon. Go the same day to the house of Josiah son of Zephaniah. [11]Take the silver and gold and make a crown, and set it on the head of the high priest, Joshua son of Jehozadak. [12]Tell him this is what the LORD Almighty says: 'Here is the man whose name is the Branch, and he will branch out from his place and build the temple of the LORD. [13]It is he who will build the temple of the LORD, and he will be clothed with majesty and will sit and rule on his throne. And he will be a priest on his throne. And there will be harmony between the two.' [14]The crown will be given to Heldai,[d] Tobijah, Jedaiah and Hen[e] son of Zephaniah as a memorial in the temple of the LORD. [15]Those who are far away will come and help to build the temple of the LORD, and you will know that the LORD Almighty has sent me to you. This will happen if you diligently obey the LORD your God."

Justice and Mercy, Not Fasting

7 In the fourth year of King Darius, the word of the LORD came to Zechariah on the fourth day of the ninth month, the month of Kislev. [2]The people of Bethel had sent Sharezer and Regem-Melech, together with their men, to entreat the LORD [3]by asking the priests of the house of the LORD Almighty and the prophets, "Should I mourn and fast in the fifth month, as I have done for so many years?"

[4]Then the word of the LORD Almighty came to me: [5]"Ask all the people of the land and the priests, 'When you fasted and mourned in the fifth and seventh months for the past seventy years, was it really for me that you fasted? [6]And when you were eating and drinking, were you not just feasting for yourselves? [7]Are these not the words the LORD proclaimed through the earlier prophets when Jerusalem and its surrounding towns were at rest and prosperous, and the Negev and the western foothills were settled?' "

[8]And the word of the LORD came again to Zechariah: [9]"This is what the LORD Almighty says: 'Administer true justice; show mercy and compassion to one another. [10]Do not oppress the widow or the fatherless, the alien or the poor. In your hearts do not think evil of each other.'

[11]"But they refused to pay attention; stubbornly they turned their backs and stopped up their ears. [12]They made their hearts as hard as flint and would not listen to the law or to the words that the LORD Almighty had sent by his Spirit through the earlier prophets. So the LORD Almighty was very angry.

[13]" 'When I called, they did not listen; so when they called, I would not listen,' says the LORD Almighty. [14]'I scattered them with a whirlwind among all the nations, where they were strangers. The land was left so desolate behind them that no one could come or go. This is how they made the pleasant land desolate.' "

The LORD Promises to Bless Jerusalem

8 Again the word of the LORD Almighty came to me. [2]This is what the LORD Almighty says: "I am very jealous for Zion; I am burning with jealousy for her."

[3]This is what the LORD says: "I will return to Zion and dwell in Jerusalem. Then

[a]5 Or *winds* [b]6 Or *horses after them* [c]8 Or *spirit* [d]14 Syriac; Hebrew *Helem* [e]14 Or *and the gracious one, the*

Jerusalem will be called the City of Truth,
and the mountain of the LORD Almighty
will be called the Holy Mountain."
4This is what the LORD Almighty says:
"Once again men and women of ripe old
age will sit in the streets of Jerusalem,
each with cane in hand because of his age.
5The city streets will be filled with boys
and girls playing there."
6This is what the LORD Almighty says:
"It may seem marvelous to the remnant of
this people at that time, but will it seem
marvelous to me?" declares the LORD Al-
mighty.
7This is what the LORD Almighty says: "I
will save my people from the countries of
the east and the west. 8I will bring them
back to live in Jerusalem; they will be my
people, and I will be faithful and righteous
to them as their God."
9This is what the LORD Almighty says:
"You who now hear these words spoken
by the prophets who were there when the
foundation was laid for the house of the
LORD Almighty, let your hands be strong
so that the temple may be built. 10Before
that time there were no wages for man or
beast. No one could go about his business
safely because of his enemy, for I had
turned every man against his neighbor.
11But now I will not deal with the remnant
of this people as I did in the past," declares
the LORD Almighty.
12"The seed will grow well, the vine will
yield its fruit, the ground will produce its
crops, and the heavens will drop their
dew. I will give all these things as an in-
heritance to the remnant of this people.
13As you have been an object of cursing
among the nations, O Judah and Israel, so
will I save you, and you will be a blessing.
Do not be afraid, but let your hands be
strong."
14This is what the LORD Almighty says:
"Just as I had determined to bring disaster
upon you and showed no pity when your
fathers angered me," says the LORD Al-
mighty, 15"so now I have determined to do
good again to Jerusalem and Judah. Do
not be afraid. 16These are the things you
are to do: Speak the truth to each other,
and render true and sound judgment in
your courts; 17do not plot evil against your
neighbor, and do not love to swear falsely.
I hate all this," declares the LORD.
18Again the word of the LORD Almighty
came to me. 19This is what the LORD Al-
mighty says: "The fasts of the fourth, fifth,
seventh and tenth months will become
joyful and glad occasions and happy festi-
vals for Judah. Therefore love truth and
peace."
20This is what the LORD Almighty says:
"Many peoples and the inhabitants of
many cities will yet come, 21and the in-
habitants of one city will go to another
and say, 'Let us go at once to entreat the
LORD and seek the LORD Almighty. I myself
am going.' 22And many peoples and pow-
erful nations will come to Jerusalem to
seek the LORD Almighty and to entreat
him."
23This is what the LORD Almighty says:
"In those days ten men from all languages
and nations will take firm hold of one Jew
by the hem of his robe and say, 'Let us go
with you, because we have heard that God
is with you.' "

Judgment on Israel's Enemies

An Oracle

9 The word of the LORD is against the
land of Hadrach
and will rest upon Damascus—
for the eyes of men and all the tribes
of Israel
are on the LORD—[a]
2and upon Hamath too, which borders
on it,
and upon Tyre and Sidon, though
they are very skillful.
3Tyre has built herself a stronghold;
she has heaped up silver like dust,
and gold like the dirt of the streets.
4But the Lord will take away her
possessions
and destroy her power on the sea,
and she will be consumed by fire.
5Ashkelon will see it and fear;
Gaza will writhe in agony,
and Ekron too, for her hope will
wither.
Gaza will lose her king
and Ashkelon will be deserted.
6Foreigners will occupy Ashdod,
and I will cut off the pride of the
Philistines.
7I will take the blood from their
mouths,
the forbidden food from between
their teeth.
Those who are left will belong to our
God

[a] 1 Or *Damascus. / For the eye of the* LORD *is on all mankind, / as well as on the tribes of Israel,*

and become leaders in Judah,
and Ekron will be like the Jebusites.
8But I will defend my house
against marauding forces.
Never again will an oppressor overrun
my people,
for now I am keeping watch.

The Coming of Zion's King

9Rejoice greatly, O Daughter of Zion!
Shout, Daughter of Jerusalem!
See, your king[a] comes to you,
righteous and having salvation,
gentle and riding on a donkey,
on a colt, the foal of a donkey.
10I will take away the chariots from
Ephraim
and the war-horses from Jerusalem,
and the battle bow will be broken.
He will proclaim peace to the nations.
His rule will extend from sea to sea
and from the River[b] to the ends of
the earth.[c]
11As for you, because of the blood of
my covenant with you,
I will free your prisoners from the
waterless pit.
12Return to your fortress, O prisoners of
hope;
even now I announce that I will
restore twice as much to you.
13I will bend Judah as I bend my bow
and fill it with Ephraim.
I will rouse your sons, O Zion,
against your sons, O Greece,
and make you like a warrior's
sword.

The Lord Will Appear

14Then the Lord will appear over them;
his arrow will flash like lightning.
The Sovereign Lord will sound the
trumpet;
he will march in the storms of the
south,
15 and the Lord Almighty will shield
them.
They will destroy
and overcome with slingstones.
They will drink and roar as with wine;
they will be full like a bowl
used for sprinkling[d] the corners of
the altar.
16The Lord their God will save them on
that day
as the flock of his people.
They will sparkle in his land
like jewels in a crown.
17How attractive and beautiful they will
be!
Grain will make the young men
thrive,
and new wine the young women.

The Lord Will Care for Judah

10 Ask the Lord for rain in the
springtime;
it is the Lord who makes the storm
clouds.
He gives showers of rain to men,
and plants of the field to everyone.
2The idols speak deceit,
diviners see visions that lie;
they tell dreams that are false,
they give comfort in vain.
Therefore the people wander like
sheep
oppressed for lack of a shepherd.

3"My anger burns against the
shepherds,
and I will punish the leaders;
for the Lord Almighty will care
for his flock, the house of Judah,
and make them like a proud horse
in battle.
4From Judah will come the
cornerstone,
from him the tent peg,
from him the battle bow,
from him every ruler.
5Together they[e] will be like mighty
men
trampling the muddy streets in
battle.
Because the Lord is with them,
they will fight and overthrow the
horsemen.

6"I will strengthen the house of Judah
and save the house of Joseph.
I will restore them
because I have compassion on
them.
They will be as though
I had not rejected them,
for I am the Lord their God
and I will answer them.
7The Ephraimites will become like
mighty men,
and their hearts will be glad as with
wine.

[a]9 Or *King* [b]10 That is, the Euphrates [c]10 Or *the end of the land* [d]15 Or *bowl, / like*
[e]4,5 Or *ruler, all of them together. / 5They*

Their children will see it and be
joyful;
their hearts will rejoice in the LORD.
8I will signal for them
and gather them in.
Surely I will redeem them;
they will be as numerous as before.
9Though I scatter them among the
peoples,
yet in distant lands they will
remember me.
They and their children will survive,
and they will return.
10I will bring them back from Egypt
and gather them from Assyria.
I will bring them to Gilead and
Lebanon,
and there will not be room enough
for them.
11They will pass through the sea of
trouble;
the surging sea will be subdued
and all the depths of the Nile will
dry up.
Assyria's pride will be brought down
and Egypt's scepter will pass away.
12I will strengthen them in the LORD
and in his name they will walk,"
declares the LORD.

11 Open your doors, O Lebanon,
so that fire may devour your
cedars!
2Wail, O pine tree, for the cedar has
fallen;
the stately trees are ruined!
Wail, oaks of Bashan;
the dense forest has been cut down!
3Listen to the wail of the shepherds;
their rich pastures are destroyed!
Listen to the roar of the lions;
the lush thicket of the Jordan is
ruined!

Two Shepherds

4This is what the LORD my God says: "Pasture the flock marked for slaughter. 5Their buyers slaughter them and go unpunished. Those who sell them say, 'Praise the LORD, I am rich!' Their own shepherds do not spare them. 6For I will no longer have pity on the people of the land," declares the LORD. "I will hand everyone over to his neighbor and his king. They will oppress the land, and I will not rescue them from their hands."

7So I pastured the flock marked for slaughter, particularly the oppressed of the flock. Then I took two staffs and called one Favor and the other Union, and I pastured the flock. 8In one month I got rid of the three shepherds.

The flock detested me, and I grew weary of them 9and said, "I will not be your shepherd. Let the dying die, and the perishing perish. Let those who are left eat one another's flesh."

10Then I took my staff called Favor and broke it, revoking the covenant I had made with all the nations. 11It was revoked on that day, and so the afflicted of the flock who were watching me knew it was the word of the LORD.

12I told them, "If you think it best, give me my pay; but if not, keep it." So they paid me thirty pieces of silver.

13And the LORD said to me, "Throw it to the potter"—the handsome price at which they priced me! So I took the thirty pieces of silver and threw them into the house of the LORD to the potter.

14Then I broke my second staff called Union, breaking the brotherhood between Judah and Israel.

15Then the LORD said to me, "Take again the equipment of a foolish shepherd. 16For I am going to raise up a shepherd over the land who will not care for the lost, or seek the young, or heal the injured, or feed the healthy, but will eat the meat of the choice sheep, tearing off their hoofs.

17"Woe to the worthless shepherd,
who deserts the flock!
May the sword strike his arm and his
right eye!
May his arm be completely
withered,
his right eye totally blinded!"

Jerusalem's Enemies to Be Destroyed

An Oracle

12 This is the word of the LORD concerning Israel. The LORD, who stretches out the heavens, who lays the foundation of the earth, and who forms the spirit of man within him, declares: 2"I am going to make Jerusalem a cup that sends all the surrounding peoples reeling. Judah will be besieged as well as Jerusalem. 3On that day, when all the nations of the earth are gathered against her, I will make Jerusalem an immovable rock for all the nations. All who try to move it will injure themselves. 4On that day I will strike every horse with panic and its rider with madness," declares the LORD. "I will keep

a watchful eye over the house of Judah,
but I will blind all the horses of the nations. 5Then the leaders of Judah will say
in their hearts, 'The people of Jerusalem
are strong, because the LORD Almighty is
their God.'

6"On that day I will make the leaders of
Judah like a firepot in a woodpile, like a
flaming torch among sheaves. They will
consume right and left all the surrounding
peoples, but Jerusalem will remain intact
in her place.

7"The LORD will save the dwellings of
Judah first, so that the honor of the house
of David and of Jerusalem's inhabitants
may not be greater than that of Judah. 8On
that day the LORD will shield those who
live in Jerusalem, so that the feeblest
among them will be like David, and the
house of David will be like God, like the
Angel of the LORD going before them. 9On
that day I will set out to destroy all the nations that attack Jerusalem.

Mourning for the One They Pierced

10"And I will pour out on the house of
David and the inhabitants of Jerusalem a
spirit[a] of grace and supplication. They
will look on[b] me, the one they have
pierced, and they will mourn for him as
one mourns for an only child, and grieve
bitterly for him as one grieves for a first-
born son. 11On that day the weeping in Je-
rusalem will be great, like the weeping of
Hadad Rimmon in the plain of Megiddo.
12The land will mourn, each clan by itself,
with their wives by themselves: the clan of
the house of David and their wives, the
clan of the house of Nathan and their
wives, 13the clan of the house of Levi and
their wives, the clan of Shimei and their
wives, 14and all the rest of the clans and
their wives.

Cleansing From Sin

13 "On that day a fountain will be
opened to the house of David and
the inhabitants of Jerusalem, to cleanse
them from sin and impurity.

2"On that day, I will banish the names
of the idols from the land, and they will be
remembered no more," declares the LORD
Almighty. "I will remove both the proph-
ets and the spirit of impurity from the
land. 3And if anyone still prophesies, his
father and mother, to whom he was born,
will say to him, 'You must die, because
you have told lies in the LORD's name.'
When he prophesies, his own parents will
stab him.

4"On that day every prophet will be
ashamed of his prophetic vision. He will
not put on a prophet's garment of hair in
order to deceive. 5He will say, 'I am not a
prophet. I am a farmer; the land has been
my livelihood since my youth.[c]' 6If
someone asks him, 'What are these
wounds on your body[d]?' he will answer,
'The wounds I was given at the house of
my friends.'

The Shepherd Struck, the Sheep Scattered

7"Awake, O sword, against my
shepherd,
against the man who is close to
me!"
declares the LORD Almighty.
"Strike the shepherd,
and the sheep will be scattered,
and I will turn my hand against the
little ones.
8In the whole land," declares the LORD,
"two-thirds will be struck down and
perish;
yet one-third will be left in it.
9This third I will bring into the fire;
I will refine them like silver
and test them like gold.
They will call on my name
and I will answer them;
I will say, 'They are my people,'
and they will say, 'The LORD is our
God.'"

The LORD Comes and Reigns

14 A day of the LORD is coming when
your plunder will be divided
among you.

2I will gather all the nations to Jerusa-
lem to fight against it; the city will be cap-
tured, the houses ransacked, and the
women raped. Half of the city will go into
exile, but the rest of the people will not be
taken from the city.

3Then the LORD will go out and fight
against those nations, as he fights in the
day of battle. 4On that day his feet will
stand on the Mount of Olives, east of Jeru-
salem, and the Mount of Olives will be
split in two from east to west, forming a
great valley, with half of the mountain

[a] 10 Or *the Spirit* [b] 10 Or *to your hands* [c] 5 Or *farmer; a man sold me in my youth* [d] 6 Or *wounds between*

moving north and half moving south.
5You will flee by my mountain valley, for
it will extend to Azel. You will flee as you
fled from the earthquake[a] in the days of
Uzziah king of Judah. Then the LORD my
God will come, and all the holy ones with
him.

6On that day there will be no light, no
cold or frost. 7It will be a unique day, with-
out daytime or nighttime—a day known
to the LORD. When evening comes, there
will be light.

8On that day living water will flow out
from Jerusalem, half to the eastern sea[b]
and half to the western sea,[c] in summer
and in winter.

9The LORD will be king over the whole
earth. On that day there will be one LORD,
and his name the only name.

10The whole land, from Geba to Rim-
mon, south of Jerusalem, will become like
the Arabah. But Jerusalem will be raised
up and remain in its place, from the Benja-
min Gate to the site of the First Gate, to
the Corner Gate, and from the Tower of
Hananel to the royal winepresses. 11It will
be inhabited; never again will it be de-
stroyed. Jerusalem will be secure.

12This is the plague with which the
LORD will strike all the nations that fought
against Jerusalem: Their flesh will rot
while they are still standing on their feet,
their eyes will rot in their sockets, and
their tongues will rot in their mouths.
13On that day men will be stricken by the
LORD with great panic. Each man will seize
the hand of another, and they will attack
each other. 14Judah too will fight at Jeru-
salem. The wealth of all the surrounding
nations will be collected—great quanti-
ties of gold and silver and clothing. 15A
similar plague will strike the horses and
mules, the camels and donkeys, and all
the animals in those camps.

16Then the survivors from all the na-
tions that have attacked Jerusalem will go
up year after year to worship the King, the
LORD Almighty, and to celebrate the Feast
of Tabernacles. 17If any of the peoples of
the earth do not go up to Jerusalem to
worship the King, the LORD Almighty, they
will have no rain. 18If the Egyptian people
do not go up and take part, they will have
no rain. The LORD[d] will bring on them the
plague he inflicts on the nations that do
not go up to celebrate the Feast of Taber-
nacles. 19This will be the punishment of
Egypt and the punishment of all the na-
tions that do not go up to celebrate the
Feast of Tabernacles.

20On that day HOLY TO THE LORD will be
inscribed on the bells of the horses, and
the cooking pots in the LORD's house will
be like the sacred bowls in front of the al-
tar. 21Every pot in Jerusalem and Judah
will be holy to the LORD Almighty, and all
who come to sacrifice will take some of
the pots and cook in them. And on that
day there will no longer be a Canaanite[e]
in the house of the LORD Almighty.

[a]5 Or 5*My mountain valley will be blocked and will extend to Azel. It will be blocked as it was blocked because of the earthquake* [b]8 That is, the Dead Sea [c]8 That is, the Mediterranean [d]18 Or *part, then the* LORD [e]21 Or *merchant*

MALACHI prophesies during the deplorable conditions described in Nehemiah 13. He calls those complacent in their spiritual life to a renewed relationship with God, promising them God's blessing if they do. As you read this book, promise the Lord that you will not be complacent in your faith but will put his will before your own concerns.

MALACHI

1 An oracle: The word of the LORD to Israel through Malachi.[a]

Jacob Loved, Esau Hated

2"I have loved you," says the LORD.
"But you ask, 'How have you loved us?'
"Was not Esau Jacob's brother?" the LORD says. "Yet I have loved Jacob, 3but Esau I have hated, and I have turned his mountains into a wasteland and left his inheritance to the desert jackals."

4Edom may say, "Though we have been crushed, we will rebuild the ruins."
But this is what the LORD Almighty says: "They may build, but I will demolish. They will be called the Wicked Land, a people always under the wrath of the LORD. 5You will see it with your own eyes and say, 'Great is the LORD—even beyond the borders of Israel!'

Blemished Sacrifices

6"A son honors his father, and a servant his master. If I am a father, where is the honor due me? If I am a master, where is the respect due me?" says the LORD Almighty. "It is you, O priests, who show contempt for my name.
"But you ask, 'How have we shown contempt for your name?'
7"You place defiled food on my altar.
"But you ask, 'How have we defiled you?'
"By saying that the LORD's table is contemptible. 8When you bring blind animals

[a] 1 *Malachi* means *my messenger.*

for sacrifice, is that not wrong? When you
sacrifice crippled or diseased animals, is
that not wrong? Try offering them to your
governor! Would he be pleased with you?
Would he accept you?" says the LORD Al-
mighty.
9"Now implore God to be gracious to
us. With such offerings from your hands,
will he accept you?"—says the LORD Al-
mighty.
10"Oh, that one of you would shut the
temple doors, so that you would not light
useless fires on my altar! I am not pleased
with you," says the LORD Almighty, "and I
will accept no offering from your hands.
11My name will be great among the
nations, from the rising to the setting
of the sun. In every place incense and
pure offerings will be brought to my
name, because my name will be great

FRIDAY

VERSE FOR THE DAY: Malachi 2:15–16

AUTHOR: Jim Smith

PASSAGE FOR THE DAY: Malachi 2:10–16

No Greener Grass

Divorce can happen to anyone. But rather than fear divorce, we should learn valuable lessons from the divorces of others and then use those lessons to strengthen our own marriages. Good marriages take work. You can't just coast, and you can't take each other for granted.

When you're tempted to consider divorce as an alternative, you need to realize that the grass *isn't* greener on the other side. Every marriage has problems, and exchanging the marriage you have now for another relationship is almost always a losing move.

It also helps to deal with your unrealistic fantasy images of marriage. Marriages cycle from enchantment to disenchantment when the fantasy dissolves and you hit reality. At that point, people either end their marriage or they get to work on some hard issues and gain some maturity. We need to work toward the goal of maturity in our marriages.

Finally, we need to watch out for societal lies about happiness. Our cultural norm is "whatever makes you happy is good." But the truth is, anyone who seeks happiness as a prime object is setting himself up for an enormous disappointment. Happiness is never obtained when that is your prime object.

MARRIAGE BUILDERS

♦ *Why is it impossible to obtain true happiness when you make it your prime goal?*

♦ *How have you worked toward the goal of maturity in your marriage?*

Additional Scripture Readings
Matthew 19:3–9; 1 Corinthians 7:10–11

Go to page 1021 for your next devotional reading.

among the nations," says the LORD
Almighty.
12"But you profane it by saying of the
Lord's table, 'It is defiled,' and of its food,
'It is contemptible.' 13And you say, 'What
a burden!' and you sniff at it contemptu-
ously," says the LORD Almighty.
"When you bring injured, crippled or
diseased animals and offer them as sacri-
fices, should I accept them from your
hands?" says the LORD. 14"Cursed is the
cheat who has an acceptable male in his
flock and vows to give it, but then sacri-
fices a blemished animal to the Lord. For
I am a great king," says the LORD Al-
mighty, "and my name is to be feared
among the nations.

Admonition for the Priests

2 "And now this admonition is for you,
O priests. 2If you do not listen, and if
you do not set your heart to honor my
name," says the LORD Almighty, "I will
send a curse upon you, and I will curse
your blessings. Yes, I have already cursed
them, because you have not set your heart
to honor me.
3"Because of you I will rebuke[a] your
descendants[b]; I will spread on your faces
the offal from your festival sacrifices, and
you will be carried off with it. 4And you
will know that I have sent you this admo-
nition so that my covenant with Levi may
continue," says the LORD Almighty. 5"My
covenant was with him, a covenant of life
and peace, and I gave them to him; this
called for reverence and he revered
me and stood in awe of my name.
6True instruction was in his mouth
and nothing false was found on his
lips. He walked with me in peace and
uprightness, and turned many from
sin.
7"For the lips of a priest ought to pre-
serve knowledge, and from his mouth
men should seek instruction—because he
is the messenger of the LORD Almighty.
8But you have turned from the way and by
your teaching have caused many to stum-
ble; you have violated the covenant with
Levi," says the LORD Almighty. 9"So I
have caused you to be despised and hu-
miliated before all the people, because
you have not followed my ways but
have shown partiality in matters of the
law."

Judah Unfaithful

10Have we not all one Father[c]? Did not
one God create us? Why do we profane
the covenant of our fathers by breaking
faith with one another?
11Judah has broken faith. A detestable
thing has been committed in Israel and in
Jerusalem: Judah has desecrated the sanc-
tuary the LORD loves, by marrying the
daughter of a foreign god. 12As for the
man who does this, whoever he may be,
may the LORD cut him off from the tents of
Jacob[d]—even though he brings offerings
to the LORD Almighty.
13Another thing you do: You flood the
LORD's altar with tears. You weep and wail
because he no longer pays attention
to your offerings or accepts them with
pleasure from your hands. 14You ask,
"Why?" It is because the LORD is acting
as the witness between you and the
wife of your youth, because you have
broken faith with her, though she is
your partner, the wife of your marriage
covenant.
15Has not ⌊the LORD⌋ made them one? In
flesh and spirit they are his. And why one?
Because he was seeking godly offspring.[e]
So guard yourself in your spirit, and do
not break faith with the wife of your
youth.
16"I hate divorce," says the LORD God of
Israel, "and I hate a man's covering him-
self[f] with violence as well as with his gar-
ment," says the LORD Almighty.
So guard yourself in your spirit, and do
not break faith.

The Day of Judgment

17You have wearied the LORD with your
words.
"How have we wearied him?" you ask.
By saying, "All who do evil are good in
the eyes of the LORD, and he is pleased
with them" or "Where is the God of jus-
tice?"
3 "See, I will send my messenger, who
will prepare the way before me. Then
suddenly the Lord you are seeking will

[a]3 Or *cut off* (see Septuagint) [b]3 Or *will blight your grain* [c]10 Or *father* [d]12 Or 12*May the LORD cut off from the tents of Jacob anyone who gives testimony in behalf of the man who does this*
[e]15 Or 15*But the one ⌊who is our father⌋ did not do this, not as long as life remained in him. And what was he seeking? An offspring from God* [f]16 Or *his wife*

WEEKENDING

LISTENING

Women and men are radically different, but it's possible to keep your differences from driving a wedge between you. Part of the solution is to shift your focus off your differences and concentrate, instead, on building your relationship. One way to shift your focus is to concentrate on listening to your mate. Consider the following questions:

1. In marriage, why might listening be more important than speaking?

2. Can you think of an occasion when, rather than listening carefully to your mate's words, you instead were formulating the next thing you wanted to say? How did that affect your ability to understand the meaning behind your spouse's words?

3. If you started concentrating more on listening and less on talking, how would that help you understand your mate better and accept the ways in which the two of you are different?

— *The* Marriage Partnership *Staff*

REVIVE

Saturday: James 1:19–27
Sunday: Proverbs 18:1–24

Go to page 1022 for your next devotional reading.

VERSE FOR THE DAY: Malachi 3:6

AUTHOR: Ron R. Lee

PASSAGE FOR THE DAY: Malachi 3:1–18

Unsettling Change

I have a friend who attended a marriage seminar with his wife. The speaker suggested that each couple in the audience rate their marriage on a scale of one to ten. (A one would mean "marginal," a ten "exceptional.") My friend assumed that he and his wife viewed their marriage the same way.

"I rated our relationship as an eight," he told me later. "But my wife gave it a four. At first it was disconcerting, but it gave us a chance to talk about why each of us rated our marriage as we did." This exercise had a positive outcome: My friend's wife was able to bring up some issues for discussion before minor irritations became major problems.

As time passes, our marriages change: There is no way to escape it. And change—whether it involves differing interests or finding that your expectations about marriage were unrealistic—can be unsettling. But it can also be the best thing that can happen to your marriage.

To make change a positive thing, we need to continue to touch base with each other on a regular basis. If we don't keep talking—honestly and openly—the changes that we find unsettling today could become damaging to our relationship tomorrow.

MARRIAGE BUILDERS

♦ *How would each of you rate your marriage on the same scale of one to ten?*

♦ *How can communication ensure that changes in your personalities will promote growth and togetherness in your relationship?*

Additional Scripture Readings
1 Samuel 15:29; Hebrews 13:8; James 1:17

Go to page 1024 for your next devotional reading.

come to his temple; the messenger of the covenant, whom you desire, will come," says the LORD Almighty.

2But who can endure the day of his coming? Who can stand when he appears? For he will be like a refiner's fire or a launderer's soap. 3He will sit as a refiner and purifier of silver; he will purify the Levites and refine them like gold and silver. Then the LORD will have men who will bring offerings in righteousness, 4and the offerings of Judah and Jerusalem will be acceptable to the LORD, as in days gone by, as in former years.

5"So I will come near to you for judgment. I will be quick to testify against sorcerers, adulterers and perjurers, against those who defraud laborers of their wages, who oppress the widows and the fatherless, and deprive aliens of justice, but do not fear me," says the LORD Almighty.

Robbing God

6"I the LORD do not change. So you, O descendants of Jacob, are not destroyed. 7Ever since the time of your forefathers you have turned away from my decrees and have not kept them. Return to me, and I will return to you," says the LORD Almighty.

"But you ask, 'How are we to return?'

8"Will a man rob God? Yet you rob me.

"But you ask, 'How do we rob you?'

"In tithes and offerings. 9You are under a curse—the whole nation of you—because you are robbing me. 10Bring the whole tithe into the storehouse, that there may be food in my house. Test me in this," says the LORD Almighty, "and see if I will not throw open the floodgates of heaven and pour out so much blessing that you will not have room enough for it. 11I will prevent pests from devouring your crops, and the vines in your fields will not cast their fruit," says the LORD Almighty. 12"Then all the nations will call you blessed, for yours will be a delightful land," says the LORD Almighty.

13"You have said harsh things against me," says the LORD.

"Yet you ask, 'What have we said against you?'

14"You have said, 'It is futile to serve God. What did we gain by carrying out his requirements and going about like mourners before the LORD Almighty? 15But now we call the arrogant blessed. Certainly the evildoers prosper, and even those who challenge God escape.' "

16Then those who feared the LORD talked with each other, and the LORD listened and heard. A scroll of remembrance was written in his presence concerning those who feared the LORD and honored his name.

17"They will be mine," says the LORD Almighty, "in the day when I make up my treasured possession.[a] I will spare them, just as in compassion a man spares his son who serves him. 18And you will again see the distinction between the righteous and the wicked, between those who serve God and those who do not.

The Day of the LORD

4 "Surely the day is coming; it will burn like a furnace. All the arrogant and every evildoer will be stubble, and that day that is coming will set them on fire," says the LORD Almighty. "Not a root or a branch will be left to them. 2But for you who revere my name, the sun of righteousness will rise with healing in its wings. And you will go out and leap like calves released from the stall. 3Then you will trample down the wicked; they will be ashes under the soles of your feet on the day when I do these things," says the LORD Almighty.

4"Remember the law of my servant Moses, the decrees and laws I gave him at Horeb for all Israel.

5"See, I will send you the prophet Elijah before that great and dreadful day of the LORD comes. 6He will turn the hearts of the fathers to their children, and the hearts of the children to their fathers; or else I will come and strike the land with a curse."

[a]17 Or *Almighty, "my treasured possession, in the day when I act*

VERSE FOR THE DAY: Malachi 4:1–2

AUTHOR: Marian V. Liautaud

PASSAGE FOR THE DAY: Malachi 4:1–6

Tested by Fire

The worst phone call I ever made was to my husband the day our house burned. Still cold from running door-to-door for help in sub-zero weather, I called from a neighbor's house to tell Dan the bad news. He'd gone to work that day, fully expecting to return to all the comforts of home. Instead he came home to complete loss. Well, not complete. What mattered most to him—me—was safe and waiting for him.

I was afraid Dan might be angry. We didn't know how the fire had started, but I felt responsible since I was the one at home when it happened. But my fears were completely unfounded. Dan embraced me with tenderness, concern and gratitude, thankful that the only injury was my sprained ankle.

As the day wore on, my shock dissipated, giving way to despair. What would we do? We'd just moved into this house five months earlier, and we didn't have family nearby or any close friends to turn to. But Dan told me that fire revealed something significant about us: In losing all of our possessions, we could see more clearly what we really have—each other and a home that can't be destroyed by fire.

That first night in a hotel, Dan and I lay entwined in our bed. As he cradled me, a salty mixture of grief and joy began to wet my pillow. Here we were without a home, yet I felt completely rooted and sheltered by his love. At that moment I discovered what it means to have a sense of place. Mine is with my husband.

MARRIAGE BUILDERS

- *What about your spouse makes you feel "at home"?*
- *How can you carve out more time for each other, apart from caring for your car, home or other material "things"?*

Additional Scripture Readings
Matthew 25:31–46; Romans 8:31–39

Go to page 1031 for your next devotional reading.

NEW TESTAMENT

MATTHEW writes this Gospel to emphasize how Jesus fulfills God's promises from the Old Testament. He includes numerous sayings of Jesus about living as one of his disciples and as a member of the church, concluding with the command of Jesus to make disciples of all nations. As you read this book, ask yourself whether you are living as a disciple of Jesus, as well as how you can tell others the story of Jesus.

MATTHEW

The Genealogy of Jesus

1 A record of the genealogy of Jesus Christ the son of David, the son of Abraham:

2 Abraham was the father of Isaac,
Isaac the father of Jacob,
Jacob the father of Judah and his brothers,
3 Judah the father of Perez and Zerah, whose mother was Tamar,
Perez the father of Hezron,
Hezron the father of Ram,
4 Ram the father of Amminadab,
Amminadab the father of Nahshon,
Nahshon the father of Salmon,
5 Salmon the father of Boaz, whose mother was Rahab,
Boaz the father of Obed, whose mother was Ruth,
Obed the father of Jesse,
6 and Jesse the father of King David.

David was the father of Solomon, whose mother had been Uriah's wife,
7 Solomon the father of Rehoboam,
Rehoboam the father of Abijah,
Abijah the father of Asa,
8 Asa the father of Jehoshaphat,
Jehoshaphat the father of Jehoram,
Jehoram the father of Uzziah,
9 Uzziah the father of Jotham,
Jotham the father of Ahaz,
Ahaz the father of Hezekiah,

[10]Hezekiah the father of Manasseh,
Manasseh the father of Amon,
Amon the father of Josiah,
[11]and Josiah the father of Jeconiah[a]
and his brothers at the time of
the exile to Babylon.

[12]After the exile to Babylon:
Jeconiah was the father of Shealtiel,
Shealtiel the father of Zerubbabel,
[13]Zerubbabel the father of Abiud,
Abiud the father of Eliakim,
Eliakim the father of Azor,
[14]Azor the father of Zadok,
Zadok the father of Akim,
Akim the father of Eliud,
[15]Eliud the father of Eleazar,
Eleazar the father of Matthan,
Matthan the father of Jacob,
[16]and Jacob the father of Joseph, the
husband of Mary, of whom was
born Jesus, who is called Christ.

[17]Thus there were fourteen generations in all from Abraham to David, fourteen from David to the exile to Babylon, and fourteen from the exile to the Christ.[b]

The Birth of Jesus Christ

[18]This is how the birth of Jesus Christ came about: His mother Mary was pledged to be married to Joseph, but before they came together, she was found to be with child through the Holy Spirit. [19]Because Joseph her husband was a righteous man and did not want to expose her to public disgrace, he had in mind to divorce her quietly.

[20]But after he had considered this, an angel of the Lord appeared to him in a dream and said, "Joseph son of David, do not be afraid to take Mary home as your wife, because what is conceived in her is from the Holy Spirit. [21]She will give birth to a son, and you are to give him the name Jesus,[c] because he will save his people from their sins."

[22]All this took place to fulfill what the Lord had said through the prophet: [23]"The virgin will be with child and will give birth to a son, and they will call him Immanuel"[d]—which means, "God with us."

[24]When Joseph woke up, he did what the angel of the Lord had commanded him and took Mary home as his wife. [25]But he had no union with her until she gave birth to a son. And he gave him the name Jesus.

The Visit of the Magi

2 After Jesus was born in Bethlehem in Judea, during the time of King Herod, Magi[e] from the east came to Jerusalem [2]and asked, "Where is the one who has been born king of the Jews? We saw his star in the east[f] and have come to worship him."

[3]When King Herod heard this he was disturbed, and all Jerusalem with him. [4]When he had called together all the people's chief priests and teachers of the law, he asked them where the Christ[g] was to be born. [5]"In Bethlehem in Judea," they replied, "for this is what the prophet has written:

[6]" 'But you, Bethlehem, in the land of Judah,
are by no means least among the rulers of Judah;
for out of you will come a ruler
who will be the shepherd of my people Israel.'[h]"

[7]Then Herod called the Magi secretly and found out from them the exact time the star had appeared. [8]He sent them to Bethlehem and said, "Go and make a careful search for the child. As soon as you find him, report to me, so that I too may go and worship him."

[9]After they had heard the king, they went on their way, and the star they had seen in the east[i] went ahead of them until it stopped over the place where the child was. [10]When they saw the star, they were overjoyed. [11]On coming to the house, they saw the child with his mother Mary, and they bowed down and worshiped him. Then they opened their treasures and presented him with gifts of gold and of incense and of myrrh. [12]And having been warned in a dream not to go back to Herod, they returned to their country by another route.

The Escape to Egypt

[13]When they had gone, an angel of the

[a]*11* That is, Jehoiachin; also in verse 12 [b]*17* Or *Messiah.* "The Christ" (Greek) and "the Messiah" (Hebrew) both mean "the Anointed One." [c]*21* *Jesus* is the Greek form of *Joshua,* which means *the* LORD *saves.* [d]*23* Isaiah 7:14 [e]*1* Traditionally *Wise Men* [f]*2* Or *star when it rose* [g]*4* Or *Messiah* [h]*6* Micah 5:2 [i]*9* Or *seen when it rose*

Lord appeared to Joseph in a dream. "Get up," he said, "take the child and his mother and escape to Egypt. Stay there until I tell you, for Herod is going to search for the child to kill him."

14So he got up, took the child and his mother during the night and left for Egypt, 15where he stayed until the death of Herod. And so was fulfilled what the Lord had said through the prophet: "Out of Egypt I called my son."[a]

16When Herod realized that he had been outwitted by the Magi, he was furious, and he gave orders to kill all the boys in Bethlehem and its vicinity who were two years old and under, in accordance with the time he had learned from the Magi. 17Then what was said through the prophet Jeremiah was fulfilled:

18"A voice is heard in Ramah,
weeping and great mourning,
Rachel weeping for her children
and refusing to be comforted,
because they are no more."[b]

The Return to Nazareth

19After Herod died, an angel of the Lord appeared in a dream to Joseph in Egypt 20and said, "Get up, take the child and his mother and go to the land of Israel, for those who were trying to take the child's life are dead."

21So he got up, took the child and his mother and went to the land of Israel. 22But when he heard that Archelaus was reigning in Judea in place of his father Herod, he was afraid to go there. Having been warned in a dream, he withdrew to the district of Galilee, 23and he went and lived in a town called Nazareth. So was fulfilled what was said through the prophets: "He will be called a Nazarene."

John the Baptist Prepares the Way

3 In those days John the Baptist came, preaching in the Desert of Judea 2and saying, "Repent, for the kingdom of heaven is near." 3This is he who was spoken of through the prophet Isaiah:

"A voice of one calling in the desert,
'Prepare the way for the Lord,
make straight paths for him.' "[c]

4John's clothes were made of camel's hair, and he had a leather belt around his waist. His food was locusts and wild honey. 5People went out to him from Jerusalem and all Judea and the whole region of the Jordan. 6Confessing their sins, they were baptized by him in the Jordan River.

7But when he saw many of the Pharisees and Sadducees coming to where he was baptizing, he said to them: "You brood of vipers! Who warned you to flee from the coming wrath? 8Produce fruit in keeping with repentance. 9And do not think you can say to yourselves, 'We have Abraham as our father.' I tell you that out of these stones God can raise up children for Abraham. 10The ax is already at the root of the trees, and every tree that does not produce good fruit will be cut down and thrown into the fire.

11"I baptize you with[d] water for repentance. But after me will come one who is more powerful than I, whose sandals I am not fit to carry. He will baptize you with the Holy Spirit and with fire. 12His winnowing fork is in his hand, and he will clear his threshing floor, gathering his wheat into the barn and burning up the chaff with unquenchable fire."

The Baptism of Jesus

13Then Jesus came from Galilee to the Jordan to be baptized by John. 14But John tried to deter him, saying, "I need to be baptized by you, and do you come to me?"

15Jesus replied, "Let it be so now; it is proper for us to do this to fulfill all righteousness." Then John consented.

16As soon as Jesus was baptized, he went up out of the water. At that moment heaven was opened, and he saw the Spirit of God descending like a dove and lighting on him. 17And a voice from heaven said, "This is my Son, whom I love; with him I am well pleased."

The Temptation of Jesus

4 Then Jesus was led by the Spirit into the desert to be tempted by the devil. 2After fasting forty days and forty nights, he was hungry. 3The tempter came to him and said, "If you are the Son of God, tell these stones to become bread."

4Jesus answered, "It is written: 'Man does not live on bread alone, but on every word that comes from the mouth of God.'[e]"

5Then the devil took him to the holy city and had him stand on the highest

[a] *15* Hosea 11:1 [b] *18* Jer. 31:15 [c] *3* Isaiah 40:3 [d] *11* Or *in* [e] *4* Deut. 8:3

point of the temple. 6"If you are the Son of God," he said, "throw yourself down. For it is written:

" 'He will command his angels
concerning you,
and they will lift you up in their
hands,
so that you will not strike your foot
against a stone.'[a]"

7Jesus answered him, "It is also written: 'Do not put the Lord your God to the test.'[b]"

8Again, the devil took him to a very high mountain and showed him all the kingdoms of the world and their splendor. 9"All this I will give you," he said, "if you will bow down and worship me."

10Jesus said to him, "Away from me, Satan! For it is written: 'Worship the Lord your God, and serve him only.'[c]"

11Then the devil left him, and angels came and attended him.

Jesus Begins to Preach

12When Jesus heard that John had been put in prison, he returned to Galilee. 13Leaving Nazareth, he went and lived in Capernaum, which was by the lake in the area of Zebulun and Naphtali— 14to fulfill what was said through the prophet Isaiah:

15"Land of Zebulun and land of
Naphtali,
the way to the sea, along the
Jordan,
Galilee of the Gentiles—
16the people living in darkness
have seen a great light;
on those living in the land of the
shadow of death
a light has dawned."[d]

17From that time on Jesus began to preach, "Repent, for the kingdom of heaven is near."

The Calling of the First Disciples

18As Jesus was walking beside the Sea of Galilee, he saw two brothers, Simon called Peter and his brother Andrew. They were casting a net into the lake, for they were fishermen. 19"Come, follow me," Jesus said, "and I will make you fishers of men." 20At once they left their nets and followed him.

21Going on from there, he saw two other brothers, James son of Zebedee and his brother John. They were in a boat with their father Zebedee, preparing their nets. Jesus called them, 22and immediately they left the boat and their father and followed him.

Jesus Heals the Sick

23Jesus went throughout Galilee, teaching in their synagogues, preaching the good news of the kingdom, and healing every disease and sickness among the people. 24News about him spread all over Syria, and people brought to him all who were ill with various diseases, those suffering severe pain, the demon-possessed, those having seizures, and the paralyzed, and he healed them. 25Large crowds from Galilee, the Decapolis,[e] Jerusalem, Judea and the region across the Jordan followed him.

The Beatitudes

5 Now when he saw the crowds, he went up on a mountainside and sat down. His disciples came to him, 2and he began to teach them, saying:

3"Blessed are the poor in spirit,
for theirs is the kingdom of heaven.
4Blessed are those who mourn,
for they will be comforted.
5Blessed are the meek,
for they will inherit the earth.
6Blessed are those who hunger and
thirst for righteousness,
for they will be filled.
7Blessed are the merciful,
for they will be shown mercy.
8Blessed are the pure in heart,
for they will see God.
9Blessed are the peacemakers,
for they will be called sons of God.
10Blessed are those who are persecuted
because of righteousness,
for theirs is the kingdom of heaven.

11"Blessed are you when people insult you, persecute you and falsely say all kinds of evil against you because of me. 12Rejoice and be glad, because great is your reward in heaven, for in the same way they persecuted the prophets who were before you.

Salt and Light

13"You are the salt of the earth. But if

[a]6 Psalm 91:11,12 [b]7 Deut. 6:16 [c]10 Deut. 6:13 [d]16 Isaiah 9:1,2 [e]25 That is, the Ten Cities

the salt loses its saltiness, how can it be
made salty again? It is no longer good for
anything, except to be thrown out and
trampled by men.
14"You are the light of the world. A city
on a hill cannot be hidden. 15Neither
do people light a lamp and put it un-
der a bowl. Instead they put it on its
stand, and it gives light to everyone in the
house. 16In the same way, let your light
shine before men, that they may see your
good deeds and praise your Father in
heaven.

The Fulfillment of the Law

17"Do not think that I have come to
abolish the Law or the Prophets; I have
not come to abolish them but to fulfill
them. 18I tell you the truth, until heaven
and earth disappear, not the smallest let-
ter, not the least stroke of a pen, will by
any means disappear from the Law until

VERSE FOR THE DAY: Matthew 5:9

AUTHOR: Ruth Senter

PASSAGE FOR THE DAY: Matthew 5:1–12

Beyond the Fairy Tale

In a poll conducted by *Psychology Today* magazine, a man married for more than twenty years responded, "Commitment means a willingness to be unhappy for a while." Such statements are not necessarily good PR for marriage. In fact, I wonder how many fairy tales would have sold had they ended simply "and they lived together ever after." Who doesn't want to be happy? There would be something wrong if I didn't desire a happy marriage.

But Jesus puts happiness in another context. "Blessed [happy] are the peacemakers," Jesus said. He didn't say, "Happy are those who have never known troubles." He said, "Happy are those who have learned to bring peace out of the trouble." That's a foreign idea in fairy tales where people live happily ever after only when conflict has been forever banished.

Marriage was created for our good, not necessarily for our happiness. God looked on his creation and pronounced it good—not easy or happy. And I suppose, despite my love for candlelight and roses, were you to ask about my marriage I would have to say, "It's been good." And according to God's standard, that's a high tribute.

MARRIAGE BUILDERS

♦ *As a couple, what are the troubles you've had that have eventually resulted in greater peace?*

♦ *As you look back over the years of your marriage, what are the things you can call "good"?*

Additional Scripture Readings
Psalm 27:13–14; 2 Corinthians 4:17; James 3:18

Go to page 1033 for your next devotional reading.

everything is accomplished. 19Anyone
who breaks one of the least of these com-
mandments and teaches others to do the
same will be called least in the kingdom of
heaven, but whoever practices and
teaches these commands will be called
great in the kingdom of heaven. 20For I tell
you that unless your righteousness sur-
passes that of the Pharisees and the teach-
ers of the law, you will certainly not enter
the kingdom of heaven.

Murder

21"You have heard that it was said to the
people long ago, 'Do not murder,[a] and
anyone who murders will be subject to
judgment.' 22But I tell you that anyone
who is angry with his brother[b] will be
subject to judgment. Again, anyone who
says to his brother, 'Raca,[c]' is answer-
able to the Sanhedrin. But anyone who
says, 'You fool!' will be in danger of the
fire of hell.

23"Therefore, if you are offering your
gift at the altar and there remember that
your brother has something against you,
24leave your gift there in front of the altar.
First go and be reconciled to your brother;
then come and offer your gift.

25"Settle matters quickly with your ad-
versary who is taking you to court. Do it
while you are still with him on the way, or
he may hand you over to the judge, and
the judge may hand you over to the offi-
cer, and you may be thrown into prison.
26I tell you the truth, you will not get out
until you have paid the last penny.[d]

Adultery

27"You have heard that it was said, 'Do
not commit adultery.'[e] 28But I tell you
that anyone who looks at a woman lustful-
ly has already committed adultery with
her in his heart. 29If your right eye causes
you to sin, gouge it out and throw it away.
It is better for you to lose one part of your
body than for your whole body to be
thrown into hell. 30And if your right hand
causes you to sin, cut it off and throw it
away. It is better for you to lose one part
of your body than for your whole body to
go into hell.

Divorce

31"It has been said, 'Anyone who di-
vorces his wife must give her a certificate
of divorce.'[f] 32But I tell you that anyone
who divorces his wife, except for marital
unfaithfulness, causes her to become an
adulteress, and anyone who marries the
divorced woman commits adultery.

Oaths

33"Again, you have heard that it was
said to the people long ago, 'Do not break
your oath, but keep the oaths you have
made to the Lord.' 34But I tell you, Do not
swear at all: either by heaven, for it is
God's throne; 35or by the earth, for it is his
footstool; or by Jerusalem, for it is the city
of the Great King. 36And do not swear by
your head, for you cannot make even one
hair white or black. 37Simply let your 'Yes'
be 'Yes,' and your 'No,' 'No'; anything be-
yond this comes from the evil one.

An Eye for an Eye

38"You have heard that it was said, 'Eye
for eye, and tooth for tooth.'[g] 39But I tell
you, Do not resist an evil person. If some-
one strikes you on the right cheek, turn to
him the other also. 40And if someone
wants to sue you and take your tunic, let
him have your cloak as well. 41If someone
forces you to go one mile, go with him two
miles. 42Give to the one who asks you, and
do not turn away from the one who wants
to borrow from you.

Love for Enemies

43"You have heard that it was said,
'Love your neighbor[h] and hate your ene-
my.' 44But I tell you: Love your enemies[i]
and pray for those who persecute you,
45that you may be sons of your Father in
heaven. He causes his sun to rise on the
evil and the good, and sends rain on the
righteous and the unrighteous. 46If you
love those who love you, what reward will
you get? Are not even the tax collectors
doing that? 47And if you greet only your
brothers, what are you doing more than
others? Do not even pagans do that? 48Be
perfect, therefore, as your heavenly Father
is perfect.

[a] *21* Exodus 20:13 [b] *22* Some manuscripts *brother without cause* [c] *22* An Aramaic term of contempt
[d] *26* Greek *kodrantes* [e] *27* Exodus 20:14 [f] *31* Deut. 24:1 [g] *38* Exodus 21:24; Lev. 24:20; Deut. 19:21 [h] *43* Lev. 19:18 [i] *44* Some late manuscripts *enemies, bless those who curse you, do good to those who hate you*

VERSE FOR THE DAY: Matthew 5:28

AUTHOR: Douglas B. DeMerchant

PASSAGE FOR THE DAY: Matthew 5:27–32

Dangerous Fantasies

Marriage doesn't kill an active imagination any more than it dampens our appreciation for members of the opposite sex. And yet, just as marriage calls us to redirect our passions exclusively toward our partners, so too it calls us to redirect our mental passions.

The place to begin is with the Biblical injunction to think on things that are true, noble, right, pure, lovely, admirable (Philippians 4:8). This calls for discernment—the ability to sort out the wholesome from the unsavory, the godly from the evil, the lovely from the stained. We need to be aware of and alert to the influences and messages all around us that promote unhealthy fantasies.

To help combat the negative effects of such influences, open communication with your spouse is essential. For example, talk to your mate about your lovemaking. If it has become routine, discuss ways to liven things up. And to help heighten the pleasure of these physical times, focus your thoughts on your spouse exclusively. Fantasizing about his or her touch, intimate moments together and physical closeness provides new energy and a greater desire to be together.

Fantasy should only be focused on your mate. It should be used to heighten and enrich the sex life in your bed, not the sex life in your head.

MARRIAGE BUILDERS

♦ *What influences and messages around us promote unhealthy fantasies?*

♦ *Talk with your spouse about your times of lovemaking. What would each of you like to be different?*

Additional Scripture Readings
Philippians 4:8; 1 John 2:15–17

Go to page 1034 for your next devotional reading.

Giving to the Needy

6 "Be careful not to do your 'acts of righteousness' before men, to be seen by them. If you do, you will have no reward from your Father in heaven.

2"So when you give to the needy, do not announce it with trumpets, as the hypocrites do in the synagogues and on the streets, to be honored by men. I tell you the truth, they have received their reward in full. 3But when you give to the needy, do not let your left hand know what your right hand is doing, 4so that your giving may be in secret. Then your Father, who

VERSE FOR THE DAY: Matthew 6:3–4

AUTHOR: Ruth Senter

PASSAGE FOR THE DAY: Matthew 6:1–7

Secret Service

We spotted Mr. Per as we backed our van into campsite number seven. He was disappearing through the white birch and pine that separated our parking spot from his. "Somebody's raked our spot," my daughter Jori said. Later, we saw a rake leaning against a Winnebago.

When we returned from a walk, we found a pile of neatly stacked logs beside our fireplace, and two coloring books lay on the picnic table.

"Somebody likes kids," was all Mr. Per said next morning when I mentioned the coloring books. The next night our lantern was lit for us when we made our way up the path from the lake. He had hung it to light the rocky way we had to walk. Mr. Per was whistling through the woods, heading toward his site just as we walked into camp.

Our lives had been touched by a man who knew something profound about service. Mr. Per demonstrated for us what Jesus taught about the true spirit of giving: ". . . Do not let your left hand know what your right hand is doing, so that your giving may be in secret. Then your Father, who sees what is done in secret, will reward you" (Matthew 6:4).

MARRIAGE BUILDERS

♦ *Why is it important to let go of any expectation for reward or recognition from your spouse when you do something kind for him or her?*

♦ *What spiritual satisfaction do you feel because God sees your "unrecognized" service toward others?*

Additional Scripture Readings
Hebrews 6:10; Matthew 6:6–18; 1 Peter 5:5

Go to page 1036 for your next devotional reading.

sees what is done in secret, will reward you.

Prayer

5"And when you pray, do not be like the hypocrites, for they love to pray standing in the synagogues and on the street corners to be seen by men. I tell you the truth, they have received their reward in full. 6But when you pray, go into your room, close the door and pray to your Father, who is unseen. Then your Father, who sees what is done in secret, will reward you. 7And when you pray, do not keep on babbling like pagans, for they think they will be heard because of their many words. 8Do not be like them, for your Father knows what you need before you ask him.

9"This, then, is how you should pray:

" 'Our Father in heaven,
hallowed be your name,
10your kingdom come,
your will be done
on earth as it is in heaven.
11Give us today our daily bread.
12Forgive us our debts,
as we also have forgiven our
debtors.
13And lead us not into temptation,
but deliver us from the evil one.[a]'

14For if you forgive men when they sin against you, your heavenly Father will also forgive you. 15But if you do not forgive men their sins, your Father will not forgive your sins.

Fasting

16"When you fast, do not look somber as the hypocrites do, for they disfigure their faces to show men they are fasting. I tell you the truth, they have received their reward in full. 17But when you fast, put oil on your head and wash your face, 18so that it will not be obvious to men that you are fasting, but only to your Father, who is unseen; and your Father, who sees what is done in secret, will reward you.

Treasures in Heaven

19"Do not store up for yourselves treasures on earth, where moth and rust destroy, and where thieves break in and steal. 20But store up for yourselves treasures in heaven, where moth and rust do not destroy, and where thieves do not break in and steal. 21For where your treasure is, there your heart will be also.

22"The eye is the lamp of the body. If your eyes are good, your whole body will be full of light. 23But if your eyes are bad, your whole body will be full of darkness. If then the light within you is darkness, how great is that darkness!

24"No one can serve two masters. Either he will hate the one and love the other, or he will be devoted to the one and despise the other. You cannot serve both God and Money.

Do Not Worry

25"Therefore I tell you, do not worry about your life, what you will eat or drink; or about your body, what you will wear. Is not life more important than food, and the body more important than clothes? 26Look at the birds of the air; they do not sow or reap or store away in barns, and yet your heavenly Father feeds them. Are you not much more valuable than they? 27Who of you by worrying can add a single hour to his life[b]?

28"And why do you worry about clothes? See how the lilies of the field grow. They do not labor or spin. 29Yet I tell you that not even Solomon in all his splendor was dressed like one of these. 30If that is how God clothes the grass of the field, which is here today and tomorrow is thrown into the fire, will he not much more clothe you, O you of little faith? 31So do not worry, saying, 'What shall we eat?' or 'What shall we drink?' or 'What shall we wear?' 32For the pagans run after all these things, and your heavenly Father knows that you need them. 33But seek first his kingdom and his righteousness, and all these things will be given to you as well. 34Therefore do not worry about tomorrow, for tomorrow will worry about itself. Each day has enough trouble of its own.

Judging Others

7 "Do not judge, or you too will be judged. 2For in the same way you judge others, you will be judged, and with the measure you use, it will be measured to you.

3"Why do you look at the speck of sawdust in your brother's eye and pay no at-

[a]13 Or *from evil*; some late manuscripts *one, / for yours is the kingdom and the power and the glory forever. Amen.* [b]27 Or *single cubit to his height*

WEEKENDING

SPONTANEITY

As they say, variety is the spice of life. If your marriage has seemed a little routine lately, trying spicing it up with some of these suggestions.

1. Sit on the same side of a restaurant booth.
2. Give your mate a foot massage.
3. Sing a song to your spouse.
4. Write out 50 reasons you're glad you're married.
5. Create your own holiday.
6. Reminisce about your first kiss or first date.
7. Go up on your roof to watch a sunset.
8. Avoid a social event at the last minute and take off together alone.
9. Photocopy a newspaper cartoon and write your own caption.
10. Go for a walk barefoot.

— *Doug Fields*

REVIVE

Saturday: Psalm 16:7–11
Sunday: Psalm 145:13–16

Go to page 1038 for your next devotional reading.

tention to the plank in your own eye?
4How can you say to your brother, 'Let me
take the speck out of your eye,' when all
the time there is a plank in your own eye?
5You hypocrite, first take the plank out of
your own eye, and then you will see clear-
ly to remove the speck from your broth-
er's eye.

6"Do not give dogs what is sacred; do
not throw your pearls to pigs. If you do,
they may trample them under their feet,
and then turn and tear you to pieces.

Ask, Seek, Knock

7"Ask and it will be given to you; seek
and you will find; knock and the door will
be opened to you. 8For everyone who asks
receives; he who seeks finds; and to him
who knocks, the door will be opened.

9"Which of you, if his son asks for
bread, will give him a stone? 10Or if he
asks for a fish, will give him a snake? 11If
you, then, though you are evil, know how
to give good gifts to your children, how
much more will your Father in heaven
give good gifts to those who ask him! 12So
in everything, do to others what you
would have them do to you, for this sums
up the Law and the Prophets.

The Narrow and Wide Gates

13"Enter through the narrow gate. For
wide is the gate and broad is the road that
leads to destruction, and many enter
through it. 14But small is the gate and nar-
row the road that leads to life, and only a
few find it.

A Tree and Its Fruit

15"Watch out for false prophets. They
come to you in sheep's clothing, but in-
wardly they are ferocious wolves. 16By
their fruit you will recognize them. Do
people pick grapes from thornbushes, or
figs from thistles? 17Likewise every good
tree bears good fruit, but a bad tree bears
bad fruit. 18A good tree cannot bear bad
fruit, and a bad tree cannot bear good
fruit. 19Every tree that does not bear good
fruit is cut down and thrown into the fire.
20Thus, by their fruit you will recognize
them.

21"Not everyone who says to me, 'Lord,
Lord,' will enter the kingdom of heaven,
but only he who does the will of my Fa-
ther who is in heaven. 22Many will say to
me on that day, 'Lord, Lord, did we not
prophesy in your name, and in your name
drive out demons and perform many mir-
acles?' 23Then I will tell them plainly, 'I
never knew you. Away from me, you evil-
doers!'

The Wise and Foolish Builders

24"Therefore everyone who hears these
words of mine and puts them into practice
is like a wise man who built his house on
the rock. 25The rain came down, the
streams rose, and the winds blew and beat
against that house; yet it did not fall, be-
cause it had its foundation on the rock.
26But everyone who hears these words of
mine and does not put them into practice
is like a foolish man who built his house
on sand. 27The rain came down, the
streams rose, and the winds blew and beat
against that house, and it fell with a great
crash."

28When Jesus had finished saying these
things, the crowds were amazed at his
teaching, 29because he taught as one who
had authority, and not as their teachers of
the law.

The Man With Leprosy

8 When he came down from the moun-
tainside, large crowds followed him.
2A man with leprosy[a] came and knelt be-
fore him and said, "Lord, if you are will-
ing, you can make me clean."

3Jesus reached out his hand and
touched the man. "I am willing," he said.
"Be clean!" Immediately he was cured[b]
of his leprosy. 4Then Jesus said to him,
"See that you don't tell anyone. But go,
show yourself to the priest and offer the
gift Moses commanded, as a testimony to
them."

The Faith of the Centurion

5When Jesus had entered Capernaum, a
centurion came to him, asking for help.
6"Lord," he said, "my servant lies at home
paralyzed and in terrible suffering."

7Jesus said to him, "I will go and heal
him."

8The centurion replied, "Lord, I do not
deserve to have you come under my roof.
But just say the word, and my servant will
be healed. 9For I myself am a man under
authority, with soldiers under me. I tell

[a]2 The Greek word was used for various diseases affecting the skin—not necessarily leprosy.
[b]3 Greek *made clean*

this one, 'Go,' and he goes; and that one,
'Come,' and he comes. I say to my servant,
'Do this,' and he does it."
10When Jesus heard this, he was aston-
ished and said to those following him, "I
tell you the truth, I have not found anyone
in Israel with such great faith. 11I say to
you that many will come from the east
and the west, and will take their places at
the feast with Abraham, Isaac and Jacob
in the kingdom of heaven. 12But the sub-
jects of the kingdom will be thrown out-
side, into the darkness, where there will
be weeping and gnashing of teeth."

VERSE FOR THE DAY: Matthew 7:11 | AUTHOR: Max Lucado | PASSAGE FOR THE DAY: Matthew 7:7–12

The Theology of Parenthood

Andrea, our three-year-old, stood at the edge of my bed. It was three in the morning. "What's wrong?" I asked.

"I need a fwashwight in my woom."

I told her the night light and the hall light were on.

"But Daddy," she objected, "what if I open my eyes and can't see anything?"

My wife explained that there had been a power failure and Andrea must have awakened in the dark. She had opened her eyes and had been unable to see anything. I picked Andrea up, got a flashlight out of the utility room, and carried her to her bed. All the while, I told her that Mom and Dad were here and that she didn't need to be afraid.

If I know that one of the privileges of fatherhood is to comfort a child, then why am I so reluctant to let my heavenly Father comfort me? Why do I think he's tired of hearing the same old stuff? Why do I think he consults his list when I ask for forgiveness and asks, "Don't you think you're going to the well a few too many times on this one?" Why don't I let my Father do for me what I am more than willing to do for my own children?

Being a father is teaching me that when I am afraid, there is a Father who is ready to comfort me. There is a Father who will hold me until I'm better, who won't go to sleep when I'm afraid of waking up and seeing the dark.

MARRIAGE BUILDERS

♦ *What parallels can you draw between your relationship with your children and God's relationship with you?*

♦ *How have you experienced the comfort of your heavenly Father?*

Additional Scripture Readings
James 1:17; Luke 11:13

Go to page 1043 for your next devotional reading.

13Then Jesus said to the centurion, "Go!
It will be done just as you believed it
would." And his servant was healed at
that very hour.

Jesus Heals Many

14When Jesus came into Peter's house,
he saw Peter's mother-in-law lying in bed
with a fever. 15He touched her hand and
the fever left her, and she got up and began to wait on him.

16When evening came, many who were
demon-possessed were brought to him,
and he drove out the spirits with a word
and healed all the sick. 17This was to fulfill
what was spoken through the prophet Isaiah:

"He took up our infirmities
and carried our diseases."[a]

The Cost of Following Jesus

18When Jesus saw the crowd around
him, he gave orders to cross to the other
side of the lake. 19Then a teacher of the
law came to him and said, "Teacher, I will
follow you wherever you go."

20Jesus replied, "Foxes have holes and
birds of the air have nests, but the Son of
Man has no place to lay his head."

21Another disciple said to him, "Lord,
first let me go and bury my father."

22But Jesus told him, "Follow me, and
let the dead bury their own dead."

Jesus Calms the Storm

23Then he got into the boat and his disciples followed him. 24Without warning, a
furious storm came up on the lake, so that
the waves swept over the boat. But Jesus
was sleeping. 25The disciples went and
woke him, saying, "Lord, save us! We're
going to drown!"

26He replied, "You of little faith, why are
you so afraid?" Then he got up and rebuked the winds and the waves, and it
was completely calm.

27The men were amazed and asked,
"What kind of man is this? Even the winds
and the waves obey him!"

The Healing of Two Demon-possessed Men

28When he arrived at the other side in
the region of the Gadarenes,[b] two demon-possessed men coming from the
tombs met him. They were so violent that
no one could pass that way. 29"What do
you want with us, Son of God?" they
shouted. "Have you come here to torture
us before the appointed time?"

30Some distance from them a large herd
of pigs was feeding. 31The demons begged
Jesus, "If you drive us out, send us into
the herd of pigs."

32He said to them, "Go!" So they came
out and went into the pigs, and the whole
herd rushed down the steep bank into the
lake and died in the water. 33Those tending the pigs ran off, went into the town
and reported all this, including what had
happened to the demon-possessed men.
34Then the whole town went out to meet
Jesus. And when they saw him, they
pleaded with him to leave their region.

Jesus Heals a Paralytic

9 Jesus stepped into a boat, crossed
over and came to his own town.
2Some men brought to him a paralytic, lying on a mat. When Jesus saw their faith,
he said to the paralytic, "Take heart, son;
your sins are forgiven."

3At this, some of the teachers of the law
said to themselves, "This fellow is blaspheming!"

4Knowing their thoughts, Jesus said,
"Why do you entertain evil thoughts in
your hearts? 5Which is easier: to say,
'Your sins are forgiven,' or to say, 'Get up
and walk'? 6But so that you may know
that the Son of Man has authority on earth
to forgive sins. . . ." Then he said to the
paralytic, "Get up, take your mat and go
home." 7And the man got up and went
home. 8When the crowd saw this, they
were filled with awe; and they praised
God, who had given such authority to
men.

The Calling of Matthew

9As Jesus went on from there, he saw a
man named Matthew sitting at the tax collector's booth. "Follow me," he told him,
and Matthew got up and followed him.

10While Jesus was having dinner at
Matthew's house, many tax collectors and
"sinners" came and ate with him and his
disciples. 11When the Pharisees saw this,
they asked his disciples, "Why does your
teacher eat with tax collectors and 'sinners'?"

12On hearing this, Jesus said, "It is not
the healthy who need a doctor, but the

[a] 17 Isaiah 53:4 [b] 28 Some manuscripts *Gergesenes*; others *Gerasenes*

sick. 13But go and learn what this means:
'I desire mercy, not sacrifice.'[a] For I have
not come to call the righteous, but sin-
ners."

Jesus Questioned About Fasting

14Then John's disciples came and asked
him, "How is it that we and the Pharisees
fast, but your disciples do not fast?"
15Jesus answered, "How can the guests
of the bridegroom mourn while he is with
them? The time will come when the bride-
groom will be taken from them; then they
will fast.
16"No one sews a patch of unshrunk
cloth on an old garment, for the patch will
pull away from the garment, making the
tear worse. 17Neither do men pour new
wine into old wineskins. If they do, the
skins will burst, the wine will run out and
the wineskins will be ruined. No, they
pour new wine into new wineskins, and
both are preserved."

A Dead Girl and a Sick Woman

18While he was saying this, a ruler came
and knelt before him and said, "My
daughter has just died. But come and put
your hand on her, and she will live."
19Jesus got up and went with him, and so
did his disciples.
20Just then a woman who had been sub-
ject to bleeding for twelve years came up
behind him and touched the edge of his
cloak. 21She said to herself, "If I only
touch his cloak, I will be healed."
22Jesus turned and saw her. "Take
heart, daughter," he said, "your faith has
healed you." And the woman was healed
from that moment.
23When Jesus entered the ruler's house
and saw the flute players and the noisy
crowd, 24he said, "Go away. The girl is not
dead but asleep." But they laughed at him.
25After the crowd had been put outside,
he went in and took the girl by the hand,
and she got up. 26News of this spread
through all that region.

Jesus Heals the Blind and Mute

27As Jesus went on from there, two
blind men followed him, calling out,
"Have mercy on us, Son of David!"
28When he had gone indoors, the blind
men came to him, and he asked them, "Do
you believe that I am able to do this?"
"Yes, Lord," they replied.
29Then he touched their eyes and said,
"According to your faith will it be done to
you"; 30and their sight was restored. Jesus
warned them sternly, "See that no one
knows about this." 31But they went out
and spread the news about him all over
that region.
32While they were going out, a man
who was demon-possessed and could not
talk was brought to Jesus. 33And when the
demon was driven out, the man who had
been mute spoke. The crowd was amazed
and said, "Nothing like this has ever been
seen in Israel."
34But the Pharisees said, "It is by the
prince of demons that he drives out de-
mons."

The Workers Are Few

35Jesus went through all the towns and
villages, teaching in their synagogues,
preaching the good news of the kingdom
and healing every disease and sickness.
36When he saw the crowds, he had com-
passion on them, because they were ha-
rassed and helpless, like sheep without a
shepherd. 37Then he said to his disciples,
"The harvest is plentiful but the workers
are few. 38Ask the Lord of the harvest,
therefore, to send out workers into his
harvest field."

Jesus Sends Out the Twelve

10 He called his twelve disciples to
him and gave them authority to
drive out evil[b] spirits and to heal every
disease and sickness.
2These are the names of the twelve
apostles: first, Simon (who is called Peter)
and his brother Andrew; James son of
Zebedee, and his brother John; 3Philip
and Bartholomew; Thomas and Matthew
the tax collector; James son of Alphaeus,
and Thaddaeus; 4Simon the Zealot and Ju-
das Iscariot, who betrayed him.
5These twelve Jesus sent out with the
following instructions: "Do not go among
the Gentiles or enter any town of the Sa-
maritans. 6Go rather to the lost sheep of
Israel. 7As you go, preach this message:
'The kingdom of heaven is near.' 8Heal the
sick, raise the dead, cleanse those who
have leprosy,[c] drive out demons. Freely
you have received, freely give. 9Do not
take along any gold or silver or copper in

[a] 13 Hosea 6:6 [b] 1 Greek *unclean* [c] 8 The Greek word was used for various diseases affecting the skin—not necessarily leprosy.

your belts; [10]take no bag for the journey,
or extra tunic, or sandals or a staff; for the
worker is worth his keep.
[11]"Whatever town or village you enter,
search for some worthy person there and
stay at his house until you leave. [12]As you
enter the home, give it your greeting. [13]If
the home is deserving, let your peace rest
on it; if it is not, let your peace return to
you. [14]If anyone will not welcome you or
listen to your words, shake the dust off
your feet when you leave that home or
town. [15]I tell you the truth, it will be more
bearable for Sodom and Gomorrah on the
day of judgment than for that town. [16]I am
sending you out like sheep among wolves.
Therefore be as shrewd as snakes and as
innocent as doves.
[17]"Be on your guard against men; they
will hand you over to the local councils
and flog you in their synagogues. [18]On my
account you will be brought before gover-
nors and kings as witnesses to them and
to the Gentiles. [19]But when they arrest
you, do not worry about what to say or
how to say it. At that time you will be giv-
en what to say, [20]for it will not be you
speaking, but the Spirit of your Father
speaking through you.
[21]"Brother will betray brother to death,
and a father his child; children will rebel
against their parents and have them put to
death. [22]All men will hate you because of
me, but he who stands firm to the end will
be saved. [23]When you are persecuted in
one place, flee to another. I tell you the
truth, you will not finish going through
the cities of Israel before the Son of Man
comes.
[24]"A student is not above his teacher,
nor a servant above his master. [25]It is
enough for the student to be like his
teacher, and the servant like his master. If
the head of the house has been called Be-
elzebub,[a] how much more the members
of his household!
[26]"So do not be afraid of them. There is
nothing concealed that will not be dis-
closed, or hidden that will not be made
known. [27]What I tell you in the dark,
speak in the daylight; what is whispered
in your ear, proclaim from the roofs. [28]Do
not be afraid of those who kill the body
but cannot kill the soul. Rather, be afraid
of the One who can destroy both soul and
body in hell. [29]Are not two sparrows sold
for a penny[b]? Yet not one of them will
fall to the ground apart from the will of
your Father. [30]And even the very hairs of
your head are all numbered. [31]So don't be
afraid; you are worth more than many
sparrows.
[32]"Whoever acknowledges me before
men, I will also acknowledge him before
my Father in heaven. [33]But whoever dis-
owns me before men, I will disown him
before my Father in heaven.
[34]"Do not suppose that I have come to
bring peace to the earth. I did not come to
bring peace, but a sword. [35]For I have
come to turn

"'a man against his father,
a daughter against her mother,
a daughter-in-law against her
mother-in-law—
36 a man's enemies will be the
members of his own
household.'[c]

[37]"Anyone who loves his father or
mother more than me is not worthy of me;
anyone who loves his son or daughter
more than me is not worthy of me; [38]and
anyone who does not take his cross and
follow me is not worthy of me. [39]Whoever
finds his life will lose it, and whoever
loses his life for my sake will find it.
[40]"He who receives you receives me,
and he who receives me receives the one
who sent me. [41]Anyone who receives a
prophet because he is a prophet will re-
ceive a prophet's reward, and anyone who
receives a righteous man because he is a
righteous man will receive a righteous
man's reward. [42]And if anyone gives even
a cup of cold water to one of these little
ones because he is my disciple, I tell you
the truth, he will certainly not lose his re-
ward."

Jesus and John the Baptist

11 After Jesus had finished instruct-
ing his twelve disciples, he went on
from there to teach and preach in the
towns of Galilee.[d]
[2]When John heard in prison what
Christ was doing, he sent his disciples [3]to
ask him, "Are you the one who was to
come, or should we expect someone
else?"
[4]Jesus replied, "Go back and report to
John what you hear and see: [5]The blind

[a]25 Greek *Beezeboul* or *Beelzeboul* [b]29 Greek *an assarion* [c]36 Micah 7:6 [d]1 Greek *in their towns*

receive sight, the lame walk, those who
have leprosy[a] are cured, the deaf hear,
the dead are raised, and the good news is
preached to the poor. 6Blessed is the man
who does not fall away on account
of me."

7As John's disciples were leaving, Jesus
began to speak to the crowd about John:
"What did you go out into the desert to
see? A reed swayed by the wind? 8If not,
what did you go out to see? A man dressed
in fine clothes? No, those who wear fine
clothes are in kings' palaces. 9Then what
did you go out to see? A prophet? Yes, I
tell you, and more than a prophet. 10This
is the one about whom it is written:

" 'I will send my messenger ahead of
you,
who will prepare your way before
you.'[b]

11I tell you the truth: Among those born of
women there has not risen anyone greater
than John the Baptist; yet he who is least
in the kingdom of heaven is greater than
he. 12From the days of John the Baptist
until now, the kingdom of heaven has
been forcefully advancing, and forceful
men lay hold of it. 13For all the Prophets
and the Law prophesied until John. 14And
if you are willing to accept it, he is the Eli-
jah who was to come. 15He who has ears,
let him hear.

16"To what can I compare this genera-
tion? They are like children sitting in the
marketplaces and calling out to others:

17" 'We played the flute for you,
and you did not dance;
we sang a dirge,
and you did not mourn.'

18For John came neither eating nor drink-
ing, and they say, 'He has a demon.' 19The
Son of Man came eating and drinking, and
they say, 'Here is a glutton and a drunk-
ard, a friend of tax collectors and "sin-
ners." ' But wisdom is proved right by her
actions."

Woe on Unrepentant Cities

20Then Jesus began to denounce the cit-
ies in which most of his miracles had been
performed, because they did not repent.
21"Woe to you, Korazin! Woe to you,
Bethsaida! If the miracles that were per-
formed in you had been performed in
Tyre and Sidon, they would have repented
long ago in sackcloth and ashes. 22But I
tell you, it will be more bearable for Tyre
and Sidon on the day of judgment than for
you. 23And you, Capernaum, will you be
lifted up to the skies? No, you will go
down to the depths.[c] If the miracles that
were performed in you had been per-
formed in Sodom, it would have remained
to this day. 24But I tell you that it will be
more bearable for Sodom on the day of
judgment than for you."

Rest for the Weary

25At that time Jesus said, "I praise you,
Father, Lord of heaven and earth, because
you have hidden these things from the
wise and learned, and revealed them to lit-
tle children. 26Yes, Father, for this was
your good pleasure.

27"All things have been committed to
me by my Father. No one knows the Son
except the Father, and no one knows the
Father except the Son and those to whom
the Son chooses to reveal him.

28"Come to me, all you who are weary
and burdened, and I will give you rest.
29Take my yoke upon you and learn from
me, for I am gentle and humble in heart,
and you will find rest for your souls. 30For
my yoke is easy and my burden is light."

Lord of the Sabbath

12 At that time Jesus went through
the grainfields on the Sabbath. His
disciples were hungry and began to pick
some heads of grain and eat them. 2When
the Pharisees saw this, they said to him,
"Look! Your disciples are doing what is
unlawful on the Sabbath."

3He answered, "Haven't you read what
David did when he and his companions
were hungry? 4He entered the house of
God, and he and his companions ate the
consecrated bread—which was not lawful
for them to do, but only for the priests. 5Or
haven't you read in the Law that on the
Sabbath the priests in the temple dese-
crate the day and yet are innocent? 6I tell
you that one[d] greater than the temple is
here. 7If you had known what these words
mean, 'I desire mercy, not sacrifice,'[e] you
would not have condemned the innocent.
8For the Son of Man is Lord of the Sab-
bath."

9Going on from that place, he went into

[a]5 The Greek word was used for various diseases affecting the skin—not necessarily leprosy. [b]10 Mal. 3:1 [c]23 Greek *Hades* [d]6 Or *something*; also in verses 41 and 42 [e]7 Hosea 6:6

their synagogue, [10]and a man with a shriveled hand was there. Looking for a reason to accuse Jesus, they asked him, "Is it lawful to heal on the Sabbath?"

[11]He said to them, "If any of you has a sheep and it falls into a pit on the Sabbath, will you not take hold of it and lift it out? [12]How much more valuable is a man than a sheep! Therefore it is lawful to do good on the Sabbath."

[13]Then he said to the man, "Stretch out your hand." So he stretched it out and it was completely restored, just as sound as the other. [14]But the Pharisees went out and plotted how they might kill Jesus.

God's Chosen Servant

[15]Aware of this, Jesus withdrew from that place. Many followed him, and he healed all their sick, [16]warning them not to tell who he was. [17]This was to fulfill what was spoken through the prophet Isaiah:

[18]"Here is my servant whom I have chosen,
the one I love, in whom I delight;

VERSE FOR THE DAY: Matthew 11:29 | AUTHOR: R. Ruth Barton | PASSAGE FOR THE DAY: Matthew 11:25–30

A Competitive Spirit

Pride is what motivates our desire to receive glory for what we do. It also tempts us to insist on being better at it than anyone else. And it's pride that makes it hard for us to rejoice in someone else's success.

In contrast, Christ's answer to anyone seeking a position of distinction in his kingdom always involves humility and servanthood. In Matthew 11:29 he says, "Take my yoke upon you and learn from me, for I am gentle and humble in heart, and you will find rest for your souls." He offers rest from the wrestling of a proud spirit. Rest from frantic human effort to make oneself feel significant, respected. Rest that comes only when we are at peace with ourselves and with God's design for our lives.

Competitive people tend to find their reward in the recognition they receive from others. They fail to realize that the approval of Christ far outweighs any recognition others can give.

MARRIAGE BUILDERS

♦ *In Matthew 11:29, Jesus says, "learn from me." Can you remember times in Christ's life when he modeled humility? gentleness? servanthood?*

♦ *How is your attitude about the areas in which you are currently serving—at home and at church?*

Additional Scripture Readings
Proverbs 11:2; 16:18; 29:23;
Galatians 6:3–4

Go to page 1044 for your next devotional reading.

VERSE FOR THE DAY: Matthew 12:19–20

AUTHOR: James Long

PASSAGE FOR THE DAY: Matthew 12:1–21

Jesus, the Righteous Husband

I looked around my living room, seeing reminders of the relationship my wife and I share. I reflected on just how much I love this woman, and I reminded myself of my desire to be all she needs in a husband. That's when this question occurred to me: What kind of husband would Jesus have made?

I flipped through the gospel of Matthew with the image in mind of Jesus as a husband. "He will not quarrel or cry out; no one will hear his voice in the streets. A bruised reed he will not break, and a smoldering wick he will not snuff out" (Matthew 12:19–20).

It was an image of strong gentleness. I thought of Jesus taking time for the children; patiently instructing his followers, though tired and hungry; touching the rotting skin of outcast lepers; weeping over a city's waywardness; calling even his betrayer "friend."

This Man felt the whole spectrum of emotion, yet always maintained self-control. He experienced success without it degenerating to egotism. He faced reversal without turning bitter. He endured temptation, but did not yield to its pressure. You could freeze any moment of his life in time and he would have no reason for regret or embarrassment.

I realized that, in a sense, every moment of my life is a moment frozen. An expression of who I am, in that instant. And I decided to devote myself to piling up moments and memories that will give my wife some small glimpse of Jesus in my life.

MARRIAGE BUILDERS

♦ *Why is it helpful to have a sense that how you behave each moment is important?*

♦ *When have you seen glimpses of Christ's character in your spouse's behavior?*

Additional Scripture Readings
Matthew 11:29; 21:5; 2 Corinthians 10:1

Go to page 1049 for your next devotional reading.

seeds, yet when it grows, it is the largest
of garden plants and becomes a tree, so
that the birds of the air come and perch in
its branches."
33He told them still another parable:
"The kingdom of heaven is like yeast that
a woman took and mixed into a large
amount[a] of flour until it worked all
through the dough."
34Jesus spoke all these things to the
crowd in parables; he did not say anything
to them without using a parable. 35So was
fulfilled what was spoken through the
prophet:

"I will open my mouth in parables,
I will utter things hidden since the
creation of the world."[b]

The Parable of the Weeds Explained

36Then he left the crowd and went into
the house. His disciples came to him and
said, "Explain to us the parable of the
weeds in the field."
37He answered, "The one who sowed
the good seed is the Son of Man. 38The
field is the world, and the good seed
stands for the sons of the kingdom. The
weeds are the sons of the evil one, 39and
the enemy who sows them is the devil.
The harvest is the end of the age, and the
harvesters are angels.
40"As the weeds are pulled up and
burned in the fire, so it will be at the end
of the age. 41The Son of Man will send out
his angels, and they will weed out of his
kingdom everything that causes sin and
all who do evil. 42They will throw them
into the fiery furnace, where there will be
weeping and gnashing of teeth. 43Then
the righteous will shine like the sun in the
kingdom of their Father. He who has ears,
let him hear.

The Parables of the Hidden Treasure and the Pearl

44"The kingdom of heaven is like trea-
sure hidden in a field. When a man found
it, he hid it again, and then in his joy went
and sold all he had and bought that field.
45"Again, the kingdom of heaven is like
a merchant looking for fine pearls.
46When he found one of great value, he
went away and sold everything he had
and bought it.

The Parable of the Net

47"Once again, the kingdom of heaven
is like a net that was let down into the lake
and caught all kinds of fish. 48When it was
full, the fishermen pulled it up on the
shore. Then they sat down and collected
the good fish in baskets, but threw the bad
away. 49This is how it will be at the end of
the age. The angels will come and sepa-
rate the wicked from the righteous 50and
throw them into the fiery furnace, where
there will be weeping and gnashing of
teeth.
51"Have you understood all these
things?" Jesus asked.
"Yes," they replied.
52He said to them, "Therefore every
teacher of the law who has been instruct-
ed about the kingdom of heaven is like the
owner of a house who brings out of his
storeroom new treasures as well as old."

A Prophet Without Honor

53When Jesus had finished these para-
bles, he moved on from there. 54Coming
to his hometown, he began teaching the
people in their synagogue, and they were
amazed. "Where did this man get this wis-
dom and these miraculous powers?" they
asked. 55"Isn't this the carpenter's son?
Isn't his mother's name Mary, and aren't
his brothers James, Joseph, Simon and Ju-
das? 56Aren't all his sisters with us? Where
then did this man get all these things?"
57And they took offense at him.
But Jesus said to them, "Only in his
hometown and in his own house is a
prophet without honor."
58And he did not do many miracles
there because of their lack of faith.

John the Baptist Beheaded

14 At that time Herod the tetrarch
heard the reports about Jesus, 2and
he said to his attendants, "This is John the
Baptist; he has risen from the dead! That
is why miraculous powers are at work in
him."
3Now Herod had arrested John and
bound him and put him in prison because
of Herodias, his brother Philip's wife, 4for
John had been saying to him: "It is not
lawful for you to have her." 5Herod want-
ed to kill John, but he was afraid of the
people, because they considered him a
prophet.

[a]33 Greek *three satas* (probably about 1/2 bushel or 22 liters) [b]35 Psalm 78:2

6On Herod's birthday the daughter of
Herodias danced for them and pleased
Herod so much 7that he promised with an
oath to give her whatever she asked.
8Prompted by her mother, she said, "Give
me here on a platter the head of John the
Baptist." 9The king was distressed, but be-
cause of his oaths and his dinner guests,
he ordered that her request be granted
10and had John beheaded in the prison.
11His head was brought in on a platter and
given to the girl, who carried it to her
mother. 12John's disciples came and took
his body and buried it. Then they went
and told Jesus.

Jesus Feeds the Five Thousand

13When Jesus heard what had hap-
pened, he withdrew by boat privately to a
solitary place. Hearing of this, the crowds
followed him on foot from the towns.
14When Jesus landed and saw a large
crowd, he had compassion on them and
healed their sick.

15As evening approached, the disciples
came to him and said, "This is a remote
place, and it's already getting late. Send
the crowds away, so they can go to the vil-
lages and buy themselves some food."

16Jesus replied, "They do not need to go
away. You give them something to eat."

17"We have here only five loaves of
bread and two fish," they answered.

18"Bring them here to me," he said.
19And he directed the people to sit down
on the grass. Taking the five loaves and
the two fish and looking up to heaven, he
gave thanks and broke the loaves. Then
he gave them to the disciples, and the dis-
ciples gave them to the people. 20They all
ate and were satisfied, and the disciples
picked up twelve basketfuls of broken
pieces that were left over. 21The number
of those who ate was about five thousand
men, besides women and children.

Jesus Walks on the Water

22Immediately Jesus made the disciples
get into the boat and go on ahead of him
to the other side, while he dismissed the
crowd. 23After he had dismissed them, he
went up on a mountainside by himself to
pray. When evening came, he was there
alone, 24but the boat was already a consid-
erable distance[a] from land, buffeted by
the waves because the wind was
against it.

25During the fourth watch of the night
Jesus went out to them, walking on the
lake. 26When the disciples saw him walk-
ing on the lake, they were terrified. "It's a
ghost," they said, and cried out in fear.

27But Jesus immediately said to them:
"Take courage! It is I. Don't be afraid."

28"Lord, if it's you," Peter replied, "tell
me to come to you on the water."

29"Come," he said.

Then Peter got down out of the boat,
walked on the water and came toward
Jesus. 30But when he saw the wind, he
was afraid and, beginning to sink, cried
out, "Lord, save me!"

31Immediately Jesus reached out his
hand and caught him. "You of little faith,"
he said, "why did you doubt?"

32And when they climbed into the boat,
the wind died down. 33Then those who
were in the boat worshiped him, saying,
"Truly you are the Son of God."

34When they had crossed over, they
landed at Gennesaret. 35And when the
men of that place recognized Jesus, they
sent word to all the surrounding country.
People brought all their sick to him 36and
begged him to let the sick just touch the
edge of his cloak, and all who touched
him were healed.

Clean and Unclean

15 Then some Pharisees and teachers
of the law came to Jesus from Jeru-
salem and asked, 2"Why do your disciples
break the tradition of the elders? They
don't wash their hands before they eat!"

3Jesus replied, "And why do you break
the command of God for the sake of your
tradition? 4For God said, 'Honor your fa-
ther and mother'[b] and 'Anyone who
curses his father or mother must be put to
death.'[c] 5But you say that if a man says
to his father or mother, 'Whatever help
you might otherwise have received from
me is a gift devoted to God,' 6he is not to
'honor his father[d]' with it. Thus you nul-
lify the word of God for the sake of your
tradition. 7You hypocrites! Isaiah was
right when he prophesied about you:

8" 'These people honor me with their
lips,
but their hearts are far from me.

[a]24 Greek *many stadia* [b]4 Exodus 20:12; Deut. 5:16 [c]4 Exodus 21:17; Lev. 20:9 [d]6 Some manuscripts *father or his mother*

[9]They worship me in vain;
their teachings are but rules taught
by men.'[a]"

[10]Jesus called the crowd to him and said, "Listen and understand. [11]What goes into a man's mouth does not make him 'unclean,' but what comes out of his mouth, that is what makes him 'unclean.' "

[12]Then the disciples came to him and asked, "Do you know that the Pharisees were offended when they heard this?"

[13]He replied, "Every plant that my heavenly Father has not planted will be pulled

[a]9 Isaiah 29:13

THURSDAY

VERSE FOR THE DAY: Matthew 14:23

AUTHOR: Bill Hybels

PASSAGE FOR THE DAY: Matthew 14:22–36

Take Care of Yourself

For many years, Christians have been taught the difference between "selfish living," which is sinful, and "selfless giving," which is righteous. But we haven't been taught to give appropriate emphasis to *self-care*—the necessity of Christians making sure their own needs are being met.

Jesus was an exceedingly giving person who, on occasion, would give out to people from morning to night. However, equally clear in Scripture are times when Jesus said, in essence, "Enough is enough; no more healing today, no more teaching. I'm heading out to the mountains, or to the Sea of Galilee." This self-care aspect of discipleship has not gotten enough affirmation.

Self-care is also harder today because it isn't built into our lifestyle, as it was for people in Jesus' time. To get from one place to another, Jesus and his disciples took long walks. When it got dark, they stopped traveling. And before they could eat they had to build a fire and wait for the coals to get hot. In that sense, times of quiet and waiting were built into their everyday lives. We don't have all those "inconveniences" these days, so we tend to pack too much activity into our days and nights. Christians need to make time for caring for themselves, personally and spiritually.

MARRIAGE BUILDERS

♦ *Why should taking time for yourself be part of the discipline of serving others?*

♦ *Where are some possible "breathing spaces" in your regular workday?*

Additional Scripture Readings
Psalm 46:10; Zechariah 2:13

Go to page 1053 for your next devotional reading.

up by the roots. 14Leave them; they are
blind guides.[a] If a blind man leads a blind
man, both will fall into a pit."

15Peter said, "Explain the parable
to us."

16"Are you still so dull?" Jesus asked
them. 17"Don't you see that whatever en-
ters the mouth goes into the stomach and
then out of the body? 18But the things that
come out of the mouth come from the
heart, and these make a man 'unclean.'
19For out of the heart come evil thoughts,
murder, adultery, sexual immorality,
theft, false testimony, slander. 20These are
what make a man 'unclean'; but eating
with unwashed hands does not make him
'unclean.' "

The Faith of the Canaanite Woman

21Leaving that place, Jesus withdrew to
the region of Tyre and Sidon. 22A Canaan-
ite woman from that vicinity came to him,
crying out, "Lord, Son of David, have mer-
cy on me! My daughter is suffering terri-
bly from demon-possession."

23Jesus did not answer a word. So his
disciples came to him and urged him,
"Send her away, for she keeps crying out
after us."

24He answered, "I was sent only to the
lost sheep of Israel."

25The woman came and knelt before
him. "Lord, help me!" she said.

26He replied, "It is not right to take the
children's bread and toss it to their dogs."

27"Yes, Lord," she said, "but even the
dogs eat the crumbs that fall from their
masters' table."

28Then Jesus answered, "Woman, you
have great faith! Your request is granted."
And her daughter was healed from that
very hour.

Jesus Feeds the Four Thousand

29Jesus left there and went along the
Sea of Galilee. Then he went up on a
mountainside and sat down. 30Great
crowds came to him, bringing the lame,
the blind, the crippled, the mute and
many others, and laid them at his feet; and
he healed them. 31The people were
amazed when they saw the mute speak-
ing, the crippled made well, the lame
walking and the blind seeing. And they
praised the God of Israel.

32Jesus called his disciples to him and
said, "I have compassion for these people;
they have already been with me three
days and have nothing to eat. I do not
want to send them away hungry, or they
may collapse on the way."

33His disciples answered, "Where could
we get enough bread in this remote place
to feed such a crowd?"

34"How many loaves do you have?"
Jesus asked.

"Seven," they replied, "and a few small
fish."

35He told the crowd to sit down on the
ground. 36Then he took the seven loaves
and the fish, and when he had given
thanks, he broke them and gave them to
the disciples, and they in turn to the peo-
ple. 37They all ate and were satisfied. Af-
terward the disciples picked up seven bas-
ketfuls of broken pieces that were left
over. 38The number of those who ate was
four thousand, besides women and chil-
dren. 39After Jesus had sent the crowd
away, he got into the boat and went to the
vicinity of Magadan.

The Demand for a Sign

16 The Pharisees and Sadducees
came to Jesus and tested him by
asking him to show them a sign from
heaven.

2He replied,[b] "When evening comes,
you say, 'It will be fair weather, for the sky
is red,' 3and in the morning, 'Today it will
be stormy, for the sky is red and overcast.'
You know how to interpret the appear-
ance of the sky, but you cannot interpret
the signs of the times. 4A wicked and adul-
terous generation looks for a miraculous
sign, but none will be given it except the
sign of Jonah." Jesus then left them and
went away.

The Yeast of the Pharisees and Sadducees

5When they went across the lake, the
disciples forgot to take bread. 6"Be care-
ful," Jesus said to them. "Be on your guard
against the yeast of the Pharisees and Sad-
ducees."

7They discussed this among themselves
and said, "It is because we didn't bring
any bread."

8Aware of their discussion, Jesus asked,
"You of little faith, why are you talking
among yourselves about having no bread?

[a] 14 Some manuscripts *guides of the blind* and all of verse 3.

[b] 2 Some early manuscripts do not have the rest of verse 2

9Do you still not understand? Don't you
remember the five loaves for the five thou-
sand, and how many basketfuls you gath-
ered? 10Or the seven loaves for the four
thousand, and how many basketfuls you
gathered? 11How is it you don't under-
stand that I was not talking to you about
bread? But be on your guard against the
yeast of the Pharisees and Sadducees."
12Then they understood that he was not
telling them to guard against the yeast
used in bread, but against the teaching of
the Pharisees and Sadducees.

Peter's Confession of Christ

13When Jesus came to the region of
Caesarea Philippi, he asked his disciples,
"Who do people say the Son of Man is?"
14They replied, "Some say John the
Baptist; others say Elijah; and still others,
Jeremiah or one of the prophets."
15"But what about you?" he asked.
"Who do you say I am?"
16Simon Peter answered, "You are the
Christ,[a] the Son of the living God."
17Jesus replied, "Blessed are you, Si-
mon son of Jonah, for this was not re-
vealed to you by man, but by my Father in
heaven. 18And I tell you that you are Pe-
ter,[b] and on this rock I will build my
church, and the gates of Hades[c] will not
overcome it.[d] 19I will give you the keys of
the kingdom of heaven; whatever you
bind on earth will be[e] bound in heaven,
and whatever you loose on earth will be[e]
loosed in heaven." 20Then he warned his
disciples not to tell anyone that he was the
Christ.

Jesus Predicts His Death

21From that time on Jesus began to ex-
plain to his disciples that he must go to
Jerusalem and suffer many things at the
hands of the elders, chief priests and
teachers of the law, and that he must be
killed and on the third day be raised to
life.
22Peter took him aside and began to re-
buke him. "Never, Lord!" he said. "This
shall never happen to you!"
23Jesus turned and said to Peter, "Get
behind me, Satan! You are a stumbling
block to me; you do not have in mind the
things of God, but the things of men."
24Then Jesus said to his disciples, "If
anyone would come after me, he must
deny himself and take up his cross and
follow me. 25For whoever wants to save
his life[f] will lose it, but whoever loses his
life for me will find it. 26What good will it
be for a man if he gains the whole world,
yet forfeits his soul? Or what can a man
give in exchange for his soul? 27For the
Son of Man is going to come in his Fa-
ther's glory with his angels, and then he
will reward each person according to what
he has done. 28I tell you the truth, some
who are standing here will not taste death
before they see the Son of Man coming in
his kingdom."

The Transfiguration

17 After six days Jesus took with him
Peter, James and John the brother
of James, and led them up a high moun-
tain by themselves. 2There he was trans-
figured before them. His face shone like
the sun, and his clothes became as white
as the light. 3Just then there appeared be-
fore them Moses and Elijah, talking with
Jesus.
4Peter said to Jesus, "Lord, it is good for
us to be here. If you wish, I will put up
three shelters—one for you, one for Mo-
ses and one for Elijah."
5While he was still speaking, a bright
cloud enveloped them, and a voice from
the cloud said, "This is my Son, whom I
love; with him I am well pleased. Listen to
him!"
6When the disciples heard this, they fell
facedown to the ground, terrified. 7But
Jesus came and touched them. "Get up,"
he said. "Don't be afraid." 8When they
looked up, they saw no one except Jesus.
9As they were coming down the moun-
tain, Jesus instructed them, "Don't tell
anyone what you have seen, until the Son
of Man has been raised from the dead."
10The disciples asked him, "Why then
do the teachers of the law say that Elijah
must come first?"
11Jesus replied, "To be sure, Elijah
comes and will restore all things. 12But I
tell you, Elijah has already come, and they
did not recognize him, but have done to
him everything they wished. In the same
way the Son of Man is going to suffer at
their hands." 13Then the disciples under-

[a] 16 Or *Messiah*; also in verse 20 [b] 18 *Peter* means *rock*. [c] 18 Or *hell* [d] 18 Or *not prove stronger than it* [e] 19 Or *have been* [f] 25 The Greek word means either *life* or *soul*; also in verse 26.

stood that he was talking to them about John the Baptist.

The Healing of a Boy With a Demon

14When they came to the crowd, a man approached Jesus and knelt before him. 15"Lord, have mercy on my son," he said. "He has seizures and is suffering greatly. He often falls into the fire or into the water. 16I brought him to your disciples, but they could not heal him."

17"O unbelieving and perverse generation," Jesus replied, "how long shall I stay with you? How long shall I put up with you? Bring the boy here to me." 18Jesus rebuked the demon, and it came out of the boy, and he was healed from that moment.

19Then the disciples came to Jesus in private and asked, "Why couldn't we drive it out?"

20He replied, "Because you have so little faith. I tell you the truth, if you have faith as small as a mustard seed, you can say to this mountain, 'Move from here to there' and it will move. Nothing will be impossible for you.[a]"

22When they came together in Galilee, he said to them, "The Son of Man is going to be betrayed into the hands of men. 23They will kill him, and on the third day he will be raised to life." And the disciples were filled with grief.

The Temple Tax

24After Jesus and his disciples arrived in Capernaum, the collectors of the two-drachma tax came to Peter and asked, "Doesn't your teacher pay the temple tax[b]?"

25"Yes, he does," he replied.

When Peter came into the house, Jesus was the first to speak. "What do you think, Simon?" he asked. "From whom do the kings of the earth collect duty and taxes—from their own sons or from others?"

26"From others," Peter answered.

"Then the sons are exempt," Jesus said to him. 27"But so that we may not offend them, go to the lake and throw out your line. Take the first fish you catch; open its mouth and you will find a four-drachma coin. Take it and give it to them for my tax and yours."

The Greatest in the Kingdom of Heaven

18 At that time the disciples came to Jesus and asked, "Who is the greatest in the kingdom of heaven?"

2He called a little child and had him stand among them. 3And he said: "I tell you the truth, unless you change and become like little children, you will never enter the kingdom of heaven. 4Therefore, whoever humbles himself like this child is the greatest in the kingdom of heaven.

5"And whoever welcomes a little child like this in my name welcomes me. 6But if anyone causes one of these little ones who believe in me to sin, it would be better for him to have a large millstone hung around his neck and to be drowned in the depths of the sea.

7"Woe to the world because of the things that cause people to sin! Such things must come, but woe to the man through whom they come! 8If your hand or your foot causes you to sin, cut it off and throw it away. It is better for you to enter life maimed or crippled than to have two hands or two feet and be thrown into eternal fire. 9And if your eye causes you to sin, gouge it out and throw it away. It is better for you to enter life with one eye than to have two eyes and be thrown into the fire of hell.

The Parable of the Lost Sheep

10"See that you do not look down on one of these little ones. For I tell you that their angels in heaven always see the face of my Father in heaven.[c]

12"What do you think? If a man owns a hundred sheep, and one of them wanders away, will he not leave the ninety-nine on the hills and go to look for the one that wandered off? 13And if he finds it, I tell you the truth, he is happier about that one sheep than about the ninety-nine that did not wander off. 14In the same way your Father in heaven is not willing that any of these little ones should be lost.

A Brother Who Sins Against You

15"If your brother sins against you,[d] go and show him his fault, just between the two of you. If he listens to you, you have won your brother over. 16But if he will not

[a]20 Some manuscripts *you.* 21*But this kind does not go out except by prayer and fasting.* [b]24 Greek *the two drachmas* [c]10 Some manuscripts *heaven.* 11*The Son of Man came to save what was lost.*
[d]15 Some manuscripts do not have *against you.*

listen, take one or two others along, so
that 'every matter may be established by
the testimony of two or three wit-
nesses.'[a] 17If he refuses to listen to them,
tell it to the church; and if he refuses to
listen even to the church, treat him as you
would a pagan or a tax collector.

18"I tell you the truth, whatever you
bind on earth will be[b] bound in heaven,
and whatever you loose on earth will be[b]
loosed in heaven.

19"Again, I tell you that if two of you on
earth agree about anything you ask for, it
will be done for you by my Father in heav-
en. 20For where two or three come togeth-
er in my name, there am I with them."

The Parable of the Unmerciful Servant

21Then Peter came to Jesus and asked,
"Lord, how many times shall I forgive my
brother when he sins against me? Up to
seven times?"

22Jesus answered, "I tell you, not seven
times, but seventy-seven times.[c]

23"Therefore, the kingdom of heaven is
like a king who wanted to settle accounts
with his servants. 24As he began the settle-

[a]16 Deut. 19:15 [b]18 Or *have been* [c]22 Or *seventy times seven*

FRIDAY

VERSE FOR THE DAY: Matthew 18:21 | AUTHOR: Lewis Smedes | PASSAGE FOR THE DAY: Matthew 18:21–35

Be a Forgiver

Jesus said, "Forgive seventy-seven times," but he didn't mean to count. What he meant was, "Be the kind of person who doesn't ask the question, 'How many times should I forgive?' Just be a forgiving person."

The proper question is not, "How often?" but rather, "Under what circumstances can I forgive?" One consideration is this: Repeated forgiving should not be confused with toleration of what's going on. We must be intolerant of evil, whether it happens to us or anyone else.

You can forgive me almost anything, but if you tolerate everything I do you will make matters between us worse. Sometimes there comes a time when one spouse will say to the other, "I cannot forgive you while this continues. It must stop or I must get out, so that I can begin to forgive."

MARRIAGE BUILDERS

♦ *What is something you know your spouse has had to forgive you for more than once?*

♦ *Describe the essential difference between forgiveness and tolerance.*

Additional Scripture Readings
Luke 17:3–4; 1 Corinthians 13:5

Go to page 1055 for your next devotional reading.

ment, a man who owed him ten thousand talents[a] was brought to him. 25Since he was not able to pay, the master ordered that he and his wife and his children and all that he had be sold to repay the debt.

26"The servant fell on his knees before him. 'Be patient with me,' he begged, 'and I will pay back everything.' 27The servant's master took pity on him, canceled the debt and let him go.

28"But when that servant went out, he found one of his fellow servants who owed him a hundred denarii.[b] He grabbed him and began to choke him. 'Pay back what you owe me!' he demanded.

29"His fellow servant fell to his knees and begged him, 'Be patient with me, and I will pay you back.'

30"But he refused. Instead, he went off and had the man thrown into prison until he could pay the debt. 31When the other servants saw what had happened, they were greatly distressed and went and told their master everything that had happened.

32"Then the master called the servant in. 'You wicked servant,' he said, 'I canceled all that debt of yours because you begged me to. 33Shouldn't you have had mercy on your fellow servant just as I had on you?' 34In anger his master turned him over to the jailers to be tortured, until he should pay back all he owed.

35"This is how my heavenly Father will treat each of you unless you forgive your brother from your heart."

Divorce

19 When Jesus had finished saying these things, he left Galilee and went into the region of Judea to the other side of the Jordan. 2Large crowds followed him, and he healed them there.

3Some Pharisees came to him to test him. They asked, "Is it lawful for a man to divorce his wife for any and every reason?"

4"Haven't you read," he replied, "that at the beginning the Creator 'made them male and female,'[c] 5and said, 'For this reason a man will leave his father and mother and be united to his wife, and the two will become one flesh'[d]? 6So they are no longer two, but one. Therefore what God has joined together, let man not separate."

7"Why then," they asked, "did Moses command that a man give his wife a certificate of divorce and send her away?"

8Jesus replied, "Moses permitted you to divorce your wives because your hearts were hard. But it was not this way from the beginning. 9I tell you that anyone who divorces his wife, except for marital unfaithfulness, and marries another woman commits adultery."

10The disciples said to him, "If this is the situation between a husband and wife, it is better not to marry."

11Jesus replied, "Not everyone can accept this word, but only those to whom it has been given. 12For some are eunuchs because they were born that way; others were made that way by men; and others have renounced marriage[e] because of the kingdom of heaven. The one who can accept this should accept it."

The Little Children and Jesus

13Then little children were brought to Jesus for him to place his hands on them and pray for them. But the disciples rebuked those who brought them.

14Jesus said, "Let the little children come to me, and do not hinder them, for the kingdom of heaven belongs to such as these." 15When he had placed his hands on them, he went on from there.

The Rich Young Man

16Now a man came up to Jesus and asked, "Teacher, what good thing must I do to get eternal life?"

17"Why do you ask me about what is good?" Jesus replied. "There is only One who is good. If you want to enter life, obey the commandments."

18"Which ones?" the man inquired.

Jesus replied, " 'Do not murder, do not commit adultery, do not steal, do not give false testimony, 19honor your father and mother,'[f] and 'love your neighbor as yourself.'[g]"

20"All these I have kept," the young man said. "What do I still lack?"

21Jesus answered, "If you want to be perfect, go, sell your possessions and give to the poor, and you will have treasure in heaven. Then come, follow me."

22When the young man heard this, he

[a] *24* That is, millions of dollars [b] *28* That is, a few dollars [c] *4* Gen. 1:27 [d] *5* Gen. 2:24
[e] *12* Or *have made themselves eunuchs* [f] *19* Exodus 20:12-16; Deut. 5:16-20 [g] *19* Lev. 19:18

WEEKENDING

TOGETHERNESS

It takes time to build a sense of togetherness in marriage. But it also requires a couple to have shared priorities, values and goals. These questions can help you discuss where you feel your marriage is right now, and what each of you can do to make togetherness a higher priority in your relationship.

1. Do you feel the two of you are doing enough things together *outside* the home?

2. If you answered "yes" to the first question, are these activities things you enjoy doing, or are they more along the lines of duties you feel obligated to fulfill?

3. If you answered "no" to the first question, what new interests, hobbies and/or ministry involvements would the two of you enjoy doing together?

— *The* Marriage Partnership *Staff*

REVIVE

Saturday: 1 Corinthians 1:4–17
Sunday: Colossians 2:2–13

Go to page 1056 for your next devotional reading.

went away sad, because he had great wealth.

23Then Jesus said to his disciples, "I tell you the truth, it is hard for a rich man to enter the kingdom of heaven. 24Again I tell you, it is easier for a camel to go through the eye of a needle than for a rich man to enter the kingdom of God."

25When the disciples heard this, they were greatly astonished and asked, "Who then can be saved?"

26Jesus looked at them and said, "With man this is impossible, but with God all things are possible."

27Peter answered him, "We have left everything to follow you! What then will there be for us?"

28Jesus said to them, "I tell you the truth, at the renewal of all things, when the Son of Man sits on his glorious throne, you who have followed me will also sit on twelve thrones, judging the twelve tribes of Israel. 29And everyone who has left houses or brothers or sisters or father or

VERSE FOR THE DAY: Matthew 19:6

AUTHOR: Ron and Jeanette Lee

PASSAGE FOR THE DAY: Matthew 19:1–11

Clones Need Not Apply

When asked about divorce, Jesus pointed out the problem with the Pharisees' question. Since marriage makes two people one, how can that new entity be separated?

When I married Jeanette, I thought oneness meant similarity. And since we agreed on values and faith, laughed at the same things and enjoyed the same friends, I figured our life together would be a snap. Then I started noticing some big differences. Jeanette saw money as something to be spent on good times, and it took her forty-five minutes to leave a party. I wanted to carve out some privacy and thought we should start saving for a house.

God didn't make us identical. He gave us individual strengths and brought us together to combine those strengths. We're not clones, but being one means we're glued together like two sheets of paper. With that bond, we're twice as strong. And because we're now one, we could never be separated without each being damaged.

God made us different, and he also made us one. Our perfect God makes no mistakes.

MARRIAGE BUILDERS

♦ *What were the differences that came as a surprise now that you are married?*

♦ *When your differences lead to conflict, how can you reach a positive solution?*

Additional Scripture Readings
Psalm 139:14; Romans 12:6; 1 Corinthians 12:4–12

Go to page 1066 for your next devotional reading.

mother[a] or children or fields for my sake
will receive a hundred times as much and
will inherit eternal life. [30]But many who
are first will be last, and many who are last
will be first.

The Parable of the Workers in the Vineyard

20 "For the kingdom of heaven is like
a landowner who went out early in
the morning to hire men to work in his
vineyard. [2]He agreed to pay them a denar-
ius for the day and sent them into his vine-
yard.

[3]"About the third hour he went out and
saw others standing in the marketplace
doing nothing. [4]He told them, 'You also go
and work in my vineyard, and I will pay
you whatever is right.' [5]So they went.

"He went out again about the sixth hour
and the ninth hour and did the same
thing. [6]About the eleventh hour he went
out and found still others standing
around. He asked them, 'Why have you
been standing here all day long doing
nothing?'

[7]" 'Because no one has hired us,' they
answered.

"He said to them, 'You also go and work
in my vineyard.'

[8]"When evening came, the owner of the
vineyard said to his foreman, 'Call the
workers and pay them their wages, begin-
ning with the last ones hired and going on
to the first.'

[9]"The workers who were hired about
the eleventh hour came and each received
a denarius. [10]So when those came who
were hired first, they expected to receive
more. But each one of them also received
a denarius. [11]When they received it, they
began to grumble against the landowner.
[12]'These men who were hired last worked
only one hour,' they said, 'and you have
made them equal to us who have borne
the burden of the work and the heat of the
day.'

[13]"But he answered one of them,
'Friend, I am not being unfair to you.
Didn't you agree to work for a denarius?
[14]Take your pay and go. I want to give the
man who was hired last the same as I gave
you. [15]Don't I have the right to do what I
want with my own money? Or are you en-
vious because I am generous?'

[16]"So the last will be first, and the first
will be last."

Jesus Again Predicts His Death

[17]Now as Jesus was going up to Jerusa-
lem, he took the twelve disciples aside
and said to them, [18]"We are going up to
Jerusalem, and the Son of Man will be be-
trayed to the chief priests and the teachers
of the law. They will condemn him to
death [19]and will turn him over to the Gen-
tiles to be mocked and flogged and crucif-
ied. On the third day he will be raised to
life!"

A Mother's Request

[20]Then the mother of Zebedee's sons
came to Jesus with her sons and, kneeling
down, asked a favor of him.

[21]"What is it you want?" he asked.

She said, "Grant that one of these two
sons of mine may sit at your right and the
other at your left in your kingdom."

[22]"You don't know what you are ask-
ing," Jesus said to them. "Can you drink
the cup I am going to drink?"

"We can," they answered.

[23]Jesus said to them, "You will indeed
drink from my cup, but to sit at my right
or left is not for me to grant. These places
belong to those for whom they have been
prepared by my Father."

[24]When the ten heard about this, they
were indignant with the two brothers.
[25]Jesus called them together and said,
"You know that the rulers of the Gentiles
lord it over them, and their high officials
exercise authority over them. [26]Not so
with you. Instead, whoever wants to be-
come great among you must be your ser-
vant, [27]and whoever wants to be first must
be your slave— [28]just as the Son of Man
did not come to be served, but to serve,
and to give his life as a ransom for many."

Two Blind Men Receive Sight

[29]As Jesus and his disciples were leav-
ing Jericho, a large crowd followed him.
[30]Two blind men were sitting by the road-
side, and when they heard that Jesus was
going by, they shouted, "Lord, Son of Da-
vid, have mercy on us!"

[31]The crowd rebuked them and told
them to be quiet, but they shouted all the
louder, "Lord, Son of David, have mercy
on us!"

[32]Jesus stopped and called them. "What
do you want me to do for you?" he asked.

[a]29 Some manuscripts *mother or wife*

33"Lord," they answered, "we want our sight."

34Jesus had compassion on them and touched their eyes. Immediately they received their sight and followed him.

The Triumphal Entry

21 As they approached Jerusalem and came to Bethphage on the Mount of Olives, Jesus sent two disciples, 2saying to them, "Go to the village ahead of you, and at once you will find a donkey tied there, with her colt by her. Untie them and bring them to me. 3If anyone says anything to you, tell him that the Lord needs them, and he will send them right away."

4This took place to fulfill what was spoken through the prophet:

5"Say to the Daughter of Zion,
'See, your king comes to you,
gentle and riding on a donkey,
on a colt, the foal of a donkey.' "[a]

6The disciples went and did as Jesus had instructed them. 7They brought the donkey and the colt, placed their cloaks on them, and Jesus sat on them. 8A very large crowd spread their cloaks on the road, while others cut branches from the trees and spread them on the road. 9The crowds that went ahead of him and those that followed shouted,

"Hosanna[b] to the Son of David!"

"Blessed is he who comes in the name of the Lord!"[c]

"Hosanna[b] in the highest!"

10When Jesus entered Jerusalem, the whole city was stirred and asked, "Who is this?"

11The crowds answered, "This is Jesus, the prophet from Nazareth in Galilee."

Jesus at the Temple

12Jesus entered the temple area and drove out all who were buying and selling there. He overturned the tables of the money changers and the benches of those selling doves. 13"It is written," he said to them, " 'My house will be called a house of prayer,'[d] but you are making it a 'den of robbers.'[e]"

14The blind and the lame came to him at the temple, and he healed them. 15But when the chief priests and the teachers of the law saw the wonderful things he did and the children shouting in the temple area, "Hosanna to the Son of David," they were indignant.

16"Do you hear what these children are saying?" they asked him.

"Yes," replied Jesus, "have you never read,

" 'From the lips of children and infants
you have ordained praise'[f]?"

17And he left them and went out of the city to Bethany, where he spent the night.

The Fig Tree Withers

18Early in the morning, as he was on his way back to the city, he was hungry. 19Seeing a fig tree by the road, he went up to it but found nothing on it except leaves. Then he said to it, "May you never bear fruit again!" Immediately the tree withered.

20When the disciples saw this, they were amazed. "How did the fig tree wither so quickly?" they asked.

21Jesus replied, "I tell you the truth, if you have faith and do not doubt, not only can you do what was done to the fig tree, but also you can say to this mountain, 'Go, throw yourself into the sea,' and it will be done. 22If you believe, you will receive whatever you ask for in prayer."

The Authority of Jesus Questioned

23Jesus entered the temple courts, and, while he was teaching, the chief priests and the elders of the people came to him. "By what authority are you doing these things?" they asked. "And who gave you this authority?"

24Jesus replied, "I will also ask you one question. If you answer me, I will tell you by what authority I am doing these things. 25John's baptism—where did it come from? Was it from heaven, or from men?"

They discussed it among themselves and said, "If we say, 'From heaven,' he will ask, 'Then why didn't you believe him?' 26But if we say, 'From men'—we are afraid of the people, for they all hold that John was a prophet."

27So they answered Jesus, "We don't know."

Then he said, "Neither will I tell you by what authority I am doing these things.

[a]5 Zech. 9:9 [b]9 A Hebrew expression meaning "Save!" which became an exclamation of praise; also in verse 15 [c]9 Psalm 118:26 [d]13 Isaiah 56:7 [e]13 Jer. 7:11 [f]16 Psalm 8:2

The Parable of the Two Sons

28"What do you think? There was a man
who had two sons. He went to the first
and said, 'Son, go and work today in the
vineyard.'
29" 'I will not,' he answered, but later he
changed his mind and went.
30"Then the father went to the other son
and said the same thing. He answered, 'I
will, sir,' but he did not go.
31"Which of the two did what his father
wanted?"
"The first," they answered.
Jesus said to them, "I tell you the truth,
the tax collectors and the prostitutes are
entering the kingdom of God ahead of
you. 32For John came to you to show you
the way of righteousness, and you did not
believe him, but the tax collectors and the
prostitutes did. And even after you saw
this, you did not repent and believe him.

The Parable of the Tenants

33"Listen to another parable: There was
a landowner who planted a vineyard. He
put a wall around it, dug a winepress in it
and built a watchtower. Then he rented
the vineyard to some farmers and went
away on a journey. 34When the harvest
time approached, he sent his servants to
the tenants to collect his fruit.
35"The tenants seized his servants; they
beat one, killed another, and stoned a
third. 36Then he sent other servants to
them, more than the first time, and the
tenants treated them the same way. 37Last
of all, he sent his son to them. 'They will
respect my son,' he said.
38"But when the tenants saw the son,
they said to each other, 'This is the heir.
Come, let's kill him and take his inheri-
tance.' 39So they took him and threw him
out of the vineyard and killed him.
40"Therefore, when the owner of the
vineyard comes, what will he do to those
tenants?"
41"He will bring those wretches to a
wretched end," they replied, "and he will
rent the vineyard to other tenants, who
will give him his share of the crop at har-
vest time."
42Jesus said to them, "Have you never
read in the Scriptures:

" 'The stone the builders rejected
has become the capstone[a];
the Lord has done this,
and it is marvelous in our eyes'[b]?

43"Therefore I tell you that the kingdom
of God will be taken away from you and
given to a people who will produce its
fruit. 44He who falls on this stone will be
broken to pieces, but he on whom it falls
will be crushed."[c]
45When the chief priests and the Phari-
sees heard Jesus' parables, they knew he
was talking about them. 46They looked for
a way to arrest him, but they were afraid
of the crowd because the people held that
he was a prophet.

The Parable of the Wedding Banquet

22 Jesus spoke to them again in para-
bles, saying: 2"The kingdom of
heaven is like a king who prepared a wed-
ding banquet for his son. 3He sent his ser-
vants to those who had been invited to the
banquet to tell them to come, but they re-
fused to come.
4"Then he sent some more servants and
said, 'Tell those who have been invited
that I have prepared my dinner: My oxen
and fattened cattle have been butchered,
and everything is ready. Come to the wed-
ding banquet.'
5"But they paid no attention and went
off—one to his field, another to his busi-
ness. 6The rest seized his servants, mis-
treated them and killed them. 7The king
was enraged. He sent his army and de-
stroyed those murderers and burned their
city.
8"Then he said to his servants, 'The
wedding banquet is ready, but those I in-
vited did not deserve to come. 9Go to the
street corners and invite to the banquet
anyone you find.' 10So the servants went
out into the streets and gathered all the
people they could find, both good and
bad, and the wedding hall was filled with
guests.
11"But when the king came in to see the
guests, he noticed a man there who was
not wearing wedding clothes. 12'Friend,'
he asked, 'how did you get in here without
wedding clothes?' The man was speech-
less.
13"Then the king told the attendants,
'Tie him hand and foot, and throw him
outside, into the darkness, where there
will be weeping and gnashing of teeth.'
14"For many are invited, but few are
chosen."

[a]42 Or *cornerstone* [b]42 Psalm 118:22,23 [c]44 Some manuscripts do not have verse 44.

Paying Taxes to Caesar

15Then the Pharisees went out and laid
plans to trap him in his words. 16They sent
their disciples to him along with the Hero-
dians. "Teacher," they said, "we know you
are a man of integrity and that you teach
the way of God in accordance with the
truth. You aren't swayed by men, because
you pay no attention to who they are.
17Tell us then, what is your opinion? Is it
right to pay taxes to Caesar or not?"

18But Jesus, knowing their evil intent,
said, "You hypocrites, why are you trying
to trap me? 19Show me the coin used for
paying the tax." They brought him a de-
narius, 20and he asked them, "Whose por-
trait is this? And whose inscription?"

21"Caesar's," they replied.

Then he said to them, "Give to Caesar
what is Caesar's, and to God what is
God's."

22When they heard this, they were
amazed. So they left him and went away.

Marriage at the Resurrection

23That same day the Sadducees, who
say there is no resurrection, came to him
with a question. 24"Teacher," they said,
"Moses told us that if a man dies without
having children, his brother must marry
the widow and have children for him.
25Now there were seven brothers among
us. The first one married and died, and
since he had no children, he left his wife
to his brother. 26The same thing happened
to the second and third brother, right on
down to the seventh. 27Finally, the wom-
an died. 28Now then, at the resurrection,
whose wife will she be of the seven, since
all of them were married to her?"

29Jesus replied, "You are in error be-
cause you do not know the Scriptures or
the power of God. 30At the resurrection
people will neither marry nor be given in
marriage; they will be like the angels in
heaven. 31But about the resurrection of
the dead—have you not read what God
said to you, 32'I am the God of Abraham,
the God of Isaac, and the God of Jacob'[a]?
He is not the God of the dead but of the
living."

33When the crowds heard this, they
were astonished at his teaching.

The Greatest Commandment

34Hearing that Jesus had silenced the
Sadducees, the Pharisees got together.
35One of them, an expert in the law, tested
him with this question: 36"Teacher, which
is the greatest commandment in the
Law?"

37Jesus replied: " 'Love the Lord your
God with all your heart and with all your
soul and with all your mind.'[b] 38This is
the first and greatest commandment.
39And the second is like it: 'Love your
neighbor as yourself.'[c] 40All the Law and
the Prophets hang on these two com-
mandments."

Whose Son Is the Christ?

41While the Pharisees were gathered to-
gether, Jesus asked them, 42"What do you
think about the Christ[d]? Whose son
is he?"

"The son of David," they replied.

43He said to them, "How is it then that
David, speaking by the Spirit, calls him
'Lord'? For he says,

44" 'The Lord said to my Lord:
"Sit at my right hand
until I put your enemies
under your feet." '[e]

45If then David calls him 'Lord,' how can
he be his son?" 46No one could say a word
in reply, and from that day on no one
dared to ask him any more questions.

Seven Woes

23 Then Jesus said to the crowds and
to his disciples: 2"The teachers of
the law and the Pharisees sit in Moses'
seat. 3So you must obey them and do ev-
erything they tell you. But do not do what
they do, for they do not practice what they
preach. 4They tie up heavy loads and put
them on men's shoulders, but they them-
selves are not willing to lift a finger to
move them.

5"Everything they do is done for men to
see: They make their phylacteries[f] wide
and the tassels on their garments long;
6they love the place of honor at banquets
and the most important seats in the syna-
gogues; 7they love to be greeted in the
marketplaces and to have men call them
'Rabbi.'

8"But you are not to be called 'Rabbi,'

[a]32 Exodus 3:6 [b]37 Deut. 6:5 [c]39 Lev. 19:18 [d]42 Or *Messiah* [e]44 Psalm 110:1
[f]5 That is, boxes containing Scripture verses, worn on forehead and arm

for you have only one Master and you are
all brothers. 9And do not call anyone on
earth 'father,' for you have one Father,
and he is in heaven. 10Nor are you to be
called 'teacher,' for you have one Teacher,
the Christ.[a] 11The greatest among you
will be your servant. 12For whoever exalts
himself will be humbled, and whoever
humbles himself will be exalted.

13"Woe to you, teachers of the law and
Pharisees, you hypocrites! You shut the
kingdom of heaven in men's faces. You
yourselves do not enter, nor will you let
those enter who are trying to.[b]

15"Woe to you, teachers of the law and
Pharisees, you hypocrites! You travel over
land and sea to win a single convert, and
when he becomes one, you make him
twice as much a son of hell as you are.

16"Woe to you, blind guides! You say,
'If anyone swears by the temple, it means
nothing; but if anyone swears by the gold
of the temple, he is bound by his oath.'
17You blind fools! Which is greater: the
gold, or the temple that makes the gold sacred? 18You also say, 'If anyone swears by
the altar, it means nothing; but if anyone
swears by the gift on it, he is bound by his
oath.' 19You blind men! Which is greater:
the gift, or the altar that makes the gift sacred? 20Therefore, he who swears by the
altar swears by it and by everything on it.
21And he who swears by the temple
swears by it and by the one who dwells in
it. 22And he who swears by heaven swears
by God's throne and by the one who sits
on it.

23"Woe to you, teachers of the law and
Pharisees, you hypocrites! You give a
tenth of your spices—mint, dill and cummin. But you have neglected the more important matters of the law—justice, mercy and faithfulness. You should have
practiced the latter, without neglecting
the former. 24You blind guides! You strain
out a gnat but swallow a camel.

25"Woe to you, teachers of the law and
Pharisees, you hypocrites! You clean the
outside of the cup and dish, but inside
they are full of greed and self-indulgence.
26Blind Pharisee! First clean the inside of
the cup and dish, and then the outside
also will be clean.

27"Woe to you, teachers of the law and
Pharisees, you hypocrites! You are like
whitewashed tombs, which look beautiful
on the outside but on the inside are full of
dead men's bones and everything unclean. 28In the same way, on the outside
you appear to people as righteous but on
the inside you are full of hypocrisy and
wickedness.

29"Woe to you, teachers of the law and
Pharisees, you hypocrites! You build
tombs for the prophets and decorate the
graves of the righteous. 30And you say, 'If
we had lived in the days of our forefathers, we would not have taken part with
them in shedding the blood of the prophets.' 31So you testify against yourselves
that you are the descendants of those who
murdered the prophets. 32Fill up, then, the
measure of the sin of your forefathers!

33"You snakes! You brood of vipers!
How will you escape being condemned to
hell? 34Therefore I am sending you prophets and wise men and teachers. Some of
them you will kill and crucify; others you
will flog in your synagogues and pursue
from town to town. 35And so upon you
will come all the righteous blood that has
been shed on earth, from the blood of
righteous Abel to the blood of Zechariah
son of Berekiah, whom you murdered between the temple and the altar. 36I tell you
the truth, all this will come upon this generation.

37"O Jerusalem, Jerusalem, you who kill
the prophets and stone those sent to you,
how often I have longed to gather your
children together, as a hen gathers her
chicks under her wings, but you were not
willing. 38Look, your house is left to you
desolate. 39For I tell you, you will not see
me again until you say, 'Blessed is he who
comes in the name of the Lord.'[c]"

Signs of the End of the Age

24 Jesus left the temple and was walking away when his disciples came
up to him to call his attention to its buildings. 2"Do you see all these things?" he
asked. "I tell you the truth, not one stone
here will be left on another; every one will
be thrown down."

3As Jesus was sitting on the Mount of
Olives, the disciples came to him privately. "Tell us," they said, "when will this
happen, and what will be the sign of your
coming and of the end of the age?"

[a]10 Or *Messiah* [b]13 Some manuscripts *to.* 14*Woe to you, teachers of the law and Pharisees, you hypocrites! You devour widows' houses and for a show make lengthy prayers. Therefore you will be punished more severely.* [c]39 Psalm 118:26

4Jesus answered: "Watch out that no
one deceives you. 5For many will come in
my name, claiming, 'I am the Christ,[a]'
and will deceive many. 6You will hear of
wars and rumors of wars, but see to it that
you are not alarmed. Such things must
happen, but the end is still to come. 7Na-
tion will rise against nation, and kingdom
against kingdom. There will be famines
and earthquakes in various places. 8All
these are the beginning of birth pains.

9"Then you will be handed over to be
persecuted and put to death, and you will
be hated by all nations because of me.
10At that time many will turn away from
the faith and will betray and hate each
other, 11and many false prophets will ap-
pear and deceive many people. 12Because
of the increase of wickedness, the love of
most will grow cold, 13but he who stands
firm to the end will be saved. 14And this
gospel of the kingdom will be preached in
the whole world as a testimony to all na-
tions, and then the end will come.

15"So when you see standing in the holy
place 'the abomination that causes desola-
tion,'[b] spoken of through the prophet
Daniel—let the reader understand—
16then let those who are in Judea flee to
the mountains. 17Let no one on the roof of
his house go down to take anything out of
the house. 18Let no one in the field go
back to get his cloak. 19How dreadful it
will be in those days for pregnant women
and nursing mothers! 20Pray that your
flight will not take place in winter or on
the Sabbath. 21For then there will be great
distress, unequaled from the beginning of
the world until now—and never to be
equaled again. 22If those days had not
been cut short, no one would survive, but
for the sake of the elect those days will be
shortened. 23At that time if anyone says to
you, 'Look, here is the Christ!' or, 'There
he is!' do not believe it. 24For false Christs
and false prophets will appear and per-
form great signs and miracles to deceive
even the elect—if that were possible.
25See, I have told you ahead of time.

26"So if anyone tells you, 'There he is,
out in the desert,' do not go out; or, 'Here
he is, in the inner rooms,' do not believe
it. 27For as lightning that comes from the
east is visible even in the west, so will be
the coming of the Son of Man. 28Wherever
there is a carcass, there the vultures will
gather.

29"Immediately after the distress of
those days

" 'the sun will be darkened,
and the moon will not give its light;
the stars will fall from the sky,
and the heavenly bodies will be
shaken.'[c]

30"At that time the sign of the Son of
Man will appear in the sky, and all the na-
tions of the earth will mourn. They will
see the Son of Man coming on the clouds
of the sky, with power and great glory.
31And he will send his angels with a loud
trumpet call, and they will gather his elect
from the four winds, from one end of the
heavens to the other.

32"Now learn this lesson from the fig
tree: As soon as its twigs get tender and its
leaves come out, you know that summer
is near. 33Even so, when you see all these
things, you know that it[d] is near, right at
the door. 34I tell you the truth, this genera-
tion[e] will certainly not pass away until all
these things have happened. 35Heaven
and earth will pass away, but my words
will never pass away.

The Day and Hour Unknown

36"No one knows about that day or
hour, not even the angels in heaven, nor
the Son,[f] but only the Father. 37As it was
in the days of Noah, so it will be at the
coming of the Son of Man. 38For in the
days before the flood, people were eating
and drinking, marrying and giving in mar-
riage, up to the day Noah entered the ark;
39and they knew nothing about what
would happen until the flood came and
took them all away. That is how it will be
at the coming of the Son of Man. 40Two
men will be in the field; one will be taken
and the other left. 41Two women will be
grinding with a hand mill; one will be tak-
en and the other left.

42"Therefore keep watch, because you
do not know on what day your Lord will
come. 43But understand this: If the owner
of the house had known at what time of
night the thief was coming, he would have
kept watch and would not have let his
house be broken into. 44So you also must
be ready, because the Son of Man will

[a]5 Or *Messiah*; also in verse 23 [b]15 Daniel 9:27; 11:31; 12:11 [c]29 Isaiah 13:10; 34:4 [d]33 Or *he* [e]34 Or *race* [f]36 Some manuscripts do not have *nor the Son.*

come at an hour when you do not expect him.

45"Who then is the faithful and wise servant, whom the master has put in charge of the servants in his household to give them their food at the proper time? 46It will be good for that servant whose master finds him doing so when he returns. 47I tell you the truth, he will put him in charge of all his possessions. 48But suppose that servant is wicked and says to himself, 'My master is staying away a long time,' 49and he then begins to beat his fellow servants and to eat and drink with drunkards. 50The master of that servant will come on a day when he does not expect him and at an hour he is not aware of. 51He will cut him to pieces and assign him a place with the hypocrites, where there will be weeping and gnashing of teeth.

The Parable of the Ten Virgins

25 "At that time the kingdom of heaven will be like ten virgins who took their lamps and went out to meet the bridegroom. 2Five of them were foolish and five were wise. 3The foolish ones took their lamps but did not take any oil with them. 4The wise, however, took oil in jars along with their lamps. 5The bridegroom was a long time in coming, and they all became drowsy and fell asleep.

6"At midnight the cry rang out: 'Here's the bridegroom! Come out to meet him!'

7"Then all the virgins woke up and trimmed their lamps. 8The foolish ones said to the wise, 'Give us some of your oil; our lamps are going out.'

9" 'No,' they replied, 'there may not be enough for both us and you. Instead, go to those who sell oil and buy some for yourselves.'

10"But while they were on their way to buy the oil, the bridegroom arrived. The virgins who were ready went in with him to the wedding banquet. And the door was shut.

11"Later the others also came. 'Sir! Sir!' they said. 'Open the door for us!'

12"But he replied, 'I tell you the truth, I don't know you.'

13"Therefore keep watch, because you do not know the day or the hour.

The Parable of the Talents

14"Again, it will be like a man going on a journey, who called his servants and entrusted his property to them. 15To one he gave five talents[a] of money, to another two talents, and to another one talent, each according to his ability. Then he went on his journey. 16The man who had received the five talents went at once and put his money to work and gained five more. 17So also, the one with the two talents gained two more. 18But the man who had received the one talent went off, dug a hole in the ground and hid his master's money.

19"After a long time the master of those servants returned and settled accounts with them. 20The man who had received the five talents brought the other five. 'Master,' he said, 'you entrusted me with five talents. See, I have gained five more.'

21"His master replied, 'Well done, good and faithful servant! You have been faithful with a few things; I will put you in charge of many things. Come and share your master's happiness!'

22"The man with the two talents also came. 'Master,' he said, 'you entrusted me with two talents; see, I have gained two more.'

23"His master replied, 'Well done, good and faithful servant! You have been faithful with a few things; I will put you in charge of many things. Come and share your master's happiness!'

24"Then the man who had received the one talent came. 'Master,' he said, 'I knew that you are a hard man, harvesting where you have not sown and gathering where you have not scattered seed. 25So I was afraid and went out and hid your talent in the ground. See, here is what belongs to you.'

26"His master replied, 'You wicked, lazy servant! So you knew that I harvest where I have not sown and gather where I have not scattered seed? 27Well then, you should have put my money on deposit with the bankers, so that when I returned I would have received it back with interest.

28" 'Take the talent from him and give it to the one who has the ten talents. 29For everyone who has will be given more, and he will have an abundance. Whoever does not have, even what he has will be taken from him. 30And throw that worthless servant outside, into the darkness, where there will be weeping and gnashing of teeth.'

[a]15 A talent was worth more than a thousand dollars.

The Sheep and the Goats

31"When the Son of Man comes in his
glory, and all the angels with him, he will
sit on his throne in heavenly glory. 32All
the nations will be gathered before him,
and he will separate the people one from
another as a shepherd separates the sheep
from the goats. 33He will put the sheep on
his right and the goats on his left.
34"Then the King will say to those on
his right, 'Come, you who are blessed by
my Father; take your inheritance, the
kingdom prepared for you since the cre-
ation of the world. 35For I was hungry and
you gave me something to eat, I was
thirsty and you gave me something to
drink, I was a stranger and you invited me
in, 36I needed clothes and you clothed me,
I was sick and you looked after me, I was
in prison and you came to visit me.'
37"Then the righteous will answer him,
'Lord, when did we see you hungry and
feed you, or thirsty and give you some-
thing to drink? 38When did we see you a
stranger and invite you in, or needing
clothes and clothe you? 39When did we
see you sick or in prison and go to visit
you?'
40"The King will reply, 'I tell you the
truth, whatever you did for one of the
least of these brothers of mine, you did
for me.'
41"Then he will say to those on his left,
'Depart from me, you who are cursed, into
the eternal fire prepared for the devil and
his angels. 42For I was hungry and you
gave me nothing to eat, I was thirsty and
you gave me nothing to drink, 43I was a
stranger and you did not invite me in, I
needed clothes and you did not clothe me,
I was sick and in prison and you did not
look after me.'
44"They also will answer, 'Lord, when
did we see you hungry or thirsty or a
stranger or needing clothes or sick or in
prison, and did not help you?'
45"He will reply, 'I tell you the truth,
whatever you did not do for one of the
least of these, you did not do for me.'
46"Then they will go away to eternal
punishment, but the righteous to eternal
life."

The Plot Against Jesus

26 When Jesus had finished saying all
these things, he said to his disci-
ples, 2"As you know, the Passover is two
days away—and the Son of Man will be
handed over to be crucified."
3Then the chief priests and the elders of
the people assembled in the palace of the
high priest, whose name was Caiaphas,
4and they plotted to arrest Jesus in some
sly way and kill him. 5"But not during the
Feast," they said, "or there may be a riot
among the people."

Jesus Anointed at Bethany

6While Jesus was in Bethany in the
home of a man known as Simon the Lep-
er, 7a woman came to him with an alabas-
ter jar of very expensive perfume, which
she poured on his head as he was recline-
ing at the table.
8When the disciples saw this, they were
indignant. "Why this waste?" they asked.
9"This perfume could have been sold at a
high price and the money given to the
poor."
10Aware of this, Jesus said to them,
"Why are you bothering this woman? She
has done a beautiful thing to me. 11The
poor you will always have with you, but
you will not always have me. 12When she
poured this perfume on my body, she did
it to prepare me for burial. 13I tell you the
truth, wherever this gospel is preached
throughout the world, what she has done
will also be told, in memory of her."

Judas Agrees to Betray Jesus

14Then one of the Twelve—the one
called Judas Iscariot—went to the chief
priests 15and asked, "What are you willing
to give me if I hand him over to you?" So
they counted out for him thirty silver
coins. 16From then on Judas watched for
an opportunity to hand him over.

The Lord's Supper

17On the first day of the Feast of Unleav-
ened Bread, the disciples came to Jesus
and asked, "Where do you want us to
make preparations for you to eat the Pass-
over?"
18He replied, "Go into the city to a cer-
tain man and tell him, 'The Teacher says:
My appointed time is near. I am going to
celebrate the Passover with my disciples
at your house.' " 19So the disciples did as
Jesus had directed them and prepared the
Passover.
20When evening came, Jesus was re-
clining at the table with the Twelve. 21And
while they were eating, he said, "I tell you
the truth, one of you will betray me."

22They were very sad and began to say
to him one after the other, "Surely not I,
Lord?"
23Jesus replied, "The one who has
dipped his hand into the bowl with me
will betray me. 24The Son of Man will go
just as it is written about him. But woe to
that man who betrays the Son of Man! It
would be better for him if he had not been
born."
25Then Judas, the one who would be-
tray him, said, "Surely not I, Rabbi?"
Jesus answered, "Yes, it is you."[a]
26While they were eating, Jesus took
bread, gave thanks and broke it, and gave
it to his disciples, saying, "Take and eat;
this is my body."
27Then he took the cup, gave thanks
and offered it to them, saying, "Drink
from it, all of you. 28This is my blood of
the[b] covenant, which is poured out for
many for the forgiveness of sins. 29I tell
you, I will not drink of this fruit of the vine
from now on until that day when I drink
it anew with you in my Father's king-
dom."
30When they had sung a hymn, they
went out to the Mount of Olives.

Jesus Predicts Peter's Denial

31Then Jesus told them, "This very
night you will all fall away on account of
me, for it is written:

" 'I will strike the shepherd,
and the sheep of the flock will be
scattered.'[c]

32But after I have risen, I will go ahead of
you into Galilee."
33Peter replied, "Even if all fall away on
account of you, I never will."
34"I tell you the truth," Jesus answered,
"this very night, before the rooster crows,
you will disown me three times."
35But Peter declared, "Even if I have to
die with you, I will never disown you."
And all the other disciples said the same.

Gethsemane

36Then Jesus went with his disciples to
a place called Gethsemane, and he said to
them, "Sit here while I go over there and
pray." 37He took Peter and the two sons of
Zebedee along with him, and he began to
be sorrowful and troubled. 38Then he said
to them, "My soul is overwhelmed with
sorrow to the point of death. Stay here and
keep watch with me."
39Going a little farther, he fell with his
face to the ground and prayed, "My Fa-
ther, if it is possible, may this cup be taken
from me. Yet not as I will, but as you will."
40Then he returned to his disciples and
found them sleeping. "Could you men not
keep watch with me for one hour?" he
asked Peter. 41"Watch and pray so that
you will not fall into temptation. The spirit
is willing, but the body is weak."
42He went away a second time and
prayed, "My Father, if it is not possible for
this cup to be taken away unless I drink it,
may your will be done."
43When he came back, he again found
them sleeping, because their eyes were
heavy. 44So he left them and went away
once more and prayed the third time, say-
ing the same thing.
45Then he returned to the disciples and
said to them, "Are you still sleeping and
resting? Look, the hour is near, and the
Son of Man is betrayed into the hands of
sinners. 46Rise, let us go! Here comes my
betrayer!"

Jesus Arrested

47While he was still speaking, Judas,
one of the Twelve, arrived. With him was
a large crowd armed with swords and
clubs, sent from the chief priests and the
elders of the people. 48Now the betrayer
had arranged a signal with them: "The one
I kiss is the man; arrest him." 49Going at
once to Jesus, Judas said, "Greetings, Rab-
bi!" and kissed him.
50Jesus replied, "Friend, do what you
came for."[d]
Then the men stepped forward, seized
Jesus and arrested him. 51With that, one
of Jesus' companions reached for his
sword, drew it out and struck the servant
of the high priest, cutting off his ear.
52"Put your sword back in its place,"
Jesus said to him, "for all who draw the
sword will die by the sword. 53Do you
think I cannot call on my Father, and he
will at once put at my disposal more than
twelve legions of angels? 54But how then
would the Scriptures be fulfilled that say
it must happen in this way?"
55At that time Jesus said to the crowd,
"Am I leading a rebellion, that you have
come out with swords and clubs to cap-

[a]25 Or *"You yourself have said it"* [b]28 Some manuscripts *the new* [c]31 Zech. 13:7 [d]50 Or *"Friend, why have you come?"*

VERSE FOR THE DAY: Matthew 26:39

AUTHOR: Alesia T. Thayer

PASSAGE FOR THE DAY: Matthew 26:36–46

Accepting God's Will

My husband and I respond differently to change. Randy loves an adventure, and I need to have my roots firmly embedded, with friends and family nearby. But we were faced with a decision to move.

"God," I questioned, "couldn't we serve you *here* just as well as in some far-away city?" There seemed to be no answer. Yet I believed that if we followed the concrete, visible guidance in our daily lives, God would honor us. He would put us in the right place at the right time.

Catherine Marshall once noted that when a person finally comes to a place in her prayer life where she says, " 'God, whatever you want for my life now, I accept it,' then God really begins to work. But first, one must give up self-will and be willing to totally accept God's will, no matter what it is."

Jesus prayed in the Garden of Gethsemane: "My Father, if it is possible, may this cup be taken from me. Yet not as I will, but as you will." From that total surrender came the most precious sacrifice ever made. Compared to such a surrender, what was I giving up?

Randy and I moved to Utah. Our new home was in a lush green valley, not the desert I had imagined. We were surrounded by loving, warm people, and even an airport close by so I could fly home occasionally. God cares for the little things in our lives—if only we'll surrender the big ones.

MARRIAGE BUILDERS

♦ *Have you ever felt God calling you to do something that you did not feel willing to do? What were the results?*

♦ *Is there anything you feel God is asking of you as a couple, but you've been dragging your feet?*

Additional Scripture Readings
Romans 12:1–3; Hebrews 13:20–21; Genesis 50:15–21

Go to page 1069 for your next devotional reading.

ture me? Every day I sat in the temple
courts teaching, and you did not arrest
me. 56But this has all taken place that the
writings of the prophets might be ful-
filled." Then all the disciples deserted him
and fled.

Before the Sanhedrin

57Those who had arrested Jesus took
him to Caiaphas, the high priest, where
the teachers of the law and the elders had
assembled. 58But Peter followed him at a
distance, right up to the courtyard of the
high priest. He entered and sat down with
the guards to see the outcome.

59The chief priests and the whole San-
hedrin were looking for false evidence
against Jesus so that they could put him to
death. 60But they did not find any, though
many false witnesses came forward.

Finally two came forward 61and de-
clared, "This fellow said, 'I am able to de-
stroy the temple of God and rebuild it in
three days.' "

62Then the high priest stood up and said
to Jesus, "Are you not going to answer?
What is this testimony that these men are
bringing against you?" 63But Jesus re-
mained silent.

The high priest said to him, "I charge
you under oath by the living God: Tell us
if you are the Christ,[a] the Son of God."

64"Yes, it is as you say," Jesus replied.
"But I say to all of you: In the future you
will see the Son of Man sitting at the right
hand of the Mighty One and coming on
the clouds of heaven."

65Then the high priest tore his clothes
and said, "He has spoken blasphemy!
Why do we need any more witnesses?
Look, now you have heard the blasphemy.
66What do you think?"

"He is worthy of death," they answered.

67Then they spit in his face and struck
him with their fists. Others slapped him
68and said, "Prophesy to us, Christ. Who
hit you?"

Peter Disowns Jesus

69Now Peter was sitting out in the court-
yard, and a servant girl came to him. "You
also were with Jesus of Galilee," she said.

70But he denied it before them all. "I
don't know what you're talking about," he
said.

71Then he went out to the gateway,
where another girl saw him and said to the
people there, "This fellow was with Jesus
of Nazareth."

72He denied it again, with an oath: "I
don't know the man!"

73After a little while, those standing
there went up to Peter and said, "Surely
you are one of them, for your accent gives
you away."

74Then he began to call down curses on
himself and he swore to them, "I don't
know the man!"

Immediately a rooster crowed. 75Then
Peter remembered the word Jesus had
spoken: "Before the rooster crows, you
will disown me three times." And he went
outside and wept bitterly.

Judas Hangs Himself

27 Early in the morning, all the chief
priests and the elders of the people
came to the decision to put Jesus to death.
2They bound him, led him away and
handed him over to Pilate, the governor.

3When Judas, who had betrayed him,
saw that Jesus was condemned, he was
seized with remorse and returned the thir-
ty silver coins to the chief priests and the
elders. 4"I have sinned," he said, "for I
have betrayed innocent blood."

"What is that to us?" they replied.
"That's your responsibility."

5So Judas threw the money into the
temple and left. Then he went away and
hanged himself.

6The chief priests picked up the coins
and said, "It is against the law to put this
into the treasury, since it is blood money."
7So they decided to use the money to buy
the potter's field as a burial place for for-
eigners. 8That is why it has been called the
Field of Blood to this day. 9Then what was
spoken by Jeremiah the prophet was ful-
filled: "They took the thirty silver coins,
the price set on him by the people of Isra-
el, 10and they used them to buy the pot-
ter's field, as the Lord commanded me."[b]

Jesus Before Pilate

11Meanwhile Jesus stood before the
governor, and the governor asked him,
"Are you the king of the Jews?"

"Yes, it is as you say," Jesus replied.

12When he was accused by the chief
priests and the elders, he gave no answer.
13Then Pilate asked him, "Don't you hear
the testimony they are bringing against
you?" 14But Jesus made no reply, not even

[a] *63* Or *Messiah*; also in verse 68 [b] *10* See Zech. 11:12,13; Jer. 19:1-13; 32:6-9.

to a single charge—to the great amazement of the governor.

15Now it was the governor's custom at
the Feast to release a prisoner chosen by
the crowd. 16At that time they had a noto-
rious prisoner, called Barabbas. 17So
when the crowd had gathered, Pilate
asked them, "Which one do you want me
to release to you: Barabbas, or Jesus who
is called Christ?" 18For he knew it was out
of envy that they had handed Jesus over
to him.

19While Pilate was sitting on the judge's
seat, his wife sent him this message:
"Don't have anything to do with that inno-
cent man, for I have suffered a great deal
today in a dream because of him."

20But the chief priests and the elders
persuaded the crowd to ask for Barabbas
and to have Jesus executed.

21"Which of the two do you want me to
release to you?" asked the governor.

"Barabbas," they answered.

22"What shall I do, then, with Jesus who
is called Christ?" Pilate asked.

They all answered, "Crucify him!"

23"Why? What crime has he commit-
ted?" asked Pilate.

But they shouted all the louder, "Cruci-
fy him!"

24When Pilate saw that he was getting
nowhere, but that instead an uproar was
starting, he took water and washed his
hands in front of the crowd. "I am inno-
cent of this man's blood," he said. "It is
your responsibility!"

25All the people answered, "Let his
blood be on us and on our children!"

26Then he released Barabbas to them.
But he had Jesus flogged, and handed him
over to be crucified.

The Soldiers Mock Jesus

27Then the governor's soldiers took
Jesus into the Praetorium and gathered
the whole company of soldiers around
him. 28They stripped him and put a scarlet
robe on him, 29and then twisted together
a crown of thorns and set it on his head.
They put a staff in his right hand and knelt
in front of him and mocked him. "Hail,
king of the Jews!" they said. 30They spit
on him, and took the staff and struck him
on the head again and again. 31After they
had mocked him, they took off the robe
and put his own clothes on him. Then
they led him away to crucify him.

The Crucifixion

32As they were going out, they met a
man from Cyrene, named Simon, and they
forced him to carry the cross. 33They came
to a place called Golgotha (which means
The Place of the Skull). 34There they of-
fered Jesus wine to drink, mixed with gall;
but after tasting it, he refused to drink it.
35When they had crucified him, they di-
vided up his clothes by casting lots.[a]
36And sitting down, they kept watch over
him there. 37Above his head they placed
the written charge against him: THIS IS
JESUS, THE KING OF THE JEWS. 38Two robbers
were crucified with him, one on his right
and one on his left. 39Those who passed
by hurled insults at him, shaking their
heads 40and saying, "You who are going to
destroy the temple and build it in three
days, save yourself! Come down from the
cross, if you are the Son of God!"

41In the same way the chief priests, the
teachers of the law and the elders mocked
him. 42"He saved others," they said, "but
he can't save himself! He's the King of Is-
rael! Let him come down now from the
cross, and we will believe in him. 43He
trusts in God. Let God rescue him now if
he wants him, for he said, 'I am the Son of
God.' " 44In the same way the robbers who
were crucified with him also heaped in-
sults on him.

The Death of Jesus

45From the sixth hour until the ninth
hour darkness came over all the land.
46About the ninth hour Jesus cried out in
a loud voice, *"Eloi, Eloi,*[b] *lama sabach-
thani?"*—which means, "My God, my
God, why have you forsaken me?"[c]

47When some of those standing there
heard this, they said, "He's calling Elijah."

48Immediately one of them ran and got
a sponge. He filled it with wine vinegar,
put it on a stick, and offered it to Jesus to
drink. 49The rest said, "Now leave him
alone. Let's see if Elijah comes to save
him."

50And when Jesus had cried out again
in a loud voice, he gave up his spirit.

51At that moment the curtain of the
temple was torn in two from top to bot-

[a]35 A few late manuscripts *lots that the word spoken by the prophet might be fulfilled: "They divided my garments among themselves and cast lots for my clothing"* (Psalm 22:18) [b]46 Some manuscripts *Eli, Eli* [c]46 Psalm 22:1

tom. The earth shook and the rocks split.
52The tombs broke open and the bodies of
many holy people who had died were
raised to life. 53They came out of the
tombs, and after Jesus' resurrection they
went into the holy city and appeared to
many people.

54When the centurion and those with
him who were guarding Jesus saw the
earthquake and all that had happened,
they were terrified, and exclaimed, "Sure-
ly he was the Son[a] of God!"

55Many women were there, watching
from a distance. They had followed Jesus

[a]54 Or *a son*

VERSE FOR THE DAY: Matthew 28:5–6

AUTHOR: Andrea Midgett

PASSAGE FOR THE DAY: Matthew 28:1–20

Easter Is True

Judy Vander Zee's physical condition began to deteriorate almost as soon as she left the hospital. Every day she was a little less able to carry out all the duties of wife, homemaker, musician and mother. Today, she spends most of her time in a motorized wheelchair.

Judy's husband, Len, a pastor, has had his own struggles. He recalls the close of a particular Easter Sunday that made a difference. Tired and tense as he washed dishes that night, he found himself thinking that no matter what he had said from the pulpit, the message of hope did not seem to square with his life. The doctors were holding out no hope for improvement in his wife's condition. Their four children needed more than they were getting from their parents.

Judy was trying to cheer him out of his grumpiness when suddenly he burst into tears. As Len began to talk, the walls between them began to crumble. Later, he turned on a recording of Handel's *Messiah*. They had listened to it many times, but it suddenly made sense to them as never before. Easter *was* true. Christ had gone through even more than what they were experiencing. And he had been victorious.

MARRIAGE BUILDERS

♦ *When have you received spiritual encouragement when you were experiencing difficulty or desperation?*

♦ *What is the power source Christians draw on as they pursue victory instead of despair?*

Additional Scripture Readings
Luke 24:1–12, 36–49; John 20:1–18

Go to page 1073 for your next devotional reading.

from Galilee to care for his needs.
56Among them were Mary Magdalene,
Mary the mother of James and Joses, and
the mother of Zebedee's sons.

The Burial of Jesus

57As evening approached, there came a
rich man from Arimathea, named Joseph,
who had himself become a disciple of
Jesus. 58Going to Pilate, he asked for
Jesus' body, and Pilate ordered that it be
given to him. 59Joseph took the body,
wrapped it in a clean linen cloth, 60and
placed it in his own new tomb that he had
cut out of the rock. He rolled a big stone
in front of the entrance to the tomb and
went away. 61Mary Magdalene and the
other Mary were sitting there opposite the
tomb.

The Guard at the Tomb

62The next day, the one after Preparation Day, the chief priests and the Pharisees went to Pilate. 63"Sir," they said, "we remember that while he was still alive that deceiver said, 'After three days I will rise again.' 64So give the order for the tomb to be made secure until the third day. Otherwise, his disciples may come and steal the body and tell the people that he has been raised from the dead. This last deception will be worse than the first."

65"Take a guard," Pilate answered. "Go, make the tomb as secure as you know how." 66So they went and made the tomb secure by putting a seal on the stone and posting the guard.

The Resurrection

28 After the Sabbath, at dawn on the first day of the week, Mary Magdalene and the other Mary went to look at the tomb.

2There was a violent earthquake, for an angel of the Lord came down from heaven and, going to the tomb, rolled back the stone and sat on it. 3His appearance was like lightning, and his clothes were white as snow. 4The guards were so afraid of him that they shook and became like dead men.

5The angel said to the women, "Do not be afraid, for I know that you are looking for Jesus, who was crucified. 6He is not here; he has risen, just as he said. Come and see the place where he lay. 7Then go quickly and tell his disciples: 'He has risen from the dead and is going ahead of you into Galilee. There you will see him.' Now I have told you."

8So the women hurried away from the tomb, afraid yet filled with joy, and ran to tell his disciples. 9Suddenly Jesus met them. "Greetings," he said. They came to him, clasped his feet and worshiped him. 10Then Jesus said to them, "Do not be afraid. Go and tell my brothers to go to Galilee; there they will see me."

The Guards' Report

11While the women were on their way, some of the guards went into the city and reported to the chief priests everything that had happened. 12When the chief priests had met with the elders and devised a plan, they gave the soldiers a large sum of money, 13telling them, "You are to say, 'His disciples came during the night and stole him away while we were asleep.' 14If this report gets to the governor, we will satisfy him and keep you out of trouble." 15So the soldiers took the money and did as they were instructed. And this story has been widely circulated among the Jews to this very day.

The Great Commission

16Then the eleven disciples went to Galilee, to the mountain where Jesus had told them to go. 17When they saw him, they worshiped him; but some doubted. 18Then Jesus came to them and said, "All authority in heaven and on earth has been given to me. 19Therefore go and make disciples of all nations, baptizing them in[a] the name of the Father and of the Son and of the Holy Spirit, 20and teaching them to obey everything I have commanded you. And surely I am with you always, to the very end of the age."

[a]19 Or *into*; see Acts 8:16; 19:5; Romans 6:3; 1 Cor. 1:13; 10:2 and Gal. 3:27.

MARK writes this Gospel to tell the basic story about Jesus. He recounts miracles, parables and other sayings of Jesus. Almost half of his book deals with the final week of Jesus' life, ending with his death on the cross and his resurrection from the dead. As you read this book, notice how full of life and emotion Jesus is and how caring he is. Note too why he came into the world—to give his life for you (Mark 10:45). God wants you to accept his Son Jesus as your own personal Savior and Lord.

MARK

John the Baptist Prepares the Way

1 The beginning of the gospel about Jesus Christ, the Son of God.[a]

2 It is written in Isaiah the prophet:

"I will send my messenger ahead of you,
who will prepare your way"[b]—
3 "a voice of one calling in the desert,
'Prepare the way for the Lord,
make straight paths for him.' "[c]

4 And so John came, baptizing in the desert region and preaching a baptism of repentance for the forgiveness of sins. 5 The whole Judean countryside and all the people of Jerusalem went out to him. Confessing their sins, they were baptized by him in the Jordan River. 6 John wore clothing made of camel's hair, with a leather belt around his waist, and he ate locusts and wild honey. 7 And this was his message: "After me will come one more powerful than I, the thongs of whose sandals I am not worthy to stoop down and

[a] 1 Some manuscripts do not have *the Son of God.*

[b] 2 Mal. 3:1 [c] 3 Isaiah 40:3

untie. 8I baptize you with[a] water, but he
will baptize you with the Holy Spirit."

The Baptism and Temptation of Jesus

9At that time Jesus came from Nazareth
in Galilee and was baptized by John in the
Jordan. 10As Jesus was coming up out of
the water, he saw heaven being torn open
and the Spirit descending on him like a
dove. 11And a voice came from heaven:
"You are my Son, whom I love; with you
I am well pleased."

12At once the Spirit sent him out into
the desert, 13and he was in the desert forty
days, being tempted by Satan. He was
with the wild animals, and angels attend-
ed him.

The Calling of the First Disciples

14After John was put in prison, Jesus
went into Galilee, proclaiming the good
news of God. 15"The time has come," he
said. "The kingdom of God is near. Repent
and believe the good news!"

16As Jesus walked beside the Sea of Gal-
ilee, he saw Simon and his brother An-
drew casting a net into the lake, for they
were fishermen. 17"Come, follow me,"
Jesus said, "and I will make you fishers of
men." 18At once they left their nets and
followed him.

19When he had gone a little farther, he
saw James son of Zebedee and his brother
John in a boat, preparing their nets.
20Without delay he called them, and they
left their father Zebedee in the boat with
the hired men and followed him.

Jesus Drives Out an Evil Spirit

21They went to Capernaum, and when
the Sabbath came, Jesus went into the
synagogue and began to teach. 22The peo-
ple were amazed at his teaching, because
he taught them as one who had authority,
not as the teachers of the law. 23Just then
a man in their synagogue who was pos-
sessed by an evil[b] spirit cried out,
24"What do you want with us, Jesus of
Nazareth? Have you come to destroy us?
I know who you are—the Holy One of
God!"

25"Be quiet!" said Jesus sternly. "Come
out of him!" 26The evil spirit shook the
man violently and came out of him with a
shriek.

27The people were all so amazed that
they asked each other, "What is this? A
new teaching—and with authority! He
even gives orders to evil spirits and they
obey him." 28News about him spread
quickly over the whole region of Galilee.

Jesus Heals Many

29As soon as they left the synagogue,
they went with James and John to the
home of Simon and Andrew. 30Simon's
mother-in-law was in bed with a fever,
and they told Jesus about her. 31So he
went to her, took her hand and helped her
up. The fever left her and she began to
wait on them.

32That evening after sunset the people
brought to Jesus all the sick and demon-
possessed. 33The whole town gathered at
the door, 34and Jesus healed many who
had various diseases. He also drove out
many demons, but he would not let the
demons speak because they knew who he
was.

Jesus Prays in a Solitary Place

35Very early in the morning, while it
was still dark, Jesus got up, left the house
and went off to a solitary place, where he
prayed. 36Simon and his companions
went to look for him, 37and when they
found him, they exclaimed: "Everyone is
looking for you!"

38Jesus replied, "Let us go somewhere
else—to the nearby villages—so I can
preach there also. That is why I have
come." 39So he traveled throughout Gali-
lee, preaching in their synagogues and
driving out demons.

A Man With Leprosy

40A man with leprosy[c] came to him
and begged him on his knees, "If you are
willing, you can make me clean."

41Filled with compassion, Jesus
reached out his hand and touched the
man. "I am willing," he said. "Be clean!"
42Immediately the leprosy left him and he
was cured.

43Jesus sent him away at once with a
strong warning: 44"See that you don't tell
this to anyone. But go, show yourself to
the priest and offer the sacrifices that Mo-
ses commanded for your cleansing, as a
testimony to them." 45Instead he went out
and began to talk freely, spreading the

[a] *8* Or *in* [b] *23* Greek *unclean*; also in verses 26 and 27 [c] *40* The Greek word was used for various diseases affecting the skin—not necessarily leprosy.

news. As a result, Jesus could no longer
enter a town openly but stayed outside in
lonely places. Yet the people still came to
him from everywhere.

Jesus Heals a Paralytic

2 A few days later, when Jesus again en-
tered Capernaum, the people heard
that he had come home. [2]So many gath-
ered that there was no room left, not even
outside the door, and he preached the
word to them. [3]Some men came, bringing
to him a paralytic, carried by four of them.
[4]Since they could not get him to Jesus be-
cause of the crowd, they made an opening
in the roof above Jesus and, after digging
through it, lowered the mat the paralyzed
man was lying on. [5]When Jesus saw their

THURSDAY

VERSE FOR THE DAY: Mark 1:35 | AUTHOR: Donna Sinclair | PASSAGE FOR THE DAY: Mark 1:35–39

Solitude and Hospitality

In our home, hospitality meant a door that was open to everyone and a welcome from me. But it also aroused a certain ambivalence. I needed to be nurturing, but I needed solitude as well. The balance was difficult to find as more people felt comfortable about accepting my breezy (and foolhardy) invitations to "drop in."

How could I have some private time? I was reading a book by Henri Nouwen when I began to find an answer. True hospitality, he says, grows out of solitude. One is rooted in the other. In solitude we can pay attention to our personal and spiritual well-being. Then we are able to reach out to others—not greedy for attention or affection—but offering ourselves to build a community of love.

I had to choose where the open-door policy began and ended. I know now that when the balance shifts too much to the "open house" side, I begin to feel sick: too much coffee, too much sitting, too much being still, and I start to fidget and wish that the visitor would leave. But when the balance falls too far in the other direction, I begin to feel isolated and empty—hungry both to care and be cared for.

The broadening and deepening that was going on as I struggled to balance these conflicting demands has been valuable for our marriage as well as for me.

MARRIAGE BUILDERS

- *What does it mean to you that Jesus took time out for prayer?*
- *How satisfied are both of you with your current balance between times of spiritual replenishment and times of outreach?*

Additional Scripture Readings
Genesis 2:1–3; Matthew 14:22–36; Psalm 46:10

Go to page 1081 for your next devotional reading.

faith, he said to the paralytic, "Son, your sins are forgiven."

[6]Now some teachers of the law were sitting there, thinking to themselves, [7]"Why does this fellow talk like that? He's blaspheming! Who can forgive sins but God alone?"

[8]Immediately Jesus knew in his spirit that this was what they were thinking in their hearts, and he said to them, "Why are you thinking these things? [9]Which is easier: to say to the paralytic, 'Your sins are forgiven,' or to say, 'Get up, take your mat and walk'? [10]But that you may know that the Son of Man has authority on earth to forgive sins . . . ." He said to the paralytic, [11]"I tell you, get up, take your mat and go home." [12]He got up, took his mat and walked out in full view of them all. This amazed everyone and they praised God, saying, "We have never seen anything like this!"

The Calling of Levi

[13]Once again Jesus went out beside the lake. A large crowd came to him, and he began to teach them. [14]As he walked along, he saw Levi son of Alphaeus sitting at the tax collector's booth. "Follow me," Jesus told him, and Levi got up and followed him.

[15]While Jesus was having dinner at Levi's house, many tax collectors and "sinners" were eating with him and his disciples, for there were many who followed him. [16]When the teachers of the law who were Pharisees saw him eating with the "sinners" and tax collectors, they asked his disciples: "Why does he eat with tax collectors and 'sinners'?"

[17]On hearing this, Jesus said to them, "It is not the healthy who need a doctor, but the sick. I have not come to call the righteous, but sinners."

Jesus Questioned About Fasting

[18]Now John's disciples and the Pharisees were fasting. Some people came and asked Jesus, "How is it that John's disciples and the disciples of the Pharisees are fasting, but yours are not?"

[19]Jesus answered, "How can the guests of the bridegroom fast while he is with them? They cannot, so long as they have him with them. [20]But the time will come when the bridegroom will be taken from them, and on that day they will fast.

[21]"No one sews a patch of unshrunk cloth on an old garment. If he does, the new piece will pull away from the old, making the tear worse. [22]And no one pours new wine into old wineskins. If he does, the wine will burst the skins, and both the wine and the wineskins will be ruined. No, he pours new wine into new wineskins."

Lord of the Sabbath

[23]One Sabbath Jesus was going through the grainfields, and as his disciples walked along, they began to pick some heads of grain. [24]The Pharisees said to him, "Look, why are they doing what is unlawful on the Sabbath?"

[25]He answered, "Have you never read what David did when he and his companions were hungry and in need? [26]In the days of Abiathar the high priest, he entered the house of God and ate the consecrated bread, which is lawful only for priests to eat. And he also gave some to his companions."

[27]Then he said to them, "The Sabbath was made for man, not man for the Sabbath. [28]So the Son of Man is Lord even of the Sabbath."

3 Another time he went into the synagogue, and a man with a shriveled hand was there. [2]Some of them were looking for a reason to accuse Jesus, so they watched him closely to see if he would heal him on the Sabbath. [3]Jesus said to the man with the shriveled hand, "Stand up in front of everyone."

[4]Then Jesus asked them, "Which is lawful on the Sabbath: to do good or to do evil, to save life or to kill?" But they remained silent.

[5]He looked around at them in anger and, deeply distressed at their stubborn hearts, said to the man, "Stretch out your hand." He stretched it out, and his hand was completely restored. [6]Then the Pharisees went out and began to plot with the Herodians how they might kill Jesus.

Crowds Follow Jesus

[7]Jesus withdrew with his disciples to the lake, and a large crowd from Galilee followed. [8]When they heard all he was doing, many people came to him from Judea, Jerusalem, Idumea, and the regions across the Jordan and around Tyre and Sidon. [9]Because of the crowd he told his disciples to have a small boat ready for him, to keep the people from crowding him. [10]For he had healed many, so that those with diseases were pushing forward to

touch him. 11Whenever the evil[a] spirits
saw him, they fell down before him and
cried out, "You are the Son of God." 12But
he gave them strict orders not to tell who
he was.

The Appointing of the Twelve Apostles

13Jesus went up on a mountainside and
called to him those he wanted, and they
came to him. 14He appointed twelve—
designating them apostles[b]—that they
might be with him and that he might send
them out to preach 15and to have authori-
ty to drive out demons. 16These are the
twelve he appointed: Simon (to whom he
gave the name Peter); 17James son of Zeb-
edee and his brother John (to them he
gave the name Boanerges, which means
Sons of Thunder); 18Andrew, Philip, Bar-
tholomew, Matthew, Thomas, James son
of Alphaeus, Thaddaeus, Simon the Zealot
19and Judas Iscariot, who betrayed him.

Jesus and Beelzebub

20Then Jesus entered a house, and
again a crowd gathered, so that he and his
disciples were not even able to eat.
21When his family heard about this, they
went to take charge of him, for they said,
"He is out of his mind."

22And the teachers of the law who came
down from Jerusalem said, "He is pos-
sessed by Beelzebub[c]! By the prince of
demons he is driving out demons."

23So Jesus called them and spoke to
them in parables: "How can Satan drive
out Satan? 24If a kingdom is divided
against itself, that kingdom cannot stand.
25If a house is divided against itself, that
house cannot stand. 26And if Satan op-
poses himself and is divided, he cannot
stand; his end has come. 27In fact, no one
can enter a strong man's house and carry
off his possessions unless he first ties up
the strong man. Then he can rob his
house. 28I tell you the truth, all the sins
and blasphemies of men will be forgiven
them. 29But whoever blasphemes against
the Holy Spirit will never be forgiven; he
is guilty of an eternal sin."

30He said this because they were saying,
"He has an evil spirit."

Jesus' Mother and Brothers

31Then Jesus' mother and brothers ar-
rived. Standing outside, they sent some-
one in to call him. 32A crowd was sitting
around him, and they told him, "Your
mother and brothers are outside looking
for you."

33"Who are my mother and my broth-
ers?" he asked.

34Then he looked at those seated in a
circle around him and said, "Here are my
mother and my brothers! 35Whoever does
God's will is my brother and sister and
mother."

The Parable of the Sower

4 Again Jesus began to teach by the
lake. The crowd that gathered around
him was so large that he got into a boat
and sat in it out on the lake, while all the
people were along the shore at the water's
edge. 2He taught them many things by
parables, and in his teaching said: 3"Lis-
ten! A farmer went out to sow his seed.
4As he was scattering the seed, some fell
along the path, and the birds came and ate
it up. 5Some fell on rocky places, where it
did not have much soil. It sprang up
quickly, because the soil was shallow.
6But when the sun came up, the plants
were scorched, and they withered be-
cause they had no root. 7Other seed fell
among thorns, which grew up and choked
the plants, so that they did not bear grain.
8Still other seed fell on good soil. It came
up, grew and produced a crop, multiply-
ing thirty, sixty, or even a hundred times."

9Then Jesus said, "He who has ears to
hear, let him hear."

10When he was alone, the Twelve and
the others around him asked him about
the parables. 11He told them, "The secret
of the kingdom of God has been given to
you. But to those on the outside every-
thing is said in parables 12so that,

" 'they may be ever seeing but never
perceiving,
and ever hearing but never
understanding;
otherwise they might turn and be
forgiven!'[d]"

13Then Jesus said to them, "Don't you
understand this parable? How then will
you understand any parable? 14The farm-
er sows the word. 15Some people are like
seed along the path, where the word is
sown. As soon as they hear it, Satan

[a] 11 Greek *unclean*; also in verse 30
[b] 14 Some manuscripts do not have *designating them apostles.*
[c] 22 Greek *Beezeboul* or *Beelzeboul*
[d] 12 Isaiah 6:9,10

comes and takes away the word that was
sown in them. 16Others, like seed sown on
rocky places, hear the word and at once
receive it with joy. 17But since they have
no root, they last only a short time. When
trouble or persecution comes because of
the word, they quickly fall away. 18Still
others, like seed sown among thorns, hear
the word; 19but the worries of this life, the
deceitfulness of wealth and the desires for
other things come in and choke the word,
making it unfruitful. 20Others, like seed
sown on good soil, hear the word, accept
it, and produce a crop—thirty, sixty or
even a hundred times what was sown."

A Lamp on a Stand

21He said to them, "Do you bring in a
lamp to put it under a bowl or a bed? In-
stead, don't you put it on its stand? 22For
whatever is hidden is meant to be dis-
closed, and whatever is concealed is
meant to be brought out into the open. 23If
anyone has ears to hear, let him hear."

24"Consider carefully what you hear,"
he continued. "With the measure you use,
it will be measured to you—and even
more. 25Whoever has will be given more;
whoever does not have, even what he has
will be taken from him."

The Parable of the Growing Seed

26He also said, "This is what the king-
dom of God is like. A man scatters seed on
the ground. 27Night and day, whether he
sleeps or gets up, the seed sprouts and
grows, though he does not know how.
28All by itself the soil produces grain—
first the stalk, then the head, then the full
kernel in the head. 29As soon as the grain
is ripe, he puts the sickle to it, because the
harvest has come."

The Parable of the Mustard Seed

30Again he said, "What shall we say the
kingdom of God is like, or what parable
shall we use to describe it? 31It is like a
mustard seed, which is the smallest seed
you plant in the ground. 32Yet when plant-
ed, it grows and becomes the largest of all
garden plants, with such big branches that
the birds of the air can perch in its shade."

33With many similar parables Jesus
spoke the word to them, as much as they
could understand. 34He did not say any-
thing to them without using a parable. But
when he was alone with his own disciples,
he explained everything.

Jesus Calms the Storm

35That day when evening came, he said
to his disciples, "Let us go over to the oth-
er side." 36Leaving the crowd behind, they
took him along, just as he was, in the boat.
There were also other boats with him. 37A
furious squall came up, and the waves
broke over the boat, so that it was nearly
swamped. 38Jesus was in the stern, sleep-
ing on a cushion. The disciples woke him
and said to him, "Teacher, don't you care
if we drown?"

39He got up, rebuked the wind and said
to the waves, "Quiet! Be still!" Then the
wind died down and it was completely
calm.

40He said to his disciples, "Why are you
so afraid? Do you still have no faith?"

41They were terrified and asked each
other, "Who is this? Even the wind and the
waves obey him!"

The Healing of a Demon-possessed Man

5 They went across the lake to the re-
gion of the Gerasenes.[a] 2When Jesus
got out of the boat, a man with an evil[b]
spirit came from the tombs to meet him.
3This man lived in the tombs, and no one
could bind him any more, not even with a
chain. 4For he had often been chained
hand and foot, but he tore the chains apart
and broke the irons on his feet. No one
was strong enough to subdue him. 5Night
and day among the tombs and in the hills
he would cry out and cut himself with
stones.

6When he saw Jesus from a distance, he
ran and fell on his knees in front of him.
7He shouted at the top of his voice, "What
do you want with me, Jesus, Son of the
Most High God? Swear to God that you
won't torture me!" 8For Jesus had said to
him, "Come out of this man, you evil
spirit!"

9Then Jesus asked him, "What is your
name?"

"My name is Legion," he replied, "for
we are many." 10And he begged Jesus
again and again not to send them out of
the area.

11A large herd of pigs was feeding on
the nearby hillside. 12The demons begged

[a] 1 Some manuscripts *Gadarenes*; other manuscripts *Gergesenes* and 13 [b] 2 Greek *unclean*; also in verses 8

Jesus, "Send us among the pigs; allow us
to go into them." 13He gave them permis-
sion, and the evil spirits came out and
went into the pigs. The herd, about two
thousand in number, rushed down the
steep bank into the lake and were
drowned.

14Those tending the pigs ran off and re-
ported this in the town and countryside,
and the people went out to see what had
happened. 15When they came to Jesus,
they saw the man who had been pos-
sessed by the legion of demons, sitting
there, dressed and in his right mind; and
they were afraid. 16Those who had seen it
told the people what had happened to the
demon-possessed man—and told about
the pigs as well. 17Then the people began
to plead with Jesus to leave their region.

18As Jesus was getting into the boat, the
man who had been demon-possessed
begged to go with him. 19Jesus did not let
him, but said, "Go home to your family
and tell them how much the Lord has
done for you, and how he has had mercy
on you." 20So the man went away and be-
gan to tell in the Decapolis[a] how much
Jesus had done for him. And all the people
were amazed.

A Dead Girl and a Sick Woman

21When Jesus had again crossed over
by boat to the other side of the lake, a
large crowd gathered around him while he
was by the lake. 22Then one of the syna-
gogue rulers, named Jairus, came there.
Seeing Jesus, he fell at his feet 23and
pleaded earnestly with him, "My little
daughter is dying. Please come and put
your hands on her so that she will be
healed and live." 24So Jesus went with
him.

A large crowd followed and pressed
around him. 25And a woman was there
who had been subject to bleeding for
twelve years. 26She had suffered a great
deal under the care of many doctors and
had spent all she had, yet instead of get-
ting better she grew worse. 27When she
heard about Jesus, she came up behind
him in the crowd and touched his cloak,
28because she thought, "If I just touch his
clothes, I will be healed." 29Immediately
her bleeding stopped and she felt in her
body that she was freed from her suffer-
ing.

30At once Jesus realized that power had
gone out from him. He turned around in
the crowd and asked, "Who touched my
clothes?"

31"You see the people crowding against
you," his disciples answered, "and yet you
can ask, 'Who touched me?' "

32But Jesus kept looking around to see
who had done it. 33Then the woman,
knowing what had happened to her, came
and fell at his feet and, trembling with
fear, told him the whole truth. 34He said to
her, "Daughter, your faith has healed you.
Go in peace and be freed from your suffer-
ing."

35While Jesus was still speaking, some
men came from the house of Jairus, the
synagogue ruler. "Your daughter is dead,"
they said. "Why bother the teacher any
more?"

36Ignoring what they said, Jesus told
the synagogue ruler, "Don't be afraid; just
believe."

37He did not let anyone follow him ex-
cept Peter, James and John the brother of
James. 38When they came to the home of
the synagogue ruler, Jesus saw a commo-
tion, with people crying and wailing loud-
ly. 39He went in and said to them, "Why
all this commotion and wailing? The child
is not dead but asleep." 40But they
laughed at him.

After he put them all out, he took the
child's father and mother and the disci-
ples who were with him, and went in
where the child was. 41He took her by the
hand and said to her, *"Talitha koum!"*
(which means, "Little girl, I say to you, get
up!"). 42Immediately the girl stood up and
walked around (she was twelve years
old). At this they were completely aston-
ished. 43He gave strict orders not to let
anyone know about this, and told them to
give her something to eat.

A Prophet Without Honor

6 Jesus left there and went to his home-
town, accompanied by his disciples.
2When the Sabbath came, he began to
teach in the synagogue, and many who
heard him were amazed.

"Where did this man get these things?"
they asked. "What's this wisdom that has
been given him, that he even does mira-
cles! 3Isn't this the carpenter? Isn't this
Mary's son and the brother of James, Jo-
seph,[b] Judas and Simon? Aren't his sis-

[a]20 That is, the Ten Cities [b]3 Greek *Joses*, a variant of *Joseph*

ters here with us?" And they took offense at him.

4Jesus said to them, "Only in his hometown, among his relatives and in his own house is a prophet without honor." 5He could not do any miracles there, except lay his hands on a few sick people and heal them. 6And he was amazed at their lack of faith.

Jesus Sends Out the Twelve

Then Jesus went around teaching from village to village. 7Calling the Twelve to him, he sent them out two by two and gave them authority over evil[a] spirits.

8These were his instructions: "Take nothing for the journey except a staff—no bread, no bag, no money in your belts. 9Wear sandals but not an extra tunic. 10Whenever you enter a house, stay there until you leave that town. 11And if any place will not welcome you or listen to you, shake the dust off your feet when you leave, as a testimony against them."

12They went out and preached that people should repent. 13They drove out many demons and anointed many sick people with oil and healed them.

John the Baptist Beheaded

14King Herod heard about this, for Jesus' name had become well known. Some were saying,[b] "John the Baptist has been raised from the dead, and that is why miraculous powers are at work in him."

15Others said, "He is Elijah."

And still others claimed, "He is a prophet, like one of the prophets of long ago."

16But when Herod heard this, he said, "John, the man I beheaded, has been raised from the dead!"

17For Herod himself had given orders to have John arrested, and he had him bound and put in prison. He did this because of Herodias, his brother Philip's wife, whom he had married. 18For John had been saying to Herod, "It is not lawful for you to have your brother's wife." 19So Herodias nursed a grudge against John and wanted to kill him. But she was not able to, 20because Herod feared John and protected him, knowing him to be a righteous and holy man. When Herod heard John, he was greatly puzzled[c]; yet he liked to listen to him.

21Finally the opportune time came. On his birthday Herod gave a banquet for his high officials and military commanders and the leading men of Galilee. 22When the daughter of Herodias came in and danced, she pleased Herod and his dinner guests.

The king said to the girl, "Ask me for anything you want, and I'll give it to you." 23And he promised her with an oath, "Whatever you ask I will give you, up to half my kingdom."

24She went out and said to her mother, "What shall I ask for?"

"The head of John the Baptist," she answered.

25At once the girl hurried in to the king with the request: "I want you to give me right now the head of John the Baptist on a platter."

26The king was greatly distressed, but because of his oaths and his dinner guests, he did not want to refuse her. 27So he immediately sent an executioner with orders to bring John's head. The man went, beheaded John in the prison, 28and brought back his head on a platter. He presented it to the girl, and she gave it to her mother. 29On hearing of this, John's disciples came and took his body and laid it in a tomb.

Jesus Feeds the Five Thousand

30The apostles gathered around Jesus and reported to him all they had done and taught. 31Then, because so many people were coming and going that they did not even have a chance to eat, he said to them, "Come with me by yourselves to a quiet place and get some rest."

32So they went away by themselves in a boat to a solitary place. 33But many who saw them leaving recognized them and ran on foot from all the towns and got there ahead of them. 34When Jesus landed and saw a large crowd, he had compassion on them, because they were like sheep without a shepherd. So he began teaching them many things.

35By this time it was late in the day, so his disciples came to him. "This is a remote place," they said, "and it's already very late. 36Send the people away so they can go to the surrounding countryside and villages and buy themselves something to eat."

[a] 7 Greek *unclean*
[b] 14 Some early manuscripts *He was saying many things*
[c] 20 Some early manuscripts *he did*

37But he answered, "You give them
something to eat."
They said to him, "That would take
eight months of a man's wages[a]! Are we
to go and spend that much on bread and
give it to them to eat?"
38"How many loaves do you have?" he
asked. "Go and see."
When they found out, they said,
"Five—and two fish."
39Then Jesus directed them to have all
the people sit down in groups on the
green grass. 40So they sat down in groups
of hundreds and fifties. 41Taking the five
loaves and the two fish and looking up to
heaven, he gave thanks and broke the
loaves. Then he gave them to his disciples
to set before the people. He also divided
the two fish among them all. 42They all ate
and were satisfied, 43and the disciples
picked up twelve basketfuls of broken
pieces of bread and fish. 44The number of
the men who had eaten was five thousand.

Jesus Walks on the Water

45Immediately Jesus made his disciples
get into the boat and go on ahead of him
to Bethsaida, while he dismissed the
crowd. 46After leaving them, he went up
on a mountainside to pray.
47When evening came, the boat was in
the middle of the lake, and he was alone
on land. 48He saw the disciples straining
at the oars, because the wind was against
them. About the fourth watch of the night
he went out to them, walking on the lake.
He was about to pass by them, 49but when
they saw him walking on the lake, they
thought he was a ghost. They cried out,
50because they all saw him and were terrified.
Immediately he spoke to them and said,
"Take courage! It is I. Don't be afraid."
51Then he climbed into the boat with
them, and the wind died down. They were
completely amazed, 52for they had not understood about the loaves; their hearts
were hardened.
53When they had crossed over, they
landed at Gennesaret and anchored there.
54As soon as they got out of the boat, people recognized Jesus. 55They ran throughout that whole region and carried the sick
on mats to wherever they heard he was.
56And wherever he went—into villages,
towns or countryside—they placed the
sick in the marketplaces. They begged
him to let them touch even the edge of his
cloak, and all who touched him were
healed.

Clean and Unclean

7 The Pharisees and some of the teachers of the law who had come from Jerusalem gathered around Jesus and 2saw
some of his disciples eating food with
hands that were "unclean," that is, unwashed. 3(The Pharisees and all the Jews
do not eat unless they give their hands a
ceremonial washing, holding to the tradition of the elders. 4When they come from
the marketplace they do not eat unless
they wash. And they observe many other
traditions, such as the washing of cups,
pitchers and kettles.[b])
5So the Pharisees and teachers of the
law asked Jesus, "Why don't your disciples live according to the tradition of the
elders instead of eating their food with
'unclean' hands?"
6He replied, "Isaiah was right when he
prophesied about you hypocrites; as it is
written:

" 'These people honor me with their
lips,
but their hearts are far from me.
7They worship me in vain;
their teachings are but rules taught
by men.'[c]

8You have let go of the commands of God
and are holding on to the traditions of
men."
9And he said to them: "You have a fine
way of setting aside the commands of God
in order to observe[d] your own traditions!
10For Moses said, 'Honor your father and
your mother,'[e] and, 'Anyone who curses
his father or mother must be put to
death.'[f] 11But you say that if a man says
to his father or mother: 'Whatever help
you might otherwise have received from
me is Corban' (that is, a gift devoted to
God), 12then you no longer let him do anything for his father or mother. 13Thus you
nullify the word of God by your tradition
that you have handed down. And you do
many things like that."
14Again Jesus called the crowd to him

[a]*37* Greek *take two hundred denarii* [b]*4* Some early manuscripts *pitchers, kettles and dining couches*
[c]*6,7* Isaiah 29:13 [d]*9* Some manuscripts *set up* [e]*10* Exodus 20:12; Deut. 5:16 [f]*10* Exodus 21:17; Lev. 20:9

and said, "Listen to me, everyone, and understand this. 15Nothing outside a man can make him 'unclean' by going into him. Rather, it is what comes out of a man that makes him 'unclean.'[a]"

17After he had left the crowd and entered the house, his disciples asked him about this parable. 18"Are you so dull?" he asked. "Don't you see that nothing that enters a man from the outside can make him 'unclean'? 19For it doesn't go into his heart but into his stomach, and then out of his body." (In saying this, Jesus declared all foods "clean.")

20He went on: "What comes out of a man is what makes him 'unclean.' 21For from within, out of men's hearts, come evil thoughts, sexual immorality, theft, murder, adultery, 22greed, malice, deceit, lewdness, envy, slander, arrogance and folly. 23All these evils come from inside and make a man 'unclean.' "

The Faith of a Syrophoenician Woman

24Jesus left that place and went to the vicinity of Tyre.[b] He entered a house and did not want anyone to know it; yet he could not keep his presence secret. 25In fact, as soon as she heard about him, a woman whose little daughter was possessed by an evil[c] spirit came and fell at his feet. 26The woman was a Greek, born in Syrian Phoenicia. She begged Jesus to drive the demon out of her daughter.

27"First let the children eat all they want," he told her, "for it is not right to take the children's bread and toss it to their dogs."

28"Yes, Lord," she replied, "but even the dogs under the table eat the children's crumbs."

29Then he told her, "For such a reply, you may go; the demon has left your daughter."

30She went home and found her child lying on the bed, and the demon gone.

The Healing of a Deaf and Mute Man

31Then Jesus left the vicinity of Tyre and went through Sidon, down to the Sea of Galilee and into the region of the Decapolis.[d] 32There some people brought to him a man who was deaf and could hardly talk, and they begged him to place his hand on the man.

33After he took him aside, away from the crowd, Jesus put his fingers into the man's ears. Then he spit and touched the man's tongue. 34He looked up to heaven and with a deep sigh said to him, "*Ephphatha!*" (which means, "Be opened!"). 35At this, the man's ears were opened, his tongue was loosened and he began to speak plainly.

36Jesus commanded them not to tell anyone. But the more he did so, the more they kept talking about it. 37People were overwhelmed with amazement. "He has done everything well," they said. "He even makes the deaf hear and the mute speak."

Jesus Feeds the Four Thousand

8 During those days another large crowd gathered. Since they had nothing to eat, Jesus called his disciples to him and said, 2"I have compassion for these people; they have already been with me three days and have nothing to eat. 3If I send them home hungry, they will collapse on the way, because some of them have come a long distance."

4His disciples answered, "But where in this remote place can anyone get enough bread to feed them?"

5"How many loaves do you have?" Jesus asked.

"Seven," they replied.

6He told the crowd to sit down on the ground. When he had taken the seven loaves and given thanks, he broke them and gave them to his disciples to set before the people, and they did so. 7They had a few small fish as well; he gave thanks for them also and told the disciples to distribute them. 8The people ate and were satisfied. Afterward the disciples picked up seven basketfuls of broken pieces that were left over. 9About four thousand men were present. And having sent them away, 10he got into the boat with his disciples and went to the region of Dalmanutha.

11The Pharisees came and began to question Jesus. To test him, they asked him for a sign from heaven. 12He sighed deeply and said, "Why does this generation ask for a miraculous sign? I tell you the truth, no sign will be given to it."

[a]15 Some early manuscripts *'unclean.' 16If anyone has ears to hear, let him hear.* [b]24 Many early manuscripts *Tyre and Sidon* [c]25 Greek *unclean* [d]31 That is, the Ten Cities

VERSE FOR THE DAY: Mark 8:8

AUTHOR: Donna Lobs

PASSAGE FOR THE DAY: Mark 8:1–13

The Bare Cupboard

One wintry Sunday, my husband, our daughter and I visited a church official and his family. Tom, Martha and their children were leaving the next morning for an extended vacation, so we helped them empty their pantry. But a short while later unexpected guests arrived.

I followed Martha into the empty kitchen, wondering if I was about to witness a loaves-and-fishes miracle. She opened the refrigerator and took out a forgotten lettuce leaf. Then she unwrapped a three-day-old loaf of French bread, saying "A few drops of water and five minutes in the oven and it will be as good as new."

A corner of the refrigerator yielded up two hard-boiled eggs, which she peeled and chopped. There was a near-empty bottle of salad dressing. Martha dribbled a few drops of water into the bottle and smacked it until a dollop fell onto the eggs. We seasoned the "egg salad," spread it on the sliced bread, and slid the sandwiches under the broiler.

Martha set the table. The sandwiches and six leftover cookies sat next to a silver teapot. "The food is ready," Martha announced.

I looked at glowing faces and listened to lively reminiscences of the past and talk of future hopes. I thought of Jesus and his disciples and their simple suppers of bread and fish. On that chilly afternoon, I saw that the spirit of sharing is the essence of true hospitality. Even if you serve egg salad on old bread.

MARRIAGE BUILDERS

♦ *How have you practiced hospitality in the last month? Have you been generous in ways that required you to trust in God?*
♦ *In God's economy, five loaves of bread and two fish could feed 5,000 people. How have you seen God provide for your family?*

Additional Scripture Readings
Matthew 14:13–21; Hebrews 13:1–2; Romans 12:11–13

Go to page 1083 for your next devotional reading.

13Then he left them, got back into the boat
and crossed to the other side.

The Yeast of the Pharisees and Herod

14The disciples had forgotten to bring
bread, except for one loaf they had with
them in the boat. 15"Be careful," Jesus
warned them. "Watch out for the yeast of
the Pharisees and that of Herod."
16They discussed this with one another
and said, "It is because we have no bread."
17Aware of their discussion, Jesus asked
them: "Why are you talking about having
no bread? Do you still not see or understand? Are your hearts hardened? 18Do
you have eyes but fail to see, and ears but
fail to hear? And don't you remember?
19When I broke the five loaves for the five
thousand, how many basketfuls of pieces
did you pick up?"
"Twelve," they replied.
20"And when I broke the seven loaves
for the four thousand, how many basketfuls of pieces did you pick up?"
They answered, "Seven."
21He said to them, "Do you still not understand?"

The Healing of a Blind Man at Bethsaida

22They came to Bethsaida, and some
people brought a blind man and begged
Jesus to touch him. 23He took the blind
man by the hand and led him outside the
village. When he had spit on the man's
eyes and put his hands on him, Jesus
asked, "Do you see anything?"
24He looked up and said, "I see people;
they look like trees walking around."
25Once more Jesus put his hands on the
man's eyes. Then his eyes were opened,
his sight was restored, and he saw everything clearly. 26Jesus sent him home, saying, "Don't go into the village.[a]"

Peter's Confession of Christ

27Jesus and his disciples went on to the
villages around Caesarea Philippi. On the
way he asked them, "Who do people say
I am?"
28They replied, "Some say John the
Baptist; others say Elijah; and still others,
one of the prophets."
29"But what about you?" he asked.
"Who do you say I am?"
Peter answered, "You are the Christ.[b]"
30Jesus warned them not to tell anyone
about him.

Jesus Predicts His Death

31He then began to teach them that the
Son of Man must suffer many things and
be rejected by the elders, chief priests and
teachers of the law, and that he must be
killed and after three days rise again. 32He
spoke plainly about this, and Peter took
him aside and began to rebuke him.
33But when Jesus turned and looked at
his disciples, he rebuked Peter. "Get behind me, Satan!" he said. "You do not
have in mind the things of God, but the
things of men."
34Then he called the crowd to him along
with his disciples and said: "If anyone
would come after me, he must deny himself and take up his cross and follow me.
35For whoever wants to save his life[c] will
lose it, but whoever loses his life for me
and for the gospel will save it. 36What
good is it for a man to gain the whole
world, yet forfeit his soul? 37Or what can
a man give in exchange for his soul? 38If
anyone is ashamed of me and my words
in this adulterous and sinful generation,
the Son of Man will be ashamed of him
when he comes in his Father's glory with
the holy angels."
9 And he said to them, "I tell you the
truth, some who are standing here
will not taste death before they see the
kingdom of God come with power."

The Transfiguration

2After six days Jesus took Peter, James
and John with him and led them up a high
mountain, where they were all alone.
There he was transfigured before them.
3His clothes became dazzling white, whiter than anyone in the world could bleach
them. 4And there appeared before them
Elijah and Moses, who were talking with
Jesus.
5Peter said to Jesus, "Rabbi, it is good
for us to be here. Let us put up three shelters—one for you, one for Moses and one
for Elijah." 6(He did not know what to say,
they were so frightened.)
7Then a cloud appeared and enveloped
them, and a voice came from the cloud:

[a]26 Some manuscripts *Don't go and tell anyone in the village* and "the Messiah" (Hebrew) both mean "the Anointed One."

[b]29 Or *Messiah.* "The Christ" (Greek)

[c]35 The Greek word means either *life* or *soul*; also in verse 36.

WEEKENDING

SERVING

At its best, marriage is a relationship in which two people serve each other, as well as others outside the marriage. But too often, the additional responsibilities of marriage, work, friends and extended family result in our investing too little energy in acts of ministry. These questions will help you consider your ministry involvements both individually *and* as a couple.

1. Are both of you satisfied with your current level of church involvement—individually and as a couple?

2. If not, is it because one or both of you feel that your gifts are not being used effectively? Because you are unsure where you might like to serve?

3. Do you feel you are devoting too little time, too much time, or the right amount of time to *individual* ministry projects? To *shared* ministry projects (serving together on church committees, co-leading a Bible study group, etc.)?

— *The* Marriage Partnership *Staff*

REVIVE

Saturday: Psalm 122:1–9
Sunday: Nehemiah 10:34–39

Go to page 1085 for your next devotional reading.

"This is my Son, whom I love. Listen to him!"

8Suddenly, when they looked around, they no longer saw anyone with them except Jesus.

9As they were coming down the mountain, Jesus gave them orders not to tell anyone what they had seen until the Son of Man had risen from the dead. 10They kept the matter to themselves, discussing what "rising from the dead" meant.

11And they asked him, "Why do the teachers of the law say that Elijah must come first?"

12Jesus replied, "To be sure, Elijah does come first, and restores all things. Why then is it written that the Son of Man must suffer much and be rejected? 13But I tell you, Elijah has come, and they have done to him everything they wished, just as it is written about him."

The Healing of a Boy With an Evil Spirit

14When they came to the other disciples, they saw a large crowd around them and the teachers of the law arguing with them. 15As soon as all the people saw Jesus, they were overwhelmed with wonder and ran to greet him.

16"What are you arguing with them about?" he asked.

17A man in the crowd answered, "Teacher, I brought you my son, who is possessed by a spirit that has robbed him of speech. 18Whenever it seizes him, it throws him to the ground. He foams at the mouth, gnashes his teeth and becomes rigid. I asked your disciples to drive out the spirit, but they could not."

19"O unbelieving generation," Jesus replied, "how long shall I stay with you? How long shall I put up with you? Bring the boy to me."

20So they brought him. When the spirit saw Jesus, it immediately threw the boy into a convulsion. He fell to the ground and rolled around, foaming at the mouth.

21Jesus asked the boy's father, "How long has he been like this?"

"From childhood," he answered. 22"It has often thrown him into fire or water to kill him. But if you can do anything, take pity on us and help us."

23" 'If you can'?" said Jesus. "Everything is possible for him who believes."

24Immediately the boy's father exclaimed, "I do believe; help me overcome my unbelief!"

25When Jesus saw that a crowd was running to the scene, he rebuked the evil[a] spirit. "You deaf and mute spirit," he said, "I command you, come out of him and never enter him again."

26The spirit shrieked, convulsed him violently and came out. The boy looked so much like a corpse that many said, "He's dead." 27But Jesus took him by the hand and lifted him to his feet, and he stood up.

28After Jesus had gone indoors, his disciples asked him privately, "Why couldn't we drive it out?"

29He replied, "This kind can come out only by prayer.[b]"

30They left that place and passed through Galilee. Jesus did not want anyone to know where they were, 31because he was teaching his disciples. He said to them, "The Son of Man is going to be betrayed into the hands of men. They will kill him, and after three days he will rise." 32But they did not understand what he meant and were afraid to ask him about it.

Who Is the Greatest?

33They came to Capernaum. When he was in the house, he asked them, "What were you arguing about on the road?" 34But they kept quiet because on the way they had argued about who was the greatest.

35Sitting down, Jesus called the Twelve and said, "If anyone wants to be first, he must be the very last, and the servant of all."

36He took a little child and had him stand among them. Taking him in his arms, he said to them, 37"Whoever welcomes one of these little children in my name welcomes me; and whoever welcomes me does not welcome me but the one who sent me."

Whoever Is Not Against Us Is for Us

38"Teacher," said John, "we saw a man driving out demons in your name and we told him to stop, because he was not one of us."

39"Do not stop him," Jesus said. "No one who does a miracle in my name can in the next moment say anything bad about me, 40for whoever is not against us is for us. 41I tell you the truth, anyone who gives you a cup of water in my name be-

[a] 25 Greek *unclean* [b] 29 Some manuscripts *prayer and fasting*

cause you belong to Christ will certainly not lose his reward.

Causing to Sin

42"And if anyone causes one of these little ones who believe in me to sin, it would be better for him to be thrown into the sea with a large millstone tied around his neck. 43If your hand causes you to sin, cut it off. It is better for you to enter life maimed than with two hands to go into hell, where the fire never goes out.[a] 45And if your foot causes you to sin, cut it off. It is better for you to enter life crippled than to have two feet and be thrown into hell.[b] 47And if your eye causes you to sin, pluck it out. It is better for you to enter the kingdom of God with one eye than to have two eyes and be thrown into hell, 48where

" 'their worm does not die,
and the fire is not quenched.'[c]

49Everyone will be salted with fire.

50"Salt is good, but if it loses its salti-

[a]43 Some manuscripts *out,* 44*where / " 'their worm does not die, / and the fire is not quenched.'*
[b]45 Some manuscripts *hell,* 46*where / " 'their worm does not die, / and the fire is not quenched.'*
[c]48 Isaiah 66:24

VERSE FOR THE DAY: Mark 9:23

AUTHOR: Stuart Briscoe

PASSAGE FOR THE DAY: Mark 9:14–27

God's Provision

Jill was asked to give a commencement address to a secular group of three hundred students and their families. She felt it was too much of a challenge. After all, she hadn't been asked to preach, and she wondered how she could give a speech that could still be used for the Lord and yet not overstep the school's boundary.

She was going to turn down the invitation, but I fished her declining letter out of her correspondence basket and told her, "What a wonderful opportunity. You have to do this."

She did such a good job that she was invited back for three or four consecutive years! And that's not all. The head of the school eventually came to the Lord, and also his wife.

Don't think in terms of impossible situations. If God calls you to some work, he equips you for it. With God, you go ahead and work in the arena of impossibility, reckoning on his resources.

MARRIAGE BUILDERS

♦ *Describe a time when you were amazed at the way God provided in some difficult, or seemingly impossible, situation.*

♦ *What aspects of serving the Lord seem frightening or threatening?*

Additional Scripture Readings
Philippians 4:13; Ephesians 3:20–21

Go to page 1087 for your next devotional reading.

ness, how can you make it salty again?
Have salt in yourselves, and be at peace
with each other."

Divorce

10 Jesus then left that place and went
into the region of Judea and across
the Jordan. Again crowds of people came
to him, and as was his custom, he taught
them.

2Some Pharisees came and tested him
by asking, "Is it lawful for a man to di-
vorce his wife?"

3"What did Moses command you?" he
replied.

4They said, "Moses permitted a man to
write a certificate of divorce and send her
away."

5"It was because your hearts were hard
that Moses wrote you this law," Jesus re-
plied. 6"But at the beginning of creation
God 'made them male and female.'[a] 7'For
this reason a man will leave his father and
mother and be united to his wife,[b] 8and
the two will become one flesh.'[c] So they
are no longer two, but one. 9Therefore
what God has joined together, let man not
separate."

10When they were in the house again,
the disciples asked Jesus about this. 11He
answered, "Anyone who divorces his wife
and marries another woman commits
adultery against her. 12And if she divorces
her husband and marries another man,
she commits adultery."

The Little Children and Jesus

13People were bringing little children to
Jesus to have him touch them, but the dis-
ciples rebuked them. 14When Jesus saw
this, he was indignant. He said to them,
"Let the little children come to me, and do
not hinder them, for the kingdom of God
belongs to such as these. 15I tell you the
truth, anyone who will not receive the
kingdom of God like a little child will nev-
er enter it." 16And he took the children in
his arms, put his hands on them and
blessed them.

The Rich Young Man

17As Jesus started on his way, a man ran
up to him and fell on his knees before
him. "Good teacher," he asked, "what
must I do to inherit eternal life?"

18"Why do you call me good?" Jesus an-
swered. "No one is good—except God
alone. 19You know the commandments:
'Do not murder, do not commit adultery,
do not steal, do not give false testimony,
do not defraud, honor your father and
mother.'[d]"

20"Teacher," he declared, "all these I
have kept since I was a boy."

21Jesus looked at him and loved him.
"One thing you lack," he said. "Go, sell ev-
erything you have and give to the poor,
and you will have treasure in heaven.
Then come, follow me."

22At this the man's face fell. He went
away sad, because he had great wealth.

23Jesus looked around and said to his
disciples, "How hard it is for the rich to
enter the kingdom of God!"

24The disciples were amazed at his
words. But Jesus said again, "Children,
how hard it is[e] to enter the kingdom of
God! 25It is easier for a camel to go
through the eye of a needle than for a rich
man to enter the kingdom of God."

26The disciples were even more
amazed, and said to each other, "Who
then can be saved?"

27Jesus looked at them and said, "With
man this is impossible, but not with God;
all things are possible with God."

28Peter said to him, "We have left every-
thing to follow you!"

29"I tell you the truth," Jesus replied,
"no one who has left home or brothers or
sisters or mother or father or children or
fields for me and the gospel 30will fail to
receive a hundred times as much in this
present age (homes, brothers, sisters,
mothers, children and fields—and with
them, persecutions) and in the age to
come, eternal life. 31But many who are
first will be last, and the last first."

Jesus Again Predicts His Death

32They were on their way up to Jerusa-
lem, with Jesus leading the way, and the
disciples were astonished, while those
who followed were afraid. Again he took
the Twelve aside and told them what was
going to happen to him. 33"We are going
up to Jerusalem," he said, "and the Son of
Man will be betrayed to the chief priests
and teachers of the law. They will con-
demn him to death and will hand him
over to the Gentiles, 34who will mock him

[a] 6 Gen. 1:27 [b] 7 Some early manuscripts do not have *and be united to his wife.* [c] 8 Gen. 2:24
[d] 19 Exodus 20:12-16; Deut. 5:16-20 [e] 24 Some manuscripts *is for those who trust in riches*

and spit on him, flog him and kill him.
Three days later he will rise."

The Request of James and John

35Then James and John, the sons of
Zebedee, came to him. "Teacher," they
said, "we want you to do for us whatever
we ask."
36"What do you want me to do for you?"
he asked.
37They replied, "Let one of us sit at your
right and the other at your left in your
glory."
38"You don't know what you are ask-
ing," Jesus said. "Can you drink the cup I
drink or be baptized with the baptism I
am baptized with?"
39"We can," they answered.
Jesus said to them, "You will drink the
cup I drink and be baptized with the bap-
tism I am baptized with, 40but to sit at my
right or left is not for me to grant. These
places belong to those for whom they
have been prepared."
41When the ten heard about this, they
became indignant with James and John.
42Jesus called them together and said,
"You know that those who are regarded as
rulers of the Gentiles lord it over them,
and their high officials exercise authority
over them. 43Not so with you. Instead,

VERSE FOR THE DAY: Mark 10:43–45

AUTHOR: Jay Kesler

PASSAGE FOR THE DAY: Mark 10:35–45

Leading by Serving

Leadership and respect can't be demanded, but they can be commanded. We command leadership and respect by earning it.

Being a spiritual leader is not as much what you *do* as what you *are*. The Bible tells us the fruit of the spirit is the hallmark of the believer. And the fruit of the spirit is love, joy, peace, patience, kindness, goodness, faithfulness, gentleness and self-control (Galatians 5:22–23). These are things we're to practice every moment of every day. When a man consistently practices walking in the spirit not just in his public life, but also when he's with his wife and children, he becomes a spiritual leader.

Jesus made it clear that Christian leadership isn't power. The essence of spiritual leadership is the same as the essence of Christianity; we are called to be servants. The man who best serves his family will be a true leader.

MARRIAGE BUILDERS

♦ *Do you agree that "being a spiritual leader is not as much what you* do *as what you* are*"? Why?*
♦ *What are some ways you can provide leadership in your marriage by serving your spouse?*

Additional Scripture Readings
1 Samuel 2:11; Galatians 5:16–18, 22–23

Go to page 1089 for your next devotional reading.

whoever wants to become great among
you must be your servant, 44and whoever
wants to be first must be slave of all. 45For
even the Son of Man did not come to be
served, but to serve, and to give his life as
a ransom for many."

Blind Bartimaeus Receives His Sight

46Then they came to Jericho. As Jesus
and his disciples, together with a large
crowd, were leaving the city, a blind man,
Bartimaeus (that is, the Son of Timaeus),
was sitting by the roadside begging.
47When he heard that it was Jesus of Naz-
areth, he began to shout, "Jesus, Son of
David, have mercy on me!"

48Many rebuked him and told him to be
quiet, but he shouted all the more, "Son of
David, have mercy on me!"

49Jesus stopped and said, "Call him."

So they called to the blind man, "Cheer
up! On your feet! He's calling you."
50Throwing his cloak aside, he jumped to
his feet and came to Jesus.

51"What do you want me to do for you?"
Jesus asked him.

The blind man said, "Rabbi, I want to
see."

52"Go," said Jesus, "your faith has
healed you." Immediately he received his
sight and followed Jesus along the road.

The Triumphal Entry

11 As they approached Jerusalem and
came to Bethphage and Bethany at
the Mount of Olives, Jesus sent two of his
disciples, 2saying to them, "Go to the vil-
lage ahead of you, and just as you enter it,
you will find a colt tied there, which no
one has ever ridden. Untie it and bring it
here. 3If anyone asks you, 'Why are you
doing this?' tell him, 'The Lord needs it
and will send it back here shortly.'"

4They went and found a colt outside in
the street, tied at a doorway. As they un-
tied it, 5some people standing there asked,
"What are you doing, untying that colt?"
6They answered as Jesus had told them to,
and the people let them go. 7When they
brought the colt to Jesus and threw their
cloaks over it, he sat on it. 8Many people
spread their cloaks on the road, while oth-
ers spread branches they had cut in the
fields. 9Those who went ahead and those
who followed shouted,

"Hosanna![a]"

"Blessed is he who comes in the name
of the Lord!"[b]

10"Blessed is the coming kingdom of
our father David!"

"Hosanna in the highest!"

11Jesus entered Jerusalem and went to
the temple. He looked around at every-
thing, but since it was already late, he
went out to Bethany with the Twelve.

Jesus Clears the Temple

12The next day as they were leaving
Bethany, Jesus was hungry. 13Seeing in
the distance a fig tree in leaf, he went to
find out if it had any fruit. When he
reached it, he found nothing but leaves,
because it was not the season for figs.
14Then he said to the tree, "May no one
ever eat fruit from you again." And his dis-
ciples heard him say it.

15On reaching Jerusalem, Jesus entered
the temple area and began driving out
those who were buying and selling there.
He overturned the tables of the money
changers and the benches of those selling
doves, 16and would not allow anyone to
carry merchandise through the temple
courts. 17And as he taught them, he said,
"Is it not written:

" 'My house will be called
a house of prayer for all nations'[c]?

But you have made it 'a den of rob-
bers.'[d]"

18The chief priests and the teachers of
the law heard this and began looking for
a way to kill him, for they feared him, be-
cause the whole crowd was amazed at his
teaching.

19When evening came, they[e] went out
of the city.

The Withered Fig Tree

20In the morning, as they went along,
they saw the fig tree withered from the
roots. 21Peter remembered and said to
Jesus, "Rabbi, look! The fig tree you
cursed has withered!"

22"Have[f] faith in God," Jesus an-
swered. 23"I tell you the truth, if anyone
says to this mountain, 'Go, throw yourself

[a] 9 A Hebrew expression meaning "Save!" which became an exclamation of praise; also in verse 10
[b] 9 Psalm 118:25,26 [c] 17 Isaiah 56:7 [d] 17 Jer. 7:11 [e] 19 Some early manuscripts *he*
[f] 22 Some early manuscripts *If you have*

into the sea,' and does not doubt in his
heart but believes that what he says will
happen, it will be done for him. 24Therefore I tell you, whatever you ask for in
prayer, believe that you have received it,
and it will be yours. 25And when you
stand praying, if you hold anything
against anyone, forgive him, so that your
Father in heaven may forgive you your
sins.[a]"

The Authority of Jesus Questioned

27They arrived again in Jerusalem, and
while Jesus was walking in the temple
courts, the chief priests, the teachers of
the law and the elders came to him. 28"By
what authority are you doing these
things?" they asked. "And who gave you
authority to do this?"

29Jesus replied, "I will ask you one
question. Answer me, and I will tell you
by what authority I am doing these things.
30John's baptism—was it from heaven, or
from men? Tell me!"

31They discussed it among themselves
and said, "If we say, 'From heaven,' he
will ask, 'Then why didn't you believe
him?' 32But if we say, 'From men' . . . ."
(They feared the people, for everyone
held that John really was a prophet.)

[a]25 Some manuscripts *sins.* 26*But if you do not forgive, neither will your Father who is in heaven forgive your sins.*

WEDNESDAY

VERSE FOR THE DAY: Mark 11:25 | AUTHOR: Lewis Smedes | PASSAGE FOR THE DAY: Mark 11:20–25

One at a Time

When forgiving your spouse for something, it's important to be concrete. Forgiveness must be so specific that before we even think about forgiving, we should write down the exact thing we need to forgive. We should not forgive someone for "being a bad person." Forgive what somebody does, not what he or she is. Piece by piece, one thing at a time.

Don't forgive a spouse for being someone who always does something wrong. I once had a habit of saying to my wife, "You always do this!" It made things difficult for Doris, because if I tried to forgive her, I would be accusing her of being the kind of person who always did something that hurt me. God can forgive wholesale, but we have to do it retail—one thing at a time.

MARRIAGE BUILDERS

♦ *Do you have a tendency to generalize specific things your spouse does wrong into character assassination?*

♦ *How can you separate what he or she* does *from who he or she* is?

Additional Scripture Readings
Matthew 6:14–15; 18:21–35;
John 20:22–23

Go to page 1091 for your next devotional reading.

33So they answered Jesus, "We don't know."

Jesus said, "Neither will I tell you by what authority I am doing these things."

The Parable of the Tenants

12 He then began to speak to them in parables: "A man planted a vineyard. He put a wall around it, dug a pit for the winepress and built a watchtower. Then he rented the vineyard to some farmers and went away on a journey. 2At harvest time he sent a servant to the tenants to collect from them some of the fruit of the vineyard. 3But they seized him, beat him and sent him away empty-handed. 4Then he sent another servant to them; they struck this man on the head and treated him shamefully. 5He sent still another, and that one they killed. He sent many others; some of them they beat, others they killed.

6"He had one left to send, a son, whom he loved. He sent him last of all, saying, 'They will respect my son.'

7"But the tenants said to one another, 'This is the heir. Come, let's kill him, and the inheritance will be ours.' 8So they took him and killed him, and threw him out of the vineyard.

9"What then will the owner of the vineyard do? He will come and kill those tenants and give the vineyard to others. 10Haven't you read this scripture:

" 'The stone the builders rejected
has become the capstone[a];
11the Lord has done this,
and it is marvelous in our eyes'[b]?"

12Then they looked for a way to arrest him because they knew he had spoken the parable against them. But they were afraid of the crowd; so they left him and went away.

Paying Taxes to Caesar

13Later they sent some of the Pharisees and Herodians to Jesus to catch him in his words. 14They came to him and said, "Teacher, we know you are a man of integrity. You aren't swayed by men, because you pay no attention to who they are; but you teach the way of God in accordance with the truth. Is it right to pay taxes to Caesar or not? 15Should we pay or shouldn't we?"

But Jesus knew their hypocrisy. "Why are you trying to trap me?" he asked. "Bring me a denarius and let me look at it." 16They brought the coin, and he asked them, "Whose portrait is this? And whose inscription?"

"Caesar's," they replied.

17Then Jesus said to them, "Give to Caesar what is Caesar's and to God what is God's."

And they were amazed at him.

Marriage at the Resurrection

18Then the Sadducees, who say there is no resurrection, came to him with a question. 19"Teacher," they said, "Moses wrote for us that if a man's brother dies and leaves a wife but no children, the man must marry the widow and have children for his brother. 20Now there were seven brothers. The first one married and died without leaving any children. 21The second one married the widow, but he also died, leaving no child. It was the same with the third. 22In fact, none of the seven left any children. Last of all, the woman died too. 23At the resurrection[c] whose wife will she be, since the seven were married to her?"

24Jesus replied, "Are you not in error because you do not know the Scriptures or the power of God? 25When the dead rise, they will neither marry nor be given in marriage; they will be like the angels in heaven. 26Now about the dead rising—have you not read in the book of Moses, in the account of the bush, how God said to him, 'I am the God of Abraham, the God of Isaac, and the God of Jacob'[d]? 27He is not the God of the dead, but of the living. You are badly mistaken!"

The Greatest Commandment

28One of the teachers of the law came and heard them debating. Noticing that Jesus had given them a good answer, he asked him, "Of all the commandments, which is the most important?"

29"The most important one," answered Jesus, "is this: 'Hear, O Israel, the Lord our God, the Lord is one.[e] 30Love the Lord your God with all your heart and with all your soul and with all your mind and with all your strength.'[f] 31The second is this:

[a]10 Or *cornerstone* [b]11 Psalm 118:22,23 [c]23 Some manuscripts *resurrection, when men rise from the dead,* [d]26 Exodus 3:6 [e]29 Or *the Lord our God is one Lord* [f]30 Deut. 6:4,5

'Love your neighbor as yourself.'[a] There
is no commandment greater than these."
32"Well said, teacher," the man replied.
"You are right in saying that God is one
and there is no other but him. 33To love
him with all your heart, with all your un-
derstanding and with all your strength,
and to love your neighbor as yourself is
more important than all burnt offerings
and sacrifices."
34When Jesus saw that he had an-
swered wisely, he said to him, "You are
not far from the kingdom of God." And
from then on no one dared ask him any
more questions.

Whose Son Is the Christ?

35While Jesus was teaching in the tem-
ple courts, he asked, "How is it that the
teachers of the law say that the Christ[b] is
the son of David? 36David himself, speak-
ing by the Holy Spirit, declared:

" 'The Lord said to my Lord:
"Sit at my right hand
until I put your enemies
under your feet." '[c]

37David himself calls him 'Lord.' How
then can he be his son?"
The large crowd listened to him with
delight.
38As he taught, Jesus said, "Watch out
for the teachers of the law. They like to
walk around in flowing robes and be
greeted in the marketplaces, 39and have
the most important seats in the syna-
gogues and the places of honor at ban-
quets. 40They devour widows' houses and

[a]31 Lev. 19:18 [b]35 Or *Messiah* [c]36 Psalm 110:1

VERSE FOR THE DAY: Mark 12:31

AUTHOR: Larry Crabb

PASSAGE FOR THE DAY: Mark 12:28–34

Committed to Love

These days, there is a widespread belief that the *real* problem people have in their relationships is they haven't learned to take care of themselves properly. I recently listened to a Christian speaker citing Jesus' teaching that we should love others as we love ourselves. He said, "We're all pretty good at loving others; our problem is loving ourselves." When I heard that, I about threw up.

I believe exactly the reverse: Scripture does not justify learning how to love yourself before you love others. What the Lord is saying is, "Love others with the same kind of commitment that you already have to loving yourself."

MARRIAGE BUILDERS

- *What do you think "loving yourself" means?*
- *Why are you responsible to love others, even if your self-esteem is sometimes low?*

Additional Scripture Readings
Romans 13:9–10; Galatians 5:14; James 2:8

Go to page 1100 for your next devotional reading.

for a show make lengthy prayers. Such men will be punished most severely."

The Widow's Offering

41Jesus sat down opposite the place where the offerings were put and watched the crowd putting their money into the temple treasury. Many rich people threw in large amounts. 42But a poor widow came and put in two very small copper coins,[a] worth only a fraction of a penny.[b]

43Calling his disciples to him, Jesus said, "I tell you the truth, this poor widow has put more into the treasury than all the others. 44They all gave out of their wealth; but she, out of her poverty, put in everything—all she had to live on."

Signs of the End of the Age

13 As he was leaving the temple, one of his disciples said to him, "Look, Teacher! What massive stones! What magnificent buildings!"

2"Do you see all these great buildings?" replied Jesus. "Not one stone here will be left on another; every one will be thrown down."

3As Jesus was sitting on the Mount of Olives opposite the temple, Peter, James, John and Andrew asked him privately, 4"Tell us, when will these things happen? And what will be the sign that they are all about to be fulfilled?"

5Jesus said to them: "Watch out that no one deceives you. 6Many will come in my name, claiming, 'I am he,' and will deceive many. 7When you hear of wars and rumors of wars, do not be alarmed. Such things must happen, but the end is still to come. 8Nation will rise against nation, and kingdom against kingdom. There will be earthquakes in various places, and famines. These are the beginning of birth pains.

9"You must be on your guard. You will be handed over to the local councils and flogged in the synagogues. On account of me you will stand before governors and kings as witnesses to them. 10And the gospel must first be preached to all nations. 11Whenever you are arrested and brought to trial, do not worry beforehand about what to say. Just say whatever is given you at the time, for it is not you speaking, but the Holy Spirit.

12"Brother will betray brother to death, and a father his child. Children will rebel against their parents and have them put to death. 13All men will hate you because of me, but he who stands firm to the end will be saved.

14"When you see 'the abomination that causes desolation'[c] standing where it[d] does not belong—let the reader understand—then let those who are in Judea flee to the mountains. 15Let no one on the roof of his house go down or enter the house to take anything out. 16Let no one in the field go back to get his cloak. 17How dreadful it will be in those days for pregnant women and nursing mothers! 18Pray that this will not take place in winter, 19because those will be days of distress unequaled from the beginning, when God created the world, until now—and never to be equaled again. 20If the Lord had not cut short those days, no one would survive. But for the sake of the elect, whom he has chosen, he has shortened them. 21At that time if anyone says to you, 'Look, here is the Christ[e]!' or, 'Look, there he is!' do not believe it. 22For false Christs and false prophets will appear and perform signs and miracles to deceive the elect—if that were possible. 23So be on your guard; I have told you everything ahead of time.

24"But in those days, following that distress,

" 'the sun will be darkened,
and the moon will not give its light;
25the stars will fall from the sky,
and the heavenly bodies will be
shaken.'[f]

26"At that time men will see the Son of Man coming in clouds with great power and glory. 27And he will send his angels and gather his elect from the four winds, from the ends of the earth to the ends of the heavens.

28"Now learn this lesson from the fig tree: As soon as its twigs get tender and its leaves come out, you know that summer is near. 29Even so, when you see these things happening, you know that it is near, right at the door. 30I tell you the truth, this generation[g] will certainly not pass away until all these things have happened. 31Heaven and earth will pass away, but my words will never pass away.

[a] *42* Greek *two lepta* [b] *42* Greek *kodrantes* [c] *14* Daniel 9:27; 11:31; 12:11 [d] *14* Or *he*; also in verse 29 [e] *21* Or *Messiah* [f] *25* Isaiah 13:10; 34:4 [g] *30* Or *race*

The Day and Hour Unknown

32"No one knows about that day or
hour, not even the angels in heaven, nor
the Son, but only the Father. 33Be on
guard! Be alert[a]! You do not know when
that time will come. 34It's like a man going
away: He leaves his house and puts his
servants in charge, each with his assigned
task, and tells the one at the door to keep
watch.
35"Therefore keep watch because you
do not know when the owner of the house
will come back—whether in the evening,
or at midnight, or when the rooster crows,
or at dawn. 36If he comes suddenly, do not
let him find you sleeping. 37What I say to
you, I say to everyone: 'Watch!' "

Jesus Anointed at Bethany

14 Now the Passover and the Feast of
Unleavened Bread were only two
days away, and the chief priests and the
teachers of the law were looking for some
sly way to arrest Jesus and kill him. 2"But
not during the Feast," they said, "or the
people may riot."
3While he was in Bethany, reclining at
the table in the home of a man known as
Simon the Leper, a woman came with an
alabaster jar of very expensive perfume,
made of pure nard. She broke the jar and
poured the perfume on his head.
4Some of those present were saying in-
dignantly to one another, "Why this waste
of perfume? 5It could have been sold for
more than a year's wages[b] and the mon-
ey given to the poor." And they rebuked
her harshly.
6"Leave her alone," said Jesus. "Why
are you bothering her? She has done a
beautiful thing to me. 7The poor you will
always have with you, and you can help
them any time you want. But you will not
always have me. 8She did what she could.
She poured perfume on my body before-
hand to prepare for my burial. 9I tell you
the truth, wherever the gospel is preached
throughout the world, what she has done
will also be told, in memory of her."
10Then Judas Iscariot, one of the
Twelve, went to the chief priests to betray
Jesus to them. 11They were delighted to
hear this and promised to give him mon-
ey. So he watched for an opportunity to
hand him over.

The Lord's Supper

12On the first day of the Feast of Unleav-
ened Bread, when it was customary to sac-
rifice the Passover lamb, Jesus' disciples
asked him, "Where do you want us to go
and make preparations for you to eat the
Passover?"
13So he sent two of his disciples, telling
them, "Go into the city, and a man carry-
ing a jar of water will meet you. Follow
him. 14Say to the owner of the house he
enters, 'The Teacher asks: Where is my
guest room, where I may eat the Passover
with my disciples?' 15He will show you a
large upper room, furnished and ready.
Make preparations for us there."
16The disciples left, went into the city
and found things just as Jesus had told
them. So they prepared the Passover.
17When evening came, Jesus arrived
with the Twelve. 18While they were recli-
ning at the table eating, he said, "I tell you
the truth, one of you will betray me—one
who is eating with me."
19They were saddened, and one by one
they said to him, "Surely not I?"
20"It is one of the Twelve," he replied,
"one who dips bread into the bowl with
me. 21The Son of Man will go just as it is
written about him. But woe to that man
who betrays the Son of Man! It would be
better for him if he had not been born."
22While they were eating, Jesus took
bread, gave thanks and broke it, and gave
it to his disciples, saying, "Take it; this is
my body."
23Then he took the cup, gave thanks
and offered it to them, and they all drank
from it.
24"This is my blood of the[c] covenant,
which is poured out for many," he said to
them. 25"I tell you the truth, I will not
drink again of the fruit of the vine until
that day when I drink it anew in the king-
dom of God."
26When they had sung a hymn, they
went out to the Mount of Olives.

Jesus Predicts Peter's Denial

27"You will all fall away," Jesus told
them, "for it is written:

" 'I will strike the shepherd,
and the sheep will be scattered.'[d]

[a]33 Some manuscripts *alert and pray* [b]5 Greek *than three hundred denarii* [c]24 Some manuscripts *the new* [d]27 Zech. 13:7

28But after I have risen, I will go ahead of
you into Galilee."
29Peter declared, "Even if all fall away,
I will not."
30"I tell you the truth," Jesus answered,
"today—yes, tonight—before the rooster
crows twice[a] you yourself will disown
me three times."
31But Peter insisted emphatically, "Even
if I have to die with you, I will never dis-
own you." And all the others said the
same.

Gethsemane

32They went to a place called Gethsem-
ane, and Jesus said to his disciples, "Sit
here while I pray." 33He took Peter, James
and John along with him, and he began to
be deeply distressed and troubled. 34"My
soul is overwhelmed with sorrow to the
point of death," he said to them. "Stay
here and keep watch."
35Going a little farther, he fell to the
ground and prayed that if possible the
hour might pass from him. 36"*Abba*,[b] Fa-
ther," he said, "everything is possible for
you. Take this cup from me. Yet not what
I will, but what you will."
37Then he returned to his disciples and
found them sleeping. "Simon," he said to
Peter, "are you asleep? Could you not
keep watch for one hour? 38Watch and
pray so that you will not fall into tempta-
tion. The spirit is willing, but the body is
weak."
39Once more he went away and prayed
the same thing. 40When he came back, he
again found them sleeping, because their
eyes were heavy. They did not know what
to say to him.
41Returning the third time, he said to
them, "Are you still sleeping and resting?
Enough! The hour has come. Look, the
Son of Man is betrayed into the hands of
sinners. 42Rise! Let us go! Here comes my
betrayer!"

Jesus Arrested

43Just as he was speaking, Judas, one of
the Twelve, appeared. With him was a
crowd armed with swords and clubs, sent
from the chief priests, the teachers of the
law, and the elders.
44Now the betrayer had arranged a sig-
nal with them: "The one I kiss is the man;
arrest him and lead him away under
guard." 45Going at once to Jesus, Judas
said, "Rabbi!" and kissed him. 46The men
seized Jesus and arrested him. 47Then one
of those standing near drew his sword and
struck the servant of the high priest, cut-
ting off his ear.
48"Am I leading a rebellion," said Jesus,
"that you have come out with swords and
clubs to capture me? 49Every day I was
with you, teaching in the temple courts,
and you did not arrest me. But the Scrip-
tures must be fulfilled." 50Then everyone
deserted him and fled.
51A young man, wearing nothing but a
linen garment, was following Jesus. When
they seized him, 52he fled naked, leaving
his garment behind.

Before the Sanhedrin

53They took Jesus to the high priest,
and all the chief priests, elders and teach-
ers of the law came together. 54Peter fol-
lowed him at a distance, right into the
courtyard of the high priest. There he sat
with the guards and warmed himself at
the fire.
55The chief priests and the whole San-
hedrin were looking for evidence against
Jesus so that they could put him to death,
but they did not find any. 56Many testified
falsely against him, but their statements
did not agree.
57Then some stood up and gave this
false testimony against him: 58"We heard
him say, 'I will destroy this man-made
temple and in three days will build anoth-
er, not made by man.'" 59Yet even then
their testimony did not agree.
60Then the high priest stood up before
them and asked Jesus, "Are you not going
to answer? What is this testimony that
these men are bringing against you?"
61But Jesus remained silent and gave no
answer.
Again the high priest asked him, "Are
you the Christ,[c] the Son of the Blessed
One?"
62"I am," said Jesus. "And you will see
the Son of Man sitting at the right hand of
the Mighty One and coming on the clouds
of heaven."
63The high priest tore his clothes. "Why
do we need any more witnesses?" he
asked. 64"You have heard the blasphemy.
What do you think?"
They all condemned him as worthy of
death. 65Then some began to spit at him;
they blindfolded him, struck him with

[a]30 Some early manuscripts do not have *twice*. [b]36 Aramaic for *Father* [c]61 Or *Messiah*

their fists, and said, "Prophesy!" And the guards took him and beat him.

Peter Disowns Jesus

66While Peter was below in the courtyard, one of the servant girls of the high priest came by. 67When she saw Peter warming himself, she looked closely at him.

"You also were with that Nazarene, Jesus," she said.

68But he denied it. "I don't know or understand what you're talking about," he said, and went out into the entryway.[a]

69When the servant girl saw him there, she said again to those standing around, "This fellow is one of them." 70Again he denied it.

After a little while, those standing near said to Peter, "Surely you are one of them, for you are a Galilean."

71He began to call down curses on himself, and he swore to them, "I don't know this man you're talking about."

72Immediately the rooster crowed the second time.[b] Then Peter remembered the word Jesus had spoken to him: "Before the rooster crows twice[c] you will disown me three times." And he broke down and wept.

Jesus Before Pilate

15 Very early in the morning, the chief priests, with the elders, the teachers of the law and the whole Sanhedrin, reached a decision. They bound Jesus, led him away and handed him over to Pilate.

2"Are you the king of the Jews?" asked Pilate.

"Yes, it is as you say," Jesus replied.

3The chief priests accused him of many things. 4So again Pilate asked him, "Aren't you going to answer? See how many things they are accusing you of."

5But Jesus still made no reply, and Pilate was amazed.

6Now it was the custom at the Feast to release a prisoner whom the people requested. 7A man called Barabbas was in prison with the insurrectionists who had committed murder in the uprising. 8The crowd came up and asked Pilate to do for them what he usually did.

9"Do you want me to release to you the king of the Jews?" asked Pilate, 10knowing it was out of envy that the chief priests had handed Jesus over to him. 11But the chief priests stirred up the crowd to have Pilate release Barabbas instead.

12"What shall I do, then, with the one you call the king of the Jews?" Pilate asked them.

13"Crucify him!" they shouted.

14"Why? What crime has he committed?" asked Pilate.

But they shouted all the louder, "Crucify him!"

15Wanting to satisfy the crowd, Pilate released Barabbas to them. He had Jesus flogged, and handed him over to be crucified.

The Soldiers Mock Jesus

16The soldiers led Jesus away into the palace (that is, the Praetorium) and called together the whole company of soldiers. 17They put a purple robe on him, then twisted together a crown of thorns and set it on him. 18And they began to call out to him, "Hail, king of the Jews!" 19Again and again they struck him on the head with a staff and spit on him. Falling on their knees, they paid homage to him. 20And when they had mocked him, they took off the purple robe and put his own clothes on him. Then they led him out to crucify him.

The Crucifixion

21A certain man from Cyrene, Simon, the father of Alexander and Rufus, was passing by on his way in from the country, and they forced him to carry the cross. 22They brought Jesus to the place called Golgotha (which means The Place of the Skull). 23Then they offered him wine mixed with myrrh, but he did not take it. 24And they crucified him. Dividing up his clothes, they cast lots to see what each would get.

25It was the third hour when they crucified him. 26The written notice of the charge against him read: THE KING OF THE JEWS. 27They crucified two robbers with him, one on his right and one on his left.[d] 29Those who passed by hurled insults at him, shaking their heads and saying, "So! You who are going to destroy the temple

[a]68 Some early manuscripts *entryway and the rooster crowed* [b]72 Some early manuscripts do not have *the second time.* [c]72 Some early manuscripts do not have *twice.* [d]27 Some manuscripts *left,* 28*and the scripture was fulfilled which says, "He was counted with the lawless ones"* (Isaiah 53:12)

and build it in three days, [30]come down
from the cross and save yourself!"
[31]In the same way the chief priests and
the teachers of the law mocked him
among themselves. "He saved others,"
they said, "but he can't save himself! [32]Let
this Christ,[a] this King of Israel, come
down now from the cross, that we may
see and believe." Those crucified with him
also heaped insults on him.

The Death of Jesus

[33]At the sixth hour darkness came over
the whole land until the ninth hour. [34]And
at the ninth hour Jesus cried out in a loud
voice, *"Eloi, Eloi, lama sabachthani?"* —
which means, "My God, my God, why
have you forsaken me?"[b]
[35]When some of those standing near
heard this, they said, "Listen, he's calling
Elijah."
[36]One man ran, filled a sponge with
wine vinegar, put it on a stick, and offered
it to Jesus to drink. "Now leave him alone.
Let's see if Elijah comes to take him
down," he said.
[37]With a loud cry, Jesus breathed his
last.
[38]The curtain of the temple was torn in
two from top to bottom. [39]And when the
centurion, who stood there in front of
Jesus, heard his cry and[c] saw how he
died, he said, "Surely this man was the
Son[d] of God!"
[40]Some women were watching from a
distance. Among them were Mary Magdalene, Mary the mother of James the younger and of Joses, and Salome. [41]In Galilee these women had followed him and cared for his needs. Many other women who had come up with him to Jerusalem were also there.

The Burial of Jesus

[42]It was Preparation Day (that is, the day before the Sabbath). So as evening approached, [43]Joseph of Arimathea, a prominent member of the Council, who was himself waiting for the kingdom of God, went boldly to Pilate and asked for Jesus' body. [44]Pilate was surprised to hear that he was already dead. Summoning the centurion, he asked him if Jesus had already died. [45]When he learned from the centurion that it was so, he gave the body to Joseph. [46]So Joseph bought some linen cloth, took down the body, wrapped it in the linen, and placed it in a tomb cut out of rock. Then he rolled a stone against the entrance of the tomb. [47]Mary Magdalene and Mary the mother of Joses saw where he was laid.

The Resurrection

16 When the Sabbath was over, Mary Magdalene, Mary the mother of James, and Salome bought spices so that they might go to anoint Jesus' body. [2]Very early on the first day of the week, just after sunrise, they were on their way to the tomb [3]and they asked each other, "Who will roll the stone away from the entrance of the tomb?"
[4]But when they looked up, they saw that the stone, which was very large, had been rolled away. [5]As they entered the tomb, they saw a young man dressed in a white robe sitting on the right side, and they were alarmed.
[6]"Don't be alarmed," he said. "You are looking for Jesus the Nazarene, who was crucified. He has risen! He is not here. See the place where they laid him. [7]But go, tell his disciples and Peter, 'He is going ahead of you into Galilee. There you will see him, just as he told you.' "
[8]Trembling and bewildered, the women went out and fled from the tomb. They said nothing to anyone, because they were afraid.

[The earliest manuscripts and some other ancient witnesses do not have Mark 16:9–20.]

[9]When Jesus rose early on the first day of the week, he appeared first to Mary Magdalene, out of whom he had driven seven demons. [10]She went and told those who had been with him and who were mourning and weeping. [11]When they heard that Jesus was alive and that she had seen him, they did not believe it.
[12]Afterward Jesus appeared in a different form to two of them while they were walking in the country. [13]These returned and reported it to the rest; but they did not believe them either.
[14]Later Jesus appeared to the Eleven as they were eating; he rebuked them for

[a] 32 Or *Messiah* [b] 34 Psalm 22:1 [c] 39 Some manuscripts do not have *heard his cry and* [d] 39 Or *a son*

their lack of faith and their stubborn refusal to believe those who had seen him after he had risen.

15He said to them, "Go into all the world and preach the good news to all creation. 16Whoever believes and is baptized will be saved, but whoever does not believe will be condemned. 17And these signs will accompany those who believe: In my name they will drive out demons; they will speak in new tongues; 18they will pick up snakes with their hands; and when they drink deadly poison, it will not hurt them at all; they will place their hands on sick people, and they will get well."

19After the Lord Jesus had spoken to them, he was taken up into heaven and he sat at the right hand of God. 20Then the disciples went out and preached everywhere, and the Lord worked with them and confirmed his word by the signs that accompanied it.

LUKE writes this Gospel to present Jesus as a Savior for the whole human race. The stories emphasize how kind and loving Jesus is to those despised by society (such as tax collectors, Samaritans, the poor, and women). He stresses the importance of prayer in Jesus' life. As you read this book, be sure that you have repented of your sins and have claimed Jesus as your own personal Savior. Ask yourself whether you show the same sort of compassion to others that Jesus showed.

LUKE

Introduction

1 Many have undertaken to draw up an
account of the things that have been
fulfilled[a] among us, [2]just as they were
handed down to us by those who from the
first were eyewitnesses and servants of
the word. [3]Therefore, since I myself have
carefully investigated everything from the
beginning, it seemed good also to me to
write an orderly account for you, most ex-
cellent Theophilus, [4]so that you may
know the certainty of the things you have
been taught.

The Birth of John the Baptist Foretold

[5]In the time of Herod king of Judea
there was a priest named Zechariah, who
belonged to the priestly division of Abi-
jah; his wife Elizabeth was also a descen-
dant of Aaron. [6]Both of them were upright
in the sight of God, observing all the
Lord's commandments and regulations
blamelessly. [7]But they had no children,
because Elizabeth was barren; and they
were both well along in years.

[8]Once when Zechariah's division was

[a]1 Or *been surely believed*

on duty and he was serving as priest before God, 9he was chosen by lot, according to the custom of the priesthood, to go into the temple of the Lord and burn incense. 10And when the time for the burning of incense came, all the assembled worshipers were praying outside.

11Then an angel of the Lord appeared to him, standing at the right side of the altar of incense. 12When Zechariah saw him, he was startled and was gripped with fear. 13But the angel said to him: "Do not be afraid, Zechariah; your prayer has been heard. Your wife Elizabeth will bear you a son, and you are to give him the name John. 14He will be a joy and delight to you, and many will rejoice because of his birth, 15for he will be great in the sight of the Lord. He is never to take wine or other fermented drink, and he will be filled with the Holy Spirit even from birth.[a] 16Many of the people of Israel will he bring back to the Lord their God. 17And he will go on before the Lord, in the spirit and power of Elijah, to turn the hearts of the fathers to their children and the disobedient to the wisdom of the righteous—to make ready a people prepared for the Lord."

18Zechariah asked the angel, "How can I be sure of this? I am an old man and my wife is well along in years."

19The angel answered, "I am Gabriel. I stand in the presence of God, and I have been sent to speak to you and to tell you this good news. 20And now you will be silent and not able to speak until the day this happens, because you did not believe my words, which will come true at their proper time."

21Meanwhile, the people were waiting for Zechariah and wondering why he stayed so long in the temple. 22When he came out, he could not speak to them. They realized he had seen a vision in the temple, for he kept making signs to them but remained unable to speak.

23When his time of service was completed, he returned home. 24After this his wife Elizabeth became pregnant and for five months remained in seclusion. 25"The Lord has done this for me," she said. "In these days he has shown his favor and taken away my disgrace among the people."

The Birth of Jesus Foretold

26In the sixth month, God sent the angel Gabriel to Nazareth, a town in Galilee, 27to a virgin pledged to be married to a man named Joseph, a descendant of David. The virgin's name was Mary. 28The angel went to her and said, "Greetings, you who are highly favored! The Lord is with you."

29Mary was greatly troubled at his words and wondered what kind of greeting this might be. 30But the angel said to her, "Do not be afraid, Mary, you have found favor with God. 31You will be with child and give birth to a son, and you are to give him the name Jesus. 32He will be great and will be called the Son of the Most High. The Lord God will give him the throne of his father David, 33and he will reign over the house of Jacob forever; his kingdom will never end."

34"How will this be," Mary asked the angel, "since I am a virgin?"

35The angel answered, "The Holy Spirit will come upon you, and the power of the Most High will overshadow you. So the holy one to be born will be called[b] the Son of God. 36Even Elizabeth your relative is going to have a child in her old age, and she who was said to be barren is in her sixth month. 37For nothing is impossible with God."

38"I am the Lord's servant," Mary answered. "May it be to me as you have said." Then the angel left her.

Mary Visits Elizabeth

39At that time Mary got ready and hurried to a town in the hill country of Judea, 40where she entered Zechariah's home and greeted Elizabeth. 41When Elizabeth heard Mary's greeting, the baby leaped in her womb, and Elizabeth was filled with the Holy Spirit. 42In a loud voice she exclaimed: "Blessed are you among women, and blessed is the child you will bear! 43But why am I so favored, that the mother of my Lord should come to me? 44As soon as the sound of your greeting reached my ears, the baby in my womb leaped for joy. 45Blessed is she who has believed that what the Lord has said to her will be accomplished!"

Mary's Song

46And Mary said:

"My soul glorifies the Lord
47 and my spirit rejoices in God my Savior,

[a] 15 Or *from his mother's womb* [b] 35 Or *So the child to be born will be called holy,*

48 for he has been mindful
of the humble state of his servant.
From now on all generations will call
me blessed,
49 for the Mighty One has done great
things for me—
holy is his name.
50 His mercy extends to those who fear
him,
from generation to generation.
51 He has performed mighty deeds
with his arm;
he has scattered those who are
proud in their inmost
thoughts.
52 He has brought down rulers from
their thrones
but has lifted up the humble.

FRIDAY

VERSE FOR THE DAY: Luke 1:38

AUTHOR: Elizabeth Cody Newenhuyse

PASSAGE FOR THE DAY: Luke 1:26–45

In God We Trust?

It's easy for us to *say* we're trusting God, but are we doing so with our fingers crossed behind our backs? God alone is sure of the future. Sometimes we need to get out of the way and let him act, to wholly trust the process to him—however events might unfold.

It's good for us to remember a couple—then engaged to be married—from 2,000 years ago who took God at his word. Mary, who conceived a son by the Holy Spirit and gave birth to the Savior, responded to the angel Gabriel: "I am the Lord's servant. May it be to me as you have said" (Luke 1:38). Joseph, who had to wonder how his fiance became pregnant, did the obedient and honorable thing: He "took Mary home as his wife" even though she was already with child (Matthew 1:24).

If push came to shove, would I be as courageous as Mary, as obedient as Joseph? Am I willing to put my life entirely in God's hands, to actually *live* as though I really trust him?

God is big enough and loving enough to take care of all our needs—including the ones we aren't even aware of. That is what makes it possible for us to rest in the confidence that he will provide.

MARRIAGE BUILDERS

♦ *Do you find it easy or difficult to trust God with your family's future? What things do you find it hard to trust to him?*

♦ *Reflect on a time when you trusted God together in the midst of difficult circumstances. What did you learn about God's lovingkindness?*

Additional Scripture Readings
Proverbs 3:5–6; Job 13:15

Go to page 1104 for your next devotional reading.

53He has filled the hungry with good
things
but has sent the rich away empty.
54He has helped his servant Israel,
remembering to be merciful
55to Abraham and his descendants
forever,
even as he said to our fathers."

56Mary stayed with Elizabeth for about three months and then returned home.

The Birth of John the Baptist

57When it was time for Elizabeth to have her baby, she gave birth to a son. 58Her neighbors and relatives heard that the Lord had shown her great mercy, and they shared her joy.

59On the eighth day they came to circumcise the child, and they were going to name him after his father Zechariah, 60but his mother spoke up and said, "No! He is to be called John."

61They said to her, "There is no one among your relatives who has that name."

62Then they made signs to his father, to find out what he would like to name the child. 63He asked for a writing tablet, and to everyone's astonishment he wrote, "His name is John." 64Immediately his mouth was opened and his tongue was loosed, and he began to speak, praising God. 65The neighbors were all filled with awe, and throughout the hill country of Judea people were talking about all these things. 66Everyone who heard this wondered about it, asking, "What then is this child going to be?" For the Lord's hand was with him.

Zechariah's Song

67His father Zechariah was filled with the Holy Spirit and prophesied:

68"Praise be to the Lord, the God of
Israel,
because he has come and has
redeemed his people.
69He has raised up a horn[a] of salvation
for us
in the house of his servant David
70(as he said through his holy prophets
of long ago),
71salvation from our enemies
and from the hand of all who hate
us—
72to show mercy to our fathers
and to remember his holy covenant,
73 the oath he swore to our father
Abraham:
74to rescue us from the hand of our
enemies,
and to enable us to serve him
without fear
75 in holiness and righteousness before
him all our days.

76And you, my child, will be called a
prophet of the Most High;
for you will go on before the Lord
to prepare the way for him,
77to give his people the knowledge of
salvation
through the forgiveness of their
sins,
78because of the tender mercy of our
God,
by which the rising sun will come
to us from heaven
79to shine on those living in darkness
and in the shadow of death,
to guide our feet into the path of
peace."

80And the child grew and became strong in spirit; and he lived in the desert until he appeared publicly to Israel.

The Birth of Jesus

2 In those days Caesar Augustus issued a decree that a census should be taken of the entire Roman world. 2(This was the first census that took place while Quirinius was governor of Syria.) 3And everyone went to his own town to register.

4So Joseph also went up from the town of Nazareth in Galilee to Judea, to Bethlehem the town of David, because he belonged to the house and line of David. 5He went there to register with Mary, who was pledged to be married to him and was expecting a child. 6While they were there, the time came for the baby to be born, 7and she gave birth to her firstborn, a son. She wrapped him in cloths and placed him in a manger, because there was no room for them in the inn.

The Shepherds and the Angels

8And there were shepherds living out in the fields nearby, keeping watch over their flocks at night. 9An angel of the Lord appeared to them, and the glory of the Lord shone around them, and they were terrified. 10But the angel said to them, "Do

[a]69 *Horn* here symbolizes strength.

not be afraid. I bring you good news of
great joy that will be for all the people.
11Today in the town of David a Savior has
been born to you; he is Christ[a] the Lord.
12This will be a sign to you: You will find
a baby wrapped in cloths and lying in a
manger."
13Suddenly a great company of the
heavenly host appeared with the angel,
praising God and saying,

14"Glory to God in the highest,
and on earth peace to men on
whom his favor rests."

15When the angels had left them and
gone into heaven, the shepherds said to
one another, "Let's go to Bethlehem and
see this thing that has happened, which
the Lord has told us about."
16So they hurried off and found Mary
and Joseph, and the baby, who was lying
in the manger. 17When they had seen him,
they spread the word concerning what
had been told them about this child, 18and
all who heard it were amazed at what the
shepherds said to them. 19But Mary trea-
sured up all these things and pondered
them in her heart. 20The shepherds re-
turned, glorifying and praising God for all
the things they had heard and seen, which
were just as they had been told.

Jesus Presented in the Temple

21On the eighth day, when it was time to
circumcise him, he was named Jesus, the
name the angel had given him before he
had been conceived.
22When the time of their purification ac-
cording to the Law of Moses had been
completed, Joseph and Mary took him to
Jerusalem to present him to the Lord 23(as
it is written in the Law of the Lord, "Every
firstborn male is to be consecrated to the
Lord"[b]), 24and to offer a sacrifice in keep-
ing with what is said in the Law of the
Lord: "a pair of doves or two young pi-
geons."[c]
25Now there was a man in Jerusalem
called Simeon, who was righteous and de-
vout. He was waiting for the consolation
of Israel, and the Holy Spirit was upon
him. 26It had been revealed to him by the
Holy Spirit that he would not die before he
had seen the Lord's Christ. 27Moved by
the Spirit, he went into the temple courts.
When the parents brought in the child
Jesus to do for him what the custom of the
Law required, 28Simeon took him in his
arms and praised God, saying:

29"Sovereign Lord, as you have
promised,
you now dismiss[d] your servant in
peace.
30For my eyes have seen your salvation,
31 which you have prepared in the
sight of all people,
32a light for revelation to the Gentiles
and for glory to your people Israel."

33The child's father and mother mar-
veled at what was said about him. 34Then
Simeon blessed them and said to Mary,
his mother: "This child is destined to
cause the falling and rising of many in Is-
rael, and to be a sign that will be spoken
against, 35so that the thoughts of many
hearts will be revealed. And a sword will
pierce your own soul too."
36There was also a prophetess, Anna,
the daughter of Phanuel, of the tribe of
Asher. She was very old; she had lived
with her husband seven years after her
marriage, 37and then was a widow until
she was eighty-four.[e] She never left the
temple but worshiped night and day, fast-
ing and praying. 38Coming up to them at
that very moment, she gave thanks to God
and spoke about the child to all who were
looking forward to the redemption of Je-
rusalem.
39When Joseph and Mary had done ev-
erything required by the Law of the Lord,
they returned to Galilee to their own town
of Nazareth. 40And the child grew and be-
came strong; he was filled with wisdom,
and the grace of God was upon him.

The Boy Jesus at the Temple

41Every year his parents went to Jerusa-
lem for the Feast of the Passover. 42When
he was twelve years old, they went up to
the Feast, according to the custom. 43After
the Feast was over, while his parents were
returning home, the boy Jesus stayed be-
hind in Jerusalem, but they were unaware
of it. 44Thinking he was in their company,
they traveled on for a day. Then they be-
gan looking for him among their relatives
and friends. 45When they did not find
him, they went back to Jerusalem to look

[a] *11* Or *Messiah.* "The Christ" (Greek) and "the Messiah" (Hebrew) both mean "the Anointed One"; also in verse 26. [b] *23* Exodus 13:2,12 [c] *24* Lev. 12:8 [d] *29* Or *promised, / now dismiss* [e] *37* Or *widow for eighty-four years*

for him. 46After three days they found him
in the temple courts, sitting among the
teachers, listening to them and asking
them questions. 47Everyone who heard
him was amazed at his understanding and
his answers. 48When his parents saw him,
they were astonished. His mother said to
him, "Son, why have you treated us like
this? Your father and I have been anxious-
ly searching for you."
49"Why were you searching for me?" he
asked. "Didn't you know I had to be in my
Father's house?" 50But they did not under-
stand what he was saying to them.
51Then he went down to Nazareth with
them and was obedient to them. But his
mother treasured all these things in her
heart. 52And Jesus grew in wisdom and
stature, and in favor with God and men.

John the Baptist Prepares the Way

3 In the fifteenth year of the reign of Ti-
berius Caesar—when Pontius Pilate
was governor of Judea, Herod tetrarch of
Galilee, his brother Philip tetrarch of Itu-
rea and Traconitis, and Lysanias tetrarch
of Abilene— 2during the high priesthood
of Annas and Caiaphas, the word of God
came to John son of Zechariah in the
desert. 3He went into all the country
around the Jordan, preaching a baptism of
repentance for the forgiveness of sins. 4As
is written in the book of the words of Isa-
iah the prophet:

"A voice of one calling in the desert,
'Prepare the way for the Lord,
make straight paths for him.
5Every valley shall be filled in,
every mountain and hill made low.
The crooked roads shall become
straight,
the rough ways smooth.
6And all mankind will see God's
salvation.' "[a]

7John said to the crowds coming out to
be baptized by him, "You brood of vipers!
Who warned you to flee from the coming
wrath? 8Produce fruit in keeping with re-
pentance. And do not begin to say to your-
selves, 'We have Abraham as our father.'
For I tell you that out of these stones God
can raise up children for Abraham. 9The
ax is already at the root of the trees, and
every tree that does not produce good
fruit will be cut down and thrown into the
fire."
10"What should we do then?" the crowd
asked.
11John answered, "The man with two
tunics should share with him who has
none, and the one who has food should do
the same."
12Tax collectors also came to be bap-
tized. "Teacher," they asked, "what
should we do?"
13"Don't collect any more than you are
required to," he told them.
14Then some soldiers asked him, "And
what should we do?"
He replied, "Don't extort money and
don't accuse people falsely—be content
with your pay."
15The people were waiting expectantly
and were all wondering in their hearts if
John might possibly be the Christ.[b]
16John answered them all, "I baptize you
with[c] water. But one more powerful than
I will come, the thongs of whose sandals
I am not worthy to untie. He will baptize
you with the Holy Spirit and with fire.
17His winnowing fork is in his hand to
clear his threshing floor and to gather the
wheat into his barn, but he will burn up
the chaff with unquenchable fire." 18And
with many other words John exhorted the
people and preached the good news to
them.
19But when John rebuked Herod the te-
trarch because of Herodias, his brother's
wife, and all the other evil things he had
done, 20Herod added this to them all: He
locked John up in prison.

The Baptism and Genealogy of Jesus

21When all the people were being bap-
tized, Jesus was baptized too. And as he
was praying, heaven was opened 22and
the Holy Spirit descended on him in bodi-
ly form like a dove. And a voice came from
heaven: "You are my Son, whom I love;
with you I am well pleased."
23Now Jesus himself was about thirty
years old when he began his ministry. He
was the son, so it was thought, of Joseph,

the son of Heli, 24the son of Matthat,
the son of Levi, the son of Melki,
the son of Jannai, the son of Joseph,
25the son of Mattathias, the son of
Amos,
the son of Nahum, the son of Esli,
the son of Naggai, 26the son of Ma-
ath,

[a]6 Isaiah 40:3-5 [b]15 Or *Messiah* [c]16 Or *in*

WEEKENDING

LOVE

The Bible offers guidance on how couples can shift the focus off their differences and concentrate, instead, on building a lasting relationship. One way is to concentrate on your own responsibility to love your spouse. Consider the following questions:

1. Scripture requires us to love our neighbors as ourselves. Since your mate qualifies as a "neighbor," how can you show love when you find your spouse's differences hard to accept?

2. Can you think of an occasion when, rather than showing love to your mate, you instead retaliated to "pay him or her back" for something? How did that affect the level of intimacy between you? How long did it take the two of you to re-establish intimacy?

3. If you concentrated on loving your spouse as you love yourself, how would it be easier for you to understand—and even appreciate—your mate, differences and all?

— *The* Marriage Partnership *Staff*

REVIVE

Saturday: James 2:8–13
Sunday: Luke 10:25–37

Go to page 1106 for your next devotional reading.

the son of Mattathias, the son of Semein,
the son of Josech, the son of Joda,
27the son of Joanan, the son of Rhesa,
the son of Zerubbabel, the son of Shealtiel,
the son of Neri, 28the son of Melki,
the son of Addi, the son of Cosam,
the son of Elmadam, the son of Er,
29the son of Joshua, the son of Eliezer,
the son of Jorim, the son of Matthat,
the son of Levi, 30the son of Simeon,
the son of Judah, the son of Joseph,
the son of Jonam, the son of Eliakim,
31the son of Melea, the son of Menna,
the son of Mattatha, the son of Nathan,
the son of David, 32the son of Jesse,
the son of Obed, the son of Boaz,
the son of Salmon,[a] the son of Nahshon,
33the son of Amminadab, the son of Ram,[b]
the son of Hezron, the son of Perez,
the son of Judah, 34the son of Jacob,
the son of Isaac, the son of Abraham,
the son of Terah, the son of Nahor,
35the son of Serug, the son of Reu,
the son of Peleg, the son of Eber,
the son of Shelah, 36the son of Cainan,
the son of Arphaxad, the son of Shem,
the son of Noah, the son of Lamech,
37the son of Methuselah, the son of Enoch,
the son of Jared, the son of Mahalalel,
the son of Kenan, 38the son of Enosh,
the son of Seth, the son of Adam,
the son of God.

The Temptation of Jesus

4 Jesus, full of the Holy Spirit, returned from the Jordan and was led by the Spirit in the desert, 2where for forty days he was tempted by the devil. He ate nothing during those days, and at the end of them he was hungry.

3The devil said to him, "If you are the Son of God, tell this stone to become bread."

4Jesus answered, "It is written: 'Man does not live on bread alone.'[c]"

5The devil led him up to a high place and showed him in an instant all the kingdoms of the world. 6And he said to him, "I will give you all their authority and splendor, for it has been given to me, and I can give it to anyone I want to. 7So if you worship me, it will all be yours."

8Jesus answered, "It is written: 'Worship the Lord your God and serve him only.'[d]"

9The devil led him to Jerusalem and had him stand on the highest point of the temple. "If you are the Son of God," he said, "throw yourself down from here. 10For it is written:

" 'He will command his angels
concerning you
to guard you carefully;
11they will lift you up in their hands,
so that you will not strike your foot
against a stone.'[e]"

12Jesus answered, "It says: 'Do not put the Lord your God to the test.'[f]"

13When the devil had finished all this tempting, he left him until an opportune time.

Jesus Rejected at Nazareth

14Jesus returned to Galilee in the power of the Spirit, and news about him spread through the whole countryside. 15He taught in their synagogues, and everyone praised him.

16He went to Nazareth, where he had been brought up, and on the Sabbath day he went into the synagogue, as was his custom. And he stood up to read. 17The scroll of the prophet Isaiah was handed to him. Unrolling it, he found the place where it is written:

18"The Spirit of the Lord is on me,
because he has anointed me
to preach good news to the poor.
He has sent me to proclaim freedom
for the prisoners
and recovery of sight for the blind,
to release the oppressed,
19 to proclaim the year of the Lord's
favor."[g]

20Then he rolled up the scroll, gave it back to the attendant and sat down. The eyes of everyone in the synagogue were fastened on him, 21and he began by saying

[a]32 Some early manuscripts *Sala* [b]33 Some manuscripts *Amminadab, the son of Admin, the son of Arni*; other manuscripts vary widely. [c]4 Deut. 8:3 [d]8 Deut. 6:13 [e]11 Psalm 91:11,12 [f]12 Deut. 6:16 [g]19 Isaiah 61:1,2

to them, "Today this scripture is fulfilled
in your hearing."
22All spoke well of him and were
amazed at the gracious words that came
from his lips. "Isn't this Joseph's son?"
they asked.
23Jesus said to them, "Surely you will
quote this proverb to me: 'Physician, heal
yourself! Do here in your hometown what
we have heard that you did in Caper-
naum.' "
24"I tell you the truth," he continued,
"no prophet is accepted in his hometown.
25I assure you that there were many wid-
ows in Israel in Elijah's time, when the sky
was shut for three and a half years and
there was a severe famine throughout the
land. 26Yet Elijah was not sent to any of
them, but to a widow in Zarephath in the
region of Sidon. 27And there were many in
Israel with leprosy[a] in the time of Elisha
the prophet, yet not one of them was
cleansed—only Naaman the Syrian."
28All the people in the synagogue were
furious when they heard this. 29They got
up, drove him out of the town, and took
him to the brow of the hill on which the
town was built, in order to throw him
down the cliff. 30But he walked right
through the crowd and went on his way.

Jesus Drives Out an Evil Spirit

31Then he went down to Capernaum, a
town in Galilee, and on the Sabbath began
to teach the people. 32They were amazed
at his teaching, because his message had
authority.
33In the synagogue there was a man

[a]27 The Greek word was used for various diseases affecting the skin—not necessarily leprosy.

VERSE FOR THE DAY:	AUTHOR:	PASSAGE FOR THE DAY:
Luke 4:18	Jill Briscoe	Luke 4:14–21

God's Call

At a recent missions conference, a young woman was asked, "How did you receive your call to missions?" She responded, "I got saved."

I love that answer! Stuart and I were both Christians when we got married, and we have used our gifts for God's kingdom because it's part of the whole package of being a Christian.

People often ask me, "How did you become a speaker? When did you get your call?" Well, I got saved, and then I couldn't shut up. One thing led to another, and here I am.

MARRIAGE BUILDERS

♦ *Since you became a Christian, what are some ways you've most enjoyed serving God?*

♦ *What responsibilities do you believe come along with being part of God's family?*

Additional Scripture Readings
2 Corinthians 5:14–15; Isaiah 6:8

Go to page 1110 for your next devotional reading.

possessed by a demon, an evil[a] spirit. He
cried out at the top of his voice, 34"Ha!
What do you want with us, Jesus of Naza-
reth? Have you come to destroy us? I
know who you are—the Holy One of
God!"
35"Be quiet!" Jesus said sternly. "Come
out of him!" Then the demon threw the
man down before them all and came out
without injuring him.
36All the people were amazed and said
to each other, "What is this teaching?
With authority and power he gives orders
to evil spirits and they come out!" 37And
the news about him spread throughout
the surrounding area.

Jesus Heals Many

38Jesus left the synagogue and went to
the home of Simon. Now Simon's mother-
in-law was suffering from a high fever,
and they asked Jesus to help her. 39So he
bent over her and rebuked the fever, and
it left her. She got up at once and began to
wait on them.
40When the sun was setting, the people
brought to Jesus all who had various
kinds of sickness, and laying his hands on
each one, he healed them. 41Moreover, de-
mons came out of many people, shouting,
"You are the Son of God!" But he rebuked
them and would not allow them to speak,
because they knew he was the Christ.[b]
42At daybreak Jesus went out to a soli-
tary place. The people were looking for
him and when they came to where he was,
they tried to keep him from leaving them.
43But he said, "I must preach the good
news of the kingdom of God to the other
towns also, because that is why I was
sent." 44And he kept on preaching in the
synagogues of Judea.[c]

The Calling of the First Disciples

5 One day as Jesus was standing by the
Lake of Gennesaret,[d] with the people
crowding around him and listening to the
word of God, 2he saw at the water's edge
two boats, left there by the fishermen,
who were washing their nets. 3He got into
one of the boats, the one belonging to Si-
mon, and asked him to put out a little
from shore. Then he sat down and taught
the people from the boat.
4When he had finished speaking, he
said to Simon, "Put out into deep water,
and let down[e] the nets for a catch."
5Simon answered, "Master, we've
worked hard all night and haven't caught
anything. But because you say so, I will let
down the nets."
6When they had done so, they caught
such a large number of fish that their nets
began to break. 7So they signaled their
partners in the other boat to come and
help them, and they came and filled both
boats so full that they began to sink.
8When Simon Peter saw this, he fell at
Jesus' knees and said, "Go away from me,
Lord; I am a sinful man!" 9For he and all
his companions were astonished at the
catch of fish they had taken, 10and so were
James and John, the sons of Zebedee, Si-
mon's partners.
Then Jesus said to Simon, "Don't be
afraid; from now on you will catch men."
11So they pulled their boats up on shore,
left everything and followed him.

The Man With Leprosy

12While Jesus was in one of the towns,
a man came along who was covered with
leprosy.[f] When he saw Jesus, he fell with
his face to the ground and begged him,
"Lord, if you are willing, you can make me
clean."
13Jesus reached out his hand and
touched the man. "I am willing," he said.
"Be clean!" And immediately the leprosy
left him.
14Then Jesus ordered him, "Don't tell
anyone, but go, show yourself to the
priest and offer the sacrifices that Moses
commanded for your cleansing, as a testi-
mony to them."
15Yet the news about him spread all the
more, so that crowds of people came to
hear him and to be healed of their sick-
nesses. 16But Jesus often withdrew to
lonely places and prayed.

Jesus Heals a Paralytic

17One day as he was teaching, Pharisees
and teachers of the law, who had come
from every village of Galilee and from Ju-
dea and Jerusalem, were sitting there.
And the power of the Lord was present for
him to heal the sick. 18Some men came
carrying a paralytic on a mat and tried to
take him into the house to lay him before

[a]*33* Greek *unclean*; also in verse 36 [b]*41* Or *Messiah* [c]*44* Or *the land of the Jews*; some manuscripts *Galilee* [d]*1* That is, Sea of Galilee [e]*4* The Greek verb is plural. [f]*12* The Greek word was used for various diseases affecting the skin—not necessarily leprosy.

Jesus. 19When they could not find a way
to do this because of the crowd, they went
up on the roof and lowered him on his
mat through the tiles into the middle of
the crowd, right in front of Jesus.
20When Jesus saw their faith, he said,
"Friend, your sins are forgiven."
21The Pharisees and the teachers of the
law began thinking to themselves, "Who
is this fellow who speaks blasphemy?
Who can forgive sins but God alone?"
22Jesus knew what they were thinking
and asked, "Why are you thinking these
things in your hearts? 23Which is easier: to
say, 'Your sins are forgiven,' or to say, 'Get
up and walk'? 24But that you may know
that the Son of Man has authority on earth
to forgive sins. . . ." He said to the para-
lyzed man, "I tell you, get up, take your
mat and go home." 25Immediately he
stood up in front of them, took what he
had been lying on and went home prais-
ing God. 26Everyone was amazed and gave
praise to God. They were filled with awe
and said, "We have seen remarkable
things today."

The Calling of Levi

27After this, Jesus went out and saw a
tax collector by the name of Levi sitting at
his tax booth. "Follow me," Jesus said to
him, 28and Levi got up, left everything and
followed him.
29Then Levi held a great banquet for
Jesus at his house, and a large crowd of
tax collectors and others were eating with
them. 30But the Pharisees and the teachers
of the law who belonged to their sect com-
plained to his disciples, "Why do you eat
and drink with tax collectors and 'sin-
ners'?"
31Jesus answered them, "It is not the
healthy who need a doctor, but the sick.
32I have not come to call the righteous, but
sinners to repentance."

Jesus Questioned About Fasting

33They said to him, "John's disciples of-
ten fast and pray, and so do the disciples
of the Pharisees, but yours go on eating
and drinking."
34Jesus answered, "Can you make the
guests of the bridegroom fast while he is
with them? 35But the time will come when
the bridegroom will be taken from them;
in those days they will fast."
36He told them this parable: "No one
tears a patch from a new garment and
sews it on an old one. If he does, he will
have torn the new garment, and the patch
from the new will not match the old.
37And no one pours new wine into old
wineskins. If he does, the new wine will
burst the skins, the wine will run out and
the wineskins will be ruined. 38No, new
wine must be poured into new wineskins.
39And no one after drinking old wine
wants the new, for he says, 'The old is bet-
ter.' "

Lord of the Sabbath

6 One Sabbath Jesus was going through
the grainfields, and his disciples be-
gan to pick some heads of grain, rub them
in their hands and eat the kernels. 2Some
of the Pharisees asked, "Why are you do-
ing what is unlawful on the Sabbath?"
3Jesus answered them, "Have you never
read what David did when he and his
companions were hungry? 4He entered
the house of God, and taking the conse-
crated bread, he ate what is lawful only for
priests to eat. And he also gave some to
his companions." 5Then Jesus said to
them, "The Son of Man is Lord of the Sab-
bath."
6On another Sabbath he went into the
synagogue and was teaching, and a man
was there whose right hand was shriveled.
7The Pharisees and the teachers of the law
were looking for a reason to accuse Jesus,
so they watched him closely to see if he
would heal on the Sabbath. 8But Jesus
knew what they were thinking and said to
the man with the shriveled hand, "Get up
and stand in front of everyone." So he got
up and stood there.
9Then Jesus said to them, "I ask you,
which is lawful on the Sabbath: to do good
or to do evil, to save life or to destroy it?"
10He looked around at them all, and
then said to the man, "Stretch out your
hand." He did so, and his hand was com-
pletely restored. 11But they were furious
and began to discuss with one another
what they might do to Jesus.

The Twelve Apostles

12One of those days Jesus went out to a
mountainside to pray, and spent the night
praying to God. 13When morning came,
he called his disciples to him and chose
twelve of them, whom he also designated
apostles: 14Simon (whom he named Pe-
ter), his brother Andrew, James, John,
Philip, Bartholomew, 15Matthew, Thomas,
James son of Alphaeus, Simon who was

called the Zealot, [16]Judas son of James,
and Judas Iscariot, who became a traitor.

Blessings and Woes

[17]He went down with them and stood
on a level place. A large crowd of his disci-
ples was there and a great number of peo-
ple from all over Judea, from Jerusalem,
and from the coast of Tyre and Sidon,
[18]who had come to hear him and to be
healed of their diseases. Those troubled
by evil[a] spirits were cured, [19]and the peo-
ple all tried to touch him, because power
was coming from him and healing them
all.

[20]Looking at his disciples, he said:

"Blessed are you who are poor,
for yours is the kingdom of God.
[21]Blessed are you who hunger now,
for you will be satisfied.
Blessed are you who weep now,
for you will laugh.
[22]Blessed are you when men hate you,
when they exclude you and insult
you
and reject your name as evil,
because of the Son of Man.

[23]"Rejoice in that day and leap for joy,
because great is your reward in heaven.
For that is how their fathers treated the
prophets.

[24]"But woe to you who are rich,
for you have already received your
comfort.
[25]Woe to you who are well fed now,
for you will go hungry.
Woe to you who laugh now,
for you will mourn and weep.
[26]Woe to you when all men speak well
of you,
for that is how their fathers treated
the false prophets.

Love for Enemies

[27]"But I tell you who hear me: Love
your enemies, do good to those who hate
you, [28]bless those who curse you, pray for
those who mistreat you. [29]If someone
strikes you on one cheek, turn to him the
other also. If someone takes your cloak,
do not stop him from taking your tunic.
[30]Give to everyone who asks you, and if
anyone takes what belongs to you, do not
demand it back. [31]Do to others as you
would have them do to you.

[32]"If you love those who love you, what
credit is that to you? Even 'sinners' love
those who love them. [33]And if you do
good to those who are good to you, what
credit is that to you? Even 'sinners' do
that. [34]And if you lend to those from
whom you expect repayment, what credit
is that to you? Even 'sinners' lend to 'sin-
ners,' expecting to be repaid in full. [35]But
love your enemies, do good to them, and
lend to them without expecting to get any-
thing back. Then your reward will be
great, and you will be sons of the Most
High, because he is kind to the ungrateful
and wicked. [36]Be merciful, just as your Fa-
ther is merciful.

Judging Others

[37]"Do not judge, and you will not be
judged. Do not condemn, and you will not
be condemned. Forgive, and you will be
forgiven. [38]Give, and it will be given to
you. A good measure, pressed down,
shaken together and running over, will be
poured into your lap. For with the mea-
sure you use, it will be measured to you."

[39]He also told them this parable: "Can a
blind man lead a blind man? Will they not
both fall into a pit? [40]A student is not
above his teacher, but everyone who is
fully trained will be like his teacher.

[41]"Why do you look at the speck of saw-
dust in your brother's eye and pay no at-
tention to the plank in your own eye?
[42]How can you say to your brother,
'Brother, let me take the speck out of your
eye,' when you yourself fail to see the
plank in your own eye? You hypocrite,
first take the plank out of your eye, and
then you will see clearly to remove the
speck from your brother's eye.

A Tree and Its Fruit

[43]"No good tree bears bad fruit, nor
does a bad tree bear good fruit. [44]Each tree
is recognized by its own fruit. People do
not pick figs from thornbushes, or grapes
from briers. [45]The good man brings good
things out of the good stored up in his
heart, and the evil man brings evil things
out of the evil stored up in his heart. For
out of the overflow of his heart his mouth
speaks.

The Wise and Foolish Builders

[46]"Why do you call me, 'Lord, Lord,'
and do not do what I say? [47]I will show

[a]18 Greek *unclean*

VERSE FOR THE DAY: Luke 6:37

AUTHOR: Kathy Tippett Henderson

PASSAGE FOR THE DAY: Luke 6:37–42

Judgment or Forgiveness?

Can we ever fully recover from the sickness of "judgmentalism"? Maybe.

First, I can reprogram my thoughts to view people differently. When I search for the image of God stamped on all God's children, a spirit of gratitude comes to me quite naturally. With a thankful heart, I can sharpen the positive image of everyone with whom I come in contact.

Second, I can confess my faults openly. At our church trio practice one Sunday, I snapped at a fellow member for being late. After church I apologized for my abruptness, and she revealed problems at home that made her ministry in music difficult. Together we worked out an alternative plan and ended up rescheduling our trio practices.

Third, I can give equal time in prayer. A man in our church was unfaithful to his wife. I spent time with his wife, in tears, anger and prayer. By week's end I realized I hadn't once prayed for her husband. He was hard to love, but perhaps prayer would have softened his heart. As I called his name in prayer, my compassion for him grew.

When a brother or sister stumbles or feels the pain of a fall, rather than reach for my judge's robe, I need to kneel down with them, sharing their hurt, and then gently seek to restore them to health and wholeness.

MARRIAGE BUILDERS

♦ *Why is the habit of negative thoughts about others dangerous for you and disappointing to God?*

♦ *In your marriage relationship, why is it important to "clear the air" by confessing wrongs and asking for forgiveness?*

Additional Scripture Readings
Galatians 6:1–5; Matthew 7:1–6; 12:34b

Go to page 1112 for your next devotional reading.

you what he is like who comes to me and hears my words and puts them into practice. 48He is like a man building a house, who dug down deep and laid the foundation on rock. When a flood came, the torrent struck that house but could not shake it, because it was well built. 49But the one who hears my words and does not put them into practice is like a man who built a house on the ground without a foundation. The moment the torrent struck that house, it collapsed and its destruction was complete."

The Faith of the Centurion

7 When Jesus had finished saying all this in the hearing of the people, he entered Capernaum. 2There a centurion's servant, whom his master valued highly, was sick and about to die. 3The centurion heard of Jesus and sent some elders of the Jews to him, asking him to come and heal his servant. 4When they came to Jesus, they pleaded earnestly with him, "This man deserves to have you do this, 5because he loves our nation and has built our synagogue." 6So Jesus went with them.

He was not far from the house when the centurion sent friends to say to him: "Lord, don't trouble yourself, for I do not deserve to have you come under my roof. 7That is why I did not even consider myself worthy to come to you. But say the word, and my servant will be healed. 8For I myself am a man under authority, with soldiers under me. I tell this one, 'Go,' and he goes; and that one, 'Come,' and he comes. I say to my servant, 'Do this,' and he does it."

9When Jesus heard this, he was amazed at him, and turning to the crowd following him, he said, "I tell you, I have not found such great faith even in Israel." 10Then the men who had been sent returned to the house and found the servant well.

Jesus Raises a Widow's Son

11Soon afterward, Jesus went to a town called Nain, and his disciples and a large crowd went along with him. 12As he approached the town gate, a dead person was being carried out—the only son of his mother, and she was a widow. And a large crowd from the town was with her. 13When the Lord saw her, his heart went out to her and he said, "Don't cry."

14Then he went up and touched the coffin, and those carrying it stood still. He said, "Young man, I say to you, get up!" 15The dead man sat up and began to talk, and Jesus gave him back to his mother.

16They were all filled with awe and praised God. "A great prophet has appeared among us," they said. "God has come to help his people." 17This news about Jesus spread throughout Judea[a] and the surrounding country.

Jesus and John the Baptist

18John's disciples told him about all these things. Calling two of them, 19he sent them to the Lord to ask, "Are you the one who was to come, or should we expect someone else?"

20When the men came to Jesus, they said, "John the Baptist sent us to you to ask, 'Are you the one who was to come, or should we expect someone else?' "

21At that very time Jesus cured many who had diseases, sicknesses and evil spirits, and gave sight to many who were blind. 22So he replied to the messengers, "Go back and report to John what you have seen and heard: The blind receive sight, the lame walk, those who have leprosy[b] are cured, the deaf hear, the dead are raised, and the good news is preached to the poor. 23Blessed is the man who does not fall away on account of me."

24After John's messengers left, Jesus began to speak to the crowd about John: "What did you go out into the desert to see? A reed swayed by the wind? 25If not, what did you go out to see? A man dressed in fine clothes? No, those who wear expensive clothes and indulge in luxury are in palaces. 26But what did you go out to see? A prophet? Yes, I tell you, and more than a prophet. 27This is the one about whom it is written:

" 'I will send my messenger ahead of you,
who will prepare your way before you.'[c]

28I tell you, among those born of women there is no one greater than John; yet the one who is least in the kingdom of God is greater than he."

29(All the people, even the tax collec-

[a]17 Or *the land of the Jews* [b]22 The Greek word was used for various diseases affecting the skin—not necessarily leprosy. [c]27 Mal. 3:1

tors, when they heard Jesus' words, acknowledged that God's way was right, because they had been baptized by John.
30But the Pharisees and experts in the law
rejected God's purpose for themselves,
because they had not been baptized by
John.)
31"To what, then, can I compare the
people of this generation? What are they
like? 32They are like children sitting in the
marketplace and calling out to each other:

" 'We played the flute for you,
and you did not dance;
we sang a dirge,
and you did not cry.'

33For John the Baptist came neither eating
bread nor drinking wine, and you say, 'He
has a demon.' 34The Son of Man came eating
and drinking, and you say, 'Here is a
glutton and a drunkard, a friend of tax collectors
and "sinners." ' 35But wisdom is
proved right by all her children."

Jesus Anointed by a Sinful Woman

36Now one of the Pharisees invited
Jesus to have dinner with him, so he went
to the Pharisee's house and reclined at the
table. 37When a woman who had lived a
sinful life in that town learned that Jesus
was eating at the Pharisee's house, she
brought an alabaster jar of perfume, 38and
as she stood behind him at his feet weeping,
she began to wet his feet with her

VERSE FOR THE DAY:	AUTHOR:	PASSAGE FOR THE DAY:
Luke 7:50	Catherine Marshall	Luke 7:36–50

Stepping Out in Faith

There is no way for us to take the first steps toward the Christian life except by faith, any more than a baby can get launched on his earthly life without blind baby-trust in his parents. We have to accept the fact of a personal relationship with Jesus Christ by faith, even as our young children accept the fact of parental love. For the child, as for the new Christian, understanding comes later.

In Jesus' ministry of healing, it seems faith was necessary *before* the divine act, not afterward. "Jesus said to the woman, 'Your faith has saved you; go in peace' " (Luke 7:50). And: "If you believe, you will receive whatever you ask for in prayer" (Matthew 21:22). Faith, then, can be defined as stepping out on trust.

We must have faith before the fact, not after. And when we take the risk of completely trusting God, we, like David in Psalm 34:8, can say, "Taste and see that the Lord is good."

MARRIAGE BUILDERS

- *What present situations or future risks are facing you now?*
- *Have you trusted them to God?*

Additional Scripture Readings
Psalm 34:8; Matthew 21:22; Luke 7:1–17

Go to page 1116 for your next devotional reading.

tears. Then she wiped them with her hair,
kissed them and poured perfume on
them.
39When the Pharisee who had invited
him saw this, he said to himself, "If this
man were a prophet, he would know who
is touching him and what kind of woman
she is—that she is a sinner."
40Jesus answered him, "Simon, I have
something to tell you."
"Tell me, teacher," he said.
41"Two men owed money to a certain
moneylender. One owed him five hun-
dred denarii,[a] and the other fifty. 42Nei-
ther of them had the money to pay him
back, so he canceled the debts of both.
Now which of them will love him more?"
43Simon replied, "I suppose the one
who had the bigger debt canceled."
"You have judged correctly," Jesus said.
44Then he turned toward the woman
and said to Simon, "Do you see this wom-
an? I came into your house. You did not
give me any water for my feet, but she wet
my feet with her tears and wiped them
with her hair. 45You did not give me a kiss,
but this woman, from the time I entered,
has not stopped kissing my feet. 46You did
not put oil on my head, but she has
poured perfume on my feet. 47Therefore,
I tell you, her many sins have been forgiv-
en—for she loved much. But he who has
been forgiven little loves little."
48Then Jesus said to her, "Your sins are
forgiven."
49The other guests began to say among
themselves, "Who is this who even for-
gives sins?"
50Jesus said to the woman, "Your faith
has saved you; go in peace."

The Parable of the Sower

8 After this, Jesus traveled about from
one town and village to another, pro-
claiming the good news of the kingdom of
God. The Twelve were with him, 2and also
some women who had been cured of evil
spirits and diseases: Mary (called Magda-
lene) from whom seven demons had
come out; 3Joanna the wife of Cuza, the
manager of Herod's household; Susanna;
and many others. These women were
helping to support them out of their own
means.
4While a large crowd was gathering and
people were coming to Jesus from town
after town, he told this parable: 5"A farmer
went out to sow his seed. As he was scat-
tering the seed, some fell along the path;
it was trampled on, and the birds of the air
ate it up. 6Some fell on rock, and when it
came up, the plants withered because
they had no moisture. 7Other seed fell
among thorns, which grew up with it and
choked the plants. 8Still other seed fell on
good soil. It came up and yielded a crop,
a hundred times more than was sown."
When he said this, he called out, "He
who has ears to hear, let him hear."
9His disciples asked him what this para-
ble meant. 10He said, "The knowledge of
the secrets of the kingdom of God has
been given to you, but to others I speak in
parables, so that,

> " 'though seeing, they may not see;
> though hearing, they may not
> understand.'[b]

11"This is the meaning of the parable:
The seed is the word of God. 12Those
along the path are the ones who hear, and
then the devil comes and takes away the
word from their hearts, so that they may
not believe and be saved. 13Those on the
rock are the ones who receive the word
with joy when they hear it, but they have
no root. They believe for a while, but in
the time of testing they fall away. 14The
seed that fell among thorns stands for
those who hear, but as they go on their
way they are choked by life's worries,
riches and pleasures, and they do not ma-
ture. 15But the seed on good soil stands for
those with a noble and good heart, who
hear the word, retain it, and by persever-
ing produce a crop.

A Lamp on a Stand

16"No one lights a lamp and hides it in
a jar or puts it under a bed. Instead, he
puts it on a stand, so that those who come
in can see the light. 17For there is nothing
hidden that will not be disclosed, and
nothing concealed that will not be known
or brought out into the open. 18Therefore
consider carefully how you listen. Whoev-
er has will be given more; whoever does
not have, even what he thinks he has will
be taken from him."

Jesus' Mother and Brothers

19Now Jesus' mother and brothers
came to see him, but they were not able to
get near him because of the crowd.

[a]41 A denarius was a coin worth about a day's wages. [b]10 Isaiah 6:9

20Someone told him, "Your mother and
brothers are standing outside, wanting to
see you."
21He replied, "My mother and brothers
are those who hear God's word and put it
into practice."

Jesus Calms the Storm

22One day Jesus said to his disciples,
"Let's go over to the other side of the
lake." So they got into a boat and set out.
23As they sailed, he fell asleep. A squall
came down on the lake, so that the boat
was being swamped, and they were in
great danger.
24The disciples went and woke him,
saying, "Master, Master, we're going to
drown!"
He got up and rebuked the wind and the
raging waters; the storm subsided, and all
was calm. 25"Where is your faith?" he
asked his disciples.
In fear and amazement they asked one
another, "Who is this? He commands even
the winds and the water, and they obey
him."

The Healing of a Demon-possessed Man

26They sailed to the region of the Gera-
senes,[a] which is across the lake from Gal-
ilee. 27When Jesus stepped ashore, he was
met by a demon-possessed man from the
town. For a long time this man had not
worn clothes or lived in a house, but had
lived in the tombs. 28When he saw Jesus,
he cried out and fell at his feet, shouting
at the top of his voice, "What do you want
with me, Jesus, Son of the Most High God?
I beg you, don't torture me!" 29For Jesus
had commanded the evil[b] spirit to come
out of the man. Many times it had seized
him, and though he was chained hand and
foot and kept under guard, he had broken
his chains and had been driven by the de-
mon into solitary places.
30Jesus asked him, "What is your
name?"
"Legion," he replied, because many de-
mons had gone into him. 31And they
begged him repeatedly not to order them
to go into the Abyss.
32A large herd of pigs was feeding there
on the hillside. The demons begged Jesus
to let them go into them, and he gave
them permission. 33When the demons
came out of the man, they went into the
pigs, and the herd rushed down the steep
bank into the lake and was drowned.
34When those tending the pigs saw
what had happened, they ran off and re-
ported this in the town and countryside,
35and the people went out to see what had
happened. When they came to Jesus, they
found the man from whom the demons
had gone out, sitting at Jesus' feet,
dressed and in his right mind; and they
were afraid. 36Those who had seen it told
the people how the demon-possessed
man had been cured. 37Then all the peo-
ple of the region of the Gerasenes asked
Jesus to leave them, because they were
overcome with fear. So he got into the
boat and left.
38The man from whom the demons had
gone out begged to go with him, but Jesus
sent him away, saying, 39"Return home
and tell how much God has done for you."
So the man went away and told all over
town how much Jesus had done for him.

A Dead Girl and a Sick Woman

40Now when Jesus returned, a crowd
welcomed him, for they were all expecting
him. 41Then a man named Jairus, a ruler
of the synagogue, came and fell at Jesus'
feet, pleading with him to come to his
house 42because his only daughter, a girl
of about twelve, was dying.
As Jesus was on his way, the crowds al-
most crushed him. 43And a woman was
there who had been subject to bleeding
for twelve years,[c] but no one could heal
her. 44She came up behind him and
touched the edge of his cloak, and imme-
diately her bleeding stopped.
45"Who touched me?" Jesus asked.
When they all denied it, Peter said,
"Master, the people are crowding and
pressing against you."
46But Jesus said, "Someone touched
me; I know that power has gone out
from me."
47Then the woman, seeing that she
could not go unnoticed, came trembling
and fell at his feet. In the presence of all
the people, she told why she had touched
him and how she had been instantly
healed. 48Then he said to her, "Daughter,
your faith has healed you. Go in peace."
49While Jesus was still speaking, some-
one came from the house of Jairus, the

[a]26 Some manuscripts *Gadarenes*; other manuscripts *Gergesenes*; also in verse 37 [b]29 Greek *unclean*
[c]43 Many manuscripts *years, and she had spent all she had on doctors*

synagogue ruler. "Your daughter is dead,"
he said. "Don't bother the teacher any
more."
50Hearing this, Jesus said to Jairus,
"Don't be afraid; just believe, and she will
be healed."
51When he arrived at the house of Jai-
rus, he did not let anyone go in with him
except Peter, John and James, and the
child's father and mother. 52Meanwhile,
all the people were wailing and mourning
for her. "Stop wailing," Jesus said. "She is
not dead but asleep."
53They laughed at him, knowing that
she was dead. 54But he took her by the
hand and said, "My child, get up!" 55Her
spirit returned, and at once she stood up.
Then Jesus told them to give her some-
thing to eat. 56Her parents were aston-
ished, but he ordered them not to tell any-
one what had happened.

Jesus Sends Out the Twelve

9 When Jesus had called the Twelve to-
gether, he gave them power and au-
thority to drive out all demons and to cure
diseases, 2and he sent them out to preach
the kingdom of God and to heal the sick.
3He told them: "Take nothing for the jour-
ney—no staff, no bag, no bread, no mon-
ey, no extra tunic. 4Whatever house you
enter, stay there until you leave that town.
5If people do not welcome you, shake the
dust off your feet when you leave their
town, as a testimony against them." 6So
they set out and went from village to vil-
lage, preaching the gospel and healing
people everywhere.
7Now Herod the tetrarch heard about
all that was going on. And he was per-
plexed, because some were saying that
John had been raised from the dead, 8oth-
ers that Elijah had appeared, and still oth-
ers that one of the prophets of long ago
had come back to life. 9But Herod said, "I
beheaded John. Who, then, is this I hear
such things about?" And he tried to see
him.

Jesus Feeds the Five Thousand

10When the apostles returned, they re-
ported to Jesus what they had done. Then
he took them with him and they withdrew
by themselves to a town called Bethsaida,
11but the crowds learned about it and fol-
lowed him. He welcomed them and spoke
to them about the kingdom of God, and
healed those who needed healing.
12Late in the afternoon the Twelve came
to him and said, "Send the crowd away so
they can go to the surrounding villages
and countryside and find food and lodg-
ing, because we are in a remote place
here."
13He replied, "You give them something
to eat."
They answered, "We have only five
loaves of bread and two fish—unless we
go and buy food for all this crowd."
14(About five thousand men were there.)
But he said to his disciples, "Have them
sit down in groups of about fifty each."
15The disciples did so, and everybody sat
down. 16Taking the five loaves and the
two fish and looking up to heaven,
he gave thanks and broke them. Then he
gave them to the disciples to set before the
people. 17They all ate and were satisfied,
and the disciples picked up twelve basket-
fuls of broken pieces that were left over.

Peter's Confession of Christ

18Once when Jesus was praying in pri-
vate and his disciples were with him, he
asked them, "Who do the crowds say
I am?"
19They replied, "Some say John the
Baptist; others say Elijah; and still others,
that one of the prophets of long ago has
come back to life."
20"But what about you?" he asked.
"Who do you say I am?"
Peter answered, "The Christ[a] of God."
21Jesus strictly warned them not to tell
this to anyone. 22And he said, "The Son of
Man must suffer many things and be re-
jected by the elders, chief priests and
teachers of the law, and he must be killed
and on the third day be raised to life."
23Then he said to them all: "If anyone
would come after me, he must deny him-
self and take up his cross daily and follow
me. 24For whoever wants to save his life
will lose it, but whoever loses his life for
me will save it. 25What good is it for a man
to gain the whole world, and yet lose or
forfeit his very self? 26If anyone is
ashamed of me and my words, the Son of
Man will be ashamed of him when he
comes in his glory and in the glory of the
Father and of the holy angels. 27I tell you
the truth, some who are standing here will

[a]20 Or *Messiah*

not taste death before they see the kingdom of God."

The Transfiguration

28 About eight days after Jesus said this,
he took Peter, John and James with him
and went up onto a mountain to pray.
29 As he was praying, the appearance of his
face changed, and his clothes became as
bright as a flash of lightning. 30 Two men,
Moses and Elijah, 31 appeared in glorious
splendor, talking with Jesus. They spoke
about his departure, which he was about
to bring to fulfillment at Jerusalem. 32 Pe-
ter and his companions were very sleepy,
but when they became fully awake, they
saw his glory and the two men standing
with him. 33 As the men were leaving
Jesus, Peter said to him, "Master, it is
good for us to be here. Let us put up three

VERSE FOR THE DAY: Luke 9:24

AUTHOR: Kevin A. and Karen Miller

PASSAGE FOR THE DAY: Luke 9:23–27

The Third Hunger

The Book of Genesis shows that marriage was meant for companionship—"It's not good for a man to be alone." It was meant for raising kids—"Be fruitful and multiply." And Genesis gives us a third glimpse into marriage: It is meant for shared, fulfilling service. God places Adam and Eve in the Garden and says, in essence, "Take care of this, you two. It's a big operation, and you'll need each other. Till, plant, replenish, create."

We hunger for this. Cooperating together. Meshing. Working as a team on something bigger than both of us. God has planted this hunger deep within every married couple. It's more than a hunger for companionship. It's more than a hunger to pour our lives into our kids. It's a third hunger, a hunger to do something significant together. We were joined to make a difference. We were married for a mission.

But too many couples, after developing companionship and having kids, may be missing one-third of what God created marriage for—serving him together. In marriage, as in other areas of life, Jesus' words hold true: In saving our lives we lose them, and in losing our lives in love to others, we drink of life more deeply.

MARRIAGE BUILDERS

♦ *How have you felt this "third hunger" as a couple?*
♦ *If you're still "hungry" to do something significant together, brainstorm some ideas for service or ministry you might begin in the coming weeks.*

Additional Scripture Readings
Matthew 10:39; 1 Samuel 12:24; 1 Peter 4:10–11

Go to page 1119 for your next devotional reading.

shelters—one for you, one for Moses and
one for Elijah." (He did not know what he
was saying.)
34While he was speaking, a cloud ap-
peared and enveloped them, and they
were afraid as they entered the cloud. 35A
voice came from the cloud, saying, "This
is my Son, whom I have chosen; listen to
him." 36When the voice had spoken, they
found that Jesus was alone. The disciples
kept this to themselves, and told no one at
that time what they had seen.

The Healing of a Boy With an Evil Spirit

37The next day, when they came down
from the mountain, a large crowd met
him. 38A man in the crowd called out,
"Teacher, I beg you to look at my son, for
he is my only child. 39A spirit seizes him
and he suddenly screams; it throws him
into convulsions so that he foams at the
mouth. It scarcely ever leaves him and is
destroying him. 40I begged your disciples
to drive it out, but they could not."
41"O unbelieving and perverse generation," Jesus replied, "how long shall I stay
with you and put up with you? Bring your
son here."
42Even while the boy was coming, the
demon threw him to the ground in a convulsion. But Jesus rebuked the evil[a] spirit, healed the boy and gave him back to his
father. 43And they were all amazed at the
greatness of God.
While everyone was marveling at all
that Jesus did, he said to his disciples,
44"Listen carefully to what I am about to
tell you: The Son of Man is going to be betrayed into the hands of men." 45But they
did not understand what this meant. It
was hidden from them, so that they did
not grasp it, and they were afraid to ask
him about it.

Who Will Be the Greatest?

46An argument started among the disciples as to which of them would be the
greatest. 47Jesus, knowing their thoughts,
took a little child and had him stand beside him. 48Then he said to them, "Whoever welcomes this little child in my name
welcomes me; and whoever welcomes me
welcomes the one who sent me. For he
who is least among you all—he is the
greatest."
49"Master," said John, "we saw a man
driving out demons in your name and we
tried to stop him, because he is not one
of us."
50"Do not stop him," Jesus said, "for
whoever is not against you is for you."

Samaritan Opposition

51As the time approached for him to be
taken up to heaven, Jesus resolutely set
out for Jerusalem. 52And he sent messengers on ahead, who went into a Samaritan
village to get things ready for him; 53but
the people there did not welcome him, because he was heading for Jerusalem.
54When the disciples James and John saw
this, they asked, "Lord, do you want us to
call fire down from heaven to destroy
them[b]?" 55But Jesus turned and rebuked
them, 56and[c] they went to another village.

The Cost of Following Jesus

57As they were walking along the road,
a man said to him, "I will follow you wherever you go."
58Jesus replied, "Foxes have holes and
birds of the air have nests, but the Son of
Man has no place to lay his head."
59He said to another man, "Follow me."
But the man replied, "Lord, first let me
go and bury my father."
60Jesus said to him, "Let the dead bury
their own dead, but you go and proclaim
the kingdom of God."
61Still another said, "I will follow you,
Lord; but first let me go back and say
good-by to my family."
62Jesus replied, "No one who puts his
hand to the plow and looks back is fit for
service in the kingdom of God."

Jesus Sends Out the Seventy-two

10 After this the Lord appointed seventy-two[d] others and sent them
two by two ahead of him to every town
and place where he was about to go. 2He
told them, "The harvest is plentiful, but
the workers are few. Ask the Lord of the
harvest, therefore, to send out workers
into his harvest field. 3Go! I am sending
you out like lambs among wolves. 4Do not

[a] 42 Greek *unclean* [b] 54 Some manuscripts *them, even as Elijah did* [c] 55,56 Some manuscripts *them. And he said, "You do not know what kind of spirit you are of, for the Son of Man did not come to destroy men's lives, but to save them." 56And* [d] 1 Some manuscripts *seventy*; also in verse 17

take a purse or bag or sandals; and do not
greet anyone on the road.
5"When you enter a house, first say,
'Peace to this house.' 6If a man of peace is
there, your peace will rest on him; if not,
it will return to you. 7Stay in that house,
eating and drinking whatever they give
you, for the worker deserves his wages.
Do not move around from house to house.
8"When you enter a town and are wel-
comed, eat what is set before you. 9Heal
the sick who are there and tell them, 'The
kingdom of God is near you.' 10But when
you enter a town and are not welcomed,
go into its streets and say, 11'Even the dust
of your town that sticks to our feet we
wipe off against you. Yet be sure of this:
The kingdom of God is near.' 12I tell you,
it will be more bearable on that day for
Sodom than for that town.
13"Woe to you, Korazin! Woe to you,
Bethsaida! For if the miracles that were
performed in you had been performed in
Tyre and Sidon, they would have repented
long ago, sitting in sackcloth and ashes.
14But it will be more bearable for Tyre and
Sidon at the judgment than for you. 15And
you, Capernaum, will you be lifted up to
the skies? No, you will go down to the
depths.[a]
16"He who listens to you listens to me;
he who rejects you rejects me; but he who
rejects me rejects him who sent me."
17The seventy-two returned with joy
and said, "Lord, even the demons submit
to us in your name."
18He replied, "I saw Satan fall like light-
ning from heaven. 19I have given you au-
thority to trample on snakes and scorpi-
ons and to overcome all the power of the
enemy; nothing will harm you. 20Howev-
er, do not rejoice that the spirits submit to
you, but rejoice that your names are writ-
ten in heaven."
21At that time Jesus, full of joy through
the Holy Spirit, said, "I praise you, Father,
Lord of heaven and earth, because you
have hidden these things from the wise
and learned, and revealed them to little
children. Yes, Father, for this was your
good pleasure.
22"All things have been committed to
me by my Father. No one knows who the
Son is except the Father, and no one
knows who the Father is except the Son
and those to whom the Son chooses to re-
veal him."
23Then he turned to his disciples and
said privately, "Blessed are the eyes that
see what you see. 24For I tell you that
many prophets and kings wanted to see
what you see but did not see it, and to
hear what you hear but did not hear it."

The Parable of the Good Samaritan

25On one occasion an expert in the law
stood up to test Jesus. "Teacher," he
asked, "what must I do to inherit eternal
life?"
26"What is written in the Law?" he re-
plied. "How do you read it?"
27He answered: " 'Love the Lord your
God with all your heart and with all your
soul and with all your strength and with
all your mind'[b]; and, 'Love your neighbor
as yourself.'[c]"
28"You have answered correctly," Jesus
replied. "Do this and you will live."
29But he wanted to justify himself, so he
asked Jesus, "And who is my neighbor?"
30In reply Jesus said: "A man was going
down from Jerusalem to Jericho, when he
fell into the hands of robbers. They
stripped him of his clothes, beat him and
went away, leaving him half dead. 31A
priest happened to be going down the
same road, and when he saw the man, he
passed by on the other side. 32So too, a Le-
vite, when he came to the place and saw
him, passed by on the other side. 33But a
Samaritan, as he traveled, came where the
man was; and when he saw him, he took
pity on him. 34He went to him and ban-
daged his wounds, pouring on oil and
wine. Then he put the man on his own
donkey, took him to an inn and took care
of him. 35The next day he took out two sil-
ver coins[d] and gave them to the innkeep-
er. 'Look after him,' he said, 'and when I
return, I will reimburse you for any extra
expense you may have.'
36"Which of these three do you think
was a neighbor to the man who fell into
the hands of robbers?"
37The expert in the law replied, "The
one who had mercy on him."
Jesus told him, "Go and do likewise."

At the Home of Martha and Mary

38As Jesus and his disciples were on
their way, he came to a village where a
woman named Martha opened her home

[a]15 Greek *Hades* [b]27 Deut. 6:5 [c]27 Lev. 19:18 [d]35 Greek *two denarii*

to him. 39She had a sister called Mary,
who sat at the Lord's feet listening to what
he said. 40But Martha was distracted by all
the preparations that had to be made. She
came to him and asked, "Lord, don't you
care that my sister has left me to do
the work by myself? Tell her to help me!"
41"Martha, Martha," the Lord answered,
"you are worried and upset about many
things, 42but only one thing is needed.[a]
Mary has chosen what is better, and it will
not be taken away from her."

[a]42 Some manuscripts *but few things are needed—or only one*

VERSE FOR THE DAY: Luke 10:40

AUTHOR: Susan M. Felch

PASSAGE FOR THE DAY: Luke 10:38–42

Undistracted Loyalty

When I think about the extremes of vigorous activity and genuine rest, I am drawn to the story of Mary and Martha. Martha is actively serving Jesus, but he rebukes her and commends Mary, instead, for choosing what is better.

Martha fits the picture of an overextended server. She had received Jesus into her home, yet, apparently, she did not welcome this opportunity for humble service. Instead, she writhed under the burden while Mary sat quietly and worshiped.

Like the disciples, Martha focused her attention on the supposed defects of others rather than on the privilege of serving her Lord. And she gave priority to tangible commitments (her work) rather than to intangible attitudes of the heart (worship).

Jesus' rebuke to Martha in no way invalidates the need for vigorous service. Mary, herself, was not passive in her devotion to Jesus. John records that later she served Jesus publicly and unashamedly (John 12:1–8). Instead, Jesus redirects Martha's attention. Martha has received him into her house and all she needs is to be focused on him—whether in serving, or in listening. The "better" way that Mary chose was not quietness *per se*, but undistracted loyalty to Jesus.

MARRIAGE BUILDERS

♦ *Which comes easier for you, a more contemplative relationship with God (like Mary's) or a more hands-on, active one (like Martha's)?*

♦ *What can you do to foster undivided loyalty to Christ, whether in quiet worship or active service?*

Additional Scripture Readings
1 Chronicles 29:17–18; John 12:1–8;
Psalm 139:23–24; 141:8

Go to page 1121 for your next devotional reading.

Jesus' Teaching on Prayer

11 One day Jesus was praying in a certain place. When he finished, one of his disciples said to him, "Lord, teach us to pray, just as John taught his disciples."

2He said to them, "When you pray, say:

" 'Father,[a]
hallowed be your name,
your kingdom come.[b]
3Give us each day our daily bread.
4Forgive us our sins,
for we also forgive everyone who
sins against us.[c]
And lead us not into temptation.[d]' "

5Then he said to them, "Suppose one of you has a friend, and he goes to him at midnight and says, 'Friend, lend me three loaves of bread, 6because a friend of mine on a journey has come to me, and I have nothing to set before him.'

7"Then the one inside answers, 'Don't bother me. The door is already locked, and my children are with me in bed. I can't get up and give you anything.' 8I tell you, though he will not get up and give him the bread because he is his friend, yet because of the man's boldness[e] he will get up and give him as much as he needs.

9"So I say to you: Ask and it will be given to you; seek and you will find; knock and the door will be opened to you. 10For everyone who asks receives; he who seeks finds; and to him who knocks, the door will be opened.

11"Which of you fathers, if your son asks for[f] a fish, will give him a snake instead? 12Or if he asks for an egg, will give him a scorpion? 13If you then, though you are evil, know how to give good gifts to your children, how much more will your Father in heaven give the Holy Spirit to those who ask him!"

Jesus and Beelzebub

14Jesus was driving out a demon that was mute. When the demon left, the man who had been mute spoke, and the crowd was amazed. 15But some of them said, "By Beelzebub,[g] the prince of demons, he is driving out demons." 16Others tested him by asking for a sign from heaven.

17Jesus knew their thoughts and said to them: "Any kingdom divided against itself will be ruined, and a house divided against itself will fall. 18If Satan is divided against himself, how can his kingdom stand? I say this because you claim that I drive out demons by Beelzebub. 19Now if I drive out demons by Beelzebub, by whom do your followers drive them out? So then, they will be your judges. 20But if I drive out demons by the finger of God, then the kingdom of God has come to you.

21"When a strong man, fully armed, guards his own house, his possessions are safe. 22But when someone stronger attacks and overpowers him, he takes away the armor in which the man trusted and divides up the spoils.

23"He who is not with me is against me, and he who does not gather with me, scatters.

24"When an evil[h] spirit comes out of a man, it goes through arid places seeking rest and does not find it. Then it says, 'I will return to the house I left.' 25When it arrives, it finds the house swept clean and put in order. 26Then it goes and takes seven other spirits more wicked than itself, and they go in and live there. And the final condition of that man is worse than the first."

27As Jesus was saying these things, a woman in the crowd called out, "Blessed is the mother who gave you birth and nursed you."

28He replied, "Blessed rather are those who hear the word of God and obey it."

The Sign of Jonah

29As the crowds increased, Jesus said, "This is a wicked generation. It asks for a miraculous sign, but none will be given it except the sign of Jonah. 30For as Jonah was a sign to the Ninevites, so also will the Son of Man be to this generation. 31The Queen of the South will rise at the judgment with the men of this generation and condemn them; for she came from the ends of the earth to listen to Solomon's wisdom, and now one[i] greater than Solomon is here. 32The men of Nineveh will stand up at the judgment with this generation and condemn it; for they repented at

[a]2 Some manuscripts *Our Father in heaven* [b]2 Some manuscripts *come. May your will be done on earth as it is in heaven.* [c]4 Greek *everyone who is indebted to us* [d]4 Some manuscripts *temptation but deliver us from the evil one* [e]8 Or *persistence* [f]11 Some manuscripts *for bread, will give him a stone; or if he asks for* [g]15 Greek *Beezeboul* or *Beelzeboul*; also in verses 18 and 19 [h]24 Greek *unclean* [i]31 Or *something*; also in verse 32

WEEKENDING

TIME

Discuss this list of time-management tips. Which ones could be put to work to help you find more time to spend with each other?

1. Remember that you manage time; it doesn't manage you.

2. Decide what's truly important and postpone or cancel a few items from your to-do list.

3. Try scheduling in reverse. Put couple time on the calendar first.

4. Eliminate something from your schedule to free up an hour or two for each other.

5. Get each other's perspective on how you're using your time.

6. Be honest about your limitations. Analyze a proposed project realistically, determining where you'll find the hours to complete it.

7. List your commitments. Then keep that list next to your phone and calendar to remind you what you're already involved in before you take on something new.

— *Louise A. Ferrebee*

REVIVE

Saturday: 1 Corinthians 10:31–33

Sunday: Colossians 3:12–17

Go to page 1124 for your next devotional reading.

the preaching of Jonah, and now one greater than Jonah is here.

The Lamp of the Body

33"No one lights a lamp and puts it in a place where it will be hidden, or under a bowl. Instead he puts it on its stand, so that those who come in may see the light. 34Your eye is the lamp of your body. When your eyes are good, your whole body also is full of light. But when they are bad, your body also is full of darkness. 35See to it, then, that the light within you is not darkness. 36Therefore, if your whole body is full of light, and no part of it dark, it will be completely lighted, as when the light of a lamp shines on you."

Six Woes

37When Jesus had finished speaking, a Pharisee invited him to eat with him; so he went in and reclined at the table. 38But the Pharisee, noticing that Jesus did not first wash before the meal, was surprised.

39Then the Lord said to him, "Now then, you Pharisees clean the outside of the cup and dish, but inside you are full of greed and wickedness. 40You foolish people! Did not the one who made the outside make the inside also? 41But give what is inside ⌊the dish⌋[a] to the poor, and everything will be clean for you.

42"Woe to you Pharisees, because you give God a tenth of your mint, rue and all other kinds of garden herbs, but you neglect justice and the love of God. You should have practiced the latter without leaving the former undone.

43"Woe to you Pharisees, because you love the most important seats in the synagogues and greetings in the marketplaces.

44"Woe to you, because you are like unmarked graves, which men walk over without knowing it."

45One of the experts in the law answered him, "Teacher, when you say these things, you insult us also."

46Jesus replied, "And you experts in the law, woe to you, because you load people down with burdens they can hardly carry, and you yourselves will not lift one finger to help them.

47"Woe to you, because you build tombs for the prophets, and it was your forefathers who killed them. 48So you testify that you approve of what your forefathers did; they killed the prophets, and you build their tombs. 49Because of this, God in his wisdom said, 'I will send them prophets and apostles, some of whom they will kill and others they will persecute.' 50Therefore this generation will be held responsible for the blood of all the prophets that has been shed since the beginning of the world, 51from the blood of Abel to the blood of Zechariah, who was killed between the altar and the sanctuary. Yes, I tell you, this generation will be held responsible for it all.

52"Woe to you experts in the law, because you have taken away the key to knowledge. You yourselves have not entered, and you have hindered those who were entering."

53When Jesus left there, the Pharisees and the teachers of the law began to oppose him fiercely and to besiege him with questions, 54waiting to catch him in something he might say.

Warnings and Encouragements

12 Meanwhile, when a crowd of many thousands had gathered, so that they were trampling on one another, Jesus began to speak first to his disciples, saying: "Be on your guard against the yeast of the Pharisees, which is hypocrisy. 2There is nothing concealed that will not be disclosed, or hidden that will not be made known. 3What you have said in the dark will be heard in the daylight, and what you have whispered in the ear in the inner rooms will be proclaimed from the roofs.

4"I tell you, my friends, do not be afraid of those who kill the body and after that can do no more. 5But I will show you whom you should fear: Fear him who, after the killing of the body, has power to throw you into hell. Yes, I tell you, fear him. 6Are not five sparrows sold for two pennies[b]? Yet not one of them is forgotten by God. 7Indeed, the very hairs of your head are all numbered. Don't be afraid; you are worth more than many sparrows.

8"I tell you, whoever acknowledges me before men, the Son of Man will also acknowledge him before the angels of God. 9But he who disowns me before men will be disowned before the angels of God. 10And everyone who speaks a word against the Son of Man will be forgiven, but anyone who blasphemes against the Holy Spirit will not be forgiven.

[a]41 Or *what you have* [b]6 Greek *two assaria*

11"When you are brought before synagogues, rulers and authorities, do not worry about how you will defend yourselves or what you will say, 12for the Holy Spirit will teach you at that time what you should say."

The Parable of the Rich Fool

13Someone in the crowd said to him, "Teacher, tell my brother to divide the inheritance with me."

14Jesus replied, "Man, who appointed me a judge or an arbiter between you?" 15Then he said to them, "Watch out! Be on your guard against all kinds of greed; a man's life does not consist in the abundance of his possessions."

16And he told them this parable: "The ground of a certain rich man produced a good crop. 17He thought to himself, 'What shall I do? I have no place to store my crops.'

18"Then he said, 'This is what I'll do. I will tear down my barns and build bigger ones, and there I will store all my grain and my goods. 19And I'll say to myself, "You have plenty of good things laid up for many years. Take life easy; eat, drink and be merry."'

20"But God said to him, 'You fool! This very night your life will be demanded from you. Then who will get what you have prepared for yourself?'

21"This is how it will be with anyone who stores up things for himself but is not rich toward God."

Do Not Worry

22Then Jesus said to his disciples: "Therefore I tell you, do not worry about your life, what you will eat; or about your body, what you will wear. 23Life is more than food, and the body more than clothes. 24Consider the ravens: They do not sow or reap, they have no storeroom or barn; yet God feeds them. And how much more valuable you are than birds! 25Who of you by worrying can add a single hour to his life[a]? 26Since you cannot do this very little thing, why do you worry about the rest?

27"Consider how the lilies grow. They do not labor or spin. Yet I tell you, not even Solomon in all his splendor was dressed like one of these. 28If that is how God clothes the grass of the field, which is here today, and tomorrow is thrown into the fire, how much more will he clothe you, O you of little faith! 29And do not set your heart on what you will eat or drink; do not worry about it. 30For the pagan world runs after all such things, and your Father knows that you need them. 31But seek his kingdom, and these things will be given to you as well.

32"Do not be afraid, little flock, for your Father has been pleased to give you the kingdom. 33Sell your possessions and give to the poor. Provide purses for yourselves that will not wear out, a treasure in heaven that will not be exhausted, where no thief comes near and no moth destroys. 34For where your treasure is, there your heart will be also.

Watchfulness

35"Be dressed ready for service and keep your lamps burning, 36like men waiting for their master to return from a wedding banquet, so that when he comes and knocks they can immediately open the door for him. 37It will be good for those servants whose master finds them watching when he comes. I tell you the truth, he will dress himself to serve, will have them recline at the table and will come and wait on them. 38It will be good for those servants whose master finds them ready, even if he comes in the second or third watch of the night. 39But understand this: If the owner of the house had known at what hour the thief was coming, he would not have let his house be broken into. 40You also must be ready, because the Son of Man will come at an hour when you do not expect him."

41Peter asked, "Lord, are you telling this parable to us, or to everyone?"

42The Lord answered, "Who then is the faithful and wise manager, whom the master puts in charge of his servants to give them their food allowance at the proper time? 43It will be good for that servant whom the master finds doing so when he returns. 44I tell you the truth, he will put him in charge of all his possessions. 45But suppose the servant says to himself, 'My master is taking a long time in coming,' and he then begins to beat the menservants and maidservants and to eat and drink and get drunk. 46The master of that servant will come on a day when he does not expect him and at an hour he is not aware of. He will cut him to pieces and

[a]25 Or *single cubit to his height*

VERSE FOR THE DAY: Luke 12:24

AUTHOR: Susan M. Bailey

PASSAGE FOR THE DAY: Luke 12:22–34

Rooms Marked "Private"

Our phone was disconnected last month because we couldn't pay our bill on time. Our mortgage is two months past due, and it will take us two years to pay off medical bills from having our third child.

Richard and I both made career moves—ones we felt God's leading to make—which cut our income in half. I left a full-time job in favor of part-time work so I could be home with our kids more, and Richard resigned his job to pursue a career in real estate. Short-term projections said we could get by on our reduced income for some time. But it's been months now, and our expenses still exceed our income.

In the past, I had rarely included God in our financial decisions. Except for the percentage we gave to the church, I had figured our money was ours and if we messed up, it was our problem. With the exception of our mortgage, we had almost no debts. But perhaps we have failed to act responsibly by not recognizing that all we have truly does come from God and that he cares about every aspect of our life, including the water bill.

If I've learned anything by being broke, it's that there are still rooms in my life marked "private." God didn't lead us down this road to punish us for failing to relinquish every area of our life to him. But somehow for me handing over the money behind Door Number One feels like the first hopeful step we've taken toward real financial freedom.

MARRIAGE BUILDERS

♦ *Review your spending during the last week. Do your expenses reflect the attitude that all you have belongs to God?*

♦ *What are other areas you might tend to keep behind a "closed door" instead of letting God have control?*

Additional Scripture Readings
Matthew 6:25–34; Psalm 145:16

Go to page 1128 for your next devotional reading.

assign him a place with the unbelievers.
47"That servant who knows his master's
will and does not get ready or does not do
what his master wants will be beaten with
many blows. 48But the one who does not
know and does things deserving punish-
ment will be beaten with few blows. From
everyone who has been given much,
much will be demanded; and from the one
who has been entrusted with much, much
more will be asked.

Not Peace but Division

49"I have come to bring fire on the
earth, and how I wish it were already kin-
dled! 50But I have a baptism to undergo,
and how distressed I am until it is com-
pleted! 51Do you think I came to bring
peace on earth? No, I tell you, but divi-
sion. 52From now on there will be five in
one family divided against each other,
three against two and two against three.
53They will be divided, father against son
and son against father, mother against
daughter and daughter against mother,
mother-in-law against daughter-in-law
and daughter-in-law against mother-in-
law."

Interpreting the Times

54He said to the crowd: "When you see
a cloud rising in the west, immediately
you say, 'It's going to rain,' and it does.
55And when the south wind blows, you
say, 'It's going to be hot,' and it is. 56Hypo-
crites! You know how to interpret the ap-
pearance of the earth and the sky. How is
it that you don't know how to interpret
this present time?
57"Why don't you judge for yourselves
what is right? 58As you are going with
your adversary to the magistrate, try hard
to be reconciled to him on the way, or he
may drag you off to the judge, and the
judge turn you over to the officer, and the
officer throw you into prison. 59I tell you,
you will not get out until you have paid
the last penny.[a]"

Repent or Perish

13 Now there were some present at
that time who told Jesus about the
Galileans whose blood Pilate had mixed
with their sacrifices. 2Jesus answered, "Do
you think that these Galileans were worse
sinners than all the other Galileans be-
cause they suffered this way? 3I tell you,
no! But unless you repent, you too will all
perish. 4Or those eighteen who died when
the tower in Siloam fell on them—do you
think they were more guilty than all the
others living in Jerusalem? 5I tell you, no!
But unless you repent, you too will all per-
ish."
6Then he told this parable: "A man had
a fig tree, planted in his vineyard, and he
went to look for fruit on it, but did not find
any. 7So he said to the man who took care
of the vineyard, 'For three years now I've
been coming to look for fruit on this fig
tree and haven't found any. Cut it down!
Why should it use up the soil?'
8" 'Sir,' the man replied, 'leave it alone
for one more year, and I'll dig around it
and fertilize it. 9If it bears fruit next year,
fine! If not, then cut it down.' "

A Crippled Woman Healed on the Sabbath

10On a Sabbath Jesus was teaching in
one of the synagogues, 11and a woman
was there who had been crippled by a
spirit for eighteen years. She was bent
over and could not straighten up at all.
12When Jesus saw her, he called her for-
ward and said to her, "Woman, you are set
free from your infirmity." 13Then he put
his hands on her, and immediately she
straightened up and praised God.
14Indignant because Jesus had healed
on the Sabbath, the synagogue ruler said
to the people, "There are six days for
work. So come and be healed on those
days, not on the Sabbath."
15The Lord answered him, "You hypo-
crites! Doesn't each of you on the Sabbath
untie his ox or donkey from the stall and
lead it out to give it water? 16Then should
not this woman, a daughter of Abraham,
whom Satan has kept bound for eighteen
long years, be set free on the Sabbath day
from what bound her?"
17When he said this, all his opponents
were humiliated, but the people were de-
lighted with all the wonderful things he
was doing.

The Parables of the Mustard Seed and the Yeast

18Then Jesus asked, "What is the king-
dom of God like? What shall I compare it
to? 19It is like a mustard seed, which a
man took and planted in his garden. It

[a]59 Greek *lepton*

grew and became a tree, and the birds of
the air perched in its branches."
20Again he asked, "What shall I com-
pare the kingdom of God to? 21It is like
yeast that a woman took and mixed into a
large amount[a] of flour until it worked all
through the dough."

The Narrow Door

22Then Jesus went through the towns
and villages, teaching as he made his way
to Jerusalem. 23Someone asked him,
"Lord, are only a few people going to be
saved?"
He said to them, 24"Make every effort to
enter through the narrow door, because
many, I tell you, will try to enter and will
not be able to. 25Once the owner of the
house gets up and closes the door, you
will stand outside knocking and pleading,
'Sir, open the door for us.'
"But he will answer, 'I don't know you
or where you come from.'
26"Then you will say, 'We ate and drank
with you, and you taught in our streets.'
27"But he will reply, 'I don't know you
or where you come from. Away from me,
all you evildoers!'
28"There will be weeping there, and
gnashing of teeth, when you see Abra-
ham, Isaac and Jacob and all the prophets
in the kingdom of God, but you your-
selves thrown out. 29People will come
from east and west and north and south,
and will take their places at the feast in the
kingdom of God. 30Indeed there are those
who are last who will be first, and first
who will be last."

Jesus' Sorrow for Jerusalem

31At that time some Pharisees came to
Jesus and said to him, "Leave this place
and go somewhere else. Herod wants to
kill you."
32He replied, "Go tell that fox, 'I will
drive out demons and heal people today
and tomorrow, and on the third day I will
reach my goal.' 33In any case, I must keep
going today and tomorrow and the next
day—for surely no prophet can die out-
side Jerusalem!
34"O Jerusalem, Jerusalem, you who kill
the prophets and stone those sent to you,
how often I have longed to gather your
children together, as a hen gathers her
chicks under her wings, but you were not
willing! 35Look, your house is left to you
desolate. I tell you, you will not see me
again until you say, 'Blessed is he who
comes in the name of the Lord.'[b]"

Jesus at a Pharisee's House

14 One Sabbath, when Jesus went to
eat in the house of a prominent
Pharisee, he was being carefully watched.
2There in front of him was a man suffering
from dropsy. 3Jesus asked the Pharisees
and experts in the law, "Is it lawful to heal
on the Sabbath or not?" 4But they re-
mained silent. So taking hold of the man,
he healed him and sent him away.
5Then he asked them, "If one of you has
a son[c] or an ox that falls into a well on
the Sabbath day, will you not immediately
pull him out?" 6And they had nothing to
say.
7When he noticed how the guests
picked the places of honor at the table, he
told them this parable: 8"When someone
invites you to a wedding feast, do not take
the place of honor, for a person more dis-
tinguished than you may have been invit-
ed. 9If so, the host who invited both of you
will come and say to you, 'Give this man
your seat.' Then, humiliated, you will
have to take the least important place.
10But when you are invited, take the low-
est place, so that when your host comes,
he will say to you, 'Friend, move up to a
better place.' Then you will be honored in
the presence of all your fellow guests.
11For everyone who exalts himself will be
humbled, and he who humbles himself
will be exalted."
12Then Jesus said to his host, "When
you give a luncheon or dinner, do not in-
vite your friends, your brothers or rela-
tives, or your rich neighbors; if you do,
they may invite you back and so you will
be repaid. 13But when you give a banquet,
invite the poor, the crippled, the lame, the
blind, 14and you will be blessed. Although
they cannot repay you, you will be repaid
at the resurrection of the righteous."

The Parable of the Great Banquet

15When one of those at the table with
him heard this, he said to Jesus, "Blessed
is the man who will eat at the feast in the
kingdom of God."
16Jesus replied: "A certain man was pre-
paring a great banquet and invited many

[a]21 Greek *three satas* (probably about 1/2 bushel or 22 liters) [b]35 Psalm 118:26 [c]5 Some manuscripts *donkey*

guests. 17At the time of the banquet he
sent his servant to tell those who had been
invited, 'Come, for everything is now
ready.'
18"But they all alike began to make ex-
cuses. The first said, 'I have just bought a
field, and I must go and see it. Please ex-
cuse me.'
19"Another said, 'I have just bought five
yoke of oxen, and I'm on my way to try
them out. Please excuse me.'
20"Still another said, 'I just got married,
so I can't come.'
21"The servant came back and reported
this to his master. Then the owner of
the house became angry and ordered his ser-
vant, 'Go out quickly into the streets and
alleys of the town and bring in the poor,
the crippled, the blind and the lame.'
22" 'Sir,' the servant said, 'what you or-
dered has been done, but there is still
room.'
23"Then the master told his servant, 'Go
out to the roads and country lanes and
make them come in, so that my house will
be full. 24I tell you, not one of those men
who were invited will get a taste of my
banquet.' "

The Cost of Being a Disciple

25Large crowds were traveling with
Jesus, and turning to them he said: 26"If
anyone comes to me and does not hate his
father and mother, his wife and children,
his brothers and sisters—yes, even his
own life—he cannot be my disciple.
27And anyone who does not carry his
cross and follow me cannot be my disci-
ple.
28"Suppose one of you wants to build a
tower. Will he not first sit down and esti-
mate the cost to see if he has enough mon-
ey to complete it? 29For if he lays the foun-
dation and is not able to finish it, everyone
who sees it will ridicule him, 30saying,
'This fellow began to build and was not
able to finish.'
31"Or suppose a king is about to go to
war against another king. Will he not first
sit down and consider whether he is able
with ten thousand men to oppose the one
coming against him with twenty thou-
sand? 32If he is not able, he will send a dele-
gation while the other is still a long way
off and will ask for terms of peace. 33In the
same way, any of you who does not give
up everything he has cannot be my disci-
ple.
34"Salt is good, but if it loses its salti-
ness, how can it be made salty again? 35It
is fit neither for the soil nor for the ma-
nure pile; it is thrown out.
"He who has ears to hear, let him hear."

The Parable of the Lost Sheep

15 Now the tax collectors and "sin-
ners" were all gathering around to
hear him. 2But the Pharisees and the
teachers of the law muttered, "This man
welcomes sinners and eats with them."
3Then Jesus told them this parable:
4"Suppose one of you has a hundred
sheep and loses one of them. Does he not
leave the ninety-nine in the open country
and go after the lost sheep until he finds
it? 5And when he finds it, he joyfully puts
it on his shoulders 6and goes home. Then
he calls his friends and neighbors together
and says, 'Rejoice with me; I have found
my lost sheep.' 7I tell you that in the same
way there will be more rejoicing in heaven
over one sinner who repents than over
ninety-nine righteous persons who do not
need to repent.

The Parable of the Lost Coin

8"Or suppose a woman has ten silver
coins[a] and loses one. Does she not light
a lamp, sweep the house and search care-
fully until she finds it? 9And when she
finds it, she calls her friends and neigh-
bors together and says, 'Rejoice with me;
I have found my lost coin.' 10In the same
way, I tell you, there is rejoicing in the
presence of the angels of God over one
sinner who repents."

The Parable of the Lost Son

11Jesus continued: "There was a man
who had two sons. 12The younger one
said to his father, 'Father, give me my
share of the estate.' So he divided his
property between them.
13"Not long after that, the younger son
got together all he had, set off for a distant
country and there squandered his wealth
in wild living. 14After he had spent every-
thing, there was a severe famine in that
whole country, and he began to be in
need. 15So he went and hired himself out
to a citizen of that country, who sent him

[a]8 Greek *ten drachmas*, each worth about a day's wages

to his fields to feed pigs. [16]He longed to fill
his stomach with the pods that the pigs
were eating, but no one gave him any-
thing.
[17]"When he came to his senses, he said,
'How many of my father's hired men have
food to spare, and here I am starving to
death! [18]I will set out and go back to my
father and say to him: Father, I have
sinned against heaven and against you. [19]I
am no longer worthy to be called your
son; make me like one of your hired men.'
[20]So he got up and went to his father.
"But while he was still a long way off,
his father saw him and was filled with
compassion for him; he ran to his son,
threw his arms around him and kissed
him.
[21]"The son said to him, 'Father, I have
sinned against heaven and against you. I

VERSE FOR THE DAY: Luke 14:11 | AUTHOR: Gary L. Thomas | PASSAGE FOR THE DAY: Luke 14:1–14

Exalting Humility

Where I fail in humility, I fail in love. That's especially true in marriage. What starts out as mutual affection can easily collapse into a contest of wills, judgment and accusation. When I'm experiencing persistent anger with my wife, Lisa, almost always I can find a point where I'm judging her, calling myself "right" and her "wrong." But Christ took away our license to judge. Humble people focus instead on changing themselves.

Humility means more than just being able to admit being wrong. Humility isn't thinking less *of* ourselves; it's thinking less *about* ourselves. Obsessing over what you *aren't* makes you as self-absorbed as the person who obsesses about what she *is*.

Jesus was humble, yet he never pretended he wasn't the Son of God. He never claimed that his mission in life wasn't important; he just used his power to serve and love rather than to dominate.

Humility gives us the strength to accept who we are, respect others and escape from an egocentric worldview in which we expect everyone (especially our spouse) to bend to our demands and desires. Humility is the Christlike spirit of becoming a servant.

MARRIAGE BUILDERS

♦ *Identify one area in which you and your spouse butt heads. How could humility play a role in resolving that conflict?*
♦ *What's the antidote for thinking too much* about *yourself?*

Additional Scripture Readings
Philippians 2:3–4; Titus 3:1–2

Go to page 1131 for your next devotional reading.

am no longer worthy to be called your son.[a]'

22"But the father said to his servants, 'Quick! Bring the best robe and put it on him. Put a ring on his finger and sandals on his feet. 23Bring the fattened calf and kill it. Let's have a feast and celebrate. 24For this son of mine was dead and is alive again; he was lost and is found.' So they began to celebrate.

25"Meanwhile, the older son was in the field. When he came near the house, he heard music and dancing. 26So he called one of the servants and asked him what was going on. 27'Your brother has come,' he replied, 'and your father has killed the fattened calf because he has him back safe and sound.'

28"The older brother became angry and refused to go in. So his father went out and pleaded with him. 29But he answered his father, 'Look! All these years I've been slaving for you and never disobeyed your orders. Yet you never gave me even a young goat so I could celebrate with my friends. 30But when this son of yours who has squandered your property with prostitutes comes home, you kill the fattened calf for him!'

31" 'My son,' the father said, 'you are always with me, and everything I have is yours. 32But we had to celebrate and be glad, because this brother of yours was dead and is alive again; he was lost and is found.' "

The Parable of the Shrewd Manager

16 Jesus told his disciples: "There was a rich man whose manager was accused of wasting his possessions. 2So he called him in and asked him, 'What is this I hear about you? Give an account of your management, because you cannot be manager any longer.'

3"The manager said to himself, 'What shall I do now? My master is taking away my job. I'm not strong enough to dig, and I'm ashamed to beg— 4I know what I'll do so that, when I lose my job here, people will welcome me into their houses.'

5"So he called in each one of his master's debtors. He asked the first, 'How much do you owe my master?'

6" 'Eight hundred gallons[b] of olive oil,' he replied.

"The manager told him, 'Take your bill, sit down quickly, and make it four hundred.'

7"Then he asked the second, 'And how much do you owe?'

" 'A thousand bushels[c] of wheat,' he replied.

"He told him, 'Take your bill and make it eight hundred.'

8"The master commended the dishonest manager because he had acted shrewdly. For the people of this world are more shrewd in dealing with their own kind than are the people of the light. 9I tell you, use worldly wealth to gain friends for yourselves, so that when it is gone, you will be welcomed into eternal dwellings.

10"Whoever can be trusted with very little can also be trusted with much, and whoever is dishonest with very little will also be dishonest with much. 11So if you have not been trustworthy in handling worldly wealth, who will trust you with true riches? 12And if you have not been trustworthy with someone else's property, who will give you property of your own?

13"No servant can serve two masters. Either he will hate the one and love the other, or he will be devoted to the one and despise the other. You cannot serve both God and Money."

14The Pharisees, who loved money, heard all this and were sneering at Jesus. 15He said to them, "You are the ones who justify yourselves in the eyes of men, but God knows your hearts. What is highly valued among men is detestable in God's sight.

Additional Teachings

16"The Law and the Prophets were proclaimed until John. Since that time, the good news of the kingdom of God is being preached, and everyone is forcing his way into it. 17It is easier for heaven and earth to disappear than for the least stroke of a pen to drop out of the Law.

18"Anyone who divorces his wife and marries another woman commits adultery, and the man who marries a divorced woman commits adultery.

The Rich Man and Lazarus

19"There was a rich man who was dressed in purple and fine linen and lived in luxury every day. 20At his gate was laid

[a]21 Some early manuscripts *son. Make me like one of your hired men.* [b]6 Greek *one hundred batous* (probably about 3 kiloliters) [c]7 Greek *one hundred korous* (probably about 35 kiloliters)

a beggar named Lazarus, covered with
sores 21and longing to eat what fell from
the rich man's table. Even the dogs came
and licked his sores.

22"The time came when the beggar died
and the angels carried him to Abraham's
side. The rich man also died and was bur-
ied. 23In hell,[a] where he was in torment,
he looked up and saw Abraham far away,
with Lazarus by his side. 24So he called to
him, 'Father Abraham, have pity on me
and send Lazarus to dip the tip of his fin-
ger in water and cool my tongue, because
I am in agony in this fire.'

25"But Abraham replied, 'Son, remem-
ber that in your lifetime you received your
good things, while Lazarus received bad
things, but now he is comforted here and
you are in agony. 26And besides all this,
between us and you a great chasm has
been fixed, so that those who want to go
from here to you cannot, nor can anyone
cross over from there to us.'

27"He answered, 'Then I beg you, fa-
ther, send Lazarus to my father's house,
28for I have five brothers. Let him warn
them, so that they will not also come to
this place of torment.'

29"Abraham replied, 'They have Moses
and the Prophets; let them listen to them.'

30" 'No, father Abraham,' he said, 'but if
someone from the dead goes to them, they
will repent.'

31"He said to him, 'If they do not listen
to Moses and the Prophets, they will not
be convinced even if someone rises from
the dead.' "

Sin, Faith, Duty

17 Jesus said to his disciples: "Things
that cause people to sin are bound
to come, but woe to that person through
whom they come. 2It would be better for
him to be thrown into the sea with a mill-
stone tied around his neck than for him to
cause one of these little ones to sin. 3So
watch yourselves.

"If your brother sins, rebuke him, and if
he repents, forgive him. 4If he sins against
you seven times in a day, and seven times
comes back to you and says, 'I repent,'
forgive him."

5The apostles said to the Lord, "In-
crease our faith!"

6He replied, "If you have faith as small
as a mustard seed, you can say to this
mulberry tree, 'Be uprooted and planted
in the sea,' and it will obey you.

7"Suppose one of you had a servant
plowing or looking after the sheep. Would
he say to the servant when he comes in
from the field, 'Come along now and sit
down to eat'? 8Would he not rather say,
'Prepare my supper, get yourself ready
and wait on me while I eat and drink; after
that you may eat and drink'? 9Would he
thank the servant because he did what he
was told to do? 10So you also, when you
have done everything you were told to do,
should say, 'We are unworthy servants;
we have only done our duty.' "

Ten Healed of Leprosy

11Now on his way to Jerusalem, Jesus
traveled along the border between Samar-
ia and Galilee. 12As he was going into a vil-
lage, ten men who had leprosy[b] met him.
They stood at a distance 13and called out
in a loud voice, "Jesus, Master, have pity
on us!"

14When he saw them, he said, "Go,
show yourselves to the priests." And as
they went, they were cleansed.

15One of them, when he saw he was
healed, came back, praising God in a loud
voice. 16He threw himself at Jesus' feet
and thanked him—and he was a Samari-
tan.

17Jesus asked, "Were not all ten
cleansed? Where are the other nine?
18Was no one found to return and give
praise to God except this foreigner?"
19Then he said to him, "Rise and go; your
faith has made you well."

The Coming of the Kingdom of God

20Once, having been asked by the Phari-
sees when the kingdom of God would
come, Jesus replied, "The kingdom of God
does not come with your careful observa-
tion, 21nor will people say, 'Here it is,' or
'There it is,' because the kingdom of God
is within[c] you."

22Then he said to his disciples, "The
time is coming when you will long to see
one of the days of the Son of Man, but you
will not see it. 23Men will tell you, 'There
he is!' or 'Here he is!' Do not go running
off after them. 24For the Son of Man in his
day[d] will be like the lightning, which
flashes and lights up the sky from one end
to the other. 25But first he must suffer

[a]23 Greek *Hades* [b]12 The Greek word was used for various diseases affecting the skin—not necessarily leprosy. [c]21 Or *among* [d]24 Some manuscripts do not have *in his day.*

many things and be rejected by this generation.

26"Just as it was in the days of Noah, so
also will it be in the days of the Son of
Man. 27People were eating, drinking, mar-
rying and being given in marriage up to
the day Noah entered the ark. Then the
flood came and destroyed them all.

28"It was the same in the days of Lot.
People were eating and drinking, buying
and selling, planting and building. 29But
the day Lot left Sodom, fire and sulfur
rained down from heaven and destroyed
them all.

30"It will be just like this on the day the
Son of Man is revealed. 31On that day no
one who is on the roof of his house, with
his goods inside, should go down to get

VERSE FOR THE DAY: Luke 17:10

AUTHOR: Martha Reapsome

PASSAGE FOR THE DAY: Luke 17:1–10

Setting Priorities

The process of godliness takes place as I learn Christlike responses to life's rough edges. One day I was feeling ill-used after completing a difficult assignment that had fallen short of others' expectations. The next day in my Bible study I read Luke 17:10. "So you also, when you have done everything you were told to do, should say, 'We are unworthy servants; we have only done our duty.' " I was reminded that I *had* fulfilled my responsibility.

Reading further, I discovered in Mark 1 that even Jesus was not always considered successful. He disappointed his friends by not doing what they expected—even when their expectations for him were good things. Peter asked him to come back and heal more people. Jesus replied that he would not because he had other priorities and must do what the Father sent him to do. Instead of meeting his friends' demands, Jesus went on to preach in other towns.

Jesus did not always live up to people's expectations because he didn't operate according to *their* agenda. His example helped me realize that I need not always be successful in other people's eyes. It gave me the courage to say "No" to demands on my time and energies that conflict with the priorities I have already set before God.

MARRIAGE BUILDERS

♦ *"Doing our duty" sounds unpleasant. What are the joys that come along when we do what is right before God?*

♦ *What are your personal and shared priorities before the Lord?*

Additional Scripture Readings
Mark 1:35–39; Galatians 1:10; Ephesians 5:8–10

Go to page 1133 for your next devotional reading.

them. Likewise, no one in the field should
go back for anything. 32Remember Lot's
wife! 33Whoever tries to keep his life will
lose it, and whoever loses his life will pre-
serve it. 34I tell you, on that night two peo-
ple will be in one bed; one will be taken
and the other left. 35Two women will be
grinding grain together; one will be taken
and the other left.[a]"

37"Where, Lord?" they asked.

He replied, "Where there is a dead
body, there the vultures will gather."

The Parable of the Persistent Widow

18 Then Jesus told his disciples a par-
able to show them that they should
always pray and not give up. 2He said: "In
a certain town there was a judge who nei-
ther feared God nor cared about men.
3And there was a widow in that town who
kept coming to him with the plea, 'Grant
me justice against my adversary.'

4"For some time he refused. But finally
he said to himself, 'Even though I don't
fear God or care about men, 5yet because
this widow keeps bothering me, I will see
that she gets justice, so that she won't
eventually wear me out with her com-
ing!' "

6And the Lord said, "Listen to what the
unjust judge says. 7And will not God bring
about justice for his chosen ones, who cry
out to him day and night? Will he keep
putting them off? 8I tell you, he will see
that they get justice, and quickly. Howev-
er, when the Son of Man comes, will he
find faith on the earth?"

The Parable of the Pharisee and the Tax Collector

9To some who were confident of their
own righteousness and looked down on
everybody else, Jesus told this parable:
10"Two men went up to the temple to
pray, one a Pharisee and the other a tax
collector. 11The Pharisee stood up and
prayed about[b] himself: 'God, I thank you
that I am not like other men—robbers,
evildoers, adulterers—or even like this
tax collector. 12I fast twice a week and give
a tenth of all I get.'

13"But the tax collector stood at a dis-
tance. He would not even look up to heav-
en, but beat his breast and said, 'God,
have mercy on me, a sinner.'

14"I tell you that this man, rather than
the other, went home justified before God.
For everyone who exalts himself will be
humbled, and he who humbles himself
will be exalted."

The Little Children and Jesus

15People were also bringing babies to
Jesus to have him touch them. When the
disciples saw this, they rebuked them.
16But Jesus called the children to him and
said, "Let the little children come to me,
and do not hinder them, for the kingdom
of God belongs to such as these. 17I tell
you the truth, anyone who will not receive
the kingdom of God like a little child will
never enter it."

The Rich Ruler

18A certain ruler asked him, "Good
teacher, what must I do to inherit eternal
life?"

19"Why do you call me good?" Jesus an-
swered. "No one is good—except God
alone. 20You know the commandments:
'Do not commit adultery, do not murder,
do not steal, do not give false testimony,
honor your father and mother.'[c]"

21"All these I have kept since I was a
boy," he said.

22When Jesus heard this, he said to
him, "You still lack one thing. Sell every-
thing you have and give to the poor, and
you will have treasure in heaven. Then
come, follow me."

23When he heard this, he became very
sad, because he was a man of great
wealth. 24Jesus looked at him and said,
"How hard it is for the rich to enter the
kingdom of God! 25Indeed, it is easier for
a camel to go through the eye of a needle
than for a rich man to enter the kingdom
of God."

26Those who heard this asked, "Who
then can be saved?"

27Jesus replied, "What is impossible
with men is possible with God."

28Peter said to him, "We have left all we
had to follow you!"

29"I tell you the truth," Jesus said to
them, "no one who has left home or wife
or brothers or parents or children for the
sake of the kingdom of God 30will fail to
receive many times as much in this age
and, in the age to come, eternal life."

[a] 35 Some manuscripts *left.* 36 *Two men will be in the field; one will be taken and the other left.* [b] 11 Or *to* [c] 20 Exodus 20:12-16; Deut. 5:16-20

Jesus Again Predicts His Death

31 Jesus took the Twelve aside and told them, "We are going up to Jerusalem, and everything that is written by the prophets about the Son of Man will be fulfilled. 32 He will be handed over to the Gentiles. They will mock him, insult him, spit on him, flog him and kill him. 33 On the third day he will rise again."

34 The disciples did not understand any of this. Its meaning was hidden from them, and they did not know what he was talking about.

VERSE FOR THE DAY: Luke 18:24

AUTHOR: Beverly J. Burch

PASSAGE FOR THE DAY: Luke 18:18–30

Stop the Money Madness

While running errands, Jill noticed a great sale. She picked out a colorful shower curtain with coordinating towels and accessories. She couldn't wait to show Greg—he wouldn't believe it.

He *didn't* believe it. How could she buy all that when they had a perfectly good shower curtain and the towels they'd received as wedding gifts just six months earlier? It wasn't their first heated argument over money. Greg and Jill had yet to develop a sense of "money oneness." They needed to learn how to forge an identity as a married couple without forfeiting their individual identities.

Moving from individual to shared control of finances can feel threatening to newlyweds who are still learning to trust one another. Because money is concrete and quantifiable, it can become the focus of conflicts that are really about something deeper. A newlywed might not feel comfortable accusing his or her mate of self-centeredness; it's easier to criticize spending instead.

Greg and Jill saw a counselor because of their constant fighting over finances. When they realized they'd really each been afraid of the other's perceived "power," they agreed that neither wanted to lord it over the other. Once they realized they weren't in danger of being controlled, they began to trust one another. Their arguments over finances didn't disappear completely, but they were able to find common ground much more easily.

MARRIAGE BUILDERS

- *When have finances been a source of conflict for you? Can you identify a deeper issue behind the money argument?*
- *In what areas of finance (giving, saving, spending) have you begun to develop "money oneness"?*

Additional Scripture Readings
Proverbs 11:28; 1 Timothy 6:6–10

Go to page 1135 for your next devotional reading.

A Blind Beggar Receives His Sight

35As Jesus approached Jericho, a blind
man was sitting by the roadside begging.
36When he heard the crowd going by, he
asked what was happening. 37They told
him, "Jesus of Nazareth is passing by."
38He called out, "Jesus, Son of David,
have mercy on me!"
39Those who led the way rebuked him
and told him to be quiet, but he shouted
all the more, "Son of David, have mercy
on me!"
40Jesus stopped and ordered the man to
be brought to him. When he came near,
Jesus asked him, 41"What do you want me
to do for you?"
"Lord, I want to see," he replied.
42Jesus said to him, "Receive your sight;
your faith has healed you." 43Immediately
he received his sight and followed Jesus,
praising God. When all the people saw it,
they also praised God.

Zacchaeus the Tax Collector

19 Jesus entered Jericho and was
passing through. 2A man was there
by the name of Zacchaeus; he was a chief
tax collector and was wealthy. 3He wanted
to see who Jesus was, but being a short
man he could not, because of the crowd.
4So he ran ahead and climbed a sycamore-
fig tree to see him, since Jesus was coming
that way.
5When Jesus reached the spot, he
looked up and said to him, "Zacchaeus,
come down immediately. I must stay at
your house today." 6So he came down at
once and welcomed him gladly.
7All the people saw this and began to
mutter, "He has gone to be the guest of a
'sinner.' "
8But Zacchaeus stood up and said to the
Lord, "Look, Lord! Here and now I give
half of my possessions to the poor, and if
I have cheated anybody out of anything, I
will pay back four times the amount."
9Jesus said to him, "Today salvation has
come to this house, because this man, too,
is a son of Abraham. 10For the Son of Man
came to seek and to save what was lost."

The Parable of the Ten Minas

11While they were listening to this, he
went on to tell them a parable, because he
was near Jerusalem and the people
thought that the kingdom of God was go-
ing to appear at once. 12He said: "A man
of noble birth went to a distant country to
have himself appointed king and then to
return. 13So he called ten of his servants
and gave them ten minas.[a] 'Put this mon-
ey to work,' he said, 'until I come back.'
14"But his subjects hated him and sent
a delegation after him to say, 'We don't
want this man to be our king.'
15"He was made king, however, and re-
turned home. Then he sent for the ser-
vants to whom he had given the money, in
order to find out what they had gained
with it.
16"The first one came and said, 'Sir,
your mina has earned ten more.'
17" 'Well done, my good servant!' his
master replied. 'Because you have been
trustworthy in a very small matter, take
charge of ten cities.'
18"The second came and said, 'Sir, your
mina has earned five more.'
19"His master answered, 'You take
charge of five cities.'
20"Then another servant came and said,
'Sir, here is your mina; I have kept it laid
away in a piece of cloth. 21I was afraid of
you, because you are a hard man. You
take out what you did not put in and reap
what you did not sow.'
22"His master replied, 'I will judge you
by your own words, you wicked servant!
You knew, did you, that I am a hard man,
taking out what I did not put in, and reap-
ing what I did not sow? 23Why then didn't
you put my money on deposit, so that
when I came back, I could have collected
it with interest?'
24"Then he said to those standing by,
'Take his mina away from him and give it
to the one who has ten minas.'
25" 'Sir,' they said, 'he already has ten!'
26"He replied, 'I tell you that to every-
one who has, more will be given, but as
for the one who has nothing, even what he
has will be taken away. 27But those ene-
mies of mine who did not want me to be
king over them—bring them here and kill
them in front of me.' "

The Triumphal Entry

28After Jesus had said this, he went on
ahead, going up to Jerusalem. 29As he ap-

[a] 13 A mina was about three months' wages.

proached Bethphage and Bethany at the
hill called the Mount of Olives, he sent
two of his disciples, saying to them, 30"Go
to the village ahead of you, and as you en-
ter it, you will find a colt tied there, which
no one has ever ridden. Untie it and
bring it here. 31If anyone asks you, 'Why
are you untying it?' tell him, 'The Lord
needs it.' "

32Those who were sent ahead went and
found it just as he had told them. 33As
they were untying the colt, its owners
asked them, "Why are you untying the
colt?"

34They replied, "The Lord needs it."

35They brought it to Jesus, threw their
cloaks on the colt and put Jesus on it. 36As
he went along, people spread their cloaks
on the road.

37When he came near the place where
the road goes down the Mount of Olives,
the whole crowd of disciples began joyful-
ly to praise God in loud voices for all the
miracles they had seen:

VERSE FOR THE DAY: Luke 19:10

AUTHOR: Bill and Gloria Gaither

PASSAGE FOR THE DAY: Luke 19:1–10

A Passion for Truth

A true Christian marriage seeks what is eternal and shares a commitment to a larger purpose. Over the years, we've been going in the same direction, and that has kept us together. Of course, we haven't always agreed on how to get there. If we hadn't both had a sense that we wanted to be open to where God was taking us, we would have had real conflict in our marriage. But we've always been able to sit down somewhere along the way and say, "What is it we're doing here? What is life about?"

We're both driven by the principle of being *in* the world but not *of* the world. We grew up seeing people attending church, dressing the right way and acting and saying all the right things, but never really affecting the world much.

But we've had a real passion to communicate the truth of Christ to all kinds of people—to infiltrate the culture through simple yet profound music that people can understand. We're of no earthly value if we don't risk getting our hands and feet dirty to try to go to where the people are.

MARRIAGE BUILDERS

♦ *Describe the difference between being* in *the world and being* of *the world.*

♦ *As a couple, what are some specific ways your "hands and feet" get "dirty" as you try to reach others with the good news?*

Additional Scripture Readings
Matthew 9:9–13; 11:19; Romans 5:8

Go to page 1138 for your next devotional reading.

38"Blessed is the king who comes in the
name of the Lord!"[a]

"Peace in heaven and glory in the
highest!"

39Some of the Pharisees in the crowd said to Jesus, "Teacher, rebuke your disciples!"

40"I tell you," he replied, "if they keep quiet, the stones will cry out."

41As he approached Jerusalem and saw the city, he wept over it 42and said, "If you, even you, had only known on this day what would bring you peace—but now it is hidden from your eyes. 43The days will come upon you when your enemies will build an embankment against you and encircle you and hem you in on every side. 44They will dash you to the ground, you and the children within your walls. They will not leave one stone on another, because you did not recognize the time of God's coming to you."

Jesus at the Temple

45Then he entered the temple area and began driving out those who were selling. 46"It is written," he said to them, " 'My house will be a house of prayer'[b]; but you have made it 'a den of robbers.'[c]"

47Every day he was teaching at the temple. But the chief priests, the teachers of the law and the leaders among the people were trying to kill him. 48Yet they could not find any way to do it, because all the people hung on his words.

The Authority of Jesus Questioned

20 One day as he was teaching the people in the temple courts and preaching the gospel, the chief priests and the teachers of the law, together with the elders, came up to him. 2"Tell us by what authority you are doing these things," they said. "Who gave you this authority?"

3He replied, "I will also ask you a question. Tell me, 4John's baptism—was it from heaven, or from men?"

5They discussed it among themselves and said, "If we say, 'From heaven,' he will ask, 'Why didn't you believe him?' 6But if we say, 'From men,' all the people will stone us, because they are persuaded that John was a prophet."

7So they answered, "We don't know where it was from."

8Jesus said, "Neither will I tell you by what authority I am doing these things."

The Parable of the Tenants

9He went on to tell the people this parable: "A man planted a vineyard, rented it to some farmers and went away for a long time. 10At harvest time he sent a servant to the tenants so they would give him some of the fruit of the vineyard. But the tenants beat him and sent him away empty-handed. 11He sent another servant, but that one also they beat and treated shamefully and sent away empty-handed. 12He sent still a third, and they wounded him and threw him out.

13"Then the owner of the vineyard said, 'What shall I do? I will send my son, whom I love; perhaps they will respect him.'

14"But when the tenants saw him, they talked the matter over. 'This is the heir,' they said. 'Let's kill him, and the inheritance will be ours.' 15So they threw him out of the vineyard and killed him.

"What then will the owner of the vineyard do to them? 16He will come and kill those tenants and give the vineyard to others."

When the people heard this, they said, "May this never be!"

17Jesus looked directly at them and asked, "Then what is the meaning of that which is written:

" 'The stone the builders rejected
has become the capstone[d]'[e]?

18Everyone who falls on that stone will be broken to pieces, but he on whom it falls will be crushed."

19The teachers of the law and the chief priests looked for a way to arrest him immediately, because they knew he had spoken this parable against them. But they were afraid of the people.

Paying Taxes to Caesar

20Keeping a close watch on him, they sent spies, who pretended to be honest. They hoped to catch Jesus in something he said so that they might hand him over to the power and authority of the governor. 21So the spies questioned him: "Teacher, we know that you speak and teach what is right, and that you do not show partiality but teach the way of God

[a]38 Psalm 118:26 [b]46 Isaiah 56:7 [c]46 Jer. 7:11 [d]17 Or *cornerstone* [e]17 Psalm 118:22

in accordance with the truth. 22Is it right
for us to pay taxes to Caesar or not?"
23He saw through their duplicity and
said to them, 24"Show me a denarius.
Whose portrait and inscription are on it?"
25"Caesar's," they replied.
He said to them, "Then give to Caesar
what is Caesar's, and to God what is
God's."
26They were unable to trap him in what
he had said there in public. And aston-
ished by his answer, they became silent.

The Resurrection and Marriage

27Some of the Sadducees, who say there
is no resurrection, came to Jesus with a
question. 28"Teacher," they said, "Moses
wrote for us that if a man's brother dies
and leaves a wife but no children, the man
must marry the widow and have children
for his brother. 29Now there were seven
brothers. The first one married a woman
and died childless. 30The second 31and
then the third married her, and in the
same way the seven died, leaving no chil-
dren. 32Finally, the woman died too.
33Now then, at the resurrection whose
wife will she be, since the seven were mar-
ried to her?"
34Jesus replied, "The people of this age
marry and are given in marriage. 35But
those who are considered worthy of tak-
ing part in that age and in the resurrection
from the dead will neither marry nor be
given in marriage, 36and they can no long-
er die; for they are like the angels. They
are God's children, since they are children
of the resurrection. 37But in the account of
the bush, even Moses showed that the
dead rise, for he calls the Lord 'the God of
Abraham, and the God of Isaac, and the
God of Jacob.'[a] 38He is not the God of the
dead, but of the living, for to him all are
alive."
39Some of the teachers of the law re-
sponded, "Well said, teacher!" 40And no
one dared to ask him any more questions.

Whose Son Is the Christ?

41Then Jesus said to them, "How is it
that they say the Christ[b] is the Son of Da-
vid? 42David himself declares in the Book
of Psalms:

" 'The Lord said to my Lord:
"Sit at my right hand
43until I make your enemies
a footstool for your feet." '[c]

44David calls him 'Lord.' How then can he
be his son?"
45While all the people were listening,
Jesus said to his disciples, 46"Beware of
the teachers of the law. They like to walk
around in flowing robes and love to be
greeted in the marketplaces and have the
most important seats in the synagogues
and the places of honor at banquets.
47They devour widows' houses and for a
show make lengthy prayers. Such men
will be punished most severely."

The Widow's Offering

21 As he looked up, Jesus saw the rich
putting their gifts into the temple
treasury. 2He also saw a poor widow put
in two very small copper coins.[d] 3"I tell
you the truth," he said, "this poor widow
has put in more than all the others. 4All
these people gave their gifts out of their
wealth; but she out of her poverty put in
all she had to live on."

Signs of the End of the Age

5Some of his disciples were remarking
about how the temple was adorned with
beautiful stones and with gifts dedicated
to God. But Jesus said, 6"As for what you
see here, the time will come when not one
stone will be left on another; every one of
them will be thrown down."
7"Teacher," they asked, "when will
these things happen? And what will be the
sign that they are about to take place?"
8He replied: "Watch out that you are
not deceived. For many will come in my
name, claiming, 'I am he,' and, 'The time
is near.' Do not follow them. 9When you
hear of wars and revolutions, do not be
frightened. These things must happen
first, but the end will not come right
away."
10Then he said to them: "Nation will
rise against nation, and kingdom against
kingdom. 11There will be great earth-
quakes, famines and pestilences in vari-
ous places, and fearful events and great
signs from heaven.
12"But before all this, they will lay
hands on you and persecute you. They
will deliver you to synagogues and pris-
ons, and you will be brought before kings
and governors, and all on account of my
name. 13This will result in your being wit-

[a] 37 Exodus 3:6 [b] 41 Or *Messiah* [c] 43 Psalm 110:1 [d] 2 Greek *two lepta*

WEEKENDING

CAREER

Work stress doesn't have to adversely affect your relationship. Use this career inventory as a starting point to find ways to help each other deal effectively with work stress.

1. How can you provide needed support to each other during times of high work stress?

2. Are you doing a good job of coping with your own work-related stress to keep it from negatively affecting your attitude at home? If not, how can you more effectively deal with work stress?

3. Are you doing enough to include each other in your respective work worlds? If not, what can each of you do to involve the other more?

4. What are your individual career goals? How can you help each other achieve those goals?

— *The* Marriage Partnership *Staff*

REVIVE

Saturday: Psalm 90:1–7
Sunday: Isaiah 30:15–18

Go to page 1142 for your next devotional reading.

nesses to them. 14But make up your mind
not to worry beforehand how you will de-
fend yourselves. 15For I will give you
words and wisdom that none of your ad-
versaries will be able to resist or contra-
dict. 16You will be betrayed even by par-
ents, brothers, relatives and friends, and
they will put some of you to death. 17All
men will hate you because of me. 18But
not a hair of your head will perish. 19By
standing firm you will gain life.

20"When you see Jerusalem being sur-
rounded by armies, you will know that its
desolation is near. 21Then let those who
are in Judea flee to the mountains, let
those in the city get out, and let those in
the country not enter the city. 22For this is
the time of punishment in fulfillment of
all that has been written. 23How dreadful
it will be in those days for pregnant wom-
en and nursing mothers! There will be
great distress in the land and wrath
against this people. 24They will fall by the
sword and will be taken as prisoners to all
the nations. Jerusalem will be trampled
on by the Gentiles until the times of the
Gentiles are fulfilled.

25"There will be signs in the sun, moon
and stars. On the earth, nations will be in
anguish and perplexity at the roaring and
tossing of the sea. 26Men will faint from
terror, apprehensive of what is coming on
the world, for the heavenly bodies will be
shaken. 27At that time they will see the
Son of Man coming in a cloud with power
and great glory. 28When these things be-
gin to take place, stand up and lift up your
heads, because your redemption is draw-
ing near."

29He told them this parable: "Look at
the fig tree and all the trees. 30When they
sprout leaves, you can see for yourselves
and know that summer is near. 31Even so,
when you see these things happening,
you know that the kingdom of God is
near.

32"I tell you the truth, this generation[a]
will certainly not pass away until all these
things have happened. 33Heaven and
earth will pass away, but my words will
never pass away.

34"Be careful, or your hearts will be
weighed down with dissipation, drunken-
ness and the anxieties of life, and that day
will close on you unexpectedly like a trap.
35For it will come upon all those who live
on the face of the whole earth. 36Be always
on the watch, and pray that you may be
able to escape all that is about to happen,
and that you may be able to stand before
the Son of Man."

37Each day Jesus was teaching at the
temple, and each evening he went out to
spend the night on the hill called the
Mount of Olives, 38and all the people
came early in the morning to hear him at
the temple.

Judas Agrees to Betray Jesus

22 Now the Feast of Unleavened
Bread, called the Passover, was ap-
proaching, 2and the chief priests and the
teachers of the law were looking for some
way to get rid of Jesus, for they were
afraid of the people. 3Then Satan entered
Judas, called Iscariot, one of the Twelve.
4And Judas went to the chief priests and
the officers of the temple guard and dis-
cussed with them how he might betray
Jesus. 5They were delighted and agreed to
give him money. 6He consented, and
watched for an opportunity to hand Jesus
over to them when no crowd was present.

The Last Supper

7Then came the day of Unleavened
Bread on which the Passover lamb had to
be sacrificed. 8Jesus sent Peter and John,
saying, "Go and make preparations for us
to eat the Passover."

9"Where do you want us to prepare for
it?" they asked.

10He replied, "As you enter the city, a
man carrying a jar of water will meet you.
Follow him to the house that he enters,
11and say to the owner of the house, 'The
Teacher asks: Where is the guest room,
where I may eat the Passover with my dis-
ciples?' 12He will show you a large upper
room, all furnished. Make preparations
there."

13They left and found things just as
Jesus had told them. So they prepared the
Passover.

14When the hour came, Jesus and his
apostles reclined at the table. 15And he
said to them, "I have eagerly desired to eat
this Passover with you before I suffer.
16For I tell you, I will not eat it again until
it finds fulfillment in the kingdom of
God."

17After taking the cup, he gave thanks
and said, "Take this and divide it among
you. 18For I tell you I will not drink again

[a]32 Or *race*

of the fruit of the vine until the kingdom
of God comes."
19And he took bread, gave thanks and
broke it, and gave it to them, saying, "This
is my body given for you; do this in re-
membrance of me."
20In the same way, after the supper he
took the cup, saying, "This cup is the new
covenant in my blood, which is poured
out for you. 21But the hand of him who is
going to betray me is with mine on the ta-
ble. 22The Son of Man will go as it has
been decreed, but woe to that man who
betrays him." 23They began to question
among themselves which of them it might
be who would do this.
24Also a dispute arose among them as to
which of them was considered to be great-
est. 25Jesus said to them, "The kings of the
Gentiles lord it over them; and those who
exercise authority over them call them-
selves Benefactors. 26But you are not to be
like that. Instead, the greatest among you
should be like the youngest, and the one
who rules like the one who serves. 27For
who is greater, the one who is at the table
or the one who serves? Is it not the one
who is at the table? But I am among you
as one who serves. 28You are those who
have stood by me in my trials. 29And I
confer on you a kingdom, just as my Fa-
ther conferred one on me, 30so that you
may eat and drink at my table in my king-
dom and sit on thrones, judging the
twelve tribes of Israel.
31"Simon, Simon, Satan has asked to sift
you[a] as wheat. 32But I have prayed for
you, Simon, that your faith may not fail.
And when you have turned back,
strengthen your brothers."
33But he replied, "Lord, I am ready to go
with you to prison and to death."
34Jesus answered, "I tell you, Peter, be-
fore the rooster crows today, you will
deny three times that you know me."
35Then Jesus asked them, "When I sent
you without purse, bag or sandals, did
you lack anything?"
"Nothing," they answered.
36He said to them, "But now if you have
a purse, take it, and also a bag; and if you
don't have a sword, sell your cloak and
buy one. 37It is written: 'And he was num-
bered with the transgressors'[b]; and I tell
you that this must be fulfilled in me. Yes,
what is written about me is reaching its
fulfillment."
38The disciples said, "See, Lord, here
are two swords."
"That is enough," he replied.

Jesus Prays on the Mount of Olives

39Jesus went out as usual to the Mount
of Olives, and his disciples followed him.
40On reaching the place, he said to them,
"Pray that you will not fall into tempta-
tion." 41He withdrew about a stone's
throw beyond them, knelt down and
prayed, 42"Father, if you are willing, take
this cup from me; yet not my will, but
yours be done." 43An angel from heaven
appeared to him and strengthened him.
44And being in anguish, he prayed more
earnestly, and his sweat was like drops of
blood falling to the ground.[c]
45When he rose from prayer and went
back to the disciples, he found them
asleep, exhausted from sorrow. 46"Why
are you sleeping?" he asked them. "Get up
and pray so that you will not fall into
temptation."

Jesus Arrested

47While he was still speaking a crowd
came up, and the man who was called Ju-
das, one of the Twelve, was leading them.
He approached Jesus to kiss him, 48but
Jesus asked him, "Judas, are you betray-
ing the Son of Man with a kiss?"
49When Jesus' followers saw what was
going to happen, they said, "Lord, should
we strike with our swords?" 50And one of
them struck the servant of the high priest,
cutting off his right ear.
51But Jesus answered, "No more of
this!" And he touched the man's ear and
healed him.
52Then Jesus said to the chief priests,
the officers of the temple guard, and the
elders, who had come for him, "Am I lead-
ing a rebellion, that you have come with
swords and clubs? 53Every day I was with
you in the temple courts, and you did not
lay a hand on me. But this is your hour—
when darkness reigns."

Peter Disowns Jesus

54Then seizing him, they led him away
and took him into the house of the high
priest. Peter followed at a distance. 55But
when they had kindled a fire in the middle

[a]31 The Greek is plural. [b]37 Isaiah 53:12 [c]44 Some early manuscripts do not have verses 43 and 44.

of the courtyard and had sat down together, Peter sat down with them. 56A servant girl saw him seated there in the firelight. She looked closely at him and said, "This man was with him."

57But he denied it. "Woman, I don't know him," he said.

58A little later someone else saw him and said, "You also are one of them."

"Man, I am not!" Peter replied.

59About an hour later another asserted, "Certainly this fellow was with him, for he is a Galilean."

60Peter replied, "Man, I don't know what you're talking about!" Just as he was speaking, the rooster crowed. 61The Lord turned and looked straight at Peter. Then Peter remembered the word the Lord had spoken to him: "Before the rooster crows today, you will disown me three times." 62And he went outside and wept bitterly.

The Guards Mock Jesus

63The men who were guarding Jesus began mocking and beating him. 64They blindfolded him and demanded, "Prophesy! Who hit you?" 65And they said many other insulting things to him.

Jesus Before Pilate and Herod

66At daybreak the council of the elders of the people, both the chief priests and teachers of the law, met together, and Jesus was led before them. 67"If you are the Christ,[a]" they said, "tell us."

Jesus answered, "If I tell you, you will not believe me, 68and if I asked you, you would not answer. 69But from now on, the Son of Man will be seated at the right hand of the mighty God."

70They all asked, "Are you then the Son of God?"

He replied, "You are right in saying I am."

71Then they said, "Why do we need any more testimony? We have heard it from his own lips."

23 Then the whole assembly rose and led him off to Pilate. 2And they began to accuse him, saying, "We have found this man subverting our nation. He opposes payment of taxes to Caesar and claims to be Christ,[b] a king."

3So Pilate asked Jesus, "Are you the king of the Jews?"

"Yes, it is as you say," Jesus replied.

4Then Pilate announced to the chief priests and the crowd, "I find no basis for a charge against this man."

5But they insisted, "He stirs up the people all over Judea[c] by his teaching. He started in Galilee and has come all the way here."

6On hearing this, Pilate asked if the man was a Galilean. 7When he learned that Jesus was under Herod's jurisdiction, he sent him to Herod, who was also in Jerusalem at that time.

8When Herod saw Jesus, he was greatly pleased, because for a long time he had been wanting to see him. From what he had heard about him, he hoped to see him perform some miracle. 9He plied him with many questions, but Jesus gave him no answer. 10The chief priests and the teachers of the law were standing there, vehemently accusing him. 11Then Herod and his soldiers ridiculed and mocked him. Dressing him in an elegant robe, they sent him back to Pilate. 12That day Herod and Pilate became friends—before this they had been enemies.

13Pilate called together the chief priests, the rulers and the people, 14and said to them, "You brought me this man as one who was inciting the people to rebellion. I have examined him in your presence and have found no basis for your charges against him. 15Neither has Herod, for he sent him back to us; as you can see, he has done nothing to deserve death. 16Therefore, I will punish him and then release him.[d]"

18With one voice they cried out, "Away with this man! Release Barabbas to us!" 19(Barabbas had been thrown into prison for an insurrection in the city, and for murder.)

20Wanting to release Jesus, Pilate appealed to them again. 21But they kept shouting, "Crucify him! Crucify him!"

22For the third time he spoke to them: "Why? What crime has this man committed? I have found in him no grounds for the death penalty. Therefore I will have him punished and then release him."

23But with loud shouts they insistently demanded that he be crucified, and their shouts prevailed. 24So Pilate decided to grant their demand. 25He released the man who had been thrown into prison for insurrection and murder, the one they

[a]67 Or *Messiah* [b]2 Or *Messiah*; also in verses 35 and 39 [c]5 Or *over the land of the Jews*
[d]16 Some manuscripts *him.* 17*Now he was obliged to release one man to them at the Feast.*

asked for, and surrendered Jesus to their will.

The Crucifixion

26As they led him away, they seized Simon from Cyrene, who was on his way in from the country, and put the cross on him and made him carry it behind Jesus. 27A large number of people followed him, including women who mourned and wailed for him. 28Jesus turned and said to them, "Daughters of Jerusalem, do not weep for me; weep for yourselves and for your children. 29For the time will come when you will say, 'Blessed are the barren women, the wombs that never bore and the breasts that never nursed!' 30Then

" 'they will say to the mountains, "Fall on us!"
and to the hills, "Cover us!" '[a]

31For if men do these things when the tree is green, what will happen when it is dry?"

32Two other men, both criminals, were also led out with him to be executed. 33When they came to the place called the Skull, there they crucified him, along with the criminals—one on his right, the other on his left. 34Jesus said, "Father, forgive them, for they do not know what they are doing."[b] And they divided up his clothes by casting lots.

35The people stood watching, and the rulers even sneered at him. They said, "He saved others; let him save himself if he is the Christ of God, the Chosen One."

36The soldiers also came up and mocked him. They offered him wine vinegar 37and said, "If you are the king of the Jews, save yourself."

38There was a written notice above him,

[a]30 Hosea 10:8 [b]34 Some early manuscripts do not have this sentence.

VERSE FOR THE DAY: Luke 23:34

AUTHOR: Philip Yancey

PASSAGE FOR THE DAY: Luke 23:26–43

Forgiveness Is Never Easy

From the gospel accounts, it seems forgiveness was not easy for God. "If you are willing, take this cup from me," Jesus prayed, contemplating the cost, and the sweat rolled off him like drops of blood. Finally, in one of his last statements before dying, he said, "Forgive them"—all of them, the Roman soldiers, the religious leaders, his disciples who had fled in darkness, you, me, who have denied him so many times—"forgive them, for they do not know what they are doing." By becoming a human being, the Son of God could truly say, with understanding, "They do not know what they are doing." He had lived among us. He understood.

MARRIAGE BUILDERS

- *What was the cost of God's forgiveness?*
- *What are some of the costs when you forgive others?*

Additional Scripture Readings
Mark 14:36; Hebrews 2:17–18; 4:15

Go to page 1146 for your next devotional reading.

which read: THIS IS THE KING OF THE JEWS.

39One of the criminals who hung there
hurled insults at him: "Aren't you the
Christ? Save yourself and us!"

40But the other criminal rebuked him.
"Don't you fear God," he said, "since you
are under the same sentence? 41We are
punished justly, for we are getting what
our deeds deserve. But this man has done
nothing wrong."

42Then he said, "Jesus, remember me
when you come into your kingdom.[a]"

43Jesus answered him, "I tell you the
truth, today you will be with me in para-
dise."

Jesus' Death

44It was now about the sixth hour, and
darkness came over the whole land until
the ninth hour, 45for the sun stopped shin-
ing. And the curtain of the temple was
torn in two. 46Jesus called out with a loud
voice, "Father, into your hands I commit
my spirit." When he had said this, he
breathed his last.

47The centurion, seeing what had hap-
pened, praised God and said, "Surely this
was a righteous man." 48When all the peo-
ple who had gathered to witness this sight
saw what took place, they beat their
breasts and went away. 49But all those
who knew him, including the women who
had followed him from Galilee, stood at a
distance, watching these things.

Jesus' Burial

50Now there was a man named Joseph,
a member of the Council, a good and up-
right man, 51who had not consented to
their decision and action. He came from
the Judean town of Arimathea and he was
waiting for the kingdom of God. 52Going
to Pilate, he asked for Jesus' body. 53Then
he took it down, wrapped it in linen cloth
and placed it in a tomb cut in the rock, one
in which no one had yet been laid. 54It was
Preparation Day, and the Sabbath was
about to begin.

55The women who had come with Jesus
from Galilee followed Joseph and saw the
tomb and how his body was laid in it.
56Then they went home and prepared
spices and perfumes. But they rested on
the Sabbath in obedience to the com-
mandment.

The Resurrection

24 On the first day of the week, very
early in the morning, the women
took the spices they had prepared and
went to the tomb. 2They found the stone
rolled away from the tomb, 3but when
they entered, they did not find the body of
the Lord Jesus. 4While they were wonder-
ing about this, suddenly two men in
clothes that gleamed like lightning stood
beside them. 5In their fright the women
bowed down with their faces to the
ground, but the men said to them, "Why
do you look for the living among the
dead? 6He is not here; he has risen! Re-
member how he told you, while he was
still with you in Galilee: 7'The Son of Man
must be delivered into the hands of sinful
men, be crucified and on the third day be
raised again.'" 8Then they remembered
his words.

9When they came back from the tomb,
they told all these things to the Eleven and
to all the others. 10It was Mary Magdalene,
Joanna, Mary the mother of James, and
the others with them who told this to the
apostles. 11But they did not believe the
women, because their words seemed to
them like nonsense. 12Peter, however, got
up and ran to the tomb. Bending over, he
saw the strips of linen lying by them-
selves, and he went away, wondering to
himself what had happened.

On the Road to Emmaus

13Now that same day two of them were
going to a village called Emmaus, about
seven miles[b] from Jerusalem. 14They
were talking with each other about every-
thing that had happened. 15As they talked
and discussed these things with each oth-
er, Jesus himself came up and walked
along with them; 16but they were kept
from recognizing him.

17He asked them, "What are you dis-
cussing together as you walk along?"

They stood still, their faces downcast.
18One of them, named Cleopas, asked
him, "Are you only a visitor to Jerusalem
and do not know the things that have hap-
pened there in these days?"

19"What things?" he asked.

"About Jesus of Nazareth," they re-
plied. "He was a prophet, powerful in
word and deed before God and all the peo-
ple. 20The chief priests and our rulers

[a] 42 Some manuscripts *come with your kingly power*

[b] 13 Greek *sixty stadia* (about 11 kilometers)

handed him over to be sentenced to death,
and they crucified him; 21but we had
hoped that he was the one who was going
to redeem Israel. And what is more, it is
the third day since all this took place. 22In
addition, some of our women amazed us.
They went to the tomb early this morning
23but didn't find his body. They came and
told us that they had seen a vision of an-
gels, who said he was alive. 24Then some
of our companions went to the tomb and
found it just as the women had said, but
him they did not see."

25He said to them, "How foolish you
are, and how slow of heart to believe all
that the prophets have spoken! 26Did not
the Christ[a] have to suffer these things
and then enter his glory?" 27And begin-
ning with Moses and all the Prophets, he
explained to them what was said in all the
Scriptures concerning himself.

28As they approached the village to
which they were going, Jesus acted as if
he were going farther. 29But they urged
him strongly, "Stay with us, for it is nearly
evening; the day is almost over." So he
went in to stay with them.

30When he was at the table with them,
he took bread, gave thanks, broke it and
began to give it to them. 31Then their eyes
were opened and they recognized him,
and he disappeared from their sight.
32They asked each other, "Were not our
hearts burning within us while he talked
with us on the road and opened the Scrip-
tures to us?"

33They got up and returned at once to
Jerusalem. There they found the Eleven
and those with them, assembled together
34and saying, "It is true! The Lord has ris-
en and has appeared to Simon." 35Then
the two told what had happened on the
way, and how Jesus was recognized by
them when he broke the bread.

Jesus Appears to the Disciples

36While they were still talking about
this, Jesus himself stood among them and
said to them, "Peace be with you."

37They were startled and frightened,
thinking they saw a ghost. 38He said to
them, "Why are you troubled, and why do
doubts rise in your minds? 39Look at my
hands and my feet. It is I myself! Touch
me and see; a ghost does not have flesh
and bones, as you see I have."

40When he had said this, he showed
them his hands and feet. 41And while they
still did not believe it because of joy and
amazement, he asked them, "Do you have
anything here to eat?" 42They gave him a
piece of broiled fish, 43and he took it and
ate it in their presence.

44He said to them, "This is what I told
you while I was still with you: Everything
must be fulfilled that is written about me
in the Law of Moses, the Prophets and the
Psalms."

45Then he opened their minds so they
could understand the Scriptures. 46He told
them, "This is what is written: The Christ
will suffer and rise from the dead on the
third day, 47and repentance and forgive-
ness of sins will be preached in his name
to all nations, beginning at Jerusalem.
48You are witnesses of these things. 49I am
going to send you what my Father has
promised; but stay in the city until you
have been clothed with power from on
high."

The Ascension

50When he had led them out to the vi-
cinity of Bethany, he lifted up his hands
and blessed them. 51While he was bless-
ing them, he left them and was taken up
into heaven. 52Then they worshiped him
and returned to Jerusalem with great joy.
53And they stayed continually at the tem-
ple, praising God.

[a]26 Or *Messiah*; also in verse 46

JOHN writes this Gospel to present Jesus, the powerful Son of God, who comes in human flesh, gives his life on the cross, and then returns to the Father—all with a view that we may believe in him and receive eternal life. His coming shows us how much the Father and the Son love us, and his parting command is that we should show the same sacrificial love to one another. As you read this book, be sure that you believe that Jesus is the Christ, the Son of God, and promise him that you will love others as he loves you.

JOHN

The Word Became Flesh

1 In the beginning was the Word, and the Word was with God, and the Word was God. 2He was with God in the beginning.

3Through him all things were made; without him nothing was made that has been made. 4In him was life, and that life was the light of men. 5The light shines in the darkness, but the darkness has not understood[a] it.

6There came a man who was sent from God; his name was John. 7He came as a witness to testify concerning that light, so that through him all men might believe. 8He himself was not the light; he came only as a witness to the light. 9The true light that gives light to every man was coming into the world.[b]

10He was in the world, and though the world was made through him, the world did not recognize him. 11He came to that

[a]5 Or *darkness, and the darkness has not overcome every man who comes into the world*

[b]9 Or *This was the true light that gives light to*

which was his own, but his own did not
receive him. 12Yet to all who received him,
to those who believed in his name, he
gave the right to become children of
God— 13children born not of natural
descent,[a] nor of human decision or
a husband's will, but born of God.
14The Word became flesh and made his
dwelling among us. We have seen his glo-
ry, the glory of the One and Only,[b] who
came from the Father, full of grace and
truth.

[a] 13 Greek *of bloods* [b] 14 Or *the Only Begotten*

VERSE FOR THE DAY: John 1:14

AUTHOR: Ruth Senter

PASSAGE FOR THE DAY: John 1:1–14

He Is Here—Anyway

God is everywhere present, so why am I surprised when I find him in unexpected places? Royalty in a barn? Sovereignty riding a common colt through the streets of Jerusalem? Peace by the bedside of my friend's mother who is dying of leukemia? Expectations are disappointed. Plans are thwarted. I do not like what life does to people and plans.

But the very essence of God is that he is here anyway. No, the conditions are not right. But he is here—perhaps even more so *because* the conditions are not right. The conditions were not right when he came. There was no room in the inn. The conditions were not right when he died. They crucified him with two criminals, one on each side. Not until he comes again will the conditions ever be right.

But "the Word became flesh and made his dwelling among us" (John 1:14). It is the height of incongruity. It is in his humanity that we catch glimpses of Christ's divinity. The shepherds came to the stable and found a King. The people lined the streets of Jerusalem for a common colt and found the Messiah. So I must go through the death of a friend and know peace. For God often chooses to couch his lessons in places and situations that don't make sense. But he is God, and he is there. I will find him, if I will but look.

MARRIAGE BUILDERS

- *When have you experienced a surprising juxtaposition of grace or peace in the middle of a marital disagreement?*
- *What are the evidences that God is present in your marriage?*

Additional Scripture Readings
Jeremiah 29:13; Luke 2:1–20; John 12:12–15

Go to page 1149 for your next devotional reading.

15John testifies concerning him. He
cries out, saying, "This was he of whom I
said, 'He who comes after me has sur-
passed me because he was before me.' "
16From the fullness of his grace we have
all received one blessing after another.
17For the law was given through Moses;
grace and truth came through Jesus
Christ. 18No one has ever seen God, but
God the One and Only,[a,b] who is at the
Father's side, has made him known.

John the Baptist Denies Being the Christ

19Now this was John's testimony when
the Jews of Jerusalem sent priests and Le-
vites to ask him who he was. 20He did not
fail to confess, but confessed freely, "I am
not the Christ.[c]"

21They asked him, "Then who are you?
Are you Elijah?"

He said, "I am not."

"Are you the Prophet?"

He answered, "No."

22Finally they said, "Who are you? Give
us an answer to take back to those who
sent us. What do you say about yourself?"

23John replied in the words of Isaiah the
prophet, "I am the voice of one calling in
the desert, 'Make straight the way for the
Lord.' "[d]

24Now some Pharisees who had been
sent 25questioned him, "Why then do you
baptize if you are not the Christ, nor Eli-
jah, nor the Prophet?"

26"I baptize with[e] water," John replied,
"but among you stands one you do not
know. 27He is the one who comes after
me, the thongs of whose sandals I am not
worthy to untie."

28This all happened at Bethany on the
other side of the Jordan, where John was
baptizing.

Jesus the Lamb of God

29The next day John saw Jesus coming
toward him and said, "Look, the Lamb of
God, who takes away the sin of the world!
30This is the one I meant when I said, 'A
man who comes after me has surpassed
me because he was before me.' 31I myself
did not know him, but the reason I came
baptizing with water was that he might be
revealed to Israel."

32Then John gave this testimony: "I saw
the Spirit come down from heaven as a
dove and remain on him. 33I would not
have known him, except that the one who
sent me to baptize with water told me,
'The man on whom you see the Spirit
come down and remain is he who will
baptize with the Holy Spirit.' 34I have seen
and I testify that this is the Son of God."

Jesus' First Disciples

35The next day John was there again
with two of his disciples. 36When he saw
Jesus passing by, he said, "Look, the
Lamb of God!"

37When the two disciples heard him say
this, they followed Jesus. 38Turning
around, Jesus saw them following and
asked, "What do you want?"

They said, "Rabbi" (which means
Teacher), "where are you staying?"

39"Come," he replied, "and you will
see."

So they went and saw where he was
staying, and spent that day with him. It
was about the tenth hour.

40Andrew, Simon Peter's brother, was
one of the two who heard what John had
said and who had followed Jesus. 41The
first thing Andrew did was to find his
brother Simon and tell him, "We have
found the Messiah" (that is, the Christ).
42And he brought him to Jesus.

Jesus looked at him and said, "You are
Simon son of John. You will be called Ce-
phas" (which, when translated, is Pe-
ter[f]).

Jesus Calls Philip and Nathanael

43The next day Jesus decided to leave
for Galilee. Finding Philip, he said to him,
"Follow me."

44Philip, like Andrew and Peter, was
from the town of Bethsaida. 45Philip found
Nathanael and told him, "We have found
the one Moses wrote about in the Law,
and about whom the prophets also
wrote—Jesus of Nazareth, the son of Jo-
seph."

46"Nazareth! Can anything good come
from there?" Nathanael asked.

"Come and see," said Philip.

[a] *18* Or *the Only Begotten* [b] *18* Some manuscripts *but the only* (or *only begotten*) *Son* [c] *20* Or *Messiah.* "The Christ" (Greek) and "the Messiah" (Hebrew) both mean "the Anointed One"; also in verse 25. [d] *23* Isaiah 40:3 [e] *26* Or *in*; also in verses 31 and 33 [f] *42* Both *Cephas* (Aramaic) and *Peter* (Greek) mean *rock.*

47When Jesus saw Nathanael approaching, he said of him, "Here is a true Israelite, in whom there is nothing false."

48"How do you know me?" Nathanael asked.

Jesus answered, "I saw you while you were still under the fig tree before Philip called you."

49Then Nathanael declared, "Rabbi, you are the Son of God; you are the King of Israel."

50Jesus said, "You believe[a] because I told you I saw you under the fig tree. You shall see greater things than that." 51He then added, "I tell you[b] the truth, you[b] shall see heaven open, and the angels of God ascending and descending on the Son of Man."

Jesus Changes Water to Wine

2 On the third day a wedding took place at Cana in Galilee. Jesus' mother was there, 2and Jesus and his disciples had also been invited to the wedding. 3When the wine was gone, Jesus' mother said to him, "They have no more wine."

4"Dear woman, why do you involve me?" Jesus replied. "My time has not yet come."

5His mother said to the servants, "Do whatever he tells you."

6Nearby stood six stone water jars, the kind used by the Jews for ceremonial washing, each holding from twenty to thirty gallons.[c]

7Jesus said to the servants, "Fill the jars with water"; so they filled them to the brim.

8Then he told them, "Now draw some out and take it to the master of the banquet."

They did so, 9and the master of the banquet tasted the water that had been turned into wine. He did not realize where it had come from, though the servants who had drawn the water knew. Then he called the bridegroom aside 10and said, "Everyone brings out the choice wine first and then the cheaper wine after the guests have had too much to drink; but you have saved the best till now."

11This, the first of his miraculous signs, Jesus performed at Cana in Galilee. He thus revealed his glory, and his disciples put their faith in him.

Jesus Clears the Temple

12After this he went down to Capernaum with his mother and brothers and his disciples. There they stayed for a few days.

13When it was almost time for the Jewish Passover, Jesus went up to Jerusalem. 14In the temple courts he found men selling cattle, sheep and doves, and others sitting at tables exchanging money. 15So he made a whip out of cords, and drove all from the temple area, both sheep and cattle; he scattered the coins of the money changers and overturned their tables. 16To those who sold doves he said, "Get these out of here! How dare you turn my Father's house into a market!"

17His disciples remembered that it is written: "Zeal for your house will consume me."[d]

18Then the Jews demanded of him, "What miraculous sign can you show us to prove your authority to do all this?"

19Jesus answered them, "Destroy this temple, and I will raise it again in three days."

20The Jews replied, "It has taken forty-six years to build this temple, and you are going to raise it in three days?" 21But the temple he had spoken of was his body. 22After he was raised from the dead, his disciples recalled what he had said. Then they believed the Scripture and the words that Jesus had spoken.

23Now while he was in Jerusalem at the Passover Feast, many people saw the miraculous signs he was doing and believed in his name.[e] 24But Jesus would not entrust himself to them, for he knew all men. 25He did not need man's testimony about man, for he knew what was in a man.

Jesus Teaches Nicodemus

3 Now there was a man of the Pharisees named Nicodemus, a member of the Jewish ruling council. 2He came to Jesus at night and said, "Rabbi, we know you are a teacher who has come from God. For no one could perform the miraculous signs you are doing if God were not with him."

3In reply Jesus declared, "I tell you the truth, no one can see the kingdom of God unless he is born again.[f]"

4"How can a man be born when he is

[a]*50* Or *Do you believe . . . ?* [b]*51* The Greek is plural. [c]*6* Greek *two to three metretes* (probably about 75 to 115 liters) [d]*17* Psalm 69:9 [e]*23* Or *and believed in him* [f]*3* Or *born from above*; also in verse 7

old?" Nicodemus asked. "Surely he cannot enter a second time into his mother's
womb to be born!"
5Jesus answered, "I tell you the truth,
no one can enter the kingdom of God unless he is born of water and the Spirit.
6Flesh gives birth to flesh, but the Spirit[a]
gives birth to spirit. 7You should not be
surprised at my saying, 'You[b] must be
born again.' 8The wind blows wherever it
pleases. You hear its sound, but you cannot tell where it comes from or where it is

[a]6 Or *but spirit* [b]7 The Greek is plural.

VERSE FOR THE DAY: John 2:9

AUTHOR: Frederick Buechner

PASSAGE FOR THE DAY: John 2:1–11

The Marriage Miracle

John tells us that turning water into wine at a wedding feast was the first sign given by Jesus. And in a way, a miracle trembles on the threshold of taking place at *every* wedding.

To give yourself away in love to another would seem to mean that you end up with less of yourself left than you had to begin with. But the miracle is that just the reverse is true. To give yourself away in love to somebody else—as a man and a woman do at a wedding—is to become for the first time yourself fully. To live not just for yourself alone anymore but for another self, to whom you swear to be true, is to come fully alive.

"For better for worse, for richer for poorer, in sickness and in health"—there will be good times and bad times both. There will be times when the vows seem all but impossible to keep. But by holding fast to each other in trust, in patience, in hope, and by holding fast also to him who has promised to be present whenever two or three are gathered in his name, the impossible becomes possible. Little by little, by grace we become human in spite of ourselves, become whole, become truly loving and lovely at last.

The glory of Christ is, in the long run, the power of Christ to adorn and beautify, to transform and hallow, the human heart.

MARRIAGE BUILDERS

♦ *In what concrete ways is your life more "full" now that you are married?*

♦ *Have there been changes in yourselves or in your relationship that you once would have thought were impossible?*

Additional Scripture Readings
Luke 10:27; Philippians 4:13

Go to page 1151 for your next devotional reading.

going. So it is with everyone born of the
Spirit."
9"How can this be?" Nicodemus asked.
10"You are Israel's teacher," said Jesus,
"and do you not understand these things?
11I tell you the truth, we speak of what we
know, and we testify to what we have
seen, but still you people do not accept
our testimony. 12I have spoken to you of
earthly things and you do not believe;
how then will you believe if I speak of
heavenly things? 13No one has ever gone
into heaven except the one who came
from heaven—the Son of Man.[a] 14Just as
Moses lifted up the snake in the desert, so
the Son of Man must be lifted up, 15that
everyone who believes in him may have
eternal life.[b]
16"For God so loved the world that he
gave his one and only Son,[c] that whoever
believes in him shall not perish but have
eternal life. 17For God did not send his Son
into the world to condemn the world, but
to save the world through him. 18Whoever
believes in him is not condemned, but
whoever does not believe stands con-
demned already because he has not be-
lieved in the name of God's one and only
Son.[d] 19This is the verdict: Light has
come into the world, but men loved dark-
ness instead of light because their deeds
were evil. 20Everyone who does evil hates
the light, and will not come into the light
for fear that his deeds will be exposed.
21But whoever lives by the truth comes
into the light, so that it may be seen plain-
ly that what he has done has been done
through God."[e]

John the Baptist's Testimony About Jesus

22After this, Jesus and his disciples
went out into the Judean countryside,
where he spent some time with them, and
baptized. 23Now John also was baptizing
at Aenon near Salim, because there was
plenty of water, and people were con-
stantly coming to be baptized. 24(This was
before John was put in prison.) 25An argu-
ment developed between some of John's
disciples and a certain Jew[f] over the mat-
ter of ceremonial washing. 26They came to
John and said to him, "Rabbi, that man
who was with you on the other side of the
Jordan—the one you testified about—
well, he is baptizing, and everyone is go-
ing to him."
27To this John replied, "A man can re-
ceive only what is given him from heaven.
28You yourselves can testify that I said, 'I
am not the Christ[g] but am sent ahead of
him.' 29The bride belongs to the bride-
groom. The friend who attends the bride-
groom waits and listens for him, and is
full of joy when he hears the bridegroom's
voice. That joy is mine, and it is now com-
plete. 30He must become greater; I must
become less.
31"The one who comes from above is
above all; the one who is from the earth
belongs to the earth, and speaks as one
from the earth. The one who comes from
heaven is above all. 32He testifies to what
he has seen and heard, but no one accepts
his testimony. 33The man who has accept-
ed it has certified that God is truthful.
34For the one whom God has sent speaks
the words of God, for God[h] gives the Spir-
it without limit. 35The Father loves the
Son and has placed everything in his
hands. 36Whoever believes in the Son has
eternal life, but whoever rejects the Son
will not see life, for God's wrath remains
on him."[i]

Jesus Talks With a Samaritan Woman

4 The Pharisees heard that Jesus was
gaining and baptizing more disciples
than John, 2although in fact it was not
Jesus who baptized, but his disciples.
3When the Lord learned of this, he left Ju-
dea and went back once more to Galilee.
4Now he had to go through Samaria. 5So
he came to a town in Samaria called Sy-
char, near the plot of ground Jacob had
given to his son Joseph. 6Jacob's well was
there, and Jesus, tired as he was from the
journey, sat down by the well. It was
about the sixth hour.
7When a Samaritan woman came to
draw water, Jesus said to her, "Will you
give me a drink?" 8(His disciples had gone
into the town to buy food.)
9The Samaritan woman said to him,
"You are a Jew and I am a Samaritan wom-
an. How can you ask me for a drink?" (For

[a] 13 Some manuscripts *Man, who is in heaven* [b] 15 Or *believes may have eternal life in him*
[c] 16 Or *his only begotten Son* [d] 18 Or *God's only begotten Son* [e] 21 Some interpreters end the quotation after verse 15. [f] 25 Some manuscripts *and certain Jews* [g] 28 Or *Messiah* [h] 34 Greek *he* [i] 36 Some interpreters end the quotation after verse 30.

VERSE FOR THE DAY: John 3:16

AUTHOR: Nate Adams

PASSAGE FOR THE DAY: John 3:16–21

Only Begotten Son

I was shaving when I heard a crash in the bedroom. The full-length mirror that was leaning against our bedroom wall must have fallen. Then I heard Caleb's scream.

I flew around the corner to see a zillion pieces of broken mirror on the floor—and Caleb, my 19-month-old, lying in the middle of it. Then I saw the blood.

The sight of my son's blood overwhelmed me. I snatched him up and scanned his body. Though the glass had been scattered all around him, the only mark was a small scratch on the inside of his left ear. Only a trickle of blood flowed, so it was apparently more fear than injury that was forcing his tears.

The interesting thing about this little crisis is now I can't read, hear or even think of John 3:16 without remembering Caleb lying in the middle of that broken glass. That most familiar Bible verse had become much too familiar, even trite to me. But now when I hear it I get a lump in my throat, thinking about what kind of determined, redemptive love could be strong enough to let an only Son cry out in pain on a cross.

A few months after Caleb's accident, our second son was born. I no longer had an "only begotten son." But as I experienced the joy of a new life and an expanded family, I realized in a fresh way that it was Jesus' death that made it possible for the Only Begotten Son to have many brothers and sisters.

MARRIAGE BUILDERS

♦ *How does having children of your own affect your perception of God's sacrifice of his only begotten son?*

♦ *How has sacrifice been part of love in your marriage relationship?*

Additional Scripture Readings
Romans 5:8–9; Hebrews 9:20–28

Go to page 1159 for your next devotional reading.

Jews do not associate with Samaritans.[a])
10Jesus answered her, "If you knew the
gift of God and who it is that asks you for
a drink, you would have asked him and he
would have given you living water."
11"Sir," the woman said, "you have
nothing to draw with and the well is deep.
Where can you get this living water? 12Are
you greater than our father Jacob, who
gave us the well and drank from it him-
self, as did also his sons and his flocks and
herds?"
13Jesus answered, "Everyone who
drinks this water will be thirsty again,
14but whoever drinks the water I give him
will never thirst. Indeed, the water I give
him will become in him a spring of water
welling up to eternal life."
15The woman said to him, "Sir, give me
this water so that I won't get thirsty and
have to keep coming here to draw water."
16He told her, "Go, call your husband
and come back."
17"I have no husband," she replied.
Jesus said to her, "You are right when
you say you have no husband. 18The fact
is, you have had five husbands, and the
man you now have is not your husband.
What you have just said is quite true."
19"Sir," the woman said, "I can see that
you are a prophet. 20Our fathers wor-
shiped on this mountain, but you Jews
claim that the place where we must wor-
ship is in Jerusalem."
21Jesus declared, "Believe me, woman,
a time is coming when you will worship
the Father neither on this mountain nor in
Jerusalem. 22You Samaritans worship
what you do not know; we worship what
we do know, for salvation is from the
Jews. 23Yet a time is coming and has now
come when the true worshipers will wor-
ship the Father in spirit and truth, for they
are the kind of worshipers the Father
seeks. 24God is spirit, and his worshipers
must worship in spirit and in truth."
25The woman said, "I know that Messi-
ah" (called Christ) "is coming. When he
comes, he will explain everything to us."
26Then Jesus declared, "I who speak to
you am he."

The Disciples Rejoin Jesus

27Just then his disciples returned and
were surprised to find him talking with a
woman. But no one asked, "What do you
want?" or "Why are you talking with her?"
28Then, leaving her water jar, the wom-
an went back to the town and said to the
people, 29"Come, see a man who told me
everything I ever did. Could this be the
Christ[b]?" 30They came out of the town
and made their way toward him.
31Meanwhile his disciples urged him,
"Rabbi, eat something."
32But he said to them, "I have food to
eat that you know nothing about."
33Then his disciples said to each other,
"Could someone have brought him food?"
34"My food," said Jesus, "is to do the
will of him who sent me and to finish his
work. 35Do you not say, 'Four months
more and then the harvest'? I tell you,
open your eyes and look at the fields!
They are ripe for harvest. 36Even now the
reaper draws his wages, even now he har-
vests the crop for eternal life, so that the
sower and the reaper may be glad togeth-
er. 37Thus the saying 'One sows and an-
other reaps' is true. 38I sent you to reap
what you have not worked for. Others
have done the hard work, and you have
reaped the benefits of their labor."

Many Samaritans Believe

39Many of the Samaritans from that
town believed in him because of the wom-
an's testimony, "He told me everything I
ever did." 40So when the Samaritans came
to him, they urged him to stay with them,
and he stayed two days. 41And because of
his words many more became believers.
42They said to the woman, "We no long-
er believe just because of what you said;
now we have heard for ourselves, and we
know that this man really is the Savior of
the world."

Jesus Heals the Official's Son

43After the two days he left for Galilee.
44(Now Jesus himself had pointed out that
a prophet has no honor in his own coun-
try.) 45When he arrived in Galilee, the Gal-
ileans welcomed him. They had seen all
that he had done in Jerusalem at the Pass-
over Feast, for they also had been there.
46Once more he visited Cana in Galilee,
where he had turned the water into wine.
And there was a certain royal official
whose son lay sick at Capernaum. 47When
this man heard that Jesus had arrived in
Galilee from Judea, he went to him and
begged him to come and heal his son, who
was close to death.

[a]9 Or *do not use dishes Samaritans have used* [b]29 Or *Messiah*

48"Unless you people see miraculous
signs and wonders," Jesus told him, "you
will never believe."
49The royal official said, "Sir, come
down before my child dies."
50Jesus replied, "You may go. Your son
will live."
The man took Jesus at his word and departed. 51While he was still on the way,
his servants met him with the news that
his boy was living. 52When he inquired as
to the time when his son got better, they
said to him, "The fever left him yesterday
at the seventh hour."
53Then the father realized that this was
the exact time at which Jesus had said to
him, "Your son will live." So he and all his
household believed.
54This was the second miraculous sign
that Jesus performed, having come from
Judea to Galilee.

The Healing at the Pool

5 Some time later, Jesus went up to Jerusalem for a feast of the Jews. 2Now
there is in Jerusalem near the Sheep Gate
a pool, which in Aramaic is called Bethesda[a] and which is surrounded by five covered colonnades. 3Here a great number of
disabled people used to lie—the blind,
the lame, the paralyzed.[b] 5One who was
there had been an invalid for thirty-eight
years. 6When Jesus saw him lying there
and learned that he had been in this condition for a long time, he asked him, "Do
you want to get well?"
7"Sir," the invalid replied, "I have no
one to help me into the pool when the water is stirred. While I am trying to get in,
someone else goes down ahead of me."
8Then Jesus said to him, "Get up! Pick
up your mat and walk." 9At once the man
was cured; he picked up his mat and
walked.
The day on which this took place was a
Sabbath, 10and so the Jews said to the
man who had been healed, "It is the Sabbath; the law forbids you to carry your
mat."
11But he replied, "The man who made
me well said to me, 'Pick up your mat and
walk.'"
12So they asked him, "Who is this fellow who told you to pick it up and walk?"
13The man who was healed had no idea
who it was, for Jesus had slipped away
into the crowd that was there.
14Later Jesus found him at the temple
and said to him, "See, you are well again.
Stop sinning or something worse may
happen to you." 15The man went away
and told the Jews that it was Jesus who
had made him well.

Life Through the Son

16So, because Jesus was doing these
things on the Sabbath, the Jews persecuted him. 17Jesus said to them, "My Father
is always at his work to this very day, and
I, too, am working." 18For this reason the
Jews tried all the harder to kill him; not
only was he breaking the Sabbath, but he
was even calling God his own Father,
making himself equal with God.
19Jesus gave them this answer: "I tell
you the truth, the Son can do nothing by
himself; he can do only what he sees his
Father doing, because whatever the Father does the Son also does. 20For the Father loves the Son and shows him all he
does. Yes, to your amazement he will
show him even greater things than these.
21For just as the Father raises the dead and
gives them life, even so the Son gives life
to whom he is pleased to give it. 22Moreover, the Father judges no one, but has entrusted all judgment to the Son, 23that all
may honor the Son just as they honor the
Father. He who does not honor the Son
does not honor the Father, who sent him.
24"I tell you the truth, whoever hears
my word and believes him who sent me
has eternal life and will not be condemned; he has crossed over from death
to life. 25I tell you the truth, a time is coming and has now come when the dead will
hear the voice of the Son of God and those
who hear will live. 26For as the Father has
life in himself, so he has granted the Son
to have life in himself. 27And he has given
him authority to judge because he is the
Son of Man.
28"Do not be amazed at this, for a time
is coming when all who are in their graves
will hear his voice 29and come out—those
who have done good will rise to live, and
those who have done evil will rise to be
condemned. 30By myself I can do nothing;

[a]2 Some manuscripts *Bethzatha*; other manuscripts *Bethsaida* [b]3 Some less important manuscripts *paralyzed—and they waited for the moving of the waters. 4From time to time an angel of the Lord would come down and stir up the waters. The first one into the pool after each such disturbance would be cured of whatever disease he had.*

I judge only as I hear, and my judgment is just, for I seek not to please myself but him who sent me.

Testimonies About Jesus

31"If I testify about myself, my testimony is not valid. 32There is another who testifies in my favor, and I know that his testimony about me is valid.

33"You have sent to John and he has testified to the truth. 34Not that I accept human testimony; but I mention it that you may be saved. 35John was a lamp that burned and gave light, and you chose for a time to enjoy his light.

36"I have testimony weightier than that of John. For the very work that the Father has given me to finish, and which I am doing, testifies that the Father has sent me. 37And the Father who sent me has himself testified concerning me. You have never heard his voice nor seen his form, 38nor does his word dwell in you, for you do not believe the one he sent. 39You diligently study[a] the Scriptures because you think that by them you possess eternal life. These are the Scriptures that testify about me, 40yet you refuse to come to me to have life.

41"I do not accept praise from men, 42but I know you. I know that you do not have the love of God in your hearts. 43I have come in my Father's name, and you do not accept me; but if someone else comes in his own name, you will accept him. 44How can you believe if you accept praise from one another, yet make no effort to obtain the praise that comes from the only God[b]?

45"But do not think I will accuse you before the Father. Your accuser is Moses, on whom your hopes are set. 46If you believed Moses, you would believe me, for he wrote about me. 47But since you do not believe what he wrote, how are you going to believe what I say?"

Jesus Feeds the Five Thousand

6 Some time after this, Jesus crossed to the far shore of the Sea of Galilee (that is, the Sea of Tiberias), 2and a great crowd of people followed him because they saw the miraculous signs he had performed on the sick. 3Then Jesus went up on a mountainside and sat down with his disciples. 4The Jewish Passover Feast was near.

5When Jesus looked up and saw a great crowd coming toward him, he said to Philip, "Where shall we buy bread for these people to eat?" 6He asked this only to test him, for he already had in mind what he was going to do.

7Philip answered him, "Eight months' wages[c] would not buy enough bread for each one to have a bite!"

8Another of his disciples, Andrew, Simon Peter's brother, spoke up, 9"Here is a boy with five small barley loaves and two small fish, but how far will they go among so many?"

10Jesus said, "Have the people sit down." There was plenty of grass in that place, and the men sat down, about five thousand of them. 11Jesus then took the loaves, gave thanks, and distributed to those who were seated as much as they wanted. He did the same with the fish.

12When they had all had enough to eat, he said to his disciples, "Gather the pieces that are left over. Let nothing be wasted." 13So they gathered them and filled twelve baskets with the pieces of the five barley loaves left over by those who had eaten.

14After the people saw the miraculous sign that Jesus did, they began to say, "Surely this is the Prophet who is to come into the world." 15Jesus, knowing that they intended to come and make him king by force, withdrew again to a mountain by himself.

Jesus Walks on the Water

16When evening came, his disciples went down to the lake, 17where they got into a boat and set off across the lake for Capernaum. By now it was dark, and Jesus had not yet joined them. 18A strong wind was blowing and the waters grew rough. 19When they had rowed three or three and a half miles,[d] they saw Jesus approaching the boat, walking on the water; and they were terrified. 20But he said to them, "It is I; don't be afraid." 21Then they were willing to take him into the boat, and immediately the boat reached the shore where they were heading.

22The next day the crowd that had stayed on the opposite shore of the lake realized that only one boat had been there, and that Jesus had not entered it with his disciples, but that they had gone away alone. 23Then some boats from Tibe-

[a] *39* Or *Study diligently* (the imperative) [b] *44* Some early manuscripts *the Only One* [c] *7* Greek *two hundred denarii* [d] *19* Greek *rowed twenty-five or thirty stadia* (about 5 or 6 kilometers)

rias landed near the place where the people had eaten the bread after the Lord had given thanks. 24Once the crowd realized that neither Jesus nor his disciples were there, they got into the boats and went to Capernaum in search of Jesus.

Jesus the Bread of Life

25When they found him on the other side of the lake, they asked him, "Rabbi, when did you get here?"

26Jesus answered, "I tell you the truth, you are looking for me, not because you saw miraculous signs but because you ate the loaves and had your fill. 27Do not work for food that spoils, but for food that endures to eternal life, which the Son of Man will give you. On him God the Father has placed his seal of approval."

28Then they asked him, "What must we do to do the works God requires?"

29Jesus answered, "The work of God is this: to believe in the one he has sent."

30So they asked him, "What miraculous sign then will you give that we may see it and believe you? What will you do? 31Our forefathers ate the manna in the desert; as it is written: 'He gave them bread from heaven to eat.'[a]"

32Jesus said to them, "I tell you the truth, it is not Moses who has given you the bread from heaven, but it is my Father who gives you the true bread from heaven. 33For the bread of God is he who comes down from heaven and gives life to the world."

34"Sir," they said, "from now on give us this bread."

35Then Jesus declared, "I am the bread of life. He who comes to me will never go hungry, and he who believes in me will never be thirsty. 36But as I told you, you have seen me and still you do not believe. 37All that the Father gives me will come to me, and whoever comes to me I will never drive away. 38For I have come down from heaven not to do my will but to do the will of him who sent me. 39And this is the will of him who sent me, that I shall lose none of all that he has given me, but raise them up at the last day. 40For my Father's will is that everyone who looks to the Son and believes in him shall have eternal life, and I will raise him up at the last day."

41At this the Jews began to grumble about him because he said, "I am the bread that came down from heaven." 42They said, "Is this not Jesus, the son of Joseph, whose father and mother we know? How can he now say, 'I came down from heaven'?"

43"Stop grumbling among yourselves," Jesus answered. 44"No one can come to me unless the Father who sent me draws him, and I will raise him up at the last day. 45It is written in the Prophets: 'They will all be taught by God.'[b] Everyone who listens to the Father and learns from him comes to me. 46No one has seen the Father except the one who is from God; only he has seen the Father. 47I tell you the truth, he who believes has everlasting life. 48I am the bread of life. 49Your forefathers ate the manna in the desert, yet they died. 50But here is the bread that comes down from heaven, which a man may eat and not die. 51I am the living bread that came down from heaven. If anyone eats of this bread, he will live forever. This bread is my flesh, which I will give for the life of the world."

52Then the Jews began to argue sharply among themselves, "How can this man give us his flesh to eat?"

53Jesus said to them, "I tell you the truth, unless you eat the flesh of the Son of Man and drink his blood, you have no life in you. 54Whoever eats my flesh and drinks my blood has eternal life, and I will raise him up at the last day. 55For my flesh is real food and my blood is real drink. 56Whoever eats my flesh and drinks my blood remains in me, and I in him. 57Just as the living Father sent me and I live because of the Father, so the one who feeds on me will live because of me. 58This is the bread that came down from heaven. Your forefathers ate manna and died, but he who feeds on this bread will live forever." 59He said this while teaching in the synagogue in Capernaum.

Many Disciples Desert Jesus

60On hearing it, many of his disciples said, "This is a hard teaching. Who can accept it?"

61Aware that his disciples were grumbling about this, Jesus said to them, "Does this offend you? 62What if you see the Son of Man ascend to where he was before! 63The Spirit gives life; the flesh counts for nothing. The words I have spoken to you are spirit[c] and they are life. 64Yet there are some of you who do not believe." For

[a] *31* Exodus 16:4; Neh. 9:15; Psalm 78:24,25 [b] *45* Isaiah 54:13 [c] *63* Or *Spirit*

Jesus had known from the beginning which of them did not believe and who would betray him. 65He went on to say, "This is why I told you that no one can come to me unless the Father has enabled him."

66From this time many of his disciples turned back and no longer followed him.

67"You do not want to leave too, do you?" Jesus asked the Twelve.

68Simon Peter answered him, "Lord, to whom shall we go? You have the words of eternal life. 69We believe and know that you are the Holy One of God."

70Then Jesus replied, "Have I not chosen you, the Twelve? Yet one of you is a devil!" 71(He meant Judas, the son of Simon Iscariot, who, though one of the Twelve, was later to betray him.)

Jesus Goes to the Feast of Tabernacles

7 After this, Jesus went around in Galilee, purposely staying away from Judea because the Jews there were waiting to take his life. 2But when the Jewish Feast of Tabernacles was near, 3Jesus' brothers said to him, "You ought to leave here and go to Judea, so that your disciples may see the miracles you do. 4No one who wants to become a public figure acts in secret. Since you are doing these things, show yourself to the world." 5For even his own brothers did not believe in him.

6Therefore Jesus told them, "The right time for me has not yet come; for you any time is right. 7The world cannot hate you, but it hates me because I testify that what it does is evil. 8You go to the Feast. I am not yet[a] going up to this Feast, because for me the right time has not yet come." 9Having said this, he stayed in Galilee.

10However, after his brothers had left for the Feast, he went also, not publicly, but in secret. 11Now at the Feast the Jews were watching for him and asking, "Where is that man?"

12Among the crowds there was widespread whispering about him. Some said, "He is a good man."

Others replied, "No, he deceives the people." 13But no one would say anything publicly about him for fear of the Jews.

Jesus Teaches at the Feast

14Not until halfway through the Feast did Jesus go up to the temple courts and begin to teach. 15The Jews were amazed and asked, "How did this man get such learning without having studied?"

16Jesus answered, "My teaching is not my own. It comes from him who sent me. 17If anyone chooses to do God's will, he will find out whether my teaching comes from God or whether I speak on my own. 18He who speaks on his own does so to gain honor for himself, but he who works for the honor of the one who sent him is a man of truth; there is nothing false about him. 19Has not Moses given you the law? Yet not one of you keeps the law. Why are you trying to kill me?"

20"You are demon-possessed," the crowd answered. "Who is trying to kill you?"

21Jesus said to them, "I did one miracle, and you are all astonished. 22Yet, because Moses gave you circumcision (though actually it did not come from Moses, but from the patriarchs), you circumcise a child on the Sabbath. 23Now if a child can be circumcised on the Sabbath so that the law of Moses may not be broken, why are you angry with me for healing the whole man on the Sabbath? 24Stop judging by mere appearances, and make a right judgment."

Is Jesus the Christ?

25At that point some of the people of Jerusalem began to ask, "Isn't this the man they are trying to kill? 26Here he is, speaking publicly, and they are not saying a word to him. Have the authorities really concluded that he is the Christ[b]? 27But we know where this man is from; when the Christ comes, no one will know where he is from."

28Then Jesus, still teaching in the temple courts, cried out, "Yes, you know me, and you know where I am from. I am not here on my own, but he who sent me is true. You do not know him, 29but I know him because I am from him and he sent me."

30At this they tried to seize him, but no one laid a hand on him, because his time had not yet come. 31Still, many in the crowd put their faith in him. They said, "When the Christ comes, will he do more miraculous signs than this man?"

32The Pharisees heard the crowd whispering such things about him. Then the

[a]8 Some early manuscripts do not have *yet*. [b]26 Or *Messiah*; also in verses 27, 31, 41 and 42

chief priests and the Pharisees sent temple guards to arrest him.

33Jesus said, "I am with you for only a short time, and then I go to the one who sent me. 34You will look for me, but you will not find me; and where I am, you cannot come."

35The Jews said to one another, "Where does this man intend to go that we cannot find him? Will he go where our people live scattered among the Greeks, and teach the Greeks? 36What did he mean when he said, 'You will look for me, but you will not find me,' and 'Where I am, you cannot come'?"

37On the last and greatest day of the Feast, Jesus stood and said in a loud voice, "If anyone is thirsty, let him come to me and drink. 38Whoever believes in me, as[a] the Scripture has said, streams of living water will flow from within him." 39By this he meant the Spirit, whom those who believed in him were later to receive. Up to that time the Spirit had not been given, since Jesus had not yet been glorified.

40On hearing his words, some of the people said, "Surely this man is the Prophet."

41Others said, "He is the Christ."

Still others asked, "How can the Christ come from Galilee? 42Does not the Scripture say that the Christ will come from David's family[b] and from Bethlehem, the town where David lived?" 43Thus the people were divided because of Jesus. 44Some wanted to seize him, but no one laid a hand on him.

Unbelief of the Jewish Leaders

45Finally the temple guards went back to the chief priests and Pharisees, who asked them, "Why didn't you bring him in?"

46"No one ever spoke the way this man does," the guards declared.

47"You mean he has deceived you also?" the Pharisees retorted. 48"Has any of the rulers or of the Pharisees believed in him? 49No! But this mob that knows nothing of the law—there is a curse on them."

50Nicodemus, who had gone to Jesus earlier and who was one of their own number, asked, 51"Does our law condemn anyone without first hearing him to find out what he is doing?"

52They replied, "Are you from Galilee, too? Look into it, and you will find that a prophet[c] does not come out of Galilee."

[The earliest manuscripts and many other ancient witnesses do not have John 7:53–8:11.]

53Then each went to his own home.

8 But Jesus went to the Mount of Olives. 2At dawn he appeared again in the temple courts, where all the people gathered around him, and he sat down to teach them. 3The teachers of the law and the Pharisees brought in a woman caught in adultery. They made her stand before the group 4and said to Jesus, "Teacher, this woman was caught in the act of adultery. 5In the Law Moses commanded us to stone such women. Now what do you say?" 6They were using this question as a trap, in order to have a basis for accusing him.

But Jesus bent down and started to write on the ground with his finger. 7When they kept on questioning him, he straightened up and said to them, "If any one of you is without sin, let him be the first to throw a stone at her." 8Again he stooped down and wrote on the ground.

9At this, those who heard began to go away one at a time, the older ones first, until only Jesus was left, with the woman still standing there. 10Jesus straightened up and asked her, "Woman, where are they? Has no one condemned you?"

11"No one, sir," she said.

"Then neither do I condemn you," Jesus declared. "Go now and leave your life of sin."

The Validity of Jesus' Testimony

12When Jesus spoke again to the people, he said, "I am the light of the world. Whoever follows me will never walk in darkness, but will have the light of life."

13The Pharisees challenged him, "Here you are, appearing as your own witness; your testimony is not valid."

14Jesus answered, "Even if I testify on my own behalf, my testimony is valid, for

[a] *37,38* Or / *If anyone is thirsty, let him come to me. / And let him drink,* 38*who believes in me. / As*
[b] *42* Greek *seed* [c] *52* Two early manuscripts *the Prophet*

I know where I came from and where I am
going. But you have no idea where I come
from or where I am going. 15You judge by
human standards; I pass judgment on no
one. 16But if I do judge, my decisions are
right, because I am not alone. I stand with
the Father, who sent me. 17In your own
Law it is written that the testimony of two
men is valid. 18I am one who testifies for
myself; my other witness is the Father,
who sent me."

19Then they asked him, "Where is your
father?"

"You do not know me or my Father,"
Jesus replied. "If you knew me, you would
know my Father also." 20He spoke these
words while teaching in the temple area
near the place where the offerings were
put. Yet no one seized him, because his
time had not yet come.

21Once more Jesus said to them, "I am
going away, and you will look for me, and
you will die in your sin. Where I go, you
cannot come."

22This made the Jews ask, "Will he kill
himself? Is that why he says, 'Where I go,
you cannot come'?"

23But he continued, "You are from be-
low; I am from above. You are of this
world; I am not of this world. 24I told you
that you would die in your sins; if you do
not believe that I am ⌊the one I claim to
be⌋,[a] you will indeed die in your sins."

25"Who are you?" they asked.

"Just what I have been claiming all
along," Jesus replied. 26"I have much to
say in judgment of you. But he who sent
me is reliable, and what I have heard from
him I tell the world."

27They did not understand that he was
telling them about his Father. 28So Jesus
said, "When you have lifted up the Son of
Man, then you will know that I am ⌊the
one I claim to be⌋ and that I do nothing on
my own but speak just what the Father
has taught me. 29The one who sent me is
with me; he has not left me alone, for I
always do what pleases him." 30Even as he
spoke, many put their faith in him.

The Children of Abraham

31To the Jews who had believed him,
Jesus said, "If you hold to my teaching,
you are really my disciples. 32Then you
will know the truth, and the truth will set
you free."

33They answered him, "We are Abra-
ham's descendants[b] and have never been
slaves of anyone. How can you say that
we shall be set free?"

34Jesus replied, "I tell you the truth, ev-
eryone who sins is a slave to sin. 35Now a
slave has no permanent place in the fami-
ly, but a son belongs to it forever. 36So if
the Son sets you free, you will be free in-
deed. 37I know you are Abraham's descen-
dants. Yet you are ready to kill me, be-
cause you have no room for my word. 38I
am telling you what I have seen in the Fa-
ther's presence, and you do what you
have heard from your father.[c]"

39"Abraham is our father," they an-
swered.

"If you were Abraham's children," said
Jesus, "then you would[d] do the things
Abraham did. 40As it is, you are deter-
mined to kill me, a man who has told you
the truth that I heard from God. Abraham
did not do such things. 41You are doing
the things your own father does."

"We are not illegitimate children," they
protested. "The only Father we have is
God himself."

The Children of the Devil

42Jesus said to them, "If God were your
Father, you would love me, for I came
from God and now am here. I have not
come on my own; but he sent me. 43Why
is my language not clear to you? Because
you are unable to hear what I say. 44You
belong to your father, the devil, and you
want to carry out your father's desire. He
was a murderer from the beginning, not
holding to the truth, for there is no truth
in him. When he lies, he speaks his native
language, for he is a liar and the father of
lies. 45Yet because I tell the truth, you do
not believe me! 46Can any of you prove
me guilty of sin? If I am telling the truth,
why don't you believe me? 47He who be-
longs to God hears what God says. The
reason you do not hear is that you do not
belong to God."

The Claims of Jesus About Himself

48The Jews answered him, "Aren't we
right in saying that you are a Samaritan
and demon-possessed?"

[a]*24* Or *I am he*; also in verse 28 [b]*33* Greek *seed*; also in verse 37 [c]*38* Or *presence. Therefore do what you have heard from the Father.* [d]*39* Some early manuscripts *"If you are Abraham's children," said Jesus, "then*

49"I am not possessed by a demon," said
Jesus, "but I honor my Father and you dis-
honor me. 50I am not seeking glory for
myself; but there is one who seeks it, and
he is the judge. 51I tell you the truth, if
anyone keeps my word, he will never see
death."
52At this the Jews exclaimed, "Now we
know that you are demon-possessed!
Abraham died and so did the prophets, yet
you say that if anyone keeps your word,
he will never taste death. 53Are you great-
er than our father Abraham? He died, and
so did the prophets. Who do you think
you are?"
54Jesus replied, "If I glorify myself,
my glory means nothing. My Father,
whom you claim as your God, is the one
who glorifies me. 55Though you do not
know him, I know him. If I said I did
not, I would be a liar like you, but I do
know him and keep his word. 56Your
father Abraham rejoiced at the thought
of seeing my day; he saw it and was
glad."
57"You are not yet fifty years old," the

FRIDAY

VERSE FOR THE DAY: John 8:50, 54

AUTHOR: R. Ruth Barton

PASSAGE FOR THE DAY: John 8:48–59

Coping With Competition

Overcoming the natural tendencies of a competitive spirit takes supernatural intervention. It must be a matter of constant petition to God.

A competitive spirit is often fed by a dissatisfied spirit. If we learn to accept God's place and plan for us, we won't need to compare ourselves with someone else. Having developed the use of gifts with humble service as our goal, we will be able to serve quietly without envying. We will be able to work in the church nursery in a spirit of service and contentment rather than wishing we were gifted like the person who leads a large Bible class. Servants in either situation can feel confident and grateful for the opportunity to serve God wherever he has placed them.

The bottom line may be our willingness to forget about who gets the glory for our service—ourselves or God. Certainly, when we learn to hand the bouquets back to God, we won't need to compare ourselves with anyone else.

MARRIAGE BUILDERS

♦ *How can you keep competition or unhealthy comparisons from creeping into your relationship with each other?*

♦ *How do contentment and acceptance of God's plan for you help curb destructive comparisons?*

Additional Scripture Readings
Proverbs 14:10; 1 Corinthians 13:4; James 4:10; Galatians 6:3–4

Go to page 1161 for your next devotional reading.

Jews said to him, "and you have seen Abraham!"

58"I tell you the truth," Jesus answered, "before Abraham was born, I am!" 59At this, they picked up stones to stone him, but Jesus hid himself, slipping away from the temple grounds.

Jesus Heals a Man Born Blind

9 As he went along, he saw a man blind from birth. 2His disciples asked him, "Rabbi, who sinned, this man or his parents, that he was born blind?"

3"Neither this man nor his parents sinned," said Jesus, "but this happened so that the work of God might be displayed in his life. 4As long as it is day, we must do the work of him who sent me. Night is coming, when no one can work. 5While I am in the world, I am the light of the world."

6Having said this, he spit on the ground, made some mud with the saliva, and put it on the man's eyes. 7"Go," he told him, "wash in the Pool of Siloam" (this word means Sent). So the man went and washed, and came home seeing.

8His neighbors and those who had formerly seen him begging asked, "Isn't this the same man who used to sit and beg?" 9Some claimed that he was.

Others said, "No, he only looks like him."

But he himself insisted, "I am the man."

10"How then were your eyes opened?" they demanded.

11He replied, "The man they call Jesus made some mud and put it on my eyes. He told me to go to Siloam and wash. So I went and washed, and then I could see."

12"Where is this man?" they asked him.

"I don't know," he said.

The Pharisees Investigate the Healing

13They brought to the Pharisees the man who had been blind. 14Now the day on which Jesus had made the mud and opened the man's eyes was a Sabbath. 15Therefore the Pharisees also asked him how he had received his sight. "He put mud on my eyes," the man replied, "and I washed, and now I see."

16Some of the Pharisees said, "This man is not from God, for he does not keep the Sabbath."

But others asked, "How can a sinner do such miraculous signs?" So they were divided.

17Finally they turned again to the blind man, "What have you to say about him? It was your eyes he opened."

The man replied, "He is a prophet."

18The Jews still did not believe that he had been blind and had received his sight until they sent for the man's parents. 19"Is this your son?" they asked. "Is this the one you say was born blind? How is it that now he can see?"

20"We know he is our son," the parents answered, "and we know he was born blind. 21But how he can see now, or who opened his eyes, we don't know. Ask him. He is of age; he will speak for himself." 22His parents said this because they were afraid of the Jews, for already the Jews had decided that anyone who acknowledged that Jesus was the Christ[a] would be put out of the synagogue. 23That was why his parents said, "He is of age; ask him."

24A second time they summoned the man who had been blind. "Give glory to God,[b]" they said. "We know this man is a sinner."

25He replied, "Whether he is a sinner or not, I don't know. One thing I do know. I was blind but now I see!"

26Then they asked him, "What did he do to you? How did he open your eyes?"

27He answered, "I have told you already and you did not listen. Why do you want to hear it again? Do you want to become his disciples, too?"

28Then they hurled insults at him and said, "You are this fellow's disciple! We are disciples of Moses! 29We know that God spoke to Moses, but as for this fellow, we don't even know where he comes from."

30The man answered, "Now that is remarkable! You don't know where he comes from, yet he opened my eyes. 31We know that God does not listen to sinners. He listens to the godly man who does his will. 32Nobody has ever heard of opening the eyes of a man born blind. 33If this man were not from God, he could do nothing."

34To this they replied, "You were steeped in sin at birth; how dare you lecture us!" And they threw him out.

Spiritual Blindness

35Jesus heard that they had thrown him

[a]22 Or *Messiah* [b]24 A solemn charge to tell the truth (see Joshua 7:19)

WEEKENDING

PRAYER

No amount of marriage seminars or sermons can replace the value of shared prayer. Discuss which of these tips could help you get started.

1. Start slowly. If praying aloud is difficult, take turns praying silently. Then end the silent prayers with a verse of Scripture prayed out loud. Or write down your prayers and share them. Eventually, try to pray freely in front of your spouse.

2. Don't get discouraged. All couples hit dry times. When staleness happens, don't stop praying.

3. Read a book on prayer together. Let someone else's thoughts on prayer jump-start your motivation.

4. Change your location. Try praying together while going for a walk or while driving together.

— *Jim Killam*

REVIVE

Saturday: 1 John 5:14–15
Sunday: Hebrews 4:14–16

Go to page 1163 for your next devotional reading.

out, and when he found him, he said, "Do you believe in the Son of Man?"

36"Who is he, sir?" the man asked. "Tell me so that I may believe in him."

37Jesus said, "You have now seen him; in fact, he is the one speaking with you."

38Then the man said, "Lord, I believe," and he worshiped him.

39Jesus said, "For judgment I have come into this world, so that the blind will see and those who see will become blind."

40Some Pharisees who were with him heard him say this and asked, "What? Are we blind too?"

41Jesus said, "If you were blind, you would not be guilty of sin; but now that you claim you can see, your guilt remains.

The Shepherd and His Flock

10 "I tell you the truth, the man who does not enter the sheep pen by the gate, but climbs in by some other way, is a thief and a robber. 2The man who enters by the gate is the shepherd of his sheep. 3The watchman opens the gate for him, and the sheep listen to his voice. He calls his own sheep by name and leads them out. 4When he has brought out all his own, he goes on ahead of them, and his sheep follow him because they know his voice. 5But they will never follow a stranger; in fact, they will run away from him because they do not recognize a stranger's voice." 6Jesus used this figure of speech, but they did not understand what he was telling them.

7Therefore Jesus said again, "I tell you the truth, I am the gate for the sheep. 8All who ever came before me were thieves and robbers, but the sheep did not listen to them. 9I am the gate; whoever enters through me will be saved.[a] He will come in and go out, and find pasture. 10The thief comes only to steal and kill and destroy; I have come that they may have life, and have it to the full.

11"I am the good shepherd. The good shepherd lays down his life for the sheep. 12The hired hand is not the shepherd who owns the sheep. So when he sees the wolf coming, he abandons the sheep and runs away. Then the wolf attacks the flock and scatters it. 13The man runs away because he is a hired hand and cares nothing for the sheep.

14"I am the good shepherd; I know my sheep and my sheep know me— 15just as the Father knows me and I know the Father—and I lay down my life for the sheep. 16I have other sheep that are not of this sheep pen. I must bring them also. They too will listen to my voice, and there shall be one flock and one shepherd. 17The reason my Father loves me is that I lay down my life—only to take it up again. 18No one takes it from me, but I lay it down of my own accord. I have authority to lay it down and authority to take it up again. This command I received from my Father."

19At these words the Jews were again divided. 20Many of them said, "He is demon-possessed and raving mad. Why listen to him?"

21But others said, "These are not the sayings of a man possessed by a demon. Can a demon open the eyes of the blind?"

The Unbelief of the Jews

22Then came the Feast of Dedication[b] at Jerusalem. It was winter, 23and Jesus was in the temple area walking in Solomon's Colonnade. 24The Jews gathered around him, saying, "How long will you keep us in suspense? If you are the Christ,[c] tell us plainly."

25Jesus answered, "I did tell you, but you do not believe. The miracles I do in my Father's name speak for me, 26but you do not believe because you are not my sheep. 27My sheep listen to my voice; I know them, and they follow me. 28I give them eternal life, and they shall never perish; no one can snatch them out of my hand. 29My Father, who has given them to me, is greater than all[d]; no one can snatch them out of my Father's hand. 30I and the Father are one."

31Again the Jews picked up stones to stone him, 32but Jesus said to them, "I have shown you many great miracles from the Father. For which of these do you stone me?"

33"We are not stoning you for any of these," replied the Jews, "but for blasphemy, because you, a mere man, claim to be God."

34Jesus answered them, "Is it not written in your Law, 'I have said you are gods'[e]? 35If he called them 'gods,' to whom the word of God came—and the Scripture cannot be broken— 36what

[a]9 Or *kept safe* [b]22 That is, Hanukkah [c]24 Or *Messiah* [d]29 Many early manuscripts *What my Father has given me is greater than all* [e]34 Psalm 82:6

about the one whom the Father set apart
as his very own and sent into the world?
Why then do you accuse me of blasphemy
because I said, 'I am God's Son'? 37Do not
believe me unless I do what my Father
does. 38But if I do it, even though you do
not believe me, believe the miracles, that
you may know and understand that the
Father is in me, and I in the Father."
39Again they tried to seize him, but he es-
caped their grasp.

40Then Jesus went back across the Jor-
dan to the place where John had been
baptizing in the early days. Here he stayed
41and many people came to him. They
said, "Though John never performed a mi-
raculous sign, all that John said about this
man was true." 42And in that place many
believed in Jesus.

The Death of Lazarus

11 Now a man named Lazarus was
sick. He was from Bethany, the vil-
lage of Mary and her sister Martha. 2This
Mary, whose brother Lazarus now lay
sick, was the same one who poured per-
fume on the Lord and wiped his feet with
her hair. 3So the sisters sent word to Jesus,
"Lord, the one you love is sick."

4When he heard this, Jesus said, "This

VERSE FOR THE DAY: John 11:33

AUTHOR: Archibald D. Hart, Ph.D.

PASSAGE FOR THE DAY: John 11:1–44

Empathy and Sympathy

If I go home from work and I'm mad at my boss, I'm apt to project that anger onto my wife. But an understanding spouse can help by saying, "Wait a minute. I really think you're projecting your anger on me, and it's inappropriate. Let's see if we can focus it back where it belongs. Do you want to tell me about whatever it is that your boss did today?"

You also need to respond with *empathy* rather than sympathy. Sympathy says, in essence, "I want to help you by feeling your pain with you." This is counterproductive since it leaves *both* of you suffering.

In contrast, empathy says "I can't feel your pain, but I want to understand it. Will you share it with me?" That gives your spouse an opportunity to unburden himself, and it prevents you from taking on his anger, hurt or pain. In the end, that can be the best way to help a spouse who is struggling with a work-related problem.

MARRIAGE BUILDERS

♦ *Why is empathy a better way to go when "bearing burdens" with your spouse?*

♦ *When has your spouse's support or fresh perspective been helpful to you in dealing with a work-related problem?*

Additional Scripture Readings
Romans 12:15–16; 2 Corinthians 1:3–4

Go to page 1169 for your next devotional reading.

sickness will not end in death. No, it is for
God's glory so that God's Son may be glo-
rified through it." 5Jesus loved Martha and
her sister and Lazarus. 6Yet when he
heard that Lazarus was sick, he stayed
where he was two more days.

7Then he said to his disciples, "Let us go
back to Judea."

8"But Rabbi," they said, "a short while
ago the Jews tried to stone you, and yet
you are going back there?"

9Jesus answered, "Are there not twelve
hours of daylight? A man who walks by
day will not stumble, for he sees by this
world's light. 10It is when he walks by
night that he stumbles, for he has no
light."

11After he had said this, he went on to
tell them, "Our friend Lazarus has fallen
asleep; but I am going there to wake
him up."

12His disciples replied, "Lord, if he
sleeps, he will get better." 13Jesus had
been speaking of his death, but his disci-
ples thought he meant natural sleep.

14So then he told them plainly, "Lazarus
is dead, 15and for your sake I am glad I
was not there, so that you may believe.
But let us go to him."

16Then Thomas (called Didymus) said
to the rest of the disciples, "Let us also go,
that we may die with him."

Jesus Comforts the Sisters

17On his arrival, Jesus found that Laza-
rus had already been in the tomb for four
days. 18Bethany was less than two miles[a]
from Jerusalem, 19and many Jews had
come to Martha and Mary to comfort
them in the loss of their brother. 20When
Martha heard that Jesus was coming, she
went out to meet him, but Mary stayed at
home.

21"Lord," Martha said to Jesus, "if you
had been here, my brother would not
have died. 22But I know that even now
God will give you whatever you ask."

23Jesus said to her, "Your brother will
rise again."

24Martha answered, "I know he will rise
again in the resurrection at the last day."

25Jesus said to her, "I am the resurrec-
tion and the life. He who believes in me
will live, even though he dies; 26and who-
ever lives and believes in me will never
die. Do you believe this?"

27"Yes, Lord," she told him, "I believe
that you are the Christ,[b] the Son of God,
who was to come into the world."

28And after she had said this, she went
back and called her sister Mary aside.
"The Teacher is here," she said, "and is
asking for you." 29When Mary heard this,
she got up quickly and went to him.
30Now Jesus had not yet entered the vil-
lage, but was still at the place where Mar-
tha had met him. 31When the Jews who
had been with Mary in the house, com-
forting her, noticed how quickly she got
up and went out, they followed her, sup-
posing she was going to the tomb to
mourn there.

32When Mary reached the place where
Jesus was and saw him, she fell at his feet
and said, "Lord, if you had been here, my
brother would not have died."

33When Jesus saw her weeping, and the
Jews who had come along with her also
weeping, he was deeply moved in spirit
and troubled. 34"Where have you laid
him?" he asked.

"Come and see, Lord," they replied.

35Jesus wept.

36Then the Jews said, "See how he
loved him!"

37But some of them said, "Could not he
who opened the eyes of the blind man
have kept this man from dying?"

Jesus Raises Lazarus From the Dead

38Jesus, once more deeply moved, came
to the tomb. It was a cave with a stone laid
across the entrance. 39"Take away the
stone," he said.

"But, Lord," said Martha, the sister of
the dead man, "by this time there is a bad
odor, for he has been there four days."

40Then Jesus said, "Did I not tell you
that if you believed, you would see the
glory of God?"

41So they took away the stone. Then
Jesus looked up and said, "Father, I thank
you that you have heard me. 42I knew that
you always hear me, but I said this for the
benefit of the people standing here, that
they may believe that you sent me."

43When he had said this, Jesus called in
a loud voice, "Lazarus, come out!" 44The
dead man came out, his hands and feet
wrapped with strips of linen, and a cloth
around his face.

Jesus said to them, "Take off the grave
clothes and let him go."

[a]18 Greek *fifteen stadia* (about 3 kilometers) [b]27 Or *Messiah*

The Plot to Kill Jesus

45Therefore many of the Jews who had
come to visit Mary, and had seen what
Jesus did, put their faith in him. 46But
some of them went to the Pharisees and
told them what Jesus had done. 47Then
the chief priests and the Pharisees called
a meeting of the Sanhedrin.
"What are we accomplishing?" they
asked. "Here is this man performing many
miraculous signs. 48If we let him go on
like this, everyone will believe in him, and
then the Romans will come and take away
both our place[a] and our nation."
49Then one of them, named Caiaphas,
who was high priest that year, spoke up,
"You know nothing at all! 50You do not re-
alize that it is better for you that one man
die for the people than that the whole na-
tion perish."
51He did not say this on his own, but as
high priest that year he prophesied that
Jesus would die for the Jewish nation,
52and not only for that nation but also for
the scattered children of God, to bring
them together and make them one. 53So
from that day on they plotted to take his
life.
54Therefore Jesus no longer moved
about publicly among the Jews. Instead
he withdrew to a region near the desert, to
a village called Ephraim, where he stayed
with his disciples.
55When it was almost time for the Jew-
ish Passover, many went up from the
country to Jerusalem for their ceremonial
cleansing before the Passover. 56They
kept looking for Jesus, and as they stood
in the temple area they asked one another,
"What do you think? Isn't he coming to
the Feast at all?" 57But the chief priests
and Pharisees had given orders that if any-
one found out where Jesus was, he should
report it so that they might arrest him.

Jesus Anointed at Bethany

12 Six days before the Passover, Jesus
arrived at Bethany, where Lazarus
lived, whom Jesus had raised from the
dead. 2Here a dinner was given in Jesus'
honor. Martha served, while Lazarus was
among those reclining at the table with
him. 3Then Mary took about a pint[b] of
pure nard, an expensive perfume; she
poured it on Jesus' feet and wiped his feet
with her hair. And the house was filled
with the fragrance of the perfume.
4But one of his disciples, Judas Iscariot,
who was later to betray him, objected,
5"Why wasn't this perfume sold and the
money given to the poor? It was worth a
year's wages.[c]" 6He did not say this be-
cause he cared about the poor but because
he was a thief; as keeper of the money
bag, he used to help himself to what was
put into it.
7"Leave her alone," Jesus replied. "⌊It
was intended⌋ that she should save this
perfume for the day of my burial. 8You
will always have the poor among you, but
you will not always have me."
9Meanwhile a large crowd of Jews
found out that Jesus was there and came,
not only because of him but also to see
Lazarus, whom he had raised from the
dead. 10So the chief priests made plans to
kill Lazarus as well, 11for on account of
him many of the Jews were going over to
Jesus and putting their faith in him.

The Triumphal Entry

12The next day the great crowd that had
come for the Feast heard that Jesus was
on his way to Jerusalem. 13They took
palm branches and went out to meet him,
shouting,

"Hosanna![d]"

"Blessed is he who comes in the name
of the Lord!"[e]

"Blessed is the King of Israel!"

14Jesus found a young donkey and sat
upon it, as it is written,

15"Do not be afraid, O Daughter of Zion;
see, your king is coming,
seated on a donkey's colt."[f]

16At first his disciples did not under-
stand all this. Only after Jesus was glori-
fied did they realize that these things had
been written about him and that they had
done these things to him.
17Now the crowd that was with him
when he called Lazarus from the tomb
and raised him from the dead continued
to spread the word. 18Many people, be-
cause they had heard that he had given
this miraculous sign, went out to meet
him. 19So the Pharisees said to one anoth-

[a]48 Or *temple* [b]3 Greek *a litra* (probably about 0.5 liter) [c]5 Greek *three hundred denarii*
[d]13 A Hebrew expression meaning "Save!" which became an exclamation of praise [e]13 Psalm 118:25, 26 [f]15 Zech. 9:9

er, "See, this is getting us nowhere. Look how the whole world has gone after him!"

Jesus Predicts His Death

20Now there were some Greeks among those who went up to worship at the Feast. 21They came to Philip, who was from Bethsaida in Galilee, with a request. "Sir," they said, "we would like to see Jesus." 22Philip went to tell Andrew; Andrew and Philip in turn told Jesus.

23Jesus replied, "The hour has come for the Son of Man to be glorified. 24I tell you the truth, unless a kernel of wheat falls to the ground and dies, it remains only a single seed. But if it dies, it produces many seeds. 25The man who loves his life will lose it, while the man who hates his life in this world will keep it for eternal life. 26Whoever serves me must follow me; and where I am, my servant also will be. My Father will honor the one who serves me.

27"Now my heart is troubled, and what shall I say? 'Father, save me from this hour'? No, it was for this very reason I came to this hour. 28Father, glorify your name!"

Then a voice came from heaven, "I have glorified it, and will glorify it again." 29The crowd that was there and heard it said it had thundered; others said an angel had spoken to him.

30Jesus said, "This voice was for your benefit, not mine. 31Now is the time for judgment on this world; now the prince of this world will be driven out. 32But I, when I am lifted up from the earth, will draw all men to myself." 33He said this to show the kind of death he was going to die.

34The crowd spoke up, "We have heard from the Law that the Christ[a] will remain forever, so how can you say, 'The Son of Man must be lifted up'? Who is this 'Son of Man'?"

35Then Jesus told them, "You are going to have the light just a little while longer. Walk while you have the light, before darkness overtakes you. The man who walks in the dark does not know where he is going. 36Put your trust in the light while you have it, so that you may become sons of light." When he had finished speaking, Jesus left and hid himself from them.

The Jews Continue in Their Unbelief

37Even after Jesus had done all these miraculous signs in their presence, they still would not believe in him. 38This was to fulfill the word of Isaiah the prophet:

> "Lord, who has believed our message
> and to whom has the arm of the
> Lord been revealed?"[b]

39For this reason they could not believe, because, as Isaiah says elsewhere:

> 40"He has blinded their eyes
> and deadened their hearts,
> so they can neither see with their
> eyes,
> nor understand with their hearts,
> nor turn—and I would heal
> them."[c]

41Isaiah said this because he saw Jesus' glory and spoke about him.

42Yet at the same time many even among the leaders believed in him. But because of the Pharisees they would not confess their faith for fear they would be put out of the synagogue; 43for they loved praise from men more than praise from God.

44Then Jesus cried out, "When a man believes in me, he does not believe in me only, but in the one who sent me. 45When he looks at me, he sees the one who sent me. 46I have come into the world as a light, so that no one who believes in me should stay in darkness.

47"As for the person who hears my words but does not keep them, I do not judge him. For I did not come to judge the world, but to save it. 48There is a judge for the one who rejects me and does not accept my words; that very word which I spoke will condemn him at the last day. 49For I did not speak of my own accord, but the Father who sent me commanded me what to say and how to say it. 50I know that his command leads to eternal life. So whatever I say is just what the Father has told me to say."

Jesus Washes His Disciples' Feet

13 It was just before the Passover Feast. Jesus knew that the time had come for him to leave this world and go to the Father. Having loved his own who were in the world, he now showed them the full extent of his love.[d]

2The evening meal was being served, and the devil had already prompted Judas Iscariot, son of Simon, to betray Jesus.

[a] *34* Or *Messiah* [b] *38* Isaiah 53:1 [c] *40* Isaiah 6:10 [d] *1* Or *he loved them to the last*

3Jesus knew that the Father had put all things under his power, and that he had come from God and was returning to God; 4so he got up from the meal, took off his outer clothing, and wrapped a towel around his waist. 5After that, he poured water into a basin and began to wash his disciples' feet, drying them with the towel that was wrapped around him.

6He came to Simon Peter, who said to him, "Lord, are you going to wash my feet?"

7Jesus replied, "You do not realize now what I am doing, but later you will understand."

8"No," said Peter, "you shall never wash my feet."

Jesus answered, "Unless I wash you, you have no part with me."

9"Then, Lord," Simon Peter replied, "not just my feet but my hands and my head as well!"

10Jesus answered, "A person who has had a bath needs only to wash his feet; his whole body is clean. And you are clean, though not every one of you." 11For he knew who was going to betray him, and that was why he said not every one was clean.

12When he had finished washing their feet, he put on his clothes and returned to his place. "Do you understand what I have done for you?" he asked them. 13"You call me 'Teacher' and 'Lord,' and rightly so, for that is what I am. 14Now that I, your Lord and Teacher, have washed your feet, you also should wash one another's feet. 15I have set you an example that you should do as I have done for you. 16I tell you the truth, no servant is greater than his master, nor is a messenger greater than the one who sent him. 17Now that you know these things, you will be blessed if you do them.

Jesus Predicts His Betrayal

18"I am not referring to all of you; I know those I have chosen. But this is to fulfill the scripture: 'He who shares my bread has lifted up his heel against me.'[a]

19"I am telling you now before it happens, so that when it does happen you will believe that I am He. 20I tell you the truth, whoever accepts anyone I send accepts me; and whoever accepts me accepts the one who sent me."

21After he had said this, Jesus was troubled in spirit and testified, "I tell you the truth, one of you is going to betray me."

22His disciples stared at one another, at a loss to know which of them he meant. 23One of them, the disciple whom Jesus loved, was reclining next to him. 24Simon Peter motioned to this disciple and said, "Ask him which one he means."

25Leaning back against Jesus, he asked him, "Lord, who is it?"

26Jesus answered, "It is the one to whom I will give this piece of bread when I have dipped it in the dish." Then, dipping the piece of bread, he gave it to Judas Iscariot, son of Simon. 27As soon as Judas took the bread, Satan entered into him.

"What you are about to do, do quickly," Jesus told him, 28but no one at the meal understood why Jesus said this to him. 29Since Judas had charge of the money, some thought Jesus was telling him to buy what was needed for the Feast, or to give something to the poor. 30As soon as Judas had taken the bread, he went out. And it was night.

Jesus Predicts Peter's Denial

31When he was gone, Jesus said, "Now is the Son of Man glorified and God is glorified in him. 32If God is glorified in him,[b] God will glorify the Son in himself, and will glorify him at once.

33"My children, I will be with you only a little longer. You will look for me, and just as I told the Jews, so I tell you now: Where I am going, you cannot come.

34"A new command I give you: Love one another. As I have loved you, so you must love one another. 35By this all men will know that you are my disciples, if you love one another."

36Simon Peter asked him, "Lord, where are you going?"

Jesus replied, "Where I am going, you cannot follow now, but you will follow later."

37Peter asked, "Lord, why can't I follow you now? I will lay down my life for you."

38Then Jesus answered, "Will you really lay down your life for me? I tell you the truth, before the rooster crows, you will disown me three times!

[a] *18* Psalm 41:9 [b] *32* Many early manuscripts do not have *If God is glorified in him.*

Jesus Comforts His Disciples

14 "Do not let your hearts be troubled. Trust in God[a]; trust also in me. [2]In my Father's house are many rooms; if it were not so, I would have told you. I am going there to prepare a place for you. [3]And if I go and prepare a place for you, I will come back and take you to be with me that you also may be where I am. [4]You know the way to the place where I am going."

Jesus the Way to the Father

[5]Thomas said to him, "Lord, we don't know where you are going, so how can we know the way?"

[6]Jesus answered, "I am the way and the truth and the life. No one comes to the Father except through me. [7]If you really knew me, you would know[b] my Father as well. From now on, you do know him and have seen him."

[8]Philip said, "Lord, show us the Father and that will be enough for us."

[9]Jesus answered: "Don't you know me, Philip, even after I have been among you such a long time? Anyone who has seen me has seen the Father. How can you say, 'Show us the Father'? [10]Don't you believe that I am in the Father, and that the Father is in me? The words I say to you are not just my own. Rather, it is the Father, living in me, who is doing his work. [11]Believe me when I say that I am in the Father and the Father is in me; or at least believe on the evidence of the miracles themselves. [12]I tell you the truth, anyone who has faith in me will do what I have been doing. He will do even greater things than these, because I am going to the Father. [13]And I will do whatever you ask in my name, so that the Son may bring glory to the Father. [14]You may ask me for anything in my name, and I will do it.

Jesus Promises the Holy Spirit

[15]"If you love me, you will obey what I command. [16]And I will ask the Father, and he will give you another Counselor to be with you forever— [17]the Spirit of truth. The world cannot accept him, because it neither sees him nor knows him. But you know him, for he lives with you and will be[c] in you. [18]I will not leave you as orphans; I will come to you. [19]Before long, the world will not see me anymore, but you will see me. Because I live, you also will live. [20]On that day you will realize that I am in my Father, and you are in me, and I am in you. [21]Whoever has my commands and obeys them, he is the one who loves me. He who loves me will be loved by my Father, and I too will love him and show myself to him."

[22]Then Judas (not Judas Iscariot) said, "But, Lord, why do you intend to show yourself to us and not to the world?"

[23]Jesus replied, "If anyone loves me, he will obey my teaching. My Father will love him, and we will come to him and make our home with him. [24]He who does not love me will not obey my teaching. These words you hear are not my own; they belong to the Father who sent me.

[25]"All this I have spoken while still with you. [26]But the Counselor, the Holy Spirit, whom the Father will send in my name, will teach you all things and will remind you of everything I have said to you. [27]Peace I leave with you; my peace I give you. I do not give to you as the world gives. Do not let your hearts be troubled and do not be afraid.

[28]"You heard me say, 'I am going away and I am coming back to you.' If you loved me, you would be glad that I am going to the Father, for the Father is greater than I. [29]I have told you now before it happens, so that when it does happen you will believe. [30]I will not speak with you much longer, for the prince of this world is coming. He has no hold on me, [31]but the world must learn that I love the Father and that I do exactly what my Father has commanded me.

"Come now; let us leave.

The Vine and the Branches

15 "I am the true vine, and my Father is the gardener. [2]He cuts off every branch in me that bears no fruit, while every branch that does bear fruit he prunes[d] so that it will be even more fruitful. [3]You are already clean because of the word I have spoken to you. [4]Remain in me, and I will remain in you. No branch can bear fruit by

[a] 1 Or *You trust in God* [b] 7 Some early manuscripts *If you really have known me, you will know*
[c] 17 Some early manuscripts *and is* [d] 2 The Greek for *prunes* also means *cleans*.

itself; it must remain in the vine. Neither
can you bear fruit unless you remain
in me.
5"I am the vine; you are the branches. If
a man remains in me and I in him, he will
bear much fruit; apart from me you can do
nothing. 6If anyone does not remain in
me, he is like a branch that is thrown
away and withers; such branches are
picked up, thrown into the fire and
burned. 7If you remain in me and my
words remain in you, ask whatever you
wish, and it will be given you. 8This is to
my Father's glory, that you bear much
fruit, showing yourselves to be my disci-
ples.
9"As the Father has loved me, so have I
loved you. Now remain in my love. 10If
you obey my commands, you will remain
in my love, just as I have obeyed my Fa-

VERSE FOR THE DAY: John 14:27

AUTHOR: Gregg Lewis

PASSAGE FOR THE DAY: John 14:23–27

Powerless to Help

I was trying to get to sleep in a treehouse fifty feet off the ground. But it wasn't anticipation of my first daylight glimpse of the remote central highlands of Papua New Guinea that kept me awake. What prevented sleep was this thought: "In eleven years of marriage I've never felt so far from my wife and young family." Not only was I separated by ten thousand miles from those I loved most, I was a rugged two-hour trip from the nearest town with a telephone system.

What if Debi needed me? It might take days for word to reach me. And then it could take another week for me to get back home. For the first time in my life I felt totally, humblingly helpless.

So I did what I too often do only after I've considered everything else: I prayed. "Lord, please watch over Debi and the kids. I know I can't do it; you'll have to keep them safe. Please."

I had committed my wife and my family to God before—on my wedding day, on the day each of my children was born, and numerous other times. But this was different. This time I had no choice but to trust God. And this time I felt God's response in the form of a reassuring peace that seemed to fill that thatched-roof treehouse.

MARRIAGE BUILDERS

♦ *When have you been in a situation in which you could trust only God for the outcome?*

♦ *Identify one or two worrisome areas in your life now that you need to trustingly release into God's control.*

Additional Scripture Readings
Psalm 46:1–3; Isaiah 41:10; 1 Peter 5:7

Go to page 1170 for your next devotional reading.

ther's commands and remain in his love.
[11]I have told you this so that my joy may
be in you and that your joy may be com-
plete. [12]My command is this: Love each
other as I have loved you. [13]Greater love
has no one than this, that he lay down his
life for his friends. [14]You are my friends if
you do what I command. [15]I no longer call
you servants, because a servant does not
know his master's business. Instead, I
have called you friends, for everything
that I learned from my Father I have made
known to you. [16]You did not choose me,
but I chose you and appointed you to go
and bear fruit—fruit that will last. Then
the Father will give you whatever you ask
in my name. [17]This is my command: Love
each other.

The World Hates the Disciples

[18]"If the world hates you, keep in mind
that it hated me first. [19]If you belonged to
the world, it would love you as its own. As
it is, you do not belong to the world, but
I have chosen you out of the world. That
is why the world hates you. [20]Remember
the words I spoke to you: 'No servant is
greater than his master.'[a] If they perse-

[a]20 John 13:16

VERSE FOR THE DAY:	AUTHOR:	PASSAGE FOR THE DAY:
John 15:4	Andrew Murray	John 15:1–8

Connected to the Vine

The branch has nothing but what it gets from the vine; you and I can have nothing but what we get from Jesus. The life of a branch is one of deep restfulness. A little branch, if it could speak, would whisper: "I have one lesson for you. With all your hurry and effort in Christ's work you never prosper. The first thing you need is to come and rest in your Lord Jesus. If you would be a true branch of Christ, the living Vine, just rest on him. Let Christ bear the responsibility."

You say, "Won't that make me slothful?" It will not. No one who learns to rest upon the living Christ can become slothful, for the closer your contact with Christ the more his Spirit of zeal and love will be borne in upon you.

MARRIAGE BUILDERS

♦ *Which of your current activities seem to take the most "hurry and effort"? How does your connection to God fit in with those pressures?*

♦ *From your own experience, what sort of balance between work and spiritual rest works best for you?*

Additional Scripture Readings
Galatians 5:22–23; Psalm 128:3;
Colossians 1:10

Go to page 1171 for your next devotional reading.

cuted me, they will persecute you also. If
they obeyed my teaching, they will obey
yours also. 21They will treat you this way
because of my name, for they do not know
the One who sent me. 22If I had not come
and spoken to them, they would not be
guilty of sin. Now, however, they have no
excuse for their sin. 23He who hates me
hates my Father as well. 24If I had not
done among them what no one else did,
they would not be guilty of sin. But now
they have seen these miracles, and yet
they have hated both me and my Father.
25But this is to fulfill what is written in

VERSE FOR THE DAY: John 15:12 | AUTHOR: Jerry Bridges | PASSAGE FOR THE DAY: John 15:9–17

Loving Jesus' Way

Marriage remains the most intense environment there is for practicing love, and no one before or since has loved more than Jesus did. He set the example for sacrificial love when he left heaven's glory to live thirty-three years of grime, dust, humanness and rejection—all without sinning—just so he could give himself up for those he loved.

For Jesus, love was a motive, not a duty. Too many times I've served my wife, Jane, out of a sense of duty or to keep peace, without the motive of love. I'm still learning what it means to love as Christ loved—how to "give myself up" when my desires and Jane's desires conflict.

Paul encouraged us to "be imitators of God, therefore, as dearly loved children and live a life of love, just as Christ loved us and gave himself up for us" (Eph. 5:1-2). The extent to which you believe you are "dearly loved" by God is the extent to which you can love others.

If Jesus were preaching about marriage today, he might say: "Remember my love and sacrifice, and do the same for each other. Let love be your motive and humility be your attitude. Love the way I did." Impossible tasks—if we didn't have our secret weapon: God's power to love, which he has freely given to his dearly loved children (see Phil. 4:13).

MARRIAGE BUILDERS

♦ *How could your sacrificial love smooth any areas of disagreement?*
♦ *Recall a time when you felt you were receiving God's love from your spouse. How did that experience help you?*

Additional Scripture Readings
John 13:31–35; 1 John 2:7–10

Go to page 1180 for your next devotional reading.

their Law: 'They hated me without reason.'[a]

[26]"When the Counselor comes, whom I will send to you from the Father, the Spirit of truth who goes out from the Father, he will testify about me. [27]And you also must testify, for you have been with me from the beginning.

16 "All this I have told you so that you will not go astray. [2]They will put you out of the synagogue; in fact, a time is coming when anyone who kills you will think he is offering a service to God. [3]They will do such things because they have not known the Father or me. [4]I have told you this, so that when the time comes you will remember that I warned you. I did not tell you this at first because I was with you.

The Work of the Holy Spirit

[5]"Now I am going to him who sent me, yet none of you asks me, 'Where are you going?' [6]Because I have said these things, you are filled with grief. [7]But I tell you the truth: It is for your good that I am going away. Unless I go away, the Counselor will not come to you; but if I go, I will send him to you. [8]When he comes, he will convict the world of guilt[b] in regard to sin and righteousness and judgment: [9]in regard to sin, because men do not believe in me; [10]in regard to righteousness, because I am going to the Father, where you can see me no longer; [11]and in regard to judgment, because the prince of this world now stands condemned.

[12]"I have much more to say to you, more than you can now bear. [13]But when he, the Spirit of truth, comes, he will guide you into all truth. He will not speak on his own; he will speak only what he hears, and he will tell you what is yet to come. [14]He will bring glory to me by taking from what is mine and making it known to you. [15]All that belongs to the Father is mine. That is why I said the Spirit will take from what is mine and make it known to you.

[16]"In a little while you will see me no more, and then after a little while you will see me."

The Disciples' Grief Will Turn to Joy

[17]Some of his disciples said to one another, "What does he mean by saying, 'In a little while you will see me no more, and then after a little while you will see me,' and 'Because I am going to the Father'?" [18]They kept asking, "What does he mean by 'a little while'? We don't understand what he is saying."

[19]Jesus saw that they wanted to ask him about this, so he said to them, "Are you asking one another what I meant when I said, 'In a little while you will see me no more, and then after a little while you will see me'? [20]I tell you the truth, you will weep and mourn while the world rejoices. You will grieve, but your grief will turn to joy. [21]A woman giving birth to a child has pain because her time has come; but when her baby is born she forgets the anguish because of her joy that a child is born into the world. [22]So with you: Now is your time of grief, but I will see you again and you will rejoice, and no one will take away your joy. [23]In that day you will no longer ask me anything. I tell you the truth, my Father will give you whatever you ask in my name. [24]Until now you have not asked for anything in my name. Ask and you will receive, and your joy will be complete.

[25]"Though I have been speaking figuratively, a time is coming when I will no longer use this kind of language but will tell you plainly about my Father. [26]In that day you will ask in my name. I am not saying that I will ask the Father on your behalf. [27]No, the Father himself loves you because you have loved me and have believed that I came from God. [28]I came from the Father and entered the world; now I am leaving the world and going back to the Father."

[29]Then Jesus' disciples said, "Now you are speaking clearly and without figures of speech. [30]Now we can see that you know all things and that you do not even need to have anyone ask you questions. This makes us believe that you came from God."

[31]"You believe at last!"[c] Jesus answered. [32]"But a time is coming, and has come, when you will be scattered, each to his own home. You will leave me all alone. Yet I am not alone, for my Father is with me.

[33]"I have told you these things, so that in me you may have peace. In this world you will have trouble. But take heart! I have overcome the world."

[a]25 Psalms 35:19; 69:4 [b]8 Or *will expose the guilt of the world* [c]31 Or *"Do you now believe?"*

Jesus Prays for Himself

17 After Jesus said this, he looked toward heaven and prayed:

"Father, the time has come. Glorify
your Son, that your Son may glorify
you. [2]For you granted him authority
over all people that he might give
eternal life to all those you have given
him. [3]Now this is eternal life: that
they may know you, the only true
God, and Jesus Christ, whom you
have sent. [4]I have brought you glory
on earth by completing the work you
gave me to do. [5]And now, Father, glo-
rify me in your presence with the glo-
ry I had with you before the world be-
gan.

Jesus Prays for His Disciples

[6]"I have revealed you[a] to those
whom you gave me out of the world.
They were yours; you gave them to
me and they have obeyed your word.
[7]Now they know that everything you
have given me comes from you. [8]For
I gave them the words you gave me
and they accepted them. They knew
with certainty that I came from you,
and they believed that you sent me. [9]I
pray for them. I am not praying for
the world, but for those you have giv-
en me, for they are yours. [10]All I have
is yours, and all you have is mine.
And glory has come to me through
them. [11]I will remain in the world no
longer, but they are still in the world,
and I am coming to you. Holy Father,
protect them by the power of your
name—the name you gave me—so
that they may be one as we are one.
[12]While I was with them, I protected
them and kept them safe by that
name you gave me. None has been
lost except the one doomed to de-
struction so that Scripture would be
fulfilled.

[13]"I am coming to you now, but I
say these things while I am still in the
world, so that they may have the full
measure of my joy within them. [14]I
have given them your word and the
world has hated them, for they are
not of the world any more than I am
of the world. [15]My prayer is not that
you take them out of the world but
that you protect them from the evil
one. [16]They are not of the world, even
as I am not of it. [17]Sanctify[b] them by
the truth; your word is truth. [18]As
you sent me into the world, I have
sent them into the world. [19]For them
I sanctify myself, that they too may
be truly sanctified.

Jesus Prays for All Believers

[20]"My prayer is not for them alone.
I pray also for those who will believe
in me through their message, [21]that
all of them may be one, Father, just as
you are in me and I am in you. May
they also be in us so that the world
may believe that you have sent me.
[22]I have given them the glory that you
gave me, that they may be one as we
are one: [23]I in them and you in me.
May they be brought to complete uni-
ty to let the world know that you sent
me and have loved them even as you
have loved me.

[24]"Father, I want those you have
given me to be with me where I am,
and to see my glory, the glory you
have given me because you loved me
before the creation of the world.

[25]"Righteous Father, though the
world does not know you, I know
you, and they know that you have
sent me. [26]I have made you known to
them, and will continue to make you
known in order that the love you
have for me may be in them and that
I myself may be in them."

Jesus Arrested

18 When he had finished praying,
Jesus left with his disciples and
crossed the Kidron Valley. On the other
side there was an olive grove, and he and
his disciples went into it.

[2]Now Judas, who betrayed him, knew
the place, because Jesus had often met
there with his disciples. [3]So Judas came to
the grove, guiding a detachment of sol-
diers and some officials from the chief
priests and Pharisees. They were carrying
torches, lanterns and weapons.

[4]Jesus, knowing all that was going to
happen to him, went out and asked them,
"Who is it you want?"

[5]"Jesus of Nazareth," they replied.
"I am he," Jesus said. (And Judas the

[a]6 Greek *your name*; also in verse 26 [b]17 Greek *hagiazo (set apart for sacred use* or *make holy)*; also in verse 19

traitor was standing there with them.)
6When Jesus said, "I am he," they drew
back and fell to the ground.
7Again he asked them, "Who is it you
want?"
And they said, "Jesus of Nazareth."
8"I told you that I am he," Jesus an-
swered. "If you are looking for me, then
let these men go." 9This happened so that
the words he had spoken would be ful-
filled: "I have not lost one of those you
gave me."[a]
10Then Simon Peter, who had a sword,
drew it and struck the high priest's ser-
vant, cutting off his right ear. (The ser-
vant's name was Malchus.)
11Jesus commanded Peter, "Put your
sword away! Shall I not drink the cup the
Father has given me?"

Jesus Taken to Annas

12Then the detachment of soldiers with
its commander and the Jewish officials ar-
rested Jesus. They bound him 13and
brought him first to Annas, who was the
father-in-law of Caiaphas, the high priest
that year. 14Caiaphas was the one who had
advised the Jews that it would be good if
one man died for the people.

Peter's First Denial

15Simon Peter and another disciple
were following Jesus. Because this disci-
ple was known to the high priest, he went
with Jesus into the high priest's court-
yard, 16but Peter had to wait outside at the
door. The other disciple, who was known
to the high priest, came back, spoke to the
girl on duty there and brought Peter in.
17"You are not one of his disciples, are
you?" the girl at the door asked Peter.
He replied, "I am not."
18It was cold, and the servants and offi-
cials stood around a fire they had made to
keep warm. Peter also was standing with
them, warming himself.

The High Priest Questions Jesus

19Meanwhile, the high priest ques-
tioned Jesus about his disciples and his
teaching.
20"I have spoken openly to the world,"
Jesus replied. "I always taught in syna-
gogues or at the temple, where all the
Jews come together. I said nothing in se-
cret. 21Why question me? Ask those who
heard me. Surely they know what I said."
22When Jesus said this, one of the offi-
cials nearby struck him in the face. "Is this
the way you answer the high priest?" he
demanded.
23"If I said something wrong," Jesus re-
plied, "testify as to what is wrong. But if I
spoke the truth, why did you strike me?"
24Then Annas sent him, still bound, to Ca-
iaphas the high priest.[b]

Peter's Second and Third Denials

25As Simon Peter stood warming him-
self, he was asked, "You are not one of his
disciples, are you?"
He denied it, saying, "I am not."
26One of the high priest's servants, a rel-
ative of the man whose ear Peter had cut
off, challenged him, "Didn't I see you with
him in the olive grove?" 27Again Peter de-
nied it, and at that moment a rooster be-
gan to crow.

Jesus Before Pilate

28Then the Jews led Jesus from Caia-
phas to the palace of the Roman governor.
By now it was early morning, and to avoid
ceremonial uncleanness the Jews did not
enter the palace; they wanted to be able to
eat the Passover. 29So Pilate came out to
them and asked, "What charges are you
bringing against this man?"
30"If he were not a criminal," they re-
plied, "we would not have handed him
over to you."
31Pilate said, "Take him yourselves and
judge him by your own law."
"But we have no right to execute any-
one," the Jews objected. 32This happened
so that the words Jesus had spoken indi-
cating the kind of death he was going to
die would be fulfilled.
33Pilate then went back inside the pal-
ace, summoned Jesus and asked him,
"Are you the king of the Jews?"
34"Is that your own idea," Jesus asked,
"or did others talk to you about me?"
35"Am I a Jew?" Pilate replied. "It was
your people and your chief priests who
handed you over to me. What is it you
have done?"
36Jesus said, "My kingdom is not of this
world. If it were, my servants would fight
to prevent my arrest by the Jews. But now
my kingdom is from another place."
37"You are a king, then!" said Pilate.
Jesus answered, "You are right in say-
ing I am a king. In fact, for this reason I

[a]9 John 6:39 [b]24 Or *(Now Annas had sent him, still bound, to Caiaphas the high priest.)*

was born, and for this I came into the world, to testify to the truth. Everyone on the side of truth listens to me."

38"What is truth?" Pilate asked. With this he went out again to the Jews and said, "I find no basis for a charge against him. 39But it is your custom for me to release to you one prisoner at the time of the Passover. Do you want me to release 'the king of the Jews'?"

40They shouted back, "No, not him! Give us Barabbas!" Now Barabbas had taken part in a rebellion.

Jesus Sentenced to be Crucified

19 Then Pilate took Jesus and had him flogged. 2The soldiers twisted together a crown of thorns and put it on his head. They clothed him in a purple robe 3and went up to him again and again, saying, "Hail, king of the Jews!" And they struck him in the face.

4Once more Pilate came out and said to the Jews, "Look, I am bringing him out to you to let you know that I find no basis for a charge against him." 5When Jesus came out wearing the crown of thorns and the purple robe, Pilate said to them, "Here is the man!"

6As soon as the chief priests and their officials saw him, they shouted, "Crucify! Crucify!"

But Pilate answered, "You take him and crucify him. As for me, I find no basis for a charge against him."

7The Jews insisted, "We have a law, and according to that law he must die, because he claimed to be the Son of God."

8When Pilate heard this, he was even more afraid, 9and he went back inside the palace. "Where do you come from?" he asked Jesus, but Jesus gave him no answer. 10"Do you refuse to speak to me?" Pilate said. "Don't you realize I have power either to free you or to crucify you?"

11Jesus answered, "You would have no power over me if it were not given to you from above. Therefore the one who handed me over to you is guilty of a greater sin."

12From then on, Pilate tried to set Jesus free, but the Jews kept shouting, "If you let this man go, you are no friend of Caesar. Anyone who claims to be a king opposes Caesar."

13When Pilate heard this, he brought Jesus out and sat down on the judge's seat at a place known as the Stone Pavement (which in Aramaic is Gabbatha). 14It was the day of Preparation of Passover Week, about the sixth hour.

"Here is your king," Pilate said to the Jews.

15But they shouted, "Take him away! Take him away! Crucify him!"

"Shall I crucify your king?" Pilate asked.

"We have no king but Caesar," the chief priests answered.

16Finally Pilate handed him over to them to be crucified.

The Crucifixion

So the soldiers took charge of Jesus. 17Carrying his own cross, he went out to the place of the Skull (which in Aramaic is called Golgotha). 18Here they crucified him, and with him two others—one on each side and Jesus in the middle.

19Pilate had a notice prepared and fastened to the cross. It read: JESUS OF NAZARETH, THE KING OF THE JEWS. 20Many of the Jews read this sign, for the place where Jesus was crucified was near the city, and the sign was written in Aramaic, Latin and Greek. 21The chief priests of the Jews protested to Pilate, "Do not write 'The King of the Jews,' but that this man claimed to be king of the Jews."

22Pilate answered, "What I have written, I have written."

23When the soldiers crucified Jesus, they took his clothes, dividing them into four shares, one for each of them, with the undergarment remaining. This garment was seamless, woven in one piece from top to bottom.

24"Let's not tear it," they said to one another. "Let's decide by lot who will get it."

This happened that the scripture might be fulfilled which said,

> "They divided my garments among them
> and cast lots for my clothing."[a]

So this is what the soldiers did.

25Near the cross of Jesus stood his mother, his mother's sister, Mary the wife of Clopas, and Mary Magdalene. 26When Jesus saw his mother there, and the disciple whom he loved standing nearby, he said to his mother, "Dear woman, here is your son," 27and to the disciple, "Here is your mother." From that time on, this disciple took her into his home.

[a]24 Psalm 22:18

The Death of Jesus

[28]Later, knowing that all was now completed, and so that the Scripture would be fulfilled, Jesus said, "I am thirsty." [29]A jar of wine vinegar was there, so they soaked a sponge in it, put the sponge on a stalk of the hyssop plant, and lifted it to Jesus' lips. [30]When he had received the drink, Jesus said, "It is finished." With that, he bowed his head and gave up his spirit.

[31]Now it was the day of Preparation, and the next day was to be a special Sabbath. Because the Jews did not want the bodies left on the crosses during the Sabbath, they asked Pilate to have the legs broken and the bodies taken down. [32]The soldiers therefore came and broke the legs of the first man who had been crucified with Jesus, and then those of the other. [33]But when they came to Jesus and found that he was already dead, they did not break his legs. [34]Instead, one of the soldiers pierced Jesus' side with a spear, bringing a sudden flow of blood and water. [35]The man who saw it has given testimony, and his testimony is true. He knows that he tells the truth, and he testifies so that you also may believe. [36]These things happened so that the scripture would be fulfilled: "Not one of his bones will be broken,"[a] [37]and, as another scripture says, "They will look on the one they have pierced."[b]

The Burial of Jesus

[38]Later, Joseph of Arimathea asked Pilate for the body of Jesus. Now Joseph was a disciple of Jesus, but secretly because he feared the Jews. With Pilate's permission, he came and took the body away. [39]He was accompanied by Nicodemus, the man who earlier had visited Jesus at night. Nicodemus brought a mixture of myrrh and aloes, about seventy-five pounds.[c] [40]Taking Jesus' body, the two of them wrapped it, with the spices, in strips of linen. This was in accordance with Jewish burial customs. [41]At the place where Jesus was crucified, there was a garden, and in the garden a new tomb, in which no one had ever been laid. [42]Because it was the Jewish day of Preparation and since the tomb was nearby, they laid Jesus there.

The Empty Tomb

20 Early on the first day of the week, while it was still dark, Mary Magdalene went to the tomb and saw that the stone had been removed from the entrance. [2]So she came running to Simon Peter and the other disciple, the one Jesus loved, and said, "They have taken the Lord out of the tomb, and we don't know where they have put him!"

[3]So Peter and the other disciple started for the tomb. [4]Both were running, but the other disciple outran Peter and reached the tomb first. [5]He bent over and looked in at the strips of linen lying there but did not go in. [6]Then Simon Peter, who was behind him, arrived and went into the tomb. He saw the strips of linen lying there, [7]as well as the burial cloth that had been around Jesus' head. The cloth was folded up by itself, separate from the linen. [8]Finally the other disciple, who had reached the tomb first, also went inside. He saw and believed. [9](They still did not understand from Scripture that Jesus had to rise from the dead.)

Jesus Appears to Mary Magdalene

[10]Then the disciples went back to their homes, [11]but Mary stood outside the tomb crying. As she wept, she bent over to look into the tomb [12]and saw two angels in white, seated where Jesus' body had been, one at the head and the other at the foot.

[13]They asked her, "Woman, why are you crying?"

"They have taken my Lord away," she said, "and I don't know where they have put him." [14]At this, she turned around and saw Jesus standing there, but she did not realize that it was Jesus.

[15]"Woman," he said, "why are you crying? Who is it you are looking for?"

Thinking he was the gardener, she said, "Sir, if you have carried him away, tell me where you have put him, and I will get him."

[16]Jesus said to her, "Mary."

She turned toward him and cried out in Aramaic, "Rabboni!" (which means Teacher).

[17]Jesus said, "Do not hold on to me, for I have not yet returned to the Father. Go instead to my brothers and tell them, 'I am

[a]*36* Exodus 12:46; Num. 9:12; Psalm 34:20 [b]*37* Zech. 12:10 [c]*39* Greek *a hundred litrai* (about 34 kilograms)

returning to my Father and your Father, to
my God and your God.' "
18Mary Magdalene went to the disciples
with the news: "I have seen the Lord!"
And she told them that he had said these
things to her.

Jesus Appears to His Disciples

19On the evening of that first day of the
week, when the disciples were together,
with the doors locked for fear of the Jews,
Jesus came and stood among them and
said, "Peace be with you!" 20After he said
this, he showed them his hands and side.
The disciples were overjoyed when they
saw the Lord.
21Again Jesus said, "Peace be with you!
As the Father has sent me, I am sending
you." 22And with that he breathed on
them and said, "Receive the Holy Spirit.
23If you forgive anyone his sins, they are
forgiven; if you do not forgive them, they
are not forgiven."

Jesus Appears to Thomas

24Now Thomas (called Didymus), one
of the Twelve, was not with the disciples
when Jesus came. 25So the other disciples
told him, "We have seen the Lord!"
But he said to them, "Unless I see the
nail marks in his hands and put my finger
where the nails were, and put my hand
into his side, I will not believe it."
26A week later his disciples were in the
house again, and Thomas was with them.
Though the doors were locked, Jesus
came and stood among them and said,
"Peace be with you!" 27Then he said to
Thomas, "Put your finger here; see my
hands. Reach out your hand and put it
into my side. Stop doubting and believe."
28Thomas said to him, "My Lord and
my God!"
29Then Jesus told him, "Because you
have seen me, you have believed; blessed
are those who have not seen and yet have
believed."
30Jesus did many other miraculous
signs in the presence of his disciples,
which are not recorded in this book. 31But
these are written that you may[a] believe
that Jesus is the Christ, the Son of God,
and that by believing you may have life in
his name.

Jesus and the Miraculous Catch of Fish

21 Afterward Jesus appeared again to
his disciples, by the Sea of Tiberi-
as.[b] It happened this way: 2Simon Peter,
Thomas (called Didymus), Nathanael
from Cana in Galilee, the sons of Zebedee,
and two other disciples were together.
3"I'm going out to fish," Simon Peter told
them, and they said, "We'll go with you."
So they went out and got into the boat, but
that night they caught nothing.
4Early in the morning, Jesus stood on
the shore, but the disciples did not realize
that it was Jesus.
5He called out to them, "Friends,
haven't you any fish?"
"No," they answered.
6He said, "Throw your net on the right
side of the boat and you will find some."
When they did, they were unable to haul
the net in because of the large number of
fish.
7Then the disciple whom Jesus loved
said to Peter, "It is the Lord!" As soon as
Simon Peter heard him say, "It is the
Lord," he wrapped his outer garment
around him (for he had taken it off) and
jumped into the water. 8The other disci-
ples followed in the boat, towing the net
full of fish, for they were not far from
shore, about a hundred yards.[c] 9When
they landed, they saw a fire of burning
coals there with fish on it, and some
bread.
10Jesus said to them, "Bring some of the
fish you have just caught."
11Simon Peter climbed aboard and
dragged the net ashore. It was full of large
fish, 153, but even with so many the net
was not torn. 12Jesus said to them, "Come
and have breakfast." None of the disciples
dared ask him, "Who are you?" They
knew it was the Lord. 13Jesus came, took
the bread and gave it to them, and did the
same with the fish. 14This was now the
third time Jesus appeared to his disciples
after he was raised from the dead.

Jesus Reinstates Peter

15When they had finished eating, Jesus
said to Simon Peter, "Simon son of John,
do you truly love me more than these?"
"Yes, Lord," he said, "you know that I
love you."

[a] *31* Some manuscripts *may continue to*
[b] *1* That is, Sea of Galilee
[c] *8* Greek *about two hundred cubits* (about 90 meters)

Jesus said, "Feed my lambs."

16Again Jesus said, "Simon son of John, do you truly love me?"

He answered, "Yes, Lord, you know that I love you."

Jesus said, "Take care of my sheep."

17The third time he said to him, "Simon son of John, do you love me?"

Peter was hurt because Jesus asked him the third time, "Do you love me?" He said, "Lord, you know all things; you know that I love you."

Jesus said, "Feed my sheep. 18I tell you the truth, when you were younger you dressed yourself and went where you wanted; but when you are old you will stretch out your hands, and someone else will dress you and lead you where you do not want to go." 19Jesus said this to indicate the kind of death by which Peter would glorify God. Then he said to him, "Follow me!"

20Peter turned and saw that the disciple whom Jesus loved was following them. (This was the one who had leaned back against Jesus at the supper and had said, "Lord, who is going to betray you?") 21When Peter saw him, he asked, "Lord, what about him?"

22Jesus answered, "If I want him to remain alive until I return, what is that to you? You must follow me." 23Because of this, the rumor spread among the brothers that this disciple would not die. But Jesus did not say that he would not die; he only said, "If I want him to remain alive until I return, what is that to you?"

24This is the disciple who testifies to these things and who wrote them down. We know that his testimony is true.

25Jesus did many other things as well. If every one of them were written down, I suppose that even the whole world would not have room for the books that would be written.

LUKE begins the second volume of his history of Christianity (Acts 1:1–3) by telling how Jesus pours out the Holy Spirit on the apostles. The Spirit in turn inspires them to spread the message of salvation from Jerusalem to Rome. In his story Luke stresses how unity and love prevail in the church and how God protects the missionaries from their enemies. As you read this book, think about how powerful the Holy Spirit still is in the church and in your own life and how God protects you against the forces of evil.

ACTS

Jesus Taken Up Into Heaven

1 In my former book, Theophilus, I wrote about all that Jesus began to do
and to teach 2until the day he was taken
up to heaven, after giving instructions
through the Holy Spirit to the apostles he
had chosen. 3After his suffering, he
showed himself to these men and gave
many convincing proofs that he was alive.
He appeared to them over a period of forty
days and spoke about the kingdom of
God. 4On one occasion, while he was eat-
ing with them, he gave them this com-
mand: "Do not leave Jerusalem, but wait
for the gift my Father promised, which
you have heard me speak about. 5For
John baptized with[a] water, but in a few
days you will be baptized with the Holy
Spirit."

6So when they met together, they asked
him, "Lord, are you at this time going to
restore the kingdom to Israel?"

[a]5 Or *in*

7He said to them: "It is not for you to
know the times or dates the Father has set
by his own authority. 8But you will re-
ceive power when the Holy Spirit comes
on you; and you will be my witnesses in
Jerusalem, and in all Judea and Samaria,
and to the ends of the earth."

9After he said this, he was taken up be-
fore their very eyes, and a cloud hid him
from their sight.

10They were looking intently up into
the sky as he was going, when suddenly
two men dressed in white stood beside
them. 11"Men of Galilee," they said, "why
do you stand here looking into the sky?
This same Jesus, who has been taken
from you into heaven, will come back in
the same way you have seen him go into
heaven."

Matthias Chosen to Replace Judas

12Then they returned to Jerusalem from
the hill called the Mount of Olives, a Sab-

VERSE FOR THE DAY: Acts 1:14 | AUTHOR: Jill and Stuart Briscoe | PASSAGE FOR THE DAY: Acts 1:1–14

Praying for Each Other

If a couple has never prayed together, they should begin simply and practically. Over breakfast, a husband might say to his wife, "What are you doing today, Dear?" The day ahead might include a dentist appointment, work at the office and tea with a recently divorced friend. The husband could then say, "Okay, I'll pray for you." He can pray about her work, the dentist appointment and that she would be a help to her friend.

Then she might ask him, "What does your day look like?" He can tell her, and she can pray through his day. Or they might do this at night, praying about what happened that day. Sometimes a couple just doesn't know what to pray; this way, they're giving each other the specific things they need prayer for.

If they have trouble coming up with additional things to pray about, they can think about other people they love. Concerns about close friends and family members can give them another common area for prayer.

MARRIAGE BUILDERS

♦ *Make a list of things you'd like to pray about together. Consider your family, friends, church, national leaders, world events, specific needs, etc.*

♦ *Break your list into several smaller lists, and try using one list each day for a short time of joint prayer.*

Additional Scripture Readings
Matthew 18:19–20; 1 John 5:14–15

Go to page 1182 for your next devotional reading.

bath day's walk[a] from the city. 13When they arrived, they went upstairs to the room where they were staying. Those present were Peter, John, James and Andrew; Philip and Thomas, Bartholomew and Matthew; James son of Alphaeus and Simon the Zealot, and Judas son of James. 14They all joined together constantly in prayer, along with the women and Mary the mother of Jesus, and with his brothers.

15In those days Peter stood up among the believers[b] (a group numbering about a hundred and twenty) 16and said, "Brothers, the Scripture had to be fulfilled which the Holy Spirit spoke long ago through the mouth of David concerning Judas, who served as guide for those who arrested Jesus— 17he was one of our number and shared in this ministry."

18(With the reward he got for his wickedness, Judas bought a field; there he fell headlong, his body burst open and all his intestines spilled out. 19Everyone in Jerusalem heard about this, so they called that field in their language Akeldama, that is, Field of Blood.)

20"For," said Peter, "it is written in the book of Psalms,

" 'May his place be deserted;
let there be no one to dwell in it,'[c]

and,

" 'May another take his place of
leadership.'[d]

21Therefore it is necessary to choose one of the men who have been with us the whole time the Lord Jesus went in and out among us, 22beginning from John's baptism to the time when Jesus was taken up from us. For one of these must become a witness with us of his resurrection."

23So they proposed two men: Joseph called Barsabbas (also known as Justus) and Matthias. 24Then they prayed, "Lord, you know everyone's heart. Show us which of these two you have chosen 25to take over this apostolic ministry, which Judas left to go where he belongs." 26Then they cast lots, and the lot fell to Matthias; so he was added to the eleven apostles.

The Holy Spirit Comes at Pentecost

2 When the day of Pentecost came, they were all together in one place. 2Suddenly a sound like the blowing of a violent wind came from heaven and filled the whole house where they were sitting. 3They saw what seemed to be tongues of fire that separated and came to rest on each of them. 4All of them were filled with the Holy Spirit and began to speak in other tongues[e] as the Spirit enabled them.

5Now there were staying in Jerusalem God-fearing Jews from every nation under heaven. 6When they heard this sound, a crowd came together in bewilderment, because each one heard them speaking in his own language. 7Utterly amazed, they asked: "Are not all these men who are speaking Galileans? 8Then how is it that each of us hears them in his own native language? 9Parthians, Medes and Elamites; residents of Mesopotamia, Judea and Cappadocia, Pontus and Asia, 10Phrygia and Pamphylia, Egypt and the parts of Libya near Cyrene; visitors from Rome 11(both Jews and converts to Judaism); Cretans and Arabs—we hear them declaring the wonders of God in our own tongues!" 12Amazed and perplexed, they asked one another, "What does this mean?"

13Some, however, made fun of them and said, "They have had too much wine.[f]"

Peter Addresses the Crowd

14Then Peter stood up with the Eleven, raised his voice and addressed the crowd: "Fellow Jews and all of you who live in Jerusalem, let me explain this to you; listen carefully to what I say. 15These men are not drunk, as you suppose. It's only nine in the morning! 16No, this is what was spoken by the prophet Joel:

17" 'In the last days, God says,
I will pour out my Spirit on all
people.
Your sons and daughters will
prophesy,
your young men will see visions,
your old men will dream dreams.
18Even on my servants, both men and
women,
I will pour out my Spirit in those
days,
and they will prophesy.
19I will show wonders in the heaven
above

[a] 12 That is, about 3/4 mile (about 1,100 meters) [b] 15 Greek *brothers* [c] 20 Psalm 69:25
[d] 20 Psalm 109:8 [e] 4 Or *languages*; also in verse 11 [f] 13 Or *sweet wine*

WEEKENDING

DAILY LIFE

If you think romance is related only to physical love, you are greatly limiting its potential. Romance can be constantly present in marriage, although its intensity will vary. There are peak moments, such as in physical lovemaking. But there are major portions of time when romance is no more intense than a quiet conversation, a smile or a gentle touch.

Daily romance is built upon qualities that each partner expresses to the other: meeting each other's needs; being tender, considerate, sensitive, thoughtful; listening to each other and learning to speak your partner's love language so that deep, intimate communication occurs. With that in mind, discuss the following questions with your mate.

1. What things do you feel make your daily life together romantic?

2. What actions on your part create romance? What actions on your spouse's part create romance?

— H. Norman Wright

REVIVE

Saturday: Ephesians 4:14–16
Sunday: Hebrews 10:19–25

Go to page 1183 for your next devotional reading.

and signs on the earth below,
blood and fire and billows of
smoke.
20 The sun will be turned to darkness
and the moon to blood
before the coming of the great and
glorious day of the Lord.
21 And everyone who calls
on the name of the Lord will be
saved.'[a]

22 "Men of Israel, listen to this: Jesus of Nazareth was a man accredited by God to you by miracles, wonders and signs, which God did among you through him, as you yourselves know. 23 This man was handed over to you by God's set purpose and foreknowledge; and you, with the help of wicked men,[b] put him to death by nailing him to the cross. 24 But God raised him from the dead, freeing him from the agony of death, because it was impossible for death to keep its hold on him. 25 David said about him:

" 'I saw the Lord always before me.

[a] 21 Joel 2:28-32 [b] 23 Or *of those not having the law* (that is, Gentiles)

VERSE FOR THE DAY: Acts 2:25–26

AUTHOR: Donald R. Harvey

PASSAGE FOR THE DAY: Acts 2:14–28

Never Shaken

Every couple faces things they'd prefer to avoid—job losses, severe illnesses, financial reversals. We call them crises, roadblocks, setbacks or tragedies, and none of these are terms of endearment. That's because these storms of life produce immense stress—and they also test our marriages.

God does not cause bad things, but he allows painful and unjust experiences. And there is a useful purpose in them. The trials of life may cause us pain, but they refine our faith in a way nothing else can (see 1 Pet. 1:6–7).

Life is hard, and you and your spouse won't be exempt. When the storms arrive, they will stress your marriage. But you can survive the storms—and even be strengthened in the process. You can do it by winning the battle before it begins by strengthening your commitment to your marriage, building your relationship with your spouse and growing a faith that embraces the big picture. God always has a future for his people.

MARRIAGE BUILDERS

♦ *Would you consider yourselves worriers or optimists when thinking about the future?*

♦ *Pray together, entrusting your concerns and anxieties to God.*

Additional Scripture Readings
Isaiah 51:1–3; 2 Corinthians 6:1–10

Go to page 1185 for your next devotional reading.

Because he is at my right hand,
I will not be shaken.
26Therefore my heart is glad and my
tongue rejoices;
my body also will live in hope,
27because you will not abandon me to
the grave,
nor will you let your Holy One see
decay.
28You have made known to me the
paths of life;
you will fill me with joy in your
presence.'[a]

29"Brothers, I can tell you confidently that the patriarch David died and was buried, and his tomb is here to this day. 30But he was a prophet and knew that God had promised him on oath that he would place one of his descendants on his throne. 31Seeing what was ahead, he spoke of the resurrection of the Christ,[b] that he was not abandoned to the grave, nor did his body see decay. 32God has raised this Jesus to life, and we are all witnesses of the fact. 33Exalted to the right hand of God, he has received from the Father the promised Holy Spirit and has poured out what you now see and hear. 34For David did not ascend to heaven, and yet he said,

" 'The Lord said to my Lord:
"Sit at my right hand
35until I make your enemies
a footstool for your feet." '[c]

36"Therefore let all Israel be assured of this: God has made this Jesus, whom you crucified, both Lord and Christ."

37When the people heard this, they were cut to the heart and said to Peter and the other apostles, "Brothers, what shall we do?"

38Peter replied, "Repent and be baptized, every one of you, in the name of Jesus Christ for the forgiveness of your sins. And you will receive the gift of the Holy Spirit. 39The promise is for you and your children and for all who are far off—for all whom the Lord our God will call."

40With many other words he warned them; and he pleaded with them, "Save yourselves from this corrupt generation." 41Those who accepted his message were baptized, and about three thousand were added to their number that day.

The Fellowship of the Believers

42They devoted themselves to the apostles' teaching and to the fellowship, to the breaking of bread and to prayer. 43Everyone was filled with awe, and many wonders and miraculous signs were done by the apostles. 44All the believers were together and had everything in common. 45Selling their possessions and goods, they gave to anyone as he had need. 46Every day they continued to meet together in the temple courts. They broke bread in their homes and ate together with glad and sincere hearts, 47praising God and enjoying the favor of all the people. And the Lord added to their number daily those who were being saved.

Peter Heals the Crippled Beggar

3 One day Peter and John were going up to the temple at the time of prayer—at three in the afternoon. 2Now a man crippled from birth was being carried to the temple gate called Beautiful, where he was put every day to beg from those going into the temple courts. 3When he saw Peter and John about to enter, he asked them for money. 4Peter looked straight at him, as did John. Then Peter said, "Look at us!" 5So the man gave them his attention, expecting to get something from them.

6Then Peter said, "Silver or gold I do not have, but what I have I give you. In the name of Jesus Christ of Nazareth, walk." 7Taking him by the right hand, he helped him up, and instantly the man's feet and ankles became strong. 8He jumped to his feet and began to walk. Then he went with them into the temple courts, walking and jumping, and praising God. 9When all the people saw him walking and praising God, 10they recognized him as the same man who used to sit begging at the temple gate called Beautiful, and they were filled with wonder and amazement at what had happened to him.

Peter Speaks to the Onlookers

11While the beggar held on to Peter and John, all the people were astonished and came running to them in the place called Solomon's Colonnade. 12When Peter saw this, he said to them: "Men of Israel, why does this surprise you? Why do you stare

[a]*28* Psalm 16:8-11 [b]*31* Or *Messiah.* "The Christ" (Greek) and "the Messiah" (Hebrew) both mean "the Anointed One"; also in verse 36. [c]*35* Psalm 110:1

at us as if by our own power or godliness
we had made this man walk? 13The God of
Abraham, Isaac and Jacob, the God of our
fathers, has glorified his servant Jesus.
You handed him over to be killed, and you
disowned him before Pilate, though he
had decided to let him go. 14You disowned
the Holy and Righteous One and asked
that a murderer be released to you. 15You
killed the author of life, but God raised
him from the dead. We are witnesses of
this. 16By faith in the name of Jesus, this
man whom you see and know was made
strong. It is Jesus' name and the faith that
comes through him that has given this
complete healing to him, as you can all
see.

17"Now, brothers, I know that you acted
in ignorance, as did your leaders. 18But
this is how God fulfilled what he had fore-
told through all the prophets, saying that
his Christ[a] would suffer. 19Repent, then,
and turn to God, so that your sins may be
wiped out, that times of refreshing may

[a]18 Or *Messiah*; also in verse 20

VERSE FOR THE DAY: Acts 2:42 | AUTHOR: Ben Patterson | PASSAGE FOR THE DAY: Acts 2:42–47

Keeping the Sabbath

The Sabbath is both a gift and a command. I'm one of those driven, goal-oriented people, and I wouldn't force myself to stop working unless God told me to. That's essentially what the Sabbath is: one day a week when your duty is to stop. It's a command that saves people like me from ourselves.

The Hebrews were commanded to keep the Sabbath in light of the fact that they had been freed from slavery in Egypt. And even today, the rationale for keeping the Sabbath is to help us remember that we're not slaves to our work or to the demands of others. We belong to God, which means we're free.

For me, the great payoff for observing the Sabbath is that it reminds me that I'm more than my work. And because I tend to be a driven person, I need to be reminded on a weekly basis that I'm not defined by my work. I belong to God, not to my work.

MARRIAGE BUILDERS

- *Would you characterize either one of you as "driven"?*
- *What kind of Sabbath habits have you developed since you married?*

Additional Scripture Readings
Deuteronomy 5:12–15; Mark 2:23—3:5

Go to page 1187 for your next devotional reading.

come from the Lord, [20]and that he may
send the Christ, who has been appointed
for you — even Jesus. [21]He must remain in
heaven until the time comes for God to re-
store everything, as he promised long ago
through his holy prophets. [22]For Moses
said, 'The Lord your God will raise up for
you a prophet like me from among your
own people; you must listen to everything
he tells you. [23]Anyone who does not listen
to him will be completely cut off from
among his people.'[a]

[24]"Indeed, all the prophets from Samuel
on, as many as have spoken, have foretold
these days. [25]And you are heirs of the
prophets and of the covenant God made
with your fathers. He said to Abraham,
'Through your offspring all peoples on
earth will be blessed.'[b] [26]When God
raised up his servant, he sent him first to
you to bless you by turning each of you
from your wicked ways."

Peter and John Before the Sanhedrin

4 The priests and the captain of the temple guard and the Sadducees came up
to Peter and John while they were speak-
ing to the people. [2]They were greatly dis-
turbed because the apostles were teaching
the people and proclaiming in Jesus the
resurrection of the dead. [3]They seized Pe-
ter and John, and because it was evening,
they put them in jail until the next day.
[4]But many who heard the message be-
lieved, and the number of men grew to
about five thousand.

[5]The next day the rulers, elders and
teachers of the law met in Jerusalem. [6]An-
nas the high priest was there, and so were
Caiaphas, John, Alexander and the other
men of the high priest's family. [7]They had
Peter and John brought before them and
began to question them: "By what power
or what name did you do this?"

[8]Then Peter, filled with the Holy Spirit,
said to them: "Rulers and elders of the
people! [9]If we are being called to account
today for an act of kindness shown to a
cripple and are asked how he was healed,
[10]then know this, you and all the people of
Israel: It is by the name of Jesus Christ of
Nazareth, whom you crucified but whom
God raised from the dead, that this man
stands before you healed. [11]He is

" 'the stone you builders rejected,
which has become the capstone.[c]'[d]

[12]Salvation is found in no one else, for
there is no other name under heaven giv-
en to men by which we must be saved."

[13]When they saw the courage of Peter
and John and realized that they were un-
schooled, ordinary men, they were aston-
ished and they took note that these men
had been with Jesus. [14]But since they
could see the man who had been healed
standing there with them, there was noth-
ing they could say. [15]So they ordered
them to withdraw from the Sanhedrin and
then conferred together. [16]"What are we
going to do with these men?" they asked.
"Everybody living in Jerusalem knows
they have done an outstanding miracle,
and we cannot deny it. [17]But to stop this
thing from spreading any further among
the people, we must warn these men to
speak no longer to anyone in this name."

[18]Then they called them in again and
commanded them not to speak or teach at
all in the name of Jesus. [19]But Peter and
John replied, "Judge for yourselves
whether it is right in God's sight to obey
you rather than God. [20]For we cannot help
speaking about what we have seen and
heard."

[21]After further threats they let them go.
They could not decide how to punish
them, because all the people were prais-
ing God for what had happened. [22]For the
man who was miraculously healed was
over forty years old.

The Believers' Prayer

[23]On their release, Peter and John went
back to their own people and reported all
that the chief priests and elders had said
to them. [24]When they heard this, they
raised their voices together in prayer to
God. "Sovereign Lord," they said, "you
made the heaven and the earth and the
sea, and everything in them. [25]You spoke
by the Holy Spirit through the mouth of
your servant, our father David:

" 'Why do the nations rage
and the peoples plot in vain?
[26]The kings of the earth take their stand
and the rulers gather together
against the Lord
and against his Anointed One.[e]'[f]

[a]23 Deut. 18:15,18,19 [b]25 Gen. 22:18; 26:4 [c]11 Or *cornerstone* [d]11 Psalm 118:22
[e]26 That is, Christ or Messiah [f]26 Psalm 2:1,2

27 Indeed Herod and Pontius Pilate met together with the Gentiles and the people[a]
of Israel in this city to conspire against
your holy servant Jesus, whom you
anointed. 28 They did what your power
and will had decided beforehand should
happen. 29 Now, Lord, consider their
threats and enable your servants to speak
your word with great boldness. 30 Stretch
out your hand to heal and perform miraculous signs and wonders through the
name of your holy servant Jesus."
31 After they prayed, the place where
they were meeting was shaken. And they

[a] 27 The Greek is plural.

VERSE FOR THE DAY: Acts 4:12–13 | AUTHOR: Ruth Senter | PASSAGE FOR THE DAY: Acts 4:1–13

An Invitation to Risk

My natural bent is toward the safe way. If I have a choice, I will not drive unknown mountain roads in the fog or walk the neighborhood after dark. And I often find myself choosing the low-risk way in other areas. I would rather swim laps at the neighborhood pool than join my husband for a game of tennis because I know I can "win" at swimming laps by myself.

But I am convinced that, as a child of God, I am called to risk. Christ's invitation to risk comes to me even as it came to his disciple, Peter, one dark and windy night on Lake Gennesaret.

"Come," Jesus called. The command seemed illogical and contained no guarantee of safety or reward. But Peter obeyed and ventured out onto the surface of the water. We do not think of Peter's risk as highly successful. "You of little faith, . . . why did you doubt?" (Matthew 14:31) Jesus chided after Peter's near-drowning. But Peter had taken a risk. Years later he would stand before a hostile crowd and declare, "There is no other name . . . by which we must be saved" (Acts 4:12). His audience marveled at his courage—courage that perhaps began to grow on a dark and windy night at sea. Without risk there is no opportunity for personal growth.

MARRIAGE BUILDERS

♦ *Think over the past few years. Name one or two risks you have taken.*

♦ *What type of personal growth resulted from having taken those risks?*

Additional Scripture Readings
Matthew 14:22–33; 2 Timothy 1:7

Go to page 1194 for your next devotional reading.

were all filled with the Holy Spirit and spoke the word of God boldly.

The Believers Share Their Possessions

32All the believers were one in heart and mind. No one claimed that any of his possessions was his own, but they shared everything they had. 33With great power the apostles continued to testify to the resurrection of the Lord Jesus, and much grace was upon them all. 34There were no needy persons among them. For from time to time those who owned lands or houses sold them, brought the money from the sales 35and put it at the apostles' feet, and it was distributed to anyone as he had need.

36Joseph, a Levite from Cyprus, whom the apostles called Barnabas (which means Son of Encouragement), 37sold a field he owned and brought the money and put it at the apostles' feet.

Ananias and Sapphira

5 Now a man named Ananias, together with his wife Sapphira, also sold a piece of property. 2With his wife's full knowledge he kept back part of the money for himself, but brought the rest and put it at the apostles' feet.

3Then Peter said, "Ananias, how is it that Satan has so filled your heart that you have lied to the Holy Spirit and have kept for yourself some of the money you received for the land? 4Didn't it belong to you before it was sold? And after it was sold, wasn't the money at your disposal? What made you think of doing such a thing? You have not lied to men but to God."

5When Ananias heard this, he fell down and died. And great fear seized all who heard what had happened. 6Then the young men came forward, wrapped up his body, and carried him out and buried him.

7About three hours later his wife came in, not knowing what had happened. 8Peter asked her, "Tell me, is this the price you and Ananias got for the land?"

"Yes," she said, "that is the price."

9Peter said to her, "How could you agree to test the Spirit of the Lord? Look! The feet of the men who buried your husband are at the door, and they will carry you out also."

10At that moment she fell down at his feet and died. Then the young men came in and, finding her dead, carried her out and buried her beside her husband. 11Great fear seized the whole church and all who heard about these events.

The Apostles Heal Many

12The apostles performed many miraculous signs and wonders among the people. And all the believers used to meet together in Solomon's Colonnade. 13No one else dared join them, even though they were highly regarded by the people. 14Nevertheless, more and more men and women believed in the Lord and were added to their number. 15As a result, people brought the sick into the streets and laid them on beds and mats so that at least Peter's shadow might fall on some of them as he passed by. 16Crowds gathered also from the towns around Jerusalem, bringing their sick and those tormented by evil[a] spirits, and all of them were healed.

The Apostles Persecuted

17Then the high priest and all his associates, who were members of the party of the Sadducees, were filled with jealousy. 18They arrested the apostles and put them in the public jail. 19But during the night an angel of the Lord opened the doors of the jail and brought them out. 20"Go, stand in the temple courts," he said, "and tell the people the full message of this new life."

21At daybreak they entered the temple courts, as they had been told, and began to teach the people.

When the high priest and his associates arrived, they called together the Sanhedrin—the full assembly of the elders of Israel—and sent to the jail for the apostles. 22But on arriving at the jail, the officers did not find them there. So they went back and reported, 23"We found the jail securely locked, with the guards standing at the doors; but when we opened them, we found no one inside." 24On hearing this report, the captain of the temple guard and the chief priests were puzzled, wondering what would come of this.

25Then someone came and said, "Look! The men you put in jail are standing in the temple courts teaching the people." 26At that, the captain went with his officers and brought the apostles. They did not

[a]16 Greek *unclean*

use force, because they feared that the people would stone them.

[27]Having brought the apostles, they made them appear before the Sanhedrin to be questioned by the high priest. [28]"We gave you strict orders not to teach in this name," he said. "Yet you have filled Jerusalem with your teaching and are determined to make us guilty of this man's blood."

[29]Peter and the other apostles replied: "We must obey God rather than men! [30]The God of our fathers raised Jesus from the dead—whom you had killed by hanging him on a tree. [31]God exalted him to his own right hand as Prince and Savior that he might give repentance and forgiveness of sins to Israel. [32]We are witnesses of these things, and so is the Holy Spirit, whom God has given to those who obey him."

[33]When they heard this, they were furious and wanted to put them to death. [34]But a Pharisee named Gamaliel, a teacher of the law, who was honored by all the people, stood up in the Sanhedrin and ordered that the men be put outside for a little while. [35]Then he addressed them: "Men of Israel, consider carefully what you intend to do to these men. [36]Some time ago Theudas appeared, claiming to be somebody, and about four hundred men rallied to him. He was killed, all his followers were dispersed, and it all came to nothing. [37]After him, Judas the Galilean appeared in the days of the census and led a band of people in revolt. He too was killed, and all his followers were scattered. [38]Therefore, in the present case I advise you: Leave these men alone! Let them go! For if their purpose or activity is of human origin, it will fail. [39]But if it is from God, you will not be able to stop these men; you will only find yourselves fighting against God."

[40]His speech persuaded them. They called the apostles in and had them flogged. Then they ordered them not to speak in the name of Jesus, and let them go.

[41]The apostles left the Sanhedrin, rejoicing because they had been counted worthy of suffering disgrace for the Name. [42]Day after day, in the temple courts and from house to house, they never stopped teaching and proclaiming the good news that Jesus is the Christ.[a]

The Choosing of the Seven

6 In those days when the number of disciples was increasing, the Grecian Jews among them complained against the Hebraic Jews because their widows were being overlooked in the daily distribution of food. [2]So the Twelve gathered all the disciples together and said, "It would not be right for us to neglect the ministry of the word of God in order to wait on tables. [3]Brothers, choose seven men from among you who are known to be full of the Spirit and wisdom. We will turn this responsibility over to them [4]and will give our attention to prayer and the ministry of the word."

[5]This proposal pleased the whole group. They chose Stephen, a man full of faith and of the Holy Spirit; also Philip, Procorus, Nicanor, Timon, Parmenas, and Nicolas from Antioch, a convert to Judaism. [6]They presented these men to the apostles, who prayed and laid their hands on them.

[7]So the word of God spread. The number of disciples in Jerusalem increased rapidly, and a large number of priests became obedient to the faith.

Stephen Seized

[8]Now Stephen, a man full of God's grace and power, did great wonders and miraculous signs among the people. [9]Opposition arose, however, from members of the Synagogue of the Freedmen (as it was called)—Jews of Cyrene and Alexandria as well as the provinces of Cilicia and Asia. These men began to argue with Stephen, [10]but they could not stand up against his wisdom or the Spirit by whom he spoke.

[11]Then they secretly persuaded some men to say, "We have heard Stephen speak words of blasphemy against Moses and against God."

[12]So they stirred up the people and the elders and the teachers of the law. They seized Stephen and brought him before the Sanhedrin. [13]They produced false witnesses, who testified, "This fellow never stops speaking against this holy place and against the law. [14]For we have heard him say that this Jesus of Nazareth will destroy this place and change the customs Moses handed down to us."

[15]All who were sitting in the Sanhedrin

[a]42 Or *Messiah*

looked intently at Stephen, and they saw that his face was like the face of an angel.

Stephen's Speech to the Sanhedrin

7 Then the high priest asked him, "Are these charges true?"

2To this he replied: "Brothers and fathers, listen to me! The God of glory appeared to our father Abraham while he was still in Mesopotamia, before he lived in Haran. 3'Leave your country and your people,' God said, 'and go to the land I will show you.'[a]

4"So he left the land of the Chaldeans and settled in Haran. After the death of his father, God sent him to this land where you are now living. 5He gave him no inheritance here, not even a foot of ground. But God promised him that he and his descendants after him would possess the land, even though at that time Abraham had no child. 6God spoke to him in this way: 'Your descendants will be strangers in a country not their own, and they will be enslaved and mistreated four hundred years. 7But I will punish the nation they serve as slaves,' God said, 'and afterward they will come out of that country and worship me in this place.'[b] 8Then he gave Abraham the covenant of circumcision. And Abraham became the father of Isaac and circumcised him eight days after his birth. Later Isaac became the father of Jacob, and Jacob became the father of the twelve patriarchs.

9"Because the patriarchs were jealous of Joseph, they sold him as a slave into Egypt. But God was with him 10and rescued him from all his troubles. He gave Joseph wisdom and enabled him to gain the goodwill of Pharaoh king of Egypt; so he made him ruler over Egypt and all his palace.

11"Then a famine struck all Egypt and Canaan, bringing great suffering, and our fathers could not find food. 12When Jacob heard that there was grain in Egypt, he sent our fathers on their first visit. 13On their second visit, Joseph told his brothers who he was, and Pharaoh learned about Joseph's family. 14After this, Joseph sent for his father Jacob and his whole family, seventy-five in all. 15Then Jacob went down to Egypt, where he and our fathers died. 16Their bodies were brought back to Shechem and placed in the tomb that Abraham had bought from the sons of Hamor at Shechem for a certain sum of money.

17"As the time drew near for God to fulfill his promise to Abraham, the number of our people in Egypt greatly increased. 18Then another king, who knew nothing about Joseph, became ruler of Egypt. 19He dealt treacherously with our people and oppressed our forefathers by forcing them to throw out their newborn babies so that they would die.

20"At that time Moses was born, and he was no ordinary child.[c] For three months he was cared for in his father's house. 21When he was placed outside, Pharaoh's daughter took him and brought him up as her own son. 22Moses was educated in all the wisdom of the Egyptians and was powerful in speech and action.

23"When Moses was forty years old, he decided to visit his fellow Israelites. 24He saw one of them being mistreated by an Egyptian, so he went to his defense and avenged him by killing the Egyptian. 25Moses thought that his own people would realize that God was using him to rescue them, but they did not. 26The next day Moses came upon two Israelites who were fighting. He tried to reconcile them by saying, 'Men, you are brothers; why do you want to hurt each other?'

27"But the man who was mistreating the other pushed Moses aside and said, 'Who made you ruler and judge over us? 28Do you want to kill me as you killed the Egyptian yesterday?'[d] 29When Moses heard this, he fled to Midian, where he settled as a foreigner and had two sons.

30"After forty years had passed, an angel appeared to Moses in the flames of a burning bush in the desert near Mount Sinai. 31When he saw this, he was amazed at the sight. As he went over to look more closely, he heard the Lord's voice: 32'I am the God of your fathers, the God of Abraham, Isaac and Jacob.'[e] Moses trembled with fear and did not dare to look.

33"Then the Lord said to him, 'Take off your sandals; the place where you are standing is holy ground. 34I have indeed seen the oppression of my people in Egypt. I have heard their groaning and have come down to set them free. Now come, I will send you back to Egypt.'[f]

35"This is the same Moses whom they

[a]*3* Gen. 12:1 [b]*7* Gen. 15:13,14 [c]*20* Or *was fair in the sight of God* [d]*28* Exodus 2:14
[e]*32* Exodus 3:6 [f]*34* Exodus 3:5,7,8,10

had rejected with the words, 'Who made
you ruler and judge?' He was sent to be
their ruler and deliverer by God himself,
through the angel who appeared to him in
the bush. 36He led them out of Egypt and
did wonders and miraculous signs in
Egypt, at the Red Sea[a] and for forty years
in the desert.

37"This is that Moses who told the Israelites, 'God will send you a prophet like me from your own people.'[b] 38He was in the assembly in the desert, with the angel who spoke to him on Mount Sinai, and with our fathers; and he received living words to pass on to us.

39"But our fathers refused to obey him. Instead, they rejected him and in their hearts turned back to Egypt. 40They told Aaron, 'Make us gods who will go before us. As for this fellow Moses who led us out of Egypt—we don't know what has happened to him!'[c] 41That was the time they made an idol in the form of a calf. They brought sacrifices to it and held a celebration in honor of what their hands had made. 42But God turned away and gave them over to the worship of the heavenly bodies. This agrees with what is written in the book of the prophets:

" 'Did you bring me sacrifices and offerings
forty years in the desert, O house of Israel?
43You have lifted up the shrine of Molech
and the star of your god Rephan,
the idols you made to worship.
Therefore I will send you into exile'[d] beyond Babylon.

44"Our forefathers had the tabernacle of the Testimony with them in the desert. It had been made as God directed Moses, according to the pattern he had seen. 45Having received the tabernacle, our fathers under Joshua brought it with them when they took the land from the nations God drove out before them. It remained in the land until the time of David, 46who enjoyed God's favor and asked that he might provide a dwelling place for the God of Jacob.[e] 47But it was Solomon who built the house for him.

48"However, the Most High does not live in houses made by men. As the prophet says:

49" 'Heaven is my throne,
and the earth is my footstool.
What kind of house will you build for me?
says the Lord.
Or where will my resting place be?
50Has not my hand made all these things?'[f]

51"You stiff-necked people, with uncircumcised hearts and ears! You are just like your fathers: You always resist the Holy Spirit! 52Was there ever a prophet your fathers did not persecute? They even killed those who predicted the coming of the Righteous One. And now you have betrayed and murdered him— 53you who have received the law that was put into effect through angels but have not obeyed it."

The Stoning of Stephen

54When they heard this, they were furious and gnashed their teeth at him. 55But Stephen, full of the Holy Spirit, looked up to heaven and saw the glory of God, and Jesus standing at the right hand of God. 56"Look," he said, "I see heaven open and the Son of Man standing at the right hand of God."

57At this they covered their ears and, yelling at the top of their voices, they all rushed at him, 58dragged him out of the city and began to stone him. Meanwhile, the witnesses laid their clothes at the feet of a young man named Saul.

59While they were stoning him, Stephen prayed, "Lord Jesus, receive my spirit." 60Then he fell on his knees and cried out, "Lord, do not hold this sin against them." When he had said this, he fell asleep.

8 And Saul was there, giving approval to his death.

The Church Persecuted and Scattered

On that day a great persecution broke out against the church at Jerusalem, and all except the apostles were scattered throughout Judea and Samaria. 2Godly men buried Stephen and mourned deeply for him. 3But Saul began to destroy the church. Going from house to house, he dragged off men and women and put them in prison.

[a] *36* That is, Sea of Reeds [b] *37* Deut. 18:15 [c] *40* Exodus 32:1 [d] *43* Amos 5:25-27 [e] *46* Some early manuscripts *the house of Jacob* [f] *50* Isaiah 66:1,2

Philip in Samaria

4Those who had been scattered
preached the word wherever they went.
5Philip went down to a city in Samaria and
proclaimed the Christ[a] there. 6When the
crowds heard Philip and saw the miracu-
lous signs he did, they all paid close atten-
tion to what he said. 7With shrieks, evil[b]
spirits came out of many, and many para-
lytics and cripples were healed. 8So there
was great joy in that city.

Simon the Sorcerer

9Now for some time a man named Si-
mon had practiced sorcery in the city and
amazed all the people of Samaria. He
boasted that he was someone great, 10and
all the people, both high and low, gave
him their attention and exclaimed, "This
man is the divine power known as the
Great Power." 11They followed him be-
cause he had amazed them for a long time
with his magic. 12But when they believed
Philip as he preached the good news of
the kingdom of God and the name of Jesus
Christ, they were baptized, both men and
women. 13Simon himself believed and
was baptized. And he followed Philip ev-
erywhere, astonished by the great signs
and miracles he saw.

14When the apostles in Jerusalem heard
that Samaria had accepted the word of
God, they sent Peter and John to them.
15When they arrived, they prayed for
them that they might receive the Holy
Spirit, 16because the Holy Spirit had not
yet come upon any of them; they had sim-
ply been baptized into[c] the name of the
Lord Jesus. 17Then Peter and John placed
their hands on them, and they received
the Holy Spirit.

18When Simon saw that the Spirit was
given at the laying on of the apostles'
hands, he offered them money 19and said,
"Give me also this ability so that everyone
on whom I lay my hands may receive the
Holy Spirit."

20Peter answered: "May your money
perish with you, because you thought you
could buy the gift of God with money!
21You have no part or share in this minis-
try, because your heart is not right before
God. 22Repent of this wickedness and
pray to the Lord. Perhaps he will forgive
you for having such a thought in your
heart. 23For I see that you are full of bitter-
ness and captive to sin."

24Then Simon answered, "Pray to the
Lord for me so that nothing you have said
may happen to me."

25When they had testified and pro-
claimed the word of the Lord, Peter and
John returned to Jerusalem, preaching the
gospel in many Samaritan villages.

Philip and the Ethiopian

26Now an angel of the Lord said to Phil-
ip, "Go south to the road—the desert
road—that goes down from Jerusalem to
Gaza." 27So he started out, and on his way
he met an Ethiopian[d] eunuch, an impor-
tant official in charge of all the treasury of
Candace, queen of the Ethiopians. This
man had gone to Jerusalem to worship,
28and on his way home was sitting in his
chariot reading the book of Isaiah the
prophet. 29The Spirit told Philip, "Go to
that chariot and stay near it."

30Then Philip ran up to the chariot and
heard the man reading Isaiah the prophet.
"Do you understand what you are read-
ing?" Philip asked.

31"How can I," he said, "unless some-
one explains it to me?" So he invited Phil-
ip to come up and sit with him.

32The eunuch was reading this passage
of Scripture:

"He was led like a sheep to the
slaughter,
and as a lamb before the shearer is
silent,
so he did not open his mouth.
33In his humiliation he was deprived of
justice.
Who can speak of his descendants?
For his life was taken from the
earth."[e]

34The eunuch asked Philip, "Tell me,
please, who is the prophet talking about,
himself or someone else?" 35Then Philip
began with that very passage of Scripture
and told him the good news about Jesus.

36As they traveled along the road, they
came to some water and the eunuch said,
"Look, here is water. Why shouldn't I be
baptized?"[f] 38And he gave orders to stop
the chariot. Then both Philip and the eu-
nuch went down into the water and Philip
baptized him. 39When they came up out

[a]5 Or *Messiah* [b]7 Greek *unclean* [c]16 Or *in* [d]27 That is, from the upper Nile region
[e]33 Isaiah 53:7,8 [f]36 Some late manuscripts *baptized?"* 37*Philip said, "If you believe with all your heart, you may." The eunuch answered, "I believe that Jesus Christ is the Son of God."*

of the water, the Spirit of the Lord suddenly took Philip away, and the eunuch did not see him again, but went on his way rejoicing. 40Philip, however, appeared at Azotus and traveled about, preaching the gospel in all the towns until he reached Caesarea.

Saul's Conversion

9 Meanwhile, Saul was still breathing out murderous threats against the Lord's disciples. He went to the high priest 2and asked him for letters to the synagogues in Damascus, so that if he found any there who belonged to the Way, whether men or women, he might take them as prisoners to Jerusalem. 3As he neared Damascus on his journey, suddenly a light from heaven flashed around him. 4He fell to the ground and heard a voice say to him, "Saul, Saul, why do you persecute me?"

5"Who are you, Lord?" Saul asked.

"I am Jesus, whom you are persecuting," he replied. 6"Now get up and go into the city, and you will be told what you must do."

7The men traveling with Saul stood there speechless; they heard the sound but did not see anyone. 8Saul got up from the ground, but when he opened his eyes he could see nothing. So they led him by the hand into Damascus. 9For three days he was blind, and did not eat or drink anything.

10In Damascus there was a disciple named Ananias. The Lord called to him in a vision, "Ananias!"

"Yes, Lord," he answered.

11The Lord told him, "Go to the house of Judas on Straight Street and ask for a man from Tarsus named Saul, for he is praying. 12In a vision he has seen a man named Ananias come and place his hands on him to restore his sight."

13"Lord," Ananias answered, "I have heard many reports about this man and all the harm he has done to your saints in Jerusalem. 14And he has come here with authority from the chief priests to arrest all who call on your name."

15But the Lord said to Ananias, "Go! This man is my chosen instrument to carry my name before the Gentiles and their kings and before the people of Israel. 16I will show him how much he must suffer for my name."

17Then Ananias went to the house and entered it. Placing his hands on Saul, he said, "Brother Saul, the Lord—Jesus, who appeared to you on the road as you were coming here—has sent me so that you may see again and be filled with the Holy Spirit." 18Immediately, something like scales fell from Saul's eyes, and he could see again. He got up and was baptized, 19and after taking some food, he regained his strength.

Saul in Damascus and Jerusalem

Saul spent several days with the disciples in Damascus. 20At once he began to preach in the synagogues that Jesus is the Son of God. 21All those who heard him were astonished and asked, "Isn't he the man who raised havoc in Jerusalem among those who call on this name? And hasn't he come here to take them as prisoners to the chief priests?" 22Yet Saul grew more and more powerful and baffled the Jews living in Damascus by proving that Jesus is the Christ.[a]

23After many days had gone by, the Jews conspired to kill him, 24but Saul learned of their plan. Day and night they kept close watch on the city gates in order to kill him. 25But his followers took him by night and lowered him in a basket through an opening in the wall.

26When he came to Jerusalem, he tried to join the disciples, but they were all afraid of him, not believing that he really was a disciple. 27But Barnabas took him and brought him to the apostles. He told them how Saul on his journey had seen the Lord and that the Lord had spoken to him, and how in Damascus he had preached fearlessly in the name of Jesus. 28So Saul stayed with them and moved about freely in Jerusalem, speaking boldly in the name of the Lord. 29He talked and debated with the Grecian Jews, but they tried to kill him. 30When the brothers learned of this, they took him down to Caesarea and sent him off to Tarsus.

31Then the church throughout Judea, Galilee and Samaria enjoyed a time of peace. It was strengthened; and encouraged by the Holy Spirit, it grew in numbers, living in the fear of the Lord.

Aeneas and Dorcas

32As Peter traveled about the country, he went to visit the saints in Lydda.

[a]22 Or *Messiah*

33There he found a man named Aeneas, a
paralytic who had been bedridden for
eight years. 34"Aeneas," Peter said to him,
"Jesus Christ heals you. Get up and take
care of your mat." Immediately Aeneas
got up. 35All those who lived in Lydda
and Sharon saw him and turned to the
Lord.

36In Joppa there was a disciple named
Tabitha (which, when translated, is Dor-
cas[a]), who was always doing good and
helping the poor. 37About that time she
became sick and died, and her body was
washed and placed in an upstairs room.
38Lydda was near Joppa; so when the dis-
ciples heard that Peter was in Lydda, they
sent two men to him and urged him,
"Please come at once!"

39Peter went with them, and when he
arrived he was taken upstairs to the room.
All the widows stood around him, crying
and showing him the robes and other
clothing that Dorcas had made while she
was still with them.

40Peter sent them all out of the room;
then he got down on his knees and
prayed. Turning toward the dead woman,
he said, "Tabitha, get up." She opened her
eyes, and seeing Peter she sat up. 41He
took her by the hand and helped her to
her feet. Then he called the believers and
the widows and presented her to them
alive. 42This became known all over Jop-
pa, and many people believed in the Lord.
43Peter stayed in Joppa for some time with
a tanner named Simon.

[a]36 Both *Tabitha* (Aramaic) and *Dorcas* (Greek) mean *gazelle*.

THURSDAY

VERSE FOR THE DAY: Acts 9:36

AUTHOR: Marylou Habecker

PASSAGE FOR THE DAY: Acts 9:32–43

A Cure for Loneliness

The story is told of a woman who went to Henrietta Mears, the great Christian educator, to tell about her loneliness. When she confessed she had few friends, Dr. Mears asked her to name the qualities that she herself would want in a friend. "Someone who would accept and not misuse me. Someone on whom I could count. One who could share my hopes and dreams," the woman replied.

Dr. Mears' advice to her was, "Go, be that kind of friend to others and you will find they will be that kind of friend to you."

We need not be lonely. It all depends on how we choose to respond to others.

MARRIAGE BUILDERS

♦ *Obviously, a spouse is more than a friend. But what characteristics make your spouse a good friend to you?*

♦ *How can you and your spouse prevent loneliness from creeping into your marriage?*

Additional Scripture Readings
Matthew 7:7–12; Psalm 62:1; Proverbs 17:17

Go to page 1202 for your next devotional reading.

Cornelius Calls for Peter

10 At Caesarea there was a man
named Cornelius, a centurion in
what was known as the Italian Regiment.
2He and all his family were devout and
God-fearing; he gave generously to those
in need and prayed to God regularly. 3One
day at about three in the afternoon he had
a vision. He distinctly saw an angel of
God, who came to him and said, "Cornelius!"
4Cornelius stared at him in fear. "What
is it, Lord?" he asked.
The angel answered, "Your prayers and
gifts to the poor have come up as a memorial offering before God. 5Now send men
to Joppa to bring back a man named Simon who is called Peter. 6He is staying
with Simon the tanner, whose house is by
the sea."
7When the angel who spoke to him had
gone, Cornelius called two of his servants
and a devout soldier who was one of his
attendants. 8He told them everything that
had happened and sent them to Joppa.

Peter's Vision

9About noon the following day as they
were on their journey and approaching
the city, Peter went up on the roof to pray.
10He became hungry and wanted something to eat, and while the meal was being
prepared, he fell into a trance. 11He saw
heaven opened and something like a large
sheet being let down to earth by its four
corners. 12It contained all kinds of four-
footed animals, as well as reptiles of the
earth and birds of the air. 13Then a voice
told him, "Get up, Peter. Kill and eat."
14"Surely not, Lord!" Peter replied. "I
have never eaten anything impure or unclean."
15The voice spoke to him a second time,
"Do not call anything impure that God has
made clean."
16This happened three times, and immediately the sheet was taken back to
heaven.
17While Peter was wondering about the
meaning of the vision, the men sent by
Cornelius found out where Simon's house
was and stopped at the gate. 18They called
out, asking if Simon who was known as
Peter was staying there.
19While Peter was still thinking about
the vision, the Spirit said to him, "Simon,
three[a] men are looking for you. 20So get
up and go downstairs. Do not hesitate to
go with them, for I have sent them."
21Peter went down and said to the men,
"I'm the one you're looking for. Why have
you come?"
22The men replied, "We have come
from Cornelius the centurion. He is a righteous and God-fearing man, who is respected by all the Jewish people. A holy
angel told him to have you come to his
house so that he could hear what you
have to say." 23Then Peter invited the men
into the house to be his guests.

Peter at Cornelius' House

The next day Peter started out with
them, and some of the brothers from Joppa went along. 24The following day he arrived in Caesarea. Cornelius was expecting them and had called together his
relatives and close friends. 25As Peter entered the house, Cornelius met him and
fell at his feet in reverence. 26But Peter
made him get up. "Stand up," he said, "I
am only a man myself."
27Talking with him, Peter went inside
and found a large gathering of people.
28He said to them: "You are well aware
that it is against our law for a Jew to associate with a Gentile or visit him. But God
has shown me that I should not call any
man impure or unclean. 29So when I was
sent for, I came without raising any objection. May I ask why you sent for me?"
30Cornelius answered: "Four days ago I
was in my house praying at this hour, at
three in the afternoon. Suddenly a man in
shining clothes stood before me 31and
said, 'Cornelius, God has heard your
prayer and remembered your gifts to the
poor. 32Send to Joppa for Simon who is
called Peter. He is a guest in the home of
Simon the tanner, who lives by the sea.'
33So I sent for you immediately, and it was
good of you to come. Now we are all here
in the presence of God to listen to everything the Lord has commanded you to
tell us."
34Then Peter began to speak: "I now realize how true it is that God does not show
favoritism 35but accepts men from every
nation who fear him and do what is right.
36You know the message God sent to the
people of Israel, telling the good news of

[a]19 One early manuscript *two*; other manuscripts do not have the number.

peace through Jesus Christ, who is Lord of
all. 37You know what has happened
throughout Judea, beginning in Galilee af-
ter the baptism that John preached—
38how God anointed Jesus of Nazareth
with the Holy Spirit and power, and how
he went around doing good and healing
all who were under the power of the devil,
because God was with him.

39"We are witnesses of everything he
did in the country of the Jews and in Jeru-
salem. They killed him by hanging him on
a tree, 40but God raised him from the dead
on the third day and caused him to be
seen. 41He was not seen by all the people,
but by witnesses whom God had already
chosen—by us who ate and drank with
him after he rose from the dead. 42He
commanded us to preach to the people
and to testify that he is the one whom God
appointed as judge of the living and the
dead. 43All the prophets testify about him
that everyone who believes in him re-
ceives forgiveness of sins through his
name."

44While Peter was still speaking these
words, the Holy Spirit came on all who
heard the message. 45The circumcised be-
lievers who had come with Peter were as-
tonished that the gift of the Holy Spirit
had been poured out even on the Gentiles.
46For they heard them speaking in
tongues[a] and praising God.

Then Peter said, 47"Can anyone keep
these people from being baptized with
water? They have received the Holy Spirit
just as we have." 48So he ordered that they
be baptized in the name of Jesus Christ.
Then they asked Peter to stay with them
for a few days.

Peter Explains His Actions

11 The apostles and the brothers
throughout Judea heard that the
Gentiles also had received the word of
God. 2So when Peter went up to Jerusa-
lem, the circumcised believers criticized
him 3and said, "You went into the house
of uncircumcised men and ate with
them."

4Peter began and explained everything
to them precisely as it had happened: 5"I
was in the city of Joppa praying, and in a
trance I saw a vision. I saw something like
a large sheet being let down from heaven
by its four corners, and it came down to
where I was. 6I looked into it and saw
four-footed animals of the earth, wild
beasts, reptiles, and birds of the air. 7Then
I heard a voice telling me, 'Get up, Peter.
Kill and eat.'

8"I replied, 'Surely not, Lord! Nothing
impure or unclean has ever entered my
mouth.'

9"The voice spoke from heaven a sec-
ond time, 'Do not call anything impure
that God has made clean.' 10This hap-
pened three times, and then it was all
pulled up to heaven again.

11"Right then three men who had been
sent to me from Caesarea stopped at the
house where I was staying. 12The Spirit
told me to have no hesitation about going
with them. These six brothers also went
with me, and we entered the man's house.
13He told us how he had seen an angel ap-
pear in his house and say, 'Send to Joppa
for Simon who is called Peter. 14He will
bring you a message through which you
and all your household will be saved.'

15"As I began to speak, the Holy Spirit
came on them as he had come on us at the
beginning. 16Then I remembered what the
Lord had said: 'John baptized with[b] wa-
ter, but you will be baptized with the Holy
Spirit.' 17So if God gave them the same gift
as he gave us, who believed in the Lord
Jesus Christ, who was I to think that I
could oppose God?"

18When they heard this, they had no
further objections and praised God, say-
ing, "So then, God has granted even the
Gentiles repentance unto life."

The Church in Antioch

19Now those who had been scattered by
the persecution in connection with Ste-
phen traveled as far as Phoenicia, Cyprus
and Antioch, telling the message only to
Jews. 20Some of them, however, men from
Cyprus and Cyrene, went to Antioch and
began to speak to Greeks also, telling
them the good news about the Lord Jesus.
21The Lord's hand was with them, and a
great number of people believed and
turned to the Lord.

22News of this reached the ears of the
church at Jerusalem, and they sent Barna-
bas to Antioch. 23When he arrived and
saw the evidence of the grace of God, he
was glad and encouraged them all to re-
main true to the Lord with all their hearts.
24He was a good man, full of the Holy Spir-

[a]46 Or *other languages* [b]16 Or *in*

it and faith, and a great number of people were brought to the Lord.

25Then Barnabas went to Tarsus to look for Saul, 26and when he found him, he brought him to Antioch. So for a whole year Barnabas and Saul met with the church and taught great numbers of people. The disciples were called Christians first at Antioch.

27During this time some prophets came down from Jerusalem to Antioch. 28One of them, named Agabus, stood up and through the Spirit predicted that a severe famine would spread over the entire Roman world. (This happened during the reign of Claudius.) 29The disciples, each according to his ability, decided to provide help for the brothers living in Judea. 30This they did, sending their gift to the elders by Barnabas and Saul.

Peter's Miraculous Escape From Prison

12 It was about this time that King Herod arrested some who belonged to the church, intending to persecute them. 2He had James, the brother of John, put to death with the sword. 3When he saw that this pleased the Jews, he proceeded to seize Peter also. This happened during the Feast of Unleavened Bread. 4After arresting him, he put him in prison, handing him over to be guarded by four squads of four soldiers each. Herod intended to bring him out for public trial after the Passover.

5So Peter was kept in prison, but the church was earnestly praying to God for him.

6The night before Herod was to bring him to trial, Peter was sleeping between two soldiers, bound with two chains, and sentries stood guard at the entrance. 7Suddenly an angel of the Lord appeared and a light shone in the cell. He struck Peter on the side and woke him up. "Quick, get up!" he said, and the chains fell off Peter's wrists.

8Then the angel said to him, "Put on your clothes and sandals." And Peter did so. "Wrap your cloak around you and follow me," the angel told him. 9Peter followed him out of the prison, but he had no idea that what the angel was doing was really happening; he thought he was seeing a vision. 10They passed the first and second guards and came to the iron gate leading to the city. It opened for them by itself, and they went through it. When they had walked the length of one street, suddenly the angel left him.

11Then Peter came to himself and said, "Now I know without a doubt that the Lord sent his angel and rescued me from Herod's clutches and from everything the Jewish people were anticipating."

12When this had dawned on him, he went to the house of Mary the mother of John, also called Mark, where many people had gathered and were praying. 13Peter knocked at the outer entrance, and a servant girl named Rhoda came to answer the door. 14When she recognized Peter's voice, she was so overjoyed she ran back without opening it and exclaimed, "Peter is at the door!"

15"You're out of your mind," they told her. When she kept insisting that it was so, they said, "It must be his angel."

16But Peter kept on knocking, and when they opened the door and saw him, they were astonished. 17Peter motioned with his hand for them to be quiet and described how the Lord had brought him out of prison. "Tell James and the brothers about this," he said, and then he left for another place.

18In the morning, there was no small commotion among the soldiers as to what had become of Peter. 19After Herod had a thorough search made for him and did not find him, he cross-examined the guards and ordered that they be executed.

Herod's Death

Then Herod went from Judea to Caesarea and stayed there a while. 20He had been quarreling with the people of Tyre and Sidon; they now joined together and sought an audience with him. Having secured the support of Blastus, a trusted personal servant of the king, they asked for peace, because they depended on the king's country for their food supply.

21On the appointed day Herod, wearing his royal robes, sat on his throne and delivered a public address to the people. 22They shouted, "This is the voice of a god, not of a man." 23Immediately, because Herod did not give praise to God, an angel of the Lord struck him down, and he was eaten by worms and died.

24But the word of God continued to increase and spread.

25When Barnabas and Saul had finished

their mission, they returned from[a] Jerusalem, taking with them John, also called Mark.

Barnabas and Saul Sent Off

13 In the church at Antioch there were prophets and teachers: Barnabas, Simeon called Niger, Lucius of Cyrene, Manaen (who had been brought up with Herod the tetrarch) and Saul. [2]While they were worshiping the Lord and fasting, the Holy Spirit said, "Set apart for me Barnabas and Saul for the work to which I have called them." [3]So after they had fasted and prayed, they placed their hands on them and sent them off.

On Cyprus

[4]The two of them, sent on their way by the Holy Spirit, went down to Seleucia and sailed from there to Cyprus. [5]When they arrived at Salamis, they proclaimed the word of God in the Jewish synagogues. John was with them as their helper.

[6]They traveled through the whole island until they came to Paphos. There they met a Jewish sorcerer and false prophet named Bar-Jesus, [7]who was an attendant of the proconsul, Sergius Paulus. The proconsul, an intelligent man, sent for Barnabas and Saul because he wanted to hear the word of God. [8]But Elymas the sorcerer (for that is what his name means) opposed them and tried to turn the proconsul from the faith. [9]Then Saul, who was also called Paul, filled with the Holy Spirit, looked straight at Elymas and said, [10]"You are a child of the devil and an enemy of everything that is right! You are full of all kinds of deceit and trickery. Will you never stop perverting the right ways of the Lord? [11]Now the hand of the Lord is against you. You are going to be blind, and for a time you will be unable to see the light of the sun."

Immediately mist and darkness came over him, and he groped about, seeking someone to lead him by the hand. [12]When the proconsul saw what had happened, he believed, for he was amazed at the teaching about the Lord.

In Pisidian Antioch

[13]From Paphos, Paul and his companions sailed to Perga in Pamphylia, where John left them to return to Jerusalem. [14]From Perga they went on to Pisidian Antioch. On the Sabbath they entered the synagogue and sat down. [15]After the reading from the Law and the Prophets, the synagogue rulers sent word to them, saying, "Brothers, if you have a message of encouragement for the people, please speak."

[16]Standing up, Paul motioned with his hand and said: "Men of Israel and you Gentiles who worship God, listen to me! [17]The God of the people of Israel chose our fathers; he made the people prosper during their stay in Egypt, with mighty power he led them out of that country, [18]he endured their conduct[b] for about forty years in the desert, [19]he overthrew seven nations in Canaan and gave their land to his people as their inheritance. [20]All this took about 450 years.

"After this, God gave them judges until the time of Samuel the prophet. [21]Then the people asked for a king, and he gave them Saul son of Kish, of the tribe of Benjamin, who ruled forty years. [22]After removing Saul, he made David their king. He testified concerning him: 'I have found David son of Jesse a man after my own heart; he will do everything I want him to do.'

[23]"From this man's descendants God has brought to Israel the Savior Jesus, as he promised. [24]Before the coming of Jesus, John preached repentance and baptism to all the people of Israel. [25]As John was completing his work, he said: 'Who do you think I am? I am not that one. No, but he is coming after me, whose sandals I am not worthy to untie.'

[26]"Brothers, children of Abraham, and you God-fearing Gentiles, it is to us that this message of salvation has been sent. [27]The people of Jerusalem and their rulers did not recognize Jesus, yet in condemning him they fulfilled the words of the prophets that are read every Sabbath. [28]Though they found no proper ground for a death sentence, they asked Pilate to have him executed. [29]When they had carried out all that was written about him, they took him down from the tree and laid him in a tomb. [30]But God raised him from the dead, [31]and for many days he was seen by those who had traveled with him from Galilee to Jerusalem. They are now his witnesses to our people.

[32]"We tell you the good news: What God promised our fathers [33]he has ful-

[a]*25* Some manuscripts *to* [b]*18* Some manuscripts *and cared for them*

filled for us, their children, by raising up
Jesus. As it is written in the second Psalm:

" 'You are my Son;
today I have become your
Father.[a]'[b]

34The fact that God raised him from the
dead, never to decay, is stated in these
words:

" 'I will give you the holy and sure
blessings promised to David.'[c]

35So it is stated elsewhere:

" 'You will not let your Holy One see
decay.'[d]

36"For when David had served God's
purpose in his own generation, he fell
asleep; he was buried with his fathers and
his body decayed. 37But the one whom
God raised from the dead did not see de-
cay.

38"Therefore, my brothers, I want you
to know that through Jesus the forgive-
ness of sins is proclaimed to you.
39Through him everyone who believes is
justified from everything you could not be
justified from by the law of Moses. 40Take
care that what the prophets have said does
not happen to you:

41" 'Look, you scoffers,
wonder and perish,
for I am going to do something in
your days
that you would never believe,
even if someone told you.'[e]"

42As Paul and Barnabas were leaving
the synagogue, the people invited them to
speak further about these things on the
next Sabbath. 43When the congregation
was dismissed, many of the Jews and de-
vout converts to Judaism followed Paul
and Barnabas, who talked with them and
urged them to continue in the grace of
God.

44On the next Sabbath almost the whole
city gathered to hear the word of the Lord.
45When the Jews saw the crowds, they
were filled with jealousy and talked abu-
sively against what Paul was saying.

46Then Paul and Barnabas answered
them boldly: "We had to speak the word
of God to you first. Since you reject it and
do not consider yourselves worthy of eter-
nal life, we now turn to the Gentiles. 47For
this is what the Lord has commanded us:

" 'I have made you[f] a light for the
Gentiles,
that you[f] may bring salvation to
the ends of the earth.'[g]"

48When the Gentiles heard this, they
were glad and honored the word of the
Lord; and all who were appointed for eter-
nal life believed.

49The word of the Lord spread through
the whole region. 50But the Jews incited
the God-fearing women of high standing
and the leading men of the city. They
stirred up persecution against Paul and
Barnabas, and expelled them from their
region. 51So they shook the dust from
their feet in protest against them and went
to Iconium. 52And the disciples were filled
with joy and with the Holy Spirit.

In Iconium

14 At Iconium Paul and Barnabas
went as usual into the Jewish syna-
gogue. There they spoke so effectively
that a great number of Jews and Gentiles
believed. 2But the Jews who refused to be-
lieve stirred up the Gentiles and poisoned
their minds against the brothers. 3So Paul
and Barnabas spent considerable time
there, speaking boldly for the Lord, who
confirmed the message of his grace by en-
abling them to do miraculous signs and
wonders. 4The people of the city were di-
vided; some sided with the Jews, others
with the apostles. 5There was a plot afoot
among the Gentiles and Jews, together
with their leaders, to mistreat them and
stone them. 6But they found out about it
and fled to the Lycaonian cities of Lystra
and Derbe and to the surrounding coun-
try, 7where they continued to preach the
good news.

In Lystra and Derbe

8In Lystra there sat a man crippled in
his feet, who was lame from birth and had
never walked. 9He listened to Paul as he
was speaking. Paul looked directly at him,
saw that he had faith to be healed 10and
called out, "Stand up on your feet!" At
that, the man jumped up and began to
walk.

11When the crowd saw what Paul had
done, they shouted in the Lycaonian lan-
guage, "The gods have come down to us

[a]33 Or *have begotten you* [b]33 Psalm 2:7 [c]34 Isaiah 55:3 [d]35 Psalm 16:10 [e]41 Hab. 1:5
[f]47 The Greek is singular. [g]47 Isaiah 49:6

in human form!" [12]Barnabas they called
Zeus, and Paul they called Hermes be-
cause he was the chief speaker. [13]The
priest of Zeus, whose temple was just out-
side the city, brought bulls and wreaths to
the city gates because he and the crowd
wanted to offer sacrifices to them.

[14]But when the apostles Barnabas and
Paul heard of this, they tore their clothes
and rushed out into the crowd, shouting:
[15]"Men, why are you doing this? We too
are only men, human like you. We are
bringing you good news, telling you to
turn from these worthless things to the
living God, who made heaven and earth
and sea and everything in them. [16]In the
past, he let all nations go their own way.
[17]Yet he has not left himself without testi-
mony: He has shown kindness by giving
you rain from heaven and crops in their
seasons; he provides you with plenty of
food and fills your hearts with joy."
[18]Even with these words, they had diffi-
culty keeping the crowd from sacrificing
to them.

[19]Then some Jews came from Antioch
and Iconium and won the crowd over.
They stoned Paul and dragged him out-
side the city, thinking he was dead. [20]But
after the disciples had gathered around
him, he got up and went back into the
city. The next day he and Barnabas left for
Derbe.

The Return to Antioch in Syria

[21]They preached the good news in that
city and won a large number of disciples.
Then they returned to Lystra, Iconium
and Antioch, [22]strengthening the disciples
and encouraging them to remain true to
the faith. "We must go through many
hardships to enter the kingdom of God,"
they said. [23]Paul and Barnabas appointed
elders[a] for them in each church and, with
prayer and fasting, committed them to the
Lord, in whom they had put their trust.
[24]After going through Pisidia, they came
into Pamphylia, [25]and when they had
preached the word in Perga, they went
down to Attalia.

[26]From Attalia they sailed back to Anti-
och, where they had been committed to
the grace of God for the work they had
now completed. [27]On arriving there, they
gathered the church together and report-
ed all that God had done through them
and how he had opened the door of faith
to the Gentiles. [28]And they stayed there a
long time with the disciples.

The Council at Jerusalem

15 Some men came down from Judea
to Antioch and were teaching the
brothers: "Unless you are circumcised, ac-
cording to the custom taught by Moses,
you cannot be saved." [2]This brought Paul
and Barnabas into sharp dispute and de-
bate with them. So Paul and Barnabas
were appointed, along with some other
believers, to go up to Jerusalem to see the
apostles and elders about this question.
[3]The church sent them on their way, and
as they traveled through Phoenicia and
Samaria, they told how the Gentiles had
been converted. This news made all the
brothers very glad. [4]When they came to
Jerusalem, they were welcomed by the
church and the apostles and elders, to
whom they reported everything God had
done through them.

[5]Then some of the believers who be-
longed to the party of the Pharisees stood
up and said, "The Gentiles must be cir-
cumcised and required to obey the law of
Moses."

[6]The apostles and elders met to consid-
er this question. [7]After much discussion,
Peter got up and addressed them: "Broth-
ers, you know that some time ago God
made a choice among you that the Gen-
tiles might hear from my lips the message
of the gospel and believe. [8]God, who
knows the heart, showed that he accepted
them by giving the Holy Spirit to them,
just as he did to us. [9]He made no distinc-
tion between us and them, for he purified
their hearts by faith. [10]Now then, why do
you try to test God by putting on the necks
of the disciples a yoke that neither we nor
our fathers have been able to bear? [11]No!
We believe it is through the grace of our
Lord Jesus that we are saved, just as they
are."

[12]The whole assembly became silent as
they listened to Barnabas and Paul telling
about the miraculous signs and wonders
God had done among the Gentiles
through them. [13]When they finished,
James spoke up: "Brothers, listen to me.
[14]Simon[b] has described to us how God at
first showed his concern by taking from
the Gentiles a people for himself. [15]The

[a]23 Or *Barnabas ordained elders*; or *Barnabas had elders elected*
[b]14 Greek *Simeon*, a variant of *Simon*; that is, Peter

words of the prophets are in agreement
with this, as it is written:

16" 'After this I will return
and rebuild David's fallen tent.
Its ruins I will rebuild,
and I will restore it,
17that the remnant of men may seek the
Lord,
and all the Gentiles who bear my
name,
says the Lord, who does these
things'[a]
18 that have been known for ages.[b]

19"It is my judgment, therefore, that we should not make it difficult for the Gentiles who are turning to God. 20Instead we should write to them, telling them to abstain from food polluted by idols, from sexual immorality, from the meat of strangled animals and from blood. 21For Moses has been preached in every city from the earliest times and is read in the synagogues on every Sabbath."

The Council's Letter to Gentile Believers

22Then the apostles and elders, with the whole church, decided to choose some of their own men and send them to Antioch with Paul and Barnabas. They chose Judas (called Barsabbas) and Silas, two men who were leaders among the brothers. 23With them they sent the following letter:

The apostles and elders, your brothers,

To the Gentile believers in Antioch, Syria and Cilicia:

Greetings.

24We have heard that some went out from us without our authorization and disturbed you, troubling your minds by what they said. 25So we all agreed to choose some men and send them to you with our dear friends Barnabas and Paul— 26men who have risked their lives for the name of our Lord Jesus Christ. 27Therefore we are sending Judas and Silas to confirm by word of mouth what we are writing. 28It seemed good to the Holy Spirit and to us not to burden you with anything beyond the following requirements:
29You are to abstain from food sacrificed to idols, from blood, from the meat of strangled animals and from sexual immorality. You will do well to avoid these things.

Farewell.

30The men were sent off and went down to Antioch, where they gathered the church together and delivered the letter. 31The people read it and were glad for its encouraging message. 32Judas and Silas, who themselves were prophets, said much to encourage and strengthen the brothers. 33After spending some time there, they were sent off by the brothers with the blessing of peace to return to those who had sent them.[c] 35But Paul and Barnabas remained in Antioch, where they and many others taught and preached the word of the Lord.

Disagreement Between Paul and Barnabas

36Some time later Paul said to Barnabas, "Let us go back and visit the brothers in all the towns where we preached the word of the Lord and see how they are doing." 37Barnabas wanted to take John, also called Mark, with them, 38but Paul did not think it wise to take him, because he had deserted them in Pamphylia and had not continued with them in the work. 39They had such a sharp disagreement that they parted company. Barnabas took Mark and sailed for Cyprus, 40but Paul chose Silas and left, commended by the brothers to the grace of the Lord. 41He went through Syria and Cilicia, strengthening the churches.

Timothy Joins Paul and Silas

16 He came to Derbe and then to Lystra, where a disciple named Timothy lived, whose mother was a Jewess and a believer, but whose father was a Greek. 2The brothers at Lystra and Iconium spoke well of him. 3Paul wanted to take him along on the journey, so he circumcised him because of the Jews who lived in that area, for they all knew that his father was a Greek. 4As they traveled from town to town, they delivered the decisions reached by the apostles and elders in Jerusalem for the people to obey. 5So the

[a]17 Amos 9:11,12 [b]17,18 Some manuscripts *things'— / 18known to the Lord for ages is his work*
[c]33 Some manuscripts *them, 34but Silas decided to remain there*

churches were strengthened in the faith and grew daily in numbers.

Paul's Vision of the Man of Macedonia

6Paul and his companions traveled throughout the region of Phrygia and Galatia, having been kept by the Holy Spirit from preaching the word in the province of Asia. 7When they came to the border of Mysia, they tried to enter Bithynia, but the Spirit of Jesus would not allow them to. 8So they passed by Mysia and went down to Troas. 9During the night Paul had a vision of a man of Macedonia standing and begging him, "Come over to Macedonia and help us." 10After Paul had seen the vision, we got ready at once to leave for Macedonia, concluding that God had called us to preach the gospel to them.

Lydia's Conversion in Philippi

11From Troas we put out to sea and sailed straight for Samothrace, and the next day on to Neapolis. 12From there we traveled to Philippi, a Roman colony and

VERSE FOR THE DAY: Acts 15:32

AUTHOR: Preston and Genie Dyer

PASSAGE FOR THE DAY: Acts 15:22–35

Be an Encourager

People tend to focus on what's wrong with the world rather than what's right, and that trickles over into our relationships. Instead of being like diamond miners who sift through the dirt looking for one gem, we sift through all the diamonds looking for a little dirt.

Most couples don't start out focusing on their partner's negative traits. When people are dating, they often say things like, "We're so much alike." But once they get married, their differences become more apparent. Whenever couples fall into judging each other's actions against personal codes of behavior, they need to understand one important truth: Differences are just differences. There is no right or wrong when it comes to personalities.

In contrast, affirming your partner's strengths goes a long way toward creating an uplifting atmosphere. Don't assume your spouse knows what his or her strengths are; point them out. The more you can express appreciation, the stronger your relationship will be. By focusing on the positives, you will be reminded just why you married the person you did.

MARRIAGE BUILDERS

♦ *Identify—and mention—some things your spouse* does *that you especially appreciate.*

♦ *What are some things you love about his or her character?*

Additional Scripture Readings
2 Thessalonians 2:16–17; Romans 12:8

Go to page 1203 for your next devotional reading.

WEEKENDING

PARTNERSHIP

At its best, marriage is a partnership in which two people serve each other. But too often, the additional responsibilities of work, household chores and church involvement result in our investing too little energy in helping each other. Going over these suggestions together will help you gain a greater understanding of what you can do to minister to each other more effectively.

What kind of support do you need from your spouse to help you nurture your spirituality?

☐ Helping you find ways to free up more time during the day for prayer and reading the Bible and devotional books.

☐ Suggesting times to read the Bible and pray together as a couple.

☐ Taking over additional household chores so you can participate in outside ministry projects.

☐ Joining you in a shared ministry activity.

☐ Other: _____

— *The* Marriage Partnership *Staff*

REVIVE

Saturday: Psalm 119:9–16
Sunday: 1 Peter 3:8–16

Go to page 1205 for your next devotional reading.

the leading city of that district of Macedonia. And we stayed there several days.

13On the Sabbath we went outside the city gate to the river, where we expected to find a place of prayer. We sat down and began to speak to the women who had gathered there. 14One of those listening was a woman named Lydia, a dealer in purple cloth from the city of Thyatira, who was a worshiper of God. The Lord opened her heart to respond to Paul's message. 15When she and the members of her household were baptized, she invited us to her home. "If you consider me a believer in the Lord," she said, "come and stay at my house." And she persuaded us.

Paul and Silas in Prison

16Once when we were going to the place of prayer, we were met by a slave girl who had a spirit by which she predicted the future. She earned a great deal of money for her owners by fortune-telling. 17This girl followed Paul and the rest of us, shouting, "These men are servants of the Most High God, who are telling you the way to be saved." 18She kept this up for many days. Finally Paul became so troubled that he turned around and said to the spirit, "In the name of Jesus Christ I command you to come out of her!" At that moment the spirit left her.

19When the owners of the slave girl realized that their hope of making money was gone, they seized Paul and Silas and dragged them into the marketplace to face the authorities. 20They brought them before the magistrates and said, "These men are Jews, and are throwing our city into an uproar 21by advocating customs unlawful for us Romans to accept or practice."

22The crowd joined in the attack against Paul and Silas, and the magistrates ordered them to be stripped and beaten. 23After they had been severely flogged, they were thrown into prison, and the jailer was commanded to guard them carefully. 24Upon receiving such orders, he put them in the inner cell and fastened their feet in the stocks.

25About midnight Paul and Silas were praying and singing hymns to God, and the other prisoners were listening to them. 26Suddenly there was such a violent earthquake that the foundations of the prison were shaken. At once all the prison doors flew open, and everybody's chains came loose. 27The jailer woke up, and when he saw the prison doors open, he drew his sword and was about to kill himself because he thought the prisoners had escaped. 28But Paul shouted, "Don't harm yourself! We are all here!"

29The jailer called for lights, rushed in and fell trembling before Paul and Silas. 30He then brought them out and asked, "Sirs, what must I do to be saved?"

31They replied, "Believe in the Lord Jesus, and you will be saved—you and your household." 32Then they spoke the word of the Lord to him and to all the others in his house. 33At that hour of the night the jailer took them and washed their wounds; then immediately he and all his family were baptized. 34The jailer brought them into his house and set a meal before them; he was filled with joy because he had come to believe in God—he and his whole family.

35When it was daylight, the magistrates sent their officers to the jailer with the order: "Release those men." 36The jailer told Paul, "The magistrates have ordered that you and Silas be released. Now you can leave. Go in peace."

37But Paul said to the officers: "They beat us publicly without a trial, even though we are Roman citizens, and threw us into prison. And now do they want to get rid of us quietly? No! Let them come themselves and escort us out."

38The officers reported this to the magistrates, and when they heard that Paul and Silas were Roman citizens, they were alarmed. 39They came to appease them and escorted them from the prison, requesting them to leave the city. 40After Paul and Silas came out of the prison, they went to Lydia's house, where they met with the brothers and encouraged them. Then they left.

In Thessalonica

17 When they had passed through Amphipolis and Apollonia, they came to Thessalonica, where there was a Jewish synagogue. 2As his custom was, Paul went into the synagogue, and on three Sabbath days he reasoned with them from the Scriptures, 3explaining and proving that the Christ[a] had to suffer and rise from the dead. "This Jesus I am proclaiming to you is the Christ,[a]" he said. 4Some of the Jews were persuaded and

[a]3 Or *Messiah*

joined Paul and Silas, as did a large number of God-fearing Greeks and not a few prominent women.

5But the Jews were jealous; so they rounded up some bad characters from the marketplace, formed a mob and started a riot in the city. They rushed to Jason's house in search of Paul and Silas in order to bring them out to the crowd.[a] 6But when they did not find them, they dragged Jason and some other brothers before the city officials, shouting: "These men who have caused trouble all over the world have now come here, 7and Jason has welcomed them into his house. They are all defying Caesar's decrees, saying that there is another king, one called Jesus." 8When they heard this, the crowd and the city officials were thrown into turmoil. 9Then they made Jason and the others post bond and let them go.

In Berea

10As soon as it was night, the brothers sent Paul and Silas away to Berea. On arriving there, they went to the Jewish syna-

[a]5 Or *the assembly of the people*

VERSE FOR THE DAY: Acts 17:11 | AUTHOR: Ruth Bell Graham | PASSAGE FOR THE DAY: Acts 17:1–15

God's Reference Point

When it comes to spiritual growth, my reference point must be the Word of God, not the advice of my friends or the experiences of other Christians. When we've lost that reference point, we're headed for trouble.

I remember reading one time about the little disc on Meads Ranch in the Dakotas. The disc is only about eight inches high, but it is the exact point through which the four sections of latitude and longitude pass. It is the reference point for every surveyor or builder in the United States.

A story is told of a group of builders who decided to build a bridge across the bay, but ignored the reference point. They came to the middle of the bridge and found that the two ends were fifteen feet apart. They had ignored the reference point, and I would lose perspective too but for the Word of God.

MARRIAGE BUILDERS

♦ *How does your decision-making process depend on God's Word?*
♦ *What creative techniques could you implement to bring more Scripture into your day (reading a few verses over dinner or just before you go to sleep; Scripture card on your desk or the refrigerator door)?*

Additional Scripture Readings
Hebrews 4:7–13; Psalm 119:9–16, 105, 129–133; Colossians 3:16–17

Go to page 1209 for your next devotional reading.

gogue. 11Now the Bereans were of more
noble character than the Thessalonians,
for they received the message with great
eagerness and examined the Scriptures
every day to see if what Paul said was true.
12Many of the Jews believed, as did also a
number of prominent Greek women and
many Greek men.

13When the Jews in Thessalonica
learned that Paul was preaching the word
of God at Berea, they went there too, agi-
tating the crowds and stirring them up.
14The brothers immediately sent Paul to
the coast, but Silas and Timothy stayed at
Berea. 15The men who escorted Paul
brought him to Athens and then left with
instructions for Silas and Timothy to join
him as soon as possible.

In Athens

16While Paul was waiting for them in
Athens, he was greatly distressed to see
that the city was full of idols. 17So he rea-
soned in the synagogue with the Jews and
the God-fearing Greeks, as well as in the
marketplace day by day with those who
happened to be there. 18A group of Epicu-
rean and Stoic philosophers began to dis-
pute with him. Some of them asked,
"What is this babbler trying to say?" Oth-
ers remarked, "He seems to be advocating
foreign gods." They said this because Paul
was preaching the good news about Jesus
and the resurrection. 19Then they took
him and brought him to a meeting of the
Areopagus, where they said to him, "May
we know what this new teaching is that
you are presenting? 20You are bringing
some strange ideas to our ears, and we
want to know what they mean." 21(All the
Athenians and the foreigners who lived
there spent their time doing nothing but
talking about and listening to the latest
ideas.)

22Paul then stood up in the meeting of
the Areopagus and said: "Men of Athens!
I see that in every way you are very reli-
gious. 23For as I walked around and
looked carefully at your objects of wor-
ship, I even found an altar with this in-
scription: TO AN UNKNOWN GOD. Now what
you worship as something unknown I am
going to proclaim to you.

24"The God who made the world and
everything in it is the Lord of heaven and
earth and does not live in temples built by
hands. 25And he is not served by human
hands, as if he needed anything, because
he himself gives all men life and breath
and everything else. 26From one man he
made every nation of men, that they
should inhabit the whole earth; and he de-
termined the times set for them and the
exact places where they should live. 27God
did this so that men would seek him and
perhaps reach out for him and find him,
though he is not far from each one of us.
28'For in him we live and move and have
our being.' As some of your own poets
have said, 'We are his offspring.'

29"Therefore since we are God's off-
spring, we should not think that the divine
being is like gold or silver or stone—an
image made by man's design and skill.
30In the past God overlooked such igno-
rance, but now he commands all people
everywhere to repent. 31For he has set a
day when he will judge the world with jus-
tice by the man he has appointed. He has
given proof of this to all men by raising
him from the dead."

32When they heard about the resurrec-
tion of the dead, some of them sneered,
but others said, "We want to hear you
again on this subject." 33At that, Paul left
the Council. 34A few men became follow-
ers of Paul and believed. Among them was
Dionysius, a member of the Areopagus,
also a woman named Damaris, and a
number of others.

In Corinth

18 After this, Paul left Athens and
went to Corinth. 2There he met a
Jew named Aquila, a native of Pontus,
who had recently come from Italy with his
wife Priscilla, because Claudius had or-
dered all the Jews to leave Rome. Paul
went to see them, 3and because he was a
tentmaker as they were, he stayed and
worked with them. 4Every Sabbath he rea-
soned in the synagogue, trying to per-
suade Jews and Greeks.

5When Silas and Timothy came from
Macedonia, Paul devoted himself exclu-
sively to preaching, testifying to the Jews
that Jesus was the Christ.[a] 6But when the
Jews opposed Paul and became abusive,
he shook out his clothes in protest and
said to them, "Your blood be on your own
heads! I am clear of my responsibility.
From now on I will go to the Gentiles."

7Then Paul left the synagogue and went
next door to the house of Titius Justus, a

[a]5 Or *Messiah;* also in verse 28

worshiper of God. 8Crispus, the synagogue ruler, and his entire household believed in the Lord; and many of the Corinthians who heard him believed and were baptized.

9One night the Lord spoke to Paul in a vision: "Do not be afraid; keep on speaking, do not be silent. 10For I am with you, and no one is going to attack and harm you, because I have many people in this city." 11So Paul stayed for a year and a half, teaching them the word of God.

12While Gallio was proconsul of Achaia, the Jews made a united attack on Paul and brought him into court. 13"This man," they charged, "is persuading the people to worship God in ways contrary to the law."

14Just as Paul was about to speak, Gallio said to the Jews, "If you Jews were making a complaint about some misdemeanor or serious crime, it would be reasonable for me to listen to you. 15But since it involves questions about words and names and your own law—settle the matter yourselves. I will not be a judge of such things." 16So he had them ejected from the court. 17Then they all turned on Sosthenes the synagogue ruler and beat him in front of the court. But Gallio showed no concern whatever.

Priscilla, Aquila and Apollos

18Paul stayed on in Corinth for some time. Then he left the brothers and sailed for Syria, accompanied by Priscilla and Aquila. Before he sailed, he had his hair cut off at Cenchrea because of a vow he had taken. 19They arrived at Ephesus, where Paul left Priscilla and Aquila. He himself went into the synagogue and reasoned with the Jews. 20When they asked him to spend more time with them, he declined. 21But as he left, he promised, "I will come back if it is God's will." Then he set sail from Ephesus. 22When he landed at Caesarea, he went up and greeted the church and then went down to Antioch.

23After spending some time in Antioch, Paul set out from there and traveled from place to place throughout the region of Galatia and Phrygia, strengthening all the disciples.

24Meanwhile a Jew named Apollos, a native of Alexandria, came to Ephesus. He was a learned man, with a thorough knowledge of the Scriptures. 25He had been instructed in the way of the Lord, and he spoke with great fervor[a] and taught about Jesus accurately, though he knew only the baptism of John. 26He began to speak boldly in the synagogue. When Priscilla and Aquila heard him, they invited him to their home and explained to him the way of God more adequately.

27When Apollos wanted to go to Achaia, the brothers encouraged him and wrote to the disciples there to welcome him. On arriving, he was a great help to those who by grace had believed. 28For he vigorously refuted the Jews in public debate, proving from the Scriptures that Jesus was the Christ.

Paul in Ephesus

19 While Apollos was at Corinth, Paul took the road through the interior and arrived at Ephesus. There he found some disciples 2and asked them, "Did you receive the Holy Spirit when[b] you believed?"

They answered, "No, we have not even heard that there is a Holy Spirit."

3So Paul asked, "Then what baptism did you receive?"

"John's baptism," they replied.

4Paul said, "John's baptism was a baptism of repentance. He told the people to believe in the one coming after him, that is, in Jesus." 5On hearing this, they were baptized into[c] the name of the Lord Jesus. 6When Paul placed his hands on them, the Holy Spirit came on them, and they spoke in tongues[d] and prophesied. 7There were about twelve men in all.

8Paul entered the synagogue and spoke boldly there for three months, arguing persuasively about the kingdom of God. 9But some of them became obstinate; they refused to believe and publicly maligned the Way. So Paul left them. He took the disciples with him and had discussions daily in the lecture hall of Tyrannus. 10This went on for two years, so that all the Jews and Greeks who lived in the province of Asia heard the word of the Lord.

11God did extraordinary miracles through Paul, 12so that even handkerchiefs and aprons that had touched him were taken to the sick, and their illnesses were cured and the evil spirits left them.

13Some Jews who went around driving out evil spirits tried to invoke the name of the Lord Jesus over those who were de-

[a]25 Or *with fervor in the Spirit* [b]2 Or *after* [c]5 Or *in* [d]6 Or *other languages*

mon-possessed. They would say, "In the name of Jesus, whom Paul preaches, I command you to come out." [14]Seven sons of Sceva, a Jewish chief priest, were doing this. [15]⌊One day⌋ the evil spirit answered them, "Jesus I know, and I know about Paul, but who are you?" [16]Then the man who had the evil spirit jumped on them and overpowered them all. He gave them such a beating that they ran out of the house naked and bleeding.

[17]When this became known to the Jews and Greeks living in Ephesus, they were all seized with fear, and the name of the Lord Jesus was held in high honor. [18]Many of those who believed now came and openly confessed their evil deeds. [19]A number who had practiced sorcery brought their scrolls together and burned them publicly. When they calculated the value of the scrolls, the total came to fifty thousand drachmas.[a] [20]In this way the word of the Lord spread widely and grew in power.

[21]After all this had happened, Paul decided to go to Jerusalem, passing through Macedonia and Achaia. "After I have been there," he said, "I must visit Rome also." [22]He sent two of his helpers, Timothy and Erastus, to Macedonia, while he stayed in the province of Asia a little longer.

The Riot in Ephesus

[23]About that time there arose a great disturbance about the Way. [24]A silversmith named Demetrius, who made silver shrines of Artemis, brought in no little business for the craftsmen. [25]He called them together, along with the workmen in related trades, and said: "Men, you know we receive a good income from this business. [26]And you see and hear how this fellow Paul has convinced and led astray large numbers of people here in Ephesus and in practically the whole province of Asia. He says that man-made gods are no gods at all. [27]There is danger not only that our trade will lose its good name, but also that the temple of the great goddess Artemis will be discredited, and the goddess herself, who is worshiped throughout the province of Asia and the world, will be robbed of her divine majesty."

[28]When they heard this, they were furious and began shouting: "Great is Artemis of the Ephesians!" [29]Soon the whole city was in an uproar. The people seized Gaius and Aristarchus, Paul's traveling companions from Macedonia, and rushed as one man into the theater. [30]Paul wanted to appear before the crowd, but the disciples would not let him. [31]Even some of the officials of the province, friends of Paul, sent him a message begging him not to venture into the theater.

[32]The assembly was in confusion: Some were shouting one thing, some another. Most of the people did not even know why they were there. [33]The Jews pushed Alexander to the front, and some of the crowd shouted instructions to him. He motioned for silence in order to make a defense before the people. [34]But when they realized he was a Jew, they all shouted in unison for about two hours: "Great is Artemis of the Ephesians!"

[35]The city clerk quieted the crowd and said: "Men of Ephesus, doesn't all the world know that the city of Ephesus is the guardian of the temple of the great Artemis and of her image, which fell from heaven? [36]Therefore, since these facts are undeniable, you ought to be quiet and not do anything rash. [37]You have brought these men here, though they have neither robbed temples nor blasphemed our goddess. [38]If, then, Demetrius and his fellow craftsmen have a grievance against anybody, the courts are open and there are proconsuls. They can press charges. [39]If there is anything further you want to bring up, it must be settled in a legal assembly. [40]As it is, we are in danger of being charged with rioting because of today's events. In that case we would not be able to account for this commotion, since there is no reason for it." [41]After he had said this, he dismissed the assembly.

Through Macedonia and Greece

20 When the uproar had ended, Paul sent for the disciples and, after encouraging them, said good-by and set out for Macedonia. [2]He traveled through that area, speaking many words of encouragement to the people, and finally arrived in Greece, [3]where he stayed three months. Because the Jews made a plot against him just as he was about to sail for Syria, he decided to go back through Macedonia. [4]He was accompanied by Sopater son of

[a]*19* A drachma was a silver coin worth about a day's wages.

Pyrrhus from Berea, Aristarchus and Secundus from Thessalonica, Gaius from Derbe, Timothy also, and Tychicus and Trophimus from the province of Asia. [5]These men went on ahead and waited for us at Troas. [6]But we sailed from Philippi after the Feast of Unleavened Bread, and five days later joined the others at Troas, where we stayed seven days.

Eutychus Raised From the Dead at Troas

[7]On the first day of the week we came together to break bread. Paul spoke to the people and, because he intended to leave the next day, kept on talking until midnight. [8]There were many lamps in the upstairs room where we were meeting. [9]Seated in a window was a young man

VERSE FOR THE DAY: Acts 20:2

AUTHOR: Archibald D. Hart, Ph.D.

PASSAGE FOR THE DAY: Acts 20:1–37

Working Too Hard

How can you keep your work from becoming the primary focus of your life? And how can you keep job stress from having a negative effect on your marriage?

First, don't let your marriage become a dumping ground for your work frustrations. If the only conversation that takes place between a husband and wife is about work, the marriage will eventually burn out. Intimacy can't grow between two people who never explore any of the deeper issues in their lives.

Second, especially with dual-career couples, guard against emotional detachment. Each spouse gets wrapped up in his or her own career, and work becomes a gauge of their self-esteem, rather than the two of them nurturing each other and reminding the other of his or her value.

In contrast, if a couple develops a habit of showing appreciation for the things they value in each other, it will help each of them see his or her value apart from their work. You have to practice affirming your partner before it will become second nature to you. Too many spouses say, "Oh, she knows I like that about her," or, "He knows I value that quality in him." No, they don't know. You need to tell your partner these things over and over.

MARRIAGE BUILDERS

♦ *What do you think is a good balance for what to share and what not to share about work?*

♦ *What is the danger of looking to work successes as a gauge for your self-esteem?*

Additional Scripture Readings
Romans 14:19; 1 Thessalonians 5:11

Go to page 1222 for your next devotional reading.

named Eutychus, who was sinking into a deep sleep as Paul talked on and on. When he was sound asleep, he fell to the ground from the third story and was picked up dead. 10Paul went down, threw himself on the young man and put his arms around him. "Don't be alarmed," he said. "He's alive!" 11Then he went upstairs again and broke bread and ate. After talking until daylight, he left. 12The people took the young man home alive and were greatly comforted.

Paul's Farewell to the Ephesian Elders

13We went on ahead to the ship and sailed for Assos, where we were going to take Paul aboard. He had made this arrangement because he was going there on foot. 14When he met us at Assos, we took him aboard and went on to Mitylene. 15The next day we set sail from there and arrived off Kios. The day after that we crossed over to Samos, and on the following day arrived at Miletus. 16Paul had decided to sail past Ephesus to avoid spending time in the province of Asia, for he was in a hurry to reach Jerusalem, if possible, by the day of Pentecost.

17From Miletus, Paul sent to Ephesus for the elders of the church. 18When they arrived, he said to them: "You know how I lived the whole time I was with you, from the first day I came into the province of Asia. 19I served the Lord with great humility and with tears, although I was severely tested by the plots of the Jews. 20You know that I have not hesitated to preach anything that would be helpful to you but have taught you publicly and from house to house. 21I have declared to both Jews and Greeks that they must turn to God in repentance and have faith in our Lord Jesus.

22"And now, compelled by the Spirit, I am going to Jerusalem, not knowing what will happen to me there. 23I only know that in every city the Holy Spirit warns me that prison and hardships are facing me. 24However, I consider my life worth nothing to me, if only I may finish the race and complete the task the Lord Jesus has given me—the task of testifying to the gospel of God's grace.

25"Now I know that none of you among whom I have gone about preaching the kingdom will ever see me again. 26Therefore, I declare to you today that I am innocent of the blood of all men. 27For I have not hesitated to proclaim to you the whole will of God. 28Keep watch over yourselves and all the flock of which the Holy Spirit has made you overseers.[a] Be shepherds of the church of God,[b] which he bought with his own blood. 29I know that after I leave, savage wolves will come in among you and will not spare the flock. 30Even from your own number men will arise and distort the truth in order to draw away disciples after them. 31So be on your guard! Remember that for three years I never stopped warning each of you night and day with tears.

32"Now I commit you to God and to the word of his grace, which can build you up and give you an inheritance among all those who are sanctified. 33I have not coveted anyone's silver or gold or clothing. 34You yourselves know that these hands of mine have supplied my own needs and the needs of my companions. 35In everything I did, I showed you that by this kind of hard work we must help the weak, remembering the words the Lord Jesus himself said: 'It is more blessed to give than to receive.' "

36When he had said this, he knelt down with all of them and prayed. 37They all wept as they embraced him and kissed him. 38What grieved them most was his statement that they would never see his face again. Then they accompanied him to the ship.

On to Jerusalem

21 After we had torn ourselves away from them, we put out to sea and sailed straight to Cos. The next day we went to Rhodes and from there to Patara. 2We found a ship crossing over to Phoenicia, went on board and set sail. 3After sighting Cyprus and passing to the south of it, we sailed on to Syria. We landed at Tyre, where our ship was to unload its cargo. 4Finding the disciples there, we stayed with them seven days. Through the Spirit they urged Paul not to go on to Jerusalem. 5But when our time was up, we left and continued on our way. All the disciples and their wives and children accompanied us out of the city, and there on the beach we knelt to pray. 6After saying good-by to each other, we went aboard the ship, and they returned home.

[a]28 Traditionally *bishops* [b]28 Many manuscripts *of the Lord*

[7]We continued our voyage from Tyre
and landed at Ptolemais, where we greet-
ed the brothers and stayed with them for
a day. [8]Leaving the next day, we reached
Caesarea and stayed at the house of Philip
the evangelist, one of the Seven. [9]He had
four unmarried daughters who prophe-
sied.

[10]After we had been there a number of
days, a prophet named Agabus came
down from Judea. [11]Coming over to us, he
took Paul's belt, tied his own hands and
feet with it and said, "The Holy Spirit says,
'In this way the Jews of Jerusalem will
bind the owner of this belt and will hand
him over to the Gentiles.' "

[12]When we heard this, we and the peo-
ple there pleaded with Paul not to go up to
Jerusalem. [13]Then Paul answered, "Why
are you weeping and breaking my heart?
I am ready not only to be bound, but also
to die in Jerusalem for the name of the
Lord Jesus." [14]When he would not be dis-
suaded, we gave up and said, "The Lord's
will be done."

[15]After this, we got ready and went up
to Jerusalem. [16]Some of the disciples from
Caesarea accompanied us and brought us
to the home of Mnason, where we were to
stay. He was a man from Cyprus and one
of the early disciples.

Paul's Arrival at Jerusalem

[17]When we arrived at Jerusalem, the
brothers received us warmly. [18]The next
day Paul and the rest of us went to see
James, and all the elders were present.
[19]Paul greeted them and reported in detail
what God had done among the Gentiles
through his ministry.

[20]When they heard this, they praised
God. Then they said to Paul: "You see,
brother, how many thousands of Jews
have believed, and all of them are zealous
for the law. [21]They have been informed
that you teach all the Jews who live
among the Gentiles to turn away from Mo-
ses, telling them not to circumcise their
children or live according to our customs.
[22]What shall we do? They will certainly
hear that you have come, [23]so do what we
tell you. There are four men with us who
have made a vow. [24]Take these men, join
in their purification rites and pay their ex-
penses, so that they can have their heads
shaved. Then everybody will know there
is no truth in these reports about you, but
that you yourself are living in obedience
to the law. [25]As for the Gentile believers,
we have written to them our decision that
they should abstain from food sacrificed
to idols, from blood, from the meat of
strangled animals and from sexual immo-
rality."

[26]The next day Paul took the men and
purified himself along with them. Then he
went to the temple to give notice of the
date when the days of purification would
end and the offering would be made for
each of them.

Paul Arrested

[27]When the seven days were nearly
over, some Jews from the province of Asia
saw Paul at the temple. They stirred up
the whole crowd and seized him, [28]shout-
ing, "Men of Israel, help us! This is the
man who teaches all men everywhere
against our people and our law and this
place. And besides, he has brought Greeks
into the temple area and defiled this holy
place." [29](They had previously seen
Trophimus the Ephesian in the city with
Paul and assumed that Paul had brought
him into the temple area.)

[30]The whole city was aroused, and the
people came running from all directions.
Seizing Paul, they dragged him from the
temple, and immediately the gates were
shut. [31]While they were trying to kill him,
news reached the commander of the Ro-
man troops that the whole city of Jerusa-
lem was in an uproar. [32]He at once took
some officers and soldiers and ran down
to the crowd. When the rioters saw the
commander and his soldiers, they stopped
beating Paul.

[33]The commander came up and arrest-
ed him and ordered him to be bound with
two chains. Then he asked who he was
and what he had done. [34]Some in the
crowd shouted one thing and some anoth-
er, and since the commander could not
get at the truth because of the uproar, he
ordered that Paul be taken into the bar-
racks. [35]When Paul reached the steps, the
violence of the mob was so great he had
to be carried by the soldiers. [36]The crowd
that followed kept shouting, "Away with
him!"

Paul Speaks to the Crowd

[37]As the soldiers were about to take
Paul into the barracks, he asked the com-
mander, "May I say something to you?"

"Do you speak Greek?" he replied.
[38]"Aren't you the Egyptian who started a

revolt and led four thousand terrorists out
into the desert some time ago?"
39Paul answered, "I am a Jew, from Tar-
sus in Cilicia, a citizen of no ordinary city.
Please let me speak to the people."
40Having received the commander's
permission, Paul stood on the steps and
motioned to the crowd. When they were
all silent, he said to them in Aramaic[a]:

22 1"Brothers and fathers, listen now
to my defense."
2When they heard him speak to them in
Aramaic, they became very quiet.
Then Paul said: 3"I am a Jew, born in
Tarsus of Cilicia, but brought up in this
city. Under Gamaliel I was thoroughly
trained in the law of our fathers and was
just as zealous for God as any of you are
today. 4I persecuted the followers of this
Way to their death, arresting both men
and women and throwing them into pris-
on, 5as also the high priest and all the
Council can testify. I even obtained letters
from them to their brothers in Damascus,
and went there to bring these people as
prisoners to Jerusalem to be punished.
6"About noon as I came near Damascus,
suddenly a bright light from heaven
flashed around me. 7I fell to the ground
and heard a voice say to me, 'Saul! Saul!
Why do you persecute me?'
8" 'Who are you, Lord?' I asked.
" 'I am Jesus of Nazareth, whom you
are persecuting,' he replied. 9My compan-
ions saw the light, but they did not under-
stand the voice of him who was speaking
to me.
10" 'What shall I do, Lord?' I asked.
" 'Get up,' the Lord said, 'and go into
Damascus. There you will be told all that
you have been assigned to do.' 11My com-
panions led me by the hand into Damas-
cus, because the brilliance of the light had
blinded me.
12"A man named Ananias came to see
me. He was a devout observer of the law
and highly respected by all the Jews living
there. 13He stood beside me and said,
'Brother Saul, receive your sight!' And at
that very moment I was able to see him.
14"Then he said: 'The God of our fathers
has chosen you to know his will and to see
the Righteous One and to hear words from
his mouth. 15You will be his witness to all
men of what you have seen and heard.
16And now what are you waiting for? Get
up, be baptized and wash your sins away,
calling on his name.'
17"When I returned to Jerusalem and
was praying at the temple, I fell into a
trance 18and saw the Lord speaking.
'Quick!' he said to me. 'Leave Jerusalem
immediately, because they will not accept
your testimony about me.'
19" 'Lord,' I replied, 'these men know
that I went from one synagogue to another
to imprison and beat those who believe in
you. 20And when the blood of your mar-
tyr[b] Stephen was shed, I stood there giv-
ing my approval and guarding the clothes
of those who were killing him.'
21"Then the Lord said to me, 'Go; I will
send you far away to the Gentiles.' "

Paul the Roman Citizen

22The crowd listened to Paul until he
said this. Then they raised their voices
and shouted, "Rid the earth of him! He's
not fit to live!"
23As they were shouting and throwing
off their cloaks and flinging dust into the
air, 24the commander ordered Paul to be
taken into the barracks. He directed that
he be flogged and questioned in order to
find out why the people were shouting at
him like this. 25As they stretched him out
to flog him, Paul said to the centurion
standing there, "Is it legal for you to flog
a Roman citizen who hasn't even been
found guilty?"
26When the centurion heard this, he
went to the commander and reported it.
"What are you going to do?" he asked.
"This man is a Roman citizen."
27The commander went to Paul and
asked, "Tell me, are you a Roman citi-
zen?"
"Yes, I am," he answered.
28Then the commander said, "I had to
pay a big price for my citizenship."
"But I was born a citizen," Paul replied.
29Those who were about to question
him withdrew immediately. The com-
mander himself was alarmed when he re-
alized that he had put Paul, a Roman citi-
zen, in chains.

Before the Sanhedrin

30The next day, since the commander
wanted to find out exactly why Paul was
being accused by the Jews, he released
him and ordered the chief priests and all
the Sanhedrin to assemble. Then he

[a]40 Or possibly *Hebrew*; also in 22:2 [b]20 Or *witness*

brought Paul and had him stand before them.

23 Paul looked straight at the Sanhedrin and said, "My brothers, I have fulfilled my duty to God in all good conscience to this day." [2]At this the high priest Ananias ordered those standing near Paul to strike him on the mouth. [3]Then Paul said to him, "God will strike you, you whitewashed wall! You sit there to judge me according to the law, yet you yourself violate the law by commanding that I be struck!"

[4]Those who were standing near Paul said, "You dare to insult God's high priest?"

[5]Paul replied, "Brothers, I did not realize that he was the high priest; for it is written: 'Do not speak evil about the ruler of your people.'[a]"

[6]Then Paul, knowing that some of them were Sadducees and the others Pharisees, called out in the Sanhedrin, "My brothers, I am a Pharisee, the son of a Pharisee. I stand on trial because of my hope in the resurrection of the dead." [7]When he said this, a dispute broke out between the Pharisees and the Sadducees, and the assembly was divided. [8](The Sadducees say that there is no resurrection, and that there are neither angels nor spirits, but the Pharisees acknowledge them all.)

[9]There was a great uproar, and some of the teachers of the law who were Pharisees stood up and argued vigorously. "We find nothing wrong with this man," they said. "What if a spirit or an angel has spoken to him?" [10]The dispute became so violent that the commander was afraid Paul would be torn to pieces by them. He ordered the troops to go down and take him away from them by force and bring him into the barracks.

[11]The following night the Lord stood near Paul and said, "Take courage! As you have testified about me in Jerusalem, so you must also testify in Rome."

The Plot to Kill Paul

[12]The next morning the Jews formed a conspiracy and bound themselves with an oath not to eat or drink until they had killed Paul. [13]More than forty men were involved in this plot. [14]They went to the chief priests and elders and said, "We have taken a solemn oath not to eat anything until we have killed Paul. [15]Now then, you and the Sanhedrin petition the commander to bring him before you on the pretext of wanting more accurate information about his case. We are ready to kill him before he gets here."

[16]But when the son of Paul's sister heard of this plot, he went into the barracks and told Paul.

[17]Then Paul called one of the centurions and said, "Take this young man to the commander; he has something to tell him." [18]So he took him to the commander.

The centurion said, "Paul, the prisoner, sent for me and asked me to bring this young man to you because he has something to tell you."

[19]The commander took the young man by the hand, drew him aside and asked, "What is it you want to tell me?"

[20]He said: "The Jews have agreed to ask you to bring Paul before the Sanhedrin tomorrow on the pretext of wanting more accurate information about him. [21]Don't give in to them, because more than forty of them are waiting in ambush for him. They have taken an oath not to eat or drink until they have killed him. They are ready now, waiting for your consent to their request."

[22]The commander dismissed the young man and cautioned him, "Don't tell anyone that you have reported this to me."

Paul Transferred to Caesarea

[23]Then he called two of his centurions and ordered them, "Get ready a detachment of two hundred soldiers, seventy horsemen and two hundred spearmen[b] to go to Caesarea at nine tonight. [24]Provide mounts for Paul so that he may be taken safely to Governor Felix."

[25]He wrote a letter as follows:

[26]Claudius Lysias,

To His Excellency, Governor Felix:

Greetings.

[27]This man was seized by the Jews and they were about to kill him, but I came with my troops and rescued him, for I had learned that he is a Roman citizen. [28]I wanted to know why they were accusing him, so I brought him to their Sanhedrin. [29]I found that the accusation had to do with questions about their law, but there was

[a]5 Exodus 22:28 [b]23 The meaning of the Greek for this word is uncertain.

no charge against him that deserved death or imprisonment. 30When I was informed of a plot to be carried out against the man, I sent him to you at once. I also ordered his accusers to present to you their case against him.

31So the soldiers, carrying out their orders, took Paul with them during the night and brought him as far as Antipatris. 32The next day they let the cavalry go on with him, while they returned to the barracks. 33When the cavalry arrived in Caesarea, they delivered the letter to the governor and handed Paul over to him. 34The governor read the letter and asked what province he was from. Learning that he was from Cilicia, 35he said, "I will hear your case when your accusers get here." Then he ordered that Paul be kept under guard in Herod's palace.

The Trial Before Felix

24 Five days later the high priest Ananias went down to Caesarea with some of the elders and a lawyer named Tertullus, and they brought their charges against Paul before the governor. 2When Paul was called in, Tertullus presented his case before Felix: "We have enjoyed a long period of peace under you, and your foresight has brought about reforms in this nation. 3Everywhere and in every way, most excellent Felix, we acknowledge this with profound gratitude. 4But in order not to weary you further, I would request that you be kind enough to hear us briefly.

5"We have found this man to be a troublemaker, stirring up riots among the Jews all over the world. He is a ringleader of the Nazarene sect 6and even tried to desecrate the temple; so we seized him. 8By[a] examining him yourself you will be able to learn the truth about all these charges we are bringing against him."

9The Jews joined in the accusation, asserting that these things were true.

10When the governor motioned for him to speak, Paul replied: "I know that for a number of years you have been a judge over this nation; so I gladly make my defense. 11You can easily verify that no more than twelve days ago I went up to Jerusalem to worship. 12My accusers did not find me arguing with anyone at the temple, or stirring up a crowd in the synagogues or anywhere else in the city. 13And they cannot prove to you the charges they are now making against me. 14However, I admit that I worship the God of our fathers as a follower of the Way, which they call a sect. I believe everything that agrees with the Law and that is written in the Prophets, 15and I have the same hope in God as these men, that there will be a resurrection of both the righteous and the wicked. 16So I strive always to keep my conscience clear before God and man.

17"After an absence of several years, I came to Jerusalem to bring my people gifts for the poor and to present offerings. 18I was ceremonially clean when they found me in the temple courts doing this. There was no crowd with me, nor was I involved in any disturbance. 19But there are some Jews from the province of Asia, who ought to be here before you and bring charges if they have anything against me. 20Or these who are here should state what crime they found in me when I stood before the Sanhedrin—21unless it was this one thing I shouted as I stood in their presence: 'It is concerning the resurrection of the dead that I am on trial before you today.' "

22Then Felix, who was well acquainted with the Way, adjourned the proceedings. "When Lysias the commander comes," he said, "I will decide your case." 23He ordered the centurion to keep Paul under guard but to give him some freedom and permit his friends to take care of his needs.

24Several days later Felix came with his wife Drusilla, who was a Jewess. He sent for Paul and listened to him as he spoke about faith in Christ Jesus. 25As Paul discoursed on righteousness, self-control and the judgment to come, Felix was afraid and said, "That's enough for now! You may leave. When I find it convenient, I will send for you." 26At the same time he was hoping that Paul would offer him a bribe, so he sent for him frequently and talked with him.

27When two years had passed, Felix was succeeded by Porcius Festus, but because Felix wanted to grant a favor to the Jews, he left Paul in prison.

[a]*6-8* Some manuscripts *him and wanted to judge him according to our law. 7But the commander, Lysias, came and with the use of much force snatched him from our hands 8and ordered his accusers to come before you. By*

The Trial Before Festus

25 Three days after arriving in the province, Festus went up from Caesarea to Jerusalem, [2]where the chief priests and Jewish leaders appeared before him and presented the charges against Paul. [3]They urgently requested Festus, as a favor to them, to have Paul transferred to Jerusalem, for they were preparing an ambush to kill him along the way. [4]Festus answered, "Paul is being held at Caesarea, and I myself am going there soon. [5]Let some of your leaders come with me and press charges against the man there, if he has done anything wrong."

[6]After spending eight or ten days with them, he went down to Caesarea, and the next day he convened the court and ordered that Paul be brought before him. [7]When Paul appeared, the Jews who had come down from Jerusalem stood around him, bringing many serious charges against him, which they could not prove.

[8]Then Paul made his defense: "I have done nothing wrong against the law of the Jews or against the temple or against Caesar."

[9]Festus, wishing to do the Jews a favor, said to Paul, "Are you willing to go up to Jerusalem and stand trial before me there on these charges?"

[10]Paul answered: "I am now standing before Caesar's court, where I ought to be tried. I have not done any wrong to the Jews, as you yourself know very well. [11]If, however, I am guilty of doing anything deserving death, I do not refuse to die. But if the charges brought against me by these Jews are not true, no one has the right to hand me over to them. I appeal to Caesar!"

[12]After Festus had conferred with his council, he declared: "You have appealed to Caesar. To Caesar you will go!"

Festus Consults King Agrippa

[13]A few days later King Agrippa and Bernice arrived at Caesarea to pay their respects to Festus. [14]Since they were spending many days there, Festus discussed Paul's case with the king. He said: "There is a man here whom Felix left as a prisoner. [15]When I went to Jerusalem, the chief priests and elders of the Jews brought charges against him and asked that he be condemned.

[16]"I told them that it is not the Roman custom to hand over any man before he has faced his accusers and has had an opportunity to defend himself against their charges. [17]When they came here with me, I did not delay the case, but convened the court the next day and ordered the man to be brought in. [18]When his accusers got up to speak, they did not charge him with any of the crimes I had expected. [19]Instead, they had some points of dispute with him about their own religion and about a dead man named Jesus who Paul claimed was alive. [20]I was at a loss how to investigate such matters; so I asked if he would be willing to go to Jerusalem and stand trial there on these charges. [21]When Paul made his appeal to be held over for the Emperor's decision, I ordered him held until I could send him to Caesar."

[22]Then Agrippa said to Festus, "I would like to hear this man myself."

He replied, "Tomorrow you will hear him."

Paul Before Agrippa

[23]The next day Agrippa and Bernice came with great pomp and entered the audience room with the high ranking officers and the leading men of the city. At the command of Festus, Paul was brought in. [24]Festus said: "King Agrippa, and all who are present with us, you see this man! The whole Jewish community has petitioned me about him in Jerusalem and here in Caesarea, shouting that he ought not to live any longer. [25]I found he had done nothing deserving of death, but because he made his appeal to the Emperor I decided to send him to Rome. [26]But I have nothing definite to write to His Majesty about him. Therefore I have brought him before all of you, and especially before you, King Agrippa, so that as a result of this investigation I may have something to write. [27]For I think it is unreasonable to send on a prisoner without specifying the charges against him."

26 Then Agrippa said to Paul, "You have permission to speak for yourself."

So Paul motioned with his hand and began his defense: [2]"King Agrippa, I consider myself fortunate to stand before you today as I make my defense against all the accusations of the Jews, [3]and especially so because you are well acquainted with all the Jewish customs and controversies. Therefore, I beg you to listen to me patiently.

[4]"The Jews all know the way I have
lived ever since I was a child, from the be-
ginning of my life in my own country, and
also in Jerusalem. [5]They have known me
for a long time and can testify, if they are
willing, that according to the strictest sect
of our religion, I lived as a Pharisee. [6]And
now it is because of my hope in what God
has promised our fathers that I am on trial
today. [7]This is the promise our twelve
tribes are hoping to see fulfilled as they
earnestly serve God day and night. O king,
it is because of this hope that the Jews are
accusing me. [8]Why should any of you
consider it incredible that God raises the
dead?

[9]"I too was convinced that I ought to do
all that was possible to oppose the name
of Jesus of Nazareth. [10]And that is just
what I did in Jerusalem. On the authority
of the chief priests I put many of the saints
in prison, and when they were put to
death, I cast my vote against them.
[11]Many a time I went from one synagogue
to another to have them punished, and I
tried to force them to blaspheme. In my
obsession against them, I even went to
foreign cities to persecute them.

[12]"On one of these journeys I was going
to Damascus with the authority and com-
mission of the chief priests. [13]About noon,
O king, as I was on the road, I saw a light
from heaven, brighter than the sun, blaz-
ing around me and my companions. [14]We
all fell to the ground, and I heard a voice
saying to me in Aramaic,[a] 'Saul, Saul,
why do you persecute me? It is hard for
you to kick against the goads.'

[15]"Then I asked, 'Who are you, Lord?'

" 'I am Jesus, whom you are persecut-
ing,' the Lord replied. [16]'Now get up and
stand on your feet. I have appeared to you
to appoint you as a servant and as a wit-
ness of what you have seen of me and
what I will show you. [17]I will rescue you
from your own people and from the Gen-
tiles. I am sending you to them [18]to open
their eyes and turn them from darkness to
light, and from the power of Satan to God,
so that they may receive forgiveness of
sins and a place among those who are
sanctified by faith in me.'

[19]"So then, King Agrippa, I was not dis-
obedient to the vision from heaven. [20]First
to those in Damascus, then to those in Je-
rusalem and in all Judea, and to the Gen-
tiles also, I preached that they should re-
pent and turn to God and prove their
repentance by their deeds. [21]That is why
the Jews seized me in the temple courts
and tried to kill me. [22]But I have had God's
help to this very day, and so I stand here
and testify to small and great alike. I am
saying nothing beyond what the prophets
and Moses said would happen— [23]that
the Christ[b] would suffer and, as the first
to rise from the dead, would proclaim
light to his own people and to the Gen-
tiles."

[24]At this point Festus interrupted Paul's
defense. "You are out of your mind, Paul!"
he shouted. "Your great learning is driving
you insane."

[25]"I am not insane, most excellent Fes-
tus," Paul replied. "What I am saying is
true and reasonable. [26]The king is familiar
with these things, and I can speak freely to
him. I am convinced that none of this has
escaped his notice, because it was not
done in a corner. [27]King Agrippa, do you
believe the prophets? I know you do."

[28]Then Agrippa said to Paul, "Do you
think that in such a short time you can
persuade me to be a Christian?"

[29]Paul replied, "Short time or long—I
pray God that not only you but all who are
listening to me today may become what I
am, except for these chains."

[30]The king rose, and with him the gov-
ernor and Bernice and those sitting with
them. [31]They left the room, and while
talking with one another, they said, "This
man is not doing anything that deserves
death or imprisonment."

[32]Agrippa said to Festus, "This man
could have been set free if he had not ap-
pealed to Caesar."

Paul Sails for Rome

27 When it was decided that we
would sail for Italy, Paul and some
other prisoners were handed over to a
centurion named Julius, who belonged to
the Imperial Regiment. [2]We boarded a
ship from Adramyttium about to sail for
ports along the coast of the province of
Asia, and we put out to sea. Aristarchus, a
Macedonian from Thessalonica, was
with us.

[3]The next day we landed at Sidon; and
Julius, in kindness to Paul, allowed him to
go to his friends so they might provide for
his needs. [4]From there we put out to sea
again and passed to the lee of Cyprus be-

[a]14 Or *Hebrew* [b]23 Or *Messiah*

cause the winds were against us. 5When
we had sailed across the open sea off the
coast of Cilicia and Pamphylia, we landed
at Myra in Lycia. 6There the centurion
found an Alexandrian ship sailing for Italy
and put us on board. 7We made slow
headway for many days and had difficulty
arriving off Cnidus. When the wind did
not allow us to hold our course, we sailed
to the lee of Crete, opposite Salmone. 8We
moved along the coast with difficulty and
came to a place called Fair Havens, near
the town of Lasea.

9Much time had been lost, and sailing
had already become dangerous because
by now it was after the Fast.[a] So Paul
warned them, 10"Men, I can see that our
voyage is going to be disastrous and bring
great loss to ship and cargo, and to our
own lives also." 11But the centurion, in-
stead of listening to what Paul said, fol-
lowed the advice of the pilot and of the
owner of the ship. 12Since the harbor was
unsuitable to winter in, the majority de-
cided that we should sail on, hoping to
reach Phoenix and winter there. This was
a harbor in Crete, facing both southwest
and northwest.

The Storm

13When a gentle south wind began to
blow, they thought they had obtained
what they wanted; so they weighed an-
chor and sailed along the shore of Crete.
14Before very long, a wind of hurricane
force, called the "northeaster," swept
down from the island. 15The ship was
caught by the storm and could not head
into the wind; so we gave way to it and
were driven along. 16As we passed to the
lee of a small island called Cauda, we were
hardly able to make the lifeboat secure.
17When the men had hoisted it aboard,
they passed ropes under the ship itself to
hold it together. Fearing that they would
run aground on the sandbars of Syrtis,
they lowered the sea anchor and let the
ship be driven along. 18We took such a vi-
olent battering from the storm that the
next day they began to throw the cargo
overboard. 19On the third day, they threw
the ship's tackle overboard with their own
hands. 20When neither sun nor stars ap-
peared for many days and the storm con-
tinued raging, we finally gave up all hope
of being saved.

21After the men had gone a long time
without food, Paul stood up before them
and said: "Men, you should have taken
my advice not to sail from Crete; then you
would have spared yourselves this dam-
age and loss. 22But now I urge you to keep
up your courage, because not one of you
will be lost; only the ship will be de-
stroyed. 23Last night an angel of the God
whose I am and whom I serve stood be-
side me 24and said, 'Do not be afraid, Paul.
You must stand trial before Caesar; and
God has graciously given you the lives of
all who sail with you.' 25So keep up your
courage, men, for I have faith in God that
it will happen just as he told me. 26Never-
theless, we must run aground on some is-
land."

The Shipwreck

27On the fourteenth night we were still
being driven across the Adriatic[b] Sea,
when about midnight the sailors sensed
they were approaching land. 28They took
soundings and found that the water was a
hundred and twenty feet[c] deep. A short
time later they took soundings again and
found it was ninety feet[d] deep. 29Fearing
that we would be dashed against the
rocks, they dropped four anchors from the
stern and prayed for daylight. 30In an at-
tempt to escape from the ship, the sailors
let the lifeboat down into the sea, pretend-
ing they were going to lower some an-
chors from the bow. 31Then Paul said to
the centurion and the soldiers, "Unless
these men stay with the ship, you cannot
be saved." 32So the soldiers cut the ropes
that held the lifeboat and let it fall away.

33Just before dawn Paul urged them all
to eat. "For the last fourteen days," he
said, "you have been in constant suspense
and have gone without food—you haven't
eaten anything. 34Now I urge you to take
some food. You need it to survive. Not one
of you will lose a single hair from his
head." 35After he said this, he took some
bread and gave thanks to God in front of
them all. Then he broke it and began to
eat. 36They were all encouraged and ate
some food themselves. 37Altogether there
were 276 of us on board. 38When they had
eaten as much as they wanted, they light-

[a] 9 That is, the Day of Atonement (Yom Kippur) [b] 27 In ancient times the name referred to an area extending well south of Italy. [c] 28 Greek *twenty orguias* (about 37 meters) [d] 28 Greek *fifteen orguias* (about 27 meters)

ened the ship by throwing the grain into the sea.

39When daylight came, they did not recognize the land, but they saw a bay with a sandy beach, where they decided to run the ship aground if they could. 40Cutting loose the anchors, they left them in the sea and at the same time untied the ropes that held the rudders. Then they hoisted the foresail to the wind and made for the beach. 41But the ship struck a sandbar and ran aground. The bow stuck fast and would not move, and the stern was broken to pieces by the pounding of the surf.

42The soldiers planned to kill the prisoners to prevent any of them from swimming away and escaping. 43But the centurion wanted to spare Paul's life and kept them from carrying out their plan. He ordered those who could swim to jump overboard first and get to land. 44The rest were to get there on planks or on pieces of the ship. In this way everyone reached land in safety.

Ashore on Malta

28 Once safely on shore, we found out that the island was called Malta. 2The islanders showed us unusual kindness. They built a fire and welcomed us all because it was raining and cold. 3Paul gathered a pile of brushwood and, as he put it on the fire, a viper, driven out by the heat, fastened itself on his hand. 4When the islanders saw the snake hanging from his hand, they said to each other, "This man must be a murderer; for though he escaped from the sea, Justice has not allowed him to live." 5But Paul shook the snake off into the fire and suffered no ill effects. 6The people expected him to swell up or suddenly fall dead, but after waiting a long time and seeing nothing unusual happen to him, they changed their minds and said he was a god.

7There was an estate nearby that belonged to Publius, the chief official of the island. He welcomed us to his home and for three days entertained us hospitably. 8His father was sick in bed, suffering from fever and dysentery. Paul went in to see him and, after prayer, placed his hands on him and healed him. 9When this had happened, the rest of the sick on the island came and were cured. 10They honored us in many ways and when we were ready to sail, they furnished us with the supplies we needed.

Arrival at Rome

11After three months we put out to sea in a ship that had wintered in the island. It was an Alexandrian ship with the figurehead of the twin gods Castor and Pollux. 12We put in at Syracuse and stayed there three days. 13From there we set sail and arrived at Rhegium. The next day the south wind came up, and on the following day we reached Puteoli. 14There we found some brothers who invited us to spend a week with them. And so we came to Rome. 15The brothers there had heard that we were coming, and they traveled as far as the Forum of Appius and the Three Taverns to meet us. At the sight of these men Paul thanked God and was encouraged. 16When we got to Rome, Paul was allowed to live by himself, with a soldier to guard him.

Paul Preaches at Rome Under Guard

17Three days later he called together the leaders of the Jews. When they had assembled, Paul said to them: "My brothers, although I have done nothing against our people or against the customs of our ancestors, I was arrested in Jerusalem and handed over to the Romans. 18They examined me and wanted to release me, because I was not guilty of any crime deserving death. 19But when the Jews objected, I was compelled to appeal to Caesar—not that I had any charge to bring against my own people. 20For this reason I have asked to see you and talk with you. It is because of the hope of Israel that I am bound with this chain."

21They replied, "We have not received any letters from Judea concerning you, and none of the brothers who have come from there has reported or said anything bad about you. 22But we want to hear what your views are, for we know that people everywhere are talking against this sect."

23They arranged to meet Paul on a certain day, and came in even larger numbers to the place where he was staying. From morning till evening he explained and declared to them the kingdom of God and tried to convince them about Jesus from the Law of Moses and from the Prophets. 24Some were convinced by what he said, but others would not believe. 25They disagreed among themselves and began to leave after Paul had made this final statement: "The Holy Spirit spoke the truth to your forefathers when he said through Isaiah the prophet:

26" 'Go to this people and say,
"You will be ever hearing but never understanding;
you will be ever seeing but never perceiving."
27For this people's heart has become calloused;
they hardly hear with their ears,
and they have closed their eyes.
Otherwise they might see with their eyes,
hear with their ears,
understand with their hearts
and turn, and I would heal them.'[a]

28"Therefore I want you to know that God's salvation has been sent to the Gentiles, and they will listen!"[b]

30For two whole years Paul stayed there in his own rented house and welcomed all who came to see him. 31Boldly and without hindrance he preached the kingdom of God and taught about the Lord Jesus Christ.

[a]27 Isaiah 6:9,10 [b]28 Some manuscripts *listen!"* 29*After he said this, the Jews left, arguing vigorously among themselves.*

PAUL, planning a mission trip to Spain (Romans 15:23–29), writes this letter to introduce himself to the church at Rome. In it he summarizes what he has been preaching about sin, Christ, and the way of salvation. Everything you need to know about God's great plan for redemption lies in these sixteen chapters. As you read the book, think about how much God loves you in sending his Son Jesus and how you can say thank you to him by the life you live.

ROMANS

1 Paul, a servant of Christ Jesus, called
to be an apostle and set apart for the
gospel of God— 2the gospel he promised
beforehand through his prophets in the
Holy Scriptures 3regarding his Son, who
as to his human nature was a descendant
of David, 4and who through the Spirit[a] of
holiness was declared with power to be
the Son of God[b] by his resurrection from
the dead: Jesus Christ our Lord. 5Through
him and for his name's sake, we received
grace and apostleship to call people from
among all the Gentiles to the obedience
that comes from faith. 6And you also are
among those who are called to belong to
Jesus Christ.

7To all in Rome who are loved by God
and called to be saints:

Grace and peace to you from God our
Father and from the Lord Jesus Christ.

Paul's Longing to Visit Rome

8First, I thank my God through Jesus
Christ for all of you, because your faith
is being reported all over the world.
9God, whom I serve with my whole heart
in preaching the gospel of his Son, is
my witness how constantly I remember
you 10in my prayers at all times; and I
pray that now at last by God's will the

[a]4 Or *who as to his spirit* [b]4 Or *was appointed to be the Son of God with power*

way may be opened for me to come to you.

11I long to see you so that I may impart to you some spiritual gift to make you strong— 12that is, that you and I may be mutually encouraged by each other's faith. 13I do not want you to be unaware, brothers, that I planned many times to come to you (but have been prevented from doing so until now) in order that I might have a harvest among you, just as I have had among the other Gentiles.

14I am obligated both to Greeks and non-Greeks, both to the wise and the foolish. 15That is why I am so eager to preach the gospel also to you who are at Rome.

16I am not ashamed of the gospel, because it is the power of God for the salvation of everyone who believes: first for the Jew, then for the Gentile. 17For in the gospel a righteousness from God is revealed, a righteousness that is by faith from first to last,[a] just as it is written: "The righteous will live by faith."[b]

God's Wrath Against Mankind

18The wrath of God is being revealed from heaven against all the godlessness and wickedness of men who suppress the truth by their wickedness, 19since what may be known about God is plain to them, because God has made it plain to them. 20For since the creation of the world God's invisible qualities—his eternal power and divine nature—have been clearly seen, being understood from what has been made, so that men are without excuse.

21For although they knew God, they neither glorified him as God nor gave thanks to him, but their thinking became futile and their foolish hearts were darkened. 22Although they claimed to be wise, they became fools 23and exchanged the glory of the immortal God for images made to look like mortal man and birds and animals and reptiles.

24Therefore God gave them over in the sinful desires of their hearts to sexual impurity for the degrading of their bodies with one another. 25They exchanged the truth of God for a lie, and worshiped and served created things rather than the Creator—who is forever praised. Amen.

26Because of this, God gave them over to shameful lusts. Even their women exchanged natural relations for unnatural ones. 27In the same way the men also abandoned natural relations with women and were inflamed with lust for one another. Men committed indecent acts with other men, and received in themselves the due penalty for their perversion.

28Furthermore, since they did not think it worthwhile to retain the knowledge of God, he gave them over to a depraved mind, to do what ought not to be done. 29They have become filled with every kind of wickedness, evil, greed and depravity. They are full of envy, murder, strife, deceit and malice. They are gossips, 30slanderers, God-haters, insolent, arrogant and boastful; they invent ways of doing evil; they disobey their parents; 31they are senseless, faithless, heartless, ruthless. 32Although they know God's righteous decree that those who do such things deserve death, they not only continue to do these very things but also approve of those who practice them.

God's Righteous Judgment

2 You, therefore, have no excuse, you who pass judgment on someone else, for at whatever point you judge the other, you are condemning yourself, because you who pass judgment do the same things. 2Now we know that God's judgment against those who do such things is based on truth. 3So when you, a mere man, pass judgment on them and yet do the same things, do you think you will escape God's judgment? 4Or do you show contempt for the riches of his kindness, tolerance and patience, not realizing that God's kindness leads you toward repentance?

5But because of your stubbornness and your unrepentant heart, you are storing up wrath against yourself for the day of God's wrath, when his righteous judgment will be revealed. 6God "will give to each person according to what he has done."[c] 7To those who by persistence in doing good seek glory, honor and immortality, he will give eternal life. 8But for those who are self-seeking and who reject the truth and follow evil, there will be wrath and anger. 9There will be trouble and distress for every human being who does evil: first for the Jew, then for the Gentile; 10but glory, honor and peace for everyone who does good: first for the Jew,

[a]17 Or *is from faith to faith* [b]17 Hab. 2:4 [c]6 Psalm 62:12; Prov. 24:12

then for the Gentile. 11For God does not
show favoritism.
12All who sin apart from the law will
also perish apart from the law, and all who
sin under the law will be judged by the
law. 13For it is not those who hear the law
who are righteous in God's sight, but it is
those who obey the law who will be de-
clared righteous. 14(Indeed, when Gen-
tiles, who do not have the law, do by na-
ture things required by the law, they are a
law for themselves, even though they do
not have the law, 15since they show that
the requirements of the law are written on
their hearts, their consciences also bear-
ing witness, and their thoughts now ac-

VERSE FOR THE DAY:
Romans 2:4

AUTHOR:
Frank Peretti

PASSAGE FOR THE DAY:
Romans 2:1–16

God's Kindness

Barbara and I were married fifteen years before we had a steady income. We were poor as dirt. We used to live in an 8-foot-by-24-foot trailer with a shack attached. It was hard looking for God's will, struggling to find the work God wanted us to do. But looking back, Barb and I would go through our poor days again in a minute. We were all we had—us and the Lord.

I marveled that Barb stuck by me all those years. I'm honored to have her along. Success, the big house—without Barb it would be empty and pointless. Remember the first couple of *Godfather* movies? They ended with some man who was rich beyond measure in money but completely devoid of human love. One of the movies even ends with the decrepit old guy sitting alone in a rocker out in the cold.

I don't want that kind of "success." At the end of my days, even if I were sitting alone on someone else's porch in a borrowed rocker, I'd be a satisfied man if I had buried my wife in peace, knowing that on her last day we were very much in love.

That would make me the richest man in the world.

MARRIAGE BUILDERS

♦ *In what ways are the two of you "rich," even if you struggle financially?*

♦ *Does your daily planner reflect a high priority on your relationship as well as the pursuit of material provision?*

Additional Scripture Readings
Micah 6:6–8; 1 Corinthians 1:25–31

Go to page 1224 for your next devotional reading.

cusing, now even defending them.) 16This will take place on the day when God will judge men's secrets through Jesus Christ, as my gospel declares.

The Jews and the Law

17Now you, if you call yourself a Jew; if you rely on the law and brag about your relationship to God; 18if you know his will and approve of what is superior because you are instructed by the law; 19if you are convinced that you are a guide for the blind, a light for those who are in the dark, 20an instructor of the foolish, a teacher of infants, because you have in the law the embodiment of knowledge and truth— 21you, then, who teach others, do you not teach yourself? You who preach against stealing, do you steal? 22You who say that people should not commit adultery, do you commit adultery? You who abhor idols, do you rob temples? 23You who brag about the law, do you dishonor God by breaking the law? 24As it is written: "God's name is blasphemed among the Gentiles because of you."[a]

25Circumcision has value if you observe the law, but if you break the law, you have become as though you had not been circumcised. 26If those who are not circumcised keep the law's requirements, will they not be regarded as though they were circumcised? 27The one who is not circumcised physically and yet obeys the law will condemn you who, even though you have the[b] written code and circumcision, are a lawbreaker.

28A man is not a Jew if he is only one outwardly, nor is circumcision merely outward and physical. 29No, a man is a Jew if he is one inwardly; and circumcision is circumcision of the heart, by the Spirit, not by the written code. Such a man's praise is not from men, but from God.

God's Faithfulness

3 What advantage, then, is there in being a Jew, or what value is there in circumcision? 2Much in every way! First of all, they have been entrusted with the very words of God.

3What if some did not have faith? Will their lack of faith nullify God's faithfulness? 4Not at all! Let God be true, and every man a liar. As it is written:

"So that you may be proved right
when you speak
and prevail when you judge."[c]

5But if our unrighteousness brings out God's righteousness more clearly, what shall we say? That God is unjust in bringing his wrath on us? (I am using a human argument.) 6Certainly not! If that were so, how could God judge the world? 7Some one might argue, "If my falsehood enhances God's truthfulness and so increases his glory, why am I still condemned as a sinner?" 8Why not say—as we are being slanderously reported as saying and as some claim that we say—"Let us do evil that good may result"? Their condemnation is deserved.

No One Is Righteous

9What shall we conclude then? Are we any better[d]? Not at all! We have already made the charge that Jews and Gentiles alike are all under sin. 10As it is written:

"There is no one righteous, not even one;
11 there is no one who understands,
no one who seeks God.
12All have turned away,
they have together become worthless;
there is no one who does good,
not even one."[e]
13"Their throats are open graves;
their tongues practice deceit."[f]
"The poison of vipers is on their lips."[g]
14 "Their mouths are full of cursing and bitterness."[h]
15"Their feet are swift to shed blood;
16 ruin and misery mark their ways,
17and the way of peace they do not know."[i]
18 "There is no fear of God before their eyes."[j]

19Now we know that whatever the law says, it says to those who are under the law, so that every mouth may be silenced and the whole world held accountable to God. 20Therefore no one will be declared righteous in his sight by observing the

[a] 24 Isaiah 52:5; Ezek. 36:22 [b] 27 Or *who, by means of a* [c] 4 Psalm 51:4 [d] 9 Or *worse*
[e] 12 Psalms 14:1-3; 53:1-3; Eccles. 7:20 [f] 13 Psalm 5:9 [g] 13 Psalm 140:3 [h] 14 Psalm 10:7
[i] 17 Isaiah 59:7,8 [j] 18 Psalm 36:1

law; rather, through the law we become conscious of sin.

Righteousness Through Faith

21But now a righteousness from God, apart from law, has been made known, to which the Law and the Prophets testify. 22This righteousness from God comes through faith in Jesus Christ to all who believe. There is no difference, 23for all have sinned and fall short of the glory of God, 24and are justified freely by his grace through the redemption that came by Christ Jesus. 25God presented him as a

THURSDAY

VERSE FOR THE DAY: Romans 3:20

AUTHOR: Ruth Senter

PASSAGE FOR THE DAY: Romans 3:9–31

The Freedom of Limits

Many years ago, our neighbors started fencing in their back yards. But not long after, I noticed that people gathered by their fences to talk. Never before, it seemed, had news flowed so freely. It seemed that fences had provided a security that promoted conversation.

Fences represent the human need for fixed limits. Sometimes boundaries make me feel secure, but sometimes they make me feel restricted. Fence me in and I immediately want freedom. I remember undergoing a tonsillectomy as a six-year-old. Things were fairly peaceful in the operating room until the nurse tried to tie my hands to the side of the table. Then the doctor had a tiger on his hands.

A part of me still resists prescribed limits, whether they be diets, speed limits or God's "Thou shalt nots." God's Word reminds me of my limits.

Freedom is not untied hands, but understanding what restraints can do for me. I need God's boundaries to show me the difference between obedience and disobedience. Through the law, Paul says in Romans 3:20, "we become conscious of sin."

I can't say I enjoy discipline. But I've learned that it provides the fences I need to truly enjoy others. Freedom is not an absence of limits but a positive attitude toward restraint.

MARRIAGE BUILDERS

♦ *One of God's boundaries for marriage is sexual fidelity and purity. How does that "limit" actually protect you and your marriage?*
♦ *What other ways have you experienced freedom as a result of limits or restraints?*

Additional Scripture Readings
Psalm 25:21; Proverbs 2:1; Micah 6:8

Go to page 1226 for your next devotional reading.

sacrifice of atonement,[a] through faith in his blood. He did this to demonstrate his justice, because in his forbearance he had left the sins committed beforehand unpunished— 26he did it to demonstrate his justice at the present time, so as to be just and the one who justifies those who have faith in Jesus.

27Where, then, is boasting? It is excluded. On what principle? On that of observing the law? No, but on that of faith. 28For we maintain that a man is justified by faith apart from observing the law. 29Is God the God of Jews only? Is he not the God of Gentiles too? Yes, of Gentiles too, 30since there is only one God, who will justify the circumcised by faith and the uncircumcised through that same faith. 31Do we, then, nullify the law by this faith? Not at all! Rather, we uphold the law.

Abraham Justified by Faith

4 What then shall we say that Abraham, our forefather, discovered in this matter? 2If, in fact, Abraham was justified by works, he had something to boast about—but not before God. 3What does the Scripture say? "Abraham believed God, and it was credited to him as righteousness."[b]

4Now when a man works, his wages are not credited to him as a gift, but as an obligation. 5However, to the man who does not work but trusts God who justifies the wicked, his faith is credited as righteousness. 6David says the same thing when he speaks of the blessedness of the man to whom God credits righteousness apart from works:

7"Blessed are they
whose transgressions are forgiven,
whose sins are covered.
8Blessed is the man
whose sin the Lord will never count
against him."[c]

9Is this blessedness only for the circumcised, or also for the uncircumcised? We have been saying that Abraham's faith was credited to him as righteousness. 10Under what circumstances was it credited? Was it after he was circumcised, or before? It was not after, but before! 11And he received the sign of circumcision, a seal of the righteousness that he had by faith while he was still uncircumcised. So then, he is the father of all who believe but have not been circumcised, in order that righteousness might be credited to them. 12And he is also the father of the circumcised who not only are circumcised but who also walk in the footsteps of the faith that our father Abraham had before he was circumcised.

13It was not through law that Abraham and his offspring received the promise that he would be heir of the world, but through the righteousness that comes by faith. 14For if those who live by law are heirs, faith has no value and the promise is worthless, 15because law brings wrath. And where there is no law there is no transgression.

16Therefore, the promise comes by faith, so that it may be by grace and may be guaranteed to all Abraham's offspring—not only to those who are of the law but also to those who are of the faith of Abraham. He is the father of us all. 17As it is written: "I have made you a father of many nations."[d] He is our father in the sight of God, in whom he believed—the God who gives life to the dead and calls things that are not as though they were.

18Against all hope, Abraham in hope believed and so became the father of many nations, just as it had been said to him, "So shall your offspring be."[e] 19Without weakening in his faith, he faced the fact that his body was as good as dead—since he was about a hundred years old—and that Sarah's womb was also dead. 20Yet he did not waver through unbelief regarding the promise of God, but was strengthened in his faith and gave glory to God, 21being fully persuaded that God had power to do what he had promised. 22This is why "it was credited to him as righteousness." 23The words "it was credited to him" were written not for him alone, 24but also for us, to whom God will credit righteousness—for us who believe in him who raised Jesus our Lord from the dead. 25He was delivered over to death for our sins and was raised to life for our justification.

Peace and Joy

5 Therefore, since we have been justified through faith, we[f] have peace with God through our Lord Jesus Christ, 2through whom we have gained access by

[a] 25 Or *as the one who would turn aside his wrath, taking away sin*
[b] 3 Gen. 15:6; also in verse 22
[c] 8 Psalm 32:1,2
[d] 17 Gen. 17:5
[e] 18 Gen. 15:5
[f] 1 Or *let us*

faith into this grace in which we now
stand. And we[a] rejoice in the hope of the
glory of God. 3Not only so, but we[a] also
rejoice in our sufferings, because we
know that suffering produces persever-
ance; 4perseverance, character; and char-
acter, hope. 5And hope does not disap-
point us, because God has poured out his
love into our hearts by the Holy Spirit,
whom he has given us.

6You see, at just the right time, when we
were still powerless, Christ died for the

[a] 2,3 Or *let us*

FRIDAY

VERSE FOR THE DAY: Romans 4:7–8

AUTHOR: Lewis B. Smedes

PASSAGE FOR THE DAY: Romans 4:1–17

What Not to Forgive

Husbands and wives shouldn't forgive everything that annoys them. There are some things that we ought *not* to forgive for two reasons: (1) they're not serious enough; and (2) they're not things for which another person is responsible.

A man once told me, "My wife has been depressed for three years. Now she only leaves her couch to fill her stomach. I can't take it. How can I forgive her?"

So I asked, "Would you forgive her if she broke her leg? It's the same thing. You don't forgive. You bear, you wait, you suffer along with her." We ought to pray for an unsung gift: the gift of magnanimity, the gift of being willing to accommodate, cope with and endure each other's weaknesses.

Other things are too trivial to forgive. Everyone has annoying behavior patterns that are better accommodated to than forgiven. For example, I have a habit of channel switching on the television. It's very annoying to my wife, Doris. But she doesn't forgive me for that. While I'm trying to improve, she basically says, "I'll put up with it."

There are things about our mates that annoy us, but we don't need to forgive them. We just need to put up with it.

MARRIAGE BUILDERS

♦ *Privately recall some of your spouse's most irksome habits. Be honest with yourself: Are these things you should try not to resent but just put up with?*

♦ *What trivial things about yourself are you glad your spouse puts up with?*

Additional Scripture Readings
Proverbs 17:9; Romans 14:13; 15:1–2

Go to page 1228 for your next devotional reading.

ungodly. 7Very rarely will anyone die for
a righteous man, though for a good man
someone might possibly dare to die. 8But
God demonstrates his own love for us in
this: While we were still sinners, Christ
died for us.

9Since we have now been justified by
his blood, how much more shall we be
saved from God's wrath through him!
10For if, when we were God's enemies, we
were reconciled to him through the death
of his Son, how much more, having been
reconciled, shall we be saved through his
life! 11Not only is this so, but we also re-
joice in God through our Lord Jesus
Christ, through whom we have now re-
ceived reconciliation.

Death Through Adam, Life Through Christ

12Therefore, just as sin entered the
world through one man, and death
through sin, and in this way death came to
all men, because all sinned— 13for before
the law was given, sin was in the world.
But sin is not taken into account when
there is no law. 14Nevertheless, death
reigned from the time of Adam to the time
of Moses, even over those who did not sin
by breaking a command, as did Adam,
who was a pattern of the one to come.

15But the gift is not like the trespass. For
if the many died by the trespass of the one
man, how much more did God's grace and
the gift that came by the grace of the one
man, Jesus Christ, overflow to the many!
16Again, the gift of God is not like the re-
sult of the one man's sin: The judgment
followed one sin and brought condemna-
tion, but the gift followed many trespasses
and brought justification. 17For if, by the
trespass of the one man, death reigned
through that one man, how much more
will those who receive God's abundant
provision of grace and of the gift of righ-
teousness reign in life through the one
man, Jesus Christ.

18Consequently, just as the result of one
trespass was condemnation for all men, so
also the result of one act of righteousness
was justification that brings life for all
men. 19For just as through the disobedi-
ence of the one man the many were made
sinners, so also through the obedience of
the one man the many will be made righ-
teous.

20The law was added so that the tres-
pass might increase. But where sin in-
creased, grace increased all the more, 21so
that, just as sin reigned in death, so also
grace might reign through righteousness
to bring eternal life through Jesus Christ
our Lord.

Dead to Sin, Alive in Christ

6 What shall we say, then? Shall we go
on sinning so that grace may in-
crease? 2By no means! We died to sin;
how can we live in it any longer? 3Or don't
you know that all of us who were baptized
into Christ Jesus were baptized into his
death? 4We were therefore buried with
him through baptism into death in order
that, just as Christ was raised from the
dead through the glory of the Father, we
too may live a new life.

5If we have been united with him like
this in his death, we will certainly also be
united with him in his resurrection. 6For
we know that our old self was crucified
with him so that the body of sin might be
done away with,[a] that we should no
longer be slaves to sin— 7because anyone
who has died has been freed from sin.

8Now if we died with Christ, we believe
that we will also live with him. 9For we
know that since Christ was raised from
the dead, he cannot die again; death no
longer has mastery over him. 10The death
he died, he died to sin once for all; but the
life he lives, he lives to God.

11In the same way, count yourselves
dead to sin but alive to God in Christ
Jesus. 12Therefore do not let sin reign in
your mortal body so that you obey its evil
desires. 13Do not offer the parts of your
body to sin, as instruments of wickedness,
but rather offer yourselves to God, as
those who have been brought from death
to life; and offer the parts of your body to
him as instruments of righteousness.
14For sin shall not be your master, be-
cause you are not under law, but under
grace.

Slaves to Righteousness

15What then? Shall we sin because we
are not under law but under grace? By no
means! 16Don't you know that when you
offer yourselves to someone to obey him
as slaves, you are slaves to the one whom
you obey—whether you are slaves to sin,
which leads to death, or to obedience,
which leads to righteousness? 17But

[a]6 Or *be rendered powerless*

WEEKENDING

TRADITIONS

Holidays can become a tug-of-war between a husband and wife who each want to celebrate special occasions the way their family did when they were growing up. But by working at it together, you can take each of your individual family traditions and come up with a new approach that is uniquely "yours." Use the following questions to get started.

1. How did your family celebrate birthdays and wedding anniversaries? Topics to consider: cakes and candles, party decorations and special meals; family celebrations or parties with friends; modest gifts or lavish presents; dinner at home or an evening out.

2. What did your family do at Thanksgiving? Easter? Advent and Christmas? Topics to consider: at home or with relatives; worship services; special meals and foods; sports; decorated eggs, Santa Claus, the Christmas tree.

— *The* Marriage Partnership *Staff*

REVIVE

Saturday: Genesis 2:20–24
Sunday: Psalm 23:1–6

Go to page 1231 for your next devotional reading.

thanks be to God that, though you used to
be slaves to sin, you wholeheartedly
obeyed the form of teaching to which you
were entrusted. 18You have been set free
from sin and have become slaves to righ-
teousness.

19I put this in human terms because you
are weak in your natural selves. Just as
you used to offer the parts of your body in
slavery to impurity and to ever-increasing
wickedness, so now offer them in slavery
to righteousness leading to holiness.
20When you were slaves to sin, you were
free from the control of righteousness.
21What benefit did you reap at that time
from the things you are now ashamed of?
Those things result in death! 22But now
that you have been set free from sin and
have become slaves to God, the benefit
you reap leads to holiness, and the result
is eternal life. 23For the wages of sin is
death, but the gift of God is eternal life
in[a] Christ Jesus our Lord.

An Illustration From Marriage

7 Do you not know, brothers—for I am
speaking to men who know the law—
that the law has authority over a man only
as long as he lives? 2For example, by law
a married woman is bound to her hus-
band as long as he is alive, but if her hus-
band dies, she is released from the law of
marriage. 3So then, if she marries another
man while her husband is still alive, she is
called an adulteress. But if her husband
dies, she is released from that law and is
not an adulteress, even though she mar-
ries another man.

4So, my brothers, you also died to the
law through the body of Christ, that you
might belong to another, to him who was
raised from the dead, in order that we
might bear fruit to God. 5For when we
were controlled by the sinful nature,[b] the
sinful passions aroused by the law were at
work in our bodies, so that we bore fruit
for death. 6But now, by dying to what
once bound us, we have been released
from the law so that we serve in the new
way of the Spirit, and not in the old way
of the written code.

Struggling With Sin

7What shall we say, then? Is the law sin?
Certainly not! Indeed I would not have
known what sin was except through the
law. For I would not have known what
coveting really was if the law had not said,
"Do not covet."[c] 8But sin, seizing the op-
portunity afforded by the commandment,
produced in me every kind of covetous
desire. For apart from law, sin is dead.
9Once I was alive apart from law; but
when the commandment came, sin
sprang to life and I died. 10I found that the
very commandment that was intended to
bring life actually brought death. 11For
sin, seizing the opportunity afforded by
the commandment, deceived me, and
through the commandment put me to
death. 12So then, the law is holy, and the
commandment is holy, righteous and
good.

13Did that which is good, then, become
death to me? By no means! But in order
that sin might be recognized as sin, it pro-
duced death in me through what was
good, so that through the commandment
sin might become utterly sinful.

14We know that the law is spiritual; but
I am unspiritual, sold as a slave to sin. 15I
do not understand what I do. For what I
want to do I do not do, but what I hate I
do. 16And if I do what I do not want to do,
I agree that the law is good. 17As it is, it is
no longer I myself who do it, but it is sin
living in me. 18I know that nothing good
lives in me, that is, in my sinful nature.[d]
For I have the desire to do what is good,
but I cannot carry it out. 19For what I do
is not the good I want to do; no, the evil
I do not want to do—this I keep on doing.
20Now if I do what I do not want to do, it
is no longer I who do it, but it is sin living
in me that does it.

21So I find this law at work: When I
want to do good, evil is right there with
me. 22For in my inner being I delight in
God's law; 23but I see another law at work
in the members of my body, waging war
against the law of my mind and making
me a prisoner of the law of sin at work
within my members. 24What a wretched
man I am! Who will rescue me from this
body of death? 25Thanks be to God—
through Jesus Christ our Lord!

So then, I myself in my mind am a slave
to God's law, but in the sinful nature a
slave to the law of sin.

Life Through the Spirit

8 Therefore, there is now no condemna-
tion for those who are in Christ

[a] 23 Or *through* [b] 5 Or *the flesh*; also in verse 25 [c] 7 Exodus 20:17; Deut. 5:21 [d] 18 Or *my flesh*

Jesus,[a] 2because through Christ Jesus the
law of the Spirit of life set me free from the
law of sin and death. 3For what the law
was powerless to do in that it was weak-
ened by the sinful nature,[b] God did by
sending his own Son in the likeness of sin-
ful man to be a sin offering.[c] And so he
condemned sin in sinful man,[d] 4in order
that the righteous requirements of the law
might be fully met in us, who do not live
according to the sinful nature but accord-
ing to the Spirit.

5Those who live according to the sinful
nature have their minds set on what that
nature desires; but those who live in ac-
cordance with the Spirit have their minds
set on what the Spirit desires. 6The mind
of sinful man[e] is death, but the mind con-
trolled by the Spirit is life and peace; 7the
sinful mind[f] is hostile to God. It does not
submit to God's law, nor can it do so.
8Those controlled by the sinful nature
cannot please God.

9You, however, are controlled not by
the sinful nature but by the Spirit, if the
Spirit of God lives in you. And if anyone
does not have the Spirit of Christ, he does
not belong to Christ. 10But if Christ is in
you, your body is dead because of sin, yet
your spirit is alive because of righteous-
ness. 11And if the Spirit of him who raised
Jesus from the dead is living in you, he
who raised Christ from the dead will also
give life to your mortal bodies through his
Spirit, who lives in you.

12Therefore, brothers, we have an obli-
gation—but it is not to the sinful nature,
to live according to it. 13For if you live ac-
cording to the sinful nature, you will die;
but if by the Spirit you put to death the
misdeeds of the body, you will live, 14be-
cause those who are led by the Spirit of
God are sons of God. 15For you did not re-
ceive a spirit that makes you a slave again
to fear, but you received the Spirit of son-
ship.[g] And by him we cry, "*Abba,*[h] Fa-
ther." 16The Spirit himself testifies with
our spirit that we are God's children.
17Now if we are children, then we are
heirs—heirs of God and co-heirs with
Christ, if indeed we share in his sufferings
in order that we may also share in his
glory.

Future Glory

18I consider that our present sufferings
are not worth comparing with the glory
that will be revealed in us. 19The creation
waits in eager expectation for the sons of
God to be revealed. 20For the creation was
subjected to frustration, not by its own
choice, but by the will of the one who sub-
jected it, in hope 21that[i] the creation it-
self will be liberated from its bondage to
decay and brought into the glorious free-
dom of the children of God.

22We know that the whole creation has
been groaning as in the pains of childbirth
right up to the present time. 23Not only so,
but we ourselves, who have the firstfruits
of the Spirit, groan inwardly as we wait ea-
gerly for our adoption as sons, the re-
demption of our bodies. 24For in this hope
we were saved. But hope that is seen is no
hope at all. Who hopes for what he al-
ready has? 25But if we hope for what we
do not yet have, we wait for it patiently.

26In the same way, the Spirit helps us in
our weakness. We do not know what we
ought to pray for, but the Spirit himself in-
tercedes for us with groans that words
cannot express. 27And he who searches
our hearts knows the mind of the Spirit,
because the Spirit intercedes for the saints
in accordance with God's will.

More Than Conquerors

28And we know that in all things God
works for the good of those who love
him,[j] who[k] have been called according
to his purpose. 29For those God foreknew
he also predestined to be conformed to
the likeness of his Son, that he might be
the firstborn among many brothers. 30And
those he predestined, he also called; those
he called, he also justified; those he justi-
fied, he also glorified.

31What, then, shall we say in response
to this? If God is for us, who can be against
us? 32He who did not spare his own Son,
but gave him up for us all—how will he
not also, along with him, graciously give
us all things? 33Who will bring any charge

[a] *1* Some later manuscripts *Jesus, who do not live according to the sinful nature but according to the Spirit,*
[b] *3* Or *the flesh*; also in verses 4, 5, 8, 9, 12 and 13 [c] *3* Or *man, for sin* [d] *3* Or *in the flesh*
[e] *6* Or *mind set on the flesh* [f] *7* Or *the mind set on the flesh* [g] *15* Or *adoption* [h] *15* Aramaic for *Father* [i] *20,21* Or *subjected it in hope.* 21*For* [j] *28* Some manuscripts *And we know that all things work together for good to those who love God* [k] *28* Or *works together with those who love him to bring about what is good—with those who*

against those whom God has chosen? It is God who justifies. 34Who is he that condemns? Christ Jesus, who died—more than that, who was raised to life—is at the right hand of God and is also interceding for us. 35Who shall separate us from the love of Christ? Shall trouble or hardship or persecution or famine or nakedness or danger or sword? 36As it is written:

"For your sake we face death all day long;
we are considered as sheep to be slaughtered."[a]

37No, in all these things we are more than conquerors through him who loved us. 38For I am convinced that neither death nor life, neither angels nor demons,[b] neither the present nor the future, nor any

[a]36 Psalm 44:22 [b]38 Or *nor heavenly rulers*

MONDAY

VERSE FOR THE DAY: Romans 8:39 | AUTHOR: Ruth Bell Graham | PASSAGE FOR THE DAY: Romans 8:31–39

Overpowering Love

I may feel stale and dry, as I sometimes do when I've gotten too busy, or I'm physically exhausted, or I haven't spent time alone with God. I may feel guilt because I haven't lived up to all the light that God has placed upon my path.

I know that I received outstanding godly training from my parents, from the small boarding school I attended in North Korea, from the Christian college I attended and from all the people God has brought into my life. Then I realize that I am not the saint that I want to be. I've been critical, unkind or lazy. Or perhaps I've broken a confidence.

At that moment Romans 8:31–39 comes into my consciousness, and I am surrounded again by an awareness of God's love. He loves me in spite of me! Sometimes I think that the less we deserve God's love, the more we have of it. I know from raising our five children that my heart went out the most to the one who was struggling the most. If I love my children with that kind of love, how much more does my heavenly Father love me even when I've fallen flat on my face?

MARRIAGE BUILDERS

♦ *When have you felt spiritually dry? When have you felt like a failure?*

♦ *How does receiving God's enduring love encourage you in times of staleness or spiritual disappointment?*

Additional Scripture Readings
1 Chronicles 16:8–34; Psalm 118:1–29; Psalm 136:1–26

Go to page 1236 for your next devotional reading.

powers, 39neither height nor depth, nor anything else in all creation, will be able to separate us from the love of God that is in Christ Jesus our Lord.

God's Sovereign Choice

9 I speak the truth in Christ—I am not lying, my conscience confirms it in the Holy Spirit— 2I have great sorrow and unceasing anguish in my heart. 3For I could wish that I myself were cursed and cut off from Christ for the sake of my brothers, those of my own race, 4the people of Israel. Theirs is the adoption as sons; theirs the divine glory, the covenants, the receiving of the law, the temple worship and the promises. 5Theirs are the patriarchs, and from them is traced the human ancestry of Christ, who is God over all, forever praised![a] Amen.

6It is not as though God's word had failed. For not all who are descended from Israel are Israel. 7Nor because they are his descendants are they all Abraham's children. On the contrary, "It is through Isaac that your offspring will be reckoned."[b] 8In other words, it is not the natural children who are God's children, but it is the children of the promise who are regarded as Abraham's offspring. 9For this was how the promise was stated: "At the appointed time I will return, and Sarah will have a son."[c]

10Not only that, but Rebekah's children had one and the same father, our father Isaac. 11Yet, before the twins were born or had done anything good or bad—in order that God's purpose in election might stand: 12not by works but by him who calls—she was told, "The older will serve the younger."[d] 13Just as it is written: "Jacob I loved, but Esau I hated."[e]

14What then shall we say? Is God unjust? Not at all! 15For he says to Moses,

> "I will have mercy on whom I have mercy,
> and I will have compassion on whom I have compassion."[f]

16It does not, therefore, depend on man's desire or effort, but on God's mercy. 17For the Scripture says to Pharaoh: "I raised you up for this very purpose, that I might display my power in you and that my name might be proclaimed in all the earth."[g] 18Therefore God has mercy on whom he wants to have mercy, and he hardens whom he wants to harden.

19One of you will say to me: "Then why does God still blame us? For who resists his will?" 20But who are you, O man, to talk back to God? "Shall what is formed say to him who formed it, 'Why did you make me like this?' "[h] 21Does not the potter have the right to make out of the same lump of clay some pottery for noble purposes and some for common use?

22What if God, choosing to show his wrath and make his power known, bore with great patience the objects of his wrath—prepared for destruction? 23What if he did this to make the riches of his glory known to the objects of his mercy, whom he prepared in advance for glory—24even us, whom he also called, not only from the Jews but also from the Gentiles? 25As he says in Hosea:

> "I will call them 'my people' who are not my people;
> and I will call her 'my loved one' who is not my loved one,"[i]

26and,

> "It will happen that in the very place where it was said to them,
> 'You are not my people,'
> they will be called 'sons of the living God.' "[j]

27Isaiah cries out concerning Israel:

> "Though the number of the Israelites be like the sand by the sea,
> only the remnant will be saved.
> 28For the Lord will carry out his sentence on earth with speed and finality."[k]

29It is just as Isaiah said previously:

> "Unless the Lord Almighty had left us descendants,
> we would have become like Sodom,
> we would have been like Gomorrah."[l]

Israel's Unbelief

30What then shall we say? That the Gentiles, who did not pursue righteousness, have obtained it, a righteousness that is by

[a]5 Or *Christ, who is over all. God be forever praised!* Or *Christ. God who is over all be forever praised!*
[b]7 Gen. 21:12 [c]9 Gen. 18:10,14 [d]12 Gen. 25:23 [e]13 Mal. 1:2,3 [f]15 Exodus 33:19
[g]17 Exodus 9:16 [h]20 Isaiah 29:16; 45:9 [i]25 Hosea 2:23 [j]26 Hosea 1:10 [k]28 Isaiah 10:22,23
[l]29 Isaiah 1:9

faith; 31but Israel, who pursued a law of
righteousness, has not attained it. 32Why
not? Because they pursued it not by faith
but as if it were by works. They stumbled
over the "stumbling stone." 33As it is writ-
ten:

"See, I lay in Zion a stone that causes
men to stumble
and a rock that makes them fall,
and the one who trusts in him will
never be put to shame."[a]

10 Brothers, my heart's desire and
prayer to God for the Israelites is
that they may be saved. 2For I can testify
about them that they are zealous for God,
but their zeal is not based on knowledge.
3Since they did not know the righteous-
ness that comes from God and sought to
establish their own, they did not submit to
God's righteousness. 4Christ is the end of
the law so that there may be righteous-
ness for everyone who believes.

5Moses describes in this way the right-
eousness that is by the law: "The man
who does these things will live by
them."[b] 6But the righteousness that is by
faith says: "Do not say in your heart, 'Who
will ascend into heaven?'[c]" (that is, to
bring Christ down) 7"or 'Who will de-
scend into the deep?'[d]" (that is, to bring
Christ up from the dead). 8But what does
it say? "The word is near you; it is in your
mouth and in your heart,"[e] that is, the
word of faith we are proclaiming: 9That if
you confess with your mouth, "Jesus is
Lord," and believe in your heart that God
raised him from the dead, you will be
saved. 10For it is with your heart that you
believe and are justified, and it is with
your mouth that you confess and are
saved. 11As the Scripture says, "Anyone
who trusts in him will never be put to
shame."[f] 12For there is no difference be-
tween Jew and Gentile—the same Lord is
Lord of all and richly blesses all who call
on him, 13for, "Everyone who calls on the
name of the Lord will be saved."[g]

14How, then, can they call on the one
they have not believed in? And how can
they believe in the one of whom they have
not heard? And how can they hear with-
out someone preaching to them? 15And
how can they preach unless they are sent?
As it is written, "How beautiful are the feet
of those who bring good news!"[h]

16But not all the Israelites accepted the
good news. For Isaiah says, "Lord, who
has believed our message?"[i] 17Conse-
quently, faith comes from hearing the
message, and the message is heard
through the word of Christ. 18But I ask:
Did they not hear? Of course they did:

"Their voice has gone out into all the
earth,
their words to the ends of the
world."[j]

19Again I ask: Did Israel not understand?
First, Moses says,

"I will make you envious by those
who are not a nation;
I will make you angry by a nation
that has no understanding."[k]

20And Isaiah boldly says,

"I was found by those who did not
seek me;
I revealed myself to those who did
not ask for me."[l]

21But concerning Israel he says,

"All day long I have held out my
hands
to a disobedient and obstinate
people."[m]

The Remnant of Israel

11 I ask then: Did God reject his peo-
ple? By no means! I am an Israelite
myself, a descendant of Abraham, from
the tribe of Benjamin. 2God did not reject
his people, whom he foreknew. Don't you
know what the Scripture says in the pas-
sage about Elijah—how he appealed to
God against Israel: 3"Lord, they have
killed your prophets and torn down your
altars; I am the only one left, and they are
trying to kill me"[n]? 4And what was God's
answer to him? "I have reserved for myself
seven thousand who have not bowed the
knee to Baal."[o] 5So too, at the present
time there is a remnant chosen by grace.
6And if by grace, then it is no longer by
works; if it were, grace would no longer be
grace.[p]

[a]33 Isaiah 8:14; 28:16 [b]5 Lev. 18:5 [c]6 Deut. 30:12 [d]7 Deut. 30:13 [e]8 Deut. 30:14
[f]11 Isaiah 28:16 [g]13 Joel 2:32 [h]15 Isaiah 52:7 [i]16 Isaiah 53:1 [j]18 Psalm 19:4
[k]19 Deut. 32:21 [l]20 Isaiah 65:1 [m]21 Isaiah 65:2 [n]3 1 Kings 19:10,14 [o]4 1 Kings 19:18
[p]6 Some manuscripts *by grace. But if by works, then it is no longer grace; if it were, work would no longer be work.*

7What then? What Israel sought so earnestly it did not obtain, but the elect did. The others were hardened, 8as it is written:

"God gave them a spirit of stupor,
eyes so that they could not see
and ears so that they could not hear,
to this very day."[a]

9And David says:

"May their table become a snare and a trap,
a stumbling block and a retribution for them.
10May their eyes be darkened so they cannot see,
and their backs be bent forever."[b]

Ingrafted Branches

11Again I ask: Did they stumble so as to fall beyond recovery? Not at all! Rather, because of their transgression, salvation has come to the Gentiles to make Israel envious. 12But if their transgression means riches for the world, and their loss means riches for the Gentiles, how much greater riches will their fullness bring!

13I am talking to you Gentiles. Inasmuch as I am the apostle to the Gentiles, I make much of my ministry 14in the hope that I may somehow arouse my own people to envy and save some of them. 15For if their rejection is the reconciliation of the world, what will their acceptance be but life from the dead? 16If the part of the dough offered as firstfruits is holy, then the whole batch is holy; if the root is holy, so are the branches.

17If some of the branches have been broken off, and you, though a wild olive shoot, have been grafted in among the others and now share in the nourishing sap from the olive root, 18do not boast over those branches. If you do, consider this: You do not support the root, but the root supports you. 19You will say then, "Branches were broken off so that I could be grafted in." 20Granted. But they were broken off because of unbelief, and you stand by faith. Do not be arrogant, but be afraid. 21For if God did not spare the natural branches, he will not spare you either.

22Consider therefore the kindness and sternness of God: sternness to those who fell, but kindness to you, provided that you continue in his kindness. Otherwise, you also will be cut off. 23And if they do not persist in unbelief, they will be grafted in, for God is able to graft them in again. 24After all, if you were cut out of an olive tree that is wild by nature, and contrary to nature were grafted into a cultivated olive tree, how much more readily will these, the natural branches, be grafted into their own olive tree!

All Israel Will Be Saved

25I do not want you to be ignorant of this mystery, brothers, so that you may not be conceited: Israel has experienced a hardening in part until the full number of the Gentiles has come in. 26And so all Israel will be saved, as it is written:

"The deliverer will come from Zion;
he will turn godlessness away from Jacob.
27And this is[c] my covenant with them
when I take away their sins."[d]

28As far as the gospel is concerned, they are enemies on your account; but as far as election is concerned, they are loved on account of the patriarchs, 29for God's gifts and his call are irrevocable. 30Just as you who were at one time disobedient to God have now received mercy as a result of their disobedience, 31so they too have now become disobedient in order that they too may now[e] receive mercy as a result of God's mercy to you. 32For God has bound all men over to disobedience so that he may have mercy on them all.

Doxology

33Oh, the depth of the riches of the wisdom and[f] knowledge of God!
How unsearchable his judgments,
and his paths beyond tracing out!
34"Who has known the mind of the Lord?
Or who has been his counselor?"[g]
35"Who has ever given to God,
that God should repay him?"[h]
36For from him and through him and to him are all things.
To him be the glory forever! Amen.

[a]8 Deut. 29:4; Isaiah 29:10 [b]10 Psalm 69:22,23 [c]27 Or *will be* [d]27 Isaiah 59:20,21; 27:9; Jer. 31:33,34 [e]31 Some manuscripts do not have *now.* [f]33 Or *riches and the wisdom and the* [g]34 Isaiah 40:13 [h]35 Job 41:11

Living Sacrifices

12 Therefore, I urge you, brothers, in view of God's mercy, to offer your bodies as living sacrifices, holy and pleasing to God—this is your spiritual[a] act of worship. [2]Do not conform any longer to the pattern of this world, but be transformed by the renewing of your mind. Then you will be able to test and approve what God's will is—his good, pleasing and perfect will.

[3]For by the grace given me I say to every one of you: Do not think of yourself more highly than you ought, but rather think of yourself with sober judgment, in accordance with the measure of faith God has given you. [4]Just as each of us has one body with many members, and these members do not all have the same function, [5]so in Christ we who are many form one body, and each member belongs to all the others. [6]We have different gifts, according to the grace given us. If a man's gift is prophesying, let him use it in proportion to his[b] faith. [7]If it is serving, let him serve; if it is teaching, let him teach; [8]if it is encouraging, let him encourage; if it is contributing to the needs of others, let him give generously; if it is leadership, let him govern diligently; if it is showing mercy, let him do it cheerfully.

Love

[9]Love must be sincere. Hate what is evil; cling to what is good. [10]Be devoted to one another in brotherly love. Honor one another above yourselves. [11]Never be lacking in zeal, but keep your spiritual fervor, serving the Lord. [12]Be joyful in hope, patient in affliction, faithful in prayer. [13]Share with God's people who are in need. Practice hospitality.

[14]Bless those who persecute you; bless and do not curse. [15]Rejoice with those who rejoice; mourn with those who mourn. [16]Live in harmony with one another. Do not be proud, but be willing to associate with people of low position.[c] Do not be conceited.

[17]Do not repay anyone evil for evil. Be careful to do what is right in the eyes of everybody. [18]If it is possible, as far as it depends on you, live at peace with everyone. [19]Do not take revenge, my friends, but leave room for God's wrath, for it is written: "It is mine to avenge; I will repay,"[d] says the Lord. [20]On the contrary:

> "If your enemy is hungry, feed him;
> if he is thirsty, give him something
> to drink.
> In doing this, you will heap burning
> coals on his head."[e]

[21]Do not be overcome by evil, but overcome evil with good.

Submission to the Authorities

13 Everyone must submit himself to the governing authorities, for there is no authority except that which God has established. The authorities that exist have been established by God. [2]Consequently, he who rebels against the authority is rebelling against what God has instituted, and those who do so will bring judgment on themselves. [3]For rulers hold no terror for those who do right, but for those who do wrong. Do you want to be free from fear of the one in authority? Then do what is right and he will commend you. [4]For he is God's servant to do you good. But if you do wrong, be afraid, for he does not bear the sword for nothing. He is God's servant, an agent of wrath to bring punishment on the wrongdoer. [5]Therefore, it is necessary to submit to the authorities, not only because of possible punishment but also because of conscience.

[6]This is also why you pay taxes, for the authorities are God's servants, who give their full time to governing. [7]Give everyone what you owe him: If you owe taxes, pay taxes; if revenue, then revenue; if respect, then respect; if honor, then honor.

Love, for the Day Is Near

[8]Let no debt remain outstanding, except the continuing debt to love one another, for he who loves his fellowman has fulfilled the law. [9]The commandments, "Do not commit adultery," "Do not murder," "Do not steal," "Do not covet,"[f] and whatever other commandment there may be, are summed up in this one rule: "Love your neighbor as yourself."[g] [10]Love does no harm to its neighbor. Therefore love is the fulfillment of the law.

[11]And do this, understanding the present time. The hour has come for you to wake up from your slumber, because

[a] 1 Or *reasonable* [b] 6 Or *in agreement with the* [c] 16 Or *willing to do menial work*
[d] 19 Deut. 32:35 [e] 20 Prov. 25:21,22 [f] 9 Exodus 20:13-15,17; Deut. 5:17-19,21 [g] 9 Lev. 19:18

our salvation is nearer now than when we
first believed. 12The night is nearly over;
the day is almost here. So let us put aside
the deeds of darkness and put on the ar-
mor of light. 13Let us behave decently, as
in the daytime, not in orgies and drunken-
ness, not in sexual immorality and de-
bauchery, not in dissension and jealousy.
14Rather, clothe yourselves with the Lord
Jesus Christ, and do not think about how
to gratify the desires of the sinful na-
ture.[a]

The Weak and the Strong

14 Accept him whose faith is weak,
without passing judgment on dis-
putable matters. 2One man's faith allows
him to eat everything, but another man,

[a]14 Or *the flesh*

VERSE FOR THE DAY: Romans 13:10 | AUTHOR: Lewis B. Smedes | PASSAGE FOR THE DAY: Romans 13:8–14

Is Love Fair?

We don't get lasting love by chance; we earn it by working at fairness. Romance can keep love alive for a shining season; but unfair love will freeze by late fall.

Fairness is at stake in every conversation, in every sharing of duties, in every argument. We need fairness in our trust; it isn't fair to let a person down. We need fairness in our talk; it isn't fair to use words that violate a person's feelings or betray a person's confidence. We need fairness when we divide the chores. We need fairness when we decide who goes out to work for a living and who stays home to mind the children.

Love is fair when it builds up both the lover and the beloved, when it increases both and diminishes neither, when it brings them close and lets them be separate, when it nourishes both and leaves neither wanting. Fair love respects the boundaries of the other person's selfhood. It postpones our most legitimate desires to meet our loved one's needs. It declines every impulse to take advantage of a weakness. Fair love does not use ancient and forgiven wrongs against us.

Our love is fair when we decline any pleasure that comes at the price of another's pain.

MARRIAGE BUILDERS

- *What do you think is a "fair" balance of closeness and separateness in your marriage?*
- *What do you think is "fair" behavior when you are disagreeing?*

Additional Scripture Readings
Proverbs 1:1–3; 3:29; 31:12

Go to page 1237 for your next devotional reading.

whose faith is weak, eats only vegetables.
3The man who eats everything must not
look down on him who does not, and the
man who does not eat everything must
not condemn the man who does, for God
has accepted him. 4Who are you to judge
someone else's servant? To his own mas-
ter he stands or falls. And he will stand,
for the Lord is able to make him stand.

5One man considers one day more sa-
cred than another; another man considers
every day alike. Each one should be fully
convinced in his own mind. 6He who re-
gards one day as special, does so to the
Lord. He who eats meat, eats to the Lord,
for he gives thanks to God; and he who
abstains, does so to the Lord and gives
thanks to God. 7For none of us lives to
himself alone and none of us dies to him-
self alone. 8If we live, we live to the Lord;
and if we die, we die to the Lord. So,
whether we live or die, we belong to the
Lord.

9For this very reason, Christ died and
returned to life so that he might be the
Lord of both the dead and the living.
10You, then, why do you judge your broth-
er? Or why do you look down on your

VERSE FOR THE DAY:
Romans 14:1

AUTHOR:
Jill and Stuart Briscoe

PASSAGE FOR THE DAY:
Romans 14:1–12

Spiritual Growth

When one spouse is experiencing more rapid spiritual growth, there's a danger of putting pressure on the other partner: "She should say grace at meals" or "He should lead the family devotions." Most people resist being told what to do! If one person is uncomfortable with something, then the spouse who is spiritually ready should go ahead to initiate and lead those activities. The point is not to nag, but to encourage one another. Encouraging literally means "putting the heart into people"—giving someone a heart or desire for something. A spouse may get encouraged as he sees the Holy Spirit work in his partner. That's a better way of encouraging each other than imposing your desires on your mate.

It all begins in being responsible for our own growing love for God. As we're absorbed in the Lord, it should be catching! It makes our partners hungry for that experience, but it does so without admonishing or pushing.

MARRIAGE BUILDERS

♦ *As you turn your attention to your own spiritual life, what is one area in which you'd like to see growth?*

♦ *Can you think of a concrete way your spouse could encourage you as you grow in that area?*

Additional Scripture Readings
1 Peter 3:1–2; Romans 15:1–5

Go to page 1239 for your next devotional reading.

brother? For we will all stand before God's judgment seat. 11It is written:

" 'As surely as I live,' says the Lord,
'every knee will bow before me;
every tongue will confess to
God.' "[a]

12So then, each of us will give an account of himself to God.

13Therefore let us stop passing judgment on one another. Instead, make up your mind not to put any stumbling block or obstacle in your brother's way. 14As one who is in the Lord Jesus, I am fully convinced that no food[b] is unclean in itself. But if anyone regards something as unclean, then for him it is unclean. 15If your brother is distressed because of what you eat, you are no longer acting in love. Do not by your eating destroy your brother for whom Christ died. 16Do not allow what you consider good to be spoken of as evil. 17For the kingdom of God is not a matter of eating and drinking, but of righteousness, peace and joy in the Holy Spirit, 18because anyone who serves Christ in this way is pleasing to God and approved by men.

19Let us therefore make every effort to do what leads to peace and to mutual edification. 20Do not destroy the work of God for the sake of food. All food is clean, but it is wrong for a man to eat anything that causes someone else to stumble. 21It is better not to eat meat or drink wine or to do anything else that will cause your brother to fall.

22So whatever you believe about these things keep between yourself and God. Blessed is the man who does not condemn himself by what he approves. 23But the man who has doubts is condemned if he eats, because his eating is not from faith; and everything that does not come from faith is sin.

15 We who are strong ought to bear with the failings of the weak and not to please ourselves. 2Each of us should please his neighbor for his good, to build him up. 3For even Christ did not please himself but, as it is written: "The insults of those who insult you have fallen on me."[c] 4For everything that was written in the past was written to teach us, so that through endurance and the encouragement of the Scriptures we might have hope.

5May the God who gives endurance and encouragement give you a spirit of unity among yourselves as you follow Christ Jesus, 6so that with one heart and mouth you may glorify the God and Father of our Lord Jesus Christ.

7Accept one another, then, just as Christ accepted you, in order to bring praise to God. 8For I tell you that Christ has become a servant of the Jews[d] on behalf of God's truth, to confirm the promises made to the patriarchs 9so that the Gentiles may glorify God for his mercy, as it is written:

"Therefore I will praise you among the Gentiles;
I will sing hymns to your name."[e]

10Again, it says,

"Rejoice, O Gentiles, with his people."[f]

11And again,

"Praise the Lord, all you Gentiles,
and sing praises to him, all you peoples."[g]

12And again, Isaiah says,

"The Root of Jesse will spring up,
one who will arise to rule over the nations;
the Gentiles will hope in him."[h]

13May the God of hope fill you with all joy and peace as you trust in him, so that you may overflow with hope by the power of the Holy Spirit.

Paul the Minister to the Gentiles

14I myself am convinced, my brothers, that you yourselves are full of goodness, complete in knowledge and competent to instruct one another. 15I have written you quite boldly on some points, as if to remind you of them again, because of the grace God gave me 16to be a minister of Christ Jesus to the Gentiles with the priestly duty of proclaiming the gospel of God, so that the Gentiles might become an offering acceptable to God, sanctified by the Holy Spirit.

17Therefore I glory in Christ Jesus in my service to God. 18I will not venture to speak of anything except what Christ has

[a] *11* Isaiah 45:23 [b] *14* Or *that nothing* [c] *3* Psalm 69:9 [d] *8* Greek *circumcision*
[e] *9* 2 Samuel 22:50; Psalm 18:49 [f] *10* Deut. 32:43 [g] *11* Psalm 117:1 [h] *12* Isaiah 11:10

accomplished through me in leading the
Gentiles to obey God by what I have said
and done— 19by the power of signs and
miracles, through the power of the Spirit.
So from Jerusalem all the way around to
Illyricum, I have fully proclaimed the gos-
pel of Christ. 20It has always been my am-
bition to preach the gospel where Christ
was not known, so that I would not be
building on someone else's foundation.
21Rather, as it is written:

"Those who were not told about him
will see,
and those who have not heard will
understand."[a]

22This is why I have often been hindered
from coming to you.

[a]21 Isaiah 52:15

VERSE FOR THE DAY: Romans 15:5–6

AUTHOR: Jill and Stuart Briscoe

PASSAGE FOR THE DAY: Romans 15:1–13

Unity and Diversity

Spiritual life in marriage needs both unity and diversity. We discovered this by trial and error. We knew that couples are supposed to read the Bible and pray together. Our problem was that we came to the Scriptures from opposite directions.

People think having mutual spirituality always means having a quiet time together, studying the Bible together and praying together. For us, studying the Bible together was an unmitigated disaster, and we found that it led more to frustration than anything else. Now we study the Scriptures independently, but we talk about what we've been learning.

We have always prayed together, but we have to be flexible. Often one of us is away, so we don't have any sort of meticulously disciplined approach. But one of the week's high points is very early on Sunday morning when we're making the half-hour drive to church. We spend that time praying, and once we get to church, we spend another thirty minutes praying before the first service.

You have to find what meshes with *your* partnership. For us, it's prayer.

MARRIAGE BUILDERS

♦ *What are the ways your approach to spiritual things is different from your spouse's?*

♦ *How can those differences be positive for developing a spiritual friendship between the two of you?*

Additional Scripture Readings
1 Corinthians 12:12–13; Ephesians 4:3–4

Go to page 1243 for your next devotional reading.

Paul's Plan to Visit Rome

23But now that there is no more place
for me to work in these regions, and since
I have been longing for many years to see
you, 24I plan to do so when I go to Spain.
I hope to visit you while passing through
and to have you assist me on my journey
there, after I have enjoyed your company
for a while. 25Now, however, I am on my
way to Jerusalem in the service of the
saints there. 26For Macedonia and Achaia
were pleased to make a contribution for
the poor among the saints in Jerusalem.
27They were pleased to do it, and indeed
they owe it to them. For if the Gentiles
have shared in the Jews' spiritual bless-
ings, they owe it to the Jews to share with
them their material blessings. 28So after I
have completed this task and have made
sure that they have received this fruit, I
will go to Spain and visit you on the way.
29I know that when I come to you, I will
come in the full measure of the blessing of
Christ.

30I urge you, brothers, by our Lord
Jesus Christ and by the love of the Spirit,
to join me in my struggle by praying to
God for me. 31Pray that I may be rescued
from the unbelievers in Judea and that my
service in Jerusalem may be acceptable to
the saints there, 32so that by God's will I
may come to you with joy and together
with you be refreshed. 33The God of peace
be with you all. Amen.

Personal Greetings

16 I commend to you our sister Phoe-
be, a servant[a] of the church in
Cenchrea. 2I ask you to receive her in the
Lord in a way worthy of the saints and to
give her any help she may need from you,
for she has been a great help to many peo-
ple, including me.

3Greet Priscilla[b] and Aquila, my fellow
workers in Christ Jesus. 4They risked
their lives for me. Not only I but all
the churches of the Gentiles are grate-
ful to them.

5Greet also the church that meets at their
house.

Greet my dear friend Epenetus, who was
the first convert to Christ in the prov-
ince of Asia.

6Greet Mary, who worked very hard for
you.

7Greet Andronicus and Junias, my rela-
tives who have been in prison with
me. They are outstanding among the
apostles, and they were in Christ be-
fore I was.

8Greet Ampliatus, whom I love in the
Lord.

9Greet Urbanus, our fellow worker in
Christ, and my dear friend Stachys.

10Greet Apelles, tested and approved in
Christ.

Greet those who belong to the house-
hold of Aristobulus.

11Greet Herodion, my relative.

Greet those in the household of Narcis-
sus who are in the Lord.

12Greet Tryphena and Tryphosa, those
women who work hard in the Lord.

Greet my dear friend Persis, another
woman who has worked very hard in
the Lord.

13Greet Rufus, chosen in the Lord, and his
mother, who has been a mother to
me, too.

14Greet Asyncritus, Phlegon, Hermes, Pat-
robas, Hermas and the brothers with
them.

15Greet Philologus, Julia, Nereus and his
sister, and Olympas and all the saints
with them.

16Greet one another with a holy kiss.

All the churches of Christ send greet-
ings.

17I urge you, brothers, to watch out for
those who cause divisions and put obsta-
cles in your way that are contrary to the
teaching you have learned. Keep away
from them. 18For such people are not serv-
ing our Lord Christ, but their own appe-
tites. By smooth talk and flattery they
deceive the minds of naive people.
19Everyone has heard about your obedi-
ence, so I am full of joy over you; but I
want you to be wise about what is good,
and innocent about what is evil.

20The God of peace will soon crush Sa-
tan under your feet.

The grace of our Lord Jesus be with
you.

21Timothy, my fellow worker, sends his
greetings to you, as do Lucius, Jason and
Sosipater, my relatives.

22I, Tertius, who wrote down this letter,
greet you in the Lord.

[a] 1 Or *deaconess* [b] 3 Greek *Prisca*, a variant of *Priscilla*

[23]Gaius, whose hospitality I and the whole church here enjoy, sends you his greetings.

Erastus, who is the city's director of public works, and our brother Quartus send you their greetings.[a]

[25]Now to him who is able to establish you by my gospel and the proclamation of Jesus Christ, according to the revelation of the mystery hidden for long ages past, [26]but now revealed and made known through the prophetic writings by the command of the eternal God, so that all nations might believe and obey him—[27]to the only wise God be glory forever through Jesus Christ! Amen.

[a]23 Some manuscripts *their greetings.* [24]*May the grace of our Lord Jesus Christ be with all of you. Amen.*

PAUL, while staying in Ephesus (Acts 19), writes this letter to the church he started in Corinth (Acts 18:1–17). He addresses various problems he has heard about and answers questions they have asked of him in a letter (see 1 Corinthians 7:1). He places a high priority on being obedient to Christ and on striving for unity, humility and love in the church. As you read this book, make a decision to seek the Lord's will in everything you do and to work hard to be humble, to love others, and to become one in spirit with your fellow believers.

1 CORINTHIANS

1 Paul, called to be an apostle of Christ Jesus by the will of God, and our brother Sosthenes,

2 To the church of God in Corinth, to those sanctified in Christ Jesus and called to be holy, together with all those everywhere who call on the name of our Lord Jesus Christ—their Lord and ours:

3 Grace and peace to you from God our Father and the Lord Jesus Christ.

Thanksgiving

4 I always thank God for you because of his grace given you in Christ Jesus. 5 For in him you have been enriched in every way—in all your speaking and in all your knowledge— 6 because our testimony about Christ was confirmed in you. 7 Therefore you do not lack any spiritual gift as you eagerly wait for our Lord Jesus Christ to be revealed. 8 He will keep you strong to the end, so that you will be

blameless on the day of our Lord Jesus
Christ. 9God, who has called you into fel-
lowship with his Son Jesus Christ our
Lord, is faithful.

Divisions in the Church

10I appeal to you, brothers, in the name
of our Lord Jesus Christ, that all of you
agree with one another so that there may
be no divisions among you and that you
may be perfectly united in mind and
thought. 11My brothers, some from
Chloe's household have informed me that
there are quarrels among you. 12What I
mean is this: One of you says, "I follow
Paul"; another, "I follow Apollos"; anoth-
er, "I follow Cephas[a]"; still another, "I
follow Christ."
13Is Christ divided? Was Paul crucified
for you? Were you baptized into[b] the
name of Paul? 14I am thankful that I did
not baptize any of you except Crispus and
Gaius, 15so no one can say that you were
baptized into my name. 16(Yes, I also bap-
tized the household of Stephanas; beyond
that, I don't remember if I baptized any-
one else.) 17For Christ did not send me to
baptize, but to preach the gospel—not

[a] 12 That is, Peter [b] 13 Or *in*; also in verse 15

VERSE FOR THE DAY: 1 Corinthians 1:7–8 | AUTHOR: Howard Hendricks | PASSAGE FOR THE DAY: 1 Corinthians 1:1–17

Welding Your Strengths

I spent the first ten years of our marriage trying to change Jeanne. I thought if she would just get organized, everything would be okay. Then one day it dawned on me that if I ever got her organized, I'd probably hate her. The thing that had attracted me to her in the first place was her warmth, her graciousness, the time she always took for people.

I finally got off this organization kick when I realized Jeanne had what I desperately needed—an ability to relax and take life as it comes. When I learned to take Jeanne's strengths and weld them with my strengths, then we were building our marriage out of each other's strengths rather than our weaknesses. We began to realize that we had a stronger unit as a couple than we could ever have as individuals.

MARRIAGE BUILDERS

♦ *If you have ever fallen into the trap of trying to change your spouse, what was the outcome?*
♦ *What strengths do you admire most in your husband or wife? How have those qualities contributed to strengthening you as a team?*

Additional Scripture Readings
Proverbs 27:17; Ecclesiastes 4:9–10; Luke 10:1–2

Go to page 1244 for your next devotional reading.

WEEKENDING

LONELINESS

To determine whether you sometimes neglect your relationships, check each statement that applies to you. Let your discoveries spark real changes in your relationships.

☐ I am sometimes reluctant to let friends or family members know about my personal struggles.

☐ When someone talks to me I can easily be distracted.

☐ When someone expresses his or her feelings, I'd rather talk about solutions than hear more about what causes those feelings.

☐ I know I should carve out more time for close friendships, but I seem to procrastinate.

☐ When I'm with people, I'm too concerned about making proper impressions.

☐ I have pressing activities that keep me from feeling at ease.

☐ It's been too long since I last sat down with friends to share personal problems.

☐ At times I avoid people because I don't want to be hassled.

— Dr. Les Carter and Dr. Frank Minirth

REVIVE

Saturday: John 21:15–17

Sunday: Galatians 6:2–10

Go to page 1246 for your next devotional reading.

with words of human wisdom, lest the cross of Christ be emptied of its power.

Christ the Wisdom and Power of God

18For the message of the cross is foolishness to those who are perishing, but to us who are being saved it is the power of God. 19For it is written:

"I will destroy the wisdom of the wise;
the intelligence of the intelligent I will frustrate."[a]

20Where is the wise man? Where is the scholar? Where is the philosopher of this age? Has not God made foolish the wisdom of the world? 21For since in the wisdom of God the world through its wisdom did not know him, God was pleased through the foolishness of what was preached to save those who believe. 22Jews demand miraculous signs and Greeks look for wisdom, 23but we preach Christ crucified: a stumbling block to Jews and foolishness to Gentiles, 24but to those whom God has called, both Jews and Greeks, Christ the power of God and the wisdom of God. 25For the foolishness of God is wiser than man's wisdom, and the weakness of God is stronger than man's strength.

26Brothers, think of what you were when you were called. Not many of you were wise by human standards; not many were influential; not many were of noble birth. 27But God chose the foolish things of the world to shame the wise; God chose the weak things of the world to shame the strong. 28He chose the lowly things of this world and the despised things—and the things that are not—to nullify the things that are, 29so that no one may boast before him. 30It is because of him that you are in Christ Jesus, who has become for us wisdom from God—that is, our righteousness, holiness and redemption. 31Therefore, as it is written: "Let him who boasts boast in the Lord."[b]

2 When I came to you, brothers, I did not come with eloquence or superior wisdom as I proclaimed to you the testimony about God.[c] 2For I resolved to know nothing while I was with you except Jesus Christ and him crucified. 3I came to you in weakness and fear, and with much trembling. 4My message and my preaching were not with wise and persuasive words, but with a demonstration of the Spirit's power, 5so that your faith might not rest on men's wisdom, but on God's power.

Wisdom From the Spirit

6We do, however, speak a message of wisdom among the mature, but not the wisdom of this age or of the rulers of this age, who are coming to nothing. 7No, we speak of God's secret wisdom, a wisdom that has been hidden and that God destined for our glory before time began. 8None of the rulers of this age understood it, for if they had, they would not have crucified the Lord of glory. 9However, as it is written:

"No eye has seen,
no ear has heard,
no mind has conceived
what God has prepared for those who love him"[d]—

10but God has revealed it to us by his Spirit.

The Spirit searches all things, even the deep things of God. 11For who among men knows the thoughts of a man except the man's spirit within him? In the same way no one knows the thoughts of God except the Spirit of God. 12We have not received the spirit of the world but the Spirit who is from God, that we may understand what God has freely given us. 13This is what we speak, not in words taught us by human wisdom but in words taught by the Spirit, expressing spiritual truths in spiritual words.[e] 14The man without the Spirit does not accept the things that come from the Spirit of God, for they are foolishness to him, and he cannot understand them, because they are spiritually discerned. 15The spiritual man makes judgments about all things, but he himself is not subject to any man's judgment:

16"For who has known the mind of the Lord
that he may instruct him?"[f]

But we have the mind of Christ.

On Divisions in the Church

3 Brothers, I could not address you as spiritual but as worldly—mere infants in Christ. 2I gave you milk, not solid food, for you were not yet ready for it. In-

[a] 19 Isaiah 29:14 [b] 31 Jer. 9:24 [c] 1 Some manuscripts *as I proclaimed to you God's mystery*
[d] 9 Isaiah 64:4 [e] 13 Or *Spirit, interpreting spiritual truths to spiritual men* [f] 16 Isaiah 40:13

VERSE FOR THE DAY: 1 Corinthians 1:27

AUTHOR: Robertson McQuilkin

PASSAGE FOR THE DAY: 1 Corinthians 1:18–31

In Sickness, In Health

My wife, Muriel, has Alzheimer's Disease. She has started speaking only in phrases and single words. But she can say one sentence: "I love you."

She not only says it, she acts it. At first, the board of the seminary where I work arranged for a companion to stay in our home so I could go to the office. During those two years, as soon as I left for the office, Muriel would take out after me. With me, she was content; without me, she was distressed, sometimes terror-stricken. The walk to school is a mile round trip. She would make that trip as many as ten times a day.

Sometimes at night, when I helped her undress, I found bloody feet. When I told our family doctor, he choked up. "Such love," he said simply. Then, after a moment, "I have a theory that the characteristics developed across the years come out at times like these."

Muriel still feeds herself, but leaves all other functions to me. Yet she is contented (which is my goal) and often bubbles with laughter. What more could I ask? I have a home full of love and laughter; many couples with their wits about them don't have that! When Muriel reaches out to me in the night hours or smiles contentedly and lovingly as she awakes, I thank the Lord for his grace to us and ask him to let me keep her.

Muriel is the joy of my life. Daily I discern new manifestations of the kind of person she is, the wife I always loved. I also see fresh manifestations of God's love—the God I long to love more fully.

MARRIAGE BUILDERS

♦ *What are some of the simple things about married life that bring you joy?*

♦ *How do your actions show the love of God to your spouse?*

Additional Scripture Readings
1 John 3:16–20; 4:16–21

Go to page 1249 for your next devotional reading.

deed, you are still not ready. 3You are still
worldly. For since there is jealousy and
quarreling among you, are you not world-
ly? Are you not acting like mere men? 4For
when one says, "I follow Paul," and anoth-
er, "I follow Apollos," are you not mere
men?

5What, after all, is Apollos? And what is
Paul? Only servants, through whom you
came to believe—as the Lord has as-
signed to each his task. 6I planted the
seed, Apollos watered it, but God made it
grow. 7So neither he who plants nor he
who waters is anything, but only God,
who makes things grow. 8The man who
plants and the man who waters have one
purpose, and each will be rewarded ac-
cording to his own labor. 9For we are
God's fellow workers; you are God's field,
God's building.

10By the grace God has given me, I laid
a foundation as an expert builder, and
someone else is building on it. But each
one should be careful how he builds.
11For no one can lay any foundation other
than the one already laid, which is Jesus
Christ. 12If any man builds on this founda-
tion using gold, silver, costly stones,
wood, hay or straw, 13his work will be
shown for what it is, because the Day will
bring it to light. It will be revealed with
fire, and the fire will test the quality of
each man's work. 14If what he has built
survives, he will receive his reward. 15If it
is burned up, he will suffer loss; he him-
self will be saved, but only as one escap-
ing through the flames.

16Don't you know that you yourselves
are God's temple and that God's Spirit
lives in you? 17If anyone destroys God's
temple, God will destroy him; for God's
temple is sacred, and you are that temple.

18Do not deceive yourselves. If any one
of you thinks he is wise by the standards
of this age, he should become a "fool" so
that he may become wise. 19For the wis-
dom of this world is foolishness in God's
sight. As it is written: "He catches the wise
in their craftiness"[a]; 20and again, "The
Lord knows that the thoughts of the wise
are futile."[b] 21So then, no more boasting
about men! All things are yours, 22whether
Paul or Apollos or Cephas[c] or the
world or life or death or the present or the
future—all are yours, 23and you are of
Christ, and Christ is of God.

Apostles of Christ

4 So then, men ought to regard us as
servants of Christ and as those en-
trusted with the secret things of God.
2Now it is required that those who have
been given a trust must prove faithful. 3I
care very little if I am judged by you or by
any human court; indeed, I do not even
judge myself. 4My conscience is clear, but
that does not make me innocent. It is the
Lord who judges me. 5Therefore judge
nothing before the appointed time; wait
till the Lord comes. He will bring to light
what is hidden in darkness and will ex-
pose the motives of men's hearts. At that
time each will receive his praise from God.

6Now, brothers, I have applied these
things to myself and Apollos for your ben-
efit, so that you may learn from us the
meaning of the saying, "Do not go beyond
what is written." Then you will not take
pride in one man over against another.
7For who makes you different from any-
one else? What do you have that you did
not receive? And if you did receive it, why
do you boast as though you did not?

8Already you have all you want! Al-
ready you have become rich! You have be-
come kings—and that without us! How I
wish that you really had become kings so
that we might be kings with you! 9For it
seems to me that God has put us apostles
on display at the end of the procession,
like men condemned to die in the arena.
We have been made a spectacle to the
whole universe, to angels as well as to
men. 10We are fools for Christ, but you are
so wise in Christ! We are weak, but you
are strong! You are honored, we are dis-
honored! 11To this very hour we go hun-
gry and thirsty, we are in rags, we are bru-
tally treated, we are homeless. 12We work
hard with our own hands. When we are
cursed, we bless; when we are persecuted,
we endure it; 13when we are slandered, we
answer kindly. Up to this moment we
have become the scum of the earth, the
refuse of the world.

14I am not writing this to shame you,
but to warn you, as my dear children.
15Even though you have ten thousand
guardians in Christ, you do not have many
fathers, for in Christ Jesus I became your
father through the gospel. 16Therefore I
urge you to imitate me. 17For this reason
I am sending to you Timothy, my son

[a] 19 Job 5:13 [b] 20 Psalm 94:11 [c] 22 That is, Peter

whom I love, who is faithful in the Lord. He will remind you of my way of life in Christ Jesus, which agrees with what I teach everywhere in every church.

18Some of you have become arrogant, as if I were not coming to you. 19But I will come to you very soon, if the Lord is willing, and then I will find out not only how these arrogant people are talking, but what power they have. 20For the kingdom of God is not a matter of talk but of power. 21What do you prefer? Shall I come to you with a whip, or in love and with a gentle spirit?

Expel the Immoral Brother!

5 It is actually reported that there is sexual immorality among you, and of a kind that does not occur even among pagans: A man has his father's wife. 2And you are proud! Shouldn't you rather have been filled with grief and have put out of your fellowship the man who did this? 3Even though I am not physically present, I am with you in spirit. And I have already passed judgment on the one who did this, just as if I were present. 4When you are assembled in the name of our Lord Jesus and I am with you in spirit, and the power of our Lord Jesus is present, 5hand this man over to Satan, so that the sinful nature[a] may be destroyed and his spirit saved on the day of the Lord.

6Your boasting is not good. Don't you know that a little yeast works through the whole batch of dough? 7Get rid of the old yeast that you may be a new batch without yeast—as you really are. For Christ, our Passover lamb, has been sacrificed. 8Therefore let us keep the Festival, not with the old yeast, the yeast of malice and wickedness, but with bread without yeast, the bread of sincerity and truth.

9I have written you in my letter not to associate with sexually immoral people—10not at all meaning the people of this world who are immoral, or the greedy and swindlers, or idolaters. In that case you would have to leave this world. 11But now I am writing you that you must not associate with anyone who calls himself a brother but is sexually immoral or greedy, an idolater or a slanderer, a drunkard or a swindler. With such a man do not even eat.

12What business is it of mine to judge those outside the church? Are you not to judge those inside? 13God will judge those outside. "Expel the wicked man from among you."[b]

Lawsuits Among Believers

6 If any of you has a dispute with another, dare he take it before the ungodly for judgment instead of before the saints? 2Do you not know that the saints will judge the world? And if you are to judge the world, are you not competent to judge trivial cases? 3Do you not know that we will judge angels? How much more the things of this life! 4Therefore, if you have disputes about such matters, appoint as judges even men of little account in the church![c] 5I say this to shame you. Is it possible that there is nobody among you wise enough to judge a dispute between believers? 6But instead, one brother goes to law against another—and this in front of unbelievers!

7The very fact that you have lawsuits among you means you have been completely defeated already. Why not rather be wronged? Why not rather be cheated? 8Instead, you yourselves cheat and do wrong, and you do this to your brothers.

9Do you not know that the wicked will not inherit the kingdom of God? Do not be deceived: Neither the sexually immoral nor idolaters nor adulterers nor male prostitutes nor homosexual offenders 10nor thieves nor the greedy nor drunkards nor slanderers nor swindlers will inherit the kingdom of God. 11And that is what some of you were. But you were washed, you were sanctified, you were justified in the name of the Lord Jesus Christ and by the Spirit of our God.

Sexual Immorality

12"Everything is permissible for me"—but not everything is beneficial. "Everything is permissible for me"—but I will not be mastered by anything. 13"Food for the stomach and the stomach for food"—but God will destroy them both. The body is not meant for sexual immorality, but for the Lord, and the Lord for the body. 14By his power God raised the Lord from the dead, and he will raise us also. 15Do you not know that your bodies are members of Christ himself? Shall I then take the members of Christ and unite them with a pros-

[a]5 Or *that his body*; or *that the flesh* [b]13 Deut. 17:7; 19:19; 21:21; 22:21,24; 24:7 [c]4 Or *matters, do you appoint as judges men of little account in the church?*

titute? Never! 16Do you not know that he
who unites himself with a prostitute is
one with her in body? For it is said, "The
two will become one flesh."[a] 17But he
who unites himself with the Lord is one
with him in spirit.

18Flee from sexual immorality. All other
sins a man commits are outside his body,
but he who sins sexually sins against his
own body. 19Do you not know that your
body is a temple of the Holy Spirit, who is
in you, whom you have received from
God? You are not your own; 20you were
bought at a price. Therefore honor God
with your body.

Marriage

7 Now for the matters you wrote about:
It is good for a man not to marry.[b]
2But since there is so much immorality,
each man should have his own wife, and
each woman her own husband. 3The husband should fulfill his marital duty to his
wife, and likewise the wife to her husband. 4The wife's body does not belong to
her alone but also to her husband. In the
same way, the husband's body does not
belong to him alone but also to his wife.
5Do not deprive each other except by mutual consent and for a time, so that you
may devote yourselves to prayer. Then
come together again so that Satan will not
tempt you because of your lack of self-
control. 6I say this as a concession, not as
a command. 7I wish that all men were as
I am. But each man has his own gift from
God; one has this gift, another has that.

8Now to the unmarried and the widows
I say: It is good for them to stay unmarried, as I am. 9But if they cannot control
themselves, they should marry, for it is
better to marry than to burn with passion.

[a] 16 Gen. 2:24 [b] 1 Or "*It is good for a man not to have sexual relations with a woman.*"

VERSE FOR THE DAY: 1 Corinthians 6:18

AUTHOR: Tim Stafford

PASSAGE FOR THE DAY: 1 Corinthians 6:18–20

Marriage's Fence

God's rule against adultery guarantees that two people who are drawn together to become "one flesh" should have no sexual competition or interference. The rule is like a fence, keeping the enemies of love outside, and so allowing the freedom to "make love" within its protective boundaries.

So partners ask, even if silently, for guarantees: "You will never leave me, will you? There cannot be someone else?" Marriage, you might say, is an instinctive institution.

Exclusivity and permanence are reflexes of love.

MARRIAGE BUILDERS

- *What led you to commit yourself in marriage to your spouse?*
- *What attitudes and actions should you avoid because they would threaten the exclusivity and permanence of your marriage?*

Additional Scripture Readings
Genesis 2:24; Matthew 5:27; Luke 16:18

Go to page 1250 for your next devotional reading.

VERSE FOR THE DAY:
1 Corinthians 7:4

AUTHOR:
Charles R. Swindoll

PASSAGE FOR THE DAY:
1 Corinthians 7:1–5

Marriage's Grace

What does it take to make a person just as charming, thoughtful and encouraging with his or her mate as with those who know only the public smile? It takes grace—the oil that lessens the friction in marriage. More times than I want to remember, I have found that it was easier to extend grace to a parishioner or one of the folks on our church staff than it was for me to treat my wife, Cynthia, with grace.

One way grace helps to build a harmonious marriage is when we face marital realities. As I study the seventh chapter of 1 Corinthians, I find that marriage requires mutual unselfishness. "The husband should fulfill his marital duty to his wife, and likewise the wife to her husband. The wife's body does not belong to her alone but also to her husband. In the same way, the husband's body does not belong to him alone but also to his wife" (1 Cor. 7:3–4).

Paul is writing in a context having to do with sexual intimacy. The application is broader, however. He is encouraging unselfishness. What does it take to operate unselfishly? It takes grace. Grace to accept, to overlook, to understand. Grace to forgive and to respect. Grace to yield one's own rights, to affirm and to restrain. Grace to give, as well as grace to receive.

A good marriage requires mutual unselfishness. It calls for grace to release rights and expect little in return.

MARRIAGE BUILDERS

♦ *Over the past years of your marriage, what were some of the "marital realities" that have been accepted or overlooked because of grace?*

♦ *Why does it take grace to receive love and kindness as well as to give it?*

Additional Scripture Readings
1 Corinthians 13:4–7; Galatians 5:22–23

Go to page 1251 for your next devotional reading.

10To the married I give this command
(not I, but the Lord): A wife must not sep-
arate from her husband. 11But if she does,
she must remain unmarried or else be rec-
onciled to her husband. And a husband
must not divorce his wife.
12To the rest I say this (I, not the Lord):
If any brother has a wife who is not a be-
liever and she is willing to live with him,
he must not divorce her. 13And if a woman
has a husband who is not a believer and
he is willing to live with her, she must not
divorce him. 14For the unbelieving hus-
band has been sanctified through his wife,

VERSE FOR THE DAY: 1 Corinthians 7:6–10

AUTHOR: Jay Kesler

PASSAGE FOR THE DAY: 1 Corinthians 7:6–16

Stand for What's Right

You can't force someone to change, or to get help, if he or she doesn't want it. Paul, speaking to the issue of unequal values among spouses, doesn't say to the woman, "Try to change your husband to be a different man." Rather, he says, "Be faithful to Christ. Carry out your marital responsibilities in the best way you can, and somehow the faithfulness of your life will speak to him in the long run" (see 1 Corinthians 7:6–10).

I watched my mother take this approach with my father over a period of about 25 years. Eventually out of respect for her Christian faith he began to seek Christ himself, and they finally achieved a true unity.

This quality of courageous patience is one of the fruits of the Holy Spirit (Gal. 5:22–23). In the King James Version, the term is "long suffering." It seems that significant character change is not possible without pain; look what it cost Christ to buy us the ability to change. Perhaps it's not possible for us to help another person grow without pain, either.

But there's a special power in the kind of suffering that takes place when a person stands, day in and day out, for what is right. It's the kind of power Jesus displayed when he was reviled but did not revile back. The person who desires change doesn't try to force it, but chooses to live the best way he or she can under the circumstances, trusting in God for daily strength and the final outcome.

MARRIAGE BUILDERS

- *Why is it so often ineffective to try to "change" your spouse?*
- *As you hope for continual improvement in your relationship, how can you trust God for the future?*

Additional Scripture Readings
Galatians 5:22–23; 1 Thessalonians 4:11–12

Go to page 1253 for your next devotional reading.

and the unbelieving wife has been sanctified through her believing husband. Otherwise your children would be unclean, but as it is, they are holy.

15But if the unbeliever leaves, let him do so. A believing man or woman is not bound in such circumstances; God has called us to live in peace. 16How do you know, wife, whether you will save your husband? Or, how do you know, husband, whether you will save your wife?

17Nevertheless, each one should retain the place in life that the Lord assigned to him and to which God has called him. This is the rule I lay down in all the churches. 18Was a man already circumcised when he was called? He should not become uncircumcised. Was a man uncircumcised when he was called? He should not be circumcised. 19Circumcision is nothing and uncircumcision is nothing. Keeping God's commands is what counts. 20Each one should remain in the situation which he was in when God called him. 21Were you a slave when you were called? Don't let it trouble you—although if you can gain your freedom, do so. 22For he who was a slave when he was called by the Lord is the Lord's freedman; similarly, he who was a free man when he was called is Christ's slave. 23You were bought at a price; do not become slaves of men. 24Brothers, each man, as responsible to God, should remain in the situation God called him to.

25Now about virgins: I have no command from the Lord, but I give a judgment as one who by the Lord's mercy is trustworthy. 26Because of the present crisis, I think that it is good for you to remain as you are. 27Are you married? Do not seek a divorce. Are you unmarried? Do not look for a wife. 28But if you do marry, you have not sinned; and if a virgin marries, she has not sinned. But those who marry will face many troubles in this life, and I want to spare you this.

29What I mean, brothers, is that the time is short. From now on those who have wives should live as if they had none; 30those who mourn, as if they did not; those who are happy, as if they were not; those who buy something, as if it were not theirs to keep; 31those who use the things of the world, as if not engrossed in them. For this world in its present form is passing away.

32I would like you to be free from concern. An unmarried man is concerned about the Lord's affairs—how he can please the Lord. 33But a married man is concerned about the affairs of this world—how he can please his wife—34and his interests are divided. An unmarried woman or virgin is concerned about the Lord's affairs: Her aim is to be devoted to the Lord in both body and spirit. But a married woman is concerned about the affairs of this world—how she can please her husband. 35I am saying this for your own good, not to restrict you, but that you may live in a right way in undivided devotion to the Lord.

36If anyone thinks he is acting improperly toward the virgin he is engaged to, and if she is getting along in years and he feels he ought to marry, he should do as he wants. He is not sinning. They should get married. 37But the man who has settled the matter in his own mind, who is under no compulsion but has control over his own will, and who has made up his mind not to marry the virgin—this man also does the right thing. 38So then, he who marries the virgin does right, but he who does not marry her does even better.[a]

39A woman is bound to her husband as long as he lives. But if her husband dies, she is free to marry anyone she wishes, but he must belong to the Lord. 40In my judgment, she is happier if she stays as she is—and I think that I too have the Spirit of God.

Food Sacrificed to Idols

8 Now about food sacrificed to idols: We know that we all possess knowledge.[b] Knowledge puffs up, but love builds up. 2The man who thinks he knows something does not yet know as he ought to know. 3But the man who loves God is known by God.

4So then, about eating food sacrificed to

[a] *36-38* Or *36If anyone thinks he is not treating his daughter properly, and if she is getting along in years, and he feels she ought to marry, he should do as he wants. He is not sinning. He should let her get married. 37But the man who has settled the matter in his own mind, who is under no compulsion but has control over his own will, and who has made up his mind to keep the virgin unmarried—this man also does the right thing. 38So then, he who gives his virgin in marriage does right, but he who does not give her in marriage does even better.* [b] *1* Or *"We all possess knowledge," as you say*

VERSE FOR THE DAY:
1 Corinthians 9:19

AUTHOR:
Kevin A. Miller

PASSAGE FOR THE DAY:
1 Corinthians 9:19–27

When Up Is Down

In the movie *The Poseidon Adventure*, the ocean liner *S.S. Poseidon* is sailing on the open sea when it encounters a huge storm. A wall of water crashes through the ballroom chandelier. Men in tuxedos and women in evening gowns scream and run. The lights go out, smoke pours into rooms and, amid all the confusion, the ship flips over.

Because of the air trapped inside the ocean liner, the ship stays afloat, but upside down. In the confusion, the passengers can't figure out what's going on. They scramble to get out, mostly by climbing the steps to the top deck. Only the top deck is now 100 feet under water. In their frantic effort to get to the top of the ship, they drown.

The survivors are the few who do what doesn't make any sense. They do the opposite of what everyone else is doing and descend into the dark belly of the ship until they reach the hull—and by doing so reach the ocean's surface.

In marriage, it's as if God has turned the ship upside-down and the only way for us to get free is to choose what doesn't make sense: We lay down our lives by serving, supporting and sacrificing for our spouses.

This kind of selflessness doesn't come naturally. That's why the Scripture has to remind me: Exaltation comes after humility. You really do have to descend into greatness.

MARRIAGE BUILDERS

- *In what ways do you enjoy serving your spouse?*
- *What aspects of serving each other require deeper sacrifice?*

Additional Scripture Readings
Matthew 20:20–28; James 3:13–18

Go to page 1255 for your next devotional reading.

idols: We know that an idol is nothing at all in the world and that there is no God but one. 5For even if there are so-called gods, whether in heaven or on earth (as indeed there are many "gods" and many "lords"), 6yet for us there is but one God, the Father, from whom all things came and for whom we live; and there is but one Lord, Jesus Christ, through whom all things came and through whom we live.

7But not everyone knows this. Some people are still so accustomed to idols that when they eat such food they think of it as having been sacrificed to an idol, and since their conscience is weak, it is defiled. 8But food does not bring us near to God; we are no worse if we do not eat, and no better if we do.

9Be careful, however, that the exercise of your freedom does not become a stumbling block to the weak. 10For if anyone with a weak conscience sees you who have this knowledge eating in an idol's temple, won't he be emboldened to eat what has been sacrificed to idols? 11So this weak brother, for whom Christ died, is destroyed by your knowledge. 12When you sin against your brothers in this way and wound their weak conscience, you sin against Christ. 13Therefore, if what I eat causes my brother to fall into sin, I will never eat meat again, so that I will not cause him to fall.

The Rights of an Apostle

9 Am I not free? Am I not an apostle? Have I not seen Jesus our Lord? Are you not the result of my work in the Lord? 2Even though I may not be an apostle to others, surely I am to you! For you are the seal of my apostleship in the Lord.

3This is my defense to those who sit in judgment on me. 4Don't we have the right to food and drink? 5Don't we have the right to take a believing wife along with us, as do the other apostles and the Lord's brothers and Cephas[a]? 6Or is it only I and Barnabas who must work for a living?

7Who serves as a soldier at his own expense? Who plants a vineyard and does not eat of its grapes? Who tends a flock and does not drink of the milk? 8Do I say this merely from a human point of view? Doesn't the Law say the same thing? 9For it is written in the Law of Moses: "Do not muzzle an ox while it is treading out the grain."[b] Is it about oxen that God is concerned? 10Surely he says this for us, doesn't he? Yes, this was written for us, because when the plowman plows and the thresher threshes, they ought to do so in the hope of sharing in the harvest. 11If we have sown spiritual seed among you, is it too much if we reap a material harvest from you? 12If others have this right of support from you, shouldn't we have it all the more?

But we did not use this right. On the contrary, we put up with anything rather than hinder the gospel of Christ. 13Don't you know that those who work in the temple get their food from the temple, and those who serve at the altar share in what is offered on the altar? 14In the same way, the Lord has commanded that those who preach the gospel should receive their living from the gospel.

15But I have not used any of these rights. And I am not writing this in the hope that you will do such things for me. I would rather die than have anyone deprive me of this boast. 16Yet when I preach the gospel, I cannot boast, for I am compelled to preach. Woe to me if I do not preach the gospel! 17If I preach voluntarily, I have a reward; if not voluntarily, I am simply discharging the trust committed to me. 18What then is my reward? Just this: that in preaching the gospel I may offer it free of charge, and so not make use of my rights in preaching it.

19Though I am free and belong to no man, I make myself a slave to everyone, to win as many as possible. 20To the Jews I became like a Jew, to win the Jews. To those under the law I became like one under the law (though I myself am not under the law), so as to win those under the law. 21To those not having the law I became like one not having the law (though I am not free from God's law but am under Christ's law), so as to win those not having the law. 22To the weak I became weak, to win the weak. I have become all things to all men so that by all possible means I might save some. 23I do all this for the sake of the gospel, that I may share in its blessings.

24Do you not know that in a race all the runners run, but only one gets the prize? Run in such a way as to get the prize. 25Everyone who competes in the games goes into strict training. They do it to get a crown that will not last; but we do it to get

[a]5 That is, Peter [b]9 Deut. 25:4

WEEKENDING

ENCOURAGEMENT

A person's self-esteem can take a real beating out in the world each day. That's why it's important for spouses to champion each other. Married partners can build each other up and create deeper trust and intimacy by expressing appreciation and encouragement. Here are three ways to get started.

1. Remind your spouse of his or her positive inner qualities.

2. Don't expect perfection—give your spouse room to be "imperfect." And if your partner tends to set unrealistically high standards, encourage him or her to be more realistic. Help your spouse affirm his or her strengths, rather than concentrate on his or her failures.

3. When others offer criticism, help your spouse determine which criticisms are legitimate and which are not. Encourage an attitude of forgiveness toward those who have been unkind or unfair.

— *The* Marriage Partnership *Staff*

REVIVE

Saturday: Romans 14:1–19
Sunday: Ephesians 5:8–21

Go to page 1257 for your next devotional reading.

a crown that will last forever. 26Therefore
I do not run like a man running aimlessly;
I do not fight like a man beating the air.
27No, I beat my body and make it my slave
so that after I have preached to others, I
myself will not be disqualified for the
prize.

Warnings From Israel's History

10 For I do not want you to be igno-
rant of the fact, brothers, that our
forefathers were all under the cloud and
that they all passed through the sea. 2They
were all baptized into Moses in the cloud
and in the sea. 3They all ate the same spir-
itual food 4and drank the same spiritual
drink; for they drank from the spiritual
rock that accompanied them, and that
rock was Christ. 5Nevertheless, God was
not pleased with most of them; their bod-
ies were scattered over the desert.

6Now these things occurred as exam-
ples[a] to keep us from setting our hearts
on evil things as they did. 7Do not be idol-
aters, as some of them were; as it is writ-
ten: "The people sat down to eat and drink
and got up to indulge in pagan revelry."[b]
8We should not commit sexual immorali-
ty, as some of them did—and in one day
twenty-three thousand of them died. 9We
should not test the Lord, as some of them
did—and were killed by snakes. 10And do
not grumble, as some of them did—and
were killed by the destroying angel.

11These things happened to them as ex-
amples and were written down as warn-
ings for us, on whom the fulfillment of the
ages has come. 12So, if you think you are
standing firm, be careful that you don't
fall! 13No temptation has seized you ex-
cept what is common to man. And God is
faithful; he will not let you be tempted be-
yond what you can bear. But when you
are tempted, he will also provide a way
out so that you can stand up under it.

Idol Feasts and the Lord's Supper

14Therefore, my dear friends, flee from
idolatry. 15I speak to sensible people;
judge for yourselves what I say. 16Is not
the cup of thanksgiving for which we give
thanks a participation in the blood of
Christ? And is not the bread that we break
a participation in the body of Christ? 17Be-
cause there is one loaf, we, who are many,
are one body, for we all partake of the one
loaf.

18Consider the people of Israel: Do not
those who eat the sacrifices participate in
the altar? 19Do I mean then that a sacrifice
offered to an idol is anything, or that an
idol is anything? 20No, but the sacrifices of
pagans are offered to demons, not to God,
and I do not want you to be participants
with demons. 21You cannot drink the cup
of the Lord and the cup of demons too;
you cannot have a part in both the Lord's
table and the table of demons. 22Are we
trying to arouse the Lord's jealousy? Are
we stronger than he?

The Believer's Freedom

23"Everything is permissible"—but not
everything is beneficial. "Everything is
permissible"—but not everything is con-
structive. 24Nobody should seek his own
good, but the good of others.

25Eat anything sold in the meat market
without raising questions of conscience,
26for, "The earth is the Lord's, and every-
thing in it."[c]

27If some unbeliever invites you to a
meal and you want to go, eat whatever is
put before you without raising questions
of conscience. 28But if anyone says to you,
"This has been offered in sacrifice," then
do not eat it, both for the sake of the man
who told you and for conscience'
sake[d]— 29the other man's conscience, I
mean, not yours. For why should my free-
dom be judged by another's conscience?
30If I take part in the meal with thankful-
ness, why am I denounced because of
something I thank God for?

31So whether you eat or drink or what-
ever you do, do it all for the glory of God.
32Do not cause anyone to stumble, wheth-
er Jews, Greeks or the church of God—
33even as I try to please everybody in ev-
ery way. For I am not seeking my own
good but the good of many, so that they
11 may be saved. 1Follow my exam-
ple, as I follow the example of
Christ.

Propriety in Worship

2I praise you for remembering me in ev-
erything and for holding to the teach-
ings,[e] just as I passed them on to you.

3Now I want you to realize that the head
of every man is Christ, and the head of the

[a]6 Or *types*; also in verse 11 [b]7 Exodus 32:6 [c]26 Psalm 24:1 [d]28 Some manuscripts *conscience' sake, for "the earth is the Lord's and everything in it"* [e]2 Or *traditions*

woman is man, and the head of Christ is
God. 4Every man who prays or prophesies
with his head covered dishonors his head.
5And every woman who prays or prophe-
sies with her head uncovered dishonors
her head—it is just as though her head
were shaved. 6If a woman does not cover
her head, she should have her hair cut off;
and if it is a disgrace for a woman to have
her hair cut or shaved off, she should cov-
er her head. 7A man ought not to cover his
head,[a] since he is the image and glory of
God; but the woman is the glory of man.
8For man did not come from woman, but

[a]4-7 Or 4Every man who prays or prophesies with long hair dishonors his head. 5And every woman who prays or prophesies with no covering of hair on her head dishonors her head—she is just like one of the "shorn women." 6If a woman has no covering, let her be for now with short hair, but since it is a disgrace for a woman to have her hair shorn or shaved, she should grow it again. 7A man ought not to have long hair

VERSE FOR THE DAY: 1 Corinthians 10:24

AUTHOR: Larry Crabb

PASSAGE FOR THE DAY: 1 Corinthians 10:23–33

Overcoming Selfishness

The temptation to focus on ourselves instead of others might very well be the most serious challenge we face in marriage. I once got home from an exhausting trip. When I walked through the door Rachael had a thousand things she wanted to tell me. I found myself annoyed, thinking, "Well, a few things happened to me today, too. And I wouldn't mind you asking a question about that."

It's my immature, demanding nature that says, "If my wife loves me, she should be sensitive to me." Instead, I should recognize that God has already shown his love and sensitivity toward me, and that should free me up to be sensitive to my wife. Whatever sensitivity others show toward me is a plus (and my wife is unusually sensitive and supportive)—but it's not something I should *demand.*

After I work hard all day, it's all right for me to *desire* that Rachael would give me a hug and ask how I'm doing. But it's wrong for me to demand or require those things. Learning to call that attitude wrong is half the battle.

MARRIAGE BUILDERS

♦ *What sensitivities does your spouse show that you are especially thankful for?*

♦ *How can you be more sensitive to the little things your spouse may need?*

Additional Scripture Readings
Philippians 2:3–4; Romans 2:7–8; 1 Corinthians 13:5

Go to page 1258 for your next devotional reading.

woman from man; [9]neither was man created for woman, but woman for man.
[10]For this reason, and because of the angels, the woman ought to have a sign of authority on her head.

[11]In the Lord, however, woman is not independent of man, nor is man independent of woman. [12]For as woman came from man, so also man is born of woman. But everything comes from God. [13]Judge for yourselves: Is it proper for a woman to pray to God with her head uncovered? [14]Does not the very nature of things teach you that if a man has long hair, it is a disgrace to him, [15]but that if a woman has long hair, it is her glory? For long hair is given to her as a covering. [16]If anyone wants to be contentious about this, we

VERSE FOR THE DAY:
1 Corinthians 11:1

AUTHOR:
Kirby and Everett Worthington

PASSAGE FOR THE DAY:
1 Corinthians 11:1–16

Looking for an Example

Carrie's six-year marriage ended in divorce. "I didn't have a chance," she said. "My parents fought constantly. They divorced when I was fifteen." Yet Carrie's twin sister, Cheryl, is still happily married.

The quality of your parents' relationship influences how you approach marriage, but it's not the sole determinant of your future happiness. If your parents had a less-than-ideal marriage, you still can choose to take positive action. You and your spouse can work together to make your marriage what God intended it to be.

Start by looking to God for guidance and support—he wants your marriage to thrive. Rely on prayer to break through the roadblocks you encounter. You also can learn from your parents' example, looking for whatever redeeming elements there were to follow and identifying what you want to avoid.

Get to know happily married couples and talk with them about what makes their marriages work. Read marriage books together or attend a church-sponsored marriage seminar or a marriage-enrichment weekend. Then, each of you take the initiative in making improvements; small changes can make a big difference.

There are no excuses! You can have a great marriage even if you grew up with lousy role models.

MARRIAGE BUILDERS

♦ *What are some good habits or traditions you picked up from your two families?*

♦ *What's one area of tension you've inherited from your parents that you'd like to see changed in your relationship?*

Additional Scripture Readings
Proverbs 2:1–11; 2 Corinthians 3:17–18

Go to page 1260 for your next devotional reading.

have no other practice—nor do the churches of God.

The Lord's Supper

17In the following directives I have no praise for you, for your meetings do more harm than good. 18In the first place, I hear that when you come together as a church, there are divisions among you, and to some extent I believe it. 19No doubt there have to be differences among you to show which of you have God's approval. 20When you come together, it is not the Lord's Supper you eat, 21for as you eat, each of you goes ahead without waiting for anybody else. One remains hungry, another gets drunk. 22Don't you have homes to eat and drink in? Or do you despise the church of God and humiliate those who have nothing? What shall I say to you? Shall I praise you for this? Certainly not!

23For I received from the Lord what I also passed on to you: The Lord Jesus, on the night he was betrayed, took bread, 24and when he had given thanks, he broke it and said, "This is my body, which is for you; do this in remembrance of me." 25In the same way, after supper he took the cup, saying, "This cup is the new covenant in my blood; do this, whenever you drink it, in remembrance of me." 26For whenever you eat this bread and drink this cup, you proclaim the Lord's death until he comes.

27Therefore, whoever eats the bread or drinks the cup of the Lord in an unworthy manner will be guilty of sinning against the body and blood of the Lord. 28A man ought to examine himself before he eats of the bread and drinks of the cup. 29For anyone who eats and drinks without recognizing the body of the Lord eats and drinks judgment on himself. 30That is why many among you are weak and sick, and a number of you have fallen asleep. 31But if we judged ourselves, we would not come under judgment. 32When we are judged by the Lord, we are being disciplined so that we will not be condemned with the world.

33So then, my brothers, when you come together to eat, wait for each other. 34If anyone is hungry, he should eat at home, so that when you meet together it may not result in judgment.

And when I come I will give further directions.

Spiritual Gifts

12 Now about spiritual gifts, brothers, I do not want you to be ignorant. 2You know that when you were pagans, somehow or other you were influenced and led astray to mute idols. 3Therefore I tell you that no one who is speaking by the Spirit of God says, "Jesus be cursed," and no one can say, "Jesus is Lord," except by the Holy Spirit.

4There are different kinds of gifts, but the same Spirit. 5There are different kinds of service, but the same Lord. 6There are different kinds of working, but the same God works all of them in all men.

7Now to each one the manifestation of the Spirit is given for the common good. 8To one there is given through the Spirit the message of wisdom, to another the message of knowledge by means of the same Spirit, 9to another faith by the same Spirit, to another gifts of healing by that one Spirit, 10to another miraculous powers, to another prophecy, to another distinguishing between spirits, to another speaking in different kinds of tongues,[a] and to still another the interpretation of tongues.[a] 11All these are the work of one and the same Spirit, and he gives them to each one, just as he determines.

One Body, Many Parts

12The body is a unit, though it is made up of many parts; and though all its parts are many, they form one body. So it is with Christ. 13For we were all baptized by[b] one Spirit into one body—whether Jews or Greeks, slave or free—and we were all given the one Spirit to drink.

14Now the body is not made up of one part but of many. 15If the foot should say, "Because I am not a hand, I do not belong to the body," it would not for that reason cease to be part of the body. 16And if the ear should say, "Because I am not an eye, I do not belong to the body," it would not for that reason cease to be part of the body. 17If the whole body were an eye, where would the sense of hearing be? If the whole body were an ear, where would the sense of smell be? 18But in fact God has arranged the parts in the body, every one of them, just as he wanted them to be. 19If they were all one part, where would

[a] *10* Or *languages*; also in verse 28 [b] *13* Or *with*; or *in*

VERSE FOR THE DAY: 1 Corinthians 12:4–6

AUTHOR: Philip Yancey

PASSAGE FOR THE DAY: 1 Corinthians 12:1–31

Feelings of Insignificance

My wife, Janet, used to direct a church-related ministry to senior citizens in Chicago. Her days were full of adventure and people. Meanwhile I would stare at a computer screen in search of the perfect word. The daily regimen of a writer is not what you'd call glamorous. The vast difference in our lives used to bother me. I tended to feel that what I did was somehow less valuable, less worthy.

But I have come to see that the differences between us—in personality, outlook and daily routine—actually represent a great strength. Janet provides me with a new set of eyes into the world. My own faith is tested as I hear of her attempts to bring hope to the lives of those who have so little. On the other hand, I can offer Janet calmness, reflection and balance.

The New Testament uses the image of a human body to illustrate the church. A body composed of many members with many gifts can accomplish far more than a one-celled organism. The same principle applies to marriage. I marvel at the difference in temperament that allows Janet to deal with situations that would probably drive me crazy. I have learned to see her work as a part of my own outreach. By serving her, and offering a listening ear, I can strengthen her and thus help assure that her vital work will continue.

MARRIAGE BUILDERS

♦ *List five differences between you and your spouse in personality, outlook and daily routine.*

♦ *How do these differences make your marriage more balanced and complete?*

Additional Scripture Readings
Proverbs 25:11; Romans 14:1; James 4:4–7

Go to page 1262 for your next devotional reading.

the body be? [20]As it is, there are many
parts, but one body.
[21]The eye cannot say to the hand, "I
don't need you!" And the head cannot say
to the feet, "I don't need you!" [22]On the
contrary, those parts of the body that
seem to be weaker are indispensable,
[23]and the parts that we think are less hon-
orable we treat with special honor. And
the parts that are unpresentable are treat-
ed with special modesty, [24]while our pre-
sentable parts need no special treatment.
But God has combined the members of
the body and has given greater honor to
the parts that lacked it, [25]so that there
should be no division in the body, but that
its parts should have equal concern for
each other. [26]If one part suffers, every part
suffers with it; if one part is honored, ev-
ery part rejoices with it.
[27]Now you are the body of Christ, and
each one of you is a part of it. [28]And in the
church God has appointed first of all apos-
tles, second prophets, third teachers, then
workers of miracles, also those having
gifts of healing, those able to help others,
those with gifts of administration, and
those speaking in different kinds of
tongues. [29]Are all apostles? Are all proph-
ets? Are all teachers? Do all work mira-
cles? [30]Do all have gifts of healing? Do all
speak in tongues[a]? Do all interpret? [31]But
eagerly desire[b] the greater gifts.

Love

And now I will show you the most ex-
cellent way.
13 If I speak in the tongues[c] of men
and of angels, but have not love, I
am only a resounding gong or a clanging
cymbal. [2]If I have the gift of prophecy and
can fathom all mysteries and all knowl-
edge, and if I have a faith that can move
mountains, but have not love, I am noth-
ing. [3]If I give all I possess to the poor and
surrender my body to the flames,[d] but
have not love, I gain nothing.
[4]Love is patient, love is kind. It does not
envy, it does not boast, it is not proud. [5]It
is not rude, it is not self-seeking, it is not
easily angered, it keeps no record of
wrongs. [6]Love does not delight in evil but
rejoices with the truth. [7]It always protects,
always trusts, always hopes, always perse-
veres.
[8]Love never fails. But where there are
prophecies, they will cease; where there
are tongues, they will be stilled; where
there is knowledge, it will pass away. [9]For
we know in part and we prophesy in part,
[10]but when perfection comes, the imper-
fect disappears. [11]When I was a child, I
talked like a child, I thought like a child,
I reasoned like a child. When I became a
man, I put childish ways behind me.
[12]Now we see but a poor reflection as in
a mirror; then we shall see face to face.
Now I know in part; then I shall know ful-
ly, even as I am fully known.
[13]And now these three remain: faith,
hope and love. But the greatest of these is
love.

Gifts of Prophecy and Tongues

14 Follow the way of love and eagerly
desire spiritual gifts, especially the
gift of prophecy. [2]For anyone who speaks
in a tongue[e] does not speak to men but
to God. Indeed, no one understands him;
he utters mysteries with his spirit.[f] [3]But
everyone who prophesies speaks to men
for their strengthening, encouragement
and comfort. [4]He who speaks in a tongue
edifies himself, but he who prophesies ed-
ifies the church. [5]I would like every one of
you to speak in tongues,[g] but I would
rather have you prophesy. He who proph-
esies is greater than one who speaks in
tongues,[g] unless he interprets, so that the
church may be edified.
[6]Now, brothers, if I come to you and
speak in tongues, what good will I be to
you, unless I bring you some revelation or
knowledge or prophecy or word of in-
struction? [7]Even in the case of lifeless
things that make sounds, such as the flute
or harp, how will anyone know what tune
is being played unless there is a distinc-
tion in the notes? [8]Again, if the trumpet
does not sound a clear call, who will get
ready for battle? [9]So it is with you. Unless
you speak intelligible words with your
tongue, how will anyone know what you
are saying? You will just be speaking into
the air. [10]Undoubtedly there are all sorts
of languages in the world, yet none of
them is without meaning. [11]If then I do

[a]30 Or *other languages* [b]31 Or *But you are eagerly desiring* [c]1 Or *languages* [d]3 Some early manuscripts *body that I may boast* [e]2 Or *another language*; also in verses 4, 13, 14, 19, 26 and 27 [f]2 Or *by the Spirit* [g]5 Or *other languages*; also in verses 6, 18, 22, 23 and 39

not grasp the meaning of what someone is
saying, I am a foreigner to the speaker,
and he is a foreigner to me. 12So it is with
you. Since you are eager to have spiritual
gifts, try to excel in gifts that build up the
church.

13For this reason anyone who speaks in
a tongue should pray that he may inter-
pret what he says. 14For if I pray in a
tongue, my spirit prays, but my mind is
unfruitful. 15So what shall I do? I will pray
with my spirit, but I will also pray with my
mind; I will sing with my spirit, but I will
also sing with my mind. 16If you are prais-
ing God with your spirit, how can one
who finds himself among those who do

VERSE FOR THE DAY:
1 Corinthians 13:7

AUTHOR:
Elisa Morgan

PASSAGE FOR THE DAY:
1 Corinthians 13:1–7

The Curse of Familiarity

In marriage, the task of communication faces a particularly hard-to-conquer curse: familiarity. We may perform for the world, but at home familiarity erodes our energy, saps our strength and cuts off our compassion—all essential ingredients to good listening.

When the phone rings, I am aware of the tone of voice that I use as I answer it, because I don't know who's on the other end. But as soon as I recognize the voice of my mom, my husband or my best friend, my tone relaxes to its usual pitch.

Our homes offer a shelter from the storms of life. But when we grow apathetic within our safe place, the familiarity that was meant to help can end up hurting. When I slip my mind into neutral because it's "just my husband" talking, I need to be reminded of what good listening is all about.

If we want to survive this era in which families are ripped apart almost as fast as they are made, we'll need to fight against the temptation to tune out at home. We need to open our ears—listen to the voices inside the walls of our homes. While good communication alone can't cure a bad marriage, it can make a big difference. If we're to love well those we love most, we'll learn to listen. By learning to really hear what our spouses are saying, we can break the curse of familiarity.

MARRIAGE BUILDERS

♦ *What benefits and pitfalls come with the familiarity that comes with being married?*

♦ *How can you improve your communication radar when it comes to listening to your spouse?*

Additional Scripture Readings
Colossians 3:12; Galatians 5:22–23

Go to page 1268 for your next devotional reading.

not understand[a] say "Amen" to your
thanksgiving, since he does not know
what you are saying? 17You may be giving
thanks well enough, but the other man is
not edified.

18I thank God that I speak in tongues
more than all of you. 19But in the church
I would rather speak five intelligible
words to instruct others than ten thousand words in a tongue.

20Brothers, stop thinking like children.
In regard to evil be infants, but in your
thinking be adults. 21In the Law it is written:

"Through men of strange tongues
and through the lips of foreigners
I will speak to this people,
but even then they will not listen to
me,"[b]
says the Lord.

22Tongues, then, are a sign, not for believers but for unbelievers; prophecy,
however, is for believers, not for unbelievers. 23So if the whole church comes together and everyone speaks in tongues,
and some who do not understand[c] or
some unbelievers come in, will they not
say that you are out of your mind? 24But
if an unbeliever or someone who does not
understand[d] comes in while everybody is
prophesying, he will be convinced by all
that he is a sinner and will be judged by
all, 25and the secrets of his heart will be
laid bare. So he will fall down and worship
God, exclaiming, "God is really among
you!"

Orderly Worship

26What then shall we say, brothers?
When you come together, everyone has a
hymn, or a word of instruction, a revelation, a tongue or an interpretation. All of
these must be done for the strengthening
of the church. 27If anyone speaks in a
tongue, two—or at the most three—
should speak, one at a time, and someone
must interpret. 28If there is no interpreter,
the speaker should keep quiet in the
church and speak to himself and God.

29Two or three prophets should speak,
and the others should weigh carefully
what is said. 30And if a revelation comes to
someone who is sitting down, the first
speaker should stop. 31For you can all
prophesy in turn so that everyone may be
instructed and encouraged. 32The spirits
of prophets are subject to the control of
prophets. 33For God is not a God of disorder but of peace.

As in all the congregations of the saints,
34women should remain silent in the
churches. They are not allowed to speak,
but must be in submission, as the Law
says. 35If they want to inquire about something, they should ask their own husbands at home; for it is disgraceful for a
woman to speak in the church.

36Did the word of God originate with
you? Or are you the only people it has
reached? 37If anybody thinks he is a
prophet or spiritually gifted, let him acknowledge that what I am writing to you
is the Lord's command. 38If he ignores
this, he himself will be ignored.[e]

39Therefore, my brothers, be eager to
prophesy, and do not forbid speaking in
tongues. 40But everything should be done
in a fitting and orderly way.

The Resurrection of Christ

15 Now, brothers, I want to remind
you of the gospel I preached to
you, which you received and on which
you have taken your stand. 2By this gospel
you are saved, if you hold firmly to the
word I preached to you. Otherwise, you
have believed in vain.

3For what I received I passed on to you
as of first importance[f]: that Christ died
for our sins according to the Scriptures,
4that he was buried, that he was raised on
the third day according to the Scriptures,
5and that he appeared to Peter,[g] and then
to the Twelve. 6After that, he appeared to
more than five hundred of the brothers at
the same time, most of whom are still living, though some have fallen asleep.
7Then he appeared to James, then to all
the apostles, 8and last of all he appeared
to me also, as to one abnormally born.

9For I am the least of the apostles and
do not even deserve to be called an apostle, because I persecuted the church of
God. 10But by the grace of God I am what
I am, and his grace to me was not without
effect. No, I worked harder than all of
them—yet not I, but the grace of God that
was with me. 11Whether, then, it was I or

[a] 16 Or *among the inquirers* [b] 21 Isaiah 28:11,12 [c] 23 Or *some inquirers* [d] 24 Or *or some inquirer* [e] 38 Some manuscripts *If he is ignorant of this, let him be ignorant* [f] 3 Or *you at the first* [g] 5 Greek *Cephas*

they, this is what we preach, and this is what you believed.

The Resurrection of the Dead

12But if it is preached that Christ has been raised from the dead, how can some of you say that there is no resurrection of the dead? 13If there is no resurrection of the dead, then not even Christ has been raised. 14And if Christ has not been raised, our preaching is useless and so is your faith. 15More than that, we are then found to be false witnesses about God, for we have testified about God that he raised Christ from the dead. But he did not raise him if in fact the dead are not raised. 16For if the dead are not raised, then Christ has not been raised either. 17And if Christ has not been raised, your faith is futile; you are still in your sins. 18Then those also who have fallen asleep in Christ are lost. 19If only for this life we have hope in Christ, we are to be pitied more than all men.

20But Christ has indeed been raised from the dead, the firstfruits of those who have fallen asleep. 21For since death came through a man, the resurrection of the dead comes also through a man. 22For as in Adam all die, so in Christ all will be made alive. 23But each in his own turn: Christ, the firstfruits; then, when he comes, those who belong to him. 24Then the end will come, when he hands over the kingdom to God the Father after he has destroyed all dominion, authority and power. 25For he must reign until he has put all his enemies under his feet. 26The last enemy to be destroyed is death. 27For he "has put everything under his feet."[a] Now when it says that "everything" has been put under him, it is clear that this does not include God himself, who put everything under Christ. 28When he has done this, then the Son himself will be made subject to him who put everything under him, so that God may be all in all.

29Now if there is no resurrection, what will those do who are baptized for the dead? If the dead are not raised at all, why are people baptized for them? 30And as for us, why do we endanger ourselves every hour? 31I die every day—I mean that, brothers—just as surely as I glory over you in Christ Jesus our Lord. 32If I fought wild beasts in Ephesus for merely human reasons, what have I gained? If the dead are not raised,

"Let us eat and drink,
for tomorrow we die."[b]

33Do not be misled: "Bad company corrupts good character." 34Come back to your senses as you ought, and stop sinning; for there are some who are ignorant of God—I say this to your shame.

The Resurrection Body

35But someone may ask, "How are the dead raised? With what kind of body will they come?" 36How foolish! What you sow does not come to life unless it dies. 37When you sow, you do not plant the body that will be, but just a seed, perhaps of wheat or of something else. 38But God gives it a body as he has determined, and to each kind of seed he gives its own body. 39All flesh is not the same: Men have one kind of flesh, animals have another, birds another and fish another. 40There are also heavenly bodies and there are earthly bodies; but the splendor of the heavenly bodies is one kind, and the splendor of the earthly bodies is another. 41The sun has one kind of splendor, the moon another and the stars another; and star differs from star in splendor.

42So will it be with the resurrection of the dead. The body that is sown is perishable, it is raised imperishable; 43it is sown in dishonor, it is raised in glory; it is sown in weakness, it is raised in power; 44it is sown a natural body, it is raised a spiritual body.

If there is a natural body, there is also a spiritual body. 45So it is written: "The first man Adam became a living being"[c]; the last Adam, a life-giving spirit. 46The spiritual did not come first, but the natural, and after that the spiritual. 47The first man was of the dust of the earth, the second man from heaven. 48As was the earthly man, so are those who are of the earth; and as is the man from heaven, so also are those who are of heaven. 49And just as we have borne the likeness of the earthly man, so shall we[d] bear the likeness of the man from heaven.

50I declare to you, brothers, that flesh and blood cannot inherit the kingdom of God, nor does the perishable inherit the imperishable. 51Listen, I tell you a mystery: We will not all sleep, but we will all

[a] *27* Psalm 8:6 [b] *32* Isaiah 22:13 [c] *45* Gen. 2:7 [d] *49* Some early manuscripts *so let us*

be changed— 52in a flash, in the twinkling
of an eye, at the last trumpet. For the
trumpet will sound, the dead will be
raised imperishable, and we will be
changed. 53For the perishable must clothe
itself with the imperishable, and the mor-
tal with immortality. 54When the perish-
able has been clothed with the imperish-
able, and the mortal with immortality,
then the saying that is written will come
true: "Death has been swallowed up in
victory."[a]

55"Where, O death, is your victory?
Where, O death, is your sting?"[b]

56The sting of death is sin, and the power
of sin is the law. 57But thanks be to God!
He gives us the victory through our Lord
Jesus Christ.

58Therefore, my dear brothers, stand
firm. Let nothing move you. Always give
yourselves fully to the work of the Lord,
because you know that your labor in the
Lord is not in vain.

The Collection for God's People

16 Now about the collection for God's
people: Do what I told the Galatian
churches to do. 2On the first day of every
week, each one of you should set aside a
sum of money in keeping with his income,
saving it up, so that when I come no col-
lections will have to be made. 3Then,
when I arrive, I will give letters of intro-
duction to the men you approve and send
them with your gift to Jerusalem. 4If it
seems advisable for me to go also, they
will accompany me.

Personal Requests

5After I go through Macedonia, I will
come to you—for I will be going through
Macedonia. 6Perhaps I will stay with you
awhile, or even spend the winter, so that
you can help me on my journey, wherever
I go. 7I do not want to see you now and
make only a passing visit; I hope to spend
some time with you, if the Lord permits.
8But I will stay on at Ephesus until Pente-
cost, 9because a great door for effective
work has opened to me, and there are
many who oppose me.

10If Timothy comes, see to it that he has
nothing to fear while he is with you, for he
is carrying on the work of the Lord, just as
I am. 11No one, then, should refuse to ac-
cept him. Send him on his way in peace so
that he may return to me. I am expecting
him along with the brothers.

12Now about our brother Apollos: I
strongly urged him to go to you with the
brothers. He was quite unwilling to go
now, but he will go when he has the op-
portunity.

13Be on your guard; stand firm in the
faith; be men of courage; be strong. 14Do
everything in love.

15You know that the household of
Stephanas were the first converts in Acha-
ia, and they have devoted themselves to
the service of the saints. I urge you, broth-
ers, 16to submit to such as these and to ev-
eryone who joins in the work, and labors
at it. 17I was glad when Stephanas, Fortu-
natus and Achaicus arrived, because they
have supplied what was lacking from you.
18For they refreshed my spirit and yours
also. Such men deserve recognition.

Final Greetings

19The churches in the province of Asia
send you greetings. Aquila and Priscilla[c]
greet you warmly in the Lord, and so does
the church that meets at their house. 20All
the brothers here send you greetings.
Greet one another with a holy kiss.

21I, Paul, write this greeting in my own
hand.

22If anyone does not love the Lord—a
curse be on him. Come, O Lord[d]!

23The grace of the Lord Jesus be with
you.

24My love to all of you in Christ Jesus.
Amen.[e]

[a]54 Isaiah 25:8 [b]55 Hosea 13:14 [c]19 Greek *Prisca*, a variant of *Priscilla* [d]22 In Aramaic the expression *Come, O Lord* is *Marana tha*. [e]24 Some manuscripts do not have *Amen*.

PAUL writes this second letter to the church in Corinth from Macedonia (Acts 20:1; 2 Corinthians 7:5), while on his way to Corinth (2 Corinthians 13:1). As the most personal of all his letters, he expresses both how exciting and how painful his life as a missionary has been. He also finds it necessary to defend himself against those who are criticizing him. As you read this letter, think about how exciting it can be to serve the Lord, but realize too that being a Christian can sometimes lead to pain and suffering.

2 CORINTHIANS

1 Paul, an apostle of Christ Jesus by the will of God, and Timothy our brother,

To the church of God in Corinth, together with all the saints throughout Achaia:

2 Grace and peace to you from God our Father and the Lord Jesus Christ.

The God of All Comfort

3 Praise be to the God and Father of our Lord Jesus Christ, the Father of compassion and the God of all comfort, 4 who comforts us in all our troubles, so that we can comfort those in any trouble with the comfort we ourselves have received from God. 5 For just as the sufferings of Christ flow over into our lives, so also through Christ our comfort overflows. 6 If we are distressed, it is for your comfort and salvation; if we are comforted, it is for your comfort, which produces in you patient endurance of the same sufferings we suffer. 7 And our hope for you is firm, because we know that just as you share in our sufferings, so also you share in our comfort.

8 We do not want you to be uninformed, brothers, about the hardships we suffered in the province of Asia. We were under great pressure, far beyond our ability to endure, so that we despaired even of life.

9Indeed, in our hearts we felt the sentence
of death. But this happened that we might
not rely on ourselves but on God, who
raises the dead. 10He has delivered us
from such a deadly peril, and he will deliver us. On him we have set our hope that
he will continue to deliver us, 11as you
help us by your prayers. Then many will
give thanks on our[a] behalf for the gracious favor granted us in answer to the
prayers of many.

Paul's Change of Plans

12Now this is our boast: Our conscience
testifies that we have conducted ourselves
in the world, and especially in our relations with you, in the holiness and sincerity that are from God. We have done so not
according to worldly wisdom but according to God's grace. 13For we do not write
you anything you cannot read or understand. And I hope that, 14as you have understood us in part, you will come to understand fully that you can boast of us just
as we will boast of you in the day of the
Lord Jesus.

15Because I was confident of this, I
planned to visit you first so that you might
benefit twice. 16I planned to visit you on
my way to Macedonia and to come back
to you from Macedonia, and then to have
you send me on my way to Judea. 17When
I planned this, did I do it lightly? Or do I
make my plans in a worldly manner so
that in the same breath I say, "Yes, yes"
and "No, no"?

18But as surely as God is faithful, our
message to you is not "Yes" and "No."
19For the Son of God, Jesus Christ, who
was preached among you by me and Silas[b] and Timothy, was not "Yes" and
"No," but in him it has always been "Yes."
20For no matter how many promises God
has made, they are "Yes" in Christ. And so
through him the "Amen" is spoken by us
to the glory of God. 21Now it is God who
makes both us and you stand firm in
Christ. He anointed us, 22set his seal of
ownership on us, and put his Spirit in our
hearts as a deposit, guaranteeing what is
to come.

23I call God as my witness that it was in
order to spare you that I did not return to
Corinth. 24Not that we lord it over your
faith, but we work with you for your joy,
because it is by faith you stand firm.

2 1So I made up my mind that I would
not make another painful visit to you.
2For if I grieve you, who is left to make me
glad but you whom I have grieved? 3I
wrote as I did so that when I came I should
not be distressed by those who ought to
make me rejoice. I had confidence in all of
you, that you would all share my joy. 4For
I wrote you out of great distress and anguish of heart and with many tears, not to
grieve you but to let you know the depth
of my love for you.

Forgiveness for the Sinner

5If anyone has caused grief, he has not
so much grieved me as he has grieved all
of you, to some extent—not to put it too
severely. 6The punishment inflicted on
him by the majority is sufficient for him.
7Now instead, you ought to forgive and
comfort him, so that he will not be overwhelmed by excessive sorrow. 8I urge
you, therefore, to reaffirm your love for
him. 9The reason I wrote you was to see
if you would stand the test and be obedient in everything. 10If you forgive anyone,
I also forgive him. And what I have forgiven—if there was anything to forgive—I
have forgiven in the sight of Christ for
your sake, 11in order that Satan might not
outwit us. For we are not unaware of his
schemes.

Ministers of the New Covenant

12Now when I went to Troas to preach
the gospel of Christ and found that the
Lord had opened a door for me, 13I still
had no peace of mind, because I did not
find my brother Titus there. So I said
good-by to them and went on to Macedonia.

14But thanks be to God, who always
leads us in triumphal procession in Christ
and through us spreads everywhere the
fragrance of the knowledge of him. 15For
we are to God the aroma of Christ among
those who are being saved and those who
are perishing. 16To the one we are the
smell of death; to the other, the fragrance
of life. And who is equal to such a task?
17Unlike so many, we do not peddle the
word of God for profit. On the contrary, in
Christ we speak before God with sincerity,
like men sent from God.

3 Are we beginning to commend ourselves again? Or do we need, like
some people, letters of recommendation

[a] 11 Many manuscripts *your* [b] 19 Greek *Silvanus*, a variant of *Silas*

to you or from you? [2]You yourselves are
our letter, written on our hearts, known
and read by everybody. [3]You show that
you are a letter from Christ, the result of
our ministry, written not with ink but with
the Spirit of the living God, not on tablets
of stone but on tablets of human hearts.
[4]Such confidence as this is ours
through Christ before God. [5]Not that we
are competent in ourselves to claim any-
thing for ourselves, but our competence
comes from God. [6]He has made us compe-
tent as ministers of a new covenant—not
of the letter but of the Spirit; for the letter
kills, but the Spirit gives life.

The Glory of the New Covenant

[7]Now if the ministry that brought death,
which was engraved in letters on stone,
came with glory, so that the Israelites
could not look steadily at the face of Mo-
ses because of its glory, fading though it
was, [8]will not the ministry of the Spirit be
even more glorious? [9]If the ministry that
condemns men is glorious, how much
more glorious is the ministry that brings
righteousness! [10]For what was glorious
has no glory now in comparison with the
surpassing glory. [11]And if what was fading
away came with glory, how much greater
is the glory of that which lasts!

VERSE FOR THE DAY: 2 Corinthians 1:20 | AUTHOR: Evelyn Christenson | PASSAGE FOR THE DAY: 2 Corinthians 1:18–22

Seeking God's Face

A faithful prayer life is a costly life. It may mean loss of sleep, missing favorite television programs, not having coffee with friends. It may even mean going through some deep waters so that we have the opportunity to learn trust.

I was in my early twenties when we lost our third baby. I'd miscarried once, had a stillborn baby, then miscarried again. At that difficult time, I took hold of Romans 8:28, which says that because I have been called by God and he loves me, he is turning everything into good for me. But to believe that promise, I had to learn to know the One who made it. And to learn to know him, I had to learn to pray.

I took that promise on faith, and for more than forty years I have watched it work in my life. It has been my anchor, my rock of granite. I know I can trust him because I know who he is. He is the God of the universe whom I have met face-to-face in prayer.

MARRIAGE BUILDERS

♦ *What life experiences have forced you to trust God more completely? What role did prayer play as you went through those times?*
♦ *How does meeting God "face-to-face" build your trust in him?*

Additional Scripture Readings
Romans 8:28; 1 Peter 3:12; 1 John 5:14

Go to page 1269 for your next devotional reading.

WEEKENDING

MONEY

Learning to respect a mate's money perspective is a great way to invest in marriage. Discuss your answers to these questions:

1. What is my own relationship with money? Does money make me feel anxious, guilty, loved, responsible, secure? What assumptions and values about money did I develop while growing up?

2. Do I ever label my spouse's money attitudes as right or wrong? How can I listen closely to pick up on his or her hurts, fears and hopes that get channeled into money? How can I begin to focus on empathizing rather than criticizing?

3. What I can learn from my spouse? How can I temporarily suspend my own biases and see what my spouse can teach me?

4. Whom could we ask for advice? Since some money conflicts are caused by not being aware of the options, who can refer us to a qualified financial advisor who will respect our priorities?

— *Beverly J. Burch*

REVIVE

Saturday: 1 Timothy 6:17–19
Sunday: Matthew 22:15–22

Go to page 1270 for your next devotional reading.

VERSE FOR THE DAY:
2 Corinthians 3:18

AUTHOR:
Jeanette and Robert Lauer

PASSAGE FOR THE DAY:
2 Corinthians 3:7–18

Mountain Climbers

By the time Beth and Phil joined our newlyweds' group, the differences between them had become nearly intolerable. Beth complained that Phil was boring and uncommunicative; Phil was tired of Beth's demands that he talk or that they do something exciting together. But over time they learned to modify their behaviors and save their marriage. Each of them changed, and each helped the other to change.

Some changes come with time: passions cool, energies wane and children and careers intrude on the amount of time a couple can spend together. Other changes occur by design, as happens when a couple sets out to alter each other's behavior.

Usually, one spouse's attempts to change the other end in failure. However, two people *can* make each other more compatible through "mutual education." Each partner helps change the other by seeking to replace one behavior with another that is more preferable. And always at the heart of mutual education is the principle of gentle persuasion, not coerced change. Any effort to help your spouse change should send the message: "I love you. I believe this change would benefit you and it will mean much to me. Would you give it a try?"

Affirm the value of change, and remember that it's a two-way street. The two of you are like mountain climbers, each lending a hand to the other, making suggestions and giving encouragement, as you work toward the same goal: A stronger, more fulfilling relationship.

MARRIAGE BUILDERS

♦ *It's clear that God wants to help people change for the better. Why do you think change is so difficult in a marriage relationship?*
♦ *Why is it so hard to help each other change? How can God help?*

Additional Scripture Readings
Ephesians 4:15–16; Philippians 2:12; Proverbs 27:17

Go to page 1272 for your next devotional reading.

12Therefore, since we have such a hope,
we are very bold. 13We are not like Moses,
who would put a veil over his face to keep
the Israelites from gazing at it while the
radiance was fading away. 14But their
minds were made dull, for to this day the
same veil remains when the old covenant
is read. It has not been removed, because
only in Christ is it taken away. 15Even to
this day when Moses is read, a veil covers
their hearts. 16But whenever anyone turns
to the Lord, the veil is taken away. 17Now
the Lord is the Spirit, and where the Spirit
of the Lord is, there is freedom. 18And we,
who with unveiled faces all reflect[a] the
Lord's glory, are being transformed into
his likeness with ever-increasing glory,
which comes from the Lord, who is the
Spirit.

Treasures in Jars of Clay

4 Therefore, since through God's mercy
we have this ministry, we do not lose
heart. 2Rather, we have renounced secret
and shameful ways; we do not use decep-
tion, nor do we distort the word of God.
On the contrary, by setting forth the truth
plainly we commend ourselves to every
man's conscience in the sight of God.
3And even if our gospel is veiled, it is
veiled to those who are perishing. 4The
god of this age has blinded the minds of
unbelievers, so that they cannot see the
light of the gospel of the glory of Christ,
who is the image of God. 5For we do not
preach ourselves, but Jesus Christ as
Lord, and ourselves as your servants for
Jesus' sake. 6For God, who said, "Let light
shine out of darkness,"[b] made his light
shine in our hearts to give us the light of
the knowledge of the glory of God in the
face of Christ.

7But we have this treasure in jars of clay
to show that this all-surpassing power is
from God and not from us. 8We are hard
pressed on every side, but not crushed;
perplexed, but not in despair; 9persecut-
ed, but not abandoned; struck down, but
not destroyed. 10We always carry around
in our body the death of Jesus, so that the
life of Jesus may also be revealed in our
body. 11For we who are alive are always
being given over to death for Jesus' sake,
so that his life may be revealed in our
mortal body. 12So then, death is at work in
us, but life is at work in you.

13It is written: "I believed; therefore I
have spoken."[c] With that same spirit of
faith we also believe and therefore speak,
14because we know that the one who
raised the Lord Jesus from the dead will
also raise us with Jesus and present us
with you in his presence. 15All this is for
your benefit, so that the grace that is
reaching more and more people may
cause thanksgiving to overflow to the glo-
ry of God.

16Therefore we do not lose heart.
Though outwardly we are wasting away,
yet inwardly we are being renewed day by
day. 17For our light and momentary trou-
bles are achieving for us an eternal glory
that far outweighs them all. 18So we fix
our eyes not on what is seen, but on what
is unseen. For what is seen is temporary,
but what is unseen is eternal.

Our Heavenly Dwelling

5 Now we know that if the earthly tent
we live in is destroyed, we have a
building from God, an eternal house in
heaven, not built by human hands.
2Meanwhile we groan, longing to be
clothed with our heavenly dwelling, 3be-
cause when we are clothed, we will not be
found naked. 4For while we are in this
tent, we groan and are burdened, because
we do not wish to be unclothed but to be
clothed with our heavenly dwelling, so
that what is mortal may be swallowed up
by life. 5Now it is God who has made us
for this very purpose and has given us the
Spirit as a deposit, guaranteeing what is to
come.

6Therefore we are always confident and
know that as long as we are at home in the
body we are away from the Lord. 7We live
by faith, not by sight. 8We are confident,
I say, and would prefer to be away from
the body and at home with the Lord. 9So
we make it our goal to please him, wheth-
er we are at home in the body or away
from it. 10For we must all appear before
the judgment seat of Christ, that each one
may receive what is due him for the things
done while in the body, whether good or
bad.

The Ministry of Reconciliation

11Since, then, we know what it is to fear
the Lord, we try to persuade men. What
we are is plain to God, and I hope it is also

[a]18 Or *contemplate* [b]6 Gen. 1:3 [c]13 Psalm 116:10

plain to your conscience. 12We are not trying to commend ourselves to you again,
but are giving you an opportunity to take
pride in us, so that you can answer those
who take pride in what is seen rather than
in what is in the heart. 13If we are out of
our mind, it is for the sake of God; if we
are in our right mind, it is for you. 14For
Christ's love compels us, because we are
convinced that one died for all, and there-
fore all died. 15And he died for all, that
those who live should no longer live for
themselves but for him who died for them
and was raised again.

16So from now on we regard no one
from a worldly point of view. Though we
once regarded Christ in this way, we do so
no longer. 17Therefore, if anyone is in
Christ, he is a new creation; the old has
gone, the new has come! 18All this is from
God, who reconciled us to himself
through Christ and gave us the ministry of
reconciliation: 19that God was reconciling
the world to himself in Christ, not count-
ing men's sins against them. And he has
committed to us the message of reconcil-
iation. 20We are therefore Christ's ambas-
sadors, as though God were making his
appeal through us. We implore you on
Christ's behalf: Be reconciled to God.

VERSE FOR THE DAY: 2 Corinthians 4:17

AUTHOR: David Myers and Thomas Ludwig

PASSAGE FOR THE DAY: 2 Corinthians 4:7–18

A Cosmic Perspective

Christian faith encourages us with the good news that our struggles will not endure forever. Authentic Christian hope is not built on a make-believe escape from life's frustrations and agonies, but it does promise that evil, deprivation and heartache are not the last word.

At the end of his *Chronicles of Narnia*, C.S. Lewis depicts heaven as the ultimate liberation from the relativity of earthly experience. Here creatures cannot feel deprived, depressed or anxious. There is no letdown after an achievement, for happiness is continually expanding. Here is "the Great Story, which no one on earth has read: which goes on forever: in which every chapter is better than the one before." This resurrection hope does not eliminate the ups and downs of day-to-day life, but it does offer a liberating cosmic perspective from which to view them.

MARRIAGE BUILDERS

- *What do you most look forward to about heaven?*
- *What things are you struggling with—as individuals, as a couple, as a family? Remember God's promise of "an eternal glory that far outweighs them all."*

Additional Scripture Readings
2 Corinthians 3:17–18; Hebrews 10:19–25; Philippians 3:12–14

Go to page 1273 for your next devotional reading.

21God made him who had no sin to be
sin[a] for us, so that in him we might be-
come the righteousness of God.
6 As God's fellow workers we urge you
not to receive God's grace in vain.
2For he says,

"In the time of my favor I heard you,
and in the day of salvation I helped
you."[b]

I tell you, now is the time of God's favor,
now is the day of salvation.

[a]21 Or *be a sin offering* [b]2 Isaiah 49:8

VERSE FOR THE DAY:
2 Corinthians 5:17

AUTHOR:
Ron R. Lee

PASSAGE FOR THE DAY:
2 Corinthians 5:16–21

Point of View

A few years ago, my pre-school-age daughter started giving a blow-by-blow account of my weekday morning ritual. "First, Dad takes a shower," she told my wife, Jeanette. "Then he gets dressed and eats breakfast. Then he brushes his teeth and gurgles (her word for 'gargles') and *then* he spits! Then he puts on his tie and does this (she runs her hand down her chest)."

Seeing my daughter act out my morning ritual was pretty entertaining. So why don't I find it amusing when, from time to time, my *wife* offers a few insightful observations regarding my behavior?

We may not want to acknowledge it, but our spouses are in an excellent position to tell us we're not the exemplary people we think we are. Over the years, Jeanette has observed a good number of things that I had somehow failed to notice about myself. My wife sees me from the outside, a vantage point that is uniquely different from my own.

The longer we're married, the more I realize how much I need Jeanette's input. Without her insight, and at times, her prodding, I could easily take the path of least resistance and miss out on a lifetime of personal growth.

MARRIAGE BUILDERS

♦ *How do you feel about having someone else get so close to the real you?*

♦ *How can the intimate knowledge of each other that you share as married Christians be an important asset to personal growth?*

Additional Scripture Readings
Proverbs 27:17; 2 Corinthians 3:18

Go to page 1276 for your next devotional reading.

Paul's Hardships

3We put no stumbling block in anyone's path, so that our ministry will not be
discredited. 4Rather, as servants of God
we commend ourselves in every way: in
great endurance; in troubles, hardships
and distresses; 5in beatings, imprison-
ments and riots; in hard work, sleepless
nights and hunger; 6in purity, understand-
ing, patience and kindness; in the Holy
Spirit and in sincere love; 7in truthful
speech and in the power of God; with
weapons of righteousness in the right
hand and in the left; 8through glory and
dishonor, bad report and good report;
genuine, yet regarded as impostors;
9known, yet regarded as unknown; dying,
and yet we live on; beaten, and yet not
killed; 10sorrowful, yet always rejoicing;
poor, yet making many rich; having noth-
ing, and yet possessing everything.
11We have spoken freely to you, Corin-
thians, and opened wide our hearts to
you. 12We are not withholding our affec-
tion from you, but you are withholding
yours from us. 13As a fair exchange—I
speak as to my children—open wide your
hearts also.

Do Not Be Yoked With Unbelievers

14Do not be yoked together with unbe-
lievers. For what do righteousness and
wickedness have in common? Or what fel-
lowship can light have with darkness?
15What harmony is there between Christ
and Belial[a]? What does a believer have in
common with an unbeliever? 16What
agreement is there between the temple of
God and idols? For we are the temple of
the living God. As God has said: "I will live
with them and walk among them, and I
will be their God, and they will be my peo-
ple."[b]

17"Therefore come out from them
and be separate,
says the Lord.
Touch no unclean thing,
and I will receive you."[c]
18"I will be a Father to you,
and you will be my sons and
daughters,
says the Lord Almighty."[d]

7 Since we have these promises, dear
friends, let us purify ourselves from
everything that contaminates body and
spirit, perfecting holiness out of reverence
for God.

Paul's Joy

2Make room for us in your hearts. We
have wronged no one, we have corrupted
no one, we have exploited no one. 3I do
not say this to condemn you; I have said
before that you have such a place in our
hearts that we would live or die with you.
4I have great confidence in you; I take
great pride in you. I am greatly encour-
aged; in all our troubles my joy knows no
bounds.
5For when we came into Macedonia,
this body of ours had no rest, but we were
harassed at every turn—conflicts on the
outside, fears within. 6But God, who com-
forts the downcast, comforted us by the
coming of Titus, 7and not only by his com-
ing but also by the comfort you had given
him. He told us about your longing for me,
your deep sorrow, your ardent concern
for me, so that my joy was greater than
ever.
8Even if I caused you sorrow by my let-
ter, I do not regret it. Though I did regret
it—I see that my letter hurt you, but only
for a little while— 9yet now I am happy,
not because you were made sorry, but be-
cause your sorrow led you to repentance.
For you became sorrowful as God intend-
ed and so were not harmed in any way by
us. 10Godly sorrow brings repentance that
leads to salvation and leaves no regret, but
worldly sorrow brings death. 11See what
this godly sorrow has produced in you:
what earnestness, what eagerness to clear
yourselves, what indignation, what alarm,
what longing, what concern, what read-
iness to see justice done. At every point
you have proved yourselves to be inno-
cent in this matter. 12So even though I
wrote to you, it was not on account of the
one who did the wrong or of the injured
party, but rather that before God you
could see for yourselves how devoted to
us you are. 13By all this we are encour-
aged.
In addition to our own encouragement,
we were especially delighted to see how
happy Titus was, because his spirit has
been refreshed by all of you. 14I had boast-
ed to him about you, and you have not
embarrassed me. But just as everything

[a] 15 Greek *Beliar*, a variant of *Belial* [b] 16 Lev. 26:12; Jer. 32:38; Ezek. 37:27 [c] 17 Isaiah 52:11; Ezek. 20:34,41 [d] 18 2 Samuel 7:14; 7:8

we said to you was true, so our boasting about you to Titus has proved to be true as well. 15And his affection for you is all the greater when he remembers that you were all obedient, receiving him with fear and trembling. 16I am glad I can have complete confidence in you.

Generosity Encouraged

8 And now, brothers, we want you to know about the grace that God has given the Macedonian churches. 2Out of the most severe trial, their overflowing joy and their extreme poverty welled up in rich generosity. 3For I testify that they gave as much as they were able, and even beyond their ability. Entirely on their own, 4they urgently pleaded with us for the privilege of sharing in this service to the saints. 5And they did not do as we expected, but they gave themselves first to the Lord and then to us in keeping with God's will. 6So we urged Titus, since he had earlier made a beginning, to bring also to completion this act of grace on your part. 7But just as you excel in everything—in faith, in speech, in knowledge, in complete earnestness and in your love for us[a]—see that you also excel in this grace of giving.

8I am not commanding you, but I want to test the sincerity of your love by comparing it with the earnestness of others. 9For you know the grace of our Lord Jesus Christ, that though he was rich, yet for your sakes he became poor, so that you through his poverty might become rich.

10And here is my advice about what is best for you in this matter: Last year you were the first not only to give but also to have the desire to do so. 11Now finish the work, so that your eager willingness to do it may be matched by your completion of it, according to your means. 12For if the willingness is there, the gift is acceptable according to what one has, not according to what he does not have.

13Our desire is not that others might be relieved while you are hard pressed, but that there might be equality. 14At the present time your plenty will supply what they need, so that in turn their plenty will supply what you need. Then there will be equality, 15as it is written: "He who gathered much did not have too much, and he who gathered little did not have too little."[b]

Titus Sent to Corinth

16I thank God, who put into the heart of Titus the same concern I have for you. 17For Titus not only welcomed our appeal, but he is coming to you with much enthusiasm and on his own initiative. 18And we are sending along with him the brother who is praised by all the churches for his service to the gospel. 19What is more, he was chosen by the churches to accompany us as we carry the offering, which we administer in order to honor the Lord himself and to show our eagerness to help. 20We want to avoid any criticism of the way we administer this liberal gift. 21For we are taking pains to do what is right, not only in the eyes of the Lord but also in the eyes of men.

22In addition, we are sending with them our brother who has often proved to us in many ways that he is zealous, and now even more so because of his great confidence in you. 23As for Titus, he is my partner and fellow worker among you; as for our brothers, they are representatives of the churches and an honor to Christ. 24Therefore show these men the proof of your love and the reason for our pride in you, so that the churches can see it.

9 There is no need for me to write to you about this service to the saints. 2For I know your eagerness to help, and I have been boasting about it to the Macedonians, telling them that since last year you in Achaia were ready to give; and your enthusiasm has stirred most of them to action. 3But I am sending the brothers in order that our boasting about you in this matter should not prove hollow, but that you may be ready, as I said you would be. 4For if any Macedonians come with me and find you unprepared, we—not to say anything about you—would be ashamed of having been so confident. 5So I thought it necessary to urge the brothers to visit you in advance and finish the arrangements for the generous gift you had promised. Then it will be ready as a generous gift, not as one grudgingly given.

Sowing Generously

6Remember this: Whoever sows sparingly will also reap sparingly, and whoever sows generously will also reap generously. 7Each man should give what he has decided in his heart to give, not reluctant-

[a]7 Some manuscripts *in our love for you* [b]15 Exodus 16:18

ly or under compulsion, for God loves a cheerful giver. 8And God is able to make all grace abound to you, so that in all things at all times, having all that you need, you will abound in every good work. 9As it is written:

"He has scattered abroad his gifts to the poor;
his righteousness endures forever."[a]

10Now he who supplies seed to the sower and bread for food will also supply and in-

[a]9 Psalm 112:9

VERSE FOR THE DAY: 2 Corinthians 9:6–7

AUTHOR: Ronald Blue

PASSAGE FOR THE DAY: 2 Corinthians 9:6–15

Why Give to God?

If the Bible told us an exact amount (or percentage) to give, it would allow us to feel that a certain portion of our income is God's and the rest is ours to do with as we please. But the truth is that God owns it all, and part of our training in obedience is learning to let him lead us in this area.

Taken together, the tithes and other offerings that are commanded in the Old Testament actually total 23 percent—not 10 percent (Numbers 18:21). The New Testament sets a higher standard for giving—the example of Christ. The new guideline for giving is found in 2 Corinthians 9:6–7: ". . . whoever sows sparingly will also reap sparingly, and whoever sows generously will also reap generously. Each man should give what he has decided in his heart to give, not reluctantly or under compulsion, for God loves a cheerful giver." And 2 Corinthians 8:12 instructs us to give in relation to our prosperity.

Couples should discuss this issue and then create their own financial plan—including a plan for giving. Giving is good when it is done prayerfully and in harmony with your spouse; when it does not cause a stumbling block for the recipient or for your spouse; and when it is done with the right attitude. But giving is *not* good if it drives a wedge between the two of you. Remember, God doesn't need your money. Giving is for *your* benefit.

MARRIAGE BUILDERS

- *How does giving benefit you?*
- *How can the two of you make sure that giving is a source of satisfaction and joy and not just an obligation or difficulty?*

Additional Scripture Readings
Numbers 18:21; 2 Corinthians 8:12

Go to page 1279 for your next devotional reading.

crease your store of seed and will enlarge
the harvest of your righteousness. 11You
will be made rich in every way so that you
can be generous on every occasion, and
through us your generosity will result in
thanksgiving to God.
12This service that you perform is not
only supplying the needs of God's people
but is also overflowing in many expres-
sions of thanks to God. 13Because of the
service by which you have proved your-
selves, men will praise God for the obedi-
ence that accompanies your confession of
the gospel of Christ, and for your genero-
sity in sharing with them and with every-
one else. 14And in their prayers for you
their hearts will go out to you, because of
the surpassing grace God has given you.
15Thanks be to God for his indescribable
gift!

Paul's Defense of His Ministry

10 By the meekness and gentleness of
Christ, I appeal to you—I, Paul,
who am "timid" when face to face with
you, but "bold" when away! 2I beg you
that when I come I may not have to be as
bold as I expect to be toward some people
who think that we live by the standards of
this world. 3For though we live in the
world, we do not wage war as the world
does. 4The weapons we fight with are not
the weapons of the world. On the con-
trary, they have divine power to demolish
strongholds. 5We demolish arguments
and every pretension that sets itself up
against the knowledge of God, and we
take captive every thought to make it obe-
dient to Christ. 6And we will be ready to
punish every act of disobedience, once
your obedience is complete.
7You are looking only on the surface of
things.[a] If anyone is confident that he be-
longs to Christ, he should consider again
that we belong to Christ just as much as
he. 8For even if I boast somewhat freely
about the authority the Lord gave us for
building you up rather than pulling you
down, I will not be ashamed of it. 9I do not
want to seem to be trying to frighten you
with my letters. 10For some say, "His let-
ters are weighty and forceful, but in per-
son he is unimpressive and his speaking
amounts to nothing." 11Such people
should realize that what we are in our let-
ters when we are absent, we will be in our
actions when we are present.
12We do not dare to classify or compare
ourselves with some who commend
themselves. When they measure them-
selves by themselves and compare them-
selves with themselves, they are not wise.
13We, however, will not boast beyond
proper limits, but will confine our boast-
ing to the field God has assigned to us, a
field that reaches even to you. 14We are
not going too far in our boasting, as would
be the case if we had not come to you, for
we did get as far as you with the gospel of
Christ. 15Neither do we go beyond our
limits by boasting of work done by oth-
ers.[b] Our hope is that, as your faith con-
tinues to grow, our area of activity among
you will greatly expand, 16so that we can
preach the gospel in the regions beyond
you. For we do not want to boast about
work already done in another man's terri-
tory. 17But, "Let him who boasts boast in
the Lord."[c] 18For it is not the one who
commends himself who is approved, but
the one whom the Lord commends.

Paul and the False Apostles

11 I hope you will put up with a little
of my foolishness; but you are al-
ready doing that. 2I am jealous for you
with a godly jealousy. I promised you to
one husband, to Christ, so that I might
present you as a pure virgin to him. 3But
I am afraid that just as Eve was deceived
by the serpent's cunning, your minds may
somehow be led astray from your sincere
and pure devotion to Christ. 4For if some-
one comes to you and preaches a Jesus
other than the Jesus we preached, or if
you receive a different spirit from the one
you received, or a different gospel from
the one you accepted, you put up with it
easily enough. 5But I do not think I am in
the least inferior to those "super-apos-
tles." 6I may not be a trained speaker, but
I do have knowledge. We have made this
perfectly clear to you in every way.
7Was it a sin for me to lower myself in
order to elevate you by preaching the gos-
pel of God to you free of charge? 8I robbed
other churches by receiving support from
them so as to serve you. 9And when I was

[a] 7 Or *Look at the obvious facts* [b] 13-15 Or *13We, however, will not boast about things that cannot be measured, but we will boast according to the standard of measurement that the God of measure has assigned us—a measurement that relates even to you. 14 . . . 15Neither do we boast about things that cannot be measured in regard to the work done by others.* [c] 17 Jer. 9:24

with you and needed something, I was not
a burden to anyone, for the brothers who
came from Macedonia supplied what I
needed. I have kept myself from being a
burden to you in any way, and will contin-
ue to do so. [10]As surely as the truth of
Christ is in me, nobody in the regions of
Achaia will stop this boasting of mine.
[11]Why? Because I do not love you? God
knows I do! [12]And I will keep on doing
what I am doing in order to cut the ground
from under those who want an opportuni-
ty to be considered equal with us in the
things they boast about.

[13]For such men are false apostles, de-
ceitful workmen, masquerading as apos-
tles of Christ. [14]And no wonder, for Satan
himself masquerades as an angel of light.
[15]It is not surprising, then, if his servants
masquerade as servants of righteousness.
Their end will be what their actions de-
serve.

Paul Boasts About His Sufferings

[16]I repeat: Let no one take me for a fool.
But if you do, then receive me just as you
would a fool, so that I may do a little
boasting. [17]In this self-confident boasting
I am not talking as the Lord would, but as
a fool. [18]Since many are boasting in the
way the world does, I too will boast. [19]You
gladly put up with fools since you are so
wise! [20]In fact, you even put up with any-
one who enslaves you or exploits you or
takes advantage of you or pushes himself
forward or slaps you in the face. [21]To my
shame I admit that we were too weak for
that!

What anyone else dares to boast
about—I am speaking as a fool—I also
dare to boast about. [22]Are they Hebrews?
So am I. Are they Israelites? So am I. Are
they Abraham's descendants? So am I.
[23]Are they servants of Christ? (I am out of
my mind to talk like this.) I am more. I
have worked much harder, been in prison
more frequently, been flogged more se-
verely, and been exposed to death again
and again. [24]Five times I received from the
Jews the forty lashes minus one. [25]Three
times I was beaten with rods, once I was
stoned, three times I was shipwrecked, I
spent a night and a day in the open sea, [26]I
have been constantly on the move. I have
been in danger from rivers, in danger from
bandits, in danger from my own country-
men, in danger from Gentiles; in danger in
the city, in danger in the country, in dan-
ger at sea; and in danger from false broth-
ers. [27]I have labored and toiled and have
often gone without sleep; I have known
hunger and thirst and have often gone
without food; I have been cold and naked.
[28]Besides everything else, I face daily the
pressure of my concern for all the
churches. [29]Who is weak, and I do not feel
weak? Who is led into sin, and I do not
inwardly burn?

[30]If I must boast, I will boast of the
things that show my weakness. [31]The God
and Father of the Lord Jesus, who is to be
praised forever, knows that I am not lying.
[32]In Damascus the governor under King
Aretas had the city of the Damascenes
guarded in order to arrest me. [33]But I was
lowered in a basket from a window in the
wall and slipped through his hands.

Paul's Vision and His Thorn

12 I must go on boasting. Although
there is nothing to be gained, I will
go on to visions and revelations from the
Lord. [2]I know a man in Christ who four-
teen years ago was caught up to the third
heaven. Whether it was in the body or out
of the body I do not know—God knows.
[3]And I know that this man—whether in
the body or apart from the body I do not
know, but God knows— [4]was caught
up to paradise. He heard inexpressible
things, things that man is not permitted to
tell. [5]I will boast about a man like that, but
I will not boast about myself, except about
my weaknesses. [6]Even if I should choose
to boast, I would not be a fool, because I
would be speaking the truth. But I refrain,
so no one will think more of me than is
warranted by what I do or say.

[7]To keep me from becoming conceited
because of these surpassingly great reve-
lations, there was given me a thorn in my
flesh, a messenger of Satan, to torment
me. [8]Three times I pleaded with the Lord
to take it away from me. [9]But he said to
me, "My grace is sufficient for you, for my
power is made perfect in weakness."
Therefore I will boast all the more gladly
about my weaknesses, so that Christ's
power may rest on me. [10]That is why, for
Christ's sake, I delight in weaknesses, in
insults, in hardships, in persecutions, in
difficulties. For when I am weak, then I
am strong.

Paul's Concern for the Corinthians

[11]I have made a fool of myself, but you
drove me to it. I ought to have been com-
mended by you, for I am not in the least

inferior to the "super-apostles," even
though I am nothing. 12The things that
mark an apostle—signs, wonders and
miracles—were done among you with
great perseverance. 13How were you infe-
rior to the other churches, except that I
was never a burden to you? Forgive me
this wrong!

14Now I am ready to visit you for the
third time, and I will not be a burden to
you, because what I want is not your pos-
sessions but you. After all, children
should not have to save up for their par-
ents, but parents for their children. 15So I
will very gladly spend for you everything
I have and expend myself as well. If I love
you more, will you love me less? 16Be that
as it may, I have not been a burden to you.

VERSE FOR THE DAY: 2 Corinthians 12:9

AUTHOR: Elizabeth Cody Newenhuyse

PASSAGE FOR THE DAY: 2 Corinthians 12:1–10

The Perfectionist Threat

We expect too much of our mates. We want them to be friend, counselor, sex playmate, prudent banker, intellectual peer. And we want marriage to offer a lifetime of unparalleled happiness.

Actually, we need to give ourselves a reality check from time to time: "Why did I marry this person, and what do I really want?" Did I marry Fritz because I wanted a resident Handy Andy? No, I married him because I couldn't imagine a future that didn't include him.

Our expectations are fed both by unrealistic media images and even by some Christian speakers and authors. We're familiar with the ideal of the perfect wife and husband: spiritual leader, gracious homemaker, involved parent. We read the books, we listen to the tapes, and we think our marriages seem terribly inadequate by comparison.

Yet the Bible doesn't chastise us with unattainable and unrealistic ideals. The Bible speaks instead of kindness and joy and gentleness and respect and serving. I know that I am married to *this* man, and this man only, to honor, to cherish, to enjoy. Instead of fretting about what our spouses are *not*—and what our marriages are lacking—we can be thankful for each other and concentrate on loving the person God has given to each of us.

MARRIAGE BUILDERS

♦ *What unrealistic expectations might you have about your spouse?*

♦ *How can you be strong when you are weak?*

Additional Scripture Readings
Colossians 3:12–14; Jude 24–25

Go to page 1283 for your next devotional reading.

Yet, crafty fellow that I am, I caught you
by trickery! 17Did I exploit you through
any of the men I sent you? 18I urged Titus
to go to you and I sent our brother with
him. Titus did not exploit you, did he? Did
we not act in the same spirit and follow
the same course?

19Have you been thinking all along that
we have been defending ourselves to you?
We have been speaking in the sight of God
as those in Christ; and everything we do,
dear friends, is for your strengthening.
20For I am afraid that when I come I may
not find you as I want you to be, and you
may not find me as you want me to be. I
fear that there may be quarreling, jealou-
sy, outbursts of anger, factions, slander,
gossip, arrogance and disorder. 21I am
afraid that when I come again my God will
humble me before you, and I will be
grieved over many who have sinned earli-
er and have not repented of the impurity,
sexual sin and debauchery in which they
have indulged.

Final Warnings

13 This will be my third visit to you.
"Every matter must be established
by the testimony of two or three wit-
nesses."[a] 2I already gave you a warning
when I was with you the second time. I
now repeat it while absent: On my return
I will not spare those who sinned earlier
or any of the others, 3since you are de-
manding proof that Christ is speaking
through me. He is not weak in dealing
with you, but is powerful among you. 4For
to be sure, he was crucified in weakness,
yet he lives by God's power. Likewise, we
are weak in him, yet by God's power we
will live with him to serve you.

5Examine yourselves to see whether
you are in the faith; test yourselves. Do
you not realize that Christ Jesus is in
you—unless, of course, you fail the test?
6And I trust that you will discover that we
have not failed the test. 7Now we pray to
God that you will not do anything wrong.
Not that people will see that we have
stood the test but that you will do what is
right even though we may seem to have
failed. 8For we cannot do anything against
the truth, but only for the truth. 9We are
glad whenever we are weak but you are
strong; and our prayer is for your perfec-
tion. 10This is why I write these things
when I am absent, that when I come I may
not have to be harsh in my use of authori-
ty—the authority the Lord gave me for
building you up, not for tearing you down.

Final Greetings

11Finally, brothers, good-by. Aim for
perfection, listen to my appeal, be of one
mind, live in peace. And the God of love
and peace will be with you.

12Greet one another with a holy kiss.
13All the saints send their greetings.

14May the grace of the Lord Jesus
Christ, and the love of God, and the fel-
lowship of the Holy Spirit be with you all.

[a] 1 Deut. 19:15

PAUL writes this letter to the churches he founded in Galatia (Acts 13:13–14:28), warning them against certain false teachers. He reminds them of the simple message of salvation by faith alone, which he and other church leaders teach, and concludes with advice on how to live a Spirit-filled life. As you read this book, be sure that you are saved by a personal faith in Jesus, and ask God's Spirit to help you walk in Christian love and peace.

GALATIANS

1 Paul, an apostle—sent not from men
nor by man, but by Jesus Christ and
God the Father, who raised him from the
dead— 2and all the brothers with me,

To the churches in Galatia:

3Grace and peace to you from God our
Father and the Lord Jesus Christ, 4who
gave himself for our sins to rescue us from
the present evil age, according to the will
of our God and Father, 5to whom be glory
for ever and ever. Amen.

No Other Gospel

6I am astonished that you are so quickly
deserting the one who called you by the
grace of Christ and are turning to a differ-
ent gospel— 7which is really no gospel at
all. Evidently some people are throwing
you into confusion and are trying to per-
vert the gospel of Christ. 8But even if we
or an angel from heaven should preach a
gospel other than the one we preached to
you, let him be eternally condemned! 9As
we have already said, so now I say again:
If anybody is preaching to you a gospel
other than what you accepted, let him be
eternally condemned!

10Am I now trying to win the approval
of men, or of God? Or am I trying to please
men? If I were still trying to please men, I
would not be a servant of Christ.

Paul Called by God

11I want you to know, brothers, that the
gospel I preached is not something that
man made up. 12I did not receive it from
any man, nor was I taught it; rather, I re-
ceived it by revelation from Jesus Christ.
13For you have heard of my previous
way of life in Judaism, how intensely I
persecuted the church of God and tried to
destroy it. 14I was advancing in Judaism
beyond many Jews of my own age and
was extremely zealous for the traditions
of my fathers. 15But when God, who set
me apart from birth[a] and called me by
his grace, was pleased 16to reveal his Son
in me so that I might preach him among
the Gentiles, I did not consult any man,
17nor did I go up to Jerusalem to see those
who were apostles before I was, but I went
immediately into Arabia and later re-
turned to Damascus.
18Then after three years, I went up to Je-
rusalem to get acquainted with Peter[b]
and stayed with him fifteen days. 19I saw
none of the other apostles—only James,
the Lord's brother. 20I assure you before
God that what I am writing you is no lie.
21Later I went to Syria and Cilicia. 22I was
personally unknown to the churches of
Judea that are in Christ. 23They only heard
the report: "The man who formerly perse-
cuted us is now preaching the faith he
once tried to destroy." 24And they praised
God because of me.

Paul Accepted by the Apostles

2 Fourteen years later I went up again to
Jerusalem, this time with Barnabas. I
took Titus along also. 2I went in response
to a revelation and set before them the
gospel that I preach among the Gentiles.
But I did this privately to those who
seemed to be leaders, for fear that I was
running or had run my race in vain. 3Yet
not even Titus, who was with me, was
compelled to be circumcised, even though
he was a Greek. 4⌊This matter arose⌋ be-
cause some false brothers had infiltrated
our ranks to spy on the freedom we have
in Christ Jesus and to make us slaves. 5We
did not give in to them for a moment, so
that the truth of the gospel might remain
with you.
6As for those who seemed to be impor-
tant—whatever they were makes no dif-
ference to me; God does not judge by ex-
ternal appearance—those men added
nothing to my message. 7On the contrary,
they saw that I had been entrusted with
the task of preaching the gospel to the
Gentiles,[c] just as Peter had been to the
Jews.[d] 8For God, who was at work in the
ministry of Peter as an apostle to the Jews,
was also at work in my ministry as an
apostle to the Gentiles. 9James, Peter[e]
and John, those reputed to be pillars, gave
me and Barnabas the right hand of fellow-
ship when they recognized the grace giv-
en to me. They agreed that we should go
to the Gentiles, and they to the Jews. 10All
they asked was that we should continue to
remember the poor, the very thing I was
eager to do.

Paul Opposes Peter

11When Peter came to Antioch, I op-
posed him to his face, because he was
clearly in the wrong. 12Before certain men
came from James, he used to eat with the
Gentiles. But when they arrived, he began
to draw back and separate himself from
the Gentiles because he was afraid of
those who belonged to the circumcision
group. 13The other Jews joined him in his
hypocrisy, so that by their hypocrisy even
Barnabas was led astray.
14When I saw that they were not acting
in line with the truth of the gospel, I said
to Peter in front of them all, "You are a
Jew, yet you live like a Gentile and not like
a Jew. How is it, then, that you force Gen-
tiles to follow Jewish customs?
15"We who are Jews by birth and not
'Gentile sinners' 16know that a man is not
justified by observing the law, but by faith
in Jesus Christ. So we, too, have put our
faith in Christ Jesus that we may be justi-
fied by faith in Christ and not by observ-
ing the law, because by observing the law
no one will be justified.
17"If, while we seek to be justified in
Christ, it becomes evident that we our-
selves are sinners, does that mean that
Christ promotes sin? Absolutely not! 18If I
rebuild what I destroyed, I prove that I am
a lawbreaker. 19For through the law I died
to the law so that I might live for God. 20I
have been crucified with Christ and I no
longer live, but Christ lives in me. The life
I live in the body, I live by faith in the Son
of God, who loved me and gave himself

[a]15 Or *from my mother's womb* [b]18 Greek *Cephas* [c]7 Greek *uncircumcised* [d]7 Greek *circumcised*; also in verses 8 and 9 [e]9 Greek *Cephas*; also in verses 11 and 14

WEEKENDING

MONEY

Our parents' example affects the way we think about money. Discuss which of these statements reflect your parents' attitudes and actions. What were the positives and negatives about their example?

1. My parents never bought anything unless they could pay cash.

2. My parents taught us about giving to God's work.

3. My mom/dad paid the bills and kept track of our family's financial situation.

4. My parents always paid off the full amount on their credit card bills.

5. My parents kept a budget.

6. My parents preferred spending money on durable goods (appliances, furniture), not on "intangibles" such as eating out or entertainment.

7. My parents hired services when possible, rather than doing it themselves.

8. To my parents, money in the bank meant security.

9. My parents viewed money as something to spend and enjoy.

— *The* Marriage Partnership *Staff*

REVIVE

Saturday: Matthew 19:16–30
Sunday: 1 Thessalonians 4:1–12

Go to page 1286 for your next devotional reading.

for me. [21]I do not set aside the grace of God, for if righteousness could be gained through the law, Christ died for nothing!"[a]

Faith or Observance of the Law

3 You foolish Galatians! Who has bewitched you? Before your very eyes Jesus Christ was clearly portrayed as crucified. [2]I would like to learn just one thing from you: Did you receive the Spirit by observing the law, or by believing what you heard? [3]Are you so foolish? After beginning with the Spirit, are you now trying to attain your goal by human effort? [4]Have you suffered so much for nothing—if it really was for nothing? [5]Does God give you his Spirit and work miracles among you because you observe the law, or because you believe what you heard?

[6]Consider Abraham: "He believed God, and it was credited to him as righteousness."[b] [7]Understand, then, that those who believe are children of Abraham. [8]The Scripture foresaw that God would justify the Gentiles by faith, and announced the gospel in advance to Abraham: "All nations will be blessed through you."[c] [9]So those who have faith are blessed along with Abraham, the man of faith.

[10]All who rely on observing the law are under a curse, for it is written: "Cursed is everyone who does not continue to do everything written in the Book of the Law."[d] [11]Clearly no one is justified before God by the law, because, "The righteous will live by faith."[e] [12]The law is not based on faith; on the contrary, "The man who does these things will live by them."[f] [13]Christ redeemed us from the curse of the law by becoming a curse for us, for it is written: "Cursed is everyone who is hung on a tree."[g] [14]He redeemed us in order that the blessing given to Abraham might come to the Gentiles through Christ Jesus, so that by faith we might receive the promise of the Spirit.

The Law and the Promise

[15]Brothers, let me take an example from everyday life. Just as no one can set aside or add to a human covenant that has been duly established, so it is in this case. [16]The promises were spoken to Abraham and to his seed. The Scripture does not say "and to seeds," meaning many people, but "and to your seed,"[h] meaning one person, who is Christ. [17]What I mean is this: The law, introduced 430 years later, does not set aside the covenant previously established by God and thus do away with the promise. [18]For if the inheritance depends on the law, then it no longer depends on a promise; but God in his grace gave it to Abraham through a promise.

[19]What, then, was the purpose of the law? It was added because of transgressions until the Seed to whom the promise referred had come. The law was put into effect through angels by a mediator. [20]A mediator, however, does not represent just one party; but God is one.

[21]Is the law, therefore, opposed to the promises of God? Absolutely not! For if a law had been given that could impart life, then righteousness would certainly have come by the law. [22]But the Scripture declares that the whole world is a prisoner of sin, so that what was promised, being given through faith in Jesus Christ, might be given to those who believe.

[23]Before this faith came, we were held prisoners by the law, locked up until faith should be revealed. [24]So the law was put in charge to lead us to Christ[i] that we might be justified by faith. [25]Now that faith has come, we are no longer under the supervision of the law.

Sons of God

[26]You are all sons of God through faith in Christ Jesus, [27]for all of you who were baptized into Christ have clothed yourselves with Christ. [28]There is neither Jew nor Greek, slave nor free, male nor female, for you are all one in Christ Jesus. [29]If you belong to Christ, then you are Abraham's seed, and heirs according to the promise.

4 What I am saying is that as long as the heir is a child, he is no different from a slave, although he owns the whole estate. [2]He is subject to guardians and trustees until the time set by his father. [3]So also, when we were children, we were in slavery under the basic principles of the world. [4]But when the time had fully come, God sent his Son, born of a woman, born under law, [5]to redeem those under law, that we might receive the full rights of

[a]*21* Some interpreters end the quotation after verse 14. [b]*6* Gen. 15:6 [c]*8* Gen. 12:3; 18:18; 22:18
[d]*10* Deut. 27:26 [e]*11* Hab. 2:4 [f]*12* Lev. 18:5 [g]*13* Deut. 21:23 [h]*16* Gen. 12:7; 13:15; 24:7
[i]*24* Or *charge until Christ came*

sons. 6Because you are sons, God sent the
Spirit of his Son into our hearts, the Spirit
who calls out, *"Abba,*[a] Father." 7So you
are no longer a slave, but a son; and since
you are a son, God has made you also an
heir.

Paul's Concern for the Galatians

8Formerly, when you did not know
God, you were slaves to those who by na-
ture are not gods. 9But now that you know
God—or rather are known by God—how
is it that you are turning back to those
weak and miserable principles? Do you
wish to be enslaved by them all over
again? 10You are observing special days
and months and seasons and years! 11I
fear for you, that somehow I have wasted
my efforts on you.

12I plead with you, brothers, become
like me, for I became like you. You have
done me no wrong. 13As you know, it was
because of an illness that I first preached
the gospel to you. 14Even though my ill-
ness was a trial to you, you did not treat
me with contempt or scorn. Instead, you
welcomed me as if I were an angel of God,
as if I were Christ Jesus himself. 15What
has happened to all your joy? I can testify
that, if you could have done so, you would
have torn out your eyes and given them to
me. 16Have I now become your enemy by
telling you the truth?

17Those people are zealous to win you
over, but for no good. What they want is
to alienate you ⌊from us⌋, so that you may
be zealous for them. 18It is fine to be zeal-
ous, provided the purpose is good, and to
be so always and not just when I am with
you. 19My dear children, for whom I am
again in the pains of childbirth until Christ
is formed in you, 20how I wish I could be
with you now and change my tone, be-
cause I am perplexed about you!

Hagar and Sarah

21Tell me, you who want to be under
the law, are you not aware of what the law
says? 22For it is written that Abraham had
two sons, one by the slave woman and the
other by the free woman. 23His son by the
slave woman was born in the ordinary
way; but his son by the free woman was
born as the result of a promise.

24These things may be taken figurative-
ly, for the women represent two cov-
enants. One covenant is from Mount Sinai
and bears children who are to be slaves:
This is Hagar. 25Now Hagar stands for
Mount Sinai in Arabia and corresponds to
the present city of Jerusalem, because she
is in slavery with her children. 26But the
Jerusalem that is above is free, and she is
our mother. 27For it is written:

"Be glad, O barren woman,
who bears no children;
break forth and cry aloud,
you who have no labor pains;
because more are the children of the
desolate woman
than of her who has a husband."[b]

28Now you, brothers, like Isaac, are
children of promise. 29At that time the son
born in the ordinary way persecuted the
son born by the power of the Spirit. It is
the same now. 30But what does the Scrip-
ture say? "Get rid of the slave woman and
her son, for the slave woman's son will
never share in the inheritance with the
free woman's son."[c] 31Therefore, broth-
ers, we are not children of the slave wom-
an, but of the free woman.

Freedom in Christ

5 It is for freedom that Christ has set us
free. Stand firm, then, and do not let
yourselves be burdened again by a yoke of
slavery.

2Mark my words! I, Paul, tell you that if
you let yourselves be circumcised, Christ
will be of no value to you at all. 3Again I
declare to every man who lets himself be
circumcised that he is obligated to obey
the whole law. 4You who are trying to be
justified by law have been alienated from
Christ; you have fallen away from grace.
5But by faith we eagerly await through the
Spirit the righteousness for which we
hope. 6For in Christ Jesus neither circum-
cision nor uncircumcision has any value.
The only thing that counts is faith ex-
pressing itself through love.

7You were running a good race. Who
cut in on you and kept you from obeying
the truth? 8That kind of persuasion does
not come from the one who calls you. 9"A
little yeast works through the whole batch
of dough." 10I am confident in the Lord
that you will take no other view. The one
who is throwing you into confusion will
pay the penalty, whoever he may be.
11Brothers, if I am still preaching circum-
cision, why am I still being persecuted? In

[a]6 Aramaic for *Father* [b]27 Isaiah 54:1 [c]30 Gen. 21:10

VERSE FOR THE DAY: Galatians 5:22–23

AUTHOR: Lyn Cryderman

PASSAGE FOR THE DAY: Galatians 5:16–25

Biblical Virtues

I began to think about the biblical virtues of kindness and gentleness after my father-in-law handed me a note he received from my wife when she was a girl. In Esther's nine-year-old handwriting were these words: "Dear Dad, Please be nice to me." If my wife had to beg one of the nicest men I know to be nice to her, maybe being nice really does matter.

The Apostle Paul urged us to be kind and gentle toward one another (Gal. 5:22–23). Sadly, I don't see either of these qualities in marriages much today. I don't see enough in my own marriage.

Is it kind to say, in front of your Bible study group, "Sorry we're late, but you know these women!" Is it gentle to assume that your wife naturally enjoys things like ironing, cooking, vacuuming and picking up the dry cleaning? Is it kind and gentle to say, "You'll never find the time, and besides, we can't afford it," when your spouse says she's thinking about graduate school?

Many spouses will tell you the cold slap of a harsh answer hurts almost as bad as the back of the hand. Maybe more.

In Galatians, Paul uses fruit as a metaphor to describe what happens when Christ's Spirit resides in our hearts. It is a funny thing, this Spirit. Give it freedom to dwell within you, and there's little room for the grouchy words and thoughtless acts that bedevil many marriages.

MARRIAGE BUILDERS

- *Privately consider ways you might evidence kindness and gentleness toward your spouse today.*
- *In what areas can you see that the indwelling Holy Spirit has born "fruit" in the way you treat your spouse?*

Additional Scripture Readings
Philippians 4:5; Ephesians 4:2; Titus 3:3–11

Go to page 1287 for your next devotional reading.

that case the offense of the cross has been
abolished. 12As for those agitators, I wish
they would go the whole way and emasculate themselves!

13You, my brothers, were called to be
free. But do not use your freedom to indulge the sinful nature[a]; rather, serve
one another in love. 14The entire law is
summed up in a single command: "Love
your neighbor as yourself."[b] 15If you
keep on biting and devouring each other,
watch out or you will be destroyed by
each other.

Life by the Spirit

16So I say, live by the Spirit, and you

[a] 13 Or *the flesh*; also in verses 16, 17, 19 and 24 [b] 14 Lev. 19:18

VERSE FOR THE DAY: Galatians 6:3–4

AUTHOR: Gary L. Thomas

PASSAGE FOR THE DAY: Galatians 6:1–10

A Good Double Standard

I spent the early days of our marriage adding up the pluses and minuses of our personality traits. The problem was, I spent too much time on my pluses and Lisa's minuses. Then I read a passage written by Puritan scholar John Owen: "The person who understands the evil in his own heart is the only person who is useful, fruitful and solid in his beliefs and obedience. Others only delude themselves and thus upset families, churches and all other relationships. In their self-pride and judgment of others, they show great inconsistency."

I felt the Lord teaching me that the happiest husband is the one who lives with a double standard—he's tough on himself and easy on his wife. I'd been deluded by my sense of self-righteousness. Rather than focusing on what Lisa could improve, I should have been on my knees, begging God to change me.

Scripture reminds us that our goal is to become more like Christ. As I grow in relationship to Christ, my wife should be able to notice at least some family resemblance. I need a holy double standard. As I become more unyielding and aggressive in attacking my own sins and weaknesses, I must extend more and more grace toward my wife in hers.

MARRIAGE BUILDERS

♦ *Have you been keeping score with an emphasis on your own plus-points and your spouse's minus ones?*
♦ *Brainstorm two or three ways you could make your spouse's life better or easier this week.*

Additional Scripture Readings
Ephesians 5:1–2; Philippians 2:5–11

Go to page 1290 for your next devotional reading.

will not gratify the desires of the sinful nature. [17]For the sinful nature desires what is contrary to the Spirit, and the Spirit what is contrary to the sinful nature. They are in conflict with each other, so that you do not do what you want. [18]But if you are led by the Spirit, you are not under law.

[19]The acts of the sinful nature are obvious: sexual immorality, impurity and debauchery; [20]idolatry and witchcraft; hatred, discord, jealousy, fits of rage, selfish ambition, dissensions, factions [21]and envy; drunkenness, orgies, and the like. I warn you, as I did before, that those who live like this will not inherit the kingdom of God.

[22]But the fruit of the Spirit is love, joy, peace, patience, kindness, goodness, faithfulness, [23]gentleness and self-control. Against such things there is no law. [24]Those who belong to Christ Jesus have crucified the sinful nature with its passions and desires. [25]Since we live by the Spirit, let us keep in step with the Spirit. [26]Let us not become conceited, provoking and envying each other.

Doing Good to All

6 Brothers, if someone is caught in a sin, you who are spiritual should restore him gently. But watch yourself, or you also may be tempted. [2]Carry each other's burdens, and in this way you will fulfill the law of Christ. [3]If anyone thinks he is something when he is nothing, he deceives himself. [4]Each one should test his own actions. Then he can take pride in himself, without comparing himself to somebody else, [5]for each one should carry his own load.

[6]Anyone who receives instruction in the word must share all good things with his instructor.

[7]Do not be deceived: God cannot be mocked. A man reaps what he sows. [8]The one who sows to please his sinful nature, from that nature[a] will reap destruction; the one who sows to please the Spirit, from the Spirit will reap eternal life. [9]Let us not become weary in doing good, for at the proper time we will reap a harvest if we do not give up. [10]Therefore, as we have opportunity, let us do good to all people, especially to those who belong to the family of believers.

Not Circumcision but a New Creation

[11]See what large letters I use as I write to you with my own hand!

[12]Those who want to make a good impression outwardly are trying to compel you to be circumcised. The only reason they do this is to avoid being persecuted for the cross of Christ. [13]Not even those who are circumcised obey the law, yet they want you to be circumcised that they may boast about your flesh. [14]May I never boast except in the cross of our Lord Jesus Christ, through which[b] the world has been crucified to me, and I to the world. [15]Neither circumcision nor uncircumcision means anything; what counts is a new creation. [16]Peace and mercy to all who follow this rule, even to the Israel of God.

[17]Finally, let no one cause me trouble, for I bear on my body the marks of Jesus.

[18]The grace of our Lord Jesus Christ be with your spirit, brothers. Amen.

[a]8 Or *his flesh, from the flesh* [b]14 Or *whom*

PAUL writes this letter from prison (Ephesians 4:1; probably in Rome, see Acts 28:30–31) to the church he started in Ephesus (Acts 19). In the first half he explains God's great plan to redeem the world through Christ, showing what this means for individual Christians and for the whole church. In the second half he gives practical advice on how to live the Christian life. As you read this book, first examine yourself to be sure that you are saved. Then move on to fight against Satan and show your love to your family, your church and your community.

EPHESIANS

1 Paul, an apostle of Christ Jesus by the will of God,

To the saints in Ephesus,[a] the faithful[b] in Christ Jesus:

2 Grace and peace to you from God our Father and the Lord Jesus Christ.

Spiritual Blessings in Christ

3 Praise be to the God and Father of our Lord Jesus Christ, who has blessed us in the heavenly realms with every spiritual blessing in Christ. 4 For he chose us in him before the creation of the world to be holy and blameless in his sight. In love 5 he[c] predestined us to be adopted as his sons through Jesus Christ, in accordance with his pleasure and will— 6 to the praise of his glorious grace, which he has freely given us in the One he loves. 7 In him we have

[a] 1 Some early manuscripts do not have *in Ephesus.* [b] 1 Or *believers who are* [c] 4,5 Or *sight in love.* 5 *He*

VERSE FOR THE DAY:
Ephesians 1:17–18

AUTHOR:
Gary J. Oliver

PASSAGE FOR THE DAY:
Ephesians 1:3–23

Friends and Lovers

Falling in love is the first, and sadly for some couples the only, season of love. Often couples confuse infatuation with love. A husband might see his wife as he'd like her to be—a warm, caring person who keeps his needs foremost in her mind. Who she truly is—a woman who can be angry with him at times—is irrelevant.

After a few years of marriage, Tina and Mike had never moved beyond infatuation. During their courtship, their romantic love seemed new, exciting, intense. They were all-absorbed in each other, seeing each other daily and talking by phone late into the night. "Our love felt so real," Tina says. "I thought those feelings would last forever."

But they didn't. After they married, Mike's sixty-hour workweeks didn't leave much time for Tina. She was preoccupied with her own job and other outside interests. Since their wedding day, they'd done little to cultivate their relationship. But love is like a plant that requires careful, long-term attention. In the romance stage of love, seeds are planted. But without constant care, romance can't grow into mature love.

Mike and Tina needed to concentrate on becoming friends as well as lovers. So they asked three other couples to pray for them, they started reading a devotional book together and they instituted date nights twice a month. By nurturing their friendship, they moved beyond the disillusionment of lost romance to a love that could carry them into the future.

MARRIAGE BUILDERS

- *What aspects of your love seem better than romance?*
- *When have romantic feelings seemed to thrive between you? How can you recreate some of those activities or events?*

Additional Scripture Readings
Colossians 1:9–14; James 1:2–5

Go to page 1292 for your next devotional reading.

redemption through his blood, the forgiveness of sins, in accordance with the riches of God's grace 8that he lavished on us with all wisdom and understanding. 9And he[a] made known to us the mystery of his will according to his good pleasure, which he purposed in Christ, 10to be put into effect when the times will have reached their fulfillment—to bring all things in heaven and on earth together under one head, even Christ.

11In him we were also chosen,[b] having been predestined according to the plan of him who works out everything in conformity with the purpose of his will, 12in order that we, who were the first to hope in Christ, might be for the praise of his glory. 13And you also were included in Christ when you heard the word of truth, the gospel of your salvation. Having believed, you were marked in him with a seal, the promised Holy Spirit, 14who is a deposit guaranteeing our inheritance until the redemption of those who are God's possession—to the praise of his glory.

Thanksgiving and Prayer

15For this reason, ever since I heard about your faith in the Lord Jesus and your love for all the saints, 16I have not stopped giving thanks for you, remembering you in my prayers. 17I keep asking that the God of our Lord Jesus Christ, the glorious Father, may give you the Spirit[c] of wisdom and revelation, so that you may know him better. 18I pray also that the eyes of your heart may be enlightened in order that you may know the hope to which he has called you, the riches of his glorious inheritance in the saints, 19and his incomparably great power for us who believe. That power is like the working of his mighty strength, 20which he exerted in Christ when he raised him from the dead and seated him at his right hand in the heavenly realms, 21far above all rule and authority, power and dominion, and every title that can be given, not only in the present age but also in the one to come. 22And God placed all things under his feet and appointed him to be head over everything for the church, 23which is his body, the fullness of him who fills everything in every way.

Made Alive in Christ

2 As for you, you were dead in your transgressions and sins, 2in which you used to live when you followed the ways of this world and of the ruler of the kingdom of the air, the spirit who is now at work in those who are disobedient. 3All of us also lived among them at one time, gratifying the cravings of our sinful nature[d] and following its desires and thoughts. Like the rest, we were by nature objects of wrath. 4But because of his great love for us, God, who is rich in mercy, 5made us alive with Christ even when we were dead in transgressions—it is by grace you have been saved. 6And God raised us up with Christ and seated us with him in the heavenly realms in Christ Jesus, 7in order that in the coming ages he might show the incomparable riches of his grace, expressed in his kindness to us in Christ Jesus. 8For it is by grace you have been saved, through faith—and this not from yourselves, it is the gift of God—9not by works, so that no one can boast. 10For we are God's workmanship, created in Christ Jesus to do good works, which God prepared in advance for us to do.

One in Christ

11Therefore, remember that formerly you who are Gentiles by birth and called "uncircumcised" by those who call themselves "the circumcision" (that done in the body by the hands of men)— 12remember that at that time you were separate from Christ, excluded from citizenship in Israel and foreigners to the covenants of the promise, without hope and without God in the world. 13But now in Christ Jesus you who once were far away have been brought near through the blood of Christ.

14For he himself is our peace, who has made the two one and has destroyed the barrier, the dividing wall of hostility, 15by abolishing in his flesh the law with its commandments and regulations. His purpose was to create in himself one new man out of the two, thus making peace, 16and in this one body to reconcile both of them to God through the cross, by which he put to death their hostility. 17He came

[a] *8,9* Or *us. With all wisdom and understanding,* 9*he*
[b] *11* Or *were made heirs*
[c] *17* Or *a spirit*
[d] *3* Or *our flesh*

and preached peace to you who were far
away and peace to those who were near.
18For through him we both have access to
the Father by one Spirit.
19Consequently, you are no longer for-
eigners and aliens, but fellow citizens
with God's people and members of God's
household, 20built on the foundation of
the apostles and prophets, with Christ
Jesus himself as the chief cornerstone.
21In him the whole building is joined to-
gether and rises to become a holy temple
in the Lord. 22And in him you too are be-
ing built together to become a dwelling in
which God lives by his Spirit.

Paul the Preacher to the Gentiles

3 For this reason I, Paul, the prisoner of
Christ Jesus for the sake of you Gen-
tiles—

THURSDAY

VERSE FOR THE DAY: Ephesians 2:10

AUTHOR: H. Norman Wright

PASSAGE FOR THE DAY: Ephesians 2:1–10

God's Preparation

Our son, Matthew, was severely retarded, and his disability taught us many things. The greatest thing we learned was that God either will prepare you for these kinds of events in your marriage in advance, or he will give you his strength at that time. In our case, God was preparing us for years, though we didn't realize it.

In seminary, my professor assigned me the topic of the Christian education of a mentally retarded child. And to complete my school-psychologist credentials, I had to put in 500 hours of work in a school district. I ended up testing and placing children with developmental disabilities. Then my church decided that since I had the experience, I should lead a Sunday school ministry to mentally impaired children.

During that time, Joyce and I had the most fascinating conversation of our marriage. One of us said, "Isn't it interesting that we've had so much exposure to retarded children and learned so much about them? Could it be that God is preparing us for something?" That was all we said, and within a year Matthew was born. God had prepared us ahead of time to be the parents Matthew would need.

MARRIAGE BUILDERS

♦ *When have you seen that God prepared you in your past to deal with some challenge in your present experience?*

♦ *How can you have assurance that God will meet your needs in the future?*

Additional Scripture Readings
Isaiah 30:21; 1 Corinthians 10:13

Go to page 1293 for your next devotional reading.

2Surely you have heard about the administration of God's grace that was given
to me for you, 3that is, the mystery made
known to me by revelation, as I have already written briefly. 4In reading this,
then, you will be able to understand my
insight into the mystery of Christ, 5which
was not made known to men in other generations as it has now been revealed by
the Spirit to God's holy apostles and
prophets. 6This mystery is that through
the gospel the Gentiles are heirs together
with Israel, members together of one
body, and sharers together in the promise
in Christ Jesus.

7I became a servant of this gospel by the
gift of God's grace given me through the
working of his power. 8Although I am less
than the least of all God's people, this
grace was given me: to preach to the Gentiles the unsearchable riches of Christ,
9and to make plain to everyone the admin-

VERSE FOR THE DAY: Ephesians 3:20–21

AUTHOR: Elizabeth Cody Newenhuyse

PASSAGE FOR THE DAY: Ephesians 3:14–21

God's Reckless Generosity

The prevailing wisdom is "a good marriage takes hard work." Well, that depends on what you mean by "work." I think there's a flaw in the work-at-your-marriage premise. It can too easily take something (your marriage) that is an astonishing gift, and bleed it of fun and grace.

One man, one woman, forever: what an incredible, audacious idea! We tend to wax so deadly earnest about ideals of commitment and fidelity that we weigh marriage down until it falls to the ground with a dull thud. Certainly these ideals are important and necessary. And yes, there are times when we need to look at our marriage and ourselves intentionally, and talk about how well (or how poorly) our life together is going.

But we should have *fun* in the doing of it. God gave us marriage to be enjoyed. I don't want to look at my husband and feel sober and dutiful: "Have you had your green vegetables today? Have we engaged in the appropriate conflict-resolution methods?" No, I want to look at my husband and grin at the amazement of it all. I want to laugh at God's reckless generosity in bringing us together—and keeping us there.

MARRIAGE BUILDERS

- *What do you most enjoy about being married?*
- *Which activities could help the two of you celebrate the joy and the fun of your life together?*

Additional Scripture Readings
Psalm 68:3–6; 1 John 3:1

Go to page 1295 for your next devotional reading.

istration of this mystery, which for ages
past was kept hidden in God, who created
all things. 10His intent was that now,
through the church, the manifold wisdom
of God should be made known to the rul-
ers and authorities in the heavenly realms,
11according to his eternal purpose which
he accomplished in Christ Jesus our Lord.
12In him and through faith in him we may
approach God with freedom and confi-
dence. 13I ask you, therefore, not to be dis-
couraged because of my sufferings for
you, which are your glory.

A Prayer for the Ephesians

14For this reason I kneel before the Fa-
ther, 15from whom his whole family[a] in
heaven and on earth derives its name. 16I
pray that out of his glorious riches he may
strengthen you with power through his
Spirit in your inner being, 17so that Christ
may dwell in your hearts through faith.
And I pray that you, being rooted and es-
tablished in love, 18may have power, to-
gether with all the saints, to grasp how
wide and long and high and deep is the
love of Christ, 19and to know this love that
surpasses knowledge—that you may be
filled to the measure of all the fullness of
God.

20Now to him who is able to do immea-
surably more than all we ask or imagine,
according to his power that is at work
within us, 21to him be glory in the church
and in Christ Jesus throughout all genera-
tions, for ever and ever! Amen.

Unity in the Body of Christ

4 As a prisoner for the Lord, then, I urge
you to live a life worthy of the calling
you have received. 2Be completely hum-
ble and gentle; be patient, bearing with
one another in love. 3Make every effort to
keep the unity of the Spirit through the
bond of peace. 4There is one body and one
Spirit— just as you were called to one
hope when you were called— 5one Lord,
one faith, one baptism; 6one God and Fa-
ther of all, who is over all and through all
and in all.

7But to each one of us grace has been
given as Christ apportioned it. 8This is
why it[b] says:

"When he ascended on high,
he led captives in his train
and gave gifts to men."[c]

9(What does "he ascended" mean except
that he also descended to the lower, earth-
ly regions[d]? 10He who descended is the
very one who ascended higher than all the
heavens, in order to fill the whole uni-
verse.) 11It was he who gave some to be
apostles, some to be prophets, some to be
evangelists, and some to be pastors and
teachers, 12to prepare God's people for
works of service, so that the body of Christ
may be built up 13until we all reach unity
in the faith and in the knowledge of the
Son of God and become mature, attaining
to the whole measure of the fullness of
Christ.

14Then we will no longer be infants,
tossed back and forth by the waves, and
blown here and there by every wind of
teaching and by the cunning and crafti-
ness of men in their deceitful scheming.
15Instead, speaking the truth in love, we
will in all things grow up into him who is
the Head, that is, Christ. 16From him the
whole body, joined and held together by
every supporting ligament, grows and
builds itself up in love, as each part does
its work.

Living as Children of Light

17So I tell you this, and insist on it in the
Lord, that you must no longer live as
the Gentiles do, in the futility of their
thinking. 18They are darkened in their
understanding and separated from the
life of God because of the ignorance
that is in them due to the hardening
of their hearts. 19Having lost all sensitiv-
ity, they have given themselves over to
sensuality so as to indulge in every kind
of impurity, with a continual lust for
more.

20You, however, did not come to know
Christ that way. 21Surely you heard of him
and were taught in him in accordance
with the truth that is in Jesus. 22You were
taught, with regard to your former way of
life, to put off your old self, which is being
corrupted by its deceitful desires; 23to be
made new in the attitude of your minds;
24and to put on the new self, created to be
like God in true righteousness and holi-
ness.

25Therefore each of you must put off
falsehood and speak truthfully to his
neighbor, for we are all members of one

[a]15 Or *whom all fatherhood* [b]8 Or *God* [c]8 Psalm 68:18 [d]9 Or *the depths of the earth*

WEEKENDING

APPRECIATION

When couples come to us for counseling, we have them list all the strengths their partner brings to the relationship before we give them an opportunity to tell us what's wrong with their spouse. Right off the bat, this gets them thinking in terms of what is good in their marriage. That's why it's good to spell out the reasons why you love your spouse. Though one of your partner's traits may drive you crazy, another may more than compensate for any shortcomings. By focusing on the positives, you will be reminded just why you married the person you did.

List at least ten traits you admire in your spouse, such as honesty, a good sense of humor, loyalty, compassion, thoughtfulness, patience or punctuality. Then think of all the reasons why you value those traits in your mate.

— Preston and Genie Dyer

REVIVE

Saturday: Romans 12:1–21
Sunday: 1 Corinthians 12:1–27

Go to page 1296 for your next devotional reading.

VERSE FOR THE DAY: Ephesians 4:26

AUTHOR: Louis McBurney, M.D.

PASSAGE FOR THE DAY: Ephesians 4:25–32

Anger Under Control

Anger is not sinful, it's a God-given emotional response to life's threats and hurts. It's not the anger itself that has moral implications, it's how you handle it.

Some people resort to verbal abuse, others take the opposite approach—withdrawing into an icy silence in an effort to bury the hurt. Sometimes the anger surfaces later in pouting or sulking, or in withholding affection, attention or cooperation. The good news is that either one of you can decide to change the established patterns. Learning to discharge your anger in non-destructive ways brings life and vitality to your marriage.

First, express your own feelings rather than hurling blame or launching a character assassination against your mate.

Second, use preambles for introducing heavy topics. Melissa and I often say, "This is not something you need to 'fix,' I just need to talk out some feelings." That gives the other person a chance to begin listening in a focused, non-defensive way.

Third, increase your "critical interval"—the time between a stimulus and a response. The old advice of counting to ten is a good way to begin dealing with a short temper. Simply delay your response until your objectivity has returned.

Finally, and most important: Kiss and make up. When the dust settles and you've heard each other out, get forgiveness into the picture. And when forgiving one another is difficult, stop to consider the alternative. Prolonged loneliness and lingering bitterness are simply not worth it.

MARRIAGE BUILDERS

♦ *Take a minute to remember and assess your own patterns of behavior when you are angry. Do you tend to assign blame, or strike back with icy silence?*

♦ *What's the best way you have found for communicating your forgiveness after a disagreement?*

Additional Scripture Readings
James 1:19; 1 Corinthians 13:5; Proverbs 15:1

Go to page 1298 for your next devotional reading.

body. 26"In your anger do not sin"[a]: Do
not let the sun go down while you are still
angry, 27and do not give the devil a foot-
hold. 28He who has been stealing must
steal no longer, but must work, doing
something useful with his own hands,
that he may have something to share with
those in need.

29Do not let any unwholesome talk
come out of your mouths, but only what
is helpful for building others up according
to their needs, that it may benefit those
who listen. 30And do not grieve the Holy
Spirit of God, with whom you were sealed
for the day of redemption. 31Get rid of all
bitterness, rage and anger, brawling and
slander, along with every form of malice.
32Be kind and compassionate to one an-
other, forgiving each other, just as in
Christ God forgave you.

5 Be imitators of God, therefore, as
dearly loved children 2and live a life of
love, just as Christ loved us and gave him-
self up for us as a fragrant offering and
sacrifice to God.

3But among you there must not be even
a hint of sexual immorality, or of any kind
of impurity, or of greed, because these are
improper for God's holy people. 4Nor
should there be obscenity, foolish talk or
coarse joking, which are out of place, but
rather thanksgiving. 5For of this you can
be sure: No immoral, impure or greedy
person—such a man is an idolater—has
any inheritance in the kingdom of Christ
and of God.[b] 6Let no one deceive you
with empty words, for because of such
things God's wrath comes on those who
are disobedient. 7Therefore do not be
partners with them.

8For you were once darkness, but now
you are light in the Lord. Live as children
of light 9(for the fruit of the light consists
in all goodness, righteousness and truth)
10and find out what pleases the Lord.
11Have nothing to do with the fruitless
deeds of darkness, but rather expose
them. 12For it is shameful even to mention
what the disobedient do in secret. 13But
everything exposed by the light becomes
visible, 14for it is light that makes every-
thing visible. This is why it is said:

"Wake up, O sleeper,
rise from the dead,
and Christ will shine on you."

15Be very careful, then, how you live—
not as unwise but as wise, 16making the
most of every opportunity, because the
days are evil. 17Therefore do not be fool-
ish, but understand what the Lord's will
is. 18Do not get drunk on wine, which
leads to debauchery. Instead, be filled
with the Spirit. 19Speak to one another
with psalms, hymns and spiritual songs.
Sing and make music in your heart to the
Lord, 20always giving thanks to God the
Father for everything, in the name of our
Lord Jesus Christ.

21Submit to one another out of rever-
ence for Christ.

Wives and Husbands

22Wives, submit to your husbands as to
the Lord. 23For the husband is the head of
the wife as Christ is the head of the
church, his body, of which he is the Sav-
ior. 24Now as the church submits to
Christ, so also wives should submit to
their husbands in everything.

25Husbands, love your wives, just as
Christ loved the church and gave himself
up for her 26to make her holy, cleansing[c]
her by the washing with water through
the word, 27and to present her to himself
as a radiant church, without stain or wrin-
kle or any other blemish, but holy and
blameless. 28In this same way, husbands
ought to love their wives as their own bod-
ies. He who loves his wife loves himself.
29After all, no one ever hated his own
body, but he feeds and cares for it, just as
Christ does the church— 30for we are
members of his body. 31"For this reason a
man will leave his father and mother and
be united to his wife, and the two will be-
come one flesh."[d] 32This is a profound
mystery—but I am talking about Christ
and the church. 33However, each one of
you also must love his wife as he loves
himself, and the wife must respect her
husband.

Children and Parents

6 Children, obey your parents in the
Lord, for this is right. 2"Honor your fa-
ther and mother"—which is the first com-
mandment with a promise— 3"that it may
go well with you and that you may enjoy
long life on the earth."[e]

4Fathers, do not exasperate your chil-

[a]26 Psalm 4:4 [b]5 Or *kingdom of the Christ and God* [c]26 Or *having cleansed* [d]31 Gen. 2:24
[e]3 Deut. 5:16

VERSE FOR THE DAY: Ephesians 5:21

AUTHOR: Annette LaPlaca

PASSAGE FOR THE DAY: Ephesians 5:21–33

Submit to One Another

There seems to be endless debate, especially *these* days, over whether a wife should still be expected to "submit" to her husband.

Sometimes I wonder if, in the heat of the battle, we aren't missing the point altogether. In the fifth chapter of Ephesians, Paul prefaces his remarks to both wives and husbands with the admonition to "submit to one another out of reverence for Christ" (v. 21). And husbands will be quick to notice that Paul gives twice as much time and attention to *their* responsibilities within the marriage than to those of their wives.

There are numerous "one another" passages in the New Testament. Love one another. Accept one another. Encourage one another. Pray for one another. And all of them, like "submit to one another," echo the bilateral nature of healthy human relationships. I have responsibilities to David within our marriage; David has responsibilities to me. When both of us are trying to obey God's Word, David's submissive kindness and godliness make it a pleasure and no strain for me to be just as submissive to him.

It's complicated, to be sure. And it's an ideal picture that we try to live out as seriously flawed human beings. But, as Paul says, "This is a profound mystery" (v. 32). That's partnership. And it's mutual submission at work.

MARRIAGE BUILDERS

♦ *What can the two of you do in the days ahead to show your respect for each other?*

♦ *Use a comprehensive concordance to explore the "one another" commands of the New Testament. Which of these would most enrich your marriage?*

Additional Scripture Readings
Colossians 3:15–25; 1 Peter 3:1–7; 1 Corinthians 11:11–12

Go to page 1301 for your next devotional reading.

dren; instead, bring them up in the training and instruction of the Lord.

Slaves and Masters

[5]Slaves, obey your earthly masters with respect and fear, and with sincerity of heart, just as you would obey Christ. [6]Obey them not only to win their favor when their eye is on you, but like slaves of Christ, doing the will of God from your heart. [7]Serve wholeheartedly, as if you were serving the Lord, not men, [8]because you know that the Lord will reward everyone for whatever good he does, whether he is slave or free.

[9]And masters, treat your slaves in the same way. Do not threaten them, since you know that he who is both their Master and yours is in heaven, and there is no favoritism with him.

The Armor of God

[10]Finally, be strong in the Lord and in his mighty power. [11]Put on the full armor of God so that you can take your stand against the devil's schemes. [12]For our struggle is not against flesh and blood, but against the rulers, against the authorities, against the powers of this dark world and against the spiritual forces of evil in the heavenly realms. [13]Therefore put on the full armor of God, so that when the day of evil comes, you may be able to stand your ground, and after you have done everything, to stand. [14]Stand firm then, with the belt of truth buckled around your waist, with the breastplate of righteousness in place, [15]and with your feet fitted with the readiness that comes from the gospel of peace. [16]In addition to all this, take up the shield of faith, with which you can extinguish all the flaming arrows of the evil one. [17]Take the helmet of salvation and the sword of the Spirit, which is the word of God. [18]And pray in the Spirit on all occasions with all kinds of prayers and requests. With this in mind, be alert and always keep on praying for all the saints.

[19]Pray also for me, that whenever I open my mouth, words may be given me so that I will fearlessly make known the mystery of the gospel, [20]for which I am an ambassador in chains. Pray that I may declare it fearlessly, as I should.

Final Greetings

[21]Tychicus, the dear brother and faithful servant in the Lord, will tell you everything, so that you also may know how I am and what I am doing. [22]I am sending him to you for this very purpose, that you may know how we are, and that he may encourage you.

[23]Peace to the brothers, and love with faith from God the Father and the Lord Jesus Christ. [24]Grace to all who love our Lord Jesus Christ with an undying love.

PAUL writes this letter to the church he started in Philippi (Acts 16:11–40). Even though he is in prison, he feels happy when he thinks of what Christ means to him and of what the Philippians are doing for him. He gives some very practical advice on how to live the Christian life. As you read this book, remember always to rejoice in the Lord and to be content, whatever the circumstances.

PHILIPPIANS

1 Paul and Timothy, servants of Christ Jesus,

To all the saints in Christ Jesus at Philippi, together with the overseers[a] and deacons:

[2]Grace and peace to you from God our Father and the Lord Jesus Christ.

Thanksgiving and Prayer

[3]I thank my God every time I remember you. [4]In all my prayers for all of you, I always pray with joy [5]because of your partnership in the gospel from the first day until now, [6]being confident of this, that he who began a good work in you will carry it on to completion until the day of Christ Jesus.

[7]It is right for me to feel this way about all of you, since I have you in my heart; for whether I am in chains or defending and confirming the gospel, all of you share in God's grace with me. [8]God can testify how I long for all of you with the affection of Christ Jesus.

[9]And this is my prayer: that your love may abound more and more in knowledge and depth of insight, [10]so that you may be able to discern what is best and may be pure and blameless until the day of Christ, [11]filled with the fruit of righteousness that

[a] *1* Traditionally *bishops*

comes through Jesus Christ—to the glory
and praise of God.

Paul's Chains Advance the Gospel

12Now I want you to know, brothers,
that what has happened to me has really
served to advance the gospel. 13As a re-
sult, it has become clear throughout the
whole palace guard[a] and to everyone else
that I am in chains for Christ. 14Because of
my chains, most of the brothers in the
Lord have been encouraged to speak the
word of God more courageously and fear-
lessly.

15It is true that some preach Christ out
of envy and rivalry, but others out of
goodwill. 16The latter do so in love, know-
ing that I am put here for the defense of
the gospel. 17The former preach Christ out
of selfish ambition, not sincerely, suppos-
ing that they can stir up trouble for me
while I am in chains.[b] 18But what does it

[a] 13 Or *whole palace* [b] 16,17 Some late manuscripts have verses 16 and 17 in reverse order.

VERSE FOR THE DAY: Philippians 1:6

AUTHOR: John A. Huffman, Jr.

PASSAGE FOR THE DAY: Philippians 1:1–11

More and Less

As a five-year-old, I accepted Jesus Christ as my Savior. At fourteen, I committed myself to Christ as Lord. And now, having entered my fifties, I still confess those initial commitments.

But I have come to a greater understanding of the richness of God's love in Jesus Christ. The testimony I could trumpet simplistically as a teenager, I now declare with a tear in my voice. In my youthful idealism, I half-believed that I really deserved God's grace and perhaps could have earned it, that I was even doing him some kind of favor to receive it. Now I am painfully aware that in spite of being created in God's image, I have self-destructive tendencies that daily cause me to depend upon the Lord's initiative on my behalf.

I realize that my hope really is based on nothing less than Jesus' blood and righteousness. Now I have committed all I know and don't know of myself to all I know and don't know of God in Jesus Christ.

MARRIAGE BUILDERS

♦ *In what specific areas have you grown in your understanding of God and in your life as a Christian?*

♦ *What are some of your hopes or goals for your future spiritual development?*

Additional Scripture Readings
2 Timothy 1:12; Jude 24–25;
Philippians 3:8

Go to page 1303 for your next devotional reading.

matter? The important thing is that in every way, whether from false motives or true, Christ is preached. And because of this I rejoice.

Yes, and I will continue to rejoice, 19for I know that through your prayers and the help given by the Spirit of Jesus Christ, what has happened to me will turn out for my deliverance.[a] 20I eagerly expect and hope that I will in no way be ashamed, but will have sufficient courage so that now as always Christ will be exalted in my body, whether by life or by death. 21For to me, to live is Christ and to die is gain. 22If I am to go on living in the body, this will mean fruitful labor for me. Yet what shall I choose? I do not know! 23I am torn between the two: I desire to depart and be with Christ, which is better by far; 24but it is more necessary for you that I remain in the body. 25Convinced of this, I know that I will remain, and I will continue with all of you for your progress and joy in the faith, 26so that through my being with you again your joy in Christ Jesus will overflow on account of me.

27Whatever happens, conduct yourselves in a manner worthy of the gospel of Christ. Then, whether I come and see you or only hear about you in my absence, I will know that you stand firm in one spirit, contending as one man for the faith of the gospel 28without being frightened in any way by those who oppose you. This is a sign to them that they will be destroyed, but that you will be saved—and that by God. 29For it has been granted to you on behalf of Christ not only to believe on him, but also to suffer for him, 30since you are going through the same struggle you saw I had, and now hear that I still have.

Imitating Christ's Humility

2 If you have any encouragement from being united with Christ, if any comfort from his love, if any fellowship with the Spirit, if any tenderness and compassion, 2then make my joy complete by being like-minded, having the same love, being one in spirit and purpose. 3Do nothing out of selfish ambition or vain conceit, but in humility consider others better than yourselves. 4Each of you should look not only to your own interests, but also to the interests of others.

5Your attitude should be the same as that of Christ Jesus:

6Who, being in very nature[b] God,
did not consider equality with God
something to be grasped,
7but made himself nothing,
taking the very nature[c] of a
servant,
being made in human likeness.
8And being found in appearance as a
man,
he humbled himself
and became obedient to death—
even death on a cross!
9Therefore God exalted him to the
highest place
and gave him the name that is
above every name,
10that at the name of Jesus every knee
should bow,
in heaven and on earth and under
the earth,
11and every tongue confess that Jesus
Christ is Lord,
to the glory of God the Father.

Shining as Stars

12Therefore, my dear friends, as you have always obeyed—not only in my presence, but now much more in my absence—continue to work out your salvation with fear and trembling, 13for it is God who works in you to will and to act according to his good purpose.

14Do everything without complaining or arguing, 15so that you may become blameless and pure, children of God without fault in a crooked and depraved generation, in which you shine like stars in the universe 16as you hold out[d] the word of life—in order that I may boast on the day of Christ that I did not run or labor for nothing. 17But even if I am being poured out like a drink offering on the sacrifice and service coming from your faith, I am glad and rejoice with all of you. 18So you too should be glad and rejoice with me.

Timothy and Epaphroditus

19I hope in the Lord Jesus to send Timothy to you soon, that I also may be cheered when I receive news about you. 20I have no one else like him, who takes a genuine interest in your welfare. 21For everyone looks out for his own interests, not those of Jesus Christ. 22But you know that Timothy has proved himself, because as a son with his father he has served with me in the work of the gospel. 23I hope, there-

[a]19 Or *salvation* [b]6 Or *in the form of* [c]7 Or *the form* [d]16 Or *hold on to*

fore, to send him as soon as I see how things go with me. [24]And I am confident in the Lord that I myself will come soon.

[25]But I think it is necessary to send back to you Epaphroditus, my brother, fellow worker and fellow soldier, who is also your messenger, whom you sent to take care of my needs. [26]For he longs for all of you and is distressed because you heard he was ill. [27]Indeed he was ill, and almost died. But God had mercy on him, and not on him only but also on me, to spare me sorrow upon sorrow. [28]Therefore I am all the more eager to send him, so that when you see him again you may be glad and I may have less anxiety. [29]Welcome him in the Lord with great joy, and honor men like him, [30]because he almost died for the work of Christ, risking his life to make up for the help you could not give me.

No Confidence in the Flesh

3 Finally, my brothers, rejoice in the Lord! It is no trouble for me to write the same things to you again, and it is a safeguard for you.

VERSE FOR THE DAY: Philippians 2:3–4

AUTHOR: Charlene Ann Baumbich

PASSAGE FOR THE DAY: Philippians 2:1–11

Loving Your Mate's Quirks

After twenty years of marriage, I've found that my husband's quirks are what I cherish the most. But in the same way, his most endearing trait can be my greatest frustration.

George is a tool-and-die engineer—precise, exacting. I am a writer—impulsive, expressive. It has taken me a while to realize that many of the fussy, overly meticulous things that George does are actually acts of love for me. For example, when I venture on a trip alone, he always readies the car. Tires checked. Gas tank topped. CB hooked up. And when he leaves for work, I lie in bed and listen as he checks the locks—making sure I'm safe.

During a period when George was unemployed, he built an office for my budding writing career. At the time, I had no published articles. But George was going to build me an office anyway. My desire to become a writer was on his list.

More importantly, *I* was on his list.

MARRIAGE BUILDERS

♦ *Name a couple of your mate's quirks that are actually expressions of his or her love for you.*

♦ *Which of your own quirks does your spouse find irritating? How can you use these to express love in a way your spouse understands?*

Additional Scripture Readings
Romans 12:10; Galatians 5:13; Ephesians 4:2; Colossians 3:13

Go to page 1304 for your next devotional reading.

[2]Watch out for those dogs, those men
who do evil, those mutilators of the flesh.
[3]For it is we who are the circumcision, we
who worship by the Spirit of God, who
glory in Christ Jesus, and who put no con-
fidence in the flesh— [4]though I myself
have reasons for such confidence.

If anyone else thinks he has reasons to
put confidence in the flesh, I have more:
[5]circumcised on the eighth day, of the
people of Israel, of the tribe of Benjamin,
a Hebrew of Hebrews; in regard to the
law, a Pharisee; [6]as for zeal, persecuting
the church; as for legalistic righteousness,
faultless.

[7]But whatever was to my profit I now
consider loss for the sake of Christ. [8]What
is more, I consider everything a loss com-
pared to the surpassing greatness of
knowing Christ Jesus my Lord, for whose
sake I have lost all things. I consider them
rubbish, that I may gain Christ [9]and be
found in him, not having a righteousness
of my own that comes from the law, but

FRIDAY

VERSE FOR THE DAY: Philippians 3:8

AUTHOR: Bonnie Shipley Rice

PASSAGE FOR THE DAY: Philippians 3:8–14

The Hard Road to Joy

No one doubts that submitting our lives to God and practicing spiritual disciplines require commitment and hard work. But it helps to recognize that they produce a surprising side effect: *joy*. In Philippians, Paul speaks about his joy. In the fellowship of the brethren, in service, even in suffering the apostle was filled with joy. How is that possible? It's possible because he had disciplined himself to know Christ.

In Philippians 3:8, Paul mentions the surpassing greatness of knowing Christ Jesus. Verse 10 mentions "the power of his resurrection." In verse 12 are the words "I press on to take hold of that for which Christ Jesus took hold of me."

Our emotional balance and spiritual maturity are conditioned upon our conceding to Christ's rule in our lives. Joy is the amazing gift he gives while we are in the process—joy here on earth, greater joy in our life with God in heaven. One day we will all stand before God. It is at that time that we will know and revel in how far we've come.

MARRIAGE BUILDERS

♦ *What have you had to lose or let go of in order to keep your goal of knowing Christ?*

♦ *When in the past month have you felt the supernatural joy of Christ?*

Additional Scripture Readings
Hosea 6:1–3; Matthew 7:7–8; Jeremiah 29:13

Go to page 1305 for your next devotional reading.

WEEKENDING

MERCY

Couples are too often blindsided by their individual differences. But it's possible to keep your differences from driving a wedge between you. One way is to concentrate on showing mercy to your spouse. Consider the following questions:

1. Considering we all have our flaws, in what ways could you do a better job of showing mercy to your spouse?

2. Can you think of an occasion when, rather than giving your mate the benefit of the doubt, you instead concluded that what your spouse had done or said was *deliberately* hurtful? If so, how did that affect your ability to view your spouse as a person who does his/her best to act out of pure motives?

3. If you concentrated on showing mercy rather than judging your mate's words, actions and habits, how would that make it easier to accept the ways you and your mate are different?

— *The* Marriage Partnership *Staff*

REVIVE

Saturday: Micah 6:1–8

Sunday: Matthew 7:1–12

Go to page 1307 for your next devotional reading.

that which is through faith in Christ—the
righteousness that comes from God and is
by faith. 10I want to know Christ and the
power of his resurrection and the fellow-
ship of sharing in his sufferings, becom-
ing like him in his death, 11and so, some-
how, to attain to the resurrection from
the dead.

Pressing on Toward the Goal

12Not that I have already obtained all
this, or have already been made perfect,
but I press on to take hold of that for
which Christ Jesus took hold of me.
13Brothers, I do not consider myself yet to
have taken hold of it. But one thing I do:
Forgetting what is behind and straining
toward what is ahead, 14I press on toward
the goal to win the prize for which God
has called me heavenward in Christ Jesus.

15All of us who are mature should take
such a view of things. And if on some
point you think differently, that too God
will make clear to you. 16Only let us live
up to what we have already attained.

17Join with others in following my ex-
ample, brothers, and take note of those
who live according to the pattern we gave
you. 18For, as I have often told you before
and now say again even with tears, many
live as enemies of the cross of Christ.
19Their destiny is destruction, their god is
their stomach, and their glory is in their
shame. Their mind is on earthly things.
20But our citizenship is in heaven. And we
eagerly await a Savior from there, the Lord
Jesus Christ, 21who, by the power that en-
ables him to bring everything under his
control, will transform our lowly bodies
so that they will be like his glorious
body.

4 Therefore, my brothers, you whom I
love and long for, my joy and crown,
that is how you should stand firm in the
Lord, dear friends!

Exhortations

2I plead with Euodia and I plead with
Syntyche to agree with each other in the
Lord. 3Yes, and I ask you, loyal yokefel-
low,[a] help these women who have con-
tended at my side in the cause of the gos-
pel, along with Clement and the rest of my
fellow workers, whose names are in the
book of life.

4Rejoice in the Lord always. I will say it
again: Rejoice! 5Let your gentleness be ev-
ident to all. The Lord is near. 6Do not be
anxious about anything, but in every-
thing, by prayer and petition, with thanks-
giving, present your requests to God.
7And the peace of God, which transcends
all understanding, will guard your hearts
and your minds in Christ Jesus.

8Finally, brothers, whatever is true,
whatever is noble, whatever is right, what-
ever is pure, whatever is lovely, whatever
is admirable—if anything is excellent or
praiseworthy—think about such things.
9Whatever you have learned or received
or heard from me, or seen in me—put it
into practice. And the God of peace will be
with you.

Thanks for Their Gifts

10I rejoice greatly in the Lord that at last
you have renewed your concern for me.
Indeed, you have been concerned, but
you had no opportunity to show it. 11I am
not saying this because I am in need, for
I have learned to be content whatever the
circumstances. 12I know what it is to be in
need, and I know what it is to have plenty.
I have learned the secret of being content
in any and every situation, whether well
fed or hungry, whether living in plenty or
in want. 13I can do everything through
him who gives me strength.

14Yet it was good of you to share in my
troubles. 15Moreover, as you Philippians
know, in the early days of your acquain-
tance with the gospel, when I set out from
Macedonia, not one church shared with
me in the matter of giving and receiving,
except you only; 16for even when I was in
Thessalonica, you sent me aid again and
again when I was in need. 17Not that I am
looking for a gift, but I am looking for
what may be credited to your account.
18I have received full payment and even
more; I am amply supplied, now that I
have received from Epaphroditus the gifts
you sent. They are a fragrant offering, an
acceptable sacrifice, pleasing to God.
19And my God will meet all your needs ac-
cording to his glorious riches in Christ
Jesus.

20To our God and Father be glory for
ever and ever. Amen.

[a]3 Or *loyal Syzygus*

VERSE FOR THE DAY: Philippians 4:11

AUTHOR: Rodney Clapp

PASSAGE FOR THE DAY: Philippians 4:10–13

Is Contentment Possible?

The problem with contentment, American-style, is that it denies our human limitations. We are encouraged to admire the supposedly "self-made" man or woman. We are taught to value self-sufficiency. And we assume that money will insulate us from chance, protect us from "the slings and arrows of outrageous fortune"—maybe even from death.

In contrast, the Apostle Paul claims he achieved contentment "in any and all circumstances." Paul's ideal of contentment is truer to life. We didn't create ourselves and we can't save ourselves from death.

In the last two chapters of Philippians, Paul describes a type of contentment that isn't based on self-sufficiency. It comes in grateful acceptance of his dependence on God and the sharing in the gifts offered by others. His contentment isn't the satiation of appetites but the taming of appetites. His contentment doesn't bring the absence of suffering; it brings the enablement to continue in service to the Kingdom of God.

Paul gave himself to something bigger and greater than himself. His life had purpose and significance beyond itself. He was not free of worry, pain or limitations, but he was content. Both joy and suffering come from beyond us and are bigger than us. Both say we are dependent and can never be complete in ourselves, that salvation and wholeness come only when we can admit we aren't self-made little gods.

It takes courage *not* to pursue contentment American-style.

MARRIAGE BUILDERS

♦ *In what areas of your life do you tend to be "self-sufficient"?*
♦ *Are certain circumstances robbing you of the peace and joy that are part of contentment? Take time today to remind each other of God's loving intentions for you and your life.*

Additional Scripture Readings
1 Timothy 6:6–8; Hebrews 13:5–8

Go to page 1310 for your next devotional reading.

Final Greetings

21Greet all the saints in Christ Jesus.
The brothers who are with me send greetings. 22All the saints send you greetings,
especially those who belong to Caesar's
household.

23The grace of the Lord Jesus Christ be
with your spirit. Amen.[a]

[a]23 Some manuscripts do not have *Amen*.

PAUL writes this letter to the church in Colosse at about the same time as he writes Ephesians. False teachers are deceiving some of those to whom he writes (Colossians 2:4). Therefore, Paul stresses the power and glory of Christ and instructs his readers on how to live as Christians. As you read this book, put your faith in this glorious Savior who died for you, and promise him that you will show Christian love and compassion to others.

COLOSSIANS

1 Paul, an apostle of Christ Jesus by the will of God, and Timothy our brother,

2 To the holy and faithful[a] brothers in Christ at Colosse:

Grace and peace to you from God our Father.[b]

Thanksgiving and Prayer

3 We always thank God, the Father of our Lord Jesus Christ, when we pray for you, 4 because we have heard of your faith in Christ Jesus and of the love you have for all the saints— 5 the faith and love that spring from the hope that is stored up for you in heaven and that you have already heard about in the word of truth, the gospel 6 that has come to you. All over the world this gospel is bearing fruit and growing, just as it has been doing among you since the day you heard it and understood God's grace in all its truth. 7 You learned it from Epaphras, our dear fellow servant, who is a faithful minister of Christ on our[c] behalf, 8 and who also told us of your love in the Spirit.

9 For this reason, since the day we heard about you, we have not stopped praying for you and asking God to fill you with the knowledge of his will through all spiritual

[a] 2 Or *believing* [b] 2 Some manuscripts *Father and the Lord Jesus Christ* [c] 7 Some manuscripts *your*

wisdom and understanding. [10]And we pray this in order that you may live a life worthy of the Lord and may please him in every way: bearing fruit in every good work, growing in the knowledge of God, [11]being strengthened with all power according to his glorious might so that you may have great endurance and patience, and joyfully [12]giving thanks to the Father, who has qualified you[a] to share in the in-

[a]12 Some manuscripts *us*

VERSE FOR THE DAY: Colossians 1:10

AUTHOR: Walter Wangerin, Jr.

PASSAGE FOR THE DAY: Colossians 1:9–14

Whom Did You Marry?

In our little apartment in St. Louis, Thanne went to bed at precisely nine o'clock every night. No matter the difference of the days, some harder and some easier. No matter the marvelous conversations she cut short to get her sleep. And she always showered first. And she always laid her clothes out neatly! Thanne's prearranged, punctilious life seemed to me a compulsive, cold routine.

I, on the other hand, was to her a stunning mess, so unpredictable as to be unreliable. And how, in the name of cleanli-godliness, could I contrive to strew dirty socks through every room of the apartment?

What had I married? A machine?

What had she married? An adolescent?

In marriage, idealization will surely run upon realization. The question is not how we might avoid this crisis, because we can't. The question, rather, is what work is required to meet the crisis and to grow by it? For if we think that this revelation of the real spouse is the final truth of our mate and our marriage—and that we've made a dreadful mistake, therefore—then we will move to alienation, one from the other. But if we take this as a natural step in the process of growing together, we may, with clear sight, move toward acceptance and accommodation of each other.

MARRIAGE BUILDERS

♦ *What are the benefits of growing together, despite your differences?*

♦ *In what ways has accepting and accommodating each other become an ongoing part of your marriage?*

Additional Scripture Readings
1 Corinthians 10:24; Philippians 2:3–4

Go to page 1313 for your next devotional reading.

heritance of the saints in the kingdom of
light. 13For he has rescued us from the do-
minion of darkness and brought us into
the kingdom of the Son he loves, 14in
whom we have redemption,[a] the forgive-
ness of sins.

The Supremacy of Christ

15He is the image of the invisible God,
the firstborn over all creation. 16For by
him all things were created: things in
heaven and on earth, visible and invisible,
whether thrones or powers or rulers or au-
thorities; all things were created by him
and for him. 17He is before all things, and
in him all things hold together. 18And he
is the head of the body, the church; he is
the beginning and the firstborn from
among the dead, so that in everything he
might have the supremacy. 19For God was
pleased to have all his fullness dwell in
him, 20and through him to reconcile to
himself all things, whether things on earth
or things in heaven, by making peace
through his blood, shed on the cross.

21Once you were alienated from God
and were enemies in your minds because
of[b] your evil behavior. 22But now he has
reconciled you by Christ's physical body
through death to present you holy in his
sight, without blemish and free from accu-
sation— 23if you continue in your faith,
established and firm, not moved from the
hope held out in the gospel. This is the
gospel that you heard and that has been
proclaimed to every creature under heav-
en, and of which I, Paul, have become a
servant.

Paul's Labor for the Church

24Now I rejoice in what was suffered for
you, and I fill up in my flesh what is still
lacking in regard to Christ's afflictions, for
the sake of his body, which is the church.
25I have become its servant by the com-
mission God gave me to present to you the
word of God in its fullness— 26the mys-
tery that has been kept hidden for ages
and generations, but is now disclosed to
the saints. 27To them God has chosen to
make known among the Gentiles the glo-
rious riches of this mystery, which is
Christ in you, the hope of glory.

28We proclaim him, admonishing and
teaching everyone with all wisdom, so
that we may present everyone perfect in
Christ. 29To this end I labor, struggling
with all his energy, which so powerfully
works in me.

2 I want you to know how much I am
struggling for you and for those at La-
odicea, and for all who have not met me
personally. 2My purpose is that they may
be encouraged in heart and united in love,
so that they may have the full riches of
complete understanding, in order that
they may know the mystery of God, name-
ly, Christ, 3in whom are hidden all the
treasures of wisdom and knowledge. 4I
tell you this so that no one may deceive
you by fine-sounding arguments. 5For
though I am absent from you in body, I
am present with you in spirit and delight
to see how orderly you are and how firm
your faith in Christ is.

Freedom From Human Regulations Through Life With Christ

6So then, just as you received Christ
Jesus as Lord, continue to live in him,
7rooted and built up in him, strengthened
in the faith as you were taught, and over-
flowing with thankfulness.

8See to it that no one takes you captive
through hollow and deceptive philoso-
phy, which depends on human tradition
and the basic principles of this world rath-
er than on Christ.

9For in Christ all the fullness of the Dei-
ty lives in bodily form, 10and you have
been given fullness in Christ, who is the
head over every power and authority. 11In
him you were also circumcised, in the put-
ting off of the sinful nature,[c] not with a
circumcision done by the hands of men
but with the circumcision done by Christ,
12having been buried with him in baptism
and raised with him through your faith in
the power of God, who raised him from
the dead.

13When you were dead in your sins and
in the uncircumcision of your sinful na-
ture,[d] God made you[e] alive with Christ.
He forgave us all our sins, 14having can-
celed the written code, with its regula-
tions, that was against us and that stood
opposed to us; he took it away, nailing it
to the cross. 15And having disarmed the
powers and authorities, he made a public
spectacle of them, triumphing over them
by the cross.[f]

16Therefore do not let anyone judge you

[a] *14* A few late manuscripts *redemption through his blood* [b] *21* Or *minds, as shown by* [c] *11* Or *the flesh* [d] *13* Or *your flesh* [e] *13* Some manuscripts *us* [f] *15* Or *them in him*

by what you eat or drink, or with regard to
a religious festival, a New Moon celebra-
tion or a Sabbath day. 17These are a shad-
ow of the things that were to come; the
reality, however, is found in Christ. 18Do
not let anyone who delights in false hu-
mility and the worship of angels disqual-
ify you for the prize. Such a person goes
into great detail about what he has seen,
and his unspiritual mind puffs him up
with idle notions. 19He has lost connec-
tion with the Head, from whom the whole
body, supported and held together by its
ligaments and sinews, grows as God
causes it to grow.

20Since you died with Christ to the basic
principles of this world, why, as though
you still belonged to it, do you submit to
its rules: 21"Do not handle! Do not taste!
Do not touch!"? 22These are all destined to
perish with use, because they are based
on human commands and teachings.
23Such regulations indeed have an appear-
ance of wisdom, with their self-imposed
worship, their false humility and their
harsh treatment of the body, but they lack
any value in restraining sensual indul-
gence.

Rules for Holy Living

3 Since, then, you have been raised
with Christ, set your hearts on things
above, where Christ is seated at the right
hand of God. 2Set your minds on things
above, not on earthly things. 3For you
died, and your life is now hidden with
Christ in God. 4When Christ, who is
your[a] life, appears, then you also will ap-
pear with him in glory.

5Put to death, therefore, whatever be-
longs to your earthly nature: sexual im-
morality, impurity, lust, evil desires and
greed, which is idolatry. 6Because of
these, the wrath of God is coming.[b] 7You
used to walk in these ways, in the life you
once lived. 8But now you must rid your-
selves of all such things as these: anger,
rage, malice, slander, and filthy language
from your lips. 9Do not lie to each other,
since you have taken off your old self with
its practices 10and have put on the new
self, which is being renewed in knowledge
in the image of its Creator. 11Here there is
no Greek or Jew, circumcised or uncir-
cumcised, barbarian, Scythian, slave or
free, but Christ is all, and is in all.

12Therefore, as God's chosen people,
holy and dearly loved, clothe yourselves
with compassion, kindness, humility,
gentleness and patience. 13Bear with each
other and forgive whatever grievances
you may have against one another. For-
give as the Lord forgave you. 14And over
all these virtues put on love, which binds
them all together in perfect unity.

15Let the peace of Christ rule in your
hearts, since as members of one body you
were called to peace. And be thankful.
16Let the word of Christ dwell in you rich-
ly as you teach and admonish one another
with all wisdom, and as you sing psalms,
hymns and spiritual songs with gratitude
in your hearts to God. 17And whatever you
do, whether in word or deed, do it all in
the name of the Lord Jesus, giving thanks
to God the Father through him.

Rules for Christian Households

18Wives, submit to your husbands, as is
fitting in the Lord.

19Husbands, love your wives and do not
be harsh with them.

20Children, obey your parents in every-
thing, for this pleases the Lord.

21Fathers, do not embitter your chil-
dren, or they will become discouraged.

22Slaves, obey your earthly masters in
everything; and do it, not only when their
eye is on you and to win their favor, but
with sincerity of heart and reverence for
the Lord. 23Whatever you do, work at it
with all your heart, as working for the
Lord, not for men, 24since you know that
you will receive an inheritance from the
Lord as a reward. It is the Lord Christ you
are serving. 25Anyone who does wrong
will be repaid for his wrong, and there is
no favoritism.

4 Masters, provide your slaves with
what is right and fair, because you
know that you also have a Master in
heaven.

Further Instructions

2Devote yourselves to prayer, being
watchful and thankful. 3And pray for us,
too, that God may open a door for our
message, so that we may proclaim the
mystery of Christ, for which I am in
chains. 4Pray that I may proclaim it clear-
ly, as I should. 5Be wise in the way you act
toward outsiders; make the most of every
opportunity. 6Let your conversation be al-
ways full of grace, seasoned with salt, so

[a]4 Some manuscripts *our* [b]6 Some early manuscripts *coming on those who are disobedient*

VERSE FOR THE DAY:
Colossians 3:18–19

AUTHOR:
Leslie Parrott

PASSAGE FOR THE DAY:
Colossians 3:12–25

Better Than Equality

The headline of a recent newspaper article caught my attention. Referring to married couples, it asked: "Are We Peers Yet?" I took the ten-question "test" that promised to tell me whether my marriage was a peer marriage (between equals), a near-peer marriage (equality is admired but still out of reach), or a traditional marriage (hierarchy places the husband at the top).

The test made me doubt my equal footing with Les. How could I be certain I had an equal say in how we spend our money? In a crisis, would my voice really carry the same weight as my husband's? Determined somehow to quantify and compare the power each of us had, my attitude resembled that of the finicky building inspector who needed to sign off before our home loan could be approved.

But soon I realized my inspection was misguided. There is no such thing as perfect equality. Even the best of peers aren't identical; we're individuals with different gifts. I realized that determining which spouse was initiating this or controlling that didn't really matter. The true measure of a marriage is not so much who has the power; it's a commitment to mutual respect and dedication to the partnership. What matters is becoming peers of the heart—listening to each other, seeking consensus in major decisions, being equally dedicated to one another's well-being.

That's the type of equality I want.

MARRIAGE BUILDERS

- *In what areas do you seem to struggle with who's in control?*
- *What would help you in seeking consensus in those areas?*

Additional Scripture Readings
Romans 8:16–17; Galatians 3:26–29

Go to page 1314 for your next devotional reading.

that you may know how to answer everyone.

Final Greetings

7Tychicus will tell you all the news about me. He is a dear brother, a faithful minister and fellow servant in the Lord. 8I am sending him to you for the express purpose that you may know about our[a] circumstances and that he may encourage your hearts. 9He is coming with Onesimus, our faithful and dear brother, who is one of you. They will tell you everything that is happening here.

[a]8 Some manuscripts *that he may know about your*

VERSE FOR THE DAY: Colossians 4:6

AUTHOR: Bill Hybels

PASSAGE FOR THE DAY: Colossians 4:2–18

Is Anyone Listening?

Each of us prefers certain "languages" to express and to accept appreciation and affection. My wife, Lynne, and I know this from experience.

For years we expressed love differently and didn't realize it. Because I appreciate people opening doors of opportunity for me, I assumed Lynne would, too. So for years I did everything I could to offer opportunities that would stimulate and inspire her. Finally she said, "Bill, I feel like you're never satisfied with what I'm doing. You're always trying to head me off in new directions. I wish that once in a while you would just put your arms around me, hold me and let me feel loved and accepted just the way I am."

Most of us mistakenly assume our spouses want to receive love the same way we do. So we use whatever language comes most naturally to us. And that usually doesn't work. I thought I was doing Lynne a favor, but in reality I was making her feel pressured and inadequate. What she actually needed was a loving embrace.

We must tell one another which love language communicates most clearly to us. Learning new ways of communicating love can transform a marriage where spouses *hope* they're loved into a marriage where they *know* they are.

MARRIAGE BUILDERS

♦ *When have you found yourselves speaking two different languages when trying to communicate about something?*

♦ *How do you communicate your love to your spouse? How clearly does your message get through?*

Additional Scripture Readings
Proverbs 25:11; Ecclesiastes 9:17; James 3:1–2

Go to page 1318 for your next devotional reading.

[10]My fellow prisoner Aristarchus sends you his greetings, as does Mark, the cousin of Barnabas. (You have received instructions about him; if he comes to you, welcome him.) [11]Jesus, who is called Justus, also sends greetings. These are the only Jews among my fellow workers for the kingdom of God, and they have proved a comfort to me. [12]Epaphras, who is one of you and a servant of Christ Jesus, sends greetings. He is always wrestling in prayer for you, that you may stand firm in all the will of God, mature and fully assured. [13]I vouch for him that he is working hard for you and for those at Laodicea and Hierapolis. [14]Our dear friend Luke, the doctor, and Demas send greetings. [15]Give my greetings to the brothers at Laodicea, and to Nympha and the church in her house.

[16]After this letter has been read to you, see that it is also read in the church of the Laodiceans and that you in turn read the letter from Laodicea.

[17]Tell Archippus: "See to it that you complete the work you have received in the Lord."

[18]I, Paul, write this greeting in my own hand. Remember my chains. Grace be with you.

PAUL writes this letter to the church he began in Thessalonica (Acts 17:1–9), shortly after leaving them and being unable to return (1 Thessalonians 2:17–18). He is excited about their Christian faith, reminds them of his intense love for them, and answers questions about what death means for a Christian. As you read this book, find comfort as a believer that when you die you will still be under God's care and will "be with the Lord forever" (1 Thessalonians 4:17).

1 THESSALONIANS

1 Paul, Silas[a] and Timothy,

To the church of the Thessalonians in God the Father and the Lord Jesus Christ:

Grace and peace to you.[b]

Thanksgiving for the Thessalonians' Faith

[2]We always thank God for all of you, mentioning you in our prayers. [3]We continually remember before our God and Father your work produced by faith, your labor prompted by love, and your endurance inspired by hope in our Lord Jesus Christ.

[4]For we know, brothers loved by God, that he has chosen you, [5]because our gospel came to you not simply with words, but also with power, with the Holy Spirit and with deep conviction. You know how we lived among you for your sake. [6]You became imitators of us and of the Lord; in spite of severe suffering, you welcomed the message with the joy given by the

[a] 1 Greek *Silvanus*, a variant of *Silas*

[b] 1 Some early manuscripts *you from God our Father and the Lord Jesus Christ*

Holy Spirit. 7And so you became a model
to all the believers in Macedonia and
Achaia. 8The Lord's message rang out
from you not only in Macedonia and
Achaia—your faith in God has become
known everywhere. Therefore we do not
need to say anything about it, 9for they
themselves report what kind of reception
you gave us. They tell how you turned to
God from idols to serve the living and true
God, 10and to wait for his Son from heaven, whom he raised from the dead—
Jesus, who rescues us from the coming
wrath.

Paul's Ministry in Thessalonica

2 You know, brothers, that our visit to
you was not a failure. 2We had previ-
ously suffered and been insulted in Philip-
pi, as you know, but with the help of our
God we dared to tell you his gospel in
spite of strong opposition. 3For the appeal
we make does not spring from error or im-
pure motives, nor are we trying to trick
you. 4On the contrary, we speak as men
approved by God to be entrusted with the
gospel. We are not trying to please men
but God, who tests our hearts. 5You know
we never used flattery, nor did we put on
a mask to cover up greed—God is our wit-
ness. 6We were not looking for praise
from men, not from you or anyone else.

As apostles of Christ we could have
been a burden to you, 7but we were gentle
among you, like a mother caring for her
little children. 8We loved you so much
that we were delighted to share with you
not only the gospel of God but our lives as
well, because you had become so dear to
us. 9Surely you remember, brothers, our
toil and hardship; we worked night and
day in order not to be a burden to anyone
while we preached the gospel of God to
you.

10You are witnesses, and so is God, of
how holy, righteous and blameless we
were among you who believed. 11For you
know that we dealt with each of you as a
father deals with his own children, 12en-
couraging, comforting and urging you to
live lives worthy of God, who calls you
into his kingdom and glory.

13And we also thank God continually
because, when you received the word of
God, which you heard from us, you ac-
cepted it not as the word of men, but as it
actually is, the word of God, which is at
work in you who believe. 14For you,
brothers, became imitators of God's
churches in Judea, which are in Christ
Jesus: You suffered from your own coun-
trymen the same things those churches
suffered from the Jews, 15who killed the
Lord Jesus and the prophets and also
drove us out. They displease God and are
hostile to all men 16in their effort to keep
us from speaking to the Gentiles so that
they may be saved. In this way they al-
ways heap up their sins to the limit. The
wrath of God has come upon them at
last.[a]

Paul's Longing to See the Thessalonians

17But, brothers, when we were torn
away from you for a short time (in person,
not in thought), out of our intense longing
we made every effort to see you. 18For we
wanted to come to you—certainly I, Paul,
did, again and again—but Satan stopped
us. 19For what is our hope, our joy, or the
crown in which we will glory in the pres-
ence of our Lord Jesus when he comes? Is
it not you? 20Indeed, you are our glory and
joy.

3 So when we could stand it no longer,
we thought it best to be left by our-
selves in Athens. 2We sent Timothy, who
is our brother and God's fellow worker[b]
in spreading the gospel of Christ, to
strengthen and encourage you in your
faith, 3so that no one would be unsettled
by these trials. You know quite well that
we were destined for them. 4In fact, when
we were with you, we kept telling you that
we would be persecuted. And it turned
out that way, as you well know. 5For this
reason, when I could stand it no longer, I
sent to find out about your faith. I was
afraid that in some way the tempter might
have tempted you and our efforts might
have been useless.

Timothy's Encouraging Report

6But Timothy has just now come to us
from you and has brought good news
about your faith and love. He has told us
that you always have pleasant memories
of us and that you long to see us, just as
we also long to see you. 7Therefore, broth-
ers, in all our distress and persecution we
were encouraged about you because of

[a]16 Or *them fully*
[b]2 Some manuscripts *brother and fellow worker*; other manuscripts *brother and God's servant*

your faith. [8]For now we really live, since
you are standing firm in the Lord. [9]How
can we thank God enough for you in re-
turn for all the joy we have in the presence
of our God because of you? [10]Night and
day we pray most earnestly that we may
see you again and supply what is lacking
in your faith.

[11]Now may our God and Father himself
and our Lord Jesus clear the way for us to
come to you. [12]May the Lord make your
love increase and overflow for each other
and for everyone else, just as ours does for
you. [13]May he strengthen your hearts so
that you will be blameless and holy in the
presence of our God and Father when our
Lord Jesus comes with all his holy ones.

Living to Please God

4 Finally, brothers, we instructed you
how to live in order to please God, as
in fact you are living. Now we ask you and

VERSE FOR THE DAY: 1 Thessalonians 2:17

AUTHOR: Jay Kesler

PASSAGE FOR THE DAY: 1 Thessalonians 2:17–20

When You're Apart

Over the years, I've done a lot of traveling. Being away from my wife, Janie, is never easy, but when we *are* together, we work hard to make our time positive and meaningful. We share our lives with each other in as much detail as possible.

I may be gone for several weeks at a time. But I know almost hour by hour what Janie is doing during that time, and she knows where I am and what I'm doing because we talk about it ahead of time. I look at my watch and calculate, "It's 8 o'clock back home; Janie's getting ready to go to church." I consciously try to put her in my mind, thinking about her activities, praying through certain situations with her. And she does the same for me.

Another thing we do when we're apart is read the same chapters in the Bible at the same time, and when I come home we talk about what we have read. This helps us continue to grow together in our emotional, spiritual and intellectual life.

Making the effort to enjoy intimacies such as these can cause you to draw closer, though there may be hundreds of miles between you.

MARRIAGE BUILDERS

♦ *How do you update each other on your individual lives—whether you're traveling or at home together?*

♦ *What specific things could each of you do to better involve each other in your individual lives?*

Additional Scripture Readings
2 Timothy 1:3–5; 1 Thessalonians 1:2–3

Go to page 1319 for your next devotional reading.

WEEKENDING

FRIENDS

Marriage partners exhibit many characteristics of good friends, but it's unreasonable to expect your spouse to be *everything* to you—to fulfill all your social needs. Talk together about the friendship you share. Then discuss your needs and goals for same-sex friendships outside your marriage. Do what you can to help one another meet these friendship goals.

1. To what extent is your spouse also your friend?

2. In what ways is your mate much *more* than a friend?

3. What role do your current outside friendships play in strengthening your marriage?

4. Do you have friends whom you can trust deeply, those you can depend on in difficult times?

5. What can you do to develop deeper friendships with one or two people outside your marriage?

— *The* Marriage Partnership *Staff*

REVIVE

Saturday: 1 Samuel 20:42
Sunday: John 15:12–13

Go to page 1320 for your next devotional reading.

urge you in the Lord Jesus to do this more
and more. 2For you know what instruc-
tions we gave you by the authority of the
Lord Jesus.

3It is God's will that you should be sanc-
tified: that you should avoid sexual immo-
rality; 4that each of you should learn to
control his own body[a] in a way that is
holy and honorable, 5not in passionate
lust like the heathen, who do not know
God; 6and that in this matter no one
should wrong his brother or take advan-
tage of him. The Lord will punish men for
all such sins, as we have already told you
and warned you. 7For God did not call us
to be impure, but to live a holy life.
8Therefore, he who rejects this instruction
does not reject man but God, who gives
you his Holy Spirit.

9Now about brotherly love we do not

[a]4 Or *learn to live with his own wife*; or *learn to acquire a wife*

VERSE FOR THE DAY: 1 Thessalonians 4:4–5

AUTHOR: Clifford and Joyce Penner

PASSAGE FOR THE DAY: 1 Thessalonians 4:1–12

Controlling Lust

The Bible teaches that we are not to lust after something that is not ours. It also teaches that what we put into our minds influences who we become. If a man even looks at a woman (other than his wife) with the intent to be with her sexually, he has committed adultery. We do not understand that to mean a man will *never* find other women attractive. Rather, we are to *limit* how we respond to those natural attractions by controlling both our thoughts and our actions.

It's true that our world bombards us with sexual images, but it is our choice whether to pursue these images or resist them. So how can we keep our mental life pure? First, we fill our sexual thoughts with creative pictures of sexual activity with our spouse. Further, we avoid sexually explicit material that is pornographic in nature. And we make ourselves accountable to someone if we can't control these impulses by ourselves.

All of these things take discipline. But they are essential if we are to maintain a pure thought life and a healthy, fulfilling sex life with our mate.

MARRIAGE BUILDERS

- *How do you strive to maintain purity in your own thought life?*
- *What are ways you could help each other avoid sexually explicit images that sometimes lead to impure thoughts?*

Additional Scripture Readings
Matthew 5:28; 1 John 2:16–17;
Exodus 20:17

Go to page 1321 for your next devotional reading.

need to write to you, for you yourselves
have been taught by God to love each other. 10And in fact, you do love all the brothers throughout Macedonia. Yet we urge you, brothers, to do so more and more.
11Make it your ambition to lead a quiet life, to mind your own business and to work with your hands, just as we told you, 12so that your daily life may win the respect of outsiders and so that you will not be dependent on anybody.

The Coming of the Lord

13Brothers, we do not want you to be ignorant about those who fall asleep, or to grieve like the rest of men, who have no hope. 14We believe that Jesus died and rose again and so we believe that God will bring with Jesus those who have fallen asleep in him. 15According to the Lord's own word, we tell you that we who are still alive, who are left till the coming of the Lord, will certainly not precede those

VERSE FOR THE DAY: 1 Thessalonians 5:18

AUTHOR: Ruth Senter

PASSAGE FOR THE DAY: 1 Thessalonians 5:1–28

Restored by Thankfulness

Following years of fruitful ministry, a pastor found himself beginning each new day with dread. Finally, the quagmire was so deep that he gave up his church and retreated to his home.

One day a former parishioner brought over a basket of fruit, and the pastor's wife asked her husband if he would write a note in response to the kindness. With considerable effort, the despondent pastor took up his pen and began writing. A trickle of warmth returned to his spirit as he wrote in praise of fruit baskets, and in praise of his former parishioner. Before the day was over, he had written also in praise of a deacon, a head usher and an organist who had never missed a Sunday in fifteen years.

His days now began to take on definition. One by one, he wrote in praise of the people in his life. Sometimes his words were blurred by his tears, but he wrote on until he once again greeted his day with zest, closed it in praise. He had moved outside himself, and life had been renewed. The pastor returned to his little village church, a whole man, restored by the spirit of thankfulness.

MARRIAGE BUILDERS

♦ *In past times of disappointment or depression, what restored you to stability and joy?*

♦ *Sometimes writing things down makes them more tangible or memorable to us. Consider keeping a daily journal of things you want to thank God for.*

Additional Scripture Readings
Psalm 100:1–5; Psalm 136:1–26; Colossians 2:6–7

Go to page 1324 for your next devotional reading.

who have fallen asleep. [16]For the Lord
himself will come down from heaven,
with a loud command, with the voice of
the archangel and with the trumpet call of
God, and the dead in Christ will rise first.
[17]After that, we who are still alive and are
left will be caught up together with them
in the clouds to meet the Lord in the air.
And so we will be with the Lord forever.
[18]Therefore encourage each other with
these words.

5 Now, brothers, about times and dates
we do not need to write to you, [2]for
you know very well that the day of the
Lord will come like a thief in the night.
[3]While people are saying, "Peace and safe-
ty," destruction will come on them sud-
denly, as labor pains on a pregnant wom-
an, and they will not escape.

[4]But you, brothers, are not in darkness
so that this day should surprise you like a
thief. [5]You are all sons of the light and
sons of the day. We do not belong to the
night or to the darkness. [6]So then, let us
not be like others, who are asleep, but let
us be alert and self-controlled. [7]For those
who sleep, sleep at night, and those who
get drunk, get drunk at night. [8]But since
we belong to the day, let us be self-con-
trolled, putting on faith and love as a
breastplate, and the hope of salvation as a
helmet. [9]For God did not appoint us to
suffer wrath but to receive salvation
through our Lord Jesus Christ. [10]He died
for us so that, whether we are awake or
asleep, we may live together with him.
[11]Therefore encourage one another and
build each other up, just as in fact you are
doing.

Final Instructions

[12]Now we ask you, brothers, to respect
those who work hard among you, who are
over you in the Lord and who admonish
you. [13]Hold them in the highest regard in
love because of their work. Live in peace
with each other. [14]And we urge you,
brothers, warn those who are idle, encour-
age the timid, help the weak, be patient
with everyone. [15]Make sure that nobody
pays back wrong for wrong, but always try
to be kind to each other and to everyone
else.

[16]Be joyful always; [17]pray continually;
[18]give thanks in all circumstances, for this
is God's will for you in Christ Jesus.

[19]Do not put out the Spirit's fire; [20]do
not treat prophecies with contempt. [21]Test
everything. Hold on to the good. [22]Avoid
every kind of evil.

[23]May God himself, the God of peace,
sanctify you through and through. May
your whole spirit, soul and body be kept
blameless at the coming of our Lord Jesus
Christ. [24]The one who calls you is faithful
and he will do it.

[25]Brothers, pray for us. [26]Greet all the
brothers with a holy kiss. [27]I charge you
before the Lord to have this letter read to
all the brothers.

[28]The grace of our Lord Jesus Christ be
with you.

PAUL writes this letter shortly after 1 Thessalonians to clarify some things that the church failed to understand in his first letter. He tells them that the antichrist is coming, but they must continue with their regular schedules until Jesus returns. As you read this book, remember that God wants you to look forward to Christ's return as well as to continue doing your daily work.

2 THESSALONIANS

1 Paul, Silas[a] and Timothy,

To the church of the Thessalonians in God our Father and the Lord Jesus Christ:

[2]Grace and peace to you from God the Father and the Lord Jesus Christ.

Thanksgiving and Prayer

[3]We ought always to thank God for you, brothers, and rightly so, because your faith is growing more and more, and the love every one of you has for each other is increasing. [4]Therefore, among God's churches we boast about your perseverance and faith in all the persecutions and trials you are enduring.

[5]All this is evidence that God's judgment is right, and as a result you will be counted worthy of the kingdom of God, for which you are suffering. [6]God is just: He will pay back trouble to those who trouble you [7]and give relief to you who are troubled, and to us as well. This will happen when the Lord Jesus is revealed from heaven in blazing fire with his powerful angels. [8]He will punish those who do not know God and do not obey the gospel of our Lord Jesus. [9]They will be punished with everlasting destruction and shut out from the presence of the Lord and from the majesty of his power [10]on the day he comes to be glorified in his holy people and to be marveled at among all those who have believed. This includes you, because you believed our testimony to you.

[a] 1 Greek *Silvanus*, a variant of *Silas*

11 With this in mind, we constantly pray
for you, that our God may count you wor-
thy of his calling, and that by his power he
may fulfill every good purpose of yours
and every act prompted by your faith.
12 We pray this so that the name of our
Lord Jesus may be glorified in you, and
you in him, according to the grace of our
God and the Lord Jesus Christ.[a]

The Man of Lawlessness

2 Concerning the coming of our Lord
Jesus Christ and our being gathered to
him, we ask you, brothers, 2 not to become
easily unsettled or alarmed by some
prophecy, report or letter supposed to
have come from us, saying that the day of
the Lord has already come. 3 Don't let any-
one deceive you in any way, for that day

[a] 12 Or *God and Lord, Jesus Christ*

VERSE FOR THE DAY:	AUTHOR:	PASSAGE FOR THE DAY:
2 Thessalonians 1:11	Evelyn Christenson	2 Thessalonians 1:1–12

Praying for One Another

It is often easier to pray *about* our mates than it is to pray *for* them. "Lord, I don't like what he (or she) is doing. . . ." That is praying *about* our spouse. But Scripture says that even if someone has despitefully used you, you are to pray *for* that person. Praying for spouses has nothing to do with our rights, how we are treated, or what the other person may be doing. It is our responsibility, no matter what the circumstances.

When I pray *for* my husband, I have the privilege of seeing God work in Chris's life as a result of my prayer. Praying for my husband also releases a source of power into his life and ministry. I am actually ministering to him through my prayers. For the eighteen years that Chris was in the pastorate, I sat in the congregation and prayed as he preached. There were times when I could almost sense God's power in Chris's sermons in proportion to my prayers.

Probably the greatest gift I have given to Chris over the fifty-two years of our marriage is that I have communed with the God of heaven on his behalf, praying for him.

MARRIAGE BUILDERS

♦ *How can praying for your spouse help insure that God's work will be done in his or her life, and not your own work?*

♦ *Write down three things your spouse would like you to be praying for this week.*

Additional Scripture Readings
1 Thessalonians 1:2–3; 1 Timothy 2:1–3; Philemon 4–7

Go to page 1325 for your next devotional reading.

will not come, until the rebellion occurs
and the man of lawlessness[a] is revealed,
the man doomed to destruction. 4He will
oppose and will exalt himself over every-
thing that is called God or is worshiped, so
that he sets himself up in God's temple,
proclaiming himself to be God.
5Don't you remember that when I was
with you I used to tell you these things?
6And now you know what is holding him
back, so that he may be revealed at the
proper time. 7For the secret power of law-
lessness is already at work; but the one
who now holds it back will continue to do
so till he is taken out of the way. 8And
then the lawless one will be revealed,
whom the Lord Jesus will overthrow with
the breath of his mouth and destroy by
the splendor of his coming. 9The coming
of the lawless one will be in accordance
with the work of Satan displayed in all
kinds of counterfeit miracles, signs and
wonders, 10and in every sort of evil that
deceives those who are perishing. They
perish because they refused to love the
truth and so be saved. 11For this reason

[a]3 Some manuscripts *sin*

VERSE FOR THE DAY: 2 Thessalonians 2:16–17

AUTHOR: Ron Hutchcraft

PASSAGE FOR THE DAY: 2 Thessalonians 2:13–17

Made to Need Each Other

Men often avoid situations in which they don't feel competent. A man may be sure of himself in his work but unsure of his skills in deeply personal relationships. If he feels unsure, he will often compensate by coming on even stronger.

I remember a time in our marriage when a one-hour trip took three hours. I insisted that I knew exactly where I was going. If Karen would suggest that we stop and ask for directions, I would suggest that she keep knitting. Finally, when I realized it was not a sign of weakness to admit need, Karen and I came up with a mutually satisfying plan: I pilot, Karen navigates. I have the wheel, Karen has the map. We have both become very good at what we do, and we get places much faster. Karen and I are made to *need* each other. No wonder we get lost if we get crowded out of each other's life.

MARRIAGE BUILDERS

♦ *Name some areas where you and your spouse have opposite, but complementary, talents or gifts.*

♦ *When has it been hard for you to let go and really depend on your spouse?*

Additional Scripture Readings
Ephesians 5:25–33; Genesis 2:18–24; Ecclesiastes 4:9–10

Go to page 1326 for your next devotional reading.

God sends them a powerful delusion so
that they will believe the lie 12and so that
all will be condemned who have not be-
lieved the truth but have delighted in
wickedness.

Stand Firm

13But we ought always to thank God for
you, brothers loved by the Lord, because
from the beginning God chose you[a] to be
saved through the sanctifying work of the

[a]13 Some manuscripts *because God chose you as his firstfruits*

VERSE FOR THE DAY: 2 Thessalonians 3:5 | AUTHOR: James Long | PASSAGE FOR THE DAY: 2 Thessalonians 3:1–5

Making Marriage Great

Harriet and I recently clicked off the 6,570th day on the nuptial odometer. Eighteen years. Good and happy. Now, the unembellished truth is: There have been a few ruts in the yellow brick road. We've felt the need for periodic tune-ups. And yet, our marriage is stronger now than last year, the year before, or even those first passionate years.

Our marriage is better, and perhaps more important, individually we are better. Her character and, I think, mine show greater depth and strength. Why, in spite of the challenges (or maybe, in part, because of them), are we still together, counting this year better than last? What makes a marriage great?

Great marriage does imply vigilance and hard work, but it does not begin there. If I want a great marriage, I must be a great "me." The instructions in God's Word, taken seriously and acted on, could revolutionize any marriage because they would revolutionize any individual.

When I ask myself, "What makes a marriage great?," must I look any further than two people who are discovering together the secrets of compassion, kindness, humility, gentleness, patience, forgiveness and love? It is on these qualities that a great marriage is built.

MARRIAGE BUILDERS

♦ *Do you feel your marriage is stronger today than it was a year ago? Why or why not?*

♦ *Doublecheck your marriage against each of the fruit of the Spirit listed in Galatians 5:22–23. How does your life reflect these qualities?*

Additional Scripture Readings
Colossians 3:12–14; Philippians 1:9–11; 2 Corinthians 4:17–18.

Go to page 1327 for your next devotional reading.

WEEKENDING

CHERISHING

Make a list of fifteen simple "cherishing behaviors" that you would enjoy receiving from your mate. Once each of you has completed your list, exchange lists with your partner and discuss what you are requesting from each other. Be sure to tell your spouse *how* you would like each behavior performed. For example, if you request a back rub, specify light skin rub or deep muscle massage, with lotion or without.

After your discussion declare the next seven days to be "Cherishing Days." Make a commitment to put your partner's list into practice. Try to accomplish as many of the behaviors as possible each day. Focus your attention and energies on what you do for your spouse, not on what he or she does for you.

— *H. Norman Wright*

REVIVE

Saturday: Philippians 2:1–11
Sunday: Galatians 5:1–15

Go to page 1330 for your next devotional reading.

Spirit and through belief in the truth. [14]He called you to this through our gospel, that you might share in the glory of our Lord Jesus Christ. [15]So then, brothers, stand firm and hold to the teachings[a] we passed on to you, whether by word of mouth or by letter.

[16]May our Lord Jesus Christ himself and God our Father, who loved us and by his grace gave us eternal encouragement and good hope, [17]encourage your hearts and strengthen you in every good deed and word.

Request for Prayer

3 Finally, brothers, pray for us that the message of the Lord may spread rapidly and be honored, just as it was with you. [2]And pray that we may be delivered from wicked and evil men, for not everyone has faith. [3]But the Lord is faithful, and he will strengthen and protect you from the evil one. [4]We have confidence in the Lord that you are doing and will continue to do the things we command. [5]May the Lord direct your hearts into God's love and Christ's perseverance.

Warning Against Idleness

[6]In the name of the Lord Jesus Christ, we command you, brothers, to keep away from every brother who is idle and does not live according to the teaching[b] you received from us. [7]For you yourselves know how you ought to follow our example. We were not idle when we were with you, [8]nor did we eat anyone's food without paying for it. On the contrary, we worked night and day, laboring and toiling so that we would not be a burden to any of you. [9]We did this, not because we do not have the right to such help, but in order to make ourselves a model for you to follow. [10]For even when we were with you, we gave you this rule: "If a man will not work, he shall not eat."

[11]We hear that some among you are idle. They are not busy; they are busybodies. [12]Such people we command and urge in the Lord Jesus Christ to settle down and earn the bread they eat. [13]And as for you, brothers, never tire of doing what is right.

[14]If anyone does not obey our instruction in this letter, take special note of him. Do not associate with him, in order that he may feel ashamed. [15]Yet do not regard him as an enemy, but warn him as a brother.

Final Greetings

[16]Now may the Lord of peace himself give you peace at all times and in every way. The Lord be with all of you.

[17]I, Paul, write this greeting in my own hand, which is the distinguishing mark in all my letters. This is how I write.

[18]The grace of our Lord Jesus Christ be with you all.

[a]15 Or *traditions* [b]6 Or *tradition*

PAUL writes this letter to young Timothy, who is serving as a pastor in Ephesus. He instructs him how to organize and run the church and how to deal with false teachers and refute what they say. As you read this book, promise God that you will not stray from true faith.

1 TIMOTHY

1 Paul, an apostle of Christ Jesus by the command of God our Savior and of Christ Jesus our hope,

2 To Timothy my true son in the faith:

Grace, mercy and peace from God the Father and Christ Jesus our Lord.

Warning Against False Teachers of the Law

3 As I urged you when I went into Macedonia, stay there in Ephesus so that you may command certain men not to teach false doctrines any longer 4 nor to devote themselves to myths and endless genealogies. These promote controversies rather than God's work—which is by faith. 5 The goal of this command is love, which comes from a pure heart and a good conscience and a sincere faith. 6 Some have wandered away from these and turned to meaningless talk. 7 They want to be teachers of the law, but they do not know what they are talking about or what they so confidently affirm.

8 We know that the law is good if one uses it properly. 9 We also know that law[a] is made not for the righteous but for lawbreakers and rebels, the ungodly and sinful, the unholy and irreligious; for those who kill their fathers or mothers, for murderers, 10 for adulterers and perverts, for slave traders and liars and perjurers—and for whatever else is contrary to the sound doctrine 11 that conforms to the glorious gospel of the blessed God, which he entrusted to me.

The Lord's Grace to Paul

12 I thank Christ Jesus our Lord, who has given me strength, that he considered me faithful, appointing me to his service. 13 Even though I was once a blasphemer and a persecutor and a violent man, I was

[a] 9 Or *that the law*

shown mercy because I acted in ignorance
and unbelief. 14The grace of our Lord was
poured out on me abundantly, along with
the faith and love that are in Christ Jesus.
15Here is a trustworthy saying that de-
serves full acceptance: Christ Jesus came
into the world to save sinners—of whom
I am the worst. 16But for that very reason
I was shown mercy so that in me, the
worst of sinners, Christ Jesus might dis-
play his unlimited patience as an example
for those who would believe on him and
receive eternal life. 17Now to the King
eternal, immortal, invisible, the only God,
be honor and glory for ever and ever.
Amen.

VERSE FOR THE DAY: 1 Timothy 1:16

AUTHOR: Bill and Lynne Hybels

PASSAGE FOR THE DAY: 1 Timothy 1:12–17

Double Trouble

Probably the most widely believed of all the marriage myths is this one: Marriage will ensure my happiness. It is almost accepted as fact that a quick walk down the center aisle will usher one into the halls of happiness. The real truth is it might, and it might not.

This myth seems ridiculous indeed when you consider the math of marriage: One sinner plus another sinner equals two sinners. Double trouble under one roof. Add a couple of young "sinnerlings" and we're talking quadruple trouble under that same single roof.

Even mature, well-adjusted, Spirit-filled believers have to work through countless areas of disparity. There is financial disparity: He wants golf clubs, she wants a dishwasher. There is recreational disparity: She wants to travel, he wants to plant a garden. There is sexual disparity: He is romantically inclined tonight, she was last night. There is social disparity: She favors her friends, he favors his. Every time you turn around there is a new area of potential disagreement.

Don't misunderstand us. Marriage can be wonderful. It can be deeply satisfying and mutually fulfilling. But, *if* it becomes that, it is because *both* partners have paid a very high price over many years to make it that way.

MARRIAGE BUILDERS

♦ *How do you react to the contention that "ensured happiness" is one of the myths of marriage?*

♦ *What are you doing to make happiness a reality in your own marriage?*

Additional Scripture Readings
Isaiah 64:6; Romans 3:22–24

Go to page 1332 for your next devotional reading.

18Timothy, my son, I give you this instruction in keeping with the prophecies once made about you, so that by following them you may fight the good fight, 19holding on to faith and a good conscience. Some have rejected these and so have shipwrecked their faith. 20Among them are Hymenaeus and Alexander, whom I have handed over to Satan to be taught not to blaspheme.

Instructions on Worship

2 I urge, then, first of all, that requests, prayers, intercession and thanksgiving be made for everyone— 2for kings and all those in authority, that we may live peaceful and quiet lives in all godliness and holiness. 3This is good, and pleases God our Savior, 4who wants all men to be saved and to come to a knowledge of the truth. 5For there is one God and one mediator between God and men, the man Christ Jesus, 6who gave himself as a ransom for all men—the testimony given in its proper time. 7And for this purpose I was appointed a herald and an apostle—I am telling the truth, I am not lying—and a teacher of the true faith to the Gentiles.

8I want men everywhere to lift up holy hands in prayer, without anger or disputing.

9I also want women to dress modestly, with decency and propriety, not with braided hair or gold or pearls or expensive clothes, 10but with good deeds, appropriate for women who profess to worship God.

11A woman should learn in quietness and full submission. 12I do not permit a woman to teach or to have authority over a man; she must be silent. 13For Adam was formed first, then Eve. 14And Adam was not the one deceived; it was the woman who was deceived and became a sinner. 15But women[a] will be saved[b] through childbearing—if they continue in faith, love and holiness with propriety.

Overseers and Deacons

3 Here is a trustworthy saying: If anyone sets his heart on being an overseer,[c] he desires a noble task. 2Now the overseer must be above reproach, the husband of but one wife, temperate, self-controlled, respectable, hospitable, able to teach, 3not given to drunkenness, not violent but gentle, not quarrelsome, not a lover of money. 4He must manage his own family well and see that his children obey him with proper respect. 5(If anyone does not know how to manage his own family, how can he take care of God's church?) 6He must not be a recent convert, or he may become conceited and fall under the same judgment as the devil. 7He must also have a good reputation with outsiders, so that he will not fall into disgrace and into the devil's trap.

8Deacons, likewise, are to be men worthy of respect, sincere, not indulging in much wine, and not pursuing dishonest gain. 9They must keep hold of the deep truths of the faith with a clear conscience. 10They must first be tested; and then if there is nothing against them, let them serve as deacons.

11In the same way, their wives[d] are to be women worthy of respect, not malicious talkers but temperate and trustworthy in everything.

12A deacon must be the husband of but one wife and must manage his children and his household well. 13Those who have served well gain an excellent standing and great assurance in their faith in Christ Jesus.

14Although I hope to come to you soon, I am writing you these instructions so that, 15if I am delayed, you will know how people ought to conduct themselves in God's household, which is the church of the living God, the pillar and foundation of the truth. 16Beyond all question, the mystery of godliness is great:

He[e] appeared in a body,[f]
was vindicated by the Spirit,
was seen by angels,
was preached among the nations,
was believed on in the world,
was taken up in glory.

Instructions to Timothy

4 The Spirit clearly says that in later times some will abandon the faith and follow deceiving spirits and things taught by demons. 2Such teachings come through hypocritical liars, whose consciences have been seared as with a hot iron. 3They forbid people to marry and order them to abstain from certain foods, which God created to be received with

[a] 15 Greek *she* [b] 15 Or *restored* [c] 1 Traditionally *bishop*; also in verse 2 [d] 11 Or *way, deaconesses* [e] 16 Some manuscripts *God* [f] 16 Or *in the flesh*

VERSE FOR THE DAY: 1 Timothy 2:13

AUTHOR: Louis McBurney, M.D.

PASSAGE FOR THE DAY: 1 Timothy 2:8–15

We Need Each Other

Adam was hanging out in the Garden of Eden when God came along and noticed that Adam was alone. That's when God realized: "This guy's never gonna make it on his own. He needs some special help."

I always had a sort of puzzled fascination with God's answer to Adam's incompleteness. Then one day I married Melissa and the curiosity grew right along with my admiration. She's up before dawn and out jogging two miles. By the time I drag myself into semiconsciousness she's read some, studied for the lessons she teaches and started breakfast. She finds time to read about five books for every one I get through, work up talks for conferences we lead and enjoy her hobby of photography.

But Melissa's greatest strength is her ability to convince me that she couldn't live without me. I know she could get along quite well on her own, but she seems comfortable with our interdependence. Even when she went skydiving recently, she made me feel that my driving her to the airport and photographing the adventure were wonderful accomplishments.

I bet that all started when Adam woke up from that nap with a sore chest wall. He was probably still wondering what happened when he laid eyes on Eve and she told him what a heroic thing he had done to give up one of his ribs just for her. And God saw that it was very good. Thank God.

MARRIAGE BUILDERS

♦ *In what areas have you and your spouse developed interdependence?*

♦ *In what areas has your teamwork improved since the early days of your marriage?*

Additional Scripture Readings
Genesis 2:18–24; 1 Corinthians 11:8–9, 12

Go to page 1333 for your next devotional reading.

thanksgiving by those who believe and
who know the truth. 4For everything God
created is good, and nothing is to be re-
jected if it is received with thanksgiving,
5because it is consecrated by the word of
God and prayer.

6If you point these things out to the
brothers, you will be a good minister of
Christ Jesus, brought up in the truths of
the faith and of the good teaching that you
have followed. 7Have nothing to do with
godless myths and old wives' tales; rather,
train yourself to be godly. 8For physical
training is of some value, but godliness

VERSE FOR THE DAY:
1 Timothy 3:2

AUTHOR:
Marsha Crockett

PASSAGE FOR THE DAY:
1 Timothy 3:1–13

True Hospitality

John and I speak two different languages when it comes to entertaining. To me a "water glass" means a cobalt blue goblet to match the dishes. To John, it's a plastic fast-food cup. We often don't see eye-to-eye on whether to use candles on a lace tablecloth or paper plates on the picnic table. But John's approach to hospitality is closer to what it should be than my cosmetic attempts to look hospitable.

To be honest, my hospitality usually revolves around me. I've entertained friends in large part for my own enjoyment rather than understanding Christ's desire to use my home to meet the needs of others. Maybe that's why the word "hospitality" shares the same root as "hospital." Real hospitality cares for others, helping them feel welcomed and loved.

My husband's open heart to both the world and to Jesus has allowed many, including me, to see Christ in our home. Some don't yet know it's Jesus they've seen, but many have asked, "What makes you so different?" I know what it is. John loves other people regardless of who they are, how they look or what they do. He knows that true hospitality isn't narrowly defined by concocted parties, friendship or comfort.

Hospitality happens when I grasp the truth that Jesus personally welcomes me to his table "while I'm yet a sinner." And with a hospitable love like that, no one minds if the plastic water glasses don't match the china.

MARRIAGE BUILDERS

- *How have your first attempts at hospitality worked out?*
- *Brainstorm some ways you'd like to open your home to others.*

Additional Scripture Readings
2 Kings 4:8–37; Luke 10:38–42

Go to page 1334 for your next devotional reading.

has value for all things, holding promise
for both the present life and the life to
come.
9This is a trustworthy saying that de-
serves full acceptance 10(and for this we
labor and strive), that we have put our
hope in the living God, who is the Savior
of all men, and especially of those who be-
lieve.
11Command and teach these things.
12Don't let anyone look down on you be-
cause you are young, but set an example
for the believers in speech, in life, in love,
in faith and in purity. 13Until I come, de-
vote yourself to the public reading of
Scripture, to preaching and to teaching.
14Do not neglect your gift, which was giv-
en you through a prophetic message when
the body of elders laid their hands on you.
15Be diligent in these matters; give
yourself wholly to them, so that everyone
may see your progress. 16Watch your life
and doctrine closely. Persevere in them,
because if you do, you will save both
yourself and your hearers.

Advice About Widows, Elders and Slaves

5 Do not rebuke an older man harshly,
but exhort him as if he were your fa-
ther. Treat younger men as brothers, 2old-

THURSDAY

VERSE FOR THE DAY: 1 Timothy 4:13–14

AUTHOR: Stuart Briscoe

PASSAGE FOR THE DAY: 1 Timothy 4:1–16

Building Confidence

I don't really think in terms of "Let's identify people's gifts and then figure out what to do with them." Instead, my approach is, "Let's figure out what needs to be done and get people doing those things. If they're good at it, it's because they're gifted."

In Jill's case, I knew her heart for serving God and people. I also saw a desperate need for more women to be taught the Bible. And when the question came up, "Why isn't somebody doing something about this?" all I said to Jill was, "Why don't you do it?" That was enough. She started the women's Bible studies, and she discovered her gift.

At times, Jill had a reticence about attempting certain things. Sometimes I'd need to say, "You can do this!" I believe in Jill even when she doesn't believe in herself. Husbands and wives should be doing that sort of thing for each other.

MARRIAGE BUILDERS

♦ *How does your spouse's confidence in you bolster your own courage?*

♦ *How have you encouraged each other to put the talents and gifts God's given you to work?*

Additional Scripture Readings
1 Corinthians 12:4–11; 2 Timothy 1:6

Go to page 1335 for your next devotional reading.

VERSE FOR THE DAY: 1 Timothy 5:4

AUTHOR: Jay Kesler

PASSAGE FOR THE DAY: 1 Timothy 5:1–16

Quantity Time

The idea of substituting quality time for quantity time doesn't work in real life. The less quantity time you find to devote to your mate, the tougher it is to *create* quality time together. If people could just sit down and say, "Now we're going to have a quality experience," maybe it would work. But real life can't be manipulated that way.

Television news, history books, even the Bible show great moments of human achievement, but they can't detail the years of preparation and work that lead up to it. In the Bible, we read about important experiences and important events, but not always the day-to-day happenings of the "before" and "after."

If we're not careful, we can try to live our lives from one great experience to another. But it can't be done. In real life, it's the mundane, day-after-day experiences that make the highlights stand out. It's the quantity time that makes possible the quality time.

Long ago, I learned that I need to use my personal time at home, where I'm close to my wife and family. If I'm going to keep my priorities consistent, the use of my "personal" time has to be as purposeful as the use of my business time. If we seek God's help in establishing and maintaining our priorities, we'll find the amounts of time it takes to strengthen our marriage.

MARRIAGE BUILDERS

♦ *Based on a list of activities that each of you makes time for on a regular basis, where does "couple time" rank in relation to the other involvements?*

♦ *What are the most common distractions that keep you from spending enough time together as a couple? What can you do this month to free up more time to do more things together?*

Additional Scripture Readings
Deuteronomy 8:1–18; 2 Peter 3:8; Psalm 31:15

Go to page 1337 for your next devotional reading.

er women as mothers, and younger women as sisters, with absolute purity.

3Give proper recognition to those widows who are really in need. 4But if a widow has children or grandchildren, these should learn first of all to put their religion into practice by caring for their own family and so repaying their parents and grandparents, for this is pleasing to God. 5The widow who is really in need and left all alone puts her hope in God and continues night and day to pray and to ask God for help. 6But the widow who lives for pleasure is dead even while she lives. 7Give the people these instructions, too, so that no one may be open to blame. 8If anyone does not provide for his relatives, and especially for his immediate family, he has denied the faith and is worse than an unbeliever.

9No widow may be put on the list of widows unless she is over sixty, has been faithful to her husband,[a] 10and is well known for her good deeds, such as bringing up children, showing hospitality, washing the feet of the saints, helping those in trouble and devoting herself to all kinds of good deeds.

11As for younger widows, do not put them on such a list. For when their sensual desires overcome their dedication to Christ, they want to marry. 12Thus they bring judgment on themselves, because they have broken their first pledge. 13Besides, they get into the habit of being idle and going about from house to house. And not only do they become idlers, but also gossips and busybodies, saying things they ought not to. 14So I counsel younger widows to marry, to have children, to manage their homes and to give the enemy no opportunity for slander. 15Some have in fact already turned away to follow Satan.

16If any woman who is a believer has widows in her family, she should help them and not let the church be burdened with them, so that the church can help those widows who are really in need.

17The elders who direct the affairs of the church well are worthy of double honor, especially those whose work is preaching and teaching. 18For the Scripture says, "Do not muzzle the ox while it is treading out the grain,"[b] and "The worker deserves his wages."[c] 19Do not entertain an accusation against an elder unless it is brought by two or three witnesses. 20Those who sin are to be rebuked publicly, so that the others may take warning.

21I charge you, in the sight of God and Christ Jesus and the elect angels, to keep these instructions without partiality, and to do nothing out of favoritism.

22Do not be hasty in the laying on of hands, and do not share in the sins of others. Keep yourself pure.

23Stop drinking only water, and use a little wine because of your stomach and your frequent illnesses.

24The sins of some men are obvious, reaching the place of judgment ahead of them; the sins of others trail behind them. 25In the same way, good deeds are obvious, and even those that are not cannot be hidden.

6 All who are under the yoke of slavery should consider their masters worthy of full respect, so that God's name and our teaching may not be slandered. 2Those who have believing masters are not to show less respect for them because they are brothers. Instead, they are to serve them even better, because those who benefit from their service are believers, and dear to them. These are the things you are to teach and urge on them.

Love of Money

3If anyone teaches false doctrines and does not agree to the sound instruction of our Lord Jesus Christ and to godly teaching, 4he is conceited and understands nothing. He has an unhealthy interest in controversies and quarrels about words that result in envy, strife, malicious talk, evil suspicions 5and constant friction between men of corrupt mind, who have been robbed of the truth and who think that godliness is a means to financial gain.

6But godliness with contentment is great gain. 7For we brought nothing into the world, and we can take nothing out of it. 8But if we have food and clothing, we will be content with that. 9People who want to get rich fall into temptation and a trap and into many foolish and harmful desires that plunge men into ruin and destruction. 10For the love of money is a root of all kinds of evil. Some people, eager for money, have wandered from the faith and pierced themselves with many griefs.

[a] 9 Or *has had but one husband* [b] 18 Deut. 25:4 [c] 18 Luke 10:7

WEEKENDING

AFFIRMATION

One reason couples have trouble sharing their spiritual lives is they haven't established a trusting and open relationship with each other. One way to enhance mutual openness and vulnerability is to remove hurtful words from your vocabulary and to focus on building each other up. Here are three ways you can express love and appreciation for each other, which should lead to a deeper level of trust and intimacy. Discuss with each other which of these would mean the most to you personally.

1. Even though you've said it before, take time regularly to reaffirm your full, unconditional love for and acceptance of your spouse.

2. Never offer criticisms or make negative comments about your spouse in front of other people. In public, be your spouse's biggest fan. Save your loving criticisms for times when the two of you are alone.

3. Eliminate all put-downs and cynicism from your humor.

— *The* Marriage Partnership *Staff*

REVIVE

Saturday: John 15:9–17

Sunday: 1 Thessalonians 3:6–13

Go to page 1338 for your next devotional reading.

Paul's Charge to Timothy

[11]But you, man of God, flee from all this, and pursue righteousness, godliness, faith, love, endurance and gentleness. [12]Fight the good fight of the faith. Take hold of the eternal life to which you were called when you made your good confession in the presence of many witnesses. [13]In the sight of God, who gives life to everything, and of Christ Jesus, who while testifying before Pontius Pilate made the good confession, I charge you [14]to keep this command without spot or blame until the appearing of our Lord Jesus Christ, [15]which God will bring about in his own time—God, the blessed and only Ruler, the King of kings and Lord of lords, [16]who alone is immortal and who lives in unap-

VERSE FOR THE DAY: 1 Timothy 6:6

AUTHOR: Ruth Senter

PASSAGE FOR THE DAY: 1 Timothy 6:6–10

Natural Wealth

Outwardly, there was little about Marjorie's missionary life in Mexico that resembled success. She had worked in a remote Indian village for thirty years, tied to a dispensary that opened its doors around the clock to pain, sickness and suffering.

The village's church was a squat square of red clay topped by layers of thatch. We'd gone there the previous night to sing and pray. Marjorie had pumped out "Amazing Grace" on her portable organ. A handful of barefoot waifs sat on the backless benches. Several men in straw sandals and white shirts led the service. Their smiling wives held squirming babies.

When the vespers had ended, Marjorie gave her own personal benediction—a warm hug to everyone present. Then she folded up her organ and we carried it down the path toward home.

"The men who led tonight were little boys I've watched grow up," she told me later. "Daniel has even been to Bible school." We sat on the bare cement of her porch and looked west toward the Sierra Madre.

"Contentment is natural wealth; luxury, artificial poverty," Socrates once said. In that isolated hamlet of central Mexico, I had witnessed contentment firsthand.

MARRIAGE BUILDERS

♦ *If "contentment is natural wealth," how rich are you as a couple and as a family?*

♦ *How do "godliness" and "contentment" combine to make the Christian's life rich?*

Additional Scripture Readings
Philippians 4:10–19; Hebrews 13:5–8; Psalm 37:3–6

Go to page 1341 for your next devotional reading.

proachable light, whom no one has seen
or can see. To him be honor and might
forever. Amen.

17Command those who are rich in this
present world not to be arrogant nor to
put their hope in wealth, which is so un-
certain, but to put their hope in God, who
richly provides us with everything for our
enjoyment. 18Command them to do good,
to be rich in good deeds, and to be gener-
ous and willing to share. 19In this way
they will lay up treasure for themselves as
a firm foundation for the coming age, so
that they may take hold of the life that is
truly life.

20Timothy, guard what has been en-
trusted to your care. Turn away from god-
less chatter and the opposing ideas of
what is falsely called knowledge, 21which
some have professed and in so doing have
wandered from the faith.

Grace be with you.

THIS second letter to Timothy is written by Paul shortly before Paul dies (2 Timothy 4:6–8). Times are difficult, both morally and spiritually, and Paul wants to encourage Timothy to persevere in his Christian faith and life. As you read this book, be sure to find your daily strength in Jesus Christ and in God's inspired word.

2 TIMOTHY

1 Paul, an apostle of Christ Jesus by the
will of God, according to the promise
of life that is in Christ Jesus,

2 To Timothy, my dear son:

Grace, mercy and peace from God the
Father and Christ Jesus our Lord.

Encouragement to Be Faithful

3 I thank God, whom I serve, as my fore-
fathers did, with a clear conscience, as
night and day I constantly remember you
in my prayers. 4 Recalling your tears, I long
to see you, so that I may be filled with joy.
5 I have been reminded of your sincere
faith, which first lived in your grandmoth-
er Lois and in your mother Eunice and, I
am persuaded, now lives in you also. 6 For
this reason I remind you to fan into flame
the gift of God, which is in you through
the laying on of my hands. 7 For God did
not give us a spirit of timidity, but a spirit
of power, of love and of self-discipline.

8 So do not be ashamed to testify about
our Lord, or ashamed of me his prisoner.
But join with me in suffering for the gos-
pel, by the power of God, 9 who has saved
us and called us to a holy life—not be-
cause of anything we have done but be-
cause of his own purpose and grace. This
grace was given us in Christ Jesus before
the beginning of time, 10 but it has now
been revealed through the appearing of
our Savior, Christ Jesus, who has de-
stroyed death and has brought life and im-
mortality to light through the gospel.
11 And of this gospel I was appointed a her-
ald and an apostle and a teacher. 12 That is
why I am suffering as I am. Yet I am not
ashamed, because I know whom I have
believed, and am convinced that he is able

to guard what I have entrusted to him for
that day.
13 What you heard from me, keep as the
pattern of sound teaching, with faith and
love in Christ Jesus. 14 Guard the good de-
posit that was entrusted to you—guard it
with the help of the Holy Spirit who lives
in us.
15 You know that everyone in the prov-
ince of Asia has deserted me, including
Phygelus and Hermogenes.
16 May the Lord show mercy to the
household of Onesiphorus, because he of-
ten refreshed me and was not ashamed of
my chains. 17 On the contrary, when he
was in Rome, he searched hard for me un-

VERSE FOR THE DAY: 2 Timothy 1:7

AUTHOR: Diane M. Langberg

PASSAGE FOR THE DAY: 2 Timothy 1:1–14

No Spirit of Timidity

God's truth—not our emotions—should be the ruling force in our lives.

Happiness, for instance, is usually rooted in circumstances that bring positive feelings. However, rejoicing is in the Lord, the One who is the same yesterday, today and forever. When Paul spoke in 2 Corinthians 4:8–9 of being troubled and persecuted, he did not exhibit happiness. But he was rejoicing in his unchangeable God.

In 2 Timothy 1:5, Paul reminds Timothy of who he is. "For this reason," based on who you are, "I remind you to fan into flame the gift of God . . . for God did not give us a spirit of timidity, but a spirit of power, of love and of self-discipline." The word "spirit" here refers to the dominant tendency of the mind.

Paul is not talking about a feeling, but an attitude of the mind. It is an attitude built upon the assumption that I am a person created by God, a joint-heir with Christ, and an important part of his Body.

It is only as we set our minds on exercising that "spirit of power, of love and of self-discipline" that emotions will cease to be the ruling force in our lives. Negative feelings will not be absent from our lives, but in spite of them, Christ will become the integrating force, enabling us to walk among negative feelings in a way that honors him.

MARRIAGE BUILDERS

- *In what situations do you feel overwhelmed by negative feelings?*
- *How do you exercise God's gift of a "spirit of power, of love and of self-discipline?"*

Additional Scripture Readings
Philippians 4:4; 2 Corinthians 4:8–9

Go to page 1343 for your next devotional reading.

til he found me. [18]May the Lord grant that
he will find mercy from the Lord on that
day! You know very well in how many
ways he helped me in Ephesus.

2 You then, my son, be strong in the
grace that is in Christ Jesus. [2]And the
things you have heard me say in the presence of many witnesses entrust to reliable
men who will also be qualified to teach
others. [3]Endure hardship with us like a
good soldier of Christ Jesus. [4]No one serving as a soldier gets involved in civilian affairs—he wants to please his commanding officer. [5]Similarly, if anyone competes
as an athlete, he does not receive the victor's crown unless he competes according
to the rules. [6]The hardworking farmer
should be the first to receive a share of the
crops. [7]Reflect on what I am saying, for
the Lord will give you insight into all this.

[8]Remember Jesus Christ, raised from
the dead, descended from David. This is
my gospel, [9]for which I am suffering even
to the point of being chained like a criminal. But God's word is not chained.
[10]Therefore I endure everything for the
sake of the elect, that they too may obtain
the salvation that is in Christ Jesus, with
eternal glory.

[11]Here is a trustworthy saying:

If we died with him,
we will also live with him;
[12]if we endure,
we will also reign with him.
If we disown him,
he will also disown us;
[13]if we are faithless,
he will remain faithful,
for he cannot disown himself.

A Workman Approved by God

[14]Keep reminding them of these things.
Warn them before God against quarreling
about words; it is of no value, and only
ruins those who listen. [15]Do your best to
present yourself to God as one approved,
a workman who does not need to be
ashamed and who correctly handles the
word of truth. [16]Avoid godless chatter, because those who indulge in it will become
more and more ungodly. [17]Their teaching
will spread like gangrene. Among them
are Hymenaeus and Philetus, [18]who have
wandered away from the truth. They say
that the resurrection has already taken
place, and they destroy the faith of some.
[19]Nevertheless, God's solid foundation
stands firm, sealed with this inscription:
"The Lord knows those who are his,"[a]
and, "Everyone who confesses the name
of the Lord must turn away from wickedness."

[20]In a large house there are articles not
only of gold and silver, but also of wood
and clay; some are for noble purposes and
some for ignoble. [21]If a man cleanses himself from the latter, he will be an instrument for noble purposes, made holy, useful to the Master and prepared to do any
good work.

[22]Flee the evil desires of youth, and pursue righteousness, faith, love and peace,
along with those who call on the Lord out
of a pure heart. [23]Don't have anything to
do with foolish and stupid arguments, because you know they produce quarrels.
[24]And the Lord's servant must not quarrel;
instead, he must be kind to everyone, able
to teach, not resentful. [25]Those who oppose him he must gently instruct, in the
hope that God will grant them repentance
leading them to a knowledge of the truth,
[26]and that they will come to their senses
and escape from the trap of the devil, who
has taken them captive to do his will.

Godlessness in the Last Days

3 But mark this: There will be terrible
times in the last days. [2]People will be
lovers of themselves, lovers of money,
boastful, proud, abusive, disobedient to
their parents, ungrateful, unholy, [3]without love, unforgiving, slanderous, without
self-control, brutal, not lovers of the good,
[4]treacherous, rash, conceited, lovers of
pleasure rather than lovers of God— [5]having a form of godliness but denying its
power. Have nothing to do with them.

[6]They are the kind who worm their way
into homes and gain control over weak-willed women, who are loaded down with
sins and are swayed by all kinds of evil
desires, [7]always learning but never able to
acknowledge the truth. [8]Just as Jannes
and Jambres opposed Moses, so also
these men oppose the truth—men of depraved minds, who, as far as the faith is
concerned, are rejected. [9]But they will not
get very far because, as in the case of
those men, their folly will be clear to everyone.

[a]19 Num. 16:5 (see Septuagint)

Paul's Charge to Timothy

10You, however, know all about my
teaching, my way of life, my purpose,
faith, patience, love, endurance, 11persecutions, sufferings—what kinds of things
happened to me in Antioch, Iconium and
Lystra, the persecutions I endured. Yet the
Lord rescued me from all of them. 12In
fact, everyone who wants to live a godly
life in Christ Jesus will be persecuted,
13while evil men and impostors will go
from bad to worse, deceiving and being
deceived. 14But as for you, continue in
what you have learned and have become
convinced of, because you know those
from whom you learned it, 15and how

VERSE FOR THE DAY: 2 Timothy 2:22

AUTHOR: Jerry B. Jenkins

PASSAGE FOR THE DAY: 2 Timothy 2:14–26

Protect Your Marriage

A tragedy occurred at a church in Michigan where a couple flirted humorously for almost ten years. They did this in front of their spouses, who laughed right along with them. Then came the day when the woman's husband was hospitalized. She needed rides back and forth, and her friend and his wife provided them. No one suspected anything, but on one of those rare occasions when it was just the man doing the driving, the wife of the sick man told him how difficult and cold her husband had been.

The flirters began to see each other on the sly. Then the day came when she told him she'd always hoped he had really meant it when he said he wished he'd met her before she was married. Suddenly, years of flirting had blossomed into an affair.

What begins as a series of seemingly small indiscretions can add up to major traps. Maybe at first it seems innocent and safe, but then you say or do something you never thought you'd say or do. That's why we all need "hedges"—precautions that we have planned out ahead of time and we adhere to in order to protect our marriages. These hedges can provide a way to avoid potentially dangerous relationships before they get started. For the benefit of every marriage, we all need to set our own ground rules. And then stick to them.

MARRIAGE BUILDERS

♦ *What are some of the "hedges"—or personal standards—you've set for yourself to avoid temptations?*
♦ *Are there ways you can team up to fight temptation?*

Additional Scripture Readings
1 Corinthians 6:18; James 4:7

Go to page 1344 for your next devotional reading.

from infancy you have known the holy
Scriptures, which are able to make you
wise for salvation through faith in Christ
Jesus. 16All Scripture is God-breathed and
is useful for teaching, rebuking, correcting
and training in righteousness, 17so that
the man of God may be thoroughly
equipped for every good work.

4 In the presence of God and of Christ
Jesus, who will judge the living and
the dead, and in view of his appearing and
his kingdom, I give you this charge:
2Preach the Word; be prepared in season
and out of season; correct, rebuke and en-
courage—with great patience and careful
instruction. 3For the time will come when
men will not put up with sound doctrine.
Instead, to suit their own desires, they will
gather around them a great number of
teachers to say what their itching ears
want to hear. 4They will turn their ears
away from the truth and turn aside to
myths. 5But you, keep your head in all sit-
uations, endure hardship, do the work of
an evangelist, discharge all the duties of
your ministry.

6For I am already being poured out like
a drink offering, and the time has come for
my departure. 7I have fought the good
fight, I have finished the race, I have kept
the faith. 8Now there is in store for me
the crown of righteousness, which the
Lord, the righteous Judge, will award to
me on that day—and not only to me,
but also to all who have longed for his
appearing.

THURSDAY

VERSE FOR THE DAY: 2 Timothy 3:14–15

AUTHOR: Martha Reapsome

PASSAGE FOR THE DAY: 2 Timothy 3:10–17

Ongoing Care

Learning about God is like going to the supermarket. The full bags come home and their contents are stored. Some food is left out for immediate use. Other items come out of storage later when they are needed. When we store the Word in our hearts daily, we have a ready supply to draw from when tomorrow's need arises.

At a time when our family experienced deep grief because of the death of one of our children, a friend prayed for me: "Holy Spirit, remind Martha of the truths about you that she already knows." What I had learned about the character of God through years of study and experience was my staying power in crisis. I was able to face tragedy with peace and confidence because over the years I had locked the resource firmly in place.

MARRIAGE BUILDERS

♦ *How does studying God's Word regularly equip you for today and for the future?*

♦ *When have you experienced peace and confidence in the face of difficulty?*

Additional Scripture Readings
2 Peter 3:11–13; 1 Samuel 12:24

Go to page 1347 for your next devotional reading.

Personal Remarks

9Do your best to come to me quickly,
10for Demas, because he loved this world,
has deserted me and has gone to Thessa-
lonica. Crescens has gone to Galatia, and
Titus to Dalmatia. 11Only Luke is with me.
Get Mark and bring him with you, be-
cause he is helpful to me in my ministry.
12I sent Tychicus to Ephesus. 13When you
come, bring the cloak that I left with Car-
pus at Troas, and my scrolls, especially
the parchments.

14Alexander the metalworker did me a
great deal of harm. The Lord will repay
him for what he has done. 15You too
should be on your guard against him, be-
cause he strongly opposed our message.

16At my first defense, no one came to
my support, but everyone deserted me.
May it not be held against them. 17But the
Lord stood at my side and gave me
strength, so that through me the message
might be fully proclaimed and all the Gen-
tiles might hear it. And I was delivered
from the lion's mouth. 18The Lord will
rescue me from every evil attack and
will bring me safely to his heavenly king-
dom. To him be glory for ever and ever.
Amen.

Final Greetings

19Greet Priscilla[a] and Aquila and the
household of Onesiphorus. 20Erastus
stayed in Corinth, and I left Trophimus
sick in Miletus. 21Do your best to get here
before winter. Eubulus greets you, and so
do Pudens, Linus, Claudia and all the
brothers.

22The Lord be with your spirit. Grace be
with you.

[a]19 Greek *Prisca*, a variant of *Priscilla*

PAUL writes to Titus, a pastor serving in Crete, to advise him both on what to teach the churches and on how to organize them, especially with false teachers around. As you read this book, note God's concern for proper order in the church and for true teaching about Christ.

TITUS

1 Paul, a servant of God and an apostle
of Jesus Christ for the faith of God's
elect and the knowledge of the truth that
leads to godliness— 2a faith and knowl-
edge resting on the hope of eternal life,
which God, who does not lie, promised
before the beginning of time, 3and at his
appointed season he brought his word to
light through the preaching entrusted to
me by the command of God our Savior,

4To Titus, my true son in our common
faith:

Grace and peace from God the Father
and Christ Jesus our Savior.

Titus' Task on Crete

5The reason I left you in Crete was
that you might straighten out what was
left unfinished and appoint[a] elders in
every town, as I directed you. 6An elder
must be blameless, the husband of but
one wife, a man whose children believe
and are not open to the charge of being
wild and disobedient. 7Since an over-
seer[b] is entrusted with God's work, he
must be blameless—not overbearing, not
quick-tempered, not given to drunken-
ness, not violent, not pursuing dishonest
gain. 8Rather he must be hospitable, one
who loves what is good, who is self-con-
trolled, upright, holy and disciplined. 9He
must hold firmly to the trustworthy mes-
sage as it has been taught, so that he can
encourage others by sound doctrine and
refute those who oppose it.

10For there are many rebellious people,
mere talkers and deceivers, especially
those of the circumcision group. 11They
must be silenced, because they are ruin-
ing whole households by teaching things
they ought not to teach—and that for the
sake of dishonest gain. 12Even one of their
own prophets has said, "Cretans are al-

[a]5 Or *ordain* [b]7 Traditionally *bishop*

VERSE FOR THE DAY: Titus 2:4–5

AUTHOR: Lyn Cryderman

PASSAGE FOR THE DAY: Titus 2:1–15

A Team Needs a Captain

Esther and I have what I'd call an egalitarian relationship with male veto privilege. It's clear to us that when two people join together, it makes no sense for one person to set her gifts and abilities aside. So we divide our duties along the lines of what we each do best. I trust Esther's ability to manage our finances, organize our household and maintain our home and cars. Since she works full-time, that means in addition to my full-time job, I cook (which I love) and help out with housecleaning (which I hate).

So does this team have a captain? What about Paul's teaching that a husband is the "head" of his wife (see Eph. 5:22–23)? We honor God's sovereignty by balancing his Old Testament design for marriage with his New Testament instructions for working it out.

God's original plan for was for two people to become one (see Gen. 2:24). For us, becoming one has meant working hard at honest and ongoing communication, defying those natural impulses to do what's best for me rather than what's best for we. When big decisions come up, if we've been diligent about becoming one, I know exactly what Esther thinks and feels about various options. If I want to love her as I love myself, I don't dare disregard her needs.

What Esther submits to then is something we've both thought through, not some personal agenda of mine that's forged in solitude. One of the best ways husbands can lead is by making sure both partners are enjoying the blessings of oneness.

MARRIAGE BUILDERS

♦ *How do you balance Paul's teaching on headship with your status as equals in the eyes of God?*

♦ *How does oneness take the threat out of the idea of submission?*

Additional Scripture Readings
Matthew 25:14–30; Romans 12:1–11

Go to page 1348 for your next devotional reading.

WEEKENDING

COMMUNICATION

Actions really do speak louder than words. Use the space below to brainstorm five ways each of you could say "I love you" without saying a word. When each of you has completed your list, decide to get busy and start acting out what you want to say.

Husband's List

1. _____
2. _____
3. _____
4. _____
5. _____

Wife's List

1. _____
2. _____
3. _____
4. _____
5. _____

— Dave and Claudia Arp

REVIVE

Saturday: Psalm 118:1–29
Sunday: Philemon 4–7

Go to page 1351 for your next devotional reading.

ways liars, evil brutes, lazy gluttons."
13This testimony is true. Therefore, re-
buke them sharply, so that they will be
sound in the faith 14and will pay no atten-
tion to Jewish myths or to the commands
of those who reject the truth. 15To the
pure, all things are pure, but to those who
are corrupted and do not believe, nothing
is pure. In fact, both their minds and con-
sciences are corrupted. 16They claim to
know God, but by their actions they deny
him. They are detestable, disobedient and
unfit for doing anything good.

What Must Be Taught to Various Groups

2 You must teach what is in accord with
sound doctrine. 2Teach the older men
to be temperate, worthy of respect, self-
controlled, and sound in faith, in love and
in endurance.

3Likewise, teach the older women to be
reverent in the way they live, not to be
slanderers or addicted to much wine, but
to teach what is good. 4Then they can
train the younger women to love their
husbands and children, 5to be self-con-
trolled and pure, to be busy at home, to be
kind, and to be subject to their husbands,
so that no one will malign the word of
God.

6Similarly, encourage the young men to
be self-controlled. 7In everything set them
an example by doing what is good. In your
teaching show integrity, seriousness 8and
soundness of speech that cannot be con-
demned, so that those who oppose you
may be ashamed because they have noth-
ing bad to say about us.

9Teach slaves to be subject to their mas-
ters in everything, to try to please them,
not to talk back to them, 10and not to steal
from them, but to show that they can be
fully trusted, so that in every way they will
make the teaching about God our Savior
attractive.

11For the grace of God that brings salva-
tion has appeared to all men. 12It teaches
us to say "No" to ungodliness and worldly
passions, and to live self-controlled, up-
right and godly lives in this present age,
13while we wait for the blessed hope—the
glorious appearing of our great God and
Savior, Jesus Christ, 14who gave himself
for us to redeem us from all wickedness
and to purify for himself a people that are
his very own, eager to do what is good.

15These, then, are the things you should
teach. Encourage and rebuke with all au-
thority. Do not let anyone despise you.

Doing What Is Good

3 Remind the people to be subject to
rulers and authorities, to be obedient,
to be ready to do whatever is good, 2to
slander no one, to be peaceable and con-
siderate, and to show true humility to-
ward all men.

3At one time we too were foolish, dis-
obedient, deceived and enslaved by all
kinds of passions and pleasures. We lived
in malice and envy, being hated and hat-
ing one another. 4But when the kindness
and love of God our Savior appeared, 5he
saved us, not because of righteous things
we had done, but because of his mercy.
He saved us through the washing of re-
birth and renewal by the Holy Spirit,
6whom he poured out on us generously
through Jesus Christ our Savior, 7so that,
having been justified by his grace, we
might become heirs having the hope of
eternal life. 8This is a trustworthy saying.
And I want you to stress these things, so
that those who have trusted in God may
be careful to devote themselves to doing
what is good. These things are excellent
and profitable for everyone.

9But avoid foolish controversies and ge-
nealogies and arguments and quarrels
about the law, because these are unprofit-
able and useless. 10Warn a divisive person
once, and then warn him a second time.
After that, have nothing to do with him.
11You may be sure that such a man is
warped and sinful; he is self-condemned.

Final Remarks

12As soon as I send Artemas or Tychi-
cus to you, do your best to come to me at
Nicopolis, because I have decided to win-
ter there. 13Do everything you can to help
Zenas the lawyer and Apollos on their
way and see that they have everything
they need. 14Our people must learn to de-
vote themselves to doing what is good, in
order that they may provide for daily ne-
cessities and not live unproductive lives.

15Everyone with me sends you greet-
ings. Greet those who love us in the faith.

Grace be with you all.

PAUL writes this brief letter to ask Philemon, a Christian brother living (probably) in Colosse, to forgive and take back Onesimus, a runaway slave who has become a Christian and is helping Paul in prison. As you read this book, be willing to forgive others, no matter what they do to you.

PHILEMON

1 Paul, a prisoner of Christ Jesus, and
Timothy our brother,

To Philemon our dear friend and fellow
worker, 2 to Apphia our sister, to Archip-
pus our fellow soldier and to the church
that meets in your home:

3 Grace to you and peace from God our
Father and the Lord Jesus Christ.

Thanksgiving and Prayer

4 I always thank my God as I remember
you in my prayers, 5 because I hear about
your faith in the Lord Jesus and your love
for all the saints. 6 I pray that you may be
active in sharing your faith, so that you
will have a full understanding of every
good thing we have in Christ. 7 Your love
has given me great joy and encourage-
ment, because you, brother, have re-
freshed the hearts of the saints.

Paul's Plea for Onesimus

8 Therefore, although in Christ I could
be bold and order you to do what you
ought to do, 9 yet I appeal to you on the
basis of love. I then, as Paul—an old man
and now also a prisoner of Christ Jesus—
10 I appeal to you for my son Onesimus,[a]
who became my son while I was in chains.
11 Formerly he was useless to you, but now
he has become useful both to you and
to me.

12 I am sending him—who is my very
heart—back to you. 13 I would have liked
to keep him with me so that he could take
your place in helping me while I am in
chains for the gospel. 14 But I did not want
to do anything without your consent, so
that any favor you do will be spontaneous
and not forced. 15 Perhaps the reason he
was separated from you for a little while

[a] 10 *Onesimus* means *useful.*

was that you might have him back for
good— [16]no longer as a slave, but better
than a slave, as a dear brother. He is very
dear to me but even dearer to you, both as
a man and as a brother in the Lord.

[17]So if you consider me a partner, wel-
come him as you would welcome me. [18]If
he has done you any wrong or owes you
anything, charge it to me. [19]I, Paul, am
writing this with my own hand. I will pay
it back—not to mention that you owe me
your very self. [20]I do wish, brother, that I
may have some benefit from you in the
Lord; refresh my heart in Christ. [21]Confi-
dent of your obedience, I write to you,
knowing that you will do even more than
I ask.

[22]And one thing more: Prepare a guest

VERSE FOR THE DAY: Philemon 20

AUTHOR: Paul Stevens

PASSAGE FOR THE DAY: Philemon 1–21

Spiritual Growth

Marriage is a source of spiritual renewal because it offers three gifts to the spiritual life: sustenance, healing and growth.

Sustenance is experienced in the context of a down-to-earth reality. My wife, Gail, knitted me a beautiful red sweater, but I accidentally left it at a conference center. Without a word, she sat down and knitted me an exact replica of the first sweater. Could God show me his love more directly than through acts like these?

Healing is received when anxieties and fears are dispelled by mutual acceptance and companionship. My first day on the job as a carpenter pushed me off the stress scale. But when I went home that night, Gail ministered to me. I was renewed by a spiritual grace through acceptance and companionship.

Growth comes through the discipline of adjusting your life to another person from whom you can never hide. I can trust Gail's hardest words to me, knowing that confrontation is not rejection but an opportunity to grow. This is one of God's direct ways of helping me mature.

God is especially present where the marriage is human, earthy, fleshly, vulnerable, painful, troubled and just plain hard. And he is also present in moments of hilarious joy or close companionship. Indeed, he deepens and sanctifies *all* these moments.

MARRIAGE BUILDERS

- *How have you seen God's love in your spouse's caring acts?*
- *When have your personal anxieties or problems been eased because of your spouse's care and attention?*

Additional Scripture Readings
Ecclesiastes 4:9–12; Proverbs 27:6; 2 Corinthians 4:16

Go to page 1356 for your next devotional reading.

room for me, because I hope to be restored to you in answer to your prayers.

23Epaphras, my fellow prisoner in Christ Jesus, sends you greetings. 24And so do Mark, Aristarchus, Demas and Luke, my fellow workers.

25The grace of the Lord Jesus Christ be with your spirit.

THE author of this letter encourages Christians who are being persecuted for their faith by pointing them to the greatness of the Son of God who became man. Christ is the full expression of God's revelation, better than anything in the Old Testament; the author warns his readers to depend on Christ alone. As you read this book, commit yourself firmly to Jesus your Intercessor, and be sure to persevere and grow daily in your Christian faith and life.

HEBREWS

The Son Superior to Angels

1 In the past God spoke to our forefathers through the prophets at many
times and in various ways, **2**but in these
last days he has spoken to us by his Son,
whom he appointed heir of all things, and
through whom he made the universe.
3The Son is the radiance of God's glory
and the exact representation of his being,
sustaining all things by his powerful
word. After he had provided purification
for sins, he sat down at the right hand of
the Majesty in heaven. **4**So he became
as much superior to the angels as the
name he has inherited is superior to
theirs.

5For to which of the angels did God ever
say,

"You are my Son;
today I have become your
Father[a]"[b]?

Or again,

"I will be his Father,
and he will be my Son"[c]?

6And again, when God brings his firstborn
into the world, he says,

[a]5 Or *have begotten you* [b]5 Psalm 2:7 [c]5 2 Samuel 7:14; 1 Chron. 17:13

"Let all God's angels worship him."[a]

7In speaking of the angels he says,

"He makes his angels winds,
his servants flames of fire."[b]

8But about the Son he says,

"Your throne, O God, will last for ever
and ever,
and righteousness will be the
scepter of your kingdom.
9You have loved righteousness and
hated wickedness;
therefore God, your God, has set
you above your companions
by anointing you with the oil of
joy."[c]

10He also says,

"In the beginning, O Lord, you laid
the foundations of the earth,
and the heavens are the work of
your hands.
11They will perish, but you remain;
they will all wear out like a
garment.
12You will roll them up like a robe;
like a garment they will be changed.
But you remain the same,
and your years will never end."[d]

13To which of the angels did God ever say,

"Sit at my right hand
until I make your enemies
a footstool for your feet"[e]?

14Are not all angels ministering spirits sent to serve those who will inherit salvation?

Warning to Pay Attention

2 We must pay more careful attention, therefore, to what we have heard, so that we do not drift away. 2For if the message spoken by angels was binding, and every violation and disobedience received its just punishment, 3how shall we escape if we ignore such a great salvation? This salvation, which was first announced by the Lord, was confirmed to us by those who heard him. 4God also testified to it by signs, wonders and various miracles, and gifts of the Holy Spirit distributed according to his will.

Jesus Made Like His Brothers

5It is not to angels that he has subjected the world to come, about which we are speaking. 6But there is a place where someone has testified:

"What is man that you are mindful of
him,
the son of man that you care for
him?
7You made him a little[f] lower than
the angels;
you crowned him with glory and
honor
8 and put everything under his
feet."[g]

In putting everything under him, God left nothing that is not subject to him. Yet at present we do not see everything subject to him. 9But we see Jesus, who was made a little lower than the angels, now crowned with glory and honor because he suffered death, so that by the grace of God he might taste death for everyone.

10In bringing many sons to glory, it was fitting that God, for whom and through whom everything exists, should make the author of their salvation perfect through suffering. 11Both the one who makes men holy and those who are made holy are of the same family. So Jesus is not ashamed to call them brothers. 12He says,

"I will declare your name to my
brothers;
in the presence of the congregation
I will sing your praises."[h]

13And again,

"I will put my trust in him."[i]

And again he says,

"Here am I, and the children God has
given me."[j]

14Since the children have flesh and blood, he too shared in their humanity so that by his death he might destroy him who holds the power of death—that is, the devil— 15and free those who all their lives were held in slavery by their fear of death. 16For surely it is not angels he helps, but Abraham's descendants. 17For this reason he had to be made like his brothers in every way, in order that he might become a merciful and faithful high

[a] 6 Deut. 32:43 (see Dead Sea Scrolls and Septuagint) [b] 7 Psalm 104:4 [c] 9 Psalm 45:6,7
[d] 12 Psalm 102:25-27 [e] 13 Psalm 110:1 [f] 7 Or *him for a little while*; also in verse 9
[g] 8 Psalm 8:4-6 [h] 12 Psalm 22:22 [i] 13 Isaiah 8:17 [j] 13 Isaiah 8:18

priest in service to God, and that he might make atonement for[a] the sins of the people. 18Because he himself suffered when he was tempted, he is able to help those who are being tempted.

Jesus Greater Than Moses

3 Therefore, holy brothers, who share in the heavenly calling, fix your thoughts on Jesus, the apostle and high priest whom we confess. 2He was faithful to the one who appointed him, just as Moses was faithful in all God's house. 3Jesus has been found worthy of greater honor than Moses, just as the builder of a house has greater honor than the house itself. 4For every house is built by someone, but God is the builder of everything. 5Moses was faithful as a servant in all God's house, testifying to what would be said in the future. 6But Christ is faithful as a son over God's house. And we are his house, if we hold on to our courage and the hope of which we boast.

Warning Against Unbelief

7So, as the Holy Spirit says:

"Today, if you hear his voice,
8 do not harden your hearts
as you did in the rebellion,
during the time of testing in the desert,
9where your fathers tested and tried me
and for forty years saw what I did.
10That is why I was angry with that generation,
and I said, 'Their hearts are always going astray,
and they have not known my ways.'
11So I declared on oath in my anger,
'They shall never enter my rest.' "[b]

12See to it, brothers, that none of you has a sinful, unbelieving heart that turns away from the living God. 13But encourage one another daily, as long as it is called Today, so that none of you may be hardened by sin's deceitfulness. 14We have come to share in Christ if we hold firmly till the end the confidence we had at first. 15As has just been said:

"Today, if you hear his voice,
do not harden your hearts
as you did in the rebellion."[c]

16Who were they who heard and rebelled? Were they not all those Moses led out of Egypt? 17And with whom was he angry for forty years? Was it not with those who sinned, whose bodies fell in the desert? 18And to whom did God swear that they would never enter his rest if not to those who disobeyed[d]? 19So we see that they were not able to enter, because of their unbelief.

A Sabbath-Rest for the People of God

4 Therefore, since the promise of entering his rest still stands, let us be careful that none of you be found to have fallen short of it. 2For we also have had the gospel preached to us, just as they did; but the message they heard was of no value to them, because those who heard did not combine it with faith.[e] 3Now we who have believed enter that rest, just as God has said,

"So I declared on oath in my anger,
'They shall never enter my rest.' "[f]

And yet his work has been finished since the creation of the world. 4For somewhere he has spoken about the seventh day in these words: "And on the seventh day God rested from all his work."[g] 5And again in the passage above he says, "They shall never enter my rest."

6It still remains that some will enter that rest, and those who formerly had the gospel preached to them did not go in, because of their disobedience. 7Therefore God again set a certain day, calling it Today, when a long time later he spoke through David, as was said before:

"Today, if you hear his voice,
do not harden your hearts."[c]

8For if Joshua had given them rest, God would not have spoken later about another day. 9There remains, then, a Sabbath-rest for the people of God; 10for anyone who enters God's rest also rests from his own work, just as God did from his. 11Let us, therefore, make every effort to enter that rest, so that no one will fall by following their example of disobedience.

12For the word of God is living and active. Sharper than any double-edged

[a] *17* Or *and that he might turn aside God's wrath, taking away* [b] *11* Psalm 95:7-11
[c] *15,7* Psalm 95:7,8 [d] *18* Or *disbelieved* [e] *2* Many manuscripts *because they did not share in the faith of those who obeyed* [f] *3* Psalm 95:11; also in verse 5 [g] *4* Gen. 2:2

sword, it penetrates even to dividing soul
and spirit, joints and marrow; it judges the
thoughts and attitudes of the heart.
13Nothing in all creation is hidden from
God's sight. Everything is uncovered and
laid bare before the eyes of him to whom
we must give account.

[a]14 Or *gone into heaven*

Jesus the Great High Priest

14Therefore, since we have a great high
priest who has gone through the heav-
ens,[a] Jesus the Son of God, let us hold
firmly to the faith we profess. 15For we do
not have a high priest who is unable to

TUESDAY

VERSE FOR THE DAY: Hebrews 4:15 | AUTHOR: Philip Yancey | PASSAGE FOR THE DAY: Hebrews 4:12–16

God Takes Our Side

Forgiveness puts the forgiver on the same side as the wrongdoer. In the novel *Viper's Tangle*, Nobel laureate François Mauriac tells of a stubborn old man who spends the last few decades of his marriage sleeping down the hall from his wife. Every night he waits for her to approach him; every night she waits for him to approach her. Neither can forgive.

And yet the novel ends in hope. Somehow this curmudgeonly old man and his timid wife have a serious talk. The wife confesses the many nights she has spent in loneliness and tears waiting for his approach. Now he no longer sees her as the *enemy*, but rather as a vulnerable human being in desperate need of love. He sees a mirror of himself, and he begins to forgive.

A similar principle was at work when God came to earth in Christ. Somehow he had to come to terms with these human creatures he desperately wanted to love—but how? On earth, living among us, he put himself on our side.

The fourth chapter of Hebrews makes explicit this mystery of incarnation: "We do not have a high priest who is unable to sympathize with our weaknesses, but we have one who has been tempted in every way, just as we are—yet was without sin" (v. 15). In Christ, God bridged the gap; he took our side all the way.

MARRIAGE BUILDERS

♦ *How does lack of forgiveness lead to loneliness in your relationship?*

♦ *How does it help to know that, because Christ was a man, God understands our longings and weaknesses?*

Additional Scripture Readings
Hebrews 2:17–18; 2 Corinthians 5:21

Go to page 1358 for your next devotional reading.

sympathize with our weaknesses, but we
have one who has been tempted in every
way, just as we are—yet was without sin.
16Let us then approach the throne of grace
with confidence, so that we may receive
mercy and find grace to help us in our
time of need.

5 Every high priest is selected from
among men and is appointed to repre-
sent them in matters related to God, to of-
fer gifts and sacrifices for sins. 2He is able
to deal gently with those who are ignorant
and are going astray, since he himself is
subject to weakness. 3This is why he has
to offer sacrifices for his own sins, as well
as for the sins of the people.

4No one takes this honor upon himself;
he must be called by God, just as Aaron
was. 5So Christ also did not take upon
himself the glory of becoming a high
priest. But God said to him,

"You are my Son;
today I have become your
Father.[a]"[b]

6And he says in another place,

"You are a priest forever,
in the order of Melchizedek."[c]

7During the days of Jesus' life on earth,
he offered up prayers and petitions with
loud cries and tears to the one who could
save him from death, and he was heard
because of his reverent submission. 8Al-
though he was a son, he learned obedi-
ence from what he suffered 9and, once
made perfect, he became the source of
eternal salvation for all who obey him
10and was designated by God to be high
priest in the order of Melchizedek.

Warning Against Falling Away

11We have much to say about this, but
it is hard to explain because you are slow
to learn. 12In fact, though by this time you
ought to be teachers, you need someone
to teach you the elementary truths of
God's word all over again. You need milk,
not solid food! 13Anyone who lives on
milk, being still an infant, is not acquaint-
ed with the teaching about righteousness.
14But solid food is for the mature, who by
constant use have trained themselves to
distinguish good from evil.

6 Therefore let us leave the elementary
teachings about Christ and go on to
maturity, not laying again the foundation
of repentance from acts that lead to
death,[d] and of faith in God, 2instruction
about baptisms, the laying on of hands,
the resurrection of the dead, and eternal
judgment. 3And God permitting, we will
do so.

4It is impossible for those who have
once been enlightened, who have tasted
the heavenly gift, who have shared in the
Holy Spirit, 5who have tasted the good-
ness of the word of God and the powers of
the coming age, 6if they fall away, to be
brought back to repentance, because[e] to
their loss they are crucifying the Son of
God all over again and subjecting him to
public disgrace.

7Land that drinks in the rain often fall-
ing on it and that produces a crop useful
to those for whom it is farmed receives the
blessing of God. 8But land that produces
thorns and thistles is worthless and is in
danger of being cursed. In the end it will
be burned.

9Even though we speak like this, dear
friends, we are confident of better things
in your case—things that accompany sal-
vation. 10God is not unjust; he will not for-
get your work and the love you have
shown him as you have helped his people
and continue to help them. 11We want
each of you to show this same diligence to
the very end, in order to make your hope
sure. 12We do not want you to become
lazy, but to imitate those who through
faith and patience inherit what has been
promised.

The Certainty of God's Promise

13When God made his promise to Abra-
ham, since there was no one greater for
him to swear by, he swore by himself,
14saying, "I will surely bless you and give
you many descendants."[f] 15And so after
waiting patiently, Abraham received what
was promised.

16Men swear by someone greater than
themselves, and the oath confirms what is
said and puts an end to all argument. 17Be-
cause God wanted to make the unchang-
ing nature of his purpose very clear to the
heirs of what was promised, he confirmed
it with an oath. 18God did this so that, by
two unchangeable things in which it is im-
possible for God to lie, we who have fled
to take hold of the hope offered to us may

[a]5 Or *have begotten you* [b]5 Psalm 2:7 [c]6 Psalm 110:4 [d]1 Or *from useless rituals* [e]6 Or *repentance while* [f]14 Gen. 22:17

VERSE FOR THE DAY: Hebrews 6:10

AUTHOR: Jill Briscoe

PASSAGE FOR THE DAY: Hebrews 6:1–12

Shared Ministry

The first time Stuart and I led a marriage seminar, I over-prepared because I felt unsure of myself. All the while I kept saying to Stuart, "When are we going to sit down and work on our message?"

The day came and we still hadn't gotten together. I remember shouting upstairs, "Do you YET know what we're going to do today?" He came down and said, "I have been so busy, Jill. We'll talk about it on the way there." Of course I burst into tears.

Stuart said, "We'll just get up there and tell the people what has happened. And then we'll talk it out." And that's what we did. We talked through the problem of our differences and brainstormed ways we could do better the next time.

Since then, our preparation habits have not changed all that much, but our attitudes have. We're much more open and understanding of the other person's way of doing things. Stuart now makes time to interact with me because he realizes I need that to feel comfortable. And I go ahead and prepare on my own, knowing Stuart is giving it thought and prayer all along and that he will draw on resources from his many years of teaching. We have adjusted to each other's needs and strengths.

It's like a game of tennis. We're on the same team and we both want to win, but his forehand is better and my backhand is better. Since the goal is to win the tournament, we help each other practice and play to our strengths.

MARRIAGE BUILDERS

♦ *What is one area where you are weak but your spouse is strong? An area where you are strong, but your spouse is not-so-strong?*
♦ *Have you been able to help each other in these areas?*

Additional Scripture Readings
Ecclesiastes 4:9–10; 2 Thessalonians 2:17

Go to page 1362 for your next devotional reading.

be greatly encouraged. [19]We have this
hope as an anchor for the soul, firm and
secure. It enters the inner sanctuary be-
hind the curtain, [20]where Jesus, who went
before us, has entered on our behalf. He
has become a high priest forever, in the
order of Melchizedek.

Melchizedek the Priest

7 This Melchizedek was king of Salem
and priest of God Most High. He met
Abraham returning from the defeat of the
kings and blessed him, [2]and Abraham
gave him a tenth of everything. First, his
name means "king of righteousness"; then
also, "king of Salem" means "king of
peace." [3]Without father or mother, with-
out genealogy, without beginning of days
or end of life, like the Son of God he re-
mains a priest forever.

[4]Just think how great he was: Even the
patriarch Abraham gave him a tenth of the
plunder! [5]Now the law requires the
descendants of Levi who become priests
to collect a tenth from the people—that is,
their brothers—even though their broth-
ers are descended from Abraham. [6]This
man, however, did not trace his descent
from Levi, yet he collected a tenth from
Abraham and blessed him who had the
promises. [7]And without doubt the lesser
person is blessed by the greater. [8]In the
one case, the tenth is collected by men
who die; but in the other case, by him who
is declared to be living. [9]One might even
say that Levi, who collects the tenth, paid
the tenth through Abraham, [10]because
when Melchizedek met Abraham, Levi
was still in the body of his ancestor.

Jesus Like Melchizedek

[11]If perfection could have been attained
through the Levitical priesthood (for on
the basis of it the law was given to the peo-
ple), why was there still need for another
priest to come—one in the order of Mel-
chizedek, not in the order of Aaron? [12]For
when there is a change of the priesthood,
there must also be a change of the law.
[13]He of whom these things are said be-
longed to a different tribe, and no one
from that tribe has ever served at the altar.
[14]For it is clear that our Lord descended
from Judah, and in regard to that tribe
Moses said nothing about priests. [15]And
what we have said is even more clear if
another priest like Melchizedek appears,
[16]one who has become a priest not on the
basis of a regulation as to his ancestry but
on the basis of the power of an indestruc-
tible life. [17]For it is declared:

"You are a priest forever,
in the order of Melchizedek."[a]

[18]The former regulation is set aside be-
cause it was weak and useless [19](for the
law made nothing perfect), and a better
hope is introduced, by which we draw
near to God.

[20]And it was not without an oath! Oth-
ers became priests without any oath, [21]but
he became a priest with an oath when God
said to him:

"The Lord has sworn
and will not change his mind:
'You are a priest forever.' "[a]

[22]Because of this oath, Jesus has become
the guarantee of a better covenant.

[23]Now there have been many of those
priests, since death prevented them from
continuing in office; [24]but because Jesus
lives forever, he has a permanent priest-
hood. [25]Therefore he is able to save com-
pletely[b] those who come to God through
him, because he always lives to intercede
for them.

[26]Such a high priest meets our need—
one who is holy, blameless, pure, set apart
from sinners, exalted above the heavens.
[27]Unlike the other high priests, he does
not need to offer sacrifices day after day,
first for his own sins, and then for the sins
of the people. He sacrificed for their sins
once for all when he offered himself. [28]For
the law appoints as high priests men who
are weak; but the oath, which came after
the law, appointed the Son, who has been
made perfect forever.

The High Priest of a New Covenant

8 The point of what we are saying is
this: We do have such a high priest,
who sat down at the right hand of the
throne of the Majesty in heaven, [2]and who
serves in the sanctuary, the true taberna-
cle set up by the Lord, not by man.

[3]Every high priest is appointed to offer
both gifts and sacrifices, and so it was nec-
essary for this one also to have something
to offer. [4]If he were on earth, he would not
be a priest, for there are already men who
offer the gifts prescribed by the law. [5]They
serve at a sanctuary that is a copy and

[a]*17,21* Psalm 110:4 [b]*25* Or *forever*

shadow of what is in heaven. This is why
Moses was warned when he was about to
build the tabernacle: "See to it that you
make everything according to the pattern
shown you on the mountain."[a] 6But the
ministry Jesus has received is as superior
to theirs as the covenant of which he is
mediator is superior to the old one, and it
is founded on better promises.
7For if there had been nothing wrong
with that first covenant, no place would
have been sought for another. 8But God
found fault with the people and said[b]:

"The time is coming, declares the
Lord,
when I will make a new covenant
with the house of Israel
and with the house of Judah.
9It will not be like the covenant
I made with their forefathers
when I took them by the hand
to lead them out of Egypt,
because they did not remain faithful
to my covenant,
and I turned away from them,
declares the Lord.
10This is the covenant I will make with
the house of Israel
after that time, declares the Lord.
I will put my laws in their minds
and write them on their hearts.
I will be their God,
and they will be my people.
11No longer will a man teach his
neighbor,
or a man his brother, saying, 'Know
the Lord,'
because they will all know me,
from the least of them to the
greatest.
12For I will forgive their wickedness
and will remember their sins no
more."[c]

13By calling this covenant "new," he has
made the first one obsolete; and what is
obsolete and aging will soon disappear.

Worship in the Earthly Tabernacle

9 Now the first covenant had regula-
tions for worship and also an earthly
sanctuary. 2A tabernacle was set up. In its
first room were the lampstand, the table
and the consecrated bread; this was called
the Holy Place. 3Behind the second cur-
tain was a room called the Most Holy
Place, 4which had the golden altar of in-
cense and the gold-covered ark of the cov-
enant. This ark contained the gold jar of
manna, Aaron's staff that had budded,
and the stone tablets of the covenant.
5Above the ark were the cherubim of the
Glory, overshadowing the atonement cov-
er.[d] But we cannot discuss these things
in detail now.
6When everything had been arranged
like this, the priests entered regularly into
the outer room to carry on their ministry.
7But only the high priest entered the inner
room, and that only once a year, and nev-
er without blood, which he offered for
himself and for the sins the people had
committed in ignorance. 8The Holy Spirit
was showing by this that the way into the
Most Holy Place had not yet been dis-
closed as long as the first tabernacle was
still standing. 9This is an illustration for
the present time, indicating that the gifts
and sacrifices being offered were not able
to clear the conscience of the worshiper.
10They are only a matter of food and drink
and various ceremonial washings—exter-
nal regulations applying until the time of
the new order.

The Blood of Christ

11When Christ came as high priest of
the good things that are already here,[e] he
went through the greater and more perfect
tabernacle that is not man-made, that is to
say, not a part of this creation. 12He did
not enter by means of the blood of goats
and calves; but he entered the Most Holy
Place once for all by his own blood, hav-
ing obtained eternal redemption. 13The
blood of goats and bulls and the ashes of
a heifer sprinkled on those who are cere-
monially unclean sanctify them so that
they are outwardly clean. 14How much
more, then, will the blood of Christ, who
through the eternal Spirit offered himself
unblemished to God, cleanse our con-
sciences from acts that lead to death,[f] so
that we may serve the living God!
15For this reason Christ is the mediator
of a new covenant, that those who are
called may receive the promised eternal
inheritance—now that he has died as a
ransom to set them free from the sins
committed under the first covenant.

[a] 5 Exodus 25:40 [b] 8 Some manuscripts may be translated *fault and said to the people.*
[c] 12 Jer. 31:31-34 [d] 5 Traditionally *the mercy seat* [e] 11 Some early manuscripts *are to come*
[f] 14 Or *from useless rituals*

16In the case of a will,[a] it is necessary
to prove the death of the one who made it,
17because a will is in force only when
somebody has died; it never takes effect
while the one who made it is living. 18This
is why even the first covenant was not put
into effect without blood. 19When Moses
had proclaimed every commandment of
the law to all the people, he took the blood
of calves, together with water, scarlet
wool and branches of hyssop, and sprin-
kled the scroll and all the people. 20He
said, "This is the blood of the covenant,
which God has commanded you to
keep."[b] 21In the same way, he sprinkled
with the blood both the tabernacle and ev-
erything used in its ceremonies. 22In fact,
the law requires that nearly everything be
cleansed with blood, and without the
shedding of blood there is no forgiveness.
23It was necessary, then, for the copies
of the heavenly things to be purified with
these sacrifices, but the heavenly things
themselves with better sacrifices than
these. 24For Christ did not enter a man-
made sanctuary that was only a copy of
the true one; he entered heaven itself,
now to appear for us in God's presence.
25Nor did he enter heaven to offer himself
again and again, the way the high priest
enters the Most Holy Place every year
with blood that is not his own. 26Then
Christ would have had to suffer many
times since the creation of the world. But
now he has appeared once for all at the
end of the ages to do away with sin by the
sacrifice of himself. 27Just as man is des-
tined to die once, and after that to face
judgment, 28so Christ was sacrificed once
to take away the sins of many people; and
he will appear a second time, not to bear
sin, but to bring salvation to those who are
waiting for him.

Christ's Sacrifice Once for All

10 The law is only a shadow of the
good things that are coming—not
the realities themselves. For this reason it
can never, by the same sacrifices repeated
endlessly year after year, make perfect
those who draw near to worship. 2If it
could, would they not have stopped being
offered? For the worshipers would have
been cleansed once for all, and would no
longer have felt guilty for their sins. 3But
those sacrifices are an annual reminder of
sins, 4because it is impossible for the
blood of bulls and goats to take away sins.
5Therefore, when Christ came into the
world, he said:

"Sacrifice and offering you did not
desire,
but a body you prepared for me;
6with burnt offerings and sin offerings
you were not pleased.
7Then I said, 'Here I am—it is written
about me in the scroll—
I have come to do your will,
O God.' "[c]

8First he said, "Sacrifices and offerings,
burnt offerings and sin offerings you did
not desire, nor were you pleased with
them" (although the law required them to
be made). 9Then he said, "Here I am, I
have come to do your will." He sets aside
the first to establish the second. 10And by
that will, we have been made holy
through the sacrifice of the body of Jesus
Christ once for all.
11Day after day every priest stands and
performs his religious duties; again and
again he offers the same sacrifices, which
can never take away sins. 12But when this
priest had offered for all time one sacrifice
for sins, he sat down at the right hand of
God. 13Since that time he waits for his ene-
mies to be made his footstool, 14because
by one sacrifice he has made perfect for-
ever those who are being made holy.
15The Holy Spirit also testifies to us
about this. First he says:

16"This is the covenant I will make with
them
after that time, says the Lord.
I will put my laws in their hearts,
and I will write them on their
minds."[d]

17Then he adds:

"Their sins and lawless acts
I will remember no more."[e]

18And where these have been forgiven,
there is no longer any sacrifice for sin.

A Call to Persevere

19Therefore, brothers, since we have
confidence to enter the Most Holy Place
by the blood of Jesus, 20by a new and liv-
ing way opened for us through the cur-
tain, that is, his body, 21and since we have

[a]16 Same Greek word as *covenant*; also in verse 17 [b]20 Exodus 24:8 [c]7 Psalm 40:6-8 (see Septuagint) [d]16 Jer. 31:33 [e]17 Jer. 31:34

a great priest over the house of God, [22]let
us draw near to God with a sincere heart
in full assurance of faith, having our
hearts sprinkled to cleanse us from a
guilty conscience and having our bodies
washed with pure water. [23]Let us hold un-
swervingly to the hope we profess, for he
who promised is faithful. [24]And let us con-
sider how we may spur one another on to-
ward love and good deeds. [25]Let us not
give up meeting together, as some are in
the habit of doing, but let us encourage
one another—and all the more as you see
the Day approaching.

[26]If we deliberately keep on sinning af-
ter we have received the knowledge of the
truth, no sacrifice for sins is left, [27]but
only a fearful expectation of judgment
and of raging fire that will consume the
enemies of God. [28]Anyone who rejected

VERSE FOR THE DAY: Hebrews 10:24–25

AUTHOR: H. Norman Wright

PASSAGE FOR THE DAY: Hebrews 10:19–25

An Encouraging Word

Each of us needs encouragement, especially from our spouse. But how can we best tell our partner "I believe in you"? A good place to start is by encouraging, giving the benefit of the doubt and thinking the best of your mate.

It's easy to be a critic, but it's much more rewarding to be an encourager. When you criticize you are standing against your spouse. When you encourage, however, you stand beside him or her. The Hebrew term for encourage conveys the idea of putting strength into someone's hands, arms or body so they can handle pressure.

In order to do a better job of encouraging, you need to become a "talent scout" by seeking out your mate's underdeveloped potential. Most of us have been conditioned instead to look for people's liabilities. Perhaps this approach makes us feel better about our own imperfections, but it's not very pleasant to live in such an environment.

Encouragement means not taking your partner for granted. Your spouse is a unique gift to you, and he or she needs constant recognition. Too many people suffer from emotional malnutrition because they are receiving too little encouragement.

MARRIAGE BUILDERS

♦ *How might you tell your partner "I believe in you" without using those words?*

♦ *In what ways has your spouse been an encouragement to you?*

Additional Scripture Readings
Proverbs 12:25; 25:11; Ephesians 4:29–32

Go to page 1364 for your next devotional reading.

the law of Moses died without mercy on
the testimony of two or three witnesses.
29How much more severely do you think
a man deserves to be punished who has
trampled the Son of God under foot, who
has treated as an unholy thing the blood
of the covenant that sanctified him, and
who has insulted the Spirit of grace? 30For
we know him who said, "It is mine to
avenge; I will repay,"[a] and again, "The
Lord will judge his people."[b] 31It is a
dreadful thing to fall into the hands of the
living God.

32Remember those earlier days after
you had received the light, when you
stood your ground in a great contest in the
face of suffering. 33Sometimes you were
publicly exposed to insult and persecu-
tion; at other times you stood side by side
with those who were so treated. 34You
sympathized with those in prison and joy-
fully accepted the confiscation of your
property, because you knew that you
yourselves had better and lasting posses-
sions.

35So do not throw away your confi-
dence; it will be richly rewarded. 36You
need to persevere so that when you have
done the will of God, you will receive
what he has promised. 37For in just a very
little while,

"He who is coming will come and will
not delay.
38 But my righteous one[c] will live by
faith.
And if he shrinks back,
I will not be pleased with him."[d]

39But we are not of those who shrink back
and are destroyed, but of those who be-
lieve and are saved.

By Faith

11 Now faith is being sure of what we
hope for and certain of what we do
not see. 2This is what the ancients were
commended for.

3By faith we understand that the uni-
verse was formed at God's command, so
that what is seen was not made out of
what was visible.

4By faith Abel offered God a better sac-
rifice than Cain did. By faith he was com-
mended as a righteous man, when God
spoke well of his offerings. And by faith
he still speaks, even though he is dead.

5By faith Enoch was taken from this life,
so that he did not experience death; he
could not be found, because God had tak-
en him away. For before he was taken, he
was commended as one who pleased God.
6And without faith it is impossible to
please God, because anyone who comes
to him must believe that he exists and that
he rewards those who earnestly seek him.

7By faith Noah, when warned about
things not yet seen, in holy fear built an
ark to save his family. By his faith he con-
demned the world and became heir of the
righteousness that comes by faith.

8By faith Abraham, when called to go to
a place he would later receive as his inher-
itance, obeyed and went, even though he
did not know where he was going. 9By
faith he made his home in the promised
land like a stranger in a foreign country;
he lived in tents, as did Isaac and Jacob,
who were heirs with him of the same
promise. 10For he was looking forward to
the city with foundations, whose architect
and builder is God.

11By faith Abraham, even though he
was past age—and Sarah herself was bar-
ren—was enabled to become a father be-
cause he[e] considered him faithful who
had made the promise. 12And so from this
one man, and he as good as dead, came
descendants as numerous as the stars in
the sky and as countless as the sand on
the seashore.

13All these people were still living by
faith when they died. They did not receive
the things promised; they only saw them
and welcomed them from a distance. And
they admitted that they were aliens and
strangers on earth. 14People who say such
things show that they are looking for a
country of their own. 15If they had been
thinking of the country they had left, they
would have had opportunity to return.
16Instead, they were longing for a better
country—a heavenly one. Therefore God
is not ashamed to be called their God, for
he has prepared a city for them.

17By faith Abraham, when God tested
him, offered Isaac as a sacrifice. He who
had received the promises was about to
sacrifice his one and only son, 18even

[a] *30* Deut. 32:35 [b] *30* Deut. 32:36; Psalm 135:14 [c] *38* One early manuscript *But the righteous*
[d] *38* Hab. 2:3,4 [e] *11* Or *By faith even Sarah, who was past age, was enabled to bear children because she*

though God had said to him, "It is through
Isaac that your offspring[a] will be reckoned."[b] 19Abraham reasoned that God
could raise the dead, and figuratively
speaking, he did receive Isaac back from
death.

20By faith Isaac blessed Jacob and Esau
in regard to their future.

21By faith Jacob, when he was dying,
blessed each of Joseph's sons, and worshiped as he leaned on the top of his staff.

22By faith Joseph, when his end was
near, spoke about the exodus of the Israelites from Egypt and gave instructions
about his bones.

23By faith Moses' parents hid him for
three months after he was born, because
they saw he was no ordinary child, and
they were not afraid of the king's edict.

24By faith Moses, when he had grown
up, refused to be known as the son of
Pharaoh's daughter. 25He chose to be mistreated along with the people of God rather than to enjoy the pleasures of sin for a
short time. 26He regarded disgrace for the
sake of Christ as of greater value than the

[a]18 Greek *seed* [b]18 Gen. 21:12

FRIDAY

VERSE FOR THE DAY: Hebrews 11:1

AUTHOR: Elizabeth Cody Newenhuyse

PASSAGE FOR THE DAY: Hebrews 11:1–39

It Takes Two to Trust

In marriage, it takes two to trust. When I decided to leave a secure job so I could stay home and write full-time, my husband, Fritz, encouraged the move. Since then, we've learned over and over the meaning of my favorite Proverb: "Trust in the Lord with all your heart and lean not on your own understanding; in all your ways acknowledge him, and he will make your paths straight" (3:5–6).

God demands that we rely totally on him; anything less is disobedience. No concern is too small, no issue too complex to bring to him.

That may be why Fritz and I, through the ups and downs of our life, have felt fundamentally confident about the future. We have tried to rise above the good news/bad news syndrome; that is, feeling great when things go well and despairing when they don't. Those emotions come and go. God's peace, which settles deep inside you, won't.

And it's available to every one of us who trusts in him—wholly.

MARRIAGE BUILDERS

♦ *What are the advantages of two people trusting the Lord together?*

♦ *How does God's peace offset up and down times?*

Additional Scripture Readings
Proverbs 3:5–6; Philippians 4:6–7

Go to page 1366 for your next devotional reading.

treasures of Egypt, because he was looking ahead to his reward. 27By faith he left Egypt, not fearing the king's anger; he persevered because he saw him who is invisible. 28By faith he kept the Passover and the sprinkling of blood, so that the destroyer of the firstborn would not touch the firstborn of Israel.

29By faith the people passed through the Red Sea[a] as on dry land; but when the Egyptians tried to do so, they were drowned.

30By faith the walls of Jericho fell, after the people had marched around them for seven days.

31By faith the prostitute Rahab, because she welcomed the spies, was not killed with those who were disobedient.[b]

32And what more shall I say? I do not have time to tell about Gideon, Barak, Samson, Jephthah, David, Samuel and the prophets, 33who through faith conquered kingdoms, administered justice, and gained what was promised; who shut the mouths of lions, 34quenched the fury of the flames, and escaped the edge of the sword; whose weakness was turned to strength; and who became powerful in battle and routed foreign armies. 35Women received back their dead, raised to life again. Others were tortured and refused to be released, so that they might gain a better resurrection. 36Some faced jeers and flogging, while still others were chained and put in prison. 37They were stoned[c]; they were sawed in two; they were put to death by the sword. They went about in sheepskins and goatskins, destitute, persecuted and mistreated — 38the world was not worthy of them. They wandered in deserts and mountains, and in caves and holes in the ground.

39These were all commended for their faith, yet none of them received what had been promised. 40God had planned something better for us so that only together with us would they be made perfect.

God Disciplines His Sons

12 Therefore, since we are surrounded by such a great cloud of witnesses, let us throw off everything that hinders and the sin that so easily entangles, and let us run with perseverance the race marked out for us. 2Let us fix our eyes on Jesus, the author and perfecter of our faith, who for the joy set before him endured the cross, scorning its shame, and sat down at the right hand of the throne of God. 3Consider him who endured such opposition from sinful men, so that you will not grow weary and lose heart.

4In your struggle against sin, you have not yet resisted to the point of shedding your blood. 5And you have forgotten that word of encouragement that addresses you as sons:

"My son, do not make light of the
Lord's discipline,
and do not lose heart when he
rebukes you,
6because the Lord disciplines those he
loves,
and he punishes everyone he
accepts as a son."[d]

7Endure hardship as discipline; God is treating you as sons. For what son is not disciplined by his father? 8If you are not disciplined (and everyone undergoes discipline), then you are illegitimate children and not true sons. 9Moreover, we have all had human fathers who disciplined us and we respected them for it. How much more should we submit to the Father of our spirits and live! 10Our fathers disciplined us for a little while as they thought best; but God disciplines us for our good, that we may share in his holiness. 11No discipline seems pleasant at the time, but painful. Later on, however, it produces a harvest of righteousness and peace for those who have been trained by it.

12Therefore, strengthen your feeble arms and weak knees. 13"Make level paths for your feet,"[e] so that the lame may not be disabled, but rather healed.

Warning Against Refusing God

14Make every effort to live in peace with all men and to be holy; without holiness no one will see the Lord. 15See to it that no one misses the grace of God and that no bitter root grows up to cause trouble and defile many. 16See that no one is sexually immoral, or is godless like Esau, who for a single meal sold his inheritance rights as the oldest son. 17Afterward, as you know, when he wanted to inherit this blessing, he was rejected. He could bring about no

[a]29 That is, Sea of Reeds [b]31 Or *unbelieving the test;* [c]37 Some early manuscripts *stoned; they were put to* [d]6 Prov. 3:11,12 [e]13 Prov. 4:26

WEEKENDING

HELPING

The Bible offers guidance on how couples can shift the focus off their differences and concentrate, instead, on building a lasting relationship. One way is to focus on bearing each other's burdens. Consider the following questions:

1. If you and your spouse worked harder at helping bear each other's burdens, in what ways do you think it would draw you closer together?

2. Can you think of an occasion when you could have done more to offer your mate needed help and encouragement when he or she was struggling? How did your failure to provide what was needed affect your spouse's view of you?

3. How could working harder at helping your mate with his or her burdens help you concentrate less on any unsettling differences that exist between you?

— *The* Marriage Partnership *Staff*

REVIVE

Saturday: Galatians 6:2–10
Sunday: Romans 15:1–13

Go to page 1368 for your next devotional reading.

change of mind, though he sought the blessing with tears.

18You have not come to a mountain that can be touched and that is burning with fire; to darkness, gloom and storm; 19to a trumpet blast or to such a voice speaking words that those who heard it begged that no further word be spoken to them, 20because they could not bear what was commanded: "If even an animal touches the mountain, it must be stoned."[a] 21The sight was so terrifying that Moses said, "I am trembling with fear."[b]

22But you have come to Mount Zion, to the heavenly Jerusalem, the city of the living God. You have come to thousands upon thousands of angels in joyful assembly, 23to the church of the firstborn, whose names are written in heaven. You have come to God, the judge of all men, to the spirits of righteous men made perfect, 24to Jesus the mediator of a new covenant, and to the sprinkled blood that speaks a better word than the blood of Abel.

25See to it that you do not refuse him who speaks. If they did not escape when they refused him who warned them on earth, how much less will we, if we turn away from him who warns us from heaven? 26At that time his voice shook the earth, but now he has promised, "Once more I will shake not only the earth but also the heavens."[c] 27The words "once more" indicate the removing of what can be shaken—that is, created things—so that what cannot be shaken may remain.

28Therefore, since we are receiving a kingdom that cannot be shaken, let us be thankful, and so worship God acceptably with reverence and awe, 29for our "God is a consuming fire."[d]

Concluding Exhortations

13 Keep on loving each other as brothers. 2Do not forget to entertain strangers, for by so doing some people have entertained angels without knowing it. 3Remember those in prison as if you were their fellow prisoners, and those who are mistreated as if you yourselves were suffering.

4Marriage should be honored by all, and the marriage bed kept pure, for God will judge the adulterer and all the sexually immoral. 5Keep your lives free from the love of money and be content with what you have, because God has said,

"Never will I leave you;
never will I forsake you."[e]

6So we say with confidence,

"The Lord is my helper; I will not be afraid.
What can man do to me?"[f]

7Remember your leaders, who spoke the word of God to you. Consider the outcome of their way of life and imitate their faith. 8Jesus Christ is the same yesterday and today and forever.

9Do not be carried away by all kinds of strange teachings. It is good for our hearts to be strengthened by grace, not by ceremonial foods, which are of no value to those who eat them. 10We have an altar from which those who minister at the tabernacle have no right to eat.

11The high priest carries the blood of animals into the Most Holy Place as a sin offering, but the bodies are burned outside the camp. 12And so Jesus also suffered outside the city gate to make the people holy through his own blood. 13Let us, then, go to him outside the camp, bearing the disgrace he bore. 14For here we do not have an enduring city, but we are looking for the city that is to come.

15Through Jesus, therefore, let us continually offer to God a sacrifice of praise—the fruit of lips that confess his name. 16And do not forget to do good and to share with others, for with such sacrifices God is pleased.

17Obey your leaders and submit to their authority. They keep watch over you as men who must give an account. Obey them so that their work will be a joy, not a burden, for that would be of no advantage to you.

18Pray for us. We are sure that we have a clear conscience and desire to live honorably in every way. 19I particularly urge you to pray so that I may be restored to you soon.

20May the God of peace, who through the blood of the eternal covenant brought back from the dead our Lord Jesus, that great Shepherd of the sheep, 21equip you with everything good for doing his will,

[a] *20* Exodus 19:12,13 [b] *21* Deut. 9:19 [c] *26* Haggai 2:6 [d] *29* Deut. 4:24 [e] *5* Deut. 31:6
[f] *6* Psalm 118:6,7

VERSE FOR THE DAY: Hebrews 12:11

AUTHOR: Kay Marshall Strom

PASSAGE FOR THE DAY: Hebrews 12:7–13

The Fruit of Pruning

A peach tree stands in our back yard. Unpruned, the tree grew big and leafy. It was loaded with peaches, although the fruit was disappointingly small and tasteless.

The year my husband, Larry, was out of work, he went to work on the tree. When I came home from school one day and saw how far back he had pruned it, I stared in shock.

"You've killed it," I cried. "Now we won't have any peaches at all."

But I was wrong. That spring the pruned branches burst forth with a beautiful blanketing of pink blossoms. Soon little green peaches replaced the blossoms. "Leave them alone," I begged. Larry ignored me and thinned the fruit.

By the end of summer the branches were so heavily laden with fruit they had to be propped up. And the peaches—how large and sweet and juicy they were. There was no denying it: The tree was far better off for the painful cutting it endured under Larry's pruning shears.

No one wants to go through troubles and suffering and pain. It was eleven months before Larry got a job. Looking back, we can only say, "Thank you, Lord, for pruning us. Thank you for teaching us to trust you. Thank you for drawing us together as a family and welding us in a way that never happened in happier times. Thank you, that after seeing each other at our worst, we still want to be together."

MARRIAGE BUILDERS

♦ *When was the last time you felt that God was "pruning" something out of your life? What was the outcome?*

♦ *When was it hardest for you to trust God during a difficult period of your life?*

Additional Scripture Readings
John 15:2–4; Ephesians 3:20–21; Psalm 145:13–17

Go to page 1371 for your next devotional reading.

and may he work in us what is pleasing to him, through Jesus Christ, to whom be glory for ever and ever. Amen.

22Brothers, I urge you to bear with my word of exhortation, for I have written you only a short letter.

23I want you to know that our brother Timothy has been released. If he arrives soon, I will come with him to see you.

24Greet all your leaders and all God's people. Those from Italy send you their greetings.

25Grace be with you all.

JAMES (a brother of Jesus) writes this letter to urge Christians to express their faith in daily living. He reminds them of what Jesus said, especially in the Sermon on the Mount (Matthew 5–7). As you read this book, ask yourself whether others can see by what you do and say that you believe in Jesus.

JAMES

1 James, a servant of God and of the Lord Jesus Christ,

To the twelve tribes scattered among the nations:

Greetings.

Trials and Temptations

2Consider it pure joy, my brothers, whenever you face trials of many kinds, 3because you know that the testing of your faith develops perseverance. 4Perseverance must finish its work so that you may be mature and complete, not lacking anything. 5If any of you lacks wisdom, he should ask God, who gives generously to all without finding fault, and it will be given to him. 6But when he asks, he must believe and not doubt, because he who doubts is like a wave of the sea, blown and tossed by the wind. 7That man should not think he will receive anything from the Lord; 8he is a double-minded man, unstable in all he does.

9The brother in humble circumstances ought to take pride in his high position. 10But the one who is rich should take pride in his low position, because he will pass away like a wild flower. 11For the sun rises with scorching heat and withers the plant; its blossom falls and its beauty is destroyed. In the same way, the rich man will fade away even while he goes about his business.

12Blessed is the man who perseveres under trial, because when he has stood the test, he will receive the crown of life that God has promised to those who love him.

13When tempted, no one should say, "God is tempting me." For God cannot be tempted by evil, nor does he tempt anyone; 14but each one is tempted when, by his own evil desire, he is dragged away and enticed. 15Then, after desire has con-

VERSE FOR THE DAY: James 1:4 | AUTHOR: Harold B. Smith | PASSAGE FOR THE DAY: James 1:1–18

Patience in Marriage

Most of us, before we're married, imagine that love will solve all our problems. But could it be that patience, more than love, is the sum and substance of a great marriage?

Our society rewards problem-solvers. Every challenge is an opportunity to be met quickly. Then comes marriage, and we problem-solvers are suddenly faced with a challenge that taxes the very essence of who we are. We think we're called to fix things when they're broken. To make things work. But then we wake up one morning to find that the person next to us is more complicated than anything we've ever had to deal with.

It is *two* people who give expression to marital oneness. Two people—usually polar opposites—who commit themselves to building a framework for physical, emotional and spiritual oneness by accepting, respecting and unconditionally loving each other. To do so, however, takes time, which means we have to be patient.

Patience in marriage works a lot like faith. It demonstrates the certainty that what we hope for—physical, emotional, spiritual oneness—is waiting for us, even though we can't yet see it. My wife and I have had more than twenty years to practice the power of patience. Of forgiving each other. Of accepting. Of instilling hope. And the longer we're married, the more practice we get. But even after years of practice, we need to be reminded that oneness is an assurance that only those with patience can hold on to—and one day realize.

MARRIAGE BUILDERS

♦ *Identify and describe a time when you tried a "quick" solution for an ongoing problem in your marriage. What happened?*

♦ *What are some other areas where patience comes into play in your relationship with each other?*

Additional Scripture Readings
Colossians 1:9–14; Proverbs 19:11; 2 Peter 1:5–7

Go to page 1373 for your next devotional reading.

ceived, it gives birth to sin; and sin, when
it is full-grown, gives birth to death.
16Don't be deceived, my dear brothers.
17Every good and perfect gift is from
above, coming down from the Father of
the heavenly lights, who does not change
like shifting shadows. 18He chose to give
us birth through the word of truth, that we
might be a kind of firstfruits of all he cre-
ated.

Listening and Doing

19My dear brothers, take note of this:
Everyone should be quick to listen, slow
to speak and slow to become angry, 20for
man's anger does not bring about the right-
eous life that God desires. 21Therefore,
get rid of all moral filth and the evil that
is so prevalent and humbly accept the
word planted in you, which can save you.
22Do not merely listen to the word, and
so deceive yourselves. Do what it says.
23Anyone who listens to the word but
does not do what it says is like a man who
looks at his face in a mirror 24and, after
looking at himself, goes away and imme-
diately forgets what he looks like. 25But
the man who looks intently into the per-
fect law that gives freedom, and continues
to do this, not forgetting what he has
heard, but doing it—he will be blessed in
what he does.
26If anyone considers himself religious
and yet does not keep a tight rein on his
tongue, he deceives himself and his reli-
gion is worthless. 27Religion that God our
Father accepts as pure and faultless is
this: to look after orphans and widows in
their distress and to keep oneself from be-
ing polluted by the world.

Favoritism Forbidden

2 My brothers, as believers in our glori-
ous Lord Jesus Christ, don't show fa-
voritism. 2Suppose a man comes into your
meeting wearing a gold ring and fine
clothes, and a poor man in shabby clothes
also comes in. 3If you show special atten-
tion to the man wearing fine clothes and
say, "Here's a good seat for you," but say
to the poor man, "You stand there" or "Sit
on the floor by my feet," 4have you not
discriminated among yourselves and be-
come judges with evil thoughts?
5Listen, my dear brothers: Has not God
chosen those who are poor in the eyes of
the world to be rich in faith and to inherit
the kingdom he promised those who love
him? 6But you have insulted the poor. Is it
not the rich who are exploiting you? Are
they not the ones who are dragging you
into court? 7Are they not the ones who are
slandering the noble name of him to
whom you belong?
8If you really keep the royal law found
in Scripture, "Love your neighbor as your-
self,"[a] you are doing right. 9But if you
show favoritism, you sin and are convict-
ed by the law as lawbreakers. 10For who-
ever keeps the whole law and yet stum-
bles at just one point is guilty of breaking
all of it. 11For he who said, "Do not com-
mit adultery,"[b] also said, "Do not mur-
der."[c] If you do not commit adultery but
do commit murder, you have become a
lawbreaker.
12Speak and act as those who are going
to be judged by the law that gives free-
dom, 13because judgment without mercy
will be shown to anyone who has not
been merciful. Mercy triumphs over judg-
ment!

Faith and Deeds

14What good is it, my brothers, if a man
claims to have faith but has no deeds? Can
such faith save him? 15Suppose a brother
or sister is without clothes and daily food.
16If one of you says to him, "Go, I wish
you well; keep warm and well fed," but
does nothing about his physical needs,
what good is it? 17In the same way, faith
by itself, if it is not accompanied by ac-
tion, is dead.
18But someone will say, "You have
faith; I have deeds."
Show me your faith without deeds, and
I will show you my faith by what I do.
19You believe that there is one God. Good!
Even the demons believe that—and shud-
der.
20You foolish man, do you want evi-
dence that faith without deeds is use-
less[d]? 21Was not our ancestor Abraham
considered righteous for what he did
when he offered his son Isaac on the altar?
22You see that his faith and his actions
were working together, and his faith was
made complete by what he did. 23And the
scripture was fulfilled that says, "Abra-

[a]8 Lev. 19:18 [b]11 Exodus 20:14; Deut. 5:18 [c]11 Exodus 20:13; Deut. 5:17 [d]20 Some early manuscripts *dead*

ham believed God, and it was credited to
him as righteousness,"[a] and he was
called God's friend. [24]You see that a per-
son is justified by what he does and not by
faith alone.

[25]In the same way, was not even Rahab
the prostitute considered righteous for
what she did when she gave lodging to the
spies and sent them off in a different di-
rection? [26]As the body without the spirit is
dead, so faith without deeds is dead.

[a]23 Gen. 15:6

Taming the Tongue

3 Not many of you should presume to
be teachers, my brothers, because you
know that we who teach will be judged
more strictly. [2]We all stumble in many
ways. If anyone is never at fault in what he
says, he is a perfect man, able to keep his
whole body in check.

[3]When we put bits into the mouths of
horses to make them obey us, we can turn
the whole animal. [4]Or take ships as an ex-

VERSE FOR THE DAY: James 3:13–14 | AUTHOR: Stephen Arterburn | PASSAGE FOR THE DAY: James 3:13–18

Genuine Intimacy

One obstacle to achieving intimacy is the array of false concepts of intimacy presented by our culture. In the eyes of the world, intimacy equals "closeness," which almost always includes being *sexually* close. The more "intimate" two people are, it is assumed, the more sexual they will be. Conversely, the more sexual two people are, the more "intimate" they are assumed to be.

Genuine intimacy *may* involve being sexual, but this is a by-product of intimacy, not the thing itself. Much sexuality is oriented to self-gratification. And even "openness" and "vulnerability" can be forms of emotional exhibitionism that serve selfish needs rather than contribute to true intimacy.

Authentic intimacy must build on authentic, biblical *love*, where the focus is taken off *my* desire, *my* needs, *my* hurts and placed on the other person's desires, needs and hurts. The joy of genuine love is not receiving but giving, not being served but serving. It involves serving others purely for *their* sake.

MARRIAGE BUILDERS

♦ *What aspects of your relationship make you feel close to, or intimate with, your spouse?*
♦ *On your own, consider additional ways you might serve your spouse today.*

Additional Scripture Readings
Mark 10:43–45; Philippians 2:3–5

Go to page 1374 for your next devotional reading.

ample. Although they are so large and are
driven by strong winds, they are steered
by a very small rudder wherever the pilot
wants to go. [5]Likewise the tongue is a
small part of the body, but it makes great
boasts. Consider what a great forest is set
on fire by a small spark. [6]The tongue also
is a fire, a world of evil among the parts of
the body. It corrupts the whole person,
sets the whole course of his life on fire,
and is itself set on fire by hell.
[7]All kinds of animals, birds, reptiles and
creatures of the sea are being tamed and
have been tamed by man, [8]but no man
can tame the tongue. It is a restless evil,
full of deadly poison.
[9]With the tongue we praise our Lord
and Father, and with it we curse men, who
have been made in God's likeness. [10]Out
of the same mouth come praise and curs-
ing. My brothers, this should not be.
[11]Can both fresh water and salt[a] water
flow from the same spring? [12]My brothers,
can a fig tree bear olives, or a grapevine
bear figs? Neither can a salt spring pro-
duce fresh water.

Two Kinds of Wisdom

[13]Who is wise and understanding
among you? Let him show it by his good
life, by deeds done in the humility that
comes from wisdom. [14]But if you harbor
bitter envy and selfish ambition in your
hearts, do not boast about it or deny the
truth. [15]Such "wisdom" does not come
down from heaven but is earthly, unspiri-
tual, of the devil. [16]For where you have
envy and selfish ambition, there you find
disorder and every evil practice.
[17]But the wisdom that comes from
heaven is first of all pure; then peace-lov-
ing, considerate, submissive, full of mercy

[a] *11* Greek *bitter* (see also verse 14)

VERSE FOR THE DAY: James 4:8 | AUTHOR: Paul Tournier | PASSAGE FOR THE DAY: James 4:1–12

To Be Understood

It is impossible to overemphasize the need people have to be listened to, to be taken seriously, to be understood. No one can develop freely and find a full life without feeling understood by at least one person. Misunderstood, one loses his self-confidence; he loses his faith in life or even in God. He who would see himself clearly must open up to a confidant. This is why God says, "It is not good that man should be alone."

MARRIAGE BUILDERS

♦ *How is fully understanding each other harder than you may have thought before you were married?*
♦ *What satisfaction do you find in knowing that God knows and understands you completely?*

Additional Scripture Readings
Psalm 139:23; 1 Corinthians 13:12

Go to page 1375 for your next devotional reading.

and good fruit, impartial and sincere.
18Peacemakers who sow in peace raise a
harvest of righteousness.

Submit Yourselves to God

4 What causes fights and quarrels
among you? Don't they come from
your desires that battle within you? 2You
want something but don't get it. You kill
and covet, but you cannot have what you
want. You quarrel and fight. You do not
have, because you do not ask God. 3When
you ask, you do not receive, because you
ask with wrong motives, that you may
spend what you get on your pleasures.
4You adulterous people, don't you
know that friendship with the world is ha-
tred toward God? Anyone who chooses to
be a friend of the world becomes an ene-
my of God. 5Or do you think Scripture
says without reason that the spirit he
caused to live in us envies intensely?[a]
6But he gives us more grace. That is why
Scripture says:

[a]5 Or *that God jealously longs for the spirit that he made to live in us*; or *that the Spirit he caused to live in us longs jealously*

VERSE FOR THE DAY: James 5:16 | AUTHOR: Evelyn Christenson | PASSAGE FOR THE DAY: James 5:13–18

Marriage Cement

An important aspect of a married person's prayer life has to be praying with your spouse. Prayer is the cement that holds a marriage together. The hurts and misunderstandings that come into all marriages melt away in the presence of a holy God. When you stand before God, there is no room for pride or anger or resentful feelings. Rather, there is power in your marriage and in your lives as the two of you agree together in prayer.

Praying with my husband, Chris, is a humbling experience. We often kneel and hold hands. When we invite the Holy God into our marriage, into our home, into our bedroom where we pray, it is bound to draw us together.

Living a life of prayer is the power source of all Christians. It provides us with the resources to be the persons God would have us be.

MARRIAGE BUILDERS

♦ *In what ways have you found prayer to be the "cement" that holds your marriage together?*

♦ *If there is any area of conflict between the two of you right now, stop and take time to pray about it together.*

Additional Scripture Readings
Matthew 18:19–20; Ephesians 6:18;
1 Timothy 2:1–4

Go to page 1376 for your next devotional reading.

WEEKENDING

LAUGHTER

Shared laughter is essential glue for holding your marriage together when the insistent pressures of life start to dictate the atmosphere of your home. Discuss and choose some of the following suggestions for making room for laughter in your relationship.

1. Look for a weekly humor column in your paper, and read it out loud to each other.

2. When something makes you laugh when the two of you are apart, call your spouse and share the fun.

3. Discover the type of humor that makes your partner laugh, then find ways to crack him or her up.

4. Watch reruns of a favorite sitcom instead of watching the nightly news.

5. Cultivate a friendship with a couple who seem to have a lot of fun and laughter in their marriage.

— *The* Marriage Partnership *Staff*

REVIVE

Saturday: Psalm 100:1–5
Sunday: Philippians 4:4

Go to page 1379 for your next devotional reading.

"God opposes the proud
but gives grace to the humble."[a]

7Submit yourselves, then, to God. Resist
the devil, and he will flee from you.
8Come near to God and he will come near
to you. Wash your hands, you sinners,
and purify your hearts, you double-mind-
ed. 9Grieve, mourn and wail. Change your
laughter to mourning and your joy to
gloom. 10Humble yourselves before the
Lord, and he will lift you up.

11Brothers, do not slander one another.
Anyone who speaks against his brother or
judges him speaks against the law and
judges it. When you judge the law, you
are not keeping it, but sitting in judgment
on it. 12There is only one Lawgiver and
Judge, the one who is able to save and de-
stroy. But you—who are you to judge
your neighbor?

Boasting About Tomorrow

13Now listen, you who say, "Today or
tomorrow we will go to this or that city,
spend a year there, carry on business and
make money." 14Why, you do not even
know what will happen tomorrow. What
is your life? You are a mist that appears for
a little while and then vanishes. 15Instead,
you ought to say, "If it is the Lord's will,
we will live and do this or that." 16As it is,
you boast and brag. All such boasting is
evil. 17Anyone, then, who knows the good
he ought to do and doesn't do it, sins.

Warning to Rich Oppressors

5 Now listen, you rich people, weep and
wail because of the misery that is
coming upon you. 2Your wealth has rot-
ted, and moths have eaten your clothes.
3Your gold and silver are corroded. Their
corrosion will testify against you and eat
your flesh like fire. You have hoarded
wealth in the last days. 4Look! The wages
you failed to pay the workmen who
mowed your fields are crying out against
you. The cries of the harvesters have
reached the ears of the Lord Almighty.
5You have lived on earth in luxury and
self-indulgence. You have fattened your-
selves in the day of slaughter.[b] 6You have
condemned and murdered innocent men,
who were not opposing you.

Patience in Suffering

7Be patient, then, brothers, until the
Lord's coming. See how the farmer waits
for the land to yield its valuable crop and
how patient he is for the autumn and
spring rains. 8You too, be patient and
stand firm, because the Lord's coming is
near. 9Don't grumble against each other,
brothers, or you will be judged. The Judge
is standing at the door!

10Brothers, as an example of patience in
the face of suffering, take the prophets
who spoke in the name of the Lord. 11As
you know, we consider blessed those who
have persevered. You have heard of Job's
perseverance and have seen what the
Lord finally brought about. The Lord is
full of compassion and mercy.

12Above all, my brothers, do not
swear—not by heaven or by earth or by
anything else. Let your "Yes" be yes, and
your "No," no, or you will be condemned.

The Prayer of Faith

13Is any one of you in trouble? He
should pray. Is anyone happy? Let him
sing songs of praise. 14Is any one of you
sick? He should call the elders of the
church to pray over him and anoint him
with oil in the name of the Lord. 15And the
prayer offered in faith will make the sick
person well; the Lord will raise him up.
If he has sinned, he will be forgiven.
16Therefore confess your sins to each oth-
er and pray for each other so that you may
be healed. The prayer of a righteous man
is powerful and effective.

17Elijah was a man just like us. He
prayed earnestly that it would not rain,
and it did not rain on the land for three
and a half years. 18Again he prayed, and
the heavens gave rain, and the earth pro-
duced its crops.

19My brothers, if one of you should
wander from the truth and someone
should bring him back, 20remember this:
Whoever turns a sinner from the error of
his way will save him from death and cov-
er over a multitude of sins.

[a]6 Prov. 3:34 [b]5 Or *yourselves as in a day of feasting*

PETER writes this letter to a group of Christians suffering for their faith, reminding them of how much Jesus suffered. He inspires them with hope for the future and shows them how to grow in their faith. As you read this book, decide to do your best to live a holy life as you look forward to the return of Jesus and to the reward he promises to give his followers.

1 PETER

1 Peter, an apostle of Jesus Christ,

To God's elect, strangers in the world, scattered throughout Pontus, Galatia, Cappadocia, Asia and Bithynia, [2]who have been chosen according to the foreknowledge of God the Father, through the sanctifying work of the Spirit, for obedience to Jesus Christ and sprinkling by his blood:

Grace and peace be yours in abundance.

Praise to God for a Living Hope

[3]Praise be to the God and Father of our Lord Jesus Christ! In his great mercy he has given us new birth into a living hope through the resurrection of Jesus Christ from the dead, [4]and into an inheritance that can never perish, spoil or fade—kept in heaven for you, [5]who through faith are shielded by God's power until the coming of the salvation that is ready to be revealed in the last time. [6]In this you greatly rejoice, though now for a little while you may have had to suffer grief in all kinds of trials. [7]These have come so that your faith—of greater worth than gold, which perishes even though refined by fire—may be proved genuine and may result in praise, glory and honor when Jesus Christ is revealed. [8]Though you have not seen him, you love him; and even though you do not see him now, you believe in him and are filled with an inexpressible and glorious joy, [9]for you are receiving the goal of your faith, the salvation of your souls.

[10]Concerning this salvation, the prophets, who spoke of the grace that was to come to you, searched intently and with the greatest care, [11]trying to find out the time and circumstances to which the Spir-

VERSE FOR THE DAY: 1 Peter 1:7

AUTHOR: Paula Corn Rinehart

PASSAGE FOR THE DAY: 1 Peter 1:3–9

Differences Strengthen Us

Somewhere between the end of our honeymoon and the birth of our first child, my husband, Stacy, and I awoke to a disturbing revelation: We had each married our opposite. How would we reconcile Stacy's punctuality and love of order with my affinity for creative confusion? Or the fact that people energized me and often exhausted him?

If, through the crucifixion, God could reconcile humanity to himself, then he can perform the amazing task of bringing a man and a woman into a harmonious union. That process, in our lives, has been characterized by a slow but radical evolution of thoughts—and not a little pain and discomfort. After much trial and error though, our individual differences have become more the glue that binds us and less the wedge that pushes us apart.

Mike Mason, in his book *The Mystery of Marriage*, uses the word "otherness" to describe the ways in which spouses are different. He observes, "Our natural tendency is to treat people as if they were not *others* at all, but merely aspects of ourselves. We do not experience them as the overwhelming, comprehensive realities which we feel ourselves to be. Compared with us, they are not quite real."

We are always growing toward the understanding that the person we married does not innately think and respond as we would. He or she is a different person, a mystery well worth the time it takes to unravel.

MARRIAGE BUILDERS

♦ *What are three ways in which your spouse thinks and responds differently than you do?*

♦ *How do you deal with each of these differences in order to live harmoniously together?*

Additional Scripture Readings
Isaiah 55:9–11; Romans 15:7

Go to page 1381 for your next devotional reading.

it of Christ in them was pointing when he predicted the sufferings of Christ and the glories that would follow. 12It was revealed to them that they were not serving themselves but you, when they spoke of the things that have now been told you by those who have preached the gospel to you by the Holy Spirit sent from heaven. Even angels long to look into these things.

Be Holy

13Therefore, prepare your minds for action; be self-controlled; set your hope fully on the grace to be given you when Jesus Christ is revealed. 14As obedient children, do not conform to the evil desires you had when you lived in ignorance. 15But just as he who called you is holy, so be holy in all you do; 16for it is written: "Be holy, because I am holy."[a]

17Since you call on a Father who judges each man's work impartially, live your lives as strangers here in reverent fear. 18For you know that it was not with perishable things such as silver or gold that you were redeemed from the empty way of life handed down to you from your forefathers, 19but with the precious blood of Christ, a lamb without blemish or defect. 20He was chosen before the creation of the world, but was revealed in these last times for your sake. 21Through him you believe in God, who raised him from the dead and glorified him, and so your faith and hope are in God.

22Now that you have purified yourselves by obeying the truth so that you have sincere love for your brothers, love one another deeply, from the heart.[b] 23For you have been born again, not of perishable seed, but of imperishable, through the living and enduring word of God. 24For,

"All men are like grass,
and all their glory is like the flowers
of the field;
the grass withers and the flowers fall,
25 but the word of the Lord stands
forever."[c]

And this is the word that was preached to you.

2 Therefore, rid yourselves of all malice and all deceit, hypocrisy, envy, and slander of every kind. 2Like newborn babies, crave pure spiritual milk, so that by it you may grow up in your salvation, 3now that you have tasted that the Lord is good.

The Living Stone and a Chosen People

4As you come to him, the living Stone—rejected by men but chosen by God and precious to him— 5you also, like living stones, are being built into a spiritual house to be a holy priesthood, offering spiritual sacrifices acceptable to God through Jesus Christ. 6For in Scripture it says:

"See, I lay a stone in Zion,
a chosen and precious cornerstone,
and the one who trusts in him
will never be put to shame."[d]

7Now to you who believe, this stone is precious. But to those who do not believe,

"The stone the builders rejected
has become the capstone,[e]"[f]

8and,

"A stone that causes men to stumble
and a rock that makes them fall."[g]

They stumble because they disobey the message—which is also what they were destined for.

9But you are a chosen people, a royal priesthood, a holy nation, a people belonging to God, that you may declare the praises of him who called you out of darkness into his wonderful light. 10Once you were not a people, but now you are the people of God; once you had not received mercy, but now you have received mercy.

11Dear friends, I urge you, as aliens and strangers in the world, to abstain from sinful desires, which war against your soul. 12Live such good lives among the pagans that, though they accuse you of doing wrong, they may see your good deeds and glorify God on the day he visits us.

Submission to Rulers and Masters

13Submit yourselves for the Lord's sake to every authority instituted among men: whether to the king, as the supreme authority, 14or to governors, who are sent by him to punish those who do wrong and to commend those who do right. 15For it is God's will that by doing good you should silence the ignorant talk of foolish men.

[a]16 Lev. 11:44,45; 19:2; 20:7 [b]22 Some early manuscripts *from a pure heart* [c]25 Isaiah 40:6-8
[d]6 Isaiah 28:16 [e]7 Or *cornerstone* [f]7 Psalm 118:22 [g]8 Isaiah 8:14

16Live as free men, but do not use your
freedom as a cover-up for evil; live as ser-
vants of God. 17Show proper respect to ev-
eryone: Love the brotherhood of believ-
ers, fear God, honor the king.

18Slaves, submit yourselves to your
masters with all respect, not only to those
who are good and considerate, but also to
those who are harsh. 19For it is commend-
able if a man bears up under the pain of
unjust suffering because he is conscious
of God. 20But how is it to your credit if you
receive a beating for doing wrong and en-
dure it? But if you suffer for doing good
and you endure it, this is commendable
before God. 21To this you were called, be-
cause Christ suffered for you, leaving you
an example, that you should follow in his
steps.

22"He committed no sin,
and no deceit was found in his
mouth."[a]

23When they hurled their insults at him,
he did not retaliate; when he suffered, he
made no threats. Instead, he entrusted
himself to him who judges justly. 24He
himself bore our sins in his body on the
tree, so that we might die to sins and live
for righteousness; by his wounds you
have been healed. 25For you were like
sheep going astray, but now you have re-
turned to the Shepherd and Overseer of
your souls.

Wives and Husbands

3 Wives, in the same way be submissive
to your husbands so that, if any of
them do not believe the word, they may
be won over without words by the behav-
ior of their wives, 2when they see the puri-
ty and reverence of your lives. 3Your

[a]22 Isaiah 53:9

TUESDAY

VERSE FOR THE DAY: 1 Peter 2:2

AUTHOR: Jill and Stuart Briscoe

PASSAGE FOR THE DAY: 1 Peter 2:1–10

Growing Up Together

Being married can "grow you up" as a person. You don't have the luxury of being self-centered when you constantly have your spouse's personality and needs to take into account.

We were both Christians when we married, but marriage has changed us. In fact, marriage will always have a profound impact on the development of both spouses' spirituality. The great evidence of spirituality is love. Well, what better arena for practicing love than in a marriage?

MARRIAGE BUILDERS

♦ *In what ways do you think you personally have "grown up" since you were married?*

♦ *How is your love for one another evidence of your spiritual life?*

Additional Scripture Readings
Ephesians 4:14–16; Hebrews 5:12–14

Go to page 1382 for your next devotional reading.

VERSE FOR THE DAY: 1 Peter 3:1

AUTHOR: Evelyn Christenson

PASSAGE FOR THE DAY: 1 Peter 3:1–7

God's Changes

When I have met God in the morning before my husband wakes up, Chris faces a different person because I have been in the presence of the God of the universe. Pressures and frustrations are replaced with praise, adoration and thankfulness. It's bound to affect my character.

I have also discovered that my prayer life can be a support and inspiration to my husband. 1 Peter 3:1–2 speaks of husbands being "won over without words" when they observe the "purity and reverence" of their wives.

Most people would rather change their spouses with words. However, when we learn to pray, we don't have to preach; we don't have to say a word. We have switched the emphasis from "Lord, change him," to "Lord, change me." As God began to change me through prayer, my husband saw a person who truly desired holiness and who was growing more Christlike.

For a long time I prayed, "Lord, make me the wife you want me to be." Then one day God said to me, "You've got the wrong emphasis. It's not 'Make me the *wife* you want me to be,' but 'Make me the wife *you* want me to be.' " The first concern for a married person is not what kind of mate his or her spouse desires. The primary issue is, rather, "Lord, what do *you* want me to be?" It calls for close communion with God to know the difference.

MARRIAGE BUILDERS

♦ *Can you pinpoint a recent time when having spent time with God improved your marriage relationship? What effect did it have?*
♦ *How can you shift your perspective from trying to change your mate to working on areas where you personally need to change?*

Additional Scripture Readings
John 13:34–35; 1 Thessalonians 4:11–12; 1 Peter 2:12

Go to page 1384 for your next devotional reading.

beauty should not come from outward
adornment, such as braided hair and the
wearing of gold jewelry and fine clothes.
4Instead, it should be that of your inner
self, the unfading beauty of a gentle and
quiet spirit, which is of great worth in
God's sight. 5For this is the way the holy
women of the past who put their hope in
God used to make themselves beautiful.
They were submissive to their own hus-
bands, 6like Sarah, who obeyed Abraham
and called him her master. You are her
daughters if you do what is right and do
not give way to fear.

7Husbands, in the same way be consid-
erate as you live with your wives, and
treat them with respect as the weaker
partner and as heirs with you of the gra-
cious gift of life, so that nothing will hin-
der your prayers.

Suffering for Doing Good

8Finally, all of you, live in harmony
with one another; be sympathetic, love as
brothers, be compassionate and humble.
9Do not repay evil with evil or insult with
insult, but with blessing, because to this
you were called so that you may inherit a
blessing. 10For,

"Whoever would love life
and see good days
must keep his tongue from evil
and his lips from deceitful speech.
11He must turn from evil and do good;
he must seek peace and pursue it.
12For the eyes of the Lord are on the
righteous
and his ears are attentive to their
prayer,
but the face of the Lord is against
those who do evil."[a]

13Who is going to harm you if you are
eager to do good? 14But even if you should
suffer for what is right, you are blessed.
"Do not fear what they fear[b]; do not be
frightened."[c] 15But in your hearts set
apart Christ as Lord. Always be prepared
to give an answer to everyone who asks
you to give the reason for the hope that
you have. But do this with gentleness and
respect, 16keeping a clear conscience, so
that those who speak maliciously against
your good behavior in Christ may be
ashamed of their slander. 17It is better, if
it is God's will, to suffer for doing good
than for doing evil. 18For Christ died for
sins once for all, the righteous for the un-
righteous, to bring you to God. He was put
to death in the body but made alive by the
Spirit, 19through whom[d] also he went
and preached to the spirits in prison
20who disobeyed long ago when God wait-
ed patiently in the days of Noah while the
ark was being built. In it only a few peo-
ple, eight in all, were saved through water,
21and this water symbolizes baptism that
now saves you also—not the removal of
dirt from the body but the pledge[e] of a
good conscience toward God. It saves you
by the resurrection of Jesus Christ, 22who
has gone into heaven and is at God's right
hand—with angels, authorities and pow-
ers in submission to him.

Living for God

4 Therefore, since Christ suffered in his
body, arm yourselves also with the
same attitude, because he who has suf-
fered in his body is done with sin. 2As a
result, he does not live the rest of his
earthly life for evil human desires, but
rather for the will of God. 3For you have
spent enough time in the past doing what
pagans choose to do—living in debauch-
ery, lust, drunkenness, orgies, carousing
and detestable idolatry. 4They think it
strange that you do not plunge with them
into the same flood of dissipation, and
they heap abuse on you. 5But they will
have to give account to him who is ready
to judge the living and the dead. 6For this
is the reason the gospel was preached
even to those who are now dead, so that
they might be judged according to men in
regard to the body, but live according to
God in regard to the spirit.

7The end of all things is near. Therefore
be clear minded and self-controlled so
that you can pray. 8Above all, love each
other deeply, because love covers over a
multitude of sins. 9Offer hospitality to one
another without grumbling. 10Each one
should use whatever gift he has received
to serve others, faithfully administering
God's grace in its various forms. 11If any-
one speaks, he should do it as one speak-
ing the very words of God. If anyone
serves, he should do it with the strength
God provides, so that in all things God
may be praised through Jesus Christ. To

[a] *12* Psalm 34:12-16 [b] *14* Or *not fear their threats* [c] *14* Isaiah 8:12 [d] *18,19* Or *alive in the spirit, 19through which* [e] *21* Or *response*

VERSE FOR THE DAY: 1 Peter 4:8

AUTHOR: Nancy Kennedy

PASSAGE FOR THE DAY: 1 Peter 4:7–11

The Romantically Impaired

I used to think expressions of love came only in velvet jeweler's boxes, rosy bouquets or boxes of Godiva chocolate. Now I'm married, and I know better.

One anniversary, I hinted for weeks about a pair of silver hoop earrings I wanted. I left the catalogue open on Barry's desk with the earrings I wanted circled in red.

Finally, the big day arrived. No silver hoops. No chocolates. No flowers. But Barry did buy me new tires. He spent the next hour washing and waxing my car. As he worked, I fumed and built my defense, in case I might be charged with murder.

But as I watched Barry scrub the dirt off my car, I remembered our first date, when he searched all over northern Maine for size-seven ice skates because he'd promised to take me skating. Then I thought about the time I hurt my back and he cleaned me up and carried me in his arms to the doctor. He also lets me drink the last Diet Pepsi, and shivers in the cold after giving me his jacket to wear.

Barry speaks his own language when it comes to love. Flowers die, and chocolate turns to fat. Barry's unconventional gifts express his love by showing concern for my safety. And even if I haven't used the snake-bite kit and road flares yet, the jumper cables have come in handy.

Before my husband finished washing my car, I grabbed a rag and helped polish the back bumper. It wasn't exactly a Hallmark commercial, but it was romantic enough—even for me.

MARRIAGE BUILDERS

- *What are some ways your spouse shows that he or she loves you?*
- *How can you appreciate your spouse's "romance language," even when it is different from your own?*

Additional Scripture Readings
Hebrews 10:24; 1 Timothy 6:18–19

Go to page 1385 for your next devotional reading.

him be the glory and the power for ever
and ever. Amen.

Suffering for Being a Christian

12Dear friends, do not be surprised at
the painful trial you are suffering, as
though something strange were happen-
ing to you. 13But rejoice that you partici-
pate in the sufferings of Christ, so that you
may be overjoyed when his glory is re-
vealed. 14If you are insulted because of the
name of Christ, you are blessed, for the
Spirit of glory and of God rests on you. 15If
you suffer, it should not be as a murderer
or thief or any other kind of criminal, or
even as a meddler. 16However, if you suf-
fer as a Christian, do not be ashamed, but
praise God that you bear that name. 17For
it is time for judgment to begin with the
family of God; and if it begins with us,
what will the outcome be for those who
do not obey the gospel of God? 18And,

FRIDAY

VERSE FOR THE DAY: 1 Peter 5:7

AUTHOR: Dave Carder

PASSAGE FOR THE DAY: 1 Peter 5:1–14

Cast Your Cares on Him

When problems crop up, couples with an idealistic view of what constitutes a "good" marriage are quick to think, "We can never be that good!" The chasm between where they are and where they think they should be seems hopelessly uncrossable.

Here's the good news: The great gulf is an illusion. A perfect marriage is impossible, and a great marriage is much easier than you think. Couples can begin getting back on track by cultivating an intimate relationship with God, depending on him for strength, comfort and courage. But spouses in habitual conflict tend to abandon any spiritual life. If this describes your marriage, get started again by each writing down three personal prayer requests, then swapping lists. Pray for each other three times a day.

After a few weeks, try a month of praying aloud in front of each other daily, thanking God for one specific character quality or blessing you see in each other.

Eventually, try asking your spouse, "What would you like me to pray for about myself?" which is an invitation for constructive criticism. But after thirty days of hearing how and why your spouse loves you, you'll know he or she is on your side.

MARRIAGE BUILDERS

- *Does conflict ever stop you from praying for your spouse? How could you get started again?*
- *Create a list of thirty of your spouse's positive character qualities, then use it in prayers of thanksgiving.*

Additional Scripture Readings
Psalm 37:3–7; Isaiah 58:11–14

Go to page 1386 for your next devotional reading.

WEEKENDING

EXPECTATIONS

Take a look at these seven areas of marital expectations. Separately, rank them in order of importance to you. Then discuss your different expectations.

1. Security: the knowledge of permanence in the relationship and of financial and material well-being.

2. Companionship: having a soul partner to share the joys and sorrows of life; also, having common areas of interest and activity that you enjoy together.

3. Sex: the oneness that comes through physical intimacy; the initiation and enjoyment of a growing physical relationship.

4. Understanding and tenderness: experiencing regularly a touch, a kiss, a wink across the room that says, "I love you, I care, I'm thinking of you."

5. Encouragement: verbal support and appreciation of your work and your efforts at home.

6. Intellectual closeness: discussing and growing together in common areas of intellectual thought.

7. Mutual activity: doing things together, such as political involvement, sports, church work, hobbies.

— *David and Claudia Arp*

REVIVE

Saturday: Ecclesiastes 4:9–12
Sunday: Galatians 6:2

Go to page 1389 for your next devotional reading.

"If it is hard for the righteous to be saved,
what will become of the ungodly and the sinner?"[a]

19So then, those who suffer according to God's will should commit themselves to their faithful Creator and continue to do good.

To Elders and Young Men

5 To the elders among you, I appeal as a fellow elder, a witness of Christ's sufferings and one who also will share in the glory to be revealed: 2Be shepherds of God's flock that is under your care, serving as overseers—not because you must, but because you are willing, as God wants you to be; not greedy for money, but eager to serve; 3not lording it over those entrusted to you, but being examples to the flock. 4And when the Chief Shepherd appears, you will receive the crown of glory that will never fade away.

5Young men, in the same way be submissive to those who are older. All of you, clothe yourselves with humility toward one another, because,

"God opposes the proud
but gives grace to the humble."[b]

6Humble yourselves, therefore, under God's mighty hand, that he may lift you up in due time. 7Cast all your anxiety on him because he cares for you.

8Be self-controlled and alert. Your enemy the devil prowls around like a roaring lion looking for someone to devour. 9Resist him, standing firm in the faith, because you know that your brothers throughout the world are undergoing the same kind of sufferings.

10And the God of all grace, who called you to his eternal glory in Christ, after you have suffered a little while, will himself restore you and make you strong, firm and steadfast. 11To him be the power for ever and ever. Amen.

Final Greetings

12With the help of Silas,[c] whom I regard as a faithful brother, I have written to you briefly, encouraging you and testifying that this is the true grace of God. Stand fast in it.

13She who is in Babylon, chosen together with you, sends you her greetings, and so does my son Mark. 14Greet one another with a kiss of love.

Peace to all of you who are in Christ.

[a] 18 Prov. 11:31 [b] 5 Prov. 3:34 [c] 12 Greek *Silvanus*, a variant of *Silas*

PETER writes a second letter because false teachers are troubling the church and disturbing the faith of some by their heresy, immorality and greed. He wants Christians to grow in the knowledge of the truth of God's Word. As you read this book, remember that God will eventually win the battle against false teaching, and promise the Lord that you will study to increase your knowledge of the Bible.

2 PETER

1 Simon Peter, a servant and apostle of Jesus Christ,

To those who through the righteousness of our God and Savior Jesus Christ have received a faith as precious as ours:

2 Grace and peace be yours in abundance through the knowledge of God and of Jesus our Lord.

Making One's Calling and Election Sure

3 His divine power has given us everything we need for life and godliness through our knowledge of him who called us by his own glory and goodness. 4 Through these he has given us his very great and precious promises, so that through them you may participate in the divine nature and escape the corruption in the world caused by evil desires.

5 For this very reason, make every effort to add to your faith goodness; and to goodness, knowledge; 6 and to knowledge, self-control; and to self-control, perseverance; and to perseverance, godliness; 7 and to godliness, brotherly kindness; and to brotherly kindness, love. 8 For if you possess these qualities in increasing measure, they will keep you from being ineffective and unproductive in your knowledge of our Lord Jesus Christ. 9 But if anyone does not have them, he is nearsighted and blind, and has forgotten that he has been cleansed from his past sins.

10 Therefore, my brothers, be all the

more eager to make your calling and election sure. For if you do these things, you will never fall, [11]and you will receive a rich welcome into the eternal kingdom of our Lord and Savior Jesus Christ.

Prophecy of Scripture

[12]So I will always remind you of these things, even though you know them and are firmly established in the truth you now have. [13]I think it is right to refresh your memory as long as I live in the tent of this body, [14]because I know that I will soon put it aside, as our Lord Jesus Christ has made clear to me. [15]And I will make every effort to see that after my departure you will always be able to remember these things.

MONDAY

VERSE FOR THE DAY: 2 Peter 1:5–7

AUTHOR: Lyn Cryderman

PASSAGE FOR THE DAY: 2 Peter 1:3–11

Common Decency

I'm a pretty good husband. Not great, but good. I come straight home from work. Help out around the house. Remember birthdays and anniversaries. In fact, my wife has a drawerful of romantic cards and notes that profess my undying love and affection.

But at the same time, I occasionally joke about burned casseroles; or play the role of the poor sap who comes home from a hard day at work and still has to clean the toilet. This is all in the spirit of good clean fun, of course. The problem is that this kind of humor can develop into an attitude. It makes orneriness a virtue and before you know it, your marriage can become a caricature.

One of my favorite novelists made one of his characters say, "What the world really needs is a little less love and a lot more common decency." Think about it. Think of all the insensitive behaviors toward our spouses we feel are covered by "love": forgetting to use words like "please" and "thank you"; coming home late from work without calling first; ignoring basic needs like encouragement, privacy, intimacy, conversation. Then think what might happen to your relationship if you began treating these needs like your marriage depended on them.

What would happen if you worked a little harder on common decency than on love?

MARRIAGE BUILDERS

♦ *Privately think back over your own interaction with your spouse over the last 24 hours. In what ways could you have offered more courtesy or encouragement?*

Additional Scripture Readings
Colossians 3:12–17; Philippians 2:4; Galatians 5:22–23

Go to page 1391 for your next devotional reading.

16We did not follow cleverly invented
stories when we told you about the power
and coming of our Lord Jesus Christ, but
we were eyewitnesses of his majesty.
17For he received honor and glory from
God the Father when the voice came to
him from the Majestic Glory, saying, "This
is my Son, whom I love; with him I am
well pleased."[a] 18We ourselves heard this
voice that came from heaven when we
were with him on the sacred mountain.

19And we have the word of the prophets
made more certain, and you will do well
to pay attention to it, as to a light shining
in a dark place, until the day dawns and
the morning star rises in your hearts.
20Above all, you must understand that no
prophecy of Scripture came about by the
prophet's own interpretation. 21For
prophecy never had its origin in the will of
man, but men spoke from God as they
were carried along by the Holy Spirit.

False Teachers and Their Destruction

2 But there were also false prophets
among the people, just as there will be
false teachers among you. They will se-
cretly introduce destructive heresies, even
denying the sovereign Lord who bought
them—bringing swift destruction on
themselves. 2Many will follow their
shameful ways and will bring the way of
truth into disrepute. 3In their greed these
teachers will exploit you with stories they
have made up. Their condemnation has
long been hanging over them, and their
destruction has not been sleeping.

4For if God did not spare angels when
they sinned, but sent them to hell,[b] put-
ting them into gloomy dungeons[c] to be
held for judgment; 5if he did not spare the
ancient world when he brought the flood
on its ungodly people, but protected
Noah, a preacher of righteousness, and
seven others; 6if he condemned the cities
of Sodom and Gomorrah by burning them
to ashes, and made them an example of
what is going to happen to the ungodly;
7and if he rescued Lot, a righteous man,
who was distressed by the filthy lives of
lawless men 8(for that righteous man, liv-
ing among them day after day, was tor-
mented in his righteous soul by the law-
less deeds he saw and heard)— 9if this is
so, then the Lord knows how to rescue
godly men from trials and to hold the un-
righteous for the day of judgment, while
continuing their punishment.[d] 10This is
especially true of those who follow the
corrupt desire of the sinful nature[e] and
despise authority.

Bold and arrogant, these men are not
afraid to slander celestial beings; 11yet
even angels, although they are stronger
and more powerful, do not bring slander-
ous accusations against such beings in the
presence of the Lord. 12But these men
blaspheme in matters they do not under-
stand. They are like brute beasts, crea-
tures of instinct, born only to be caught
and destroyed, and like beasts they too
will perish.

13They will be paid back with harm for
the harm they have done. Their idea of
pleasure is to carouse in broad daylight.
They are blots and blemishes, reveling in
their pleasures while they feast with
you.[f] 14With eyes full of adultery, they
never stop sinning; they seduce the unsta-
ble; they are experts in greed—an ac-
cursed brood! 15They have left the straight
way and wandered off to follow the way of
Balaam son of Beor, who loved the wages
of wickedness. 16But he was rebuked for
his wrongdoing by a donkey—a beast
without speech—who spoke with a man's
voice and restrained the prophet's mad-
ness.

17These men are springs without water
and mists driven by a storm. Blackest
darkness is reserved for them. 18For they
mouth empty, boastful words and, by ap-
pealing to the lustful desires of sinful hu-
man nature, they entice people who are
just escaping from those who live in error.
19They promise them freedom, while they
themselves are slaves of depravity—for a
man is a slave to whatever has mastered
him. 20If they have escaped the corruption
of the world by knowing our Lord and
Savior Jesus Christ and are again entan-
gled in it and overcome, they are worse off
at the end than they were at the begin-
ning. 21It would have been better for them
not to have known the way of righteous-
ness, than to have known it and then to
turn their backs on the sacred command
that was passed on to them. 22Of them the
proverbs are true: "A dog returns to its

[a] 17 Matt. 17:5; Mark 9:7; Luke 9:35 [b] 4 Greek *Tartarus* [c] 4 Some manuscripts *into chains of darkness* [d] 9 Or *unrighteous for punishment until the day of judgment* [e] 10 Or *the flesh* [f] 13 Some manuscripts *in their love feasts*

vomit,"[a] and, "A sow that is washed goes back to her wallowing in the mud."

The Day of the Lord

3 Dear friends, this is now my second letter to you. I have written both of them as reminders to stimulate you to wholesome thinking. [2]I want you to recall the words spoken in the past by the holy prophets and the command given by our Lord and Savior through your apostles.

[3]First of all, you must understand that in the last days scoffers will come, scoffing and following their own evil desires. [4]They will say, "Where is this 'coming' he promised? Ever since our fathers died, everything goes on as it has since the beginning of creation." [5]But they deliberately forget that long ago by God's word the heavens existed and the earth was formed out of water and by water. [6]By these waters also the world of that time was deluged and destroyed. [7]By the same word the present heavens and earth are re-

[a]22 Prov. 26:11

VERSE FOR THE DAY: 2 Peter 3:9

AUTHOR: Dr. Frances White

PASSAGE FOR THE DAY: 2 Peter 3:8–16

Learning to Wait

How willing are we to be still and patiently wait rather than insist on fast results? Are we secure enough *not* to feel we have to see the results we desire?

Leaving the choice for results with the individual frees us from the awesome task of being omniscient and deciding an individual's fate for him or her. Most people know what they might best do to resolve an issue once they're able to identify the feelings that are hindering them. One of the most valuable contributions we can make is to learn to *listen* to them. Reflecting back in a different but accurate form what they have said enables them to trust us and therefore express deeper feelings—some of which they may not have been fully aware of. Their emotions will gradually unravel and start to make sense.

However, if we feel the need to assume the ultimate responsibility for others, it increases our stress and shows a lack of respect for others as adults capable of making their own decisions.

MARRIAGE BUILDERS

♦ *How patient are you when you have to wait for your spouse to learn something?*

♦ *In what ways can you pattern your marriage relationship after God's loving acceptance?*

Additional Scripture Readings
Matthew 19:16–30; Ephesians 4:1–6; Proverbs 19:8, 11

Go to page 1395 for your next devotional reading.

served for fire, being kept for the day of judgment and destruction of ungodly men.

[8]But do not forget this one thing, dear friends: With the Lord a day is like a thousand years, and a thousand years are like a day. [9]The Lord is not slow in keeping his promise, as some understand slowness. He is patient with you, not wanting anyone to perish, but everyone to come to repentance.

[10]But the day of the Lord will come like a thief. The heavens will disappear with a roar; the elements will be destroyed by fire, and the earth and everything in it will be laid bare.[a]

[11]Since everything will be destroyed in this way, what kind of people ought you to be? You ought to live holy and godly lives [12]as you look forward to the day of God and speed its coming.[b] That day will bring about the destruction of the heavens by fire, and the elements will melt in the heat. [13]But in keeping with his promise we are looking forward to a new heaven and a new earth, the home of righteousness.

[14]So then, dear friends, since you are looking forward to this, make every effort to be found spotless, blameless and at peace with him. [15]Bear in mind that our Lord's patience means salvation, just as our dear brother Paul also wrote you with the wisdom that God gave him. [16]He writes the same way in all his letters, speaking in them of these matters. His letters contain some things that are hard to understand, which ignorant and unstable people distort, as they do the other Scriptures, to their own destruction.

[17]Therefore, dear friends, since you already know this, be on your guard so that you may not be carried away by the error of lawless men and fall from your secure position. [18]But grow in the grace and knowledge of our Lord and Savior Jesus Christ. To him be glory both now and forever! Amen.

[a]10 Some manuscripts *be burned up* [b]12 Or *as you wait eagerly for the day of God to come*

JOHN writes this first letter to emphasize some of the same themes as his Gospel (such as "walking in the light," "knowing the truth," and "loving one another"). He does so because antichrists are promoting false views of the Son of God. As you read this book, realize how much God wants you to fight sin, to love others and to believe in the true Jesus for eternal life.

1 JOHN

The Word of Life

1 That which was from the beginning,
which we have heard, which we have
seen with our eyes, which we have looked
at and our hands have touched—this
we proclaim concerning the Word of
life. 2The life appeared; we have seen it
and testify to it, and we proclaim to
you the eternal life, which was with the
Father and has appeared to us. 3We
proclaim to you what we have seen and
heard, so that you also may have fellow-
ship with us. And our fellowship is with
the Father and with his Son, Jesus
Christ. 4We write this to make our[a] joy
complete.

Walking in the Light

5This is the message we have heard
from him and declare to you: God is light;
in him there is no darkness at all. 6If we
claim to have fellowship with him yet
walk in the darkness, we lie and do not
live by the truth. 7But if we walk in the
light, as he is in the light, we have fellow-
ship with one another, and the blood of
Jesus, his Son, purifies us from all[b] sin.
8If we claim to be without sin, we de-
ceive ourselves and the truth is not in us.
9If we confess our sins, he is faithful and
just and will forgive us our sins and purify
us from all unrighteousness. 10If we claim
we have not sinned, we make him out to

[a]4 Some manuscripts *your* [b]7 Or *every*

be a liar and his word has no place in our lives.

2 My dear children, I write this to you so that you will not sin. But if anybody does sin, we have one who speaks to the Father in our defense—Jesus Christ, the Righteous One. [2]He is the atoning sacrifice for our sins, and not only for ours but also for[a] the sins of the whole world.

[3]We know that we have come to know him if we obey his commands. [4]The man who says, "I know him," but does not do what he commands is a liar, and the truth is not in him. [5]But if anyone obeys his word, God's love[b] is truly made complete in him. This is how we know we are in him: [6]Whoever claims to live in him must walk as Jesus did.

[7]Dear friends, I am not writing you a new command but an old one, which you have had since the beginning. This old command is the message you have heard. [8]Yet I am writing you a new command; its truth is seen in him and you, because the darkness is passing and the true light is already shining.

[9]Anyone who claims to be in the light but hates his brother is still in the darkness. [10]Whoever loves his brother lives in the light, and there is nothing in him[c] to make him stumble. [11]But whoever hates his brother is in the darkness and walks around in the darkness; he does not know where he is going, because the darkness has blinded him.

[12]I write to you, dear children,
because your sins have been
forgiven on account of his
name.
[13]I write to you, fathers,
because you have known him who
is from the beginning.
I write to you, young men,
because you have overcome the evil
one.
I write to you, dear children,
because you have known the
Father.
[14]I write to you, fathers,
because you have known him who
is from the beginning.
I write to you, young men,
because you are strong,
and the word of God lives in you,
and you have overcome the evil
one.

Do Not Love the World

[15]Do not love the world or anything in the world. If anyone loves the world, the love of the Father is not in him. [16]For everything in the world—the cravings of sinful man, the lust of his eyes and the boasting of what he has and does—comes not from the Father but from the world. [17]The world and its desires pass away, but the man who does the will of God lives forever.

Warning Against Antichrists

[18]Dear children, this is the last hour; and as you have heard that the antichrist is coming, even now many antichrists have come. This is how we know it is the last hour. [19]They went out from us, but they did not really belong to us. For if they had belonged to us, they would have remained with us; but their going showed that none of them belonged to us.

[20]But you have an anointing from the Holy One, and all of you know the truth.[d] [21]I do not write to you because you do not know the truth, but because you do know it and because no lie comes from the truth. [22]Who is the liar? It is the man who denies that Jesus is the Christ. Such a man is the antichrist—he denies the Father and the Son. [23]No one who denies the Son has the Father; whoever acknowledges the Son has the Father also.

[24]See that what you have heard from the beginning remains in you. If it does, you also will remain in the Son and in the Father. [25]And this is what he promised us—even eternal life.

[26]I am writing these things to you about those who are trying to lead you astray. [27]As for you, the anointing you received from him remains in you, and you do not need anyone to teach you. But as his anointing teaches you about all things and as that anointing is real, not counterfeit—just as it has taught you, remain in him.

Children of God

[28]And now, dear children, continue in him, so that when he appears we may be confident and unashamed before him at his coming.

[29]If you know that he is righteous, you

[a]2 Or *He is the one who turns aside God's wrath, taking away our sins, and not only ours but also*
[b]5 Or *word, love for God* [c]10 Or *it* [d]20 Some manuscripts *and you know all things*

know that everyone who does what is
right has been born of him.
3 How great is the love the Father has
lavished on us, that we should be
called children of God! And that is what
we are! The reason the world does not
know us is that it did not know him. 2Dear
friends, now we are children of God, and
what we will be has not yet been made
known. But we know that when he ap-
pears,[a] we shall be like him, for we shall
see him as he is. 3Everyone who has this
hope in him purifies himself, just as he is
pure.
4Everyone who sins breaks the law; in
fact, sin is lawlessness. 5But you know
that he appeared so that he might take
away our sins. And in him is no sin. 6No
one who lives in him keeps on sinning. No
one who continues to sin has either seen
him or known him.
7Dear children, do not let anyone lead
you astray. He who does what is right is
righteous, just as he is righteous. 8He who
does what is sinful is of the devil, because
the devil has been sinning from the begin-
ning. The reason the Son of God appeared
was to destroy the devil's work. 9No one

[a]2 Or *when it is made known*

VERSE FOR THE DAY: 1 John 3:18

AUTHOR: Dale Evans Rogers

PASSAGE FOR THE DAY: 1 John 3:11–20

A Miracle of Commitment

It is unrealistic to assume that two completely different personalities can blend together in marriage without going through difficulties. But if both marriage partners *want* to make it work, a miracle as great as parting the Red Sea can happen.

Our feelings can change from day to day, and even from hour to hour. As a result, there are times when we must *will* to affirm and express our love to our mate. There are times when we don't *feel* very loving. Misunderstandings over matters like money or disciplining of children or work pressures can create rifts. In the heat of those disagreements harsh words are spoken, and they cut deeply.

It is in the moments when feelings of love change to anger and hostility that true commitment holds us steady.

MARRIAGE BUILDERS

♦ *What do you think are the essential factors that hold today's marriages together?*

♦ *Reread 1 John 3:18. In what ways have you lived out this verse before your spouse?*

Additional Scripture Readings
Ephesians 4:31–32; Romans 12:10; 1 John 4:7–21

Go to page 1396 for your next devotional reading.

who is born of God will continue to sin,
because God's seed remains in him; he
cannot go on sinning, because he has
been born of God. [10]This is how we know
who the children of God are and who the
children of the devil are: Anyone who
does not do what is right is not a child of
God; nor is anyone who does not love his
brother.

Love One Another

[11]This is the message you heard from
the beginning: We should love one another.
[12]Do not be like Cain, who belonged to
the evil one and murdered his brother.
And why did he murder him? Because his
own actions were evil and his brother's
were righteous. [13]Do not be surprised, my
brothers, if the world hates you. [14]We
know that we have passed from death to
life, because we love our brothers. Anyone
who does not love remains in death.
[15]Anyone who hates his brother is a murderer,
and you know that no murderer has
eternal life in him.

[16]This is how we know what love is:
Jesus Christ laid down his life for us. And
we ought to lay down our lives for our
brothers. [17]If anyone has material possessions
and sees his brother in need but has
no pity on him, how can the love of God
be in him? [18]Dear children, let us not love
with words or tongue but with actions and
in truth. [19]This then is how we know that
we belong to the truth, and how we set
our hearts at rest in his presence [20]whenever
our hearts condemn us. For God is
greater than our hearts, and he knows everything.

[21]Dear friends, if our hearts do not con-

THURSDAY

VERSE FOR THE DAY:	AUTHOR:	PASSAGE FOR THE DAY:
1 John 4:8	Ruth Bell Graham	1 John 4:7–21

Perfect Love

When I stop to think of all that love should be—accepting, forgiving, supporting, strengthening—God is all that and more. He is perfect love.

I have to chuckle when I read back over my early letters and poems to Bill. My love for him was so idealistic. The expectations that I had for him were so lofty, so unfair. And I think sometimes that wives have expectations for their husbands that only the Lord could live up to. But when I visualize everything that love is or could be, I have the perfect picture of the love God has for me. And that is refreshing.

MARRIAGE BUILDERS

♦ *How would you describe the love you have for your spouse?*
♦ *Share with each other examples of married couples who have modeled love for you. What lessons from their love could you learn to apply to your own marriage?*

Additional Scripture Readings
John 3:16–17; 16:27; 2 John 6

Go to page 1397 for your next devotional reading.

VERSE FOR THE DAY: 1 John 5:14–15

AUTHOR: Catherine Marshall

PASSAGE FOR THE DAY: 1 John 5:13–21

Dare to Trust

I learned my first real lesson in trusting God totally when I was a teenager. By the time I reached my senior year in high school, my father had taken several cuts in his meager minister's salary. I had been accepted by a college, but college now seemed out of the question.

One evening Mother said quietly, "I believe it is God's will for you to go to college, or else he would not have given you the mental equipment. Furthermore, all resources are at God's disposal. Do you believe that?"

"Yes—I think I do."

"Much of what happens to us in life depends on where we place our faith," she said. "If we deposit it in God, then we're on sure ground."

She opened the Bible to 1 John 5:14–15. "'. . . If we ask anything according to his will, he hears us,'" she read. "'And if we know that he hears us—whatever we ask—we know that we have what we asked of him.' Let's claim that promise right now for the resources for your college." And so we knelt by the bed and prayed.

When the answer came, it was from an unlikely source: the New Deal administration of Franklin Roosevelt. Mother was offered a job with the Federal Writer's Project, which asked her to help record the history of our country. Her salary would cover the amount needed for my college expenses with a little to spare. And since history had always been one of Mother's loves, her new job could not have been more to her liking!

MARRIAGE BUILDERS

♦ *When has God answered your prayers in ways you could never have anticipated?*

♦ *Do you believe that all resources are at God's disposal? How does that affect your family's financial planning?*

Additional Scripture Readings
Matthew 18:19–20; Matthew 21:22;
2 Chronicles 7:14–16

Go to page 1399 for your next devotional reading.

demn us, we have confidence before God
22and receive from him anything we ask,
because we obey his commands and do
what pleases him. 23And this is his com-
mand: to believe in the name of his Son,
Jesus Christ, and to love one another as he
commanded us. 24Those who obey his
commands live in him, and he in them.
And this is how we know that he lives in
us: We know it by the Spirit he gave us.

Test the Spirits

4 Dear friends, do not believe every
spirit, but test the spirits to see whether they are from God, because many false
prophets have gone out into the world.
2This is how you can recognize the Spirit
of God: Every spirit that acknowledges
that Jesus Christ has come in the flesh is
from God, 3but every spirit that does not
acknowledge Jesus is not from God. This
is the spirit of the antichrist, which you
have heard is coming and even now is already in the world.

4You, dear children, are from God and
have overcome them, because the one
who is in you is greater than the one who
is in the world. 5They are from the world
and therefore speak from the viewpoint of
the world, and the world listens to them.
6We are from God, and whoever knows
God listens to us; but whoever is not from
God does not listen to us. This is how we
recognize the Spirit[a] of truth and the
spirit of falsehood.

God's Love and Ours

7Dear friends, let us love one another,
for love comes from God. Everyone who
loves has been born of God and knows
God. 8Whoever does not love does not
know God, because God is love. 9This is
how God showed his love among us: He
sent his one and only Son[b] into the world
that we might live through him. 10This is
love: not that we loved God, but that he
loved us and sent his Son as an atoning
sacrifice for[c] our sins. 11Dear friends,
since God so loved us, we also ought to
love one another. 12No one has ever seen
God; but if we love one another, God lives
in us and his love is made complete in us.

13We know that we live in him and he
in us, because he has given us of his Spirit.
14And we have seen and testify that the
Father has sent his Son to be the Savior of
the world. 15If anyone acknowledges that
Jesus is the Son of God, God lives in him
and he in God. 16And so we know and rely
on the love God has for us.

God is love. Whoever lives in love lives
in God, and God in him. 17In this way, love
is made complete among us so that we
will have confidence on the day of judgment, because in this world we are like
him. 18There is no fear in love. But perfect
love drives out fear, because fear has to do
with punishment. The one who fears is
not made perfect in love.

19We love because he first loved us. 20If
anyone says, "I love God," yet hates his
brother, he is a liar. For anyone who does
not love his brother, whom he has seen,
cannot love God, whom he has not seen.
21And he has given us this command:
Whoever loves God must also love his
brother.

Faith in the Son of God

5 Everyone who believes that Jesus is
the Christ is born of God, and everyone who loves the father loves his child as
well. 2This is how we know that we love
the children of God: by loving God and
carrying out his commands. 3This is love
for God: to obey his commands. And his
commands are not burdensome, 4for everyone born of God overcomes the world.
This is the victory that has overcome the
world, even our faith. 5Who is it that overcomes the world? Only he who believes
that Jesus is the Son of God.

6This is the one who came by water and
blood—Jesus Christ. He did not come by
water only, but by water and blood. And
it is the Spirit who testifies, because the
Spirit is the truth. 7For there are three that
testify: 8the[d] Spirit, the water and the
blood; and the three are in agreement.
9We accept man's testimony, but God's
testimony is greater because it is the testimony of God, which he has given about
his Son. 10Anyone who believes in the Son
of God has this testimony in his heart.
Anyone who does not believe God has
made him out to be a liar, because he has
not believed the testimony God has given

[a]*6* Or *spirit* [b]*9* Or *his only begotten Son* [c]*10* Or *as the one who would turn aside his wrath, taking away* [d]*7,8* Late manuscripts of the Vulgate *testify in heaven: the Father, the Word and the Holy Spirit, and these three are one. 8And there are three that testify on earth: the* (not found in any Greek manuscript before the sixteenth century)

WEEKENDING

WORK

Because of work, less time and energy is left over for your marriage relationship. To help you gain greater insight into the role of work in your and your spouse's lives, discuss your responses to the following statements.

1. My work situation is unsatisfactory, but the situation is not likely to improve.

2. I feel that one (or both) of us should consider changing jobs.

3. My spouse's job is more important than mine.

4. I sometimes experience envy over my mate's job.

5. I don't feel that my spouse understands the pressures I face at work.

Discuss your responses. Do you find any tensions or frustrations related to one or both of your jobs? If so, try to pinpoint the causes. Discuss these issues together to see if you can gain greater insight into what each of you is feeling—then work on some solutions.

— *The* Marriage Partnership *Staff*

REVIVE

Saturday: 1 Corinthians 3:10–15
Sunday: 2 Thessalonians 3:1–13

Go to page 1402 for your next devotional reading.

about his Son. [11]And this is the testimony:
God has given us eternal life, and this life
is in his Son. [12]He who has the Son has
life; he who does not have the Son of God
does not have life.

Concluding Remarks

[13]I write these things to you who be-
lieve in the name of the Son of God so that
you may know that you have eternal life.
[14]This is the confidence we have in ap-
proaching God: that if we ask anything ac-
cording to his will, he hears us. [15]And if
we know that he hears us—whatever we
ask—we know that we have what we
asked of him.

[16]If anyone sees his brother commit a
sin that does not lead to death, he should
pray and God will give him life. I refer to
those whose sin does not lead to death.
There is a sin that leads to death. I am not
saying that he should pray about that.
[17]All wrongdoing is sin, and there is sin
that does not lead to death.

[18]We know that anyone born of God
does not continue to sin; the one who was
born of God keeps him safe, and the evil
one cannot harm him. [19]We know that we
are children of God, and that the whole
world is under the control of the evil one.
[20]We know also that the Son of God has
come and has given us understanding, so
that we may know him who is true. And
we are in him who is true—even in his
Son Jesus Christ. He is the true God and
eternal life.

[21]Dear children, keep yourselves from
idols.

JOHN writes this second letter to warn the church to stand firm against false teachers and to keep loving other Christians. As you read this book, learn how to stand up for your Lord whenever you encounter false teachers.

2 JOHN

1 The elder,

To the chosen lady and her children,
whom I love in the truth—and not I only,
but also all who know the truth— 2 because of the truth, which lives in us and
will be with us forever:

3 Grace, mercy and peace from God the
Father and from Jesus Christ, the Father's
Son, will be with us in truth and love.

4 It has given me great joy to find some
of your children walking in the truth, just
as the Father commanded us. 5 And now,
dear lady, I am not writing you a new
command but one we have had from the
beginning. I ask that we love one another.
6 And this is love: that we walk in obedi-
ence to his commands. As you have heard
from the beginning, his command is that
you walk in love.
7 Many deceivers, who do not acknowl-
edge Jesus Christ as coming in the flesh,
have gone out into the world. Any such
person is the deceiver and the antichrist.
8 Watch out that you do not lose what you
have worked for, but that you may be re-
warded fully. 9 Anyone who runs ahead
and does not continue in the teaching of
Christ does not have God; whoever con-
tinues in the teaching has both the Father
and the Son. 10 If anyone comes to you and
does not bring this teaching, do not take
him into your house or welcome him.
11 Anyone who welcomes him shares in
his wicked work.

12 I have much to write to you, but I do
not want to use paper and ink. Instead, I
hope to visit you and talk with you face to
face, so that our joy may be complete.

13 The children of your chosen sister
send their greetings.

VERSE FOR THE DAY:
2 John 10

AUTHOR:
Elizabeth Cody Newenhuyse

PASSAGE FOR THE DAY:
2 John 1–13

Spiritual Pollution

Mindlessness is a dangerous form of spiritual pollution. Scripture adjures us to dwell on what is true, noble, right, pure, lovely, admirable (Phil. 4:8). A mind is a terrible thing to trash, but that's what happens when brains and spirits are crammed full of media trivia: the latest slang, current music groups, T-shirt sentiments, celebrity gossip.

The world is full of stuff we *don't* need to know, which crowds out the things we ought to know and are better off for knowing. One of the most profound insights I've heard on the media-and-discernment issue came from my pastor, John Benson, preaching from 2 John: "If anyone comes to you and does not bring this teaching [of Christ as God incarnate], do not take him into your house or welcome him" (v. 10). Our pastor further posed the question: Who or what do we welcome into our homes? Who or what is *un*welcome?

This warning applies to our media consumption and the mental pollution that comes with it. The best response to the purveyors of garbage is a slammed door.

MARRIAGE BUILDERS

♦ *In what practical ways could God's standards help you in monitoring what comes into your home via television or other media?*
♦ *What do you do to refresh your mind when impure or unwholesome thoughts seem to get stuck there?*

Additional Scripture Readings
Romans 12:1–2; Philippians 4:8

Go to page 1404 for your next devotional reading.

JOHN writes this third letter to commend a church leader for his hospitality and to warn against another one who is unfriendly and even cruel. As you read this book, think how you can act as a friend toward other Christians.

3 JOHN

1 The elder,

To my dear friend Gaius, whom I love in the truth.

2 Dear friend, I pray that you may enjoy good health and that all may go well with you, even as your soul is getting along well. 3 It gave me great joy to have some brothers come and tell about your faithfulness to the truth and how you continue to walk in the truth. 4 I have no greater joy than to hear that my children are walking in the truth.

5 Dear friend, you are faithful in what you are doing for the brothers, even though they are strangers to you. 6 They have told the church about your love. You will do well to send them on their way in a manner worthy of God. 7 It was for the sake of the Name that they went out, receiving no help from the pagans. 8 We ought therefore to show hospitality to such men so that we may work together for the truth.

9 I wrote to the church, but Diotrephes, who loves to be first, will have nothing to do with us. 10 So if I come, I will call attention to what he is doing, gossiping maliciously about us. Not satisfied with that, he refuses to welcome the brothers. He also stops those who want to do so and puts them out of the church.

11 Dear friend, do not imitate what is evil but what is good. Anyone who does what is good is from God. Anyone who does what is evil has not seen God. 12 Demetrius is well spoken of by everyone—and even by the truth itself. We also speak well of him, and you know that our testimony is true.

13 I have much to write you, but I do not want to do so with pen and ink. 14 I hope to see you soon, and we will talk face to face.

Peace to you. The friends here send their greetings. Greet the friends there by name.

VERSE FOR THE DAY:
3 John 11

AUTHOR:
Tom Anderson

PASSAGE FOR THE DAY:
3 John 1–14

The Love Experiment

As we drove to our rented beach cottage, I vowed that for the two weeks of our vacation I would be the loving husband Evelyn had always wanted. No ifs, ands or buts.

I had often been a selfish husband, but I worked hard, and I figured I deserve a bit of coddling. But I had to admit that I often failed to show love to my wife, Evelyn. I would chide her for her tardiness or insist on the TV channel I wanted to watch. At times, I would throw out day-old newspapers knowing Evelyn still wanted to read them. Now we were on vacation and I decided, "for two weeks all that will change."

And it did, from the moment I kissed Evelyn at the door and said, "Honey, that new yellow sweater looks great on you." She seemed surprised, and pleased.

After our long drive to the cottage, I wanted to sit and read. Evelyn suggested we take a walk. I started to refuse, but then I thought, "Evelyn is expressing a desire to spend time alone with me." We walked on the beach.

So it went: Two weeks of not calling the office; a visit to the shell museum (though I usually hate museums); holding my tongue while Evelyn made us late for a dinner date. The whole vacation passed relaxed and happy, so much so that I made a new vow to keep remembering 1 Peter 3:7 when we went home again. I would continue to *choose* to love my wife!

MARRIAGE BUILDERS

♦ *What loving behaviors have become more natural over the years of your marriage?*

♦ *Are you doing all you can to express your love in ways your spouse can recognize?*

Additional Scripture Readings
Ephesians 5:25–33; Colossians 3:19; 1 Peter 3:7

Go to page 1406 for your next devotional reading.

JUDE (a brother of Jesus and James) writes this short letter to warn Christians against false teachers in the church and to urge them to strengthen their faith and love. As you read this book, begin to grow in faith and love by depending on the Father, Son and Holy Spirit.

JUDE

1 Jude, a servant of Jesus Christ and a
brother of James,

To those who have been called, who are
loved by God the Father and kept by[a]
Jesus Christ:

2 Mercy, peace and love be yours in
abundance.

The Sin and Doom of Godless Men

3 Dear friends, although I was very eager
to write to you about the salvation we
share, I felt I had to write and urge you to
contend for the faith that was once for all
entrusted to the saints. 4 For certain men
whose condemnation was written about[b]
long ago have secretly slipped in among
you. They are godless men, who change
the grace of our God into a license for immorality and deny Jesus Christ our only
Sovereign and Lord.

5 Though you already know all this, I
want to remind you that the Lord[c] delivered his people out of Egypt, but later destroyed those who did not believe. 6 And
the angels who did not keep their positions of authority but abandoned their
own home—these he has kept in darkness, bound with everlasting chains for
judgment on the great Day. 7 In a similar
way, Sodom and Gomorrah and the surrounding towns gave themselves up to
sexual immorality and perversion. They
serve as an example of those who suffer
the punishment of eternal fire.

8 In the very same way, these dreamers
pollute their own bodies, reject authority
and slander celestial beings. 9 But even the
archangel Michael, when he was disputing with the devil about the body of Moses, did not dare to bring a slanderous accusation against him, but said, "The Lord

[a] 1 Or *for*; or *in Jesus*
[b] 4 Or *men who were marked out for condemnation*
[c] 5 Some early manuscripts

rebuke you!" [10]Yet these men speak abusively against whatever they do not understand; and what things they do understand by instinct, like unreasoning animals—these are the very things that destroy them.

[11]Woe to them! They have taken the way of Cain; they have rushed for profit into Balaam's error; they have been destroyed in Korah's rebellion.

[12]These men are blemishes at your love feasts, eating with you without the slightest qualm—shepherds who feed only themselves. They are clouds without rain, blown along by the wind; autumn trees, without fruit and uprooted—twice dead. [13]They are wild waves of the sea, foaming up their shame; wandering stars, for whom blackest darkness has been reserved forever.

[14]Enoch, the seventh from Adam, prophesied about these men: "See, the Lord is coming with thousands upon thousands of his holy ones [15]to judge everyone, and to convict all the ungodly of all the ungodly acts they have done in the ungodly way, and of all the harsh words ungodly sinners have spoken against him." [16]These men are grumblers and faultfinders; they follow their own evil desires; they boast about themselves and flatter others for their own advantage.

A Call to Persevere

[17]But, dear friends, remember what the apostles of our Lord Jesus Christ foretold. [18]They said to you, "In the last times there will be scoffers who will follow their own ungodly desires." [19]These are the men who divide you, who follow mere natural instincts and do not have the Spirit.

[20]But you, dear friends, build yourselves up in your most holy faith and pray in the Holy Spirit. [21]Keep yourselves in

VERSE FOR THE DAY: Jude 24–25

AUTHOR: Judith Briles

PASSAGE FOR THE DAY: Jude 17–25

Keeping Your Balance

Even a man or woman who is in tune with God's leading will struggle to maintain a balanced life. There are going to be times when each of us is out of step at work or in our personal lives. Just being open and receptive to the fact that life is not going to be perfect helps bring perspective back into a busy person's life.

God may not provide us with a perfectly ordered life, but what he does provide is himself, his presence and open doors that bring us closer to being productive, positive and realistic Christians.

MARRIAGE BUILDERS

♦ *In what areas does perfectionism creep into your goals for your marriage?*

♦ *How can you relax and depend on God's presence as a third partner in your marriage team?*

Additional Scripture Readings
Isaiah 30:21; Micah 6:8

Go to page 1412 for your next devotional reading.

God's love as you wait for the mercy of
our Lord Jesus Christ to bring you to eter-
nal life.
22Be merciful to those who doubt;
23snatch others from the fire and save
them; to others show mercy, mixed with
fear—hating even the clothing stained by
corrupted flesh.

Doxology

24To him who is able to keep you from
falling and to present you before his glori-
ous presence without fault and with great
joy— 25to the only God our Savior be glo-
ry, majesty, power and authority, through
Jesus Christ our Lord, before all ages, now
and forevermore! Amen.

JOHN, banished to the island of Patmos, writes what Christ reveals to him in order to comfort Christians suffering for their faith. Through visions of God in control of both the present and the future, he offers them hope, assuring them that in the end Christ will achieve victory over Satan, who is doomed to eternal punishment. As you read this book, rejoice in the awesome power of Christ, and remember that regardless of what happens now or in the future, nothing can ever separate you from his love.

REVELATION

Prologue

1 The revelation of Jesus Christ, which God gave him to show his servants what must soon take place. He made it known by sending his angel to his servant John, 2 who testifies to everything he saw—that is, the word of God and the testimony of Jesus Christ. 3 Blessed is the one who reads the words of this prophecy, and blessed are those who hear it and take to heart what is written in it, because the time is near.

Greetings and Doxology

4 John,

To the seven churches in the province of Asia:

Grace and peace to you from him who is, and who was, and who is to come, and from the seven spirits[a] before his throne,

[a] 4 Or *the sevenfold Spirit*

5and from Jesus Christ, who is the faithful
witness, the firstborn from the dead, and
the ruler of the kings of the earth.

To him who loves us and has freed us
from our sins by his blood, 6and has made
us to be a kingdom and priests to serve his
God and Father—to him be glory and
power for ever and ever! Amen.

7Look, he is coming with the clouds,
and every eye will see him,
even those who pierced him;
and all the peoples of the earth will
mourn because of him.
So shall it be! Amen.

8"I am the Alpha and the Omega," says
the Lord God, "who is, and who was, and
who is to come, the Almighty."

One Like a Son of Man

9I, John, your brother and companion
in the suffering and kingdom and patient
endurance that are ours in Jesus, was on
the island of Patmos because of the word
of God and the testimony of Jesus. 10On
the Lord's Day I was in the Spirit, and I
heard behind me a loud voice like a trum-
pet, 11which said: "Write on a scroll what
you see and send it to the seven churches:
to Ephesus, Smyrna, Pergamum, Thyatira,
Sardis, Philadelphia and Laodicea."

12I turned around to see the voice that
was speaking to me. And when I turned I
saw seven golden lampstands, 13and
among the lampstands was someone "like
a son of man,"[a] dressed in a robe reach-
ing down to his feet and with a golden
sash around his chest. 14His head and hair
were white like wool, as white as snow,
and his eyes were like blazing fire. 15His
feet were like bronze glowing in a furnace,
and his voice was like the sound of rush-
ing waters. 16In his right hand he held sev-
en stars, and out of his mouth came a
sharp double-edged sword. His face was
like the sun shining in all its brilliance.

17When I saw him, I fell at his feet as
though dead. Then he placed his right
hand on me and said: "Do not be afraid. I
am the First and the Last. 18I am the Living
One; I was dead, and behold I am alive for
ever and ever! And I hold the keys of
death and Hades.

19"Write, therefore, what you have
seen, what is now and what will take place
later. 20The mystery of the seven stars that
you saw in my right hand and of the seven
golden lampstands is this: The seven stars
are the angels[b] of the seven churches,
and the seven lampstands are the seven
churches.

To the Church in Ephesus

2 "To the angel[c] of the church in Ephe-
sus write:

These are the words of him who
holds the seven stars in his right hand
and walks among the seven golden
lampstands: 2I know your deeds,
your hard work and your persever-
ance. I know that you cannot tolerate
wicked men, that you have tested
those who claim to be apostles but
are not, and have found them false.
3You have persevered and have en-
dured hardships for my name, and
have not grown weary.

4Yet I hold this against you: You
have forsaken your first love. 5Re-
member the height from which you
have fallen! Repent and do the things
you did at first. If you do not repent,
I will come to you and remove your
lampstand from its place. 6But you
have this in your favor: You hate the
practices of the Nicolaitans, which I
also hate.

7He who has an ear, let him hear
what the Spirit says to the churches.
To him who overcomes, I will give
the right to eat from the tree of life,
which is in the paradise of God.

To the Church in Smyrna

8"To the angel of the church in Smyrna
write:

These are the words of him who is
the First and the Last, who died and
came to life again. 9I know your af-
flictions and your poverty—yet you
are rich! I know the slander of those
who say they are Jews and are not,
but are a synagogue of Satan. 10Do
not be afraid of what you are about to
suffer. I tell you, the devil will put
some of you in prison to test you, and
you will suffer persecution for ten
days. Be faithful, even to the point of
death, and I will give you the crown
of life.

11He who has an ear, let him hear
what the Spirit says to the churches.

[a] 13 Daniel 7:13 [b] 20 Or *messengers* [c] 1 Or *messenger*; also in verses 8, 12 and 18

He who overcomes will not be hurt at
all by the second death.

To the Church in Pergamum

12"To the angel of the church in Pergamum write:

These are the words of him who
has the sharp, double-edged sword.
13I know where you live—where Sa-
tan has his throne. Yet you remain
true to my name. You did not re-
nounce your faith in me, even in the
days of Antipas, my faithful witness,
who was put to death in your city—
where Satan lives.
14Nevertheless, I have a few things
against you: You have people there
who hold to the teaching of Balaam,
who taught Balak to entice the Israel-
ites to sin by eating food sacrificed to
idols and by committing sexual im-
morality. 15Likewise you also have
those who hold to the teaching of the
Nicolaitans. 16Repent therefore! Oth-
erwise, I will soon come to you and
will fight against them with the
sword of my mouth.
17He who has an ear, let him hear
what the Spirit says to the churches.
To him who overcomes, I will give
some of the hidden manna. I will also
give him a white stone with a new
name written on it, known only to
him who receives it.

To the Church in Thyatira

18"To the angel of the church in Thyatira write:

These are the words of the Son of
God, whose eyes are like blazing fire
and whose feet are like burnished
bronze. 19I know your deeds, your
love and faith, your service and per-
severance, and that you are now do-
ing more than you did at first.
20Nevertheless, I have this against
you: You tolerate that woman Jeze-
bel, who calls herself a prophetess.
By her teaching she misleads my ser-
vants into sexual immorality and the
eating of food sacrificed to idols. 21I
have given her time to repent of her
immorality, but she is unwilling. 22So
I will cast her on a bed of suffering,
and I will make those who commit
adultery with her suffer intensely,
unless they repent of her ways. 23I
will strike her children dead. Then all
the churches will know that I am he
who searches hearts and minds, and
I will repay each of you according to
your deeds. 24Now I say to the rest of
you in Thyatira, to you who do not
hold to her teaching and have not
learned Satan's so-called deep secrets
(I will not impose any other burden
on you): 25Only hold on to what you
have until I come.
26To him who overcomes and does
my will to the end, I will give authori-
ty over the nations—

27'He will rule them with an iron
scepter;
he will dash them to pieces
like pottery'[a]—

just as I have received authority from
my Father. 28I will also give him the
morning star. 29He who has an ear, let
him hear what the Spirit says to the
churches.

To the Church in Sardis

3 "To the angel[b] of the church in Sardis write:

These are the words of him who
holds the seven spirits[c] of God and
the seven stars. I know your deeds;
you have a reputation of being alive,
but you are dead. 2Wake up!
Strengthen what remains and is
about to die, for I have not found
your deeds complete in the sight of
my God. 3Remember, therefore, what
you have received and heard; obey it,
and repent. But if you do not wake
up, I will come like a thief, and you
will not know at what time I will
come to you.
4Yet you have a few people in Sar-
dis who have not soiled their clothes.
They will walk with me, dressed in
white, for they are worthy. 5He who
overcomes will, like them, be dressed
in white. I will never blot out his
name from the book of life, but will
acknowledge his name before my Fa-
ther and his angels. 6He who has an
ear, let him hear what the Spirit says
to the churches.

[a] 27 Psalm 2:9 [b] 1 Or *messenger*; also in verses 7 and 14 [c] 1 Or *the sevenfold Spirit*

To the Church in Philadelphia

7"To the angel of the church in Philadelphia write:

These are the words of him who is holy and true, who holds the key of David. What he opens no one can shut, and what he shuts no one can open. 8I know your deeds. See, I have placed before you an open door that no one can shut. I know that you have little strength, yet you have kept my word and have not denied my name. 9I will make those who are of the synagogue of Satan, who claim to be Jews though they are not, but are liars—I will make them come and fall down at your feet and acknowledge that I have loved you. 10Since you have kept my command to endure patiently, I will also keep you from the hour of trial that is going to come upon the whole world to test those who live on the earth.

11I am coming soon. Hold on to what you have, so that no one will take your crown. 12Him who overcomes I will make a pillar in the temple of my God. Never again will he leave it. I will write on him the name of my God and the name of the city of my God, the new Jerusalem, which is coming down out of heaven from my God; and I will also write on him my new name. 13He who has an ear, let him hear what the Spirit says to the churches.

To the Church in Laodicea

14"To the angel of the church in Laodicea write:

These are the words of the Amen, the faithful and true witness, the ruler of God's creation. 15I know your deeds, that you are neither cold nor hot. I wish you were either one or the other! 16So, because you are lukewarm—neither hot nor cold—I am about to spit you out of my mouth. 17You say, 'I am rich; I have acquired wealth and do not need a thing.' But you do not realize that you are wretched, pitiful, poor, blind and naked. 18I counsel you to buy from me gold refined in the fire, so you can become rich; and white clothes to wear, so you can cover your shameful nakedness; and salve to put on your eyes, so you can see.

19Those whom I love I rebuke and discipline. So be earnest, and repent. 20Here I am! I stand at the door and knock. If anyone hears my voice and opens the door, I will come in and eat with him, and he with me.

21To him who overcomes, I will give the right to sit with me on my throne, just as I overcame and sat down with my Father on his throne. 22He who has an ear, let him hear what the Spirit says to the churches."

The Throne in Heaven

4 After this I looked, and there before me was a door standing open in heaven. And the voice I had first heard speaking to me like a trumpet said, "Come up here, and I will show you what must take place after this." 2At once I was in the Spirit, and there before me was a throne in heaven with someone sitting on it. 3And the one who sat there had the appearance of jasper and carnelian. A rainbow, resembling an emerald, encircled the throne. 4Surrounding the throne were twenty-four other thrones, and seated on them were twenty-four elders. They were dressed in white and had crowns of gold on their heads. 5From the throne came flashes of lightning, rumblings and peals of thunder. Before the throne, seven lamps were blazing. These are the seven spirits[a] of God. 6Also before the throne there was what looked like a sea of glass, clear as crystal.

In the center, around the throne, were four living creatures, and they were covered with eyes, in front and in back. 7The first living creature was like a lion, the second was like an ox, the third had a face like a man, the fourth was like a flying eagle. 8Each of the four living creatures had six wings and was covered with eyes all around, even under his wings. Day and night they never stop saying:

"Holy, holy, holy
is the Lord God Almighty,
who was, and is, and is to come."

9Whenever the living creatures give glory, honor and thanks to him who sits on the throne and who lives for ever and ever, 10the twenty-four elders fall down before

[a]5 Or *the sevenfold Spirit*

him who sits on the throne, and worship
him who lives for ever and ever. They lay
their crowns before the throne and say:

11"You are worthy, our Lord and God,
to receive glory and honor and
power,
for you created all things,
and by your will they were created
and have their being."

The Scroll and the Lamb

5 Then I saw in the right hand of him
who sat on the throne a scroll with
writing on both sides and sealed with seven seals. 2And I saw a mighty angel proclaiming in a loud voice, "Who is worthy to break the seals and open the scroll?" 3But no one in heaven or on earth or under the earth could open the scroll or even look inside it. 4I wept and wept because no one was found who was worthy to open the scroll or look inside. 5Then one of the elders said to me, "Do not weep! See, the Lion of the tribe of Judah, the Root of David, has triumphed. He is able to open the scroll and its seven seals."

VERSE FOR THE DAY: Revelation 2:26

AUTHOR: Donald R. Harvey

PASSAGE FOR THE DAY: Revelation 2:18–29

Becoming Overcomers

Couples need to guard against the "Teflon mentality"—an expectation that pain, stress and hardship will slide right off. Christians do feel pain and stress, but we don't have to be overwhelmed by them.

Hard times will come, but the real battle is won or lost *before* a crisis occurs. A marriage that crumbles under pressure is like a china cup with a hairline crack. While the cup sits on a table, the crack goes unnoticed. But when the cup is held up to the light, the tiny crack becomes visible. The light doesn't cause the crack; it illuminates a fracture that already exists.

Marriages that weather the storms of life share at least three characteristics. First, the couples are committed to marriage as a sacred institution. Second, they're committed to each other and not just to marriage. Third, couples with a vital faith and commitment to God make it for the long haul. You can win the battle before it begins!

MARRIAGE BUILDERS

♦ *Given these three couple characteristics, are you ready for whatever your future may hold?*

♦ *What stresses are you facing together right now?*

Additional Scripture Readings
Romans 8:28–39; 1 Peter 1:6–7

Go to page 1415 for your next devotional reading.

6Then I saw a Lamb, looking as if it had
been slain, standing in the center of the
throne, encircled by the four living cre-
atures and the elders. He had seven horns
and seven eyes, which are the seven spir-
its[a] of God sent out into all the earth. 7He
came and took the scroll from the right
hand of him who sat on the throne. 8And
when he had taken it, the four living cre-
atures and the twenty-four elders fell down
before the Lamb. Each one had a harp and
they were holding golden bowls full of in-
cense, which are the prayers of the saints.
9And they sang a new song:

"You are worthy to take the scroll
and to open its seals,
because you were slain,
and with your blood you purchased
men for God
from every tribe and language and
people and nation.
10You have made them to be a kingdom
and priests to serve our God,
and they will reign on the earth."

11Then I looked and heard the voice of
many angels, numbering thousands upon
thousands, and ten thousand times ten
thousand. They encircled the throne and
the living creatures and the elders. 12In a
loud voice they sang:

"Worthy is the Lamb, who was slain,
to receive power and wealth and
wisdom and strength
and honor and glory and praise!"

13Then I heard every creature in heaven
and on earth and under the earth and on
the sea, and all that is in them, singing:

"To him who sits on the throne and to
the Lamb
be praise and honor and glory and
power,
for ever and ever!"

14The four living creatures said, "Amen,"
and the elders fell down and worshiped.

The Seals

6 I watched as the Lamb opened the
first of the seven seals. Then I heard
one of the four living creatures say in a
voice like thunder, "Come!" 2I looked, and
there before me was a white horse! Its rid-
er held a bow, and he was given a crown,
and he rode out as a conqueror bent on
conquest.

3When the Lamb opened the second
seal, I heard the second living creature
say, "Come!" 4Then another horse came
out, a fiery red one. Its rider was given
power to take peace from the earth and to
make men slay each other. To him was
given a large sword.

5When the Lamb opened the third seal,
I heard the third living creature say,
"Come!" I looked, and there before me
was a black horse! Its rider was holding a
pair of scales in his hand. 6Then I heard
what sounded like a voice among the four
living creatures, saying, "A quart[b] of
wheat for a day's wages,[c] and three
quarts of barley for a day's wages,[c] and
do not damage the oil and the wine!"

7When the Lamb opened the fourth
seal, I heard the voice of the fourth living
creature say, "Come!" 8I looked, and there
before me was a pale horse! Its rider was
named Death, and Hades was following
close behind him. They were given power
over a fourth of the earth to kill by sword,
famine and plague, and by the wild beasts
of the earth.

9When he opened the fifth seal, I saw
under the altar the souls of those who had
been slain because of the word of God and
the testimony they had maintained.
10They called out in a loud voice, "How
long, Sovereign Lord, holy and true, until
you judge the inhabitants of the earth and
avenge our blood?" 11Then each of them
was given a white robe, and they were told
to wait a little longer, until the number of
their fellow servants and brothers who
were to be killed as they had been was
completed.

12I watched as he opened the sixth seal.
There was a great earthquake. The sun
turned black like sackcloth made of goat
hair, the whole moon turned blood red,
13and the stars in the sky fell to earth, as
late figs drop from a fig tree when shaken
by a strong wind. 14The sky receded like
a scroll, rolling up, and every mountain
and island was removed from its place.

15Then the kings of the earth, the
princes, the generals, the rich, the mighty,
and every slave and every free man hid in
caves and among the rocks of the moun-
tains. 16They called to the mountains and
the rocks, "Fall on us and hide us from the
face of him who sits on the throne and
from the wrath of the Lamb! 17For the

[a]6 Or *the sevenfold Spirit* [b]6 Greek *a choinix* (probably about a liter) [c]6 Greek *a denarius*

great day of their wrath has come, and
who can stand?"

144,000 Sealed

7 After this I saw four angels standing at
the four corners of the earth, holding
back the four winds of the earth to prevent
any wind from blowing on the land or on
the sea or on any tree. 2Then I saw another angel coming up from the east, having
the seal of the living God. He called out in
a loud voice to the four angels who had
been given power to harm the land and
the sea: 3"Do not harm the land or the sea
or the trees until we put a seal on the foreheads of the servants of our God." 4Then
I heard the number of those who were
sealed: 144,000 from all the tribes of Israel.

5From the tribe of Judah 12,000 were
sealed,
from the tribe of Reuben 12,000,
from the tribe of Gad 12,000,
6from the tribe of Asher 12,000,
from the tribe of Naphtali 12,000,
from the tribe of Manasseh 12,000,
7from the tribe of Simeon 12,000,
from the tribe of Levi 12,000,
from the tribe of Issachar 12,000,
8from the tribe of Zebulun 12,000,
from the tribe of Joseph 12,000,
from the tribe of Benjamin 12,000.

The Great Multitude in White Robes

9After this I looked and there before me
was a great multitude that no one could
count, from every nation, tribe, people
and language, standing before the throne
and in front of the Lamb. They were wearing white robes and were holding palm
branches in their hands. 10And they cried
out in a loud voice:

"Salvation belongs to our God,
who sits on the throne,
and to the Lamb."

11All the angels were standing around the
throne and around the elders and the four
living creatures. They fell down on their
faces before the throne and worshiped
God, 12saying:

"Amen!
Praise and glory
and wisdom and thanks and honor
and power and strength
be to our God for ever and ever.
Amen!"

13Then one of the elders asked me,
"These in white robes—who are they, and
where did they come from?"
14I answered, "Sir, you know."
And he said, "These are they who have
come out of the great tribulation; they
have washed their robes and made them
white in the blood of the Lamb. 15Therefore,

"they are before the throne of God
and serve him day and night in his
temple;
and he who sits on the throne will
spread his tent over them.
16Never again will they hunger;
never again will they thirst.
The sun will not beat upon them,
nor any scorching heat.
17For the Lamb at the center of the
throne will be their shepherd;
he will lead them to springs of
living water.
And God will wipe away every tear
from their eyes."

The Seventh Seal and the Golden Censer

8 When he opened the seventh seal,
there was silence in heaven for about
half an hour.
2And I saw the seven angels who stand
before God, and to them were given seven
trumpets.
3Another angel, who had a golden censer, came and stood at the altar. He was
given much incense to offer, with the
prayers of all the saints, on the golden altar before the throne. 4The smoke of the
incense, together with the prayers of the
saints, went up before God from the angel's hand. 5Then the angel took the censer, filled it with fire from the altar, and
hurled it on the earth; and there came
peals of thunder, rumblings, flashes of
lightning and an earthquake.

The Trumpets

6Then the seven angels who had the
seven trumpets prepared to sound them.
7The first angel sounded his trumpet,
and there came hail and fire mixed with
blood, and it was hurled down upon the
earth. A third of the earth was burned up,
a third of the trees were burned up, and all
the green grass was burned up.
8The second angel sounded his trumpet, and something like a huge mountain,

all ablaze, was thrown into the sea. A third
of the sea turned into blood, 9a third of the
living creatures in the sea died, and a third
of the ships were destroyed.
10The third angel sounded his trumpet,
and a great star, blazing like a torch, fell
from the sky on a third of the rivers and
on the springs of water— 11the name of
the star is Wormwood.[a] A third of the
waters turned bitter, and many people
died from the waters that had become bitter.
12The fourth angel sounded his trumpet, and a third of the sun was struck, a
third of the moon, and a third of the stars,
so that a third of them turned dark. A third
of the day was without light, and also a
third of the night.
13As I watched, I heard an eagle that
was flying in midair call out in a loud

[a] 11 That is, Bitterness

VERSE FOR THE DAY: Revelation 7:17

AUTHOR: Diane Eble

PASSAGE FOR THE DAY: Revelation 7:9–17

Mystery of Faith

I know a 76-year-old woman whose husband died after fifty-four years of marriage. Sam had been sick for two years before he died, and his wife was beside him the whole time. In the end, he couldn't speak, so he wasn't able to say good-bye to her. She grieved over that. But God comforted her, she said, by showing her that everything that needed to be spoken had been said over their fifty-four years together.

"Somehow," she told me, "God takes the awfulness out of each experience and sets you on your way."

The mystery of faith: We trust God, and "somehow he takes the awfulness out of" the tragedy. What seemed unbearable ahead of time will somehow become bearable if and when the time comes.

In the end, I'm helpless to shield myself or my loved ones from the unthinkable. Yet there is this: the determination to apply faith to every present experience, easy and hard, pleasant and painful, so that if the floods cover me, I will not be swept away (see Isaiah 43:2).

MARRIAGE BUILDERS

♦ *Why is it so hard not to "borrow trouble" from tomorrow by worrying?*

♦ *How have you experienced God's grace in moments of sorrow or trouble?*

Additional Scripture Readings
Isaiah 43:2; 2 Corinthians 4:7–18

Go to page 1423 for your next devotional reading.

voice: "Woe! Woe! Woe to the inhabitants
of the earth, because of the trumpet blasts
about to be sounded by the other three an-
gels!"

9 The fifth angel sounded his trumpet,
and I saw a star that had fallen from
the sky to the earth. The star was given
the key to the shaft of the Abyss. 2When
he opened the Abyss, smoke rose from it
like the smoke from a gigantic furnace.
The sun and sky were darkened by the
smoke from the Abyss. 3And out of the
smoke locusts came down upon the earth
and were given power like that of scorpi-
ons of the earth. 4They were told not to
harm the grass of the earth or any plant or
tree, but only those people who did not
have the seal of God on their foreheads.
5They were not given power to kill them,
but only to torture them for five months.
And the agony they suffered was like that
of the sting of a scorpion when it strikes
a man. 6During those days men will seek
death, but will not find it; they will long to
die, but death will elude them.

7The locusts looked like horses pre-
pared for battle. On their heads they wore
something like crowns of gold, and their
faces resembled human faces. 8Their hair
was like women's hair, and their teeth
were like lions' teeth. 9They had breast-
plates like breastplates of iron, and the
sound of their wings was like the thunder-
ing of many horses and chariots rushing
into battle. 10They had tails and stings like
scorpions, and in their tails they had pow-
er to torment people for five months.
11They had as king over them the angel of
the Abyss, whose name in Hebrew is
Abaddon, and in Greek, Apollyon.[a]

12The first woe is past; two other woes
are yet to come.

13The sixth angel sounded his trumpet,
and I heard a voice coming from the
horns[b] of the golden altar that is before
God. 14It said to the sixth angel who had
the trumpet, "Release the four angels who
are bound at the great river Euphrates."
15And the four angels who had been kept
ready for this very hour and day and
month and year were released to kill a
third of mankind. 16The number of the
mounted troops was two hundred million.
I heard their number.

17The horses and riders I saw in my vi-
sion looked like this: Their breastplates
were fiery red, dark blue, and yellow as
sulfur. The heads of the horses resembled
the heads of lions, and out of their mouths
came fire, smoke and sulfur. 18A third of
mankind was killed by the three plagues
of fire, smoke and sulfur that came out of
their mouths. 19The power of the horses
was in their mouths and in their tails; for
their tails were like snakes, having heads
with which they inflict injury.

20The rest of mankind that were not
killed by these plagues still did not repent
of the work of their hands; they did not
stop worshiping demons, and idols of
gold, silver, bronze, stone and wood—
idols that cannot see or hear or walk.
21Nor did they repent of their murders,
their magic arts, their sexual immorality
or their thefts.

The Angel and the Little Scroll

10 Then I saw another mighty angel
coming down from heaven. He was
robed in a cloud, with a rainbow above his
head; his face was like the sun, and his
legs were like fiery pillars. 2He was hold-
ing a little scroll, which lay open in his
hand. He planted his right foot on the sea
and his left foot on the land, 3and he gave
a loud shout like the roar of a lion. When
he shouted, the voices of the seven thun-
ders spoke. 4And when the seven thun-
ders spoke, I was about to write; but I
heard a voice from heaven say, "Seal up
what the seven thunders have said and do
not write it down."

5Then the angel I had seen standing on
the sea and on the land raised his right
hand to heaven. 6And he swore by him
who lives for ever and ever, who created
the heavens and all that is in them, the
earth and all that is in it, and the sea and
all that is in it, and said, "There will be no
more delay! 7But in the days when the
seventh angel is about to sound his trum-
pet, the mystery of God will be accom-
plished, just as he announced to his ser-
vants the prophets."

8Then the voice that I had heard from
heaven spoke to me once more: "Go, take
the scroll that lies open in the hand of the
angel who is standing on the sea and on
the land."

9So I went to the angel and asked him
to give me the little scroll. He said to me,
"Take it and eat it. It will turn your stom-
ach sour, but in your mouth it will be as
sweet as honey." 10I took the little scroll

[a] *11 Abaddon* and *Apollyon* mean *Destroyer.* [b] *13* That is, projections

from the angel's hand and ate it. It tasted
as sweet as honey in my mouth, but when
I had eaten it, my stomach turned sour.
11Then I was told, "You must prophesy
again about many peoples, nations, lan-
guages and kings."

The Two Witnesses

11 I was given a reed like a measuring
rod and was told, "Go and measure
the temple of God and the altar, and count
the worshipers there. 2But exclude the
outer court; do not measure it, because it
has been given to the Gentiles. They will
trample on the holy city for 42 months.
3And I will give power to my two wit-
nesses, and they will prophesy for 1,260
days, clothed in sackcloth." 4These are the
two olive trees and the two lampstands
that stand before the Lord of the earth. 5If
anyone tries to harm them, fire comes
from their mouths and devours their ene-
mies. This is how anyone who wants to
harm them must die. 6These men have
power to shut up the sky so that it will not
rain during the time they are prophesying;
and they have power to turn the waters
into blood and to strike the earth with ev-
ery kind of plague as often as they want.
7Now when they have finished their tes-
timony, the beast that comes up from the
Abyss will attack them, and overpower
and kill them. 8Their bodies will lie in the
street of the great city, which is figurative-
ly called Sodom and Egypt, where also
their Lord was crucified. 9For three and a
half days men from every people, tribe,
language and nation will gaze on their
bodies and refuse them burial. 10The in-
habitants of the earth will gloat over them
and will celebrate by sending each other
gifts, because these two prophets had tor-
mented those who live on the earth.
11But after the three and a half days a
breath of life from God entered them, and
they stood on their feet, and terror struck
those who saw them. 12Then they heard a
loud voice from heaven saying to them,
"Come up here." And they went up to
heaven in a cloud, while their enemies
looked on.
13At that very hour there was a severe
earthquake and a tenth of the city col-
lapsed. Seven thousand people were
killed in the earthquake, and the survivors
were terrified and gave glory to the God of
heaven.
14The second woe has passed; the third
woe is coming soon.

The Seventh Trumpet

15The seventh angel sounded his trum-
pet, and there were loud voices in heaven,
which said:

"The kingdom of the world has
become the kingdom of our
Lord and of his Christ,
and he will reign for ever and ever."

16And the twenty-four elders, who were
seated on their thrones before God, fell on
their faces and worshiped God, 17saying:

"We give thanks to you, Lord God
Almighty,
the One who is and who was,
because you have taken your great
power
and have begun to reign.
18The nations were angry;
and your wrath has come.
The time has come for judging the
dead,
and for rewarding your servants the
prophets
and your saints and those who
reverence your name,
both small and great—
and for destroying those who destroy
the earth."

19Then God's temple in heaven was
opened, and within his temple was seen
the ark of his covenant. And there came
flashes of lightning, rumblings, peals of
thunder, an earthquake and a great hail-
storm.

The Woman and the Dragon

12 A great and wondrous sign ap-
peared in heaven: a woman
clothed with the sun, with the moon un-
der her feet and a crown of twelve stars on
her head. 2She was pregnant and cried out
in pain as she was about to give birth.
3Then another sign appeared in heaven:
an enormous red dragon with seven heads
and ten horns and seven crowns on his
heads. 4His tail swept a third of the stars
out of the sky and flung them to the earth.
The dragon stood in front of the woman
who was about to give birth, so that he
might devour her child the moment it was
born. 5She gave birth to a son, a male
child, who will rule all the nations with an
iron scepter. And her child was snatched
up to God and to his throne. 6The woman
fled into the desert to a place prepared for

her by God, where she might be taken care of for 1,260 days.

7And there was war in heaven. Michael and his angels fought against the dragon, and the dragon and his angels fought back. 8But he was not strong enough, and they lost their place in heaven. 9The great dragon was hurled down—that ancient serpent called the devil, or Satan, who leads the whole world astray. He was hurled to the earth, and his angels with him.

10Then I heard a loud voice in heaven say:

"Now have come the salvation and the power and the kingdom of our God,
and the authority of his Christ.
For the accuser of our brothers,
who accuses them before our God day and night,
has been hurled down.
11They overcame him
by the blood of the Lamb
and by the word of their testimony;
they did not love their lives so much as to shrink from death.
12Therefore rejoice, you heavens
and you who dwell in them!
But woe to the earth and the sea,
because the devil has gone down to you!
He is filled with fury,
because he knows that his time is short."

13When the dragon saw that he had been hurled to the earth, he pursued the woman who had given birth to the male child. 14The woman was given the two wings of a great eagle, so that she might fly to the place prepared for her in the desert, where she would be taken care of for a time, times and half a time, out of the serpent's reach. 15Then from his mouth the serpent spewed water like a river, to overtake the woman and sweep her away with the torrent. 16But the earth helped the woman by opening its mouth and swallowing the river that the dragon had spewed out of his mouth. 17Then the dragon was enraged at the woman and went off to make war against the rest of her offspring—those who obey God's commandments and hold to the testimony of Jesus.

13 1And the dragon[a] stood on the shore of the sea.

The Beast out of the Sea

And I saw a beast coming out of the sea. He had ten horns and seven heads, with ten crowns on his horns, and on each head a blasphemous name. 2The beast I saw resembled a leopard, but had feet like those of a bear and a mouth like that of a lion. The dragon gave the beast his power and his throne and great authority. 3One of the heads of the beast seemed to have had a fatal wound, but the fatal wound had been healed. The whole world was astonished and followed the beast. 4Men worshiped the dragon because he had given authority to the beast, and they also worshiped the beast and asked, "Who is like the beast? Who can make war against him?"

5The beast was given a mouth to utter proud words and blasphemies and to exercise his authority for forty-two months. 6He opened his mouth to blaspheme God, and to slander his name and his dwelling place and those who live in heaven. 7He was given power to make war against the saints and to conquer them. And he was given authority over every tribe, people, language and nation. 8All inhabitants of the earth will worship the beast—all whose names have not been written in the book of life belonging to the Lamb that was slain from the creation of the world.[b]

9He who has an ear, let him hear.

10If anyone is to go into captivity,
into captivity he will go.
If anyone is to be killed[c] with the sword,
with the sword he will be killed.

This calls for patient endurance and faithfulness on the part of the saints.

The Beast out of the Earth

11Then I saw another beast, coming out of the earth. He had two horns like a lamb, but he spoke like a dragon. 12He exercised all the authority of the first beast on his behalf, and made the earth and its inhabitants worship the first beast, whose fatal wound had been healed. 13And he performed great and miraculous signs, even causing fire to come down from heaven to earth in full view of men. 14Because of the

[a] *1* Some late manuscripts *And I* [b] *8* Or *written from the creation of the world in the book of life belonging to the Lamb that was slain* [c] *10* Some manuscripts *anyone kills*

signs he was given power to do on behalf
of the first beast, he deceived the inhabi-
tants of the earth. He ordered them to set
up an image in honor of the beast who
was wounded by the sword and yet lived.
15He was given power to give breath to the
image of the first beast, so that it could
speak and cause all who refused to wor-
ship the image to be killed. 16He also
forced everyone, small and great, rich and
poor, free and slave, to receive a mark on
his right hand or on his forehead, 17so that
no one could buy or sell unless he had the
mark, which is the name of the beast or
the number of his name.

18This calls for wisdom. If anyone has
insight, let him calculate the number of
the beast, for it is man's number. His
number is 666.

The Lamb and the 144,000

14 Then I looked, and there before me
was the Lamb, standing on Mount
Zion, and with him 144,000 who had his
name and his Father's name written on
their foreheads. 2And I heard a sound
from heaven like the roar of rushing wa-
ters and like a loud peal of thunder. The
sound I heard was like that of harpists
playing their harps. 3And they sang a new
song before the throne and before the four
living creatures and the elders. No one
could learn the song except the 144,000
who had been redeemed from the earth.
4These are those who did not defile them-
selves with women, for they kept them-
selves pure. They follow the Lamb wher-
ever he goes. They were purchased from
among men and offered as firstfruits to
God and the Lamb. 5No lie was found in
their mouths; they are blameless.

The Three Angels

6Then I saw another angel flying in mid-
air, and he had the eternal gospel to pro-
claim to those who live on the earth—to
every nation, tribe, language and people.
7He said in a loud voice, "Fear God and
give him glory, because the hour of his
judgment has come. Worship him who
made the heavens, the earth, the sea and
the springs of water."

8A second angel followed and said,
"Fallen! Fallen is Babylon the Great,
which made all the nations drink the mad-
dening wine of her adulteries."

9A third angel followed them and said
in a loud voice: "If anyone worships the
beast and his image and receives his mark
on the forehead or on the hand, 10he, too,
will drink of the wine of God's fury, which
has been poured full strength into the cup
of his wrath. He will be tormented with
burning sulfur in the presence of the holy
angels and of the Lamb. 11And the smoke
of their torment rises for ever and ever.
There is no rest day or night for those who
worship the beast and his image, or for
anyone who receives the mark of his
name." 12This calls for patient endurance
on the part of the saints who obey God's
commandments and remain faithful to
Jesus.

13Then I heard a voice from heaven say,
"Write: Blessed are the dead who die in
the Lord from now on."

"Yes," says the Spirit, "they will rest
from their labor, for their deeds will fol-
low them."

The Harvest of the Earth

14I looked, and there before me was a
white cloud, and seated on the cloud was
one "like a son of man"[a] with a crown of
gold on his head and a sharp sickle in his
hand. 15Then another angel came out of
the temple and called in a loud voice to
him who was sitting on the cloud, "Take
your sickle and reap, because the time to
reap has come, for the harvest of the earth
is ripe." 16So he who was seated on the
cloud swung his sickle over the earth, and
the earth was harvested.

17Another angel came out of the temple
in heaven, and he too had a sharp sickle.
18Still another angel, who had charge of
the fire, came from the altar and called in
a loud voice to him who had the sharp
sickle, "Take your sharp sickle and gather
the clusters of grapes from the earth's
vine, because its grapes are ripe." 19The
angel swung his sickle on the earth, gath-
ered its grapes and threw them into the
great winepress of God's wrath. 20They
were trampled in the winepress outside
the city, and blood flowed out of the press,
rising as high as the horses' bridles for a
distance of 1,600 stadia.[b]

Seven Angels With Seven Plagues

15 I saw in heaven another great and
marvelous sign: seven angels with
the seven last plagues—last, because with
them God's wrath is completed. 2And I

[a] *14* Daniel 7:13 [b] *20* That is, about 180 miles (about 300 kilometers)

saw what looked like a sea of glass mixed
with fire and, standing beside the sea,
those who had been victorious over the
beast and his image and over the number
of his name. They held harps given them
by God [3]and sang the song of Moses the
servant of God and the song of the Lamb:

"Great and marvelous are your deeds,
Lord God Almighty.
Just and true are your ways,
King of the ages.
[4]Who will not fear you, O Lord,
and bring glory to your name?
For you alone are holy.
All nations will come
and worship before you,
for your righteous acts have been
revealed."

[5]After this I looked and in heaven the
temple, that is, the tabernacle of the Testi-
mony, was opened. [6]Out of the temple
came the seven angels with the seven
plagues. They were dressed in clean, shin-
ing linen and wore golden sashes around
their chests. [7]Then one of the four living
creatures gave to the seven angels seven
golden bowls filled with the wrath of God,
who lives for ever and ever. [8]And the tem-
ple was filled with smoke from the glory
of God and from his power, and no one
could enter the temple until the seven
plagues of the seven angels were com-
pleted.

The Seven Bowls of God's Wrath

16 Then I heard a loud voice from the
temple saying to the seven angels,
"Go, pour out the seven bowls of God's
wrath on the earth."

[2]The first angel went and poured out
his bowl on the land, and ugly and painful
sores broke out on the people who had the
mark of the beast and worshiped his im-
age.

[3]The second angel poured out his bowl
on the sea, and it turned into blood like
that of a dead man, and every living thing
in the sea died.

[4]The third angel poured out his bowl on
the rivers and springs of water, and they
became blood. [5]Then I heard the angel in
charge of the waters say:

"You are just in these judgments,
you who are and who were, the
Holy One,
because you have so judged;
[6]for they have shed the blood of your
saints and prophets,
and you have given them blood to
drink as they deserve."

[7]And I heard the altar respond:

"Yes, Lord God Almighty,
true and just are your judgments."

[8]The fourth angel poured out his bowl
on the sun, and the sun was given power
to scorch people with fire. [9]They were
seared by the intense heat and they
cursed the name of God, who had control
over these plagues, but they refused to re-
pent and glorify him.

[10]The fifth angel poured out his bowl on
the throne of the beast, and his kingdom
was plunged into darkness. Men gnawed
their tongues in agony [11]and cursed the
God of heaven because of their pains and
their sores, but they refused to repent of
what they had done.

[12]The sixth angel poured out his bowl
on the great river Euphrates, and its water
was dried up to prepare the way for the
kings from the East. [13]Then I saw three
evil[a] spirits that looked like frogs; they
came out of the mouth of the dragon, out
of the mouth of the beast and out of the
mouth of the false prophet. [14]They are
spirits of demons performing miraculous
signs, and they go out to the kings of the
whole world, to gather them for the battle
on the great day of God Almighty.

[15]"Behold, I come like a thief! Blessed is
he who stays awake and keeps his clothes
with him, so that he may not go naked and
be shamefully exposed."

[16]Then they gathered the kings together
to the place that in Hebrew is called Arma-
geddon.

[17]The seventh angel poured out his
bowl into the air, and out of the temple
came a loud voice from the throne, saying,
"It is done!" [18]Then there came flashes of
lightning, rumblings, peals of thunder and
a severe earthquake. No earthquake like it
has ever occurred since man has been on
earth, so tremendous was the quake.
[19]The great city split into three parts, and
the cities of the nations collapsed. God re-
membered Babylon the Great and gave
her the cup filled with the wine of the fury
of his wrath. [20]Every island fled away and
the mountains could not be found. [21]From

[a]13 Greek *unclean*

the sky huge hailstones of about a hundred pounds each fell upon men. And they cursed God on account of the plague of hail, because the plague was so terrible.

The Woman on the Beast

17 One of the seven angels who had the seven bowls came and said to me, "Come, I will show you the punishment of the great prostitute, who sits on many waters. [2]With her the kings of the earth committed adultery and the inhabitants of the earth were intoxicated with the wine of her adulteries."

[3]Then the angel carried me away in the Spirit into a desert. There I saw a woman sitting on a scarlet beast that was covered with blasphemous names and had seven heads and ten horns. [4]The woman was dressed in purple and scarlet, and was glittering with gold, precious stones and pearls. She held a golden cup in her hand, filled with abominable things and the filth of her adulteries. [5]This title was written on her forehead:

MYSTERY
BABYLON THE GREAT
THE MOTHER OF PROSTITUTES
AND OF THE ABOMINATIONS OF THE EARTH.

[6]I saw that the woman was drunk with the blood of the saints, the blood of those who bore testimony to Jesus.

When I saw her, I was greatly astonished. [7]Then the angel said to me: "Why are you astonished? I will explain to you the mystery of the woman and of the beast she rides, which has the seven heads and ten horns. [8]The beast, which you saw, once was, now is not, and will come up out of the Abyss and go to his destruction. The inhabitants of the earth whose names have not been written in the book of life from the creation of the world will be astonished when they see the beast, because he once was, now is not, and yet will come.

[9]"This calls for a mind with wisdom. The seven heads are seven hills on which the woman sits. [10]They are also seven kings. Five have fallen, one is, the other has not yet come; but when he does come, he must remain for a little while. [11]The beast who once was, and now is not, is an eighth king. He belongs to the seven and is going to his destruction.

[12]"The ten horns you saw are ten kings who have not yet received a kingdom, but who for one hour will receive authority as kings along with the beast. [13]They have one purpose and will give their power and authority to the beast. [14]They will make war against the Lamb, but the Lamb will overcome them because he is Lord of lords and King of kings—and with him will be his called, chosen and faithful followers."

[15]Then the angel said to me, "The waters you saw, where the prostitute sits, are peoples, multitudes, nations and languages. [16]The beast and the ten horns you saw will hate the prostitute. They will bring her to ruin and leave her naked; they will eat her flesh and burn her with fire. [17]For God has put it into their hearts to accomplish his purpose by agreeing to give the beast their power to rule, until God's words are fulfilled. [18]The woman you saw is the great city that rules over the kings of the earth."

The Fall of Babylon

18 After this I saw another angel coming down from heaven. He had great authority, and the earth was illuminated by his splendor. [2]With a mighty voice he shouted:

"Fallen! Fallen is Babylon the Great!
She has become a home for demons
and a haunt for every evil[a] spirit,
a haunt for every unclean and
detestable bird.
[3]For all the nations have drunk
the maddening wine of her
adulteries.
The kings of the earth committed
adultery with her,
and the merchants of the earth grew
rich from her excessive
luxuries."

[4]Then I heard another voice from heaven say:

"Come out of her, my people,
so that you will not share in her
sins,
so that you will not receive any of
her plagues;
[5]for her sins are piled up to heaven,
and God has remembered her
crimes.
[6]Give back to her as she has given;

[a]2 Greek *unclean*

pay her back double for what she has done.
Mix her a double portion from her own cup.
7Give her as much torture and grief as the glory and luxury she gave herself.
In her heart she boasts,
'I sit as queen; I am not a widow, and I will never mourn.'
8Therefore in one day her plagues will overtake her:
death, mourning and famine.
She will be consumed by fire,
for mighty is the Lord God who judges her.

9"When the kings of the earth who committed adultery with her and shared her luxury see the smoke of her burning, they will weep and mourn over her. 10Terrified at her torment, they will stand far off and cry:

" 'Woe! Woe, O great city,
O Babylon, city of power!
In one hour your doom has come!'

11"The merchants of the earth will weep and mourn over her because no one buys their cargoes any more— 12cargoes of gold, silver, precious stones and pearls; fine linen, purple, silk and scarlet cloth; every sort of citron wood, and articles of every kind made of ivory, costly wood, bronze, iron and marble; 13cargoes of cinnamon and spice, of incense, myrrh and frankincense, of wine and olive oil, of fine flour and wheat; cattle and sheep; horses and carriages; and bodies and souls of men.

14"They will say, 'The fruit you longed for is gone from you. All your riches and splendor have vanished, never to be recovered.' 15The merchants who sold these things and gained their wealth from her will stand far off, terrified at her torment. They will weep and mourn 16and cry out:

" 'Woe! Woe, O great city,
dressed in fine linen, purple and scarlet,
and glittering with gold, precious stones and pearls!
17In one hour such great wealth has been brought to ruin!'

"Every sea captain, and all who travel by ship, the sailors, and all who earn their living from the sea, will stand far off. 18When they see the smoke of her burning, they will exclaim, 'Was there ever a city like this great city?' 19They will throw dust on their heads, and with weeping and mourning cry out:

" 'Woe! Woe, O great city,
where all who had ships on the sea became rich through her wealth!
In one hour she has been brought to ruin!
20Rejoice over her, O heaven!
Rejoice, saints and apostles and prophets!
God has judged her for the way she treated you.' "

21Then a mighty angel picked up a boulder the size of a large millstone and threw it into the sea, and said:

"With such violence
the great city of Babylon will be thrown down,
never to be found again.
22The music of harpists and musicians, flute players and trumpeters,
will never be heard in you again.
No workman of any trade
will ever be found in you again.
The sound of a millstone
will never be heard in you again.
23The light of a lamp
will never shine in you again.
The voice of bridegroom and bride
will never be heard in you again.
Your merchants were the world's great men.
By your magic spell all the nations were led astray.
24In her was found the blood of prophets and of the saints,
and of all who have been killed on the earth."

Hallelujah!

19 After this I heard what sounded like the roar of a great multitude in heaven shouting:

"Hallelujah!
Salvation and glory and power belong to our God,
2 for true and just are his judgments.
He has condemned the great prostitute who corrupted the earth by her adulteries.
He has avenged on her the blood of his servants."

3And again they shouted:

"Hallelujah!

WEEKENDING

RELAXATION

Life gets crowded, and it seems that the daily pressures and responsibilities take priority. But time for relaxing together is essential for maintaining your connection as husband and wife. Discuss the following ideas for taking more time to kick back and relax.

1. Take half a vacation day to sleep in and have breakfast in bed together.

2. Skip your Saturday chores and take a trip to the zoo or other fun place.

3. Wash the car together (wear something that can get wet).

4. Get out your calendars and schedule an overnight away from home.

5. If most of your time with church friends is spent on ministry projects, invite them over for a game night.

— *The* Marriage Partnership *Staff*

REVIVE

Saturday: Isaiah 30:15; 32:18
Sunday: Genesis 2:1–2

The smoke from her goes up for ever
and ever."

4The twenty-four elders and the four
living creatures fell down and worshiped
God, who was seated on the throne. And
they cried:

"Amen, Hallelujah!"

5Then a voice came from the throne,
saying:

"Praise our God,
all you his servants,
you who fear him,
both small and great!"

6Then I heard what sounded like a great
multitude, like the roar of rushing waters
and like loud peals of thunder, shouting:

"Hallelujah!
For our Lord God Almighty reigns.
7Let us rejoice and be glad
and give him glory!
For the wedding of the Lamb has
come,
and his bride has made herself
ready.
8Fine linen, bright and clean,
was given her to wear."
(Fine linen stands for the righteous acts of
the saints.)

9Then the angel said to me, "Write:
'Blessed are those who are invited to the
wedding supper of the Lamb!' " And he
added, "These are the true words of God."
10At this I fell at his feet to worship him.
But he said to me, "Do not do it! I am a
fellow servant with you and with your
brothers who hold to the testimony of
Jesus. Worship God! For the testimony of
Jesus is the spirit of prophecy."

The Rider on the White Horse

11I saw heaven standing open and there
before me was a white horse, whose rider
is called Faithful and True. With justice he
judges and makes war. 12His eyes are like
blazing fire, and on his head are many
crowns. He has a name written on him
that no one knows but he himself. 13He is
dressed in a robe dipped in blood, and his
name is the Word of God. 14The armies of
heaven were following him, riding on
white horses and dressed in fine linen,
white and clean. 15Out of his mouth
comes a sharp sword with which to strike
down the nations. "He will rule them with
an iron scepter."[a] He treads the wine-
press of the fury of the wrath of God Al-
mighty. 16On his robe and on his thigh he
has this name written:

KING OF KINGS AND LORD OF LORDS.

17And I saw an angel standing in the
sun, who cried in a loud voice to all the
birds flying in midair, "Come, gather to-
gether for the great supper of God, 18so
that you may eat the flesh of kings, gener-
als, and mighty men, of horses and their
riders, and the flesh of all people, free and
slave, small and great."
19Then I saw the beast and the kings of
the earth and their armies gathered to-
gether to make war against the rider on
the horse and his army. 20But the beast
was captured, and with him the false
prophet who had performed the miracu-
lous signs on his behalf. With these signs
he had deluded those who had received
the mark of the beast and worshiped his
image. The two of them were thrown alive
into the fiery lake of burning sulfur. 21The
rest of them were killed with the sword
that came out of the mouth of the rider on
the horse, and all the birds gorged them-
selves on their flesh.

The Thousand Years

20 And I saw an angel coming down
out of heaven, having the key to
the Abyss and holding in his hand a great
chain. 2He seized the dragon, that ancient
serpent, who is the devil, or Satan, and
bound him for a thousand years. 3He
threw him into the Abyss, and locked and
sealed it over him, to keep him from de-
ceiving the nations anymore until the
thousand years were ended. After that, he
must be set free for a short time.
4I saw thrones on which were seated
those who had been given authority to
judge. And I saw the souls of those who
had been beheaded because of their testi-
mony for Jesus and because of the word
of God. They had not worshiped the beast
or his image and had not received his
mark on their foreheads or their hands.
They came to life and reigned with Christ
a thousand years. 5(The rest of the dead
did not come to life until the thousand
years were ended.) This is the first resur-
rection. 6Blessed and holy are those who
have part in the first resurrection. The sec-

[a] *15* Psalm 2:9

ond death has no power over them, but they will be priests of God and of Christ and will reign with him for a thousand years.

Satan's Doom

7When the thousand years are over, Satan will be released from his prison 8and will go out to deceive the nations in the four corners of the earth—Gog and Magog—to gather them for battle. In number they are like the sand on the seashore. 9They marched across the breadth of the earth and surrounded the camp of God's people, the city he loves. But fire came down from heaven and devoured them. 10And the devil, who deceived them, was thrown into the lake of burning sulfur, where the beast and the false prophet had been thrown. They will be tormented day and night for ever and ever.

The Dead Are Judged

11Then I saw a great white throne and him who was seated on it. Earth and sky fled from his presence, and there was no place for them. 12And I saw the dead, great and small, standing before the throne, and books were opened. Another book was opened, which is the book of life. The dead were judged according to what they had done as recorded in the books. 13The sea gave up the dead that were in it, and death and Hades gave up the dead that were in them, and each person was judged according to what he had done. 14Then death and Hades were thrown into the lake of fire. The lake of fire is the second death. 15If anyone's name was not found written in the book of life, he was thrown into the lake of fire.

The New Jerusalem

21 Then I saw a new heaven and a new earth, for the first heaven and the first earth had passed away, and there was no longer any sea. 2I saw the Holy City, the new Jerusalem, coming down out of heaven from God, prepared as a bride beautifully dressed for her husband. 3And I heard a loud voice from the throne saying, "Now the dwelling of God is with men, and he will live with them. They will be his people, and God himself will be with them and be their God. 4He will wipe every tear from their eyes. There will be no more death or mourning or crying or pain, for the old order of things has passed away."

5He who was seated on the throne said, "I am making everything new!" Then he said, "Write this down, for these words are trustworthy and true."

6He said to me: "It is done. I am the Alpha and the Omega, the Beginning and the End. To him who is thirsty I will give to drink without cost from the spring of the water of life. 7He who overcomes will inherit all this, and I will be his God and he will be my son. 8But the cowardly, the unbelieving, the vile, the murderers, the sexually immoral, those who practice magic arts, the idolaters and all liars—their place will be in the fiery lake of burning sulfur. This is the second death."

9One of the seven angels who had the seven bowls full of the seven last plagues came and said to me, "Come, I will show you the bride, the wife of the Lamb." 10And he carried me away in the Spirit to a mountain great and high, and showed me the Holy City, Jerusalem, coming down out of heaven from God. 11It shone with the glory of God, and its brilliance was like that of a very precious jewel, like a jasper, clear as crystal. 12It had a great, high wall with twelve gates, and with twelve angels at the gates. On the gates were written the names of the twelve tribes of Israel. 13There were three gates on the east, three on the north, three on the south and three on the west. 14The wall of the city had twelve foundations, and on them were the names of the twelve apostles of the Lamb.

15The angel who talked with me had a measuring rod of gold to measure the city, its gates and its walls. 16The city was laid out like a square, as long as it was wide. He measured the city with the rod and found it to be 12,000 stadia[a] in length, and as wide and high as it is long. 17He measured its wall and it was 144 cubits[b] thick,[c] by man's measurement, which the angel was using. 18The wall was made of jasper, and the city of pure gold, as pure as glass. 19The foundations of the city walls were decorated with every kind of precious stone. The first foundation was jasper, the second sapphire, the third chalcedony, the fourth emerald, 20the fifth sardonyx, the sixth carnelian, the seventh

[a] 16 That is, about 1,400 miles (about 2,200 kilometers)
[b] 17 That is, about 200 feet (about 65 meters)
[c] 17 Or *high*

chrysolite, the eighth beryl, the ninth topaz, the tenth chrysoprase, the eleventh jacinth, and the twelfth amethyst.[a] 21The twelve gates were twelve pearls, each gate made of a single pearl. The great street of the city was of pure gold, like transparent glass.

22I did not see a temple in the city, because the Lord God Almighty and the Lamb are its temple. 23The city does not need the sun or the moon to shine on it, for the glory of God gives it light, and the Lamb is its lamp. 24The nations will walk by its light, and the kings of the earth will bring their splendor into it. 25On no day will its gates ever be shut, for there will be no night there. 26The glory and honor of the nations will be brought into it. 27Nothing impure will ever enter it, nor will anyone who does what is shameful or deceitful, but only those whose names are written in the Lamb's book of life.

The River of Life

22 Then the angel showed me the river of the water of life, as clear as crystal, flowing from the throne of God and of the Lamb 2down the middle of the great street of the city. On each side of the river stood the tree of life, bearing twelve crops of fruit, yielding its fruit every month. And the leaves of the tree are for the healing of the nations. 3No longer will there be any curse. The throne of God and of the Lamb will be in the city, and his servants will serve him. 4They will see his face, and his name will be on their foreheads. 5There will be no more night. They will not need the light of a lamp or the light of the sun, for the Lord God will give them light. And they will reign for ever and ever.

6The angel said to me, "These words are trustworthy and true. The Lord, the God of the spirits of the prophets, sent his angel to show his servants the things that must soon take place."

Jesus Is Coming

7"Behold, I am coming soon! Blessed is he who keeps the words of the prophecy in this book."

8I, John, am the one who heard and saw these things. And when I had heard and seen them, I fell down to worship at the feet of the angel who had been showing them to me. 9But he said to me, "Do not do it! I am a fellow servant with you and with your brothers the prophets and of all who keep the words of this book. Worship God!"

10Then he told me, "Do not seal up the words of the prophecy of this book, because the time is near. 11Let him who does wrong continue to do wrong; let him who is vile continue to be vile; let him who does right continue to do right; and let him who is holy continue to be holy."

12"Behold, I am coming soon! My reward is with me, and I will give to everyone according to what he has done. 13I am the Alpha and the Omega, the First and the Last, the Beginning and the End.

14"Blessed are those who wash their robes, that they may have the right to the tree of life and may go through the gates into the city. 15Outside are the dogs, those who practice magic arts, the sexually immoral, the murderers, the idolaters and everyone who loves and practices falsehood.

16"I, Jesus, have sent my angel to give you[b] this testimony for the churches. I am the Root and the Offspring of David, and the bright Morning Star."

17The Spirit and the bride say, "Come!" And let him who hears say, "Come!" Whoever is thirsty, let him come; and whoever wishes, let him take the free gift of the water of life.

18I warn everyone who hears the words of the prophecy of this book: If anyone adds anything to them, God will add to him the plagues described in this book. 19And if anyone takes words away from this book of prophecy, God will take away from him his share in the tree of life and in the holy city, which are described in this book.

20He who testifies to these things says, "Yes, I am coming soon."

Amen. Come, Lord Jesus.

21The grace of the Lord Jesus be with God's people. Amen.

[a] *20* The precise identification of some of these precious stones is uncertain. [b] *16* The Greek is plural.

WEIGHTS AND MEASURES

The figures of the table are calculated on the basis of a shekel equaling 11.5 grams, a cubit equaling 18 inches and an ephah equaling 22 liters. The quart referred to is either a dry quart (slightly larger than a liter) or a liquid quart (slightly smaller than a liter), whichever is applicable. The ton referred to in the footnotes is the American ton of 2,000 pounds.

This table is based upon the best available information, but it is not intended to be mathematically precise; like the measurement equivalents in the footnotes, it merely gives approximate amounts and distances. Weights and measures differed somewhat at various times and places in the ancient world. There is uncertainty particularly about the ephah and the bath; further discoveries may give more light on these units of capacity.

		BIBLICAL UNIT	APPROXIMATE AMERICAN EQUIVALENT	APPROXIMATE METRIC EQUIVALENT
WEIGHTS	talent	*(60 minas)*	75 pounds	34 kilograms
	mina	*(50 shekels)*	1 1/4 pounds	0.6 kilogram
	shekel	*(2 bekas)*	2/5 ounce	11.5 grams
	pim	*(2/3 shekel)*	1/3 ounce	7.6 grams
	beka	*(10 gerahs)*	1/5 ounce	5.5 grams
	gerah		1/50 ounce	0.6 gram
LENGTH	cubit		18 inches	0.5 meter
	span		9 inches	23 centimeters
	handbreadth		3 inches	8 centimeters
CAPACITY Dry Measure	cor [homer]	*(10 ephahs)*	6 bushels	220 liters
	lethek	*(5 ephahs)*	3 bushels	110 liters
	ephah	*(10 omers)*	3/5 bushel	22 liters
	seah	*(1/3 ephah)*	7 quarts	7.3 liters
	omer	*(1/10 ephah)*	2 quarts	2 liters
	cab	*(1/18 ephah)*	1 quart	1 liter
Liquid Measure	bath	*(1 ephah)*	6 gallons	22 liters
	hin	*(1/6 bath)*	4 quarts	4 liters
	log	*(1/72 bath)*	1/3 quart	0.3 liter

Page 563: Taken from an interview with Lewis B. Smedes, by James D. Berkley, that originally appeared in the Winter 1991 issue of *Marriage Partnership* magazine. Copyright © 1991 by James D. Berkley. Used by permission of the author.

Page 571: Taken from an unpublished interview with Max Lucado, by Ron R. Lee. Copyright © 2000 by Max Lucado and Christianity Today, Inc. Used by permission.

Page 574: Taken from a Marriage Builders exercise created by the staff of *Marriage Partnership* magazine. Copyright © 1993 by Christianity Today, Inc. Used by permission.

Page 577: Taken from an article by Gregg Lewis that originally appeared in the Fall 1989 issue of *Marriage Partnership* magazine. Copyright © 1989 by Christianity Today, Inc. Used by permission.

Page 580: Taken from an article by Elizabeth Cody Newenhuyse that originally appeared in the Winter 1993 issue of *Marriage Partnership* magazine. Copyright © 1993 by Elizabeth Cody Newenhuyse. Used by permission of the author.

Page 583: Taken from an article by Lyn Cryderman that originally appeared in the Fall 1989 issue of *Marriage Partnership* magazine. Copyright © 1989 by Lyn Cryderman. Used by permission of the author.

Page 587: Taken from an article by Ruth Ann Polston that originally appeared in the March/April 1986 issue of *Partnership* magazine. Copyright © 1986 by Ruth Ann Polston. Used by permission of the author.

Page 590: Taken from an interview with Evelyn Christenson, by Phyllis E. Alsdurf, that originally appeared in the March/April 1985 issue of *Partnership* magazine. Copyright © 1985 by Phyllis E. Alsdurf. Used by permission of the author.

Page 591: Taken from an article by Nancy Kennedy that originally appeared in the Spring 1998 issue of *Marriage Partnership* magazine. Copyright © 1998 by Nancy Kennedy. Used by permission of the author.

Page 592: Taken from an article by Beverly J. Burch that originally appeared in the Winter 1997 issue of *Marriage Partnership* magazine. Copyright © 1997 by Beverly J. Burch. Used by permission of the author.

Page 594: Taken from MARRIAGE: FOR BETTER OR FOR WORSE, by Diana and David Garland. Copyright © 1989 Broadman Press, Nashville, Tennessee. Used by permission.

Page 606: Taken from CHARLIE'S VICTORY, by Charlie and Lucy Wedemeyer with Gregg Lewis. Copyright © 1993 by Charlie and Lucy Wedemeyer. Used by permission of Zondervan Publishing House, Grand Rapids, Michigan.

Page 617: Taken from an interview with Gary Smalley, by Ron R. Lee, that originally appeared in the Spring 1997 issue of *Marriage Partnership* magazine. Copyright © 1997 by Christianity Today, Inc. Used by permission.

Page 621: Taken from an article by Ben Patterson that originally appeared in the Fall 1990 issue of *Marriage Partnership* magazine. Copyright © 1990 by Ben Patterson. Used by permission of the author.

Page 626: Taken from IN-LAWS/OUTLAWS: HOW TO MAKE PEACE WITH HIS FAMILY AND YOURS, by Penny Bilofsky and Fredda Sacharow. Copyright © 1991 by Benny Bilofsky and Fredda Sacharow. Used by permission of Villard Books, a division of Random House, Inc.

Page 629: Taken from an interview with David and Claudia Arp, by Annette LaPlaca, that originally appeared in the Spring 1994 issue of *Marriage Partnership* magazine. Copyright © 1994 by Christianity Today, Inc. Used by permission.

Page 637: Taken from an interview with Walter Wangerin, Jr., by Annette LaPlaca, that originally appeared in the Fall 1996 issue of *Marriage Partnership* magazine. Copyright © 1996 by Christianity Today, Inc. Used by permission.

Page 644: Taken from an article by Elizabeth Cody Newenhuyse that originally appeared in the Winter 1993 issue of *Marriage Partnership* magazine. Copyright © 1993 by Elizabeth Cody Newenhuyse. Used by permission of the author.

Page 650: Taken from an article by Ruth Senter that originally appeared in the March/April 1987 issue of *Partnership* magazine. Copyright © 1987 by Christianity Today, Inc. Used by permission.

Page 652: Taken from THE FIRST YEARS OF FOREVER, by Ed Wheat, M.D., and Gloria Okes Perkins. Copyright © 1988 by Ed Wheat. Used by permission of Zondervan Publishing House, Grand Rapids, Michigan.

Page 653: Taken from LOVE THAT LASTS, by Gary and Betsy Ricucci. Copyright © 1992 by People of Destiny International. Used by permission.

Page 655: Taken from an interview with Jeanne Hendricks, by Ruth Senter, that originally appeared in the May/June 1985 issue of *Partnership* magazine. Copyright © 1985 by Christianity Today, Inc. Used by permission.

Page 657: Taken from an article by Harold B. Smith that originally appeared in the Fall 1994 issue of *Marriage Partnership* magazine. Copyright © 1994 by Christianity Today, Inc. Used by permission.

Page 662: Taken from TRAITS OF A LASTING MARRIAGE, by Jim and Sally Conway. Copyright © 1991 by Jim and Sally Conway. Used by permission of InterVarsity Press, Downers Grove, Illinois.

Page 664: Taken from WELCOME HOME, DAVEY, by Dave Roever and Harold Fickett. Copyright © 1986 by Dave Roever. Used by permission of the authors. Published by Word, Inc., Dallas, Texas.

Page 668: Taken from an article by Alison A. McCaughan that originally appeared in the January/February 1985 issue of *Partnership* magazine. Copyright © 1985 by Alison A. McCaughan. Used by permission of the author.

Page 670: Taken from a Marriage Builders exercise created by the staff of *Marriage Partnership* magazine. Copyright © 1994 by Christianity Today, Inc. Used by permission.

Page 672: Taken from an interview with Dennis and Lucy Guernsey, by Scott W. Bolinder, that originally appeared in the Spring 1988 issue of *Marriage Partnership* magazine. Copyright © 1988 by Christianity Today, Inc. Used by permission.

Page 674: Taken from an interview with Jim and Sally Conway, by Ron R. Lee, that originally appeared in the Winter 1993 issue of *Marriage Partnership* magazine. Copyright © 1993 by Christianity Today, Inc. Used by permission.

Page 679: Taken from an article by Scott M. Stanley that originally appeared in the Winter 1996 issue of *Marriage Partnership* magazine. Copyright © 1996 by Scott M. Stanley. Used by permission of the author.

Page 682: Taken from an article by Elisa Morgan that originally appeared in the September/October 1985 issue of *Partnership* magazine. Copyright © 1985 by Elisa Morgan. Used by permission of the author.

Page 686: Taken from an article by Marian V. Liautaud that originally appeared in the Winter 1991 issue of *Marriage Partnership* magazine. Copyright © 1991 by Christianity Today, Inc. Used by permission.

Page 687: Taken from an article by Robert Moeller that originally appeared in the Spring 1999 issue of *Marriage Partnership* magazine. Copyright © 1999 by Robert Moeller. Used by permission of the author.

Page 689: Taken from STRIKE THE ORIGINAL MATCH, by Charles R. Swindoll. Copyright © 1980 by Multnomah Press. Used by permission of Zondervan Puplishing House, Grand Rapids, Michigan.

Page 691: Taken from PEACEFUL LIVING IN A STRESSFUL WORLD, by Ron Hutchcraft. Copyright © 1984 by Ron Hutchcraft. Used by permission of Thomas Nelson Publishers, Nashville, Tennessee.

Page 693: Taken from an article by Win Couchman that originally appeared in the Spring 1992 issue of *Marriage Partnership* magazine. Copyright © 1992 by Win Couchman. Used by permission of the author.

Page 697: Taken from an article by Elizabeth Cody Newenhuyse that originally appeared in the Fall 1991 issue of *Marriage Partnership* magazine. Copyright © 1991 by Christianity Today, Inc. Used by permission.

Page 699: Taken from an article by Les and Leslie Parrott that originally appeared in the Winter 1995 issue of *Marriage Partnership* magazine. Copyright © 1995 by Les and Leslie Parrott. Used by permission of the authors.

Page 701: Taken from 52 SIMPLE WAYS TO GIVE YOUR SPIRITUAL LIFE A LIFT, by Jan Dargatz. Copyright © 1991 by Jan Dargatz. Used by permission of Oliver Nelson, a division of Thomas Nelson Publishers, Nashville, Tennessee.

Page 703: Taken from an interview with Jill Briscoe, by Ruth Senter, that originally appeared in the March/April 1985 issue of *Partnership* magazine. Copyright © 1985 by Christianity Today, Inc. Used by permission.

Page 705: Taken from an interview with Will Willimon, by Michael G. Maudlin, that originally appeared in the Spring 1990 issue of *Marriage Partnership* magazine. Copyright © 1990 by Michael G. Maudlin. Used by permission of the author.

Page 707: Taken from an article by Jeanette and Robert Lauer that originally appeared in the Summer 1991 issue of *Marriage Partnership* magazine. Copyright © 1991 by Jeanette and Robert Lauer. Used by permission of the author.

Page 708: Taken from an article by Luci Shaw that originally appeared in the Summer 1990 issue of *Marriage Partnership* magazine. Copyright © 1990 by Luci Shaw. Used by permission of the author.

Page 715: Taken from an article by Jim Smith that originally appeared in the Summer 1992 issue of *Marriage Partnership* magazine. Copyright © 1992 by the estate of Jim Smith. Used by permission.

Page 717: Taken from HOLDING ON TO ROMANCE, by H. Norman Wright. Copyright © 1987, 1992 by Regal Books, a division of Gospel Light, Ventura, California. Used by permission.

Page 719: Taken from an article by Tim Stafford that originally appeared in the Summer 1988 issue of *Marriage Partnership* magazine. Copyright © 1988 by Tim Stafford. Used by permission of the author.

Page 731: Taken from an article by Bonnie Shipley Rice that originally appeared in the May/June 1985 issue of *Partnership* magazine. Copyright © 1985 by Christianity Today, Inc. Used by permission.

Page 733: Taken from "Prayer and the Jealous God," an article by Henri J.M. Nouwen that originally appeared in the June 1985 issue of the *New Oxford Review*. Copyright © 1985 by the *New Oxford Review*. Used by permission of Henri J.M. Nouwen.

Page 750: Taken from THE ADVENTURE OF BEING A WIFE, by Ruth Stafford Peale. Copyright © by Ruth Stafford Peale. Used by permission of the author. Published by Prentice-Hall.

Page 751: Taken from PEACEFUL LIVING IN A STRESSFUL WORLD, by Ron Hutchcraft. Copyright © 1984 by Ron Hutchcraft. Used by permission of Thomas Nelson Publishers, Nashville, Tennessee.

Page 756: Taken from a Marriage Builders exercise created by the staff of *Marriage Partnership* magazine. Copyright © 1993 by Christianity Today, Inc. Used by permission.

Page 760: Taken from an article by Les and Leslie Parrott that originally appeared in Winter 1998 issue of *Marriage Partnership* magazine. Copyright © 1998 by Les and Leslie Parrott. Used by permission of the authors.

Page 763: Taken from an interview with Vic and Betsey Glavach, by Gregg Lewis, that originally appeared in the Winter 1991 issue of *Marriage Partnership* magazine. Copyright © 1991 by Christianity Today, Inc. Used by permission.

Page 766: Taken from an article by Diane Eble that originally appeared in the Spring 1992 issue of *Marriage Partnership* magazine. Copyright © 1992 by Diane Eble. Used by permission of the author.

Page 771: Taken from an article by Les and Leslie Parrott that originally appeared in Summer 1999 issue of *Marriage Partnership* magazine. Copyright © 1999 by Les and Leslie Parrott. Used by permission of the authors.

Page 779: Taken from an article by Diane M. Langberg that originally appeared in the November/December 1985 issue of *Partnership* magazine. Copyright © 1985 by Diane M. Langberg. Used by permission of the author.

Page 781: Taken from 52 WAYS TO SHOW AGING PARENTS YOU CARE, by Todd Temple and Tracy Green. Copyright © 1991 by Todd Temple and Tracy Green. Used by permission of Oliver Nelson, a division of Thomas Nelson Publishers.

Page 782: Taken from an article by Louis McBurney, M.D., that originally appeared in the Summer 1998 issue of *Marriage Partnership* magazine. Copyright © 1998 by Louis McBurney, M.D. Used by permission of the author.

Page 786: Taken from TRAITS OF A LASTING MARRIAGE, by Jim and Sally Conway. Copyright © 1991 by Jim and Sally Conway. Used by permission of InterVarsity Press, Downers Grove, Illinois.

Page 788: Taken from an article by Elisa Morgan that originally appeared in the September/October 1985 issue of *Partnership* magazine. Copyright © 1985 by Elisa Morgan. Used by permission of the author.

Page 791: Taken from an article by Mary Ellen Williams Ton that originally appeared in the May/June 1985 issue of *Partnership* magazine. Copyright © 1985 by Mary Ellen Williams Ton. Used by permission of the author.

Page 799: Taken from an article by Tim Stafford that originally appeared in the Fall 1988 issue of *Marriage Partnership* magazine. Copyright © 1988 by Tim Stafford. Used by permission of the author.

Page 803: Taken from THE QUESTIONS BOOK FOR MARRIAGE INTIMACY, by Dennis and Barbara Rainey. Copyright © 1988 by Dennis and Barbara Rainey. Used by permission of Dennis and Barbara Rainey, the FAMILY MINISTRY, Little Rock, Arkansas.

Page 805: Taken from WHAT MY PARENTS DID RIGHT, compiled and edited by Gloria Gaither, Star Song Publishing Group, P.O.Box 150009, Nashville, Tennessee. Copyright © 1991 by Gloria Gaither. Used by permission.

Page 808: Taken from an article by Diane Eble that originally appeared in the Winter 1991 issue of *Marriage Partnership* magazine. Copyright © 1991 by Diane Eble. Used by permission of the author.

Page 821: Taken from an interview with Mark and Angela Lewis, by Gregg Lewis, that originally appeared in the Summer 1990 issue of *Marriage Partnership* magazine. Copyright © 1990 by Christianity Today, Inc. Used by permission.

Page 827: Taken from an interview with Howard and Jeanne Hendricks, by Ruth Senter, that originally appeared in the May/June 1985 issue of *Partnership* magazine. Copyright © 1985 by Christianity Today, Inc. Used by permission.

Page 834: Taken from an article by Ben Patterson that originally appeared in the Fall 1990 issue of *Marriage Partnership* magazine. Copyright © 1990 by Ben Patterson. Used by permission of the author.

Page 837: Written by Jeron Frame. Copyright © 1994 by Christianity Today, Inc. Used by permission.

Page 842: Taken from an article by John W. Kennedy that originally appeared in the Winter 1997 issue of *Marriage Partnership* magazine. Copyright © 1997 by Christianity Today, Inc. Used by permission.

Page 871: Taken from an article by Ruth Senter that originally appeared in the September/October 1985 issue of *Partnership* magazine. Copyright © 1985 by Christianity Today, Inc. Used by permission.

Page 873: Taken from an article by Jay Kesler that originally appeared in the Winter 1993 issue of *Marriage Partnership* magazine. Copyright © 1993 by Jay Kesler. Used by permission of the author.

Page 883: Taken from an interview with Lewis B. Smedes, by James D. Berkley, that originally appeared in the Winter 1991 issue of *Marriage Partnership* magazine. Copyright © 1991 by James D. Berkley. Used by permission of the author.

Page 909: Written by David and Annette LaPlaca. Copyright © 1994 by Christianity Today, Inc. Used by permission.

Page 922: Taken from an article by Kaye V. Cook that originally appeared in the Spring 1994 issue of *Marriage Partnership* magazine. Copyright © 1994 by Kaye V. Cook. Used by permission of the author.

Page 932: Taken from an interview with Jim and Sally Conway, by Ron R. Lee, that originally appeared in the Winter 1993 issue of *Marriage Partnership* magazine. Copyright © 1993 by Christianity Today, Inc. Used by permission.

Page 935: Taken from THE TABLE OF INWARDNESS, by Calvin Miller. Copyright © 1984 by InterVarsity Christian Fellowship of the USA. Used by permission of InterVarsity Press, Downers Grove, Illinois.

Page 938: Taken from an interview with Jill and Stuart Briscoe, by Annette LaPlaca, that originally appeared in the Fall 1993 issue of *Marriage Partnership* magazine. Copyright © 1993 by Christianity Today, Inc. Used by permission.

Page 942: Taken from an interview with Jill and Stuart Briscoe, by Annette LaPlaca, that originally appeared in the Fall 1993 issue of *Marriage Partnership* magazine. Copyright © 1993 by Christianity Today, Inc. Used by permission.

Page 946: Taken from an article by Jim Smith that originally appeared in the Summer 1992 issue of *Marriage Partnership* magazine. Copyright © 1992 by the estate of Jim Smith. Used by permission.

Page 948: Taken from a Marriage Builders exercise created by the staff of *Marriage Partnership* magazine. Copyright © 1993 by Christianity Today, Inc. Used by permission.

Page 951: Taken from an article by Joni Eareckson Tada that originally appeared in the January/February 1988 issue of *Marriage Partnership* magazine. Copyright © 1988 by Joni Eareckson Tada. Used by permission of the author.

Page 956: Taken from an article by Tim Stafford that originally appeared in the Fall 1988 issue of *Marriage Partnership* magazine. Copyright © 1988 by Tim Stafford. Used by permission of the author.

Page 962: Taken from an article by Keith Stonehocker that originally appeared in the Fall 1992 issue of *Marriage Partnership* magazine. Copyright © 1992 by Christianity Today, Inc. Used by permission.

Page 967: Taken from an article by Richard Capen that originally appeared in the Winter 1991 issue of *Marriage Partnership* magazine. Copyright © 1991 by Richard Capen. Used by permission of the author.

Page 974: Written by Ron R. Lee. Copyright © 2000 by Christianity Today, Inc. Used by permission.

Page 975: Taken from a Marriage Builders exercise by Harold B. Smith. Copyright © 1990 by Christianity Today, Inc. Used by permission.

Page 978: Taken from an article by Wonda Layton that originally appeared in the January/February 1985 issue of *Partnership* magazine. Copyright © 1985 by Wonda Layton. Used by permission of the author.

Page 986: Taken from an article by Charlene Ann Baumbich that originally appeared in the Winter 1990 issue of *Marriage Partnership* magazine. Copyright © 1990 by Charlene Ann Baumbich. Used by permission of the author.

Page 987: Taken from an unpublished interview with Max Lucado, by Ron R. Lee. Copyright © 2000 by Max Lucado and Christianity Today, Inc. Used by permission.

Page 990: Taken from THE GRACE AWAKENING, by Charles R. Swindoll. Copyright © 1990 by Charles R. Swindoll. Published by Word Inc., Dallas, Texas. Used by permission.

Page 995: Taken from THE IMITATION OF CHRIST, by Thomas à Kempis.

Page 997: Written by Jeron Frame. Copyright © 1994 by Christianity Today, Inc. Used by permission.

Page 1001: Taken from an article by Charlene Ann Baumbich that originally appeared in the Winter 1990 issue of *Marriage Partnership* magazine. Copyright © 1990 by Charlene Ann Baumbich. Used by permission of the author.

Page 1003: Taken from MARRIAGE SPIRITUALITY: TEN DISCIPLINES FOR COUPLES WHO LOVE GOD, by Paul Stevens. Copyright © 1989 by Paul Stevens. Used by permission of InterVarsity Press, Downers Grove, Illinois.

Page 1006: Written by Ron and Jeanette Lee. Copyright © 2000 by Christianity Today, Inc. Used by permission.

Page 1011: Taken from an article by Win Couchman that originally appeared in the Spring 1992 issue of *Marriage Partnership* magazine. Copyright © 1992 by Win Couchman. Used by permission of the author.

Page 1019: Taken from an interview with Jim Smith, by Annette LaPlaca, that originally appeared in the Spring 1993 issue of *Marriage Partnership* magazine. Copyright © 1993 by Christianity Today, Inc.

Page 1021: Taken from a Marriage Builders exercise created by the staff of *Marriage Partnership* magazine. Copyright © 1994 by Christianity Today, Inc.

Page 1022: Taken from an article by Ron R. Lee that originally appeared in the Spring 1990 issue of *Marriage Partnership* magazine. Copyright © 1990 by Christianity Today, Inc.

Page 1024: Taken from an article by Marian V. Liautaud that originally appeared in the Winter 1996 issue of *Marriage Partnership* magazine. Copyright © 1996 by Marian V. Liautaud. Used by permission of the author.

Page 1031: Taken from an article by Ruth Senter that originally appeared in the September/October 1985 issue of *Partnership* magazine. Copyright © 1985 by Christianity Today, Inc. Used by permission.

Page 1033: Taken from an article by Douglas B. DeMerchant that originally appeared in the Winter 1991 issue of *Marriage Partnership* magazine. Copyright © 1991 by Douglas B. DeMerchant. Used by permission of the author.

Page 1034: Taken from an article by Ruth Senter that originally appeared in the July/August 1986 issue of *Partnership* magazine. Copyright © 1986 by Christianity Today, Inc. Used by permission.

Page 1036: Taken from CREATIVE ROMANCE, by Doug Fields. Copyright © 1991 by Doug Fields. Used by permission of the author. Published by Harvest House Publishers, Eugene, Oregon.

Page 1038: Taken from THE APPLAUSE OF HEAVEN, by Max Lucado. Copyright © 1990 by Max Lucado. Used by permission of Word, Inc., Dallas, Texas.

Page 1043: Taken from an article by R. Ruth Barton that originally appeared in the March/April 1985 issue of *Partnership* magazine. Copyright © 1985 by R. Ruth Barton. Used by permission of the author.

Page 1044: Taken from an article by James Long that originally appeared in the Spring 1990 issue of *Marriage Partnership* magazine. Copyright © 1990 by James Long. Used by permission of the author.

Page 1049: Taken from an interview with Bill Hybels, by Ron R. Lee, that originally appeared in the Fall 1991 issue of *Marriage Partnership* magazine. Copyright © 1991 by Christianity Today, Inc. Used by permission.

Page 1053: Taken from an interview with Lewis B. Smedes, by James D. Berkley, that originally appeared in the Winter 1991 issue of *Marriage Partnership* magazine. Copyright © 1991 by James D. Berkley. Used by permission of the author.

Page 1055: Taken from a Marriage Builders exercise created by the staff of *Marriage Partnership* magazine. Copyright © 1993 by Christianity Today, Inc. Used by permission.

Page 1056: Written by Ron R. Lee. Copyright © 2000 by Christianity Today, Inc. Used by permission.

Page 1066: Taken from an article by Alesia T. Thayer that originally appeared in the September/October 1984 issue of *Partnership* magazine. Copyright © 1984 by Alesia T. Thayer. Used by permission of the author.

Page 1069: Taken from an article by Andrea Midgett that originally appeared in the Fall 1991 issue of *Marriage Partnership* magazine. Copyright © 1991 by Andrea Midgett. Used by permission of the author.

Page 1073: Taken from THE PASTOR'S WIFE TODAY, by Donna Sinclair. Copyright © 1981 by Abingdon Press. Used by permission.

Page 1081: Taken from an article by Donna Lobs that originally appeared in the January/February 1984 issue of *Partnership* magazine. Copyright © 1984 by Donna Lobs. Used by permission of the author.

Page 1083: Taken from a Marriage Builders exercise created by the staff of *Marriage Partnership* magazine. Copyright © 1992 by Christianity Today, Inc. Used by permission.

Page 1085: Taken from an interview with Stuart and Jill Briscoe, by Annette LaPlaca, that originally appeared in the Fall 1993 issue of *Marriage Partnership* magazine. Copyright © 1993 by Christianity Today, Inc. Used by permission.

Page 1087: Taken from an article by Jay Kesler that originally appeared in the Winter 1989 issue of *Marriage Partnership* magazine. Copyright © 1989 by Jay Kesler. Used by permission of the author.

Page 1089: Taken from an interview with Lewis B. Smedes, by James D. Berkley, that originally appeared in the Winter 1991 issue of *Marriage Partnership* magazine. Copyright © 1991 by James D. Berkley. Used by permission of the author.

Page 1091: Taken from an interview with Larry Crabb, by Gregg Lewis, that originally appeared in the Spring 1991 issue of *Marriage Partnership* magazine. Copyright © 1991 by Christianity Today, Inc. Used by permission.

Page 1100: Taken from an article by Elizabeth Cody Newenhuyse that originally appeared in the Spring 1993 issue of *Marriage Partnership* magazine. Copyright © 1993 by Elizabeth Cody Newenhuyse. Used by permission of the author.

Page 1104: Taken from a Marriage Builders exercise created by the staff of *Marriage Partnership* magazine. Copyright © 1994 by Christianity Today, Inc. Used by permission.

Page 1106: Taken from an interview with Jill and Stuart Briscoe, by Annette LaPlaca, that originally appeared in the Fall 1993 issue of *Marriage Partnership* magazine. Copyright © 1993 by Christianity Today, Inc. Used by permission.

Page 1110: Taken from an article by Kathy Tippett Henderson that originally appeared in the January/February 1985 issue of *Partnership* magazine. Copyright © 1985 by Kathy Tippett Henderson. Used by permission of the author.

Page 1112: Taken from BEYOND OURSELVES, by Catherine Marshall. Copyright © 1961 by Catherine Marshall. Used by permission of Chosen Books, Fleming H. Revell, a division of Baker Book House.

Page 1116: Taken from MORE THAN YOU & ME, by Kevin A. Miller and Karen Miller. Copyright © 1994 by Kevin A. Miller and Karen Miller. Used by permission of Focus on the Family Publishing, Colorado Springs, Colorado.

Page 1119: Taken from an article by Susan M. Felch that originally appeared in the November/December 1985 issue of *Partnership* magazine. Copyright © 1985 by Susan M. Felch. Used by permission of the author.

Page 1121: Taken from an article by Louise A. Ferrebee that originally appeared in the Summer 1998 issue of *Marriage Partnership* magazine. Copyright © 1998 by Christianity Today, Inc. Used by permission.

Page 1124: Taken from an article by Susan M. Bailey that originally appeared in the Spring 1991 issue of *Marriage Partnership* magazine. Copyright © 1991 by Christianity Today, Inc. Used by permission.

Page 1128: Taken from an article by Gary L. Thomas that originally appeared in the Winter 1999 issue of *Marriage Partnership* magazine. Copyright © 1999 by Gary L. Thomas. Used by permission of the author.

Page 1131: Taken from an article by Martha Reapsome that originally appeared in the March/April 1985 issue of *Partnership* magazine. Copyright © 1985 by Martha Reapsome. Used by permission of the author.

Page 1133: Taken from an article by Beverly J. Burch that originally appeared in the Spring 1997 issue of *Marriage Partnership* magazine. Copyright © 1997 by Beverly J. Burch. Used by permission of the author.

Page 1135: Taken from an interview with Bill and Gloria Gaither, by Harold B. Smith and Elizabeth Cody Newenhuyse, that originally appeared in the Spring 1992 issue of *Marriage Partnership* magazine. Copyright © 1992 by Christianity Today, Inc. Used by permission.

Page 1138: Taken from a Marriage Builders exercise created by the staff of *Marriage Partnership* magazine. Copyright © 1993 by Christianity Today, Inc. Used by permission.

Page 1142: Taken from an article by Philip Yancey that originally appeared in the April 8, 1991, edition of *Christianity Today* magazine. Copyright © 1991 by Philip Yancey. Used by permission of the author.

Page 1146: Taken from an article by Ruth Senter that originally appeared in the November/December 1986 issue of *Partnership* magazine. Copyright © 1986 by Christianity Today, Inc. Used by permission.

Page 1149: Taken from A ROOM CALLED REMEMBER, by Frederick Buechner. Copyright © 1984 by Frederick Buechner. Used by permission of HarperSanFrancisco, a division of HarperCollins Publishers, Inc.

Page 1151: Taken from ENERGIZERS, by Nate Adams. Copyright © 1993 by Nate Adams. Used by permission of Zondervan Publishing House.

Page 1159: Taken from an article by R. Ruth Barton that originally appeared in the March/April 1985 issue of *Partnership* magazine. Copyright © 1985 by R. Ruth Barton. Used by permission of the author.

Page 1161: Taken from an article by Jim Killam that originally appeared in the Winter 1998 issue of *Marriage Partnership* magazine. Copyright © 1998 by Jim Killam. Used by permission of the author.

Page 1163: Taken from an article by Archibald D. Hart, Ph.D., that originally appeared in the Fall 1991 issue of *Marriage Partnership* magazine. Copyright © 1991 by Archibald D. Hart, Ph.D.. Used by permission of the author.

Page 1169: Taken from an article by Gregg Lewis that originally appeared in the Summer 1989 issue of *Marriage Partnership* magazine. Copyright © 1989 by Christianity Today, Inc. Used by permission.

Page 1170: Taken from ABSOLUTE SURRENDER, by Andrew Murray. Used by permission of Christian Literature Crusade, Inc.

Page 1171: Taken from an article by Jerry Bridges and Annette LaPlaca that originally appeared in the Summer 1996 issue of *Marriage Partnership* magazine. Copyright © 1996 by Jerry Bridges and Christianity Today, Inc. Used by permission.

Page 1180: Taken from an interview with Jill and Stuart Briscoe, by Annette LaPlaca, that originally appeared in the Fall 1993 issue of *Marriage Partnership* magazine. Copyright © 1993 by Christianity Today, Inc. Used by permission.

Page 1182: Taken from HOLDING ON TO ROMANCE, by H. Norman Wright. Copyright © 1987, 1992 by Regal Books, a division of Gospel Light, Ventura, California. Used by permission.

Page 1183: Taken from an article by Donald R. Harvey that originally appeared in the Winter 1996 issue of *Marriage Partnership* magazine. Copyright © 1996 by Donald R. Harvey. Used by permission of the author.

Page 1185: Taken from an interview with Ben Patterson, by Ron R. Lee, that originally appeared in the Fall 1994 issue of *Marriage Partnership* magazine. Copyright © 1994 by Christianity Today, Inc. Used by permission.

Page 1187: Taken from an article by Ruth Senter that originally appeared in the March/April 1986 issue of *Partnership* magazine. Copyright © 1986 by Christianity Today, Inc. Used by permission.

Page 1194: Taken from an article by Marylou Habecker that originally appeared in the May/June 1986 issue of *Partnership* magazine. Copyright © 1986 by Marylou Habecker. Used by permission of the author.

Page 1202: Taken from an article by Preston and Genie Dyer that originally appeared in the Fall 1992 issue of *Marriage Partnership* magazine. Copyright © 1992 by Preston and Genie Dyer. Used by permission of the author.

Page 1203: Taken from a Marriage Builders exercise created by the staff of *Marriage Partnership* magazine. Copyright © 1992 by Christianity Today, Inc. Used by permission.

Page 1205: Taken from an interview with Ruth Bell Graham, by Ruth Senter, that originally appeared in the July/August 1984 issue of *Partnership* magazine. Copyright © 1984 by Christianity Today, Inc. Used by permission.

Page 1209: Taken from an article by Archibald D. Hart, Ph.D., that originally appeared in the Fall 1991 issue of *Marriage Partnership* magazine. Copyright © 1991 by Archibald D. Hart, Ph.D.. Used by permission of the author.

Page 1222: Taken from a profile of Frank and Barbara Peretti, by Annette LaPlaca, that originally appeared in the Spring 1996 issue of *Marriage Partnership* magazine. Copyright © 1996 by Christianity Today, Inc. Used by permission.

Page 1224: Taken from an article by Ruth Senter that originally appeared in the July/August 1985 issue of *Partnership* magazine. Copyright © 1985 by Christianity Today, Inc. Used by permission.

Page 1226: Taken from an interview with Lewis B. Smedes, by James D. Berkley, that originally appeared in the Winter 1991 issue of *Marriage Partnership* magazine. Copyright © 1991 by James D. Berkley. Used by permission of the author.

Page 1228: Taken from a Marriage Builders exercise created by the staff of *Marriage Partnership* magazine. Copyright © 1993 by Christianity Today, Inc. Used by permission.

Page 1231: Taken from an interview with Ruth Bell Graham, by Ruth Senter, that originally appeared in the July/August 1984 issue of *Partnership* magazine. Copyright © 1984 by Christianity Today, Inc. Used by permission.

Page 1236: Taken from A PRETTY GOOD PERSON, by Lewis B. Smedes. Copyright © 1990 by Lewis B. Smedes. Used by permission of HarperCollins Publishers.

Page 1237: Taken from an interview with Jill and Stuart Briscoe, by Annette LaPlaca, that originally appeared in the Fall 1993 issue of *Marriage Partnership* magazine. Copyright © 1993 by Christianity Today, Inc. Used by permission.

Page 1239: Taken from an interview with Jill and Stuart Briscoe, by Annette LaPlaca, that originally appeared in the Fall 1993 issue of *Marriage Partnership* magazine. Copyright © 1993 by Christianity Today, Inc. Used by permission.

Page 1243: Taken from an interview with Howard and Jeanne Hendricks, by Ruth Senter, that originally appeared in the May/June 1985 issue of *Partnership* magazine. Copyright © 1985 by Christianity Today, Inc. Used by permission.

Page 1244: Taken from THE ANGER WORKBOOK, by Dr. Les Carter and Dr. Frank Minirth. Copyright © 1993 by Dr. Les Carter and Dr. Frank Minirth. Used by permission of Thomas Nelson Publishers, Nashville, Tennessee.

Page 1246: Taken from an article by Robertson McQuilkin that first appeared in *Christianity Today* magazine. Copyright © 1990 by Robertson McQuilkin. Used by permission of the author.

Page 1249: Taken from an article by Tim Stafford that originally appeared in the Winter 1989 issue of *Marriage Partnership* magazine. Copyright © 1989 by Tim Stafford. Used by permission of the author.

Page 1250: Taken from THE GRACE AWAKENING, by Charles R. Swindoll. Copyright © 1990 by Charles R. Swindoll. Used by permission of Word, Inc., Dallas, Texas.

Page 1251: Taken from an article by Jay Kesler that originally appeared in the Spring 1992 issue of *Marriage Partnership* magazine. Copyright © 1992 by Jay Kesler. Used by permission of the author.

Page 1253: Taken from an article by Kevin A. Miller that originally appeared in the Fall 1996 issue of *Marriage Partnership* magazine. Copyright © 1996 by Christianity Today, Inc. Used by permission.

Page 1255: Taken from a Marriage Builders exercise created by the staff of *Marriage Partnership* magazine. Copyright © 1993 by Christianity Today, Inc. Used by permission.

Page 1257: Taken from an interview with Larry Crabb, by Gregg Lewis, that originally appeared in the Spring 1991 issue of *Marriage Partnership* magazine. Copyright © 1991 by Christianity Today, Inc. Used by permission.

Page 1258: Taken from an article by R. Kirby Worthington and Everett L. Worthington, Jr., that originally appeared in the Fall 1996 issue of *Marriage Partnership* magazine. Copyright © 1996 by R. Kirby Worthington and Everett L. Worthington, Jr. Used by permission of the authors.

Page 1260: Taken from an article by Philip Yancey that originally appeared in the Spring 1989 issue of *Marriage Partnership* magazine. Copyright © 1989 by Philip Yancey. Used by permission of the author.

Page 1262: Taken from an article by Elisa Morgan that originally appeared in the September/October 1985 issue of *Partnership* magazine. Copyright © 1985 by Elisa Morgan. Used by permission of the author.

Page 1268: Taken from an interview with Evelyn Christenson, by Phyllis E. Alsdurf, that originally appeared in the March/April 1985 issue of *Partnership* magazine. Copyright © 1985 by Phyllis E. Alsdurf. Used by permission of the author.

Page 1269: Taken from an article by Beverly J. Burch that originally appeared in the Spring 1997 issue of *Marriage Partnership* magazine. Copyright © 1997 by Beverly J. Burch. Used by permission of the author.

Page 1270: Taken from an article by Jeanette and Robert Lauer that originally appeared in the Fall 1992 issue of *Marriage Partnership* magazine. Copyright © 1992 by Jeanette and Robert Lauer. Used by permission of the authors.

Page 1272: Taken from THE HUMAN CONNECTION, by Martin Bolt and David Myers. Copyright © 1984 by Martin Bolt and David Myers. Used by permission of David Myers and Thomas Ludwig. Published by InterVarsity Press, Downers Grove, Illinois.

Page 1273: Taken from an article by Ron R. Lee that originally appeared in the Spring 1993 issue of *Marriage Partnership* magazine. Copyright © 1993 by Christianity Today, Inc. Used by permission.

Page 1276: Taken from an article by Ron Blue that originally appeared in the Fall 1993 issue of *Marriage Partnership* magazine. Copyright © 1993 by Ron Blue. Used by permission of the author.

Page 1279: Taken from an article by Elizabeth Cody Newenhuyse that originally appeared in the July/August 1990 issue of *Today's Christian Woman* magazine. Copyright © 1990 by Elizabeth Cody Newenhuyse. Used by permission of the author.

Page 1283: Taken from a Marriage Builders exercise created by the staff of *Marriage Partnership* magazine. Copyright © 1992 by Christianity Today, Inc. Used by permission.

Page 1286: Taken from an article by Lyn Cryderman that originally appeared in the Spring 1992 issue of *Marriage Partnership* magazine. Copyright © 1992 by Lyn Cryderman. Used by permission of the author.

Page 1287: Taken from an article by Gary L. Thomas that originally appeared in the Spring 1997 issue of *Marriage Partnership* magazine. Copyright © 1997 by Gary L. Thomas. Used by permission of the author.

Page 1290: Taken from an article by Gary J. Oliver that originally appeared in the Summer 1998 issue of *Marriage Partnership* magazine. Copyright © 1998 by Gary J. Oliver. Used by permission of the author.

Page 1292: Taken from an interview with H. Norman Wright, by Kenneth H. Sidey, that originally appeared in the Fall 1990 issue of *Marriage Partnership* magazine. Copyright © 1990 by Kenneth H. Sidey. Used by permission of the author.

Page 1293: Taken from an article by Elizabeth Cody Newenhuyse that originally appeared in the Summer 1990 issue of *Marriage Partnership* magazine. Copyright © 1990 by Christianity Today, Inc. Used by permission.

READING PLAN

This reading plan gives you a structured pattern for reading through the entire Bible in one year.

DATE	PASSAGE
January 1	Genesis 1–4
January 2	Genesis 5–8
January 3	Genesis 9–12
January 4	Genesis 13–17
January 5	Genesis 18–20
January 6	Genesis 21–23
January 7	Genesis 24–25
January 8	Genesis 26–28
January 9	Genesis 29–31
January 10	Genesis 32–35
January 11	Genesis 36–38
January 12	Genesis 39–41
January 13	Genesis 42–43
January 14	Genesis 44–46
January 15	Genesis 47–50
January 16	Exodus 1–4
January 17	Exodus 5–7
January 18	Exodus 8–10
January 19	Exodus 11–13
January 20	Exodus 14–16
January 21	Exodus 17–20
January 22	Exodus 21–23
January 23	Exodus 24–27
January 24	Exodus 28–30
January 25	Exodus 31–34
January 26	Exodus 35–37
January 27	Exodus 38–40
January 28	Leviticus 1–4
January 29	Leviticus 5–7
January 30	Leviticus 8–10
January 31	Leviticus 11–13
February 1	Leviticus 14–15
February 2	Leviticus 16–18
February 3	Leviticus 19–21
February 4	Leviticus 22–23
February 5	Leviticus 24–25
February 6	Leviticus 26–27
February 7	Numbers 1–2
February 8	Numbers 3–4
February 9	Numbers 5–6
February 10	Numbers 7
February 11	Numbers 8–10
February 12	Numbers 11–13
February 13	Numbers 14–15
February 14	Numbers 16–18
February 15	Numbers 19–21
February 16	Numbers 22–24
February 17	Numbers 25–26
February 18	Numbers 27–29
February 19	Numbers 30–32
February 20	Numbers 33–36
February 21	Deuteronomy 1–2
February 22	Deuteronomy 3–4
February 23	Deuteronomy 5–8
February 24	Deuteronomy 9–11
February 25	Deuteronomy 12–15
February 26	Deuteronomy 16–19
February 27	Deuteronomy 20–23
February 28	Deuteronomy 24–27
March 1	Deuteronomy 28–29
March 2	Deuteronomy 30–32
March 3	Deuteronomy 33–34
March 4	Joshua 1–4
March 5	Joshua 5–7
March 6	Joshua 8–10
March 7	Joshua 11–13
March 8	Joshua 14–17
March 9	Joshua 18–20
March 10	Joshua 21–22
March 11	Joshua 23–24
March 12	Judges 1–3
March 13	Judges 4–5
March 14	Judges 6–8
March 15	Judges 9–10
March 16	Judges 11–13
March 17	Judges 14–16
March 18	Judges 17–19
March 19	Judges 20–21
March 20	Ruth 1–4
March 21	1 Samuel 1–3
March 22	1 Samuel 4–7
March 23	1 Samuel 8–12
March 24	1 Samuel 13–14
March 25	1 Samuel 15–16
March 26	1 Samuel 17–18
March 27	1 Samuel 19–21
March 28	1 Samuel 22–24
March 29	1 Samuel 25–27
March 30	1 Samuel 28–31
March 31	2 Samuel 1–3
April 1	2 Samuel 4–7
April 2	2 Samuel 8–11
April 3	2 Samuel 12–13
April 4	2 Samuel 14–16
April 5	2 Samuel 17–19
April 6	2 Samuel 20–22
April 7	2 Samuel 23–24
April 8	1 Kings 1–2
April 9	1 Kings 3–5
April 10	1 Kings 6–7
April 11	1 Kings 8–9
April 12	1 Kings 10–12
April 13	1 Kings 13–15
April 14	1 Kings 16–18
April 15	1 Kings 19–20
April 16	1 Kings 21–22
April 17	2 Kings 1–3

DATE	PASSAGE
April 18	2 Kings 4–5
April 19	2 Kings 6–8
April 20	2 Kings 9–10
April 21	2 Kings 11–13
April 22	2 Kings 14–16
April 23	2 Kings 17–18
April 24	2 Kings 19–21
April 25	2 Kings 22–23
April 26	2 Kings 24–25
April 27	1 Chronicles 1–2
April 28	1 Chronicles 3–4
April 29	1 Chronicles 5–6
April 30	1 Chronicles 7–9
May 1	1 Chronicles 10–12
May 2	1 Chronicles 13–16
May 3	1 Chronicles 17–19
May 4	1 Chronicles 20–23
May 5	1 Chronicles 24–26
May 6	1 Chronicles 27–29
May 7	2 Chronicles 1–4
May 8	2 Chronicles 5–7
May 9	2 Chronicles 8–11
May 10	2 Chronicles 12–16
May 11	2 Chronicles 17–20
May 12	2 Chronicles 21–24
May 13	2 Chronicles 25–28
May 14	2 Chronicles 29–31
May 15	2 Chronicles 32–34
May 16	2 Chronicles 35–36
May 17	Ezra 1–4
May 18	Ezra 5–7
May 19	Ezra 8–10
May 20	Nehemiah 1–3
May 21	Nehemiah 4–7
May 22	Nehemiah 8–9
May 23	Nehemiah 10–11
May 24	Nehemiah 12–13
May 25	Esther 1–3
May 26	Esther 4–7
May 27	Esther 8–10
May 28	Job 1–4
May 29	Job 5–8
May 30	Job 9–12
May 31	Job 13–16
June 1	Job 17–20
June 2	Job 21–24
June 3	Job 25–30
June 4	Job 31–34
June 5	Job 35–38
June 6	Job 39–42
June 7	Psalms 1–8
June 8	Psalms 9–17
June 9	Psalms 18–21
June 10	Psalms 22–27
June 11	Psalms 28–33
June 12	Psalms 34–37
June 13	Psalms 38–42
June 14	Psalms 43–49
June 15	Psalms 50–55
June 16	Psalms 56–61
June 17	Psalms 62–68
June 18	Psalms 69–72
June 19	Psalms 73–77
June 20	Psalms 78–80
June 21	Psalms 81–88
June 22	Psalms 89–94
June 23	Psalms 95–103
June 24	Psalms 104–106
June 25	Psalms 107–111
June 26	Psalms 112–118
June 27	Psalm 119
June 28	Psalms 120–133
June 29	Psalms 134–140
June 30	Psalms 141–150
July 1	Proverbs 1–3
July 2	Proverbs 4–7
July 3	Proverbs 8–11
July 4	Proverbs 12–14
July 5	Proverbs 15–17
July 6	Proverbs 18–20
July 7	Proverbs 21–23
July 8	Proverbs 24–26
July 9	Proverbs 27–29
July 10	Proverbs 30–31
July 11	Ecclesiastes 1–4
July 12	Ecclesiastes 5–8
July 13	Ecclesiastes 9–12
July 14	Song of Songs 1–4
July 15	Song of Songs 5–8
July 16	Isaiah 1–3
July 17	Isaiah 4–8
July 18	Isaiah 9–11
July 19	Isaiah 12–14
July 20	Isaiah 15–19
July 21	Isaiah 20–24
July 22	Isaiah 25–28
July 23	Isaiah 29–31
July 24	Isaiah 32–34
July 25	Isaiah 35–37
July 26	Isaiah 38–40
July 27	Isaiah 41–43
July 28	Isaiah 44–46
July 29	Isaiah 47–49
July 30	Isaiah 50–52
July 31	Isaiah 53–56
August 1	Isaiah 57–59
August 2	Isaiah 60–63
August 3	Isaiah 64–66
August 4	Jeremiah 1–3
August 5	Jeremiah 4–5
August 6	Jeremiah 6–8
August 7	Jeremiah 9–11
August 8	Jeremiah 12–14
August 9	Jeremiah 15–17
August 10	Jeremiah 18–21
August 11	Jeremiah 22–24
August 12	Jeremiah 25–27
August 13	Jeremiah 28–30
August 14	Jeremiah 31–32
August 15	Jeremiah 33–36
August 16	Jeremiah 37–39
August 17	Jeremiah 40–43
August 18	Jeremiah 44–46
August 19	Jeremiah 47–48
August 20	Jeremiah 49
August 21	Jeremiah 50
August 22	Jeremiah 51–52
August 23	Lamentations 1–2
August 24	Lamentations 3–5
August 25	Ezekiel 1–4

DATE	PASSAGE
August 26	Ezekiel 5–8
August 27	Ezekiel 9–12
August 28	Ezekiel 13–15
August 29	Ezekiel 16–17
August 30	Ezekiel 18–20
August 31	Ezekiel 21–22
September 1	Ezekiel 23–24
September 2	Ezekiel 25–27
September 3	Ezekiel 28–30
September 4	Ezekiel 31–32
September 5	Ezekiel 33–35
September 6	Ezekiel 36–38
September 7	Ezekiel 39–40
September 8	Ezekiel 41–43
September 9	Ezekiel 44–46
September 10	Ezekiel 47–48
September 11	Daniel 1–3
September 12	Daniel 4–5
September 13	Daniel 6–8
September 14	Daniel 9–12
September 15	Hosea 1–4
September 16	Hosea 5–9
September 17	Hosea 10–14
September 18	Joel 1–3
September 19	Amos 1–4
September 20	Amos 5–9
September 21	Obadiah and Jonah
September 22	Micah 1–4
September 23	Micah 5–7
September 24	Nahum 1–3
September 25	Habakkuk 1–3
September 26	Zephaniah 1–3
September 27	Haggai
September 28	Zechariah 1–5
September 29	Zechariah 6–10
September 30	Zechariah 11–14
October 1	Malachi 1–4
October 2	Matthew 1–4
October 3	Matthew 5–6
October 4	Matthew 7–9
October 5	Matthew 10–11
October 6	Matthew 12–13
October 7	Matthew 14–17
October 8	Matthew 18–20
October 9	Matthew 21–22
October 10	Matthew 23–24
October 11	Matthew 25–26
October 12	Matthew 27–28
October 13	Mark 1–3
October 14	Mark 4–5
October 15	Mark 6–7
October 16	Mark 8–9
October 17	Mark 10–11
October 18	Mark 12–13
October 19	Mark 14
October 20	Mark 15–16
October 21	Luke 1–2
October 22	Luke 3–4
October 23	Luke 5–6
October 24	Luke 7–8
October 25	Luke 9–10
October 26	Luke 11–12
October 27	Luke 13–15
October 28	Luke 16–18
October 29	Luke 19–20
October 30	Luke 21–22
October 31	Luke 23–24
November 1	John 1–2
November 2	John 3–4
November 3	John 5–6
November 4	John 7–8
November 5	John 9–10
November 6	John 11–12
November 7	John 13–15
November 8	John 16–17
November 9	John 18–19
November 10	John 20–21
November 11	Acts 1–3
November 12	Acts 4–5
November 13	Acts 6–7
November 14	Acts 8–9
November 15	Acts 10–11
November 16	Acts 12–13
November 17	Acts 14–15
November 18	Acts 16–17
November 19	Acts 18–19
November 20	Acts 20–21
November 21	Acts 22–23
November 22	Acts 24–26
November 23	Acts 27–28
November 24	Romans 1–3
November 25	Romans 4–7
November 26	Romans 8–10
November 27	Romans 11–14
November 28	Romans 15–16
November 29	1 Corinthians 1–4
November 30	1 Corinthians 5–9
December 1	1 Corinthians 10–13
December 2	1 Corinthians 14–16
December 3	2 Corinthians 1–4
December 4	2 Corinthians 5–9
December 5	2 Corinthians 10–13
December 6	Galatians 1–3
December 7	Galatians 4–6
December 8	Ephesians 1–6
December 9	Philippians 1–4
December 10	Colossians 1–4
December 11	1 Thessalonians 1–5
December 12	2 Thessalonians 1–3
December 13	1 Timothy 1–6
December 14	2 Timothy 1–4
December 15	Titus and Philemon
December 16	Hebrews 1–4
December 17	Hebrews 5–8
December 18	Hebrews 9–10
December 19	Hebrews 11–13
December 20	James 1–5
December 21	1 Peter 1–5
December 22	2 Peter 1–3
December 23	1 John 1–5
December 24	2, 3 John, Jude
December 25	Revelation 1–3
December 26	Revelation 4–7
December 27	Revelation 8–11
December 28	Revelation 12–14
December 29	Revelation 15–17
December 30	Revelation 18–19
December 31	Revelation 20–22

AUTHOR BIOGRAPHIES

This index gives information about the contributors and tells where their devotions can be found.

Nate Adams is vice-president for mobilization and mission education with the North American Mission Board of the Southern Baptist Convention. He and his wife, Beth, have been married fourteen years. They live with their sons in Georgia. *A devotion is found on page 1151.*

Tom Anderson and his wife, Evelyn, live in Bernardsville, New Jersey, where Tom is a semi-retired private investor. The Andersons have been married twenty-six years and are the parents of two children. *A devotion is found on page 1404.*

David and Claudia Arp are partners in their ministry to married couples, Marriage Alive International, Inc. Married thirty-seven years and the parents of three adult sons, the Arps live in Knoxville, Tennessee. *Devotions are found on pages 42, 547, 629, 1348, 1386.*

Stephen Arterburn is co-founder of New Life Clinic and a popular conference and radio speaker. He is the author of numerous books, including *Surprised by God* (Nelson) and *Seven Keys to Spiritual Renewal* (Tyndale), written with David Stoop. Stephen and his wife, Sandy, have been married seventeen years and have one child. *A devotion is found on page 1373.*

Susan M. Bailey is a penname for a freelance writer and editor living in the Midwest. She has been married thirteen years and has four children. *A devotion is found on page 1124.*

R. Ruth Barton is a freelance writer and speaker. She and her husband, Chris, live with their three daughters in Wheaton, Illinois. They have been married eighteen years. *Devotions are found on pages 1043, 1159.*

Charlene Ann Baumbich is a speaker and the author of *Don't Miss Your Kids!* and *How to Eat Humble Pie and Not Get Indigestion* (both published by InterVarsity Press). She and her husband, George, live in Glen Ellyn, Illinois, and they are the parents of two grown sons. *Devotions are found on pages 986, 1001, 1303.*

Penny Bilofsky, M.S.S., L.S.W., is a psychotherapist in private practice in Cherry Hill, New Jersey, and Philadelphia, and a lecturer at Rutgers University and the Philadelphia University of the Arts. She and her husband, Allan, live in New Jersey with their two daughters. *A devotion is found on page 626.*

Ron Blue is the founder and managing partner of Ronald Blue & Company, a financial planning and assets management company based in Atlanta. He is the author of several books, including *Master Your Money* (Thomas Nelson), and *Taming the Money Monster* (Focus on the Family). Ron and his wife, Judy, have five children and have been married thirty-four years. *Devotions are found on pages 7, 130, 1276.*

Ernest Boyer, Jr., was one of America's foremost educators and the author of several books, including *A Way in the World* (HarperSanFrancisco). He and his wife, Kathryn, were the parents of four grown children. *A devotion is found on page 421.*

Jerry Bridges is a representative in student ministry with the Navigators, based in Colorado Springs, Colorado. Jerry has two adult children. He and his wife, Jane, live in Colorado. *A devotion is found on page 1171.*

Judith Briles, Ph.D., a former financial planner, is an author and speaker. She and her husband, John Maling, have been married twenty-six years. They live in Denver, Colorado. *A devotion is found on page 1406.*

Jill and Stuart Briscoe are well-known Bible teachers and the authors of more than forty books. Stuart has been senior pastor of Elmbrook Church, near Milwaukee, since 1970. In the forty-one years they have been married, the Briscoes have served in youth work, adult ministries and preaching and teaching around the world. They are the parents of three adult children. *Devotions are found on pages 326, 560, 703, 938, 942, 1085, 1106, 1180, 1237, 1239, 1334, 1358, 1381.*

Frederick Buechner is the author of numerous award-winning books, including *A Room Called Remember* (HarperSanFrancisco). A former Presbyterian clergyman, Buechner is now a distinguished lecturer. He and his wife, Judith, have been married forty-three years and are the parents of three adult children. *A devotion is found on page 1149.*

Beverly J. Burch is a psychotherapist with Summit Clinical Services in Wheaton, Illinois. With Truman Esau, M.D., she is the author of *Partners in Progress* and *Making Marriage Work* (both published by Victor Books). She and her husband, John, have two daughters. *Devotions are found on pages 592, 1133, 1269.*

Richard "Dick" Capen, Jr., is an author, speaker and business consultant who served as U.S. Ambassador to Spain during the Bush administration. He has received the U.S. Defense Department's highest civilian decoration, the Distinguished Service Medal. Dick and Joan Capen have been married for thirty-seven years and are the parents of three children. They live in Rancho Santa Fe, California. *A devotion is found on page 967.*

Dave Carder is the assistant pastor of counseling ministries at First Evangelical Free Church in Fullerton, California, and the author of *Torn Asunder: Recovering from Extra-Marital Affairs* (Moody). He and his wife, Ronnie, have four children. *A devotion is found on page 1385.*

Les Carter, Ph.D., is a psychotherapist at the Minirth Clinic in Richardson, Texas, and the author of thirteen books. He and his wife, Leigh Ann, are the parents of three children. They live in the Dallas area. *Devotions are found on pages 334, 1244.*

Gary Chapman, Ph.D., is a counselor, seminar leader and the author of numerous books, including *The Five Love Languages* (Northfield). He is senior associate pastor and director of family life at Calvary Baptist Church in Winston-Salem, North Carolina. He and his wife, Karolyn, have been married thirty-eight years. *A devotion is found on page 55.*

Evelyn Christenson conducts prayer seminars throughout the world. A well-known author and speaker, she is president of Evelyn Christenson Ministries and chairman of the board of the United Prayer Ministry. She and her husband, Chris, have been married fifty-seven years and have three grown children. *Devotions are found on pages 590, 1268, 1324, 1375, 1382.*

Rodney Clapp is editorial director of Brazos Press and the author of several books, including *Peculiar People* (InterVarsity). He and his wife, Sandy, live with their daughter in the Chicago area. The Clapps have been married twenty-two years. *A devotion is found on page 1307.*

Charles Colson is the founder and president of Prison Fellowship and the author of numerous books. The former White House aide to President Richard Nixon is the father of three adult children. Charles and Patty Colson have been married thirty-five years. *A devotion is found on page 805.*

Kaye V. Cook, Ph.D., is professor of psychology at Gordon College in Wenham, Massachusetts. She is co-author with Lance Lee, Ph.D., of *Man & Woman, Alone & Together* (BridgePoint). *A devotion is found on p. 922.*

Jim Conway, Ph.D., is director of Midlife Dimensions, a counseling center in Fullerton, California, which he founded with his wife, **Sally Conway,** who died in 1997. The Conways wrote numerous books together, including *When a Mate Wants Out: Secrets for Saving a Marriage* (Zondervan) and *Traits of a Lasting Marriage* (InterVarsity). *Devotions are found on pages 519, 662, 674, 786, 932.*

Win Couchman is a speaker and counselor and the author of *Don't Call Me Spry!* (Shaw). Win and her husband, Bob, have been married fifty-six years and are the parents of four grown children. The Couchmans live in Menomonee Falls, Wisconsin. *Devotions are found on pages 438, 693, 1011.*

Larry Crabb, Jr., Ph.D., is a psychologist, educator, speaker and the author of several books, including *The Safest Place on Earth* (Word). He is a professor at Colorado Christian University in Lakewood, Colorado. Larry and his wife, Rachael, have been married thirty-three years and have two grown sons. *Devotions are found on pages 184, 1091, 1257.*

Marsha Crockett is a freelance writer and the author of *Weaving a Life of Prayer* (InterVarsity) and *Sanctuary* (Bethany). She and her husband, John, have been married sixteen years. They live with their two daughters in Arizona. *A devotion is found on page 1333.*

Lyn Cryderman is a writer and editor and associate publisher at Zondervan Publishing House. A former newspaper photographer, magazine editor and hog farmer, he and his wife, Esther, live with their four children in Caledonia, Michigan. *Devotions are found on pages 583, 1286, 1347, 1389.*

Jan Dargatz is the editor or author of more than 150 books. She is the dean of a study program through the American Christian Trust at Hebrew University in Jerusalem. *A devotion is found on page 418.*

Douglas B. DeMerchant, Psy.D., is a clinical psychologist in private practice in Wheaton, Illinois. He and his wife, Claudette, have been married eighteen years and have two children. *A devotion is found on page 1033.*

Kamilla Denman is teaching English and American literature while she completes doctoral work at Harvard University. She and her husband, Scott, have been married twenty-one years. They live with their two children in Brookline, Massachusetts. *A devotion is found on page 9.*

Preston and Genie Dyer bring more than thirty years experience in marriage and family enrichment, therapy, education and research to the classroom at Baylor University in Waco, Texas. Genie is a professor and family life educator; Preston is a professor and clinical social worker. The Dyers have co-authored numerous articles and books. Married thirty-nine years, they have two children. *Devotions are found on pages 1202, 1295.*

Diane Eble, a speaker and writer, is the author of *Abundant Gifts* (Tyndale). She and her husband, Gene, live with their two children in Winfield, Illinois. They have been married nineteen years. *Devotions are found on pages 766, 808, 1415.*

Lowell and Carol Erdahl are the co-authors of *Be Good to Each Other* (Augsburg/Fortress). Recently retired, Lowell was bishop of the St. Paul area synod of the Evangelical Lutheran Church in America. Carol is co-owner of The Red Balloon Bookshop, which primarily sells children's literature. The Erdahls have been married forty-five years and have three children. *A devotion is found on page 471.*

Susan M. Felch is associate professor of English at Calvin College in Grand Rapids, Michigan. She and her husband, Douglas, have been married twenty-five years. *A devotion is found on page 1119.*

Louise A. Ferrebee is print promotions coordinator for the B & B Media Group. She and her husband, Tom, have been married sixteen years. They live with their two sons in the Chicago area. *A devotion is found on page 1121.*

Harold Fickett has written several books, including *The Holy Fool* (Shaw) and *Flannery O'Connor: Images of Grace* (Eerdmans). He is a fellow in the Center for Christian Writers at Friends University in Wichita, Kansas. *A devotion is found on page 664.*

Doug Fields is a youth pastor, speaker and writer in Mission Viejo, California, and the founder of Making Young Lives Count, an organization that provides youth-ministry tools to churches. Doug and his wife, Cathy, have been married fourteen years and have three children. *A devotion is found on page 1036.*

John Fischer is an author, musician and speaker. He is the author of *12 Steps for the Recovering Pharisee (Like Me)* (Bethany). He lives with his wife, Marti, and their two children in California. The Fischers have been married twenty-four years. *A devotion is found on page 286.*

Jeron Frame is a freelance writer and editor living in Paoli, Pennsylvania. Her husband, Randy, is also a writer and editor. They have been married sixteen years and have three daughters. *A devotion is found on page 997.*

Bill and Gloria Gaither are popular Christian recording artists and songwriters living in Alexandria, Indiana. Gloria is also an author, while Bill is busy with the Gaither Vocal Band. The Gaithers have been married thirty-seven years and have three grown children. *A devotion is found on page 1135.*

Diana R. and David E. Garland are co-authors of *Marriage: For Better or for Worse* (Broadman) and *Beyond Companionship* (Westminster). The Garlands have two children. *A devotion is found on page 594.*

Betsey Glavach is a retirement counselor living in Wheaton, Illinois. She and her husband, Vic, have been married twenty-nine years and have three children. *A devotion is found on page 763.*

David L. Goetz is new product manager for Leadership Resources at Christianity Today, Inc. He and his wife, Jana, have been married eight years and have two children. *A devotion is found on page 512.*

Ruth Bell Graham is a writer and the wife of evangelist Billy Graham. The Grahams have been married fifty-six years and are the parents of five adult children. They reside in Montreat, North Carolina. *Devotions are found on pages 1205, 1231, 1396.*

Tracy Green is the executive producer of "Noonday," a daily news and talk show. She is the author of numerous magazine articles and the co-author of *52 Ways to Show Aging Parents You Care.* She lives in Atlanta. *A devotion is found on page 781.*

Dennis and Lucy Guernsey were married more than thirty-six years at the time of Dennis's death in 1996. Lucy is director of alumni and church relations at Fuller Theological Seminary. *A devotion is found on page 672.*

Marylou Habecker and her husband, Eugene, have been married thirty-one years and have three children. *A devotion is found on page 1194.*

Janis Long Harris is a senior editor at Tyndale House Publishers and the author of *Secrets of People Who Love Their Work* (InterVarsity). She and her husband, Paul, have been married twenty-one years. They live with their two children in River Forest, Illinois. *Devotions are found on pages 168, 189.*

Archibald Hart, Ph.D., is a clinical psychologist in the Graduate School of Psychology at Fuller Theological Seminary. He is the author of several books, including *The Anxiety Cure* (Word) and *Healing Life's Hidden Addictions* (Servant). Arch and Kathleen Hart have been married forty-five years and have three children. *Devotions are found on pages 1163, 1209.*

Donald R. Harvey, Ph.D., is a marriage therapist in private practice and associate professor of graduate psychology at Trevecca Nazarene University in Nashville. He is the author of several books on marriage. He and Jan have been married twenty-seven years and have two grown children. *Devotions are found on pages 1183, 1412.*

Kathy Tippett Henderson is a music teacher in Greenville, North Carolina. She and her husband, Doug, have been married thirty years and have three children. *Devotions are found on pages 447, 1110.*

Howard and Jeanne Hendricks have been married fifty-two years and are the parents of four grown children. Jeanne is a homemaker, and Howard is distinguished professor and chairman of the Center for Christian Leadership at Dallas Theological Seminary. *Devotions are found on pages 4, 458, 655, 827, 1243.*

John A. Huffman, Jr., is senior pastor of St. Andrew's Presbyterian Church in Newport Beach, California, and serves as chairman of the board of World Vision. He and his wife, Anne, have been married thirty-five years; two of their three children are living. *A devotion is found on page 1301.*

Ron Hutchcraft is an author, radio host, speaker and executive director of Metropolitan New York/New Jersey Youth for Christ. He and his wife, Karen, live with their three children in Wayne, New Jersey. *Devotions are found on pages 691, 751, 1325.*

Bill Hybels is senior pastor of Willow Creek Community Church in South Barrington, Illinois. A speaker and writer, he is on the board of directors for Focus on the Family and is former chaplain of the Chicago Bears. Bill's wife, **Lynne Hybels,** occasionally teams up with Bill on writing projects. They have been married twenty-five years and have two children. *Devotions are found on pages 93, 1049, 1314, 1330.*

Jerry B. Jenkins is the co-author, with Tim LaHaye, of the bestselling Left Behind series and is writer-in-residence at Moody Bible Institute in Chicago. Married for twenty-eight years, Jerry and his wife, Dianna, have three sons. *A devotion is found on page 1343.*

Thomas à Kempis was a fifteenth-century German Augustinian monk and priest who wrote the devotional classic *The Imitation of Christ. A devotion is found on page 995.*

John W. Kennedy is managing editor of the division of Foreign Missions for the Assemblies of God. He and his wife, Patty, live in Springfield, Missouri, with their three children. *A devotion is found on page 842.*

Nancy Kennedy is a freelance writer and the author of several books, including *Prayers God Always Answers* (WaterBrook). She and her husband, Barry, have been married twenty-four years and have two children. The Kennedys live in Florida. *Devotions are found on pages 591, 1384.*

Jay Kesler is a former pastor, an author, a radio host and the president of Taylor University in Upland, Indiana. The parents of three children, Jay and his wife, Janie, have been married forty-two years. *Devotions are found on pages 873, 1087, 1251, 1318, 1335.*

Jim Killam is a journalist and college media adviser at Northern Illinois University. He and his wife, Lauren, have been married fourteen years and live in Rockford, Illinois, with their three children. *A devotion appears on page 1161.*

Gary D. Kinnaman, D.Min., is senior minister of Word of Grace Church in Mesa, Arizona. He is the author of *Learning to Love the One You Marry* (Vine). He and his wife, Marilyn, have been married twenty-eight years and have three children. *A devotion is found on page 186.*

Diane M. Langberg, Ph.D., is a psychologist and the director of Diane Langberg, Ph.D., & Associates in Philadelphia, Pennsylvania. She and her husband, Ronald, have two children. *Devotions are found on pages 779, 1341.*

Annette LaPlaca is senior associate editor of *Marriage Partnership* magazine and the author of several books. **David LaPlaca** is a book designer and musician. The LaPlacas live in West Chicago, Illinois, with their two children. *Devotions are found on pages 244, 502, 909, 1298.*

Jeanette C. Lauer, Ph.D., and **Robert H. Lauer,** Ph.D., are research professors with U.S. International University and full-time writers. The Lauers have been married forty-five years and have three children. They reside in San Diego. *Devotions are found on pages 707, 1270.*

Wonda Layton is a freelance writer and former teacher. She and her husband, Larry, a retired American Baptist minister, have two children (one deceased) and two grandchildren. They have been married fifty-five years and live in Edmonds, Washington. *A devotion is found on page 978.*

Ron and Jeanette Lee have been married twenty years and have one daughter. Ron is a former newspaper reporter who now works as editor of *Marriage Partnership* magazine and executive editor of *Christian Parenting Today* magazine. Jeanette is an event planner and substitute teacher. *Devotions are found on pages 251, 337, 974, 1006, 1022, 1056, 1273.*

Gregg Lewis is an editor and prolific author of books and magazine articles. He and his wife, Deborah, have been married twenty-six years and have five children. The Lewis family resides in Rome, Georgia. *Devotions are found on pages 577, 1169.*

Mark Lewis experienced a spiritual reawakening after surviving the devastation of Hurricane Hugo on the island of St. Croix. After finishing seminary in Kentucky, he and his wife, Angela, returned to the Caribbean where they serve as missionaries with World Gospel Mission. *A devotion is found on page 821.*

Marian V. Liautaud is a freelance writer and co-owner, with her husband, Dan, of two Big Mike's Super Subs sandwich shops. The Liautauds live in Minneapolis with their four sons. *Devotions are found on pages 686, 1024.*

Donna Lobs is a deacon in the Episcopal Diocese of Central Florida. She and her husband, Richard, have been married thirty-six years and have four children and six grandchildren. *A devotion is found on page 1081.*

James Long is a journalist and the author of several books. He studied at Grace Theological Seminary in Indiana and has had ministries with teenagers, street people and the bereaved. Jim and his wife, Harriet, have been married twenty-seven years. They have two sons. *Devotions are found on pages 1044, 1326.*

Max Lucado is senior minister of Oak Hills Church of Christ in San Antonio, Texas, and the bestselling author of numerous books, including *When Christ Comes* (Word) and *Because I Love You* (Crossway). Max and his wife, Denalyn, have been married eighteen years and have three daughters. *Devotions are found on pages 571, 987, 1038.*

Thomas Ludwig is a writer and professor of psychology at Hope College in Holland, Michigan. He and his wife, Debra, have been married twenty-seven years and have two children. *Devotions are found on pages 280, 1272.*

Catherine Marshall was the popular author of *A Man Called Peter,* a biography of her first husband, U.S. Senate chaplain Peter Marshall, and the best-selling novel *Christy.* She shared a writing and speaking ministry with her second husband, Leonard LeSourd, who was editor of *Guideposts* magazine. *Devotions are found on pages 1112, 1397.*

Richard E. Matteson, Ed.D., is a clinical psychologist in private practice in the Chicago area. He and his wife, Janet, have been married forty-one years and have four grown children. A devotion is found on page 189.

Louis McBurney, M.D., is a psychiatrist and co-founder of Marble Retreat in Marble, Colorado. Louis and his wife, Melissa, have been married thirty-eight years and counsel clergy couples at Marble Retreat. They are the parents of three grown children. *Devotions are found on pages 782, 1296, 1332.*

Alison A. McCaughan is editor of one of the official magazines of the Presbyterian Church in Ireland. She is also a part-time teacher of English and history. Alison is the wife of Rev. James McCaughan, minister of First Dunboe Presbyterian Church in Castlerock, Northern Ireland. The McCaughans have been married nineteen years and have three children. *A devotion is found on page 668.*

Robertson McQuilkin is the chancellor and former president of Columbia Bible College and Seminary in Columbia, South Carolina. A well-known speaker and writer, he and his wife, Muriel, are the parents of six children (one deceased). *A devotion is found on page 1246.*

Paul A. Mickey is the co-author with William Proctor of *12 Keys to a Better Marriage* (Bristol House). He is a retired professor, a family counselor and serves as a financial advisor for churches. He and his wife, Jane, have been married thirty-seven years. *A devotion is found on page 81.*

Andrea Midgett is a freelance writer and editor living in South Bend, Indiana. She and her husband, David Lodge, have been married fourteen years and are the parents of three children. *Devotions are found on pages 345, 1069.*

Calvin Miller, a former pastor, is now dean at Samford University in Birmingham, Alabama. His many books include *The Singer Trilogy, The Taste of Joy* and *A Hunger for Meaning.* Calvin and Barbara Miller have been married forty years and have two children. *Devotions are found on pages 414, 935.*

Kevin A. and Karen Miller, LCSW, have been married eighteen years. Kevin is vice-president for editorial development at Christianity Today, Inc. Karen is a marriage-and-family therapist. The Millers live with their two children in Wheaton, Illinois. *Devotions are found on pages 1116, 1253.*

Frank Minirth, M.D., is a psychiatrist and the president and co-founder of the Minirth Clinic in Richardson, Texas. Frank and Mary Alice Minirth have been married twenty-six years and are the parents of five children. The Minirths live in Dallas. *Devotions are found on pages 334, 1244.*

Robert Moeller is pastor of the First Evangelical Free Church of Chicago. Together with his wife,

Cheryl, he is the author of *Marriage Minutes* (Moody). Bob and Cheryl have been married twenty years and have six children. *A devotion is found on page 687.*

Elisa Morgan is the president and CEO of MOPS International (Mothers of Preschoolers). She is a writer and speaker and host of a radio ministry. Elisa's husband, Evan, heads Sky Media, which markets CD-ROMs and internet Bible education. The Morgans have been married twenty years and have two children. *Devotions are found on pages 682, 788, 1262.*

Andrew Murray, a Scottish preacher, ministered in South Africa for more than fifty years until his death in 1917. The devotion represented here is taken from *Absolute Surrender,* a collection of lectures delivered in London in preparation for an evangelistic crusade. *That devotion is found on page 1170.*

David Myers is a writer and the John Dirk Werkman professor of psychology at Hope College in Holland, Michigan. He and his wife, Carol, have been married thirty-six years and are the parents of three children. *Devotions are found on pages 280, 1272.*

Elizabeth Cody Newenhuyse is a speaker and the author of several books, including *Sometimes I Feel Like Running Away from Home* (Bethany) and *Great Expectations of a Hopeless Romantic* (Victor). She and her husband, Fritz, have been married twenty-one years. *Devotions are found on pages 284, 387, 558, 580, 644, 697.*

Henri J.M. Nouwen taught for nearly two decades at the Theological Institute in Utrecht, Holland, and at the Universities of Notre Dame, Yale and Harvard in the United States. Until his recent death, he shared his life with mentally handicapped people at the L'Arche Community of Daybreak in Toronto, Ontario. A few of his many books are *The Return of the Prodigal Son, In the Name of Jesus* and *The Life of the Beloved. Devotions are found on pages 181, 481, 733.*

Gary J. Oliver, Ph.D., is executive director of the Center for Marriage and Family Studies and professor of psychology and practical theology at John Brown University in Siloam Springs, Arkansas. He and his wife, Carrie, have been married nineteen years and have three sons. *A devotion is found on page 1290.*

Anne Ortlund is an author and conference speaker with Renewal Ministries based in Newport Beach, California. Her husband, Ray Ortland, is a retired Presbyterian minister. They are the parents of four adult children. *A devotion is found on page 30.*

Les Parrott III, Ph.D., and **Leslie Parrott,** Ed.D., are co-directors of the Center for Relationship Development at Seattle Pacific University and the co-authors of numerous books, including *Saving Your Marriage Before It Starts* (Zondervan). The Parrotts have been married fifteen years and have one son. *Devotions are found on pages 390, 476, 699, 760, 771, 1313.*

Ben Patterson, formerly a parish pastor, is dean of the chapel at Hope College in Holland, Michigan. He is the author of several books, including *Deepening Your Conversation with God* (Bethany). Ben and his wife, Lauretta, have been married twenty-eight years and have four children. *Devotions are found on pages 507, 621, 834, 1185.*

Ruth Stafford Peale is publisher and the chairman of the board for Guideposts, Inc. She and her husband, the late Dr. Norman Vincent Peale, were married more than sixty years. Mrs. Peale lives in Pawling, New York. *A devotion is found on page 750.*

Clifford Penner, Ph.D., a clinical psychologist, and his wife, **Joyce Penner,** R.N., M.N., a clinical nurse specialist, are sex therapists practicing in Pasadena, California. They are the authors of *The Gift of Sex, Restoring the Pleasure* and *Sex Facts for the Family* (all published by Word). The Penners have been married thirty-five years and are the parents of three children. *A devotion is found on page 1320.*

Gloria Oakes Perkins, a writer and biblical counselor, has co-authored several books with Ed Wheat, including *Intended for Pleasure, Love Life for Every Married Couple* and *How to Save Your Marriage Alone.* She and her husband, Dan, have been married forty-five years and are the parents of two sons. *A devotion is found on page 652.*

Frank Peretti is a bestselling novelist. He and his wife, Barbara, have been married twenty-seven years. *A devotion is found on page 1222.*

Ruth Ann Polston is an author and speaker and the wife of a minister. Ruth Ann and Don Polston have been married fifty years and are the parents of two children. They live in Indianapolis. *A devotion is found on page 587.*

Dennis and Barbara Rainey are co-founders of FamilyLife, a marriage and family ministry based in Little Rock, Arkansas. The Raineys, who have been married twenty-seven years, often write and speak together. They are the parents of six children. *A devotion is found on page 803.*

Martha Reapsome is an author and the midwest director of Neighborhood Bible Studies. Her most recent study guide is *Treasures* (Neighborhood Bible Studies). She and her husband of thirty-seven years, Jim, are the parent of two children. *Devotions are found on pages 545, 1131, 1344.*

Bonnie Shipley Rice, now deceased, was an editorial administrator at Christianity Today, Inc. She and her husband, John, were married more than forty years and were the parents of four grown children.*Devotions are found on pages 731, 1304.*

Gary and Betsy Ricucci are the co-authors of *Love That Lasts* (People of Destiny). Gary is a pastor who works with couples at Covenant Life Church in Gaithersburg, Maryland. Gary and Betsey have been married twenty-two years and have four children. *A devotion is found on page 653.*

Paula Rinehart and her husband, Stacy, are authors of *Choices: Finding God's Way in Dating, Sex, Singleness and Marriage* (NavPress). Paula is a counselor and freelance writer. The Rineharts have been married twenty-six years. They live with their two children in Raleigh, North Carolina. *A devotion is found on page 1379.*

Dave Roever and his wife, Brenda, have two children and have been married thirty-two years. *A devotion is found on page 664.*

Dale Evans Rogers is the author of numerous books. She has made more than 5,000 appearances for charities on behalf of abused, orphaned and mentally handicapped children. She and Roy were married more than fifty years at the time of his death. Mrs. Rogers resides in California. *A devotion is found on page 1395.*

Martha Russi is a pen name for a writer living in the Midwest. She has been married twenty-seven years and is the mother of two grown sons. *A devotion is found on page 490.*

Fredda Sacharow is an editor and freelance writer whose work appears frequently in *The New York Times*. The winner of numerous national writing awards, she lives in New Jersey with her husband, Steven, and their daughter. *A devotion is found on page 626.*

Charles M. Sell is a well-known conference and seminar speaker on the topics of marriage and the family. He is the author of several books, including *Spiritual Intimacy for Couples* (Crossway) and *Unfinished Business* (Zondervan). He is professor of Christian education at Trinity Evangelical Divinity School. "Chick" and Ginger Sell live in Grayslake, Illinois. *A devotion is found on page 159.*

Ruth Senter is a freelance writer and a popular author of Christian books. She and her husband, Mark, have been married thirty-four years and have two grown children. *Devotions are found on pages 215, 264, 542, 650, 871, 1031, 1034, 1146, 1187, 1224, 1321, 1338.*

Luci Shaw is a poet, author, lecturer and writer-in-residence at Regent College. She and her husband, John Hoyte, live in Menlo Park, California. She is the mother of five adult children. *A devotion is found on page 708.*

Donna Sinclair lives with her husband, Jim, and their three children in North Bay, Ontario. She is senior writer for *The United Church Observer*. She and Jim have three children. *A devotion is found on page 1073.*

Gary Smalley is a nationally known author and speaker who serves as president of Smalley Relationship Center in Branson, Missouri. Norma, his wife of thirty-five years, serves with him in the ministry. They are parents of three grown children. *A devotion is found on page 617.*

Lewis B. Smedes, Ph.D., is professor emeritus of theology and ethics at Fuller Theological Seminary. He is the author of numerous books, including *The Art of Forgiving, Love within Limits* and *Caring and Commitment* (all published by HarperSanFrancisco). He and his wife, Doris, have three children. *Devotions are found on pages 120, 563, 883, 1053, 1089, 1226, 1236.*

Hannah Whitall Smith was an American Quaker philanthropist and author. She was a well-known speaker in the late 1800s and an ardent advocate for peace, temperance and women's suffrage. Smith wrote hundreds of religious tracts and a number of books. *A devotion is found on page 548.*

Harold B. Smith is corporate vice president for Christianity Today, Inc. He and his wife, Judy, have two sons and live in the Chicago area. *Devotions are found on pages 657, 975, 1371.*

Jim Smith was a marriage and family counselor who served as executive director of the Highland Park Presbyterian Church Family Life Counseling Center in Dallas. He was the author of several books, including *Learning to Live with the One You Love* (Tyndale). *Devotions are found on pages 715, 946, 1019.*

Beth Spring is a freelance journalist living in McLean, Virginia. She has written numerous magazine articles and is co-author, with Ed Larson, of the book *Euthanasia: Spiritual, Medical & Legal Issues in Terminal Health Care* (Multnomah). Beth and her husband, Jeff, have two children. *A devotion is found on page 179.*

Tim Stafford is senior writer for *Christianity Today* magazine and is the author of a number of books, including *As Our Years Increase* (HarperCollins). He and Popie, his wife of twenty-two years, live in California and have three children. *Devotions are found on pages 3, 77, 719, 799, 956, 1249.*

Scott M. Stanley, Ph.D., is a clinical psychologist specializing in marriage research. He is co-director of the Center for Marital and Family Studies at the University of Denver and the author of several books, including *The Heart of Commitment* (Nelson) and *A Lasting Promise* (Jossey-Bass). *Devotions are found on pages 149, 679.*

Paul Stevens is the author of *Marriage Sprituality* (InterVarsity) and *Disciplines of the Hungry Heart* (Shaw). He is academic dean and associate professor of applied theology at Regent College in Vancouver, British Columbia. He and his wife, Gail, spend a portion of each year ministering in Kenya. Their three children are grown and married. *Devotions are found on pages 1003, 1351.*

Keith Stonehocker is senior vice-president of Christianity Today, Inc., and former publisher of *Marriage Partnership* magazine. He and Carolyn, his wife of twenty-five years, have one son and live in the Chicago area. *A devotion is found on page 962.*

Kay Marshall Strom is the author of several books, including *Called to Care* (InterVarsity). After losing her first husband to a long-term illness, she married an old friend, also widowed. She and Dan Klein have, between them, four adult children. They live in Santa Barbara, California. *A devotion is found on page 1368.*

Paul W. Swets is author of *How to Talk So Your Teenager Will Listen* (Word). He serves as minister of congregational care at Second Presbyterian Church (PCUSA) in Memphis, Tennessee. He and his wife, Janiece, have two children. *A devotion is found on page 510.*

Charles R. Swindoll is a well-known author and speaker who serves as senior pastor of Stonebriar Community Church in Frisco, Texas. He also is president of Dallas Theological Seminary. He and his wife, Cynthia, have been married forty-five years and have four grown children. *Devotions are found on pages 689, 990, 1250.*

Joni Eareckson Tada is a well-known speaker, author, artist and advocate for persons with disabilities who serves as president and CEO of JAF (Joni and Friends) Ministries. She and Ken, her husband of sixteen years, live in California. *A devotion is found on page 951.*

Todd Temple is co-founder and executive director of 10 TO 20, a company that produces national events and conferences for students. He is the author and co-author of several books, including *Creative Dating.* A devotion is found on page 781.

Alesia T. Thayer is a writer for American College Testing and Reed Reference Publishing Company and Educational Testing Service. Alesia and her husband, Randall, live in Owensborough, Kentucky, with their three children. *A devotion is found on page 1066.*

Gary L. Thomas is the author of several books, including *Sacred Marriage* and *Seeking the Face of God* (both published by Harvest House). He and his wife, Lisa, have been married fifteen years and have three children. *Devotions are found on pages 1128, 1287.*

Mary Ellen Williams Ton is doing graduate work in counseling at Christian Theological Seminary. She and her husband, Eugene, have four grown children and live in Indianapolis. *A devotion is found on page 791.*

Paul Tournier was a Swiss physician and counselor whose prolific writing inspired and encouraged Christians around the world. Among others, the Christian doctor wrote *The Meaning of Persons* (Harper) and *To Understand Each Other* (John Knox). Paul Tournier was married to Nelly Bouvier and they were the parents of two children. He married again shortly before his death in 1986. *A devotion is found on page 1374.*

John Trent, Ph.D., is a well-known author, speaker and marriage and family counselor who serves as president of Encouraging Words, based in Phoenix. He is author of a number of books, including *Life Mapping* and *Choosing to Live the Blessing* (both published by WaterBrook). John and his wife, Cindy, have been married twenty years and have two children. *A devotion is found on page 50.*

Walter Wangerin, Jr., is a columnist, author and lecturer and professor of English at Valparaiso University. He has published numerous volumes of short stories, novels and nonfiction works, including *As for Me and My House* (Thomas Nelson). Walter and Thanne Wangerin have been married thirty-one years and are the parents of four children. *Devotions are found on pages 637, 1310.*

Charlie and Lucy Wedemeyer are co-authors, with Gregg Lewis, of *Charlie's Victory* (Zondervan), the story of Charlie's ongoing battle with Lou Gehrig's disease. Lucy is a real estate broker. The Wedemeyers have two children. *A devotion is found on page 606.*

Ed Wheat, M.D., is a retired family physician and certified sex therapist. He has helped thousands of troubled couples improve their love lives and build happier marriages with his unique counseling methods. Dr. Wheat and his wife, Gaye, live in Springdale, Arkansas. *A devotion is found on page 652.*

Dr. Frances White, recently retired, was professor of clinical psychology at the Wheaton College Graduate School in Illinois. *A devotion is found on page 1391.*

Marti Winchell Williams is a missionary nurse. She and her husband, Raymond, have been married twenty-one years and are the parents of three children. *A devotion is found on page 60.*

Will Willimon is dean of the chapel at Duke University in Durham, North Carolina. A United Methodist minister, he also teaches at Duke University Divinity School, writes books and speaks at conferences. He and his wife; Patsy, have two children. *Devotions are found on pages 111, 705.*

R. Kirby Worthington and Everett L. Worthington, Jr., Ph.D., have been married twenty-nine years and are the parents of four children. Kirby is a child development specialist working at the Canterbury Community Nursery School at Virginia Commonwealth University. Everett is a professor and chair of the psychology department at the same university. *A devotion is found on page 1258.*

H. Norman Wright is the author of more than fifty books, the founder and director of Christian Marriage Enrichment and a pastoral counselor on staff at the Rolling Hills Covenant Church in California. Norm and his wife, Joyce, have been married thirty-nine years. *Devotions are found on pages 267, 717, 1182, 1292, 1327, 1362.*

Philip Yancey has written a number of books, including *What's So Amazing about Grace* and *The Jesus I Never Knew* (both published by Zondervan). Philip and Janet Yancey have been married twenty-nine years and live in Evergreen, Colorado. *Devotions are found on pages 537, 1142, 1260, 1356.*

Susan Alexander Yates is a columnist for *Today's Christian Woman* magazine and the author of several books, including *What Really Matters at Home* (Word), co-authored with her husband, John, a pastor in Falls Church, Virginia. They have been married thirty years and have five children. *A devotion is found on page 435.*

Ravi Zacharias is an internationally recognized apologist, evangelist and president of Ravi Zacharias International Ministries based in Norcross, Georgia. He and and his wife, Margaret, have been married twenty-seven years and have three children. *Devotions are found on pages 191, 309.*

SUBJECT INDEX

The subjects covered in the devotions are many and varied. This subject index will help you locate material on just about any topic or issue of interest, or about any problem confronting you.

SUBJECT	PAGE
Acceptance	111
	751
	788
	791
	827
	1104
	1194
	1226
	1303
	1310
Accountability	1273
Achievement	1335
Adjustments	1310
Adultery	77
	799
	1033
	1249
	1343
Affection	771
Affirmation	55
	1202
	1295
	1337
Agreement	967
Anger	149
	563
	594
	617
	1296
Anniversary	1326
Appreciation	1209
	1262
	1295
Arguing	1296
Attitudes	997
Betrayal	782
Blessing	909
Caring	946
Change	50
	111
	186
	264
	542
	705
	791
	978
	1001
	1022
	1270
	1382
Character	670

SUBJECT	PAGE
Cherishing	1253
	1327
Children	1034
	1151
	1273
	1292
Choices	808
	1404
Christ	1142
	1146
Christlikeness	693
	1044
Church	1083
Comfort	1038
	1344
Commitment	168
	345
	387
	435
	606
	664
	719
	946
	956
	967
	986
	1031
	1091
	1149
	1246
	1301
	1395
Communication	42
	149
	510
	512
	547
	653
	655
	674
	682
	689
	691
	705
	707
	788
	803
	873
	932
	946
	975

SUBJECT	PAGE
	1021
	1022
	1314
	1348
	1384
Comparing	1159
Comparison	1260
Compassion	799
	956
Competition	1159
Confession	590
Confidence	244
Conflict	149
	594
	679
	687
	689
	1133
	1296
Confrontation	512
	1053
Contentment	280
	951
	1307
	1338
Control	1133
	1313
Cooperation	1116
Counseling	490
Courage	215
	421
	1100
	1187
Courtesy	771
	1389
	1404
Courtship	771
	946
Covenant	421
	435
Creation	3
Creativity	717
	1182
Crisis	93
	808
	962
Criticism	1001
	1362
Death, preparing for	708
Decision-making	458
	471
	687
	932
Depression	655
Devotional life	9
	30
	326
	438
	545
	731
	935
	1375
	1382
Differences	267
	670
	715
	1056
	1104
	1228
	1260
	1303
	1305
	1366
	1371
	1379
Disagreements	687
Disappointment	558
Discernment	337
Discipline	1224
Discouragement	345
	697
	1321
Disillusionment	286
	1290
Diversity	1239
Divorce	390
	1001
	1019
	1056
Double standard	1287
Doubt	519
Downscaling	93
Easter	1069
Empathy	592
	974
	1163
Encouragement	179
	547
	560
	662
	701
	703
	1069
	1202
	1209
	1255
	1270
	1314
	1334
	1337
	1362
Enjoyment	672
	1293
Equality	1313
Evangelism	191
Example	1283
Exclusivity	1249
Expectations	922
	1131
	1279
	1386
	1396

SUBJECT	PAGE
Fairness	1236
Faith	184
	244
	519
	548
	558
	587
	733
	766
	837
	842
	956
	1112
	1146
	1222
	1237
	1268
	1272
	1301
	1364
	1368
	1385
	1415
Faithfulness	387
	652
	657
	719
	871
	1246
Familiarity	286
Family	50
	626
	1335
Family time	948
Fantasies	1033
Fantasy	1019
Fatigue	580
	644
Fears	481
	733
Feelings	986
	1395
Fidelity	168
	435
	1249
Fighting	689
Finances	7
	130
	763
	1124
	1276
Forgiveness	50
	120
	490
	537
	563
	590
	799
	873
	883
	1053
	1089
	1142
	1226
	1296
	1356
Friendship	189
	438
	1194
	1244
	1290
	1319
Fruit of the Spirit	1326
Fun	629
	672
	1293
	1376
Future	834
Gender differences	674
	932
	975
Generosity	1081
Gentleness	1286
Gifts	4
	1384
Giving	7
	130
	1151
	1276
Goals	502
	574
	756
	1055
	1319
	1386
Godliness	1131
God's anger	251
God's call	458
God's care	1066
God's faithfulness	587
God's goodness	184
	760
God's jealousy	181
God's judgment	251
God's leading	60
God's love	791
	1231
	1396
God's mercy	251
God's power	1344
God's provision	1344
God's sovereignty	842
God's sufficiency	1066
God's unchangeableness	1341
God's will	244
	458
	471
	668
	750
	1066
	1222
God's Word	326

SUBJECT	PAGE
	545
	560
	703
	1205
Goodness	693
Grace	571
	637
	951
	987
	990
Gratitude	571
	617
	621
	1321
Growth	264
	577
	705
	1326
Guidance	668
	750
Habits	771
Happiness	186
	1019
	1287
	1330
Headship	1333
Healing	390
	1351
Helping	781
	962
	1366
Holidays	1228
Holiness	186
Holy Spirit	693
	1011
Honesty	512
	805
Home	309
	1024
Honor	617
Hope	558
	637
	1272
Hospitality	191
	309
	1073
	1081
	1333
Housework	922
Humility	779
	995
	1043
	1128
	1159
	1171
	1287
Husband	1044
Idealism	1385
Idealization	1310
Identity	679
Illness	519
	606
	652
	664
	1069
	1246
Incarnation	1146
Incompleteness	1332
Independence	592
Individuality	1243
	1313
Infatuation	1290
In-laws	626
	679
Interaction	803
Intercession	1324
Interdependence	1038
	1332
Intimacy	3
	512
	592
	707
	708
	771
	935
	1318
	1373
	1374
	1375
Joy	621
	629
	733
	1304
	1341
Judging	447
	1110
	1128
	1287
Justice	537
Kindness	974
	1286
	1404
Knowledge	337
Laughter	629
	1376
Leadership	1087
Learning	650
Leisure	418
	756
	1423
Limits	1224
Listening	510
	653
	655
	691
	788
	1021
	1262
	1391
Loneliness	334
	1244
Love	652

SUBJECT	PAGE
	827
	1091
	1171
	1236
	1250
	1298
	1384
Love languages	55
Love, unconditional	719
	1151
Love, voluntary	345
Lust	1320
Magic	871
Manipulation	502
Marriage	1031
Maturity	1381
Meditation	545
Memories	490
	1044
Mentors	1258
Mercy	1305
Ministry	215
	942
	1034
	1083
	1085
	1106
	1112
	1116
	1135
	1187
	1397
Miracle	1149
Misfortune	542
Mission	1106
Money	1133
	1222
	1269
	1283
Needs	786
	1049
Nurture	334
Obedience	9
	215
	284
	668
	750
	978
	1006
	1066
	1187
	1304
Observation	1273
Oneness	1333
	1056
Optimism	591
Overcoming	1183
	1412
Pain	1183
Parenting	1038
	1151
	1292
Parents	781
Partnership	3
	1011
Patience	251
	577
	1371
	1391
Peace	951
	1169
Peers	1313
Perfectionism	1279
Personal growth	1273
Pornography	782
Power	1375
Practicing love	1381
Prayer	30
	181
	284
	438
	476
	481
	750
	938
	1011
	1049
	1161
	1180
	1239
	1268
	1324
	1375
	1382
	1385
Preparation	1292
Pride	974
	1043
Priorities	87
	574
	1006
	1024
	1121
	1385
Privacy	1003
Problem-solving	591
Protection	1169
	1343
Provision	548
	763
	909
	1085
	1100
	1124
	1397
Reconciliation	563
Rejection	779
Relaxation	418
	1036
	1185
	1423
Renewal	580

SUBJECT	PAGE
	1351
Resentment	621
	883
Respect	662
	689
	1087
	1128
	1251
Responsibilities	1038
Rest	81
	548
	644
	1170
	1185
Restoration	1110
Revenge	120
Risk	264
Risks	1187
Role models	1258
Roles	1313
	1333
Romance	267
	717
	771
	1182
Sabbath	1185
Sacrifice	974
	1171
Salvation	1151
	1301
Scheduling	580
	946
	1121
Secrets	708
Security	264
Self-discipline	1292
Self-esteem	701
	1255
Selfishness	699
	1253
	1257
Self-sufficiency	1307
Sensitivity	1236
	1257
Separation	1318
Servanthood	1043
	1338
Service	942
	1087
	1170
	1307
Service, shared	191
	309
	699
	1333
Serving	1034
	1036
	1081
	1083
	1119
	1203
	1253
	1366
	1373
Sex	77
	715
	997
	1033
	1250
	1320
Sexual differences	715
Sexuality	159
	657
Sharing	1038
Silence	995
Sin	251
	414
Solitude	583
	1073
Spiritual disciplines	731
Spiritual dryness	1231
Spiritual gifts	1085
	1106
	1334
Spiritual growth	186
	476
	731
	1161
	1205
	1287
	1351
	1385
Spiritual life	181
	686
	1003
	1203
	1237
	1239
	1337
	1381
Spiritual pollution	1402
Spirituality	837
Strength	1268
	1379
Strengths	1358
Stress	542
	1138
	1412
Stubbornness	1325
Submission	1066
	1298
	1304
	1347
Suffering	421
	507
	664
	766
	821
	1368
	1415
Support	1270
	1334

SUBJECT PAGE
Talents 1106
Teamwork 4
. 502
. 679
. 682
. 687
. 781
. 942
. 1038
. 1133
. 1038
. 1243
. 1313
. 1325
. 1333
. 1358
Temptation 1343
Thankfulness 280
Thanksgiving 821
Thought life 1320
. 1402
Thoughtfulness 1389
Time 81
. 418
. 606
. 1121
. 1335
. 1399
Togetherness 81
. 583
. 1376
Tolerance 990
Traditions 1228
Traveling 1318
Trouble 990
. 1183
. 1412
Trust 4
. 390
. 481
. 637
. 662

SUBJECT PAGE
. 760
. 842
. 1100
. 1268
. 1364
. 1368
. 1397
Truth 708
. 805
Truthfulness 705
Unbeliever, married to an 1251
Understanding 337
. 786
. 1374
Unity 87
. 1055
. 1239
Unselfishness 1091
Vulnerability 476
. 592
. 751
Waiting 60
. 834
. 1391
Wisdom 337
. 650
. 697
Work 781
. 948
. 1038
. 1138
. 1163
. 1185
. 1292
. 1399
Working together 179
Worry 1364
Worship 30
. 414
. 1119
Youth 650

